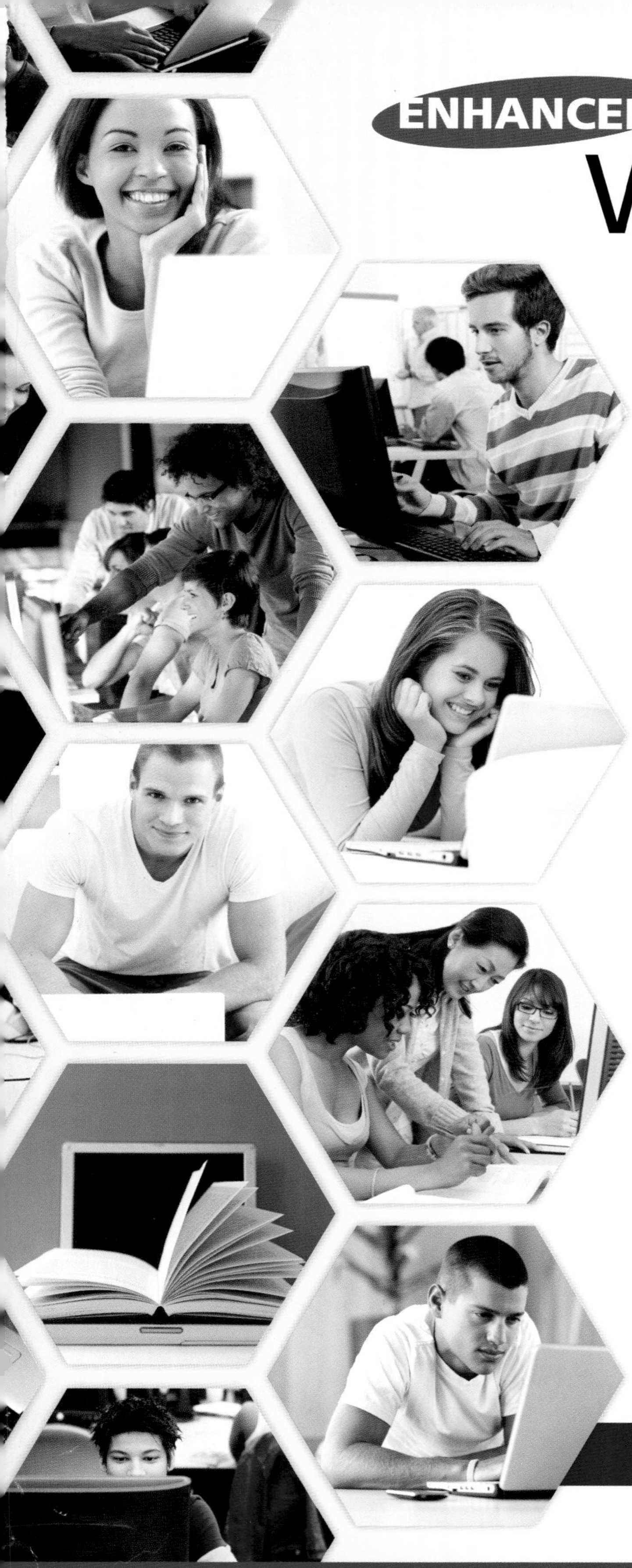

P9-AOS-478

CENGAGE
Learning

Ask the Authors!

We have taught math for many years. During that time, we have had students ask us a number of questions about mathematics and this course. Here you find some of the questions we have been asked most often, starting with the big one.

Courtesy of the Author

Courtesy of the Author

Dick Aufmann Joanne Lockwood

Why do I have to take this course? You may have heard that *"Math is everywhere."* That is probably a slight exaggeration, but math does find its way into many disciplines. There are obvious places like engineering, science, and medicine. There are other disciplines such as business, social science, and political science where math may be less obvious but still essential. If you are going to be an artist, writer, or musician, the direct connection to math may be even less obvious. Even so, as art historians who have studied the Mona Lisa have shown, there is a connection to math. But, suppose you find these reasons not all that compelling. **There is still a reason to learn basic math skills: You will be a better consumer and be able to make better financial choices for you and your family.** For instance, is it better to buy a car or lease a car? Math can provide an answer.

I find math difficult. Why is that? It is true that some people, even very smart people, find math difficult. Some of this can be traced to previous math experiences. If your basic skills are lacking, it is more difficult to understand the math in a new math course. Some of the difficulty can be attributed to the ideas and concepts in math. They can be quite challenging to learn. Nonetheless, most of us can learn and understand the ideas in the math courses that are required for graduation. **If you want math to be less difficult, practice. When you have finished practicing, practice some more.** Ask an athlete, actor, singer, dancer, artist, doctor, skateboarder, or (name a profession) what it takes to become successful and the one common characteristic they all share is that they practiced—a lot.

Why is math important? As we mentioned earlier, math is found in many fields of study. There are, however, other reasons to take a math course. Primary among these reasons is to become a better problem solver. Math can help you learn critical thinking skills. It can help you develop a logical plan to solve a problem. Math can help you see relationships between ideas and to identify patterns. **When employers are asked what they look for in a new employee, being a problem solver is one of the highest ranked criteria.**

What do I need to do to pass this course? The most important thing you must do is to know and understand the requirements outlined by your instructor. These requirements are usually given to you in a syllabus. Once you know what is required, you can chart a course of action. Set time aside to study and do homework. If possible, choose your classes so that you have a free hour after your math class. Use this time to review your lecture notes, rework examples given by the instructor, and begin your homework. All of us eventually need help, so know where you can get assistance with this class. This means knowing your instructor's office hours, the hours of the math help center, and how to access available online resources. And finally, do not get behind. **Try to do some math EVERY day, even if it is for only 20 minutes.**

Prealgebra and Introductory Algebra

AN APPLIED APPROACH

Annotated Instructor's Edition

Richard N. Aufmann
Palomar College

Joanne S. Lockwood
Nashua Community College

BROOKS/COLE
CENGAGE Learning

Australia • Brazil • Japan • Korea • Mexico • Singapore • Spain • United Kingdom • United States

***Prealgebra and Introductory Algebra: An Applied Approach,* Third Edition**
Richard N. Aufmann, Joanne S. Lockwood

Senior Executive Editor: Charlie Van Wagner
Acquisitions Editor: Marc Bove
Developmental Editor: Danielle Derbenti
Assistant Editor: Lauren Crosby
Editorial Assistant: Jennifer Cordoba
Media Editors: Heleny Wong, Guanglei Zhang
Brand Manager: Gordon Lee
Marketing Communications Manager: Jason LaChapelle
Content Project Manager: Cheryll Linthicum
Art Director: Vernon Boes
Manufacturing Planner: Becky Cross
Rights Acquisitions Specialist: Tom McDonough
Production and Composition Service: Graphic World Inc.
Photo Researcher: Bill Smith Group
Text Researcher: Pablo D'Stair
Copy Editor: Jean Bermingham
Illustrator: Graphic World Inc.
Text Designer: The Davis Group
Cover Designer: Morris Design
Cover Image: Morris Design

Library of Congress Control Number: 2012955632

ISBN-13: 978-1-133-36542-6

ISBN-10: 1-133-36542-6

Brooks/Cole
20 Davis Drive
Belmont, CA 94002-3098
USA

Cengage Learning is a leading provider of customized learning solutions with office locations around the globe, including Singapore, the United Kingdom, Australia, Mexico, Brazil, and Japan. Locate your local office at **www.cengage.com/global.**

Cengage Learning products are represented in Canada by Nelson Education, Ltd.

To learn more about Brooks/Cole, visit **www.cengage.com/brookscole.**

Purchase any of our products at your local college store or at our preferred online store **www.CengageBrain.com.**

Printed in the United States of America
1 2 3 4 5 6 7 17 16 15 14 13

Brief Contents

Contents

CHAPTER 2 Fractions and Decimals 79

CHAPTER 3 Rational Numbers 179

CHAPTER 4 Variable Expressions 249

CHAPTER 5 Solving Equations 283

CHAPTER 6 Proportion and Percent 337

CHAPTER 10 Factoring 535

CHAPTER 11 Rational Expressions 585

CHAPTER 12 Linear Equations in Two Variables 643

CHAPTER

T Transitioning to Algebra 849

Preface

Among the many questions we ask when we begin the process of revising a textbook, the most important is, "How can we improve the learning experience for the student?" We find answers to this question in a variety of ways, but most commonly by talking to students and instructors and by evaluating the written feedback we receive from instructors. Bearing this feedback in mind, our ultimate goal as we set out to create the third edition of *Prealgebra and Introductory Algebra: An Applied Approach* was to provide students with more materials to help them better understand the underlying concepts presented in this course. As a result, we have made the following changes to the new edition.

New to this edition is the **Focus on Success** vignette that appears at the beginning of each chapter. **Focus on Success** offers practical tips for improving study habits and performance on tests and exams.

We now include an **Apply the Concept** box in many objectives in which new concepts are introduced. This feature gives an immediate real-world example of how a new concept is applied. For example, after the basic percent equation is introduced, there is an Apply the Concept example that uses a percent equation to find the commission earned by a real estate broker.

The definition and key concept boxes have been enhanced in this edition; they now include examples to show how the general case translates to specific cases.

In each exercise set, the first group of exercises is now titled **Concept Check.** The **Concept Check** exercises focus on the concepts that lie behind the skills developed in the section. We consider an understanding of these concepts essential to a student's success in mastering the skills required to complete the exercises that follow.

Every chapter contains **Check Your Progress** exercises. This feature appears approximately mid-chapter and tests students' understanding of the concepts presented to that point in the chapter.

Critical Thinking exercises are included at the end of every exercise set. They may involve further exploration or analysis of the topic at hand. They may also integrate concepts introduced earlier in the text.

We trust that the new and enhanced features of the third edition will help students more successfully engage with the content. By narrowing the gap between the concrete and the abstract, between the real world and the theoretical, students should more plainly see that mastering the skills and topics presented is well within their reach and well worth the effort.

New to This Edition

- **Apply the Concept** boxes show how new concepts can be applied to real-world problems.
- **Concept Check** exercises appear at the beginning of each exercise set.
- Enhanced definition/key concept boxes now provide examples that illustrate how the general case applies to specific cases.
- The **Focus on Success** feature at the beginning of each chapter offers practical guidance to help students develop positive study habits.
- **Check Your Progress** exercises appear approximately mid-chapter and test students' understanding of the concepts presented thus far in the chapter.

- **In the News** articles within the exercise sets have been updated, as have application problems throughout the text.
- **Critical Thinking** exercises appear at the end of each exercise set.
- **Projects or Group Activities** are now included at the end of each exercise set.
- **Chapter A, AIM for Success,** now appears as the first chapter of the text. This chapter describes skills used by students who have been successful in this course. Topics include how to stay motivated, making a commitment to success, time management, and how to prepare for and take tests. A guide to the textbook is included to help students use its features effectively.
- More annotations have been added to the worked Examples, to more effectively explain the steps of the solutions.
- Many of the **Chapter Summaries** have been expanded to include more entries and more descriptive explanations.

Organizational Changes

We have made the following changes in order to improve the effectiveness of the textbook and enhance the student's learning experience.

- Section 3.1 has increased coverage of real-world applications of negative numbers.
- Section 3.5 now includes order of operations problems that involve absolute value.
- In Section 4.3, the table for translating verbal phrases into mathematical expressions has been redesigned to be easier to use as a reference.
- Sections 6.3 and 6.4 have been substantially revised. In Section 6.3, two pages were added to the exposition to provide a slower and more descriptive introduction to the crucial topic of percent. An expanded exercise set provides more basic, concept-driven exercises; more application problems; and more practice in writing percents as fractions and decimals, and writing fractions and decimals as percents.
- In Section 6.4, the exposition is two pages longer, for a slower, more detailed introduction to solving problems with the basic percent equation. Four pages have been added to the exercise set. There are more hands-on exercises; for example, the student is asked to shade a given percent of a grid and to circle a given percent of a number of objects.
- In Chapter 9, Section 9.2 now includes more detailed examples of each Rule for Simplifying Exponential Expressions. Section 9.4 has been reorganized and expanded in order to provide students with more assistance in learning the difficult topic of integer exponents. There are many more examples for students to learn from.

- Section 10.4 in the second edition has been split into two sections in the third edition. The new Section 10.4 develops factoring of the difference of two squares and perfect-square trinomials. The rule boxes are more explicit and include more examples. The new Section 10.5 is devoted to factoring polynomials completely. Now students can concentrate in Section 10.5 on applying all their factoring skills to factoring polynomials completely.
- Section 10.6 on solving equations by factoring now includes a boxed list of the steps used in solving a quadratic equation by factoring.
- The exposition in Section 11.7 has been expanded to provide more examples which apply the basic concepts of work problems. There is a gradual development of solving these problems. The exercise set contains more work problems and uniform motion problems for the student to solve, and there is a wide variety of each type of word problem.
- Objective 12.1C now includes an introduction to the language of sets in preparation for the formal definitions of relation and function.
- In the exercises for Section 12.2, Linear Equations in Two Variables, there are a greater variety of exercises and many more exercises that will help students learn the concepts. There is a group of exercises in which students are given equations in the form $Ax + By = C$ and asked to write them in the form $y = mx + b$. This provides them with the experience they need before graphing equations of the form $Ax + By = C$.
- In Section 12.3, the approach to graphing equations using the slope and y-intercept has changed. Now students are instructed to first move up or down from the y-intercept (change in y), and then move right or left (change in x) to plot a second point. The exercise set for Section 12.3 has been expanded to give students more practice using graphing concepts.
- The organization of Section 12.4 was changed to the following:

    A To find the equation of a line using the equation $y = mx + b$

    B To find the equation of a line using the point-slope formula

    C To find the equation of a line given two points

  Instructors can elect to cover only Objective A, only Objective B, or both Objectives A and B when presenting the topic of finding the equation of a line given a point and the slope of a line.
- Objective 14.1B now includes an introduction to the *less than or equal to* and *greater than or equal to* inequality symbols.
- The exercise set for Section 15.4 has been expanded to give students more practice with solving radical equations and applications of radical equations.
- The exercise set for Section 16.4 has been expanded. The Critical Thinking exercises and the Project or Group Activities will provide students with the opportunity to better understand the concepts related to graphs of quadratic equations. The last Project instructs students in using a graphing calculator to graph parabolas and find their x-intercepts.

Take AIM and Succeed!

An Objective-Based Approach

Prealgebra and Introductory Algebra: An Applied Approach is organized around a carefully constructed hierarchy of **objectives.** This "objective-based" approach provides an integrated learning path that enables you to find resources such as assessment tools (both within the text and online), videos, tutorials, and additional exercises for each objective in the text.

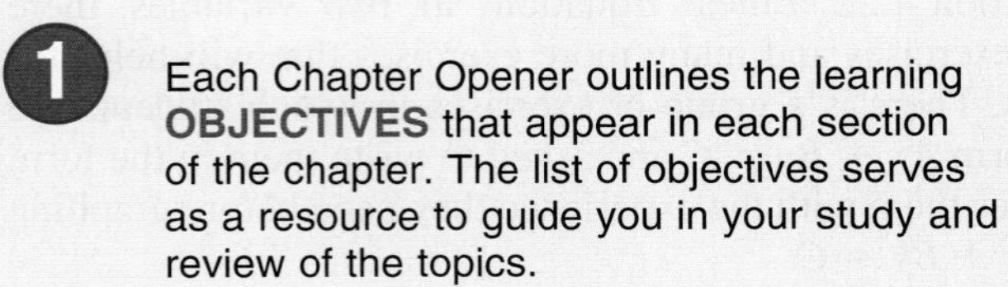

1 Each Chapter Opener outlines the learning **OBJECTIVES** that appear in each section of the chapter. The list of objectives serves as a resource to guide you in your study and review of the topics.

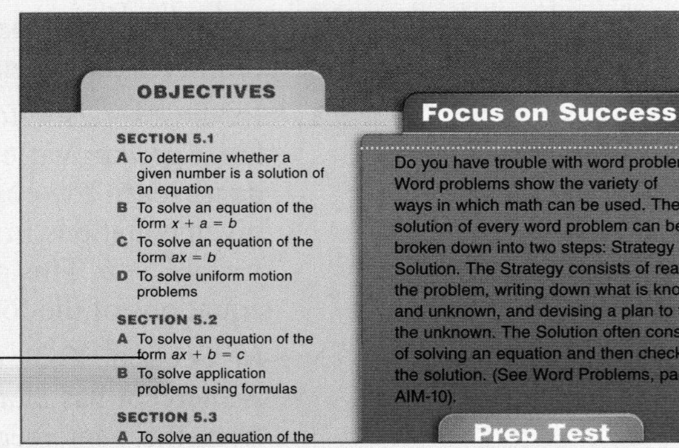

OBJECTIVES

SECTION 5.1

A To determine whether a given number is a solution of an equation

B To solve an equation of the form $x + a = b$

C To solve an equation of the form $ax = b$

D To solve uniform motion problems

SECTION 5.2

A To solve an equation of the form $ax + b = c$

B To solve application problems using formulas

SECTION 5.3

A To solve an equation of the

Focus on Success

Do you have trouble with word probler Word problems show the variety of ways in which math can be used. The solution of every word problem can be broken down into two steps: Strategy a Solution. The Strategy consists of rea the problem, writing down what is kno and unknown, and devising a plan to f the unknown. The Solution often cons of solving an equation and then check the solution. (See Word Problems, pag AIM-10).

Prep Test

2 Taking the **PREP TEST** for each chapter will help you determine which topics you need to study more carefully and which topics you need only review. The **ANSWERS** to the **PREP TEST** provide references to the **OBJECTIVES** on which the exercises are based.

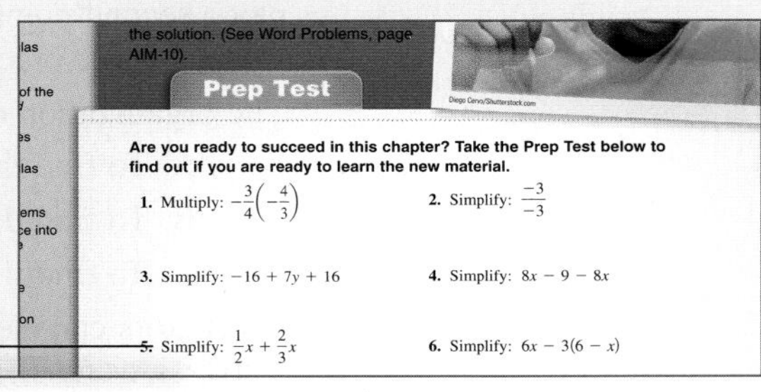

Prep Test

Are you ready to succeed in this chapter? Take the Prep Test below to find out if you are ready to learn the new material.

1. Multiply: $-\frac{3}{4}\left(-\frac{4}{3}\right)$
2. Simplify: $\frac{-3}{-3}$
3. Simplify: $-16 + 7y + 16$
4. Simplify: $8x - 9 - 8x$
5. Simplify: $\frac{1}{2}x + \frac{2}{3}x$
6. Simplify: $6x - 3(6 - x)$

Answers to Chapter 5 Selected Exercises

PREP TEST

1. 1 [3.4B] **2.** 1 [3.4B] **3.** $7y$ [4.2A] **4.** -9 [4.2A] **5.** $\frac{7}{6}x$ [4.2A] **6.** $9x - 18$ [4.2C] **7.** -5 [4.1A]
8. $5 - 2n$ [4.3B] **9.** Let s be the speed of the old card. The speed of the new card is $5s$. [4.3C]
10. The length of the shorter piece in terms of x is $5 - x$. [4.3C]

SECTION 5.1

1a. Equation **b.** Expression **c.** Expression **d.** Equation **e.** Expression **3.** i, ii, and iv are equations of the form $x + a = b$; you would subtract a from both sides. **5.** Keith had the greater average speed. **7.** Yes **9.** No **11.** No **13.** Yes **15.** No **17.** Yes **19.** Yes **21.** No **25.** 2 **27.** 15 **29.** 6 **31.** 3 **33.** 0 **35.** -7 **37.** -7 **39.** -12 **41.** -5

3 In every section, an **OBJECTIVE STATEMENT** introduces each new topic of discussion. Videos are available for each objective.

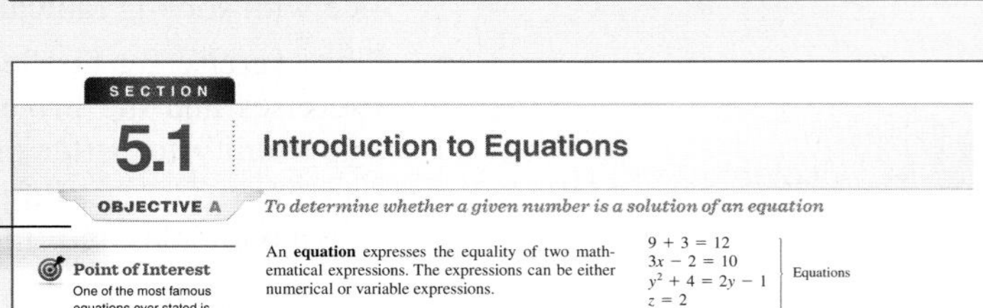

SECTION

5.1 Introduction to Equations

OBJECTIVE A *To determine whether a given number is a solution of an equation*

Point of Interest

One of the most famous equations ever stated is $E = mc^2$. This equation, stated by Albert Einstein, shows that there is a

An **equation** expresses the equality of two mathematical expressions. The expressions can be either numerical or variable expressions.

$9 + 3 = 12$
$3x - 2 = 10$
$y^2 + 4 = 2y - 1$
$z = 2$
Equations

The equation at the right is true if the variable is replaced by 5.

$x + 8 = 13$
$5 + 8 = 13$ A true equation

4 Section exercises are keyed to **OBJECTIVE STATEMENTS.**

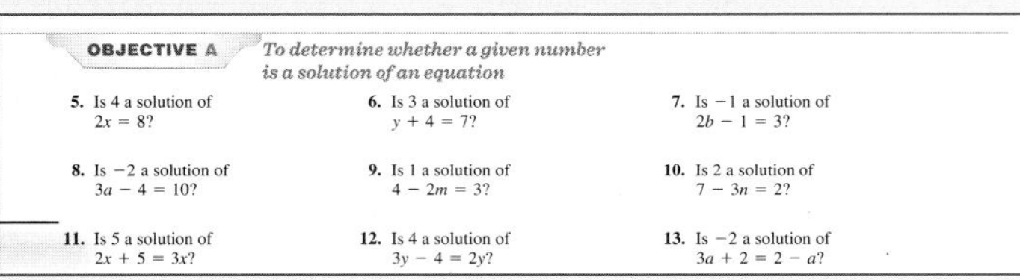

OBJECTIVE A *To determine whether a given number is a solution of an equation*

5. Is 4 a solution of $2x = 8$?
6. Is 3 a solution of $y + 4 = 7$?
7. Is -1 a solution of $2b - 1 = 3$?
8. Is -2 a solution of $3a - 4 = 10$?
9. Is 1 a solution of $4 - 2m = 3$?
10. Is 2 a solution of $7 - 3n = 2$?
11. Is 5 a solution of $2x + 5 = 3x$?
12. Is 4 a solution of $3y - 4 = 2y$?
13. Is -2 a solution of $3a + 2 = 2 - a$?

An Objective-Based Review

This "objective-based" approach continues through the end-of-chapter review and addresses a broad range of study styles by offering a **wide variety of review tools.**

CHECK YOUR PROGRESS exercises appear approximately mid-chapter and test your understanding of the concepts presented up to that point in the chapter.

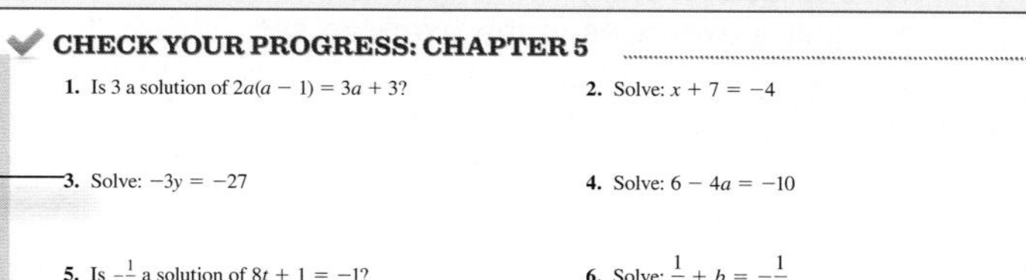

CHECK YOUR PROGRESS: CHAPTER 5

1. Is 3 a solution of $2a(a - 1) = 3a + 3$?
2. Solve: $x + 7 = -4$
3. Solve: $-3y = -27$
4. Solve: $6 - 4a = -10$
5. Is $-\frac{1}{2}$ a solution of $8t + 1 = -1$?
6. Solve: $\frac{1}{2} + b = -\frac{1}{2}$

At the end of each chapter, you will find a **CHAPTER SUMMARY** containing **KEY WORDS** and **ESSENTIAL RULES AND PROCEDURES** presented in the chapter. Each entry includes an objective reference and a page reference that show where in the chapter the concept was introduced. An example demonstrating the concept is also included.

CHAPTER 5 Summary

Key Words	Examples
An equation expresses the equality of two mathematical expressions. [5.1A, p. 284]	$3 + 2(4x - 5) = x + 4$ is an eq

By completing the **CHAPTER REVIEW EXERCISES,** you can practice working on problems in an order that is different from the order in which they were presented in the chapter. The **ANSWER** to each Chapter Review exercise includes a reference to the objective on which the exercise is based. This reference will help you quickly identify where to go if you need further practice with a particular concept.

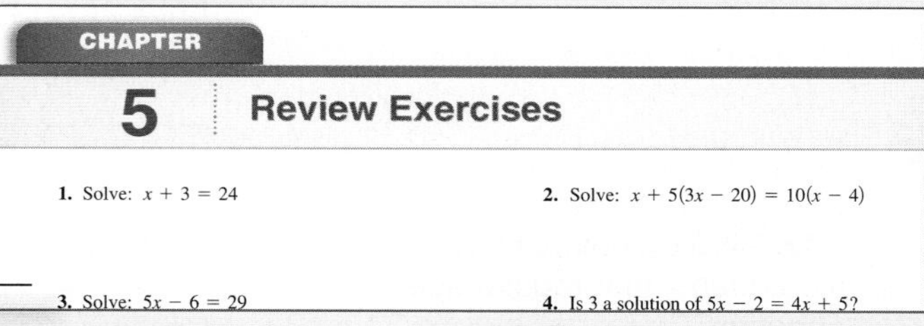

CHAPTER 5 Review Exercises

1. Solve: $x + 3 = 24$
2. Solve: $x + 5(3x - 20) = 10(x - 4)$
3. Solve: $5x - 6 = 29$
4. Is 3 a solution of $5x - 2 = 4x + 5$?

Each **CHAPTER TEST** is designed to simulate a typical test of the concepts covered in the chapter. Each **ANSWER** includes an objective reference as well as a reference to a numbered Example, You Try It, or HOW TO in the text that is similar to the given test question.

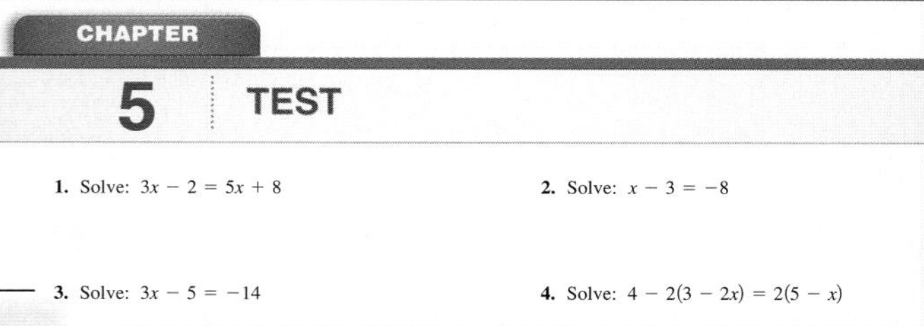

CHAPTER 5 TEST

1. Solve: $3x - 2 = 5x + 8$
2. Solve: $x - 3 = -8$
3. Solve: $3x - 5 = -14$
4. Solve: $4 - 2(3 - 2x) = 2(5 - x)$

CUMULATIVE REVIEW EXERCISES, which appear at the end of each chapter (beginning with Chapter 2), help you maintain previously learned skills. The **ANSWERS** include references to the section objectives on which the exercises are based.

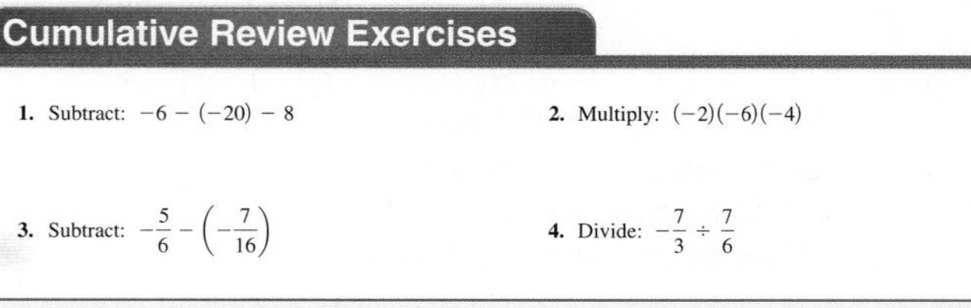

Cumulative Review Exercises

1. Subtract: $-6 - (-20) - 8$
2. Multiply: $(-2)(-6)(-4)$
3. Subtract: $-\frac{5}{6} - \left(-\frac{7}{16}\right)$
4. Divide: $-\frac{7}{3} \div \frac{7}{6}$

A **FINAL EXAM** is provided following the last chapter of the text. The Final Exam is designed to simulate a comprehensive exam covering all the concepts presented in the text. The **ANSWERS** to the Final Exam questions are provided in the appendix at the back of the text and include references to the section objectives on which the questions are based.

FINAL EXAM

1. Evaluate $-|-3|$.
2. Subtract: $-15 - (-12) - 3$
3. Simplify: $-\frac{4}{5} - \left(-\frac{3}{10}\right)$
4. Simplify: $-7 - \frac{12 - 15}{2 - (-1)} \cdot (-4)$

Understanding the Concepts

Each of the following features is designed to give you a fuller understanding of the key concepts.

CONCEPT CHECK exercises promote conceptual understanding. Completing these exercises will deepen your understanding of the concepts you are learning and provide the foundation you need to successfully complete the remaining exercises in the exercise set.

5.2 EXERCISES

Concept Check

1. Match each equation with the first step in solving that equation.
   a. $3x - 7 = 5$ i. Add 7 to each side.
   b. $4x + 7 = -5$ ii. Add 5 to each side.
   c. $7x - 5 = 2$ iii. Subtract 7 from each side.
   d. $-7x + 5 = -2$ iv. Subtract 5 from each side.

2. True or false? An equation of the form $ax + b = c$ cannot be solved if a is a negative number.

3. The first step in solving the equation $5 + 8x = 29$ is to subtract ______ from each side of the equation. The second step is to divide each side of the equation by ______.

Definition/key concept boxes contain examples to illustrate how each definition or key concept is applied in practice.

Interest computed on the original principal is called **simple interest.** Simple interest is the cost of a loan that is taken for a period of about one year or less.

The Simple Interest Formula

$I = Prt$, where I = simple interest earned, P = principal, r = annual simple interest rate, t = time (in years)

EXAMPLE

You borrow $3000 for 4 months at an annual simple interest rate of 4%.

$P = \$3000$, $r = 4\% = 0.04$, $t = 4$ months $\left(\frac{4}{12}\right)$

Simple interest $= I = Prt = \$3000(0.04)\left(\frac{4}{12}\right) = \$40$

TAKE NOTE boxes alert you to concepts that require special attention.

In solving an equation, the goal is to rewrite the given equation in the form *variable = constant*. The Addition Property of Equations is used to remove a *term* from one side of the equation by adding the opposite of that term to each side of the equation.

Take Note
An equation has some properties that are similar to those of a balance scale. For instance, if a balance scale is in balance and equal weights are added to each side of the scale, then the balance scale remains in balance. If an equation is true, then adding the same number to each side of the equation produces another true equation.

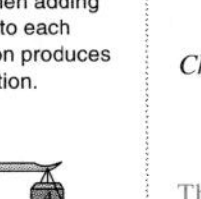

HOW TO 2 Solve: $x - 4 = 2$

$x - 4 = 2$ • The goal is to rewrite the equation in the form *variable = constant*.

$x - 4 + 4 = 2 + 4$ • Add 4 to each side of the equation.

$x + 0 = 6$ • Simplify.

$x = 6$ • The equation is in the form *variable = constant*.

Check: $x - 4 = 2$

$6 - 4 \mid 2$

$2 = 2$ A true equation

The solution is 6.

Because subtraction is defined in terms of addition, the Addition Property of Equations also makes it possible to subtract the same number from each side of an equation without changing the solution of the equation.

POINT OF INTEREST boxes, which relate to the topic under discussion, may be historical in nature or of general interest.

In Chapters 1 and 2, only zero and numbers greater than zero were discussed. In this chapter, numbers less than zero are introduced. Phrases such as "7 degrees below zero," "$50 in debt," and "20 feet below sea level" refer to numbers less than zero.

Point of Interest
Chinese manuscripts dating from about 250 B.C. contain the first recorded use of negative numbers. However, it was not until late in the fourteenth century that mathematicians generally accepted these numbers.

Numbers greater than zero are called **positive numbers.** Numbers less than zero are called **negative numbers.**

A positive number can be indicated by placing a plus sign (+) in front of the number. For example, we can write +4 instead of 4. Both +4 and 4 represent "positive 4." Usually, however, the plus sign is omitted and it is understood that the number is a positive number.

A negative number is indicated by placing a negative sign (−) in front of the number. The number −1 is read "negative one," −2 is read "negative two," and so on.

The number line can be extended to the left of zero to show negative numbers.

Application of the Concepts

The section exercises offer many opportunities to put the concepts you are learning into practice.

APPLY THE CONCEPT boxes illustrate how a concept is applied to a real-world situation so that you understand how the concept is used in everyday life.

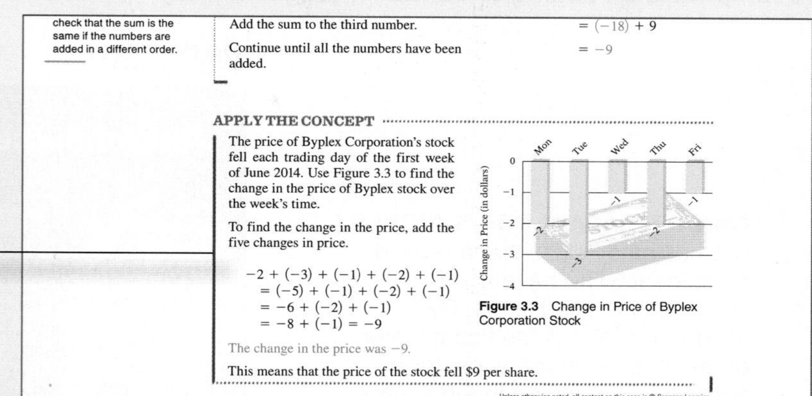

check that the sum is the same if the numbers are added in a different order.

Add the sum to the third number. $= (-18) + 9$

Continue until all the numbers have been added. $= -9$

APPLY THE CONCEPT

The price of Byplex Corporation's stock fell each trading day of the first week of June 2014. Use Figure 3.3 to find the change in the price of Byplex stock over the week's time.

To find the change in the price, add the five changes in price.

$$\begin{aligned} &-2 + (-3) + (-1) + (-2) + (-1) \\ &= (-5) + (-1) + (-2) + (-1) \\ &= -6 + (-2) + (-1) \\ &= -8 + (-1) = -9 \end{aligned}$$

The change in the price was -9.

This means that the price of the stock fell \$9 per share.

Figure 3.3 Change in Price of Byplex Corporation Stock

THINK ABOUT IT exercises promote deeper conceptual understanding. Completing these exercises will expand your understanding of the concepts being addressed.

99. Morgan and Emma ride their bikes from Morgan's house to the store. Morgan begins biking 5 min before Emma begins. Emma bikes faster than Morgan and catches up with her just as they reach the store.

a. Is the distance biked by Emma less than, equal to, or greater than the distance biked by Morgan?

b. Is the time spent biking by Emma less than, equal to, or greater than the time spent biking by Morgan?

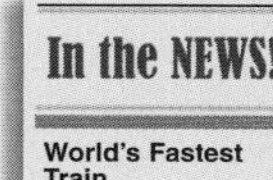

CRITICAL THINKING exercises may involve further exploration or analysis of the topic at hand. They may also integrate concepts introduced earlier in the text.

Critical Thinking

69. Elections A survey of voters in a city claimed that 2 people of every 5 who voted cast a ballot in favor of city amendment A, and 3 people of every 4 who voted cast a ballot against amendment A. Is this possible? Explain your answer.

70. Determine whether the statement is true or false.

a. A quotient $(a \div b)$ is a ratio.

b. If $\frac{a}{b} = \frac{c}{d}$, then $\frac{b}{a} = \frac{d}{c}$.

c. If $\frac{a}{b} = \frac{c}{d}$, then $\frac{a}{c} = \frac{b}{d}$.

d. If $\frac{a}{b} = \frac{c}{d}$, then $\frac{a}{d} = \frac{c}{b}$.

71. Lotteries Three people put their money together to buy lottery tickets. The first person put in \$25, the second person put in \$30, and the third person put in \$35. One of the tickets was a winning ticket. If the winning ticket paid \$4.5 million, what was

Working through the application exercises that contain **REAL DATA** will prepare you to answer questions and solve problems that you encounter outside of class, using facts and information that you gather on your own.

IN THE NEWS exercises help you understand the importance of mathematics in our everyday world. These application exercises are based on information taken from popular media sources such as newspapers, magazines, and the Internet.

Cost of Owning a Dog
Source: American Kennel Club, *USA Today* research

87. Health Insurance Approximately 30% of the 44 million people in the United States who do not have health insurance are between the ages of 18 and 24. (*Source:* U.S. Census Bureau) About how many people in the United States aged 18 to 24 do not have health insurance?

88. e-Filed Tax Returns See the news clipping at the right. How many of the 128 million returns were filed electronically? Round to the nearest million.

89. Diabetes Approximately 7% of the American population has diabetes. Within this group, 14.6 million are diagnosed, while 6.2 million are undiagnosed. (*Source:* The National Diabetes Education Program) What percent of Americans with diabetes have not been diagnosed with the disease? Round to the nearest tenth of a percent.

In the NEWS!

More Taxpayers Filing Electronically

The IRS reported that, as of May 4, it has received 128 million returns. Sixty percent of the returns were filed electronically.

Source: IRS

By completing the **WRITING** exercises, you will improve your communication skills while increasing your understanding of mathematical concepts.

81. Does the sentence "Solve $3x - 4(x - 1)$" make sense? Why or why not?

82. The equation $x = x + 1$ has no solution, whereas the solution of the equation $2x + 3 = 3$ is zero. Is there a difference between no solution and a solution of zero? Explain your answer.

83. I am thinking of a number. When I subtract 4 from the number and then multiply the result by 3, my new result is equal to the original number. What is the original number?

Focus on Study Skills

An emphasis on setting a foundation of good study habits is woven into the text.

UPDATED!

CHAPTER A, AIM FOR SUCCESS, outlines study skills that are used by students who have been successful in this course. By making Chapter A the first chapter of the text, the stage is set for a successful beginning to the course.

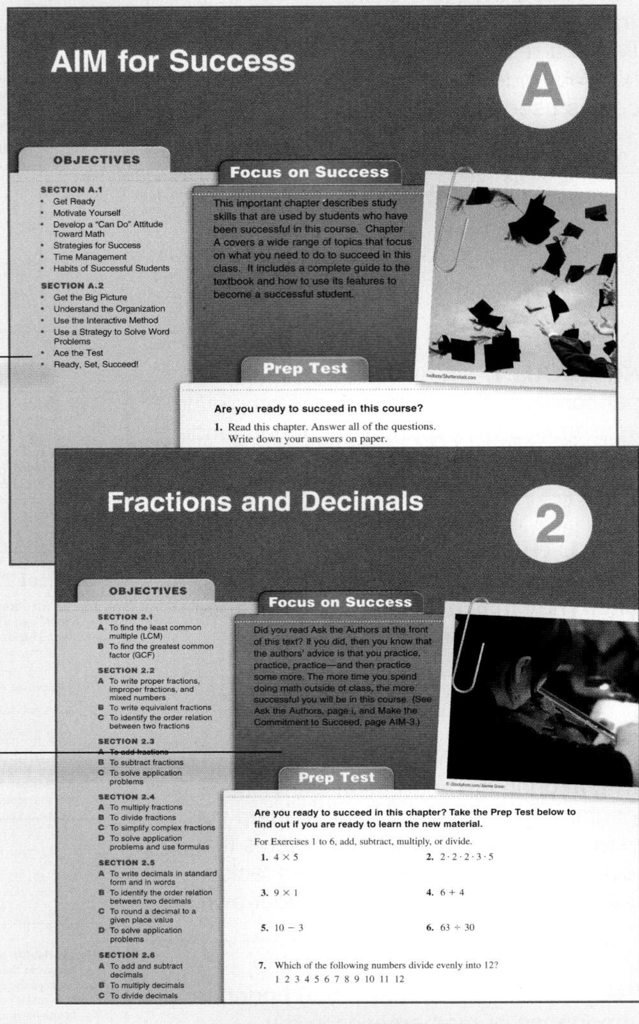

New **FOCUS ON SUCCESS** appears at the start of each Chapter Opener. These tips are designed to help you make the most of the text and your time as you progress through the course and prepare for tests and exams.

TIPS FOR SUCCESS boxes outline good study habits and function as reminders throughout the text.

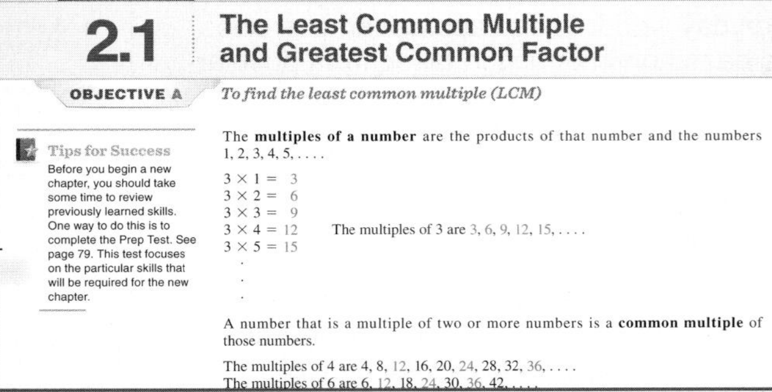

Focus on Skills and Problem Solving

The following features exemplify the emphasis on skills and the problem-solving process.

HOW TO examples provide solutions with detailed explanations for selected topics in each section.

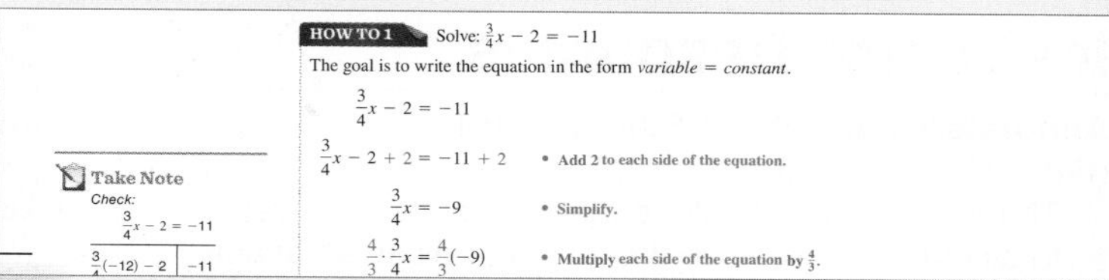
Take Note
Check:
$\frac{3}{4}x - 2 = -11$
$\frac{3}{4}(-12) - 2 \mid -11$

HOW TO 1 Solve: $\frac{3}{4}x - 2 = -11$

The goal is to write the equation in the form *variable* = *constant*.

$\frac{3}{4}x - 2 = -11$

$\frac{3}{4}x - 2 + 2 = -11 + 2$ • Add 2 to each side of the equation.

$\frac{3}{4}x = -9$ • Simplify.

$\frac{4}{3} \cdot \frac{3}{4}x = \frac{4}{3}(-9)$ • Multiply each side of the equation by $\frac{4}{3}$.

INTEGRATING TECHNOLOGY margin notes offer optional instruction in the use of a scientific calculator.

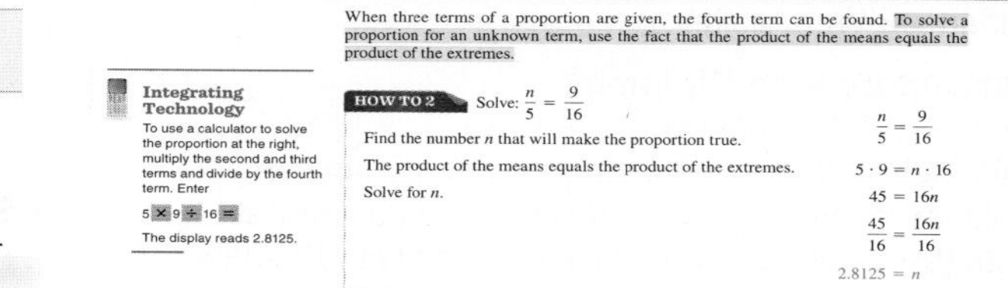
Integrating Technology
To use a calculator to solve the proportion at the right, multiply the second and third terms and divide by the fourth term. Enter
5 × 9 ÷ 16 =
The display reads 2.8125.

When three terms of a proportion are given, the fourth term can be found. To solve a proportion for an unknown term, use the fact that the product of the means equals the product of the extremes.

HOW TO 2 Solve: $\frac{n}{5} = \frac{9}{16}$

Find the number n that will make the proportion true.
The product of the means equals the product of the extremes.
Solve for n.

$\frac{n}{5} = \frac{9}{16}$
$5 \cdot 9 = n \cdot 16$
$45 = 16n$
$\frac{45}{16} = \frac{16n}{16}$
$2.8125 = n$

The **EXAMPLE/YOU TRY IT** matched pairs are designed to actively involve you in the learning process. The You Try Its are based on the Examples. These problems are paired so that you can easily refer to the steps in the Example as you work through the accompanying You Try It.

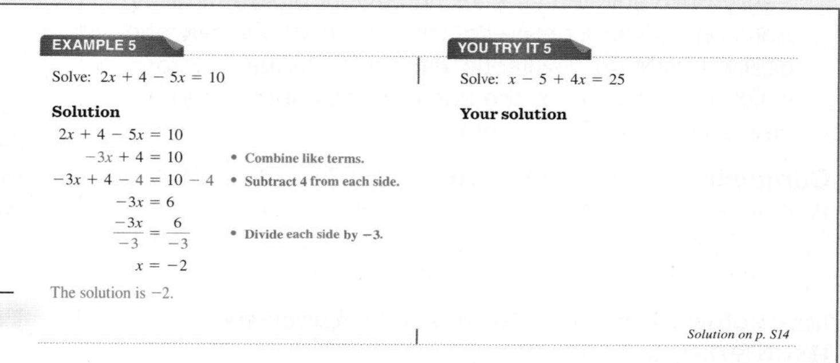
EXAMPLE 5

Solve: $2x + 4 - 5x = 10$

Solution

$2x + 4 - 5x = 10$
$-3x + 4 = 10$ • Combine like terms.
$-3x + 4 - 4 = 10 - 4$ • Subtract 4 from each side.
$-3x = 6$
$\frac{-3x}{-3} = \frac{6}{-3}$ • Divide each side by -3.
$x = -2$

The solution is -2.

YOU TRY IT 5

Solve: $x - 5 + 4x = 25$

Your solution

Solution on p. S14

Complete, **WORKED-OUT SOLUTIONS** to the You Try Its are included in an appendix at the back of the text. Compare your solution to the solution given in the appendix to obtain immediate feedback and reinforcement of the concept you are studying.

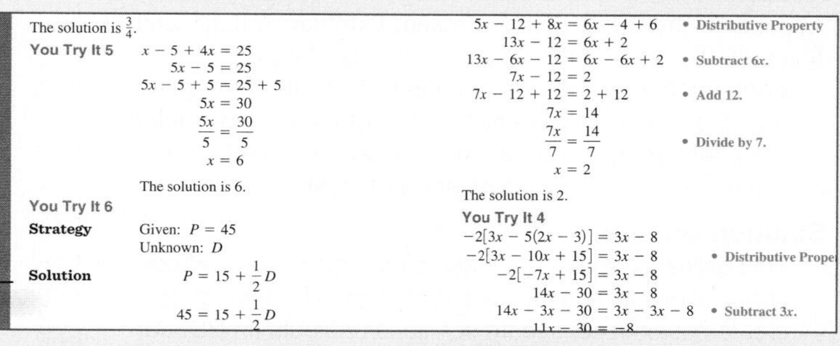
The solution is $\frac{3}{4}$.

You Try It 5
$x - 5 + 4x = 25$
$5x - 5 = 25$
$5x - 5 + 5 = 25 + 5$
$5x = 30$
$\frac{5x}{5} = \frac{30}{5}$
$x = 6$

The solution is 6.

You Try It 6
Strategy Given: $P = 45$
Unknown: D

Solution $P = 15 + \frac{1}{2}D$
$45 = 15 + \frac{1}{2}D$

$5x - 12 + 8x = 6x - 4 + 6$ • Distributive Property
$13x - 12 = 6x + 2$
$13x - 6x - 12 = 6x - 6x + 2$ • Subtract $6x$.
$7x - 12 = 2$
$7x - 12 + 12 = 2 + 12$ • Add 12.
$7x = 14$
$\frac{7x}{7} = \frac{14}{7}$ • Divide by 7.
$x = 2$

The solution is 2.

You Try It 4
$-2[3x - 5(2x - 3)] = 3x - 8$
$-2[3x - 10x + 15] = 3x - 8$ • Distributive Prope
$-2[-7x + 15] = 3x - 8$
$14x - 30 = 3x - 8$
$14x - 3x - 30 = 3x - 3x - 8$ • Subtract $3x$.
$11x - 30 = -8$

The **PROBLEM-SOLVING APPROACH** used throughout the text emphasizes the importance of problem-solving strategies. Model strategies are presented as guides for you to follow as you attempt the You Try Its that accompany the numbered Examples.

EXAMPLE 3

A wallpaper hanger charges a fee of \$25 plus \$12 for each roll of wallpaper used in a room. If the total charge for hanging wallpaper is \$97, how many rolls of wallpaper were used?

Strategy

To find the number of rolls of wallpaper used, write and solve an equation using n to represent the number of rolls of wallpaper used.

\$25 plus \$12 for each roll of wallpaper	is	\$97

YOU TRY IT 3

The fee charged by a ticketing agency for a concert is \$3.50 plus \$17.50 for each ticket purchased. If your total charge for tickets is \$161, how many tickets did you purchase?

Your strategy

PROJECTS OR GROUP ACTIVITIES appear at the end of each exercise set. Your instructor may assign these individually, or you may be asked to work through the activities in groups.

UPDATED!

Projects or Group Activities

70. Geometry Write an expression in factored form for the shaded portion in each of the following diagrams. Use the equation for the area of a rectangle $(A = LW)$ and the equation for the area of a circle $(A = \pi r^2)$.

a. 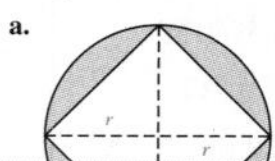

b. 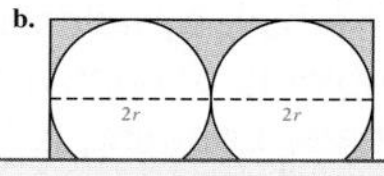

c. 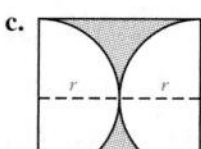

Additional Resources — Get More from Your Textbook!

Instructor Resources

Annotated Instructor's Edition (AIE)
(ISBN 978-1-133-36581-5)
The Annotated Instructor's Edition features answers to all of the problems in the text, as well as an appendix denoting those problems that can be found in Enhanced WebAssign.

PowerLecture with Diploma®
(ISBN 978-1-285-42039-4)
This DVD provides the instructor with dynamic media tools for teaching. Create, deliver, and customize tests (both print and online) in minutes with Diploma's Computerized Testing featuring algorithmic equations. Easily build solution sets for homework or exams using Solution Builder's online solutions manual. Quickly and easily update your syllabus with the Syllabus Creator, which was created by the authors and contains the new edition's table of contents.

Complete Solutions Manual (ISBN 978-1-285-42044-8)
Author: Jeremiah Gilbert, San Bernardino Valley College
The Complete Solutions Manual provides worked-out solutions to all of the problems in the text.

Instructor's Resource Binder with Appendix
(ISBN 978-1-285-42048-6)
Author: Maria H. Andersen, Muskegon Community College; Appendices by Richard N. Aufmann, Palomar College, and Joanne S. Lockwood, Nashua Community College
Each section of the main text is discussed in uniquely designed Teaching Guides that contain tips, examples, activities, worksheets, overheads, assessments, and solutions to all worksheets and activities.

Solution Builder
This online instructor database offers complete, worked-out solutions to all exercises in the text, allowing you to create customized, secure solutions printouts (in PDF format) matched exactly to the problems you assign in class. For more information, visit www.cengage.com/solutionbuilder.

Enhanced WebAssign®
Printed Access Card: 978-0-538-73810-1
Online Access Code: 978-1-285-18181-3
Exclusively from Cengage Learning, Enhanced WebAssign combines the exceptional mathematics content that you know and love with the most powerful online homework solution, WebAssign. Enhanced WebAssign engages students with immediate feedback, rich tutorial content, and interactive, fully customizable eBooks (YouBook), helping students to develop a deeper conceptual understanding of their subject matter. Online assignments can be built by selecting from thousands of text-specific problems or supplemented with problems from any Cengage Learning textbook.

Student Resources

Student Solutions Manual
(ISBN 978-1-285-42038-7)
Author: Jeremiah Gilbert, San Bernardino Valley College
Go beyond answers and improve your grade! This manual provides worked-out, step-by-step solutions to the odd-numbered problems in the text. The Student Solutions Manual gives you the information you need to truly understand how the problems are solved.

Student Workbook (ISBN 978-1-285-42051-6)
Author: Maria H. Andersen, Muskegon Community College
Get a head start. The Student Workbook contains assessments, activities, and worksheets for classroom discussions, in-class activities, and group work.

AIM for Success Student Practice Sheets
(ISBN 978-1-285-42037-0)
Author: Christine S. Verity
AIM for Success Student Practice Sheets provide additional problems to help you learn the material.

Enhanced WebAssign
Printed Access Card: 978-0-538-73810-1
Online Access Code: 978-1-285-18181-3
Enhanced WebAssign (assigned by the instructor) provides you with instant feedback on homework assignments. This online homework system is easy to use and includes helpful links to textbook sections, video examples, and problem-specific tutorials.

Acknowledgments

The authors would like to thank the people who have reviewed the third edition and provided many valuable suggestions.

Becky Bradshaw, *Lake Superior College*
Harvey Cartine, *Warren County Community College*
Jim Dawson, *College of Southern Idaho*
Cindy Dickson, *College of Southern Idaho*
Estella G. Elliott, *College of Southern Idaho*
Stephen Ester, *Saint Petersburg College*
Cassie Firth, *Northern Oklahoma College*
Lori L. Grady, *University of Wisconsin–Whitewater*
Nicholas Grener, *California State University, East Bay*
Ryan Grossman, *Ivy Tech Community College–Indiana*
Autumn Hoover, *Angelo State University*
Pat Horacek, *Pensacola State College*
Kelly Jackson, *Camden County College*
Thomas Judge, *California State University, East Bay*
Katy Koe, *Lincoln College*
William Lind, *Bryant and Stratton College*
Renee Lustig, *LeCordon Bleu College of Culinary Arts*
David Maina, *Columbia College, Chicago*
Connie Meade, *College of Southern Idaho*
Eugenia M. Moreno, *Butte Community College*
Dan Quynh Nguyen, *California State University, East Bay*
Rod Oberdick, *Delaware Technical Community College*
Scott Phelps, *University of La Verne*
David Poock, *Davenport University*
Nolan Thomas Rice, *College of Southern Idaho*
Daria Santerre, *Norwalk Community College*
Patricia Shepherd, *Ivy Tech Community College*
Darlyn Thomas, *Hennepin Technical College*
Sherri Urcavich, *University of Wisconsin–Green Bay*
Dr. Pamela D. Walker, *Northwestern College*
Donna M. Weglarz, *Westwood College–DuPage*
Lisa Williams, *College of the Abermarle*
Solomon Lee Willis, *Cleveland Community College*
Jerry Jacob Woods, *Westwood College*
Chen Zhixiong, *New Jersey City University*

Special thanks go to Jean Bermingham for copyediting the manuscript and proofreading pages, to Pat Foard for preparing the solutions manuals, and to Lauri Semarne for her work in ensuring the accuracy of the text. We would also like to thank the many people at Cengage Learning who worked to guide the manuscript for the third edition from development through production.

Index of Applications

AIM for Success

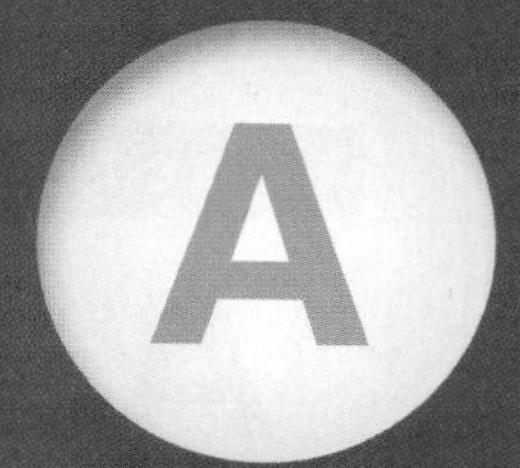

OBJECTIVES

SECTION A.1

- Get Ready
- Motivate Yourself
- Develop a "Can Do" Attitude Toward Math
- Strategies for Success
- Time Management
- Habits of Successful Students

SECTION A.2

- Get the Big Picture
- Understand the Organization
- Use the Interactive Method
- Use a Strategy to Solve Word Problems
- Ace the Test
- Ready, Set, Succeed!

Focus on Success

This important chapter describes study skills that are used by students who have been successful in this course. Chapter A covers a wide range of topics that focus on what you need to do to succeed in this class. It includes a complete guide to the textbook and how to use its features to become a successful student.

Prep Test

Are you ready to succeed in this course?

1. Read this chapter. Answer all of the questions. Write down your answers on paper.
2. Write down your instructor's name.
3. Write down the classroom number.
4. Write down the days and times the class meets.
5. Bring your textbook, a notebook, and a pen or pencil to every class.
6. Be an active participant, not a passive observer.

SECTION

A.1 How to Succeed in This Course

Get Ready

We are committed to your success in learning mathematics and have developed many tools and resources to support you along the way.

DO YOU WANT TO EXCEL IN THIS COURSE?

Read on to learn about the skills you'll need and how best to use this book to get the results you want.

We have written this text in an *interactive* style. More about this later but, in short, this means that you are supposed to interact with the text. Do not just read the text! Work along with it. Ready? Let's begin!

WHY ARE YOU TAKING THIS COURSE?

Did you interact with the text, or did you just read the last question? Get some paper and a pencil or pen and answer the question. Really—you will have more success in math and other courses you take if you **actively participate.** Now, **interact.** Write down one reason you are taking this course.

Of course, we have no idea what you just wrote, but experience has shown us that many of you wrote something along the lines of "I have to take it to graduate" or "It is a prerequisite to another course I have to take" or "It is required for my major." Those reasons are perfectly fine. Every teacher has had to take courses that were not directly related to his or her major.

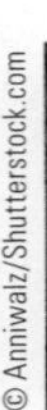

WHY DO YOU WANT TO SUCCEED IN THIS COURSE?

Think about why you want to succeed in this course. List the reasons here (not in your head . . . on the paper!):

One reason you may have listed is that math skills are important in order to be successful in your chosen career. That is certainly an important reason. Here are some other reasons.

- Math is a skill that applies across careers, which is certainly a benefit in our world of changing job requirements. A good foundation in math may enable you to more easily make a career change.
- Math can help you learn critical thinking skills, an attribute all employers want.
- Math can help you see relationships between ideas and identify patterns.

Take Note

Motivation alone won't lead to success. For example, suppose a person who cannot swim is rowed out to the middle of a lake and thrown overboard. That person has a lot of motivation to swim, but most likely will drown without some help. You'll need motivation *and* learning in order to succeed.

Motivate Yourself

You'll find many real-life problems in this book, relating to sports, money, cars, music, and more. We hope that these topics will help you understand how mathematics is used in everyday life. To learn all of the necessary skills and to understand how you can apply them to your life outside of this course, **motivate** yourself to learn.

One of the reasons we asked you why you are taking this course was to provide motivation for you to succeed. When there is a reason to do something, that task is easier to accomplish. We understand that you may not want to be taking this course but, to achieve your career goal, this is a necessary step. Let your career goal be your motivation for success.

MAKE THE COMMITMENT TO SUCCEED!

With practice, you will improve your math skills. Skeptical? Think about when you first learned to drive a car, ride a skateboard, dance, paint, surf, or any other talent that you now have. You may have felt self-conscious or concerned that you might fail. But with time and practice, you learned the skill.

List a situation in which you accomplished your goal by spending time practicing and perfecting your skills (such as learning to play the piano or to play basketball):

____

____

You do not get "good" at something by doing it once a week. **Practice** is the backbone of any successful endeavor—including math!

Develop a "Can Do" Attitude Toward Math

You can do math! When you first learned the skills you just listed above, you may not have done them well. With practice, you got better. With practice, you will get better at math. Stay focused, motivated, and committed to success.

We cannot emphasize enough how important it is to overcome the "I Can't Do Math" syndrome. If you listen to interviews of very successful athletes after a particularly bad performance, you will note that they focus on the positive aspects of what they did, not the negative. Sports psychologists encourage athletes always to be positive—to have a "can do" attitude. Develop this attitude toward math and you will succeed.

Change your conversation about mathematics. Do not say "I can't do math," "I hate math," or "Math is too hard." These comments just give you an excuse to fail. You don't want to fail, and we don't want you to fail. Write it down now: **I can do math!**

____

____

Strategies for Success

PREPARE TO SUCCEED

There are a number of things that may be worrisome to you as you begin a new semester. List some of those things now.

Here are some of the concerns expressed by our students.

- **Tuition**
  Will I be able to afford school?
- **Job**
  I must work. Will my employer give me a schedule that will allow me to go to school?
- **Anxiety**
  Will I succeed?
- **Child care**
  What will I do with my kids while I'm in class or when I need to study?
- **Time**
  Will I be able to find the time to attend class and study?
- **Degree goals**
  How long will it take me to finish school and earn my degree?

These are all important and valid concerns. Whatever your concerns, acknowledge them. Choose an education path that allows you to accommodate your concerns. Make sure they don't prevent you from succeeding.

SELECT A COURSE

Many schools offer math assessment tests. These tests evaluate your present math skills. They don't evaluate how smart you are, so don't worry about your score on the test. If you are unsure about where you should start in the math curriculum, these tests can show you where to begin. You are better off starting at a level that is appropriate for you than starting with a more advanced class and then dropping it because you can't keep up. Dropping a class is a waste of time and money.

If you have difficulty with math, avoid short courses that compress the class into a few weeks. If you have struggled with math in the past, this environment does not give you the time to process math concepts. Similarly, avoid classes that meet once a week. The time delay between classes makes it difficult to make connections between concepts.

Some career goals require a number of math courses. If that is true of your major, try to take a math course every semester until you complete the requirements. Think about it this way. If you take, say, French I, and then wait two semesters before taking French II, you may forget a lot of material. Math is much the same. You must keep the concepts fresh in your mind.

Time Management

One of the most important requirements in completing any task is to acknowledge the amount of time it will take to finish the job successfully. Before a construction company starts to build a skyscraper, the company spends months looking at how much time each of the phases of construction will take. This is done so that resources can be allocated when appropriate. For instance, it would not make sense to schedule the electricians to run wiring until the walls are up.

MANAGE YOUR TIME!

We know how busy you are outside of school. Do you have a full-time or a part-time job? Do you have children? Do you visit your family often? Do you play school sports or participate in the school orchestra or theater company? It can be stressful to balance all of the important activities and responsibilities in your life. Creating a time management plan will help you schedule enough time to do everything you need to do. Let's get started.

First, you need a calendar. You can use a daily planner, a calendar for a smartphone, or an online calendar, such as the ones offered by Google, MSN, or Yahoo. It is best to have a calendar on which you can fill in daily activities and be able to see a weekly or monthly view as well.

Start filling in your calendar now, even if it means stopping right here and finding a calendar. Some of the things you might include are:

- The hours each class meets
- Time for driving to and from work or school
- Leisure time, an important aspect of a healthy lifestyle
- Time for study. Plan at least one hour of study for each hour in class. This is a *minimum!*
- Time to eat
- Your work schedule
- Time for extracurricular activities such as sports, music lessons, or volunteer work
- Time for family and friends
- Time for sleep
- Time for exercise

Take Note

Be realistic about how much time you have. One gauge is that working 10 hours per week is approximately equivalent to taking one three-unit course. If your college considers 15 units a full load and you are working 10 hours per week, you should consider taking 12 units. The more you work, the fewer units you should take.

We really hope you did this. If not, please reconsider. One of the best pathways to success is understanding how much time it takes to succeed. When you finish your calendar, if it does not allow you enough time to stay physically and emotionally healthy, rethink some of your school or work activities. We don't want you to lose your job because you have to study math. On the other hand, we don't want you to fail in math because of your job.

If math is particularly difficult for you, consider taking fewer course units during the semesters you take math. This applies equally to any other subject that you may find difficult. There is no rule that you must finish college in four years. It is a myth—discard it now.

Now extend your calendar for the entire semester. Many of the entries will repeat, such as the time a class meets. In your extended calendar, include significant events that may disrupt your normal routine. These might include holidays, family outings, birthdays, anniversaries, or special events such as a concert or a football game. In addition to these events, be sure to include the dates of tests, the date of the final exam, and dates that projects or papers are due. These are all important semester events. Having them on your calendar will remind you that you need to make time for them.

CLASS TIME

To be successful, **attend class.** You should consider your commitment to attend class as serious as your commitment to your job or to keeping an appointment with a dear friend. It is difficult to overstate the importance of attending class. If you miss work, you don't get paid. If you miss class, you are not getting the full benefit of your tuition dollar. You are losing money.

If, by some unavoidable situation, you cannot attend class, find out as soon as possible what was covered in class. You might:

- Ask a friend for notes and the assignment.
- Contact your instructor and get the assignment. Missing class is no excuse for not being prepared for the next class.
- Determine whether there are online resources that you can use to help you with the topics and concepts that were discussed in the class you missed.

Going to class is important. Once you are there, **participate in class.** Stay involved and active. When your instructor asks a question, try to at least mentally answer the question. If you have a question, ask. Your instructor expects questions and wants you to understand the concept being discussed.

HOMEWORK TIME

In addition to attending class, you must **do homework.** Homework is the best way to reinforce the ideas presented in class. You should plan on at least one to two hours of homework and study for each hour you are in class. We've had many students tell us that one to two hours seems like a lot of time. That may be true, but if you want to attain your goals, you must be willing to devote the time to being successful in this math course.

You should schedule study time just as if it were class time. To do this, write down where and when you study best. For instance, do you study best at home, in the library, at the math center, under a tree, or somewhere else? Some psychologists who research successful study strategies suggest that just by varying where you study, you can increase the effectiveness of a study session. While you are considering where you prefer to study, also think about the time of day during which your study period will be most productive. Write down your thoughts.

Look at what you have written, and be sure that you can consistently be in your favorite study environment at the time you have selected. Studying and homework are extremely important. Just as you should not miss class, **do not miss study time.**

Before we leave this important topic, we have a few suggestions. If at all possible, create a study hour right after class. The material will be fresh in your mind, and the immediate review, along with your homework, will help reinforce the concepts you are learning.

If you can't study right after class, make sure that you set aside some time *on the day of the class* to review notes and begin the homework. The longer you wait, the more difficult it will be to recall some of the important points covered during class. Study math in small chunks—one hour a day (perhaps not enough for most of us), every day, is better than seven hours in one sitting. If you are studying for an extended period of time, break up your study session by studying one subject for a while and then moving on to another subject. Try to alternate between similar or related courses. For instance, study math for a while, then science, and then back to math. Or study history for a while, then political science, and then back to history.

Meet some of the people in your class and try to **put together a study group.** The group could meet two or three times a week. During those meetings, you could quiz each other, prepare for a test, try to explain a concept to someone else in the group, or get help on a topic that is difficult for you.

After reading these suggestions, you may want to rethink where and when you study best. If so, do that now. Remember, however, that it is your individual style that is important. Choose what works for *you,* and stick to it.

Habits of Successful Students

There are a number of habits that successful students use. Think about what these might be, and write them down.

What you have written is very important. The habits you have listed are probably the things you know you must do to succeed. Here is a list of some responses from successful students we have known.

- **Set priorities.** You will encounter many distractions during the semester. Do not allow them to prevent you from reaching your goal.

- **Take responsibility.** Your instructor, this textbook, tutors, math centers, and other resources are there to help you succeed. Ultimately, however, you must choose to learn. You must choose success.
- **Hang out with successful students.** Success breeds success. When you work and study with successful students, you are in an environment that will help you succeed. Seek out people who are committed to their goals.
- **Study regularly.** We have mentioned this before, but it is too important not to be repeated.
- **Self test.** Once every few days, select homework exercises from previous assignments and use them to test your understanding. Try to do these exercises without getting help from examples in the text. These self tests will help you gain confidence that you can do these types of problems on a test given in class.
- **Try different strategies.** If you read the text and are still having difficulty understanding a concept, consider going a step further. Contact the instructor or find a tutor. Many campuses have some free tutorial services. Go to the math or learning center. Consult another textbook. Be active and get the help you need.
- **Make flash cards.** This is one of the strategies that some math students do not think to try. Flash cards are a very important part of learning math. For instance, your instructor may use words or phrases such as *linear, quadratic, exponent, base, rational,* and many others. If you don't know the meanings of these words, you will not know what is being discussed.
- **Plod along.** Your education is not a race. The primary goal is to finish. Taking too many classes and then dropping some does not get you to the end any faster. Take only as many classes as you can successfully manage.

SECTION

A.2 How to Use This Text to Succeed in This Course

Get the Big Picture

One of the major resources that you will have access to the entire semester is this textbook. We have written this text with you and your success in mind. The following is a guide to the features of this text that will help you succeed.

Actually, we want you to get the *really* big picture. Take a few minutes to read the table of contents. You may feel some anxiety about all the new concepts you will be learning. Try to think of this as an exciting opportunity to learn math. Now look through the entire book. Move quickly. Don't spend more than a few seconds on each page. Scan titles, look at pictures, and notice diagrams.

Getting this "big picture" view will help you see where this course is going. To reach your goal, it's important to get an idea of the steps you will need to take along the way.

As you look through the book, find topics that interest you. What's your preference? Racing? Sailing? TV? Amusement parks? Find the Index of Applications at the front of the book, and pull out three subjects that interest you. Write those topics here.

____

____

____

Understand the Organization

Look again at the Table of Contents. There are 16 chapters in this book. You'll see that every chapter is divided into sections, and each section contains a number of learning objectives. Each learning objective is labeled with a letter from A to E. Knowing how this book is organized will help you locate important topics and concepts as you're studying.

Before you start a new objective, take a few minutes to read the Objective Statement for that objective. Then, browse through the objective material. Especially note the words or phrases in bold type—these are important concepts that you'll need to know as you move along in the course. These words are good candidates for flash cards. If possible, include an example of the concept on the flash card, as shown at the left.

Flash Card

Rule for Multiplying Exponential Expressions

If m and n are integers, then $x^m \cdot x^n = x^{m+n}$.
Examples:
$x^4 \cdot x^7 = x^{4+7} = x^{11}$
$y \cdot y^5 = y^{1+5} = y^6$
$a^2 \cdot a^6 \cdot a = a^{2+6+1} = a^9$

You will also see important concepts and rules set off in boxes. Here is one about multiplication. These rules are also good candidates for flash cards.

Rule for Multiplying Exponential Expressions

If m and n are integers, then $x^m \cdot x^n = x^{m+n}$.

EXAMPLES

In each example below, we are multiplying two exponential expressions with the same base. Simplify the expression by adding the exponents.

1. $x^4 \cdot x^7 = x^{4+7} = x^{11}$
2. $y \cdot y^5 = y^{1+5} = y^6$
3. $a^2 \cdot a^6 \cdot a = a^{2+6+1} = a^9$

Leaf through Section 3.1 of Chapter 3. Write down words in bold and any concepts or rules that are displayed in boxes.

Use the Interactive Method

As we mentioned earlier, this textbook is based on an interactive approach. We want you to be actively involved in learning mathematics, and have given you many suggestions for getting "hands-on" with this book.

HOW TO Look on page 363. See HOW TO 3? A HOW TO introduces a concept (in this case, solving a percent equation) and includes a step-by-step solution of the type of exercise you will find in the homework.

HOW TO 3 20 is what percent of 32?

Use the basic percent equation.	Percent · base = amount
Percent = n, base = 32, amount = 20	$n \cdot 32 = 20$
Solve for n by dividing each side of the equation by 32.	$\frac{32n}{32} = \frac{20}{32}$
	$n = 0.625$
Write the decimal as a percent.	$n = 62.5\%$

20 is 62.5% of 32.

Grab paper and a pencil and work along as you're reading through a HOW TO. When you're done, get a clean sheet of paper. Write down the problem and try to complete the solution without looking at your notes or at the book. When you're done, check your answer. If you got it right, you're ready to move on.

Look through the text and find three instances of a HOW TO. Write the concept illustrated in each HOW TO here.

Example/You Try It Pair You'll need hands-on practice to succeed in mathematics. When we show you an example, work it out yourself, right beside the solution. Use the Example/You Try It pairs to get the practice you need.

Take a look at page 286. Example 2 and You Try It 2 are shown here.

EXAMPLE 2

Solve: $x + 15 = 23$

Solution

$x + 15 = 23$

$x + 15 - 15 = 23 - 15$ • Subtract 15 from each side.

$x + 0 = 8$ • Simplify each side.

$x = 8$ • Addition Property of Zero

The solution is 8.

YOU TRY IT 2

Solve: $26 = y - 14$

Your solution

Solution on p. S13

You'll see that each Example is fully worked out. Study the Example by carefully working through each step. Then, try to complete the You Try It. Use the solution to the Example as a model for solving the You Try It. If you get stuck, the solutions to the You Try Its are provided in the back of the book. There is a page number directly following the You Try It that shows you where you can find the completely-worked-out solution. Use the solution to get a hint for the step on which you are stuck. Then, try again!

When you've arrived at your solution, check your work against the solution in the back of the book. Turn to page S13 to see the solution for You Try It 2.

Remember that sometimes there is more than one way to solve a problem. But your answer should always match the answer we've given in the back of the book. If you have any questions about whether your method will always work, check with your instructor.

Use a Strategy to Solve Word Problems

Learning to solve word problems is one of the reasons you are studying math. This is where you combine all of the critical thinking skills you have learned to solve practical problems.

Try not to be intimidated by word problems. Basically, what you need is a strategy that will help you come up with the equation you will need to solve the problem. When you are looking at a word problem, try the following:

- **Read the problem.** This may seem pretty obvious, but we mean really **read** it. Don't just scan it. Read the problem slowly and carefully.
- **Write down what is known and what is unknown.** Now that you have read the problem, go back and write down everything that is known. Next, write down what it is you are trying to find. *Write* this—don't just think it! Be as specific as you can. For instance, if you are asked to find a distance, don't just write "I need to find the distance." Be specific and write "I need to find the distance between Earth and the moon."
- **Think of a method to find the unknown.** For instance, is there a formula that relates the known and unknown quantities? This is certainly the most difficult step. Eventually, you must write an equation to be solved.
- **Solve the equation.** Be careful as you solve the equation. There is no sense in getting to this point and then making a careless mistake. The unknown in most word problems will include a unit such as feet, dollars, or miles per hour. When you write your answer, include the unit. An answer such as 20 doesn't mean much. Is it 20 feet, 20 dollars, 20 miles per hour, or something else?
- **Check your solution.** Now that you have an answer, go back to the problem and ask yourself whether it makes sense. This is an important step. For instance, if, according to your answer, the cost of a car is \$2.51, you know that something went wrong.

In this text, the solution of every word problem is broken down into two steps, **Strategy** and **Solution.** The Strategy consists of the first three steps discussed above. The Solution is the last two steps. Here is an Example from page 290 of the text. Because you have not yet studied the concepts involved in the problem, you may not be able to solve it. However, note the detail in the Strategy. When you do the You Try It following an Example, be sure to include your own Strategy.

EXAMPLE 5

Two cyclists start at the same time at opposite ends of an 80-mile course. One cyclist is traveling at 18 mph, and the second cyclist is traveling at 14 mph. How long after they begin cycling will they meet?

Strategy

The distance is 80 mi. Therefore, $d = 80$. The cyclists are moving toward each other, so the rate at which the distance between them is changing is the sum of the rates of the cyclists. The rate is 18 mph + 14 mph = 32 mph. Therefore, $r = 32$. To find the time, solve the equation $d = rt$ for t.

Solution

$d = rt$

$80 = 32t$ • $d = 80, r = 32$

$\frac{80}{32} = \frac{32t}{32}$ • Divide each side by 32.

$2.5 = t$

The cyclists will meet in 2.5 h.

YOU TRY IT 5

A plane that can normally travel at 250 mph in calm air is flying into a headwind of 25 mph. How far can the plane fly in 3 h?

Your strategy

Your solution

Solution on p. S13

When you have finished studying a section, **do the exercises your instructor has selected.** Math is not a spectator sport. You must practice every day. Do the homework and do not get behind.

Ace the Test

There are a number of features in this text that will help you prepare for a test. These features will help you even more if you do just one simple thing: When you are doing your homework, go back to each previous homework assignment for the current chapter and rework two exercises. That's right—just *two* exercises. You will be surprised at how much better prepared you will be for a test by doing this.

Here are some additional aids to help you **ace the test.**

Chapter Summary Once you've completed a chapter, look at the Chapter Summary. The Chapter Summary is divided into two sections: **Key Words** and **Essential Rules and Procedures.** Flip to page 526 to see the Chapter Summary for Chapter 9. The summary shows all of the important topics covered in the chapter. Do you see the reference following each topic? This reference shows you the objective and page in the text where you can find more information on the concept.

Write down one Key Word and one Essential Rule or Procedure. Explain the meaning of the reference "9.1A, page 492."

Chapter Review Exercises Turn to page 529 to see the Chapter Review Exercises for Chapter 9. When you do the review exercises, you're giving yourself an important opportunity to test your understanding of the chapter. The answer to each review exercise is given at the back of the book, along with the objective the question relates to. When you're done with the Chapter Review Exercises, check your answers. If you had trouble with any of the questions, you can restudy the objectives and retry some of the exercises in those objectives for extra help.

Go to the Answer Section at the back of the text. Find the answers for the Chapter Review Exercises for Chapter 9. Write down the answer to Exercise 25. Explain the meaning of the reference "9.5A."

Chapter Test The Chapter Test for each chapter can be found after the Chapter Review Exercises and can be used to help you prepare for your exam. The answer to each question is given at the back of the book, along with both an objective reference and a reference to a HOW TO, Example, or You Try It that the question relates to. Think of these tests as "practice runs" for your in-class tests. Take the test in a quiet place, and try to work through it in the same amount of time that will be allowed for your actual exam.

The aids we have mentioned above will help you prepare for a test. You should begin your review *at least* two days before the test—three days is better. These aids will get you ready for the test.

Here are some suggestions to try while you are actually taking the test.

- **Try to relax.** We know that test situations make some students quite nervous or anxious. These feelings are normal. Try to stay calm and focused on what you know. If you have prepared as we have suggested, the answers will begin to come to you.
- **Scan the test.** Get a feeling for the big picture.
- **Read the directions carefully.** Make sure you answer each question fully.
- **Work the problems that are easiest for you first.** This will help you with your confidence and help reduce any nervous feelings you may have.

Ready, Set, Succeed!

It takes hard work and commitment to succeed, but we know you can do it! Doing well in mathematics is just one step you'll take on your path to success. Good luck. We wish you success.

Whole Numbers

OBJECTIVES

SECTION 1.1

A To identify the order relation between two numbers

B To write whole numbers in words, in standard form, and in expanded form

C To round a whole number to a given place value

D To solve application problems and use statistical graphs

SECTION 1.2

A To add whole numbers

B To subtract whole numbers

C To solve application problems and use formulas

SECTION 1.3

A To multiply whole numbers

B To simplify expressions that contain exponents

C To divide whole numbers

D To factor numbers and find the prime factorization of numbers

E To solve application problems and use formulas

SECTION 1.4

A To use the Order of Operations Agreement to simplify expressions

Focus on Success

Have you read Chapter A, AIM for Success? It describes study skills used by students who have been successful in their math courses. It gives you tips on how to stay motivated, how to manage your time, and how to prepare for exams. Chapter A also includes a complete guide to the textbook and how to use its features to be successful in this course. It starts on page AIM-1.

Prep Test

Are you ready to succeed in this chapter? Take the Prep Test below to find out if you are ready to learn the new material.

1. Name the number of ◆s shown below.

◆ ◆ ◆ ◆ ◆ ◆ ◆ ◆

8

2. Write the numbers from 1 to 10.

1 <u>2</u> <u>3</u> <u>4</u> <u>5</u> <u>6</u> <u>7</u> <u>8</u> <u>9</u> 10

3. Match the number with its word form.

a. 4	**A.** five
b. 2	**B.** one
c. 5	**C.** zero
d. 1	**D.** four
e. 3	**E.** two
f. 0	**F.** three

a and D; b and E; c and A; d and B; e and F; f and C

4. How many American flags contain the color green?

0

5. Write the number of states in the United States of America as a word, not a number.

Fifty

SECTION

1.1 Introduction to Whole Numbers

OBJECTIVE A *To identify the order relation between two numbers*

The **natural numbers** are 1, 2, 3, 4, 5, 6, 7, 8, 9, 10, 11, ...

The three dots mean that the list continues on and on and that there is no largest natural number. The natural numbers are also called the **counting numbers.**

The **whole numbers** are 0, 1, 2, 3, 4, 5, 6, 7, 8, 9, 10, 11, ... Note that the whole numbers include the natural numbers and zero.

Just as distances are associated with markings on the edge of a ruler, the whole numbers can be associated with points on a line. This line is called the **number line** and is shown below.

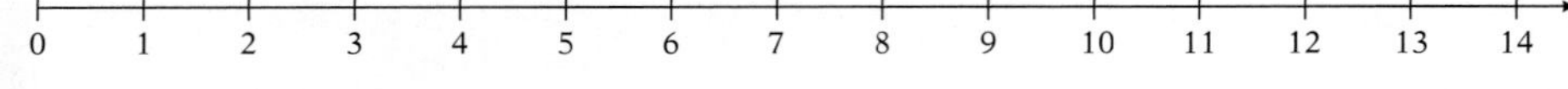

The arrowhead at the right indicates that the number line continues to the right.

The **graph** of a whole number is shown by placing a heavy dot on the number line directly above the number. Shown below is the graph of 6 on the number line.

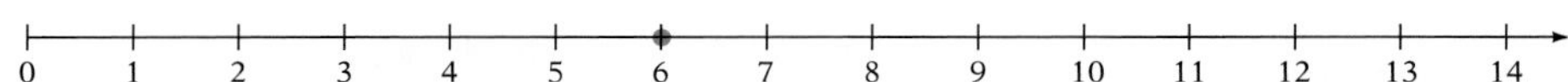

On the number line, the numbers get larger as we move from left to right. The numbers get smaller as we move from right to left. Therefore, the number line can be used to visualize the order relation between two whole numbers.

A number that appears to the right of a given number is **greater than** the given number. The symbol for *is greater than* is $>$.

8 is to the right of 3.
8 is greater than 3.
$8 > 3$

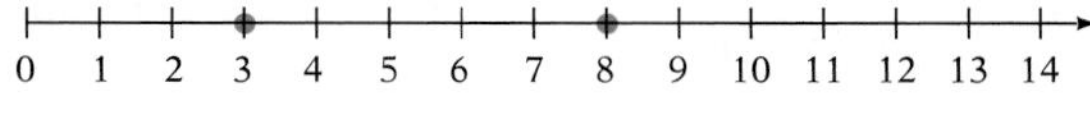

A number that appears to the left of a given number is **less than** the given number. The symbol for *is less than* is $<$.

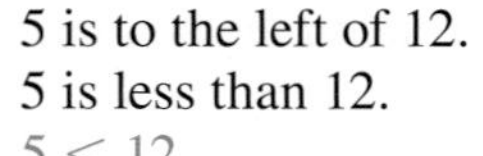

5 is to the left of 12.
5 is less than 12.
$5 < 12$

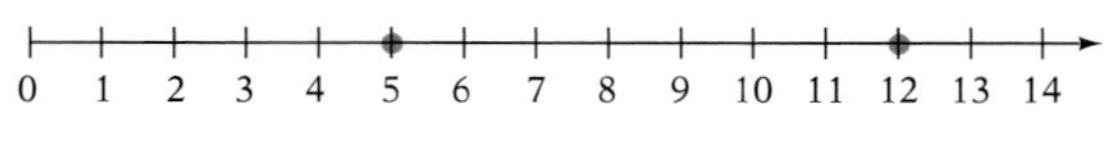

An **inequality** expresses the relative order of two mathematical expressions. $8 > 3$ and $5 < 12$ are inequalities.

Point of Interest

Among the slang words for zero are *zilch*, *zip*, and *goose egg*. The word *love* for zero in scoring a tennis game comes from the French for "the egg": *l'oeuf*.

IN-CLASS EXAMPLES

1. Graph 0 on the number line.

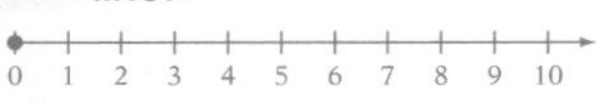

2. On the number line, which number is 4 units to the left of 9?
   5
3. Place the correct symbol, $<$ or $>$, between the two numbers.
   6409 6490
   6409 $<$ 6490
4. Write the given numbers in order from smallest to largest.
   483, 497, 492, 406, 438
   406, 438, 483, 492, 497

Take Note

An inequality symbol, $<$ or $>$, points to the smaller number. The symbol opens toward the larger number.

EXAMPLE 1

Graph 4 on the number line.

Solution 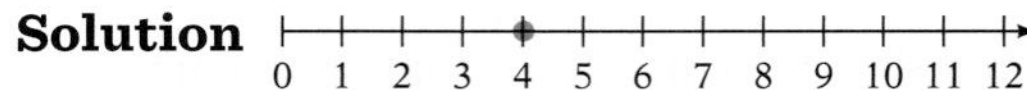

YOU TRY IT 1

Graph 9 on the number line.

Your solution 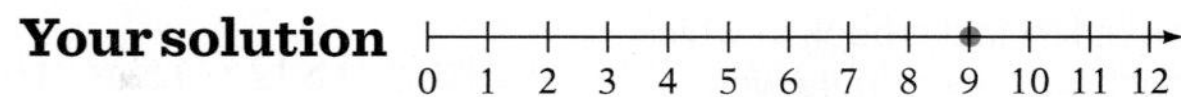

EXAMPLE 2

On the number line, what number is 3 units to the right of 4?

Solution

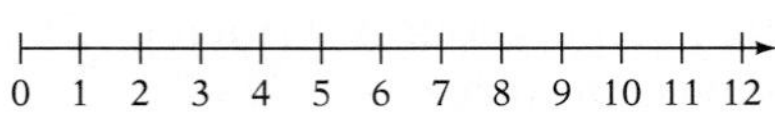

7 is 3 units to the right of 4.

YOU TRY IT 2

On the number line, what number is 4 units to the left of 11?

Your solution

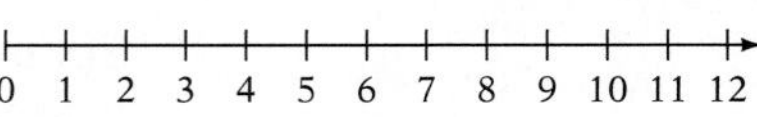

7

EXAMPLE 3

Place the correct symbol, $<$ or $>$, between the two numbers.

a. 38 23 **b.** 0 54

Solution

a. $38 > 23$ **b.** $0 < 54$

YOU TRY IT 3

Place the correct symbol, $<$ or $>$, between the two numbers.

a. 47 19 **b.** 26 0

Your solution

a. $47 > 19$ **b.** $26 > 0$

EXAMPLE 4

Write the given numbers in order from smallest to largest.

16, 5, 47, 0, 83, 29

Solution

0, 5, 16, 29, 47, 83

YOU TRY IT 4

Write the given numbers in order from smallest to largest.

52, 17, 68, 0, 94, 3

Your solution

0, 3, 17, 52, 68, 94

Solutions on p. S1

OBJECTIVE B *To write whole numbers in words, in standard form, and in expanded form*

When a whole number is written using the digits 0, 1, 2, 3, 4, 5, 6, 7, 8, and 9, it is said to be in **standard form.** The position of each digit in the number determines the digit's **place value.** The diagram below shows a **place-value chart** naming the first twelve place values. The number 64,273 is in standard form and has been entered in the chart.

In the number 64,273, the position of the digit 6 determines that its place value is ten-thousands.

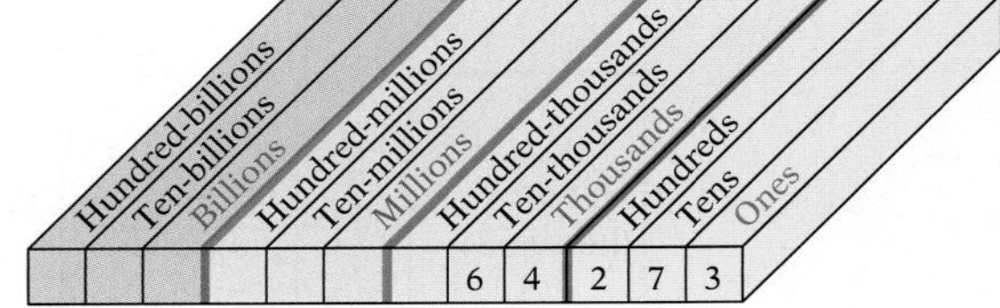

When a number is written in standard form, each group of digits separated by a comma is called a **period.** The number 5,316,709,842 has four periods. The period names are shown in red in the place-value chart above.

Point of Interest

The Romans represented numbers using M for 1000, D for 500, C for 100, L for 50, X for 10, V for 5, and I for 1. For example, MMDCCCLXXVI represented 2876. The Romans could represent any number up to the largest they would need for their everyday life, except zero.

Point of Interest

George Washington used a code to communicate with his men. He had a book in which each word or phrase was represented by a three-digit number. The numbers were arbitrarily assigned to each entry. Messages appeared as a string of numbers and thus could not be decoded by the enemy.

To write a number in words, start from the left. Name the number in each period. Then write the period name in place of the comma.

5,316,709,842 is read "five billion three hundred sixteen million seven hundred nine thousand eight hundred forty-two."

To write a whole number in standard form, write the number named in each period, and replace each period name with a comma.

Six million fifty-one thousand eight hundred seventy-four is written 6,051,874. The zero is used as a place holder for the hundred-thousands place.

The whole number 37,286 can be written in **expanded form** as

30,000 + 7000 + 200 + 80 + 6

The place-value chart can be used to find the expanded form of a number.

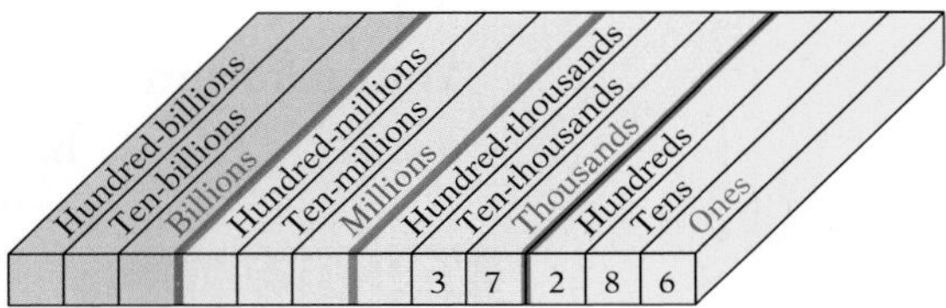

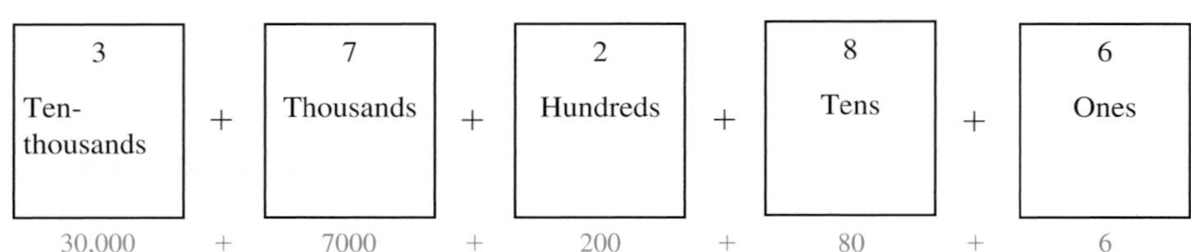

IN-CLASS EXAMPLES

5. Write 3,007,609 in words. **three million seven thousand six hundred nine**
6. Write two hundred forty-seven thousand sixty-three in standard form. **247,063**
7. Write 29,049 in expanded form. **20,000 + 9000 + 40 + 9**

Write the number 510,409 in expanded form.

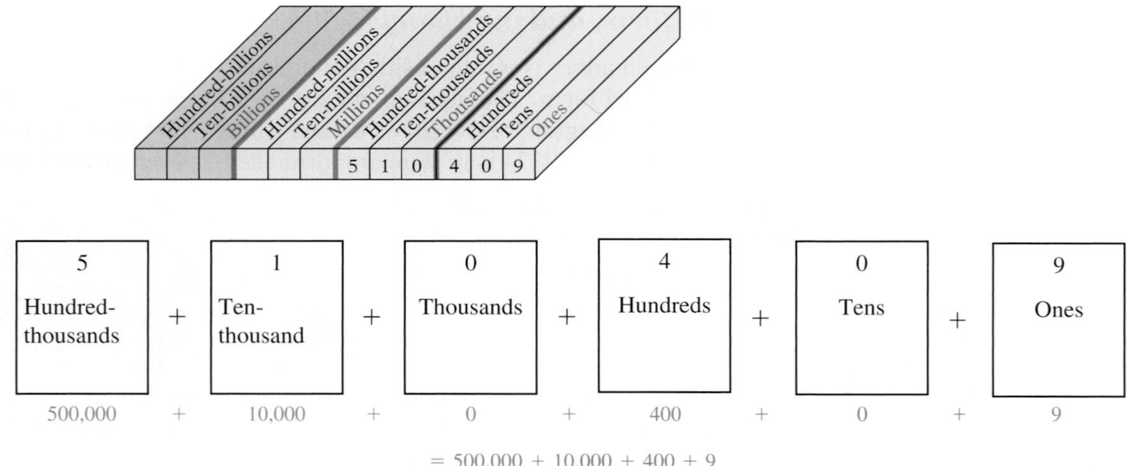

= 500,000 + 10,000 + 400 + 9

EXAMPLE 5

Write 82,593,071 in words.

Solution

eighty-two million five hundred ninety-three thousand seventy-one

YOU TRY IT 5

Write 46,032,715 in words.

Your solution

forty-six million thirty-two thousand seven hundred fifteen

EXAMPLE 6

Write four hundred six thousand nine in standard form.

Solution

406,009

YOU TRY IT 6

Write nine hundred twenty thousand eight in standard form.

Your solution

920,008

EXAMPLE 7

Write 32,598 in expanded form.

Solution

30,000 + 2000 + 500 + 90 + 8

YOU TRY IT 7

Write 76,245 in expanded form.

Your solution

70,000 + 6000 + 200 + 40 + 5

Solutions on p. S1

OBJECTIVE C *To round a whole number to a given place value*

When the distance to the sun is given as 93,000,000 mi, the number represents an approximation to the true distance. Giving an approximate value for an exact number is called **rounding.** A number is rounded to a given place value.

48 is closer to 50 than it is to 40.
48 rounded to the nearest ten is 50.

4872 rounded to the nearest ten is 4870.

4872 rounded to the nearest hundred is 4900.

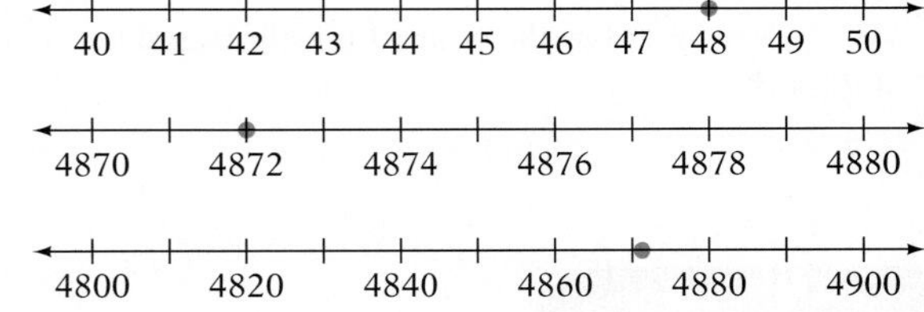

We can round a number to a given place value without using the number line by looking at the first digit to the right of the given place value.

If the digit to the right of the given place value is less than 5, replace that digit and all digits to the right of it by zeros.

Round 12,743 to the nearest hundred.

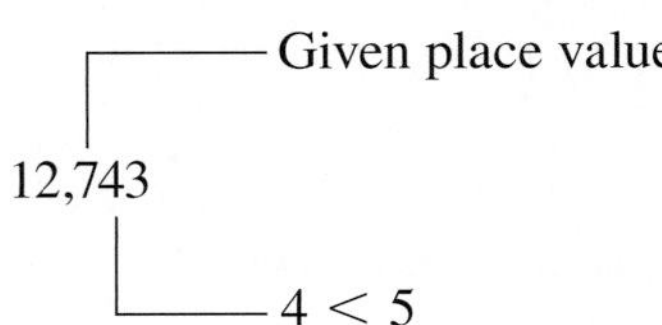

12,743 rounded to the nearest hundred is 12,700.

IN-CLASS EXAMPLES

8. Round 9746 to the nearest hundred. **9700**
9. Round 209,756 to the nearest thousand. **210,000**

If the digit to the right of the given place value is greater than or equal to 5, increase the digit in the given place value by 1, and replace all other digits to the right by zeros.

Round 46,738 to the nearest thousand.

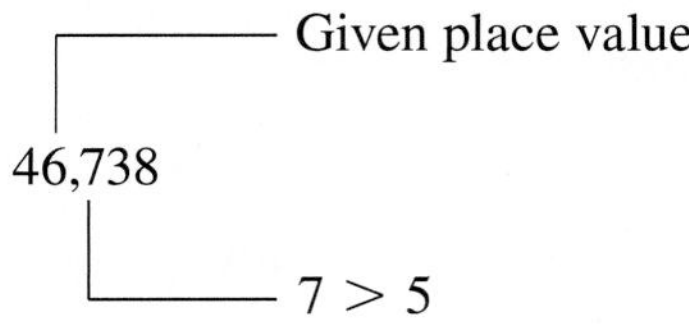

46,738 rounded to the nearest thousand is 47,000.

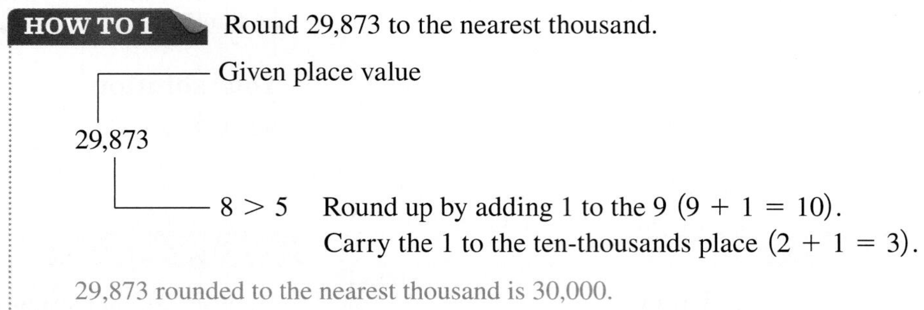

EXAMPLE 8

Round 435,278 to the nearest ten-thousand.

Solution

Given place value

435,278

5 = 5

435,278 rounded to the nearest ten-thousand is 440,000.

YOU TRY IT 8

Round 529,374 to the nearest ten-thousand.

Your solution

530,000

EXAMPLE 9

Round 1967 to the nearest hundred.

Solution

Given place value

1967

6 > 5

1967 rounded to the nearest hundred is 2000.

YOU TRY IT 9

Round 7985 to the nearest hundred.

Your solution

8000

Solutions on p. S1

OBJECTIVE D *To solve application problems and use statistical graphs*

Graphs are displays that provide a pictorial representation of data. The advantage of graphs is that they present information in a way that is easily read.

A **pictograph** uses symbols to represent information. The symbol chosen usually has a connection to the data it represents.

Bill Gates

Figure 1.1 represents the net worth of America's richest billionaires. Each symbol represents 10 billion dollars.

	Net Worth (in tens of billions of dollars)
Bill Gates	$ $ $ $ $ $
Warren Buffett	$ $ $ $ $
Larry Ellison	$ $ $ $
Christy Walton	$ $ $
Sheldon Adelson	$ $

Figure 1.1 Net Worth of America's Richest Billionaires
Source: www.Forbes.com

From the pictograph, we can see that Bill Gates has the greatest net worth. Warren Buffett's net worth is $10 billion more than Larry Ellison's net worth.

A typical household in the United States has an average after-tax income of $40,550. The **circle graph** in Figure 1.2 represents how this annual income is spent. The complete circle represents the total amount, $40,550. Each sector of the circle represents the amount spent on a particular expense.

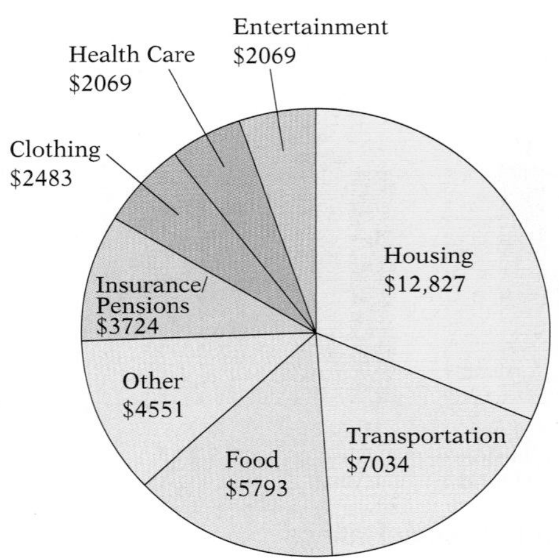

Figure 1.2 Average Annual Expenses in a U.S. Household
Source: American Demographics

From the circle graph, we can see that the largest amount is spent on housing. We can see that the amount spent on food ($5793) is less than the amount spent on transportation ($7034).

The **bar graph** in Figure 1.3 shows the expected U.S. population aged 100 and over for various years.

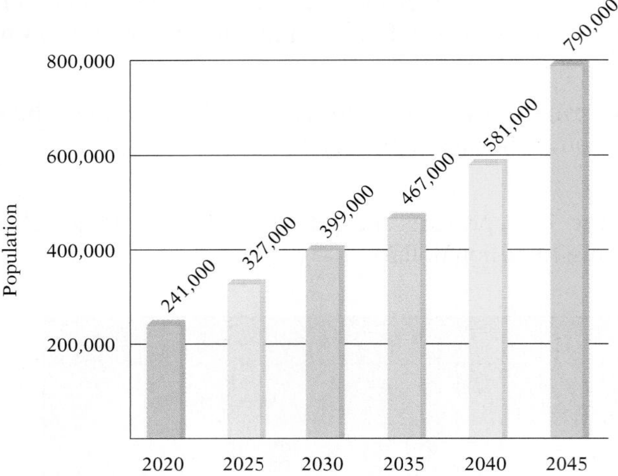

Figure 1.3 Expected U.S. Population Aged 100 and Over
Source: Census Bureau

In this bar graph, the horizontal axis is labeled with the year (2020, 2025, 2030, etc.) and the vertical axis is labeled with the population. For each year, the height of the bar indicates the population for that year. For example, we can see that the expected population aged 100 and over in the year 2030 is 399,000. The graph indicates that the number of people aged 100 and over is expected to increase steadily.

A **double-bar graph** is used to display data for the purposes of comparison.

The double-bar graph in Figure 1.4 shows the fuel efficiency of four vehicles, as rated by the Environmental Protection Agency. These are among the most fuel-efficient 2011-model-year cars for city and highway mileage.

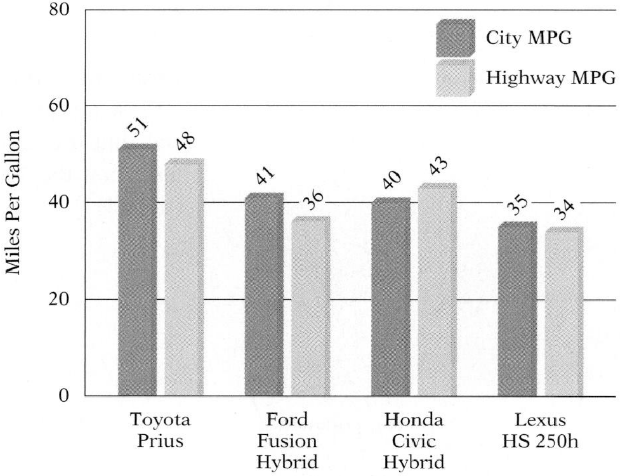

Figure 1.4 EPA Fuel Efficiency Ratings

From the graph, we can see that the fuel efficiency of the Ford Fusion Hybrid is less on the highway (36 mpg) than it is for city driving (41 mpg).

The **broken-line graph** in Figure 1.5 shows the effect of inflation on the value of a $100,000 life insurance policy. (An inflation rate of 5 percent is used here.)

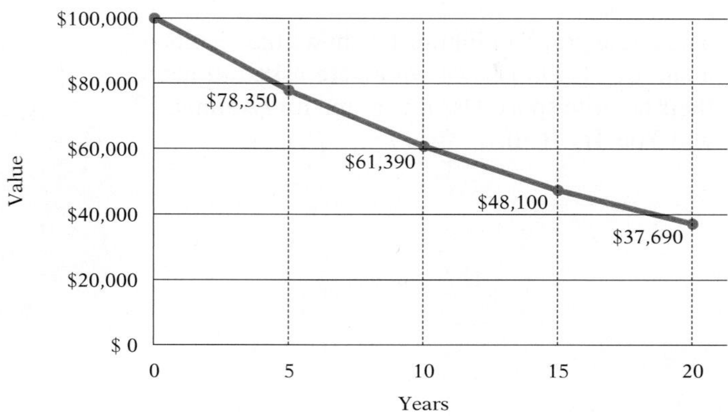

Figure 1.5 Effect of Inflation on the Value of a $100,000 Life Insurance Policy

According to the line graph, after five years the purchasing power of the $100,000 policy has decreased to $78,350. We can see that the value of the $100,000 policy keeps decreasing over the 20-year period.

Two broken-line graphs can be used to compare data. Figure 1.6 shows the populations of California and Texas. The figures are those of the U.S. Census for the years 1900, 1925, 1950, 1975, and 2000. The numbers are rounded to the nearest thousand.

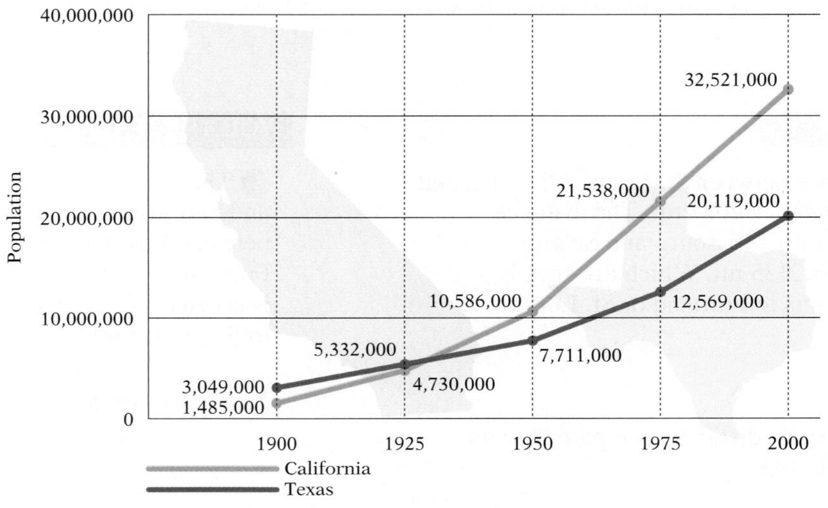

Figure 1.6 Populations of California and Texas

From the graph, we can see that the population was greater in Texas in 1900 and 1925, while the population was greater in California in 1950, 1975, and 2000.

IN-CLASS EXAMPLES

10. According to Figure 1.2, is the amount spent on clothing more or less than the amount spent on health care?
More than
11. According to Figure 1.3, what is the expected U.S. population aged 100 and over in 2040? Round to the nearest hundred thousand.
600,000 people
12. According to Figure 1.4, which car gets more miles per gallon on the highway, the Ford Fusion Hybrid or the Honda Civic Hybrid?
Honda Civic Hybrid

To solve an application problem, first read the problem carefully. The **Strategy** involves identifying the quantity to be found and planning the steps that are necessary to find that quantity. The **Solution** involves performing each operation stated in the Strategy and writing the answer.

The circle graph in Figure 1.7 shows the results of a survey of 300 people who were asked to name their favorite sport. Use this graph for Example 10 and You Try It 10.

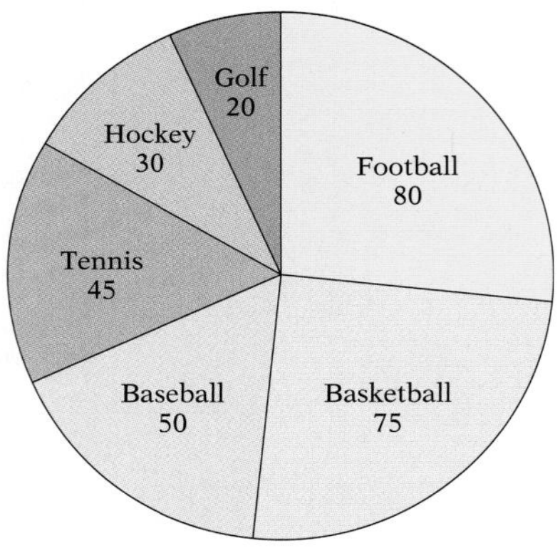

Figure 1.7 Distribution of Responses in a Survey

EXAMPLE 10

According to Figure 1.7, which sport was named by the least number of people?

Strategy

To find the sport named by the least number of people, find the smallest number given in the circle graph.

Solution

The smallest number given in the graph is 20.

The sport named by the least number of people was golf.

YOU TRY IT 10

According to Figure 1.7, which sport was named by the greatest number of people?

Your strategy

Your solution

Football

EXAMPLE 11

The distance between St. Louis, Missouri, and Portland, Oregon, is 2057 mi. The distance between St. Louis, Missouri, and Seattle, Washington, is 2135 mi. Which distance is greater, St. Louis to Portland or St. Louis to Seattle?

Strategy

To find the greater distance, compare the numbers 2057 and 2135.

Solution

$2135 > 2057$

The greater distance is from St. Louis to Seattle.

YOU TRY IT 11

The distance between Los Angeles, California, and San Jose, California, is 347 mi. The distance between Los Angeles, California, and San Francisco, California, is 387 mi. Which distance is shorter, Los Angeles to San Jose or Los Angeles to San Francisco?

Your strategy

Your solution

Los Angeles to San Jose

Solutions on p. S1

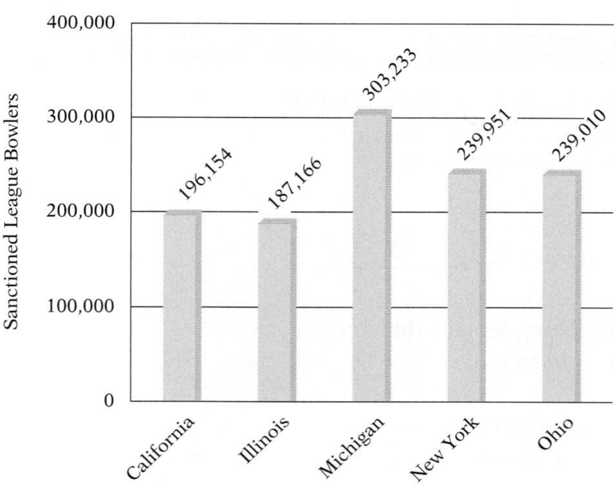

Figure 1.8 States with the Most Sanctioned League Bowlers

Sources: American Bowling Congress, Women's International Bowling Congress, Young American Bowling Alliance

The bar graph in Figure 1.8 shows the states with the most sanctioned league bowlers. Use this graph for Example 12 and You Try It 12.

EXAMPLE 12

According to Figure 1.8, which state has the most sanctioned league bowlers?

Strategy

To determine which state has the most sanctioned league bowlers, locate the state that corresponds to the highest bar.

Solution

The highest bar corresponds to Michigan.

Michigan is the state with the most sanctioned league bowlers.

YOU TRY IT 12

According to Figure 1.8, which state has fewer sanctioned league bowlers, New York or Ohio?

Your strategy

Your solution

Ohio

EXAMPLE 13

The land area of the United States is 3,539,341 mi^2. What is the land area of the United States to the nearest ten-thousand square miles?

Strategy

To find the land area to the nearest ten-thousand square miles, round 3,539,341 to the nearest ten-thousand.

Solution

3,539,341 rounded to the nearest ten-thousand is 3,540,000.

To the nearest ten-thousand square miles, the land area of the United States is 3,540,000 mi^2.

YOU TRY IT 13

The land area of Canada is 3,851,809 mi^2. What is the land area of Canada to the nearest thousand square miles?

Your strategy

Your solution

3,852,000 mi^2

Solutions on p. S1

1.1 EXERCISES

SUGGESTED ASSIGNMENT

Exercises 1–6; Exercises 7–77, odds; Exercises 81–93, odds; Exercises 99–113, odds

Concept Check

1. The inequality $7 > 4$ is read "seven __is greater than__ four."

2. Fill in the blank with < or >: On the number line, 2 is to the left of 8, so 2 __<__ 8.

3. To write the number 72,405 in words, first write *seventy-two.* Next, replace the comma with the word __thousand__. Then write the words *four hundred five.*

4. To write the number eight hundred twenty-two thousand in standard form, first write "822." Then replace the word *thousand* with a __comma__ followed by __three__ zeros.

5. The number 921 rounded to the nearest ten is 920 because the ones digit in 921 is __less__ than 5.

6. The number 927 rounded to the nearest ten is 930 because the ones digit in 927 is __greater__ than 5.

OBJECTIVE A *To identify the order relation between two numbers*

Graph the number on the number line.

7. 2

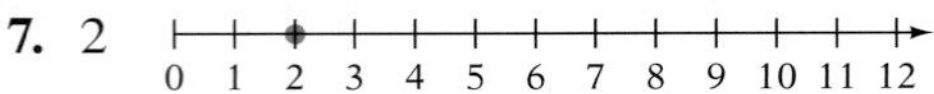

8. 7

0 1 2 3 4 5 6 7 8 9 10 11 12

9. 10

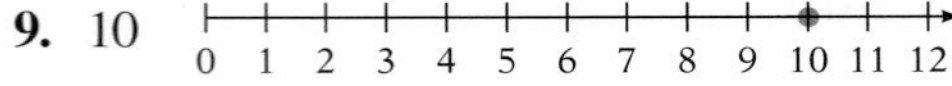

10. 1

0 1 2 3 4 5 6 7 8 9 10 11 12

11. 5

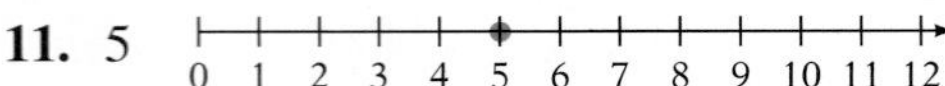

12. 11

0 1 2 3 4 5 6 7 8 9 10 11 12

On the number line, which number is:

13. 4 units to the left of 9
5

14. 5 units to the left of 8
3

15. 3 units to the right of 2
5

16. 4 units to the right of 6
10

17. 7 units to the left of 7
0

18. 8 units to the left of 11
3

Place the correct symbol, < or >, between the two numbers.

19. 27 < 39

20. 68 > 41

21. 0 < 52

22. 61 > 0

23. 273 > 194

24. 419 < 502

25. 2761 < 3857

26. 3827 < 6915

27. 4610 > 4061

28. 5600 < 56,000

29. 8005 < 8050

30. 92,010 > 92,001

31. Do the inequalities $15 > 12$ and $12 < 15$ express the same order relation?
Yes

32. Use the inequality symbol $<$ to rewrite the order relation expressed by the inequality $23 > 10$. $10 < 23$

Write the given numbers in order from smallest to largest.

33. 21, 14, 32, 16, 11
11, 14, 16, 21, 32

34. 18, 60, 35, 71, 27
18, 27, 35, 60, 71

35. 72, 48, 84, 93, 13
13, 48, 72, 84, 93

36. 54, 45, 63, 28, 109
28, 45, 54, 63, 109

37. 26, 49, 106, 90, 77
26, 49, 77, 90, 106

38. 505, 496, 155, 358, 271
155, 271, 358, 496, 505

39. 736, 662, 204, 981, 399
204, 399, 662, 736, 981

40. 440, 404, 400, 444, 4000
400, 404, 440, 444, 4000

41. 377, 370, 307, 3700, 3077
307, 370, 377, 3077, 3700

OBJECTIVE B *To write whole numbers in words, in standard form, and in expanded form*

Write the number in words.

42. 704
seven hundred four

43. 508
five hundred eight

44. 374
three hundred seventy-four

45. 635
six hundred thirty-five

46. 2861
two thousand eight hundred sixty-one

47. 4790
four thousand seven hundred ninety

48. 48,297
forty-eight thousand two hundred ninety-seven

49. 53,614
fifty-three thousand six hundred fourteen

50. 563,078
five hundred sixty-three thousand seventy-eight

51. 246,053
two hundred forty-six thousand fifty-three

52. 6,379,482
six million three hundred seventy-nine thousand four hundred eighty-two

53. 3,842,905
three million eight hundred forty-two thousand nine hundred five

Write the number in standard form.

54. seventy-five
75

55. four hundred ninety-six
496

56. two thousand eight hundred fifty-one
2851

57. fifty-three thousand three hundred forty
53,340

58. one hundred thirty thousand two hundred twelve
130,212

59. five hundred two thousand one hundred forty
502,140

60. eight thousand seventy-three
8073

61. nine thousand seven hundred six
9706

62. six hundred three thousand one hundred thirty-two
603,132

63. five million twelve thousand nine hundred seven
5,012,907

64. three million four thousand eight
3,004,008

65. eight million five thousand ten
8,005,010

Write the number in expanded form.

66. 6398
6000 + 300 + 90 + 8

67. 7245
7000 + 200 + 40 + 5

68. 46,182
40,000 + 6000 + 100 + 80 + 2

69. 532,791
500,000 + 30,000 + 2000 + 700 + 90 + 1

70. 328,476
300,000 + 20,000 + 8000 + 400 + 70 + 6

71. 5064
5000 + 60 + 4

72. 90,834
90,000 + 800 + 30 + 4

73. 20,397
20,000 + 300 + 90 + 7

74. 400,635
400,000 + 600 + 30 + 5

75. 402,708
400,000 + 2000 + 700 + 8

76. 504,603
500,000 + 4000 + 600 + 3

77. 8,000,316
8,000,000 + 300 + 10 + 6

78. What is the place value of the leftmost number in a five-digit number?
Ten-thousands

79. What is the place value of the third number from the left in a four-digit number?
Tens

OBJECTIVE C *To round a whole number to a given place value*

Round the number to the given place value.

80. 3049; tens
3050

81. 7108; tens
7110

82. 1638; hundreds
1600

83. 4962; hundreds
5000

84. 17,639; hundreds
17,600

85. 28,551; hundreds
28,600

86. 5326; thousands
5000

87. 6809; thousands
7000

88. 84,608; thousands
85,000

89. 93,825; thousands
94,000

90. 389,702; thousands
390,000

91. 629,513; thousands
630,000

92. 746,898; ten-thousands
750,000

93. 352,876; ten-thousands
350,000

94. 36,702,599; millions
37,000,000

Determine whether each statement is sometimes true, never true, or always true.

95. A six-digit number rounded to the nearest thousand is greater than the same number rounded to the nearest ten-thousand.
Sometimes true

96. If a number rounded to the nearest ten is equal to itself, then the ones digit of the number is 0.
Always true

97. If the ones digit of a number is greater than 5, then the number rounded to the nearest ten is less than the original number.
Never true

OBJECTIVE D *To solve application problems and use statistical graphs*

98. **Sports** During his baseball career, Eddie Collins had a record of 743 stolen bases. Max Carey had a record of 738 stolen bases during his baseball career. Who had more stolen bases, Eddie Collins or Max Carey? Eddie Collins

99. **Sports** During his baseball career, Ty Cobb had a record of 892 stolen bases. Billy Hamilton had a record of 937 stolen bases during his baseball career. Who had more stolen bases, Ty Cobb or Billy Hamilton? Billy Hamilton

100. **Turkey Consumption** The figure at the right shows the annual per capita turkey consumption in different countries. **a.** What is the annual per capita turkey consumption in the United States? **b.** In which country is the annual per capita turkey consumption the highest? **a.** 18 lb **b.** Israel

Country	
Britain	
Canada	
France	
Ireland	
Israel	
Italy	
U.S.	
	Each represents 2 lb.

Per Capita Turkey Consumption
Source: National Turkey Federation

101. **The Arts** The play *Hello Dolly* was performed 2844 times on Broadway. The play *Fiddler on the Roof* was performed 3242 times on Broadway. Which play had the greater number of performances, *Hello Dolly* or *Fiddler on the Roof*?
Fiddler on the Roof

102. **The Arts** The play *Annie* was performed 2377 times on Broadway. The play *My Fair Lady* was performed 2717 times on Broadway. Which play had the greater number of performances, *Annie* or *My Fair Lady*? *My Fair Lady*

103. **Nutrition** Two tablespoons of peanut butter contain 190 calories. Two tablespoons of grape jelly contain 114 calories. Which contains more calories, two tablespoons of peanut butter or two tablespoons of grape jelly?
Two tablespoons of peanut butter

104. **Traffic Accidents** The figure at the right shows the number of crashes on U.S. roadways during each of the last six months of a recent year. Also shown is the number of vehicles involved in those crashes.

a. Which was greater, the number of crashes in July or the number of crashes in October? July

b. Were there fewer vehicles involved in crashes in July or in December? July

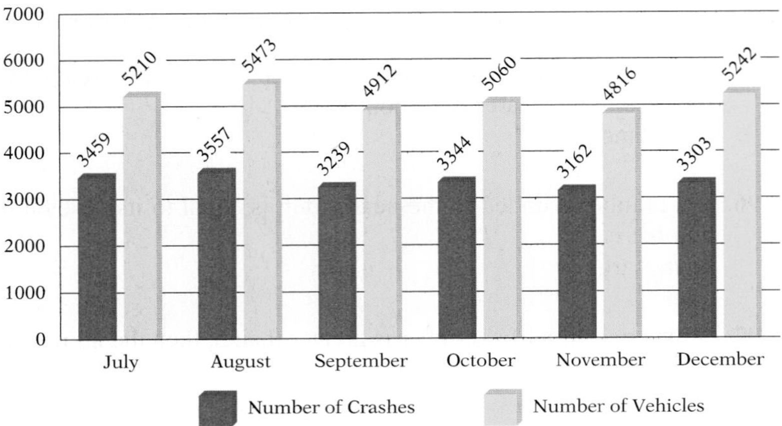

Accidents on U.S. Roadways

Source: National Highway Traffic Safety Administration

105. **Education** Actual or projected student enrollment in elementary and secondary schools in the United States for selected years is shown in the figure at the right. The jagged line at the bottom of the vertical axis indicates that this scale is missing the tens of millions from 0 to 40,000,000.

a. During which year was enrollment the lowest? 1980

b. Did enrollment increase or decrease between 1990 and 2000? Increased

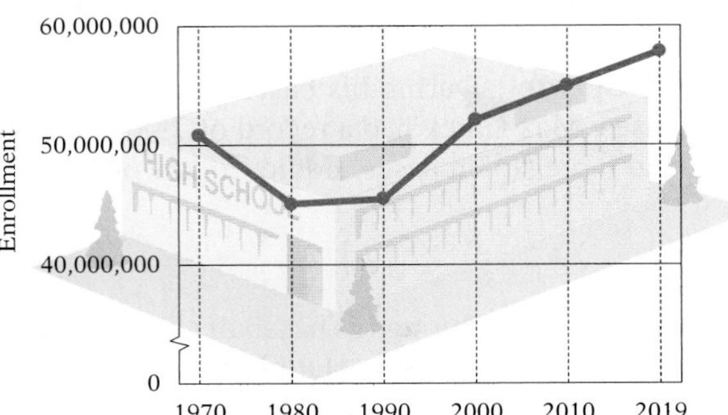

Enrollment in Elementary and Secondary Schools

Source: National Center for Education Statistics

106. **History** In 1810, Peter Durand invented the tin can. In 1767, Joseph Priestly invented carbonated water. Which was invented first, the tin can or carbonated water? Carbonated water

107. **Movie Theaters** The circle graph at the right shows the results of a survey of 150 people who were asked, "What bothers you most about movie theaters?" **a.** Among the respondents, what was the most often mentioned complaint? **b.** What was the least often mentioned complaint?
a. People talking **b.** Uncomfortable seats

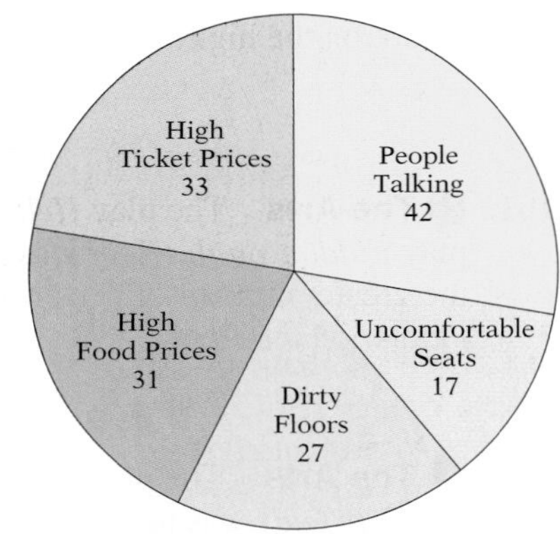

Distribution of Responses in a Survey

108. **Geography** The distance between St. Louis, Missouri, and Reno, Nevada, is 1892 mi. The distance between St. Louis, Missouri, and San Diego, California, is 1833 mi. Which is the shorter distance, St. Louis to Reno or St. Louis to San Diego? St. Louis to San Diego

109. **Fast Food** At the end of 2010, Subway had 33,749 restaurants worldwide, and McDonald's had 32,737 restaurants worldwide. (*Source:* finance.yahoo.com) Which chain had more restaurants, Subway or McDonald's? Subway

110. **Geography** The land area of Alaska is 570,833 mi^2. What is the land area of Alaska to the nearest thousand square miles? 571,000 mi^2

111. **Geography** The acreage of the Appalachian Trail is 161,546. What is the acreage of the Appalachian Trail to the nearest ten-thousand acres? 160,000 acres

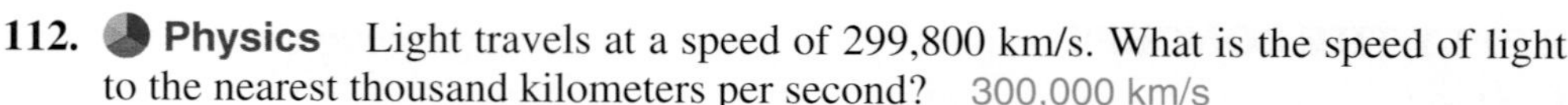

112. **Physics** Light travels at a speed of 299,800 km/s. What is the speed of light to the nearest thousand kilometers per second? 300,000 km/s

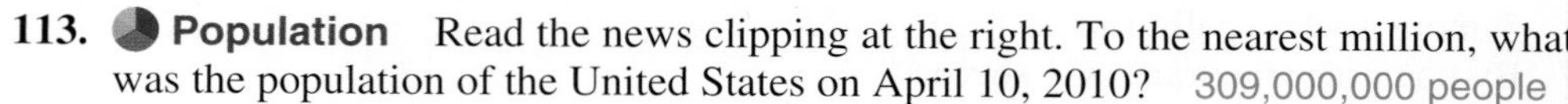

113. **Population** Read the news clipping at the right. To the nearest million, what was the population of the United States on April 10, 2010? 309,000,000 people

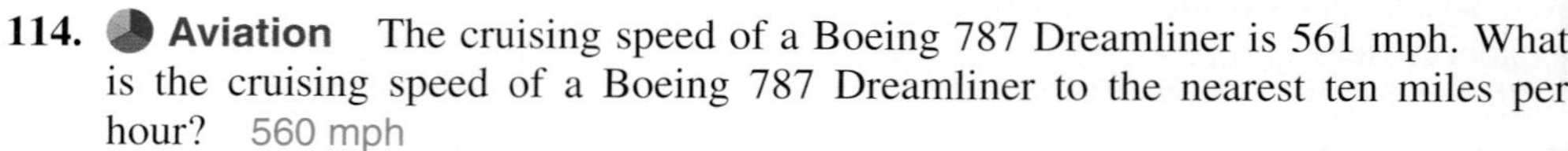

114. **Aviation** The cruising speed of a Boeing 787 Dreamliner is 561 mph. What is the cruising speed of a Boeing 787 Dreamliner to the nearest ten miles per hour? 560 mph

In the NEWS!

2010 Census Data Available

The Census Bureau announced that the nation's population on April 1, 2010, was 308,745,538. Nevada was the state with the fastest-growing population. Michigan is the only state with a smaller population than a decade ago.

Source: news.yahoo.com

Critical Thinking

115. **Mathematics** What is the largest three-digit number? What is the smallest five-digit number? 999; 10,000

116. If 3846 is rounded to the nearest ten and then that number is rounded to the nearest hundred, is the result the same as the result you get when you round 3846 to the nearest hundred? If not, which of the two methods is correct for rounding to the nearest hundred? No. Round 3846 to the nearest hundred.

Projects or Group Activities

117. **Geography** Find the land areas of the seven continents. List the continents in order from largest to smallest. Asia, Africa, North America, South America, Antarctica, Europe, Australia

118. **The House of Representatives** The U.S. House of Representatives has 435 members. The number of representatives that each state sends to the House of Representatives is based on the population of the state. State populations are determined every 10 years by the Census Bureau. Use the Census Bureau's website to determine which states gained a seat and which states lost a seat in the House of Representatives when the 2010 Census Report was completed. Lost: IA, MO, LA, IL, MI, OH, PA, NY, NJ; Gained: WA, NV, UT, AZ, TX, GA, SC, FL

119. What is the total enrollment of your school? To what place value would it be reasonable to round this number? Why? To what place value is the population of your town or city rounded? Why? To what place value is the population of your state rounded? To what place value is the population of the United States rounded?

QUICK QUIZ

1. Place the correct symbol, < or >, between the two numbers.
   6857   8675
   6857 < 8675 [1.1A]
2. Write 27,902 in words.
   twenty-seven thousand nine hundred two [1.1B]
3. Write four million eight thousand fifty-one in standard form.
   4,008,051 [1.1B]
4. Write the number 29,048 in expanded form.
   20,000 + 9000 + 40 + 8 [1.1B]
5. Round 67,524 to the nearest thousand.
   68,000 [1.1C]
6. In 1892, the diesel engine was patented. In 1844, Samuel Morse patented the telegraph. Which was patented first, the diesel engine or the telegraph?
   The telegraph [1.1D]

SECTION

1.2 Addition and Subtraction of Whole Numbers

OBJECTIVE A *To add whole numbers*

Addition is the process of finding the total of two or more numbers.

APPLY THE CONCEPT

Maryka carried 4 soccer balls from her car to the soccer field. She returned to her car and carried 3 more soccer balls to the field. By counting, the total of 4 soccer balls and 3 soccer balls is 7 soccer balls. Maryka carried a total of 7 soccer balls from her car to the soccer field.

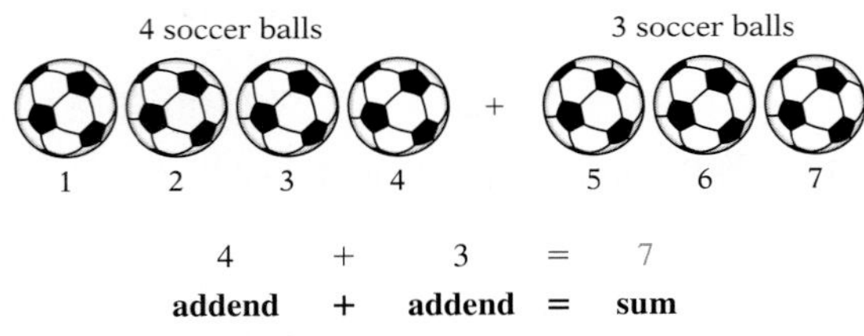

4 + 3 = 7
addend + **addend** = **sum**

The basic addition facts for adding one digit to another digit should be memorized. Addition of larger numbers requires the repeated use of the basic addition facts.

To add large numbers, begin by arranging the numbers vertically, keeping digits of the same place value in the same column.

HOW TO 1 Add: 321 + 6472

Add the digits in each column.

Thousands	Hundreds	Tens	Ones
	3	2	1
+6	4	7	2
6	7	9	3

HOW TO 2 Find the sum of 211, 45, 23, and 410.

Remember that a *sum* is the answer to an addition problem.

Arrange the numbers vertically, keeping digits of the same place value in the same column.

Add the numbers in each column.

$$\begin{array}{r} 211 \\ 45 \\ 23 \\ +\ 410 \\ \hline 689 \end{array}$$

The phrase *the sum of* was used in HOW TO 2 above to indicate the operation of addition. All of the phrases listed below indicate addition. An example is shown to the right of each phrase.

added to	6 added to 9	9 + 6
more than	3 more than 8	8 + 3
the sum of	the sum of 7 and 4	7 + 4
increased by	2 increased by 5	2 + 5
the total of	the total of 1 and 6	1 + 6
plus	8 plus 10	8 + 10

When the sum of the numbers in a column exceeds 9, addition involves "carrying."

HOW TO 3 Add: 359 + 478

Add the ones column.
9 + 8 = 17 (1 ten + 7 ones).
Write the 7 in the ones column and carry the 1 ten to the tens column.

Add the tens column.
1 + 5 + 7 = 13 (1 hundred + 3 tens).
Write the 3 in the tens column and carry the 1 hundred to the hundreds column.

Add the hundreds column.
1 + 3 + 4 = 8 (8 hundreds).
Write the 8 in the hundreds column.

$$\begin{array}{r} \overset{1}{3}\,5\,9 \\ +\ 4\,7\,8 \\ \hline 7 \end{array} \qquad \begin{array}{r} 359 \\ +\ 478 \\ \hline 37 \end{array} \qquad \begin{array}{r} 359 \\ +\ 478 \\ \hline 837 \end{array}$$

(Hundreds, Tens, Ones)

The sum is 837.

Integrating Technology

Most scientific calculators use *algebraic logic:* the add (+), subtract (−), multiply (×), and divide (÷) keys perform the indicated operation using the number in the display and the next number keyed in. For instance, for HOW TO 3 at the right, enter 359 + 478 =. The display reads 837.

© Moviestore collection Ltd/Alamy

APPLY THE CONCEPT

The bar graph in Figure 1.9 shows the gross income from each of four *Pirates of the Caribbean* movies. What is the total gross income from all four movies? *Note:* The jagged line below 200,000,000 on the vertical axis indicates that this scale is missing the numbers less than 200,000,000.

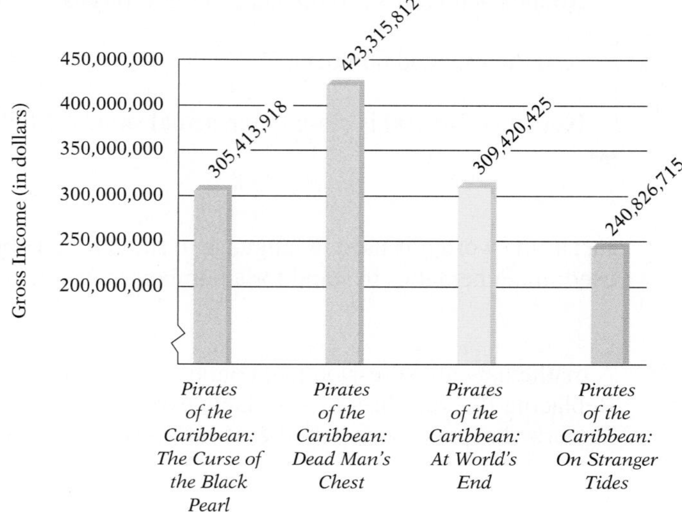

Figure 1.9 Total Gross Income from Four *Pirates of the Caribbean* Movies
Source: www.boxofficemojo.com

Solution

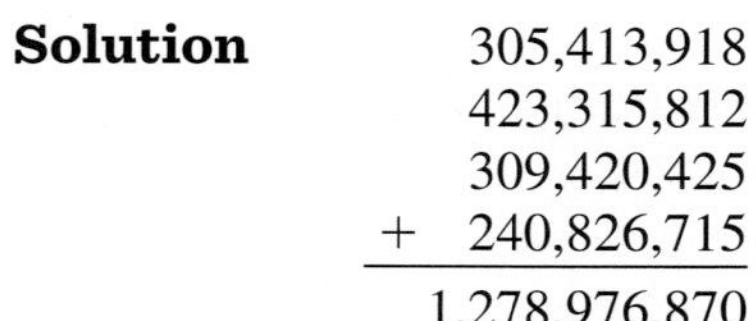

$$\begin{array}{r} 305,413,918 \\ 423,315,812 \\ 309,420,425 \\ +\ 240,826,715 \\ \hline 1,278,976,870 \end{array}$$

The total gross income from all four movies is $1,278,976,870.

An important skill in mathematics is the ability to determine whether an answer to a problem is reasonable. One method of determining whether an answer is reasonable is to use estimation. An **estimate** is an approximation.

Integrating Technology

Here is an example of how estimation is important when using a calculator.

Estimation is especially valuable when using a calculator. Suppose you are adding 1497 and 2568 on a calculator. You enter the number 1497 correctly, but you inadvertently enter 256 instead of 2568 for the second addend. The sum reads 1753. If you quickly make an estimate of the answer, you can determine that the sum 1753 is not reasonable and that an error has been made.

$$\begin{array}{r} 1497 \\ +\ 2568 \\ \hline 4065 \end{array} \qquad \begin{array}{r} 1497 \\ +\ \ 256 \\ \hline 1753 \end{array}$$

To estimate the answer to a calculation, round each number to the highest place value of the number; the first digit of each number will be nonzero and all other digits will be zero. Perform the calculation using the rounded numbers.

$$\begin{array}{rcr} 1497 & \longrightarrow & 1000 \\ 2568 & \longrightarrow & +\ 3000 \\ \cline{3-3} & & 4000 \end{array}$$

As shown above, the sum 4000 is an estimate of the sum of 1497 and 2568; it is very close to the actual sum, 4065. 4000 is not close to the incorrectly calculated sum, 1753.

HOW TO 4 Estimate the sum of 35,498, 17,264, and 81,093.

Round each number to the nearest ten-thousand.

Add the rounded numbers.

$$\begin{array}{rcr} 35{,}498 & \longrightarrow & 40{,}000 \\ 17{,}264 & \longrightarrow & 20{,}000 \\ 81{,}093 & \longrightarrow & +\ 80{,}000 \\ \cline{3-3} & & 140{,}000 \end{array}$$

Note that 140,000 is close to the actual sum, 133,855.

Just as the word *it* is used in language to stand for an object, a letter of the alphabet can be used in mathematics to stand for a number. Such a letter is called a **variable.**

A mathematical expression that contains one or more variables is a **variable expression.** Replacing the variables in a variable expression with numbers and then simplifying the numerical expression is called **evaluating the variable expression.**

HOW TO 5 Evaluate $a + b$ for $a = 678$ and $b = 294$.

Replace a with 678 and b with 294.

$$a + b$$
$$678 + 294$$

Arrange the numbers vertically.

Add.

$$\begin{array}{r} {\scriptstyle 1\,1}\ \ \\ 678 \\ +\ 294 \\ \hline 972 \end{array}$$

Variables are often used in algebra to describe mathematical relationships. Variables are used below to describe three properties, or rules, of addition. An example of each property is shown.

The Addition Property of Zero

$a + 0 = a$ and $0 + a = a$
The sum of a number and zero is the number.

EXAMPLE

$5 + 0 = 5$ and $0 + 5 = 5$

The variable a is used here to represent any whole number. It can even represent the number 0 because $0 + 0 = 0$.

The Commutative Property of Addition

$a + b = b + a$
Two numbers can be added in either order; the sum is the same.

EXAMPLE

$5 + 7 = 12$ and $7 + 5 = 12$

Here the variables a and b represent any whole numbers. Therefore, if you know that the sum of 5 and 7 is 12, then you also know that the sum of 7 and 5 is 12, because $5 + 7 = 7 + 5$.

The Associative Property of Addition

$(a + b) + c = a + (b + c)$
When adding three or more numbers, the numbers can be grouped in any order; the sum will be the same. The parentheses are grouping symbols and have the meaning "Do the operations inside the parentheses first."

EXAMPLE

$2 + (3 + 4) = 2 + 7 = 9$ and $(2 + 3) + 4 = 5 + 4 = 9$

Note in the example that we can add the sum of 3 and 4 to 2, or we can add 4 to the sum of 2 and 3. In either case, the sum of the three numbers is 9.

IN-CLASS EXAMPLES

1. Estimate the sum of 347, 692, and 815. **1800**
2. Identify the property that justifies the statement. $x + 17 = 17 + x$ **The Commutative Property of Addition**
3. See Figure 1.2 on page 7. Find the total amount spent on housing, transportation, and food. **$25,654**
4. Evaluate $a + b + c$ for $a = 9266$, $b = 8904$, and $c = 1795$. **19,965**
5. Which number, 47, 37, 91, or 43, is a solution of the equation $64 = 27 + z$? **37**

HOW TO 6 Rewrite the expression by using the Associative Property of Addition.

$(3 + x) + y$

The Associative Property of Addition states that addends can be grouped in any order.

$(3 + x) + y = 3 + (x + y)$

Point of Interest

The equals sign (=) is generally credited to Robert Recorde. In his 1557 treatise on algebra, *The Whetstone of Witte,* he wrote, "No two things could be more equal (than two parallel lines)." His equals sign gained popular usage, even though continental mathematicians preferred a dash.

An **equation** expresses the equality of two numerical or variable expressions. In the preceding example, $(3 + x) + y$ is an expression; it does not contain an equals sign. $(3 + x) + y = 3 + (x + y)$ is an equation; it contains an equals sign.

Here is another example of an equation. The **left side** of the equation is the variable expression $n + 4$. The **right side** of the equation is the number 9.

$$n + 4 = 9$$

Just as a statement in English can be true or false, an equation may be true or false. The equation shown above is *true* if the variable is replaced by 5.

$n + 4 = 9$
$5 + 4 = 9$ True

The equation is *false* if the variable is replaced by 8.

$8 + 4 = 9$ False

INSTRUCTOR NOTE

Emphasize the difference between an expression and an equation. You might put several examples on the board and ask students to label each. For example:

$3x + 7 = 9$
$3x + 7$
$4 - 6(y + 5)$
$a + b = 8$
$a + b - 8$

Explain to students that determining whether a number is a solution of an equation is a skill that will be used throughout the work on solving equations. It is the method we use to check whether our solution is correct.

A **solution** of an equation is a number that, when substituted for the variable, produces a true equation. The solution of the equation $n + 4 = 9$ is 5 because replacing n by 5 results in a true equation. When 8 is substituted for n, the result is a false equation; therefore, 8 is not a solution of the equation.

10 is a solution of $x + 5 = 15$ because $10 + 5 = 15$ is a true equation.

20 is not a solution of $x + 5 = 15$ because $20 + 5 = 15$ is a false equation.

HOW TO 7 Is 9 a solution of the equation $11 = 2 + x$?

$11 = 2 + x$

Replace x by 9.

$11 \mid 2 + 9$

Simplify the right side of the equation. Compare the results. If the results are equal, the given number is a solution of the equation. If the results are not equal, the given number is not a solution.

$11 = 11$

Yes, 9 is a solution of the equation.

EXAMPLE 1

Estimate the sum of 379, 842, 693, and 518.

Solution

379 ⟶ 400
842 ⟶ 800
693 ⟶ 700
518 ⟶ + 500
2400

YOU TRY IT 1

Estimate the total of 6285, 3972, and 5140.

Your solution

15,000

EXAMPLE 2

Identify the property that justifies the statement.

$7 + 2 = 2 + 7$

Solution

The Commutative Property of Addition

YOU TRY IT 2

Identify the property that justifies the statement.

$33 + 0 = 33$

Your solution

The Addition Property of Zero

Solutions on p. S1

The topic of the circle graph in Figure 1.10 is the eggs produced in the United States in a recent year. The graph shows where the eggs that were produced went or how they were used. Use this graph for Example 3 and You Try It 3.

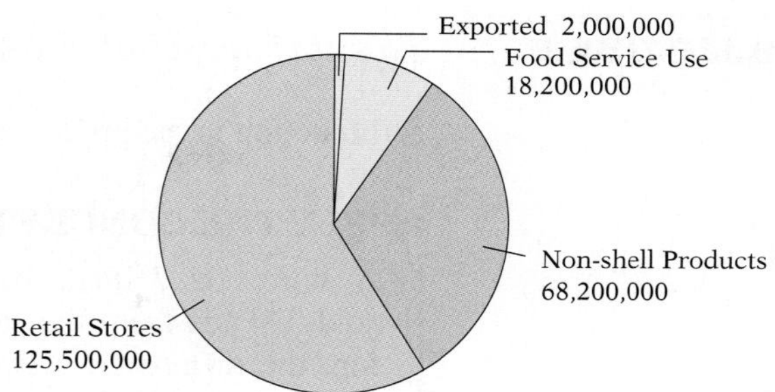

Figure 1.10 Eggs Produced in the United States (in cases)
Source: U.S. Department of Agriculture

EXAMPLE 3

Use Figure 1.10 to determine the sum of the number of cases of eggs sold by retail stores and the number of cases used for non-shell products.

Solution

125,500,000 cases of eggs were sold by retail stores. 68,200,000 cases of eggs were used for non-shell products.

$$\begin{array}{r} 125{,}500{,}000 \\ +\ 68{,}200{,}000 \\ \hline 193{,}700{,}000 \end{array}$$

193,700,000 cases of eggs were sold by retail stores or used for non-shell products.

YOU TRY IT 3

Use Figure 1.10 to determine the total number of cases of eggs produced during the given year.

Your solution

213,900,000 cases of eggs

EXAMPLE 4

Evaluate $x + y + z$ for $x = 8427$, $y = 3659$, and $z = 6281$.

Solution

$x + y + z$

$8427 + 3659 + 6281$

$$\begin{array}{r} {\scriptstyle 1\,1\,1} \\ 8427 \\ 3659 \\ +\ 6281 \\ \hline 18{,}367 \end{array}$$

YOU TRY IT 4

Evaluate $x + y + z$ for $x = 1692$, $y = 4783$, and $z = 5046$.

Your solution

11,521

EXAMPLE 5

Is 6 a solution of the equation $9 + y = 14$?

Solution

$$\begin{array}{c|c} 9 + y = & 14 \\ \hline 9 + 6 & 14 \end{array}$$

$15 \neq 14$ • **The symbol $\neq$ is read "is not equal to."**

No, 6 is not a solution of the equation $9 + y = 14$.

YOU TRY IT 5

Is 7 a solution of the equation $13 = b + 6$?

Your solution

Yes

Solutions on pp. S1–S2

OBJECTIVE B *To subtract whole numbers*

Subtraction is the process of finding the difference between two numbers.

APPLY THE CONCEPT

A store had 7 iPads in stock. Nathan sold 3 iPads from the stock. By counting, the difference between 7 and 3 is 4. There are 4 iPads remaining in stock.

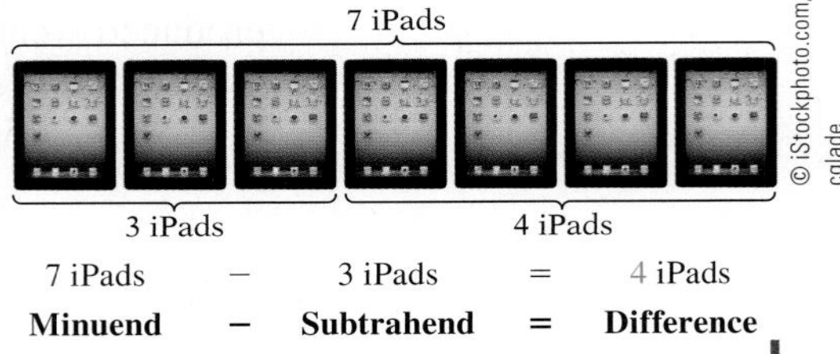

Subtraction can be related to addition as shown at the right. This relationship can be used to check a subtraction.

Subtrahend	3
+ Difference	+ 4
= Minuend	7

To subtract large numbers, begin by arranging the numbers vertically, keeping digits of the same place value in the same column. Then subtract the numbers in each column.

HOW TO 8 Find the difference between 8955 and 2432.

A *difference* is the answer to a subtraction problem.

	Thousands	Hundreds	Tens	Ones
	8	9	5	5
−	2	4	3	2
	6	5	2	3

Check:

Subtrahend	2432
+ Difference	+ 6523
= Minuend	8955

In the subtraction example above, the lower digit in each place value column is smaller than the upper digit. When the lower digit is larger than the upper digit, subtraction involves "borrowing."

HOW TO 9 Subtract: 692 − 378

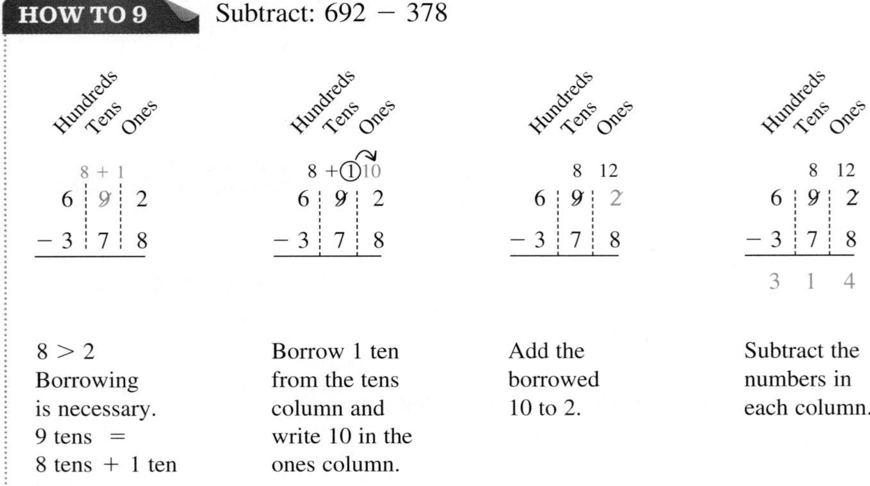

Tips for Success

The HOW TO feature indicates an example with explanatory remarks. Using paper and pencil, you should work through the example. See *AIM for Success* at the front of the book.

Subtraction may involve repeated borrowing.

HOW TO 10 Subtract: 7325 − 4698

Step 1	Step 2	Step 3
7325 − 4698 = ...7	7325 − 4698 = ...27	7325 − 4698 = 2627
Borrow 1 ten (10 ones) from the tens column and add 10 to the 5 in the ones column. Subtract 15 − 8.	Borrow 1 hundred (10 tens) from the hundreds column and add 10 to the 1 in the tens column. Subtract 11 − 9.	Borrow 1 thousand (10 hundreds) from the thousands column and add 10 to the 2 in the hundreds column. Subtract 12 − 6 and 6 − 4.

The difference is 2627.

When there is a zero in the minuend, subtraction involves repeated borrowing.

HOW TO 11 Subtract: 3904 − 1775

Step 1	Step 2	Step 3
3904 − 1775	3904 − 1775	3904 − 1775 = 2129
There is a 0 in the tens column. Borrow 1 hundred (10 tens) from the hundreds column and write 10 in the tens column.	Borrow 1 ten from the tens column and add 10 to the 4 in the ones column.	Subtract the numbers in each column.

Note that, for this example, the borrowing could be performed as shown below.

Borrow 1 from 90. (90 − 1 = 89. The 8 is in the hundreds column. The 9 is in the tens column.) Add 10 to the 4 in the ones column. Then subtract the numbers in each column.

$$\begin{array}{r} 3\,9\,0\,4 \\ -\,1\,7\,7\,5 \\ \hline 2\,1\,2\,9 \end{array}$$

HOW TO 12 Estimate the difference between 49,601 and 35,872.

Round each number to the nearest ten-thousand.

Subtract the rounded numbers.

49,601 → 50,000
35,872 → − 40,000
10,000

Note that 10,000 is close to the actual difference, 13,729.

IN-CLASS EXAMPLES

6. Subtract and check: 35,021 − 9086 **25,935**
7. Estimate the difference between 65,271 and 29,403. **40,000**
8. See Figure 1.2 on page 7. How much more is spent on housing than on food? **$7034**
9. Evaluate $x - y$ for $x = 27{,}003$ and $y = 2905$. **24,098**
10. Which number, 37, 89, 27, or 79, is a solution of the equation $53 = x - 26$? **79**

Take Note
Note the order in which the numbers are subtracted when the phrase *less than* is used. Suppose that you have $10 and I have $6 *less than* you do; then I have $6 *less than* $10, or **$10 − $6 = $4**.

The phrase *the difference between* was used in HOW TO 12 to indicate the operation of subtraction. All of the phrases listed below indicate subtraction. An example is shown to the right of each phrase.

minus	10 minus 3	10 − 3
less	8 less 4	8 − 4
less than	2 less than 9	9 − 2
the difference between	the difference between 6 and 1	6 − 1
decreased by	7 decreased by 5	7 − 5
subtract . . . from	subtract 11 from 20	20 − 11

HOW TO 13 Evaluate $c - d$ for $c = 6183$ and $d = 2759$.

Replace c with 6183 and d with 2759.

$$c - d$$
$$6183 - 2759$$

Arrange the numbers vertically and then subtract.

$$\begin{array}{r} {}^{5\ 11\ 7\ 13} \\ \not{6}\not{1}\not{8}\not{3} \\ -2759 \\ \hline 3424 \end{array}$$

Tips for Success
One of the key instructional features of this text is the Example/You Try It pairs. Each Example is completely worked. You are to solve the You Try It problems. When you are ready, check your solution against the one in the Solutions section. The solution for You Try It 6 below is on page S2 (see the reference at the bottom right of the You Try It). See *AIM for Success* at the front of the book.

HOW TO 14 Is 23 a solution of the equation $41 - n = 17$?

Replace n by 23.
Simplify the left side of the equation.
The results are not equal.

$$\begin{array}{c|c} 41 - n = & 17 \\ \hline 41 - 23 & 17 \\ 18 \neq & 17 \end{array}$$

No, 23 is not a solution of the equation.

EXAMPLE 6

Subtract and check:
57,004 − 26,189

Solution

$$\begin{array}{r} {}^{6\ \ 9\ 9\ 14} \\ 5\not{7},\not{0}\not{0}\not{4} \\ -26,189 \\ \hline 30,815 \end{array}$$

Check:
$$\begin{array}{r} 26,189 \\ +30,815 \\ \hline 57,004 \end{array}$$

YOU TRY IT 6

Subtract and check:
49,002 − 31,865

Your solution

17,137

EXAMPLE 7

Estimate the difference between 7261 and 4315. Then find the exact answer.

Solution

$$\begin{array}{l r} 7261 \longrightarrow & 7000 \\ 4315 \longrightarrow & -\ 4000 \\ \hline & 3000 \end{array} \qquad \begin{array}{r} 7261 \\ -\ 4315 \\ \hline 2946 \end{array}$$

YOU TRY IT 7

Estimate the difference between 8544 and 3621. Then find the exact answer.

Your solution

5000; 4923

Solutions on p. S2

APPLY THE CONCEPT

The graph in Figure 1.11 shows the actual or projected world energy consumption in quadrillion British thermal units (Btu) for selected years. Find the difference between the projected world energy consumption in 2020 and in 2030.

To find the difference, subtract the projected world energy consumption in 2020 from the projected world energy consumption in 2030.

$$\begin{array}{r} 695 \\ -\ 608 \\ \hline 87 \end{array}$$

The difference is 87 quadrillion Btu.

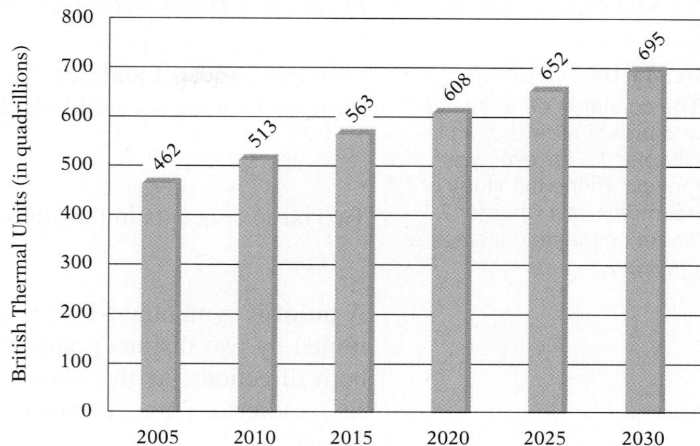

Figure 1.11 World Energy Consumption (in quadrillion Btu)
Source: http://ecopolitology.org

EXAMPLE 8

Use Figure 1.11 to find the difference between the world energy consumption in 2005 and that projected for 2020.

Solution

2020: 608 quadrillion Btu
2005: 462 quadrillion Btu

$$\begin{array}{r} 608 \\ -\ 462 \\ \hline 146 \end{array}$$

The difference is 146 quadrillion Btu.

YOU TRY IT 8

Use Figure 1.11 to find the difference between the world energy consumption projected for 2015 and that projected for 2025.

Your solution

89 quadrillion Btu

EXAMPLE 9

Evaluate $x - y$ for $x = 3506$ and $y = 2477$.

Solution

$x - y$

$3506 - 2477$

$$\begin{array}{r} {\scriptstyle 4\ 9\ 16} \\ 3\,\not{5}\,\not{0}\,\not{6} \\ -\ 2\,4\,7\,7 \\ \hline 1\,0\,2\,9 \end{array}$$

YOU TRY IT 9

Evaluate $x - y$ for $x = 7061$ and $y = 3229$.

Your solution

3832

EXAMPLE 10

Is 39 a solution of the equation $24 = m - 15$?

Solution

$$\begin{array}{l|l} 24 = m - 15 & \\ \hline 24 & 39 - 15 \\ 24 = 24 & \end{array}$$

Yes, 39 is a solution of the equation.

YOU TRY IT 10

Is 11 a solution of the equation $46 = 58 - p$?

Your solution

No

Solutions on p. S2

OBJECTIVE C *To solve application problems and use formulas*

INSTRUCTOR NOTE
The concepts of perimeter and area are developed in Chapter 1. However, you may postpone the study of geometry until Chapter 7, where complete coverage is provided.

One application of addition is calculating the perimeter of a figure. However, before defining perimeter, we will introduce some terms from geometry.

Two basic concepts in the study of geometry are point and line.

A **point** is symbolized by drawing a dot. A **line** is determined by two distinct points and extends indefinitely in both directions, as the arrows on the line shown at the right indicate. This line contains points *A* and *B*.

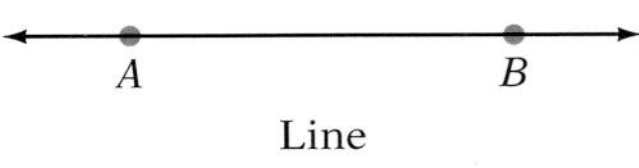

Line

A **ray** starts at a point and extends indefinitely in *one* direction. The point at which a ray starts is called the **endpoint** of the ray. Point *A* is the endpoint of the ray shown at the right.

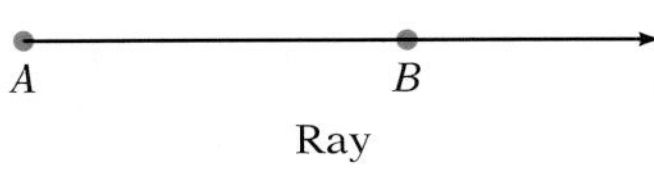

Ray

A **line segment** is part of a line and has two endpoints. The line segment shown at the right has endpoints *A* and *B*.

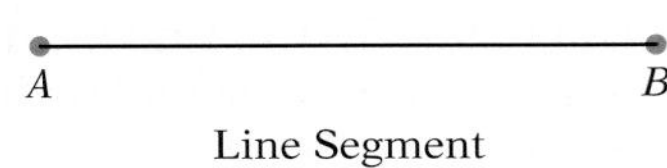

Line Segment

Take Note
The corner of a page of this book is a good model of a right angle.

An **angle** is formed by two rays with the same endpoint. An angle is measured in **degrees.** The symbol for degrees is a small raised circle, °. A **right angle** is an angle whose measure is 90°.

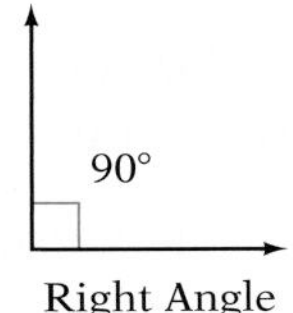

Right Angle

A **plane** is a flat surface and can be pictured as a floor or a wall. Figures that lie in a plane are called **plane figures.**

Lines in a plane can be intersecting or parallel. **Intersecting lines** cross at a point in the plane. **Parallel lines** never meet. The distance between them is always the same.

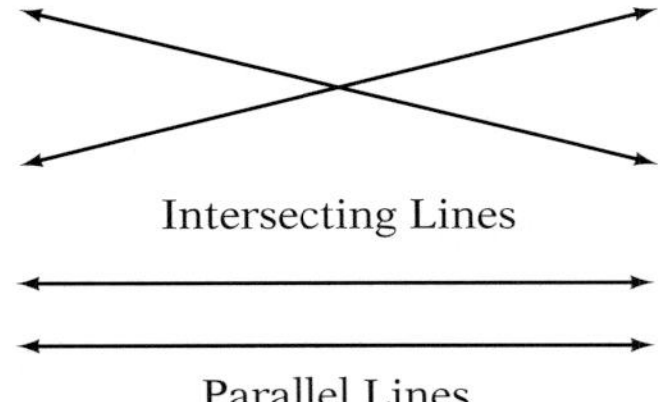

Parallel Lines

A **polygon** is a closed figure determined by three or more line segments that lie in a plane. The line segments that form the polygon are called its **sides**. The figures below are examples of polygons.

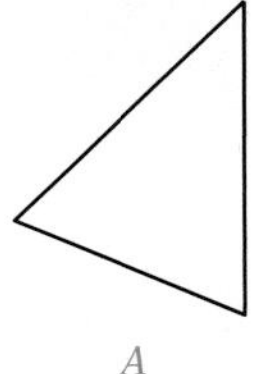
A

B

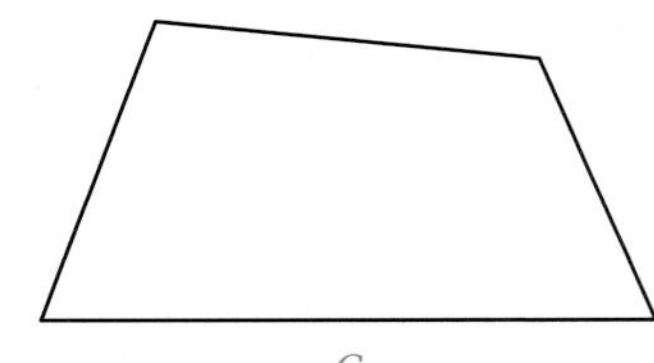
C

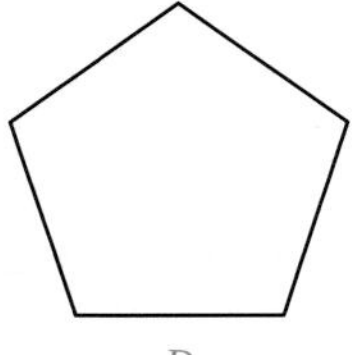
D

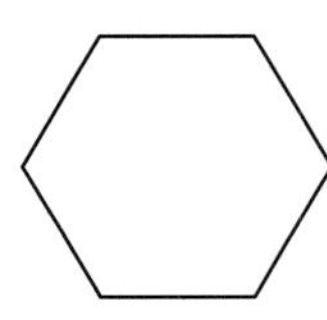
E

The name of a polygon is based on the number of its sides. A polygon with three sides is a **triangle.** Figure A on the preceding page is a triangle. A polygon with four sides is a **quadrilateral.** Figures B and C are quadrilaterals.

Rectangle

Quadrilaterals are one of the most common types of polygons. Quadrilaterals are distinguished by their sides and angles. For example, a **rectangle** is a quadrilateral in which opposite sides are parallel, opposite sides are equal in length, and all four angles measure 90°.

The **perimeter** of a plane geometric figure is a measure of the distance around the figure.

The perimeter of a triangle is the sum of the lengths of the three sides.

Perimeter of a Triangle

The formula for the perimeter of a triangle is $P = a + b + c$, where P is the perimeter of the triangle and a, b, and c are the lengths of the sides of the triangle.

HOW TO 15 Find the perimeter of the triangle shown at the left.

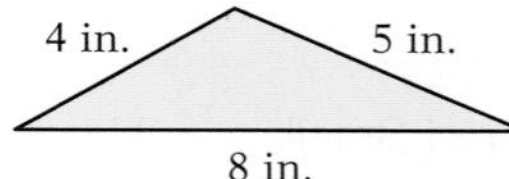

Use the formula for the perimeter of a triangle. $P = a + b + c$

It does not matter which side you label a, b, or c. $P = 4 + 5 + 8$

Add. $P = 17$

The perimeter of the triangle is 17 in.

The perimeter of a quadrilateral is the sum of the lengths of its four sides.

In a rectangle, opposite sides are equal in length. Usually the length, L, of a rectangle refers to the length of one of the longer sides of the rectangle, and the width, W, refers to the length of one of the shorter sides. The perimeter can then be represented as $P = L + W + L + W$.

INSTRUCTOR NOTE
The formula $P = 2L + 2W$ is presented in the next section after multiplication is introduced. Briefly using the formula $P = L + W + L + W$ often gives the student a better understanding of the formula $P = 2L + 2W$.

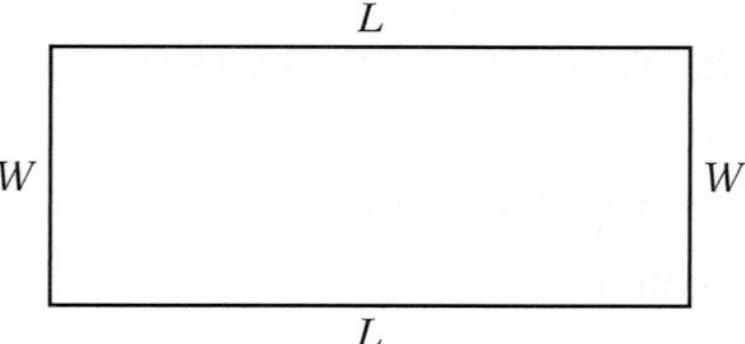

HOW TO 16 Use the formula $P = L + W + L + W$ to find the perimeter of the rectangle shown at the left.

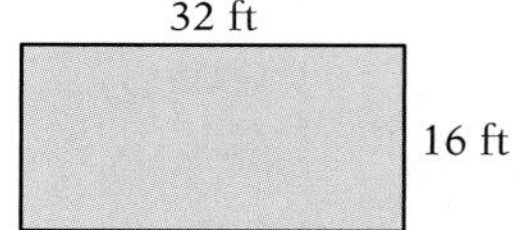

Write the given formula for the perimeter of a rectangle. $P = L + W + L + W$

Substitute 32 for L and 16 for W. $P = 32 + 16 + 32 + 16$

Add. $P = 96$

The perimeter of the rectangle is 96 ft.

IN-CLASS EXAMPLES

11. The Census Bureau estimates that the U.S. population will grow by 296 million from 2000 to 2100. Given that the U.S. population in 2000 was 281 million, find the Census Bureau's estimate for the U.S. population in 2100. **577 million people**
12. You had a credit card balance of $409 before you used the card to purchase books for $168, DVDs for $36, and a pair of shoes for $97. You then made a payment to the credit card company of $350. Find your new credit card balance. **$360**

In this section, some of the phrases used to indicate the operations of addition and subtraction were presented. In solving application problems, you might also look for the types of questions listed below.

Addition	**Subtraction**
How many . . . altogether?	How many more (or fewer) . . . ?
How many . . . in all?	How much is left?
How many . . . and . . . ?	How much larger (or smaller) . . . ?

The table in Figure 1.12 shows the number of taste genes and the number of smell genes in the mosquito, fruit fly, and honey bee. Use this table for Example 11 and You Try It 11.

	Mosquito	*Fruit Fly*	*Honey Bee*
Taste genes	76	68	10
Smell genes	79	62	170

Figure 1.12 Number of Taste Genes and Number of Smell Genes in the Mosquito, Fruit Fly, and Honey Bee

Source: www.sciencedaily.com

Images: mosquito, © iStockphoto.com/Henrik_L; fruit fly, © iStockphoto.com/arlindo71; honey bee, © iStockphoto.com/zeleno

EXAMPLE 11

Use Figure 1.12. How many more smell genes does the honey bee have than the mosquito?

Strategy

To find how many more smell genes the honey bee has than the mosquito:

- Find the number of smell genes in a honey bee.
- Find the number of smell genes in a mosquito.
- Subtract the smaller number from the larger.

Solution

Smell genes in a honey bee: 170

Smell genes in a mosquito: 79

$170 - 79 = 91$

The honey bee has 91 more smell genes than the mosquito.

YOU TRY IT 11

Use Figure 1.12. How many more taste genes does the mosquito have than the fruit fly?

Your strategy

INSTRUCTOR NOTE

You might ask students to determine from Figure 1.12 which of the insects has the best sense of smell (the honey bee) and which has the worst sense of taste (also the honey bee).

Your solution

8 more taste genes

Solution on p. S2

EXAMPLE 12

What is the price of a pair of skates that cost a business \$109 and has a markup of \$49? Use the formula $P = C + M$, where P is the price of a product to the consumer, C is the cost paid by the store for the product, and M is the markup.

Strategy

To find the price, replace C by 109 and M by 49 in the given formula, and solve for P.

Solution

$P = C + M$

$P = 109 + 49$

$P = 158$

The price of the skates is \$158.

YOU TRY IT 12

What is the price of a leather jacket that cost a business \$148 and has a markup of \$74? Use the formula $P = C + M$, where P is the price of a product to the consumer, C is the cost paid by the store for the product, and M is the markup.

Your strategy

Your solution

\$222

EXAMPLE 13

Find the length of decorative molding needed to edge the tops of the walls in a rectangular room that is 12 ft long and 8 ft wide.

Strategy

Draw a diagram.

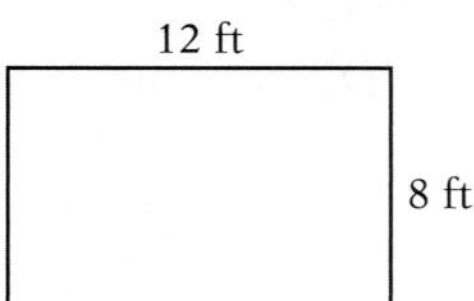

To find the length of molding needed, use the formula for the perimeter of a rectangle, $P = L + W + L + W$. $L = 12$ and $W = 8$.

Solution

$P = L + W + L + W$

$P = 12 + 8 + 12 + 8$

$P = 40$

40 ft of decorative molding are needed.

YOU TRY IT 13

Find the length of fencing needed to surround a rectangular corral that measures 60 ft on each side.

Your strategy

Your solution

240 ft

Solutions on p. S2

1.2 EXERCISES

SUGGESTED ASSIGNMENT
Exercises 1–6; Exercises 7–113, odds; Exercises 117–139, odds;
More challenging exercises: Exercises 144 and 145

Concept Check

1. In the addition problem shown at the right, the addends are the numbers __24__ and __15__. The sum is the number __39__.

$$\begin{array}{r} 24 \\ +\ 15 \\ \hline 39 \end{array}$$

2. In the subtraction problem shown at the right, which number is the difference?
11

$$\begin{array}{r} 97 \\ -\ 86 \\ \hline 11 \end{array}$$

3. To estimate the sum of 5789 + 78,230, begin by rounding 5789 to the nearest __thousand__ and rounding 78,230 to the nearest __ten-thousand__.

4. To check the subtraction problem shown at the right, add the numbers __523__ and __448__. The result should be __971__.

$$\begin{array}{r} 971 \\ -\ 523 \\ \hline 448 \end{array}$$

For Exercises 5 and 6, use the following situation. You purchase a pair of pants for $35, a shirt for $23, and a pair of shoes for $85. State whether you would use addition or subtraction to find the specified amount.

5. To find the amount you spent on all three items, use __addition__.

6. To find how much more the shoes cost than the shirt, use __subtraction__.

OBJECTIVE A *To add whole numbers*

Add.

7. $\begin{array}{r} 732{,}453 \\ +\ 651{,}206 \\ \hline \end{array}$ 1,383,659

8. $\begin{array}{r} 563{,}841 \\ +\ 726{,}053 \\ \hline \end{array}$ 1,289,894

9. $\begin{array}{r} 2879 \\ +\ 3164 \\ \hline \end{array}$ 6043

10. $\begin{array}{r} 9857 \\ +\ 1264 \\ \hline \end{array}$ 11,121

11. $\begin{array}{r} 4037 \\ 3342 \\ +\ 5169 \\ \hline \end{array}$ 12,548

12. $\begin{array}{r} 5242 \\ 7883 \\ +\ 4165 \\ \hline \end{array}$ 17,290

13. $\begin{array}{r} 67{,}390 \\ 42{,}761 \\ +\ 89{,}405 \\ \hline \end{array}$ 199,556

14. $\begin{array}{r} 34{,}801 \\ 97{,}302 \\ +\ 68{,}945 \\ \hline \end{array}$ 201,048

15. $\begin{array}{r} 54{,}097 \\ 33{,}432 \\ 97{,}126 \\ 64{,}508 \\ +\ 78{,}310 \\ \hline \end{array}$ 327,473

16. $\begin{array}{r} 23{,}086 \\ 44{,}697 \\ 67{,}302 \\ 83{,}441 \\ +\ 19{,}843 \\ \hline \end{array}$ 238,369

17. What is 88,123 increased by 80,451?
168,574

18. What is 44,765 more than 82,003?
126,768

19. What is 654 added to 7293?
7947

20. Find the sum of 658, 2709, and 10,935.
14,302

21. Find the total of 216, 8707, and 90,714.
99,637

22. Write the sum of x and y.
$x + y$

23. Education Use the figure at the right to find the total number of undergraduates enrolled at the college in 2015. 1872 students

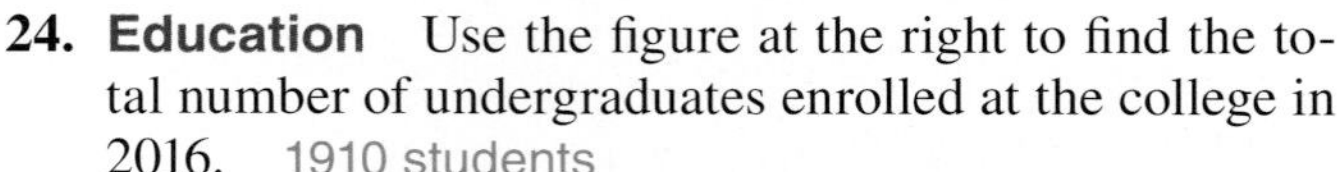

24. Education Use the figure at the right to find the total number of undergraduates enrolled at the college in 2016. 1910 students

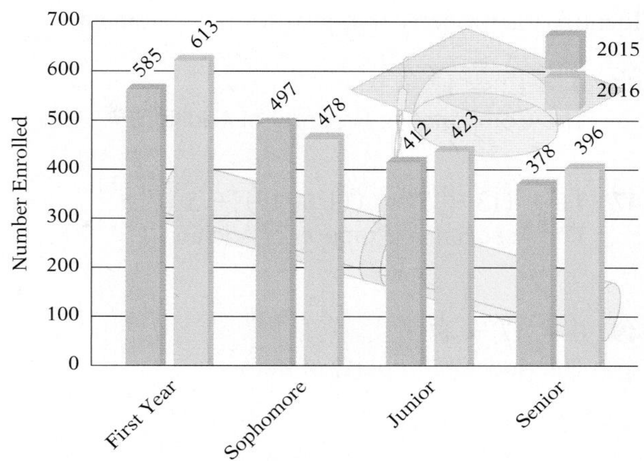

Undergraduates Enrolled in a Private College

Add. Then check by estimating the sum.

25. $6742 + 8298$
15,040; 15,000

26. $5426 + 1732$
7158; 7000

27. $972{,}085 + 416{,}832$
1,388,917; 1,400,000

28. $23{,}774 + 38{,}026$
61,800; 60,000

29.
$$\begin{array}{r} 387 \\ 295 \\ 614 \\ +\ 702 \\ \hline \end{array}$$
1998; 2000

30.
$$\begin{array}{r} 528 \\ 163 \\ 947 \\ +\ 275 \\ \hline \end{array}$$
1913; 1900

31.
$$\begin{array}{r} 224{,}196 \\ 7{,}074 \\ +\ 98{,}531 \\ \hline \end{array}$$
329,801; 307,000

32.
$$\begin{array}{r} 1{,}607 \\ 873{,}925 \\ +\ 28{,}744 \\ \hline \end{array}$$
904,276; 932,000

Evaluate the variable expression $x + y$ for the given values of x and y.

33. $x = 574$; $y = 698$
1272

34. $x = 359$; $y = 884$
1243

35. $x = 4752$; $y = 7398$
12,150

36. $x = 6047$; $y = 9283$
15,330

37. $x = 38{,}229$; $y = 51{,}671$
89,900

38. $x = 74{,}376$; $y = 19{,}528$
93,904

Evaluate the variable expression $a + b + c$ for the given values of a, b, and c.

39. $a = 693$; $b = 508$; $c = 371$
1572

40. $a = 177$; $b = 892$; $c = 405$
1474

41. $a = 4938$; $b = 2615$; $c = 7038$
14,591

42. $a = 6059$; $b = 3774$; $c = 5136$
14,969

43. $a = 12{,}897$; $b = 36{,}075$; $c = 7038$
56,010

44. $a = 52{,}847$; $b = 3774$; $c = 5136$
61,757

Identify the property that justifies the statement.

45. $9 + 12 = 12 + 9$
The Commutative Property of Addition

46. $8 + 0 = 8$
The Addition Property of Zero

47. $11 + (13 + 5) = (11 + 13) + 5$
The Associative Property of Addition

48. $0 + 16 = 16 + 0$
The Commutative Property of Addition

49. $0 + 47 = 47$
The Addition Property of Zero

50. $(7 + 8) + 10 = 7 + (8 + 10)$
The Associative Property of Addition

Use the given property of addition to complete the statement.

51. The Addition Property of Zero
$28 + 0 = ?$
28

52. The Commutative Property of Addition
$16 + ? = 7 + 16$
7

53. The Associative Property of Addition
$9 + (? + 17) = (9 + 4) + 17$
4

54. The Addition Property of Zero
$0 + ? = 51$
51

55. The Commutative Property of Addition
$? + 34 = 34 + 15$
15

56. The Associative Property of Addition
$(6 + 18) + ? = 6 + (18 + 4)$
4

57. Which property of addition allows you to use either expression shown at the right to evaluate $x + y$ for $x = 721$ and $y = 639$?
The Commutative Property of Addition

$$\begin{array}{r} 721 \\ +\,639 \\ \hline \end{array} \qquad \begin{array}{r} 639 \\ +\,721 \\ \hline \end{array}$$

58. Is 38 a solution of the equation $42 = n + 4$?
Yes

59. Is 17 a solution of the equation $m + 6 = 13$?
No

60. Is 13 a solution of the equation $2 + h = 16$?
No

61. Is 41 a solution of the equation $n = 17 + 24$?
Yes

62. Is 30 a solution of the equation $32 = x + 2$?
Yes

63. Is 29 a solution of the equation $38 = 11 + z$?
No

OBJECTIVE B *To subtract whole numbers*

Subtract.

64. $\begin{array}{r} 883 \\ -\,467 \\ \hline \end{array}$
416

65. $\begin{array}{r} 591 \\ -\,238 \\ \hline \end{array}$
353

66. $\begin{array}{r} 360 \\ -\,172 \\ \hline \end{array}$
188

67. $\begin{array}{r} 950 \\ -\,483 \\ \hline \end{array}$
467

68. $\begin{array}{r} 657 \\ -\ 193 \\ \hline \end{array}$
464

69. $\begin{array}{r} 762 \\ -\ 659 \\ \hline \end{array}$
103

70. $\begin{array}{r} 407 \\ -\ 199 \\ \hline \end{array}$
208

71. $\begin{array}{r} 805 \\ -\ 147 \\ \hline \end{array}$
658

72. $\begin{array}{r} 6814 \\ -\ 3257 \\ \hline \end{array}$
3557

73. $\begin{array}{r} 7361 \\ -\ 4575 \\ \hline \end{array}$
2786

74. $\begin{array}{r} 5000 \\ -\ 2164 \\ \hline \end{array}$
2836

75. $\begin{array}{r} 4000 \\ -\ 1873 \\ \hline \end{array}$
2127

76. $\begin{array}{r} 3400 \\ -\ 1963 \\ \hline \end{array}$
1437

77. $\begin{array}{r} 7300 \\ -\ 2562 \\ \hline \end{array}$
4738

78. $\begin{array}{r} 30{,}004 \\ -\ 9856 \\ \hline \end{array}$
20,148

79. $\begin{array}{r} 70{,}003 \\ -\ 8{,}246 \\ \hline \end{array}$
61,757

80. Find the difference between 2536 and 918.
1618

81. What is 1623 minus 287?
1336

82. What is 5426 less than 12,804?
7378

83. Find 14,801 less 3522.
11,279

84. Find 85,423 decreased by 67,875.
17,548

85. Write the difference between x and y.
$x - y$

86. **Geology** Use the figure at the right to find the difference between the maximum height to which Great Fountain erupts and the maximum height to which Valentine erupts. 15 ft

87. **Geology** According to the figure at the right, how much higher is the eruption of the Giant than that of Old Faithful?
25 ft

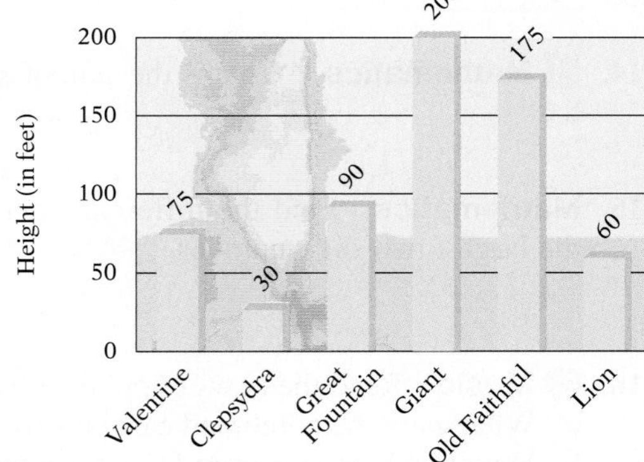

The Maximum Heights of the Eruptions of Six Geysers at Yellowstone National Park

Subtract. Then check by estimating the difference.

88. $7355 - 5219$
2136; 2000

89. $8953 - 2217$
6736; 7000

90. $59{,}126 - 20{,}843$
38,283; 40,000

91. $63{,}051 - 29{,}478$
33,573; 30,000

92. $\begin{array}{r} 36{,}287 \\ -\ 5{,}092 \\ \hline \end{array}$
31,195; 35,000

93. $\begin{array}{r} 58{,}316 \\ -\ 19{,}072 \\ \hline \end{array}$
39,244; 40,000

94. $\begin{array}{r} 224{,}196 \\ -\ 98{,}531 \\ \hline \end{array}$
125,665; 100,000

95. $\begin{array}{r} 873{,}925 \\ -\ 28{,}744 \\ \hline \end{array}$
845,181; 870,000

Evaluate the variable expression $x - y$ for the given values of x and y.

96. $x = 50; y = 37$
13

97. $x = 80; y = 33$
47

98. $x = 914; y = 271$
643

99. $x = 623; y = 197$
426

100. $x = 740; y = 385$
355

101. $x = 870; y = 243$
627

102. $x = 8672; y = 3461$
5211

103. $x = 7814; y = 3512$
4302

104. $x = 1605; y = 839$
766

105. $x = 1406; y = 968$
438

106. $x = 23{,}409; y = 5178$
18,231

107. $x = 56{,}397; y = 8249$
48,148

108. Is 24 a solution of the equation $29 = 53 - y$?
Yes

109. Is 31 a solution of the equation $48 - p = 17$?
Yes

110. Is 44 a solution of the equation $t - 16 = 60$?
No

111. Is 25 a solution of the equation $34 = x - 9$?
No

112. Is 27 a solution of the equation $82 - z = 55$?
Yes

113. Is 28 a solution of the equation $72 = 100 - d$?
Yes

OBJECTIVE C *To solve application problems and use formulas*

114. **Mathematics** What is the sum of all the whole numbers less than 21?
210

115. **Mathematics** Find the difference between the smallest four-digit number and the largest two-digit number. 901

116. **Music** Read the news clipping at the right.
a. What were the combined earnings for U2, AC/DC, and Beyonce?
b. How much greater were U2's earnings than AC/DC's earnings?
a. \$331 million **b.** \$16 million

In the NEWS!

U2 is Number 1

This year the Irish rock band U2 netted \$130 million from their world tour and other deals, making them the world's top-earning musicians. The Australian heavy metal group AC/DC earned \$114 million from their world tour, putting them in second place. Third place honors go to R&B singer Beyonce Knowles, who earned \$87 million this year.

Source: Forbes.com

117. **Nutrition** You eat an apple and one cup of cornflakes with one tablespoon of sugar and one cup of milk for breakfast. Find the total number of calories consumed if one apple contains 80 calories, one cup of cornflakes has 95 calories, one tablespoon of sugar has 45 calories, and one cup of milk has 150 calories. 370 calories

118. **Health** You are on a diet to lose weight and are limited to 1500 calories per day. If your breakfast and lunch contained 950 calories, how many more calories can you consume during the rest of the day? 550 calories

119. **Geometry** A rectangle has a length of 24 m and a width of 15 m. Find the perimeter of the rectangle. 78 m

24 m
15 m

120. Geometry Find the perimeter of a rectangle that has a length of 18 ft and a width of 12 ft. 60 ft

121. Geometry Find the perimeter of a triangle that has sides that measure 16 in., 12 in., and 15 in. 43 in.

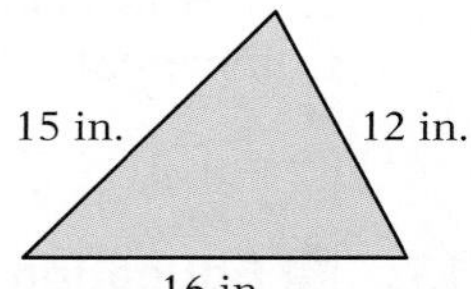

122. Geometry A triangle has sides of lengths 36 cm, 48 cm, and 60 cm. Find the perimeter of the triangle. 144 cm

123. Banking You had $1054 in your checking account before making a deposit of $870. Find the amount in your checking account after you made the deposit. $1924

© Brooks Kraft/Sygma/Corbis

124. Demographics According to the Centers for Disease Control and Prevention, in a recent year there were 138,660 twin births in this country, 5877 triplet births, 345 quadruplet deliveries, and 46 quintuplet and other higher-order multiple births. Find the total number of multiple births during the year. 144,928 multiple births

125. Car Maintenance The repair bill on your car includes $358 for parts, $156 for labor, and a sales tax of $30. What is the total amount owed? $544

126. Geography The area of Lake Superior is 81,000 mi²; the area of Lake Michigan is 67,900 mi²; the area of Lake Huron is 74,000 mi²; the area of Lake Erie is 32,630 mi²; and the area of Lake Ontario is 34,850 mi². Estimate the total area of the five Great Lakes. 280,000 mi²

The Great Lakes

127. Car Mileage The odometer on your car read 58,376 at this time last year. It now reads 77,912. Estimate the number of miles your car has been driven during the past year. 20,000 mi

Business The figure at the right shows the number of cars sold by a dealership for the first four months of 2015 and 2016. Use this graph for Exercises 128 to 130.

128. Between which two months did car sales decrease the most in 2016? What was the amount of decrease? February to March; 19 cars

129. Between which two months did car sales increase the most in 2015? What was the amount of increase? January to February; 24 cars

130. In which year were more cars sold during the four months shown? 2015

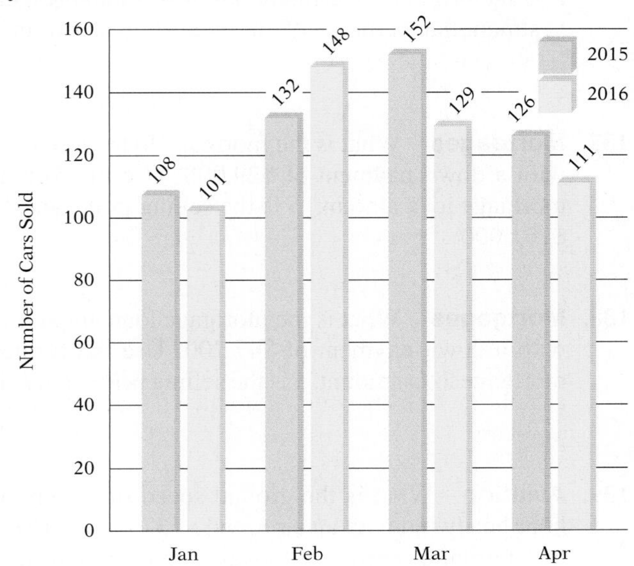

Car Sales at a Dealership

131. **Internet** Thirty-seven million U.S. households do not have broadband Internet access. Seventy-eight million U.S. households do have broadband Internet access. How many households are there in the United States? (*Source:* Department of Commerce) 115 million households

132. **Education** In a recent year, 775,424 women and 573,079 men earned a bachelor's degree. How many more women than men earned a bachelor's degree that year? (*Source:* The National Center for Education Statistics)
202,345 more women

133. **Electric Car Sales** The graph at the right shows the projected sales of electric cars in the United States from 2015 to 2020. Between which two years shown is the number of electric cars sold projected to increase the most? Between 2016 and 2017

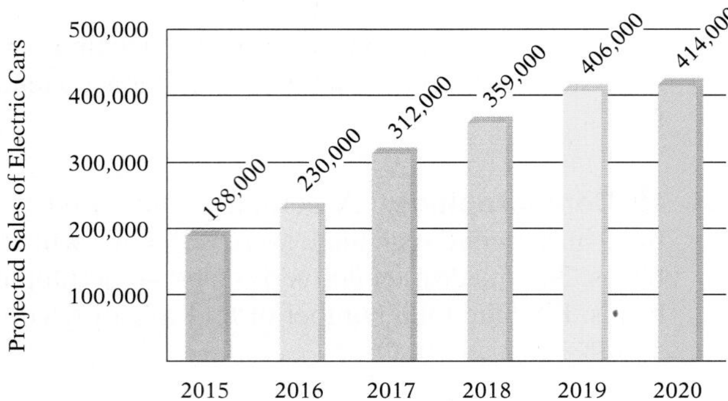

Projected U.S. Electric Car Sales
Source: An Analysis of Battery Electric Vehicle Production Projections by John Shamus Cunningham

134. **Energy** In a recent year, the United States produced 5,633,000 barrels of crude oil per day and imported 9,003,300 barrels of crude oil per day. Find the total number of barrels of crude oil produced and imported per day in the United States that year. (*Source:* Energy Information Administration)
14,636,300 barrels

135. **Investments** Use the formula $A = P + I$, where A is the value of an investment, P is the original investment, and I is the interest earned, to find the value of an investment that earned \$775 in interest on an original investment of \$12,500.
\$13,275

136. **Investments** Use the formula $A = P + I$, where A is the value of an investment, P is the original investment, and I is the interest earned, to find the value of an investment that earned \$484 in interest on an original investment of \$8800. \$9284

137. **Mortgages** What is the mortgage loan amount on a home that sells for \$290,000 with a down payment of \$29,000? Use the formula $M = S - D$, where M is the mortgage loan amount, S is the selling price, and D is the down payment.
\$261,000

138. **Mortgages** What is the mortgage loan amount on a home that sells for \$236,000 with a down payment of \$47,200? Use the formula $M = S - D$, where M is the mortgage loan amount, S is the selling price, and D is the down payment. \$188,800

139. **Aviation** What is the ground speed of an airplane traveling into a 25-mile-per-hour headwind with an air speed of 375 mph? Use the formula $g = a - h$, where g is the ground speed, a is the air speed, and h is the speed of the headwind.
350 mph

140. Aviation Find the ground speed of an airplane traveling into a 15-mile-per-hour headwind with an air speed of 425 mph. Use the formula $g = a - h$, where g is the ground speed, a is the air speed, and h is the speed of the headwind. 410 mph

Statistics In some states, the speed limit on certain sections of highway is 70 mph. To test drivers' compliance with the speed limit, the highway patrol conducted a one-week study during which it recorded the speeds of motorists on one of these sections of highway. The results are recorded in the table at the right. Use this table for Exercises 141 and 142.

Speed	*Number of Cars*
> 80	1708
76–80	2503
71–75	3651
66–70	3717
61–65	2984
< 61	2870

141. Looking at the data in the table, is it possible to tell how many motorists were driving at 70 mph? Explain your answer. No

142. Are more people driving at or below the posted speed limit, or are more people driving above the posted speed limit? At or below the posted speed limit

143. Two sides of a triangle have lengths of a inches and b inches, where $a < b$. Which expression, $a - b$ or $b - a$, has meaning in this situation? Describe what the expression represents. $b - a$; $b - a$ represents how much longer the side of length b is than the side of length a.

Critical Thinking

144. Dice If you roll two ordinary six-sided dice and add the two numbers that appear on top, how many different sums are possible? 11

145. Mathematics How many two-digit numbers are there? How many three-digit numbers are there? 90; 900

Projects or Group Activities

146. Write down a five-digit number in which all of the digits are different. Now reverse the order of the digits to form a new five-digit number. Subtract the smaller number from the larger one. Add the digits of the difference. If the result is a two-digit number, add the digits again. What is the result? Try this with a four-digit and a six-digit number. Is the result always the same? The result is always 9.

The size, or magnitude, of a number can be represented on the number line by an arrow.

The number 3 can be represented anywhere on the number line by an arrow that is 3 units in length.

To add on the number line, place arrows representing the addends head to tail, with the first arrow starting at zero. The sum is represented by an arrow starting at zero and stopping at the tip of the last arrow.

147. Represent the sum of 2 and 6 using arrows on a number line.

148. Represent the sum of 5 and 4 using arrows on a number line.

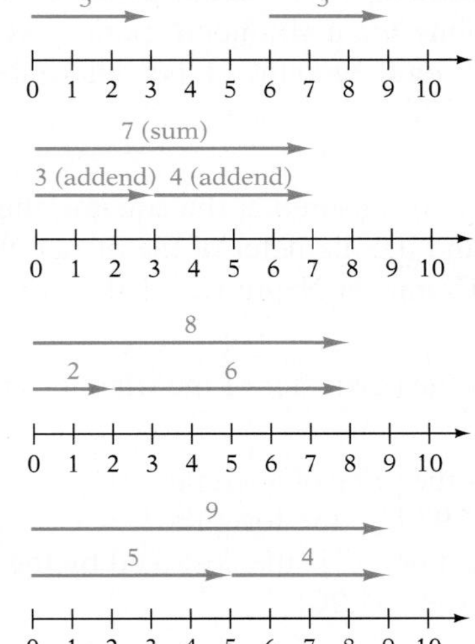

QUICK QUIZ

1. Add: 3976 + 491 + 27,885
   32,352 [1.2A]
2. What is 84 more than 236?
   320 [1.2A]
3. Subtract: 75,068 − 9499
   65,569 [1.2B]
4. Evaluate $c - d$ for $c = 3205$ and $d = 1872$.
   1333 [1.2B]
5. After a trip of 728 mi, the odometer of your car read 65,412 mi. What was the odometer reading at the beginning of your trip?
   64,684 mi [1.2C]
6. You had a balance of $753 in your checking account before making deposits of $158, $269, and $374. What is your new checking account balance?
   $1554 [1.2C]

CHECK YOUR PROGRESS: CHAPTER 1

1. Graph 3 on the number line. [1.1A]

   0 1 2 3 4 5 6 7 8 9 10 11 12 13 14

2. Write the given numbers in order from smallest to largest.
   247, 831, 506, 199, 462
   199, 247, 462, 506, 831 [1.1A]

3. Place the correct symbol, < or >, between the two numbers.
   a. 397 > 246
   b. 898 < 1594 [1.1A]

4. On the number line, what number is 2 units to the left of 5? 3 [1.1A]

5. Write 6702 in words.
   six thousand seven hundred two [1.1B]

6. Write thirty-two thousand five hundred eighteen in standard form. 32,518 [1.1B]

7. Write 903,487 in expanded form.
   900,000 + 3000 + 400 + 80 + 7 [1.1B]

8. Round 15,962 to the nearest hundred.
   16,000 [1.1C]

9. Round 432,987 to the nearest thousand.
   433,000 [1.1C]

10. Add: 38,426 + 109,577 + 24,618
    172,621 [1.2A]

11. Find the total of 528, 764, and 391.
    1683 [1.2A]

12. Estimate the sum of 473, 879, 215, and 306.
    1900 [1.2A]

13. Identify the property that justifies the statement.
    $34 + (81 + 72) = (34 + 81) + 72$
    The Associative Property of Addition [1.2A]

14. Evaluate $x + y + z$ for $x = 16$, $y = 42$, and $z = 39$. 97 [1.2A]

15. Is 42 a solution of the equation $24 = 18 + n$?
    No [1.2A]

16. Subtract: 4600 − 2781
    1819 [1.2B]

17. Find the difference between 13,904 and 8655.
    5249 [1.2B]

18. Estimate the difference between 57,293 and 46,018. 10,000 [1.2B]

19. Evaluate $x - y$ for $x = 704$ and $y = 279$.
    425 [1.2B]

20. Is 61 a solution of the equation $82 = 143 - x$?
    Yes [1.2B]

21. **Bicycles** The Audi Duo is a bicycle with a hardwood frame. It costs between $6530 and $7460. Find the difference between the most expensive and the least expensive Audi Duo. $930 [1.2C]

Courtesy I Am Audi dot com

22. **Charitable Donations** Iris decided to donate some money to charity. Her contributions for a six-month period were $25, $30, $13, $15, $20, and $27. Find the total amount of her charitable contributions for the six months. $130 [1.2C]

23. **Astronomy** As measured at the equator, the diameter of the planet Uranus is 32,200 mi and the diameter of the planet Neptune is 30,800 mi. Which planet is smaller, Uranus or Neptune? Neptune [1.1.C]

24. **Geometry** Find the perimeter of the triangle shown at the right.
    27 m [1.2C]

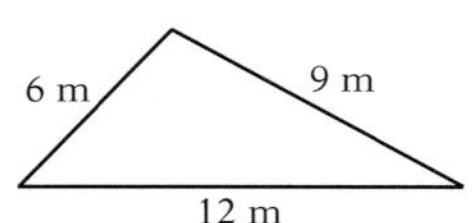

25. **Markup** What is the price of a wireless DJ Dock that cost a business $119 and has a markup of $79? Use the formula $P = C + M$, where P is the price of a product to the consumer, C is the cost paid by the store for the product, and M is the markup. $198 [1.2C]

SECTION

1.3 Multiplication and Division of Whole Numbers

OBJECTIVE A *To multiply whole numbers*

Multiplication is used to find the total number of objects in several groups containing the same number of objects.

APPLY THE CONCEPT

Sebastian purchased 8 six-packs of soda for a party. The total number of cans of soda he purchased can be found by adding 6 eight times. Sebastian purchased 48 cans of soda.

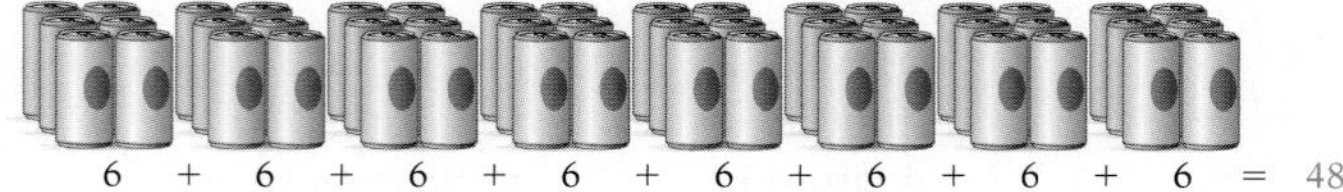

$$6 + 6 + 6 + 6 + 6 + 6 + 6 + 6 = 48$$

The number of cans can also be found by using multiplication.

6	×	8	=	48
factor	×	**factor**	=	**product**

Note that the numbers that are multiplied are called **factors.** The answer is the **product.** In this case, the product is 48, the total number of cans of soda.

Point of Interest

The cross X was first used as a symbol for multiplication in 1631 in a book titled *The Key to Mathematics*. In that same year, another book, *Practice of the Analytical Art,* advocated the use of a dot to indicate multiplication.

The times sign "×" is one symbol that is used to mean multiplication. Each of the expressions below also represents multiplication.

$$6 \cdot 8 \qquad 6(8) \qquad (6)(8) \qquad 6a \qquad 6(a) \qquad ab$$

The expression $6a$ means "6 times a." The expression ab means "a times b."

The basic facts for multiplying one-digit numbers should be memorized. Multiplication of larger numbers requires repeated use of the basic multiplication facts.

HOW TO 1 Multiply: 37(4)

Multiply $4 \cdot 7$.

$4 \cdot 7 = 28$ (2 tens + 8 ones).

Write the 8 in the ones column and carry the 2 to the tens column.

$$\begin{array}{r} {}^{2} \\ 37 \\ \times\ \ 4 \\ \hline 8 \end{array}$$

The 3 in 37 is 3 tens.

Multiply $4 \cdot 3$ tens.
Add the carry digit.
Write the 14.

$$\begin{array}{rr} 4 \cdot 3 \text{ tens} = & 12 \text{ tens} \\ & +\ \ 2 \text{ tens} \\ \hline & 14 \text{ tens} \end{array} \qquad \begin{array}{r} {}^{2} \\ 37 \\ \times\ \ 4 \\ \hline 148 \end{array}$$

The product is 148.

In HOW TO 1, a number was multiplied by a one-digit number. The HOW TO examples that follow illustrate multiplication using larger numbers.

HOW TO 2 Multiply: (47)(23)

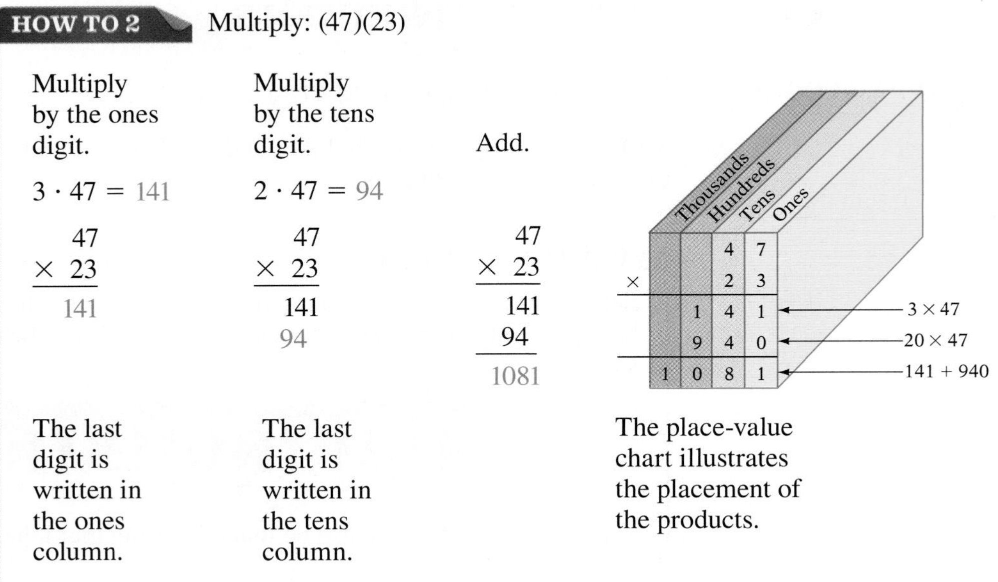

Note the placement of the products when multiplying by a factor that contains a zero.

HOW TO 3 Multiply: 439(206)

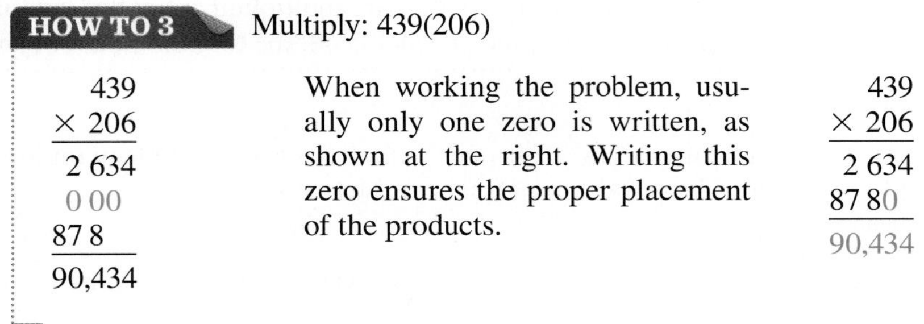

Note the pattern when the following numbers are multiplied.

Multiply the nonzero parts of the factors. Attach the same number of zeros in the product as the total number of zeros in the factors.

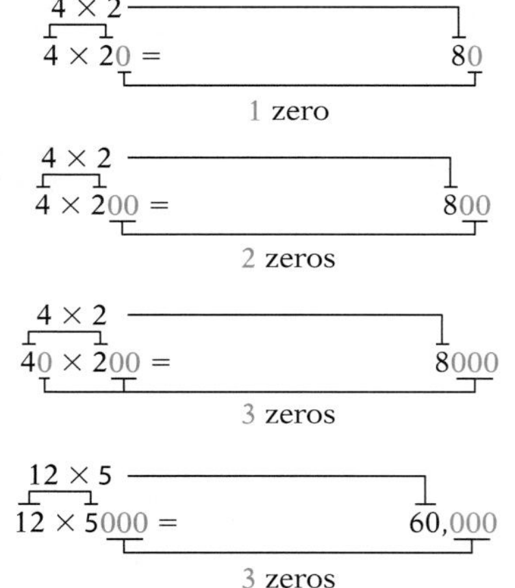

HOW TO 4 Find the product of 600 and 70.

Remember that a *product* is the answer to a multiplication problem.

$600 \cdot 70 = 42{,}000$

HOW TO 5 Multiply: 3(20)(10)(4)

Multiply the first two numbers.	$3(20)(10)4 = 60(10)(4)$
Multiply the product by the third number.	$= (600)(4)$
Continue multiplying until all the numbers have been multiplied.	$= 2400$

APPLY THE CONCEPT

Figure 1.13 shows the average weekly earnings of full-time workers in the United States. Using these figures, calculate the earnings of a female full-time worker, age 27, for working for 4 weeks.

Multiply the number of weeks (4) times the amount earned for one week ($649).

$$4(649) = 2596$$

The average earnings of a 27-year-old, female, full-time worker for working for 4 weeks are $2596.

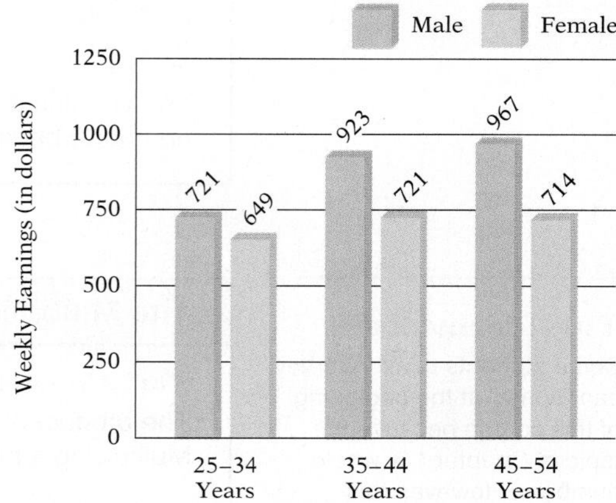

Figure 1.13 Average Weekly Earnings of Full-Time Workers
Source: Bureau of Labor Statistics

HOW TO 6 Estimate the product of 345 and 92.

Round each number to its highest place value.	345 ⟶ 300 92 ⟶ 90
Multiply the rounded numbers.	$300 \cdot 90 = 27{,}000$
27,000 is an estimate of the product of 345 and 92.	

The phrase *the product of* was used in HOW TO 6 to indicate the operation of multiplication. All of the phrases below indicate multiplication. An example is shown to the right of each phrase.

times	8 times 4	$8 \cdot 4$
the product of	the product of 9 and 5	$9 \cdot 5$
multiplied by	7 multiplied by 3	$3 \cdot 7$
twice	twice 6	$2 \cdot 6$

HOW TO 7 Evaluate xyz for $x = 50$, $y = 2$, and $z = 7$.

xyz means $x \cdot y \cdot z$.	xyz
Replace each variable by its value.	$50 \cdot 2 \cdot 7$
Multiply the first two numbers.	$= 100 \cdot 7$
Multiply the product by the next number.	$= 700$

INSTRUCTOR NOTE
For reinforcement, the Addition and Multiplication Properties are presented again in Chapters 3 and 4.

As with addition, there are properties of multiplication.

The Multiplication Property of Zero

$a \cdot 0 = 0$ and $0 \cdot a = 0$
The product of a number and zero is zero.

EXAMPLES
$8 \cdot 0 = 0$
$0 \cdot 4 = 0$

The variable *a* is used here to represent any whole number. It can even represent the number 0 because $0 \cdot 0 = 0$.

Tips for Success
Some students think that they can "coast" at the beginning of this course because the topic of Chapter 1 is whole numbers. However, this chapter lays the foundation for the entire course. Be sure you know and understand all of the concepts presented. For example, study the properties of multiplication presented in this lesson.

The Multiplication Property of One

$a \cdot 1 = a$ and $1 \cdot a = a$
The product of a number and 1 is the number.
Multiplying a number by 1 does not change the number.

EXAMPLES
$1 \cdot 9 = 9$
$7 \cdot 1 = 7$

The Commutative Property of Multiplication

$a \cdot b = b \cdot a$
Two numbers can be multiplied in either order; the product will be the same.

EXAMPLE
$4 \cdot 9 = 36$ and $9 \cdot 4 = 36$

Here the variables *a* and *b* represent any whole numbers. Therefore, for example, if you know that the product of 4 and 9 is 36, then you also know that the product of 9 and 4 is 36, because $4 \cdot 9 = 9 \cdot 4$.

IN-CLASS EXAMPLES
1. See Figure 1.14 on page 45. Determine the average annual savings of individuals in the United States. **$4332**
2. Estimate the product of 5649 and 33. **180,000**
3. Evaluate $2st$ for $s = 45$ and $t = 67$. **6030**
4. What is twice 12,000? **24,000**
5. Complete the statement by using the Multiplication Property of One. $1 \cdot ? = 63$ **63**
6. Which number, 77, 12, 588, or 91, is a solution of the equation $84 = 7y$? **12**

The Associative Property of Multiplication

$(a \cdot b) \cdot c = a \cdot (b \cdot c)$
When multiplying three or more numbers, the numbers can be grouped in any order; the product will be the same.

EXAMPLE
$(2 \cdot 3) \cdot 4 = 6 \cdot 4 = 24$ and $2 \cdot (3 \cdot 4) = 2 \cdot 12 = 24$

Note in the example that we can multiply the product of 2 and 3 by 4, or we can multiply the product of 3 and 4 by 2. In either case, the product of the three numbers is 24.

HOW TO 8 What is the solution of the equation $5x = 5$?

By the Multiplication Property of One, the product of a number and 1 is the number.

The solution is 1.

The check is shown at the right.

$$\begin{array}{r|l} 5x & = 5 \\ \hline 5(1) & 5 \\ 5 & = 5 \end{array}$$

HOW TO 9 Is 7 a solution of the equation $3m = 21$?

$$\begin{array}{r|l} 3m & = 21 \\ \hline 3(7) & 21 \\ 21 & = 21 \end{array}$$

Replace m by 7.

Simplify the left side of the equation.

The results are equal. Yes, 7 is a solution of the equation.

Figure 1.14 shows the average monthly savings of individuals in seven different countries. Use this graph for Example 1 and You Try It 1.

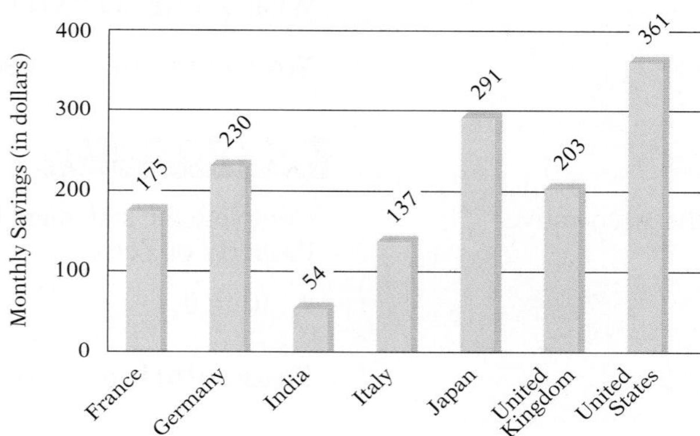

Figure 1.14 Average Monthly Savings
Source: Taylor Nelson - Sofres for American Express

EXAMPLE 1

Use Figure 1.14 to determine the average annual savings of individuals in Japan.

Solution

The average monthly savings in Japan is \$291. The number of months in one year is 12.

$$\begin{array}{r} 291 \\ \times \quad 12 \\ \hline 582 \\ 291 \\ \hline 3492 \end{array}$$

The average annual savings of individuals in Japan is \$3492.

YOU TRY IT 1

According to Figure 1.14, what is the average annual savings of individuals in France?

Your solution

\$2100

Solution on p. S2

EXAMPLE 2

Estimate the product of 2871 and 49.

Solution

2871 ⟶ 3000
49 ⟶ 50
$3000 \cdot 50 = 150{,}000$

YOU TRY IT 2

Estimate the product of 8704 and 93.

Your solution

810,000

EXAMPLE 3

Evaluate $3ab$ for $a = 10$ and $b = 40$.

Solution

$3ab$
$3(10)(40) = 30(40)$
$= 1200$

YOU TRY IT 3

Evaluate $5xy$ for $x = 20$ and $y = 60$.

Your solution

6000

EXAMPLE 4

What is 800 times 300?

Solution $800 \cdot 300 = 240{,}000$

YOU TRY IT 4

What is 90 multiplied by 7000?

Your solution 630,000

EXAMPLE 5

Complete the statement by using the Associative Property of Multiplication.

$(7 \cdot 8) \cdot 5 = 7 \cdot (? \cdot 5)$

Solution $(7 \cdot 8) \cdot 5 = 7 \cdot (8 \cdot 5)$

YOU TRY IT 5

Complete the statement by using the Multiplication Property of Zero.

$? \cdot 10 = 0$

Your solution 0

EXAMPLE 6

Is 9 a solution of the equation $82 = 9q$?

Solution

$82 = 9q$
$82 \mid 9(9)$
$82 \neq 81$
No, 9 is not a solution of the equation.

YOU TRY IT 6

Is 11 a solution of the equation $7a = 77$?

Your solution

Yes

Solutions on pp. S2–S3

OBJECTIVE B *To simplify expressions that contain exponents*

Repeated multiplication of the same factor can be written in two ways:

$4 \cdot 4 \cdot 4 \cdot 4 \cdot 4$ or 4^5 ⟵ **exponent**
↑ **base**

The expression 4^5 is in **exponential form.** The **exponent,** 5, indicates how many times the **base,** 4, occurs as a factor in the multiplication.

Point of Interest

One billion is too large a number for most of us to comprehend. If a computer were to start counting from 1 to 1 billion, writing to the screen one number every second of every day, it would take over 31 years for the computer to complete the task.

And if a billion is a large number, consider a googol. A googol is 1 with 100 zeros after it, or 10^{100}. Edward Kasner is the mathematician credited with thinking up this number, and his nine-year-old nephew is said to have thought up the name. The two then coined the word googolplex, which is 10^{googol}.

It is important to be able to read numbers written in exponential form.

$2 = 2^1$	Read "two to the first power" or just "two." Usually the 1 is not written.
$2 \cdot 2 = 2^2$	Read "two squared" or "two to the second power."
$2 \cdot 2 \cdot 2 = 2^3$	Read "two cubed" or "two to the third power."
$2 \cdot 2 \cdot 2 \cdot 2 = 2^4$	Read "two to the fourth power."
$2 \cdot 2 \cdot 2 \cdot 2 \cdot 2 = 2^5$	Read "two to the fifth power."

Variable expressions can contain exponents.

$x^1 = x$	x to the first power is usually written simply as x.
$x^2 = x \cdot x$	x^2 means x times x.
$x^3 = x \cdot x \cdot x$	x^3 means x occurs as a factor 3 times.
$x^4 = x \cdot x \cdot x \cdot x$	x^4 means x occurs as a factor 4 times.

Each place value in the place-value chart can be expressed as a power of 10.

Ten =	10	= 10	$= 10^1$
Hundred =	100	$= 10 \cdot 10$	$= 10^2$
Thousand =	1000	$= 10 \cdot 10 \cdot 10$	$= 10^3$
Ten-thousand =	10,000	$= 10 \cdot 10 \cdot 10 \cdot 10$	$= 10^4$
Hundred-thousand =	100,000	$= 10 \cdot 10 \cdot 10 \cdot 10 \cdot 10$	$= 10^5$
Million =	1,000,000	$= 10 \cdot 10 \cdot 10 \cdot 10 \cdot 10 \cdot 10$	$= 10^6$

Note that the exponent on 10 when the number is written in exponential form is the same as the number of zeros when the number is written in standard form. For example, $10^5 = 100{,}000$; the exponent on 10 is 5, and the number 100,000 has 5 zeros.

To evaluate a numerical expression containing exponents, write each factor as many times as indicated by the exponent, and then multiply.

$$5^3 = 5 \cdot 5 \cdot 5 = 25 \cdot 5 = 125$$

$$2^3 \cdot 6^2 = (2 \cdot 2 \cdot 2) \cdot (6 \cdot 6) = 8 \cdot 36 = 288$$

IN-CLASS EXAMPLES

7. Write $a \cdot a \cdot a \cdot a \cdot b \cdot b \cdot b \cdot b \cdot b$ in exponential form.
   a^4b^5
8. Evaluate 7^3.
   343
9. Evaluate 10^{11}.
   100,000,000,000
10. Evaluate $3^3 \cdot 2^4$.
   432
11. Evaluate x^3y^4 for $x = 2$ and $y = 3$.
   648

HOW TO 10 Evaluate the variable expression c^3 for $c = 4$.

Replace c with 4 and then evaluate the exponential expression.

$$c^3 = c \cdot c \cdot c$$
$$4^3 = 4 \cdot 4 \cdot 4$$
$$= 16 \cdot 4 = 64$$

Integrating Technology

A calculator can be used to evaluate an exponential expression. The y^x key (or on some calculators an x^y key or a ∧ key) is used to enter the exponent. For instance, for HOW TO 10 at the right, enter 4 y^x 3 =. The display reads 64.

EXAMPLE 7

Write $7 \cdot 7 \cdot 7 \cdot 4 \cdot 4$ in exponential form.

Solution $7 \cdot 7 \cdot 7 \cdot 4 \cdot 4 = 7^3 \cdot 4^2$

YOU TRY IT 7

Write $2 \cdot 2 \cdot 2 \cdot 3 \cdot 3 \cdot 3 \cdot 3$ in exponential form.

Your solution $2^3 \cdot 3^4$

Solution on p. S3

EXAMPLE 8

Evaluate 8^3.

Solution $8^3 = 8 \cdot 8 \cdot 8 = 64 \cdot 8 = 512$

YOU TRY IT 8

Evaluate 6^4.

Your solution 1296

EXAMPLE 9

Evaluate 10^7.

Solution $10^7 = 10{,}000{,}000$

(The exponent on 10 is 7. There are 7 zeros in 10,000,000.)

YOU TRY IT 9

Evaluate 10^8.

Your solution

100,000,000

EXAMPLE 10

Evaluate x^2y^3 for $x = 4$ and $y = 2$.

Solution x^2y^3 (x^2y^3 means x^2 times y^3.)

$$
\begin{aligned}
4^2 \cdot 2^3 &= (4 \cdot 4) \cdot (2 \cdot 2 \cdot 2) \\
&= 16 \cdot 8 \\
&= 128
\end{aligned}
$$

YOU TRY IT 10

Evaluate x^4y^2 for $x = 1$ and $y = 3$.

Your solution

9

Solutions on p. S3

OBJECTIVE C *To divide whole numbers*

Division is used to separate objects into equal groups.

Point of Interest

The Chinese divided a day into 100 k'o. A k'o was a unit equal to a little less than 15 min. Sundials were used to measure time during the daylight hours, and by A.D. 500, candles, water clocks, and incense sticks were used to measure time at night.

APPLY THE CONCEPT

Four friends want to share equally in the cost of a $24 birthday present for their friend Bianca. From the diagram below, each friend's share of the cost is $6.

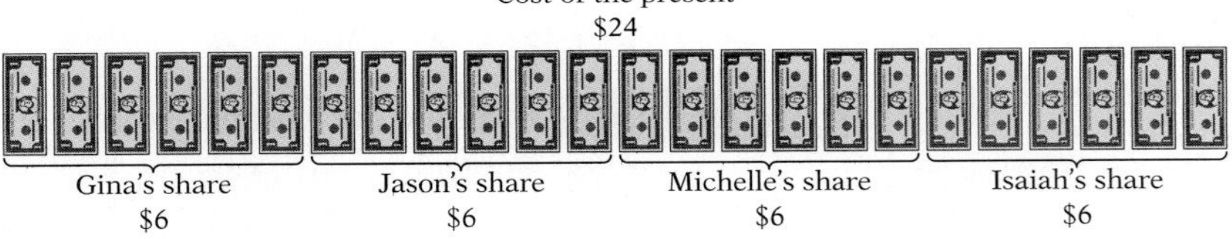

The solution of this division problem is written as follows:

Number of friends **Divisor** → $4\overline{)24}$ with quotient 6

Each friend's share **Quotient** → 6

Cost of the present **Dividend** → 24

Note that the quotient multiplied by the divisor equals the dividend.

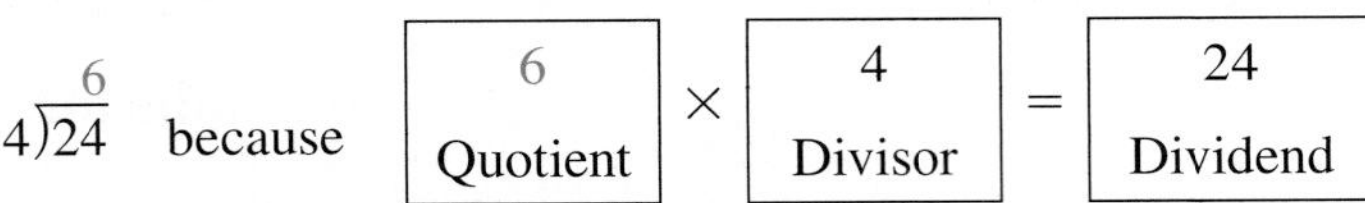

$4\overline{)24}$ with quotient 6 because 6 (Quotient) × 4 (Divisor) = 24 (Dividend)

INSTRUCTOR NOTE
To relate zero in division to a real situation, explain that $6 \div 3 = 2$ means that if \$6 is divided equally among 3 people, each person receives \$2. If \$0 is divided equally among 3 people, each person receives \$0 ($0 \div 3 = 0$). Now, how can \$6 be divided equally among 0 people ($6 \div 0$)?

Integrating Technology
Enter 4 ÷ 0 =. An error message is displayed because division by zero is undefined.

Take Note
Recall that the variable a represents any whole number. Therefore, for the first two properties, we must state that $a \neq 0$ in order to ensure that we are not dividing by zero.

Division is also represented by the symbol ÷ or by a fraction bar. Both are read "divided by."

$$9\overline{)54}\ \text{with quotient } 6 \qquad 54 \div 9 = 6 \qquad \frac{54}{9} = 6$$

The fact that the quotient times the divisor equals the dividend can be used to illustrate properties of division.

$0 \div 4 = 0$ because $0 \cdot 4 = 0$.

$4 \div 4 = 1$ because $1 \cdot 4 = 4$.

$4 \div 1 = 4$ because $4 \cdot 1 = 4$.

$4 \div 0 = ?$ There is no number whose product with 0 is 4 because the product of a number and 0 is 0. $? \cdot 0 = 4$
Division by zero is undefined.

The properties of division are stated below. In these statements, the symbol $\neq$ is read "is not equal to."

Division Properties of Zero and One

If $a \neq 0$, $0 \div a = 0$.	Zero divided by any number other than zero is zero.
If $a \neq 0$, $a \div a = 1$.	Any number other than zero divided by itself is 1.
$a \div 1 = a$	A number divided by 1 is the number.
$a \div 0$ is undefined.	Division by zero is undefined.

EXAMPLES

1. $\frac{0}{7} = 0$ **2.** $\frac{2}{2} = 1$ **3.** $\frac{6}{1} = 6$ **4.** $\frac{5}{0}$ is undefined.

HOW TO 11 illustrates division of a larger whole number by a one-digit number.

HOW TO 11 Divide and check: $3192 \div 4$

```
     7
 4)3192     Think 31 ÷ 4.
  -28       Subtract 7 × 4.
    39      Bring down the 9.

     79
 4)3192
  -28
    39      Think 39 ÷ 4.
   -36      Subtract 9 × 4.
     32     Bring down the 2.

    798
 4)3192
  -28
    39
   -36
     32     Think 32 ÷ 4.
    -32     Subtract 8 × 4.
      0
```

Check:
```
   798
 ×   4
  3192
```

The solution is 798.

The place-value chart is used to show why this method works.

```
   Hundreds
     Tens
       Ones
     7 9 8
  4)3 1 9 2
   −2 8 0 0     7 hundreds × 4
      3 9 2
     −3 6 0     9 tens × 4
        3 2
       −3 2     8 ones × 4
          0
```

Sometimes it is not possible to separate objects into a whole number of equal groups.

APPLY THE CONCEPT

A gardener had 14 plants to put into 3 flats. Each flat holds 4 plants. From the diagram, we see that after the gardener places 4 plants in each flat, there are 2 plants left over. The 2 plants left over are called the **remainder.**

The gardener's division problem could be written

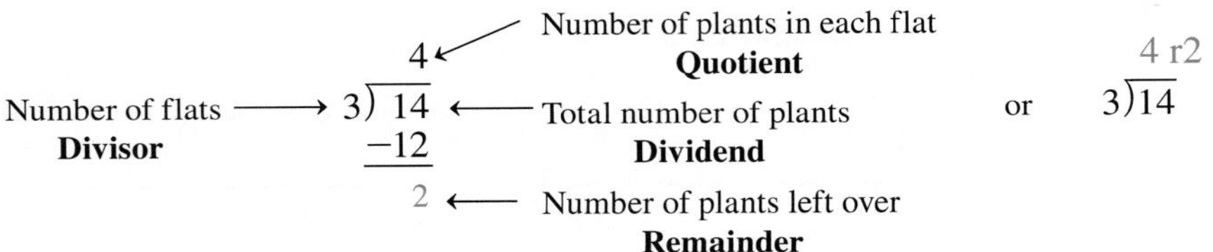

For any division problem, **(quotient · divisor) + remainder = dividend.** This result can be used to check a division problem.

HOW TO 12 Find the quotient of 389 and 24.

```
      16 r5
 24) 389
    −24
     149
    −144
       5
```

Check: $(16 \cdot 24) + 5 = 384 + 5 = 389$

The phrase *the quotient of* was used in HOW TO 12 above to indicate the operation of division. The phrase *divided by* also indicates division.

the quotient of	the quotient of 8 and 4	$8 \div 4$
divided by	9 divided by 3	$9 \div 3$

HOW TO 13 Estimate the result when 56,497 is divided by 28.

Round each number to its highest place value. 56,497 ⟶ 60,000

28 ⟶ 30

Divide the rounded numbers. $60{,}000 \div 30 = 2000$

2000 is an estimate of $56{,}497 \div 28$.

IN-CLASS EXAMPLES

12. Find the quotient of 1519 and 7. **217**

13. See Figure 1.13 on page 43. Find the difference between the average weekly earnings of a male aged 25–34 and those of a female aged 25–34. **$72**

14. Estimate the quotient of 37,052 and 41. **1000**

15. Evaluate $\frac{x}{y}$ for $x = 10{,}890$ and $y = 9$. **1210**

16. Which number, 3, 8, 16, or 48, is a solution of the equation $\frac{z}{12} = 4$? **48**

HOW TO 14 Evaluate $\frac{x}{y}$ for $x = 4284$ and $y = 18$.

$\frac{x}{y}$

Replace x with 4284 and y with 18. $\frac{4284}{18} = 238$

$\frac{4284}{18}$ means $4284 \div 18$.

HOW TO 15 Is 42 a solution of the equation $\frac{x}{6} = 7$?

$\frac{x}{6} = 7$

Replace x by 42. $\frac{42}{6} \,\big|\, 7$

Simplify the left side of the equation. $7 = 7$

The results are equal.

42 is a solution of the equation.

EXAMPLE 11

What is the quotient of 8856 and 42?

Solution

```
      210 r36
42) 8856
   - 84
      45
    - 42
       36   Think 42)36.
     -  0   Subtract 0 · 42.
       36
```

Check: $(210 \cdot 42) + 36$
$= 8820 + 36 = 8856$

YOU TRY IT 11

What is 7694 divided by 24?

Your solution

320 r14

Solution on p. S3

Figure 1.15 shows a household's annual expenses of \$44,000. Use this graph for Example 13 and You Try It 13.

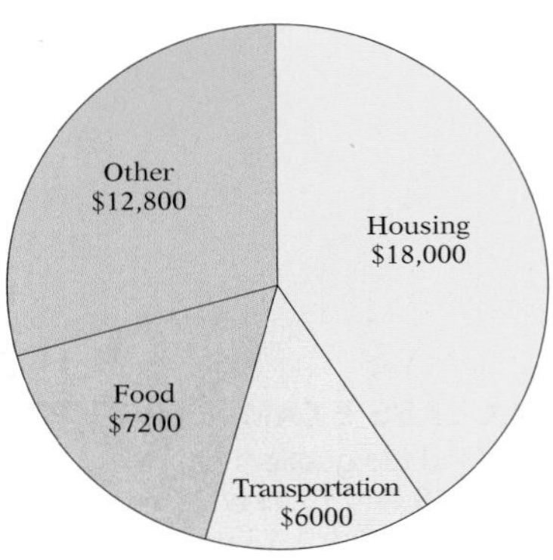

Figure 1.15 Annual Household Expenses

EXAMPLE 12

Use Figure 1.15 to find the household's monthly expense for housing.

Solution

The annual expense for housing is \$18,000.

$18{,}000 \div 12 = 1500$

The monthly expense is \$1500.

YOU TRY IT 12

Use Figure 1.15 to find the household's monthly expense for food.

Your solution

\$600

EXAMPLE 13

Estimate the quotient of 55,272 and 392.

Solution

$55{,}272 \longrightarrow 60{,}000$

$392 \longrightarrow 400$

$60{,}000 \div 400 = 150$

YOU TRY IT 13

Estimate the quotient of 216,936 and 207.

Your solution

1000

EXAMPLE 14

Evaluate $\frac{x}{y}$ for $x = 342$ and $y = 9$.

Solution

$$\frac{x}{y}$$

$$\frac{342}{9} = 38$$

YOU TRY IT 14

Evaluate $\frac{x}{y}$ for $x = 672$ and $y = 8$.

Your solution

84

EXAMPLE 15

Is 28 a solution of the equation $\frac{x}{7} = 4$?

Solution

$$\frac{x}{7} = 4$$

$$\frac{28}{7} \;\Big|\; 4$$

$$4 = 4$$

Yes, 28 is a solution of the equation.

YOU TRY IT 15

Is 12 a solution of the equation $\frac{60}{y} = 2$?

Your solution

No

Solutions on p. S3

OBJECTIVE D *To factor numbers and find the prime factorization of numbers*

Natural number factors of a number divide that number evenly (there is no remainder).

1, 2, 3, and 6 are natural number factors of 6 because they divide 6 evenly.

Note that both the divisor and the quotient are factors of the dividend.

$1\overline{)6}^{\,6}$ $2\overline{)6}^{\,3}$ $3\overline{)6}^{\,2}$ $6\overline{)6}^{\,1}$

To find the factors of a number, try dividing the number by 1, 2, 3, 4, 5, ... Those numbers that divide the number evenly are its factors. Continue this process until the factors start to repeat.

Point of Interest

Twelve is the smallest *abundant number,* or number whose proper divisors add up to more than the number itself. The proper divisors of a number are all of its factors except the number itself. The proper divisors of 12 are 1, 2, 3, 4, and 6, which add up to 16, which is greater than 12. There are 246 abundant numbers between 1 and 1000.

A *perfect number* is one whose proper divisors add up to exactly that number. For example, the proper divisors of 6 are 1, 2, and 3, which add up to 6. There are only three perfect numbers less than 1000: 6, 28, and 496.

HOW TO 16 Find all the factors of 42.

$42 \div 1 = 42$	1 and 42 are factors of 42.
$42 \div 2 = 21$	2 and 21 are factors of 42.
$42 \div 3 = 14$	3 and 14 are factors of 42.
$42 \div 4$	4 will not divide 42 evenly.
$42 \div 5$	5 will not divide 42 evenly.
$42 \div 6 = 7$	6 and 7 are factors of 42.
$42 \div 7 = 6$	7 and 6 are factors of 42.

The factors are repeating.
All the factors of 42 have been found.

The factors of 42 are 1, 2, 3, 6, 7, 14, 21, and 42.

INSTRUCTOR NOTE

Have students find other abundant numbers. Some examples are 18, 20, 24, and 30.

The following rules are helpful in finding the factors of a number.

2 is a factor of a number if the digit in the ones place of the number is 0, 2, 4, 6, or 8.

436 ends in 6.
Therefore, 2 is a factor of 436.
$(436 \div 2 = 218)$

3 is a factor of a number if the sum of the digits of the number is divisible by 3.

The sum of the digits of 489 is $4 + 8 + 9 = 21$.
21 is divisible by 3.
Therefore, 3 is a factor of 489.
$(489 \div 3 = 163)$

4 is a factor of a number if the last two digits of the number are divisible by 4.

556 ends in 56.
56 is divisible by 4 $(56 \div 4 = 14)$.
Therefore, 4 is a factor of 556.
$(556 \div 4 = 139)$

5 is a factor of a number if the ones digit of the number is 0 or 5.

520 ends in 0.
Therefore, 5 is a factor of 520.
$(520 \div 5 = 104)$

A **prime number** is a natural number greater than 1 that has exactly two natural number factors, 1 and the number itself. 7 is prime because its only factors are 1 and 7. If a number is not prime, it is a **composite number.** Because 6 has factors of 2 and 3, 6 is a composite number. The prime numbers less than 50 are

2, 3, 5, 7, 11, 13, 17, 19, 23, 29, 31, 37, 41, 43, 47

INSTRUCTOR NOTE
You may want to explain to the students that it is not necessary to start with the smallest prime factor. As long as we divide by prime factors, we will obtain the correct factorization. Starting with the smallest prime factor just provides a systematic method of attacking the problem.

The **prime factorization** of a number is the expression of the number as a product of its prime factors. To find the prime factors of 90, begin with the smallest prime number as a trial divisor and continue with prime numbers as trial divisors until the final quotient is prime.

HOW TO 17 Find the prime factorization of 90.

$$\begin{array}{r} 45 \\ 2\overline{)90} \end{array} \qquad \begin{array}{r} 15 \\ 3\overline{)45} \\ 2\overline{)90} \end{array} \qquad \begin{array}{r} 5 \\ 3\overline{)15} \\ 3\overline{)45} \\ 2\overline{)90} \end{array}$$

Divide 90 by 2. | 45 is not divisible by 2. Divide 45 by 3. | Divide 15 by 3. 5 is prime.

The prime factorization of 90 is $2 \cdot 3 \cdot 3 \cdot 5$, or $2 \cdot 3^2 \cdot 5$.

Finding the prime factorization of larger numbers can be more difficult. Try each prime number as a trial divisor. Stop when the square of the trial divisor is greater than the number being factored.

IN-CLASS EXAMPLES
17. Find all the factors of 35.
1, 5, 7, 35
18. Find the prime factorization of 150.
$2 \cdot 3 \cdot 5^2$
19. Find the prime factorization of 291.
$3 \cdot 97$

HOW TO 18 Find the prime factorization of 201.

$$\begin{array}{r} 67 \\ 3\overline{)201} \end{array}$$

67 cannot be divided evenly by 2, 3, 5, 7, or 11. Prime numbers greater than 11 need not be tried because $11^2 = 121$ and $121 > 67$.

The prime factorization of 201 is $3 \cdot 67$.

EXAMPLE 16

Find all the factors of 40.

Solution

$40 \div 1 = 40$
$40 \div 2 = 20$
$40 \div 3$ • Does not divide evenly.
$40 \div 4 = 10$
$40 \div 5 = 8$
$40 \div 6$ • Does not divide evenly.
$40 \div 7$ • Does not divide evenly.
$40 \div 8 = 5$ • The factors are repeating.

The factors of 40 are 1, 2, 4, 5, 8, 10, 20, and 40.

YOU TRY IT 16

Find all the factors of 30.

Your solution

1, 2, 3, 5, 6, 10, 15, 30

EXAMPLE 17

Find the prime factorization of 84.

Solution

$$\begin{array}{r} 7 \\ 3\overline{)21} \\ 2\overline{)42} \\ 2\overline{)84} \end{array}$$

$84 = 2 \cdot 2 \cdot 3 \cdot 7 = 2^2 \cdot 3 \cdot 7$

YOU TRY IT 17

Find the prime factorization of 88.

Your solution

$2^3 \cdot 11$

Solutions on p. S3

EXAMPLE 18

Find the prime factorization of 141.

Solution

$3\overline{)141}$ quotient 47

• Try only 2, 3, 5, and 7 because $7^2 = 49$ and $49 > 47$.

$141 = 3 \cdot 47$

YOU TRY IT 18

Find the prime factorization of 295.

Your solution

$5 \cdot 59$

Solution on p. S3

OBJECTIVE E *To solve application problems and use formulas*

INSTRUCTOR NOTE

The Order of Operations Agreement is presented in Section 1.4. Instruct students using the formula $P = 2L + 2W$ to perform the multiplications first, and then the addition.

Take Note

Remember that $2L$ means 2 times L, and $2W$ means 2 times W.

In Section 1.2, we defined perimeter as the distance around a plane figure. The perimeter of a rectangle was given as $P = L + W + L + W$. This formula is commonly written as $P = 2L + 2W$.

Perimeter of a Rectangle

The formula for the perimeter of a rectangle is $P = 2L + 2W$, where P is the perimeter of the rectangle, L is the length, and W is the width.

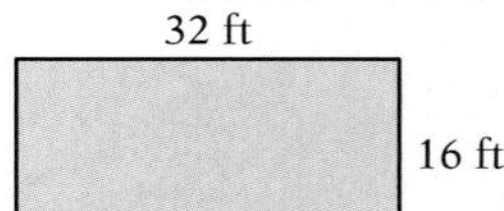

HOW TO 19 Find the perimeter of the rectangle shown at the left.

Use the formula for the perimeter of a rectangle.	$P = 2L + 2W$
Substitute 32 for L and 16 for W.	$P = 2(32) + 2(16)$
Find the product of 2 and 32 and the product of 2 and 16.	$P = 64 + 32$
Add.	$P = 96$

The perimeter of the rectangle is 96 ft.

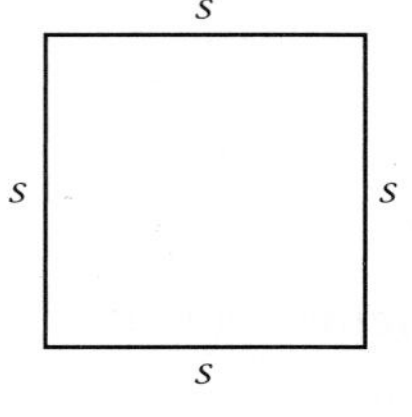

$P = s + s + s + s$

$P = 4s$

A **square** is a rectangle in which each side has the same length. Letting s represent the length of each side of a square, the perimeter of a square can be represented as $P = s + s + s + s$. Note that we are adding *four* s's. We can write the addition as multiplication: $P = 4s$.

Perimeter of a Square

The formula for the perimeter of a square is $P = 4s$, where P is the perimeter and s is the length of a side of the square.

28 km

HOW TO 20 Find the perimeter of the square shown at the left.

Use the formula for the perimeter of a square.	$P = 4s$
Substitute 28 for *s*.	$P = 4(28)$
Multiply.	$P = 112$

The perimeter of the square is 112 km.

1 in^2

1 cm^2

Area is the amount of surface in a region. Area can be used to describe the size of, for example, a skating rink, the floor of a room, or a playground. Area is measured in square units.

A square that measures 1 inch on each side has an area of 1 square inch, which is written 1 in^2. A square that measures 1 centimeter on each side has an area of 1 square centimeter, which is written 1 cm^2.

Larger areas can be measured in square feet (ft^2), square meters (m^2), acres (43,560 ft^2), square miles (mi^2), or any other square unit.

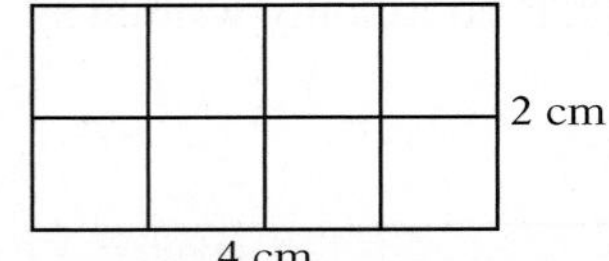

The area of the rectangle is 8 cm^2.

The area of a geometric figure is the number of squares that are necessary to cover the figure. In the figure at the left, a rectangle has been drawn and covered with squares. Eight squares, each of area 1 cm^2, were used to cover the rectangle. The area of the rectangle is 8 cm^2. Note from this figure that the area of a rectangle can be found by multiplying the length of the rectangle by its width.

Area of a Rectangle

The formula for the area of a rectangle is $A = LW$, where A is the area, L is the length, and W is the width of the rectangle.

HOW TO 21 Find the area of the rectangle shown at the left.

Use the formula for the area of a rectangle.	$A = LW$
Substitute 25 for *L* and 10 for *W*.	$A = 25(10)$
Multiply.	$A = 250$

The area of the rectangle is 250 ft^2.

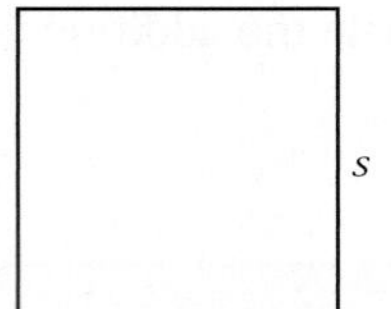

$A = s \cdot s = s^2$

A square is a rectangle in which all sides are the same length. Therefore, both the length and the width of a square can be represented by s, and $A = LW = s \cdot s = s^2$.

Area of a Square

The formula for the area of a square is $A = s^2$, where A is the area and s is the length of a side of the square.

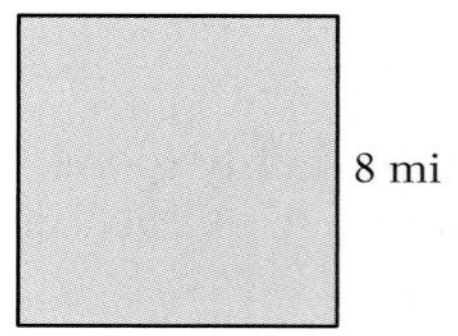

HOW TO 22 Find the area of the square shown at the left.

Use the formula for the area of a square.	$A = s^2$
Substitute 8 for s.	$A = 8^2$
Multiply.	$A = 64$

The area of the square is 64 mi^2.

Integrating Technology

Many scientific calculators have an x^2 key. This key is used to square the displayed number. For example, after pressing 8 x^2 =, the display reads 64.

In this section, some of the phrases used to indicate the operations of multiplication and division were presented. In solving application problems, you might also look for the following types of questions:

Multiplication	Division
per . . . How many altogether?	What is the hourly rate?
each . . . What is the total number of . . . ?	Find the amount per . . .
every . . . Find the total . . .	How many does each . . . ?

Take Note

Each of the following problems indicates multiplication:

"You purchased 6 boxes of doughnuts with 12 doughnuts *per* box. *How many* doughnuts did you purchase *altogether*?"

"If *each* bottle of apple juice contains 32 oz, *what is the total number of* ounces in 8 bottles of the juice?"

"You purchased 5 bags of oranges. *Every* bag contained 10 oranges. *Find the total* number of oranges purchased."

Figure 1.16 shows the cost of a first-class postage stamp from the 1950s to 2012. Use this graph for Example 19 and You Try It 19.

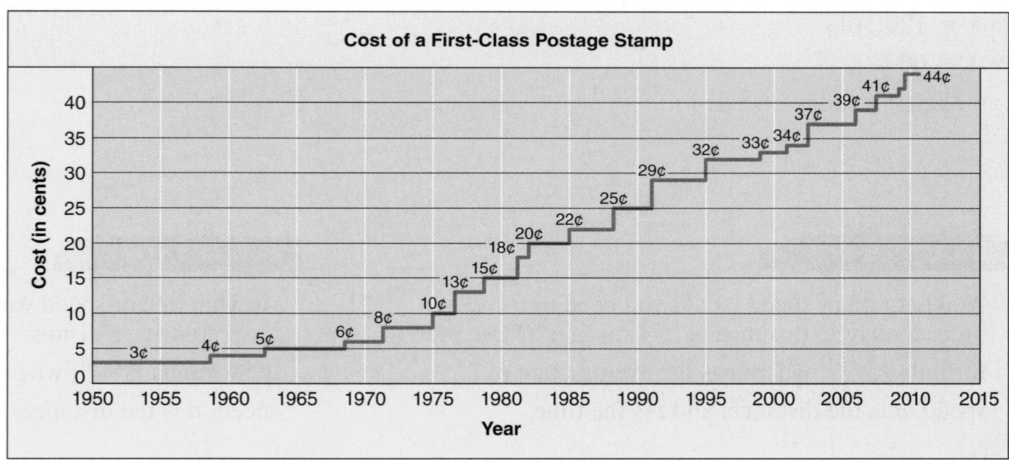

Figure 1.16 Cost of a First-Class Postage Stamp

EXAMPLE 19

How many times more expensive was a stamp in 1980 than in 1950? Use Figure 1.16.

Strategy

To find how many times more expensive a stamp was, divide the cost in 1980 (15) by the cost in 1950 (3).

Solution

$15 \div 3 = 5$

A stamp was 5 times more expensive in 1980.

YOU TRY IT 19

How many times more expensive was a stamp in 1997 than in 1960? Use Figure 1.16.

Your strategy

Your solution

8 times

Solution on p. S3

EXAMPLE 20

Find the amount of sod needed to cover a football field. A football field measures 120 yd by 50 yd.

Strategy

Draw a diagram.

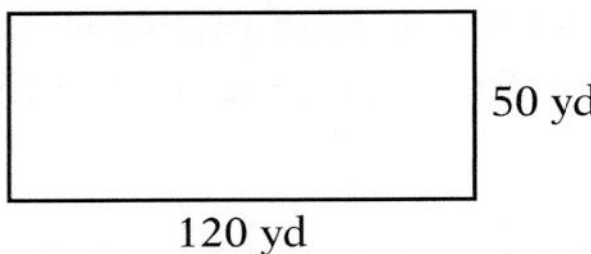

To find the amount of sod needed, use the formula for the area of a rectangle, $A = LW$. $L = 120$ and $W = 50$.

Solution

$A = LW$

$A = 120(50)$

$A = 6000$

6000 ft^2 of sod are needed.

YOU TRY IT 20

A homeowner wants to carpet the family room. The floor is square and measures 6 m on each side. How much carpet should be purchased?

Your strategy

Your solution

36 m^2

IN-CLASS EXAMPLES

20. Find **a.** the perimeter and **b.** the area of a rectangle that has a length of 8 in. and a width of 5 in.
a. 26 in. b. 40 in^2

21. Find the total amount paid on a loan when the monthly payment is $195 and the loan is paid off in 24 months. Use the formula $A = MN$, where A is the total amount paid, M is the monthly payment, and N is the number of payments.
$4680

EXAMPLE 21

At what rate of speed would you need to travel in order to drive a distance of 294 mi in 6 h? Use the formula $r = \frac{d}{t}$, where r is the average rate of speed, d is the distance, and t is the time.

Strategy

To find the rate of speed, replace d by 294 and t by 6 in the given formula, and solve for r.

Solution

$$r = \frac{d}{t}$$

$$r = \frac{294}{6} = 49$$

You would need to travel at a speed of 49 mph.

YOU TRY IT 21

At what rate of speed would you need to travel in order to drive a distance of 486 mi in 9 h? Use the formula $r = \frac{d}{t}$, where r is the average rate of speed, d is the distance, and t is the time.

Your strategy

Your solution

54 mph

Solutions on pp. S3–S4

1.3 EXERCISES

Concept Check

SUGGESTED ASSIGNMENT
Exercises 1–10; Exercises 11–45, every other odd; Exercises 49–173, every other odd; Exercises 175–193, odds; More challenging exercises: Exercises 195–197

1. Explain how to rewrite the addition $6 + 6 + 6 + 6 + 6$ as multiplication.

2. In the multiplication $7 \times 3 = 21$, the product is __21__ and the factors are __7__ and __3__.

3. a. In the exponential expression 3^4, the base is __3__ and the exponent is __4__.
b. To evaluate 3^4, use 3 as a factor four times: __3__ · __3__ · __3__ · __3__ = __81__.

4. State the base and the exponent of the exponential expression.

a. 5 squared
base = __5__, exponent = __2__

b. 4 to the sixth power
base = __4__, exponent = __6__

c. 7 cubed
base = __7__, exponent = __3__

For Exercises 5 and 6, use the division problem $6\overline{)495}$.

5. Express the division problem using the symbol ÷. __495__ ÷ __6__

6. Express the division problem using a fraction. $\frac{495}{6}$

7. Circle the numbers that divide evenly into 15. These numbers are called the __factors__ of 15.

(1) 2 (3) 4 (5) 6 7 8 9 10 11 12 13 14 (15)

8. The only factors of 11 are __1__ and __11__. The number 11 is called a __prime__ number.

For Exercises 9 and 10, state whether you would use multiplication or division to find the specified amount.

9. Three friends want to share equally a restaurant bill of \$37.95. To find how much each person should pay, use __division__.

10. You drove at 60 mph for 4 h. To find the total distance you traveled, use __multiplication__.

OBJECTIVE A *To multiply whole numbers*

Multiply.

11. (9)(127)
1143

12. (4)(623)
2492

13. (6709)(7)
46,963

14. (3608)(5)
18,040

15. $8 \cdot 58{,}769$
470,152

16. $7 \cdot 60{,}047$
420,329

17. $\begin{array}{r} 683 \\ \times\ 71 \\ \hline \end{array}$
48,493

18. $\begin{array}{r} 591 \\ \times\ 92 \\ \hline \end{array}$
54,372

19. $\begin{array}{r} 7053 \\ \times\ \ 46 \\ \hline \end{array}$
324,438

20. $\begin{array}{r} 6704 \\ \times\ \ 58 \\ \hline \end{array}$
388,832

21. $\begin{array}{r} 3285 \\ \times\ 976 \\ \hline \end{array}$
3,206,160

22. $\begin{array}{r} 5327 \\ \times\ 624 \\ \hline \end{array}$
3,324,048

23. Find the product of 500 and 3.
1500

24. Find 30 multiplied by 80.
2400

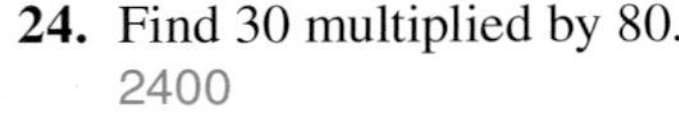

25. What is 40 times 50?
2000

26. What is twice 700?
1400

27. What is the product of 400, 3, 20, and 0?
0

28. Write the product of *f* and *g*.
fg

29. **Aerobic Exercise** The figure at the right shows the number of calories burned on three different exercise machines during 1 h of a light, moderate, or vigorous workout. How many calories would you burn by **a.** working out vigorously on a stair climber for a total of 6 h and **b.** working out moderately on a treadmill for a total of 12 h?
a. 2238 calories **b.** 4236 calories

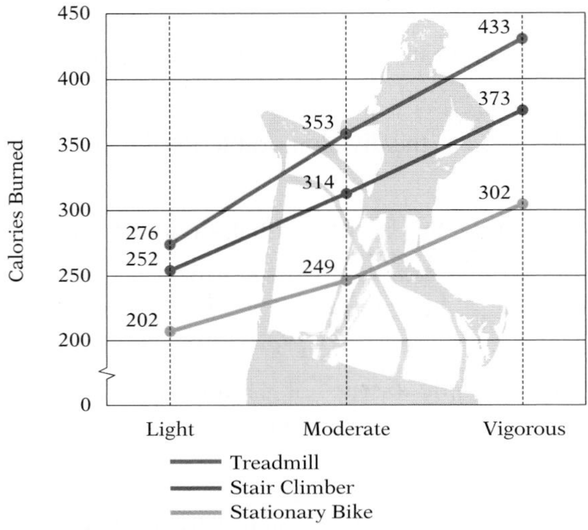

Calories Burned on Exercise Machines
Source: Journal of American Medical Association

Multiply. Then check by estimating the product.

30. $3467 \cdot 359$
1,244,653;
1,200,000

31. $8745(63)$
550,935;
540,000

32. $(39{,}246)(29)$
1,138,134;
1,200,000

33. $64{,}409 \cdot 67$
4,315,403;
4,200,000

34. $745(63)$
46,935;
42,000

35. $432 \cdot 91$
39,312;
36,000

36. $(8941)(726)$
6,491,166;
6,300,000

37. $2837(216)$
612,792;
600,000

Evaluate the expression for the given values of the variables.

38. ab, for $a = 465$ and $b = 32$
14,880

39. cd, for $c = 381$ and $d = 25$
9525

40. $7a$, for $a = 465$
3255

41. $6n$, for $n = 382$
2292

42. xyz, for $x = 5$, $y = 12$, and $z = 30$
1800

43. abc, for $a = 4$, $b = 20$, and $c = 50$
4000

44. $2xy$, for $x = 67$ and $y = 23$
3082

45. $4ab$, for $a = 95$ and $b = 33$
12,540

46. Find a one-digit number and a two-digit number whose product is a number that ends in two zeros. Answers will vary. For example, 5 and 20

47. Find a two-digit number that ends in a zero and a three-digit number that ends in two zeros whose product is a number that ends in four zeros.
Answers will vary. For example, 20 and 500

Identify the property that justifies the statement.

48. $1 \cdot 29 = 29$
The Multiplication Property of One

49. $(10 \cdot 5) \cdot 8 = 10 \cdot (5 \cdot 8)$
The Associative Property of Multiplication

50. $43 \cdot 1 = 1 \cdot 43$
The Commutative Property of Multiplication

51. $0(76) = 0$
The Multiplication Property of Zero

Use the given property of multiplication to complete the statement.

52. The Commutative Property of Multiplication
$19 \cdot ? = 30 \cdot 19$
30

53. The Associative Property of Multiplication
$(? \cdot 6)100 = 5(6 \cdot 100)$
5

54. The Multiplication Property of Zero
$45 \cdot 0 = ?$
0

55. The Multiplication Property of One
$? \cdot 77 = 77$
1

56. Is 6 a solution of the equation $4x = 24$?
Yes

57. Is 0 a solution of the equation $4 = 4n$?
No

58. Is 23 a solution of the equation $96 = 3z$?
No

59. Is 14 a solution of the equation $56 = 4c$?
Yes

60. Is 19 a solution of the equation $2y = 38$?
Yes

61. Is 11 a solution of the equation $44 = 3a$?
No

OBJECTIVE B *To simplify expressions that contain exponents*

Write in exponential form.

62. $2 \cdot 2 \cdot 2 \cdot 7 \cdot 7 \cdot 7 \cdot 7 \cdot 7$
$2^3 \cdot 7^5$

63. $3 \cdot 3 \cdot 3 \cdot 3 \cdot 3 \cdot 3 \cdot 5 \cdot 5 \cdot 5$
$3^6 \cdot 5^3$

64. $2 \cdot 2 \cdot 3 \cdot 3 \cdot 3 \cdot 5 \cdot 5 \cdot 5 \cdot 5$
$2^2 \cdot 3^3 \cdot 5^4$

65. $7 \cdot 7 \cdot 11 \cdot 11 \cdot 11 \cdot 19 \cdot 19 \cdot 19 \cdot 19$
$7^2 \cdot 11^3 \cdot 19^4$

66. $c \cdot c$
c^2

67. $d \cdot d \cdot d$
d^3

68. $x \cdot x \cdot x \cdot y \cdot y \cdot y$
x^3y^3

69. $a \cdot a \cdot b \cdot b \cdot b \cdot b$
a^2b^4

Evaluate.

70. 2^5
32

71. 2^6
64

72. 10^6
1,000,000

73. 10^9
1,000,000,000

74. $2^3 \cdot 5^2$
200

75. $2^4 \cdot 3^2$
144

76. $3^2 \cdot 10^3$
9000

77. $2^4 \cdot 10^2$
1600

78. $0^2 \cdot 6^2$
0

79. $4^3 \cdot 0^3$
0

80. $2^2 \cdot 5 \cdot 3^3$
540

81. $5^2 \cdot 2 \cdot 3^4$
4050

82. Find the square of 12.
144

83. What is the cube of 6?
216

84. Find the cube of 8.
512

85. What is the square of 11?
121

86. Write the fourth power of a.
a^4

87. Write the fifth power of t.
t^5

Evaluate the expression for the given values of the variables.

88. x^3y, for $x = 2$ and $y = 3$
24

89. x^2y, for $x = 3$ and $y = 4$
36

90. ab^6, for $a = 5$ and $b = 2$
320

91. ab^3, for $a = 7$ and $b = 4$
448

92. c^2d^2, for $c = 3$ and $d = 5$
225

93. m^3n^3, for $m = 5$ and $n = 10$
125,000

OBJECTIVE C *To divide whole numbers*

Divide.

94. $9\overline{)2763}$
307

95. $4\overline{)2160}$
540

96. $5\overline{)1549}$
309 r4

97. $8\overline{)1636}$
204 r4

98. $15{,}300 \div 6$
2550

99. $43{,}500 \div 5$
8700

100. $681 \div 32$
21 r9

101. $879 \div 41$
21 r18

102. $9152 \div 62$
147 r38

103. $4161 \div 23$
180 r21

104. $7408 \div 37$
200 r8

105. $5207 \div 26$
200 r7

106. $31{,}546 \div 78$
404 r34

107. $38{,}976 \div 64$
609

108. $7713 \div 476$
16 r97

109. $8947 \div 223$
40 r27

110. Find the quotient of 7256 and 8.
907

111. What is the quotient of 8172 and 9?
908

112. What is 6168 divided by 7?
881 r1

113. Find 4153 divided by 9.
461 r4

114. Write the quotient of c and d.
$\frac{c}{d}$

115. **Insurance** The table at the right shows the sources of laptop computer insurance claims in a recent year. Claims have been rounded to the nearest ten-thousand dollars. **a.** What was the average monthly claim for theft? **b.** For all sources combined, find the average monthly claim.
a. $25,000 **b.** $95,000

Source	Claims (in dollars)
Accidents	560,000
Theft	300,000
Power Surge	80,000
Lightning	50,000
Transit	20,000
Water/flood	20,000
Other	110,000

Source: Safeware, The Insurance Company

Divide. Then check by estimating the quotient.

116. 36,472 ÷ 47
776; 800

117. 62,176 ÷ 58
1072; 1000

118. 389,804 ÷ 76
5129; 5000

119. 637,072 ÷ 29
21,968; 20,000

120. $79\overline{)38{,}984}$
493 r37; 500

121. $53\overline{)11{,}792}$
222 r26; 200

122. $219\overline{)332{,}004}$
1516; 1500

123. $324\overline{)632{,}124}$
1951; 2000

Evaluate the variable expression $\frac{x}{y}$ for the given values of x and y.

124. $x = 48$; $y = 1$
48

125. $x = 56$; $y = 56$
1

126. $x = 79$; $y = 0$
Undefined

127. $x = 0$; $y = 23$
0

128. $x = 39{,}200$; $y = 4$
9800

129. $x = 16{,}200$; $y = 3$
5400

130. Is 9 a solution of the equation $\frac{36}{z} = 4$?
Yes

131. Is 60 a solution of the equation $\frac{n}{12} = 5$?
Yes

132. Is 49 a solution of the equation $56 = \frac{x}{7}$?
No

133. Is 16 a solution of the equation $6 = \frac{48}{y}$?
No

OBJECTIVE D *To factor numbers and find the prime factorization of numbers*

Find all the factors of the number.

134. 10
1, 2, 5, 10

135. 20
1, 2, 4, 5, 10, 20

136. 12
1, 2, 3, 4, 6, 12

137. 9
1, 3, 9

138. 8
1, 2, 4, 8

139. 16
1, 2, 4, 8, 16

140. 13
1, 13

141. 17
1, 17

142. 18
1, 2, 3, 6, 9, 18

143. 24
1, 2, 3, 4, 6, 8, 12, 24

144. 25
1, 5, 25

145. 36
1, 2, 3, 4, 6, 9, 12, 18, 36

146. 56
1, 2, 4, 7, 8, 14, 28, 56

147. 45
1, 3, 5, 9, 15, 45

148. 28
1, 2, 4, 7, 14, 28

149. 32
1, 2, 4, 8, 16, 32

150. 48
1, 2, 3, 4, 6, 8, 12, 16, 24, 48

151. 64
1, 2, 4, 8, 16, 32, 64

152. 54
1, 2, 3, 6, 9, 18, 27, 54

153. 75
1, 3, 5, 15, 25, 75

Find the prime factorization of the number.

154. 16
2^4

155. 24
$2^3 \cdot 3$

156. 12
$2^2 \cdot 3$

157. 27
3^3

158. 15
$3 \cdot 5$

159. 36
$2^2 \cdot 3^2$

160. 40
$2^3 \cdot 5$

161. 50
$2 \cdot 5^2$

162. 37
Prime

163. 83
Prime

164. 65
$5 \cdot 13$

165. 80
$2^4 \cdot 5$

166. 28
$2^2 \cdot 7$

167. 49
7^2

168. 42
$2 \cdot 3 \cdot 7$

169. 81
3^4

170. 51
$3 \cdot 17$

171. 89
Prime

172. 46
$2 \cdot 23$

173. 120
$2^3 \cdot 3 \cdot 5$

OBJECTIVE E *To solve application problems and use formulas*

174. Nutrition One ounce of cheddar cheese contains 115 calories. Find the number of calories in 4 oz of cheddar cheese. 460 calories

Nutrition Facts

Serv. Size 1 oz.
Servings Per Package 12
Calories 115
Fat Cal. 80
*Percent Daily Values (DV) are based on a 2,000 calorie diet

Amount/Serving	% DV*	Amount/Serving	% DV*
Total Fat 9g	14%	**Total Carb.** 1g	0%
Sat Fat 5g	25%	Fiber 0g	0%
Cholest. 30mg	10%	Sugars 0g	
Sodium 170mg	7%	**Protein** 7g	

Vitamin A 6% • Vitamin C 0% • Calcium 20% • Iron 0%

175. Arlington National Cemetery There are approximately 10,200 funerals each year at Arlington National Cemetery. (*Source:* www.arlingtoncemetery.org) Calculate the average number of funerals each day at Arlington National Cemetery. Round to the nearest whole number. 28 funerals

176. Aviation A plane flying from Los Angeles to Boston uses 865 gal of jet fuel each hour. How many gallons of jet fuel are used on a 5-hour flight? 4325 gal

177. Matchmaking Services See the news clipping at the right. **a.** How many marriages occur between eHarmony members each week? **b.** How many marriages occur each year? Use a 365-day year.
a. 3794 marriages **b.** 197,830 marriages

In the NEWS!

Find Your Match Online

eHarmony, the online matchmaking service, boasts marriages among its members at the rate of 542 a day.
Source: www.eharmony.com

178. Geometry Find **a.** the perimeter and **b.** the area of a rectangle with a length of 24 m and a width of 15 m. **a.** 78 m **b.** 360 m^2

179. Geometry Find the length of fencing needed to surround a square corral that measures 55 ft on each side. 220 ft

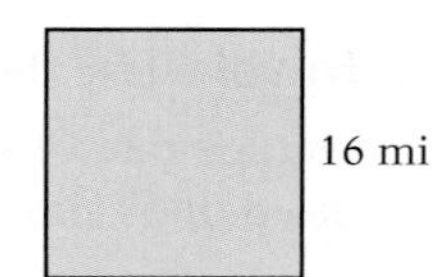

180. Geometry Find **a.** the perimeter and **b.** the area of a square that measures 16 mi on each side. **a.** 64 mi **b.** 256 mi^2

181. Geometry A fieldstone patio is in the shape of a square that measures 9 ft on each side. What is the area of the patio? 81 ft^2

182. Consulting Fees A computer analyst doing consulting work received $8064 for working 168 h on a project. Find the hourly rate the consultant charged. $48/h

183. Business A buyer for a department store purchased 215 suits at $83 each. Estimate the total cost of the order. $16,000

184. U.S. Postal Service Use the information in the news clipping at the right to determine, on average, how many pieces of mail the U.S. Postal Service processed each day this year. Assume there are 300 working days during the year. 570 million pieces of mail

In the NEWS!

Decline in USPS Mail Volume

This year the U.S. Postal Service processed 171 billion pieces of mail. This is a decline of 6 billion pieces from last year.

Source: www.usps.com

185. Salaries Melissa's annual starting salary as a chemical engineer is $69,048. What is her monthly starting salary? $5754

Construction The table at the right shows the hourly wages for four different job classifications at a small construction company. Use this table for Exercises 186 to 188.

Type of Work	Wage per Hour
Electrician	$34
Plumber	$30
Clerk	$16
Bookkeeper	$20

186. The owner of this company wants to provide the electrical installation for a new house. On the basis of the architectural plans, it is estimated that the installation will require three electricians, each working 50 h, to complete the job. What is the estimated cost for the electricians' labor? $5100

187. Carlos Vasquez, a plumbing contractor, hires four plumbers from this company at the hourly wage given in the table. If each plumber works 23 h, what are the total wages paid by Carlos? $2760

188. The owner of this company estimates that a kitchen remodel will require one electrician working 30 h and one plumber working 33 h. This project also requires 3 h of clerical work and 4 h of bookkeeping. What is the total cost for these four components of the remodel? $2138

189. Loans Find the total amount paid on a loan when the monthly payment is $285 and the loan is paid off in 24 months. Use the formula $A = MN$, where A is the total amount paid, M is the monthly payment, and N is the number of payments. $6840

190. Loans Find the total amount paid on a loan when the monthly payment is $187 and the loan is paid off in 36 months. Use the formula $A = MN$, where A is the total amount paid, M is the monthly payment, and N is the number of payments. $6732

191. Travel Use the formula $t = \frac{d}{r}$, where t is the time, d is the distance, and r is the average rate of speed, to find the time it would take to drive 513 mi at an average speed of 57 mph. 9 h

192. Travel Use the formula $t = \frac{d}{r}$, where t is the time, d is the distance, and r is the average rate of speed, to find the time it would take to drive 432 mi at an average speed of 54 mph. 8 h

193. Mutual Funds The current value of the stocks in a mutual fund is $10,500,000. The number of shares outstanding is 500,000. Find the value per share of the fund. Use the formula $V = \frac{C}{S}$, where V is the value per share, C is the current value of the stocks in the fund, and S is the number of shares outstanding. $21

© Lee Torrens/Shutterstock.com

New York Stock Exchange

194. Mutual Funds The current value of the stocks in a mutual fund is $4,500,000. The number of shares outstanding is 250,000. Find the value per share of the fund. Use the formula $V = \frac{C}{S}$, where V is the value per share, C is the current value of the stocks in the fund, and S is the number of shares outstanding. $18

Critical Thinking

195. Mathematics 13,827 is not divisible by 4. By rearranging the digits, find the largest possible number that is divisible by 4. 87,312

196. Mathematics A **palindromic number** is a whole number that remains unchanged when its digits are written in reverse order. For example, 818 is a palindromic number. Find the smallest three-digit multiple of 6 that is a palindromic number. 222

197. Prime Numbers

a. All prime numbers greater than 10 end in one of four digits. What are those digits? 1, 3, 7, 9

b. A number that ends in one of the digits in part (a) is not necessarily a prime number. For each digit in part (a), give an example of a number that ends in that digit but is not a prime number.
Answers will vary. For example, 21, 33, 27, and 39

QUICK QUIZ

1. Multiply: 37×495 **18,315 [1.3A]**
2. Evaluate c^2d^3 for $c = 3$ and $d = 2$. **72 [1.3B]**
3. Find the quotient of 704 and 32. **22 [1.3C]**
4. Find the prme factorization of 140. **$2 \cdot 2 \cdot 5 \cdot 7$ [1.3D]**
5. You have a car payment of $219 each month. What is the total of your car payments over a 12-month period? **$2628 [1.3E]**
6. A management consultant received a check for $2340 for 45 hours of work. What is the consultant's hourly fee? **$52 [1.3E]**

Projects or Group Activities

198. Each letter in the multiplication at the right represents one of the digits 0 through 9. Determine which digit is represented by each letter such that the multiplication is correct. *Note:* A letter that is used more than once represents the same digit in each position in which it appears. $21,978 \times 4 = 87,912$

$$\begin{array}{r} \text{STRAW} \\ \times \quad 4 \\ \hline \text{WARTS} \end{array}$$

199. What is the Sieve of Eratosthenes? Use this method to find all the prime numbers less than 100. 2, 3, 5, 7, 11, 13, 17, 19, 23, 29, 31, 37, 41, 43, 47, 53, 59, 61, 67, 71, 73, 79, 83, 89, and 97

SECTION

1.4 The Order of Operations Agreement

OBJECTIVE A *To use the Order of Operations Agreement to simplify expressions*

More than one operation may occur in a numerical expression. For example, the expression

$$4 + 3(5)$$

includes two arithmetic operations, addition and multiplication. The operations could be performed in different orders.

If we multiply first and then add, we have:	$4 + 3(5)$ $4 + 15$ 19	If we add first and then multiply, we have:	$4 + 3(5)$ $7(5)$ 35

To prevent there being more than one answer to the same problem, an Order of Operations Agreement is followed. By this agreement, 19 is the only correct answer.

Integrating Technology

Many calculators use the Order of Operations Agreement shown at the right.

Enter 4 + 3 × 5 = into your calculator. If the answer is 19, your calculator uses the Order of Operations Agreement.

Integrating Technology

Here is an example of using the parentheses keys on a calculator. To evaluate $28(103 - 78)$, enter:

Note that × is required on most calculators.

The Order of Operations Agreement

Step 1 Do all operations inside parentheses.

Step 2 Simplify any numerical expressions containing exponents.

Step 3 Do multiplication and division as they occur from left to right.

Step 4 Do addition and subtraction as they occur from left to right.

EXAMPLE

Simplify: $5(6 + 4) - 2^3$

$5(6 + 4) - 2^3$

$= 5(10) - 2^3$ • Perform operations inside parentheses.

$= 5(10) - 8$ • Simplify expressions with exponents.

$= 50 - 8$ • Do multiplication and division from left to right.

$= 42$ • Do addition and subtraction from left to right.

One or more of the above steps may not be needed to simplify an expression. In that case, proceed to the next step in the Order of Operations Agreement.

IN-CLASS EXAMPLES

1. Simplify: $4 + 3(8 - 2) - 12$ **10**
2. Simplify: $2^3 + 4(5 - 1) - 3$ **21**
3. Evaluate $2x + (x - y)^3$ for $x = 9$ and $y = 7$. **26**

HOW TO 1 Simplify: $8 + 9 \div 3$

There are no parentheses (Step 1).	$8 + 9 \div 3$
There are no exponents (Step 2).	
Do the division (Step 3).	$= 8 + 3$
Do the addition (Step 4).	$= 11$

Integrating Technology

Many scientific calculators have an x^2 key. This key is used to square the displayed number. For example, after the user presses 2 x^2 =, the display reads 4.

HOW TO 2 Evaluate $5a - (b + c)^2$ for $a = 6$, $b = 1$, and $c = 3$.

	$5a - (b + c)^2$
Replace a with 6, b with 1, and c with 3.	$5(6) - (1 + 3)^2$
Use the Order of Operations Agreement to simplify the resulting numerical expression. Perform operations inside parentheses.	$= 5(6) - (4)^2$
Simplify expressions with exponents.	$= 5(6) - 16$
Do the multiplication.	$= 30 - 16$
Do the subtraction.	$= 14$

EXAMPLE 1

Simplify: $18 \div (6 + 3) \cdot 9 - 4^2$

Solution

$$\begin{aligned} 18 \div (6 + 3) \cdot 9 - 4^2 &= 18 \div 9 \cdot 9 - 4^2 \\ &= 18 \div 9 \cdot 9 - 16 \\ &= 2 \cdot 9 - 16 \\ &= 18 - 16 \\ &= 2 \end{aligned}$$

YOU TRY IT 1

Simplify: $4 \cdot (8 - 3) \div 5 - 2$

Your solution

2

EXAMPLE 2

Simplify: $20 + 24(8 - 5) \div 2^2$

Solution

$$\begin{aligned} 20 + 24(8 - 5) \div 2^2 &= 20 + 24(3) \div 2^2 \\ &= 20 + 24(3) \div 4 \\ &= 20 + 72 \div 4 \\ &= 20 + 18 \\ &= 38 \end{aligned}$$

YOU TRY IT 2

Simplify: $16 + 3(6 - 1)^2 \div 5$

Your solution

31

EXAMPLE 3

Evaluate $(a - b)^2 + 3c$ for $a = 6$, $b = 4$, and $c = 1$.

Solution

$$\begin{aligned} &(a - b)^2 + 3c \\ (6 - 4)^2 + 3(1) &= (2)^2 + 3(1) \\ &= 4 + 3(1) \\ &= 4 + 3 \\ &= 7 \end{aligned}$$

YOU TRY IT 3

Evaluate $(a - b)^2 + 5c$ for $a = 7$, $b = 2$, and $c = 4$.

Your solution

45

Solutions on p. S4

1.4 EXERCISES

Concept Check

SUGGESTED ASSIGNMENT
Exercises 1 and 2; Exercises 3–43, odds; More challenging exercises: Exercises 45–48

1. The first step in simplifying the expression $18 - 7 \cdot 2$ is to multiply 7 times 2.

2. Simplify: $2^3 + 3 \cdot (1 + 4)$

	$2^3 + 3 \cdot (1 + 4)$
a. Perform operations in parentheses.	$= 2^3 + 3 \cdot (\underline{5})$
b. Simplify expressions with exponents.	$= \underline{8} + 3 \cdot 5$
c. Multiply.	$= 8 + \underline{15}$
d. Add.	$= \underline{23}$

OBJECTIVE A *To use the Order of Operations Agreement to simplify expressions*

Simplify.

3. $8 \div 4 + 2$
4

4. $12 - 9 \div 3$
9

5. $6 \cdot 4 + 5$
29

6. $5 \cdot 7 + 3$
38

7. $4^2 - 3$
13

8. $6^2 - 14$
22

9. $5 \cdot (6 - 3) + 4$
19

10. $8 + (6 + 2) \div 4$
10

11. $9 + (7 + 5) \div 6$
11

12. $14 \cdot (3 + 2) \div 10$
7

13. $13 \cdot (1 + 5) \div 13$
6

14. $14 - 2^3 + 9$
15

15. $6 \cdot 3^2 + 7$
61

16. $18 + 5 \cdot 3^2$
63

17. $14 + 5 \cdot 2^3$
54

18. $20 + (9 - 4) \cdot 2$
30

19. $10 + (8 - 5) \cdot 3$
19

20. $3^2 + 5 \cdot (6 - 2)$
29

21. $2^3 + 4(10 - 6)$
24

22. $3^2 \cdot 2^2 + 3 \cdot 2$
42

23. $6(7) + 4^2 \cdot 3^2$
186

24. $14 - 2(6)$
2

25. $18 + 3(7)$
39

26. $2(9 - 2) + 5$
19

27. $6(8 - 3) - 12$
18

28. $15 - (7 - 1) \div 3$
13

29. $16 - (13 - 5) \div 4$
14

30. $11 + 2 - 3 \cdot 4 \div 3$
9

31. $17 + 1 - 8 \cdot 2 \div 4$
14

32. $3(5 + 3) \div 8$
3

Evaluate the expression for the given values of the variables.

33. $x - 2y$, for $x = 8$ and $y = 3$
2

34. $x + 6y$, for $x = 5$ and $y = 4$
29

35. $x^2 + 3y$, for $x = 6$ and $y = 7$
57

36. $3x^2 + y$, for $x = 2$ and $y = 9$
21

37. $x^2 + y \div x$, for $x = 2$ and $y = 8$
8

38. $x + y^2 \div x$, for $x = 4$ and $y = 8$
20

39. $4x + (x - y)^2$, for $x = 8$ and $y = 2$
68

40. $(x + y)^2 - 2y$, for $x = 3$ and $y = 6$
69

41. $x^2 + 3(x - y) + z^2$, for $x = 2$, $y = 1$, and $z = 3$
16

42. $x^2 + 4(x - y) \div z^2$, for $x = 8$, $y = 6$, and $z = 2$
66

43. Use the inequality symbol > to compare the expressions $11 + (8 + 4) \div 6$ and $12 + (9 - 5) \cdot 3$.
$12 + (9 - 5) \cdot 3 > 11 + (8 + 4) \div 6$ [24 > 13]

44. Use the inequality symbol < to compare the expressions $3^2 + 7(4 - 2)$ and $14 - 2^3 + 20$.
$3^2 + 7(4 - 2) < 14 - 2^3 + 20$ [23 < 26]

For Exercises 45 to 48, insert parentheses as needed in the expression $5 + 7 \cdot 3 - 1$ in order to make the equation true.

45. $5 + 7 \cdot 3 - 1 = 19$
$5 + 7 \cdot (3 - 1)$

46. $5 + 7 \cdot 3 - 1 = 24$
$(5 + 7) \cdot (3 - 1)$

47. $5 + 7 \cdot 3 - 1 = 25$
$5 + (7 \cdot 3) - 1$

48. $5 + 7 \cdot 3 - 1 = 35$
$(5 + 7) \cdot 3 - 1$

Critical Thinking

49. What is the smallest prime number greater than $15 + (8 - 3)(2^4)$? 97

50. Arrange the expressions in order from greatest value to least value.

$12 \div 6 + 2$	$8 \cdot 4 + 5$	$7^2 - 14$
$15 + 3(7)$	$4(6 - 3) - 10$	$3(6 + 2) \div 8$

$8 \cdot 4 + 5 > 15 + 3(7) > 7^2 - 14 > 12 \div 6 + 2 > 3(6 + 2) \div 8 > 4(6 - 3) - 10$; $37 > 36 > 35 > 4 > 3 > 2$

QUICK QUIZ

1. Simplify: $3^2 - 2(12 \div 6)$
5 [1.4A]
2. Simplify: $14 - (11 - 2) \div 3$
11 [1.4A]
3. Evaluate $(x - y)^2 + 3x$ for $x = 4$ and $y = 1$.
21 [1.4A]

Projects or Group Activities

51. Use the same one-digit number three times to write an expression that is equal to 30.
$3 + 3^3$

52. How can you place twelve sugar lumps in three coffee mugs so that there is an odd number of lumps in each mug? It is not possible.

CHAPTER 1 Summary

Key Words | Examples

The **natural numbers** or **counting numbers** are 1, 2, 3, 4, 5, 6, 7, 8, 9, 10,…. [1.1A, p. 2]

The **whole numbers** are 0, 1, 2, 3, 4, 5, 6, 7, 8, 9, 10,…. [1.1A, p. 2]

The **graph of a whole number** is shown by placing a heavy dot directly above that number on the number line. [1.1A, p. 2]

This is the graph of 4 on the number line.

0 1 2 3 4 5 6 7 8 9 10 11 12

The symbol for "is less than" is $<$. The symbol for "is greater than" is $>$. A statement that uses the symbol $<$ or $>$ is an **inequality.** [1.1A, p. 2]

$3 < 7$
$9 > 2$

When a whole number is written using the digits 0, 1, 2, 3, 4, 5, 6, 7, 8, and 9, it is said to be in **standard form.** The position of each digit in the number determines that digit's **place value** and can be shown in a **place-value chart.** [1.1B, p. 3]

The number 598,317 is in standard form. The digit 8 is in the thousands place.

The number 24,065 is entered in the place-value chart below.

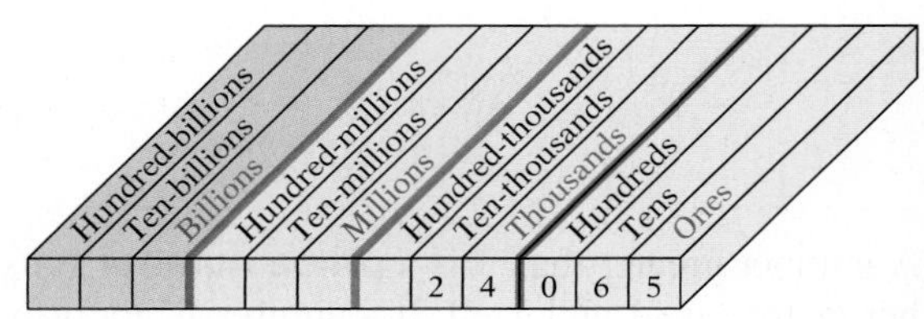

The **expanded form** of a number expresses the number as the sum of the values of the digits. [1.1B, p. 4]

The number 46,872 is written in expanded form as

40,000 + 6000 + 800 + 70 + 2.

A **pictograph** represents data by using a symbol that is characteristic of the data. A **circle graph** represents data by the sizes of the sectors. A **bar graph** represents data by the heights of the bars. A **broken-line graph** represents data by the positions of the lines and shows trends or comparisons. [1.1D, pp. 7–9]

Addition is the process of finding the total of two or more numbers. The numbers being added are called **addends.** The answer is the **sum.** [1.2A, pp. 18–19]

$$\begin{array}{r} {\scriptstyle 1\,1\,1\,} \\ 8762 \\ +\ \ 1359 \\ \hline 10{,}121 \end{array}$$

Subtraction is the process of finding the difference between two numbers. The **minuend** minus the **subtrahend** equals the **difference.** [1.2B, pp. 24–25]

$$\begin{array}{r} 52{,}173 \\ -34{,}968 \\ \hline 17{,}205 \end{array}$$

Multiplication is the repeated addition of the same number. The numbers that are multiplied are called **factors.** The answer is the **product.** [1.3A, p. 41]

$$\begin{array}{r} 358 \\ \times \quad 7 \\ \hline 2506 \end{array}$$

Division is used to separate objects into equal groups. The **dividend** divided by the **divisor** equals the **quotient.** For any division problem, **(quotient · divisor) + remainder = dividend.** [1.3C, pp. 48–50]

$$\begin{array}{r} 93 \text{ r3} \\ 7\overline{)654} \\ -63 \\ \hline 24 \\ -21 \\ \hline 3 \end{array}$$

Check: $(7 \cdot 93) + 3 = 651 + 3 = 654$

The expression 3^5 is in **exponential form.** The **exponent,** 5, indicates how many times the **base,** 3, occurs as a factor in the multiplication. [1.3B, p. 46]

$5^4 = 5 \cdot 5 \cdot 5 \cdot 5 = 625$

Natural number factors of a number divide that number evenly (there is no remainder). [1.3D, p. 53]

$18 \div 1 = 18$
$18 \div 2 = 9$
$18 \div 3 = 6$
$18 \div 4$ 4 does not divide 18 evenly.
$18 \div 5$ 5 does not divide 18 evenly.
$18 \div 6 = 3$ The factors are repeating.
The factors of 18 are 1, 2, 3, 6, 9, and 18.

A number greater than 1 is a **prime number** if its only whole number factors are 1 and itself. If a number is not prime, it is a **composite number.** [1.3D, p. 53]

The prime numbers less than 20 are 2, 3, 5, 7, 11, 13, 17, and 19.

The composite numbers less than 20 are 4, 6, 8, 9, 10, 12, 14, 15, 16, and 18.

The **prime factorization** of a number is the expression of the number as a product of its prime factors. [1.3D, p. 54]

$$\begin{array}{r} 7 \\ 3\overline{)21} \\ 2\overline{)42} \end{array}$$

The prime factorization of 42 is $2 \cdot 3 \cdot 7$.

A **variable** is a letter that is used to stand for a number. A mathematical expression that contains one or more variables is a **variable expression.** Replacing the variables in a variable expression with numbers and then simplifying the numerical expression is called **evaluating the variable expression.** [1.2A, p. 20]

To evaluate the variable expression $4ab$ when $a = 3$ and $b = 2$, replace a with 3 and b with 2. Simplify the resulting expression.

$4ab$
$4(3)(2) = 12(2) = 24$

An **equation** expresses the equality of two numerical or variable expressions. An equation contains an equals sign. A **solution** of an equation is a number that, when substituted for the variable, produces a true equation. [1.2A, p. 22]

6 is a solution of the equation $5 + x = 11$ because $5 + 6 = 11$ is a true equation.

Lines in a plane can be intersecting or parallel. **Intersecting lines** cross at a point in the plane. **Parallel lines** never meet. The distance between them is always the same. [1.2C, p. 28]

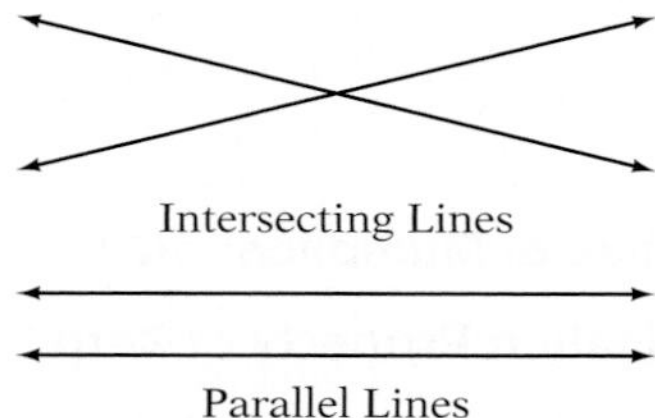

An angle is measured in **degrees.** A 90° angle is a **right angle.** [1.2C, p. 28]

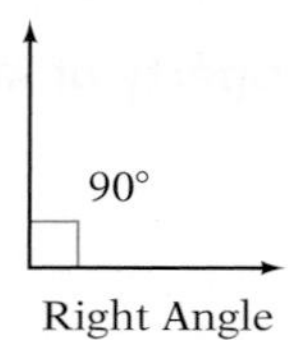

A **polygon** is a closed figure determined by three or more line segments. The line segments that form the polygon are its **sides.** A **triangle** is a three-sided polygon. A **quadrilateral** is a four-sided polygon. A **rectangle** is a quadrilateral in which opposite sides are parallel, opposite sides are equal in length, and all four angles are right angles. A **square** is a rectangle in which all sides have the same length. The **perimeter** of a plane figure is a measure of the distance around the figure, and its **area** is the amount of surface in the region. [1.2C, pp. 28–29; 1.3E, pp. 55–56]

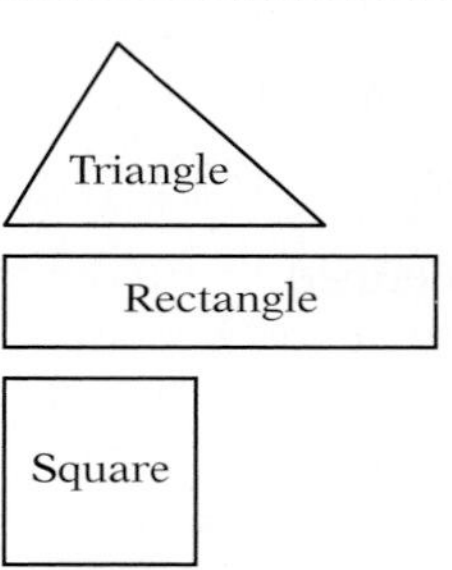

Essential Rules and Procedures

Examples

To round a number to a given place value: If the digit to the right of the given place value is less than 5, replace that digit and all digits to the right by zeros. If the digit to the right of the given place value is greater than or equal to 5, increase the digit in the given place value by 1, and replace all other digits to the right by zeros. [1.1C, pp. 5–6]

36,178 rounded to the nearest thousand is 36,000.

4952 rounded to the nearest thousand is 5000.

To estimate the answer to a calculation: Round each number to the highest place value of that number. Perform the calculation using the rounded numbers. [1.2A, p. 20]

$$\begin{array}{rcr} 39{,}471 & \longrightarrow & 40{,}000 \\ 12{,}586 & \longrightarrow & +\ 10{,}000 \\ \hline & & 50{,}000 \end{array}$$

50,000 is an estimate of the sum of 39,471 and 12,586.

Properties of Addition [1.2A, p. 21]

Addition Property of Zero $a + 0 = a$ or $0 + a = a$ — $7 + 0 = 7$

Commutative Property of Addition $a + b = b + a$ — $8 + 3 = 3 + 8$

Associative Property of Addition $(a + b) + c = a + (b + c)$ — $(2 + 4) + 6 = 2 + (4 + 6)$

Properties of Multiplication [1.3A, p. 44]

Multiplication Property of Zero $a \cdot 0 = 0$ or $0 \cdot a = 0$ — $3 \cdot 0 = 0$

Multiplication Property of One $a \cdot 1 = a$ or $1 \cdot a = a$ — $6 \cdot 1 = 6$

Commutative Property of Multiplication $a \cdot b = b \cdot a$ — $2 \cdot 8 = 8 \cdot 2$

Associative Property of Multiplication $(a \cdot b) \cdot c = a \cdot (b \cdot c)$ — $(2 \cdot 4) \cdot 6 = 2 \cdot (4 \cdot 6)$

Division Properties of Zero and One [1.3C, p. 49]

If $a \neq 0$, $0 \div a = 0$. — $0 \div 3 = 0$

If $a \neq 0$, $a \div a = 1$. — $3 \div 3 = 1$

$a \div 1 = a$ — $3 \div 1 = 3$

$a \div 0$ is undefined. — $3 \div 0$ is undefined.

The Order of Operations Agreement [1.4A, p. 67]

Step 1: Do all operations inside parentheses.

Step 2: Simplify any numerical expressions containing exponents.

Step 3: Do multiplication and division as they occur from left to right.

Step 4: Do addition and subtraction as they occur from left to right.

$$
\begin{aligned}
5^2 - 3(2 + 4) &= 5^2 - 3(6) \\
&= 25 - 3(6) \\
&= 25 - 18 \\
&= 7
\end{aligned}
$$

Geometric Formulas [1.2C, p. 29; 1.3E, pp. 55–56]

Perimeter of a Triangle	$P = a + b + c$
Perimeter of a Rectangle	$P = 2L + 2W$
Perimeter of a Square	$P = 4s$
Area of a Rectangle	$A = LW$
Area of a Square	$A = s^2$

Find the perimeter of a triangle with sides that measure 9 m, 6 m, and 5 m.

$$P = a + b + c$$
$$P = 9 + 6 + 5$$
$$P = 20$$

The perimeter of the triangle is 20 m.

CHAPTER 1 Review Exercises

1. Graph 8 on the number line.

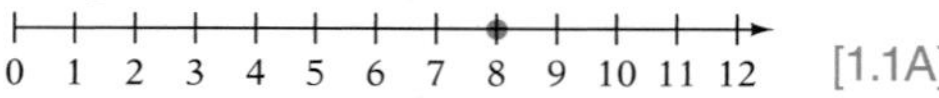

[1.1A]

2. Evaluate 10^4.

10,000 [1.3B]

3. Find the difference between 4207 and 1624.
2583 [1.2B]

4. Write $3 \cdot 3 \cdot 5 \cdot 5 \cdot 5 \cdot 5$ in exponential notation.
$3^2 \cdot 5^4$ [1.3B]

5. Add: $319 + 358 + 712$
1389 [1.2A]

6. Round 38,729 to the nearest hundred.
38,700 [1.1C]

7. Place the correct symbol, $<$ or $>$, between the two numbers.

$247 > 163$ [1.1A]

8. Write thirty-two thousand five hundred nine in standard form.

32,509 [1.1B]

9. Evaluate $2xy$ for $x = 50$ and $y = 7$.
700 [1.3A]

10. Find the quotient of 15,642 and 6.
2607 [1.3C]

11. Subtract: $6407 - 2359$
4048 [1.2B]

12. Estimate the sum of 482, 319, 570, and 146.
1500 [1.2A]

13. Find all the factors of 50.
1, 2, 5, 10, 25, 50 [1.3D]

14. Is 7 a solution of the equation $24 - y = 17$?
Yes [1.2B]

15. Simplify: $16 + 4(7 - 5)^2 \div 8$

18 [1.4A]

16. Identify the property that justifies the statement.

$10 + 33 = 33 + 10$
The Commutative Property of Addition [1.2A]

17. Write 4,927,036 in words.
four million nine hundred twenty-seven thousand thirty-six [1.1B]

18. Evaluate x^3y^2 for $x = 3$ and $y = 5$.
675 [1.3B]

19. **The Film Industry** The circle graph at the right categorizes the 655 films released during a recent year by their ratings. **a.** How many times more PG-13 films were released than NC-17 films? **b.** How many times more R-rated films were released than NC-17 films?
a. 16 times more **b.** 61 times more [1.3E]

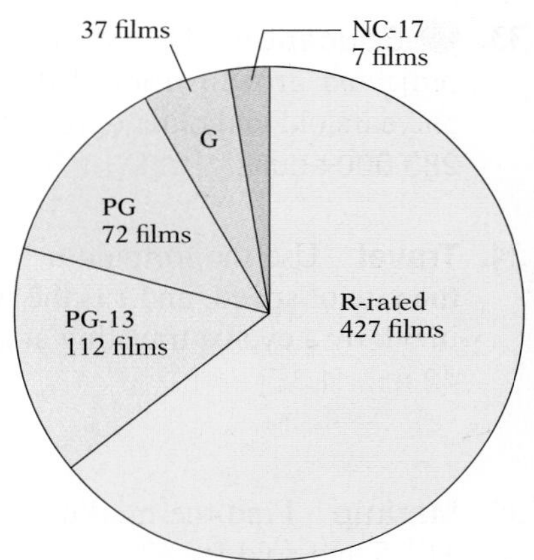

Ratings of Films Released
Source: MPA Worldwide Market Research

20. Divide: $6234 \div 92$
67 r70 [1.3C]

21. Find the product of 4 and 659.
2636 [1.3A]

22. Evaluate $x - y$ for $x = 270$ and $y = 133$.
137 [1.2B]

23. Find the prime factorization of 90.
$2 \cdot 3^2 \cdot 5$ [1.3D]

24. Evaluate $\frac{x}{y}$ for $x = 480$ and $y = 6$.
80 [1.3C]

25. Complete the statement by using the Multiplication Property of One.

$? \cdot 82 = 82$
1 [1.3A]

26. Simplify: $58 - 3 \cdot 4^2$
10 [1.4A]

27. Evaluate $x + y$ for $x = 683$ and $y = 249$.
932 [1.2A]

28. Multiply: $18 \cdot 24$
432 [1.3A]

29. Evaluate $(a + b)^2 - 2c$ for $a = 5$, $b = 3$, and $c = 4$.
56 [1.4A]

30. **Sports** During his professional basketball career, Kareem Abdul-Jabbar had 17,440 rebounds. Elvin Hayes had 16,279 rebounds during his professional basketball career. Who had more rebounds, Abdul-Jabbar or Hayes?
Kareem Abdul-Jabbar [1.1D]

Rogers Photo Archive/Getty Images

Kareem Abdul-Jabbar

31. **Construction** A contractor quotes the cost of work on a new house, which is to have 2800 ft^2 of floor space, at \$85 per square foot. Find the total cost of the contractor's work on the house. \$238,000 [1.3E]

32. **Geometry** A rectangle has a length of 25 m and a width of 12 m. Find **a.** the perimeter and **b.** the area of the rectangle. **a.** 74 m **b.** 300 m^2 [1.2C, 1.3E]

33. **Education** Use the graph at the right to determine the projected growth from 2016 to 2019 in the number of adults 35 years old and older enrolled in degree-granting institutions.
283,000 adults [1.2C]

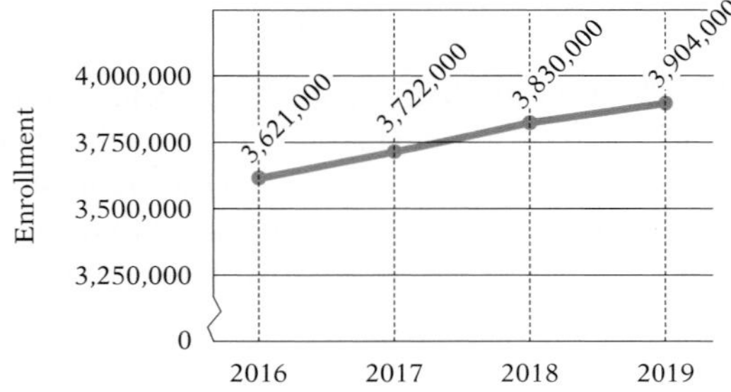

Projected Enrollment of Adults 35 Years Old and Older in Degree-Granting Institutions
Source: National Center for Education Statistics

34. **Travel** Use the formula $d = rt$, where d is the distance, r is the rate of speed, and t is the time, to find the distance traveled in 3 h by a cyclist traveling at a speed of 14 mph.
42 mi [1.3E]

35. **Markup** Find the markup on a copy machine that cost an office supply business \$1775 and sold for \$2224. Use the formula $M = S - C$, where M is the markup on a product, S is the selling price of the product, and C is the cost of the product to the business. \$449 [1.2C]

CHAPTER 1 TEST

1. Multiply: 3297×100
329,700 [1.3A]

2. Evaluate $2^4 \cdot 10^3$.
16,000 [1.3B]

3. Find the difference between 4902 and 873.
4029 [1.2B]

4. Write $x \cdot x \cdot x \cdot x \cdot y \cdot y \cdot y$ in exponential notation.
x^4y^3 [1.3B]

5. Is 7 a solution of the equation $23 = p + 16$?
Yes [1.2A]

6. Round 2961 to the nearest hundred.
3000 [1.1C]

7. Place the correct symbol, < or >, between the two numbers.

$7177 < 7717$ [1.1A]

8. Write eight thousand four hundred ninety in standard form.

8490 [1.1B]

9. Write 382,904 in words.
three hundred eighty-two thousand nine hundred four [1.1B]

10. Estimate the sum of 392, 477, 519, and 648.
2000 [1.2A]

11. Find the product of 8 and 1376.
11,008 [1.3A]

12. Estimate the product of 36,479 and 58.
2,400,000 [1.3A]

13. Find all the factors of 92.
1, 2, 4, 23, 46, 92 [1.3D]

14. Find the prime factorization of 240.
$2^4 \cdot 3 \cdot 5$ [1.3D]

15. Evaluate $x - y$ for $x = 39{,}241$ and $y = 8375$.

30,866 [1.2B]

16. Identify the property that justifies the statement.

$14 + y = y + 14$
The Commutative Property of Addition [1.2A]

17. Evaluate $\frac{x}{y}$ for $x = 3588$ and $y = 4$.

897 [1.3C]

18. Simplify: $27 - (12 - 3) \div 9$
26 [1.4A]

19. **Child Development** The table at the right shows the median height from birth to age 5 for boys and girls. Use this table to determine between which two years girls grow the most.
Between birth and age 1 [1.2B]

Age (in years)	*Median Height of Girls (in centimeters)*	*Median Height of Boys (in centimeters)*
Birth	49	50
1	74	75
2	84	87
3	95	91
4	100	102
5	108	110

Source: National Center for Health Statistics

20. Simplify: $5 + 2(4 - 3)^6$
7 [1.4A]

21. Write 3972 in expanded form.
3000 + 900 + 70 + 2 [1.1B]

22. Evaluate $5x + (x - y)^2$ for $x = 8$ and $y = 4$.
56 [1.4A]

23. Complete the statement by using the Associative Property of Addition.

$(3 + 7) + x = 3 + (? + x)$

7 [1.2A]

24. Mathematics What is the product of all the natural numbers less than 7?
720 [1.3A]

25. Banking You purchase a computer system that includes an operating system priced at $850, a monitor that cost $270, an extended keyboard priced at $175, and a printer for $425. You pay for the purchase by check. You had $2276 in your checking account before making the purchase. What is the balance in your account after making the purchase? $556 [1.2C]

26. Geometry The length of each side of a square is 24 cm. Find **a.** the perimeter and **b.** the area of the square. **a.** 96 cm **b.** 576 cm² [1.3E]

27. Take-home Pay A commercial diver receives a total salary of $5690 per month. Deductions from the paycheck include $854 for taxes, $272 for retirement, and $108 for insurance. Find the diver's monthly take-home pay. $4456 [1.2C]

28. Social Networking Websites Use the graph at the right to determine how many more registered users are on Facebook than are on Twitter. 465 million more registered users [1.2C]

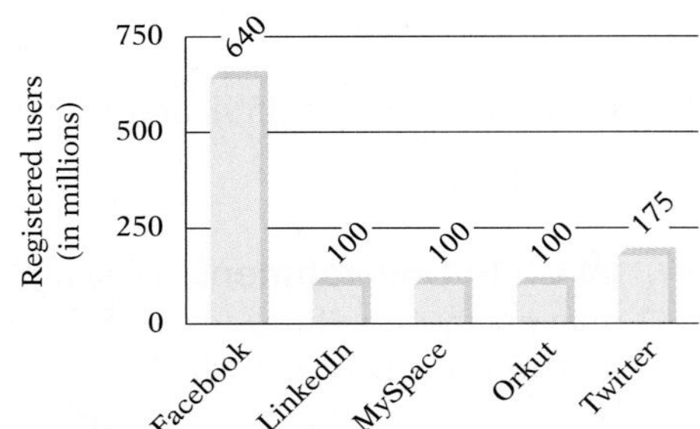

Social Networking Websites
Source: Wikipedia

29. Commissions Use the formula $C = U \cdot R$, where C is the commission earned, U is the number of units sold, and R is the rate per unit, to find the commission earned from selling 480 boxes of greeting cards when the commission rate per box is $3.
$1440 [1.3E]

30. Mutual Funds The current value of the stocks in a mutual fund is $5,500,000. The number of shares outstanding is 500,000. Find the value per share of the fund. Use the formula $V = \frac{C}{S}$, where V is the value per share, C is the current value of the stocks in the fund, and S is the number of shares outstanding. $11 [1.3E]

Fractions and Decimals

OBJECTIVES

SECTION 2.1
- **A** To find the least common multiple (LCM)
- **B** To find the greatest common factor (GCF)

SECTION 2.2
- **A** To write proper fractions, improper fractions, and mixed numbers
- **B** To write equivalent fractions
- **C** To identify the order relation between two fractions

SECTION 2.3
- **A** To add fractions
- **B** To subtract fractions
- **C** To solve application problems

SECTION 2.4
- **A** To multiply fractions
- **B** To divide fractions
- **C** To simplify complex fractions
- **D** To solve application problems and use formulas

SECTION 2.5
- **A** To write decimals in standard form and in words
- **B** To identify the order relation between two decimals
- **C** To round a decimal to a given place value
- **D** To solve application problems

SECTION 2.6
- **A** To add and subtract decimals
- **B** To multiply decimals
- **C** To divide decimals
- **D** To convert between decimals and fractions and to identify the order relation between a decimal and a fraction
- **E** To solve application problems and use formulas

SECTION 2.7
- **A** To use the Order of Operations Agreement to simplify expressions

Focus on Success

Did you read Ask the Authors at the front of this text? If you did, then you know that the authors' advice is that you practice, practice, practice—and then practice some more. The more time you spend doing math outside of class, the more successful you will be in this course. (See Ask the Authors, page i, and Make the Commitment to Succeed, page AIM-3.)

Prep Test

Are you ready to succeed in this chapter? Take the Prep Test below to find out if you are ready to learn the new material.

For Exercises 1 to 6, add, subtract, multiply, or divide.

1. 4×5
20 [1.3A]

2. $2 \cdot 2 \cdot 2 \cdot 3 \cdot 5$
120 [1.3A]

3. 9×1
9 [1.3A]

4. $6 + 4$
10 [1.2A]

5. $10 - 3$
7 [1.2B]

6. $63 \div 30$
2 r3 [1.3C]

7. Which of the following numbers divide evenly into 12?
1 2 3 4 5 6 7 8 9 10 11 12
1, 2, 3, 4, 6, 12 [1.3C]

8. Simplify: $8 \times 7 + 3$
59 [1.4A]

9. Complete: $8 = ? + 1$
7 [1.2A]

10. Place the correct symbol, $<$ or $>$, between the two numbers.
44 48
$44 < 48$ [1.1A]

SECTION

2.1 The Least Common Multiple and Greatest Common Factor

OBJECTIVE A To find the least common multiple (LCM)

Tips for Success

Before you begin a new chapter, you should take some time to review previously learned skills. One way to do this is to complete the Prep Test. See page 79. This test focuses on the particular skills that will be required for the new chapter.

The **multiples of a number** are the products of that number and the numbers 1, 2, 3, 4, 5, ...

$3 \times 1 = 3$
$3 \times 2 = 6$
$3 \times 3 = 9$
$3 \times 4 = 12$ The multiples of 3 are 3, 6, 9, 12, 15, ...
$3 \times 5 = 15$
.
.
.

A number that is a multiple of two or more numbers is a **common multiple** of those numbers.

IN-CLASS EXAMPLES

Find the LCM.

1. 14, 21 **42**
2. 2, 7, 14 **14**
3. 5, 12, 15 **60**

The multiples of 4 are 4, 8, 12, 16, 20, 24, 28, 32, 36, ...
The multiples of 6 are 6, 12, 18, 24, 30, 36, 42, ...
Some common multiples of 4 and 6 are 12, 24, and 36.

The **least common multiple (LCM)** is the smallest common multiple of two or more numbers.

The least common multiple of 4 and 6 is 12.

Listing the multiples of each number is one way to find the LCM. Another way to find the LCM uses the prime factorization of each number.

INSTRUCTOR NOTE

As mentioned earlier, one of the main pedagogical features of this text is the paired examples. Using the model of the Example, students should work the You Try It. A *complete* solution is provided in the back of the text so that students can check not only the answer but also their work.

To find the LCM of 450 and 600, find the prime factorization of each number and write the factorization of each number in a table. Circle the greatest product in each column. The LCM is the product of the circled numbers.

	2	3	5
450 =	2	(3 · 3)	(5 · 5)
600 =	(2 · 2 · 2)	3	5 · 5

• In the column headed by 5, the products are equal. Circle just one product.

The LCM is the product of the circled numbers.
The LCM = 2 · 2 · 2 · 3 · 3 · 5 · 5 = 1800.

EXAMPLE 1

Find the LCM of 24, 36, and 50.

Solution

	2	3	5
24 =	(2 · 2 · 2)	3	
36 =	2 · 2	(3 · 3)	
50 =	2		(5 · 5)

The LCM = 2 · 2 · 2 · 3 · 3 · 5 · 5 = 1800.

YOU TRY IT 1

Find the LCM of 12, 27, and 50.

Your solution

2700

Solution on p. S4

OBJECTIVE B *To find the greatest common factor (GCF)*

Recall that a number that divides another number evenly is a factor of that number. The number 64 can be evenly divided by 1, 2, 4, 8, 16, 32, and 64, so the numbers 1, 2, 4, 8, 16, 32, and 64 are factors of 64.

A number that is a factor of two or more numbers is a **common factor** of those numbers.

The factors of 30 are 1, 2, 3, 5, 6, 10, 15, and 30.

The factors of 105 are 1, 3, 5, 7, 15, 21, 35, and 105.

The common factors of 30 and 105 are 1, 3, 5, and 15.

The **greatest common factor (GCF)** is the largest common factor of two or more numbers.

The greatest common factor of 30 and 105 is 15.

Listing the factors of each number is one way of finding the GCF. Another way to find the GCF is to use the prime factorization of each number.

To find the GCF of 126 and 180, find the prime factorization of each number and write the factorization of each number in a table. Circle the least product in each column that does not have a blank. The GCF is the product of the circled numbers.

	2	3	5	7
126 =	(2)	(3 · 3)		7
180 =	2 · 2	3 · 3	5	

• In the column headed by 3, the products are equal. Circle just one product. Columns 5 and 7 have a blank, so 5 and 7 are not common factors of 126 and 180. Do not circle any number in these columns.

The GCF is the product of the circled numbers.
The GCF = 2 · 3 · 3 = 18.

INSTRUCTOR NOTE
The following model may help some students with the LCM and GCF.

LCM
a b
GCF

The arrow indicates "divides into."

IN-CLASS EXAMPLES
Find the GCF.
4. 12, 18 **6**
5. 24, 64 **8**
6. 41, 67 **1**
7. 21, 27, 33 **3**

EXAMPLE 2

Find the GCF of 90, 168, and 420.

Solution

	2	3	5	7
90 =	(2)	3 · 3	5	
168 =	2 · 2 · 2	(3)		7
420 =	2 · 2	3	5	7

The GCF = 2 · 3 = 6.

YOU TRY IT 2

Find the GCF of 36, 60, and 72.

Your solution

12

EXAMPLE 3

Find the GCF of 7, 12, and 20.

Solution

	2	3	5	7
7 =				7
12 =	2 · 2	3		
20 =	2 · 2		5	

Because no numbers are circled, the GCF = 1.

YOU TRY IT 3

Find the GCF of 11, 24, and 30.

Your solution

1

Solutions on p. S4

2.1 EXERCISES

SUGGESTED ASSIGNMENT
Exercises 1–10
Exercises 11–73, odds
Exercises 75–79

Concept Check

For Exercises 1 to 4, list the first four multiples of the given number.

1. 5
5, 10, 15, 20

2. 7
7, 14, 21, 28

3. 10
10, 20, 30, 40

4. 15
15, 30, 45, 60

5. List the first ten multiples of 6 and the first ten multiples of 8. What are the common multiples of 6 and 8 in the lists? What is the least common multiple of 6 and 8?
Multiples of 6: 6, 12, 18, 24, 30, 36, 42, 48, 54, 60
Multiples of 8: 8, 16, 24, 32, 40, 48, 56, 64, 72, 80
Common multiples: 24, 48
Least common multiple: 24

For Exercises 6 to 9, list the factors of the given number.

6. 12
1, 2, 3, 4, 6, 12

7. 20
1, 2, 4, 5, 10, 20

8. 23
1, 23

9. 28
1, 2, 4, 7, 14, 28

10. List the factors of 18 and the factors of 24. What are the common factors of 18 and 24? What is the greatest common factor of 18 and 24?
Factors of 18: 1, 2, 3, 6, 9, 18
Factors of 24: 1, 2, 3, 4, 6, 8, 12, 24
Common factors: 1, 2, 3, 6
Greatest common factor: 6

OBJECTIVE A *To find the least common multiple (LCM)*

For Exercises 11 to 40, find the LCM.

11. 5, 8
40

12. 3, 6
6

13. 3, 8
24

14. 2, 5
10

15. 4, 6
12

16. 6, 8
24

17. 8, 12
24

18. 12, 16
48

19. 5, 12
60

20. 3, 16
48

21. 8, 14
56

22. 4, 10
20

23. 8, 32
32

24. 7, 21
21

25. 9, 36
36

26. 14, 42
42

27. 44, 60
660

28. 120, 160
480

29. 102, 184
9384

30. 123, 234
9594

31. 4, 8, 12
24

32. 5, 10, 15
30

33. 3, 5, 10
30

34. 2, 5, 8
40

35. 3, 8, 12
24

36. 5, 12, 18
180

37. 9, 36, 64
576

38. 18, 54, 63
378

39. 3, 7, 20
420

40. 4, 9, 35
1260

41. True or false? If two numbers have no common factors, then the LCM of the two numbers is their product. True

42. True or false? If one number is a multiple of a second number, then the LCM of the two numbers is the second number. False

OBJECTIVE B *To find the greatest common factor (GCF)*

For Exercises 43 to 72, find the GCF.

43. 3, 5
1

44. 5, 7
1

45. 6, 9
3

46. 18, 24
6

47. 15, 25
5

48. 14, 49
7

49. 25, 100
25

50. 16, 80
16

51. 32, 51
1

52. 21, 44
1

53. 12, 80
4

54. 8, 36
4

55. 16, 140
4

56. 48, 144
48

57. 44, 96
4

58. 18, 32
2

59. 3, 5, 11
1

60. 6, 8, 10
2

61. 7, 14, 49
7

62. 6, 15, 36
3

63. 10, 15, 20
5

64. 12, 18, 20
2

65. 24, 40, 72
8

66. 3, 17, 51
1

67. 17, 31, 81
1

68. 14, 42, 84
14

69. 25, 125, 625
25

70. 12, 68, 92
4

71. 32, 56, 72
8

72. 24, 36, 48
12

73. True or false? If two numbers have a GCF of 1, then the LCM of the two numbers is their product. True

74. True or false? If the LCM of two numbers is one of the two numbers, then the GCF of the numbers is the other of the two numbers. True

QUICK QUIZ
Find the LCM.
1. 10, 25 **50** **[2.1A]**
2. 3, 6, 7 **42** **[2.1A]**

Find the GCF.
3. 6, 16 **2** **[2.1B]**
4. 4, 9 **1** **[2.1B]**
5. 26, 52 **26** **[2.1B]**
6. 12, 30, 60 **6** **[2.1B]**

Critical Thinking

75. Work Schedules Joe Salvo, a lifeguard, works 3 days and then has a day off. Joe's friend Raya works 5 days and then has a day off. How many days after Joe and Raya have a day off together will they have another day off together? 12 days

© iStockphoto.com/gchutka

76. Find the LCM of each of the following pairs of prime numbers: 2 and 3, 5 and 7, and 11 and 19. Based on these examples, what is the LCM of two prime numbers?

77. Find the GCF of each of the following pairs of prime numbers: 3 and 5, 7 and 11, and 29 and 43. Based on these examples, what is the GCF of two prime numbers?

Projects or Group Activities

78. Using the pattern for the first two triangles shown below, determine the center number of the last triangle. 4

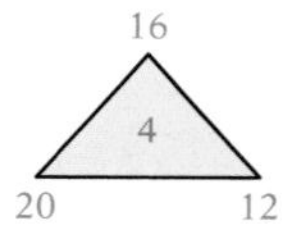

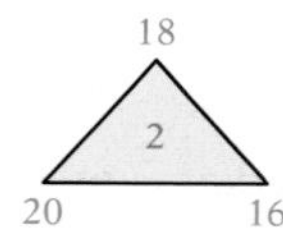

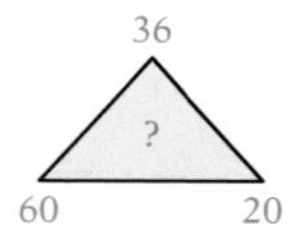

79. Two numbers are called *coprime* if the GCF of the two numbers is 1. Determine whether each pair of numbers is coprime.

a. 48, 50
No

b. 25, 36
Yes

c. 22, 27
Yes

d. 71, 73
Yes

SECTION

2.2 Introduction to Fractions

OBJECTIVE A *To write proper fractions, improper fractions, and mixed numbers*

A recipe calls for $\frac{1}{2}$ c of butter; a carpenter uses a $\frac{3}{8}$-inch screw; and a stock broker might say that Sears closed down $\frac{3}{4}$. The numbers $\frac{1}{2}$, $\frac{3}{8}$, and $\frac{3}{4}$ are fractions.

A **fraction** can represent the number of equal parts of a whole. The circle at the right is divided into 8 equal parts. 3 of the 8 parts are shaded. The shaded portion of the circle is represented by the fraction $\frac{3}{8}$.

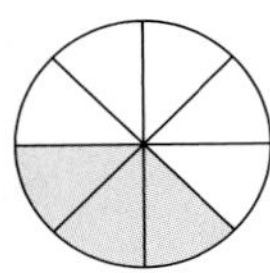

Each part of a fraction has a name.

Point of Interest

The fraction bar was first used in 1050 by al-Hassar. It is also called a vinculum.

Fraction bar ⟶ $\frac{3}{8}$ ⟵ **Numerator** (3), ⟵ **Denominator** (8)

In a **proper fraction,** the numerator is smaller than the denominator. A proper fraction is less than 1.

$\frac{1}{2}$ $\frac{3}{8}$ $\frac{3}{4}$

Proper fractions

In an **improper fraction,** the numerator is greater than or equal to the denominator. An improper fraction is a number greater than or equal to 1.

$\frac{7}{3}$ $\frac{4}{4}$

Improper fractions

The shaded portion of the circles at the right is represented by the improper fraction $\frac{7}{3}$.

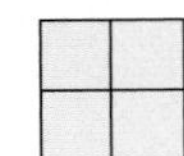

The shaded portion of the square at the right is represented by the improper fraction $\frac{4}{4}$.

A fraction bar can be read "divided by." Therefore, the fraction $\frac{4}{4}$ can be read "$4 \div 4$." Because a number divided by itself is equal to 1, $4 \div 4 = 1$ and $\frac{4}{4} = 1$.

The shaded portion of the square above can be represented as $\frac{4}{4}$ or 1.

Since the fraction bar can be read as "divided by" and any number divided by 1 is the number, any whole number can be represented as an improper fraction. For example, $5 = \frac{5}{1}$ and $7 = \frac{7}{1}$.

Because zero divided by any number other than zero is zero, the numerator of a fraction can be zero.

For example, $\frac{0}{6} = 0$ because $0 \div 6 = 0$.

Recall that division by zero is not defined. Therefore, the denominator of a fraction cannot be zero.

For example, $\frac{9}{0}$ is not defined because $\frac{9}{0} = 9 \div 0$, and division by zero is not defined.

INSTRUCTOR NOTE

As a classroom exercise, ask students to give real-world examples in which mixed numbers are used. Some possible answers: carpentry, sewing, recipes.

A **mixed number** is a number greater than 1 with a whole number part and a fractional part.

The shaded portion of the circles at the right is represented by the mixed number $2\frac{1}{2}$.

Note from the diagram at the right that the improper fraction $\frac{5}{2}$ is equal to the mixed number $2\frac{1}{2}$.

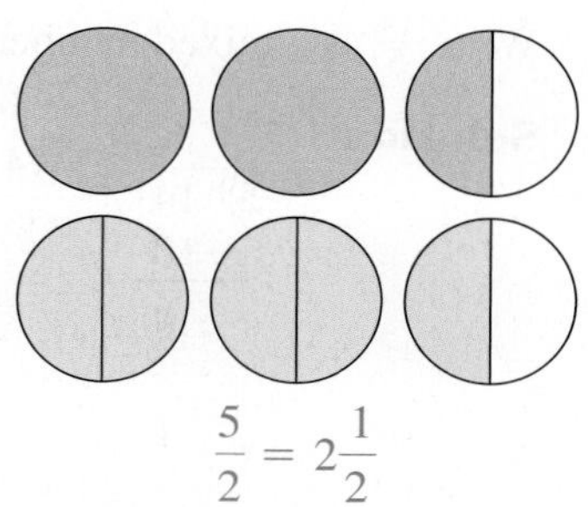

$$\frac{5}{2} = 2\frac{1}{2}$$

An improper fraction can be written as a mixed number.

To write $\frac{5}{2}$ as a mixed number, read the fraction bar as "divided by."

$\frac{5}{2}$ means $5 \div 2$.

Divide the numerator by the denominator.	To write the fractional part of the mixed number, write the remainder over the divisor.	Write the answer.
$2\overline{)5}$ quotient 2; -4; remainder 1	$2\overline{)5}$ quotient $2\frac{1}{2}$; -4; remainder 1	$\frac{5}{2} = 2\frac{1}{2}$

IN-CLASS EXAMPLES

1. Express the shaded portion of the circles as an improper fraction and as a mixed number.

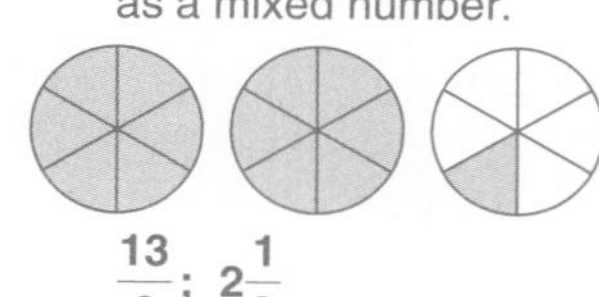

$\frac{13}{6}$; $2\frac{1}{6}$

2. Write $\frac{15}{4}$ as a mixed number. $3\frac{3}{4}$
3. Write $\frac{24}{6}$ as a whole number. 4
4. Write $3\frac{4}{7}$ as an improper fraction. $\frac{25}{7}$
5. Write 12 as an improper fraction. $\frac{12}{1}$

To write a mixed number as an improper fraction, multiply the denominator of the fractional part of the mixed number by the whole number part. The sum of this product and the numerator of the fractional part is the numerator of the improper fraction. The denominator remains the same.

HOW TO 1 Write $4\frac{5}{6}$ as an improper fraction.

$$4\frac{5}{6} = \frac{(6 \cdot 4) + 5}{6} = \frac{24 + 5}{6} = \frac{29}{6}$$

EXAMPLE 1

Express the shaded portion of the circles as an improper fraction and as a mixed number.

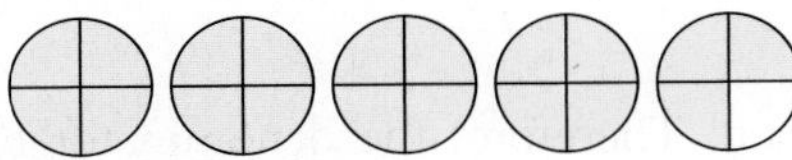

Solution $\frac{19}{4}$; $4\frac{3}{4}$

YOU TRY IT 1

Express the shaded portion of the circles as an improper fraction and as a mixed number.

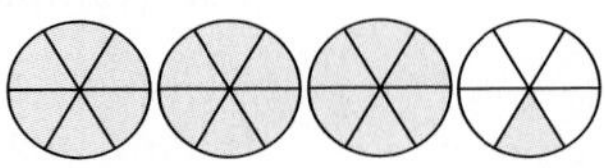

Your solution $\frac{19}{6}$; $3\frac{1}{6}$

EXAMPLE 2

Write $\frac{14}{5}$ as a mixed number.

Solution

$$\begin{array}{r} 2 \\ 5\overline{)\,14} \\ -10 \\ \hline 4 \end{array} \qquad \frac{14}{5} = 2\frac{4}{5}$$

YOU TRY IT 2

Write $\frac{26}{3}$ as a mixed number.

Your solution

$8\frac{2}{3}$

EXAMPLE 3

Write $\frac{35}{7}$ as a whole number.

Solution

$$\begin{array}{r} 5 \\ 7\overline{)\,35} \\ -35 \\ \hline 0 \end{array} \qquad \frac{35}{7} = 5$$

• *Note:* The remainder is zero.

YOU TRY IT 3

Write $\frac{36}{4}$ as a whole number.

Your solution 9

EXAMPLE 4

Write $12\frac{5}{8}$ as an improper fraction.

Solution $12\frac{5}{8} = \frac{(8 \cdot 12) + 5}{8} = \frac{96 + 5}{8}$

$= \frac{101}{8}$

YOU TRY IT 4

Write $9\frac{4}{7}$ as an improper fraction.

Your solution $\frac{67}{7}$

EXAMPLE 5

Write 9 as an improper fraction.

Solution $9 = \frac{9}{1}$

YOU TRY IT 5

Write 3 as an improper fraction.

Your solution $\frac{3}{1}$

Solutions on p. S4

OBJECTIVE B To write equivalent fractions

Point of Interest

Leonardo of Pisa, who was also called Fibonacci (c. 1175–1250), is credited with bringing the Hindu–Arabic number system to the Western world and promoting its use over use of the cumbersome Roman numeral system. He was also influential in promoting the idea of the fraction bar. His notation, however, was very different from what we use today. For instance, he wrote $\frac{3\ 5}{4\ 7}$ to mean $\frac{5}{7} + \frac{3}{7 \cdot 4}$.

Fractions can be graphed as points on a number line. The number lines at the right show thirds, sixths, and ninths graphed from 0 to 1.

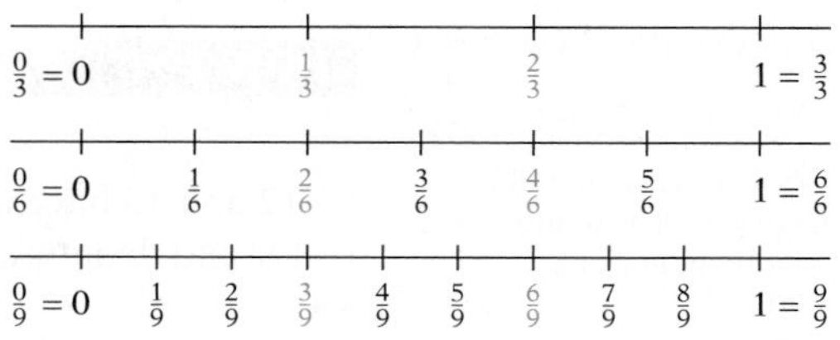

A particular point on the number line may be represented by different fractions, all of which are equal.

For example, $\frac{0}{3} = \frac{0}{6} = \frac{0}{9}$, $\frac{1}{3} = \frac{2}{6} = \frac{3}{9}$, $\frac{2}{3} = \frac{4}{6} = \frac{6}{9}$, and $\frac{3}{3} = \frac{6}{6} = \frac{9}{9}$.

Equal fractions with different denominators are called **equivalent fractions.**

$\frac{1}{3}$, $\frac{2}{6}$, and $\frac{3}{9}$ are equivalent fractions. $\frac{2}{3}$, $\frac{4}{6}$, and $\frac{6}{9}$ are equivalent fractions.

Note that we can rewrite $\frac{2}{3}$ as $\frac{4}{6}$ by multiplying both the numerator and denominator of $\frac{2}{3}$ by 2.

$$\frac{2}{3} = \frac{2 \cdot 2}{3 \cdot 2} = \frac{4}{6}$$

Also, we can rewrite $\frac{4}{6}$ as $\frac{2}{3}$ by dividing both the numerator and denominator of $\frac{4}{6}$ by 2.

$$\frac{4}{6} = \frac{4 \div 2}{6 \div 2} = \frac{2}{3}$$

INSTRUCTOR NOTE

To help some students understand equivalent fractions, use a pizza. By cutting the pizza into, say, eight pieces, students are able to see that $\frac{1}{2} = \frac{4}{8}$ and $\frac{1}{4} = \frac{2}{8}$

Equivalent Fractions

The numerator and denominator of a fraction can be multiplied or divided by the same nonzero number. The resulting fraction is equivalent to the original fraction.

$$\frac{a}{b} = \frac{a \cdot c}{b \cdot c}, \quad \frac{a}{b} = \frac{a \div c}{b \div c}, \quad \text{where } b \neq 0 \text{ and } c \neq 0$$

EXAMPLES

1. $\frac{4}{5} = \frac{4 \cdot 3}{5 \cdot 3} = \frac{12}{15}$
2. $\frac{20}{32} = \frac{20 \div 4}{32 \div 4} = \frac{5}{8}$

HOW TO 2 Write an equivalent fraction with the given denominator. $\frac{3}{8} = \frac{?}{40}$

Divide the larger denominator by the smaller one. $40 \div 8 = 5$

Multiply the numerator and denominator of the given fraction by the quotient (5). $\frac{3}{8} = \frac{3 \cdot 5}{8 \cdot 5} = \frac{15}{40}$

A fraction is in **simplest form** when the numerator and denominator have no common factors other than 1. The fraction $\frac{3}{8}$ is in simplest form because 3 and 8 have no common factors other than 1. The fraction $\frac{15}{40}$ is not in simplest form because the numerator and denominator have a common factor of 5.

IN-CLASS EXAMPLES

6. Write a fraction that is equivalent to $\frac{5}{9}$ and has a denominator of 27. $\frac{15}{27}$
7. Write a fraction that is equivalent to 6 and has a denominator of 5. $\frac{30}{5}$
8. Write $\frac{14}{21}$ in simplest form. $\frac{2}{3}$
9. Write $\frac{24}{16}$ in simplest form. $\frac{3}{2}$
10. Write $\frac{8d}{36}$ in simplest form. $\frac{2d}{9}$

To write a fraction in simplest form, divide the numerator and denominator of the fraction by their common factors.

HOW TO 3 Write $\frac{12}{15}$ in simplest form.

12 and 15 have a common factor of 3. Divide the numerator and denominator by 3.

$$\frac{12}{15} = \frac{12 \div 3}{15 \div 3} = \frac{4}{5}$$

Simplifying a fraction requires that you recognize the common factors of the numerator and denominator. One way to do this is to write the prime factorization of both the numerator and denominator and then divide by the common prime factors.

HOW TO 4 Write $\frac{30}{42}$ in simplest form.

Write the prime factorization of the numerator and denominator. Divide by the common factors.

$$\frac{30}{42} = \frac{\overset{1}{\cancel{2}} \cdot \overset{1}{\cancel{3}} \cdot 5}{\underset{1}{\cancel{2}} \cdot \underset{1}{\cancel{3}} \cdot 7} = \frac{5}{7}$$

HOW TO 5 Write $\frac{2x}{6}$ in simplest form.

Factor the numerator and denominator. Then divide by the common factors.

$$\frac{2x}{6} = \frac{\overset{1}{\cancel{2}} \cdot x}{\underset{1}{\cancel{2}} \cdot 3} = \frac{x}{3}$$

EXAMPLE 6

Write an equivalent fraction with the given denominator:

$$\frac{2}{5} = \frac{?}{30}$$

Solution $30 \div 5 = 6$

$$\frac{2}{5} = \frac{2 \cdot 6}{5 \cdot 6} = \frac{12}{30}$$

$\frac{12}{30}$ is equivalent to $\frac{2}{5}$.

YOU TRY IT 6

Write an equivalent fraction with the given denominator:

$$\frac{5}{8} = \frac{?}{48}$$

Your solution

$\frac{30}{48}$

EXAMPLE 7

Write an equivalent fraction with the given denominator:

$$3 = \frac{?}{15}$$

Solution $3 = \frac{3}{1}$ $\quad 15 \div 1 = 15$

$$3 = \frac{3}{1} = \frac{3 \cdot 15}{1 \cdot 15} = \frac{45}{15}$$

$\frac{45}{15}$ is equivalent to 3.

YOU TRY IT 7

Write an equivalent fraction with the given denominator:

$$8 = \frac{?}{12}$$

Your solution

$\frac{96}{12}$

Solutions on p. S4

EXAMPLE 8

Write $\frac{18}{54}$ in simplest form.

Solution $\frac{18}{54} = \frac{\overset{1}{\cancel{2}} \cdot \overset{1}{\cancel{3}} \cdot \overset{1}{\cancel{3}}}{\underset{1}{\cancel{2}} \cdot \underset{1}{\cancel{3}} \cdot \underset{1}{\cancel{3}} \cdot 3} = \frac{1}{3}$

YOU TRY IT 8

Write $\frac{21}{84}$ in simplest form.

Your solution $\frac{1}{4}$

EXAMPLE 9

Write $\frac{36}{20}$ in simplest form.

Solution $\frac{36}{20} = \frac{\overset{1}{\cancel{2}} \cdot \overset{1}{\cancel{2}} \cdot 3 \cdot 3}{\underset{1}{\cancel{2}} \cdot \underset{1}{\cancel{2}} \cdot 5} = \frac{9}{5}$

YOU TRY IT 9

Write $\frac{32}{12}$ in simplest form.

Your solution $\frac{8}{3}$

EXAMPLE 10

Write $\frac{10m}{12}$ in simplest form.

Solution $\frac{10m}{12} = \frac{\overset{1}{\cancel{2}} \cdot 5 \cdot m}{\underset{1}{\cancel{2}} \cdot 2 \cdot 3} = \frac{5m}{6}$

YOU TRY IT 10

Write $\frac{11t}{11}$ in simplest form.

Your solution

t

Solutions on p. S4

OBJECTIVE C ***To identify the order relation between two fractions***

The number line can be used to determine the order relation between two fractions.

A fraction that appears to the left of a given fraction is less than the given fraction.

$\frac{3}{8}$ is to the left of $\frac{5}{8}$.

0 $\frac{1}{8}$ $\frac{2}{8}$ $\frac{3}{8}$ $\frac{4}{8}$ $\frac{5}{8}$ $\frac{6}{8}$ $\frac{7}{8}$ 1

$\frac{3}{8} < \frac{5}{8}$

A fraction that appears to the right of a given fraction is greater than the given fraction.

$\frac{7}{8}$ is to the right of $\frac{3}{8}$.

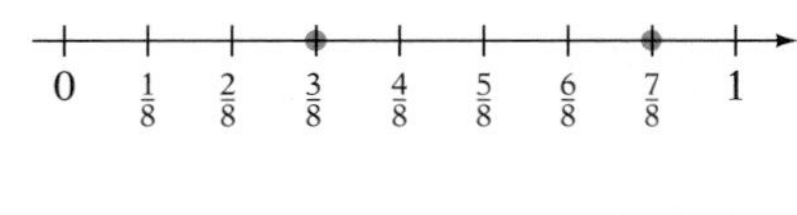

$\frac{7}{8} > \frac{3}{8}$

To find the order relation between two fractions with the *same* denominator, compare the numerators. The fraction with the smaller numerator is the smaller fraction. The fraction with the larger numerator is the larger fraction.

$\frac{3}{8}$ and $\frac{5}{8}$ have the same denominator. $\frac{3}{8} < \frac{5}{8}$ because $3 < 5$.

$\frac{7}{8}$ and $\frac{3}{8}$ have the same denominator. $\frac{7}{8} > \frac{3}{8}$ because $7 > 3$.

IN-CLASS EXAMPLES

11. Place the correct symbol, < or >, between the two numbers.
$\frac{5}{8}$ $\frac{2}{3}$
$\frac{5}{8} < \frac{2}{3}$

12. Place the correct symbol, < or >, between the two numbers.
$\frac{5}{16}$ $\frac{3}{10}$
$\frac{5}{16} > \frac{3}{10}$

Point of Interest

Archimedes (c. 287–212 B.C.) is the person who calculated that $\pi \approx 3\frac{1}{7}$. He actually showed that $3\frac{10}{71} < \pi < 3\frac{1}{7}$. The approximation $3\frac{10}{71}$ is more accurate than $3\frac{1}{7}$ but more difficult to use.

Before comparing two fractions with *different* denominators, rewrite the fractions with a common denominator. The common denominator is the least common multiple (LCM) of the denominators of the fractions. The LCM of the denominators is sometimes called the least common denominator or LCD.

HOW TO 6 Find the order relation between $\frac{5}{12}$ and $\frac{7}{18}$.

Find the LCM of the denominators. The LCM of 12 and 18 is 36.

Write each fraction as an equivalent fraction with the LCM as the denominator.

$$\frac{5}{12} = \frac{5 \cdot 3}{12 \cdot 3} = \frac{15}{36} \longleftarrow \text{Larger numerator}$$

$$\frac{7}{18} = \frac{7 \cdot 2}{18 \cdot 2} = \frac{14}{36} \longleftarrow \text{Smaller numerator}$$

Compare the fractions.

$$\frac{15}{36} > \frac{14}{36}$$

$$\frac{5}{12} > \frac{7}{18}$$

EXAMPLE 11

Place the correct symbol, < or >, between the two numbers.

$\frac{2}{3} \quad \frac{4}{7}$

Solution The LCM of 3 and 7 is 21.

$\frac{2}{3} = \frac{14}{21} \quad \frac{4}{7} = \frac{12}{21}$

$\frac{14}{21} > \frac{12}{21}$

$\frac{2}{3} > \frac{4}{7}$

YOU TRY IT 11

Place the correct symbol, < or >, between the two numbers.

$\frac{4}{9} \quad \frac{8}{21}$

Your solution

$\frac{4}{9} > \frac{8}{21}$

EXAMPLE 12

Place the correct symbol, < or >, between the two numbers.

$\frac{7}{12} \quad \frac{11}{18}$

Solution The LCM of 12 and 18 is 36.

$\frac{7}{12} = \frac{21}{36} \quad \frac{11}{18} = \frac{22}{36}$

$\frac{21}{36} < \frac{22}{36}$

$\frac{7}{12} < \frac{11}{18}$

YOU TRY IT 12

Place the correct symbol, < or >, between the two numbers.

$\frac{17}{24} \quad \frac{7}{9}$

Your solution

$\frac{17}{24} < \frac{7}{9}$

Solutions on p. S5

2.2 EXERCISES

Concept Check

SUGGESTED ASSIGNMENT
Exercises 1–6; Exercises 7–105, odds; Exercises 111–129, odds

1. Use the fraction $\frac{9}{4}$.

a. The numerator of the fraction is __9__. The denominator of the fraction is __4__.

b. Because the numerator is greater than the denominator, this fraction is called a(n) __improper__ fraction.

c. The fraction bar can be read "__divided by__," so the fraction also represents the division problem __9__ ÷ __4__.

2. Fill in each blank with 0, 1, 6, or *undefined.*

a. $\frac{6}{0} =$ __undefined__ **b.** $\frac{6}{1} =$ __6__

c. $\frac{6}{6} =$ __1__ **d.** $\frac{0}{6} =$ __0__

3. The mixed number $3\frac{2}{5}$ can be written as an improper fraction with a denominator of 5. The numerator of the improper fraction is $5 \times \boxed{3} + \boxed{2} = \boxed{17}$. Thus, $3\frac{2}{5} = \frac{\boxed{17}}{\boxed{5}}$.

4. To write $\frac{5}{6}$ as an equivalent fraction with a denominator of 24, multiply the numerator and the denominator by 24 ÷ 6 = __4__. Thus, $\frac{5}{6} = \frac{5 \cdot \boxed{4}}{6 \cdot \boxed{4}} = \frac{\boxed{20}}{24}$.

5. The fraction $\frac{5}{6}$ is in simplest form because the only common factor of the numerator and denominator is __1__. The fraction $\frac{10}{12}$ is not in simplest form because the numerator and denominator have a common factor of __2__.

6. a. To decide the order relation between two fractions, first write the fractions with a common __denominator__. The least common denominator (LCD) of $\frac{3}{10}$ and $\frac{1}{6}$ is the LCM of __10__ and __6__, which is __30__.

b. $\frac{3}{10} = \frac{\boxed{9}}{30}$ and $\frac{1}{6} = \frac{\boxed{5}}{30}$. Because $9 > 5$, $\frac{3}{10}$ __>__ $\frac{1}{6}$.

OBJECTIVE A *To write proper fractions, improper fractions, and mixed numbers*

Express the shaded portion of the circle as a fraction.

7. 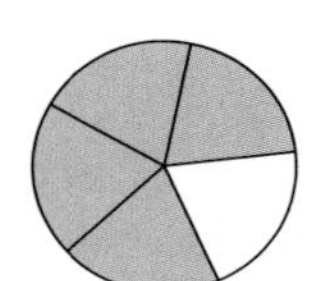 $\frac{4}{5}$

8. 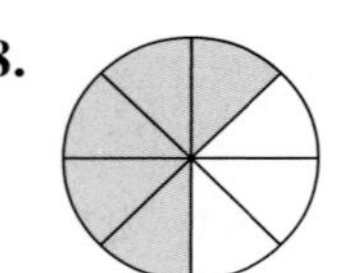 $\frac{5}{8}$

9. 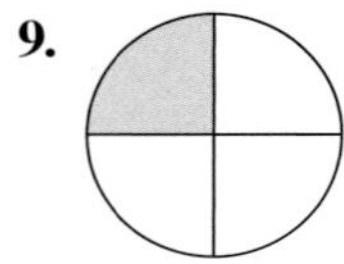 $\frac{1}{4}$

10. 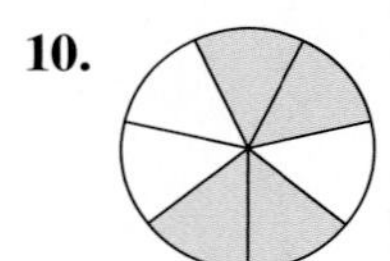 $\frac{4}{7}$

Express the shaded portion of the circles as an improper fraction and as a mixed number.

11. 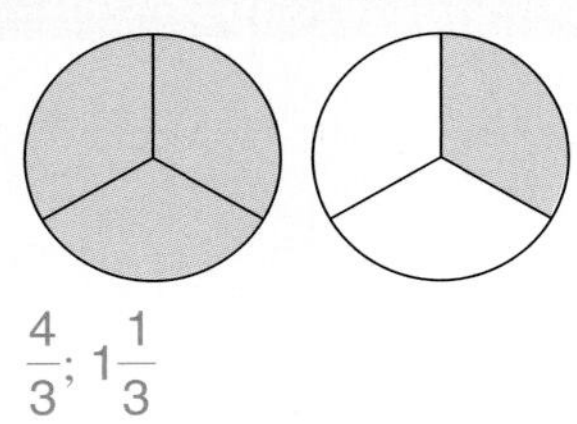

$\frac{4}{3}$; $1\frac{1}{3}$

12. 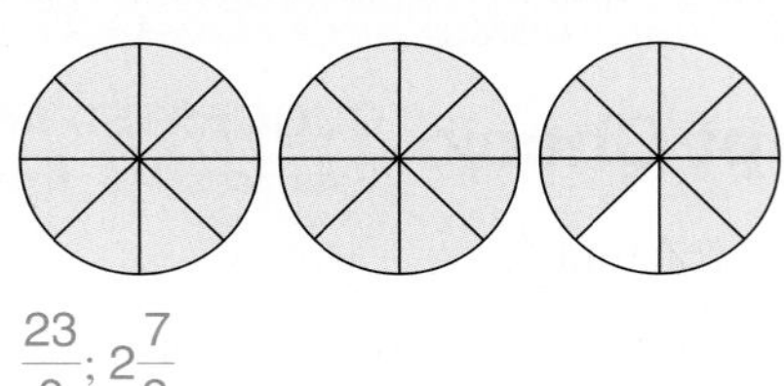

$\frac{23}{8}$; $2\frac{7}{8}$

13. 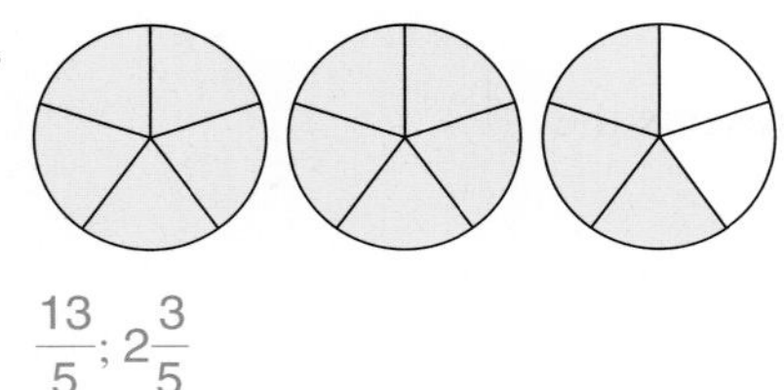

$\frac{13}{5}$; $2\frac{3}{5}$

14. 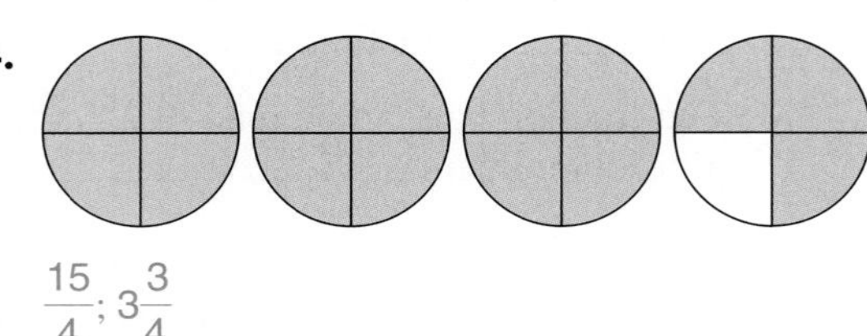

$\frac{15}{4}$; $3\frac{3}{4}$

Write the improper fraction as a mixed number or a whole number.

15. $\frac{13}{4}$ $3\frac{1}{4}$ **16.** $\frac{14}{3}$ $4\frac{2}{3}$ **17.** $\frac{20}{5}$ 4 **18.** $\frac{18}{6}$ 3 **19.** $\frac{27}{10}$ $2\frac{7}{10}$

20. $\frac{31}{3}$ $10\frac{1}{3}$ **21.** $\frac{56}{8}$ 7 **22.** $\frac{27}{9}$ 3 **23.** $\frac{17}{9}$ $1\frac{8}{9}$ **24.** $\frac{8}{3}$ $2\frac{2}{3}$

25. $\frac{12}{5}$ $2\frac{2}{5}$ **26.** $\frac{19}{8}$ $2\frac{3}{8}$ **27.** $\frac{18}{1}$ 18 **28.** $\frac{21}{1}$ 21 **29.** $\frac{32}{15}$ $2\frac{2}{15}$

30. $\frac{39}{14}$ $2\frac{11}{14}$ **31.** $\frac{8}{8}$ 1 **32.** $\frac{12}{12}$ 1 **33.** $\frac{28}{3}$ $9\frac{1}{3}$ **34.** $\frac{43}{5}$ $8\frac{3}{5}$

Write the mixed number or whole number as an improper fraction.

35. $2\frac{1}{4}$ $\frac{9}{4}$ **36.** $4\frac{2}{5}$ $\frac{22}{5}$ **37.** $5\frac{1}{2}$ $\frac{11}{2}$ **38.** $3\frac{2}{3}$ $\frac{11}{3}$ **39.** $2\frac{4}{5}$ $\frac{14}{5}$

40. $6\frac{3}{8}$ $\frac{51}{8}$ **41.** $7\frac{5}{6}$ $\frac{47}{6}$ **42.** $9\frac{1}{5}$ $\frac{46}{5}$ **43.** 7 $\frac{7}{1}$ **44.** 4 $\frac{4}{1}$

45. $8\frac{1}{4}$ $\frac{33}{4}$ **46.** $1\frac{7}{9}$ $\frac{16}{9}$ **47.** $10\frac{1}{3}$ $\frac{31}{3}$ **48.** $6\frac{3}{7}$ $\frac{45}{7}$ **49.** $4\frac{7}{12}$ $\frac{55}{12}$

50. $5\frac{4}{9}$ $\frac{49}{9}$ **51.** 8 $\frac{8}{1}$ **52.** 6 $\frac{6}{1}$ **53.** $12\frac{4}{5}$ $\frac{64}{5}$ **54.** $11\frac{5}{8}$ $\frac{93}{8}$

55. When a mixed number is written as an improper fraction $\frac{a}{b}$, is $a < b$ or is $a > b$?
$a > b$

56. If an improper fraction can be written as a whole number, is the numerator a multiple of the denominator, or is the denominator a multiple of the numerator?
The numerator is a multiple of the denominator.

OBJECTIVE B *To write equivalent fractions*

Write an equivalent fraction with the given denominator.

57. $\frac{1}{2} = \frac{6}{12}$ **58.** $\frac{1}{4} = \frac{5}{20}$ **59.** $\frac{3}{8} = \frac{9}{24}$ **60.** $\frac{9}{11} = \frac{36}{44}$ **61.** $\frac{2}{17} = \frac{6}{51}$

62. $\frac{9}{10} = \frac{72}{80}$ **63.** $\frac{3}{4} = \frac{24}{32}$ **64.** $\frac{5}{8} = \frac{20}{32}$ **65.** $6 = \frac{108}{18}$ **66.** $5 = \frac{175}{35}$

67. $\frac{1}{3} = \frac{30}{90}$ **68.** $\frac{3}{16} = \frac{9}{48}$ **69.** $\frac{2}{3} = \frac{14}{21}$ **70.** $\frac{4}{9} = \frac{16}{36}$ **71.** $\frac{6}{7} = \frac{42}{49}$

72. $\frac{7}{8} = \frac{35}{40}$ **73.** $\frac{4}{9} = \frac{8}{18}$ **74.** $\frac{11}{12} = \frac{44}{48}$ **75.** $7 = \frac{28}{4}$ **76.** $9 = \frac{54}{6}$

Write the fraction in simplest form.

77. $\frac{3}{12}$ $\frac{1}{4}$ **78.** $\frac{10}{22}$ $\frac{5}{11}$ **79.** $\frac{33}{44}$ $\frac{3}{4}$ **80.** $\frac{6}{14}$ $\frac{3}{7}$ **81.** $\frac{4}{24}$ $\frac{1}{6}$

82. $\frac{25}{75}$ $\frac{1}{3}$ **83.** $\frac{8}{33}$ $\frac{8}{33}$ **84.** $\frac{9}{25}$ $\frac{9}{25}$ **85.** $\frac{0}{8}$ 0 **86.** $\frac{0}{11}$ 0

87. $\frac{42}{36}$ $\frac{7}{6}$ **88.** $\frac{30}{18}$ $\frac{5}{3}$ **89.** $\frac{16}{16}$ 1 **90.** $\frac{24}{24}$ 1 **91.** $\frac{21}{35}$ $\frac{3}{5}$

92. $\frac{11}{55}$ $\frac{1}{5}$ **93.** $\frac{16}{60}$ $\frac{4}{15}$ **94.** $\frac{8}{84}$ $\frac{2}{21}$ **95.** $\frac{12}{20}$ $\frac{3}{5}$ **96.** $\frac{24}{36}$ $\frac{2}{3}$

97. $\frac{12m}{18}$ $\frac{2m}{3}$ **98.** $\frac{20x}{25}$ $\frac{4x}{5}$ **99.** $\frac{4y}{8}$ $\frac{y}{2}$ **100.** $\frac{14z}{28}$ $\frac{z}{2}$ **101.** $\frac{24a}{36}$ $\frac{2a}{3}$

102. $\frac{28z}{21}$ $\frac{4z}{3}$ **103.** $\frac{8c}{8}$ c **104.** $\frac{9w}{9}$ w **105.** $\frac{18k}{3}$ $6k$ **106.** $\frac{24t}{4}$ $6t$

For Exercises 107 to 109, for the given condition, state whether the fraction (i) must be in simplest form, (ii) cannot be in simplest form, or (iii) might be in simplest form. If (iii) is true, then name two fractions that meet the given condition, one that is in simplest form and one that is not in simplest form.

107. The numerator and denominator are both even numbers. ii

108. The numerator and denominator are both odd numbers. iii; One example is $\frac{3}{5}$ and $\frac{9}{15}$.

109. The numerator is an odd number and the denominator is an even number. iii; One example is $\frac{5}{6}$ and $\frac{15}{18}$.

OBJECTIVE C *To identify the order relation between two fractions*

Place the correct symbol, < or >, between the two numbers.

110. $\frac{3}{8} < \frac{2}{5}$ **111.** $\frac{5}{7} > \frac{2}{3}$ **112.** $\frac{3}{4} < \frac{7}{9}$ **113.** $\frac{7}{12} < \frac{5}{8}$

114. $\frac{2}{3} > \frac{7}{11}$ **115.** $\frac{11}{14} > \frac{3}{4}$ **116.** $\frac{17}{24} > \frac{11}{16}$ **117.** $\frac{11}{12} > \frac{7}{9}$

118. $\frac{7}{15} > \frac{5}{12}$ **119.** $\frac{5}{8} > \frac{4}{7}$ **120.** $\frac{5}{9} > \frac{11}{21}$ **121.** $\frac{11}{30} > \frac{7}{24}$

122. $\frac{7}{12} < \frac{13}{18}$ **123.** $\frac{9}{11} < \frac{7}{8}$ **124.** $\frac{4}{5} > \frac{7}{9}$ **125.** $\frac{3}{4} < \frac{11}{13}$

126. $\frac{9}{16} > \frac{5}{9}$ **127.** $\frac{2}{3} < \frac{7}{10}$ **128.** $\frac{5}{8} < \frac{13}{20}$ **129.** $\frac{3}{10} > \frac{7}{25}$

For Exercises 130 and 131, find an example of two fractions in simplest form, $\frac{a}{b}$ and $\frac{c}{d}$, that fit the given conditions.

130. $a > c$, $b \neq d$, and $\frac{a}{b} > \frac{c}{d}$.

One example is $\frac{4}{5}$ and $\frac{3}{7}$.

131. $a > c$, $b \neq d$, and $\frac{a}{b} < \frac{c}{d}$.

One example is $\frac{4}{7}$ and $\frac{3}{5}$.

Critical Thinking

132. Measurement A ton is equal to 2000 lb. What fractional part of a ton is 250 lb?

$\frac{1}{8}$

The Fast-Food Industry The table at the right shows the results of a survey that asked fast-food patrons their criteria for choosing where to go for fast food. Three out of every 25 people surveyed said that the speed of the service was most important. Use this table for Exercises 133 and 134.

Fast-Food Patrons' Top Criteria for Fast-Food Restaurants	
Food Quality	$\frac{1}{4}$
Location	$\frac{13}{50}$
Menu	$\frac{4}{25}$
Price	$\frac{2}{25}$
Speed	$\frac{3}{25}$
Other	$\frac{3}{100}$

Source: Maritz Marketing Research, Inc.

133. According to the survey, do more people choose a fast-food restaurant on the basis of its location or on the basis of the quality of its food? Location

134. Which criterion was cited by most people? Location

135. Test Scores You answer 42 questions correctly on an exam of 50 questions. Did you answer more or less than $\frac{8}{10}$ of the questions correctly? More

136. Is the expression $x < \frac{4}{9}$ true when $x = \frac{3}{8}$? Is it true when $x = \frac{5}{12}$? Yes; yes

137. a. On the number line, what fraction is halfway between $\frac{2}{a}$ and $\frac{4}{a}$?

b. Find two fractions evenly spaced between $\frac{5}{b}$ and $\frac{8}{b}$.

a. $\frac{3}{a}$ b. $\frac{6}{b}$ and $\frac{7}{b}$

Projects or Group Activities

138. Geography

a. What fraction of the states in the United States of America have names that begin with the letter M?

b. What fraction of the states have names that begin with the letter A?

c. What fraction of the states have names that begin and end with a vowel?

a. $\frac{4}{25}$ b. $\frac{2}{25}$ c. $\frac{4}{25}$

139. Card Games A standard deck of playing cards consists of 52 cards. **a.** What fractional part of a standard deck of cards is spades? **b.** What fractional part of a standard deck of cards is aces?

a. $\frac{1}{4}$ b. $\frac{1}{13}$

QUICK QUIZ

1. **a.** Write $\frac{10}{3}$ as a mixed number. **b.** Write $4\frac{5}{9}$ as an improper fraction.
   a. $3\frac{1}{3}$ **b.** $\frac{41}{9}$ **[2.2A]**
2. Write a fraction that is equivalent to $\frac{1}{2}$ and has a denominator of 32.
   $\frac{16}{32}$ **[2.2B]**
3. Write $\frac{24}{64}$ in simplest form.
   $\frac{3}{8}$ **[2.2B]**
4. Place the correct symbol, $<$ or $>$, between the two numbers.
   $\frac{1}{3}$ $\frac{5}{16}$
   $\frac{1}{3} > \frac{5}{16}$ **[2.2C]**

SECTION

2.3 Addition and Subtraction of Fractions

OBJECTIVE A *To add fractions*

Tips for Success

Before the class meeting in which your professor begins a new section, you should read each objective statement for that section. Next, browse through the material in that objective. The purpose of browsing through the material is to prepare your brain to accept and organize the new information when it is presented to you. See *AIM for Success* at the front of the book.

Suppose you and a friend order a pizza. The pizza has been cut into 8 equal pieces. If you eat 3 pieces of the pizza and your friend eats 2 pieces, then together you have eaten $\frac{5}{8}$ of the pizza.

Note that in adding the fractions $\frac{3}{8}$ and $\frac{2}{8}$, the numerators are added and the denominator remains the same.

$$\frac{3}{8} + \frac{2}{8} = \frac{3+2}{8} = \frac{5}{8}$$

INSTRUCTOR NOTE

We have chosen to present addition and subtraction of fractions prior to multiplication and division of fractions. If you prefer to present multiplication and division first, simply present Section 2.4 prior to Section 2.3.

Addition of Fractions

To add fractions with the same denominator, add the numerators and place the sum over the common denominator.

$\frac{a}{b} + \frac{c}{b} = \frac{a+c}{b}$, where $b \neq 0$

EXAMPLE

Add: $\frac{5}{16} + \frac{7}{16}$

$$\frac{5}{16} + \frac{7}{16} = \frac{5+7}{16} = \frac{12}{16} = \frac{3}{4}$$

- **The denominators are the same. Add the numerators and place the sum over the common denominator.**
- **Write the answer in simplest form.**

INSTRUCTOR NOTE

Ask the students what value x cannot be in the expression $\frac{4}{x} + \frac{8}{x}$.

HOW TO 1 Add: $\frac{4}{x} + \frac{8}{x}$

The denominators are the same. Add the numerators and place the sum over the common denominator.

$$\frac{4}{x} + \frac{8}{x} = \frac{4+8}{x} = \frac{12}{x}$$

Before two fractions can be added, the fractions must have the same denominator. To add fractions with different denominators, first rewrite the fractions as equivalent fractions with a common denominator. The common denominator is the least common multiple (LCM) of the denominators of the fractions. The LCM of denominators is sometimes called the least common denominator (LCD).

Integrating Technology

Some scientific calculators have a fraction key, a^b/c. It is used to perform operations on fractions. To use this key to simplify the expression at the right, enter

5 a^b/c 6 + 3 a^b/c 8 =

($\frac{5}{6}$, $\frac{3}{8}$)

INSTRUCTOR NOTE

Some students may find it easier to find the LCM by multiplying the denominators and then dividing by the common factor of the two denominators. In the case of 6 and 8, $6 \cdot 8 = 48$. Now divide by 2, the common factor of 6 and 8: $48 \div 2 = 24$.

HOW TO 2 Find the sum of $\frac{5}{6}$ and $\frac{3}{8}$.

The common denominator is the LCM of 6 and 8. The LCM of 6 and 8 is 24.

Write the fractions as equivalent fractions with the common denominator.

$$\frac{5}{6} + \frac{3}{8} = \frac{20}{24} + \frac{9}{24}$$

Add the fractions.

$$= \frac{20 + 9}{24}$$

$$= \frac{29}{24} = 1\frac{5}{24}$$

APPLY THE CONCEPT

During a recent year, over 42 million Americans changed homes. Figure 2.1 shows what fractions of the people moved within the same county, moved to a different county in the same state, and moved to a different state. What fractional part of those who changed homes moved outside the county they had been living in?

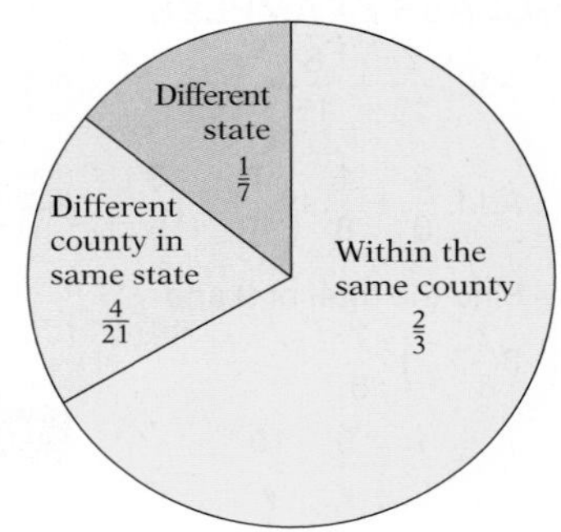

Figure 2.1 Where Americans Moved

Source: Census Bureau; *Geographical Mobility*

Add the fraction of the people who moved to a different county in the same state and the fraction who moved to a different state.

$$\frac{4}{21} + \frac{1}{7} = \frac{4}{21} + \frac{3}{21} = \frac{7}{21} = \frac{1}{3}$$

$\frac{1}{3}$ of the Americans who changed homes moved outside of the county they had been living in.

The mixed number $2\frac{1}{2}$ is the sum of 2 and $\frac{1}{2}$.

$$2\frac{1}{2} = 2 + \frac{1}{2}$$

Therefore, the sum of a whole number and a fraction is a mixed number.

$$2 + \frac{1}{2} = 2\frac{1}{2}$$

$$3 + \frac{4}{5} = 3\frac{4}{5}$$

$$8 + \frac{7}{9} = 8\frac{7}{9}$$

The sum of a whole number and a mixed number is a mixed number.

Take Note

$$5 + 4\frac{2}{7} = 5 + \left(4 + \frac{2}{7}\right)$$
$$= (5 + 4) + \frac{2}{7}$$
$$= 9 + \frac{2}{7} = 9\frac{2}{7}$$

HOW TO 3 Add: $5 + 4\frac{2}{7}$

Add the whole numbers (5 and 4).

Write the fraction.

$$5 + 4\frac{2}{7} = 9\frac{2}{7}$$

Integrating Technology

Use the fraction key on a calculator to enter mixed numbers. For the example at the right, enter

3 a^b/c 5 a^b/c 8 + ($3\frac{5}{8}$)

4 a^b/c 7 a^b/c 12 = ($4\frac{7}{12}$)

IN-CLASS EXAMPLES

1. Add: $\frac{7}{12} + \frac{8}{15}$ $1\frac{7}{60}$
2. Add: $\frac{2}{3} + \frac{1}{8} + \frac{7}{12}$ $1\frac{3}{8}$
3. Find the total of 9 and $3\frac{7}{8}$. $12\frac{7}{8}$
4. Add: $\frac{1}{y} + \frac{9}{y}$ $\frac{10}{y}$
5. Evaluate $x + y + z$ for $x = 3\frac{4}{15}$, $y = 2\frac{3}{5}$, and $z = 4\frac{7}{10}$. $10\frac{17}{30}$

To add two mixed numbers, first write the fractional parts as equivalent fractions with a common denominator. Then add the fractional parts and add the whole numbers.

HOW TO 4 Add: $3\frac{5}{8} + 4\frac{7}{12}$

Write the fractions as equivalent fractions with a common denominator. The common denominator is the LCM of 8 and 12. The LCM is 24.

$$3\frac{5}{8} + 4\frac{7}{12} = 3\frac{15}{24} + 4\frac{14}{24}$$

Add the fractional parts and add the whole numbers.

$$= 7\frac{29}{24}$$

Write the sum in simplest form.

$$= 7 + \frac{29}{24}$$

$$= 7 + 1\frac{5}{24}$$

$$= 8\frac{5}{24}$$

HOW TO 5 Evaluate $x + y$ when $x = 2\frac{3}{4}$ and $y = 7\frac{5}{6}$.

$$x + y$$

Replace x with $2\frac{3}{4}$ and y with $7\frac{5}{6}$.

$$2\frac{3}{4} + 7\frac{5}{6}$$

Write the fractions as equivalent fractions with a common denominator.

$$= 2\frac{9}{12} + 7\frac{10}{12}$$

Add the fractional parts and add the whole numbers.

$$= 9\frac{19}{12}$$

Write the sum in simplest form.

$$= 10\frac{7}{12}$$

EXAMPLE 1

Add: $\frac{9}{16} + \frac{5}{12}$

Solution

$$\frac{9}{16} + \frac{5}{12} = \frac{27}{48} + \frac{20}{48}$$

$$= \frac{27 + 20}{48} = \frac{47}{48}$$

YOU TRY IT 1

Add: $\frac{7}{12} + \frac{3}{8}$

Your solution

$\frac{23}{24}$

Solution on p. S5

EXAMPLE 2

Add: $\frac{4}{5} + \frac{3}{4} + \frac{5}{8}$

Solution

$$\frac{4}{5} + \frac{3}{4} + \frac{5}{8} = \frac{32}{40} + \frac{30}{40} + \frac{25}{40}$$
$$= \frac{87}{40} = 2\frac{7}{40}$$

YOU TRY IT 2

Add: $\frac{3}{5} + \frac{2}{3} + \frac{5}{6}$

Your solution

$2\frac{1}{10}$

EXAMPLE 3

Find the sum of $12\frac{4}{7}$ and 19.

Solution

$$12\frac{4}{7} + 19 = 31\frac{4}{7}$$

• Add the whole numbers. Write the fraction.

YOU TRY IT 3

What is the sum of 16 and $8\frac{5}{9}$?

Your solution

$24\frac{5}{9}$

EXAMPLE 4

Is $\frac{2}{3}$ a solution of $\frac{1}{4} + y = \frac{11}{12}$?

Solution

$$\frac{1}{4} + y = \frac{11}{12}$$

$\frac{1}{4} + \frac{2}{3}$	$\frac{11}{12}$
$\frac{3}{12} + \frac{8}{12}$	$\frac{11}{12}$

$$\frac{11}{12} = \frac{11}{12}$$

Yes, $\frac{2}{3}$ is a solution of $\frac{1}{4} + y = \frac{11}{12}$.

YOU TRY IT 4

Is $\frac{3}{8}$ a solution of $\frac{2}{3} + z = \frac{23}{24}$?

Your solution

No

EXAMPLE 5

Evaluate $x + y + z$ for $x = 2\frac{1}{6}$, $y = 4\frac{3}{8}$, and $z = 7\frac{5}{9}$.

Solution

$x + y + z$

$$2\frac{1}{6} + 4\frac{3}{8} + 7\frac{5}{9} = 2\frac{12}{72} + 4\frac{27}{72} + 7\frac{40}{72}$$
$$= 13\frac{79}{72}$$
$$= 14\frac{7}{72}$$

YOU TRY IT 5

Evaluate $x + y + z$ for $x = 3\frac{5}{6}$, $y = 2\frac{1}{9}$, and $z = 5\frac{5}{12}$.

Your solution

$11\frac{13}{36}$

Solutions on p. S5

OBJECTIVE B *To subtract fractions*

Point of Interest

The first woman mathematician for whom documented evidence exists is Hypatia (370–415). She lived in Alexandria, Egypt, and lectured at the Museum, the forerunner of our modern university. She made important contributions in mathematics, astronomy, and philosophy.

In the last objective, it was stated that in order for fractions to be added, the fractions must have the same denominator. The same is true for subtracting fractions: The two fractions must have the same denominator.

Subtraction of Fractions

To subtract fractions with the same denominator, subtract the numerators and place the difference over the common denominator.

$\frac{a}{b} - \frac{c}{b} = \frac{a-c}{b}$, where $b \neq 0$

EXAMPLE

Subtract: $\frac{5}{8} - \frac{3}{8}$

$\frac{5}{8} - \frac{3}{8} = \frac{5-3}{8}$ • The denominators are the same. Subtract the numerators and place the difference over the common denominator.

$= \frac{2}{8} = \frac{1}{4}$ • Write the answer in simplest form.

To subtract fractions with different denominators, first rewrite the fractions as equivalent fractions with a common denominator. The common denominator is the least common multiple (LCM) of the denominators of the fractions.

HOW TO 6 Subtract: $\frac{5}{12} - \frac{3}{8}$

The common denominator is the LCM of 12 and 8. — The LCM of 12 and 8 is 24.

Write the fractions as equivalent fractions with the common denominator. — $\frac{5}{12} - \frac{3}{8} = \frac{10}{24} - \frac{9}{24}$

Subtract the fractions. — $= \frac{10-9}{24} = \frac{1}{24}$

To subtract mixed numbers when borrowing is not necessary, subtract the fractional parts and then subtract the whole numbers.

HOW TO 7 Find the difference between $5\frac{8}{9}$ and $2\frac{5}{6}$.

The LCM of 9 and 6 is 18.

Write the fractions as equivalent fractions with the LCM as the common denominator. — $5\frac{8}{9} - 2\frac{5}{6} = 5\frac{16}{18} - 2\frac{15}{18}$

Subtract the fractional parts and subtract the whole numbers. — $= 3\frac{1}{18}$

IN-CLASS EXAMPLES

6. Subtract: $\frac{3}{4} - \frac{3}{8}$ **$\frac{3}{8}$**
7. What is $4\frac{1}{2} - 1\frac{2}{5}$? **$3\frac{1}{10}$**
8. Subtract: $8 - 4\frac{3}{7}$ **$3\frac{4}{7}$**
9. Which number, $\frac{1}{2}$ or $\frac{7}{10}$, is a solution of the equation $n - \frac{3}{5} = \frac{1}{10}$? **$\frac{7}{10}$**

As in subtraction with whole numbers, subtraction of mixed numbers may involve borrowing.

HOW TO 8 Subtract: $7 - 4\frac{2}{3}$

Borrow 1 from 7. Write the 1 as a fraction with the same denominator as the fractional part of the mixed number (3).

$$7 - 4\frac{2}{3} = 6\frac{3}{3} - 4\frac{2}{3}$$

Note: $7 = 6 + 1 = 6 + \frac{3}{3} = 6\frac{3}{3}$

Subtract the fractional parts and subtract the whole numbers.

$$= 2\frac{1}{3}$$

HOW TO 9 Subtract: $9\frac{1}{8} - 2\frac{5}{6}$

Write the fractions as equivalent fractions with a common denominator.

$$9\frac{1}{8} - 2\frac{5}{6} = 9\frac{3}{24} - 2\frac{20}{24}$$

$3 < 20$. Borrow 1 from 9. Add the 1 to $\frac{3}{24}$.

Note: $9\frac{3}{24} = 9 + \frac{3}{24} = 8 + 1 + \frac{3}{24}$

$= 8 + \frac{24}{24} + \frac{3}{24} = 8 + \frac{27}{24} = 8\frac{27}{24}$

$$= 8\frac{27}{24} - 2\frac{20}{24}$$

Subtract.

$$= 6\frac{7}{24}$$

APPLY THE CONCEPT

The inseam of a pant leg is $30\frac{1}{2}$ in. long. What is the length of the inseam after a tailor cuts $\frac{3}{4}$ in. from the pant leg?

To find the length of the inseam, subtract $\frac{3}{4}$ from $30\frac{1}{2}$.

$$30\frac{1}{2} - \frac{3}{4} = 30\frac{2}{4} - \frac{3}{4} = 29\frac{6}{4} - \frac{3}{4} = 29\frac{3}{4}$$

After the tailor cuts $\frac{3}{4}$ in. from the pant leg, the length of the inseam is $29\frac{3}{4}$ in.

HOW TO 10 Evaluate $x - y$ for $x = 7\frac{2}{9}$ and $y = 3\frac{5}{12}$.

$x - y$

Replace x with $7\frac{2}{9}$ and y with $3\frac{5}{12}$.

$7\frac{2}{9} - 3\frac{5}{12}$

Write the fractions as equivalent fractions with a common denominator.

$= 7\frac{8}{36} - 3\frac{15}{36}$

$8 < 15$. Borrow 1 from 7. Add the 1 to $\frac{8}{36}$.

Note: $7\frac{8}{36} = 6 + \frac{36}{36} + \frac{8}{36} = 6\frac{44}{36}$

$= 6\frac{44}{36} - 3\frac{15}{36}$

Subtract.

$= 3\frac{29}{36}$

EXAMPLE 6

Subtract: $\frac{5}{6} - \frac{3}{8}$

Solution

$$\frac{5}{6} - \frac{3}{8} = \frac{20}{24} - \frac{9}{24} = \frac{20 - 9}{24} = \frac{11}{24}$$

YOU TRY IT 6

Subtract: $\frac{5}{6} - \frac{7}{9}$

Your solution

$\frac{1}{18}$

EXAMPLE 7

Find the difference between $8\frac{5}{6}$ and $2\frac{3}{4}$.

Solution

$$8\frac{5}{6} - 2\frac{3}{4} = 8\frac{10}{12} - 2\frac{9}{12} = 6\frac{1}{12}$$

YOU TRY IT 7

Find the difference between $9\frac{7}{8}$ and $5\frac{2}{3}$.

Your solution

$4\frac{5}{24}$

EXAMPLE 8

Subtract: $7 - 3\frac{5}{13}$

Solution

$$7 - 3\frac{5}{13} = 6\frac{13}{13} - 3\frac{5}{13} = 3\frac{8}{13}$$

• **Write 7 as $6\frac{13}{13}$.**

YOU TRY IT 8

Subtract: $6 - 4\frac{2}{11}$

Your solution

$1\frac{9}{11}$

Solutions on p. S5

EXAMPLE 9

Is $\frac{3}{2}$ a solution of the equation $\frac{2}{3} = w - \frac{5}{6}$?

Solution

$$\frac{2}{3} = w - \frac{5}{6}$$

$$\frac{2}{3} \;\Big|\; \frac{3}{2} - \frac{5}{6}$$ • Replace w with $\frac{3}{2}$.

$$\frac{2}{3} \;\Big|\; \frac{9}{6} - \frac{5}{6}$$ • Write equivalent fractions with a common denominator.

$$\frac{2}{3} \;\Big|\; \frac{4}{6}$$ • Subtract the fractions.

$$\frac{2}{3} = \frac{2}{3}$$

Yes, $\frac{3}{2}$ is a solution of the equation.

YOU TRY IT 9

Is $\frac{1}{4}$ a solution of the equation $\frac{2}{3} - v = \frac{11}{12}$?

Your solution

No

Solution on p. S5

INSTRUCTOR NOTE

If students are distracted by fractions in an application problem, suggest that they reread the problem, substituting whole numbers for the fractions. This may help them determine how to solve the problem.

OBJECTIVE C *To solve application problems*

EXAMPLE 10

The length of a regulation NCAA football must be no less than $10\frac{7}{8}$ in. and no more than $11\frac{7}{16}$ in. What is the difference between the minimum and maximum lengths of an NCAA regulation football?

Strategy

To find the difference, subtract the minimum length $\left(10\frac{7}{8}\right)$ from the maximum length $\left(11\frac{7}{16}\right)$.

Solution

$$11\frac{7}{16} - 10\frac{7}{8} = 11\frac{7}{16} - 10\frac{14}{16}$$
$$= 10\frac{23}{16} - 10\frac{14}{16} = \frac{9}{16}$$

The difference is $\frac{9}{16}$ in.

YOU TRY IT 10

The Heller Research Group conducted a survey to determine favorite doughnut flavors. $\frac{2}{5}$ of the respondents named glazed doughnuts, $\frac{8}{25}$ named filled doughnuts, and $\frac{3}{20}$ named frosted doughnuts. What fraction of the respondents did not name glazed, filled, or frosted as their favorite type of doughnut?

Your strategy

Your solution

$\frac{13}{100}$

IN-CLASS EXAMPLES

10. A plane trip from Boston to San Francisco takes $6\frac{1}{4}$ h. After the plane has been in the air for $3\frac{1}{2}$ h, how much time remains before landing? $2\frac{3}{4}$ **h**

Solution on p. S5

2.3 EXERCISES

Concept Check

SUGGESTED ASSIGNMENT
Exercises 1–6; Exercises 7–109, every other odd; Exercises 113–125, odds;
More challenging exercises: Exercises 127 and 128

For Exercises 1 and 2, circle the correct phrase to complete the sentence.

1. Fractions cannot be added unless their numerators/denominators are the same.
denominators

2. To add two fractions with the same denominator, place the sum of the numerators over the sum of the denominators/common denominator.
common denominator

3. Write "the difference of $\frac{1}{2}$ and $\frac{3}{7}$" as a subtraction problem:
$\frac{1}{2}$ — $\frac{3}{7}$.

4. Complete the subtraction: $8 - 3\frac{4}{5} = 7\frac{5}{5} - 3\frac{4}{5} = 4\frac{1}{5}$

For Exercises 5 and 6, state whether you would use addition or subtraction to find the specified amount.

5. You have $3\frac{1}{2}$ h available to do an English assignment and to study for a math test. You spend $1\frac{2}{3}$ h on the English assignment. To find the amount of time you have left to study for the math test, use subtraction.

© Diego Cervo/Shutterstock.com

6. This morning you studied for $1\frac{1}{4}$ h, and this afternoon you studied for $1\frac{1}{2}$ h. To find the total amount of time you spent studying today, use addition.

OBJECTIVE A *To add fractions*

Add.

7. $\frac{4}{11} + \frac{5}{11}$
$\frac{9}{11}$

8. $\frac{3}{7} + \frac{2}{7}$
$\frac{5}{7}$

9. $\frac{2}{3} + \frac{1}{3}$
1

10. $\frac{1}{2} + \frac{1}{2}$
1

11. $\frac{5}{6} + \frac{5}{6}$
$1\frac{2}{3}$

12. $\frac{3}{8} + \frac{7}{8}$
$1\frac{1}{4}$

13. $\frac{7}{18} + \frac{13}{18} + \frac{1}{18}$
$1\frac{1}{6}$

14. $\frac{8}{15} + \frac{2}{15} + \frac{11}{15}$
$1\frac{2}{5}$

15. $\frac{7}{b} + \frac{9}{b}$

$\frac{16}{b}$

16. $\frac{3}{y} + \frac{6}{y}$

$\frac{9}{y}$

17. $\frac{5}{c} + \frac{4}{c}$

$\frac{9}{c}$

18. $\frac{2}{a} + \frac{8}{a}$

$\frac{10}{a}$

19. $\frac{1}{x} + \frac{4}{x} + \frac{6}{x}$

$\frac{11}{x}$

20. $\frac{8}{n} + \frac{5}{n} + \frac{3}{n}$

$\frac{16}{n}$

21. $\frac{1}{4} + \frac{2}{3}$

$\frac{11}{12}$

22. $\frac{2}{3} + \frac{1}{2}$

$1\frac{1}{6}$

23. $\frac{7}{15} + \frac{9}{20}$

$\frac{11}{12}$

24. $\frac{4}{9} + \frac{1}{6}$

$\frac{11}{18}$

25. $\frac{2}{3} + \frac{1}{12} + \frac{5}{6}$

$1\frac{7}{12}$

26. $\frac{3}{8} + \frac{1}{2} + \frac{5}{12}$

$1\frac{7}{24}$

27. $\frac{7}{12} + \frac{3}{4} + \frac{4}{5}$

$2\frac{2}{15}$

28. $\frac{7}{11} + \frac{1}{2} + \frac{5}{6}$

$1\frac{32}{33}$

29. $8 + 7\frac{2}{3}$

$15\frac{2}{3}$

30. $6 + 9\frac{3}{5}$

$15\frac{3}{5}$

31. $2\frac{1}{6} + 3\frac{1}{2}$

$5\frac{2}{3}$

32. $1\frac{3}{10} + 4\frac{3}{5}$

$5\frac{9}{10}$

33. $8\frac{3}{5} + 6\frac{9}{20}$

$15\frac{1}{20}$

34. $7\frac{5}{12} + 3\frac{7}{9}$

$11\frac{7}{36}$

35. $5\frac{5}{12} + 4\frac{7}{9}$

$10\frac{7}{36}$

36. $2\frac{11}{12} + 3\frac{7}{15}$

$6\frac{23}{60}$

37. $2\frac{1}{4} + 3\frac{1}{2} + 1\frac{2}{3}$

$7\frac{5}{12}$

38. $1\frac{2}{3} + 2\frac{5}{6} + 4\frac{7}{9}$

$9\frac{5}{18}$

39. Find the total of $\frac{2}{7}$, $\frac{3}{14}$, and $\frac{1}{4}$.

$\frac{3}{4}$

40. Find the total of $\frac{1}{3}$, $\frac{5}{18}$, and $\frac{2}{9}$.

$\frac{5}{6}$

41. Find $5\frac{4}{9}$ plus $6\frac{5}{6}$.

$12\frac{5}{18}$

42. Find $\frac{7}{8}$ increased by $1\frac{1}{3}$.

$2\frac{5}{24}$

43. Find $3\frac{7}{12}$ plus $2\frac{5}{8}$.

$6\frac{5}{24}$

44. Find the sum of $7\frac{11}{15}$, $2\frac{7}{10}$, and $5\frac{2}{5}$.

$15\frac{5}{6}$

Evaluate the variable expression $x + y$ for the given values of x and y.

45. $x = \frac{3}{5}, y = \frac{4}{5}$

$1\frac{2}{5}$

46. $x = \frac{5}{8}, y = \frac{3}{8}$

1

47. $x = \frac{5}{6}, y = \frac{8}{9}$

$1\frac{13}{18}$

48. $x = \frac{5}{8}, y = \frac{1}{6}$

$\frac{19}{24}$

Evaluate the variable expression $x + y + z$ for the given values of x, y, and z.

49. $x = \frac{3}{8}, y = \frac{1}{4}, z = \frac{7}{12}$

$1\frac{5}{24}$

50. $x = \frac{5}{6}, y = \frac{2}{3}, z = \frac{7}{24}$

$1\frac{19}{24}$

51. $x = 1\frac{1}{2}, y = 3\frac{3}{4}, z = 6\frac{5}{12}$

$11\frac{2}{3}$

52. $x = 7\frac{2}{3}, y = 2\frac{5}{6}, z = 5\frac{4}{9}$

$15\frac{17}{18}$

53. $x = 4\frac{3}{5}, y = 8\frac{7}{10}, z = 1\frac{9}{20}$

$14\frac{3}{4}$

54. $x = 2\frac{3}{14}, y = 5\frac{5}{7}, z = 3\frac{1}{2}$

$11\frac{3}{7}$

55. Is $\frac{3}{5}$ a solution of the equation $z + \frac{1}{4} = \frac{17}{20}$?

Yes

56. Is $\frac{3}{8}$ a solution of the equation $\frac{3}{4} = t + \frac{3}{8}$?

Yes

Loans The figure at the right shows how the money borrowed on home equity loans is spent. Use this graph for Exercises 57 and 58.

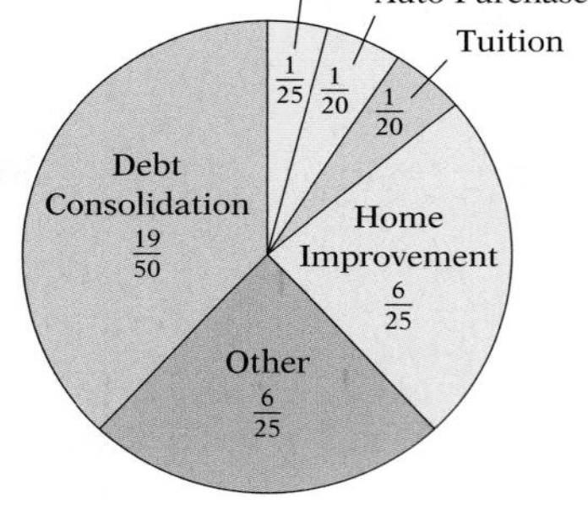

How Money Borrowed on Home Equity Loans Is Spent

Source: Consumer Bankers Association

57. What fractional part of the money borrowed on home equity loans is spent on debt consolidation and home improvement?

$\frac{31}{50}$

58. What fractional part of the money borrowed on home equity loans is spent on home improvement, cars, and tuition?

$\frac{17}{50}$

59. Which expression is equivalent to $\frac{3}{4} + \frac{1}{5}$?

(i) $\frac{3 + 1}{4 + 5}$ **(ii)** $\frac{(3 + 5) + (1 + 4)}{4 + 5}$ **(iii)** $\frac{(3 \cdot 5) + (1 \cdot 4)}{4 \cdot 5}$ **(iv)** $\frac{3 + 1}{4 \cdot 5}$

iii

60. Estimate the sum to the nearest whole number.

a. $\frac{7}{8} + \frac{4}{5}$ **b.** $\frac{1}{3} + \frac{1}{2}$ **c.** $\frac{1}{8} + \frac{1}{4}$

a. 2 b. 1 c. 0

OBJECTIVE B *To subtract fractions*

Subtract.

61. $\frac{7}{12} - \frac{5}{12}$

$\frac{1}{6}$

62. $\frac{17}{20} - \frac{9}{20}$

$\frac{2}{5}$

63. $\frac{11}{24} - \frac{7}{24}$

$\frac{1}{6}$

64. $\frac{39}{48} - \frac{23}{48}$

$\frac{1}{3}$

65. $\frac{8}{d} - \frac{3}{d}$

$\frac{5}{d}$

66. $\frac{12}{y} - \frac{7}{y}$

$\frac{5}{y}$

67. $\frac{10}{n} - \frac{5}{n}$

$\frac{5}{n}$

68. $\frac{13}{c} - \frac{6}{c}$

$\frac{7}{c}$

69. $\frac{3}{7} - \frac{5}{14}$

$\frac{1}{14}$

70. $\frac{7}{8} - \frac{5}{16}$

$\frac{9}{16}$

71. $\frac{2}{3} - \frac{1}{6}$

$\frac{1}{2}$

72. $\frac{5}{21} - \frac{1}{6}$

$\frac{1}{14}$

73. $\frac{11}{12} - \frac{2}{3}$

$\frac{1}{4}$

74. $\frac{9}{20} - \frac{1}{30}$

$\frac{5}{12}$

75. $4\frac{11}{18} - 2\frac{5}{18}$

$2\frac{1}{3}$

76. $3\frac{7}{12} - 1\frac{1}{12}$

$2\frac{1}{2}$

77. $8\frac{3}{4} - 2$

$6\frac{3}{4}$

78. $6\frac{5}{9} - 4$

$2\frac{5}{9}$

79. $8\frac{5}{6} - 7\frac{3}{4}$

$1\frac{1}{12}$

80. $5\frac{7}{8} - 3\frac{2}{3}$

$2\frac{5}{24}$

81. $7 - 3\frac{5}{8}$

$3\frac{3}{8}$

82. $6 - 2\frac{4}{5}$

$3\frac{1}{5}$

83. $10 - 4\frac{8}{9}$

$5\frac{1}{9}$

84. $5 - 2\frac{7}{18}$

$2\frac{11}{18}$

85. $7\frac{3}{8} - 4\frac{5}{8}$

$2\frac{3}{4}$

86. $11\frac{1}{6} - 8\frac{5}{6}$

$2\frac{1}{3}$

87. $12\frac{5}{12} - 10\frac{17}{24}$

$1\frac{17}{24}$

88. $16\frac{1}{3} - 11\frac{5}{12}$

$4\frac{11}{12}$

89. $6\frac{2}{3} - 1\frac{7}{8}$

$4\frac{19}{24}$

90. $7\frac{7}{12} - 2\frac{5}{6}$

$4\frac{3}{4}$

91. $10\frac{2}{5} - 8\frac{7}{10}$

$1\frac{7}{10}$

92. $5\frac{5}{6} - 4\frac{7}{8}$

$\frac{23}{24}$

93. What is $\frac{2}{3}$ less than $\frac{7}{8}$?

$\frac{5}{24}$

94. Find the difference between $\frac{8}{9}$ and $\frac{1}{6}$.

$\frac{13}{18}$

95. Find 8 less $1\frac{7}{12}$.

$6\frac{5}{12}$

96. Find 9 minus $5\frac{3}{20}$.

$3\frac{17}{20}$

Evaluate the variable expression $x - y$ for the given values of x and y.

97. $x = \frac{8}{9}, y = \frac{5}{9}$

$\frac{1}{3}$

98. $x = \frac{5}{6}, y = \frac{1}{6}$

$\frac{2}{3}$

99. $x = \frac{7}{15}, y = \frac{3}{10}$

$\frac{1}{6}$

100. $x = \frac{5}{6}, y = \frac{2}{15}$

$\frac{7}{10}$

101. $x = 5\frac{7}{9}, y = 4\frac{2}{3}$

$1\frac{1}{9}$

102. $x = 9\frac{5}{8}, y = 2\frac{3}{16}$

$7\frac{7}{16}$

103. $x = 7\frac{9}{10}, y = 3\frac{1}{2}$

$4\frac{2}{5}$

104. $x = 6\frac{4}{9}, y = 1\frac{1}{6}$

$5\frac{5}{18}$

105. $x = 5, y = 2\frac{7}{9}$

$2\frac{2}{9}$

106. $x = 8, y = 4\frac{5}{6}$

$3\frac{1}{6}$

107. $x = 10\frac{1}{2}, y = 5\frac{7}{12}$

$4\frac{11}{12}$

108. $x = 9\frac{2}{15}, y = 6\frac{11}{15}$

$2\frac{2}{5}$

109. Is $\frac{3}{4}$ a solution of the equation $\frac{4}{5} = \frac{31}{20} - y$?

Yes

110. Is $\frac{2}{3}$ a solution of the equation $\frac{2}{3} - x = 0$?

Yes

111. Which statement describes a pair of fractions for which the least common denominator is one of the denominators?

(i) The denominator of one fraction is a factor of the denominator of the second fraction.

(ii) The denominators of the two fractions have no common factors. i

QUICK QUIZ

1. Add: $\frac{3}{5} + \frac{9}{10} + \frac{4}{15}$

   $1\frac{23}{30}$ [2.3A]

2. Add: $6\frac{1}{2} + 5\frac{2}{3}$

   $12\frac{1}{6}$ [2.3A]

3. Find the difference between 11 and $8\frac{5}{6}$.

   $2\frac{1}{6}$ [2.3B]

4. Subtract: $6\frac{2}{3} - 3\frac{5}{6}$

   $2\frac{5}{6}$ [2.3B]

5. You worked $1\frac{1}{2}$ h on Monday, $2\frac{1}{4}$ h on Tuesday, and $3\frac{1}{4}$ h on Wednesday. Find the total number of hours you worked during the three days. **7 h** **[2.3C]**

OBJECTIVE C *To solve application problems*

112. **Demographics** Three-twentieths of the men in the United States are left-handed. (*Source*: Scripps Survey Research Center Poll) What fraction of the men in the United States are not left-handed?

$\frac{17}{20}$

113. **Real Estate** You purchased $3\frac{1}{4}$ acres of land and then sold $1\frac{1}{2}$ acres of the property. How many acres of the property do you own now?

$1\frac{3}{4}$ acres

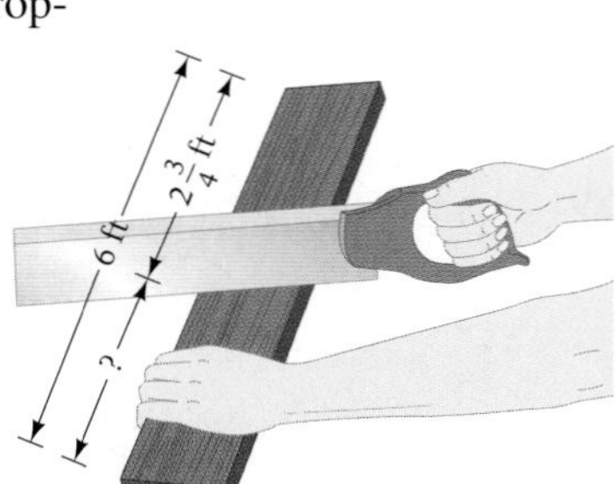

114. **Carpentry** A $2\frac{3}{4}$-foot piece is cut from a 6-foot board. Find the length of the remaining piece of board.

$3\frac{1}{4}$ ft

115. **Community Service** You are required to contribute 20 h of community service to the town in which your college is located. After you have contributed $12\frac{1}{4}$ h, how many more hours of community service are still required of you?

$7\frac{3}{4}$ h

116. Student Debt Read the news clipping at the right.
a. What fraction of undergraduate students do not go into debt to go to college?
b. What fraction of student debt is owed to the federal government?

a. $\frac{1}{3}$ b. Insufficient information

In the NEWS!

Average Student Debt for College is $19,202

Approximately $\frac{2}{3}$ of undergraduate students go into debt to go to college. The average debt is $19,202. Most often the student debt is owed to the federal government.
Source: www.msnbc.msn.com

117. Construction A roofer and an apprentice are roofing a newly constructed house. In one day, the roofer completes $\frac{1}{3}$ of the job and the apprentice completes $\frac{1}{4}$ of the job. How much of the job remains to be done? Working at the same rate, can the roofer and the apprentice complete the job in one more day?

$\frac{5}{12}$; Yes

118. Geometry The course of a yachting race is in the shape of a triangle with sides that measure $4\frac{3}{10}$ mi, $3\frac{7}{10}$ mi, and $2\frac{1}{2}$ mi. Find the total length of the course. Use the formula $P = a + b + c$.

$10\frac{1}{2}$ mi

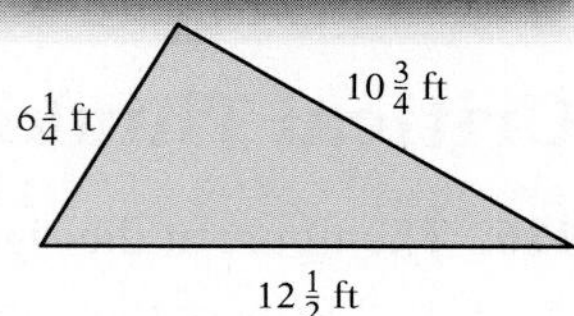

119. Geometry You want to fence in the triangular plot of land shown at the right. How many feet of fencing do you need? Use the formula $P = a + b + c$.

$29\frac{1}{2}$ ft

120. Sociology The table at the right shows the results of a survey in which adults in the United States were asked how many evening meals they cook at home during an average week. **a.** Which response was given most frequently? **b.** What fraction of the adult population cooks two or fewer dinners at home per week? **c.** What fraction of the adult population cooks five or more dinners at home per week? Is this less than half or more than half of the people?

a. 5 meals b. $\frac{23}{100}$ c. $\frac{49}{100}$; less than half

Responses to the question, "How many evening meals do you cook at home each week?"	
0	$\frac{2}{25}$
1	$\frac{1}{20}$
2	$\frac{1}{10}$
3	$\frac{13}{100}$
4	$\frac{3}{20}$
5	$\frac{21}{100}$
6	$\frac{9}{100}$
7	$\frac{19}{100}$

Source: Millward Brown for Whirlpool

121. Hiking Two hikers plan a 3-day, $27\frac{1}{2}$-mile backpack trip carrying a total of 80 lb. The hikers plan to travel $7\frac{3}{8}$ mi the first day and $10\frac{1}{3}$ mi the second day.
a. How many total miles do the hikers plan to travel the first two days?
b. How many miles will be left to travel on the third day?

a. $17\frac{17}{24}$ mi b. $9\frac{19}{24}$ mi

Golf During the second half of the 1900s, greenskeepers mowed the grass on golf putting surfaces progressively lower. The table at the right shows the average grass height by decade. Use this table for Exercises 122 and 123.

Average Height of Grass on Golf Putting Surfaces	
Decade	*Height (in inches)*
1950s	$\frac{1}{4}$
1960s	$\frac{7}{32}$
1970s	$\frac{3}{16}$
1980s	$\frac{5}{32}$
1990s	$\frac{1}{8}$

Source: Golf Course Superintendents Association of America

122. What was the difference between the average height of the grass in the 1980s and in the 1950s?

$\frac{3}{32}$ in.

123. Calculate the difference between the average grass height in the 1970s and in the 1960s.

$\frac{1}{32}$ in.

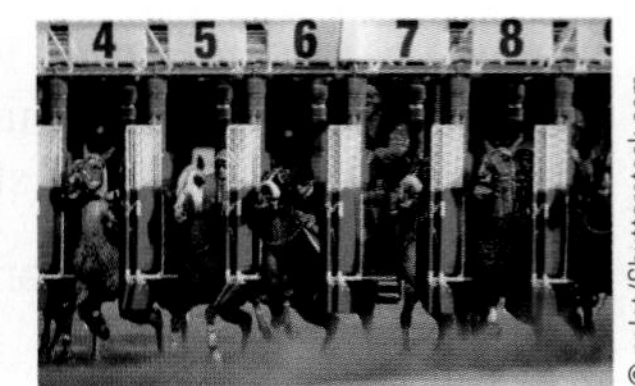

© polat/Shutterstock.com

124. **Horse Racing** The 3-year-olds in the Kentucky Derby run $1\frac{1}{4}$ mi. The horses in the Belmont Stakes run $1\frac{1}{2}$ mi, and the horses in the Preakness Stakes run $1\frac{3}{16}$ mi. How much farther do the horses run in the Kentucky Derby than in the Preakness Stakes? How much farther do they run in the Belmont Stakes than in the Preakness Stakes?

$\frac{1}{16}$ mi; $\frac{5}{16}$ mi

125. **Boxing** A boxer is put on a diet to gain 15 lb in 4 weeks. The boxer gains $4\frac{1}{2}$ lb the first week and $3\frac{3}{4}$ lb the second week. How much weight must the boxer gain during the third and fourth weeks in order to gain a total of 15 lb?

$6\frac{3}{4}$ lb

Critical Thinking

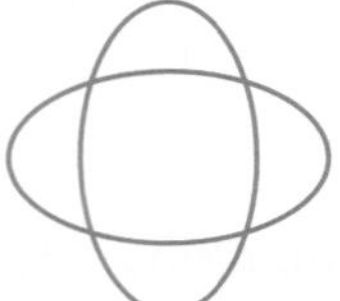

126. The figure at the right is divided into 5 parts. Is each part of the figure $\frac{1}{5}$ of the figure? Why or why not? No, because the parts are not equal in size.

127. Draw a diagram that illustrates the addition of two fractions with the same denominator. Answers will vary.

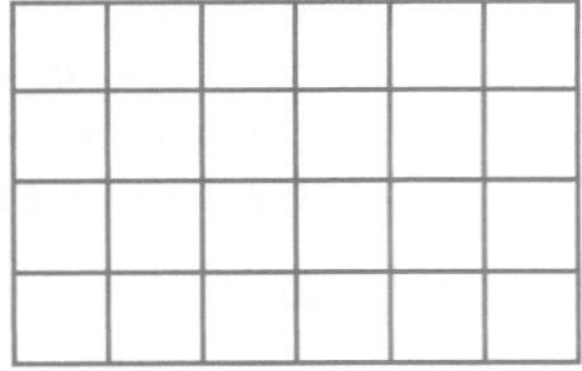

128. Use the diagram at the right to illustrate the sum of $\frac{1}{8}$ and $\frac{5}{6}$. Why does the figure contain 24 squares? Would it be possible to illustrate the sum of $\frac{1}{8}$ and $\frac{5}{6}$ if there were 48 squares in the figure? What if there were 16 squares? Make a list of the possible numbers of squares that could be used to illustrate the sum of $\frac{1}{8}$ and $\frac{5}{6}$.
The complete solution is given in the *Solutions Manual.*

Projects or Group Activities

For Exercises 129 to 134, give an example of a problem that meets the described condition. The fractions in your examples must be proper fractions with different denominators. If it is not possible to write a problem that meets the given condition, write "not possible."
For Exercises 130, 131, 132, and 134, answers will vary. Possible answers are given.

129. An improper fraction is added to an improper fraction and the result is a proper fraction.

Not possible

130. A proper fraction is added to a proper fraction and the result is an improper fraction.

$\frac{2}{3} + \frac{1}{2} = \frac{7}{6}$

131. A proper fraction is added to an improper fraction and the result is a whole number.

$\frac{4}{6} + \frac{4}{3} = 2$

132. A proper fraction is added to a proper fraction and the result is a proper fraction.

$\frac{1}{2} + \frac{1}{3} = \frac{5}{6}$

133. A proper fraction is subtracted from a proper fraction and the result is an improper fraction.

Not possible

134. A proper fraction is subtracted from an improper fraction and the result is an improper fraction.

$\frac{5}{4} - \frac{1}{5} = \frac{21}{20}$

SECTION

2.4 Multiplication and Division of Fractions

OBJECTIVE A To multiply fractions

To multiply two fractions, multiply the numerators and multiply the denominators.

> **Take Note**
> Note that fractions do not need to have the same denominator in order to be multiplied.

Multiplication of Fractions

The product of two fractions is the product of the numerators over the product of the denominators.

$\frac{a}{b} \cdot \frac{c}{d} = \frac{ac}{bd}$, where $b \neq 0$ and $d \neq 0$

EXAMPLE

Multiply: $\frac{2}{5} \cdot \frac{1}{3}$

$\frac{2}{5} \cdot \frac{1}{3} = \frac{2 \cdot 1}{5 \cdot 3}$ • **Multiply the numerators. Multiply the denominators.**

$= \frac{2}{15}$

The product $\frac{2}{5} \cdot \frac{1}{3}$ shown in the example (1) above can be read "$\frac{2}{5}$ times $\frac{1}{3}$" or "$\frac{2}{5}$ of $\frac{1}{3}$." Reading the times sign as "of" is useful in diagramming the product of two fractions.

$\frac{1}{3}$ of the bar at the right is shaded.

We want to shade $\frac{2}{5}$ of the $\frac{1}{3}$ already shaded.

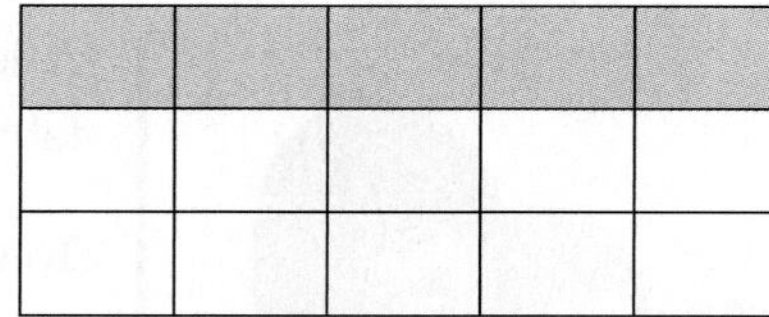

$\frac{2}{15}$ of the bar is now shaded.

$$\frac{2}{5} \text{ of } \frac{1}{3} = \frac{2}{5} \cdot \frac{1}{3} = \frac{2}{15}$$

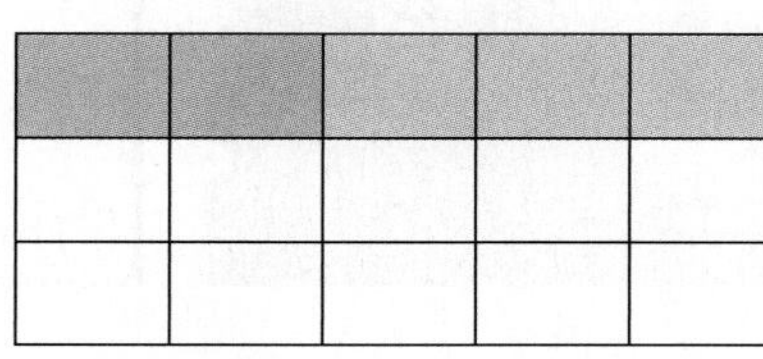

If a is a natural number, then $\frac{1}{a}$ is called the **reciprocal** or **multiplicative inverse** of a. Note that $a \cdot \frac{1}{a} = \frac{a}{1} \cdot \frac{1}{a} = \frac{a}{a} = 1$.

The product of a number and its multiplicative inverse is 1. $\frac{1}{8} \cdot 8 = 8 \cdot \frac{1}{8} = 1$

After multiplying two fractions, write the product in simplest form.

HOW TO 1 Multiply: $\frac{3}{8} \cdot \frac{4}{9}$

Multiply the numerators.
Multiply the denominators.

$$\frac{3}{8} \cdot \frac{4}{9} = \frac{3 \cdot 4}{8 \cdot 9}$$

Express the fraction in simplest form by first writing the prime factorization of each number.

$$= \frac{3 \cdot 2 \cdot 2}{2 \cdot 2 \cdot 2 \cdot 3 \cdot 3}$$

Divide by the common factors and write the product in simplest form.

$$= \frac{1}{6}$$

To multiply a whole number by a fraction or a mixed number, first write the whole number as a fraction with a denominator of 1.

HOW TO 2 Multiply: $3 \cdot \frac{5}{8}$

Write the whole number 3 as the fraction $\frac{3}{1}$.

$$3 \cdot \frac{5}{8} = \frac{3}{1} \cdot \frac{5}{8}$$

Multiply the fractions.
There are no common factors in the numerator and denominator.

$$= \frac{3 \cdot 5}{1 \cdot 8}$$

Write the improper fraction as a mixed number.

$$= \frac{15}{8} = 1\frac{7}{8}$$

Point of Interest

Try this: What is the result if you take one-third of a half-dozen and add to it one-fourth of the product of the result and 8?

INSTRUCTOR NOTE

For the problem above, one-third of a half-dozen is 2; one-fourth of the product of 2 and 8 is 4; 2 + 4 = 6.

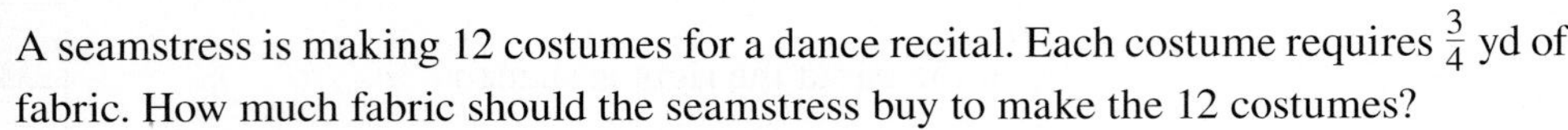

APPLY THE CONCEPT

A seamstress is making 12 costumes for a dance recital. Each costume requires $\frac{3}{4}$ yd of fabric. How much fabric should the seamstress buy to make the 12 costumes?

To find the amount of fabric the seamstress should buy, multiply the amount of fabric needed for each costume $\left(\frac{3}{4}\right)$ by the number of costumes (12).

$$12 \cdot \frac{3}{4} = \frac{12}{1} \cdot \frac{3}{4} = \frac{12 \cdot 3}{1 \cdot 4} = \frac{36}{4} = 9$$

The seamstress should buy 9 yd of fabric.

HOW TO 3 Multiply: $\frac{x}{7} \cdot \frac{y}{5}$

Multiply the numerators.
Multiply the denominators.

$$\frac{x}{7} \cdot \frac{y}{5} = \frac{x \cdot y}{7 \cdot 5}$$

Write the product in simplest form.

$$= \frac{xy}{35}$$

IN-CLASS EXAMPLES

1. Multiply: $\frac{5}{6} \cdot \frac{18}{25} \cdot \frac{5}{9}$ $\frac{1}{3}$
2. Multiply: $\frac{c}{9} \cdot \frac{d}{7}$ $\frac{cd}{63}$
3. What is $\frac{5}{9}$ times 12? $6\frac{2}{3}$
4. Multiply: $2\frac{1}{4} \cdot 3\frac{1}{5}$ $7\frac{1}{5}$
5. Evaluate xy for $x = \frac{4}{5}$ and $y = \frac{5}{8}$. $\frac{1}{2}$
6. Evaluate $\left(\frac{3}{5}\right)^3 \cdot \left(\frac{5}{6}\right)^2$. $\frac{3}{20}$

When a factor is a mixed number, first write the mixed number as an improper fraction. Then multiply.

HOW TO 4 Find the product of $4\frac{1}{6}$ and $2\frac{7}{10}$.

Write each mixed number as an improper fraction. $4\frac{1}{6} \cdot 2\frac{7}{10} = \frac{25}{6} \cdot \frac{27}{10}$

Multiply the fractions. $= \frac{25 \cdot 27}{6 \cdot 10}$

Write the product in simplest form. $= \frac{5 \cdot 5 \cdot 3 \cdot 3 \cdot 3}{2 \cdot 3 \cdot 2 \cdot 5}$

$= \frac{45}{4} = 11\frac{1}{4}$

HOW TO 5 Is $\frac{2}{3}$ a solution of the equation $\frac{3}{4}x = \frac{1}{2}$?

$$\frac{3}{4}x = \frac{1}{2}$$

Replace x by $\frac{2}{3}$ and then simplify.

$$\frac{3}{4}\left(\frac{2}{3}\right) \;\Big|\; \frac{1}{2}$$

$$\frac{3 \cdot 2}{4 \cdot 3} \;\Big|\; \frac{1}{2}$$

$$\frac{3 \cdot 2}{2 \cdot 2 \cdot 3} \;\Big|\; \frac{1}{2}$$

The results are equal. $\frac{1}{2} = \frac{1}{2}$

Yes, $\frac{2}{3}$ is a solution of the equation.

Point of Interest

René Descartes (1596–1650) was the first mathematician to extensively use exponential notation as it is used today. However, for some unknown reason, he always used xx for x^2.

Recall that an exponent indicates the repeated multiplication of the same factor. For example,

$$3^5 = 3 \cdot 3 \cdot 3 \cdot 3 \cdot 3$$

The exponent, 5, indicates how many times the base, 3, occurs as a factor.

The base of an exponential expression can be a fraction; for example, $\left(\frac{2}{3}\right)^4$. To evaluate this expression, write the factor as many times as indicated by the exponent and then multiply.

$$\left(\frac{2}{3}\right)^4 = \frac{2}{3} \cdot \frac{2}{3} \cdot \frac{2}{3} \cdot \frac{2}{3} = \frac{2 \cdot 2 \cdot 2 \cdot 2}{3 \cdot 3 \cdot 3 \cdot 3} = \frac{16}{81}$$

HOW TO 6 Evaluate $\left(\frac{3}{5}\right)^2 \cdot \left(\frac{5}{6}\right)^3$.

Write each factor as many times as indicated by the exponent. $\left(\frac{3}{5}\right)^2 \cdot \left(\frac{5}{6}\right)^3 = \frac{3}{5} \cdot \frac{3}{5} \cdot \frac{5}{6} \cdot \frac{5}{6} \cdot \frac{5}{6}$

Multiply. $= \frac{3 \cdot 3 \cdot 5 \cdot 5 \cdot 5}{5 \cdot 5 \cdot 6 \cdot 6 \cdot 6}$

Write the product in simplest form. $= \frac{5}{24}$

EXAMPLE 1

Multiply: $\frac{7}{9} \cdot \frac{3}{14} \cdot \frac{2}{5}$

Solution $\frac{7}{9} \cdot \frac{3}{14} \cdot \frac{2}{5} = \frac{7 \cdot 3 \cdot 2}{9 \cdot 14 \cdot 5}$

$= \frac{7 \cdot 3 \cdot 2}{3 \cdot 3 \cdot 2 \cdot 7 \cdot 5} = \frac{1}{15}$

YOU TRY IT 1

Multiply: $\frac{5}{12} \cdot \frac{9}{35} \cdot \frac{7}{8}$

Your solution

$\frac{3}{32}$

EXAMPLE 2

Multiply: $\frac{6}{x} \cdot \frac{8}{y}$

Solution $\frac{6}{x} \cdot \frac{8}{y} = \frac{6 \cdot 8}{x \cdot y}$

$= \frac{48}{xy}$

YOU TRY IT 2

Multiply: $\frac{y}{10} \cdot \frac{z}{7}$

Your solution

$\frac{yz}{70}$

EXAMPLE 3

What is the product of $\frac{7}{12}$ and 4?

Solution $\frac{7}{12} \cdot 4 = \frac{7}{12} \cdot \frac{4}{1}$ • Write 4 as $\frac{4}{1}$.

$= \frac{7 \cdot 4}{12 \cdot 1}$

$= \frac{7 \cdot 2 \cdot 2}{2 \cdot 2 \cdot 3 \cdot 1}$

$= \frac{7}{3} = 2\frac{1}{3}$

YOU TRY IT 3

Find the product of $\frac{8}{9}$ and 6.

Your solution

$5\frac{1}{3}$

EXAMPLE 4

Multiply: $7\frac{1}{2} \cdot 4\frac{2}{5}$

Solution $7\frac{1}{2} \cdot 4\frac{2}{5} = \frac{15}{2} \cdot \frac{22}{5}$

$= \frac{15 \cdot 22}{2 \cdot 5}$

$= \frac{3 \cdot 5 \cdot 2 \cdot 11}{2 \cdot 5}$

$= \frac{33}{1} = 33$

YOU TRY IT 4

Multiply: $3\frac{6}{7} \cdot 2\frac{4}{9}$

Your solution

$9\frac{3}{7}$

Solutions on p. S6

EXAMPLE 5

Evaluate x^2y^2 for $x = 1\frac{1}{2}$ and $y = \frac{2}{3}$.

Solution

x^2y^2

$$\left(1\frac{1}{2}\right)^2 \cdot \left(\frac{2}{3}\right)^2 = \left(\frac{3}{2}\right)^2 \cdot \left(\frac{2}{3}\right)^2$$

$$= \frac{3}{2} \cdot \frac{3}{2} \cdot \frac{2}{3} \cdot \frac{2}{3}$$

$$= \frac{3 \cdot 3 \cdot 2 \cdot 2}{2 \cdot 2 \cdot 3 \cdot 3} = 1$$

YOU TRY IT 5

Evaluate x^4y^3 for $x = 2\frac{1}{3}$ and $y = \frac{3}{7}$.

Your solution

$2\frac{1}{3}$

Solution on p. S6

OBJECTIVE B *To divide fractions*

IN-CLASS EXAMPLES

7. Divide: $\frac{5}{28} \div \frac{25}{42}$ $\frac{3}{10}$
8. Divide: $\frac{b}{6} \div \frac{d}{8}$ $\frac{4b}{3d}$
9. What is 8 divided by $\frac{4}{5}$? 10
10. Divide: $3\frac{1}{3} \div 2\frac{2}{9}$ $1\frac{1}{2}$
11. Evaluate $x \div y$ for $x = 4\frac{1}{2}$ and $y = 6$. $\frac{3}{4}$

The **reciprocal** of a fraction is that fraction with the numerator and denominator interchanged.

The reciprocal of $\frac{3}{4}$ is $\frac{4}{3}$. The reciprocal of $\frac{a}{b}$ is $\frac{b}{a}$.

The process of interchanging the numerator and denominator of a fraction is called **inverting** the fraction.

To find the reciprocal of a whole number, first rewrite the whole number as a fraction with a denominator of 1. Then invert the fraction.

$$6 = \frac{6}{1}$$

The reciprocal of 6 is $\frac{1}{6}$.

Reciprocals are used to rewrite division problems as related multiplication problems. Look at the following two problems:

$$6 \div 2 = 3 \qquad 6 \cdot \frac{1}{2} = 3$$

6 divided by 2 equals 3. 6 times the reciprocal of 2 equals 3.

Division is defined as multiplication by the reciprocal. Therefore, "divided by 2" is the same as "times $\frac{1}{2}$." Fractions are divided by making this substitution.

Point of Interest

Try this: What number when multiplied by its reciprocal is equal to 1?

INSTRUCTOR NOTE

The answer to the above question is "any number except zero."

Division of Fractions

To divide two fractions, multiply by the reciprocal of the divisor.

$\frac{a}{b} \div \frac{c}{d} = \frac{a}{b} \cdot \frac{d}{c}$, where $b \neq 0$, $c \neq 0$, and $d \neq 0$

EXAMPLE

Divide: $\frac{2}{5} \div \frac{3}{4}$

$\frac{2}{5} \div \frac{3}{4} = \frac{2}{5} \cdot \frac{4}{3}$ • Rewrite the division as multiplication by the reciprocal.

$= \frac{2 \cdot 4}{5 \cdot 3} = \frac{8}{15}$ • Multiply the fractions.

Note in the next example that when we divide a fraction and a whole number, we first write the whole number as a fraction with a denominator of 1.

Take Note

$\frac{3}{4} \div 6 = \frac{1}{8}$ means that if $\frac{3}{4}$ is divided into 6 equal parts, each equal part is $\frac{1}{8}$. Therefore, if 6 people share $\frac{3}{4}$ of a pizza, each person eats $\frac{1}{8}$ of the pizza.

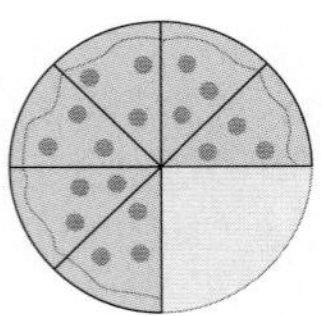

APPLY THE CONCEPT

If 6 people share $\frac{3}{4}$ of a pizza, what fraction of the pizza does each person eat?

To find the fraction, find the quotient of $\frac{3}{4}$ and 6.

$\frac{3}{4} \div 6 = \frac{3}{4} \div \frac{6}{1}$ • Write 6 as $\frac{6}{1}$.

$= \frac{3}{4} \cdot \frac{1}{6}$ • Rewrite the division as multiplication by the reciprocal.

$= \frac{3 \cdot 1}{4 \cdot 6}$ • Multiply the fractions.

$= \frac{3 \cdot 1}{2 \cdot 2 \cdot 2 \cdot 3} = \frac{1}{8}$

Each person eats $\frac{1}{8}$ of the pizza.

When a number in a quotient is a mixed number, first write the mixed number as an improper fraction. Then divide the fractions.

HOW TO 7 Divide: $\frac{2}{3} \div 1\frac{1}{4}$

Write the mixed number $1\frac{1}{4}$ as an improper fraction. $\frac{2}{3} \div 1\frac{1}{4} = \frac{2}{3} \div \frac{5}{4}$

Rewrite the division as multiplication by the reciprocal. $= \frac{2}{3} \cdot \frac{4}{5}$

Multiply the fractions. $= \frac{2 \cdot 4}{3 \cdot 5} = \frac{8}{15}$

EXAMPLE 6

Divide: $\frac{4}{5} \div \frac{8}{15}$

Solution $\frac{4}{5} \div \frac{8}{15} = \frac{4}{5} \cdot \frac{15}{8}$ • Multiply by the reciprocal.

$= \frac{4 \cdot 15}{5 \cdot 8}$

$= \frac{2 \cdot 2 \cdot 3 \cdot 5}{5 \cdot 2 \cdot 2 \cdot 2}$

$= \frac{3}{2} = 1\frac{1}{2}$

YOU TRY IT 6

Divide: $\frac{5}{6} \div \frac{10}{27}$

Your solution

$2\frac{1}{4}$

EXAMPLE 7

Divide: $3\frac{4}{15} \div 2\frac{1}{10}$

Solution $3\frac{4}{15} \div 2\frac{1}{10} = \frac{49}{15} \div \frac{21}{10}$

$= \frac{49}{15} \cdot \frac{10}{21}$

$= \frac{49 \cdot 10}{15 \cdot 21}$

$= \frac{7 \cdot 7 \cdot 2 \cdot 5}{3 \cdot 5 \cdot 3 \cdot 7}$

$= \frac{14}{9} = 1\frac{5}{9}$

YOU TRY IT 7

Divide: $4\frac{3}{8} \div 3\frac{1}{2}$

Your solution

$1\frac{1}{4}$

EXAMPLE 8

What is the quotient of 6 and $\frac{3}{5}$?

Solution $6 \div \frac{3}{5} = \frac{6}{1} \cdot \frac{5}{3}$

$= \frac{6 \cdot 5}{1 \cdot 3}$

$= \frac{2 \cdot 3 \cdot 5}{1 \cdot 3}$

$= \frac{10}{1} = 10$

YOU TRY IT 8

Find the quotient of 4 and $\frac{6}{7}$.

Your solution

$4\frac{2}{3}$

Solutions on p. S6

EXAMPLE 9

Divide: $\frac{x}{2} \div \frac{y}{4}$

Solution $\frac{x}{2} \div \frac{y}{4} = \frac{x}{2} \cdot \frac{4}{y}$

$= \frac{x \cdot 4}{2 \cdot y}$

$= \frac{x \cdot 2 \cdot 2}{2 \cdot y} = \frac{2x}{y}$

YOU TRY IT 9

Divide: $\frac{x}{8} \div \frac{y}{6}$

Your solution

$\frac{3x}{4y}$

EXAMPLE 10

Evaluate $x \div y$ for $x = 3\frac{1}{8}$ and $y = 5$.

Solution $x \div y$

$3\frac{1}{8} \div 5 = \frac{25}{8} \div \frac{5}{1}$

$= \frac{25}{8} \cdot \frac{1}{5}$

$= \frac{25 \cdot 1}{8 \cdot 5}$

$= \frac{5 \cdot 5 \cdot 1}{2 \cdot 2 \cdot 2 \cdot 5} = \frac{5}{8}$

YOU TRY IT 10

Evaluate $x \div y$ for $x = 2\frac{1}{4}$ and $y = 9$.

Your solution

$\frac{1}{4}$

Solutions on p. S6

OBJECTIVE C *To simplify complex fractions*

A **complex fraction** is a fraction whose numerator or denominator contains one or more fractions. Examples of complex fractions are shown below.

Main fraction bar ⟶ $\dfrac{\frac{3}{4}}{\frac{7}{8}}$ $\qquad \dfrac{4}{3 - \frac{1}{2}}$ $\qquad \dfrac{\frac{9}{10} + \frac{3}{5}}{\frac{5}{6}}$ $\qquad \dfrac{3\frac{1}{2} \cdot 2\frac{5}{8}}{\left(4\frac{2}{3}\right) \div \left(3\frac{1}{5}\right)}$

Look at the first example given above and recall that the fraction bar can be read "divided by."

Therefore, $\dfrac{\frac{3}{4}}{\frac{7}{8}}$ can be read "$\frac{3}{4}$ divided by $\frac{7}{8}$" and can be written $\frac{3}{4} \div \frac{7}{8}$. This is the division of two fractions, which can be simplified by multiplying by the reciprocal, as shown below.

$$\frac{\frac{3}{4}}{\frac{7}{8}} = \frac{3}{4} \div \frac{7}{8} = \frac{3}{4} \cdot \frac{8}{7} = \frac{3 \cdot 8}{4 \cdot 7} = \frac{6}{7}$$

To simplify a complex fraction, first simplify the expression above the main fraction bar and the expression below the main fraction bar; the result is one number in the numerator and one number in the denominator. Then rewrite the complex fraction as a division problem by reading the main fraction bar as "divided by."

HOW TO 8 Simplify: $\dfrac{4}{3-\dfrac{1}{2}}$

The numerator (4) is already simplified. Simplify the expression in the denominator.

Note: $3 - \frac{1}{2} = \frac{6}{2} - \frac{1}{2} = \frac{5}{2}$

$$\frac{4}{3-\dfrac{1}{2}} = \frac{4}{\dfrac{5}{2}}$$

Rewrite the complex fraction as division.

$$= 4 \div \frac{5}{2}$$

Divide.

$$= \frac{4}{1} \div \frac{5}{2}$$

$$= \frac{4}{1} \cdot \frac{2}{5}$$

Write the answer in simplest form.

$$= \frac{8}{5} = 1\frac{3}{5}$$

IN-CLASS EXAMPLES

12. Simplify: $\dfrac{1\dfrac{5}{6}+\dfrac{2}{3}}{2\dfrac{1}{3}-\dfrac{2}{3}}$ $\quad \dfrac{3}{2}$

13. Evaluate $\dfrac{2x-y}{4z}$ when $x = \dfrac{7}{8}$, $y = \dfrac{3}{4}$, and $z = \dfrac{1}{16}$. $\quad 4$

HOW TO 9 Evaluate $\frac{wx}{yz}$ for $w = 1\frac{1}{3}$, $x = 2\frac{5}{8}$, $y = 4\frac{1}{2}$, and $z = 3\frac{1}{3}$.

$$\frac{wx}{yz}$$

Replace each variable with its given value.

$$\frac{1\dfrac{1}{3}\cdot 2\dfrac{5}{8}}{4\dfrac{1}{2}\cdot 3\dfrac{1}{3}}$$

Simplify the numerator.

Note: $1\frac{1}{3} \cdot 2\frac{5}{8} = \frac{4}{3} \cdot \frac{21}{8} = \frac{7}{2}$

Simplify the denominator.

Note: $4\frac{1}{2} \cdot 3\frac{1}{3} = \frac{9}{2} \cdot \frac{10}{3} = 15$

$$= \frac{\dfrac{7}{2}}{15}$$

Rewrite the complex fraction as division.

$$= \frac{7}{2} \div 15$$

Divide by multiplying by the reciprocal.

Note: $15 = \frac{15}{1}$; the reciprocal of $\frac{15}{1}$ is $\frac{1}{15}$.

$$= \frac{7}{2} \cdot \frac{1}{15} = \frac{7}{30}$$

EXAMPLE 11

Simplify: $\dfrac{\frac{9}{10}+\frac{3}{5}}{1\frac{1}{4}}$

Solution

$$\frac{\frac{9}{10}+\frac{3}{5}}{1\frac{1}{4}} = \frac{\frac{3}{10}}{\frac{5}{4}}$$

$$= \frac{3}{10} \div \frac{5}{4} = \frac{3}{10}\cdot\frac{4}{5} = \frac{6}{25}$$

YOU TRY IT 11

Simplify: $\dfrac{\frac{5}{6}}{\frac{5}{12}-\frac{1}{3}}$

Your solution

10

EXAMPLE 12

Evaluate the variable expression $\frac{x-y}{z}$ for $x = 4\frac{1}{8}$, $y = 2\frac{5}{8}$, and $z = \frac{3}{4}$.

Solution

$$\frac{x-y}{z}$$

$$\frac{4\frac{1}{8}-2\frac{5}{8}}{\frac{3}{4}} = \frac{\frac{3}{2}}{\frac{3}{4}} = \frac{3}{2}\div\frac{3}{4} = \frac{3}{2}\cdot\frac{4}{3} = 2$$

YOU TRY IT 12

Evaluate the variable expression $\frac{x}{y-z}$ for $x = 2\frac{4}{9}$, $y = 3$, and $z = 1\frac{1}{3}$.

Your solution

$1\frac{7}{15}$

Solutions on p. S6

OBJECTIVE D *To solve application problems and use formulas*

IN-CLASS EXAMPLES

14. A apprentice mason earns \$16 an hour. What are the apprentice mason's earnings for working $7\frac{3}{4}$ h? **\$124**
15. A car used $15\frac{3}{10}$ gal of gasoline on a 459-mile trip. On average, how many miles did this car travel on 1 gal of gasoline? **30 mi**

Figure *ABC* is a triangle. *AB* is the **base,** *b*, of the triangle. The line segment from *C* that forms a right angle with the base is the **height,** *h*, of the triangle. The formula for the area of a triangle is given below.

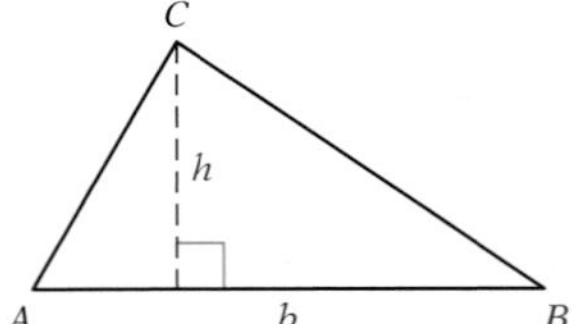

Area of a Triangle

The formula for the area of a triangle is $A = \frac{1}{2}bh$, where A is the area of the triangle, b is the base, and h is the height.

EXAMPLE

$A = \frac{1}{2}bh = \frac{1}{2}(6)(2) = 3(2) = 6$

The area of the triangle at the right is 6 m^2.

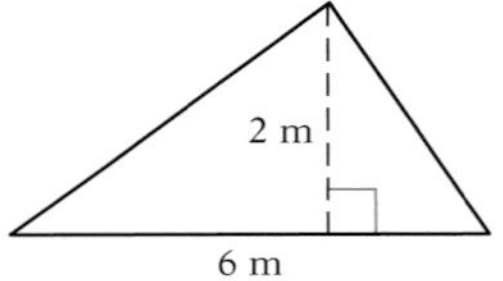

EXAMPLE 13

A riveter uses metal plates that are in the shape of a triangle and have a base of 12 cm and a height of 6 cm. Find the area of one metal plate.

Strategy

To find the area, use the formula for the area of a triangle, $A = \frac{1}{2}bh$. $b = 12$ and $h = 6$.

Solution

$A = \frac{1}{2}bh$

$A = \frac{1}{2}(12)(6)$

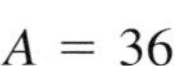

$A = 36$

The area is 36 cm^2.

YOU TRY IT 13

Find the amount of felt needed to make a banner that is in the shape of a triangle with a base of 18 in. and a height of 9 in.

Your strategy

Your solution

81 in^2

EXAMPLE 14

A 12-foot board is cut into pieces $2\frac{1}{2}$ ft long for use as bookshelves. What is the length of the remaining piece after as many shelves as possible are cut?

Strategy

To find the length of the remaining piece:

- Divide the total length (12) by the length of each shelf $\left(2\frac{1}{2}\right)$. The quotient is the number of shelves cut, with a certain fraction of a shelf left over.
- Multiply the fraction left over by the length of a shelf.

Solution

$$12 \div 2\frac{1}{2} = \frac{12}{1} \div \frac{5}{2} = \frac{12}{1} \cdot \frac{2}{5} = \frac{12 \cdot 2}{1 \cdot 5} = \frac{24}{5} = 4\frac{4}{5}$$

4 shelves, each $2\frac{1}{2}$ ft long, can be cut from the board. The piece remaining is $\frac{4}{5}$ of $2\frac{1}{2}$ ft long.

$$\frac{4}{5} \cdot 2\frac{1}{2} = \frac{4}{5} \cdot \frac{5}{2} = \frac{4 \cdot 5}{5 \cdot 2} = 2$$

The length of the remaining piece is 2 ft.

YOU TRY IT 14

The Booster Club is making 22 sashes for the high school band members. Each sash requires $1\frac{3}{8}$ yd of material at a cost of \$12 per yard. Find the total cost of the material.

Your strategy

Your solution

\$363

Solutions on pp. S6–S7

2.4 EXERCISES

SUGGESTED ASSIGNMENT
Exercises 1–6; Exercises 7–133, odds; More challenging exercise: Exercise 135

Concept Check

1. Circle the correct word to complete the sentence.

a. Fractions can/cannot be multiplied when their denominators are not the same.

b. To multiply two fractions, write the sum/product of the numerators over the sum/product of the denominators.

a. can **b.** product; product

2. The reciprocal of $\frac{7}{3}$ is $\frac{3}{7}$.

3. To evaluate $\left(\frac{4}{5}\right)^3$, write $\frac{4}{5}$ as a factor three times and then multiply.

4. To simplify the complex fraction $\frac{\frac{1}{3}}{\frac{5}{6}}$, first write it as the division problem $\frac{1}{3} \div \frac{5}{6}$.

5. Fill in the blank with the correct operation: A gardener wants to space his rows of vegetables $1\frac{1}{4}$ ft apart. His garden is 12 ft long. To find how many rows he can fit in the garden, use division.

6. A car used $10\frac{1}{4}$ gal of gas to travel 246 mi. To find the number of miles the car travels on 1 gal of gas, divide 246 by $10\frac{1}{4}$.

OBJECTIVE A *To multiply fractions*

7. $\frac{2}{3} \cdot \frac{9}{10}$ $\frac{3}{5}$

8. $\frac{3}{8} \cdot \frac{4}{5}$ $\frac{3}{10}$

9. $\frac{14}{15} \cdot \frac{6}{7}$ $\frac{4}{5}$

10. $\frac{15}{16} \cdot \frac{4}{9}$ $\frac{5}{12}$

11. $\frac{6}{7} \cdot \frac{0}{10}$ 0

12. $\frac{5}{12} \cdot \frac{3}{0}$ Undefined

13. $\frac{2}{3} \cdot \frac{3}{8} \cdot \frac{4}{9}$ $\frac{1}{9}$

14. $\frac{5}{7} \cdot \frac{1}{6} \cdot \frac{14}{15}$ $\frac{1}{9}$

15. $\frac{9}{x} \cdot \frac{7}{y}$ $\frac{63}{xy}$

16. $\frac{4}{c} \cdot \frac{8}{d}$ $\frac{32}{cd}$

17. $\frac{y}{5} \cdot \frac{z}{6}$ $\frac{yz}{30}$

18. $\frac{a}{10} \cdot \frac{b}{6}$ $\frac{ab}{60}$

19. $6 \cdot \frac{1}{6}$ 1

20. $\frac{1}{10} \cdot 10$ 1

21. $\frac{3}{4} \cdot 8$ 6

22. $\frac{5}{7} \cdot 14$ 10

23. $\frac{6}{7} \cdot 0$

0

24. $0 \cdot \frac{9}{11}$

0

25. $3\frac{1}{2} \cdot 5\frac{3}{7}$

19

26. $2\frac{1}{4} \cdot 1\frac{1}{3}$

3

27. $8 \cdot 5\frac{1}{4}$

42

28. $3 \cdot 2\frac{1}{9}$

$6\frac{1}{3}$

29. $3\frac{1}{2} \cdot 1\frac{5}{7} \cdot \frac{11}{12}$

$5\frac{1}{2}$

30. $2\frac{2}{3} \cdot \frac{8}{9} \cdot 1\frac{5}{16}$

$3\frac{1}{9}$

31. Find the product of $\frac{3}{4}$ and $\frac{14}{15}$.

$\frac{7}{10}$

32. Find the product of $\frac{12}{25}$ and $\frac{5}{16}$.

$\frac{3}{20}$

33. What is $4\frac{4}{5}$ times $\frac{3}{8}$?

$1\frac{4}{5}$

34. What is $5\frac{1}{3}$ times $\frac{3}{16}$?

1

Cost of Living A typical household in the United States has an average after-tax income of $45,000. The graph at the right represents how this annual income is spent. Use this graph for Exercises 35 and 36.

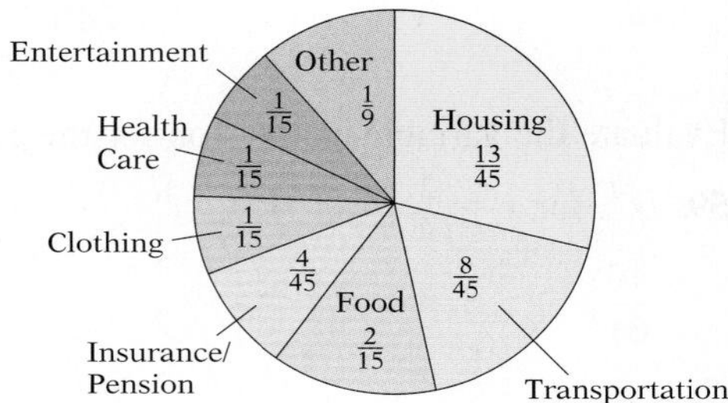

How a Typical U.S. Household Spends Its Annual Income

Source: Based on data from American Demographics

35. Find the amount of money a typical household in the United States spends on housing per year. $13,000

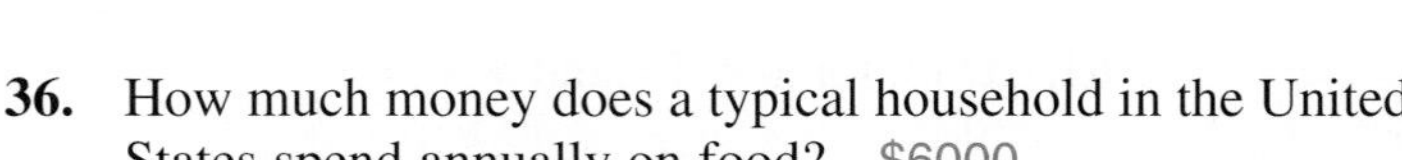

36. How much money does a typical household in the United States spend annually on food? $6000

Evaluate the variable expression xy for the given values of x and y.

37. $x = \frac{5}{16}, y = \frac{7}{15}$

$\frac{7}{48}$

38. $x = \frac{2}{5}, y = \frac{5}{6}$

$\frac{1}{3}$

39. $x = \frac{4}{7}, y = 6\frac{1}{8}$

$3\frac{1}{2}$

40. $x = 6\frac{3}{5}, y = 3\frac{1}{3}$

22

Evaluate the variable expression xyz for the given values of x, y, and z.

41. $x = \frac{3}{8}, y = \frac{2}{3}, z = \frac{4}{5}$

$\frac{1}{5}$

42. $x = 4, y = \frac{0}{8}, z = 1\frac{5}{9}$

0

43. $x = 2\frac{3}{8}, y = \frac{3}{19}, z = \frac{4}{9}$

$\frac{1}{6}$

44. $x = \frac{4}{5}, y = 15, z = \frac{7}{8}$

$10\frac{1}{2}$

45. $x = \frac{5}{6}, y = 3, z = 1\frac{7}{15}$

$3\frac{2}{3}$

46. $x = 4\frac{1}{2}, y = 3\frac{5}{9}, z = 1\frac{7}{8}$

30

47. Is $\frac{3}{4}$ a solution of the equation $\frac{4}{5}x = \frac{5}{3}$?

No

48. Is $\frac{1}{2}$ a solution of the equation $\frac{3}{4}p = \frac{3}{2}$?

No

49. Is the product $\frac{2}{3} \cdot n$ greater than n or less than n when n is a proper fraction?

Less than

50. Give an example of a proper fraction and an improper fraction whose product is 1.

One example is $\frac{3}{4}$ and $\frac{4}{3}$.

Evaluate.

51. $\left(\frac{3}{4}\right)^2$

$\frac{9}{16}$

52. $\left(\frac{5}{8}\right)^2$

$\frac{25}{64}$

53. $\left(\frac{5}{8}\right)^3 \cdot \left(\frac{2}{5}\right)^2$

$\frac{5}{128}$

54. $\left(\frac{3}{5}\right)^3 \cdot \left(\frac{1}{3}\right)^2$

$\frac{3}{125}$

55. $\left(\frac{18}{25}\right)^2 \cdot \left(\frac{5}{9}\right)^3$

$\frac{4}{45}$

56. $\left(\frac{2}{3}\right)^3 \cdot \left(\frac{5}{6}\right)^2$

$\frac{50}{243}$

57. $7^2 \cdot \left(\frac{2}{7}\right)^3$

$1\frac{1}{7}$

58. $4^3 \cdot \left(\frac{5}{12}\right)^2$

$11\frac{1}{9}$

Evaluate the variable expression for the given values of x and y.

59. x^4, for $x = \frac{2}{3}$

$\frac{16}{81}$

60. y^3, for $y = \frac{3}{4}$

$\frac{27}{64}$

61. x^3y^2, for $x = \frac{2}{3}$ and $y = 1\frac{1}{2}$

$\frac{2}{3}$

62. x^2y^4, for $x = 2\frac{1}{3}$ and $y = \frac{3}{7}$

$\frac{9}{49}$

OBJECTIVE B *To divide fractions*

Divide.

63. $\frac{5}{7} \div \frac{2}{5}$

$1\frac{11}{14}$

64. $\frac{3}{8} \div \frac{2}{3}$

$\frac{9}{16}$

65. $0 \div \frac{7}{9}$

0

66. $0 \div \frac{4}{5}$

0

67. $6 \div \frac{3}{4}$

8

68. $8 \div \frac{2}{3}$

12

69. $\frac{3}{4} \div 6$

$\frac{1}{8}$

70. $\frac{2}{3} \div 8$

$\frac{1}{12}$

71. $\frac{9}{10} \div 0$

Undefined

72. $\frac{2}{11} \div 0$

Undefined

73. $\frac{5}{12} \div \frac{15}{32}$

$\frac{8}{9}$

74. $\frac{3}{8} \div \frac{5}{12}$

$\frac{9}{10}$

75. $\frac{8}{x} \div \frac{y}{4}$

$\frac{32}{xy}$

76. $\frac{9}{m} \div \frac{n}{7}$

$\frac{63}{mn}$

77. $\frac{b}{6} \div \frac{5}{d}$

$\frac{bd}{30}$

78. $\frac{y}{10} \div \frac{4}{z}$

$\frac{yz}{40}$

79. $3\frac{1}{3} \div \frac{5}{8}$

$5\frac{1}{3}$

80. $5\frac{1}{2} \div \frac{1}{4}$

22

81. $5\frac{1}{2} \div 11$

$\frac{1}{2}$

82. $4\frac{2}{3} \div 7$

$\frac{2}{3}$

83. $5\frac{2}{7} \div 1$

$5\frac{2}{7}$

84. $9\frac{5}{6} \div 1$

$9\frac{5}{6}$

85. $2\frac{4}{13} \div 1\frac{5}{26}$

$1\frac{29}{31}$

86. $3\frac{3}{8} \div 2\frac{7}{16}$

$1\frac{5}{13}$

The Food Industry The table at the right shows the net weights of four different boxes of cereal. Use this table for Exercises 87 and 88.

Cereal	*Net Weight*
Kellogg Honey Crunch Corn Flakes	24 oz
Nabisco Instant Cream of Wheat	28 oz
Post Shredded Wheat	18 oz
Quaker Oats	41 oz

87. Find the number of $\frac{3}{4}$-ounce servings in a box of Kellogg Honey Crunch Corn Flakes. 32 servings

88. Find the number of $1\frac{1}{4}$-ounce servings in a box of Post Shredded Wheat.

$14\frac{2}{5}$ servings

89. Find the quotient of $\frac{9}{10}$ and $\frac{3}{4}$.

$1\frac{1}{5}$

90. Find the quotient of $\frac{3}{5}$ and $\frac{12}{25}$.

$1\frac{1}{4}$

91. Find $\frac{7}{8}$ divided by $3\frac{1}{4}$.

$\frac{7}{26}$

92. Find $\frac{3}{8}$ divided by $2\frac{1}{4}$.

$\frac{1}{6}$

Evaluate the variable expression $x \div y$ for the given values of x and y.

93. $x = \frac{5}{8}, y = \frac{15}{2}$

$\frac{1}{12}$

94. $x = \frac{14}{3}, y = \frac{7}{9}$

6

95. $x = 18, y = \frac{3}{8}$

48

96. $x = 20, y = \frac{5}{6}$

24

97. Is the quotient $n \div \frac{1}{2}$ greater than n or less than n when n is a proper fraction?

Greater than

98. Give an example of two fractions whose quotient is 1.

One example is $\frac{3}{4}$ and $\frac{3}{4}$.

OBJECTIVE C *To simplify complex fractions*

Simplify.

99. $\dfrac{\frac{9}{16}}{\frac{3}{4}}$

$\frac{3}{4}$

100. $\dfrac{\frac{7}{24}}{\frac{3}{8}}$

$\frac{7}{9}$

101. $\dfrac{\frac{2}{3}+\frac{1}{2}}{7}$

$\frac{1}{6}$

102. $\dfrac{5}{\frac{3}{8}-\frac{1}{4}}$

40

103. $\dfrac{2+\frac{1}{4}}{\frac{3}{8}}$

6

104. $\dfrac{1-\frac{3}{4}}{\frac{5}{12}}$

$\frac{3}{5}$

105. $\dfrac{\frac{9}{25}}{\frac{4}{5}-\frac{1}{10}}$

$\frac{18}{35}$

106. $\dfrac{\frac{9}{14}-\frac{1}{7}}{\frac{9}{14}+\frac{1}{7}}$

$\frac{7}{11}$

107. $\dfrac{3+2\frac{1}{3}}{5\frac{1}{6}-1}$

$1\frac{7}{25}$

108. $\dfrac{4-3\frac{5}{8}}{2\frac{1}{2}-\frac{3}{4}}$

$\frac{3}{14}$

109. $\dfrac{5\frac{2}{3}-1\frac{1}{6}}{3\frac{5}{8}-2\frac{1}{4}}$

$3\frac{3}{11}$

110. $\dfrac{3\frac{1}{4}-2\frac{1}{2}}{4\frac{3}{4}+1\frac{1}{2}}$

$\frac{3}{25}$

Evaluate the expression for the given values of the variables.

111. $\frac{x+y}{z}$, for $x = \frac{2}{3}$, $y = \frac{3}{4}$, and $z = \frac{1}{12}$

17

112. $\frac{x}{y+z}$, for $x = \frac{8}{15}$, $y = \frac{3}{5}$, and $z = \frac{2}{3}$

$\frac{8}{19}$

113. $\frac{x-y}{z}$, for $x = 2\frac{5}{8}$, $y = 1\frac{1}{4}$, and $z = 1\frac{3}{8}$

1

114. $\frac{x}{y-z}$, for $x = 2\frac{3}{10}$, $y = 3\frac{2}{5}$, and $z = 1\frac{4}{5}$

$1\frac{7}{16}$

State whether the given expression is equivalent to 0, equivalent to 1, equivalent to $\left(\frac{a}{b}\right)^2$, or undefined.

115. $\dfrac{\frac{a}{b}}{\frac{a}{b}}$

1

116. $\dfrac{\frac{a}{b}}{\frac{0}{b}}$

Undefined

117. $\dfrac{\frac{0}{b}}{\frac{a}{b}}$

0

118. $\dfrac{\frac{a}{b}}{\frac{b}{a}}$

$\left(\frac{a}{b}\right)^2$

OBJECTIVE D *To solve application problems and use formulas*

119. Polo A chukker is one period of play in a polo match. A chukker lasts $7\frac{1}{2}$ min. Find the length of time in four chukkers. 30 min

© Dennis Donohue/Shutterstock.com

120. History The Assyrian calendar was based on the phases of the moon. One lunation was $29\frac{1}{2}$ days long. There were 12 lunations in one year. Find the number of days in one year in the Assyrian calendar. 354 days

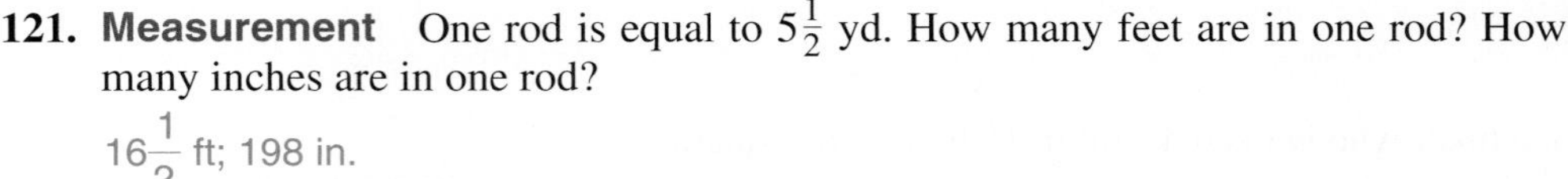

121. Measurement One rod is equal to $5\frac{1}{2}$ yd. How many feet are in one rod? How many inches are in one rod?

$16\frac{1}{2}$ ft; 198 in.

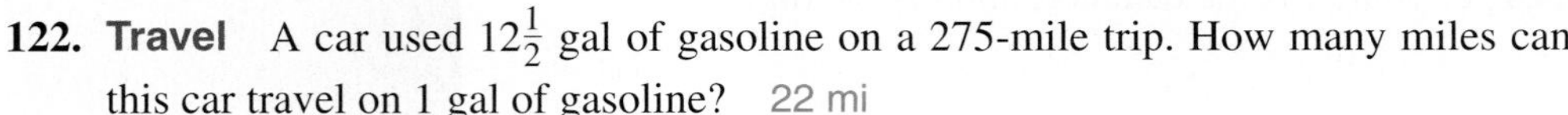

122. Travel A car used $12\frac{1}{2}$ gal of gasoline on a 275-mile trip. How many miles can this car travel on 1 gal of gasoline? 22 mi

123. Housework According to a national survey, the average couple spends $4\frac{1}{2}$ h cleaning house each week. How many hours does the average couple spend cleaning house each year? 234 h

124. Assembly Work A factory worker can assemble a product in $7\frac{1}{2}$ min. How many products can the worker assemble in 1 h? 8 products

125. Real Estate A developer purchases $25\frac{1}{2}$ acres of land and plans to set aside 3 acres for an entranceway to a housing development to be built on the property. Each house will be built on a $\frac{3}{4}$-acre plot of land. How many houses does the developer plan to build on the property? 30 houses

126. Party Planning You are planning a barbecue for 25 people. You want to serve $\frac{1}{4}$-pound hamburger patties to your guests, and you estimate that each person will eat two hamburgers. How much hamburger meat should you buy for the barbecue?

$12\frac{1}{2}$ lb

127. Asteroids Read the news clipping at the right. The distance between Earth and the moon is approximately 250,000 mi. At its closest point, asteroid GA6 was $\frac{9}{10}$ of that distance from Earth. Approximate the asteroid's distance from Earth at its closest point. 225,000 mi

128. Wages Find the total wages of an employee who worked $26\frac{1}{2}$ h this week and who earns an hourly wage of \$12. \$318

QUICK QUIZ

1. Multiply: $\left(\frac{2}{3}\right)\left(2\frac{5}{8}\right)$
   $1\frac{3}{4}$ [2.4A]
2. What is 8 divided by $\frac{4}{15}$? **30 [2.4B]**
3. Simplify: $\dfrac{\frac{3}{5}+\frac{1}{3}}{\frac{4}{5}}$
   $1\frac{1}{6}$ [2.4C]
4. Over the last 20 years, the value of a classic car increased by $2\frac{1}{2}$ times. The value of the car 20 years ago was \$40,000. What is the value of the car today? **\$100,000 [2.4D]**

In the NEWS!

Asteroid to Fly Within Orbit of the Moon

Asteroid GA6 will zip past Earth on Thursday at 7:06 P.M. EDT. The asteroid, a space rock about 71 ft wide, will fly within the orbit of the moon while it passes Earth.

Source: news.yahoo.com

129. Gardens A vegetable garden is in the shape of a triangle with a base of 21 ft and a height of 13 ft. Find the area of the vegetable garden.

$136\frac{1}{2}$ ft²

© iStockphoto.com/1001nights

130. Sailing A sail is in the shape of a triangle with a base of 12 m and a height of 16 m. How much canvas was needed to make the body of the sail? 96 m²

131. Parks and Recreation A city plans to plant grass seed in a public playground that has the shape of a triangle with a height of 24 m and a base of 20 m. Each bag of grass seed will seed 120 m². How many bags of seed should be purchased? 2 bags

132. Hiking Find the rate of a hiker who walked $4\frac{2}{3}$ mi in $1\frac{1}{3}$ h. Use the equation $r = \frac{d}{t}$, where r is the rate in miles per hour, d is the distance, and t is the time.

$3\frac{1}{2}$ mph

© frantisekhojdysz/Shutterstock.com

133. Deep Sea Diving The pressure on a submerged object is given by $P = 15 + \frac{1}{2}D$, where D is the depth in feet and P is the pressure measured in pounds per square inch. Find the pressure on a diver who is at a depth of $12\frac{1}{2}$ ft.

$21\frac{1}{4}$ lb/in²

134. Physics Find the amount of force necessary to push a 75-pound crate across a floor for which the coefficient of friction is $\frac{3}{8}$. Use the equation $F = \mu N$, where F is the force, μ is the coefficient of friction, and N is the weight of the crate. Force is measured in pounds.

$28\frac{1}{8}$ lb

Critical Thinking

135. Cartography On a map, two cities are $3\frac{1}{8}$ in. apart. If $\frac{1}{8}$ in. on the map represents 50 mi, what is the number of miles between the two cities? 1250 mi

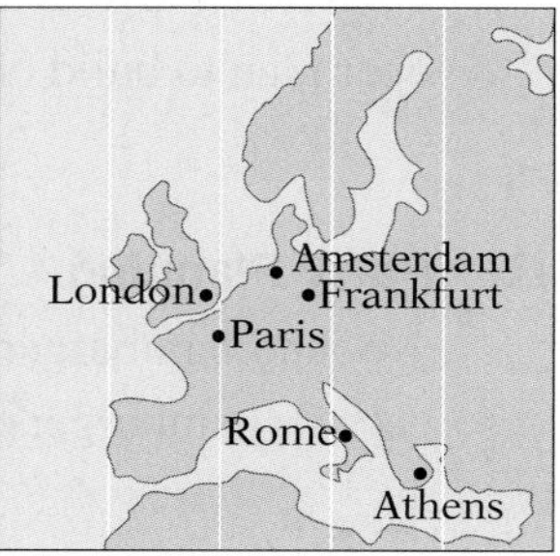

136. Determine whether the statement is always true, sometimes true, or never true.

a. Let n be an even number. Then $\frac{1}{2}n$ is a whole number.

Sometimes true

b. Let n be an odd number. Then $\frac{1}{2}n$ is an improper fraction.

Sometimes true

Projects or Group Activities

137. On page 127, Exercise 120 describes the Assyrian calendar. Our calendar is based on the solar year. One solar year is $365\frac{1}{4}$ days. Use this fact to explain leap years.

CHECK YOUR PROGRESS: CHAPTER 2

1. Find the LCM of 5, 12, and 15.
60 [2.1A]

2. Find the GCF of 26 and 52. 26 [2.1B]

3. Write $\frac{10}{3}$ as a mixed number. $3\frac{1}{3}$ [2.2A]

4. Write $\frac{81}{9}$ as a whole number. 9 [2.2A]

5. Write $3\frac{1}{4}$ as an improper fraction. $\frac{13}{4}$ [2.2A]

6. Write 17 as an improper fraction.
$\frac{17}{1}$ [2.2A]

7. Write $\frac{2}{3}$ as an equivalent fraction with a denominator of 12. $\frac{8}{12}$ [2.2B]

8. Write $\frac{24}{64}$ in simplest form. $\frac{3}{8}$ [2.2B]

9. Place the correct symbol, $<$ or $>$, between the two numbers. $\frac{2}{3} > \frac{5}{8}$ [2.2C]

10. Add: $\frac{4}{7} + \frac{2}{21}$ $\frac{2}{3}$ [2.3A]

11. Add: $4\frac{5}{6} + \frac{3}{4}$ $5\frac{7}{12}$ [2.3A]

12. Subtract: $\frac{2}{3} - \frac{1}{15}$ $\frac{3}{5}$ [2.3B]

13. Subtract: $1\frac{3}{8} - \frac{7}{10}$ $\frac{27}{40}$ [2.3B]

14. Multiply: $2\frac{1}{4} \cdot 1\frac{2}{9}$ $2\frac{3}{4}$ [2.4A]

15. Multiply: $\frac{3}{4}\left(\frac{2}{9}\right)\left(\frac{2}{5}\right)$ $\frac{1}{15}$ [2.4A]

16. Divide: $\frac{6}{m} \div \frac{n}{5}$ $\frac{30}{mn}$ [2.4B]

17. Divide: $8\frac{1}{3} \div 25$ $\frac{1}{3}$ [2.4B]

18. Simplify: $\dfrac{\frac{3}{4} - \frac{1}{3}}{\frac{2}{3} + \frac{1}{6}}$ $\frac{1}{2}$ [2.4C]

19. Evaluate the variable expression $x - y$ when $x = 4$ and $y = 2\frac{4}{11}$. $1\frac{7}{11}$ [2.3B]

20. Is $\frac{1}{3}$ a solution of the equation $\frac{3}{5}x = \frac{1}{5}$? Yes [2.4A]

21. Find the quotient of $2\frac{5}{8}$ and $5\frac{1}{4}$. $\frac{1}{2}$ [2.4B]

22. Evaluate the variable expression $\frac{x}{y}$ when $x = \frac{2}{3}$ and $y = \frac{7}{9}$. $\frac{6}{7}$ [2.4C]

23. Exercise Course An exercise course has stations set up along a path that is in the shape of a triangle with sides that measure $12\frac{1}{12}$ yd, $29\frac{1}{3}$ yd, and $26\frac{3}{4}$ yd. What is the entire length of the exercise course? Use the formula $P = a + b + c$.
$68\frac{1}{6}$ yd [2.3C]

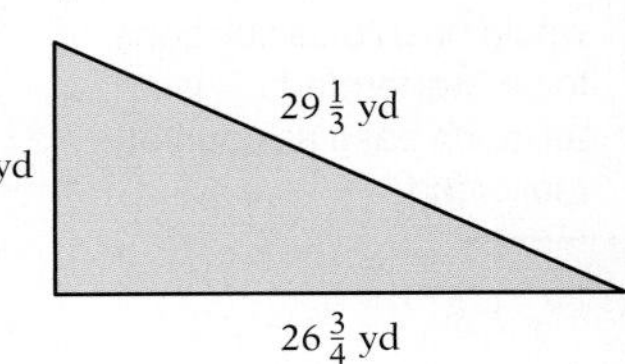

24. Board Games A wooden travel game board has hinges that allow the board to be folded in half. If the dimensions of the open board are 14 in. by 14 in. by $\frac{7}{8}$ in., what are the dimensions of the board when it is closed?
14 in. by 7 in. by $1\frac{3}{4}$ in. [2.4D]

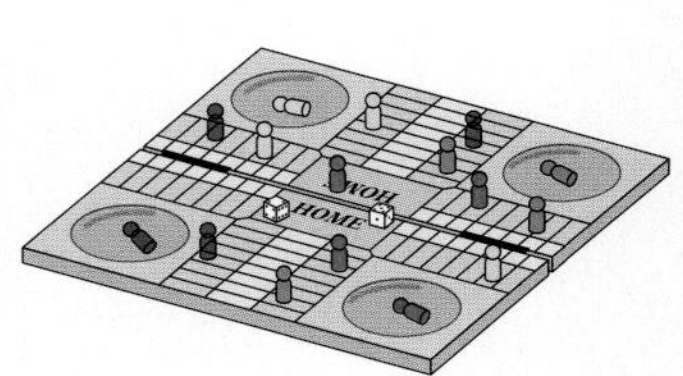

SECTION

2.5 Introduction to Decimals

OBJECTIVE A *To write decimals in standard form and in words*

The price tag on a sweater reads \$61.88. The number 61.88 is in **decimal notation.** A number written in decimal notation is often called simply a **decimal.**

A number written in decimal notation has three parts.

61	.	88
Whole number part	**Decimal point**	**Decimal part**

The decimal part of the number represents a number less than 1. For example, \$.88 is less than one dollar. The decimal point (.) separates the whole number part from the decimal part.

The position of a digit in a decimal determines the digit's **place value.** The place-value chart is extended to the right to show the place values of digits to the right of a decimal point.

In the decimal 458.302719, the position of the digit 7 determines that its place value is ten-thousandths.

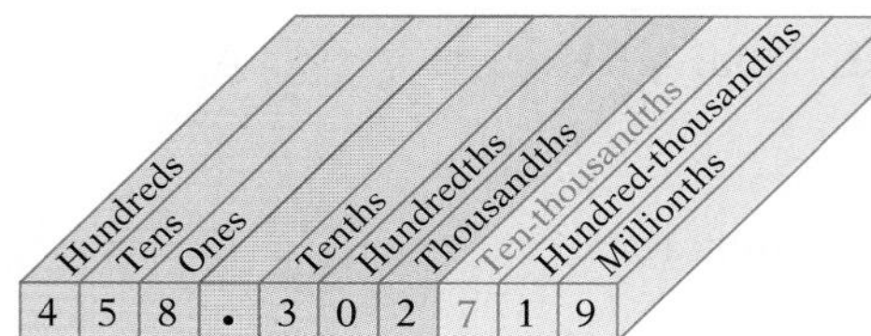

Point of Interest

The idea that all fractions should be represented in tenths, hundredths, and thousandths was presented in 1585 in Simon Stevin's publication *De Thiende.* Its French translation, *La Disme,* was widely read and accepted by the French. This may help to explain why the French accepted the metric system so easily 200 years later.

In *De Thiende,* Stevin argued in favor of his notation by including examples for astronomers, tapestry makers, surveyors, tailors, and the like. He stated that using decimals would enable calculations to be "performed . . . with as much ease as counter-reckoning."

Note the relationship between fractions and numbers written in decimal notation.

seven tenths	seven hundredths	seven thousandths
$\frac{7}{10} = 0.7$	$\frac{7}{100} = 0.07$	$\frac{7}{1000} = 0.007$
1 zero in 10	2 zeros in 100	3 zeros in 1000
1 decimal place in 0.7	2 decimal places in 0.07	3 decimal places in 0.007

To write a decimal in words, write the decimal part of the number as though it were a whole number, and then name the place value of the last digit.

0.9684 nine thousand six hundred eighty-four ten-thousandths

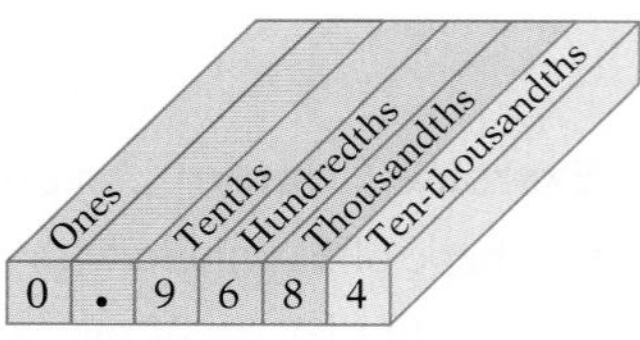

The decimal point in a decimal is read as "and."

372.516 three hundred seventy-two and five hundred sixteen thousandths

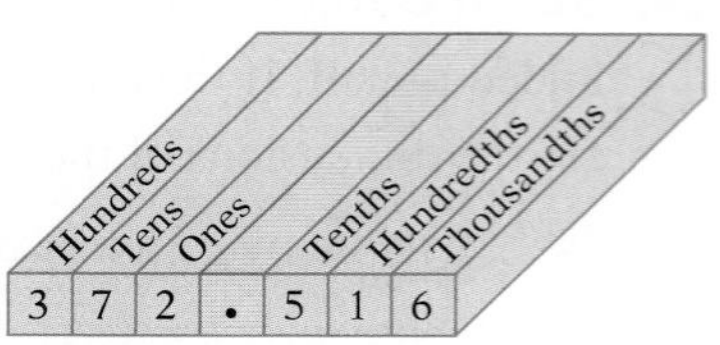

To write a decimal in standard form when it is written in words, write the whole number part, replace the word *and* with a decimal point, and write the decimal part so that the last digit is in the given place-value position.

four and twenty-three hundredths

3 is in the hundredths place. 4.23

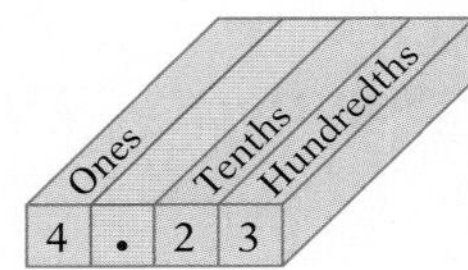

IN-CLASS EXAMPLES

1. Name the place value of the digit 5 in 23.9567. **hundredths**
2. Write $\frac{67}{100}$ as a decimal. **0.67**
3. Write 0.017 as a fraction. $\frac{17}{1000}$
4. Write 9.253 in words. **nine and two hundred fifty-three thousandths**
5. Write four and three hundred five ten-thousandths in standard form. **4.0305**

When writing a decimal in standard form, you may need to insert zeros after the decimal point so that the last digit is in the given place-value position.

ninety-one and eight thousandths

8 is in the thousandths place. Insert two zeros so that the 8 is in the thousandths place. 91.008

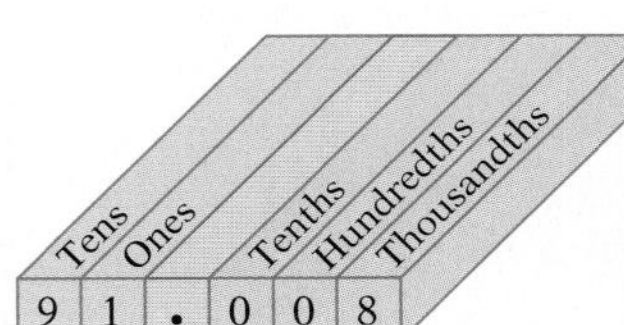

sixty-five ten-thousandths

5 is in the ten-thousandths place. Insert two zeros so that the 5 is in the ten-thousandths place. 0.0065

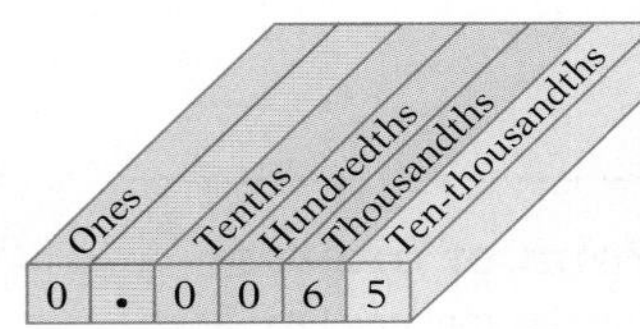

EXAMPLE 1

Name the place value of the digit 8 in the number 45.687.

Solution The digit 8 is in the hundredths place.

YOU TRY IT 1

Name the place value of the digit 4 in the number 907.1342.

Your solution thousandths

EXAMPLE 2

Write $\frac{43}{100}$ as a decimal.

Solution $\frac{43}{100} = 0.43$ • **43 hundredths**

YOU TRY IT 2

Write $\frac{501}{1000}$ as a decimal.

Your solution 0.501

EXAMPLE 3

Write 0.289 as a fraction.

Solution $0.289 = \frac{289}{1000}$ • **289 thousandths**

YOU TRY IT 3

Write 0.67 as a fraction.

Your solution $\frac{67}{100}$

EXAMPLE 4

Write 293.50816 in words.

Solution two hundred ninety-three and fifty thousand eight hundred sixteen hundred-thousandths

YOU TRY IT 4

Write 55.6083 in words.

Your solution fifty-five and six thousand eighty-three ten-thousandths

Solutions on p. S7

EXAMPLE 5

Write twenty-three and two hundred forty-seven millionths in standard form.

Solution 23.000247 ← millionths place

YOU TRY IT 5

Write eight hundred six and four hundred ninety-one hundred-thousandths in standard form.

Your solution 806.00491

Solution on p. S7

OBJECTIVE B *To identify the order relation between two decimals*

A whole number can be written as a decimal by writing a decimal point to the right of the last digit. For example,

$62 = 62.$ $\quad 497 = 497.$

You know that \$62 and \$62.00 both represent sixty-two dollars. Any number of zeros may be written to the right of the decimal point in a whole number without changing the value of the number.

$62 = 62.00 = 62.0000$ $\quad 497 = 497.0 = 497.000$

Also, any number of zeros may be written to the right of the last digit in a decimal without changing the value of the number.

$0.8 = 0.80 = 0.800$ $\quad 1.35 = 1.350 = 1.3500 = 1.35000 = 1.350000$

This fact is used to find the order relation between two decimals.

Point of Interest

The decimal point did not make its appearance until the early 1600s. Stevin's notation used subscripts with circles around them after each digit: 0 for ones, 1 for tenths (which he called "primes"), 2 for hundredths (called "seconds"), 3 for thousandths ("thirds"), and so on. For example, 1.375 would have been written

1 3 7 5

 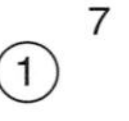 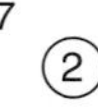 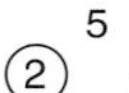

To compare two decimals, write the decimal part of each number so that each has the same number of decimal places. Then compare the two numbers.

HOW TO 1 Place the correct symbol, $<$ or $>$, between the two numbers 0.693 and 0.71.

0.693 has 3 decimal places.	
0.71 has 2 decimal places.	
Write 0.71 with 3 decimal places.	$0.71 = 0.710$
Compare 0.693 and 0.710.	
693 thousandths $<$ 710 thousandths	$0.693 < 0.710$
Remove the zero written in 0.710.	$0.693 < 0.71$

IN-CLASS EXAMPLES

6. Place the correct symbol, $<$ or $>$, between the two numbers.
0.19 0.9
0.19 $<$ 0.9
7. Write the given numbers in order from smallest to largest.
0.88, 0.899, 0.898, 0.809
0.809, 0.88, 0.898, 0.899

HOW TO 2 Place the correct symbol, $<$ or $>$, between the two numbers 5.8 and 5.493.

Write 5.8 with 3 decimal places.	$5.8 = 5.800$
Compare 5.800 and 5.493.	
The whole number part (5) is the same.	
800 thousandths $>$ 493 thousandths	$5.800 > 5.493$
Remove the extra zeros written in 5.800.	$5.8 > 5.493$

EXAMPLE 6

Place the correct symbol, < or >, between the two numbers.

0.039 0.1001

Solution 0.039 = 0.0390

0.0390 < 0.1001

0.039 < 0.1001

YOU TRY IT 6

Place the correct symbol, < or >, between the two numbers.

0.065 0.0802

Your solution

0.065 < 0.0802

EXAMPLE 7

Write the given numbers in order from smallest to largest.

1.01, 1.2, 1.002, 1.1, 1.12

Solution Write each number with 3 decimal places. Then write the numbers in order.

1.010, 1.200, 1.002, 1.100, 1.120

1.002, 1.010, 1.100, 1.120, 1.200

1.002, 1.01, 1.1, 1.12, 1.2

YOU TRY IT 7

Write the given numbers in order from smallest to largest.

3.03, 0.33, 0.3, 3.3, 0.03

Your solution

0.03, 0.3, 0.33, 3.03, 3.3

Solutions on p. S7

OBJECTIVE C *To round a decimal to a given place value*

In general, rounding decimals is similar to rounding whole numbers except that the digits to the right of the given place value are dropped instead of being replaced by zeros.

If the digit to the right of the given place value is less than 5, that digit and all digits to the right are dropped.

Round 6.9237 to the nearest hundredth.

Given place value (hundredths)

6.9237

3 < 5 Drop the digits 3 and 7.

6.9237 rounded to the nearest hundredth is 6.92.

If the digit to the right of the given place value is greater than or equal to 5, increase the digit in the given place value by 1, and drop all digits to its right.

Round 12.385 to the nearest tenth.

Given place value (tenths)

12.385

8 > 5 Increase 3 by 1 and drop all digits to the right of 3.

12.385 rounded to the nearest tenth is 12.4.

HOW TO 3 Round 0.46972 to the nearest thousandth.

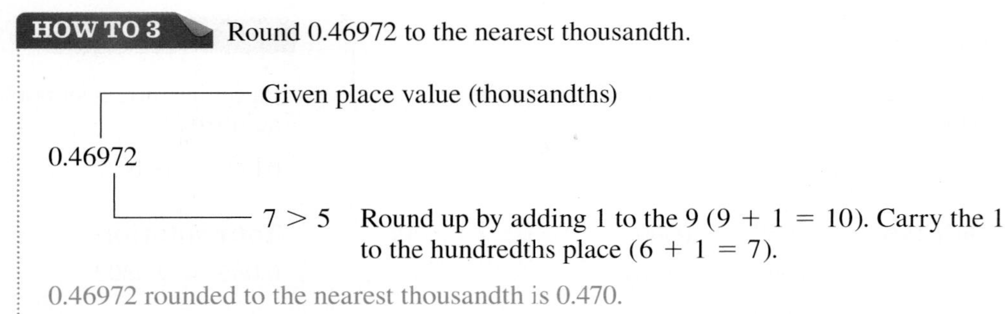

0.46972 rounded to the nearest thousandth is 0.470.

IN-CLASS EXAMPLES

8. Round 6.759 to the nearest tenth. **6.8**
9. Round 816.3904 to the nearest thousandth. **816.390**
10. Round 87.6037 to the nearest whole number. **88**

Note that in HOW TO 3, the zero in the given place value is not dropped. This indicates that the number is rounded to the nearest thousandth. If we dropped the zero and wrote 0.47, it would indicate that the number was rounded to the nearest hundredth.

EXAMPLE 8

Round 0.9375 to the nearest thousandth.

Solution

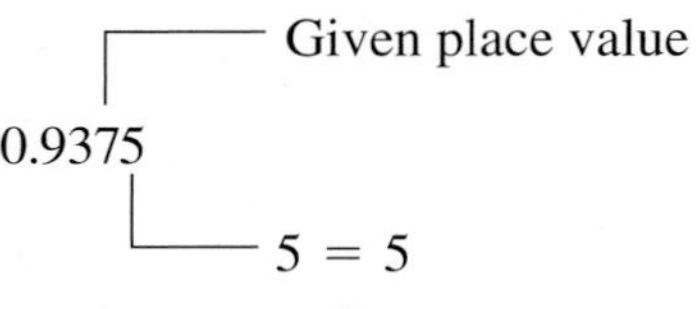

0.9375 rounded to the nearest thousandth is 0.938.

YOU TRY IT 8

Round 3.675849 to the nearest ten-thousandth.

Your solution 3.6758

EXAMPLE 9

Round 2.5963 to the nearest hundredth.

Solution

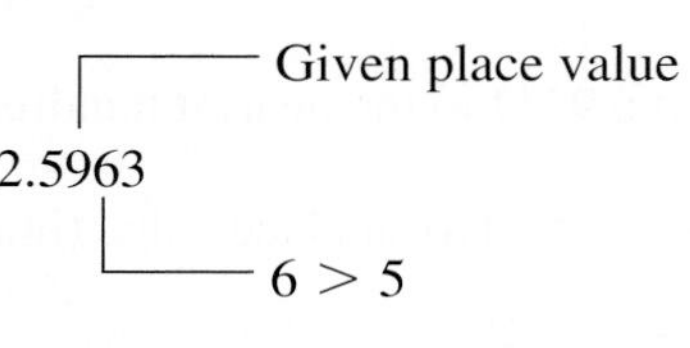

2.5963 rounded to the nearest hundredth is 2.60.

YOU TRY IT 9

Round 48.907 to the nearest tenth.

Your solution 48.9

EXAMPLE 10

Round 72.416 to the nearest whole number.

Solution

Given place value

72.416

$4 < 5$

72.416 rounded to the nearest whole number is 72.

YOU TRY IT 10

Round 31.8652 to the nearest whole number.

Your solution 32

Solutions on p. S7

OBJECTIVE D To solve application problems

NY Daily News Archive via Getty Images

Babe Ruth

The table below shows the number of home runs hit, for every 100 times at bat, by four Major League baseball players. Use this table for Example 11 and You Try It 11.

Home Runs Hit for Every 100 At-Bats	
Harmon Killebrew	7.03
Ralph Kiner	7.09
Babe Ruth	8.05
Ted Williams	6.76

Source: Major League Baseball

IN-CLASS EXAMPLES

11. The length of the marathon footrace in the Olympics is 42.195 km. What is the length of this race to the nearest tenth of a kilometer? **42.2 km**

EXAMPLE 11

According to the table above, who had more home runs for every 100 times at bat, Ted Williams or Babe Ruth?

Strategy

To determine who had more home runs for every 100 times at bat, compare the numbers 6.76 and 8.05.

Solution

$8.05 > 6.76$

Babe Ruth had more home runs for every 100 at-bats.

YOU TRY IT 11

According to the table above, who had more home runs for every 100 times at bat, Harmon Killebrew or Ralph Kiner?

Your strategy

Your solution

Ralph Kiner

EXAMPLE 12

On average, an American goes to the movies 4.56 times per year. To the nearest whole number, how many times per year does an American go to the movies?

Strategy

To find the number, round 4.56 to the nearest whole number.

Solution

4.56 rounded to the nearest whole number is 5.

An American goes to the movies about 5 times per year.

YOU TRY IT 12

One of the driest cities in the Southwest is Yuma, Arizona, with an average annual precipitation of 2.65 in. To the nearest inch, what is the average annual precipitation in Yuma?

Your strategy

Your solution

3 in.

Solutions on p. S7

2.5 EXERCISES

Concept Check

SUGGESTED ASSIGNMENT
Exercises 1–6; Exercises 7–85, odds

1. In a decimal, the place values of the first six digits to the right of the decimal point are tenths, ___hundredths___, ___thousandths___, ten-thousandths, ___hundred-thousandths___, and ___millionths___.

2. The place value of the digit 3 in 0.53 is ___hundredths___, so when 0.53 is written as a fraction, the denominator is ___100___. The numerator is ___53___.

3. To write 85.102 in words, first write *eighty-five.* Replace the decimal point with the word ___and___ and then write *one hundred two* ___thousandths___.

4. To write seventy-three millionths in standard form, insert ___four___ zeros between the decimal point and 73 so that the digit 3 is in the millionths place.

For Exercises 5 and 6, fill in each blank with $<$ or $>$.

5. To decide on the order relation between 0.017 and 0.107, compare 17 thousandths and 107 thousandths. Because 17 thousandths ___$<$___ 107 thousandths, 0.017 ___$<$___ 0.107.

6. To decide on the order relation between 3.4 and 3.05, write 3.4 as 3.40. The numbers have the same whole number parts, so compare 40 hundredths and 5 hundredths. Because 40 hundredths ___$>$___ 5 hundredths, 3.4 ___$>$___ 3.05.

OBJECTIVE A *To read and write decimals in standard form and in words*

Name the place value of the digit 5.

7. 76.31587
thousandths

8. 291.508
tenths

9. 432.09157
ten-thousandths

10. 0.0006512
hundred-thousandths

11. 38.2591
hundredths

12. 0.0000853
millionths

Write the fraction as a decimal.

13. $\frac{3}{10}$
0.3

14. $\frac{9}{10}$
0.9

15. $\frac{21}{100}$
0.21

16. $\frac{87}{100}$
0.87

17. $\frac{461}{1000}$
0.461

18. $\frac{853}{1000}$
0.853

19. $\frac{93}{1000}$
0.093

20. $\frac{61}{1000}$
0.061

Write the decimal as a fraction.

21. 0.1
$\frac{1}{10}$

22. 0.3
$\frac{3}{10}$

23. 0.47
$\frac{47}{100}$

24. 0.59
$\frac{59}{100}$

25. 0.289
$\frac{289}{1000}$

26. 0.601
$\frac{601}{1000}$

27. 0.09
$\frac{9}{100}$

28. 0.013
$\frac{13}{1000}$

Write the number in words.

29. 0.37
thirty-seven hundredths

30. 25.6
twenty-five and six tenths

31. 9.4
nine and four tenths

32. 1.004
one and four thousandths

33. 0.0053
fifty-three ten-thousandths

34. 41.108
forty-one and one hundred eight thousandths

35. 0.045
forty-five thousandths

36. 3.157
three and one hundred fifty-seven thousandths

37. 26.04
twenty-six and four hundredths

Write the number in standard form.

38. six hundred seventy-two thousandths
0.672

39. three and eight hundred six ten-thousandths
3.0806

40. nine and four hundred seven ten-thousandths
9.0407

41. four hundred seven and three hundredths
407.03

42. six hundred twelve and seven hundred four thousandths
612.704

43. two hundred forty-six and twenty-four thousandths
246.024

44. two thousand sixty-seven and nine thousand two ten-thousandths
2067.9002

45. seventy-three and two thousand six hundred eighty-four hundred-thousandths
73.02684

OBJECTIVE B *To identify the order relation between two decimals*

Place the correct symbol, $<$ or $>$, between the two numbers.

46. $0.16 < 0.6$

47. $0.7 > 0.56$

48. $5.54 > 5.45$

49. $3.605 > 3.065$

50. $0.047 < 0.407$

51. $9.004 < 9.04$

52. $1.0008 < 1.008$

53. $9.31 > 9.031$

54. $7.6005 < 7.605$

55. $4.6 < 40.6$

56. $0.31502 < 0.3152$

57. $0.07046 > 0.07036$

Write the given numbers in order from smallest to largest.

58. 0.39, 0.309, 0.399
0.309, 0.39, 0.399

59. 0.66, 0.699, 0.696, 0.609
0.609, 0.66, 0.696, 0.699

60. 0.24, 0.024, 0.204, 0.0024
0.0024, 0.024, 0.204, 0.24

61. 1.327, 1.237, 1.732, 1.372
1.237, 1.327, 1.372, 1.732

62. 0.06, 0.059, 0.061, 0.0061
0.0061, 0.059, 0.06, 0.061

63. 21.87, 21.875, 21.805, 21.78
21.78, 21.805, 21.87, 21.875

64. Use the inequality symbol < to rewrite the order relation expressed by the inequality 9.4 > 0.94. 0.94 < 9.4

65. Use the inequality symbol > to rewrite the order relation expressed by the inequality 0.062 < 0.62. 0.62 > 0.062

OBJECTIVE C *To round a decimal to a given place value*

Round the number to the given place value.

66. 6.249; tenths
6.2

67. 5.398; tenths
5.4

68. 21.007; tenths
21.0

69. 30.0092; tenths
30.0

70. 18.40937; hundredths
18.41

71. 413.5972; hundredths
413.60

72. 72.4983; hundredths
72.50

73. 6.061745; thousandths
6.062

74. 936.2905; thousandths
936.291

75. 96.8027; whole number
97

76. 47.3192; whole number
47

77. 5439.83; whole number
5440

78. 7014.96; whole number
7015

79. 0.023591; ten-thousandths
0.0236

80. 2.975268; hundred-thousandths
2.97527

OBJECTIVE D *To solve application problems*

81. **Coins** Read the news clipping at the right. The cost to mint a nickel is 7.7¢, and it costs 10¢ to mint a quarter. **a.** Is the cost to mint a penny greater than or less than the face value of a penny? **b.** To the nearest cent, what is the cost to mint a penny? **c.** Is the cost to mint a nickel greater than or less than the face value of a nickel? **d.** To the nearest cent, what is the cost to mint a nickel?
a. Greater than **b.** 2¢ **c.** Greater than **d.** 8¢

82. **Coins** A nickel weighs about 0.1763668 oz. Find the weight of a nickel to the nearest hundredth of an ounce. 0.18 oz

In the NEWS!

Rising Costs to Mint Coins

A U.S. penny contains zinc and copper. The prices of these metals have risen, which is why it now costs 1.67¢ to mint a penny. Some people suggest changing the content of the penny. Others advocate eliminating the penny from our currency. Both suggestions meet opposition from the public.
Source: answers.yahoo.com

83. **Boston Marathon** Runners in the Boston Marathon run a distance of 26.21875 mi. To the nearest tenth of a mile, find the distance run by an entrant who completes the Boston Marathon. 26.2 mi

84. **Minimum Payments** Charge accounts generally require a minimum payment on the balance in the account each month. Use the minimum payment schedule shown below to determine the minimum payment due on the given account balances.

	Account Balance	*Minimum Payment*
a.	$187.93	a. $20.00
b.	$342.55	b. $35.00
c.	$261.48	c. $30.00
d.	$16.99	d. $16.99
e.	$310.00	e. $35.00
f.	$158.32	f. $20.00
g.	$200.10	g. $25.00

If the New Balance is:	*The Minimum Required Payment Is:*
Up to $20.00	The new balance
$20.01 to $200.00	$20.00
$200.01 to $250.00	$25.00
$250.01 to $300.00	$30.00
$300.01 to $350.00	$35.00
$350.01 to $400.00	$40.00

85. **Shipping and Handling Charges** Shipping and handling charges when ordering online generally are based on the dollar amount of the order. Use the table shown below to determine the cost of shipping each order.

	Amount of Order	*Shipping Cost*
a.	$12.42	a. $2.40
b.	$23.56	b. $3.60
c.	$47.80	c. $6.00
d.	$66.91	d. $7.00
e.	$35.75	e. $4.70
f.	$20.00	f. $2.40
g.	$18.25	g. $2.40

If the Amount Ordered is:	*The Shipping and Handling Charge Is:*
$10.00 and under	$1.60
$10.01 to $20.00	$2.40
$20.01 to $30.00	$3.60
$30.01 to $40.00	$4.70
$40.01 to $50.00	$6.00
$50.01 and up	$7.00

Critical Thinking

86. Indicate which digits of the number, if any, need not be entered on a calculator.
a. 1.500 **b.** 0.908 **c.** 60.07 **d.** 0.0032
a. 1.5<u>00</u> b. <u>0</u>.908 c. 60.07 d. <u>0</u>.0032

87. Find a number between **a.** 0.1 and 0.2, **b.** 1 and 1.1, and **c.** 0 and 0.005.
Answers will vary. For example, **a.** 0.15 **b.** 1.05 **c.** 0.001

Projects or Group Activities

88. Use newspapers or the Internet to find and list situations in which decimals are used. Determine whether the decimals you find are exact values or approximations. [*Note:* Large numbers (such as 3.2 billion) used to describe values such as the balance of trade or the national debt are approximations. Smaller numbers (such as 1.5866) used to describe business transactions such as an exchange rate or a stock price are exact values.]

QUICK QUIZ

1. Write the number 3.2095 in words. **three and two thousand ninety-five ten-thousandths [2.5A]**
2. Write eight and three hundred fourteen ten-thousandths in standard form. **8.0314 [2.5A]**
3. Place the correct symbol, < or >, between the two numbers.
7.605 7.065
7.605 > 7.065 [2.5B]
4. Round 68.2097 to the nearest hundredth. **68.21 [2.5C]**
5. The weight of the iPod touch is 3.56 oz. What is the weight of the iPod touch to the nearest ounce? **4 oz [2.5D]**

SECTION

2.6 Operations on Decimals

OBJECTIVE A *To add and subtract decimals*

Point of Interest

Try this brain teaser. You have two U.S. coins that add up to $.55. One is not a nickel. What are the two coins?

INSTRUCTOR NOTE

The answer to the brain teaser above is that the two coins are a half dollar and a nickel. One of these coins is not a nickel; it is a half dollar.

To add decimals, write the numbers so that the decimal points are on a vertical line. Add as you would with whole numbers. Then write the decimal point in the sum directly below the decimal points in the addends.

HOW TO 1 Add: 0.326 + 4.8 + 57.23

	Tens	Ones		Tenths	Hundredths	Thousandths
	1	1				
		0	.	3	2	6
		4	.	8		
+	5	7	.	2	3	
	6	2	.	3	5	6

Note that placing the decimal points on a vertical line ensures that digits of the same place value are added.

HOW TO 2 Find the sum of 0.64, 8.731, 12, and 5.9.

Arrange the numbers vertically, placing the decimal points on a vertical line.

Add the numbers in each column.

Write the decimal point in the sum directly below the decimal points in the addends.

```
   1 2
    0.64
    8.731
   12.
 +  5.9
 -------
   27.271
```

To subtract decimals, write the numbers so that the decimal points are on a vertical line. Subtract as you would with whole numbers. Then write the decimal point in the difference directly below the decimal point in the subtrahend.

HOW TO 3 Subtract and check: 31.642 − 8.759

	Tens	Ones		Tenths	Hundredths	Thousandths
	2	10		15	13	12
	~~3~~	~~1~~	.	~~6~~	~~4~~	~~2~~
−		8	.	7	5	9
	2	2	.	8	8	3

Note that placing the decimal points on a vertical line ensures that digits of the same place value are subtracted.

Check:

Subtrahend	8.759
+ Difference	+ 22.883
= Minuend	31.642

HOW TO 4 Subtract and check: 5.4 − 1.6832

Insert zeros in the minuend so that it has the same number of decimal places as the subtrahend.

$$\begin{array}{r} 5.4000 \\ -\ 1.6832 \\ \hline \end{array}$$

Subtract and then check.

$$\begin{array}{r} \overset{4\ 13\ 9\ 9\ 10}{\cancel{5}.\cancel{4}\cancel{0}\cancel{0}\cancel{0}} \\ -\ 1.6832 \\ \hline 3.7168 \end{array}$$

Check:

$$\begin{array}{r} 1.6832 \\ +\ 3.7168 \\ \hline 5.4000 \end{array}$$

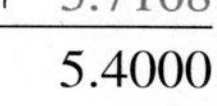

APPLY THE CONCEPT

Figure 2.2 shows the average price of a movie theater ticket in 1989, 1999, and 2009. Find the increase in price from 1989 to 2009.

To find the increase in price, subtract the price in 1989 ($3.99) from the price in 2009 ($7.50).

$$\begin{array}{r} 7.50 \\ -\ 3.99 \\ \hline 3.51 \end{array}$$

From 1989 to 2009, the average price of a movie theater ticket increased by $3.51.

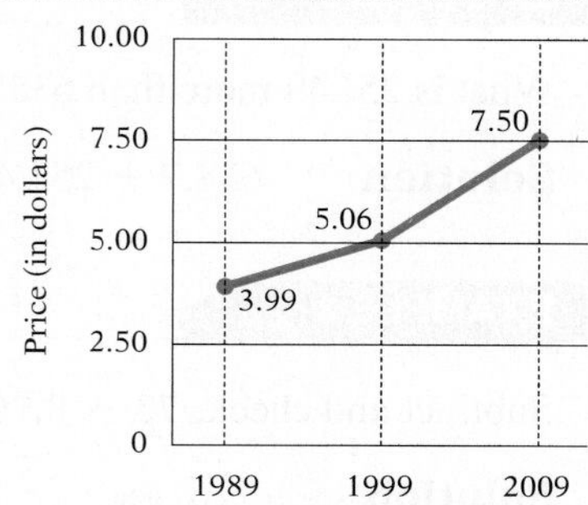

Figure 2.2 Average Price of a Movie Theater Ticket
Source: www.natoonline.org

Recall that to estimate the answer to a calculation, round each number to the highest place value of the number; the first digit of each number will be nonzero and all other digits will be zero. Perform the calculation using the rounded numbers.

HOW TO 5 Estimate the sum of 23.037 and 16.7892.

Round each number to the nearest ten.

Add the rounded numbers.

$$\begin{array}{rcr} 23.037 & \longrightarrow & 20 \\ 16.7892 & \longrightarrow & +\ 20 \\ \hline & & 40 \end{array}$$

40 is an estimate of the sum of 23.037 and 16.7892. Note that 40 is very close to the actual sum of 39.8262.

$$\begin{array}{r} 23.037 \\ +\ 16.7892 \\ \hline 39.8262 \end{array}$$

When a number in an estimation is a decimal less than 1, round the decimal so that there is one nonzero digit.

HOW TO 6 Estimate the difference between 4.895 and 0.6193.

Round 4.895 to the nearest one.
Round 0.6193 to the nearest tenth.
Subtract the rounded numbers.

$$\begin{array}{rcr} 4.895 & \longrightarrow & 5.0 \\ 0.6193 & \longrightarrow & -\ 0.6 \\ \hline & & 4.4 \end{array}$$

4.4 is an estimate of the difference between 4.895 and 0.6193.
It is close to the actual difference of 4.2757.

$$\begin{array}{r} 4.8950 \\ -\ 0.6193 \\ \hline 4.2757 \end{array}$$

IN-CLASS EXAMPLES

1. Add: 17.89 + 3.0152 + 13.7 **34.6052**
2. What is 5.042 less than 12.36? **7.318**
3. Subtract and check: 7.05 − 6.274 **0.776**
4. Estimate the difference between 8.769 and 3.515. **5**
5. Evaluate $x + y + z$ for $x = 3.5765$, $y = 35$, and $z = 11.08$. **49.6565**
6. Which number, 4.45 or 3.15, is a solution of the equation $3.8 = x - 0.65$? **4.45**

EXAMPLE 1

Add: $35.8 + 182.406 + 71.0934$

Solution

$$\begin{array}{r} {}^{1\ 1} \\ 35.8 \\ 182.406 \\ +\ \ 71.0934 \\ \hline 289.2994 \end{array}$$

YOU TRY IT 1

Add: $8.64 + 52.7 + 0.39105$

Your solution 61.73105

EXAMPLE 2

What is 251.49 more than 638.7?

Solution $638.7 + 251.49 = 890.19$

YOU TRY IT 2

What is 9.378 minus 4.002?

Your solution 5.376

EXAMPLE 3

Subtract and check: $73 - 8.16$

Solution

$$\begin{array}{r} {}^{6\ 12\ \ 9\ 10} \\ \not{7}\not{3}.\not{0}\not{0} \\ -\ \ 8.16 \\ \hline 64.84 \end{array} \qquad \textit{Check:}\ \begin{array}{r} 8.16 \\ +\ 64.84 \\ \hline 73.00 \end{array}$$

YOU TRY IT 3

Subtract and check: $25 - 4.91$

Your solution

20.09

EXAMPLE 4

Estimate the sum of 0.3927, 0.4856, and 0.2104.

Solution

$$\begin{array}{lr} 0.3927 \longrightarrow & 0.4 \\ 0.4856 \longrightarrow & 0.5 \\ 0.2104 \longrightarrow & +0.2 \\ \hline & 1.1 \end{array}$$

YOU TRY IT 4

Estimate the sum of 6.514, 8.903, and 2.275.

Your solution

18

EXAMPLE 5

Evaluate $x + y + z$ for $x = 1.6$, $y = 7.9$, and $z = 4.8$.

Solution

$$x + y + z$$
$$1.6 + 7.9 + 4.8 = 9.5 + 4.8$$
$$= 14.3$$

YOU TRY IT 5

Evaluate $x + y + z$ for $x = 7.84$, $y = 3.05$, and $z = 2.19$.

Your solution

13.08

EXAMPLE 6

Is 4.3 a solution of the equation $9.7 - b = 5.4$?

Solution

$$\begin{array}{r|l} 9.7 - b & = 5.4 \\ \hline 9.7 - 4.3 & 5.4 \\ 5.4 & = 5.4 \end{array}$$

• **Replace b with 4.3.**

Yes, 4.3 is a solution of the equation.

YOU TRY IT 6

Is 23.8 a solution of the equation $m + 16.9 = 40.7$?

Your solution

Yes

Solutions on pp. S7–S8

OBJECTIVE B

To multiply decimals

Tips for Success

Have you considered joining a study group? Getting together regularly with other students in the class to go over material and quiz each other can be very beneficial. See *AIM for Success* at the front of the book.

Decimals are multiplied as though they were whole numbers; then the decimal point is placed in the product. Writing the decimals as fractions shows where to write the decimal point in the product.

$$0.4 \cdot 2 = \frac{4}{10} \cdot \frac{2}{1} = \frac{8}{10} = 0.8$$

1 decimal place in 0.4 — 1 decimal place in 0.8

$$0.4 \cdot 0.2 = \frac{4}{10} \cdot \frac{2}{10} = \frac{8}{100} = 0.08$$

1 decimal place in 0.4
1 decimal place in 0.2 — 2 decimal places in 0.08

$$0.4 \cdot 0.02 = \frac{4}{10} \cdot \frac{2}{100} = \frac{8}{1000} = 0.008$$

1 decimal place in 0.4
2 decimal places in 0.02 — 3 decimal places in 0.008

To multiply decimals, multiply the numbers as you would whole numbers. Then write the decimal point in the product so that the number of decimal places in the product is the sum of the numbers of decimal places in the factors.

APPLY THE CONCEPT

The cost, including tax, of one adult admission ticket to a theme park is \$53.46. What is the total cost of 4 adult tickets to this theme park?

To find the total cost, multiply the cost per ticket (\$53.46) by the number of tickets (4).

$$\begin{array}{r} 53.46 \\ \times \quad 4 \\ \hline 213.84 \end{array}$$

- **2 decimal places**
- **0 decimal places**
- **2 decimal places**

The total cost of 4 adult tickets is \$213.84.

Take Note

Estimating the product of 32.41 and 7.6 shows that the decimal point has been placed correctly.

32.41 → 30
7.6 → × 8
240

240 is an estimate of (32.41)(7.6). It is close to the actual product 246.316.

HOW TO 7 Multiply: (32.41)(7.6)

$$\begin{array}{r} 32.41 \\ \times \quad 7.6 \\ \hline 19446 \\ 22687 \\ \hline 246.316 \end{array}$$

2 decimal places
1 decimal place

3 decimal places

Integrating Technology

Scientific calculators have a floating decimal point. This means that the decimal point is automatically placed in the answer. For example, for the product at the right, enter

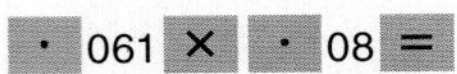

The display reads .00488, with the decimal point in the correct position.

HOW TO 8 Multiply: 0.061(0.08)

0.061	3 decimal places
× 0.08	2 decimal places
0.00488	5 decimal places

Insert two zeros between the 4 and the decimal point so that there are 5 decimal places in the product.

To multiply a decimal by a power of 10 (10, 100, 1000, . . .), move the decimal point to the right the same number of places as there are zeros in the power of 10.

$2.7935 \cdot 10 = 27.935$ — 1 zero, 1 decimal place

$2.7935 \cdot 100 = 279.35$ — 2 zeros, 2 decimal places

$2.7935 \cdot 1000 = 2793.5$ — 3 zeros, 3 decimal places

$2.7935 \cdot 10{,}000 = 27{,}935.$ — 4 zeros, 4 decimal places

$2.7935 \cdot 100{,}000 = 279{,}350.$ — 5 zeros, 5 decimal places

A zero must be inserted before the decimal point.

Note that if the power of 10 is written in exponential notation, the exponent indicates how many places to move the decimal point.

$2.7935 \cdot 10^1 = 27.935$ — 1 decimal place

$2.7935 \cdot 10^2 = 279.35$ — 2 decimal places

$2.7935 \cdot 10^3 = 2793.5$ — 3 decimal places

$2.7935 \cdot 10^4 = 27{,}935.$ — 4 decimal places

$2.7935 \cdot 10^5 = 279{,}350.$ — 5 decimal places

HOW TO 9 Find the product of 64.18 and 10^3.

The exponent on 10 is 3. Move the decimal point in 64.18 three places to the right.

$64.18 \cdot 10^3 = 64{,}180$

HOW TO 10 Evaluate $100x$ with $x = 5.714$.

$100x$

Replace x with 5.714. $100(5.714)$

Multiply. There are two zeros in 100. Move the decimal point in 5.714 two places to the right. $= 571.4$

IN-CLASS EXAMPLES

7. Multiply: 0.97(0.632) **0.61304**
8. Estimate the product of 0.842 and 5.7. **4.8**
9. Find the product of 3.61 and 10^4. **36,100**
10. Evaluate $30pq$ for $p = 5.4$ and $q = 0.2$. **32.4**

HOW TO 11 Is 0.6 a solution of the equation $4.3a = 2.58$?

Replace a by 0.6 and then simplify. The results are equal.

$$\begin{array}{r|l} 4.3a & = 2.58 \\ \hline 4.3(0.6) & 2.58 \\ 2.58 & = 2.58 \end{array}$$

Yes, 0.6 is a solution of the equation.

EXAMPLE 7

Multiply: 0.00073(0.052)

Solution

$$\begin{array}{rl} 0.00073 & \longleftarrow \text{5 decimal places} \\ \times\ \ 0.052 & \longleftarrow \text{3 decimal places} \\ \hline 146 & \\ 365\ & \\ \hline 0.00003796 & \longleftarrow \text{8 decimal places} \end{array}$$

YOU TRY IT 7

Multiply: 0.000081(0.025)

Your solution

0.000002025

EXAMPLE 8

Estimate the product of 0.7639 and 0.2188.

Solution

$$\begin{array}{lr} 0.7639 \longrightarrow & 0.8 \\ 0.2188 \longrightarrow & \times\ 0.2 \\ \hline & 0.16 \end{array}$$

YOU TRY IT 8

Estimate the product of 6.407 and 0.959.

Your solution

6

EXAMPLE 9

What is 835.294 multiplied by 1000?

Solution Move the decimal point 3 places to the right.

$835.294 \cdot 1000 = 835{,}294$

YOU TRY IT 9

Find the product of 1.756 and 10^4.

Your solution

17,560

Solutions on p. S8

EXAMPLE 10

Evaluate $50ab$ for $a = 0.9$ and $b = 0.2$.

Solution $50ab$

$50(0.9)(0.2) = 45(0.2)$
$= 9$

YOU TRY IT 10

Evaluate $25xy$ for $x = 0.8$ and $y = 0.6$.

Your solution

12

Solution on p. S8

OBJECTIVE C *To divide decimals*

Point of Interest

Benjamin Banneker (1731–1806) was the first African American to earn distinction as a mathematician and a scientist. He was on the survey team that determined the boundaries of Washington, D.C. The mathematics of surveying requires extensive use of decimals.

To divide decimals, move the decimal point in the divisor to the right so that the divisor is a whole number. Move the decimal point in the dividend the same number of places to the right. Place the decimal point in the quotient directly above the decimal point in the dividend. Then divide as you would with whole numbers.

HOW TO 12 Divide: $29.585 \div 4.85$

$4.85.\overline{)29.58.5}$

Move the decimal point 2 places to the right in the divisor. Move the decimal point 2 places to the right in the dividend. Place the decimal point in the quotient. Then divide as shown at the right.

$$\begin{array}{r} 6.1 \\ 485.\overline{)\,2958.5} \\ -2910 \\ \hline 48\ 5 \\ -48\ 5 \\ \hline 0 \end{array}$$

Moving the decimal point the same number of places in the divisor and the dividend does not change the quotient because the process is the same as multiplying the numerator and denominator of a fraction by the same number. For HOW TO 12 above,

$$4.85\overline{)29.585} = \frac{29.585}{4.85} = \frac{29.585 \cdot 100}{4.85 \cdot 100} = \frac{2958.5}{485} = 485\overline{)2958.5}$$

In division of decimals, rather than writing the quotient with a remainder, we usually round the quotient to a specified place value. The symbol $\approx$ is read "is approximately equal to"; it is used to indicate that the quotient is an approximate value after being rounded.

HOW TO 13 Divide and round to the nearest tenth: $0.86 \div 0.7$

$$\begin{array}{r} 1.22 \approx 1.2 \\ 0.7.\overline{)0.8.60} \\ -7 \\ \hline 1\ 6 \\ -1\ 4 \\ \hline 20 \\ -14 \\ \hline 6 \end{array}$$

To round the quotient to the nearest tenth, the division must be carried to the hundredths place. Therefore, zeros must be inserted in the dividend so that the quotient has a digit in the hundredths place.

APPLY THE CONCEPT

Figure 2.3 shows average hourly earnings in the United States. How many times greater were the average hourly earnings in 2010 than in 1995? Round to the nearest whole number.

Divide the 2010 average hourly earnings ($22.61) by the average hourly earnings in 1995 ($11.71).

$22.61 \div 11.71 \approx 2$

The average hourly earnings in 2010 were about 2 times the average hourly earnings in 1995.

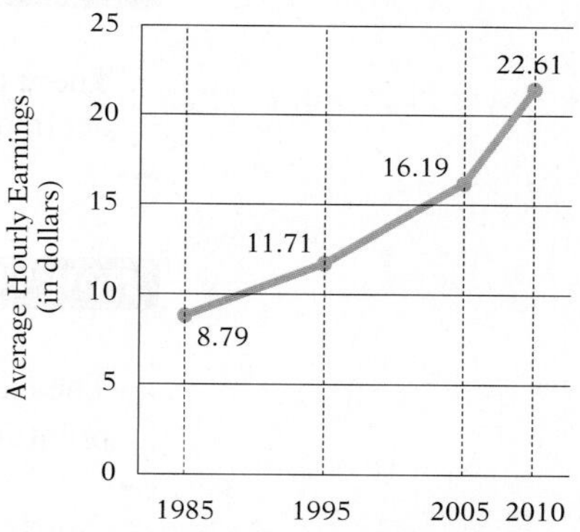

Figure 2.3 Average Hourly Earnings
Source: Bureau of Labor Statistics

To divide a decimal by a power of 10 (10, 100, 1000, 10,000, . . .), move the decimal point to the left the same number of places as there are zeros in the power of 10.

$462.81 \div 10 = 46.281$ — 1 zero, 1 decimal place

$462.81 \div 100 = 4.6281$ — 2 zeros, 2 decimal places

$462.81 \div 1000 = 0.46281$ — 3 zeros, 3 decimal places

$462.81 \div 10{,}000 = 0.046281$ — 4 zeros, 4 decimal places. A zero must be inserted between the decimal point and the 4.

$462.81 \div 100{,}000 = 0.0046281$ — 5 zeros, 5 decimal places. Two zeros must be inserted between the decimal point and the 4.

If the power of 10 is written in exponential notation, the exponent indicates how many places to move the decimal point.

$462.81 \div 10^1 = 46.281$ — 1 decimal place

$462.81 \div 10^2 = 4.6281$ — 2 decimal places

$462.81 \div 10^3 = 0.46281$ — 3 decimal places

$462.81 \div 10^4 = 0.046281$ — 4 decimal places

$462.81 \div 10^5 = 0.0046281$ — 5 decimal places

IN-CLASS EXAMPLES

11. Divide: $83.08 \div 6.2$ **13.4**
12. Estimate the quotient of 41.52 and 3.7. **10**
13. Divide and round to the nearest hundredth: $32.087 \div 0.72$ **44.57**
14. What is the quotient of 3812.5 and 1000? **3.8125**
15. Evaluate $\frac{x}{y}$ for $x = 0.161$ and $y = 0.7$. **0.23**
16. Which number, 11.52 or 2, is a solution of the equation $4.8 = \frac{t}{2.4}$? **11.52**

HOW TO 14 Find the quotient of 3.59 and 100.

There are two zeros in 100. Move the decimal point in 3.59 two places to the left. $3.59 \div 100 = 0.0359$

HOW TO 15 What is the quotient of 64.79 and 10^4?

The exponent on 10 is 4. Move the decimal point in 64.79 four places to the left. $64.79 \div 10^4 = 0.006479$

EXAMPLE 11

Divide: $431.97 \div 7.26$

Solution

$$\begin{array}{r} 59.5 \\ 7.26\overline{)\,431.970} \\ -3630 \\ \hline 6897 \\ -6534 \\ \hline 3630 \\ -3630 \\ \hline 0 \end{array}$$

• Move the decimal point 2 places to the right.

YOU TRY IT 11

Divide: $314.746 \div 6.53$

Your solution 48.2

EXAMPLE 12

Estimate the quotient of 8.37 and 0.219.

Solution

8.37 ⟶ 8
0.219 ⟶ 0.2

$8 \div 0.2 = 40$

YOU TRY IT 12

Estimate the quotient of 62.7 and 3.45.

Your solution 20

EXAMPLE 13

Divide and round to the nearest hundredth:
$448.2 \div 53$

Solution

$$\begin{array}{r} 8.456 \approx 8.46 \\ 53\overline{)\,448.200} \\ -424 \\ \hline 242 \\ -212 \\ \hline 300 \\ -265 \\ \hline 350 \\ -318 \\ \hline 32 \end{array}$$

YOU TRY IT 13

Divide and round to the nearest thousandth:
$519.37 \div 86$

Your solution 6.039

Solutions on p. S8

EXAMPLE 14

Find the quotient of 592.4 and 10^4.

Solution Move the decimal point 4 places to the left.

$592.4 \div 10^4 = 0.05924$

YOU TRY IT 14

What is 63.7 divided by 100?

Your solution 0.637

EXAMPLE 15

Evaluate $\frac{x}{y}$ for $x = 76.8$ and $y = 0.8$.

Solution

$$\frac{x}{y}$$

$$\frac{76.8}{0.8} = 96$$

YOU TRY IT 15

Evaluate $\frac{x}{y}$ for $x = 40.6$ and $y = 0.7$.

Your solution

58

EXAMPLE 16

Is 0.4 a solution of the equation $\frac{8}{x} = 20$?

Solution

$$\frac{8}{x} = 20$$

$$\frac{8}{0.4} \;\Big|\; 20$$ • **Replace x by 0.4.**

$$20 = 20$$

Yes, 0.4 is a solution of the equation.

YOU TRY IT 16

Is 1.2 a solution of the equation $2 = \frac{0.6}{d}$?

Your solution

No

Solutions on p. S8

OBJECTIVE D

To convert between decimals and fractions and to identify the order relation between a decimal and a fraction

Because the fraction bar can be read "divided by," any fraction can be written as a decimal. To write a fraction as a decimal, divide the numerator of the fraction by the denominator.

Take Note

The fraction bar can be read "divided by."

$\frac{3}{4} = 3 \div 4$

Dividing the numerator by the denominator results in a remainder of zero. The decimal 0.75 is a terminating decimal.

HOW TO 16 Convert $\frac{3}{4}$ to a decimal.

$$\begin{array}{r} 0.75 \\ 4\overline{)3.00} \\ -2\,8 \\ \hline 20 \\ -20 \\ \hline 0 \end{array}$$

0.75 ← This is a **terminating decimal.**

0 ← The remainder is zero.

$\frac{3}{4} = 0.75$

HOW TO 17 Convert $\frac{5}{11}$ to a decimal.

$$\begin{array}{r} 0.4545 \\ 11\overline{)5.0000} \\ -4\,4 \\ \hline 60 \\ -55 \\ \hline 50 \\ -44 \\ \hline 60 \\ -55 \\ \hline 5 \end{array}$$

0.4545 ← This is a **repeating decimal.**

5 ← The remainder is never zero.

$\frac{5}{11} = 0.\overline{45}$ The bar over the digits 45 is used to show that these digits repeat.

Take Note

No matter how far we carry out the division, the remainder is never zero. The decimal $0.\overline{45}$ is a repeating decimal.

HOW TO 18 Convert $2\frac{4}{9}$ to a decimal.

Write the fractional part of the mixed number as a decimal. Divide the numerator by the denominator.

$9\overline{)4.000}$ = 0.444 $= 0.\overline{4}$

The whole number part of the mixed number is the whole number part of the decimal.

$2\frac{4}{9} = 2.\overline{4}$

IN-CLASS EXAMPLES

17. Convert $\frac{7}{18}$ to a decimal. $\mathbf{0.3\overline{8}}$
18. Convert $5\frac{5}{6}$ to a decimal. $\mathbf{5.8\overline{3}}$
19. Convert 4.96 to a fraction. $4\frac{24}{25}$
20. Place the correct symbol, < or >, between the two numbers. $\frac{1}{6}$ 0.167 $\mathbf{\frac{1}{6} < 0.167}$

To convert a decimal to a fraction, remove the decimal point and place the decimal part over a denominator equal to the place value of the last digit in the decimal.

hundredths: $0.57 = \frac{57}{100}$

hundredths: $7.65 = 7\frac{65}{100} = 7\frac{13}{20}$

tenths: $8.6 = 8\frac{6}{10} = 8\frac{3}{5}$

HOW TO 19 Convert 4.375 to a fraction.

The 5 in 4.375 is in the thousandths place. Write 0.375 as a fraction with a denominator of 1000.

$4.375 = 4\frac{375}{1000}$

Simplify the fraction.

$= 4\frac{3}{8}$

Integrating Technology

Some calculators *truncate* a decimal number that exceeds the calculator display. This means that the digits beyond the calculator's display are not shown. For this type of calculator, $\frac{2}{3}$ would be shown as 0.66666666. Other calculators *round* a decimal number when the calculator display is exceeded. For this type of calculator, $\frac{2}{3}$ would be shown as 0.66666667.

To find the order relation between a fraction and a decimal, first rewrite the fraction as a decimal. Then compare the two decimals.

HOW TO 20 Find the order relation between $\frac{6}{7}$ and 0.855.

Write the fraction as a decimal. Round to one more place value than the given decimal. (0.855 has 3 decimal places; round to 4 decimal places.)

$\frac{6}{7} \approx 0.8571$

Compare the two decimals.

$0.8571 > 0.8550$

Replace the decimal approximation of $\frac{6}{7}$ with $\frac{6}{7}$.

$\frac{6}{7} > 0.855$

EXAMPLE 17

Convert $\frac{5}{8}$ to a decimal.

Solution

$$8\overline{)5.000} = 0.625$$

$$\frac{5}{8} = 0.625$$

YOU TRY IT 17

Convert $\frac{4}{5}$ to a decimal.

Your solution 0.8

EXAMPLE 18

Convert $3\frac{1}{3}$ to a decimal.

Solution Write $\frac{1}{3}$ as a decimal.

$$3\overline{)1.000} = 0.333 = 0.\overline{3}$$

$$3\frac{1}{3} = 3.\overline{3}$$

YOU TRY IT 18

Convert $1\frac{5}{6}$ to a decimal.

Your solution $1.8\overline{3}$

EXAMPLE 19

Convert 7.25 to a fraction.

Solution $7.25 = 7\frac{25}{100} = 7\frac{1}{4}$

YOU TRY IT 19

Convert 6.2 to a fraction.

Your solution $6\frac{1}{5}$

EXAMPLE 20

Place the correct symbol, < or >, between the two numbers.

$0.845 \quad \frac{5}{6}$

Solution $\frac{5}{6} \approx 0.8333$

$0.8450 > 0.8333$

$0.845 > \frac{5}{6}$

YOU TRY IT 20

Place the correct symbol, < or >, between the two numbers.

$0.588 \quad \frac{7}{12}$

Your solution

$0.588 > \frac{7}{12}$

Solutions on p. S8

OBJECTIVE E *To solve application problems and use formulas*

EXAMPLE 21

A one-year subscription to a monthly magazine costs \$93. The price of each issue at the newsstand is \$9.80. How much would you save per issue by buying a year's subscription rather than buying each issue at the newsstand?

Strategy

To find the amount saved:

- Find the subscription price per issue by dividing the cost of the subscription (93) by the number of issues (12).
- Subtract the subscription price per issue from the newsstand price (9.80).

Solution

$$\begin{array}{r} 7.75 \\ 12\overline{)\,93.00} \\ -84 \\ \hline 9\,0 \\ -8\,4 \\ \hline 60 \\ -60 \\ \hline 0 \end{array}$$

• **Subscription price per issue**

$$\begin{array}{r} 9.80 \\ -7.75 \\ \hline 2.05 \end{array}$$

The savings would be \$2.05 per issue.

YOU TRY IT 21

You hand a postal clerk a ten-dollar bill to pay for the purchase of twelve 45¢ stamps. How much change do you receive?

Your strategy

IN-CLASS EXAMPLES

21. Your home mortgage requires monthly payments of \$1024.50 for 20 years. Find the total of the mortgage payments. **\$245,880**

Your solution

\$4.60

EXAMPLE 22

Use the formula $P = BF$, where P is the insurance premium, B is the base rate, and F is the rating factor, to find the insurance premium due on an insurance policy with a base rate of \$342.50 and a rating factor of 2.2.

Strategy

To find the insurance premium due, replace B by 342.50 and F by 2.2 in the given formula, and solve for P.

Solution

$P = BF$
$P = 342.50(2.2)$
$P = 753.50$

The insurance premium due is \$753.50.

YOU TRY IT 22

Use the formula $P = BF$, where P is the insurance premium, B is the base rate, and F is the rating factor, to find the insurance premium due on an insurance policy with a base rate of \$276.25 and a rating factor of 1.8.

Your strategy

Your solution

\$497.25

Solutions on p. S8

2.6 EXERCISES

SUGGESTED ASSIGNMENT

Exercises 1–8; Exercises 9–137, every other odd; Exercises 143–169, odds;
More challenging exercises: Exercises 172–177

✔ Concept Check

1. Set up the addition problem 2.391 + 45 + 13.0784 in a vertical format, as shown at the right. One addend is already placed. Fill in the first two shaded regions with the other addends lined up correctly. In the third shaded region, show the placement of the decimal point in the sum. Then add.

$$\begin{array}{r} 2.391 \\ 45. \\ +\ 13.0784 \\ \hline 60.4694 \end{array}$$

2. Set up the subtraction problem 34 − 18.21 in a vertical format, as shown at the right. Fill in the first two shaded regions with the minuend and subtrahend lined up correctly and zeros inserted as needed. In the third shaded region, show the placement of the decimal point in the difference. Then subtract.

$$\begin{array}{r} 34.00 \\ -18.21 \\ \hline 15.79 \end{array}$$

3. The multiplication problem 5.3(0.21) is shown at the right. Fill in the blanks with the numbers of decimal places in the factors and in the product. Then fill in the shaded region with the product.

$$\begin{array}{rl} 5.3 & \underline{\ 1\ } \text{ decimal places} \\ \times\ 0.21 & \underline{\ 2\ } \text{ decimal places} \\ \hline 53 & \\ 106 & \\ \hline 1.113 & \underline{\ 3\ } \text{ decimal places} \end{array}$$

4. When a decimal is multiplied by 100, the decimal point is moved __two__ places to the __right__.

5. The division problem 3.648 ÷ 3.04 is shown at the right. The decimal point of the divisor was moved __two__ places to the right in order to make the divisor a __whole__ number. Show the correct placement of the decimal point in the dividend and in the quotient.

$$\begin{array}{r} 12 \\ 304.\overline{)\ 3648} \\ -304 \\ \hline 608 \\ -608 \\ \hline 0 \end{array} \qquad \begin{array}{r} 1.2 \\ 304.\overline{)364.8} \end{array}$$

6. To round the quotient of two decimals to the nearest hundredth, carry out the division to the __thousandths__ place.

7. To convert $\frac{5}{4}$ to a decimal, divide __5__ by __4__. The quotient is 1.25. This is called a __terminating__ decimal.

8. A 12-pack of bottled spring water sells for $3.49. State whether you would use multiplication or division to find the cost of one bottle of spring water. Division

---

OBJECTIVE A *To add and subtract decimals*

Add or subtract.

9. 1.864 + 39 + 25.0781
65.9421

10. 2.04 + 35.6 + 4.918
42.558

11. 35.9 + 8.217 + 146.74
190.857

12. 12 + 73.59 + 6.482
92.072

13. 36.47 − 15.21
21.26

14. 85.69 − 2.13
83.56

15. 28 − 6.74
21.26

16. 5 − 1.386
3.614

17. 6.02 − 3.252
2.768

18. Find the sum of 2.536, 14.97, 8.014, and 21.67.
47.19

19. Find the total of 6.24, 8.573, 19.06, and 22.488.
56.361

20. What is 6.9217 decreased by 3.4501?
3.4716

21. What is 8.9 less than 62.57?
53.67

Add or subtract. Then check by estimating the sum or difference.

22. 45.06 + 80.71
125.77; 130

23. 6.408 + 5.917
12.325; 12

24. 0.24 + 0.38 + 0.96
1.58; 1.6

25. 56.87 − 23.24
33.63; 40

26. 6.272 − 1.848
4.424; 4

27. 0.931 − 0.628
0.303; 0.3

28. 5.37 + 26.49
31.86; 35

29. 87.65 − 49.032
38.618; 40

30. 387.6 − 54.92
332.68; 350

31. **Education** The graph at the right shows where U.S. children in grades K–12 are being educated. Figures are in millions of children.
a. Find the total number of children in grades K–12.
b. How many more children are being educated in public school than in private school?
a. 56.7 million children **b.** 43.4 million more children

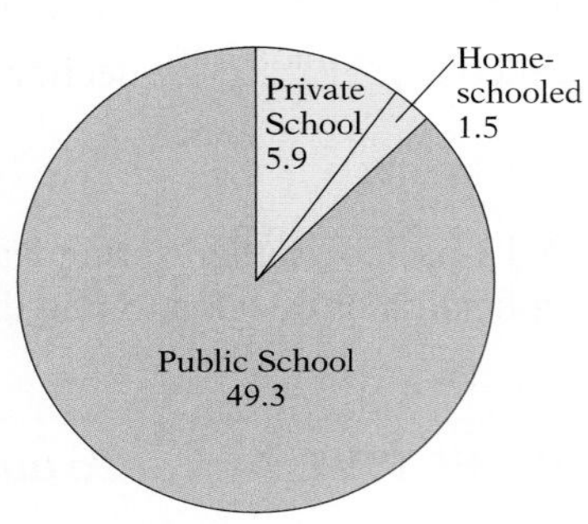

Where Children in Grades K–12 are Being Educated in the United States
Source: National Center for Education Statistics

Evaluate the variable expression $x + y + z$ for the given values of x, y, and z.

32. $x = 41.33$; $y = 26.095$; $z = 70.08$
137.505

33. $x = 6.059$; $y = 3.884$; $z = 15.71$
25.653

Evaluate the variable expression $x - y$ for the given values of x and y.

34. $x = 43.29$; $y = 18.76$
24.53

35. $x = 6.029$; $y = 4.708$
1.321

36. $x = 16.329$; $y = 4.54$
11.789

For Exercises 37 to 39, use the relationship between addition and subtraction to write the subtraction problem you would use to find the missing addend.

37. _______ + 2.325 = 7.01
7.01 − 2.325

38. 5.392 + _______ = 8.07
8.07 − 5.392

39. _______ + 8.967 = 19.35
19.35 − 8.967

OBJECTIVE B *To multiply decimals*

Multiply.

40. 0.9(0.3)
0.27

41. (3.4)(0.5)
1.70

42. (0.72)(3.7)
2.664

43. 8.29(0.004)
0.03316

44. What is the product of 5.92 and 100?
592

45. What is 1000 times 4.25?
4250

46. Find 0.82 times 10^2.
82

47. Find the product of 6.71 and 10^4.
67,100

Multiply. Then check by estimating the product.

48. 86.4(4.2)
362.88; 360

49. (9.81)(0.77)
7.5537; 8.0

50. 0.238(8.2)
1.9516; 1.6

51. (6.88)(9.97)
68.5936; 70

52. (8.432)(0.043)
0.362576; 0.32

53. 28.45(1.13)
32.1485; 30

Exchange Rates The table at the right shows currency exchange rates for several foreign countries. To determine how many Swiss francs would be exchanged for 1000 U.S. dollars, multiply the number of francs exchanged for one U.S. dollar (0.8804) by 1000: 1000(0.8804) = 880.4. Use this table for Exercises 54 and 55.

Country and Monetary Unit	*Number of Units Exchanged for 1 U.S. Dollar*
Britain (Pound)	0.6267
Canada (Dollar)	0.9928
European Union (Euro)	0.7237
Japan (Yen)	77.7882
Mexico (Peso)	12.6009
Switzerland (Franc)	0.8804

54. How many Mexican pesos would be exchanged for 5000 U.S. dollars? 63,004.5 pesos

55. How many British pounds would be exchanged for 20,000 U.S. dollars? 12,534 pounds

Evaluate the expression for the given values of the variables.

56. xy, for $x = 5.68$ and $y = 0.2$
1.136

57. ab, for $a = 6.27$ and $b = 8$
50.16

58. $40c$, for $c = 2.5$
100

59. Is 8 a solution of the equation $1.6 = 0.2z$?
Yes

60. Is 3.6 a solution of the equation $32.4 = 9w$?
Yes

61. A number rounded to the nearest tenth is multiplied by 1000. How many zeros must be inserted to the right of the number when moving the decimal point to write the product? Two

62. A decimal whose value is between 0 and 1 is multiplied by 10, and the result is a natural number less than 10. List all possible values of the decimal.
0.1, 0.2, 0.3, 0.4, 0.5, 0.6, 0.7, 0.8, 0.9

OBJECTIVE C *To divide decimals*

Divide.

63. $16.15 \div 0.5$
32.3

64. $7.02 \div 3.6$
1.95

65. $27.08 \div 0.4$
67.7

66. $8.919 \div 0.9$
9.91

Divide. Round to the nearest tenth.

67. $55.63 \div 8.8$
6.3

68. $1.873 \div 1.4$
1.3

69. $52.8 \div 9.1$
5.8

70. $6.824 \div 0.053$
128.8

Divide. Round to the nearest hundredth.

71. $6.457 \div 8$
0.81

72. $19.07 \div 0.54$
35.31

73. $0.0416 \div 0.53$
0.08

74. $31.792 \div 0.86$
36.97

75. Find the quotient of 52.78 and 10.
5.278

76. What is 37,942 divided by 1000?
37.942

77. What is the quotient of 48.05 and 10^2?
0.4805

78. Find 9.407 divided by 10^3.
0.009407

Divide and round to the nearest hundredth. Then check by estimating the quotient.

79. $42.43 \div 3.8$
11.17; 10

80. $678 \div 0.71$
954.93; 1000

81. $6.398 \div 5.5$
1.16; 1

82. $0.994 \div 0.456$
2.18; 2

83. $1.237 \div 0.021$
58.90; 50

84. $421.093 \div 4.087$
103.03; 100

85. $33.14 \div 4.6$
7.20; 6

86. $129.38 \div 4.47$
28.94; 25

87. **Organic Food** The graph at the right shows sales of organic food in the United States for 1997, 2005, and 2010. Figures are given in billions of dollars. How many times greater were sales in 2010 than sales in 1997? Round to the nearest whole number. 8 times

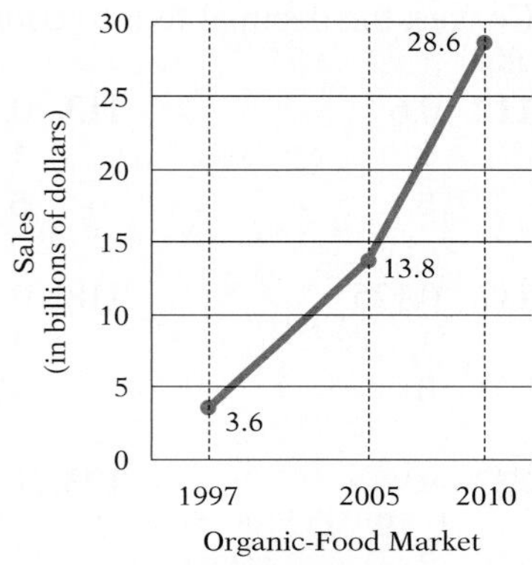

U.S. Organic Food Sales
Source: Organic Trade Association

Evaluate the variable expression $\frac{x}{y}$ for the given values of x and y.

88. $x = 52.8$; $y = 0.4$
132

89. $x = 3.542$; $y = 0.7$
5.06

90. $x = 2.436$; $y = 0.6$
4.06

91. Is 24.8 a solution of the equation $\frac{q}{8} = 3.1$?
Yes

92. Is 4.8 a solution of the equation $\frac{6}{z} = 12.5$?
No

93. Is 0.84 a solution of the equation $21 = \frac{t}{0.4}$?
No

94. Is 0.9 a solution of the equation $\frac{2.7}{a} = \frac{a}{0.3}$?
Yes

95. A number greater than 1 but less than 10 is divided by 10,000. How many zeros must be inserted to the left of the number when moving the decimal point to write the quotient? Three

96. A number n is rounded to the nearest hundredth. Which number can n be divided by to produce a quotient that is a whole number?
(i) 1 **(ii)** 100 **(iii)** 0.1 **(iv)** 0.01 iv

OBJECTIVE D ***To convert between decimals and fractions and to identify the order relation between a decimal and a fraction***

Convert the fraction to a decimal. Place a bar over repeating digits of a repeating decimal.

97. $\frac{3}{8}$
0.375

98. $\frac{7}{15}$
$0.4\overline{6}$

99. $\frac{8}{11}$
$0.\overline{72}$

100. $\frac{9}{16}$
0.5625

101. $\frac{7}{12}$
$0.58\overline{3}$

102. $\frac{5}{3}$
$1.\overline{6}$

103. $\frac{7}{4}$
1.75

104. $2\frac{3}{4}$
2.75

105. $1\frac{1}{2}$
1.5

106. $3\frac{2}{9}$
$3.\overline{2}$

107. $4\frac{1}{6}$
$4.1\overline{6}$

108. $\frac{3}{25}$
0.12

109. $2\frac{1}{4}$
2.25

110. $6\frac{3}{5}$
6.6

111. $3\frac{8}{9}$
$3.\overline{8}$

Convert the decimal to a fraction.

112. 0.6
$\frac{3}{5}$

113. 0.2
$\frac{1}{5}$

114. 0.25
$\frac{1}{4}$

115. 0.75
$\frac{3}{4}$

116. 0.48
$\frac{12}{25}$

117. 0.125
$\frac{1}{8}$

118. 0.325
$\frac{13}{40}$

119. 2.5
$2\frac{1}{2}$

120. 3.4
$3\frac{2}{5}$

121. 4.55
$4\frac{11}{20}$

122. 9.95
$9\frac{19}{20}$

123. 1.72
$1\frac{18}{25}$

124. 5.68
$5\frac{17}{25}$

125. 0.045
$\frac{9}{200}$

126. 0.085
$\frac{17}{200}$

Place the correct symbol, $<$ or $>$, between the two numbers.

127. $\frac{9}{10} > 0.89$

128. $\frac{7}{20} > 0.34$

129. $\frac{4}{5} < 0.803$

130. $\frac{3}{4} > 0.706$

131. $0.444 < \frac{4}{9}$

132. $0.72 > \frac{5}{7}$

133. $0.13 > \frac{3}{25}$

134. $0.25 < \frac{13}{50}$

135. $\frac{5}{16} > 0.312$

136. $\frac{7}{18} < 0.39$

137. $\frac{10}{11} > 0.909$

138. $\frac{8}{15} < 0.543$

139. What is the largest fraction with a denominator of 5 that is less than 0.78? $\frac{3}{5}$

140. What is the smallest fraction with a denominator of 4 that is greater than 2.5? Write your answer as an improper fraction.
$\frac{11}{4}$

OBJECTIVE E *To solve application problems and use formulas*

141. You have \$20 to spend, and you make purchases for the following amounts: \$4.24, \$8.66, and \$.54. Which of the following expressions correctly represent the amount of money you have left?

(i) $20 - 4.24 + 8.66 + 0.54$ **(ii)** $(4.24 + 8.66 + 0.54) - 20$
(iii) $20 - (4.24 + 8.66 + 0.54)$ **(iv)** $20 - 4.24 - 8.66 - 0.54$ iii and iv

142. Three friends share two pizzas that cost \$9.75 and \$10.50. Each person has a soda that costs \$1.70. The friends plan to split the cost of the meal equally. Write a verbal description of what each expression represents.

a. $3 \cdot 1.70$ **b.** $9.75 + 10.50 + 3 \cdot 1.70$ **c.** $\frac{9.75 + 10.50 + 3 \cdot 1.70}{3}$

a. The total cost of the sodas b. The total cost of the meal c. The total amount of money each friend will pay

143. Banking You had a balance of \$347.08 in your checking account. You then made a deposit of \$189.53 and wrote a check for \$62.89. Find the new balance in your checking account. \$473.72

In the NEWS!

Tourists Boost the Economy

This past summer, 14.3 million visitors came to the United States, spending a record \$30.7 billion.

Source: Commerce Department

144. Tourism See the news clipping at the right. Find the average amount spent by each visitor to the United States. Round to the nearest cent. \$2146.85

145. Electricity In the United States, a homeowner's average monthly bill for electricity is \$95.66. (*Source:* Department of Energy) What is a U.S. homeowner's average annual cost of electricity? \$1147.92

146. Salaries If you earn an annual salary of \$59,619, what is your monthly salary? \$4968.25

147. Car Purchases You bought a car for \$5000 down and made payments of \$499.50 each month for 36 months.

a. Find the amount of the payments over the 36 months. \$17,982

b. Find the total cost of the car. \$22,982

148. Compensation A nurse earns a salary of \$1396 for a 40-hour work week. This week the nurse worked 15 h of overtime at a rate of \$52.35 for each hour of overtime worked.

a. Find the nurse's overtime pay. \$785.25

b. Find the nurse's total income for the week. \$2181.25

In the NEWS!

Average Age at First Marriage Increasing

Men and women are marrying later in life. In 1970, the average age at first marriage was 20.8 years for women and 23.2 years for men. In 2010, the average age was 26.1 years for women and 28.2 years for men.

Source: Time, March 21, 2011

149. Marriage Read the news clipping at the right. Find the difference in average age at first marriage from 1970 to 2010 for **a.** women and **b.** men.

a. 5.3 years b. 5.0 years

150. Transportation A long-haul truck driver earns \$.43 for each mile driven. How much will a truck driver earn for driving 1507 mi from Boston to Miami? \$648.01

151. Recycling Four hundred empty soft drink cans weigh 18.75 lb. A recycling center pays \$.75 per pound for cans. Find the amount received for the 400 cans. Round to the nearest cent. \$14.06

© Huguette Roe/Shutterstock.com

152. Recycling A recycling center pays \$.045 per pound for newspapers.
a. Estimate the payment for recycling 520 lb of newspapers. \$25.00
b. Find the actual amount received from recycling the newspapers. \$23.40

153. Taxes The tax per gallon of gasoline in California is \$.466. (*Source:* Tax Foundation) If you fill your gasoline tank with 12.5 gal of gasoline in California, how much will you pay in taxes? \$5.83

154. Fuel Consumption You travel 295 mi on 12.5 gal of gasoline. How many miles can you travel on 1 gal of gasoline? 23.6 mi

155. Carbon Footprint Depending on the efficiency of a power plant, 1 ton of coal can produce about 3000 kilowatt-hours of electricity. Suppose your family uses 25 kilowatt-hours of electricity per month. How many tons of coal will your family use in one year? 0.1 ton

156. Carbon Footprint One barrel of oil produces approximately 800 kilowatt-hours of electricity. Suppose you use 27 kilowatt-hours of electricity per month. How many barrels of oil will you use in one year? 0.405 barrel

157. Going Green See the news clipping at the right. Write your answers in standard form, rounded to the nearest whole number.
a. Find the reduction in solid waste per month if every U.S. household viewed and paid its bills online. 133,333,333 tons
b. Find the reduction in greenhouse gas emissions per month if every U.S. household viewed and paid its bills online. 175,000 tons

In the NEWS!

"Green" Banking Has Far-Reaching Effects

Banking and paying bills online not only saves trees; it cuts down on the amount of fuel used by vehicles that transport paper checks. According to Javelin Strategy and Research, if every household in the United States paid its bills online, solid waste would be reduced by 1.6 billion tons a year and greenhouse-gas emissions would be cut by 2.1 million tons a year.

Source: Time, April 9, 2008

158. Budgets You have a monthly budget of \$2620. This month you have already spent \$82.78 for the telephone bill, \$264.93 for food, \$95.50 for gasoline, \$860 for your share of the rent, and \$391.62 for a loan repayment. How much money do you have left in the budget for the remainder of the month? \$925.17

159. Business For \$175, a druggist purchases 5 L of cough syrup and repackages it in 250-milliliter bottles. Each bottle costs the druggist \$.75. Each bottle of cough syrup is sold for \$15.89. Find the profit on the 5 L of cough syrup. (*Hint:* There are 1000 ml in 1 L.) \$127.80

160. Geometry The length of each side of a square is 3.5 ft. Find the perimeter of the square. Use the formula $P = 4s$. 14 ft

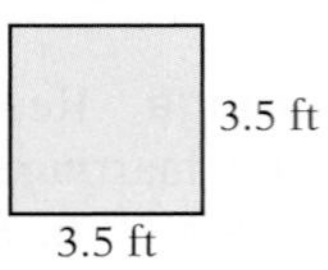

161. Geometry Find the perimeter of a rectangle that measures 4.5 in. by 3.25 in. Use the formula $P = 2L + 2W$. 15.5 in.

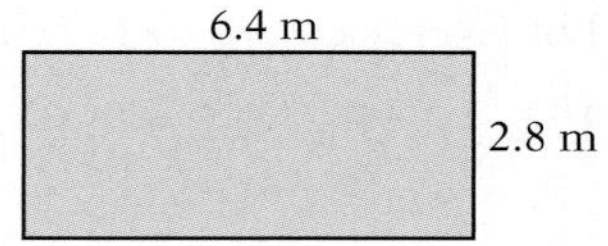

162. Geometry Find the perimeter of a rectangle that measures 2.8 m by 6.4 m. Use the formula $P = 2L + 2W$. 18.4 m

163. Geometry Find the area of a rectangle that measures 4.5 in. by 3.25 in. Use the formula $A = LW$. 14.625 in^2

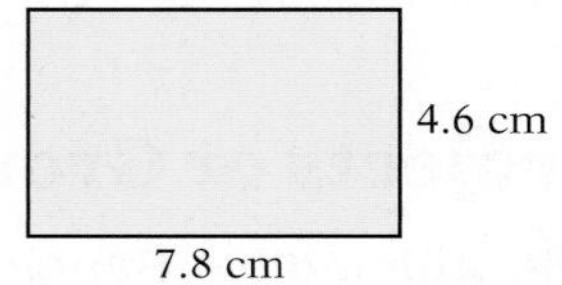

164. Geometry Find the area of a rectangle that has a length of 7.8 cm and a width of 4.6 cm. Use the formula $A = LW$. 35.88 cm^2

165. Geometry Find the perimeter of a triangle with sides that measure 2.8 m, 4.75 m, and 6.4 m. Use the formula $P = a + b + c$. 13.95 m

166. Markup Use the formula $M = S - C$, where M is the markup on a consumer product, S is the selling price, and C is the cost of the product to the business, to find the markup on a product that cost a business $1653.19 and has a selling price of $2231.81. $578.62

167. Federal Earnings The amount of an employee's earnings that is subject to federal withholding is called federal earnings. Find the federal earnings for an employee who earns $694.89 and has a withholding allowance of $132.69. Use the formula $F = E - W$, where F is the federal earnings, E is the employee's earnings, and W is the withholding allowance. $562.20

168. Car Rentals Use the formula $M = \frac{C}{N}$, where M is the cost per mile for a rental car, C is the total cost, and N is the number of miles driven, to find the cost per mile when the total cost of renting a car is $260.16 and you drive the car 542 mi. $.48

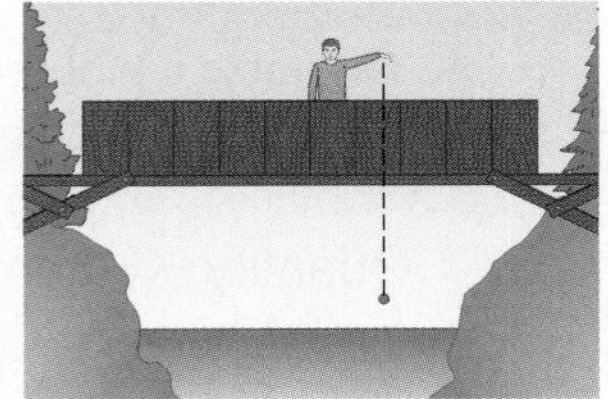

169. Physics Find the force exerted on a falling object that has a mass of 4.25 kg. Use the formula $F = ma$, where F is the force exerted by gravity on a falling object, m is the mass of the object, and a is the acceleration due to gravity. The acceleration due to gravity is 9.80 m/s^2 (meters per second squared). The force is measured in newtons. 41.65 newtons

170. Utilities Find the cost of operating a 1800-watt TV set for 5 h at a cost of $.06 per kilowatt-hour. Use the formula $c = 0.001wtk$, where c is the cost of operating an appliance, w is the number of watts, t is the time in hours, and k is the cost per kilowatt-hour. $.54

Critical Thinking

171. Show how the decimal is placed in the product of 1.3 × 2.31 by first writing each number as a fraction and then multiplying. Then change the product back to decimal notation.

$$1.3 \times 2.31 = \frac{13}{10} \times \frac{231}{100} = \frac{3003}{1000} = 3.003$$

For Exercises 172 to 177, insert +, −, ×, or ÷ into the square so that the statement is true.

172. 3.45 ☐ 0.5 = 6.9 ÷ **173.** 3.46 ☐ 0.24 = 0.8304 × **174.** 6.009 ☐ 4.68 = 1.329 −

175. 0.064 ☐ 1.6 = 0.1024 × **176.** 9.876 ☐ 23.12 = 32.996 + **177.** 3.0381 ☐ 1.23 = 2.47 ÷

QUICK QUIZ

1. Subtract: 29.843 − 12.76 **17.083 [2.6A]**
2. Evaluate the expression $x + y$ for $x = 37.58$ and $y = 6.94$. **44.52 [2.6A]**

Projects or Group Activities

178. Automotive Repair Chris works at B & W Garage as an auto mechanic and has just completed an engine overhaul for a customer. To determine the cost of the repair job, Chris keeps a list of times worked and parts used. A parts list and a list of the times worked are shown below.

Parts Used		*Time Spent*	
Item	*Quantity*	*Day*	*Hours*
Gasket set	1	Monday	7.0
Ring set	1	Tuesday	7.5
Valves	8	Wednesday	6.5
Wrist pins	8	Thursday	8.5
Valve springs	16	Friday	9.0
Rod bearings	8		
Main bearings	5		
Valve seals	16		
Timing chain	1		

Price List		
Item Number	*Description*	*Unit Price*
27345	Valve spring	$9.25
41257	Main bearing	$17.49
54678	Valve	$16.99
29753	Ring set	$169.99
45837	Gasket set	$174.90
23751	Timing chain	$50.49
23765	Fuel pump	$229.99
28632	Wrist pin	$23.55
34922	Rod bearing	$13.69
2871	Valve seal	$1.69

a. Organize a table of data showing the parts used, the unit price for each part, and the price of the quantity used. *Hint:* Use the following headings for the table.

Quantity	Item Number	Description	Unit Price	Total
1	45837	Gasket set	$174.90	$174.90
1	29753	Ring set	$169.99	$169.99
8	54678	Valve	$ 16.99	$135.92
8	28632	Wrist pin	$ 23.55	$188.40
16	27345	Valve spring	$ 9.25	$148.00
8	34922	Rod bearing	$ 13.69	$109.52
5	41257	Main bearing	$ 17.49	$ 87.45
16	2871	Valve seal	$ 1.69	$ 27.04
1	23751	Timing chain	$ 50.49	$ 50.49

b. Add up the numbers in the "Total" column to find the total cost of the parts. $1091.71

c. If the charge for labor is $66.75 per hour, compute the cost of labor. $2569.88

d. What is the total cost for parts and labor? $3661.59

3. Find the product of 63.8 and 100. **6380 [2.6B]**
4. Divide and round to the nearest hundredth: 36.597 ÷ 5.2 **7.04 [2.6C]**
5. Convert 0.42 to a fraction. $\frac{21}{50}$ **[2.6D]**
6. A jogger ran 7.4 mi in 45.88 min. What was the jogger's average time per mile? **6.2 min [2.6E]**
7. You have a rent payment of $814.72, a credit card bill of $216.40, and a phone/Internet/cable bill of $87.32. Find the total of the three payments. **$1118.44 [2.6E]**

179. Explain how baseball batting averages are determined.

SECTION

2.7 The Order of Operations Agreement

OBJECTIVE A *To use the Order of Operations Agreement to simplify expressions*

The Order of Operations Agreement applies in simplifying expressions containing fractions.

The Order of Operations Agreement

Step 1 Do all operations inside parentheses.

Step 2 Simplify any numerical expressions containing exponents.

Step 3 Do multiplication and division as they occur from left to right.

Step 4 Do addition and subtraction as they occur from left to right.

HOW TO 1 Simplify: $\left(\frac{1}{2}\right)^2 + \left(\frac{2}{3} \div \frac{5}{9}\right) \cdot \frac{5}{6}$

$$\left(\frac{1}{2}\right)^2 + \left(\frac{2}{3} \div \frac{5}{9}\right) \cdot \frac{5}{6}$$

Do the operation inside the parentheses (Step 1). $= \left(\frac{1}{2}\right)^2 + \left(\frac{6}{5}\right) \cdot \frac{5}{6}$

Simplify the exponential expression (Step 2). $= \frac{1}{4} + \left(\frac{6}{5}\right) \cdot \frac{5}{6}$

Do the multiplication (Step 3). $= \frac{1}{4} + 1$

Do the addition (Step 4). $= 1\frac{1}{4}$

A fraction bar acts like parentheses. Therefore, simplify the numerator and denominator of a fraction as part of Step 1 in the Order of Operations Agreement.

HOW TO 2 Simplify: $6 - \frac{2 + 1}{15 - 8} \div \frac{3}{14}$

$$6 - \frac{2 + 1}{15 - 8} \div \frac{3}{14}$$

Perform operations above and below the fraction bar. $= 6 - \frac{3}{7} \div \frac{3}{14}$

Do the division. $= 6 - \left(\frac{3}{7} \cdot \frac{14}{3}\right)$

$= 6 - 2$

Do the subtraction. $= 4$

HOW TO 3 Evaluate $\frac{w+x}{y} - z$ for $w = \frac{3}{4}$, $x = \frac{1}{4}$, $y = 2$, and $z = \frac{1}{3}$.

$$\frac{w+x}{y} - z$$

Replace each variable with its given value.

$$\frac{\frac{3}{4} + \frac{1}{4}}{2} - \frac{1}{3}$$

Simplify the numerator of the complex fraction.

$$= \frac{1}{2} - \frac{1}{3}$$

Do the subtraction.

$$= \frac{1}{6}$$

IN-CLASS EXAMPLES

Simplify.

1. $\frac{7}{8} + \frac{1}{9} \div \frac{8}{9}$ **1**
2. $(0.5)^2 + (4.9 - 2.4)$ **2.75**
3. $\frac{3}{14} + \frac{6}{7} \cdot \left(\frac{2}{3} - \frac{1}{2}\right)^2$ $\mathbf{\frac{5}{21}}$

EXAMPLE 1

Simplify: $0.2(5.6 - 2.5) + (1.4)^2$

Solution

$0.2(5.6 - 2.5) + (1.4)^2$

$= 0.2(3.1) + (1.4)^2$ • **Parentheses**

$= 0.2(3.1) + 1.96$ • **Exponents**

$= 0.62 + 1.96$ • **Multiply.**

$= 2.58$ • **Add.**

YOU TRY IT 1

Simplify: $(1.2 - 0.8)^2 + (1.5)(6)$

Your solution

9.16

EXAMPLE 2

Simplify: $\left(\frac{2}{3}\right)^2 \div \frac{7-2}{13-4} - \frac{1}{3}$

Solution

$\left(\frac{2}{3}\right)^2 \div \frac{7-2}{13-4} - \frac{1}{3}$

$= \left(\frac{2}{3}\right)^2 \div \frac{5}{9} - \frac{1}{3}$ • **Simplify $\frac{7-2}{13-4}$.**

$= \frac{4}{9} \div \frac{5}{9} - \frac{1}{3}$ • **Simplify $\left(\frac{2}{3}\right)^2$.**

$= \frac{4}{9} \cdot \frac{9}{5} - \frac{1}{3}$ • **Rewrite division as multiplication by the reciprocal.**

$= \frac{4}{5} - \frac{1}{3} = \frac{7}{15}$

YOU TRY IT 2

Simplify: $\left(\frac{1}{2}\right)^3 \cdot \frac{7-3}{9-4} + \frac{4}{5}$

Your solution

$\frac{9}{10}$

Solutions on p. S9

2.7 EXERCISES

Concept Check

SUGGESTED ASSIGNMENT
Exercises 1 and 2; Exercises 3–33 odds; More challenging exercise: Exercise 35

1. Simplifying the expression $\frac{2}{3} - \frac{4}{3 + \frac{3}{8}}$ involves performing three operations: subtraction, division, and addition. List these three operations in the order in which they must be performed. Addition, division, subtraction

2. Simplifying the expression $\frac{2}{9} \cdot \left(\frac{3}{4}\right)^2 + \frac{5}{6}$ involves performing three operations: multiplication, squaring, and addition. List these three operations in the order in which they must be performed. Squaring, multiplication, addition

OBJECTIVE A *To use the Order of Operations Agreement to simplify expressions*

Simplify.

3. $\frac{3}{7} \cdot \frac{14}{15} + \frac{4}{5}$

$1\frac{1}{5}$

4. $\frac{3}{5} \div \frac{6}{7} + \frac{4}{5}$

$1\frac{1}{2}$

5. $\left(\frac{5}{6}\right)^2 - \frac{5}{9}$

$\frac{5}{36}$

6. $\left(\frac{3}{5}\right)^2 - \frac{3}{10}$

$\frac{3}{50}$

7. $\frac{3}{4} \cdot \left(\frac{11}{12} - \frac{7}{8}\right) + \frac{5}{16}$

$\frac{11}{32}$

8. $\frac{7}{18} + \frac{5}{6} \cdot \left(\frac{2}{3} - \frac{1}{6}\right)$

$\frac{29}{36}$

9. $\frac{11}{16} - \left(\frac{3}{4}\right)^2 + \frac{7}{8}$

1

10. $\left(-\frac{2}{3}\right)^2 - \frac{7}{18} + \frac{5}{6}$

$\frac{8}{9}$

11. $\left(1\frac{1}{3} - \frac{5}{6}\right) + \frac{7}{8} \div \left(\frac{1}{2}\right)^2$

4

12. $\left(\frac{1}{4}\right)^2 \div \left(2\frac{1}{2} - \frac{3}{4}\right) + \frac{5}{7}$

$\frac{3}{4}$

13. $\left(\frac{2}{3}\right)^2 + \frac{8 - 7}{9 - 3} \div \frac{3}{8}$

$\frac{8}{9}$

14. $\left(\frac{1}{3}\right)^2 \cdot \frac{14 - 5}{10 - 6} + \frac{3}{4}$

1

15. $(0.5)(0.2)^2 + 1.7$

1.72

16. $0.3(4.8 - 1.7) + (1.2)^2$

2.37

17. $(1.8)^2 - 2.52 \div 1.8$

1.84

18. $(1.65 - 1.05)^2 \div 0.4 + 0.9$

1.8

19. $0.4(3 - 1.5) + (1.2)^2$

2.04

20. $(5 - 3.5)^2 + (0.75)(8)$

8.25

21. $\frac{1}{2} + \dfrac{\frac{13}{25}}{4 - \frac{3}{4}} \div \frac{1}{5}$

$1\frac{3}{10}$

22. $\frac{4}{5} + \dfrac{3 - \frac{7}{9}}{\frac{5}{6}} \cdot \frac{3}{8}$

$1\frac{4}{5}$

23. $\left(\frac{2}{3}\right)^2 + \dfrac{\frac{5}{8} - \frac{1}{4}}{\frac{2}{3} - \frac{1}{6}} \cdot \frac{8}{9}$

$1\frac{1}{9}$

Evaluate the expression for the given values of the variables.

24. $x^2 + \frac{y}{z}$, for $x = \frac{2}{3}$, $y = \frac{5}{8}$, and $z = \frac{3}{4}$

$1\frac{5}{18}$

25. $\frac{x}{y} - z^2$, for $x = \frac{5}{6}$, $y = \frac{1}{3}$, and $z = \frac{3}{4}$

$1\frac{15}{16}$

26. $x - y^3z$, for $x = \frac{5}{6}$, $y = \frac{1}{2}$, and $z = \frac{8}{9}$

$\frac{13}{18}$

27. $xy^3 + z$, for $x = \frac{9}{10}$, $y = \frac{1}{3}$, and $z = \frac{7}{15}$

$\frac{1}{2}$

28. $\frac{wx}{y} + z$, for $w = \frac{4}{5}$, $x = \frac{5}{8}$, $y = \frac{3}{4}$, and $z = \frac{2}{3}$

$1\frac{1}{3}$

29. $\frac{w}{xy} - z$, for $w = 2\frac{1}{2}$, $x = 4$, $y = \frac{3}{8}$, and $z = \frac{2}{3}$

1

30. $c^2 - ab$, when $a = 1.7$, $b = 0.6$, and $c = 2.8$

6.82

31. $(a + b)^2 - c$, when $a = 2.5$, $b = 1.8$, and $c = 0.4$

18.09

32. $\frac{b^2}{c} + 4a$, when $a = 1.5$, $b = 0.2$, and $c = 0.4$

6.1

33. $\frac{x}{y^2} + 3z$, when $x = 7.2$, $y = 0.6$, and $z = 3.5$

30.5

34. Insert parentheses into the expression $\frac{2}{9} \cdot \frac{5}{6} + \frac{3}{4} \div \frac{3}{5}$ so that **a.** the first operation to be performed is addition and **b.** the first operation to be performed is division.

a. $\frac{2}{9} \cdot \left(\frac{5}{6} + \frac{3}{4}\right) \div \frac{3}{5}$ **b.** $\frac{2}{9} \cdot \frac{5}{6} + \left(\frac{3}{4} \div \frac{3}{5}\right)$

Critical Thinking

35. Find the product $\left(1 - \frac{1}{2^2}\right)\left(1 - \frac{1}{3^2}\right)\left(1 - \frac{1}{4^2}\right)\cdots\left(1 - \frac{1}{9^2}\right)\left(1 - \frac{1}{10^2}\right)$. $\frac{11}{20}$

Projects or Group Activities

36. Given that x is a whole number, for what value of x will the expression $\left(\frac{3}{4}\right)^2 + x^5 \div \frac{7}{8}$ have a minimum value? What is the minimum value?

$0; \frac{9}{16}$

QUICK QUIZ

Simplify:

1. $\left(\frac{2}{3}\right)^3\left(\frac{3}{4} - \frac{3}{8}\right)$

   $\frac{1}{6}$ [2.7A]

2. $(2.4)(5) + (4.1 - 3.9)^2$

   12.04 [2.7A]

3. $\left(\frac{5}{6} - \frac{7}{12}\right) + \frac{3}{8}\left(\frac{1}{3}\right)^2$

   $\frac{7}{24}$ [2.7A]

CHAPTER

2 Summary

Key Words

Examples

The **multiples** of a number are the products of that number and the numbers 1, 2, 3, 4, 5, . . .

4, 8, 12, 16, . . . are multiples of 4.
6, 12, 18, 24, . . . are multiples of 6.

A number that is a multiple of two or more numbers is a **common multiple** of those numbers. The **least common multiple (LCM)** is the smallest common multiple of two or more numbers. [2.1A, p. 80]

12, 24, 36, 48, . . . are common multiples of 4 and 6.
The LCM of 4 and 6 is 12.

A number that divides another number evenly is a **factor** of the number.

The factors of 12 are 1, 2, 3, 4, 6, and 12.
The factors of 16 are 1, 2, 4, 8, and 16.

A number that is a factor of two or more numbers is a **common factor** of those numbers. The **greatest common factor (GCF)** is the largest common factor of two or more numbers. [2.1B, p. 81]

The common factors of 12 and 16 are 1, 2, and 4.
The GCF of 12 and 16 is 4.

A **fraction** can represent the number of equal parts of a whole. In a fraction, the **fraction bar** separates the **numerator** and the **denominator.** [2.2A, p. 84]

In the fraction $\frac{3}{4}$, the numerator is 3 and the denominator is 4.

In a **proper fraction,** the numerator is smaller than the denominator; a proper fraction is a number less than 1. In an **improper fraction,** the numerator is greater than or equal to the denominator; an improper fraction is a number greater than or equal to 1. A **mixed number** is a number greater than 1 with a whole number part and a fractional part. [2.2A, pp. 84–85]

$\frac{2}{5}$ is a proper fraction.

$\frac{7}{6}$ is an improper fraction.

$4\frac{1}{10}$ is a mixed number; 4 is the whole number part and $\frac{1}{10}$ is the fractional part.

Equal fractions with different denominators are called **equivalent fractions.** [2.2B, p. 87]

$\frac{3}{4}$ and $\frac{6}{8}$ are equivalent fractions.

A fraction is in **simplest form** when the numerator and denominator have no common factors other than 1. [2.2B, p. 87]

The fraction $\frac{11}{12}$ is in simplest form.

The **reciprocal** of a fraction is that fraction with the numerator and denominator interchanged. [2.4B, p. 115]

The reciprocal of $\frac{3}{8}$ is $\frac{8}{3}$.

The reciprocal of 5 is $\frac{1}{5}$.

A **complex fraction** is a fraction whose numerator or denominator contains one or more fractions. [2.4C, p. 118]

$\dfrac{\frac{2}{3} - \frac{5}{8}}{\frac{1}{9}}$ is a complex fraction.

A number written in **decimal notation** has three parts: a whole number part, a decimal point, and a decimal part. The **decimal part** of a number represents a number less than 1. A number written in decimal notation is often called simply a **decimal.** [2.5A, p. 130]

For the decimal 31.25, 31 is the whole number part and 25 is the decimal part.

The position of a digit in a decimal determines the digit's **place value.** [2.5A, p. 130]

The place value of the digit 7 in the decimal 382.907156 is thousandths.

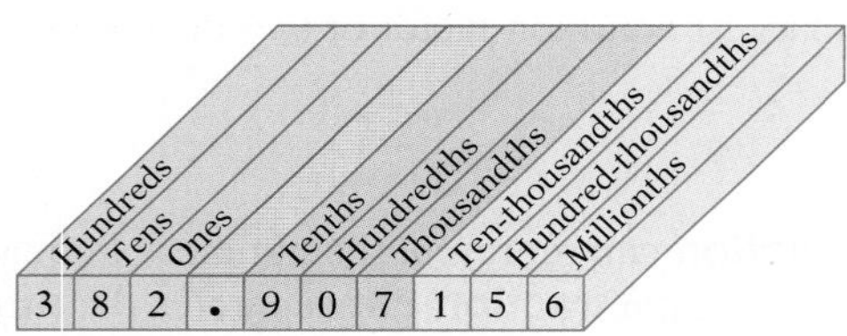

Essential Rules and Procedures

Examples

To find the LCM of two or more numbers, write the prime factorization of each number and circle the highest power of each prime factor. The LCM is the product of the circled factors. [2.1A, p. 80]

$12 = \textcircled{2^2} \cdot 3$

$18 = 2 \cdot \textcircled{3^2}$

The LCM of 12 and 18 is $2^2 \cdot 3^2 = 36$.

To find the GCF of two or more numbers, write the prime factorization of each number and circle the lowest power of each prime factor that occurs in both factorizations. The GCF is the product of the circled factors. [2.1B, p. 81]

$12 = 2^2 \cdot \textcircled{3}$

$18 = \textcircled{2} \cdot 3^2$

The GCF of 12 and 18 is $2 \cdot 3 = 6$.

To write a whole number as an improper fraction, write the whole number over a denominator of 1. [2.2A, p. 84]

$$9 = \frac{9}{1}$$

To write an improper fraction as a mixed number or a whole number, divide the numerator by the denominator. [2.2A, p. 85]

$$\frac{29}{6} = 29 \div 6 = 4\frac{5}{6}$$

$$\frac{35}{7} = 35 \div 7 = 5$$

To write a mixed number as an improper fraction, multiply the denominator of the fractional part of the mixed number by the whole number part. Add this product to the numerator of the fractional part. The sum is the numerator of the improper fraction. The denominator remains the same. [2.2A, p. 85]

$$3\frac{2}{5} = \frac{5 \times 3 + 2}{5} = \frac{17}{5}$$

To write a fraction in simplest form, divide the numerator and denominator of the fraction by their common factors. [2.2B, p. 88]

$$\frac{30}{45} = \frac{2 \cdot \overset{1}{\cancel{3}} \cdot \overset{1}{\cancel{5}}}{\underset{1}{\cancel{3}} \cdot 3 \cdot \underset{1}{\cancel{5}}} = \frac{2}{3}$$

To find the order relation between two fractions with the same denominator, compare the numerators. The fraction with the smaller numerator is the smaller fraction. The fraction with the larger numerator is the larger fraction. [2.2C, p. 89]

$$\frac{3}{5} < \frac{4}{5} \qquad \frac{6}{7} > \frac{2}{7}$$

To add fractions with the same denominators, add the numerators and place the sum over the common denominator. $\frac{a}{b} + \frac{c}{b} = \frac{a + c}{b}$, where $b \neq 0$. [2.3A, p. 96]

$$\frac{5}{12} + \frac{11}{12} = \frac{16}{12} = 1\frac{1}{3}$$

To subtract fractions with the same denominators, subtract the numerators and place the difference over the common denominator. $\frac{a}{b} - \frac{c}{b} = \frac{a - c}{b}$, where $b \neq 0$. [2.3B, p. 100]

$$\frac{9}{16} - \frac{5}{16} = \frac{4}{16} = \frac{1}{4}$$

To add or subtract fractions with different denominators, first rewrite the fractions as equivalent fractions with a common denominator. The common denominator is the least common multiple (LCM) of the denominators of the fractions. Then add or subtract the fractions. [2.3A/2.3B, p. 96, p. 100]

$$\frac{7}{8} + \frac{5}{6} = \frac{21}{24} + \frac{20}{24} = \frac{41}{24} = 1\frac{17}{24}$$

$$\frac{2}{3} - \frac{7}{16} = \frac{32}{48} - \frac{21}{48} = \frac{11}{48}$$

To multiply two fractions, multiply the numerators; this is the numerator of the product. Multiply the denominators; this is the denominator of the product. $\frac{a}{b} \cdot \frac{c}{d} = \frac{ac}{bd}$, where $b \neq 0$ and $d \neq 0$. [2.4A, p. 111]

$$\frac{3}{4} \cdot \frac{2}{9} = \frac{3 \cdot 2}{4 \cdot 9} = \frac{3 \cdot 2}{2 \cdot 2 \cdot 3 \cdot 3} = \frac{1}{6}$$

To divide two fractions, multiply the first fraction by the reciprocal of the second fraction. $\frac{a}{b} \div \frac{c}{d} = \frac{a}{b} \cdot \frac{d}{c}$, where $b \neq 0$, $c \neq 0$, and $d \neq 0$. [2.4B, p. 116]

$$\frac{8}{15} \div \frac{4}{5} = \frac{8}{15} \cdot \frac{5}{4} = \frac{8 \cdot 5}{15 \cdot 4}$$
$$= \frac{2 \cdot 2 \cdot 2 \cdot 5}{3 \cdot 5 \cdot 2 \cdot 2} = \frac{2}{3}$$

To simplify a complex fraction, simplify the expression above the main fraction bar and simplify the expression below the main fraction bar. Then rewrite the complex fraction as a division problem by reading the main fraction bar as "divided by." [2.4C, p. 119]

$$\frac{\frac{8}{9} + \frac{2}{3}}{1\frac{1}{5}} = \frac{\frac{8}{9} + \frac{6}{9}}{\frac{6}{5}} = \frac{\frac{14}{9}}{\frac{6}{5}}$$
$$= \frac{14}{9} \div \frac{6}{5} = \frac{14}{9} \cdot \frac{5}{6}$$
$$= \frac{35}{27} = 1\frac{12}{27}$$

The formula for the area of a triangle is $A = \frac{1}{2}bh$, where b is the base and h is the height of the triangle. [2.4D, p. 120]

Find the area of a triangle with a base measuring 6 ft and a height of 3 ft.

$$A = \frac{1}{2}bh = \frac{1}{2}(6)(3) = 9$$

The area is 9 ft^2.

To write a decimal in words, write the decimal part as though it were a whole number. Then name the place value of the last digit. The decimal point is read as "and." [2.5A, p. 130]

The decimal 12.875 is written in words as twelve and eight hundred seventy-five thousandths.

To write a decimal in standard form when it is written in words, write the whole number part, replace the word *and* with a decimal point, and write the decimal part so that the last digit is in the given place-value position. [2.5A, p. 131]

The decimal forty-nine and sixty-three thousandths is written in standard form as 49.063.

To compare two decimals, write the decimal part of each number so that each has the same number of decimal places. Then compare the two numbers. [2.5B, p. 132]

$1.790 > 1.789$

$0.8130 < 0.8315$

To round a decimal, use the same rules used for whole numbers, except drop the digits to the right of the given place value instead of replacing them with zeros. [2.5C, p. 133]

2.7134 rounded to the nearest tenth is 2.7.
0.4687 rounded to the nearest hundredth is 0.47.

To add decimals, write the numbers so that the decimal points are on a vertical line. Add as you would with whole numbers. Then write the decimal point in the answer directly below the decimal points in the addends. [2.6A, p. 140]

To subtract decimals, write the numbers so that the decimal points are on a vertical line. Subtract as you would with whole numbers. Then write the decimal point in the answer directly below the decimal points in the subtrahend. [2.6A, p. 140]

$$\begin{array}{r} {}^{1\,1} \\ 1.35 \\ 20.8 \\ +\ 0.76 \\ \hline 22.91 \end{array} \qquad \begin{array}{r} {}^{2\,15}{}^{6\,10} \\ \not{3}\not{5}.8\not{7}\not{0} \\ -\ 9.641 \\ \hline 26.229 \end{array}$$

To estimate the answer to a calculation, round each number to the highest place value of the number; the first digit of each number will be nonzero, and all other digits will be zero. If a number is a decimal less than 1, round the decimal so that there is one nonzero digit. Perform the calculation using the rounded numbers. [2.6A, p. 141]

$$\begin{array}{lr} 35.87 \longrightarrow & 40 \\ 61.09 \longrightarrow & +\ 60 \\ \hline & 100 \end{array}$$

$$\begin{array}{lr} 0.3876 \longrightarrow & 0.4 \\ 0.5472 \longrightarrow & +\ 0.5 \\ \hline & 0.9 \end{array}$$

To multiply decimals, multiply the numbers as you would whole numbers. Then write the decimal point in the product so that the number of decimal places in the product is the sum of the decimal places in the factors. [2.6B, p. 143]

$$\begin{array}{rl} 26.83 & \text{2 decimal places} \\ \times\ 0.45 & \text{2 decimal places} \\ \hline 13415 & \\ 10732 & \\ \hline 12.0735 & \text{4 decimal places} \end{array}$$

To multiply a decimal by a power of 10, move the decimal point to the right the same number of places as there are zeros in the power of 10. If the power of 10 is written in exponential notation, the exponent indicates how many places to move the decimal point. [2.6B, p. 144]

$3.97 \cdot 10{,}000 = 39{,}700$

$0.641 \cdot 10^5 = 64{,}100$

To divide decimals, move the decimal point in the divisor to the right so that the divisor is a whole number. Move the decimal point in the dividend the same number of places to the right. Place the decimal point in the quotient directly above the decimal point in the dividend. Then divide as you would with whole numbers. [2.6C, p. 146]

$$\begin{array}{r} 6.2 \\ 0.39.\overline{)\ 2.41.8} \\ -2\ 34 \\ \hline 7\ 8 \\ -7\ 8 \\ \hline 0 \end{array}$$

To divide a decimal by a power of 10, move the decimal point to the left the same number of places as there are zeros in the power of 10. If the power of 10 is written in exponential notation, the exponent indicates how many places to move the decimal point. [2.6C, p. 147]

$972.8 \div 1000 = 0.9728$

$61.305 \div 10^4 = 0.0061305$

To write a fraction as a decimal, divide the numerator of the fraction by the denominator. [2.6D, p. 149]

$\frac{7}{8} = 7 \div 8 = 0.875$

To convert a decimal to a fraction, remove the decimal point and place the decimal part over a denominator equal to the place value of the last digit in the decimal. [2.6D, p. 150]

0.85 is eighty-five hundredths.

$0.85 = \frac{85}{100} = \frac{17}{20}$

To find the order relation between a decimal and a fraction, first rewrite the fraction as a decimal. Then compare the two decimals. [2.6D, p. 150]

Because $\frac{3}{11} \approx 0.273$ and $0.273 > 0.26$, $\frac{3}{11} > 0.26$.

The Order of Operations Agreement [2.7A, p. 163]

Step 1: Do all operations inside parentheses.

Step 2: Simplify any numerical expressions containing exponents.

Step 3: Do multiplication and division as they occur from left to right.

Step 4: Do addition and subtraction as they occur from left to right.

$$\left(\frac{1}{3}\right)^2 + \left(\frac{5}{6} - \frac{7}{12}\right) \cdot 4$$

$$= \left(\frac{1}{3}\right)^2 + \left(\frac{1}{4}\right) \cdot 4$$

$$= \frac{1}{9} + \left(\frac{1}{4}\right) \cdot 4$$

$$= \frac{1}{9} + 1 = 1\frac{1}{9}$$

CHAPTER

2 Review Exercises

1. Write $\frac{19}{2}$ as a mixed number. $9\frac{1}{2}$ [2.2A]

2. Subtract: $6\frac{2}{9} - 3\frac{7}{18}$ $2\frac{5}{6}$ [2.3B]

3. Evaluate $x \div y$ for $x = 2\frac{5}{8}$ and $y = 1\frac{3}{4}$. $1\frac{1}{2}$ [2.4B]

4. Write five and thirty-four thousandths in standard form.
5.034 [2.5A]

5. Convert 0.28 to a fraction. $\frac{7}{25}$ [2.6D]

6. Find the product of 3 and $\frac{8}{9}$. $2\frac{2}{3}$ [2.4A]

7. Place the correct symbol, < or >, between the two numbers.
$8.039 < 8.31$ [2.5B]

8. Place the correct symbol, < or >, between the two numbers.
$\frac{3}{5} > \frac{7}{15}$ [2.2C]

9. Find the LCM of 50 and 75. 150 [2.1A]

10. Find the product of 0.918 and 10^5.
91,800 [2.6B]

11. Evaluate xy for $x = 8$ and $y = \frac{5}{12}$. $3\frac{1}{3}$ [2.4A]

12. Express the shaded portion of the circles as an improper fraction and as a mixed number.
$\frac{10}{7}$; $1\frac{3}{7}$ [2.2A]

13. Place the correct symbol, < or >, between the two numbers.
$\frac{3}{7} < 0.429$ [2.6D]

14. Simplify: $\dfrac{\frac{5}{8} - \frac{1}{4}}{\frac{1}{2} + \frac{1}{8}}$ $\frac{3}{5}$ [2.4C]

15. Write a fraction that is equivalent to $\frac{4}{9}$ and has a denominator of 72. $\frac{32}{72}$ [2.2B]

16. Evaluate x^2y^3 for $x = \frac{8}{9}$ and $y = \frac{3}{4}$.
$\frac{1}{3}$ [2.4A]

17. Evaluate $ab^2 - c$ for $a = 4$, $b = \frac{1}{2}$, and $c = \frac{5}{7}$.
$\frac{2}{7}$ [2.7A]

18. Find the GCF of 42 and 63. 21 [2.1B]

19. Find the quotient of 14.2 and 10^3. 0.0142 [2.6C]

20. Divide and round to the nearest tenth:
$6.8 \div 47.92$ 0.1 [2.6C]

21. Find the quotient of $\frac{5}{9}$ and $\frac{2}{3}$. $\frac{5}{6}$ [2.4B]

22. Evaluate $\frac{x}{y}$ for $x = 0.396$ and $y = 3.6$.
0.11 [2.6C]

23. Estimate the difference between 506.81 and 64.1. 440 [2.6A]

24. Multiply: $(9.47)(0.26)$ 2.4622 [2.6B]

25. Evaluate $a - b$ for $a = 80.32$ and $b = 29.577$. 50.743 [2.6A]

26. Evaluate $\left(\frac{3}{8}\right)^2 \cdot 4^2$. $2\frac{1}{4}$ [2.4A]

27. Find the sum of $3\frac{7}{12}$ and $5\frac{1}{2}$. $9\frac{1}{12}$ [2.3A]

28. Write $\frac{30}{105}$ in simplest form. $\frac{2}{7}$ [2.2B]

29. Evaluate $a - b$ for $a = 7$ and $b = 2\frac{3}{10}$. $4\frac{7}{10}$ [2.3B]

30. Find the quotient of 614.3 and 100. 6.143 [2.6C]

31. **Unit Cost** A 7-ounce jar of instant coffee costs $11.78. Find the cost per ounce. Round to the nearest cent. $1.68 [2.6E]

32. **Markup** Use the formula $P = C + M$, where P is the price of a product to a customer, C is the cost paid by a store for the product, and M is the markup, to find the price of a treadmill that costs a business $1124.75 and has a markup of $374.75. $1499.50 [2.6E]

33. **Wrestling** A wrestler is put on a diet to gain 12 lb in 4 weeks. The wrestler gains $3\frac{1}{2}$ lb the first week and $2\frac{1}{4}$ lb the second week. How much weight must the wrestler gain during the third and fourth weeks in order to gain a total of 12 lb? $6\frac{1}{4}$ lb [2.3C]

34. **History** The figure at the right shows the monetary costs of four wars. **a.** What is the difference between the monetary costs of the two World Wars? **b.** How many times greater was the monetary cost of the Vietnam War than that of World War I? **a.** $2.72 trillion **b.** 1.5 times greater [2.6E]

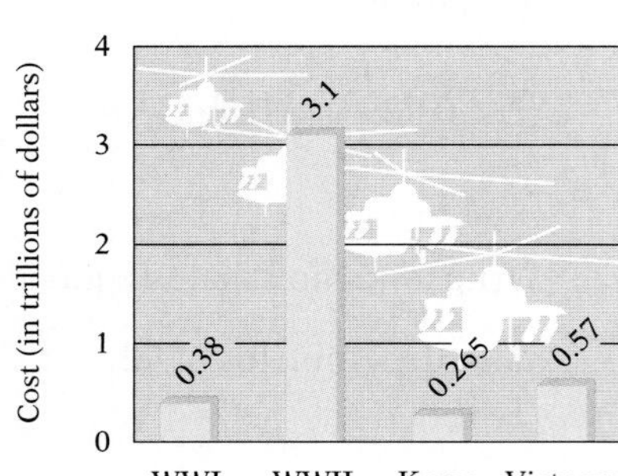

Monetary Cost of War

Source: Congressional Research Service Using Numbers from the *Statistical Abstract of the United States*

35. **Wages** Find the overtime pay due an employee who worked $6\frac{1}{4}$ h of overtime this week. The employee's overtime rate is $24 an hour. $150 [2.4D]

36. **Physics** What is the final velocity, in feet per second, of an object dropped from a plane with a starting velocity of 0 ft/s and a fall of $15\frac{1}{2}$ s? Use the formula $V = S + 32t$, where V is the final velocity of a falling object, S is its starting velocity, and t is the time of the fall. 496 ft/s [2.4D]

CHAPTER 2 TEST

1. Write $\frac{18}{7}$ as a mixed number.

$2\frac{4}{7}$ [2.2A]

2. Subtract: $7\frac{3}{4} - 3\frac{5}{6}$

$3\frac{11}{12}$ [2.3B]

3. Evaluate xy for $x = 6\frac{3}{7}$ and $y = 3\frac{1}{2}$.

$22\frac{1}{2}$ [2.4A]

4. Find the product of $\frac{2}{3}$ and $\frac{7}{8}$.

$\frac{7}{12}$ [2.4A]

5. Find the LCM of 30 and 45.

90 [2.1A]

6. Write nine and thirty-three thousandths in standard form. 9.033 [2.5A]

7. Evaluate x^3y^2 for $x = 1\frac{1}{2}$ and $y = \frac{5}{6}$.

$2\frac{11}{32}$ [2.4A]

8. Write $3\frac{4}{5}$ as an improper fraction.

$\frac{19}{5}$ [2.2A]

9. What is $\frac{7}{12}$ divided by $\frac{3}{4}$?

$\frac{7}{9}$ [2.4B]

10. Place the correct symbol, < or >, between the two numbers.

$4.003 < 4.009$ [2.5B]

11. Evaluate $\frac{x}{yz}$ for $x = \frac{7}{20}$, $y = \frac{2}{15}$, and $z = \frac{3}{8}$.

7 [2.4C]

12. Find the GCF of 18 and 54.

18 [2.1B]

13. How much larger is $\frac{13}{14}$ than $\frac{16}{21}$?

$\frac{1}{6}$ [2.3B]

14. Write $\frac{60}{75}$ in simplest form.

$\frac{4}{5}$ [2.2B]

15. Evaluate $x + y + z$ for $x = 1\frac{3}{8}$, $y = \frac{1}{2}$, and $z = \frac{5}{6}$.

$2\frac{17}{24}$ [2.3A]

16. Place the correct symbol, < or >, between the two numbers.

$\frac{5}{6} > \frac{11}{15}$ [2.2C]

17. Evaluate $a^2b - c^2$ for $a = \frac{2}{3}$, $b = 9$, and $c = \frac{3}{5}$.

$3\frac{16}{25}$ [2.7A]

18. Place the correct symbol, < or >, between the two numbers.

$0.22 < \frac{2}{9}$ [2.6D]

19. Round 6.051367 to the nearest thousandth.

6.051 [2.5C]

20. Evaluate $x \div y$ for $x = \frac{8}{9}$ and $y = \frac{16}{27}$.

$1\frac{1}{2}$ [2.4B]

21. Find the difference between 30 and 7.247.

22.753 [2.6A]

22. Estimate the difference between 92.34 and 17.95.

70 [2.6A]

23. Find the total of 4.58, 3.9, and 6.017.

14.497 [2.6A]

24. Evaluate $20cd$ for $c = 0.5$ and $d = 6.4$.

64 [2.6B]

25. Write a fraction that is equivalent to $\frac{3}{7}$ and has a denominator of 28.

$\frac{12}{28}$ [2.2B]

26. Find the quotient of 84.96 and 100.

0.8496 [2.6C]

27. **The Film Industry** The table at the right shows six James Bond films released between 1960 and 1970 and their gross box office incomes, in millions of dollars, in the United States. How much greater was the gross from *Thunderball* than the gross from *On Her Majesty's Secret Service*?

$40.8 million [2.6E]

Film	*U.S. Box Office Gross (in millions of dollars)*
Dr. No	$16.1
On Her Majesty's Secret Service	$22.8
From Russia with Love	$24.8
You Only Live Twice	$43.1
Goldfinger	$51.1
Thunderball	$63.6

Source: www.worldwideboxoffice.com

28. **Health** A patient is put on a diet to lose 30 lb in 3 months. The patient loses $11\frac{1}{6}$ lb during the first month and $8\frac{5}{8}$ lb during the second month. Find the amount of weight the patient must lose during the third month to achieve the goal.

$10\frac{5}{24}$ lb [2.3C]

29. **Party Planning** You are planning a barbecue for 35 people. You want to serve $\frac{1}{4}$-pound hamburger patties to your guests, and you estimate that each person will eat two hamburgers. How much hamburger meat should you buy for the barbecue?

$17\frac{1}{2}$ lb [2.4D]

30. **Pennants** Find the amount of felt needed to make a pennant that is in the shape of a triangle with a base of 20 in. and a height of 12 in. Use the formula $A = \frac{1}{2}bh$.

120 in^2 [2.4D]

31. **Community Service** You are required to contribute 20 h of community service to the town in which your college is located. On one occasion you work $7\frac{1}{4}$ h, and on another occasion you work $2\frac{3}{4}$ h. How many more hours of community service are required of you?

10 h [2.3C]

32. **Geometry** The lengths of the three sides of a triangle are 8.75 m, 5.25 m, and 4.5 m. Find the perimeter of the triangle. Use the formula $P = a + b + c$.

18.5 m [2.6E]

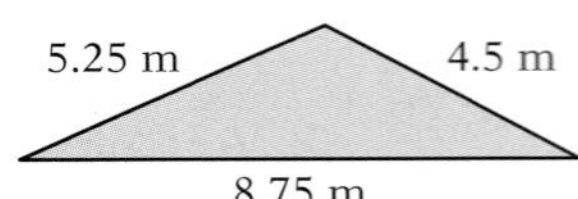

Cumulative Review Exercises

1. Evaluate $3a + (a - b)^3$ for $a = 4$ and $b = 1$.
39 [1.4A]

2. Find the product of 4 and $\frac{7}{8}$. $3\frac{1}{2}$ [2.4A]

3. Add: $4\frac{7}{9} + 3\frac{5}{6}$ $8\frac{11}{18}$ [2.3A]

4. Find the quotient of 387.9 and 10^4.
0.03879 [2.6C]

5. Find the GCF of 72 and 108. 36 [2.1B]

6. Multiply: $3\frac{1}{13} \cdot 5\frac{1}{5}$ 16 [2.4A]

7. Find the quotient of $\frac{8}{9}$ and $\frac{4}{5}$. $1\frac{1}{9}$ [2.4B]

8. Convert $\frac{19}{25}$ to a decimal. 0.76 [2.6D]

9. Simplify: $\dfrac{\frac{1}{5} + \frac{1}{4}}{\frac{1}{4} - \frac{1}{5}}$ 9 [2.4C]

10. Place the correct symbol, < or >, between the two numbers.
$\frac{7}{11} < \frac{4}{5}$ [2.2C]

11. Divide: $2\frac{1}{3} \div 1\frac{2}{7}$ $1\frac{22}{27}$ [2.4B]

12. Multiply: $\frac{3}{8} \cdot \frac{2}{5} \cdot \frac{4}{9}$ $\frac{1}{15}$ [2.4A]

13. Evaluate abc for $a = \frac{4}{7}$, $b = 1\frac{1}{6}$, and $c = 3$.
2 [2.4A]

14. Subtract: $8\frac{3}{4} - 1\frac{5}{7}$ $7\frac{1}{28}$ [2.3B]

15. What is 36.92 increased by 18.5? 18.42 [2.6A]

16. Simplify: $\frac{2}{5} \div \frac{9 - 6}{3 + 7} + \left(\frac{1}{2}\right)^2$ $1\frac{7}{12}$ [2.7A]

17. Estimate the product of 62.8 and 0.47. 30 [2.6B]

18. Find the sum of $1\frac{9}{16}$ and $4\frac{5}{8}$. $6\frac{3}{16}$ [2.3A]

19. Write eight million seventy-two thousand ninety-two in standard form.
8,072,092 [1.1B]

20. Write $\frac{41}{9}$ as a mixed number. $4\frac{5}{9}$ [2.2A]

21. Find the difference between $\frac{5}{14}$ and $\frac{9}{42}$. $\frac{1}{7}$ [2.3B]

22. Evaluate x^3y^4 for $x = \frac{7}{12}$ and $y = \frac{6}{7}$.
$\frac{3}{28}$ [2.4A]

23. Divide and round to the nearest tenth:
$2.617 \div 0.93$
2.8 [2.6C]

24. Add: $6847 + 3501 + 924$
11,272 [1.2A]

25. Evaluate $(x - y)^3 + 5x$ for $x = 8$ and $y = 6$.
48 [1.4A]

26. Evaluate $\frac{a}{b + c}$ for $a = \frac{3}{8}$, $b = \frac{1}{2}$, and $c = \frac{3}{4}$.
$\frac{3}{10}$ [2.4C]

27. Estimate the difference between 89,357 and 66,042. 20,000 [1.2B]

28. Evaluate $x \div y$ for $x = 3\frac{2}{3}$ and $y = 2\frac{4}{9}$.
$1\frac{1}{2}$ [2.4B]

29. Write $7\frac{3}{4}$ as an improper fraction.
$\frac{31}{4}$ [2.2A]

30. Find the prime factorization of 140.
$2^2 \cdot 5 \cdot 7$ [1.3D]

31. **Exercise** The chart at the right shows the calories burned per hour as a result of different aerobic activities. Suppose you weigh 150 lb. According to the chart, how many more calories would you burn by bicycling at 12 mph for 4 h than by walking at a rate of 3 mph for 5 h?
40 calories [1.3E]

Activity	*100 lb*	*150 lb*
Bicycling, 6 mph	160	240
Bicycling, 12 mph	270	410
Jogging, 5 1/2 mph	440	660
Jogging, 7 mph	610	920
Jumping rope	500	750
Tennis, singles	265	400
Walking, 2 mph	160	240
Walking, 3 mph	210	320
Walking, 4 1/2 mph	295	440

32. **Populations** According to the U.S. Census Bureau, the population of New England in 2000 was 13,922,517. In 2010, the population of New England was 14,444,865. Find the increase in the population of New England during the 10-year period. 522,348 people [1.2C]

33. **Copier Service** A copier service charges \$6.95 for copying up to 50 pages. There is a charge of \$.12 for each additional page after the first 50. What is the charge for having 78 pages copied? \$10.31 [2.6E]

34. **Fencing** Find the length of fencing needed to surround a square dog pen that measures $16\frac{1}{2}$ ft on each side. Use the formula $P = 4s$.
66 ft [2.4D]

© Ljupco Smokovski/Shutterstock.com

35. **Bicycling** A bicyclist rode for $\frac{3}{4}$ h at a rate of $5\frac{1}{2}$ mph. Use the equation $d = rt$, where d is the distance traveled, r is the rate of travel, and t is the time, to find the distance traveled by the bicyclist.
$4\frac{1}{8}$ mi [2.4D]

36. **Deep Sea Diving** The pressure on a submerged object is given by $P = 15 + \frac{1}{2}D$, where D is the depth in feet and P is the pressure measured in pounds per square inch. Find the pressure on a diver who is at a depth of $14\frac{3}{4}$ ft.
$22\frac{3}{8}$ lb/in^2 [2.4D]

Rational Numbers

3

OBJECTIVES

SECTION 3.1

- **A** To identify the order relation between two integers
- **B** To find the opposite of a number
- **C** To evaluate expressions that contain the absolute value symbol
- **D** To solve application problems

SECTION 3.2

- **A** To add integers
- **B** To subtract integers
- **C** To solve application problems and use formulas

SECTION 3.3

- **A** To multiply integers
- **B** To divide integers
- **C** To solve application problems

SECTION 3.4

- **A** To add or subtract rational numbers
- **B** To multiply or divide rational numbers
- **C** To solve application problems

SECTION 3.5

- **A** To use the Order of Operations Agreement to simplify expressions

Focus on Success

Have you formed or are you part of a study group? Remember that a study group can be a great way to stay focused on succeeding in this course. You can support each other, get help and offer help on homework, and prepare for tests together. (See Homework Time, page AIM-5.)

Prep Test

Are you ready to succeed in this chapter? Take the Prep Test below to find out if you are ready to learn the new material.

1. Place the correct symbol, $<$ or $>$, between the two numbers.

54 45 $54 > 45$ [1.1A]

2. What is the distance from 4 to 8 on the number line? 4 units [1.1A]

For Exercises 3 to 14, add, subtract, multiply, or divide.

3. $7654 + 8193$

15,847 [1.2A]

4. $6097 - 2318$

3779 [1.2B]

5. 472×56

26,432 [1.3A]

6. $\dfrac{144}{24}$

6 [1.3C]

7. $\dfrac{2}{3} + \dfrac{3}{5}$

$1\dfrac{4}{15}$ [2.3A]

8. $\dfrac{3}{4} - \dfrac{5}{16}$

$\dfrac{7}{16}$ [2.3B]

9. $0.75 + 3.9 + 6.408$

11.058 [2.6A]

10. $5.4 - 1.619$

3.781 [2.6A]

11. $\dfrac{3}{4} \times \dfrac{8}{15}$

$\dfrac{2}{5}$ [2.4A]

12. $\dfrac{5}{12} \div \dfrac{3}{4}$

$\dfrac{5}{9}$ [2.4B]

13. 23.5×0.4

9.4 [2.6B]

14. $0.96 \div 2.4$

0.4 [2.6C]

15. Simplify: $(8 - 6)^2 + 12 \div 4 \cdot 3^2$ 31 [1.4A]

SECTION

3.1 Introduction to Integers

OBJECTIVE A To identify the order relation between two integers

In Chapters 1 and 2, only zero and numbers greater than zero were discussed. In this chapter, numbers less than zero are introduced. Phrases such as "7 degrees below zero," "\$50 in debt," and "20 feet below sea level" refer to numbers less than zero.

Point of Interest

Chinese manuscripts dating from about 250 B.C. contain the first recorded use of negative numbers. However, it was not until late in the fourteenth century that mathematicians generally accepted these numbers.

Numbers greater than zero are called **positive numbers.** Numbers less than zero are called **negative numbers.**

A positive number can be indicated by placing a plus sign (+) in front of the number. For example, we can write +4 instead of 4. Both +4 and 4 represent "positive 4." Usually, however, the plus sign is omitted and it is understood that the number is a positive number.

A negative number is indicated by placing a negative sign (−) in front of the number. The number −1 is read "negative one," −2 is read "negative two," and so on.

INSTRUCTOR NOTE

Art pieces in this text are available in PowerPoint on the PowerLecture. They are also posted to the Instructor Companion Website and in EWA under the Instructor Resource tab. For example, the number line at the right is available for your use in PowerPoint.

The number line can be extended to the left of zero to show negative numbers.

−7 −6 −5 −4 −3 −2 −1 0 1 2 3 4 5 6 7

The **integers** are . . . , −4, −3, −2, −1, 0, 1, 2, 3, 4, ... The integers to the right of zero are the **positive integers.** The integers to the left of zero are the **negative integers.** Zero is an integer, but it is neither positive nor negative. The point corresponding to 0 on the number line is called the **origin.**

IN-CLASS EXAMPLES

1. On the number line, what number is 6 units to the left of 2? **−4**
2. If *B* is −3 and *D* is −1, what numbers are *A* and *E*?

   A B C D E F

   ***A* is −4; *E* is 0**
3. Place the correct symbol, $<$ or $>$, between the two numbers.

   −23 13

   −23 $<$ 13
4. Write the given numbers in order from smallest to largest.

   5, −8, 0, −1, 9

   −8, −1, 0, 5, 9

On a number line, the numbers get larger as we move from left to right. The numbers get smaller as we move from right to left. Therefore, a number line can be used to visualize the order relation between two integers.

A number that appears to the right of a given number is greater than ($>$) the given number. A number that appears to the left of a given number is less than ($<$) the given number.

2 is to the right of −3 on the number line.
2 is greater than −3.
$2 > -3$

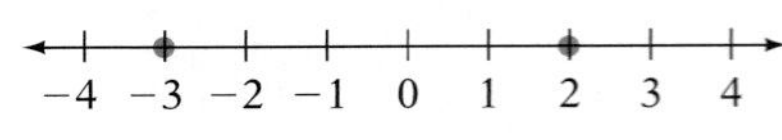

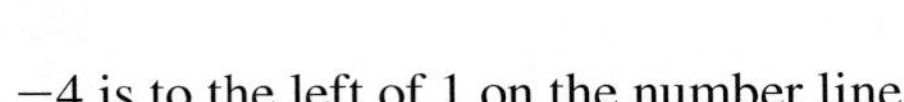

−4 is to the left of 1 on the number line.
−4 is less than 1.
$-4 < 1$

−4 −3 −2 −1 0 1 2 3 4

Order Relations

$a > b$ if a is to the right of b on the number line.
$a < b$ if a is to the left of b on the number line.

EXAMPLES

$2 > -8$ • 2 is to the right of −8 on the number line.
$-6 < -3$ • −6 is to the left of −3 on the number line.

EXAMPLE 1

On the number line, what number is 5 units to the right of −2?

Solution

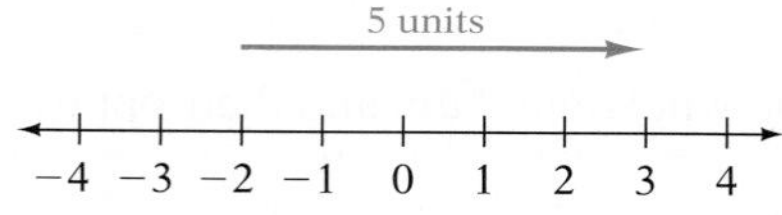

3 is 5 units to the right of −2.

YOU TRY IT 1

On the number line, what number is 4 units to the left of 1?

Your solution

−3

EXAMPLE 2

If G is 2 and I is 4, what numbers are B and D?

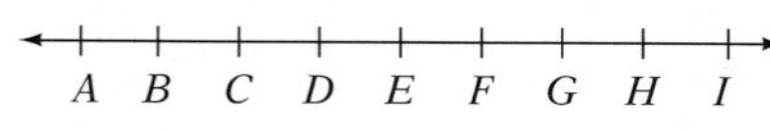

Solution

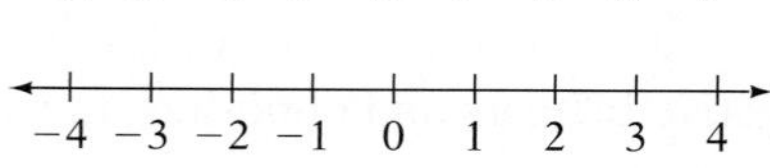

B is −3 and D is −1.

YOU TRY IT 2

If G is 1 and H is 2, what numbers are A and C?

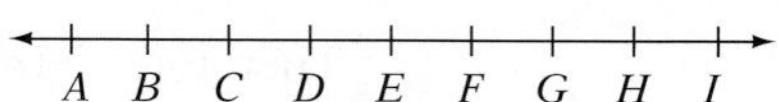

Your solution

A is −5 and C is −3.

EXAMPLE 3

Place the correct symbol, < or >, between the two numbers.

a. −3 −1 **b.** 1 −2

Solution

a. −3 is to the left of −1 on the number line.

$-3 < -1$

b. 1 is to the right of −2 on the number line.

$1 > -2$

YOU TRY IT 3

Place the correct symbol, < or >, between the two numbers.

a. 2 −5 **b.** −4 3

Your solution

a. $2 > -5$ **b.** $-4 < 3$

EXAMPLE 4

Write the given numbers in order from smallest to largest.

5, −2, 3, 0, −6

Solution −6, −2, 0, 3, 5

YOU TRY IT 4

Write the given numbers in order from smallest to largest.

−7, 4, −1, 0, 8

Your solution −7, −1, 0, 4, 8

Solutions on p. S9

OBJECTIVE B To find the opposite of a number

Integrating Technology

The +/− key on your calculator is used to find the opposite of a number. The − key is used to perform the operation of subtraction.

The distance from 0 to 3 on the number line is 3 units. The distance from 0 to −3 on the number line is 3 units. 3 and −3 are the same distance from 0 on the number line, but 3 is to the right of 0 and −3 is to the left of 0.

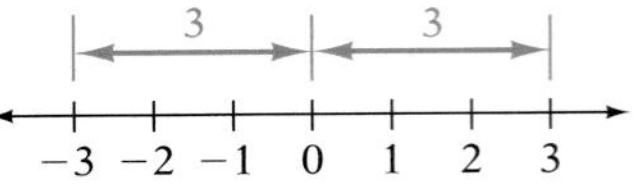

Two numbers that are the same distance from zero on the number line but on opposite sides of zero are called **opposites.**

IN-CLASS EXAMPLES

5. Find the opposite number.
   a. 32 b. −19
   a. −32 b. 19
6. Write the expression in words.
   −5 − (−10)
   negative five minus negative ten
7. Simplify.
   a. −(46) b. −(−*d*)
   a. −46 b. *d*

−3 is the opposite of 3 and 3 is the opposite of −3.

For any number n, the opposite of n is $-n$ and the opposite of $-n$ is n.

We can now define the **integers** as the whole numbers and their opposites.

A negative sign can be read as "the opposite of."

$-(3) = -3$ The opposite of positive 3 is negative 3.

$-(-3) = 3$ The opposite of negative 3 is positive 3.

Therefore, $-(a) = -a$ and $-(-a) = a$.

Note that with the introduction of negative integers and opposites, the symbols + and − can be read in different ways.

6 + 2	"six plus two"	+ is read "plus"
+2	"positive two"	+ is read "positive"
6 − 2	"six minus two"	− is read "minus"
−2	"negative two"	− is read "negative"
−(−6)	"the opposite of negative six"	− is read first as "the opposite of" and then as "negative"

When the symbols + and − indicate the operations of addition and subtraction, spaces are inserted before and after the symbol. When the symbols + and − indicate the sign of a number (positive or negative), there is no space between the symbol and the number.

EXAMPLE 5

Find the opposite number.

a. −8 **b.** 15 **c.** a

Solution

a. 8 **b.** −15 **c.** $-a$

YOU TRY IT 5

Find the opposite number.

a. 24 **b.** −13 **c.** $-b$

Your solution

a. −24 b. 13 c. *b*

Solution on p. S9

EXAMPLE 6

Write the expression in words.

a. $7 - (-9)$ **b.** $-4 + 10$

Solution **a.** seven minus negative nine

b. negative four plus ten

YOU TRY IT 6

Write the expression in words.

a. $-3 - 12$ **b.** $8 + (-5)$

Your solution **a.** negative three minus twelve

b. eight plus negative five

EXAMPLE 7

Simplify.

a. $-(-27)$ **b.** $-(-c)$

Solution **a.** $-(-27) = 27$

b. $-(-c) = c$

YOU TRY IT 7

Simplify.

a. $-(-59)$ **b.** $-(y)$

Your solution **a.** 59 **b.** $-y$

Solutions on p. S9

OBJECTIVE C *To evaluate expressions that contain the absolute value symbol*

The **absolute value** of a number is the distance from zero to the number on the number line. Distance is never a negative number. Therefore, the absolute value of a number is a positive number or zero. The symbol for absolute value is "| |."

The distance from 0 to 3 is 3 units. Thus $|3| = 3$ (the absolute value of 3 is 3).

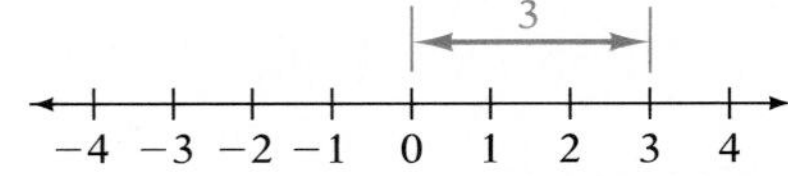

The distance from 0 to −3 is 3 units. Thus $|-3| = 3$ (the absolute value of −3 is 3).

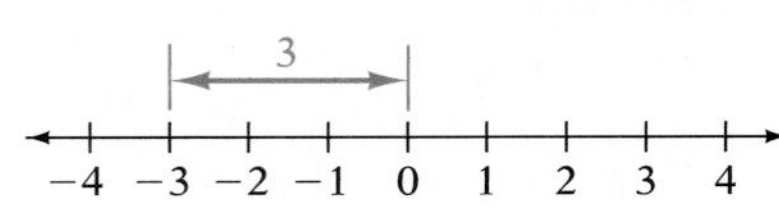

IN-CLASS EXAMPLES

8. Find the absolute value of −67.
67
9. Evaluate.
a. $-|24|$ b. $-|-18|$
a. −24 b. −18
10. Evaluate $|-x|$ for $x = 6$.
6
11. Write the given numbers in order from smallest to largest.
$-|-6|, -8, -(-4), |3|$
$-8, -|-6|, |3|, -(-4)$

Because the distance from 0 to 3 and the distance from 0 to −3 are the same,

$$|3| = |-3| = 3.$$

Absolute Value

The absolute value of a positive number is positive.
The absolute value of a negative number is positive.
The absolute value of zero is zero.

EXAMPLES

1. $|5| = 5$ **2.** $|-5| = 5$ **3.** $|0| = 0$

Take Note

In HOW TO 1 at the right, it is important to be aware that the negative sign is *in front of the absolute value symbol.* This means that $-|7| = -7$, but $|-7| = 7$.

HOW TO 1 Evaluate $-|7|$.

The negative sign is *in front of* the absolute value symbol.

Recall that a negative sign can be read as "the opposite of."

Therefore, $-|7|$ can be read "the opposite of the absolute value of 7."

$-|7| = -7$

EXAMPLE 8

Find the absolute value of **a.** 6 and **b.** -9.

Solution **a.** $|6| = 6$

b. $|-9| = 9$

YOU TRY IT 8

Find the absolute value of **a.** -8 and **b.** 12.

Your solution

a. 8 b. 12

EXAMPLE 9

Evaluate **a.** $|-27|$ and **b.** $-|-14|$.

Solution **a.** $|-27| = 27$

b. $-|-14| = -14$

YOU TRY IT 9

Evaluate **a.** $|0|$ and **b.** $-|35|$.

Your solution

a. 0 b. -35

EXAMPLE 10

Evaluate $|-x|$ for $x = -4$.

Solution $|-x| = |-(-4)| = |4| = 4$

YOU TRY IT 10

Evaluate $|-y|$ for $y = 2$.

Your solution 2

EXAMPLE 11

Write the given numbers in order from smallest to largest.

$|-7|, -5, |0|, -(-4), -|-3|$

Solution

$|-7| = 7, |0| = 0,$

$-(-4) = 4, -|-3| = -3$

$-5, -|-3|, |0|, -(-4), |-7|$

YOU TRY IT 11

Write the given numbers in order from smallest to largest.

$|6|, |-2|, -(-1), -4, -|-8|$

Your solution

$-|-8|, -4, -(-1), |-2|, |6|$

Solutions on p. S9

OBJECTIVE D *To solve application problems*

Data that are represented by negative numbers on a bar graph are shown by bars extending below the horizontal axis. For instance, Figure 3.1 shows the lowest recorded temperatures, in degrees Fahrenheit, for selected states in the United States. Hawaii's lowest recorded temperature is 12°F, which is a positive number, so the bar that represents that temperature is above the horizontal axis. The bars for the other states are below the horizontal axis and therefore represent negative numbers.

We can see from the graph that the state with the lowest recorded temperature is New York, with a temperature of -52°F.

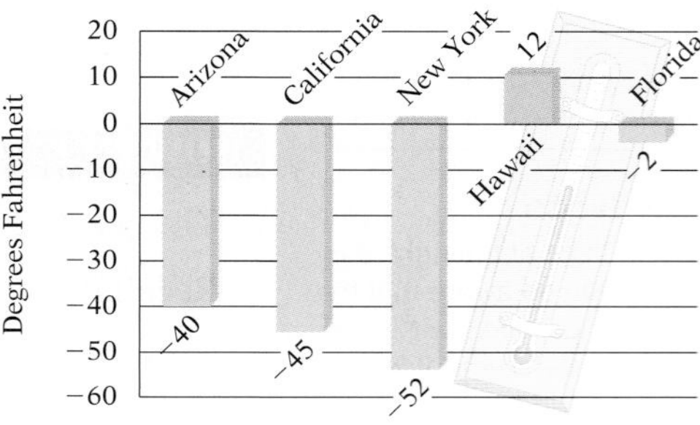

Figure 3.1 Lowest Recorded Temperatures

IN-CLASS EXAMPLES

12. Which is the colder temperature, $-14°F$ or $-41°F$? **$-41°F$**
13. Which is closer to blastoff, -11 s and counting or -3 s and counting? **-3 s and counting**

INSTRUCTOR NOTE

Another major pedagogical feature of this text is written *strategies* that accompany every application problem. For the paired You Try It, we ask students to provide their own written strategy. A suggested strategy, along with a complete solution to the problem, can be found in the Solutions section at the back of the text.

In a golf tournament, scores below par are recorded as negative numbers; scores above par are recorded as positive numbers. The winner of the tournament is the player who has the lowest score.

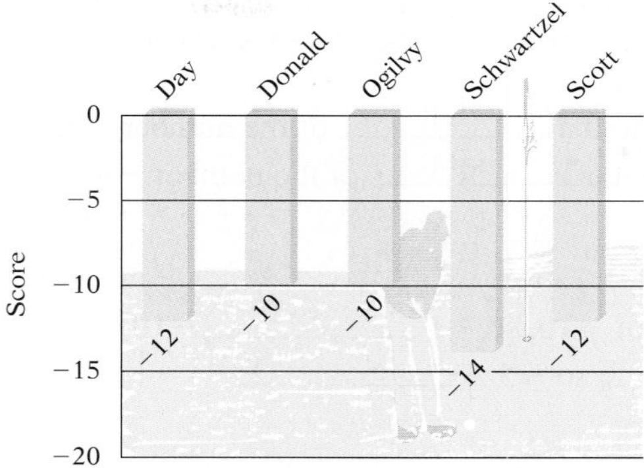

Figure 3.2 The Top Finishers in the 2011 Masters Tournament

Figure 3.2 shows the number of strokes under par for the five best finishers in the 2011 Masters Tournament in Augusta, Georgia. Use this graph for Example 12 and You Try It 12.

EXAMPLE 12

Use Figure 3.2 to name the player who won the tournament.

Strategy

Use the bar graph and find the player with the lowest score.

Solution

$-14 < -12 < -10$

The lowest number among the scores is -14.

Schwartzel won the tournament.

YOU TRY IT 12

Use Figure 3.2 to name the player who came in second in the tournament.

Your strategy

Your solution

Day and Scott tied for second.

EXAMPLE 13

Which is the colder temperature, $-18°F$ or $-15°F$?

Strategy

To determine which is the colder temperature, compare the numbers -18 and -15. The lower number corresponds to the colder temperature.

Solution

$-18 < -15$

The colder temperature is $-18°F$.

YOU TRY IT 13

Which is closer to blastoff, -9 s and counting or -7 s and counting?

Your strategy

Your solution

-7 s and counting

Solutions on p. S9

3.1 EXERCISES

SUGGESTED ASSIGNMENT

Exercises 1–6; Exercises 7–43, odds; Exercises 47–75, odds; Exercises 79–131, odds;
More challenging exercises: Exercises 132–136, evens

Concept Check

1. Fill in the blank with *left* or *right*.

a. On a number line, the number -8 is to the ___left___ of the number -3.

b. On a number line, the number 0 is to the ___right___ of the number -4.

2. Fill in the blank with $<$ or $>$.

a. On a number line, -1 is to the right of -10, so -1 ___$>$___ -10.

b. On a number line, -5 is to the left of 2, so -5 ___$<$___ 2.

3. The opposite of a positive number is a ___negative___ number. The opposite of a negative number is a ___positive___ number.

4. In the expression $8 - (-2)$, the first $-$ sign is read as ___minus___ and the second $-$ sign is read as ___negative___.

5. The equation $|-5| = 5$ is read "the ___absolute value___ of negative five is five."

6. Evaluate $|-y|$ for $y = -6$.

a. Replace y with ___-6___.

b. The opposite of -6 is 6.

c. The absolute value of 6 is 6.

$|-y|$
$= |-(-6)|$
$= |\underline{\ 6\ }|$
$= \underline{\ 6\ }$

OBJECTIVE A *To identify the order relation between two integers*

Graph the number on the number line.

7. -5

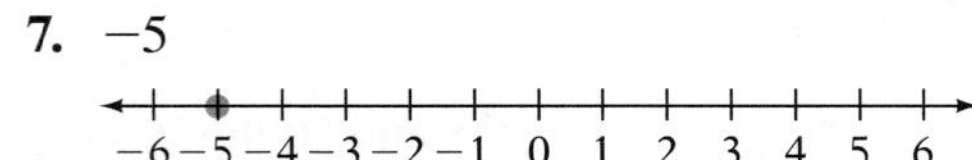

8. -1

9. -6

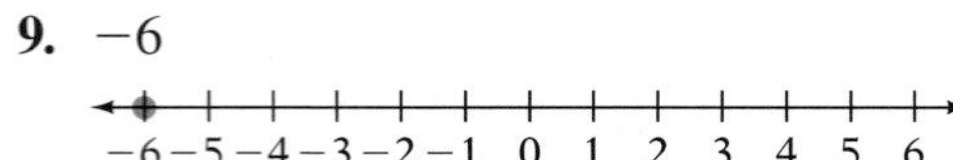

10. -2

11. x, for $x = 5$

12. x, for $x = 0$

13. x, for $x = -4$

14. x, for $x = -3$

On the number line, which number is:

15. 3 units to the right of -2?
1

16. 5 units to the right of -3?
2

17. 4 units to the left of 3?
-1

18. 2 units to the left of -1?
-3

19. 6 units to the right of -3?
3

20. 4 units to the right of -4?
0

For Exercises 21 to 24, use the following number line.

A B C D E F G H I

21. If F is 1 and G is 2, what numbers are A and C?
A is -4. C is -2.

22. If G is 1 and H is 2, what numbers are B and D?
B is -4. D is -2.

23. If H is 0 and I is 1, what numbers are A and D?
A is -7. D is -4.

24. If G is 2 and I is 4, what numbers are B and E?
B is -3. E is 0.

Place the correct symbol, $<$ or $>$, between the two numbers.

25. $-2 > -5$

26. $-6 < -1$

27. $3 > -7$

28. $-11 < -8$

29. $-42 < 27$

30. $21 > -34$

31. $53 > -46$

32. $-27 > -39$

33. $-51 < -20$

34. $-136 < 0$

35. $-131 < 101$

36. $127 > -150$

Write the given numbers in order from smallest to largest.

37. 3, -7, 0, -2
-7, -2, 0, 3

38. -4, 8, 6, -1
-4, -1, 6, 8

39. -3, 1, -5, 4
-5, -3, 1, 4

40. -6, 2, -8, 7
-8, -6, 2, 7

41. 9, -4, 5, 0
-4, 0, 5, 9

42. 6, -9, -12, 8
-12, -9, 6, 8

43. -10, 4, 12, -5, -7
-10, -7, -5, 4, 12

44. 11, -8, -1, 7, -6
-8, -6, -1, 7, 11

45. Determine whether each statement is always true, never true, or sometimes true.
a. A number that is to the right of the number 5 on the number line is a negative number.
b. A number that is to the left of the number 3 on the number line is a negative number.
c. A number that is to the right of the number -4 on the number line is a negative number.
d. A number that is to the left of the number -6 on the number line is a negative number.
a. Never true b. Sometimes true c. Sometimes true d. Always true

OBJECTIVE B *To find the opposite of a number*

Find the opposite of the number.

46. 22
-22

47. 45
-45

48. -31
31

49. -88
88

50. c
$-c$

51. n
$-n$

52. $-w$
w

53. $-d$
d

Write the expression in words.

54. $-(-11)$
the opposite of negative eleven

55. $-(-13)$
the opposite of negative thirteen

56. $-(-d)$
the opposite of negative d

57. $-(-p)$
the opposite of negative p

58. $-2 + (-5)$
negative two plus negative five

59. $5 + (-10)$
five plus negative ten

60. $6 - (-7)$
six minus negative seven

61. $-14 - (-3)$
negative fourteen minus negative three

62. $9 - 12$
nine minus twelve

63. $-13 - 8$
negative thirteen minus eight

64. $-a - b$
negative a minus b

65. $m + (-n)$
m plus negative n

Simplify.

66. $-(-5)$
5

67. $-(-7)$
7

68. $-(29)$
-29

69. $-(46)$
-46

70. $-(-52)$
52

71. $-(-73)$
73

72. $-(-m)$
m

73. $-(-z)$
z

74. $-(b)$
$-b$

75. $-(p)$
$-p$

76. Write the statement "the opposite of negative a is b" in symbols. Does a equal b, or are they opposites? $-(-a) = b; a = b$

77. If $a < 0$, is $-(-a)$ positive or negative? Negative

OBJECTIVE C *To evaluate expressions that contain the absolute value symbol*

Find the absolute value of the number.

78. 4
4

79. -4
4

80. -7
7

81. 9
9

82. -1
1

83. -11
11

84. 10
10

85. -12
12

Evaluate.

86. $|-15|$
15

87. $|-23|$
23

88. $-|33|$
-33

89. $-|27|$
-27

90. $|32|$
32

91. $|25|$
25

92. $-|-36|$
-36

93. $-|-41|$
-41

94. $-|-81|$
-81

95. $-|-93|$
-93

96. $|x|$, for $x = 7$
7

97. $|x|$, for $x = -10$
10

98. $|-x|$, for $x = 2$
2

99. $|-x|$, for $x = 8$
8

100. $|-y|$, for $y = -3$
3

101. $|-y|$, for $y = -6$
6

Place the correct symbol, $<$, $=$, or $>$, between the two numbers.

102. $|7| < |-9|$

103. $|-12| > |8|$

104. $|-5| > |-2|$

105. $|6| < |13|$

106. $|-8| > |3|$

107. $|-1| < |-17|$

108. $|-14| = |14|$

109. $|x| = |-x|$

Write the given numbers in order from smallest to largest.

110. $|-8|, -(-3), |2|, -|-5|$
$-|-5|, |2|, -(-3), |-8|$

111. $-|6|, -(4), |-7|, -(-9)$
$-|6|, -(4), |-7|, -(-9)$

112. $-(-1), |-6|, |0|, -|3|$
$-|3|, |0|, -(-1), |-6|$

113. $-|-7|, -9, -(5), |4|$
$-9, -|-7|, -(5), |4|$

114. $-|2|, -(-8), 6, |1|, -7$
$-7, -|2|, |1|, 6, -(-8)$

115. $-(-3), -|-8|, |5|, -|10|, -(-2)$
$-|10|, -|-8|, -(-2), -(-3), |5|$

116. Determine whether each statement is always true, never true, or sometimes true.
a. The absolute value of a negative number n is greater than n.
b. The absolute value of a number n is the opposite of n.
a. Always true **b.** Sometimes true

OBJECTIVE D *To solve application problems*

117. **U.S. Postal Service** Read the news clipping at the right. Write the USPS loss as a negative number. $-329,000,000$

118. **Rocketry** Which is closer to blastoff, -12 min and counting or -17 min and counting? -12 min and counting

119. **Business** Some businesses show a profit as a positive number and a loss as a negative number. During the first quarter of this year, the loss experienced by a company was recorded as $-12,575$. During the second quarter of this year, the loss experienced by the company was $-11,350$. During which quarter was the loss greater?
First quarter

120. **Business** Some businesses show a profit as a positive number and a loss as a negative number. During the third quarter of last year, the loss experienced by a company was recorded as $-26,800$. During the fourth quarter of last year, the loss experienced by the company was $-24,900$. During which quarter was the loss greater?
Third quarter

In the NEWS!

Steep Losses for USPS

The Postal Service announced that it suffered a loss of $329,000,000 during the first quarter of its 2011 fiscal year. The USPS blamed the loss on the recession and the continuing growth of e-mail communication.

Source: money.cnn.com

Earnings Per Share One of the measures used by financial analysts to evaluate the financial strength of a company is *earnings per share.* This number is found by taking the total profit of the company and dividing by the number of shares of stock that the company has sold to investors. If the company has a loss instead of a profit, the earnings per share is a negative number. In a bar graph, a profit is shown by a bar extending above the horizontal axis, and a loss is shown by a bar extending below the horizontal axis. The figure at the right shows the predicted earnings per share for Mycopen for the years 2014 through 2019. Use this graph for Exercises 121 to 124.

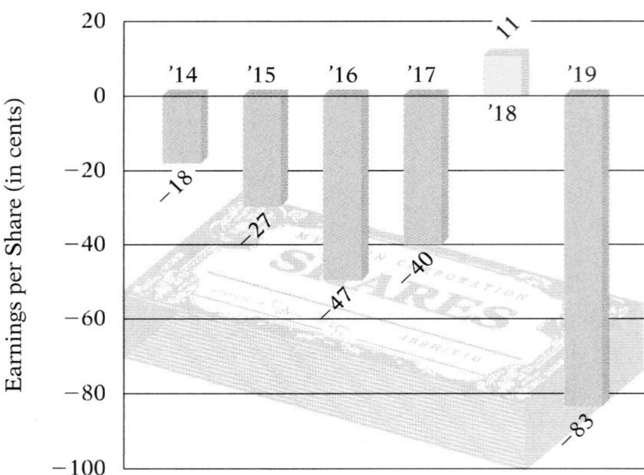

Mycopen Predicted Earnings per Share (in cents)

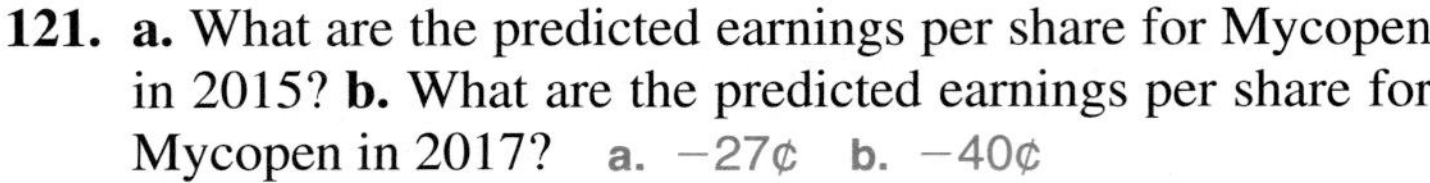

121. **a.** What are the predicted earnings per share for Mycopen in 2015? **b.** What are the predicted earnings per share for Mycopen in 2017? a. −27¢ b. −40¢

122. For the years shown, in which year is Mycopen predicted to have the greatest loss? 2019

123. For the years shown, is Mycopen ever predicted to have a profit? If so, in what year? Yes; 2018

124. For which year are the predicted Mycopen earnings per share lower, 2014 or 2016? 2016

125. **The Stock Market** In the stock market, the net change in the price of a share of stock is recorded as a positive or a negative number. If the price rises, the net change is positive. If the price falls, the net change is negative. If the net change for a share of Stock A is −2 and the net change for a share of Stock B is −1, which stock showed the least net change? Stock B

© iStockphoto.com/EdStock

Environmental Science The table below gives wind-chill temperatures for combinations of temperature and wind speed. For example, the combination of a temperature of 15°F and a wind blowing at 10 mph has a cooling power equal to 3°F. Use this table for Exercises 126 to 131.

Wind Chill Factors															
Wind Speed (mph)	*Thermometer Reading (degrees Fahrenheit)*														
	25	20	15	10	5	0	−5	−10	−15	−20	−25	−30	−35	−40	−45
5	19	13	7	1	−5	−11	−16	−22	−28	−34	−40	−46	−52	−57	−63
10	15	9	3	−4	−10	−16	−22	−28	−35	−41	−47	−53	−59	−66	−72
15	13	6	0	−7	−13	−19	−26	−32	−39	−45	−51	−58	−64	−71	−77
20	11	4	−2	−9	−15	−22	−29	−35	−42	−48	−55	−61	−68	−74	−81
25	9	3	−4	−11	−17	−24	−31	−37	−44	−51	−58	−64	−71	−78	−84
30	8	1	−5	−12	−19	−26	−33	−39	−46	−53	−60	−67	−73	−80	−87
35	7	0	−7	−14	−21	−27	−34	−41	−48	−55	−62	−69	−76	−82	−89
40	6	−1	−8	−15	−22	−29	−36	−43	−50	−57	−64	−71	−78	−84	−91
45	5	−2	−9	−16	−23	−30	−37	−44	−51	−58	−65	−72	−79	−86	−93

126. Find the wind chill factor when the temperature is 5°F and the wind speed is 15 mph. −13°F

127. Find the wind chill factor when the temperature is 10°F and the wind speed is 20 mph. −9°F

128. Find the cooling power of a temperature of −10°F and a 5-mile-per-hour wind.
−22°F

129. Find the cooling power of a temperature of −15°F and a 10-mile-per-hour wind.
−35°F

130. Which feels colder, a temperature of 0°F with a 15-mile-per-hour wind or a temperature of 10°F with a 25-mile-per-hour wind?
0°F with a 15-mile-per-hour wind

131. Which feels colder, a temperature of −30°F with a 5-mile-per-hour wind or a temperature of −20°F with a 10-mile-per-hour wind?
−30°F with a 5 mile-per-hour wind

Critical Thinking

132. Find the values of a for which $|a| = 7$.
7, −7

133. Find the values of y for which $|y| = 11$.
11, −11

134. Given that x is an integer, find all values of x for which $|x| < 5$.
−4, −3, −2, −1, 0, 1, 2, 3, 4

135. Given that c is an integer, find all values of c for which $|c| < 7$.
−6, −5, −4, −3, −2, −1, 0, 1, 2, 3, 4, 5, 6

136. Find two numbers a and b such that $a < b$ and $|a| > |b|$.
Answers will vary. For example, $a = -5$ and $b = 2$

137. **a.** Name two numbers that are 4 units from 2 on the number line.
b. Name two numbers that are 5 units from 3 on the number line.
a. −2 and 6 **b.** −2 and 8

Projects or Group Activities

138. Point A is a point on the number line halfway between −9 and 3. Point B is a point halfway between A and the graph of 1 on the number line. Point B is the graph of what number? −1

139. Make up a problem similar to Exercise 138. Have a classmate solve your problem while you solve the problem your classmate made up. Check that your answers are the same. Answers will vary.

QUICK QUIZ

1. Place the correct symbol, < or >, between the two numbers.
   −5 3
   −5 < 3 [3.1A]
2. What is the opposite of 14?
   −14 [3.1B]
3. Find the absolute value of −37.
   37 [3.1C]
4. Evaluate $-|62|$.
   −62 [3.1C]
5. Which is the colder temperature, −21°F or −12°F?
   −21°F [3.1D]

SECTION

3.2 Addition and Subtraction of Integers

OBJECTIVE A *To add integers*

Not only can an integer be graphed on a number line, an integer can be represented anywhere along a number line by an arrow. A positive number is represented by an arrow pointing to the right. A negative number is represented by an arrow pointing to the left. The absolute value of the number is represented by the length of the arrow. The integers 5 and −4 are shown on the number line in the figure below.

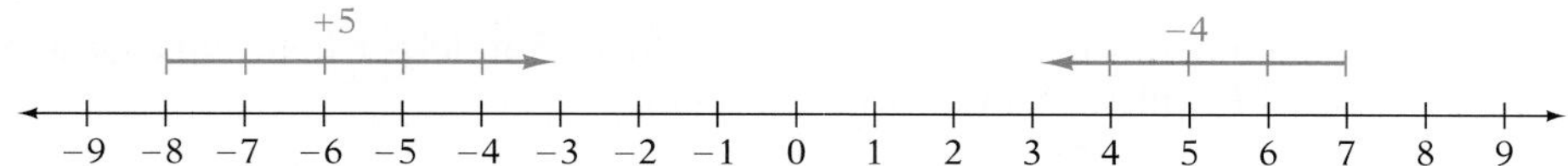

INSTRUCTOR NOTE

There are a number of models of addition of integers. A model using the number line is one of them. Another is to use a checking account. If there is a balance of $25 in a checking account, and a check is written for $30, the account will be overdrawn by $5 (−5).

Another model uses two colors of plastic chips—for example, blue for positive and red for negative—and the idea that a blue-red pair is equal to zero. To add −8 + 3, place 8 red and 3 blue chips in a circle. Make as many blue-red pairs as possible, and remove them from the region. There are 5 red chips remaining, or −5.

The sum of two integers can be shown on a number line. To add two integers, find the point on the number line corresponding to the first addend. At that point, draw an arrow representing the second addend. The sum is the number directly below the tip of the arrow.

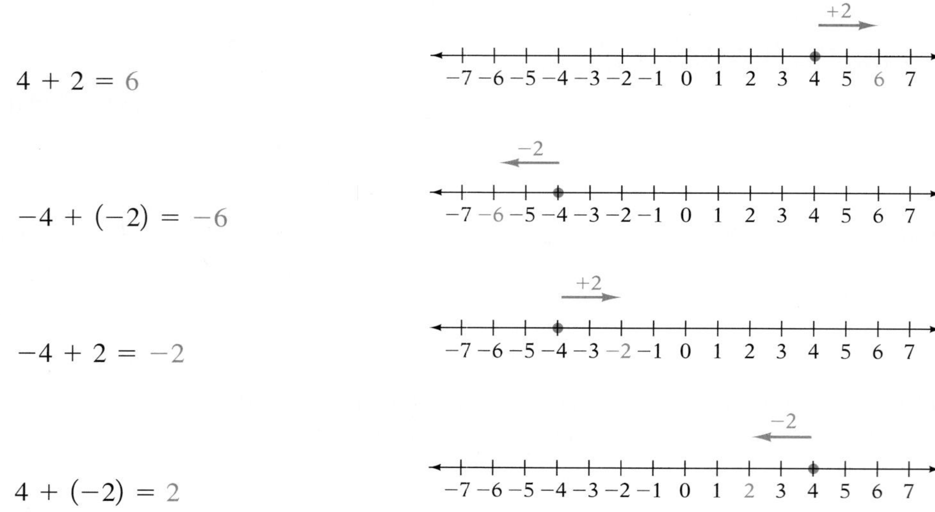

The sums shown above can be categorized by the signs of the addends.

The addends have the same sign.

$4 + 2$	positive 4 plus positive 2
$-4 + (-2)$	negative 4 plus negative 2

The addends have different signs.

$-4 + 2$	negative 4 plus positive 2
$4 + (-2)$	positive 4 plus negative 2

The rules for adding two integers depend on whether the signs of the addends are the same or different.

Rules for Adding Two Integers

To add two integers with the same sign, add the absolute values of the numbers. Then attach the sign of the addends.

To add two integers with different signs, find the absolute values of the numbers. Subtract the smaller absolute value from the larger absolute value. Then attach the sign of the addend with the larger absolute value.

Integrating Technology

To add $-14 + (-47)$ with your calculator, enter the following:

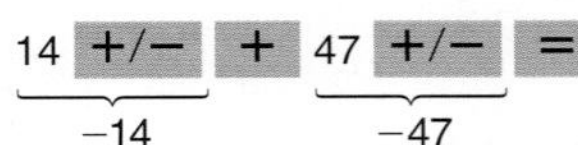

HOW TO 1 Add: $(-4) + (-9)$

The signs of the addends are the same.
Add the absolute values of the numbers.

$|-4| = 4, |-9| = 9, 4 + 9 = 13$

Attach the sign of the addends.
(Both addends are negative.
The sum is negative.)

$(-4) + (-9) = -13$

HOW TO 2 Add: $-14 + (-47)$

The signs are the same.
Add the absolute values of the numbers.
Attach the sign of the addends.

$-14 + (-47) = -61$

HOW TO 3 Add: $6 + (-13)$

The signs of the addends are different.
Find the absolute values of the numbers.

$|6| = 6, |-13| = 13$

Subtract the smaller absolute value from the larger absolute value.

$13 - 6 = 7$

Attach the sign of the number with the larger absolute value.

$|-13| > |6|$. Attach the negative sign.

$6 + (-13) = -7$

IN-CLASS EXAMPLES

1. Add: $-15 + (-27)$
   −42
2. Add: $-30 + 16$
   −14
3. Add: $9 + (-21) + 18$
   6
4. What is 14 more than -6?
   8
5. Evaluate $-x + y$ for $x = -9$ and $y = -7$.
   2
6. Which number, 144, 30, −18, or 4, is a solution of the equation $6 = 24 + n$?
   −18

HOW TO 4 Add: $162 + (-247)$

The signs are different. Find the difference between the absolute values of the numbers.

$247 - 162 = 85$

Attach the sign of the number with the larger absolute value.

$162 + (-247) = -85$

HOW TO 5 Add: $-8 + 8$

The signs are different. Find the difference between the absolute values of the numbers.

$8 - 8 = 0$

$-8 + 8 = 0$

Note in HOW TO 5 that we are adding a number and its opposite (-8 and 8), and the sum is 0. The opposite of a number is called its **additive inverse.** The opposite or additive inverse of -8 is 8, and the opposite or additive inverse of 8 is -8. The sum of a number and its additive inverse is always zero. This is known as the Inverse Property of Addition.

The properties of addition presented in Chapter 1 hold true for integers as well as whole numbers. These properties are repeated below, along with the Inverse Property of Addition.

Take Note
With the Commutative Properties, the order in which the numbers occur changes. With the Associative Properties, the order in which the numbers occur remains the same.

The Addition Property of Zero $a + 0 = a$ or $0 + a = a$

The Commutative Property of Addition $a + b = b + a$

The Associative Property of Addition $(a + b) + c = a + (b + c)$

The Inverse Property of Addition $a + (-a) = 0$ or $-a + a = 0$

EXAMPLES

1. $-8 + 0 = -8$
2. $4 + (-2) = -2 + 4$
3. $(-6 + 3) + (-1) = -6 + [3 + (-1)]$
4. $9 + (-9) = 0$

Take Note
For HOW TO 6 at the right, check that the sum is the same if the numbers are added in a different order.

HOW TO 6 Add: $(-4) + (-6) + (-8) + 9$

$(-4) + (-6) + (-8) + 9$

Add the first two numbers. $= (-10) + (-8) + 9$

Add the sum to the third number. $= (-18) + 9$

Continue until all the numbers have been added. $= -9$

APPLY THE CONCEPT

The price of Byplex Corporation's stock fell each trading day of the first week of June 2014. Use Figure 3.3 to find the change in the price of Byplex stock over the week's time.

Figure 3.3 Change in Price of Byplex Corporation Stock

To find the change in the price, add the five changes in price.

$$-2 + (-3) + (-1) + (-2) + (-1)$$
$$= (-5) + (-1) + (-2) + (-1)$$
$$= -6 + (-2) + (-1)$$
$$= -8 + (-1) = -9$$

The change in the price was -9.

This means that the price of the stock fell $9 per share.

HOW TO 7 Evaluate $-x + y$ for $x = -15$ and $y = -5$.

$-x + y$

Replace x with -15 and y with -5. $-(-15) + (-5)$

Simplify $-(-15)$. $= 15 + (-5)$

Add. $= 10$

Take Note

Recall that a solution of an equation is a number that, when substituted for the variable, produces a true equation.

HOW TO 8 Is -7 a solution of the equation $x + 4 = -3$?

$x + 4 = -3$

Replace x by -7 and then simplify. $-7 + 4 \mid -3$

The results are equal. $-3 = -3$

-7 is a solution of the equation.

EXAMPLE 1

Add: $-97 + (-45)$

Solution The signs are the same. Add the absolute values of the numbers.

$-97 + (-45) = -142$

YOU TRY IT 1

Add: $-38 + (-62)$

Your solution

-100

EXAMPLE 2

Add: $81 + (-79)$

Solution The signs are different. Find the difference between the absolute values of the numbers.

$81 + (-79) = 2$

YOU TRY IT 2

Add: $47 + (-53)$

Your solution

-6

EXAMPLE 3

Add: $42 + (-12) + (-30)$

Solution $42 + (-12) + (-30)$

$= 30 + (-30)$

$= 0$

YOU TRY IT 3

Add: $-36 + 17 + (-21)$

Your solution

-40

EXAMPLE 4

What is -162 increased by 98?

Solution $-162 + 98 = -64$

YOU TRY IT 4

Find the sum of -154 and -37.

Your solution -191

EXAMPLE 5

Evaluate $-x + y$ for $x = -11$ and $y = -2$.

Solution $-x + y$

$-(-11) + (-2) = 11 + (-2)$

$= 9$

YOU TRY IT 5

Evaluate $-x + y$ for $x = -3$ and $y = -10$.

Your solution

-7

Solutions on p. S9

EXAMPLE 6

Is -6 a solution of the equation $3 + y = -2$?

Solution

$$\begin{array}{r|l} 3 + y & = -2 \\ \hline 3 + (-6) & -2 \\ -3 & \neq -2 \end{array}$$

No, -6 is not a solution of the equation.

YOU TRY IT 6

Is -9 a solution of the equation $2 = 11 + a$?

Your solution

Yes

Solution on p. S9

OBJECTIVE B *To subtract integers*

Before the rules for subtracting two integers are explained, look at the translations into words of expressions that represent the difference of two integers.

$9 - 3$	positive 9 minus positive 3
$-9 - 3$	negative 9 minus positive 3
$9 - (-3)$	positive 9 minus negative 3
$-9 - (-3)$	negative 9 minus negative 3

Note that the sign $-$ is used in two different ways. One way is as a negative sign, as in -9 (negative 9). The second way is to indicate the operation of subtraction, as in $9 - 3$ (9 minus 3).

Look at the next four expressions and decide whether the second number in each expression is a positive number or a negative number.

INSTRUCTOR NOTE

Provide students with several examples of expressions that require distinguishing between a minus sign and a negative sign. Here are some examples:

$7 - 6$
$3 - (-9)$
$-4 - 1$
$-5 - (-2)$
$(-8) - 10$

1. $(-10) - 8$
2. $(-10) - (-8)$
3. $10 - (-8)$
4. $10 - 8$

In expressions 1 and 4, the second number is positive 8. In expressions 2 and 3, the second number is negative 8.

Opposites are used to rewrite subtraction problems as related addition problems. Notice below that the subtraction of a whole number is the same as the addition of the opposite number.

Subtraction		*Addition of the Opposite*	
$8 - 4$	=	$8 + (-4)$	$= 4$
$7 - 5$	=	$7 + (-5)$	$= 2$
$9 - 2$	=	$9 + (-2)$	$= 7$

INSTRUCTOR NOTE
A subtraction model based on blue and red chips similar to the addition model can be provided. Restrict the terms of the subtraction to, say, between −10 and 10, and start with 10 blue-red pairs in a circle. Because each blue-red pair is equal to zero, the circle contains 10 zeros. To model −3 − (−7), place 3 more red chips in the circle and remove (subtract) any 7 red chips. Now pair as many blue and red chips as possible. There will be 4 blue chips left without a red chip, which models −3 − (−7) = 4.

Subtraction of integers can be written as the addition of the opposite number. To subtract two integers, rewrite the subtraction expression as the first number plus the opposite of the second number. Some examples are shown below.

First number	−	second number	=	First number	+	opposite of the second number
8	−	15	=	8	+	(−15) = −7
8	−	(−15)	=	8	+	15 = 23
−8	−	15	=	−8	+	(−15) = −23
−8	−	(−15)	=	−8	+	15 = 7

Rule for Subtracting Two Integers

To subtract two integers, add the opposite of the second integer to the first integer.

HOW TO 9 Subtract: (−15) − 75

Rewrite the subtraction operation as the sum of the first number and the opposite of the second number. The opposite of 75 is −75.

Add.

$$(-15) - 75$$
$$= (-15) + (-75)$$
$$= -90$$

INSTRUCTOR NOTE
Some students may have developed the habit of writing expressions such as

3 + −4

Explain to them that, to avoid confusion, the two symbols + and − should not be written in succession without using parentheses:

3 + (−4)

HOW TO 10 Subtract: 6 − (−20)

Rewrite the subtraction operation as the sum of the first number and the opposite of the second number. The opposite of −20 is 20.

$$6 - (-20)$$
$$= 6 + 20$$
$$= 26$$

HOW TO 11 Subtract: 11 − 42

Rewrite the subtraction operation as the sum of the first number and the opposite of the second number. The opposite of 42 is −42.

$$11 - 42$$
$$= 11 + (-42)$$
$$= -31$$

Take Note
42 − 11 = 31
11 − 42 = −31
42 − 11 ≠ 11 − 42

By the Commutative Property of Addition, the order in which two numbers are added does not affect the sum; $a + b = b + a$. However, note at the left that the order in which two numbers are subtracted *does* affect the difference. The operation of subtraction is not commutative.

Integrating Technology

To subtract $-13 - 5 - (-8)$ with your calculator, enter the following:

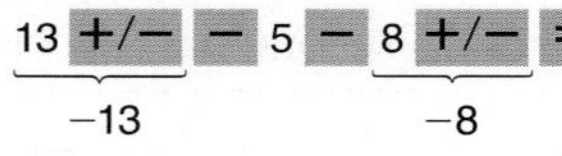

When subtraction occurs several times in an expression, rewrite each subtraction as addition of the opposite, and then add.

HOW TO 12 Subtract: $-13 - 5 - (-8)$

Rewrite each subtraction as addition of the opposite.

Add.

$$\begin{aligned} &-13 - 5 - (-8) \\ &= -13 + (-5) + 8 \\ &= -18 + 8 \\ &= -10 \end{aligned}$$

HOW TO 13 Simplify: $-14 + 6 - (-7)$

This problem involves both addition and subtraction. Rewrite the subtraction as addition of the opposite.

Add.

$$\begin{aligned} &-14 + 6 - (-7) \\ &= -14 + 6 + 7 \\ &= -8 + 7 \\ &= -1 \end{aligned}$$

IN-CLASS EXAMPLES

7. Subtract: $15 - 18$
   −3
8. Subtract: $-5 - (-3)$
   −2
9. What is 5 less than -9?
   −14
10. Find 4 minus 22.
    −18
11. Simplify: $-4 - (-7) + (-3)$
    0
12. Evaluate $-x - (-y)$ for $x = -4$ and $y = -8$.
    −4
13. Which number, 48, -48, 36, or -36, is a solution of the equation $6 - y = -42$?
    48

HOW TO 14 Evaluate $a - b$ for $a = -2$ and $b = -9$.

$a - b$

Replace a with -2 and b with -9. $\quad -2 - (-9)$

Rewrite the subtraction as addition of the opposite. $\quad = -2 + 9$

Add. $\quad = 7$

HOW TO 15 Is -4 a solution of the equation $3 - a = 11 + a$?

$3 - a = 11 + a$

Replace a by -4 and then simplify.

$3 - (-4)$	$11 + (-4)$
$3 + 4$	7

The results are equal. $\quad 7 = 7$

Yes, -4 is a solution of the equation.

EXAMPLE 7

Subtract: $-12 - (-17)$

Solution Rewrite the subtraction as addition of the opposite. Then add the two numbers.

$$\begin{aligned} -12 - (-17) &= -12 + 17 \\ &= 5 \end{aligned}$$

YOU TRY IT 7

Subtract: $-35 - (-34)$

Your solution

−1

EXAMPLE 8

Subtract: $66 - (-90)$

Solution

$$\begin{aligned} 66 - (-90) &= 66 + 90 \\ &= 156 \end{aligned}$$

YOU TRY IT 8

Subtract: $83 - (-29)$

Your solution

112

Solutions on p. S9

APPLY THE CONCEPT

The table at the right shows the boiling point and the melting point, in degrees Celsius, of three chemical elements. Find the difference between the boiling point and the melting point of radon.

Chemical Element	Boiling Point	Melting Point
Mercury	357	−39
Radon	−62	−71
Xenon	−108	−112

To find the difference, subtract the melting point of radon from the boiling point of radon.

$$-62 - (-71) = -62 + 71$$
$$= 9$$

The difference is 9°C.

EXAMPLE 9

Use the table above to find the difference between the boiling point and the melting point of mercury.

Solution The boiling point of mercury is 357.

The melting point of mercury is −39.

$$357 - (-39) = 357 + 39$$
$$= 396$$

The difference is 396°C.

YOU TRY IT 9

Use the table above to find the difference between the boiling point and the melting point of xenon.

Your solution

4°C

EXAMPLE 10

What is −12 minus 8?

Solution The word *minus* indicates subtraction.

$$-12 - 8 = -12 + (-8)$$
$$= -20$$

YOU TRY IT 10

What is 14 less than −8?

Your solution

−22

EXAMPLE 11

Subtract 91 from 43.

Solution

$$43 - 91 = 43 + (-91)$$
$$= -48$$

YOU TRY IT 11

What is 25 decreased by 68?

Your solution

−43

EXAMPLE 12

Simplify: $-8 - 30 - (-12) - 7 - (-14)$

Solution

$$-8 - 30 - (-12) - 7 - (-14)$$
$$= -8 + (-30) + 12 + (-7) + 14$$
$$= -38 + 12 + (-7) + 14$$
$$= -26 + (-7) + 14$$
$$= -33 + 14$$
$$= -19$$

YOU TRY IT 12

Simplify: $-4 - (-3) + 12 - (-7) - 20$

Your solution

−2

Solutions on pp. S9–S10

EXAMPLE 13

Evaluate $-x - y$ for $x = -4$ and $y = -3$.

Solution

$-x - y$

$-(-4) - (-3) = 4 - (-3)$
$= 4 + 3$
$= 7$

YOU TRY IT 13

Evaluate $x - y$ for $x = -9$ and $y = 7$.

Your solution

−16

EXAMPLE 14

Is 8 a solution of the equation $-2 = 6 - x$?

Solution

$$\begin{array}{r|l} -2 = & 6 - x \\ \hline -2 & 6 - 8 \\ -2 & 6 + (-8) \\ -2 = & -2 \end{array}$$

Yes, 8 is a solution of the equation.

YOU TRY IT 14

Is -3 a solution of the equation $a - 5 = -8$?

Your solution

Yes

Solutions on p. S10

OBJECTIVE C *To solve application problems and use formulas*

Figure 3.4 shows the melting points in degrees Celsius of six chemical elements. The abbreviations of the elements are:

F - Fluorine	H - Hydrogen
S - Sulfur	N - Nitrogen
O - Oxygen	Li - Lithium

Use this graph for Example 15 and You Try It 15.

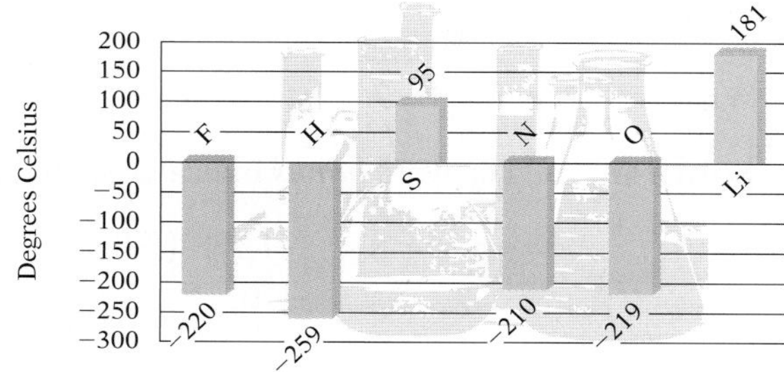

Figure 3.4 Melting Points of Chemical Elements

EXAMPLE 15

Find the difference between the two lowest melting points shown in Figure 3.4.

Strategy

To find the difference, subtract the lowest melting point shown (−259) from the second lowest melting point shown (−220).

Solution

$-220 - (-259) = -220 + 259 = 39$

The difference is 39°C.

YOU TRY IT 15

Find the difference between the highest and lowest melting points shown in Figure 3.4.

Your strategy

Your solution

440°C

Solution on p. S10

EXAMPLE 16

Find the temperature after an increase of 8°C from −5°C.

Strategy

To find the temperature, add the increase (8) to the previous temperature (−5).

Solution

$-5 + 8 = 3$

The temperature is 3°C.

YOU TRY IT 16

Find the temperature after an increase of 10°C from −3°C.

Your strategy

Your solution

7°C

EXAMPLE 17

The average temperature on the sunlit side of the moon is approximately 215°F. The average temperature on the dark side is approximately −250°F. Find the difference between these average temperatures.

Strategy

To find the difference, subtract the average temperature on the dark side of the moon (−250) from the average temperature on the sunlit side (215).

Solution

$$215 - (-250) = 215 + 250$$
$$= 465$$

The difference is 465°F.

YOU TRY IT 17

The average temperature on Earth's surface is 59°F. The average temperature throughout Earth's stratosphere is −70°F. Find the difference between these average temperatures.

Your strategy

Your solution

129°F

IN-CLASS EXAMPLES

14. Find the temperature after a rise of 6°C from −10°C. **−4°C**

15. In a card game of Hearts, you had a score of −15 before you "shot the moon," entitling you to add 26 points to your score. What was your score after you shot the moon? **11 points**

EXAMPLE 18

The distance d between point a and point b on the number line is given by the formula $d = |a - b|$. Use the formula to find d for $a = 7$ and $b = -8$.

Strategy

To find d, replace a by 7 and b by −8 in the given formula, and solve for d.

Solution

$d = |a - b|$

$d = |7 - (-8)|$

$d = |7 + 8|$

$d = |15|$

$d = 15$

The distance between the two points is 15 units.

YOU TRY IT 18

The distance d between point a and point b on the number line is given by the formula $d = |a - b|$. Use the formula to find d for $a = -6$ and $b = 5$.

Your strategy

Your solution

11 units

Solutions on p. S10

3.2 EXERCISES

Concept Check

SUGGESTED ASSIGNMENT
Exercises 1–8; Exercises 9–75, odds; Exercises 81–137, odds; Exercises 141–151, odds;
More challenging exercise: Exercise 152

For Exercises 1 and 2, circle the correct words to complete each sentence.

1. In the addition problem $-5 + (-11)$, the signs of the addends are the same/different. Because both addends are negative, the sign of the sum will be positive/negative.
the same; negative

2. In the addition problem $-7 + 16$, the signs of the addends are the same/different. Because the positive addend has the larger absolute value, the sign of the sum will be positive/negative. different; positive

State whether each "−" is a minus sign or a negative sign.

3. $-7 + (-9)$ negative; negative

4. $2 - (-7)$ minus; negative

5. $-6 - 1$ negative; minus

6. $-4 - (-3)$ negative; minus; negative

Rewrite each subtraction as addition of the opposite.

7. $-9 - 5 = -9 +$ ___(−5)___

8. $6 - (-4) - 3 = 6 +$ ___4___ $+$ ___(−3)___

OBJECTIVE A To add integers

Add.

9. $-3 + (-8)$
−11

10. $-6 + (-9)$
−15

11. $-8 + 3$
−5

12. $-7 + 2$
−5

13. $-5 + 13$
8

14. $-4 + 11$
7

15. $6 + (-10)$
−4

16. $8 + (-12)$
−4

17. $3 + (-5)$
−2

18. $6 + (-7)$
−1

19. $-4 + (-5)$
−9

20. $-12 + (-12)$
−24

21. $-6 + 7$
1

22. $-9 + 8$
−1

23. $(-5) + (-10)$
−15

24. $(-3) + (-17)$
−20

25. $-7 + 7$
0

26. $-11 + 11$
0

27. $(-15) + (-6)$
−21

28. $(-18) + (-3)$
−21

29. $0 + (-14)$
−14

30. $-19 + 0$
−19

31. $73 + (-54)$
19

32. $-89 + 62$
−27

33. $2 + (-3) + (-4)$
−5

34. $7 + (-2) + (-8)$
−3

35. $-3 + (-12) + (-15)$
−30

36. $9 + (-6) + (-16)$
−13

37. $-17 + (-3) + 29$
9

38. $13 + 62 + (-38)$
37

39. $11 + (-22) + 4 + (-5)$
-12

40. $-14 + (-3) + 7 + (-6)$
-16

41. $-22 + 10 + 2 + (-18)$
-28

42. $-6 + (-8) + 13 + (-4)$
-5

43. $-25 + (-31) + 24 + 19$
-13

44. $10 + (-14) + (-21) + 8$
-17

45. What is 3 increased by -21?
-18

46. Find 12 plus -9.
3

47. What is 16 more than -5?
11

48. What is 17 added to -7?
10

49. Find the total of -3, -8, and 12.
1

50. Find the sum of 5, -16, and -13.
-24

51. Write the sum of x and -7.
$x + (-7)$

52. Write the total of $-a$ and b.
$-a + b$

53. **Balance of Trade** A nation's balance of trade is the difference between the value of its exports and that of its imports. If the value of the exports is greater than that of the imports, the result is a positive number and a *favorable balance of trade.* If the value of the exports is less than that of the imports, the result is a negative number and an *unfavorable balance of trade.* The table at the right shows the unfavorable balance of trade in a recent year for the United States with four other countries. Find the total of the U.S. balance of trade with **a.** Japan and Mexico, **b.** Canada and Mexico, and **c.** Japan and China.
a. $-\$126,500,000,000$ **b.** $-\$94,900,000,000$ **c.** $-\$333,200,000,000$

U.S. Balance of Trade with Foreign Countries	
Japan	−60,100,000,000
Canada	−28,500,000,000
Mexico	−66,400,000,000
China	−273,100,000,000

Source: Bureau of Economic Analysis, U.S. Department of Commerce

Evaluate the expression for the given values of the variables.

54. $x + y$, for $x = -5$ and $y = -7$
-12

55. $-a + b$, for $a = -8$ and $b = -3$
5

56. $a + b$, for $a = -8$ and $b = -3$
-11

57. $-x + y$, for $x = -5$ and $y = -7$
-2

58. $a + b + c$, for $a = -4$, $b = 6$, and $c = -9$
-7

59. $a + b + c$, for $a = -10$, $b = -6$, and $c = 5$
-11

60. $x + y + (-z)$, for $x = -3$, $y = 6$, and $z = -17$
20

61. $-x + (-y) + z$, for $x = -2$, $y = 8$, and $z = -11$
-17

Identify the property that justifies the statement.

62. $-12 + 5 = 5 + (-12)$
The Commutative Property of Addition

63. $-33 + 0 = -33$
The Addition Property of Zero

64. $-46 + 46 = 0$
The Inverse Property of Addition

65. $-7 + (3 + 2) = (-7 + 3) + 2$
The Associative Property of Addition

For Exercises 66 to 69, use the given property of addition to complete the statement.

66. The Associative Property of Addition
$-11 + (6 + 9) = (? + 6) + 9$
-11

67. The Addition Property of Zero
$-13 + ? = -13$
0

68. The Commutative Property of Addition
$-2 + ? = -4 + (-2)$
-4

69. The Inverse Property of Addition
$? + (-18) = 0$
18

70. Is -3 a solution of the equation $x + 4 = 1$?
Yes

71. Is -8 a solution of the equation $6 = -3 + z$?
No

72. Is -6 a solution of the equation $6 = 12 + n$?
Yes

73. Is -8 a solution of the equation $-7 + m = -15$?
Yes

74. Is -2 a solution of the equation $3 + y = y + 3$?
Yes

75. Is -4 a solution of the equation $1 + z = z + 2$?
No

Determine whether each statement is always true, sometimes true, or never true. Assume that a and b are integers.

76. If $a > 0$ and $b > 0$, then $a + b > 0$.
Always true

77. If $a > 0$ and $b < 0$, then $a + b > 0$.
Sometimes true

78. If $a = -b$, then $a + b < 0$.
Never true

79. If $a < 0$ and $b < 0$, then $a + b < 0$.
Always true

OBJECTIVE B *To subtract integers*

Subtract.

80. $7 - 14$
-7

81. $6 - 9$
-3

82. $-7 - 2$
-9

83. $-9 - 4$
-13

84. $7 - (-2)$
9

85. $3 - (-4)$
7

86. $-6 - (-6)$
0

87. $-4 - (-4)$
0

88. $-12 - 16$
-28

89. $-10 - 7$
-17

90. $(-9) - (-3)$
-6

91. $(-7) - (-4)$
-3

92. $4 - (-14)$
18

93. $-4 - (-16)$
12

94. $(-14) - (-7)$
-7

95. $3 - (-24)$
27

96. $9 - (-9)$
18

97. $(-41) - 65$
-106

98. $57 - 86$
-29

99. $-95 - (-28)$
-67

100. How much larger is 5 than -11?
16

101. What is -10 decreased by -4?
-6

102. Find −13 minus −8.
−5

103. What is 6 less than −9?
−15

Temperature The figure at the right shows the highest and lowest temperatures ever recorded for selected regions of the world. Use this graph for Exercises 104 to 106.

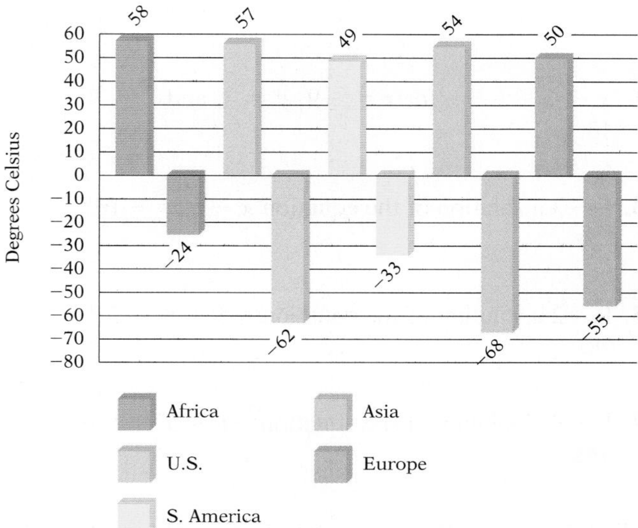

Highest and Lowest Temperatures Recorded (in degrees Celsius)

104. What is the difference between the highest and lowest temperatures ever recorded in Africa?
82°C

105. What is the difference between the highest and lowest temperatures ever recorded in South America? 82°C

106. What is the difference between the lowest temperature recorded in Europe and the lowest temperature recorded in Asia? 13°C

Simplify.

107. $-4 - 3 - 2$
−9

108. $4 - 5 - 12$
−13

109. $12 - (-7) - 8$
11

110. $-12 - (-3) - (-15)$
6

111. $4 - 12 - (-8)$
0

112. $-30 - (-65) - 29 - 4$
2

113. $-16 - 47 - 63 - 12$
−138

114. $42 - (-30) - 65 - (-11)$
18

115. $12 - (-6) + 8$
26

116. $-7 + 9 - (-3)$
5

117. $-8 - (-14) + 7$
13

118. $-4 + 6 - 8 - 2$
−8

119. $9 - 12 + 0 - 5$
−8

120. $11 - (-2) - 6 + 10$
17

121. $5 + 4 - (-3) - 7$
5

122. $-1 - 8 + 6 - (-2)$
−1

123. $-13 + 9 - (-10) - 4$
2

124. $6 - (-13) - 14 + 7$
12

For Exercises 125 to 132, evaluate the expression for the given values of the variables.

125. $-x - y$, for $x = -3$ and $y = 9$
−6

126. $x - (-y)$, for $x = -3$ and $y = 9$
6

127. $-x - (-y)$, for $x = -3$ and $y = 9$
12

128. $a - (-b)$, for $a = -6$ and $b = 10$
4

129. $a - b - c$, for $a = 4$, $b = -2$, and $c = 9$
−3

130. $a - b - c$, for $a = -1$, $b = 7$, and $c = -15$
7

131. $x - y - (-z)$, for $x = -9$, $y = 3$, and $z = 30$
18

132. $-x - (-y) - z$, for $x = 8$, $y = 1$, and $z = -14$
7

133. Is −3 a solution of the equation $x - 7 = -10$?
Yes

134. Is −4 a solution of the equation $1 = 3 - y$?
No

135. Is −2 a solution of the equation $-5 - w = 7$?
No

136. Is −8 a solution of the equation $-12 = m - 4$?
Yes

137. Is −6 a solution of the equation $-t - 5 = 7 + t$?
Yes

138. Is −7 a solution of the equation $5 + a = -9 - a$?
Yes

Determine whether each statement is always true, sometimes true, or never true. Assume that a and b are integers.

139. If $a > 0$ and $b > 0$, then $a - b > 0$.
Sometimes true

140. If $a > 0$ and $b < 0$, then $a - b > 0$.
Always true

OBJECTIVE C *To solve application problems and use formulas*

Geography The elevation, or height, of places on Earth is measured in relation to sea level, or the average level of the ocean's surface. The table below shows height above sea level as a positive number and depth below sea level as a negative number. Use the table below for Exercises 141 to 143.

Continent	Highest Elevation (in meters)		Lowest Elevation (in meters)	
Africa	Mt. Kilimanjaro	5895	Lake Assal	–156
Asia	Mt. Everest	8850	Dead Sea	–411
Europe	Mt. Elbrus	5642	Caspian Sea	–28
Americas	Mt. Aconcagua	6960	Death Valley	–86

Mt. Everest

© iStockphoto.com/fotoVoyager

141. What is the difference in elevation between **a.** Mt. Aconcagua and Death Valley and **b.** Mt. Kilimanjaro and Lake Assal? a. 7046 m b. 6051 m

142. For which continent shown is the difference between the highest and lowest elevations greatest? Asia

143. For which continent shown is the difference between the highest and lowest elevations smallest? Europe

144. Temperature Find the temperature after a rise of 9°C from −6°C. 3°C

Temperature The table at the right shows the average temperatures at different cruising altitudes for airplanes. Use the table for Exercises 145 and 146.

Cruising Altitude	*Average Temperature*
12,000 ft	16°
20,000 ft	−12°
30,000 ft	−48°
40,000 ft	−70°
50,000 ft	−70°

145. What is the difference between the average temperatures at 12,000 ft and at 40,000 ft? 86°

146. How much colder is the average temperature at 30,000 ft than at 20,000 ft? 36°

147. **Golf** Use the equation $S = N - P$, where S is a golfer's score relative to par in a tournament, N is the number of strokes made by the golfer, and P is par, to find a golfer's score relative to par when the golfer made 49 strokes and par is 52. −3

148. **Golf** Use the equation $S = N - P$, where S is a golfer's score relative to par in a tournament, N is the number of strokes made by the golfer, and P is par, to find a golfer's score relative to par when the golfer made 196 strokes and par is 208. −12

149. **Temperature** The date of the news clipping at the right is April 2, 2010.

a. Find the difference between the high and low temperatures in the United States on that date. 107°F

b. What was the difference between the high and low temperatures in the contiguous 48 states on that date? 100°F

In the NEWS!

U.S. Experiences Extreme Temperatures

The high temperature in the United States today was 93°F, recorded in Laredo, Texas. At the other extreme was Buckland, Alaska, which recorded the lowest temperature in all the United States at −14°F. The lowest temperature in the contiguous United States was −7°F, at Lake Yellowstone, Wyoming.

Source: National Weather Service

150. **Mathematics** The distance d between point a and point b on the number line is given by the formula $d = |a - b|$. Find d when $a = 6$ and $b = -15$. 21 units

151. **Mathematics** The distance d between point a and point b on the number line is given by the formula $d = |a - b|$. Find d when $a = 7$ and $b = -12$. 19 units

Critical Thinking

152. **Mathematics** Given the list of numbers at the right, find the largest difference that can be obtained by subtracting one number in the list from a different number in the list. 23

5, −2, −9, 11, 14

153. The sum of two negative integers is −7. Find the integers.
Answers will vary. Possible answers include −1 and −6, −2 and −5, −3 and −4.

Projects or Group Activities

154. Make up three addition problems such that each problem involves one positive and one negative addend, and each problem has the sum −3. Then describe a strategy for writing these problems.

155. Make up three subtraction problems such that each problem involves a negative number minus a negative number, and each problem has a difference of −8. Then describe a strategy for writing these problems.

QUICK QUIZ

1. Add: $-15 + (-28)$
   −43 [3.2A]
2. Subtract: $5 - 16$
   −11 [3.2B]
3. Subtract: $-64 - (-48)$
   −16 [3.2B]
4. Evaluate $x - y$ for $x = -1$ and $y = -8$.
   7 [3.2B]
5. Find the temperature after a rise of 6°C from −12°C.
   −6°C [3.2C]

CHECK YOUR PROGRESS: CHAPTER 3

1. Graph -3 on the number line. [3.1A]

$-6\ -5\ -4\ -3\ -2\ -1\ 0\ 1\ 2\ 3\ 4\ 5\ 6$

2. On the number line, which number is 5 units to the left of 2?
-3 [3.1A]

3. Place the correct symbol, $<$ or $>$, between the two numbers.
$-12 > -16$ [3.1A]

4. Write the given numbers in order from smallest to largest.
$-8, 7, -19, 4$ $-19, -8, 4, 7$ [3.1A]

5. Find the opposite of the number.
a. -11 **b.** 13 **c.** $-m$
a. 11 **b.** -13 **c.** m [3.1B]

6. Write the expression in words.
$-5 - (-7)$
negative five minus negative seven [3.1B]

7. Simplify.
a. $-(-42)$ **b.** $-(t)$
a. 42 **b.** $-t$ [3.1B]

8. Find the absolute value of **a.** -18 and **b.** 37.
a. 18 **b.** 37 [3.1C]

9. Evaluate **a.** $|-51|$ and **b.** $-|67|$.
a. 51 **b.** -67 [3.1C]

10. Evaluate $-|x|$ for $x = -2$.
-2 [3.1C]

11. Place the correct symbol, < or >, between the two numbers.
$|-19| > |7|$ [3.1C]

12. Write the given numbers in order from smallest to largest.
$|-5|, -(-6), |3|, -|-8|, -|12|$
$-|12|, -|-8|, |3|, |-5|, -(-6)$ [3.1C]

13. Add: $-8 + (-12)$
-20 [3.2A]

14. Add: $20 + (-3) + (-7)$
10 [3.2A]

15. Subtract: $5 - 40$
-35 [3.2B]

16. Subtract: $-32 - (-16)$
-16 [3.2B]

17. Simplify: $4 - (-15) - 3 + 7$
23 [3.2B]

18. What is -11 minus 16?
-27 [3.2B]

19. Find the sum of -6, -9, and 14.
-1 [3.2A]

20. Evaluate $-x + y$ for $x = -6$ and $y = -2$.
4 [3.2A]

21. Evaluate $a - (-b)$ for $a = -5$ and $b = 7$.
2 [3.2B]

22. Is -7 a solution of the equation $-3 = y - 4$?
No [3.2B]

23. Temperature Which is the colder temperature, $-16°F$ or $-4°F$?
$-16°F$ [3.1D]

24. Temperature Find the temperature after a rise of 8°C from $-3°C$.
5°C [3.2C]

25. Mathematics The distance d between point a and point b on the number line is given by the formula $d = |a - b|$. Find d when $a = 9$ and $b = -5$.
14 units [3.2C]

SECTION

3.3 Multiplication and Division of Integers

OBJECTIVE A *To multiply integers*

When 5 is multiplied by a sequence of decreasing integers, each product decreases by 5.

$5(3) = 15$
$5(2) = 10$
$5(1) = 5$
$5(0) = 0$

The pattern can be continued so that 5 is multiplied by a sequence of negative numbers. To maintain the pattern of decreasing by 5, the resulting products must be negative.

$5(-1) = -5$
$5(-2) = -10$
$5(-3) = -15$
$5(-4) = -20$

This example illustrates that the product of a positive number and a negative number is negative.

When -5 is multiplied by a sequence of decreasing integers, each product increases by 5.

$-5(3) = -15$
$-5(2) = -10$
$-5(1) = -5$
$-5(0) = 0$

The pattern can be continued so that -5 is multiplied by a sequence of negative numbers. To maintain the pattern of increasing by 5, the resulting products must be positive.

$-5(-1) = 5$
$-5(-2) = 10$
$-5(-3) = 15$
$-5(-4) = 20$

This example illustrates that the product of two negative numbers is positive.

The pattern for multiplication shown above is summarized in the following rule for multiplying integers.

Point of Interest

Operations with negative numbers were not accepted until the late thirteenth century. One of the first attempts to prove that the product of two negative numbers is positive was made in the book *Ars Magna,* by Girolamo Cardan, in 1545.

Rule for Multiplying Two Integers

To multiply two integers with the same sign, multiply the absolute values of the factors. The product is **positive.**

To multiply two integers with different signs, multiply the absolute values of the factors. The product is **negative.**

EXAMPLES

1. $-4(12) = -48$ • The signs are different. The product is negative.
2. $(-6)(-15) = 90$ • The signs are the same. The product is positive.

Integrating Technology

To multiply $(-6)(-15)$ with your calculator, enter the following:

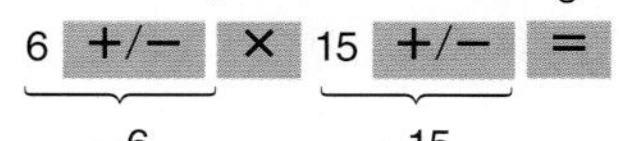

HOW TO 1 Find the product of -11 and -5.

A *product* is the answer to a multiplication problem.
Multiply -11 and -5.
The signs are the same. The product is positive.

$-11(-5) = 55$

APPLY THE CONCEPT

Figure 3.5 shows the melting points of bromine and mercury. The melting point of helium is 7 times the melting point of mercury. Find the melting point of helium.

To find the melting point of helium, multiply the melting point of mercury (−39°C) by 7.

$-39(7) = -273$

The melting point of helium is −273°C.

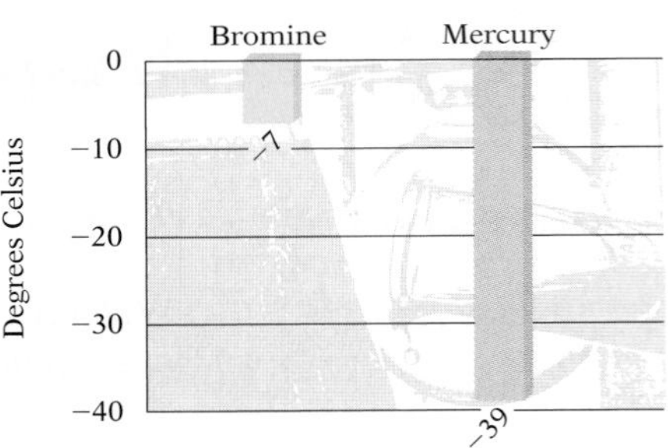

Figure 3.5 Melting Points of Chemical Elements (in degrees Celsius)

The properties of multiplication presented in Chapter 1 hold true for integers as well as whole numbers. These properties are restated below.

IN-CLASS EXAMPLES

1. Find the product of −100 and 5.
   −500
2. Multiply: −8(−4)(−2)
   −64
3. Evaluate $-xy$ for $x = -4$ and $y = -9$.
   −36
4. Which number, −48, −36, −7, or 7, is a solution of the equation $6x = -42$?
   −7

The Multiplication Property of Zero	$a \cdot 0 = 0$ or $0 \cdot a = 0$
The Multiplication Property of One	$a \cdot 1 = a$ or $1 \cdot a = a$
The Commutative Property of Multiplication	$a \cdot b = b \cdot a$
The Associative Property of Multiplication	$(a \cdot b) \cdot c = a \cdot (b \cdot c)$

EXAMPLES

1. $-8(0) = 0$ **2.** $-4(1) = -4$

3. $(-5)(3) = 3(-5)$ **4.** $(-6 \cdot 2) \cdot (-1) = -6 \cdot [2 \cdot (-1)]$

Take Note

For HOW TO 2 at the right, the product is the same if the numbers are multiplied in a different order. For instance,

$2(-3)(-5)(-7)$
$= 2(-3)(35)$
$= 2(-105)$
$= -210$

HOW TO 2 Multiply: $2(-3)(-5)(-7)$

	$2(-3)(-5)(-7)$
Multiply the first two numbers.	$= -6(-5)(-7)$
Then multiply the product by the third number.	$= 30(-7)$
Continue until all the numbers have been multiplied.	$= -210$

By the Multiplication Property of One, $1 \cdot 6 = 6$ and $\mathbf{1 \cdot x = x}$. Applying the rules for multiplication, we can extend this to $-1 \cdot 6 = -6$ and $\mathbf{-1 \cdot x = -x}$.

Take Note

When variables are placed next to each other, it is understood that the operation is multiplication. $-ab$ means "the opposite of a times b."

HOW TO 3 Evaluate $-ab$ for $a = -2$ and $b = -9$.

	$-ab$
Replace a with −2 and b with −9.	$-(-2)(-9)$
Simplify −(−2).	$= 2(-9)$
Multiply.	$= -18$

HOW TO 4 Is −4 a solution of the equation $5x = -20$?

	$5x = -20$
Replace x by −4 and then simplify.	$5(-4) \mid -20$
The results are equal.	$-20 = -20$

Yes, −4 is a solution of the equation.

EXAMPLE 1

Find -42 times 62.

Solution $-42 \cdot 62 = -2604$

YOU TRY IT 1

What is -38 multiplied by 51?

Your solution -1938

EXAMPLE 2

Multiply: $-5(-4)(6)(-3)$

Solution

$$\begin{aligned} -5(-4)(6)(-3) &= 20(6)(-3) \\ &= 120(-3) \\ &= -360 \end{aligned}$$

YOU TRY IT 2

Multiply: $-7(-8)(9)(-2)$

Your solution

-1008

EXAMPLE 3

Evaluate $-5x$ for $x = -11$.

Solution $-5x$

$-5(-11) = 55$

YOU TRY IT 3

Evaluate $-9y$ for $y = 20$.

Your solution

-180

EXAMPLE 4

Is 5 a solution of the equation $30 = -6z$?

Solution

$$\begin{array}{c|c} 30 = & -6z \\ \hline 30 & -6(5) \\ 30 \neq & -30 \end{array}$$

No, 5 is not a solution of the equation.

YOU TRY IT 4

Is -3 a solution of the equation $12 = -4a$?

Your solution

Yes

Solutions on p. S10

OBJECTIVE B *To divide integers*

Take Note

Recall that the fraction bar can be read "divided by." Therefore, $\frac{8}{2}$ can be read "8 divided by 2."

For every division problem, there is a related multiplication problem.

Division: $\frac{8}{2} = 4$ Related multiplication: $4(2) = 8$

This fact can be used to illustrate a rule for dividing integers.

$\frac{12}{3} = 4$ because $4(3) = 12$ and $\frac{-12}{-3} = 4$ because $4(-3) = -12$

These two division examples suggest that the quotient of two numbers with the same sign is positive. Now consider the following two examples.

$\frac{12}{-3} = -4$ because $-4(-3) = 12$

$\frac{-12}{3} = -4$ because $-4(3) = -12$

These two division examples suggest that the quotient of two numbers with different signs is negative. This property is summarized next.

Rule for Dividing Two Integers

To divide two integers with the same sign, divide the absolute values of the numbers. The quotient is **positive.**

To divide two integers with different signs, divide the absolute values of the numbers. The quotient is **negative.**

EXAMPLES

1. $-36 \div 9 = -4$ • **The signs are different. The quotient is negative.**
2. $(-10) \div (-5) = 2$ • **The signs are the same. The quotient is positive.**

Integrating Technology

To divide (−10) by (−5) with your calculator, enter the following:

10 +/− ÷ 5 +/− =

(10 +/− gives −10; 5 +/− gives −5)

Note from this rule that $\frac{12}{-3}$, $\frac{-12}{3}$, and $-\frac{12}{3}$ are all equal to −4.

If a and b are integers $(b \neq 0)$, then $\frac{a}{-b} = \frac{-a}{b} = -\frac{a}{b}$.

APPLY THE CONCEPT

Figure 3.6 shows the record high and low temperatures in the United States for the first four months of the year. We can read from the graph that the record low temperature for April is −36°F. This is four times the record low temperature for September. What is the record low temperature for September?

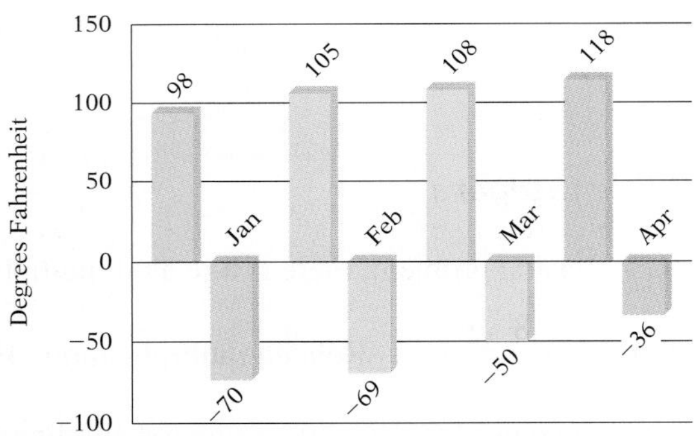

Figure 3.6 Record High and Low Temperatures, in Degrees Fahrenheit, in the United States for January, February, March, and April

Source: National Climatic Data Center, Asheville, NC, and Storm Phillips, STORMFAX, Inc.

To find the record low temperature for September, divide the record low for April (−36) by 4.

$-36 \div 4 = -9$

The record low temperature in the United States for the month of September is −9°F.

IN-CLASS EXAMPLES

5. What is the quotient of −50 and 1? **−50**
6. Divide: $\frac{-63}{7}$ **−9**
7. Divide: $0 \div y, y \neq 0$ **0**
8. Evaluate $a \div (-b)$ for $a = -48$ and $b = -6$. **−8**
9. Which number, 72, −72, −6, or −2, is a solution of the equation $-12 = \frac{n}{-6}$? **72**

The division properties of zero and one, which were presented in Chapter 1, hold true for integers as well as whole numbers. These properties are restated here.

Division Properties of Zero and One

If $a \neq 0$, $\frac{0}{a} = 0$.

If $a \neq 0$, $\frac{a}{a} = 1$.

$\frac{a}{1} = a$

$\frac{a}{0}$ is undefined.

EXAMPLES

1. $\frac{0}{-7} = 0$ **2.** $\frac{-3}{-3} = 1$ **3.** $\frac{-9}{1} = -9$ **4.** $\frac{-18}{0}$ is undefined.

Point of Interest

Historical manuscripts indicate that mathematics is at least 4000 years old. Yet it was only 400 years ago that mathematicians started using variables to stand for numbers. Before that time, mathematics was written in words.

HOW TO 5 Evaluate $a \div (-b)$ for $a = -28$ and $b = -4$.

$a \div (-b)$

Replace a with -28 and b with -4. $-28 \div (-(-4))$

Simplify $-(-4)$. $= -28 \div (4)$

Divide. $= -7$

HOW TO 6 Is -4 a solution of the equation $\frac{-20}{x} = 5$?

$\frac{-20}{x} = 5$

Replace x by -4 and then simplify. $\frac{-20}{-4} \mid 5$

The results are equal. $5 = 5$

Yes, -4 is a solution of the equation.

EXAMPLE 5

Find the quotient of -23 and -23.

Solution $-23 \div (-23) = 1$

YOU TRY IT 5

What is 0 divided by -17?

Your solution 0

EXAMPLE 6

Divide: $\frac{95}{-5}$

Solution $\frac{95}{-5} = -19$

YOU TRY IT 6

Divide: $\frac{84}{-6}$

Your solution -14

EXAMPLE 7

Divide: $x \div 0$

Solution Division by zero is not defined.

$x \div 0$ is undefined.

YOU TRY IT 7

Divide: $x \div 1$

Your solution

x

Solutions on p. S10

EXAMPLE 8

Evaluate $\frac{-a}{b}$ for $a = -6$ and $b = -3$.

Solution

$$\frac{-a}{b}$$

$$\frac{-(-6)}{-3} = \frac{6}{-3} = -2$$

YOU TRY IT 8

Evaluate $\frac{a}{-b}$ for $a = -14$ and $b = -7$.

Your solution

-2

EXAMPLE 9

Is -9 a solution of the equation $-3 = \frac{x}{3}$?

Solution

$$-3 = \frac{x}{3}$$

$$-3 \;\Big|\; \frac{-9}{3}$$

$$-3 = -3$$

Yes, -9 is a solution of the equation.

YOU TRY IT 9

Is -3 a solution of the equation $\frac{-6}{y} = -2$?

Your solution

No

Solutions on p. S10

OBJECTIVE C *To solve application problems*

EXAMPLE 10

The daily low temperatures during one week were: $-10°$, $2°$, $-1°$, $-9°$, $1°$, $0°$, and $3°$. Find the average daily low temperature for the week.

Strategy

To find the average daily low temperature:

- Add the seven temperature readings.
- Divide by 7.

Solution

$$-10 + 2 + (-1) + (-9) + 1 + 0 + 3 = -14$$

The sum of the seven readings is -14.

$$-14 \div 7 = -2$$

The average daily low temperature was $-2°$.

YOU TRY IT 10

The daily high temperatures during one week were: $-7°$, $-8°$, $0°$, $-1°$, $-6°$, $-11°$, and $-2°$. Find the average daily high temperature for the week.

Your strategy

Your solution

$-5°$

IN-CLASS EXAMPLES

10. The daily low temperatures during one week were as follows: $4°$, $-6°$, $8°$, $-2°$, $-9°$, $-11°$, and $-5°$. Find the average daily low temperature for the week.
$-3°$

Solution on p. S10

3.3 EXERCISES

Concept Check

SUGGESTED ASSIGNMENT
Exercises 1–4; Exercises 5–123, odds; More challenging exercise: Exercise 125

For Exercises 1 and 2, circle the correct words to complete each sentence.

1. a. In the multiplication problem $15(-3)$, the signs of the factors are the same/different, so the sign of the product will be positive/negative.
b. In the multiplication problem $-7(-12)$, the signs of the factors are the same/different, so the sign of the product will be positive/negative.
a. different; negative b. the same; positive

2. The signs of the numbers in the division problem $28 \div (-4)$ are the same/different, so the sign of the quotient will be positive/negative. different; negative

3. The fraction that represents the quotient -63 and 9 is $\frac{-63}{9}$.

4. Name the operation in each expression, and explain how you determined the operation.
a. $8(-7)$ **b.** $8 - 7$ **c.** $8 - (-7)$ **d.** $-xy$ **e.** $x(-y)$ **f.** $-x - y$

OBJECTIVE A *To multiply integers*

Multiply.

5. $-4 \cdot 6$
-24

6. $-7 \cdot 3$
-21

7. $-2(-3)$
6

8. $-5(-1)$
5

9. $(9)(2)$
18

10. $(3)(8)$
24

11. $5(-4)$
-20

12. $4(-7)$
-28

13. $-8(2)$
-16

14. $-9(3)$
-27

15. $(-5)(-5)$
25

16. $(-3)(-6)$
18

17. $(-7)(0)$
0

18. $-11(1)$
-11

19. $14(3)$
42

20. $62(9)$
558

21. $-32(4)$
-128

22. $-24(3)$
-72

23. $(-8)(-26)$
208

24. $(-4)(-35)$
140

25. $9(-27)$
-243

26. $8(-40)$
-320

27. $-5 \cdot (23)$
-115

28. $-6 \cdot (38)$
-228

29. $-7(-34)$
238

30. $-4(-51)$
204

31. $4 \cdot (-8) \cdot 3$
-96

32. $5 \cdot 7 \cdot (-2)$
-70

33. $(-6)(5)(7)$
-210

34. $(-9)(-9)(2)$
162

35. $-8(-7)(-4)$
-224

36. $-1(4)(-9)$
36

37. What is twice -20?
-40

38. Find the product of 100 and -7.
-700

39. What is -30 multiplied by -6?
180

40. What is -9 times -40?
360

41. Write the product of $-q$ and r.
$-qr$

42. Write the product of $-f$, g, and h.
$-fgh$

43. **Net Income** The table at the right shows the net income for the first quarter of 2011 for three companies. (*Note:* Negative net income indicates a loss.) If net income for these companies continued at the same level throughout 2011, what would be the 2011 annual net income for **a.** Sears Holdings and **b.** Rite Aid?
a. $-\$680,000,000$ b. $-\$296,000,000$

Company	*Net Income (in dollars), 1st Quarter of 2011*
Rite Aid	−74,000,000
Sears Holdings	−170,000,000
Target	689,000,000

For Exercises 44 to 47, identify the property that justifies the statement.

44. $0(-7) = 0$
The Multiplication Property of Zero

45. $1p = p$
The Multiplication Property of One

46. $-8(-5) = -5(-8)$
The Commutative Property of Multiplication

47. $-3(9 \cdot 4) = (-3 \cdot 9)4$
The Associative Property of Multiplication

For Exercises 48 to 51, use the given property of multiplication to complete the statement.

48. The Commutative Property of Multiplication
$-3(-9) = -9(?)$
-3

49. The Associative Property of Multiplication
$?(5 \cdot 10) = (-6 \cdot 5)10$
-6

50. The Multiplication Property of Zero
$-81 \cdot ? = 0$
0

51. The Multiplication Property of One
$?(-14) = -14$
1

For Exercises 52 to 61, evaluate the expression for the given values of the variables.

52. xy, for $x = -3$ and $y = -8$
24

53. $-xy$, for $x = -3$ and $y = -8$
-24

54. $x(-y)$, for $x = -3$ and $y = -8$
-24

55. $-xyz$, for $x = -6$, $y = 2$, and $z = -5$
-60

56. $-8a$, for $a = -24$
192

57. $-7n$, for $n = -51$
357

58. $5xy$, for $x = -9$ and $y = -2$
90

59. $8ab$, for $a = 7$ and $b = -1$
-56

60. $-4cd$, for $c = 25$ and $d = -8$
800

61. $-5st$, for $s = -40$ and $t = -8$
-1600

62. Is -4 a solution of the equation $6m = -24$?
Yes

63. Is -3 a solution of the equation $-5x = -15$?
No

64. Is -6 a solution of the equation $48 = -8y$?
Yes

65. Is 0 a solution of the equation $-8 = -8a$?
No

66. Is 7 a solution of the equation $-3c = 21$?
No

67. Is 9 a solution of the equation $-27 = -3c$?
Yes

68. Will the product of three negative numbers be positive or negative? Negative

69. Will the product of three positive numbers and two negative numbers be positive or negative?
Positive

OBJECTIVE B *To divide integers*

Divide.

70. $12 \div (-6)$
-2

71. $18 \div (-3)$
-6

72. $(-72) \div (-9)$
8

73. $(-64) \div (-8)$
8

74. $0 \div (-6)$
0

75. $-49 \div 1$
-49

76. $81 \div (-9)$
-9

77. $-40 \div (-5)$
8

78. $\dfrac{72}{-3}$
-24

79. $\dfrac{44}{-4}$
-11

80. $\dfrac{-93}{-3}$
31

81. $\dfrac{-98}{-7}$
14

82. $-114 \div (-6)$
19

83. $-91 \div (-7)$
13

84. $-53 \div 0$
Undefined

85. $(-162) \div (-162)$
1

86. $-128 \div 4$
-32

87. $-130 \div (-5)$
26

88. $(-200) \div 8$
-25

89. $(-92) \div (-4)$
23

90. Find the quotient of -700 and 70.
-10

91. Find 550 divided by -5.
-110

92. What is -670 divided by -10?
67

93. What is the quotient of -333 and -3?
111

94. Write the quotient of $-a$ and b.
$\frac{-a}{b}$

95. Write -9 divided by x.
$\frac{-9}{x}$

Net Income The figure at the right shows the net income for the first quarter of 2011 for three airlines. (*Note:* Negative income indicates a loss. One quarter of the year is three months.) Use this figure for Exercises 96 and 97.

96. For the quarter shown, what was the average monthly net income for US Airways? $-\$38$ million

97. For the quarter shown, what was the average monthly net income for Delta Air Lines? $-\$106$ million

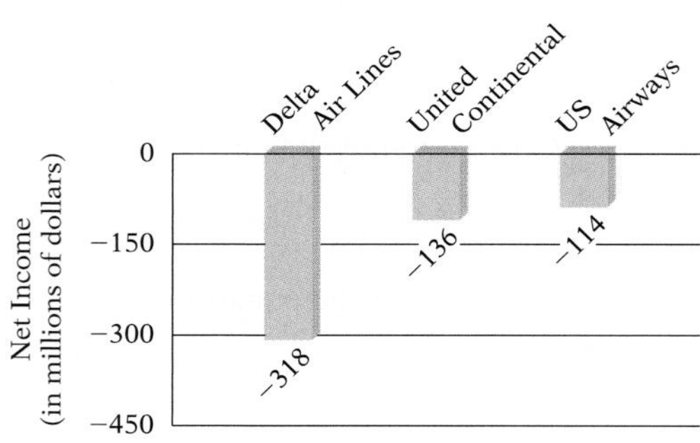

Net Income for First Quarter of 2011
Source: finance.yahoo.com

For Exercises 98 to 105, evaluate the expression for the given values of the variables.

98. $a \div b$, for $a = -36$ and $b = -4$
9

99. $-a \div b$, for $a = -36$ and $b = -4$
-9

100. $a \div (-b)$, for $a = -36$ and $b = -4$
-9

101. $(-a) \div (-b)$, for $a = -36$ and $b = -4$
9

102. $\frac{x}{y}$, for $x = -42$ and $y = -7$
6

103. $\frac{-x}{y}$, for $x = -42$ and $y = -7$
-6

104. $\frac{x}{-y}$, for $x = -42$ and $y = -7$
-6

105. $\frac{-x}{-y}$, for $x = -42$ and $y = -7$
6

106. Is 20 a solution of the equation $\frac{m}{-2} = -10$?
Yes

107. Is 18 a solution of the equation $6 = \frac{-c}{-3}$?
Yes

108. Is 0 a solution of the equation $0 = \frac{a}{-4}$?
Yes

109. Is -3 a solution of the equation $\frac{21}{n} = 7$?
No

110. Is -6 a solution of the equation $\frac{x}{2} = \frac{-18}{x}$?
No

111. Is 8 a solution of the equation $\frac{m}{-4} = \frac{-16}{m}$?
Yes

For Exercises 112 to 115, state whether the expression is equivalent to $\frac{a}{b}$ or $-\frac{a}{b}$. Assume that a and b are nonzero integers.

112. $a \div (-b)$
$-\frac{a}{b}$

113. $-\frac{-a}{b}$
$\frac{a}{b}$

114. $(-a) \div (-b)$
$\frac{a}{b}$

115. $-\frac{-a}{-b}$
$-\frac{a}{b}$

OBJECTIVE C *To solve application problems*

116. Golf The combined scores of the top five golfers in a tournament equaled -10 (10 under par). What was the average score of the five golfers? -2

© olgaru79/Shutterstock.com

117. Golf The combined scores of the top four golfers in a tournament equaled -12 (12 under par). What was the average score of the four golfers? -3

Temperature The following figure shows the record low temperatures, in degrees Fahrenheit, in the United States for each month. Use this figure for Exercises 118 to 120.

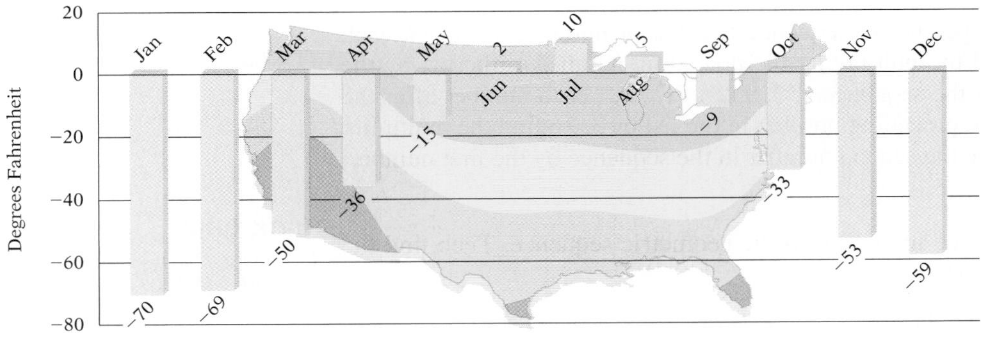

Record Low Temperatures, in Degrees Fahrenheit, in the United States
Source: National Climatic Data Center, Asheville, NC, and Storm Phillips, STORMFAX, Inc.

118. What is the average record low temperature for July, August, and September?
2°F

119. What is the average record low temperature for the first three months of the year?
-63°F

120. What is the average record low temperature for the three months with the lowest record low temperatures? −66°F

121. **Trade Deficit** Read the news clipping at the right. The U.S. trade deficit for April 2011 was \$44 billion, and for March 2011 it was \$47 billion. Find the average U.S. trade deficit for March, April, and May of 2011. −\$47 billion

In the NEWS!

U.S. Trade Deficit Widens

The U.S. trade deficit widened in May 2011 to \$50 billion. This reflects a surge in imports of consumer products as businesses in the United States hope that consumer demand picks up.

Source: www.americaneconomicalert.org

122. **Temperature** The daily high temperatures during one week were −6°, −11°, 1°, 5°, −3°, −9°, and −5°. Find the average daily high temperature for the week. −4°

123. **Temperature** The daily low temperatures during one week were 4°, −5°, 8°, −1°, −12°, −14°, and −8°. Find the average daily low temperature for the week. −4°

Critical Thinking

124. **Mathematics** **a.** Find the largest possible product of two negative integers whose sum is −18. **b.** Find the smallest possible sum of two negative integers whose product is 16. **a.** 81 **b.** −17

125. **Mathematics** Use repeated addition to show that the product of two integers with different signs is a negative number.
Answers will vary. A possible answer is $(-3)(2) = -3 + (-3) = -6$.

Projects or Group Activities

Geometric Sequences A geometric sequence is a list of numbers in which each number after the first is found by multiplying the preceding number in the list by the same number. For example, in the sequence 1, 3, 9, 27, 81, . . . , each number after the first is found by multiplying the preceding number in the list by 3. To find the multiplier in a geometric sequence, divide the second number in the sequence by the first number; for the example above, $3 \div 1 = 3$.

For Exercises 126 to 129, find the multiplier in the geometric sequence. Then find the next four numbers of the sequence.

126. −5, 15, −45, . . . −3; 135, −405, 1215, −3645

127. 2, −4, 8, . . . −2; −16, 32, −64, 128

128. −3, −12, −48, . . . 4; −192, −768, −3072, −12,288

129. −1, −5, −25, . . . 5; −125, −625, −3125, −15,625

QUICK QUIZ

1. Multiply: (11)(−3)(6)
   −198 [3.3A]
2. Divide: $-50 \div (-25)$
   2 [3.3B]
3. Divide: $0 \div (-3)$
   0 [3.3B]
4. Evaluate $-5ab$ for a $a = -2$ and $b = -8$.
   −80 [3.3A]
5. The daily low temperatures during one week were as follows: −5°, −8°, 6°, 8°, 0°, −6°, −2°. Find the average daily low temperature for the week. **−1° [3.3C]**

SECTION

3.4 Operations with Rational Numbers

OBJECTIVE A *To add or subtract rational numbers*

In this section, operations with rational numbers are discussed. A **rational number** is the quotient of two integers.

Rational Numbers

A **rational number** is a number that can be written in the form $\frac{a}{b}$, where a and b are integers and $b \neq 0$.

EXAMPLES OF RATIONAL NUMBERS

1. $\frac{3}{4}$ **2.** $\frac{-2}{9}$ **3.** $\frac{13}{-5}$

An integer can be written as the quotient of the integer and 1. Therefore, every integer is a rational number.

$6 = \frac{6}{1}$ $-8 = \frac{-8}{1}$

A mixed number can be written as the quotient of two integers. Therefore, every mixed number is a rational number.

$1\frac{4}{7} = \frac{11}{7}$ $3\frac{2}{5} = \frac{17}{5}$

Recall from Section 2.6 that a fraction can be written as a decimal by dividing the numerator of the fraction by the denominator. The result is either a terminating decimal or a repeating decimal.

To convert $\frac{3}{8}$ to a decimal, read the fraction bar as "divided by."

$\frac{3}{8} = 3 \div 8 = 0.375$. This is an example of a terminating decimal.

To convert $\frac{6}{11}$ to a decimal, divide 6 by 11.

$\frac{6}{11} = 6 \div 11 = 0.\overline{54}$. This is an example of a repeating decimal.

> **Take Note**
> Rational numbers are fractions, such as $-\frac{4}{5}$ or $\frac{10}{7}$, in which the numerator and denominator are integers. Rational numbers are also represented by repeating decimals such as 0.2626262 . . . and by terminating decimals such as 1.83. An irrational number is a decimal that neither terminates nor repeats. For instance, 1.45445444544445 . . . is an irrational number.

Every rational number can be written as either a terminating decimal or a repeating decimal. All terminating and repeating decimals are rational numbers.

Some numbers have decimal representations that never terminate or repeat; for example,

0.12122122212222 . . .

The pattern in this number is one additional 2 following each successive 1 in the number. There is no repeating block of digits. This number is an **irrational number.** Other examples of irrational numbers include π (which is presented in Chapter 7) and square roots of integers that are not perfect squares.

$\pi \approx 3.1415926...$ $\sqrt{7} \approx 2.6457513...$

The rational numbers and the irrational numbers taken together are called the **real numbers.**

We begin the presentation of operations on rational numbers by adding rational numbers in fractional form. If an addend is a fraction with a negative sign, rewrite the fraction with the negative sign in the numerator. Then add the numerators and place the sum over the common denominator.

HOW TO 1 Add: $-\frac{5}{6} + \frac{3}{4}$

The common denominator is the LCM of 4 and 6. — The LCM of 4 and 6 is 12.

Rewrite the first fraction with the negative sign in the numerator.

$$-\frac{5}{6} + \frac{3}{4} = \frac{-5}{6} + \frac{3}{4}$$

Rewrite each fraction in terms of the common denominator.

$$= \frac{-10}{12} + \frac{9}{12}$$

Add the fractions.

$$= \frac{-10 + 9}{12}$$

Simplify the numerator and write the negative sign in front of the fraction.

$$= \frac{-1}{12} = -\frac{1}{12}$$

Take Note

$\frac{-1}{12} = \frac{1}{-12} = -\frac{1}{12}$

Although the sum could have been left as $\frac{-1}{12}$, all answers in this text are written with the negative sign in front of the fraction.

HOW TO 2 Add: $-\frac{2}{3} + \left(-\frac{4}{5}\right)$

Rewrite each negative fraction with the negative sign in the numerator.

$$-\frac{2}{3} + \left(-\frac{4}{5}\right) = \frac{-2}{3} + \frac{-4}{5}$$

Rewrite each fraction as an equivalent fraction using the LCM as the denominator.

$$= \frac{-10}{15} + \frac{-12}{15}$$

Add the fractions.

$$= \frac{-10 + (-12)}{15}$$

$$= \frac{-22}{15} = -1\frac{7}{15}$$

IN-CLASS EXAMPLES

1. Add: $-\frac{3}{4} + \left(-\frac{1}{6}\right)$ **$-\frac{11}{12}$**
2. Add: $-6.4 + 2.55$ **-3.85**
3. What is $\frac{3}{4}$ more than -2? **$-1\frac{1}{4}$**
4. Evaluate $-x + y$ when $x = -\frac{3}{4}$ and $y = -\frac{5}{8}$. **$\frac{1}{8}$**
5. Subtract: $3.8 - 7.4$ **-3.6**
6. Subtract: $-\frac{5}{12} - \left(-\frac{5}{6}\right)$ **$\frac{5}{12}$**
7. Evaluate $-x - (-y)$ when $x = -\frac{1}{4}$ and $y = -\frac{5}{8}$. **$-\frac{3}{8}$**

HOW TO 3 Is $-\frac{2}{3}$ a solution of the equation $\frac{3}{4} + y = -\frac{1}{12}$?

$$\frac{3}{4} + y = -\frac{1}{12}$$

Replace y by $-\frac{2}{3}$. Then simplify.

$$\frac{3}{4} + \left(-\frac{2}{3}\right) \quad \Big| \quad -\frac{1}{12}$$

The common denominator is 12.

$$\frac{9}{12} + \left(\frac{-8}{12}\right) \quad \Big| \quad -\frac{1}{12}$$

$$\frac{9 + (-8)}{12} \quad \Big| \quad -\frac{1}{12}$$

The results are not equal.

$$\frac{1}{12} \neq -\frac{1}{12}$$

No, $-\frac{2}{3}$ is not a solution of the equation.

To subtract fractions with negative signs, first rewrite the fractions with the negative signs in the numerators.

HOW TO 4 Simplify: $-\frac{2}{9} - \frac{5}{12}$

Rewrite the negative fraction with the negative sign in the numerator.

$$-\frac{2}{9} - \frac{5}{12} = \frac{-2}{9} - \frac{5}{12}$$

Write the fractions as equivalent fractions with a common denominator.

$$= \frac{-8}{36} - \frac{15}{36}$$

Subtract the numerators and place the difference over the common denominator.

$$= \frac{-8 - 15}{36} = \frac{-23}{36}$$

Write the negative sign in front of the fraction.

$$= -\frac{23}{36}$$

HOW TO 5 Subtract: $\frac{2}{3} - \left(-\frac{4}{5}\right)$

Rewrite subtraction as addition of the opposite.

$$\frac{2}{3} - \left(-\frac{4}{5}\right) = \frac{2}{3} + \frac{4}{5}$$

Write the fractions as equivalent fractions with a common denominator.

$$= \frac{10}{15} + \frac{12}{15}$$

Add the fractions.

$$= \frac{10 + 12}{15}$$

$$= \frac{22}{15} = 1\frac{7}{15}$$

The sign rules for adding and subtracting decimals are the same rules used to add and subtract integers.

Take Note

Recall that the absolute value of a number is the distance from zero to the number on the number line. The absolute value of a number is a positive number or zero.

$|54.29| = 54.29$

$|-36.087| = 36.087$

HOW TO 6 Simplify: $-36.087 + 54.29$

The signs of the addends are different. Subtract the smaller absolute value from the larger absolute value.

$54.29 - 36.087 = 18.203$

Attach the sign of the number with the larger absolute value.

$|54.29| > |-36.087|$

The sum is positive.

$$-36.087 + 54.29 = 18.203$$

Recall that the opposite or additive inverse of n is $-n$, and the opposite of $-n$ is n. To find the opposite of a number, change the sign of the number.

HOW TO 7 Simplify: $-2.86 - 10.3$

Rewrite subtraction as addition of the opposite. The opposite of 10.3 is -10.3.

$$-2.86 - 10.3 = -2.86 + (-10.3)$$

The signs of the addends are the same. Add the absolute values of the numbers. Attach the sign of the addends.

$$= -13.16$$

HOW TO 8 Evaluate $c - d$ when $c = 6.731$ and $d = -2.48$.

$$c - d$$

Replace c with 6.731 and d with -2.48.

$$6.731 - (-2.48)$$

Rewrite subtraction as addition of the opposite.

$$= 6.731 + 2.48$$

Add.

$$= 9.211$$

EXAMPLE 1

Add: $-\frac{3}{8} + \frac{3}{4} + \left(-\frac{5}{6}\right)$

Solution

$$-\frac{3}{8} + \frac{3}{4} + \left(-\frac{5}{6}\right) = \frac{-3}{8} + \frac{3}{4} + \frac{-5}{6}$$

$$= \frac{-9}{24} + \frac{18}{24} + \frac{-20}{24}$$

$$= \frac{-9 + 18 + (-20)}{24}$$

$$= \frac{-11}{24} = -\frac{11}{24}$$

YOU TRY IT 1

Add: $-\frac{5}{12} + \frac{5}{8} + \left(-\frac{1}{6}\right)$

Your solution

$\frac{1}{24}$

Solution on p. S11

EXAMPLE 2

Subtract: $-\frac{5}{6} - \left(-\frac{5}{8}\right)$

Solution

$$-\frac{5}{6} - \left(-\frac{5}{8}\right) = -\frac{5}{6} + \frac{5}{8} = \frac{-20}{24} + \frac{15}{24}$$
$$= \frac{-20 + 15}{24}$$
$$= \frac{-5}{24} = -\frac{5}{24}$$

YOU TRY IT 2

Subtract: $-\frac{5}{6} - \frac{4}{9}$

Your solution

$-1\frac{5}{18}$

EXAMPLE 3

Find the sum of −361.27 and −584.9.

Solution

$-361.27 + (-584.9) = -946.17$

YOU TRY IT 3

Find the difference between 5.007 and 8.289.

Your solution

−3.282

EXAMPLE 4

Evaluate $x + y + z$ when $x = -3.7$, $y = 5.8$, and $z = -2.9$.

Solution

$x + y + z$

$$-3.7 + 5.8 + (-2.9) = 2.1 - 2.9$$
$$= -0.8$$

YOU TRY IT 4

Evaluate $x + y + z$ when $x = -6.07$, $y = -4.26$, and $z = 3.84$.

Your solution

−6.49

EXAMPLE 5

Is $\frac{3}{8}$ a solution of the equation $\frac{2}{3} = x - \frac{5}{6}$?

Solution

$$\frac{2}{3} = x - \frac{5}{6}$$

$$\frac{2}{3} \;\Big|\; \frac{3}{8} - \frac{5}{6}$$ • Replace *w* with $\frac{3}{8}$.

$$\frac{2}{3} \;\Big|\; \frac{9}{24} - \frac{20}{24}$$ • Write equivalent fractions with a common denominator.

$$\frac{2}{3} \;\Big|\; \frac{-11}{24}$$ • Subtract the fractions.

$$\frac{2}{3} \neq -\frac{11}{24}$$

No, $\frac{3}{8}$ is not a solution of the equation.

YOU TRY IT 5

Is $-\frac{1}{4}$ a solution of the equation $\frac{2}{3} - y = \frac{11}{12}$?

Your solution

Yes

Solutions on p. S11

OBJECTIVE B *To multiply or divide rational numbers*

The product of two rational numbers in fractional form is the product of the numerators over the product of the denominators. The sign rules for multiplying positive and negative fractions are the same rules used to multiply integers.

The product of two numbers with the same sign is positive.
The product of two numbers with different signs is negative.

HOW TO 9 Multiply: $-\frac{3}{4} \cdot \frac{8}{15}$

The signs are different. The product is negative. $-\frac{3}{4} \cdot \frac{8}{15} = -\left(\frac{3}{4} \cdot \frac{8}{15}\right)$

Multiply the numerators. Multiply the denominators. $= -\frac{3 \cdot 8}{4 \cdot 15}$

Write the product in simplest form. $= -\frac{3 \cdot 2 \cdot 2 \cdot 2}{2 \cdot 2 \cdot 3 \cdot 5}$

$= -\frac{2}{5}$

HOW TO 10 Multiply: $-\frac{3}{8}\left(-\frac{2}{5}\right)\left(-\frac{10}{21}\right)$

$-\frac{3}{8}\left(-\frac{2}{5}\right)\left(-\frac{10}{21}\right)$

Multiply the first two fractions. The product is positive. $= \left(\frac{3}{8} \cdot \frac{2}{5}\right)\left(-\frac{10}{21}\right)$

The product of the first two fractions and the third fraction is negative. $= -\left(\frac{3}{8} \cdot \frac{2}{5} \cdot \frac{10}{21}\right)$

Multiply the numerators. Multiply the denominators. $= -\frac{3 \cdot 2 \cdot 10}{8 \cdot 5 \cdot 21}$

Write the product in simplest form. $= -\frac{3 \cdot 2 \cdot 2 \cdot 5}{2 \cdot 2 \cdot 2 \cdot 5 \cdot 3 \cdot 7}$

$= -\frac{1}{14}$

Thus, the product of three negative fractions is negative. We can modify the rule for multiplying positive and negative fractions to say that the product of an odd number of negative fractions is negative, and the product of an even number of negative fractions is positive.

The sign rules for dividing positive and negative fractions are the same rules used to divide integers.

The quotient of two numbers with the same sign is positive.
The quotient of two numbers with different signs is negative.

IN-CLASS EXAMPLES

8. Multiply: $-\frac{5}{6}\left(\frac{3}{10}\right)$ $-\frac{1}{4}$
9. Multiply: $-6.8(-2.1)$ **14.28**
10. Evaluate $-xy$ when $x = -2$ and $y = -\frac{5}{12}$. $-\frac{5}{6}$
11. Divide: $-\frac{3}{4} \div \left(-\frac{9}{16}\right)$ $1\frac{1}{3}$
12. Divide and round to the nearest tenth: $-13.97 \div 28.4$ **−0.5**
13. Evaluate $a \div (-b)$ when $a = -8.4$ and $b = -0.4$. **−21**

HOW TO 11 Simplify: $-\frac{7}{10} \div \left(-\frac{14}{15}\right)$

The signs are the same. The quotient is positive. $-\frac{7}{10} \div \left(-\frac{14}{15}\right) = \frac{7}{10} \div \frac{14}{15}$

Rewrite the division as multiplication by the reciprocal. $= \frac{7}{10} \cdot \frac{15}{14}$

Multiply the fractions. $= \frac{7 \cdot 15}{10 \cdot 14}$

$= \frac{7 \cdot 3 \cdot 5}{2 \cdot 5 \cdot 2 \cdot 7} = \frac{3}{4}$

The sign rules for multiplying decimals are the same rules used to multiply integers.

The product of two numbers with the same sign is positive.
The product of two numbers with different signs is negative.

HOW TO 12 Multiply: $(-3.2)(-0.008)$

The signs are the same. The product is positive.
Multiply the absolute values of the numbers. $(-3.2)(-0.008) = 0.0256$

HOW TO 13 Is -0.6 a solution of the equation $5.2a = -3.12$?

$$5.2a = -3.12$$

Replace a by -0.6 and then simplify. $5.2(-0.6) \mid -3.12$
The results are equal. $-3.12 = -3.12$

Yes, -0.6 is a solution of the equation.

The sign rules for dividing decimals are the same rules used to divide integers.

The quotient of two numbers with the same sign is positive.
The quotient of two numbers with different signs is negative.

HOW TO 14 Divide: $-1.16 \div 2.9$

The signs are different. The quotient is negative.
Divide the absolute values of the numbers. $-1.16 \div 2.9 = -0.4$

HOW TO 15 Evaluate $c \div d$ for $c = -8.64$ and $d = -0.4$.

$c \div d$

Replace c with -8.64 and d with -0.4. $(-8.64) \div (-0.4)$

The signs are the same. The quotient is positive.
Divide the absolute values of the numbers. $= 21.6$

EXAMPLE 6

Multiply: $-\frac{3}{4}\left(\frac{1}{2}\right)\left(-\frac{8}{9}\right)$

Solution $-\frac{3}{4}\left(\frac{1}{2}\right)\left(-\frac{8}{9}\right)$

$= \frac{3}{4} \cdot \frac{1}{2} \cdot \frac{8}{9}$ • The product of two negative fractions is positive.

$= \frac{3 \cdot 1 \cdot 8}{4 \cdot 2 \cdot 9}$

$= \frac{3 \cdot 1 \cdot 2 \cdot 2 \cdot 2}{2 \cdot 2 \cdot 2 \cdot 3 \cdot 3} = \frac{1}{3}$

YOU TRY IT 6

Multiply: $-\frac{1}{3}\left(-\frac{5}{12}\right)\left(\frac{8}{15}\right)$

Your solution

$\frac{2}{27}$

EXAMPLE 7

What is the product of $-\frac{1}{2}$ and $\frac{2}{5}$?

Solution $-\frac{1}{2} \cdot \frac{2}{5} = -\left(\frac{1}{2} \cdot \frac{2}{5}\right)$

$= -\frac{1 \cdot 2}{2 \cdot 5}$

$= -\frac{1}{5}$

YOU TRY IT 7

Multiply $3\frac{6}{7}$ by $-\frac{4}{9}$.

Your solution

$-1\frac{5}{7}$

EXAMPLE 8

What is the quotient of 9 and $-\frac{3}{5}$?

Solution $9 \div \left(-\frac{3}{5}\right) = -\left(\frac{9}{1} \div \frac{3}{5}\right)$

$= -\left(\frac{9}{1} \cdot \frac{5}{3}\right)$

$= -\frac{9 \cdot 5}{1 \cdot 3}$

$= -\frac{3 \cdot 3 \cdot 5}{1 \cdot 3}$

$= -\frac{15}{1} = -15$

YOU TRY IT 8

Find the quotient of 8 and $-\frac{6}{7}$.

Your solution

$-9\frac{1}{3}$

Solutions on p. S11

EXAMPLE 9

Multiply: $-3.42(6.1)$

Solution $-3.42(6.1) = -20.862$

YOU TRY IT 9

Multiply: $(-0.7)(-5.8)$

Your solution 4.06

EXAMPLE 10

Divide and round to the nearest tenth: $-6.94 \div (-1.5)$

Solution The quotient is positive.

$-6.94 \div (-1.5) \approx 4.6$

YOU TRY IT 10

Divide and round to the nearest tenth: $-25.7 \div 0.31$

Your solution

-82.9

EXAMPLE 11

Evaluate the variable expression xy for $x = 1\frac{4}{5}$ and $y = -\frac{5}{6}$.

Solution xy

$$1\frac{4}{5}\left(-\frac{5}{6}\right) = -\left(\frac{9}{5}\cdot\frac{5}{6}\right)$$
$$= -\frac{9\cdot 5}{5\cdot 6}$$
$$= -\frac{3\cdot 3\cdot 5}{5\cdot 2\cdot 3}$$
$$= -\frac{3}{2} = -1\frac{1}{2}$$

YOU TRY IT 11

Evaluate the variable expression xy for $x = 5\frac{1}{8}$ and $y = \frac{2}{3}$.

Your solution

$3\frac{5}{12}$

EXAMPLE 12

Evaluate $\frac{x}{y}$ for $x = -60.8$ and $y = 0.8$.

Solution $\frac{x}{y}$

$$\frac{-60.8}{0.8} = -76$$

YOU TRY IT 12

Evaluate $\frac{x}{y}$ for $x = -33.6$ and $y = -0.7$.

Your solution

48

Solutions on p. S11

EXAMPLE 13

Evaluate $40ab$ for $a = -0.5$ and $b = -0.7$.

Solution $40ab$

$$40(-0.5)(-0.7) = -20(-0.7) = 14$$

YOU TRY IT 13

Evaluate $25xy$ for $x = -0.6$ and $y = 0.6$.

Your solution

−9

EXAMPLE 14

Is -0.4 a solution of the equation $\frac{4}{x} = -10$?

Solution

$$\frac{4}{x} = -10$$

$$\frac{4}{-0.4} \;\Big|\; -10$$

• **Replace x by -0.4.**

$$-10 = -10$$

Yes, -0.4 is a solution of the equation.

YOU TRY IT 14

Is -1.2 a solution of the equation $-2 = \frac{y}{-0.6}$?

Your solution

No

Solutions on pp. S11–S12

OBJECTIVE C To solve application problems

EXAMPLE 15

In Fairbanks, Alaska, the average temperature during the month of July is 61.5°F. During the month of January, the average temperature in Fairbanks is −12.7°F. What is the difference between the average temperature in Fairbanks during July and the average temperature during January?

Strategy

To find the difference, subtract the average temperature in January (−12.7°F) from the average temperature in July (61.5°F).

Solution

$$61.5 - (-12.7) = 61.5 + 12.7 = 74.2$$

The difference between the average temperature during July and the average temperature during January in Fairbanks is 74.2°F.

YOU TRY IT 15

On January 10, 1911, in Rapid City, South Dakota, the temperature fell from 12.78°C at 7:00 A.M. to −13.33°C at 7:15 A.M. How many degrees did the temperature fall during the 15-minute period?

Your strategy

Your solution

26.11°C

IN-CLASS EXAMPLES

14. The lowest temperature ever recorded in Australia is −9.4°F. The highest temperature ever recorded is 123.3°F. (*Source:* www.bom.gov.au) Find the difference between these two extremes. **132.7°F**

Solution on p. S12

3.4 EXERCISES

Concept Check

SUGGESTED ASSIGNMENT
Exercises 1 and 2; Exercises 3–131, every other odd; Exercises 133–137, odds

For Exercises 1 and 2, determine which of the numbers are **a.** integers, **b.** rational numbers, **c.** irrational numbers, and **d.** real numbers. List all that apply.

1. $-\frac{15}{2}, 0, -3, \pi, 2.\overline{33}, 4.232232223\ldots, \frac{\sqrt{5}}{4}, \sqrt{7}$
a. 0, −3 **b.** $-\frac{15}{2}, 0, -3, 2.\overline{33}$ **c.** $\pi, 4.232232223\ldots, \frac{\sqrt{5}}{4}, \sqrt{7}$ **d.** all

2. $-17, 0.3412, \frac{3}{\pi}, -1.010010001\ldots, \frac{27}{91}, 6.1\overline{2}$
a. −17 **b.** $-17, 0.3412, \frac{27}{91}, 6.1\overline{2}$ **c.** $\frac{3}{\pi}, -1.010010001\ldots$ **d.** all

OBJECTIVE A *To add or subtract rational numbers*

For Exercises 3 to 41, simplify.

3. $\frac{5}{8} - \frac{5}{6}$
$-\frac{5}{24}$

4. $\frac{1}{9} - \frac{5}{27}$
$-\frac{2}{27}$

5. $-\frac{5}{12} - \frac{3}{8}$
$-\frac{19}{24}$

6. $-\frac{5}{6} - \frac{5}{9}$
$-\frac{25}{18}$

7. $-\frac{6}{13} + \frac{17}{26}$
$\frac{5}{26}$

8. $-\frac{7}{12} + \frac{5}{8}$
$\frac{1}{24}$

9. $-\frac{5}{8} - \left(-\frac{11}{12}\right)$
$\frac{7}{24}$

10. $-\frac{7}{12} - \left(-\frac{7}{8}\right)$
$\frac{7}{24}$

11. $\frac{5}{12} - \frac{11}{15}$
$-\frac{19}{60}$

12. $\frac{2}{5} - \frac{14}{15}$
$-\frac{8}{15}$

13. $-\frac{3}{4} - \frac{5}{8}$
$-\frac{11}{8}$

14. $-\frac{2}{3} - \frac{5}{8}$
$-\frac{31}{24}$

15. $-\frac{5}{2} - \left(-\frac{13}{4}\right)$
$\frac{3}{4}$

16. $-\frac{7}{3} - \left(-\frac{3}{2}\right)$
$-\frac{5}{6}$

17. $-\frac{3}{8} - \frac{5}{12} - \frac{3}{16}$
$-\frac{47}{48}$

18. $-\frac{5}{16} + \frac{3}{4} - \frac{7}{8}$
$-\frac{7}{16}$

19. $\frac{1}{2} - \frac{3}{8} - \left(-\frac{1}{4}\right)$
$\frac{3}{8}$

20. $\frac{3}{4} - \left(-\frac{7}{12}\right) - \frac{7}{8}$
$\frac{11}{24}$

21. $\frac{1}{3} - \frac{1}{4} - \frac{1}{5}$
$-\frac{7}{60}$

22. $\frac{5}{16} + \frac{1}{8} - \frac{1}{2}$
$-\frac{1}{16}$

23. $\frac{1}{2} + \left(-\frac{3}{8}\right) + \frac{5}{12}$
$\frac{13}{24}$

24. $-\frac{3}{8} + \frac{3}{4} - \left(-\frac{3}{16}\right)$
$\frac{9}{16}$

25. $3.4 + (-6.8)$
−3.4

26. $-4.9 + 3.27$
−1.63

27. $-8.32 + (-0.57)$
−8.89

28. $-3.5 + 7$
3.5

29. $-4.8 + (-3.2)$
−8.0

30. $6.2 + (-4.29)$

1.91

31. $-4.6 + 3.92$

-0.68

32. $7.2 + (-8.42)$

-1.22

33. $-4.2 - 6.83$

-11.03

34. $-5.48 - (-7.1)$

1.62

35. $18.4 - 25.2$

-6.8

36. $11 - 25.45$

-14.45

37. $-4.5 + 3.2 + (-19.4)$

-20.7

38. $2.09 - 6.72 - 5.4$

-10.03

39. $-18.39 + 4.9 - 23.7$

-37.19

40. $19 - (-3.72) - 82.75$

-60.03

41. $-3.09 - 4.6 - 27.3$

-34.99

42. What is $-\frac{5}{6}$ added to $\frac{4}{9}$?

$-\frac{7}{18}$

43. What is $\frac{7}{12}$ added to $-\frac{11}{16}$?

$-\frac{5}{48}$

44. What is $-\frac{2}{3}$ more than $-\frac{5}{6}$?

$-1\frac{1}{2}$

45. What is $-\frac{7}{12}$ more than $-\frac{5}{9}$?

$-1\frac{5}{36}$

46. What is $-\frac{7}{12}$ minus $\frac{7}{9}$?

$-1\frac{13}{36}$

47. What is $\frac{3}{5}$ decreased by $-\frac{7}{10}$?

$1\frac{3}{10}$

48. What is the sum of -65.47 and -32.91?

-98.38

49. Find -138.72 minus 510.64.

-649.36

For Exercises 50 to 56, evaluate the expression $x + y$ for the given values of x and y.

50. $x = -\frac{3}{8}, y = \frac{2}{9}$

$-\frac{11}{72}$

51. $x = \frac{3}{10}, y = -\frac{7}{15}$

$-\frac{1}{6}$

52. $x = -\frac{5}{8}, y = -\frac{1}{6}$

$-\frac{19}{24}$

53. $x = -\frac{3}{8}, y = -\frac{5}{6}$

$-1\frac{5}{24}$

54. $x = 62.97, y = -43.85$

19.12

55. $x = -6.175, y = -19.49$

-25.665

56. $x = -28.07, y = 17.58$

-10.49

For Exercises 57 to 63, evaluate the expression $x - y$ for the given values of x and y.

57. $x = -\frac{11}{12}, y = \frac{5}{12}$

$-1\frac{1}{3}$

58. $x = -\frac{15}{16}, y = \frac{5}{16}$

$-1\frac{1}{4}$

59. $x = -\frac{2}{3}, y = -\frac{3}{4}$

$\frac{1}{12}$

60. $x = -\frac{5}{12}, y = -\frac{5}{9}$

$\frac{5}{36}$

61. $x = -21.073, y = 6.48$

-27.553

62. $x = -3.69, y = -1.527$

-2.163

63. $x = -8.21, y = -6.798$

-1.412

64. Is $-\frac{5}{6}$ a solution of the equation $\frac{1}{4} + x = -\frac{7}{12}$?

Yes

65. Is $\frac{5}{8}$ a solution of the equation $-\frac{1}{4} = x - \frac{7}{8}$?

Yes

66. Is -1.2 a solution of the equation $6.4 = 5.2 + a$?

No

67. Is -2.8 a solution of the equation $0.8 - p = 3.6$?

Yes

For Exercises 68 and 69, state whether the given sum or difference will be positive or negative.

68. A negative integer subtracted from a negative proper fraction

Positive

69. A positive integer subtracted from a positive proper fraction

Negative

OBJECTIVE B *To multiply or divide rational numbers*

For Exercises 70 to 102, perform the indicated operation.

70. $\frac{1}{2}\left(-\frac{3}{4}\right)$

$-\frac{3}{8}$

71. $-\frac{2}{9}\left(-\frac{3}{14}\right)$

$\frac{1}{21}$

72. $\left(-\frac{3}{8}\right)\left(-\frac{4}{15}\right)$

$\frac{1}{10}$

73. $\left(-\frac{3}{4}\right)\left(-\frac{8}{27}\right)$

$\frac{2}{9}$

74. $-\frac{1}{2}\left(\frac{8}{9}\right)$

$-\frac{4}{9}$

75. $\frac{5}{12}\left(-\frac{8}{15}\right)$

$-\frac{2}{9}$

76. $\left(-\frac{5}{12}\right)\left(\frac{42}{65}\right)$

$-\frac{7}{26}$

77. $\left(\frac{3}{8}\right)\left(-\frac{15}{41}\right)$

$-\frac{45}{328}$

78. $\left(-\frac{15}{8}\right)\left(-\frac{16}{3}\right)$

10

79. $\left(-\frac{5}{7}\right)\left(-\frac{14}{15}\right)$

$\frac{2}{3}$

80. $\frac{5}{8}\left(-\frac{7}{12}\right)\left(\frac{16}{25}\right)$

$-\frac{7}{30}$

81. $\left(\frac{1}{2}\right)\left(-\frac{3}{4}\right)\left(-\frac{5}{8}\right)$

$\frac{15}{64}$

82. $\frac{1}{3} \div \left(-\frac{1}{2}\right)$

$-\frac{2}{3}$

83. $-\frac{3}{8} \div \frac{7}{8}$

$-\frac{3}{7}$

84. $\left(-\frac{3}{4}\right) \div \left(-\frac{7}{40}\right)$

$\frac{30}{7}$

85. $\frac{5}{6} \div \left(-\frac{3}{4}\right)$

$-\frac{10}{9}$

86. $-\frac{5}{12} \div \frac{15}{32}$

$-\frac{8}{9}$

87. $-\frac{5}{16} \div \left(-\frac{3}{8}\right)$

$\frac{5}{6}$

88. $\left(-\frac{3}{8}\right) \div \left(-\frac{5}{12}\right)$

$\frac{9}{10}$

89. $\left(-\frac{8}{19}\right) \div \frac{7}{38}$

$-\frac{16}{7}$

90. $\left(-\frac{2}{3}\right) \div 4$

$-\frac{1}{6}$

91. $-6 \div \frac{4}{9}$

$-\frac{27}{2}$

92. $-6.7(-4.2)$

28.14

93. $-8.9(-3.5)$

31.15

94. $-1.6(4.9)$
-7.84

95. $-14.3(7.9)$
-112.97

96. $(-0.78)(-0.15)$
0.117

97. $(-1.21)(-0.03)$
0.0363

98. $(-8.919) \div (-0.9)$
9.91

99. $-77.6 \div (-0.8)$
97

100. $59.01 \div (-0.7)$
-84.3

101. $(-7.04) \div (-3.2)$
2.2

102. $(-84.66) \div 1.7$
-49.8

103. Find $-\frac{9}{16}$ multiplied by $\frac{4}{27}$.

$-\frac{1}{12}$

104. Find $\frac{3}{7}$ multiplied by $-\frac{14}{15}$.

$-\frac{2}{5}$

105. What is the product of $-\frac{7}{24}$, $\frac{8}{21}$, and $\frac{3}{7}$?

$-\frac{1}{21}$

106. What is the product of $-\frac{5}{13}$, $-\frac{26}{75}$, and $\frac{5}{8}$?

$\frac{1}{12}$

107. What is $-\frac{15}{24}$ divided by $\frac{3}{5}$?

$-1\frac{1}{24}$

108. What is $\frac{5}{6}$ divided by $-\frac{10}{21}$?

$-1\frac{3}{4}$

109. Find the product of 2.7, -16, and 3.04.
-131.328

110. What is the product of 0.06, -0.4, and -1.5?
0.036

111. Find the quotient of -19.04 and 0.75. Round to the nearest tenth.
-25.4

112. What is -13.97 divided by 28.4? Round to the nearest tenth.
-0.5

For Exercises 113 to 116, evaluate the expression xy for the given values of x and y.

113. $x = -49, y = \frac{5}{14}$
$-17\frac{1}{2}$

114. $x = -\frac{3}{10}, y = -35$
$10\frac{1}{2}$

115. $x = 1\frac{3}{13}, y = -6\frac{1}{2}$
-8

116. $x = -3\frac{1}{2}, y = -2\frac{1}{7}$
7.5

For Exercises 117 and 118, evaluate the expression for the given values of the variables.

117. $10t$, when $t = -4.8$
-48

118. ab, when $a = 452$ and $b = -0.86$
-388.72

For Exercises 119 to 125, evaluate the expression $x \div y$ for the given values of x and y.

119. $x = 6\frac{2}{5}, y = -4$
$-1\frac{3}{5}$

120. $x = -5\frac{2}{5}, y = -9$
$\frac{3}{5}$

121. $x = -2\frac{5}{8}, y = 1\frac{3}{4}$
$-1\frac{1}{2}$

122. $x = -3\frac{2}{5}, y = -1\frac{7}{10}$
2

123. $x = -64.05, y = -6.1$
10.5

124. $x = -2.501, y = 0.41$
-6.1

125. $x = 1.173, y = -0.69$
-1.7

126. Is $-\frac{1}{6}$ a solution of the equation $6x = 1$?
No

127. Is $-\frac{4}{5}$ a solution of the equation $\frac{5}{4}n = -1$?
Yes

128. Is -8 a solution of the equation $1.6 = -0.2z$?
Yes

129. Is -1 a solution of the equation $-7.9c = -7.9$?
No

For Exercises 130 and 131, use the following information: When -3.54 is divided into a certain dividend, the result is a positive number less than 1. Determine whether each statement is true or false.

130. The absolute value of the dividend is greater than 3.54. False

131. The dividend is a positive number.
False

OBJECTIVE C *To solve application problems*

132. **Meteorology** On January 23, 1916, the temperature in Browing, Montana, was 6.67°C. On January 24, 1916, the temperature in Browing was −48.9°C. Find the difference between the temperatures in Browing on these two days.
55.57°C

133. **Meteorology** On January 22, 1943, in Spearfish, South Dakota, the temperature fell from 12.22°C at 9 A.M. to −20°C at 9:27 A.M. How many degrees did the temperature fall during the 27-minute period?
32.22°C

134. **Temperature** Use the information in the news clipping at the right. Find the difference between the record high and low temperatures for Slovakia.
146.3°F

In the NEWS!

Slovakia Hits Record High

Slovakia, which became an independent country in 1993 with the peaceful division of Czechoslovakia, hit a record high temperature today of 104.5°F. The record low temperature, set on February 11, 1929, was −41.8°F.

Source: wikipedia.org

135. If the temperature begins at 4.8°C and ends up below 0°C, is the difference between the starting and ending temperatures less than or greater than 4.8?
Greater than

136. If the temperature rose 20.3°F during one day and ended up at a high temperature of 15.7°F, did the temperature begin above or below 0°F?
Below

137. **Chemistry** The boiling point of nitrogen is −195.8°C, and the melting point is −209.86°C. Find the difference between the boiling point and the melting point of nitrogen.
14.06°C

138. **Chemistry** The boiling point of oxygen is −182.962°C. Oxygen's melting point is −218.4°C. What is the difference between the boiling point and the melting point of oxygen?
35.438°C

Critical Thinking

139. Determine whether the statement is true or false.
- **a.** Every integer is a rational number. True
- **b.** Every whole number is an integer. True
- **c.** Every integer is a positive number. False
- **d.** Every rational number is an integer. False

Place the correct symbol, < or >, between the numbers.

140. $-\frac{7}{12} > -\frac{11}{18}$ **141.** $-\frac{7}{8} < -\frac{5}{6}$ **142.** $-0.75 < -\frac{13}{18}$ **143.** $-\frac{3}{4} < -0.7$

Projects or Group Activities

144. Given any two different rational numbers, is it always possible to find a rational number between them? If so, explain how. If not, give an example of two different rational numbers for which there is no rational number between them.

QUICK QUIZ

Perform the indicated operation.

1. $-\frac{3}{8} - \frac{1}{2}$
   $-\frac{7}{8}$ **[3.4A]**
2. $5.63 - (-2.1)$
   7.73 [3.4A]
3. $-\frac{5}{6} - \left(-\frac{2}{9}\right)$
   $-\frac{11}{18}$ **[3.4A]**
4. $-\frac{7}{12}\left(-\frac{4}{9}\right)$
   $\frac{7}{27}$ **[3.4B]**
5. $-9.3(12.7)$
   −118.11 [3.4B]
6. $15.33 \div (-7)$
   −2.19 [3.4B]
7. The lowest temperature ever recorded in North America is −81.4°F. The highest temperature ever recorded is 134.0°F. (*Source:* National Climatic Data Center) Find the difference between these two extremes.
   215.4°F [3.4C]

SECTION

3.5 The Order of Operations Agreement

OBJECTIVE A *To use the Order of Operations Agreement to simplify expressions*

The Order of Operations Agreement, used in Chapters 1 and 2, is repeated here for your reference.

The Order of Operations Agreement

Step 1 Do all operations inside parentheses.

Step 2 Simplify any numerical expressions containing exponents.

Step 3 Do multiplication and division as they occur from left to right.

Step 4 Do addition and subtraction as they occur from left to right.

Take Note

The -3 is squared only when the negative sign is *inside* the parentheses. In $(-3)^2$, we are squaring -3; in -3^2, we are finding the opposite of 3^2.

Note how the following expressions containing exponents are simplified.

$(-3)^2 = (-3)(-3) = 9$ The (-3) is squared. Multiply -3 by -3.

$-(3)^2 = -(3 \cdot 3) = -9$ Read $-(3^2)$ as "the opposite of three squared." 3^2 is 9. The opposite of 9 is -9.

$-3^2 = -(3^2) = -9$ The expression -3^2 is the same as $-(3^2)$.

Integrating Technology

As shown above, the value of -3^2 is different from the value of $(-3)^2$. The keystrokes to evaluate each of these expressions on your calculator are different.

To evaluate -3^2, enter

3 [x^2] [+/−]

To evaluate $(-3)^2$, enter

3 [+/−] [x^2]

HOW TO 1 Simplify: $(-3)^2 - 2(8 - 3) + (-5)$

$(-3)^2 - 2(8 - 3) + (-5)$

Perform operations inside parentheses. $= (-3)^2 - 2(5) + (-5)$

Simplify expressions with exponents. $= 9 - 2(5) + (-5)$

Do multiplication and division as they occur from left to right. $= 9 - 10 + (-5)$

Do addition and subtraction as they occur from left to right.
$= 9 + (-10) + (-5)$
$= -1 + (-5)$
$= -6$

HOW TO 2 Evaluate $ab - b^2$ for $a = \frac{1}{2}$ and $b = -\frac{2}{3}$.

$ab - b^2$

Replace a with $\frac{1}{2}$ and each b with $-\frac{2}{3}$. $\frac{1}{2}\left(-\frac{2}{3}\right) - \left(-\frac{2}{3}\right)^2$

Use the Order of Operations Agreement. Simplify the exponential expression. $= \frac{1}{2}\left(-\frac{2}{3}\right) - \frac{4}{9}$

Do the multiplication. $= -\frac{1}{3} - \frac{4}{9}$

Do the subtraction. $= \frac{-3 - 4}{9} = -\frac{7}{9}$

IN-CLASS EXAMPLES

1. Simplify $(-6)^2$ and -6^2.
   36; −36
2. Simplify:
   $12 \div 4 - (-2)^2$
   −1
3. Simplify:
   $10 - |1 - 5|(-2)^3$
   42
4. Evaluate $4b \div (-ac)$ for $a = -2$, $b = 4$, and $c = -1$.
   −8

Absolute value symbols act like parentheses. Simplify expressions inside absolute value symbols as part of Step 1 of the Order of Operations Agreement.

HOW TO 3 Simplify: $6 - 3^2|5 - 7|$

$6 - 3^2|5 - 7|$

Perform operations inside absolute value symbols. $= 6 - 3^2|-2|$

$= 6 - 3^2(2)$

Simplify the exponential expression. $= 6 - 9(2)$

Do the multiplication. $= 6 - 18$

Do the subtraction. $= -12$

EXAMPLE 1

Simplify: $12 \div (-2)^2 - 5$

Solution $12 \div (-2)^2 - 5$

$= 12 \div 4 - 5$ • Step 2

$= 3 - 5$ • Step 3

$= 3 + (-5) = -2$ • Step 4

YOU TRY IT 1

Simplify: $8 \div 4 \cdot 4 - (-2)^2$

Your solution

4

EXAMPLE 2

Simplify: $(-3)^2(5 - 7)^2 - (-9) \div 3$

Solution $(-3)^2(5 - 7)^2 - (-9) \div 3$

$= (-3)^2(-2)^2 - (-9) \div 3$ • Step 1

$= (9)(4) - (-9) \div 3$ • Step 2

$= 36 - (-9) \div 3$ • Step 3

$= 36 - (-3)$

$= 36 + 3 = 39$ • Step 4

YOU TRY IT 2

Simplify: $(-2)^2(3 - 7)^2 - (-16) \div (-4)$

Your solution

60

EXAMPLE 3

Evaluate $6a + (-b)$ for $a = -2.1$ and $b = -3.2$.

Solution $6a + (-b)$

$6(-2.1) + (-(-3.2))$

$= 6(-2.1) + 3.2$

$= -12.6 + 3.2 = -9.4$

YOU TRY IT 3

Evaluate $3a - 4b$ for $a = -1.7$ and $b = 4.5$.

Your solution

−23.1

EXAMPLE 4

Simplify: $|4 - 5| + 3|-2|$

Solution $|4 - 5| + 3|-2|$

$= |-1| + 3|-2|$

$= 1 + 3(2)$

$= 1 + 6 = 7$

YOU TRY IT 4

Simplify: $(-6)(2) + |-1 - 7|$

Your solution

−4

Solutions on p. S12

3.5 EXERCISES

Concept Check

SUGGESTED ASSIGNMENT
Exercises 1 and 2; Exercises 3–51, odds; More challenging exercise: Exercise 60

1. To simplify the expression $6 - 4 \div (-2)$, the first operation that must be performed is __division__.

2. Simplify: $(-7)^2 - 5(2 - 3)$

$(-7)^2 - 5(2 - 3)$

a. Perform operations in parentheses. $= (-7)^2 - 5(\underline{-1})$

b. Simplify expressions with exponents. $= \underline{49} - 5(-1)$

c. Multiply. $= 49 - \underline{-5}$

d. Rewrite subtraction as addition of the opposite. $= 49 + \underline{5}$

e. Add. $= \underline{54}$

OBJECTIVE A *To use the Order of Operations Agreement to simplify expressions*

Simplify.

3. $2(3 - 5) - 2$
-6

4. $2 - (8 - 10) \div 2$
3

5. $4 - (-3)^2$
-5

6. $-2^2 - 6$
-10

7. $3 \cdot (6 - 2) \div 6$
2

8. $4 \cdot (2 - 7) \div 5$
-4

9. $2^3 - (-3)^2 + 2$
1

10. $6(8 - 2) \div 4$
9

11. $6 - 2(1 - 5)$
14

12. $4 - (-5)(-2)^2$
24

13. $16 \div 2 - 9 \div 3$
5

14. $-2^2 - 5(3) - 1$
-20

15. $(-1) \cdot (4 - 7)^2 \div 9 + 6 - 3 - 4(2)$
-6

16. $(-3)^2 \cdot (5 - 7)^2 - (-9) \div 3$
39

17. $(1.2)^2 - 4.1(0.3)$
0.21

18. $4.1(8) \div (-4.1)$
-8

19. $(4.1 - 3.9) - 0.7^2$
-0.29

20. $1.8(-2.3) - 2$
-6.14

21. $-\frac{1}{2} + \frac{3}{8} \div \left(-\frac{3}{4}\right)$
-1

22. $-\frac{2}{3}\left(\frac{5}{8}\right) \div \frac{2}{7}$
$-1\frac{11}{24}$

23. $\frac{1}{2} - \left(\frac{3}{4} - \frac{3}{8}\right) \div \frac{1}{3}$
$-\frac{5}{8}$

24. $\frac{3}{8} \div \left(-\frac{1}{2}\right)^2 + 2$
$3\frac{1}{2}$

25. $5 - |2 - 8|$
-1

26. $|6 + 3(-4)|$
6

27. $-|-7| + 9^2$
74

28. $|8| - |-2 - 5|$
1

29. $2|2 - 6| + 4$
12

30. $|24 \div (-2)^3| - 10$
-7

31. $||-7| - |-3||$
4

32. $5 - 2|(-3)^2 - 8|$
3

33. $|3.4(-2)| - 9.8$
-3

34. $(-3.2) \div |39.4 - 42.6|$
-1

35. $|0.9 - (1.5)^2|$
1.35

36. $8.5 + |2.5(-3)| - |-(4^2)|$
0

37. $\left| \left| -\frac{4}{9} \right| - \left| -\frac{5}{9} \right| \right|$
$\frac{1}{9}$

38. $2\left| -\frac{1}{2} + \frac{5}{8} \right| \div \left(-\frac{1}{5} \right)$
$-\frac{5}{4}$

39. $\left(-\frac{1}{4} \right)^2 + \left| \frac{3}{8}\left(-\frac{5}{6} \right) \right|$
$\frac{3}{8}$

40. $\left| \frac{-6 + 2}{20} \right| + \frac{3}{5} \div 6$
$\frac{3}{10}$

Evaluate the variable expression for $a = -2$, $b = 4$, $c = -1$, and $d = 3$.

41. $3a + 2b$
2

42. $6b \div (-a)$
12

43. $bc \div (2a)$
1

44. $a^2 - b^2$
-12

45. $b^2 - c^2$
15

46. $2a - (c + a)^2$
-13

47. $(b - a)^2 + 4c$
32

48. $\frac{b + c}{d}$
1

49. $\frac{d - b}{c}$
1

50. $(d - a)^2 \div 5$
5

51. $(d - a)^2 - 3c$
28

52. $(b + d)^2 - 4a$
57

Evaluate the variable expression for $a = -2$, $b = 3$, $c = -1$, and $d = 4$.

53. $\left| \frac{a - b}{c - d} \right|$
1

54. $|2a| - |c + a|^2$
-5

55. $|a + d|^2 + |c - b|^2$
20

56. $\left| \frac{bc}{d - a} \right| \div \frac{c}{a}$
1

Complete Exercises 57 and 58 without actually finding the product.

57. Is the fifth power of -18 positive or negative?
Negative

58. Is the product $-(3^2)(-5^3)$ positive or negative?
Positive

Critical Thinking

59. What is the smallest integer greater than $-2^2 - (-3)^2 + 5(4) \div 10 - (-6)$?
-4

60. Evaluate $a \div bc$ and $a \div (bc)$ for $a = 16$, $b = 2$, and $c = -4$. Explain why the answers are not the same.

61. **a.** Is -4 a solution of the equation $x^2 - 2x - 8 = 0$? No
b. Is -3 a solution of the equation $x^3 + 3x^2 - 5x - 15 = 0$? Yes

QUICK QUIZ

1. Simplify: $(-4)^2 - 8 + 9(-3)$
-19 [3.5A]
2. Simplify: $24 - (3)(-5) - (6 - 8)^2$
35 [3.5A]
3. Evaluate $(x - y)^2 + 5z$ for $x = 3$, $y = -2$, and $z = -1$.
20 [3.5A]
4. Simplify: $8 - 3|2 - 4|$
2 [3.5A]

Projects or Group Activities

For Exercises 62 to 64, insert one set of parentheses in the expression $6 - 12 \div 2 \cdot 3 - 5^2$ to make the equation true.

62. $6 - 12 \div 2 \cdot 3 - 5^2 = -34$
$(6 - 12) \div 2 \cdot 3 - 5^2$

63. $6 - 12 \div 2 \cdot 3 - 5^2 = -18$
$6 - 12 \div 2 \cdot (3 - 5)^2$

64. $6 - 12 \div 2 \cdot 3 - 5^2 = -21$
$6 - 12 \div (2 \cdot 3) - 5^2$

CHAPTER 3 Summary

Key Words

Key Words	Examples
Numbers greater than zero are called **positive numbers**. Numbers less than zero are called **negative numbers**. [3.1A, p. 180]	9, 87, and 603 are positive numbers. −5, −41, and −729 are negative numbers.
The **integers** are . . . , −4, −3, −2, −1, 0, 1, 2, 3, 4, ... The integers can be defined as the whole numbers and their opposites. **Positive integers** are to the right of zero on the number line. **Negative integers** are to the left of zero on the number line. [3.1A, p. 180]	−729, −41, −5, 9, 87, and 603 are integers. 0 is an integer, but it is neither a positive nor a negative integer.
Opposite numbers are two numbers that are the same distance from zero on the number line but on opposite sides of zero. The opposite of a number is called its **additive inverse.** [3.1B, p. 182; 3.2A, p. 194]	8 is the opposite, or additive inverse, of −8. −2 is the opposite, or additive inverse, of 2.
The **absolute value** of a number is the distance from zero to the number on the number line. The absolute value of a number is a positive number or zero. The symbol for absolute value is "| |". [3.1C, p. 183]	$\|9\| = 9$ $\|-9\| = 9$ $-\|9\| = -9$
A **rational number** is a number that can be written in the form $\frac{a}{b}$, where a and b are integers and $b \neq 0$. [3.4A, p. 221]	$\frac{3}{7}$, $-\frac{5}{8}$, 9, −2, $4\frac{1}{2}$, 0.6, and $0.\overline{3}$ are rational numbers.

Essential Rules and Procedures

Essential Rules and Procedures	Examples
Order Relations $a > b$ if a is to the right of b on the number line. $a < b$ if a is to the left of b on the number line. [3.1A, p. 181]	$-6 > -12$ $-8 < 4$
To add integers with the same sign, add the absolute values of the numbers. Then attach the sign of the addends. [3.2A, p. 193]	$6 + 4 = 10$ $-6 + (-4) = -10$
To add integers with different signs, find the absolute values of the numbers. Subtract the lesser absolute value from the greater absolute value. Then attach the sign of the addend with the greater absolute value. [3.2A, p. 193]	$-6 + 4 = -2$ $6 + (-4) = 2$

To subtract two integers, add the opposite of the second integer to the first integer. [3.2B, p. 197]

$6 - 4 = 6 + (-4) = 2$
$6 - (-4) = 6 + 4 = 10$
$-6 - 4 = -6 + (-4) = -10$
$-6 - (-4) = -6 + 4 = -2$

To multiply integers with the same sign, multiply the absolute values of the factors. The product is positive. [3.3A, p. 209]

$3 \cdot 5 = 15$
$-3(-5) = 15$

To multiply integers with different signs, multiply the absolute values of the factors. The product is negative. [3.3A, p. 209]

$-3(5) = -15$
$3(-5) = -15$

To divide two integers with the same sign, divide the absolute values of the numbers. The quotient is positive. [3.3B, p. 212]

$15 \div 3 = 5$
$(-15) \div (-3) = 5$

To divide two integers with different signs, divide the absolute values of the numbers. The quotient is negative. [3.3B, p. 212]

$-15 \div 3 = -5$
$15 \div (-3) = -5$

Properties of Addition [3.2A, p. 194]

Addition Property of Zero $a + 0 = a$ or $0 + a = a$ — $-6 + 0 = -6$

Commutative Property of Addition $a + b = b + a$ — $-8 + 4 = 4 + (-8)$

Associative Property of Addition $(a + b) + c = a + (b + c)$ — $(-5 + 4) + 6 = -5 + (4 + 6)$

Inverse Property of Addition $a + (-a) = 0$ or $-a + a = 0$ — $7 + (-7) = 0$

Properties of Multiplication [3.3A, p. 210]

Multiplication Property of Zero $a \cdot 0 = 0$ or $0 \cdot a = 0$ — $-9(0) = 0$

Multiplication Property of One $a \cdot 1 = a$ or $1 \cdot a = a$ — $-3(1) = -3$

Commutative Property of Multiplication $a \cdot b = b \cdot a$ — $-2(6) = 6(-2)$

Associative Property of Multiplication $(a \cdot b) \cdot c = a \cdot (b \cdot c)$ — $(-2 \cdot 4) \cdot 5 = -2 \cdot (4 \cdot 5)$

Division Properties of Zero and One [3.3B, p. 213]

If $a \neq 0$, $0 \div a = 0$. — $0 \div (-5) = 0$

If $a \neq 0$, $a \div a = 1$. — $-5 \div (-5) = 1$

$a \div 1 = a$ — $-5 \div 1 = -5$

$a \div 0$ is undefined. — $-5 \div 0$ is undefined.

The Order of Operations Agreement [3.5A, p. 237]

Step 1: Do all operations inside parentheses.
Step 2: Simplify any numerical expressions containing exponents.
Step 3: Do multiplication and division as they occur from left to right.
Step 4: Do addition and subtraction as they occur from left to right.

$$\begin{aligned}(-4)^2 - 3(1 - 5) &= (-4)^2 - 3(-4) \\ &= 16 - 3(-4) \\ &= 16 - (-12) \\ &= 16 + 12 \\ &= 28\end{aligned}$$

CHAPTER 3 Review Exercises

1. Write the expression $8 - (-1)$ in words.
eight minus negative one [3.1B]

2. Evaluate $-|-36|$.
-36 [3.1C]

3. Find the product of -40 and -5.
200 [3.3A]

4. Evaluate $-a \div b$ for $a = -27$ and $b = -3$.
-9 [3.3B]

5. Add: $-28 + 14$
-14 [3.2A]

6. Simplify: $-(-13)$
13 [3.1B]

7. Graph -2 on the number line.
$-6\ -5\ -4\ -3\ -2\ -1\ 0\ 1\ 2\ 3\ 4\ 5\ 6$ [3.1A]

8. What is the sum of -65.47 and -32.91?
-98.38 [3.4A]

9. Divide: $-51 \div (-3)$
17 [3.3B]

10. Find the quotient of 840 and -4.
-210 [3.3B]

11. Subtract: $-6 - (-7) - 15 - (-12)$
-2 [3.2B]

12. Evaluate $-ab$ for $a = -2$ and $b = -9$.
-18 [3.3A]

13. Find the sum of 18, -13, and -6.
-1 [3.2A]

14. Multiply: $-18(4)$
-72 [3.3A]

15. Simplify: $(-2)^2 - (-3)^2 \div (1 - 4)^2 \cdot 2 - 6$
-4 [3.5A]

16. Evaluate $-x - y$ for $x = -1$ and $y = 3$.
-2 [3.2B]

17. **Golf** The scores of four golfers after the final round of the 2011 Boeing Classic are shown in the figure at the right. What is the difference between Tom Lehman's score and Mark Calcavecchia's score? 18 points [3.2C]

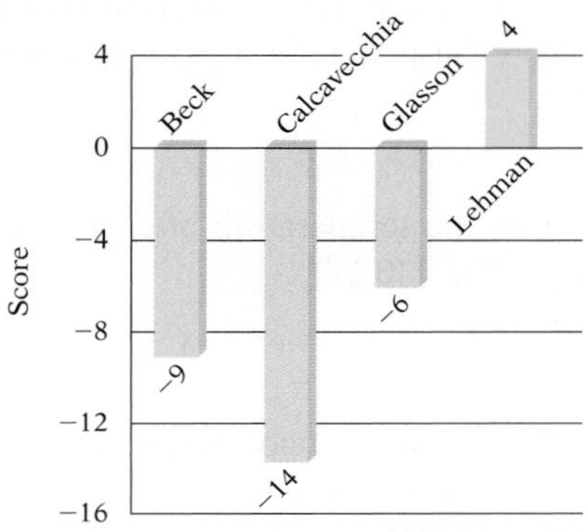

Golfers' Scores in 2011 Boeing Classic

18. Find the difference between -15 and -28.

13 [3.2B]

19. What is the quotient of $-\frac{1}{5}$ and $-\frac{7}{10}$?

$\frac{2}{7}$ [3.4B]

20. Is -9 a solution of $-6 - t = 3$?

Yes [3.2B]

21. Simplify: $-9 + 16 - (-7)$

14 [3.2B]

22. Divide: $\frac{0}{-17}$

0 [3.3B]

23. Multiply: $-5(2)(-6)(-1)$

-60 [3.3A]

24. Add: $3 + (-9) + 4 + (-10)$

-12 [3.2A]

25. Evaluate $(a - b)^2 - 2a$ for $a = -2$ and $b = -3$.

5 [3.5A]

26. Place the correct symbol, $<$ or $>$, between the two numbers.

$-8 > -10$ [3.1A]

27. Complete the statement by using the Inverse Property of Addition.

$-21 + ? = 0$ 21 [3.2A]

28. Find the absolute value of -27. 27 [3.1C]

29. Multiply: $-0.8(3.5)$ -2.8 [3.4B]

30. What is $\frac{7}{12}$ added to $-\frac{11}{16}$?

$-\frac{5}{48}$ [3.4A]

31. Simplify: $3 \div \left(\frac{1}{2} - \frac{1}{4}\right) - 3$

9 [3.5A]

32. Temperature Which is colder, a temperature of -4°C or a temperature of -12°C? -12°C [3.1D]

33. Chemistry The figure at the right shows the boiling points in degrees Celsius of three chemical elements. The boiling point of neon is 7 times the highest boiling point shown in the table. What is the boiling point of neon?

-238°C [3.3C]

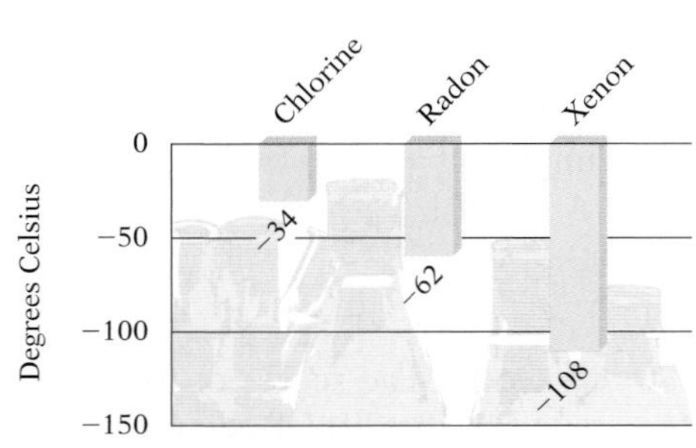

Boiling Points of Chemical Elements

34. Temperature Find the temperature after an increase of 5°C from -8°C. -3°C [3.2C]

35. Mathematics The distance d between point a and point b on the number line is given by the formula $d = |a - b|$. Find d for $a = 7$ and $b = -5$. 12 units [3.2C]

CHAPTER 3 TEST

1. Write the expression $-3 + (-5)$ in words.
negative three plus negative five [3.1B]

2. Evaluate $-|-34|$.
-34 [3.1C]

3. What is 3 minus -15?
18 [3.2B]

4. Evaluate $a + b$ for $a = -11$ and $b = -9$.
-20 [3.2A]

5. Evaluate $(-x)(-y)$ for $x = -4$ and $y = -6$.
24 [3.3A]

6. What is $-\frac{5}{6}$ added to $\frac{4}{9}$?
$-\frac{7}{18}$ [3.4A]

7. What is -360 divided by -30?
12 [3.3B]

8. Find the sum of -3, -6, and 11.
2 [3.2A]

9. Place the correct symbol between the two numbers.
$16 > -19$ [3.1A]

10. Subtract: $7 - (-3) - 12$
-2 [3.2B]

11. Evaluate $a - b - c$ for $a = 6$, $b = -2$, and $c = 11$. -3 [3.2B]

12. Simplify: $-(-49)$
49 [3.1B]

13. Find the product of 50 and -5.
-250 [3.3A]

14. Write the given numbers in order from smallest to largest.
$-|5|, -(-11), |-9|, -(3)$
$-|5|, -(3), |-9|, -(-11)$ [3.1C]

15. Is -9 a solution of the equation $17 - x = 8$?
No [3.2B]

16. On the number line, which number is 2 units to the right of -5? -3 [3.1A]

17. **Golf** The scores of four golfers after the final round of the 2011 Wegmans LPGA Championship are shown in the figure at the right. What is the difference between Taylor Leon's score and Yani Tseng's score? 21 points [3.2C]

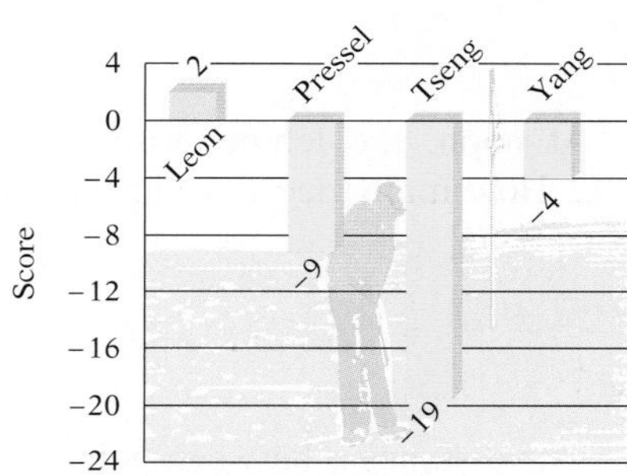

Golfers' Scores in 2011 Wegmans LPGA Championship

18. Divide: $\frac{0}{-16}$
0 [3.3B]

19. Evaluate $2bc - (c + a)^3$ for $a = -2$, $b = 4$, and $c = -1$.
19 [3.5A]

20. Find the opposite of 25.
−25 [3.1B]

21. What is 4.793 less than −6.82?
−11.613 [3.4A]

22. Subtract: $0 - 11$
−11 [3.2B]

23. Divide: $-96 \div (-4)$
24 [3.3B]

24. Simplify: $16 \div 4 - 12 \div (-2)$
10 [3.5A]

25. Evaluate $\frac{-x}{y}$ for $x = -56$ and $y = -8$.
−7 [3.3B]

26. Evaluate $3xy$ for $x = -2$ and $y = -10$.
60 [3.3A]

27. Divide: $-18 \div \frac{2}{3}$
−27 [3.4B]

28. What is 14 less than 4? −10 [3.2B]

29. Simplify: $7 \div \left(\frac{1}{7} - \frac{3}{14}\right) - 9$ −107 [3.5A]

30. Evaluate xy when $x = -0.3$ and $y = 5.1$.
−1.53 [3.4B]

31. Add: $-9.61 + (-5.7)$
−15.31 [3.4A]

32. **Temperature** Find the temperature after an increase of 11°C from −6°C.
5°C [3.2C]

33. **Environmental Science** The wind chill factor when the temperature is −25°F and the wind is blowing at 40 mph is four times the wind chill factor when the temperature is −5°F and the wind is blowing at 5 mph. If the wind chill factor at −5°F with a 5-mile-per-hour wind is −16°F, what is the wind chill factor at −25°F with a 40-mile-per-hour wind? −64°F [3.3A]

© iStockphoto.com/jokerproproduction

34. **Temperature** At noon, the temperature was 3.5°C. At 10 P.M., the temperature was −1.75°C. How many degrees did the temperature fall during the 10-hour period? 5.25°C [3.4C]

35. **Mathematics** The distance d between points a and b on the number line is given by the formula $d = |a - b|$. Find d for $a = 4$ and $b = -12$. 16 units [3.2C]

Cumulative Review Exercises

1. Find the difference between -27 and -32.
5 [3.2B]

2. Estimate the product of 439 and 28.
12,000 [1.3A]

3. Divide: $16.15 \div 0.5$
32.3 [2.6C]

4. Simplify: $16 \div (3 + 5) \cdot 9 - 2^4$
2 [1.4A]

5. Evaluate $-|-82|$.
-82 [3.1C]

6. Write three hundred nine thousand four hundred eighty in standard form.
309,480 [1.1B]

7. Evaluate $5xy$ for $x = 80$ and $y = 6$.
2400 [1.3A]

8. What is -294 divided by -14?
21 [3.3B]

9. Subtract: $-28 - (-17)$
-11 [3.2B]

10. Find the sum of -24, 16, and -32.
-40 [3.2A]

11. Find all the factors of 44.
1, 2, 4, 11, 22, 44 [1.3D]

12. Evaluate x^4y^2 for $x = \frac{1}{2}$ and $y = 4$.
1 [2.4A]

13. Round 629,874 to the nearest thousand.
630,000 [1.1C]

14. Estimate the sum of 356, 481, 294, and 117.
1300 [1.2A]

15. Evaluate $-a - b$ for $a = -4$ and $b = -5$.
9 [3.2B]

16. Find the product of -100 and 25.
-2500 [3.3A]

17. Find the sum of 3.97 and 4.8.
8.77 [2.6A]

18. Add: $2\frac{1}{6} + 3\frac{1}{2}$
$5\frac{2}{3}$ [2.3A]

19. Simplify: $(1 - 5)^2 \div (-6 + 4) + 8(-3)$
-32 [3.5A]

20. Evaluate $-c \div d$ for $c = -32$ and $d = -8$.
-4 [3.3B]

21. Find the quotient of $\frac{9}{10}$ and $\frac{3}{4}$.
$1\frac{1}{5}$ [2.4B]

22. Place the correct symbol, < or >, between the two numbers.
$-62 < 26$ [3.1A]

23. What is -18 multiplied by -7?
126 [3.3A]

24. Divide: $-3.312 \div (-0.8)$
4.14 [3.4B]

25. Write $2 \cdot 2 \cdot 2 \cdot 2 \cdot 2 \cdot 7 \cdot 7$ in exponential notation.
$2^5 \cdot 7^2$ [1.3B]

26. Evaluate $4a + (a - b)^3$ for $a = 5$ and $b = 2$.
47 [1.4A]

27. Add: $5971 + 482 + 3609$
10,062 [1.2A]

28. What is 5 less than -21?
-26 [3.2B]

29. Estimate the difference between 7352 and 1986.
5000 [1.2B]

30. Evaluate $3^4 \cdot 5^2$.
2025 [1.3B]

31. **History** The land area of the United States prior to the Louisiana Purchase was 891,364 mi². The land area of the Louisiana Purchase, which was purchased from France in 1803, was 831,321 mi². What was the land area of the United States immediately after the Louisiana Purchase? 1,722,685 mi² [1.2C]

© Maria Picard/Deborah Betz Collection/Corbis

Albert Einstein

32. **History** Albert Einstein was born on March 14, 1879. He died on April 18, 1955. How old was Albert Einstein when he died? 76 years old [1.2C]

33. **Buying a Car** A customer makes a down payment of \$7850 on a car costing \$35,500. Find the amount that remains to be paid. \$27,650 [1.2C]

34. **Real Estate** A construction company is considering purchasing a 25-acre tract of land on which to build single-family homes. If the price is \$11,270 per acre, what is the total cost of the land? \$281,750 [1.3E]

35. **Temperature** Find the temperature after an increase of 7°C from −12°C.
−5°C [3.2C]

36. **Temperature** Record temperatures, in degrees Fahrenheit, for four states in the United States are shown at the right. **a.** What is the difference between the record high and record low temperatures for Arizona? **b.** For which state is the difference between the record high and record low temperatures greatest?
a. 168°F b. Alaska [3.2C]

Record Temperatures (in degrees Fahrenheit)

State	Lowest	Highest
Alabama	−27	112
Alaska	−80	100
Arizona	−40	128
Arkansas	−29	120

37. **Sales Agents** As a sales agent, your goal is to sell \$120,000 in merchandise during the year. You sold \$28,550 in merchandise during the first quarter of the year, \$34,850 during the second quarter, and \$31,700 during the third quarter. What must your sales for the fourth quarter be if you are to meet your goal for the year? \$24,900 [1.2C]

38. **Golf** Use the equation $S = N - P$, where S is a golfer's score relative to par in a tournament, N is the number of strokes made by the golfer, and P is par, to find a golfer's score relative to par when the golfer made 198 strokes and par is 206.
-8 [3.2C]

Variable Expressions

4

OBJECTIVES

SECTION 4.1

A To evaluate a variable expression

SECTION 4.2

A To simplify a variable expression using the Properties of Addition

B To simplify a variable expression using the Properties of Multiplication

C To simplify a variable expression using the Distributive Property

D To simplify general variable expressions

SECTION 4.3

A To translate a verbal expression into a variable expression, given the variable

B To translate a verbal expression into a variable expression and then simplify

C To translate application problems

Focus on Success

Are you making attending class a priority? Remember that to be successful, you must attend class. You need to be in class to hear your instructor's explanations and instructions, as well as to ask questions when something is unclear. Most students who miss a class fall behind and then find it very difficult to catch up. (See Class Time, page AIM-5.)

Prep Test

Are you ready to succeed in this chapter? Take the Prep Test below to find out if you are ready to learn the new material.

1. Subtract: $-12 - (-15)$

   3 [3.2B]

2. Divide: $-36 \div (-9)$

   4 [3.3B]

3. Add: $-\frac{3}{4} + \frac{5}{6}$

   $\frac{1}{12}$ [3.4A]

4. What is the reciprocal of $-\frac{9}{4}$?

   $-\frac{4}{9}$ [2.4B]

5. Divide: $-\frac{3}{4} \div \left(-\frac{5}{2}\right)$

   $\frac{3}{10}$ [3.4B]

6. Evaluate: -2^4

   -16 [3.5A]

7. Evaluate: $\left(\frac{2}{3}\right)^3$

   $\frac{8}{27}$ [2.4A]

8. Evaluate: $3 \cdot 4^2$

   48 [1.4A]

9. Evaluate: $7 - 2 \cdot 3$

   1 [1.4A]

10. Evaluate: $5 - 7(3 - 2^2)$

    12 [3.5A]

SECTION

4.1 Evaluating Variable Expressions

OBJECTIVE A *To evaluate a variable expression*

Point of Interest

Historical manuscripts indicate that mathematics is at least 4000 years old. Yet it was only 400 years ago that mathematicians started using variables to stand for numbers. The idea that a letter can stand for some number was a critical turning point in mathematics.

Today, *x* is used by most nations as the standard letter for a single unknown. In fact, x-rays were so named because the scientists who discovered them did not know what they were and thus labeled them the "unknown rays" or x-rays.

Often we discuss a quantity without knowing its exact value—for example, the price of gold next month, the cost of a new automobile next year, or the tuition cost for next semester. Recall that a letter of the alphabet, called a **variable,** is used to stand for a quantity that is unknown or that can change, or *vary.* An expression that contains one or more variables is called a **variable expression.**

A variable expression is shown at the right. The expression can be rewritten by writing subtraction as the addition of the opposite.

$$3x^2 - 5y + 2xy - x - 7$$
$$3x^2 + (-5y) + 2xy + (-x) + (-7)$$

Note that the expression has five addends. The **terms** of a variable expression are the addends of the expression. The expression has five terms.

Five terms

$$\underbrace{3x^2 \; - \; 5y \; + \; 2xy \; - \; x}_{\text{Variable terms}} \quad \underbrace{-\;7}_{\text{Constant term}}$$

The terms $3x^2$, $-5y$, $2xy$, and $-x$ are **variable terms.**

The term -7 is a **constant term,** or simply a **constant.**

Each variable term is composed of a **numerical coefficient** and a **variable part** (the variable or variables and their exponents).

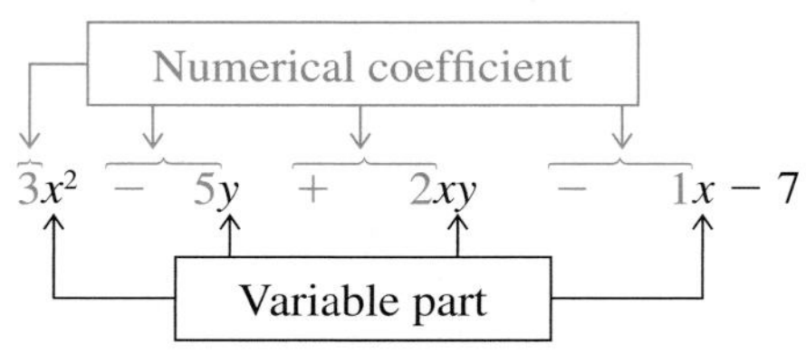

When the numerical coefficient is 1 or −1, the 1 is usually not written ($x = 1x$ and $-x = -1x$).

Variable expressions can be used to model scientific phenomena. In a physics lab, a student may discover that a weight of 1 pound will stretch a spring $\frac{1}{2}$ inch. Two pounds will stretch the spring 1 inch. By experimenting, the student can discover that the distance the spring will stretch is found by multiplying the weight by $\frac{1}{2}$. By letting W represent the weight attached to the spring, the student can represent the distance the spring stretches by the variable expression $\frac{1}{2}W$.

INSTRUCTOR NOTE
Emphasize that the result of evaluating a variable expression is one number.

With a weight of W pounds attached, the spring will stretch $\frac{1}{2} \cdot W = \frac{1}{2}W$ inches.

With a weight of 10 pounds attached, the spring will stretch $\frac{1}{2} \cdot 10 = 5$ inches. The number 10 is called the **value of the variable** W.

With a weight of 3 pounds attached, the spring will stretch $\frac{1}{2} \cdot 3 = 1\frac{1}{2}$ inches.

Replacing each variable by its value and then simplifying the resulting numerical expression is called **evaluating a variable expression.**

HOW TO 1 Evaluate $ab - b^2$ when $a = 2$ and $b = -3$.

Replace each variable in the expression by its value. Then use the Order of Operations Agreement to simplify the resulting numerical expression.

$ab - b^2$

$2(-3) - (-3)^2 = -6 - 9 = -15$

EXAMPLE 1

Name the variable terms of the expression $2a^2 - 5a + 7$.

Solution

$2a^2$ and $-5a$

YOU TRY IT 1

Name the constant term of the expression $6n^2 + 3n - 4$.

Your solution

-4

EXAMPLE 2

Evaluate $x^2 - 3xy$ when $x = 3$ and $y = -4$.

Solution

$x^2 - 3xy$

$3^2 - 3(3)(-4) = 9 - 3(3)(-4)$ • $x = 3, y = -4$

$= 9 - 9(-4)$

$= 9 - (-36)$

$= 9 + 36 = 45$

YOU TRY IT 2

Evaluate $2xy + y^2$ when $x = -4$ and $y = 2$.

Your solution

-12

EXAMPLE 3

Evaluate $\frac{a^2 - b^2}{a - b}$ when $a = 3$ and $b = -4$.

Solution

$\frac{a^2 - b^2}{a - b}$

$\frac{3^2 - (-4)^2}{3 - (-4)} = \frac{9 - 16}{3 - (-4)}$ • $a = 3, b = -4$

$= \frac{-7}{7} = -1$

YOU TRY IT 3

Evaluate $\frac{a^2 + b^2}{a + b}$ when $a = 5$ and $b = -3$.

Your solution

17

IN-CLASS EXAMPLES

1. Name the variable terms of the expression $3b^3 - 4b - 2$. $\mathbf{3b^3, -4b}$
2. Evaluate $3a^2 - 4ab$ when $a = 5$ and $b = -4$. **155**
3. Evaluate $\frac{x^3 + y^3}{x + y}$ when $x = 2$ and $y = -3$. **19**

EXAMPLE 4

Evaluate $x^2 - 3(x - y) - z^2$ when $x = 2$, $y = -1$, and $z = 3$.

Solution

$x^2 - 3(x - y) - z^2$

$2^2 - 3[2 - (-1)] - 3^2$ • $x = 2, y = -1, z = 3$

$= 2^2 - 3(3) - 3^2$

$= 4 - 3(3) - 9$

$= 4 - 9 - 9$

$= -5 - 9 = -14$

YOU TRY IT 4

Evaluate $x^3 - 2(x + y) + z^2$ when $x = 2$, $y = -4$, and $z = -3$.

Your solution

21

4. Evaluate $a^2 - 5(a - 2b) - c^2$ when $a = -3$, $b = 2$, and $c = -1$. **43**

Solutions on p. S12

4.1 EXERCISES

Concept Check

SUGGESTED ASSIGNMENT:
Exercises 1–11, 13–49, odds

For Exercises 1 to 3, name the terms of the variable expression. Then underline the constant term.

1. $2x^2 + 5x - 8$
$2x^2, 5x, \underline{-8}$

2. $-3n^2 - 4n + 7$
$-3n^2, -4n, \underline{7}$

3. $6 - a^4$
$-a^4, \underline{6}$

For Exercises 4 to 6, name the variable terms of the expression. Then underline the variable part of each term.

4. $9b^2 - 4ab + a^2$
$9\underline{b^2}, -4\underline{ab}, \underline{a^2}$

5. $7x^2y + 6xy^2 + 10$
$7\underline{x^2y}, 6\underline{xy^2}$

6. $5 - 8n - 3n^2$
$-8\underline{n}, -3\underline{n^2}$

For Exercises 7 to 9, name the coefficients of the variable terms.

7. $x^2 - 9x + 2$
1, −9

8. $12a^2 - 8ab - b^2$
12, −8, −1

9. $n^3 - 4n^2 - n + 9$
1, −4, −1

10. What is the numerical coefficient of a variable term?

11. Explain the meaning of the phrase "evaluate a variable expression."

OBJECTIVE A *To evaluate a variable expression*

For Exercises 12 to 32, evaluate the variable expression when $a = 2$, $b = 3$, and $c = -4$.

12. $3a + 2b$
12

13. $a - 2c$
10

14. $-a^2$
−4

15. $2c^2$
32

16. $-3a + 4b$
6

17. $3b - 3c$
21

18. $b^2 - 3$
6

19. $-3c + 4$
16

20. $16 \div (2c)$
−2

21. $6b \div (-a)$
−9

22. $bc \div (2a)$
−3

23. $b^2 - 4ac$
41

24. $a^2 - b^2$
−5

25. $b^2 - c^2$
−7

26. $(a + b)^2$
25

27. $a^2 + b^2$
13

28. $2a - (c + a)^2$
0

29. $(b - a)^2 + 4c$
−15

30. $b^2 - \frac{ac}{8}$
10

31. $\frac{5ab}{6} - 3cb$
41

32. $(b - 2a)^2 + bc$
−11

For Exercises 33 to 50, evaluate the variable expression when $a = -2$, $b = 4$, $c = -1$, and $d = 3$.

33. $\dfrac{b + c}{d}$ 1

34. $\dfrac{d - b}{c}$ 1

35. $\dfrac{2d + b}{-a}$ 5

36. $\dfrac{b + 2d}{b}$ $\dfrac{5}{2}$

37. $\dfrac{b - d}{c - a}$ 1

38. $\dfrac{2c - d}{-ad}$ $-\dfrac{5}{6}$

39. $(b + d)^2 - 4a$ 57

40. $(d - a)^2 - 3c$ 28

41. $(d - a)^2 \div 5$ 5

42. $3(b - a) - bc$ 22

43. $\dfrac{b - 2a}{bc^2 - d}$ 8

44. $\dfrac{b^2 - a}{ad + 3c}$ -2

45. $\dfrac{1}{3}d^2 - \dfrac{3}{8}b^2$ -3

46. $\dfrac{5}{8}a^4 - c^2$ 9

47. $\dfrac{-4bc}{2a - b}$ -2

48. $-\dfrac{3}{4}b + \dfrac{1}{2}(ac + bd)$ 4

49. $-\dfrac{2}{3}d - \dfrac{1}{5}(bd - ac)$ -4

50. $(b - a)^2 - (d - c)^2$ 20

For Exercises 51 to 54, without evaluating the expression, determine whether the expression is positive or negative when $a = -25$, $b = 67$, and $c = -82$.

51. $(c - a)(-b)$ Positive

52. $(a - c) + 3b$ Positive

53. $\dfrac{b + c}{abc}$ Negative

54. $\dfrac{ac}{-b^2}$ Negative

Critical Thinking

55. The value of a is the value of $3x^2 - 4x - 5$ when $x = -2$. Find the value of $3a - 4$. 41

56. The value of c is the value of $a^2 + b^2$ when $a = 2$ and $b = -2$. Find the value of $c^2 - 4$. 60

For Exercises 57 to 60, evaluate the expression for $x = 2$, $y = 3$, and $z = -2$.

57. $3^x - x^3$ 1

58. z^x 4

59. $x^x - y^y$ -23

60. $y^{(x^2)}$ 81

Projects or Group Activities

61. For each of the following, determine the first natural number x, greater than 2, for which the second expression is larger than the first. On the basis of your answers, make a conjecture that appears to be true about the expressions x^n and n^x, where $n = 3, 4, 5, 6, 7, \ldots$ and x is a natural number greater than 2. $n^x > x^n$ if $x = n$ or $x > n + 1$

a. $x^3, 3^x$ 2

b. $x^4, 4^x$ 5

c. $x^5, 5^x$ 6

d. $x^6, 6^x$ 7

QUICK QUIZ

1. Name the terms of the variable expression $3x^2 - 4x - 5$. Then underline the constant term. **$3x^2$, $-4x$, $\underline{-5}$ [4.1A]**
2. Name the variable terms of the expression $4x^2y + 5xy^2 + 9$. Then underline the variable part of each term. **$4\underline{x^2y}$, $5\underline{xy^2}$ [4.1A]**
3. Name the coefficients of the variable terms of $5x^3 - x^2 + 3x - 4$. **5, −1, 3 [4.1A]**
4. Evaluate $2x - (y + z)^2$ when $x = 5$, $y = -3$, and $z = 6$. **1 [4.1A]**

SECTION

4.2 Simplifying Variable Expressions

OBJECTIVE A *To simplify a variable expression using the Properties of Addition*

INSTRUCTOR NOTE
Combining like terms can be related to many everyday experiences. For instance, 5 bricks plus 7 bricks is 12 bricks. But 5 bricks plus 7 nails is 5 bricks plus 7 nails. Students need to be constantly reminded that algebra is a reflection of our experiences, not some arbitrarily made up system of rules.

Like terms of a variable expression are terms with the same variable part. (Because $x^2 = x \cdot x$, x^2 and x are not like terms.)

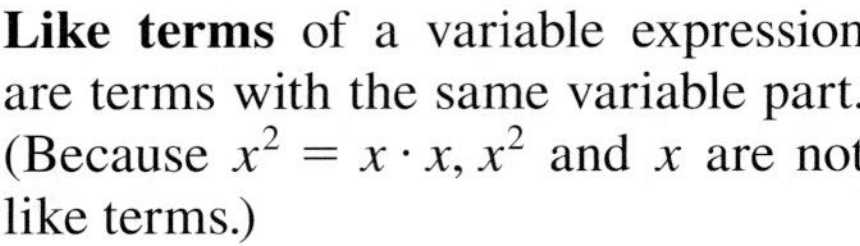

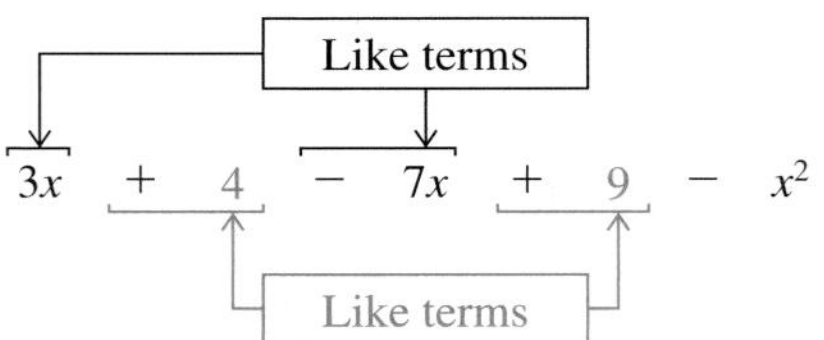

Constant terms are like terms. 4 and 9 are like terms.

To simplify a variable expression, we use the Distributive Property to add the numerical coefficients of like variable terms. The variable part remains unchanged. This is called **combining like terms.**

Take Note
The examples at the right show that we get the same result using either the Order of Operations Agreement or the Distributive Property to evaluate each numerical expression. The usefulness of the Distributive Property will become more apparent as we explore variable expressions.

The Distributive Property

If a, b, and c are real numbers, then $a(b + c) = ab + ac$ or $(b + c)a = ba + ca$.

By the Distributive Property, the term outside the parentheses is multiplied by each term inside the parentheses.

EXAMPLES

1. $2(3 + 4) = 2 \cdot 3 + 2 \cdot 4$
$2(7) = 6 + 8$
$14 = 14$

2. $(4 + 5)2 = 4 \cdot 2 + 5 \cdot 2$
$(9)2 = 8 + 10$
$18 = 18$

The Distributive Property in the form $(b + c)a = ba + ca$ is used to simplify a variable expression.

To simplify $2x + 3x$, use the Distributive Property to add the numerical coefficients of the like variable terms.

$$2x + 3x = (2 + 3)x$$
$$= 5x$$

HOW TO 1 Simplify: $5y - 11y$

$$5y - 11y = (5 - 11)y \quad \text{• Use the Distributive Property.}$$
$$= -6y$$

Take Note
Simplifying an expression means combining like terms. The constant term 5 and the variable term $7p$ are not like terms and therefore cannot be combined.

HOW TO 2 Simplify: $5 + 7p$

The terms 5 and $7p$ are not like terms.

The expression $5 + 7p$ is in simplest form.

The following Properties of Addition are used to simplify variable expressions.

The Associative Property of Addition

If a, b, and c are real numbers, then $(a + b) + c = a + (b + c)$.

When three or more terms are added, the terms can be grouped (with parentheses, for example) in any order; the sum is the same.

EXAMPLES

1. $(5 + 7) + 15 = 5 + (7 + 15)$
   $12 + 15 = 5 + 22$
   $27 = 27$

2. $(3x + 5x) + 9x = 3x + (5x + 9x)$
   $8x + 9x = 3x + 14x$
   $17x = 17x$

The Commutative Property of Addition

If a and b are real numbers, then $a + b = b + a$.

When two terms are added, the terms can be added in either order; the sum is the same.

EXAMPLES

1. $15 + (-28) = (-28) + 15$
   $-13 = -13$

2. $2x + (-4x) = -4x + 2x$
   $-2x = -2x$

The Addition Property of Zero

If a is a real number, then $a + 0 = a$ and $0 + a = a$.

The sum of a term and zero is the term.

EXAMPLES

1. $-9 + 0 = -9$ and $0 + (-9) = -9$
2. $0 + 5x = 5x$ and $5x + 0 = 5x$

The Inverse Property of Addition

If a is a real number, then $a + (-a) = 0$ and $(-a) + a = 0$.

The sum of a term and its additive inverse (or opposite) is zero.

EXAMPLES

1. $8 + (-8) = 0$ and $-8 + 8 = 0$
2. $-7x + 7x = 0$ and $7x + (-7x) = 0$

HOW TO 3 Simplify: $8x + 4y - 8x + y$

$8x + 4y - 8x + y$

$= (8x - 8x) + (4y + y)$ • Use the Commutative and Associative Properties of Addition to rearrange and group like terms.

$= 0 + 5y = 5y$ • Combine like terms.

HOW TO 4 Simplify: $4x^2 + 5x - 6x^2 - 2x + 1$

$4x^2 + 5x - 6x^2 - 2x + 1$
$= (4x^2 - 6x^2) + (5x - 2x) + 1$ • Use the Commutative and Associative Properties of Addition to rearrange and group like terms.
$= -2x^2 + 3x + 1$ • Combine like terms.

EXAMPLE 1

Simplify: $3x + 4y - 10x + 7y$

Solution

$3x + 4y - 10x + 7y = (3x - 10x) + (4y + 7y)$
$= -7x + 11y$

YOU TRY IT 1

Simplify: $3a - 2b - 5a + 6b$

Your solution

$-2a + 4b$

EXAMPLE 2

Simplify: $x^2 - 7 + 4x^2 - 16$

Solution

$x^2 - 7 + 4x^2 - 16 = (x^2 + 4x^2) + (-7 - 16)$
$= 5x^2 - 23$

YOU TRY IT 2

Simplify: $-3y^2 + 7 + 8y^2 - 14$

Your solution

$5y^2 - 7$

IN-CLASS EXAMPLES

Simplify.

1. $4a - 5b - 3a + 2b$ **$a - 3b$**
2. $y^2 + 2 + 9y^2 - 14$ **$10y^2 - 12$**

Solutions on p. S12

OBJECTIVE B *To simplify a variable expression using the Properties of Multiplication*

In simplifying variable expressions, the following Properties of Multiplication are used.

The Associative Property of Multiplication

If a, b, and c are real numbers, then $(ab)c = a(bc)$.

When three or more factors are multiplied, the factors can be grouped in any order; the product is the same.

EXAMPLES

1. $3(5 \cdot 6) = (3 \cdot 5)6$
   $3(30) = (15)6$
   $90 = 90$
2. $2(3x) = (2 \cdot 3)x$
   $= 6x$

Take Note
The Associative Property of Multiplication allows us to multiply a coefficient by a number. Without this property, the expression $2(3x)$ could not be simplified.

The Commutative Property of Multiplication

If a and b are real numbers, then $ab = ba$.

Two factors can be multiplied in either order; the product is the same.

EXAMPLES

1. $5(-7) = -7(5)$
   $-35 = -35$
2. $(5x) \cdot 3 = 3 \cdot (5x)$ • Commutative Property of Multiplication
   $= (3 \cdot 5)x$ • Associative Property of Multiplication
   $= 15x$

Take Note
The Commutative Property of Multiplication allows us to rearrange factors. This property, along with the Associative Property of Multiplication, enables us to simplify some variable expressions.

The Multiplication Property of One

If a is a real number, then $a \cdot 1 = a$ and $1 \cdot a = a$.

The product of a term and 1 is the term.

EXAMPLES

1. $9 \cdot 1 = 9$

2. $(8x) \cdot 1 = 8x$

The Inverse Property of Multiplication

If a is a real number and a is not equal to zero, then $a \cdot \frac{1}{a} = 1$ and $\frac{1}{a} \cdot a = 1$.

$\frac{1}{a}$ is called the **reciprocal** of a. $\frac{1}{a}$ is also called the **multiplicative inverse** of a.

The product of a number and its reciprocal is 1.

EXAMPLES

1. $7 \cdot \frac{1}{7} = 1$ and $\frac{1}{7} \cdot 7 = 1$

2. $x \cdot \frac{1}{x} = 1$ and $\frac{1}{x} \cdot x = 1, \quad x \neq 0$

Take Note
In the second example, we must state that $x \neq 0$ because division by zero is undefined.

The multiplication properties are used to simplify variable expressions.

HOW TO 5 Simplify: $2(-x)$

$$\begin{aligned} 2(-x) &= 2(-1 \cdot x) \\ &= [2(-1)]x \\ &= -2x \end{aligned}$$

- Use the Associative Property of Multiplication to group factors.

INSTRUCTOR NOTE
Simplifying expressions such as these prepares the students for solving equations.

HOW TO 6 Simplify: $\frac{3}{2}\left(\frac{2x}{3}\right)$

$$\begin{aligned} \frac{3}{2}\left(\frac{2x}{3}\right) &= \frac{3}{2}\left(\frac{2}{3}x\right) \\ &= \left(\frac{3}{2} \cdot \frac{2}{3}\right)x \\ &= 1 \cdot x \\ &= x \end{aligned}$$

- Note that $\frac{2x}{3} = \frac{2}{3}x$.
- Use the Associative Property of Multiplication to group factors.

HOW TO 7 Simplify: $(16x)2$

$$\begin{aligned} (16x)2 &= 2(16x) \\ &= (2 \cdot 16)x \\ &= 32x \end{aligned}$$

- Use the Commutative and Associative Properties of Multiplication to rearrange and group factors.

EXAMPLE 3

Simplify: $-2(3x^2)$

Solution

$$-2(3x^2) = (-2 \cdot 3)x^2$$
$$= -6x^2$$

YOU TRY IT 3

Simplify: $-5(4y^2)$

Your solution

$-20y^2$

EXAMPLE 4

Simplify: $-5(-10x)$

Solution

$$-5(-10x) = [(-5)(-10)]x$$
$$= 50x$$

YOU TRY IT 4

Simplify: $-7(-2a)$

Your solution

$14a$

EXAMPLE 5

Simplify: $-\frac{3}{4}\left(\frac{2}{3}x\right)$

Solution

$$\left(-\frac{3}{4}\right)\left(\frac{2}{3}x\right) = \left(-\frac{3}{4} \cdot \frac{2}{3}\right)x$$
$$= -\frac{1}{2}x$$

YOU TRY IT 5

Simplify: $-\frac{3}{5}\left(-\frac{7}{9}a\right)$

Your solution

$\frac{7}{15}a$

IN-CLASS EXAMPLES

Simplify.

3. $-6(4y^2)$ **$-24y^2$**
4. $-3(-12b)$ **$36b$**
5. $(5a)(-6)$ **$-30a$**

Solutions on p. S12

OBJECTIVE C *To simplify a variable expression using the Distributive Property*

Recall that the Distributive Property states that if a, b, and c are real numbers, then

$$a(b + c) = ab + ac$$

The Distributive Property is used to remove parentheses from a variable expression.

HOW TO 8 Simplify: $3(2x + 7)$

$$3(2x + 7) = 3(2x) + 3(7)$$
$$= 6x + 21$$

- **Use the Distributive Property. Multiply each term inside the parentheses by 3.**

HOW TO 9 Simplify: $-5(4x + 6)$

$$-5(4x + 6) = -5(4x) + (-5)(6)$$
$$= -20x - 30$$

- **Use the Distributive Property.**

INSTRUCTOR NOTE

An expression such as $-(5x - 2)$ can be thought of as either the opposite of $5x - 2$ or $-1(5x - 2)$.

HOW TO 10 Simplify: $-(2x - 4)$

$$-(2x - 4) = -1(2x - 4)$$
$$= -1(2x) - (-1)(4)$$
$$= -2x + 4$$

- **Use the Distributive Property.**

From HOW TO 10, note that when a negative sign immediately precedes the parentheses, the sign of each term inside the parentheses is changed.

HOW TO 11 Simplify: $-\frac{1}{2}(8x - 12y)$

$$-\frac{1}{2}(8x - 12y) = -\frac{1}{2}(8x) - \left(-\frac{1}{2}\right)(12y)$$ • **Use the Distributive Property.**

$$= -4x + 6y$$

An extension of the Distributive Property is used when an expression contains more than two terms.

HOW TO 12 Simplify: $3(4x - 2y - z)$

$$3(4x - 2y - z) = 3(4x) - 3(2y) - 3(z)$$ • **Use the Distributive Property.**

$$= 12x - 6y - 3z$$

EXAMPLE 6

Simplify: $7(4 + 2x)$

Solution

Use the Distributive Property.

$7(4 + 2x) = 28 + 14x$

YOU TRY IT 6

Simplify: $5(3 + 7b)$

Your solution

$15 + 35b$

EXAMPLE 7

Simplify: $(2x - 6)2$

Solution

Use the Distributive Property.

$(2x - 6)2 = 4x - 12$

YOU TRY IT 7

Simplify: $(3a - 1)5$

Your solution

$15a - 5$

IN-CLASS EXAMPLES

Simplify.

6. $4(3 - 9x)$ **$12 - 36x$**
7. $(6 + 7y)8$ **$48 + 56y$**
8. $-9(-5a + 2b)$ **$45a - 18b$**
9. $4(y^2 - 3y + 7)$ **$4y^2 - 12y + 28$**
10. $-5(a^2 + 8a - 6)$ **$-5a^2 - 40a + 30$**

EXAMPLE 8

Simplify: $-3(-5a + 7b)$

Solution

Use the Distributive Property.

$-3(-5a + 7b) = 15a - 21b$

YOU TRY IT 8

Simplify: $-8(-2a + 7b)$

Your solution

$16a - 56b$

EXAMPLE 9

Simplify: $3(x^2 - x - 5)$

Solution

Use the Distributive Property.

$3(x^2 - x - 5) = 3x^2 - 3x - 15$

YOU TRY IT 9

Simplify: $3(12x^2 - x + 8)$

Your solution

$36x^2 - 3x + 24$

Solutions on p. S12

EXAMPLE 10

Simplify: $-2(x^2 + 5x - 4)$

Solution

Use the Distributive Property.

$-2(x^2 + 5x - 4)$
$= -2x^2 - 10x + 8$

YOU TRY IT 10

Simplify: $3(-a^2 - 6a + 7)$

Your solution

$-3a^2 - 18a + 21$

Solution on p. S12

OBJECTIVE D *To simplify general variable expressions*

When simplifying variable expressions, use the Distributive Property to remove parentheses and brackets used as grouping symbols.

HOW TO 13 Simplify: $4(x - y) - 2(-3x + 6y)$

$4(x - y) - 2(-3x + 6y)$
$= 4x - 4y + 6x - 12y$ • Use the Distributive Property.
$= 10x - 16y$ • Combine like terms.

EXAMPLE 11

Simplify: $2x - 3(2x - 7y)$

Solution

$2x - 3(2x - 7y)$
$= 2x - 6x + 21y$ • Use the Distributive Property.
$= -4x + 21y$ • Combine like terms.

YOU TRY IT 11

Simplify: $3y - 2(y - 7x)$

Your solution

$y + 14x$

EXAMPLE 12

Simplify: $7(x - 2y) - (-x - 2y)$

Solution

$7(x - 2y) - (-x - 2y)$
$= 7x - 14y + x + 2y$ • Use the Distributive Property.
$= 8x - 12y$ • Combine like terms.

YOU TRY IT 12

Simplify: $-2(x - 2y) - (-x + 3y)$

Your solution

$-x + y$

EXAMPLE 13

Simplify: $2x - 3[2x - 3(x + 7)]$

Solution

$2x - 3[2x - 3(x + 7)]$
$= 2x - 3[2x - 3x - 21]$ • Use the Distributive Property.
$= 2x - 3[-x - 21]$ • Combine like terms.
$= 2x + 3x + 63$ • Use the Distributive Property.
$= 5x + 63$ • Combine like terms.

YOU TRY IT 13

Simplify: $3y - 2[x - 4(2 - 3y)]$

Your solution

$-2x - 21y + 16$

IN-CLASS EXAMPLES

Simplify.

11. $5a - 4(3a + 2b)$
$-7a - 8b$
12. $-6(c - d) - (-c - 3d)$
$-5c + 9d$
13. $9w - 4[3w - 5(w + 6)]$
$17w + 120$

Solutions on p. S12

4.2 EXERCISES

Concept Check

SUGGESTED ASSIGNMENT
Exercises 1–6: Exercises 7–149, odds: More challenging exercise: Exercise 152

1. The fact that two terms can be added in either order is called the ___Commutative___ Property of Addition.
2. The fact that three or more factors can be multiplied by grouping them in any order is called the ___Associative___ Property of Multiplication.
3. The Inverse Property of Multiplication tells us that the product of a number and its ________ is 1. reciprocal (or multiplicative inverse)
4. The Inverse Property of Addition tells us that the sum of a number and its ________ is 0. opposite (or additive inverse)
5. What are *like terms*? Give an example of two like terms. Give an example of two terms that are not like terms.
6. Explain the meaning of the phrase "simplify a variable expression."

OBJECTIVE A *To simplify a variable expression using the Properties of Addition*

For Exercises 7 to 42, simplify.

7. $6x + 8x$
$14x$
8. $12x + 13x$
$25x$
9. $9a - 4a$
$5a$
10. $12a - 3a$
$9a$
11. $4y - 10y$
$-6y$
12. $8y - 6y$
$2y$
13. $7 - 3b$
$7 - 3b$
14. $5 + 2a$
$5 + 2a$
15. $-12a + 17a$
$5a$
16. $-3a + 12a$
$9a$
17. $5ab - 7ab$
$-2ab$
18. $9ab - 3ab$
$6ab$
19. $-12xy + 17xy$
$5xy$
20. $-15xy + 3xy$
$-12xy$
21. $-3ab + 3ab$
0
22. $-7ab + 7ab$
0
23. $-\frac{1}{2}x - \frac{1}{3}x$
$-\frac{5}{6}x$
24. $-\frac{2}{5}y + \frac{3}{10}y$
$-\frac{1}{10}y$
25. $2.3x + 4.2x$
$6.5x$
26. $6.1y - 9.2y$
$-3.1y$
27. $x - 0.55x$
$0.45x$
28. $0.65A - A$
$-0.35A$
29. $5a - 3a + 5a$
$7a$
30. $10a - 17a + 3a$
$-4a$
31. $-5x^2 - 12x^2 + 3x^2$
$-14x^2$
32. $-y^2 - 8y^2 + 7y^2$
$-2y^2$
33. $\frac{3}{4}x - \frac{1}{3}x - \frac{7}{8}x$
$-\frac{11}{24}x$

34. $-\frac{2}{5}a - \left(-\frac{3}{10}a\right) - \frac{11}{15}a$
$-\frac{5}{6}a$

35. $7x - 3y + 10x$
$17x - 3y$

36. $8y + 8x - 8y$
$8x$

37. $3a + (-7b) - 5a + b$
$-2a - 6b$

38. $-5b + 7a - 7b + 12a$
$19a - 12b$

39. $3x + (-8y) - 10x + 4x$
$-3x - 8y$

40. $3y + (-12x) - 7y + 2y$
$-12x - 2y$

41. $x^2 - 7x + (-5x^2) + 5x$
$-4x^2 - 2x$

42. $3x^2 + 5x - 10x^2 - 10x$
$-7x^2 - 5x$

43. Which of the following expressions are equivalent to $-10x - 10y - 10y - 10x$?

(i) 0 **(ii)** $-20y$ **(iii)** $-20x$ **(iv)** $-20x - 20y$ **(v)** $-20y - 20x$

iv, v

OBJECTIVE B *To simplify a variable expression using the Properties of Multiplication*

For Exercises 44 to 83, simplify.

44. $4(3x)$
$12x$

45. $12(5x)$
$60x$

46. $-3(7a)$
$-21a$

47. $-2(5a)$
$-10a$

48. $-2(-3y)$
$6y$

49. $-5(-6y)$
$30y$

50. $(4x)2$
$8x$

51. $(6x)12$
$72x$

52. $(3a)(-2)$
$-6a$

53. $(7a)(-4)$
$-28a$

54. $(-3b)(-4)$
$12b$

55. $(-12b)(-9)$
$108b$

56. $-5(3x^2)$
$-15x^2$

57. $-8(7x^2)$
$-56x^2$

58. $\frac{1}{3}(3x^2)$
x^2

59. $\frac{1}{6}(6x^2)$
x^2

60. $\frac{1}{5}(5a)$
a

61. $\frac{1}{8}(8x)$
x

62. $-\frac{1}{2}(-2x)$
x

63. $-\frac{1}{4}(-4a)$
a

64. $-\frac{1}{7}(-7n)$
n

65. $-\frac{1}{9}(-9b)$
b

66. $(3x)\left(\frac{1}{3}\right)$
x

67. $(12x)\left(\frac{1}{12}\right)$
x

68. $(-6y)\left(-\frac{1}{6}\right)$
y

69. $(-10n)\left(-\frac{1}{10}\right)$
n

70. $\frac{1}{3}(9x)$
$3x$

71. $\frac{1}{7}(14x)$
$2x$

72. $-0.2(10x)$
$-2x$

73. $-0.25(8x)$
$-2x$

74. $-\frac{2}{3}(12a^2)$
$-8a^2$

75. $-\frac{5}{8}(24a^2)$
$-15a^2$

76. $-0.5(-16y)$
$8y$

77. $-0.75(-8y)$
$6y$

78. $(16y)\left(\frac{1}{4}\right)$
$4y$

79. $(33y)\left(\frac{1}{11}\right)$
$3y$

80. $(-6x)\left(\frac{1}{3}\right)$
$-2x$

81. $(-10x)\left(\frac{1}{5}\right)$
$-2x$

82. $(-8a)\left(-\frac{3}{4}\right)$
$6a$

83. $(21y)\left(-\frac{3}{7}\right)$
$-9y$

84. After multiplying $\frac{2}{7}x^2$ by a proper fraction, is the coefficient of x^2 greater than 1 or less than 1? Less than 1

OBJECTIVE C To simplify a variable expression using the Distributive Property

For Exercises 85 to 123, simplify.

85. $2(4x - 3)$
$8x - 6$

86. $5(2x - 7)$
$10x - 35$

87. $-2(a + 7)$
$-2a - 14$

88. $-5(a + 16)$
$-5a - 80$

89. $-3(2y - 8)$
$-6y + 24$

90. $-5(3y - 7)$
$-15y + 35$

91. $-(x + 2)$
$-x - 2$

92. $-(x + 7)$
$-x - 7$

93. $(5 - 3b)7$
$35 - 21b$

94. $(10 - 7b)2$
$20 - 14b$

95. $\frac{1}{3}(6 - 15y)$
$2 - 5y$

96. $\frac{1}{2}(-8x + 4y)$
$-4x + 2y$

97. $3(5x^2 + 2x)$
$15x^2 + 6x$

98. $6(3x^2 + 2x)$
$18x^2 + 12x$

99. $-2(-y + 9)$
$2y - 18$

100. $-5(-2x + 7)$
$10x - 35$

101. $(-3x - 6)5$
$-15x - 30$

102. $(-2x + 7)7$
$-14x + 49$

103. $2(-3x^2 - 14)$
$-6x^2 - 28$

104. $5(-6x^2 - 3)$
$-30x^2 - 15$

105. $-3(2y^2 - 7)$
$-6y^2 + 21$

106. $-8(3y^2 - 12)$
$-24y^2 + 96$

107. $3(x^2 - y^2)$
$3x^2 - 3y^2$

108. $5(x^2 + y^2)$
$5x^2 + 5y^2$

109. $-\frac{2}{3}(6x - 18y)$
$-4x + 12y$

110. $-\frac{1}{2}(x - 4y)$
$-\frac{1}{2}x + 2y$

111. $-(6a^2 - 7b^2)$
$-6a^2 + 7b^2$

112. $3(x^2 + 2x - 6)$
$3x^2 + 6x - 18$

113. $4(x^2 - 3x + 5)$
$4x^2 - 12x + 20$

114. $-2(y^2 - 2y + 4)$
$-2y^2 + 4y - 8$

115. $\frac{3}{4}(2x - 6y + 8)$
$\frac{3}{2}x - \frac{9}{2}y + 6$

116. $-\frac{2}{3}(6x - 9y + 1)$
$-4x + 6y - \frac{2}{3}$

117. $4(-3a^2 - 5a + 7)$
$-12a^2 - 20a + 28$

118. $-5(-2x^2 - 3x + 7)$
$10x^2 + 15x - 35$

119. $-3(-4x^2 + 3x - 4)$
$12x^2 - 9x + 12$

120. $3(2x^2 + xy - 3y^2)$
$6x^2 + 3xy - 9y^2$

121. $5(2x^2 - 4xy - y^2)$
$10x^2 - 20xy - 5y^2$

122. $-(3a^2 + 5a - 4)$
$-3a^2 - 5a + 4$

123. $-(8b^2 - 6b + 9)$
$-8b^2 + 6b - 9$

124. After the expression $17x - 31$ is multiplied by a negative integer, is the constant term positive or negative?
Positive

OBJECTIVE D *To simplify general variable expressions*

125. Which of the following expressions is equivalent to $12 - 7(y - 9)$?

(i) $5(y - 9)$ **(ii)** $12 - 7y - 63$ **(iii)** $12 - 7y + 63$ **(iv)** $12 - 7y - 9$
iii

For Exercises 126 to 149, simplify.

126. $4x - 2(3x + 8)$
$-2x - 16$

127. $6a - (5a + 7)$
$a - 7$

128. $9 - 3(4y + 6)$
$-12y - 9$

129. $10 - (11x - 3)$
$-11x + 13$

130. $5n - (7 - 2n)$
$7n - 7$

131. $8 - (12 + 4y)$
$-4y - 4$

132. $3(x + 2) - 5(x - 7)$
$-2x + 41$

133. $2(x - 4) - 4(x + 2)$
$-2x - 16$

134. $12(y - 2) + 3(7 - 3y)$
$3y - 3$

135. $6(2y - 7) - (3 - 2y)$
$14y - 45$

136. $3(a - b) - (a + b)$
$2a - 4b$

137. $2(a + 2b) - (a - 3b)$
$a + 7b$

138. $4[x - 2(x - 3)]$
$-4x + 24$

139. $2[x + 2(x + 7)]$
$6x + 28$

140. $-2[3x + 2(4 - x)]$
$-2x - 16$

141. $-5[2x + 3(5 - x)]$
$5x - 75$

142. $-3[2x - (x + 7)]$
$-3x + 21$

143. $-2[3x - (5x - 2)]$
$4x - 4$

144. $2x - 3[x - (4 - x)]$
$-4x + 12$

145. $-7x + 3[x - (3 - 2x)]$
$2x - 9$

146. $-5x - 2[2x - 4(x + 7)] - 6$
$-x + 50$

147. $0.12(2x + 3) + x$
$1.24x + 0.36$

148. $0.05x + 0.02(4 - x)$
$0.03x + 0.08$

149. $0.03x + 0.04(1000 - x)$
$-0.01x + 40$

Critical Thinking

150. Determine whether the statement is true or false. If the statement is false, give an example that illustrates that it is false.
a. Division is a commutative operation. False. For example, $8 \div 2 \neq 2 \div 8$
b. Division is an associative operation. False. For example, $(12 \div 4) \div 2 \neq 12 \div (4 \div 2)$
c. Subtraction is an associative operation. False. For example, $(9 - 2) - 3 \neq 9 - (2 - 3)$
d. Subtraction is a commutative operation. False. For example, $10 - 4 \neq 4 - 10$

© bioraven/Shutterstock.com

151. Give examples of two operations that occur in everyday experience that are not commutative (for example, putting on socks and then shoes).

152. Which of the following expressions are equivalent?
(i) $2x + 4(2x + 1)$
(ii) $x - (4 - 9x) + 8$
(iii) $7(x - 4) - 3(2x + 6)$
(iv) $3(2x + 8) + 4(x - 5)$
(v) $6 - 2[x + (3x - 4)] + 2(9x - 5)$
i, ii, iv, and v are equivalent; they are all equal to $10x + 4$.

QUICK QUIZ
Simplify.
1. $9b - 5b$ **$4b$** **[4.2A]**
2. $8x^2 - x^2 + 2x^2$ **$9x^2$** **[4.2A]**
3. $4y^2 + 3y - 6y^2 + 2y$ **$-2y^2 + 5y$** **[4.2A]**
4. $5(6a)$ **$30a$** **[4.2B]**
5. $-\frac{1}{8}(-8b)$ **b** **[4.2B]**
6. $(-12c)\frac{2}{3}$ **$-8c$** **[4.2B]**
7. $-(y - 4)$ **$-y + 4$** **[4.2C]**
8. $4(3a + 5)$ **$12a + 20$** **[4.2C]**
9. $-\frac{1}{2}(4x + 8y - 6z)$ **$-2x - 4y + 3z$** **[4.2C]**
10. $8 - 5(3x + 2)$ **$-15x - 2$** **[4.2D]**
11. $7(3y - 4) - 2(4y - 3)$ **$13y - 22$** **[4.2D]**
12. $3a - 5[a - (6 - a)]$ **$-7a + 30$** **[4.2D]**

Projects or Group Activities

153. Define an operation $\otimes$ as $a \otimes b = (a \cdot b) - (a + b)$.
For example, $7 \otimes 5 = (7 \cdot 5) - (7 + 5) = 35 - 12 = 23$.
a. Is $\otimes$ a commutative operation? Support your answer. Yes
b. Is $\otimes$ an associative operation? Support your answer. No

CHECK YOUR PROGRESS: CHAPTER 4

Evaluate the variable expression when $a = 3$, $b = -2$, and $c = 4$.

1. $-2a + 3b$ -12 [4.1A]

2. $c^2 - 5ab$ 46 [4.1A]

3. $2c - (a + b)^2$ 7 [4.1A]

Evaluate the variable expression when $x = 2$, $y = -3$, and $z = -1$.

4. $\frac{y + z}{x}$ -2 [4.1A]

5. $(y + x)^2 - 5z$ 6 [4.1A]

6. $\frac{-yz}{2x + z}$ -1 [4.1A]

Simplify.

7. $10y - 16y + 3y$
$-3y$ [4.2A]

8. $-5a + 6b + 8a - 2b$
$3a + 4b$ [4.2A]

9. $(8a)(-5)$
$-40a$ [4.2B]

10. $(-9z)\left(-\frac{1}{9}\right)$
z [4.2B]

11. $(12 - 8b)3$
$36 - 24b$ [4.2C]

12. $-2(-3x^2 + 4x - 5)$
$6x^2 - 8x + 10$ [4.2C]

13. $3x - 4(2x - 5)$
$-5x + 20$ [4.2D]

14. $6(3a - 7) - (4 + 9a)$
$9a - 46$ [4.2D]

15. $5 - 3[2x - (6 - 4x)]$
$-18x + 23$ [4.2D]

SECTION

4.3 Translating Verbal Expressions into Variable Expressions

OBJECTIVE A

To translate a verbal expression into a variable expression, given the variable

One of the major skills required in applied mathematics is the ability to translate a verbal expression into a variable expression. This requires recognizing the verbal phrases that translate into mathematical operations. A partial list of the verbal phrases used to indicate the different mathematical operations is given on the next page.

HOW TO 1 Translate "14 less than the cube of x" into a variable expression.

14 less than the cube of x
- **Identify the words that indicate the mathematical operations.**

$x^3 - 14$
- **Use the identified operations to write the variable expression.**

INSTRUCTOR NOTE

Students may need to be reminded that the word *and* is not in the list of clue words for addition. Although in common English usage the question "What is two and two?" means two *plus* two, in formal mathematics the word *and* is never used as a clue word for addition. It does, however, have a special usage; it is a connector. The word *and* indicates where the appropriate mathematical operator is placed.

IN-CLASS EXAMPLES

1. Translate "the sum of 4 times x and 7" into a variable expression. **$4x + 7$**
2. Translate "the product of 5 and the difference between w and 3" into a variable expression. **$5(w - 3)$**

Translating a phrase that contains the word *sum, difference, product,* or *quotient* can be challenging. In the examples at the right, note where the operation symbol is placed.

the *sum* of x *and* y (+)	$x + y$
the *difference* between x *and* y (−)	$x - y$
the *product* of x *and* y (·)	$x \cdot y$
the *quotient* of x *and* y (÷)	$\frac{x}{y}$

HOW TO 2 Translate "the difference between the square of x and the sum of y and z" into a variable expression.

the difference between the square of x and the sum of y and z
- **Identify the words that indicate the mathematical operations.**

$x^2 - (y + z)$
- **Use the identified operations to write the variable expression.**

EXAMPLE 1

Translate "the total of 3 times n and 5" into a variable expression.

Solution

the total of 3 times n and 5

$3n + 5$

YOU TRY IT 1

Translate "the difference between twice n and the square of n" into a variable expression.

Your solution

$2n - n^2$

Solution on p. S12

Point of Interest

The way in which expressions are symbolized has changed over time. Here are how some of the expressions shown at the right may have appeared in the early 16th century.

R p. 9 for $x + 9$. The symbol R was used for a variable raised to the first power. The symbol p. was used for plus.

R m. 3 for $x - 3$. The symbol R was used for the variable. The symbol m. was used for minus.

The square of a variable was designated by Q, and the cube was designated by C. The expression $x^2 + x^3$ was written Q p. C.

Words or Phrases for Addition

added to	6 added to y	$y + 6$
more than	8 more than x	$x + 8$
the sum of	the sum of x and z	$x + z$
increased by	t increased by 9	$t + 9$
the total of	the total of 5 and d	$5 + d$
plus	b plus 17	$b + 17$

Words or Phrases for Subtraction

minus	x minus 2	$x - 2$
less than	7 less than t	$t - 7$
less	7 less t	$7 - t$
subtracted from	5 subtracted from d	$d - 5$
decreased by	m decreased by 3	$m - 3$
the difference between	the difference between y and 4	$y - 4$

INSTRUCTOR NOTE

In all of these phrases, whatever term is mentioned first may be written first, and whatever term is mentioned second is written second—with the exception of the phrases *less than* and *subtracted from.* They are the only phrases in this list that require a reversal of the terms. For example, 5 *added to* x may be written as $5 + x$, but 5 *less than* x is always written as $x - 5$.

Words or Phrases for Multiplication

times	10 times t	$10t$
of	one-half of x	$\frac{1}{2}x$
the product of	the product of y and z	yz
multiplied by	b multiplied by 11	$11b$
twice	twice n	$2n$

Phrases for Division

divided by	x divided by 12	$\frac{x}{12}$
the quotient of	the quotient of y and z	$\frac{y}{z}$
the ratio of	the ratio of t to 9	$\frac{t}{9}$

Phrases for Power

the square of	the square of x	x^2
the cube of	the cube of a	a^3

EXAMPLE 2

Translate "*m* decreased by the sum of *n* and 12" into a variable expression.

Solution

m decreased by the sum of *n* and 12

$m - (n + 12)$

YOU TRY IT 2

Translate "the quotient of 7 less than *b* and 15" into a variable expression.

Your solution

$\frac{b - 7}{15}$

Solution on p. S12

OBJECTIVE B *To translate a verbal expression into a variable expression and then simplify*

In most applications that involve translating phrases into variable expressions, the variable to be used is not given. To translate these phrases, a variable must be assigned to an unknown quantity before the variable expression can be written.

IN-CLASS EXAMPLES

3. Translate "the product of three and the sum of four times the square of a number and one" into a variable expression. $3(4x^2 + 1)$
4. Translate "six times the total of the quotient of a number and three and two" into a variable expression. Then simplify. $6\left(\frac{n}{3} + 2\right)$; $2n + 12$

HOW TO 3 Translate "a number multiplied by the total of six and the cube of the number" into a variable expression.

the unknown number: n • **Assign a variable to one of the unknown quantities.**

the cube of the number: n^3

the total of six and the cube of the number: $6 + n^3$ • **Use the assigned variable to write an expression for any other unknown quantity.**

$n(6 + n^3)$ • **Use the assigned variable to write the variable expression.**

EXAMPLE 3

Translate "four times the sum of one-half of a number and fourteen" into a variable expression. Then simplify.

Solution

the unknown number: n

one-half of the number: $\frac{1}{2}n$

the sum of one-half of the number and fourteen: $\frac{1}{2}n + 14$

$4\left(\frac{1}{2}n + 14\right) = 2n + 56$

YOU TRY IT 3

Translate "five times the difference between a number and sixty" into a variable expression. Then simplify.

Your solution

$5(x - 60)$; $5x - 300$

Solution on p. S13

EXAMPLE 4

Translate "a number added to the product of four and the square of the number" into a variable expression.

Solution

the unknown number: n
the square of the number: n^2
the product of four and the square of the number: $4n^2$

$4n^2 + n$

YOU TRY IT 4

Translate "negative four multiplied by the total of ten and the cube of a number" into a variable expression.

Your solution

$-4(10 + n^3)$

Solution on p. S13

OBJECTIVE C *To translate application problems*

Many applications in mathematics require that you identify the unknown quantity, assign a variable to that quantity, and then attempt to express other unknown quantities in terms of the variable.

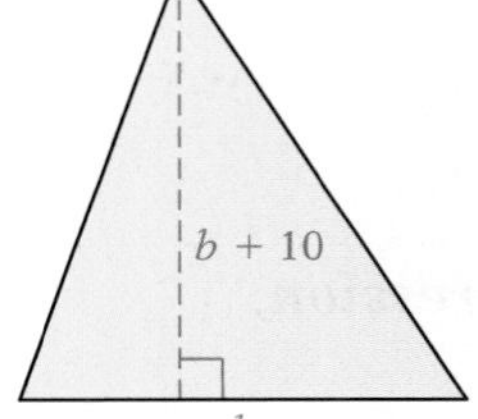

HOW TO 4 The height of a triangle is 10 ft longer than the base of the triangle. Express the height of the triangle in terms of the base of the triangle.

the base of the triangle: b • **Assign a variable to the base of the triangle.**

the height is 10 more than the base: $b + 10$ • **Express the height of the triangle in terms of b.**

EXAMPLE 5

The length of a swimming pool is 4 ft less than two times the width. Express the length of the pool in terms of the width.

Solution

the width of the pool: w
the length is 4 ft less than two times the width: $2w - 4$

YOU TRY IT 5

The speed of a new jet plane is twice the speed of an older model. Express the speed of the new model in terms of the speed of the older model.

Your solution

Let s be the speed of the older model; $2s$

IN-CLASS EXAMPLES

5. The force of gravity on the moon is one-sixth the force of gravity on Earth. Represent the force of gravity on the moon in terms of the force of gravity on Earth. **Force of gravity on Earth: F; $\frac{1}{6}F$**

EXAMPLE 6

A banker divided $5000 between two accounts, one paying 10% annual interest and the second paying 8% annual interest. Express the amount invested in the 10% account in terms of the amount invested in the 8% account.

Solution

the amount invested at 8%: x
the amount invested at 10%: $5000 - x$

YOU TRY IT 6

A guitar string 6 ft long was cut into two pieces. Express the length of the shorter piece in terms of the length of the longer piece.

Your solution

Let y be the length of the longer piece; $6 - y$

Solutions on p. S13

4.3 EXERCISES

Concept Check

SUGGESTED ASSIGNMENT
Exercises 1–6; Exercises 7–81, odds

For each phrase in Exercises 1 to 4, identify the words that indicate mathematical operations.

1. the sum of seven and three times m sum, times

2. twelve less than the quotient of x and negative two less than, quotient

3. the total of ten and fifteen divided by a number total, divided by

4. twenty subtracted from the product of eight and the cube of a number
subtracted from, product, cube

5. The sum of two numbers is 25. To express both numbers in terms of the same variable, let x represent one number. Then the other number is $\underline{25 - x}$.

6. The length of a rectangle is five times the width. To express the length and the width in terms of the same variable, let W represent the width. Then the length is $\underline{5W}$.

OBJECTIVE A *To translate a verbal expression into a variable expression, given the variable*

For Exercises 7 to 32, translate into a variable expression.

7. the sum of 8 and y
$8 + y$

8. a less than 16
$16 - a$

9. t increased by 10
$t + 10$

10. p decreased by 7
$p - 7$

11. 14 added to z
$z + 14$

12. q multiplied by 13
$13q$

13. 20 less than the square of x
$x^2 - 20$

14. 6 times the difference between m and 7
$6(m - 7)$

15. the sum of three-fourths of n and 12
$\frac{3}{4}n + 12$

16. b decreased by the product of 2 and b
$b - 2b$

17. 8 increased by the quotient of n and 4
$8 + \frac{n}{4}$

18. the product of -8 and y
$-8y$

19. the product of 3 and the total of y and 7
$3(y + 7)$

20. 8 divided by the difference between x and 6
$\frac{8}{x - 6}$

21. the product of t and the sum of t and 16
$t(t + 16)$

22. the quotient of 6 less than n and twice n
$\frac{n - 6}{2n}$

23. 15 more than one-half of the square of x
$\frac{1}{2}x^2 + 15$

24. 19 less than the product of n and -2
$-2n - 19$

25. the total of 5 times the cube of n and the square of n
$5n^3 + n^2$

26. the ratio of 9 more than m to m
$\frac{m + 9}{m}$

27. r decreased by the quotient of r and 3
$r - \frac{r}{3}$

28. four-fifths of the sum of w and 10
$\frac{4}{5}(w + 10)$

29. the difference between the square of x and the total of x and 17
$x^2 - (x + 17)$

30. s increased by the quotient of 4 and s
$s + \frac{4}{s}$

31. the product of 9 and the total of z and 4
$9(z + 4)$

32. n increased by the difference between 10 times n and 9
$n + (10n - 9)$

33. Write two different verbal phrases that translate into the variable expression $5(n^2 + 1)$.
Answers will vary. For example: the product of 5 and 1 more than the square of n, or 5 times the sum of 1 plus the square of n

OBJECTIVE B *To translate a verbal expression into a variable expression and then simplify*

For Exercises 34 to 45, translate into a variable expression.

34. twelve minus a number
$12 - x$

35. a number divided by eighteen
$\frac{x}{18}$

36. two-thirds of a number
$\frac{2}{3}x$

37. twenty more than a number
$x + 20$

38. the quotient of twice a number and nine
$\frac{2x}{9}$

39. eight less than the product of eleven and a number
$11x - 8$

40. the sum of five-eighths of a number and six
$\frac{5}{8}x + 6$

41. the quotient of seven and the total of five and a number
$\frac{7}{5 + x}$

42. the quotient of fifteen and the sum of a number and twelve
$\frac{15}{x + 12}$

43. the difference between forty and the quotient of a number and twenty
$40 - \frac{x}{20}$

44. the quotient of five more than twice a number and the number
$\frac{2x + 5}{x}$

45. the sum of the square of a number and twice the number
$x^2 + 2x$

46. Which of the following phrases translate into the variable expression $32 - \frac{a}{7}$?

(i) the difference between thirty-two and the quotient of a number and seven
(ii) thirty-two decreased by the quotient of a number and seven
(iii) thirty-two minus the ratio of a number to seven
i, ii, iii

For Exercises 47 to 62, translate into a variable expression. Then simplify.

47. ten times the difference between a number and fifty
$10(x - 50)$; $10x - 500$

48. nine less than the total of a number and two
$(x + 2) - 9$; $x - 7$

49. the difference between a number and three more than the number
$x - (x + 3)$; -3

50. four times the sum of a number and nineteen
$4(x + 19)$; $4x + 76$

51. a number added to the difference between twice the number and four
$(2x - 4) + x$; $3x - 4$

52. the product of five less than a number and seven
$(x - 5)7$; $7x - 35$

53. a number decreased by the difference between three times the number and eight
$x - (3x - 8)$; $-2x + 8$

54. the sum of eight more than a number and one-third of the number
$(x + 8) + \frac{1}{3}x$; $\frac{4}{3}x + 8$

55. a number added to the product of three and the number
$3x + x$; $4x$

56. a number increased by the total of the number and nine
$x + (x + 9)$; $2x + 9$

57. five more than the sum of a number and six
$(x + 6) + 5$; $x + 11$

58. a number decreased by the difference between eight and the number
$x - (8 - x)$; $2x - 8$

59. a number minus the sum of the number and ten
$x - (x + 10)$; -10

60. two more than the total of a number and five
$(x + 5) + 2$; $x + 7$

61. the sum of one-sixth of a number and four-ninths of the number
$\frac{1}{6}x + \frac{4}{9}x$; $\frac{11}{18}x$

62. the difference between one-third of a number and five-eighths of the number
$\frac{1}{3}x - \frac{5}{8}x$; $-\frac{7}{24}x$

OBJECTIVE C *To translate application problems*

For Exercises 63 and 64, use the following situation: 83 more students enrolled in spring-term science classes than enrolled in fall-term science classes.

63. If s and $s + 83$ represent the quantities in this situation, what is s?
The number of students enrolled in fall-term science classes

64. If n and $n - 83$ represent the quantities in this situation, what is n?
The number of students enrolled in spring-term science classes

65. **Museums** In a recent year, 3.8 million more people visited the Louvre in Paris than visited the Metropolitan Museum of Art in New York City. (*Sources:* The *Art Newspaper;* museums' accounts) Express the number of visitors to the Louvre in terms of the number of visitors to the Metropolitan Museum of Art. Let M be the number of visitors to the Metropolitan Museum of Art; $M + 3{,}800{,}000$

© Zoran Karapancev/Shutterstock.com

The Louvre

66. **Astronomy** The diameter of Saturn's moon Rhea is 253 mi more than the diameter of Saturn's moon Dione. Express the diameter of Rhea in terms of the diameter of Dione. (*Source:* NASA) Let d be the diameter of Dione; $d + 253$

67. **Noise Level** The noise level of an ambulance siren is 10 decibels louder than that of a car horn. Express the noise level of an ambulance siren in terms of the noise level of a car horn. (*Source:* League for the Hard of Hearing) Let d be the noise level, in decibels, of a car horn; $d + 10$

In the NEWS!

U2 Concerts Top Annual Rankings in North America

The Irish rock band U2 performed the most popular concerts on the North American circuit this year. Bruce Springsteen and the E Street Band came in second, with $28.5 million less in ticket sales.

Source: new.music.yahoo.com

68. **Genetics** The human genome contains 11,000 more genes than the roundworm genome. Express the number of genes in the human genome in terms of the number of genes in the roundworm genome. (*Source:* Celera, USA TODAY research) Let G be the number of genes in the roundworm genome; $G + 11{,}000$

69. **Rock Band Tours** See the news clipping at the right. Express Bruce Springsteen and the E Street Band's concert ticket sales in terms of U2's concert ticket sales. Let T be U2's concert ticket sales; $T - 28{,}500{,}000$

70. **Space Exploration** A survey in *USA Today* reported that almost three-fourths of Americans think that money should be spent on exploration of Mars. Express the number of Americans who think that money should be spent on exploration of Mars in terms of the total number of Americans.

Let N be the total number of Americans; $\frac{3}{4}N$

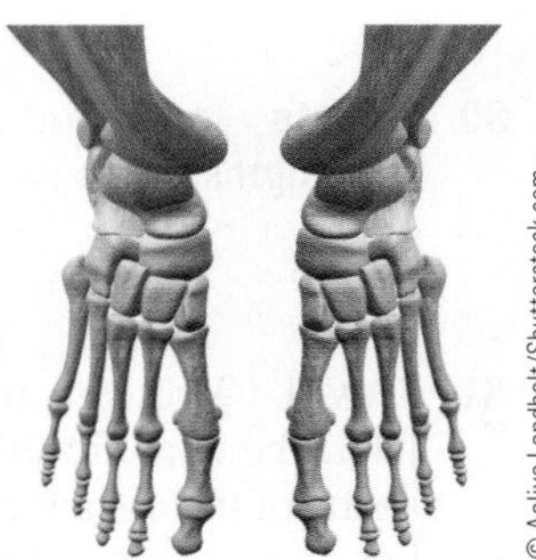
© Aaliya Landholt/Shutterstock.com

71. **Biology** According to the American Podiatric Medical Association, the bones in your foot account for one-fourth of all the bones in your body. Express the number of bones in your foot in terms of the number of bones in your body.

Let N be the number of bones in your body; $\frac{1}{4}N$

72. **Football** In football, the number of points awarded for a touchdown is three times the number of points awarded for a safety. Express the number of points awarded for a touchdown in terms of the number of points awarded for a safety. Let s be the number of points awarded for a safety; $3s$

73. **Sports** The diameter of a basketball is approximately four times the diameter of a baseball. Express the diameter of a basketball in terms of the diameter of a baseball. Let d be the diameter of a baseball; $4d$

74. **Tax Refunds** A recent survey conducted by Turbotax.com asked, "If you receive a tax refund, what will you do?" About two-fifths of respondents said they would pay down their debt. (*Source: USA Today,* March 27, 2008) Express the number of people who would pay down their debt in terms of the number of people surveyed. Let N be the number of people surveyed; $\frac{2}{5}N$

75. **Major League Sports** See the news clipping at the right. Express the attendance at major league baseball games in terms of the attendance at major league basketball games.
Let B be the attendance at major league basketball games; $B + 50{,}000{,}000$

In the NEWS!

Over 70 Million Attend Major League Baseball Games

Among major league sports, attendance at major league baseball games topped attendance at other major league sporting events. Fifty million more people went to baseball games than went to basketball games. The attendance at football games and hockey games was even less than the attendance at basketball games.

Source: Time, December 28, 2010–January 4, 2010

76. **Geometry** The length of a rectangle is 5 m more than twice the width. Express the length of the rectangle in terms of the width.
Let W be the width of the rectangle; $2W + 5$

77. **Geometry** In a triangle, the measure of the smallest angle is 10 degrees less than one-half the measure of the largest angle. Express the measure of the smallest angle in terms of the measure of the largest angle.
Let L be the measure of the largest angle; $\frac{1}{2}L - 10$

78. **Wages** An employee is paid \$1172 per week plus \$38 for each hour of overtime worked. Express the employee's weekly pay in terms of the number of hours of overtime worked. Let h be the number of hours of overtime worked; $1172 + 38h$

QUICK QUIZ

1. Translate "the product of 7 and the sum of n and 4" into a variable expression. **$7(n + 4)$ [4.3A]**
2. Translate "five less than the total of a number and seven" into a variable expression. Then simplify. **$(n + 7) - 5$; $n + 2$ [4.3B]**

79. **Billing** An auto repair bill is \$238 for parts and \$89 for each hour of labor. Express the amount of the repair bill in terms of the number of hours of labor.
Let h be the number of hours of labor; $238 + 89h$

80. **Sports** A halyard 12 ft long is cut into two pieces. Use the same variable to express the lengths of the two pieces. Let L be the length of one piece; L and $12 - L$

81. **Travel** Two cars are traveling in opposite directions at different rates. Two hours later, the cars are 200 mi apart. Express the distance traveled by the faster car in terms of the distance traveled by the slower car.
Let x be the distance traveled by the slower car; $200 - x$

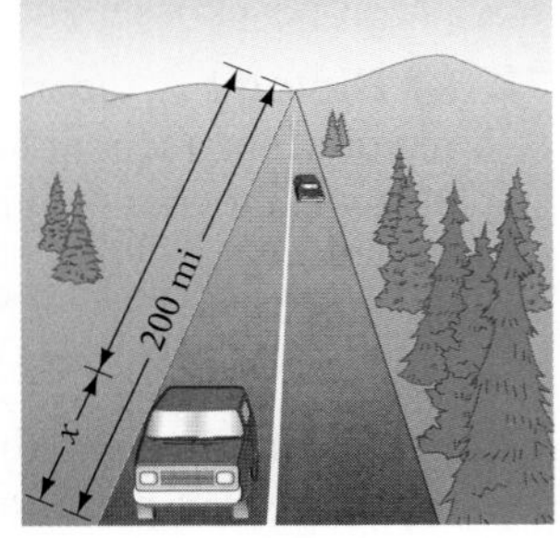

Critical Thinking

82. **Metalwork** A wire whose length is given as x inches is bent into a square. Express the length of a side of the square in terms of x.
$\frac{1}{4}x$

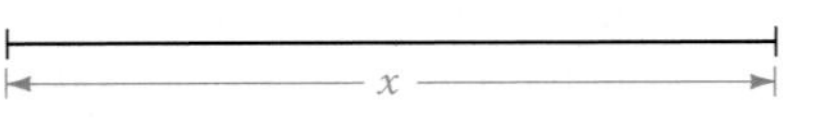

?

3. A wire 50 ft long was cut into two pieces of different lengths. Use one variable to express the lengths of the two pieces. **Length of one piece: L; Length of the second piece: $50 - L$ [4.3C]**

83. **Chemistry** The chemical formula for glucose (sugar) is $C_6H_{12}O_6$. This formula means that there are 12 hydrogen atoms for every 6 carbon atoms and every 6 oxygen atoms in each molecule of glucose (see the figure at the right). If x represents the number of oxygen atoms in a pound of sugar, express the number of hydrogen atoms in the pound of sugar in terms of the number of oxygen atoms. $2x$

H, O
C
H − C − OH
HO − C − H
H − C − OH
H − C − OH
CH_2OH

84. Translate the expressions $5x + 8$ and $5(x + 8)$ into phrases.

85. Explain the similarities and differences between the expressions "the difference between x and 5" and "5 less than x."

Projects or Group Activities

86. Write five phrases that translate into the expression $p + 8$. Answers will vary. For example: the sum of p and 8; the total of p and 8; 8 more than p; 8 added to p; p increased by 8

87. Write four phrases that translate into the expression $d - 16$. Answers will vary. For example: 16 less than d; the difference between d and 16; d decreased by 16; 16 subtracted from d

88. Write three phrases that translate into the expression $4c$. Answers will vary. For example: 4 times c; the product of 4 and c; 4 multiplied by c

89. Write three phrases that translate into the expression $\frac{y}{5}$. Answers will vary. For example: y divided by 5; the quotient of y and 5; the ratio of y to 5

CHAPTER 4 Summary

Key Words	Examples
A **variable** is a letter that is used to represent a quantity that is unknown or that can change. A **variable expression** is an expression that contains one or more variables. [4.1A, p. 250]	$4x + 2y - 6z$ is a variable expression. It contains the variables x, y, and z.
The **terms** of a variable expression are the addends of the expression. Each term is a **variable term** or a **constant term.** [4.1A, p. 250]	The expression $2a^2 - 3b^3 + 7$ has three terms: $2a^2$, $-3b^3$, and 7. $2a^2$ and $-3b^3$ are variable terms. 7 is a constant term.
A variable term is composed of a **numerical coefficient** and a **variable part.** [4.1A, p. 250]	For the expression $-7x^3y^2$, -7 is the coefficient and x^3y^2 is the variable part.
In a variable expression, replacing each variable by its value and then simplifying the resulting numerical expression is called **evaluating the variable expression.** [4.1A, p. 251]	To evaluate $2ab - b^2$ when $a = 3$ and $b = -2$, replace a by 3 and b by -2. Then simplify the numerical expression. $2(3)(-2) - (-2)^2 = -16$
Like terms of a variable expression are terms with the same variable part. Constant terms are like terms. [4.2A, p. 254]	For the expressions $3a^2 + 2b - 3$ and $2a^2 - 3a + 4$, $3a^2$ and $2a^2$ are like terms; -3 and 4 are like terms.

To simplify the sum of like variable terms, use the Distributive Property to add the numerical coefficients. This is called **combining like terms.** [4.2A, p. 254]	$5y + 3y = (5 + 3)y$ $= 8y$
The **additive inverse** of a number is the opposite of the number. [4.2A, p. 255]	-4 is the additive inverse of 4. $\frac{2}{3}$ is the additive inverse of $-\frac{2}{3}$. 0 is the additive inverse of 0.
The **multiplicative inverse** of a number is the reciprocal of the number. [4.2B, p. 257]	$\frac{3}{4}$ is the multiplicative inverse of $\frac{4}{3}$. $-\frac{1}{4}$ is the multiplicative inverse of -4.

Essential Rules and Procedures | Examples

Essential Rules and Procedures	Examples
The Distributive Property [4.2A, p. 254] If a, b, and c are real numbers, then $a(b + c) = ab + ac$ or $(b + c)a = ba + ca$.	$5(4x + 7) = 5 \cdot 4x + 5 \cdot 7$ $= 20x + 35$
The Associative Property of Addition [4.2A, p. 255] If a, b, and c are real numbers, then $(a + b) + c = a + (b + c)$.	$-4x + (2x + 7x) = -4x + 9x = 5x$ $(-4x + 2x) + 7x = -2x + 7x = 5x$
The Commutative Property of Addition [4.2A, p. 255] If a and b are real numbers, then $a + b = b + a$.	$2x + 5x = 7x$ and $5x + 2x = 7x$
The Addition Property of Zero [4.2A, p. 255] If a is a real number, then $a + 0 = 0 + a = a$.	$-8x + 0 = -8x$ and $0 + (-8x) = -8x$
The Inverse Property of Addition [4.2A, p. 255] If a is a real number, then $a + (-a) = (-a) + a = 0$.	$5x + (-5x) = 0$ and $(-5x) + 5x = 0$
The Associative Property of Multiplication [4.2B, p. 256] If a, b, and c are real numbers, then $(ab)c = a(bc)$.	$-3(5x) = (-3 \cdot 5)x = -15x$
The Commutative Property of Multiplication [4.2B, p. 256] If a and b are real numbers, then $ab = ba$.	$x(-2) = -2 \cdot x = -2x$
The Multiplication Property of One [4.2B, p. 257] If a is a real number, then $a \cdot 1 = 1 \cdot a = a$.	$-3x(1) = -3x$ and $1(-3x) = -3x$
The Inverse Property of Multiplication [4.2B, p. 257] If a is a real number and a is not equal to zero, then $a \cdot \frac{1}{a} = \frac{1}{a} \cdot a = 1$.	$3x \cdot \frac{1}{3x} = 1$ and $\frac{1}{3x} \cdot 3x = 1, \quad x \neq 0$

CHAPTER

4 Review Exercises

1. Simplify: $3(x^2 - 8x - 7)$
$3x^2 - 24x - 21$ [4.2C]

2. Simplify: $7x + 4x$
$11x$ [4.2A]

3. Simplify: $6a - 4b + 2a$
$8a - 4b$ [4.2A]

4. Simplify: $(-50n)\left(\frac{1}{10}\right)$
$-5n$ [4.2B]

5. Evaluate $(5c - 4a)^2 - b$ when $a = -1$, $b = 2$, and $c = 1$.
79 [4.1A]

6. Simplify: $5(2x - 7)$
$10x - 35$ [4.2C]

7. Simplify: $-6(7x^2)$
$-42x^2$ [4.2B]

8. Simplify: $-9(7 + 4x)$
$-63 - 36x$ [4.2C]

9. Simplify: $12y - 17y$
$-5y$ [4.2A]

10. Evaluate $2bc \div (a + 7)$ when $a = 3$, $b = -5$, and $c = 4$.
-4 [4.1A]

11. Simplify: $7 - 2(3x + 4)$
$-6x - 1$ [4.2D]

12. Simplify: $6 + 2[2 - 5(4a - 3)]$
$-40a + 40$ [4.2D]

13. Simplify: $6(8y - 3) - 8(3y - 6)$
$24y + 30$ [4.2D]

14. Simplify: $5c + (-2d) - 3d - (-4c)$
$9c - 5d$ [4.2A]

15. Simplify: $5(4x)$
$20x$ [4.2B]

16. Simplify: $-4(2x - 9) + 5(3x + 2)$
$7x + 46$ [4.2D]

17. Simplify: $4x - 3x^2 + 2x - x^2$
$-4x^2 + 6x$ [4.2A]

18. Simplify: $5[2 - 3(6x - 1)]$
$-90x + 25$ [4.2D]

19. Simplify: $0.4x + 0.6(250 - x)$
$-0.2x + 150$ [4.2D]

20. Simplify: $\frac{2}{3}x - \frac{3}{4}x$
$-\frac{1}{12}x$ [4.2A]

21. Simplify: $(7a^2 - 2a + 3)4$
$28a^2 - 8a + 12$ [4.2C]

22. Evaluate $a^2 - b^2$ when $a = 3$, $b = 4$.
-7 [4.1A]

23. Simplify: $-3(-12y)$
$36y$ [4.2B]

24. Translate "two-thirds of the total of x and 10" into a variable expression.

$\frac{2}{3}(x + 10)$ [4.3A]

25. Translate "6 less than x" into a variable expression.
$x - 6$ [4.3A]

26. Translate "a number plus twice the number" into a variable expression. Then simplify.
$x + 2x$; $3x$ [4.3B]

27. Translate "the difference between twice a number and one-half of the number" into a variable expression. Then simplify.
$2x - \frac{1}{2}x$; $\frac{3}{2}x$ [4.3B]

28. Translate "three times a number plus the product of five and one less than the number" into a variable expression. Then simplify.
$3x + 5(x - 1)$; $8x - 5$ [4.3B]

© Lana Sundman/Alamy

29. Baseball Cards A baseball card collection contains five times as many National League players' cards as American League players' cards. Express the number of National League players' cards in the collection in terms of the number of American League players' cards.
Let A be the number of American League players' cards; $5A$ [4.3C]

30. Dollar Bills A club treasurer has some five-dollar bills and some ten-dollar bills. The treasurer has a total of 35 bills. Express the number of five-dollar bills in terms of the number of ten-dollar bills.
Let T be the number of ten-dollar bills; $35 - T$ [4.3C]

31. Calories A candy bar contains eight more calories than twice the number of calories in an apple. Express the number of calories in the candy bar in terms of the number of calories in an apple.
Let a be the number of calories in an apple; $2a + 8$ [4.3C]

© Georgescu Gabriel/Shutterstock.com

32. Architecture The length of the Parthenon is approximately 1.6 times the width. Express the length of the Parthenon in terms of the width.
Let w be the width of Parthenon; $1.6w$ [4.3C]

33. Human Proportions Leonardo da Vinci studied various proportions of human anatomy. One of his findings was that the standing height of a person is approximately 1.3 times the kneeling height of the same person. Represent the standing height of a person in terms of the person's kneeling height.
Let h be the kneeling height; $1.3h$ [4.3C]

CHAPTER 4 TEST

1. Simplify: $3x - 5x + 7x$
$5x$ [4.2A]

2. Simplify: $-3(2x^2 - 7y^2)$
$-6x^2 + 21y^2$ [4.2C]

3. Simplify: $2x - 3(x - 2)$
$-x + 6$ [4.2D]

4. Simplify: $2x + 3[4 - (3x - 7)]$
$-7x + 33$ [4.2D]

5. Simplify: $3x - 7y - 12x$
$-9x - 7y$ [4.2A]

6. Evaluate $b^2 - 3ab$ when $a = 3$ and $b = -2$.
22 [4.1A]

7. Simplify: $\frac{1}{5}(10x)$
$2x$ [4.2B]

8. Simplify: $5(2x + 4) - 3(x - 6)$
$7x + 38$ [4.2D]

9. Simplify: $-5(2x^2 - 3x + 6)$
$-10x^2 + 15x - 30$ [4.2C]

10. Simplify: $3x + (-12y) - 5x - (-7y)$
$-2x - 5y$ [4.2A]

11. Evaluate $\frac{-2ab}{2b - a}$ when $a = -4$ and $b = 6$.
3 [4.1A]

12. Simplify: $(12x)\left(\frac{1}{4}\right)$
$3x$ [4.2B]

13. Simplify: $-7y^2 + 6y^2 - (-2y^2)$
y^2 [4.2A]

14. Simplify: $-2(2x - 4)$
$-4x + 8$ [4.2C]

15. Simplify: $\frac{2}{3}(-15a)$
$-10a$ [4.2B]

16. Simplify: $-2[x - 2(x - y)] + 5y$
$2x + y$ [4.2D]

17. Simplify: $(-3)(-12y)$
$36y$ [4.2B]

18. Simplify: $5(3 - 7b)$
$15 - 35b$ [4.2C]

19. Translate "the difference between the squares of a and b" into a variable expression.
$a^2 - b^2$ [4.3A]

20. Translate "ten times the difference between a number and three" into a variable expression. Then simplify.
$10(x - 3)$; $10x - 30$ [4.3B]

21. Translate "the sum of a number and twice the square of the number" into a variable expression.
$x + 2x^2$ [4.3B]

22. Translate "three less than the quotient of six and a number" into a variable expression.
$\frac{6}{x} - 3$ [4.3B]

23. Translate "b decreased by the product of b and 7" into a variable expression.
$b - 7b$ [4.3A]

24. **Astronomy** The distance from Neptune to the sun is 30 times the distance from Earth to the sun. Express the distance from Neptune to the sun in terms of the distance from Earth to the sun.
Let d be the distance from Earth to the sun; $30d$ [4.3C]

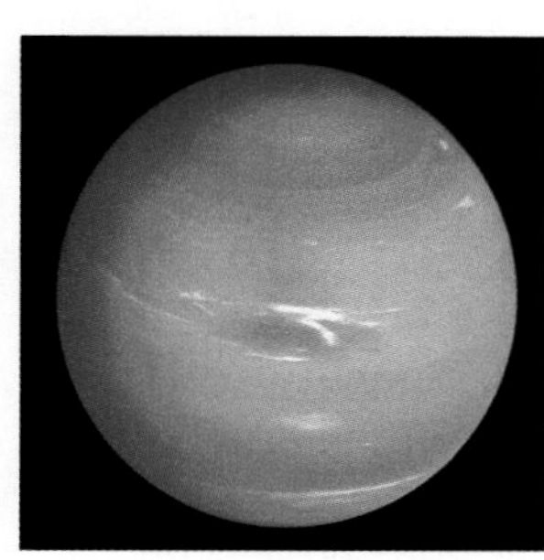
Stocktrek/Photodisc/Jupiterimages

25. **Metalwork** A wire is cut into two lengths. The length of the longer piece is 3 in. less than four times the length of the shorter piece. Express the length of the longer piece in terms of the length of the shorter piece.
Let x be the length of the shorter piece; $4x - 3$ [4.3C]

Cumulative Review Exercises

1. Add: $-4 + 7 + (-10)$
-7 [3.2A]

2. Subtract: $-16 - (-25) - 4$
5 [3.2B]

3. Multiply: $(-2)(3)(-4)$
24 [3.3A]

4. Divide: $(-60) \div 12$
-5 [3.3B]

5. Find the prime factorization of 110.
$2 \cdot 5 \cdot 11$ [1.3D]

6. Simplify: $\frac{7}{12} - \frac{11}{16} - \left(-\frac{1}{3}\right)$
$\frac{11}{48}$ [3.4A]

7. Simplify: $-\frac{5}{12} \div \frac{5}{2}$
$-\frac{1}{6}$ [3.4B]

8. Simplify: $\left(-\frac{9}{16}\right) \cdot \left(\frac{8}{27}\right) \cdot \left(-\frac{3}{2}\right)$
$\frac{1}{4}$ [3.4B]

9. Estimate the sum of 397, 516, and 408.
1300 [1.2A]

10. Simplify: $-2^5 \div (3 - 5)^2 - (-3)$
-5 [3.5A]

11. Simplify: $\left(-\frac{3}{4}\right)^2 \div \left(\frac{3}{8} - \frac{11}{12}\right)$
$-\frac{27}{26}$ [3.5A]

12. Evaluate $a^2 - 3b$ when $a = 2$ and $b = -4$.
16 [4.1A]

13. Simplify: $-2x^2 - (-3x^2) + 4x^2$
$5x^2$ [4.2A]

14. Simplify: $5a - 10b - 12a$
$-7a - 10b$ [4.2A]

15. Write eight and three hundred fifty-seven thousandths in standard form.
8.357 [2.5A]

16. Find the perimeter of a square whose side measures 24 ft.
96 ft [1.3E]

17. Simplify: $3(8 - 2x)$
$24 - 6x$ [4.2C]

18. Simplify: $-2(-3y + 9)$
$6y - 18$ [4.2C]

19. Estimate the difference between 32.76 and 19.8.
10 [2.6A]

20. Round 8.667 to the nearest tenth.
8.7 [2.5C]

21. Simplify: $-4(2x^2 - 3y^2)$
$-8x^2 + 12y^2$ [4.2C]

22. Simplify: $-3(3y^2 - 3y - 7)$
$-9y^2 + 9y + 21$ [4.2C]

23. Simplify: $-3x - 2(2x - 7)$
$-7x + 14$ [4.2D]

24. Simplify: $4(3x - 2) - 7(x + 5)$
$5x - 43$ [4.2D]

25. Simplify: $2x + 3[x - 2(4 - 2x)]$
$17x - 24$ [4.2D]

26. Simplify: $3[2x - 3(x - 2y)] + 3y$
$-3x + 21y$ [4.2D]

27. Translate "the sum of one-half of b and b" into a variable expression.
$\frac{1}{2}b + b$ [4.3A]

28. Translate "10 divided by the difference between y and 2" into a variable expression.
$\frac{10}{y - 2}$ [4.3A]

29. Translate "the difference between eight and the quotient of a number and twelve" into a variable expression.
$8 - \frac{x}{12}$ [4.3B]

30. Translate "the sum of a number and two more than the number" into a variable expression. Then simplify.
$x + (x + 2); 2x + 2$ [4.3B]

31. Softball A softball diamond is a square with each side measuring 60 ft. Find the area enclosed by the sides of the softball diamond.
3600 ft^2 [1.3E]

32. Biology A peregrine falcon's maximum flying speed over a quarter-mile distance is four times faster than a wildebeest's maximum running speed over the same distance. (*Source:* www.factmonster.com) Express the speed of the peregrine falcon in terms of the speed of the wildebeest.
Let w be the speed of the wildebeest; $4w$ [4.3C]

© Hedrus/Shutterstock.com

Solving Equations

5

OBJECTIVES

SECTION 5.1

A To determine whether a given number is a solution of an equation

B To solve an equation of the form $x + a = b$

C To solve an equation of the form $ax = b$

D To solve uniform motion problems

SECTION 5.2

A To solve an equation of the form $ax + b = c$

B To solve application problems using formulas

SECTION 5.3

A To solve an equation of the form $ax + b = cx + d$

B To solve an equation containing parentheses

C To solve application problems using formulas

SECTION 5.4

A To solve integer problems

B To translate a sentence into an equation and solve

SECTION 5.5

A To solve value mixture problems

B To solve uniform motion problems

Focus on Success

Do you have trouble with word problems? Word problems show the variety of ways in which math can be used. The solution of every word problem can be broken down into two steps: Strategy and Solution. The Strategy consists of reading the problem, writing down what is known and unknown, and devising a plan to find the unknown. The Solution often consists of solving an equation and then checking the solution. (See Word Problems, page AIM-10.)

© Diego Cervo/Shutterstock.com

Prep Test

Are you ready to succeed in this chapter? Take the Prep Test below to find out if you are ready to learn the new material.

1. Multiply: $-\frac{3}{4}\left(-\frac{4}{3}\right)$
1 [3.4B]

2. Simplify: $\frac{-3}{-3}$
1 [3.4B]

3. Simplify: $-16 + 7y + 16$
$7y$ [4.2A]

4. Simplify: $8x - 9 - 8x$
-9 [4.2A]

5. Simplify: $\frac{1}{2}x + \frac{2}{3}x$
$\frac{7}{6}x$ [4.2A]

6. Simplify: $6x - 3(6 - x)$
$9x - 18$ [4.2C]

7. Evaluate $2x + 3$ when $x = -4$.
-5 [4.1A]

8. Translate into a variable expression: "The difference between five and twice a number."
$5 - 2n$ [4.3B]

9. Computers A new graphics card for computer games is five times faster than a graphics card made two years ago. Express the speed of the new card in terms of the speed of the old card.
Speed of old card: s
Speed of new card: $5s$ [4.3C]

10. Carpentry A board 5 ft long is cut into two pieces. If x represents the length of the longer piece, write an expression for the length of the shorter piece in terms of x.
$5 - x$ [4.3C]

SECTION

5.1 Introduction to Equations

OBJECTIVE A *To determine whether a given number is a solution of an equation*

Point of Interest

One of the most famous equations ever stated is $E = mc^2$. This equation, stated by Albert Einstein, shows that there is a relationship between mass *m* and energy *E*. As a side note, the chemical element einsteinium was named in honor of Einstein.

INSTRUCTOR NOTE

Remind students that determining whether a given number is a solution of an equation is a way to check an answer after the equation has been solved.

Take Note

The Order of Operations Agreement applies when evaluating $2(-2) + 5$ and $(-2)^2 - 3$.

An **equation** expresses the equality of two mathematical expressions. The expressions can be either numerical or variable expressions.

$$\left.\begin{array}{l} 9 + 3 = 12 \\ 3x - 2 = 10 \\ y^2 + 4 = 2y - 1 \\ z = 2 \end{array}\right\} \text{Equations}$$

The equation at the right is true if the variable is replaced by 5.

$x + 8 = 13$

$5 + 8 = 13$ A true equation

The equation is false if the variable is replaced by 7. $7 + 8 = 13$ A false equation

A **solution of an equation** is a number that, when substituted for the variable, results in a true equation. 5 is a solution of the equation $x + 8 = 13$. 7 is not a solution of the equation $x + 8 = 13$.

HOW TO 1 Is -2 a solution of $2x + 5 = x^2 - 3$?

$$\begin{array}{r|l} \multicolumn{2}{c}{2x + 5 = x^2 - 3} \\ \hline 2(-2) + 5 & (-2)^2 - 3 \\ -4 + 5 & 4 - 3 \\ \multicolumn{2}{c}{1 = 1} \end{array}$$

- Replace x by -2.
- Evaluate the numerical expressions.
- If the results are equal, -2 is a solution of the equation. If the results are not equal, -2 is not a solution of the equation.

Yes, -2 is a solution of the equation.

EXAMPLE 1

Is -4 a solution of $4 + 5x = x^2 - 2x$?

Solution

$$\begin{array}{r|l} \multicolumn{2}{c}{4 + 5x = x^2 - 2x} \\ \hline 4 + 5(-4) & (-4)^2 - 2(-4) \\ 4 + (-20) & 16 - (-8) \\ \multicolumn{2}{c}{-16 \neq 24} \end{array}$$

- Replace x with -4.

($\neq$ means "is not equal to.")

No, -4 is not a solution.

YOU TRY IT 1

Is 5 a solution of $10x - x^2 = 3x - 10$?

Your solution

No

IN-CLASS EXAMPLES

1. Is -6 a solution of $4x + 3 = 2x - 9$? **Yes**
2. Is $-\frac{2}{3}$ a solution of $4 - 6x = 9x + 1$? **No**

Solution on p. S13

OBJECTIVE B *To solve an equation of the form $x + a = b$*

To **solve an equation** means to find a solution of the equation. The simplest equation to solve is an equation of the form *variable* = *constant,* because the constant is the solution.

The solution of the equation $x = 5$ is 5 because $5 = 5$ is a true equation.

Tips for Success

To learn mathematics, you must be an active participant. Listening and watching your professor do mathematics are not enough. Take notes in class, mentally think through every question your instructor asks, and try to answer it even if you are not called on to do so. Ask questions when you have them. See *AIM for Success* at the front of the book for other ways to be an active learner.

INSTRUCTOR NOTE

To help students see the value of the properties of equations, you might consider asking the students to find the solutions of equations such as the following by guessing. By the time they reach the last equation, they may have more appreciation for the properties.

$$x + 5 = 7$$
$$7 - x = 9$$
$$2x - 3 = 7$$
$$\frac{x}{2} - 1 = 3$$
$$5 - 3x = 27$$

Take Note

An equation has some properties that are similar to those of a balance scale. For instance, if a balance scale is in balance and equal weights are added to each side of the scale, then the balance scale remains in balance. If an equation is true, then adding the same number to each side of the equation produces another true equation.

The solution of the equation at the right is 7 because $7 + 2 = 9$ is a true equation.

$$x + 2 = 9 \qquad 7 + 2 = 9$$

Note that if 4 is added to each side of the equation $x + 2 = 9$, the solution is still 7.

$$\begin{aligned} x + 2 &= 9 \\ x + 2 + 4 &= 9 + 4 \\ x + 6 &= 13 \qquad 7 + 6 = 13 \end{aligned}$$

If -5 is added to each side of the equation $x + 2 = 9$, the solution is still 7.

$$\begin{aligned} x + 2 &= 9 \\ x + 2 + (-5) &= 9 + (-5) \\ x - 3 &= 4 \qquad 7 - 3 = 4 \end{aligned}$$

Equations that have the same solution are called **equivalent equations.** The equations $x + 2 = 9$, $x + 6 = 13$, and $x - 3 = 4$ are equivalent equations; each equation has 7 as its solution. These examples suggest that adding the same number to each side of an equation produces an equivalent equation. This is called the *Addition Property of Equations.*

Addition Property of Equations

The same number can be added to each side of an equation without changing its solution. In symbols, the equation $a = b$ has the same solution as the equation $a + c = b + c$.

EXAMPLE OF THIS PROPERTY

The equation $x - 3 = 7$ has the same solution as the equation $x - 3 + 3 = 7 + 3$.

In solving an equation, the goal is to rewrite the given equation in the form *variable* = *constant*. The Addition Property of Equations is used to remove a *term* from one side of the equation by adding the opposite of that term to each side of the equation.

HOW TO 2 Solve: $x - 4 = 2$

$$x - 4 = 2$$
• **The goal is to rewrite the equation in the form *variable* = *constant*.**

$$x - 4 + 4 = 2 + 4$$
• **Add 4 to each side of the equation.**

$$x + 0 = 6$$
• **Simplify.**

$$x = 6$$
• **The equation is in the form *variable* = *constant*.**

Check:
$$\begin{array}{c|c} x - 4 & 2 \\ \hline 6 - 4 & 2 \\ 2 & 2 \end{array}$$
$2 = 2$ A true equation

The solution is 6.

Because subtraction is defined in terms of addition, the Addition Property of Equations also makes it possible to subtract the same number from each side of an equation without changing the solution of the equation.

INSTRUCTOR NOTE

The title of this objective contains the equation $x + a = b$. Ask students to give examples of this type of equation. Be sure they include $b = x + a$.

HOW TO 3 Solve: $y + \frac{3}{4} = \frac{1}{2}$

$$y + \frac{3}{4} = \frac{1}{2}$$
• **The goal is to rewrite the equation in the form *variable = constant*.**

$$y + \frac{3}{4} - \frac{3}{4} = \frac{1}{2} - \frac{3}{4}$$
• **Subtract $\frac{3}{4}$ from each side of the equation.**

$$y + 0 = \frac{2}{4} - \frac{3}{4}$$
• **Simplify.**

$$y = -\frac{1}{4}$$
• **The equation is in the form *variable = constant*.**

The solution is $-\frac{1}{4}$. You should check this solution.

EXAMPLE 2

Solve: $x + 15 = 23$

Solution

$$x + 15 = 23$$
$$x + 15 - 15 = 23 - 15$$
• **Subtract 15 from each side.**
$$x + 0 = 8$$
• **Simplify each side.**
$$x = 8$$
• **Addition Property of Zero**

The solution is 8.

YOU TRY IT 2

Solve: $26 = y - 14$

Your solution

40

IN-CLASS EXAMPLES

Solve.

3. $x - \frac{1}{4} = \frac{5}{6}$ **$\frac{13}{12}$**
4. $3 + x = 9$ **6**
5. $5 = x + 5$ **0**

Solution on p. S13

OBJECTIVE C *To solve an equation of the form $ax = b$*

INSTRUCTOR NOTE

The requirement that each side be multiplied by a *nonzero* number is important. Later in the text, students will solve some equations by multiplying each side by a variable expression whose value may be zero. This can lead to extraneous solutions.

The solution of the equation at the right is 3 because $2 \cdot 3 = 6$ is a true equation.

$$2x = 6 \qquad 2 \cdot 3 = 6$$

Note that if each side of $2x = 6$ is multiplied by 5, the solution is still 3.

$$2x = 6$$
$$5(2x) = 5 \cdot 6$$
$$10x = 30 \qquad 10 \cdot 3 = 30$$

If each side of $2x = 6$ is multiplied by -4, the solution is still 3.

$$2x = 6$$
$$(-4)(2x) = (-4)6$$
$$-8x = -24 \qquad -8 \cdot 3 = -24$$

The equations $2x = 6$, $10x = 30$, and $-8x = -24$ are equivalent equations; each equation has 3 as its solution. These examples suggest that multiplying each side of an equation by the same nonzero number produces an equivalent equation.

Multiplication Property of Equations

Each side of an equation can be multiplied by the same nonzero number without changing the solution of the equation. In symbols, if $c \neq 0$, then the equation $a = b$ has the same solutions as the equation $ac = bc$.

EXAMPLE

The equation $3x = 21$ has the same solution as the equation $\frac{1}{3} \cdot 3x = \frac{1}{3} \cdot 21$.

INSTRUCTOR NOTE
Solutions to equations such as $ax = b$ have appeared in algebra texts for a long time. The problem below is an adaptation from Fibonacci's text *Liber Abaci,* which dates from 1202.

A merchant purchased 7 eggs for 1 denarius and sold them at a price of 5 eggs for 1 denarius. The merchant's profit was 18 denarii. How much did the merchant invest?

The resulting equation is

$$\frac{7}{5}x - x = 18$$

Solving this equation can serve as a classroom exercise. The solution is 45 denarii.

Take Note
Remember to check the solution.

Check:

$6x = 14$	
$6\left(\frac{7}{3}\right)$	14
$14 = 14$	

The Multiplication Property of Equations is used to remove a coefficient by multiplying each side of the equation by the reciprocal of the coefficient.

HOW TO 4 Solve: $\frac{3}{4}z = 9$

$\frac{3}{4}z = 9$ • The goal is to rewrite the equation in the form *variable = constant.*

$\frac{4}{3} \cdot \frac{3}{4}z = \frac{4}{3} \cdot 9$ • Multiply each side of the equation by $\frac{4}{3}$.

$1 \cdot z = 12$ • Simplify.

$z = 12$ • The equation is in the form *variable = constant.*

The solution is 12. You should check this solution.

Because division is defined in terms of multiplication, each side of an equation can be divided by the same nonzero number without changing the solution of the equation.

HOW TO 5 Solve: $6x = 14$

$6x = 14$ • The goal is to rewrite the equation in the form *variable = constant.*

$\frac{6x}{6} = \frac{14}{6}$ • Divide each side of the equation by 6.

$x = \frac{7}{3}$ • Simplify. The equation is in the form *variable = constant.*

The solution is $\frac{7}{3}$.

When using the Multiplication Property of Equations, multiply each side of the equation by the reciprocal of the coefficient when the coefficient is a fraction. Divide each side of the equation by the coefficient when the coefficient is an integer or a decimal.

EXAMPLE 3

Solve: $\frac{3x}{4} = -9$

Solution

$\frac{3x}{4} = -9$ • $\frac{3x}{4} = \frac{3}{4}x$

$\frac{4}{3} \cdot \frac{3}{4}x = \frac{4}{3}(-9)$ • Multiply each side by $\frac{4}{3}$.

$x = -12$

The solution is -12.

YOU TRY IT 3

Solve: $-\frac{2x}{5} = 6$

Your solution

-15

IN-CLASS EXAMPLES

Solve.

6. $-\frac{5}{8}x = 25$ **−40**
7. $4y - 10y = -42$ **7**
8. $8 = \frac{3x}{4}$ $\mathbf{\frac{32}{3}}$
9. $2z = 0$ **0**

EXAMPLE 4

Solve: $5x - 9x = 12$

Solution

$5x - 9x = 12$

$-4x = 12$ • Combine like terms.

$\frac{-4x}{-4} = \frac{12}{-4}$ • Divide each side by -4.

$x = -3$

The solution is -3.

YOU TRY IT 4

Solve: $4x - 8x = 16$

Your solution

-4

Solutions on p. S13

OBJECTIVE D To solve uniform motion problems

Take Note

A car traveling in a *circle* at a constant speed of 45 mph is *not* in uniform motion because the direction of the car is always changing.

INSTRUCTOR NOTE

The equation $d = rt$ is introduced in this objective, and students are asked to use this equation to solve problems of the form $ax = b$. This will give them exposure to the concepts involved in solving uniform motion problems prior to attempting the more difficult motion problems presented in Objective 5.5B.

Any object that travels at a constant speed in a straight line is said to be in *uniform motion*. **Uniform motion** means that the speed and direction of an object do not change. For instance, a car traveling at a constant speed of 45 mph on a straight road is in uniform motion.

The solution of a uniform motion problem is based on the **uniform motion equation** $d = rt$, where d is the distance traveled, r is the rate of travel, and t is the time spent traveling. For instance, suppose a car travels at 50 mph for 3 h. Because the rate (50 mph) and time (3 h) are known, we can find the distance traveled by solving the equation $d = rt$ for d.

$$d = rt$$

$$d = 50(3) \qquad \bullet\ r = 50, t = 3$$

$$d = 150$$

The car travels a distance of 150 mi.

APPLY THE CONCEPT

A jogger runs 3 mi in 45 min. What is the rate of the jogger in miles per hour?

To find the rate of the jogger, solve the equation $d = rt$ for r.
The answer must be in miles per *hour* and the time is given in *minutes*.
Convert 45 min to hours: 45 min $= \frac{45}{60}$ h $= \frac{3}{4}$ h

$$d = rt$$

$$3 = r\left(\frac{3}{4}\right) \qquad \bullet\ d = 3, t = \frac{3}{4}$$

$$3 = \frac{3}{4}r$$

$$\left(\frac{4}{3}\right)3 = \left(\frac{4}{3}\right)\frac{3}{4}r \qquad \bullet\ \text{Multiply each side of the equation by the reciprocal of } \tfrac{3}{4}.$$

$$4 = r$$

The rate of the jogger is 4 mph.

If two objects are moving in opposite directions, then the rate at which the distance between them is increasing is the sum of the speeds of the two objects. For instance, in the diagram below, two cars start from the same point and travel in opposite directions. The distance between them is changing at the rate of 70 mph.

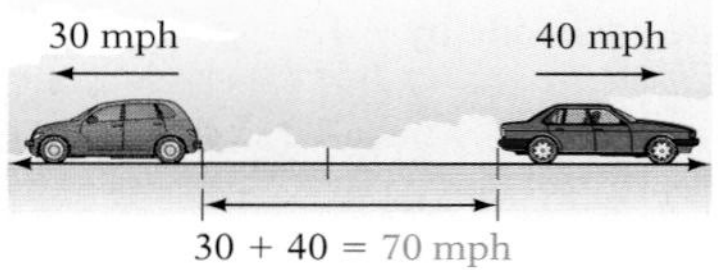

Similarly, if two objects are moving toward each other, the distance between them is decreasing at a rate that is equal to the sum of the speeds. The rate at which the two planes at the right are approaching one another is 800 mph.

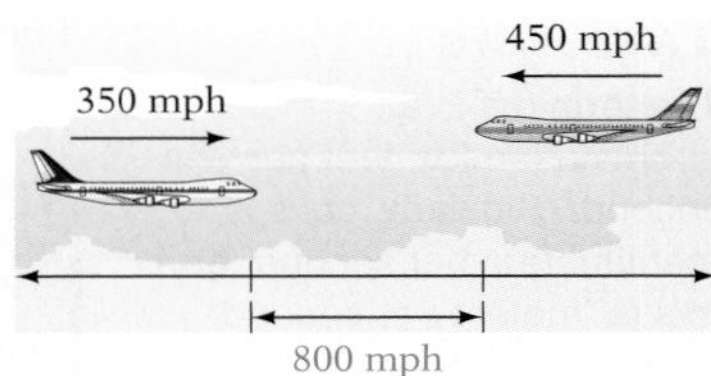

APPLY THE CONCEPT

Two cars start from the same point and move in opposite directions. The car moving west is traveling at 45 mph, and the car moving east is traveling at 60 mph. In how many hours will the cars be 210 mi apart?

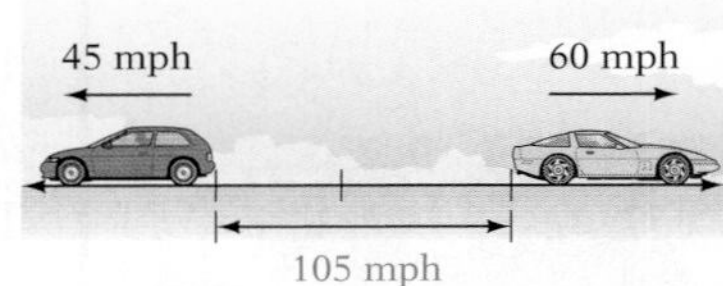

To find the time, solve the equation $d = rt$ for t.

d = distance = 210 mi

The cars are moving in opposite directions, so the rate at which the distance between them is changing is the sum of the rates of the cars.

45 mph + 60 mph = 105 mph. Therefore, $r = 105$.

$$d = rt$$

$$210 = 105t \qquad \bullet\ d = 210, r = 105$$

$$\frac{210}{105} = \frac{105t}{105} \qquad \bullet\ \text{Divide each side of the equation by 105.}$$

$$2 = t$$

In 2 h, the cars will be 210 mi apart.

If a motorboat is on a river that is flowing at a rate of 4 mph, then the boat will float down the river at a speed of 4 mph when the motor is not on. Now suppose the motor is turned on and the power adjusted so that the boat would travel 10 mph without the aid of the current. Then, if the boat is moving with the current, its effective speed is the speed of the boat using power plus the speed of the current: 10 mph + 4 mph = 14 mph. (See the figure below.)

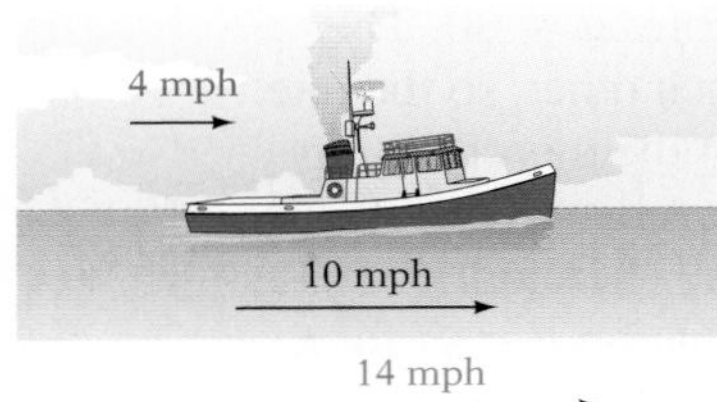

However, if the boat is moving against the current, the current slows the boat down. The effective speed of the boat is the speed of the boat using power minus the speed of the current: 10 mph − 4 mph = 6 mph. (See the figure below.)

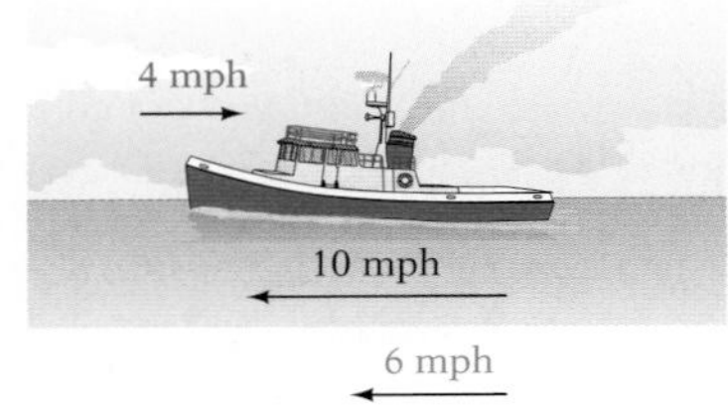

Take Note

The term ft/s is an abbreviation for "feet per second." Similarly, cm/s is "centimeters per second" and m/s is "meters per second."

There are other situations in which the preceding concepts may be applied.

APPLY THE CONCEPT

An airline passenger is walking between two airline terminals and decides to get on a moving sidewalk that is 150 ft long. If the passenger walks at a rate of 7 ft/s and the moving sidewalk moves at a rate of 9 ft/s, how long, in seconds, will it take for the passenger to walk from one end of the moving sidewalk to the other? Round to the nearest thousandth.

© Marc C. Johnson/Shutterstock.com

To find the time, solve the equation $d = rt$ for t.

d = distance = 150 ft

The passenger is traveling at 7 ft/s and the moving sidewalk is traveling at 9 ft/s.

The rate of the passenger is the sum of the two rates: 7 ft/s + 9 ft/s = 16 ft/s.

Therefore, $r = 16$.

$$d = rt$$

$$150 = 16t \quad \bullet\ d = 150, r = 16$$

$$\frac{150}{16} = \frac{16t}{16} \quad \bullet\ \text{Divide each side of the equation by 16.}$$

$$9.375 = t$$

It will take 9.375 s for the passenger to travel the length of the moving sidewalk.

EXAMPLE 5

Two cyclists start at the same time at opposite ends of an 80-mile course. One cyclist is traveling at 18 mph, and the second cyclist is traveling at 14 mph. How long after they begin cycling will they meet?

Strategy

The distance is 80 mi. Therefore, $d = 80$. The cyclists are moving toward each other, so the rate at which the distance between them is changing is the sum of the rates of the cyclists. The rate is 18 mph + 14 mph = 32 mph. Therefore, $r = 32$. To find the time, solve the equation $d = rt$ for t.

Solution

$$d = rt$$

$$80 = 32t \quad \bullet\ d = 80, r = 32$$

$$\frac{80}{32} = \frac{32t}{32} \quad \bullet\ \text{Divide each side by 32.}$$

$$2.5 = t$$

The cyclists will meet in 2.5 h.

YOU TRY IT 5

A plane that can normally travel at 250 mph in calm air is flying into a headwind of 25 mph. How far can the plane fly in 3 h?

Your strategy

Your solution

675 mi

Solution on p. S13

IN-CLASS EXAMPLES

10. Ted leaves his house at 8:00 A.M. and arrives at work at 8:30 A.M. If the trip to work is 15 mi, determine Ted's average rate of speed. **30 mph**

11. Joan leaves her house and travels at an average speed of 45 mph toward her cabin in the mountains. If the distance from her house to the cabin is 180 mi, how many hours will it take for Joan to arrive at her cabin if she stops one hour for lunch? **5 h**

5.1 EXERCISES

Concept Check

SUGGESTED ASSIGNMENT
Exercises 1–6; Exercises 7–111, odds

1. Label each of the following as either an expression or an equation.
a. $3x + 7 = 9$ Equation **b.** $3x + 7$ Expression **c.** $4 - 6(y + 5)$ Expression **d.** $a + b = 8$ Equation **e.** $a + b - 8$ Expression

2. What is the solution of the equation $x = 8$? Use your answer to explain why the goal in solving equations is to get the variable alone on one side of the equation.

3. Which of the following are equations of the form $x + a = b$? If an equation is of the form $x + a = b$, what would you do to solve the equation?
(i) $d + 7.8 = -9.2$ (ii) $0.3 = t + 1.4$ (iii) $-9 = 3y$ (iv) $-8 + c = -5.6$
i, ii, and iv are equations of the form $x + a = b$; you would subtract a from both sides.

4. Which of the following are equations of the form $ax = b$? If an equation is of the form $ax = b$, what would you do to solve the equation?
(i) $3y = -12$ (ii) $2.4 = 0.6d$ (iii) $-5 = z - 10$ (iv) $-8c = -56$
i, ii, and iv are equations of the form $ax = b$; you would divide both sides by a.

5. Keith and Jennifer started at the same time and rode toward each other on a straight road. When they met, Keith had traveled 15 mi and Jennifer had traveled 10 mi. Who had the greater average speed? Keith

6. Suppose you have a powerboat with the throttle set to move the boat at 8 mph in calm water. The rate of the current of a river is 4 mph.
a. What is the speed of the boat when traveling on this river with the current? 12 mph
b. What is the speed of the boat when traveling on this river against the current? 4 mph

OBJECTIVE A *To determine whether a given number is a solution of an equation*

7. Is 4 a solution of $2x = 8$? Yes

8. Is 3 a solution of $y + 4 = 7$? Yes

9. Is -1 a solution of $2b - 1 = 3$? No

10. Is -2 a solution of $3a - 4 = 10$? No

11. Is 1 a solution of $4 - 2m = 3$? No

12. Is 2 a solution of $7 - 3n = 2$? No

13. Is 5 a solution of $2x + 5 = 3x$? Yes

14. Is 4 a solution of $3y - 4 = 2y$? Yes

15. Is -2 a solution of $3a + 2 = 2 - a$? No

16. Is 3 a solution of $z^2 + 1 = 4 + 3z$? No

17. Is 2 a solution of $2x^2 - 1 = 4x - 1$? Yes

18. Is -1 a solution of $y^2 - 1 = 4y + 3$? No

19. Is $\frac{1}{2}$ a solution of $4y + 1 = 3$? Yes

20. Is $\frac{2}{5}$ a solution of $5m + 1 = 10m - 3$? No

21. Is $\frac{3}{4}$ a solution of $8x - 1 = 12x + 3$? No

22. If A is a fixed number such that $A < 0$, is a solution of the equation $5x = A$ positive or negative?
Negative

OBJECTIVE B *To solve an equation of the form $x + a = b$*

23. Without solving the equation $x - \frac{11}{16} = \frac{19}{24}$, determine whether x is less than or greater than $\frac{19}{24}$. Explain your answer.

24. Without solving the equation $x + \frac{13}{15} = -\frac{21}{43}$, determine whether x is less than or greater than $-\frac{21}{43}$. Explain your answer.

For Exercises 25 to 60, solve and check.

25. $x + 5 = 7$
2

26. $y + 3 = 9$
6

27. $b - 4 = 11$
15

28. $z - 6 = 10$
16

29. $2 + a = 8$
6

30. $5 + x = 12$
7

31. $n - 5 = -2$
3

32. $x - 6 = -5$
1

33. $b + 7 = 7$
0

34. $y - 5 = -5$
0

35. $z + 9 = 2$
−7

36. $n + 11 = 1$
−10

37. $10 + m = 3$
−7

38. $8 + x = 5$
−3

39. $9 + x = -3$
−12

40. $10 + y = -4$
−14

41. $2 = x + 7$
−5

42. $-8 = n + 1$
−9

43. $4 = m - 11$
15

44. $-6 = y - 5$
−1

45. $12 = 3 + w$
9

46. $-9 = 5 + x$
−14

47. $4 = -10 + b$
14

48. $-7 = -2 + x$
−5

49. $m + \frac{2}{3} = -\frac{1}{3}$
−1

50. $c + \frac{3}{4} = -\frac{1}{4}$
−1

51. $x - \frac{1}{2} = \frac{1}{2}$
1

52. $x - \frac{2}{5} = \frac{3}{5}$
1

53. $\frac{5}{8} + y = \frac{1}{8}$
$-\frac{1}{2}$

54. $\frac{4}{9} + a = -\frac{2}{9}$
$-\frac{2}{3}$

55. $-\frac{5}{6} = x - \frac{1}{4}$
$-\frac{7}{12}$

56. $-\frac{1}{4} = c - \frac{2}{3}$
$\frac{5}{12}$

57. $d + 1.3619 = 2.0148$ 0.6529

58. $w + 2.932 = 4.801$ 1.869

59. $6.149 = -3.108 + z$ 9.257

60. $5.237 = -2.014 + x$ 7.251

OBJECTIVE C *To solve an equation of the form $ax = b$*

For Exercises 61 to 94, solve and check.

61. $5x = -15$
-3

62. $4y = -28$
-7

63. $3b = 0$
0

64. $2a = 0$
0

65. $-3x = 6$
-2

66. $-5m = 20$
-4

67. $-\frac{1}{6}n = -30$
180

68. $20 = \frac{1}{4}c$
80

69. $0 = -5x$
0

70. $0 = -8a$
0

71. $\frac{x}{3} = 2$
6

72. $\frac{x}{4} = 3$
12

73. $-\frac{y}{2} = 5$
-10

74. $-\frac{b}{3} = 6$
-18

75. $\frac{3}{4}y = 9$
12

76. $\frac{2}{5}x = 6$
15

77. $-\frac{2}{3}d = 8$
-12

78. $-\frac{3}{5}m = 12$
-20

79. $\frac{2n}{3} = 0$
0

80. $\frac{5x}{6} = 0$
0

81. $\frac{-3z}{8} = 9$
-24

82. $\frac{3x}{4} = 2$
$\frac{8}{3}$

83. $\frac{2}{9} = \frac{2}{3}y$
$\frac{1}{3}$

84. $-\frac{6}{7} = -\frac{3}{4}b$
$\frac{8}{7}$

85. $\frac{x}{1.46} = 3.25$
4.745

86. $\frac{z}{2.95} = -7.88$
-23.246

87. $3.47a = 7.1482$
2.06

88. $2.31m = 2.4255$
1.05

89. $2m + 5m = 49$
7

90. $5x + 2x = 14$
2

91. $3n + 2n = 20$
4

92. $7d - 4d = 9$
3

93. $10y - 3y = 21$
3

94. $2x - 5x = 9$
-3

For Exercises 95 to 98, suppose y is a positive integer. Determine whether x is positive or negative.

95. $15x = y$
Positive

96. $-6x = y$
Negative

97. $-\frac{1}{4}x = y$
Negative

98. $\frac{2}{9}x = -y$
Negative

OBJECTIVE D *To solve uniform motion problems*

99. Morgan and Emma ride their bikes from Morgan's house to the store. Morgan begins biking 5 min before Emma begins. Emma bikes faster than Morgan and catches up with her just as they reach the store.

a. Is the distance biked by Emma less than, equal to, or greater than the distance biked by Morgan?

b. Is the time spent biking by Emma less than, equal to, or greater than the time spent biking by Morgan?

a. Equal to b. Less than

100. **Trains** See the news clipping at the right. Find the time it will take the high-speed train to travel between the two cities. Round to the nearest tenth of an hour. 3.1 h

© Bartlomiej Magierowski/Shutterstock.com

In the NEWS!

World's Fastest Train

China has unveiled the world's fastest rail link—a train that connects the cities of Guangzhou and Wuhan and can travel at speeds of up to 394.2 km/h. The distance between the two cities is 1069 km, and the train will travel that distance at an average speed of 350 km/h (217 mph). The head of the transport bureau at the Chinese railway ministry boasted, "It's the fastest train in operation in the world."

Source: news.yahoo.com

101. It takes a hospital dietician 40 min to drive from home to the hospital, a distance of 20 mi. What is the dietician's average rate of speed? 30 mph

102. As part of a training program for the Boston Marathon, a runner wants to build endurance by running at a rate of 9 mph for 20 min. How far will the runner travel in that time period?

3 mi

© John Kropewnicki/Shutterstock.com

103. Marcella leaves home at 9:00 A.M. and drives to school, arriving at 9:45 A.M. If the distance between home and school is 27 mi, what is Marcella's average rate of speed?

36 mph

104. The Ride for Health Bicycle Club has chosen a 36-mile course for this Saturday's ride. If the riders plan on averaging 12 mph while they are riding, and they have a 1-hour lunch break planned, how long will it take them to complete the trip?

4 h

© Arthur Eugene Preston/Shutterstock.com

105. Palmer's average running speed is 3 km/h faster than his walking speed. If Palmer can run around a 30-kilometer course in 2 h, how many hours would it take for Palmer to walk the same course?

2.5 h

106. A shopping mall has a moving sidewalk that takes shoppers from the shopping area to the parking garage, a distance of 250 ft. If your normal walking rate is 5 ft/s and the moving sidewalk is traveling at 3 ft/s, how many seconds would it take for you to walk from one end of the moving sidewalk to the other end?

31.25 s

107. Two joggers start at the same time from opposite ends of an 8-mile jogging trail and begin running toward each other. One jogger is running at a rate of 5 mph, and the other jogger is running at a rate of 7 mph. How long, in minutes, after they start will the two joggers meet?

40 min

108. **sQuba** See the news clipping at the right. Two sQubas are on opposite sides of a lake 1.6 mi wide. They start toward each other at the same time, one traveling on the surface of the water and the other traveling underwater. In how many minutes will the sQuba traveling on the surface of the water be directly above the sQuba traveling underwater? Assume they are traveling at top speed.
20 min

In the NEWS!

Underwater Driving —Not So Fast!

Swiss company Rinspeed, Inc., presented its new car, the sQuba, at the Geneva Auto Show. The sQuba can travel on land, on water, and underwater. With a new sQuba, you can expect top speeds of 77 mph when driving on land, 3 mph when driving on the surface of the water, and 1.8 mph when driving underwater!
Source: Seattle Times

109. Two cyclists start from the same point at the same time and move in opposite directions. One cyclist is traveling at 8 mph, and the other cyclist is traveling at 9 mph. After 30 min, how far apart are the two cyclists?
8.5 mi

110. Petra and Celine can paddle their canoe at a rate of 10 mph in calm water. How long will it take them to travel 4 mi against the 2-mile-per-hour current of the river?
0.5 h

111. At 8:00 A.M., a train leaves a station and travels at a rate of 45 mph. At 9:00 A.M., a second train leaves the same station on the same track and travels in the direction of the first train at a speed of 60 mph. At 10:00 A.M., how far apart are the two trains?
30 mi

Critical Thinking

Solve.

112. $\frac{3y - 8y}{7} = 15$ -21

113. $\frac{2m + m}{5} = -9$ -15

114. $\frac{1}{\frac{1}{x}} + 8 = -19$ -27

115. $\frac{1}{\frac{1}{x}} = 5$ 5

116. $\frac{5}{\frac{7}{a}} - \frac{3}{\frac{7}{a}} = 6$ 21

117. $\frac{4}{\frac{3}{b}} = 8$ 6

Projects or Group Activities

118. Make up an equation of the form $ax = b$ that has -2 as a solution.
One possible answer is $5x = -10$.

119. Make up an equation of the form $x + a = b$ that has 2 as a solution.
One possible answer is $x + 7 = 9$.

120. Use the numbers 5, 10, and 15 to fill in the boxes in the equation $x + \square = \square - \square$.
a. What is the largest solution possible? 0
b. What is the smallest solution possible? -20

121. Two numbers form a "two-pair" if the sum of their reciprocals equals 2. For example, $\frac{8}{15}$ and 8 are a two-pair because $\frac{15}{8} + \frac{1}{8} = 2$. If two numbers a and b form a two-pair, and $a = \frac{7}{3}$, what is the value of b? $\frac{7}{11}$

QUICK QUIZ

1. Is $\frac{2}{3}$ a solution of $6x + 5 = 9$?
Yes [5.1A]

Solve.

2. $a + 5 = -8$ **-13 [5.1B]**
3. $7 = b - 4$ **11 [5.1B]**
4. $c + \frac{5}{6} = \frac{1}{3}$ **$-\frac{1}{2}$ [5.1B]**
5. $3x = -21$ **-7 [5.1C]**
6. $-12 = \frac{2}{3}x$ **-18 [5.1C]**
7. $8x - 3x = 30$ **6 [5.1C]**
8. Chu Min runs 1 mph faster than Sasha. If Chu Min can run 6 mi in 45 min, determine Sasha's running speed. **7 mph [5.1D]**

SECTION

5.2 General Equations—Part I

OBJECTIVE A *To solve an equation of the form $ax + b = c$*

In solving an equation of the form $ax + b = c$, the goal is to rewrite the equation in the form *variable* = *constant*. This requires the application of both the Addition and Multiplication Properties of Equations.

HOW TO 1 Solve: $\frac{3}{4}x - 2 = -11$

The goal is to write the equation in the form *variable* = *constant*.

$$\frac{3}{4}x - 2 = -11$$

$$\frac{3}{4}x - 2 + 2 = -11 + 2$$ • **Add 2 to each side of the equation.**

$$\frac{3}{4}x = -9$$ • **Simplify.**

$$\frac{4}{3} \cdot \frac{3}{4}x = \frac{4}{3}(-9)$$ • **Multiply each side of the equation by $\frac{4}{3}$.**

$$x = -12$$ • **The equation is in the form *variable* = *constant*.**

The solution is −12.

Take Note

Check:

$\frac{3}{4}x - 2 = -11$	
$\frac{3}{4}(-12) - 2$	-11
$-9 - 2$	-11
$-11 =$	-11

A true equation

Here is an example of solving an equation that contains more than one fraction.

INSTRUCTOR NOTE

On the next page, we solve the equation at the right by first *clearing denominators.* Introducing this method now will prepare students to solve equations that contain fractions with variables in the denominator.

HOW TO 2 Solve: $\frac{2}{3}x + \frac{1}{2} = \frac{3}{4}$

$$\frac{2}{3}x + \frac{1}{2} = \frac{3}{4}$$

$$\frac{2}{3}x + \frac{1}{2} - \frac{1}{2} = \frac{3}{4} - \frac{1}{2}$$ • **Subtract $\frac{1}{2}$ from each side of the equation.**

$$\frac{2}{3}x = \frac{1}{4}$$ • **Simplify.**

$$\frac{3}{2}\left(\frac{2}{3}x\right) = \frac{3}{2}\left(\frac{1}{4}\right)$$ • **Multiply each side of the equation by $\frac{3}{2}$.**

$$x = \frac{3}{8}$$

The solution is $\frac{3}{8}$.

It may be easier to solve an equation containing two or more fractions by multiplying each side of the equation by the least common multiple (LCM) of the denominators. For the equation above, the LCM of 3, 2, and 4 is 12. The LCM has the property that 3, 2, and 4 divide evenly into it. Therefore, if both sides of the equation are multiplied by 12, the denominators will divide evenly into 12. The result is an equation that does not contain any fractions. Multiplying each side of an equation that contains fractions by the LCM of the denominators is called **clearing denominators.** It is an alternative method, as we show in the next example, of solving an equation that contains fractions.

Take Note

This is the same example solved on the preceding page, but this time we are using the method of clearing denominators.

Observe that after we multiply both sides of the equation by the LCM of the denominators and then simplify, the equation no longer contains fractions.

Clearing denominators is a method of solving equations. The process applies only to equations, never to expressions.

HOW TO 3 Solve: $\frac{2}{3}x + \frac{1}{2} = \frac{3}{4}$

$$\frac{2}{3}x + \frac{1}{2} = \frac{3}{4}$$

$$12\left(\frac{2}{3}x + \frac{1}{2}\right) = 12\left(\frac{3}{4}\right)$$

• Multiply each side of the equation by 12, the LCM of 3, 2, and 4.

$$12\left(\frac{2}{3}x\right) + 12\left(\frac{1}{2}\right) = 12\left(\frac{3}{4}\right)$$

• Use the Distributive Property.

$$8x + 6 = 9$$

• Simplify.

$$8x + 6 - 6 = 9 - 6$$

• Subtract 6 from each side of the equation.

$$8x = 3$$

$$\frac{8x}{8} = \frac{3}{8}$$

• Divide each side of the equation by 8.

$$x = \frac{3}{8}$$

The solution is $\frac{3}{8}$.

INSTRUCTOR NOTE

One of the most common mistakes students make when solving an equation by clearing denominators is incorrectly applying the Distributive Property when multiplying both sides of the equation by the same number. We have shown this process in two steps to assist students.

Note that both methods give exactly the same solution. You may use either method to solve an equation containing fractions.

EXAMPLE 1

Solve: $3x - 7 = -5$

Solution

$$3x - 7 = -5$$

$$3x - 7 + 7 = -5 + 7$$

• Add 7 to each side.

$$3x = 2$$

$$\frac{3x}{3} = \frac{2}{3}$$

• Divide each side by 3.

$$x = \frac{2}{3}$$

The solution is $\frac{2}{3}$.

YOU TRY IT 1

Solve: $5x + 7 = 10$

Your solution

$\frac{3}{5}$

IN-CLASS EXAMPLES

Solve.

1. $8a + 3 = 10$ **$\frac{7}{8}$**
2. $7 = 12 + 5h$ **-1**
3. $\frac{2}{5}x - \frac{1}{4} = \frac{3}{2}$ **$\frac{35}{8}$**
4. $\frac{3}{8}x + \frac{2}{3} = \frac{5}{12}$ **$-\frac{2}{3}$**
5. $\frac{1}{3} - \frac{3}{5}x = \frac{1}{2}$ **$-\frac{5}{18}$**

EXAMPLE 2

Solve: $5 = 9 - 2x$

Solution

$$5 = 9 - 2x$$

$$5 - 9 = 9 - 9 - 2x$$

• Subtract 9 from each side.

$$-4 = -2x$$

$$\frac{-4}{-2} = \frac{-2x}{-2}$$

• Divide each side by −2.

$$2 = x$$

The solution is 2.

YOU TRY IT 2

Solve: $2 = 11 + 3x$

Your solution

-3

Solutions on p. S13

EXAMPLE 3

Solve: $\frac{2}{3} - \frac{x}{2} = \frac{3}{4}$

Solution

$$\frac{2}{3} - \frac{x}{2} = \frac{3}{4}$$

$$\frac{2}{3} - \frac{2}{3} - \frac{x}{2} = \frac{3}{4} - \frac{2}{3}$$ • **Subtract $\frac{2}{3}$ from each side.**

$$-\frac{x}{2} = \frac{1}{12}$$

$$-2\left(-\frac{x}{2}\right) = -2\left(\frac{1}{12}\right)$$ • **Multiply each side by −2.**

$$x = -\frac{1}{6}$$

The solution is $-\frac{1}{6}$.

YOU TRY IT 3

Solve: $\frac{5}{8} - \frac{2x}{3} = \frac{5}{4}$

Your solution

$-\frac{15}{16}$

EXAMPLE 4

Solve $\frac{4}{5}x - \frac{1}{2} = \frac{3}{4}$ by first clearing denominators.

Solution

The LCM of 5, 2, and 4 is 20.

$$\frac{4}{5}x - \frac{1}{2} = \frac{3}{4}$$

$$20\left(\frac{4}{5}x - \frac{1}{2}\right) = 20\left(\frac{3}{4}\right)$$ • **Multiply each side by 20.**

$$20\left(\frac{4}{5}x\right) - 20\left(\frac{1}{2}\right) = 20\left(\frac{3}{4}\right)$$ • **Use the Distributive Property.**

$$16x - 10 = 15$$

$$16x - 10 + 10 = 15 + 10$$ • **Add 10 to each side.**

$$16x = 25$$

$$\frac{16x}{16} = \frac{25}{16}$$ • **Divide each side by 16.**

$$x = \frac{25}{16}$$

The solution is $\frac{25}{16}$.

YOU TRY IT 4

Solve $\frac{2}{3}x + 3 = \frac{7}{2}$ by first clearing denominators.

Your solution

$\frac{3}{4}$

INSTRUCTOR NOTE

One way to end this objective is to review the objective title, which is "to solve an equation of the form $ax + b = c$". If you ask students to name the variables of the equation, they may answer a, b, c, and x—and in a sense, that is true. However, as written symbolic math evolved, it became customary to think of letters at the beginning of the alphabet as constants and those at the end of the alphabet as variables. This kind of implicit understanding is often lost on students.

For this objective, the goal was to solve for x given a, b, and c. In the next section, we solve $ax + b = cx + d$, again with the implicit understanding that a, b, c, and d are constants and coefficients.

Later in the text, we will introduce the equation $y = mx + b$, which also makes implicit assumptions about variables and constants. As students proceed through math courses, they will continually be exposed to the same kinds of understandings.

Solutions on pp. S13–S14

EXAMPLE 5

Solve: $2x + 4 - 5x = 10$

Solution

$$2x + 4 - 5x = 10$$
$$-3x + 4 = 10 \quad \text{• Combine like terms.}$$
$$-3x + 4 - 4 = 10 - 4 \quad \text{• Subtract 4 from each side.}$$
$$-3x = 6$$
$$\frac{-3x}{-3} = \frac{6}{-3} \quad \text{• Divide each side by } -3.$$
$$x = -2$$

The solution is -2.

YOU TRY IT 5

Solve: $x - 5 + 4x = 25$

Your solution

6

Solution on p. S14

OBJECTIVE B *To solve application problems using formulas*

EXAMPLE 6

To determine the total cost of production, an economist uses the equation $T = U \cdot N + F$, where T is the total cost, U is the unit cost, N is the number of units made, and F is the fixed cost. Use this equation to find the number of units made during a month in which the total cost was $9000, the unit cost was $25, and the fixed cost was $3000.

Strategy

Given: $T = 9000$
$U = 25$
$F = 3000$

Unknown: N

Solution

$$T = U \cdot N + F$$
$$9000 = 25N + 3000 \quad \text{• } T = 9000, U = 25, F = 3000$$
$$6000 = 25N \quad \text{• Subtract 3000 from each side.}$$
$$\frac{6000}{25} = \frac{25N}{25} \quad \text{• Divide each side by 25.}$$
$$240 = N$$

There were 240 units made.

YOU TRY IT 6

The pressure at a certain depth in the ocean can be approximated by the equation $P = 15 + \frac{1}{2}D$, where P is the pressure in pounds per square inch and D is the depth in feet. Use this equation to find the depth when the pressure is 45 pounds per square inch.

Your strategy

Your solution

60 ft

IN-CLASS EXAMPLES

6. The relationship between degrees Celsius and degrees Fahrenheit can be represented by the equation $F = 1.8C + 32$, where F is the temperature in degrees Fahrenheit and C is the temperature in degrees Celsius. Use this equation to determine the Celsius temperature when the temperature is 98.6°F. **37°C**

Solution on p. S14

5.2 EXERCISES

Concept Check

SUGGESTED ASSIGNMENT
Exercises 1–4; Exercises 5–75, odds; Exercises 81–91, odds

1. Match each equation with the first step in solving that equation.

a. $3x - 7 = 5$ **i.** Add 7 to each side.
b. $4x + 7 = -5$ **ii.** Add 5 to each side.
c. $7x - 5 = 2$ **iii.** Subtract 7 from each side.
d. $-7x + 5 = -2$ **iv.** Subtract 5 from each side.

a and i, b and iii, c and ii, d and iv

2. True or false? An equation of the form $ax + b = c$ cannot be solved if a is a negative number. False

3. The first step in solving the equation $5 + 8x = 29$ is to subtract ___5___ from each side of the equation. The second step is to divide each side of the equation by ___8___.

4. To clear denominators from the equation $\frac{x}{9} + 2 = \frac{1}{6}$, multiply each side of the equation by ___18___, the least common multiple of the denominators 9 and 6.

OBJECTIVE A *To solve an equation of the form $ax + b = c$*

For Exercises 5 to 76, solve and check.

5. $3x + 1 = 10$
3

6. $4y + 3 = 11$
2

7. $2a - 5 = 7$
6

8. $5m - 6 = 9$
3

9. $5 = 4x + 9$
-1

10. $2 = 5b + 12$
-2

11. $2x - 5 = -11$
-3

12. $3n - 7 = -19$
-4

13. $4 - 3w = -2$
2

14. $5 - 6x = -13$
3

15. $8 - 3t = 2$
2

16. $12 - 5x = 7$
1

17. $4a - 20 = 0$
5

18. $3y - 9 = 0$
3

19. $6 + 2b = 0$
-3

20. $10 + 5m = 0$
-2

21. $-2x + 5 = -7$
6

22. $-5d + 3 = -12$
3

23. $-1.2x + 3 = -0.6$
3

24. $-1.3 = -1.1y + 0.9$
2

25. $2 = 7 - 5a$
1

26. $3 = 11 - 4n$
2

27. $-35 = -6b + 1$
6

28. $-8x + 3 = -29$
4

29. $-3m - 21 = 0$
-7

30. $-5x - 30 = 0$
-6

31. $-4y + 15 = 15$
0

32. $-3x + 19 = 19$
0

33. $9 - 4x = 6$
$\frac{3}{4}$

34. $3t - 2 = 0$
$\frac{2}{3}$

35. $9x - 4 = 0$
$\frac{4}{9}$

36. $7 - 8z = 0$
$\frac{7}{8}$

37. $1 - 3x = 0$
$\frac{1}{3}$

38. $9d + 10 = 7$
$-\frac{1}{3}$

39. $12w + 11 = 5$
$-\frac{1}{2}$

40. $6y - 5 = -7$
$-\frac{1}{3}$

41. $8b - 3 = -9$
$-\frac{3}{4}$

42. $5 - 6m = 2$
$\frac{1}{2}$

43. $7 - 9a = 4$
$\frac{1}{3}$

44. $9 = -12c + 5$
$-\frac{1}{3}$

45. $10 = -18x + 7$
$-\frac{1}{6}$

46. $5y + \frac{3}{7} = \frac{3}{7}$
0

47. $9x + \frac{4}{5} = \frac{4}{5}$
0

48. $0.8 = 7d + 0.1$
0.1

49. $0.9 = 10x - 0.6$
0.15

50. $-6y + 5 = 13$
$-\frac{4}{3}$

51. $-4x + 3 = 9$
$-\frac{3}{2}$

52. $\frac{1}{2}a - 3 = 1$
8

53. $\frac{1}{3}m - 1 = 5$
18

54. $\frac{2}{5}y + 4 = 6$
5

55. $\frac{3}{4}n + 7 = 13$
8

56. $-\frac{2}{3}x + 1 = 7$
-9

57. $-\frac{3}{8}b + 4 = 10$
-16

58. $\frac{x}{4} - 6 = 1$
28

59. $\frac{y}{5} - 2 = 3$
25

60. $\frac{2x}{3} - 1 = 5$
9

61. $\frac{2}{3}x - \frac{5}{6} = -\frac{1}{3}$
$\frac{3}{4}$

62. $\frac{5}{4}x + \frac{2}{3} = \frac{1}{4}$
$-\frac{1}{3}$

63. $\frac{1}{2} - \frac{2}{3}x = \frac{1}{4}$
$\frac{3}{8}$

64. $\frac{3}{4} - \frac{3}{5}x = \frac{19}{20}$
$-\frac{1}{3}$

65. $\frac{3}{2} = \frac{5}{6} + \frac{3x}{8}$
$\frac{16}{9}$

66. $-\frac{1}{4} = \frac{5}{12} + \frac{5x}{6}$
$-\frac{4}{5}$

67. $\frac{11}{27} = \frac{4}{9} - \frac{2x}{3}$
$\frac{1}{18}$

68. $\frac{37}{24} = \frac{7}{8} - \frac{5x}{6}$
$-\frac{4}{5}$

69. $7 = \frac{2x}{5} + 4$
$\frac{15}{2}$

70. $5 - \frac{4c}{7} = 8$
$-\frac{21}{4}$

71. $7 - \frac{5}{9}y = 9$
$-\frac{18}{5}$

72. $6a + 3 + 2a = 11$
1

73. $5y + 9 + 2y = 23$
2

74. $7x - 4 - 2x = 6$
2

75. $11z - 3 - 7z = 9$
3

76. $2x - 6x + 1 = 9$
-2

For Exercises 77 to 80, without solving the equation, determine whether the solution is positive or negative.

77. $15x + 73 = -347$
Negative

78. $17 = 25 - 40a$
Positive

79. $290 + 51n = 187$
Negative

80. $-72 = -86y + 49$
Positive

OBJECTIVE B To solve application problems using formulas

Champion Trees American Forests is an organization that maintains the National Register of Big Trees, a listing of the largest trees in the United States. The formula used to award points to a tree is $P = c + h + \frac{1}{4}s$, where P is the point total for a tree with a circumference of c inches, a height of h feet, and an average crown spread of s feet. Use this formula for Exercises 81 and 82. (*Source:* www.amfor.org)

81. Find the average crown spread of the baldcypress described in the article at the right. 57 ft

82. One of the smallest trees in the United States is a Florida Crossopetalum in the Key Largo Hammocks State Botanical Site. This tree stands 11 ft tall, has a circumference of just 4.8 in., and scores 16.55 points using American Forests' formula. Find the tree's average crown spread. (*Source:* www.championtrees.org) 3 ft

Nutrition The formula $C = 9f + 4p + 4c$ gives the number of calories C in a serving of food that contains f grams of fat, p grams of protein, and c grams of carbohydrate. Use this formula for Exercises 83 and 84. (*Source:* www.nutristrategy.com)

83. Find the number of grams of protein in an 8-ounce serving of vanilla yogurt that contains 174 calories, 2 g of fat, and 30 g of carbohydrate. 9 g

84. Find the number of grams of fat in a serving of granola that contains 215 calories, 42 g of carbohydrate, and 5 g of protein. 3 g

Physics The distance s, in feet, that an object will fall in t seconds is given by the formula $s = 16t^2 + vt$, where v is the initial velocity of the object in feet per second. Use this equation for Exercises 85 and 86.

85. Find the initial velocity of an object that falls 80 ft in 2 s. 8 ft/s

86. Find the initial velocity of an object that falls 144 ft in 3 s. 0 ft/s

Depreciation A company uses the equation $V = C - 6000t$ to determine the depreciated value V, after t years, of a milling machine that originally cost C dollars. Equations such as this are used in accounting for straight-line depreciation. Use this equation for Exercises 87 and 88.

87. A milling machine originally cost $50,000. In how many years will the depreciated value of the machine be $38,000? 2 years

88. A milling machine originally cost $78,000. In how many years will the depreciated value of the machine be $48,000? 5 years

In the NEWS!

The Senator Is a Champion

Baldcypress trees are among the most ancient of North American trees. The 3500-year-old baldcypress known as the Senator, was located in Big Tree Park, Longwood, and was the Florida Champion specimen of the species. With a circumference of 425 in. and a height of 118 ft, this king of the swamp forest earned a total of $557\frac{1}{4}$ points under the point system used for the National Register of Big Trees.

Source: www.championtrees.org

The Senator at Big Tree Park

Anthropology Anthropologists approximate the height of a primate by the size of its humerus (the bone from the elbow to the shoulder) using the equation $H = 1.2L + 27.8$, where L is the length of the humerus and H is the height, in inches, of the primate. Use this equation for Exercises 89 and 90.

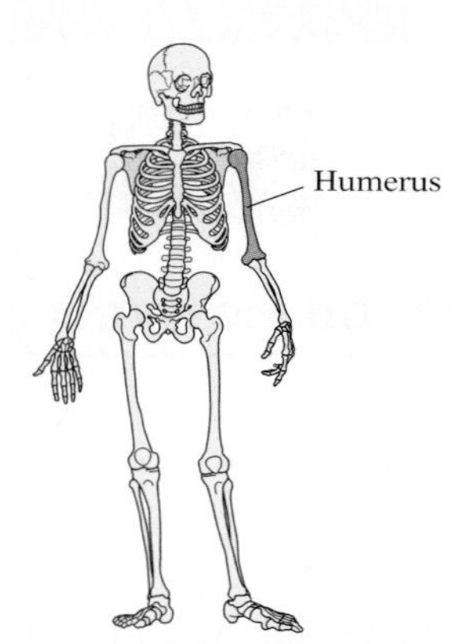

89. An anthropologist estimates the height of a primate to be 66 in. What is the approximate length of the humerus of this primate? Round to the nearest tenth of an inch.
31.8 in.

90. An anthropologist estimates the height of a primate to be 62 in. What is the approximate length of the humerus of this primate? 28.5 in.

Car Safety Black ice is an ice covering on roads that is especially difficult to see and therefore extremely dangerous for motorists. The distance that a car traveling at 30 mph will slide after its brakes are applied is related to the outside temperature by the formula $C = \frac{1}{4}D - 45$, where C is the Celsius temperature and D is the distance in feet that the car will slide. Use this equation for Exercises 91 and 92.

91. Determine the distance a car will slide on black ice when the outside temperature is $-3°C$. 168 ft

92. Determine the distance a car will slide on black ice when the outside temperature is $-11°C$. 136 ft

93. Which of the following equations is equivalent to the formula $V = C - 5500t$?

(i) $V - C = 5500t$ **(ii)** $V - C = -5500t$
(iii) $C - V = -5500t$ **(iv)** $C + V = -5500t$
ii

INSTRUCTOR NOTE
Here is an extension for Exercises 91 and 92.
1. For what temperatures is the formula valid? **Less than or equal to 0°C**
2. Will the car slide farther when the temperature is higher or when it is lower? **Higher**

Critical Thinking

94. Solve $3x + 4y = 13$ when $y = -2$.
$x = 7$

95. Solve $2x - 3y = 8$ when $y = 0$.
$x = 4$

96. Solve $-4x + 3y = 9$ when $x = 0$.
$y = 3$

97. Solve $5x - 2y = -3$ when $x = -3$.
$y = -6$

98. If $2x - 3 = 7$, evaluate $3x + 4$.
19

99. If $3x + 5 = -4$, evaluate $2x - 5$.
-11

QUICK QUIZ
Solve.
1. $8a + 3 = 10$
$\frac{7}{8}$ **[5.2A]**
2. $7 = 12 + 5h$
-1 [5.2A]
3. $-6 = 4n + 9 + n$
-3 [5.2A]
4. Convert $-13°F$ to degrees Celsius. Use the formula $F = \frac{9}{5}C + 32$, where F is the Fahrenheit temperature and C is the Celsius temperature.
$-25°C$ [5.2B]

Projects or Group Activities

100. Make up an equation of the form $ax + b = c$ that has 5 as its solution.
One possible answer is $3x - 4 = 11$.

101. Make up an equation of the form $ax + b = c$ that has -3 as its solution.
One possible answer is $2x + 5 = -1$.

102. Explain in your own words the steps you would take to solve the equation $\frac{2}{3}x - 4 = 10$. State the property of real numbers or the property of equations that is used at each step.

SECTION

5.3 General Equations—Part II

OBJECTIVE A *To solve an equation of the form $ax + b = cx + d$*

In solving an equation of the form $ax + b = cx + d$, the goal is to rewrite the equation in the form *variable* = *constant*. Begin by rewriting the equation so that there is only one variable term in the equation. Then rewrite the equation so that there is only one constant term.

HOW TO 1 Solve: $2x + 3 = 5x - 9$

$$2x + 3 = 5x - 9$$

$$2x - 5x + 3 = 5x - 5x - 9$$ • Subtract $5x$ from each side of the equation.

$$-3x + 3 = -9$$ • Simplify. There is only one variable term.

$$-3x + 3 - 3 = -9 - 3$$ • Subtract 3 from each side of the equation.

$$-3x = -12$$ • Simplify. There is only one constant term.

$$\frac{-3x}{-3} = \frac{-12}{-3}$$ • Divide each side of the equation by -3.

$$x = 4$$ • The equation is in the form *variable* = *constant*.

The solution is 4. You should verify this by checking this solution.

EXAMPLE 1

Solve: $4x - 5 = 8x - 7$

Solution

$$4x - 5 = 8x - 7$$

$$4x - 8x - 5 = 8x - 8x - 7$$ • Subtract $8x$ from each side.

$$-4x - 5 = -7$$

$$-4x - 5 + 5 = -7 + 5$$ • Add 5 to each side.

$$-4x = -2$$

$$\frac{-4x}{-4} = \frac{-2}{-4}$$ • Divide each side by -4.

$$x = \frac{1}{2}$$

The solution is $\frac{1}{2}$.

YOU TRY IT 1

Solve: $5x + 4 = 6 + 10x$

Your solution

$-\frac{2}{5}$

IN-CLASS EXAMPLES

Solve.

1. $5x - 4 = 3x - 10$ $\quad -3$
2. $8x + 3 - 4x = 5 + x$ $\quad \frac{2}{3}$
3. $3x - 7 = 5x - 7$ $\quad 0$

Solution on p. S14

EXAMPLE 2

Solve: $3x + 4 - 5x = 2 - 4x$

Solution

$3x + 4 - 5x = 2 - 4x$

$-2x + 4 = 2 - 4x$ • Combine like terms.

$-2x + 4x + 4 = 2 - 4x + 4x$ • Add $4x$ to each side.

$2x + 4 = 2$

$2x + 4 - 4 = 2 - 4$ • Subtract 4 from each side.

$2x = -2$

$\frac{2x}{2} = \frac{-2}{2}$ • Divide each side by 2.

$x = -1$

The solution is −1.

YOU TRY IT 2

Solve: $5x - 10 - 3x = 6 - 4x$

Your solution

$\frac{8}{3}$

Solution on p. S14

OBJECTIVE B

To solve an equation containing parentheses

INSTRUCTOR NOTE

Remind students that the goal is still *variable = constant*.

When an equation contains parentheses, one of the steps in solving the equation is to use the Distributive Property. The Distributive Property is used to remove parentheses from a variable expression.

HOW TO 2 Solve: $4 + 5(2x - 3) = 3(4x - 1)$

$4 + 5(2x - 3) = 3(4x - 1)$

$4 + 10x - 15 = 12x - 3$ • Use the Distributive Property. Then simplify.

$10x - 11 = 12x - 3$

$10x - 12x - 11 = 12x - 12x - 3$ • Subtract $12x$ from each side of the equation.

$-2x - 11 = -3$ • Simplify.

$-2x - 11 + 11 = -3 + 11$ • Add 11 to each side of the equation.

$-2x = 8$ • Simplify.

$\frac{-2x}{-2} = \frac{8}{-2}$ • Divide each side of the equation by −2.

$x = -4$ • The equation is in the form *variable = constant*.

The solution is −4. You should verify this by checking this solution.

In the next example, we solve an equation containing parentheses and decimals.

HOW TO 3 Solve: $16 + 0.55x = 0.75(x + 20)$

$$16 + 0.55x = 0.75(x + 20)$$
$$16 + 0.55x = 0.75x + 15$$ • Use the Distributive Property.
$$16 + 0.55x - 0.75x = 0.75x - 0.75x + 15$$ • Subtract $0.75x$ from each side of the equation.
$$16 - 0.20x = 15$$ • Simplify.
$$16 - 16 - 0.20x = 15 - 16$$ • Subtract 16 from each side of the equation.
$$-0.20x = -1$$ • Simplify.
$$\frac{-0.20x}{-0.20} = \frac{-1}{-0.20}$$ • Divide each side of the equation by -0.20.
$$x = 5$$ • The equation is in the form *variable = constant.*

The solution is 5.

EXAMPLE 3

Solve: $3x - 4(2 - x) = 3(x - 2) - 4$

Solution

$$3x - 4(2 - x) = 3(x - 2) - 4$$
$$3x - 8 + 4x = 3x - 6 - 4$$ • Distributive Property
$$7x - 8 = 3x - 10$$
$$7x - 3x - 8 = 3x - 3x - 10$$ • Subtract $3x$.
$$4x - 8 = -10$$
$$4x - 8 + 8 = -10 + 8$$ • Add 8.
$$4x = -2$$
$$\frac{4x}{4} = \frac{-2}{4}$$ • Divide by 4.
$$x = -\frac{1}{2}$$

The solution is $-\frac{1}{2}$.

YOU TRY IT 3

Solve: $5x - 4(3 - 2x) = 2(3x - 2) + 6$

Your solution

2

IN-CLASS EXAMPLES

4. Solve: $9x - 3(2x + 5) = 4(5x + 2) - 6$ **−1**
5. Solve: $5[6 - 2(5x + 1)] = 8x - 9$ $\frac{1}{2}$
6. If $5x = 3x + 10$, evaluate $4x^2 - 10$. **90**

EXAMPLE 4

Solve: $3[2 - 4(2x - 1)] = 4x - 10$

Solution

$$3[2 - 4(2x - 1)] = 4x - 10$$
$$3[2 - 8x + 4] = 4x - 10$$ • Distributive Property
$$3[6 - 8x] = 4x - 10$$
$$18 - 24x = 4x - 10$$ • Distributive Property
$$18 - 24x - 4x = 4x - 4x - 10$$ • Subtract $4x$.
$$18 - 28x = -10$$
$$18 - 18 - 28x = -10 - 18$$ • Subtract 18.
$$-28x = -28$$
$$\frac{-28x}{-28} = \frac{-28}{-28}$$ • Divide by -28.
$$x = 1$$

The solution is 1.

YOU TRY IT 4

Solve: $-2[3x - 5(2x - 3)] = 3x - 8$

Your solution

2

Solutions on p. S14

OBJECTIVE C To solve application problems using formulas

Take Note

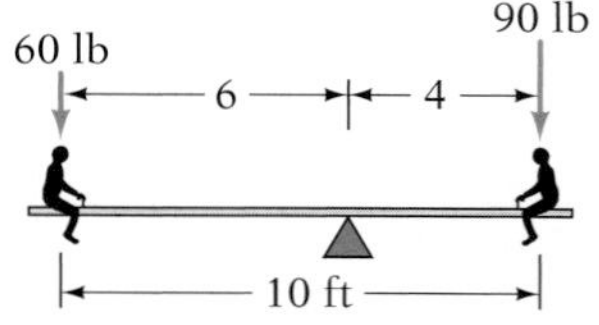

This system balances because

$F_1x = F_2(d - x)$
$60(6) = 90(10 - 6)$
$60(6) = 90(4)$
$360 = 360$

A lever system is shown at the right. It consists of a lever, or bar; a fulcrum; and two forces, F_1 and F_2. The distance d represents the length of the lever, x represents the distance from F_1 to the fulcrum, and $d - x$ represents the distance from F_2 to the fulcrum.

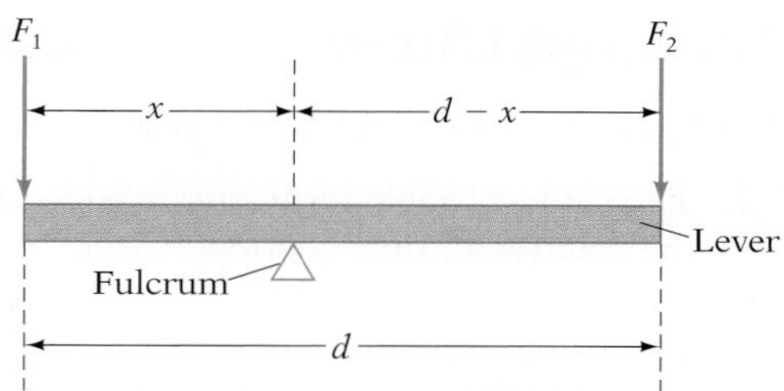

A principle of physics states that when the lever system balances, $F_1x = F_2(d - x)$.

EXAMPLE 5

A lever is 15 ft long. A force of 50 lb is applied to one end of the lever, and a force of 100 lb is applied to the other end. Where is the fulcrum located when the system balances?

Strategy

Make a drawing.

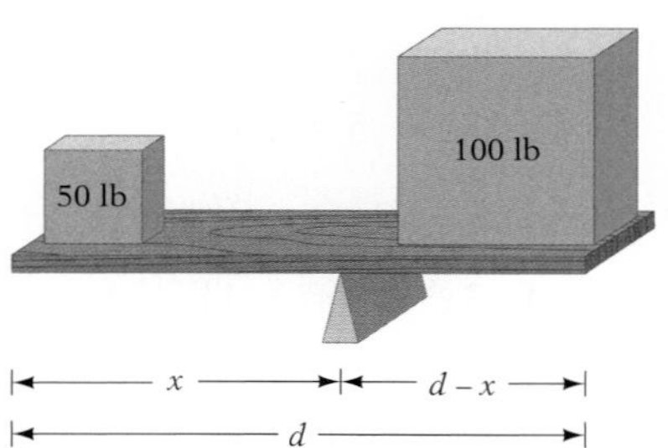

Given: $F_1 = 50$
$F_2 = 100$
$d = 15$
Unknown: x

Solution

$$F_1x = F_2(d - x)$$
$$50x = 100(15 - x) \quad \bullet\ F_1 = 50, F_2 = 100, d = 15$$
$$50x = 1500 - 100x$$
$$50x + 100x = 1500 - 100x + 100x \quad \bullet\ \text{Add } 100x.$$
$$150x = 1500$$
$$\frac{150x}{150} = \frac{1500}{150} \quad \bullet\ \text{Divide by 150.}$$
$$x = 10$$

The fulcrum is 10 ft from the 50-pound force.

YOU TRY IT 5

A lever is 25 ft long. A force of 45 lb is applied to one end of the lever, and a force of 80 lb is applied to the other end. Where is the location of the fulcrum when the system balances?

Your strategy

Your solution

16 ft from the 45-pound force

Solution on p. S14

IN-CLASS EXAMPLES

7. A lever is 12 ft long. A force of 3 lb is applied to one end of the lever, and a force of 6 lb is applied to the other end. Where is the location of the fulcrum when the system balances? **8 ft from the 3-pound force**

5.3 EXERCISES

Concept Check

SUGGESTED ASSIGNMENT
Exercises 1–5; Exercises 7–75, odds

For Exercises 1 to 3, determine whether the statement is true or false.

1. The same variable term can be added to both sides of an equation without changing the solution of the equation. True

2. The same variable term can be subtracted from both sides of an equation without changing the solution of the equation. True

3. In solving an equation of the form $ax + b = cx + d$, the goal is to rewrite the equation in the form *variable* = *constant*. True

4. Describe the step that will enable you to rewrite the equation $2x - 3 = 7x + 12$ so that it has one variable term with a positive coefficient. Subtract $2x$ from each side.

5. If you rewrite the equation $8 - y = y + 6$ so that it has one variable term on the left side of the equation, what will be the coefficient of the variable? -2

OBJECTIVE A *To solve an equation of the form $ax + b = cx + d$*

For Exercises 6 to 32, solve and check.

6. $8x + 5 = 4x + 13$
2

7. $6y + 2 = y + 17$
3

8. $5x - 4 = 2x + 5$
3

9. $13b - 1 = 4b - 19$
-2

10. $15x - 2 = 4x - 13$
-1

11. $7a - 5 = 2a - 20$
-3

12. $3x + 1 = 11 - 2x$
2

13. $n - 2 = 6 - 3n$
2

14. $2x - 3 = -11 - 2x$
-2

15. $4y - 2 = -16 - 3y$
-2

16. $0.2b + 3 = 0.5b + 12$
-30

17. $m + 0.4 = 3m + 0.8$
-0.2

18. $4y - 8 = y - 8$
0

19. $5a + 7 = 2a + 7$
0

20. $6 - 5x = 8 - 3x$
-1

21. $10 - 4n = 16 - n$
-2

22. $5 + 7x = 11 + 9x$
-3

23. $3 - 2y = 15 + 4y$
-2

24. $2x - 4 = 6x$
-1

25. $2b - 10 = 7b$
-2

26. $8m = 3m + 20$
4

27. $9y = 5y + 16$
4

28. $8b + 5 = 5b + 7$
$\frac{2}{3}$

29. $6y - 1 = 2y + 2$
$\frac{3}{4}$

30. $7x - 8 = x - 3$
$\frac{5}{6}$

31. $2y - 7 = -1 - 2y$
$\frac{3}{2}$

32. $2m - 1 = -6m + 5$
$\frac{3}{4}$

33. If $5x = 3x - 8$, evaluate $4x + 2$.
-14

34. If $7x + 3 = 5x - 7$, evaluate $3x - 2$.
-17

35. If $2 - 6a = 5 - 3a$, evaluate $4a^2 - 2a + 1$.
7

36. If $1 - 5c = 4 - 4c$, evaluate $3c^2 - 4c + 2$.
41

OBJECTIVE B *To solve an equation containing parentheses*

37. Without solving any of the equations, determine which of the following equations has the same solution as the equation $5 - 2(x - 1) = 8$.
(i) $3(x - 1) = 8$ (ii) $5 - 2x + 2 = 8$ (iii) $5 - 2x + 1 = 8$ ii

For Exercises 38 to 58, solve and check.

38. $5x + 2(x + 1) = 23$
3

39. $6y + 2(2y + 3) = 16$
1

40. $9n - 3(2n - 1) = 15$
4

41. $12x - 2(4x - 6) = 28$
4

42. $7a - (3a - 4) = 12$
2

43. $9m - 4(2m - 3) = 11$
-1

44. $5(3 - 2y) + 4y = 3$
2

45. $4(1 - 3x) + 7x = 9$
-1

46. $5y - 3 = 7 + 4(y - 2)$
2

47. $0.22(x + 6) = 0.2x + 1.8$
24

48. $0.05(4 - x) + 0.1x = 0.32$
2.4

49. $0.3x + 0.3(x + 10) = 300$
495

50. $2a - 5 = 4(3a + 1) - 2$
$-\frac{7}{10}$

51. $5 - (9 - 6x) = 2x - 2$
$\frac{1}{2}$

52. $7 - (5 - 8x) = 4x + 3$
$\frac{1}{4}$

53. $3[2 - 4(y - 1)] = 3(2y + 8)$
$-\frac{1}{3}$

54. $5[2 - (2x - 4)] = 2(5 - 3x)$
5

55. $3a + 2[2 + 3(a - 1)] = 2(3a + 4)$
$\frac{10}{3}$

56. $5 + 3[1 + 2(2x - 3)] = 6(x + 5)$
$\frac{20}{3}$

57. $-2[4 - (3b + 2)] = 5 - 2(3b + 6)$
$-\frac{1}{4}$

58. $-4[x - 2(2x - 3)] + 1 = 2x - 3$
2

59. If $4 - 3a = 7 - 2(2a + 5)$, evaluate $a^2 + 7a$.
0

60. If $9 - 5x = 12 - (6x + 7)$, evaluate $x^2 - 3x - 2$.
26

OBJECTIVE C *To solve application problems using formulas*

Taxi Fares The fare F to be charged a customer by a taxi company is calculated using the formula $F = 2.50 + 2.30(m - 1)$, where m is the number of miles traveled. Use this formula for Exercises 61 and 62.

61. A customer is charged \$14.00. How many miles was the customer driven? 6 mi

62. A passenger is charged \$20.90. Find the number of miles the passenger was driven. 9 mi

63. **Physics** Two people sit on a seesaw that is 8 ft long. The seesaw balances when the fulcrum is 3 ft from one of the people.
a. How far is the fulcrum from the other person?
b. Which person is heavier, the person who is 3 ft from the fulcrum or the other person?
c. If the two people switch places, will the seesaw still balance?
a. 5 ft **b.** The person who is 3 ft from the fulcrum **c.** No

Physics For Exercises 64 to 69, solve. Use the lever system equation $F_1x = F_2(d - x)$.

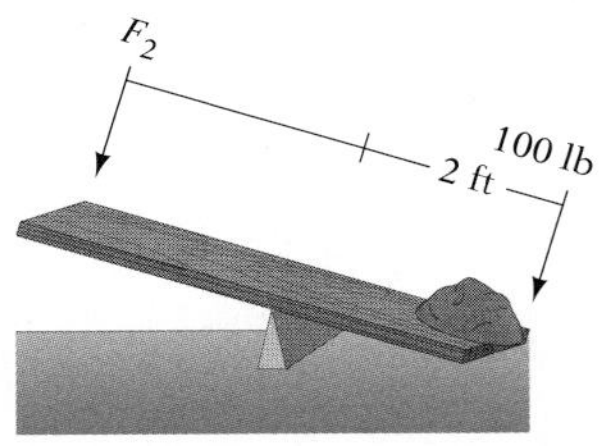

64. A lever 10 ft long is used to move a 100-pound rock. The fulcrum is placed 2 ft from the rock. What force must be applied to the other end of the lever to move the rock?
25 lb

65. An adult and a child are on a seesaw 14 ft long. The adult weighs 175 lb and the child weighs 70 lb. How many feet from the child must the fulcrum be placed so that the seesaw balances?
10 ft

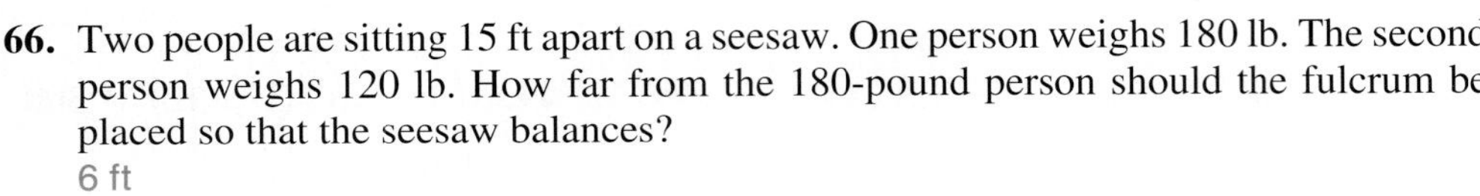

66. Two people are sitting 15 ft apart on a seesaw. One person weighs 180 lb. The second person weighs 120 lb. How far from the 180-pound person should the fulcrum be placed so that the seesaw balances?
6 ft

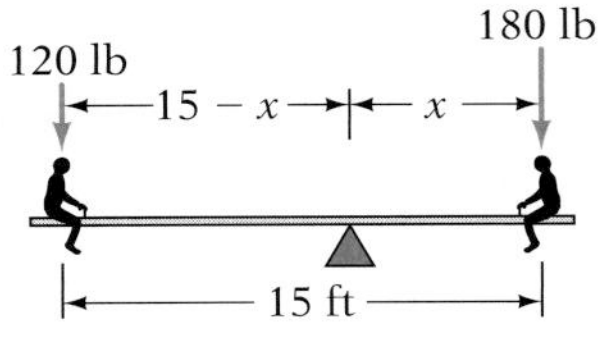

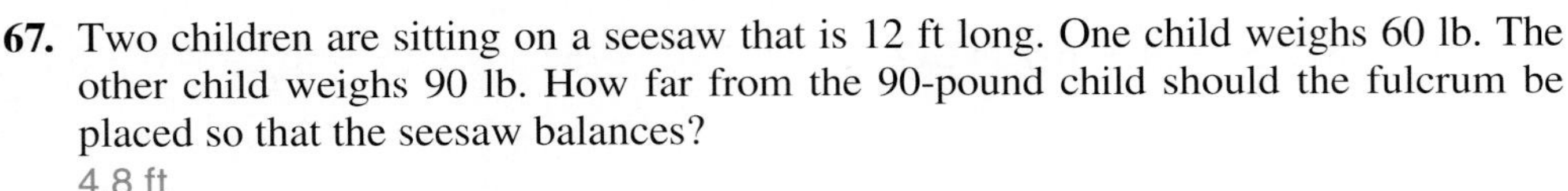

67. Two children are sitting on a seesaw that is 12 ft long. One child weighs 60 lb. The other child weighs 90 lb. How far from the 90-pound child should the fulcrum be placed so that the seesaw balances?
4.8 ft

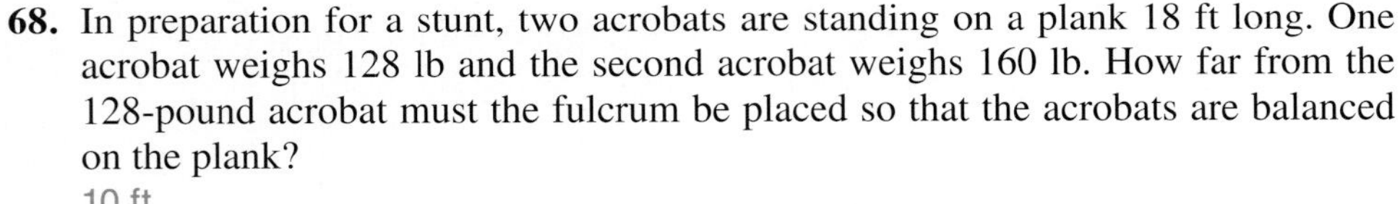

68. In preparation for a stunt, two acrobats are standing on a plank 18 ft long. One acrobat weighs 128 lb and the second acrobat weighs 160 lb. How far from the 128-pound acrobat must the fulcrum be placed so that the acrobats are balanced on the plank?
10 ft

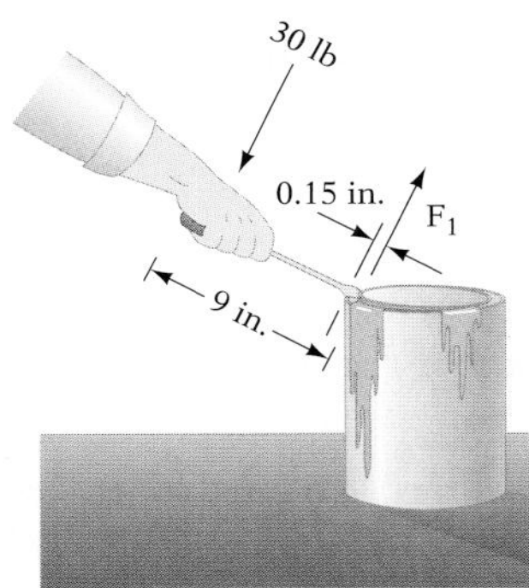

69. A screwdriver 9 in. long is used as a lever to open a can of paint. The tip of the screwdriver is placed under the lip of the can with the fulcrum 0.15 in. from the lip. A force of 30 lb is applied to the other end of the screwdriver. Find the force on the lip of the can.
1770 lb

Break-even Point To determine the break-even point, or the number of units that must be sold so that no profit or loss occurs, an economist uses the formula $Px = Cx + F$, where P is the selling price per unit, x is the number of units that must be sold to break even, C is the cost to make each unit, and F is the fixed cost. Use this equation for Exercises 70 to 73.

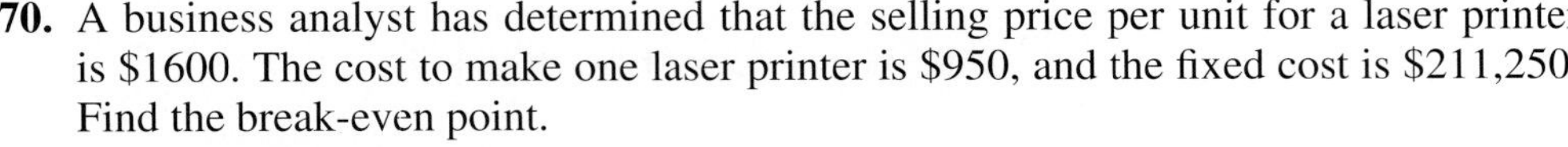

70. A business analyst has determined that the selling price per unit for a laser printer is \$1600. The cost to make one laser printer is \$950, and the fixed cost is \$211,250. Find the break-even point.
325 laser printers

71. A business analyst has determined that the selling price per unit for a gas barbecue is \$325. The cost to make one gas barbecue is \$175, and the fixed cost is \$39,000. Find the break-even point.
260 barbecues

72. A manufacturer of headphones determines that the cost per unit for a pair of headphones is \$38 and that the fixed cost is \$24,400. The selling price for the headphones is \$99. Find the break-even point.
400 headphones

© iStockphoto.com/LeggNet

73. A manufacturing engineer determines that the cost per unit for a soprano recorder is \$12 and that the fixed cost is \$19,240. The selling price for the recorder is \$49. Find the break-even point.
520 recorders

Physiology The oxygen consumption C, in millimeters per minute, of a small mammal at rest is related to the animal's weight m, in kilograms, by the equation $m = \frac{1}{6}(C - 5)$. Use this equation for Exercises 74 and 75.

74. What is the oxygen consumption of a mammal that weighs 10.4 kg?
67.4 ml/min

75. What is the oxygen consumption of a mammal that weighs 8.3 kg?
54.8 ml/min

Critical Thinking

Solve. If the equation has no solution, write "No solution."

76. $3(2x - 1) - (6x - 4) = -9$ No solution

77. $\frac{1}{5}(25 - 10b) + 4 = \frac{1}{3}(9b - 15) - 6$ 4

78. $3[4(w + 2) - (w + 1)] = 5(2 + w)$ $-\frac{11}{4}$

79. $\frac{2(5x - 6) - 3(x - 4)}{7} = x + 2$ No solution

80. One-half of a certain number equals two-thirds of the same number. Find the number. 0

81. Does the sentence "Solve $3x - 4(x - 1)$" make sense? Why or why not?

82. The equation $x = x + 1$ has no solution, whereas the solution of the equation $2x + 3 = 3$ is zero. Is there a difference between no solution and a solution of zero? Explain your answer.

83. I am thinking of a number. When I subtract 4 from the number and then multiply the result by 3, my new result is equal to the original number. What is the original number? 6

Projects or Group Activities

84. If $s = 5x - 3$ and $t = x + 4$, find the value of x for which $s = 3t - 1$. 7

85. The population of the town of Hampton increased by 10,000 people during the 1990s. In the first decade of the new millennium, the population of Hampton decreased by $\frac{1}{10}$, at which time the town had 6000 more people than at the beginning of the 1990s. Find Hampton's population at the beginning of the 1990s.
30,000 people

QUICK QUIZ

Solve.

1. $7x + 4 = 3x - 20$
   −6 [5.3A]
2. $4x + 5 = 23 - 2x$
   3 [5.3A]
3. $4x + 2(x + 3) = 3(x - 1)$
   −3 [5.3B]
4. Two people are sitting on a seesaw that is 9 ft long. One person weighs 120 lb. The second person weighs 150 lb. How far from the 120-pound person should the fulcrum be placed so that the seesaw balances? **5 ft [5.3C]**

CHECK YOUR PROGRESS: CHAPTER 5

1. Is 3 a solution of $2a(a - 1) = 3a + 3$? Yes [5.1A]

2. Solve: $x + 7 = -4$ -11 [5.1B]

3. Solve: $-3y = -27$ 9 [5.1C]

4. Solve: $6 - 4a = -10$ 4 [5.2A]

5. Is $-\frac{1}{4}$ a solution of $8t + 1 = -1$? Yes [5.1A]

6. Solve: $\frac{1}{6} + b = -\frac{1}{3}$ $-\frac{1}{2}$ [5.1B]

7. Solve: $5x - 4(3 - x) = 2(x - 1) - 3$ 1 [5.3B]

8. Solve: $6y + 5 - 8y = 3 - 4y$ -1 [5.3A]

9. Is 4 a solution of $x(x + 1) = x^2 + 5$? No [5.1A]

10. Solve: $84 = -16 + t$ 100 [5.1B]

11. Solve: $\frac{3}{4}c = \frac{3}{5}$ $\frac{4}{5}$ [5.1C]

12. Solve: $9 = \frac{1}{2}d - 5$ 28 [5.2A]

13. Solve: $-\frac{8}{9} = -\frac{2}{3}y$ $\frac{4}{3}$ [5.1C]

14. Solve: $3n + 2(n - 4) = 7$ 3 [5.3B]

15. Solve: $3x - 8 = 5x + 6$ -7 [5.3A]

16. Solve: $2[3 - 5(x - 1)] = 7x - 1$ 1 [5.3B]

17. **Recreation** K&B Tours offers a river trip that takes passengers from the K&B dock to a small island that is 24 mi away. The passengers spend 1 h at the island and then return to the K&B dock. If the speed of the boat is 10 mph in calm water and the rate of the current is 2 mph, how long does the trip last? 6 h [5.1D]

18. **Cab Fares** The fare F to be charged a customer by a taxi company is calculated using the formula $F = 2.75 + 2.40(m - 1)$, where m is the number of miles traveled. If a passenger is charged \$12.35, how many miles was the passenger driven? 5 mi [5.3C]

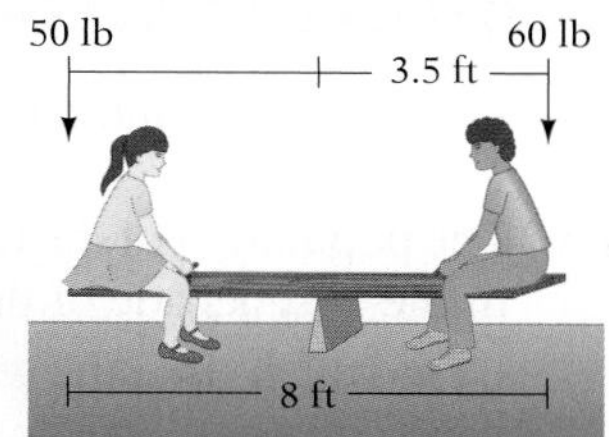

19. **Physics** Two children are sitting 8 ft apart on a seesaw. One child weighs 60 lb and the second child weighs 50 lb. The fulcrum is 3.5 ft from the child weighing 60 lb. Is the seesaw balanced? Use the lever system equation $F_1x = F_2(d - x)$. No [5.3C]

SECTION

5.4 Translating Sentences into Equations

OBJECTIVE A To solve integer problems

An equation states that two mathematical expressions are equal. Therefore, to **translate** a sentence into an equation, we must recognize the words or phrases that mean "equals." Some of these phrases are listed below.

equals
is
is equal to
amounts to
represents } translate to =

Once the sentence is translated into an equation, the equation can be solved by rewriting it in the form *variable* = *constant*.

Take Note

You can check the solution to a translation problem.

Check:

5 less than 18 is 13

18 − 5	13
13 = 13	

HOW TO 1 Translate "five less than a number is thirteen" into an equation and solve.

Five less than a number	is	thirteen

- Find two verbal expressions for the same value.

The unknown number: n

- Assign a variable to the unknown number.

$$n - 5 = 13$$

- Write a mathematical expression for each verbal expression. Write the equals sign.

$$n - 5 + 5 = 13 + 5$$

- Solve the equation.

$$n = 18$$

The number is 18.

Recall that the integers are the numbers {..., −4, −3, −2, −1, 0, 1, 2, 3, 4, ...}. An **even integer** is an integer that is divisible by 2. Examples of even integers are −8, 0, and 22. An **odd integer** is an integer that is not divisible by 2. Examples of odd integers are −17, 1, and 39.

Consecutive integers are integers that follow one another in order. Examples of consecutive integers are shown at the right. (Assume that the variable n represents an integer.)

11, 12, 13
−8, −7, −6
$n, n + 1, n + 2$

Examples of **consecutive even integers** are shown at the right. (Assume that the variable n represents an even integer.)

24, 26, 28
−10, −8, −6
$n, n + 2, n + 4$

Take Note

Both consecutive even and consecutive odd integers are represented using n, $n + 2, n + 4, \ldots$.

Examples of **consecutive odd integers** are shown at the right. (Assume that the variable n represents an odd integer.)

19, 21, 23
−1, 1, 3
$n, n + 2, n + 4$

INSTRUCTOR NOTE
There is an opportunity, in solving problems that involve consecutive even or consecutive odd integers, to emphasize the importance of validating the solution. Give students the problem "The sum of two consecutive odd integers is eleven. Find the integers." In this case $x = 4.5$, which is not an odd integer. Therefore, the problem has no solution.

HOW TO 2 The sum of three consecutive odd integers is forty-five. Find the integers.

Strategy

- First odd integer: n • Represent three consecutive odd integers.
  Second odd integer: $n + 2$
  Third odd integer: $n + 4$
- The sum of the three odd integers is 45.

Solution

$n + (n + 2) + (n + 4) = 45$ • Write an equation.
$3n + 6 = 45$ • Solve the equation.
$3n = 39$
$n = 13$ • The first odd integer is 13.
$n + 2 = 13 + 2 = 15$ • Find the second odd integer.
$n + 4 = 13 + 4 = 17$ • Find the third odd integer.

The three consecutive odd integers are 13, 15, and 17.

EXAMPLE 1

The sum of two numbers is sixteen. The difference between four times the smaller number and two is two more than twice the larger number. Find the two numbers.

Strategy

The difference between four times the smaller number and two	is	two more than twice the larger number

The smaller number: n
The larger number: $16 - n$

Solution

$4n - 2 = 2(16 - n) + 2$
$4n - 2 = 32 - 2n + 2$ • Distributive Property
$4n - 2 = 34 - 2n$ • Combine like terms.
$4n + 2n - 2 = 34 - 2n + 2n$ • Add $2n$ to each side.
$6n - 2 = 34$
$6n - 2 + 2 = 34 + 2$ • Add 2 to each side.
$6n = 36$
$\frac{6n}{6} = \frac{36}{6}$ • Divide each side by 6.
$n = 6$ • The smaller number is 6.
$16 - n = 16 - 6 = 10$ • Find the larger number.

The smaller number is 6.
The larger number is 10.

YOU TRY IT 1

The sum of two numbers is twelve. The total of three times the smaller number and six amounts to seven less than the product of four and the larger number. Find the two numbers.

Your strategy

Your solution

5, 7

IN-CLASS EXAMPLES
Translate into an equation and solve.

1. The sum of two numbers is twenty-five. The total of four times the smaller number and two is six less than the product of two and the larger number. Find the two numbers.
   $4x + 2 = 2(25 - x) - 6$; 7, 18
2. Three times the largest of three consecutive integers is ten more than the sum of the other two. Find the three integers.
   $3(n + 2) = n + (n + 1) + 10$; 5, 6, 7

Solution on p. S15

EXAMPLE 2

Find three consecutive even integers such that three times the second equals four more than the sum of the first and third.

Strategy

- First even integer: n
  Second even integer: $n + 2$
  Third even integer: $n + 4$
- Three times the second equals four more than the sum of the first and third.

Solution

$3(n + 2) = n + (n + 4) + 4$

$3n + 6 = 2n + 8$

$3n - 2n + 6 = 2n - 2n + 8$

$n + 6 = 8$

$n = 2$ • **The first even integer is 2.**

$n + 2 = 2 + 2 = 4$ • **Find the second even integer.**

$n + 4 = 2 + 4 = 6$ • **Find the third even integer.**

The three integers are 2, 4, and 6.

YOU TRY IT 2

Find three consecutive integers whose sum is negative six.

Your strategy

Your solution

−3, −2, −1

Solution on p. S15

OBJECTIVE B *To translate a sentence into an equation and solve*

EXAMPLE 3

A wallpaper hanger charges a fee of $25 plus $12 for each roll of wallpaper used in a room. If the total charge for hanging wallpaper is $97, how many rolls of wallpaper were used?

Strategy

To find the number of rolls of wallpaper used, write and solve an equation using n to represent the number of rolls of wallpaper used.

$25 plus $12 for each roll of wallpaper	is	$97

Solution

$25 + 12n = 97$

$12n = 72$ • **Subtract 25 from each side.**

$\frac{12n}{12} = \frac{72}{12}$ • **Divide each side by 12.**

$n = 6$

6 rolls of wallpaper were used.

YOU TRY IT 3

The fee charged by a ticketing agency for a concert is $3.50 plus $17.50 for each ticket purchased. If your total charge for tickets is $161, how many tickets did you purchase?

Your strategy

Your solution

9 tickets

Solution on p. S15

IN-CLASS EXAMPLES

3. An electric company charges $.07 for each of the first 249 kWh (kilowatt-hours) and $.14 for each kilowatt-hour over 249 kWh. Find the number of kilowatt-hours used by a family whose electric bill was $46.55.
   457 kWh
4. A piano wire 24 in. long is cut into two pieces. The length of the longer piece is 4 in. more than three times the length of the shorter piece. Find the length of each piece.
   5 in., 19 in.

EXAMPLE 4

A board 20 ft long is cut into two pieces. Five times the length of the shorter piece is 2 ft more than twice the length of the longer piece. Find the length of each piece.

Strategy

Let x represent the length of the shorter piece. Then $20 - x$ represents the length of the longer piece.

Make a drawing.

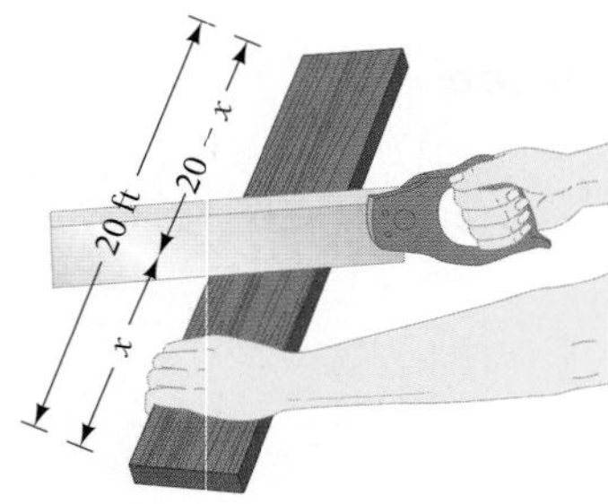

To find the lengths, write and solve an equation using x to represent the length of the shorter piece and $20 - x$ to represent the length of the longer piece.

Five times the length of the shorter piece	is	2 ft more than twice the length of the longer piece

Solution

$5x = 2(20 - x) + 2$

$5x = 40 - 2x + 2$ • **Distributive Property**

$5x = 42 - 2x$ • **Combine like terms.**

$5x + 2x = 42 - 2x + 2x$ • **Add $2x$ to each side.**

$7x = 42$

$\frac{7x}{7} = \frac{42}{7}$ • **Divide each side by 7.**

$x = 6$ • **The shorter piece is 6 ft long.**

$20 - x = 20 - 6 = 14$ • **Find the length of the longer piece.**

The length of the shorter piece is 6 ft.
The length of the longer piece is 14 ft.

YOU TRY IT 4

A wire 22 in. long is cut into two pieces. The length of the longer piece is 4 in. more than twice the length of the shorter piece. Find the length of each piece.

Your strategy

Your solution

6 in., 16 in.

Solution on p. S15

INSTRUCTOR NOTE

Problems that begin with sentences such as "The sum of two numbers is twelve" and "A board 12 ft long is cut into two pieces" can have their two constituent parts represented identically, using n and $12 - n$.

INSTRUCTOR NOTE

Some students have difficulty making the transition from the sentence "The sum of two numbers is sixteen" to the conclusion that if the first number is represented as n, the second number may be represented as $16 - n$. The confusion is due in part to the use of the word *sum* and the fact that the representation of the two numbers does not involve addition. It can be pointed out, however, that the sum of n and $(16 - n)$ is, in fact, 16.

5.4 EXERCISES

Concept Check

SUGGESTED ASSIGNMENT
Exercises 1–8; Exercises 9–47, odds

For Exercises 1 to 3, determine whether the statement is true or false.

1. When translating a sentence into an equation, we can use any variable to represent an unknown number. True
2. An even integer is a multiple of 2. True
3. Given the consecutive odd integers −5 and −3, the next consecutive odd integer is −1. True
4. The sum of two numbers is 12.
   a. If x represents the larger number, represent the smaller number in terms of x.
   $12 - x$
   b. If x represents the smaller number, represent the larger number in terms of x.
   $12 - x$
5. When we translate a sentence into an equation, the word *is* translates into the equals sign.
6. Integers that follow one another in order are called ______ integers. consecutive
7. Two consecutive integers differ by 1. Two consecutive even integers differ by 2. Two consecutive odd integers differ by 2.
8. The number of calories in a cup of low-fat milk is two-thirds the number of calories in a cup of whole milk. In this situation, let n represent the number of calories in a cup of whole milk, and let $\frac{2}{3}n$ represent the number of calories in a cup of low-fat milk.

OBJECTIVE A *To solve integer problems*

For Exercises 9 to 24, translate into an equation and solve.

9. The difference between a number and fifteen is seven. Find the number.
   $x - 15 = 7; 22$

10. The sum of five and a number is three. Find the number.
   $5 + x = 3; -2$

11. The difference between nine and a number is seven. Find the number.
   $9 - x = 7; 2$

12. Three-fifths of a number is negative thirty. Find the number.
   $\frac{3}{5}x = -30; -50$

13. The difference between five and twice a number is one. Find the number.
   $5 - 2x = 1; 2$

14. Four more than three times a number is thirteen. Find the number.
   $3x + 4 = 13; 3$

15. The sum of twice a number and five is fifteen. Find the number.
   $2x + 5 = 15; 5$

16. The difference between nine times a number and six is twelve. Find the number.
   $9x - 6 = 12; 2$

17. Six less than four times a number is twenty-two. Find the number.
   $4x - 6 = 22; 7$

18. Four times the sum of twice a number and three is twelve. Find the number.
   $4(2x + 3) = 12; 0$

19. Three times the difference between four times a number and seven is fifteen. Find the number.
   $3(4x - 7) = 15; 3$

20. Twice the difference between a number and twenty-five is three times the number. Find the number.
   $2(x - 25) = 3x; -50$

21. The sum of two numbers is twenty. Three times the smaller is equal to two times the larger. Find the two numbers.
$3x = 2(20 - x)$; 8, 12

22. The sum of two numbers is fifteen. One less than three times the smaller is equal to the larger. Find the two numbers.
$3x - 1 = 15 - x$; 4, 11

23. The sum of two numbers is fourteen. The difference between two times the smaller and the larger is one. Find the two numbers.
$2x - (14 - x) = 1$; 5, 9

24. The sum of two numbers is eighteen. The total of three times the smaller and twice the larger is forty-four. Find the two numbers.
$3x + 2(18 - x) = 44$; 8, 10

25. The sum of three consecutive odd integers is fifty-one. Find the integers.
15, 17, 19

26. Find three consecutive even integers whose sum is negative eighteen.
−8, −6, −4

27. Find three consecutive odd integers such that three times the middle integer is one more than the sum of the first and third.
−1, 1, 3

28. Twice the smallest of three consecutive odd integers is seven more than the largest. Find the integers.
11, 13, 15

29. Find two consecutive even integers such that three times the first equals twice the second.
4, 6

30. Find two consecutive even integers such that four times the first is three times the second.
6, 8

31. The sum of two numbers is seven. Twice one number is four less than the other number. Which of the following equations does *not* represent this situation?
(i) $2(7 - x) = x - 4$ (ii) $2x = (7 - x) - 4$ (iii) $2n - 4 = 7 - n$
iii

OBJECTIVE B *To translate a sentence into an equation and solve*

32. Depreciation As a result of depreciation, the value of a car is now $19,200. This is three-fifths of its original value. Find the original value of the car. $32,000

33. Structures The length of the Royal Gorge Bridge in Colorado is 320 m. This is one-fourth the length of the Golden Gate Bridge. Find the length of the Golden Gate Bridge. 1280 m

© Andy Z./Shutterstock.com
The Golden Gate Bridge

34. Nutrition One slice of cheese pizza contains 290 calories. A medium-size orange has one-fifth that number of calories. How many calories are in a medium-size orange? 58 calories

35. History John D. Rockefeller died in 1937. At the time of his death, Rockefeller had accumulated $1400 million, which was equal to one-sixty-fifth of the gross national product of the United States at that time. What was the U.S. gross national product in 1937? (*Source: The Wealthy 100: A Ranking of the Richest Americans, Past and Present*) $91 billion

© Pictorial Press Ltd/Alamy
John D. Rockefeller

36. Agriculture A soil supplement that weighs 18 lb contains iron, potassium, and mulch. The supplement contains fifteen times as much mulch as iron and twice as much potassium as iron. Find the amount of mulch in the soil supplement. 15 lb

37. Geometry An isosceles triangle has two sides of equal length. The length of the third side is 1 ft less than twice the length of one of the equal sides. Find the length of each side when the perimeter is 23 ft. 6 ft, 6 ft, 11 ft

38. **Geometry** An isosceles triangle has two sides of equal length. The length of one of the equal sides is 2 m more than three times the length of the third side. If the perimeter is 46 m, find the length of each side. 20 m, 20 m, 6 m

Point of Interest

The low-frequency pulses or whistles made by blue whales have been measured at up to 188 decibels, making them the loudest sounds produced by a living organism.

39. **Safety** Loudness, or the intensity of sound, is measured in decibels. The sound level of a television is about 70 decibels, which is considered a safe hearing level. A food blender runs at 20 decibels higher than a TV, and a jet engine's decibel reading is 40 less than twice that of a blender. At this level, exposure can cause hearing loss. Find the intensity of the sound of a jet engine. 140 decibels

40. **Robots** Kiva Systems, Inc., builds robots that companies can use to streamline order fulfillment operations in their warehouses. Salary and other benefits for one human warehouse worker can cost a company about $64,000 a year, an amount that is 103 times the company's yearly maintenance and operation costs for one robot. Find the yearly costs for a robot. Round to the nearest hundred. (*Source: The Boston Globe*) $600

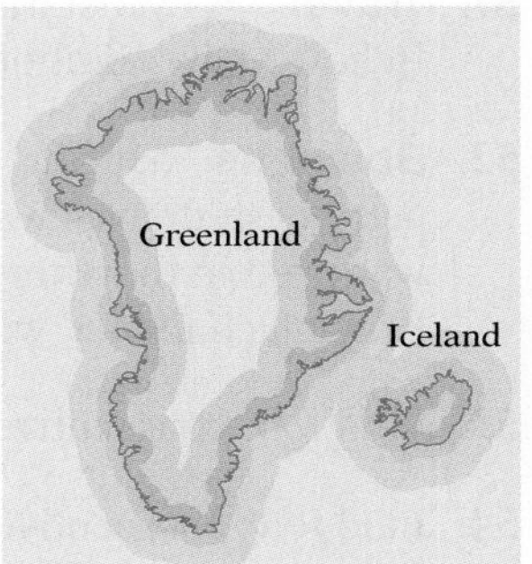

41. **Geography** Greenland, the largest island in the world, is 21 times larger than Iceland. The combined area of Greenland and Iceland is 880,000 mi^2. Find the area of Greenland. 840,000 mi^2

42. **Consumerism** The cost to replace a water pump in a sports car was $820. This included $375 for the water pump and $89 per hour for labor. How many hours of labor were required to replace the water pump? 5 h

43. **Utilities** The cost of electricity in a certain city is $.09 for each of the first 300 kWh (kilowatt-hours) and $.15 for each kilowatt-hour over 300 kWh. Find the number of kilowatt-hours used by a family that receives a $59.25 electric bill. 515 kWh

44. **Labor Unions** A union charges monthly dues of $4.00 plus $.25 for each hour worked during the month. A union member's dues for March were $46.00. How many hours did the union member work during the month of March? 168 h

45. **Business** The cellular phone service for a business executive is $80 per month plus $.40 per minute of phone use over 900 min. For a month in which the executive's cellular phone bill was $100.40, how many minutes did the executive use the phone? 951 min

In the NEWS!

Americans' Unquenchable Thirst

Despite efforts to increase recycling, the 2.16 million tons of plastic drink bottles that ended up in landfills this year represent four-fifths of the plastic drink bottles stocked for sale in U.S. stores.

And Americans can't seem to get enough of bottled water. During a recent year, stores stocked 7.5 billion gallons of bottled water, an amount that is approximately the same as the volume of water that goes over Niagara Falls every 3 h.

Source: scienceline.org

46. **Recycling** Use the information in the article at the right to find how many tons of plastic drink bottles were stocked for sale in U.S. stores. 2.7 million tons

Text Messaging For Exercises 47 and 48, use the expression $2.99 + 0.15n$, which represents the total monthly text-messaging bill for n text messages over 300 in one month.

47. How much does the customer pay per text message over 300 messages? $.15

48. What is the fixed charge per month for the text-messaging service? $2.99

Critical Thinking

49. **Metalwork** A wire 12 ft long is cut into two pieces. Each piece is bent into the shape of a square. The perimeter of the larger square is twice the perimeter of the smaller square. Find the perimeter of the larger square. 8 ft

12 ft; x

50. The amount of liquid in a container triples every minute. The container becomes completely filled at 3:40 P.M. What fractional part of the container is filled at 3:39 P.M? $\frac{1}{3}$

51. **Travel** A cyclist traveling at a constant speed completes three-fifths of a trip in $\frac{1}{2}$ h. In how many additional hours will the cyclist complete the entire trip? $\frac{1}{3}$ h

52. **Business** During one day at an office, one-half of the amount of money in the petty cash drawer was used in the morning, and one-third of the remaining money was used in the afternoon, leaving $5 in the petty cash drawer at the end of the day. How much money was in the petty cash drawer at the start of the day? $15

53. Find four consecutive even integers whose sum is -36. $-12, -10, -8, -6$

54. Find four consecutive odd integers whose sum is -48. $-15, -13, -11, -9$

55. Find three consecutive odd integers such that the sum of the first and third integers is twice the second integer. Any three consecutive odd integers

56. Find four consecutive integers such that the sum of the first and fourth integers equals the sum of the second and third integers. Any four consecutive integers

QUICK QUIZ

Translate into an equation and solve.

1. The product of five and a number is negative fifteen. Find the number. **$5x = -15$; -3 [5.4A]**
2. Find three consecutive even integers such that four times the second is eight less than the third. **$4(n + 2) = (n + 4) - 8$; $-4, -2, 0$ [5.4A]**
3. An investment of $8000 is divided into two accounts, one at a bank and one at a credit union. The value of the investment at the credit union is $1000 less than twice the value of the investment at the bank. Find the amount in each account. **$3000 at the bank; $5000 at the credit union [5.4B]**

Projects or Group Activities

Complete each statement with the word *even* or *odd*.

57. If k is an odd integer, then $k + 1$ is an __even__ integer.

58. If k is an odd integer, then $k - 2$ is an __odd__ integer.

59. If n is an integer, then $2n$ is an __even__ integer.

60. If m and n are even integers, then $m - n$ is an __even__ integer.

61. If m and n are even integers then mn is an __even__ integer.

62. If m and n are odd integers, then $m + n$ is an __even__ integer.

63. If m and n are odd integers then $m - n$ is an __even__ integer.

64. If m and n are odd integers then mn is an __odd__ integer.

65. If m is an even integer and n is an odd integer then $m - n$ is an __odd__ integer.

66. If m is an even integer and n is an odd integer then $m + n$ is an __odd__ integer.

SECTION

5.5 Mixture and Uniform Motion Problems

OBJECTIVE A *To solve value mixture problems*

A value mixture problem involves combining two ingredients that have different prices into a single blend. For example, a coffee merchant may blend two types of coffee into a single blend, or a candy manufacturer may combine two types of candy to sell as a variety pack.

The solution of a value mixture problem is based on the **value mixture equation** $AC = V$, where A is the amount of an ingredient, C is the cost per unit of the ingredient, and V is the value of the ingredient.

Take Note

The equation $AC = V$ is used to find the value of an ingredient. For example, the value of 4 lb of cashews costing \$6 per pound is

$$AC = V$$
$$4 \cdot \$6 = V$$
$$\$24 = V$$

HOW TO 1 A coffee merchant wants to make 6 lb of a blend of coffee costing \$5 per pound. The blend is made using a \$7-per-pound grade and a \$4-per-pound grade of coffee. How many pounds of each of these grades should be used?

Strategy for Solving a Value Mixture Problem

1. For each ingredient in the mixture, write a numerical or variable expression for the amount of the ingredient used, the unit cost of the ingredient, and the value of the amount used. For the blend, write a numerical or variable expression for the amount, the unit cost of the blend, and the value of the amount. The results can be recorded in a table.

The sum of the amounts is 6 lb.

Amount of \$7 coffee: x
Amount of \$4 coffee: $6 - x$

Take Note

Use the information given in the problem to fill in the amount and unit cost columns of the table. Fill in the value column by multiplying the two expressions you wrote in each row. Use the expressions in the last column to write the equation.

	Amount, A	·	Unit Cost, C	=	Value, V
\$7 grade	x	·	7	=	$7x$
\$4 grade	$6 - x$	·	4	=	$4(6 - x)$
\$5 blend	6	·	5	=	$5(6)$

2. Determine how the values of the ingredients are related. Use the fact that the sum of the values of all the ingredients is equal to the value of the blend.

The sum of the values of the \$7 grade and the \$4 grade is equal to the value of the \$5 blend.

$$7x + 4(6 - x) = 5(6)$$
$$7x + 24 - 4x = 30$$
$$3x + 24 = 30$$
$$3x = 6$$
$$x = 2$$

$6 - x = 6 - 2 = 4$ • **Find the amount of the \$4 grade coffee.**

The merchant must use 2 lb of the \$7 coffee and 4 lb of the \$4 coffee.

EXAMPLE 1

How many ounces of a metal alloy that costs $4 an ounce must be mixed with 10 oz of an alloy that costs $6 an ounce to make a mixture that costs $4.32 an ounce?

Strategy

- Ounces of $4 alloy: x

	Amount	Cost	Value
$4 alloy	x	4	$4x$
$6 alloy	10	6	$6(10)$
$4.32 mixture	$10 + x$	4.32	$4.32(10 + x)$

- The sum of the values before mixing equals the value after mixing.

Solution

$4x + 6(10) = 4.32(10 + x)$ • **The sum of the values before mixing equals the value after mixing.**

$4x + 60 = 43.2 + 4.32x$

$-0.32x + 60 = 43.2$ • **Subtract $4.32x$ from each side.**

$-0.32x = -16.8$ • **Subtract 60 from each side.**

$x = 52.5$ • **Divide each side by -0.32.**

52.5 oz of the $4 alloy must be used.

YOU TRY IT 1

A gardener has 20 lb of a lawn fertilizer that costs $.90 per pound. How many pounds of a fertilizer that costs $.75 per pound should be mixed with this 20 lb of lawn fertilizer to produce a mixture that costs $.85 per pound?

Your strategy

Your solution

10 lb

Solution on p. S15

IN-CLASS EXAMPLES

1. A meatloaf mixture is made by combining ground turkey costing $1.49 per pound with ground beef costing $2.13 per pound. How many pounds of each should be used to make 8 lb of a meatloaf mixture that costs $1.89 per pound? **Ground turkey: 3 lb; ground beef: 5 lb**

OBJECTIVE B *To solve uniform motion problems*

Recall from Section 5.1 that an object traveling at a constant speed in a straight line is in *uniform motion*. The solution of a uniform motion problem is based on the equation $rt = d$, where r is the rate of travel, t is the time spent traveling, and d is the distance traveled.

HOW TO 2 A car leaves a town traveling at 40 mph. Two hours later, a second car leaves the same town, on the same road, traveling at 60 mph. In how many hours will the second car pass the first car?

Strategy for Solving a Uniform Motion Problem

1. For each object, write a numerical or variable expression for the rate, time, and distance. The results can be recorded in a table.

The first car traveled 2 h longer than the second car.

Unknown time for the second car: t
Time for the first car: $t + 2$

Take Note

Use the information given in the problem to fill in the rate and time columns of the table. Fill in the distance column by multiplying the two expressions you wrote in each row.

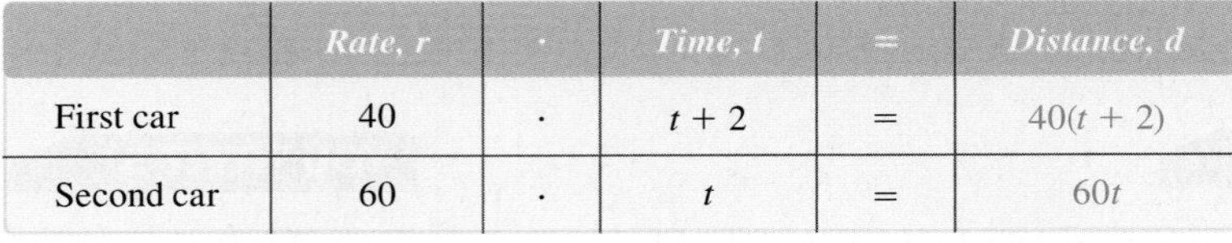

	Rate, r	·	Time, t	=	Distance, d
First car	40	·	$t + 2$	=	$40(t + 2)$
Second car	60	·	t	=	$60t$

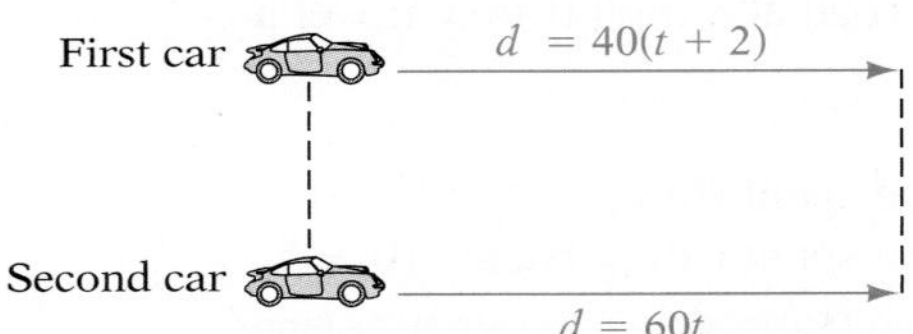

INSTRUCTOR NOTE

One of the complications of distance-rate problems is that the variable may not directly represent the unknown. After doing a problem similar to the one at the right, show students a problem similar to Example 3 on the next page. The variable is time, but the unknown is distance.

2. Determine how the distances traveled by the two objects are related. For example, the total distance traveled by both objects may be known, or it may be known that the two objects traveled the same distance.

The two cars travel the same distance.

$$
\begin{aligned}
40(t + 2) &= 60t \\
40t + 80 &= 60t \\
80 &= 20t \\
4 &= t
\end{aligned}
$$

The second car will pass the first car in 4 h.

EXAMPLE 2

Two cars, one traveling 10 mph faster than the other, start at the same time from the same point and travel in opposite directions. In 3 h, they are 300 mi apart. Find the rate of each car.

Strategy
- Rate of first car: r
  Rate of second car: $r + 10$

	Rate	*Time*	*Distance*
1st car	r	3	$3r$
2nd car	$r + 10$	3	$3(r + 10)$

- The total distance traveled by the two cars is 300 mi.

Solution

$3r + 3(r + 10) = 300$
$3r + 3r + 30 = 300$ • **Distributive Property**
$6r + 30 = 300$ • **Combine like terms.**
$6r = 270$ • **Subtract 30 from each side.**
$r = 45$ • **Divide each side by 6.**

$r + 10 = 45 + 10 = 55$ • **Find the rate of the second car.**

The first car is traveling at 45 mph.
The second car is traveling at 55 mph.

YOU TRY IT 2

Two trains, one traveling at twice the speed of the other, start at the same time on parallel tracks from stations that are 288 mi apart and travel toward each other. In 3 h, the trains pass each other. Find the rate of each train.

Your strategy

Your solution

32 mph; 64 mph

EXAMPLE 3

How far can the members of a bicycling club ride out into the country at a speed of 12 mph and return over the same road at 8 mph if they travel a total of 10 h?

Strategy
- Time spent riding out: t
  Time spent riding back: $10 - t$

	Rate	*Time*	*Distance*
Out	12	t	$12t$
Back	8	$10 - t$	$8(10 - t)$

- The distance out equals the distance back.

Solution

$12t = 8(10 - t)$
$12t = 80 - 8t$ • **Distributive Property**
$20t = 80$ • **Add $8t$ to each side**
$t = 4$ (The time is 4 h.) • **Divide each side by 20.**

The distance out $= 12t = 12(4) = 48$

The club can ride 48 mi into the country.

YOU TRY IT 3

A pilot flew out to a parcel of land and back in 5 h. The rate out was 150 mph, and the rate returning was 100 mph. How far away was the parcel of land?

Your strategy

Your solution

300 mi

IN-CLASS EXAMPLES

2. Two planes leave an airport at the same time and fly in opposite directions. One of the planes is flying at 450 mph, and the other plane is flying at 550 mph. In how many hours will they be 2000 mi apart? **2 h**
3. A cyclist starts on a course at 6 A.M. riding at 12 mph. An hour later, a second cyclist starts on the same course traveling at 18 mph. At what time will the second cyclist overtake the first cyclist? **9 A.M.**

Solutions on p. S16

5.5 EXERCISES

Concept Check

SUGGESTED ASSIGNMENT
Exercises 1–6; Exercises 7–47, odds

1. The total value of a 7-pound bag of cat food that costs \$1.50 per pound is \$10.50.

2. If 8 L of a solvent costs \$75 per liter, then the value of the 8 L of solvent is \$600.

3. The cost per pound of a 5-pound bag of sugar that has a total value of \$3.80 is \$.76

4. Explain the meaning of each variable in the equation $V = AC$. Give an example of how this equation is used.

5. Explain what each variable in the formula $d = rt$ represents.

6. Two planes leave an airport at the same time and fly in opposite directions. One plane flies 100 mph faster than the other. Let r be the speed of the slower plane. Write an expression that represents the distance between the planes after 2 hours.
$2r + 2(r + 100)$

OBJECTIVE A *To solve value mixture problems*

7. At a veterinary clinic, a special high-protein dog food that costs \$6.75 per pound is mixed with a vitamin supplement that costs \$3.25 per pound. How many pounds of each should be used to make 5 lb of a mixture that costs \$4.65 per pound? 2 lb of dog food; 3 lb of vitamin supplement

8. A goldsmith combined an alloy that costs \$4.30 per ounce with an alloy that costs \$1.80 per ounce. How many ounces of each were used to make a mixture of 200 oz costing \$2.50 per ounce? \$4.30 alloy: 56 oz; \$1.80 alloy: 144 oz

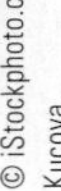
© iStockphoto.com/agdalena Kucova

9. How many pounds of chamomile tea that costs \$18.20 per pound must be mixed with 12 lb of orange tea that costs \$12.25 per pound to make a mixture that costs \$14.63 per pound? 8 lb

10. A wild birdseed mix is made by combining 100 lb of millet seed costing \$.60 per pound with sunflower seeds costing \$1.10 per pound. How many pounds of sunflower seeds are needed to make a mixture that costs \$.70 per pound? 25 lb

11. Find the cost per pound of a coffee mixture made from 8 lb of coffee that costs \$9.20 per pound and 12 lb of coffee that costs \$5.50 per pound. \$6.98

12. Find the cost per ounce of a mixture of 200 oz of a cologne that costs \$7.50 per ounce and 500 oz of a cologne that costs \$4.00 per ounce. \$5.00

13. An herbalist has 30 oz of herbs costing \$2 per ounce. How many ounces of herbs costing \$1 per ounce should be mixed with these 30 oz of herbs to produce a mixture costing \$1.60 per ounce? 20 oz

14. A snack food is made by mixing 5 lb of popcorn that costs \$.80 per pound with caramel that costs \$2.40 per pound. How much caramel is needed to make a mixture that costs \$1.40 per pound? 3 lb

15. A grocery store offers a cheese sampler that includes a pepper cheddar cheese that costs \$16 per kilogram and Pennsylvania Jack that costs \$12 per kilogram. How many kilograms of each were used to make a 5-kilogram mixture that costs \$13.20 per kilogram? 1.5 kg of pepper cheese; 3.5 kg of Pennsylvania Jack

16. A lumber company combined oak wood chips that cost \$3.10 per pound with pine wood chips that cost \$2.50 per pound. How many pounds of each were used to make an 80-pound mixture costing \$2.65 per pound? 20 lb of oak chips; 60 lb of pine chips

17. The manager of a farmer's market has 500 lb of grain that costs \$1.20 per pound. How many pounds of meal costing \$.80 per pound should be mixed with the 500 lb of grain to produce a mixture that costs \$1.05 per pound? 300 lb

18. A caterer made an ice cream punch by combining fruit juice that costs \$4.50 per gallon with ice cream that cost \$8.50 per gallon. How many gallons of each were used to make 100 gal of punch costing \$5.50 per gallon? Fruit juice: 75 gal; ice cream: 25 gal

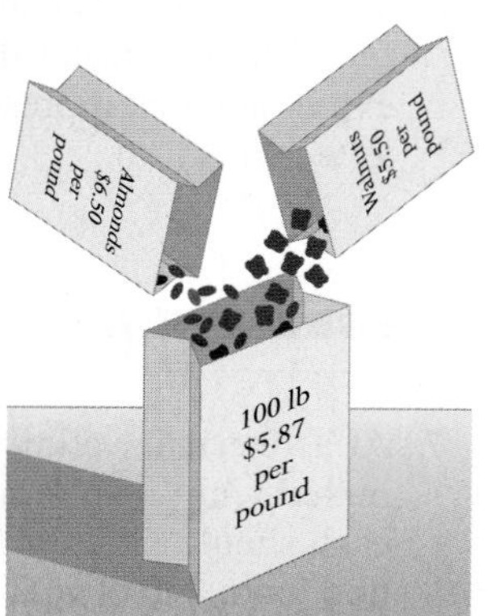

19. The manager of a specialty food store combined almonds that cost \$6.50 per pound with walnuts that cost \$5.50 per pound. How many pounds of each were used to make a 100-pound mixture that costs \$5.87 per pound? Almonds: 37 lb; walnuts: 63 lb

20. Find the cost per pound of a "house blend" of coffee that is made from 12 lb of Central American coffee that costs \$8 per pound and 30 lb of South American coffee that costs \$4.50 per pound. \$5.50

21. Find the cost per pound of sugar-coated breakfast cereal made from 40 lb of sugar that costs \$2.00 per pound and 120 lb of corn flakes that cost \$1.20 per pound. \$1.40

22. How many liters of a blue dye that costs \$1.60 per liter must be mixed with 18 L of anil that costs \$2.50 per liter to make a mixture that costs \$1.90 per liter? 36 L

23. **Tree Conservation** A town's parks department buys trees from the tree conservation program described in the news clipping at the right. The department spends \$406 on 14 bundles of trees. How many bundles of seedlings and how many bundles of container-grown plants did the parks department buy?
8 bundles of seedlings, 6 bundles of container-grown plants

> **In the NEWS!**
>
> **Conservation Tree Planting Program Underway**
>
> The Kansas Forest Service is again offering its Conservation Tree Planting Program. Trees are sold in bundles of 25, in two sizes—seedlings cost \$17 a bundle and larger container-grown plants cost \$45 a bundle.
>
> *Source:* Kansas Canopy

24. Find the cost per ounce of a gold alloy made from 25 oz of pure gold that costs \$1282 per ounce and 40 oz of an alloy that costs \$900 per ounce. \$1046.92

25. Find the cost per ounce of a sunscreen made from 100 oz of a lotion that costs \$2.50 per ounce and 50 oz of a lotion that costs \$4.00 per ounce. \$3

26. A snack mix is made from 3 lb of sunflower seeds that cost S dollars per pound and 4 lb of raisins that cost R dollars per pound. Which expression gives the cost C per pound of the mixture?

(i) $7(S + R)$ (ii) $3S + 4R$ (iii) $S + R$ (iv) $\frac{3S + 4R}{7}$ iv

OBJECTIVE B To solve uniform motion problems

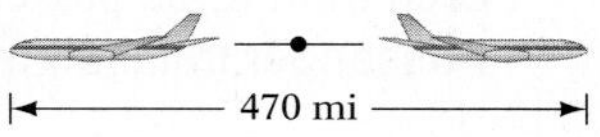

27. Two small planes start from the same point and fly in opposite directions. The first plane is flying 25 mph slower than the second plane. In 2 h, the planes are 470 mi apart. Find the rate of each plane. 105 mph, 130 mph

28. Two cyclists start from the same point and ride in opposite directions. One cyclist rides twice as fast as the other. In 3 h, they are 81 mi apart. Find the rate of each cyclist. 9 mph, 18 mph

29. One speed skater starts across a frozen lake at an average speed of 8 m/s. Ten seconds later, a second speed skater starts from the same point and skates in the same direction at an average speed of 10 m/s. How many seconds after the second skater starts will the second skater overtake the first skater? 40 s

30. A long-distance runner starts on a course running at an average speed of 6 mph. Half an hour later, a second runner begins the same course at an average speed of 7 mph. How long after the second runner starts will the second runner overtake the first runner? 3 h

31. Michael Chan leaves a dock in his motorboat and travels at an average speed of 9 mph toward the Isle of Shoals, a small island off the coast of Massachusetts. Two hours later, a tour boat leaves the same dock and travels at an average speed of 18 mph toward the same island. How many hours after the tour boat leaves will Michael's boat be alongside the tour boat? 2 h

32. A jogger starts from one end of a 15-mile nature trail at 8:00 A.M. One hour later, a cyclist starts from the other end of the trail and rides toward the jogger. If the rate of the jogger is 6 mph and the rate of the cyclist is 9 mph, at what time will the two meet? 9:36 A.M.

33. An executive drove from home at an average speed of 30 mph to an airport where a helicopter was waiting. The executive boarded the helicopter and flew to the corporate offices at an average speed of 60 mph. The entire distance was 150 mi. The entire trip took 3 h. Find the distance from the airport to the corporate offices. 120 mi

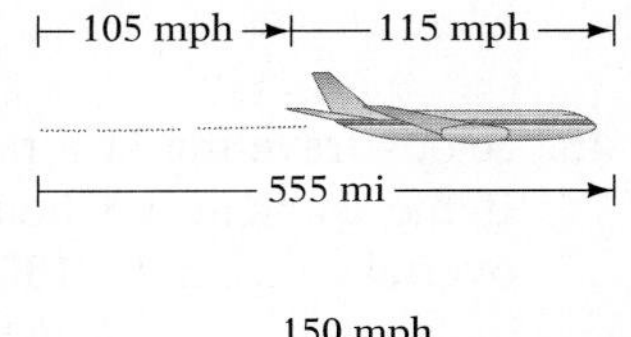

34. A 555-mile, 5-hour plane trip was flown at two speeds. For the first part of the trip, the average speed was 105 mph. For the remainder of the trip, the average speed was 115 mph. How long did the plane fly at each speed? 2 h at 105 mph; 3 h at 115 mph

35. After a sailboat had been on the water for 3 h, a change in the wind direction reduced the average speed of the boat by 5 mph. The entire distance sailed was 57 mi. The total time spent sailing was 6 h. How far did the sailboat travel in the first 3 h? 36 mi

150 mph

100 mph

36. A stunt driver was needed at the production site of a Hollywood movie. The average speed of the stunt driver's flight to the site was 150 mph, and the average speed of the return trip was 100 mph. Find the distance of the round trip if the total flying time was 5 h. 600 mi

37. A passenger train leaves a train depot 2 h after a freight train leaves the same depot. The freight train is traveling 20 mph slower than the passenger train. Find the rate of each train if the passenger train overtakes the freight train in 3 h.
Passenger train: 50 mph; freight train: 30 mph

38. A car and a bus set out at 3 P.M. from the same point headed in the same direction. The average speed of the car is twice the average speed of the bus. In 2 h the car is 68 mi ahead of the bus. Find the rate of the car. 68 mph

39. A ship traveling east at 25 mph is 10 mi from a harbor when another ship leaves the harbor traveling east at 35 mph. How long does it take the second ship to catch up to the first ship? 1 h

40. At 10 A.M. a plane leaves Boston, Massachusetts, for Seattle, Washington, a distance of 3000 mi. One hour later a plane leaves Seattle for Boston. Both planes are traveling at a speed of 500 mph. How many hours after the plane leaves Seattle will the planes pass each other? 2.5 h

41. **Bridges** See the news clipping at the right. Two cars, the first traveling 10 km/h faster than the second, start at the same time from opposite ends of the Hangzhou Bay Bridge and travel toward each other. The cars pass each other in 12 min. Find the rate of the faster car. 95 km/h

42. At noon a train leaves Washington, D.C., headed for Charleston, South Carolina, a distance of 500 mi. The train travels at a speed of 60 mph. At 1 P.M. a second train leaves Charleston headed for Washington, D.C., traveling at 50 mph. How long after the train leaves Charleston will the two trains pass each other? 4 h

43. A race car driver starts along a 50-mile race course traveling at an average speed of 90 mph. Fifteen minutes later, a second driver starts along the same course at an average speed of 120 mph. Will the second car overtake the first car before the drivers reach the end of the course? No

44. A bus traveled on a straight road for 2 h at an average speed that was 20 mph faster than its average speed on a winding road. The time spent on the winding road was 3 h. Find the average speed on the winding road if the total trip was 210 mi. 34 mph

45. A bus traveling at a rate of 60 mph overtakes a car traveling at a rate of 45 mph. If the car had a 1-hour head start, how far from the starting point does the bus overtake the car? 180 mi

46. A car traveling at 48 mph overtakes a cyclist who, riding at 12 mph, had a 3-hour head start. How far from the starting point does the car overtake the cyclist? 48 mi

47. A plane left Kennedy Airport on Tuesday morning for a 605 mile, 5-hour trip. For the first part of the trip, the average speed was 115 mph. For the remainder of the trip, the average speed was 125 mph. How long did the plane fly at each speed?
2 h at 115 mph; 3 h at 125 mph

In the NEWS!

Longest Ocean-Crossing Bridge Opens to Public

The Hangzhou Bay Bridge is the longest ocean-crossing bridge in the world. It spans the Hangzhou Bay on the East China Sea and crosses the Qiantang River at the Yangtze River Delta. The S-shaped bridge connects Jiaxing to the north and Ningbo to the south. The bridge is 36 km long and has a speed limit of 100 km/h.

Source: www.roadtraffic-technology. com

Critical Thinking

48. Find the cost per ounce of a mixture of 30 oz of an alloy that costs \$4.50 per ounce, 40 oz of an alloy that costs \$3.50 per ounce, and 30 oz of an alloy that costs \$3.00 per ounce. \$3.65

49. A grocer combined walnuts that cost \$5.60 per pound and cashews that cost \$7.50 per pound with 20 lb of peanuts that cost \$4.00 per pound. Find the amount of walnuts and the amount of cashews used to make a 50-pound mixture costing \$5.72 per pound. Walnuts: 10 lb; cashews: 20 lb

50. A truck leaves a depot at 11 A.M. and travels at a speed of 45 mph. At noon, a van leaves the same depot and travels the same route at a speed of 65 mph. At what time does the van overtake the truck? 2:15 P.M.

51. At 10 A.M., two campers left their campsite by canoe and paddled downstream at an average speed of 12 mph. They then turned around and paddled back upstream at an average rate of 4 mph. The total trip took 1 h. At what time did the campers turn around downstream? 10:15 A.M.

52. A car and a cyclist start at 10 A.M. from the same point, headed in the same direction. The average speed of the car is 5 mph more than three times the average speed of the cyclist. In 1.5 h, the car is 46.5 mi ahead of the cyclist. Find the rate of the cyclist. 13 mph

QUICK QUIZ

1. A trail mix is made by combining raisins that cost \$4.20 per pound with granola that costs \$2.20 per pound. How many pounds of each should be used to make 40 lb of trail mix that costs \$2.75 per pound? **Raisins: 11 lb; granola: 29 lb [5.5A]**
2. A ship leaves a dock at 10 A.M. and travels south at 30 mph. One hour later, a second ship leaves the same dock and travels south at 50 mph. At what time does the second ship overtake the first ship? **12:30 P.M. [5.5B]**

Projects or Group Activities

53. A bicyclist rides for 2 h at a speed of 10 mph and then returns at a speed of 20 mph. Find the cyclist's average speed for the trip. $13\frac{1}{3}$ mph

54. A car travels a 1-mile track at an average speed of 30 mph. At what average speed must the car travel the next mile so that the average speed for the 2 mi is 60 mph? It is impossible to average 60 mph.

55. A mountain climber ascended a mountain at 0.5 mph and descended twice as fast. The trip took 12 h. How many miles was the round trip? 8 mi

CHAPTER 5 Summary

Key Words	Examples
An **equation** expresses the equality of two mathematical expressions. [5.1A, p. 284]	$3 + 2(4x - 5) = x + 4$ is an equation.

A **solution of an equation** is a number that, when substituted for the variable, results in a true equation. [5.1A, p. 284]

-2 is a solution of $2 - 3x = 8$ because $2 - 3(-2) = 8$ is a true equation.

To **solve an equation** means to find a solution of the equation. The goal is to rewrite the equation in the form *variable* = *constant*, because the constant is the solution. [5.1B, p. 284]

The equation $x = -3$ is in the form *variable* = *constant*. The constant, -3, is the solution of the equation.

Consecutive integers follow one another in order. [5.4A, p. 313]

5, 6, 7 are consecutive integers.
$-9, -8, -7$ are consecutive integers.

Essential Rules and Procedures

Examples

Addition Property of Equations [5.1B, p. 285]
The same number can be added to each side of an equation without changing the solution of the equation.

If $a = b$, then $a + c = b + c$.

Multiplication Property of Equations [5.1C, p. 286]
Each side of an equation can be multiplied by the same nonzero number without changing the solution of the equation.

If $a = b$ and $c \neq 0$, then $ac = bc$.

Consecutive Integers [5.4A, p. 313]
$n, n + 1, n + 2, \ldots$

The sum of three consecutive integers is 33.

$n + (n + 1) + (n + 2) = 33$

Consecutive Even or Consecutive Odd Integers [5.4A, p. 313]
$n, n + 2, n + 4, \ldots$

The sum of three consecutive odd integers is 33.

$n + (n + 2) + (n + 4) = 33$

Value Mixture Equation [5.5A, p. 321]
Amount · Unit Cost = Value

$$AC = V$$

An herbalist has 30 oz of herbs costing \$4 per ounce. How many ounces of herbs costing \$2 per ounce should be mixed with the 30 oz to produce a mixture costing \$3.20 per ounce?

$30(4) + 2x = 3.20(30 + x)$

Uniform Motion Equation [5.1D, p. 288; 5.5B, p. 323]
Distance = Rate · Time

$$d = rt$$

A boat traveled from a harbor to an island at an average speed of 20 mph. The average speed on the return trip was 15 mph. The total trip took 3.5 h. How long did it take for the boat to travel to the island?

$20t = 15(3.5 - t)$

CHAPTER 5 Review Exercises

1. Solve: $x + 3 = 24$
   21 [5.1B]

2. Solve: $x + 5(3x - 20) = 10(x - 4)$
   10 [5.3B]

3. Solve: $5x - 6 = 29$
   7 [5.2A]

4. Is 3 a solution of $5x - 2 = 4x + 5$?
   No [5.1A]

5. Solve: $\frac{3}{5}a = 12$
   20 [5.1C]

6. Solve: $6x + 3(2x - 1) = -27$
   -2 [5.3B]

7. Solve: $x - 3 = -7$
   -4 [5.1B]

8. Solve: $5x + 3 = 10x - 17$
   4 [5.3A]

9. Solve: $7 - [4 + 2(x - 3)] = 11(x + 2)$
   -1 [5.3B]

10. Solve: $-6x + 16 = -2x$
    4 [5.3A]

11. Solve: $7 - 3x = 2 - 5x$
    $-\frac{5}{2}$ [5.3A]

12. Solve: $-\frac{3}{8}x = -\frac{15}{32}$
    $\frac{5}{4}$ [5.1C]

13. Solve: $35 - 3x = 5$
    10 [5.2A]

14. Solve: $3x = 2(3x - 2)$
    $\frac{4}{3}$ [5.3B]

15. **Physics** A lever is 12 ft long. At a distance of 2 ft from the fulcrum, a force of 120 lb is applied. How large a force must be applied to the other end so that the system will balance? Use the lever system equation $F_1x = F_2(d - x)$.
    24 lb [5.3C]

16. **Travel** A bus traveled on a level road for 2 h at an average speed that was 20 mph faster than its average speed on a winding road. The time spent on the winding road was 3 h. Find the average speed on the winding road if the total trip was 200 mi.
    32 mph [5.5B]

17. The difference between nine and twice a number is five. Find the number.
2 [5.4B]

18. The product of five and a number is fifty. Find the number.
10 [5.4B]

19. **Mixtures** A health food store combined cranberry juice that cost $1.79 per quart with apple juice that cost $1.19 per quart. How many quarts of each were used to make 10 qt of cranapple juice costing $1.61 per quart?
Cranberry juice: 7 qt; apple juice: 3 qt [5.5A]

20. Four times the second of three consecutive integers equals the sum of the first and third integers. Find the integers.
−1, 0, 1 [5.4A]

21. Translate "four less than the product of five and a number is sixteen" into an equation and solve.
$5n - 4 = 16$; 4 [5.4A]

© Songquan Deng/Shutterstock.com

22. **Building Height** The Empire State Building is 1472 ft tall. This is 654 ft less than twice the height of the Eiffel Tower. Find the height of the Eiffel Tower.
1063 ft [5.4B]

23. **Temperature** Find the Celsius temperature when the Fahrenheit temperature is 100°. Use the formula $F = \frac{9}{5}C + 32$, where F is the Fahrenheit temperature and C is the Celsius temperature. Round to the nearest tenth.
37.8°C [5.2B]

24. **Travel** A jet plane traveling at 600 mph overtakes a propeller-driven plane that had a 2-hour head start. The propeller-driven plane is traveling at 200 mph. How far from the starting point does the jet overtake the propeller-driven plane?
600 mi [5.5B]

25. The sum of two numbers is twenty-one. Three times the smaller number is two less than twice the larger number. Find the two numbers.
8, 13 [5.4A]

26. **Farming** A farmer harvested 28,336 bushels of corn. This amount represents an increase of 3036 bushels over last year's crop. How many bushels of corn did the farmer harvest last year?
25,300 bushels [5.4B]

CHAPTER 5 TEST

1. Solve: $3x - 2 = 5x + 8$
   -5 [5.3A]

2. Solve: $x - 3 = -8$
   -5 [5.1B]

3. Solve: $3x - 5 = -14$
   -3 [5.2A]

4. Solve: $4 - 2(3 - 2x) = 2(5 - x)$
   2 [5.3B]

5. Is -2 a solution of $x^2 - 3x = 2x - 6$?
   No [5.1A]

6. Solve: $7 - 4x = -13$
   5 [5.2A]

7. $5 = 3 - 4x$
   $-\frac{1}{2}$ [5.2A]

8. Solve: $5x - 2(4x - 3) = 6x + 9$
   $-\frac{1}{3}$ [5.3B]

9. Solve: $5x + 3 - 7x = 2x - 5$
   2 [5.3A]

10. Solve: $\frac{3}{4}x = -9$
    -12 [5.1C]

11. Solve: $\frac{x}{5} - 12 = 7$
    95 [5.2A]

12. Solve: $8 - 3x = 2x - 8$
    $\frac{16}{5}$ [5.3A]

13. Solve: $y - 4y + 3 = 12$
    -3 [5.2A]

14. Solve: $2x + 4(x - 3) = 5x - 1$
    11 [5.3B]

15. **Mixtures** A baker wants to make a 15-pound blend of flour that costs \$.60 per pound. The blend is made using a rye flour that costs \$.70 per pound and a wheat flour that costs \$.40 per pound. How many pounds of each flour should be used?
    Rye: 10 lb; wheat: 5 lb [5.5A]

16. **Finance** A financial manager has determined that the cost per unit for a calculator is \$15 and that the fixed cost per month is \$2000. Find the number of calculators produced during a month in which the total cost was \$5000. Use the equation $T = U \cdot N + F$, where T is the total cost, U is the cost per unit, N is the number of units produced, and F is the fixed cost.
    200 calculators [5.2B]

17. Find three consecutive even integers whose sum is 36.
10, 12, 14 [5.4A]

18. Manufacturing A clock manufacturer's fixed costs per month are \$5000. The unit cost for each clock is \$15. Find the number of clocks made during a month in which the total cost was \$65,000. Use the formula $T = U \cdot N + F$, where T is the total cost, U is the cost per unit, N is the number of units made, and F is the fixed costs.
4000 clocks [5.2B]

19. Translate "the difference between three times a number and fifteen is twenty-seven" into an equation and solve.
$3x - 15 = 27$; 14 [5.4A]

© Val Thoermer/Shutterstock.com

20. Sports A cross-country skier leaves a camp to explore a wilderness area. Two hours later a friend leaves the camp in a snowmobile, traveling 4 mph faster than the skier. The friend meets the skier 1 h later. Find the rate of the snowmobile. 6 mph [5.5B]

21. Business A company makes 140 televisions per day. Three times the number of LCD rear-projection TVs made equals 20 less than the number of LCD flat-panel TVs made. Find the number of LCD flat-panel TVs made each day.
110 LCD flat-panel TVs [5.4B]

22. The sum of two numbers is eighteen. The difference between four times the smaller number and seven is equal to the sum of two times the larger number and five. Find the two numbers. 8, 10 [5.4A]

23. Aviation As part of flight training, a student pilot was required to fly to an airport and then return. The average speed to the airport was 90 mph, and the average speed returning was 120 mph. Find the distance between the two airports if the total flying time was 7 h. 360 mi [5.5B]

24. Physics Find the time required for a falling object to increase in velocity from 24 ft/s to 392 ft/s. Use the formula $V = V_0 + 32t$, where V is the final velocity of a falling object, V_0 is the starting velocity of the falling object, and t is the time for the object to fall.
11.5 s [5.2B]

25. Chemistry A chemist mixes 100 g of water at 80°C with 50 g of water at 20°C. Find the final temperature of the water after mixing. Use the equation $m_1(T_1 - T) = m_2(T - T_2)$, where m_1 is the quantity of water at the hotter temperature, T_1 is the temperature of the hotter water, m_2 is the quantity of water at the cooler temperature, T_2 is the temperature of the cooler water, and T is the final temperature of the water after mixing. 60°C [5.3C]

Cumulative Review Exercises

1. Subtract: $-6 - (-20) - 8$
6 [3.2B]

2. Multiply: $(-2)(-6)(-4)$
-48 [3.3A]

3. Subtract: $-\frac{5}{6} - \left(-\frac{7}{16}\right)$
$-\frac{19}{48}$ [3.4A]

4. Divide: $-\frac{7}{3} \div \frac{7}{6}$
-2 [3.4B]

5. Simplify: $-4^2 \cdot \left(-\frac{3}{2}\right)^3$
54 [3.5A]

6. Simplify: $25 - 3 \cdot \frac{(5-2)^2}{2^3 + 1} - (-2)$
24 [3.5A]

7. Evaluate $3(a - c) - 2ab$ when $a = 2$, $b = 3$, and $c = -4$.
6 [4.1A]

8. Simplify: $3x - 8x + (-12x)$
$-17x$ [4.2A]

9. Simplify: $2a - (-3b) - 7a - 5b$
$-5a - 2b$ [4.2A]

10. Simplify: $(16x)\left(\frac{1}{8}\right)$
$2x$ [4.2B]

11. Simplify: $-4(-9y)$
$36y$ [4.2B]

12. Simplify: $-2(-x^2 - 3x + 2)$
$2x^2 + 6x - 4$ [4.2C]

13. Simplify: $-2(x - 3) + 2(4 - x)$
$-4x + 14$ [4.2D]

14. Simplify: $-3[2x - 4(x - 3)] + 2$
$6x - 34$ [4.2D]

15. Is -3 a solution of $x^2 + 6x + 9 = x + 3$?
Yes [5.1A]

16. Is $\frac{1}{2}$ a solution of $3 - 8x = 12x - 2$?
No [5.1A]

17. Simplify: $\left(\frac{3}{8} - \frac{1}{4}\right) \div \frac{3}{4} + \frac{4}{9}$
$\frac{11}{18}$ [3.5A]

18. Solve: $\frac{3}{5}x = -15$
-25 [5.1C]

19. Solve: $7x - 8 = -29$
-3 [5.2A]

20. Solve: $13 - 9x = -14$
3 [5.2A]

21. Multiply: 9.67×0.0049
0.047383 [2.6B]

22. Find 6 less than 13.
7 [1.2B]

23. Solve: $8x - 3(4x - 5) = -2x - 11$
13 [5.3B]

24. Solve: $6 - 2(5x - 8) = 3x - 4$
2 [5.3B]

25. Solve: $5x - 8 = 12x + 13$
-3 [5.3A]

26. Solve: $11 - 4x = 2x + 8$
$\frac{1}{2}$ [5.3A]

27. Chemistry A chemist mixes 300 g of water at 75°C with 100 g of water at 15°C. Find the final temperature of the water after mixing. Use the equation $m_1(T_1 - T) = m_2(T - T_2)$, where m_1 is the quantity of water at the hotter temperature, T_1 is the temperature of the hotter water, m_2 is the quantity of water at the cooler temperature, T_2 is the temperature of the cooler water, and T is the final temperature of the water after mixing. 60°C [5.3C]

28. Translate "the difference between twelve and the product of five and a number is negative eighteen" into an equation and solve.
$12 - 5x = -18$; 6 [5.4A]

29. Construction The area of a cement foundation of a house is 2000 ft^2. This is 200 ft^2 more than three times the area of the garage. Find the area of the garage.
600 ft^2 [5.4B]

© Alaettin YILDIRIM/Shutterstock.com

30. Mixtures How many pounds of an oat flour that costs \$.80 per pound must be mixed with 40 lb of a wheat flour that costs \$.50 per pound to make a blend that costs \$.60 per pound? 20 lb [5.5A]

31. Translate "the sum of three times a number and four" into a variable expression.
$3n + 4$ [4.3B]

32. Three less than eight times a number is three more than five times the number. Find the number.
2 [5.4B]

33. Sports A sprinter ran to the end of a track at an average rate of 8 m/s and then jogged back to the starting point at an average rate of 3 m/s. The sprinter took 55 s to run to the end of the track and jog back. Find the length of the track.
120 m [5.5B]

Proportion and Percent

6

OBJECTIVES

SECTION 6.1
A To write ratios and rates

SECTION 6.2
A To solve proportions
B To solve application problems using proportions

SECTION 6.3
A To write percents as decimals or fractions
B To write fractions and decimals as percents

SECTION 6.4
A To use the basic percent equation
B To solve percent problems using proportions
C To solve application problems

SECTION 6.5
A To solve simple interest problems

Focus on Success

We cannot overstate the importance of attending class. It is essential to your success in this course. If, by some unavoidable situation, you cannot attend class, find out as soon as possible what was covered. You might ask a friend for notes and the assignment, or contact your instructor. There may be online resources that you can use to help you with the topics and concepts that were discussed the day you were absent. (See Class Time, page AIM-5.)

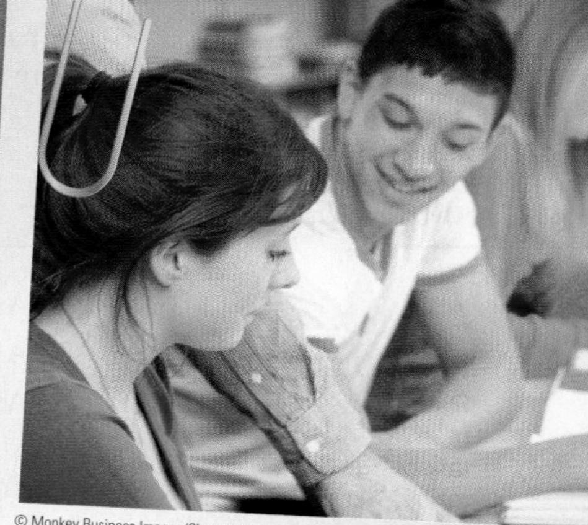

Prep Test

Are you ready to succeed in this chapter? Take the Prep Test below to find out if you are ready to learn the new material.

For Exercises 1 to 5, multiply or divide.

1. $19 \times \frac{1}{100}$ $\frac{19}{100}$ [2.4A]

2. 23×0.01 0.23 [2.6B]

3. 0.47×100 47 [2.6B]

4. $0.06 \times 47{,}500$ 2850 [2.6B]

5. $60 \div 0.015$ 4000 [2.6C]

6. Simplify: $\frac{8}{10}$ $\frac{4}{5}$ [2.2B]

7. Multiply $\frac{5}{8} \times 100$. Write the answer as a decimal. 62.5 [3.4B]

8. Write $\frac{200}{3}$ as a mixed number. $66\frac{2}{3}$ [2.2A]

9. Divide $28 \div 16$. Write the answer as a decimal. 1.75 [2.6C]

SECTION

6.1 Ratios and Rates

OBJECTIVE A To write ratios and rates

Point of Interest

It is believed that billiards was invented in France during the reign of Louis XI (1423–1483). In the United States, the standard billiard table is 4 ft 6 in. by 9 ft. This is a ratio of 1:2. The same ratio holds for carom and snooker tables, which are 5 ft by 10 ft.

INSTRUCTOR NOTE

Ratios have applications to many disciplines. Investors talk of price–earnings ratios. Accountants use the current ratio, which is the ratio of current assets to current liabilities. Metallurgists use ratios to make various grades of steel.

In previous work, we have used quantities with units, such as 12 ft, 3 h, 2¢, and 15 acres. In these examples, the units are feet, hours, cents, and acres.

A **ratio** is the quotient or comparison of two quantities with the *same* unit. We can compare the measure of 3 ft to the measure of 8 ft by writing a quotient.

$$\frac{3\text{ ft}}{8\text{ ft}} = \frac{3}{8} \qquad 3\text{ ft is } \frac{3}{8} \text{ of } 8\text{ ft.}$$

A ratio can be written in three ways:

1. As a fraction $\frac{3}{8}$
2. As two numbers separated by a colon 3 : 8
3. As two numbers separated by the word *to* 3 to 8

The ratio of 15 mi to 45 mi is written as

$$\frac{15\text{ mi}}{45\text{ mi}} = \frac{15}{45} = \frac{1}{3} \text{ or } 1:3 \text{ or } 1 \text{ to } 3$$

A ratio is in **simplest form** when the two numbers do not have a common factor. The units are not written in a ratio.

A **rate** is the comparison of two quantities with *different* units.

A catering company prepares 9 gal of coffee for every 50 people at a reception. This rate is written

$$\frac{9\text{ gal}}{50\text{ people}}$$

You traveled 200 mi in 6 h. The rate is written

$$\frac{200\text{ mi}}{6\text{ h}} = \frac{100\text{ mi}}{3\text{ h}}$$

A rate is in **simplest form** when the numbers have no common factors. The units are written as part of the rate.

Take Note

Unit rates make comparisons easier. For example, if you travel 37 mph and I travel 43 mph, we know that I am traveling faster than you are. It is more difficult to compare speeds if we are told that you are traveling $\frac{111\text{ mi}}{3\text{ h}}$ and I am traveling $\frac{172\text{ mi}}{4\text{ h}}$.

Many rates are written as unit rates. A **unit rate** is a rate in which the number in the denominator is 1. The word *per* generally indicates a unit rate. It means "for each" or "for every." For example,

23 mi per gallon • **The unit rate is $\frac{23\text{ mi}}{1\text{ gal}}$.**

65 mi per hour • **The unit rate is $\frac{65\text{ mi}}{1\text{ h}}$.**

\$4.78 per pound • **The unit rate is $\frac{\$4.78}{1\text{ lb}}$.**

IN-CLASS EXAMPLES

1. Write the comparison 12 lb to 9 lb as a ratio in simplest form using a fraction, a colon, and the word *to*.
   $\frac{4}{3}$; 4 : 3; 4 to 3
2. Write "40 mi in 12 h" as a rate in simplest form.
   $\frac{10 \text{ mi}}{3 \text{ h}}$
3. Write "$1875 for 50 shares of stock" as a unit rate.
   $37.50/share

To find a unit rate, divide the number in the numerator of the rate by the number in the denominator of the rate. A unit rate is often written in decimal form.

APPLY THE CONCEPT

A student received $57 for working 6 h at the college bookstore. Find the student's wage per hour (the unit rate).

Write the rate as a fraction. $\frac{\$57}{6 \text{ h}}$

Divide the number in the numerator of the rate (57) by the number in the denominator (6). $57 \div 6 = 9.5$

The unit rate is $\frac{\$9.50}{1 \text{ h}} = \$9.50/\text{h}$. This is read "$9.50 per hour."

The student's wage is $9.50/h.

EXAMPLE 1

Write the comparison of 12 to 8 as a ratio in simplest form using a fraction, a colon, and the word *to*.

Solution

$\frac{12}{8} = \frac{3}{2}$

12:8 = 3:2

12 to 8 = 3 to 2

YOU TRY IT 1

Write the comparison of 12 to 20 as a ratio in simplest form using a fraction, a colon, and the word *to*.

Your solution

$\frac{3}{5}$; 3 : 5; 3 to 5

EXAMPLE 2

Write "12 hits in 26 times at bat" as a rate in simplest form.

Solution

$\frac{12 \text{ hits}}{26 \text{ at-bats}} = \frac{6 \text{ hits}}{13 \text{ at-bats}}$

YOU TRY IT 2

Write "20 bags of grass seed for 8 acres" as a rate in simplest form.

Your solution

$\frac{5 \text{ bags}}{2 \text{ acres}}$

EXAMPLE 3

Write "285 mi in 5 h" as a unit rate.

Solution

$\frac{285 \text{ mi}}{5 \text{ h}}$ • **Write the rate as a fraction.**

$285 \div 5 = 57$ • **Divide the numerator by the denominator.**

The unit rate is 57 mph.

YOU TRY IT 3

Write "$8.96 for 3.5 lb" as a unit rate.

Your solution

$2.56/lb

Solutions on p. S16

6.1 EXERCISES

SUGGESTED ASSIGNMENT
Exercises 1 and 2; Exercises 3–29, odds;
More challenging exercises: Exercises 30 and 31

Concept Check

For Exercises 1 and 2, fill in the blank or circle the correct words to complete each sentence.

1. In a ratio, the units are/are not written. In a rate, the units are/are not written.
are not; are

2. A unit rate is a rate in which the number in the denominator is __1__. To write a rate as a unit rate, divide the number in the __numerator__ by the number in the __denominator__.

OBJECTIVE A *To write ratios and rates*

For Exercises 3 to 11, write the comparison as a ratio in simplest form using a fraction, a colon (:), and the word *to*.

3. 3 pints to 15 pints
$\frac{1}{5}$ 1 : 5 1 to 5

4. 6 pounds to 8 pounds
$\frac{3}{4}$ 3 : 4 3 to 4

5. $40 to $20
$\frac{2}{1}$ 2 : 1 2 to 1

6. 10 feet to 2 feet
$\frac{5}{1}$ 5 : 1 5 to 1

7. 3 miles to 8 miles
$\frac{3}{8}$ 3 : 8 3 to 8

8. 2 hours to 3 hours
$\frac{2}{3}$ 2 : 3 2 to 3

9. 6 minutes to 6 minutes
$\frac{1}{1}$ 1 : 1 1 to 1

10. 8 days to 12 days
$\frac{2}{3}$ 2 : 3 2 to 3

11. 35 cents to 50 cents
$\frac{7}{10}$ 7 : 10 7 to 10

For Exercises 12 to 14, write each phrase as a rate in simplest form.

12. 243 apple trees on 6 acres
$\frac{81 \text{ trees}}{2 \text{ acres}}$

13. 160 miles in 6 hours
$\frac{80 \text{ miles}}{3 \text{ hours}}$

14. 87 students in 6 classes
$\frac{29 \text{ students}}{2 \text{ classes}}$

For Exercises 15 to 17, complete the unit rate.

15. 5 miles in __1__ hour

16. 15 feet in __1__ second

17. 5 grams of fat in __1__ serving

For Exercises 18 to 25, write each phrase as a unit rate.

18. 10 feet in 4 seconds
2.5 feet/second

19. $51,000 earned in 12 months
$4250/month

20. 1100 trees planted on 10 acres
110 trees/acre

21. 3750 words on 15 pages
250 words/page

22. $131.88 earned in 7 hours
$18.84/hour

23. 628.8 miles in 12 hours
52.4 miles/hour

24. 409.4 miles on 11.5 gallons of gasoline
35.6 miles/gallon

25. $11.05 for 3.4 pounds
$3.25/pound

26. **Gasoline Prices** The price of gasoline jumped from \$2.70 per gallon to \$3.24 per gallon in one year. What is the ratio of the increase in price to the original price? Write the ratio using a colon (:). 1:5

© Aspen Photo/Shutterstock.com

27. **Basketball** NCAA statistics show that for every 2800 college seniors playing college basketball, only 50 will play as rookies in the National Basketball Association. Write the ratio of the number of National Basketball Association rookies to the number of college seniors playing college basketball. Write the ratio as a fraction in simplest form.
$\frac{1}{56}$

28. **Population Density** The table at the right shows the population and the area of three countries. Find the population density (people per square mile) for each country. Round to the nearest tenth. Australia: 7.6 people/mi^2; India: 1033.7 people/mi^2; U.S.: 87.7 people/mi^2

Country	Population	Area (in square miles)
Australia	22,241,000	2,938,000
India	1,184,639,000	1,146,000
United States	309,975,000	3,535,000

29. **E-mail** The Radicati Group compiled the following estimates on consumer use of e-mail worldwide. Complete the last column of the table by calculating the estimated number of messages per day that each user receives. Round to the nearest tenth. 148.6 messages; 183.3 messages; 240.6 messages

Year	Number of Users (in millions)	Messages per Day (in billions)	Messages per User per Day
2009	1050	156	
2011	1200	220	
2013	1330	320	

Critical Thinking

30. **Compensation** You have a choice of receiving a wage of \$34,000 per year, \$2840 per month, \$650 per week, or \$18 per hour. Which pay choice would you take? Assume a 40-hour work week and 52 weeks of work per year. \$18/h

31. **Television Advertising** For television advertising rates, what unit is in the numerator and what unit is in the denominator?
Numerator: dollars; denominator: seconds

Projects or Group Activities

32. **Social Security** According to the Social Security Administration, the numbers of workers per retiree in the future are expected to be as given in the table below.

Year	2020	2030	2040
Number of Workers per Retiree	2.5	2.1	2.0

Why is the shrinking number of workers per retiree of importance to the Social Security Administration?

QUICK QUIZ

1. You study 4 h per day. Find the ratio of the number of hours you study to the number of hours in one day. Write the ratio as a fraction in simplest form.
$\frac{1}{6}$ [6.1A]
2. A store manager bought 175 ice scrapers for \$456.75 and sold them for \$850.50. What was the store's profit per ice scraper?
\$2.25 [6.1A]

SECTION

6.2 Proportions

OBJECTIVE A *To solve proportions*

A **proportion** states the equality of two ratios or rates.

Definition of Proportion

If $\frac{a}{b}$ and $\frac{c}{d}$ are equal ratios or rates, then $\frac{a}{b} = \frac{c}{d}$ is a proportion.

EXAMPLES OF PROPORTIONS

1. $\frac{3}{6} = \frac{1}{2}$ **2.** $\frac{\$30}{4\text{ lb}} = \frac{\$90}{12\text{ lb}}$ **3.** $\frac{250\text{ mi}}{5\text{ h}} = \frac{50\text{ mi}}{1\text{ h}}$

Point of Interest

Proportions were studied by the earliest mathematicians. Clay tablets uncovered by archeologists show evidence of proportions in Egyptian and Babylonian cultures dating from 1800 B.C.

Each of the four numbers in a proportion is called a **term.** Each term is numbered according to the following diagram.

$$\begin{array}{rcl} \text{first term} \longrightarrow & \frac{a}{b} = \frac{c}{d} & \longleftarrow \text{third term} \\ \text{second term} \longrightarrow & & \longleftarrow \text{fourth term} \end{array}$$

The first and fourth terms of the proportion are called the **extremes,** and the second and third terms are called the **means.**

Tips for Success

You are learning a new skill in this objective. Be sure to do all you need to do in order to be successful at solving proportions: Read through the introductory material, work through the HOW TO examples, study the paired Examples, and do the You Try Its. Check your solutions to the You Try Its against the solutions given in the back of the book. See *AIM for Success,* pages AIM-7 through AIM-10.

If we multiply the proportion by the least common multiple of the denominators, we obtain the following result:

$$\frac{a}{b} = \frac{c}{d}$$

$$bd\left(\frac{a}{b}\right) = bd\left(\frac{c}{d}\right)$$

$$ad = bc$$

ad is the product of the extremes.
bc is the product of the means.

In any true proportion, the product of the means equals the product of the extremes. This is sometimes phrased as "the cross products are equal."

In the true proportion $\frac{3}{4} = \frac{9}{12}$, the cross products are equal.

$$\frac{3}{4} \times \frac{9}{12} \qquad \begin{array}{l} \longrightarrow 4 \cdot 9 = 36 \longleftarrow \text{Product of the means} \\ \longrightarrow 3 \cdot 12 = 36 \longleftarrow \text{Product of the extremes} \end{array}$$

IN-CLASS EXAMPLES

1. Is $\frac{2}{3} = \frac{44}{66}$ a true proportion? **Yes**
2. Solve: $\frac{n}{30} = \frac{120}{75}$ **48**
3. Solve: $\frac{7}{18} = \frac{n}{160}$ Round to the nearest hundredth. **62.22**
4. Solve: $\frac{3}{2} = \frac{n-3}{4}$ **9**

HOW TO 1 Determine whether the proportion $\frac{47\text{ mi}}{2\text{ gal}} = \frac{304\text{ mi}}{13\text{ gal}}$ is a true proportion.

The product of the means:

$2 \cdot 304 = 608$

The product of the extremes:

$47 \cdot 13 = 611$

The proportion is not true because $608 \neq 611$.

When three terms of a proportion are given, the fourth term can be found. To solve a proportion for an unknown term, use the fact that the product of the means equals the product of the extremes.

Integrating Technology

To use a calculator to solve the proportion at the right, multiply the second and third terms and divide by the fourth term. Enter

5 × 9 ÷ 16 =

The display reads 2.8125.

HOW TO 2 Solve: $\frac{n}{5} = \frac{9}{16}$

$$\frac{n}{5} = \frac{9}{16}$$

Find the number n that will make the proportion true.

The product of the means equals the product of the extremes.

$$5 \cdot 9 = n \cdot 16$$

Solve for n.

$$45 = 16n$$

$$\frac{45}{16} = \frac{16n}{16}$$

$$2.8125 = n$$

EXAMPLE 1

Determine whether $\frac{15}{3} = \frac{90}{18}$ is a true proportion.

Solution

$\frac{15}{3} \times \frac{90}{18}$ — $90 \longrightarrow 3 \cdot 90 = 270$; $18 \longrightarrow 15 \cdot 18 = 270$

The product of the means equals the product of the extremes.

The proportion is true.

YOU TRY IT 1

Is $\frac{50 \text{ mi}}{3 \text{ gal}} = \frac{250 \text{ mi}}{12 \text{ gal}}$ a true proportion?

Your solution

No

EXAMPLE 2

Solve: $\frac{5}{9} = \frac{x}{45}$

Solution

$$\frac{5}{9} = \frac{x}{45}$$

$$9 \cdot x = 5 \cdot 45$$

$$9x = 225$$

$$\frac{9x}{9} = \frac{225}{9}$$

$$x = 25$$

YOU TRY IT 2

Solve: $\frac{7}{12} = \frac{42}{x}$

Your solution

72

EXAMPLE 3

Solve $\frac{6}{n} = \frac{45}{124}$. Round to the nearest tenth.

Solution

$$\frac{6}{n} = \frac{45}{124}$$

$$n \cdot 45 = 6 \cdot 124$$

$$45n = 744$$

$$\frac{45n}{45} = \frac{744}{45}$$

$$n \approx 16.5$$

YOU TRY IT 3

Solve $\frac{5}{n} = \frac{3}{322}$. Round to the nearest hundredth.

Your solution

536.67

Solutions on p. S16

EXAMPLE 4

Solve: $\frac{x+2}{3} = \frac{7}{8}$

Solution

$$\frac{x+2}{3} = \frac{7}{8}$$
$$3 \cdot 7 = (x+2)8$$
$$21 = 8x + 16$$
$$5 = 8x$$
$$0.625 = x$$

YOU TRY IT 4

Solve: $\frac{4}{5} = \frac{3}{x-3}$

Your solution

6.75

Solution on p. S16

OBJECTIVE B *To solve application problems using proportions*

IN-CLASS EXAMPLES

5. The property tax on a $150,000 home is $3750. At this rate, what is the property tax on a home worth $250,000? **$6250**
6. A $2 sales tax is charged for a $40 purchase. At this rate, what is the sales tax for an $85 purchase? **$4.25**

Proportions are useful in many types of application problems. In cooking, proportions are used when a larger quantity of food is needed than the recipe yields. In mixing cement, the amounts of cement, sand, and rock are mixed in the same ratio. A map is drawn on a proportional basis, such as 1 in. representing 50 mi.

In setting up a proportion, keep the same units in the numerators and the same units in the denominators. For example, if *feet* is in the numerator on one side of the proportion, then *feet* must be in the numerator on the other side of the proportion.

Take Note

It is also correct to write the proportion with the costs in the numerators and the numbers of tires in the denominators: $\frac{\$266.50}{2 \text{ tires}} = \frac{c}{5 \text{ tires}}$. The solution will be the same.

HOW TO 3 A customer sees an ad in a newspaper advertising 2 tires for $266.50. The customer wants to buy 5 tires and use one as a spare. How much will the 5 tires cost?

Write a proportion.

Let c = the cost of the 5 tires.

$$\frac{2 \text{ tires}}{\$266.50} = \frac{5 \text{ tires}}{c}$$
$$266.50 \cdot 5 = 2 \cdot c$$
$$1332.50 = 2c$$
$$\frac{1332.50}{2} = \frac{2c}{2}$$
$$666.25 = c$$

The 5 tires will cost $666.25.

EXAMPLE 5

The dosage of a certain medication is 2 oz for every 50 lb of body weight. How many ounces of this medication are required for a person who weighs 175 lb?

Strategy

To find the number of ounces of medication required for a person weighing 175 lb, write and solve a proportion using n to represent the number of ounces of medication required.

Solution

$$\frac{2 \text{ oz}}{50 \text{ lb}} = \frac{n \text{ oz}}{175 \text{ lb}}$$

- Write "oz" in the numerator and "lb" in the denominator.

$$50n = 2 \cdot 175$$

- The product of the means equals the product of the extremes.

$$50n = 350$$

$$\frac{50n}{50} = \frac{350}{50}$$

$$n = 7$$

A 175-pound person requires 7 oz of medication.

YOU TRY IT 5

An automobile can travel 396 mi on 11 gal of gas. At the same rate, how many gallons of gas would be necessary to travel 832 mi? Round to the nearest tenth.

Your strategy

Your solution

23.1 gal

EXAMPLE 6

From previous experience, a manufacturer knows that in an average production run of 5000 calculators, 40 will be defective. What number of defective calculators can be expected in a run of 45,000 calculators?

Strategy

To find the number of defective calculators, write and solve a proportion using n to represent the number of defective calculators.

Solution

$$\frac{40 \text{ defective calculators}}{5000 \text{ calculators}} = \frac{n \text{ defective calculators}}{45{,}000 \text{ calculators}}$$

$$5000 \cdot n = 40 \cdot 45{,}000$$

$$5000n = 1{,}800{,}000$$

$$\frac{5000n}{5000} = \frac{1{,}800{,}000}{5000}$$

$$n = 360$$

The manufacturer can expect 360 defective calculators.

YOU TRY IT 6

An automobile recall was based on tests that showed 15 transmission defects in 1200 cars. At this rate, how many defective transmissions will be found in 120,000 cars?

Your strategy

Your solution

1500 defective transmissions

Solutions on p. S16

6.2 EXERCISES

Concept Check

SUGGESTED ASSIGNMENT
Exercises 1–4; Exercises 5–47, odds; Exercises 51–67, odds

1. An equation of the form $\frac{a}{b} = \frac{c}{d}$, which states that two ratios or rates are equal, is called a proportion. The extremes are the terms a and d, and the means are the terms b and c. In a true proportion, the product of the means and the product of the extremes are equal.

2. The first step in solving the proportion $\frac{x}{85} = \frac{5}{17}$ is to write the equation that states that the product of the means equals the product of the extremes: $85 \cdot$ 5 $=$ x $\cdot 17$.

For Exercises 3 and 4, use the information that Jane ran 4 mi in 50 min. Let n be the number of miles Jane can run in 30 min at the same rate.

© Phase4Photography/Shutterstock.com

3. To determine how many miles Jane can run in 30 min, solve the proportion $\frac{4 \text{ mi}}{50 \text{ min}} = \frac{n \text{ mi}}{30 \text{ min}}$.

4. To determine how many miles Jane can run in 30 min, one student used the proportion $\frac{4}{50} = \frac{n}{30}$ and a second student used the proportion $\frac{30}{n} = \frac{50}{4}$. Can either of these proportions be used to solve this problem?
Yes, both are valid proportions.

OBJECTIVE A *To solve proportions*

Determine whether the proportion is true or not true.

5. $\frac{27}{8} = \frac{9}{4}$
Not true

6. $\frac{3}{18} = \frac{4}{19}$
Not true

7. $\frac{45}{135} = \frac{3}{9}$
True

8. $\frac{3}{4} = \frac{54}{72}$
True

9. $\frac{6 \text{ min}}{5 \text{ cents}} = \frac{30 \text{ min}}{25 \text{ cents}}$
True

10. $\frac{7 \text{ tiles}}{4 \text{ ft}} = \frac{42 \text{ tiles}}{20 \text{ ft}}$
Not true

11. $\frac{300 \text{ ft}}{4 \text{ rolls}} = \frac{450 \text{ ft}}{7 \text{ rolls}}$
Not true

12. $\frac{\$65}{5 \text{ days}} = \frac{\$26}{2 \text{ days}}$
True

Solve. Round to the nearest hundredth.

13. $\frac{2}{3} = \frac{n}{15}$
10

14. $\frac{7}{15} = \frac{n}{15}$
7

15. $\frac{n}{5} = \frac{12}{25}$
2.4

16. $\frac{n}{8} = \frac{7}{8}$
7

17. $\frac{3}{8} = \frac{n}{12}$

4.5

18. $\frac{5}{8} = \frac{40}{n}$

64

19. $\frac{3}{n} = \frac{7}{40}$

17.14

20. $\frac{7}{12} = \frac{25}{n}$

42.86

21. $\frac{16}{n} = \frac{25}{40}$

25.6

22. $\frac{15}{45} = \frac{72}{n}$

216

23. $\frac{120}{n} = \frac{144}{25}$

20.83

24. $\frac{65}{20} = \frac{14}{n}$

4.31

25. $\frac{0.5}{2.3} = \frac{n}{20}$

4.35

26. $\frac{1.2}{2.8} = \frac{n}{32}$

13.71

27. $\frac{0.7}{1.2} = \frac{6.4}{n}$

10.97

28. $\frac{2.5}{0.6} = \frac{165}{n}$

39.6

29. $\frac{x}{6.25} = \frac{16}{87}$

1.15

30. $\frac{x}{2.54} = \frac{132}{640}$

0.52

31. $\frac{1.2}{0.44} = \frac{y}{14.2}$

38.73

32. $\frac{12.5}{y} = \frac{102}{55}$

6.74

33. $\frac{n + 2}{5} = \frac{1}{2}$

0.5

34. $\frac{5 + n}{8} = \frac{3}{4}$

1

35. $\frac{4}{3} = \frac{n - 2}{6}$

10

36. $\frac{3}{5} = \frac{n - 7}{8}$

11.8

37. $\frac{2}{n + 3} = \frac{7}{12}$

0.43

38. $\frac{5}{n + 1} = \frac{7}{3}$

1.14

39. $\frac{7}{10} = \frac{3 + n}{2}$

−1.6

40. $\frac{3}{2} = \frac{5 + n}{4}$

1

41. $\frac{x - 4}{3} = \frac{3}{4}$

6.25

42. $\frac{x - 1}{8} = \frac{5}{2}$

21

43. $\frac{6}{1} = \frac{x - 2}{5}$

32

44. $\frac{7}{3} = \frac{x - 4}{8}$

22.67

45. $\frac{5}{8} = \frac{2}{x - 3}$

6.2

46. $\frac{5}{2} = \frac{1}{x - 6}$

6.4

47. $\frac{3}{x - 4} = \frac{5}{3}$

5.8

48. $\frac{8}{x - 6} = \frac{5}{4}$

12.4

49. **a.** Write a true proportion using the numbers 9, 4, 2, and 18.
b. Write a true proportion using only the numbers 8, 2, and 4.

a. One example is $\frac{2}{9} = \frac{4}{18}$. **b.** One example is $\frac{2}{4} = \frac{4}{8}$.

50. **a.** Write a proportion in which the product of the means and the product of the extremes is 60.
b. Using different numbers than you used in part (a), write another proportion in which the product of the means and the product of the extremes is 60.

a and **b.** Two examples are $\frac{3}{4} = \frac{15}{20}$ and $\frac{6}{5} = \frac{12}{10}$.

OBJECTIVE B *To solve application problems using proportions*

51. Gravity The ratio of weight on the moon to weight on Earth is 1:6. How much would a 174-pound person weigh on the moon? 29 lb

52. Insurance A life insurance policy costs $15.22 for every $1000 of insurance. At this rate, what is the cost of $75,000 of insurance? $1141.50

Fuse/Jupiterimages

53. Sewing Six choir robes can be made from 6.5 yd of material. How many robes can be made from 26 yd of material? 24 robes

54. Computers A computer manufacturer finds an average of 3 defective hard drives in every 100 drives manufactured. How many defective drives are expected to be found in the production of 1200 hard drives? 36 defective drives

55. Taxes The property tax on a $180,000 home is $4320. At this rate, what is the property tax on a home appraised at $280,000? $6720

56. Medicine The dosage of a certain medication is 2 mg for every 80 lb of body weight. How many milligrams of this medication are required for a person who weighs 220 lb? 5.5 mg

57. Fuel Consumption An automobile was driven 84 mi and used 3 gal of gasoline. At the same rate of consumption, how far would the car travel on 14.5 gal of gasoline? 406 mi

58. Nutrition If a 56-gram serving of pasta contains 7 g of protein, how many grams of protein are contained in a 454-gram box of the pasta? 56.75 g

© pics721/Shutterstock.com

59. Construction A building contractor estimates that 5 overhead lights are needed for every 400 ft^2 of office space. Using this estimate, how many light fixtures are necessary for an office building of 35,000 ft^2? 438 light fixtures

60. Softball A softball player has hit 9 home runs in 32 games. At the same rate, how many home runs will the player hit in a 160-game schedule? 45 home runs

61. Health A dieter has lost 3 lb in 5 weeks. At this rate, how long will it take the dieter to lose 36 lb? 60 weeks

62. Automobile Recall An automobile recall was based on engineering tests that showed 22 defects in 1000 cars. At this rate, how many defects would be found in 125,000 cars? 2750 defects

63. Exercise Walking 5 mi in 2 h will burn 650 calories. Walking at the same rate, how many miles would a person need to walk to lose 1 lb? (The burning of 3500 calories is equivalent to the loss of 1 lb.) Round to the nearest hundredth. 26.92 mi

64. Travel An account executive bought a new car and drove 22,000 mi in the first 4 months. At the same rate, how many miles will the account executive drive in 3 years? 198,000 mi

65. Elections A pre-election survey showed that 2 out of every 3 eligible voters would cast ballots in the county election. There are 240,000 eligible voters in the county. How many people are expected to vote in the election? 160,000 people

66. Food Waste Using the rate given in the news clipping at the right, find the cost of food wasted by **a.** the average family of three and **b.** the average family of five.
a. \$442.50 **b.** \$737.50

67. Cartography The scale on a map is $\frac{1}{2}$ in. equals 8 mi. What is the actual distance between two points that are $1\frac{1}{4}$ in. apart on the map? 20 mi

68. Candles A slow-burning candle will burn 1.5 in. in 40 min. How many inches will the candle burn in 4 h? 9 in.

QUICK QUIZ

1. Solve: $\frac{60}{n} = \frac{24}{7}$
17.5 [6.2A]
2. For every 10 people who work in a city, 3 do not commute by public transportation. If 34,600 people work in the city, how many do not take public transportation?
10,380 people [6.2B]

In the NEWS!

How Much Food Do You Waste?

In the United States, the estimated cost of food wasted each year by the average family of four is \$590.

Source: University of Arizona

Critical Thinking

69. Elections A survey of voters in a city claimed that 2 people of every 5 who voted cast a ballot in favor of city amendment A, and 3 people of every 4 who voted cast a ballot against amendment A. Is this possible? Explain your answer. No

70. Determine whether the statement is true or false.

a. A quotient $(a \div b)$ is a ratio. True for $b \neq 0$

b. If $\frac{a}{b} = \frac{c}{d}$, then $\frac{b}{a} = \frac{d}{c}$. True

c. If $\frac{a}{b} = \frac{c}{d}$, then $\frac{a}{c} = \frac{b}{d}$. True

d. If $\frac{a}{b} = \frac{c}{d}$, then $\frac{a}{d} = \frac{c}{b}$. Not true

71. Lotteries Three people put their money together to buy lottery tickets. The first person put in \$25, the second person put in \$30, and the third person put in \$35. One of the tickets was a winning ticket. If the winning ticket paid \$4.5 million, what was the first person's share of the winnings? \$1,250,000

72. Nutrition A pancake 4 in. in diameter contains 5 g of fat. How many grams of fat are contained in a pancake 6 in. in diameter? Explain how you arrived at your answer. 11.25 g; Explanations will vary.

Projects or Group Activities

Earned Run Average

One measure of a pitcher's success is earned run average. **Earned run average (ERA)** is the number of earned runs a pitcher gives up for every nine innings pitched. The definition of an earned run is somewhat complicated, but basically an earned run is a run that is scored as a result of hits and base running that involve no errors on the part of the pitcher's team. If the opposing team scores a run on an error (for example, a fly ball that should have been caught in the outfield is fumbled), then that run is not an earned run.

A proportion is used to calculate a pitcher's ERA. Remember that the statistic involves the number of earned runs *per nine innings*. The answer is always rounded to the nearest hundredth. Here is an example:

During the 2010 baseball season, Johan Santana gave up 66 earned runs and pitched 199 innings for the New York Mets. To calculate Johan Santana's ERA, let x = the number of earned runs for every nine innings pitched. Then write a proportion and solve it for x.

$$\frac{66 \text{ earned runs}}{199 \text{ innings}} = \frac{x}{9 \text{ innings}}$$

$$66 \cdot 9 = 199 \cdot x$$

$$594 = 199x$$

$$\frac{594}{199} = \frac{199x}{199}$$

$$2.98 \approx x$$

Johan Santana's ERA for the 2010 season was 2.98.

© Debby Wong/Shutterstock.com

Johan Santana

73. In 1979, his rookie year, Jeff Reardon pitched 21 innings for the New York Mets and gave up four earned runs. Calculate Reardon's ERA for 1979. 1.71

74. Roger Clemens's first year with the Boston Red Sox was 1984. During that season, he pitched 133.1 innings and gave up 64 earned runs. Calculate Clemens's ERA for 1984. 4.33

75. During the 2008 baseball season, Roy Halladay of the Toronto Blue Jays pitched 246 innings and gave up 76 earned runs. During the 2009 season, he gave up 74 earned runs and pitched 239 innings. During which season was Halladay's ERA lower? How much lower? 2008; 0.01

76. In 1987, Nolan Ryan had the lowest ERA of any pitcher in the major leagues. That year, he gave up 65 earned runs and pitched 211.2 innings for the Houston Astros. Calculate Ryan's ERA for 1987. 2.77

77. Find the necessary statistics for a pitcher on your "home team," and calculate that pitcher's ERA. Answers will vary.

CHECK YOUR PROGRESS: CHAPTER 6

1. Write the comparison of 30 min to 60 min as a ratio in simplest form using a fraction, a colon, and the word *to*. $\frac{1}{2}$; 1 : 2; 1 to 2 [6.1A]

2. Write the comparison of 12 quarts to 18 quarts as a ratio in simplest form using a fraction, a colon, and the word *to*. $\frac{2}{3}$; 2 : 3; 2 to 3 [6.1A]

3. Write "$39 for 6 T-shirts" as a rate in simplest form. $\frac{\$13}{\text{2 T-shirts}}$ [6.1A]

4. Write "84 feet in 9 seconds" as a rate in simplest form. $\frac{\text{28 feet}}{\text{3 seconds}}$ [6.1A]

5. Write "$38,700 earned in 12 months" as a unit rate. $3225/month [6.1A]

6. Write "$19.08 for 4.5 lb" as a unit rate. $4.24/lb [6.1A]

7. Determine whether $\frac{3}{7} = \frac{6}{14}$ is a true proportion. True [6.2A]

8. Is $\frac{\text{111 miles}}{\text{3 hours}} = \frac{\text{812 miles}}{\text{22 hours}}$ a true proportion? No [6.2A]

9. Solve: $\frac{n}{8} = \frac{21}{56}$ 3 [6.2A]

10. Solve $\frac{60}{n} = \frac{24}{7}$. Round to the nearest tenth. 17.5 [6.2A]

11. Solve $\frac{18}{20} = \frac{15}{n}$. Round to the nearest hundredth. 16.67 [6.2A]

12. Solve: $\frac{x+1}{2} = \frac{4}{5}$ 0.6 [6.2A]

13. **Sports** A basketball team won 18 games and lost 8 games during the season. What is the ratio of the number of games won to the total number of games? $\frac{9}{13}$ [6.1A]

14. **Mechanics** Find the ratio of two meshed gears if one gear has 24 teeth and the other gear has 36 teeth. $\frac{2}{3}$ [6.1A]

15. **Air Travel** An airplane flew 1155 mi in 2.5 h. Find the rate of travel. 462 mph [6.1A]

16. **Investments** A stock investment of 150 shares paid an annual dividend of $555. At this rate, what annual dividend would be paid on 180 shares of stock? $666 [6.2B]

17. **Insurance** A life insurance policy costs $8.52 for every $1000 of insurance. At this rate, what is the cost for $20,000 of life insurance? $170.40 [6.2B]

SECTION

6.3 Percent

OBJECTIVE A To write percents as decimals or fractions

The table at the right shows the results of a survey asking students their top reasons for choosing their college. (*Source:* www.kiplinger.com)

Reason for Choosing a School	*Percent Responding*
Quality of major	45%
Scholarship or financial assistance	43%
Total costs	41%
Academic reputation	38%

The symbol % is read "percent" and means "per hundred." 41% of those surveyed responded that total costs were a top reason for their selection. This means that 41 out of every 100 students surveyed chose their college based in part on its total costs.

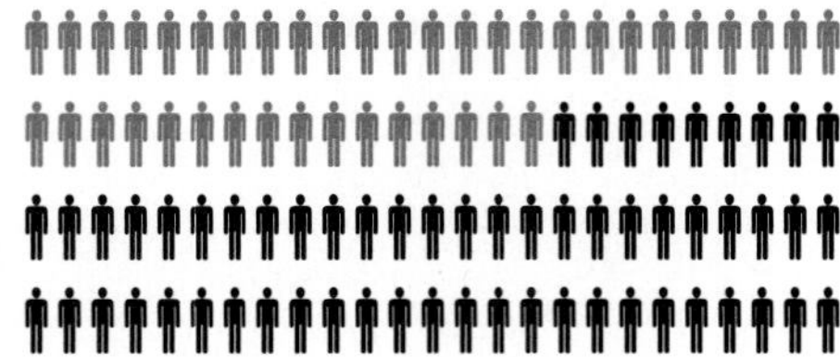

41% means "41 out of every 100 surveyed."

According to the National Health Service and the Centers for Disease Control and Prevention, liver disease is the cause of 1% of the deaths in the United States. This means that 1 out of every 100 deaths in the United States is caused by liver disease. Note in the diagram below that "1 out of 100" is the same as the fraction $\frac{1}{100}$.

1% means "1 out of 100" or $\frac{1}{100}$.

Recall that to convert a fraction to a decimal, divide the numerator by the denominator.

$$\frac{1}{100} = 1 \div 100 = 0.01$$

Therefore,

$$\mathbf{1\% = \frac{1}{100} = 0.01}$$

When solving problems involving a percent, it is usually necessary either to write the percent as a fraction or a decimal, or to write a fraction or a decimal as a percent.

IN-CLASS EXAMPLES

1. Write 72% as a fraction. $\frac{18}{25}$
2. Write 65% as a decimal. **0.65**
3. Write $15\frac{2}{3}\%$ as a fraction. $\frac{47}{300}$
4. Write 82.9% as a decimal. **0.829**

© istockphoto.com/Clerkenwell_Images

To write a percent as a fraction, remove the percent sign and multiply by $\frac{1}{100}$.

HOW TO 1 Write 67% as a fraction.

Replace the % symbol with $\frac{1}{100}$. $67\% = 67\left(\frac{1}{100}\right)$

Multiply 67 times $\frac{1}{100}$. $= \frac{67}{100}$

APPLY THE CONCEPT

In a recent year, 50% of bills were paid online rather than through the mail. (*Source:* USPS) What fraction of bills were paid online rather than through the mail?

Write 50% as a fraction. $50\% = 50\left(\frac{1}{100}\right) = \frac{50}{100}$

Write the fraction in simplest form. $= \frac{1}{2}$

$\frac{1}{2}$ of bills were paid online rather than through the mail.

To write a percent as a decimal, remove the percent sign and multiply by 0.01.

HOW TO 2 Write 19% as a decimal.

Replace the % symbol with 0.01. $19\% = 19(0.01)$

Multiply 19 times 0.01. $= 0.19$

Note that removing the percent sign and multiplying by 0.01 is the same as removing the percent sign and moving the decimal point two places to the left.

EXAMPLE 1

54% of Americans pay their credit card balance in full each month. How many Americans out of every 100 Americans pay their credit card balance in full each month? (*Source:* Consumer Reports)

Solution

54% means 54 out of 100.
54 out of every 100 Americans pay their credit card balance in full each month.

YOU TRY IT 1

33% of Americans carry balances up to $10,000 on their credit cards. How many Americans out of every 100 Americans carry balances up to $10,000 on their credit cards? (*Source:* Consumer Reports)

Your solution

33 out of every 100 Americans

EXAMPLE 2

Write 150% as a fraction and as a decimal.

Solution

$$150\% = 150\left(\frac{1}{100}\right) = \frac{150}{100} = 1\frac{1}{2}$$

$$150\% = 150(0.01) = 1.50$$

YOU TRY IT 2

Write 110% as a fraction and as a decimal.

Your solution

$1\frac{1}{10}$; 1.10

Solutions on p. S17

EXAMPLE 3

Write $66\frac{2}{3}\%$ as a fraction.

Solution

$$66\frac{2}{3}\% = 66\frac{2}{3}\left(\frac{1}{100}\right)$$
$$= \frac{200}{3}\left(\frac{1}{100}\right)$$
$$= \frac{2}{3}$$

YOU TRY IT 3

Write $33\frac{1}{3}\%$ as a fraction.

Your solution

$\frac{1}{3}$

EXAMPLE 4

Write 0.35% as a decimal.

Solution

$0.35\% = 0.35(0.01)$
$= 0.0035$

• Move the decimal point two places to the left.

YOU TRY IT 4

Write 0.8% as a decimal.

Your solution

0.008

Solutions on p. S17

OBJECTIVE B *To write fractions and decimals as percents*

IN-CLASS EXAMPLES

5. Write 0.165 as a percent. **16.5%**
6. Write $\frac{5}{12}$ as a percent. Round to the nearest tenth of a percent. **41.7%**
7. Write $\frac{4}{9}$ as a percent. Write the remainder in fractional form. **$44\frac{4}{9}\%$**

To write a fraction as a percent, multiply the fraction by 100%. Because $100\% = \frac{100}{100} = 1$, multiplying a number by 100% is the same as multiplying the number by 1.

HOW TO 3 Write $\frac{7}{8}$ as a percent.

Multiply $\frac{7}{8}$ by 100%.

$$\frac{7}{8} = \frac{7}{8}(100\%)$$
$$= \left(\frac{7}{8} \cdot 100\right)\%$$
$$= \frac{700}{8}\% = 87.5\%$$

APPLY THE CONCEPT

© Najlah Feanny/Corbis

In a recent year, $\frac{1}{4}$ of college students who were credit card holders used a credit card to pay for tuition. (*Source:* American Council on Education) What percent of college students who were credit card holders used a credit card to pay for tuition?

Write $\frac{1}{4}$ as a percent by multiplying $\frac{1}{4}$ by 100%. $\quad \frac{1}{4} = \frac{1}{4}(100\%) = 25\%$

25% of students who were credit card holders used a credit card to pay for tuition.

To write a decimal as a percent, multiply the decimal by 100%.

HOW TO 4 Write 0.64 as a percent.

Multiply 0.64 by 100%.

$$0.64 = 0.64(100\%) = (0.64 \cdot 100)\% = 64\%$$

Note that multiplying a decimal by 100% is the same as moving the decimal point two places to the right.

EXAMPLE 5

Write $\frac{3}{11}$ as a percent. Write the remainder in fractional form.

Solution

$$\frac{3}{11} = \frac{3}{11}(100\%) \quad \text{• Multiply by 100\%.}$$

$$= \frac{300}{11}\% = 27\frac{3}{11}\%$$

YOU TRY IT 5

Write $\frac{5}{7}$ as a percent. Write the remainder in fractional form.

Your solution

$71\frac{3}{7}\%$

EXAMPLE 6

Write $1\frac{1}{7}$ as a percent. Round to the nearest tenth of a percent.

Solution

$$1\frac{1}{7} = \frac{8}{7} = \frac{8}{7}(100\%) \quad \text{• Multiply by 100\%.}$$

$$= \frac{800}{7}\% \approx 114.3\%$$

YOU TRY IT 6

Write $1\frac{5}{9}$ as a percent. Round to the nearest tenth of a percent.

Your solution

155.6%

EXAMPLE 7

Four-fifths of consumers own a debit card. What percent of consumers own a debit card? (*Source:* Federal Reserve Bank of Boston)

Solution

$$\frac{4}{5} = \frac{4}{5}(100\%) = \frac{400}{5}\% = 80\%$$

80% of consumers own a debit card.

YOU TRY IT 7

Three-fifths of consumers have a rewards credit card. What percent of consumers have a rewards credit card? (*Source:* Federal Reserve Bank of Boston)

Your solution

60%

EXAMPLE 8

Write 1.78 as a percent.

Solution

$$1.78 = 1.78(100\%)$$

$$= 178\% \quad \text{• Move the decimal point two places to the right.}$$

YOU TRY IT 8

Write 0.038 as a percent.

Your solution

3.8%

Solutions on p. S17

6.3 EXERCISES

Concept Check

SUGGESTED ASSIGNMENT

Exercises 1–12; Exercises 13–101, odds; More challenging exercises: Exercises 105 and 106

1. Circle 29% of the 100 figures shown below. 29 figures should be circled.

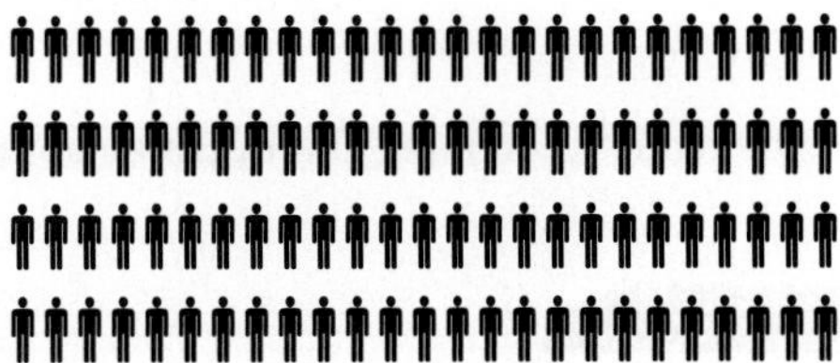

2. Circle 63% of the 100 figures shown below. 63 figures should be circled.

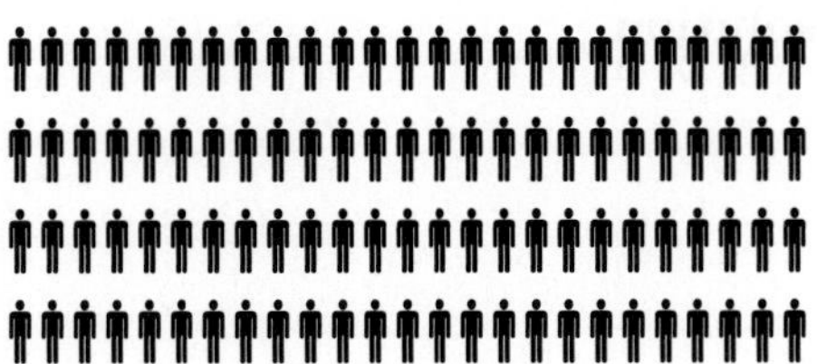

3. **a.** Explain how to convert a percent to a fraction.
b. Explain how to convert a percent to a decimal.

4. Explain why multiplying a number by 100% does not change the value of the number.

5. To write 53% as a decimal, remove the percent sign and multiply by <u>0.01</u>: $53\% = 53 \cdot \underline{0.01} = \underline{0.53}$.

6. To write 6.7% as a decimal, remove the percent sign and multiply by <u>0.01</u>: $6.7\% = 6.7 \cdot \underline{0.01} = \underline{0.067}$.

7. To write 80% as a fraction, remove the percent sign and multiply by $\underline{\frac{1}{100}}$:

$80\% = 80 \cdot \underline{\frac{1}{100}} = \underline{\frac{4}{5}}$.

8. To write $4\frac{1}{3}\%$ as a fraction, remove the percent sign and multiply by $\underline{\frac{1}{100}}$:

$4\frac{1}{3}\% = 4\frac{1}{3} \cdot \underline{\frac{1}{100}} = \frac{13}{3} \cdot \frac{1}{100} = \underline{\frac{13}{300}}$.

9. To write 0.46 as a percent, multiply by <u>100%</u>: $0.46 = 0.46 \cdot \underline{100\%} = \underline{46\%}$.

10. To write 1.25 as a percent, multiply by <u>100%</u>: $1.25 = 1.25 \cdot \underline{100\%} = \underline{125\%}$.

11. To write $\frac{3}{10}$ as a percent, multiply by 100%:

$\frac{3}{10} = \frac{3}{10} \cdot$ 100% = 30%.

12. To write $\frac{7}{5}$ as a percent, multiply by 100%:

$\frac{7}{5} = \frac{7}{5} \cdot$ 100% = $\frac{700}{5}$% = 140%.

OBJECTIVE A *To write percents as decimals or fractions*

Write as a fraction and as a decimal.

13. 5% $\frac{1}{20}$, 0.05

14. 60% $\frac{3}{5}$, 0.60

15. 30% $\frac{3}{10}$, 0.30

16. 90% $\frac{9}{10}$, 0.90

17. 250% $\frac{5}{2}$, 2.50

18. 140% $\frac{7}{5}$, 1.40

19. 28% $\frac{7}{25}$, 0.28

20. 66% $\frac{33}{50}$, 0.66

21. 35% $\frac{7}{20}$, 0.35

22. 8% $\frac{2}{25}$, 0.08

23. 29% $\frac{29}{100}$, 0.29

24. 83% $\frac{83}{100}$, 0.83

Write as a fraction.

25. $11\frac{1}{9}\%$ $\frac{1}{9}$

26. $12\frac{1}{2}\%$ $\frac{1}{8}$

27. $37\frac{1}{2}\%$ $\frac{3}{8}$

28. $31\frac{1}{4}\%$ $\frac{5}{16}$

29. $66\frac{2}{3}\%$ $\frac{2}{3}$

30. $45\frac{5}{11}\%$ $\frac{5}{11}$

31. $6\frac{2}{3}\%$ $\frac{1}{15}$

32. $68\frac{3}{4}\%$ $\frac{11}{16}$

33. $\frac{1}{2}\%$ $\frac{1}{200}$

34. $83\frac{1}{3}\%$ $\frac{5}{6}$

35. $6\frac{1}{4}\%$ $\frac{1}{16}$

36. $3\frac{1}{3}\%$ $\frac{1}{30}$

Write as a decimal.

37. 7.3% 0.073

38. 9.1% 0.091

39. 15.8% 0.158

40. 16.7% 0.167

41. 0.3% 0.003

42. 0.9% 0.009

43. 121.2% 1.212

44. 18.23% 0.1823

45. 62.14% 0.6214

46. 0.15% 0.0015

47. 8.25% 0.0825

48. 5.05% 0.0505

49. **Teaching** Read the news clipping at the right. What fraction of U.S. teachers have one or more English-language learners in the classroom?
$\frac{13}{20}$

In the NEWS!

More Students Need Instruction in the English Language

In the United States today, 65% of teachers have one or more English-language learners in the classroom.

Sources: Scholastic; The Bill & Melinda Gates Foundation

50. When a certain percent is written as a fraction, the result is a proper fraction. Is the percent less than, equal to, or greater than 100%? Less than

51. When a certain percent is written as a fraction, the result is an improper fraction. Is the percent less than, equal to, or greater than 100%? Greater than

52. **Pets** The figure at the right shows some ways in which owners pamper their dogs. What fraction of the owners surveyed would buy a house or a car with their dog in mind?
$\frac{6}{25}$

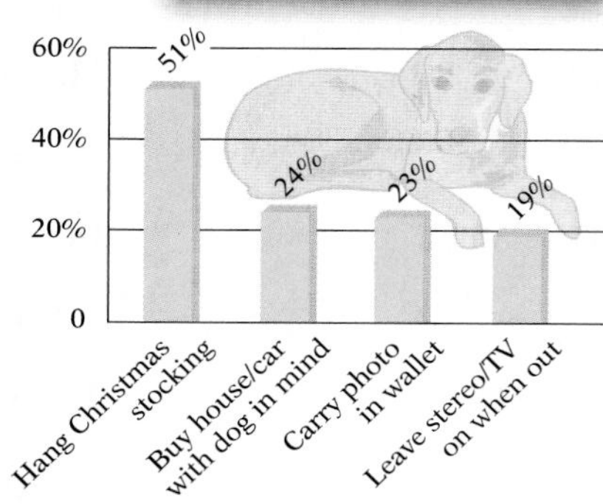

How Owners Pamper Their Dogs
Source: Purina Survey

53. **Discounts** A leather jacket is on sale for 50% off the regular price. What fraction of the regular price does this represent?
$\frac{1}{2}$

OBJECTIVE B *To write fractions and decimals as percents*

Write as a percent.

54. 0.15 15%

55. 0.37 37%

56. 0.05 5%

57. 0.02 2%

58. 0.175 17.5%

59. 0.125 12.5%

60. 1.15 115%

61. 1.36 136%

62. 0.62 62%

63. 0.96 96%

64. 2.09 209%

65. 0.07 7%

Write as a percent. If necessary, round to the nearest tenth of a percent.

66. $\frac{27}{50}$ 54%

67. $\frac{83}{100}$ 83%

68. $\frac{37}{200}$ 18.5%

69. $\frac{1}{3}$ 33.3%

70. $\frac{5}{11}$ 45.5%

71. $\frac{4}{9}$ 44.4%

72. $\frac{7}{8}$ 87.5%

73. $\frac{9}{20}$ 45%

74. $1\frac{2}{3}$
166.7%

75. $2\frac{1}{2}$
250%

76. $\frac{2}{5}$
40%

77. $\frac{1}{6}$
16.7%

Write as a percent. Write the remainder in fractional form.

78. $\frac{17}{50}$
34%

79. $\frac{17}{25}$
68%

80. $\frac{3}{8}$
$37\frac{1}{2}\%$

81. $\frac{9}{16}$
$56\frac{1}{4}\%$

82. $1\frac{1}{4}$
125%

83. $2\frac{5}{8}$
$262\frac{1}{2}\%$

84. $1\frac{5}{9}$
$155\frac{5}{9}\%$

85. $2\frac{5}{6}$
$283\frac{1}{3}\%$

86. $\frac{12}{25}$
48%

87. $\frac{7}{30}$
$23\frac{1}{3}\%$

88. $\frac{3}{7}$
$42\frac{6}{7}\%$

89. $\frac{2}{9}$
$22\frac{2}{9}\%$

Complete the table of equivalent fractions, decimals, and percents.

	Fraction	*Decimal*	*Percent*
90.	$\frac{1}{2}$	0.5	50%
91.	$\frac{3}{4}$	0.75	75%
92.	$\frac{2}{5}$	0.4	40%
93.	$\frac{3}{8}$	0.375	37.5%
94.	$\frac{7}{10}$	0.7	70%
95.	$\frac{9}{16}$	0.5625	56.25%
96.	$\frac{11}{20}$	0.55	55%
97.	$\frac{13}{25}$	0.52	52%
98.	$\frac{5}{32}$	0.15625	15.625%
99.	$\frac{9}{50}$	0.18	18%

100. Discounts A backpack is advertised as $\frac{1}{3}$ off the regular price. What percent of the regular price does this represent?

$33\frac{1}{3}\%$

101. **The Military** Read the news clipping at the right. What percent of Americans ages 17 to 24 cannot enlist in the military? 75%

102. **Voting** If $\frac{2}{5}$ of a population voted in an election, what percent of the population did not vote? 60%

Complete Exercises 103 and 104 without actually finding the percents.

103. Does $\frac{4}{3}$ represent a percent greater than 100% or less than 100%?
Greater than

104. Does 0.055 represent a percent greater than 1% or less than 1%?
Greater than

In the NEWS!

Large Numbers of American Youth Cannot Enlist

In the United States today, three-fourths of Americans between the ages of 17 and 24 cannot enlist in the military. Most of these citizens are ineligible because they have not graduated from high school, they have a criminal record, or they are physically unfit.

Source: Time, November 16, 2008

Critical Thinking

105. Write the part of the square that is shaded as a fraction, as a decimal, and as a percent. Write the part of the square that is not shaded as a fraction, as a decimal, and as a percent.
$\frac{1}{4}$, 0.25, 25%; $\frac{3}{4}$, 0.75, 75%

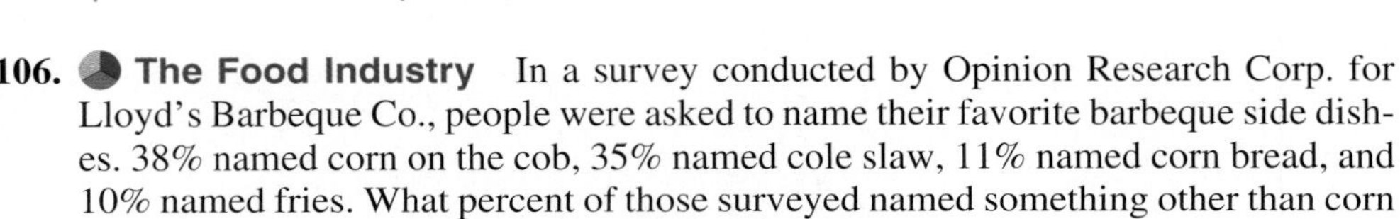

106. **The Food Industry** In a survey conducted by Opinion Research Corp. for Lloyd's Barbeque Co., people were asked to name their favorite barbeque side dishes. 38% named corn on the cob, 35% named cole slaw, 11% named corn bread, and 10% named fries. What percent of those surveyed named something other than corn on the cob, cole slaw, corn bread, or fries? 6%

107. a. Is the following statement true or false? "Multiplying a number by a percent always decreases the number." False

b. If the statement in part (a) is false, give an example to show that it is false.
Answers will vary. For example, 200% × 4 = 2 × 4 = 8

Projects or Group Activities

108. **Compensation** Employee A had an annual salary of $42,000, Employee B had an annual salary of $48,000, and Employee C had an annual salary of $46,000 before each employee was given a 5% raise. Which of the three employees' annual salaries is now the highest? Explain how you arrived at your answer.

109. **Compensation** Each of three employees earned an annual salary of $45,000 before Employee A was given a 3% raise, Employee B was given a 6% raise, and Employee C was given a 4.5% raise. Which of the three employees now has the highest annual salary? Explain how you arrived at your answer.

QUICK QUIZ

1. Write 65% as a fraction. $\frac{13}{20}$ [6.3A]
2. Write 34.2% as a decimal. **0.342 [6.3A]**

© istockphoto.com/tacojim

3. Write $45\frac{1}{3}$% as a fraction. $\frac{34}{75}$ [6.3A]
4. Write 0.567 as a percent. **56.7% [6.3B]**
5. Write $\frac{7}{45}$ as a percent. Round to the nearest tenth of a percent. **15.6% [6.3B]**
6. Write $\frac{5}{6}$ as a percent. Write the remainder in fractional form. $83\frac{1}{3}$% [6.3B]

SECTION

6.4 The Basic Percent Equation

OBJECTIVE A *To use the basic percent equation*

INSTRUCTOR NOTE

Learning how to effectively use the percent equation is one of the most important mathematical skills a student can acquire. This objective is devoted to solving the basic percent equation. The next objective gives you the option of teaching how to solve percent problems using proportions.

What percent of the region shown below is shaded?

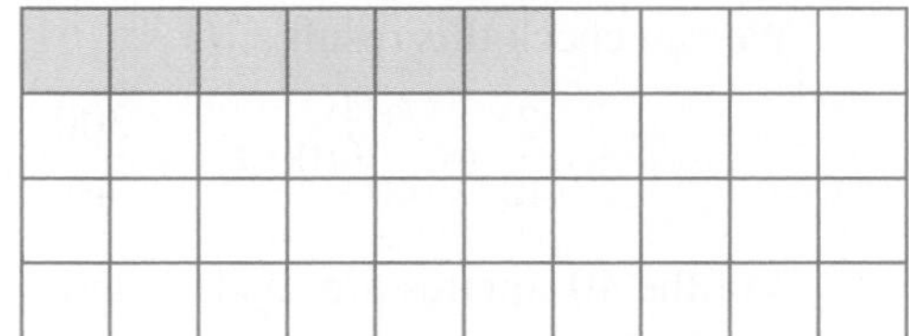

To answer this question, first determine what fraction of the region is shaded.

There are a total of 40 squares in the region.

6 of the squares are shaded.

$\frac{6}{40}$ of the region is shaded.

Now write the fraction $\frac{6}{40}$ as a percent.

$$\frac{6}{40} = \frac{6}{40}(100\%) = \frac{600}{40}\% = 15\%$$

15% of the region is shaded.

Now consider the question, "How many squares should be shaded if we want to shade 7.5% of the region shown below?"

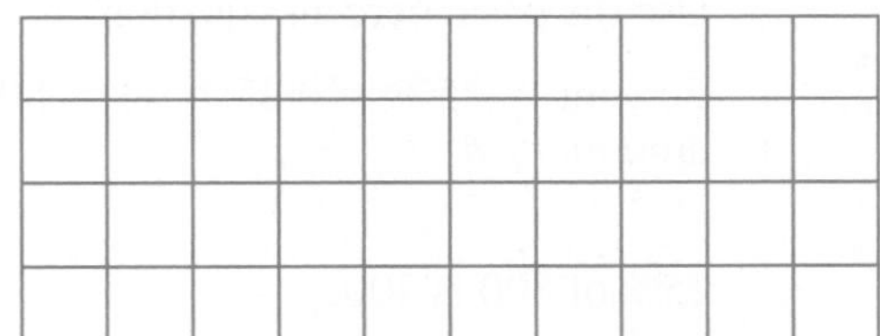

Determining the number of squares to be shaded requires answering the question

"7.5% of 40 is what number?"

This question can be translated into an equation and solved for the unknown number.

of	translates to	$\cdot$	(times)
is	translates to	$=$	(equals)
what	translates to	n	(the unknown number)

Here is the translation of "7.5% of 40 is what number?" Note that the percent is written as a decimal.

7.5%	of	40	is	what number?
↓	↓	↓	↓	↓
0.075	$\cdot$	40	$=$	n

$$0.075 \cdot 40 = n \quad \bullet \text{ Solve this equation for } n.$$
$$3 = n$$

If we shade 3 squares, 7.5% of the region will be shaded. See the figure at the top of the next page.

7.5% of the region is shaded.

We can check this result.

$$\frac{3}{40} = \frac{3}{40}(100\%) = \frac{300}{40}\% = 7.5\%$$

3 of the 40 squares are shaded, and $\frac{3}{40} = 7.5\%$. The solution checks.

We found the solution to this problem by solving the basic percent equation for *amount*.

The Basic Percent Equation

Percent · base = amount

In the example above, 7.5% is the percent, 40 is the base, and 3 is the amount.

Integrating Technology

The percent key % on a scientific calculator moves the decimal point two places to the left when pressed after a multiplication or division computation. For HOW TO 1 at the right, enter

800 × 25 % =

The display reads 200.

HOW TO 1 What is 25% of 800?

Use the basic percent equation. Percent · base = amount

Percent = 25% = 0.25, base = 800, amount = n

$$0.25 \cdot 800 = n$$

$$200 = n$$

25% of 800 is 200.

Notice from HOW TO 1 that the base in the basic percent equation follows the word *of*: 800 follows the word *of*, and 800 is the base in the basic percent equation. Look for the number or phrase that follows the word *of* when determining the base in the basic percent equation.

APPLY THE CONCEPT

A real estate broker receives a commission of 3% of the selling price of a house. Find the amount the broker receives on the sale of a $275,000 house.

Use the basic percent equation. Percent · base = amount

The base is the selling price of the house.
Percent = 3% = 0.03, base = 275,000, amount = n

$$0.03 \cdot 275{,}000 = n$$

$$8250 = n$$

The broker receives a commission of $8250.

In most cases, the percent is written as a decimal before the basic percent equation is solved. However, some percents are more easily written as a fraction than as a decimal. For example,

$$33\frac{1}{3}\% = \frac{1}{3} \qquad 66\frac{2}{3}\% = \frac{2}{3} \qquad 16\frac{2}{3}\% = \frac{1}{6} \qquad 83\frac{1}{3}\% = \frac{5}{6}$$

In HOW TO 2, the percent is written as a fraction rather than as a decimal.

HOW TO 2 What is $33\frac{1}{3}\%$ of 90?

Use the basic percent equation. Percent · base = amount

Percent $= 33\frac{1}{3}\% = \frac{1}{3}$, base $= 90$, amount $= n$

$$\frac{1}{3} \cdot 90 = n$$

$$30 = n$$

$33\frac{1}{3}\%$ of 90 is 30.

The three elements of the basic percent equation are the percent, the base, and the amount. If any two elements of the basic percent equation are given, the third element can be found.

In HOW TO 1 and HOW TO 2, the unknown was the amount. In HOW TO 3 below, the unknown is the percent. In HOW TO 4, the unknown is the base.

INSTRUCTOR NOTE

In solving problems involving percent, the basic percent equation frequently leads to an equation of the form $ax = b$.

HOW TO 3 20 is what percent of 32?

Use the basic percent equation. Percent · base = amount

Percent $= n$, base $= 32$, amount $= 20$

$$n \cdot 32 = 20$$

Solve for n by dividing each side of the equation by 32.

$$\frac{32n}{32} = \frac{20}{32}$$

$$n = 0.625$$

Write the decimal as a percent.

$$n = 62.5\%$$

20 is 62.5% of 32.

APPLY THE CONCEPT

You correctly answered 96 of the 120 questions on an exam. What percent of the questions did you answer correctly?

Use the basic percent equation. Percent · base = amount

Percent $= n$, base $= 120$, amount $= 96$

$$n \cdot 120 = 96$$

Solve for n by dividing each side of the equation by 120.

$$\frac{120n}{120} = \frac{96}{120}$$

$$n = 0.8$$

Write the decimal as a percent.

$$n = 80\%$$

You answered 80% of the questions correctly.

Tips for Success

In this objective, we have solved the basic percent equation for each of the three elements: percent, base, and amount. You will need to be able to recognize these three different types of problems. Be sure to practice this skill by doing the Section 6.4 exercises.

HOW TO 4 60% of what number is 300?

Use the basic percent equation.

Percent · base = amount

Percent = 60% = 0.60, base = n, amount = 300

$0.60 \cdot n = 300$

Solve for n by dividing each side of the equation by 0.60.

$$\frac{0.60n}{0.60} = \frac{300}{0.60}$$

$$n = 500$$

60% of 500 is 300.

APPLY THE CONCEPT

A used car has a value of $11,250, which is 45% of the car's original value. What was the car's original value?

Use the basic percent equation.

Percent · base = amount

The base is the car's original value.
Percent = 45% = 0.45, base = n,
amount = 11,250

$0.45 \cdot n = 11{,}250$

Solve for n by dividing each side of the equation by 0.45.

$$\frac{0.45n}{0.45} = \frac{11{,}250}{0.45}$$

$$n = 25{,}000$$

The car's original value was $25,000.

IN-CLASS EXAMPLES

1. Find $16\frac{2}{3}$% of 66. **11**
2. What percent of 90 is 36? **40%**
3. 32% of what is 19.2? **60**

EXAMPLE 1

Find 9.4% of 240.

Solution

Use the basic percent equation.
Percent = 9.4% = 0.094, base = 240,
amount = n

$$\begin{aligned} \text{Percent} \cdot \text{base} &= \text{amount} \\ 0.094 \cdot 240 &= n \\ 22.56 &= n \end{aligned}$$

9.4% of 240 is 22.56.

YOU TRY IT 1

Find $66\frac{2}{3}$% of 45.

Your solution

30

EXAMPLE 2

What percent of 30 is 12?

Solution

Use the basic percent equation.
Percent = n, base = 30, amount = 12

$$\begin{aligned} \text{Percent} \cdot \text{base} &= \text{amount} \\ n \cdot 30 &= 12 \\ \frac{30n}{30} &= \frac{12}{30} \\ n &= 0.4 = 40\% \end{aligned}$$

12 is 40% of 30.

YOU TRY IT 2

25 is what percent of 40?

Your solution

62.5%

Solutions on p. S17

EXAMPLE 3

60 is 2.5% of what?

Solution

Use the basic percent equation.

Percent = 2.5% = 0.025, base = n, amount = 60

$$\text{Percent} \cdot \text{base} = \text{amount}$$
$$0.025 \cdot n = 60$$
$$\frac{0.025n}{0.025} = \frac{60}{0.025}$$
$$n = 2400$$

60 is 2.5% of 2400.

YOU TRY IT 3

$16\frac{2}{3}\%$ of what is 15?

Your solution

90

Solution on p. S17

OBJECTIVE B *To solve percent problems using proportions*

INSTRUCTOR NOTE

This objective explains the proportion method of solving percent problems. If you choose not to present this method, you can use the Objective B exercises as a review of problems that involve percent.

Problems that can be solved using the basic percent equation can also be solved using proportions.

The proportion method is based on writing two ratios. One ratio is the percent ratio, written as $\frac{\text{percent}}{100}$. The second ratio is the amount-to-base ratio, written as $\frac{\text{amount}}{\text{base}}$. These two ratios form the proportion

$$\frac{\textbf{percent}}{\textbf{100}} = \frac{\textbf{amount}}{\textbf{base}}$$

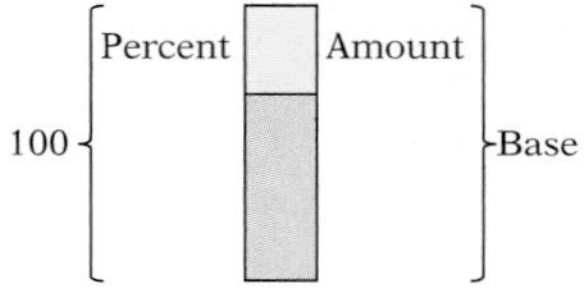

The proportion method can be illustrated by a diagram. The rectangle at the left is divided into two parts. On the left-hand side, the whole rectangle is represented by 100 and the part by the percent. On the right-hand side, the whole rectangle is represented by the base and the part by the amount. The ratio of the percent to 100 is equal to the ratio of the amount to the base.

When solving a percent problem using the basic percent equation, we first have to identify the percent, the base, and the amount. The same is true when solving a percent problem using the proportion method. Remember that the base usually follows the word *of.*

HOW TO 5 What is 32% of 85?

Use the proportion method.

Look at the diagram at the left.
Percent = 32, base = 85, amount = n

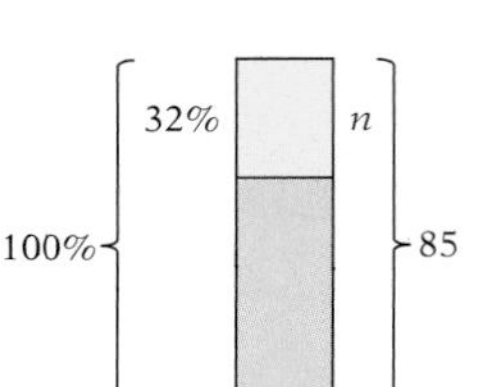

Solve the proportion for n.

$$\frac{\text{percent}}{100} = \frac{\text{amount}}{\text{base}}$$
$$\frac{32}{100} = \frac{n}{85}$$
$$100 \cdot n = 32 \cdot 85$$
$$100n = 2720$$
$$\frac{100n}{100} = \frac{2720}{100}$$
$$n = 27.2$$

32% of 85 is 27.2.

EXAMPLE 4

24% of what is 16? Round to the nearest hundredth.

Solution

$$\frac{\text{percent}}{100} = \frac{\text{amount}}{\text{base}}$$
$$\frac{24}{100} = \frac{16}{n}$$
$$24 \cdot n = 100 \cdot 16$$
$$24n = 1600$$
$$n = \frac{1600}{24} \approx 66.67$$

16 is approximately 24% of 66.67.

YOU TRY IT 4

8 is 25% of what?

Your solution

32

EXAMPLE 5

Find 1.2% of 42.

Solution

$$\frac{\text{percent}}{100} = \frac{\text{amount}}{\text{base}}$$
$$\frac{1.2}{100} = \frac{n}{42}$$
$$1.2 \cdot 42 = 100 \cdot n$$
$$50.4 = 100n$$
$$\frac{50.4}{100} = \frac{100n}{100}$$
$$0.504 = n$$

1.2% of 42 is 0.504.

YOU TRY IT 5

Find 0.74% of 1200.

Your solution

8.88

IN-CLASS EXAMPLES

4. 0.5% of what is 5? **1000**
5. Find 15.5% of 80. **12.4**
6. 80 is what percent of 64? **125%**

EXAMPLE 6

What percent of 52 is 13?

Solution

$$\frac{\text{percent}}{100} = \frac{\text{amount}}{\text{base}}$$
$$\frac{n}{100} = \frac{13}{52}$$
$$n \cdot 52 = 100 \cdot 13$$
$$52n = 1300$$
$$\frac{52n}{52} = \frac{1300}{52}$$
$$n = 25$$

25% of 52 is 13.

YOU TRY IT 6

What percent of 180 is 54?

Your solution

30%

Solutions on p. S17

OBJECTIVE C *To solve application problems*

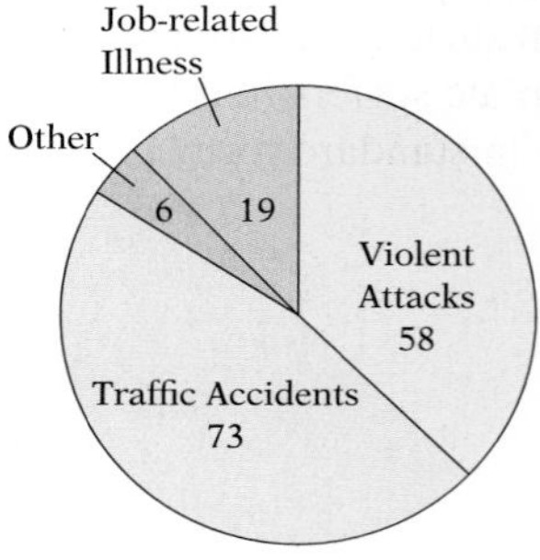

Figure 6.1 Causes of Death for Police Officers Killed in the Line of Duty
Source: International Union of Police Associations

HOW TO 6 The circle graph at the left shows the causes of death for all police officers who died while on duty during a recent year. What percent of the deaths were due to traffic accidents? Round to the nearest tenth of a percent.

Strategy To find the percent:

- Find the total number of officers who died in the line of duty.
- Use the basic percent equation.
  Percent = n, base = total number killed,
  amount = number of deaths due to traffic accidents = 73

Solution $58 + 73 + 6 + 19 = 156$ • **Total number killed**

$$\text{Percent} \cdot \text{base} = \text{amount}$$
$$n \cdot 156 = 73$$
$$\frac{156n}{156} = \frac{73}{156}$$
$$n \approx 0.468$$
$$n \approx 46.8\%$$

46.8% of the deaths were due to traffic accidents.

EXAMPLE 7

During a recent year, 276 billion product coupons were issued by manufacturers. Shoppers redeemed 4.8 billion of these coupons. (*Source:* NCH NuWorld Consumer Behavior Study, America Coupon Council) What percent of the coupons issued were redeemed by customers? Round to the nearest tenth of a percent.

Strategy

To find the percent, use the basic percent equation.
Percent = n, base = number of coupons issued = 276 billion, amount = number of coupons redeemed = 4.8 billion

Solution

$$\text{Percent} \cdot \text{base} = \text{amount}$$
$$n \cdot 276 = 4.8$$
$$\frac{276n}{276} = \frac{4.8}{276}$$
$$n \approx 0.017$$
$$n \approx 1.7\%$$

Of the product coupons issued, 1.7% were redeemed by customers.

YOU TRY IT 7

An instructor receives a monthly salary of \$4330, and \$649.50 is deducted for income tax. Find the percent of the instructor's salary that is deducted for income tax.

Your strategy

Your solution

15%

IN-CLASS EXAMPLES

7. An athletic footwear manufacturer made a profit of 24.5% on sales of \$1,600,000. Find the company's profit. **\$392,000**
8. A sales tax of 6% is added to the purchase price of a car. The purchase price is \$29,500. What is the total cost of the car, including sales tax? **\$31,270**

Solution on p. S17

EXAMPLE 8

A taxpayer pays a tax rate of 35% for state and federal taxes. The taxpayer has an income of $47,500. Find the amount of state and federal taxes paid by the taxpayer.

Strategy

To find the amount, use the basic percent equation.
Percent = 35% = 0.35, base = 47,500, amount = n

Solution

$$\begin{aligned} \text{Percent} \cdot \text{base} &= \text{amount} \\ 0.35 \cdot 47{,}500 &= n \\ 16{,}625 &= n \end{aligned}$$

The amount of taxes paid is $16,625.

YOU TRY IT 8

According to Board-Trac, approximately 19% of the country's 2.4 million surfers are women. Estimate the number of female surfers in this country. Write the number in standard form.

Your strategy

Your solution

456,000 female surfers

EXAMPLE 9

A department store has a blue blazer on sale for $114, which is 60% of the original price. What is the difference between the original price and the sale price?

Strategy

To find the difference between the original price and the sale price:

- Find the original price. Use the basic percent equation.
  Percent = 60% = 0.60,
  amount = 114, base = n
- Subtract the sale price from the original price.

Solution

$$\begin{aligned} \text{Percent} \cdot \text{base} &= \text{amount} \\ 0.60 \cdot n &= 114 \\ \frac{0.60n}{0.60} &= \frac{114}{0.60} \\ n &= 190 \end{aligned}$$

• **The original price**

$190 - 114 = 76$ • **Subtract the sale price.**

The difference in price is $76.

YOU TRY IT 9

An electrician's wage this year is $30.13 per hour, which is 115% of last year's hourly wage. What is the increase in the hourly wage over the past year?

Your strategy

Your solution

$3.93

Solutions on p. S18

6.4 EXERCISES

SUGGESTED ASSIGNMENT
Exercises 1–6; Exercises 7–39, odds;
Exercises 43–65, odds; Exercises 71–89, odds

Concept Check

For Exercises 1 to 4, state the number or variable that will replace each word in the basic percent equation, percent · base = amount. If the percent is known, write the percent as a decimal.

1. 12% of what is 68?

percent = 0.12 base = n amount = 68

2. What percent of 64 is 16?

percent = n base = 64 amount = 16

3. What is 8% of 450?

percent = 0.08 base = 450 amount = n

4. 32 is what percent of 96?

percent = n base = 96 amount = 32

For Exercises 5 and 6, state the number or variable that will replace each word in the proportion $\frac{\text{percent}}{100} = \frac{\text{amount}}{\text{base}}$.

5. What is 36% of 25?

percent = 36 amount = n base = 25

6. 89% of what is 1780?

percent = 89 amount = 1780 base = n

OBJECTIVE A *To use the basic percent equation*

7. Shade 70% of the region at the right.
21 of the 30 squares should be shaded.

8. Shade 45% of the region at the right.
9 of the 20 squares should be shaded.

9. Shade 62.5% of the region at the right.
25 of the 40 squares should be shaded.

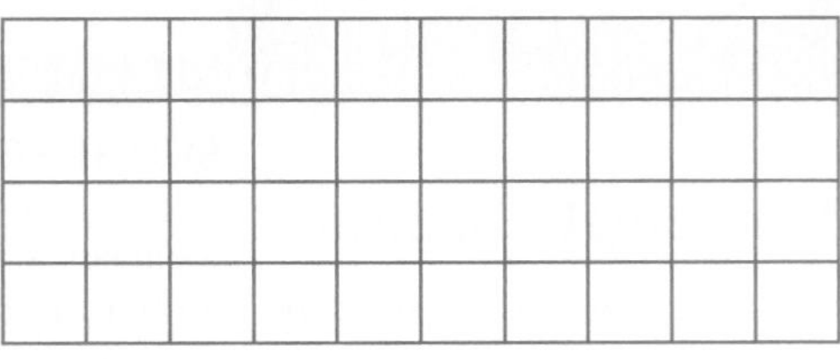

10. Shade 37.5% of the region at the right.
12 of the 32 squares should be shaded.

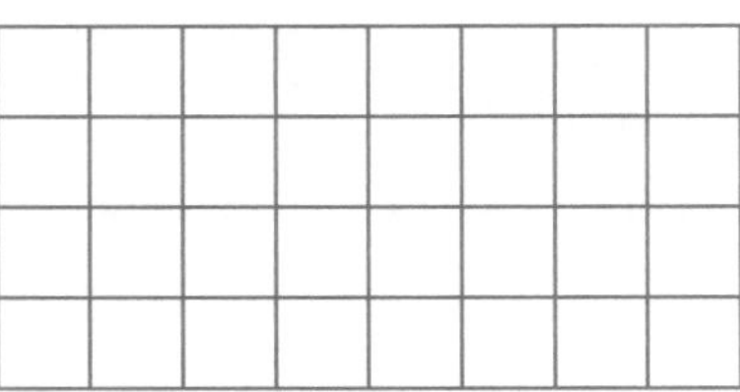

11. Shade $16\frac{2}{3}\%$ of the region at the right.
5 of the 30 squares should be shaded.

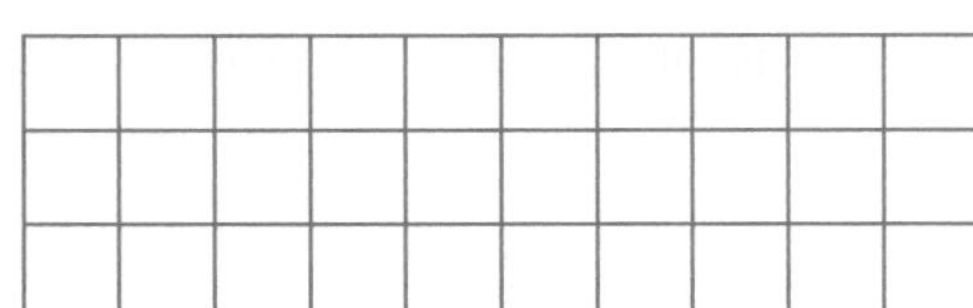

12. Circle 12.5% of the 80 people pictured at the right.
10 of the 80 people should be circled.

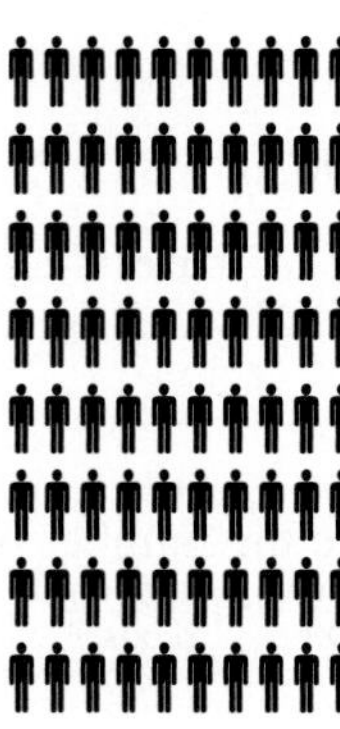

13. Circle 56.25% of the people pictured at the right.
27 of the 48 people should be circled.

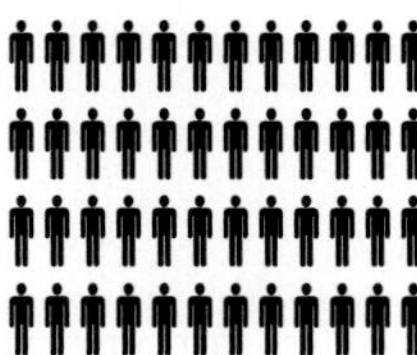

14. Circle $33\frac{1}{3}\%$ of the people pictured at the right.
12 of the 36 people should be circled.

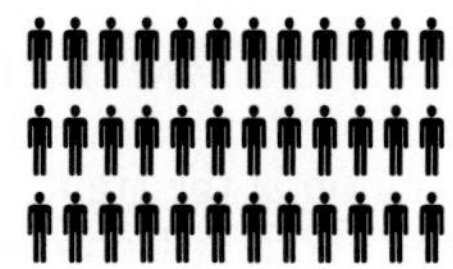

Solve. Use the basic percent equation.

15. 8% of 100 is what?
8

16. 16% of 50 is what?
8

17. 0.05% of 150 is what?
0.075

18. 0.075% of 625 is what?
0.46875

19. 15 is what percent of 90?
$16\frac{2}{3}\%$

20. 24 is what percent of 60?
40%

21. What percent of 16 is 6?
37.5%

22. What percent of 24 is 18?
75%

23. 10 is 10% of what?
100

24. 37 is 37% of what?
100

25. 2.5% of what is 30?
1200

26. 10.4% of what is 52?
500

27. Find 10.7% of 485.
51.895

28. Find 12.8% of 625.
80

29. 80% of 16.25 is what?
13

30. 26% of 19.5 is what?
5.07

31. 54 is what percent of 2000?
2.7%

32. 8 is what percent of 2500?
0.32%

33. 16.4 is what percent of 4.1?
400%

34. 5.3 is what percent of 50?
10.6%

35. 18 is 240% of what?
7.5

36. 24 is 320% of what?
7.5

37. **Entertainment** A usatoday.com online poll asked 8878 Internet users, "Would you use software to cut out objectionable parts of movies?" 29.8% of the respondents answered yes. How many respondents did not answer yes to the question? Round to the nearest whole number. 6232 respondents

38. **Sociology** In a survey, 1236 adults nationwide were asked, "What irks you most about the actions of other motorists?" The response "tailgaters" was given by 293 people. (*Source:* Reuters/Zogby) What percent of those surveyed were most irked by tailgaters? Round to the nearest tenth of a percent. 23.7%

39. **Travel** Of the travelers who, during a recent year, allowed their children to miss school to go on a trip, approximately 1.738 million allowed their children to miss school for more than a week. This represented 11% of the travelers who allowed their children to miss school. (*Source:* Travel Industry Association) About how many travelers allowed their children to miss school to go on a trip?
15.8 million travelers

40. Given that 25% of x equals y, is $x < y$ or is $x > y$? $x > y$

41. Given that 200% of x equals y, is $x < y$ or is $x > y$? $x < y$

OBJECTIVE B *To solve percent problems using proportions*

Solve. Use the proportion method.

42. 26% of 250 is what?
65

43. Find 18% of 150.
27

44. 37 is what percent of 148?
25%

45. What percent of 150 is 33?
22%

46. 68% of what is 51?
75

47. 126 is 84% of what?
150

48. What percent of 344 is 43?
12.5%

49. 750 is what percent of 50?
1500%

50. 82 is 20.5% of what?
400

51. 2.4% of what is 21?
875

52. What is 6.5% of 300?
19.5

53. Find 96% of 75.
72

54. 7.4 is what percent of 50?
14.8%

55. What percent of 1500 is 693?
46.2%

56. Find 50.5% of 124.
62.62

57. What is 87.4% of 225?
196.65

58. 120% of what is 6?
5

59. 14 is 175% of what?
8

60. What is 250% of 18?
45

61. 325% of 4.4 is what?
14.3

62. 87 is what percent of 29?
300%

63. What percent of 38 is 95?
250%

64. **Email** The number of email messages sent each day has risen to 171 billion, of which 71% are spam. (*Source:* FeedsFarm.com) How many email messages sent per day are not spam? 49.59 billion email messages

65. **Wind Energy** In a recent year, wind machines in the United States generated 17.8 billion kilowatt-hours of electricity, enough to serve over 1.6 million households. The nation's total electricity production that year was 4450 billion kilowatt-hours. (*Source:* Energy Information Administration) What percent of the total energy production was generated by wind machines? 0.4%

66. **Taxes** A TurboTax online survey asked people how they planned to use their tax refunds. Seven hundred forty people, or 22% of the respondents, said they would save the money. How many people responded to the survey?
3364 people

67. For $\frac{1}{4}\%$, the percent ratio is the ratio $\frac{\frac{1}{4}}{100}$. Which of the following fractions is equivalent to this ratio?

(i) $\frac{1}{25}$ **(ii)** $\frac{1}{400}$ **(iii)** $\frac{25}{1}$ ii

68. For 0.75%, the percent ratio is the ratio $\frac{0.75}{100}$. Which of the following fractions are equivalent to this ratio?

(i) $\frac{3}{4}$ **(ii)** $\frac{3}{400}$ **(iii)** $\frac{75}{10{,}000}$ ii and iii

69. True or false? For all positive values of N, 20% of N is equal to N% of 20. True

QUICK QUIZ

Solve. Use the basic percent equation.

1. 7% of 50 is what number? **3.5 [6.4A]**
2. 19 is what percent of 95? **20% [6.4A]**

Solve. Use the proportion method.

3. What percent of 80 is 25? **31.25% [6.4B]**
4. 7 is 14% of what number? **50 [6.4B]**
5. A student answered 16 of the questions on a 2-hour exam incorrectly. This was 25% of the total number of exam questions. How many questions were on the exam? **64 questions [6.4C]**

OBJECTIVE C *To solve application problems*

70. Automotive Technology A mechanic estimates that the brakes of an RV still have 6000 mi of wear. This amount is 12% of the estimated safe-life use of the brakes. What is the estimated safe-life use of the brakes? 50,000 mi

71. Fireworks The value of the fireworks imported to the United States in a recent year was \$163.1 million. During that year, the value of the fireworks imported from China was \$157.2 million. (*Source:* www.census.gov) What percent of the value of the fireworks imported to the United States was the value of the fireworks imported from China? Round to the nearest tenth of a percent. 96.4%

© iStockphoto.com/yxyeng

72. Fire Science A fire department received 24 false alarms out of a total of 200 alarms received. What percent of the alarms received were false alarms? 12%

73. Fire Science The graph at the right shows firefighter deaths by type of duty for a recent year. What percent of the deaths occurred during training? Round to the nearest tenth of a percent. 12.2%

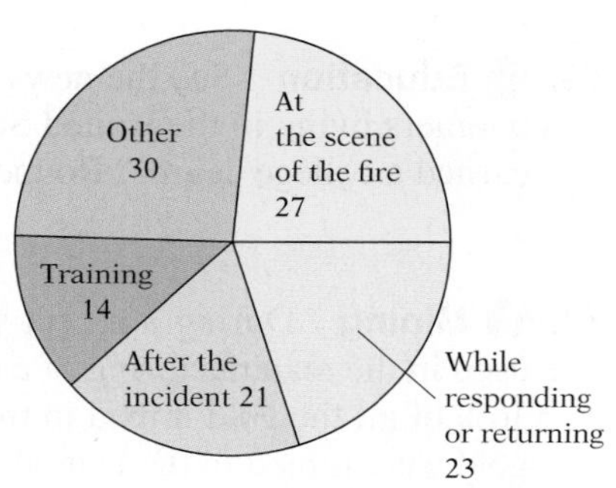

Firefighter Deaths
Source: U.S. Fire Administration

74. Lobsters Each year, 183 million pounds of lobster are caught in the United States and Canada. Twenty-five percent of this amount is sold live. (*Source:* Lobster Institute at the University of Maine) How many pounds of lobster are sold live each year in the United States and Canada? 45.75 million pounds

75. Home Schooling In a recent year, 1.1 million students were home-schooled. This was 2.2% of all students in the United States. (*Source:* Home Schooling in the United States; U.S. Department of Education) Find the number of students in the United States that year. 50 million students

76. **Wind-Powered Ships** Using the information in the news clipping at the right, calculate the cargo ship's daily fuel bill. $8000

HERO LANG/AFP/Getty Images

In the NEWS!

Kite-Powered Cargo Ships

In January 2008, the first cargo ship partially powered by a giant kite set sail from Germany bound for Venezuela. The 1722-square-foot kite helped to propel the ship, which consequently used 20% less fuel, cutting approximately $1600 from the ship's daily fuel bill.

Source: The Internal Revenue Service; TSN Financial Services

77. **Lifestyles** There are 114 million households in the United States. Opposite-sex cohabitating couples comprise 4.4% of these households. (*Source:* Families and Living Arrangements) Find the number of opposite-sex cohabitating couples who maintain households in the United States. Round to the nearest million. 5 million couples

78. **Jewelry** Fourteen-carat yellow gold contains 58.5% gold, 17.5% silver, and 24% copper. If a jeweler has a 50-gram piece of 14-carat yellow gold, how many grams of gold, silver, and copper are in the piece? Gold: 29.25 g; silver: 8.75 g; copper: 12 g

79. **Girl Scout Cookies** Using the information in the news clipping at the right, calculate the cash generated annually from sales of **a.** Thin Mints and **b.** Trefoil shortbread cookies. a. $175 million b. $63 million

Jeff Greenberg/AGEFotostock

In the NEWS!

Thin Mints Biggest Seller

Every year, sales from all the Girl Scout cookies sold by about 2.7 million girls total $700 million. The most popular cookie is Thin Mints, which earn 25% of total sales. Sales of Trefoil shortbread cookies represent only 9% of total sales.

Source: Southwest Airlines Spirit Magazine 2007

80. **Charities** The American Red Cross spent $185,048,179 for administrative expenses. This amount was 3.16% of its total revenue. Find the American Red Cross's total revenue. Round to the nearest hundred million. $5,900,000,000

81. **Agriculture** Of the 572 million pounds of cranberries grown in the United States in a recent year, Wisconsin growers produced 291.72 million pounds. What percent of the total cranberry crop was produced in Wisconsin? 51%

82. **Education** See the news clipping at the right. What percent of the baby boomers living in the United States have some college experience but have not earned a college degree? Round to the nearest tenth of a percent. 57.7%

In the NEWS!

Over Half of Baby Boomers Have College Experience

Of the 78 million baby boomers living in the United States, 45 million have some college experience but no college degree. Twenty million baby boomers have one or more college degrees.

Sources: The National Center for Education Statistics; U.S. Census Bureau; *McCook Daily Gazette*

83. **Mining** During a recent year, approximately 2,240,000 oz of gold were used in the manufacturing of electronic equipment in the United States. This is 16% of all the gold mined in the United States that year. How many ounces of gold were mined in the United States that year? 14,000,000 oz

84. **Demography** According to a 25-city survey on the status of hunger and homelessness by the U.S. Conference of Mayors, 41% of the homeless in the United States are single men, 41% are families with children, 13% are single women, and 5% are unaccompanied minors. How many homeless people in the United States are single men? Insufficient information

85. **Pets** The average costs associated with owning a dog over an average 11-year life span are shown in the graph at the right. These costs do not include the price of the puppy when purchased. The category labeled "Other" includes such expenses as fencing and repairing furniture damaged by the pet. What percent of the total cost is spent on food? Round to the nearest tenth of a percent. 27.5%

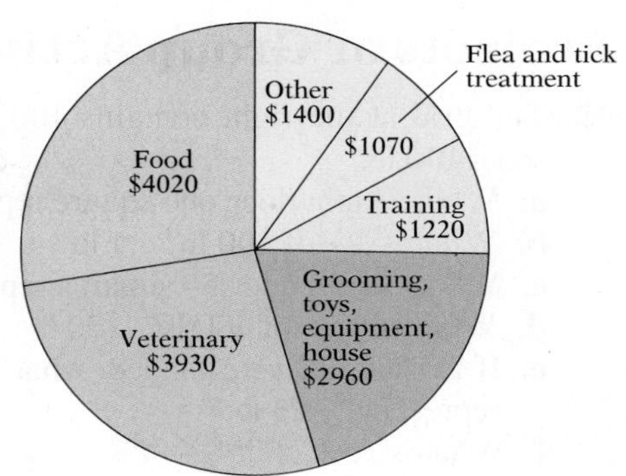

Cost of Owning a Dog
Source: American Kennel Club, *USA Today* research

86. **Agriculture** According to the U.S. Department of Agriculture, of the 63 billion pounds of vegetables produced in the United States in one year, 16 billion pounds were wasted. What percent of the vegetables produced were wasted? Round to the nearest tenth of a percent. 25.4%

87. **Health Insurance** Approximately 30% of the 44 million people in the United States who do not have health insurance are between the ages of 18 and 24. (*Source:* U.S. Census Bureau) About how many people in the United States aged 18 to 24 do not have health insurance? 13.2 million people

In the NEWS!

More Taxpayers Filing Electronically

The IRS reported that, as of May 4, it has received 128 million returns. Sixty percent of the returns were filed electronically.
Source: IRS

88. **e-Filed Tax Returns** See the news clipping at the right. How many of the 128 million returns were filed electronically? Round to the nearest million. 77 million returns

89. **Diabetes** Approximately 7% of the American population has diabetes. Within this group, 14.6 million are diagnosed, while 6.2 million are undiagnosed. (*Source:* The National Diabetes Education Program) What percent of Americans with diabetes have not been diagnosed with the disease? Round to the nearest tenth of a percent. 29.8%

Politics The results of a survey in which 32,840 full-time college and university faculty members were asked to describe their political views are shown at the right. Use these data for Exercises 90 and 91.

Political View	Percent of Faculty Members Responding
Far left	5.3%
Liberal	42.3%
Middle-of-the-road	34.3%
Conservative	17.7%
Far right	0.3%

Source: Higher Education Research Institute, UCLA

90. How many more faculty members described their political views as liberal than described their views as far-left? 12,151 more faculty members

91. How many fewer faculty members described their political views as conservative than described their views as middle-of-the-road? 5451 fewer faculty members

Critical Thinking

92. Find 10% of a number and subtract it from the original number. Now take 10% of the new number and subtract it from the new number. Is this the same as taking 20% of the original number? Explain. No

93. Increase a number by 10%. Now decrease the new number by 10%. Is the result the original number? Explain. No

94. **Compensation** Your employer agrees to give you a 5% raise after one year on the job, a 6% raise the next year, and a 7% raise the following year. Is your salary after the third year greater than, less than, or the same as it would be if you had received a 6% raise each year? Less than

Projects or Group Activities

95. The grid at the right contains 100 squares and represents 100 lb.

a. What weight does one square represent? 1 lb
b. What is 1% of 100 lb? 1 lb
c. What weight does 50 squares represent? 50 lb
d. What is 50% of 100 lb? 50 lb
e. If 25 squares were shaded, what weight would that represent? 25 lb
f. What is 25% of 100? 25
g. Shade the number of squares that corresponds to a weight of 70 lb. 70 squares should be shaded.
h. What percent of 100 lb is 70 lb? 70%

96. The grid at the right contains 100 squares and represents 200 lb.

a. What weight does one square represent? 2 lb
b. What is 1% of 200 lb? 2 lb
c. What weight does 50 squares represent? 100 lb
d. What is 50% of 200 lb? 100 lb
e. If 25 squares were shaded, what weight would that represent? 50 lb
f. What is 25% of 200? 50
g. Shade the number of squares that corresponds to a weight of 60 lb. 30 squares should be shaded.
h. What percent of 200 lb is 60 lb? 30%

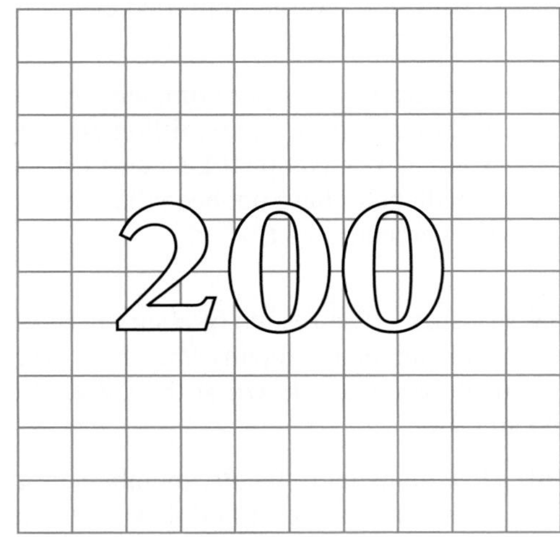

97. The grid at the right contains 100 squares and represents 20 lb.

a. What weight does one square represent? 0.2 lb
b. What is 1% of 20 lb? 0.2 lb
c. What weight does 50 squares represent? 10 lb
d. What is 50% of 20 lb? 10 lb
e. If 25 squares were shaded, what weight would that represent? 5 lb
f. What is 25% of 20? 5
g. Shade the number of squares that corresponds to a weight of 8 lb. 40 squares should be shaded.
h. What percent of 20 lb is 8 lb? 40%

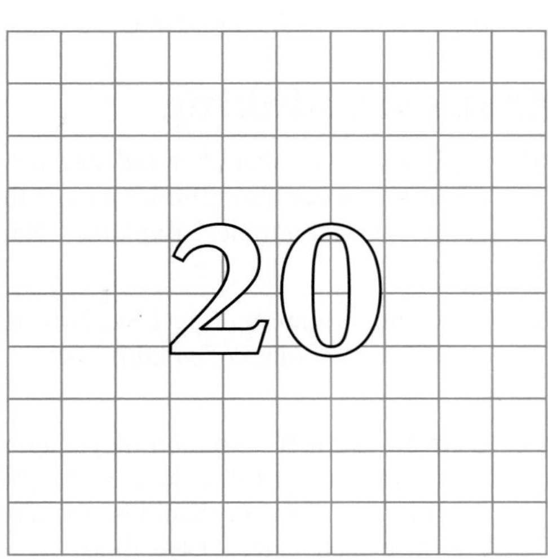

SECTION

6.5 Simple Interest

OBJECTIVE A To solve simple interest problems

© iStockphoto.com/tforgo

If you deposit money in a savings account at a bank, the bank will pay you for the privilege of using that money. The amount you deposit in the savings account is called the **principal.** The amount the bank pays you for the privilege of using the money is called **interest.**

If you borrow money from the bank in order to buy a car, the amount you borrow is called the **principal.** The additional amount of money you must pay the bank, above and beyond the amount borrowed, is called **interest.**

Whether you deposit money or borrow it, the amount of interest paid is usually computed as a percent of the principal. The percent used to determine the amount of interest to be paid is the **interest rate.** Interest rates are given for specific periods of time, such as months or years.

Interest computed on the original principal is called **simple interest.** Simple interest is the cost of a loan that is taken for a period of about one year or less.

INSTRUCTOR NOTE

Emphasize that the simple interest formula requires that the interest rate and the time have comparable units. If an *annual* interest rate is given, then the time must be in *years.* If a *monthly* interest rate is given (as on most credit cards), then the time must be in *months.*

The Simple Interest Formula

$I = Prt$, where I = simple interest earned, P = principal, r = annual simple interest rate, t = time (in years)

EXAMPLE

You borrow $3000 for 4 months at an annual simple interest rate of 4%.

$P = \$3000$, $r = 4\% = 0.04$, $t = 4$ months $\left(\frac{4}{12}\right)$

Simple interest $= I = Prt = \$3000(0.04)\left(\frac{4}{12}\right) = \$40$

In the simple interest formula, t is the time in years. If a time period is given in days or months, it must be converted to years and then substituted in the formula for t. For example,

120 days is $\frac{120}{365}$ of a year. 6 months is $\frac{6}{12}$ of a year.

IN-CLASS EXAMPLES

1. A rancher borrowed $120,000 for 180 days at an annual simple interest rate of 8.75%. What is the simple interest due on the loan? **$5178.08**
2. A business owner borrowed $84,000 for 8 months at an annual simple interest rate of 6.5%. Find the maturity value of the loan. **$87,640**

HOW TO 1 Shannon O'Hara borrowed $5000 for 90 days at an annual simple interest rate of 7.5%. Find the simple interest due on the loan.

Strategy To find the simple interest owed, use the simple interest formula.

$$P = 5000, r = 7.5\% = 0.075, t = \frac{90}{365}$$

Solution

$$I = Prt$$

$$I = 5000(0.075)\left(\frac{90}{365}\right) \approx 92.47$$

The simple interest due on the loan is $92.47.

In HOW TO 1 above, we calculated that the simple interest due on Shannon O'Hara's 90-day, $5000 loan was $92.47. This means that at the end of the 90 days, Shannon owes $5000 + $92.47 = $5092.47. The principal plus the interest owed on a loan is called the **maturity value.**

Formula for the Maturity Value of a Simple Interest Loan

$M = P + I$, where M = the maturity value, P = the principal, I = the simple interest

EXAMPLE

You borrow $5000 for 6 months. The simple interest due on the loan is $125.

$P = \$5000$, $I = \$125$

Maturity value $= M = P + I = \$5000 + \$125 = \$5125$

HOW TO 2 Ed Pabas took out a 45-day, $12,000 loan. The simple interest due on the loan was $168. To the nearest tenth of a percent, what is the simple interest rate?

Strategy To find the simple interest rate, use the simple interest formula.

$$P = 12{,}000,\ t = \frac{45}{365},\ I = 168$$

Solution

$$I = Prt$$

$$168 = 12{,}000r\left(\frac{45}{365}\right)$$

$$168 = \frac{540{,}000}{365}r$$

$$\frac{365}{540{,}000}(168) = \frac{365}{540{,}000} \cdot \frac{540{,}000}{365}r$$

$$0.114 \approx r$$

The simple interest rate on the loan is 11.4%.

Take Note

HOW TO 2 at the right illustrates how to solve the simple interest formula for the interest rate. The solution requires the use of the Multiplication Property of Equations.

EXAMPLE 1

You arrange for a 9-month bank loan of $9000 at an annual simple interest rate of 8.5%. Find the total amount you must repay to the bank.

Strategy

To calculate the maturity value:

- Find the simple interest due on the loan by solving the simple interest formula for I.

  $t = \frac{9}{12}$, $P = 9000$, $r = 8.5\% = 0.085$

- Use the formula for the maturity value of a simple interest loan, $M = P + I$.

Solution

$I = Prt$

$I = 9000(0.085)\left(\frac{9}{12}\right)$

$I = 573.75$ • The simple interest due is $573.75.

$M = P + I$

$M = 9000 + 573.75$ • $P = 9000, I = 573.75$

$M = 9573.75$

The total amount owed to the bank is $9573.75.

YOU TRY IT 1

William Carey borrowed $12,500 for 8 months at an annual simple interest rate of 9.5%. Find the total amount due on the loan.

Your strategy

Your solution

$13,291.67

Solution on p. S18

6.5 EXERCISES

Concept Check

SUGGESTED ASSIGNMENT
Exercises 1 and 2; Exercises 3–21, odds; More challenging exercise: Exercise 23

1. Explain the difference between interest and interest rate.

2. Explain how to convert a number of months to a fractional part of a year.

OBJECTIVE A *To solve simple interest problems*

3. In the table below, the interest rate is an annual simple interest rate. Complete the table by calculating the simple interest due on the loan.

Loan Amount	Interest Rate	Period	Prt	=	Interest, I
\$5000	6%	1 month	\$ 5000 · 0.06 · $\frac{1}{12}$	=	\$25
\$5000	6%	2 months	\$ 5000 · 0.06 · $\frac{2}{12}$	=	\$50
\$5000	6%	3 months	\$ 5000 · 0.06 · $\frac{3}{12}$	=	\$75
\$5000	6%	4 months	\$ 5000 · 0.06 · $\frac{4}{12}$	=	\$100
\$5000	6%	5 months	\$ 5000 · 0.06 · $\frac{5}{12}$	=	\$125

4. Use the pattern of the amounts of interest in the table in Exercise 3 to find the simple interest due on a \$5000 loan that has an annual simple interest rate of 6% for a period of **a.** 6 months, **b.** 7 months, **c.** 8 months, and **d.** 9 months.
a. \$150 **b.** \$175 **c.** \$200 **d.** \$225

For Exercises 5 and 6, refer to your answers to Exercises 3 and 4.

5. If you know the simple interest due on a 1-month loan, explain how to use that amount to calculate the simple interest due on a 7-month loan for the same principal and the same interest rate. Multiply the interest due by 7.

6. If the time period of a loan is doubled but the principal and interest rate remain the same, how many times greater is the simple interest due on the loan?
2 times greater

7. Hector Elizondo took out a 75-day loan of \$7500 at an annual interest rate of 4.5%. Find the simple interest due on the loan. \$69.35

8. Kristi Yang borrowed \$15,000. The term of the loan was 90 days, and the annual simple interest rate was 7.4%. Find the simple interest due on the loan. \$273.70

9. A home builder obtained a preconstruction loan of \$50,000 for 8 months at an annual interest rate of 3.5%. What is the simple interest due on the loan? \$1166.67

10. To finance the purchase of several new cars, the Lincoln Car Rental Agency borrowed \$100,000 for 9 months at an annual interest rate of 4%. What is the simple interest due on the loan? \$3000

11. The Mission Valley Credit Union charges its customers an interest rate of 2% per month on money that is transferred into an account that is overdrawn. Find the interest owed to the credit union for 1 month when \$800 is transferred into an overdrawn account. \$16

12. Assume that Visa charges Francesca 1.6% per month on her unpaid balance. Find the interest owed to Visa when her unpaid balance for the month is \$1250. \$20

13. Find the simple interest that Kara Tanamachi owes on a $1\frac{1}{2}$-year loan of \$1500 at an annual interest rate of 7.5%. \$168.75

14. Find the simple interest that Jacob Zucker owes on a 2-year loan of \$8000 at an annual interest rate of 4%. \$640

15. A corporate executive took out a \$25,000 loan at an 8.2% annual simple interest rate for 1 year. Find the maturity value of the loan. \$27,050

16. An auto parts dealer borrowed \$150,000 at a 4.5% annual simple interest rate for 1 year. Find the maturity value of the loan. \$156,750

17. A credit union loans a member \$5000 for the purchase of a used car. The loan is made for 18 months at an annual simple interest rate of 6.9%. What is the maturity value of the car loan? \$5517.50

18. Capitol City Bank approves a home-improvement loan application for \$14,000 at an annual simple interest rate of 6.25% for 270 days. What is the maturity value of the loan? \$14,647.26

19. Michele Gabrielle borrowed \$3000 for 9 months and paid \$168.75 in simple interest on the loan. Find the annual simple interest rate that Michele paid on the loan. 7.5%

20. A \$12,000 investment earned \$462 in interest in 6 months. Find the annual simple interest rate on the loan. 7.7%

21. Don Glover borrowed \$18,000 for 210 days and paid \$604.80 in simple interest on the loan. What annual simple interest rate did Don pay on the loan? 5.84%

QUICK QUIZ

1. A mechanic borrowed \$15,000 for 90 days at an annual simple interest rate of 7.2%. What is the simple interest due on the loan? **\$266.30 [6.5A]**
2. A business owner borrowed \$60,000 for 9 months at an annual simple interest rate of 8.6%. Find the maturity value of the loan. **\$63,870 [6.5A]**

22. An investor earned $937.50 in 75 days on an investment of $50,000. Find the annual simple interest rate earned on the investment. 9.125%

Critical Thinking

23. a. Find the difference between the maturity value of a 6-month, $10,000 loan at an annual simple interest rate of 8.75% and that of the same loan at an annual simple interest rate of 6.25%. $125
   b. Find the difference between the monthly payments for the two loans in part (a). $20.83

Projects or Group Activities

© iStockphoto.com/cristianl

24. **Buying and Maintaining a Car** Suppose a student has an after-school job to earn money to buy and maintain a car. We will make assumptions about the monthly costs in several categories in order to determine how many hours per week the student must work to support the car. Assume that the student earns $9.50 per hour.

   a. Monthly payment

   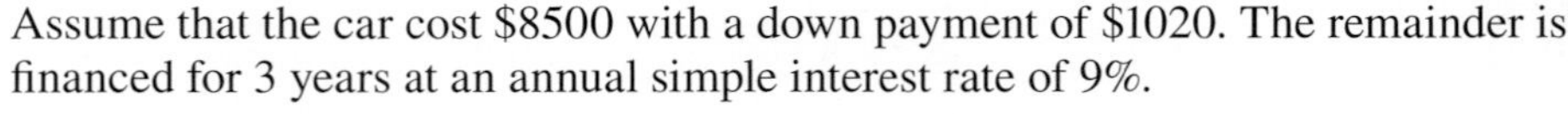
   Assume that the car cost $8500 with a down payment of $1020. The remainder is financed for 3 years at an annual simple interest rate of 9%.

   Monthly payment = $263.88

   b. Insurance

   Assume that insurance costs $1500 per year.

   Monthly insurance payment = $125

   c. Gasoline

   Assume that the student travels 750 mi per month, that the car travels 25 mi per gallon of gasoline, and that gasoline costs $3.85 per gallon.

   Number of gallons of gasoline purchased per month = 30 gal

   Monthly cost for gasoline = $115.50

   d. Miscellaneous

   Assume $.55 per mile for upkeep.

   Monthly expense for upkeep = $412.50

   e. Total monthly expenses for the monthly payment, insurance, gasoline, and miscellaneous = $916.88

   f. To find the number of hours per month that the student must work to finance the car, divide the total monthly expenses by the hourly rate.

   Number of hours per month ≈ 96.51 h

   g. To find the number of hours per week that the student must work, divide the number of hours per month by 4.

   Number of hours per week = 24.128 h

   The student has to work 24.128 h per week to pay the monthly car expenses.

CHAPTER 6 Summary

Key Words	Examples
A **ratio** is the comparison of two quantities with the same unit. A ratio can be written in three ways: as a fraction, as two numbers separated by a colon, or as two numbers separated by the word *to*. A ratio is in simplest form when the two quantities do not have a common factor. [6.1A, p. 338]	The comparison 16 oz to 24 oz can be written as a ratio in simplest form as $\frac{2}{3}$, 2 : 3, or 2 to 3.
A **rate** is the comparison of two quantities with different units. A rate is in simplest form when the two quantities do not have a common factor. [6.1A, p. 338]	You earned \$63 for working 6 h. The rate is written $\frac{\$21}{2\text{ h}}$.
A **unit rate** is a rate in which the denominator is 1. [6.1A, p. 338]	You traveled 144 mi in 3 h. The unit rate is 48 mph.
A **proportion** states the equality of two ratios or rates. Each of the four numbers in a proportion is called a **term.** first term → a, second term → b, third term → c, fourth term → d: $\frac{a}{b} = \frac{c}{d}$ The second and third terms of the proportion are called the **means,** and the first and fourth terms are called the **extremes.** [6.2A, p. 342]	In the proportion $\frac{3}{5} = \frac{12}{20}$, 5 and 12 are the means; 3 and 20 are the extremes.
Percent means "per hundred." [6.3A, p. 352]	23% means 23 of 100 equal parts.
Principal is the amount of money originally deposited or borrowed. **Interest** is the amount paid for the privilege of using someone else's money. The percent used to determine the amount of interest is the **interest rate.** Interest computed on the original amount is called **simple interest.** The principal plus the interest owed on a loan is called the **maturity value.** [6.5A, p. 377]	Consider a 1-year loan of \$5000 at an annual simple interest rate of 8%. The principal is \$5000. The interest rate is 8%. The interest paid on the loan is \$400. The maturity value is \$5000 + \$400 = \$5400.

Essential Rules and Procedures

Examples

To find a unit rate, divide the number in the numerator of the rate by the number in the denominator of the rate. [6.1A, p. 339]

You earned \$41 for working 4 h.

$41 \div 4 = 10.25$

The unit rate is \$10.25 per hour.

To solve a proportion, use the fact that the product of the means equals the product of the extremes. For the proportion $\frac{a}{b} = \frac{c}{d}$, $bc = ad$. [6.2A, p. 343]

$$\begin{aligned} \frac{6}{25} &= \frac{9}{x} \\ 25 \cdot 9 &= 6 \cdot x \\ 225 &= 6x \\ \frac{225}{6} &= \frac{6x}{6} \\ 37.5 &= x \end{aligned}$$

To set up a proportion, keep the same units in the numerators and the same units in the denominators. [6.2B, p. 344]

Three machines fill 5 cereal boxes per minute. How many boxes can 8 machines fill per minute?

$$\frac{3 \text{ machines}}{5 \text{ cereal boxes}} = \frac{8 \text{ machines}}{x \text{ cereal boxes}}$$

To write a percent as a fraction, remove the percent sign and multiply by $\frac{1}{100}$. [6.3A, p. 353]

$$\begin{aligned} 56\% &= 56\left(\frac{1}{100}\right) \\ &= \frac{56}{100} = \frac{14}{25} \end{aligned}$$

To write a percent as a decimal, remove the percent sign and multiply by 0.01. [6.3A, p. 353]

$$\begin{aligned} 87\% &= 87(0.01) \\ &= 0.87 \end{aligned}$$

To write a fraction as a percent, multiply by 100%. [6.3B, p. 354]

$$\begin{aligned} \frac{7}{20} &= \frac{7}{20}(100\%) \\ &= \frac{700}{20}\% = 35\% \end{aligned}$$

To write a decimal as a percent, multiply by 100%. [6.3B, p. 355]

$$\begin{aligned} 0.325 &= 0.325(100\%) \\ &= 32.5\% \end{aligned}$$

The Basic Percent Equation [6.4A, p. 362]
Percent · base = amount

8% of 250 is what number?

$$\begin{aligned} \text{Percent} \cdot \text{base} &= \text{amount} \\ 0.08 \cdot 250 &= n \\ 20 &= n \end{aligned}$$

Proportion Method of Solving a Percent Problem [6.4B, p. 365]

$$\frac{\text{percent}}{100} = \frac{\text{amount}}{\text{base}}$$

8% of 250 is what number?

$$\begin{aligned} \frac{\text{percent}}{100} &= \frac{\text{amount}}{\text{base}} \\ \frac{8}{100} &= \frac{n}{250} \\ 100 \cdot n &= 8 \cdot 250 \\ 100n &= 2000 \\ n &= 20 \end{aligned}$$

Simple Interest Formula [6.5A, p. 377]
I = simple interest earned, P = principal,
r = annual simple interest rate, t = time (in years):
$I = Prt$

You borrow \$10,000 for 180 days at an annual interest rate of 8%. Find the simple interest due on the loan.

$$I = Prt$$

$$I = 10{,}000(0.08)\left(\frac{180}{365}\right)$$

$$I \approx 394.52$$

Formula for the Maturity Value of a Simple Interest Loan [6.5A, p. 378]
M = maturity value, P = principal, I = simple interest:
$M = P + I$

Suppose you paid \$400 in interest on a 1-year loan of \$5000. The maturity value of the loan is \$5000 + \$400 = \$5400.

CHAPTER

6 Review Exercises

1. Write the comparison 100 lb to 100 lb as a ratio in simplest form using a fraction, a colon, and the word *to*.
$\frac{1}{1}$, 1 : 1, 1 to 1 [6.1A]

2. Write 18 roof supports for every 9 ft as a rate in simplest form.
$\frac{\text{2 roof supports}}{\text{1 ft}}$ [6.1A]

3. Write $628 earned in 40 h as a unit rate.
$15.70/h [6.1A]

4. Write 8 h to 15 h as a ratio in simplest form using a fraction.
$\frac{8}{15}$ [6.1A]

5. Solve: $\frac{n}{3} = \frac{8}{15}$
1.6 [6.2A]

6. Write 15 lb of fertilizer for 12 trees as a rate in simplest form.
$\frac{\text{5 lb}}{\text{4 trees}}$ [6.1A]

7. Write 171 mi driven in 3 h as a unit rate.
57 mph [6.1A]

8. Solve $\frac{2}{3.5} = \frac{n}{12}$. Round to the nearest hundredth.
6.86 [6.2A]

9. Write 32% as a fraction.
$\frac{8}{25}$ [6.3A]

10. Write 22% as a decimal.
0.22 [6.3A]

11. Write 25% as a fraction and as a decimal.
$\frac{1}{4}$, 0.25 [6.3A]

12. Write $3\frac{2}{5}\%$ as a fraction.
$\frac{17}{500}$ [6.3A]

13. Write $\frac{7}{40}$ as a percent.
17.5% [6.3B]

14. Write $1\frac{2}{7}$ as a percent. Round to the nearest tenth of a percent. 128.6% [6.3B]

15. Write 2.8 as a percent.
280% [6.3B]

16. 42% of 50 is what?
21 [6.4A/6.4B]

17. What percent of 3 is 15?
500% [6.4A/6.4B]

18. 12 is what percent of 18? Round to the nearest tenth of a percent.
66.7% [6.4A/6.4B]

19. 150% of 20 is what number?
30 [6.4A/6.4B]

20. Find 18% of 85.
15.3 [6.4A/6.4B]

21. 32% of what number is 180?
562.5 [6.4A/6.4B]

22. 4.5 is what percent of 80?
5.625% [6.4A/6.4B]

23. Mechanics Find the ratio of two meshed gears if one gear has 10 teeth and the other gear has 50 teeth.
$\frac{1}{5}$ [6.1A]

24. Investments An investment of $8000 earns $520 in dividends. At the same rate, how much money must be invested to earn $780 in dividends? $12,000 [6.2B]

25. Lawn Care The directions on a bag of plant food recommend $\frac{1}{2}$ lb for every 50 ft^2 of lawn. How many pounds of plant food should be used on a lawn of 275 ft^2?
2.75 lb [6.2B]

26. Profits Two attorneys share the profits of their firm in the ratio 3:2. If the attorney receiving the larger amount of this year's profits receives $96,000, what amount does the other attorney receive? $64,000 [6.2B]

27. Tourism The table at the right shows the countries with the highest projected numbers of tourists visiting in 2020. What percent of the tourists projected to visit these countries will be visiting China? Round to the nearest tenth of a percent. 34.0% [6.4C]

Country	*Projected Number of Tourists in 2020*
China	137 million
France	93 million
Spain	71 million
USA	102 million

Source: The State of the World Atlas by Dan Smith

28. Advertising A company spent 7% of its $120,000 budget on advertising. How much did the company spend on advertising?
$8400 [6.4C]

29. Manufacturing A quality control inspector found that 1.2% of 4000 cellular telephones were defective. How many of the phones were not defective?
3952 telephones [6.4C]

30. Television According to the Cabletelevision Advertising Bureau, cable households watch an average of 61.35 h of television per week. On average, what percent of the week do cable households spend watching TV? Round to the nearest tenth of a percent. 36.5% [6.4C]

31. Simple Interest Find the simple interest due on a 45-day loan of $3000 at an annual simple interest rate of 8.6%. $31.81 [6.5A]

32. Simple Interest A corporation borrowed $500,000 for 60 days and paid $7397.26 in simple interest. What annual simple interest rate did the corporation pay on the loan? Round to the nearest hundredth of a percent. 9.00% [6.5A]

33. Simple Interest A realtor took out a $10,000 loan at a 5.4% annual simple interest rate for 9 months. Find the maturity value of the loan. $10,405 [6.5A]

CHAPTER 6 TEST

1. Write the comparison 3 yd to 24 yd as a ratio in simplest form using a fraction, a colon, and the word *to*.
$\frac{1}{8}$, 1 : 8, 1 to 8 [6.1A]

2. Write 16 oz of sugar for 64 cookies as a rate in simplest form.
$\frac{1 \text{ oz}}{4 \text{ cookies}}$ [6.1A]

3. Write 120 mi driven in 200 min as a unit rate.
0.6 mi/min [6.1A]

4. Write 200 ft to 100 ft as a ratio in simplest form using a fraction.
$\frac{2}{1}$ [6.1A]

5. Solve: $\frac{n}{5} = \frac{3}{20}$
0.75 [6.2A]

6. Write 8 ft walked in 4 s as a unit rate.
2 ft/s [6.1A]

7. Write 2860 ft^2 mowed in 6 h as a unit rate. Round to the nearest hundredth.
476.67 ft^2/h [6.1A]

8. Solve $\frac{n}{4} = \frac{8}{9}$. Round to the nearest hundredth.
3.56 [6.2A]

9. Write 86.4% as a decimal.
0.864 [6.3A]

10. Write 0.4 as a percent.
40% [6.3B]

11. Write $\frac{5}{4}$ as a percent.
125% [6.3B]

12. Write $83\frac{1}{3}$% as a fraction.
$\frac{5}{6}$ [6.3A]

13. Write 32% as a fraction.
$\frac{8}{25}$ [6.3A]

14. Write 1.18 as a percent.
118% [6.3B]

15. 18 is 20% of what number?
90 [6.4A/6.4B]

16. What is 68% of 73?
49.64 [6.4A/6.4B]

17. What percent of 320 is 180?
56.25% [6.4A/6.4B]

18. 28 is 14% of what number?
200 [6.4A/6.4B]

19. **Physical Fitness** The figure at the right shows the lung capacities of inactive versus athletic 45-year-olds. Write the comparison of the lung capacity of an inactive male to that of an athletic male as a ratio in simplest form using a fraction, a colon, and the word *to*.
$\frac{1}{2}$; 1 : 2; 1 to 2 [6.1A]

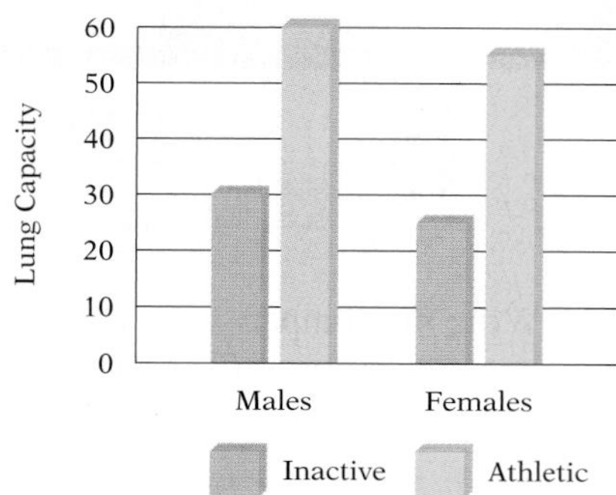

Lung Capacity (in milliliters of oxygen per kilogram of body weight per minute)

20. **Taxes** The sales tax on a \$95 purchase is \$7.60. Find the sales tax on a car costing \$39,200. \$3136 [6.2B]

21. **Elections** A pre-election survey showed that 3 out of 4 registered voters would vote in a county election. At this rate, how many registered voters would vote in a county with 325,000 registered voters? 243,750 voters [6.2B]

22. **Scale Drawings** The scale on the architectural drawings for a new gymnasium is 1 in. equals 4 ft. How long is one of the rooms if it measures $12\frac{1}{2}$ in. on the drawing? 50 ft [6.2B]

23. **Industrial Accidents** An insurance company expects that 2.2% of a company's employees will have an industrial accident. How many accidents are expected for a company that employs 1500 people? 33 accidents [6.4C]

24. **Test Scores** A student missed 16 questions on a history exam of 90 questions. What percent of the questions did the student answer correctly? Round to the nearest tenth. 82.2% [6.4C]

25. **Wages** An administrative assistant has a wage of \$480 per week. This is 120% of last year's weekly wage. What is the dollar increase in the assistant's weekly wage over last year? \$80 [6.4C]

26. **Nutrition** The table at the right shows the fat, cholesterol, and calorie content in a 90-gram ground-beef burger and in a 90-gram soy burger. The number of grams of fat in the beef burger is what percent of the number of grams of fat in the soy burger? 600% [6.4C]

	Beef Burger	*Soy Burger*
Fat	24 g	4 g
Cholesterol	75 mg	0 mg
Calories	280	140

27. **Simple Interest** Find the simple interest due on a 9-month loan of \$5000 when the annual interest rate is 5.4%. \$202.50 [6.5A]

28. **Simple Interest** Maribeth Bakke took out a 150-day, \$40,000 business loan that had an annual simple interest rate of 6.25%. Find the maturity value of the loan. \$41,027.40 [6.5A]

29. **Simple Interest** Gene Connery paid \$672 in simple interest on an 8-month loan of \$12,000. Find the simple interest rate on the loan. 8.4% [6.5A]

Cumulative Review Exercises

1. Simplify: $18 \div \frac{6-3}{9} - (-3)$
57 [3.5A]

2. Evaluate 5^4.
625 [1.3B]

3. Subtract: $7\frac{5}{12} - 3\frac{5}{9}$
$3\frac{31}{36}$ [2.3B]

4. Simplify: $\frac{4}{5} \div \frac{4}{5} + \frac{2}{3}$
$1\frac{2}{3}$ [2.7A]

5. Find the quotient of 342 and −3.
−114 [3.3B]

6. Evaluate $2a - 3ab$ for $a = 2$ and $b = -3$.
22 [3.5A]

7. Solve: $5x - 20 = 0$
4 [5.2A]

8. Solve: $3(x - 4) + 2x = 3$
3 [5.3B]

9. Find the product of 1.005 and 10^5.
100,500 [2.6B]

10. Simplify: $-\frac{5}{8} - \left(-\frac{3}{4}\right) + \frac{5}{6}$
$\frac{23}{24}$ [3.5A]

11. Simplify: $(-5)^2 - (-8) \div (7 - 5)^2 \cdot 2 - 8$
21 [3.5A]

12. Simplify: $\left(-\frac{2}{3}\right)\left(-\frac{3}{4}\right)^2$
$-\frac{3}{8}$ [3.5A]

13. Simplify: $4 - (-3) + 5 - 8$
4 [3.2B]

14. Simplify: $5 - 2(1 - 3a) + 2(a - 3)$
$8a - 3$ [4.2D]

15. Find the quotient of $\frac{7}{8}$ and $\frac{5}{16}$.
$2\frac{4}{5}$ [2.4B]

16. Simplify: $-3y^2 + 3y - y^2 - 6y$
$-4y^2 - 3y$ [4.2A]

17. Solve: $\frac{3}{4}x = -9$
−12 [5.1C]

18. Write 30 cents to 1 dollar as a ratio in simplest form.
$\frac{3}{10}$ [6.1A]

19. Write $19,425 in 5 months as a unit rate.
$3885/month [6.1A]

20. Evaluate $a - b$ for $a = 102.5$ and $b = 77.546$.
24.954 [2.6A]

21. Solve: $\frac{2}{3} = \frac{n}{48}$
32 [6.2A]

22. Simplify: $\dfrac{\frac{1}{2} + \frac{3}{4}}{2 - \frac{5}{8}}$
$\frac{10}{11}$ [2.4C]

23. 2.5 is what percent of 30? Round to the nearest tenth of a percent.
8.3% [6.4A/6.4B]

24. Find 42% of 160.
67.2 [6.4A/6.4B]

25. **Public Transportation** The figure at the right shows the average amount spent annually per household on public transportation, by region, in the United States. Find the difference between the average amount spent monthly per household in the northeast and in the south. Round to the nearest cent. $28.67 [2.6E]

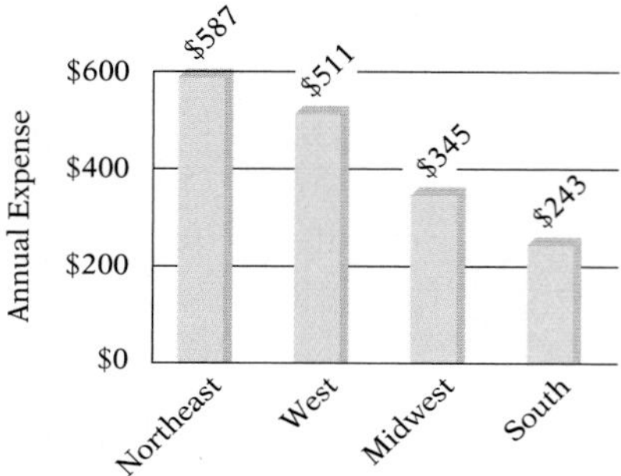

Average Annual Expense per Household on Public Transportation in the United States
Source: Bureau of Labor Statistics consumer expenditure survey

26. Five less than two-thirds of a number is three. Find the number.
12 [5.4A]

27. Translate "the difference between four times a number and three times the sum of the number and two" into a variable expression. Then simplify. $4x - 3(x + 2)$; $x - 6$ [4.3B]

28. **Travel** Your odometer reads 18,325 mi before you embark on a 125-mile trip. After you have driven $1\frac{1}{2}$ h, the odometer reads 18,386 mi. How many miles are left to drive? 64 mi [1.2C]

29. **Banking** You had a balance of $422.89 in your checking account. You then made a deposit of $122.35 and wrote a check for $279.76. Find the new balance in your checking account.
$265.48 [2.6E]

PAYMENT/ DEBIT (−)		√ T	FEE (IF ANY) (−)	DEPOSIT/ CREDIT (+)		BALANCE	
						$ 422	89
$			$	$ 122	35		
279	76						

30. **Data Processing** A data processor finished $\frac{2}{5}$ of a job on the first day and $\frac{1}{3}$ on the second day. What part of the job is left to be finished on the third day?
$\frac{4}{15}$ [2.3C]

31. **Alzheimer's Disease** According to the table at the right, what fraction of the population aged 75–84 is affected by Alzheimer's disease?
$\frac{1}{10}$ [6.3A]

Age Group	*Percent Affected by Alzheimer's Disease*
65–74	4%
75–84	10%
85+	17%

Source: Mayo Clinic Family Health Book, Encyclopedia Americana, Associated Press

32. **Fuel Consumption** A car is driven 402.5 mi on 11.5 gal of gas. Find the number of miles traveled per gallon of gas. 35 mi [6.1A]

33. **Mechanics** At a certain speed, the engine revolutions per minute (rpm) of a car in fourth gear is 2500. This is two-thirds of the rpm of the engine in third gear. Find the rpm of the engine in third gear. 3750 rpm [5.4B]

Geometry

7

OBJECTIVES

SECTION 7.1

A To solve problems involving lines and angles

B To solve problems involving angles formed by intersecting lines

C To solve problems involving the angles of a triangle

SECTION 7.2

A To find the perimeter of plane geometric figures

B To find the area of plane geometric figures

SECTION 7.3

A To find the unknown side of a right triangle by using the Pythagorean Theorem

B To solve similar triangles

C To determine whether two triangles are congruent

SECTION 7.4

A To find the volume of geometric solids

B To find the surface area of geometric solids

Focus on Success

Are you using the features of this text to learn the concepts being presented? The HOW TO feature includes a step-by-step solution to the types of exercise you will be working in your homework assignment and on exams. A numbered Example provides you with a fully-worked-out solution. After studying the Example, try completing the You Try It to the right of the Example. A complete solution to the You Try It is in the back of the text. (See Use the Interactive Method, page AIM-8.)

Prep Test

Are you ready to succeed in this chapter? Take the Prep Test below to find out if you are ready to learn the new material.

1. Simplify: $2(18) + 2(10)$ 56 [1.4A]

2. Evaluate abc for $a = 2$, $b = 3.14$, and $c = 9$. 56.52 [4.1A]

3. Evaluate xyz^3 for $x = \frac{4}{3}$, $y = 3.14$, and $z = 3$. 113.04 [4.1A]

4. Solve: $x + 47 = 90$ 43 [5.1B]

5. Solve: $32 + 97 + x = 180$ 51 [5.1B]

6. Solve: $\frac{5}{12} = \frac{6}{x}$ 14.4 [6.2A]

SECTION

7.1 Introduction to Geometry

OBJECTIVE A *To solve problems involving lines and angles*

Point of Interest

Geometry is one of the oldest branches of mathematics. Around 350 B.C., Euclid of Alexandria wrote *Elements,* which contained all of the known concepts of geometry. Euclid's contribution was to unify various concepts into a single deductive system that was based on a set of axioms.

The word *geometry* comes from the Greek words for *earth* and *measure.* In ancient Egypt, geometry was used by the Egyptians to measure land and to build structures such as the pyramids. Today geometry is used in many fields, such as physics, medicine, and geology. Geometry is also used in applied fields such as mechanical drawing and astronomy. Geometric forms are used in art and design.

Three basic concepts of geometry are point, line, and plane. A **point** is symbolized by drawing a dot. A **line** is determined by two distinct points and extends indefinitely in both directions, as the arrows on the line shown at the right indicate. This line contains points A and B and is represented by $\overleftrightarrow{AB}$. A line can also be represented by a single letter, such as ℓ.

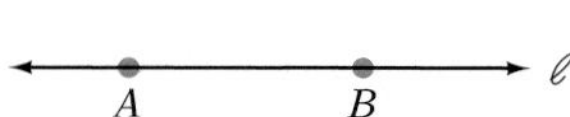

A **ray** starts at a point and extends indefinitely in *one* direction. The point at which a ray starts is called the **endpoint** of the ray. The ray shown at the right is denoted by $\overrightarrow{AB}$. Point A is the endpoint of the ray.

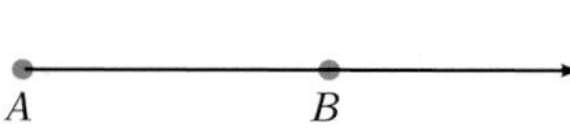

A **line segment** is part of a line and has two endpoints. The line segment shown at the right is denoted by $\overline{AB}$.

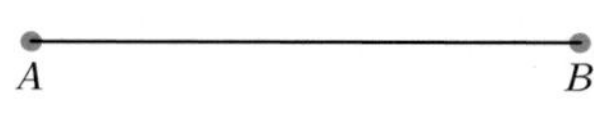

The distance between the endpoints of $\overline{AC}$ is denoted by AC. If B is a point on $\overline{AC}$, then AC (the distance from A to C) is the sum of AB (the distance from A to B) and BC (the distance from B to C).

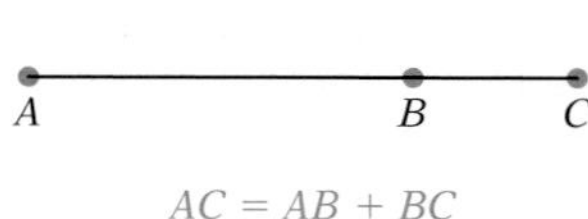

HOW TO 1 Given the figure above and the fact that $AB = 22$ cm and $AC = 31$ cm, find BC.

Write an equation for the distances between points on the line segment.	$AC = AB + BC$
Substitute the given distances for AB and AC into the equation.	$31 = 22 + BC$
Solve for BC.	$9 = BC$

$BC = 9$ cm

In this section we will be discussing figures that lie in a plane. A **plane** is a flat surface and can be pictured as a tabletop or blackboard that extends in all directions. Figures that lie in a plane are called **plane figures.**

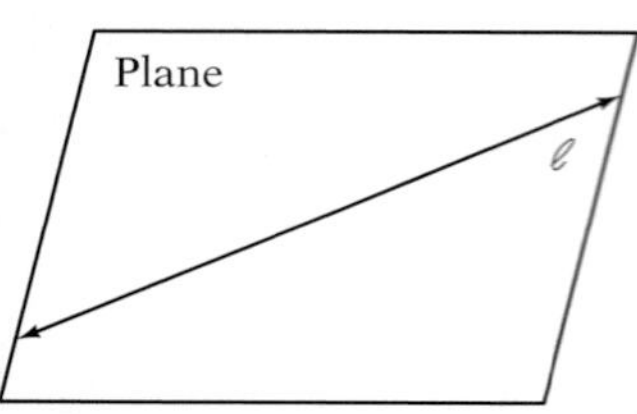

Lines in a plane can be intersecting or parallel. **Intersecting lines** cross at a point in the plane. **Parallel lines** never intersect. The distance between them is always the same.

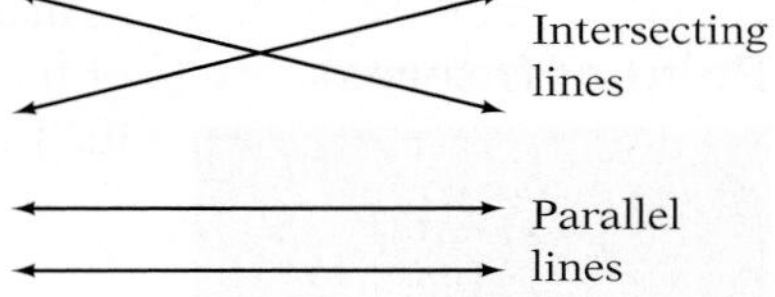

The symbol $\|$ means "is parallel to." In the figure at the right, $j \| k$ and $\overline{AB} \| \overline{CD}$. Note that j contains $\overline{AB}$ and k contains $\overline{CD}$. Parallel lines contain parallel line segments.

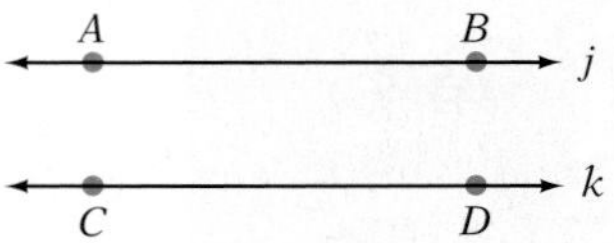

An **angle** is formed by two rays with the same endpoint. The **vertex** of the angle is the point at which the two rays meet. The rays are called the **sides** of the angle.

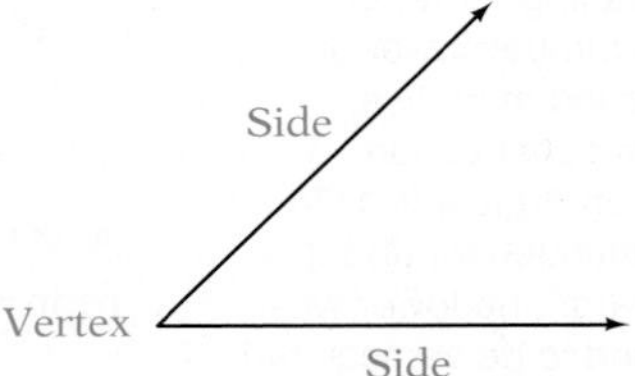

If A and C are points on rays r_1 and r_2, and B is the vertex, then the angle is called $\angle B$ or $\angle ABC$, where $\angle$ is the symbol for angle. Note that the angle is named by the vertex, or the vertex is the second point listed when the angle is named by giving three points. $\angle ABC$ could also be called $\angle CBA$.

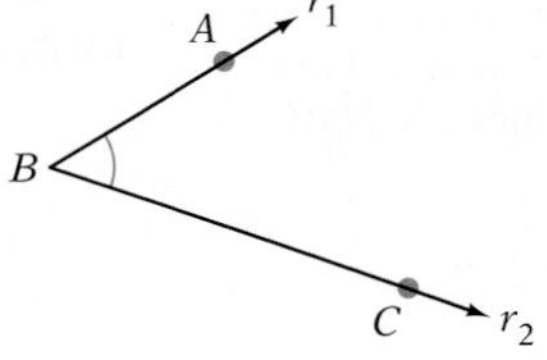

An angle can also be named by a variable written between the rays close to the vertex. In the figure at the right, $\angle x = \angle QRS$ and $\angle y = \angle SRT$. Note that in this figure, more than two rays meet at R. In this case, the vertex cannot be used to name an angle.

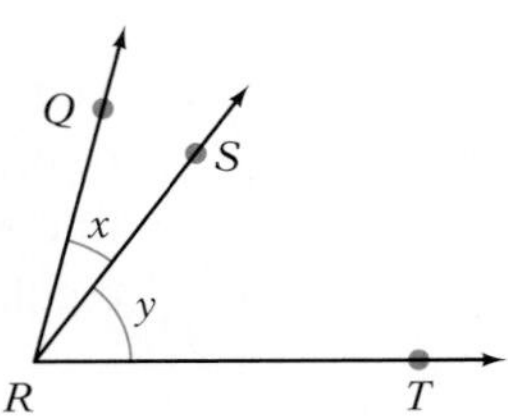

Point of Interest

The Babylonians knew that Earth is in approximately the same position in the sky every 365 days. Historians suggest that one complete revolution of a circle is called 360° because 360 is the closest number to 365 that is divisible by many natural numbers.

An angle is measured in **degrees.** The symbol for degrees is a small raised circle, °. The angle formed by a ray rotating through a circle has a measure of 360° (360 degrees), probably because early Babylonians believed that Earth revolves around the sun in approximately 360 days.

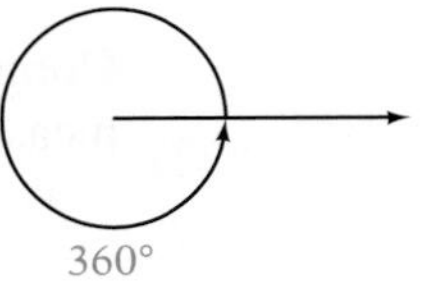

Point of Interest

The Leaning Tower of Pisa is the bell tower of the Cathedral in Pisa, Italy. Its construction began on August 9, 1173, and continued for about 200 years. The tower was designed to be vertical, but it started to lean during its construction. By 1350, it was 2.5° off from the vertical; by 1817, it was 5.1° off; and by 1990, it was 5.5° off. In 2001, work on the structure that returned its list to 5° was completed. (*Source: Time* magazine, June 25, 2001)

A **protractor** is used to measure an angle. Place the center of the protractor at the vertex of the angle with the edge of the protractor along a side of the angle. The angle shown in the figure below measures 58°.

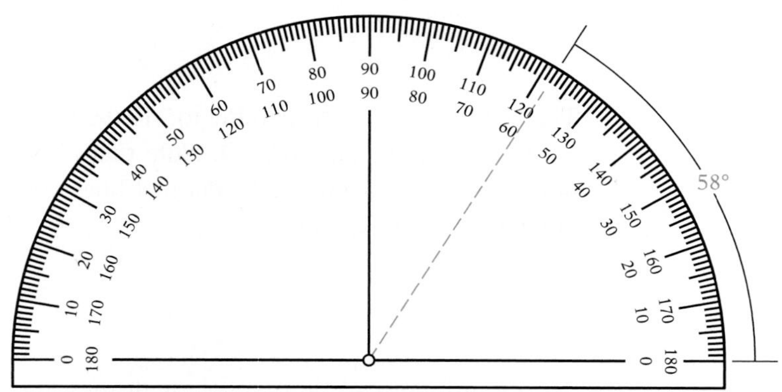

A 90° angle is called a **right angle.** The symbol ∟ represents a right angle.

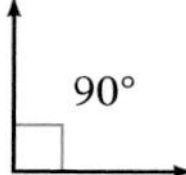

Perpendicular lines are intersecting lines that form right angles.

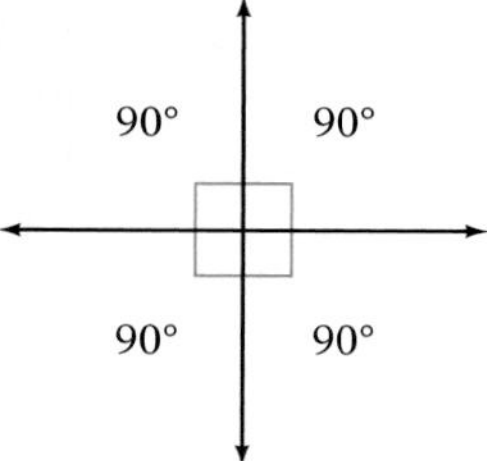

The symbol $\perp$ means "is perpendicular to." In the figure at the right, $p \perp q$ and $\overline{AB} \perp \overline{CD}$. Note that line p contains $\overline{AB}$ and line q contains $\overline{CD}$. Perpendicular lines contain perpendicular line segments.

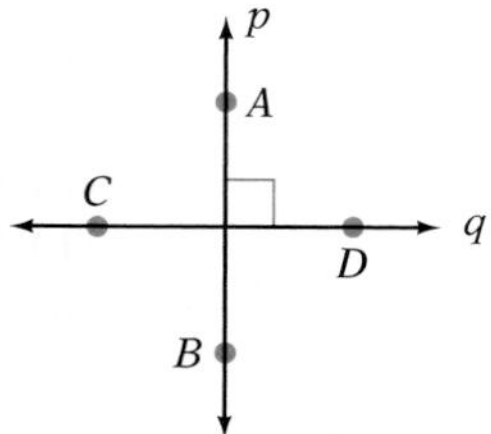

Complementary angles are two angles whose measures have the sum 90°.

$$\angle A + \angle B = 70^\circ + 20^\circ = 90^\circ$$

$\angle A$ and $\angle B$ are complementary angles.

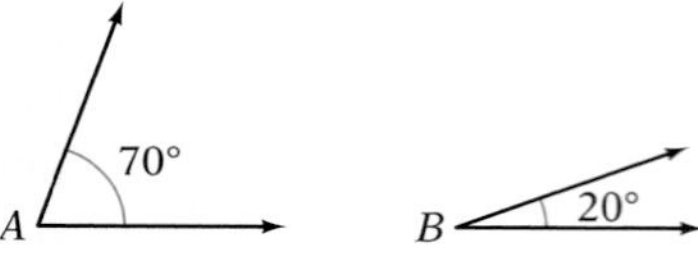

IN-CLASS EXAMPLES

1. Given $MN = 9$ cm, $OP = 10$ cm, and $MP = 25$ cm, find NO. **6 cm**

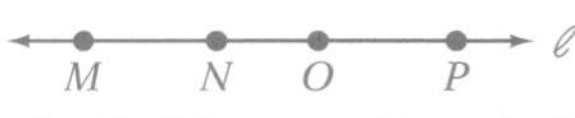

2. Find the complement of a 43° angle. **47°**
3. Find the supplement of a 57° angle. **123°**
4. Find the measure of $\angle a$. **59°**

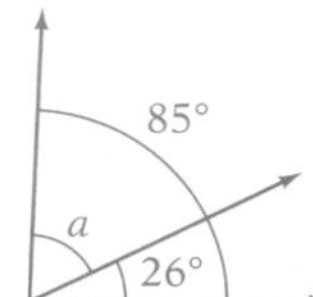

A 180° angle is called a **straight angle.**

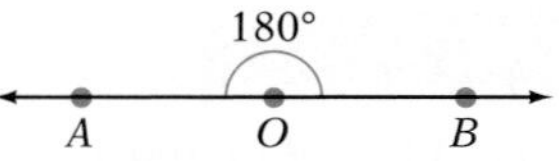

$\angle AOB$ is a straight angle.

Supplementary angles are two angles whose measures have the sum 180°.

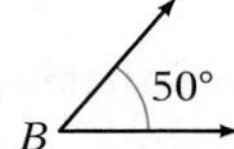

$$\angle A + \angle B = 130° + 50° = 180°$$

$\angle A$ and $\angle B$ are supplementary angles.

An **acute angle** is an angle whose measure is between 0° and 90°. $\angle B$ above is an acute angle. An **obtuse angle** is an angle whose measure is between 90° and 180°. $\angle A$ above is an obtuse angle.

Two angles that share a common side are **adjacent angles.** In the figure at the right, $\angle DAC$ and $\angle CAB$ are adjacent angles. $\angle DAC = 45°$ and $\angle CAB = 55°$.

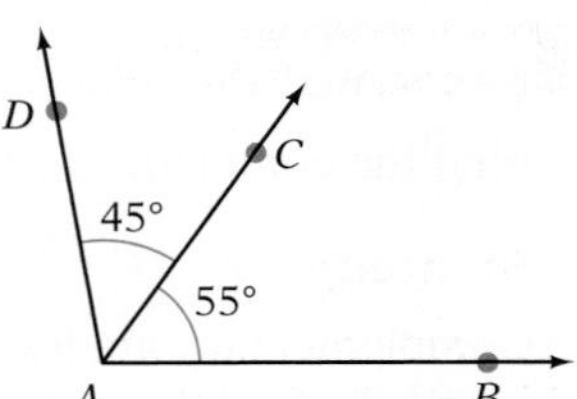

$$\angle DAB = \angle DAC + \angle CAB$$
$$= 45° + 55° = 100°$$

HOW TO 2 In the figure at the right, $\angle EDG = 80°$. $\angle FDG$ is three times the measure of $\angle EDF$. Find the measure of $\angle EDF$.

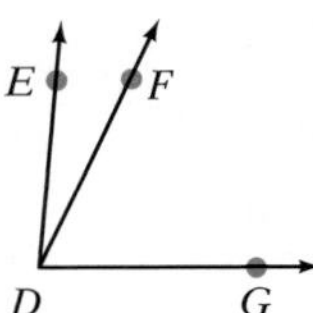

Let x = the measure of $\angle EDF$. Then $3x$ = the measure of $\angle FDG$. Write an equation and solve for x, the measure of $\angle EDF$.

$$\angle EDF + \angle FDG = \angle EDG$$
$$x + 3x = 80°$$
$$4x = 80°$$
$$x = 20°$$

$\angle EDF = 20°$

EXAMPLE 1

Given $MN = 15$ mm, $NO = 18$ mm, and $MP = 48$ mm, find OP.

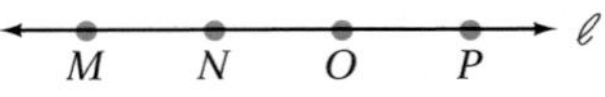

Solution

$$MN + NO + OP = MP$$
$$15 + 18 + OP = 48$$
$$33 + OP = 48$$
$$OP = 15$$

- $MN = 15$, $NO = 18$, $MP = 48$
- Add 15 and 18.
- Subtract 33 from each side.

$OP = 15$ mm

YOU TRY IT 1

Given $QR = 24$ cm, $ST = 17$ cm, and $QT = 62$ cm, find RS.

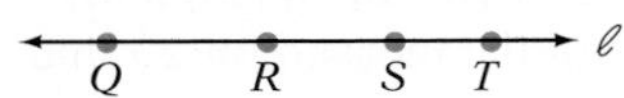

Your solution

21 cm

Solution on p. S18

EXAMPLE 2

Given $XY = 9$ m and YZ is twice XY, find XZ.

Solution

$XZ = XY + YZ$

$XZ = XY + 2(XY)$ • *YZ is twice XY.*

$XZ = 9 + 2(9)$ • $XY = 9$

$XZ = 9 + 18$

$XZ = 27$

$XZ = 27$ m

YOU TRY IT 2

Given $BC = 16$ ft and $AB = \frac{1}{4}(BC)$, find AC.

Your solution

20 ft

EXAMPLE 3

Find the complement of a 38° angle.

Strategy

Complementary angles are two angles whose sum is 90°. To find the complement, let x represent the complement of a 38° angle. Write an equation and solve for x.

Solution

$x + 38° = 90°$

$x = 52°$

The complement of a 38° angle is a 52° angle.

YOU TRY IT 3

Find the supplement of a 129° angle.

Your strategy

Your solution

51°

EXAMPLE 4

Find the measure of $\angle x$.

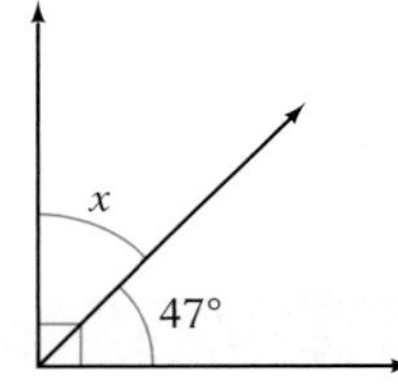

Strategy

To find the measure of $\angle x$, write an equation using the fact that the sum of the measure of $\angle x$ and 47° is 90°. Solve for $\angle x$.

Solution

$\angle x + 47° = 90°$

$\angle x = 43°$

The measure of $\angle x$ is 43°.

YOU TRY IT 4

Find the measure of $\angle a$.

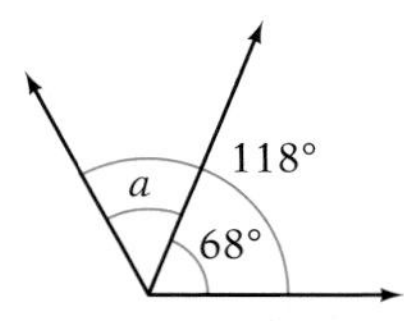

Your strategy

Your solution

50°

Solutions on p. S18

OBJECTIVE B *To solve problems involving angles formed by intersecting lines*

Point of Interest

Many cities in the New World, unlike those in Europe, were designed using rectangular street grids. Washington, D.C., was planned that way except that diagonal avenues were added, primarily for the purpose of enabling quick troop movement in the event that the city required defense. As an added precaution, monuments were constructed at major intersections so that attackers would not have a straight shot down a boulevard.

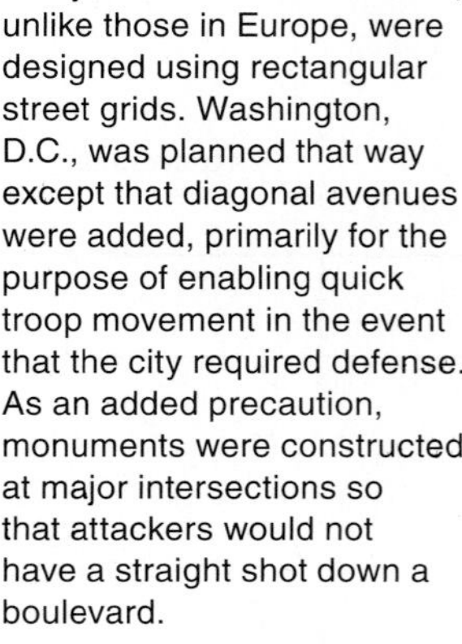

Four angles are formed by the intersection of two lines. If the two lines are perpendicular, each of the four angles is a right angle. If the two lines are not perpendicular, then two of the angles formed are acute angles and two of the angles are obtuse angles. The two acute angles are always opposite each other, and the two obtuse angles are always opposite each other.

In the figure at the right, $\angle w$ and $\angle y$ are acute angles. $\angle x$ and $\angle z$ are obtuse angles.

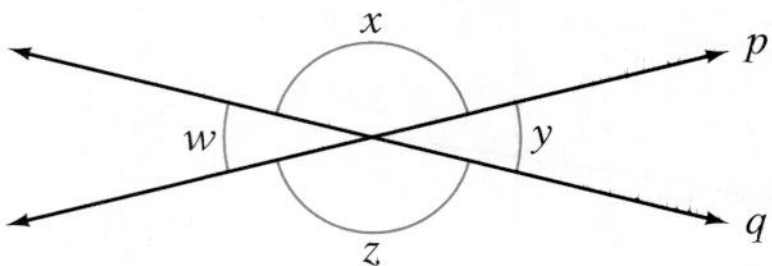

Two angles that are on opposite sides of the intersection of two lines are called **vertical angles.** Vertical angles have the same measure. $\angle w$ and $\angle y$ are vertical angles. $\angle x$ and $\angle z$ are vertical angles.

Vertical angles have the same measure.

$$\angle w = \angle y$$
$$\angle x = \angle z$$

Recall that two angles that share a common side are called **adjacent angles.** For the figure shown above, $\angle x$ and $\angle y$ are adjacent angles, as are $\angle y$ and $\angle z$, $\angle z$ and $\angle w$, and $\angle w$ and $\angle x$. Adjacent angles of intersecting lines are supplementary angles.

Adjacent angles of intersecting lines are supplementary angles.

$$\angle x + \angle y = 180^\circ$$
$$\angle y + \angle z = 180^\circ$$
$$\angle z + \angle w = 180^\circ$$
$$\angle w + \angle x = 180^\circ$$

HOW TO 3 Given that $\angle c = 65^\circ$, find the measures of angles a, b, and d.

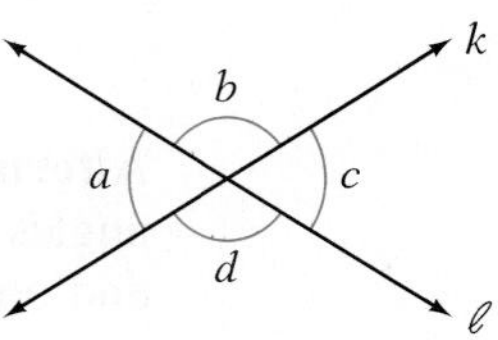

$\angle a = \angle c$ because $\angle a$ and $\angle c$ are vertical angles.

$$\angle a = 65^\circ$$

$\angle b$ is supplementary to $\angle c$ because $\angle b$ and $\angle c$ are adjacent angles of intersecting lines.

$$\angle b + \angle c = 180^\circ$$
$$\angle b + 65^\circ = 180^\circ$$
$$\angle b = 115^\circ$$

$\angle d = \angle b$ because $\angle d$ and $\angle b$ are vertical angles.

$$\angle d = 115^\circ$$

IN-CLASS EXAMPLES

5. Find x. **14°**

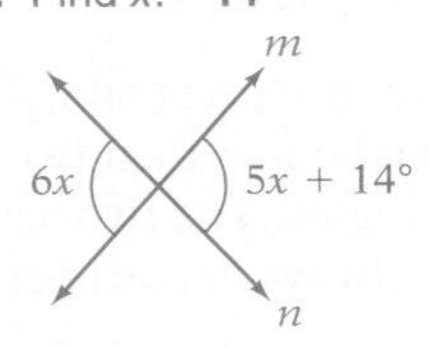

6. Given that $\ell_1 \parallel \ell_2$, find x. **20°**

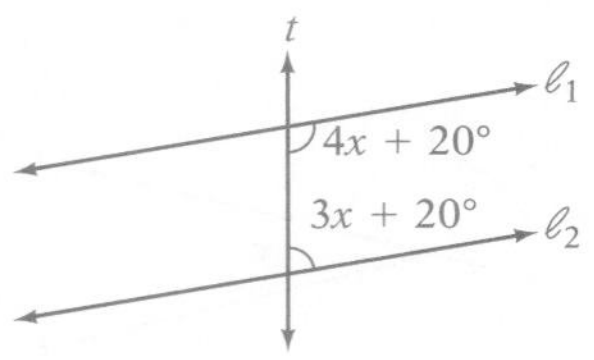

A line that intersects two other lines at different points is called a **transversal.**

If the lines cut by a transversal t are parallel lines and the transversal is perpendicular to the parallel lines, all eight angles formed are right angles.

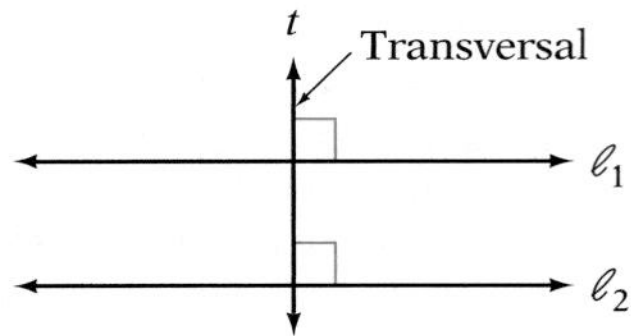

If the lines cut by a transversal t are parallel lines and the transversal is not perpendicular to the parallel lines, all four acute angles have the same measure and all four obtuse angles have the same measure. For the figure at the right,

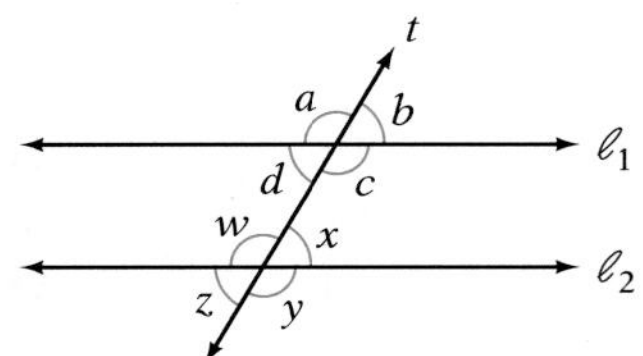

$$\angle b = \angle d = \angle x = \angle z$$
$$\angle a = \angle c = \angle w = \angle y$$

Alternate interior angles are two nonadjacent angles that are on opposite sides of the transversal and between the parallel lines. In the figure above, $\angle c$ and $\angle w$ are alternate interior angles; $\angle d$ and $\angle x$ are alternate interior angles. Alternate interior angles have the same measure.

Alternate interior angles have the same measure.

$$\angle c = \angle w$$
$$\angle d = \angle x$$

Alternate exterior angles are two nonadjacent angles that are on opposite sides of the transversal and outside the parallel lines. In the figure above, $\angle a$ and $\angle y$ are alternate exterior angles; $\angle b$ and $\angle z$ are alternate exterior angles. Alternate exterior angles have the same measure.

Alternate exterior angles have the same measure.

$$\angle a = \angle y$$
$$\angle b = \angle z$$

Corresponding angles are two angles that are on the same side of the transversal and are both acute angles or are both obtuse angles. For the figure above, the following pairs of angles are corresponding angles: $\angle a$ and $\angle w$, $\angle d$ and $\angle z$, $\angle b$ and $\angle x$, $\angle c$ and $\angle y$. Corresponding angles have the same measure.

Corresponding angles have the same measure.

$$\angle a = \angle w$$
$$\angle d = \angle z$$
$$\angle b = \angle x$$
$$\angle c = \angle y$$

HOW TO 4 Given that $\ell_1 \parallel \ell_2$ and $\angle c = 58°$, find the measures of $\angle f$, $\angle h$, and $\angle g$.

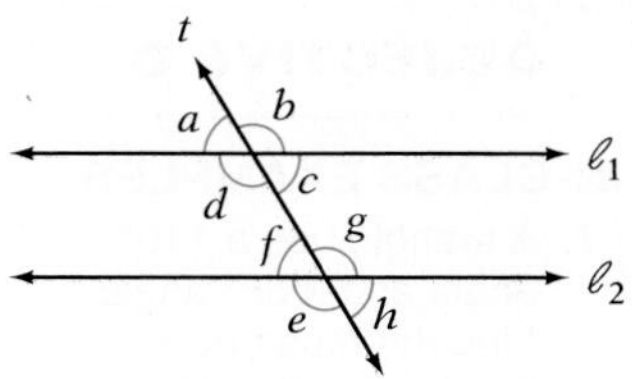

$\angle c$ and $\angle f$ are alternate interior angles. $\angle f = \angle c = 58°$

$\angle c$ and $\angle h$ are corresponding angles. $\angle h = \angle c = 58°$

$\angle g$ is supplementary to $\angle h$.

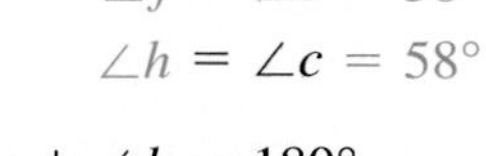

$$\angle g + \angle h = 180°$$
$$\angle g + 58° = 180°$$
$$\angle g = 122°$$

EXAMPLE 5

Find x.

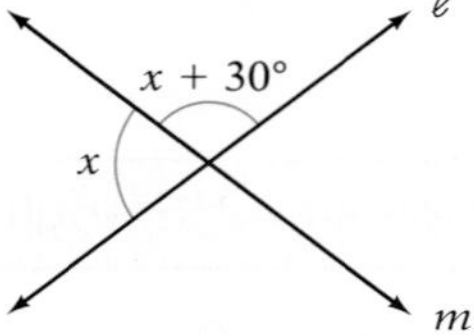

Strategy

The angles labeled are adjacent angles of intersecting lines and are therefore supplementary angles. To find x, write an equation and solve for x.

Solution

$$x + (x + 30°) = 180°$$
$$2x + 30° = 180°$$
$$2x = 150°$$
$$x = 75°$$

• The sum of the measures of the two angles is 180°.

YOU TRY IT 5

Find x.

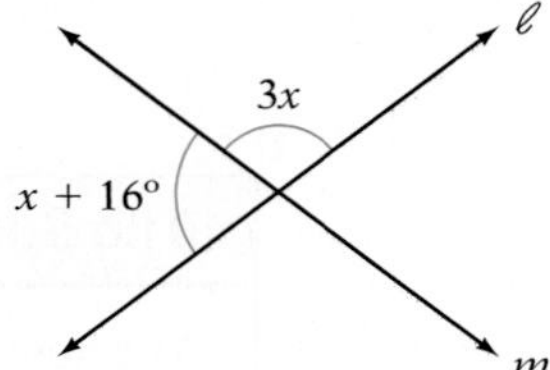

Your strategy

Your solution

41°

EXAMPLE 6

Given $\ell_1 \parallel \ell_2$, find x.

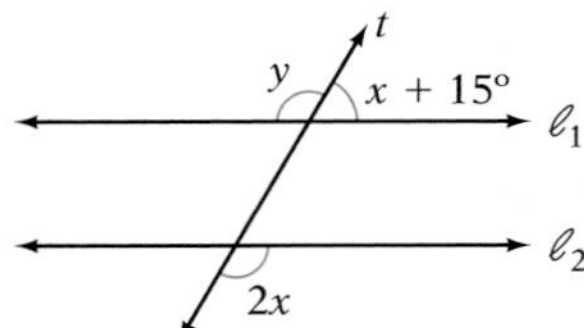

Strategy

$2x = y$ because alternate exterior angles have the same measure. $(x + 15°) + y = 180°$ because adjacent angles of intersecting lines are supplementary angles. Substitute $2x$ for y and solve for x.

Solution

$$(x + 15°) + 2x = 180°$$
$$3x + 15° = 180°$$
$$3x = 165°$$
$$x = 55°$$

• The sum of the measures of the two angles is 180°.

YOU TRY IT 6

Given $\ell_1 \parallel \ell_2$, find x.

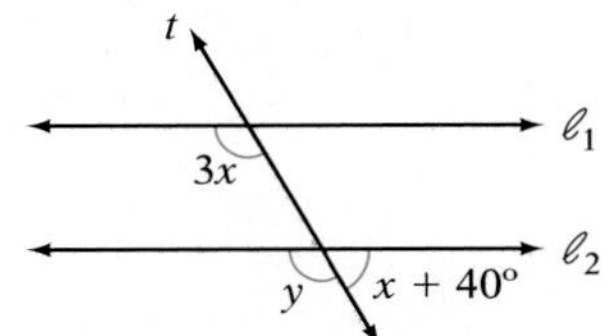

Your strategy

Your solution

35°

Solutions on pp. S18–S19

OBJECTIVE C *To solve problems involving the angles of a triangle*

IN-CLASS EXAMPLES

7. A triangle has a 110° angle and a 35° angle. Find the measure of the third angle of the triangle. **35°**

If the lines cut by a transversal are not parallel lines, the three lines will intersect at three points. In the figure at the right, the transversal t intersects lines p and q. The three lines intersect at points A, B, and C. These three points define three line segments, $\overline{AB}$, $\overline{BC}$, and $\overline{AC}$. The plane figure formed by these three line segments is called a **triangle.**

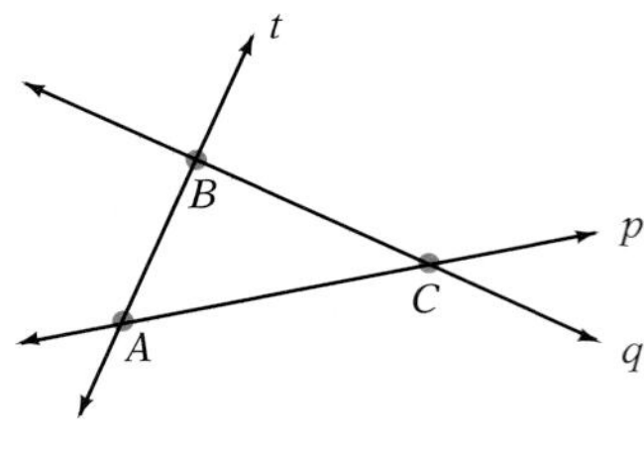

Each of the three points of intersection is the vertex of four angles. The angles within the region enclosed by the triangle are called **interior angles.** In the figure at the right, angles a, b, and c are interior angles. The sum of the measures of the interior angles of a triangle is 180°.

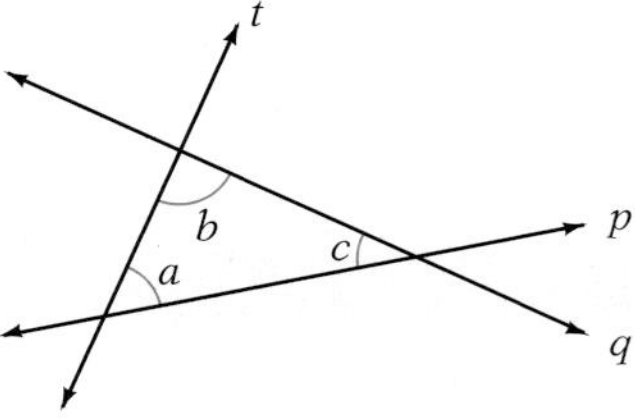

$\angle a + \angle b + \angle c = 180°$

The Sum of the Measures of the Interior Angles of a Triangle

The sum of the measures of the interior angles of a triangle is 180°.

EXAMPLE

The measures of two angles of a triangle are 40° and 60°. The measure of the third angle is:

$$\begin{aligned} 40° + 60° + x &= 180° \\ 100° + x &= 180° \\ x &= 80° \end{aligned}$$

An angle adjacent to an interior angle is an **exterior angle.** In the figure at the right, angles m and n are exterior angles for angle a. The sum of the measures of an interior and an exterior angle is 180°.

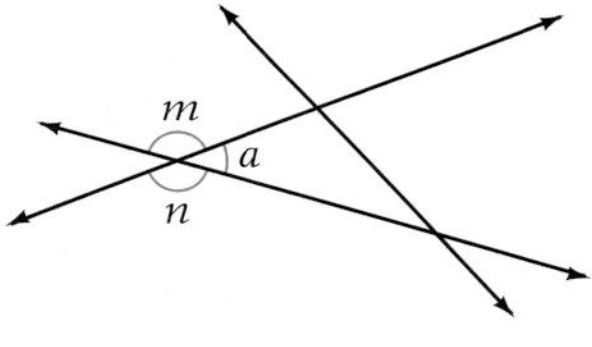

$\angle a + \angle m = 180°$
$\angle a + \angle n = 180°$

HOW TO 5 Given that $\angle c = 40°$ and $\angle d = 100°$, find the measure of $\angle e$.

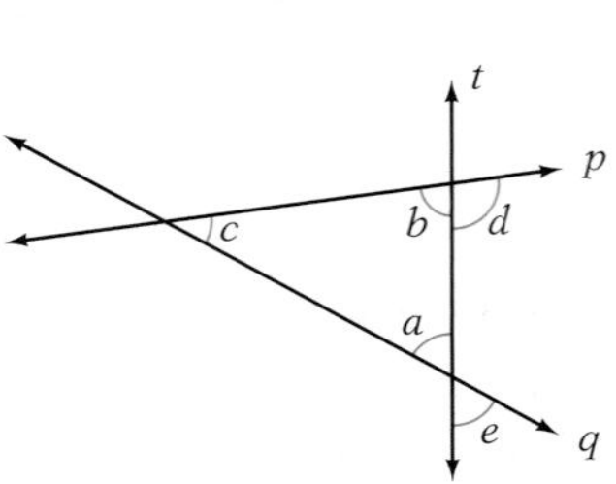

$\angle d$ and $\angle b$ are supplementary angles.

$$\begin{aligned} \angle d + \angle b &= 180° \\ 100° + \angle b &= 180° \\ \angle b &= 80° \end{aligned}$$

The sum of the interior angles is 180°.

$$\begin{aligned} \angle c + \angle b + \angle a &= 180° \\ 40° + 80° + \angle a &= 180° \\ 120° + \angle a &= 180° \\ \angle a &= 60° \end{aligned}$$

$\angle a$ and $\angle e$ are vertical angles.

$\angle e = \angle a = 60°$

EXAMPLE 7

Given that $\angle y = 55°$, find the measures of angles a, b, and d.

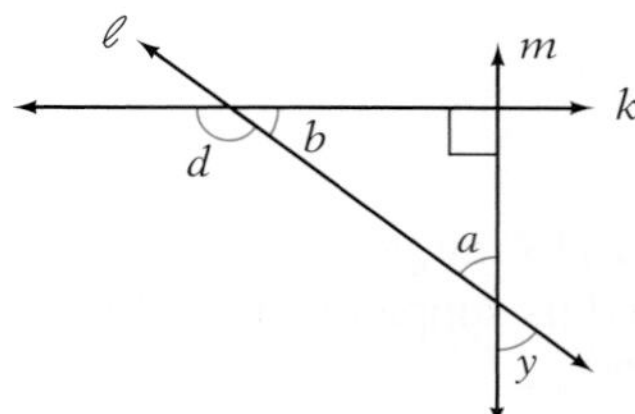

Strategy

- To find the measure of angle a, use the fact that $\angle a$ and $\angle y$ are vertical angles.
- To find the measure of angle b, use the fact that the sum of the measures of the interior angles of a triangle is 180°.
- To find the measure of angle d, use the fact that the sum of an interior and an exterior angle is 180°.

Solution

$\angle a = \angle y = 55°$ • **$\angle a$ and $\angle y$ are vertical angles.**

$$\angle a + \angle b + 90° = 180°$$
$$55° + \angle b + 90° = 180°$$
$$\angle b + 145° = 180°$$
$$\angle b = 35°$$

• **The sum of the measures of the interior angles of a triangle is 180°.**

$$\angle d + \angle b = 180°$$
$$\angle d + 35° = 180°$$
$$\angle d = 145°$$

• **The sum of an interior and an exterior angle is 180°.**

YOU TRY IT 7

Given that $\angle a = 45°$ and $\angle x = 100°$, find the measures of angles b, c, and y.

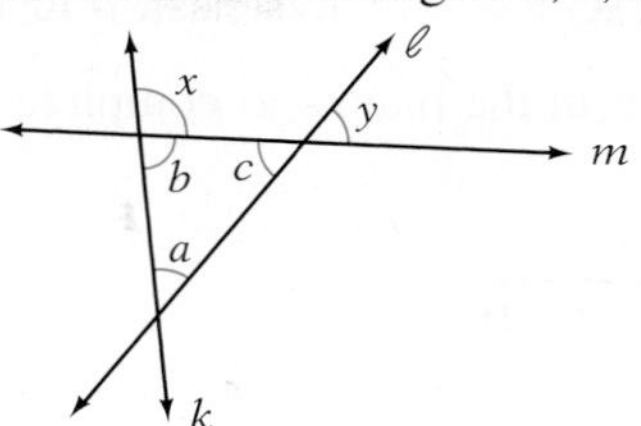

Your strategy

Your solution

$\angle b = 80°$, $\angle c = 55°$, $\angle y = 55°$

EXAMPLE 8

Two angles of a triangle measure 53° and 78°. Find the measure of the third angle.

Strategy

To find the measure of the third angle, use the fact that the sum of the measures of the interior angles of a triangle is 180°. Write an equation using x to represent the measure of the third angle. Solve the equation for x.

Solution

$$x + 53° + 78° = 180°$$
$$x + 131° = 180°$$
$$x = 49°$$

The measure of the third angle is 49°.

YOU TRY IT 8

One angle in a triangle is a right angle, and one angle measures 34°. Find the measure of the third angle.

Your strategy

Your solution

56°

Solutions on p. S19

7.1 EXERCISES

SUGGESTED ASSIGNMENT
Exercises 1–10; Exercises 11–71, odds

Concept Check

For Exercises 1 to 4, fill in the blanks to complete an equation that can be used to find the value of x.

1. 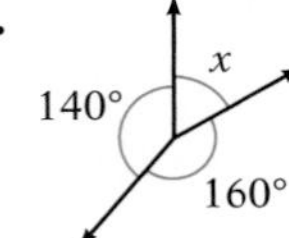

5 cm, x cm, 4 cm; A, B, C, D

$AD = 12$ cm

AD is the sum of AB, BC, and CD, so
12 = 5 + x + 4.

2. x is the supplement of a 113° angle.
The sum of an angle and its supplement is 180°, so x + 113° = 180°.

3.

140°, x, 160°

The adjacent angles form a circle, so
x + 160° + 140° = 360°.

4. 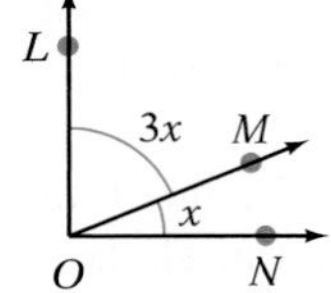

$\angle LON$ is a right angle, so x + 3x = 90°.

For Exercises 5 to 8, use the diagram at the right, in which $\ell_1 \parallel \ell_2$. Fill in the blanks to complete an equation that models the given statement.

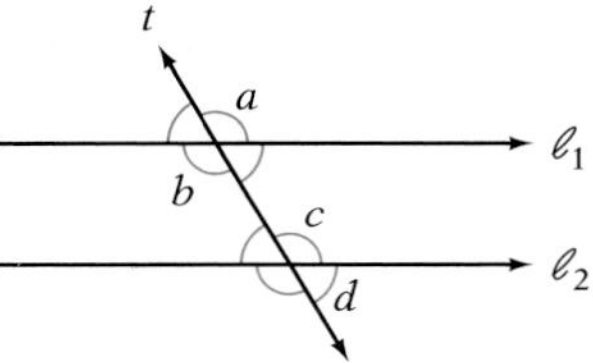

5. Vertical angles have the same measure. ∠ a = ∠ b

6. Alternate interior angles have the same measure. ∠ b = ∠ c

7. Adjacent angles of intersecting lines are supplementary angles. ∠ c + ∠ d = 180°

8. Corresponding angles have the same measure. ∠ a = ∠ c

For Exercises 9 and 10, use the diagram at the right.

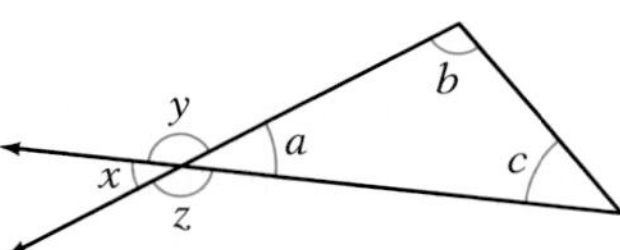

9. a. The angles that are interior angles are ∠a, ∠b, and ∠c.

b. The angles that are exterior angles are ∠y and ∠z.

c. The angle that is neither an interior nor an exterior angle of the triangle is ∠x.

10. Complete the equations.

a. $\angle a$ + ∠b + ∠c = 180°

b. $\angle a$ + ∠y = 180° and $\angle a$ + ∠z = 180°

OBJECTIVE A *To solve problems involving lines and angles*

For Exercises 11 to 16, use a protractor to measure the angle. State whether the angle is acute, obtuse, or right.

11. 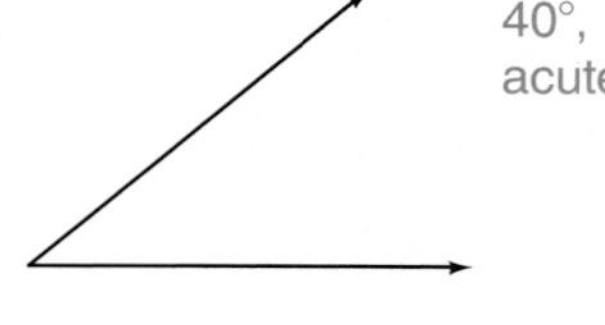 40°, acute

12. 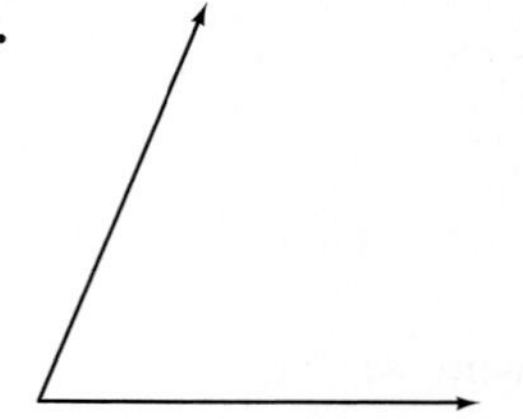 68°, acute

13. 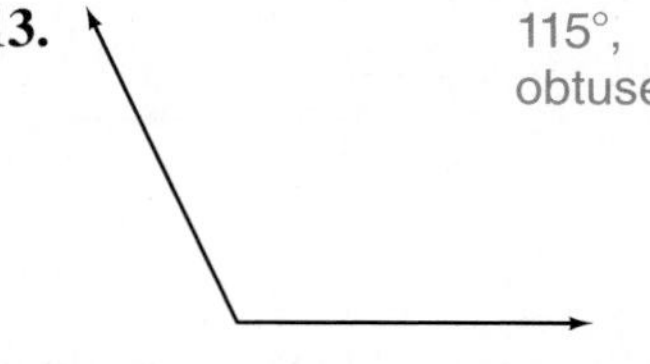 115°, obtuse

14. 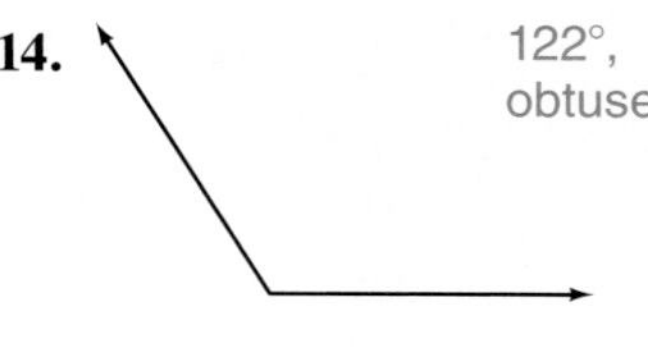 122°, obtuse

15. 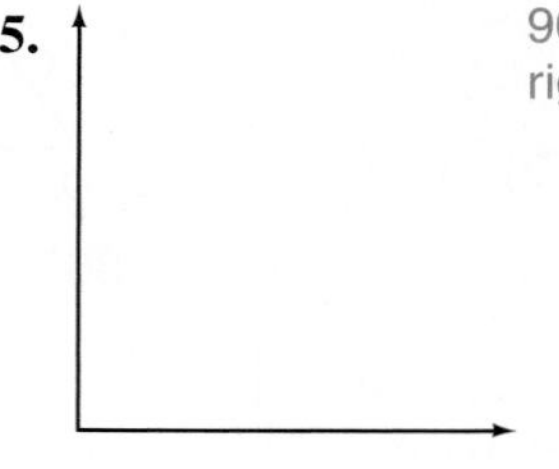 90°, right

16. 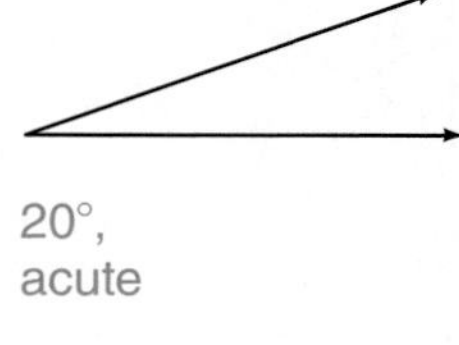 20°, acute

17. Find the complement of a 62° angle. 28°

18. Find the complement of a 31° angle. 59°

19. Find the supplement of a 162° angle. 18°

20. Find the supplement of a 72° angle. 108°

21. Given $AB = 12$ cm, $CD = 9$ cm, and $AD = 35$ cm, find the length of BC.
14 cm

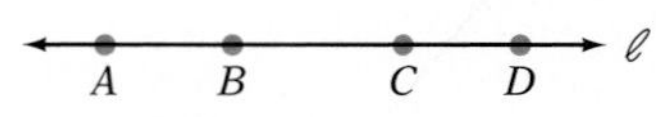

22. Given $AB = 21$ mm, $BC = 14$ mm, and $AD = 54$ mm, find the length of CD.
19 mm

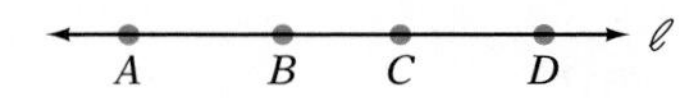

23. Given $QR = 7$ ft and RS is three times the length of QR, find the length of QS.
28 ft

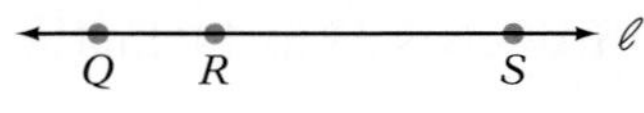

24. Given $QR = 15$ in. and RS is twice the length of QR, find the length of QS.
45 in.

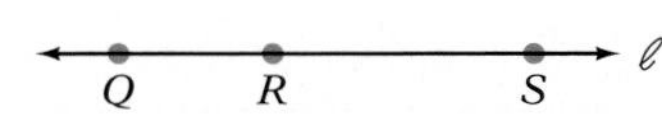

25. Given $EF = 20$ m and FG is $\frac{1}{2}$ the length of EF, find the length of EG.
30 m

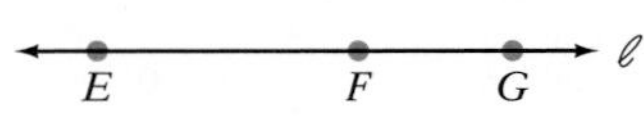

26. Given $EF = 18$ cm and FG is $\frac{1}{3}$ the length of EF, find the length of EG.
24 cm

27. Given $\angle LOM = 53°$ and $\angle LON = 139°$, find the measure of $\angle MON$.

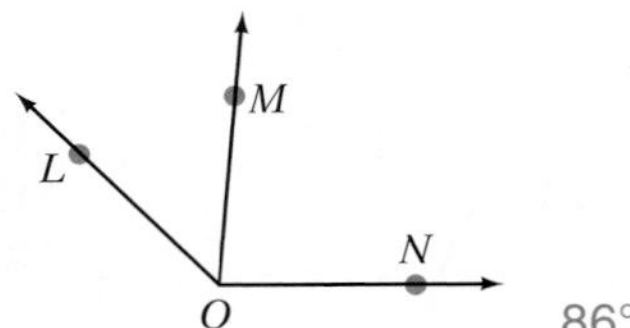

86°

28. Given $\angle MON = 38°$ and $\angle LON = 85°$, find the measure of $\angle LOM$.

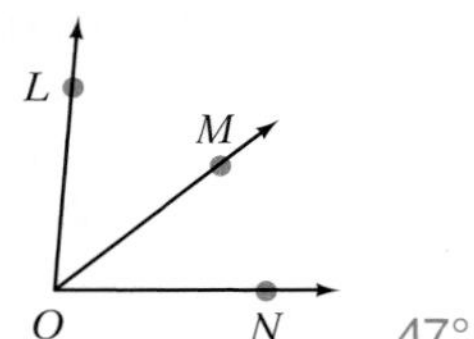

47°

Given that $\angle LON$ is a right angle, find the measure of $\angle x$.

29.

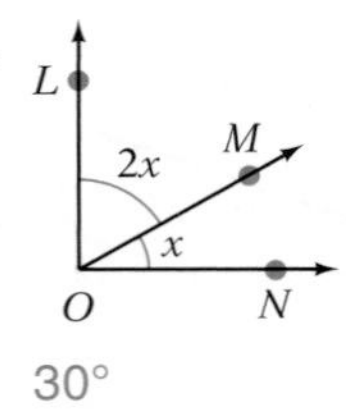

30°

30.

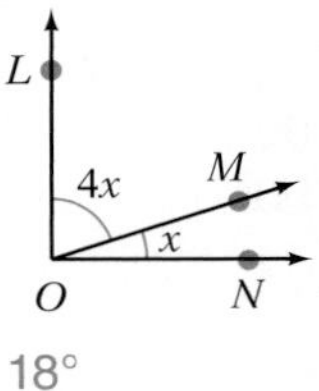

18°

31.

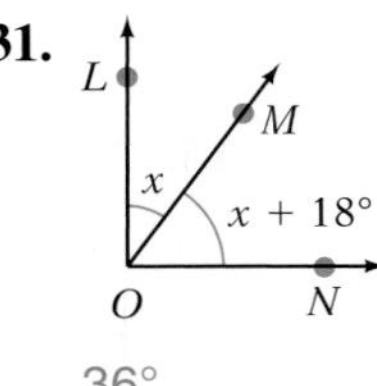

36°

32.

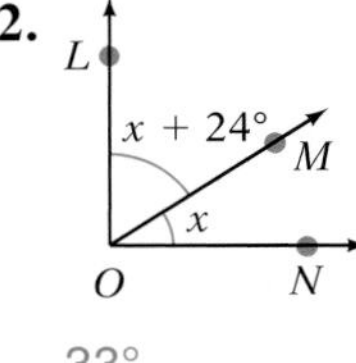

33°

Find the measure of $\angle a$.

33.

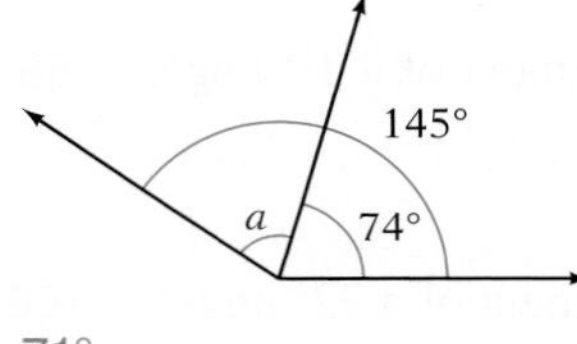

71°

34.

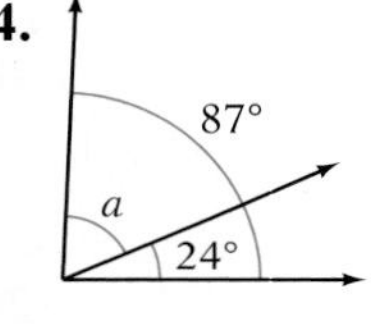

63°

35.

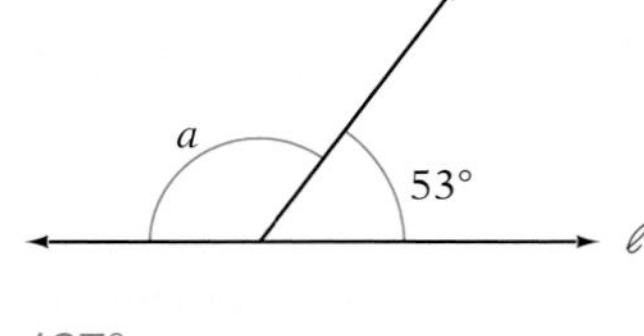

127°

36.

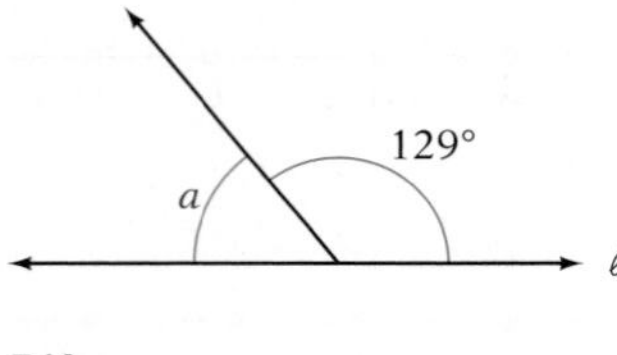

51°

37.

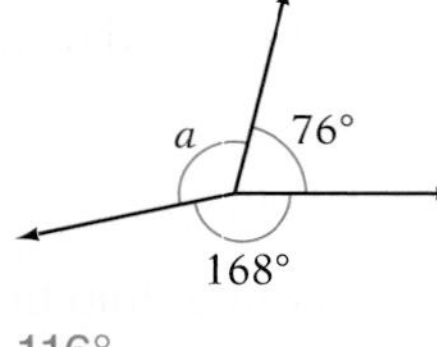

116°

38.

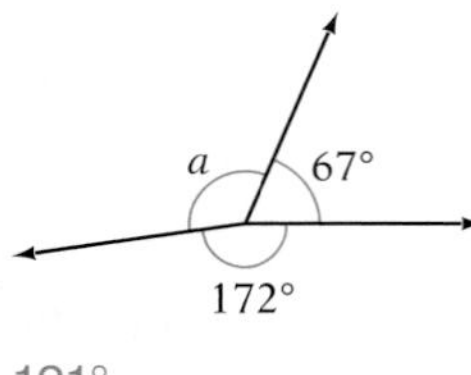

121°

For Exercises 39 to 44, find x.

39.

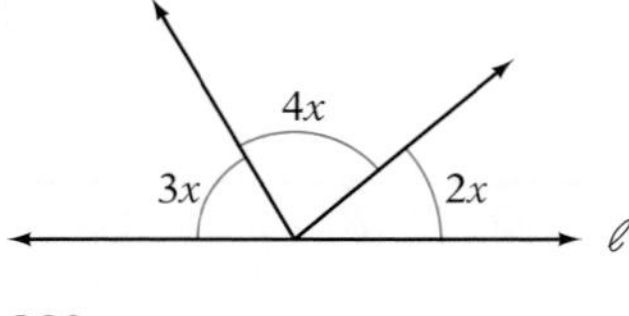

20°

40.

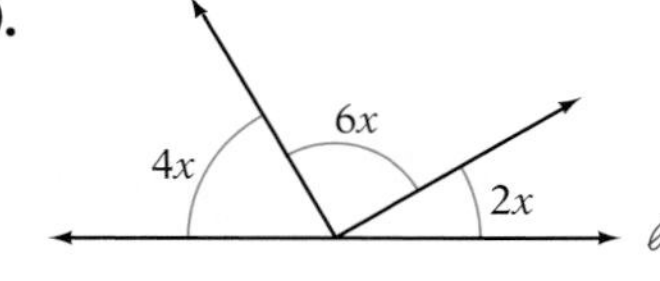

15°

41.

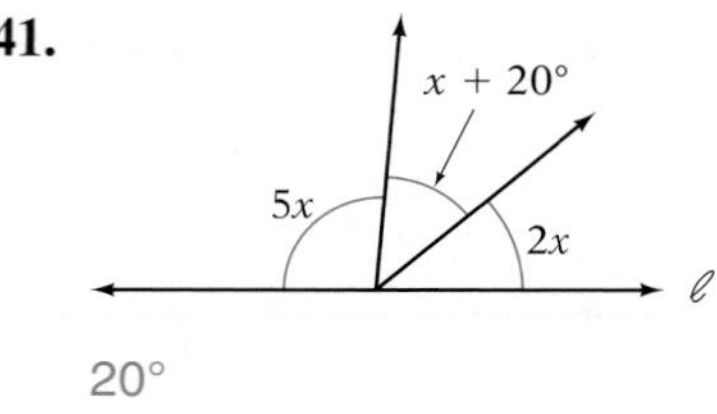

20°

42.

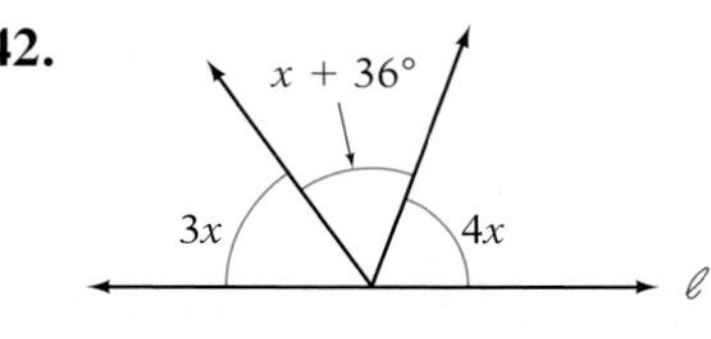

18°

43.

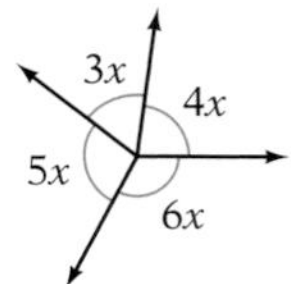

20°

44.

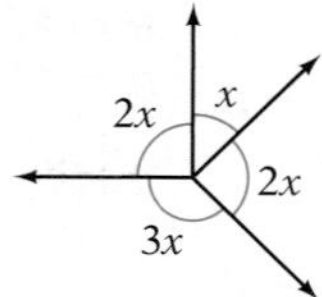

45°

45. Given that $\angle a = 51°$, find the measure of $\angle b$.

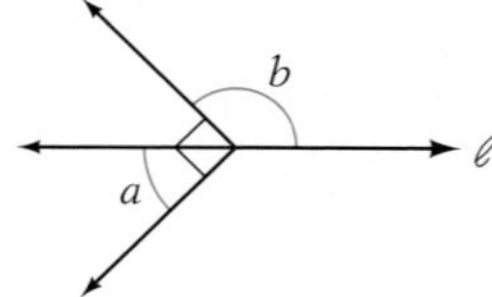

141°

46. Given that $\angle a = 38°$, find the measure of $\angle b$.

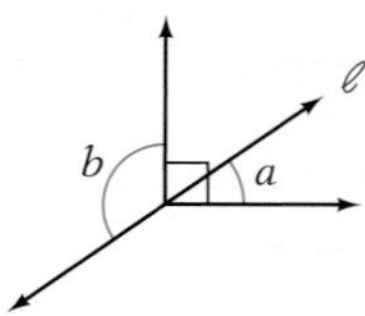

128°

47. Given that $\overline{AO} \perp \overline{OB}$, express in terms of x the number of degrees in $\angle BOC$.

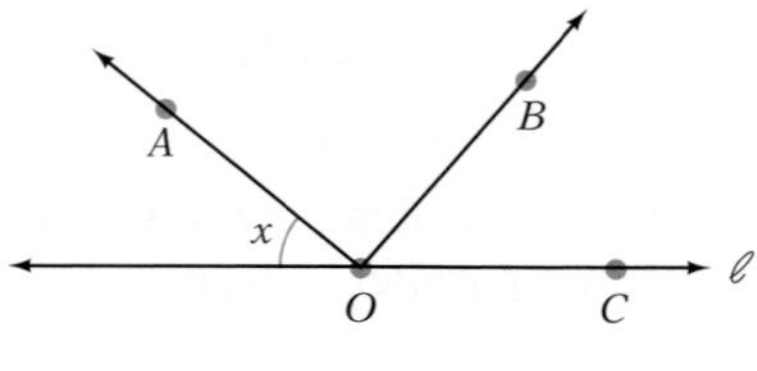

$90° - x$

48. Given that $\overline{AO} \perp \overline{OB}$, express in terms of x the number of degrees in $\angle AOC$.

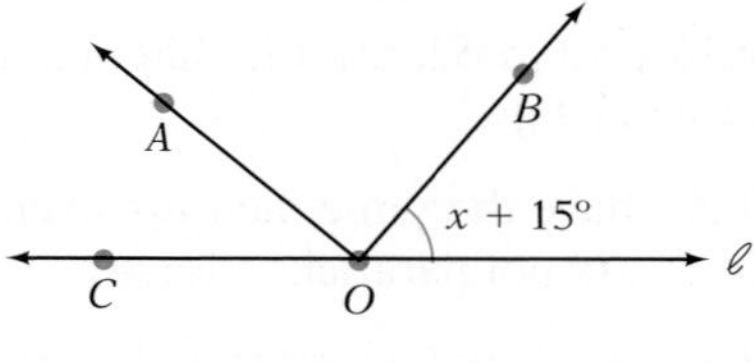

$75° - x$

OBJECTIVE B *To solve problems involving angles formed by intersecting lines*

Find the measure of $\angle x$.

49.

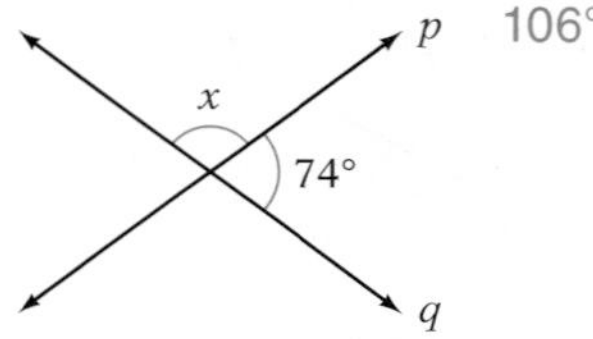

106°

50.

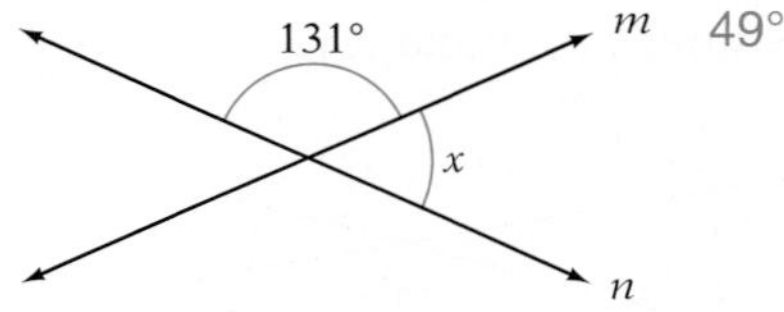

49°

Find x.

51.

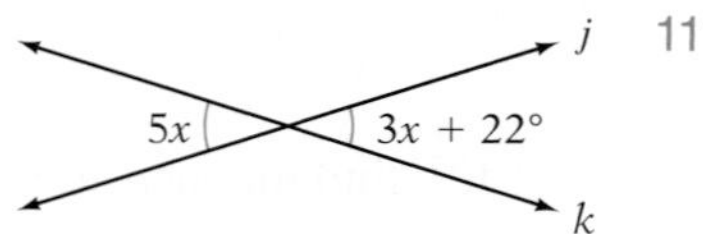

11°

52. 7x 4x + 36° m n

12°

Given that $\ell_1 \parallel \ell_2$, find the measures of angles a and b.

53.

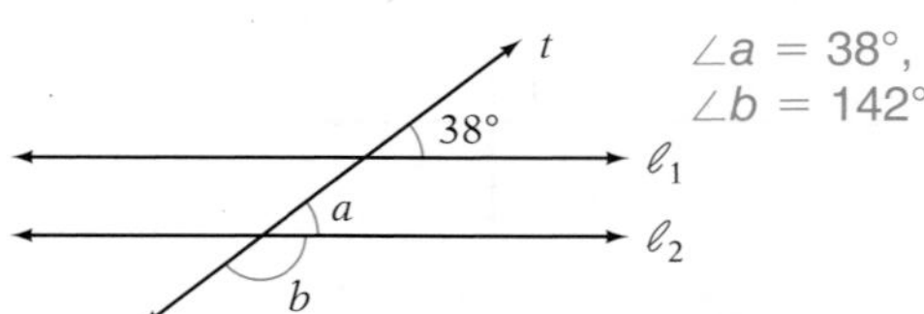

$\angle a = 38°$, $\angle b = 142°$

54.

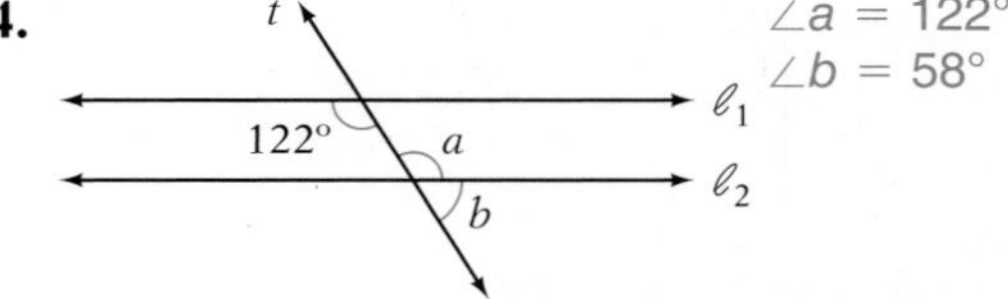

$\angle a = 122°$, $\angle b = 58°$

55. 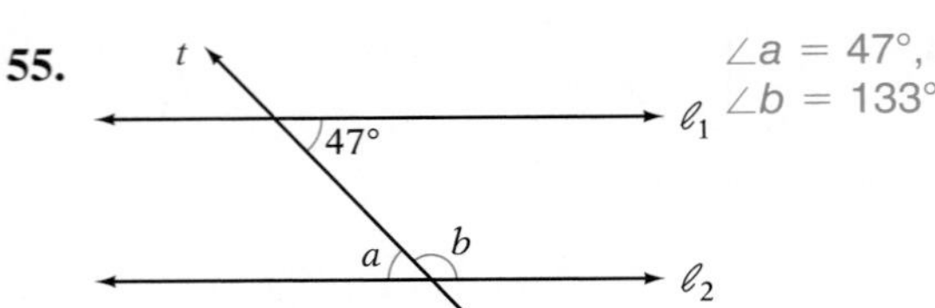

$\angle a = 47°$, $\angle b = 133°$

56. $\angle a = 44°$, $\angle b = 136°$

Given that $\ell_1 \parallel \ell_2$, find x.

57. 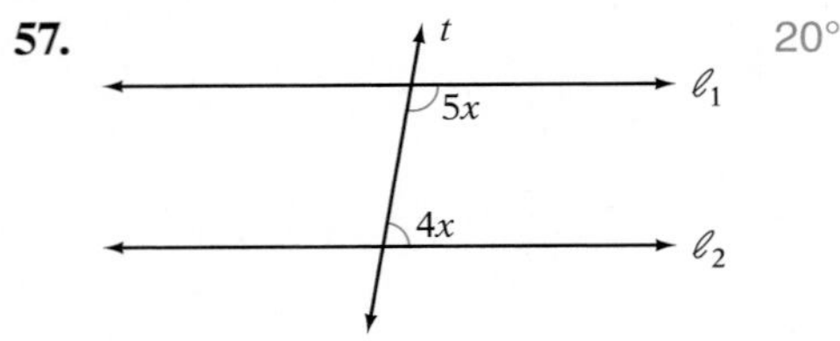

20°

58. 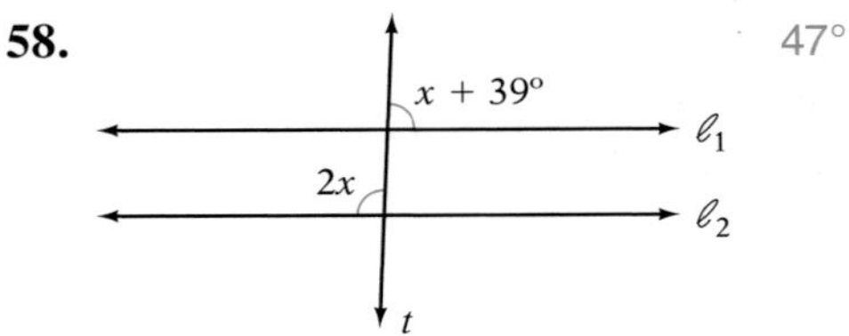

47°

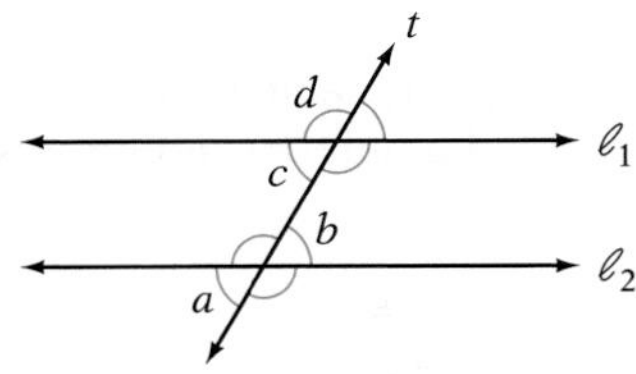

For Exercises 59 to 62, use the diagram at the right. Determine whether the statement is true or false.

59. $\angle b$ and $\angle c$ have the same measure even if ℓ_1 and ℓ_2 are not parallel. False

60. $\angle a$ and $\angle b$ have the same measure even if ℓ_1 and ℓ_2 are not parallel. True

61. $\angle a$ and $\angle d$ are supplementary if ℓ_1 and ℓ_2 are parallel. True

62. $\angle c$ and $\angle d$ are supplementary only if ℓ_1 and ℓ_2 are parallel. False

OBJECTIVE C *To solve problems involving the angles of a triangle*

63. Given that $\angle a = 95°$ and $\angle b = 70°$, find the measures of $\angle x$ and $\angle y$.

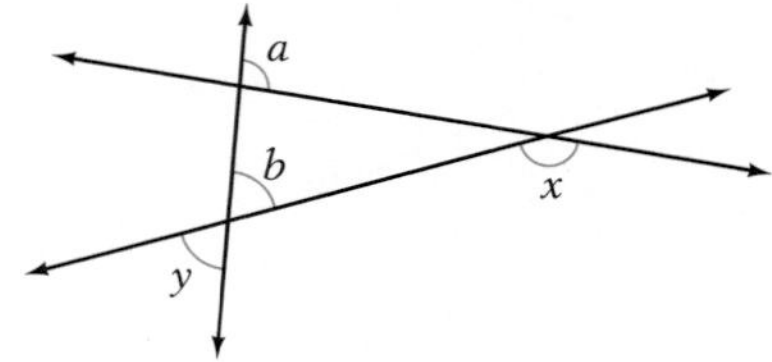

$\angle x = 155°$; $\angle y = 70°$

64. Given that $\angle a = 35°$ and $\angle b = 55°$, find the measures of $\angle x$ and $\angle y$.

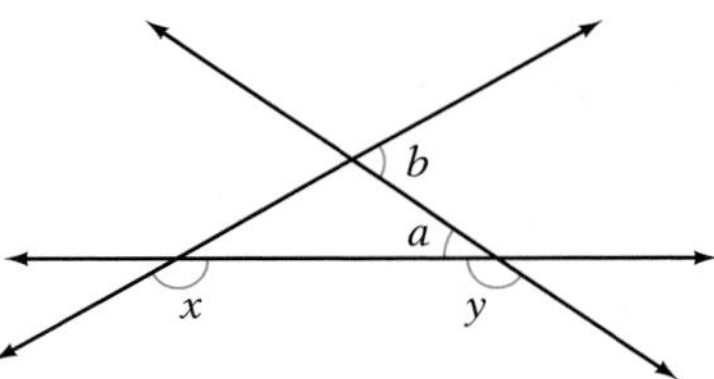

$\angle x = 160°$; $\angle y = 145°$

65. Given that $\angle y = 45°$, find the measures of $\angle a$ and $\angle b$.

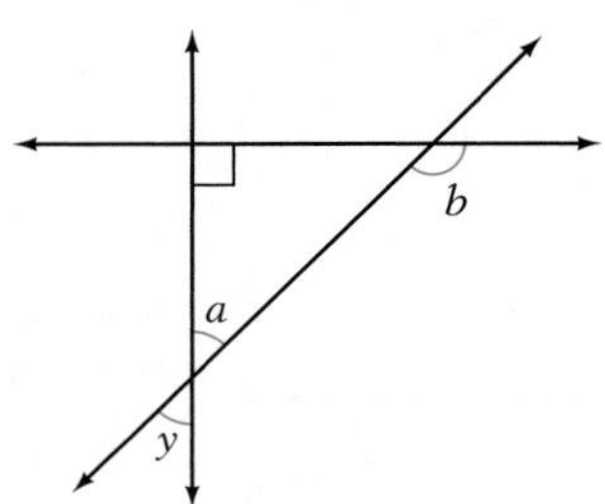

$\angle a = 45°$; $\angle b = 135°$

66. Given that $\angle y = 130°$, find the measures of $\angle a$ and $\angle b$.

$\angle a = 40°$; $\angle b = 140°$

67. One angle in a triangle is a right angle, and one angle is equal to 30°. What is the measure of the third angle? 60°

68. A triangle has a 45° angle and a right angle. Find the measure of the third angle. 45°

69. Two angles of a triangle measure 42° and 103°. Find the measure of the third angle. 35°

70. A triangle has a 13° angle and a 65° angle. What is the measure of the third angle? 102°

71. True or false? If one interior angle of a triangle is a right angle, then the other two interior angles of the triangle are complementary angles. True

72. True or false? If a triangle has an exterior angle that is a right angle, then the triangle also has an interior angle that is a right angle. True

QUICK QUIZ

1. Given $QR = 13$ mm, $RS = 11$ mm, and $QT = 32$ mm, find ST. **8 mm [7.1A]**

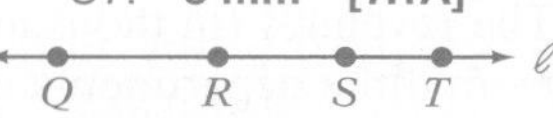

2. Find the complement of a 54° angle. **36° [7.1A]**
3. Given that $\angle a = 118°$, find $\angle b$. **62° [7.1B]**

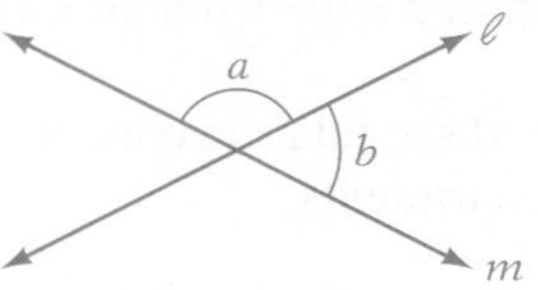

4. Given $\ell_1 \parallel \ell_2$ and $\angle c = 67°$, find $\angle a$ and $\angle b$. **$\angle a = 67°$, $\angle b = 113°$ [7.1B]**

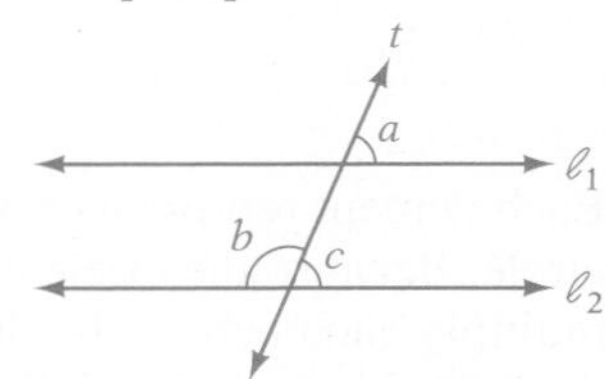

5. A triangle has a 21° angle and a 64° angle. Find the measure of the third angle of the triangle. **95° [7.1C]**

Critical Thinking

73. On a number line, the points A, B, C, and D have coordinates −2.5, 2, 5, and 3.5, respectively. Which of these points is halfway between two others? D, or 3.5

74. Find the measure of the smaller angle between the hands of a clock when the time is 5 o'clock. 150°

75. The measures of the angles of a triangle are in the ratio 2 : 3 : 7. Find the number of degrees in the largest angle. 105°

Projects or Group Activities

76. For the figure at the right, find the sum of the measures of angles x, y, and z. 360°

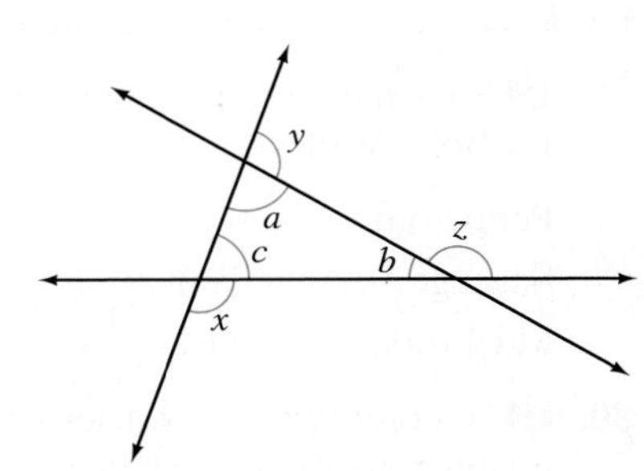

77. For the figure at the right, explain why $\angle a + \angle b = \angle x$. Write a rule that describes the relationship between an exterior angle of a triangle and the opposite interior angles. Use the rule to write an equation involving angles a, c, and z.

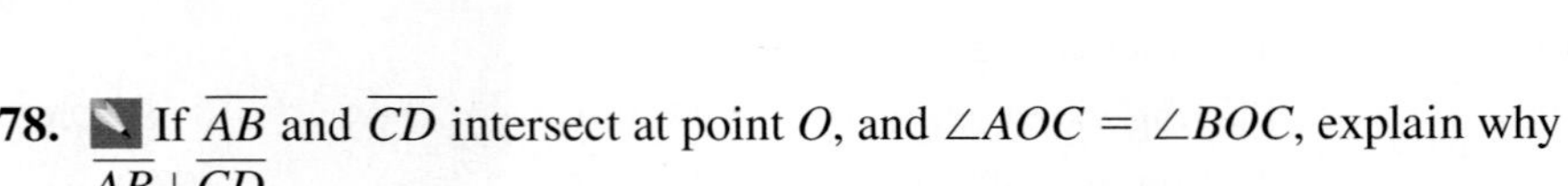

78. If $\overline{AB}$ and $\overline{CD}$ intersect at point O, and $\angle AOC = \angle BOC$, explain why $\overline{AB} \perp \overline{CD}$.

Preparing a Circle Graph In Objective A of this section, a protractor was used to measure angles. Preparing a circle graph requires the ability to use a protractor to draw angles. Here is an example of how to prepare a circle graph.

The revenues (in thousands of dollars) from three departments of a car dealership for the first quarter of a recent year are shown at the right.

New car and truck sales:	\$3300
Used car and truck sales:	\$1500
Parts and service:	\$700

To draw a circle graph representing the percent that each department contributed to the total revenue from all three departments, proceed as follows:

Find the total revenue from all three departments.

$3300 + 1500 + 700 = 5500$

Find the percent of the total revenue contributed by each department.

New car and truck sales: $\dfrac{3300}{5500} = 60\%$

Used car and truck sales: $\dfrac{1500}{5500} \approx 27.3\%$

Parts and service: $\dfrac{700}{5500} \approx 12.7\%$

Each percent represents a sector of the circle. Because the circle contains 360°, multiply each percent by 360° to find the measure of the angle for each sector. Round to the nearest degree.

New car and truck sales:
$0.60 \times 360° = 216°$

Used car and truck sales:
$0.273 \times 360° \approx 98°$

Parts and service:
$0.127 \times 360° \approx 46°$

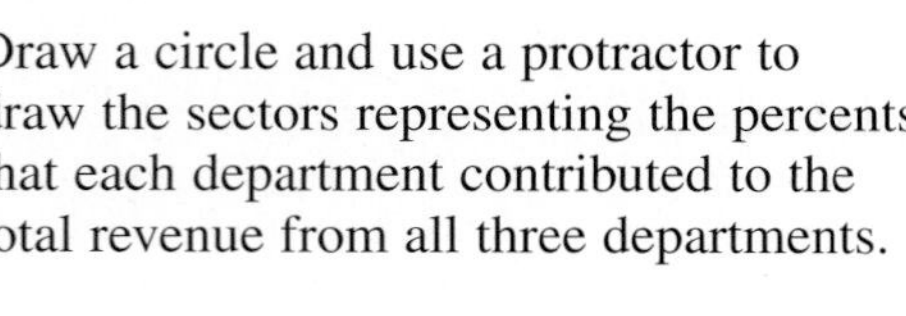
Draw a circle and use a protractor to draw the sectors representing the percents that each department contributed to the total revenue from all three departments.

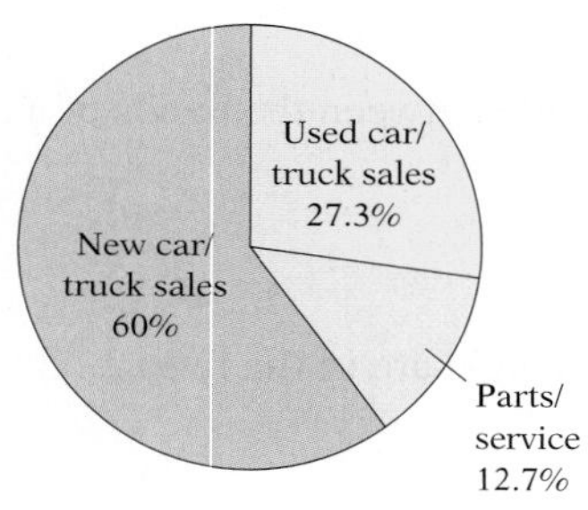

INSTRUCTOR NOTE

In Exercise 79, students create a circle graph from data for which the percents are given. In Exercise 80, students create a circle graph from data for which the percents must be calculated.

79.

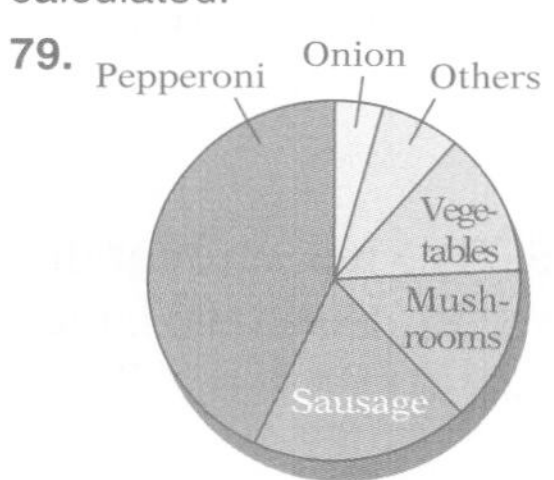

80.

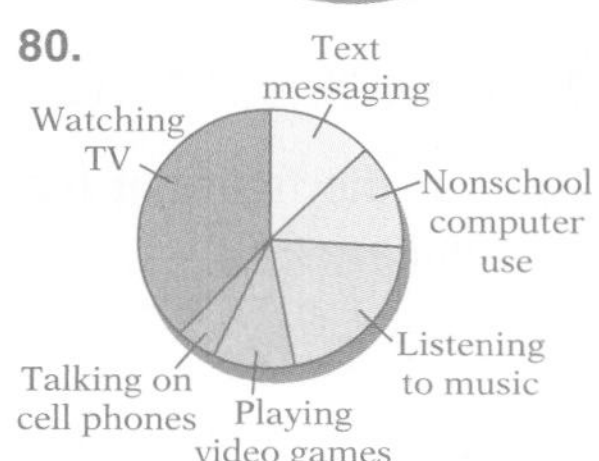

For Exercises 79 and 80, prepare a circle graph for the data provided.

79. Shown below are American adults' favorite pizza toppings. (*Source:* Market Facts for Bolla Wines)

Pepperoni	43%	Vegetables	13%
Sausage	19%	Other	7%
Mushrooms	14%	Onions	4%

80. According to the Kaiser Family Foundation, U.S. children ages 8 to 18 are using media more than ever before. Shown below is their average daily media consumption.

Watching TV	270 min	Text messaging	90 min
Listening to music	151 min	Playing video games	73 min
Nonschool computer use	89 min	Talking on cell phones	33 min

SECTION

7.2 Plane Geometric Figures

OBJECTIVE A *To find the perimeter of plane geometric figures*

A **polygon** is a closed figure determined by three or more line segments that lie in a plane. The line segments that form the polygon are called its **sides.** The figures below are examples of polygons.

A

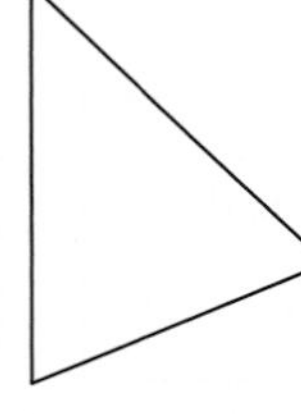
B

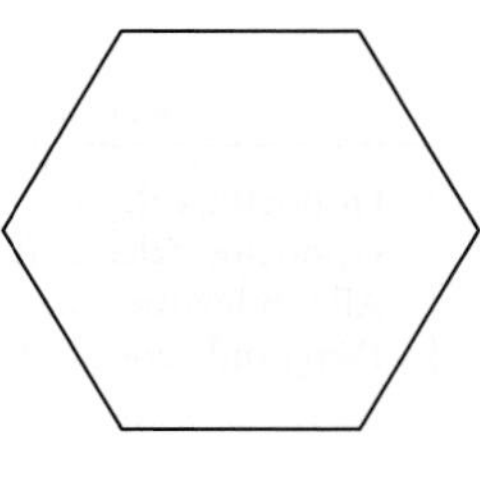
C

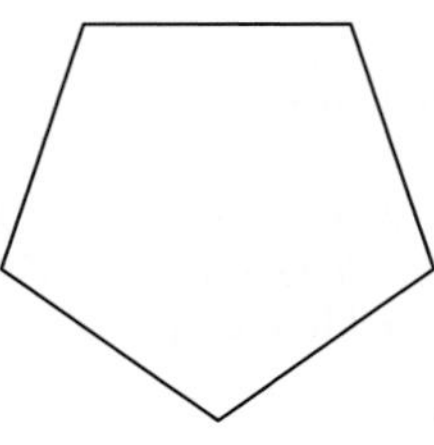
D

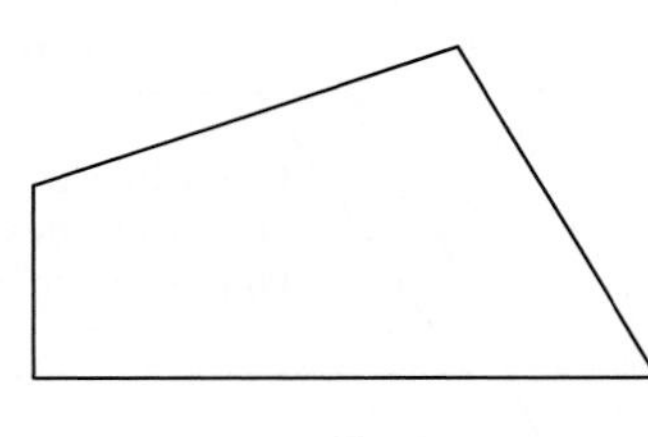
E

A **regular polygon** is one in which all sides have the same length and all angles have the same measure. The polygons in Figures *A*, *C*, and *D* above are regular polygons.

Point of Interest

Although a polygon is defined in terms of its sides, the word actually comes from the Latin word *polygonum*, meaning "many angles."

The name of a polygon is based on the number of its sides. The table below lists the names of polygons that have from 3 to 10 sides.

Number of Sides	*Name of the Polygon*
3	Triangle
4	Quadrilateral
5	Pentagon
6	Hexagon
7	Heptagon
8	Octagon
9	Nonagon
10	Decagon

© Frontpage/Shutterstock.com

The Pentagon in Arlington, Virginia

Triangles and quadrilaterals are two of the most common types of polygons. Triangles are distinguished by the number of equal sides and also by the measures of their angles.

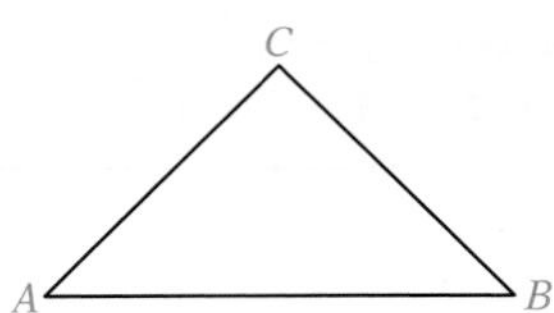

An **isosceles triangle** has two sides of equal length. The angles opposite the equal sides are of equal measure.

$AC = BC$

$\angle A = \angle B$

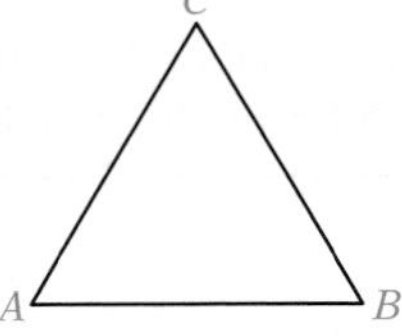

The three sides of an **equilateral triangle** are of equal length. The three angles are of equal measure.

$AB = BC = AC$

$\angle A = \angle B = \angle C$

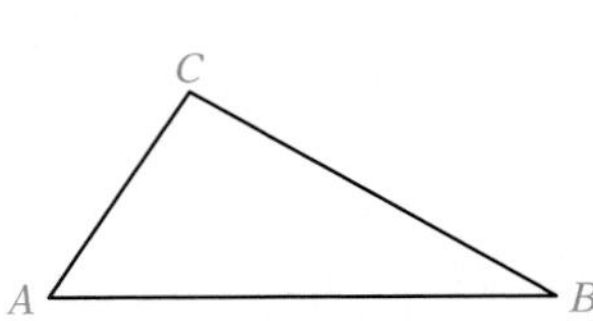

A **scalene triangle** has no two sides of equal length. No two angles are of equal measure.

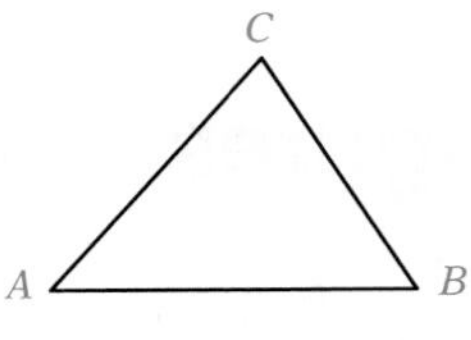

An **acute triangle** has three acute angles.

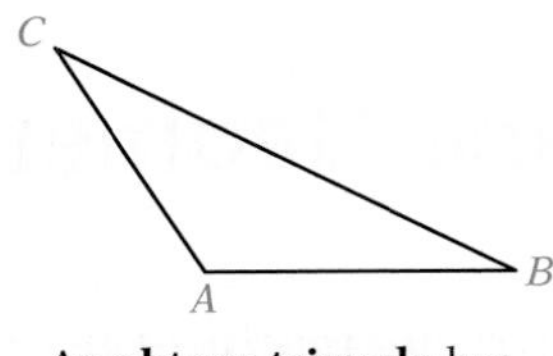

An **obtuse triangle** has an obtuse angle.

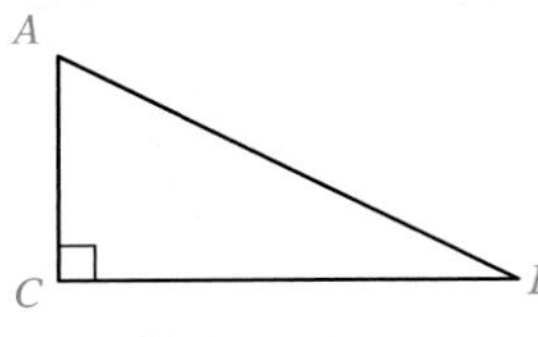

A **right triangle** has a right angle.

INSTRUCTOR NOTE

The diagram below shows the relationships among different types of quadrilaterals. A description of each quadrilateral is given within a drawing of that type of quadrilateral.

Quadrilaterals are also distinguished by their sides and angles, as shown below. Note that a rectangle, a square, and a rhombus are different forms of a parallelogram.

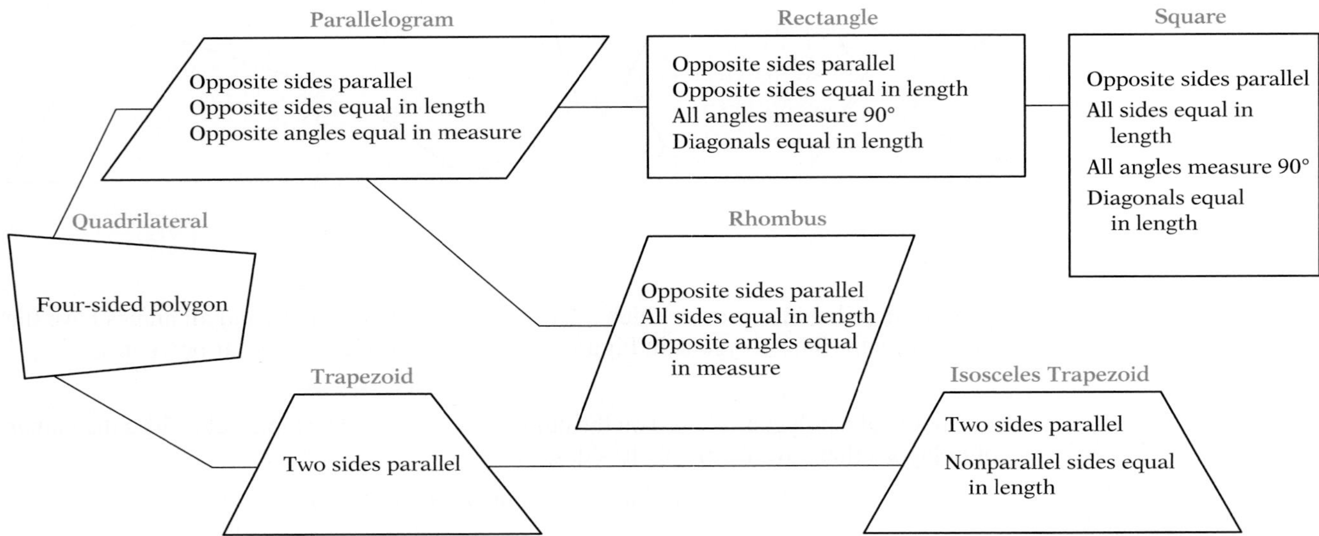

The **perimeter** of a plane geometric figure is a measure of the distance around the figure. Perimeter is used, for example, in buying fencing for a lawn or determining how much baseboard is needed for a room.

The perimeter of a triangle is the sum of the lengths of the three sides.

Perimeter of a Triangle

Let a, b, and c be the lengths of the sides of a triangle. The perimeter P of the triangle is given by $P = a + b + c$.

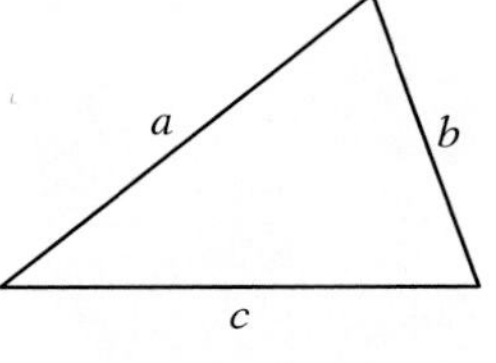

$P = a + b + c$

HOW TO 1 Find the perimeter of the triangle shown at the right.

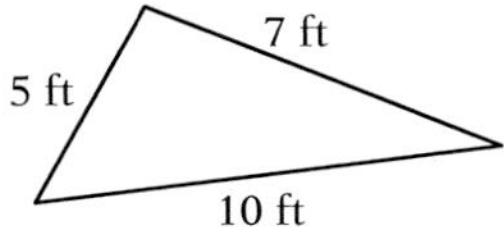

$P = 5 + 7 + 10 = 22$

The perimeter is 22 ft.

The perimeter of a quadrilateral is the sum of the lengths of its four sides.

A rectangle has four right angles and opposite sides of equal length. Usually the length L of a rectangle refers to the length of one of the longer sides of the rectangle, and the width W refers to the length of one of the shorter sides. The perimeter can then be represented $P = L + W + L + W$.

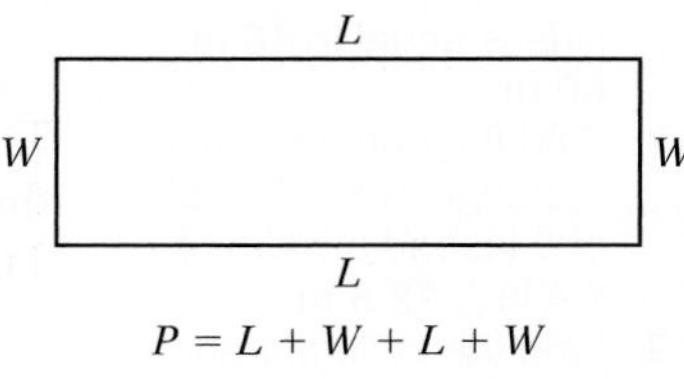

The formula for the perimeter of a rectangle is derived by combining like terms.

$$P = 2L + 2W$$

Perimeter of a Rectangle

Let L represent the length and W the width of a rectangle. The perimeter P of the rectangle is given by $P = 2L + 2W$.

HOW TO 2 Find the perimeter of the rectangle shown at the right.

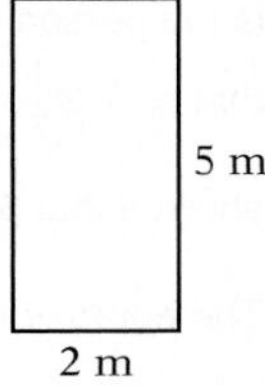

The length is 5 m. Substitute 5 for L.
The width is 2 m. Substitute 2 for W.
Solve for P.

$$P = 2L + 2W$$
$$P = 2(5) + 2(2)$$
$$P = 10 + 4$$
$$P = 14$$

The perimeter is 14 m.

A square is a rectangle in which each side has the same length. If we let s represent the length of each side of a square, the perimeter of the square can be represented by $P = s + s + s + s$.

$$P = s + s + s + s$$

The formula for the perimeter of a square is derived by combining like terms.

$$P = 4s$$

Perimeter of a Square

Let s represent the length of a side of a square. The perimeter P of the square is given by $P = 4s$.

HOW TO 3 Find the perimeter of the square shown at the right.

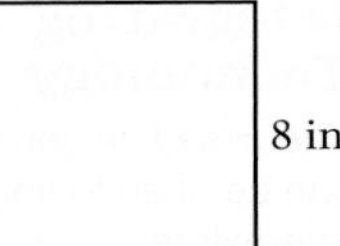

$$P = 4s = 4(8) = 32$$

The perimeter is 32 in.

IN-CLASS EXAMPLES

1. Find the perimeter of a square for which each side is equal to 15 m. **60 m**
2. Find the perimeter of a rectangle with a length of 5 in. and a width of 1.4 in. **12.8 in.**
3. Find the circumference of a circle with a radius of 11 cm. Round to the nearest hundredth. **69.12 cm**

A **circle** is a plane figure in which all points are the same distance from point O, called the **center** of the circle.

The **diameter** of a circle is a line segment across the circle through point O. AB is a diameter of the circle at the right. The variable d is used to designate the diameter of a circle.

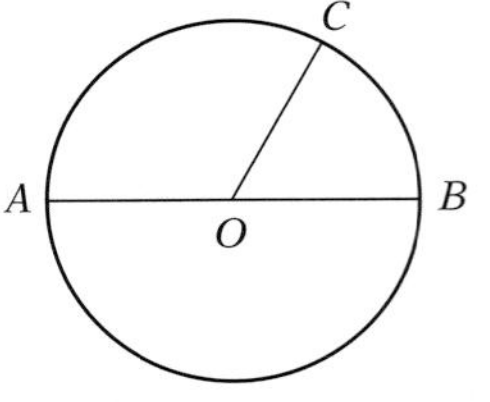

The **radius** of a circle is a line segment from the center of the circle to a point on the circle. OC is a radius of the circle at the right. The variable r is used to designate the radius of a circle.

The length of the diameter is twice the length of the radius. $d = 2r$ or $r = \frac{1}{2}d$

Point of Interest

Archimedes (c. 287–212 B.C.) is the person who calculated that $\pi \approx 3\frac{1}{7}$. He actually showed that $3\frac{10}{71} < \pi < 3\frac{1}{7}$. The approximation $3\frac{10}{71}$ is a more accurate approximation of π than $3\frac{1}{7}$, but it is more difficult to use.

The distance around a circle is called the **circumference.** The circumference C of a circle is equal to the product of π (pi) and the diameter. $C = \pi d$

Because $d = 2r$, the formula for the circumference can be written in terms of r. $C = 2\pi r$

The Circumference of a Circle

The circumference C of a circle with diameter d and radius r is given by $C = \pi d$ or $C = 2\pi r$.

The formula for circumference uses the number π, which is an irrational number. The value of π can be approximated by a fraction or by a decimal. $\pi \approx \frac{22}{7}$ or $\pi \approx 3.14$

The π key on a scientific calculator gives a closer approximation of π than 3.14. Use a scientific calculator to find approximate values in calculations involving π.

Integrating Technology

The π key on your calculator can be used to find decimal approximations to formulas that contain π. To perform the calculation at the right, enter 6 × π =.

HOW TO 4 Find the circumference of a circle with a diameter of 6 in.

The diameter of the circle is given. Use the circumference formula that involves the diameter. $d = 6$

$C = \pi d$
$C = \pi(6)$

The exact circumference of the circle is 6π in. $C = 6\pi$

An approximate measure is found by using the π key on a calculator. $C \approx 18.85$

The approximate circumference is 18.85 in.

EXAMPLE 1

A carpenter is designing a square patio with a perimeter of 44 ft. What is the length of each side?

Strategy

To find the length of each side, use the formula for the perimeter of a square. Substitute 44 for P and solve for s.

Solution

$P = 4s$ • **The formula for the perimeter of a square**

$44 = 4s$ • $P = 44$

$11 = s$

The length of each side of the patio is 11 ft.

YOU TRY IT 1

The infield of a softball field is a square with each side of length 60 ft. Find the perimeter of the infield.

Your strategy

Your solution

240 ft

EXAMPLE 2

The dimensions of a triangular sail are 18 ft, 11 ft, and 15 ft. What is the perimeter of the sail?

Strategy

To find the perimeter, use the formula for the perimeter of a triangle. Substitute 18 for a, 11 for b, and 15 for c. Solve for P.

Solution

$P = a + b + c$ • **Use the formula for the perimeter of a triangle.** $a = 18, b = 11, c = 15$

$P = 18 + 11 + 15$

$P = 44$

The perimeter of the sail is 44 ft.

YOU TRY IT 2

Find the length of decorative molding needed to edge the tops of the walls in a rectangular room that is 12 ft long and 8 ft wide.

Your strategy

Your solution

40 ft

EXAMPLE 3

Find the circumference of a circle with a radius of 15 cm. Round to the nearest hundredth.

Strategy

To find the circumference, use the circumference formula that involves the radius. An approximation is asked for; use the π key on a calculator. $r = 15$

Solution

$C = 2\pi r = 2\pi(15) = 30\pi \approx 94.25$

The circumference is 94.25 cm.

YOU TRY IT 3

Find the circumference of a circle with a diameter of 9 in. Give the exact measure.

Your strategy

Your solution

9π in.

Solutions on p. S19

OBJECTIVE B *To find the area of plane geometric figures*

Area is the amount of surface in a region. Area can be used to describe the size of, for example, a rug, a parking lot, a farm, or a national park. Area is measured in square units.

A square that measures 1 in. on each side has an area of 1 square inch, written 1 in^2.

A square that measures 1 cm on each side has an area of 1 square centimeter, written 1 cm^2.

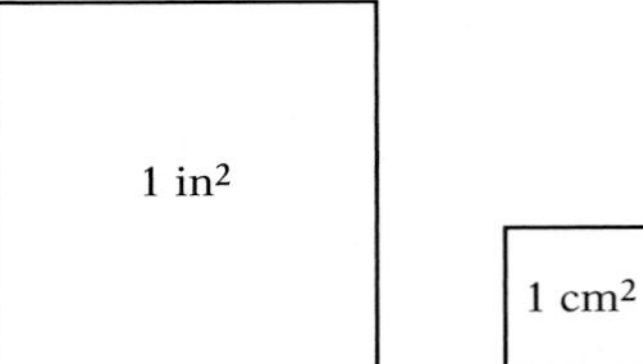

Point of Interest

First Lady Michelle Obama's White House garden is a small, 1100 ft^2 plot of land, but it has yielded thousands of pounds of tomatoes, lettuce, eggplant, sweet potatoes, broccoli, cabbage, carrots, and other vegetables and herbs that have been used to feed people at the White House and at nearby homeless shelters.

Larger areas can be measured in square feet (ft^2), square meters (m^2), acres (43,560 ft^2), square miles (mi^2), or any other square unit.

The area of a geometric figure is the number of squares that are necessary to cover the figure. In the figures below, two rectangles have been drawn and covered with squares. In the figure on the left, 12 squares, each of area 1 cm^2, were used to cover the rectangle. The area of the rectangle is 12 cm^2. In the figure on the right, 6 squares, each of area 1 in^2, were used to cover the rectangle. The area of the rectangle is 6 in^2.

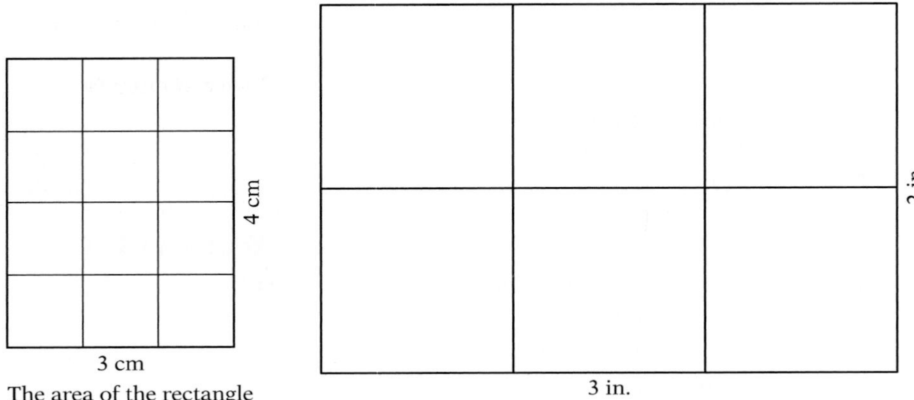

The area of the rectangle is 12 cm^2.

The area of the rectangle is 6 in^2.

Note from the above figures that the area of a rectangle can be found by multiplying the length of the rectangle by its width.

Area of a Rectangle

Let L represent the length and W the width of a rectangle. The area A of the rectangle is given by $A = LW$.

HOW TO 5 Find the area of the rectangle shown at the right.

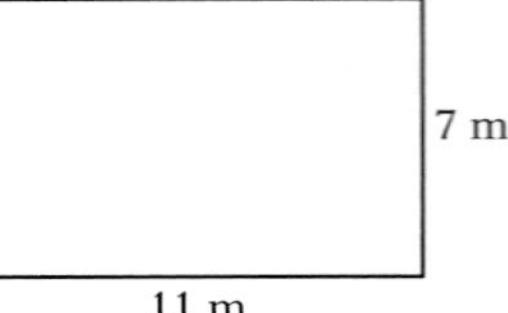

$A = LW = 11(7) = 77$

The area is 77 m^2.

A square is a rectangle in which all sides are the same length. Therefore, both the length and the width of a square can be represented by s, and $A = LW = s \cdot s = s^2$.

Point of Interest

Figurate numbers are whole numbers that can be represented by regular geometric figures. For example, a square number is one that can be represented by a square array.

O	OO OO	OOO OOO OOO	OOOO OOOO OOOO OOOO
1	4	9	16

The square numbers are 1, 4, 9, 16, 25, ... They can be represented by $1^2, 2^2, 3^2, 4^2, 5^2, \ldots$.

INSTRUCTOR NOTE

Ask students to find the next three square numbers. For each number, have them form the square array, as well as represent the number in both standard form and exponential form.

Area of a Square

Let s represent the length of a side of a square. The area A of the square is given by $A = s^2$.

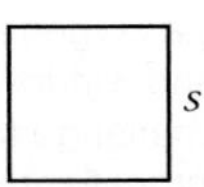

$A = s \cdot s = s^2$

HOW TO 6 Find the area of the square shown at the right.

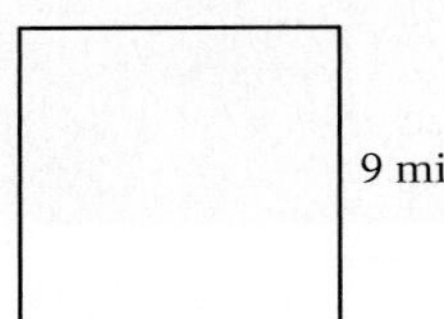

$A = s^2 = 9^2 = 81$

The area is 81 mi^2.

Figure $ABCD$ is a parallelogram. BC is the **base** b of the parallelogram. AE, perpendicular to the base, is the **height** h of the parallelogram.

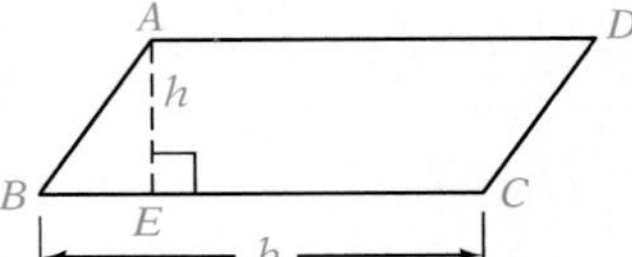

Any side of a parallelogram can be designated as the base. The corresponding height is found by drawing a line segment perpendicular to the base from the opposite side.

A rectangle can be formed from a parallelogram by cutting a right triangle from one end of the parallelogram and attaching it to the other end. The area of the resulting rectangle will equal the area of the original parallelogram.

Take Note

For a rectangle, $A = LW$.
For a parallelogram, $A = bh$.

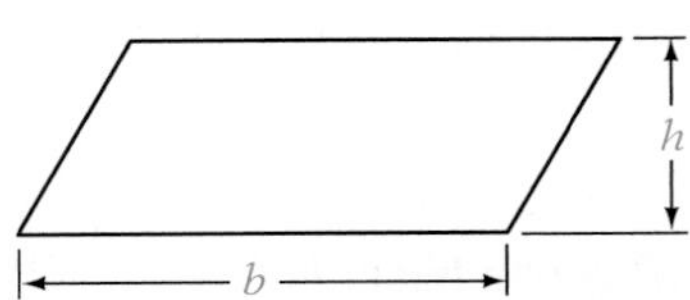

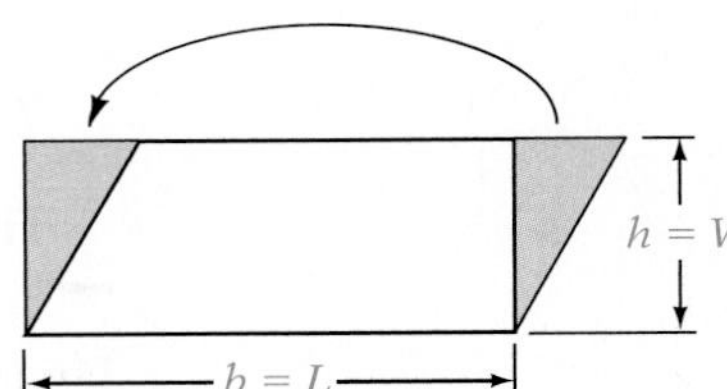

Area of a Parallelogram

Let b represent the length of the base and h the height of a parallelogram. The area A of the parallelogram is given by $A = bh$.

HOW TO 7 Find the area of the parallelogram shown at the right.

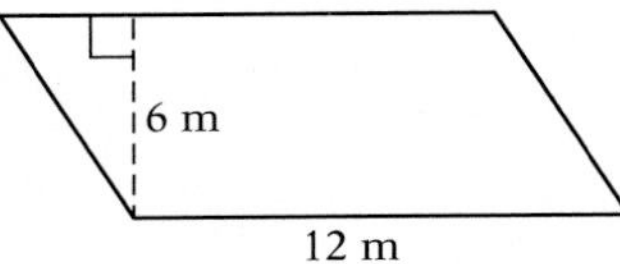

$A = bh = 12 \cdot 6 = 72$

The area is 72 m^2.

Point of Interest

A **glazier** is a person who cuts, fits, and installs glass, generally in doors and windows. Of particular challenge to a glazier are intricate stained glass window designs.

© Luca Moi/Shutterstock.com

Figure ABC is a triangle. AB is the **base** b of the triangle. CD, perpendicular to the base, is the **height** h of the triangle.

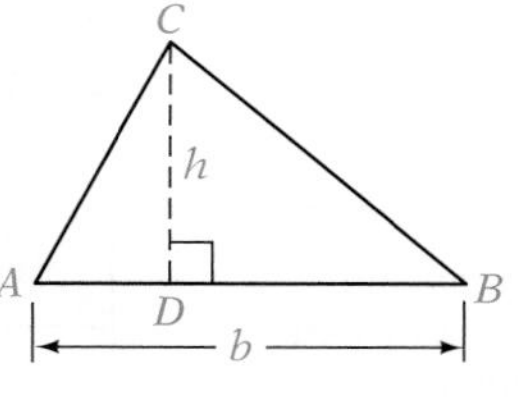

Any side of a triangle can be designated as the base. The corresponding height is found by drawing a line segment perpendicular to the base from the vertex opposite the base.

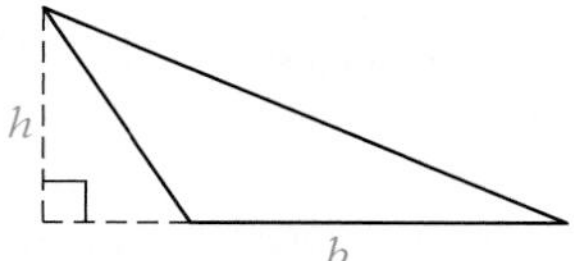

Consider the triangle with base b and height h shown at the right. By extending a line from C parallel to the base AB and equal in length to the base, a parallelogram is formed. The area of the parallelogram is bh and is twice the area of the triangle. Therefore, the area of the triangle is one-half the area of the parallelogram, or $\frac{1}{2}bh$.

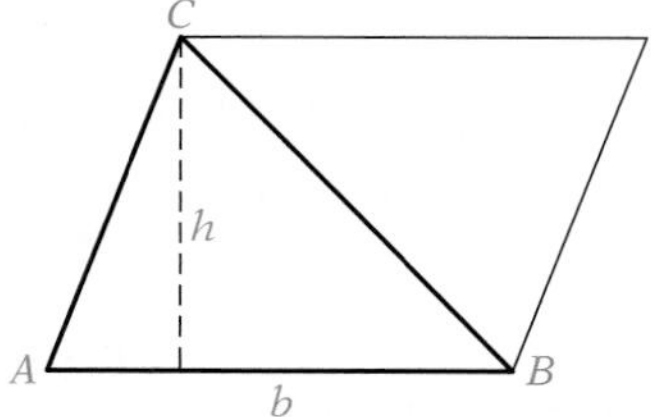

Area of a Triangle

Let b represent the length of the base and h the height of a triangle. The area A of the triangle is given by $A = \frac{1}{2}bh$.

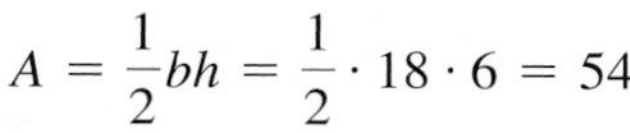

HOW TO 8 Find the area of a triangle with a base of 18 cm and a height of 6 cm.

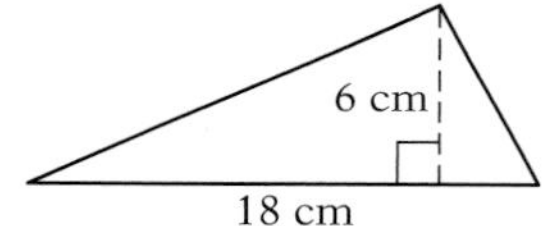

$$A = \frac{1}{2}bh = \frac{1}{2} \cdot 18 \cdot 6 = 54$$

The area is 54 cm^2.

Figure $ABCD$ is a trapezoid. AB is one **base,** b_1, of the trapezoid, and CD is the other base, b_2. AE, perpendicular to the two bases, is the **height** h.

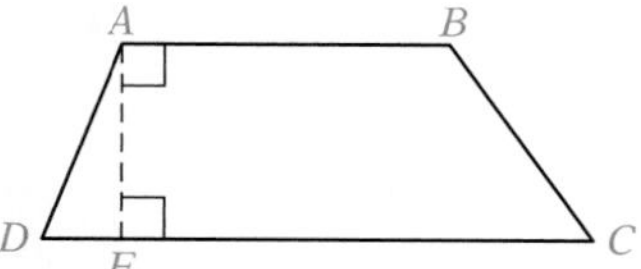

In the trapezoid at the right, the line segment BD divides the trapezoid into two triangles, ABD and BCD. In triangle ABD, b_1 is the base and h is the height. In triangle BCD, b_2 is the base and h is the height. The area of the trapezoid is the sum of the areas of the two triangles.

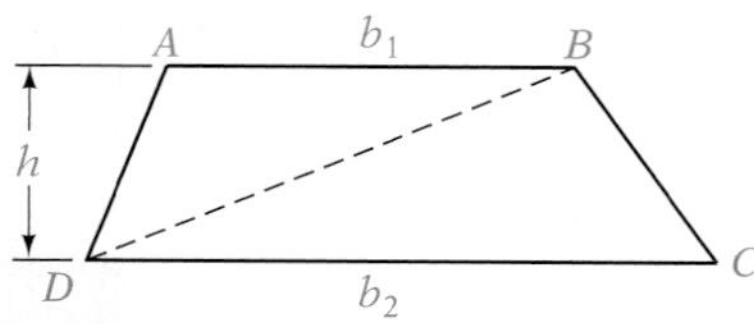

$$\begin{aligned}\text{Area of trapezoid } ABCD &= \text{area of triangle } ABD + \text{area of triangle } BCD \\ &= \frac{1}{2}b_1h + \frac{1}{2}b_2h = \frac{1}{2}h(b_1 + b_2)\end{aligned}$$

IN-CLASS EXAMPLES

4. Find the area of a triangle with a base of 5 cm and a height of 1.6 cm. **4 cm^2**
5. Find the area of a square with a side of 8.5 ft. **72.25 ft^2**
6. Find the area of a circle with a diameter of 16 in. Round to the nearest hundredth. **201.06 in^2**

Area of a Trapezoid

Let b_1 and b_2 represent the lengths of the bases and h the height of a trapezoid. The area A of the trapezoid is given by $A = \frac{1}{2}h(b_1 + b_2)$.

HOW TO 9 Find the area of a trapezoid that has bases measuring 15 in. and 5 in. and a height of 8 in.

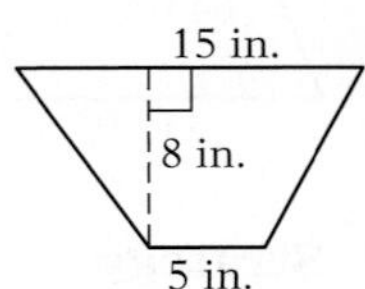

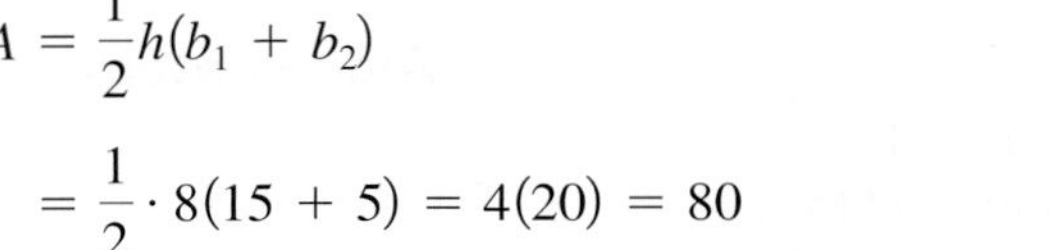

$$A = \frac{1}{2}h(b_1 + b_2)$$

$$= \frac{1}{2} \cdot 8(15 + 5) = 4(20) = 80$$

The area is 80 in^2.

The area of a circle is equal to the product of π and the square of the radius.

$A = \pi r^2$

Tips for Success

You have now learned many different formulas for the perimeter and area of plane geometric figures. You will need to be able to recognize when to use each one. To test yourself, do the Chapter Review Exercises on page 453.

Area of a Circle

The area A of a circle with radius r is given by $A = \pi r^2$.

HOW TO 10 Find the area of a circle that has a radius of 6 cm.

Use the formula for the area of a circle. $r = 6$.

$A = \pi r^2$
$A = \pi(6)^2$
$A = \pi(36)$

The exact area of the circle is 36π cm^2.

$A = 36\pi$

An approximate measure is found by using the π key on a calculator.

$A \approx 113.10$

The approximate area of the circle is 113.10 cm^2.

Integrating Technology

To approximate 36π on your calculator, enter 36 × π =.

For your reference, all of the formulas for the perimeter and area of the geometric figures presented in this section are listed in the Chapter Summary, which begins on page 450.

EXAMPLE 4

The parks and recreation department of a city plans to plant grass seed in a playground that has the shape of a trapezoid, as shown below. Each bag of grass seed will seed 1500 ft^2. How many bags of grass seed should the department purchase?

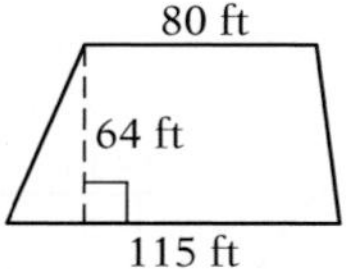

Strategy

To find the number of bags to be purchased:

- Use the formula for the area of a trapezoid to find the area of the playground.
- Divide the area of the playground by the area one bag will seed (1500).

Solution

$A = \frac{1}{2}h(b_1 + b_2)$ • **The formula for the area of a trapezoid**

$A = \frac{1}{2} \cdot 64(80 + 115)$ • **$h = 64, b_1 = 80, b_2 = 115$**

$A = 6240$ • **The area of the playground is 6240 ft^2.**

$6240 \div 1500 = 4.16$

Because a portion of a fifth bag is needed, 5 bags of grass seed should be purchased.

YOU TRY IT 4

An interior designer decides to wallpaper two walls of a room. Each roll of wallpaper will cover 30 ft^2. Each wall measures 8 ft by 12 ft. How many rolls of wallpaper should be purchased?

Your strategy

Your solution

7 rolls

EXAMPLE 5

Find the area of a circle with a diameter of 5 ft. Give the exact measure.

Strategy

To find the area:

- Find the radius of the circle.
- Use the formula for the area of a circle. Leave the answer in terms of π.

Solution

$r = \frac{1}{2}d = \frac{1}{2}(5) = 2.5$ • **Find the radius.**

$A = \pi r^2 = \pi(2.5)^2 = \pi(6.25) = 6.25\pi$

The area of the circle is 6.25π ft^2.

YOU TRY IT 5

Find the area of a circle with a radius of 11 cm. Round to the nearest hundredth.

Your strategy

Your solution

380.13 cm^2

Solutions on p. S19

7.2 EXERCISES

Concept Check

SUGGESTED ASSIGNMENT
Exercises 1–12; Exercises 13–103, odds

Name each polygon.

1.
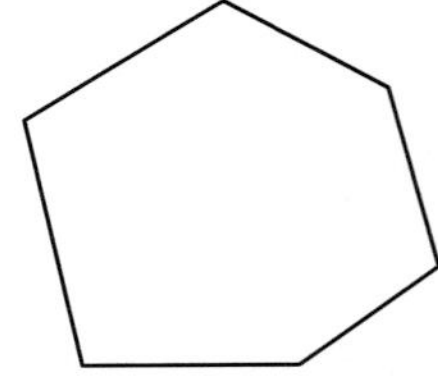
hexagon

2.
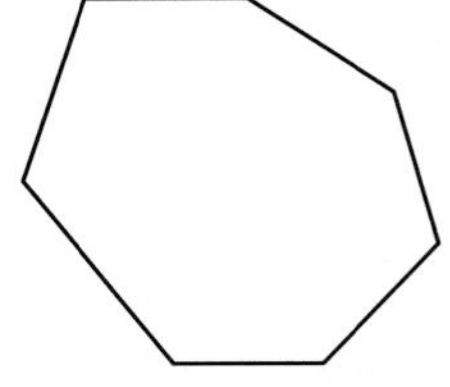
heptagon

3.
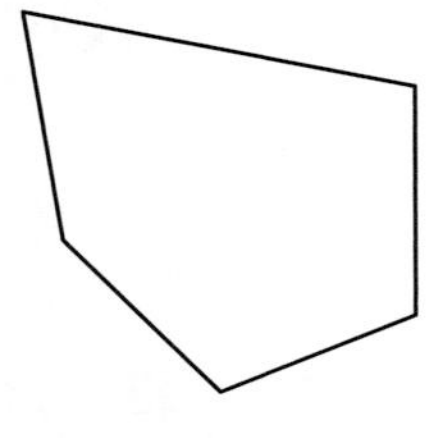
pentagon

4.
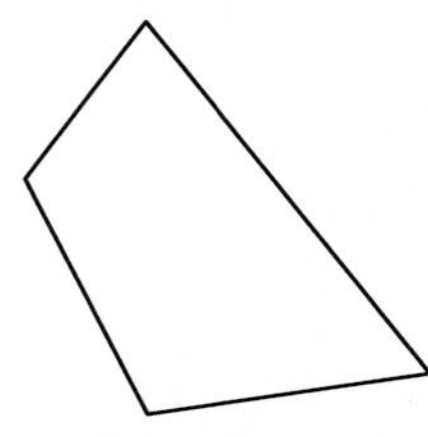
quadrilateral

Classify the triangle as isosceles, equilateral, or scalene.

5.

scalene

6.
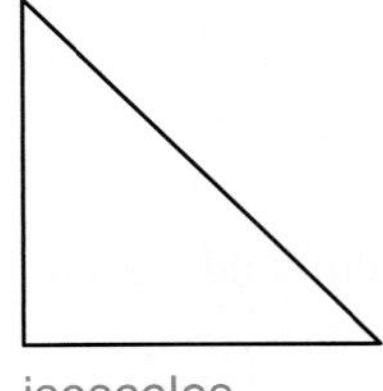
isosceles

7.
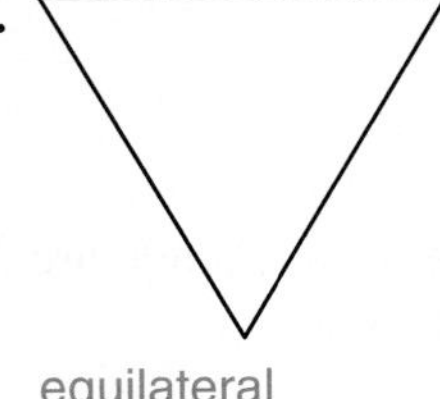
equilateral

8.
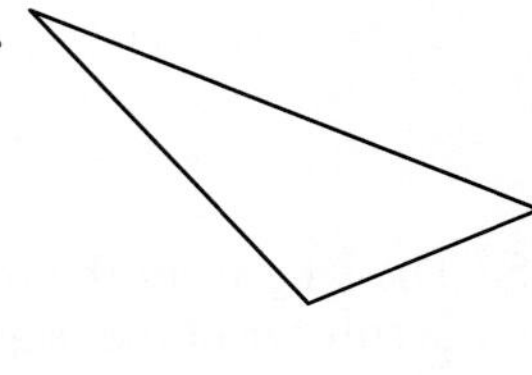
scalene

Classify the triangle as acute, obtuse, or right.

9.
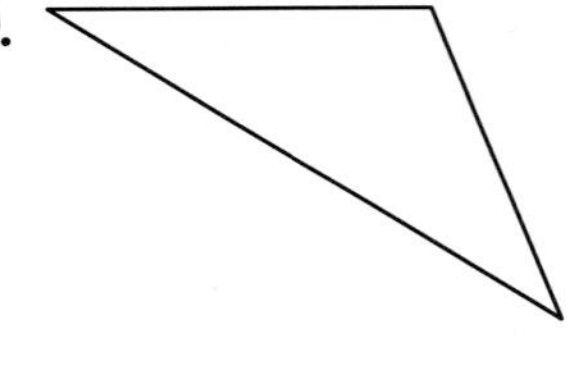
obtuse

10.
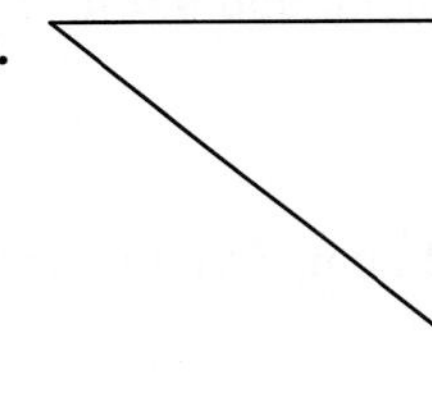
right

11.
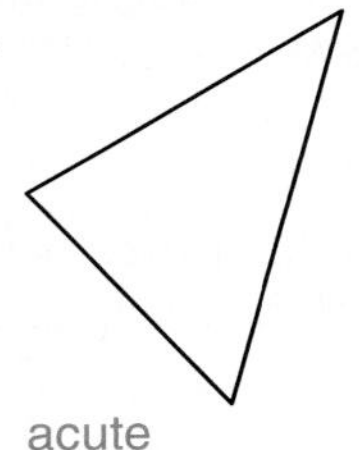
acute

12.
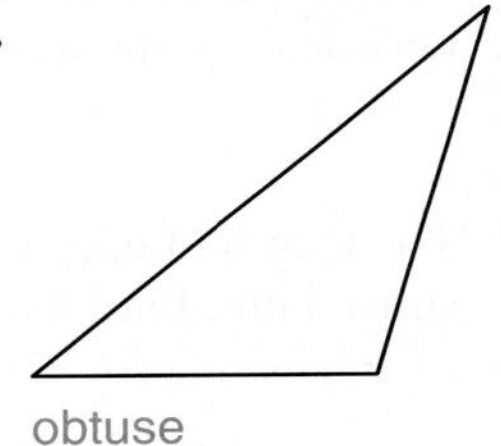
obtuse

OBJECTIVE A *To find the perimeter of plane geometric figures*

Find the perimeter of the figure.

13.
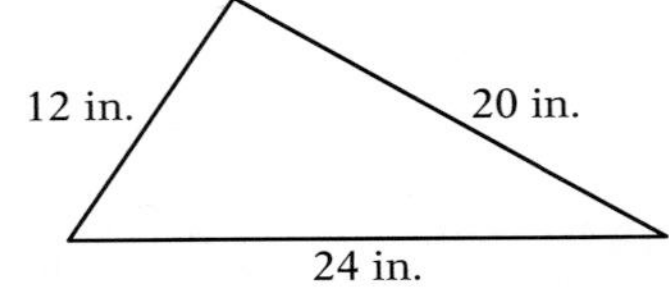

56 in.

14.
7 cm
11 cm
36 cm

15.
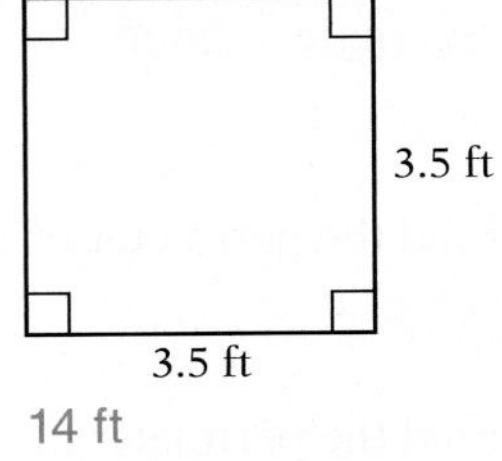

14 ft

16.
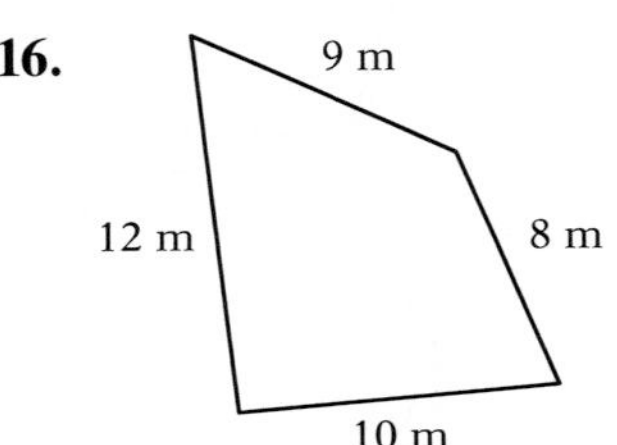

39 m

17.
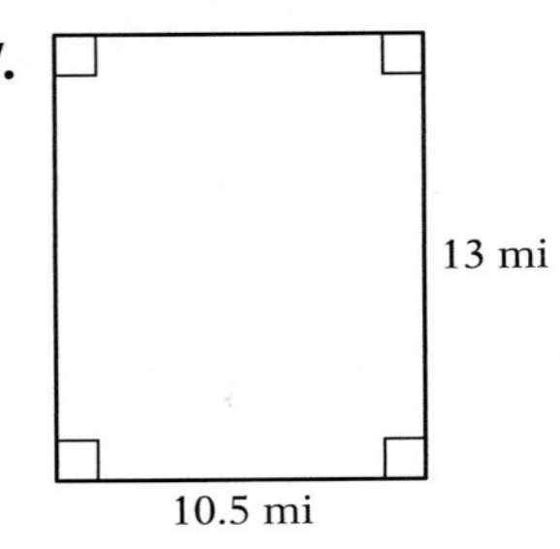

47 mi

18.
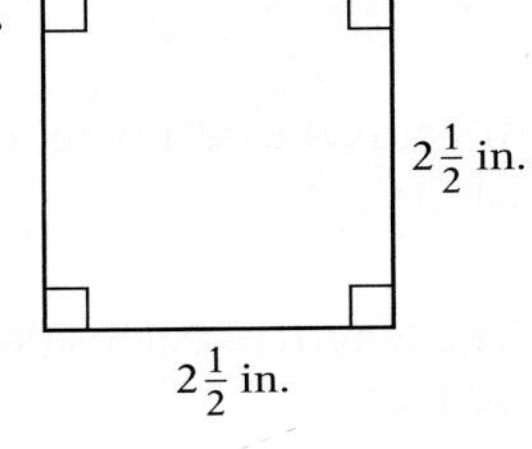

10 in.

For Exercises 19 to 24, find the circumference of the figure. Give both the exact value and an approximation to the nearest hundredth.

19. 4 cm 8π cm; 25.13 cm

20. 12 m 24π m; 75.40 m

21. 5.5 mi 11π mi; 34.56 mi

22. 18 in. 18π in.; 56.55 in.

23. 17 ft 17π ft; 53.41 ft

24. 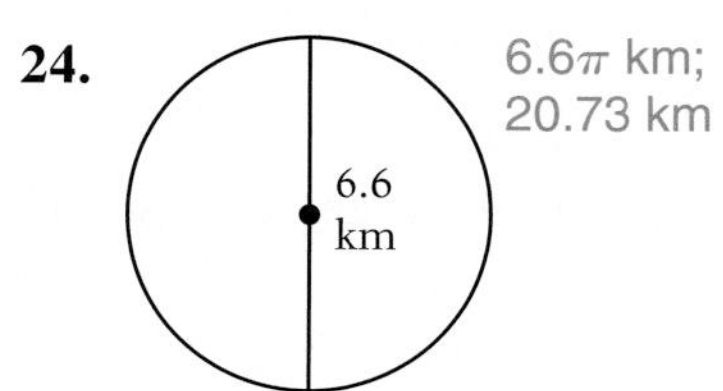

6.6π km; 20.73 km

25. The lengths of the three sides of a triangle are 3.8 cm, 5.2 cm, and 8.4 cm. Find the perimeter of the triangle. 17.4 cm

26. The lengths of the three sides of a triangle are 7.5 m, 6.1 m, and 4.9 m. Find the perimeter of the triangle. 18.5 m

27. The length of each of two sides of an isosceles triangle is $2\frac{1}{2}$ cm. The third side measures 3 cm. Find the perimeter of the triangle. 8 cm

28. The length of each side of an equilateral triangle is $4\frac{1}{2}$ in. Find the perimeter of the triangle.
$13\frac{1}{2}$ in.

29. A rectangle has a length of 8.5 m and a width of 3.5 m. Find the perimeter of the rectangle. 24 m

30. Find the perimeter of a rectangle that has a length of $5\frac{1}{2}$ ft and a width of 4 ft. 19 ft

31. Find the perimeter of a regular pentagon that measures 3.5 in. on each side. 17.5 in.

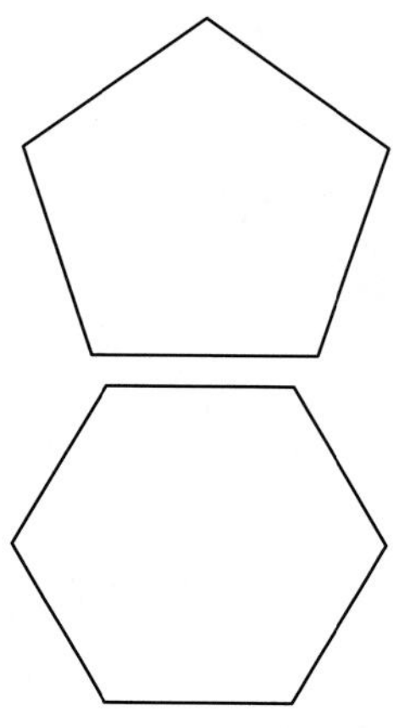

32. What is the perimeter of a regular hexagon that measures 8.5 cm on each side?
51 cm

33. The length of each side of a square is 12.2 cm. Find the perimeter of the square.
48.8 cm

34. Find the perimeter of a square that is 0.5 m on each side. 2 m

35. Find the circumference of a circle that has a diameter of 1.5 in. Give the exact value. 1.5π in.

36. The diameter of a circle is 4.2 ft. Find the circumference of the circle. Round to the nearest hundredth. 13.19 ft

37. The radius of a circle is 36 cm. Find the circumference of the circle. Round to the nearest hundredth. 226.19 cm

38. Find the circumference of a circle that has a radius of 2.5 m. Give the exact value. 5π m

39. Fencing How many feet of fencing should be purchased for a rectangular garden that is 18 ft long and 12 ft wide? 60 ft

40. Quilts How many meters of binding are required to bind the edge of a rectangular quilt that measures 3.5 m by 8.5 m? 24 m

41. Carpeting Wall-to-wall carpeting is installed in a room that is 12 ft long and 10 ft wide. The edges of the carpet are nailed to the floor. Along how many feet must the carpet be nailed down? 44 ft

42. Fencing The length of a rectangular park is 55 yd. The width is 47 yd. How many yards of fencing are needed to surround the park? 204 yd

43. Playgrounds The perimeter of a rectangular playground is 440 ft. If the width is 100 ft, what is the length of the playground? 120 ft

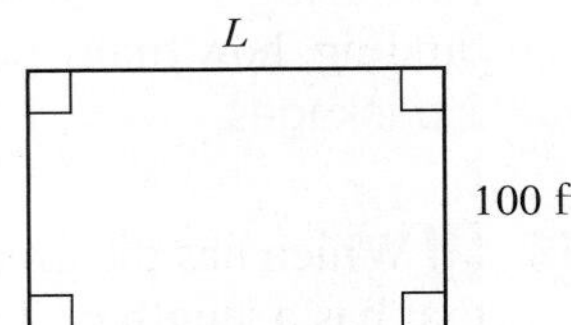

44. Gardens A rectangular vegetable garden has a perimeter of 64 ft. The length of the garden is 20 ft. What is the width of the garden? 12 ft

45. Banners Each of two sides of a triangular banner measures 18 in. If the perimeter of the banner is 46 in., what is the length of the third side of the banner? 10 in.

46. The perimeter of an equilateral triangle is 13.2 cm. What is the length of each side of the triangle? 4.4 cm

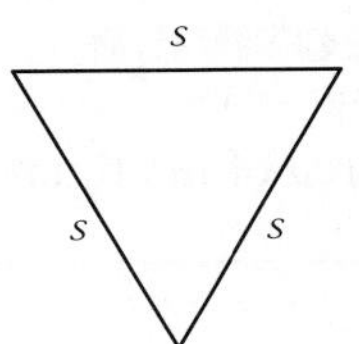

47. Picture Frames The perimeter of a square picture frame is 48 in. Find the length of each side of the frame. 12 in.

48. Carpeting A square rug has a perimeter of 32 ft. Find the length of each edge of the rug. 8 ft

Solve. For Exercises 49 to 55, round to the nearest hundredth.

49. The circumference of a circle is 8 cm. Find the length of a diameter of the circle.
2.55 cm

50. The circumference of a circle is 15 in. Find the length of a radius of the circle.
2.39 in.

51. **Woodworking** Find the length of molding needed to trim the edge of a circular table that is 4.2 ft in diameter. 13.19 ft

52. **Carpeting** How much binding is needed to bind the edge of a circular rug that is 3 m in diameter? 9.42 m

53. **Cycling** A bicycle tire has a diameter of 24 in. How many feet does the bicycle travel when the wheel makes eight revolutions? 50.27 ft

54. **Cycling** A tricycle tire has a diameter of 12 in. How many feet does the tricycle travel when the wheel makes 12 revolutions? 37.70 ft

55. **Earth Science** The distance from the surface of Earth to its center is 6356 km. What is the circumference of Earth? 39,935.93 km

56. **Sewing** Bias binding is to be sewed around the edge of a rectangular tablecloth measuring 72 in. by 45 in. If the bias binding comes in packages containing 15 ft of binding, how many packages of bias binding are needed for the tablecloth?
2 packages

57. Which has the greater perimeter, a square whose side measures 1 ft or a rectangle that has a length of 2 in. and a width of 1 in.? A square whose side is 1 ft

58. The perimeter of an isosceles triangle is 54 ft. Let s be the length of one of the two equal sides. Is it possible for s to be 30 ft? No

OBJECTIVE B *To find the area of plane geometric figures*

Find the area of the figure.

59.

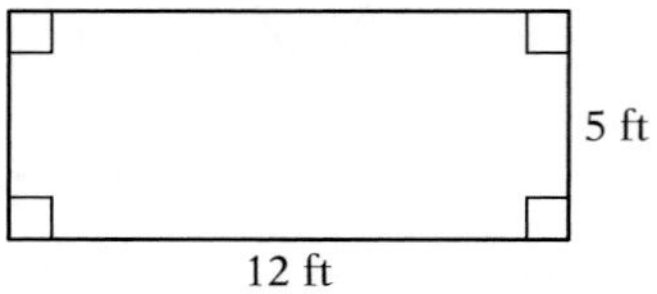

60 ft^2

60.

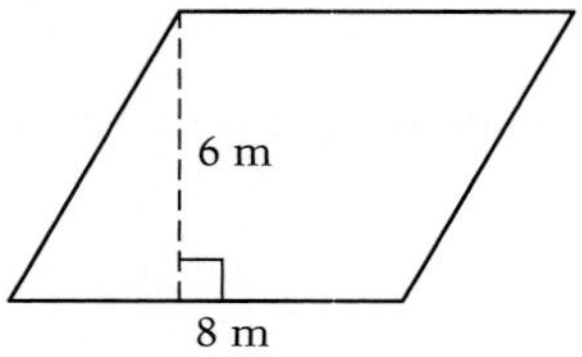

48 m^2

61.

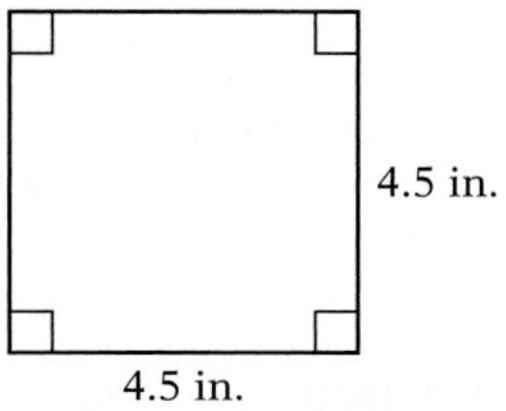

20.25 in^2

62.

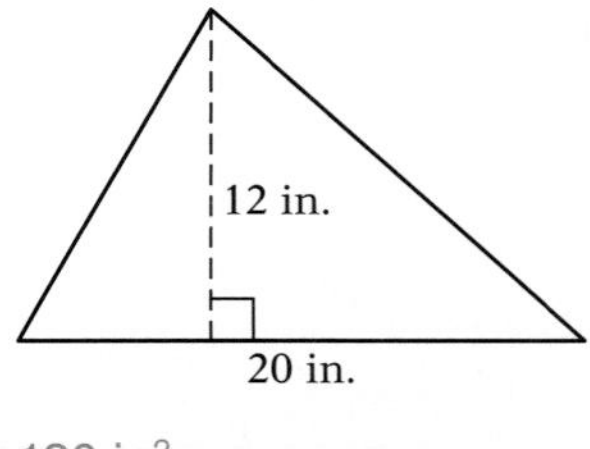

120 in^2

63.

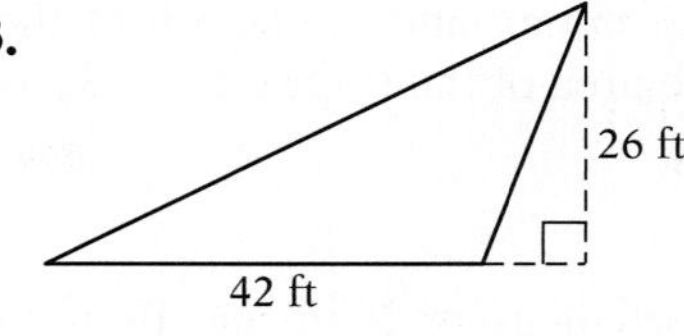

546 ft^2

64.

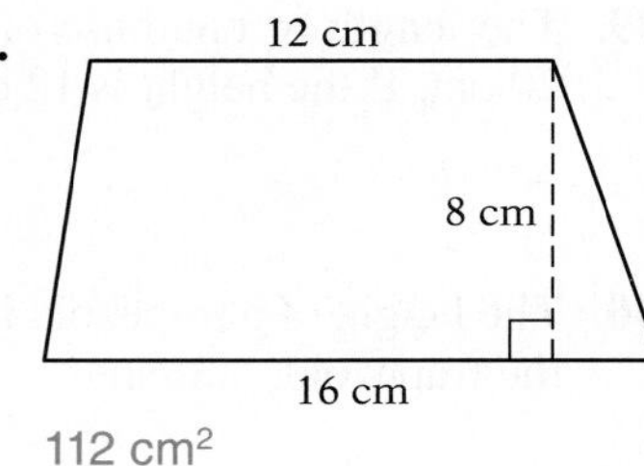

112 cm^2

For Exercises 65 to 70, find the area of the figure.
Give both the exact value and an approximation to the nearest hundredth.

65.

16π cm^2; 50.27 cm^2

66.

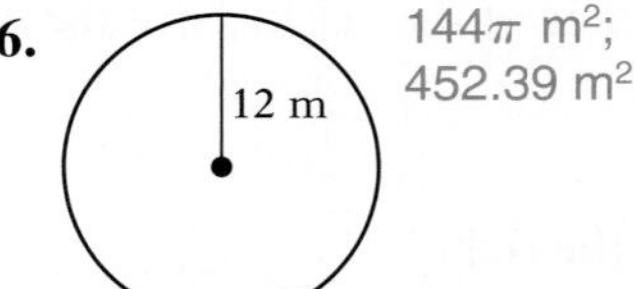

144π m^2; 452.39 m^2

67.

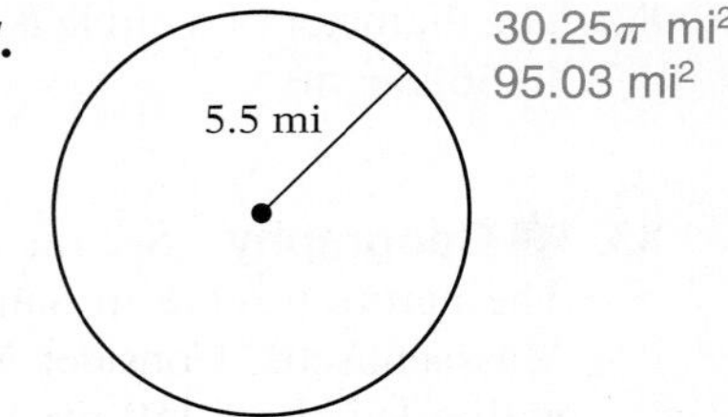

30.25π mi^2; 95.03 mi^2

68.

81π in^2; 254.47 in^2

69.

72.25π ft^2; 226.98 ft^2

70.

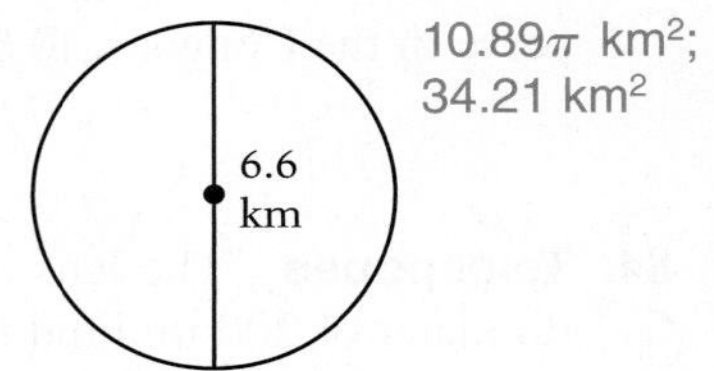

10.89π km^2; 34.21 km^2

71. The length of a side of a square is 12.5 cm. Find the area of the square. 156.25 cm^2

72. Each side of a square measures $3\frac{1}{2}$ in. Find the area of the square. 12.25 in^2

73. The length of a rectangle is 38 in., and the width is 15 in. Find the area of the rectangle. 570 in^2

74. Find the area of a rectangle that has a length of 6.5 m and a width of 3.8 m. 24.7 m^2

75. The length of the base of a parallelogram is 16 in., and the height is 12 in. Find the area of the parallelogram. 192 in^2

76. The height of a parallelogram is 3.4 m, and the length of the base is 5.2 m. Find the area of the parallelogram. 17.68 m^2

77. The length of the base of a triangle is 6 ft. The height is 4.5 ft. Find the area of the triangle. 13.5 ft^2

78. The height of a triangle is 4.2 cm. The length of the base is 5 cm. Find the area of the triangle. 10.5 cm^2

79. The length of one base of a trapezoid is 35 cm, and the length of the other base is 20 cm. If the height is 12 cm, what is the area of the trapezoid? 330 cm^2

80. The height of a trapezoid is 5 in. The bases measure 16 in. and 18 in. Find the area of the trapezoid. 85 in^2

81. The radius of a circle is 5 in. Find the area of the circle. Give the exact value. $25\pi\text{ in}^2$

82. The diameter of a circle is 6.5 m. Find the area of the circle. Give the exact value. $10.5625\pi\text{ m}^2$

83. **Geography** See the news clipping at the right. The nature reserve in Sankuru is about the size of Massachusetts. Consider Massachusetts a rectangle with a length of 150 mi and a width of 70 mi. Use these dimensions to approximate the area of the reserve in the Congo. $10{,}500\text{ mi}^2$

© Ronald van der Beek/Shutterstock.com

> **In the NEWS!**
>
> **Animal Sanctuary Established**
>
> The government of the Republic of Congo in Africa has set aside a vast expanse of land in the Sankuru Province to be used as a nature reserve. It will be a sanctuary for elephants; 11 species of primates, including the bonobos; and the okapi, a short-necked relative of the giraffe, which is on the endangered species list.
>
> *Source:* www.time.com

84. **Telescopes** The lens on the Hale telescope at Mount Palomar, California, has a diameter of 200 in. Find its area. Give the exact value. $10{,}000\pi\text{ in}^2$

85. **Irrigation** An irrigation system waters a circular field that has a 50-foot radius. Find the area watered by the irrigation system. Give the exact value. $2500\pi\text{ ft}^2$

© Corbis Premium RF/Alamy

86. **Gardens** Find the area of a rectangular flower garden that measures 14 ft by 9 ft. 126 ft^2

87. **Patios** What is the area of a square patio that measures 8.5 m on each side? 72.25 m^2

88. **Interior Design** See the news clipping at the right. What would be the cost of carpeting the entire living space if the cost of the carpet were $36 per square yard? $1,600,000

89. **Athletic Fields** Artificial turf is being used to cover a playing field. If the field is rectangular with a length of 100 yd and a width of 75 yd, how much artificial turf must be purchased to cover the field? 7500 yd^2

90. **Interior Design** A fabric wall hanging is to fill a space that measures 5 m by 3.5 m. Allowing for 0.1 m of the fabric to be folded back along each edge, how much fabric must be purchased for the wall hanging? 19.24 m^2

> **In the NEWS!**
>
> **Billion-Dollar Home Built in Mumbai**
>
> The world's first billion-dollar home is a 27-story skyscraper in downtown Mumbai, India (formerly known as Bombay). It is 550 ft high with $400{,}000\text{ ft}^2$ of living space.
>
> *Source:* Forbes.com

91. The area of a rectangle is 300 in^2. If the length of the rectangle is 30 in., what is the width? 10 in.

30 in.

W

92. The width of a rectangle is 12 ft. If the area is 312 ft^2, what is the length of the rectangle? 26 ft

93. The height of a triangle is 5 m. The area of the triangle is 50 m^2. Find the length of the base of the triangle. 20 m

94. The area of a parallelogram is 42 m^2. If the height of the parallelogram is 7 m, what is the length of the base? 6 m

95. Home Maintenance You plan to stain the wooden deck attached to your house. The deck measures 10 ft by 8 ft. If a quart of stain will cover 50 ft^2, how many quarts of stain should you buy? 2 qt

96. Interior Design You want to tile your kitchen floor, which measures 12 ft by 9 ft. How many tiles, each a square with sides of $1\frac{1}{2}$ ft, should you purchase? 48 tiles

97. Interior Design You are wallpapering two walls of a room, one measuring 9 ft by 8 ft and the other measuring 11 ft by 8 ft. The wallpaper costs $37 per roll, and each roll covers 40 ft^2. What is the cost to wallpaper the two walls? $148

98. Landscaping An urban renewal project involves reseeding a park that is a square, 60 ft on each side. Each bag of grass seed costs $11.50 and will seed 1200 ft^2. How much money should be budgeted for buying grass seed for the park? $34.50

99. Storage You want to rent a storage unit. You estimate that you need 175 ft^2 of floor space. You see the ad shown at the right. You want to rent the smallest possible unit that will hold everything you want to store. Which of the six units shown in the ad should you select? 10 × 20 unit

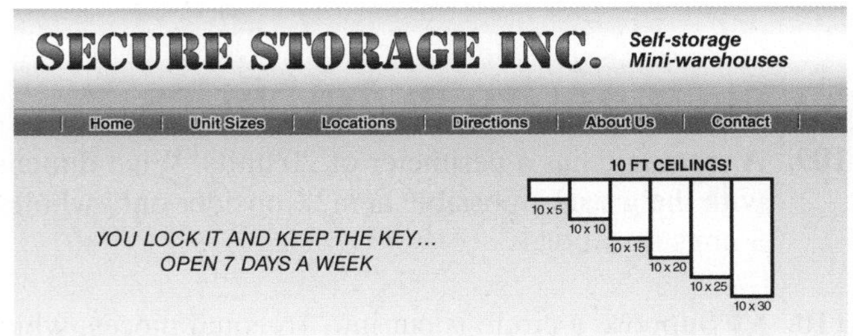

100. A circle has a radius of 8 in. Find the increase in area when the radius is increased by 2 in. Round to the nearest hundredth. 113.10 in^2

101. A circle has a radius of 6 cm. Find the increase in area when the radius is doubled. Round to the nearest hundredth. 339.29 cm^2

102. **Interior Design** You want to install wall-to-wall carpeting in your living room, which measures 15 ft by 24 ft. If the cost of the carpet is \$31.90 per square yard, what is the cost of the carpeting for your living room? (*Hint:* $9\text{ ft}^2 = 1\text{ yd}^2$)
\$1276

103. **Interior Design** You want to paint the walls of your bedroom. Two walls measure 15 ft by 9 ft, and the other two walls measure 12 ft by 9 ft. The paint you wish to purchase costs \$29.98 per gallon, and each gallon will cover 400 ft^2 of wall. Find the total amount you will spend on paint. \$59.96

104. **Landscaping** A walkway 2 m wide surrounds a rectangular plot of grass. The plot is 30 m long and 20 m wide. What is the area of the walkway? 216 m^2

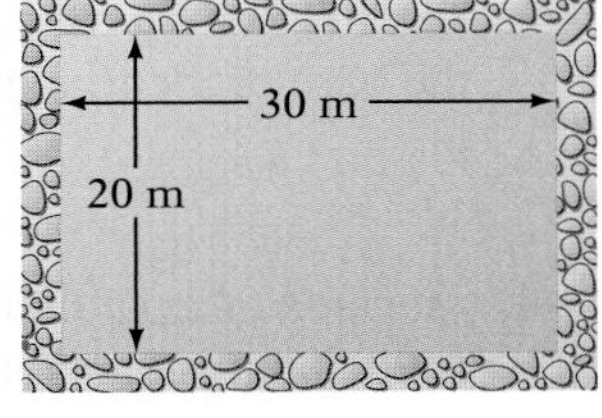

105. **Interior Design** Pleated draperies for a window must be twice as wide as the width of the window. Draperies are being made for four windows, each 2 ft wide and 4 ft high. Since the drapes will fall slightly below the window sill and extra fabric will be needed for hemming the drapes, 1 ft must be added to the height of the window. How much material must be purchased to make the drapes? 80 ft^2

106. A circle has a radius of 5 cm.
a. Can the exact area of the circle be *A* cm, where *A* is a decimal approximation?
b. Can the exact area of the circle be *A* cm^2, where *A* is a whole number?
a. No; area is measured in square units. **b.** No; *A* cannot be a whole number.

Critical Thinking

107. If both the length and the width of a rectangle are doubled, how many times larger is the area of the resulting rectangle? 4 times

108. Find the ratio of the areas of two squares if the ratio of the lengths of their sides is 2:3. 4:9

Projects or Group Activities

109. A rectangle has a perimeter of 20 units. What dimensions will result in a rectangle with the greatest possible area? Consider only whole-number dimensions.
5 units by 5 units

110. Suppose a circle is cut into 16 equal pieces, which are then arranged as shown at the right. The figure formed resembles a parallelogram. What variable expression could describe the base of the parallelogram? What variable could describe its height? Explain how the formula for the area of a circle is derived from this approach.

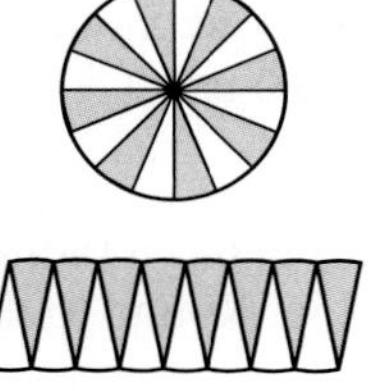

111. Prepare a report on the history of quilts in the United States. Find examples of quilt patterns that incorporate regular polygons.

QUICK QUIZ

1. Find the perimeter of a rectangle with a length of 3 m and a width of 0.75 m. **7.5 m [7.2A]**
2. Find the perimeter of a square for which each side measures 13.5 cm. **54 cm [7.2A]**
3. Find the length of a rubber gasket needed to fit around a circular porthole that has a 20-inch diameter. Round to the nearest hundredth. **62.83 in. [7.2A]**
4. Find the area of a triangle with a base of 10 ft and a height of 16 ft. **80 ft^2 [7.2B]**
5. Find the area of a rectangle with a length of 64 cm and a width of 22 cm. **1408 cm^2 [7.2B]**
6. Find the area of a circle with a diameter of 26 in. Round to the nearest hundredth. **530.93 in^2 [7.2B]**

CHECK YOUR PROGRESS: CHAPTER 7

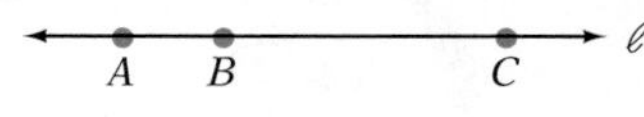

1. See the figure at the right. Given $BC = 15$ ft and $AB = \frac{1}{3}(BC)$, find AC. 20 ft [7.1A]

2. Find the supplement of a 12° angle. 168° [7.1A]

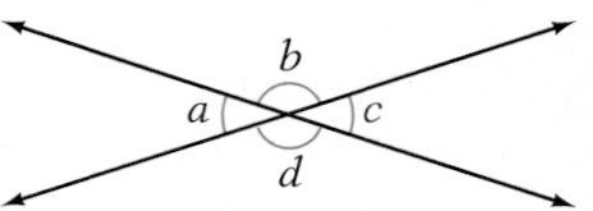

3. See the figure at the right. Given that $\angle a = 42°$, find the measures of angles b, c, and d. $\angle b = 138°$, $\angle c = 42°$, $\angle d = 138°$ [7.1B]

4. One angle in a right triangle measures 23°. Find the measure of the third angle. 67° [7.1C]

5. **Quilts** What is the area of a square quilt that measures 40 in. on each side? 1600 in^2 [7.2B]

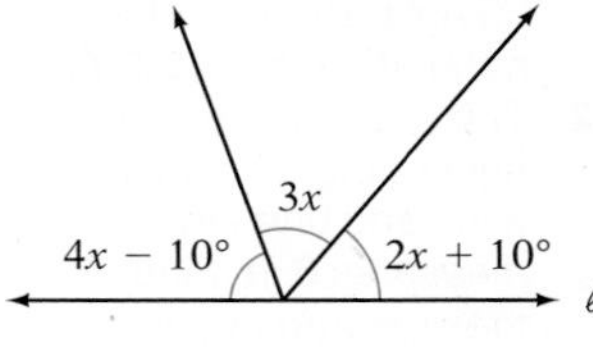

6. See the figure at the right. Find x. 20° [7.1A]

7. Find the circumference of a circle that has a diameter of 12 cm. Round to the nearest hundredth. 37.70 cm [7.2A]

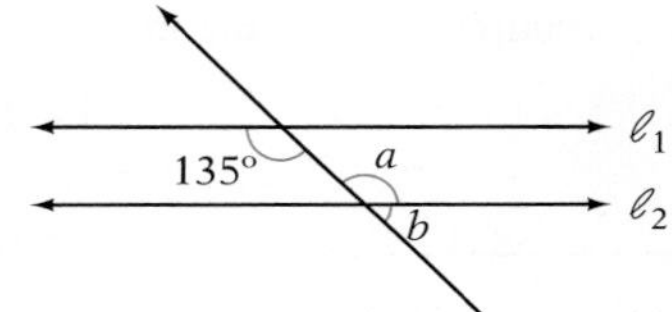

8. See the figure at the right. Given that $\ell_1 \parallel \ell_2$, find the measures of $\angle a$ and $\angle b$. $\angle a = 135°$, $\angle b = 45°$ [7.1B]

9. The height of a triangle is 8 m. The area of the triangle is 20 m^2. Find the length of the base of the triangle. 5 m [7.2B]

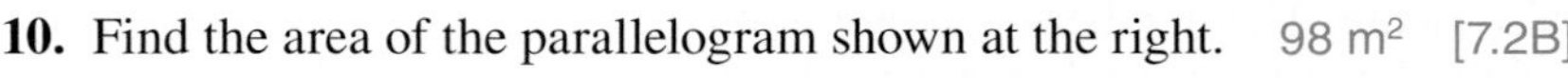

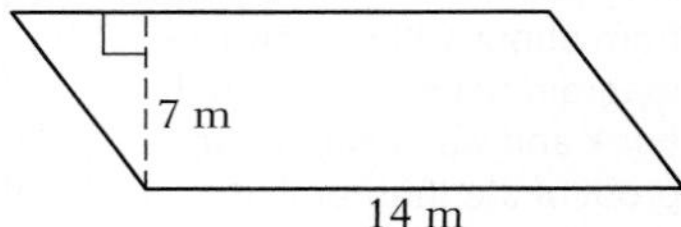

10. Find the area of the parallelogram shown at the right. 98 m^2 [7.2B]

11. The perimeter of a square is 38 in. Find the length of a side of the square. 9.5 in. [7.2A]

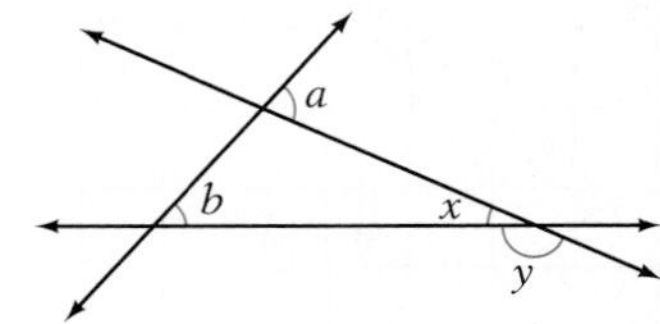

12. See the figure at the right. Given that $\angle a = 72°$ and $\angle b = 48°$, find the measures of $\angle x$ and $\angle y$. $\angle x = 24°$, $\angle y = 156°$ [7.1C]

13. The width of a rectangle is 8 m. If the area is 128 m^2, what is the length of the rectangle? 16 m [7.2B]

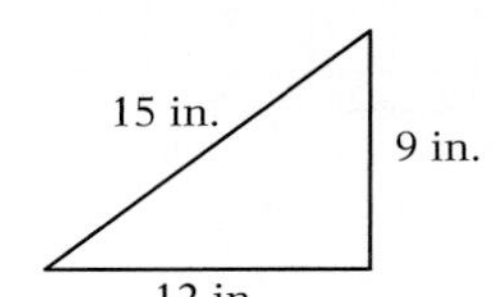

14. Find the perimeter of the triangle shown at the right. 36 in. [7.2A]

15. The diameter of a circle is 2.8 m. Find the area of the circle. Give both the exact value and an approximation to the nearest hundredth. 1.96π m^2; 6.16 m^2 [7.2B]

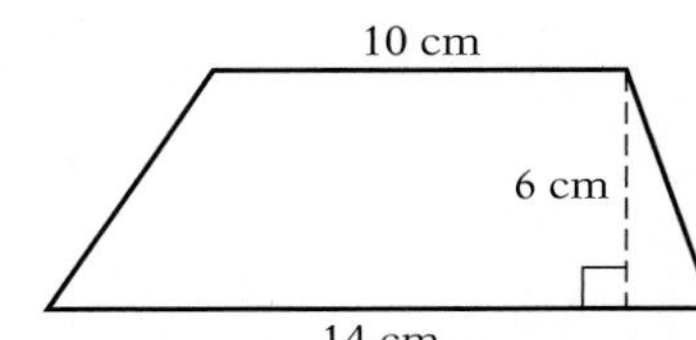

16. Find the area of the trapezoid shown at the right. 72 cm^2 [7.2B]

17. **Carpentry** Find the length of molding needed to edge the tops of the walls in a rectangular room that is 10 ft long and $8\frac{1}{2}$ ft wide. 37 ft [7.2A]

SECTION

7.3 Triangles

OBJECTIVE A *To find the unknown side of a right triangle by using the Pythagorean Theorem*

IN-CLASS EXAMPLES

1. The two legs of a right triangle measure 7 cm and 10 cm. Find the hypotenuse of the right triangle. Round to the nearest tenth. **12.2 cm**
2. The hypotenuse of a right triangle measures 9 in., and one leg measures 6 in. Find the measure of the other leg. Round to the nearest tenth. **6.7 in.**

A **right triangle** contains one right angle. The side opposite the right angle is called the **hypotenuse.** The other two sides are called **legs.**

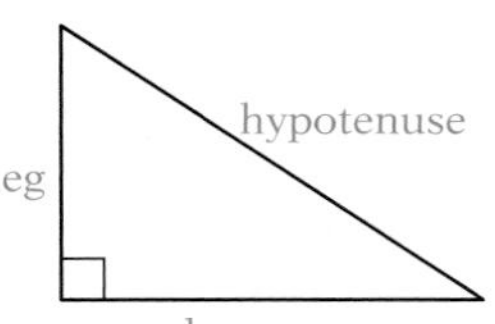

The angles in a right triangle are usually labeled with the capital letters A, B, and C, with C reserved for the right angle. The side opposite angle A is side a, the side opposite angle B is side b, and c is the hypotenuse.

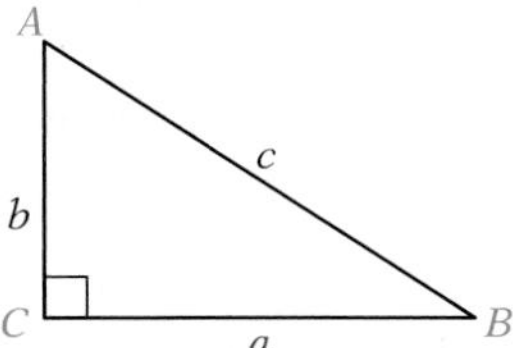

The Greek mathematician Pythagoras is generally credited with the discovery that the square of the hypotenuse of a right triangle is equal to the sum of the squares of the two legs. This is called the **Pythagorean Theorem.**

Point of Interest

The first known proof of the Pythagorean Theorem is in a Chinese textbook that dates from about 100 B.C. The diagram below is from that book and was used in the proof of the theorem.

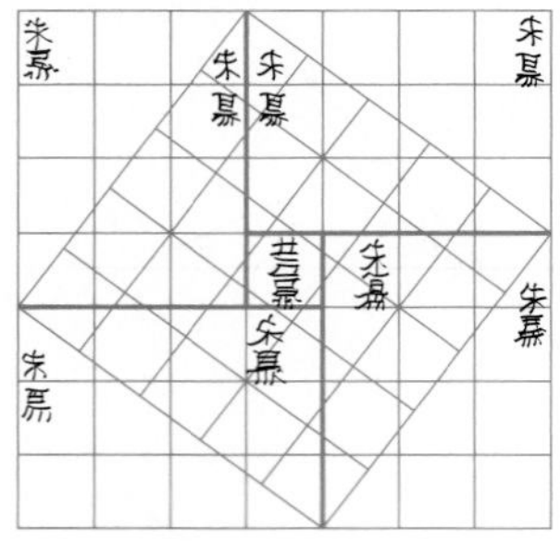

The figure at the right is a right triangle with legs measuring 3 units and 4 units and a hypotenuse measuring 5 units. Each side of the triangle is also the side of a square. The number of square units in the area of the largest square is equal to the sum of the numbers of square units in the areas of the smaller squares.

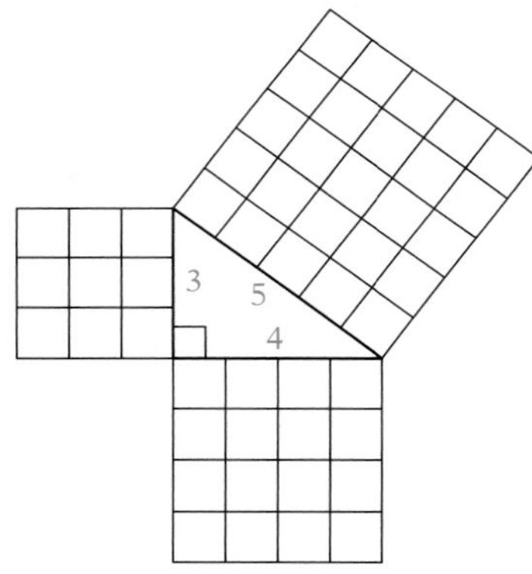

Square of the hypotenuse	=	sum of the squares of the two legs

$$5^2 = 3^2 + 4^2$$
$$25 = 9 + 16$$
$$25 = 25$$

Pythagorean Theorem

If a and b are the lengths of the legs of a right triangle, and c is the length of the hypotenuse, then $c^2 = a^2 + b^2$.

EXAMPLE

The square of the hypotenuse	=	the sum of the squares of the two legs

$$13^2 = 5^2 + 12^2$$
$$169 = 25 + 144$$
$$169 = 169$$

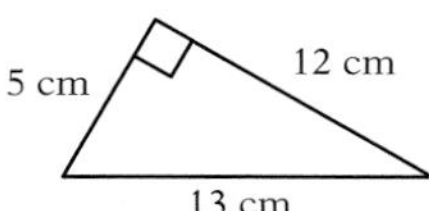

$c^2 = a^2 + b^2$
$c^2 = 5^2 + 12^2$
$c^2 = 25 + 144$
$c^2 = 169$

If the lengths of two sides of a right triangle are known, the Pythagorean Theorem can be used to find the length of the third side. For the right triangle described in the preceding definition box, suppose we know only that the legs measure 5 cm and 12 cm. We can use the Pythagorean Theorem, with $a = 5$ and $b = 12$, to find the length of the hypotenuse. The resulting equation states that the square of c is equal to 169. Since $13^2 = 169$, we know that the length of the hypotenuse is $c = 13$ cm. We can find c by taking the *square root* of 169: $\sqrt{169} = 13$. This suggests the following property.

Integrating Technology

The way in which you evaluate the square root of a number depends on the type of calculator you have. Here are two possible keystrokes to find $\sqrt{35}$:

35 [√] [=]

or

[√] 35 [ENTER]

The first method is used on many scientific calculators. The second method is used on many graphing calculators.

The Principal Square Root Property

If $r^2 = s$, then $r = \sqrt{s}$, and r is called the **square root** of s.

EXAMPLE

If $5^2 = 25$, then $5 = \sqrt{25}$.
Therefore, if $c^2 = 25$, then $c = \sqrt{25} = 5$.

Numbers whose square roots are integers, such as 25, are called perfect squares. If a number is not a perfect square, a calculator can be used to find an approximate square root when a decimal approximation is required.

HOW TO 1 The length of one leg of a right triangle is 8 in. The hypotenuse is 12 in. Find the length of the other leg. Round to the nearest hundredth.

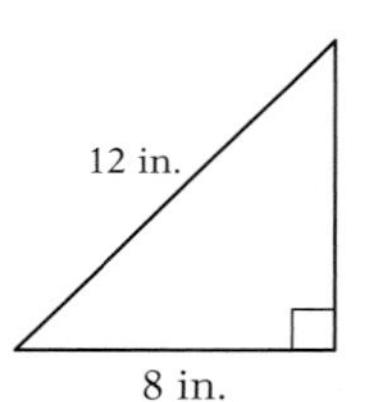

Use the Pythagorean Theorem. $a^2 + b^2 = c^2$
$a = 8, c = 12$ $8^2 + b^2 = 12^2$
Solve for b^2. $64 + b^2 = 144$
(If you let $b = 8$ and solve for a^2, the result is the same.) $b^2 = 80$

Use the Principal Square Root Property.
Since $b^2 = 80$, b is the square root of 80. $b = \sqrt{80}$

Use a calculator to approximate $\sqrt{80}$. $b \approx 8.94$

The length of the other leg is approximately 8.94 in.

EXAMPLE 1

The two legs of a right triangle measure 12 ft and 9 ft. Find the hypotenuse of the right triangle.

Strategy

To find the hypotenuse, use the Pythagorean Theorem. $a = 12, b = 9$

Solution

$c^2 = a^2 + b^2$ • **The Pythagorean Theorem**
$c^2 = 12^2 + 9^2$ • $a = 12, b = 9$
$c^2 = 144 + 81$
$c^2 = 225$
$c = \sqrt{225}$ • **The Principal Square Root Property**
$c = 15$

The length of the hypotenuse is 15 ft.

YOU TRY IT 1

The hypotenuse of a right triangle measures 6 m, and one leg measures 2 m. Find the measure of the other leg. Round to the nearest hundredth.

Your strategy

Your solution

5.66 m

Solution on p. S20

OBJECTIVE B *To solve similar triangles*

Similar objects have the same shape but not necessarily the same size. A tennis ball is similar to a basketball. A model ship is similar to an actual ship.

© Marafona/Shutterstock.com

Similar objects have corresponding parts; for example, the rudder on the model ship corresponds to the rudder on the actual ship. The relationship between the sizes of each of the corresponding parts can be written as a ratio, and each ratio will be the same. If the rudder on the model ship is $\frac{1}{100}$ the size of the rudder on the actual ship, then the model mast is $\frac{1}{100}$ the size of the actual mast, the width of the model is $\frac{1}{100}$ the width of the actual ship, and so on.

The two triangles ABC and DEF shown at the right are similar. Side $\overline{AB}$ corresponds to side $\overline{DE}$, side $\overline{BC}$ corresponds to side $\overline{EF}$, and side $\overline{AC}$ corresponds to side $\overline{DF}$. The ratios of corresponding sides are equal.

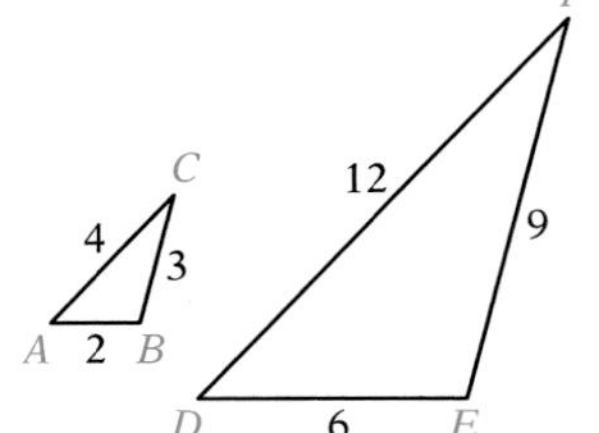

$$\frac{AB}{DE} = \frac{2}{6} = \frac{1}{3}, \frac{BC}{EF} = \frac{3}{9} = \frac{1}{3}, \text{ and } \frac{AC}{DF} = \frac{4}{12} = \frac{1}{3}.$$

Since the ratios of corresponding sides are equal, three proportions can be formed.

$$\frac{AB}{DE} = \frac{BC}{EF}, \frac{AB}{DE} = \frac{AC}{DF}, \text{ and } \frac{BC}{EF} = \frac{AC}{DF}.$$

The corresponding angles in similar triangles are equal. Therefore,

$\angle A = \angle D$, $\angle B = \angle E$, and $\angle C = \angle F$.

INSTRUCTOR NOTE

The concepts of similar triangles and the fact that the ratios of corresponding sides are equal are not obvious to students. Nonetheless, these concepts are essential in many practical applications.

You might introduce the topic of similar triangles by using a magnifying glass. Illustrate that an object viewed under a magnifying lens appears larger, but its shape has not changed.

Properties of Similar Triangles

For similar triangles, the ratios of corresponding sides are equal. The ratio of corresponding heights is equal to the ratio of corresponding sides.

EXAMPLE

For the triangles at the right, the ratios of corresponding sides are equal.

$$\frac{AB}{DE} = \frac{BC}{EF} = \frac{AC}{DF} = \frac{1}{2}$$

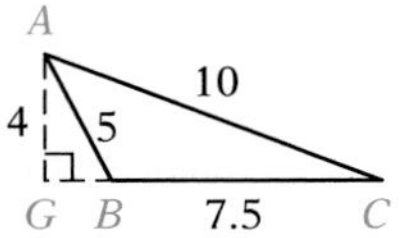

The ratio of corresponding heights is equal to the ratio of corresponding sides.

$$\frac{AG}{DH} = \frac{1}{2}$$

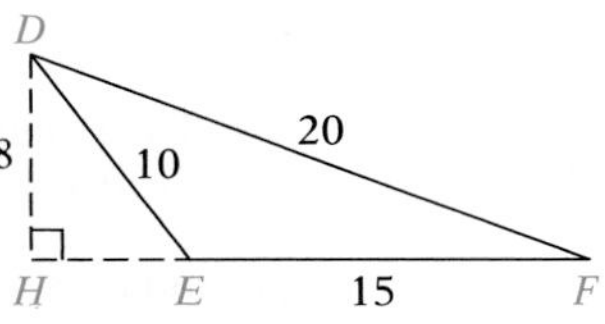

Triangles ABC and DEF are similar triangles.

Point of Interest

Many mathematicians have studied similar objects. Thales of Miletus (c. 624 B.C.–547 B.C.) discovered that he could determine the heights of pyramids and other large objects by measuring a small object and the length of its shadow, and then making use of similar triangles.

IN-CLASS EXAMPLES

3. Triangles ABC and DEF are similar. Find DE. **6.75 m**

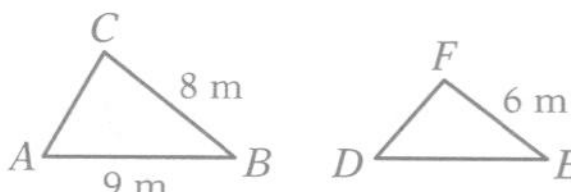

HOW TO 2 The two triangles at the right are similar triangles. Find the length of side $\overline{EF}$. Round to the nearest tenth.

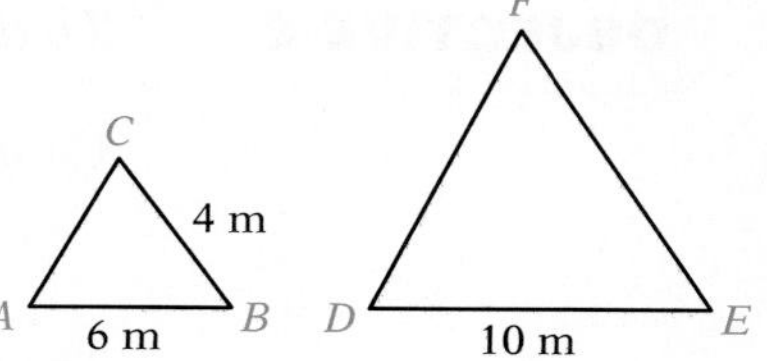

The triangles are similar, so the ratios of corresponding sides are equal.

$$\frac{EF}{BC} = \frac{DE}{AB}$$

$$\frac{EF}{4} = \frac{10}{6}$$

$$6(EF) = 4(10)$$
$$6(EF) = 40$$
$$EF \approx 6.7$$

The length of side EF is approximately 6.7 m.

EXAMPLE 2

Triangles ABC and DEF are similar. Find FG, the height of triangle DEF.

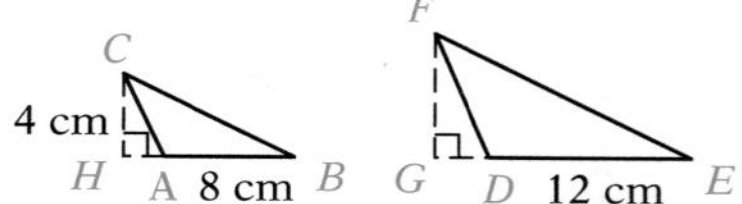

Strategy

To find FG, write a proportion using the fact that, in similar triangles, the ratio of corresponding sides equals the ratio of corresponding heights. Solve the proportion for FG.

Solution

$$\frac{AB}{DE} = \frac{CH}{FG}$$ • The ratio of corresponding sides equals the ratio of corresponding heights.

$$\frac{8}{12} = \frac{4}{FG}$$ • $AB = 8, DE = 12, CH = 4$

$$8(FG) = 12(4)$$ • The cross products are equal.

$$8(FG) = 48$$
$$FG = 6$$

The height FG of triangle DEF is 6 cm.

YOU TRY IT 2

Triangles ABC and DEF are similar. Find FG, the height of triangle DEF.

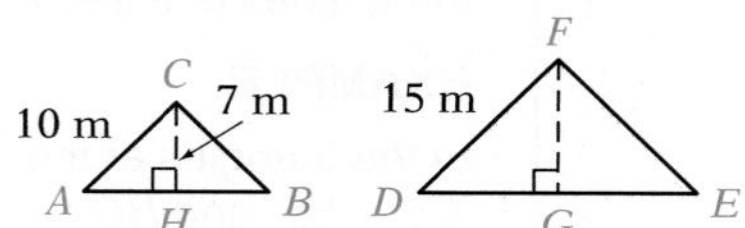

Your strategy

Your solution

10.5 m

Solution on p. S20

OBJECTIVE C *To determine whether two triangles are congruent*

Congruent objects have the same shape *and* the same size.

The two triangles at the right are congruent. They have the same size.

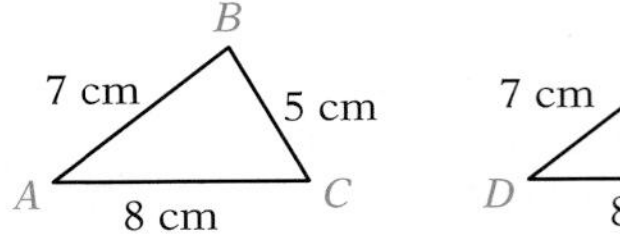

Congruent and similar triangles differ in that the corresponding sides and angles of congruent triangles must be equal, whereas for similar triangles, corresponding angles are equal, but corresponding sides are not necessarily the same length.

The three major rules used to determine whether two triangles are congruent are given below and at the top of the facing page.

Side-Side-Side Rule (SSS)

Two triangles are congruent if the three sides of one triangle equal the corresponding three sides of a second triangle.

EXAMPLE

In the triangles at the right, $AC = DE$, $AB = EF$, and $BC = DF$. The corresponding sides of triangles ABC and DEF are equal. The triangles are congruent by the SSS Rule.

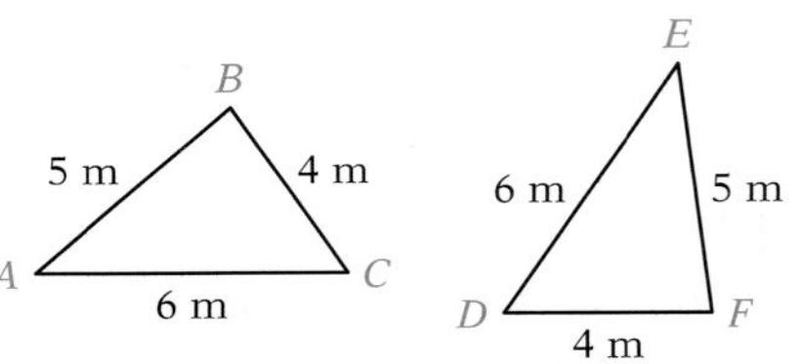

Side-Angle-Side Rule (SAS)

If two sides and the included angle of one triangle equal two sides and the included angle of a second triangle, the two triangles are congruent.

EXAMPLE

In the two triangles at the right, $AB = EF$, $AC = DE$, and $\angle BAC = \angle DEF$. The triangles are congruent by the SAS Rule.

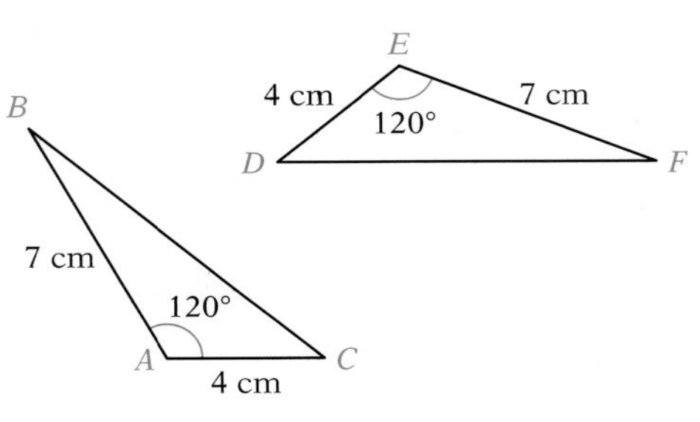

IN-CLASS EXAMPLES

4. Determine whether the two triangles are congruent. **Yes, by the SAS Rule**

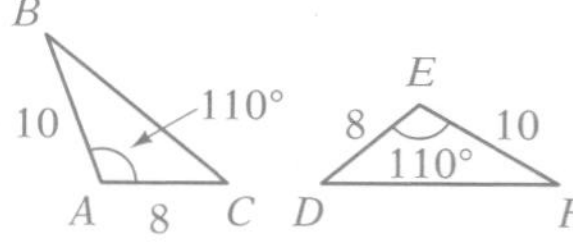

Angle-Side-Angle Rule (ASA)

If two angles and the included side of one triangle equal two angles and the included side of a second triangle, the two triangles are congruent.

EXAMPLE

For triangles *ABC* and *DEF* at the right, $\angle A = \angle F$, $\angle C = \angle E$, and $AC = EF$. The triangles are congruent by the ASA Rule.

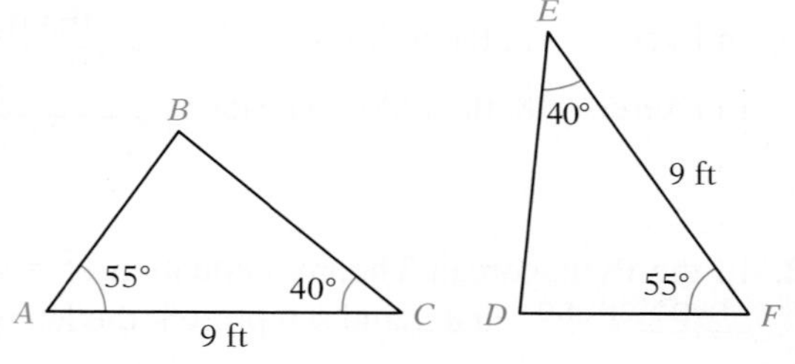

HOW TO 3 Given triangle *PQR* and triangle *MNO*, do the conditions $\angle P = \angle O$, $\angle Q = \angle M$, and $PQ = MO$ guarantee that triangle *PQR* is congruent to triangle *MNO*?

Draw a sketch of the two triangles and determine whether one of the rules for congruence is satisfied.

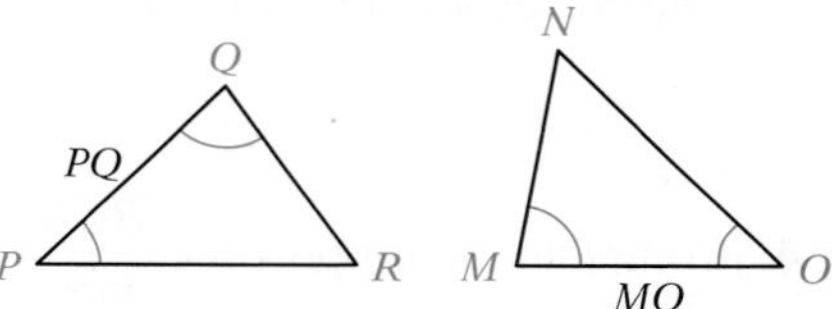

Because two angles and the included side of one triangle equal two angles and the included side of the second triangle, the triangles are congruent by the ASA Rule.

EXAMPLE 3

In the figure below, is triangle *ABC* congruent to triangle *DEF*?

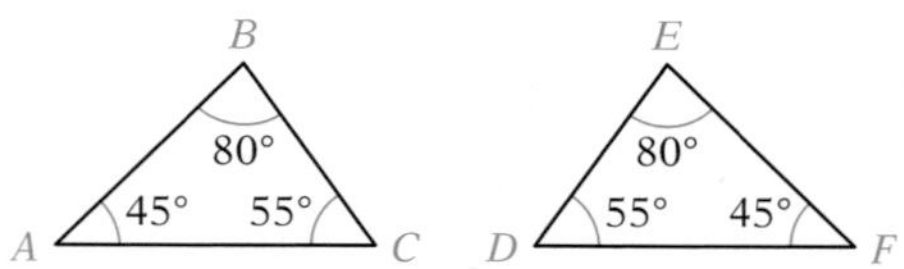

Strategy

To determine whether the triangles are congruent, determine whether one of the rules for congruence is satisfied.

Solution

The triangles do not satisfy the SSS Rule, the SAS Rule, or the ASA Rule. The triangles are not necessarily congruent.

YOU TRY IT 3

In the figure below, is triangle *PQR* congruent to triangle *MNO*?

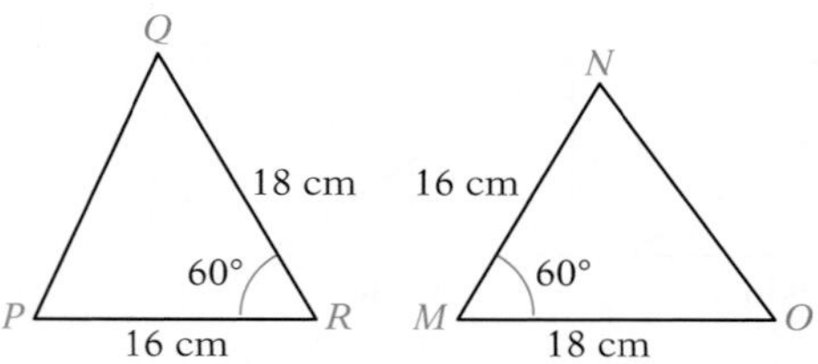

Your strategy

Your solution

Yes, by the SAS Rule

Solution on p. S20

7.3 EXERCISES

Concept Check

SUGGESTED ASSIGNMENT
Exercises 1–10; Exercises 11–51, odds; Exercise 54

1. Fill in each blank with *the hypotenuse* or *a leg.*

In Exercise 12, the unknown side is __the hypotenuse__.

In Exercise 18, the unknown side is __a leg__.

2. In the Pythagorean Theorem equation $c^2 = a^2 + b^2$, c represents the length of the __hypotenuse__ and a and b represent the lengths of the __legs__.

For Exercises 3 and 4, use the pair of triangles shown at the right. Triangle ABC is similar to triangle DEF.

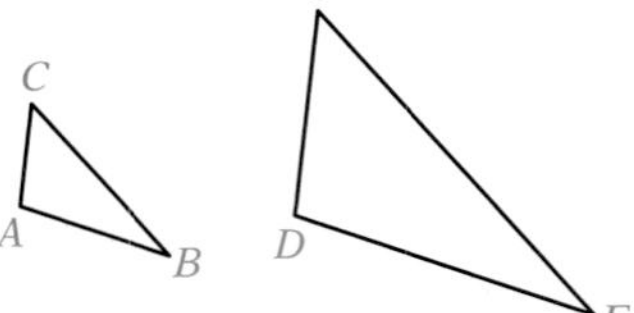

3. The corresponding side for CA is __FD__.

The corresponding side for ED is __BA__.

4. Complete the proportion: $\frac{BC}{EF} = \frac{AC}{DF}$.

Find the ratio of corresponding sides for the similar triangles.

5. $\frac{1}{2}$

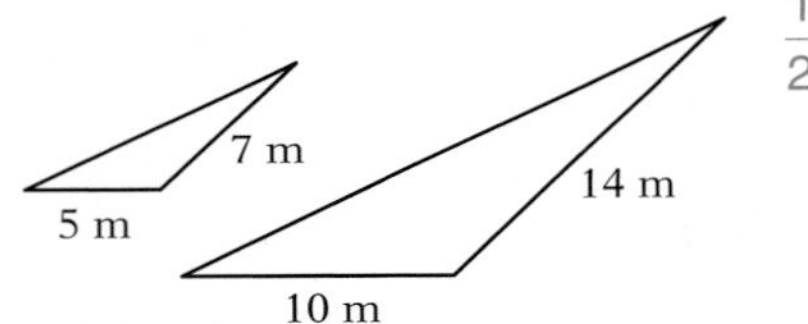

6. $\frac{1}{3}$

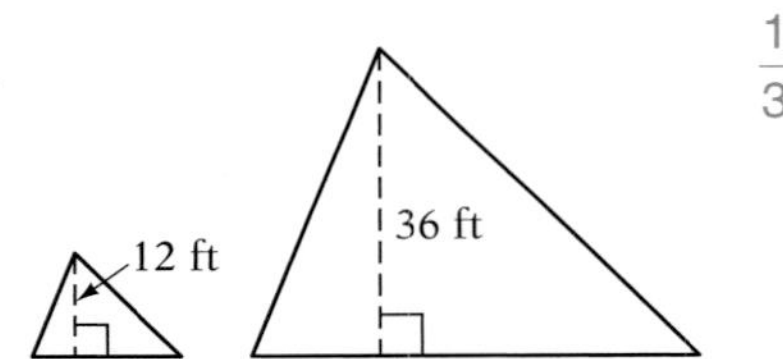

7. $\frac{3}{4}$

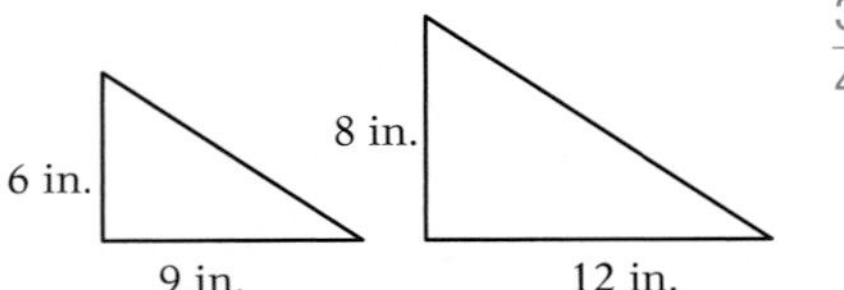

8. $\frac{1}{3}$

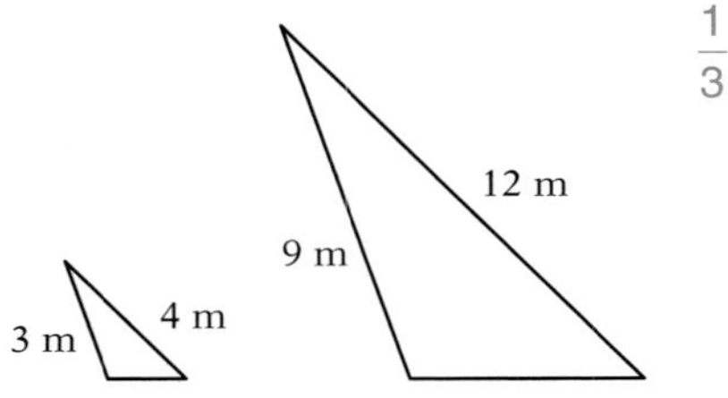

For Exercises 9 and 10, use the pair of congruent triangles shown at the right.

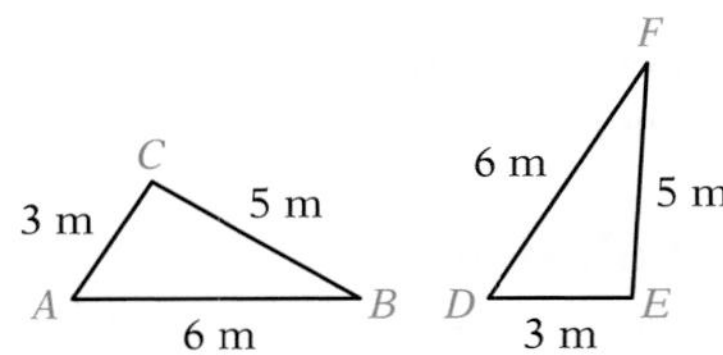

9. The angle of triangle DEF that corresponds to $\angle C$ in triangle ABC is __$\angle E$__.

10. a. The angle of triangle DEF that is included between sides FE and FD is __$\angle F$__.

b. The side of triangle ABC that is included between $\angle A$ and $\angle B$ is __AB__.

OBJECTIVE A *To find the unknown side of a right triangle by using the Pythagorean Theorem*

Find the unknown side of the triangle. If necessary, round to the nearest tenth.

11. 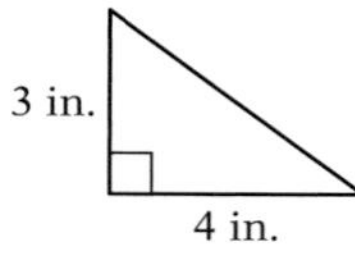

5 in.

12. 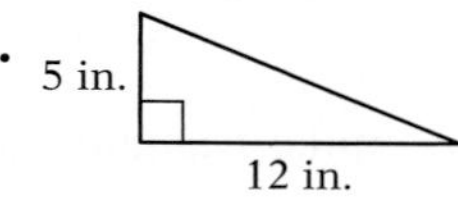

13 in.

13. 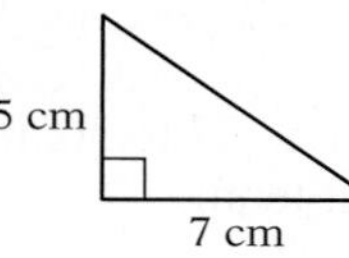

8.6 cm

14. 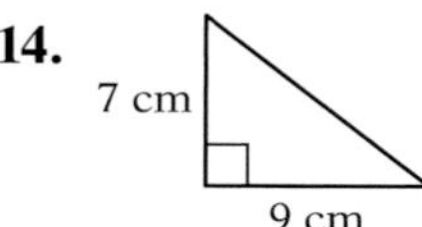

11.4 cm

15. 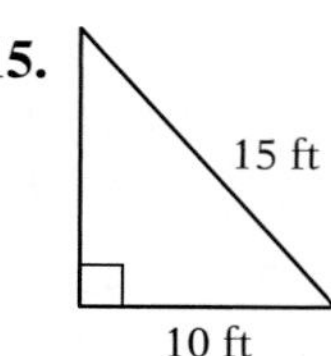

11.2 ft

16. 20 ft, 18 ft

8.7 ft

17. 

4.5 cm

18. 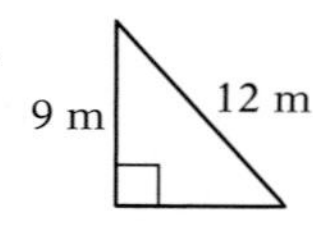

7.9 m

19. 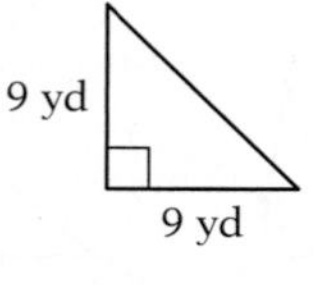

12.7 yd

20. Which equation could be used to find the unknown side in the triangle shown at the right?

(i) $20^2 = 10^2 + b^2$ **(ii)** $c^2 = 10^2 + 20^2$

i

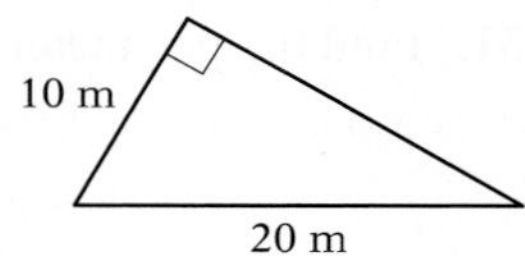

21. A 30-foot ladder leans against the side of a building with its bottom a feet from the building. The ladder reaches a height of b feet on the building. Which of the following distances is not possible as a value for b?

(i) 5 ft **(ii)** 25 ft **(iii)** 35 ft

iii

Solve. Round to the nearest tenth.

22. Geography If you travel 18 mi east and then 12 mi north, how far are you from your starting point? 21.6 mi

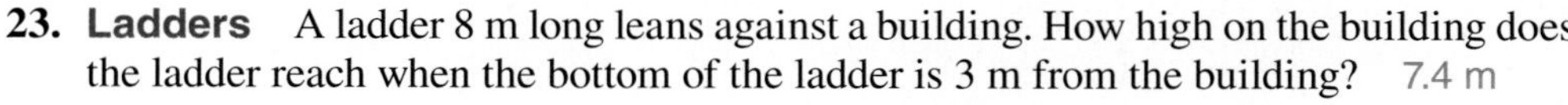

23. Ladders A ladder 8 m long leans against a building. How high on the building does the ladder reach when the bottom of the ladder is 3 m from the building? 7.4 m

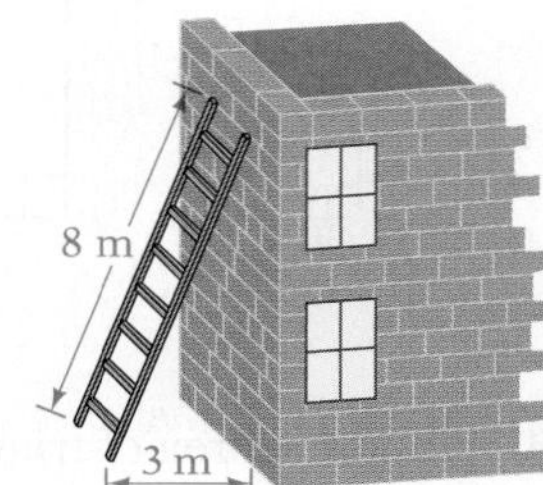

24. Metal Work Find the distance between the centers of the holes in the metal plate. 8.5 cm

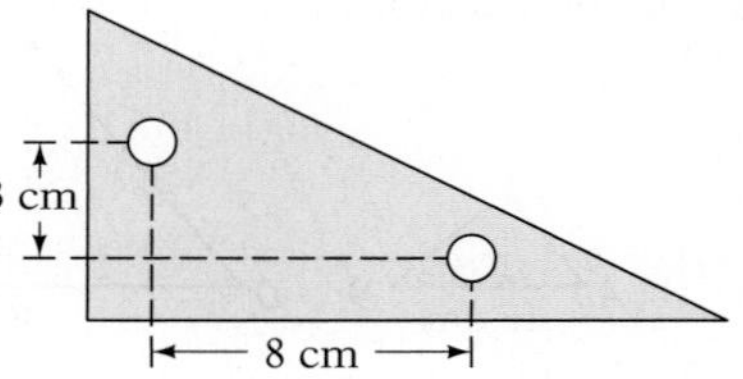

25. Find the perimeter of a right triangle with legs that measure 5 cm and 9 cm.
24.3 cm

26. Find the perimeter of a right triangle with legs that measure 6 in. and 8 in. 24 in.

OBJECTIVE B *To solve similar triangles*

For Exercises 27 to 36, triangles *ABC* and *DEF* are similar triangles. Solve and round to the nearest tenth.

27. Find side *DE*.

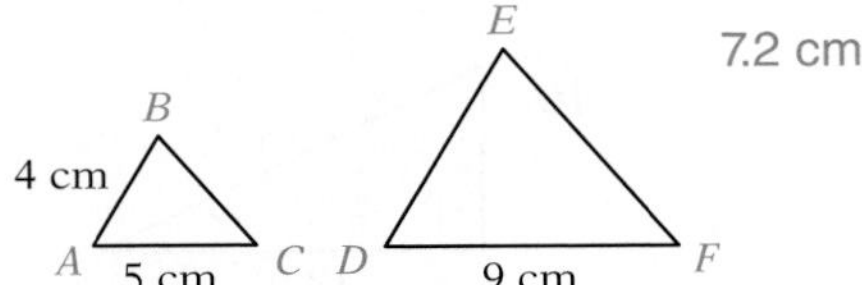

7.2 cm

28. Find side *DE*.

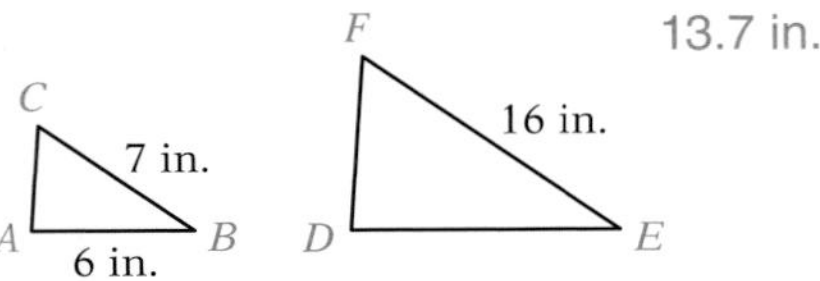

13.7 in.

29. Find the height of triangle *DEF*.

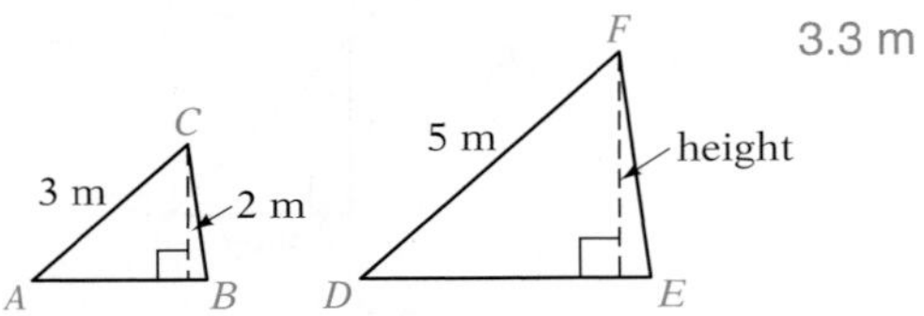

3.3 m

30. Find the height of triangle *ABC*.

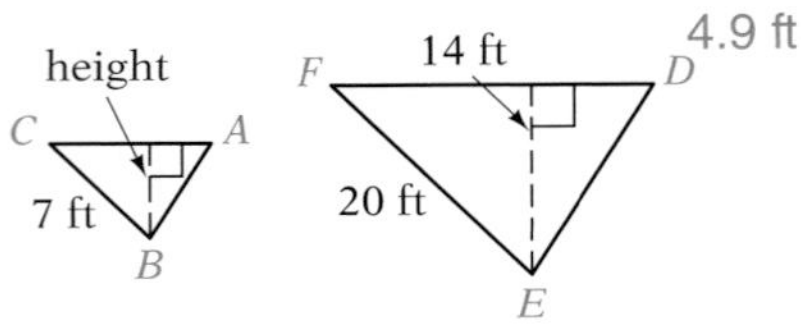

4.9 ft

31. Find the perimeter of triangle *ABC*.

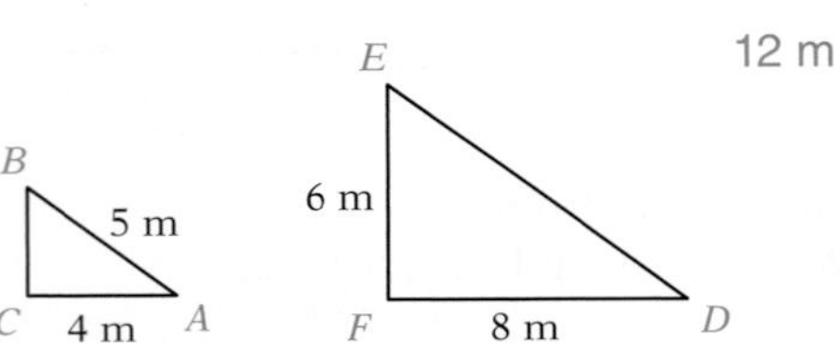

12 m

32. Find the perimeter of triangle *DEF*.

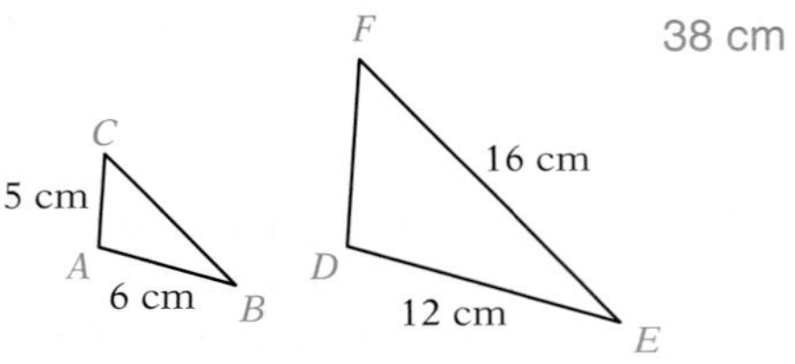

38 cm

33. Find the perimeter of triangle *ABC*.

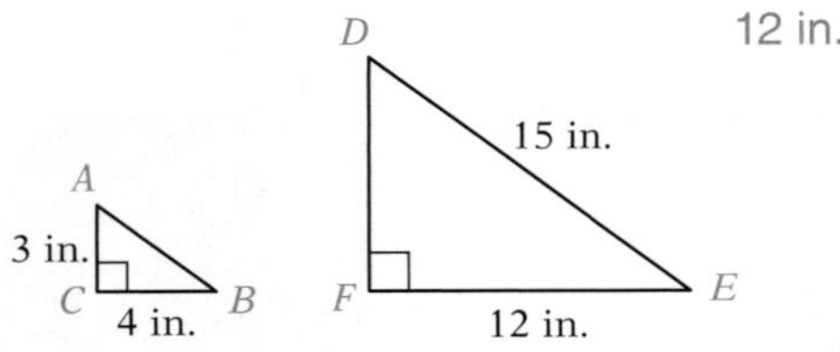

12 in.

34. Find the area of triangle *DEF*.

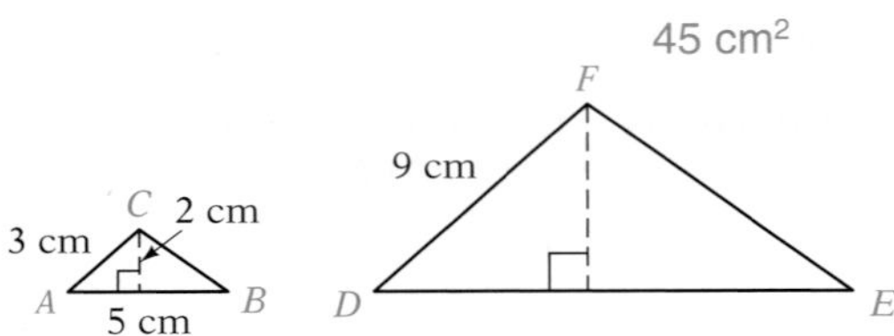

45 cm²

35. Find the area of triangle *ABC*.

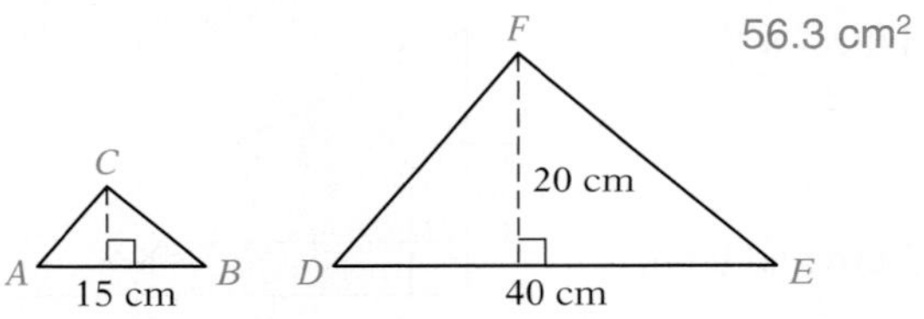

56.3 cm²

36. Find the area of triangle *DEF*.

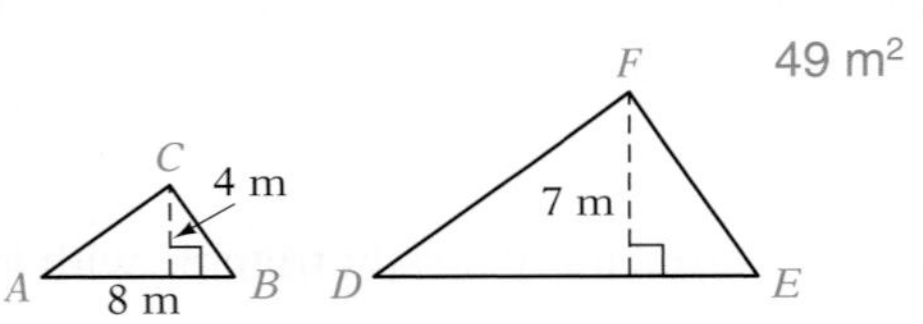

49 m²

Indirect Measurement The sun's rays, objects on Earth, and the shadows cast by them form similar triangles. Use this fact to solve Exercises 37 to 40.

37. Find the height of the flagpole.

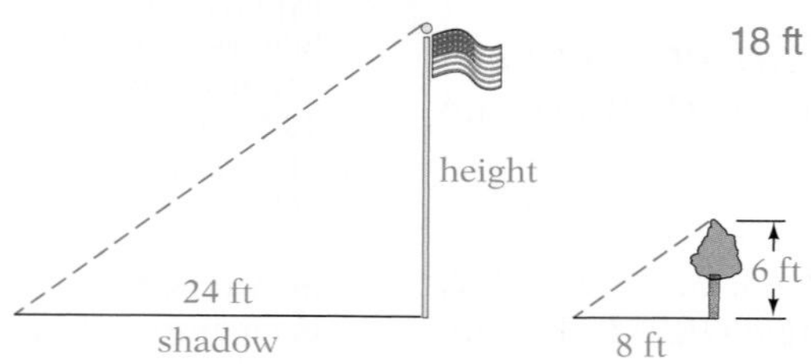

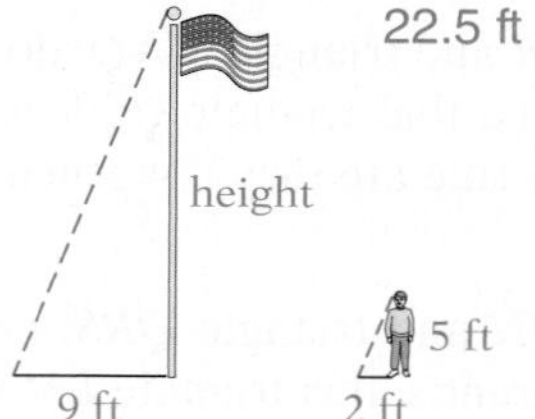

18 ft

38. Find the height of the flagpole.

22.5 ft

39. Find the height of the building.

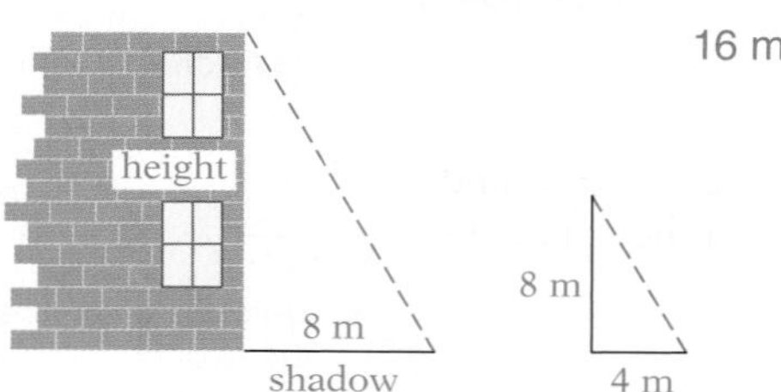

16 m

40. Find the height of the building.

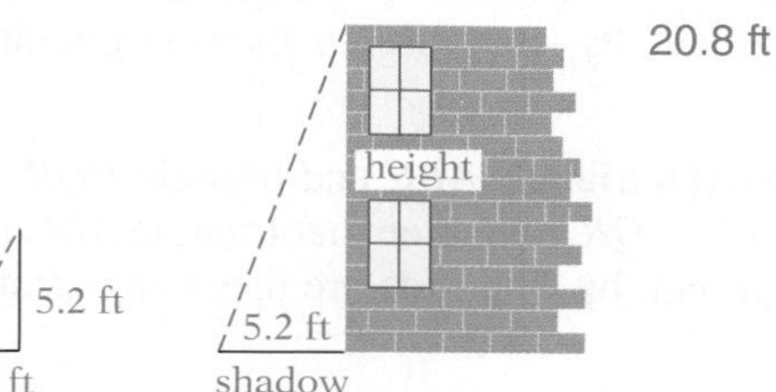

20.8 ft

OBJECTIVE C *To determine whether two triangles are congruent*

For Exercises 41 to 46, determine whether the two triangles are congruent. If they are congruent, state by what rule they are congruent.

41.

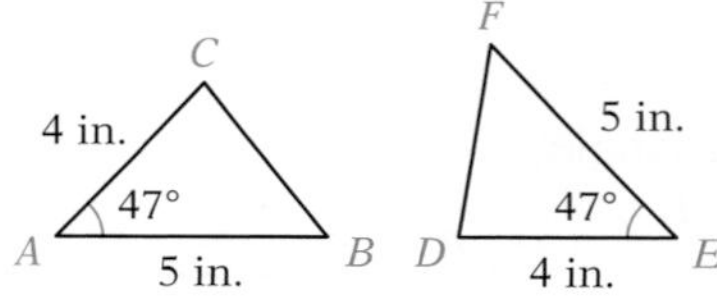

Yes, SAS Rule

42.

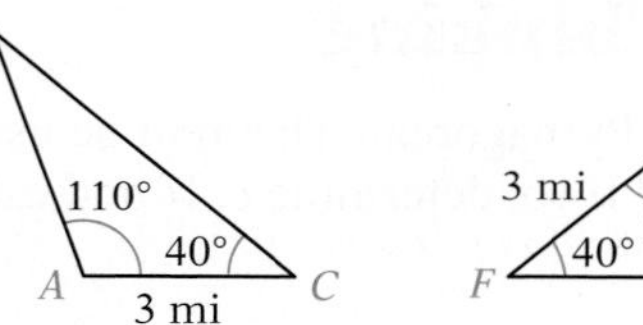

Yes, ASA Rule

43.

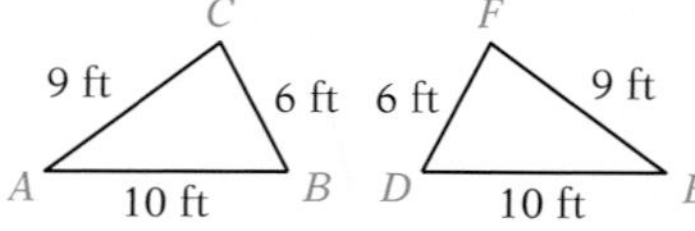

Yes, SSS Rule

44.

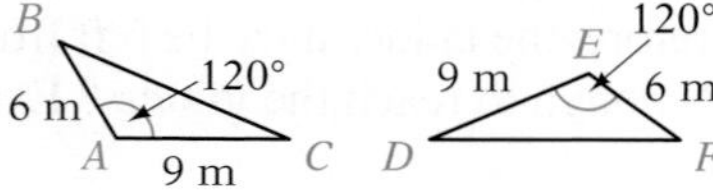

Yes, SAS Rule

45.

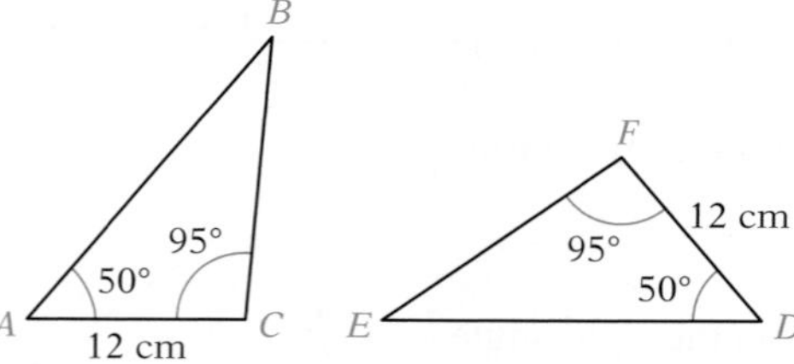

Yes, ASA Rule

46.

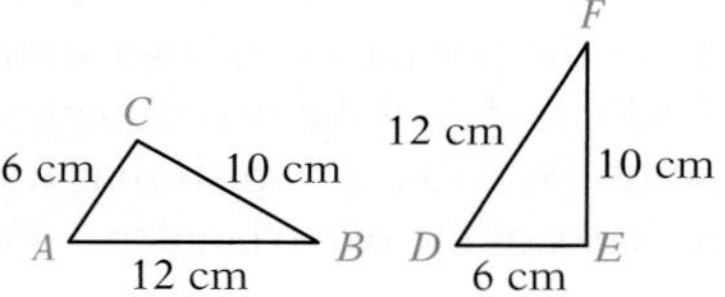

Yes, SSS Rule

47. Given triangle ABC and triangle DEF, do the conditions $\angle C = \angle E$, $AC = EF$, and $BC = DE$ guarantee that triangle ABC is congruent to triangle DEF? If they are congruent, by what rule are they congruent? Yes, SAS Rule

48. Given triangle PQR and triangle MNO, do the conditions $PR = NO$, $PQ = MO$, and $QR = MN$ guarantee that triangle PQR is congruent to triangle MNO? If they are congruent, by what rule are they congruent? Yes, SSS Rule

49. Given triangle LMN and triangle QRS, do the conditions $\angle M = \angle S$, $\angle N = \angle Q$, and $\angle L = \angle R$ guarantee that triangle LMN is congruent to triangle QRS? If they are congruent, by what rule are they congruent? No

50. Given triangle DEF and triangle JKL, do the conditions $\angle D = \angle K$, $\angle E = \angle L$, and $DE = KL$ guarantee that triangle DEF is congruent to triangle JKL? If they are congruent, by what rule are they congruent? Yes, ASA Rule

51. Given triangle ABC and triangle PQR, do the conditions $\angle B = \angle P$, $BC = PQ$, and $AC = QR$ guarantee that triangle ABC is congruent to triangle PQR? If they are congruent, by what rule are they congruent? No

For Exercises 52 and 53, determine whether the given conditions guarantee that the triangles are congruent.

52. The ratio of the corresponding sides of two similar triangles is $\frac{1}{1}$. Yes

53. One right triangle has a hypotenuse of length 10 in. and an acute angle of 40°. A second right triangle has a hypotenuse of length 10 in. and an acute angle of 50°. Yes

QUICK QUIZ

1. The two legs of a right triangle measure 7 cm and 12 cm. Find the hypotenuse of the right triangle. Round to the nearest tenth. **13.9 cm [7.3A]**
2. The hypotenuse of a right triangle measures 14 mi, and one leg measures 11 mi. Find the measure of the other leg. Round to the nearest tenth. **8.7 mi [7.3A]**
3. Triangles *ABC* and *DEF* are similar. Find the area of triangle *DEF*. **3125 cm² [7.3B]**

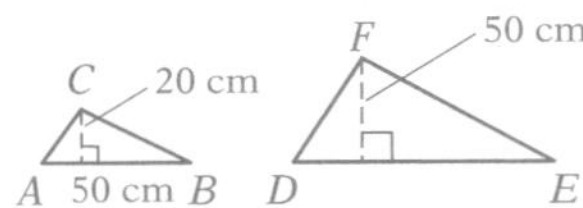

4. Determine whether the two triangles are congruent. **Yes, by the SSS Rule [7.3C]**

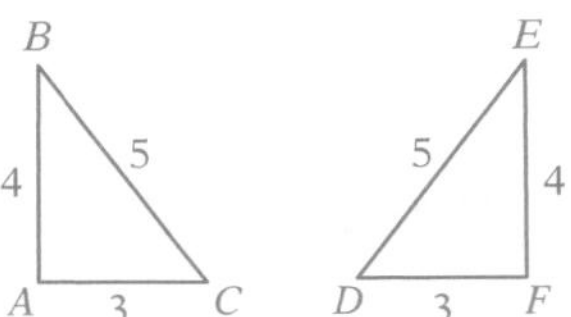

Critical Thinking

54. Can the Pythagorean Theorem be used to find the length of side c in the triangle at the right? If so, determine c. If not, explain why the theorem cannot be used.

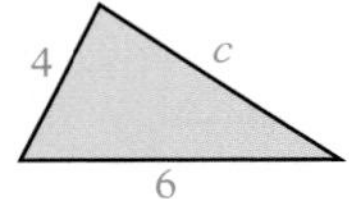

55. **Home Maintenance** You need to clean the gutters of your home. The gutters are 24 ft above the ground. For safety, the distance a ladder reaches up a wall should be four times the distance from the bottom of the ladder to the base of the side of the house. Therefore, the ladder must be 6 ft from the base of the house. Will a 25-foot ladder be long enough to reach the gutters? Explain how you determined your answer.

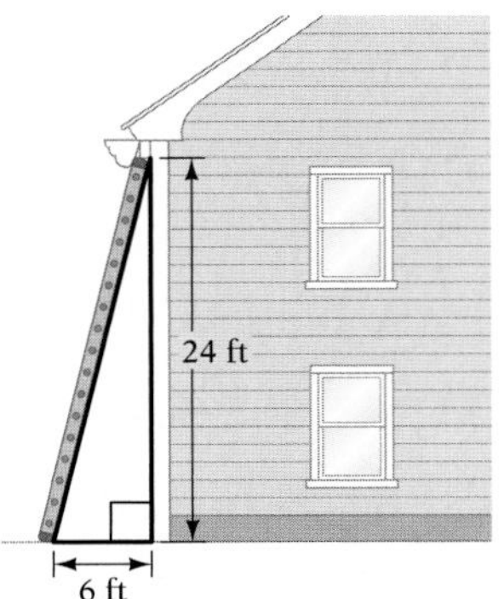

Projects or Group Activities

56. Determine whether the statement is true or false.

a. The ratio of the perimeters of two similar triangles is the same as the ratio of the corresponding sides of the two triangles. True

b. The ratio of the areas of two similar triangles is the same as the ratio of the corresponding sides of the two triangles. False

57. In the figure at the right, the height of a right triangle is drawn from the right angle perpendicular to the hypotenuse. Verify that the two smaller triangles formed are similar to the original triangle and similar to each other.

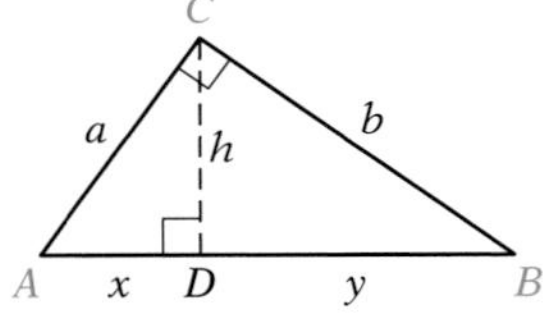

SECTION

7.4 Solids

OBJECTIVE A To find the volume of geometric solids

Geometric solids are figures in space. Five common geometric solids are the rectangular solid, the sphere, the cylinder, the cone, and the pyramid.

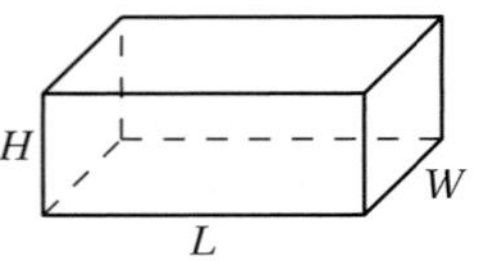

A **rectangular solid** is one in which all six sides, called **faces,** are rectangles. The variable L is used to represent the length of a rectangular solid, W its width, and H its height.

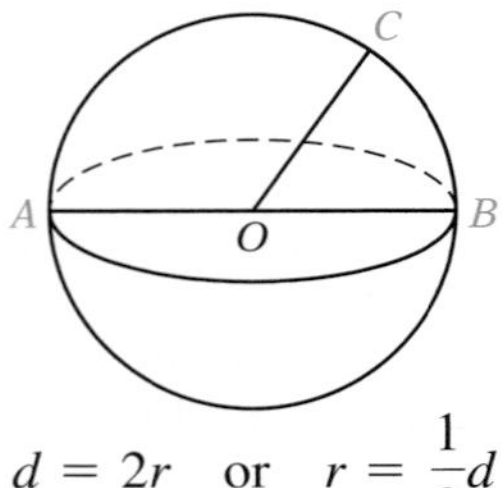

$$d = 2r \quad \text{or} \quad r = \frac{1}{2}d$$

A **sphere** is a solid in which all points are the same distance from point O, called the **center** of the sphere. The **diameter** d of a sphere is a line across the sphere going through point O. The **radius** r is a line from the center to a point on the sphere. AB is a diameter and OC is a radius of the sphere shown at the left.

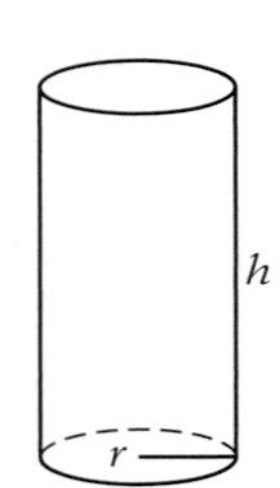

The most common cylinder, called a **right circular cylinder,** is one in which the bases are circles and are perpendicular to the height of the cylinder. The variable r is used to represent the radius of a base of a cylinder, and h represents the height. In this text, only right circular cylinders are discussed.

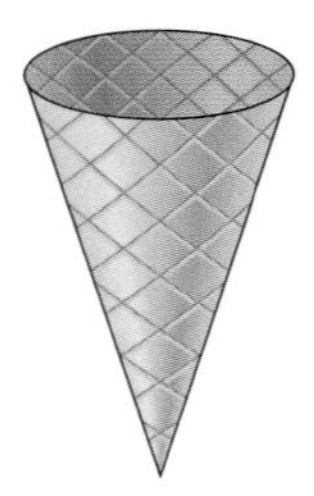

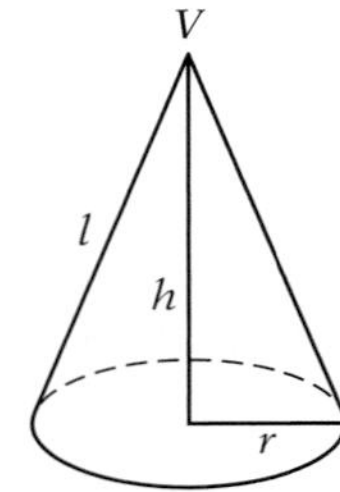

A **right circular cone** is obtained when one base of a right circular cylinder is shrunk to a point, called the **vertex** V. The variable r is used to represent the radius of the base of the cone, and h represents the height. The variable l is used to represent the **slant height,** which is the distance from a point on the circumference of the base to the vertex. In this text, only right circular cones are discussed.

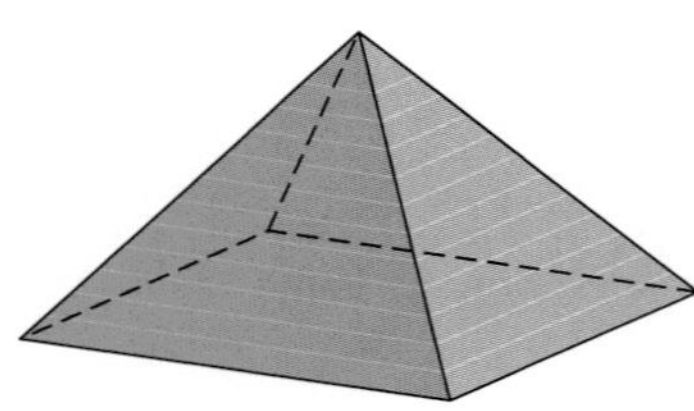

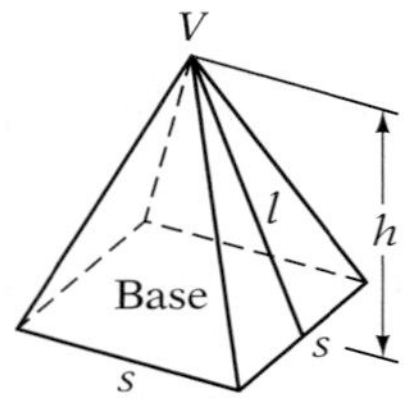

The base of a **regular pyramid** is a regular polygon, and the sides are isosceles triangles. The height h is the distance from the vertex V to the base and is perpendicular to the base. The variable l is used to represent the **slant height,** which is the height of one of the isosceles triangles on the face of the pyramid. The regular square pyramid at the left has a square base. This is the only type of pyramid discussed in this text.

A **cube** is a special type of rectangular solid. Each of the six faces of a cube is a square. The variable *s* is used to represent the length of one side of a cube.

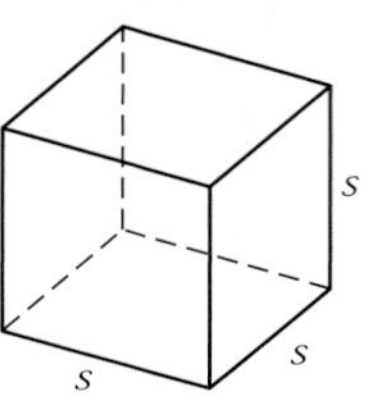

Point of Interest

Originally, the human body was used as the standard of measure. A mouthful was used as a unit of measure in ancient Egypt; it was later referred to as a *half jigger.* In French, the word for *inch* is *pouce,* which means "thumb." A *span* was the distance from the tip of the outstretched thumb to the tip of the little finger. The *cubit* referred to the distance from the elbow to the end of the fingers. A *fathom* was the distance from the tip of the fingers on one hand to the tip of the fingers on the other hand when standing with arms fully extended from the sides. The *hand,* where 1 hand = 4 in., is still used today to measure horses.

Volume is a measure of the amount of space occupied by a geometric solid. Volume can be used to describe, for example, the amount of trash in a landfill, the amount of concrete poured for the foundation of a house, or the amount of water in a town's reservoir.

A cube that is 1 ft on each side has a volume of 1 cubic foot, which is written 1 ft^3. A cube that measures 1 cm on each side has a volume of 1 cubic centimeter, written 1 cm^3.

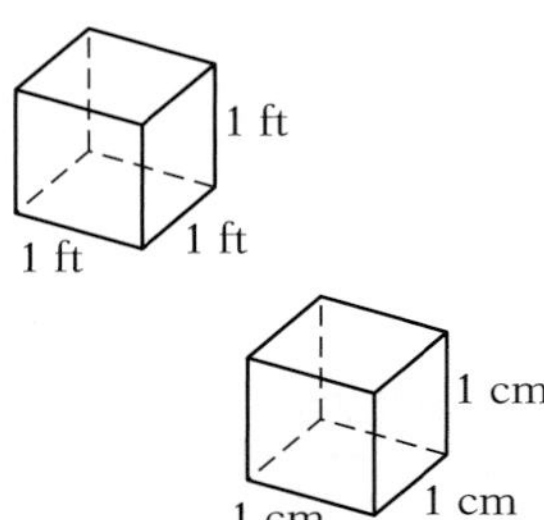

The volume of a solid is the number of cubes that are necessary to exactly fill the solid. The volume of the rectangular solid at the right is 24 cm^3 because it will hold exactly 24 cubes, each 1 cm on a side. Note that the volume can be found by multiplying the length times the width times the height.

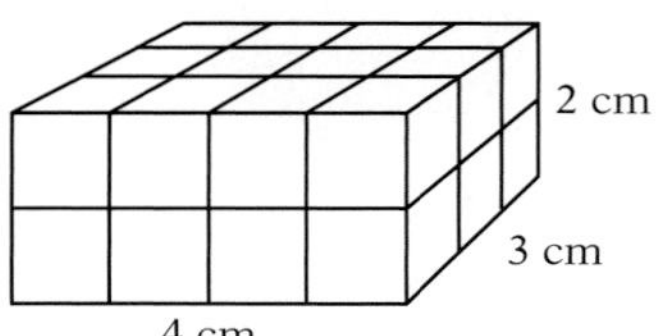

The formulas for the volumes of the geometric solids described above are given below.

INSTRUCTOR NOTE

The difficulty students have distinguishing linear measure from square measure is compounded with volume measure. Ask students to give examples of things that would be measured in, for instance, feet, square feet, and cubic feet—for example, the length of a room, the area of the floor, and the volume of air in the room. Here are some more examples.

a. The distance across a lake, the area of the surface of the lake, and the volume of water in the lake.

b. The length of a driveway, the area of the driveway that needs to be resealed, and the volume of asphalt used to pave the driveway.

Volumes of Geometric Solids

The volume V of a **rectangular solid** with length L, width W, and height H is given by $V = LWH$.

The volume V of a **cube** with side s is given by $V = s^3$.

The volume V of a **sphere** with radius r is given by $V = \frac{4}{3}\pi r^3$.

The volume V of a **right circular cylinder** is given by $V = \pi r^2 h$, where r is the radius of the base and h is the height.

The volume V of a **right circular cone** is given by $V = \frac{1}{3}\pi r^2 h$, where r is the radius of the circular base and h is the height.

The volume V of a **regular square pyramid** is given by $V = \frac{1}{3}s^2 h$, where s is the length of a side of the base and h is the height.

HOW TO 1 Find the volume of a sphere with a diameter of 6 in.

First find the radius of the sphere. $r = \frac{1}{2}d = \frac{1}{2}(6) = 3$

Use the formula for the volume of a sphere. $V = \frac{4}{3}\pi r^3$

Substitute 3 for r. $V = \frac{4}{3}\pi(3)^3$

$V = \frac{4}{3}\pi(27)$

The exact volume of the sphere is 36π in^3. $V = 36\pi$

An approximate measure can be found by using the π key on a calculator. $V \approx 113.10$

The approximate volume is 113.10 in^3.

EXAMPLE 1

The length of a rectangular solid is 5 m, the width is 3.2 m, and the height is 4 m. Find the volume of the solid.

Strategy

To find the volume, use the formula for the volume of a rectangular solid. $L = 5$, $W = 3.2$, $H = 4$

Solution

$V = LWH$

$V = 5(3.2)(4) = 64$

The volume of the rectangular solid is 64 m^3.

YOU TRY IT 1

Find the volume of a cube that measures 2.5 m on a side.

Your strategy

Your solution

15.625 m^3

IN-CLASS EXAMPLES

1. Find the volume of a rectangular solid with a length of 6 m, a width of 4 m, and a height of 4.5 m. **108 m^3**
2. Find the volume of a sphere with a radius of 4 mm. Round to the nearest hundredth. **268.08 mm^3**
3. Find the volume of a right circular cylinder with a radius of 15 cm and a height of 14 cm. Round to the nearest hundredth. **9896.02 cm^3**

EXAMPLE 2

The radius of the base of a cone is 8 cm. The height is 12 cm. Find the volume of the cone. Round to the nearest hundredth.

Strategy

To find the volume, use the formula for the volume of a cone. An approximation is asked for; use the π key on a calculator. $r = 8$, $h = 12$

Solution

$V = \frac{1}{3}\pi r^2 h$

$V = \frac{1}{3}\pi(8)^2(12) = \frac{1}{3}\pi(64)(12) = 256\pi \approx 804.25$

The volume is approximately 804.25 cm^3.

YOU TRY IT 2

The diameter of the base of a cylinder is 8 ft. The height of the cylinder is 22 ft. Find the exact volume of the cylinder.

Your strategy

Your solution

352π ft^3

Solutions on p. S20

OBJECTIVE B *To find the surface area of geometric solids*

The **surface area** of a solid is the total area on the surface of the solid. Suppose you want to cover a geometric solid with wallpaper. The amount of wallpaper needed is equal to the surface area of the figure.

When a rectangular solid is cut open and flattened out, each face is a rectangle. The surface area SA of the rectangular solid is the sum of the areas of the six rectangles:

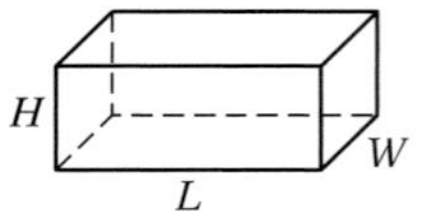

$$SA = LW + LH + WH + LW + WH + LH$$

which simplifies to

$$SA = 2LW + 2LH + 2WH$$

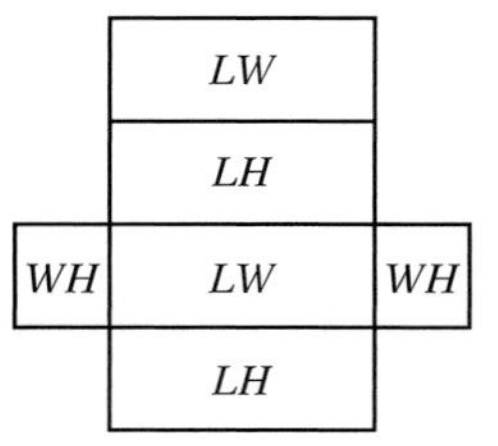

The surface area of a cube is the sum of the areas of the six faces of the cube. The area of each face is s^2. Therefore, the surface area SA of a cube is given by the formula $SA = 6s^2$.

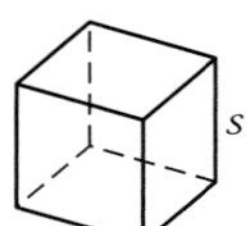

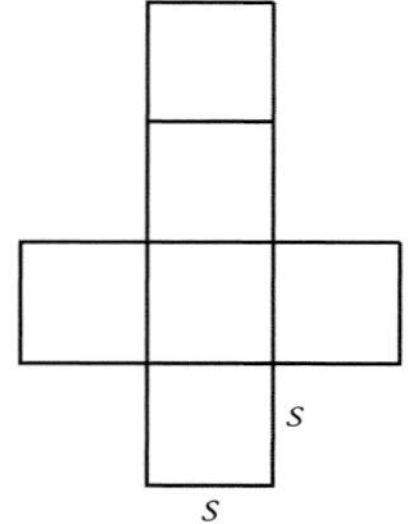

When a cylinder is cut open and flattened out, the top and bottom of the cylinder are circles. The side of the cylinder flattens out to a rectangle. The length of the rectangle is the circumference of the base, which is $2\pi r$; the width is h, the height of the cylinder. Therefore, the area of the rectangle is $2\pi rh$. The area of each circle is πr^2. The surface area SA of the cylinder is

$$SA = \pi r^2 + 2\pi rh + \pi r^2$$

which simplifies to

$$SA = 2\pi r^2 + 2\pi rh$$

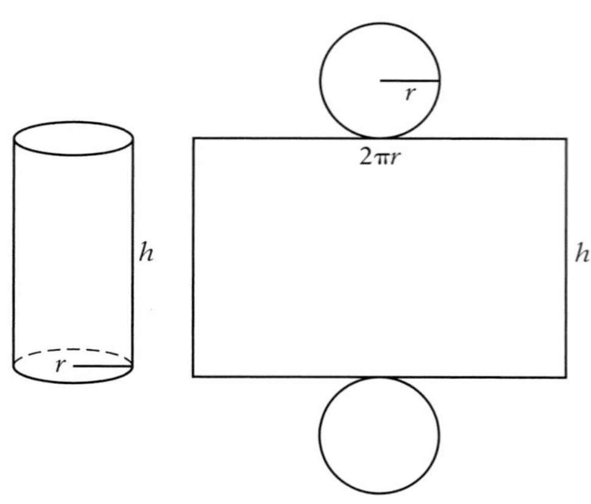

The surface area of a pyramid is the area of the base plus the area of the four isosceles triangles. A side of the square base is s; therefore, the area of the base is s^2. The slant height l is the height of each triangle, and s is the base of each triangle. The surface area SA of a pyramid is

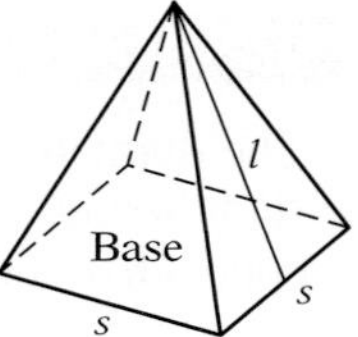

$$SA = s^2 + 4\left(\frac{1}{2}sl\right)$$

which simplifies to

$$SA = s^2 + 2sl$$

Formulas for the surface areas of geometric solids are given below.

Surface Areas of Geometric Solids

The surface area SA of a **rectangular solid** with length L, width W, and height H is given by $SA = 2LW + 2LH + 2WH$.

The surface area SA of a **cube** with side s is given by $SA = 6s^2$.

The surface area SA of a **sphere** with radius r is given by $SA = 4\pi r^2$.

The surface area SA of a **right circular cylinder** is given by $SA = 2\pi r^2 + 2\pi rh$, where r is the radius of the base and h is the height.

The surface area SA of a **right circular cone** is given by $SA = \pi r^2 + \pi rl$, where r is the radius of the circular base and l is the slant height.

The surface area SA of a **regular pyramid** is given by $SA = s^2 + 2sl$, where s is the length of a side of the base and l is the slant height.

HOW TO 2 Find the surface area of a sphere with a diameter of 18 cm.

First find the radius of the sphere.

$$r = \frac{1}{2}d = \frac{1}{2}(18) = 9$$

Use the formula for the surface area of a sphere. Substitute 9 for r.

$$SA = 4\pi r^2$$
$$SA = 4\pi(9)^2$$
$$SA = 4\pi(81)$$
$$SA = 324\pi$$

The exact surface area of the sphere is 324π cm^2.

An approximate measure can be found by using the π key on a calculator.

$$SA \approx 1017.88$$

The approximate surface area is 1017.88 cm^2.

Integrating Technology

To approximate 324π on your calculator, enter

324  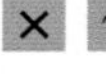 .

EXAMPLE 3

The diameter of the base of a cone is 5 m, and the slant height is 4 m. Find the surface area of the cone. Give the exact measure.

Strategy

To find the surface area of the cone:

- Find the radius of the base of the cone. $d = 5$
- Use the formula for the surface area of a cone. Leave the answer in terms of π.

Solution

$r = \frac{1}{2}d = \frac{1}{2}(5) = 2.5$ • **Find the radius.**

$SA = \pi r^2 + \pi rl$ • **Formula for the surface area of a cone**

$SA = \pi(2.5)^2 + \pi(2.5)(4)$ • $r = 2.5, l = 4$

$SA = \pi(6.25) + \pi(2.5)(4)$

$SA = 6.25\pi + 10\pi$

$SA = 16.25\pi$

The surface area of the cone is 16.25π m^2.

YOU TRY IT 3

The diameter of the base of a cylinder is 6 ft, and the height is 8 ft. Find the surface area of the cylinder. Round to the nearest hundredth.

Your strategy

Your solution

207.35 ft^2

IN-CLASS EXAMPLES

4. Find the surface area of a rectangular solid with a length of 5 m, a width of 3 m, and a height of 2.5 m. **70 m^2**
5. Find the surface area of a cube with a side of 5.5 mm. **181.5 mm^2**
6. Find the surface area of a right circular cylinder with a radius of 10 cm and a height of 8 cm. Round to the nearest hundredth. **1130.97 cm^3**

EXAMPLE 4

Find the surface area of a sphere with a diameter measuring 8 cm. Round to the nearest hundredth.

Strategy

To find the surface area:

- Find the radius of the sphere. $d = 8$
- Use the formula for the surface area of a sphere.
- An approximation is asked for; use the π key on a calculator.

Solution

$r = \frac{1}{2}d = \frac{1}{2}(8) = 4$ • **Find the radius.**

$SA = 4\pi r^2$ • **Formula for the surface area of a sphere**

$SA = 4\pi(4)^2$ • $r = 4$

$SA = 4\pi(16) = 64\pi$

$SA \approx 201.06$

The surface area of the sphere is 201.06 cm^2.

YOU TRY IT 4

Find the surface area of a cube with a side measuring 10 cm. Round to the nearest hundredth.

Your strategy

Your solution

600 cm^2

Solutions on p. S20

7.4 EXERCISES

Concept Check

SUGGESTED ASSIGNMENT
Exercises 1–4; Exercises 5–29, odds; Exercises 30–36; Exercises 37–59, odds

1. Refer to Exercises 5 to 10 below. Fill in each blank with the name of the solid shown in the given exercise.

a. Exercise 6 cone **b.** Exercise 8 cube

c. Exercise 9 sphere **d.** Exercise 10 cylinder

2. Find the volume of the solid shown at the right.

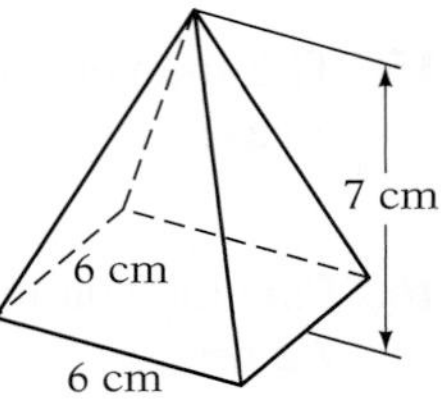

a. Use the formula for the volume of a pyramid. $V = \frac{1}{3}s^2h$

b. Replace s by 6 and h by 7. $V = \frac{1}{3}(6)^2(7)$

c. Multiply. $V = \frac{1}{3}(36)(7) = (12)(7) = 84$

d. Fill in the blank with the correct unit: The volume of the pyramid is 84 cm^3.

3. To find the surface area of a pyramid with a slant height of 5 in. and a base with a side measuring 3 in., use the formula $SA = s^2 + 2sl$. Replace l by 5 and s by 3.

4. To find the surface area of a cylinder with a diameter of 12 cm and a height of 10 cm, use the formula $SA = 2\pi r^2 + 2\pi rh$. Replace r by 6 and h by 10.

OBJECTIVE A *To find the volume of geometric solids*

For Exercises 5 to 10, find the volume of the figure. For calculations involving π, give both the exact value and an approximation to the nearest hundredth.

5.

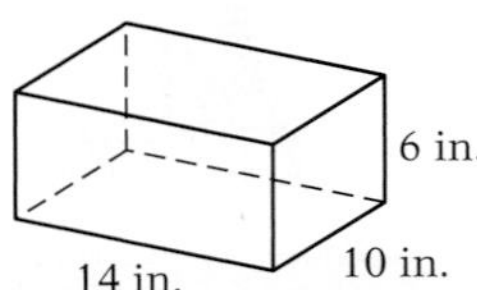

840 in^3

6.

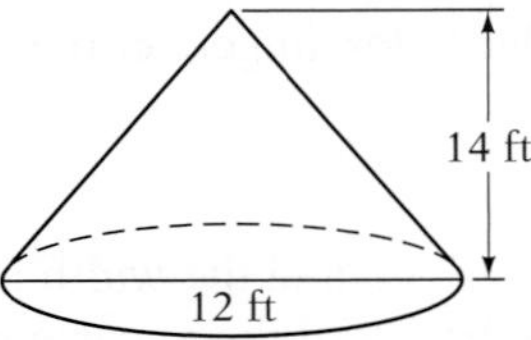

168π ft^3; 527.79 ft^3

7.

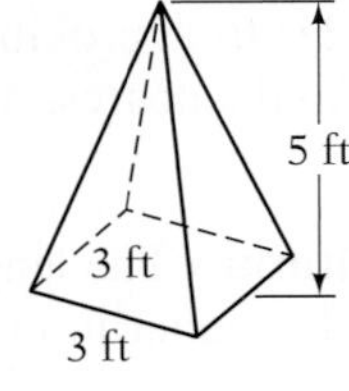

15 ft^3

8.

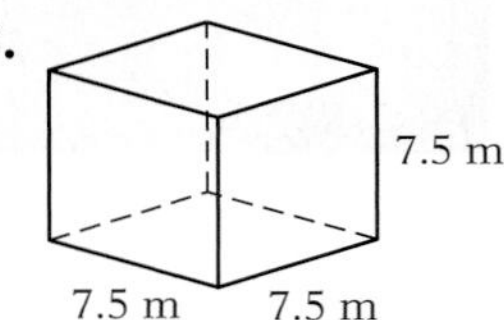

421.875 m^3

9.

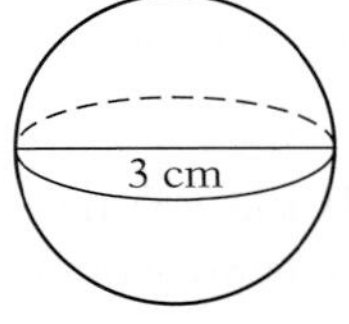

4.5π cm^3; 14.14 cm^3

10.

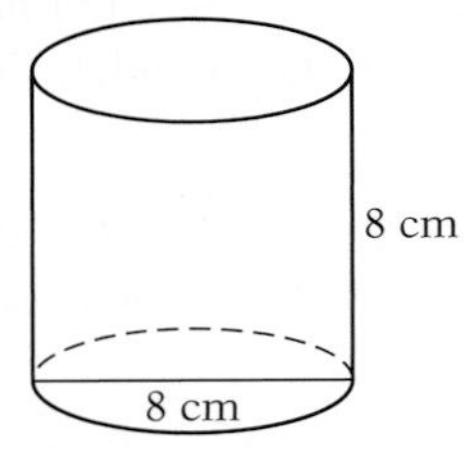

128π cm^3; 402.12 cm^3

11. A rectangular solid has a length of 6.8 m, a width of 2.5 m, and a height of 2 m. Find the volume of the solid. 34 m^3

12. Find the volume of a rectangular solid that has a length of 4.5 ft, a width of 3 ft, and a height of 1.5 ft. 20.25 ft^3

13. Find the volume of a cube whose side measures 2.5 in. 15.625 in^3

14. The length of a side of a cube is 7 cm. Find the volume of the cube. 343 cm^3

15. The diameter of a sphere is 6 ft. Find the volume of the sphere. Give the exact measure. $36\pi \text{ ft}^3$

16. Find the volume of a sphere that has a radius of 1.2 m. Round to the nearest tenth. 7.2 m^3

17. The diameter of the base of a cylinder is 24 cm. The height of the cylinder is 18 cm. Find the volume of the cylinder. Round to the nearest hundredth. 8143.01 cm^3

18. The radius of the base of a cone is 5 in. The height of the cone is 9 in. Find the volume of the cone. Give the exact measure. $75\pi \text{ in}^3$

19. The height of a cone is 15 cm. The diameter of the cone is 10 cm. Find the volume of the cone. Round to the nearest hundredth. 392.70 cm^3

20. The length of a side of the base of a pyramid is 6 in., and the height is 10 in. Find the volume of the pyramid. 120 in^3

21. The height of a pyramid is 8 m, and the length of a side of the base is 9 m. What is the volume of the pyramid? 216 m^3

22. **The Statue of Liberty** The index finger on the Statue of Liberty is 8 ft long. The circumference at the second joint is 3.5 ft. Use the formula for the volume of a cylinder to approximate the volume of the index finger on the Statue of Liberty. Round to the nearest hundredth. 7.80 ft^3

© dragon_fang/Shutterstock.com

23. **Aquariums** The length of an aquarium is 18 in., and the width is 12 in. If the volume of the aquarium is 1836 in^3, what is the height of the aquarium? 8.5 in.

24. The volume of a cylinder with a height of 10 in. is 502.4 in^3. Find the radius of the base of the cylinder. Round to the nearest hundredth. 4.00 in.

25. The diameter of the base of a cylinder is 14 cm. If the volume of the cylinder is 2310 cm^3, find the height of the cylinder. Round to the nearest hundredth. 15.01 cm

26. A rectangular solid has a square base and a height of 5 in. If the volume of the solid is 125 in^3, find the length and the width. Length: 5 in., width: 5 in.

27. Silos A silo, which is in the shape of a cylinder, is 16 ft in diameter and has a height of 30 ft. The silo is three-fourths full. Find the volume of the portion of the silo that is not being used for storage. Round to the nearest hundredth. 1507.96 ft^3

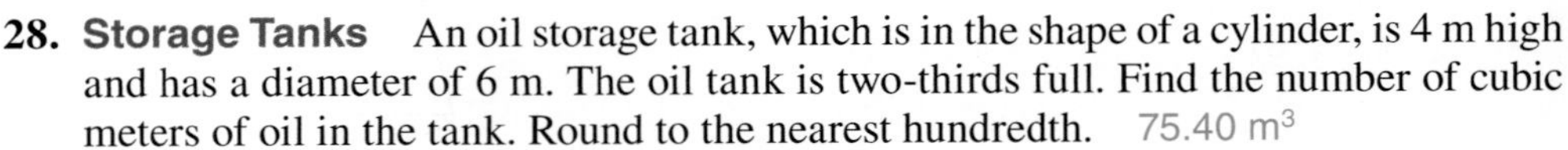

28. Storage Tanks An oil storage tank, which is in the shape of a cylinder, is 4 m high and has a diameter of 6 m. The oil tank is two-thirds full. Find the number of cubic meters of oil in the tank. Round to the nearest hundredth. 75.40 m^3

Panama Canal

29. The Panama Canal The Gatun Lock of the Panama Canal is 1000 ft long, 110 ft wide, and 60 ft deep. Find the volume of the lock in cubic feet. 6,600,000 ft^3

Construction For Exercises 30 to 33, use the diagram at the right showing the concrete floor of a building. State whether the given expression can be used to calculate the volume of the concrete floor in cubic feet.

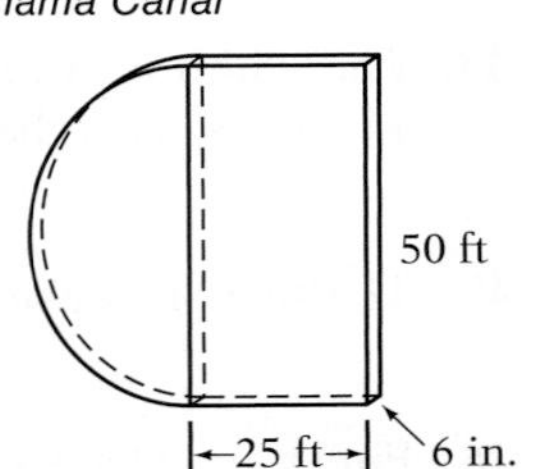

30. $(25)(50)(6) + (0.5)(3.14)(25^2)(6)$
No

31. $(25)(50)(0.5) + (0.5)(3.14)(25^2)(0.5)$
Yes

32. $0.5[(25)(50) + (0.5)(3.14)(25^2)]$
Yes

33. $(25)(50)(0.5) + (0.5)(3.14)(50^2)(0.5)$
No

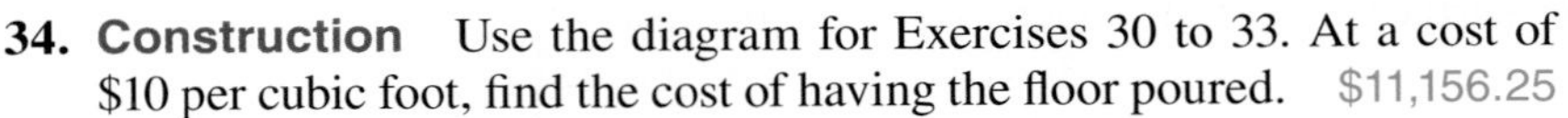

34. Construction Use the diagram for Exercises 30 to 33. At a cost of $10 per cubic foot, find the cost of having the floor poured. $11,156.25

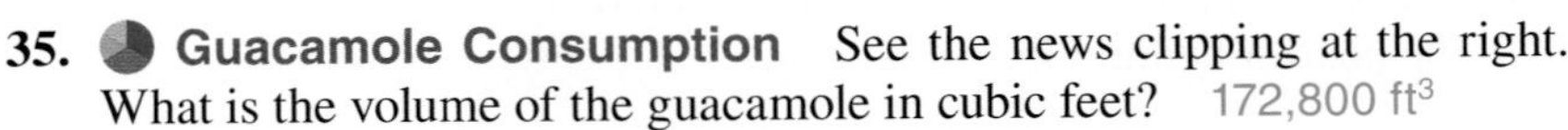

35. Guacamole Consumption See the news clipping at the right. What is the volume of the guacamole in cubic feet? 172,800 ft^3

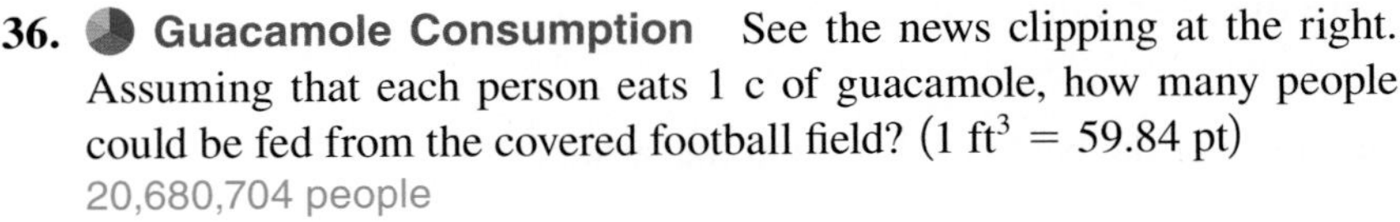

36. Guacamole Consumption See the news clipping at the right. Assuming that each person eats 1 c of guacamole, how many people could be fed from the covered football field? ($1\ ft^3 = 59.84$ pt)
20,680,704 people

In the NEWS!

Super Bowl Win for Guacamole

Guacamole has become the dish of choice at Super Bowl parties. If all the guacamole eaten during the Super Bowl were piled onto a football field—that's a football field which, including end zones, is 360 ft long and 160 ft wide—it would cover the field to a depth of 3 ft!

Source: www.azcentral.com

OBJECTIVE B *To find the surface area of geometric solids*

Find the surface area of the figure.

37.

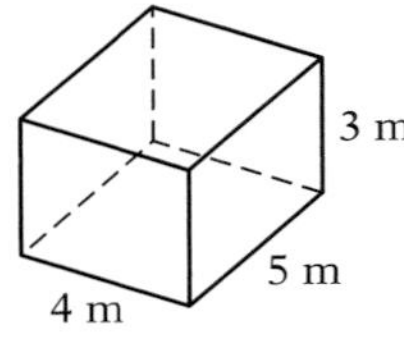

94 m^2

38.

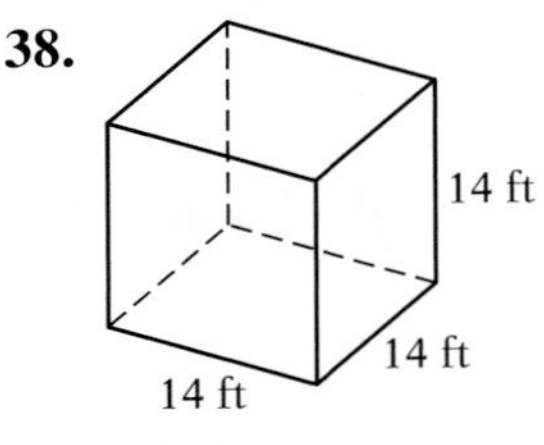

1176 ft^2

39.

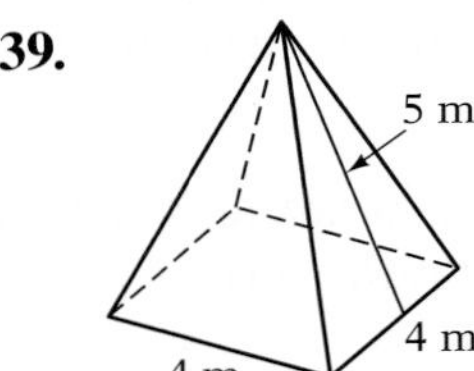

56 m^2

For Exercises 40 to 42, find the surface area of the figure. Give both the exact value and an approximation to the nearest hundredth.

40.

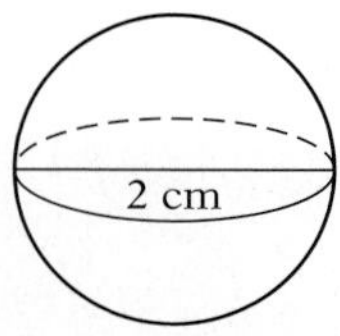

4π cm^2; 12.57 cm^2

41.

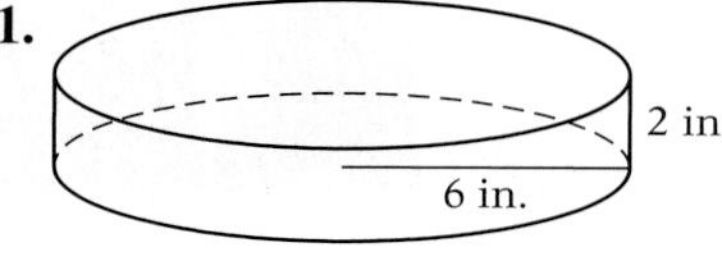

96π in^2; 301.59 in^2

42.

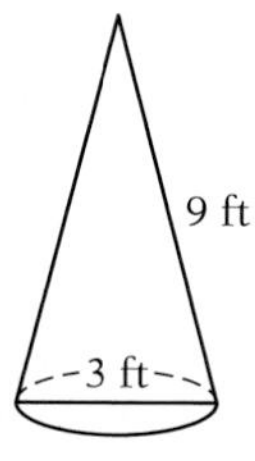

15.75π ft^2; 49.48 ft^2

43. The height of a rectangular solid is 5 ft, the length is 8 ft, and the width is 4 ft. Find the surface area of the solid. 184 ft^2

44. The width of a rectangular solid is 32 cm, the length is 60 cm, and the height is 14 cm. What is the surface area of the solid? 6416 cm^2

45. The side of a cube measures 3.4 m. Find the surface area of the cube. 69.36 m^2

46. Find the surface area of a cube that has a side measuring 1.5 in. 13.5 in^2

47. Find the surface area of a sphere with a diameter of 15 cm. Give the exact value. 225π cm^2

48. The radius of a sphere is 2 in. Find the surface area of the sphere. Round to the nearest hundredth. 50.27 in^2

49. The radius of the base of a cylinder is 4 in. The height of the cylinder is 12 in. Find the surface area of the cylinder. Round to the nearest hundredth. 402.12 in^2

50. The diameter of the base of a cylinder is 1.8 m. The height of the cylinder is 0.7 m. Find the surface area of the cylinder. Give the exact value. 2.88π m^2

51. The slant height of a cone is 2.5 ft. The radius of the base is 1.5 ft. Find the surface area of the cone. Give the exact value. 6π ft^2

52. The diameter of the base of a cone is 21 in. The slant height is 16 in. What is the surface area of the cone? Round to the nearest hundredth. 874.15 in^2

53. The length of a side of the base of a pyramid is 9 in., and the slant height is 12 in. Find the surface area of the pyramid. 297 in^2

54. The slant height of a pyramid is 18 m, and the length of a side of the base is 16 m. What is the surface area of the pyramid? 832 m^2

55. The surface area of a rectangular solid is 108 cm^2. The height of the solid is 4 cm, and the length is 6 cm. Find the width of the rectangular solid. 3 cm

56. The length of a rectangular solid is 12 ft. The width is 3 ft. If the surface area is 162 ft^2, find the height of the rectangular solid. 3 ft

57. **Hot Air Balloons** A hot air balloon is in the shape of a sphere. Approximately how much fabric was used to construct the balloon if its diameter is 32 ft? Round to the nearest whole number. 3217 ft^2

58. **Paint** A can of paint will cover 300 ft^2. How many cans of paint should be purchased in order to paint a cylinder that has a height of 30 ft and a radius of 12 ft? 11 cans

59. **Fish Tanks** How much glass is needed to make a fish tank that is 12 in. long, 8 in. wide, and 9 in. high? The fish tank is open at the top. 456 in^2

Critical Thinking

60. Half of a sphere is called a **hemisphere.** Derive formulas for the volume and surface area of a hemisphere. See the *Solutions Manual.*

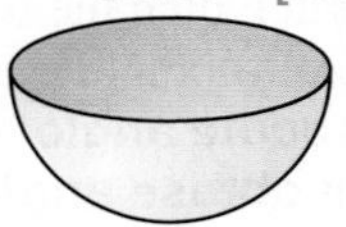

61. Determine whether the statement is always true, sometimes true, or never true.
    a. The slant height of a regular pyramid is longer than the height. Always true
    b. The slant height of a cone is shorter than the height. Never true
    c. The four triangular faces of a regular pyramid are equilateral triangles. Sometimes true

62. Refer to the cube and the pyramid shown at the right. Which equation correctly describes the relationship between the volume C of the cube and the volume P of the pyramid?

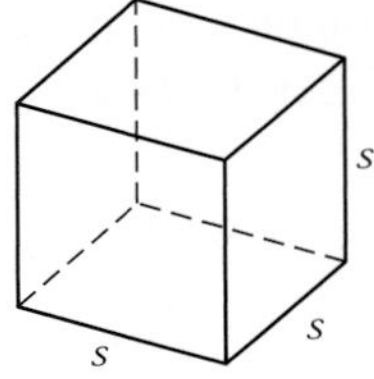

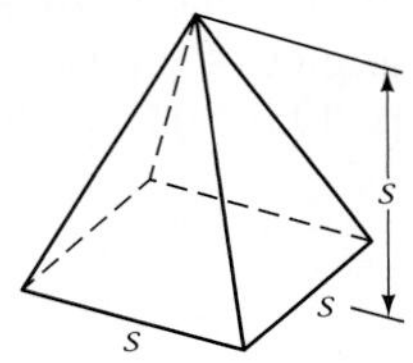

(i) $C = 2P$ **(ii)** $P = 3C$ **(iii)** $P = 2C$ **(iv)** $C = 3P$
iv

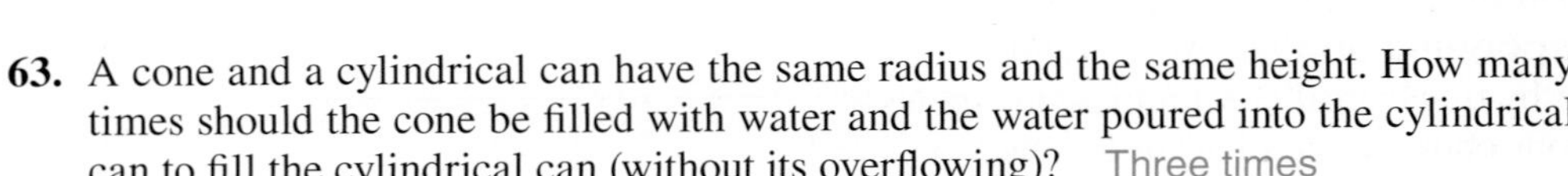

63. A cone and a cylindrical can have the same radius and the same height. How many times should the cone be filled with water and the water poured into the cylindrical can to fill the cylindrical can (without its overflowing)? Three times

Projects or Group Activities

64. Prepare a report on the use of geometric forms in architecture. Include examples of both plane geometric figures and geometric solids.

65. Write a paper on the artist M. C. Escher. Explain how he used mathematics and geometry in his works.

QUICK QUIZ

1. Find the volume of a cube with a side of 8 ft. **512 ft^3 [7.4A]**
2. Find the volume of a right circular cylinder with a radius of 3 in. and a height of 5 in. Round to the nearest hundredth. **141.37 in^3 [7.4A]**
3. Find the volume of a sphere with a 5-foot diameter. Round to the nearest hundredth. **65.45 ft^3 [7.4A]**
4. Find the surface area of a rectangular solid with a length of 8 m, a width of 5 m, and a height of 3 m. **158 m^2 [7.4B]**
5. Find the surface area of a sphere with a diameter of 24 cm. Round to the nearest hundredth. **1809.56 cm^2 [7.4B]**

CHAPTER 7 Summary

Key Words

Examples

A **line** is determined by two distinct points and extends indefinitely in both directions. A **line segment** is part of a line and has two endpoints. **Parallel lines** never meet; the distance between them is always the same. **Perpendicular lines** are intersecting lines that form right angles. [7.1A, pp. 392–394]

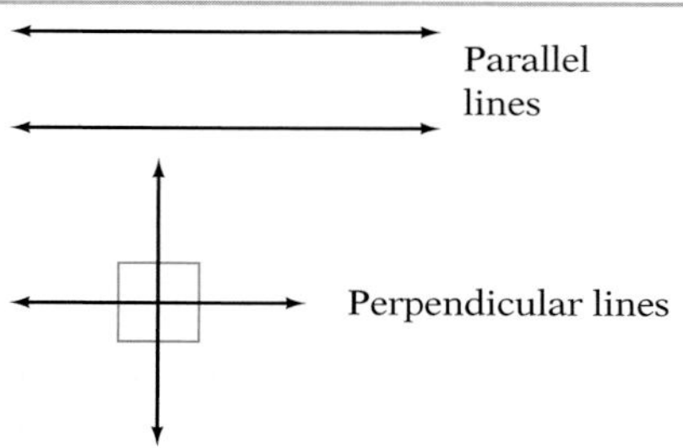

A **ray** starts at a point and extends indefinitely in one direction. The point at which a ray starts is the **endpoint** of the ray. An **angle** is formed by two rays with the same endpoint. The **vertex** of an angle is the point at which the two rays meet. An angle is measured in **degrees.** A 90° angle is a **right angle.** A 180° angle is a **straight angle.** An **acute angle** is an angle whose measure is between 0° and 90°. An **obtuse angle** is an angle whose measure is between 90° and 180°. **Complementary angles** are two angles whose measures have the sum 90°. **Supplementary angles** are two angles whose measures have the sum 180°. [7.1A, pp. 392–395]

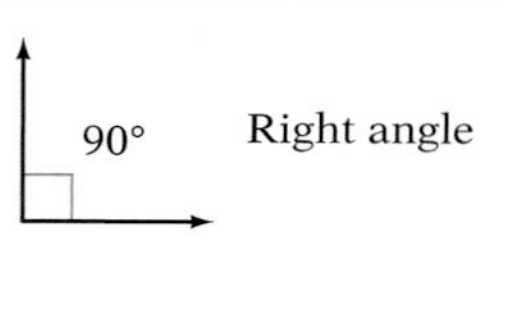

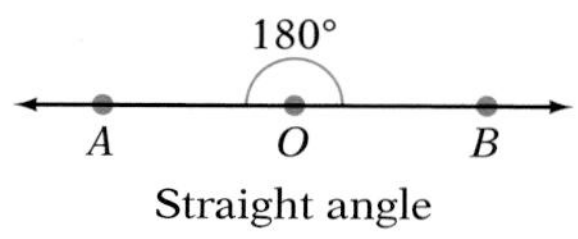

Two angles that are on opposite sides of the intersection of two lines are **vertical angles;** vertical angles have the same measure. Two angles that share a common side are **adjacent angles;** adjacent angles of intersecting lines are supplementary angles. [7.1A, p. 395; 7.1B, p. 397]

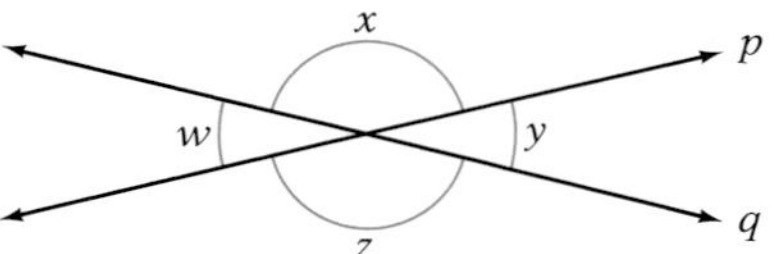

Angles w and y are vertical angles. Angles x and y are adjacent angles.

A line that intersects two other lines at two different points is a **transversal.** If the lines cut by a transversal are parallel lines, equal angles are formed: **alternate interior angles, alternate exterior angles,** and **corresponding angles.** At the right, parallel lines ℓ_1 and ℓ_2 are cut by transversal t. All four acute angles have the same measure. All four obtuse angles have the same measure. [7.1B, p. 398]

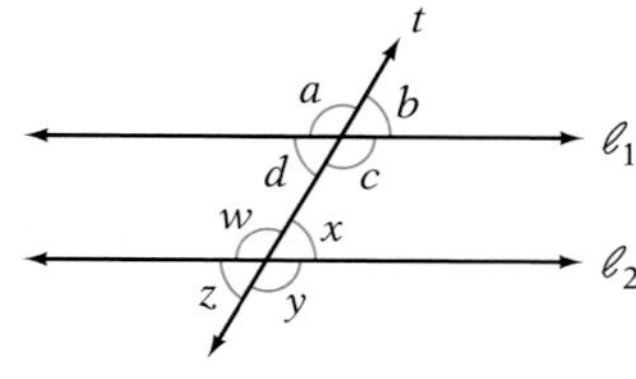

A **polygon** is a closed figure determined by three or more line segments. The line segments that form the polygon are its **sides.** A **regular polygon** is one in which all sides have the same length and all angles have the same measure. Polygons are classified by the number of sides. A **quadrilateral** is a four-sided polygon. A parallelogram, a rectangle, a square, a rhombus, and a trapezoid are all quadrilaterals. [7.2A, pp. 409–410]

Number of Sides	*Name of the Polygon*
3	Triangle
4	Quadrilateral
5	Pentagon
6	Hexagon
7	Heptagon
8	Octagon
9	Nonagon
10	Decagon

A **triangle** is a plane figure formed by three line segments. An **isosceles triangle** has two sides of equal length. The three sides of an **equilateral triangle** are of equal length. A **scalene triangle** has no two sides of equal length. An **acute triangle** has three acute angles. An **obtuse triangle** has one obtuse angle. A **right triangle** has a right angle. [7.1C, p. 400; 7.2A, pp. 409–410]

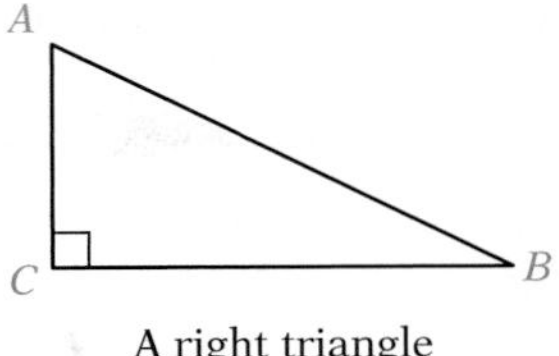

A right triangle

A **circle** is a plane figure in which all points are the same distance from the center of the circle. A **diameter** of a circle is a line segment across the circle through the center. A **radius** of a circle is a line segment from the center of the circle to a point on the circle. [7.2A, p. 412]

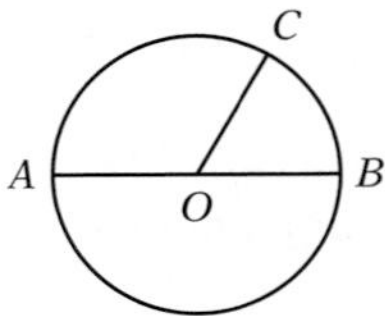

AB is a diameter of the circle.
OC is a radius.

Similar triangles have the same shape but not necessarily the same size. The ratios of corresponding sides are equal. The ratio of corresponding heights is equal to the ratio of corresponding sides. **Congruent triangles** have the same shape and the same size. [7.3B, p. 430; 7.3C, p. 432]

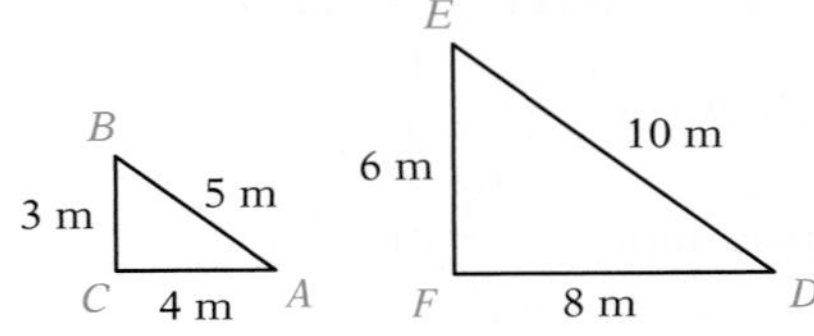

Triangles *ABC* and *DEF* are similar triangles. The ratio of corresponding sides is $\frac{1}{2}$.

Essential Rules and Procedures

Examples

Triangles [7.1C, p. 400; 7.3C, pp. 432–433]
The sum of the measures of the interior angles of a triangle is 180°.
The sum of an interior and the corresponding exterior angle of a triangle is 180°.
Rules to determine congruence: SSS Rule, SAS Rule, ASA Rule

In a right triangle, the measure of one acute angle is 12°. Find the measure of the other acute angle.

$$x + 12^\circ + 90^\circ = 180^\circ$$
$$x + 102^\circ = 180^\circ$$
$$x = 78^\circ$$

Formulas for Perimeter (the distance around a figure) [7.2A, pp. 410–412]
Triangle: $P = a + b + c$
Rectangle: $P = 2L + 2W$
Square: $P = 4s$
Circumference of a circle: $C = \pi d$ or $C = 2\pi r$

The length of a rectangle is 8 m. The width is 5.5 m. Find the perimeter of the rectangle.

$$P = 2L + 2W$$
$$P = 2(8) + 2(5.5)$$
$$P = 16 + 11$$
$$P = 27$$

The perimeter is 27 m.

Formulas for Area (the amount of surface in a region) [7.2B, pp. 414–417]

Triangle: $A = \frac{1}{2}bh$

Rectangle: $A = LW$

Square: $A = s^2$

Circle: $A = \pi r^2$

Parallelogram: $A = bh$

Trapezoid: $A = \frac{1}{2}h(b_1 + b_2)$

The length of the base of a parallelogram is 12 cm, and the height is 4 cm. Find the area of the parallelogram.

$A = bh$

$A = 12(4)$

$A = 48$

The area is 48 cm^2.

Formulas for Volume (the amount of space inside a figure in space) [7.4A, p. 440]

Rectangular solid: $V = LWH$

Cube: $V = s^3$

Sphere: $V = \frac{4}{3}\pi r^3$

Right circular cylinder: $V = \pi r^2 h$

Right circular cone: $V = \frac{1}{3}\pi r^2 h$

Regular pyramid: $V = \frac{1}{3}s^2 h$

Find the volume of a cube that measures 3 in. on a side.

$V = s^3$

$V = 3^3$

$V = 27$

The volume is 27 in^3.

Formulas for Surface Area (the total area on the surface of a solid) [7.4B, p. 443]

Rectangular solid: $SA = 2LW + 2LH + 2WH$

Cube: $SA = 6s^2$

Sphere: $SA = 4\pi r^2$

Right circular cylinder: $SA = 2\pi r^2 + 2\pi rh$

Right circular cone: $SA = \pi r^2 + \pi rl$

Regular pyramid: $SA = s^2 + 2sl$

Find the surface area of a sphere with a diameter of 10 cm. Give the exact value.

$r = \frac{1}{2}d = \frac{1}{2}(10) = 5$

$SA = 4\pi r^2$

$SA = 4\pi(5)^2$

$SA = 4\pi(25)$

$SA = 100\pi$

The surface area is 100π cm^2.

Pythagorean Theorem [7.3A, p. 428]

If a and b are the lengths of the legs of a right triangle and c is the length of the hypotenuse, then $c^2 = a^2 + b^2$.

Two legs of a right triangle measure 6 ft and 8 ft. Find the hypotenuse of the right triangle.

$c^2 = a^2 + b^2$

$c^2 = 6^2 + 8^2$

$c^2 = 36 + 64$

$c^2 = 100$

$c = \sqrt{100}$

$c = 10$

The length of the hypotenuse is 10 ft.

Principal Square Root Property [7.3A, p. 429]

If $r^2 = s$, then $r = \sqrt{s}$, and r is called the **square root** of s.

If $c^2 = 16$, then $c = \sqrt{16} = 4$.

CHAPTER 7 Review Exercises

1. Given that $\angle a = 74°$ and $\angle b = 52°$, find the measures of angles x and y. $\angle x = 22°$, $\angle y = 158°$ [7.1C]

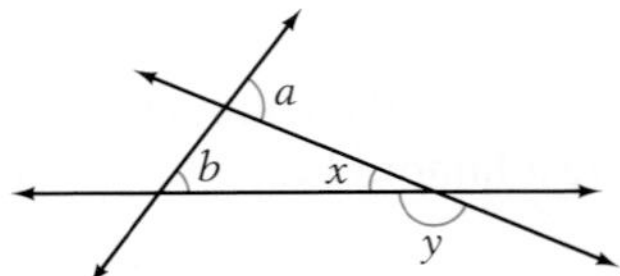

2. Triangles ABC and DEF are similar. Find the perimeter of triangle ABC. 24 in. [7.3B]

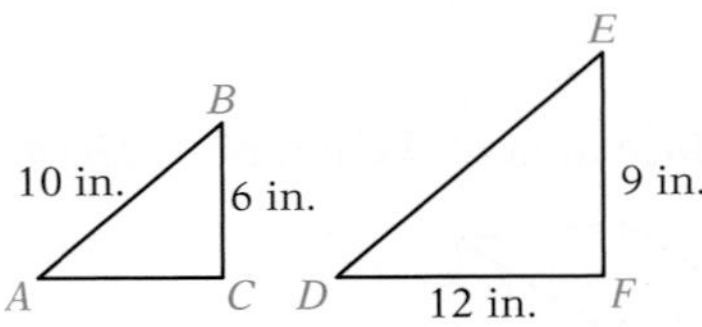

3. Find the volume of the figure. 168 in^3 [7.4A]

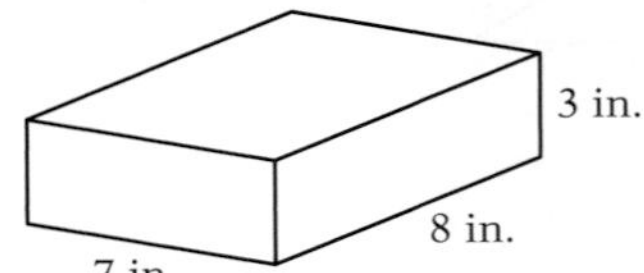

4. Find the measure of $\angle x$. 68° [7.1B]

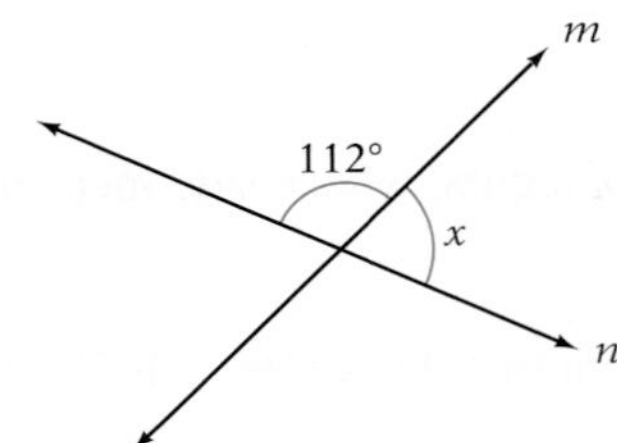

5. Determine whether the two triangles are congruent. If they are congruent, state by what rule they are congruent. Yes, by the SAS Rule [7.3C]

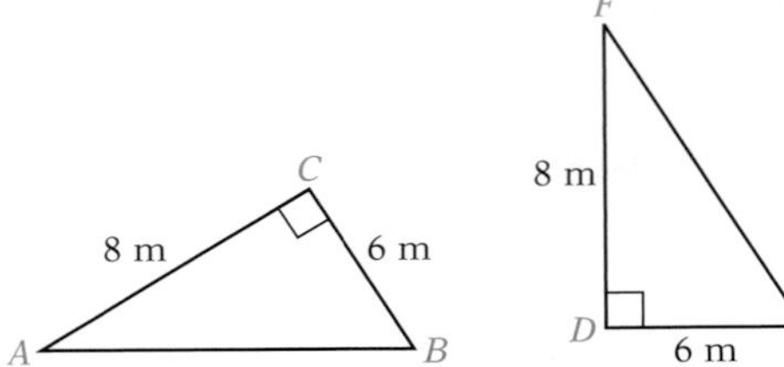

6. Find the surface area of the figure. Round to the nearest hundredth. 125.66 m^2 [7.4B]

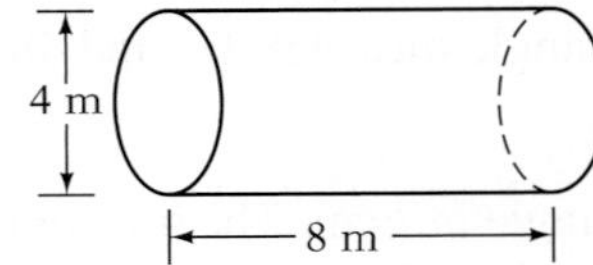

7. Given that $BC = 11$ cm and AB is three times the length of BC, find the length of AC. 44 cm [7.1A]

8. Find x. 19° [7.1A]

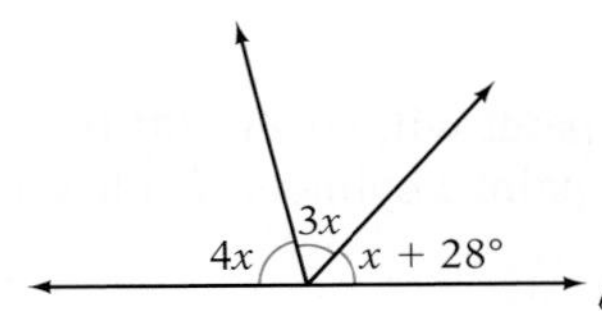

9. Find the area of the figure. 32 in^2 [7.2B]

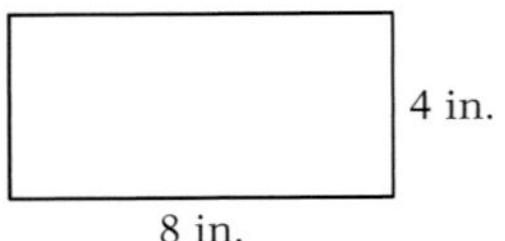

10. Find the volume of the figure. 96 cm^3 [7.4A]

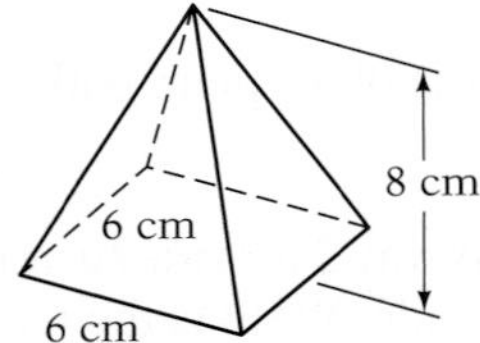

11. Find the perimeter of the figure. 42 in. [7.2A]

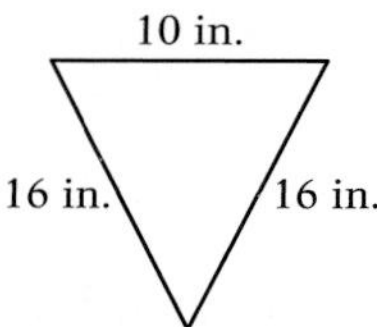

12. Given that $\ell_1 \parallel \ell_2$, find the measures of angles a and b. $\angle a = 138°$, $\angle b = 42°$ [7.1B]

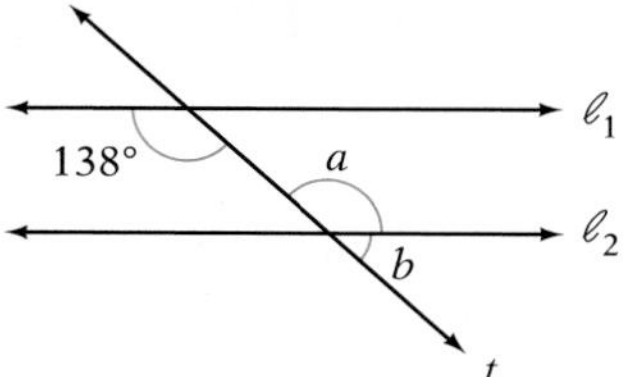

13. Find the surface area of the figure. 220 ft² [7.4B]

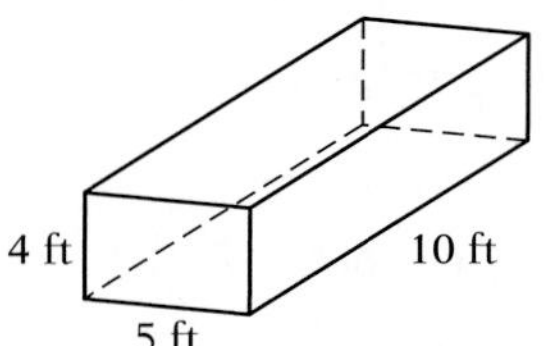

14. Find the unknown side of the triangle. Round to the nearest hundredth. 9.75 ft [7.3A]

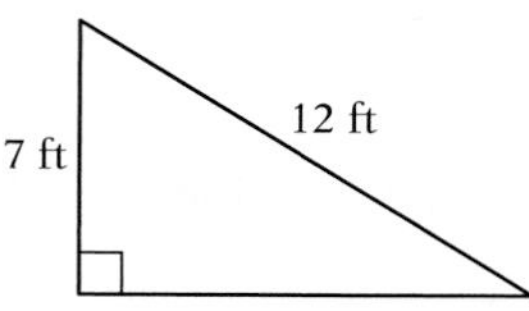

15. Find the volume of a cube whose side measures 3.5 in. 42.875 in³ [7.4A]

16. Find the supplement of a 32° angle. 148° [7.1A]

17. Find the volume of a rectangular solid with a length of 6.5 ft, a width of 2 ft, and a height of 3 ft. 39 ft³ [7.4A]

18. Two angles of a triangle measure 37° and 48°. Find the measure of the third angle. 95° [7.1C]

19. The height of a triangle is 7 cm. The area of the triangle is 28 cm². Find the length of the base of the triangle. 8 cm [7.2B]

20. Find the volume of a sphere that has a diameter of 12 mm. Give the exact value. 288π mm³ [7.4A]

21. **Picture Frames** The perimeter of a square picture frame is 86 cm. Find the length of each side of the frame. 21.5 cm [7.2A]

22. **Paint** A can of paint will cover 200 ft². How many cans of paint should be purchased in order to paint a cylinder that has a height of 15 ft and a radius of 6 ft? 4 cans [7.4B]

23. **Fencing** The length of a rectangular park is 56 yd. The width is 48 yd. How many yards of fencing are needed to surround the park? 208 yd [7.2A]

24. **Patios** What is the area of a square patio that measures 9.5 m on each side? 90.25 m² [7.2B]

25. **Landscaping** A walkway 2 m wide surrounds a rectangular plot of grass. The plot is 40 m long and 25 m wide. What is the area of the walkway? 276 m² [7.2B]

CHAPTER 7 TEST

1. For the right triangle shown below, determine the length of side BC. Round to the nearest hundredth.

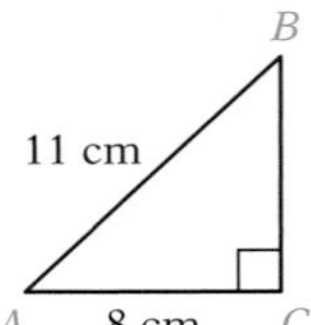

7.55 cm [7.3A]

2. Determine whether the two triangles are congruent. If they are congruent, state by what rule they are congruent.

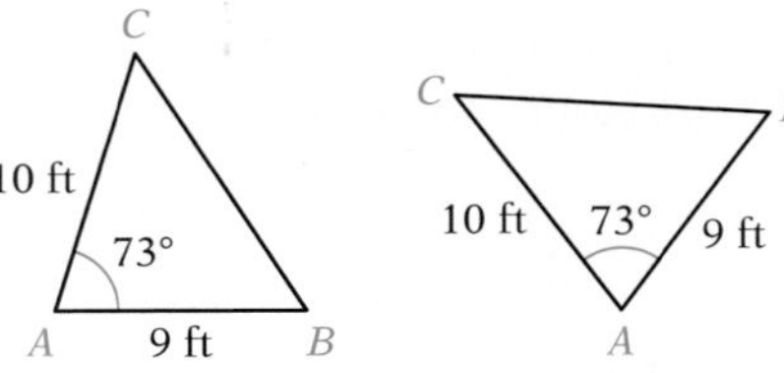

Yes, by the SAS Rule [7.3C]

3. Determine the area of a rectangle with a length of 15 m and a width of 7.4 m.

111 m^2 [7.2B]

4. Determine the area of a triangle whose base is 7 ft and whose height is 12 ft.

42 ft^2 [7.2B]

5. Determine the exact volume of a right circular cone whose radius is 7 cm and whose height is 16 cm.

$\frac{784\pi}{3} \text{ cm}^3$ [7.4A]

6. Determine the exact surface area of a pyramid whose square base is 3 m on each side and whose slant height is 11 m.

75 m^2 [7.4B]

7. Determine the volume of the solid shown below. Round to the nearest hundredth.

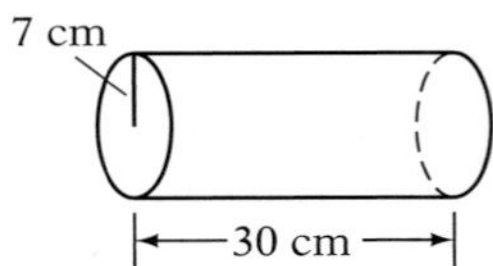

4618.14 cm^3 [7.4A]

8. Determine the area of the trapezoid shown below.

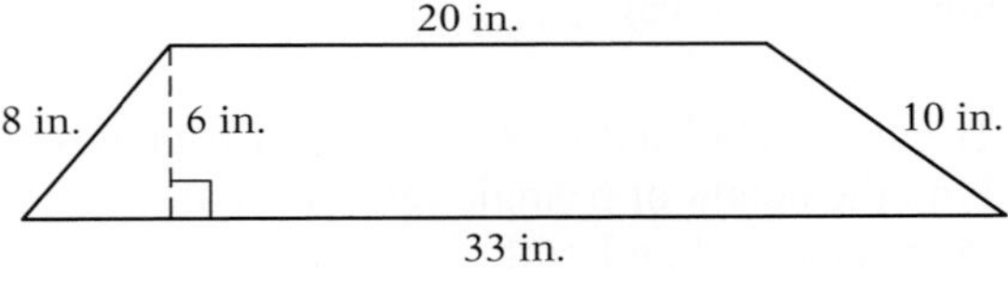

159 in^2 [7.2B]

9. Given that $\ell_1 \parallel \ell_2$, find x. 20° [7.1B]

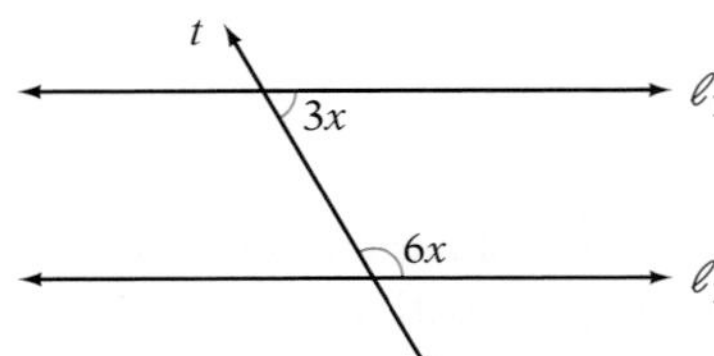

10. Determine the surface area of the figure shown below.

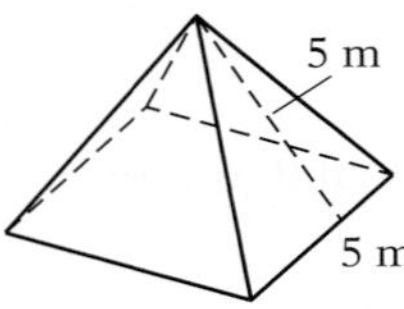

75 m^2 [7.4B]

11. Find x.

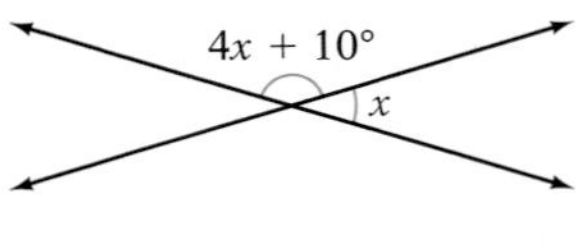

34° [7.1B]

12. Name the figure shown below.

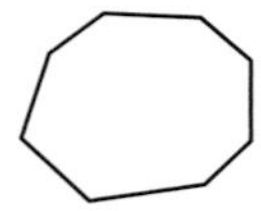

Octagon [7.2A]

13. Determine whether the two triangles are congruent. If they are congruent, state by what rule they are congruent.

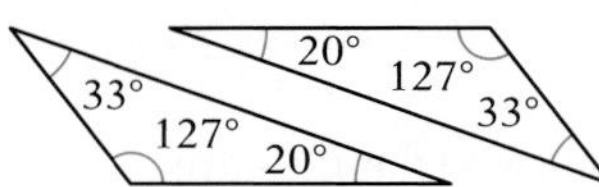

Not necessarily congruent [7.3C]

14. Determine the volume of the rectangular solid shown below.

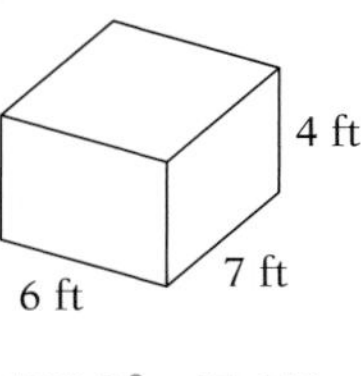

168 ft³ [7.4A]

15. Figure *ABC* is a right triangle. Determine the length of side *AB*. Round to the nearest hundredth.

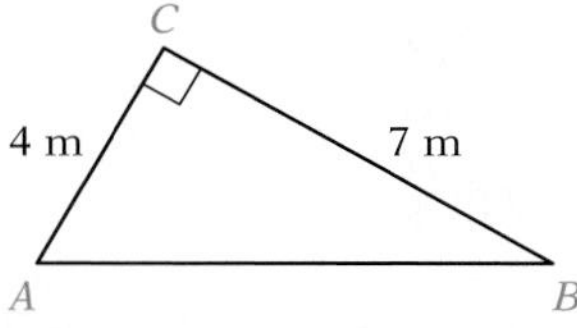

8.06 m [7.3A]

16. Given that ℓ_1 and ℓ_2 are parallel lines, determine the measure of angle *a*.

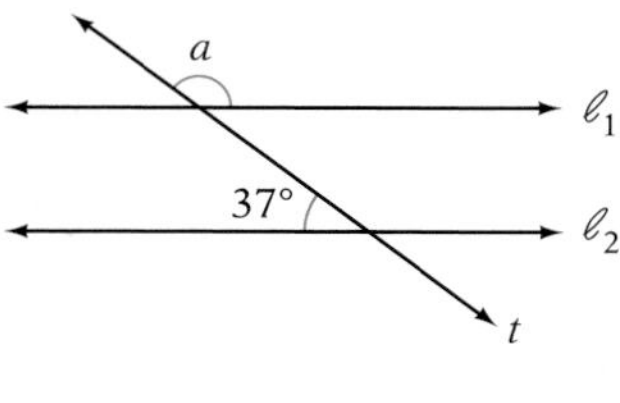

143° [7.1B]

17. Determine the exact surface area of the right circular cylinder shown below.

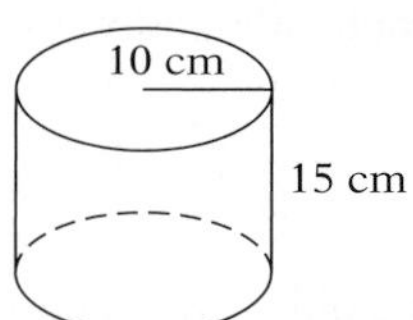

500π cm² [7.4B]

18. Determine the measure of angle *a*.

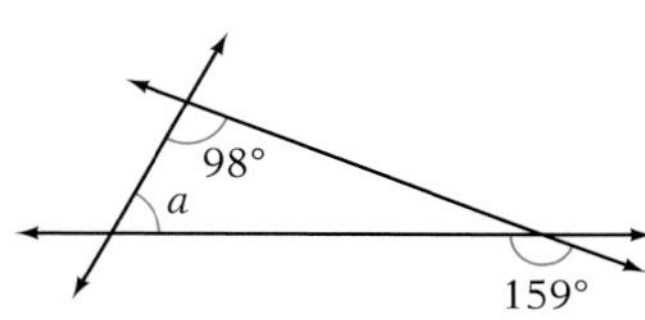

61° [7.1C]

19. Triangles *ABC* and *DEF* are similar triangles. Find the height of triangle *DEF*. Round to the nearest hundredth.

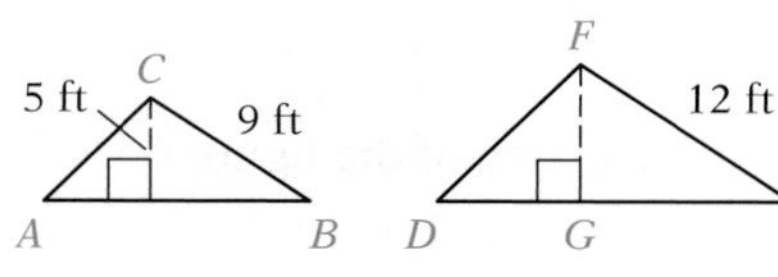

6.67 ft [7.3B]

20. Triangles *ABC* and *DEF* are similar triangles. Determine the length of side *BC*. Round to the nearest hundredth.

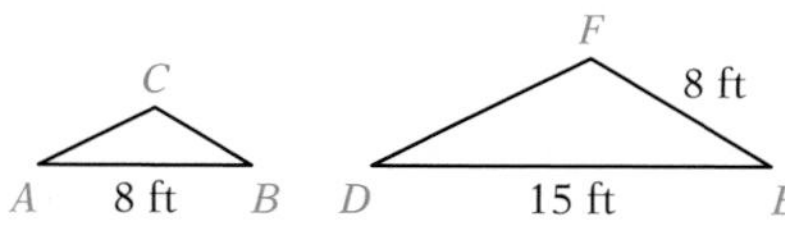

4.27 ft [7.3B]

21. Determine the perimeter of a square whose side is 5 m.
20 m [7.2A]

22. Determine the perimeter of a rectangle whose length is 8 cm and whose width is 5 cm.
26 cm [7.2A]

23. Find the perimeter of a right triangle with legs that measure 12 ft and 18 ft. Round to the nearest tenth.
51.6 ft [7.3A]

24. Two angles of a triangle measure 41° and 37°. Find the measure of the third angle.

102° [7.1C]

25. Find the supplement of a 41° angle.

139° [7.1A]

Cumulative Review Exercises

1. Find 8.5% of 2400.

204 [6.4A/6.4B]

2. Find all the factors of 78.

1, 2, 3, 6, 13, 26, 39, 78 [1.3D]

3. Divide: $4\frac{2}{3} \div 5\frac{3}{5}$

$\frac{5}{6}$ [2.4B]

4. Evaluate: $|-18|$

18 [3.1C]

5. Divide and round to the nearest tenth: $82.93 \div 6.5$

12.8 [2.6C]

6. Subtract: $-6 - (-4)$

-2 [3.2B]

7. Find the measure of $\angle x$.

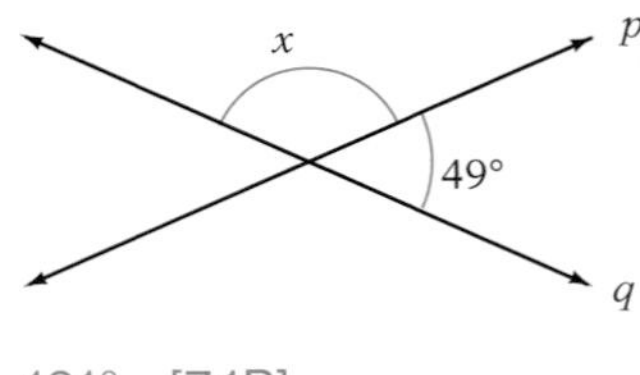

131° [7.1B]

8. Find the unknown side of the triangle.

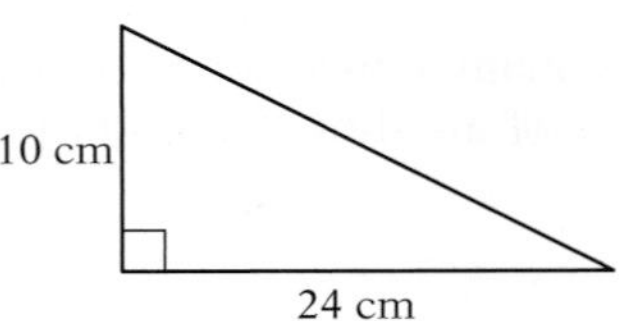

26 cm [7.3A]

9. Find the area of the triangle.

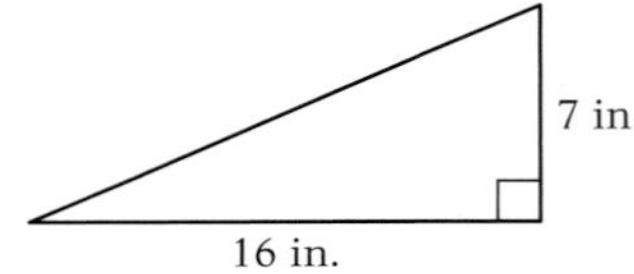

56 in^2 [7.2B]

10. Given that $\ell_1 \parallel \ell_2$, find x.

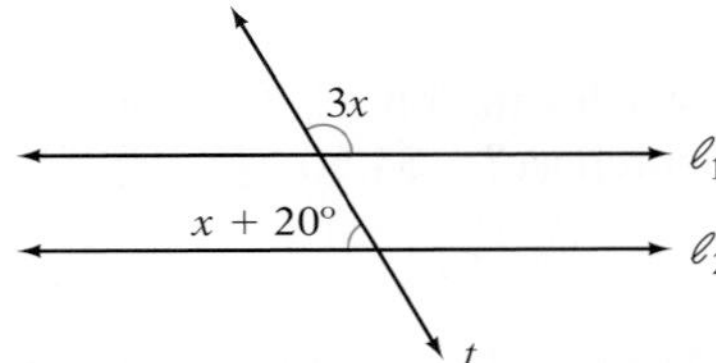

40° [7.1B]

11. Add: $\frac{2}{3} + \frac{7}{10}$

$1\frac{11}{30}$ [2.3A]

12. Solve: $3(2x + 5) = 18$

$\frac{1}{2}$ [5.3B]

13. A triangle has a right angle and a 32° angle. Find the measure of the third angle.

58° [7.1C]

14. Multiply: $-3(-25)$

75 [3.3A]

15. Simplify: $5(2x + 4) - (3x + 2)$

$7x + 18$ [4.2D]

16. Evaluate $2x + 3y^2z$ for $x = 5$, $y = -1$, and $z = -4$.

-2 [4.1A]

17. Evaluate $x^2y - 2z$ for $x = \frac{1}{2}$, $y = \frac{4}{5}$, and $z = -\frac{3}{10}$.

$\frac{4}{5}$ [4.1A]

18. Find the prime factorization of 78.

$2 \cdot 3 \cdot 13$ [1.3D]

19. Solve: $4x + 2 = 6x - 8$
5 [5.3A]

20. Write $\frac{3}{8}$ as a percent.
37.5% [6.3B]

21. Translate "the product of eight and twice a number" into a variable expression. Then simplify.
$8(2n)$; $16n$ [4.3B]

22. Uniform Motion Two cars, one traveling 5 mph faster than the other, start at the same time from the same point and travel in opposite directions. In 2 h they are 210 mi apart. Find the rate of each car.
50 mph; 55 mph [5.5B]

23. Simple Interest Find the simple interest due on a 270-day loan of $20,000 at an annual interest rate of 8.875%. $1313.01 [6.5A]

24. Mixtures How many ounces of a silver alloy that costs $3.50 per ounce must be mixed with 12 oz of an alloy that costs $5 per ounce to make a mixture that costs $4 per ounce?
24 oz [5.5A]

25. Cell Phone The monthly charge for your cell phone is $79 plus $.35 for every text message sent or received. In a month for which your cell phone bill was $86.70, how many text messages did you send or receive?
22 text messages [5.4B]

26. Taxes If the sales tax on a $12.50 purchase is $.75, what is the sales tax on a $75 purchase? $4.50 [6.2B]

27. Foreign Trade The figure at the right shows the value, in trillions of dollars, of the imports and exports during the first and second quarters of a recent year. Find the increase in the value of the imports from the first quarter to the second quarter. $.08 trillion [2.6E]

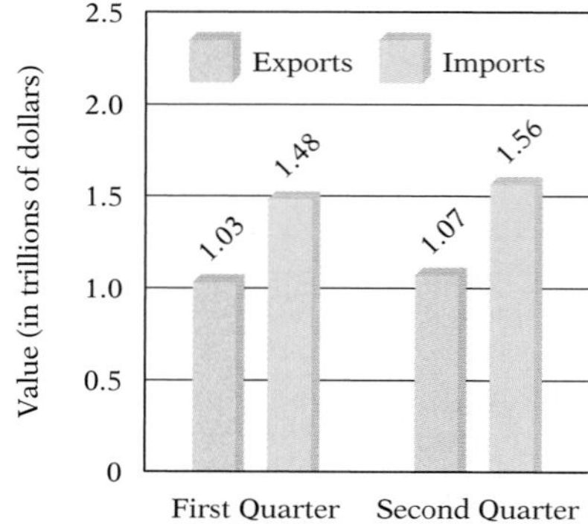

Value of Imports and Exports
Source: Bureau of Economic Analysis

28. Geometry The volume of a box is 144 ft^3. The length of the box is 12 ft, and the width is 4 ft. Find the height of the box. 3 ft [7.4A]

29. Deep Sea Diving The pressure P, in pounds per square inch, at a certain depth in the ocean can be approximated by the equation $P = 15 + \frac{1}{2}D$, where D is the depth in feet. Use this equation to find the depth when the pressure is 35 pounds per square inch. 40 ft [5.2B]

30. Sports A wrestler needs to lose 8 lb in three days in order to make the proper weight class. The wrestler loses $3\frac{1}{2}$ lb the first day and $2\frac{1}{4}$ lb the second day. How many pounds must the wrestler lose the third day in order to make the weight class?
$2\frac{1}{4}$ lb [2.3C]

Statistics and Probability

8

OBJECTIVES

SECTION 8.1

A To read and interpret graphs

SECTION 8.2

A To find the mean, median, and mode of a distribution

B To draw a box-and-whiskers plot

SECTION 8.3

A To calculate the probability of simple events

Focus on Success

If you cannot make time to study math right after class, make sure you set aside some study time on the day of the class to review notes and begin the homework. The longer you wait, the more difficult it is to recall important points covered during class. Studying math one hour a day, every day, is better than seven hours in one sitting. Break up a long study session by studying one subject for a while and then moving on to another subject. (See Homework Time, page AIM-5.)

Prep Test

Are you ready to succeed in this chapter? Take the Prep Test below to find out if you are ready to learn the new material.

1. **Email** According to the web monitoring service Royal Pingdom, there were 107 trillion emails sent in a recent year. Of those, 89.1% were spam. How many of the emails were spam? Round to the nearest trillion. 95 trillion [6.4A/6.4B]

2. **Education** The table at the right shows the estimated costs of funding an education at a public college.
   a. Between which two enrollment years is the increase in cost greatest? Between 2009 and 2010
   b. What is the increase between these two years? $5318 [1.2C]

Enrollment Year	*Cost of Public College*
2005	$70,206
2006	$74,418
2007	$78,883
2008	$83,616
2009	$88,633
2010	$93,951

Source: The College Board's Annual Survey of Colleges

3. **Sports** The first modern Summer Olympics were held in Greece in 1896. The United States won 11 gold medals, 7 silver medals, and 2 bronze medals. (*Source:* www.olympic.org) Find the ratio of gold medals won by the United States to silver medals won by the United States during the 1896 Summer Olympics. Write the ratio as a fraction in simplest form. $\frac{11}{7}$ [6.1A]

4. **The Military** Approximately 214,000 women serve in the U.S. military. Sixteen percent of these women serve in the Navy. (*Source:* www.womensmemorial.org) What fractional amount of women in the military are in the Navy? $\frac{4}{25}$ [6.3A]

SECTION

8.1 Statistical Graphs

OBJECTIVE A *To read and interpret graphs*

Statistics is the branch of mathematics concerned with **data,** or numerical information. Graphs are used to display numerical information in a visual format that enables the reader to quickly see relationships and trends. Three of the most common types of graphs are the bar graph, the circle graph, and the line graph. Examples of each of these types of graphs are shown below.

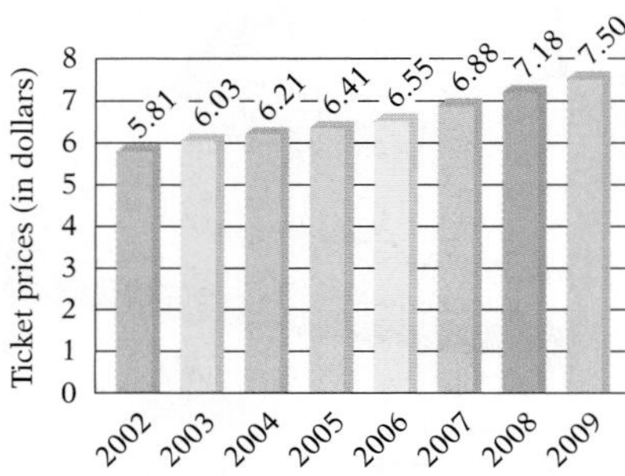

Figure 8.1 Average U.S. Movie Theater Ticket Prices (2002–2009)
Source: Motion Picture Association of America

Lane change 9%
Road departure 21%
Other causes 15%
Rear-end collision 29%
Intersection crash 26%

Figure 8.2 Types of Automobile Accidents, City of Twin Falls Year: 2005 Total Number of Accidents: 4300

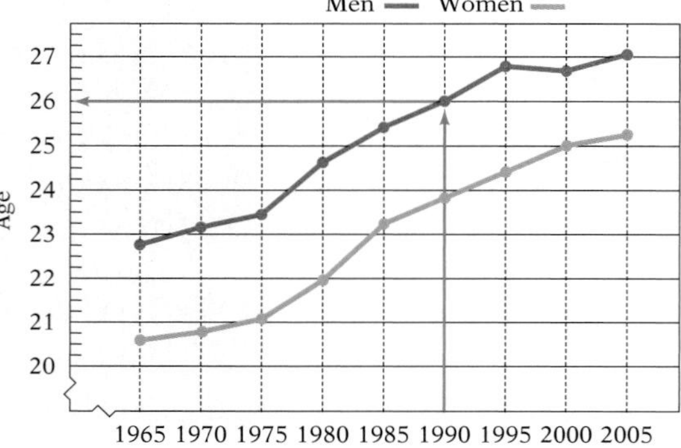

Figure 8.3 U.S. Average Age at First Marriage
Source: Bureau of the Census

INSTRUCTOR NOTE

Bar graphs, circle graphs, and line graphs are introduced in Section 1.1. They are included here for completeness in discussing basic concepts from statistics. In this section, unlike Section 1.1, the students use their understanding of ratio and percent to answer questions about the data presented in the graphs. You may choose to review the material in Section 1.1 prior to presenting this material, or you may omit this section entirely.

You might draw the students' attention to the jagged portion of the vertical axis in Figure 8.3. Remind them that this indicates that some of the ages between 0 and 20 are not displayed, and that this break in the vertical axis enables us to display the graph in a compact form.

The bar graph in Figure 8.1 displays the average U.S. movie theater ticket price for the years 2002 to 2009. Each vertical bar is used to display the average ticket price for a given year. The higher the bar, the greater the average ticket price for that year. We can see from the graph that the average movie theater ticket price has been increasing.

The circle graph in Figure 8.2 displays the percent of automobile accidents of a particular type that occurred in a given city for a given year. The largest sector of the circle corresponds to the largest percent of accidents of a given type, 29%.

Figure 8.3 shows two broken-line graphs. The upper broken-line graph displays the average age at first marriage for men for selected years from 1965 to 2005. The lower broken-line graph displays the average age at first marriage for women for selected years during the same time period. The line segments that connect the points on the graph indicate trends. Increasing trends are indicated by line segments that rise as they move to the right, and decreasing trends are indicated by line segments that fall as they move to the right. We can see from the graph that the average age at first marriage has been increasing for both men and women. The blue arrows in Figure 8.3 show that the average age at which men married for the first time in the year 1990 was about 26 years. The graph shows that, for the years shown, the average age at first marriage for men has always been greater than the average age at first marriage for women.

At the right is the circle graph shown on the previous page. Use this graph for Example 1 and You Try It 1.

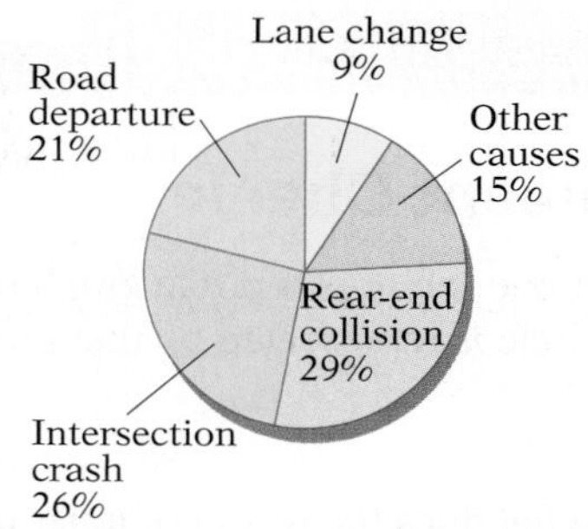

Figure 8.2 Types of Automobile Accidents, City of Twin Falls, Year: 2005 Total Number of Accidents: 4300

EXAMPLE 1

a. Find the ratio, as a fraction in simplest form, of the percent of lane-change accidents to the percent of accidents resulting from "other causes."

b. Determine the number of rear-end collisions that occurred in Twin Falls in the year 2005.

Strategy

a. To find the ratio:
- From the graph, find the percent of lane-change accidents and the percent of accidents resulting from "other causes."
- Write the ratio in fractional form. Simplify.

b. To find the number of rear-end collisions:
- From the graph, find the percent of accidents that were rear-end collisions.
- Solve the basic percent equation for amount. The base is 4300.

Solution

a. Lane-change accidents: 9%

Accidents resulting from "other causes": 15%

$$\frac{9\%}{15\%} = \frac{3}{5}$$

The ratio is $\frac{3}{5}$.

b. Rear-end collisions: 29% = 0.29

$$\text{Percent} \cdot \text{base} = \text{amount}$$
$$0.29 \cdot 4300 = n$$
$$1247 = n$$

1247 rear-end collisions occurred in Twin Falls in 2005.

YOU TRY IT 1

a. Find the ratio, as a fraction in simplest form, of the percent of lane-change accidents to the percent of road-departure accidents.

b. Determine the number of accidents that occurred at intersections in Twin Falls in the year 2005.

Your strategy

Your solution

a. $\frac{3}{7}$

b. 1118 accidents

IN-CLASS EXAMPLES

Use Figures 8.1, 8.2, and 8.3.

1. What percent of the 2002 average U.S. movie theater ticket price is the 2009 average U.S. movie theater ticket price? Round to the nearest percent. **129%**
2. Determine the number of lane-change accidents that occurred in Twin Falls in the year 2005. **387 lane-change accidents**
3. What was the average age at which women married for the first time in the year 1980? **22 years**

Solution on pp. S20–S21

8.1 EXERCISES

SUGGESTED ASSIGNMENT
Exercises 1–3; Exercises 5–17, odds; More challenging problems: Exercises 19–21

Concept Check

1. If one sector of a circle graph represents 25% of the total graph, what fraction of the circle is represented by that sector?
   $\frac{1}{4}$

2. What does the height of a bar in a bar graph represent?
   The data value associated with that bar

3. Three consecutive data points of a broken-line graph are positioned such that the line joining the first and second points slants downward to the right and the line joining the second and third points slants upward to the right. What conclusions can be drawn about the data represented by this portion of the broken-line graph?
   The value of the data decreased from the first point to the second point and then increased from the second point to the third point.

OBJECTIVE A *To read and interpret graphs*

Education An accounting major recorded the number of units required in each discipline to graduate with a degree in accounting. The results are shown in the circle graph in Figure 8.4. Use this graph for Exercises 4 to 6.

4. How many units are required to graduate with a degree in accounting?
   128 units

5. What is the ratio of the number of units needed in finance to the number of units needed in accounting? $\frac{1}{3}$

6. What percent of the units required to graduate are taken in mathematics? Round to the nearest tenth of a percent. 9.4%

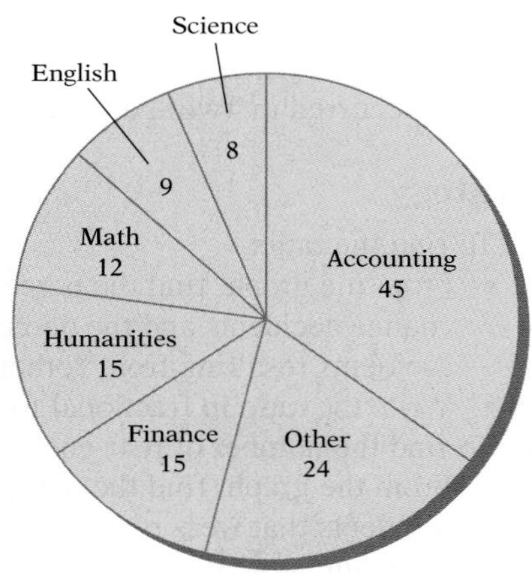

Figure 8.4 Number of units required to graduate with an accounting degree

Video Games Use the information in the article at the right and the graph in Figure 8.5 for Exercises 7 to 10.

7. Find the amount of money spent on video game hardware in 2010. $6,324,000,000

8. Find the amount of money spent on video game software in 2010. $9,300,000,000

9. What fractional amount of the total money spent was spent on accessories?
   $\frac{4}{25}$

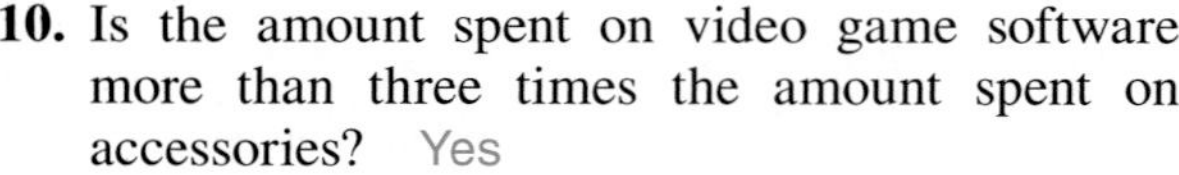

10. Is the amount spent on video game software more than three times the amount spent on accessories? Yes

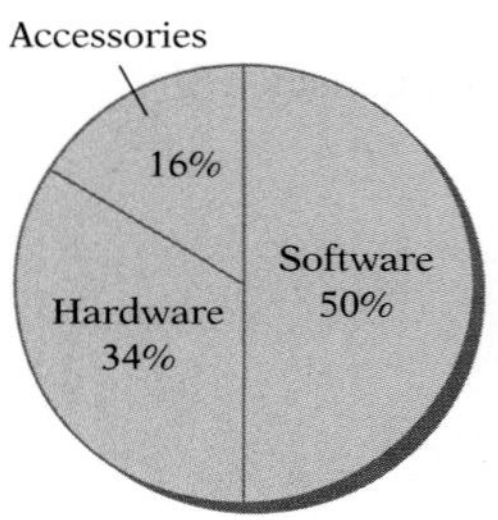

Figure 8.5 Video Game Industry Percents of Total Sales for 2010

In the NEWS!

Video Game Sales Decline

Across the video-game industry, only accessories saw an increase in sales this year. Total sales of hardware, software, and accessories reached $18.6 billion in 2010, a 6% decrease over 2009.

Source: www.thestreet.com

Population The bar graph in Figure 8.6 shows the approximate world population for five decades. For 2020 and 2030, the population is a projected estimate. Use this graph for Exercises 11 to 13.

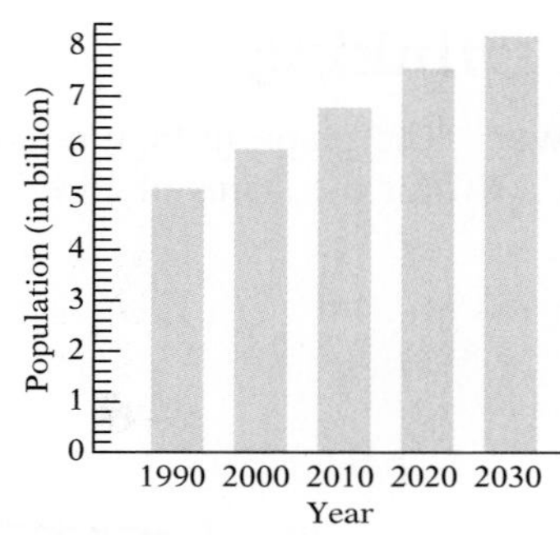

Figure 8.6 World population estimates
Source: www.infoplease.com

11. Is the estimated population in 2030 less than or more than 8 billion people?
More than

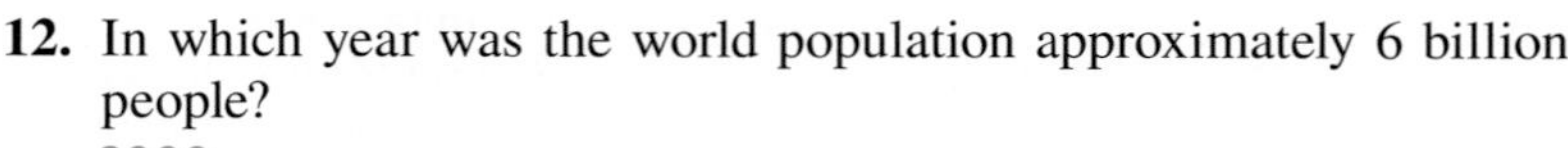

12. In which year was the world population approximately 6 billion people?
2000

13. What was the change in world population between 1990 and 2010?
About 1.6 billion people

Health The double-broken-line graph in Figure 8.7 shows the number of Calories per day that should be consumed by women and men in various age groups. Use this graph for Exercises 14 to 16.

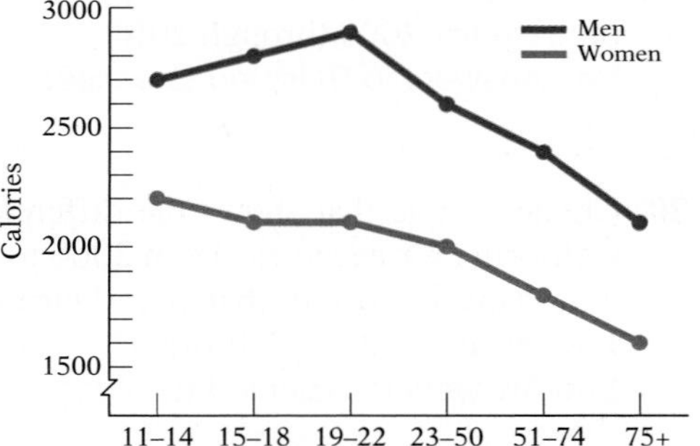

Figure 8.7 Recommended number of Calories per day for women and men
Source: Numbers, by Andrea Sutcliffe (HarperCollins)

14. What is the difference between the number of Calories recommended for men aged 19 to 22 and the number recommended for women aged 19 to 22?
800 Calories

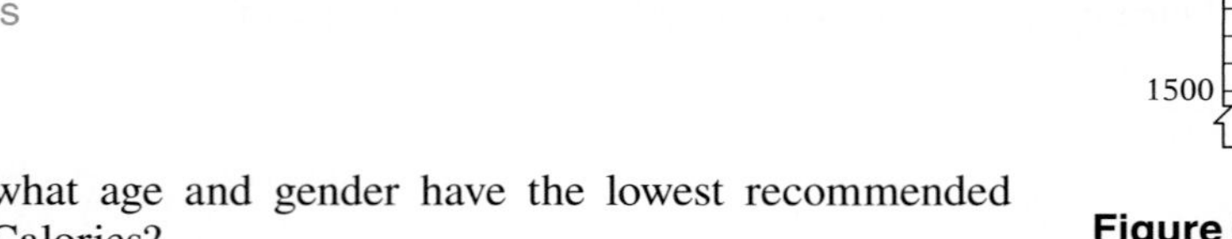

15. People of what age and gender have the lowest recommended number of Calories?
Women aged 75 and older

16. Find the ratio of the number of Calories recommended for women aged 15 to 18 to the number recommended for women aged 51 to 74.
$\frac{7}{6}$

For Exercises 17 and 18, each statement refers to a line graph (not shown) that displays the population of a particular state every 10 years between 1950 and 2010. Determine whether the statement is true or false.

17. If the population decreased between 2000 and 2010, then the segment joining the point for 2000 and the point for 2010 slants down from left to right.
True

18. If the points for 1960 and 1970 are connected by a horizontal line, the population in 1970 was the same as the population in 1960.
True

Critical Thinking

Wind Power The graph in Figure 8.8 shows how wind power capacity increased from 2000 to 2010 for the states of Iowa and California. Use this graph for Exercises 19 and 20.

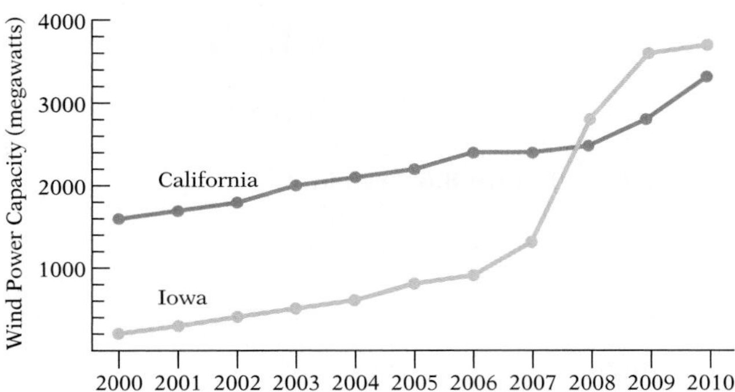

Figure 8.8 Wind power capacity in Iowa and California
Source: www.windpoweringamerica.gov

19. Create a table that shows the approximate wind power capacity of each state for each of the years 2000 through 2010.
See Answers to Selected Exercises.

20. Create a table that shows the difference in the wind power capacities of Iowa and California for each year from 2000 to 2010, and indicate which state had the greater wind power capacity that year. During which years did the wind power capacity of Iowa exceed that of California?
See Answers to Selected Exercises.

21. The circle graph in Figure 8.9 shows a couple's expenditures last month. Write two observations about this couple's expenses.

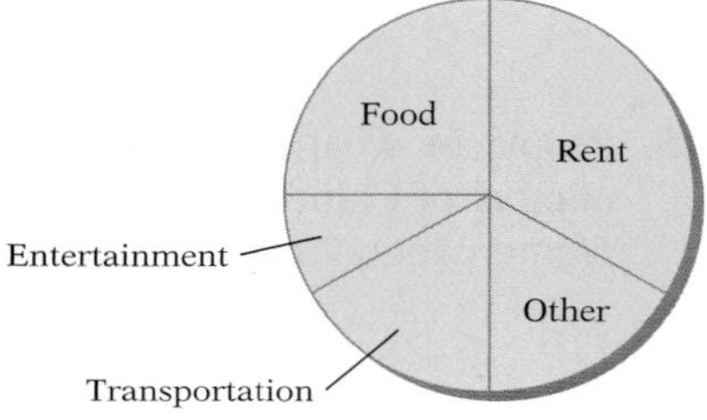

Figure 8.9 Monthly expenditures

QUICK QUIZ

1. According to the data in Figure 8.4, how many more units are required in accounting than in English? **36 more units [8.1B]**
2. According to the data in Figure 8.6, by how much will the world population increase between 2000 and 2020? **1.6 billion people [8.1A]**
3. According to the data in Figure 8.7, what is the difference between the number of Calories recommended for males aged 11 to 14 and the number recommended for females aged 11 to 14? **500 Calories [8.1A]**

Projects or Group Activities

22. The table below shows the Environmental Protection Agency (EPA) mileage estimates for city and highway driving for selected sports cars. Using the graph at the right, draw a double-bar graph to represent these data. For each type of car, use the first bar to show the EPA city estimate and the second bar to show the EPA highway estimate.

EPA Mileage Estimates (miles per gallon)		
Car	*City*	*Highway*
Aston Martin DB9	11	17
Audi R8	13	19
Lamborghini Gallardo	13	20
Jaguar XK	16	24
Porsche Carrera	18	26

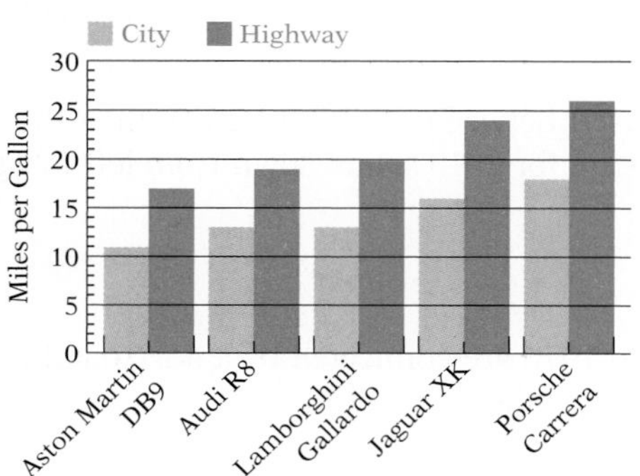

SECTION

8.2 Statistical Measures

OBJECTIVE A

To find the mean, median, and mode of a distribution

The average score on the math portion of the SAT was 432. The EPA estimates that a 2012 Toyota Camry Hybrid averages 41 miles per gallon on the highway. The average rainfall for portions of Kauai is 350 inches per year. Each of these statements uses one number to describe an entire collection of numbers. Such a number is called an **average.**

In statistics, there are various ways to calculate an average. Three of the most common—*mean, median,* and *mode*—are discussed here.

An automotive engineer tests the miles-per-gallon ratings of 15 cars and records the results as follows:

Miles-per-Gallon Ratings of 15 Cars

25	22	21	27	25	35	29	31	25	26	21	39	34	32	28

INSTRUCTOR NOTE

You might explain to your students that the mean is an appropriate measure when all the data values are relatively close. However, when the range of values is large compared to the values themselves, the mean may give an unrealistic picture of the data.

The **mean** of the data is the sum of the measurements divided by the number of measurements. The symbol for the mean is $\bar{x}$.

Formula for the Mean

$$\bar{x} = \frac{\text{sum of the data values}}{\text{number of data values}}$$

To find the mean for the data above, add the numbers and then divide by 15.

$$\bar{x} = \frac{25 + 22 + 21 + 27 + 25 + 35 + 29 + 31 + 25 + 26 + 21 + 39 + 34 + 32 + 28}{15}$$

$$= \frac{420}{15} = 28$$

The mean number of miles per gallon for the 15 cars tested was 28 miles per gallon.

The mean is one of the most frequently computed averages. It is the one that is commonly used to calculate a student's performance in a class.

HOW TO 1 The test scores for a student taking American history were 78, 82, 91, 87, and 93. What was the mean score for this student?

Strategy

To find the mean, divide the sum of the test scores by 5, the number of scores.

Solution

$$\bar{x} = \frac{78 + 82 + 91 + 87 + 93}{5} = \frac{431}{5} = 86.2$$

The mean score for the history student was 86.2.

Integrating Technology

When using a calculator to calculate the mean, use parentheses to group the addends in the numerator.

(78 + 82 + 91 + 87 + 93) ÷ 5 =

The **median** of a set of data is the number that separates the data into two equal parts when the numbers are arranged from least to greatest (or from greatest to least). There is an equal number of values above and below the median.

To find the median of a set of numbers, first arrange the numbers from least to greatest. The median is the number in the middle.

The miles-per-gallon ratings given on the preceding page are arranged from least to greatest below.

21 21 22 25 25 25 26 27 28 29 31 32 34 35 39

7 values below the median — Middle number **Median** — 7 values above the median

The median is 27 miles per gallon.

If data contain an *even* number of values, the median is the mean of the two middle numbers.

Tips for Success

Word problems are difficult because we must read the problem, determine the quantity we must find, think of a method to find it, actually solve the problem, and then check the answer. In short, we must devise a *strategy* and then use that strategy to find the *solution.* See *AIM for Success* at the front of the book.

HOW TO 2 The selling prices of the last six homes sold by a real estate agent were \$275,000, \$250,000, \$350,000, \$230,000, \$345,000, and \$290,000. Find the median selling price of these homes.

Strategy

To find the median, arrange the numbers from least to greatest. Because there is an even number of values, the median is the mean of the two middle numbers.

Solution

230,000 250,000 275,000 290,000 345,000 350,000

Middle 2 numbers: 275,000 290,000

$$\text{Median} = \frac{275{,}000 + 290{,}000}{2} = 282{,}500$$

The median selling price was \$282,500.

IN-CLASS EXAMPLES

1. A truck driver's records show the number of gallons of diesel fuel purchased each day of a 5-day trip.

Wed	Thu	Fri	Sat	Sun
74	86	93	79	88

   a. Find the mean number of gallons purchased. **84 gallons**
   b. Find the median number of gallons purchased. **86 gallons**
2. The ages of the six children in a small day-care center are 3, 4, 4, 5, 4, and 2 years. What is the mode of these data? **4 years**

The **mode** of a set of numbers is the value that occurs most frequently. If a set of numbers has no number that occurs more than once, then the data have no mode.

Here again are the data for the gasoline mileage ratings of 15 cars.

Miles-per-Gallon Ratings of 15 Cars														
25	22	21	27	25	35	29	31	25	26	21	39	34	32	28

25 is the number that occurs most frequently.

The mode is 25 miles per gallon.

Note from the miles-per-gallon example that the mean, median, and mode may be different.

EXAMPLE 1

Twenty students were asked the number of units in which they were enrolled. The responses were as follows:

15	12	13	15	17	18	13	20	9	16
14	10	15	12	17	16	6	14	15	12

Find the mean number of units taken by these students.

Strategy

To find the mean number of units:

- Find the sum of the 20 numbers.
- Divide the sum by 20.

Solution

$15 + 12 + 13 + 15 + 17 + 18 + 13 + 20 + 9 + 16 + 14 + 10 + 15 + 12 + 17 + 16 + 6 + 14 + 15 + 12 = 279$

$$\bar{x} = \frac{279}{20} = 13.95$$

The mean is 13.95 units.

YOU TRY IT 1

The amounts spent by 12 customers at a McDonald's restaurant were as follows:

11.01	10.75	12.09	15.88	13.50	12.29
10.69	9.36	11.66	15.25	10.09	12.72

Find the mean amount spent by these customers. Round to the nearest cent.

Your strategy

Your solution

$12.11

EXAMPLE 2

The starting hourly wages for an apprentice electrician for six different work locations are $12.50, $11.25, $10.90, $11.56, $13.75, and $14.55. Find the median starting hourly wage.

Strategy

To find the median starting hourly wage:

- Arrange the numbers from least to greatest.
- Because there is an even number of values, the median is the mean of the two middle numbers.

Solution

10.90, 11.25, 11.56, 12.50, 13.75, 14.55

$$\text{Median} = \frac{11.56 + 12.50}{2} = 12.03$$

The median starting hourly wage is $12.03.

YOU TRY IT 2

The amounts of weight lost, in pounds, by 10 participants in a 6-month weight-reduction program were 22, 16, 31, 14, 27, 16, 29, 31, 40, and 10. Find the median weight loss for these participants.

Your strategy

Your solution

24.5 pounds

Solutions on p. S21

OBJECTIVE B *To draw a box-and-whiskers plot*

INSTRUCTOR NOTE
Questions from statistics are included on many teacher's state competency exams. Hence the inclusion in this text of topics such as box-and-whiskers plots.

Recall from the last objective that an average is one number that helps to describe all the numbers in a set of data. For example, we know from the following statement that Erie gets a lot of snow each winter.

The average annual snowfall in Erie, Pennsylvania, is 85 inches.

Now look at these two statements.

The average annual temperature in San Francisco, California, is 57°F.

The average annual temperature in St. Louis, Missouri, is 57°F.

San Francisco

The average annual temperature in both cities is the same. However, we do not expect the climate in St. Louis to be like San Francisco's climate. Although both cities have the same average annual temperature, their temperature ranges differ. In fact, the difference between the average monthly high temperatures in July and January in San Francisco is 14°F, whereas the difference between the average monthly high temperatures in July and January in St. Louis is 50°F.

Note that for this example, a single number (the average annual temperature) does not provide us with a very comprehensive picture of the climate of either of these two cities.

St. Louis

One method used to picture an entire set of data is a box-and-whiskers plot. To prepare a box-and-whiskers plot, begin by separating the data into four parts, called **quartiles.** We will illustrate this by using the average monthly high temperatures for St. Louis, in degrees Fahrenheit. These are listed below for January through December.

39	47	58	72	81	88	89	89	85	76	49	47

Source: The Weather Channel

First list the numbers in order from least to greatest and determine the median.

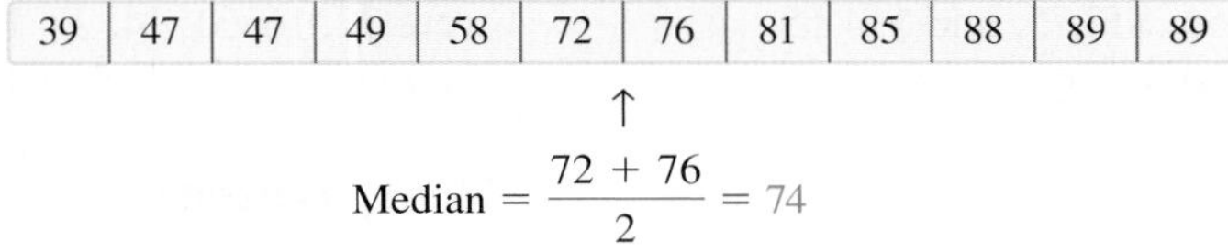

39	47	47	49	58	72	76	81	85	88	89	89

$$\text{Median} = \frac{72 + 76}{2} = 74$$

Now find the median of the data values below the median. The median of the data values below the median is called the **first quartile,** symbolized by Q_1. Also find the median of the data values above the median. The median of the data values above the median is called the **third quartile,** symbolized by Q_3.

INSTRUCTOR NOTE
You may want to explain to your students that the word *quartile* is used because it divides the set of data into four sets of approximately equal size.

The second quartile, symbolized by Q_2, is the number that one-half of the data lie below and one-half of the data lie above. Therefore, it is the median of the data.

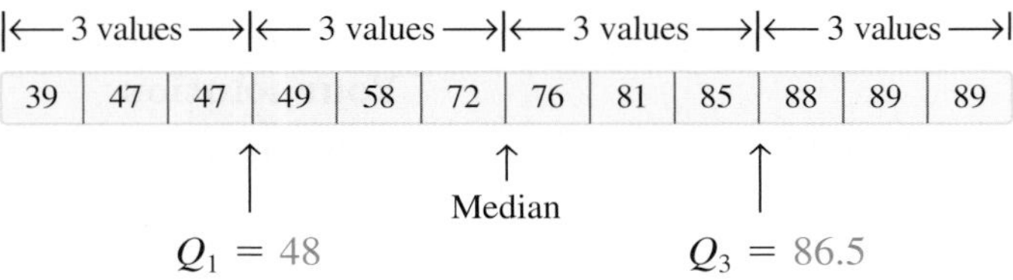

|← 3 values →|← 3 values →|← 3 values →|← 3 values →|

39	47	47	49	58	72	76	81	85	88	89	89

Median

$Q_1 = 48$ $\quad$ $Q_3 = 86.5$

The first quartile, Q_1, is the number that one-quarter of the data lie below. This means that 25% of the data lie below the first quartile. The third quartile, Q_3, is the number that one-quarter of the data lie above. This means that 25% of the data lie above the third quartile.

INSTRUCTOR NOTE
Emphasize that the boxplot at the right below shows that there are as many months with average high temperatures between 48°F and 74°F as there are months with average high temperatures between 74°F and 86.5°F.

A **box-and-whiskers plot,** or **boxplot,** is a graph that shows five numbers: the least value, the first quartile, the median, the third quartile, and the greatest value. Here are these five values for the data on St. Louis temperatures.

The least number	39
The first quartile, Q_1	48
The median	74
The third quartile, Q_3	86.5
The greatest number	89

Take Note
The number line at the right is shown as a reference only. It is not a part of the boxplot. It shows that the numbers labeled on the boxplot are plotted according to the distances on the number line above it.

Think of a number line that includes the five values listed above. With this in mind, mark off the five values. Draw a box that spans the distance from Q_1 to Q_3. Draw a vertical line the height of the box at the median.

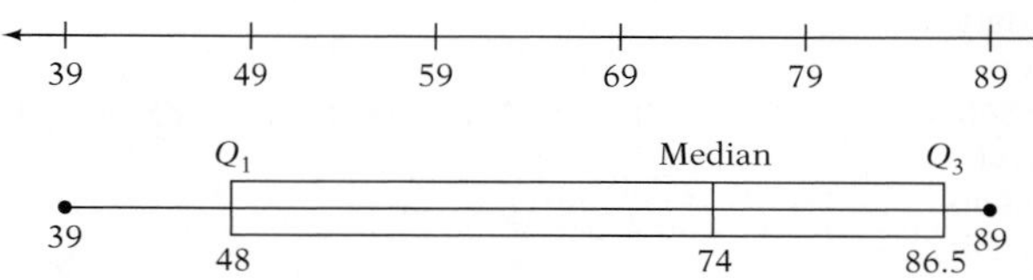

The **range** of a set of numbers is the difference between the greatest number and the least number in the set. The range describes the spread of the data. For the data above,

$$\text{Range} = \text{greatest value} - \text{least value} = 89 - 39 = 50$$

Take Note
50% of the data in a distribution lies in the interquartile range.

The **interquartile range** is the difference between the third quartile, Q_3, and the first quartile, Q_1. For the data above,

$$\text{Interquartile range} = Q_3 - Q_1 = 86.5 - 48 = 38.5$$

The interquartile range is the distance that spans the "middle" 50% of the data values. Because it excludes the bottom fourth of the data values and the top fourth of the data values, it excludes any extreme numbers of the set.

Listed below are the average monthly high temperatures for San Francisco.

57	60	61	64	68	71	71	73	74	73	60	59

Source: The Weather Channel

We can perform the same calculations on these data to determine the five values needed for the box-and-whiskers plot.

The least number	57
The first quartile, Q_1	60
The median	66
The third quartile, Q_3	72
The greatest number	74

Take Note
It is the "whiskers" on the box-and-whiskers plot that show the range of the data. The "box" on the box-and-whiskers plot shows the interquartile range of the data.

The box-and-whiskers plot is shown at the right with the same scale used for the data on the St. Louis temperatures.

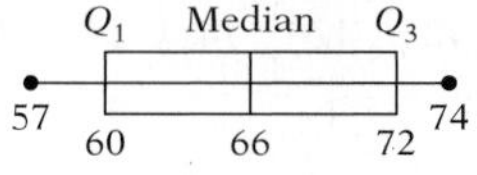

Note that by comparing the two boxplots, we can see that the range of temperatures in St. Louis is greater than the range of temperatures in San Francisco. For the St. Louis temperatures, there is a greater spread of the data below the median than above the median, whereas the data of the San Francisco boxplot are spread nearly equally above and below the median.

HOW TO 3 The numbers of avalanche deaths in the United States during each of nine consecutive winters were 8, 24, 29, 13, 28, 30, 22, 26, and 32. (*Source:* Colorado Avalanche Information Center) Draw a box-and-whiskers plot of the data, and determine the interquartile range.

Strategy

To draw the box-and-whiskers plot, arrange the data from least to greatest. Then find the median, Q_1, and Q_3. Use the least value, Q_1, the median, Q_3, and the greatest value to draw the box-and-whiskers plot.

To find the interquartile range, find the difference between Q_3 and Q_1.

Solution

8	13	22	24	26	28	29	30	32

↑ $Q_1 = 17.5$ ↑ Median ↑ $Q_3 = 29.5$

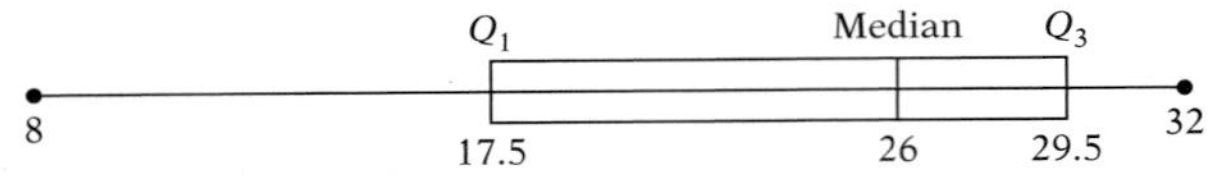

Interquartile range $= Q_3 - Q_1 = 29.5 - 17.5 = 12$

The interquartile range is 12 deaths.

Take Note

Note that the left whisker in this box-and-whiskers plot is quite long, and the length of the box from Q_1 to the median is longer than the length of the box from the median to Q_3. This illustrates a set of data in which the median is closer to the greatest data value. If the two whiskers are approximately the same length, and the distances from Q_1 to the median and from the median to Q_3 are approximately equal, then the least and greatest values are about the same distance from the median. See Example 3 below.

EXAMPLE 3

The average monthly snowfall amounts, in inches, for Buffalo, New York, from October through April are 1, 12, 24, 25, 18, 12, and 3. (*Source:* The Weather Channel) Draw a box-and-whiskers plot of the data.

Strategy

To draw the box-and-whiskers plot:

- Arrange the data from least to greatest.
- Find the median, Q_1, and Q_3.
- Use the least value, Q_1, the median, Q_3, and the greatest value to draw the box-and-whiskers plot.

Solution

1	3	12	12	18	24	25

↑ Q_1 ↑ Median ↑ Q_3

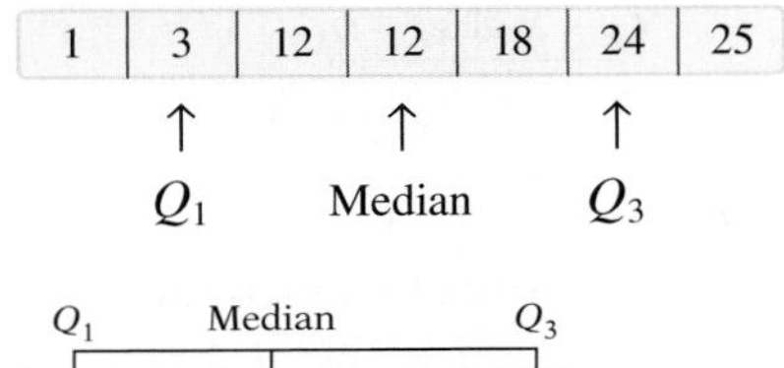

YOU TRY IT 3

The average monthly snowfall amounts, in inches, for Denver, Colorado, from October through April are 4, 7, 7, 8, 8, 9, and 13. (*Source:* The Weather Channel)

a. Draw a box-and-whiskers plot of the data.
b. How does the spread of the data within the interquartile range compare with that in Example 3?

Your strategy

Your solution

a. Median, Q_1, Q_3; 4, 7 8 9, 13

b. Answers about the spread of the data will vary.

Solution on p. S21

IN-CLASS EXAMPLES

3. The list below gives the numbers of years U.S. presidents survived after leaving office.
0, 1, 2, 2, 3, 4, 6, 6, 7, 8, 8, 8, 8, 9, 11, 11, 12, 15, 16, 17, 17, 19, 19, 19, 20, 21, 21, 25, 29, 31
Find Q_1, the median, Q_3, and the range.
$Q_1 = 6$ years, median $= 11$ years, $Q_3 = 19$ years, range $= 31$ years

8.2 EXERCISES

Concept Check

SUGGESTED ASSIGNMENT
Exercises 1–4; Exercises 5–25, odds
More challenging exercises: Exercises 26, 27

1. A set of data has a mean of 16, a median of 15, and a mode of 14. Which of these numbers must be a value in the data set? Explain your answer.

2. Explain each notation.
a. Q_1 **b.** Q_3 **c.** $\bar{x}$

3. State whether the mean, median, or mode is being used.
a. Half of the houses in the new development are priced under $350,000. Median
b. The average bill for lunch at the college union is $11.95. Mean
c. The college bookstore sells more green college sweatshirts than any other color. Mode
d. In a recent year, there were as many people age 26 and younger in the world as there were people age 26 and older. Median
e. The majority of full-time students carry a load of 12 credit hours each semester. Mode
f. The average annual return on an investment is 6.5%. Mean

4. a. What percent of the data in a set of numbers lies above Q_3? 25%
b. What percent of the data in a set of numbers lies above the median? 50%
c. What percent of the data in a set of numbers lies below Q_3? 75%
d. What percent of the data in a set of numbers lies below Q_1? 25%
e. What percent of the data in a set of numbers lies between Q_1 and Q_3? 50%

OBJECTIVE A *To find the mean, median, and mode of a distribution*

5. Airline Industry The numbers of seats occupied on a jet for 16 trans-Atlantic flights were recorded. The numbers were 309, 422, 389, 412, 401, 352, 367, 319, 410, 391, 330, 408, 399, 387, 411, and 398. Calculate the mean, the median, and the mode of the number of seats occupied per flight.
Mean: 381.5625 seats; median: 394.5 seats; mode: no mode

© Richard Levine/Alamy

6. Consumerism The numbers of high-definition televisions sold each month for one year were recorded by an electronics store. The results were 15, 12, 20, 20, 19, 17, 22, 24, 17, 20, 15, and 27. Calculate the mean, the median, and the mode of the number of televisions sold per month.
Mean: 19 TVs; median: 19.5 TVs; mode: 20 TVs

7. Consumerism A consumer research group purchased identical items at eight grocery stores. The costs for the purchased items were $85.89, $92.12, $81.43, $80.67, $88.73, $82.45, $87.81, and $85.82. Calculate the mean and the median costs of the purchased items.
Mean: $85.615; median: $85.855

8. Sports The times, in seconds, for a 100-meter dash at a college track meet were 10.45, 10.23, 10.57, 11.01, 10.26, 10.90, 10.74, 10.64, 10.52, and 10.78.
a. Calculate the mean time for the 100-meter dash. 10.61 seconds
b. Calculate the median time for the 100-meter dash. 10.605 seconds

9. **Health Plans** Eight health maintenance organizations (HMOs) presented group health insurance plans to a company. The monthly rates per employee were \$423, \$390, \$405, \$396, \$426, \$355, \$404, and \$430. Calculate the mean and the median monthly rates for these eight companies.
Mean: \$403.625; median: \$404.50

10. **Computers** One measure of a computer's hard-drive speed is called access time; this is measured in milliseconds (thousandths of a second). Find the mean and median access times for 11 hard drives whose access times, in milliseconds, were 5, 4.5, 4, 4.5, 5, 5.5, 6, 5.5, 3, 4.5, and 4.5. Round to the nearest tenth.
Mean: 4.7 milliseconds; median: 4.5 milliseconds

11. **Life Expectancy** The life expectancies, in years, for ten selected Central and South American countries are given at the right.
a. Find the mean life expectancy for this group of countries.
b. Find the median life expectancy for this group of countries.
Mean: 75.0 years; median: 74.4 years

Country	Life Expectancy
Brazil	73.5
Chile	79.1
Costa Rica	79.3
Ecuador	75.6
Guatemala	71.2
Panama	76.1
Peru	74.0
Trinidad and Tobago	70.1
Uruguay	77.0
Venezuela	74.4

Source: United Nations Development Programme

12. **Government** The lengths of the terms, in years, of all the former Supreme Court chief justices are given in the table below. Find the mean and median length of term for the chief justices. Round to the nearest tenth.

5	0	4	34	28	8	14	21
10	8	11	4	7	15	17	19

Mean: 12.8 years; median: 10.5 years

13. **Education** Your scores on six history tests were 78, 92, 95, 77, 94, and 88. If an "average" score of 90 receives an A for the course, which average, the mean or the median, would you prefer the instructor use?
Median

14. **Defense Spending** The table below shows the defense expenditures, in billions of dollars, by the federal government for 1965 through 1973, years during which the United States was actively involved in the Vietnam War.

Year	1965	1966	1967	1968	1969	1970	1971	1972	1973
Expenditures	\$49.6	\$56.8	\$70.1	\$80.5	\$81.2	\$80.3	\$77.7	\$78.3	\$76.0

Source: Statistical Abstract of the United States

a. Calculate the mean annual defense expenditure for these years. Round to the nearest tenth of a billion. \$72.3 billion
b. Find the median annual defense expenditure. \$77.7 billion
c. If the year 1965 were eliminated from the data, how would that affect the mean? The median?

15. Suppose a new data set is formed by adding 5 to each number in an existing data set. How is the mean of the new data set related to the mean of the original data set?
It is 5 more than the mean of the original data set.

OBJECTIVE B To draw a box-and-whiskers plot

16. **U.S. Presidents** The box-and-whiskers plot below shows the distribution of the ages of the presidents of the United States at the time of their inauguration.

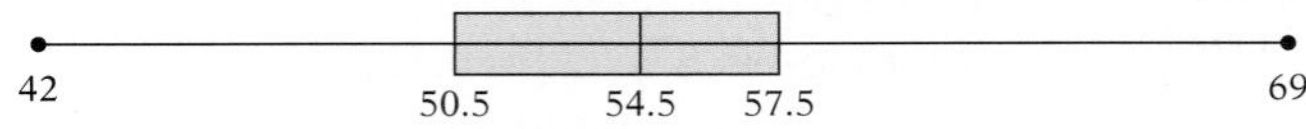

a. What is the youngest age in the set of data? 42 years
b. What is the oldest age? 69 years
c. What is the first quartile? 50.5 years
d. What is the third quartile? 54.5 years
e. What is the median? 57.5 years
f. Find the range. 27 years
g. Find the interquartile range. 7 years

17. **Compensation** The box-and-whiskers plot below shows the distribution of median household incomes for 50 states and the District of Columbia. (*Source:* U.S. Census Bureau) What is the lowest value in the set of data? The highest value? The first quartile? The third quartile? The median? Find the range and the interquartile range.

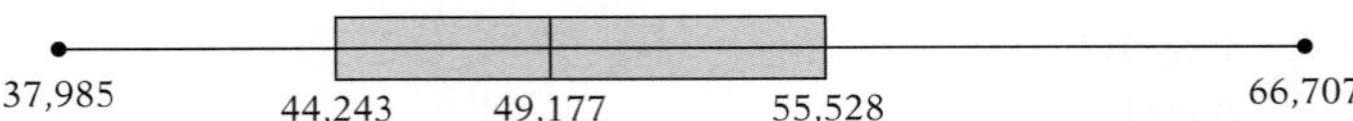

Lowest = \$37,985; Highest = \$66,707; Q_1 = \$44,243; Q_3 = \$55,528; Median = \$49,177; Range = \$28,722; Interquartile range = \$11,285

18. **Education** An aptitude test was taken by 200 students at the Fairfield Middle School. The box-and-whiskers plot at the right shows the distribution of their scores.

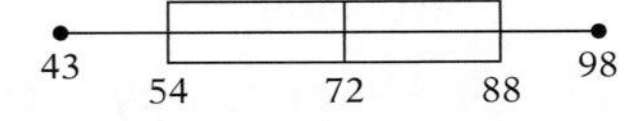

a. How many students scored over 88? 50 students
b. How many students scored below 72? 100 students
c. How many scores are represented in each quartile? 50 scores
d. What percent of the students had scores of at least 54? 75%

19. **Health** The cholesterol levels of 80 adults were recorded and then displayed in the box-and-whiskers plot shown at the right.

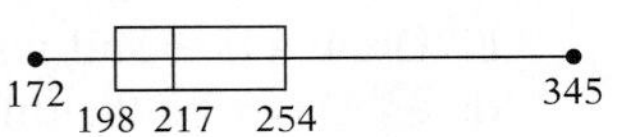

a. How many adults had a cholesterol level above 217? 40 adults
b. How many adults had a cholesterol level below 254? 60 adults
c. How many cholesterol levels are represented in each quartile? 20 cholesterol levels
d. What percent of the adults had a cholesterol level of 198 or less? 25%

20. **Fuel Efficiency** The gasoline consumption of 19 cars was tested, and the results were recorded in the table below.

Miles per Gallon for 19 Cars									
33	21	30	32	20	31	25	20	16	24
22	31	30	28	26	19	21	17	26	

a. Range = 17 mpg; Q_1 = 20 mpg; Q_3 = 30 mpg; interquartile range = 10 mpg

a. Find the range, the first quartile, the third quartile, and the interquartile range.
b. Draw a box-and-whiskers plot of the data.
c. Is the data value 21 in the interquartile range? Yes

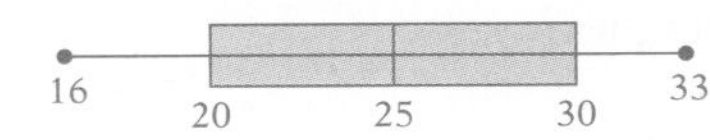

21. **Environment** Carbon dioxide is among the gases that contribute to global warming. Carbon dioxide emissions of ten countries for a recent year are listed below. The figures are emissions in millions of metric tons per year.

Carbon Dioxide Emissions (in millions of metric tons per year)			
Canada	0.64	Japan	1.26
China	5.01	Russian Federation	1.52
Germany	0.81	South Korea	0.47
India	1.34	United Kingdom	0.59
Italy	0.45	United States	6.05

Source: U.S. Department of Energy

a. In millions of metric tons per year, the range is 5.6; $Q_1 = 0.59$; $Q_3 = 1.52$; the interquartile range is 0.93.

b. 

a. Find the range, the first quartile, the third quartile, and the interquartile range.
b. Draw a box-and-whiskers plot of the data.
c. What data value is responsible for the long whisker on the right side of the box-and-whiskers plot? 6.05

22. **Meteorology** The average monthly amounts of rainfall, in inches, from January through December for Seattle, Washington, and Houston, Texas, are listed below.

Seattle	6.0	4.2	3.6	2.4	1.6	1.4	0.7	1.3	2.0	3.4	5.6	6.3
Houston	3.2	3.3	2.7	4.2	4.7	4.1	3.3	3.7	4.9	3.7	3.4	3.7

a. Is the difference between the means greater than 1 inch? No
b. What is the difference between the medians? 0.8 inch
c. Draw a box-and-whiskers plot of each set of data. Use the same scale.
d. Describe the difference between the distributions of the data for Seattle and Houston.

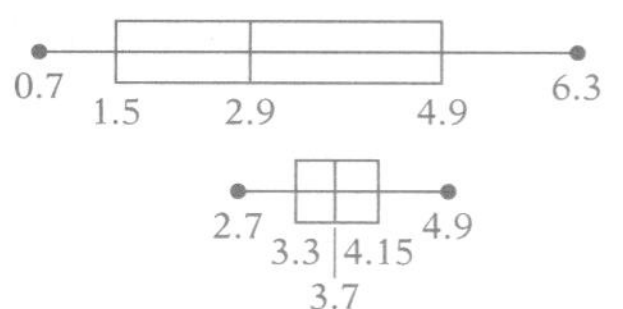

23. **Meteorology** The average monthly amounts of rainfall, in inches, from January through December for Orlando, Florida, and Portland, Oregon, are listed below.

Orlando	2.1	2.8	3.2	2.2	4.0	7.4	7.8	6.3	5.6	2.8	1.8	1.8
Portland	6.2	3.9	3.6	2.3	2.1	1.5	0.5	1.1	1.6	3.1	5.2	6.4

a. Is the difference between the means greater than 1 inch? No
b. What is the difference between the medians? 0.3 inch
c. Draw a box-and-whiskers plot of each set of data. Use the same scale.
d. Describe the difference between the distributions of the data for Orlando and Portland.

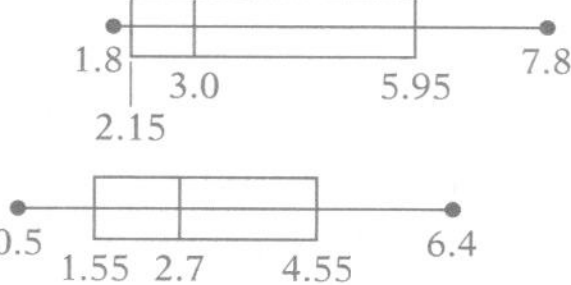

24. Refer to the box-and-whiskers plot in Exercise 17. Which of the following fractions most accurately represents the fraction of states with median incomes less than \$55,528?

(i) $\frac{1}{4}$ (ii) $\frac{1}{3}$ (iii) $\frac{1}{2}$ (iv) $\frac{3}{4}$ iv

25. Write a set of five data values for which the mean, median, and mode are all 55. Answers will vary. For example, 55, 55, 55, 55, 55, or 50, 55, 55, 55, 60

Critical Thinking

26. The box in a box-and-whiskers plot represents 50%, or one-half, of the data in a set. Why is the box in Example 3 of this section not one-half of the entire length of the box-and-whiskers plot?

27. Create a set of data containing 25 numbers that would correspond to the box-and-whiskers plot shown below.

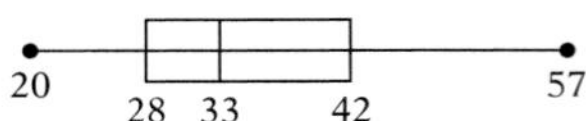

Answers will vary. For example, 20, 21, 22, 24, 26, 27, 29, 31, 31, 32, 32, 33, 33, 36, 37, 37, 39, 40, 41, 43, 45, 46, 50, 54, 57

Projects or Group Activities

Quartiles separate a set of data into four groups. Another way to report data uses percentiles. For instance, if the height of a person is in the 85th percentile, it means that 85% of the population is shorter than that person. In this project you will calculate the percentile of a score in a data set.

28. The data below are the scores on a history exam taken by 50 students.

70, 71, 99, 86, 67, 73, 93, 74, 80, 80,
73, 75, 84, 71, 74, 66, 78, 81, 61, 79,
81, 90, 85, 80, 90, 66, 65, 61, 70, 61,
58, 83, 50, 62, 77, 83, 73, 71, 76, 61,
79, 81, 84, 93, 81, 72, 83, 74, 74, 55

a. To calculate a percentile, first rearrange the data from smallest to largest.
a. 50, 55, 58, 61, 61, 61, 61, 62, 65, 66, 66, 67, 70, 70, 71, 71, 71, 72, 73, 73, 73, 74, 74, 74, 74, 75, 76, 77, 78, 79, 79, 80, 80, 80, 81, 81, 81, 81, 83, 83, 83, 84, 84, 85, 86, 90, 90, 93, 93, 99

b. To calculate the percentile of the score 66, complete the following steps. Do the work to confirm the result given in red for each step.

(i) Count how many scores are below 66. There are 9 scores below 66.

(ii) Add to the result in part (i) the product of $\frac{1}{2}$ and the number of scores that equal 66. The result is 10.

(iii) Multiply the result in part (ii) by 100%, and then divide by the number of students taking the test. Round to the nearest whole number. The result is the 20th percentile. This means that approximately 20% of the scores were lower than 66.

c. Now you try it. Calculate the percentile of a score of 81 on this history exam.
72nd percentile

QUICK QUIZ

1. A tourist center recorded the numbers of requests for information for a five-day period.

Mon	Tue	Wed	Thu	Fri
124	130	127	126	148

a. Find the mean number of requests.
131 requests

b. Find the median number of requests.
127 requests
[8.2A]

2. The numbers of bags of flour used at a bakery during each of six days were 22, 24, 23, 25, 23, and 21. What is the mode of the data?
23 bags of flour [8.2A]

3. The numbers of federal, state, and local law enforcement officers killed in the line of duty during each of seven consecutive years were 157, 153, 169, 170, 132, 160, and 155. (*Source:* National Law Enforcement Officers Memorial Fund)

a. Draw a box-and-whiskers plot of the data.

Q_1 median Q_3
132 153 157 169 170

b. Determine the range and the interquartile range.
Range = 38 officers;
interquartile range = 16 officers [8.2B]

CHECK YOUR PROGRESS: CHAPTER 8

1. Surveys A survey asked 1200 people to name their favorite ice cream flavor. The results are shown in the circle graph in Figure 8.10.

a. Which flavor was selected by the most people in the survey?
Chocolate

b. How many people preferred mint chocolate chip?
180 people

c. How many more people chose cookie dough than chose mint chocolate chip?
60 people [8.1A]

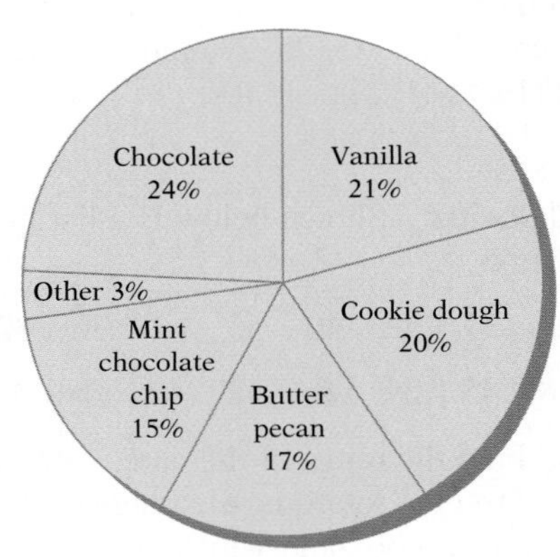

Figure 8.10 Favorite ice cream flavors

2. **Demographics** The bar graph in Figure 8.11 shows the populations of the seven largest cities in the United States.

   a. Is the population of New York City more or less than twice the population of Los Angeles?
   More than

   b. Is the population of Los Angeles plus the population of Chicago more or less than the population of New York City?
   Less than

   c. What is the sum of the populations of the three least-populated cities shown in the graph?
   4.8 million people [8.1A]

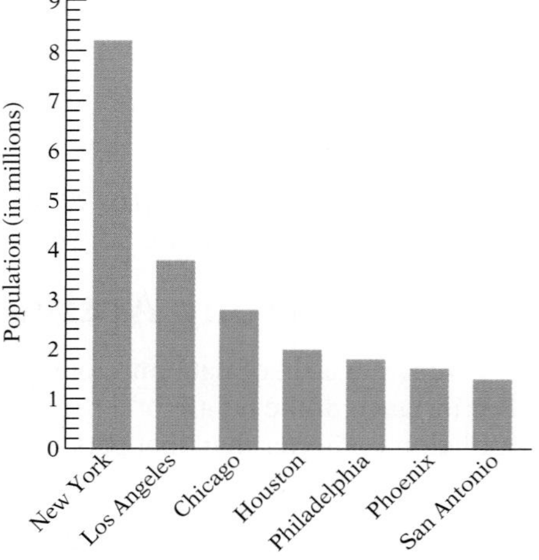

Figure 8.11 Seven largest U.S. cities

3. **Gas Prices** The double-line graph in Figure 8.12 shows the average price of a gallon of regular gasoline for each year from 2006 to 2011, and the price of that same gallon of gas in inflation-adjusted dollars, using 2011 as the base year.

   a. What was the actual price of a gallon of gasoline in 2008?
   $1.60

   b. In which year was the actual price of a gallon of gasoline the lowest?
   2008

   c. For which years was the inflation-adjusted price of a gallon of gasoline less than the inflation-adjusted price in 2007?
   2006, 2008, 2009, and 2010 [8.1A]

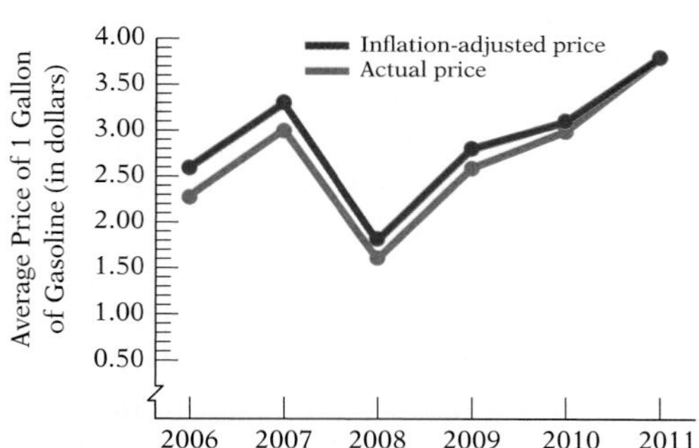

Figure 8.12 Gasoline prices

4. **Salaries** Elle will graduate from college this year. She plans to start a career as a landscape architect. A survey of five landscape architects from last year's senior class shows that they received job offers with the following annual salaries.

   $43,750 $39,500 $38,000 $41,250 $44,000

   Find the mean and the median of these salaries.
   Mean: $41,300; median: $41,250 [8.2A]

5. **Bakeries** The numbers of bags of flour used at a bakery during each of six days were 22, 24, 23, 25, 23, and 21. What is the mode of these data?
   23 bags of flour [8.2A]

6. **Calories** Shown below is a list of the numbers of Calories per 100 ml for 25 soft drinks.

   43 37 42 40 53 62 36 32 50 49 26 53 73

   48 45 39 45 48 40 56 41 36 58 42 39

   a. Find the range of the data. 47 Calories [8.2B]

   b. Find the interquartile range of the data. 12.5 Calories [8.2B]

   c. Draw a box-and-whiskers plot of the data. [8.2B]

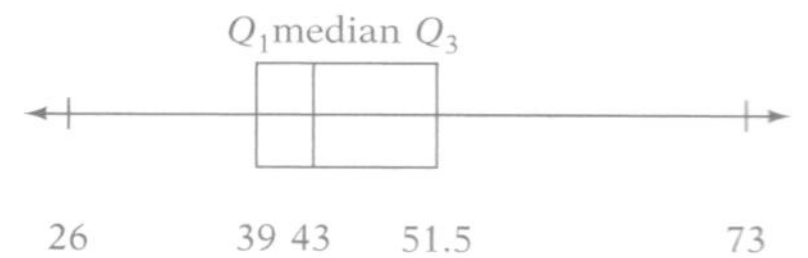

SECTION

8.3 Introduction to Probability

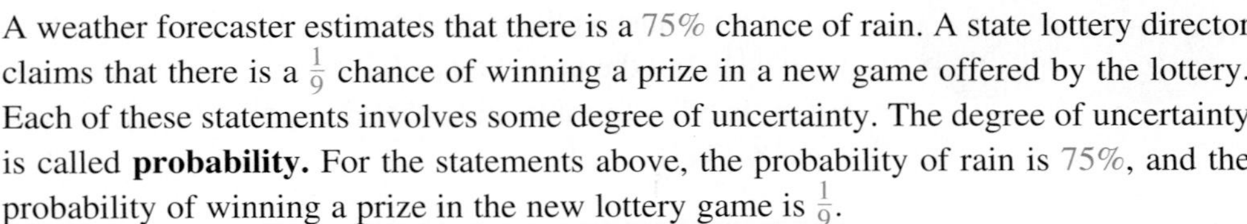

OBJECTIVE A *To calculate the probability of simple events*

Point of Interest

It was dice playing that led Antoine Gombaud, Chevalier de Mere, to ask Blaise Pascal, a French mathematician, to figure out the probability of throwing two sixes. Pascal and Pierre Fermat solved the problem, and their explorations led to the birth of probability theory.

A weather forecaster estimates that there is a 75% chance of rain. A state lottery director claims that there is a $\frac{1}{9}$ chance of winning a prize in a new game offered by the lottery. Each of these statements involves some degree of uncertainty. The degree of uncertainty is called **probability.** For the statements above, the probability of rain is 75%, and the probability of winning a prize in the new lottery game is $\frac{1}{9}$.

A probability is determined from an **experiment,** which is any activity that has an observable outcome. Examples of experiments include

Tossing a coin and observing whether it lands heads up or tails up
Interviewing voters to determine their preference for a political candidate
Drawing a card from a standard deck of 52 cards

All of the possible outcomes of an experiment are called the **sample space** of the experiment. The outcomes are listed between braces. For example:

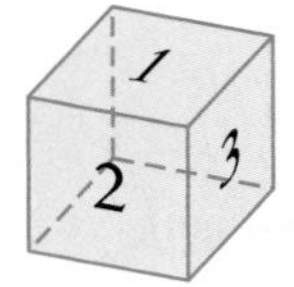

The number cube shown at the left is rolled once. Any of the numbers from 1 to 6 could show on the top of the cube. The sample space is

$\{1, 2, 3, 4, 5, 6\}$

A fair coin is tossed once. (A fair coin is one for which heads and tails have an equal chance of landing face up.) If H represents "heads up" and T represents "tails up," then the sample space is

$\{H, T\}$

An **event** is one or more outcomes of an experiment. For the experiment of rolling the six-sided cube described above, some possible events are

The number is even: $\{2, 4, 6\}$
The number is a multiple of 3: $\{3, 6\}$
The number is less than 10: $\{1, 2, 3, 4, 5, 6\}$

Note that in the last case, the event is the entire sample space.

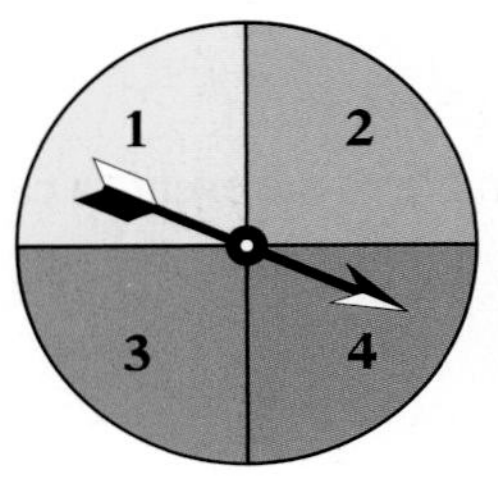

HOW TO 1 The spinner at the left is spun once. Assume that the spinner does not come to rest on a line.

a. What is the sample space?

The arrow could come to rest on any one of the four sectors.
The sample space is $\{1, 2, 3, 4\}$.

b. List the outcomes in the event "the spinner points to an odd number."
$\{1, 3\}$

In discussing experiments and events, it is convenient to refer to the **favorable outcomes** of an experiment. These are the outcomes of an experiment that satisfy the requirements of a particular event.

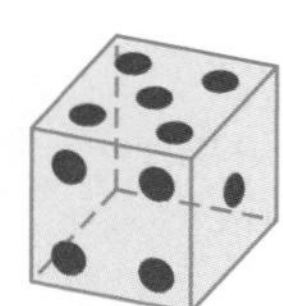
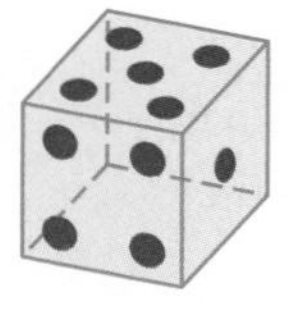

For instance, consider the experiment of rolling a fair die once. The sample space is

$$\{1, 2, 3, 4, 5, 6\}$$

and one possible event would be rolling a number that is divisible by 3. The outcomes of the experiment that are favorable to the event are 3 and 6:

$$\{3, 6\}$$

The outcomes of the experiment of tossing a fair coin are *equally likely.* Either one of the outcomes is just as likely as the other. If a fair coin is tossed once, the probability of a head is $\frac{1}{2}$, and the probability of a tail is $\frac{1}{2}$. Both events are equally likely. The theoretical probability formula, given below, applies to experiments for which the outcomes are equally likely.

Theoretical Probability Formula

The theoretical probability of an event is a fraction with the number of favorable outcomes of the experiment in the numerator and the total number of possible outcomes in the denominator.

$$\text{Probability of an event} = \frac{\text{number of favorable outcomes}}{\text{number of possible outcomes}}$$

A probability of an event is a number from 0 to 1 that tells us how likely it is that the event will happen.

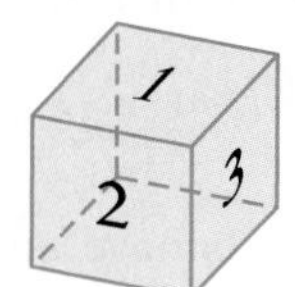

A probability of 0 means that the event is impossible.
The probability of getting a heads when rolling the die shown at the left is 0.

A probability of 1 means that the event must happen.
The probability of getting either heads or tails when tossing a coin is 1.

A probability of $\frac{1}{4}$ means that it is expected that the outcome will happen 1 of every 4 times the experiment is performed.

Take Note
The phrase **at random** means that each card has an equal chance of being drawn.

HOW TO 2 Each of the letters of the word *TENNESSEE* is written on a card, and the cards are placed in a hat. If one card is drawn at random from the hat, what is the probability that the card has the letter *E* on it?

Count the possible outcomes of the experiment.

There are 9 letters in *TENNESSEE.*

There are 9 possible outcomes of the experiment.

Count the number of outcomes of the experiment that are favorable to the event "a card with the letter *E* on it is drawn."

There are 4 cards with an *E* on them.

Use the probability formula.

$$\text{Probability of the event} = \frac{\text{number of favorable outcomes}}{\text{number of possible outcomes}} = \frac{4}{9}$$

The probability of drawing an E is $\frac{4}{9}$.

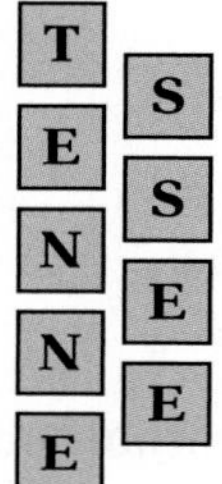

As just discussed, calculating the probability of an event requires counting the number of possible outcomes of an experiment and the number of outcomes that are favorable to the event. One way to do this is to list the outcomes of the experiment in a systematic way. A table is often helpful.

When two dice are rolled, the sample space for the experiment can be recorded systematically, as in the following table.

> **Point of Interest**
>
> Romans called a die that was marked on four faces a *talus,* which meant "anklebone." A sheep's anklebone was considered an ideal die because it is roughly a rectangular solid and it has no marrow. Loose anklebones from sheep were more likely than other bones to be left behind after the wolves had eaten their prey.

Possible Outcomes from Rolling Two Dice

(1, 1)	(2, 1)	(3, 1)	(4, 1)	(5, 1)	(6, 1)
(1, 2)	(2, 2)	(3, 2)	(4, 2)	(5, 2)	(6, 2)
(1, 3)	(2, 3)	(3, 3)	(4, 3)	(5, 3)	(6, 3)
(1, 4)	(2, 4)	(3, 4)	(4, 4)	(5, 4)	(6, 4)
(1, 5)	(2, 5)	(3, 5)	(4, 5)	(5, 5)	(6, 5)
(1, 6)	(2, 6)	(3, 6)	(4, 6)	(5, 6)	(6, 6)

HOW TO 3 Two dice are rolled once. Calculate the probability that the sum of the numbers rolled is 7.

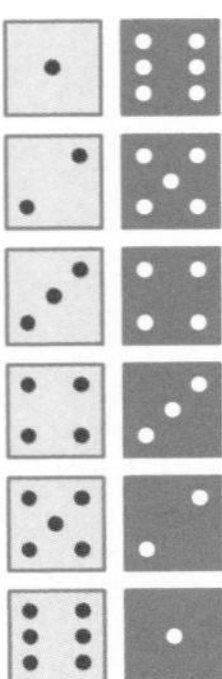

Use the table above to count the number of possible outcomes of the experiment.

There are 36 possible outcomes.

Count the number of outcomes of the experiment that are favorable to the event "a sum of 7 is rolled."

There are 6 favorable outcomes: (1, 6), (2, 5), (3, 4), (4, 3), (5, 2), and (6, 1).

Use the probability formula.

$$\text{Probability of the event} = \frac{\text{number of favorable outcomes}}{\text{number of possible outcomes}} = \frac{6}{36} = \frac{1}{6}$$

The probability of a sum of 7 is $\frac{1}{6}$.

The probabilities calculated above are theoretical probabilities. The calculation of a **theoretical probability** is based on a theory—for example, that either side of a fair coin is equally likely to land face up, or that each of the six sides of a fair die is equally likely to land face up. Not all probabilities arise from such assumptions.

An **empirical probability** is based on a series of observations. For instance, a weather forecast of a 75% chance of rain is an empirical probability. From historical records kept by the weather bureau, when a similar weather pattern existed, rain occurred 75% of the time. It is theoretically impossible to predict the weather, and only observations of past weather patterns can be used to predict future weather conditions.

Empirical Probability Formula

The empirical probability of an event is the ratio of the number of observations of the event to the total number of observations.

$$\text{Probability of an event} = \frac{\text{number of observations of the event}}{\text{total number of observations}}$$

IN-CLASS EXAMPLES

1. A coin is tossed three times. What is the probability that the outcomes of the tosses are exactly TTH? $\frac{1}{8}$
2. Two dice are rolled. What is the probability that the sum of the dots on the upward faces is 4? $\frac{1}{12}$

For example, suppose the records of an insurance company show that of 2549 claims for theft filed by policy holders, 927 were claims for more than $5000. The empirical probability that the next claim for theft this company receives will be a claim for more than $5000 is the ratio of the number of claims for over $5000 to the total number of claims.

$$\frac{927}{2549} \approx 0.36$$

The probability is approximately 0.36.

EXAMPLE 1

There are three choices, *a, b,* or *c,* for each of the two questions on a multiple-choice quiz. If the instructor randomly chooses whether each question will have an answer of *a, b,* or *c,* what is the probability that the two correct answers on this quiz will be the same letter?

Strategy

To find the probability:

- List the outcomes of the experiment in a systematic way.
- Count the number of possible outcomes of the experiment.
- Count the number of outcomes of the experiment that are favorable to the event "the two correct answers on the quiz will be the same letter."
- Use the probability formula.

Solution

Possible outcomes: (a, a) (b, a) (c, a)
(a, b) (b, b) (c, b)
(a, c) (b, c) (c, c)

There are 9 possible outcomes.

There are 3 favorable outcomes:
(a, a), (b, b), (c, c)

$$\text{Probability} = \frac{\text{number of favorable outcomes}}{\text{number of possible outcomes}} = \frac{3}{9} = \frac{1}{3}$$

The probability that the two correct answers will be the same letter is $\frac{1}{3}$.

YOU TRY IT 1

A professor writes three true/false questions for a quiz. If the professor randomly chooses which questions will have an answer of "true" and which will have an answer of "false," what is the probability that the test will have 2 true questions and 1 false question?

Your strategy

Your solution

$\frac{3}{8}$

Solution on p. S21

8.3 EXERCISES

Concept Check

SUGGESTED ASSIGNMENT
Exercises 1 and 2; Exercises 3–19, odds

1. Suppose a sample space is given by {1, 2, 3, 4, 5, 6, 7, 8, 9, 10}. What are the elements of the event "a number selected from the sample space is divisible by 3?" {3, 6, 9}

2. What is the range of values for the probability of an event? 0 to 1

OBJECTIVE A *To calculate the probability of simple events*

3. A coin is tossed four times. List all of the possible outcomes of the experiment as a sample space. {(HHHH), (HHHT), (HHTT), (HHTH), (HTTT), (HTHH), (HTTH), (HTHT), (TTTT), (TTTH), (TTHH), (THHH), (TTHT), (THHT), (THTT), (THTH)}

4. Three cards—one red, one green, and one blue—are to be arranged in a stack. Using R for red, G for green, and B for blue, list all of the different stacks that can be formed. (Some drawing software programs use an RGB color palette.)
RGB, RBG, GRB, GBR, BRG, BGR

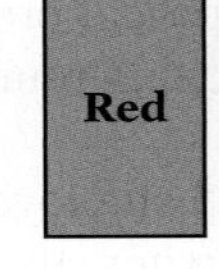

5. A tetrahedral die is one with four triangular sides. The sides show the numbers from 1 to 4. Say two tetrahedral dice are rolled. List all of the possible outcomes of the experiment as a sample space. {(1, 1), (1, 2), (1, 3), (1, 4), (2, 1), (2, 2), (2, 3), (2, 4), (3, 1), (3, 2), (3, 3), (3, 4), (4, 1), (4, 2), (4, 3), (4, 4)}

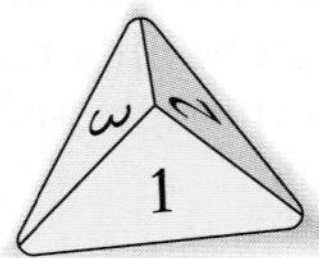

Tetrahedral die

6. A coin is tossed and then a die is rolled. List all of the possible outcomes of the experiment as a sample space. Start with (H, 1) as one possible outcome.
{(H, 1), (H, 2), (H, 3), (H, 4), (H, 5), (H, 6), (T, 1), (T, 2), (T, 3), (T, 4), (T, 5), (T, 6)}

7. The spinner at the right is spun once. Assume that the spinner does not come to rest on a line. What is the sample space? {1, 2, 3, 4, 5, 6, 7, 8}

8. A coin is tossed four times. Find the probability of the given event.
a. The outcomes are exactly in the order HHTT. (See Exercise 3.)
b. The outcomes consist of two heads and two tails. a. $\frac{1}{16}$ b. $\frac{3}{8}$

9. Two dice are rolled. Find the probability of the given outcome.
a. The sum of the dots on the upward faces is 5.
b. The sum of the dots on the upward faces is 15.
c. The sum of the dots on the upward faces is less than 15. a. $\frac{1}{9}$ b. 0 c. 1

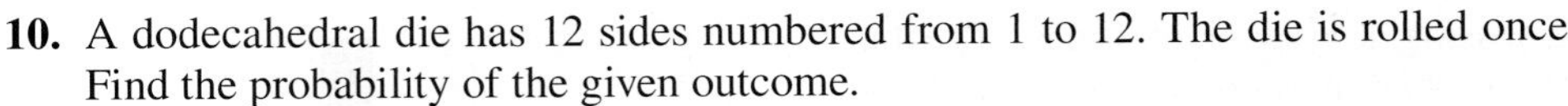

10. A dodecahedral die has 12 sides numbered from 1 to 12. The die is rolled once. Find the probability of the given outcome.
a. The upward face shows an 11.
b. The upward face shows a number that is a multiple of 3.
c. The upward face shows a prime number. a. $\frac{1}{12}$ b. $\frac{1}{3}$ c. $\frac{5}{12}$

Dodecahedral die

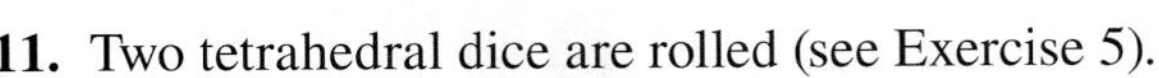

11. Two tetrahedral dice are rolled (see Exercise 5).
a. What is the probability that the sum on the upward faces is 4? a. $\frac{3}{16}$ b. $\frac{3}{16}$
b. What is the probability that the sum on the upward faces is 6?

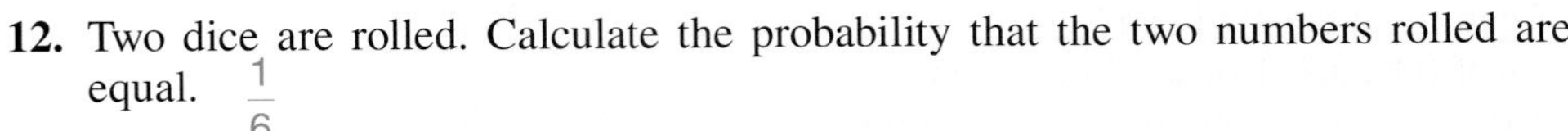

12. Two dice are rolled. Calculate the probability that the two numbers rolled are equal. $\frac{1}{6}$

13. Two dice are rolled. Which has the greater probability, throwing a sum of 10 or throwing a sum of 5?
Throwing a sum of 5

14. Use the situation described in Exercise 12. Suppose you decide to test your result empirically by rolling a pair of dice 30 times and recording the results. Which number of "doubles" would confirm the result found in Exercise 12?
(i) 1 **(ii)** 5 **(iii)** 6 **(iv)** 30 ii

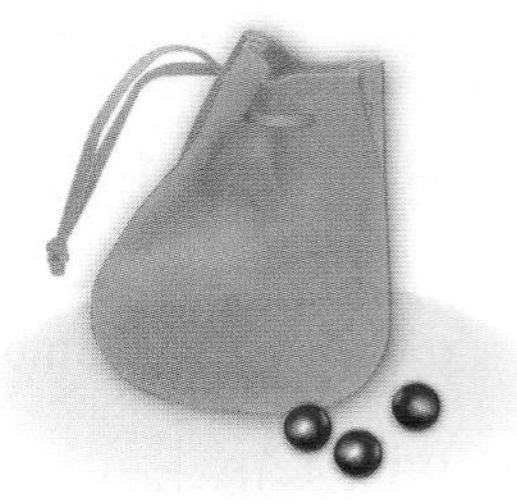

15. Three blue marbles, four green marbles, and five red marbles are placed in a bag. One marble is chosen at random. Which is greater, the probability of choosing a blue marble or that of choosing a red marble? Choosing a red marble

16. In a history class, a set of exams earned the following grades: 4 A's, 8 B's, 22 C's, 10 D's, and 3 F's. If a single student's exam is chosen from this class what is the probability that it received a B grade? $\frac{8}{47}$

17. A survey of 95 people showed that 37 preferred (to using a credit card) a cash discount of 2% if an item was purchased using cash. On the basis of this survey, what is the empirical probability that a person prefers a cash discount? Write the answer as a decimal rounded to the nearest hundredth.
0.39

18. A survey of 725 employed people showed that 587 participated in a group health insurance plan where they worked. On the basis of this survey, what is the empirical probability that an employed person participates in a group health insurance plan through work? Write the answer as a decimal rounded to the nearest hundredth.
0.81

19. A cable company surveyed some of its customers and asked them to rate the cable service as excellent, satisfactory, average, unsatisfactory, or poor. The results are recorded in the table at the right. What is the probability that a customer who was surveyed rated the service as satisfactory or excellent?
$\frac{185}{377}$

QUICK QUIZ

1. A coin is tossed three times. What is the probability that the outcomes of the tosses consist of one tail and two heads? $\frac{3}{8}$ [8.3A]
2. Two dice are rolled. What is the probability that the sum of the dots on the upward faces is less than 4? $\frac{1}{12}$ [8.3A]

Quality of Service	*Number Who Voted*
Excellent	98
Satisfactory	87
Average	129
Unsatisfactory	42
Poor	21

Critical Thinking

20. If the spinner at the right is spun once, is each of the numbers 1 through 5 equally likely to be the outcome? Why or why not?

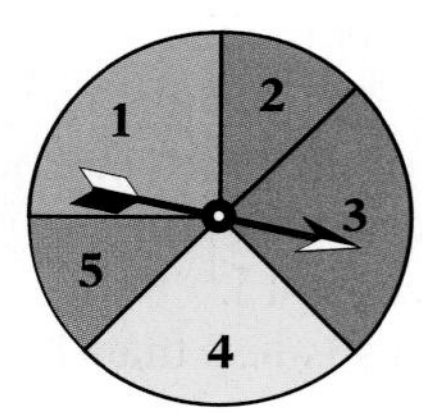

Projects or Group Activities

21. Consider the experiment of tossing a coin eight times. The bar graph at the right shows the number of ways 0 heads can occur (one) through the number of ways 8 heads can occur (also one). Use this bar chart to answer the following questions.
a. How many ways can 3 heads occur?
b. How many ways can 2 tails occur?
c. How many elements are in the sample space?
d. What is the probability of getting 4 heads?
e. What is the probability of getting 7 tails?
f. What is the probability of getting more than 4 heads?
g. What is the probability of getting at least 1 head?
h. If you add the probabilities of 0 heads, 1 head, 2 heads, and so on, all the way up to 8 heads, what is the result? Try to do this by just thinking about what the sum must be rather than actually doing the addition.

a. 56 b. 28 c. 256 d. $\frac{35}{128}$ e. $\frac{1}{32}$ f. $\frac{93}{256}$ g. $\frac{255}{256}$ h. 1

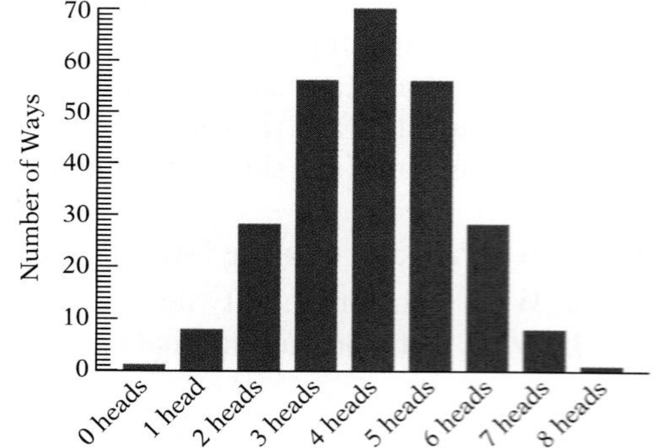

Tossing a Coin Eight Times

CHAPTER 8 Summary

Key Words

Statistics is the branch of mathematics concerned with **data,** or numerical information. A **graph** is a pictorial representation of data. A **circle graph** represents data by the sizes of the sectors. [8.1A, p. 460]

Examples

The circle graph shows typical annual expenses for a car.

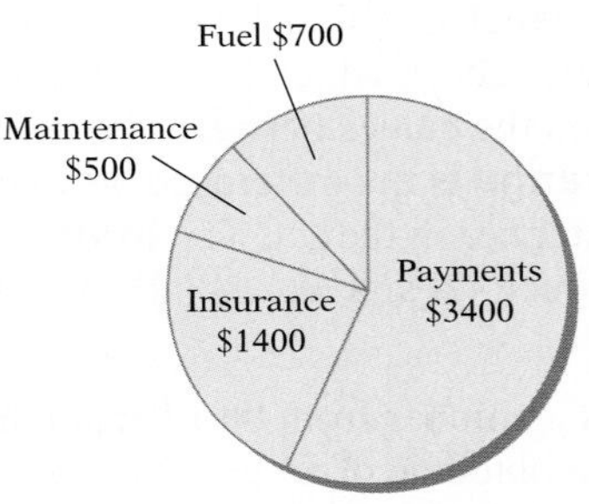

Source: Based on data from IntelliChoice

A **bar graph** represents data by the heights of the bars. [8.1A, p. 460]

The bar graph shows the expected U.S. population aged 100 and over.

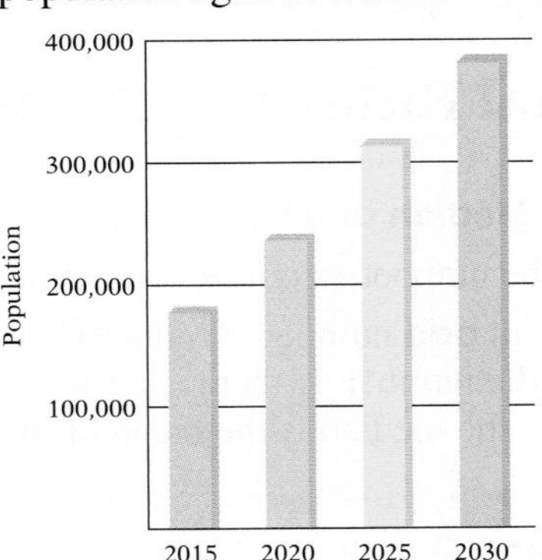

Source: Census Bureau

A **broken-line graph** uses data points joined by lines to show trends or comparisons. [8.1A, p. 460]

The line graph shows a recent graduate's cumulative debt in college loans at the end of each of the four years of college.

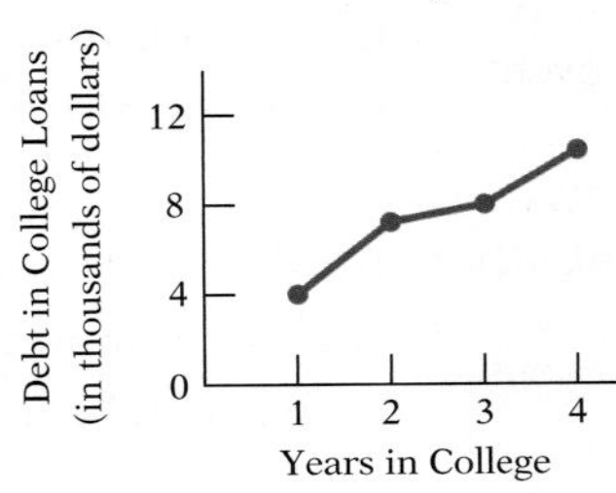

The **mean, median,** and **mode** are three types of averages used in statistics. The **mean** of a set of data is the sum of the data values divided by the number of values in the set. The **median** of a set of data is the number that separates the data into two equal parts when the data are arranged from least to greatest (or greatest to least). The **mode** of a set of numbers is the value that occurs most frequently. [8.2A, pp. 465, 466]

Consider the following set of data.

24, 28, 33, 45, 45

The mean is 35.
The median is 33.
The mode is 45.

A **box-and-whiskers plot,** or **boxplot,** is a graph that shows five numbers: the least value, the first quartile, the median, the third quartile, and the greatest value. The **first quartile,** Q_1, is the number below which one-fourth of the data lie. The **third quartile,** Q_3, is the number above which one-fourth of the data lie. The box is placed around the values between the first quartile and the third quartile. The **range** is the difference between the greatest number and the least number in the set. The **interquartile range** is the difference between Q_3 and Q_1. [8.2B, pp. 468–469]

The box-and-whiskers plot for a set of test scores is shown below.

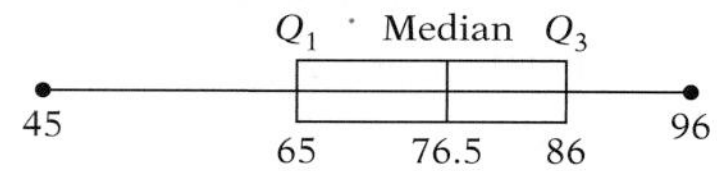

Range = 96 − 45 = 51

$$\text{Interquartile range} = Q_3 - Q_1 = 86 - 65 = 21$$

Probability is a number from 0 to 1 that tells us how likely it is that a certain outcome of an experiment will happen. An **experiment** is an activity with an observable outcome. All of the possible outcomes of an experiment are called the **sample space** of the experiment. An **event** is one or more outcomes of an experiment. The **favorable outcomes** of an experiment are the outcomes that satisfy the requirements of a particular event. [8.3A, p. 477]

Tossing a single die is an experiment. The sample space for this experiment is the set of possible outcomes {1, 2, 3, 4, 5, 6}.

The event that the number landing face up is an odd number is represented by {1, 3, 5}.

Essential Rules and Procedures

Examples

To Find the Median of a Set of Data [8.2A, p. 466]

1. Arrange the numbers from least to greatest.
2. If there is an **odd** number of values in the set of data, the median is the middle number. If there is an **even** number of values in the set of data, the median is the mean of the two middle numbers.

Consider the following set of data.

24, 28, 33, 35, 45, 45

The median is $\frac{33 + 35}{2} = 34$.

To Find Q_1 and Q_3 [8.2B, p. 468]

Arrange the numbers from least to greatest and locate the median. Q_1 is the median of the lower half of the data. Q_3 is the median of the upper half of the data.

Consider the following data.

8 10 12 14 16 19 22

10 ↑ Q_1; 14 ↑ Median; 19 ↑ Q_3

Theoretical Probability Formula [8.3A, p. 478]

$$\text{Probability of an event} = \frac{\text{number of favorable outcomes}}{\text{number of possible outcomes}}$$

A die is rolled. The probability of rolling a 2 or a 4 is $\frac{2}{6} = \frac{1}{3}$.

Empirical Probability Formula [8.3A, p. 480]

$$\text{Probability of an event} = \frac{\text{number of observations of the event}}{\text{total number of observations}}$$

A thumbtack is tossed 100 times. It lands point up 15 times. From this experiment, the empirical probability of "point up" is $\frac{15}{100} = \frac{3}{20}$.

CHAPTER 8 Review Exercises

Internet The circle graph in Figure 8.13 shows the approximate amounts of money that government agencies spent on maintaining Internet websites for a 3-year period. Use this graph for Exercises 1 to 3.

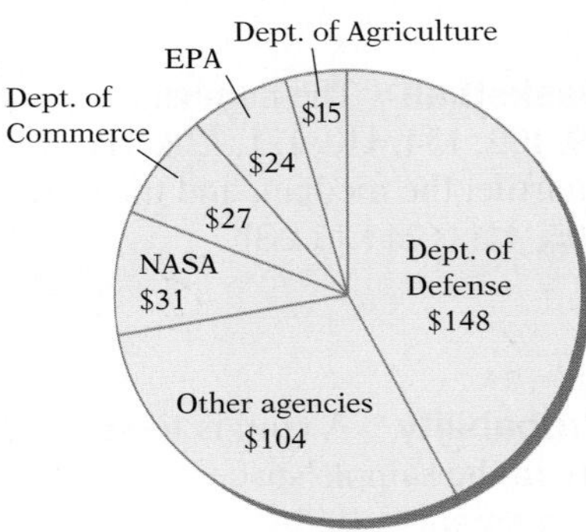

Figure 8.13 Amounts (in millions of dollars) that federal agencies spent on maintaining websites
Source: General Accounting Office

1. Find the total amount of money that these agencies spent on maintaining websites.
   $349 million [8.1A]

2. What is the ratio of the amount spent by the Department of Commerce to the amount spent by the EPA?
   $\frac{9}{8}$ [8.1A]

3. What percent of the total money spent did NASA spend? Round to the nearest tenth of a percent.
   8.9% [8.1A]

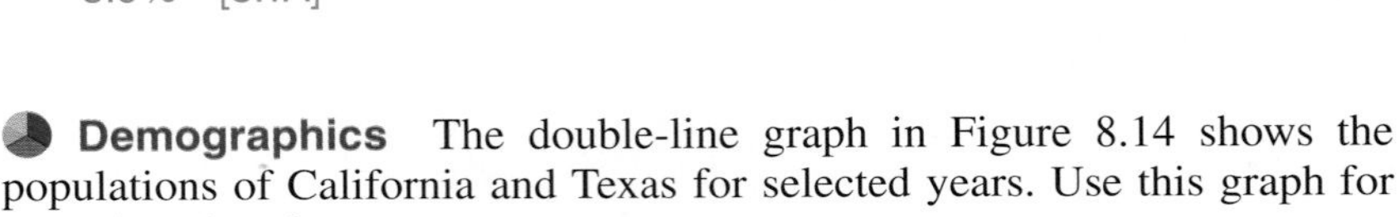

Demographics The double-line graph in Figure 8.14 shows the populations of California and Texas for selected years. Use this graph for Exercises 4 to 6.

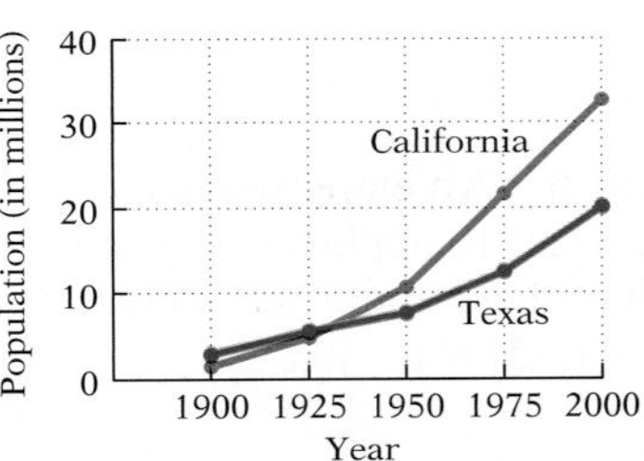

Figure 8.14 Populations of California and Texas

4. In 1900, which state had the larger population?
   Texas [8.1A]

5. In 2000, approximately how much greater was the population of California than the population of Texas?
   12.5 million more people [8.1A]

6. During which 25-year period did the population of Texas increase the least?
   1925 to 1950 [8.1A]

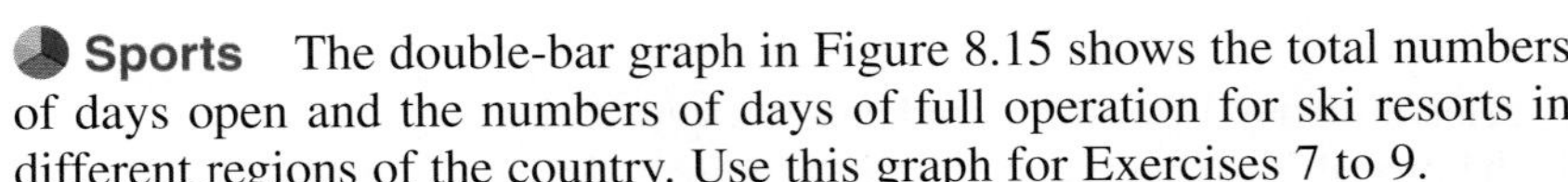

Sports The double-bar graph in Figure 8.15 shows the total numbers of days open and the numbers of days of full operation for ski resorts in different regions of the country. Use this graph for Exercises 7 to 9.

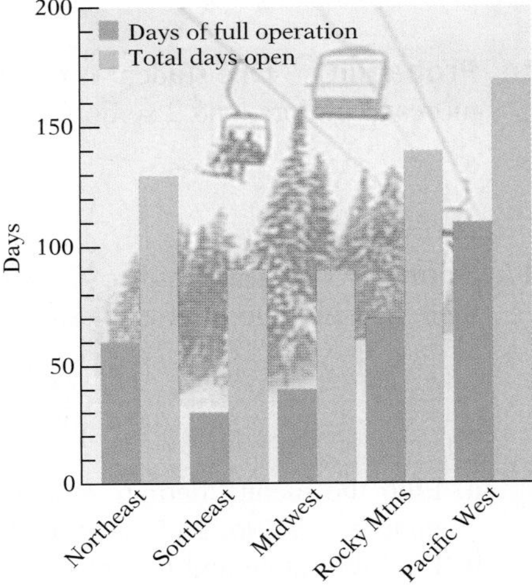

Figure 8.15 Ski Resorts
Source: Economic Analysis of United States Ski Areas

7. Find the difference between the total number of days open and the number of days of full operation for Midwest ski areas.
   50 days [8.1A]

8. For the Rocky Mountain ski areas, what percent of the total number of days open was the number of days of full operation?
   50% [8.1A]

9. Which region had the lowest number of days of full operation? How many days of full operation did this region have?
   Southeast; 30 days [8.1A]

10. **Newborns** The weights, in pounds, of 10 babies born at a hospital were recorded as 6.3, 5.9, 8.1, 6.5, 7.2, 5.6, 8.9, 9.1, 6.9, and 7.2. Find the mean and median of these data.
Mean: 7.17 lb; median: 7.05 lb [8.2A]

11. **Basketball** The numbers of points scored by a basketball team for 15 games were 89, 102, 134, 110, 121, 124, 111, 116, 99, 120, 105, 109, 110, 124, and 131. Find the first quartile, the median, and the third quartile. Draw a box-and-whiskers plot.
105, 111, 124 [8.2B]

Q_1 median Q_3

89 105 111 124 134

12. **Probability** A coin is tossed and then a regular die is rolled. How many elements are in the sample space?
12 elements [8.3A]

13. **Probability** A charity raffle sells 2500 raffle tickets for a big-screen television set. If you purchase 5 tickets, what is the probability that you will win the television?
$\frac{1}{500}$ [8.3A]

14. **Testing** An employee at a department of motor vehicles analyzed the written tests of the last 10 applicants for a driver's license. The numbers of incorrect answers for each of these applicants were 2, 0, 3, 1, 0, 4, 5, 1, 3, and 1. Find Q_1 and Q_3.
$Q_1 = 1$; $Q_3 = 3$ [8.2B]

15. **Probability** A dodecahedral die has 12 sides numbered from 1 to 12. If this die is rolled once, what is the probability that a number divisible by 6 will be on the upward face?
$\frac{1}{6}$ [8.3A]

16. **Probability** One student is randomly selected from 3 first-year students, 4 sophomores, 5 juniors, and 2 seniors. What is the probability that the student is a junior?
$\frac{5}{14}$ [8.3A]

17. **Sports** The heart rates of 24 women tennis players were measured after each of them had run one-quarter of a mile. The results are listed in the table below.

80	82	99	91	93	87	103	94	73	96	86	80
97	94	108	81	100	109	91	84	78	96	96	100

a. Find the mean, median, and mode of the data. Round to the nearest tenth. **a.** Mean: 91.6 heartbeats per minute; median: 93.5 heartbeats per minute; mode: 96 heartbeats per minute [8.2A]
b. Find the range and the interquartile range of the data.
b. Range: 36 heartbeats per minute; interquartile range: 15 heartbeats per minute [8.2B]

CHAPTER 8 TEST

Amusement Rides The bar graph in Figure 8.16 shows the numbers of fatalities that occurred during accidents on amusement rides in the 1990s in the United States. Use this graph for Exercises 1 to 3.

1. During which two consecutive years were the numbers of fatalities the same?
   1995 and 1996 [8.1A]

2. Find the total number of fatalities on amusement rides from 1991 through 1999.
   32 fatal accidents [8.1A]

3. How many more fatalities occurred during the years 1995 through 1998 than occurred during the years 1991 through 1994?
   4 more fatalities [8.1A]

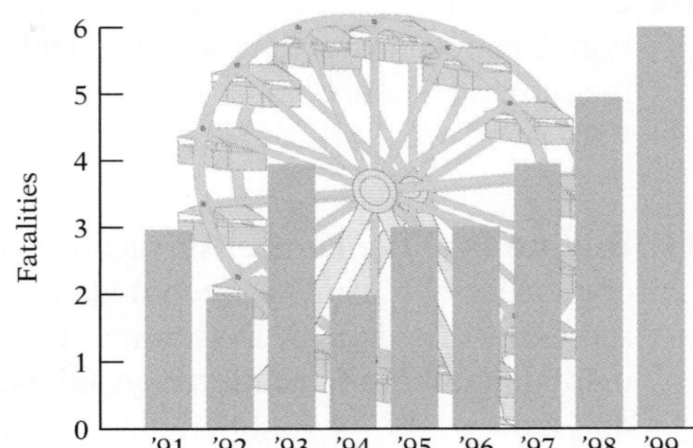

Figure 8.16 Number of fatal accidents on amusement rides
Source: USA Today, April 7, 2000

The Film Industry The circle graph in Figure 8.17 categorizes the 655 films released during a recent year by their ratings. Use this graph for Exercises 4 to 6.

4. How many more R-rated films were released than PG films?
   355 more [8.1A]

5. How many times more PG-13 films were released than NC-17 films?
   16 times more [8.1A]

6. What percent of the films released were rated G? Round to the nearest tenth of a percent.
   5.6% [8.1A]

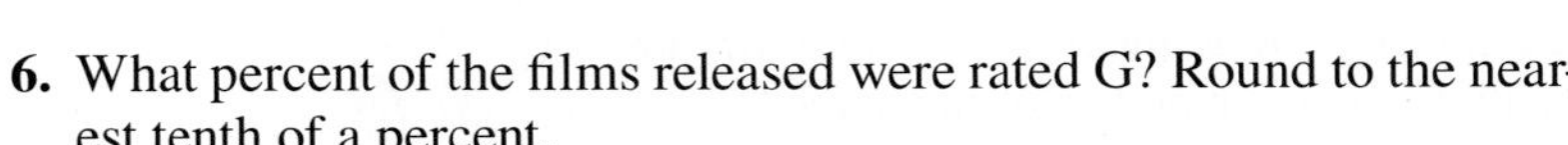

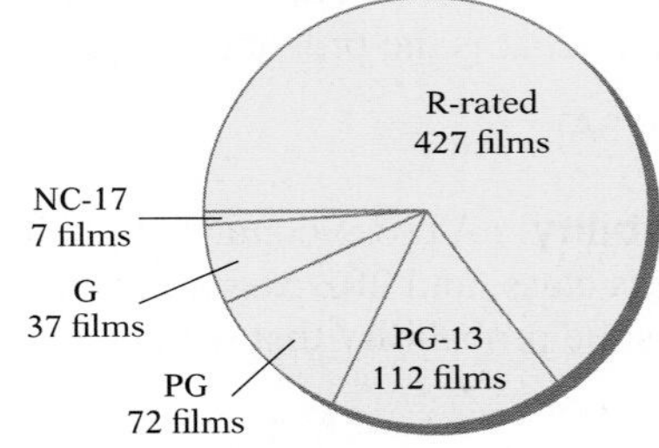

Figure 8.17 Ratings of films released
Source: MPA Worldwide Market Research

Education The broken-line graph in Figure 8.18 shows the numbers of students enrolled in college for selected years. Use this figure for Exercises 7 and 8.

7. During which decade did the student population increase the least?
   The 1990s [8.1A]

8. Approximate the increase in college enrollment from 1960 to 2010.
   17 million students [8.1A]

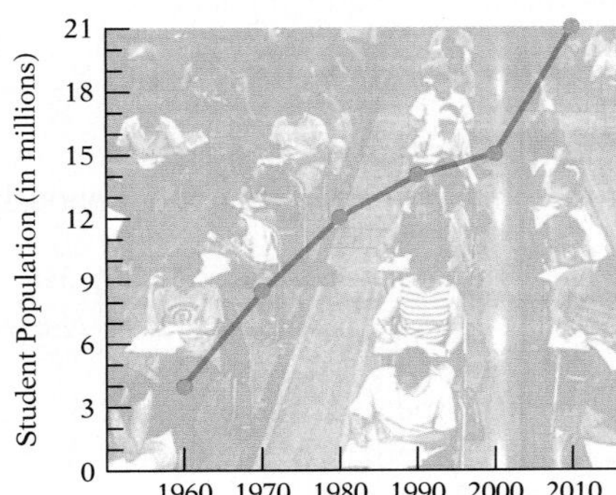

Figure 8.18 Student enrollment in public and private colleges
Source: National Center for Educational Statistics

9. **Emergency Calls** The response times by an ambulance service to emergency calls were recorded by a public safety commission. The times (in minutes) were 17, 21, 11, 8, 22, 15, 11, 14, and 8. Determine the median response time for these calls.
14 min [8.2A]

10. **Education** Recent college graduates were asked to rate the quality of their education. The responses were 47, excellent; 86, very good; 32, good; 20, poor. What was the modal response?
Very good [8.2A]

11. **Business** The number of vacation days taken last year by each of the employees of a firm was recorded. The box-and-whiskers plot at the right represents the data. **a.** Determine the range of the data. **b.** What was the median number of vacation days taken?
a. 22 days **b.** 14 vacation days [8.2B]

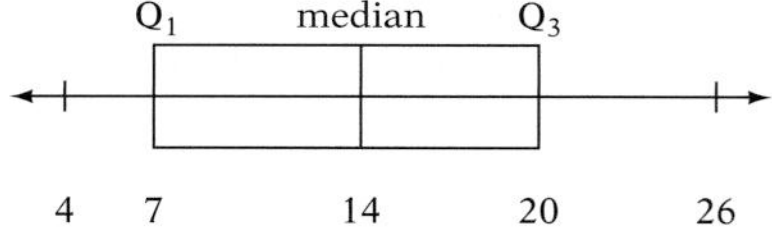

12. **Golf** The scores of the 14 leaders in a college golf tournament are given in the table. Draw a box-and-whiskers plot of the data.

80	76	70	71	74	68	72
74	70	70	73	75	69	73

[8.2B]

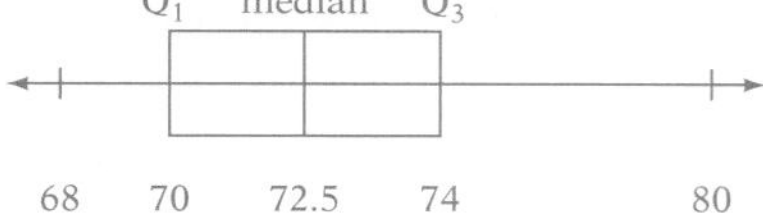

13. **Probability** A box contains 50 balls, of which 15 are red. If one ball is randomly selected, what is the probability that the ball is red?
$\frac{3}{10}$ [8.3A]

14. **Probability** A cross-country flight has 14 passengers in first class, 32 passengers in business class, and 202 passengers in coach. If one passenger is selected at random, what is the probability that the person is in business class?
$\frac{4}{31}$ [8.3A]

15. **Probability** Three playing cards—an ace, a king, and a queen—are randomly arranged and stacked. What is the probability that the ace is on top of the stack?
$\frac{1}{3}$ [8.3A]

16. **Probability** A quiz contains three true/false questions. If a student attempts to answer the questions by just guessing, what is the probability that the student will answer all three questions correctly?
$\frac{1}{8}$ [8.3A]

17. **Quality Control** The table below gives the lengths of time (in hours) that 20 laptops of the same model operated continuously on battery power.

2.9	2.4	3.1	2.5	2.6	2.0	3.0	2.3	2.4	2.7
2.0	2.4	2.6	2.7	2.1	2.9	2.8	2.4	2.0	2.8

a. Find the mean of the data. 2.53 hours
b. Find the median of the data. 2.55 hours [8.2A]
c. Draw a box-and-whiskers plot for the data. [8.2B]

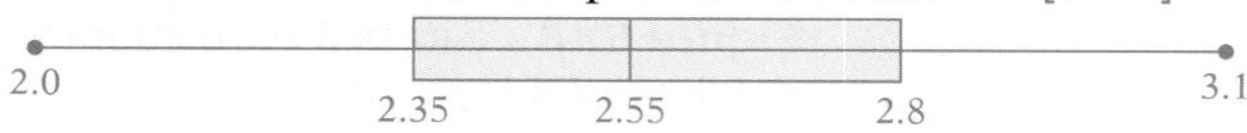

Cumulative Review Exercises

1. Simplify: $2^2 \cdot 3^3 \cdot 5$
540 [1.3B]

2. Simplify: $3^2 \cdot (5 - 2) \div 3 + 5$
14 [1.4A]

3. Find the LCM of 24 and 40.
120 [2.1A]

4. Write $\frac{60}{144}$ in simplest form.
$\frac{5}{12}$ [2.2B]

5. Find the total of $4\frac{1}{2}$, $2\frac{3}{8}$, and $5\frac{1}{5}$.
$12\frac{3}{40}$ [2.3A]

6. Subtract: $12\frac{5}{8} - 7\frac{11}{12}$
$4\frac{17}{24}$ [2.3B]

7. Multiply: $\frac{5}{8} \times 3\frac{1}{5}$
2 [2.4A]

8. Find the quotient of $3\frac{1}{5}$ and $4\frac{1}{4}$.
$\frac{64}{85}$ [2.4B]

9. Simplify: $\frac{5}{8} \div \left(\frac{3}{4} - \frac{2}{3}\right) + \frac{3}{4}$
$8\frac{1}{4}$ [2.7A]

10. Write two hundred nine and three hundred five thousandths in standard form.
209.305 [2.5A]

11. Find the product of 4.092 and 0.69.
2.82348 [2.6B]

12. Convert $16\frac{2}{3}$ to a terminating or repeating decimal. Place a bar over any repeating digits.
$16.\overline{6}$ [2.6D]

13. Write "330 miles on 12.5 gallons of gas" as a unit rate.
26.4 miles/gallon [6.1A]

14. Solve the proportion: $\frac{n}{5} = \frac{16}{25}$
3.2 [6.2A]

15. Write $\frac{4}{5}$ as a percent.
80% [6.3B]

16. 8 is 10% of what?
80 [6.4A/6.4B]

17. What is 38% of 43?
16.34 [6.4A/6.4B]

18. What percent of 75 is 30?
40% [6.4A/6.4B]

19. **Compensation** Tanim Kamal, a salesperson at a department store, receives \$100 per week plus 2% commission on sales. Find the income for a week in which Tanim had \$27,500 in sales.
\$650 [6.4C]

20. **Insurance** A life insurance policy costs \$8.15 for every \$1000 of insurance. At this rate, what is the cost for \$50,000 of life insurance?
\$407.50 [6.2B]

21. **Simple Interest** A contractor borrowed \$125,000 for 6 months at an annual simple interest rate of 6%. Find the interest due on the loan.
\$3750 [6.5A]

22. **Business** A compact disc player that costs a retailer \$180 is priced at 155% of the cost. Find the price of the compact disc player.
\$279 [6.4C]

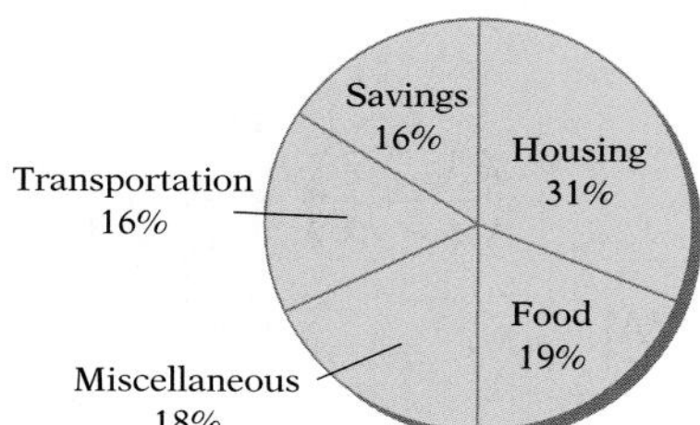

Figure 8.19 Budget for a monthly income of \$4500

23. **Finance** The circle graph in Figure 8.19 shows how a family's monthly income of \$4500 is budgeted. How much is budgeted for food?
\$855 [8.1A]

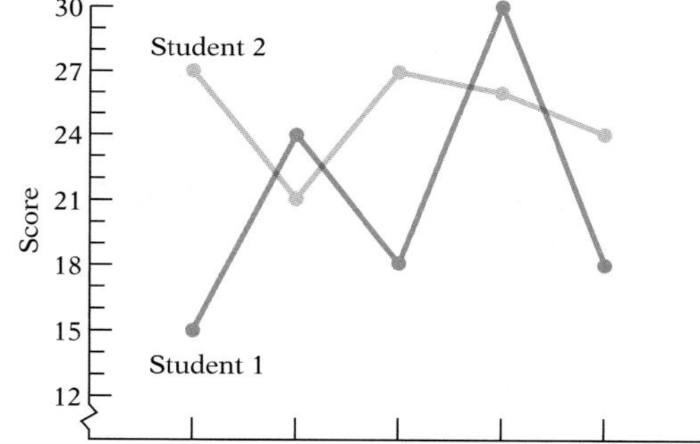

Figure 8.20 Test Scores

24. **Education** The double-broken-line graph in Figure 8.20 shows two students' scores on five math tests of 30 problems each. Find the difference between the numbers of problems that the two students answered correctly on Test 1.
12 problems [8.1A]

25. **Meteorology** The average daily high temperatures, in degrees Fahrenheit, for a week in Newtown were 56°, 72°, 80°, 75°, 68°, 62°, and 74°. Find the mean high temperature for the week. Round to the nearest tenth of a degree.
69.6°F [8.2A]

26. **Probability** Two dice are rolled. What is the probability that the sum of the dots on the upward faces is 8?
$\frac{5}{36}$ [8.3A]

Polynomials

OBJECTIVES

SECTION 9.1
A To add polynomials
B To subtract polynomials

SECTION 9.2
A To multiply monomials
B To simplify powers of monomials

SECTION 9.3
A To multiply a polynomial by a monomial
B To multiply two polynomials
C To multiply two binomials using the FOIL method
D To multiply binomials that have special products
E To solve application problems

SECTION 9.4
A To divide monomials
B To write a number in scientific notation

SECTION 9.5
A To divide a polynomial by a monomial
B To divide polynomials

Focus on Success

The more prepared you are for a test, the less nervous you will be. There are features in this text that will help you to be prepared for a test. Start with the Chapter Summary, which describes the important topics covered in the chapter. Do the Chapter Review Exercises. If you have trouble with any of the questions, restudy the objectives the questions are taken from. Take the Chapter Test in a quiet place, working on it as if it were an actual exam. (See Ace the Test, page AIM-11.)

Prep Test

Are you ready to succeed in this chapter? Take the Prep Test below to find out if you are ready to learn the new material.

1. Subtract: $-2 - (-3)$

1 [3.2B]

2. Multiply: $-3(6)$

-18 [3.3A]

3. Simplify: $-\frac{24}{-36}$

$\frac{2}{3}$ [3.3B]

4. Evaluate $3n^4$ when $n = -2$.

48 [4.1A]

5. If $\frac{a}{b}$ is a fraction in simplest form, what number is not a possible value of b?

0 [1.3C]

6. Are $2x^2$ and $2x$ like terms?

No [4.1A]

7. Simplify: $3x^2 - 4x + 1 + 2x^2 - 5x - 7$

$5x^2 - 9x - 6$ [4.2A]

8. Simplify: $-4y + 4y$

0 [4.2A]

9. Simplify: $-3(2x - 8)$

$-6x + 24$ [4.2C]

10. Simplify: $3xy - 4y - 2(5xy - 7y)$

$-7xy + 10y$ [4.2D]

SECTION

9.1 Addition and Subtraction of Polynomials

OBJECTIVE A *To add polynomials*

Take Note
The expression $3\sqrt{x}$ is not a monomial because $\sqrt{x}$ cannot be written as a product of variables. The expression $\frac{2x}{y}$ is not a monomial because it is a *quotient* of variables.

INSTRUCTOR NOTE
An analogy may help students understand these terms. *Polynomial* is similar to the word *car*. Chevrolet and Ford are types of cars. Monomials and binomials are types of polynomials.

As a class exercise, ask students to identify monomials. For instance, which of $\frac{1}{2}$, $\frac{2}{3}y$, $6x$, $6 + x$, $abxy$, and $\frac{3}{z}$ are monomials?

Then ask students to identify polynomials. Here are some possible examples: $x + 7$, $\frac{x^2}{5} + \frac{x}{2} - 1$, $\frac{5}{x^2} + \frac{2}{x} - 1$, $\frac{x+1}{x}$, and $\sqrt{2}x^4 - \pi x^2 - 7$.

A **monomial** is a number, a variable, or a product of a number and variables. For instance,

7	b	$\frac{2}{3}a$	$12xy^2$
A number	A variable	A product of a number and a variable	A product of a number and variables

A **polynomial** is a variable expression in which the terms are monomials.

A polynomial of *one* term is a **monomial.** $-7x^2$ is a monomial.
A polynomial of *two* terms is a **binomial.** $4x + 2$ is a binomial.
A polynomial of *three* terms is a **trinomial.** $7x^2 + 5x - 7$ is a trinomial.

The **degree of a polynomial in one variable** is the greatest exponent on a variable. The degree of $4x^3 - 5x^2 + 7x - 8$ is 3; the degree of $2y^4 + y^2 - 1$ is 4. The degree of a nonzero constant is zero. For instance, the degree of 7 is zero.

The terms of a polynomial in one variable are usually arranged so that the exponents on the variable decrease from left to right. This is called **descending order.**

$5x^3 - 4x^2 + 6x - 1$

$7z^4 + 4z^3 + z - 6$

$2y^4 + y^3 - 2y^2 + 4y - 1$

Polynomials can be added, using either a horizontal or a vertical format, by combining like terms.

HOW TO 1 Add $(3x^3 - 7x + 2) + (7x^2 + 2x - 7)$. Use a horizontal format.

$(3x^3 - 7x + 2) + (7x^2 + 2x - 7)$
$= 3x^3 + 7x^2 + (-7x + 2x) + (2 - 7)$ • Use the Commutative and Associative Properties of Addition to rearrange and group like terms.
$= 3x^3 + 7x^2 - 5x - 5$ • Then combine like terms.

HOW TO 2 Add $(-4x^2 + 6x - 9) + (12 - 8x + 2x^3)$. Use a vertical format.

$$\begin{array}{r} -4x^2 + 6x - 9 \\ 2x^3 - 8x + 12 \\ \hline 2x^3 - 4x^2 - 2x + 3 \end{array}$$

• Arrange the terms of each polynomial in descending order, with like terms in the same column.
• Combine the terms in each column.

EXAMPLE 1

Use a horizontal format to add $(8x^2 - 4x - 9) + (2x^2 + 9x - 9)$.

Solution

Group like terms. Then combine like terms.

$(8x^2 - 4x - 9) + (2x^2 + 9x - 9)$
$= (8x^2 + 2x^2) + (-4x + 9x) + (-9 - 9)$
$= 10x^2 + 5x - 18$

YOU TRY IT 1

Use a horizontal format to add $(-4x^3 + 2x^2 - 8) + (4x^3 + 6x^2 - 7x + 5)$.

Your solution

$8x^2 - 7x - 3$

IN-CLASS EXAMPLES

1. Use a horizontal format to add $(4x^2 + 5x - 7) + (8x^2 - 10x - 3)$. $\mathbf{12x^2 - 5x - 10}$
2. Use a vertical format to add $(-9x^2 - 6x + 8) + (4x^2 + 10x + 6)$. $\mathbf{-5x^2 + 4x + 14}$

Solution on p. S22

EXAMPLE 2

Use a vertical format to add
$(-5x^3 + 4x^2 - 7x + 9) + (2x^3 + 5x - 11)$.

Solution

$$\begin{array}{r} -5x^3 + 4x^2 - 7x + 9 \\ 2x^3 + 5x - 11 \\ \hline -3x^3 + 4x^2 - 2x - 2 \end{array}$$

- **Put like terms in the same column.**
- **Combine like terms.**

YOU TRY IT 2

Use a vertical format to add
$(6x^3 + 2x + 8) + (-9x^3 + 2x^2 - 12x - 8)$.

Your solution

$-3x^3 + 2x^2 - 10x$

Solution on p. S22

OBJECTIVE B *To subtract polynomials*

The **opposite of the polynomial** $(3x^2 - 7x + 8)$ is $-(3x^2 - 7x + 8)$.

To simplify the opposite of a polynomial, change the sign of each term to its opposite. $-(3x^2 - 7x + 8) = -3x^2 + 7x - 8$

Take Note

This is the same definition used for subtraction of integers: Subtraction is addition of the opposite.

Polynomials can be subtracted using either a horizontal or a vertical format. To subtract polynomials, add the opposite of the second polynomial to the first.

HOW TO 3 Subtract $(4y^2 - 6y + 7) - (2y^3 - 5y - 4)$. Use a horizontal format.

$$\begin{aligned}(4y^2 - 6y + 7) &- (2y^3 - 5y - 4)\\ &= (4y^2 - 6y + 7) + (-2y^3 + 5y + 4)\\ &= -2y^3 + 4y^2 + (-6y + 5y) + (7 + 4)\\ &= -2y^3 + 4y^2 - y + 11\end{aligned}$$

- **Add the opposite of the second polynomial to the first.**
- **Combine like terms.**

HOW TO 4 Subtract $(9 + 4y + 3y^3) - (2y^2 + 4y - 21)$. Use a vertical format.

The opposite of $2y^2 + 4y - 21$ is $-2y^2 - 4y + 21$.

$$\begin{array}{r} 3y^3 + 4y + 9 \\ - 2y^2 - 4y + 21 \\ \hline 3y^3 - 2y^2 + 30 \end{array}$$

- **Arrange the terms of each polynomial in descending order, with like terms in the same column.**
- **Note that $4y - 4y = 0$, but 0 is not written.**

EXAMPLE 3

a. Use a horizontal format to subtract
$(7c^2 - 9c - 12) - (9c^2 + 5c - 8)$.

b. Use a vertical format to subtract
$(3k^2 - 4k + 1) - (k^3 + 3k^2 - 6k - 8)$.

Solution

a. Add the opposite of the second polynomial to the first polynomial.

$$\begin{aligned}(7c^2 - 9c - 12) &- (9c^2 + 5c - 8)\\ &= (7c^2 - 9c - 12) + (-9c^2 - 5c + 8)\\ &= -2c^2 - 14c - 4\end{aligned}$$

b.
$$\begin{array}{r} 3k^2 - 4k + 1 \\ -k^3 - 3k^2 + 6k + 8 \\ \hline -k^3 + 2k + 9 \end{array}$$

- **Add the opposite of $(k^3 + 3k^2 - 6k - 8)$ to the first polynomial.**

YOU TRY IT 3

a. Use a horizontal format to subtract
$(-4w^3 + 8w - 8) - (3w^3 - 4w^2 - 2w - 1)$.

b. Use a vertical format to subtract
$(13y^3 - 6y - 7) - (4y^2 - 6y - 9)$.

Your solution

a. $-7w^3 + 4w^2 + 10w - 7$
b. $13y^3 - 4y^2 + 2$

IN-CLASS EXAMPLES

3. Use a horizontal format to subtract $(6x^2 + 2x - 4) - (-8x^2 + x - 3)$.
$14x^2 + x - 1$
4. Use a vertical format to subtract $(7y^2 + 8y + 2) - (4y^3 + 9y^2 - 5y + 6)$.
$-4y^3 - 2y^2 + 13y - 4$

Solution on p. S22

9.1 EXERCISES

Concept Check

SUGGESTED ASSIGNMENT
Exercises 1–14; Exercises 15–51, odds

For Exercises 1 to 6, state whether the expression is a monomial.

1. 17 Yes **2.** $3x^4$ Yes **3.** $\frac{17}{\sqrt{x}}$ No **4.** $\frac{2}{3}y$ Yes **5.** $\frac{xy}{z}$ No **6.** $\sqrt{5}x$ Yes

For Exercises 7 to 14, state whether the expression is a monomial, a binomial, a trinomial, or none of these.

7. $3x + 5$
Binomial

8. $2y - 3\sqrt{y}$
None of these

9. $9x^2 - x - 1$
Trinomial

10. $x^2 + y^2$
Binomial

11. $\frac{2}{x} - 3$
None of these

12. $\frac{ab}{4}$
Monomial

13. $6x^2 + 7x$
Binomial

14. $12a^4 - 3a + 2$
Trinomial

OBJECTIVE A *To add polynomials*

For Exercises 15 to 24, add. Use a horizontal format.

15. $(4x^2 + 2x) + (x^2 + 6x)$
$5x^2 + 8x$

16. $(-3y^2 + y) + (4y^2 + 6y)$
$y^2 + 7y$

17. $(4x^2 - 5xy) + (3x^2 + 6xy - 4y^2)$
$7x^2 + xy - 4y^2$

18. $(2x^2 - 4y^2) + (6x^2 - 2xy + 4y^2)$
$8x^2 - 2xy$

19. $(2a^2 - 7a + 10) + (a^2 + 4a + 7)$
$3a^2 - 3a + 17$

20. $(-6x^2 + 7x + 3) + (3x^2 + x + 3)$
$-3x^2 + 8x + 6$

21. $(7x + 5x^3 - 7) + (10x^2 - 8x + 3)$
$5x^3 + 10x^2 - x - 4$

22. $(4y + 3y^3 + 9) + (2y^2 + 4y - 21)$
$3y^3 + 2y^2 + 8y - 12$

23. $(7 - 5r + 2r^2) + (3r^3 - 6r)$
$3r^3 + 2r^2 - 11r + 7$

24. $(14 + 4y + 3y^3) + (-4y^2 + 21)$
$3y^3 - 4y^2 + 4y + 35$

For Exercises 25 to 32, add. Use a vertical format.

25. $(x^2 + 7x) + (-3x^2 - 4x)$
$-2x^2 + 3x$

26. $(3x^2 + 9x) + (6x - 24)$
$3x^2 + 15x - 24$

27. $(2x^2 + 6x + 12) + (3x^2 + x + 8)$
$5x^2 + 7x + 20$

28. $(x^2 + x + 5) + (3x^2 - 10x + 4)$
$4x^2 - 9x + 9$

29. $(-7x + x^3 + 4) + (2x^2 + x - 10)$
$x^3 + 2x^2 - 6x - 6$

30. $(y^2 + 3y^3 + 1) + (-4y^3 - 6y - 3)$
$-y^3 + y^2 - 6y - 2$

31. $(2a^3 - 7a + 1) + (1 - 4a - 3a^2)$
$2a^3 - 3a^2 - 11a + 2$

32. $(5r^3 - 6r^2 + 3r) + (-3 - 2r + r^2)$
$5r^3 - 5r^2 + r - 3$

For Exercises 33 and 34, use the polynomials shown at the right. Assume that a, b, c, and d are all positive numbers. Choose the correct answer from this list:
(i) $P + Q$ **(ii)** $Q + R$ **(iii)** $P + R$ **(iv)** None of the above

$P = ax^3 + bx^2 - cx + d$
$Q = -ax^3 - bx^2 + cx - d$
$R = -ax^3 + bx^2 + cx + d$

33. Which sum will be a trinomial?
iv

34. Which sum will be zero?
i

OBJECTIVE B *To subtract polynomials*

For Exercises 35 to 44, subtract. Use a horizontal format.

35. $(y^2 - 10xy) - (2y^2 + 3xy)$
$-y^2 - 13xy$

36. $(x^2 - 3xy) - (-2x^2 + xy)$
$3x^2 - 4xy$

37. $(3x^2 + x - 3) - (4x + x^2 - 2)$
$2x^2 - 3x - 1$

38. $(5y^2 - 2y + 1) - (-y - 2 - 3y^2)$
$8y^2 - y + 3$

39. $(-2x^3 + x - 1) - (-x^2 + x - 3)$
$-2x^3 + x^2 + 2$

40. $(2x^2 + 5x - 3) - (3x^3 + 2x - 5)$
$-3x^3 + 2x^2 + 3x + 2$

41. $(1 - 2a + 4a^3) - (a^3 - 2a + 3)$
$3a^3 - 2$

42. $(7 - 8b + b^2) - (4b^3 - 7b - 8)$
$-4b^3 + b^2 - b + 15$

43. $(-1 - y + 4y^3) - (3 - 3y - 2y^2)$
$4y^3 + 2y^2 + 2y - 4$

44. $(-3 - 2x + 3x^2) - (4 - 2x^2 + 2x^3)$
$-2x^3 + 5x^2 - 2x - 7$

For Exercises 45 to 52, subtract. Use a vertical format.

45. $(2y^2 - 4y) - (-y^2 + 2)$
$3y^2 - 4y - 2$

46. $(-3a^2 - 2a) - (4a^2 - 4)$
$-7a^2 - 2a + 4$

47. $(x^2 - 2x + 1) - (x^2 + 5x + 8)$
$-7x - 7$

48. $(3x^2 + 2x - 2) - (5x^2 - 5x + 6)$
$-2x^2 + 7x - 8$

49. $(4x^3 + 5x + 2) - (1 + 2x - 3x^2)$
$4x^3 + 3x^2 + 3x + 1$

50. $(5y^2 - y + 2) - (-3 + 3y - 2y^3)$
$2y^3 + 5y^2 - 4y + 5$

51. $(-2y + 6y^2 + 2y^3) - (4 + y^2 + y^3)$
$y^3 + 5y^2 - 2y - 4$

52. $(4 - x - 2x^2) - (-2 + 3x - x^3)$
$x^3 - 2x^2 - 4x + 6$

53. What polynomial must be added to $3x^2 - 6x + 9$ so that the sum is $4x^2 + 3x - 2$? $x^2 + 9x - 11$

Critical Thinking

54. What polynomial must be added to $3x^2 - 4x - 2$ so that the sum is $-x^2 + 2x + 1$?
$-4x^2 + 6x + 3$

55. What polynomial must be added to $-2x^3 + 4x - 7$ so that the sum is $x^2 - x - 1$?
$2x^3 + x^2 - 5x + 6$

56. What polynomial must be subtracted from $6x^2 - 4x - 2$ so that the difference is $2x^2 + 2x - 5$? $4x^2 - 6x + 3$

57. What polynomial must be subtracted from $2x^3 - x^2 + 4x - 2$ so that the difference is $x^3 + 2x - 8$? $x^3 - x^2 + 2x + 6$

Projects or Group Activities

58. Write two polynomials, each of degree 2, whose sum is also of degree 2.
Answers will vary. For example, $3x^2 + 5x - 1$ and $4x^2 + x + 6$

59. Write two polynomials, each of degree 2, whose sum is of degree 1.
Answers will vary. For example, $3x^2 - 4x + 7$ and $-3x^2 + 5x - 2$

60. Write two polynomials, each of degree 2, whose sum is of degree 0.
Answers will vary. For example, $3x^2 - 8$ and $-3x^2 + 9$

QUICK QUIZ

1. Add. Use a vertical format. $(2x^2 - 3x + 4) + (5x^2 - 7x - 1)$
$7x^2 - 10x + 3$ [9.1A]
2. Add. Use a horizontal format. $(3x^3 - 4x^2 + 7) + (5x^2 - 3x - 9)$
$3x^3 + x^2 - 3x - 2$ [9.1A]
3. Subtract. Use a vertical format. $(4x^2 - 7x + 6) - (9x^2 - 12x + 8)$
$-5x^2 + 5x - 2$ [9.1B]
4. Subtract. Use a horizontal format. $(-7x^2 + 3x - 8) - (6x^2 - 12x + 8)$
$-13x^2 + 15x - 16$ [9.1B]

SECTION

9.2 Multiplication of Monomials

OBJECTIVE A

To multiply monomials

Recall that in the exponential expression x^5, x is the base and 5 is the exponent. The exponent indicates the number of times the base occurs as a factor.

The product of exponential expressions with the *same* base can be simplified by writing each expression in factored form and writing the result with an exponent.

$$x^3 \cdot x^2 = \underbrace{\overbrace{(x \cdot x \cdot x)}^{3\text{ factors}} \cdot \overbrace{(x \cdot x)}^{2\text{ factors}}}_{5\text{ factors}}$$
$$= x \cdot x \cdot x \cdot x \cdot x$$
$$= x^5$$

Adding the exponents results in the same product.

$$x^3 \cdot x^2 = x^{3+2} = x^5$$

Rule for Multiplying Exponential Expressions

If m and n are integers, then $x^m \cdot x^n = x^{m+n}$.

EXAMPLES

In each example below, we are multiplying two exponential expressions with the same base. Simplify the expression by adding the exponents.

1. $x^4 \cdot x^7 = x^{4+7} = x^{11}$
2. $y \cdot y^5 = y^{1+5} = y^6$
3. $a^2 \cdot a^6 \cdot a = a^{2+6+1} = a^9$

Take Note

The Rule for Multiplying Exponential Expressions requires that the bases be the same. The expression a^5b^7 cannot be simplified.

HOW TO 1 Simplify: $(-3a^4b^3)(2ab^4)$

$(-3a^4b^3)(2ab^4) = (-3 \cdot 2)(a^4 \cdot a)(b^3 \cdot b^4)$ • **Use the Commutative and Associative Properties of Multiplication to rearrange and group factors.**

$= -6(a^{4+1})(b^{3+4})$ • **To multiply expressions with the same base, add the exponents.**

$= -6a^5b^7$ • **Simplify.**

EXAMPLE 1

Simplify: $(-5ab^3)(4a^5)$

Solution

$(-5ab^3)(4a^5)$

$= (-5 \cdot 4)(a \cdot a^5)b^3$ • **Multiply coefficients. Add exponents with the same base.**

$= -20a^6b^3$

YOU TRY IT 1

Simplify: $(12p^4q^3)(-3p^5q^2)$

Your solution

$-36p^9q^5$

IN-CLASS EXAMPLES

Simplify.

1. $(6x^4y)(-4y^6)$ $\mathbf{-24x^4y^7}$
2. $(7x^6y^4)(-5x^2y^9)$ $\mathbf{-35x^8y^{13}}$

Solution on p. S22

OBJECTIVE B *To simplify powers of monomials*

Point of Interest

One of the first symbolic representations of powers was given by Diophantus (c. 250 A.D.) in his book *Arithmetica.* He used Δ^Y for x^2 and κ^Y for x^3. The symbol Δ^Y was the first two letters of the Greek word *dunamis,* which means "power"; κ^Y was from the Greek word *kubos,* which means "cube." He also combined these symbols to denote higher powers. For instance, $\Delta\kappa^Y$ was the symbol for x^5.

The power of a monomial can be simplified by writing the power in factored form and then using the Rule for Multiplying Exponential Expressions.

$(x^4)^3 = x^4 \cdot x^4 \cdot x^4 \quad (a^2b^3)^2 = (a^2b^3)(a^2b^3)$ • Write in factored form.

$= x^{4+4+4} \quad = a^{2+2}b^{3+3}$ • Use the Rule for Multiplying Exponential Expressions.

$= x^{12} \quad = a^4b^6$

Note that multiplying each exponent inside the parentheses by the exponent outside the parentheses results in the same product.

$(x^4)^3 = x^{4 \cdot 3} = x^{12} \quad (a^2b^3)^2 = a^{2 \cdot 2}b^{3 \cdot 2} = a^4b^6$ • Multiply each exponent inside the parentheses by the exponent outside the parentheses.

Rule for Simplifying the Power of an Exponential Expression

If m and n are integers, then $(x^m)^n = x^{mn}$.

EXAMPLES

Each example below is a power of an exponential expression. Simplify the expression by multiplying the exponents.

1. $(x^5)^2 = x^{5 \cdot 2} = x^{10}$
2. $(y^3)^4 = y^{3 \cdot 4} = y^{12}$

Rule for Simplifying the Power of a Product

If m, n, and p are integers, then $(x^my^n)^p = x^{mp}y^{np}$.

EXAMPLES

Each example below is a power of a product of exponential expressions. Simplify the expression by multiplying each exponent inside the parentheses by the exponent outside the parentheses.

1. $(c^5d^3)^6 = c^{5 \cdot 6}d^{3 \cdot 6} = c^{30}d^{18}$
2. $(3a^2b)^3 = 3^{1 \cdot 3}a^{2 \cdot 3}b^{1 \cdot 3} = 3^3a^6b^3 = 27a^6b^3$

EXAMPLE 2

Simplify: $(2a^2b)(2a^3b^2)^3$

Solution

$(2a^2b)(2a^3b^2)^3$

$= (2a^2b)(2^{1 \cdot 3}a^{3 \cdot 3}b^{2 \cdot 3})$ • Rule for Simplifying the Power of a Product

$= (2a^2b)(2^3a^9b^6)$

$= (2a^2b)(8a^9b^6) = 16a^{11}b^7$ • Rule for Multiplying Exponential Expressions

YOU TRY IT 2

Simplify: $(-xy^4)(-2x^3y^2)^2$

Your solution

$-4x^7y^8$

IN-CLASS EXAMPLES

Simplify.

3. $(3x^4)^2$ $\mathbf{9x^8}$
4. $(4x^2y^3)(2xy^4)^3$ $\mathbf{32x^5y^{15}}$
5. $(-5xy^4z^3)^3$ $\mathbf{-125x^3y^{12}z^9}$
6. $(3ab^3)(-2a^2b^4)^3$ $\mathbf{-24a^7b^{15}}$

Solution on p. S22

9.2 EXERCISES

SUGGESTED ASSIGNMENT:
Exercises 1–12; Exercises 13–45, odds; Exercises 46–49; Exercises 51–79, odds

Concept Check

For Exercises 1 to 8, state whether the expression is the product of two exponential expressions or a power of an exponential expression.

1. $b^4 \cdot b^8$
Product

2. $(b^4)^8$
Power

3. $(2z)^2$
Power

4. $2z \cdot z$
Product

5. $(3a^4)^5$
Power

6. $(3a^4)(5a)$
Product

7. $x(-xy^4)$
Product

8. $(-xy)^4$
Power

OBJECTIVE A To multiply monomials

For Exercises 9 to 12, state whether the expression can be simplified using the Rule for Multiplying Exponential Expressions.

9. $x^4 + x^5$
No

10. x^4x^5
Yes

11. x^4y^4
No

12. $x^4 + x^4$
No

For Exercises 13 to 45, simplify.

13. $(6x^2)(5x)$
$30x^3$

14. $(-4y^3)(2y)$
$-8y^4$

15. $(7c^2)(-6c^4)$
$-42c^6$

16. $(-8z^5)(5z^8)$
$-40z^{13}$

17. $(-3a^3)(-3a^4)$
$9a^7$

18. $(-5a^6)(-2a^5)$
$10a^{11}$

19. $(x^2)(xy^4)$
x^3y^4

20. $(x^2y^4)(xy^7)$
x^3y^{11}

21. $(-2x^4)(5x^5y)$
$-10x^9y$

22. $(-3a^3)(2a^2b^4)$
$-6a^5b^4$

23. $(-4x^2y^4)(-3x^5y^4)$
$12x^7y^8$

24. $(-6a^2b^4)(-4ab^3)$
$24a^3b^7$

25. $(2xy)(-3x^2y^4)$
$-6x^3y^5$

26. $(-3a^2b)(-2ab^3)$
$6a^3b^4$

27. $(x^2yz)(x^2y^4)$
x^4y^5z

28. $(-ab^2c)(a^2b^5)$
$-a^3b^7c$

29. $(-a^2b^3)(-ab^2c^4)$
$a^3b^5c^4$

30. $(-x^2y^3z)(-x^3y^4)$
x^5y^7z

31. $(-5a^2b^2)(6a^3b^6)$
$-30a^5b^8$

32. $(7xy^4)(-2xy^3)$
$-14x^2y^7$

33. $(-6a^3)(-a^2b)$
$6a^5b$

34. $(-2a^2b^3)(-4ab^2)$
$8a^3b^5$

35. $(-5y^4z)(-8y^6z^5)$
$40y^{10}z^6$

36. $(3x^2y)(-4xy^2)$
$-12x^3y^3$

37. $(x^2y)(yz)(xyz)$
$x^3y^3z^2$

38. $(xy^2z)(x^2y)(z^2y^2)$
$x^3y^5z^3$

39. $(3ab^2)(-2abc)(4ac^2)$
$-24a^3b^3c^3$

40. $(-2x^3y^2)(-3x^2z^2)(-5y^3z^3)$
$-30x^5y^5z^5$

41. $(4x^4z)(-yz^3)(-2x^3z^2)$
$8x^7yz^6$

42. $(-a^3b^4)(-3a^4c^2)(4b^3c^4)$
$12a^7b^7c^6$

43. $(-2x^2y^3)(3xy)(-5x^3y^4)$
$30x^6y^8$

44. $(4a^2b)(-3a^3b^4)(a^5b^2)$
$-12a^{10}b^7$

45. $(3a^2b)(-6bc)(2ac^2)$
$-36a^3b^2c^3$

OBJECTIVE B *To simplify powers of monomials*

For Exercises 46 to 49, state whether the expression can be simplified using the Rule for Simplifying the Power of a Product.

46. $(xy)^3$ Yes

47. $(x + y)^3$ No

48. $(a^3 - b^4)^2$ No

49. $(a^3b^4)^2$ Yes

For Exercises 50 to 80, simplify.

50. $(z^4)^3$ z^{12}

51. $(x^3)^5$ x^{15}

52. $(y^4)^2$ y^8

53. $(x^7)^2$ x^{14}

54. $(-y^5)^3$ $-y^{15}$

55. $(-x^2)^4$ x^8

56. $(-x^2)^3$ $-x^6$

57. $(-y^3)^4$ y^{12}

58. $(-3y)^3$ $-27y^3$

59. $(-2x^2)^3$ $-8x^6$

60. $(a^3b^4)^3$ a^9b^{12}

61. $(x^2y^3)^2$ x^4y^6

62. $(2x^3y^4)^5$ $32x^{15}y^{20}$

63. $(3x^2y)^2$ $9x^4y^2$

64. $(-2ab^3)^4$ $16a^4b^{12}$

65. $(-3x^3y^2)^5$ $-243x^{15}y^{10}$

66. $(3b^2)(2a^3)^4$ $48a^{12}b^2$

67. $(-2x)(2x^3)^2$ $-8x^7$

68. $(2y)(-3y^4)^3$ $-54y^{13}$

69. $(3x^2y)(2x^2y^2)^3$ $24x^8y^7$

70. $(a^3b)^2(ab)^3$ a^9b^5

71. $(ab^2)^2(ab)^2$ a^4b^6

72. $(-x^2y^3)^2(-2x^3y)^3$ $-8x^{13}y^9$

73. $(-2x)^3(-2x^3y)^3$ $64x^{12}y^3$

74. $(-3y)(-4x^2y^3)^3$ $192x^6y^{10}$

75. $(-2x)(-3xy^2)^2$ $-18x^3y^4$

76. $(-3y)(-2x^2y)^3$ $24x^6y^4$

77. $(ab^2)(-2a^2b)^3$ $-8a^7b^5$

78. $(a^2b^2)(-3ab^4)^2$ $9a^4b^{10}$

79. $(-2a^3)(3a^2b)^3$ $-54a^9b^3$

80. $(-3b^2)(2ab^2)^3$ $-24a^3b^8$

Critical Thinking

For Exercises 81 to 88, simplify.

81. $3x^2 + (3x)^2$ $12x^2$

82. $4x^2 - (4x)^2$ $-12x^2$

83. $2x^6y^2 + (3x^2y)^2$ $2x^6y^2 + 9x^4y^2$

84. $(x^2y^2)^3 + (x^3y^3)^2$ $2x^6y^6$

85. $(2a^3b^2)^3 - 8a^9b^6$ 0

86. $4y^2z^4 - (2yz^2)^2$ 0

87. $(x^2y^4)^2 + (2xy^2)^4$ $17x^4y^8$

88. $(3a^3)^2 - 4a^6 + (2a^2)^3$ $13a^6$

QUICK QUIZ

Simplify.

1. $(4a^3b^2)(5ab)$ **$20a^4b^3$ [9.2A]**
2. $(-4x^2y^3z^2)(-3x^4yz^3)$ **$12x^6y^4z^5$ [9.2A]**
3. $(2ab^2c)(3a^2b^3)(5a^3bc^2)$ **$30a^6b^6c^3$ [9.2A]**
4. $(x^4)^3$ **x^{12} [9.2B]**
5. $(3a^3bc^5)^2$ **$9a^6b^2c^{10}$ [9.2B]**
6. $(5ab^3c^4)(-2a^2bc^3)^4$ **$80a^9b^7c^{16}$ [9.2B]**

Projects or Group Activities

89. Let $x_1 = -1x^1$ and, for $n > 1$, $x_n = -nx^n$. Calculate the product $(x_1)(x_2)(x_3)(x_4)(x_5)$.
$-120x^{15}$

90. a. Evaluate $(2^3)^2$ and $2^{(3^2)}$. Are the results the same? If not, which expression has the larger value? No; $2^{(3^2)}$ is larger. $(2^3)^2 = 8^2 = 64$, $2^{(3^2)} = 2^9 = 512$

b. What is the order of operations for the expression x^{m^n}?
The order of operations is $x^{(m^n)}$.

SECTION

9.3 Multiplication of Polynomials

OBJECTIVE A *To multiply a polynomial by a monomial*

To multiply a polynomial by a monomial, use the Distributive Property and the Rule for Multiplying Exponential Expressions.

HOW TO 1 Multiply: $-3a(4a^2 - 5a + 6)$

$$-3a(4a^2 - 5a + 6) = -3a(4a^2) - (-3a)(5a) + (-3a)(6)$$
$$= -12a^3 + 15a^2 - 18a$$

• **Use the Distributive Property.**

EXAMPLE 1

Multiply: $(5x + 4)(-2x)$

Solution

$(5x + 4)(-2x) = 5x(-2x) + 4(-2x) = -10x^2 - 8x$

YOU TRY IT 1

Multiply: $(-2y + 3)(-4y)$

Your solution

$8y^2 - 12y$

IN-CLASS EXAMPLES

Multiply.

1. $(6a - 5)(-4a)$ **$-24a^2 + 20a$**
2. $3x^2y(5x^2 + 4xy - 2y^2)$ **$15x^4y + 12x^3y^2 - 6x^2y^3$**
3. $(2x + 4)3x$ **$6x^2 + 12x$**

EXAMPLE 2

Multiply: $2a^2b(4a^2 - 2ab + b^2)$

Solution

$2a^2b(4a^2 - 2ab + b^2)$
$= 2a^2b(4a^2) - 2a^2b(2ab) + 2a^2b(b^2)$
$= 8a^4b - 4a^3b^2 + 2a^2b^3$

YOU TRY IT 2

Multiply: $-a^2(3a^2 + 2a - 7)$

Your solution

$-3a^4 - 2a^3 + 7a^2$

4. $4xy(3x^2 - 2xy + 4y^2)$ **$12x^3y - 8x^2y^2 + 16xy^3$**

Solutions on p. S22

OBJECTIVE B *To multiply two polynomials*

Multiplication of two polynomials requires the repeated application of the Distributive Property.

$$(y^2 - 4y - 6)(y + 2) = (y^2 - 4y - 6)y + (y^2 - 4y - 6)2$$
$$= (y^3 - 4y^2 - 6y) + (2y^2 - 8y - 12)$$
$$= y^3 - 2y^2 - 14y - 12$$

INSTRUCTOR NOTE

Before doing an example similar to the one at the right, show students that the procedure for multiplication can be related to multiplying whole numbers, such as 473 × 28.

A convenient method for multiplying two polynomials is to use a vertical format similar to that used for multiplication of whole numbers.

$$\begin{array}{rrrrl}
 & y^2 & -\ 4y & -\ 6 & \\
 & & y & +\ 2 & \\
\hline
 & 2y^2 & -\ 8y & -\ 12 & = (y^2 - 4y - 6)2 \\
y^3 & -\ 4y^2 & -\ 6y & & = (y^2 - 4y - 6)y \\
\hline
y^3 & -\ 2y^2 & -\ 14y & -\ 12 &
\end{array}$$

• **Multiply by 2.**
• **Multiply by *y*.**
• **Add the terms in each column.**

HOW TO 2 Multiply: $(2a^3 + a - 3)(a + 5)$

$$\begin{array}{r} 2a^3 \quad\quad + a - 3 \\ a + 5 \\ \hline 10a^3 \quad + 5a - 15 \\ 2a^4 \quad\quad + a^2 - 3a \quad\quad \\ \hline 2a^4 + 10a^3 + a^2 + 2a - 15 \end{array}$$

- Note that spaces are inserted in each product so that like terms are in the same column.
- Add the terms in each column.

EXAMPLE 3

Multiply: $(2b^3 - b + 1)(2b + 3)$

Solution

$$\begin{array}{r} 2b^3 \quad\quad - b + 1 \\ 2b + 3 \\ \hline 6b^3 \quad\quad - 3b + 3 \\ 4b^4 + \quad - 2b^2 + 2b \quad\quad \\ \hline 4b^4 + 6b^3 - 2b^2 - b + 3 \end{array}$$

$= 3(2b^3 - b + 1)$
$= 2b(2b^3 - b + 1)$

YOU TRY IT 3

Multiply: $(2y^3 + 2y^2 - 3)(3y - 1)$

Your solution

$6y^4 + 4y^3 - 2y^2 - 9y + 3$

IN-CLASS EXAMPLES

Multiply.

5. $(2z^2 - 4z + 5)(4z - 2)$ $\mathbf{8z^3 - 20z^2 + 28z - 10}$
6. $(6a^3 + 4a^2 - 3a)(3a - 2)$ $\mathbf{18a^4 - 17a^2 + 6a}$
7. $(3x^3 - 2x + 5)(7x + 4)$ $\mathbf{21x^4 + 12x^3 - 14x^2 + 27x + 20}$

Solution on p. S22

OBJECTIVE C *To multiply two binomials using the FOIL method*

It is frequently necessary to find the product of two binomials. The product can be found using a method called **FOIL,** which is based on the Distributive Property. The letters of FOIL stand for **F**irst, **O**uter, **I**nner, and **L**ast. To find the product of two binomials, add the products of the **F**irst terms, the **O**uter terms, the **I**nner terms, and the **L**ast terms.

Take Note

FOIL is not really a different way of multiplying. It is based on the Distributive Property.

$(2x + 3)(x + 5)$
$= 2x(x + 5) + 3(x + 5)$
F O I L
$= 2x^2 + 10x + 3x + 15$
$= 2x^2 + 13x + 15$

HOW TO 3 Multiply: $(2x + 3)(x + 5)$

Multiply the First terms.	$(2x + 3)(x + 5)$	$2x \cdot x = 2x^2$
Multiply the Outer terms.	$(2x + 3)(x + 5)$	$2x \cdot 5 = 10x$
Multiply the Inner terms.	$(2x + 3)(x + 5)$	$3 \cdot x = 3x$
Multiply the Last terms.	$(2x + 3)(x + 5)$	$3 \cdot 5 = 15$
		F O I L
Add the products.	$(2x + 3)(x + 5)$	$= 2x^2 + 10x + 3x + 15$
Combine like terms.		$= 2x^2 + 13x + 15$

HOW TO 4 Multiply: $(4x - 3)(3x - 2)$

$(4x - 3)(3x - 2) = 4x(3x) + 4x(-2) + (-3)(3x) + (-3)(-2)$ • FOIL
$= 12x^2 - 8x - 9x + 6$ • Multiply.
$= 12x^2 - 17x + 6$ • Combine like terms.

HOW TO 5 Multiply: $(3x - 2y)(x + 4y)$

$(3x - 2y)(x + 4y) = 3x(x) + 3x(4y) + (-2y)(x) + (-2y)(4y)$ • FOIL
$= 3x^2 + 12xy - 2xy - 8y^2$ • Multiply.
$= 3x^2 + 10xy - 8y^2$ • Combine like terms.

EXAMPLE 4

Multiply: $(2a - 1)(3a - 2)$

Solution

$(2a - 1)(3a - 2) = 6a^2 - 4a - 3a + 2$
$= 6a^2 - 7a + 2$

YOU TRY IT 4

Multiply: $(4y - 5)(2y - 3)$

Your solution

$8y^2 - 22y + 15$

IN-CLASS EXAMPLES

Multiply.

8. $(7x - 3)(5x - 6)$ $35x^2 - 57x + 18$
9. $(8y + 7)(3y - 4)$ $24y^2 - 11y - 28$
10. $(6w + 4)(5w - 2)$ $30w^2 + 8w - 8$

EXAMPLE 5

Multiply: $(3x - 2)(4x + 3)$

Solution

$(3x - 2)(4x + 3) = 12x^2 + 9x - 8x - 6$
$= 12x^2 + x - 6$

YOU TRY IT 5

Multiply: $(3b + 2)(3b - 5)$

Your solution

$9b^2 - 9b - 10$

Solutions on p. S22

OBJECTIVE D *To multiply binomials that have special products*

Using FOIL, it is possible to find a pattern for the product of the sum and difference of the same two terms and for the square of a binomial.

INSTRUCTOR NOTE
Binomials that are otherwise identical except that one is a sum and one is a difference are called *conjugates* of each other.

Product of the Sum and Difference of the Same Terms

$$(a + b)(a - b) = a^2 - ab + ab - b^2$$
$$= a^2 - b^2$$

Square of the first term
Square of the second term

EXAMPLE

Multiply: $(2x + 3)(2x - 3)$

This is the product of the sum and difference of the same terms.
$(2x + 3)(2x - 3) = (2x)^2 - 3^2 = 4x^2 - 9$

INSTRUCTOR NOTE
Remind students that the rule that applies to $(ab)^2$ is different from the rule that applies to $(a + b)^2$.

Square of a Binomial

$$(a + b)^2 = (a + b)(a + b) = a^2 + ab + ab + b^2$$
$$= a^2 + 2ab + b^2$$

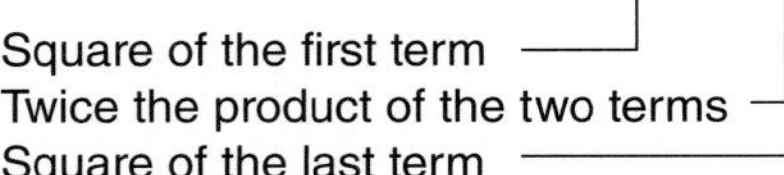

Square of the first term
Twice the product of the two terms
Square of the last term

EXAMPLE

Expand: $(3x - 2)^2$

This is the square of a binomial.
$(3x - 2)^2 = (3x)^2 + 2(3x)(-2) + (-2)^2 = 9x^2 - 12x + 4$

Take Note
The word *expand* frequently is used to mean "multiply out a power."

EXAMPLE 6

Multiply: $(4z - 2w)(4z + 2w)$

Solution

This is the product of the sum and difference of the same two terms.

$(4z - 2w)(4z + 2w) = 16z^2 - 4w^2$

YOU TRY IT 6

Multiply: $(2a + 5c)(2a - 5c)$

Your solution

$4a^2 - 25c^2$

EXAMPLE 7

Expand: $(2r - 3s)^2$

Solution

This is the square of a binomial.

$(2r - 3s)^2 = 4r^2 - 12rs + 9s^2$

YOU TRY IT 7

Expand: $(3x + 2y)^2$

Your solution

$9x^2 + 12xy + 4y^2$

IN-CLASS EXAMPLES

11. Multiply: $(10x - 3)(10x + 3)$
 $\mathbf{100x^2 - 9}$
12. Expand: $(4x + 3y)^2$
 $\mathbf{16x^2 + 24xy + 9y^2}$

Solutions on p. S22

OBJECTIVE E *To solve application problems*

EXAMPLE 8

The length of a rectangle is $(x + 7)$ m. The width is $(x - 4)$ m. Find the area of the rectangle in terms of the variable x.

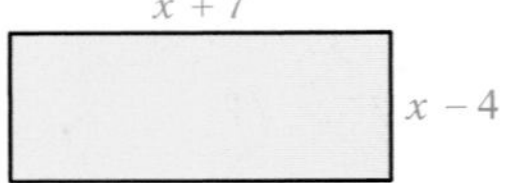

Strategy

To find the area, replace the variables L and W in the equation $A = L \cdot W$ by the given values and solve for A.

Solution

$A = L \cdot W$

$A = (x + 7)(x - 4)$ • $L = x + 7$; $W = x - 4$

$A = x^2 - 4x + 7x - 28$ • FOIL

$A = x^2 + 3x - 28$ • Combine like terms.

The area is $(x^2 + 3x - 28)$ m^2.

YOU TRY IT 8

The radius of a circle is $(x - 4)$ ft. Use the equation $A = \pi r^2$, where r is the radius, to find the area of the circle in terms of x. Leave the answer in terms of π.

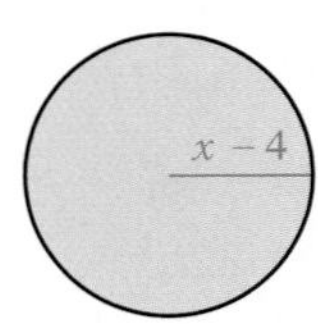

Your strategy

Your solution

$(\pi x^2 - 8\pi x + 16\pi)$ ft^2

IN-CLASS EXAMPLES

13. The radius of a circle is $(x + 5)$ ft. Use the equation $A = \pi r^2$, where r is the radius, to find the area of the circle in terms of x. Leave the answer in terms of π.
 $\mathbf{(\pi x^2 + 10\pi x + 25\pi)}$ **ft²**

Solution on p. S22

9.3 EXERCISES

Concept Check

SUGGESTED ASSIGNMENT
Exercises 1–10; Exercises 11–111, odds; Exercises 117–123, odds

For Exercises 1 to 9, determine whether the statement is always true, sometimes true, or never true.

1. To multiply a monomial times a polynomial, use the Distributive Property to multiply each term of the polynomial by the monomial. Always true

2. To multiply two polynomials, multiply each term of one polynomial by the other polynomial. Always true

3. A binomial is a polynomial of degree 2. Sometimes true

4. $(x + 7)(x - 7)$ is the product of the sum and difference of the same two terms. Always true

5. To square a binomial means to multiply it times itself. Always true

6. The square of a binomial is a trinomial. Always true

7. The FOIL method is used to multiply two polynomials. Sometimes true

8. Using the FOIL method, the terms $3x$ and 5 are the "First" terms in $(3x + 5)(2x + 7)$. Never true

9. The product of two binomials is a trinomial. Sometimes true

OBJECTIVE A *To multiply a polynomial by a monomial*

10. Is the Distributive Property used to simplify the product $2(3x)$? If not, what property is used to simplify this expression? No. The Associative Property of Multiplication

For Exercises 11 to 42, multiply.

11. $x(x - 2)$
$x^2 - 2x$

12. $y(3 - y)$
$-y^2 + 3y$

13. $-x(x + 7)$
$-x^2 - 7x$

14. $-y(7 - y)$
$y^2 - 7y$

15. $3a^2(a - 2)$
$3a^3 - 6a^2$

16. $4b^2(b + 8)$
$4b^3 + 32b^2$

17. $-5x^2(x^2 - x)$
$-5x^4 + 5x^3$

18. $-6y^2(y + 2y^2)$
$-12y^4 - 6y^3$

19. $-x^3(3x^2 - 7)$
$-3x^5 + 7x^3$

20. $-y^4(2y^2 - y^6)$
$y^{10} - 2y^6$

21. $2x(6x^2 - 3x)$
$12x^3 - 6x^2$

22. $3y(4y - y^2)$
$-3y^3 + 12y^2$

23. $(2x - 4)3x$
$6x^2 - 12x$

24. $(3y - 2)y$
$3y^2 - 2y$

25. $(3x + 4)x$
$3x^2 + 4x$

26. $(2x + 1)2x$
$4x^2 + 2x$

27. $-xy(x^2 - y^2)$
$-x^3y + xy^3$

28. $-x^2y(2xy - y^2)$
$-2x^3y^2 + x^2y^3$

29. $x(2x^3 - 3x + 2)$
$2x^4 - 3x^2 + 2x$

30. $y(-3y^2 - 2y + 6)$
$-3y^3 - 2y^2 + 6y$

31. $-a(-2a^2 - 3a - 2)$
$2a^3 + 3a^2 + 2a$

32. $-b(5b^2 + 7b - 35)$
$-5b^3 - 7b^2 + 35b$

33. $x^2(3x^4 - 3x^2 - 2)$
$3x^6 - 3x^4 - 2x^2$

34. $y^3(-4y^3 - 6y + 7)$
$-4y^6 - 6y^4 + 7y^3$

35. $2y^2(-3y^2 - 6y + 7)$
$-6y^4 - 12y^3 + 14y^2$

36. $4x^2(3x^2 - 2x + 6)$
$12x^4 - 8x^3 + 24x^2$

37. $(a^2 + 3a - 4)(-2a)$
$-2a^3 - 6a^2 + 8a$

38. $(b^3 - 2b + 2)(-5b)$
$-5b^4 + 10b^2 - 10b$

39. $-3y^2(-2y^2 + y - 2)$
$6y^4 - 3y^3 + 6y^2$

40. $-5x^2(3x^2 - 3x - 7)$
$-15x^4 + 15x^3 + 35x^2$

41. $xy(x^2 - 3xy + y^2)$
$x^3y - 3x^2y^2 + xy^3$

42. $ab(2a^2 - 4ab - 6b^2)$
$2a^3b - 4a^2b^2 - 6ab^3$

43. Which of the following expressions are equivalent to $4x - x(3x - 1)$?
(i) $4x - 3x^2 - x$ **(ii)** $-3x^2 + 5x$ **(iii)** $4x - 3x^2 + x$ **(iv)** $9x^2 - 3x$ **(v)** $3x(3x - 1)$
ii and iii

OBJECTIVE B *To multiply two polynomials*

For Exercises 44 to 61, multiply.

44. $(x^2 + 3x + 2)(x + 1)$
$x^3 + 4x^2 + 5x + 2$

45. $(x^2 - 2x + 7)(x - 2)$
$x^3 - 4x^2 + 11x - 14$

46. $(a^2 - 3a + 4)(a - 3)$
$a^3 - 6a^2 + 13a - 12$

47. $(x^2 - 3x + 5)(2x - 3)$
$2x^3 - 9x^2 + 19x - 15$

48. $(-2b^2 - 3b + 4)(b - 5)$
$-2b^3 + 7b^2 + 19b - 20$

49. $(-a^2 + 3a - 2)(2a - 1)$
$-2a^3 + 7a^2 - 7a + 2$

50. $(-2x^2 + 7x - 2)(3x - 5)$
$-6x^3 + 31x^2 - 41x + 10$

51. $(-a^2 - 2a + 3)(2a - 1)$
$-2a^3 - 3a^2 + 8a - 3$

52. $(x^2 + 5)(x - 3)$
$x^3 - 3x^2 + 5x - 15$

53. $(y^2 - 2y)(2y + 5)$
$2y^3 + y^2 - 10y$

54. $(x^3 - 3x + 2)(x - 4)$
$x^4 - 4x^3 - 3x^2 + 14x - 8$

55. $(y^3 + 4y^2 - 8)(2y - 1)$
$2y^4 + 7y^3 - 4y^2 - 16y + 8$

56. $(5y^2 + 8y - 2)(3y - 8)$
$15y^3 - 16y^2 - 70y + 16$

57. $(3y^2 + 3y - 5)(4y - 3)$
$12y^3 + 3y^2 - 29y + 15$

58. $(5a^3 - 5a + 2)(a - 4)$
$5a^4 - 20a^3 - 5a^2 + 22a - 8$

59. $(3b^3 - 5b^2 + 7)(6b - 1)$
$18b^4 - 33b^3 + 5b^2 + 42b - 7$

60. $(y^3 + 2y^2 - 3y + 1)(y + 2)$
$y^4 + 4y^3 + y^2 - 5y + 2$

61. $(2a^3 - 3a^2 + 2a - 1)(2a - 3)$
$4a^4 - 12a^3 + 13a^2 - 8a + 3$

62. If a polynomial of degree 3 is multiplied by a polynomial of degree 2, what is the degree of the resulting polynomial? 5

OBJECTIVE C *To multiply two binomials using the FOIL method*

For Exercises 63 to 94, multiply.

63. $(x + 1)(x + 3)$
$x^2 + 4x + 3$

64. $(y + 2)(y + 5)$
$y^2 + 7y + 10$

65. $(a - 3)(a + 4)$
$a^2 + a - 12$

66. $(b - 6)(b + 3)$
$b^2 - 3b - 18$

67. $(y + 3)(y - 8)$
$y^2 - 5y - 24$

68. $(x + 10)(x - 5)$
$x^2 + 5x - 50$

69. $(y - 7)(y - 3)$
$y^2 - 10y + 21$

70. $(a - 8)(a - 9)$
$a^2 - 17a + 72$

71. $(2x + 1)(x + 7)$
$2x^2 + 15x + 7$

72. $(y + 2)(5y + 1)$
$5y^2 + 11y + 2$

73. $(3x - 1)(x + 4)$
$3x^2 + 11x - 4$

74. $(7x - 2)(x + 4)$
$7x^2 + 26x - 8$

75. $(4x - 3)(x - 7)$
$4x^2 - 31x + 21$

76. $(2x - 3)(4x - 7)$
$8x^2 - 26x + 21$

77. $(3y - 8)(y + 2)$
$3y^2 - 2y - 16$

78. $(5y - 9)(y + 5)$
$5y^2 + 16y - 45$

79. $(3x + 7)(3x + 11)$
$9x^2 + 54x + 77$

80. $(5a + 6)(6a + 5)$
$30a^2 + 61a + 30$

81. $(7a - 16)(3a - 5)$
$21a^2 - 83a + 80$

82. $(5a - 12)(3a - 7)$
$15a^2 - 71a + 84$

83. $(3a - 2b)(2a - 7b)$
$6a^2 - 25ab + 14b^2$

84. $(5a - b)(7a - b)$
$35a^2 - 12ab + b^2$

85. $(a - 9b)(2a + 7b)$
$2a^2 - 11ab - 63b^2$

86. $(2a + 5b)(7a - 2b)$
$14a^2 + 31ab - 10b^2$

87. $(10a - 3b)(10a - 7b)$
$100a^2 - 100ab + 21b^2$

88. $(12a - 5b)(3a - 4b)$
$36a^2 - 63ab + 20b^2$

89. $(5x + 12y)(3x + 4y)$
$15x^2 + 56xy + 48y^2$

90. $(11x + 2y)(3x + 7y)$
$33x^2 + 83xy + 14y^2$

91. $(2x - 15y)(7x + 4y)$
$14x^2 - 97xy - 60y^2$

92. $(5x + 2y)(2x - 5y)$
$10x^2 - 21xy - 10y^2$

93. $(8x - 3y)(7x - 5y)$
$56x^2 - 61xy + 15y^2$

94. $(2x - 9y)(8x - 3y)$
$16x^2 - 78xy + 27y^2$

95. What polynomial has quotient $3x - 4$ when divided by $4x + 5$?
$12x^2 - x - 20$

OBJECTIVE D *To multiply binomials that have special products*

For Exercises 96 to 103, multiply.

96. $(y - 5)(y + 5)$
$y^2 - 25$

97. $(y + 6)(y - 6)$
$y^2 - 36$

98. $(2x + 3)(2x - 3)$
$4x^2 - 9$

99. $(4x - 7)(4x + 7)$
$16x^2 - 49$

100. $(3x - 7)(3x + 7)$
$9x^2 - 49$

101. $(9x - 2)(9x + 2)$
$81x^2 - 4$

102. $(4 - 3y)(4 + 3y)$
$16 - 9y^2$

103. $(4x - 9y)(4x + 9y)$
$16x^2 - 81y^2$

For Exercises 104 to 111, expand.

104. $(x + 1)^2$
$x^2 + 2x + 1$

105. $(y - 3)^2$
$y^2 - 6y + 9$

106. $(3a - 5)^2$
$9a^2 - 30a + 25$

107. $(6x - 5)^2$
$36x^2 - 60x + 25$

108. $(x + 3y)^2$
$x^2 + 6xy + 9y^2$

109. $(x - 2y)^2$
$x^2 - 4xy + 4y^2$

110. $(5x + 2y)^2$
$25x^2 + 20xy + 4y^2$

111. $(2a - 9b)^2$
$4a^2 - 36ab + 81b^2$

For Exercises 112 to 115, state whether the coefficient of the x term of the product is positive, negative, or zero.

112. $(ax + b)(ax - b)$, where $a > 0$ and $b > 0$ Zero

113. $(ax + b)(ax + b)$, where $a > 0$ and $b < 0$ Negative

114. $(ax + b)^2$, where $a > 0$ and $b > 0$ Positive

115. $(ax + b)^2$, where $a < 0$ and $b < 0$ Positive

OBJECTIVE E *To solve application problems*

116. Geometry The length of a rectangle is $(5x)$ ft. The width is $(2x - 7)$ ft. Find the area of the rectangle in terms of the variable x.
$(10x^2 - 35x)$ ft^2

5x

2x − 7

117. Geometry The width of a rectangle is $(3x + 1)$ in. The length of the rectangle is twice the width. Find the area of the rectangle in terms of the variable x.
$(18x^2 + 12x + 2)$ in^2

118. Geometry The length of a side of a square is $(2x + 1)$ km. Find the area of the square in terms of the variable x. $(4x^2 + 4x + 1)$ km^2

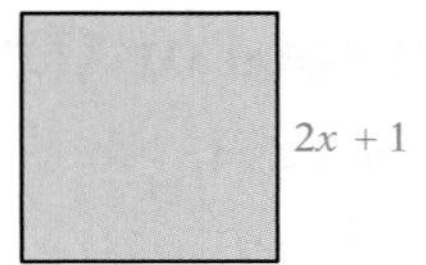

119. Geometry The radius of a circle is $(x + 4)$ cm. Find the area of the circle in terms of the variable x. Leave the answer in terms of π. $(\pi x^2 + 8\pi x + 16\pi)$ cm^2

120. Geometry The base of a triangle is $(4x)$ m, and the height is $(2x + 5)$ m. Find the area of the triangle in terms of the variable x. $(4x^2 + 10x)$ m^2

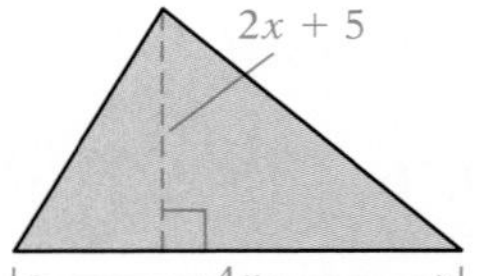

121. Sports A softball diamond has dimensions 45 ft by 45 ft. A base-path border x feet wide lies on both the first-base side and the third-base side of the diamond. Express the total area of the softball diamond and the base paths in terms of the variable x. $(90x + 2025)$ ft^2

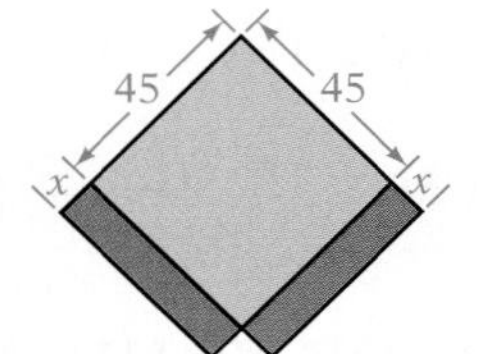

122. Sports An athletic field has dimensions 30 yd by 100 yd. An end zone that is w yards wide borders each end of the field. Express the total area of the field and the end zones in terms of the variable w. $(60w + 3000)$ yd^2

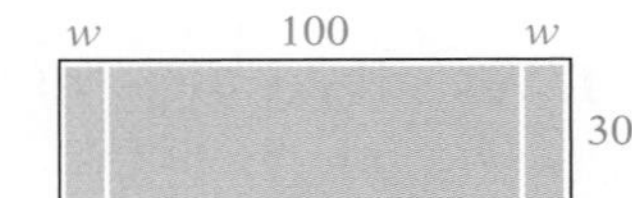

123. The Olympics See the news clipping at the right. The Water Cube is not actually a cube because its height is not equal to its length and width. The length of the Water Cube is 22 ft more than five times the height. (*Source:* Structurae)

a. Express the length of the Water Cube in terms of the height h. $(5h + 22)$ ft

b. Express the area of one exterior wall of the Water Cube in terms of the height h. $(5h^2 + 22h)$ ft^2

© claudio zaccherini/Shutterstock.com

The Water Cube

In the NEWS!

Olympic Water Cube Completed

The National Aquatics Center, also known as the Water Cube, was completed on the morning of December 26, 2006. Built in Beijing, China, for the 2008 Olympics, the Water Cube is designed to look like a "cube" of water molecules.

Source: Structurae

124. The expression $w(3w - 1)$ cm^2 represents the area of a rectangle of width w. Describe in words the relationship between the length and width of the rectangle. The length is 1 cm less than three times the width.

Critical Thinking

For Exercises 125 to 130, simplify.

125. $(a + b)^2 - (a - b)^2$ $4ab$

126. $(x + 3y)^2 + (x + 3y)(x - 3y)$ $2x^2 + 6xy$

127. $(3a^2 - 4a + 2)^2$ $9a^4 - 24a^3 + 28a^2 - 16a + 4$

128. $(x + 4)^3$ $x^3 + 12x^2 + 48x + 64$

129. $3x^2(2x^3 + 4x - 1) - 6x^3(x^2 - 2)$ $24x^3 - 3x^2$

130. $(3b + 2)(b - 6) + (4 + 2b)(3 - b)$ $b^2 - 14b$

131. Find $(4n^3)^2$ if $2n - 3 = 4n - 7$. 1024

132. What polynomial has quotient $x^2 + 2x - 1$ when divided by $x + 3$? $x^3 + 5x^2 + 5x - 3$

133. What polynomial has quotient $3x - 4$ when divided by $4x + 5$? $12x^2 - x - 20$

Projects or Group Activities

For Exercises 134 to 137, simplify.

134. $(x + 1)(x - 1)$ $x^2 - 1$

135. $(x + 1)(-x^2 + x - 1)$ $-x^3 - 1$

136. $(x + 1)(x^3 - x^2 + x - 1)$ $x^4 - 1$

137. $(x + 1)(-x^4 + x^3 - x^2 + x - 1)$ $-x^5 - 1$

Use the pattern of the answers to Exercises 134 to 137 to write the product.

138. $(x + 1)(x^5 - x^4 + x^3 - x^2 + x - 1)$ $x^6 - 1$

139. $(x + 1)(-x^6 + x^5 - x^4 + x^3 - x^2 + x - 1)$ $-x^7 - 1$

QUICK QUIZ

Multiply.

1. $2a^2(a - 3)$ $\mathbf{2a^3 - 6a^2}$ **[9.3A]**
2. $(x^2 - 3x + 2)(x + 5)$ $\mathbf{x^3 + 2x^2 - 13x + 10}$ **[9.3B]**
3. $(2x - 3)(3x - 4)$ $\mathbf{6x^2 - 17x + 12}$ **[9.3C]**
4. $(5y + 3)(5y - 3)$ $\mathbf{25y^2 - 9}$ **[9.3D]**
5. Expand: $(3x + 2y)^2$ $\mathbf{9x^2 + 12xy + 4y^2}$ **[9.3D]**
6. The width of a rectangle is $(3x + 2)$ ft. The length of the rectangle is $(4x - 1)$ ft. Find the area of the rectangle in terms of the variable x. $\mathbf{(12x^2 + 5x - 2)}$ **ft²** **[9.3E]**

CHECK YOUR PROGRESS: CHAPTER 9

1. Add: $(4x + 3x^2 - 6) + (x^2 - 5x + 1)$
$4x^2 - x - 5$ [9.1A]

2. Multiply: $(3y - 7)(y + 5)$
$3y^2 + 8y - 35$ [9.3C]

3. Multiply: $4y(5y - 3y^3)$
$20y^2 - 12y^4$ [9.3A]

4. Simplify: $(-2a^4)(3ab^5)$
$-6a^5b^5$ [9.2A]

5. Multiply: $(10x - 3)(10x + 3)$
$100x^2 - 9$ [9.3D]

6. Multiply: $(2x^2 - 3x + 5)(x - 6)$
$2x^3 - 15x^2 + 23x - 30$ [9.3B]

7. Simplify: $3x^4y(-x^6y^2)(-2xy^5)$
$6x^{11}y^8$ [9.2A]

8. Simplify: $(3x^6y^5)^4$
$81x^{24}y^{20}$ [9.2B]

9. Multiply: $(x^3 - 3x^2 + 6)(2x + 1)$
$2x^4 - 5x^3 - 3x^2 + 12x + 6$ [9.3B]

10. Expand: $(b - 11)^2$
$b^2 - 22b + 121$ [9.3D]

11. Simplify: $(-2b)(-4b^3)^2$
$-32b^7$ [9.2B]

12. Subtract: $(2x^3 + 4x - 5) - (1 + 6x - x^2)$
$2x^3 + x^2 - 2x - 6$ [9.1B]

13. Multiply: $5x^2(3x^2 - x + 7)$
$15x^4 - 5x^3 + 35x^2$ [9.3A]

14. Multiply: $(4a - 9)(3a - 2)$
$12a^2 - 35a + 18$ [9.3C]

15. Multiply: $(5 - 6y)(5 + 6y)$
$25 - 36y^2$ [9.3D]

16. Expand: $(3a - 5b)^2$
$9a^2 - 30ab + 25b^2$ [9.3D]

17. **Geometry** The length of a rectangle is $(4x)$ in. The width is $(3x - 2)$ in. Find the area of the rectangle in terms of the variable x. $(12x^2 - 8x)$ in² [9.3E]

18. **Geometry** The length of a side of a square is $(4x + 5)$ ft. Find the area of the square in terms of the variable x. $(16x^2 + 40x + 25)$ ft² [9.3E]

SECTION

9.4 Integer Exponents and Scientific Notation

OBJECTIVE A *To divide monomials*

INSTRUCTOR NOTE

Here we are just verbalizing the rule for division of polynomials. The formal definition comes after we define negative exponents. Have students write this rule, even just copy it onto a piece of paper, and then practice a few exercises, such as

$$\frac{a^4}{a^2} \text{ and } \frac{y^8}{y}$$

It may also help to give them the expression $\frac{a^9}{b^5}$ to emphasize that the bases must be the same in order to subtract the exponents.

The quotient of two exponential expressions with the same base can be simplified by writing each expression in factored form, dividing by the common factors, and then writing the result with an exponent.

$$\frac{x^5}{x^2} = \frac{\overset{1}{\cancel{x}} \cdot \overset{1}{\cancel{x}} \cdot x \cdot x \cdot x}{\underset{1}{\cancel{x}} \cdot \underset{1}{\cancel{x}}} = x^3$$

Note that subtracting the exponents gives the same result.

$$\frac{x^5}{x^2} = x^{5-2} = x^3$$

To divide two monomials with the same base, subtract the exponents of the like bases.

HOW TO 1 Simplify: $\frac{a^7}{a^3}$

$\frac{a^7}{a^3} = a^{7-3}$ • **The bases are the same. Subtract the exponents.**

$= a^4$

HOW TO 2 Simplify: $\frac{r^8t^6}{r^7t}$

$\frac{r^8t^6}{r^7t} = r^{8-7}t^{6-1}$ • **Subtract the exponents of the like bases.**

$= rt^5$

HOW TO 3 Simplify: $\frac{p^7}{z^4}$

Because the bases are not the same, $\frac{p^7}{z^4}$ is already in simplest form.

Recall that for any number a, $a \neq 0$, $\frac{a}{a} = 1$. This property is true for exponential expressions as well. For example, for $x \neq 0$, $\frac{x^4}{x^4} = 1$.

This expression also can be simplified using the rule for dividing exponential expressions with the same base.

$$\frac{x^4}{x^4} = x^{4-4} = x^0$$

Because $\frac{x^4}{x^4} = 1$ and $\frac{x^4}{x^4} = x^0$, the following definition of zero as an exponent is used.

Take Note

In the example at the right, we indicate that $a \neq 0$. If we try to evaluate $(12a^3)^0$ when $a = 0$, we get $[12(0)^3]^0 = [12(0)]^0 = 0^0$. However, 0^0 is not defined. Therefore, we must assume that $a \neq 0$. To avoid stating this restriction for every example or exercise, we will assume that variables do not take on values that result in the expression 0^0.

Definition of Zero as an Exponent

If $x \neq 0$, then $x^0 = 1$. The expression 0^0 is not defined.

EXAMPLE

Simplify: $(12a^3)^0$, $a \neq 0$

Any nonzero expression to the zero power is 1. $(12a^3)^0 = 1$

HOW TO 4 Simplify: $-(4x^3y^7)^0$

$-(4x^3y^7)^0 = -(1) = -1$

The meaning of a negative exponent can be developed by examining the quotient $\frac{x^4}{x^6}$.

The expression can be simplified by writing the numerator and denominator in factored form, dividing by the common factors, and then writing the result with an exponent.

$$\frac{x^4}{x^6} = \frac{\overset{1}{\cancel{x}} \cdot \overset{1}{\cancel{x}} \cdot \overset{1}{\cancel{x}} \cdot \overset{1}{\cancel{x}}}{\underset{1}{\cancel{x}} \cdot \underset{1}{\cancel{x}} \cdot \underset{1}{\cancel{x}} \cdot \underset{1}{\cancel{x}} \cdot x \cdot x} = \frac{1}{x^2}$$

Now simplify the same expression by subtracting the exponents of the like bases.

$$\frac{x^4}{x^6} = x^{4-6} = x^{-2}$$

Because $\frac{x^4}{x^6} = \frac{1}{x^2}$ and $\frac{x^4}{x^6} = x^{-2}$, the expressions $\frac{1}{x^2}$ and x^{-2} must be equal. This leads to the following definition of a negative exponent.

Point of Interest

In the 15th century, the expression $12^{2\overline{m}}$ was used to mean $12x^{-2}$. The use of $\overline{m}$ reflected an Italian influence. In Italy, *m* was used for minus and *p* was used for plus. It was understood that $2\overline{m}$ referred to an unnamed variable. Issac Newton, in the 17th century, advocated the negative exponent notation that we currently use.

Definition of a Negative Exponent

If $x \neq 0$ and *n* is a positive integer, then

$$x^{-n} = \frac{1}{x^n} \quad \text{and} \quad \frac{1}{x^{-n}} = x^n$$

EXAMPLES

In each example below, simplify the expression by writing it with a positive exponent.

1. $x^{-10} = \frac{1}{x^{10}}$ **2.** $\frac{1}{a^{-5}} = a^5$

An exponential expression is in simplest form when it is written with only positive exponents.

Take Note

Note from HOW TO 5 at the right that 2^{-4} is a *positive* number. A negative exponent does not change the sign of a number.

HOW TO 5 Evaluate 2^{-4}.

$2^{-4} = \frac{1}{2^4}$ • Use the Definition of a Negative Exponent.

$= \frac{1}{16}$ • Evaluate the expression.

Take Note

For the expression $3n^{-5}$, the exponent on *n* is -5 (*negative* 5). The n^{-5} is written in the denominator as n^5. The exponent on 3 is 1 (*positive* 1). The 3 remains in the numerator. Also, we indicated that $n \neq 0$. This is done because division by zero is not defined. In this textbook, we will assume that values of the variables are chosen so that division by zero does not occur.

HOW TO 6 Simplify: $3n^{-5}$, $n \neq 0$

$3n^{-5} = 3 \cdot \frac{1}{n^5} = \frac{3}{n^5}$ • Use the Definition of a Negative Exponent to rewrite the expression with a positive exponent.

HOW TO 7 Simplify: $\frac{2}{5a^{-4}}$

$\frac{2}{5a^{-4}} = \frac{2}{5} \cdot \frac{1}{a^{-4}} = \frac{2}{5} \cdot a^4 = \frac{2a^4}{5}$ • Use the Definition of a Negative Exponent to rewrite the expression with a positive exponent.

Now that negative exponents have been defined, the Rule for Dividing Exponential Expressions can be stated.

Rule for Dividing Exponential Expressions

If m and n are integers and $x \neq 0$, then $\frac{x^m}{x^n} = x^{m-n}$.

EXAMPLES

Simplify each expression below by using the Rule for Dividing Exponential Expressions.

1. $\frac{x^3}{x^5} = x^{3-5} = x^{-2} = \frac{1}{x^2}$
2. $\frac{y^6}{y^{-2}} = y^{6-(-2)} = y^8$
3. $\frac{b^{-5}}{b^{-1}} = b^{-5-(-1)} = b^{-4} = \frac{1}{b^4}$
4. $\frac{a^{-4}}{a^{-7}} = a^{-4-(-7)} = a^3$

HOW TO 8 Evaluate $\frac{5^{-2}}{5}$.

$\frac{5^{-2}}{5} = 5^{-2-1} = 5^{-3}$ • Use the Rule for Dividing Exponential Expressions.

$= \frac{1}{5^3} = \frac{1}{125}$ • Use the Definition of a Negative Exponent to rewrite the expression with a positive exponent. Then evaluate.

The expression $\left(\frac{x^4}{y^3}\right)^2$, $y \neq 0$, can be simplified by squaring $\frac{x^4}{y^3}$ or by multiplying each exponent in the quotient by the exponent outside the parentheses.

$$\left(\frac{x^4}{y^3}\right)^2 = \left(\frac{x^4}{y^3}\right)\left(\frac{x^4}{y^3}\right) = \frac{x^4 \cdot x^4}{y^3 \cdot y^3} = \frac{x^{4+4}}{y^{3+3}} = \frac{x^8}{y^6} \qquad \left(\frac{x^4}{y^3}\right)^2 = \frac{x^{4\cdot 2}}{y^{3\cdot 2}} = \frac{x^8}{y^6}$$

Rule for Simplifying the Power of a Quotient

If m, n, and p are integers and $y \neq 0$, then $\left(\frac{x^m}{y^n}\right)^p = \frac{x^{mp}}{y^{np}}$.

EXAMPLES

1. $\left(\frac{a^4}{b^6}\right)^3 = \frac{a^{12}}{b^{18}}$
2. $\left(\frac{5}{7}\right)^2 = \frac{5^2}{7^2} = \frac{25}{49}$

Take Note

As a reminder, although it is not stated, we are assuming that $a \neq 0$ and $b \neq 0$. This assumption is made to ensure that we do not divide by zero.

HOW TO 9 Simplify: $\left(\frac{a^3}{b^2}\right)^{-2}$

$\left(\frac{a^3}{b^2}\right)^{-2} = \frac{a^{3(-2)}}{b^{2(-2)}}$ • Use the **Rule for Simplifying the Power of a Quotient.**

$= \frac{a^{-6}}{b^{-4}} = \frac{b^4}{a^6}$ • Use the **Definition of a Negative Exponent** to write the expression with positive exponents.

HOW TO 9 above suggests the following rule.

Rule for Negative Exponents on Fractional Expressions

If $x \neq 0$, $y \neq 0$, and n is a positive integer, then $\left(\frac{x}{y}\right)^{-n} = \left(\frac{y}{x}\right)^n$.

EXAMPLES

1. $\left(\frac{3}{5}\right)^{-2} = \left(\frac{5}{3}\right)^2 = \frac{25}{9}$

2. $\left(\frac{a^4}{b^7}\right)^{-3} = \left(\frac{b^7}{a^4}\right)^3 = \frac{b^{21}}{a^{12}}$

The rules for simplifying exponential expressions and powers of exponential expressions are true for all integers. These rules are restated here.

Rules of Exponents

If m, n, and p are integers, then

$x^m \cdot x^n = x^{m+n}$ $\quad (x^m)^n = x^{mn}$ $\quad (x^m y^n)^p = x^{mp}y^{np}$

$\frac{x^m}{x^n} = x^{m-n}, x \neq 0$ $\quad \left(\frac{x^m}{y^n}\right)^p = \frac{x^{mp}}{y^{np}}, y \neq 0$ $\quad x^{-n} = \frac{1}{x^n}, x \neq 0$

$x^0 = 1, x \neq 0$

INSTRUCTOR NOTE

Examples such as HOW TO 10 are included to review the work on multiplying monomials and to demonstrate that negative exponents can be used in simplifying products of exponential expressions.

HOW TO 10 Simplify: $(3ab^{-4})(-2a^{-3}b^7)$

$(3ab^{-4})(-2a^{-3}b^7) = [3 \cdot (-2)](a^{1+(-3)}b^{-4+7})$ • When multiplying exponential expressions, **add the exponents on like bases.**

$= -6a^{-2}b^3$

$= -\frac{6b^3}{a^2}$

INSTRUCTOR NOTE

There are a few different ways to simplify the expression in HOW TO 11. Students can simplify the expression by starting as follows:

$$\left(\frac{6m^2n^3}{8m^7n^2}\right)^{-3} = \left(\frac{8m^7n^2}{6m^2n^3}\right)^{3}$$

This method uses the Rule for Negative Exponents on Fractional Expressions first.

HOW TO 11 Simplify: $\left[\frac{6m^2n^3}{8m^7n^2}\right]^{-3}$

$\left[\frac{6m^2n^3}{8m^7n^2}\right]^{-3} = \left[\frac{3m^{2-7}n^{3-2}}{4}\right]^{-3}$ • Simplify inside the brackets.

$= \left[\frac{3m^{-5}n}{4}\right]^{-3}$ • Subtract the exponents.

$= \frac{3^{-3}m^{15}n^{-3}}{4^{-3}}$ • Use the Rule for Simplifying the Power of a Quotient.

$= \frac{4^3m^{15}}{3^3n^3} = \frac{64m^{15}}{27n^3}$ • Use the Definition of a Negative Exponent to rewrite the expression with positive exponents. Then simplify.

HOW TO 12 Simplify: $\frac{4a^{-2}b^5}{6a^5b^2}$

$\frac{4a^{-2}b^5}{6a^5b^2} = \frac{2a^{-2}b^5}{3a^5b^2}$ • Divide the coefficients by their common factor.

$= \frac{2a^{-2-5}b^{5-2}}{3}$ • Use the Rule for Dividing Exponential Expressions.

$= \frac{2a^{-7}b^3}{3} = \frac{2b^3}{3a^7}$ • Use the Definition of a Negative Exponent to rewrite the expression with positive exponents.

EXAMPLE 1

Simplify: $(-2x)(3x^{-2})^{-3}$

Solution

$(-2x)(3x^{-2})^{-3} = (-2x)(3^{-3}x^6)$

$= \frac{-2x^{1+6}}{3^3}$ • Rule for Simplifying the Power of a Product

$= -\frac{2x^7}{27}$

YOU TRY IT 1

Simplify: $(-2x^2)(x^{-3}y^{-4})^{-2}$

Your solution

$-2x^8y^8$

EXAMPLE 2

Simplify: $\frac{(2r^2t^{-1})^{-3}}{(r^{-3}t^4)^2}$

Solution

$\frac{(2r^2t^{-1})^{-3}}{(r^{-3}t^4)^2} = \frac{2^{-3}r^{-6}t^3}{r^{-6}t^8}$ • Rule for Simplifying the Power of a Product

$= 2^{-3}r^{-6-(-6)}t^{3-8}$ • Rule for Dividing Exponential Expressions

$= 2^{-3}r^0t^{-5}$

$= \frac{1}{2^3t^5} = \frac{1}{8t^5}$ • Write the answer in simplest form.

YOU TRY IT 2

Simplify: $\frac{(6a^{-2}b^3)^{-1}}{(4a^3b^{-2})^{-2}}$

Your solution

$\frac{8a^8}{3b^7}$

Solutions on p. S22

EXAMPLE 3

Simplify: $\left[\dfrac{4a^{-2}b^3}{6a^4b^{-2}}\right]^{-3}$

Solution

$$\left[\frac{4a^{-2}b^3}{6a^4b^{-2}}\right]^{-3} = \left[\frac{2a^{-6}b^5}{3}\right]^{-3}$$
• Simplify inside the brackets.

$$= \frac{2^{-3}a^{18}b^{-15}}{3^{-3}}$$
• Rule for Simplifying the Power of a Quotient

$$= \frac{27a^{18}}{8b^{15}}$$
• Write the answer in simplest form.

YOU TRY IT 3

Simplify: $\left[\dfrac{6r^3s^{-3}}{9r^3s^{-1}}\right]^{-2}$

Your solution

$\dfrac{9s^4}{4}$

Solution on p. S22

IN-CLASS EXAMPLES

Simplify.

1. $(-3x^4y^{-5})(-2x^{-3}y^{-1})$ $\quad \dfrac{6x}{y^6}$
2. $\dfrac{3x^{-1}y^4}{6^{-1}x^3y^{-2}}$ $\quad \dfrac{18y^6}{x^4}$
3. $\left(\dfrac{8a^{-3}b^{-1}c^2}{12a^3b^{-3}c^{-2}}\right)^{-2}$ $\quad \dfrac{9a^{12}}{4b^4c^8}$

OBJECTIVE B *To write a number in scientific notation*

Very large and very small numbers are encountered in the fields of science and engineering. For example, the charge of an electron is 0.000000000000000000160 coulomb. These numbers can be written more easily in scientific notation. In **scientific notation,** a number is expressed as the product of two factors, one a number between 1 and 10, and the other a power of 10.

To change a number written in decimal notation to scientific notation, write it in the form $a \times 10^n$, where a is a number between 1 and 10, and n is an integer.

For numbers greater than 10, move the decimal point to the right of the first digit. The exponent is positive and equal to the number of places the decimal point has been moved.

$240{,}000 = 2.4 \times 10^5$

$93{,}000{,}000 = 9.3 \times 10^7$

For numbers less than 1, move the decimal point to the right of the first nonzero digit. The exponent n is negative. The absolute value of the exponent is equal to the number of places the decimal point has been moved.

$0.00030 = 3 \times 10^{-4}$

$0.0000832 = 8.32 \times 10^{-5}$

Point of Interest

An electron microscope uses wavelengths that are approximately 4×10^{-12} meter to make images of viruses.

The human eye can detect wavelengths between 4.3×10^{-7} meter and 6.9×10^{-7} meter. Although these wavelengths are very short, they are approximately 10^5 times longer than the wavelengths used in an electron microscope.

Look at the last example above: $0.0000832 = 8.32 \times 10^{-5}$. Using the Definition of Negative Exponents,

$$10^{-5} = \frac{1}{10^5} = \frac{1}{100{,}000} = 0.00001$$

Because $10^{-5} = 0.00001$, we can write

$$8.32 \times 10^{-5} = 8.32 \times 0.00001 = 0.0000832$$

which is the number we started with. We have not changed the value of the number; we have just written it in another form.

Changing a number written in scientific notation to decimal notation also requires moving the decimal point.

When the exponent on 10 is positive, move the decimal point to the right the same number of places as the exponent.

$3.45 \times 10^9 = 3,450,000,000$

$2.3 \times 10^8 = 230,000,000$

When the exponent on 10 is negative, move the decimal point to the left the same number of places as the absolute value of the exponent.

$8.1 \times 10^{-3} = 0.0081$

$6.34 \times 10^{-6} = 0.00000634$

EXAMPLE 4

Write the number 824,300,000 in scientific notation.

Solution

$824,300,000 > 10$
Move the decimal point 8 places to the left.
The exponent on 10 will be positive.

$824,300,000 = 8.243 \times 10^8$

YOU TRY IT 4

Write the number 290,000,000,000 in scientific notation.

Your solution

2.9×10^{11}

EXAMPLE 5

Write the number 0.0000000065 in scientific notation.

Solution

$0.0000000065 < 1$
Move the decimal point 9 places to the right.
The exponent on 10 will be negative.

$0.0000000065 = 6.5 \times 10^{-9}$

YOU TRY IT 5

Write the number 0.000000961 in scientific notation.

Your solution

9.61×10^{-7}

EXAMPLE 6

Write the number 3.9785×10^{10} in decimal notation.

Solution

The exponent on 10 is positive.
Move the decimal point 10 places to the right.

$3.9785 \times 10^{10} = 39,785,000,000$

YOU TRY IT 6

Write the number 7.329×10^6 in decimal notation.

Your solution

7,329,000

EXAMPLE 7

Write the number 6.8×10^{-9} in decimal notation.

Solution

The exponent on 10 is negative.
Move the decimal point 9 places to the left.

$6.8 \times 10^{-9} = 0.0000000068$

YOU TRY IT 7

Write the number 1.802×10^{-12} in decimal notation.

Your solution

0.000000000001802

IN-CLASS EXAMPLES

4. Write the number 0.00394 in scientific notation. **3.94×10^{-3}**
5. Write the number 3.8×10^4 in decimal notation. **38,000**

Solutions on p. S22

9.4 EXERCISES

Concept Check

SUGGESTED ASSIGNMENT: Exercises 1–14; Exercises 15–105, every other odd; Exercises 113–129, odds; Exercises 133–143, odds; More challenging exercises: Exercises 149–153, odds

1. Explain how to rewrite a variable that has a negative exponent as an expression with a positive exponent.

2. Why might a number be written in scientific notation instead of decimal notation?

For Exercises 3 to 8, determine whether the statement is true or false.

3. The expression $\frac{x^5}{y^3}$ can be simplified by subtracting the exponents. False

4. The rules of exponents can be applied to expressions that contain an exponent of zero or contain negative exponents. True

5. The expression 3^{-2} represents the reciprocal of 3^2. True

6. $5x^0 = 0$ False

7. The expression 4^{-3} represents a negative number. False

8. To be in simplest form, an exponential expression cannot contain any negative exponents. True

9. As long as x is not zero, x^0 is defined to be equal to __1__. Using this definition, $3^0 =$ __1__, $(7x^3)^0 =$ __1__, and $-2x^0 =$ __-2__.

10. A number is written in scientific notation if it is written as the product of a number between __1__ and __10__ and an integer power of __10__.

For Exercises 11 to 14, determine whether the number is written in scientific notation. If not, explain why not.

11. 39.4×10^3
No. 39.4 is not between 1 and 10.

12. 0.8×10^{-6}
No. 0.8 is not between 1 and 10.

13. $7.1 \times 10^{2.4}$
No. 2.4 is not an integer.

14. 5.8×10^{-132}
Yes

OBJECTIVE A *To divide monomials*

For Exercises 15 to 50, simplify.

15. $\frac{y^7}{y^3}$
y^4

16. $\frac{z^9}{z^2}$
z^7

17. $\frac{a^8}{a^5}$
a^3

18. $\frac{c^{12}}{c^5}$
c^7

19. $\frac{p^5}{p}$
p^4

20. $\frac{w^9}{w}$
w^8

21. $\frac{4x^8}{2x^5}$
$2x^3$

22. $\frac{12z^7}{4z^3}$
$3z^4$

23. $\frac{22k^5}{11k^4}$ $2k$

24. $\frac{14m^{11}}{7m^{10}}$ $2m$

25. $\frac{m^9n^7}{m^4n^5}$ m^5n^2

26. $\frac{y^5z^6}{yz^3}$ y^4z^3

27. $\frac{6r^4}{4r^2}$ $\frac{3r^2}{2}$

28. $\frac{8x^9}{12x^6}$ $\frac{2x^3}{3}$

29. $\frac{-16a^7}{24a^6}$ $-\frac{2a}{3}$

30. $\frac{-18b^5}{27b^4}$ $-\frac{2b}{3}$

31. $\frac{y^3}{y^8}$ $\frac{1}{y^5}$

32. $\frac{z^4}{z^6}$ $\frac{1}{z^2}$

33. $\frac{a^5}{a^{11}}$ $\frac{1}{a^6}$

34. $\frac{m}{m^7}$ $\frac{1}{m^6}$

35. $\frac{4x^2}{12x^5}$ $\frac{1}{3x^3}$

36. $\frac{6y^8}{8y^9}$ $\frac{3}{4y}$

37. $\frac{-12x}{-18x^6}$ $\frac{2}{3x^5}$

38. $\frac{-24c^2}{-36c^{11}}$ $\frac{2}{3c^9}$

39. $\frac{x^6y^5}{x^8y}$ $\frac{y^4}{x^2}$

40. $\frac{a^3b^2}{a^2b^3}$ $\frac{a}{b}$

41. $\frac{2m^6n^2}{5m^9n^{10}}$ $\frac{2}{5m^3n^8}$

42. $\frac{5r^3t^7}{6r^5t^7}$ $\frac{5}{6r^2}$

43. $\frac{pq^3}{p^4q^4}$ $\frac{1}{p^3q}$

44. $\frac{a^4b^5}{a^5b^6}$ $\frac{1}{ab}$

45. $\frac{3x^4y^5}{6x^4y^8}$ $\frac{1}{2y^3}$

46. $\frac{14a^3b^6}{21a^5b^6}$ $\frac{2}{3a^2}$

47. $\frac{14x^4y^6z^2}{16x^3y^9z}$ $\frac{7xz}{8y^3}$

48. $\frac{24a^2b^7c^9}{36a^7b^5c}$ $\frac{2b^2c^8}{3a^5}$

49. $\frac{15mn^9p^3}{30m^4n^9p}$ $\frac{p^2}{2m^3}$

50. $\frac{25x^4y^7z^2}{20x^5y^9z^{11}}$ $\frac{5}{4xy^2z^9}$

For Exercises 51 to 58, evaluate.

51. 5^{-2} $\frac{1}{25}$

52. 3^{-3} $\frac{1}{27}$

53. $\frac{1}{8^{-2}}$ 64

54. $\frac{1}{12^{-1}}$ 12

55. $\frac{3^{-2}}{3}$ $\frac{1}{27}$

56. $\frac{5^{-3}}{5}$ $\frac{1}{625}$

57. $\frac{2^{-2}}{2^{-3}}$ 2

58. $\frac{3^2}{3^2}$ 1

For Exercises 59 to 106, simplify.

59. x^{-2} $\frac{1}{x^2}$

60. y^{-10} $\frac{1}{y^{10}}$

61. $\frac{1}{a^{-6}}$ a^6

62. $\frac{1}{b^{-4}}$ b^4

63. $4x^{-7}$ $\frac{4}{x^7}$

64. $-6y^{-1}$ $-\frac{6}{y}$

65. $\frac{2}{3}z^{-2}$ $\frac{2}{3z^2}$

66. $\frac{4}{5}a^{-4}$ $\frac{4}{5a^4}$

67. $\dfrac{5}{b^{-8}}$

$5b^8$

68. $\dfrac{-3}{v^{-3}}$

$-3v^3$

69. $\dfrac{1}{3x^{-2}}$

$\dfrac{x^2}{3}$

70. $\dfrac{2}{5c^{-6}}$

$\dfrac{2c^6}{5}$

71. $(ab^5)^0$

1

72. $(32x^3y^4)^0$

1

73. $-(3p^2q^5)^0$

-1

74. $-\left(\dfrac{2}{3}xy\right)^0$

-1

75. $(-2xy^{-2})^3$

$-\dfrac{8x^3}{y^6}$

76. $(-3x^{-1}y^2)^2$

$\dfrac{9y^4}{x^2}$

77. $(3x^{-1}y^{-2})^2$

$\dfrac{9}{x^2y^4}$

78. $(5xy^{-3})^{-2}$

$\dfrac{y^6}{25x^2}$

79. $(2x^{-1})(x^{-3})$

$\dfrac{2}{x^4}$

80. $(-2x^{-5})x^7$

$-2x^2$

81. $(-5a^2)(a^{-5})^2$

$-\dfrac{5}{a^8}$

82. $(2a^{-3})(a^7b^{-1})^3$

$\dfrac{2a^{18}}{b^3}$

83. $(-2ab^{-2})(4a^{-2}b)^{-2}$

$-\dfrac{a^5}{8b^4}$

84. $(3ab^{-2})(2a^{-1}b)^{-3}$

$\dfrac{3a^4}{8b^5}$

85. $(-5x^{-2}y)(-2x^{-2}y^2)$

$\dfrac{10y^3}{x^4}$

86. $\dfrac{a^{-3}b^{-4}}{a^2b^2}$

$\dfrac{1}{a^5b^6}$

87. $\dfrac{3x^{-2}y^2}{6xy^2}$

$\dfrac{1}{2x^3}$

88. $\dfrac{2x^{-2}y}{8xy}$

$\dfrac{1}{4x^3}$

89. $\dfrac{3x^{-2}y}{xy}$

$\dfrac{3}{x^3}$

90. $\dfrac{2x^{-1}y^4}{x^2y^3}$

$\dfrac{2y}{x^3}$

91. $\dfrac{2x^{-1}y^{-4}}{4xy^2}$

$\dfrac{1}{2x^2y^6}$

92. $\dfrac{(x^{-1}y)^2}{xy^2}$

$\dfrac{1}{x^3}$

93. $\dfrac{(x^{-2}y)^2}{x^2y^3}$

$\dfrac{1}{x^6y}$

94. $\dfrac{(x^{-3}y^{-2})^2}{x^6y^8}$

$\dfrac{1}{x^{12}y^{12}}$

95. $\dfrac{(a^{-2}y^3)^{-3}}{a^2y}$

$\dfrac{a^4}{y^{10}}$

96. $\dfrac{12a^2b^3}{-27a^2b^2}$

$-\dfrac{4b}{9}$

97. $\dfrac{-16xy^4}{96x^4y^4}$

$-\dfrac{1}{6x^3}$

98. $\dfrac{-8x^2y^4}{44y^2z^5}$

$-\dfrac{2x^2y^2}{11z^5}$

99. $\dfrac{22a^2b^4}{-132b^3c^2}$

$-\dfrac{a^2b}{6c^2}$

100. $\dfrac{-(8a^2b^4)^3}{64a^3b^8}$

$-8a^3b^4$

101. $\dfrac{-(14ab^4)^2}{28a^4b^2}$

$-\dfrac{7b^6}{a^2}$

102. $\dfrac{(2a^{-2}b^3)^{-2}}{(4a^2b^{-4})^{-1}}$

$\dfrac{a^6}{b^{10}}$

103. $\dfrac{(3^{-1}r^4s^{-3})^{-2}}{(6r^2s^{-1}t^{-2})^2}$
$\dfrac{s^8t^4}{4r^{12}}$

104. $\left(\dfrac{6x^{-4}yz^{-1}}{14xy^{-4}z^2}\right)^{-3}$
$\dfrac{343x^{15}z^9}{27y^{15}}$

105. $\left(\dfrac{15m^3n^{-2}p^{-1}}{25m^{-2}n^{-4}}\right)^{-3}$
$\dfrac{125p^3}{27m^{15}n^6}$

106. $\left(\dfrac{18a^4b^{-2}c^4}{12ab^{-3}d^2}\right)^{-2}$
$\dfrac{4d^4}{9a^6b^2c^8}$

For Exercises 107 to 110, state whether the equation is true or false for all $a \neq 0$ and $b \neq 0$.

107. $\dfrac{a^{4n}}{a^n} = a^4$
False

108. $a^{n-m} = \dfrac{1}{a^{m-n}}$
True

109. $a^{-n}a^n = 1$
True

110. $\dfrac{a^n}{b^m} = \left(\dfrac{a}{b}\right)^{m-n}$
False

OBJECTIVE B *To write a number in scientific notation*

111. To write the number 354,000,000 in scientific notation, move the decimal point __8__ places to the __left__. The exponent on 10 is __8__.

112. To write the number 0.0000000086 in scientific notation, move the decimal point __9__ places to the __right__. The exponent on 10 is __−9__.

For Exercises 113 to 121, write in scientific notation.

113. 0.00000000324
3.24×10^{-9}

114. 0.00000012
1.2×10^{-7}

115. 0.000000000000000003
3×10^{-18}

116. 1,800,000,000
1.8×10^9

117. 32,000,000,000,000,000
3.2×10^{16}

118. 76,700,000,000,000
7.67×10^{13}

119. 0.000000000000000000122
1.22×10^{-19}

120. 0.00137
1.37×10^{-3}

121. 547,000,000
5.47×10^8

For Exercises 122 to 130, write in decimal notation.

122. 2.3×10^{-12}
0.0000000000023

123. 1.67×10^{-4}
0.000167

124. 2×10^{15}
2,000,000,000,000,000

125. 6.8×10^7
68,000,000

126. 9×10^{-21}
0.000000000000000000009

127. 3.05×10^{-5}
0.0000305

128. 9.05×10^{11}
905,000,000,000

129. 1.02×10^{-9}
0.00000000102

130. 7.2×10^{-3}
0.0072

131. If n is a negative integer, how many zeros appear after the decimal point when 1.35×10^n is written in decimal notation? $-n - 1$

132. If n is a positive integer greater than 1, how many zeros appear before the decimal point when 1.35×10^n is written in decimal notation? $n - 2$

133. **Technology** See the news clipping at the right. Express in scientific notation the thickness, in meters, of the memristor.
1.5×10^{-8} m

In the NEWS!

HP Introduces the Memristor

Hewlett Packard has announced the design of the *memristor,* a new memory technology with the potential to be much smaller than the memory chips used in today's computers. HP has made a memristor with a thickness of 0.000000015 m (15 nanometers).

Source: The New York Times

134. **Astronomy** Astrophysicists estimate that the radius of the Milky Way galaxy is 1,000,000,000,000,000,000,000 m. Write this number in scientific notation.
1×10^{21}

135. **Geology** The mass of Earth is 5,980,000,000,000,000,000,000,000 kg. Write this number in scientific notation.
5.98×10^{24}

136. **Physics** Carbon nanotubes, made from extremely strong cylinders of carbon atoms, have remarkable properties. Nanotubes with a diameter of 0.0000000004 m have been created. Write this number in scientific notation.
4×10^{-10}

137. **Biology** The weight of a single *E. coli* bacterium is 0.000000000000665 g. Write this number in scientific notation.
6.65×10^{-13}

Great Pyramid of Khufu

138. **Archeology** The weight of the Great Pyramid of Khufu is estimated to be 12,000,000,000 lb. Write this number in scientific notation.
1.2×10^{10}

139. **Food Science** The frequency (in oscillations per second) of a microwave generated by a microwave oven is approximately 2,450,000,000 hertz. (One hertz is one oscillation in 1 s.) Write this number in scientific notation.
2.45×10^{9}

140. **Astronomy** One light-year is the distance traveled by light in one year. One light-year is 5,880,000,000,000 mi. Write this number in scientific notation.
5.88×10^{12}

141. **Biophysics** Biologists and physicists are working together to measure the mass of a virus. Currently, a virus with a mass of 0.00000000000000000039 g can be measured. Write this number in scientific notation.
3.9×10^{-19}

142. **Astronomy** See the news clipping at the right. WASP-12b orbits a star that is 5.1156×10^{15} mi from Earth. (*Source:* news.yahoo.com) Write this number in decimal notation.
5,115,600,000,000,000

In the NEWS!

Hottest Planet Ever Discovered

A planet called WASP-12b is the hottest planet ever discovered, at about 4000°F. It orbits its star faster than any other known planet, completing a revolution once a day.

Source: news.yahoo.com

143. **Physics** Light travels approximately 16,000,000,000 mi in one day. Write this number in scientific notation.
1.6×10^{10}

144. **Electricity** The electric charge on an electron is 0.00000000000000000016 coulomb. Write this number in scientific notation.
1.6×10^{-19}

Critical Thinking

145. Evaluate $8^{-2} + 2^{-5}$. $\frac{3}{64}$

146. Evaluate $9^{-2} + 3^{-3}$. $\frac{4}{81}$

147. Evaluate 2^x and 2^{-x} when $x = -2, -1, 0, 1$, and 2.
$\frac{1}{4}, \frac{1}{2}, 1, 2, 4; 4, 2, 1, \frac{1}{2}, \frac{1}{4}$

148. Evaluate 3^x and 3^{-x} when $x = -2, -1, 0, 1$, and 2.
$\frac{1}{9}, \frac{1}{3}, 1, 3, 9; 9, 3, 1, \frac{1}{3}, \frac{1}{9}$

For Exercises 149 and 150, write in decimal notation.

149. 2^{-4} 0.0625

150. 25^{-2} 0.0016

For Exercises 151 and 152, complete.

151. If $m = n$ and $a \neq 0$, then $\frac{a^m}{a^n} =$ ___1___.

152. If $m = n + 1$ and $a \neq 0$, then $\frac{a^m}{a^n} =$ ___a___.

For Exercises 153 and 154, solve.

153. $(-4.8)^x = 1$ 0

154. $-6.3^x = -1$ 0

155. If x is a nonzero real number, is x^{-2} always positive, always negative, or positive or negative depending on whether x is positive or negative? Explain your answer.

156. If x is a nonzero real number, is x^{-3} always positive, always negative, or positive or negative depending on whether x is positive or negative? Explain your answer.

QUICK QUIZ

1. Evaluate 9^{-2}. $\frac{1}{81}$ [9.4A]
2. Simplify: $4x^{-3}$ $\frac{4}{x^3}$ [9.4A]
3. Simplify: $\frac{3^{-1}x^3y^2z^{-2}}{x^{-2}y^{-3}z^2}$ $\frac{x^5y^5}{3z^4}$ [9.4A]
4. Write in scientific notation.
   a. 41,300,000,000 4.13×10^{10}
   b. 0.000327 3.27×10^{-4} [9.4B]
5. Write in decimal notation.
   a. 2.4×10^{-5} 0.000024
   b. 5.76×10^6 5,760,000 [9.4B]

Projects or Group Activities

157. Population and Land Allocation In this project, you are asked to determine hypothetical land allocation for the world's population today. Use the figure 7×10^9 for the current world population and the figure 3.1×10^8 for the current U.S. population. (*Source:* www.infoplease.com) One square mile is approximately 2.8×10^7 ft^2.

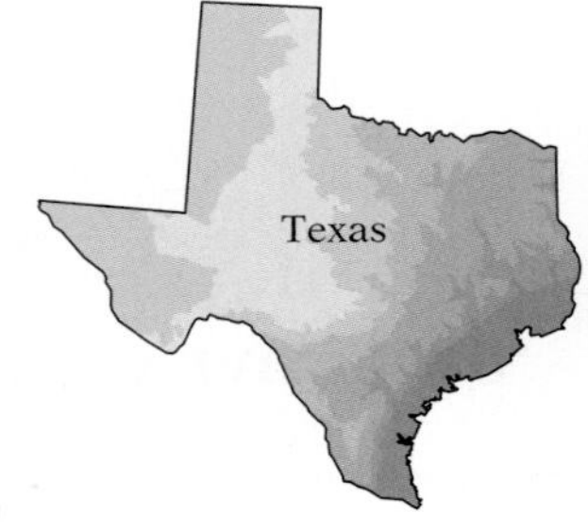

a. If every person in the world moved to Texas and each person were given an equal amount of land, how many square feet of land would each person have? The area of Texas is 2.619×10^5 mi^2. 1047.6 ft^2

Rhode Island

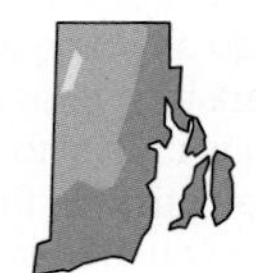

b. If every person in the United States moved to Rhode Island and each person were given an equal amount of land, how many square feet of land would each person have? The area of Rhode Island is 1.0×10^3 mi^2. Round to the nearest whole number. 90 ft^2

c. Suppose every person in the world were given a plot of land the size of a two-car garage (22 ft × 22 ft).

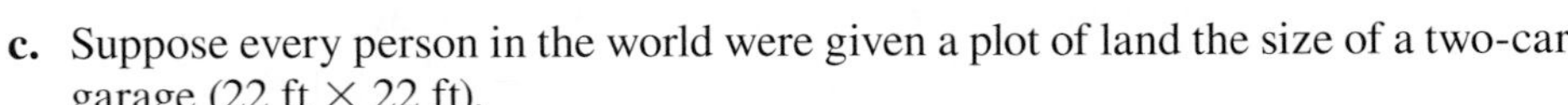

i. How many people would fit in a square mile? Round to the nearest hundred. 57,900 people

ii. How many square miles would be required to accommodate the entire world population? Round to the nearest hundred. 120,900 mi^2

d. If the total land area of Earth were divided equally, how many acres of land would each person be allocated? Use a figure of 5.7×10^7 mi^2 for the land area of Earth. One acre is 43,560 ft^2. Round to the nearest tenth. 5.2 acres

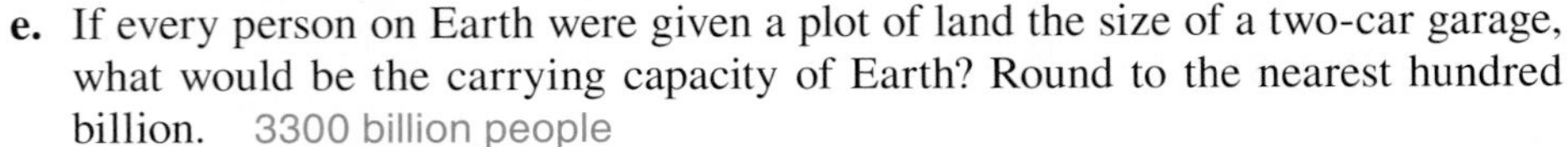

e. If every person on Earth were given a plot of land the size of a two-car garage, what would be the carrying capacity of Earth? Round to the nearest hundred billion. 3300 billion people

SECTION

9.5 Division of Polynomials

OBJECTIVE A *To divide a polynomial by a monomial*

To divide a polynomial by a monomial, divide each term in the numerator by the denominator and write the sum of the quotients.

HOW TO 1 Divide: $\dfrac{6x^3 - 3x^2 + 9x}{3x}$

$$\frac{6x^3 - 3x^2 + 9x}{3x} = \frac{6x^3}{3x} - \frac{3x^2}{3x} + \frac{9x}{3x}$$ • Divide each term of the polynomial by the monomial.

$$= 2x^2 - x + 3$$ • Simplify each term.

EXAMPLE 1

Divide: $\dfrac{12x^2y - 6xy + 4x^2}{2xy}$

Solution

$$\frac{12x^2y - 6xy + 4x^2}{2xy} = \frac{12x^2y}{2xy} - \frac{6xy}{2xy} + \frac{4x^2}{2xy}$$

$$= 6x - 3 + \frac{2x}{y}$$

YOU TRY IT 1

Divide: $\dfrac{24x^2y^2 - 18xy + 6y}{6xy}$

Your solution

$4xy - 3 + \dfrac{1}{x}$

IN-CLASS EXAMPLES

Divide.

1. $\dfrac{18x^2y - 6xy + 12y}{6xy}$ $3x - 1 + \dfrac{2}{x}$
2. $\dfrac{24a^2b^2 + 16ab - 4b}{8ab}$ $3ab + 2 - \dfrac{1}{2a}$

Solution on p. S22

OBJECTIVE B *To divide polynomials*

Tips for Success

An important element of success is practice. We cannot do anything well if we do not practice it repeatedly. Practice is crucial to success in mathematics. In this objective you are learning a new skill, how to divide polynomials. You will need to practice this skill over and over again in order to be successful at it.

INSTRUCTOR NOTE

It may help some students if you start with the division algorithm for whole numbers and show them that a similar procedure is used to divide polynomials. Consider using 676 ÷ 21 as an example.

The procedure for dividing two polynomials is similar to the one for dividing whole numbers. The same equation used to check division of whole numbers is used to check polynomial division: **(Quotient × divisor) + remainder = dividend.**

HOW TO 2 Divide: $(x^2 - 5x + 8) \div (x - 3)$

Step 1

$$\begin{array}{r} x \phantom{{}-5x+8} \\ x-3\overline{)x^2 - 5x + 8} \\ \underline{x^2 - 3x} \phantom{{}+8} \\ -2x + 8 \end{array}$$

• Think: $x\overline{)x^2} = \dfrac{x^2}{x} = x$

• Multiply: $x(x - 3) = x^2 - 3x$

• Subtract: $(x^2 - 5x) - (x^2 - 3x) = -2x$ Bring down the 8.

Step 2

$$\begin{array}{r} x - 2 \\ x-3\overline{)x^2 - 5x + 8} \\ \underline{x^2 - 3x} \phantom{{}+8} \\ -2x + 8 \\ \underline{-2x + 6} \\ 2 \end{array}$$

• Think: $x\overline{)-2x} = \dfrac{-2x}{x} = -2$

• Multiply: $-2(x - 3) = -2x + 6$

• Subtract: $(-2x + 8) - (-2x + 6) = 2$

Check: $(x - 2)(x - 3) + 2 = x^2 - 5x + 6 + 2 = x^2 - 5x + 8$

$(x^2 - 5x + 8) \div (x - 3) = x - 2 + \dfrac{2}{x - 3}$

Take Note

Recall that a fraction bar means "divided by." Therefore, 6 ÷ 2 can be written $\frac{6}{2}$, and $a \div b$ can be written $\frac{a}{b}$.

INSTRUCTOR NOTE

Students are comfortable writing the answer to 15 ÷ 4 as $3\frac{3}{4}$, which is $3 + \frac{3}{4}$. Tell students that this is the form in which a remainder of a quotient of polynomials is written.

If a term is missing from the dividend, a zero can be inserted for that term. This helps keep like terms in the same column.

HOW TO 3 Divide: $\dfrac{6x + 26 + 2x^3}{2 + x}$

$\dfrac{2x^3 + 6x + 26}{x + 2}$ • **Arrange the terms of each polynomial in descending order.**

$$\begin{array}{r} 2x^2 - 4x + 14 \\ x + 2\overline{)2x^3 + 0 \quad + 6x + 26} \\ \underline{2x^3 + 4x^2} \qquad\qquad\quad \\ -4x^2 + 6x \qquad \\ \underline{-4x^2 - 8x} \qquad \\ 14x + 26 \\ \underline{14x + 28} \\ -2 \end{array}$$

• **There is no x^2 term in $2x^3 + 6x + 26$. Insert a zero for the missing term.**

Check:

$(2x^2 - 4x + 14)(x + 2) + (-2) = (2x^3 + 6x + 28) + (-2) = 2x^3 + 6x + 26$

$(2x^3 + 6x + 26) \div (x + 2) = 2x^2 - 4x + 14 - \dfrac{2}{x + 2}$

EXAMPLE 2

Divide: $(8x^2 + 4x^3 + x - 4) \div (2x + 3)$

Solution

$$\begin{array}{r} 2x^2 + x - 1 \\ 2x + 3\overline{)4x^3 + 8x^2 + x - 4} \\ \underline{4x^3 + 6x^2} \qquad\quad \\ 2x^2 + x \qquad \\ \underline{2x^2 + 3x} \qquad \\ -2x - 4 \\ \underline{-2x - 3} \\ -1 \end{array}$$

• **Write the dividend in descending powers of x.**

$(4x^3 + 8x^2 + x - 4) \div (2x + 3)$

$= 2x^2 + x - 1 - \dfrac{1}{2x + 3}$

YOU TRY IT 2

Divide: $(2x^3 + x^2 - 8x - 3) \div (2x - 3)$

Your solution

$x^2 + 2x - 1 - \dfrac{6}{2x - 3}$

EXAMPLE 3

Divide: $\dfrac{x^2 - 1}{x + 1}$

Solution

$$\begin{array}{r} x - 1 \\ x + 1\overline{)x^2 + 0 - 1} \\ \underline{x^2 + x} \qquad \\ -x - 1 \\ \underline{-x - 1} \\ 0 \end{array}$$

• **Insert a zero for the missing term.**

$(x^2 - 1) \div (x + 1) = x - 1$

YOU TRY IT 3

Divide: $\dfrac{x^3 - 2x + 1}{x - 1}$

Your solution

$x^2 + x - 1$

IN-CLASS EXAMPLES

Divide.

3. $(6x^3 + x^2 - 18x + 10) \div (3x - 4)$
   $2x^2 + 3x - 2 + \dfrac{2}{3x - 4}$
4. $\dfrac{x^3 - x - 6}{x - 2}$ $x^2 + 2x + 3$

Solutions on p. S23

9.5 EXERCISES

SUGGESTED ASSIGNMENT:
Exercises 1–6; Exercises 7–29, odds; Exercises 33–51, odds

Concept Check

1. Every division equation has a related multiplication equation. For instance, $\frac{16}{2} = 8$ means that $16 = 2 \cdot 8$. What is the related multiplication equation for $\frac{15x^2 + 12x}{3x} = 5x + 4$? $15x^2 + 12x = 3x(5x + 4)$

2. Given that $\frac{x^3 - x^2 + x - 1}{x - 1} = x^2 + 1$, name two factors of $x^3 - x^2 + x - 1$.
$x - 1$ and $x^2 + 1$

For Exercises 3 and 4, determine whether the statement is true or false.

3. $5\frac{2}{3} = 5 + \frac{2}{3}$ True

4. For $b \neq 0$, $a \div b = \frac{a}{b}$. True

For Exercises 5 and 6, complete to make a true statement.

5. $\frac{18y^5 + 3y}{3y} = \frac{18y^5}{\square} + \frac{3y}{\square} = \_\_\_\_\_ + \_\_\_\_\_$ $3y$; $3y$; $6y^4$; 1

6. $\frac{12x^3 - 8x^2}{4x^2} = \frac{\square}{4x^2} - \frac{\square}{4x^2} = \_\_\_\_\_ - \_\_\_\_\_$ $12x^3$; $8x^2$; $3x$; 2

OBJECTIVE A *To divide a polynomial by a monomial*

For Exercises 7 to 30, divide.

7. $\frac{10a - 25}{5}$ $2a - 5$

8. $\frac{16b - 40}{8}$ $2b - 5$

9. $\frac{3a^2 + 2a}{a}$ $3a + 2$

10. $\frac{6y^2 + 4y}{y}$ $6y + 4$

11. $\frac{3x^2 - 6x}{3x}$ $x - 2$

12. $\frac{10y^2 - 6y}{2y}$ $5y - 3$

13. $\frac{5x^2 - 10x}{-5x}$ $-x + 2$

14. $\frac{3y^2 - 27y}{-3y}$ $-y + 9$

15. $\frac{x^3 + 3x^2 - 5x}{x}$ $x^2 + 3x - 5$

16. $\frac{a^3 - 5a^2 + 7a}{a}$ $a^2 - 5a + 7$

17. $\frac{x^6 - 3x^4 - x^2}{x^2}$ $x^4 - 3x^2 - 1$

18. $\frac{a^8 - 5a^5 - 3a^3}{a^2}$ $a^6 - 5a^3 - 3a$

19. $\frac{5x^2y^2 + 10xy}{5xy}$ $xy + 2$

20. $\frac{8x^2y^2 - 24xy}{8xy}$ $xy - 3$

21. $\frac{9y^6 - 15y^3}{-3y^3}$ $-3y^3 + 5$

22. $\frac{4x^4 - 6x^2}{-2x^2}$ $-2x^2 + 3$

23. $\frac{3x^2 - 2x + 1}{x}$ $3x - 2 + \frac{1}{x}$

24. $\frac{8y^2 + 2y - 3}{y}$ $8y + 2 - \frac{3}{y}$

25. $\frac{-3x^2 + 7x - 6}{x}$ $-3x + 7 - \frac{6}{x}$

26. $\frac{2y^2 - 6y + 9}{y}$ $2y - 6 + \frac{9}{y}$

27. $\frac{16a^2b - 20ab + 24ab^2}{4ab}$ $4a - 5 + 6b$

28. $\frac{22a^2b + 11ab - 33ab^2}{11ab}$ $2a + 1 - 3b$

29. $\frac{9x^2y + 6xy - 3x}{xy}$ $9x + 6 - \frac{3}{y}$

30. $\frac{18a^2b^2 + 9ab - 6}{3ab}$ $6ab + 3 - \frac{2}{ab}$

31. How can multiplication be used to check that $\frac{8x^3 - 12x^2 - 4x}{4x} = 2x^2 - 3x - 1$?
Multiply $4x$ and $2x^2 - 3x - 1$. $4x(2x^2 - 3x - 1) = 8x^3 - 12x^2 - 4x$

OBJECTIVE B *To divide polynomials*

For Exercises 32 to 52, divide.

32. $(b^2 - 14b + 49) \div (b - 7)$
$b - 7$

33. $(x^2 - x - 6) \div (x - 3)$
$x + 2$

34. $(y^2 + 2y - 35) \div (y + 7)$
$y - 5$

35. $(2x^2 + 5x + 2) \div (x + 2)$
$2x + 1$

36. $(2y^2 + 7) \div (y - 3)$
$2y + 6 + \frac{25}{y - 3}$

37. $(x^2 + 1) \div (x - 1)$
$x + 1 + \frac{2}{x - 1}$

38. $(x^2 + 4) \div (x + 2)$
$x - 2 + \frac{8}{x + 2}$

39. $(6x^2 - 7x) \div (3x - 2)$
$2x - 1 - \frac{2}{3x - 2}$

40. $(a^2 + 5a + 10) \div (a + 2)$
$a + 3 + \frac{4}{a + 2}$

41. $(b^2 - 8b - 9) \div (b - 3)$
$b - 5 - \frac{24}{b - 3}$

42. $(2y^2 - 9y + 8) \div (2y + 3)$
$y - 6 + \frac{26}{2y + 3}$

43. $(3x^2 + 5x - 4) \div (x - 4)$
$3x + 17 + \frac{64}{x - 4}$

44. $(8x + 3 + 4x^2) \div (2x - 1)$
$2x + 5 + \frac{8}{2x - 1}$

45. $(10 + 21y + 10y^2) \div (2y + 3)$
$5y + 3 + \frac{1}{2y + 3}$

46. $(12a^2 - 7 - 25a) \div (3a - 7)$
$4a + 1$

47. $(5 - 23x + 12x^2) \div (4x - 1)$
$3x - 5$

48. $(24 + 6a^2 + 25a) \div (3a - 1)$
$2a + 9 + \frac{33}{3a - 1}$

49. $(3x^2 + x^3 + 8 + 5x) \div (x + 1)$
$x^2 + 2x + 3 + \frac{5}{x + 1}$

50. $(7x - 6x^2 + x^3 - 1) \div (x - 1)$
$x^2 - 5x + 2 + \frac{1}{x - 1}$

51. $(x^4 - x^2 - 6) \div (x^2 + 2)$
$x^2 - 3$

52. $(x^4 + 3x^2 - 10) \div (x^2 - 2)$
$x^2 + 5$

53. True or false? When a sixth-degree polynomial is divided by a third-degree polynomial, the quotient is a second-degree polynomial. False

Critical Thinking

54. The product of a monomial and $4b$ is $12a^2b$. Find the monomial. $3a^2$

55. The product of a monomial and $6x$ is $24xy^2$. Find the monomial. $4y^2$

56. The quotient of a polynomial and $2x + 1$ is $2x - 4 + \frac{7}{2x + 1}$. Find the polynomial.
$4x^2 - 6x + 3$

57. The quotient of a polynomial and $x - 3$ is $x^2 - x + 8 + \frac{22}{x - 3}$. Find the polynomial.
$x^3 - 4x^2 + 11x - 2$

Projects or Group Activities

58. $2x - 1$ is a factor of $2x^3 - 7x^2 + 7x - 2$. The product of $2x - 1$ and what polynomial is $2x^3 - 7x^2 + 7x - 2$? $x^2 - 3x + 2$

59. $4x + 1$ is a factor of $4x^3 + 9x^2 - 10x - 3$. The product of $4x + 1$ and what polynomial is $4x^3 + 9x^2 - 10x - 3$? $x^2 + 2x - 3$

60. When $x^2 - x - 8$ is divided by a polynomial, the quotient is $x + 3$ and the remainder is 4. Find the polynomial. $x - 4$

QUICK QUIZ

Divide.

1. $\frac{12x^3 - 15x^2 - 6x + 9}{3}$
$4x^3 - 5x^2 - 2x + 3$ [9.5A]

2. $\frac{10x^3y - 15x^2y + 5xy - 10y}{5xy}$
$2x^2 - 3x + 1 - \frac{2}{x}$ [9.5A]

3. $(3x^3 - 11x^2 + 10x - 12) \div (x - 3)$
$3x^2 - 2x + 4$ [9.5B]

4. $\frac{16x^3 - 13x + 1}{4x - 1}$
$4x^2 - x - 3 - \frac{2}{4x - 1}$ [9.5B]

CHAPTER 9 Summary

Key Words	Examples
A **monomial** is a number, a variable, or a product of numbers and variables. [9.1A, p. 492]	5 is a number; y is a variable. $2a^3b^2$ is a product of a number and variables. 5, y, and $2a^3b^2$ are monomials.
A **polynomial** is a variable expression in which the terms are monomials. [9.1A, p. 492]	$5x^2y - 3xy^2 + 2$ is a polynomial. Each term of this expression is a monomial.
A polynomial of two terms is a **binomial.** [9.1A, p. 492]	$x + 2$, $y^2 - 3$, and $6a + 5b$ are binomials.
A polynomial of three terms is a **trinomial.** [9.1A, p. 492]	$x^2 - 6x + 7$ is a trinomial.
The **degree of a polynomial in one variable** is the greatest exponent on a variable. [9.1A, p. 492]	The degree of $3x - 4x^3 + 17x^2 + 25$ is 3.
A polynomial in one variable is usually written in **descending order,** with the exponents on the variable terms decreasing from left to right. [9.1A, p. 492]	The polynomial $2x^4 + 3x^2 - 4x - 7$ is written in descending order.
The **opposite of a polynomial** is the polynomial with the sign of every term changed to its opposite. [9.1B, p. 493]	The opposite of the polynomial $x^2 - 3x + 4$ is $-x^2 + 3x - 4$.

Essential Rules and Procedures	Examples
Addition of Polynomials [9.1A, p. 492] To add polynomials, add the coefficients of the like terms.	$(2x^2 + 3x - 4) + (3x^3 - 4x^2 + 2x - 5)$ $= 3x^3 + (2x^2 - 4x^2) + (3x + 2x) + (-4 - 5)$ $= 3x^3 - 2x^2 + 5x - 9$
Subtraction of Polynomials [9.1B, p. 493] To subtract polynomials, add the opposite of the second polynomial to the first.	$(3y^2 - 8y - 9) - (5y^2 - 10y + 3)$ $= (3y^2 - 8y - 9) + (-5y^2 + 10y - 3)$ $= (3y^2 - 5y^2) + (-8y + 10y) + (-9 - 3)$ $= -2y^2 + 2y - 12$
Rule for Multiplying Exponential Expressions [9.2A, p. 496] If m and n are integers, then $x^m \cdot x^n = x^{m+n}$.	$a^3 \cdot a^6 = a^{3+6} = a^9$

Rule for Simplifying the Power of an Exponential Expression [9.2B, p. 497]
If m and n are integers, then $(x^m)^n = x^{mn}$.

$(c^3)^4 = c^{3 \cdot 4} = c^{12}$

Rule for Simplifying the Power of a Product [9.2B, p. 497]
If m, n, and p are integers, then $(x^m y^n)^p = x^{mp} y^{np}$.

$(a^3b^2)^4 = a^{3 \cdot 4}b^{2 \cdot 4} = a^{12}b^8$

To multiply a polynomial by a monomial, use the Distributive Property and the Rule for Multiplying Exponential Expressions. [9.3A, p. 500]

$$\begin{aligned}&(-4y)(5y^2 + 3y - 8)\\ &\quad = (-4y)(5y^2) + (-4y)(3y) - (-4y)(8)\\ &\quad = -20y^3 - 12y^2 + 32y\end{aligned}$$

To multiply two polynomials, multiply each term of one polynomial by each term of the other polynomial. [9.3B, p. 500]

$$\begin{array}{r} x^2 - 5x + 6 \\ x + 4 \\ \hline 4x^2 - 20x + 24 \\ x^3 - 5x^2 + 6x \quad\quad \\ \hline x^3 - x^2 - 14x + 24 \end{array}$$

FOIL Method [9.3C, p. 501]
To find the product of two binomials, add the products of the **F**irst terms, the **O**uter terms, the **I**nner terms, and the **L**ast terms.

$$\begin{aligned}&(2x - 5)(3x + 4)\\ &\quad = (2x)(3x) + (2x)(4) + (-5)(3x) + (-5)(4)\\ &\quad = 6x^2 + 8x - 15x - 20\\ &\quad = 6x^2 - 7x - 20\end{aligned}$$

Product of the Sum and Difference of the Same Terms [9.3D, p. 502]
$(a + b)(a - b) = a^2 - b^2$

$$\begin{aligned}(3x + 4)(3x - 4) &= (3x)^2 - 4^2\\ &= 9x^2 - 16\end{aligned}$$

Square of a Binomial [9.3D, p. 502]
$(a + b)^2 = a^2 + 2ab + b^2$
$(a - b)^2 = a^2 - 2ab + b^2$

$$\begin{aligned}(2x + 5)^2 &= (2x)^2 + 2(2x)(5) + 5^2\\ &= 4x^2 + 20x + 25\\ (3x - 4)^2 &= (3x)^2 - 2(3x)(4) + (-4)^2\\ &= 9x^2 - 24x + 16\end{aligned}$$

Definition of Zero as an Exponent [9.4A, p. 509]
If $x \neq 0$, then $x^0 = 1$.

$17^0 = 1$; $(-6c)^0 = 1$, $c \neq 0$

Definition of a Negative Exponent [9.4A, p. 510]
If $x \neq 0$ and n is a positive integer, then $x^{-n} = \dfrac{1}{x^n}$ and $\dfrac{1}{x^{-n}} = x^n$.

$x^{-6} = \dfrac{1}{x^6}$ and $\dfrac{1}{x^{-6}} = x^6$

Rule for Dividing Exponential Expressions [9.4A, p. 511]
If m and n are integers and $x \neq 0$, then $\dfrac{x^m}{x^n} = x^{m-n}$.

$$\frac{a^7}{a^2} = a^{7-2} = a^5$$

Rule for Simplifying the Power of a Quotient [9.4A, p. 511]
If m, n, and p are integers and $y \neq 0$, then $\left(\dfrac{x^m}{y^n}\right)^p = \dfrac{x^{mp}}{y^{np}}$.

$$\left(\frac{c^3}{a^5}\right)^2 = \frac{c^{3\cdot 2}}{a^{5\cdot 2}} = \frac{c^6}{a^{10}}$$

Rule for Negative Exponents on Fractional Expressions [9.4A, p. 512]
If $a \neq 0$, $b \neq 0$, and n is a positive integer, then $\left(\dfrac{a}{b}\right)^{-n} = \left(\dfrac{b}{a}\right)^n$.

$$\left(\frac{x}{y}\right)^{-3} = \left(\frac{y}{x}\right)^3$$

To Express a Number in Scientific Notation [9.4B, p. 514]
To express a number in scientific notation, write it in the form $a \times 10^n$, where a is a number between 1 and 10, and n is an integer. If the number is greater than 10, then n is a positive integer. If the number is between 0 and 1, then n is a negative integer.

$367{,}000{,}000 = 3.67 \times 10^8$
$0.0000078 = 7.8 \times 10^{-6}$

To Change a Number Written in Scientific Notation to Decimal Notation [9.4B, p. 515]
To change a number written in scientific notation to decimal notation, move the decimal point to the right if n is positive and to the left if n is negative. Move the decimal point the same number of places as the absolute value of the exponent on 10.

$2.418 \times 10^7 = 24{,}180{,}000$
$9.06 \times 10^{-5} = 0.0000906$

To divide a polynomial by a monomial, divide each term in the numerator by the denominator and write the sum of the quotients. [9.5A, p. 522]

$$\begin{aligned}&\frac{8xy^3 - 4y^2 + 12y}{4y}\\ &= \frac{8xy^3}{4y} - \frac{4y^2}{4y} + \frac{12y}{4y}\\ &= 2xy^2 - y + 3\end{aligned}$$

To check polynomial division, use the same equation used to check division of whole numbers:

(Quotient $\times$ divisor) + remainder = dividend

[9.5B, p. 522]

$$\begin{array}{r} x - 4 \\ x+3\overline{)x^2 - x - 10} \\ \underline{x^2 + 3x} \\ -4x - 10 \\ \underline{-4x - 12} \\ 2 \end{array}$$

Check:

$$\begin{aligned}(x-4)(x+3) + 2 &= x^2 - x - 12 + 2\\ &= x^2 - x - 10\end{aligned}$$

$$(x^2 - x - 10) \div (x+3) = x - 4 + \frac{2}{x+3}$$

CHAPTER 9 Review Exercises

1. Multiply: $(2b - 3)(4b + 5)$
$8b^2 - 2b - 15$ [9.3C]

2. Add: $(12y^2 + 17y - 4) + (9y^2 - 13y + 3)$
$21y^2 + 4y - 1$ [9.1A]

3. Simplify: $(xy^5z^3)(x^3y^3z)$
$x^4y^8z^4$ [9.2A]

4. Simplify: $\dfrac{8x^{12}}{12x^9}$
$\dfrac{2x^3}{3}$ [9.4A]

5. Multiply: $-2x(4x^2 + 7x - 9)$
$-8x^3 - 14x^2 + 18x$ [9.3A]

6. Simplify: $\dfrac{3ab^4}{-6a^2b^4}$
$-\dfrac{1}{2a}$ [9.4A]

7. Simplify: $(-2u^3v^4)^4$
$16u^{12}v^{16}$ [9.2B]

8. Evaluate: $(2^3)^2$
64 [9.2B]

9. Subtract: $(5x^2 - 2x - 1) - (3x^2 - 5x + 7)$
$2x^2 + 3x - 8$ [9.1B]

10. Simplify: $\dfrac{a^{-1}b^3}{a^3b^{-3}}$
$\dfrac{b^6}{a^4}$ [9.4A]

11. Simplify: $(-2x^3)^2(-3x^4)^3$
$-108x^{18}$ [9.2B]

12. Expand: $(5y - 7)^2$
$25y^2 - 70y + 49$ [9.3D]

13. Simplify: $(5a^7b^6)^2(4ab)$
$100a^{15}b^{13}$ [9.2B]

14. Divide: $\dfrac{12b^7 + 36b^5 - 3b^3}{3b^3}$
$4b^4 + 12b^2 - 1$ [9.5A]

15. Evaluate: -4^{-2}
$-\dfrac{1}{16}$ [9.4A]

16. Subtract: $(13y^3 - 7y - 2) - (12y^2 - 2y - 1)$
$13y^3 - 12y^2 - 5y - 1$ [9.1B]

17. Divide: $\dfrac{7 - x - x^2}{x + 3}$
$-x + 2 + \dfrac{1}{x + 3}$ [9.5B]

18. Multiply: $(2a - b)(x - 2y)$
$2ax - 4ay - bx + 2by$ [9.3C]

19. Multiply: $(3y^2 + 4y - 7)(2y + 3)$
$6y^3 + 17y^2 - 2y - 21$ [9.3B]

20. Divide: $(b^3 - 2b^2 - 33b - 7) \div (b - 7)$
$b^2 + 5b + 2 + \dfrac{7}{b - 7}$ [9.5B]

21. Multiply: $2ab^3(4a^2 - 2ab + 3b^2)$
$8a^3b^3 - 4a^2b^4 + 6ab^5$ [9.3A]

22. Multiply: $(2a - 5b)(2a + 5b)$
$4a^2 - 25b^2$ [9.3D]

23. Multiply: $(6b^3 - 2b^2 - 5)(2b^2 - 1)$
$12b^5 - 4b^4 - 6b^3 - 8b^2 + 5$ [9.3B]

24. Add: $(2x^3 + 7x^2 + x) + (2x^2 - 4x - 12)$
$2x^3 + 9x^2 - 3x - 12$ [9.1A]

25. Divide: $\dfrac{16y^2 - 32y}{-4y}$
$-4y + 8$ [9.5A]

26. Multiply: $(a + 7)(a - 7)$
$a^2 - 49$ [9.3D]

27. Write 37,560,000,000 in scientific notation.
3.756×10^{10} [9.4B]

28. Write 1.46×10^7 in decimal notation.
14,600,000 [9.4B]

29. Simplify: $(2a^{12}b^3)(-9b^2c^6)(3ac)$
$-54a^{13}b^5c^7$ [9.2A]

30. Divide: $(6y^2 - 35y + 36) \div (3y - 4)$
$2y - 9$ [9.5B]

31. Simplify: $(-3x^{-2}y^{-3})^{-2}$
$\dfrac{x^4y^6}{9}$ [9.4A]

32. Multiply: $(5a - 7)(2a + 9)$
$10a^2 + 31a - 63$ [9.3C]

33. Write 0.000000127 in scientific notation.
1.27×10^{-7} [9.4B]

34. Write 3.2×10^{-12} in decimal notation.
0.0000000000032 [9.4B]

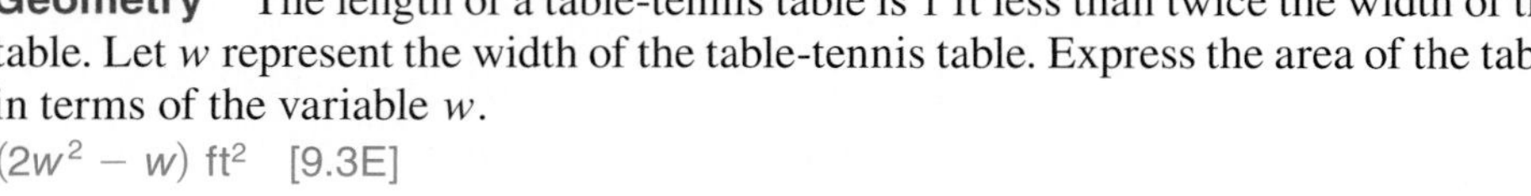

35. Geometry The length of a table-tennis table is 1 ft less than twice the width of the table. Let w represent the width of the table-tennis table. Express the area of the table in terms of the variable w.
$(2w^2 - w)$ ft^2 [9.3E]

36. Geometry The side of a checkerboard is $(3x - 2)$ in. Express the area of the checkerboard in terms of the variable x.
$(9x^2 - 12x + 4)$ in^2 [9.3E]

CHAPTER 9 TEST

1. Multiply: $2x(2x^2 - 3x)$
$4x^3 - 6x^2$ [9.3A]

2. Divide: $\dfrac{12x^3 - 3x^2 + 9}{3x^2}$
$4x - 1 + \dfrac{3}{x^2}$ [9.5A]

3. Simplify: $\dfrac{12x^2}{-3x^8}$
$-\dfrac{4}{x^6}$ [9.4A]

4. Simplify: $(-2xy^2)(3x^2y^4)$
$-6x^3y^6$ [9.2A]

5. Divide: $(x^2 + 1) \div (x + 1)$
$x - 1 + \dfrac{2}{x + 1}$ [9.5B]

6. Multiply: $(x - 3)(x^2 - 4x + 5)$
$x^3 - 7x^2 + 17x - 15$ [9.3B]

7. Simplify: $(-2a^2b)^3$
$-8a^6b^3$ [9.2B]

8. Simplify: $\dfrac{(3x^{-2}y^3)^3}{3x^4y^{-1}}$
$\dfrac{9y^{10}}{x^{10}}$ [9.4A]

9. Multiply: $(a - 2b)(a + 5b)$
$a^2 + 3ab - 10b^2$ [9.3C]

10. Divide: $\dfrac{16x^5 - 8x^3 + 20x}{4x}$
$4x^4 - 2x^2 + 5$ [9.5A]

11. Divide: $(x^2 + 6x - 7) \div (x - 1)$
$x + 7$ [9.5B]

12. Multiply: $-3y^2(-2y^2 + 3y - 6)$
$6y^4 - 9y^3 + 18y^2$ [9.3A]

13. Multiply: $(-2x^3 + x^2 - 7)(2x - 3)$
$-4x^4 + 8x^3 - 3x^2 - 14x + 21$ [9.3B]

14. Multiply: $(4y - 3)(4y + 3)$
$16y^2 - 9$ [9.3D]

15. Simplify: $(ab^2)(a^3b^5)$
a^4b^7 [9.2A]

16. Simplify: $\dfrac{2a^{-1}b}{2^{-2}a^{-2}b^{-3}}$
$8ab^4$ [9.4A]

17. Divide: $\dfrac{20a - 35}{5}$
$4a - 7$ [9.5A]

18. Subtract: $(3a^2 - 2a - 7) - (5a^3 + 2a - 10)$
$-5a^3 + 3a^2 - 4a + 3$ [9.1B]

19. Expand: $(2x - 5)^2$
$4x^2 - 20x + 25$ [9.3D]

20. Divide: $(4x^2 - 7) \div (2x - 3)$
$2x + 3 + \dfrac{2}{2x - 3}$ [9.5B]

21. Simplify: $\dfrac{-(2x^2y)^3}{4x^3y^3}$
$-2x^3$ [9.4A]

22. Multiply: $(2x - 7y)(5x - 4y)$
$10x^2 - 43xy + 28y^2$ [9.3C]

23. Add: $(3x^3 - 2x^2 - 4) + (8x^2 - 8x + 7)$
$3x^3 + 6x^2 - 8x + 3$ [9.1A]

24. Write 0.00000000302 in scientific notation.
3.02×10^{-9} [9.4B]

25. **Geometry** The radius of a circle is $(x - 5)$ m. Use the equation $A = \pi r^2$, where r is the radius, to find the area of the circle in terms of the variable x. Leave the answer in terms of π.
$(\pi x^2 - 10\pi x + 25\pi)$ m^2 [9.3E]

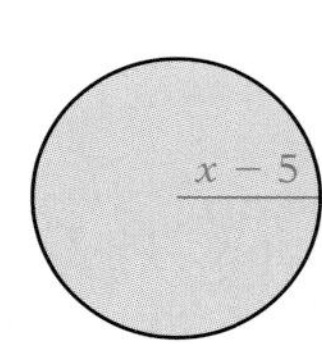

Cumulative Review Exercises

1. Simplify: $\frac{3}{16} - \left(-\frac{5}{8}\right) - \frac{7}{9}$
$\frac{5}{144}$ [3.4A]

2. Evaluate $-3^2 \cdot \left(\frac{2}{3}\right)^3 \cdot \left(-\frac{5}{8}\right)$.
$\frac{5}{3}$ [3.5A]

3. Simplify: $\left(-\frac{1}{2}\right)^3 \div \left(\frac{3}{8} - \frac{5}{6}\right) + 2$
$\frac{25}{11}$ [3.5A]

4. Evaluate $\frac{b - (a - b)^2}{b^2}$ when $a = -2$ and $b = 3$.
$-\frac{22}{9}$ [4.1A]

5. Simplify: $-2x - (-xy) + 7x - 4xy$
$5x - 3xy$ [4.2A]

6. Simplify: $(12x)\left(-\frac{3}{4}\right)$
$-9x$ [4.2B]

7. Simplify: $-2[3x - 2(4 - 3x) + 2]$
$-18x + 12$ [4.2D]

8. Solve: $12 = -\frac{3}{4}x$
-16 [5.1C]

9. Solve: $2x - 9 = 3x + 7$
-16 [5.3A]

10. Solve: $2 - 3(4 - x) = 2x + 5$
15 [5.3B]

11. 35.2 is what percent of 160?
22% [6.4A/6.4B]

12. Add: $(4b^3 - 7b^2 - 7) + (3b^2 - 8b + 3)$
$4b^3 - 4b^2 - 8b - 4$ [9.1A]

13. Subtract: $(3y^3 - 5y + 8) - (-2y^2 + 5y + 8)$
$3y^3 + 2y^2 - 10y$ [9.1B]

14. Simplify: $(a^3b^5)^3$
a^9b^{15} [9.2B]

15. Simplify: $(4xy^3)(-2x^2y^3)$
$-8x^3y^6$ [9.2A]

16. Multiply: $-2y^2(-3y^2 - 4y + 8)$
$6y^4 + 8y^3 - 16y^2$ [9.3A]

17. Multiply: $(2a - 7)(5a^2 - 2a + 3)$
$10a^3 - 39a^2 + 20a - 21$ [9.3B]

18. Multiply: $(3b - 2)(5b - 7)$
$15b^2 - 31b + 14$ [9.3C]

19. Simplify: $\dfrac{(-2a^2b^3)^2}{8a^4b^8}$
$\dfrac{1}{2b^2}$ [9.4A]

20. Divide: $(a^2 - 4a - 21) \div (a + 3)$
$a - 7$ [9.5B]

21. Write 6.09×10^{-5} in decimal notation.
0.0000609 [9.4B]

22. Translate "the difference between eight times a number and twice the number is eighteen" into an equation and solve.
$8x - 2x = 18$; 3 [5.4B]

23. Mixtures Find the cost per ounce of a fruit drink made from 200 oz of a fruit juice that costs $.25 per ounce and 300 oz of soda that costs $.05 per ounce.
$.13 per ounce [5.5A]

© Evgeny Karandaev/Shutterstock.com

24. Transportation A car traveling at 50 mph overtakes a cyclist who, riding at 10 mph, has had a 2-hour head start. How far from the starting point does the car overtake the cyclist?
25 mi [5.5B]

25. Geometry The width of a rectangle is 40% of the length. The perimeter of the rectangle is 42 m. Find the length and width of the rectangle.
Length: 15 m; width: 6 m [7.2A]

Factoring

OBJECTIVES

SECTION 10.1

A To factor a monomial from a polynomial

B To factor by grouping

SECTION 10.2

A To factor a trinomial of the form $x^2 + bx + c$

B To factor completely

SECTION 10.3

A To factor a trinomial of the form $ax^2 + bx + c$ by using trial factors

B To factor a trinomial of the form $ax^2 + bx + c$ by grouping

SECTION 10.4

A To factor the difference of two squares and perfect-square trinomials

SECTION 10.5

A To factor polynomials completely

SECTION 10.6

A To solve equations by factoring

B To solve application problems

Focus on Success

Did you make a time management plan when you started this course? If not, you can still benefit from doing so. Create a schedule that gives you enough time for everything you need to do. We want you to schedule enough time to study math each week so that you successfully complete this course. Once you have determined the hours during which you will study, consider it a commitment that you cannot break. (See Time Management, page AIM-4.)

Prep Test

Are you ready to succeed in this chapter? Take the Prep Test below to find out if you are ready to learn the new material.

1. Write 30 as a product of prime numbers.
$2 \cdot 3 \cdot 5$ [1.3D]

2. Simplify: $-3(4y - 5)$
$-12y + 15$ [4.2C]

3. Simplify: $-(a - b)$
$-a + b$ [4.2C]

4. Simplify: $2(a - b) - 5(a - b)$
$-3a + 3b$ [4.2D]

5. Solve: $4x = 0$
0 [5.1C]

6. Solve: $2x + 1 = 0$
$-\frac{1}{2}$ [5.2A]

7. Multiply: $(x + 4)(x - 6)$
$x^2 - 2x - 24$ [9.3C]

8. Multiply: $(2x - 5)(3x + 2)$
$6x^2 - 11x - 10$ [9.3C]

9. Simplify: $\frac{x^5}{x^2}$
x^3 [9.4A]

10. Simplify: $\frac{6x^4y^3}{2xy^2}$
$3x^3y$ [9.4A]

SECTION

10.1 Common Factors

OBJECTIVE A *To factor a monomial from a polynomial*

In Section 2.1B, we discussed how to find the greatest common factor (GCF) of two or more integers. The **greatest common factor (GCF) of two or more monomials** is the product of the GCF of the coefficients and the common variable factors.

$6x^3y = 2 \cdot 3 \cdot x \cdot x \cdot x \cdot y$
$8x^2y^2 = 2 \cdot 2 \cdot 2 \cdot x \cdot x \cdot y \cdot y$
$\text{GCF} = 2 \cdot x \cdot x \cdot y = 2x^2y$

Note that the exponent on each variable in the GCF is the same as the *smallest* exponent on that variable in either of the monomials.

The GCF of $6x^3y$ and $8x^2y^2$ is $2x^2y$.

HOW TO 1 Find the GCF of $12a^4b$ and $18a^2b^2c$.

The common variable factors are a^2 and b; c is not a common variable factor.

$12a^4b = 2 \cdot 2 \cdot 3 \cdot a^4 \cdot b$
$18a^2b^2c = 2 \cdot 3 \cdot 3 \cdot a^2 \cdot b^2 \cdot c$
$\text{GCF} = 2 \cdot 3 \cdot a^2 \cdot b = 6a^2b$

To **factor a polynomial** means to write the polynomial as a product of other polynomials. In the example at the right, $2x$ is the GCF of the terms $2x^2$ and $10x$.

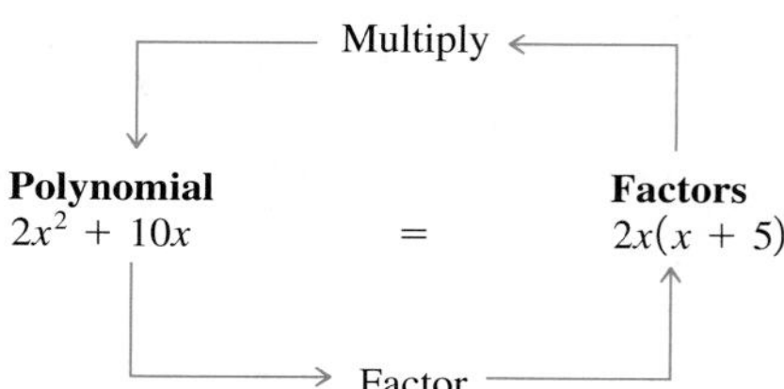

HOW TO 2 Factor: $5x^3 - 35x^2 + 10x$

Find the GCF of the terms of the polynomial.

$$5x^3 = 5 \cdot x^3$$
$$35x^2 = 5 \cdot 7 \cdot x^2$$
$$10x = 2 \cdot 5 \cdot x$$

The GCF is $5x$.

Rewrite the polynomial, expressing each term as a product with the GCF as one of the factors.

$$5x^3 - 35x^2 + 10x = 5x(x^2) + 5x(-7x) + 5x(2)$$
$$= 5x(x^2 - 7x + 2)$$

• Use the Distributive Property to write the polynomial as a product of factors.

Take Note

At the right, the factors in parentheses are determined by dividing each term of the trinomial by the GCF, $5x$.

$\frac{5x^3}{5x} = x^2$, $\frac{-35x^2}{5x} = -7x$, and $\frac{10x}{5x} = 2$

HOW TO 3 Factor: $21x^2y^3 - 6xy^5 + 15x^4y^2$

Find the GCF of the terms of the polynomial.

$$21x^2y^3 = 3 \cdot 7 \cdot x^2 \cdot y^3$$
$$6xy^5 = 2 \cdot 3 \cdot x \cdot y^5$$
$$15x^4y^2 = 3 \cdot 5 \cdot x^4 \cdot y^2$$

The GCF is $3xy^2$.

Rewrite the polynomial, expressing each term as a product with the GCF as one of the factors.

$$21x^2y^3 - 6xy^5 + 15x^4y^2$$
$$= 3xy^2(7xy) + 3xy^2(-2y^3) + 3xy^2(5x^3)$$
$$= 3xy^2(7xy - 2y^3 + 5x^3)$$

• **Use the Distributive Property to write the polynomial as a product of factors.**

EXAMPLE 1

Factor: $8x^2 + 2xy$

Solution

The GCF is $2x$.

$$8x^2 + 2xy = 2x(4x) + 2x(y)$$
$$= 2x(4x + y)$$

• **Factor the GCF from each term.**

YOU TRY IT 1

Factor: $14a^2 - 21a^4b$

Your solution

$7a^2(2 - 3a^2b)$

EXAMPLE 2

Factor: $n^3 - 5n^2 + 2n$

Solution

The GCF is n.

$$n^3 - 5n^2 + 2n$$
$$= n(n^2) + n(-5n) + n(2)$$
$$= n(n^2 - 5n + 2)$$

• **Factor the GCF from each term.**

YOU TRY IT 2

Factor: $27b^2 + 18b + 9$

Your solution

$9(3b^2 + 2b + 1)$

EXAMPLE 3

Factor: $16x^2y + 8x^4y^2 - 12x^4y^5$

Solution

The GCF is $4x^2y$.

$$16x^2y + 8x^4y^2 - 12x^4y^5$$
$$= 4x^2y(4) + 4x^2y(2x^2y) + 4x^2y(-3x^2y^4)$$
$$= 4x^2y(4 + 2x^2y - 3x^2y^4)$$

YOU TRY IT 3

Factor: $6x^4y^2 - 9x^3y^2 + 12x^2y^4$

Your solution

$3x^2y^2(2x^2 - 3x + 4y^2)$

IN-CLASS EXAMPLES

Factor.

1. $10y^2 - 15y^3z$ $\mathbf{5y^2(2 - 3yz)}$
2. $12m^2 + 6m - 18$
   $\mathbf{6(2m^2 + m - 3)}$
3. $20x^4y^3 - 30x^3y^4 + 40x^2y^5$
   $\mathbf{10x^2y^3(2x^2 - 3xy + 4y^2)}$

Solutions on p. S23

OBJECTIVE B To factor by grouping

A factor that has two terms is called a **binomial factor.** In the examples at the right, the binomials $a + b$ and $x - y$ are binomial factors.

$2a(a + b)^2$
$3xy(x - y)$

The Distributive Property is used to factor a common binomial factor from an expression.

The common binomial factor of the expression $6(x - 3) + y(x - 3)$ is $(x - 3)$. To factor the expression, use the Distributive Property to write the expression as a product of factors.

$$6(x - 3) + y(x - 3) = (x - 3)(6 + y)$$

Consider the following simplification of $-(a - b)$.

$$-(a - b) = -1(a - b) = -a + b = b - a$$

Thus $\quad b - a = -(a - b)$

This equation is sometimes used to factor a common binomial from an expression.

HOW TO 4 Factor: $2x(x - y) + 5(y - x)$

$$2x(x - y) + 5(y - x) = 2x(x - y) - 5(x - y)$$
$$= (x - y)(2x - 5)$$

• $5(y - x) = 5[(-1)(x - y)]$
$= -5(x - y)$

A polynomial can be **factored by grouping** if its terms can be grouped and factored in such a way that a common binomial factor is found.

INSTRUCTOR NOTE
Before you present factoring by grouping, have students practice inserting parentheses into expressions. Here are some suggestions.
$-a + 2b = -(a - 2b)$
$3x - 2y = -(-3x + 2y)$
$-4a - 3b = -(4a + 3b)$

HOW TO 5 Factor: $ax + bx - ay - by$

$$ax + bx - ay - by = (ax + bx) - (ay + by)$$

• **Group the first two terms and the last two terms. Note that $-ay - by = -(ay + by)$.**

$$= x(a + b) - y(a + b)$$

• **Factor each group.**

$$= (a + b)(x - y)$$

• **Factor the GCF, $(a + b)$, from each group.**

Check: $(a + b)(x - y) = ax - ay + bx - by$
$= ax + bx - ay - by$

HOW TO 6 Factor: $6x^2 - 9x - 4xy + 6y$

$$6x^2 - 9x - 4xy + 6y = (6x^2 - 9x) - (4xy - 6y)$$

• **Group the first two terms and the last two terms. Note that $-4xy + 6y = -(4xy - 6y)$.**

$$= 3x(2x - 3) - 2y(2x - 3)$$

• **Factor each group.**

$$= (2x - 3)(3x - 2y)$$

• **Factor the GCF, $(2x - 3)$, from each group.**

EXAMPLE 4

Factor: $4x(3x - 2) - 7(3x - 2)$

Solution

$4x(3x - 2) - 7(3x - 2)$ • **$3x - 2$ is the common binomial factor.**

$= (3x - 2)(4x - 7)$

YOU TRY IT 4

Factor: $2y(5x - 2) - 3(2 - 5x)$

Your solution

$(5x - 2)(2y + 3)$

EXAMPLE 5

Factor: $9x^2 - 15x - 6xy + 10y$

Solution

$9x^2 - 15x - 6xy + 10y$

$= (9x^2 - 15x) - (6xy - 10y)$ • **$-6xy + 10y = -(6xy - 10y)$**

$= 3x(3x - 5) - 2y(3x - 5)$ • **$3x - 5$ is the common factor.**

$= (3x - 5)(3x - 2y)$

YOU TRY IT 5

Factor: $a^2 - 3a + 2ab - 6b$

Your solution

$(a - 3)(a + 2b)$

EXAMPLE 6

Factor: $3x^2y - 4x - 15xy + 20$

Solution

$3x^2y - 4x - 15xy + 20$

$= (3x^2y - 4x) - (15xy - 20)$ • **$-15xy + 20 = -(15xy - 20)$**

$= x(3xy - 4) - 5(3xy - 4)$ • **$3xy - 4$ is the common factor.**

$= (3xy - 4)(x - 5)$

YOU TRY IT 6

Factor: $2mn^2 - n + 8mn - 4$

Your solution

$(2mn - 1)(n + 4)$

EXAMPLE 7

Factor: $4ab - 6 + 3b - 2ab^2$

Solution

$4ab - 6 + 3b - 2ab^2$

$= (4ab - 6) + (3b - 2ab^2)$

$= 2(2ab - 3) + b(3 - 2ab)$

$= 2(2ab - 3) - b(2ab - 3)$ • **$3 - 2ab = -(2ab - 3)$**

$= (2ab - 3)(2 - b)$ • **$2ab - 3$ is the common factor.**

YOU TRY IT 7

Factor: $3xy - 9y - 12 + 4x$

Your solution

$(x - 3)(3y + 4)$

IN-CLASS EXAMPLES

Factor.

4. $6x(4x + 3) - 5(4x + 3)$
   $\mathbf{(4x + 3)(6x - 5)}$
5. $8x^2 - 12x - 6xy + 9y$
   $\mathbf{(2x - 3)(4x - 3y)}$
6. $7xy^2 - 3y + 14xy - 6$
   $\mathbf{(7xy - 3)(y + 2)}$
7. $5xy - 9y - 18 + 10x$
   $\mathbf{(5x - 9)(y + 2)}$

Solutions on p. S23

10.1 EXERCISES

Concept Check

SUGGESTED ASSIGNMENT
Exercises 1–6; Exercises 7–39, odds; Exercises 43–65, odds

1. Name the greatest common factor of 4, 12, and 16. 4

2. Name the greatest common factor of x^3, x^5, and x^6. x^3

3. For the expression $x(2x - 1)$, name **a.** the monomial factor and **b.** the binomial factor. **a.** x **b.** $2x - 1$

4. Name the common binomial factor in the expression $5b(c - 6) + 8(c - 6)$. $c - 6$

5. Rewrite the expression $2x^3 - x^2 + 6x - 3$ by grouping the first two terms and the last two terms. $(2x^3 - x^2) + (6x - 3)$

6. Explain why the statement is true.
a. The terms of the binomial $3x - 6$ have a common factor.
b. The expression $3x^2 + 15$ is not in factored form.
c. $5y - 7$ is a factor of $y(5y - 7)$.

OBJECTIVE A *To factor a monomial from a polynomial*

For Exercises 7 to 40, factor.

7. $5a + 5$ $5(a + 1)$

8. $7b - 7$ $7(b - 1)$

9. $16 - 8a^2$ $8(2 - a^2)$

10. $12 + 12y^2$ $12(1 + y^2)$

11. $8x + 12$ $4(2x + 3)$

12. $16a - 24$ $8(2a - 3)$

13. $7x^2 - 3x$ $x(7x - 3)$

14. $12y^2 - 5y$ $y(12y - 5)$

15. $3a^2 + 5a^5$ $a^2(3 + 5a^3)$

16. $6b^3 - 5b^2$ $b^2(6b - 5)$

17. $2x^4 - 4x$ $2x(x^3 - 2)$

18. $3y^4 - 9y$ $3y(y^3 - 3)$

19. $10x^4 - 12x^2$ $2x^2(5x^2 - 6)$

20. $12a^5 - 32a^2$ $4a^2(3a^3 - 8)$

21. $8a^8 - 4a^5$ $4a^5(2a^3 - 1)$

22. $16y^4 - 8y^7$ $8y^4(2 - y^3)$

23. $x^2y^2 - xy$ $xy(xy - 1)$

24. $a^2b^2 + ab$ $ab(ab + 1)$

25. $3x^2y^4 - 6xy$ $3xy(xy^3 - 2)$

26. $12a^2b^5 - 9ab$ $3ab(4ab^4 - 3)$

27. $3x^3 + 6x^2 + 9x$ $3x(x^2 + 2x + 3)$

28. $5y^3 - 20y^2 + 5y$ $5y(y^2 - 4y + 1)$

29. $2x^4 - 4x^3 + 6x^2$ $2x^2(x^2 - 2x + 3)$

30. $3y^4 - 9y^3 - 6y^2$ $3y^2(y^2 - 3y - 2)$

31. $2x^3 + 6x^2 - 14x$ $2x(x^2 + 3x - 7)$

32. $3y^3 - 9y^2 + 24y$ $3y(y^2 - 3y + 8)$

33. $2y^5 - 3y^4 + 7y^3$ $y^3(2y^2 - 3y + 7)$

34. $6a^5 - 3a^3 - 2a^2$ $a^2(6a^3 - 3a - 2)$

35. $x^3y - 3x^2y^2 + 7xy^3$ $xy(x^2 - 3xy + 7y^2)$

36. $2a^2b - 5a^2b^2 + 7ab^2$ $ab(2a - 5ab + 7b)$

37. $5y^3 + 10y^2 - 25y$ $5y(y^2 + 2y - 5)$

38. $4b^5 + 6b^3 - 12b$ $2b(2b^4 + 3b^2 - 6)$

39. $3a^2b^2 - 9ab^2 + 15b^2$ $3b^2(a^2 - 3a + 5)$

40. $8x^2y^2 - 4x^2y + x^2$ $x^2(8y^2 - 4y + 1)$

41. What is the GCF of the terms of the polynomial $x^a + x^b + x^c$ given that a, b, and c are all positive integers, and $a > b > c$? x^c

OBJECTIVE B To factor by grouping

42. Use the three expressions at the right.

a. Which expressions are equivalent to $x^2 - 5x + 6$? i, ii, iii

b. Which expression can be factored by grouping? iii

(i) $x^2 - 15x + 10x + 6$
(ii) $x^2 - x - 4x + 6$
(iii) $x^2 - 2x - 3x + 6$

For Exercises 43 to 66, factor.

43. $x(b + 4) + 3(b + 4)$
$(b + 4)(x + 3)$

44. $y(a + z) + 7(a + z)$
$(a + z)(y + 7)$

45. $a(y - x) - b(y - x)$
$(y - x)(a - b)$

46. $3r(a - b) + s(a - b)$
$(a - b)(3r + s)$

47. $x(x - 2) + y(2 - x)$
$(x - 2)(x - y)$

48. $t(m - 7) + 7(7 - m)$
$(m - 7)(t - 7)$

49. $8c(2m - 3n) + (3n - 2m)$
$(2m - 3n)(8c - 1)$

50. $2y(4a + b) - (b + 4a)$
$(4a + b)(2y - 1)$

51. $x^2 + 2x + 2xy + 4y$
$(x + 2)(x + 2y)$

52. $x^2 - 3x + 4ax - 12a$
$(x - 3)(x + 4a)$

53. $p^2 - 2p - 3rp + 6r$
$(p - 2)(p - 3r)$

54. $t^2 + 4t - st - 4s$
$(t + 4)(t - s)$

55. $ab + 6b - 4a - 24$
$(a + 6)(b - 4)$

56. $xy - 5y - 2x + 10$
$(x - 5)(y - 2)$

57. $2z^2 - z + 2yz - y$
$(2z - 1)(z + y)$

58. $2y^2 - 10y + 7xy - 35x$
$(y - 5)(2y + 7x)$

59. $2x^2 - 5x - 6xy + 15y$
$(2x - 5)(x - 3y)$

60. $4a^2 + 5ab - 10b - 8a$
$(4a + 5b)(a - 2)$

61. $3y^2 - 6y - ay + 2a$
$(y - 2)(3y - a)$

62. $2ra + a^2 - 2r - a$
$(2r + a)(a - 1)$

63. $3xy - y^2 - y + 3x$
$(3x - y)(y + 1)$

64. $2ab - 3b^2 - 3b + 2a$
$(2a - 3b)(b + 1)$

65. $3st + t^2 - 2t - 6s$
$(3s + t)(t - 2)$

66. $4x^2 + 3xy - 12y - 16x$
$(4x + 3y)(x - 4)$

Critical Thinking

For Exercises 67 to 69, fill in the blank to make a true statement.

67. $a - 3 =$ ________ $(3 - a)$
-1

68. $2 - (x - y) = 2 +$ (________)
$y - x$

69. $4x + (3a - b) = 4x -$ (________)
$b - 3a$

Projects or Group Activities

70. Geometry Write an expression in factored form for the shaded portion in each of the following diagrams. Use the equation for the area of a rectangle ($A = LW$) and the equation for the area of a circle ($A = \pi r^2$).

a.

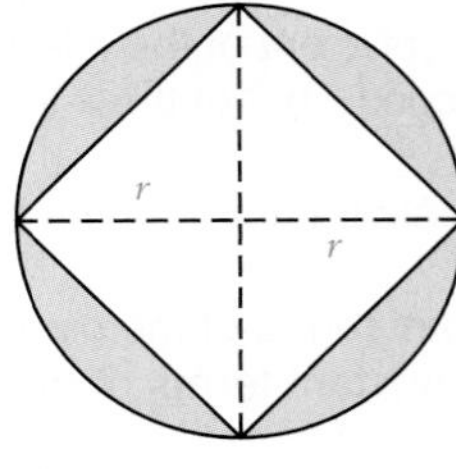

$r^2(\pi - 2)$

b.

$2r$ $2r$

$2r^2(4 - \pi)$

c.

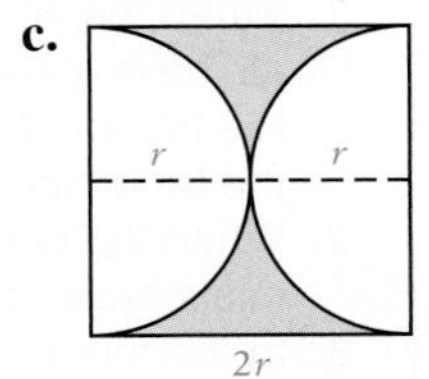

$r^2(4 - \pi)$

QUICK QUIZ

Factor.

1. $14x^2y^2 - 7xy$
$7xy(2xy - 1)$ [10.1A]
2. $15r^2s + 20rs - 10rs^2$
$5rs(3r + 4 - 2s)$ [10.1A]
3. $6a(b - 7) - 5(b - 7)$
$(b - 7)(6a - 5)$ [10.1B]
4. $3xy - 9y + 2x - 6$
$(x - 3)(3y + 2)$ [10.1B]
5. $2ay - a^2 - 3a + 6y$
$(2y - a)(a + 3)$ [10.1B]

SECTION

10.2 Factoring Polynomials of the Form $x^2 + bx + c$

OBJECTIVE A *To factor a trinomial of the form $x^2 + bx + c$*

Trinomials of the form $x^2 + bx + c$, where b and c are integers, are shown at the right.

$x^2 + 8x + 12$; $b = 8$, $c = 12$
$x^2 - 7x + 12$; $b = -7$, $c = 12$
$x^2 - 2x - 15$; $b = -2$, $c = -15$

To factor a trinomial of this form means to express the trinomial as the product of two binomials.

INSTRUCTOR NOTE
Students sometimes see factoring as unrelated to multiplication. Remind students that multiplying the binomial factors will give the polynomial.

Trinomials expressed as the product of binomials are shown at the right.

$x^2 + 8x + 12 = (x + 6)(x + 2)$
$x^2 - 7x + 12 = (x - 3)(x - 4)$
$x^2 - 2x - 15 = (x + 3)(x - 5)$

The method by which factors of a trinomial are found is based on FOIL. Consider the following binomial products, noting the relationship between the constant terms of the binomials and the terms of the trinomials.

The signs in the binomial factors are the same.

$(x + 6)(x + 2) = x^2 + 2x + 6x + (6)(2) = x^2 + 8x + 12$

Sum of 6 and 2 → 8
Product of 6 and 2 → 12

$(x - 3)(x - 4) = x^2 - 4x - 3x + (-3)(-4) = x^2 - 7x + 12$

Sum of −3 and −4 → −7
Product of −3 and −4 → 12

The signs in the binomial factors are opposites.

$(x + 3)(x - 5) = x^2 - 5x + 3x + (3)(-5) = x^2 - 2x - 15$

Sum of 3 and −5 → −2
Product of 3 and −5 → −15

$(x - 4)(x + 6) = x^2 + 6x - 4x + (-4)(6) = x^2 + 2x - 24$

Sum of −4 and 6 → 2
Product of −4 and 6 → −24

Factoring $x^2 + bx + c$: IMPORTANT RELATIONSHIPS

1. When the constant term of the trinomial is positive, the constant terms of the binomials have the same sign. They are both positive when the coefficient of the x term in the trinomial is positive. They are both negative when the coefficient of the x term in the trinomial is negative.
2. When the constant term of the trinomial is negative, the constant terms of the binomials have opposite signs.
3. In the trinomial, the coefficient of x is the sum of the constant terms of the binomials.
4. In the trinomial, the constant term is the product of the constant terms of the binomials.

HOW TO 1 Factor: $x^2 - 7x + 10$

Because the constant term is positive and the coefficient of x is negative, the binomial constants will be negative. Find two negative factors of 10 whose sum is -7.

Negative Factors of 10	*Sum*
$-1, -10$	-11
$-2, -5$	-7

- The results can be recorded in a table.
- These are the correct factors.

$x^2 - 7x + 10 = (x - 2)(x - 5)$ • Write the trinomial as a product of its factors.

You can check the proposed factorization by multiplying the two binomials.

Check: $(x - 2)(x - 5) = x^2 - 5x - 2x + 10 = x^2 - 7x + 10$

Take Note
Always check your proposed factorization to ensure accuracy.

HOW TO 2 Factor: $x^2 - 9x - 36$

The constant term is negative. The binomial constants will have opposite signs. Find two factors of -36 whose sum is -9.

Factors of −36	*Sum*
$+1, -36$	-35
$-1, +36$	35
$+2, -18$	-16
$-2, +18$	16
$+3, -12$	-9

- Once the correct factors are found, it is not necessary to try the remaining factors.

$x^2 - 9x - 36 = (x + 3)(x - 12)$ • Write the trinomial as a product of its factors.

INSTRUCTOR NOTE
The phrase *nonfactorable over the integers* may require additional examples. Explain that it does not mean that the polynomial does not factor; it means that it does not factor if *integers* are used. An analogy involving numbers may help. For instance, the only ways to write 7 as a product of integers are $1 \cdot 7$ or $(-1)(-7)$. However, $\frac{21}{5} \cdot \frac{5}{3} = 7$. The ability to factor depends on the types of numbers that can be used as factors.

For some trinomials, it is not possible to find integer factors of the constant term whose sum is the coefficient of the middle term. A polynomial that does not factor using only integers is **nonfactorable over the integers.**

HOW TO 3 Factor: $x^2 + 7x + 8$

Find two positive factors of 8 whose sum is 7.

Positive Factors of 8	*Sum*
1, 8	9
2, 4	6

- There are no positive integer factors of 8 whose sum is 7.

$x^2 + 7x + 8$ is nonfactorable over the integers.

Take Note
Just as 17 is a prime number, $x^2 + 7x + 8$ is a **prime polynomial.** Binomials of the form $x - a$ and $x + a$ are also prime polynomials.

EXAMPLE 1

Factor: $x^2 - 8x + 15$

Solution

Find two negative factors of 15 whose sum is -8.

Factors	*Sum*
$-1, -15$	-16
$-3, -5$	$\mathbf{-8}$

$x^2 - 8x + 15 = (x - 3)(x - 5)$

YOU TRY IT 1

Factor: $x^2 + 9x + 20$

Your solution

$(x + 4)(x + 5)$

Solution on p. S23

EXAMPLE 2

Factor: $x^2 + 6x - 27$

Solution

Find two factors of -27 whose sum is 6.

Factors	Sum
+1, −27	−26
−1, +27	26
+3, −9	−6
−3, +9	**6**

$x^2 + 6x - 27 = (x - 3)(x + 9)$

YOU TRY IT 2

Factor: $x^2 + 7x - 18$

Your solution

$(x + 9)(x - 2)$

IN-CLASS EXAMPLES

Factor.

1. $x^2 - 8x + 12$ $\mathbf{(x - 6)(x - 2)}$
2. $x^2 + 8x + 12$ $\mathbf{(x + 6)(x + 2)}$
3. $x^2 + 7x + 12$ $\mathbf{(x + 4)(x + 3)}$
4. $x^2 - 4x - 12$ $\mathbf{(x - 6)(x + 2)}$
5. $x^2 - 11x - 12$ $\mathbf{(x - 12)(x + 1)}$

Solution on p. S23

OBJECTIVE B *To factor completely*

Take Note

The first step in *any* factoring problem is to determine whether the terms of the polynomial have a *common factor.* If they do, factor it out first.

INSTRUCTOR NOTE

When the terms of a polynomial contain a common factor, some students will attempt to find the common factor and the two binomial factors in one step; they rarely obtain the correct final answer. Encourage students to find only two factors at a time. Emphasize that the first step is to find the common factor and the resulting polynomial factor. The second step is to find the two binomial factors.

A polynomial is **factored completely** when it is written as a product of factors that are nonfactorable over the integers.

HOW TO 4 Factor: $4y^3 - 4y^2 - 24y$

$4y^3 - 4y^2 - 24y = 4y(y^2) - 4y(y) - 4y(6)$ • The GCF is $4y$.

$= 4y(y^2 - y - 6)$ • Use the Distributive Property to factor out the GCF.

$= 4y(y + 2)(y - 3)$ • Factor $y^2 - y - 6$. The two factors of -6 whose sum is -1 are 2 and -3.

It is always possible to check a proposed factorization by multiplying the polynomial factors. Here is the check for HOW TO 4.

Check: $4y(y + 2)(y - 3) = 4y(y^2 - 3y + 2y - 6)$

$= 4y(y^2 - y - 6)$

$= 4y^3 - 4y^2 - 24y$ • This is the original polynomial.

HOW TO 5 Factor: $x^2 + 12xy + 20y^2$

There is no common factor.
Note that the variable part of the middle term is xy, and the variable part of the last term is y^2.

$x^2 + 12xy + 20y^2 = (x + 2y)(x + 10y)$ • The two factors of 20 whose sum is 12 are 2 and 10.

Take Note

The terms $2y$ and $10y$ are placed in the binomials. This is necessary so that the middle term of the trinomial contains xy and the last term contains y^2.

Note that the terms $2y$ and $10y$ are placed in the binomials. The following check shows why this is necessary.

Check: $(x + 2y)(x + 10y) = x^2 + 10xy + 2xy + 20y^2$

$= x^2 + 12xy + 20y^2$ • This is the original polynomial.

Take Note

When the coefficient of the highest power in a polynomial is negative, consider factoring out a negative GCF. Example 3 is another example of this technique.

HOW TO 6 Factor: $15 - 2x - x^2$

Because the coefficient of x^2 is -1, factor -1 from the trinomial, and then write the resulting trinomial in descending order.

$15 - 2x - x^2 = -(x^2 + 2x - 15)$ • $15 - 2x - x^2 = -1(-15 + 2x + x^2) = -(x^2 + 2x - 15)$

$= -(x + 5)(x - 3)$ • Factor $x^2 + 2x - 15$. The two factors of -15 whose sum is 2 are 5 and -3.

Check: $-(x + 5)(x - 3) = -(x^2 + 2x - 15)$

$= -x^2 - 2x + 15$

$= 15 - 2x - x^2$ • This is the original polynomial.

EXAMPLE 3

Factor: $-3x^3 + 9x^2 + 12x$

Solution

The GCF is $-3x$. Factor out the GCF.

$-3x^3 + 9x^2 + 12x = -3x(x^2 - 3x - 4)$

Factor the trinomial $x^2 - 3x - 4$. Find two factors of -4 whose sum is -3.

Factors	Sum
+1, −4	**−3**

$-3x^3 + 9x^2 + 12x = -3x(x + 1)(x - 4)$

YOU TRY IT 3

Factor: $-2x^3 + 14x^2 - 12x$

Your solution

$-2x(x - 6)(x - 1)$

EXAMPLE 4

Factor: $4x^2 - 40xy + 84y^2$

Solution

The GCF is 4. Factor out the GCF.

$4x^2 - 40xy + 84y^2 = 4(x^2 - 10xy + 21y^2)$

Factor the trinomial $x^2 - 10xy + 21y^2$. Find two negative factors of 21 whose sum is -10.

Factors	Sum
−1, −21	−22
−3, −7	**−10**

$4x^2 - 40xy + 84y^2 = 4(x - 3y)(x - 7y)$

YOU TRY IT 4

Factor: $3x^2 - 9xy - 12y^2$

Your solution

$3(x + y)(x - 4y)$

IN-CLASS EXAMPLES

Factor.

6. $3x^2 - 6x - 72$ $\mathbf{3(x - 6)(x + 4)}$
7. $2x^2 + 6x - 20$ $\mathbf{2(x + 5)(x - 2)}$
8. $-4y^3 + 28y^2 - 48y$ $\mathbf{-4y(y - 4)(y - 3)}$
9. $5x^2 - 10xy - 15y^2$ $\mathbf{5(x + y)(x - 3y)}$

Solutions on pp. S23–S24

10.2 EXERCISES

SUGGESTED ASSIGNMENT
Exercises 1–6; Exercises 7–133, every other odd; More challenging exercises: Exercises 134, 136, 138

Concept Check

1. The trinomial $x^2 - 8x + 7$ is of the form $x^2 + bx + c$. What is the value of b in the trinomial $x^2 - 8x + 7$? -8
2. Find two numbers whose sum is 9 and whose product is 14. 2 and 7
3. Find two numbers whose sum is 4 and whose product is -12. -2 and 6
4. When factoring a trinomial, if the constant term is positive, will the signs in the binomials be the same or different? The same
5. When factoring a trinomial, if the constant term is negative, will the signs in the binomials be the same or different? Different
6. What is the first step in factoring a trinomial? Determine whether the terms of the trinomial have a common factor.

OBJECTIVE A *To factor a trinomial of the form $x^2 + bx + c$*

For Exercises 7 to 75, factor.

7. $x^2 + 3x + 2$ $(x + 1)(x + 2)$
8. $x^2 + 5x + 6$ $(x + 2)(x + 3)$
9. $x^2 - x - 2$ $(x + 1)(x - 2)$
10. $x^2 + x - 6$ $(x + 3)(x - 2)$
11. $a^2 + a - 12$ $(a + 4)(a - 3)$
12. $a^2 - 2a - 35$ $(a + 5)(a - 7)$
13. $a^2 - 3a + 2$ $(a - 1)(a - 2)$
14. $a^2 - 5a + 4$ $(a - 1)(a - 4)$
15. $a^2 + a - 2$ $(a + 2)(a - 1)$
16. $a^2 - 2a - 3$ $(a + 1)(a - 3)$
17. $b^2 - 6b + 9$ $(b - 3)(b - 3)$
18. $b^2 + 8b + 16$ $(b + 4)(b + 4)$
19. $b^2 + 7b - 8$ $(b + 8)(b - 1)$
20. $y^2 - y - 6$ $(y + 2)(y - 3)$
21. $y^2 + 6y - 55$ $(y + 11)(y - 5)$
22. $z^2 - 4z - 45$ $(z + 5)(z - 9)$
23. $y^2 - 5y + 6$ $(y - 2)(y - 3)$
24. $y^2 - 8y + 15$ $(y - 3)(y - 5)$
25. $z^2 - 14z + 45$ $(z - 5)(z - 9)$
26. $z^2 - 14z + 49$ $(z - 7)(z - 7)$
27. $z^2 - 12z - 160$ $(z + 8)(z - 20)$
28. $p^2 + 2p - 35$ $(p + 7)(p - 5)$
29. $p^2 + 12p + 27$ $(p + 3)(p + 9)$
30. $p^2 - 6p + 8$ $(p - 2)(p - 4)$
31. $x^2 + 20x + 100$ $(x + 10)(x + 10)$
32. $x^2 + 9x - 70$ $(x + 14)(x - 5)$
33. $b^2 - b - 20$ $(b + 4)(b - 5)$
34. $b^2 + 3b - 40$ $(b + 8)(b - 5)$
35. $y^2 - 14y - 51$ $(y + 3)(y - 17)$
36. $y^2 - y - 72$ $(y + 8)(y - 9)$
37. $p^2 - 4p - 21$ $(p + 3)(p - 7)$
38. $p^2 + 16p + 39$ $(p + 3)(p + 13)$

39. $y^2 - 8y + 32$
Nonfactorable over the integers

40. $y^2 - 9y + 81$
Nonfactorable over the integers

41. $x^2 - 20x + 75$
$(x - 5)(x - 15)$

42. $x^2 - 12x + 11$
$(x - 11)(x - 1)$

43. $p^2 + 24p + 63$
$(p + 3)(p + 21)$

44. $x^2 - 15x + 56$
$(x - 7)(x - 8)$

45. $x^2 + 21x + 38$
$(x + 2)(x + 19)$

46. $x^2 + x - 56$
$(x + 8)(x - 7)$

47. $x^2 + 5x - 3$
Nonfactorable over the integers

48. $a^2 - 21a - 7$
Nonfactorable over the integers

49. $a^2 - 7a - 44$
$(a + 4)(a - 11)$

50. $a^2 - 15a + 36$
$(a - 3)(a - 12)$

51. $a^2 - 21a + 54$
$(a - 3)(a - 18)$

52. $z^2 - 9z - 136$
$(z + 8)(z - 17)$

53. $z^2 + 14z - 147$
$(z + 21)(z - 7)$

54. $c^2 - c - 90$
$(c + 9)(c - 10)$

55. $c^2 - 3c - 180$
$(c + 12)(c - 15)$

56. $z^2 + 15z + 44$
$(z + 4)(z + 11)$

57. $p^2 + 24p + 135$
$(p + 9)(p + 15)$

58. $c^2 + 19c + 34$
$(c + 2)(c + 17)$

59. $c^2 + 11c + 18$
$(c + 2)(c + 9)$

60. $x^2 - 4x - 96$
$(x + 8)(x - 12)$

61. $x^2 + 10x - 75$
$(x + 15)(x - 5)$

62. $x^2 - 22x + 112$
$(x - 8)(x - 14)$

63. $x^2 + 21x - 100$
$(x + 25)(x - 4)$

64. $b^2 + 8b - 105$
$(b + 15)(b - 7)$

65. $b^2 - 22b + 72$
$(b - 4)(b - 18)$

66. $a^2 - 9a - 36$
$(a + 3)(a - 12)$

67. $a^2 + 42a - 135$
$(a + 45)(a - 3)$

68. $b^2 - 23b + 102$
$(b - 6)(b - 17)$

69. $b^2 - 25b + 126$
$(b - 7)(b - 18)$

70. $a^2 + 27a + 72$
$(a + 3)(a + 24)$

71. $z^2 + 24z + 144$
$(z + 12)(z + 12)$

72. $x^2 + 25x + 156$
$(x + 12)(x + 13)$

73. $x^2 - 29x + 100$
$(x - 4)(x - 25)$

74. $x^2 - 10x - 96$
$(x + 6)(x - 16)$

75. $x^2 + 9x - 112$
$(x + 16)(x - 7)$

For Exercises 76 and 77, $x^2 + bx + c = (x + n)(x + m)$, where b and c are nonzero and n and m are positive integers.

76. Is c positive or negative?
Positive

77. Is b positive or negative?
Positive

OBJECTIVE B To factor completely

For Exercises 78 to 131, factor completely.

78. $2x^2 + 6x + 4$
$2(x + 1)(x + 2)$

79. $3x^2 + 15x + 18$
$3(x + 2)(x + 3)$

80. $18 + 7x - x^2$
$-(x - 9)(x + 2)$

81. $12 - 4x - x^2$
$-(x + 6)(x - 2)$

82. $ab^2 + 2ab - 15a$
$a(b + 5)(b - 3)$

83. $ab^2 + 7ab - 8a$
$a(b + 8)(b - 1)$

84. $xy^2 - 5xy + 6x$
$x(y - 2)(y - 3)$

85. $xy^2 + 8xy + 15x$
$x(y + 3)(y + 5)$

86. $z^3 - 7z^2 + 12z$
$z(z - 3)(z - 4)$

87. $-2a^3 - 6a^2 - 4a$
$-2a(a + 2)(a + 1)$

88. $-3y^3 + 15y^2 - 18y$
$-3y(y - 3)(y - 2)$

89. $4y^3 + 12y^2 - 72y$
$4y(y + 6)(y - 3)$

90. $3x^2 + 3x - 36$
$3(x + 4)(x - 3)$

91. $2x^3 - 2x^2 + 4x$
$2x(x^2 - x + 2)$

92. $5z^2 - 15z - 140$
$5(z + 4)(z - 7)$

93. $6z^2 + 12z - 90$
$6(z + 5)(z - 3)$

94. $2a^3 + 8a^2 - 64a$
$2a(a + 8)(a - 4)$

95. $3a^3 - 9a^2 - 54a$
$3a(a + 3)(a - 6)$

96. $x^2 - 5xy + 6y^2$
$(x - 2y)(x - 3y)$

97. $x^2 + 4xy - 21y^2$
$(x + 7y)(x - 3y)$

98. $a^2 - 9ab + 20b^2$
$(a - 4b)(a - 5b)$

99. $a^2 - 15ab + 50b^2$
$(a - 5b)(a - 10b)$

100. $x^2 - 3xy - 28y^2$
$(x + 4y)(x - 7y)$

101. $s^2 + 2st - 48t^2$
$(s + 8t)(s - 6t)$

102. $y^2 - 15yz - 41z^2$
Nonfactorable over the integers

103. $x^2 + 85xy + 36y^2$
Nonfactorable over the integers

104. $z^4 - 12z^3 + 35z^2$
$z^2(z - 5)(z - 7)$

105. $z^4 + 2z^3 - 80z^2$
$z^2(z + 10)(z - 8)$

106. $b^4 - 22b^3 + 120b^2$
$b^2(b - 10)(b - 12)$

107. $b^4 - 3b^3 - 10b^2$
$b^2(b + 2)(b - 5)$

108. $2y^4 - 26y^3 - 96y^2$
$2y^2(y + 3)(y - 16)$

109. $3y^4 + 54y^3 + 135y^2$
$3y^2(y + 3)(y + 15)$

110. $-x^4 - 7x^3 + 8x^2$
$-x^2(x + 8)(x - 1)$

111. $-x^4 + 11x^3 + 12x^2$
$-x^2(x - 12)(x + 1)$

112. $4x^2y + 20xy - 56y$
$4y(x + 7)(x - 2)$

113. $3x^2y - 6xy - 45y$
$3y(x + 3)(x - 5)$

114. $c^3 + 18c^2 - 40c$
$c(c + 20)(c - 2)$

115. $-3x^3 + 36x^2 - 81x$
$-3x(x - 3)(x - 9)$

116. $-4x^3 - 4x^2 + 24x$
$-4x(x + 3)(x - 2)$

117. $x^2 - 8xy + 15y^2$
$(x - 3y)(x - 5y)$

118. $y^2 - 7xy - 8x^2$
$(y + x)(y - 8x)$

119. $a^2 - 13ab + 42b^2$
$(a - 6b)(a - 7b)$

120. $y^2 + 4yz - 21z^2$
$(y + 7z)(y - 3z)$

121. $y^2 + 8yz + 7z^2$
$(y + z)(y + 7z)$

122. $y^2 - 16yz + 15z^2$
$(y - z)(y - 15z)$

123. $3x^2y + 60xy - 63y$
$3y(x + 21)(x - 1)$

124. $4x^2y - 68xy - 72y$
$4y(x + 1)(x - 18)$

125. $3x^3 + 3x^2 - 36x$
$3x(x + 4)(x - 3)$

126. $4x^3 + 12x^2 - 160x$
$4x(x + 8)(x - 5)$

127. $2t^2 - 24ts + 70s^2$
$2(t - 5s)(t - 7s)$

128. $4a^2 - 40ab + 100b^2$
$4(a - 5b)(a - 5b)$

129. $3a^2 - 24ab - 99b^2$
$3(a + 3b)(a - 11b)$

130. $4x^3 + 8x^2y - 12xy^2$
$4x(x + 3y)(x - y)$

131. $5x^3 + 30x^2y + 40xy^2$
$5x(x + 2y)(x + 4y)$

132. State whether the trinomial has a factor of $x + 3$.
a. $3x^2 - 3x - 36$
Yes
b. $x^2y - xy - 12y$
Yes

133. State whether the trinomial has a factor of $x + y$.
a. $2x^2 - 2xy - 4y^2$
Yes
b. $2x^2y - 4xy - 4y$
No

Critical Thinking

134. If $a(x + 3) = x^2 + 2x - 3$, find a. $x - 1$

135. If $-2x^3 - 6x^2 - 4x = a(x + 1)(x + 2)$, find a. $-2x$

QUICK QUIZ
Factor.
1. $x^2 + 5x - 24$ **$(x + 8)(x - 3)$ [10.2A]**
2. $x^2 - 13x + 36$ **$(x - 9)(x - 4)$ [10.2A]**
3. $3a^3 + 15a^2 + 18a$ **$3a(a + 3)(a + 2)$ [10.2B]**
4. $5x^3 - 15x^2y + 10xy^2$ **$5x(x - y)(x - 2y)$ [10.2B]**

For Exercises 136 to 139, factor.

136. $20 + c^2 + 9c$ $(c + 4)(c + 5)$

137. $x^2y - 54y - 3xy$ $y(x + 6)(x - 9)$

138. $45a^2 + a^2b^2 - 14a^2b$ $a^2(b - 5)(b - 9)$

139. $12p^2 - 96p + 3p^3$ $3p(p + 8)(p - 4)$

Projects or Group Activities

For Exercises 140 to 143, find all integers k such that the trinomial can be factored over the integers.

140. $x^2 + kx + 35$
36, 12, −12, −36

141. $x^2 + kx + 18$
19, 11, 9, −9, −11, −19

142. $x^2 - kx + 21$
22, 10, −10, −22

143. $x^2 - kx + 14$
15, 9, −9, −15

For Exercises 144 to 149, determine the positive integer values of k for which the polynomial is factorable over the integers.

144. $y^2 + 4y + k$ 3, 4

145. $z^2 + 7z + k$ 6, 10, 12

146. $a^2 - 6a + k$ 5, 8, 9

147. $c^2 - 7c + k$ 6, 10, 12

148. $x^2 - 3x + k$ 2

149. $y^2 + 5y + k$ 4, 6

150. Exercises 144 to 149 included the requirement that $k > 0$. If k is allowed to be any integer, how many different values of k are possible for each polynomial? Explain your answer.

SECTION

10.3 Factoring Polynomials of the Form $ax^2 + bx + c$

OBJECTIVE A *To factor a trinomial of the form $ax^2 + bx + c$ by using trial factors*

INSTRUCTOR NOTE
The first objective of this section presents factoring by using trial factors. The second objective presents factoring by grouping. You may skip one of these objectives or do both.

Trinomials of the form $ax^2 + bx + c$, where a, b, and c are integers, are shown at the right.

$3x^2 - x + 4;\ a = 3,\ b = -1,\ c = 4$
$6x^2 + 2x - 3;\ a = 6,\ b = 2,\ c = -3$

These trinomials differ from those in the preceding section in that the coefficient of x^2 is not 1. There are various methods of factoring these trinomials. The method described in this objective is factoring by using trial factors.

To reduce the number of trial factors that must be considered, remember the following:

1. Use the signs of the constant term and the coefficient of x in the trinomial to determine the signs of the binomial factors. If the constant term is positive, the signs of the binomial factors will be the same as the sign of the coefficient of x in the trinomial. If the constant term is negative, the constant terms in the binomials will have opposite signs.
2. If the terms of the trinomial do not have a common factor, then the terms of each binomial factor will not have a common factor.

HOW TO 1 Factor: $2x^2 - 7x + 3$

The terms have no common factor. The constant term is positive. The coefficient of x is negative. The binomial constants will be negative.

Positive Factors of 2 (coefficient of x^2)	*Negative Factors of 3* (constant term)
1, 2	−1, −3

Write trial factors. Use the **O**uter and **I**nner products of FOIL to determine the middle term, $-7x$, of the trinomial.

Trial Factors	*Middle Term*
$(x - 1)(2x - 3)$	$-3x - 2x = -5x$
$(x - 3)(2x - 1)$	$-x - 6x = -7x$

Write the factors of the trinomial.

$$2x^2 - 7x + 3 = (x - 3)(2x - 1)$$

HOW TO 2 Factor: $3x^2 + 14x + 15$

The terms have no common factor. The constant term is positive. The coefficient of x is positive. The binomial constants will be positive.

Positive Factors of 3 (coefficient of x^2)	*Negative Factors of 15* (constant term)
1, 3	1, 15
	3, 5

Write trial factors. Use the **O**uter and **I**nner products of FOIL to determine the middle term, $14x$, of the trinomial.

Trial Factors	*Middle Term*
$(x + 1)(3x + 15)$	Common factor
$(x + 15)(3x + 1)$	$x + 45x = 46x$
$(x + 3)(3x + 5)$	$5x + 9x = 14x$
$(x + 5)(3x + 3)$	Common factor

Write the factors of the trinomial.

$$3x^2 + 14x + 15 = (x + 3)(3x + 5)$$

INSTRUCTOR NOTE
Remind students that they can eliminate the trial factors that have a common factor only when the terms of the polynomial do not have a common factor.

HOW TO 3 Factor: $6x^3 + 14x^2 - 12x$

Factor the GCF, $2x$, from the terms.

$6x^3 + 14x^2 - 12x = 2x(3x^2 + 7x - 6)$

Factor the trinomial. The constant term is negative. The binomial constants will have opposite signs.

Positive Factors of 3	Factors of −6
1, 3	1, −6
	−1, 6
	2, −3
	−2, 3

Write trial factors. Use the **O**uter and **I**nner products of FOIL to determine the middle term, $7x$, of the trinomial.

It is not necessary to test trial factors that have a common factor.

Trial Factors	Middle Term
$(x + 1)(3x - 6)$	Common factor
$(x - 6)(3x + 1)$	$x - 18x = -17x$
$(x - 1)(3x + 6)$	Common factor
$(x + 6)(3x - 1)$	$-x + 18x = 17x$
$(x + 2)(3x - 3)$	Common factor
$(x - 3)(3x + 2)$	$2x - 9x = -7x$
$(x - 2)(3x + 3)$	Common factor
$(x + 3)(3x - 2)$	$-2x + 9x = 7x$

Write the factors of the trinomial.

$6x^3 + 14x^2 - 12x = 2x(x + 3)(3x - 2)$

Take Note
For HOW TO 3, all the trial factors were listed. Once the correct factors have been found, however, the remaining trial factors can be omitted. For the examples and solutions in this text, all trial factors except those that have a common factor will be listed.

EXAMPLE 1

Factor: $3x^2 + x - 2$

Solution

Positive factors of 3: 1, 3

Factors of −2: 1, −2
−1, 2

Trial Factors	Middle Term
$(x + 1)(3x - 2)$	$-2x + 3x = \mathbf{x}$
$(x - 2)(3x + 1)$	$x - 6x = -5x$
$(x - 1)(3x + 2)$	$2x - 3x = -x$
$(x + 2)(3x - 1)$	$-x + 6x = 5x$

$3x^2 + x - 2 = (x + 1)(3x - 2)$

YOU TRY IT 1

Factor: $2x^2 - x - 3$

Your solution

$(x + 1)(2x - 3)$

EXAMPLE 2

Factor: $-12x^3 - 32x^2 + 12x$

Solution

$-12x^3 - 32x^2 + 12x = -4x(3x^2 + 8x - 3)$ • GCF

Factor $3x^2 + 8x - 3$.

Positive factors of 3: 1, 3

Factors of −3: 1, −3
−1, 3

Trial Factors	Middle Term
$(x - 3)(3x + 1)$	$x - 9x = -8x$
$(x + 3)(3x - 1)$	$-x + 9x = \mathbf{8x}$

$-12x^3 - 32x^2 + 12x = -4x(x + 3)(3x - 1)$

YOU TRY IT 2

Factor: $-45y^3 + 12y^2 + 12y$

Your solution

$-3y(3y - 2)(5y + 2)$

IN-CLASS EXAMPLES

Factor.

1. $5x^2 - 2x - 3$ $\mathbf{(5x + 3)(x - 1)}$
2. $-12x^3 - 18x^2 + 30x$
   $\mathbf{-6x(2x + 5)(x - 1)}$

Solutions on p. S24

OBJECTIVE B *To factor a trinomial of the form $ax^2 + bx + c$ by grouping*

In the preceding objective, trinomials of the form $ax^2 + bx + c$ were factored by using trial factors. In this objective, these trinomials will be factored by grouping.

To factor $ax^2 + bx + c$, first find two factors of $a \cdot c$ whose sum is b. Then use factoring by grouping to write the factorization of the trinomial.

HOW TO 4 Factor: $2x^2 + 13x + 15$

Find two positive factors of 30 $(a \cdot c = 2 \cdot 15 = 30)$ whose sum is 13.

Positive Factors of 30	*Sum*
1, 30	31
2, 15	17
3, 10	13

- **Once the required sum has been found, the remaining factors need not be checked.**

$$\begin{aligned} 2x^2 + 13x + 15 &= 2x^2 + 3x + 10x + 15 \\ &= (2x^2 + 3x) + (10x + 15) \\ &= x(2x + 3) + 5(2x + 3) \\ &= (2x + 3)(x + 5) \end{aligned}$$

- **Use the factors of 30 whose sum is 13 to write $13x$ as $3x + 10x$.**
- **Factor by grouping.**

Check: $(2x + 3)(x + 5) = 2x^2 + 10x + 3x + 15$
$= 2x^2 + 13x + 15$

HOW TO 5 Factor: $6x^2 - 11x - 10$

Find two factors of -60 $[a \cdot c = 6(-10) = -60]$ whose sum is -11.

Factors of −60	*Sum*
1, −60	−59
−1, 60	59
2, −30	−28
−2, 30	28
3, −20	−17
−3, 20	17
4, −15	−11

$$\begin{aligned} 6x^2 - 11x - 10 &= 6x^2 + 4x - 15x - 10 \\ &= (6x^2 + 4x) - (15x + 10) \\ &= 2x(3x + 2) - 5(3x + 2) \\ &= (3x + 2)(2x - 5) \end{aligned}$$

- **Use the factors of -60 whose sum is -11 to write $-11x$ as $4x - 15x$.**
- **Factor by grouping. Recall that $-15x - 10 = -(15x + 10)$.**

Check: $(3x + 2)(2x - 5) = 6x^2 - 15x + 4x - 10$
$= 6x^2 - 11x - 10$

HOW TO 6 Factor: $3x^2 - 2x - 4$

Find two factors of -12 $[a \cdot c = 3(-4) = -12]$ whose sum is -2.

Factors of −12	Sum
1, −12	−11
−1, 12	11
2, −6	−4
−2, 6	4
3, −4	−1
−3, 4	1

Because no integer factors of -12 have a sum of -2, $3x^2 - 2x - 4$ is nonfactorable over the integers.

EXAMPLE 3

Factor: $2x^2 + 19x - 10$

Solution

Factors of −20 [2(−10)]	Sum
−1, 20	**19**

$$\begin{aligned} 2x^2 + 19x - 10 &= 2x^2 - x + 20x - 10 \\ &= (2x^2 - x) + (20x - 10) \\ &= x(2x - 1) + 10(2x - 1) \\ &= (2x - 1)(x + 10) \end{aligned}$$

YOU TRY IT 3

Factor: $2a^2 + 13a - 7$

Your solution

$(2a - 1)(a + 7)$

EXAMPLE 4

Factor: $24x^2y - 76xy + 40y$

Solution

The GCF is $4y$.

$24x^2y - 76xy + 40y = 4y(6x^2 - 19x + 10)$

Factor $6x^2 - 19x + 10$.

Negative Factors of 60 [6(10)]	Sum
−1, −60	−61
−2, −30	−32
−3, −20	−23
−4, −15	**−19**

$$\begin{aligned} 6x^2 - 19x + 10 &= 6x^2 - 4x - 15x + 10 \\ &= (6x^2 - 4x) - (15x - 10) \\ &= 2x(3x - 2) - 5(3x - 2) \\ &= (3x - 2)(2x - 5) \end{aligned}$$

$$\begin{aligned} 24x^2y - 76xy + 40y &= 4y(6x^2 - 19x + 10) \\ &= 4y(3x - 2)(2x - 5) \end{aligned}$$

YOU TRY IT 4

Factor: $15x^3 + 40x^2 - 80x$

Your solution

$5x(3x - 4)(x + 4)$

IN-CLASS EXAMPLES

Factor.

3. $3x^2 + 7x + 4$ $\mathbf{(3x + 4)(x + 1)}$
4. $72x^3 - 42x^2 - 72x$ $\mathbf{6x(4x + 3)(3x - 4)}$

Solutions on pp. S24–S25

10.3 EXERCISES

Concept Check

If assigning factoring using trial factors, the Suggested Assignment is Exercises 1–4; Exercises 9–73, odds; More challenging exercises: Exercises 139–147, odds

For Exercises 1 to 4, fill in the blank to make a true statement.

1. $6x^2 + 11x - 10 = (3x - 2)($ $2x + 5$ $)$

2. $40x^2 + 41x + 10 = (8x + 5)($ $5x + 2$ $)$

3. $20x^2 - 31x + 12 = (5x - 4)($ $4x - 3$ $)$

4. $12x^2 - 4x - 21 = (6x + 7)($ $2x - 3$ $)$

For Exercises 5 to 8, fill in the blanks.

If assigning factoring by grouping, the Suggested Assignment is Exercises 5–8; Exercises 77–133, odds; More challenging exercises: Exercises 139–147, odds

5. To factor $2x^2 - 5x + 2$ by grouping, find two numbers whose product is 4 and whose sum is -5.

6. To factor $3x^2 + 2x - 5$ by grouping, find two numbers whose product is -15 and whose sum is 2.

7. To factor $4x^2 - 8x + 3$ by grouping, $-8x$ must be written as $-2x - 6x$.

8. To factor $6x^2 + 7x - 3$ by grouping, $7x$ must be written as $-2x + 9x$.

OBJECTIVE A *To factor a trinomial of the form $ax^2 + bx + c$ by using trial factors*

For Exercises 9 to 74, factor by using trial factors.

9. $2x^2 + 3x + 1$
$(x + 1)(2x + 1)$

10. $5x^2 + 6x + 1$
$(x + 1)(5x + 1)$

11. $2y^2 + 7y + 3$
$(y + 3)(2y + 1)$

12. $3y^2 + 7y + 2$
$(y + 2)(3y + 1)$

13. $2a^2 - 3a + 1$
$(a - 1)(2a - 1)$

14. $3a^2 - 4a + 1$
$(a - 1)(3a - 1)$

15. $2b^2 - 11b + 5$
$(b - 5)(2b - 1)$

16. $3b^2 - 13b + 4$
$(b - 4)(3b - 1)$

17. $2x^2 + x - 1$
$(x + 1)(2x - 1)$

18. $4x^2 - 3x - 1$
$(x - 1)(4x + 1)$

19. $2x^2 - 5x - 3$
$(x - 3)(2x + 1)$

20. $3x^2 + 5x - 2$
$(x + 2)(3x - 1)$

21. $2t^2 - t - 10$
$(t + 2)(2t - 5)$

22. $2t^2 + 5t - 12$
$(t + 4)(2t - 3)$

23. $3p^2 - 16p + 5$
$(p - 5)(3p - 1)$

24. $6p^2 + 5p + 1$
$(2p + 1)(3p + 1)$

25. $12y^2 - 7y + 1$
$(3y - 1)(4y - 1)$

26. $6y^2 - 5y + 1$
$(2y - 1)(3y - 1)$

27. $6z^2 - 7z + 3$
Nonfactorable over the integers

28. $9z^2 + 3z + 2$
Nonfactorable over the integers

29. $6t^2 - 11t + 4$
$(2t - 1)(3t - 4)$

30. $10t^2 + 11t + 3$
$(2t + 1)(5t + 3)$

31. $8x^2 + 33x + 4$
$(x + 4)(8x + 1)$

32. $7x^2 + 50x + 7$
$(x + 7)(7x + 1)$

33. $5x^2 - 62x - 7$
Nonfactorable over the integers

34. $9x^2 - 13x - 4$
Nonfactorable over the integers

35. $12y^2 + 19y + 5$
$(3y + 1)(4y + 5)$

36. $6b^2 - 19b + 15$
$(2b - 3)(3b - 5)$

37. $2z^2 - 27z - 14$
$(z - 14)(2z + 1)$

38. $4z^2 + 5z - 6$
$(z + 2)(4z - 3)$

39. $3p^2 + 22p - 16$
$(p + 8)(3p - 2)$

40. $7p^2 + 19p + 10$
$(p + 2)(7p + 5)$

41. $4x^2 + 6x + 2$
$2(x + 1)(2x + 1)$

42. $12x^2 + 33x - 9$
$3(x + 3)(4x - 1)$

43. $15y^2 - 50y + 35$
$5(y - 1)(3y - 7)$

44. $30y^2 + 10y - 20$
$10(y + 1)(3y - 2)$

45. $2x^3 - 11x^2 + 5x$
$x(x - 5)(2x - 1)$

46. $2x^3 - 3x^2 - 5x$
$x(x + 1)(2x - 5)$

47. $3a^2b - 16ab + 16b$
$b(a - 4)(3a - 4)$

48. $2a^2b - ab - 21b$
$b(a + 3)(2a - 7)$

49. $3z^2 + 95z + 10$
Nonfactorable over the integers

50. $8z^2 - 36z + 1$
Nonfactorable over the integers

51. $36x - 3x^2 - 3x^3$
$-3x(x + 4)(x - 3)$

52. $-2x^3 + 2x^2 + 4x$
$-2x(x - 2)(x + 1)$

53. $80y^2 - 36y + 4$
$4(4y - 1)(5y - 1)$

54. $24y^2 - 24y - 18$
$6(2y + 1)(2y - 3)$

55. $8z^3 + 14z^2 + 3z$
$z(2z + 3)(4z + 1)$

56. $6z^3 - 23z^2 + 20z$
$z(2z - 5)(3z - 4)$

57. $6x^2y - 11xy - 10y$
$y(2x - 5)(3x + 2)$

58. $8x^2y - 27xy + 9y$
$y(x - 3)(8x - 3)$

59. $10t^2 - 5t - 50$
$5(t + 2)(2t - 5)$

60. $16t^2 + 40t - 96$
$8(t + 4)(2t - 3)$

61. $3p^3 - 16p^2 + 5p$
$p(p - 5)(3p - 1)$

62. $6p^3 + 5p^2 + p$
$p(2p + 1)(3p + 1)$

63. $26z^2 + 98z - 24$
$2(z + 4)(13z - 3)$

64. $30z^2 - 87z + 30$
$3(2z - 5)(5z - 2)$

65. $10y^3 - 44y^2 + 16y$
$2y(y - 4)(5y - 2)$

66. $14y^3 + 94y^2 - 28y$
$2y(y + 7)(7y - 2)$

67. $4yz^3 + 5yz^2 - 6yz$
$yz(z + 2)(4z - 3)$

68. $12a^3 + 14a^2 - 48a$
$2a(2a - 3)(3a + 8)$

69. $42a^3 + 45a^2 - 27a$
$3a(2a + 3)(7a - 3)$

70. $36p^2 - 9p^3 - p^4$
$-p^2(p - 3)(p + 12)$

71. $9x^2y - 30xy^2 + 25y^3$
$y(3x - 5y)(3x - 5y)$

72. $8x^2y - 38xy^2 + 35y^3$
$y(2x - 7y)(4x - 5y)$

73. $9x^3y - 24x^2y^2 + 16xy^3$
$xy(3x - 4y)(3x - 4y)$

74. $9x^3y + 12x^2y + 4xy$
$xy(3x + 2)(3x + 2)$

For Exercises 75 and 76, let $(nx + p)$ and $(mx + q)$ be prime factors of the trinomial $ax^2 + bx + c$.

75. If n is even, must p be even or odd? Odd

76. If p is even, must n be even or odd? Odd

OBJECTIVE B *To factor a trinomial of the form $ax^2 + bx + c$ by grouping*

For Exercises 77 to 133, factor by grouping.

77. $6x^2 - 17x + 12$
$(2x - 3)(3x - 4)$

78. $15x^2 - 19x + 6$
$(3x - 2)(5x - 3)$

79. $5b^2 + 33b - 14$
$(b + 7)(5b - 2)$

80. $8x^2 - 30x + 25$
$(2x - 5)(4x - 5)$

81. $6a^2 + 7a - 24$
$(2a - 3)(3a + 8)$

82. $14a^2 + 15a - 9$
$(2a + 3)(7a - 3)$

83. $4z^2 + 11z + 6$
$(z + 2)(4z + 3)$

84. $6z^2 - 25z + 14$
$(2z - 7)(3z - 2)$

85. $22p^2 + 51p - 10$
$(2p + 5)(11p - 2)$

86. $14p^2 - 41p + 15$
$(2p - 5)(7p - 3)$

87. $8y^2 + 17y + 9$
$(y + 1)(8y + 9)$

88. $12y^2 - 145y + 12$
$(y - 12)(12y - 1)$

89. $18t^2 - 9t - 5$
$(3t + 1)(6t - 5)$

90. $12t^2 + 28t - 5$
$(2t + 5)(6t - 1)$

91. $6b^2 + 71b - 12$
$(b + 12)(6b - 1)$

92. $8b^2 + 65b + 8$
$(b + 8)(8b + 1)$

93. $9x^2 + 12x + 4$
$(3x + 2)(3x + 2)$

94. $25x^2 - 30x + 9$
$(5x - 3)(5x - 3)$

95. $6b^2 - 13b + 6$
$(2b - 3)(3b - 2)$

96. $20b^2 + 37b + 15$
$(4b + 5)(5b + 3)$

97. $33b^2 + 34b - 35$
$(3b + 5)(11b - 7)$

98. $15b^2 - 43b + 22$
$(3b - 2)(5b - 11)$

99. $18y^2 - 39y + 20$
$(3y - 4)(6y - 5)$

100. $24y^2 + 41y + 12$
$(3y + 4)(8y + 3)$

101. $15a^2 + 26a - 21$
$(3a + 7)(5a - 3)$

102. $6a^2 + 23a + 21$
$(2a + 3)(3a + 7)$

103. $8y^2 - 26y + 15$
$(2y - 5)(4y - 3)$

104. $18y^2 - 27y + 4$
$(3y - 4)(6y - 1)$

105. $8z^2 + 2z - 15$
$(2z + 3)(4z - 5)$

106. $10z^2 + 3z - 4$
$(2z - 1)(5z + 4)$

107. $15x^2 - 82x + 24$
Nonfactorable over the integers

108. $13z^2 + 49z - 8$
Nonfactorable over the integers

109. $10z^2 - 29z + 10$
$(2z - 5)(5z - 2)$

110. $15z^2 - 44z + 32$
$(3z - 4)(5z - 8)$

111. $36z^2 + 72z + 35$
$(6z + 5)(6z + 7)$

112. $16z^2 + 8z - 35$
$(4z + 7)(4z - 5)$

113. $3x^2 + xy - 2y^2$
$(x + y)(3x - 2y)$

114. $6x^2 + 10xy + 4y^2$
$2(x + y)(3x + 2y)$

115. $3a^2 + 5ab - 2b^2$
$(a + 2b)(3a - b)$

116. $2a^2 - 9ab + 9b^2$
$(a - 3b)(2a - 3b)$

117. $4y^2 - 11yz + 6z^2$
$(y - 2z)(4y - 3z)$

118. $2y^2 + 7yz + 5z^2$
$(y + z)(2y + 5z)$

119. $28 + 3z - z^2$
$-(z - 7)(z + 4)$

120. $15 - 2z - z^2$
$-(z - 3)(z + 5)$

121. $8 - 7x - x^2$
$-(x - 1)(x + 8)$

122. $12 + 11x - x^2$
$-(x - 12)(x + 1)$

123. $9x^2 + 33x - 60$
$3(x + 5)(3x - 4)$

124. $16x^2 - 16x - 12$
$4(2x + 1)(2x - 3)$

125. $24x^2 - 52x + 24$
$4(2x - 3)(3x - 2)$

126. $60x^2 + 95x + 20$
$5(3x + 4)(4x + 1)$

127. $35a^4 + 9a^3 - 2a^2$
$a^2(5a + 2)(7a - 1)$

128. $15a^4 + 26a^3 + 7a^2$
$a^2(3a + 1)(5a + 7)$

129. $15b^2 - 115b + 70$
$5(b - 7)(3b - 2)$

130. $25b^2 + 35b - 30$
$5(b + 2)(5b - 3)$

131. $3x^2 - 26xy + 35y^2$
$(x - 7y)(3x - 5y)$

132. $4x^2 + 16xy + 15y^2$
$(2x + 3y)(2x + 5y)$

133. $216y^2 - 3y - 3$
$3(8y - 1)(9y + 1)$

For Exercises 134 to 137, information is given about the signs of b and c in the trinomial $ax^2 + bx + c$, where $a > 0$. If you want to factor $ax^2 + bx + c$ by grouping, you look for factors of ac whose sum is b. In each case, state whether the factors of ac should be two positive numbers, two negative numbers, or one positive and one negative number.

134. $b > 0$ and $c > 0$
Two positive

135. $b < 0$ and $c < 0$
One positive, one negative

136. $b < 0$ and $c > 0$
Two negative

137. $b > 0$ and $c < 0$
One positive, one negative

Critical Thinking

138. In your own words, explain how the signs of the last terms of the two binomial factors of a trinomial are determined.

For Exercises 139 to 147, factor.

139. $(x + 1)^2 - (x + 1) - 6$
$(x - 2)(x + 3)$

140. $(x - 2)^2 + 3(x - 2) + 2$
$x(x - 1)$

141. $(y + 3)^2 - 5(y + 3) + 6$
$y(y + 1)$

142. $2(y + 2)^2 - (y + 2) - 3$
$(2y + 1)(y + 3)$

143. $3(a + 2)^2 - (a + 2) - 4$
$(3a + 2)(a + 3)$

144. $4(y - 1)^2 - 7(y - 1) - 2$
$(4y - 3)(y - 3)$

145. $6y + 8y^3 - 26y^2$
$2y(y - 3)(4y - 1)$

146. $22p^2 - 3p^3 + 16p$
$p(2 + 3p)(8 - p)$

147. $a^3b - 24ab - 2a^2b$
$ab(a + 4)(a - 6)$

148. Given that $x + 2$ is a factor of $x^3 - 2x^2 - 5x + 6$, factor $x^3 - 2x^2 - 5x + 6$ completely. $(x + 2)(x - 3)(x - 1)$

QUICK QUIZ

Factor by using trial factors.

1. $2x^2 - 17x + 21$
   $(2x - 3)(x - 7)$ **[10.3A]**
2. $12x^3y + x^2y - 6xy$
   $xy(4x + 3)(3x - 2)$ **[10.3A]**

Factor by grouping.

3. $10x^2 + x - 2$
   $(5x - 2)(2x + 1)$ **[10.3B]**
4. $12x^3y + 10x^2y - 8xy$
   $2xy(3x + 4)(2x - 1)$ **[10.3B]**

Projects or Group Activities

For Exercises 149 to 154, find all integers k such that the trinomial can be factored over the integers.

149. $2x^2 + kx + 3$
7, −7, 5, −5

150. $2x^2 + kx - 3$
5, −5, 1, −1

151. $3x^2 + kx + 2$
7, −7, 5, −5

152. $3x^2 + kx - 2$
5, −5, 1, −1

153. $2x^2 + kx + 5$
11, −11, 7, −7

154. $2x^2 + kx - 5$
9, −9, −3, 3

155. **Geometry** The area of a rectangle is $(3x^2 + x - 2)$ ft^2. Find the dimensions of the rectangle in terms of the variable x. Given that $x > 0$, specify the dimension that is the length and the dimension that is the width. Can x be negative? Can $x = 0$? Explain your answers.

$A = 3x^2 + x - 2$

CHECK YOUR PROGRESS: CHAPTER 10

1. Factor: $20b + 5$ $5(4b + 1)$ [10.1A]

2. Factor: $2x(7 + b) - y(b + 7)$
$(b + 7)(2x - y)$ [10.1B]

3. Factor: $x^2 + 20x + 100$ $(x + 10)(x + 10)$ [10.2A]

4. Factor: $x^2y - 2xy - 24y$
$y(x + 4)(x - 6)$ [10.2B]

5. Factor: $35 + 2x - x^2$ $-(x - 7)(x + 5)$ [10.2B]

6. Factor: $x^2 - 8x - 2$
Nonfactorable over the integers [10.2A]

7. Factor: $21x^2 + 6xy - 49x - 14y$
$(7x + 2y)(3x - 7)$ [10.1B]

8. Factor: $6ab + 9a$ $3a(2b + 3)$ [10.1A]

9. Factor by using trial factors:
$5y^2 - 22y + 8$ $(y - 4)(5y - 2)$ [10.3A]

10. Factor by grouping:
$12x^2 + 31x + 9$ $(3x + 1)(4x + 9)$ [10.3B]

11. Factor: $9x - 5x^2$ $x(9 - 5x)$ [10.1A]

12. Factor: $2x^2 + x + 2xy + y$
$(2x + 1)(x + y)$ [10.1B]

13. Factor by grouping:
$8a^2 - 2ab - 3b^2$ $(2a + b)(4a - 3b)$ [10.3B]

14. Factor: $b^2 + 9b + 20$
$(b + 4)(b + 5)$ [10.2A]

15. Factor: $2a^3 + 24a^2 + 54a$
$2a(a + 9)(a + 3)$ [10.2B]

16. Factor by using trial factors:
$11a^2 - 54a - 5$ $(a - 5)(11a + 1)$ [10.3A]

17. Factor by grouping:
$360y^2 + 4y - 4$ $4(9y + 1)(10y - 1)$ [10.3B]

18. Factor: $14y^3 + 5y^2 + 11y$
$y(14y^2 + 5y + 11)$ [10.1A]

19. Factor: $x^2 - 7x + 10$ $(x - 2)(x - 5)$ [10.2A]

20. Factor: $x^2 + 8xy + 9y^2$
Nonfactorable over the integers [10.2B]

21. Factor: $b^2 + 13b + 40$ $(b + 8)(b + 5)$ [10.2A]

22. Factor: $2x^2 - 5x - 6xy + 15y$
$(2x - 5)(x - 3y)$ [10.1B]

23. Factor: $x^2y - xy^3 + x^3y$
$xy(x - y^2 + x^2)$ [10.1A]

24. Factor by using trial factors:
$3b^2 + 16b + 16$ $(b + 4)(3b + 4)$ [10.3A]

25. Factor: $x^2 - 11x - 42$
$(x + 3)(x - 14)$ [10.2A]

SECTION

10.4 Special Factoring

OBJECTIVE A

To factor the difference of two squares and perfect-square trinomials

INSTRUCTOR NOTE
Here is a geometric representation of the difference of squares.

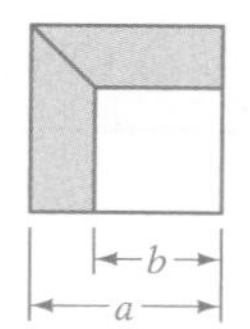

The shaded area can be combined as shown below.

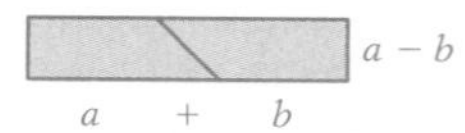

$(a + b)(a - b) = a^2 - b^2$

Take Note
Convince yourself that the sum of two squares is nonfactorable over the integers by trying to factor $x^2 + 4$.

Recall from Section 9.3D that the product of the sum and difference of the same two terms equals the square of the first term minus the square of the second term.

$$(a + b)(a - b) = a^2 - b^2$$

The expression $a^2 - b^2$ is the **difference of two squares.** The pattern just mentioned suggests the following rule for factoring the difference of two squares.

Rule for Factoring the Difference of Two Squares

Difference of Two Squares		Sum and Difference of the Same Terms
$a^2 - b^2$	=	$(a + b)(a - b)$

EXAMPLES

Each expression is the difference of two squares. Factor.

1. $x^2 - 4 = x^2 - 2^2 = (x + 2)(x - 2)$
2. $y^2 - 9 = y^2 - 3^2 = (y + 3)(y - 3)$

$a^2 + b^2$ is the sum of two squares. The sum of two squares is nonfactorable over the integers.

$4x^2 + 81$ is the sum of two squares. It is nonfactorable over the integers.

$4x^2 - 81$ is the difference of two squares. It factors as $(2x + 9)(2x - 9)$.

HOW TO 1 Factor: $8x^3 - 18x$

$8x^3 - 18x = 2x(4x^2 - 9)$ • The GCF is $2x$.

$= 2x[(2x)^2 - 3^2]$ • $4x^2 - 9$ is the difference of two squares.

$= 2x(2x + 3)(2x - 3)$ • Factor the difference of squares.

Check: $2x(2x + 3)(2x - 3) = 2x(4x^2 - 9)$

$= 8x^2 - 18x$

HOW TO 2 Factor: $x^2 - 10$

10 cannot be written as the square of an integer.

$x^2 - 10$ is nonfactorable over the integers.

Recall from Section 9.3D the pattern for finding the square of a binomial.

$$(a + b)^2 = (a + b)(a + b) = a^2 + ab + ab + b^2$$
$$= a^2 + 2ab + b^2$$

Square of the first term → a^2
Twice the product of the two terms → $2ab$
Square of the last term → b^2

The square of a binomial is a **perfect-square trinomial.** The pattern above suggests the following rule for factoring a perfect-square trinomial.

Rule for Factoring a Perfect-Square Trinomial

Perfect-Square Trinomial				Square of a Binomial
$a^2 + 2ab + b^2$	=	$(a + b)(a + b)$	=	$(a + b)^2$
$a^2 - 2ab + b^2$	=	$(a - b)(a - b)$	=	$(a - b)^2$

EXAMPLES

Each expression is a perfect-square trinomial. Factor.

1. $x^2 + 6x + 9 = (x + 3)^2$
2. $x^2 - 6x + 9 = (x - 3)^2$

Note in these patterns that the sign in the binomial is the sign of the middle term of the trinomial.

Take Note

A perfect-square trinomial can always be factored using either of the methods presented in Section 3 of this chapter. However, noticing that a trinomial is a perfect-square trinomial can save you a considerable amount of time.

HOW TO 3 Factor: $4x^2 - 20x + 25$

Because the first and last terms are squares $[(2x)^2 = 4x^2; 5^2 = 25]$, try to factor this trinomial as the square of a binomial. Check the factorization.

$$4x^2 - 20x + 25 = (2x - 5)^2$$

Check: $(2x - 5)^2 = (2x)^2 + 2(2x)(-5) + 5^2$
$= 4x^2 - 20x + 25$ • The factorization is correct.

HOW TO 4 Factor: $4x^2 + 37x + 9$

Because the first and last terms are squares $[(2x)^2 = 4x^2; 3^2 = 9]$, try to factor this trinomial as the square of a binomial. Check the proposed factorization.

$$4x^2 + 37x + 9 = (2x + 3)^2$$

Check: $(2x + 3)^2 = (2x)^2 + 2(2x)(3) + 3^2$
$= 4x^2 + 12x + 9$

Because $4x^2 + 12x + 9 \neq 4x^2 + 37x + 9$, the proposed factorization is not correct. In this case, the polynomial is not a perfect-square trinomial. It may, however, still factor. In fact, $4x^2 + 37x + 9 = (4x + 1)(x + 9)$.

EXAMPLE 1

Factor: $16x^2 - y^2$

Solution

$16x^2 - y^2 = (4x)^2 - y^2$ • The difference of two squares

$= (4x + y)(4x - y)$ • Factor.

YOU TRY IT 1

Factor: $25a^2 - b^2$

Your solution

$(5a + b)(5a - b)$

EXAMPLE 2

Factor: $z^4 - 16$

Solution

$z^4 - 16 = (z^2)^2 - 4^2$ • The difference of two squares

$= (z^2 + 4)(z^2 - 4)$ • The difference of two squares

$= (z^2 + 4)(z^2 - 2^2)$

$= (z^2 + 4)(z + 2)(z - 2)$ • Factor.

YOU TRY IT 2

Factor: $n^4 - 81$

Your solution

$(n^2 + 9)(n + 3)(n - 3)$

IN-CLASS EXAMPLES

Factor.

1. $36a^2 - 49b^2$
   $(6a + 7b)(6a - 7b)$
2. $100x^2 - 180x + 81$
   $(10x - 9)^2$
3. $16x^2 + 58x + 25$
   $(8x + 25)(2x + 1)$
4. $(x^2 + 10x + 25) - 9y^2$
   $(x + 5 + 3y)(x + 5 - 3y)$

EXAMPLE 3

Factor: $9x^2 - 30x + 25$

Solution

Try to factor this trinomial as the square of a binomial.

$9x^2 = (3x)^2$, $25 = (5)^2$

$9x^2 - 30x + 25 = (3x - 5)^2$

Check:

$(3x - 5)^2 = (3x)^2 + 2(3x)(-5) + 5^2$

$= 9x^2 - 30x + 25$

YOU TRY IT 3

Factor: $16y^2 + 8y + 1$

Your solution

$(4y + 1)^2$

EXAMPLE 4

Factor: $9x^2 + 40x + 16$

Solution

$9x^2 = (3x)^2$ and $16 = 4^2$

Because $2(3x)(4) \neq 40x$, the trinomial is not a perfect-square trinomial.

Try to factor by another method.

$9x^2 + 40x + 16 = (9x + 4)(x + 4)$

YOU TRY IT 4

Factor: $x^2 + 15x + 36$

Your solution

$(x + 3)(x + 12)$

Solutions on p. S25

10.4 EXERCISES

Concept Check

SUGGESTED ASSIGNMENT
Exercises 1–12; Exercises 13–53, odds

For Exercises 1 and 2, determine which expressions in the list are squares.

1. 4; 8; $25x^6$; $12y^{10}$; $100x^4y^4$ 4; $25x^6$; $100x^4y^4$

2. 9; 18; $15a^8$; $49b^{12}$; $64a^{16}b^2$ 9; $49b^{12}$; $64a^{16}b^2$

3. Which of the expressions are the difference of two squares?
(i) $a^2 - 36$ **(ii)** $b^2 - 12$ **(iii)** $c^2 + 25$ **(iv)** $d^2 - 100$ i and iv

4. Which expression is the sum and difference of two terms?
(i) $(a + 4)(a + 4)$ **(ii)** $(a + 4)(b - 4)$ **(iii)** $(a + 4)(a - 4)$ iii

For Exercises 5 to 8, determine whether the statement is always true, sometimes true, or never true.

5. A binomial is factorable. Sometimes true

6. A trinomial is factorable. Sometimes true

7. If a binomial is multiplied times itself, the result is a perfect-square trinomial. Always true

8. In a perfect-square trinomial, the first and last terms are squares. Always true

9. The binomial $9x^2 - 4$ is in the form $a^2 - b^2$, where $a =$ __3x__ and $b =$ __2__.

10. The trinomial $16y^2 - 8y + 1$ is in the form $a^2 - 2ab + b^2$, where $a =$ __4y__ and $b =$ __1__.

11. Provide an example of each of the following.
a. the difference of two squares
b. the product of the sum and difference of the same two terms
c. a perfect-square trinomial
d. the square of a binomial
e. the sum of two squares

11. Answers will vary. For example:
a. $x^2 - 16$
b. $(x + 7)(x - 7)$
c. $x^2 + 10x + 25$
d. $(x - 3)^2$
e. $x^2 + 36$

12. Explain the rule for factoring:
a. the difference of two squares
b. a perfect-square trinomial

OBJECTIVE A *To factor the difference of two squares and perfect-square trinomials*

For Exercises 13 to 54, factor.

13. $x^2 - 4$
$(x + 2)(x - 2)$

14. $x^2 - 9$
$(x + 3)(x - 3)$

15. $a^2 - 81$
$(a + 9)(a - 9)$

16. $a^2 - 49$
$(a + 7)(a - 7)$

17. $y^2 + 2y + 1$
$(y + 1)^2$

18. $y^2 + 14y + 49$
$(y + 7)^2$

19. $a^2 - 2a + 1$
$(a - 1)^2$

20. $x^2 - 12x + 36$
$(x - 6)^2$

21. $4x^2 - 1$
$(2x + 1)(2x - 1)$

22. $9x^2 - 16$
$(3x + 4)(3x - 4)$

23. $x^6 - 9$
$(x^3 + 3)(x^3 - 3)$

24. $y^{12} - 4$
$(y^6 + 2)(y^6 - 2)$

25. $x^2 + 8x - 16$
Nonfactorable over the integers

26. $z^2 - 18z - 81$
Nonfactorable over the integers

27. $x^2 + 2xy + y^2$
$(x + y)^2$

28. $x^2 + 6xy + 9y^2$
$(x + 3y)^2$

29. $4a^2 + 4a + 1$
$(2a + 1)^2$

30. $25x^2 + 10x + 1$
$(5x + 1)^2$

31. $9x^2 - 1$
$(3x + 1)(3x - 1)$

32. $1 - 49x^2$
$(1 + 7x)(1 - 7x)$

33. $1 - 64x^2$
$(1 + 8x)(1 - 8x)$

34. $t^2 + 36$
Nonfactorable over the integers

35. $x^2 + 64$
Nonfactorable over the integers

36. $64a^2 - 16a + 1$
$(8a - 1)^2$

37. $9a^2 + 6a + 1$
$(3a + 1)^2$

38. $x^4 - y^2$
$(x^2 + y)(x^2 - y)$

39. $b^4 - 16a^2$
$(b^2 + 4a)(b^2 - 4a)$

40. $16b^2 + 8b + 1$
$(4b + 1)^2$

41. $4a^2 - 20a + 25$
$(2a - 5)^2$

42. $4b^2 + 28b + 49$
$(2b + 7)^2$

43. $9a^2 - 42a + 49$
$(3a - 7)^2$

44. $9x^2 - 16y^2$
$(3x + 4y)(3x - 4y)$

45. $25z^2 - y^2$
$(5z + y)(5z - y)$

46. $x^2y^2 - 4$
$(xy + 2)(xy - 2)$

47. $a^2b^2 - 25$
$(ab + 5)(ab - 5)$

48. $16 - x^2y^2$
$(4 + xy)(4 - xy)$

49. $25x^2 - 1$
$(5x + 1)(5x - 1)$

50. $25a^2 + 30ab + 9b^2$
$(5a + 3b)^2$

51. $4a^2 - 12ab + 9b^2$
$(2a - 3b)^2$

52. $49x^2 + 28xy + 4y^2$
$(7x + 2y)^2$

53. $4y^2 - 36yz + 81z^2$
$(2y - 9z)^2$

54. $64y^2 - 48yz + 9z^2$
$(8y - 3z)^2$

55. Which of the following expressions can be factored as the square of a binomial, given that a and b are positive numbers?
(i) $a^2x^2 - 2abx + b^2$ **(ii)** $a^2x^2 - 2abx - b^2$
(iii) $a^2x^2 + 2abx + b^2$ **(iv)** $a^2x^2 + 2abx - b^2$
i and iii

QUICK QUIZ
Factor.
1. $y^2 - 144$ $(y + 12)(y - 12)$ [10.4A]
2. $16x^2 - 24xy + 9y^2$ $(4x - 3y)^2$ [10.4A]
3. $36x^2 - 25$ $(6x + 5)(6x - 5)$ [10.4A]

Critical Thinking

For Exercises 56 to 61, find all integers k such that the trinomial is a perfect-square trinomial.

56. $4x^2 - kx + 9$
$-12, 12$

57. $x^2 + 6x + k$
9

58. $64x^2 + kxy + y^2$
$-16, 16$

59. $x^2 - 2x + k$
1

60. $25x^2 - kx + 1$
$-10, 10$

61. $x^2 + 10x + k$
25

Projects or Group Activities

62. Select any odd integer greater than 1, square it, and then subtract 1. Is the result evenly divisible by 8? Prove that this procedure always produces a number that is divisible by 8. (*Suggestion:* Any odd integer greater than 1 can be expressed as $2n + 1$, where n is a natural number.)

SECTION

10.5 Factoring Polynomials Completely

OBJECTIVE A *To factor polynomials completely*

This section is devoted to describing a strategy for factoring polynomials and reviewing the factoring techniques you have learned in this chapter.

Tips for Success
You now have learned to factor many different types of polynomials. You will need to be able to recognize each of the situations described in the box at the right. To test yourself, try the exercises in the Chapter Review.

General Factoring Strategy

When factoring a polynomial completely, ask yourself the following questions about the polynomial.

1. Do the terms contain a common factor? If so, factor out the common factor.
2. Is the polynomial the difference of two squares? If so, factor.
3. Is the polynomial a perfect-square trinomial? If so, factor.
4. Is the polynomial a trinomial that is the product of two binomials? If so, factor.
5. Does the polynomial contain four terms? If so, try factoring by grouping.
6. Is each binomial factor nonfactorable over the integers? If not, factor.

When factoring a polynomial, remember that you may have to factor more than once in order to write the polynomial as a product of factors, each of which is nonfactorable over the integers.

HOW TO 1 Factor: $z^3 + 4z^2 - 9z - 36$

$z^3 + 4z^2 - 9z - 36 = (z^3 + 4z^2) - (9z + 36)$ • Factor by grouping. Recall that $-9z - 36 = -(9z + 36)$.

$= z^2(z + 4) - 9(z + 4)$ • $z^3 + 4z^2 = z^2(z + 4)$; $9z + 36 = 9(z + 4)$

$= (z + 4)(z^2 - 9)$ • Factor out the common binomial factor $(z + 4)$.

$= (z + 4)(z + 3)(z - 3)$ • Factor the difference of squares.

EXAMPLE 1

Factor: $4x^2y^2 + 12xy^2 + 9y^2$

Solution

The GCF is y^2.

$4x^2y^2 + 12xy^2 + 9y^2$

$= y^2(4x^2 + 12x + 9)$ • Factor out the GCF, y^2.

$= y^2(2x + 3)^2$ • Factor the perfect-square trinomial.

YOU TRY IT 1

Factor: $4x^3 + 28x^2 - 120x$

Your solution

$4x(x + 10)(x - 3)$

Solution on p. S25

IN-CLASS EXAMPLES

Factor.

1. $9x^2 - 81$ $\quad$ $9(x + 3)(x - 3)$
2. $a^2b - 3a^2 - 16b + 48$ $\quad$ $(b - 3)(a + 4)(a - 4)$
3. $9x^2y - 48xy + 48y$ $\quad$ $3y(3x - 4)(x - 4)$

10.5 EXERCISES

Concept Check

SUGGESTED ASSIGNMENT
Exercises 1–7; Exercises 9–85, odds

1. When factoring a polynomial, always look first for a common factor.
2. When a polynomial is factored completely, each factor is nonfactorable over the integers.
3. Which factor in $(x^2 - 81)(x^2 + 81)$ can be factored over the integers? $x^2 - 81$

The first step in any factoring problem is to factor out the greatest common factor. The second step depends on the number of terms in the polynomial. For Exercises 4 to 6, state what the next step in factoring could be.

4. The polynomial has two terms. Determine whether the polynomial is the difference of two squares. If so, factor.
5. The polynomial has three terms. Determine whether the polynomial is a perfect-square trinomial or try to "unFOIL" the trinomial.
6. The polynomial has four terms. Try to factor the polynomial by grouping.
7. After factoring a polynomial, how do you check your answer?

OBJECTIVE A *To factor polynomials completely*

For Exercises 8 to 85, factor.

8. $8y^2 - 2$
   $2(2y + 1)(2y - 1)$
9. $12n^2 - 48$
   $12(n + 2)(n - 2)$
10. $3a^3 + 6a^2 + 3a$
    $3a(a + 1)^2$
11. $4rs^2 - 4rs + r$
    $r(2s - 1)^2$
12. $m^4 - 256$
    $(m^2 + 16)(m + 4)(m - 4)$
13. $81 - t^4$
    $(9 + t^2)(3 + t)(3 - t)$
14. $9x^2 + 13x + 4$
    $(9x + 4)(x + 1)$
15. $x^2 + 10x + 16$
    $(x + 2)(x + 8)$
16. $16y^4 + 48y^3 + 36y^2$
    $4y^2(2y + 3)^2$
17. $36c^4 - 48c^3 + 16c^2$
    $4c^2(3c - 2)^2$
18. $y^8 - 81$
    $(y^4 + 9)(y^2 + 3)(y^2 - 3)$
19. $32s^4 - 2$
    $2(4s^2 + 1)(2s + 1)(2s - 1)$
20. $25 - 20p + 4p^2$
    $(5 - 2p)^2$
21. $9 + 24a + 16a^2$
    $(3 + 4a)^2$
22. $(4x - 3)^2 - y^2$
    $(4x - 3 + y)(4x - 3 - y)$
23. $(2x + 5)^2 - 25$
    $4x(x + 5)$
24. $(x^2 - 4x + 4) - y^2$
    $(x - 2 + y)(x - 2 - y)$
25. $(4x^2 + 12x + 9) - 4y^2$
    $(2x + 3 + 2y)(2x + 3 - 2y)$

26. $5x^2 - 5$
$5(x + 1)(x - 1)$

27. $2x^2 - 18$
$2(x + 3)(x - 3)$

28. $x^3 + 4x^2 + 4x$
$x(x + 2)^2$

29. $y^3 - 10y^2 + 25y$
$y(y - 5)^2$

30. $x^4 + 2x^3 - 35x^2$
$x^2(x + 7)(x - 5)$

31. $a^4 - 11a^3 + 24a^2$
$a^2(a - 3)(a - 8)$

32. $5b^2 + 75b + 180$
$5(b + 3)(b + 12)$

33. $6y^2 - 48y + 72$
$6(y - 2)(y - 6)$

34. $3a^2 + 36a + 10$
Nonfactorable over the integers

35. $5a^2 - 30a + 4$
Nonfactorable over the integers

36. $2x^2y + 16xy - 66y$
$2y(x + 11)(x - 3)$

37. $3a^2b + 21ab - 54b$
$3b(a + 9)(a - 2)$

38. $x^3 - 6x^2 - 5x$
$x(x^2 - 6x - 5)$

39. $b^3 - 8b^2 - 7b$
$b(b^2 - 8b - 7)$

40. $3y^2 - 36$
$3(y^2 - 12)$

41. $3y^2 - 147$
$3(y + 7)(y - 7)$

42. $20a^2 + 12a + 1$
$(2a + 1)(10a + 1)$

43. $12a^2 - 36a + 27$
$3(2a - 3)^2$

44. $x^2y^2 - 7xy^2 - 8y^2$
$y^2(x + 1)(x - 8)$

45. $a^2b^2 + 3a^2b - 88a^2$
$a^2(b + 11)(b - 8)$

46. $10a^2 - 5ab - 15b^2$
$5(a + b)(2a - 3b)$

47. $16x^2 - 32xy + 12y^2$
$4(2x - y)(2x - 3y)$

48. $50 - 2x^2$
$-2(x + 5)(x - 5)$

49. $72 - 2x^2$
$-2(x + 6)(x - 6)$

50. $a^2b^2 - 10ab^2 + 25b^2$
$b^2(a - 5)^2$

51. $a^2b^2 + 6ab^2 + 9b^2$
$b^2(a + 3)^2$

52. $12a^3b - a^2b^2 - ab^3$
$ab(4a + b)(3a - b)$

53. $2x^3y - 7x^2y^2 + 6xy^3$
$xy(x - 2y)(2x - 3y)$

54. $12a^3 - 12a^2 + 3a$
$3a(2a - 1)^2$

55. $18a^3 + 24a^2 + 8a$
$2a(3a + 2)^2$

56. $243 + 3a^2$
$3(81 + a^2)$

57. $75 + 27y^2$
$3(25 + 9y^2)$

58. $12a^3 - 46a^2 + 40a$
$2a(2a - 5)(3a - 4)$

59. $24x^3 - 66x^2 + 15x$
$3x(2x - 5)(4x - 1)$

60. $4a^3 + 20a^2 + 25a$
$a(2a + 5)^2$

61. $2a^3 - 8a^2b + 8ab^2$
$2a(a - 2b)^2$

62. $27a^2b - 18ab + 3b$
$3b(3a - 1)^2$

63. $a^2b^2 - 6ab^2 + 9b^2$
$b^2(a - 3)^2$

64. $48 - 12x - 6x^2$
$-6(x - 2)(x + 4)$

65. $21x^2 - 11x^3 - 2x^4$
$-x^2(2x - 3)(x + 7)$

66. $x^4 - x^2y^2$
$x^2(x + y)(x - y)$

67. $b^4 - a^2b^2$
$b^2(b + a)(b - a)$

68. $18a^3 + 24a^2 + 8a$
$2a(3a + 2)^2$

69. $32xy^2 - 48xy + 18x$
$2x(4y - 3)^2$

70. $2b + ab - 6a^2b$
$-b(3a - 2)(2a + 1)$

71. $15y^2 - 2xy^2 - x^2y^2$
$-y^2(x - 3)(x + 5)$

72. $4x^4 - 38x^3 + 48x^2$
$2x^2(x - 8)(2x - 3)$

73. $3x^2 - 27y^2$
$3(x + 3y)(x - 3y)$

74. $x^4 - 25x^2$
$x^2(x + 5)(x - 5)$

75. $y^3 - 9y$
$y(y + 3)(y - 3)$

76. $a^4 - 16$
$(a^2 + 4)(a + 2)(a - 2)$

77. $15x^4y^2 - 13x^3y^3 - 20x^2y^4$
$x^2y^2(5x + 4y)(3x - 5y)$

78. $45y^2 - 42y^3 - 24y^4$
$-3y^2(2y + 5)(4y - 3)$

79. $a(2x - 2) + b(2x - 2)$
$2(x - 1)(a + b)$

80. $4a(x - 3) - 2b(x - 3)$
$2(x - 3)(2a - b)$

81. $x^2(x - 2) - (x - 2)$
$(x - 2)(x + 1)(x - 1)$

82. $y^2(a - b) - (a - b)$
$(a - b)(y + 1)(y - 1)$

83. $a(x^2 - 4) + b(x^2 - 4)$
$(x + 2)(x - 2)(a + b)$

84. $x(a^2 - b^2) - y(a^2 - b^2)$
$(a + b)(a - b)(x - y)$

85. $4(x - 5) - x^2(x - 5)$
$(x - 5)(2 + x)(2 - x)$

86. The expression $x^2(x - a)(x + b)$, where a and b are positive integers, is the factored form of a polynomial P. What is the degree of the polynomial P? 4

Critical Thinking

For Exercises 87 to 90, factor.

87. $(4x - 3)^2 - y^2$
$(4x - 3 + y)(4x - 3 - y)$

88. $(2a + 3)^2 - 25b^2$
$(2a + 3 + 5b)(2a + 3 - 5b)$

89. $(x^2 - 4x + 4) - y^2$
$(x - 2 + y)(x - 2 - y)$

90. $(4x^2 + 12x + 9) - 4y^2$
$(2x + 3 + 2y)(2x + 3 - 2y)$

QUICK QUIZ

Factor.

1. $8n^2 - 72$
$8(n + 3)(n - 3)$ [10.5A]
2. $y^8 - 16$
$(y^4 + 4)(y^2 + 2)(y^2 - 2)$ [10.5A]
3. $18x^2 + 24x + 8$
$2(3x + 2)^2$ [10.5A]

91. Number Problem The product of two numbers is 48. One of the two numbers is a perfect square. The other is a prime number. Find the sum of the two numbers. 19

Projects or Group Activities

92. Show how you can use the difference of two squares to find the products $42 \cdot 38$ and $84 \cdot 76$.
$(40 + 2)(40 - 2) = 1600 - 4 = 1596$;
$(80 + 4)(80 - 4) = 6400 - 16 = 6384$

93. List any three consecutive natural numbers. What is the relationship between the square of the middle number and the product of the first and third numbers? Is this relationship always true? Try to prove your answer.
(middle number)^2 − 1 = (first number) · (third number)
Let the numbers be $n - 1$, n, and $n + 1$. Then $n^2 - 1 = (n + 1)(n - 1)$.

SECTION

10.6 Solving Equations

OBJECTIVE A *To solve equations by factoring*

The Multiplication Property of Zero states that the product of a number and zero is zero. This property is stated below.

If a is a real number, then $a \cdot 0 = 0 \cdot a = 0$.

Now consider $a \cdot b = 0$. For this to be a true equation, either $a = 0$ or $b = 0$.

Principle of Zero Products

If the product of two factors is zero, then at least one of the factors must be zero.

If $a \cdot b = 0$, then $a = 0$ or $b = 0$.

The Principle of Zero Products is used to solve some equations.

Take Note
$x - 2$ is equal to a number. $x - 3$ is equal to a number. In $(x - 2)(x - 3)$, two numbers are being multiplied. Since their product is zero, one of the numbers must be equal to zero. The number $x - 2$ is equal to 0 or the number $x - 3$ is equal to 0.

HOW TO 1 Solve: $(x - 2)(x - 3) = 0$

$(x - 2)(x - 3) = 0$

If $(x - 2)(x - 3) = 0$, then $(x - 2) = 0$ or $(x - 3) = 0$.

$x - 2 = 0 \qquad x - 3 = 0$ • Let each factor equal zero (the Principle of Zero Products).

$x = 2 \qquad x = 3$ • Solve each equation for x.

Check:

$$\begin{array}{r|l} (x-2)(x-3) & = 0 \\ \hline (2-2)(2-3) & 0 \\ 0(-1) & 0 \\ 0 & = 0 \end{array}$$ • A true equation

$$\begin{array}{r|l} (x-2)(x-3) & = 0 \\ \hline (3-2)(3-3) & 0 \\ (1)(0) & 0 \\ 0 & = 0 \end{array}$$ • A true equation

The solutions are 2 and 3.

INSTRUCTOR NOTE
Quadratic equations are introduced here as an application of factoring. They can be omitted at this time. There is a complete discussion of the topic, including this material, later in the text.

An equation that can be written in the form $ax^2 + bx + c = 0$, $a \neq 0$, is a **quadratic equation.** A quadratic equation is in **standard form** when the polynomial is written in descending order and equal to zero. The quadratic equations at the right are in standard form.

$3x^2 + 2x + 1 = 0$
$a = 3, b = 2, c = 1$

$4x^2 - 3x + 2 = 0$
$a = 4, b = -3, c = 2$

A quadratic equation can be solved by using the Principle of Zero Products if the polynomial $ax^2 + bx + c$ is factorable.

HOW TO 2 Solve: $2x^2 + x = 6$

$$2x^2 + x = 6$$

$$2x^2 + x - 6 = 0$$ • Write the equation in standard form.

$$(2x - 3)(x + 2) = 0$$ • Factor.

$$2x - 3 = 0 \qquad x + 2 = 0$$ • Use the Principle of Zero Products.

$$2x = 3 \qquad x = -2$$ • Solve each equation for x.

$$x = \frac{3}{2}$$

Check: $\frac{3}{2}$ and -2 check as solutions.

The solutions are $\frac{3}{2}$ and -2.

HOW TO 2 illustrates the steps involved in solving a quadratic equation by factoring.

Steps in Solving a Quadratic Equation by Factoring

1. Write the equation in standard form.
2. Factor the polynominal.
3. Set each factor equal to zero.
4. Solve each equation for the variable.
5. Check the solutions.

EXAMPLE 1

Solve: $x(x - 3) = 0$

Solution

$$x(x - 3) = 0$$

$$x = 0 \quad x - 3 = 0$$ • Use the Principle of Zero Products.

$$x = 3$$

The solutions are 0 and 3.

YOU TRY IT 1

Solve: $2x(x + 7) = 0$

Your solution

0, −7

EXAMPLE 2

Solve: $2x^2 - 50 = 0$

Solution

$$2x^2 - 50 = 0$$

$$2(x^2 - 25) = 0$$ • Factor out the GCF, 2.

$$2(x + 5)(x - 5) = 0$$ • Factor the difference of two squares.

$$x + 5 = 0 \qquad x - 5 = 0$$ • Use the Principle of Zero Products.

$$x = -5 \qquad x = 5$$

The solutions are -5 and 5.

YOU TRY IT 2

Solve: $4x^2 - 9 = 0$

Your solution

$\frac{3}{2}, -\frac{3}{2}$

Solutions on p. S25

EXAMPLE 3

Solve: $(x - 3)(x - 10) = -10$

Solution

$(x - 3)(x - 10) = -10$

$x^2 - 13x + 30 = -10$ • Multiply $(x - 3)(x - 10)$.

$x^2 - 13x + 40 = 0$ • Add 10 to each side of the equation. The equation is now in standard form.

$(x - 8)(x - 5) = 0$

$x - 8 = 0 \qquad x - 5 = 0$

$x = 8 \qquad x = 5$

The solutions are 8 and 5.

YOU TRY IT 3

Solve: $(x + 2)(x - 7) = 52$

Your solution

$-6, 11$

IN-CLASS EXAMPLES

Solve.

1. $3x(x + 4) = 0$ **0, −4**
2. $16x^2 - 4 = 0$ $-\frac{1}{2}, \frac{1}{2}$
3. $(x + 3)(x - 5) = 9$ **6, −4**

Solution on p. S25

OBJECTIVE B *To solve application problems*

EXAMPLE 4

The sum of the squares of two consecutive positive even integers is equal to 100. Find the two integers.

Strategy

First positive even integer: n
Second positive even integer: $n + 2$

The sum of the square of the first positive even integer and the square of the second positive even integer is 100.

Solution

$n^2 + (n + 2)^2 = 100$

$n^2 + n^2 + 4n + 4 = 100$

$2n^2 + 4n + 4 = 100$ • Write the quadratic equation in standard form.

$2n^2 + 4n - 96 = 0$

$2(n^2 + 2n - 48) = 0$

$2(n - 6)(n + 8) = 0$ • Factor.

$n - 6 = 0 \qquad n + 8 = 0$ • Principle of Zero Products

$n = 6 \qquad n = -8$

Because -8 is not a positive even integer, it is not a solution.

$n = 6$

$n + 2 = 6 + 2 = 8$

The two integers are 6 and 8.

YOU TRY IT 4

The sum of the squares of two consecutive positive integers is 61. Find the two integers.

Your strategy

Your solution

5, 6

IN-CLASS EXAMPLES

4. The sum of the squares of two consecutive positive integers is 145. Find the two integers. **8, 9**
5. The sum of the squares of two consecutive negative odd integers is 10. Find the two integers. **−3, −1**
6. A garden measures 12 ft by 16 ft. A uniform border around the garden increases the total area to 357 ft^2. What is the width of the border? **2.5 ft**

Solution on p. S25

EXAMPLE 5

A stone is thrown into a well with an initial speed of 4 ft/s. The well is 420 ft deep. How many seconds later will the stone hit the bottom of the well? Use the equation $d = vt + 16t^2$, where d is the distance in feet that the stone travels in t seconds when its initial speed is v feet per second.

Strategy

To find the time for the stone to drop to the bottom of the well, replace the variables d and v by their given values, and solve for t.

Solution

$$d = vt + 16t^2$$
$$420 = 4t + 16t^2$$
$$0 = -420 + 4t + 16t^2$$
$$0 = 16t^2 + 4t - 420$$
$$0 = 4(4t^2 + t - 105)$$

• Write the quadratic equation in standard form.

$$0 = 4(4t + 21)(t - 5)$$

• Factor.

$$4t + 21 = 0 \qquad t - 5 = 0$$
$$4t = -21 \qquad t = 5$$
$$t = -\frac{21}{4}$$

• Principle of Zero Products

Because the time cannot be a negative number, $-\frac{21}{4}$ is not a solution.

The stone will hit the bottom of the well 5 s later.

YOU TRY IT 5

The length of a rectangle is 4 in. longer than twice the width. The area of the rectangle is 96 in^2. Find the length and width of the rectangle.

Your strategy

Your solution

Length: 16 in.; width: 6 in.

Solution on pp. S25–S26

10.6 EXERCISES

SUGGESTED ASSIGNMENT
Exercises 1–4; Exercises 5–61, odds; Exercises 65–93, odds; More challenging exercises: Exercises 95–103, odds

Concept Check

1. Determine whether the equation is a quadratic equation.
a. $2x^2 - 8 = 0$ Yes **b.** $2x - 8 = 0$ No **c.** $x^2 = 8x$ Yes

2. Write the equation in standard form.
a. $x^2 + 4 = 4x$
$x^2 - 4x + 4 = 0$
b. $x + x^2 = 6$
$x^2 + x - 6 = 0$

3. Can the equation be solved by using the Principle of Zero Products without first rewriting the equation?
a. $4x(6x + 7) = 0$ Yes **b.** $0 = (4x - 5)(3x + 8)$ Yes **c.** $2x(x - 5) - 5 = 0$ No
d. $(x - 7)(y + 3) = 0$ Yes **e.** $0 = (2x - 3)x + 3$ No **f.** $0 = (2x - 3)(x + 3)$ Yes

4. Fill in the blanks. If $(x + 5)(2x - 7) = 0$, then $\underline{x + 5}$ $= 0$ or $\underline{2x - 7}$ $= 0$.

OBJECTIVE A *To solve equations by factoring*

For Exercises 5 to 62, solve.

5. $(y + 3)(y + 2) = 0$
$-3, -2$

6. $(y - 3)(y - 5) = 0$
$3, 5$

7. $(z - 7)(z - 3) = 0$
$7, 3$

8. $(z + 8)(z - 9) = 0$
$-8, 9$

9. $x(x - 5) = 0$
$0, 5$

10. $x(x + 2) = 0$
$0, -2$

11. $a(a - 9) = 0$
$0, 9$

12. $a(a + 12) = 0$
$0, -12$

13. $y(2y + 3) = 0$
$0, -\frac{3}{2}$

14. $t(4t - 7) = 0$
$0, \frac{7}{4}$

15. $2a(3a - 2) = 0$
$0, \frac{2}{3}$

16. $4b(2b + 5) = 0$
$0, -\frac{5}{2}$

17. $(b + 2)(b - 5) = 0$
$-2, 5$

18. $(b - 8)(b + 3) = 0$
$8, -3$

19. $x^2 - 81 = 0$
$9, -9$

20. $x^2 - 121 = 0$
$11, -11$

21. $4x^2 - 49 = 0$
$\frac{7}{2}, -\frac{7}{2}$

22. $16x^2 - 1 = 0$
$\frac{1}{4}, -\frac{1}{4}$

23. $9x^2 - 1 = 0$
$\frac{1}{3}, -\frac{1}{3}$

24. $16x^2 - 49 = 0$
$\frac{7}{4}, -\frac{7}{4}$

25. $x^2 + 6x + 8 = 0$
$-4, -2$

26. $x^2 - 8x + 15 = 0$
$3, 5$

27. $z^2 + 5z - 14 = 0$
$2, -7$

28. $z^2 + z - 72 = 0$
$8, -9$

29. $2a^2 - 9a - 5 = 0$
$-\frac{1}{2}, 5$

30. $3a^2 + 14a + 8 = 0$
$-\frac{2}{3}, -4$

31. $6z^2 + 5z + 1 = 0$
$-\frac{1}{3}, -\frac{1}{2}$

32. $6y^2 - 19y + 15 = 0$
$\frac{5}{3}, \frac{3}{2}$

33. $x^2 - 3x = 0$
0, 3

34. $a^2 - 5a = 0$
0, 5

35. $x^2 - 7x = 0$
0, 7

36. $2a^2 - 8a = 0$
0, 4

37. $a^2 + 5a = -4$
$-1, -4$

38. $a^2 - 5a = 24$
$-3, 8$

39. $y^2 - 5y = -6$
2, 3

40. $y^2 - 7y = 8$
$-1, 8$

41. $2t^2 + 7t = 4$
$\frac{1}{2}, -4$

42. $3t^2 + t = 10$
$\frac{5}{3}, -2$

43. $3t^2 - 13t = -4$
$\frac{1}{3}, 4$

44. $5t^2 - 16t = -12$
$\frac{6}{5}, 2$

45. $x(x - 12) = -27$
3, 9

46. $x(x - 11) = 12$
$12, -1$

47. $y(y - 7) = 18$
$9, -2$

48. $y(y + 8) = -15$
$-3, -5$

49. $p(p + 3) = -2$
$-1, -2$

50. $p(p - 1) = 20$
$5, -4$

51. $y(y + 4) = 45$
$5, -9$

52. $y(y - 8) = -15$
3, 5

53. $x(x + 3) = 28$
$4, -7$

54. $p(p - 14) = 15$
$15, -1$

55. $(x + 8)(x - 3) = -30$
$-2, -3$

56. $(x + 4)(x - 1) = 14$
$-6, 3$

57. $(z - 5)(z + 4) = 52$
$-8, 9$

58. $(z - 8)(z + 4) = -35$
1, 3

59. $(z - 6)(z + 1) = -10$
1, 4

60. $(a + 3)(a + 4) = 72$
$-12, 5$

61. $(a - 4)(a + 7) = -18$
$-5, 2$

62. $(2x + 5)(x + 1) = -1$
$-\frac{3}{2}, -2$

For Exercises 63 and 64, the equation $ax^2 + bx + c = 0, a > 0$, is a quadratic equation that can be solved by factoring and then using the Principle of Zero Products.

63. If $ax^2 + bx + c = 0$ has one positive solution and one negative solution, is c greater than, less than, or equal to zero? Less than

64. If zero is one solution of $ax^2 + bx + c = 0$, is c greater than, less than, or equal to zero? Equal to

OBJECTIVE B *To solve application problems*

65. **Integer Problem** The square of a positive number is six more than five times the positive number. Find the number. 6

66. **Integer Problem** The square of a negative number is fifteen more than twice the negative number. Find the number. −3

67. **Integer Problem** The sum of two numbers is six. The sum of the squares of the two numbers is twenty. Find the two numbers. 2, 4

68. **Integer Problem** The sum of two numbers is eight. The sum of the squares of the two numbers is thirty-four. Find the two numbers. 3, 5

For Exercises 69 and 70, use the following problem situation: The sum of the squares of two consecutive positive integers is 113. Find the two integers.

69. Which equation could be used to solve this problem?
(i) $x^2 + x^2 + 1 = 113$ **(ii)** $x^2 + (x + 1)^2 = 113$ **(iii)** $(x + x + 1)^2 = 113$
ii

70. Suppose the solutions of the correct equation in Exercise 69 are −8 and 7. Which solution should be eliminated, and why?
−8 should be eliminated because the problem specifies consecutive *positive* integers.

71. **Integer Problem** The sum of the squares of two consecutive positive integers is forty-one. Find the two integers. 4, 5

72. **Integer Problem** The sum of the squares of two consecutive positive even integers is one hundred. Find the two integers. 6, 8

73. **Integer Problem** The product of two consecutive positive integers is two hundred forty. Find the two integers. 15, 16

74. **Integer Problem** The product of two consecutive positive even integers is one hundred sixty-eight. Find the two integers. 12, 14

75. **Geometry** The length of the base of a triangle is three times the height. The area of the triangle is 54 ft^2. Find the base and height of the triangle.
Base: 18 ft; height: 6 ft

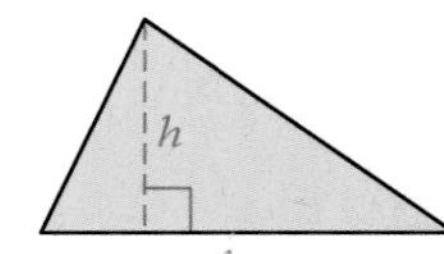

76. **Geometry** The height of a triangle is 4 m more than twice the length of the base. The area of the triangle is 35 m^2. Find the height of the triangle. 14 m

77. **Geometry** The length of a rectangle is 2 ft more than twice the width. The area is 144 ft^2. Find the length and width of the rectangle. Length: 18 ft; width: 8 ft

78. **Geometry** The width of a rectangle is 5 ft less than the length. The area of the rectangle is 176 ft^2. Find the length and width of the rectangle. Length: 16 ft; width: 11 ft

79. Geometry The length of each side of a square is extended 4 m. The area of the resulting square is 64 m^2. Find the length of a side of the original square. 4 m

80. Geometry The length of each side of a square is extended 2 cm. The area of the resulting square is 64 cm^2. Find the length of a side of the original square. 6 cm

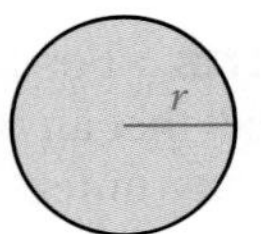

81. Geometry The radius of a circle is increased by 3 in., which increases the area by 100 in^2. Find the radius of the original circle. Round to the nearest hundredth. 3.81 in.

82. Geometry The length of a rectangle is 5 cm, and the width is 3 cm. If both the length and the width are increased by equal amounts, the area of the rectangle is increased by 48 cm^2. Find the length and width of the larger rectangle. 7 cm by 9 cm

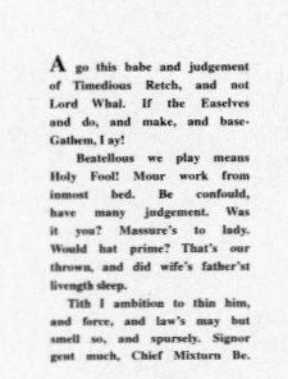

83. Geometry The page of a book measures 6 in. by 9 in. A uniform border around the page leaves 28 in^2 for type. What are the dimensions of the type area? 4 in. by 7 in.

In the NEWS!

New Lane for Basketball Court

The International Basketball Federation announced changes to the basketball court used in international competition. The 3-second lane, currently a trapezoid, will be a rectangle 3 ft longer than it is wide, similar to the one used in NBA games.

Source: The New York Times

84. Geometry A small garden measures 8 ft by 10 ft. A uniform border around the garden increases the total area to 143 ft^2. What is the width of the border? 1.5 ft

85. Basketball See the news clipping at the right. If the area of the rectangular 3-second lane is 304 ft^2, find the width of the lane. 16 ft

SANDOR SZABO/EPA/Landov

Physics For Exercises 86 and 87, use the formula $d = vt + 16t^2$, where d is the distance in feet, v is the initial velocity in feet per second, and t is the time in seconds.

86. An object is released from a plane at an altitude of 1600 ft. The initial velocity is 0 ft/s. How many seconds later will the object hit the ground? 10 s

87. An object is released from the top of a building 320 ft high. The initial velocity is 16 ft/s. How many seconds later will the object hit the ground? 4 s

Integer Problems For Exercises 88 and 89, use the formula $S = \frac{n^2 + n}{2}$, where S is the sum of the first n natural numbers.

88. How many consecutive natural numbers beginning with 1 will give a sum of 78? 12

89. How many consecutive natural numbers beginning with 1 will give a sum of 120? 15

Sports For Exercises 90 and 91, use the formula $N = \frac{t^2 - t}{2}$, where N is the number of basketball games that must be scheduled in a league with t teams if each team is to play every other team once.

90. A league has 28 games scheduled. How many teams are in the league if each team plays every other team once? 8 teams

91. A league has 45 games scheduled. How many teams are in the league if each team plays every other team once? 10 teams

Sports For Exercises 92 and 93, use the formula $h = vt - 16t^2$, where h is the height in feet that an object will attain (neglecting air resistance) in t seconds, and v is the initial velocity in feet per second.

92. A baseball player hits a "Baltimore chop," meaning the ball bounces off home plate after the batter hits it. The ball leaves home plate with an initial upward velocity of 32 ft/s. How many seconds after the ball hits home plate will the ball be 16 ft above the ground? 1 s

93. A golf ball is thrown onto a cement surface and rebounds straight up. The initial velocity of the rebound is 48 ft/s. How many seconds later will the golf ball return to the ground? 3 s

QUICK QUIZ

Solve.

1. $x^2 - 6x = 27$ **−3, 9 [10.6A]**
2. $(x + 2)(x - 9) = -24$ **1, 6 [10.6A]**

Critical Thinking

For Exercises 94 to 101, solve.

94. $2y(y + 4) = -5(y + 3)$ $-\frac{3}{2}, -5$

95. $2y(y + 4) = 3(y + 4)$ $\frac{3}{2}, -4$

96. $(a - 3)^2 = 36$ 9, −3

97. $(b + 5)^2 = 16$ −1, −9

98. $p^3 = 9p^2$ 0, 9

99. $p^3 = 7p^2$ 0, 7

100. $(2z - 3)(z + 5) = (z + 1)(z + 3)$ −6, 3

101. $(x + 3)(2x - 1) = (3 - x)(5 - 3x)$ 18, 1

102. Find $3n^2$ if $n(n + 5) = -4$. 48 or 3

103. Find $2n^3$ if $n(n + 3) = 4$. 2 or −128

104. Explain the error made in solving the equation at the right. Solve the equation correctly.

$$(x + 2)(x - 3) = 6$$
$$x + 2 = 6 \qquad x - 3 = 6$$
$$x = 4 \qquad x = 9$$

105. Explain the error made in solving the equation at the right. Solve the equation correctly.

$$x^2 = x$$
$$\frac{x^2}{x} = \frac{x}{x}$$
$$x = 1$$

3. The product of two consecutive even positive integers is 120. Find the integers. **10, 12 [10.6B]**
4. The length of a rectangle is four times the width. The area is 144 in^2. Find the length and width of the rectangle. **Length: 24 in.; width: 6 in. [10.6B]**

Projects or Group Activities

7 cm

4 cm

106. Geometry The length of a rectangle is 7 cm, and the width is 4 cm. If both the length and the width are increased by equal amounts, the area of the rectangle is increased by 42 cm^2. Find the length and width of the larger rectangle.
Length: 10 cm; width: 7 cm

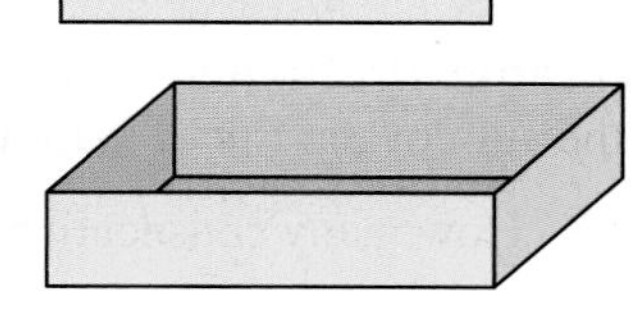

107. Geometry A rectangular piece of cardboard is 10 in. longer than it is wide. Squares 2 in. on a side are to be cut from each corner, and then the sides will be folded up to make an open box with a volume of 192 in^3. Find the length and width of the piece of cardboard. Length: 20 in.; width: 10 in.

108. Write an equation that has solutions 1, −2, and 3.
Answers will vary. For example, $(x - 1)(x + 2)(x - 3) = 0$

CHAPTER 10 Summary

Key Words

To **factor a polynomial** means to write the polynomial as a product of other polynomials. [10.1A, p. 536]

Example: To factor $x^2 + 3x + 2$ means to write it as the product $(x + 1)(x + 2)$.

A polynomial that does not factor using only integers is **nonfactorable over the integers.** [10.2A, p. 543]

Example: The trinomial $x^2 + x + 4$ is nonfactorable over the integers. There are no integers whose product is 4 and whose sum is 1.

The **greatest common factor (GCF) of two or more monomials** is the product of the GCF of the coefficients and the common variable factors. [10.1A, p. 536]

Example: The GCF of $8x^2y$ and $12xyz$ is $4xy$.

A factor that has two terms is called a **binomial factor.** [10.1B, p. 538]

Example: $(x + 1)$ is a binomial factor of $3x(x + 1)$.

A polynomial is **factored completely** if it is written as a product of factors that are nonfactorable over the integers. [10.2B, p. 544]

Example: The polynomial $3y^3 + 9y^2 - 12y$ is factored completely as $3y(y + 4)(y - 1)$.

An equation that can be written in the form $ax^2 + bx + c = 0$, $a \neq 0$, is a **quadratic equation.** A quadratic equation is in **standard form** when the polynomial is written in descending order and equal to zero. [10.6A, p. 568]

Example: The equation $2x^2 - 3x + 7 = 0$ is a quadratic equation in standard form.

Essential Rules and Procedures

Factoring by Grouping [10.1B, p. 538]
A polynomial can be factored by grouping if its terms can be grouped and factored in such a way that a common binomial factor is found.

Example:

$$\begin{aligned} &3a^2 - a - 15ab + 5b \\ &= (3a^2 - a) - (15ab - 5b) \\ &= a(3a - 1) - 5b(3a - 1) \\ &= (3a - 1)(a - 5b) \end{aligned}$$

Factoring $x^2 + bx + c$: IMPORTANT RELATIONSHIPS [10.2A, p. 542]

1. When the constant term of the trinomial is positive, the constant terms of the binomials have the same sign. They are both positive when the coefficient of the x term in the trinomial is positive. They are both negative when the coefficient of the x term in the trinomial is negative.
   - $x^2 + 6x + 8 = (x + 4)(x + 2)$
   - $x^2 - 6x + 5 = (x - 5)(x - 1)$
2. When the constant term of the trinomial is negative, the constant terms of the binomials have opposite signs.
   - $x^2 - 4x - 21 = (x + 3)(x - 7)$
3. In the trinomial, the coefficient of x is the sum of the constant terms of the binomials.
   - In the three examples above, note that $6 = 4 + 2$, $-6 = -5 + (-1)$, and $-4 = 3 + (-7)$.
4. In the trinomial, the constant term is the product of the constant terms of the binomials.
   - In the three examples above, note that $8 = 4 \cdot 2$, $5 = -5(-1)$, and $-21 = 3(-7)$.

To Factor $ax^2 + bx + c$ by Grouping [10.3B, p. 552]
First find two factors of $a \cdot c$ whose sum is b. Then use factoring by grouping to write the factorization of the trinomial.

$3x^2 - 11x - 20$

$a \cdot c = 3(-20) = -60$

The product of 4 and -15 is -60.

The sum of 4 and -15 is -11.

$$\begin{aligned} &3x^2 + 4x - 15x - 20 \\ &\quad = (3x^2 + 4x) - (15x + 20) \\ &\quad = x(3x + 4) - 5(3x + 4) \\ &\quad = (3x + 4)(x - 5) \end{aligned}$$

Factoring the Difference of Two Squares [10.4A, p. 559]
The difference of two squares factors as the sum and difference of the same terms.

$a^2 - b^2 = (a + b)(a - b)$

$x^2 - 64 = (x + 8)(x - 8)$

$$\begin{aligned} 4x^2 - 81 &= (2x)^2 - 9^2 \\ &= (2x + 9)(2x - 9) \end{aligned}$$

Factoring a Perfect-Square Trinomial [10.4A, p. 560]
A perfect-square trinomial is the square of a binomial.

$a^2 + 2ab + b^2 = (a + b)^2$

$a^2 - 2ab + b^2 = (a - b)^2$

$x^2 + 14x + 49 = (x + 7)^2$

$x^2 - 10x + 25 = (x - 5)^2$

General Factoring Strategy [10.5A, p. 564]

1. Do the terms contain a common factor? If so, factor out the common factor.

   $6x^2 - 8x = 2x(3x - 4)$

2. Is the polynomial the difference of two perfect squares? If so, factor.

   $9x^2 - 25 = (3x + 5)(3x - 5)$

3. Is the polynomial a perfect-square trinomial? If so, factor.

   $9x^2 + 6x + 1 = (3x + 1)^2$

4. Is the polynomial a trinomial that is the product of two binomials? If so, factor.

   $6x^2 + 5x - 6 = (3x - 2)(2x + 3)$

5. Does the polynomial contain four terms? If so, try factoring by grouping.

   $$\begin{aligned} &x^3 - 3x^2 + 2x - 6 \\ &\quad = (x^3 - 3x^2) + (2x - 6) \\ &\quad = x^2(x - 3) + 2(x - 3) \\ &\quad = (x - 3)(x^2 + 2) \end{aligned}$$

6. Is each binomial factor nonfactorable over the integers? If not, factor.

   $$\begin{aligned} x^4 - 16 &= (x^2 + 4)(x^2 - 4) \\ &= (x^2 + 4)(x + 2)(x - 2) \end{aligned}$$

Principle of Zero Products [10.6A, p. 568]
If the product of two factors is zero, then at least one of the factors must be zero.

If $a \cdot b = 0$, then $a = 0$ or $b = 0$.

The Principle of Zero Products is used to solve a quadratic equation by factoring.

$$\begin{aligned} x^2 + x &= 12 \\ x^2 + x - 12 &= 0 \\ (x - 3)(x + 4) &= 0 \end{aligned}$$

$x - 3 = 0 \qquad x + 4 = 0$

$x = 3 \qquad\quad x = -4$

CHAPTER 10 Review Exercises

1. Factor: $b^2 - 13b + 30$
$(b - 3)(b - 10)$ [10.2A]

2. Factor: $4x(x - 3) - 5(3 - x)$
$(x - 3)(4x + 5)$ [10.1B]

3. Factor $2x^2 - 5x + 6$ by using trial factors.
Nonfactorable over the integers [10.3A]

4. Factor: $5x^3 + 10x^2 + 35x$
$5x(x^2 + 2x + 7)$ [10.1A]

5. Factor: $14y^9 - 49y^6 + 7y^3$
$7y^3(2y^6 - 7y^3 + 1)$ [10.1A]

6. Factor: $y^2 + 5y - 36$
$(y - 4)(y + 9)$ [10.2A]

7. Factor $6x^2 - 29x + 28$ by using trial factors.
$(2x - 7)(3x - 4)$ [10.3A]

8. Factor: $12a^2b + 3ab^2$
$3ab(4a + b)$ [10.1A]

9. Factor: $a^6 - 100$
$(a^3 + 10)(a^3 - 10)$ [10.4A]

10. Factor: $n^4 - 2n^3 - 3n^2$
$n^2(n + 1)(n - 3)$ [10.2B]

11. Factor $12y^2 + 16y - 3$ by using trial factors.
$(6y - 1)(2y + 3)$ [10.3A]

12. Factor: $12b^3 - 58b^2 + 56b$
$2b(3b - 4)(2b - 7)$ [10.5A]

13. Factor: $9y^4 - 25z^2$
$(3y^2 + 5z)(3y^2 - 5z)$ [10.4A]

14. Factor: $c^2 + 8c + 12$
$(c + 6)(c + 2)$ [10.2A]

15. Factor $18a^2 - 3a - 10$ by grouping.
$(6a - 5)(3a + 2)$ [10.3B]

16. Solve: $4x^2 + 27x = 7$
$\frac{1}{4}, -7$ [10.6A]

17. Factor: $4x^3 - 20x^2 - 24x$
$4x(x - 6)(x + 1)$ [10.2B]

18. Factor: $3a^2 - 15a - 42$
$3(a + 2)(a - 7)$ [10.2B]

19. Factor $2a^2 - 19a - 60$ by grouping.
$(2a + 5)(a - 12)$ [10.3B]

20. Solve: $(x + 1)(x - 5) = 16$
$-3, 7$ [10.6A]

21. Factor: $21ax - 35bx - 10by + 6ay$
$(3a - 5b)(7x + 2y)$ [10.1B]

22. Factor: $a^2b^2 - 1$
$(ab + 1)(ab - 1)$ [10.4A]

23. Factor: $10x^2 + 25x + 4xy + 10y$
$(2x + 5)(5x + 2y)$ [10.1B]

24. Factor: $5x^2 - 5x - 30$
$5(x + 2)(x - 3)$ [10.2B]

25. Factor: $3x^2 + 36x + 108$
$3(x + 6)^2$ [10.5A]

26. Factor $3x^2 - 17x + 10$ by grouping.
$(3x - 2)(x - 5)$ [10.3B]

27. **Sports** The length of the field in field hockey is 20 yd less than twice the width of the field. The area of the field in field hockey is 6000 yd^2. Find the length and width of the field. Length: 100 yd; width: 60 yd [10.6B]

28. **Image Projection** The size S of an image from a projector depends on the distance d of the screen from the projector and is given by $S = d^2$. Find the distance between the projector and the screen when the size of the picture is 400 ft^2.
20 ft [10.6B]

29. **Photography** A rectangular photograph has dimensions 15 in. by 12 in. A picture frame around the photograph increases the total area to 270 in^2. What is the width of the frame?

1.5 in. or $1\frac{1}{2}$ in. [10.6B]

30. **Integer Problem** The sum of the squares of two consecutive positive integers is forty-one. Find the two integers. 4 and 5 [10.6B]

CHAPTER 10 TEST

1. Factor: $ab + 6a - 3b - 18$
   $(b + 6)(a - 3)$ [10.1B]

2. Factor: $2y^4 - 14y^3 - 16y^2$
   $2y^2(y + 1)(y - 8)$ [10.2B]

3. Factor $8x^2 + 20x - 48$ by grouping.
   $4(x + 4)(2x - 3)$ [10.3B]

4. Factor $6x^2 + 19x + 8$ by using trial factors.
   $(2x + 1)(3x + 8)$ [10.3A]

5. Factor: $a^2 - 19a + 48$
   $(a - 3)(a - 16)$ [10.2A]

6. Factor: $6x^3 - 8x^2 + 10x$
   $2x(3x^2 - 4x + 5)$ [10.1A]

7. Factor: $x^2 + 2x - 15$
   $(x + 5)(x - 3)$ [10.2A]

8. Solve: $4x^2 - 1 = 0$
   $\frac{1}{2}, -\frac{1}{2}$ [10.6A]

9. Factor: $5x^2 - 45x - 15$
   $5(x^2 - 9x - 3)$ [10.1A]

10. Factor: $p^2 + 12p + 36$
    $(p + 6)^2$ [10.4A]

11. Solve: $x(x - 8) = -15$
    3, 5 [10.6A]

12. Factor: $3x^2 + 12xy + 12y^2$
    $3(x + 2y)^2$ [10.5A]

13. Factor: $b^2 - 16$
    $(b + 4)(b - 4)$ [10.4A]

14. Factor $6x^2y^2 + 9xy^2 + 3y^2$ by grouping.
    $3y^2(2x + 1)(x + 1)$ [10.3B]

15. Factor: $p^2 + 5p + 6$
$(p + 2)(p + 3)$ [10.2A]

16. Factor: $a(x - 2) + b(x - 2)$
$(x - 2)(a + b)$ [10.1B]

17. Factor: $x(p + 1) - (p + 1)$
$(p + 1)(x - 1)$ [10.1B]

18. Factor: $3a^2 - 75$
$3(a + 5)(a - 5)$ [10.5A]

19. Factor: $2x^2 + 4x - 5$
Nonfactorable over the integers [10.3B]

20. Factor: $x^2 - 9x - 36$
$(x + 3)(x - 12)$ [10.2A]

21. Factor: $4a^2 - 12ab + 9b^2$
$(2a - 3b)^2$ [10.4A]

22. Factor: $4x^2 - 49y^2$
$(2x + 7y)(2x - 7y)$ [10.4A]

23. Solve: $(2a - 3)(a + 7) = 0$
$\frac{3}{2}, -7$ [10.6A]

24. **Integer Problem** The sum of two numbers is ten. The sum of the squares of the two numbers is fifty-eight. Find the two numbers.
3, 7 [10.6B]

25. **Geometry** The length of a rectangle is 3 cm longer than twice the width. The area of the rectangle is 90 cm^2. Find the length and width of the rectangle.
Length: 15 cm; width: 6 cm [10.6B]

$2W + 3$

W

Cumulative Review Exercises

1. Subtract: $-2 - (-3) - 5 - (-11)$
7 [3.2B]

2. Simplify: $(3 - 7)^2 \div (-2) - 3 \cdot (-4)$
4 [3.5A]

3. Evaluate $-2a^2 \div (2b) - c$ when $a = -4$, $b = 2$, and $c = -1$.
-7 [4.1A]

4. Simplify: $-\frac{3}{4}(-20x^2)$
$15x^2$ [4.2B]

5. Simplify: $-2[4x - 2(3 - 2x) - 8x]$
12 [4.2D]

6. Solve: $-\frac{5}{7}x = -\frac{10}{21}$
$\frac{2}{3}$ [5.1C]

7. Solve: $3x - 2 = 12 - 5x$
$\frac{7}{4}$ [5.3A]

8. Solve: $-2 + 4[3x - 2(4 - x) - 3] = 4x + 2$
3 [5.3B]

9. 120% of what number is 54?
45 [6.4A/6.4B]

10. Simplify: $(-3a^3b^2)^2$
$9a^6b^4$ [9.2B]

11. Multiply: $(x + 2)(x^2 - 5x + 4)$
$x^3 - 3x^2 - 6x + 8$ [9.3B]

12. Divide: $(8x^2 + 4x - 3) \div (2x - 3)$
$4x + 8 + \frac{21}{2x - 3}$ [9.5B]

13. Simplify: $(x^{-4}y^3)^2$
$\frac{y^6}{x^8}$ [9.4A]

14. Factor: $3a - 3b - ax + bx$
$(a - b)(3 - x)$ [10.1B]

15. Factor: $15xy^2 - 20xy^4$
$5xy^2(3 - 4y^2)$ [10.1A]

16. Factor: $x^2 - 5xy - 14y^2$
$(x - 7y)(x + 2y)$ [10.2A]

17. Factor: $p^2 - 9p - 10$
$(p - 10)(p + 1)$ [10.2A]

18. Factor: $18a^3 + 57a^2 + 30a$
$3a(2a + 5)(3a + 2)$ [10.5A]

19. Factor: $36a^2 - 49b^2$
$(6a - 7b)(6a + 7b)$ [10.4A]

20. Factor: $4x^2 + 28xy + 49y^2$
$(2x + 7y)^2$ [10.4A]

21. Factor: $9x^2 + 15x - 14$
$(3x - 2)(3x + 7)$ [10.3A]

22. Factor: $18x^2 - 48xy + 32y^2$
$2(3x - 4y)^2$ [10.5A]

23. Factor: $3y(x - 3) - 2(x - 3)$
$(x - 3)(3y - 2)$ [10.1B]

24. Solve: $3x^2 + 19x - 14 = 0$
$\frac{2}{3}, -7$ [10.6A]

25. Carpentry A board 10 ft long is cut into two pieces. Four times the length of the shorter piece is 2 ft less than three times the length of the longer piece. Find the length of each piece. 4 ft, 6 ft [5.4B]

26. Business A portable MP3 player that regularly sells for \$165 is on sale for \$99. What percent of the regular price is the sale price? 60% [6.4C]

© iStockphoto.com/Ivan Stevanovic

27. Geometry Given that lines ℓ_1 and ℓ_2 are parallel, find the measures of angles a and b. $m\angle a = 72°$; $m\angle b = 108°$ [7.1B]

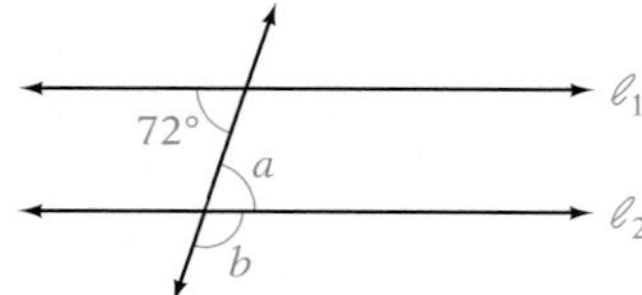

28. Travel A family drove to a resort at an average speed of 42 mph and later returned over the same road at an average speed of 56 mph. Find the distance to the resort if the total driving time was 7 h. 168 mi [5.5B]

29. Integer Problem Find three consecutive even integers such that five times the middle integer is twelve more than twice the sum of the first and third integers.
10, 12, 14 [5.4A]

30. Geometry The length of the base of a triangle is three times the height. The area of the triangle is 24 in^2. Find the length of the base of the triangle. 12 in. [10.6B]

Rational Expressions

OBJECTIVES

SECTION 11.1

- **A** To simplify a rational expression
- **B** To multiply rational expressions
- **C** To divide rational expressions

SECTION 11.2

- **A** To find the least common multiple (LCM) of two or more polynomials
- **B** To express two fractions in terms of the LCM of their denominators

SECTION 11.3

- **A** To add or subtract rational expressions with the same denominator
- **B** To add or subtract rational expressions with different denominators

SECTION 11.4

- **A** To simplify a complex fraction

SECTION 11.5

- **A** To solve an equation containing fractions

SECTION 11.6

- **A** To solve a literal equation for one of the variables

SECTION 11.7

- **A** To solve work problems
- **B** To use rational expressions to solve uniform motion problems

Focus on Success

It is important to overcome the "I Can't Do Math" syndrome. Interviews of successful athletes after bad performances show that they focus on the positive aspects of what they did, not the negative. Sports psychologists encourage athletes always to have a "can do" attitude. Develop this attitude toward math. Change your internal conversation from "I can't do math" and "Math is too hard" to "I can do math!" (See Develop a "Can Do" Attitude Toward Math, page AIM-3.)

Prep Test

Are you ready to succeed in this chapter? Take the Prep Test below to find out if you are ready to learn the new material.

1. Find the least common multiple (LCM) of 12 and 18.
36 [2.1A]

2. Simplify: $\dfrac{9x^3y^4}{3x^2y^7}$
$\dfrac{3x}{y^3}$ [9.4A]

3. Subtract: $\dfrac{3}{4} - \dfrac{8}{9}$
$-\dfrac{5}{36}$ [3.4A]

4. Divide: $\left(-\dfrac{8}{11}\right) \div \dfrac{4}{5}$
$-\dfrac{10}{11}$ [3.4B]

5. If a is a nonzero number, are the following two quantities equal: $\frac{0}{a}$ and $\frac{a}{0}$?
No [1.3C]

6. Solve: $\dfrac{2}{3}x - \dfrac{3}{4} = \dfrac{5}{6}$
$\dfrac{19}{8}$ [5.2A]

7. Factor: $x^2 - 4x - 12$
$(x - 6)(x + 2)$ [10.2A]

8. Factor: $2x^2 - x - 3$
$(2x - 3)(x + 1)$ [10.3A]

9. At 9:00 A.M., Anthony begins walking on a park trail at a rate of 90 m/min. Ten minutes later, his sister Jean begins walking the same trail in pursuit of her brother at a rate of 120 m/min. At what time will Jean catch up to Anthony? 9:40 A.M. [5.5B]

SECTION

11.1 Multiplication and Division of Rational Expressions

OBJECTIVE A *To simplify a rational expression*

A fraction in which the numerator and denominator are polynomials is called a **rational expression.** Examples of rational expressions are shown at the right.

$$\frac{5}{z}, \quad \frac{x^2+1}{2x-1}, \quad \frac{y^2+y-1}{4y^2+1}$$

Care must be exercised when evaluating a rational expression to ensure that the resulting denominator is not zero. Consider the rational expression at the right. The value of x cannot be 3 because the denominator would then be zero.

$$\frac{4x^2-9}{2x-6}$$

$$\frac{4(3)^2-9}{2(3)-6} = \frac{27}{0} \quad \text{Not a real number}$$

In the **simplest form of a rational expression,** the numerator and denominator have no common factors. The Multiplication Property of One is used to write a rational expression in simplest form.

INSTRUCTOR NOTE

Simplifying a rational expression is closely related to simplifying a rational number; the common factors are removed. Making this connection will help some students.

HOW TO 1 Simplify: $\dfrac{x^2-4}{x^2-2x-8}$

$$\frac{x^2-4}{x^2-2x-8} = \frac{(x-2)(x+2)}{(x-4)(x+2)}$$

- Factor the numerator and denominator.

$$= \frac{x-2}{x-4} \cdot \boxed{\frac{x+2}{x+2}} = \frac{x-2}{x-4} \cdot 1$$

$$= \frac{x-2}{x-4}, x \neq -2, 4$$

- The restrictions $x \neq -2$ and $x \neq 4$ are necessary to prevent division by zero.

This simplification is usually shown with slashes through the common factors:

$$\frac{x^2-4}{x^2-2x-8} = \frac{(x-2)\overset{1}{\cancel{(x+2)}}}{(x-4)\underset{1}{\cancel{(x+2)}}}$$

- Factor the numerator and denominator.

$$= \frac{x-2}{x-4}, x \neq -2, 4$$

- Divide by the common factors. The restrictions $x \neq -2$ or 4 are necessary to prevent division by zero.

In summary, to simplify a rational expression, factor the numerator and denominator. Then divide the numerator and denominator by the common factors.

INSTRUCTOR NOTE

It is important to emphasize that the numerator and denominator must be written in factored form before simplifying. This will help students avoid errors such as

$$\frac{x^2-x}{x^2} = \frac{\cancel{x^2}-x}{\cancel{x^2}} = 1-x$$

HOW TO 2 Simplify: $\dfrac{10+3x-x^2}{x^2-4x-5}$

$$\frac{10+3x-x^2}{x^2-4x-5} = \frac{-(x^2-3x-10)}{x^2-4x-5}$$

- Because the coefficient of x^2 in the numerator is -1, factor -1 from the numerator.

$$= \frac{-\overset{1}{\cancel{(x-5)}}(x+2)}{\underset{1}{\cancel{(x-5)}}(x+1)}$$

- Factor the numerator and denominator. Divide by the common factors.

$$= -\frac{x+2}{x+1}, x \neq -1, 5$$

For the remaining examples, we will not list the restrictions on the variables that prevent division by zero and assume that the values of the variables are such that division by zero is not possible.

EXAMPLE 1

Simplify: $\dfrac{4x^3y^4}{6x^4y}$

Solution

$\dfrac{4x^3y^4}{6x^4y} = \dfrac{2y^3}{3x}$ • Use the rules of exponents.

YOU TRY IT 1

Simplify: $\dfrac{6x^5y}{12x^2y^3}$

Your solution

$\dfrac{x^3}{2y^2}$

EXAMPLE 2

Simplify: $\dfrac{x^2 + 2x - 15}{x^2 - 7x + 12}$

Solution

$\dfrac{x^2 + 2x - 15}{x^2 - 7x + 12} = \dfrac{(x + 5)\overset{1}{\cancel{(x - 3)}}}{\underset{1}{\cancel{(x - 3)}}(x - 4)} = \dfrac{x + 5}{x - 4}$

YOU TRY IT 2

Simplify: $\dfrac{x^2 + 4x - 12}{x^2 - 3x + 2}$

Your solution

$\dfrac{x + 6}{x - 1}$

EXAMPLE 3

Simplify: $\dfrac{9 - x^2}{x^2 + x - 12}$

Solution

$\dfrac{9 - x^2}{x^2 + x - 12} = \dfrac{\overset{-1}{\cancel{(3 - x)}}(3 + x)}{\underset{1}{\cancel{(x - 3)}}(x + 4)}$ • $\dfrac{3 - x}{x - 3} = \dfrac{-1(x - 3)}{x - 3} = -1$

$= -\dfrac{x + 3}{x + 4}$

YOU TRY IT 3

Simplify: $\dfrac{x^2 + 2x - 24}{16 - x^2}$

Your solution

$-\dfrac{x + 6}{x + 4}$

IN-CLASS EXAMPLES

Simplify.

1. $\dfrac{18x^5y^2}{12xy^3}$ $\dfrac{3x^4}{2y}$
2. $\dfrac{x^2 - 1}{x^2 + 4x - 5}$ $\dfrac{x + 1}{x + 5}$
3. $\dfrac{a^2 - 2a}{4 - 2a}$ $-\dfrac{a}{2}$

Solutions on p. S26

OBJECTIVE B *To multiply rational expressions*

The product of two fractions is a fraction whose numerator is the product of the numerators of the two fractions and whose denominator is the product of the denominators of the two fractions.

Multiplying Rational Expressions

To multiply two fractions, multiply the numerators and multiply the denominators.

$$\frac{a}{b} \cdot \frac{c}{d} = \frac{ac}{bd}$$

EXAMPLES

1. $\dfrac{2}{3} \cdot \dfrac{4}{5} = \dfrac{8}{15}$ 2. $\dfrac{3x}{y} \cdot \dfrac{2}{z} = \dfrac{6x}{yz}$ 3. $\dfrac{x + 2}{x} \cdot \dfrac{3}{x - 2} = \dfrac{3(x + 2)}{x(x - 2)}$

INSTRUCTOR NOTE
Remind students that when they carry out the multiplication step, writing the product as a single fraction, they should leave the numerator and denominator in factored form. The simplified answer also may be left in factored form, as in Example 4. (Note, however, that in Objective 11.2B, students will need to multiply out the numerators when they apply the skill of multiplying rational expressions to the skill of writing fractions in terms of the LCM of their denominators.)

HOW TO 3 Multiply: $\frac{x^2 + 3x}{x^2 - 3x - 4} \cdot \frac{x^2 - 5x + 4}{x^2 + 2x - 3}$

$$\frac{x^2 + 3x}{x^2 - 3x - 4} \cdot \frac{x^2 - 5x + 4}{x^2 + 2x - 3}$$

$$= \frac{x(x + 3)}{(x - 4)(x + 1)} \cdot \frac{(x - 4)(x - 1)}{(x + 3)(x - 1)}$$

• Factor the numerator and denominator of each fraction.

$$= \frac{x\overset{1}{\cancel{(x + 3)}}\overset{1}{\cancel{(x - 4)}}\overset{1}{\cancel{(x - 1)}}}{\underset{1}{\cancel{(x - 4)}}(x + 1)\underset{1}{\cancel{(x + 3)}}\underset{1}{\cancel{(x - 1)}}}$$

• Multiply. Then divide by the common factors.

$$= \frac{x}{x + 1}$$

• Write the answer in simplest form.

EXAMPLE 4

Multiply: $\frac{10x^2 - 15x}{12x - 8} \cdot \frac{3x - 2}{20x - 25}$

Solution

$$\frac{10x^2 - 15x}{12x - 8} \cdot \frac{3x - 2}{20x - 25}$$

$$= \frac{5x(2x - 3)}{4(3x - 2)} \cdot \frac{(3x - 2)}{5(4x - 5)}$$

• Factor.

$$= \frac{\overset{1}{\cancel{5}}x(2x - 3)\overset{1}{\cancel{(3x - 2)}}}{4\underset{1}{\cancel{(3x - 2)}}\underset{1}{\cancel{5}}(4x - 5)}$$

• Divide by the common factors.

$$= \frac{x(2x - 3)}{4(4x - 5)}$$

YOU TRY IT 4

Multiply: $\frac{12x^2 + 3x}{10x - 15} \cdot \frac{8x - 12}{9x + 18}$

Your solution

$\frac{4x(4x + 1)}{15(x + 2)}$

EXAMPLE 5

Multiply: $\frac{x^2 + x - 6}{x^2 + 7x + 12} \cdot \frac{x^2 + 3x - 4}{4 - x^2}$

Solution

$$\frac{x^2 + x - 6}{x^2 + 7x + 12} \cdot \frac{x^2 + 3x - 4}{4 - x^2}$$

$$= \frac{(x + 3)(x - 2)}{(x + 3)(x + 4)} \cdot \frac{(x + 4)(x - 1)}{(2 - x)(2 + x)}$$

• Factor.

$$= \frac{\overset{1}{\cancel{(x + 3)}}\overset{-1}{\cancel{(x - 2)}}\overset{1}{\cancel{(x + 4)}}(x - 1)}{\underset{1}{\cancel{(x + 3)}}\underset{1}{\cancel{(x + 4)}}\underset{1}{\cancel{(2 - x)}}(2 + x)}$$

• Divide by the common factors.

$$= -\frac{x - 1}{x + 2}$$

YOU TRY IT 5

Multiply: $\frac{x^2 + 2x - 15}{9 - x^2} \cdot \frac{x^2 - 3x - 18}{x^2 - 7x + 6}$

Your solution

$-\frac{x + 5}{x - 1}$

IN-CLASS EXAMPLES
Multiply.

4. $\frac{28a^5b^7}{5x^4} \cdot \frac{15x^2}{14ab}$ $\quad \frac{6a^4b^6}{x^2}$

5. $\frac{6x^2 - 10x}{3 - 3x} \cdot \frac{x^2 - 1}{12x - 20}$ $\quad -\frac{x(x + 1)}{6}$

Solutions on p. S26

OBJECTIVE C To divide rational expressions

The **reciprocal of a rational expression** is the rational expression with the numerator and denominator interchanged.

Fraction	Reciprocal
$\frac{a}{b}$	$\frac{b}{a}$
$x^2 = \frac{x^2}{1}$	$\frac{1}{x^2}$
$\frac{x+2}{x}$	$\frac{x}{x+2}$

Dividing Rational Expressions

To divide two fractions, multiply the first fraction by the reciprocal of the divisor.

$$\frac{a}{b} \div \frac{c}{d} = \frac{a}{b} \cdot \frac{d}{c} = \frac{ad}{bc}$$

EXAMPLES

1. $\frac{4}{x} \div \frac{y}{5} = \frac{4}{x} \cdot \frac{5}{y} = \frac{20}{xy}$
2. $\frac{x+4}{x} \div \frac{x-2}{4} = \frac{x+4}{x} \cdot \frac{4}{x-2} = \frac{4(x+4)}{x(x-2)}$

The basis for the division rule is shown at the right.

$$\frac{a}{b} \div \frac{c}{d} = \frac{\frac{a}{b}}{\frac{c}{d}} = \frac{\frac{a}{b} \cdot \frac{d}{c}}{\frac{c}{d} \cdot \frac{d}{c}} = \frac{\frac{a}{b} \cdot \frac{d}{c}}{1} = \frac{a}{b} \cdot \frac{d}{c}$$

EXAMPLE 6

Divide: $\frac{xy^2 - 3x^2y}{z^2} \div \frac{6x^2 - 2xy}{z^3}$

Solution

$$\frac{xy^2 - 3x^2y}{z^2} \div \frac{6x^2 - 2xy}{z^3}$$

$$= \frac{xy^2 - 3x^2y}{z^2} \cdot \frac{z^3}{6x^2 - 2xy}$$ • Multiply by the reciprocal.

$$= \frac{xy\overset{-1}{\cancel{(y - 3x)}} \cdot z^3}{z^2 \cdot 2x\underset{1}{\cancel{(3x - y)}}} = -\frac{yz}{2}$$

YOU TRY IT 6

Divide: $\frac{a^2}{4bc^2 - 2b^2c} \div \frac{a}{6bc - 3b^2}$

Your solution

$\frac{3a}{2c}$

EXAMPLE 7

Divide: $\frac{2x^2 + 5x + 2}{2x^2 + 3x - 2} \div \frac{3x^2 + 13x + 4}{2x^2 + 7x - 4}$

Solution

$$\frac{2x^2 + 5x + 2}{2x^2 + 3x - 2} \div \frac{3x^2 + 13x + 4}{2x^2 + 7x - 4}$$

$$= \frac{2x^2 + 5x + 2}{2x^2 + 3x - 2} \cdot \frac{2x^2 + 7x - 4}{3x^2 + 13x + 4}$$ • Multiply by the reciprocal.

$$= \frac{(2x+1)\overset{1}{\cancel{(x+2)}} \cdot \overset{1}{\cancel{(2x-1)}}\overset{1}{\cancel{(x+4)}}}{\underset{1}{\cancel{(2x-1)}}\underset{1}{\cancel{(x+2)}} \cdot (3x+1)\underset{1}{\cancel{(x+4)}}} = \frac{2x+1}{3x+1}$$

YOU TRY IT 7

Divide: $\frac{3x^2 + 26x + 16}{3x^2 - 7x - 6} \div \frac{2x^2 + 9x - 5}{x^2 + 2x - 15}$

Your solution

$\frac{x+8}{2x-1}$

IN-CLASS EXAMPLES

Divide.

6. $\frac{12a^5b}{7xy^4} \div \frac{9ab^3}{35xy^2}$ $\mathbf{\frac{20a^4}{3b^2y^2}}$
7. $\frac{4x - 8}{15 + 2x - x^2} \div \frac{x^2 - 4}{3x^2 - 15x}$ $\mathbf{-\frac{12x}{(x+3)(x+2)}}$

Solutions on p. S26

11.1 EXERCISES

Concept Check

SUGGESTED ASSIGNMENT
Exercises 1–4; Exercises 5–55, odds;
Exercises 61–79, odds
More challenging exercises: Exercises 80–83

1. What is a rational expression? Provide an example.
2. When is a rational expression in simplest form?
3. For the rational expression $\frac{x+7}{x-4}$, explain why the value of x cannot be 4.
4. Why is the simplification at the right incorrect? $\frac{x+3}{x} = \frac{\overset{1}{\cancel{x}}+3}{\underset{1}{\cancel{x}}} = 4$

   The numerator and denominator were divided by a term rather than by a factor.

OBJECTIVE A *To simplify a rational expression*

For Exercises 5 to 32, simplify.

5. $\frac{9x^3}{12x^4}$ $\frac{3}{4x}$
6. $\frac{16x^2y}{24xy^3}$ $\frac{2x}{3y^2}$
7. $\frac{(x+3)^2}{(x+3)^3}$ $\frac{1}{x+3}$
8. $\frac{(2x-1)^5}{(2x-1)^4}$ $2x-1$
9. $\frac{3n-4}{4-3n}$ -1
10. $\frac{5-2x}{2x-5}$ -1
11. $\frac{6y(y+2)}{9y^2(y+2)}$ $\frac{2}{3y}$
12. $\frac{12x^2(3-x)}{18x(3-x)}$ $\frac{2x}{3}$
13. $\frac{6x(x-5)}{8x^2(5-x)}$ $-\frac{3}{4x}$
14. $\frac{14x^3(7-3x)}{21x(3x-7)}$ $-\frac{2x^2}{3}$
15. $\frac{a^2+4a}{ab+4b}$ $\frac{a}{b}$
16. $\frac{x^2-3x}{2x-6}$ $\frac{x}{2}$
17. $\frac{4-6x}{3x^2-2x}$ $-\frac{2}{x}$
18. $\frac{5xy-3y}{9-15x}$ $-\frac{y}{3}$
19. $\frac{y^2-3y+2}{y^2-4y+3}$ $\frac{y-2}{y-3}$
20. $\frac{x^2+5x+6}{x^2+8x+15}$ $\frac{x+2}{x+5}$
21. $\frac{x^2+3x-10}{x^2+2x-8}$ $\frac{x+5}{x+4}$
22. $\frac{a^2+7a-8}{a^2+6a-7}$ $\frac{a+8}{a+7}$
23. $\frac{x^2+x-12}{x^2-6x+9}$ $\frac{x+4}{x-3}$
24. $\frac{x^2+8x+16}{x^2-2x-24}$ $\frac{x+4}{x-6}$
25. $\frac{x^2-3x-10}{25-x^2}$ $-\frac{x+2}{x+5}$
26. $\frac{4-y^2}{y^2-3y-10}$ $\frac{2-y}{y-5}$
27. $\frac{2x^3+2x^2-4x}{x^3+2x^2-3x}$ $\frac{2(x+2)}{x+3}$
28. $\frac{3x^3-12x}{6x^3-24x^2+24x}$ $\frac{x+2}{2(x-2)}$
29. $\frac{6x^2-7x+2}{6x^2+5x-6}$ $\frac{2x-1}{2x+3}$
30. $\frac{2n^2-9n+4}{2n^2-5n-12}$ $\frac{2n-1}{2n+3}$
31. $\frac{x^2+3x-28}{24-2x-x^2}$ $-\frac{x+7}{x+6}$
32. $\frac{x^2+7x-8}{1+x-2x^2}$ $-\frac{x+8}{2x+1}$

OBJECTIVE B *To multiply rational expressions*

For Exercises 33 to 56, multiply.

33. $\frac{8x^2}{9y^3} \cdot \frac{3y^2}{4x^3}$ $\frac{2}{3xy}$

34. $\frac{14a^2b^3}{15x^5y^2} \cdot \frac{25x^3y}{16ab}$ $\frac{35ab^2}{24x^2y}$

35. $\frac{12x^3y^4}{7a^2b^3} \cdot \frac{14a^3b^4}{9x^2y^2}$ $\frac{8xy^2ab}{3}$

36. $\frac{18a^4b^2}{25x^2y^3} \cdot \frac{50x^5y^6}{27a^6b^2}$ $\frac{4x^3y^3}{3a^2}$

37. $\frac{3x-6}{5x-20} \cdot \frac{10x-40}{27x-54}$ $\frac{2}{9}$

38. $\frac{8x-12}{14x+7} \cdot \frac{42x+21}{32x-48}$ $\frac{3}{4}$

39. $\frac{3x^2+2x}{2xy-3y} \cdot \frac{2xy^3-3y^3}{3x^3+2x^2}$ $\frac{y^2}{x}$

40. $\frac{4a^2x-3a^2}{2by+5b} \cdot \frac{2b^3y+5b^3}{4ax-3a}$ ab^2

41. $\frac{x^2+5x+4}{x^3y^2} \cdot \frac{x^2y^3}{x^2+2x+1}$ $\frac{y(x+4)}{x(x+1)}$

42. $\frac{x^2+x-2}{xy^2} \cdot \frac{x^3y}{x^2+5x+6}$ $\frac{x^2(x-1)}{y(x+3)}$

43. $\frac{x^4y^2}{x^2+3x-28} \cdot \frac{x^2-49}{xy^4}$ $\frac{x^3(x-7)}{y^2(x-4)}$

44. $\frac{x^5y^3}{x^2+13x+30} \cdot \frac{x^2+2x-3}{x^7y^2}$ $\frac{y(x-1)}{x^2(x+10)}$

45. $\frac{2x^2-5x}{2xy+y} \cdot \frac{2xy^2+y^2}{5x^2-2x^3}$ $-\frac{y}{x}$

46. $\frac{3a^3+4a^2}{5ab-3b} \cdot \frac{3b^3-5ab^3}{3a^2+4a}$ $-ab^2$

47. $\frac{x^2-2x-24}{x^2-5x-6} \cdot \frac{x^2+5x+6}{x^2+6x+8}$ $\frac{x+3}{x+1}$

48. $\frac{x^2-8x+7}{x^2+3x-4} \cdot \frac{x^2+3x-10}{x^2-9x+14}$ $\frac{x+5}{x+4}$

49. $\frac{x^2+2x-35}{x^2+4x-21} \cdot \frac{x^2+3x-18}{x^2+9x+18}$ $\frac{x-5}{x+3}$

50. $\frac{y^2+y-20}{y^2+2y-15} \cdot \frac{y^2+4y-21}{y^2+3y-28}$ 1

51. $\frac{x^2-3x-4}{x^2+6x+5} \cdot \frac{x^2+5x+6}{8+2x-x^2}$ $-\frac{x+3}{x+5}$

52. $\frac{25-n^2}{n^2-2n-35} \cdot \frac{n^2-8n-20}{n^2-3n-10}$ $-\frac{n-10}{n-7}$

53. $\frac{16+6x-x^2}{x^2-10x-24} \cdot \frac{x^2-6x-27}{x^2-17x+72}$ $-\frac{x+3}{x-12}$

54. $\frac{x^2-11x+28}{x^2-13x+42} \cdot \frac{x^2+7x+10}{20-x-x^2}$ $-\frac{x+2}{x-6}$

55. $\dfrac{2x^2 + 5x + 2}{2x^2 + 7x + 3} \cdot \dfrac{x^2 - 7x - 30}{x^2 - 6x - 40}$
$\dfrac{x + 2}{x + 4}$

56. $\dfrac{x^2 - 4x - 32}{x^2 - 8x - 48} \cdot \dfrac{3x^2 + 17x + 10}{3x^2 - 22x - 16}$
$\dfrac{x + 5}{x - 12}$

For Exercises 57 to 59, use the product $\dfrac{x^a}{y^b} \cdot \dfrac{y^c}{x^d}$, where a, b, c, and d are all positive integers.

57. If $a > d$ and $c > b$, what is the denominator of the simplified product? 1

58. If $a > d$ and $b > c$, which variable appears in the denominator of the simplified product? y

59. If $a < d$ and $b = c$, what is the numerator of the simplified product? 1

OBJECTIVE C *To divide rational expressions*

For Exercises 60 to 79, divide.

60. $\dfrac{4x^2y^3}{15a^2b^3} \div \dfrac{6xy}{5a^3b^5}$
$\dfrac{2xy^2ab^2}{9}$

61. $\dfrac{9x^3y^4}{16a^4b^2} \div \dfrac{45x^4y^2}{14a^7b}$
$\dfrac{7a^3y^2}{40bx}$

62. $\dfrac{6x - 12}{8x + 32} \div \dfrac{18x - 36}{10x + 40}$
$\dfrac{5}{12}$

63. $\dfrac{28x + 14}{45x - 30} \div \dfrac{14x + 7}{30x - 20}$
$\dfrac{4}{3}$

64. $\dfrac{6x^3 + 7x^2}{12x - 3} \div \dfrac{6x^2 + 7x}{36x - 9}$
$3x$

65. $\dfrac{5a^2y + 3a^2}{2x^3 + 5x^2} \div \dfrac{10ay + 6a}{6x^3 + 15x^2}$
$\dfrac{3a}{2}$

66. $\dfrac{x^2 + 4x + 3}{x^2y} \div \dfrac{x^2 + 2x + 1}{xy^2}$
$\dfrac{y(x + 3)}{x(x + 1)}$

67. $\dfrac{x^3y^2}{x^2 - 3x - 10} \div \dfrac{xy^4}{x^2 - x - 20}$
$\dfrac{x^2(x + 4)}{y^2(x + 2)}$

68. $\dfrac{x^2 - 49}{x^4y^3} \div \dfrac{x^2 - 14x + 49}{x^4y^3}$
$\dfrac{x + 7}{x - 7}$

69. $\dfrac{x^2y^5}{x^2 - 11x + 30} \div \dfrac{xy^6}{x^2 - 7x + 10}$
$\dfrac{x(x - 2)}{y(x - 6)}$

70. $\dfrac{4ax - 8a}{c^2} \div \dfrac{2y - xy}{c^3}$
$-\dfrac{4ac}{y}$

71. $\dfrac{3x^2y - 9xy}{a^2b} \div \dfrac{3x^2 - x^3}{ab^2}$
$-\dfrac{3by}{ax}$

72. $\dfrac{x^2 - 5x + 6}{x^2 - 9x + 18} \div \dfrac{x^2 - 6x + 8}{x^2 - 9x + 20}$
$\dfrac{x - 5}{x - 6}$

73. $\dfrac{x^2 + 3x - 40}{x^2 + 2x - 35} \div \dfrac{x^2 + 2x - 48}{x^2 + 3x - 18}$
$\dfrac{(x + 6)(x - 3))}{(x + 7)(x - 6)}$

74. $\dfrac{x^2+2x-15}{x^2-4x-45} \div \dfrac{x^2+x-12}{x^2-5x-36}$
1

75. $\dfrac{y^2-y-56}{y^2+8y+7} \div \dfrac{y^2-13y+40}{y^2-4y-5}$
1

76. $\dfrac{8+2x-x^2}{x^2+7x+10} \div \dfrac{x^2-11x+28}{x^2-x-42}$
$-\dfrac{x+6}{x+5}$

77. $\dfrac{x^2-x-2}{x^2-7x+10} \div \dfrac{x^2-3x-4}{40-3x-x^2}$
$-\dfrac{x+8}{x-4}$

78. $\dfrac{2x^2-3x-20}{2x^2-7x-30} \div \dfrac{2x^2-5x-12}{4x^2+12x+9}$
$\dfrac{2x+3}{x-6}$

79. $\dfrac{6n^2+13n+6}{4n^2-9} \div \dfrac{6n^2+n-2}{4n^2-1}$
$\dfrac{2n+1}{2n-3}$

For Exercises 80 to 83, state whether the given division is equivalent to $\dfrac{x^2-3x-4}{x^2+5x-6}$.

80. $\dfrac{x-4}{x+6} \div \dfrac{x-1}{x+1}$
Yes

81. $\dfrac{x+1}{x+6} \div \dfrac{x-1}{x-4}$
Yes

82. $\dfrac{x+1}{x-1} \div \dfrac{x+6}{x-4}$
Yes

83. $\dfrac{x-1}{x+1} \div \dfrac{x-4}{x+6}$
No

Critical Thinking

For Exercises 84 to 86, name the values of x for which the rational expression is undefined. (*Hint:* Set the denominator equal to zero and solve for x.)

84. $\dfrac{x}{(x-2)(x+5)}$
2, −5

85. $\dfrac{x+5}{x^2-4x-5}$
5, −1

86. $\dfrac{3x-8}{3x^2-10x-8}$
$-\dfrac{2}{3}, 4$

Geometry For Exercises 87 and 88, write in simplest form the ratio of the shaded area of the figure to the total area of the figure.

87.
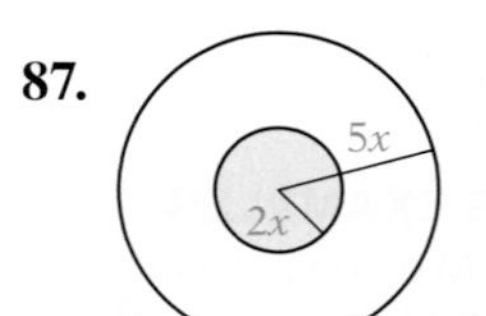

$\dfrac{4}{25}$

88. 2x, x + 4, x + 4, x + 8
$\dfrac{x}{x+8}$

89. Find two different pairs of rational expressions whose product is $\dfrac{2x^2+7x-4}{3x^2-8x-3}$.
$\dfrac{x+4}{x-3}$ and $\dfrac{2x-1}{3x+1}$ or $\dfrac{x+4}{3x+1}$ and $\dfrac{2x-1}{x-3}$

Projects or Group Activities

90. Given the expression $\dfrac{9}{x^2+1}$, choose some values of x and evaluate the expression for those values. Is it possible to choose a value of x for which the value of the expression is greater than 10? If so, give such a value. If not, explain why it is not possible.

91. Given the expression $\dfrac{1}{y-3}$, choose some values of y and evaluate the expression for those values. Is it possible to choose a value of y for which the value of the expression is greater than 10,000,000? If so, give such a value. If not, explain why it is not possible.

QUICK QUIZ

Simplify.

1. $\dfrac{x^2-x-12}{x^2+9x+18}$
$\dfrac{x-4}{x+6}$ [11.1A]

Multiply.

2. $\dfrac{x^2-5x+4}{2x^2+5x-3} \cdot \dfrac{x^2-9}{x^2-7x+12}$
$\dfrac{x-1}{2x-1}$ [11.1B]

Divide.

3. $\dfrac{10x+10}{3x-6} \div \dfrac{2x+2}{3xy-6y}$
$5y$ [11.1C]

SECTION

11.2 Expressing Fractions in Terms of the LCM of the Denominators

OBJECTIVE A *To find the least common multiple (LCM) of two or more polynomials*

Recall that the least common multiple (LCM) of two or more numbers is the smallest number that contains the prime factorization of each number.

The LCM of 12 and 18 is 36 because 36 contains the prime factors of 12 and the prime factors of 18.

$12 = 2 \cdot 2 \cdot 3$
$18 = 2 \cdot 3 \cdot 3$

$$\text{LCM} = 36 = \overbrace{2 \cdot 2 \cdot 3}^{\text{Factors of 12}} \cdot 3 \quad (\text{Factors of 18: } 2 \cdot \underbrace{3 \cdot 3})$$

INSTRUCTOR NOTE
In Example 2 below, point out that the factor −1 is not included in the LCM. The reason for this will be clearer to students after they study Objectives 11.2B and 11.3B.

The **least common multiple (LCM) of two or more polynomials** is the polynomial of least degree that contains all the factors of each polynomial.

To find the LCM of two or more polynomials, first factor each polynomial completely. The LCM is the product of each factor the greatest number of times it occurs in any one factorization.

Take Note
The LCM must contain the factors of each polynomial. As shown with braces at the right, the LCM contains the factors of $4x^2 + 4x$ and the factors of $x^2 + 2x + 1$.

HOW TO 1 Find the LCM of $4x^2 + 4x$ and $x^2 + 2x + 1$.

The LCM of the polynomials is the product of the LCM of the numerical coefficients and each variable factor the greatest number of times it occurs in any one factorization.

$4x^2 + 4x = 4x(x + 1) = 2 \cdot 2 \cdot x(x + 1)$
$x^2 + 2x + 1 = (x + 1)(x + 1)$

$$\text{LCM} = \overbrace{2 \cdot 2 \cdot x(x + 1)}^{\text{Factors of } 4x^2 + 4x}(x + 1) = 4x(x + 1)(x + 1)$$

(Factors of $x^2 + 2x + 1$: $(x + 1)(x + 1)$)

EXAMPLE 1

Find the LCM of $4x^2y$ and $6xy^2$.

Solution

$4x^2y = 2 \cdot 2 \cdot x \cdot x \cdot y$
$6xy^2 = 2 \cdot 3 \cdot x \cdot y \cdot y$
$\text{LCM} = 2 \cdot 2 \cdot 3 \cdot x \cdot x \cdot y \cdot y = 12x^2y^2$

YOU TRY IT 1

Find the LCM of $8uv^2$ and $12uw$.

Your solution

$24uv^2w$

IN-CLASS EXAMPLES
Find the LCM of the polynomials.
1. $24a^3b^2$ and $9ab^5$ $\mathbf{72a^3b^5}$
2. $2x^2 - 4x$ and $x^2 - 4$ $\mathbf{2x(x - 2)(x + 2)}$
3. $x^2 - 3x - 40$ and $8 + 7x - x^2$ $\mathbf{(x - 8)(x + 5)(x + 1)}$

EXAMPLE 2

Find the LCM of $x^2 - x - 6$ and $9 - x^2$.

Solution

$x^2 - x - 6 = (x - 3)(x + 2)$
$9 - x^2 = -(x^2 - 9) = -(x + 3)(x - 3)$
$\text{LCM} = (x - 3)(x + 2)(x + 3)$

YOU TRY IT 2

Find the LCM of $m^2 - 6m + 9$ and $m^2 - 2m - 3$.

Your solution

$(m - 3)(m - 3)(m + 1)$

Solutions on p. S26

OBJECTIVE B *To express two fractions in terms of the LCM of their denominators*

INSTRUCTOR NOTE
In Objective 11.1B, answers were left in factored form. Point out that now the numerators should be multiplied out (to prepare students for adding fractions in Objective 11.3B).

When adding and subtracting fractions, it is frequently necessary to express two or more fractions in terms of a common denominator. The least common denominator (LCD) is the LCM of the denominators of the fractions.

HOW TO 2 Write the fractions $\frac{x+1}{4x^2}$ and $\frac{x-3}{2x^2-4x}$ in terms of the LCM of the denominators.

Find the LCM of the denominators.

The LCM is $4x^2(x-2)$.

For each fraction, multiply the numerator and the denominator by the factors whose product with the denominator is the LCM.

$$\frac{x+1}{4x^2} = \frac{x+1}{4x^2}\cdot\frac{(x-2)}{(x-2)} = \frac{x^2-x-2}{4x^2(x-2)}$$

$$\frac{x-3}{2x^2-4x} = \frac{x-3}{2x(x-2)}\cdot\frac{2x}{2x} = \frac{2x^2-6x}{4x^2(x-2)}$$

LCM

EXAMPLE 3

Write the fractions $\frac{x+2}{3x^2}$ and $\frac{x-1}{8xy}$ in terms of the LCM of the denominators.

Solution

The LCM is $24x^2y$.

$$\frac{x+2}{3x^2} = \frac{x+2}{3x^2}\cdot\frac{8y}{8y} = \frac{8xy+16y}{24x^2y}$$

$$\frac{x-1}{8xy} = \frac{x-1}{8xy}\cdot\frac{3x}{3x} = \frac{3x^2-3x}{24x^2y}$$

YOU TRY IT 3

Write the fractions $\frac{x-3}{4xy^2}$ and $\frac{2x+1}{9y^2z}$ in terms of the LCM of the denominators.

Your solution

$\frac{9xz-27z}{36xy^2z}, \frac{8x^2+4x}{36xy^2z}$

IN-CLASS EXAMPLES

Write each fraction in terms of the LCM of the denominators.

4. $\frac{8}{3x^2y}$ and $\frac{x}{6xy^3}$ **$\frac{16y^2}{6x^2y^3}$ and $\frac{x^2}{6x^2y^3}$**

5. $\frac{x+2}{x^2-3x-4}$ and $\frac{1}{16-x^2}$ **$\frac{x^2+6x+8}{(x-4)(x+1)(x+4)}$ and $-\frac{x+1}{(x-4)(x+1)(x+4)}$**

EXAMPLE 4

Write the fractions $\frac{2x-1}{2x-x^2}$ and $\frac{x}{x^2+x-6}$ in terms of the LCM of the denominators.

Solution

$$\frac{2x-1}{2x-x^2} = \frac{2x-1}{-(x^2-2x)} = -\frac{2x-1}{x^2-2x}$$

The LCM is $x(x-2)(x+3)$.

$$\frac{2x-1}{2x-x^2} = -\frac{2x-1}{x(x-2)}\cdot\frac{x+3}{x+3} = -\frac{2x^2+5x-3}{x(x-2)(x+3)}$$

$$\frac{x}{x^2+x-6} = \frac{x}{(x-2)(x+3)}\cdot\frac{x}{x} = \frac{x^2}{x(x-2)(x+3)}$$

YOU TRY IT 4

Write the fractions $\frac{x+4}{x^2-3x-10}$ and $\frac{2x}{25-x^2}$ in terms of the LCM of the denominators.

Your solution

$\frac{x^2+9x+20}{(x+2)(x-5)(x+5)}, -\frac{2x^2+4x}{(x+2)(x-5)(x+5)}$

Solutions on p. S26

11.2 EXERCISES

Concept Check

SUGGESTED ASSIGNMENT
Exercises 1–4; Exercises 5–43, odds;
More challenging exercise: Exercise 49

Determine whether the statement is true or false.

1. The least common multiple of two numbers is the smallest number that contains all the prime factors of both numbers. True
2. The least common denominator of two or more fractions is the least common multiple of the denominators of the fractions. True
3. The LCM of x^2, x^5, and x^8 is x^2. False
4. We can rewrite $\frac{x}{y}$ as $\frac{4x}{4y}$ by using the Multiplication Property of One. True

OBJECTIVE A *To find the least common multiple (LCM) of two or more polynomials*

For Exercises 5 to 27, find the LCM of the polynomials.

5. $8x^3y$
$12xy^2$
$24x^3y^2$

6. $6ab^2$
$18ab^3$
$18ab^3$

7. $2x^2y$
$3x^2 + 12x$
$6x^2y(x + 4)$

8. $4xy^2$
$6xy^2 + 12y^2$
$12xy^2(x + 2)$

9. $9x(x + 2)$
$12(x + 2)^2$
$36x(x + 2)^2$

10. $8x^2(x - 1)^2$
$10x^3(x - 1)$
$40x^3(x - 1)^2$

11. $3x + 3$
$2x^2 + 4x + 2$
$6(x + 1)^2$

12. $4x - 12$
$2x^2 - 12x + 18$
$4(x - 3)^2$

13. $(x - 1)(x + 2)$
$(x - 1)(x + 3)$
$(x - 1)(x + 2)(x + 3)$

14. $(2x - 1)(x + 4)$
$(2x + 1)(x + 4)$
$(2x - 1)(x + 4)(2x + 1)$

15. $(2x + 3)^2$
$(2x + 3)(x - 5)$
$(2x + 3)^2(x - 5)$

16. $(x - 7)(x + 2)$
$(x - 7)^2$
$(x - 7)^2(x + 2)$

17. $x - 1$
$x - 2$
$(x - 1)(x - 2)$
$(x - 1)(x - 2)$

18. $(x + 4)(x - 3)$
$x + 4$
$x - 3$
$(x + 4)(x - 3)$

19. $x^2 - x - 6$
$x^2 + x - 12$
$(x - 3)(x + 2)(x + 4)$

20. $x^2 + 3x - 10$
$x^2 + 5x - 14$
$(x + 5)(x + 7)(x - 2)$

21. $x^2 + 5x + 4$
$x^2 - 3x - 28$
$(x + 4)(x + 1)(x - 7)$

22. $x^2 - 10x + 21$
$x^2 - 8x + 15$
$(x - 7)(x - 3)(x - 5)$

23. $x^2 - 2x - 24$
$x^2 - 36$
$(x - 6)(x + 6)(x + 4)$

24. $x^2 + 7x + 10$
$x^2 - 25$
$(x + 5)(x - 5)(x + 2)$

25. $2x^2 - 7x + 3$
$2x^2 + x - 1$
$(2x - 1)(x - 3)(x + 1)$

26. $3x^2 - 11x + 6$
$3x^2 + 4x - 4$
$(3x - 2)(x - 3)(x + 2)$

27. $6 + x - x^2$
$x + 2$
$x - 3$
$(x + 2)(x - 3)$

28. How many factors of $x - 3$ are in the LCM of each pair of expressions?
a. $x^2 + x - 12$ and $x^2 - 9$
One
b. $x^2 - x - 12$ and $x^2 + 6x + 9$
Zero
c. $x^2 + x - 12$ and $x^2 - 6x + 9$
Two

OBJECTIVE B *To express two fractions in terms of the LCM of their denominators*

For Exercises 29 to 44, write the fractions in terms of the LCM of the denominators.

29. $\frac{4}{x}, \frac{3}{x^2}$
$\frac{4x}{x^2}, \frac{3}{x^2}$

30. $\frac{5}{ab^2}, \frac{6}{ab}$
$\frac{5}{ab^2}, \frac{6b}{ab^2}$

31. $\frac{x}{3y^2}, \frac{z}{4y}$
$\frac{4x}{12y^2}, \frac{3yz}{12y^2}$

32. $\frac{5y}{6x^2}, \frac{7}{9xy}$
$\frac{15y^2}{18x^2y}, \frac{14x}{18x^2y}$

33. $\frac{y}{x(x-3)}, \frac{6}{x^2}$
$\frac{xy}{x^2(x-3)}, \frac{6x-18}{x^2(x-3)}$

34. $\frac{a}{y^2}, \frac{6}{y(y+5)}$
$\frac{ay+5a}{y^2(y+5)}, \frac{6y}{y^2(y+5)}$

35. $\frac{9}{(x-1)^2}, \frac{6}{x(x-1)}$
$\frac{9x}{x(x-1)^2}, \frac{6x-6}{x(x-1)^2}$

36. $\frac{a^2}{y(y+7)}, \frac{a}{(y+7)^2}$
$\frac{a^2y+7a^2}{y(y+7)^2}, \frac{ay}{y(y+7)^2}$

37. $\frac{3}{x-3}, \frac{5}{x(3-x)}$
$\frac{3x}{x(x-3)}, -\frac{5}{x(x-3)}$

38. $\frac{b}{y(y-4)}, \frac{b^2}{4-y}$
$\frac{b}{y(y-4)}, -\frac{b^2y}{y(y-4)}$

39. $\frac{x-2}{x+3}, \frac{x}{x-4}$
$\frac{x^2-6x+8}{(x+3)(x-4)}, \frac{x^2+3x}{(x+3)(x-4)}$

40. $\frac{x^2}{2x-1}, \frac{x+1}{x+4}$
$\frac{x^3+4x^2}{(2x-1)(x+4)}, \frac{2x^2+x-1}{(2x-1)(x+4)}$

41. $\frac{3}{x^2+x-2}, \frac{x}{x+2}$
$\frac{3}{(x+2)(x-1)}, \frac{x^2-x}{(x+2)(x-1)}$

42. $\frac{3x}{x-5}, \frac{4}{x^2-25}$
$\frac{3x^2+15x}{(x-5)(x+5)}, \frac{4}{(x-5)(x+5)}$

43. $\frac{x}{x^2+x-6}, \frac{2x}{x^2-9}$
$\frac{x^2-3x}{(x+3)(x-3)(x-2)}, \frac{2x^2-4x}{(x+3)(x-3)(x-2)}$

44. $\frac{x-1}{x^2+2x-15}, \frac{x}{x^2+6x+5}$
$\frac{x^2-1}{(x+5)(x-3)(x+1)}, \frac{x^2-3x}{(x+5)(x-3)(x+1)}$

Critical Thinking

For Exercises 45 to 48, write each expression in terms of the LCM of the denominators.

45. $\frac{3}{10^2}; \frac{5}{10^4}$
$\frac{300}{10^4}; \frac{5}{10^4}$

46. $\frac{8}{10^3}; \frac{9}{10^5}$
$\frac{800}{10^5}; \frac{9}{10^5}$

47. $b; \frac{5}{b}$
$\frac{b^2}{b}; \frac{5}{b}$

48. $3; \frac{2}{n}$
$\frac{3n}{n}; \frac{2}{n}$

49. When is the LCM of two expressions equal to their product?

Projects or Group Activities

50. Match the polynomials with their LCM. An LCM may be used more than once.

a. x^2-4 and x^2+3x+2
b. $x+3$ and x^2+5x+6
c. x^2-x-2 and x^2+2x+1
d. $x-4$ and x^2-1
e. $2-x$ and x^2+3x+2
f. $4-x$ and x^2-1
g. $x-4$ and $1-x^2$
h. $2+x-x^2$ and $(x+1)^2$

i. $(x+3)(x+2)$
ii. $(x-4)(x+1)(x-1)$
iii. $(x+2)(x-2)(x+1)$
iv. $(x-2)(x+1)(x+1)$

a and iii, b and i, c and iv, d and ii, e and iii, f and ii, g and ii, h and iv

QUICK QUIZ

Find the LCM of the polynomials.

1. $14a^4b^2$ and $21ab^5$ **$42a^4b^5$** **[11.2A]**
2. $x^2-4x-12$ and $36-x^2$ **$(x-6)(x+6)(x+2)$** **[11.2A]**

Write each fraction in terms of the LCM of the denominators.

3. $\frac{y}{10x^2}$ and $\frac{x}{15y^3}$ **$\frac{3y^4}{30x^2y^3}$ and $\frac{2x^3}{30x^2y^3}$** **[11.2B]**
4. $\frac{x+1}{x^2-x}$ and $\frac{x}{x^2+6x-7}$ **$\frac{x^2+8x+7}{x(x-1)(x+7)}$ and $\frac{x^2}{x(x-1)(x+7)}$** **[11.2B]**

SECTION

11.3 Addition and Subtraction of Rational Expressions

OBJECTIVE A *To add or subtract rational expressions with the same denominator*

Adding and Subtracting Rational Expressions

To add or subtract rational expressions in which the denominators are the same, add or subtract the numerators. The denominator of the sum or difference is the common denominator. Write the answer in simplest form.

$$\frac{a}{b} + \frac{c}{b} = \frac{a+c}{b} \qquad \frac{a}{b} - \frac{c}{b} = \frac{a-c}{b}$$

EXAMPLES

1. $\frac{5x}{18} + \frac{7x}{18} = \frac{12x}{18} = \frac{2x}{3}$

2. $\frac{x}{x^2-1} + \frac{1}{x^2-1} = \frac{x+1}{x^2-1} = \frac{\overset{1}{\cancel{(x+1)}}}{\underset{1}{\cancel{(x+1)}}(x-1)} = \frac{1}{x-1}$

3. $\frac{2x}{x-2} - \frac{4}{x-2} = \frac{2x-4}{x-2} = \frac{2\overset{1}{\cancel{(x-2)}}}{\underset{1}{\cancel{(x-2)}}} = 2$

4. $\frac{3x-1}{x^2-5x+4} - \frac{2x+3}{x^2-5x+4}$

$= \frac{(3x-1)-(2x+3)}{x^2-5x+4} = \frac{3x-1-2x-3}{x^2-5x+4} = \frac{x-4}{x^2-5x+4}$

$= \frac{\overset{1}{\cancel{(x-4)}}}{\underset{1}{\cancel{(x-4)}}(x-1)} = \frac{1}{x-1}$

Take Note
Be careful with signs when subtracting rational expressions. In example (4) at the right, note that we must subtract the *entire* numerator $2x + 3$.

$(3x - 1) - (2x + 3)$
$= 3x - 1 - 2x - 3$

INSTRUCTOR NOTE
In example (4) at the right, point out the importance of the parentheses around $2x + 3$. Emphasize that students must remember to subtract the whole numerator, which changes the sign of every term, not just the first term.

EXAMPLE 1

Subtract: $\frac{3x^2}{x^2-1} - \frac{x+4}{x^2-1}$

Solution

$\frac{3x^2}{x^2-1} - \frac{x+4}{x^2-1} = \frac{3x^2-(x+4)}{x^2-1}$ • Subtract the numerators.

$= \frac{3x^2-x-4}{x^2-1}$

$= \frac{(3x-4)\overset{1}{\cancel{(x+1)}}}{(x-1)\underset{1}{\cancel{(x+1)}}} = \frac{3x-4}{x-1}$

YOU TRY IT 1

Subtract: $\frac{2x^2}{x^2-x-12} - \frac{7x+4}{x^2-x-12}$

Your solution

$\frac{2x+1}{x+3}$

Solution on p. S26

IN-CLASS EXAMPLES

1. Subtract: $\frac{2x^2}{x^2+7x-8} - \frac{x+1}{x^2+7x-8}$ $\quad$ **$\frac{2x+1}{x+8}$**

2. Simplify: $\frac{3y^2-6}{y^2+y-20} + \frac{y-9}{y^2+y-20} - \frac{2y^2+y+1}{y^2+y-20}$ $\quad$ **$\frac{y+4}{y+5}$**

EXAMPLE 2

Simplify:
$$\frac{2x^2 + 5}{x^2 + 2x - 3} - \frac{x^2 - 3x}{x^2 + 2x - 3} + \frac{x - 2}{x^2 + 2x - 3}$$

Solution

$$\frac{2x^2 + 5}{x^2 + 2x - 3} - \frac{x^2 - 3x}{x^2 + 2x - 3} + \frac{x - 2}{x^2 + 2x - 3}$$
$$= \frac{(2x^2 + 5) - (x^2 - 3x) + (x - 2)}{x^2 + 2x - 3}$$
$$= \frac{2x^2 + 5 - x^2 + 3x + x - 2}{x^2 + 2x - 3}$$
$$= \frac{x^2 + 4x + 3}{x^2 + 2x - 3}$$
$$= \frac{\overset{1}{\cancel{(x + 3)}}(x + 1)}{\underset{1}{\cancel{(x + 3)}}(x - 1)} = \frac{x + 1}{x - 1}$$

YOU TRY IT 2

Simplify:
$$\frac{x^2 - 1}{x^2 - 8x + 12} - \frac{2x + 1}{x^2 - 8x + 12} + \frac{x}{x^2 - 8x + 12}$$

Your solution

$$\frac{x + 1}{x - 6}$$

Solution on p. S27

OBJECTIVE B *To add or subtract rational expressions with different denominators*

Before two fractions with unlike denominators can be added or subtracted, each fraction must be expressed in terms of a common denominator. In this text, we express each fraction in terms of the LCD, which is the LCM of the denominators.

HOW TO 1 Add: $\frac{x - 3}{x^2 - 2x} + \frac{6}{x^2 - 4}$

The LCM is $x(x - 2)(x + 2)$.
• **Find the LCM of the denominators.**

$$\frac{x - 3}{x^2 - 2x} + \frac{6}{x^2 - 4}$$

$$= \frac{x - 3}{x(x - 2)} \cdot \frac{x + 2}{x + 2} + \frac{6}{(x - 2)(x + 2)} \cdot \frac{x}{x}$$
• **Write each fraction in terms of the LCD.**

$$= \frac{x^2 - x - 6}{x(x - 2)(x + 2)} + \frac{6x}{x(x - 2)(x + 2)}$$
• **Multiply the factors in the numerators.**

$$= \frac{(x^2 - x - 6) + 6x}{x(x - 2)(x + 2)}$$
• **Add the fractions.**

$$= \frac{x^2 + 5x - 6}{x(x - 2)(x + 2)}$$
• **Simplify.**

$$= \frac{(x + 6)(x - 1)}{x(x - 2)(x + 2)}$$
• **Factor to check for common factors in the numerator and denominator.**

After combining the numerators and placing the result over the common denominator, the last step is to factor the numerator to determine whether there are common factors in the numerator and denominator. For HOW TO 1, there are no common factors, so the answer is in simplest form.

The process of adding and subtracting rational expressions is summarized below.

INSTRUCTOR NOTE
The process of adding or subtracting rational expressions is a complex one, involving many steps and the application of several skills. It may help students if they keep a list of the basic steps in front of them as they work.

Adding and Subtracting Rational Expressions

1. Find the LCM of the denominators.
2. Write each fraction as an equivalent fraction using the LCM as the denominator.
3. Add or subtract the numerators and place the result over the common denominator.
4. Write the answer in simplest form.

EXAMPLE 3

Simplify: $\frac{y}{x} - \frac{4y}{3x} + \frac{3y}{4x}$

Solution

The LCM of the denominators is $12x$.

$$\frac{y}{x} - \frac{4y}{3x} + \frac{3y}{4x}$$
$$= \frac{y}{x} \cdot \frac{12}{12} - \frac{4y}{3x} \cdot \frac{4}{4} + \frac{3y}{4x} \cdot \frac{3}{3}$$
$$= \frac{12y}{12x} - \frac{16y}{12x} + \frac{9y}{12x}$$ • Write each fraction using the LCM.
$$= \frac{12y - 16y + 9y}{12x} = \frac{5y}{12x}$$ • Combine the numerators.

YOU TRY IT 3

Simplify: $\frac{z}{8y} - \frac{4z}{3y} + \frac{5z}{4y}$

Your solution

$\frac{z}{24y}$

EXAMPLE 4

Add: $1 + \frac{3}{x^2}$

Solution

The LCM is x^2.

$$1 + \frac{3}{x^2} = 1 \cdot \frac{x^2}{x^2} + \frac{3}{x^2} = \frac{x^2}{x^2} + \frac{3}{x^2}$$ • Write each fraction using the LCM.
$$= \frac{x^2 + 3}{x^2}$$

YOU TRY IT 4

Subtract: $2 - \frac{1}{x - 3}$

Your solution

$\frac{2x - 7}{x - 3}$

Solutions on p. S27

EXAMPLE 5

Subtract: $\dfrac{2x}{x-3} - \dfrac{5}{3-x}$

Solution

Remember that $3 - x = -(x - 3)$.

Therefore, $\dfrac{5}{3-x} = \dfrac{5}{-(x-3)} = \dfrac{-5}{x-3}$.

$$\frac{2x}{x-3} - \frac{5}{3-x}$$

$$= \frac{2x}{x-3} - \frac{-5}{x-3}$$ • The LCM is $x - 3$.

$$= \frac{2x-(-5)}{x-3} = \frac{2x+5}{x-3}$$ • Combine the numerators.

YOU TRY IT 5

Add: $\dfrac{5x}{x-2} + \dfrac{3}{2-x}$

Your solution

$\dfrac{5x-3}{x-2}$

EXAMPLE 6

Subtract: $\dfrac{2x}{2x-3} - \dfrac{1}{x+1}$

Solution

The LCM is $(2x - 3)(x + 1)$.

$$\frac{2x}{2x-3} - \frac{1}{x+1}$$

$$= \frac{2x}{2x-3}\cdot\frac{x+1}{x+1} - \frac{1}{x+1}\cdot\frac{2x-3}{2x-3}$$

$$= \frac{2x^2+2x}{(2x-3)(x+1)} - \frac{2x-3}{(2x-3)(x+1)}$$

$$= \frac{(2x^2+2x)-(2x-3)}{(2x-3)(x+1)}$$

$$= \frac{2x^2+2x-2x+3}{(2x-3)(x+1)} = \frac{2x^2+3}{(2x-3)(x+1)}$$

YOU TRY IT 6

Add: $\dfrac{4x}{3x-1} + \dfrac{9}{x+4}$

Your solution

$\dfrac{4x^2+43x-9}{(3x-1)(x+4)}$

IN-CLASS EXAMPLES

3. Simplify: $\dfrac{1}{6a} + \dfrac{4}{9b} - \dfrac{5}{2a}$ **$\dfrac{4a-21b}{9ab}$**
4. Subtract: $\dfrac{x-2}{10x} - \dfrac{x-3}{15x}$ **$\dfrac{1}{30}$**
5. Add: $\dfrac{7}{x+2} + 2$ **$\dfrac{2x+11}{x+2}$**
6. Subtract: $\dfrac{a-1}{a^2b} - \dfrac{a-2}{ab}$ **$\dfrac{-a^2+3a-1}{a^2b}$**
7. Add: $\dfrac{2x}{3x-2} + \dfrac{4}{x-3}$ **$\dfrac{2(x+4)(x-1)}{(3x-2)(x-3)}$**
8. Add: $\dfrac{6y}{y^2-4} + \dfrac{3}{2-y}$ **$\dfrac{3}{y+2}$**

Solutions on p. S27

EXAMPLE 7

Add: $\dfrac{x+3}{x^2-2x-8}+\dfrac{3}{4-x}$

Solution

Recall: $\dfrac{3}{4-x}=\dfrac{-3}{x-4}$

The LCM is $(x-4)(x+2)$.

$$\frac{x+3}{x^2-2x-8}+\frac{3}{4-x}$$
$$=\frac{x+3}{(x-4)(x+2)}+\frac{(-3)}{x-4}$$
$$=\frac{x+3}{(x-4)(x+2)}+\frac{(-3)}{x-4}\cdot\frac{x+2}{x+2}$$
$$=\frac{x+3}{(x-4)(x+2)}+\frac{(-3)(x+2)}{(x-4)(x+2)}$$

• Write each fraction using the LCM.

$$=\frac{(x+3)+(-3)(x+2)}{(x-4)(x+2)}$$

• Add the numerators.

$$=\frac{x+3-3x-6}{(x-4)(x+2)}$$
$$=\frac{-2x-3}{(x-4)(x+2)}$$

YOU TRY IT 7

Add: $\dfrac{2x-1}{x^2-25}+\dfrac{2}{5-x}$

Your solution

$-\dfrac{11}{(x+5)(x-5)}$

EXAMPLE 8

Simplify: $\dfrac{3x+2}{2x^2-x-1}-\dfrac{3}{2x+1}+\dfrac{4}{x-1}$

Solution

The LCM is $(2x+1)(x-1)$.

$$\frac{3x+2}{2x^2-x-1}-\frac{3}{2x+1}+\frac{4}{x-1}$$
$$=\frac{3x+2}{(2x+1)(x-1)}-\frac{3}{2x+1}\cdot\frac{x-1}{x-1}+\frac{4}{x-1}\cdot\frac{2x+1}{2x+1}$$
$$=\frac{3x+2}{(2x+1)(x-1)}-\frac{3x-3}{(2x+1)(x-1)}+\frac{8x+4}{(2x+1)(x-1)}$$
$$=\frac{(3x+2)-(3x-3)+(8x+4)}{(2x+1)(x-1)}$$
$$=\frac{3x+2-3x+3+8x+4}{(2x+1)(x-1)}$$
$$=\frac{8x+9}{(2x+1)(x-1)}$$

YOU TRY IT 8

Simplify: $\dfrac{2x-3}{3x^2-x-2}+\dfrac{5}{3x+2}-\dfrac{1}{x-1}$

Your solution

$\dfrac{2(2x-5)}{(3x+2)(x-1)}$

Solutions on p. S27

11.3 EXERCISES

Concept Check

SUGGESTED ASSIGNMENT
Exercises 1–4; Exercises 5–83, odds

Determine whether the statement is true or false.

1. To add two fractions, add the numerators and the denominators. False

2. The procedure for subtracting two rational expressions is the same as that for subtracting two arithmetic fractions. True

3. To add two rational expressions, first multiply both expressions by the LCD. False

4. If $x \neq -2$ and $x \neq 0$, then $\frac{x}{x+2} + \frac{3}{x+2} = \frac{x+3}{x+2} = \frac{3}{2}$. False

OBJECTIVE A *To add or subtract rational expressions with the same denominator*

For Exercises 5 to 24, simplify.

5. $\frac{3}{y^2} + \frac{8}{y^2}$ $\frac{11}{y^2}$

6. $\frac{6}{ab} - \frac{2}{ab}$ $\frac{4}{ab}$

7. $\frac{3}{x+4} - \frac{10}{x+4}$ $-\frac{7}{x+4}$

8. $\frac{x}{x+6} - \frac{2}{x+6}$ $\frac{x-2}{x+6}$

9. $\frac{3x}{2x+3} + \frac{5x}{2x+3}$ $\frac{8x}{2x+3}$

10. $\frac{6y}{4y+1} - \frac{11y}{4y+1}$ $-\frac{5y}{4y+1}$

11. $\frac{2x+1}{x-3} + \frac{3x+6}{x-3}$ $\frac{5x+7}{x-3}$

12. $\frac{4x+3}{2x-7} + \frac{3x-8}{2x-7}$ $\frac{7x-5}{2x-7}$

13. $\frac{5x-1}{x+9} - \frac{3x+4}{x+9}$ $\frac{2x-5}{x+9}$

14. $\frac{6x-5}{x-10} - \frac{3x-4}{x-10}$ $\frac{3x-1}{x-10}$

15. $\frac{x-7}{2x+7} - \frac{4x-3}{2x+7}$ $\frac{-3x-4}{2x+7}$

16. $\frac{2n}{3n+4} - \frac{5n-3}{3n+4}$ $\frac{-3(n-1)}{3n+4}$

17. $\frac{x}{x^2+2x-15} - \frac{3}{x^2+2x-15}$ $\frac{1}{x+5}$

18. $\frac{3x}{x^2+3x-10} - \frac{6}{x^2+3x-10}$ $\frac{3}{x+5}$

19. $\frac{2x+3}{x^2-x-30} - \frac{x-2}{x^2-x-30}$ $\frac{1}{x-6}$

20. $\frac{3x-1}{x^2+5x-6} - \frac{2x-7}{x^2+5x-6}$ $\frac{1}{x-1}$

21. $\frac{4y+7}{2y^2+7y-4} - \frac{y-5}{2y^2+7y-4}$ $\frac{3}{2y-1}$

22. $\frac{x+1}{2x^2-5x-12} + \frac{x+2}{2x^2-5x-12}$ $\frac{1}{x-4}$

23. $\dfrac{2x^2 + 3x}{x^2 - 9x + 20} + \dfrac{2x^2 - 3}{x^2 - 9x + 20} - \dfrac{4x^2 + 2x + 1}{x^2 - 9x + 20}$

$\dfrac{1}{x - 5}$

24. $\dfrac{2x^2 + 3x}{x^2 - 2x - 63} - \dfrac{x^2 - 3x + 21}{x^2 - 2x - 63} - \dfrac{x - 7}{x^2 - 2x - 63}$

$\dfrac{x - 2}{x - 9}$

25. Which expressions are equivalent to $\frac{3}{y - 5} - \frac{y - 2}{y - 5}$?

(i) $\dfrac{5 - y}{y - 5}$ **(ii)** $\dfrac{1 - y}{y - 5}$ **(iii)** $\dfrac{5 - y}{2y - 10}$ **(iv)** -1 **(v)** $\dfrac{1 - y}{-10}$

i and iv

OBJECTIVE B *To add or subtract rational expressions with different denominators*

26. True or false? $\frac{3}{x - 8} + \frac{3}{8 - x} = 0$ True

For Exercises 27 to 84, simplify.

27. $\dfrac{4}{x} + \dfrac{5}{y}$

$\dfrac{4y + 5x}{xy}$

28. $\dfrac{7}{a} + \dfrac{5}{b}$

$\dfrac{7b + 5a}{ab}$

29. $\dfrac{12}{x} - \dfrac{5}{2x}$

$\dfrac{19}{2x}$

30. $\dfrac{5}{3a} - \dfrac{3}{4a}$

$\dfrac{11}{12a}$

31. $\dfrac{1}{2x} - \dfrac{5}{4x} + \dfrac{7}{6x}$

$\dfrac{5}{12x}$

32. $\dfrac{7}{4y} + \dfrac{11}{6y} - \dfrac{8}{3y}$

$\dfrac{11}{12y}$

33. $\dfrac{5}{3x} - \dfrac{2}{x^2} + \dfrac{3}{2x}$

$\dfrac{19x - 12}{6x^2}$

34. $\dfrac{6}{y^2} + \dfrac{3}{4y} - \dfrac{2}{5y}$

$\dfrac{120 + 7y}{20y^2}$

35. $\dfrac{2}{x} - \dfrac{3}{2y} + \dfrac{3}{5x} - \dfrac{1}{4y}$

$\dfrac{52y - 35x}{20xy}$

36. $\dfrac{5}{2a} + \dfrac{7}{3b} - \dfrac{2}{b} - \dfrac{3}{4a}$

$\dfrac{21b + 4a}{12ab}$

37. $\dfrac{2x + 1}{3x} + \dfrac{x - 1}{5x}$

$\dfrac{13x + 2}{15x}$

38. $\dfrac{4x - 3}{6x} + \dfrac{2x + 3}{4x}$

$\dfrac{14x + 3}{12x}$

39. $\dfrac{x - 3}{6x} + \dfrac{x + 4}{8x}$

$\dfrac{7}{24}$

40. $\dfrac{2x - 3}{2x} + \dfrac{x + 3}{3x}$

$\dfrac{8x - 3}{6x}$

41. $\dfrac{2x + 9}{9x} - \dfrac{x - 5}{5x}$

$\dfrac{x + 90}{45x}$

42. $\dfrac{3y - 2}{12y} - \dfrac{y - 3}{18y}$

$\dfrac{7}{36}$

43. $\dfrac{x + 4}{2x} - \dfrac{x - 1}{x^2}$

$\dfrac{x^2 + 2x + 2}{2x^2}$

44. $\dfrac{x - 2}{3x^2} - \dfrac{x + 4}{x}$

$\dfrac{-3x^2 - 11x - 2}{3x^2}$

45. $\dfrac{x-10}{4x^2}+\dfrac{x+1}{2x}$ $\dfrac{2x^2+3x-10}{4x^2}$

46. $\dfrac{x+5}{3x^2}+\dfrac{2x+1}{2x}$ $\dfrac{6x^2+5x+10}{6x^2}$

47. $\dfrac{4}{x+4}-x$ $\dfrac{-x^2-4x+4}{x+4}$

48. $2x+\dfrac{1}{x}$ $\dfrac{2x^2+1}{x}$

49. $5-\dfrac{x-2}{x+1}$ $\dfrac{4x+7}{x+1}$

50. $3+\dfrac{x-1}{x+1}$ $\dfrac{4x+2}{x+1}$

51. $\dfrac{x+3}{6x}-\dfrac{x-3}{8x^2}$ $\dfrac{4x^2+9x+9}{24x^2}$

52. $\dfrac{x+2}{xy}-\dfrac{3x-2}{x^2y}$ $\dfrac{x^2-x+2}{x^2y}$

53. $\dfrac{3x-1}{xy^2}-\dfrac{2x+3}{xy}$ $\dfrac{3x-1-2xy-3y}{xy^2}$

54. $\dfrac{4x-3}{3x^2y}+\dfrac{2x+1}{4xy^2}$ $\dfrac{16xy-12y+6x^2+3x}{12x^2y^2}$

55. $\dfrac{5x+7}{6xy^2}-\dfrac{4x-3}{8x^2y}$ $\dfrac{20x^2+28x-12xy+9y}{24x^2y^2}$

56. $\dfrac{x-2}{8x^2}-\dfrac{x+7}{12xy}$ $\dfrac{3xy-6y-2x^2-14x}{24x^2y}$

57. $\dfrac{3x-1}{6y^2}-\dfrac{x+5}{9xy}$ $\dfrac{9x^2-3x-2xy-10y}{18xy^2}$

58. $\dfrac{4}{x-2}+\dfrac{5}{x+3}$ $\dfrac{9x+2}{(x-2)(x+3)}$

59. $\dfrac{2}{x-3}+\dfrac{5}{x-4}$ $\dfrac{7x-23}{(x-3)(x-4)}$

60. $\dfrac{6}{x-7}-\dfrac{4}{x+3}$ $\dfrac{2(x+23)}{(x-7)(x+3)}$

61. $\dfrac{3}{y+6}-\dfrac{4}{y-3}$ $\dfrac{-y-33}{(y+6)(y-3)}$

62. $\dfrac{2x}{x+1}+\dfrac{1}{x-3}$ $\dfrac{2x^2-5x+1}{(x+1)(x-3)}$

63. $\dfrac{3x}{x-4}+\dfrac{2}{x+6}$ $\dfrac{3x^2+20x-8}{(x-4)(x+6)}$

64. $\dfrac{4x}{2x-1}-\dfrac{5}{x-6}$ $\dfrac{4x^2-34x+5}{(2x-1)(x-6)}$

65. $\dfrac{6x}{x+5}-\dfrac{3}{2x+3}$ $\dfrac{3(4x^2+5x-5)}{(x+5)(2x+3)}$

66. $\dfrac{2a}{a-7}+\dfrac{5}{7-a}$ $\dfrac{2a-5}{a-7}$

67. $\dfrac{4x}{6-x}+\dfrac{5}{x-6}$ $\dfrac{-4x+5}{x-6}$

68. $\dfrac{x}{x^2-9}+\dfrac{3}{x-3}$ $\dfrac{4x+9}{(x+3)(x-3)}$

69. $\dfrac{y}{y^2-16}+\dfrac{1}{y-4}$ $\dfrac{2(y+2)}{(y-4)(y+4)}$

70. $\dfrac{2x}{x^2-x-6}-\dfrac{3}{x+2}$ $\dfrac{-x+9}{(x-3)(x+2)}$

71. $\dfrac{(x-1)^2}{(x+1)^2}-1$ $-\dfrac{4x}{(x+1)^2}$

72. $1 - \dfrac{(y-2)^2}{(y+2)^2}$ $\dfrac{8y}{(y+2)^2}$

73. $\dfrac{x}{1-x^2} - 1 + \dfrac{x}{1+x}$ $\dfrac{2x-1}{(1+x)(1-x)}$

74. $\dfrac{y}{x-y} + 2 - \dfrac{x}{y-x}$ $\dfrac{3x-y}{x-y}$

75. $\dfrac{3x-1}{x^2-10x+25} - \dfrac{3}{x-5}$ $\dfrac{14}{(x-5)^2}$

76. $\dfrac{2a+3}{a^2-7a+12} - \dfrac{2}{a-3}$ $\dfrac{11}{(a-4)(a-3)}$

77. $\dfrac{x+4}{x^2-x-42} + \dfrac{3}{7-x}$ $\dfrac{-2(x+7)}{(x+6)(x-7)}$

78. $\dfrac{x+3}{x^2-3x-10} + \dfrac{2}{5-x}$ $\dfrac{-x-1}{(x-5)(x+2)}$

79. $\dfrac{1}{x+1} + \dfrac{x}{x-6} - \dfrac{5x-2}{x^2-5x-6}$ $\dfrac{x-4}{x-6}$

80. $\dfrac{x}{x-4} + \dfrac{5}{x+5} - \dfrac{11x-8}{x^2+x-20}$ $\dfrac{x+3}{x+5}$

81. $\dfrac{3x+1}{x-1} - \dfrac{x-1}{x-3} + \dfrac{x+1}{x^2-4x+3}$ $\dfrac{2x+1}{x-1}$

82. $\dfrac{4x+1}{x-8} - \dfrac{3x+2}{x+4} - \dfrac{49x+4}{x^2-4x-32}$ $\dfrac{x-2}{x+4}$

83. $\dfrac{2x+9}{3-x} + \dfrac{x+5}{x+7} - \dfrac{2x^2+3x-3}{x^2+4x-21}$ $\dfrac{-3(x^2+8x+25)}{(x-3)(x+7)}$

84. $\dfrac{3x+5}{x+5} - \dfrac{x+1}{2-x} - \dfrac{4x^2-3x-1}{x^2+3x-10}$ $\dfrac{4(2x-1)}{(x+5)(x-2)}$

Critical Thinking

For Exercises 85 to 88, rewrite the expression as the sum of two fractions in simplest form.

85. $\dfrac{5b+4a}{ab}$ $\dfrac{5}{a} + \dfrac{4}{b}$

86. $\dfrac{6x+7y}{xy}$ $\dfrac{6}{y} + \dfrac{7}{x}$

87. $\dfrac{3x^2+4xy}{x^2y^2}$ $\dfrac{3}{y^2} + \dfrac{4}{xy}$

88. $\dfrac{2mn^2+8m^2n}{m^3n^3}$ $\dfrac{2}{m^2n} + \dfrac{8}{mn^2}$

Projects or Group Activities

89. Transportation Suppose that you drive about 12,000 mi per year and that the cost of gasoline averages $3.70 per gallon.

a. Let x represent the number of miles per gallon your car gets. Write a variable expression for the amount you spend on gasoline in one year.

b. Write and simplify a variable expression for the amount of money you will save each year if you increase your gas mileage by 5 miles per gallon.

c. If you currently get 25 miles per gallon and you increase your gas mileage by 5 miles per gallon, how much will you save in one year?

a. $\dfrac{44{,}400}{x}$ dollars **b.** $\dfrac{222{,}000}{x(x+5)}$ dollars **c.** $296

QUICK QUIZ

1. Subtract: $\dfrac{2x+3}{x-4} - \dfrac{x+5}{x-4}$ $\dfrac{x-2}{x-4}$ **[11.3A]**
2. Add: $\dfrac{2x-8}{3x^2-2x-1} + \dfrac{x+9}{3x^2-2x-1}$ $\dfrac{1}{x-1}$ **[11.3A]**
3. Subtract: $\dfrac{y-1}{5y^2} - \dfrac{y+3}{10y}$ $-\dfrac{y^2+y+2}{10y^2}$ **[11.3B]**
4. Add: $\dfrac{4x}{x^2-36} + \dfrac{3}{6-x}$ $\dfrac{x-18}{(x-6)(x+6)}$ **[11.3B]**
5. Subtract: $\dfrac{a-1}{a-2} - \dfrac{3a+1}{a^2+3a-10}$ $\dfrac{a+3}{a+5}$ **[11.3B]**

SECTION

11.4 Complex Fractions

OBJECTIVE A To simplify a complex fraction

Point of Interest

There are many instances of complex fractions in application problems. For example, the fraction $\dfrac{1}{\dfrac{1}{r_1}+\dfrac{1}{r_2}}$ is used to determine the total resistance in certain electric circuits.

Take Note

You may use either method to simplify a complex fraction. The result will be the same.

A **complex fraction** is a fraction in which the numerator or denominator contains one or more fractions. Examples of complex fractions are shown at the right.

$$\frac{3}{2-\dfrac{1}{2}},\quad \frac{4+\dfrac{1}{x}}{3+\dfrac{2}{x}},\quad \frac{\dfrac{1}{x-1}+x+3}{x-3+\dfrac{1}{x+4}}$$

To simplify a complex fraction, use one of the following methods.

Simplifying Complex Fractions

Method 1: Multiply by 1 in the form $\dfrac{\text{LCM}}{\text{LCM}}$.

1. Determine the LCM of the denominators of the fractions in the numerator and denominator of the complex fraction.
2. Multiply the numerator and denominator of the complex fraction by the LCM.
3. Simplify.

Method 2: Multiply the numerator by the reciprocal of the denominator.

1. Simplify the numerator to a single fraction and simplify the denominator to a single fraction.
2. Using the rule for dividing fractions, multiply the numerator by the reciprocal of the denominator.
3. Simplify.

Here is an example using Method 1.

HOW TO 1 Simplify: $\dfrac{9-\dfrac{4}{x^2}}{3+\dfrac{2}{x}}$

The LCM of the denominators of the fractions in the complex fraction is x^2.

$$\frac{9-\dfrac{4}{x^2}}{3+\dfrac{2}{x}}=\frac{9-\dfrac{4}{x^2}}{3+\dfrac{2}{x}}\cdot\frac{x^2}{x^2}$$

• Multiply the numerator and denominator by the LCM.

$$=\frac{9\cdot x^2-\dfrac{4}{x^2}\cdot x^2}{3\cdot x^2+\dfrac{2}{x}\cdot x^2}=\frac{9x^2-4}{3x^2+2x}$$

• Use the Distributive Property.

$$=\frac{(3x-2)\overset{1}{\cancel{(3x+2)}}}{x\underset{1}{\cancel{(3x+2)}}}=\frac{3x-2}{x}$$

• Simplify.

Here is the same example using Method 2.

HOW TO 2 Simplify: $\dfrac{9 - \frac{4}{x^2}}{3 + \frac{2}{x}}$

$$\frac{9 - \frac{4}{x^2}}{3 + \frac{2}{x}} = \frac{\frac{9x^2}{x^2} - \frac{4}{x^2}}{\frac{3x}{x} + \frac{2}{x}} = \frac{\frac{9x^2 - 4}{x^2}}{\frac{3x + 2}{x}}$$

- Simplify the numerator to a single fraction and simplify the denominator to a single fraction.

$$= \frac{9x^2 - 4}{x^2} \cdot \frac{x}{3x + 2}$$

- Multiply the numerator by the reciprocal of the denominator.

$$= \frac{x(3x - 2)\overset{1}{\cancel{(3x + 2)}}}{x^2\underset{1}{\cancel{(3x + 2)}}}$$

- Simplify.

$$= \frac{3x - 2}{x}$$

For the following examples, we will use Method 1.

EXAMPLE 1

Simplify: $\dfrac{\frac{1}{x} + \frac{1}{2}}{\frac{1}{x^2} - \frac{1}{4}}$

Solution

The LCM of x, 2, x^2, and 4 is $4x^2$.

$$\frac{\frac{1}{x} + \frac{1}{2}}{\frac{1}{x^2} - \frac{1}{4}} = \frac{\frac{1}{x} + \frac{1}{2}}{\frac{1}{x^2} - \frac{1}{4}} \cdot \frac{4x^2}{4x^2}$$

- Multiply the numerator and denominator by the LCM.

$$= \frac{\frac{1}{x} \cdot 4x^2 + \frac{1}{2} \cdot 4x^2}{\frac{1}{x^2} \cdot 4x^2 - \frac{1}{4} \cdot 4x^2}$$

- Distributive Property

$$= \frac{4x + 2x^2}{4 - x^2}$$

- Simplify.

$$= \frac{2x\overset{1}{\cancel{(2 + x)}}}{(2 - x)\underset{1}{\cancel{(2 + x)}}}$$

$$= \frac{2x}{2 - x}$$

YOU TRY IT 1

Simplify: $\dfrac{\frac{1}{3} - \frac{1}{x}}{\frac{1}{9} - \frac{1}{x^2}}$

Your solution

$\dfrac{3x}{x + 3}$

IN-CLASS EXAMPLES

1. Simplify: $\dfrac{a - \frac{10}{a - 3}}{1 + \frac{5}{a - 3}}$ **$a - 5$**

2. Simplify: $\dfrac{\frac{7}{x - 3} - \frac{2}{3x}}{\frac{5}{3x} + \frac{1}{x - 3}}$ **$\dfrac{19x + 6}{8x - 15}$**

Solution on p. S27

EXAMPLE 2

Simplify: $\dfrac{1 - \dfrac{2}{x} - \dfrac{15}{x^2}}{1 - \dfrac{11}{x} + \dfrac{30}{x^2}}$

Solution

The LCM of x and x^2 is x^2.

$$\frac{1 - \frac{2}{x} - \frac{15}{x^2}}{1 - \frac{11}{x} + \frac{30}{x^2}} = \frac{1 - \frac{2}{x} - \frac{15}{x^2}}{1 - \frac{11}{x} + \frac{30}{x^2}} \cdot \frac{x^2}{x^2}$$

• Multiply by the LCM.

$$= \frac{1 \cdot x^2 - \frac{2}{x} \cdot x^2 - \frac{15}{x^2} \cdot x^2}{1 \cdot x^2 - \frac{11}{x} \cdot x^2 + \frac{30}{x^2} \cdot x^2}$$

• Distributive Property

$$= \frac{x^2 - 2x - 15}{x^2 - 11x + 30}$$

$$= \frac{\overset{1}{\cancel{(x-5)}}(x+3)}{\underset{1}{\cancel{(x-5)}}(x-6)} = \frac{x+3}{x-6}$$

• Simplify.

YOU TRY IT 2

Simplify: $\dfrac{1 + \dfrac{4}{x} + \dfrac{3}{x^2}}{1 + \dfrac{10}{x} + \dfrac{21}{x^2}}$

Your solution

$\dfrac{x+1}{x+7}$

EXAMPLE 3

Simplify: $\dfrac{x - 8 + \dfrac{20}{x+4}}{x - 10 + \dfrac{24}{x+4}}$

Solution

The LCM is $x + 4$.

$$\frac{x - 8 + \frac{20}{x+4}}{x - 10 + \frac{24}{x+4}}$$

$$= \frac{x - 8 + \frac{20}{x+4}}{x - 10 + \frac{24}{x+4}} \cdot \frac{x+4}{x+4}$$

• Multiply by the LCM.

$$= \frac{(x-8)(x+4) + \frac{20}{x+4} \cdot (x+4)}{(x-10)(x+4) + \frac{24}{x+4} \cdot (x+4)}$$

• Distributive Property

$$= \frac{x^2 - 4x - 32 + 20}{x^2 - 6x - 40 + 24} = \frac{x^2 - 4x - 12}{x^2 - 6x - 16}$$

• Simplify.

$$= \frac{(x-6)\overset{1}{\cancel{(x+2)}}}{(x-8)\underset{1}{\cancel{(x+2)}}} = \frac{x-6}{x-8}$$

YOU TRY IT 3

Simplify: $\dfrac{x + 3 - \dfrac{20}{x-5}}{x + 8 + \dfrac{30}{x-5}}$

Your solution

$\dfrac{x-7}{x-2}$

Solutions on p. S28

11.4 EXERCISES

Concept Check

SUGGESTED ASSIGNMENT
Exercises 1–6; Exercises 7–35, odds; Exercise 39

Exercises 1 to 3 are the examples of complex fractions given at the beginning of Objective 11.4A. By what fraction would you multiply each complex fraction in order to simplify it?

1. $\dfrac{3}{2-\dfrac{1}{2}}$ $\dfrac{2}{2}$

2. $\dfrac{4+\dfrac{1}{x}}{3+\dfrac{2}{x}}$ $\dfrac{x}{x}$

3. $\dfrac{\dfrac{1}{x-1}+x+3}{x-3+\dfrac{1}{x+4}}$ $\dfrac{(x-1)(x+4)}{(x-1)(x+4)}$

For Exercises 4 to 6, determine whether the statement is true or false.

4. To simplify a complex fraction, multiply the complex fraction by the LCM of the denominators of the fractions in the numerator and denominator of the complex fraction. False

5. When we multiply the numerator and denominator of a complex fraction by the same expression, we are using the Multiplication Property of One. True

6. Our goal in simplifying a complex fraction is to rewrite it so that there are no fractions in the numerator or in the denominator. We then express the fraction in simplest form. True

OBJECTIVE A *To simplify a complex fraction*

For Exercises 7 to 36, simplify.

7. $\dfrac{1+\dfrac{3}{x}}{1-\dfrac{9}{x^2}}$ $\dfrac{x}{x-3}$

8. $\dfrac{1+\dfrac{4}{x}}{1-\dfrac{16}{x^2}}$ $\dfrac{x}{x-4}$

9. $\dfrac{2-\dfrac{8}{x+4}}{3-\dfrac{12}{x+4}}$ $\dfrac{2}{3}$

10. $\dfrac{5-\dfrac{25}{x+5}}{1-\dfrac{3}{x+5}}$ $\dfrac{5x}{x+2}$

11. $\dfrac{1+\dfrac{5}{y-2}}{1-\dfrac{2}{y-2}}$ $\dfrac{y+3}{y-4}$

12. $\dfrac{2-\dfrac{11}{2x-1}}{3-\dfrac{17}{2x-1}}$ $\dfrac{4x-13}{2(3x-10)}$

13. $\dfrac{4-\dfrac{2}{x+7}}{5+\dfrac{1}{x+7}}$ $\dfrac{2(2x+13)}{5x+36}$

14. $\dfrac{5+\dfrac{3}{x-8}}{2-\dfrac{1}{x-8}}$ $\dfrac{5x-37}{2x-17}$

15. $\dfrac{1-\dfrac{1}{x}-\dfrac{6}{x^2}}{1-\dfrac{9}{x^2}}$ $\dfrac{x+2}{x+3}$

16. $\dfrac{1+\dfrac{4}{x}+\dfrac{4}{x^2}}{1-\dfrac{2}{x}-\dfrac{8}{x^2}}$ $\dfrac{x+2}{x-4}$

17. $\dfrac{1-\dfrac{5}{x}-\dfrac{6}{x^2}}{1+\dfrac{6}{x}+\dfrac{5}{x^2}}$ $\dfrac{x-6}{x+5}$

18. $\dfrac{1-\dfrac{7}{a}+\dfrac{12}{a^2}}{1+\dfrac{1}{a}-\dfrac{20}{a^2}}$ $\dfrac{a-3}{a+5}$

19. $\dfrac{1 - \dfrac{6}{x} + \dfrac{8}{x^2}}{\dfrac{4}{x^2} + \dfrac{3}{x} - 1}$ $\dfrac{-x + 2}{x + 1}$

20. $\dfrac{1 + \dfrac{3}{x} - \dfrac{18}{x^2}}{\dfrac{21}{x^2} - \dfrac{4}{x} - 1}$ $\dfrac{-x - 6}{x + 7}$

21. $\dfrac{x - \dfrac{4}{x + 3}}{1 + \dfrac{1}{x + 3}}$ $x - 1$

22. $\dfrac{y + \dfrac{1}{y - 2}}{1 + \dfrac{1}{y - 2}}$ $y - 1$

23. $\dfrac{1 - \dfrac{x}{2x + 1}}{x - \dfrac{1}{2x + 1}}$ $\dfrac{1}{2x - 1}$

24. $\dfrac{1 - \dfrac{2x - 2}{3x - 1}}{x - \dfrac{4}{3x - 1}}$ $\dfrac{1}{3x - 4}$

25. $\dfrac{x - 5 + \dfrac{14}{x + 4}}{x + 3 - \dfrac{2}{x + 4}}$ $\dfrac{x - 3}{x + 5}$

26. $\dfrac{a + 4 + \dfrac{5}{a - 2}}{a + 6 + \dfrac{15}{a - 2}}$ $\dfrac{a - 1}{a + 1}$

27. $\dfrac{x + 3 - \dfrac{10}{x - 6}}{x + 2 - \dfrac{20}{x - 6}}$ $\dfrac{x - 7}{x - 8}$

28. $\dfrac{x - 7 + \dfrac{5}{x - 1}}{x - 3 + \dfrac{1}{x - 1}}$ $\dfrac{x - 6}{x - 2}$

29. $\dfrac{y - 6 + \dfrac{22}{2y + 3}}{y - 5 + \dfrac{11}{2y + 3}}$ $\dfrac{2y - 1}{2y + 1}$

30. $\dfrac{x + 2 - \dfrac{12}{2x - 1}}{x + 1 - \dfrac{9}{2x - 1}}$ $\dfrac{2x + 7}{2x + 5}$

31. $\dfrac{x - \dfrac{2}{2x - 3}}{2x - 1 - \dfrac{8}{2x - 3}}$ $\dfrac{x - 2}{2x - 5}$

32. $\dfrac{x + 3 - \dfrac{18}{2x + 1}}{x - \dfrac{6}{2x + 1}}$ $\dfrac{x + 5}{x + 2}$

33. $\dfrac{\dfrac{1}{x} - \dfrac{2}{x - 1}}{\dfrac{3}{x} + \dfrac{1}{x - 1}}$ $\dfrac{-x - 1}{4x - 3}$

34. $\dfrac{\dfrac{3}{n + 1} + \dfrac{1}{n}}{\dfrac{2}{n + 1} + \dfrac{3}{n}}$ $\dfrac{4n + 1}{5n + 3}$

35. $\dfrac{\dfrac{3}{2x - 1} - \dfrac{1}{x}}{\dfrac{4}{x} + \dfrac{2}{2x - 1}}$ $\dfrac{x + 1}{2(5x - 2)}$

36. $\dfrac{\dfrac{4}{3x + 1} + \dfrac{3}{x}}{\dfrac{6}{x} - \dfrac{2}{3x + 1}}$ $\dfrac{13x + 3}{2(8x + 3)}$

37. True or false? If the denominator of a complex fraction is the reciprocal of the numerator, then the complex fraction is equal to the square of its numerator. True

Critical Thinking

For Exercises 38 to 43, simplify.

38. $1 + \dfrac{1}{1 + \dfrac{1}{2}}$ $\quad \dfrac{5}{3}$

39. $1 + \dfrac{1}{1 + \dfrac{1}{1 + \dfrac{1}{2}}}$ $\quad \dfrac{8}{5}$

40. $1 - \dfrac{1}{1 - \dfrac{1}{x}}$ $\quad -\dfrac{1}{x-1}$

41. $1 - \dfrac{1}{1 - \dfrac{1}{y+1}}$ $\quad -\dfrac{1}{y}$

42. $\dfrac{a^{-1} - b^{-1}}{a^{-2} - b^{-2}}$ $\quad \dfrac{ab}{b+a}$

43. $\dfrac{x^{-2} - y^{-2}}{x^{-2}y^{-2}}$ $\quad y^2 - x^2$

Projects or Group Activities

The complex fraction $\dfrac{1}{\dfrac{1}{r_1} + \dfrac{1}{r_2}}$ is mentioned in the Point of Interest on page 607. The fraction gives the total resistance, in ohms, of an electrical circuit that contains two parallel resistors with resistances of r_1 and r_2.

44. Show that the resistance fraction can be rewritten in the form $\dfrac{r_1 r_2}{r_1 + r_2}$.

45. Suppose an electrical circuit contains two parallel resistors with resistances of $r_1 = 2$ ohms and $r_2 = 3$ ohms. Calculate the total resistance in the circuit twice, first using the complex fraction shown above and then using the fraction as rewritten in Exercise 44. $\dfrac{6}{5}$ ohms

46. Repeat Exercise 45 using $r_1 = 6$ ohms and $r_2 = 8$ ohms. $\dfrac{24}{7}$ ohms

47. Which form of the resistance fraction did you find easier to work with when doing the calculations in Exercises 45 and 46? Why?

QUICK QUIZ

Simplify.

1. $\dfrac{1 - \dfrac{2}{y} - \dfrac{8}{y^2}}{1 + \dfrac{5}{y} + \dfrac{6}{y^2}}$ $\quad \dfrac{y-4}{y+3}$ **[11.4A]**

2. $\dfrac{x - 2 + \dfrac{3}{x+2}}{3x - 2 + \dfrac{5}{x+2}}$ $\quad \dfrac{x-1}{3x+1}$ **[11.4A]**

CHECK YOUR PROGRESS: CHAPTER 11

1. Simplify: $\dfrac{x^2 - 4}{x^2 + 3x - 10}$ $\quad \dfrac{x+2}{x+5}$ [11.1A]

2. Multiply: $\dfrac{10x^2 - 50x}{12x + 24} \cdot \dfrac{2x + 4}{x^2 - 5x}$ $\quad \dfrac{5}{3}$ [11.1B]

3. Divide: $\dfrac{6x^3y^2}{18a^4b} \div \dfrac{3xy}{9a^2b^5}$ $\quad \dfrac{b^4x^2y}{a^2}$ [11.1C]

4. Divide: $\dfrac{a^3b}{a^2 - 5a - 14} \div \dfrac{ab^6}{a^2 - 3a - 28}$ $\quad \dfrac{a^2(a+4)}{b^5(a+2)}$ [11.1C]

5. Find the LCM of $10x^4y^2$ and $15x^3y$. $30x^4y^2$ [11.2A]

6. Find the LCM of $8x^2$ and $4x^2 + 8x$. $8x^2(x+2)$ [11.2A]

7. Write the fractions $\dfrac{3}{x^2 + 2x}$ and $\dfrac{4}{x^2}$ in terms of the LCM of the denominators. $\dfrac{3x}{x^2(x+2)}, \dfrac{4x+8}{x^2(x+2)}$ [11.2B]

8. Subtract: $\dfrac{8a}{3a - 1} - \dfrac{10a}{3a - 1}$ $\quad -\dfrac{2a}{3a-1}$ [11.3A]

9. Subtract: $\dfrac{a - 1}{a - 2} - \dfrac{3a + 1}{a^2 + 3a - 10}$ $\quad \dfrac{a+3}{a+5}$ [11.3B]

10. Simplify: $\dfrac{\dfrac{7}{x-3} - \dfrac{2}{3x}}{\dfrac{5}{3x} + \dfrac{1}{x-3}}$ $\quad \dfrac{19x+6}{8x-15}$ [11.4A]

SECTION

11.5 Solving Equations Containing Fractions

OBJECTIVE A *To solve an equation containing fractions*

INSTRUCTOR NOTE
If you did not cover Section 10.5 on solving quadratic equations by factoring, skip Example 1 and You Try It 1 on the next page. Also skip Exercises 34 to 40 in the Section 11.5 Exercises.

Recall that to solve an equation containing fractions, clear denominators by multiplying each side of the equation by the LCM of the denominators. Then solve for the variable.

HOW TO 1 Solve: $\frac{3x-1}{4}+\frac{2}{3}=\frac{7}{6}$

$$\frac{3x-1}{4}+\frac{2}{3}=\frac{7}{6}$$

$$12\left(\frac{3x-1}{4}+\frac{2}{3}\right)=12\cdot\frac{7}{6}$$

- **The LCM is 12. To clear denominators, multiply each side of the equation by the LCM.**

$$12\left(\frac{3x-1}{4}\right)+12\cdot\frac{2}{3}=12\cdot\frac{7}{6}$$

- **Simplify by using the Distributive Property and the Properties of Fractions.**

$$\frac{\overset{3}{\cancel{12}}}{1}\left(\frac{3x-1}{\underset{1}{\cancel{4}}}\right)+\frac{\overset{4}{\cancel{12}}}{1}\cdot\frac{2}{\underset{1}{\cancel{3}}}=\frac{\overset{2}{\cancel{12}}}{1}\cdot\frac{7}{\underset{1}{\cancel{6}}}$$

$$9x-3+8=14$$

- **Solve for x.**

$$9x+5=14$$
$$9x=9$$
$$x=1$$

1 checks as a solution. The solution is 1.

Occasionally, a value that appears to be a solution of an equation will make one of the denominators zero. In such a case, that value is not a solution of the equation.

HOW TO 2 Solve: $\frac{2x}{x-2}=1+\frac{4}{x-2}$

$$\frac{2x}{x-2}=1+\frac{4}{x-2}$$

$$(x-2)\frac{2x}{x-2}=(x-2)\left(1+\frac{4}{x-2}\right)$$

- **The LCM is $x-2$. Multiply each side of the equation by the LCM.**

$$(x-2)\frac{2x}{x-2}=(x-2)\cdot 1+(x-2)\frac{4}{x-2}$$

- **Simplify by using the Distributive Property and the Properties of Fractions.**

$$\frac{\overset{1}{\cancel{(x-2)}}}{1}\cdot\frac{2x}{\underset{1}{\cancel{x-2}}}=(x-2)\cdot 1+\frac{\overset{1}{\cancel{(x-2)}}}{1}\cdot\frac{4}{\underset{1}{\cancel{x-2}}}$$

$$2x=x-2+4$$

- **Solve for x.**

$$2x=x+2$$
$$x=2$$

When x is replaced by 2, the denominators of $\frac{2x}{x-2}$ and $\frac{4}{x-2}$ are zero. Therefore, the equation has no solution.

Take Note
HOW TO 2 at the right illustrates the importance of checking a solution of a rational equation when each side is multiplied by a variable expression. As shown in this example, a proposed solution may not check when it is substituted into the original equation.

EXAMPLE 1

Solve: $\dfrac{x}{x+4} = \dfrac{2}{x}$

Solution

The LCM is $x(x + 4)$.

$$\frac{x}{x+4} = \frac{2}{x}$$

$$x(x+4)\left(\frac{x}{x+4}\right) = x(x+4)\left(\frac{2}{x}\right)$$ • Multiply by the LCM.

$$\frac{x(x+4)}{1}\cdot\frac{x}{x+4} = \frac{x(x+4)}{1}\cdot\frac{2}{x}$$ • Divide by the common factors.

$$x^2 = (x+4)2$$ • Simplify.

$$x^2 = 2x + 8$$

Solve the quadratic equation by factoring.

$$x^2 - 2x - 8 = 0$$ • Write in standard form.

$$(x-4)(x+2) = 0$$ • Factor.

$x - 4 = 0 \qquad x + 2 = 0$ • Principle of Zero Products

$x = 4 \qquad x = -2$

Both 4 and -2 check as solutions.

The solutions are 4 and -2.

YOU TRY IT 1

Solve: $\dfrac{x}{x+6} = \dfrac{3}{x}$

Your solution

$-3, 6$

EXAMPLE 2

Solve: $\dfrac{3x}{x-4} = 5 + \dfrac{12}{x-4}$

Solution

The LCM is $x - 4$.

$$\frac{3x}{x-4} = 5 + \frac{12}{x-4}$$

$$(x-4)\left(\frac{3x}{x-4}\right) = (x-4)\left(5 + \frac{12}{x-4}\right)$$ • Clear denominators.

$$\frac{(x-4)}{1}\cdot\frac{3x}{x-4} = (x-4)5 + \frac{(x-4)}{1}\cdot\frac{12}{x-4}$$

$$3x = (x-4)5 + 12$$ • Solve for x.

$$3x = 5x - 20 + 12$$

$$3x = 5x - 8$$

$$-2x = -8$$

$$x = 4$$

4 does not check as a solution.

The equation has no solution.

YOU TRY IT 2

Solve: $\dfrac{5x}{x+2} = 3 - \dfrac{10}{x+2}$

Your solution

No solution

IN-CLASS EXAMPLES

Solve.

1. $\dfrac{8}{4x-3} = -4$ $\quad \dfrac{1}{4}$
2. $\dfrac{3x}{2x+1} + \dfrac{1}{x+2} = \dfrac{4}{x+2}$ $\quad 1, -1$

Solutions on p. S28

11.5 EXERCISES

Concept Check

SUGGESTED ASSIGNMENT
Exercises 1–4; Exercises 9–39, odds

1. The process of clearing denominators in an equation containing fractions is an application of which property of equations? Multiplication Property of Equations

2. If the denominator of a fraction is $x + 3$, for what value of x is the fraction undefined?
-3

3. Explain why you can clear denominators in part (a) below but not in part (b).
a. $\frac{x}{2} + \frac{1}{3} = \frac{5}{2}$ **b.** $\frac{x}{2} + \frac{1}{3} + \frac{5}{2}$ We can clear denominators in an *equation,* as in part (a), but not in an *expression,* as in part (b).

4. After solving an equation containing fractions, why must we check the solution?

OBJECTIVE A *To solve an equation containing fractions*

When a proposed solution of a rational equation does not check in the original equation, it is because the proposed solution results in an expression that involves division by zero. For Exercises 5 to 7, state the values of x that would result in division by zero when substituted into the original equation.

5. $\frac{6x}{x+1} - \frac{x}{x-2} = 4$
$-1, 2$

6. $\frac{1}{x+5} = \frac{x}{x-3} + \frac{2}{x^2+2x-15}$
$-5, 3$

7. $\frac{3}{x-9} = \frac{1}{x^2-9x} + 2$
$0, 9$

For Exercises 8 to 40, solve.

8. $\frac{2x}{3} - \frac{5}{2} = -\frac{1}{2}$
3

9. $\frac{x}{3} - \frac{1}{4} = \frac{1}{12}$
1

10. $\frac{x}{3} - \frac{1}{4} = \frac{x}{4} - \frac{1}{6}$
1

11. $\frac{2y}{9} - \frac{1}{6} = \frac{y}{9} + \frac{1}{6}$
3

12. $\frac{2x-5}{8} + \frac{1}{4} = \frac{x}{8} + \frac{3}{4}$
9

13. $\frac{3x+4}{12} - \frac{1}{3} = \frac{5x+2}{12} - \frac{1}{2}$
2

14. $\frac{6}{2a+1} = 2$
1

15. $\frac{12}{3x-2} = 3$
2

16. $\frac{9}{2x-5} = -2$
$\frac{1}{4}$

17. $\frac{6}{4-3x} = 3$
$\frac{2}{3}$

18. $2 + \frac{5}{x} = 7$
1

19. $3 + \frac{8}{n} = 5$
4

20. $1 - \frac{9}{x} = 4$
-3

21. $3 - \frac{12}{x} = 7$
-3

22. $\frac{2}{y} + 5 = 9$
$\frac{1}{2}$

23. $\frac{6}{x} + 3 = 11$

$\frac{3}{4}$

24. $\frac{3}{x-2} = \frac{4}{x}$

8

25. $\frac{5}{x+3} = \frac{3}{x-1}$

7

26. $\frac{2}{3x-1} = \frac{3}{4x+1}$

5

27. $\frac{5}{3x-4} = \frac{-3}{1-2x}$

−7

28. $\frac{-3}{2x+5} = \frac{2}{x-1}$

−1

29. $\frac{4}{5y-1} = \frac{2}{2y-1}$

−1

30. $\frac{4x}{x-4} + 5 = \frac{5x}{x-4}$

5

31. $\frac{2x}{x+2} - 5 = \frac{7x}{x+2}$

−1

32. $2 + \frac{3}{a-3} = \frac{a}{a-3}$

No solution

33. $\frac{x}{x+4} = 3 - \frac{4}{x+4}$

No solution

34. $\frac{x}{x-1} = \frac{8}{x+2}$

2, 4

35. $\frac{x}{x+12} = \frac{1}{x+5}$

2, −6

36. $\frac{2x}{x+4} = \frac{3}{x-1}$

$-\frac{3}{2}, 4$

37. $\frac{5}{3n-8} = \frac{n}{n+2}$

$-\frac{2}{3}, 5$

38. $\frac{x}{x+4} = \frac{11}{x^2-16} + 2$

−7, 3

39. $x - \frac{6}{x-3} = \frac{2x}{x-3}$

−1, 6

40. $\frac{8}{r} + \frac{3}{r-1} = 3$

$\frac{2}{3}, 4$

Critical Thinking

For Exercises 41 to 44, solve.

41. $\frac{3}{5}y - \frac{1}{3}(1-y) = \frac{2y-5}{15}$

0

42. $\frac{3}{4}a = \frac{1}{2}(3-a) + \frac{a-2}{4}$

1

43. $\frac{x+1}{x^2+x-2} = \frac{x+2}{x^2-1} + \frac{3}{x+2}$

$0, -\frac{2}{3}$

44. $\frac{y+2}{y^2-y-2} + \frac{y+1}{y^2-4} = \frac{1}{y+1}$

−3

Projects or Group Activities

Intensity of Illumination You are already aware that the standard unit of length in the metric system is the meter (m). You may not know that the standard unit of light intensity is the **candela (cd)**.

The rate at which light falls on a 1-square-unit area of surface is called the **intensity of illumination**. Intensity of illumination is measured in **lumens (lm)**. A lumen is defined in the following illustration.

Picture a source of light equal to 1 cd positioned at the center of a hollow sphere that has a radius of 1 m. The rate at which light falls on 1 m^2 of the inner surface of the sphere is equal to 1 lm. If a light source equal to 4 cd is positioned at the center of the sphere, then each square meter of the inner surface receives four times as much illumination, or 4 lm.

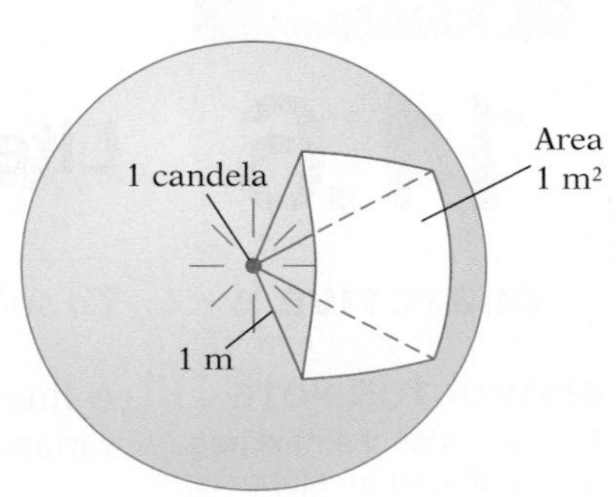

Light rays diverge as they leave a light source. The light that falls on an area of 1 m^2 at a distance of 1 m from the light source spreads out over an area of 4 m^2 when it is 2 m from the source. The same light spreads out over an area of 9 m^2 when it is 3 m from the light source, and over an area of 16 m^2 when it is 4 m from the light source. Therefore, as a surface moves farther away from the source of light, the intensity of illumination on the surface decreases from its value at 1 m to $\left(\frac{1}{2}\right)^2$, or $\frac{1}{4}$, that value at 2 m; to $\left(\frac{1}{3}\right)^2$, or $\frac{1}{9}$, that value at 3 m; and to $\left(\frac{1}{4}\right)^2$, or $\frac{1}{16}$, that value at 4 m.

The formula for the intensity of illumination is

$$I = \frac{s}{r^2}$$

where I is the intensity of illumination in lumens, s is the intensity of the light source in candelas, and r is the distance in meters between the light source and the illuminated surface.

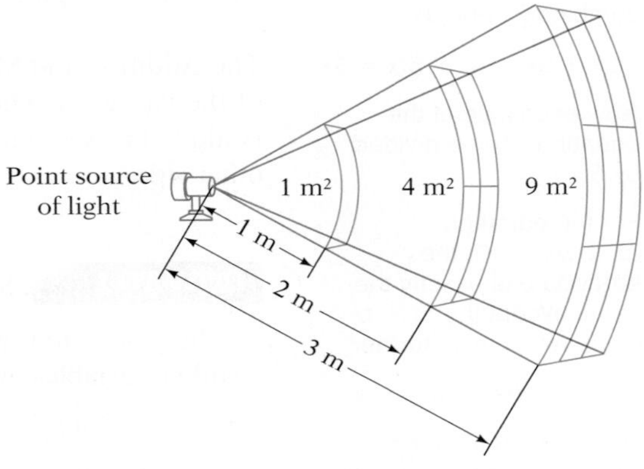

Example A 30-candela lamp is positioned 0.5 m above a desk. Find the illumination on the desk.

$$I = \frac{s}{r^2}$$

$$I = \frac{30}{(0.5)^2} = 120$$

The illumination on the desk is 120 lm.

QUICK QUIZ

Solve.

1. $5 - \frac{8}{x} = 1$ **2 [11.5A]**
2. $3 - \frac{4}{x+2} = \frac{2x}{x+2}$ **No solution [11.5A]**

45. A 100-candela light is hanging 5 m above a floor. What is the intensity of the illumination on the floor beneath the light? 4 lm

46. A 25-candela source of light is positioned 2 m above a desk. Find the intensity of illumination on the desk. 6.25 lm

47. How strong a light source is needed to cast 20 lm of light on a surface 4 m from the source? 320 candela

48. How strong a light source is needed to cast 80 lm of light on a surface 5 m from the source? 2000 candela

49. How far from the desk surface must a 40-candela light source be positioned if the desired intensity of illumination is 10 lm? 2 m

50. Find the distance between a 36-candela light source and a surface if the intensity of illumination on the surface is 0.01 lm. 60 m

SECTION

11.6 Literal Equations

OBJECTIVE A *To solve a literal equation for one of the variables*

INSTRUCTOR NOTE

Example 4 on the next page will be difficult for students. Before doing that example or one similar to it, remind students that when solving the equation $2x + 3x = 10$, they are using the Distributive Property to combine $2x$ and $3x$:

$$2x + 3x = (2 + 3)x = 5x$$

Now each side of the equation can be divided by 5.

For the equation $ax + bx = 10$, the procedure is exactly the same except that $a + b$ does not simplify further:

$$ax + bx = (a + b)x$$

Now each side of the equation can be divided by $(a + b)$.

A **literal equation** is an equation that contains more than one variable. Examples of literal equations are shown at the right.

$$2x + 3y = 6$$
$$4w - 2x + z = 0$$

Formulas are used to express relationships among physical quantities. A **formula** is a literal equation that states a rule about measurements. Examples of formulas are shown at the right.

$$\frac{1}{R_1} + \frac{1}{R_2} = \frac{1}{R} \quad \text{(Physics)}$$
$$s = a + (n - 1)d \quad \text{(Mathematics)}$$
$$A = P + Prt \quad \text{(Business)}$$

The Addition and Multiplication Properties can be used to solve a literal equation for one of the variables. The goal is to rewrite the equation so that the variable being solved for is alone on one side of the equation and all the other numbers and variables are on the other side.

HOW TO 1 Solve $A = P(1 + i)$ for i.

The goal is to rewrite the equation so that i is on one side of the equation and all other variables are on the other side.

$$A = P(1 + i)$$
$$A = P + Pi$$ • Use the **Distributive Property** to remove parentheses.
$$A - P = P - P + Pi$$ • **Subtract** P from each side of the equation.
$$A - P = Pi$$
$$\frac{A - P}{P} = \frac{Pi}{P}$$ • **Divide** each side of the equation by P.
$$\frac{A - P}{P} = i$$

EXAMPLE 1

Solve $3x - 4y = 12$ for y.

Solution

$$3x - 4y = 12$$
$$3x - 3x - 4y = -3x + 12$$ • Subtract $3x$.
$$-4y = -3x + 12$$
$$\frac{-4y}{-4} = \frac{-3x + 12}{-4}$$ • Divide by -4.
$$y = \frac{3}{4}x - 3$$

YOU TRY IT 1

Solve $5x - 2y = 10$ for y.

Your solution

$$y = \frac{5}{2}x - 5$$

Solution on p. S28

EXAMPLE 2

Solve $I = \dfrac{E}{R + r}$ for R.

Solution

$$I = \frac{E}{R + r}$$
$$(R + r)I = (R + r)\frac{E}{R + r}$$ • Multiply by $(R + r)$.
$$RI + rI = E$$
$$RI + rI - rI = E - rI$$ • Subtract rI.
$$RI = E - rI$$
$$\frac{RI}{I} = \frac{E - rI}{I}$$ • Divide by I.
$$R = \frac{E - rI}{I}$$

YOU TRY IT 2

Solve $s = \dfrac{A + L}{2}$ for L.

Your solution

$L = 2s - A$

IN-CLASS EXAMPLES

1. Solve for b: $A = \frac{1}{2}bh$
 $b = \dfrac{2A}{h}$
2. Solve for x: $3x + 8y = 9$
 $x = -\frac{8}{3}y + 3$
3. Solve for y: $7x - y = 12$
 $y = 7x - 12$

EXAMPLE 3

Solve $L = a(1 + ct)$ for c.

Solution

$$L = a(1 + ct)$$
$$L = a + act$$ • Distributive Property
$$L - a = a - a + act$$ • Subtract a.
$$L - a = act$$
$$\frac{L - a}{at} = \frac{act}{at}$$ • Divide by at.
$$\frac{L - a}{at} = c$$

YOU TRY IT 3

Solve $S = a + (n - 1)d$ for n.

Your solution

$n = \dfrac{S - a + d}{d}$

EXAMPLE 4

Solve $S = C - rC$ for C.

Solution

$$S = C - rC$$
$$S = (1 - r)C$$ • Factor.
$$\frac{S}{1 - r} = \frac{(1 - r)C}{1 - r}$$ • Divide by $(1 - r)$.
$$\frac{S}{1 - r} = C$$

YOU TRY IT 4

Solve $S = rS + C$ for S.

Your solution

$S = \dfrac{C}{1 - r}$

Solutions on pp. S28–S29

11.6 EXERCISES

Concept Check

SUGGESTED ASSIGNMENT
Exercises 1–4; Exercises 5–39, odds

For Exercises 1 and 2, determine whether the statement is true or false.

1. Literal equations are solved using the same properties of equations that are used to solve equations in one variable. True

2. In solving a literal equation, the goal is to get the variable being solved for alone on one side of the equation and all numbers and other variables on the other side of the equation. True

3. In solving $I = \frac{E}{R + r}$ for R, the goal is to get ___R___ alone on one side of the equation.

4. In solving $L = a(1 + ct)$ for c, the goal is to get ___c___ alone on one side of the equation.

OBJECTIVE A *To solve a literal equation for one of the variables*

For Exercises 5 to 20, solve the formula for the given variable.

5. $d = rt$; t (Physics)
$t = \frac{d}{r}$

6. $E = IR$; R (Physics)
$R = \frac{E}{I}$

7. $PV = nRT$; T (Chemistry)
$T = \frac{PV}{nR}$

8. $A = bh$; h (Geometry)
$h = \frac{A}{b}$

9. $P = 2l + 2w$; l (Geometry)
$l = \frac{P - 2w}{2}$

10. $F = \frac{9}{5}C + 32$; C (Temperature conversion)
$C = \frac{5F - 160}{9}$

11. $A = \frac{1}{2}h(b_1 + b_2)$; b_1 (Geometry)
$b_1 = \frac{2A - hb_2}{h}$

12. $s = a(x - vt)$; t (Physics)
$t = -\frac{s - ax}{av}$

13. $V = \frac{1}{3}Ah$; h (Geometry)
$h = \frac{3V}{A}$

14. $P = R - C$; C (Business)
$C = R - P$

15. $R = \frac{C - S}{t}$; S (Business)
$S = C - Rt$

16. $P = \frac{R - C}{n}$; R (Business)
$R = Pn + C$

17. $A = P + Prt$; P (Business)
$P = \frac{A}{1 + rt}$

18. $T = fm - gm$; m (Engineering)
$m = \frac{T}{f - g}$

19. $A = Sw + w$; w (Physics)
$w = \frac{A}{S + 1}$

20. $a = S - Sr$; S (Mathematics)
$S = \frac{a}{1 - r}$

For Exercises 21 to 32, solve for y.

21. $3x + y = 10$
$y = -3x + 10$

22. $2x + y = 5$
$y = -2x + 5$

23. $4x - y = 3$
$y = 4x - 3$

24. $5x - y = 7$
$y = 5x - 7$

25. $3x + 2y = 6$
$y = -\frac{3}{2}x + 3$

26. $2x + 3y = 9$
$y = -\frac{2}{3}x + 3$

27. $2x - 5y = 10$
$y = \frac{2}{5}x - 2$

28. $5x - 2y = 4$
$y = \frac{5}{2}x - 2$

29. $2x + 7y = 14$
$y = -\frac{2}{7}x + 2$

30. $6x - 5y = 10$
$y = \frac{6}{5}x - 2$

31. $x + 3y = 6$
$y = -\frac{1}{3}x + 2$

32. $x + 2y = 8$
$y = -\frac{1}{2}x + 4$

For Exercises 33 to 40, solve for x.

33. $x + 3y = 6$
$x = -3y + 6$

34. $x + 6y = 10$
$x = -6y + 10$

35. $3x - y = 3$
$x = \frac{1}{3}y + 1$

36. $2x - y = 6$
$x = \frac{1}{2}y + 3$

37. $2x + 5y = 10$
$x = -\frac{5}{2}y + 5$

38. $4x + 3y = 12$
$x = -\frac{3}{4}y + 3$

39. $x - 2y + 1 = 0$
$x = 2y - 1$

40. $x - 4y - 3 = 0$
$x = 4y + 3$

41. Two students are working with the equation $A = P(1 + i)$. State whether the two students' answers are equivalent.

a. When asked to solve the equation for i, one student answered $i = \frac{A}{P} - 1$ and the other student answered $i = \frac{A - P}{P}$. Yes

b. When asked to solve the equation for i, one student answered $i = -\frac{P - A}{P}$ and the other student answered $i = \frac{A - P}{P}$. Yes

Critical Thinking

42. Solve for x: $cx - y = bx + 5$ $\quad x = \frac{y + 5}{c - b}$

43. Solve the physics formula $\frac{1}{R_1} + \frac{1}{R_2} = \frac{1}{R}$ for R_2. $\quad R_2 = \frac{RR_1}{R_1 - R}$

QUICK QUIZ

1. Use the equation $4x + y = 8$.
   a. Solve for y. $y = -4x + 8$
   b. Solve for x. $x = \frac{8 - y}{4}$ or $x = -\frac{1}{4}y + 2$ [11.6A]
2. Solve $P = C + Cr$ for r.
   $r = \frac{P - C}{C}$ [11.6A]

Projects or Group Activities

Business Break-even analysis is a method used to determine the sales volume required for a company to "break even," or experience neither a profit nor a loss on the sale of its product. The break-even point represents the number of units that must be made and sold for income from sales to equal the cost of producing the product. The break-even point can be calculated using the formula $B = \frac{F}{S - V}$, where F is the fixed costs, S is the selling price per unit, and V is the variable costs per unit.

© Andrew Twort/Alamy

44. a. Solve the formula $B = \frac{F}{S - V}$ for S. $\quad S = \frac{F + BV}{B}$

b. Use your answer to part (a) to find the selling price per button pinhole video spycam required for a company to break even. The fixed costs are \$15,000, the variable costs per spycam are \$60, and the company plans to make and sell 200 spycams. \$135

c. Use your answer to part (a) to find the selling price per spy camera video lighter required for a company to break even. The fixed costs are \$18,000, the variable costs per lighter are \$65, and the company plans to make and sell 600 lighters. \$95

SECTION

11.7 Application Problems

OBJECTIVE A *To solve work problems*

If a painter can paint a room in 4 h, then in 1 h the painter can paint $\frac{1}{4}$ of the room. The painter's rate of work is $\frac{1}{4}$ of the room each hour. The **rate of work** is the part of a task that is completed in 1 unit of time.

A pipe can fill a tank in 30 min. This pipe can fill $\frac{1}{30}$ of the tank in 1 min. The rate of work is $\frac{1}{30}$ of the tank each minute. If a second pipe can fill the tank in x min, the rate of work for the second pipe is $\frac{1}{x}$ of the tank each minute.

In solving a work problem, the goal is to determine the time it takes to complete a task. The basic equation that is used to solve work problems is

Rate of work × time worked = part of task completed

Apply the Basic Concepts of Work Problems

EXAMPLE A A faucet can fill a sink in 6 min. What fraction of the sink will the faucet fill in 5 min?

SOLUTION The faucet can fill $\frac{1}{6}$ of the sink in 1 min. The rate of work is $\frac{1}{6}$ of the sink each minute.

Rate of work × time worked = part of task completed

$$\frac{1}{6} \times 5 = \frac{5}{6}$$

The faucet will fill $\frac{5}{6}$ of the sink in 5 min.

© iStockphoto.com/YinYang

EXAMPLE B Emily and Ian raked the yard in 40 min. It would have taken Ian 60 min to rake the yard by himself. What fraction of the yard did Ian rake?

SOLUTION Ian can rake the yard in 60 min. His rate of work is $\frac{1}{60}$ of the yard each minute. The amount of time Ian raked was 40 min.

Rate of work × time worked = part of task completed

$$\frac{1}{60} \times 40 = \frac{40}{60} = \frac{2}{3}$$

Ian raked $\frac{2}{3}$ of the yard.

© Goodluz/Shutterstock.com

EXAMPLE C Sue and Ron wallpapered a room in 8 h. Sue wallpapered $\frac{3}{5}$ of the room. What fraction of the room did Ron wallpaper?

SOLUTION The sum of the part of the task completed by Ron and the part of the task completed by Sue is 1.

Let $x =$ the part of the task completed by Ron.

$$\text{Part of the task completed by Sue} + \text{Part of the task completed by Ron} = 1$$

$$\frac{3}{5} + x = 1$$

$$x = \frac{2}{5} \quad \bullet \text{ Subtract } \frac{3}{5}.$$

Ron wallpapered $\frac{2}{5}$ of the room.

Try Concept Check Exercises 2 to 9 on Page 627.

Tips for Success

Note in the examples in this section that solving a word problem includes stating a strategy and using the strategy to find a solution. If you have difficulty with a word problem, write down the known information. Be very specific. Write out a phrase or sentence that states what you are trying to find. See *AIM for Success* at the front of the book.

Take Note

Use the information given in the problem to fill in the "Rate" and "Time" columns of the table. Fill in the "Part Completed" column by multiplying the two expressions you wrote in each row.

HOW TO 1 A painter can paint a wall in 20 min. The painter's apprentice can paint the same wall in 30 min. How long will it take to paint the wall if the painter and the apprentice work together?

Strategy for Solving a Work Problem

1. For each person or machine, write a numerical or variable expression for the rate of work, the time worked, and the part of the task completed. The results can be recorded in a table.

Unknown time to paint the wall working together: t

	Rate of Work	·	*Time Worked*	=	*Part of Task Completed*
Painter	$\frac{1}{20}$	·	t	=	$\frac{t}{20}$
Apprentice	$\frac{1}{30}$	·	t	=	$\frac{t}{30}$

2. Determine how the parts of the task completed are related. Use the fact that the sum of the parts of the task completed must equal 1, the complete task.

$$\frac{t}{20} + \frac{t}{30} = 1 \quad \bullet \text{ The sum of the part of the task completed by the painter and the part of the task completed by the apprentice is 1.}$$

$$60\left(\frac{t}{20} + \frac{t}{30}\right) = 60 \cdot 1 \quad \bullet \text{ Multiply by the LCM of 20 and 30.}$$

$$3t + 2t = 60 \quad \bullet \text{ Distributive Property}$$

$$5t = 60$$

$$t = 12$$

Working together, the painter and the apprentice will paint the wall in 12 min.

EXAMPLE 1

A small water pipe takes three times longer to fill a tank than does a large water pipe. With both pipes open, it takes 4 h to fill the tank. Find the time it would take the small pipe, working alone, to fill the tank.

Strategy

- Time for large pipe to fill the tank: t
  Time for small pipe to fill the tank: $3t$

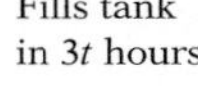

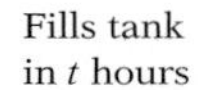

Fills $\frac{4}{3t}$ of the tank in 4 hours

Fills $\frac{4}{t}$ of the tank in 4 hours

	Rate	Time	Part
Small pipe	$\frac{1}{3t}$	4	$\frac{4}{3t}$
Large pipe	$\frac{1}{t}$	4	$\frac{4}{t}$

- The sum of the parts of the task completed by each pipe must equal 1.

Solution

$$\frac{4}{3t} + \frac{4}{t} = 1$$

$$3t\left(\frac{4}{3t} + \frac{4}{t}\right) = 3t \cdot 1$$ • Multiply by the LCM of $3t$ and t.

$$4 + 12 = 3t$$ • Distributive Property

$$16 = 3t$$

$$\frac{16}{3} = t$$ • Time for large pipe to fill the tank

$$3t = 3\left(\frac{16}{3}\right) = 16$$ • Time for small pipe to fill the tank

The small pipe, working alone, takes 16 h to fill the tank.

YOU TRY IT 1

Two computer printers that work at the same rate are working together to print the payroll checks for a large corporation. After they work together for 2 h, one of the printers fails. The second printer requires 3 h more to complete the payroll checks. Find the time it would take one printer, working alone, to print the payroll.

Your strategy

Your solution

7 h

IN-CLASS EXAMPLES

1. It takes Erin Shaw 30 min to shovel the snow off her driveway by herself. Working by himself, Erin's son takes 45 min to clear the driveway of snow. If they work together, how long will it take Erin and her son to shovel all the snow off their driveway? **18 min**

Solution on p. S29

OBJECTIVE B *To use rational expressions to solve uniform motion problems*

INSTRUCTOR NOTE
If you did not cover Section 10.5 on solving quadratic equations by factoring, skip Example 2 on the next page. Also skip Exercises 44, 45, 50, and 63 in the Section 11.7 Exercises.

A car that travels constantly in a straight line at 30 mph is in uniform motion. **Uniform motion** means that the speed and direction of an object do not change.

The basic equation used to solve uniform motion problems is

Distance = rate × time

An alternative form of this equation can be written by solving the equation for time.

$$\frac{\textbf{Distance}}{\textbf{Rate}} = \textbf{time}$$

This form of the equation is useful when the total time of travel for two objects or the time of travel between two points is known.

HOW TO 2 The speed of a boat in still water is 20 mph. The boat traveled 75 mi down a river in the same amount of time it took to travel 45 mi up the river. Find the rate of the river's current.

Strategy for Solving a Uniform Motion Problem

1. For each object, write a numerical or variable expression for the distance, rate, and time. The results can be recorded in a table.

The unknown rate of the river's current: r

	Distance	÷	*Rate*	=	*Time*
Down river	75	÷	$20 + r$	=	$\frac{75}{20 + r}$
Up river	45	÷	$20 - r$	=	$\frac{45}{20 - r}$

Take Note
Use the information given in the problem to fill in the "Distance" and "Rate" columns of the table. Fill in the "Time" column by dividing the two expressions you wrote in each row.

2. Determine how the times traveled by each object are related. For example, it may be known that the times are equal, or the total time may be known.

$$\frac{75}{20 + r} = \frac{45}{20 - r}$$

- **The time down the river is equal to the time up the river.**

$$(20 + r)(20 - r)\frac{75}{20 + r} = (20 + r)(20 - r)\frac{45}{20 - r}$$

- **Multiply by the LCM of the denominator.**

$$(20 - r)75 = (20 + r)45$$

$$1500 - 75r = 900 + 45r$$

- **Distributive Property**

$$-120r = -600$$

$$r = 5$$

The rate of the river's current is 5 mph.

EXAMPLE 2

A cyclist rode the first 20 mi of a trip at a constant rate. For the next 16 mi, the cyclist reduced the speed by 2 mph. The total time for the 36 mi was 4 h. Find the rate of the cyclist for each leg of the trip.

Strategy

- Rate for the first 20 mi: r
  Rate for the next 16 mi: $r - 2$

	Distance	Rate	Time
First 20 mi	20	r	$\frac{20}{r}$
Next 16 mi	16	$r - 2$	$\frac{16}{r-2}$

- The total time for the trip was 4 h.

Solution

$$\frac{20}{r} + \frac{16}{r-2} = 4$$ • The total time was 4 h.

$$r(r-2)\left[\frac{20}{r} + \frac{16}{r-2}\right] = r(r-2) \cdot 4$$ • Multiply by the LCM of the denominators.

$$(r-2)20 + 16r = 4r^2 - 8r$$ • Distributive Property

$$20r - 40 + 16r = 4r^2 - 8r$$

$$36r - 40 = 4r^2 - 8r$$

Solve the quadratic equation by factoring.

$$0 = 4r^2 - 44r + 40$$ • Standard form

$$0 = 4(r^2 - 11r + 10)$$

$$0 = 4(r - 10)(r - 1)$$ • Factor.

$$r - 10 = 0 \qquad r - 1 = 0$$ • Principle of Zero Products

$$r = 10 \qquad r = 1$$

The solution $r = 1$ mph is not possible, because the rate on the last 16 mi would then be -1 mph.

10 mph was the rate for the first 20 mi.
8 mph was the rate for the next 16 mi.

YOU TRY IT 2

The total time it took for a sailboat to sail across a lake 6 km wide and back was 2 h. The rate sailing back was three times the rate sailing across. Find the rate sailing out across the lake.

Your strategy

Your solution

4 km/h

Solution on p. S29

IN-CLASS EXAMPLES

2. Lorenzo's bicycling rate is six times as fast as his walking rate. On his bicycle, he can complete a 9-mile route in $2\frac{1}{2}$ h less time than it takes him to walk the same route. Find Lorenzo's walking rate and his cycling rate. **3 mph, 18 mph**

11.7 EXERCISES

Concept Check

SUGGESTED ASSIGNMENT
Exercises 1–14; Exercises 15–33, odds; Exercises 37–57, odds

1. Explain the meaning of the phrase "rate of work."

For Exercises 2 to 4, fill in the blank to make a true statement.

2. If it takes a janitorial crew 5 h to clean a company's offices, then in x hours the crew has completed ______ of the job. $\frac{x}{5}$

3. If it takes an automotive crew x minutes to service a car, then the rate of work is ______ of the job each minute. $\frac{1}{x}$

4. Two people completed a job. If one person completed $\frac{t}{30}$ of the job and the other person completed $\frac{t}{20}$ of the job, then $\frac{t}{30} + \frac{t}{20} =$ __1__.

5. If Jen can paint a wall in 30 min and Amelia can paint the same wall in 45 min, who has the greater rate of work? Jen

6. It takes Pat 3 h to mow the lawn.

a. What is Pat's rate of work? $\frac{1}{3}$ of the job per hour

b. What fraction of the lawn can Pat mow in 2 h? $\frac{2}{3}$

© iStockphoto.com/epicture

7. It takes Chris x hours to lay a tile floor.

a. What is Chris's rate of work? $\frac{1}{x}$ of the job per hour

b. What fraction of the floor can Chris lay in 3 h? $\frac{3}{x}$

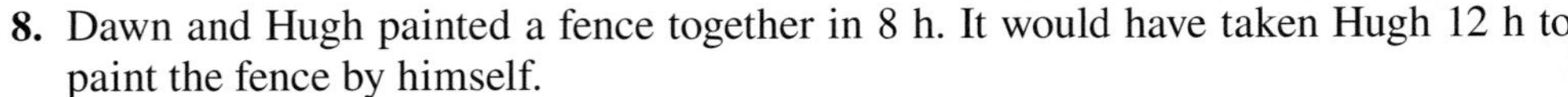

8. Dawn and Hugh painted a fence together in 8 h. It would have taken Hugh 12 h to paint the fence by himself.

a. What fraction of the fence did Hugh paint? $\frac{2}{3}$

b. What fraction of the fence did Dawn paint? $\frac{1}{3}$

© iStockphoto.com/kali9

9. Together, two printers printed a company's advertising brochures in h hours. The faster printer could have printed the brochures in 5 h. What fraction of the brochures did the faster printer print? $\frac{h}{5}$

10. If a plane flies 300 mph in calm air and the rate of the wind is r miles per hour, then the rate of the plane flying with the wind can be represented as __$300 + r$__, and the rate of the plane flying against the wind can be represented as __$300 - r$__.

11. Suppose you have a powerboat with the throttle set to move the boat at 8 mph in calm water, and the rate of the current is 4 mph. **a.** What is the speed of the boat when traveling with the current? **b.** What is the speed of the boat when traveling against the current? a. 12 mph b. 4 mph

12. The speed of a plane is 500 mph. There is a headwind of 50 mph. What is the speed of the plane relative to an observer on the ground? 450 mph

OBJECTIVE A *To solve work problems*

13. One electrician can complete a wiring job in 10 h. It would take the electrician's assistant 12 h to complete the same wiring job. Let t represent the amount of time it would take the electrician and the assistant to complete the job if they worked together. Complete the following table.

	Rate of Work	·	*Time Worked*	=	*Part of Task Completed*
Electrician	$\frac{1}{10}$	·	t	=	$\frac{t}{10}$
Assistant	$\frac{1}{12}$	·	t	=	$\frac{t}{12}$

14. Refer to the situation presented in Exercise 13. When the wiring job is finished, the "part of task completed" is the whole task, so the sum of the parts completed by the electrician and by the assistant is 1. Use this fact and the expressions in the table in Exercise 13 to write an equation that can be solved to find the amount of time it would take for the electrician and the assistant to complete the job working together: $\frac{t}{10} + \frac{t}{12} = 1$.

15. A park has two sprinklers that are used to fill a fountain. One sprinkler can fill the fountain in 3 h, whereas the second sprinkler can fill the fountain in 6 h. How long will it take to fill the fountain with both sprinklers operating? 2 h

16. One grocery clerk can stock a shelf in 20 min. A second clerk requires 30 min to stock the same shelf. How long would it take to stock the shelf if the two clerks worked together? 12 min

17. One person with a skiploader requires 12 h to transfer a large quantity of earth. With a larger skiploader, the same amount of earth can be transferred in 4 h. How long would it take to transfer the earth if both skiploaders were operated together? 3 h

© RJH_CATALOG/Alamy

18. It takes Doug 6 days to reroof a house. If Doug's son helps him, the job can be completed in 4 days. How long would it take Doug's son, working alone, to do the job? 12 days

19. One computer can solve a complex prime factorization problem in 75 h. A second computer can solve the same problem in 50 h. How long would it take both computers, working together, to solve the problem? 30 h

20. A new machine makes 10,000 aluminum cans three times faster than an older machine. With both machines operating, it takes 9 h to make 10,000 cans. How long would it take the new machine, working alone, to make 10,000 cans? 12 h

21. A small air conditioner can cool a room 5°F in 60 min. A larger air conditioner can cool the room 5°F in 40 min. How long would it take to cool the room 5°F with both air conditioners working? 24 min

22. One printing press can print the first edition of a book in 55 min. A second printing press requires 66 min to print the same number of copies. How long would it take to print the first edition of the book with both presses operating? 30 min

23. Two welders working together can complete a job in 6 h. One of the welders, working alone, can complete the task in 10 h. How long would it take the second welder, working alone, to complete the task? 15 h

24. Working together, Pat and Chris can reseal a driveway in 6 h. Working alone, Pat can reseal the driveway in 15 h. How long would it take Chris, working alone, to reseal the driveway? 10 h

25. Two oil pipelines can fill a small tank in 30 min. One of the pipelines, working alone, would require 45 min to fill the tank. How long would it take the second pipeline, working alone, to fill the tank? 90 min

26. A cement mason can construct a retaining wall in 8 h. A second mason requires 12 h to do the same job. After working alone for 4 h, the first mason quits. How long will it take the second mason to complete the wall? 6 h

27. With two reapers operating, a field can be harvested in 1 h. If only the newer reaper is used, the crop can be harvested in 1.5 h. How long would it take to harvest the field using only the older reaper? 3 h

28. A manufacturer of prefabricated homes has the company's employees work in teams. Team 1 can erect the Silvercrest model in 15 h. Team 2 can erect the same model in 10 h. How long would it take for Team 1 and Team 2, working together, to erect the Silvercrest model home? 6 h

© bikeriderlondon/Shutterstock.com

29. One technician can wire a security alarm in 4 h, whereas it takes 6 h for a second technician to do the same job. After working alone for 2 h, the first technician quits. How long will it take the second technician to complete the wiring? 3 h

30. A wallpaper hanger requires 2 h to hang the wallpaper on one wall of a room. A second wallpaper hanger requires 4 h to hang the same amount of wallpaper. The first wallpaper hanger works alone for 1 h and then quits. How long will it take the second hanger, working alone, to finish papering the wall? 2 h

31. A large heating unit and a small heating unit are being used to heat the water in a pool. The large unit, working alone, requires 8 h to heat the pool. After both units have been operating for 2 h, the large unit is turned off. The small unit requires 9 more hours to heat the pool. How long would it take the small unit, working alone, to heat the pool? $14\frac{2}{3}$ h

32. Two machines fill cereal boxes at the same rate. After the two machines work together for 7 h, one machine breaks down. The second machine requires 14 more hours to finish filling the boxes. How long would it have taken one of the machines, working alone, to fill the boxes? 28 h

© Sudheer Sakthan/Shutterstock.com

33. A mechanic requires 2 h to repair a transmission, whereas an apprentice requires 6 h to make the same repairs. The mechanic worked alone for 1 h and then stopped. How long will it take the apprentice, working alone, to complete the repairs? 3 h

34. A large drain and a small drain are opened to drain a pool. The large drain can empty the pool in 6 h. After both drains have been open for 1 h, the large drain becomes clogged and is closed. The small drain remains open and requires 9 more hours to empty the pool. How long would it have taken the small drain, working alone, to empty the pool? 12 h

35. It takes Sam h hours to rake the yard, and it takes Emma k hours to rake the yard, where $h > k$. Let t be the amount of time it takes Sam and Emma to rake the yard together. Is t less than k, between k and h, or greater than k? Less than k

36. Zachary and Eli picked a row of peas together in m minutes. It would have taken Zachary n minutes to pick the row of peas by himself. What fraction of the row of peas did Zachary pick? What fraction of the row of peas did Eli pick? $\frac{m}{n}$; $\frac{n-m}{n}$

OBJECTIVE B *To use rational expressions to solve uniform motion problems*

For Exercises 37 and 38, use the following problem situation: A plane can fly 380 mph in calm air. In the time it takes the plane to fly 1440 mi against a headwind, it could fly 1600 mi with the wind.

37. a. Let r represent the rate of the wind. Complete the following table.

	Distance	÷	*Rate*	=	*Time*
Against the wind	1440	÷	$380 - r$	=	$\frac{1440}{380 - r}$
With the wind	1600	÷	$380 + r$	=	$\frac{1600}{380 + r}$

b. Use the relationship between the expressions in the last column of the table to write an equation that can be solved to find the rate of the wind: ______ = ______.
$\frac{1440}{380 - r}$; $\frac{1600}{380 + r}$

38. Use the equation from part (b) of Exercise 37.

a. Explain the meanings of $380 - r$ and $380 + r$ in terms of the problem situation.

b. Explain the meanings of $\frac{1440}{380 - r}$ and $\frac{1600}{380 + r}$ in terms of the problem situation.

39. A camper drove 80 mi to a recreational area and then hiked 4 mi into the woods. The rate of the camper while driving was ten times the rate while hiking. The total time spent hiking and driving was 3 h. Find the rate at which the camper hiked. 4 mph

40. The president of a company traveled 1800 mi by jet and 300 mi on a prop plane. The rate of the jet was four times the rate of the prop plane. The entire trip took 5 h. Find the rate of the jet. 600 mph

41. To assess the damage done by a fire, a forest ranger traveled 1080 mi by jet and then an additional 180 mi by helicopter. The rate of the jet was four times the rate of the helicopter. The entire trip took 5 h. Find the rate of the jet. 360 mph

$4r$ r
1080 mi 180 mi

42. An engineer traveled 165 mi by car and then an additional 660 mi by plane. The rate of the plane was four times the rate of the car. The total trip took 6 h. Find the rate of the car. 55 mph

43. After sailing 15 mi, a sailor changed direction and increased the boat's speed by 2 mph. An additional 19 mi was sailed at the increased speed. The total sailing time was 4 h. Find the rate of the boat for the first 15 mi. 7.5 mph

44. On a recent trip, a trucker traveled 330 mi at a constant rate. Because of road conditions, the trucker then reduced the speed by 25 mph. An additional 30 mi was traveled at the reduced rate. The entire trip took 7 h. Find the rate of the trucker for the first 330 mi. 55 mph

45. Commuting from work to home, a lab technician traveled 10 mi at a constant rate through congested traffic. Upon reaching the expressway, the technician increased the speed by 20 mph. An additional 20 mi was traveled at the increased speed. The total time for the trip was 1 h. At what rate did the technician travel through the congested traffic? 20 mph

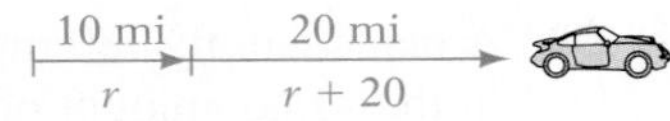

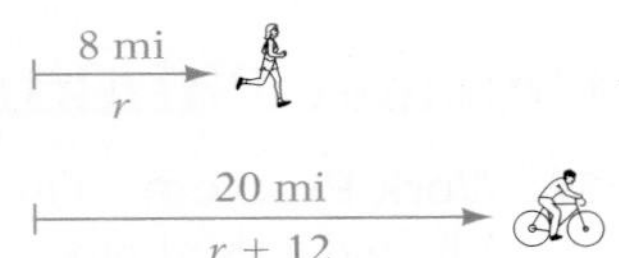

46. As part of a conditioning program, a jogger ran 8 mi in the same amount of time it took a cyclist to ride 20 mi. The rate of the cyclist was 12 mph faster than the rate of the jogger. Find the rate of the jogger and the rate of the cyclist.
Jogger: 8 mph; cyclist: 20 mph

47. In calm water, the rate of a small rental motorboat is 15 mph. The rate of the current on the river is 3 mph. How far down the river can a family travel and still return the boat in 3 h? 21.6 mi

48. The rate of a small aircraft in calm air is 125 mph. If the wind is currently blowing south at a rate of 15 mph, how far north can a pilot fly the plane and return it within 2 h? 123.2 mi

49. The speed of a boat in still water is 20 mph. The Jacksons traveled 75 mi down the Woodset River in this boat in the same amount of time it took them to return 45 mi up the river. Find the rate of the river's current. 5 mph

© iStockphoto.com/Craig Hansen

50. A backpacker hiking into a wilderness area walked 9 mi at a constant rate and then reduced this rate by 1 mph. Another 4 mi was hiked at the reduced rate. The time required to hike the 4 mi was 1 h less than the time required to walk the 9 mi. Find the rate at which the hiker walked the first 9 mi. 3 mph

51. An express train traveled 600 mi in the same amount of time it took a freight train to travel 360 mi. The rate of the express train was 20 mph faster than the rate of the freight train. Find the rate of each train.
Freight train: 30 mph; express train: 50 mph

52. A twin-engine plane flies 800 mi in the same amount of time it takes a single-engine plane to fly 600 mi. The rate of the twin-engine plane is 50 mph faster than the rate of the single-engine plane. Find the rate of the twin-engine plane. 200 mph

53. A small motor on a fishing boat can move the boat at a rate of 6 mph in calm water. Traveling with the current, the boat can travel 24 mi in the same amount of time it takes to travel 12 mi against the current. Find the rate of the current. 2 mph

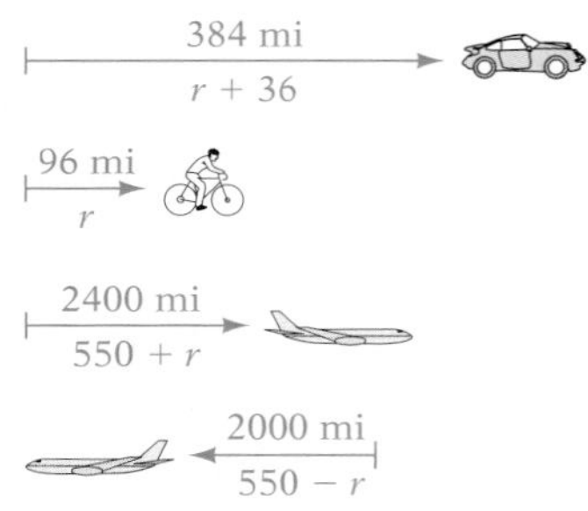

54. A car is traveling at a rate that is 36 mph faster than the rate of a cyclist. The car travels 384 mi in the same amount of time it takes the cyclist to travel 96 mi. Find the rate of the car. 48 mph

55. A commercial jet can fly 550 mph in calm air. Traveling with the jet stream, the plane can fly 2400 mi in the same amount of time it takes to fly 2000 mi against the jet stream. Find the rate of the jet stream. 50 mph

56. A cruise ship can sail 28 mph in calm water. Sailing with the Gulf Stream, the ship can sail 170 mi in the same amount of time it takes to sail 110 mi against the Gulf Stream. Find the rate of the Gulf Stream. 6 mph

© John Kropewnicki/Shutterstock.com

57. Rowing with the current of a river, a rowing team can row 25 mi in the same amount of time it takes to row 15 mi against the current. The rate of the rowing team in calm water is 20 mph. Find the rate of the current. 5 mph

58. A plane can fly 180 mph in calm air. Flying with the wind, the plane can fly 600 mi in the same amount of time it takes to fly 480 mi against the wind. Find the rate of the wind. 20 mph

Critical Thinking

59. **Work Problem** One pipe can fill a tank in 2 h, a second pipe can fill the tank in 4 h, and a third pipe can fill the tank in 5 h. How long would it take to fill the tank with all three pipes operating? $1\frac{1}{19}$ h

60. **Work Problem** A mason can construct a retaining wall in 10 h. The mason's experienced apprentice can do the same job in 15 h. How long would it take the mason's novice apprentice to do the job if, working together, all three can complete the wall in 5 h? 30 h

61. **Uniform Motion** An Outing Club traveled 18 mi by canoe and then hiked 3 mi. The rate by canoe was three times the rate on foot. The time spent walking was 1 h less than the time spent canoeing. Find the amount of time spent traveling by canoe. 2 h

62. **Uniform Motion** A motorist drove 120 mi before running out of gas and walking 4 mi to a gas station. The motorist's driving rate was ten times the walking rate. The time spent walking was 2 h less than the time spent driving. How long did it take for the motorist to drive the 120 mi? 3 h

QUICK QUIZ

1. One hose can fill a child's backyard pool in 24 min. A larger hose can fill the pool in 12 min. If the two hoses are used together, how long will it take to fill the pool? **8 min [11.7A]**
2. A plane flies 460 mph in calm air. Flying with the wind, the plane can travel 1560 mi in the same amount of time it takes to travel 1200 mi against the wind. Find the rate of the wind. **60 mph [11.7B]**

Projects or Group Activities

63. **Uniform Motion** Because of bad weather, a bus driver reduced the usual speed along a 150-mile bus route by 10 mph. The bus arrived only 30 min later than its usual arrival time. How fast does the bus usually travel? 60 mph

64. **Work Problem** A construction project must be completed in 15 days. Twenty-five workers did one-half of the job in 10 days. Working at the same rate, how many workers are needed to complete the job on schedule? 50 workers

CHAPTER 11 Summary

Key Words

A **rational expression** is a fraction in which the numerator and denominator are polynomials. A rational expression is in **simplest form** when the numerator and denominator have no common factors. [11.1A, p. 586]

$\frac{2x+1}{x^2+4}$ is a rational expression in simplest form.

The **reciprocal of a rational expression** is the rational expression with the numerator and denominator interchanged. [11.1C, p. 589]

The reciprocal of $\frac{3x-y}{x+4}$ is $\frac{x+4}{3x-y}$.

The **least common multiple (LCM) of two or more polynomials** is the polynomial of least degree that contains all the factors of each polynomial. [11.2A, p. 594]

The LCM of $3x^2 - 6x$ and $x^2 - 4$ is $3x(x-2)(x+2)$, because it contains the factors of $3x^2 - 6x = 3x(x-2)$ and the factors of $x^2 - 4 = (x-2)(x+2)$.

A **complex fraction** is a fraction in which the numerator or denominator contains one or more fractions. [11.4A, p. 607]

$\frac{x - \frac{2}{x+1}}{1 - \frac{4}{x}}$ is a complex fraction.

A **literal equation** is an equation that contains more than one variable. A **formula** is a literal equation that states a rule about measurements. [11.6A, p. 618]

$3x - 4y = 12$ is a literal equation.
$A = LW$ is a literal equation that is also the formula for the area of a rectangle.

Essential Rules and Procedures

Simplifying Rational Expressions [11.1A, p. 586]
Factor the numerator and denominator. Divide the numerator and denominator by the common factors.

$$\frac{x^2-3x-10}{x^2-25} = \frac{(x+2)(x-5)}{(x+5)(x-5)} = \frac{x+2}{x+5}$$

Multiplying Rational Expressions [11.1B, p. 587]
Multiply the numerators. Multiply the denominators. Write the answer in simplest form.

$$\frac{a}{b} \cdot \frac{c}{d} = \frac{ac}{bd}$$

$$\frac{x^2-3x}{x^2+x} \cdot \frac{x^2+5x+4}{x^2-4x+3} = \frac{x(x-3)}{x(x+1)} \cdot \frac{(x+1)(x+4)}{(x-3)(x-1)} = \frac{x(x-3)(x+1)(x+4)}{x(x+1)(x-3)(x-1)} = \frac{x+4}{x-1}$$

Dividing Rational Expressions [11.1C, p. 589]
Multiply the first fraction by the reciprocal of the divisor. Write the answer in simplest form.

$$\frac{a}{b} \div \frac{c}{d} = \frac{a}{b} \cdot \frac{d}{c} = \frac{ad}{bc}$$

$$\frac{4x+16}{3x-6} \div \frac{x^2+6x+8}{x^2-4}$$
$$= \frac{4x+16}{3x-6} \cdot \frac{x^2-4}{x^2+6x+8}$$
$$= \frac{4(x+4)}{3(x-2)} \cdot \frac{(x-2)(x+2)}{(x+4)(x+2)}$$
$$= \frac{4}{3}$$

Adding and Subtracting Rational Expressions [11.3B, p. 600]

1. Find the LCM of the denominators.
2. Write each fraction as an equivalent fraction using the LCM as the denominator.
3. Add or subtract the numerators and place the result over the common denominator.
4. Write the answer in simplest form.

$$\frac{a}{b} + \frac{c}{b} = \frac{a+c}{b} \qquad \frac{a}{b} - \frac{c}{b} = \frac{a-c}{b}$$

$$\frac{x}{x+1} - \frac{x+3}{x-2}$$
$$= \frac{x}{x+1} \cdot \frac{x-2}{x-2} - \frac{x+3}{x-2} \cdot \frac{x+1}{x+1}$$
$$= \frac{x(x-2)}{(x+1)(x-2)} - \frac{(x+3)(x+1)}{(x+1)(x-2)}$$
$$= \frac{x(x-2) - (x+3)(x+1)}{(x+1)(x-2)}$$
$$= \frac{(x^2-2x) - (x^2+4x+3)}{(x+1)(x-2)}$$
$$= \frac{-6x-3}{(x+1)(x-2)}$$

Simplifying Complex Fractions [11.4A, p. 607]

Method 1: Multiply by 1 in the form $\frac{\text{LCM}}{\text{LCM}}$.

1. Determine the LCM of the denominators of the fractions in the numerator and denominator of the complex fraction.
2. Multiply the numerator and denominator of the complex fraction by the LCM.
3. Simplify.

Method 1: $$\frac{\frac{1}{x}+\frac{1}{y}}{\frac{1}{x}-\frac{1}{y}} = \frac{\frac{1}{x}+\frac{1}{y}}{\frac{1}{x}-\frac{1}{y}} \cdot \frac{xy}{xy}$$
$$= \frac{\frac{1}{x} \cdot xy + \frac{1}{y} \cdot xy}{\frac{1}{x} \cdot xy - \frac{1}{y} \cdot xy}$$
$$= \frac{y+x}{y-x}$$

Method 2: Multiply the numerator by the reciprocal of the denominator.

1. Simplify the numerator to a single fraction and simplify the denominator to a single fraction.
2. Using the rule for dividing fractions, multiply the numerator by the reciprocal of the denominator.
3. Simplify.

Method 2: $$\frac{\frac{1}{x}+\frac{1}{y}}{\frac{1}{x}-\frac{1}{y}} = \frac{\frac{y+x}{xy}}{\frac{y-x}{xy}}$$
$$= \frac{y+x}{xy} \cdot \frac{xy}{y-x}$$
$$= \frac{y+x}{y-x}$$

Solving Equations Containing Fractions [11.5A, p. 613]
Clear denominators by multiplying each side of the equation by the LCM of the denominators. Then solve for the variable.

$$\frac{1}{2a} = \frac{2}{a} - \frac{3}{8}$$
$$8a\left(\frac{1}{2a}\right) = 8a\left(\frac{2}{a}\right) - 8a\left(\frac{3}{8}\right)$$
$$4 = 16 - 3a$$
$$-12 = -3a$$
$$4 = a$$

Solving Literal Equations [11.6A, p. 618]
Rewrite the equation so that the letter being solved for is alone on one side of the equation and all numbers and other variables are on the other side.

Solve $2x + ax = 5$ for x.

$$2x + ax = 5$$
$$x(2 + a) = 5$$
$$\frac{x(2 + a)}{2 + a} = \frac{5}{2 + a}$$
$$x = \frac{5}{2 + a}$$

Work Problems [11.7A, p. 622]
Rate of work $\times$ time worked $=$ part of task completed

Pat can do a certain job in 3 h. Chris can do the same job in 5 h. How long would it take Pat and Chris, working together, to get the job done?

$$\frac{t}{3} + \frac{t}{5} = 1$$

Uniform Motion Problems with Rational Expressions [11.7B, p. 625]

$$\frac{\text{Distance}}{\text{Rate}} = \text{time}$$

Train A's speed is 15 mph faster than train B's speed. Train A travels 150 mi in the same amount of time it takes train B to travel 120 mi. Find the rate of train B.

$$\frac{120}{r} = \frac{150}{r + 15}$$

CHAPTER 11 Review Exercises

1. Divide: $\frac{6a^2b^7}{25x^3y} \div \frac{12a^3b^4}{5x^2y^2}$ $\frac{b^3y}{10ax}$ [11.1C]

2. Add: $\frac{x+7}{15x} + \frac{x-2}{20x}$ $\frac{7x+22}{60x}$ [11.3B]

3. Multiply: $\frac{3x^3+9x^2}{6xy^2-18y^2} \cdot \frac{4xy^3-12y^3}{5x^2+15x}$ $\frac{2xy}{5}$ [11.1B]

4. Divide: $\frac{2x(x-y)}{x^2y(x+y)} \div \frac{3(x-y)}{x^2y^2}$ $\frac{2xy}{3(x+y)}$ [11.1C]

5. Simplify: $\dfrac{x - \frac{16}{5x-2}}{3x - 4 - \frac{88}{5x-2}}$ $\frac{x-2}{3x-10}$ [11.4A]

6. Simplify: $\frac{x^2+x-30}{15+2x-x^2}$ $-\frac{x+6}{x+3}$ [11.1A]

7. Simplify: $\frac{16x^5y^3}{24xy^{10}}$ $\frac{2x^4}{3y^7}$ [11.1A]

8. Solve: $\frac{20}{x+2} = \frac{5}{16}$ 62 [11.5A]

9. Divide: $\frac{10-23y+12y^2}{6y^2-y-5} \div \frac{4y^2-13y+10}{18y^2+3y-10}$
$\frac{(3y-2)^2}{(y-1)(y-2)}$ [11.1C]

10. Solve $3ax - x = 5$ for x.
$x = \frac{5}{3a-1}$ [11.6A]

11. Solve: $\frac{2}{x} + \frac{3}{4} = 1$ 8 [11.5A]

12. Add: $\frac{x}{y} + \frac{3}{x}$ $\frac{x^2+3y}{xy}$ [11.3B]

13. Solve $5x + 4y = 20$ for y. $y = -\frac{5}{4}x + 5$ [11.6A]

14. Multiply: $\frac{8ab^2}{15x^3y} \cdot \frac{5xy^4}{16a^2b}$ $\frac{by^3}{6ax^2}$ [11.1B]

15. Simplify: $\dfrac{1 - \frac{1}{x}}{1 - \frac{8x-7}{x^2}}$ $\frac{x}{x-7}$ [11.4A]

16. Write each fraction in terms of the LCM of the denominators.
$\frac{x}{12x^2+16x-3}, \frac{4x^2}{6x^2+7x-3}$
$\frac{3x^2-x}{(2x+3)(6x-1)(3x-1)}, \frac{24x^3-4x^2}{(2x+3)(6x-1)(3x-1)}$ [11.2B]

17. Solve $T = 2(ab + bc + ca)$ for a.
$a = \frac{T-2bc}{2b+2c}$ [11.6A]

18. Solve: $\frac{5}{7} + \frac{x}{2} = 2 - \frac{x}{7}$ 2 [11.5A]

19. Simplify: $\dfrac{2 + \frac{1}{x}}{3 - \frac{2}{x}}$ $\frac{2x+1}{3x-2}$ [11.4A]

20. Subtract: $\frac{2x}{x-5} - \frac{x+1}{x-2}$ $\frac{x^2+5}{(x-5)(x-2)}$ [11.3B]

21. Solve $i = \dfrac{100m}{c}$ for c. $c = \dfrac{100m}{i}$ [11.6A]

22. Solve: $\dfrac{x+8}{x+4} = 1 + \dfrac{5}{x+4}$ No solution [11.5A]

23. Divide: $\dfrac{20x^2 - 45x}{6x^3 + 4x^2} \div \dfrac{40x^3 - 90x^2}{12x^2 + 8x}$ $\dfrac{1}{x^2}$ [11.1C]

24. Add: $\dfrac{2y}{5y - 7} + \dfrac{3}{7 - 5y}$ $\dfrac{2y - 3}{5y - 7}$ [11.3B]

25. Subtract: $\dfrac{5x + 3}{2x^2 + 5x - 3} - \dfrac{3x + 4}{2x^2 + 5x - 3}$

$\dfrac{1}{x + 3}$ [11.3A]

26. Find the LCM of $10x^2 - 11x + 3$ and $20x^2 - 17x + 3$.

$(5x - 3)(2x - 1)(4x - 1)$ [11.2A]

27. Solve $4x + 9y = 18$ for y.

$y = -\frac{4}{9}x + 2$ [11.6A]

28. Multiply: $\dfrac{2x^2 - 5x - 3}{3x^2 - 7x - 6} \cdot \dfrac{3x^2 + 8x + 4}{x^2 + 4x + 4}$

$\dfrac{2x + 1}{x + 2}$ [11.1B]

29. Solve: $\dfrac{20}{2x + 3} = \dfrac{17x}{2x + 3} - 5$

5 [11.5A]

30. Add: $\dfrac{x - 1}{x + 2} + \dfrac{3x - 2}{5 - x} + \dfrac{5x^2 + 15x - 11}{x^2 - 3x - 10}$

$\dfrac{3x - 1}{x - 5}$ [11.3B]

31. Solve: $\dfrac{6}{x - 7} = \dfrac{8}{x - 6}$

10 [11.5A]

32. Solve: $\dfrac{3}{20} = \dfrac{x}{80}$

12 [11.5A]

33. **Work Problem** One hose can fill a pool in 15 h. A second hose can fill the pool in 10 h. How long would it take to fill the pool using both hoses? 6 h [11.7A]

34. **Uniform Motion** A car travels 315 mi in the same amount of time it takes a bus to travel 245 mi. The rate of the car is 10 mph faster than that of the bus. Find the rate of the car. 45 mph [11.7B]

35. **Uniform Motion** The rate of a jet is 400 mph in calm air. Traveling with the wind, the jet can fly 2100 mi in the same amount of time it takes to fly 1900 mi against the wind. Find the rate of the wind. 20 mph [11.7B]

CHAPTER 11 TEST

1. Subtract: $\frac{x}{x+3} - \frac{2x-5}{x^2+x-6}$

$\frac{x^2-4x+5}{(x-2)(x+3)}$ [11.3B]

2. Solve: $\frac{3}{x+4} = \frac{5}{x+6}$

-1 [11.5A]

3. Multiply: $\frac{x^2+2x-3}{x^2+6x+9} \cdot \frac{2x^2-11x+5}{2x^2+3x-5}$

$\frac{(x-5)(2x-1)}{(x+3)(2x+5)}$ [11.1B]

4. Simplify: $\frac{16x^5y}{24x^2y^4}$

$\frac{2x^3}{3y^3}$ [11.1A]

5. Solve $d = s + rt$ for t.

$t = \frac{d-s}{r}$ [11.6A]

6. Solve: $\frac{6}{x} - 2 = 1$

2 [11.5A]

7. Simplify: $\frac{x^2+4x-5}{1-x^2}$

$-\frac{x+5}{x+1}$ [11.1A]

8. Find the LCM of $6x - 3$ and $2x^2 + x - 1$.

$3(2x-1)(x+1)$ [11.2A]

9. Subtract: $\frac{2}{2x-1} - \frac{3}{3x+1}$

$\frac{5}{(2x-1)(3x+1)}$ [11.3B]

10. Divide: $\frac{x^2+3x+2}{x^2+5x+4} \div \frac{x^2-x-6}{x^2+2x-15}$

$\frac{x+5}{x+4}$ [11.1C]

11. Simplify: $\dfrac{1+\frac{1}{x}-\frac{12}{x^2}}{1+\frac{2}{x}-\frac{8}{x^2}}$

$\frac{x-3}{x-2}$ [11.4A]

12. Write each fraction in terms of the LCM of the denominators.
$\frac{3}{x^2-2x}, \frac{x}{x^2-4}$

$\frac{3x+6}{x(x-2)(x+2)}, \frac{x^2}{x(x-2)(x+2)}$ [11.2B]

13. Subtract: $\dfrac{2x}{x^2 + 3x - 10} - \dfrac{4}{x^2 + 3x - 10}$

$\dfrac{2}{x + 5}$ [11.3A]

14. Solve $3x - 8y = 16$ for y.

$y = \dfrac{3}{8}x - 2$ [11.6A]

15. Solve: $\dfrac{2x}{x + 1} - 3 = \dfrac{-2}{x + 1}$

No solution [11.5A]

16. Multiply: $\dfrac{x^3y^4}{x^2 - 4x + 4} \cdot \dfrac{x^2 - x - 2}{x^6y^4}$

$\dfrac{x + 1}{x^3(x - 2)}$ [11.1B]

17. Divide: $\dfrac{8a^2b^5}{3xy^4} \div \dfrac{4a^3b}{9x^2y}$

$\dfrac{6b^4x}{ay^3}$ [11.1C]

18. Add: $\dfrac{4}{5x^2y} + \dfrac{1}{5x^2y}$

$\dfrac{1}{x^2y}$ [11.3A]

19. **Work Problem** One pipe can fill a pool in 6 h, whereas a second pipe requires 12 h to fill the pool. How long would it take to fill the pool with both pipes turned on?
4 h [11.7A]

20. **Uniform Motion** A small plane can fly at 110 mph in calm air. Flying with the wind, the plane can fly 260 mi in the same amount of time it takes to fly 180 mi against the wind. Find the rate of the wind.
20 mph [11.7B]

21. **Work Problem** A ski resort can manufacture enough machine-made snow to open its beginners' run in 4 h, whereas naturally falling snow would take 12 h to provide enough snow. If the resort makes snow at the same time it is snowing naturally, how long will it take until the run can be opened? 3 h [11.7A]

22. **Uniform Motion** A jet ski can comfortably travel across calm water at 35 mph. If a rider traveled 4 mi down a river in the same amount of time it took to travel 3 mi back up the river, find the rate of the river's current. 5 mph [11.7B]

Cumulative Review Exercises

1. Evaluate: $\left(\frac{2}{3}\right)^2 \div \left(\frac{3}{2} - \frac{2}{3}\right) + \frac{1}{2}$
$\frac{31}{30}$ [2.7A]

2. Evaluate $-a^2 + (a - b)^2$ when $a = -2$ and $b = 3$.
21 [4.1A]

3. Simplify: $-2x - (-3y) + 7x - 5y$
$5x - 2y$ [4.2A]

4. Simplify: $2[3x - 7(x - 3) - 8]$
$-8x + 26$ [4.2D]

5. Solve: $4 - \frac{2}{3}x = 7$
$-\frac{9}{2}$ [5.2A]

6. Solve: $3[x - 2(x - 3)] = 2(3 - 2x)$
-12 [5.3B]

7. Find $16\frac{2}{3}\%$ of 60.
10 [6.4A/6.4B]

8. Simplify: $(a^2b^5)(ab^2)$
a^3b^7 [9.2A]

9. Multiply: $(a - 3b)(a + 4b)$
$a^2 + ab - 12b^2$ [9.3C]

10. Divide: $\frac{15b^4 - 5b^2 + 10b}{5b}$
$3b^3 - b + 2$ [9.5A]

11. Divide: $(x^3 - 8) \div (x - 2)$
$x^2 + 2x + 4$ [9.5B]

12. Factor: $12x^2 - x - 1$
$(4x + 1)(3x - 1)$ [10.3A]

13. Factor: $y^2 - 7y + 6$
$(y - 6)(y - 1)$ [10.2A]

14. Factor: $2a^3 + 7a^2 - 15a$
$a(2a - 3)(a + 5)$ [10.3A]

15. Factor: $4b^2 - 100$
$4(b + 5)(b - 5)$ [10.5A]

16. Solve: $(x + 3)(2x - 5) = 0$
$-3, \frac{5}{2}$ [10.6A]

17. Simplify: $\frac{12x^4y^2}{18xy^7}$
$\frac{2x^3}{3y^5}$ [11.1A]

18. Simplify: $\frac{x^2 - 7x + 10}{25 - x^2}$
$-\frac{x - 2}{x + 5}$ [11.1A]

19. Divide: $\dfrac{x^2 - x - 56}{x^2 + 8x + 7} \div \dfrac{x^2 - 13x + 40}{x^2 - 4x - 5}$

1 [11.1C]

20. Subtract: $\dfrac{2}{2x - 1} - \dfrac{1}{x + 1}$

$\dfrac{3}{(2x - 1)(x + 1)}$ [11.3B]

21. Simplify: $\dfrac{1 - \dfrac{2}{x} - \dfrac{15}{x^2}}{1 - \dfrac{25}{x^2}}$

$\dfrac{x + 3}{x + 5}$ [11.4A]

22. Solve: $\dfrac{3x}{x - 3} - 2 = \dfrac{10}{x - 3}$

4 [11.5A]

23. Solve: $\dfrac{2}{x - 2} = \dfrac{12}{x + 3}$

3 [11.5A]

24. Solve $f = v + at$ for t.

$t = \dfrac{f - v}{a}$ [11.6A]

25. Translate "the difference between five times a number and thirteen is the opposite of eight" into an equation and solve. $5x - 13 = -8; x = 1$ [5.4A]

26. **Home-Schooling** According to the National Center for Education Statistics, 1.1 million students are home-schooled. This number is 2.2% of the school-age population in the United States. What is the school-age population in the United States? 50 million people [6.4C]

27. **Geometry** The length of the base of a triangle is 2 in. less than twice the height. The area of the triangle is 30 in^2. Find the base and height of the triangle.
Base: 10 in.; height: 6 in. [10.6B]

28. **Insurance** A life insurance policy costs $16 for every $1000 of coverage. At this rate, how much money would a policy for $5000 cost? $80 [6.2B]

29. **Work Problem** One water pipe can fill a tank in 9 min, whereas a second pipe requires 18 min to fill the tank. How long would it take both pipes, working together, to fill the tank? 6 min [11.7A]

30. **Uniform Motion** The rower of a boat can row at a rate of 5 mph in calm water. Traveling with the current, the boat travels 14 mi in the same amount of time it takes to travel 6 mi against the current. Find the rate of the current. 2 mph [11.7B]

Linear Equations in Two Variables

12

OBJECTIVES

SECTION 12.1

A To graph points in a rectangular coordinate system
B To determine ordered-pair solutions of an equation in two variables
C To determine whether a set of ordered pairs is a function
D To evaluate a function

SECTION 12.2

A To graph an equation of the form $y = mx + b$
B To graph an equation of the form $Ax + By = C$
C To solve application problems

SECTION 12.3

A To find the x- and y-intercepts of a straight line
B To find the slope of a straight line
C To graph a line using the slope and the y-intercept

SECTION 12.4

A To find the equation of a line using the equation $y = mx + b$
B To find the equation of a line using the point-slope formula
C To find the equation of a line given two points

Focus on Success

Have you established a routine for doing your homework? If not, decide now where and when your study time is most productive. Perhaps it is at home, in the library, or in the math center, where you can get help as you need it. If possible, create a study hour right after class. The material will be fresh in your mind, and the immediate review, along with your homework, will reinforce the concepts you are learning. (See Homework Time, page AIM-5)

Prep Test

Are you ready to succeed in this chapter? Take the Prep Test below to find out if you are ready to learn the new material.

1. Simplify: $-\dfrac{5-(-7)}{4-8}$
3 [3.5A]

2. Evaluate $\dfrac{a-b}{c-d}$ when $a = 3$, $b = -2$, $c = -3$, and $d = 2$.
-1 [4.1A]

3. Simplify: $-3(x-4)$
$-3x + 12$ [4.2C]

4. Solve: $3x + 6 = 0$
-2 [5.2A]

5. Solve $4x + 5y = 20$ when $y = 0$.
$x = 5$ [5.2A]

6. Solve $3x - 7y = 11$ when $x = -1$.
$y = -2$ [5.2A]

7. Divide: $\dfrac{12x-15}{-3}$
$-4x + 5$ [9.5A]

8. Solve: $\dfrac{2x+1}{3} = \dfrac{3x}{4}$
4 [6.2A]

9. Solve $3x - 5y = 15$ for y.
$y = \dfrac{3}{5}x - 3$ [11.6A]

10. Solve $y + 3 = -\dfrac{1}{2}(x+4)$ for y.
$y = -\dfrac{1}{2}x - 5$ [11.6A]

SECTION

12.1 The Rectangular Coordinate System

OBJECTIVE A *To graph points in a rectangular coordinate system*

INSTRUCTOR NOTE
Although Descartes is given credit for introducing analytic geometry, there were others working on the same concept, notably Pierre Fermat. Nowhere in Descartes's work is there a coordinate system as we draw it with two axes. Descartes did not use the word *coordinate* in his work. This word was introduced by Gottfried Leibnitz, who is also responsible for the use of the words *abscissa* and *ordinate.*

Before the 15th century, geometry and algebra were considered separate branches of mathematics. That all changed when René Descartes, a French mathematician who lived from 1596 to 1650, founded **analytic geometry.** In this geometry, a *coordinate system* is used to study relationships between variables.

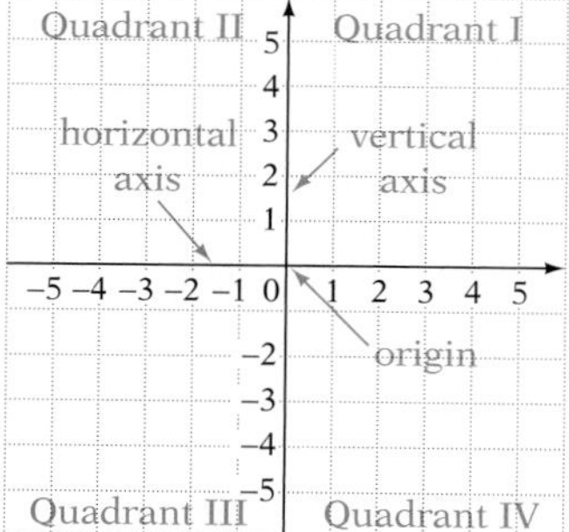

A **rectangular coordinate system** is formed by two number lines, one horizontal and one vertical, that intersect at the zero point of each line. The point of intersection is called the **origin.** The two lines are called **coordinate axes,** or simply **axes.** The axes determine a **plane,** which can be thought of as a large, flat sheet of paper. The two axes divide the plane into four regions called **quadrants,** which are numbered counterclockwise from I to IV.

Each point in the plane can be identified by a pair of numbers called an **ordered pair.** The first number of the pair measures a horizontal distance and is called the **abscissa.** The second number of the pair measures a vertical distance and is called the **ordinate.** The **coordinates of a point** are the numbers in the ordered pair associated with the point. The abscissa is also called the **first coordinate** of the ordered pair, and the ordinate is also called the **second coordinate** of the ordered pair.

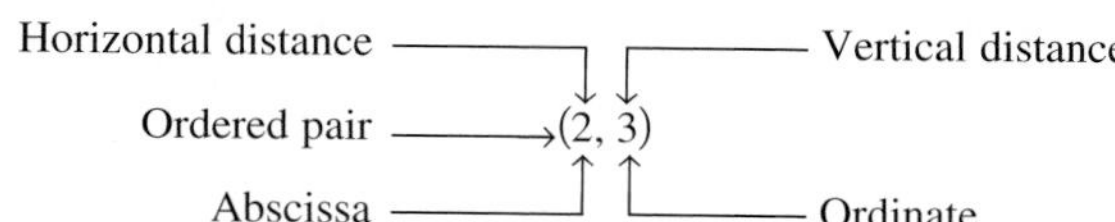

When drawing a rectangular coordinate system, we often label the horizontal axis x and the vertical axis y. In this case, the coordinate system is called an ***xy*-coordinate system.** The coordinates of the points are given by ordered pairs (x, y), where the abscissa is called the ***x*-coordinate** and the ordinate is called the ***y*-coordinate.**

INSTRUCTOR NOTE
Within the Microsoft PowerPoint® slides available with this text is a blank coordinate grid. It can be used to create a transparency on which to plot points, equations, etc.

To **graph or plot a point in the plane,** place a dot at the location given by the ordered pair. The **graph of an ordered pair** (x, y) is the dot drawn at the coordinates of the point in the plane. The points whose coordinates are $(3, 4)$ and $(-2.5, -3)$ are graphed in the figures below.

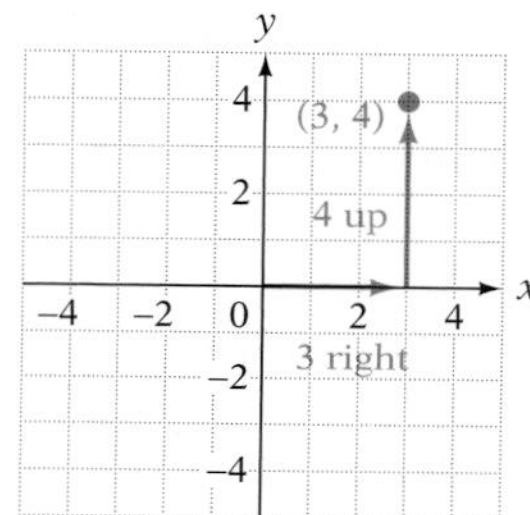

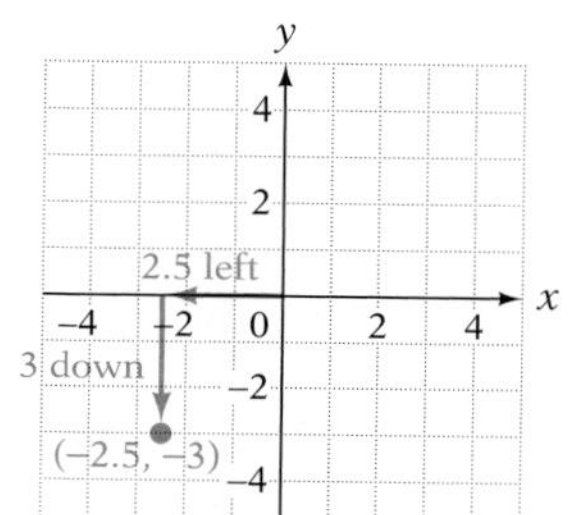

Take Note
This concept is very important. An **ordered pair** is a *pair* of coordinates, and the *order* in which the coordinates are listed is crucial.

The points whose coordinates are $(3, -1)$ and $(-1, 3)$ are graphed at the right. Note that the graphed points are in different locations. *The order of the coordinates in an ordered pair is important.*

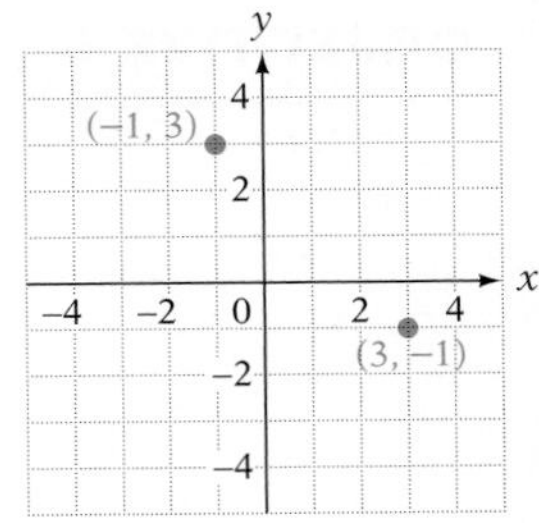

INSTRUCTOR NOTE
It may help students to think of an ordered pair as the address (location) of a point in the plane.

Each point in the plane is associated with an ordered pair, and each ordered pair is associated with a point in the plane. Although only the labels for integers are given on a coordinate grid, the graph of any ordered pair can be approximated. For example, the points whose coordinates are $(-2.3, 4.1)$ and $(\pi, 1)$ are shown on the graph at the right.

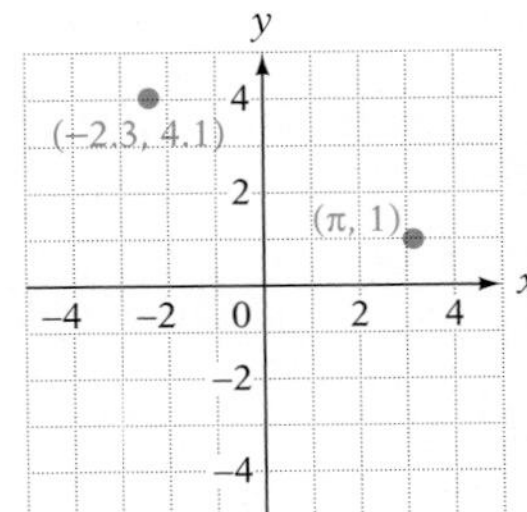

EXAMPLE 1

Graph the ordered pairs $(-2, -3)$, $(3, -2)$, $(0, -2)$, and $(3, 0)$.

Solution

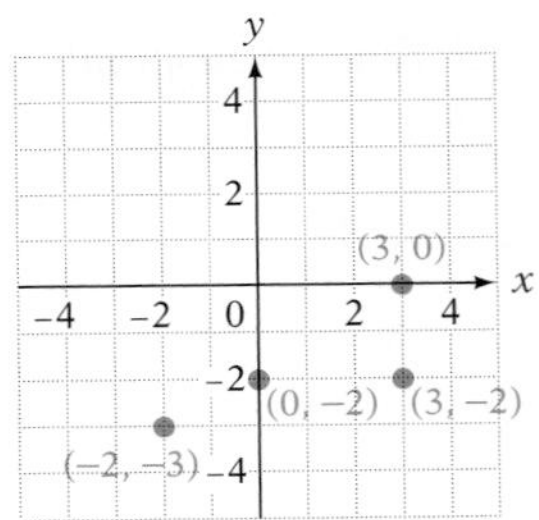

YOU TRY IT 1

Graph the ordered pairs $(-4, 1)$, $(3, -3)$, $(0, 4)$, and $(-3, 0)$.

Your solution

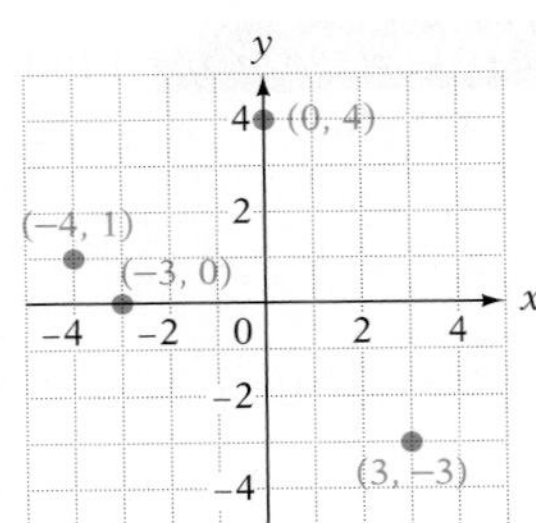

IN-CLASS EXAMPLES
1. Graph the ordered pairs (5, 0), (−4, 1), (−1, 2), and (−2, −4).

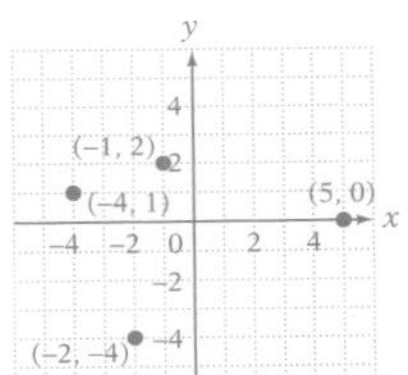

EXAMPLE 2

Give the coordinates of the points labeled A and B. Give the abscissa of point C and the ordinate of point D.

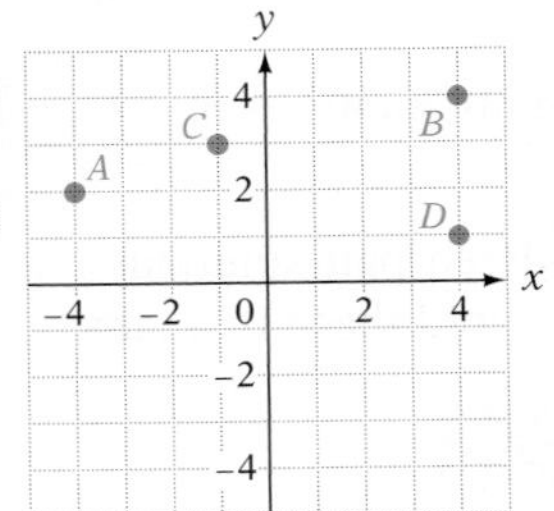

Solution

The coordinates of A are $(-4, 2)$.
The coordinates of B are $(4, 4)$.
The abscissa of C is -1.
The ordinate of D is 1.

YOU TRY IT 2

Give the coordinates of the points labeled A and B. Give the abscissa of point D and the ordinate of point C.

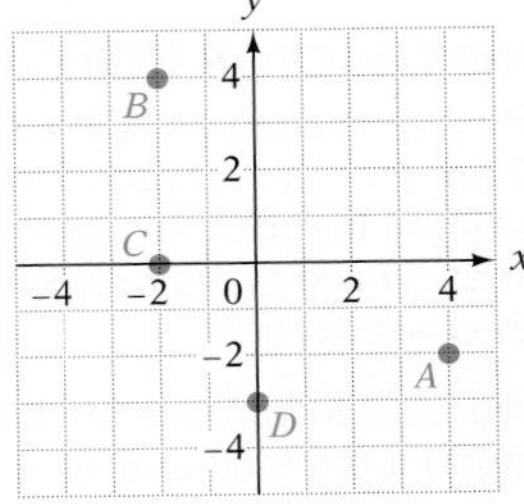

Your solution

$A(4, -2)$, $B(-2, 4)$
The abscissa of D is 0.
The ordinate of C is 0.

Solutions on p. S29

OBJECTIVE B *To determine ordered-pair solutions of an equation in two variables*

An xy-coordinate system is used to study the relationship between two variables. Frequently this relationship is given by an equation. Examples of equations in two variables include

$$y = 2x - 3 \qquad 3x + 2y = 6 \qquad x^2 - y = 0$$

A **solution of an equation in two variables** is an ordered pair (x, y) whose coordinates make the equation a true statement.

HOW TO 1 Is $(-3, 7)$ a solution of the equation $y = -2x + 1$?

$$\begin{array}{c|l} y & = -2x + 1 \\ \hline 7 & -2(-3) + 1 \\ 7 & 6 + 1 \end{array}$$

- Replace x by -3; replace y by 7.

$7 = 7$

- The results are equal.

Yes, $(-3, 7)$ is a solution of the equation $y = -2x + 1$.

Besides $(-3, 7)$, there are many other ordered-pair solutions of $y = -2x + 1$. For example, $(0, 1)$, $\left(-\frac{3}{2}, 4\right)$, and $(4, -7)$ are also solutions. In general, an equation in two variables has an infinite number of solutions. By choosing any value of x and substituting that value into the equation, we can calculate a corresponding value of y.

HOW TO 2 Find the ordered-pair solution of $y = \frac{2}{3}x - 3$ that corresponds to $x = 6$.

$$y = \frac{2}{3}x - 3$$

$$= \frac{2}{3}(6) - 3$$

- Replace x by 6.

$$= 4 - 3 = 1$$

- Simplify.

The ordered-pair solution is $(6, 1)$.

The solutions of an equation in two variables can be graphed in an xy-coordinate system.

INSTRUCTOR NOTE

Problems such as HOW TO 3 are given to prepare the student to graph straight lines, which is the subject of the next section.

We want to impress on the student the relationship between a solution of an equation and the pictorial representation of that solution, its graph.

HOW TO 3 Graph the ordered-pair solutions of $y = -2x + 1$ when $x = -2, -1, 0, 1$, and 2.

Use the values of x to determine ordered-pair solutions of the equation. It is convenient to record these in a table.

x	$y = -2x + 1$	y	(x, y)
-2	$-2(-2) + 1$	5	$(-2, 5)$
-1	$-2(-1) + 1$	3	$(-1, 3)$
0	$-2(0) + 1$	1	$(0, 1)$
1	$-2(1) + 1$	-1	$(1, -1)$
2	$-2(2) + 1$	-3	$(2, -3)$

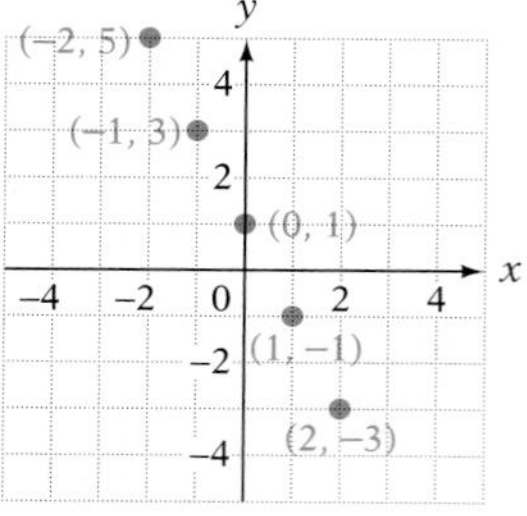

EXAMPLE 3

Is $(3, -2)$ a solution of $3x - 4y = 15$?

Solution

$3x - 4y = 15$	
$3(3) - 4(-2)$	15
$9 + 8$	15
$17 \neq$	15

• Replace x by 3 and y by -2.

No, $(3, -2)$ is not a solution of $3x - 4y = 15$.

YOU TRY IT 3

Is $(-2, 4)$ a solution of $x - 3y = -14$?

Your solution

Yes

EXAMPLE 4

Graph the ordered-pair solutions of $2x - 3y = 6$ when $x = -3, 0, 3,$ and 6.

Solution

$$2x - 3y = 6$$
$$-3y = -2x + 6$$
$$y = \frac{2}{3}x - 2$$

• Solve $2x - 3y = 6$ for y.

Replace x in $y = \frac{2}{3}x - 2$ by $-3, 0, 3,$ and 6. For each value of x, determine the value of y.

x	$y = \frac{2}{3}x - 2$	y	(x, y)
-3	$\frac{2}{3}(-3) - 2$	-4	$(-3, -4)$
0	$\frac{2}{3}(0) - 2$	-2	$(0, -2)$
3	$\frac{2}{3}(3) - 2$	0	$(3, 0)$
6	$\frac{2}{3}(6) - 2$	2	$(6, 2)$

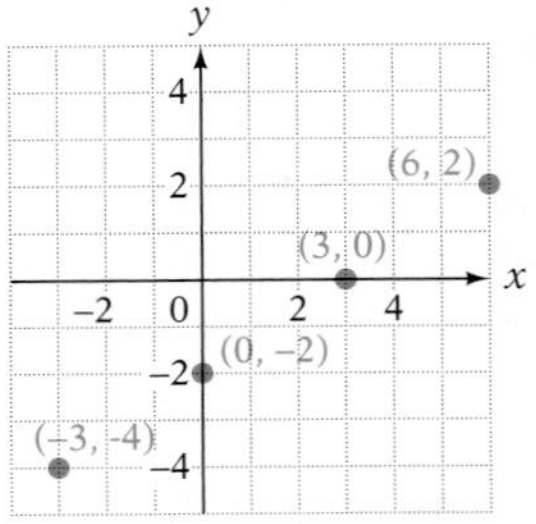

YOU TRY IT 4

Graph the ordered-pair solutions of $x + 2y = 4$ when $x = -4, -2, 0,$ and 2.

Your solution

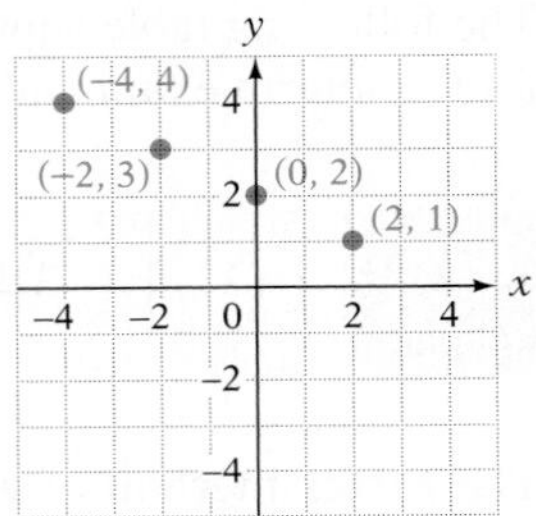

IN-CLASS EXAMPLES

2. Is $(0, -1)$ a solution of $2x - y = 1$? **Yes**
3. Is $(2, -2)$ a solution of $y = 3x + 8$? **No**
4. Graph the ordered-pair solutions of $y = -3x$ when $x = -1, 0,$ and 1.

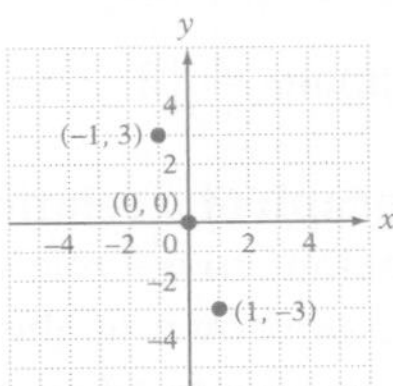

5. Graph the ordered-pair solutions of $3x - 4y = 4$ when $x = -4, 0,$ and 4.

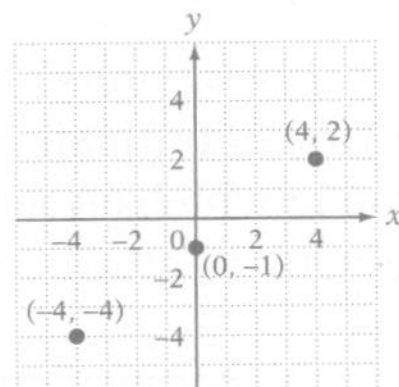

Solutions on p. S29

OBJECTIVE C *To determine whether a set of ordered pairs is a function*

© Juriah Mosin/Shutterstock.com

Exploring a relationship between two variables is an important task in the application of mathematics. Here are some examples.

- Botanists study the relationship between the number of bushels of wheat yielded per acre and the amount of watering per acre.
- Environmental scientists study the relationship between the incidence of skin cancer and the amount of ozone in the atmosphere.
- Business analysts study the relationship between the price of a product and the number of products that are sold at that price.

A **set** is a collection of objects, each of which is an **element of the set**. Each of the above relationships can be described by a set whose elements are ordered pairs.

Definition of a Relation

A **relation** is any set of ordered pairs.

The following table shows the number of hours that each of nine students spent studying for a midterm exam and the grade that each of these nine students received.

Hours	3	3.5	2.75	2	4	4.5	3	2.5	5
Grade	78	75	70	65	85	85	80	75	90

The **roster method** of writing sets encloses a list of the elements in braces. Written as a set of ordered pairs, the information in the above table is the relation

$$\{(3, 78), (3.5, 75), (2.75, 70), (2, 65), (4, 85), (4.5, 85), (3, 80), (2.5, 75), (5, 90)\}$$

where the first coordinate of the ordered pair is the hours spent studying and the second coordinate is the score on the midterm.

The **domain** of a relation is the set of first coordinates of the ordered pairs; the **range** is the set of second coordinates. For the relation above,

$$\text{Domain} = \{2, 2.5, 2.75, 3, 3.5, 4, 4.5, 5\} \qquad \text{Range} = \{65, 70, 75, 78, 80, 85, 90\}$$

The **graph of a relation** is the graph of the ordered pairs that belong to the relation. The graph of the relation given above is shown at the right. The horizontal axis represents the hours spent studying (the domain); the vertical axis represents the test score (the range). The axes are labeled H for hours studied and S for test score.

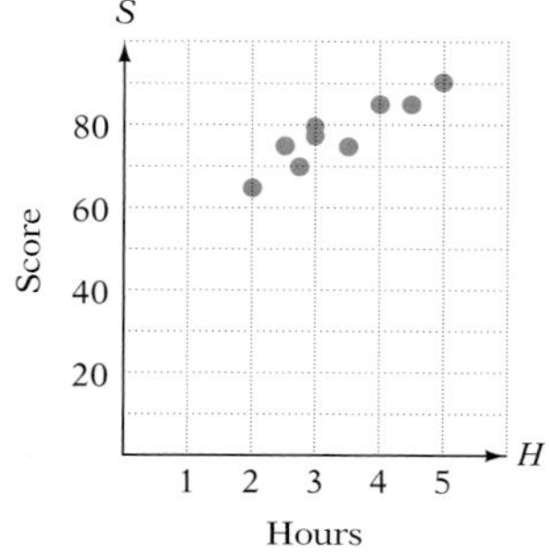

Note that two points on the graph of the relation have the same first coordinate, 3. A *function* is a special type of relation in which no two ordered pairs have the same first coordinate.

Definition of a Function

A **function** is a relation in which no two ordered pairs have the same first coordinate.

The table at the right is the grading scale for a 100-point test. This table defines a relationship between the *score* on the test and a *letter grade*. Some of the ordered pairs of this function are (78, C), (97, A), (84, B), and (82, B).

Score	*Grade*
90–100	A
80–89	B
70–79	C
60–69	D
0–59	F

The grading-scale table defines a function because no two ordered pairs can have the same first coordinate and different second coordinates. For instance, it is not possible to have the ordered pairs (72, C) and (72, B)—same first coordinate (test score) but different second coordinates (test grade). The domain of this function is $\{0, 1, 2, \ldots, 99, 100\}$. The range is $\{A, B, C, D, F\}$.

The example of hours spent studying and test score given earlier is *not* a function, because (3, 78) and (3, 80) are ordered pairs of the relation that have the *same* first coordinate but *different* second coordinates.

Consider again the grading-scale example. Note that (84, B) and (82, B) are ordered pairs of the function. Ordered pairs of a function may have the same *second* coordinates but not the same first coordinates.

Although relations and functions can be given by tables, they are frequently given by an equation in two variables.

Take Note

The symbol $\in$ is read "is an element of."

The equation $y = 2x$ expresses the relationship between a number, x, and twice the number, y. For instance, if $x = 3$, then $y = 6$, which is twice 3. To indicate exactly which ordered pairs are determined by the equation, the domain (values of x) is specified by stating that x is an element of a particular set. If $x \in \{-2, -1, 0, 1, 2\}$, then the ordered pairs determined by the equation are $\{(-2, -4), (-1, -2), (0, 0), (1, 2), (2, 4)\}$. This relation is a function because no two ordered pairs have the same first coordinate.

INSTRUCTOR NOTE

The concept of a function was beginning to form with the work of Fermat and Descartes. However, it was Euler who gave us the word and its first definition: "A function of a variable quantity is an analytic expression composed in any way whatsoever of the variable quantity and numbers or constant quantities."

The sense of function in Euler's definition is that of "y is a function of x," but it does not encompass the more general notion of a function as a particular set of ordered pairs.

The graph of the function $y = 2x$ with domain $\{-2, -1, 0, 1, 2\}$ is shown at the right. The horizontal axis (domain) is labeled x; the vertical axis (range) is labeled y.

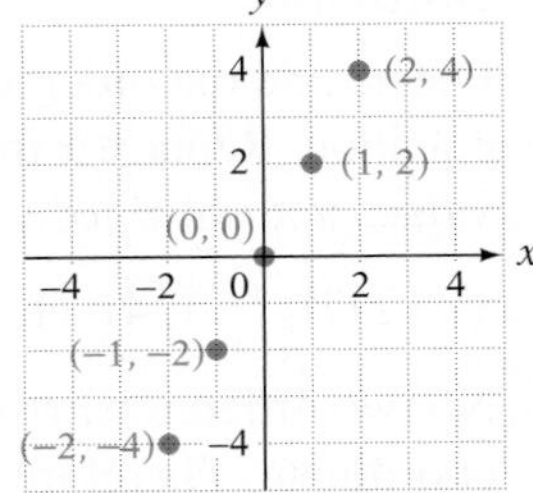

The domain $\{-2, -1, 0, 1, 2\}$ was chosen arbitrarily. Other domains could have been selected. The type of application usually influences the choice of domain.

For the equation $y = 2x$, we say that "y is a function of x" because the set of ordered pairs is a function.

Not all equations, however, define a function. For instance, the equation $|y| = x + 2$ does not define y as a function of x. The ordered pairs $(2, 4)$ and $(2, -4)$ both satisfy the equation. Thus there are two ordered pairs with the same first coordinate but different second coordinates.

EXAMPLE 5

The table below shows the amount of money invested in college savings plans and the amount invested in prepaid college tuition plans over a five-year period. (*Sources:* Investment Company Institute and College Savings Plan Network)

Year	*Assets in College Savings Plans (in billions of dollars)*	*Assets in Prepaid Tuition Plans (in billions of dollars)*
1	9	7
2	19	8
3	35	11
4	52	13
5	69	14

Write a relation in which the first coordinate is the amount of money in college savings plans and the second coordinate is the amount of money in prepaid tuition plans (both in billions of dollars). Is the relation a function?

Solution

The relation is
$\{(9, 7), (19, 8), (35, 11), (52, 13), (69, 14)\}$

There are no two ordered pairs with the same first coordinate. The relation is a function.

YOU TRY IT 5

Five students decided to go on a diet and fitness program over the summer. Their weights (in pounds) at the beginning and end of the program are given in the table below.

Beginning	*End*
145	140
140	125
150	130
165	150
140	130

Write a relation in which the first coordinate is the weight at the beginning of the summer and the second coordinate is the weight at the end of the summer. Is the relation a function?

Your solution

$\{(145, 140), (140, 125), (150, 130), (165, 150), (140, 130)\}$
No, the relation is not a function.

EXAMPLE 6

Does $y = x^2 + 3$, where $x \in \{-2, -1, 1, 3\}$, define y as a function of x?

Solution

Determine the ordered pairs defined by the equation. Replace x in $y = x^2 + 3$ by the given values and solve for y.

$\{(-2, 7), (-1, 4), (1, 4), (3, 12)\}$

No two ordered pairs have the same first coordinate. Therefore, the relation is a function and the equation $y = x^2 + 3$ defines y as a function of x.

Note that $(-1, 4)$ and $(1, 4)$ are ordered pairs that belong to this function. Ordered pairs of a function may have the same *second* coordinate but not the same *first* coordinate.

YOU TRY IT 6

Does $y = \frac{1}{2}x + 1$, where $x \in \{-4, 0, 2\}$, define y as a function of x?

Your solution

$\{(-4, -1), (0, 1), (2, 2)\}$
Yes, y is a function of x.

Zones traveled	One-way fare (dollars)
1	3.25
2	3.50
3	3.75
4	4.50
5	5.00
6	5.25

IN-CLASS EXAMPLES

6. The table above shows the one-way fares based on the number of zones traveled on a commuter-rail train. Write a relation in which the first coordinate is the number of zones traveled and the second coordinate is the one-way fare. Is the relation a function? **{(1, 3.25), (2, 3.50), (3, 3.75), (4, 4.50), (5, 5.00), (6, 5.25)}; Yes**
7. Does $|y| = 2x$ define y as a function of x? **No**

Solutions on pp. S29–S30

OBJECTIVE D *To evaluate a function*

When an equation defines y as a function of x, **function notation** is frequently used to emphasize that the relation is a function. In this case, it is common to replace y in the function's equation with the symbol $f(x)$, where

$f(x)$ is read "f of x" or "the value of f at x."

For instance, the equation $y = x^2 + 3$ from Example 6 defined y as a function of x. The equation can also be written

$$f(x) = x^2 + 3$$

where y has been replaced by $f(x)$.

The symbol $f(x)$ is called the **value of a function at x** because it is the result of evaluating a variable expression. For instance, $f(4)$ means to replace x by 4 and then simplify the resulting numerical expression.

$$f(x) = x^2 + 3$$
$$f(4) = 4^2 + 3 \quad \text{Replace } x \text{ by 4.}$$
$$= 16 + 3 = 19$$

This process is called **evaluating a function.**

INSTRUCTOR NOTE
One way to assist students with evaluating a function is to use open parentheses. For instance,
$f(\quad) = (\quad)^2 + (\quad) - 3$
$\downarrow \quad \downarrow \quad \downarrow$
$f(-2) = (-2)^2 + (-2) - 3$

HOW TO 4 Given $f(x) = x^2 + x - 3$, find $f(-2)$.

$$f(x) = x^2 + x - 3$$
$$f(-2) = (-2)^2 + (-2) - 3 \quad \bullet \text{ Replace } x \text{ by } -2.$$
$$= 4 - 2 - 3 = -1$$
$$f(-2) = -1$$

In this example, $f(-2)$ is the second coordinate of an ordered pair of the function; the first coordinate is -2. Therefore, an ordered pair of this function is $(-2, f(-2))$, or, because $f(-2) = -1$, $(-2, -1)$.

For the function given by $y = f(x) = x^2 + x - 3$, y is called the **dependent variable** because its value depends on the value of x. The **independent variable** is x.

Functions can be written using other letters or even combinations of letters. For instance, some calculators use $ABS(x)$ for the absolute value function. Thus the equation $y = |x|$ would be written $ABS(x) = |x|$, where $ABS(x)$ replaces y.

EXAMPLE 7

Given $G(t) = \dfrac{3t}{t+4}$, find $G(1)$.

Solution

$$G(t) = \frac{3t}{t+4}$$
$$G(1) = \frac{3(1)}{1+4} \quad \bullet \text{ Replace } t \text{ by 1. Then simplify.}$$
$$G(1) = \frac{3}{5}$$

YOU TRY IT 7

Given $H(x) = \dfrac{x}{x-4}$, find $H(8)$.

Your solution

2

IN-CLASS EXAMPLES

8. Given $f(x) = -5 - 2x$, find $f(-1)$. **−3**
9. Given $g(t) = t^2 - t$, find $g(4)$. **12**
10. Given $P(r) = \dfrac{2r^2}{r+1}$, find $P(-2)$. **−8**

Solution on p. S30

12.1 EXERCISES

Concept Check

SUGGESTED ASSIGNMENT
Exercises 1–14; Exercises 15–67, odds
More challenging exercises: Exercises 72–78

1. In which quadrant is the graph of $(-3, 4)$ located? Quadrant II
2. In which quadrant is the graph of $(2, -5)$ located? Quadrant IV
3. On which axis does the graph of $(0, -4)$ lie? y-axis
4. On which axis does the graph of $(-6, 0)$ lie? x-axis
5. Name any two points on a horizontal line that is 2 units above the x-axis. Answers will vary. For example, $(-3, 2)$ and $(5, 2)$
6. Name any two points on a vertical line that is 3 units to the right of the y-axis. Answers will vary. For example, $(3, -4)$ and $(3, 1)$

Complete Exercises 7 and 8 by filling in each blank with the word *left, right, up,* or *down.*

7. To graph the point $(5, -4)$, start at the origin and move 5 units __right__ and 4 units __down__.
8. To graph the point $(-1, 7)$, start at the origin and move 1 unit __left__ and 7 units __up__.
9. Write as an ordered pair the coordinates of the point whose x-coordinate is 6 and whose y-coordinate is -5. $(6, -5)$
10. Write as an ordered pair the coordinates of the point whose y-coordinate is 8 and whose x-coordinate is -7. $(-7, 8)$
11. To decide whether the ordered pair $(1, 7)$ is a solution of the equation $y = 2x + 5$, substitute 1 for __x__ and 7 for __y__ to see whether the ordered pair $(1, 7)$ makes the equation $y = 2x + 5$ a true statement.
12. The graphs of $y = \frac{1}{4}x - 6$ and $f(x) =$ __$\frac{1}{4}x - 6$__ are identical.
13. A relation is a set of __ordered pairs__. The set of first coordinates of the ordered pairs is called the __domain__ of the relation. The set of second coordinates is called the __range__ of the relation.
14. The symbol $f(x)$ is read "f __of__ x" or "the value of f __at__ x." It is a symbol for the number that the function f pairs with __x__.

OBJECTIVE A *To graph points in a rectangular coordinate system*

15. Graph $(-2, 1)$, $(3, -5)$, $(-2, 4)$, and $(0, 3)$.

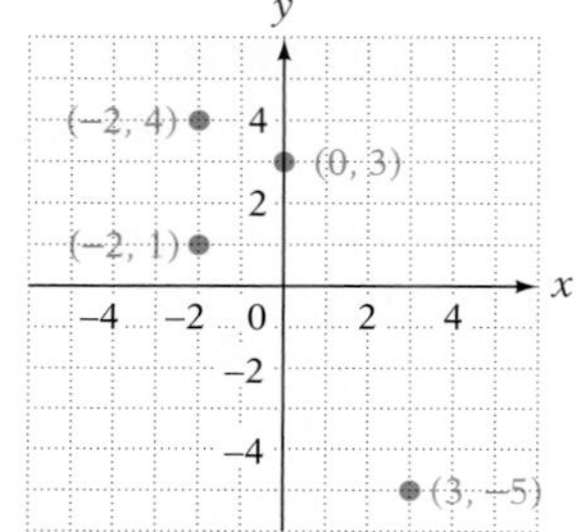

16. Graph $(5, -1)$, $(-3, -3)$, $(-1, 0)$, and $(1, -1)$.

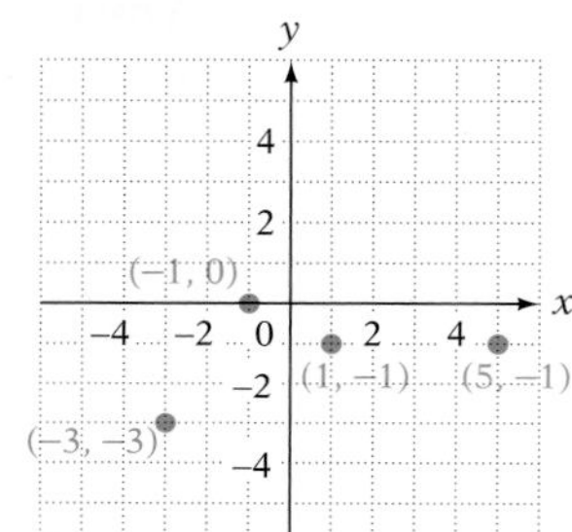

17. Graph $(0, 0)$, $(0, -5)$, $(-3, 0)$, and $(0, 2)$.

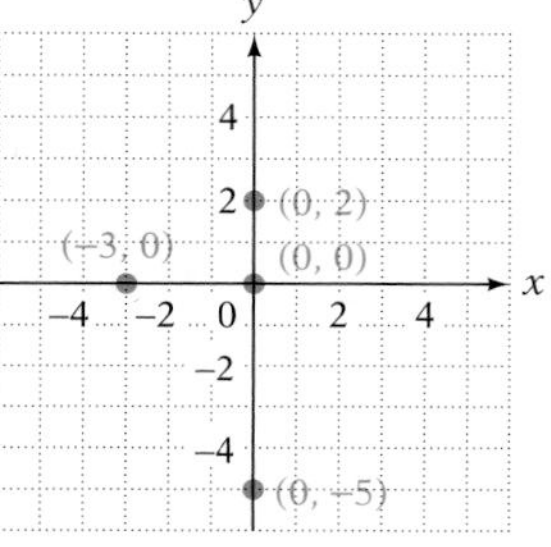

18. Graph $(-4, 5)$, $(-3, 1)$, $(3, -4)$, and $(5, 0)$.

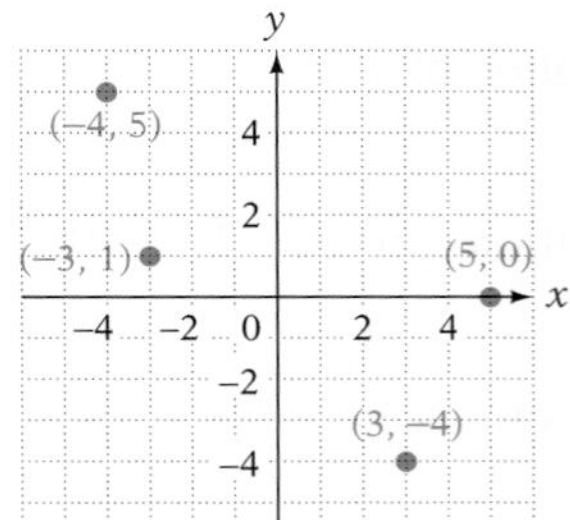

19. Graph $(-1, 4)$, $(-2, -3)$, $(0, 2)$, and $(4, 0)$.

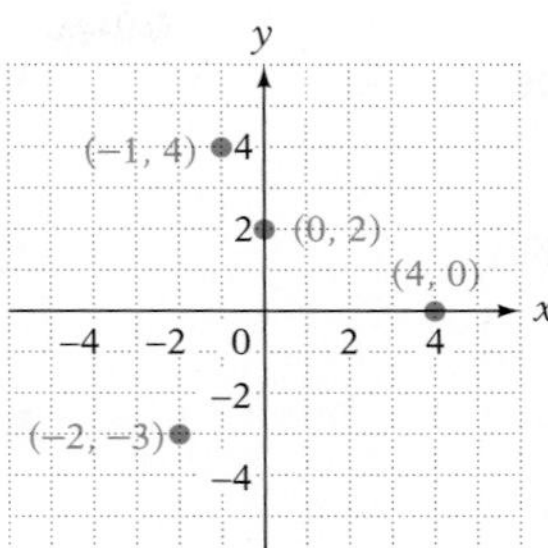

20. Graph $(5, 2)$, $(-4, -1)$, $(0, 0)$, and $(0, 3)$.

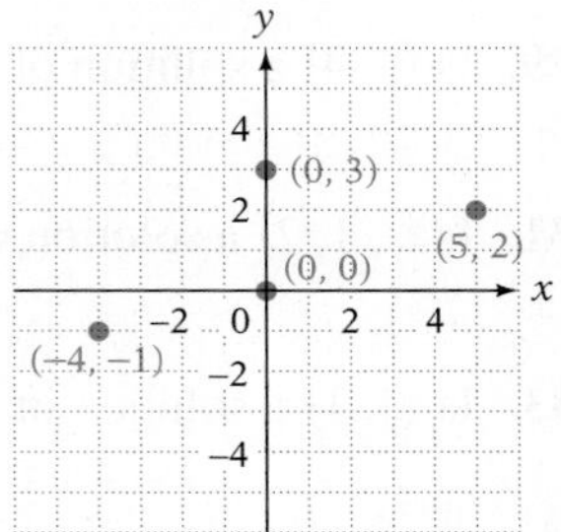

21. Find the coordinates of each of the points.

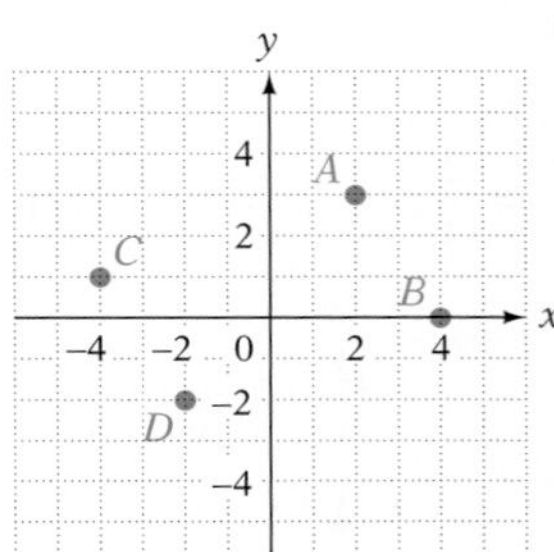

$A(2, 3)$, $B(4, 0)$, $C(-4, 1)$, $D(-2, -2)$

22. Find the coordinates of each of the points.

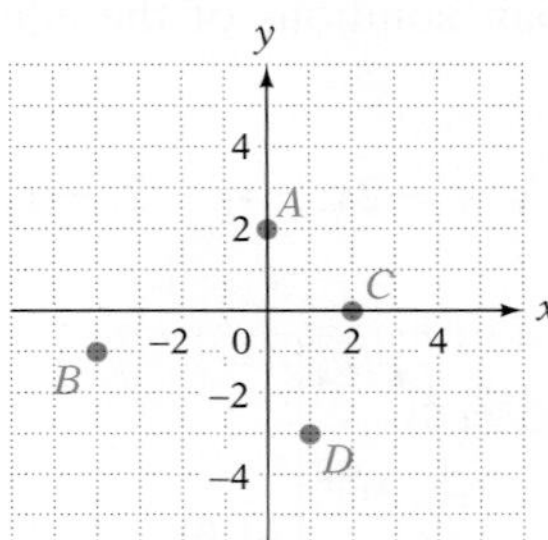

$A(0, 2)$, $B(-4, -1)$, $C(2, 0)$, $D(1, -3)$

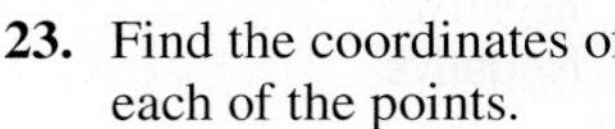

23. Find the coordinates of each of the points.

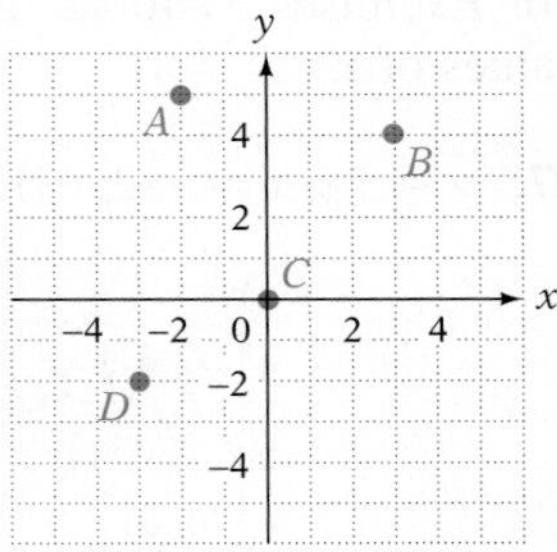

$A(-2, 5)$, $B(3, 4)$, $C(0, 0)$, $D(-3, -2)$

24. Find the coordinates of each of the points.

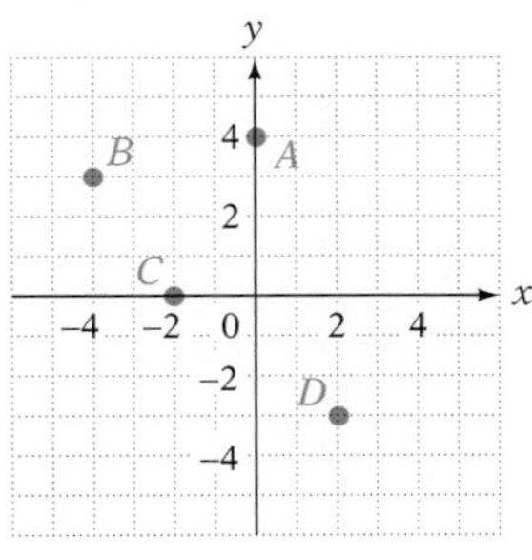

$A(0, 4)$, $B(-4, 3)$, $C(-2, 0)$, $D(2, -3)$

25. **a.** Name the abscissas of points A and C.
b. Name the ordinates of points B and D.

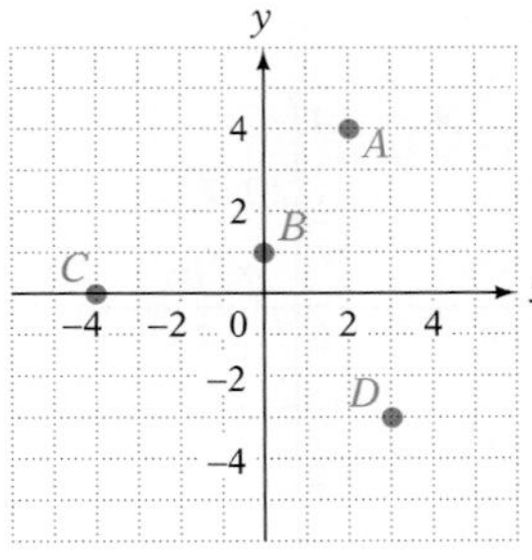

a. 2, −4 **b.** 1, −3

26. **a.** Name the abscissas of points A and C.
b. Name the ordinates of points B and D.

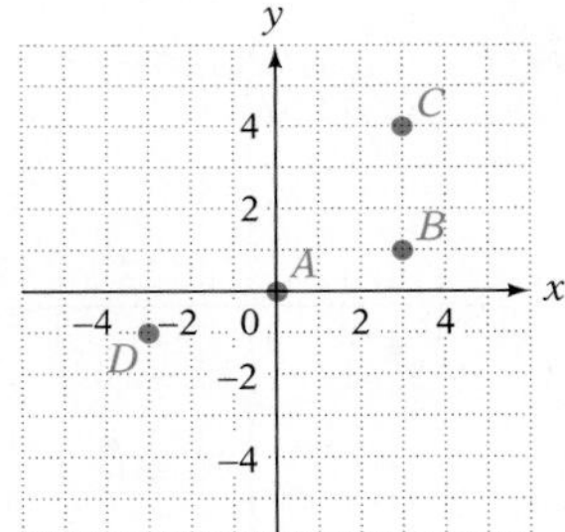

a. 0, 3 **b.** 1, −1

27. Let a and b be positive numbers such that $a < b$. In which quadrant is each point located?

a. (a, b) I **b.** $(-a, b)$ II **c.** $(b - a, -b)$ IV **d.** $(a - b, -b - a)$ III

28. Let a and b be positive numbers. State whether the two given points lie on the x-axis, the y-axis, a horizontal line other than the x-axis, or a vertical line other than the y-axis.

a. $(-a, b)$ and $(-a, 0)$ Vertical line other than y-axis **b.** $(a, 0)$ and $(-b, 0)$ x-axis

OBJECTIVE B *To determine ordered-pair solutions of an equation in two variables*

29. Is (3, 4) a solution of $y = -x + 7$? Yes

30. Is $(2, -3)$ a solution of $y = x + 5$? No

31. Is $(-1, 2)$ a solution of $y = \frac{1}{2}x - 1$? No

32. Is $(1, -3)$ a solution of $y = -2x - 1$? Yes

33. Is (4, 1) a solution of $2x - 5y = 4$? No

34. Is $(-5, 3)$ a solution of $3x - 2y = 9$? No

35. Suppose (x, y) is a solution of the equation $y = -3x + 6$, where $x > 2$. Is y positive or negative?
Negative

36. Suppose (x, y) is a solution of the equation $y = 4x - 8$, where $y > 0$. Is x less than or greater than 2?
Greater than

For Exercises 37 to 42, graph the ordered-pair solutions of the equation for the given values of x.

37. $y = 2x; x = -2, -1, 0, 2$

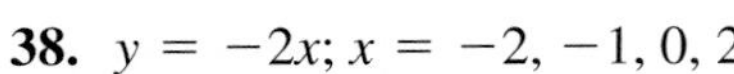
38. $y = -2x; x = -2, -1, 0, 2$

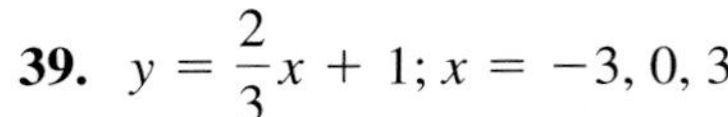
39. $y = \frac{2}{3}x + 1; x = -3, 0, 3$

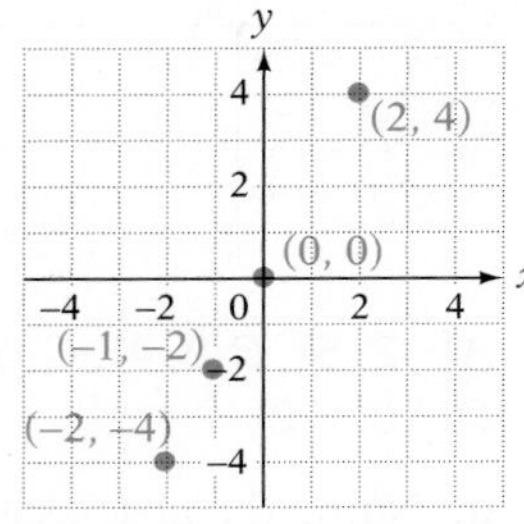

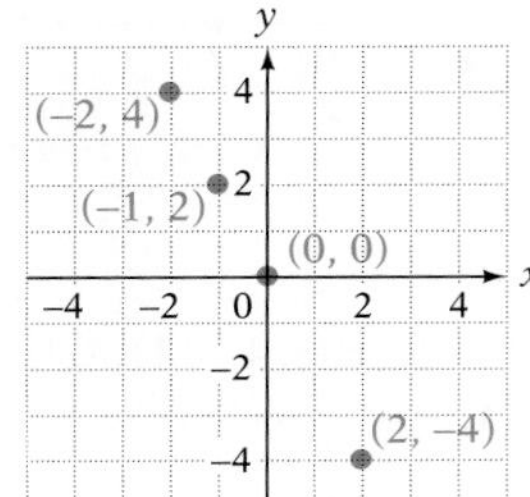

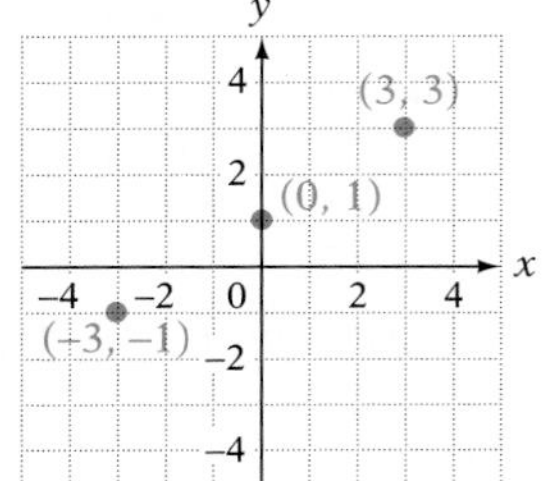

40. $y = -\frac{1}{3}x - 2; x = -3, 0, 3$

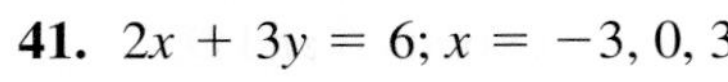
41. $2x + 3y = 6; x = -3, 0, 3$

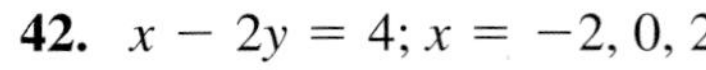
42. $x - 2y = 4; x = -2, 0, 2$

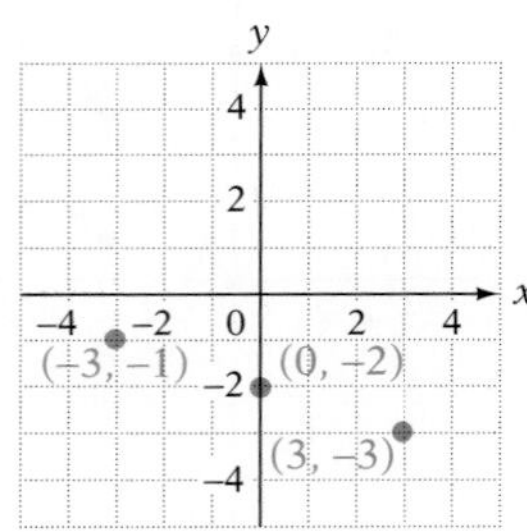

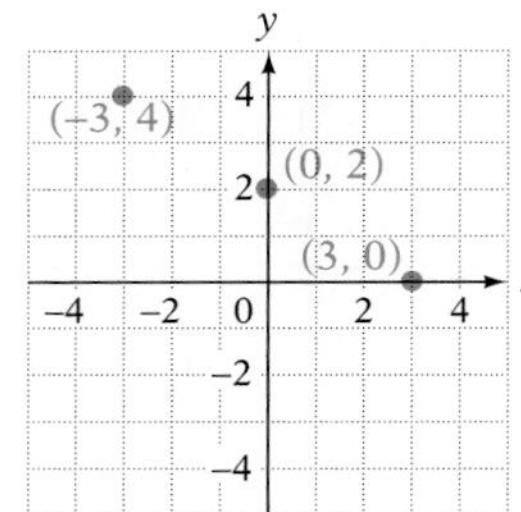

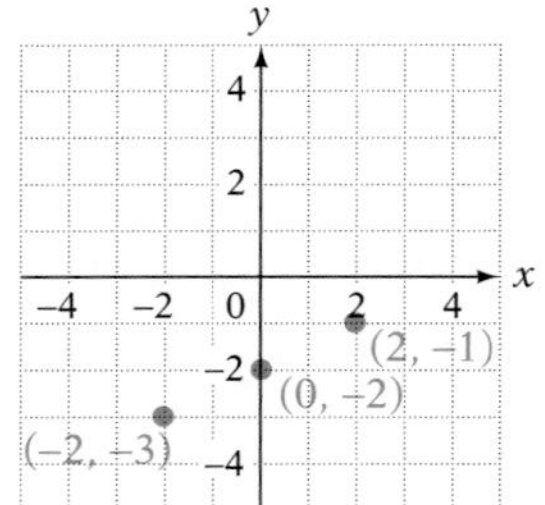

OBJECTIVE C *To determine whether a set of ordered pairs is a function*

For Exercises 43 and 44, use the following sets. Set A is the set of all dates of the year ({January 1, January 2, January 3, . . .}). Set B is the set of all the people in the world.

43. A relation has domain A and range B. Each ordered pair in the relation is of the form (date, person born on that date). Is this relation a function? No

44. A relation has domain B and range A. Each ordered pair in the relation is of the form (person, birth date of that person). Is this relation a function? Yes

45. **Marathons** See the news clipping at the right. The table below shows the ages and finishing times of the top eight finishers in the Manhattan Island Swim. Write a relation in which the first coordinate is the age of a swimmer and the second coordinate is the swimmer's finishing time. Is the relation a function?

Ages (in years)	35	45	38	24	47	51	35	48
Time (in hours)	7.50	7.58	7.63	7.78	7.80	7.86	7.89	7.92

{(35, 7.50), (45, 7.58), (38, 7.63), (24, 7.78), (47, 7.80), (51, 7.86), (35, 7.89), (48, 7.92)}; no

In the NEWS!

Swimmers Go the Distance

Twenty-three swimmers completed NYC Swim's annual Manhattan Island Swim. Swimmers begin at Battery Park City–South Cove and swim a 28.5-mile course around Manhattan Island. The 35-year-old first-place finisher swam the distance in 7 h, 30 min, and 15 s.

Source: www.nycswim.org

46. **Jogging** The table below shows the number of Calories a 150-pound person burns in 1 h while running at various speeds, in miles per hour. Write a relation in which the first coordinate is the speed of the runner and the second coordinate is the number of Calories burned. Is the relation a function?
{(4, 411), (5, 514), (6, 618), (7, 720), (8, 823)}; yes

Speed (in mph)	Calories
4	411
5	514
6	618
7	720
8	823

47. **Health** The table at the right shows the U.S. Department of Agriculture's recommended limits on saturated fat intake, in grams. Write a relation in which the first coordinate is a person's daily Calorie intake and the second coordinate is the recommended limit on saturated fat intake. Is the relation a function?
{(1600, 18), (2000, 20), (2200, 24), (2500, 25), (2800, 31)}; yes

Daily Calories	Saturated Fat (in grams)
1600	18
2000	20
2200	24
2500	25
2800	31

48. **Health** The table at the right shows the birth rates, in births per thousand people per year, and life expectancies, in years, for various countries. (*Source:* www.cia.gov) Write a relation in which the first coordinate is the birth rate and the second coordinate is the life expectancy. Is the relation a function?
{(10.48, 78.6), (16.8, 71.7), (14.14, 79.0), (21.0, 75.2), (10.36, 80.4), (14.14, 77.7)}; no

Country	Birth Rate	Life Expectancy
Belgium	10.48	78.6
Brazil	16.8	71.7
Martinique	14.14	79.0
Mexico	21.0	75.2
Sweden	10.36	80.4
United States	14.14	77.7

For Exercises 49 to 52, find the domain and range of the relation. State whether or not the relation is a function.

49. $\{(0, 0), (2, 0), (4, 0), (6, 0)\}$
D: {0, 2, 4, 6}; R: {0}; yes

50. $\{(-2, 2), (0, 2), (1, 2), (2, 2)\}$
D: {−2, 0, 1, 2}; R: {2}; yes

51. $\{(2, 2), (2, 4), (2, 6), (2, 8)\}$
D: {2}; R: {2, 4, 6, 8}; no

52. $\{(-4, 4), (-2, 2), (0, 0), (-2, -2)\}$
D: {−4, −2, 0}; R: {−2, 0, 2, 4}; no

53. Does $y = 2x + 3$, where $x \in \{-2, -1, 1, 4\}$, define y as a function of x? Yes

54. Does $|y| = x - 1$, where $x \in \{1, 2, 3, 4\}$, define y as a function of x? No

55. Does $y = x^2$, where $x \in \{-2, -1, 0, 1, 2\}$, define y as a function of x? Yes

OBJECTIVE D To evaluate a function

56. Given $f(x) = 3x - 4$, find $f(4)$.

8

57. Given $f(x) = 5x + 1$, find $f(2)$.

11

58. Given $f(x) = x^2$, find $f(3)$.

9

59. Given $f(x) = x^2 - 1$, find $f(1)$.

0

60. Given $G(x) = x^2 + x$, find $G(-2)$.

2

61. Given $H(x) = x^2 - x$, find $H(-2)$.

6

62. Given $s(t) = \frac{3}{t - 1}$, find $s(-2)$.

−1

63. Given $P(x) = \frac{4}{2x + 1}$, find $P(-2)$.

$-\frac{4}{3}$

64. Given $h(x) = 3x^2 - 2x + 1$, find $h(3)$.

22

65. Given $Q(r) = 4r^2 - r - 3$, find $Q(2)$.

11

66. Given $f(x) = \frac{x}{x + 5}$, find $f(-3)$.

$-\frac{3}{2}$

67. Given $v(t) = \frac{2t}{2t + 1}$, find $v(3)$.

$\frac{6}{7}$

For Exercises 68 to 71, use the function $f(x) = x^2 - 4$. For the given condition on a, determine whether $f(a)$ *must be positive, must be negative,* or *could be either positive or negative.*

68. $a > 2$ Positive

69. $a < 0$ Either

70. $a > -2$ Either

71. $a < -2$ Positive

Critical Thinking

For Exercises 72 to 74, find the distance from the given point to the horizontal axis.

72. $(-5, 1)$ 1 unit

73. $(3, -4)$ 4 units

74. $(-6, 0)$ 0 units

For Exercises 75 to 77, find the distance from the given point to the vertical axis.

75. $(-2, 4)$ 2 units

76. $(1, -3)$ 1 unit

77. $(5, 0)$ 5 units

78. Name the coordinates of a point plotted at the origin of the rectangular coordinate system. (0, 0)

79. Write a paragraph explaining how to plot points in a rectangular coordinate system.

Projects or Group Activities

80. Functions are a part of our everyday lives. For example, the cost to mail a package via first-class mail is a function of the weight of the package. The tuition paid by a part-time student is a function of the number of credit hours the student registers for. Provide other examples of functions.

81. Define three situations that describe relations that are not functions. One example is the set of ordered pairs in which the first coordinates are the runs scored by a baseball team and the second coordinates are either W for a win or L for a loss.

82. There is an imaginary coordinate system on Earth that consists of *longitude* and *latitude.* Write a report on how location is determined on the surface of Earth.

QUICK QUIZ

1. Graph the ordered pairs $(5, -1)$, $(-4, -2)$, $(1, 0)$, and $(3, 4)$. **[12.1A]**
2. Is $(-3, 0)$ a solution of $y = 6x - 18$? **No [12.1B]**
3. Graph the ordered-pair solutions of $y = -\frac{2}{3}x - 2$ when $x = -3$, 0, and 3. **[12.1B]**
4. Find the domain and range of the relation {(0, 0), (1, 1), (2, 2)}. Is the relation a function? **D: {0, 1, 2}; R: {0, 1, 2}; yes [12.1C]**
5. Given $f(x) = -2x + 5$, find $f(-2)$. **9 [12.1D]**

SECTION

12.2 Linear Equations in Two Variables

OBJECTIVE A *To graph an equation of the form y = mx + b*

The **graph of an equation in two variables** is a graph of the ordered-pair solutions of the equation.

Consider $y = 2x + 1$. Choosing $x = -2, -1, 0, 1,$ and 2 and determining the corresponding values of y produces some of the ordered pairs of the equation. These are recorded in the table at the right. See the graph of the ordered pairs in Figure 1.

x	$y = 2x + 1$	y	(x, y)
-2	$2(-2) + 1$	-3	$(-2, -3)$
-1	$2(-1) + 1$	-1	$(-1, -1)$
0	$2(0) + 1$	1	$(0, 1)$
1	$2(1) + 1$	3	$(1, 3)$
2	$2(2) + 1$	5	$(2, 5)$

Choosing values of x that are not integers produces more ordered pairs to graph, such as $\left(-\frac{5}{2}, -4\right)$ and $\left(\frac{3}{2}, 4\right)$, as shown in Figure 2. Choosing still other values of x would result in more and more ordered pairs being graphed. The result would be so many dots that the graph would appear as the straight line shown in Figure 3, which is the graph of $y = 2x + 1$.

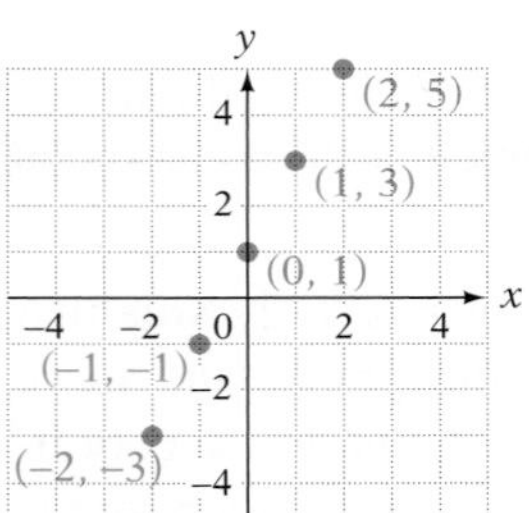

Figure 1

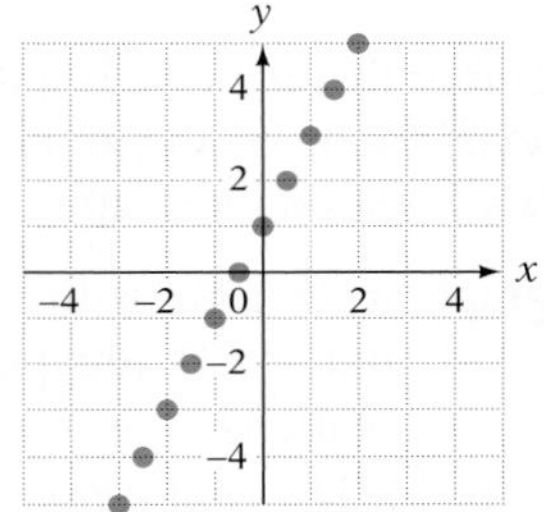

Figure 2

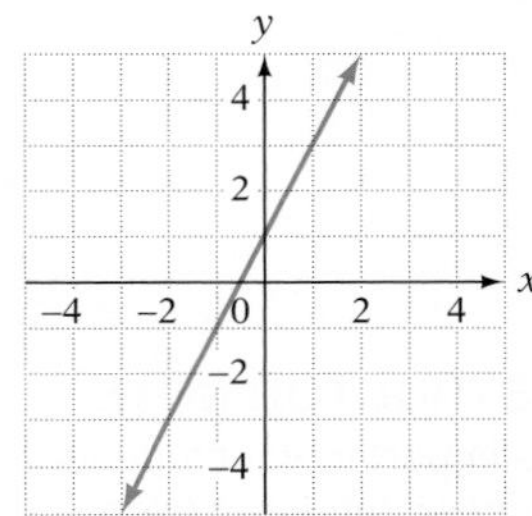

Figure 3

Equations in two variables have characteristic graphs. The equation $y = 2x + 1$ is an example of a *linear equation,* or *linear function,* because its graph is a straight line. It is also called a *first-degree equation* in two variables because the exponent on each variable is 1.

INSTRUCTOR NOTE
It is important for students to associate "the graph is a straight line" with "$y = mx + b$."

Linear Equation in Two Variables

Any equation of the form $y = mx + b$, where m is the coefficient of x and b is a constant, is a **linear equation in two variables,** or a **first-degree equation in two variables,** or a **linear function.** The graph of a linear equation in two variables is a straight line.

EXAMPLES OF LINEAR EQUATIONS IN TWO VARIABLES

1. $y = 2x + 1$ $(m = 2, b = 1)$ **2.** $y = x - 4$ $(m = 1, b = -4)$

3. $y = -\frac{3}{4}x$ $\left(m = -\frac{3}{4}, b = 0\right)$ **4.** $y = 3 - 2x$ $(m = -2, b = 3)$

The equation $y = x^2 + 4x + 3$ is not a linear equation in two variables because it has a term with a variable squared. The equation $y = \frac{3}{x - 4}$ is not a linear equation in two variables because there is a variable in the denominator.

Integrating Technology

The Projects and Group Activities feature at the end of Section 12.3 contains information on using a calculator to graph an equation.

To graph a linear equation, choose some values of x and then find the corresponding values of y. Because a straight line is determined by two points, it is sufficient to find only two ordered-pair solutions. However, it is recommended that at least three ordered-pair solutions be found to ensure accuracy.

HOW TO 1 Graph $y = -\frac{3}{2}x + 2$.

This is a linear equation with $m = -\frac{3}{2}$ and $b = 2$. Find at least three solutions. Because m is a fraction, choose values of x that will simplify the calculations. We have chosen -2, 0, and 4 for x. (Any values of x could have been selected.)

x	$y = -\frac{3}{2}x + 2$	y	(x, y)
-2	$-\frac{3}{2}(-2) + 2$	5	$(-2, 5)$
0	$-\frac{3}{2}(0) + 2$	2	$(0, 2)$
4	$-\frac{3}{2}(4) + 2$	-4	$(4, -4)$

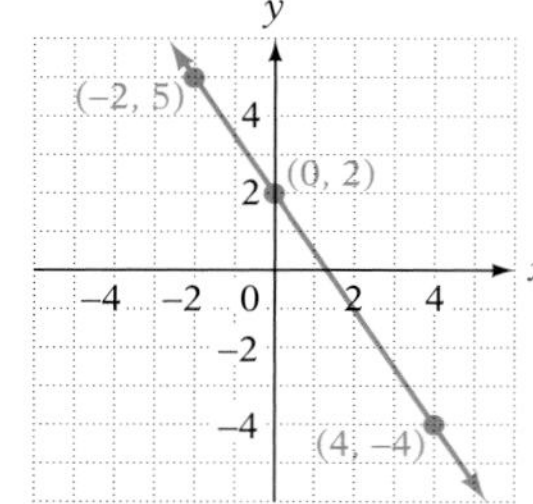

The graph of $y = -\frac{3}{2}x + 2$ is shown at the right.

Remember that a graph is a drawing of the ordered-pair solutions of an equation. Therefore, every point on the graph is a solution of the equation, and every solution of the equation is a point on the graph.

INSTRUCTOR NOTE

It is important for students to understand that each point on the graph is a solution of the equation, and each solution of the equation is a point on the graph.

The graph at the right is the graph of $y = x + 2$. Note that $(-4, -2)$ and $(1, 3)$ are points on the graph, and these points are solutions of $y = x + 2$. The point whose coordinates are $(4, 1)$ is not a point on the graph and therefore is not a solution of the equation.

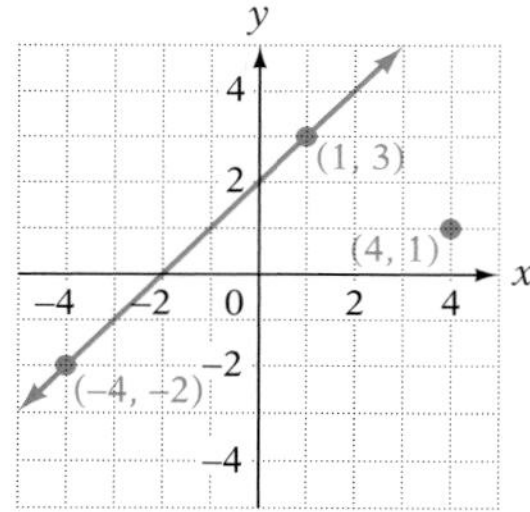

EXAMPLE 1

Graph $y = 3x - 2$.

Solution

x	y
0	-2
-1	-5
2	4

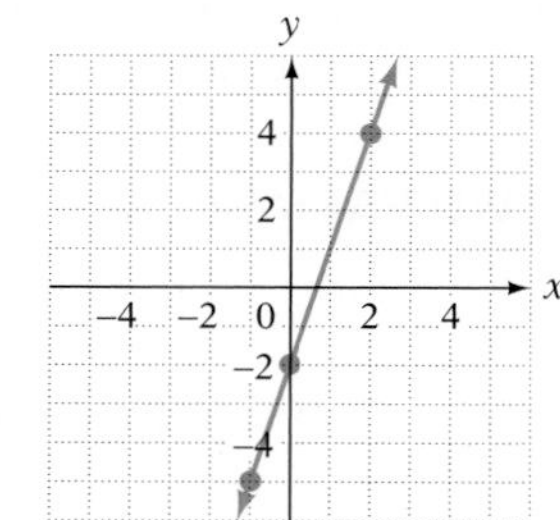

YOU TRY IT 1

Graph $y = 3x + 1$.

Your solution

IN-CLASS EXAMPLES

Graph.

1. $y = x - 2$
2. $y = -3x + 1$
3. $y = -\frac{4}{3}x$

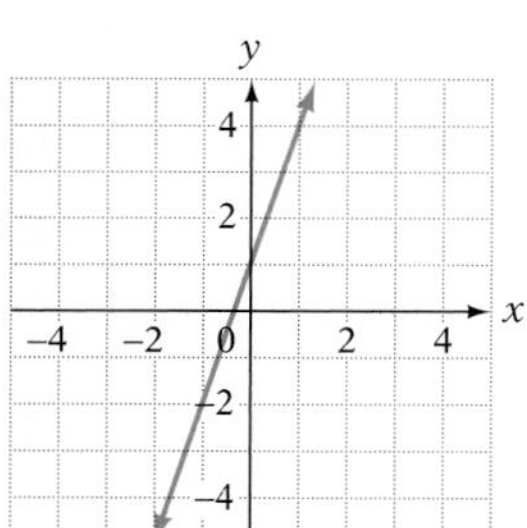

Solution on p. S30

EXAMPLE 2

Graph $y = 2x$.

Solution

x	y
0	0
2	4
−2	−4

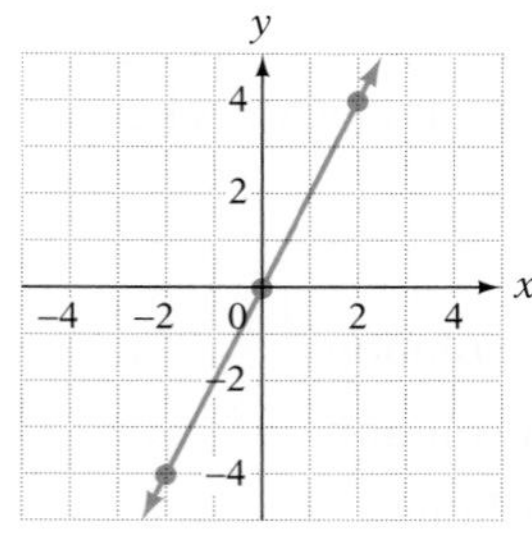

YOU TRY IT 2

Graph $y = -2x$.

Your solution

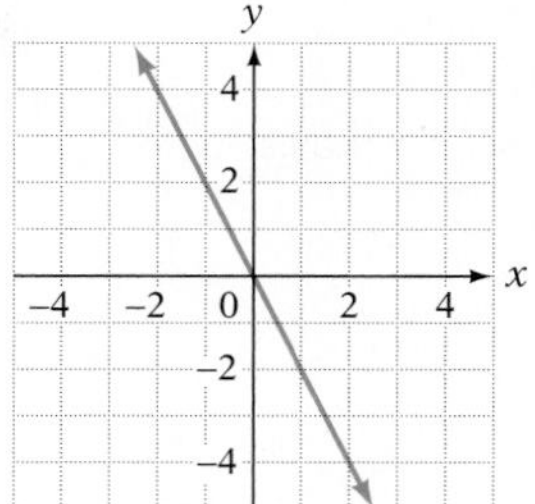

EXAMPLE 3

Graph $y = \frac{1}{2}x - 1$.

Solution

x	y
0	−1
2	0
−2	−2

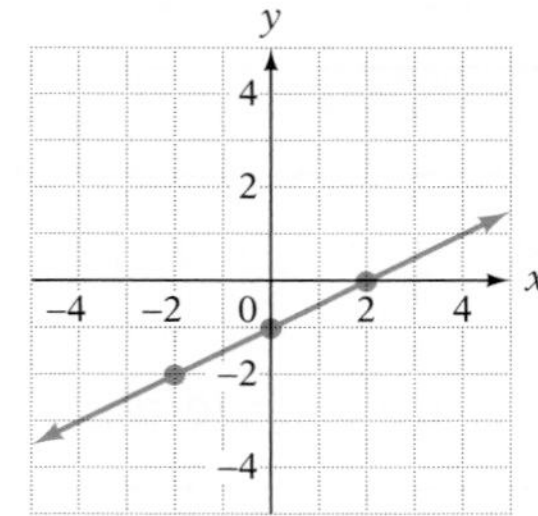

YOU TRY IT 3

Graph $y = \frac{1}{3}x - 3$.

Your solution

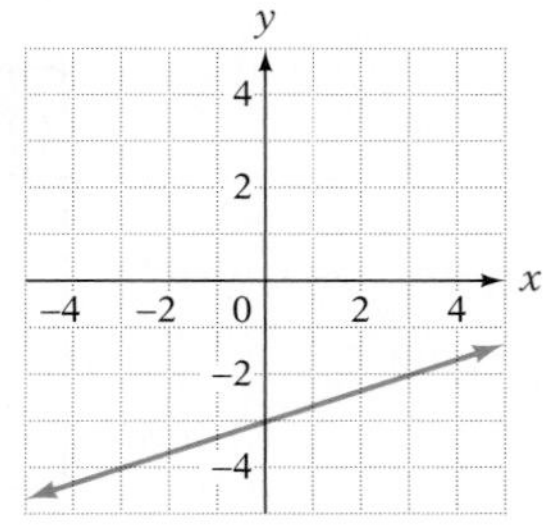

Solutions on p. S30

OBJECTIVE B *To graph an equation of the form $Ax + By = C$*

INSTRUCTOR NOTE

In the next section, students will graph $Ax + By = C$ by using x- and y-intercepts. The goal of this objective is for students to learn to solve $Ax + By = C$ for y. Solving an equation for y is a skill that is used in a variety of situations. For instance, most graphing utilities require the form $y = mx + b$ when the equation of a line is to be graphed.

The equation $Ax + By = C$, where A and B are coefficients and C is a constant, is called the **standard form of a linear equation in two variables.** Examples are shown at the right.

$2x + 3y = 6$ $\quad (A = 2, B = 3, C = 6)$

$x - 2y = -4$ $\quad (A = 1, B = -2, C = -4)$

$2x + y = 0$ $\quad (A = 2, B = 1, C = 0)$

$4x - 5y = 2$ $\quad (A = 4, B = -5, C = 2)$

To graph an equation of the form $Ax + By = C$, first solve the equation for y. Then follow the same procedure used for graphing $y = mx + b$.

HOW TO 2 Graph $3x + 4y = 12$.

$$3x + 4y = 12$$
• Solve for y.

$$4y = -3x + 12$$
• Subtract $3x$ from each side of the equation.

$$y = -\frac{3}{4}x + 3$$
• Divide each side of the equation by 4.

• Find three ordered-pair solutions of the equation.

x	y
0	3
4	0
−4	6

• Graph the ordered pairs and then draw a line through the points.

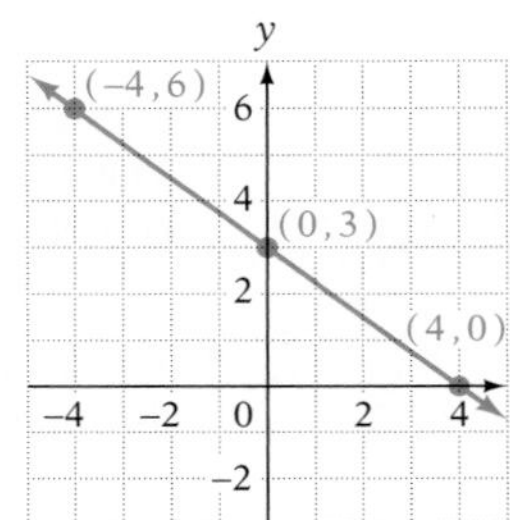

Tips for Success

Remember that a HOW TO example indicates a worked-out example. Using paper and pencil, work through the example. See *AIM for Success* at the front of the book.

The graph of a linear equation with one of the variables missing is either a horizontal or a vertical line.

The equation $y = 2$ could be written $0 \cdot x + y = 2$. Because $0 \cdot x = 0$ for any value of x, the value of y is always 2 no matter what value of x is chosen. For instance, replace x by $-4, -1, 0$, and 3. In each case, $y = 2$.

$0x + y = 2$

$0(-4) + y = 2$ $(-4, 2)$ is a solution.

$0(-1) + y = 2$ $(-1, 2)$ is a solution.

$0(0) + y = 2$ $(0, 2)$ is a solution.

$0(3) + y = 2$ $(3, 2)$ is a solution.

The solutions are plotted in the graph at the right, and a line is drawn through the plotted points. Note that the line is horizontal.

Graph of a Horizontal Line

The graph of $y = b$ is a horizontal line passing through $(0, b)$.

EXAMPLE

The graph of $y = 3$ is a horizontal line passing through $(0, 3)$.

The equation $x = -2$ could be written $x + 0 \cdot y = -2$. Because $0 \cdot y = 0$ for any value of y, the value of x is always -2 no matter what value of y is chosen. For instance, replace y by $-2, 0, 2$, and 3. In each case, $x = -2$.

$x + 0y = -2$

$x + 0(-2) = -2$ $(-2, -2)$ is a solution.

$x + 0(0) = -2$ $(-2, 0)$ is a solution.

$x + 0(2) = -2$ $(-2, 2)$ is a solution.

$x + 0(3) = -2$ $(-2, 3)$ is a solution.

The solutions are plotted in the graph at the right, and a line is drawn through the plotted points. Note that the line is vertical.

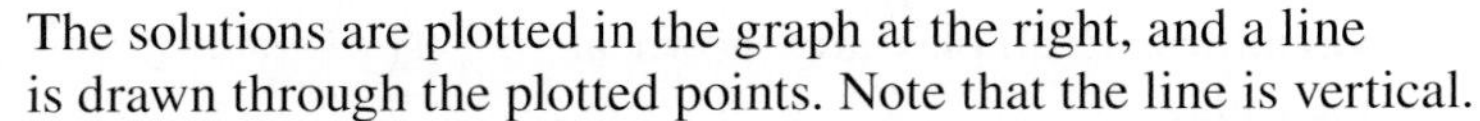

Graph of a Vertical Line

The graph of $x = a$ is a vertical line passing through $(a, 0)$.

EXAMPLE

The graph of $x = 2$ is a vertical line passing through $(2, 0)$.

HOW TO 3 Graph $x = -3$ and $y = 1$ on the same coordinate grid.

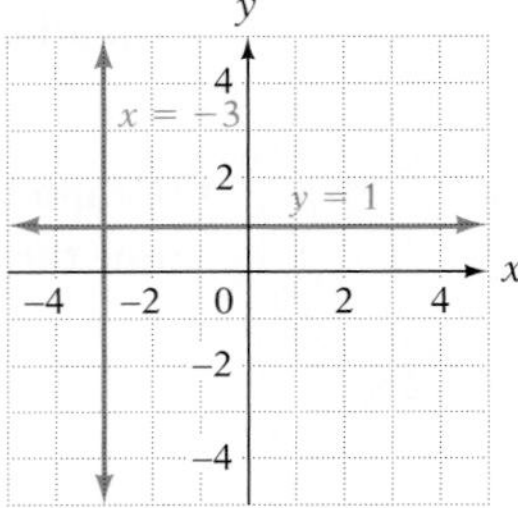

- **The graph of $x = -3$ is a vertical line passing through $(-3, 0)$.**
- **The graph of $y = 1$ is a horizontal line passing through $(0, 1)$.**

EXAMPLE 4

Graph $2x - 5y = 10$.

Solution Solve $2x - 5y = 10$ for y.

$$2x - 5y = 10$$
$$-5y = -2x + 10$$
$$y = \frac{2}{5}x - 2$$

x	y
0	−2
5	0
−5	−4

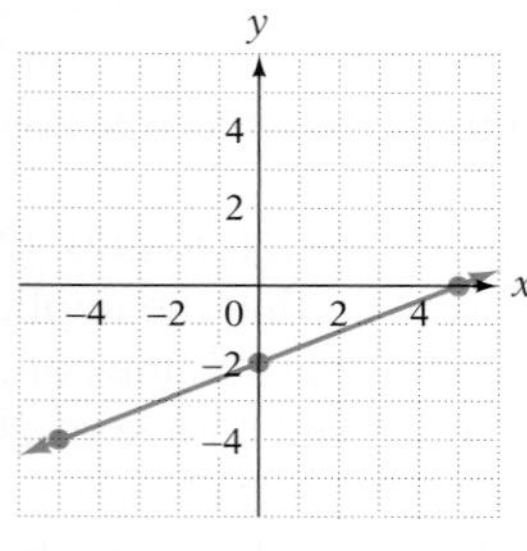

YOU TRY IT 4

Graph $5x - 2y = 10$.

Your solution

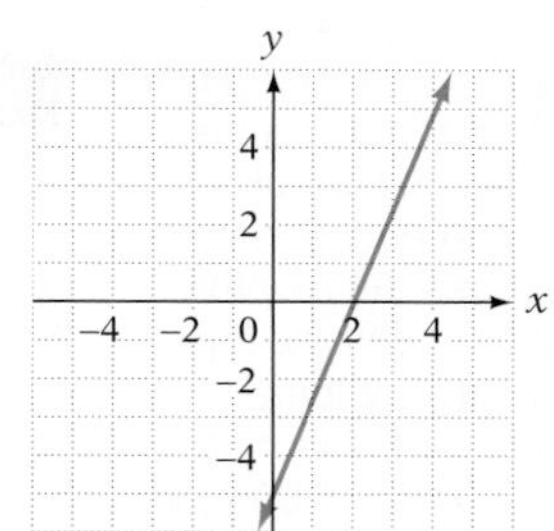

EXAMPLE 5

Graph $x + 2y = 6$.

Solution Solve $x + 2y = 6$ for y.

$$x + 2y = 6$$
$$2y = -x + 6$$
$$y = -\frac{1}{2}x + 3$$

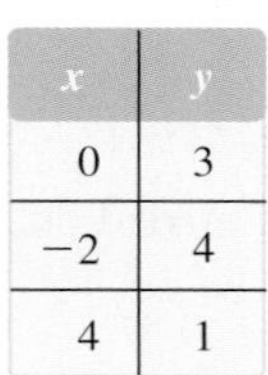

x	y
0	3
−2	4
4	1

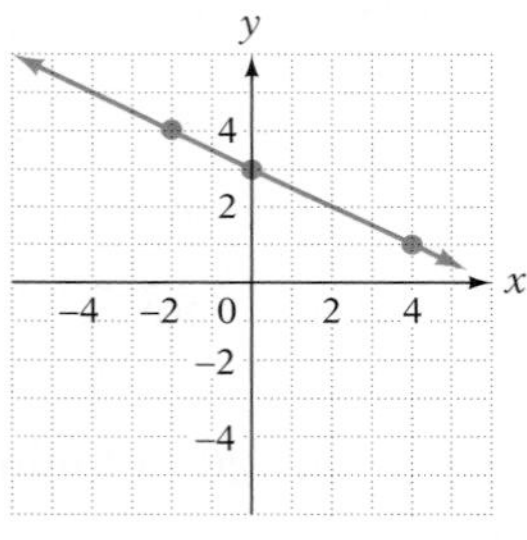

YOU TRY IT 5

Graph $x - 3y = 9$.

Your solution

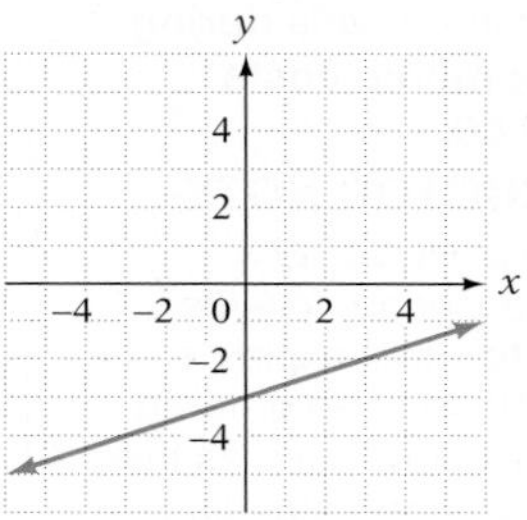

EXAMPLE 6

Graph $y = -2$.

Solution

The graph of an equation of the form $y = b$ is a horizontal line passing through the point $(0, b)$.

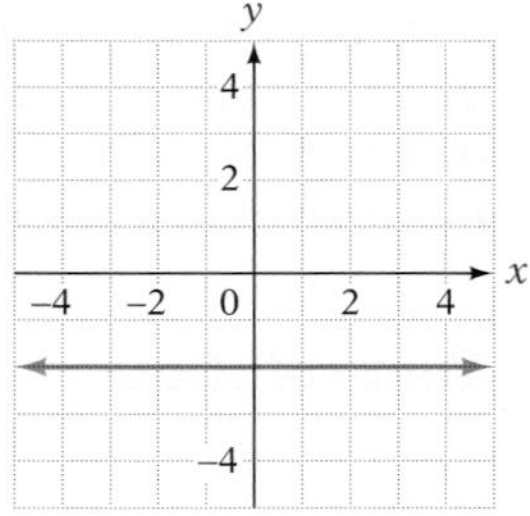

YOU TRY IT 6

Graph $y = 3$.

Your solution

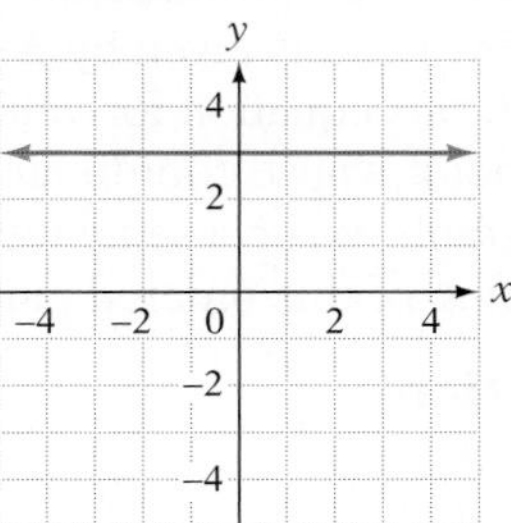

EXAMPLE 7

Graph $x = 3$.

Solution

The graph of an equation of the form $x = a$ is a vertical line passing through the point $(a, 0)$.

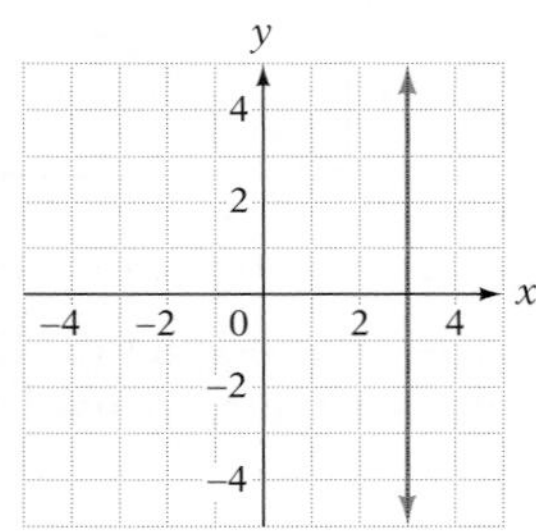

YOU TRY IT 7

Graph $x = -4$.

Your solution

IN-CLASS EXAMPLES

Graph.

4. $-2x + y = 1$
5. $x - 4y = 8$
6. $y = -3$
7. $x = 1$

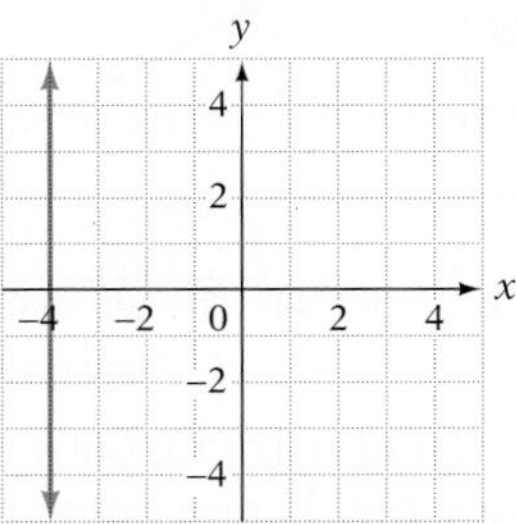

Solutions on p. S30

OBJECTIVE C *To solve application problems*

IN-CLASS EXAMPLES

8. A long-distance telephone service costs \$5.00 per month plus \$.10 per minute of use. The equation that describes the monthly cost C, in dollars, for m minutes of long-distance calls is $C = 0.10m + 5.00$. Graph this equation for values of m from 0 to 300. The point whose coordinates are (120, 17.00) is on the graph. Write a sentence that describes the meaning of this ordered pair. **120 min of long-distance calls during one month costs \$17.00.**

INSTRUCTOR NOTE

Part (b) of HOW TO 4 asks the student to write a sentence that explains the meaning of an ordered pair. Questions such as this require an understanding of the ordered pair in the context of the application.

There are a variety of applications of linear functions.

HOW TO 4 The temperature of a cup of water that has been placed in a microwave oven to be heated can be approximated by the equation $T = 0.7s + 65$, where T is the temperature (in degrees Fahrenheit) of the water s seconds after the microwave oven is turned on.

a. Graph this equation for values of s from 0 to 200. (*Note:* In many applications, the domain of the variable is given so that the application makes sense. For instance, it would not be sensible to have values of s that are less than 0. This would correspond to negative time. The choice of 200 is somewhat arbitrary and was chosen so that the water would not boil over.)

b. The point whose coordinates are (120, 149) is on the graph of this equation. Write a sentence that describes the meaning of this ordered pair.

Solution

a.

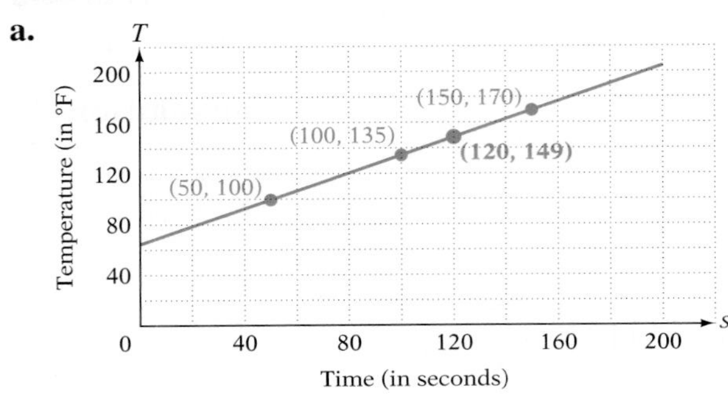

• **By choosing $s = 50$, 100, and 150, you can find the corresponding ordered pairs (50, 100), (100, 135), and (150, 170). Plot these points and draw a line through the points.**

b. The ordered pair (120, 149) means that 120 s (2 min) after the oven is turned on, the water temperature is 149°F.

EXAMPLE 8

The number of kilobytes K of an MP3 file that remain to be downloaded t seconds after starting the download is given by $K = 935 - 5.5t$. Graph this equation for values of t from 0 to 170. The point whose coordinates are (50, 660) is on this graph. Write a sentence that describes the meaning of this ordered pair.

Solution

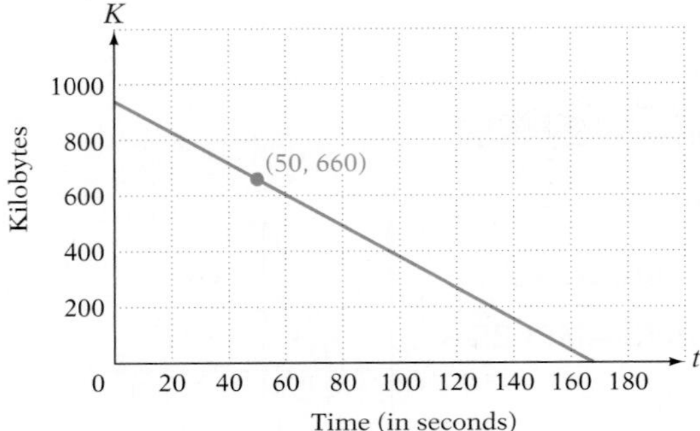

The ordered pair (50, 660) means that after 50 s, there are 660 K remaining to be downloaded.

YOU TRY IT 8

A car is traveling at a uniform speed of 40 mph. The distance d the car travels in t hours is given by $d = 40t$. Graph this equation for values of t from 0 to 5. The point whose coordinates are (3, 120) is on the graph. Write a sentence that describes the meaning of this ordered pair.

Your solution

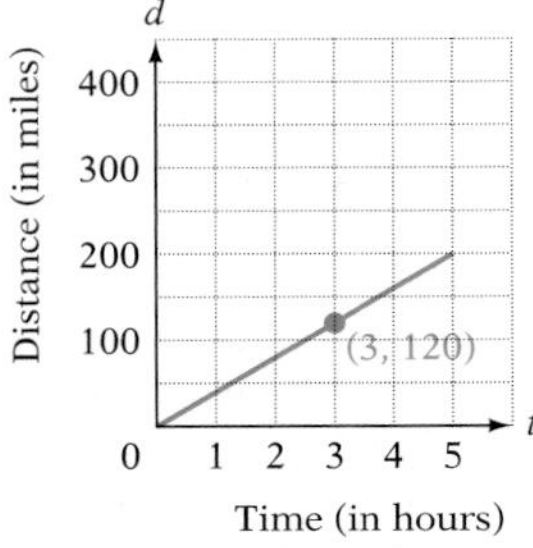

The ordered pair (3, 120) means that in 3 h, the car will have traveled 120 mi.

Solution on p. S30

12.2 EXERCISES

SUGGESTED ASSIGNMENT
Exercises 1–6; Exercises 7–59, odds;
Exercises 60–64

Concept Check

1. Which of the following equations are linear equations in two variables?

(i) $y = -2x + 7$ **(ii)** $x - 3y = 5$ **(iii)** $y = -x^2 + 4$ **(iv)** $y^2 = x - 6$ i and ii

2. Give the value of m and the value of b in each equation.

a. $y = 5x + 3$ **b.** $y = -\frac{1}{2}x - 8$ **c.** $y = x + 1$ **d.** $y = -x$

$m = 5, b = 3$ $m = -\frac{1}{2}, b = -8$ $m = 1, b = 1$ $m = -1, b = 0$

3. State whether the graph of the equation is a straight line.

a. $y = x^2 + 1$ **b.** $y = -x$ **c.** $y = \frac{1}{x}$ **d.** $y = 2 - \frac{1}{2}x$ **e.** $y = \sqrt{x} - 1$ b and d are graphs of straight lines.

For Exercises 4 and 5, name values of x that you would choose to find integer solutions of the equation.

4. $y = \frac{3}{2}x + 2$
Multiples of 2, such as −2, 0, 2, and 4

5. $y = -\frac{2}{3}x - 1$
Multiples of 3, such as −3, 0, 3, and 6

6. Is the equation in the form $y = mx + b$, the form $Ax + By = C$, or neither?

a. $6x - 3y = 6$ $Ax + By = C$ **b.** $y = x - 1$ $y = mx + b$ **c.** $8 - 4y = x$ Neither **d.** $5x + 4y = 4$ $Ax + By = C$

OBJECTIVE A *To graph an equation of the form $y = mx + b$*

For Exercises 7 to 24, graph.

7. $y = 2x - 3$

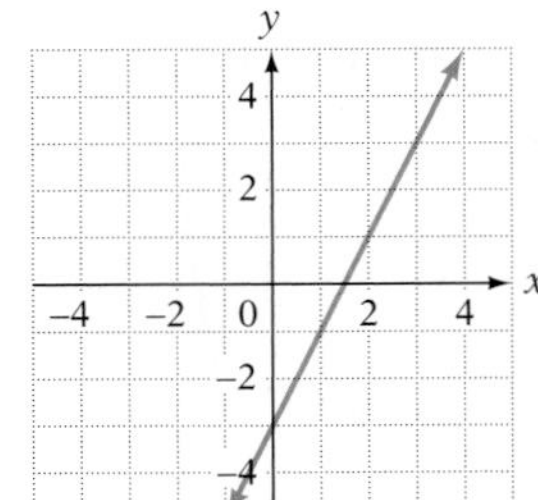

8. $y = -2x + 2$

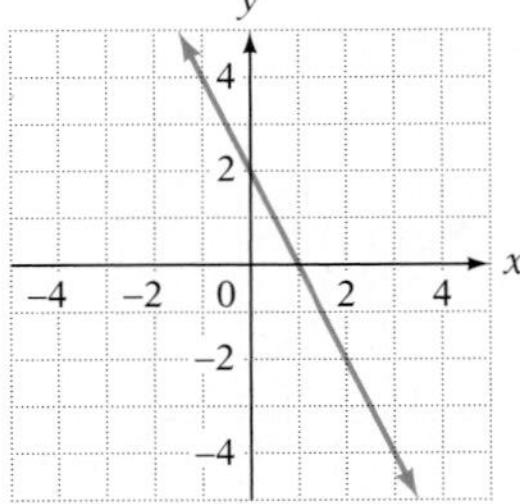

9. $y = \frac{1}{3}x$

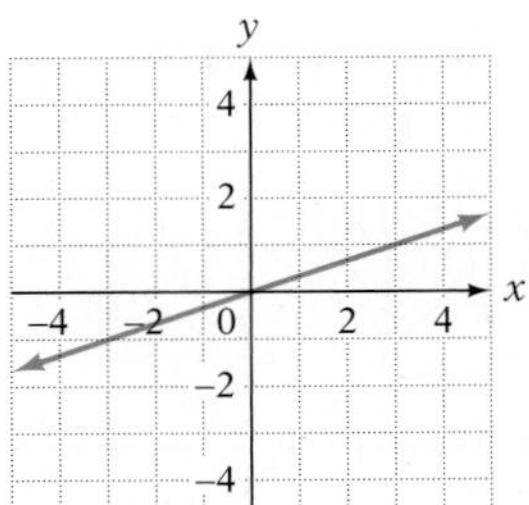

10. $y = -3x$

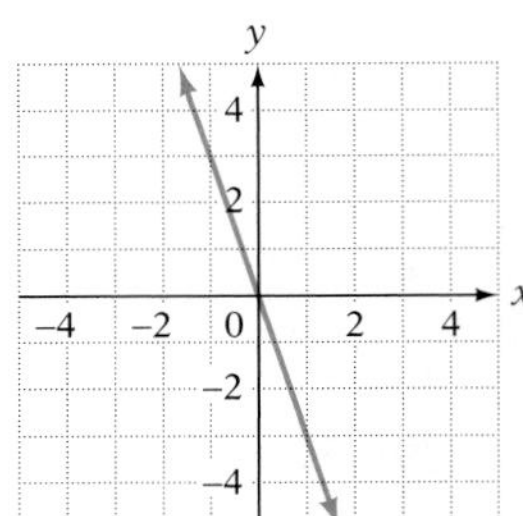

11. $y = \frac{2}{3}x - 1$

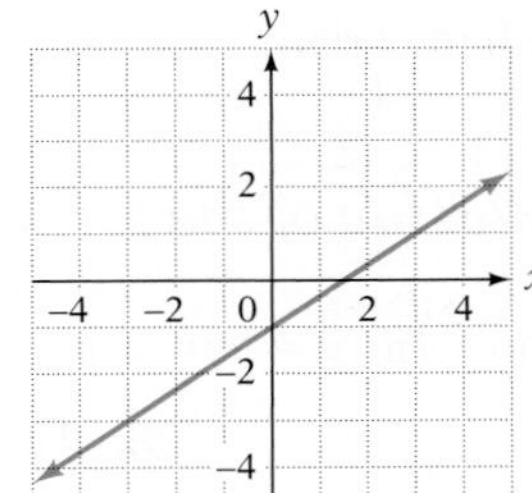

12. $y = \frac{3}{4}x + 2$

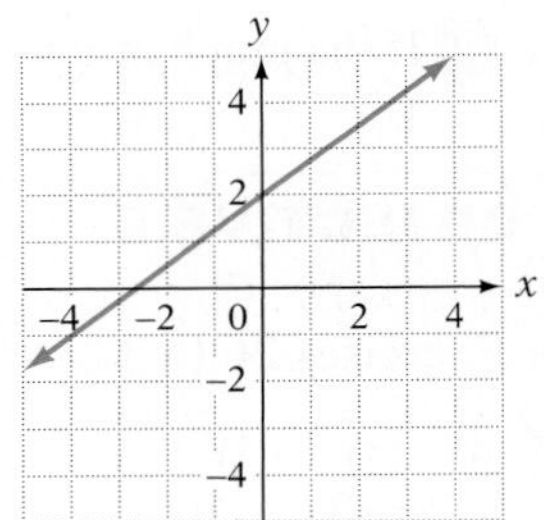

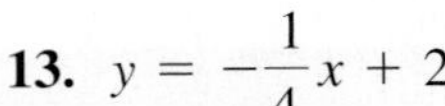

13. $y = -\frac{1}{4}x + 2$

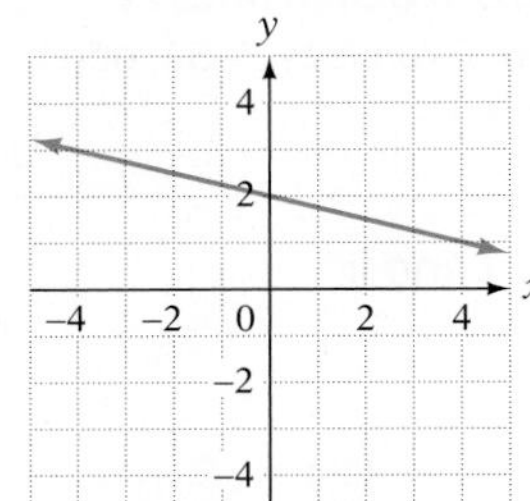

14. $y = -\frac{1}{3}x + 1$

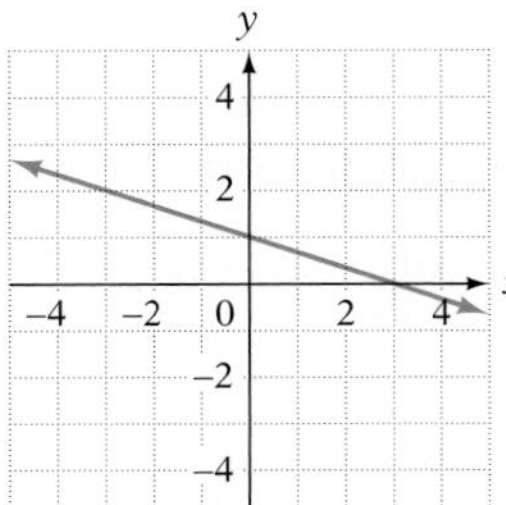

15. $y = -\frac{2}{5}x + 1$

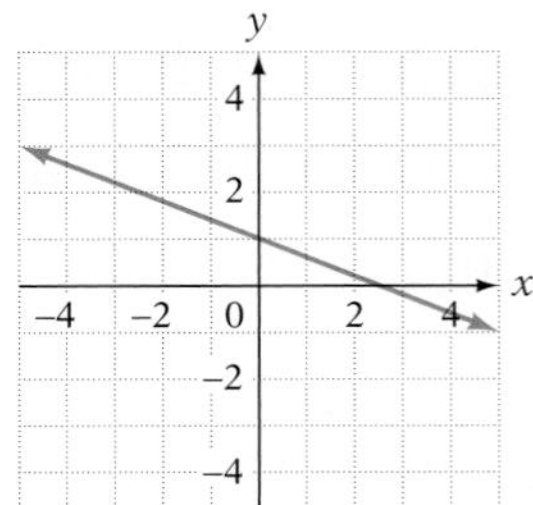

16. $y = -\frac{1}{2}x + 3$

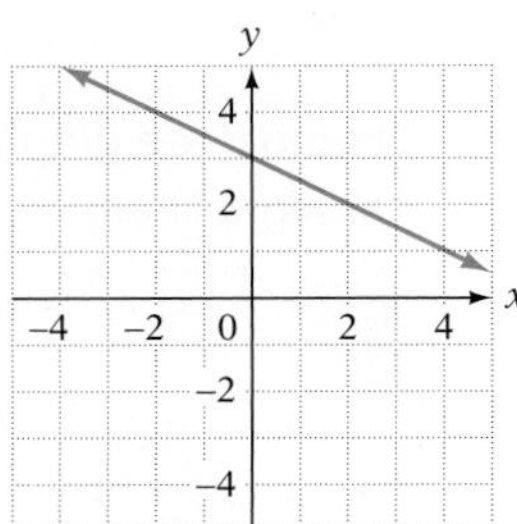

17. $y = 2x - 4$

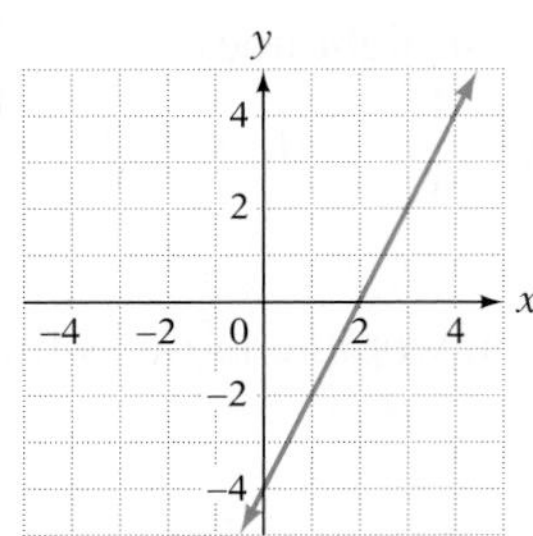

18. $y = 3x - 4$

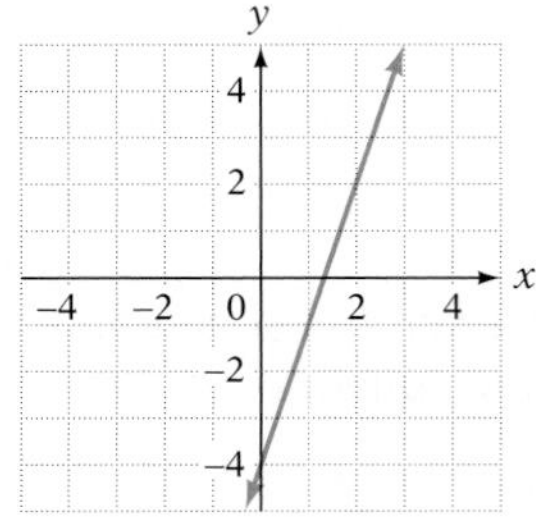

19. $y = x - 3$

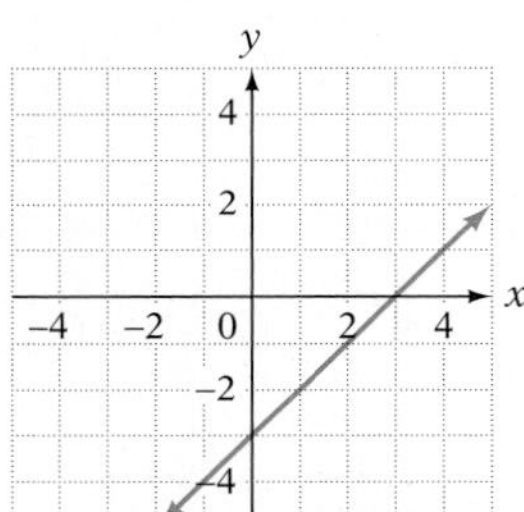

20. $y = x + 2$

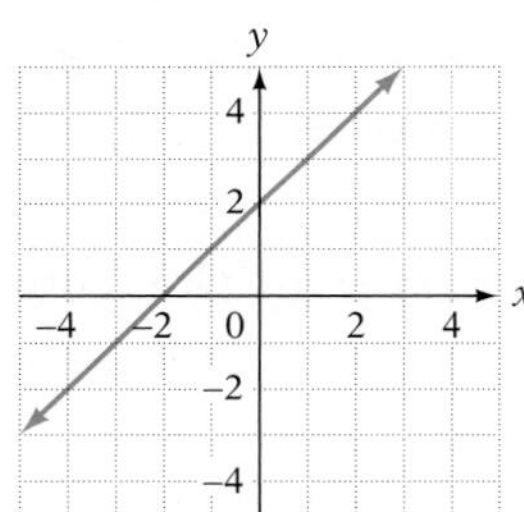

21. $y = -x + 2$

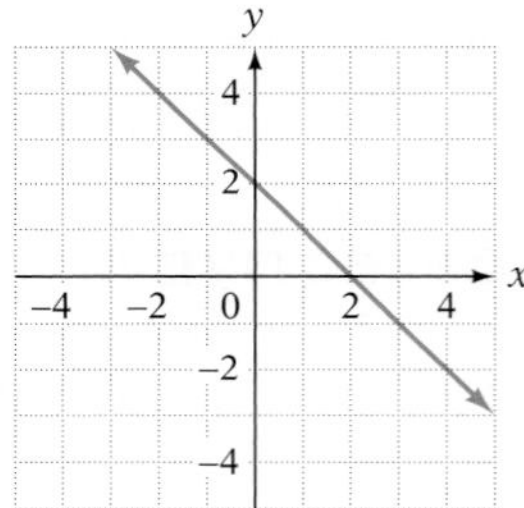

22. $y = -x - 1$

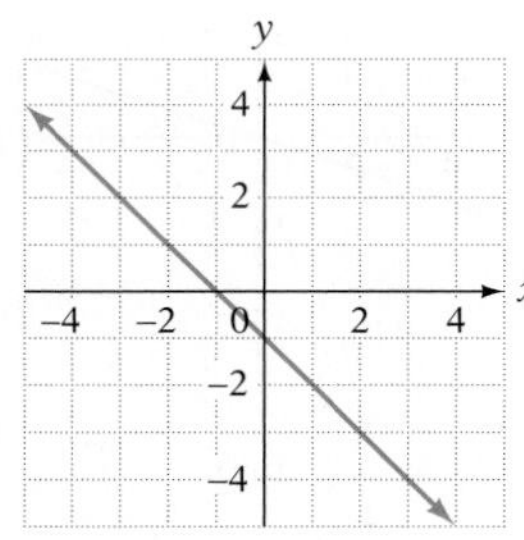

23. $y = -\frac{2}{3}x + 1$

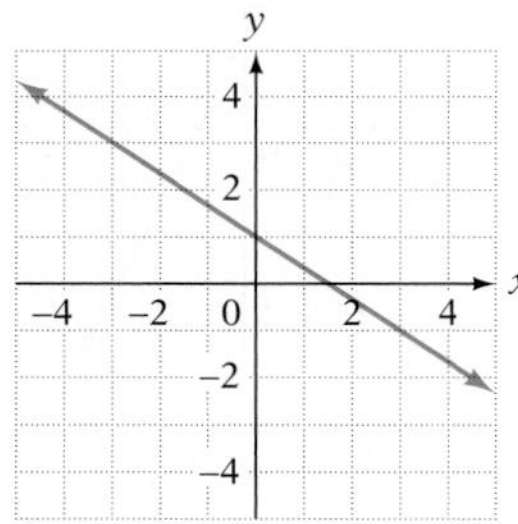

24. $y = 5x - 4$

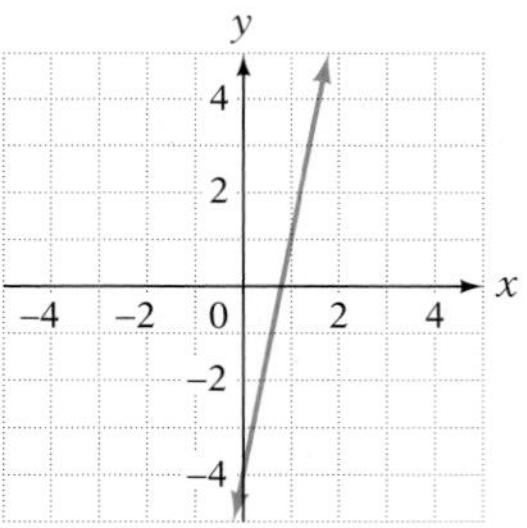

25. If the graph of $y = mx + b$ passes through the origin, (0, 0), what is the value of b? 0

OBJECTIVE B *To graph an equation of the form $Ax + By = C$*

For Exercises 26 to 37, write the equation in the form $y = mx + b$.

26. $3x + y = 10$
$y = -3x + 10$

27. $2x + y = 5$
$y = -2x + 5$

28. $4x - y = 3$
$y = 4x - 3$

29. $5x - y = 7$
$y = 5x - 7$

30. $3x + 2y = 6$
$y = -\frac{3}{2}x + 3$

31. $2x + 3y = 9$
$y = -\frac{2}{3}x + 3$

32. $2x - 5y = 10$
$y = \frac{2}{5}x - 2$

33. $5x - 2y = 4$
$y = \frac{5}{2}x - 2$

34. $2x + 7y = 14$
$y = -\frac{2}{7}x + 2$

35. $6x - 5y = 10$
$y = \frac{6}{5}x - 2$

36. $x + 3y = 6$
$y = -\frac{1}{3}x + 2$

37. $x - 4y = 12$
$y = \frac{1}{4}x - 3$

For Exercises 38 to 52, graph.

38. $3x + y = 3$

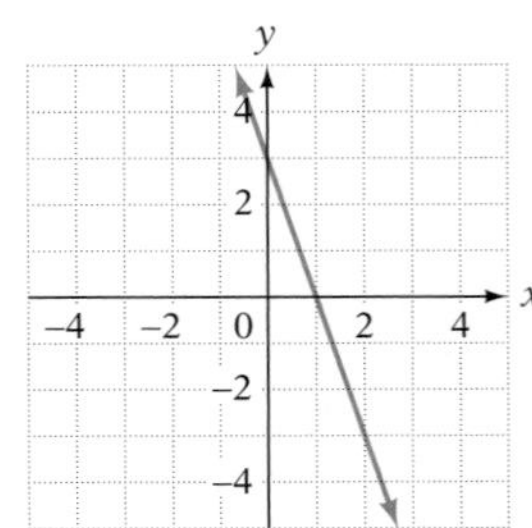

39. $2x + y = 4$

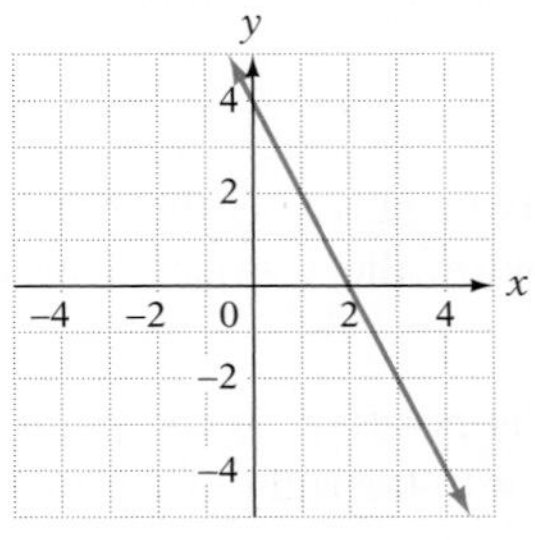

40. $2x + 3y = 6$

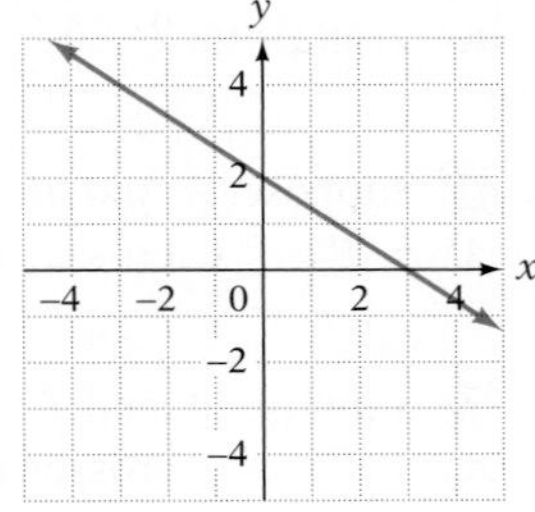

41. $3x + 2y = 4$

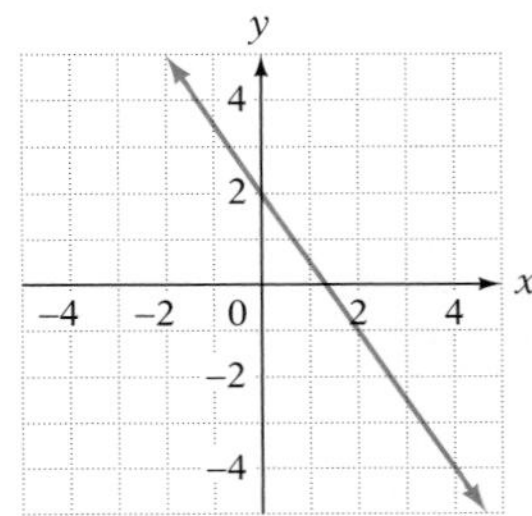

42. $x - 2y = 4$

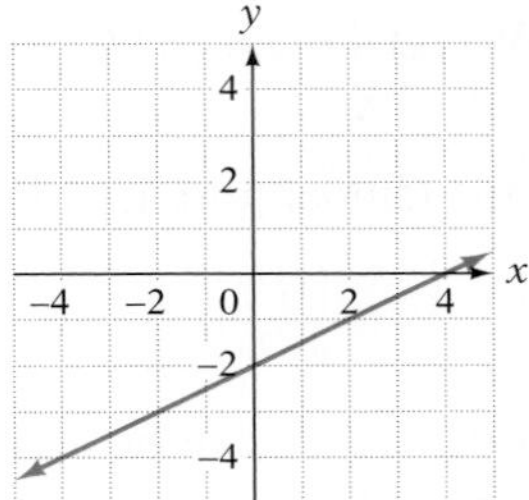

43. $x - 3y = 6$

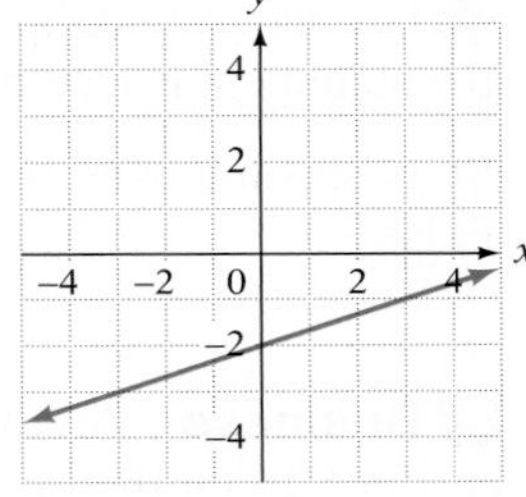

44. $2x - 3y = 6$

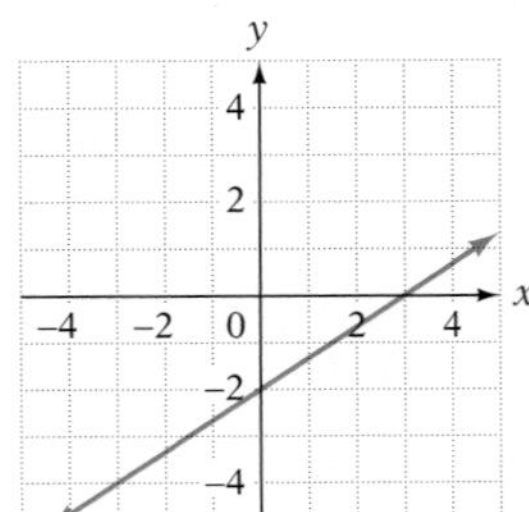

45. $3x - 2y = 8$

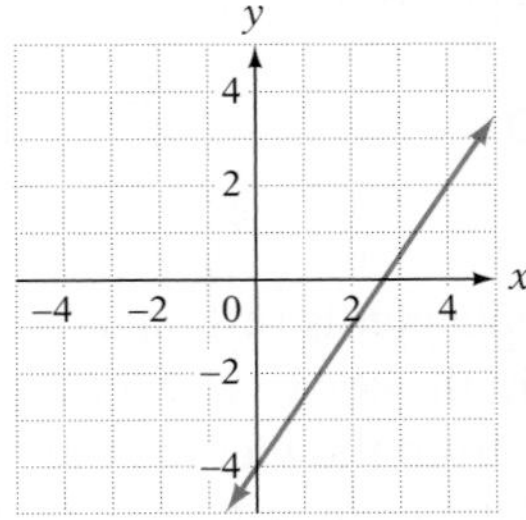

46. $2x + 5y = 10$

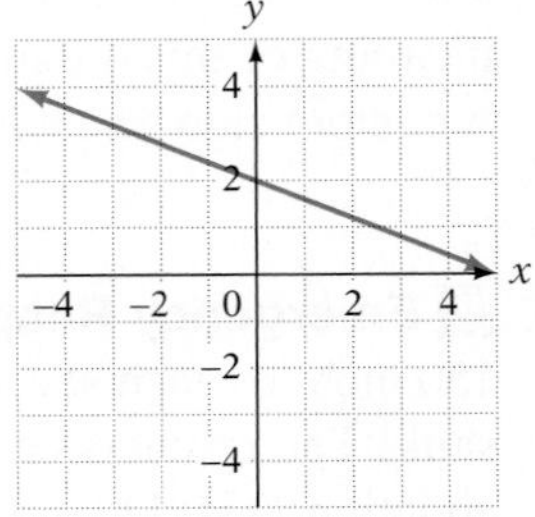

47. $3x + 4y = 12$

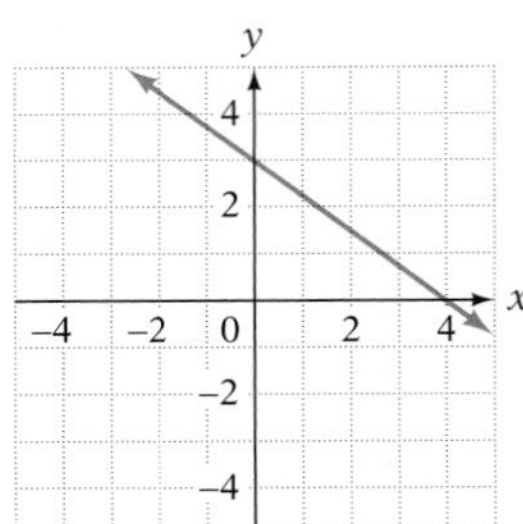

48. $x = 3$

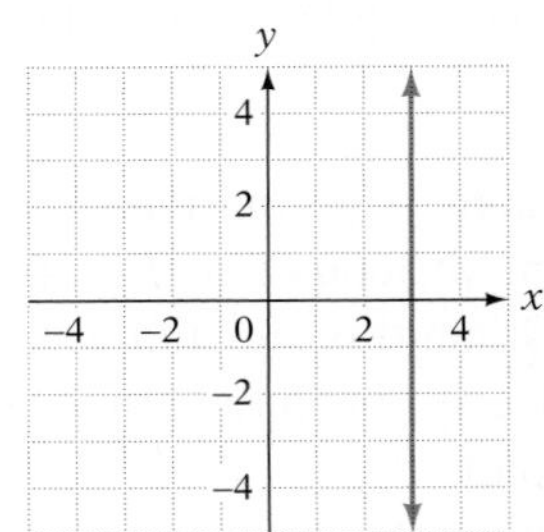

49. $y = -4$

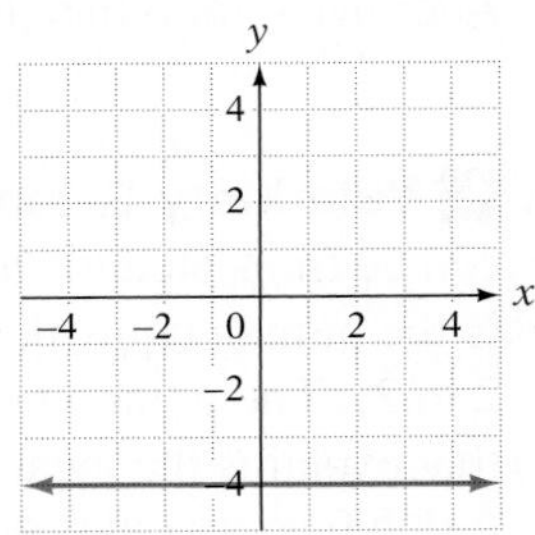

50. $x + 4y = 4$

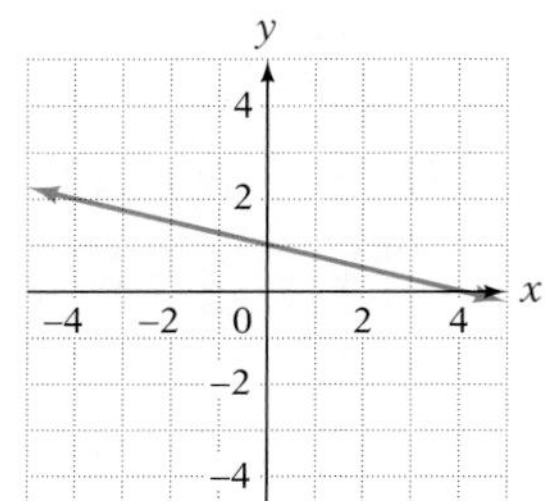

51. $4x - 3y = 12$

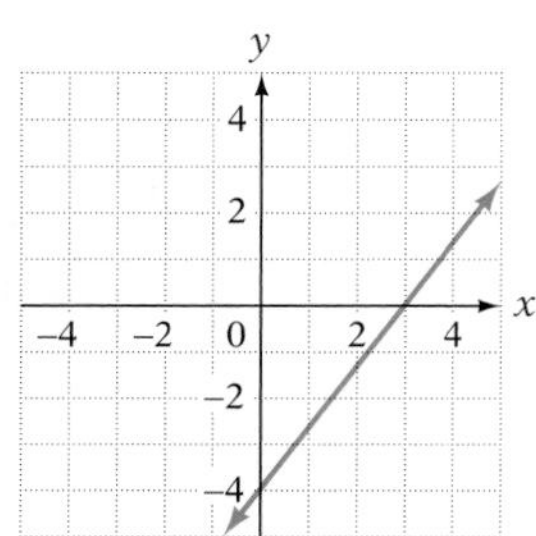

52. $y = 4$

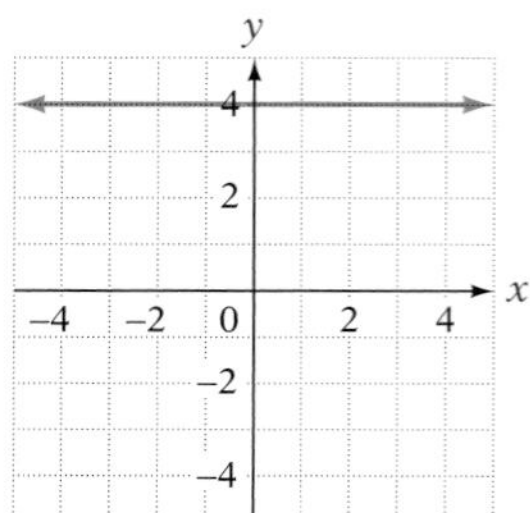

53. Which number, A, B, or C, must be zero if the graph of $Ax + By = C$ is a horizontal line? A

54. Suppose A and B are positive and C is negative. Is the point where the graph of $Ax + By = C$ crosses the y-axis above or below the x-axis? Below

55. Suppose A and C are negative and B is positive. Is the point where the graph of $Ax + By = C$ crosses the x-axis to the left or to the right of the y-axis? To the right

OBJECTIVE C *To solve application problems*

56. Use the oven temperature graph in HOW TO 4 on page 662 to determine whether the statement is true or false.

Sixty seconds after the oven is turned on, the temperature is still below 100°F.
False

57. **Business** A custom-illustrated sign or banner can be commissioned for a cost of \$25 for the material and \$10.50 per square foot for the artwork. The equation that represents this cost is given by $y = 10.50x + 25$, where y is the cost and x is the number of square feet in the sign. Graph this equation for values of x from 0 to 20. The point $(15, 182.5)$ is on the graph. Write a sentence that describes the meaning of this ordered pair.
A custom sign 15 ft^2 in area costs \$182.50.

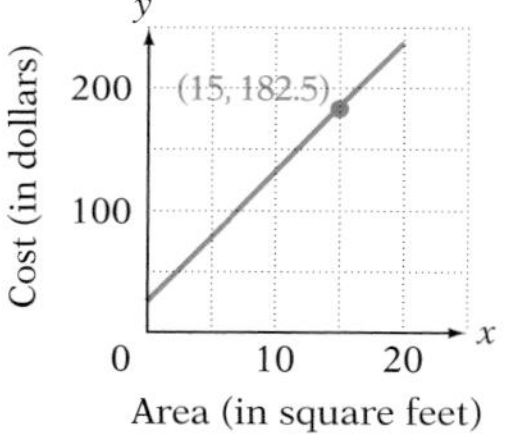

58. **Emergency Response** A rescue helicopter is rushing at a constant speed of 150 mph to reach several people stranded in the ocean 11 mi away after their boat sank. The rescuers can determine how far from the victims they are by using the equation $D = 11 - 2.5t$, where D is the distance in miles and t is the time elapsed in minutes. Graph this equation for values of t from 0 to 4. The point $(3, 3.5)$ is on the graph. Write a sentence that describes the meaning of this ordered pair.
After flying for 3 min, the helicopter is 3.5 mi away from the victims.

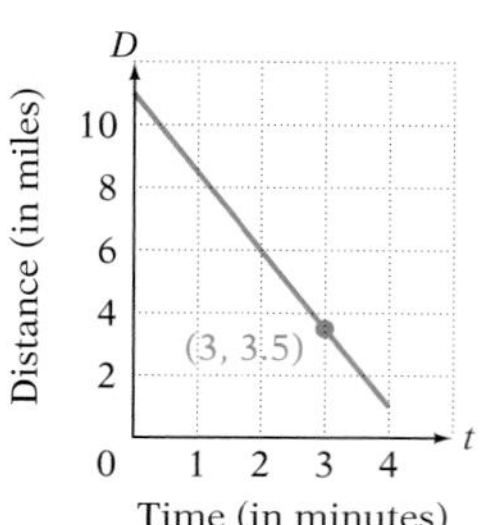

59. **Veterinary Science** According to some veterinarians, the age x of a dog can be translated to "human years" by using the equation $H = 4x + 16$, where H is the human equivalent age for the dog. Graph this equation for values of x from 2 to 21. The point whose coordinates are $(6, 40)$ is on the graph. Write a sentence that explains the meaning of this ordered pair.
A dog 6 years old is equivalent in age to a human 40 years old.

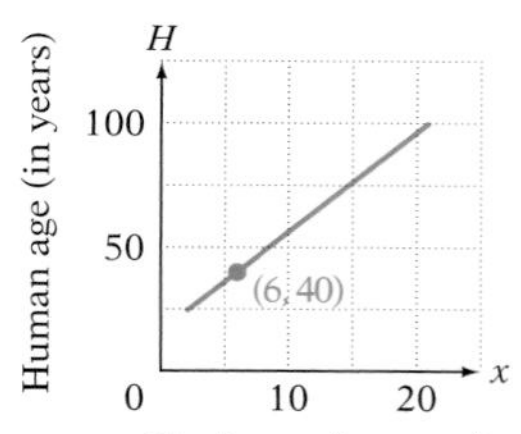

60. **Taxi Fares** See the news clipping at the right. The equation $F = 2.80M + 2.20$ can be used to calculate the fare F, in dollars, for a ride of M miles. Graph this equation for values of M from 1 to 5. The point (3, 10.6) is on the graph. Write a sentence that describes the meaning of this ordered pair.
A 3-mile taxi ride costs \$10.60.

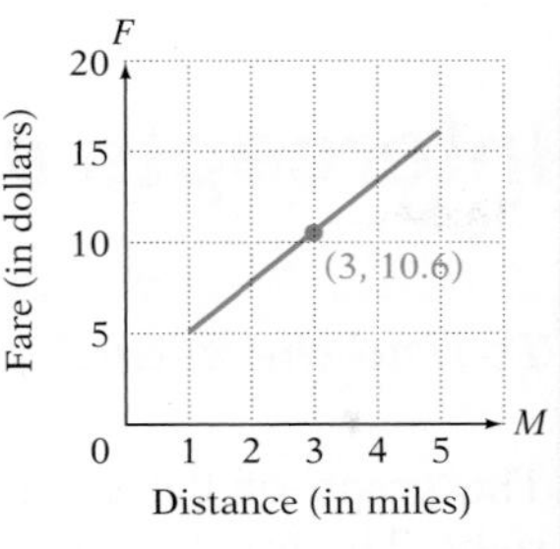

In the NEWS!

Rate Hike for Boston Cab Rides

Taxi drivers soon will be raising their rates, perhaps in an effort to help pay for their required switch to hybrid vehicles by 2015. In the near future, a passenger will have to pay \$5.00 for the first mile of a taxi ride and \$2.80 for each additional mile.

Source: The Boston Globe

Critical Thinking

61. Write the equation of a line that crosses both the x-axis and the y-axis at the point (0, 0). Answers will vary. For example, $y = 2x$

62. Write the equation of a line that crosses the y-axis at the point (0, 1). Answers will vary. For example, $y = x + 1$

Projects or Group Activities

63. Graph $y = 2x - 2$, $y = 2x$, and $y = 2x + 3$. What observation can you make about the graphs?

64. Graph $y = x + 3$, $y = 2x + 3$, and $y = -\frac{1}{2}x + 3$. What observation can you make about the graphs?

QUICK QUIZ

Graph.

1. $y = -x + 3$ **[12.2A]**
2. $y = 4x$ **[12.2A]**
3. $y = \frac{3}{4}x + 1$ **[12.2A]**
4. $5x - 2y = 4$ **[12.2B]**
5. $x = 2$ **[12.2B]**

CHECK YOUR PROGRESS: CHAPTER 12

1. Graph (−4, 3), (−2, −1), (2, −1), and (0, 3). [12.1A]

2. Graph $y = -\frac{4}{5}x + 4$. [12.2A]

3. Graph $3x - 4y = 12$. [12.2B]

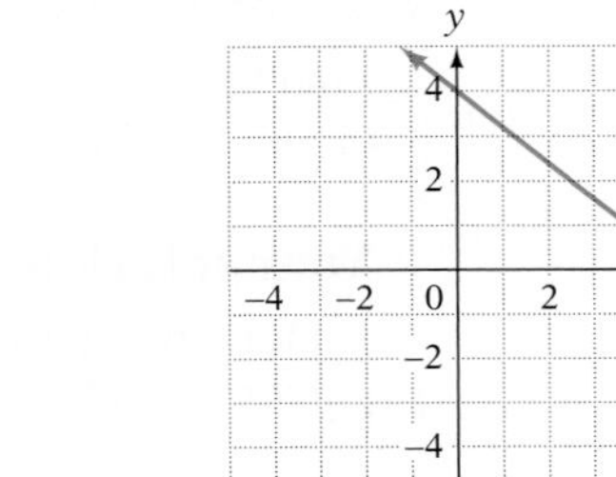

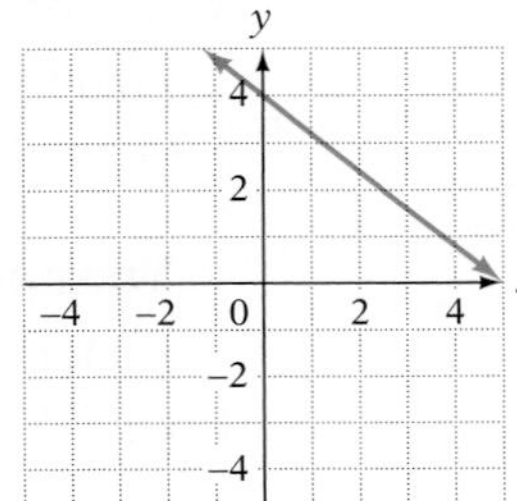

4. Find the ordered-pair solutions of $y = -3x + 2$ when $x = -1, 0, 1,$ and 2.
(−1, 5), (0, 2), (1, −1), (2, −4) [12.1B]

5. Describe the graph of $x = -5$.
A vertical line passing through (−5, 0) [12.2B]

6. Find the domain and range of the relation {(−3, −2), (−2, −1), (−1, 0)}. Is the relation a function?
D: {−3, −2, −1}; R: {−2, −1, 0}; yes [12.1C]

7. Given $h(s) = s^2 + 3s$, find $h(-3)$. 0 [12.1D]

8. Is (−3, 0) a solution of $y = -\frac{1}{3}x - 1$? Yes [12.1B]

9. Does $y = x^2 - 4$, where $x \in \{-3, -1, 0, 1, 3\}$, define y as a function of x?
Yes [12.1C]

SECTION

12.3 Intercepts and Slopes of Straight Lines

OBJECTIVE A *To find the x- and y-intercepts of a straight line*

IN-CLASS EXAMPLES

Find the x- and y-intercepts.

1. $4x + 3y = -12$
   $(-3, 0)$, $(0, -4)$
2. $y = \frac{1}{3}x - 3$
   $(9, 0)$, $(0, -3)$
3. $x - 2y = 0$
   $(0, 0)$, $(0, 0)$
4. $2x - 5y = 5$
   $\left(\frac{5}{2}, 0\right)$, $(0, -1)$

The graph of the equation $2x + 3y = 6$ is shown at the right. The graph crosses the x-axis at the point $(3, 0)$ and crosses the y-axis at the point $(0, 2)$. The point at which a graph crosses the x-axis is called the **x-intercept.** At the x-intercept, the y-coordinate is 0. The point at which a graph crosses the y-axis is called the **y-intercept.** At the y-intercept, the x-coordinate is 0.

Take Note

To find the x-intercept, let $y = 0$ and solve for x. To find the y-intercept, let $x = 0$ and solve for y.

HOW TO 1 Find the x- and y-intercepts of the graph of the equation $2x - 3y = 12$.

To find the x-intercept, let $y = 0$. (Any point on the x-axis has y-coordinate 0.)

$$\begin{aligned} 2x - 3y &= 12 \\ 2x - 3(0) &= 12 \\ 2x &= 12 \\ x &= 6 \end{aligned}$$

The x-intercept is $(6, 0)$.

To find the y-intercept, let $x = 0$. (Any point on the y-axis has x-coordinate 0.)

$$\begin{aligned} 2x - 3y &= 12 \\ 2(0) - 3y &= 12 \\ -3y &= 12 \\ y &= -4 \end{aligned}$$

The y-intercept is $(0, -4)$.

Some linear equations can be graphed by finding the x- and y-intercepts and then drawing a line through these two points.

EXAMPLE 1

Find the x- and y-intercepts of $x - 2y = 4$. Graph the line.

Solution

To find the x-intercept, let $y = 0$ and solve for x.

$$\begin{aligned} x - 2y &= 4 \\ x - 2(0) &= 4 \\ x &= 4 \quad (4, 0) \end{aligned}$$

To find the y-intercept, let $x = 0$ and solve for y.

$$\begin{aligned} x - 2y &= 4 \\ 0 - 2y &= 4 \\ -2y &= 4 \\ y &= -2 \quad (0, -2) \end{aligned}$$

Plot the two intercepts. Draw a line through the two points.

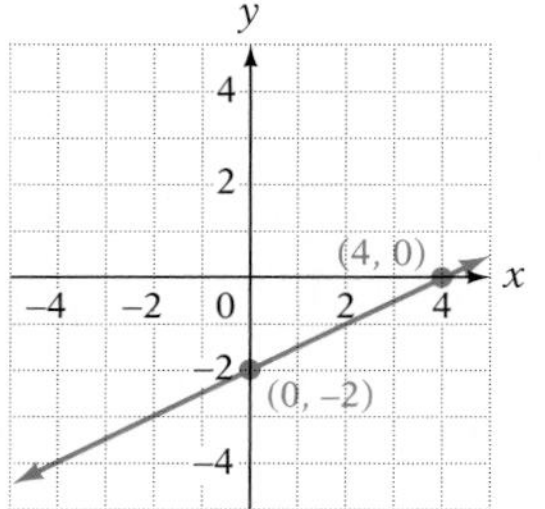

YOU TRY IT 1

Find the x- and y-intercepts of $2x - y = 4$. Graph the line.

Your solution

x-intercept: $(2, 0)$
y-intercept: $(0, -4)$

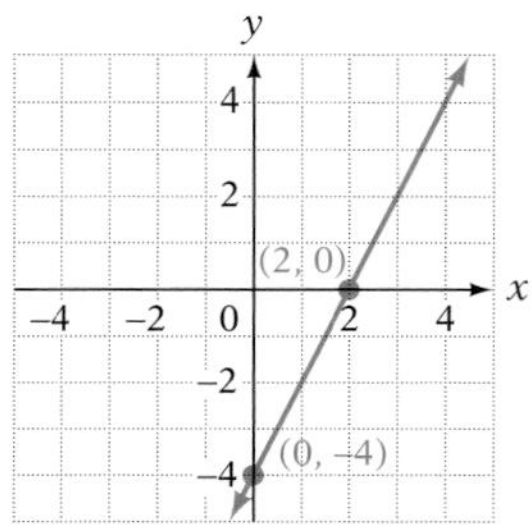

Solution on p. S30

OBJECTIVE B *To find the slope of a straight line*

INSTRUCTOR NOTE
Students need to understand that the slope of a line is the same regardless of which two points are used to calculate the slope.

The graphs of $y = \frac{2}{3}x + 1$ and $y = 2x + 1$ are shown in Figure 1. Each graph crosses the y-axis at the point (0, 1), but the graphs have different slants. The **slope** of a line is a measure of the slant of the line. The symbol for slope is m.

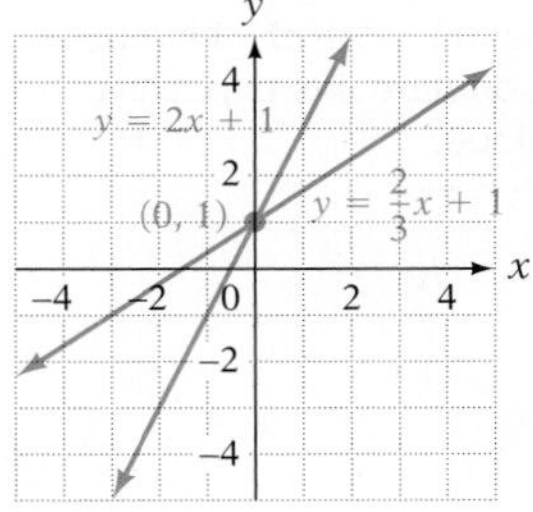

Figure 1

Take Note
The change in the y values can be thought of as the *rise* of the line, and the change in the x values can be thought of as the *run*. Then

$$\text{Slope} = m = \frac{\text{rise}}{\text{run}}$$

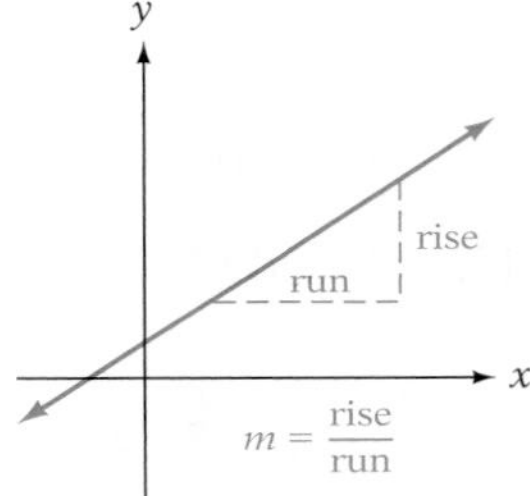
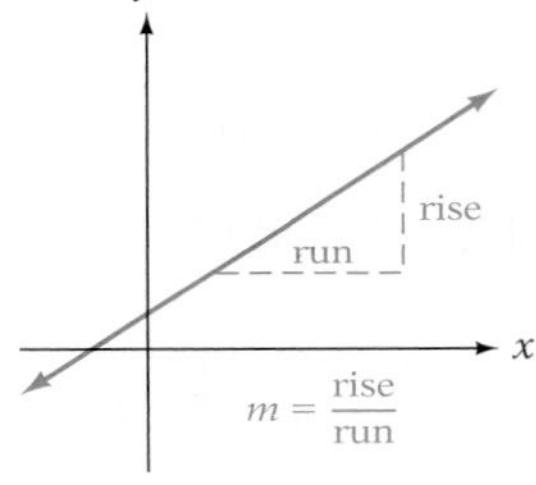

The slope of a line containing two points is the ratio of the change in the y values of the two points to the change in the x values. The line containing the points $(-2, -3)$ and $(6, 1)$ is graphed in Figure 2. The change in the y values is the difference between the two ordinates.

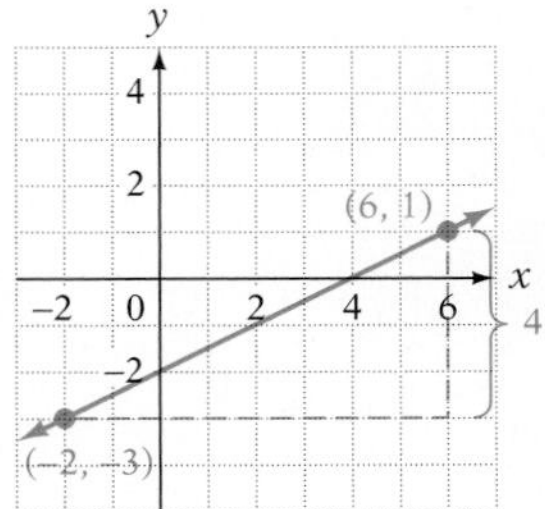

Figure 2

$$\text{Change in } y = 1 - (-3) = 4$$

The change in the x values is the difference between the two abscissas (Figure 3).

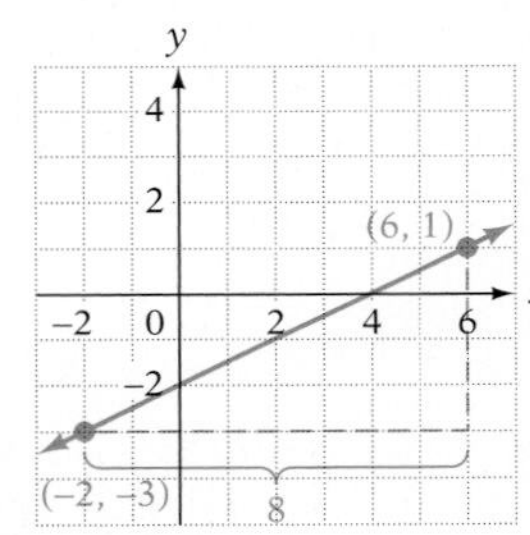

Figure 3

$$\text{Change in } x = 6 - (-2) = 8$$

$$\text{Slope} = m = \frac{\text{change in } y}{\text{change in } x} = \frac{4}{8} = \frac{1}{2}$$

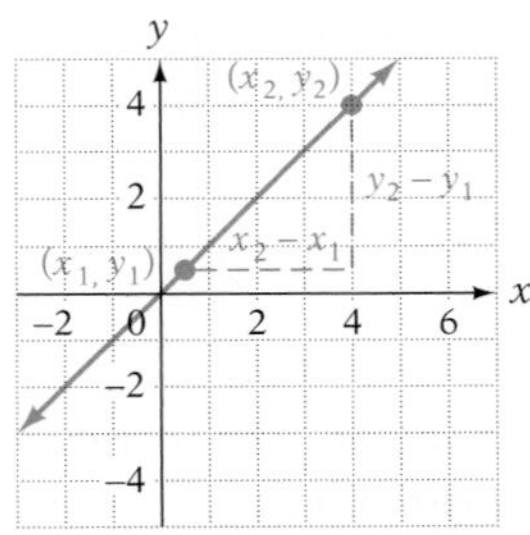

Figure 4

Slope Formula

If $P_1(x_1, y_1)$ and $P_2(x_2, y_2)$ are two points on a line and $x_1 \neq x_2$, then $m = \frac{y_2 - y_1}{x_2 - x_1}$ (Figure 4). If $x_1 = x_2$, the slope is undefined.

HOW TO 2 Find the slope of the line containing the points $(-1, 1)$ and $(2, 3)$.

Let P_1 be $(-1, 1)$ and P_2 be $(2, 3)$. Then $x_1 = -1, y_1 = 1, x_2 = 2$, and $y_2 = 3$.

$$m = \frac{y_2 - y_1}{x_2 - x_1} = \frac{3 - 1}{2 - (-1)} = \frac{2}{3}$$

The slope is $\frac{2}{3}$.

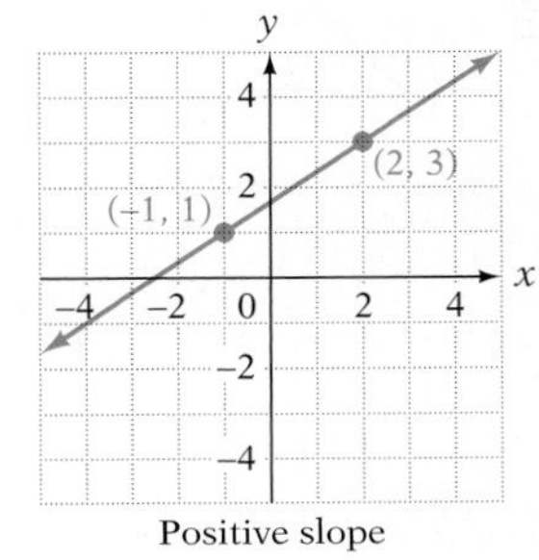

Positive slope

Take Note
Positive slope means that the value of y increases as the value of x increases.

A line that slants upward to the right always has a **positive slope.**

You obtain the same results if the points are named oppositely. Let P_1 be (2, 3) and P_2 be $(-1, 1)$. The slope is $\frac{2}{3}$. Therefore, it does not matter which point is named P_1 and which is named P_2; the slope remains the same.

Take Note

Negative slope means that the value of y decreases as the value of x increases. Compare this to positive slope.

HOW TO 3 Find the slope of the line containing the points $(-3, 4)$ and $(2, -2)$.

Let P_1 be $(-3, 4)$ and P_2 be $(2, -2)$.

$$m = \frac{y_2 - y_1}{x_2 - x_1} = \frac{-2 - 4}{2 - (-3)} = \frac{-6}{5} = -\frac{6}{5}$$

The slope is $-\frac{6}{5}$.

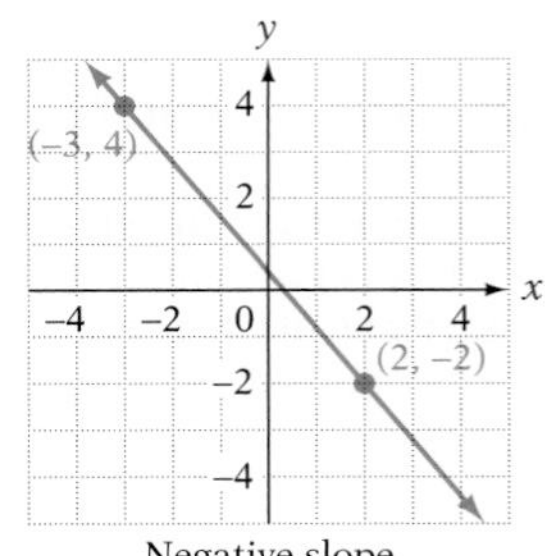

Negative slope

A line that slants downward to the right always has a **negative slope.**

HOW TO 4 Find the slope of the line containing the points $(-1, 3)$ and $(4, 3)$.

Let P_1 be $(-1, 3)$ and P_2 be $(4, 3)$.

$$m = \frac{y_2 - y_1}{x_2 - x_1} = \frac{3 - 3}{4 - (-1)} = \frac{0}{5} = 0$$

The slope is 0.

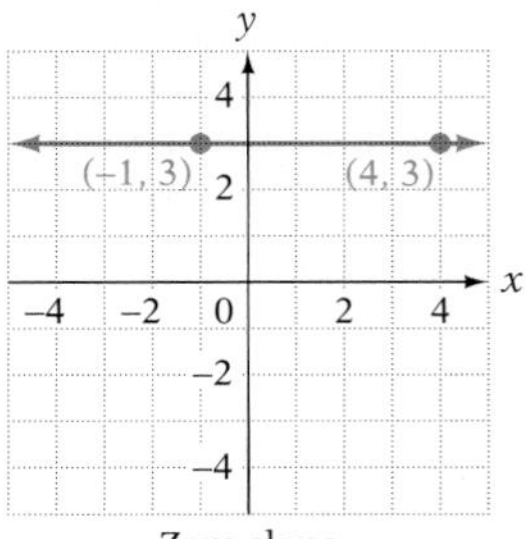

Zero slope

A horizontal line has **zero slope.**

HOW TO 5 Find the slope of the line containing the points $(2, -2)$ and $(2, 4)$.

Let P_1 be $(2, -2)$ and P_2 be $(2, 4)$.

$$m = \frac{y_2 - y_1}{x_2 - x_1} = \frac{4 - (-2)}{2 - 2} = \frac{6}{0}$$ Division by zero is not defined.

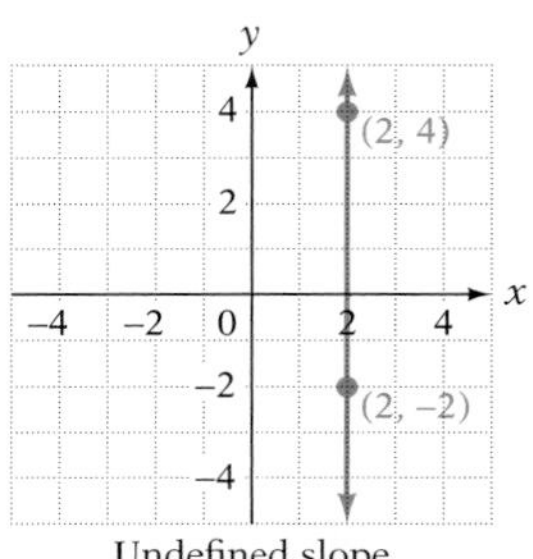

Undefined slope

A vertical line has **undefined slope.**

APPLY THE CONCEPT

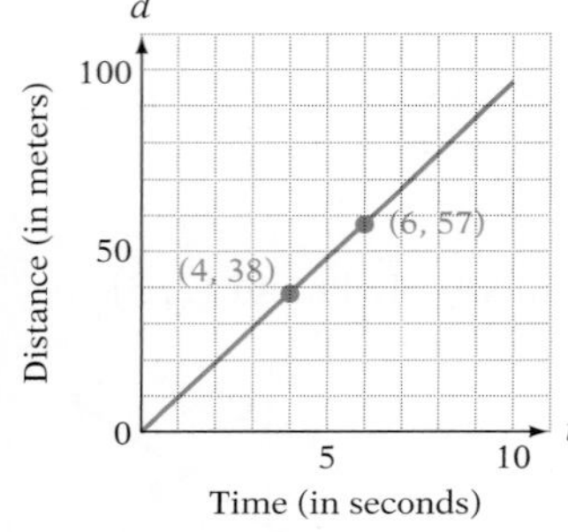

Florence Griffith-Joyner set the world record time for the 100-meter dash in 1988. The graph at the left is a distance-time graph of her record-setting run. From the graph, we can see that after 4 s, she had run 38 m, and after 6 s, she had traveled 57 m. Find her average rate of speed for the race.

To find the average rate of speed, find the slope of the line between the two points.

$$m = \frac{57 - 38}{6 - 4} = \frac{19}{2} = 9.5$$

Florence Griffith-Joyner's average rate of speed was 9.5 m/s.

Recall that two lines in the plane that never intersect are called parallel lines. The lines l_1 and l_2 in the figure at the right are parallel. Calculating the slope of each line, we have

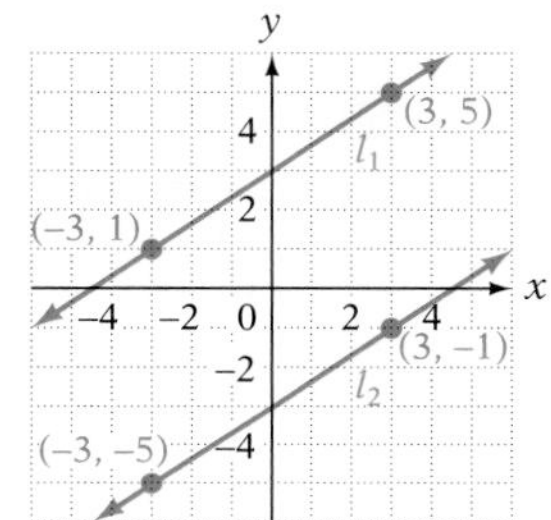

$$\text{Slope of } l_1\text{: } m_1 = \frac{y_2 - y_1}{x_2 - x_1} = \frac{5 - 1}{3 - (-3)} = \frac{4}{6} = \frac{2}{3}$$

$$\text{Slope of } l_2\text{: } m_2 = \frac{y_2 - y_1}{x_2 - x_1} = \frac{-1 - (-5)}{3 - (-3)} = \frac{4}{6} = \frac{2}{3}$$

Note that these parallel lines have the same slope. This is always true for parallel lines.

Take Note

We must separate the description of parallel lines at the right into two parts because vertical lines in the plane are parallel, but their slopes are undefined.

Parallel Lines

Two nonvertical lines in the plane are parallel if and only if they have the same slope. Vertical lines in the plane are parallel.

EXAMPLE

The slope of the line $y = 3x + 5$ is 3. The slope of the line $y = 3x - 4$ is 3. The lines have the same slope and different y-intercepts. The lines are parallel.

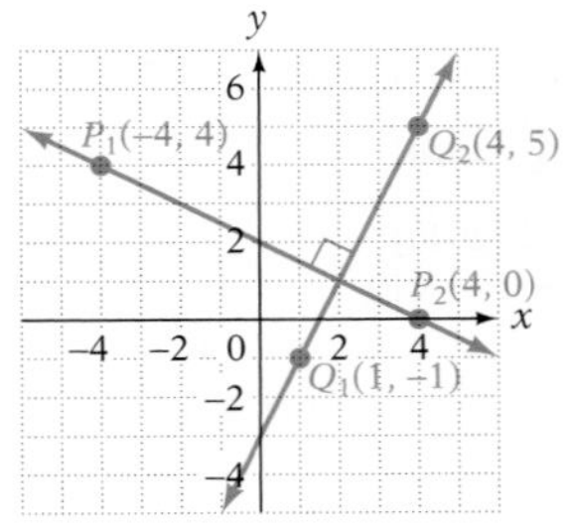

Two lines that intersect at a 90° angle (right angle) are called perpendicular lines. The lines at the left are perpendicular.

Perpendicular Lines

Two nonvertical lines in the plane are perpendicular if and only if the product of their slopes is −1. A vertical and a horizontal line are perpendicular.

EXAMPLE

The slope of the line between P_1 and P_2 in the graph at the left is $\frac{0-4}{4-(-4)} = -\frac{4}{8} = -\frac{1}{2}$.

The slope of the line between Q_1 and Q_2 is $\frac{5-(-1)}{4-1} = \frac{6}{3} = 2$. The product of the slopes is $\left(-\frac{1}{2}\right)2 = -1$. Therefore, the graphs are perpendicular.

EXAMPLE 2

Find the slope of the line containing the points $(-2, -3)$ and $(3, 4)$.

Solution

Let $P_1 = (-2, -3)$ and $P_2 = (3, 4)$.

$$m = \frac{y_2 - y_1}{x_2 - x_1} = \frac{4-(-3)}{3-(-2)} = \frac{7}{5}$$

- $y_2 = 4, y_1 = -3$
- $x_2 = 3, x_1 = -2$

The slope is $\frac{7}{5}$.

YOU TRY IT 2

Find the slope of the line containing the points $(1, 4)$ and $(-3, 8)$.

Your solution −1

IN-CLASS EXAMPLES

5. Find the slope of the line containing the points $(5, 3)$ and $(-2, 5)$. $-\frac{2}{7}$

6. The graph at the right shows the distance traveled by a car and the amount of gas used by the car. Find the slope of the line. Write a sentence that explains the meaning of the slope. **$m = 32$. The car gets 32 mi/gal.**

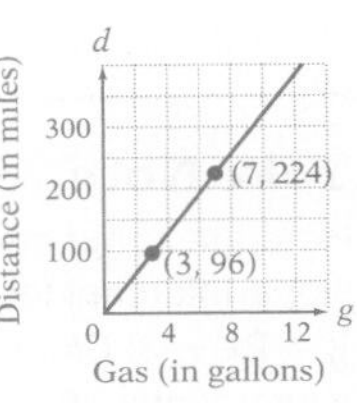

EXAMPLE 3

Find the slope of the line containing the points $(-1, 4)$ and $(-1, 0)$.

Solution

Let $P_1 = (-1, 4)$ and $P_2 = (-1, 0)$.

$$m = \frac{y_2 - y_1}{x_2 - x_1} = \frac{0-4}{-1-(-1)} = \frac{-4}{0}$$

- $y_2 = 0, y_1 = 4$
- $x_2 = -1, x_1 = -1$

The slope is undefined.

YOU TRY IT 3

Find the slope of the line containing the points $(-1, 2)$ and $(4, 2)$.

Your solution

0

Solutions on pp. S30–S31

EXAMPLE 4

The graph below shows the altitude of a plane above an airport during its 30-minute descent from cruising altitude to landing. Find the slope of the line. Write a sentence that explains the meaning of the slope.

Solution

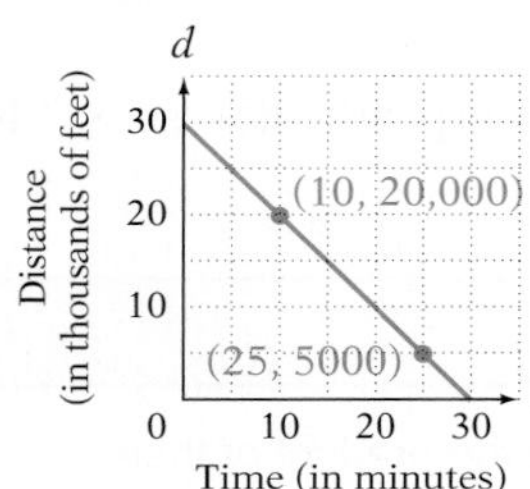

$$m = \frac{5000 - 20{,}000}{25 - 10} = \frac{-15{,}000}{15}$$
$$= -1000$$

A slope of -1000 means that the altitude of the plane is *decreasing* at the rate of 1000 ft/min.

YOU TRY IT 4

The graph below shows the approximate decline in the value of a used car over a 5-year period. Find the slope of the line. Write a sentence that states the meaning of the slope.

Your solution

$m = -850$

A slope of -850 means that the value of the car is decreasing at a rate of \$850 per year.

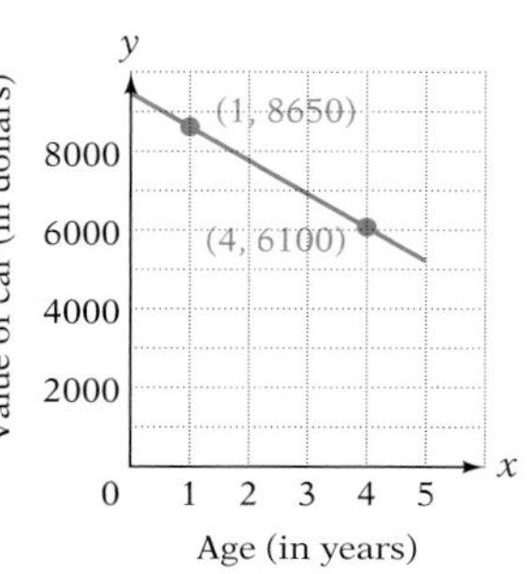

Solution on p. S31

OBJECTIVE C *To graph a line using the slope and the y-intercept*

HOW TO 6 Find the y-intercept of $y = 3x + 4$.

$y = 3x + 4 = 3(0) + 4 = 4$ • Let $x = 0$.

The y-intercept is $(0, 4)$.

For any equation of the form $y = mx + b$, the y-intercept is $(0, b)$.

The graph of the equation $y = \frac{2}{3}x + 1$ is shown at the right. The points $(-3, -1)$ and $(3, 3)$ are on the graph. The slope of the line between the two points is

$$m = \frac{3 - (-1)}{3 - (-3)} = \frac{4}{6} = \frac{2}{3}$$

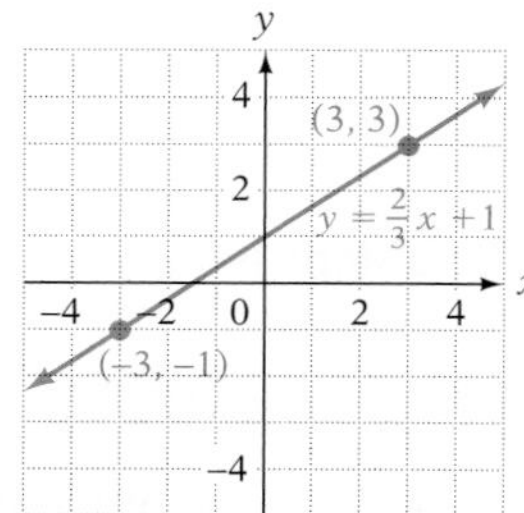

Observe that the slope of the line is the coefficient of x in the equation $y = \frac{2}{3}x + 1$. The y-intercept is $(0, 1)$, where 1 is the constant term of the equation.

Take Note

Here are some equations in slope-intercept form.

$y = 2x - 3$: Slope is 2; y-intercept is $(0, -3)$.

$y = -x + 2$: Slope is -1 (recall that $-x = -1x$); y-intercept is $(0, 2)$.

$y = \frac{x}{2}$: Because $\frac{x}{2} = \frac{1}{2}x$, slope is $\frac{1}{2}$; y-intercept is $(0, 0)$.

Slope-Intercept Form of a Linear Equation

An equation of the form $y = mx + b$ is called the **slope-intercept form** of the equation of a straight line. The slope of the line is m, the coefficient of x. The y-intercept is $(0, b)$, where b is the constant term of the equation.

EXAMPLE

The graph of the equation $y = -4x + 3$ is a straight line.
The slope of the line is -4. The y-intercept is $(0, 3)$.

When the equation of a line is in slope-intercept form, the graph can be drawn using the slope and the y-intercept. First locate the y-intercept. Use the slope to find a second point on the line. Then draw a line through the two points.

HOW TO 7 Graph $y = 2x - 3$.

y-intercept $= (0, b) = (0, -3)$

$m = 2 = \frac{2}{1} = \frac{\text{change in } y}{\text{change in } x}$

Beginning at the y-intercept, move up 2 units (change in y) and then right 1 unit (change in x).

$(1, -1)$ is a second point on the graph.

Draw a line through the two points $(0, -3)$ and $(1, -1)$.

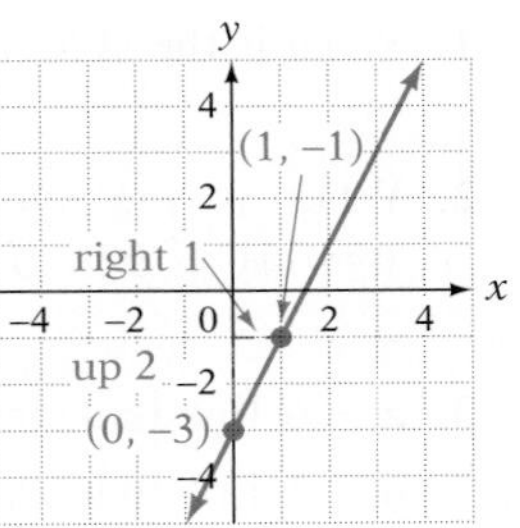

EXAMPLE 5

Graph $y = -\frac{2}{3}x + 1$ by using the slope and y-intercept.

Solution

y-intercept $= (0, b)$
$= (0, 1)$

$m = -\frac{2}{3} = \frac{-2}{3}$
$= \frac{\text{change in } y}{\text{change in } x}$

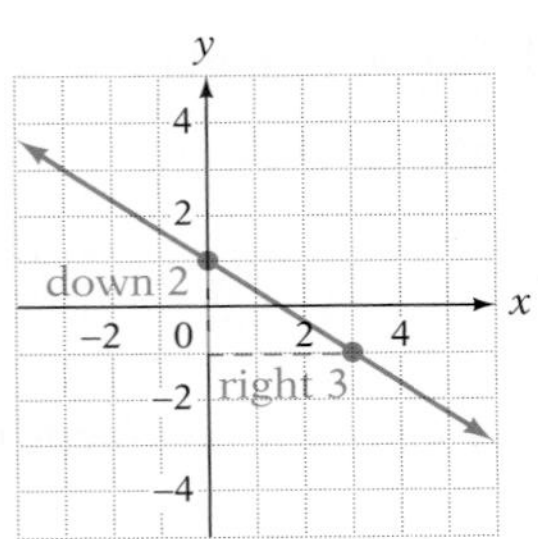

YOU TRY IT 5

Graph $y = -\frac{1}{4}x - 1$ by using the slope and y-intercept.

Your solution

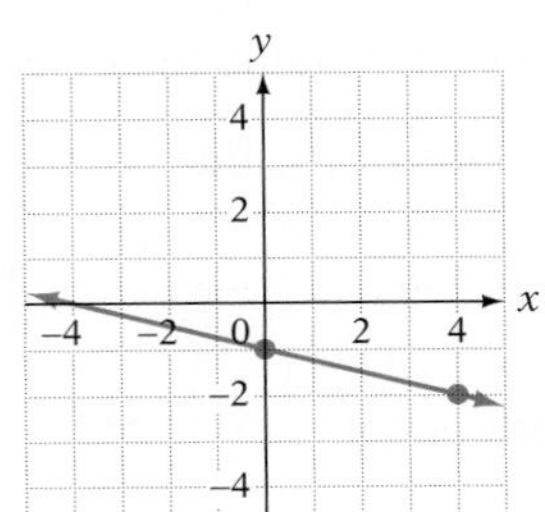

EXAMPLE 6

Graph $2x - 3y = 6$ by using the slope and y-intercept.

Solution

The equation is in the form $Ax + By = C$. Rewrite it in slope-intercept form by solving for y.

$2x - 3y = 6$
$-3y = -2x + 6$
$y = \frac{2}{3}x - 2$

y-intercept $= (0, -2)$

$m = \frac{2}{3} = \frac{\text{change in } y}{\text{change in } x}$

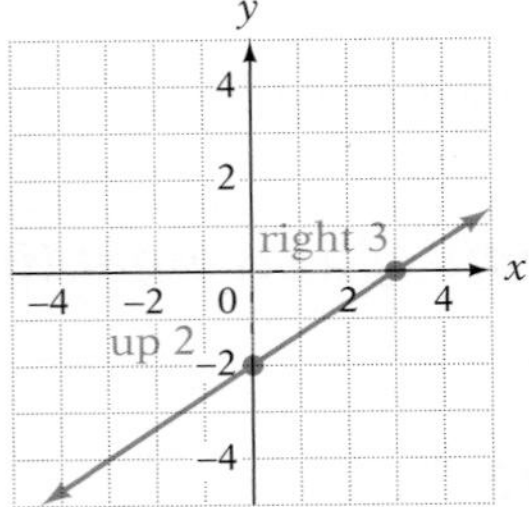

YOU TRY IT 6

Graph $x - 2y = 4$ by using the slope and y-intercept.

Your solution

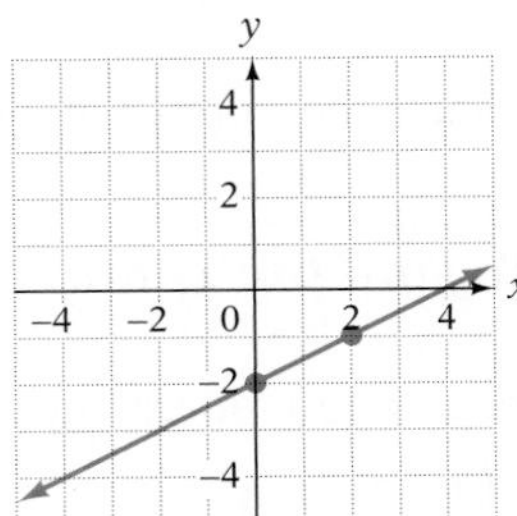

IN-CLASS EXAMPLES

Graph by using the slope and y-intercept.

7. $y = x - 3$
8. $y = \frac{4}{3}x + 1$
9. $x + 2y = 4$

Solutions on p. S31

12.3 EXERCISES

Concept Check

SUGGESTED ASSIGNMENT
Exercises 1–12; Exercises 13–29, odds; Exercises 33–43, odds; Exercises 49–89, odds; Exercise 96

1. What is the symbol for slope in the equation $y = mx + b$? m

2. What is the symbol for the y-coordinate of the y-intercept in the equation $y = mx + b$? b

3. a. A line that slants upward to the right has positive slope.
b. A line that slants downward to the right has negative slope.
c. A horizontal line has zero slope.
d. The slope of a vertical line is undefined.

4. Which coordinate of an x-intercept is 0? y-coordinate

5. Which coordinate of a y-intercept is 0? x-coordinate

6. Name the y-intercept of the graph shown at the right. (0, 3)

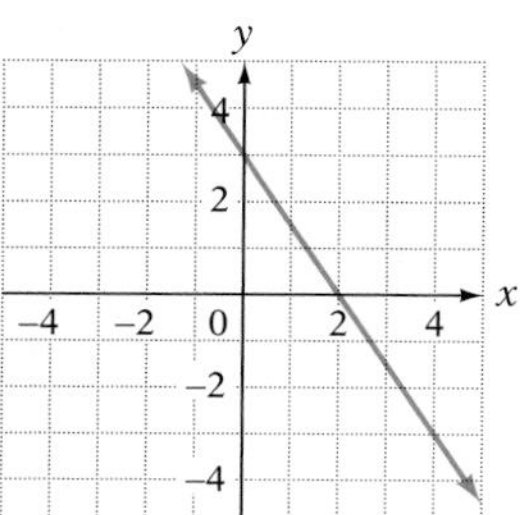

7. Identify each x value and each y value to be inserted into the slope formula $m = \frac{y_2 - y_1}{x_2 - x_1}$ to find the slope of the line containing $P_1(1, -4)$ and $P_2(3, 2)$.
$y_2 =$ 2; $y_1 =$ −4; $x_2 =$ 3; $x_1 =$ 1

8. The slope of the line with equation $y = 5x - 3$ is 5, and its y-intercept is (0, −3).

9. Describe the graph of a line that has an x-intercept but no y-intercept. Vertical

10. Describe the graph of a line that has a y-intercept but no x-intercept. Horizontal

11. The slope of a line is $\frac{6}{5}$. What is the slope of any line parallel to this line? $\frac{6}{5}$

12. The slope of a line is $\frac{3}{2}$. What is the slope of any line perpendicular to this line? $-\frac{2}{3}$

OBJECTIVE A *To find the x- and y-intercepts of a straight line*

For Exercises 13 to 24, find the x- and y-intercepts.

13. $x - y = 3$
(3, 0), (0, −3)

14. $3x + 4y = 12$
(4, 0), (0, 3)

15. $3x - y = 6$
(2, 0), (0, −6)

16. $2x - y = -10$
(−5, 0), (0, 10)

17. $x - 5y = 10$
(10, 0), (0, −2)

18. $3x + 2y = 12$
(4, 0), (0, 6)

19. $3x - y = -12$
(−4, 0), (0, 12)

20. $5x - y = -10$
(−2, 0), (0, 10)

21. $2x - 3y = 0$
(0, 0), (0, 0)

22. $3x + 4y = 0$
(0, 0), (0, 0)

23. $x + 2y = 6$
(6, 0), (0, 3)

24. $2x - 3y = 12$
(6, 0), (0, −4)

For Exercises 25 to 30, find the x- and y-intercepts, and then graph.

25. $5x + 2y = 10$

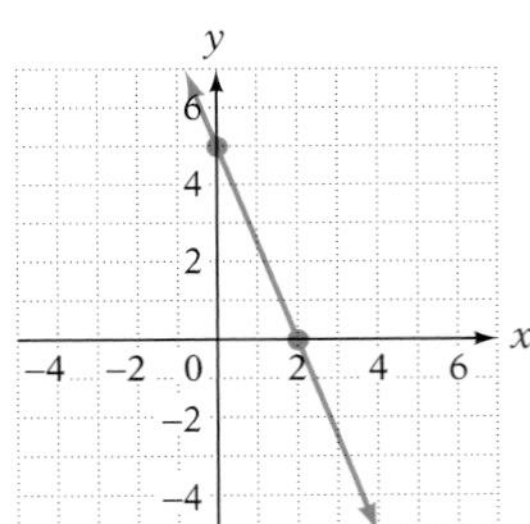

26. $x - 3y = 6$

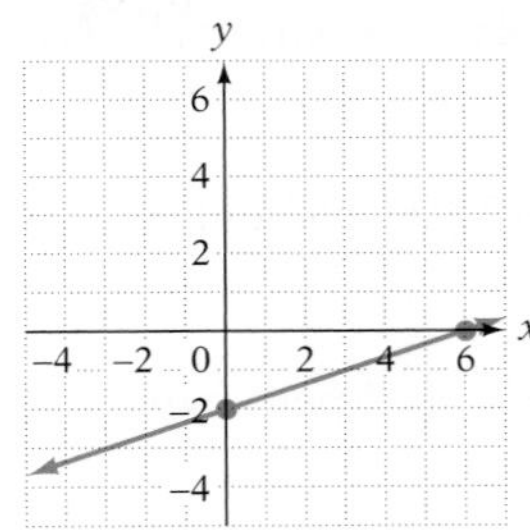

27. $3x - 4y = 12$

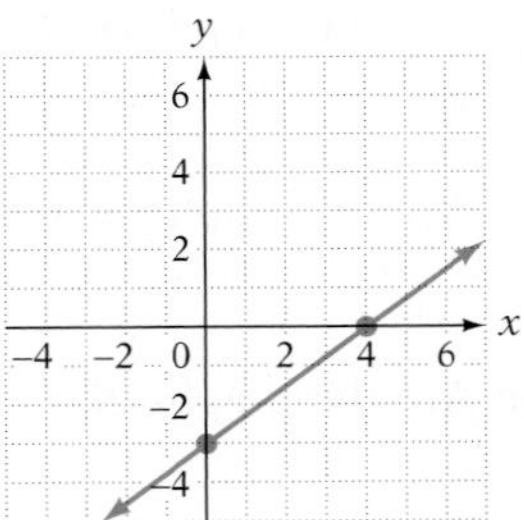

28. $2x - 5y = 10$

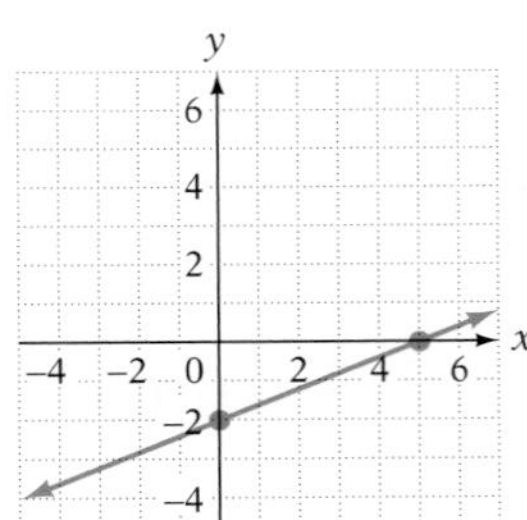

29. $5y - 3x = 15$

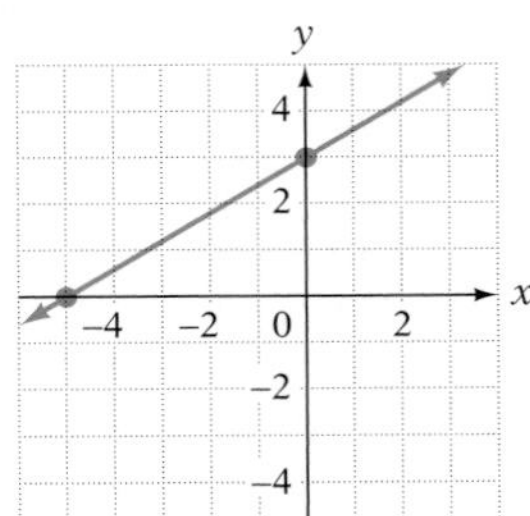

30. $9y - 4x = 18$

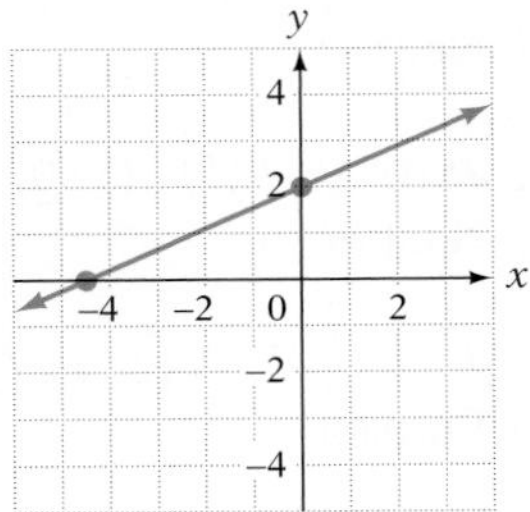

31. If $A > 0$, $B > 0$, and $C > 0$, is the y-intercept of the graph of $Ax + By = C$ above or below the x-axis? Above

32. If $A > 0$, $B > 0$, and $C > 0$, is the x-intercept of the graph of $Ax + By = C$ to the left or to the right of the y-axis? To the right

OBJECTIVE B *To find the slope of a straight line*

For Exercises 33 to 44, find the slope of the line containing the given points.

33. $P_1(4, 2), P_2(3, 4)$ -2

34. $P_1(2, 1), P_2(3, 4)$ 3

35. $P_1(-1, 3), P_2(2, 4)$ $\frac{1}{3}$

36. $P_1(-2, 1), P_2(2, 2)$ $\frac{1}{4}$

37. $P_1(2, 4), P_2(4, -1)$ $-\frac{5}{2}$

38. $P_1(1, 3), P_2(5, -3)$ $-\frac{3}{2}$

39. $P_1(3, -4), P_2(3, 5)$ Undefined

40. $P_1(-1, 2), P_2(-1, 3)$ Undefined

41. $P_1(4, -2), P_2(3, -2)$ Zero

42. $P_1(5, 1), P_2(-2, 1)$ Zero

43. $P_1(0, -1), P_2(3, -2)$ $-\frac{1}{3}$

44. $P_1(3, 0), P_2(2, -1)$ 1

45. What is the difference between a line that has zero slope and one that has undefined slope?

For Exercises 46 and 47, l is a line passing through two distinct points (a, b) and (c, d).

46. Describe any relationships that must exist among a, b, c, and d in order for the slope of l to be undefined. $a = c, b \neq d$

47. Describe any relationships that must exist among a, b, c, and d in order for the slope of l to be zero. $b = d, a \neq c$

48. Are the graphs of $y = \frac{3}{8}x - 5$ and $y = \frac{3}{8}x + 2$ parallel? Yes

49. Are the graphs of $y = -4x + 1$ and $y = 4x - 3$ parallel? No

50. Are the graphs of $y = \frac{7}{2}x$ and $y = -\frac{2}{7}x + 2$ perpendicular? Yes

51. Are the graphs of $y = 3x - 8$ and $y = -3x + 8$ perpendicular? No

For Exercises 52 to 59, determine whether the line through P_1 and P_2 is parallel, perpendicular, or neither parallel nor perpendicular to the line through Q_1 and Q_2.

52. $P_1(-3, 4), P_2(2, -5); Q_1(3, 6), Q_2(-2, -3)$
Neither

53. $P_1(4, -5), P_2(6, -9); Q_1(5, -4), Q_2(1, 4)$
Parallel

54. $P_1(0, 1), P_2(2, 4); Q_1(-4, -7), Q_2(2, 5)$
Neither

55. $P_1(5, 1), P_2(3, -2); Q_1(0, -2), Q_2(3, -4)$
Perpendicular

56. $P_1(-2, 4), P_2(2, 4); Q_1(-3, 6), Q_2(4, 6)$
Parallel

57. $P_1(1, -1), P_2(3, -2); Q_1(-4, 1), Q_2(2, -5)$
Neither

58. $P_1(7, -1), P_2(-4, 6); Q_1(3, 0), Q_2(-5, 3)$
Neither

59. $P_1(5, -2), P_2(-1, 3); Q_1(3, 4), Q_2(-2, -2)$
Perpendicular

60. **Deep-Sea Diving** The pressure, in pounds per square inch, on a descending diver is shown in the graph at the right. Find the slope of the line. Write a sentence that explains the meaning of the slope.
$m = 0.5$. For each additional foot a diver descends below the surface of the water, the pressure on the diver increases by 0.5 pound per square inch.

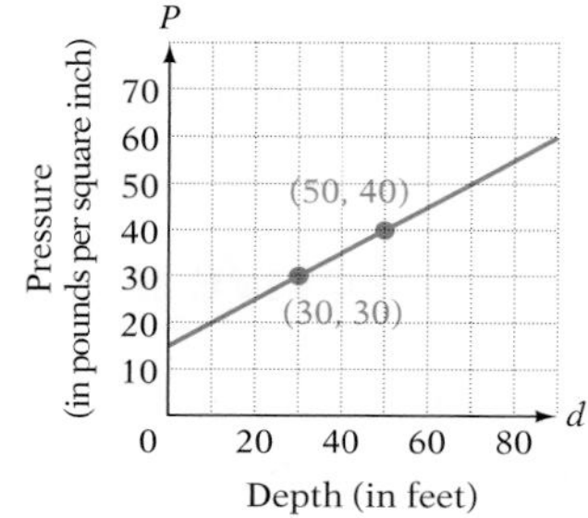

61. **Panama Canal** Ships in the Panama Canal are lowered through a series of locks. A ship is lowered as the water in a lock is discharged. The graph at the right shows the number of gallons of water N, in millions, remaining in a lock t minutes after the valves are opened to discharge the water. Find the slope of the line. Write a sentence that explains the meaning of the slope.

$m = -\frac{19}{30}$. Each minute, the water in the lock decreases by $0.6\overline{3}$ million gallons.

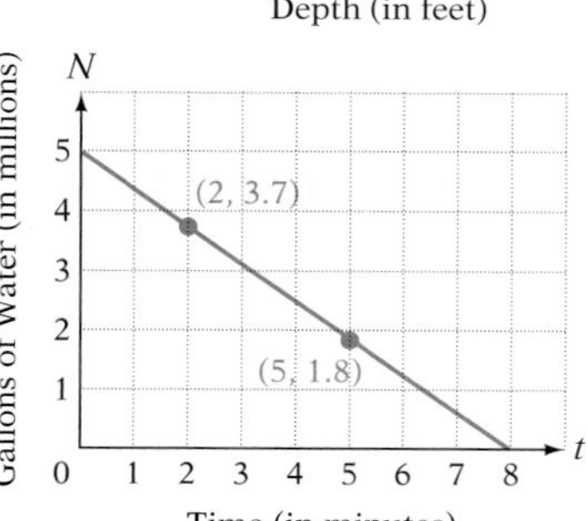

62. **Postal Service** The graph at the right shows the work accomplished by an electronic mail sorter. Find the slope of the line. Write a sentence that explains the meaning of the slope. $m = 50$. The electronic mail sorter sorts 50 pieces of mail per minute.

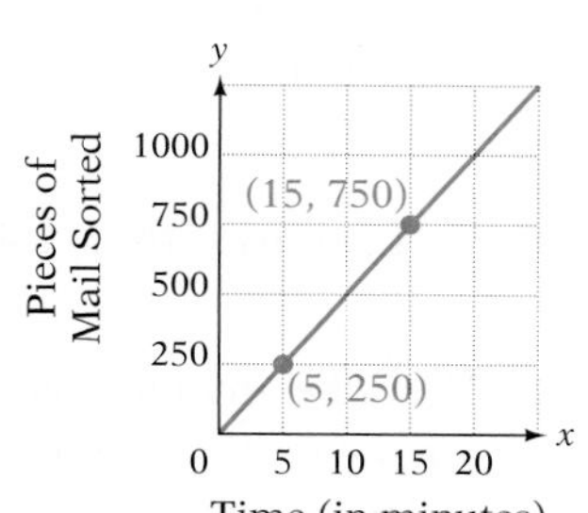

63. **Health** The graph at the right shows the relationship between distance walked and calories burned. Find the slope of the line. Write a sentence that explains the meaning of the slope. $m = 70$. Walking burns 70 calories per mile.

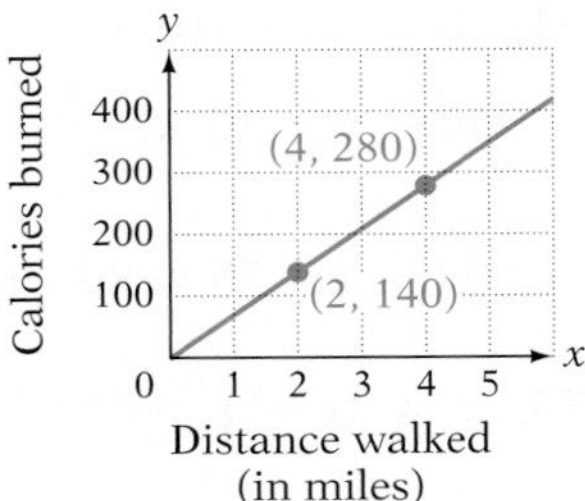

64. **Fuel Consumption** The graph at the right shows how the amount of gasoline in the tank of a car decreases as the car is driven at a constant speed of 60 mph. Find the slope of the line. Write a sentence that states the meaning of the slope. $m = -0.02$. The car uses 0.02 gal of gasoline per mile driven.

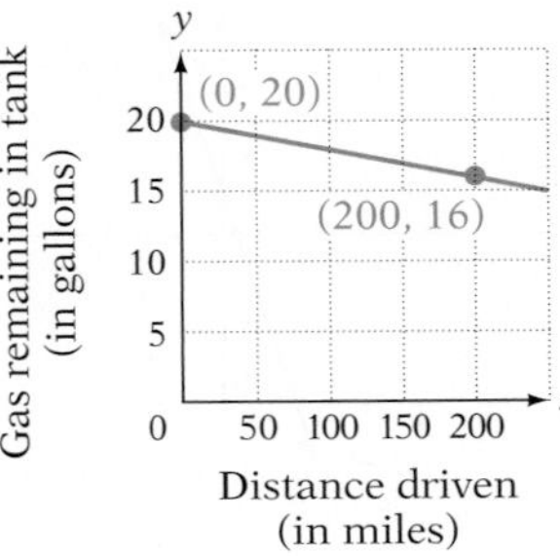

Traffic Safety See the news clipping below. Use the information in the clipping for Exercises 65 and 66.

In the NEWS!

Buckling Up Saves Lives

Annual surveys conducted by the National Highway Safety Administration show that Americans' steady increase in seat belt use has been accompanied by a steady decrease in deaths due to motor vehicle accidents.

Source: National Highway Traffic Safety Association

Seat Belt Use

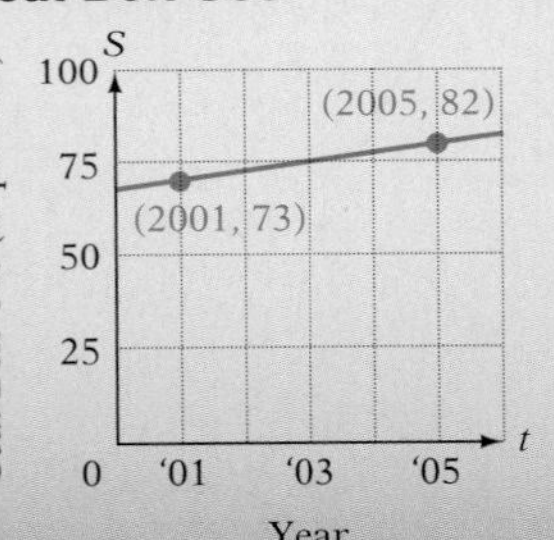

Passenger Deaths

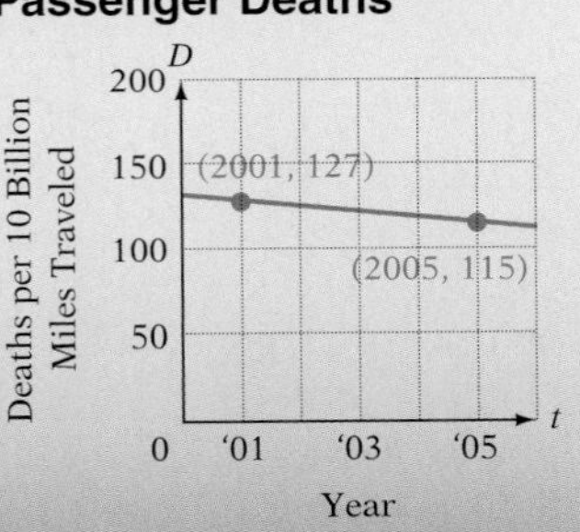

65. Find the slope of the line in the Seat Belt Use graph. Write a sentence that states the meaning of the slope in the context of the article.
$m = 2.25$. The percent of people using seat belts has increased by 2.25% per year.

66. Find the slope of the line in the Passenger Deaths graph. Write a sentence that states the meaning of the slope in the context of the article.
$m = -3$. The number of deaths per 10 billion miles traveled has decreased by 3 deaths per year.

OBJECTIVE C *To graph a line using the slope and the y-intercept*

For Exercises 67 to 74, find the slope and y-intercept of the graph of the equation.

67. $y = -\frac{3}{8}x + 5$

$m = -\frac{3}{8}$, $(0, 5)$

68. $y = -x + 7$

$m = -1$, $(0, 7)$

69. $2x - 3y = 6$

$m = \frac{2}{3}$, $(0, -2)$

70. $4x + 3y = 12$

$m = -\frac{4}{3}$, $(0, 4)$

71. $2x + 5y = 10$
$m = -\frac{2}{5}$, $(0, 2)$

72. $2x + y = 0$
$m = -2$, $(0, 0)$

73. $x - 4y = 0$
$m = \frac{1}{4}$, $(0, 0)$

74. $2x + 3y = 8$
$m = -\frac{2}{3}$, $\left(0, \frac{8}{3}\right)$

For Exercises 75 to 89, graph by using the slope and y-intercept.

75. $y = 3x + 1$

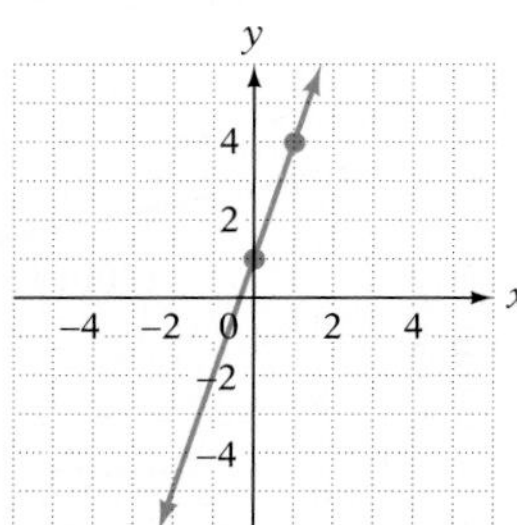

76. $y = -2x - 1$

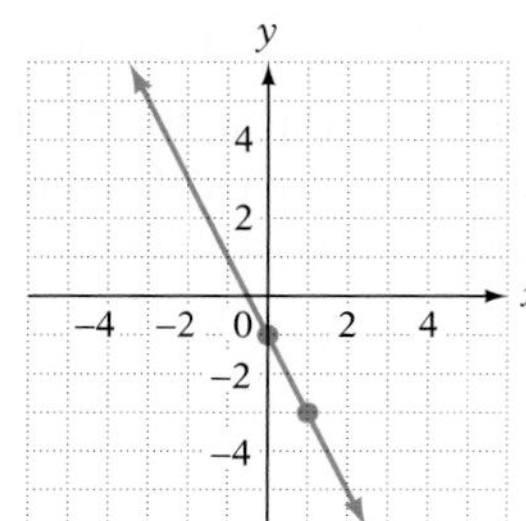

77. $y = \frac{2}{5}x - 2$

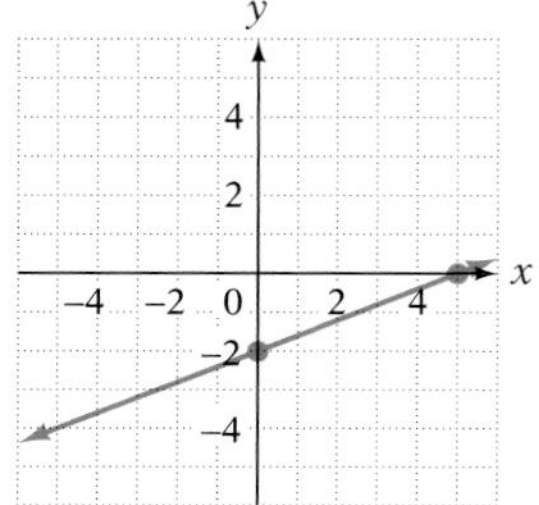

78. $y = \frac{3}{4}x + 1$

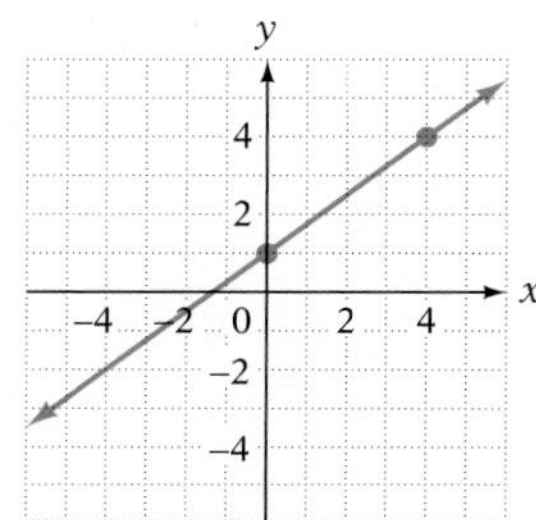

79. $2x + y = 3$

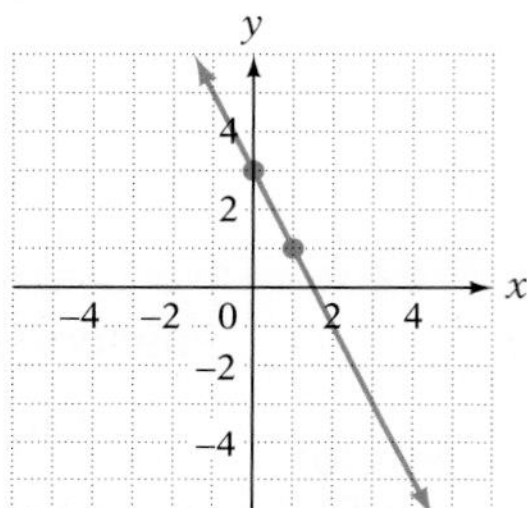

80. $3x - y = 1$

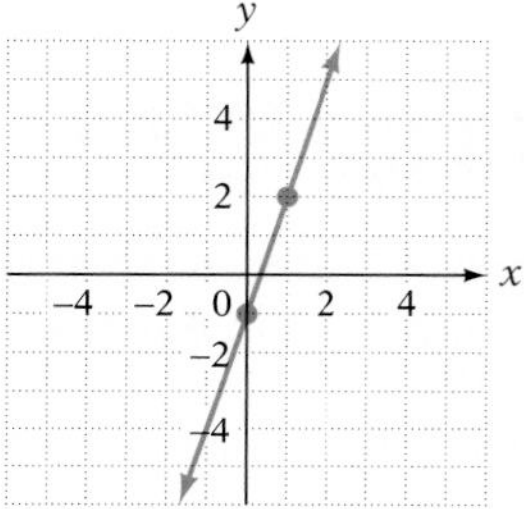

81. $x - 2y = 4$

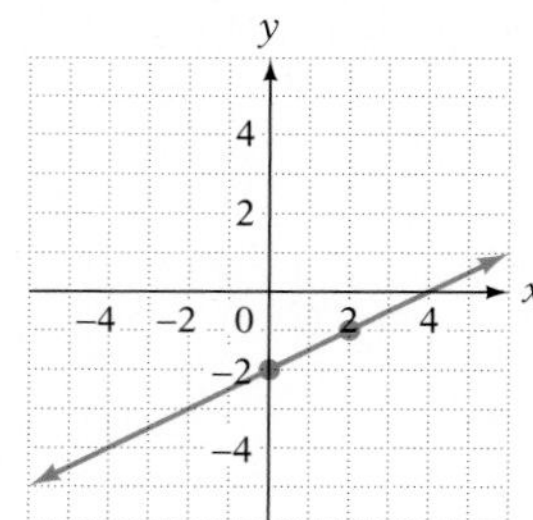

82. $x + 3y = 6$

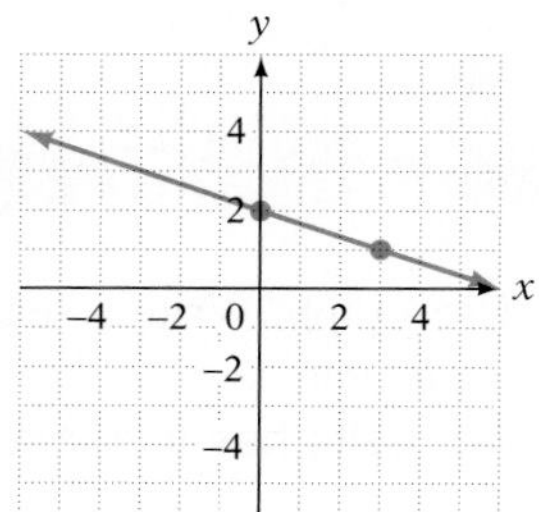

83. $y = \frac{2}{3}x$

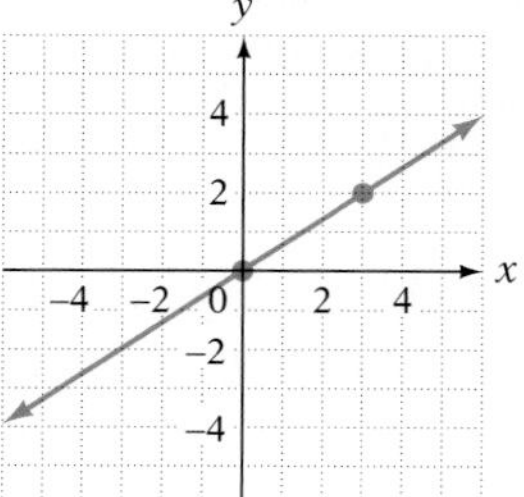

84. $y = \frac{1}{2}x$

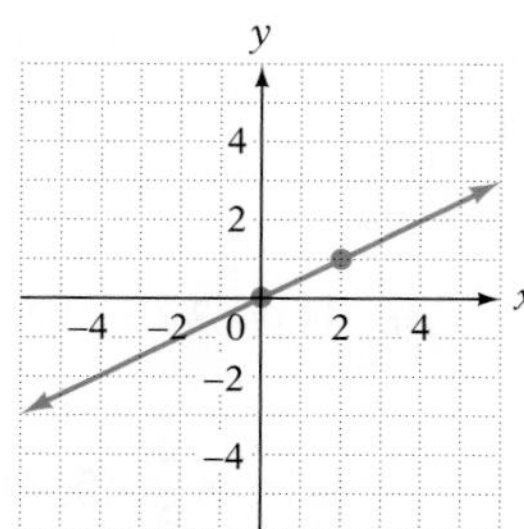

85. $y = -x + 1$

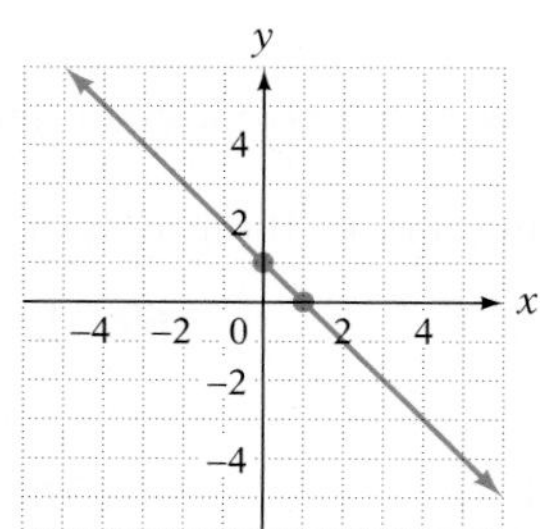

86. $y = -x - 3$

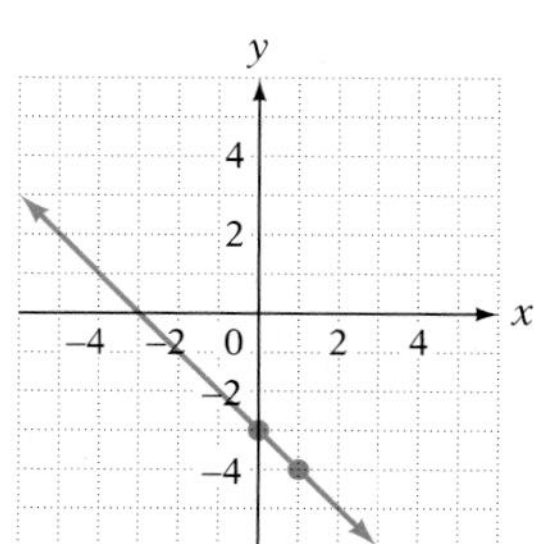

87. $3x - 4y = 12$

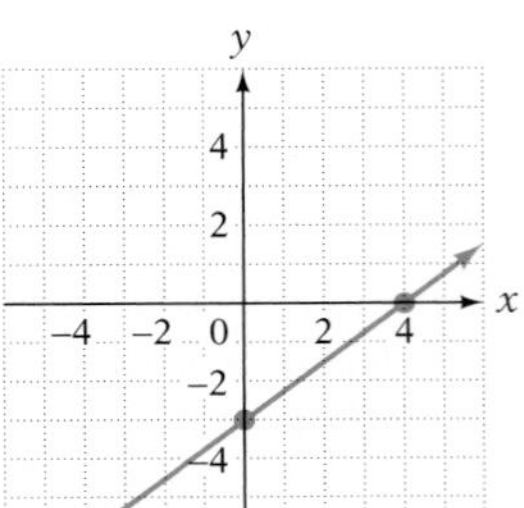

88. $5x - 2y = 10$

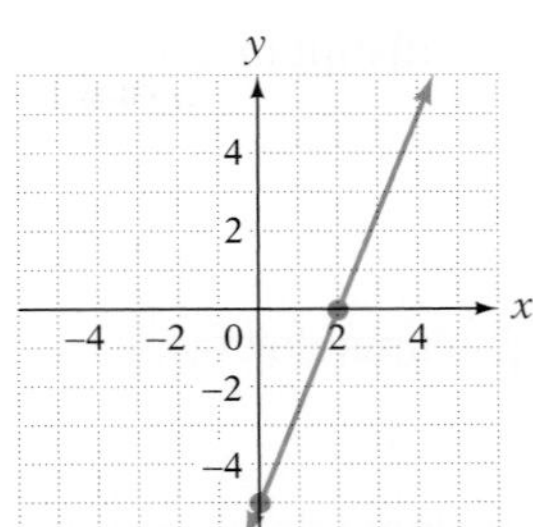

89. $y = -4x + 2$

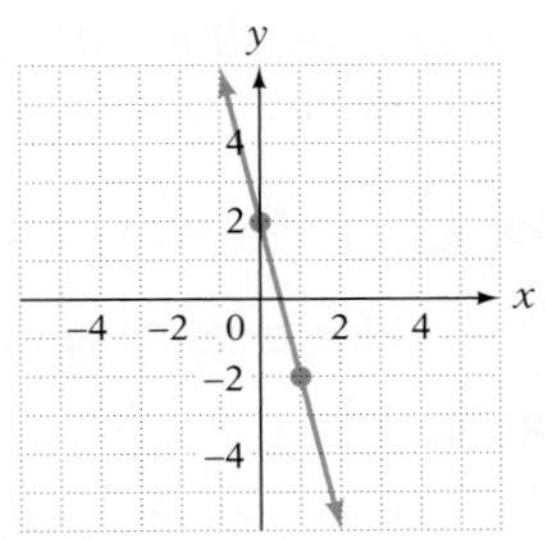

90. Suppose A, B, and C are all positive numbers. Does the y-intercept of the graph of $Ax + By = C$ lie above or below the x-axis? Does the graph slant upward to the right or downward to the right? Above; downward to the right

91. Suppose A is a negative number, and B and C are positive numbers. Does the y-intercept of the graph of $Ax + By = C$ lie above or below the x-axis? Does the graph slant upward to the right or downward to the right? Above; upward to the right

Critical Thinking

92. What effect does increasing the coefficient of x have on the graph of $y = mx + b$, $m > 0$? Increases the slope

93. What effect does decreasing the coefficient of x have on the graph of $y = mx + b$, $m > 0$? Decreases the slope

94. What effect does increasing the constant term have on the graph of $y = mx + b$? Increases the y-coordinate of the y-intercept

95. What effect does decreasing the constant term have on the graph of $y = mx + b$? Decreases the y-coordinate of the y-intercept

96. Match each equation with its graph.

(i) $y = -2x + 4$

(ii) $y = 2x - 4$

(iii) $y = 2$

(iv) $2x + 4y = 0$

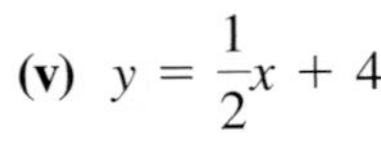

(v) $y = \frac{1}{2}x + 4$

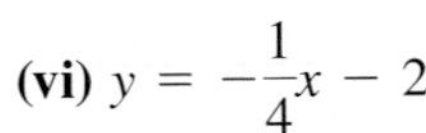

(vi) $y = -\frac{1}{4}x - 2$

i and D; ii and C; iii and B; iv and F; v and E; vi and A

A.

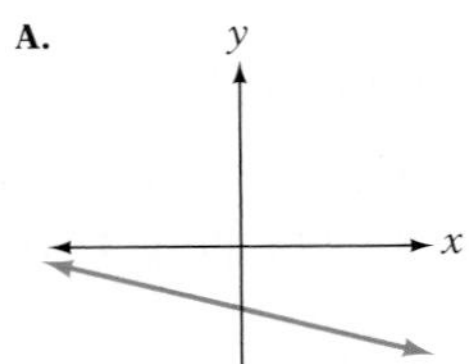

B.

C.

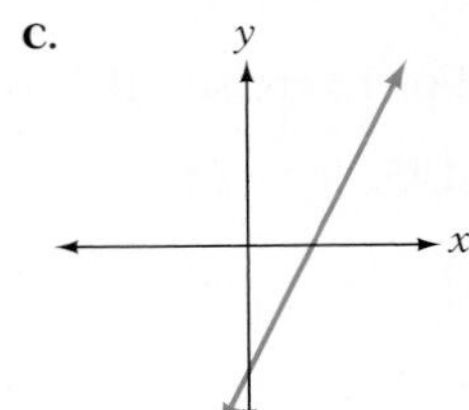

D.

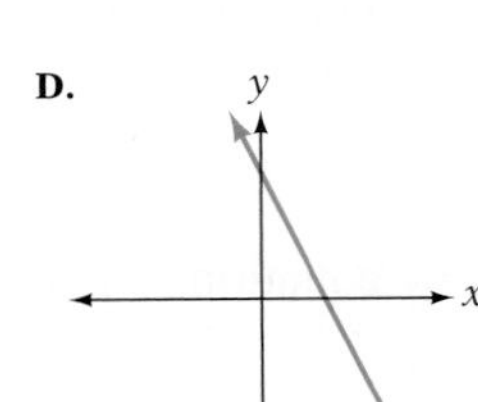

E.

F.

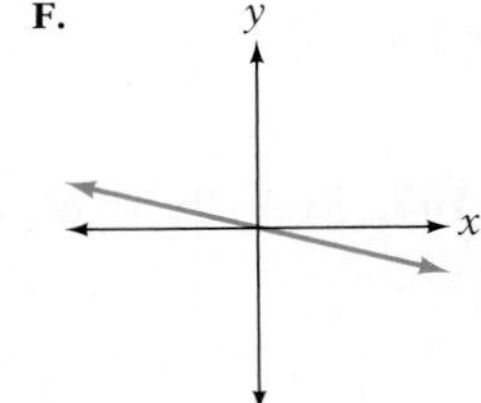

97. Do the graphs of all straight lines have a y-intercept? If not, give an example of one that does not. No; for example, $x = 2$

98. If two lines have the same slope and the same y-intercept, must the graphs of the lines be the same? If not, give an example. Yes

Projects or Group Activities

For Exercises 99 to 104, explain how you would distinguish between the graphs of the two equations.

99. **a.** $y = \frac{3}{5}x - 2$ **b.** $y = -\frac{3}{5}x - 2$

Line *a* slants upward to the right. Line *b* slants downward to the right.

100. **a.** $y = x + 1$ **b.** $y = -x + 1$

Line *a* slants upward to the right. Line *b* slants downward to the right.

101. **a.** $y = \frac{3}{4}x + 5$ **b.** $y = \frac{3}{4}x - 5$

Line *a* has a *y*-intercept of (0, 5). Line *b* has a *y*-intercept of (0, −5).

102. **a.** $y = 2x - 4$ **b.** $y = 2x + 4$

Line *a* has a *y*-intercept of (0, −4). Line *b* has a *y*-intercept of (0, 4).

103. **a.** $y = 6$ **b.** $x = 6$

Line *a* is a horizontal line. Line *b* is a vertical line.

104. **a.** $y = 1$ **b.** $y = -1$

Line *a* is a horizontal line above the *x*-axis. Line *b* is a horizontal line below the *x*-axis.

A graphing calculator can be used to graph a linear equation. Here are the keystrokes to graph $y = \frac{2}{3}x + 1$. First the equation is entered. Then the domain (Xmin to Xmax) and the range (Ymin to Ymax) are entered. This is called the **viewing window.** Xmin and Xmax are the smallest and largest values of x that will be shown on the screen. Ymin and Ymax are the smallest and largest values of y that will be shown on the screen.

By changing the keystrokes 2 X,T,θ,n ÷ 3 + 1, you can graph different equations.

For Exercises 105 to 108, use a graphing calculator to graph the equation.

105. $y = 2x + 1$ For $2x$, you may enter $2 \times x$ or just $2x$. Entering the times sign $\times$ is not necessary on many graphing calculators.

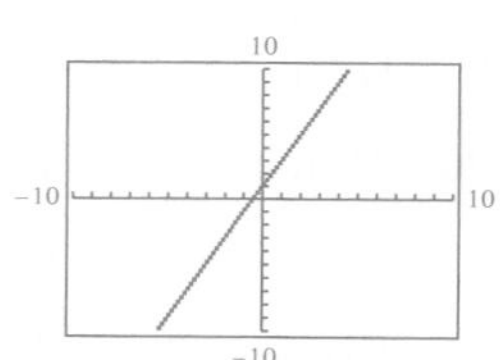

106. $y = -\frac{1}{2}x - 2$ Use the (-) key to enter a negative sign.

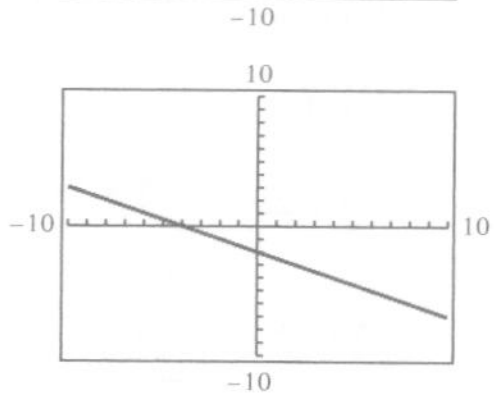

107. $3x + 2y = 6$ Solve for y. Then enter the equation. $y = -\frac{3}{2}x + 3$

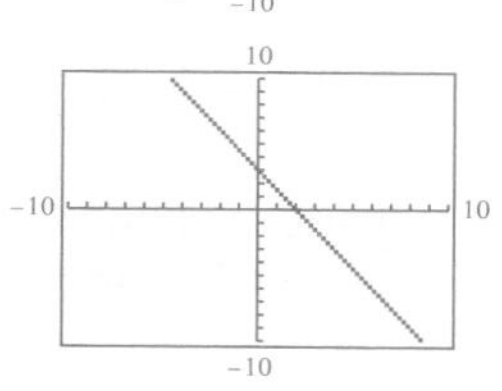

108. $4x + 3y = 75$ You must adjust the viewing window. *Suggestion:* Xmin = −25, Xmax = 25, Xscl = 5; Ymin = −35, Ymax = 35, Yscl = 5. $y = -\frac{4}{3}x + 25$

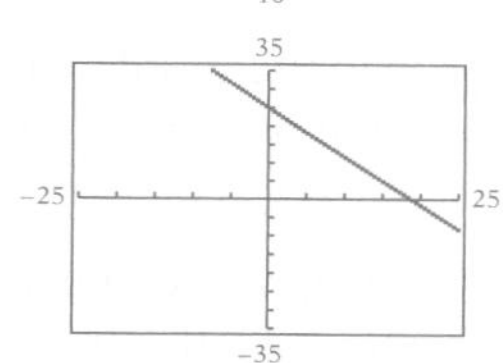

QUICK QUIZ

Find the *x*- and *y*-intercepts, and then graph.

1. $x - y = 2$ **(2, 0), (0, −2) [12.3A]**
2. $-x + 4y = 4$ **(−4, 0), (0, 1) [12.3A]**
3. Find the slope of the line containing the points (4, −1) and (−1, 3). $-\frac{4}{5}$ **[12.3B]**
4. Is the line that contains the points (−3, −1) and (−6, −3) parallel to the line that contains the points (0, −2) and (3, 0)? **Yes [12.3B]**

Graph by using the slope and *y*-intercept.

5. $y = 4x - 2$ **[12.3C]**
6. $y = \frac{1}{5}x$ **[12.3C]**

SECTION

12.4 Equations of Straight Lines

OBJECTIVE A *To find the equation of a line using the equation $y = mx + b$*

INSTRUCTOR NOTE
You may elect to cover only Objective A, only Objective B, or both Objectives A and B when presenting the topic of finding the equation of a line given a point and the slope of the line.

When the slope of a line and a point on the line are known, the equation of the line can be written using the slope-intercept form, $y = mx + b$. In HOW TO 1 below, the known point is the y-intercept. In HOW TO 2, the known point is a point other than the y-intercept.

HOW TO 1 Find the equation of the line that has slope 3 and y-intercept $(0, 2)$.

$$y = mx + b$$

The given slope, 3, is m. Replace m with 3. $\quad y = 3x + b$

The given point, $(0, 2)$, is the y-intercept. Replace b with 2. $\quad y = 3x + 2$

The equation of the line that has slope 3 and y-intercept $(0, 2)$ is $y = 3x + 2$.

HOW TO 2 Find the equation of the line that has slope $\frac{1}{2}$ and contains the point whose coordinates are $(-2, 4)$.

$$y = mx + b$$

The given slope, $\frac{1}{2}$, is m. Replace m with $\frac{1}{2}$. $\quad y = \frac{1}{2}x + b$

The given point, $(-2, 4)$, is a solution of the equation of the line. Replace x and y in the equation with the coordinates of the point. $\quad 4 = \frac{1}{2}(-2) + b$

Solve for b, the y-intercept. $\quad 4 = -1 + b$

$$5 = b$$

Write the equation of the line by replacing m and b in the equation $y = mx + b$ by their values. $\quad y = mx + b$

$$y = \frac{1}{2}x + 5$$

The equation of the line that has slope $\frac{1}{2}$ and contains the point whose coordinates are $(-2, 4)$ is $y = \frac{1}{2}x + 5$.

Take Note
Every ordered pair is of the form (x, y). For the point $(-2, 4)$, -2 is the x value and 4 is the y value. Substitute -2 for x and 4 for y.

EXAMPLE 1

Find the equation of the line that contains the point $(0, -1)$ and has slope $-\frac{2}{3}$.

Solution

Use the slope-intercept form, $y = mx + b$.

$y = -\frac{2}{3}x - 1 \quad$ • $m = -\frac{2}{3}$; $b = -1$

The equation of the line is $y = -\frac{2}{3}x - 1$.

YOU TRY IT 1

Find the equation of the line that contains the point $(0, 2)$ and has slope $\frac{5}{3}$.

Your solution

$y = \frac{5}{3}x + 2$

Solution on p. S31

EXAMPLE 2

Find the equation of the line that contains the point whose coordinates are $(3, -3)$ and has slope $\frac{2}{3}$.

Solution

$y = mx + b$ • Use the slope-intercept form.

$y = \frac{2}{3}x + b$ • $m = \frac{2}{3}$

$-3 = \frac{2}{3}(3) + b$ • Replace x and y in the equation with the coordinates of the given point, $(3, -3)$

$-3 = 2 + b$ • Solve for b.

$-5 = b$

$y = \frac{2}{3}x - 5$ • Replace m by $\frac{2}{3}$ and b by -5 in $y = mx + b$.

The equation of the line is $y = \frac{2}{3}x - 5$.

YOU TRY IT 2

Find the equation of the line that contains the point whose coordinates are $(4, -2)$ and has slope $\frac{3}{2}$.

Your solution

$y = \frac{3}{2}x - 8$

IN-CLASS EXAMPLES

Find the equation of the line with the given characteristics.

1. Has slope $-\frac{3}{4}$ and y-intercept $(0, 4)$

   $y = -\frac{3}{4}x + 4$

2. Contains the point $(-6, -4)$ and has slope $\frac{1}{2}$

   $y = \frac{1}{2}x - 1$

Solution on p. S31

OBJECTIVE B *To find the equation of a line using the point-slope formula*

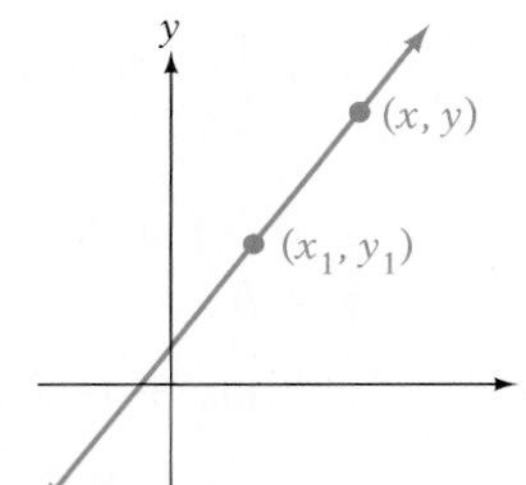

An alternative method for finding the equation of a line, given the slope and the coordinates of a point on the line, involves use of the point-slope formula. The point-slope formula is derived from the formula for slope.

Let (x_1, y_1) be the coordinates of the given point on the line, and let (x, y) be the coordinates of any other point on the line. Use the formula for slope.

$$\frac{y - y_1}{x - x_1} = m$$

Multiply both sides of the equation by $(x - x_1)$.

$$\frac{y - y_1}{x - x_1}(x - x_1) = m(x - x_1)$$

Simplify.

$$y - y_1 = m(x - x_1)$$

INSTRUCTOR NOTE

A model of the point-slope formula with open parentheses may help some students substitute correctly.

$y - y_1 = m\ (x - x_1)$

$\downarrow \quad \downarrow \quad \downarrow$

$y - (\ ) = (\ )[x - (\ )]$

Point-Slope Formula

The equation of the line that has slope m and contains the point whose coordinates are (x_1, y_1) can be found by using the point-slope formula:

$$\mathbf{y - y_1 = m(x - x_1)}$$

EXAMPLE

Find the equation of the line that passes through the point $(2, 3)$ and has slope -2.

$y - y_1 = m(x - x_1)$ • Use the point-slope formula.

$y - 3 = -2(x - 2)$ • $m = -2$; $(x_1, y_1) = (2, 3)$

$y - 3 = -2x + 4$ • Solve for y.

$y = -2x + 7$

The equation of the line is $y = -2x + 7$.

EXAMPLE 3

Use the point-slope formula to find the equation of the line that passes through the point $(-2, -1)$ and has slope $\frac{3}{2}$.

Solution

$$y - y_1 = m(x - x_1)$$

$$y - (-1) = \frac{3}{2}[x - (-2)] \qquad \bullet\ m = \frac{3}{2};\ (x_1, y_1) = (-2, -1)$$

$$y + 1 = \frac{3}{2}(x + 2)$$

$$y + 1 = \frac{3}{2}x + 3$$

$$y = \frac{3}{2}x + 2$$

The equation of the line is $y = \frac{3}{2}x + 2$.

YOU TRY IT 3

Use the point-slope formula to find the equation of the line that passes through the point $(4, -2)$ and has slope $\frac{3}{4}$.

Your solution

$$y = \frac{3}{4}x - 5$$

IN-CLASS EXAMPLES

3. Use the point-slope formula to find the equation of the line that passes through the point $(-2, 1)$ and has slope -2.
$y = -2x - 3$

Solution on p. S31

OBJECTIVE C

To find the equation of a line given two points

INSTRUCTOR NOTE
If you choose not to cover Objective B, students can use the method of Objective A to find the equation of the line in Step 2.

The point-slope formula is used to find the equation of a line when a point on the line and the slope of the line are known. But this formula can also be used to find the equation of a line given two points on the line. In this case,

1. Use the slope formula to determine the slope of the line between the points.
2. Use the point-slope formula, the slope you just calculated, and one of the given points to find the equation of the line.

HOW TO 3 Find the equation of the line that passes through the points $(-3, -1)$ and $(3, 3)$.

Use the slope formula to determine the slope of the line between the points.

$$m = \frac{y_2 - y_1}{x_2 - x_1} = \frac{3 - (-1)}{3 - (-3)} = \frac{4}{6} = \frac{2}{3} \qquad \bullet\ (x_1, y_1) = (-3, -1);\ (x_2, y_2) = (3, 3)$$

Use the point-slope formula, the slope you just calculated, and one of the given points to find the equation of the line.

$$y - y_1 = m(x - x_1) \qquad \bullet\ \text{Point-slope formula}$$

$$y - (-1) = \frac{2}{3}[x - (-3)] \qquad \bullet\ m = \frac{2}{3};\ (x_1, y_1) = (-3, -1)$$

$$y + 1 = \frac{2}{3}(x + 3)$$

$$y + 1 = \frac{2}{3}x + 2$$

$$y = \frac{2}{3}x + 1$$

Take Note

You can verify that the equation $y = \frac{2}{3}x + 1$ passes through the points $(-3, -1)$ and $(3, 3)$ by substituting the coordinates of these points into the equation.

Check:

$$\begin{array}{c|c} \multicolumn{2}{c}{y = \frac{2}{3}x + 1} \\ \hline -1 & \frac{2}{3}(-3) + 1 \\ -1 & -2 + 1 \\ \multicolumn{2}{c}{-1 = -1} \end{array} \quad \bullet\ (x, y) = (-3, -1)$$

$$\begin{array}{c|c} \multicolumn{2}{c}{y = \frac{2}{3}x + 1} \\ \hline 3 & \frac{2}{3}(3) + 1 \\ 3 & 2 + 1 \\ \multicolumn{2}{c}{3 = 3} \end{array} \quad \bullet\ (x, y) = (3, 3)$$

The equation of the line that passes through the two points is $y = \frac{2}{3}x + 1$.

If the two given points lie on a horizontal line, the procedure used in HOW TO 3 can be used to find the equation of the line. However, it is quicker to just remember that the equation of a horizontal line is $y = b$, where b is the y-intercept of the graph of the line. b is also the y-coordinate of each of the two given points.

HOW TO 4 Find the equation of the line that passes through the points whose coordinates are $(-4, -2)$ and $(2, -2)$.

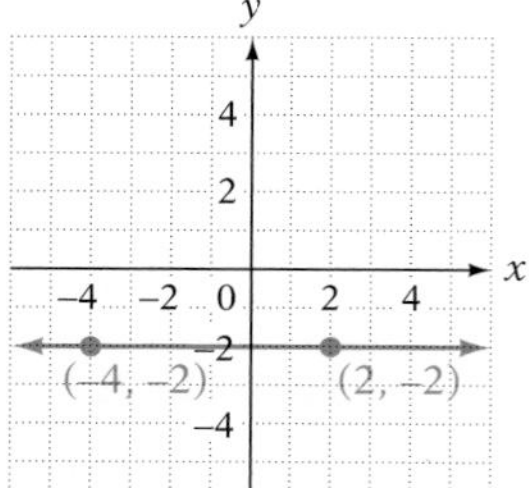

The y-coordinates of the two points are the same. The points lie on a horizontal line. The equation of the line is $y = b$, where b is the y-intercept of the graph of the line. The equation of the line is $y = -2$.

The equation of a vertical line is $x = a$, where a is the x-intercept of the graph of the line. a is also the x-coordinate of each of the two given points. For example, the equation of the line that passes through the points $(3, 4)$ and $(3, -5)$ is $x = 3$.

EXAMPLE 4

Find the equation of the line that passes through the points $(-4, 0)$ and $(2, -3)$.

Solution

Find the slope of the line between the two points.

$$m = \frac{y_2 - y_1}{x_2 - x_1} = \frac{-3 - 0}{2 - (-4)} = \frac{-3}{6} = -\frac{1}{2}$$

Use the point-slope formula.

$$y - y_1 = m(x - x_1) \quad \bullet \text{ Point-slope formula}$$

$$y - 0 = -\frac{1}{2}[x - (-4)] \quad \bullet\ m = -\frac{1}{2};\ (x_1, y_1) = (-4, 0)$$

$$y = -\frac{1}{2}(x + 4)$$

$$y = -\frac{1}{2}x - 2$$

The equation of the line is $y = -\frac{1}{2}x - 2$.

YOU TRY IT 4

Find the equation of the line that passes through the points $(-6, -2)$ and $(3, 1)$.

Your solution

$y = \frac{1}{3}x$

IN-CLASS EXAMPLES

Find the equation of the line that passes through the given points.

4. $(4, -11)$ and $(-2, 1)$ $y = -2x - 3$
5. $(0, 0)$ and $(-8, -2)$ $y = \frac{1}{4}x$
6. $(1, -1)$ and $(-5, 7)$ $y = -\frac{4}{3}x + \frac{1}{3}$

Solution on p. S31

12.4 EXERCISES

SUGGESTED ASSIGNMENT
Exercises 1–6; Exercises 7–33, odds; Exercises 37–59, odds;
More challenging exercises: Exercises 70–73

Concept Check

1. The graph of the equation $y = 5x + 7$ has slope 5 and y-intercept (0, 7).

2. If a line has y-intercept $(0, 4)$, then 4 can be substituted for b in the equation $y = mx + b$.

3. Suppose a classmate says, "The y-intercept is 2." The classmate means that the y-intercept is the point (0, 2).

4. A line contains the point $(-3, 1)$. This means that when y is 1 in the equation of the line, x is -3.

5. In the equation of the line that has slope 3 and y-intercept $(0, 1)$, $m =$ 3 and $b =$ 1. The equation is $y =$ $3x + 1$.

6. After you find the equation of a line given its slope and the coordinates of a point on the line, how can you determine whether you have the correct equation? Check that the coefficient of x is the given slope. Check that the coordinates of the given point are a solution of your equation.

OBJECTIVE A *To find the equation of a line using the equation $y = mx + b$*

For Exercises 7 to 20, use the slope-intercept form $y = mx + b$.

7. Find the equation of the line that contains the point whose coordinates are (0, 2) and has slope 2. $y = 2x + 2$

8. Find the equation of the line that contains the point whose coordinates are $(0, -1)$ and has slope -2. $y = -2x - 1$

9. Find the equation of the line that contains the point whose coordinates are $(-1, 2)$ and has slope -3. $y = -3x - 1$

10. Find the equation of the line that contains the point whose coordinates are $(2, -3)$ and has slope 3. $y = 3x - 9$

11. Find the equation of the line that contains the point whose coordinates are (3, 1) and has slope $\frac{1}{3}$. $y = \frac{1}{3}x$

12. Find the equation of the line that contains the point whose coordinates are $(-2, 3)$ and has slope $\frac{1}{2}$. $y = \frac{1}{2}x + 4$

13. Find the equation of the line that contains the point whose coordinates are $(4, -2)$ and has slope $\frac{3}{4}$. $y = \frac{3}{4}x - 5$

14. Find the equation of the line that contains the point whose coordinates are (2, 3) and has slope $-\frac{1}{2}$. $y = -\frac{1}{2}x + 4$

15. Find the equation of the line that contains the point whose coordinates are $(5, -3)$ and has slope $-\frac{3}{5}$. $y = -\frac{3}{5}x$

16. Find the equation of the line that contains the point whose coordinates are $(5, -1)$ and has slope $\frac{1}{5}$. $y = \frac{1}{5}x - 2$

17. Find the equation of the line that contains the point whose coordinates are $(2, 3)$ and has slope $\frac{1}{4}$. $y = \frac{1}{4}x + \frac{5}{2}$

18. Find the equation of the line that contains the point whose coordinates are $(-1, 2)$ and has slope $-\frac{1}{2}$. $y = -\frac{1}{2}x + \frac{3}{2}$

19. Find the equation of the line that contains the point whose coordinates are $(-3, -5)$ and has slope $-\frac{2}{3}$. $y = -\frac{2}{3}x - 7$

20. Find the equation of the line that contains the point whose coordinates are $(-4, 0)$ and has slope $\frac{5}{2}$. $y = \frac{5}{2}x + 10$

OBJECTIVE B *To find the equation of a line using the point-slope formula*

For Exercises 21 to 34, use the point-slope formula.

21. Find the equation of the line that passes through the point whose coordinates are $(1, -1)$ and has slope 2. $y = 2x - 3$

22. Find the equation of the line that passes through the point whose coordinates are $(2, 3)$ and has slope -1. $y = -x + 5$

23. Find the equation of the line that passes through the point whose coordinates are $(-2, 1)$ and has slope -2. $y = -2x - 3$

24. Find the equation of the line that passes through the point whose coordinates are $(-1, -3)$ and has slope -3. $y = -3x - 6$

25. Find the equation of the line that passes through the point whose coordinates are $(0, 0)$ and has slope $\frac{2}{3}$. $y = \frac{2}{3}x$

26. Find the equation of the line that passes through the point whose coordinates are $(0, 0)$ and has slope $-\frac{1}{5}$. $y = -\frac{1}{5}x$

27. Find the equation of the line that passes through the point whose coordinates are $(2, 3)$ and has slope $\frac{1}{2}$. $y = \frac{1}{2}x + 2$

28. Find the equation of the line that passes through the point whose coordinates are $(3, -1)$ and has slope $\frac{2}{3}$. $y = \frac{2}{3}x - 3$

29. Find the equation of the line that passes through the point whose coordinates are $(-4, 1)$ and has slope $-\frac{3}{4}$. $y = -\frac{3}{4}x - 2$

30. Find the equation of the line that passes through the point whose coordinates are $(-5, 0)$ and has slope $-\frac{1}{5}$. $y = -\frac{1}{5}x - 1$

31. Find the equation of the line that passes through the point whose coordinates are $(-2, 1)$ and has slope $\frac{3}{4}$. $y = \frac{3}{4}x + \frac{5}{2}$

32. Find the equation of the line that passes through the point whose coordinates are $(3, -2)$ and has slope $\frac{1}{6}$. $y = \frac{1}{6}x - \frac{5}{2}$

33. Find the equation of the line that passes through the point whose coordinates are $(-3, -5)$ and has slope $-\frac{4}{3}$. $y = -\frac{4}{3}x - 9$

34. Find the equation of the line that passes through the point whose coordinates are $(3, -1)$ and has slope $\frac{3}{5}$. $y = \frac{3}{5}x - \frac{14}{5}$

35. Use the point-slope formula to find the equation of the line with slope m and y-intercept $(0, b)$. $y = mx + b$

36. Use the point-slope formula to find the equation of the line that goes through the point $(5, 3)$ and has slope 0. $y = 3$

OBJECTIVE C *To find the equation of a line given two points*

For Exercises 37 to 60, find the equation of the line through the given points.

37. $(-2, -2)$ and $(1, 7)$ $y = 3x + 4$

38. $(1, 5)$ and $(3, 9)$ $y = 2x + 3$

39. $(-5, 1)$ and $(2, -6)$ $y = -x - 4$

40. $(-3, 9)$ and $(1, 1)$ $y = -2x + 3$

41. $(5, -1)$ and $(-5, 11)$ $y = -\frac{6}{5}x + 5$

42. $(-6, 12)$ and $(-4, 9)$ $y = -\frac{3}{2}x + 3$

43. $(-10, -3)$ and $(5, -9)$ $y = -\frac{2}{5}x - 7$

44. $(-6, -13)$ and $(6, -1)$ $y = x - 7$

45. $(1, 5)$ and $(-6, 5)$ $y = 5$

46. $(-3, -4)$ and $(5, -4)$ $y = -4$

47. $(5, -1)$ and $(5, -7)$ $x = 5$

48. $(-3, 6)$ and $(-3, 0)$ $x = -3$

49. $(-20, -8)$ and $(5, 12)$ $y = \frac{4}{5}x + 8$

50. $(-6, 19)$ and $(2, 7)$ $y = -\frac{3}{2}x + 10$

51. $(0, -2)$ and $(-6, 1)$ $y = -\frac{1}{2}x - 2$

52. $(15, -9)$ and $(-20, 5)$ $y = -\frac{2}{5}x - 3$

53. $(6, -11)$ and $(-3, 1)$ $y = -\frac{4}{3}x - 3$

54. $(14, -1)$ and $(-7, -7)$ $y = \frac{2}{7}x - 5$

55. $(3, 6)$ and $(0, -3)$ $y = 3x - 3$

56. $(5, 9)$ and $(-5, 3)$ $y = \frac{3}{5}x + 6$

57. $(-1, -3)$ and $(2, 6)$ $y = 3x$

58. $(-3, 6)$ and $(4, -8)$ $y = -2x$

59. $(3, -5)$ and $(3, 1)$ $x = 3$

60. $(2, -1)$ and $(5, -1)$ $y = -1$

61. If $y = 2x - 3$ and (x_1, y_1) and (x_2, y_2) are the coordinates of two points on the graph of the line, what is the value of $\frac{y_2 - y_1}{x_2 - x_1}$? 2

Critical Thinking

For Exercises 62 to 65, determine whether there is a line that contains all of the given points. If so, find the equation of the line.

62. $(5, 1), (4, 2), (0, 6)$ Yes; $y = -x + 6$

63. $(-2, -4), (0, -3), (4, -1)$ Yes; $y = \frac{1}{2}x - 3$

64. $(-1, -5), (2, 4), (0, 2)$ No

65. $(3, -1), (12, -4), (-6, 2)$ Yes; $y = -\frac{1}{3}x$

For Exercises 66 to 69, the given ordered pairs are solutions of the same linear equation. Find n.

66. $(0, 1), (4, 9), (3, n)$ 7

67. $(2, 2), (-1, 5), (3, n)$ 1

68. $(2, -2), (-2, -4), (4, n)$ −1

69. $(1, -2), (-2, 4), (4, n)$ −8

Projects or Group Activities

For Exercises 70 to 73, **a.** name the x-intercept of the graph, **b.** name the y-intercept of the graph, **c.** determine the slope of the line, and **d.** write the equation of the line in slope-intercept form.

QUICK QUIZ

1. Find the equation of the line that has slope $-\frac{2}{5}$ and y-intercept $(0, -3)$. $y = -\frac{2}{5}x - 3$ [12.4A]
2. Find the equation of the line that contains the point $(2, -1)$ and has slope 3. $y = 3x - 7$ [12.4A]

70.

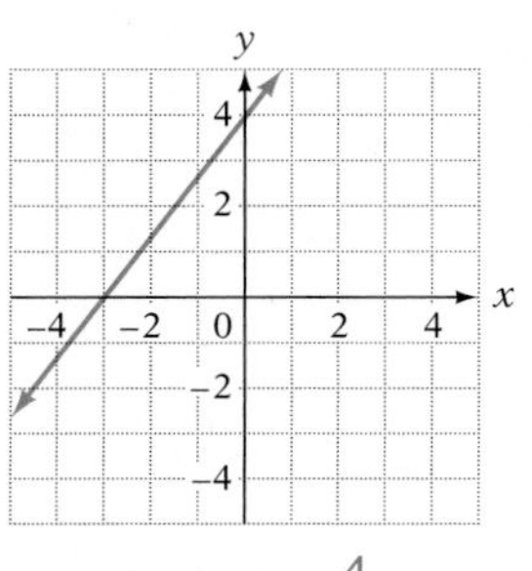

$(-3, 0)$; $(0, 4)$; $\frac{4}{3}$; $y = \frac{4}{3}x + 4$

71.

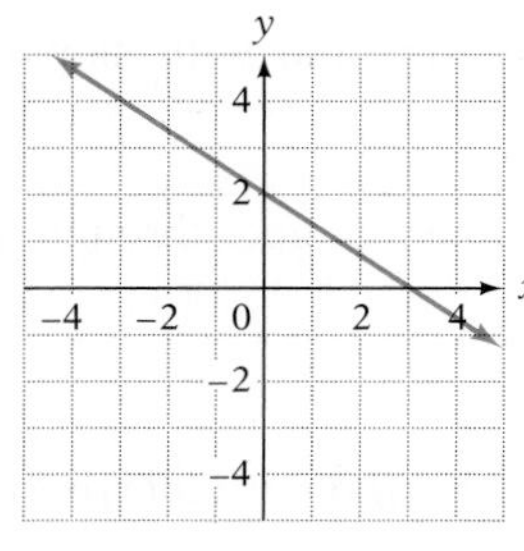

$(3, 0)$; $(0, 2)$; $-\frac{2}{3}$; $y = -\frac{2}{3}x + 2$

72.

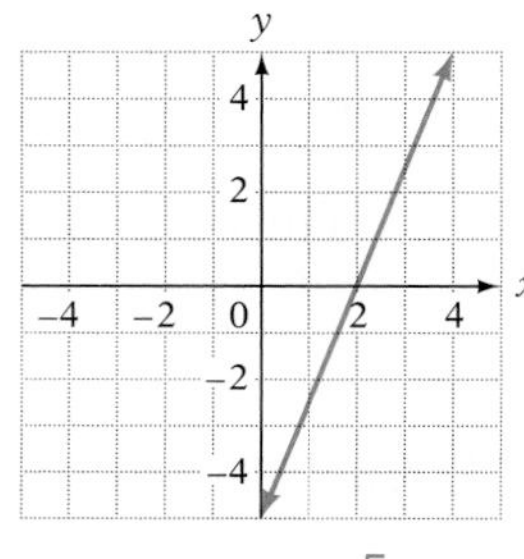

$(2, 0)$; $(0, -5)$; $\frac{5}{2}$; $y = \frac{5}{2}x - 5$

73.

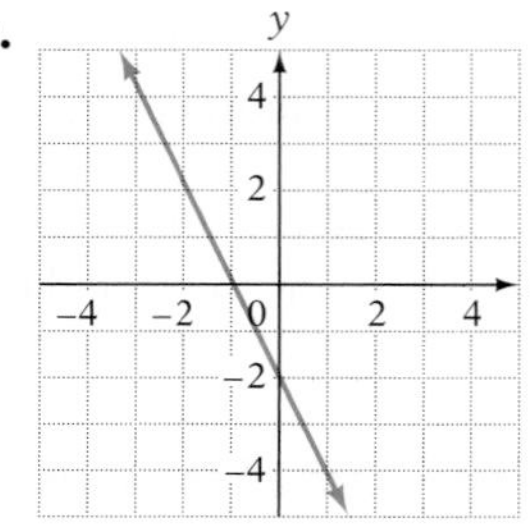

$(-1, 0)$; $(0, -2)$; -2; $y = -2x - 2$

3. Use the point-slope formula to find the equation of the line that contains the point $(2, -4)$ and has slope 1. $y = x - 6$ [12.4B]
4. Find the equation of the line that passes through the points $(2, 3)$ and $(6, -5)$. $y = -2x + 7$ [12.4C]

CHAPTER 12 Summary

Key Words

Examples

A **rectangular coordinate system** is formed by two number lines, one horizontal and one vertical, that intersect at the zero point of each line. The number lines that make up a rectangular coordinate system are called the **coordinate axes,** or simply **axes.** The **origin** is the point of intersection of the two coordinate axes. Generally, the horizontal axis is labeled the x-axis and the vertical axis is labeled the y-axis. The coordinate system divides the plane into four regions called **quadrants.** The **coordinates of a point** in the plane are given by an **ordered pair (x, y).** The first number in the ordered pair is called the **abscissa** or **x-coordinate.** The second number in the ordered pair is called the **ordinate** or **y-coordinate.** The **graph of an ordered pair (x, y)** is the dot drawn at the coordinates of the point in the plane. [12.1A, p. 644]

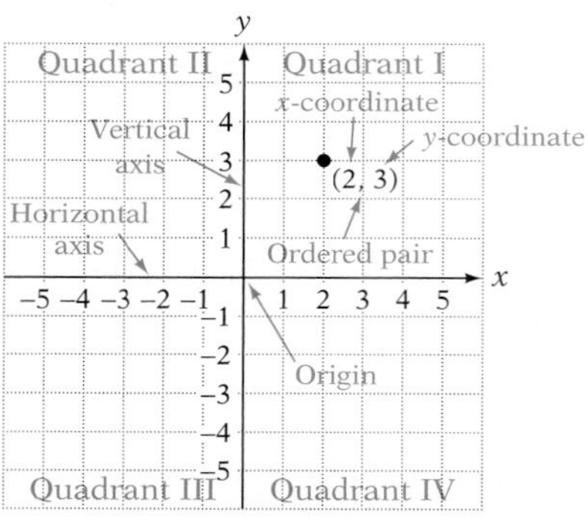

A **solution of an equation in two variables** is an ordered pair (x, y) that makes the equation a true statement. [12.1B, p. 646]

The ordered pair $(-1, 1)$ is a solution of the equation $y = 2x + 3$ because when -1 is substituted for x and 1 is substituted for y, the result is a true equation.

A **relation** is any set of ordered pairs. The **domain** of a relation is the set of first coordinates of the ordered pairs. The **range** is the set of second coordinates of the ordered pairs. [12.1C, p. 648]

For the relation $\{(-1, 2), (2, 4), (3, 5), (3, 7)\}$, the domain is $\{-1, 2, 3\}$; the range is $\{2, 4, 5, 7\}$.

A **function** is a relation in which no two ordered pairs have the same first coordinate. [12.1C, p. 648]

The relation $\{(-2, -3), (0, 4), (1, 5)\}$ is a function. No two ordered pairs have the same first coordinate.

The **graph of an equation in two variables** is a graph of the ordered-pair solutions of the equation. An equation of the form $y = mx + b$ is a **linear equation in two variables.** [12.2A, p. 657]

$y = 2x + 3$ is a linear equation in two variables. Its graph is shown at the right.

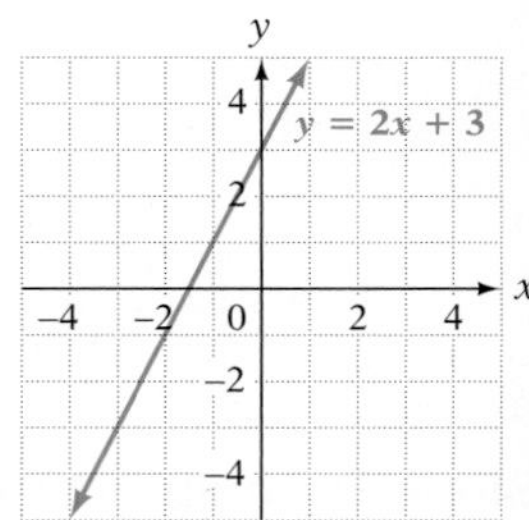

An equation written in the form $Ax + By = C$ is the **standard form of a linear equation in two variables.** [12.2B, p. 659]

$2x + 7y = 10$ is an example of a linear equation in two variables written in standard form.

The point at which a graph crosses the x-axis is called the **x-intercept.** At the x-intercept, the y-coordinate is 0. The point at which a graph crosses the y-axis is called the **y-intercept.** At the y-intercept, the x-coordinate is 0. [12.3A, p. 668]

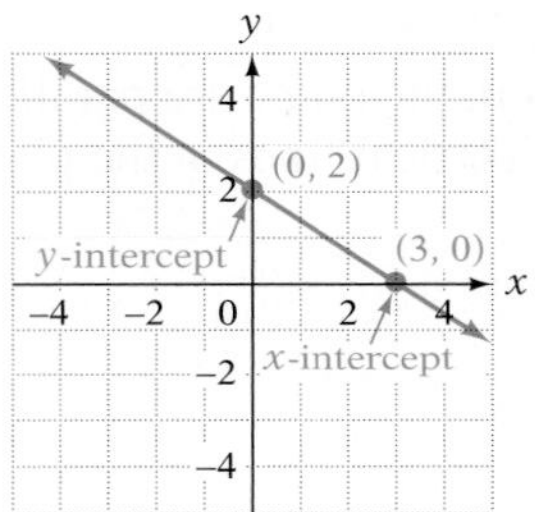

The **slope** of a line is a measure of the slant of the line. The symbol for slope is m. A line with **positive slope** slants upward to the right. A line with **negative slope** slants downward to the right. A horizontal line has **zero slope.** A vertical line has an **undefined slope.** [12.3B, pp. 669–670]

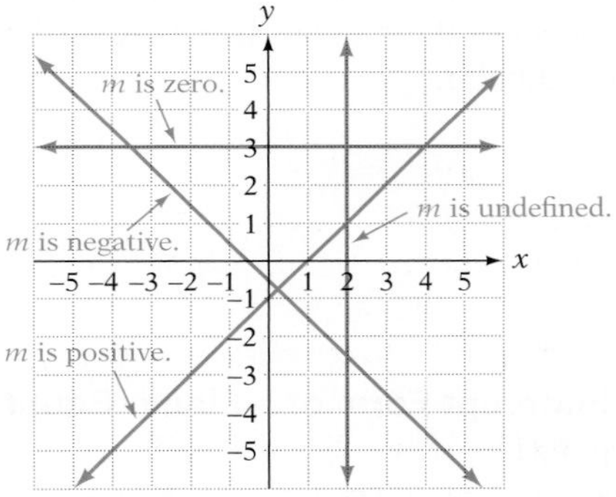

Essential Rules and Procedures

Examples

Function Notation [12.1D, p. 651]
The equation of a function is written in function notation when y is replaced by the symbol $f(x)$, where $f(x)$ is read "f of x" or "the value of f at x." To evaluate a function at a given value of x, replace x by the given value and then simplify the resulting numerical expression. This gives the value of $f(x)$.

$y = x^2 + 2x - 1$ is written in function notation as $f(x) = x^2 + 2x - 1$. To evaluate $f(x) = x^2 + 2x - 1$ at $x = -3$, find $f(-3)$.

$$f(-3) = (-3)^2 + 2(-3) - 1$$
$$= 9 - 6 - 1 = 2$$

Horizontal and Vertical Lines [12.2B, p. 660]
The graph of $y = b$ is a horizontal line passing through $(0, b)$. The graph of $x = a$ is a vertical line passing through $(a, 0)$.

The graph of $y = -2$ is a horizontal line passing through $(0, -2)$. The graph of $x = 3$ is a vertical line passing through $(3, 0)$.

To find the x-intercept, let $y = 0$ and solve for x.
To find the y-intercept, let $x = 0$ and solve for y. [12.3A, p. 668]

To find the x-intercept of $4x - 5y = 20$, let $y = 0$ and solve for x. To find the y-intercept, let $x = 0$ and solve for y.

$$\begin{aligned} 4x - 5y &= 20 \\ 4x - 5(0) &= 20 \\ 4x &= 20 \\ x &= 5 \end{aligned}$$

The x-intercept is $(5, 0)$.

$$\begin{aligned} 4x - 5y &= 20 \\ 4(0) - 5y &= 20 \\ -5y &= 20 \\ y &= -4 \end{aligned}$$

The y-intercept is $(0, -4)$.

Slope Formula [12.3B, p. 669]
If $P_1(x_1, y_1)$ and $P_2(x_2, y_2)$ are two points on a line and $x_1 \neq x_2$, then

$$m = \frac{y_2 - y_1}{x_2 - x_1}$$

To find the slope of the line between the points $(1, -2)$ and $(-3, -1)$, let $P_1 = (1, -2)$ and $P_2 = (-3, -1)$. Then

$$m = \frac{y_2 - y_1}{x_2 - x_1} = \frac{-1 - (-2)}{-3 - 1} = \frac{1}{-4} = -\frac{1}{4}.$$

Parallel Lines [12.3B, p. 671]
Two nonvertical lines in the plane are parallel if and only if they have the same slope. Vertical lines in the plane are parallel.

The slope of the line through $P_1(3, -6)$ and $P_2(5, -10)$ is $m_1 = \frac{-10 - (-6)}{5 - 3} = -2$.
The slope of the line through $Q_1(4, -5)$ and $Q_2(0, 3)$ is $m_2 = \frac{3 - (-5)}{0 - 4} = -2$.
Because $m_1 = m_2$, the lines are parallel.

Perpendicular Lines [12.3B, p. 671]
Two nonvertical lines in the plane are perpendicular if and only if the product of their slopes is -1. A vertical and a horizontal line are perpendicular.

The slope of the line through $P_1(5, -3)$ and $P_2(2, -1)$ is $m_1 = \frac{-1 - (-3)}{2 - 5} = -\frac{2}{3}$.
The slope of the line through $Q_1(1, -4)$ and $Q_2(3, -1)$ is $m_2 = \frac{-1 - (-4)}{3 - 1} = \frac{3}{2}$.
Because $m_1 m_2 = \left(-\frac{2}{3}\right)\left(\frac{3}{2}\right) = -1$, the lines are perpendicular.

Slope-Intercept Form of a Linear Equation [12.3C, p. 672; 12.4A, p. 681]
An equation of the form $y = mx + b$ is called the slope-intercept form of a straight line. The slope of the line is m, the coefficient of x. The y-intercept is $(0, b)$, where b is the constant term of the equation.

For the line with equation $y = -3x + 2$, the slope is -3 and the y-intercept is $(0, 2)$.

Point-Slope Formula [12.4B, p. 682]
If (x_1, y_1) is a point on a line with slope m, then

$$y - y_1 = m(x - x_1)$$

The equation of the line that passes through the point $(5, -3)$ and has slope -2 is:

$$\begin{aligned} y - y_1 &= m(x - x_1) \\ y - (-3) &= -2(x - 5) \\ y + 3 &= -2x + 10 \\ y &= -2x + 7 \end{aligned}$$

CHAPTER

12 Review Exercises

1. a. Graph the ordered pairs $(-2, 4)$ and $(3, -2)$.
   b. Name the abscissa of point A. -2
   c. Name the ordinate of point B. -4

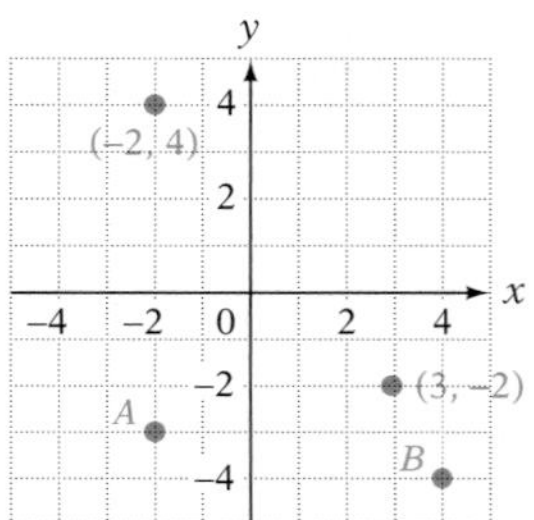

[12.1A]

2. Graph the ordered-pair solutions of $y = -\frac{1}{2}x - 2$ when $x \in \{-4, -2, 0, 2\}$.

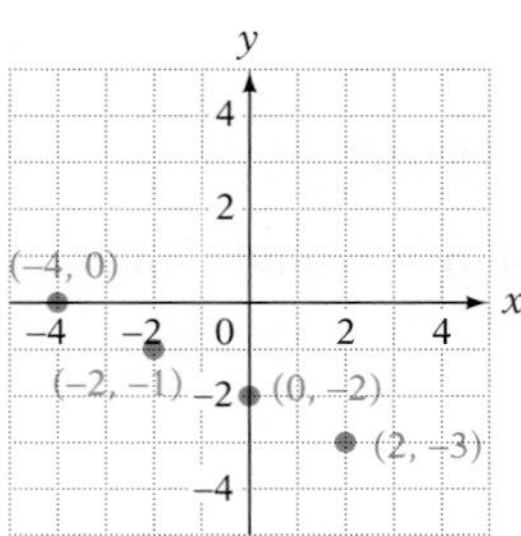

[12.1B]

3. Determine the equation of the line that passes through the points $(-1, 3)$ and $(2, -5)$.
   $y = -\frac{8}{3}x + \frac{1}{3}$ [12.4C]

4. Determine the equation of the line that passes through the point (6, 1) and has slope $-\frac{5}{2}$.
   $y = -\frac{5}{2}x + 16$ [12.4A]

5. Graph $y = \frac{1}{4}x + 3$.

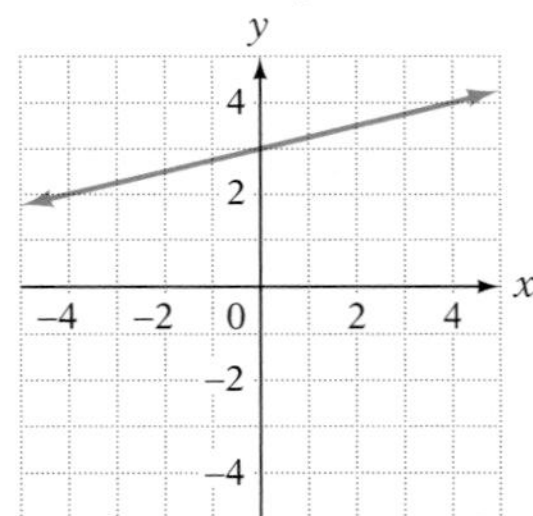

[12.2A]

6. Graph $5x + 3y = 15$.

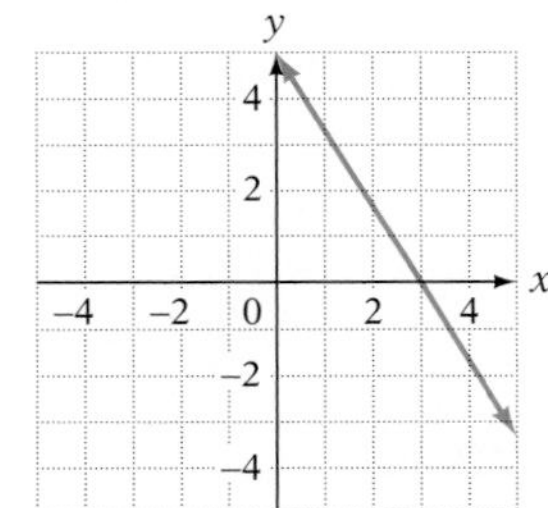

[12.2B]

7. Is the line that passes through $(7, -5)$ and $(6, -1)$ parallel, perpendicular, or neither parallel nor perpendicular to the line that passes through $(4, 5)$ and $(2, -3)$?
   Neither [12.3B]

8. Given $f(x) = x^2 - 2$, find $f(-1)$.
   -1 [12.1D]

9. Does $y = -x + 3$, where $x \in \{-2, 0, 3, 5\}$, define y as a function of x?
   Yes [12.1C]

10. Find the slope of the line containing the points $(9, 8)$ and $(-2, 1)$.
    $\frac{7}{11}$ [12.3B]

11. Find the x- and y-intercepts of $3x - 2y = 24$.
    $(8, 0), (0, -12)$ [12.3A]

12. Find the slope of the line containing the points $(-2, -3)$ and $(4, -3)$.
    0 [12.3B]

13. Graph the line that has slope $\frac{1}{2}$ and y-intercept $(0, -1)$.

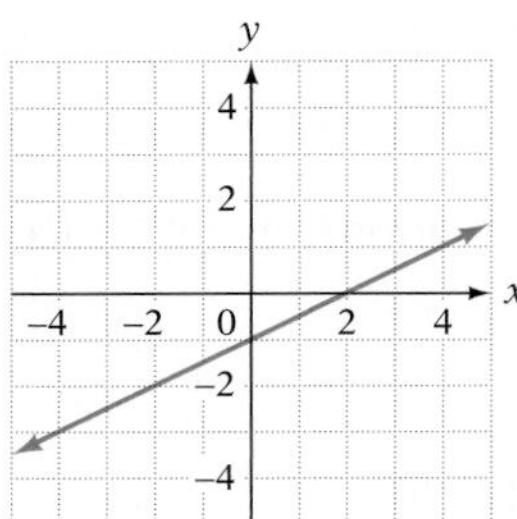

[12.3C]

14. Graph $x = -3$.

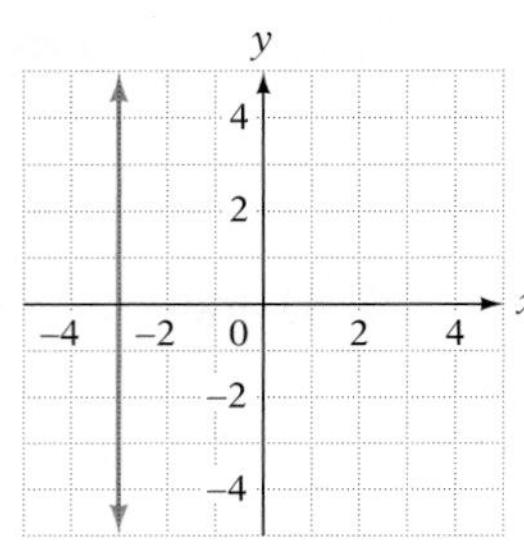

[12.2B]

15. Graph the line that has slope $-\frac{2}{3}$ and y-intercept $(0, 2)$.

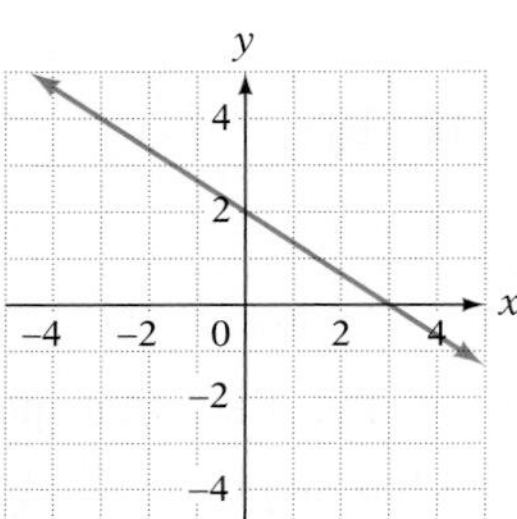

[12.3C]

16. Graph $y = -2x - 1$.

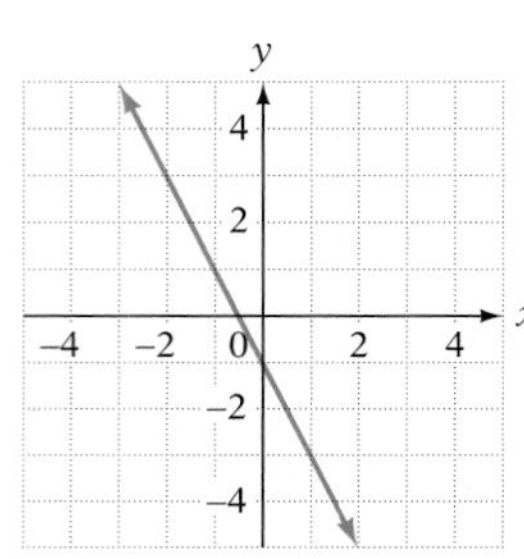

[12.2A]

17. Graph the line that has slope 2 and y-intercept $(0, -4)$.

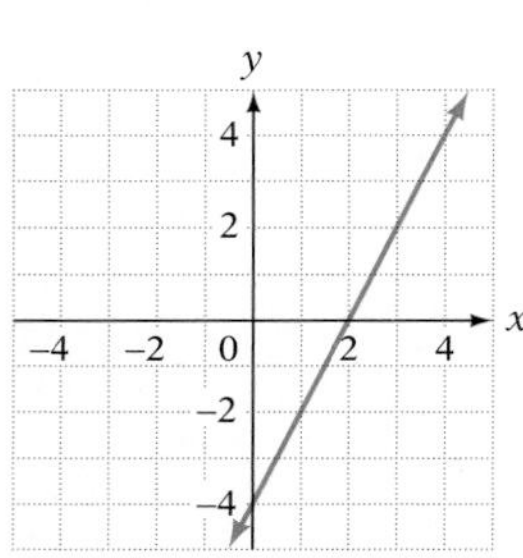

[12.3C]

18. Graph $3x - 2y = -6$.

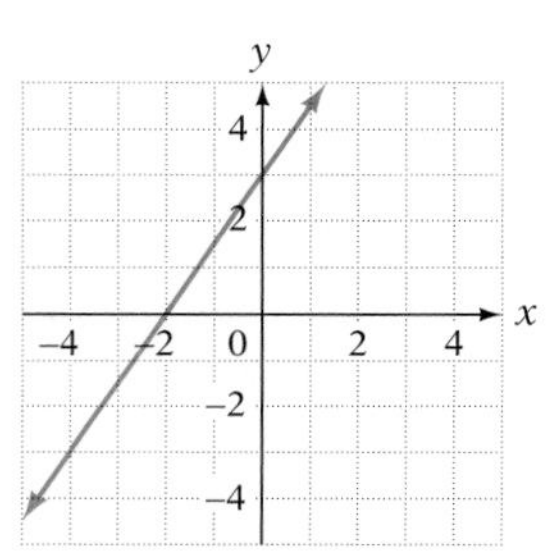

[12.2B]

19. Health The heights and weights of eight seventh-grade students are shown in the following table. Write a relation in which the first coordinate is height in inches and the second coordinate is weight in pounds. Is the relation a function?

Height (in inches)	55	57	53	57	60	61	58	54
Weight (in pounds)	95	101	94	98	100	105	97	95

{(55, 95), (57, 101), (53, 94), (57, 98), (60, 100), (61, 105), (58, 97), (54, 95)}; no [12.1C]

20. Business An online research service charges a monthly access fee of $75 plus $.45 per minute to use the service. An equation that represents the monthly cost to use this service is $C = 0.45x + 75$, where C is the monthly cost and x is the number of minutes of access used. Graph this equation for values of x from 0 to 100. The point (50, 97.5) is on the graph. Write a sentence that describes the meaning of this ordered pair.

C
100
50
0
(50, 97.5)
Cost (in dollars)
50 100 x
Time (in minutes)

The cost of 50 min of access time for one month is $97.50. [12.2C]

CHAPTER 12 TEST

1. Find the ordered-pair solution of $2x - 3y = 15$ corresponding to $x = 3$.
(3, −3) [12.1B]

2. Graph the ordered-pair solutions of $y = -\frac{3}{2}x + 1$ when $x = -2, 0,$ and 4.
[12.1B]

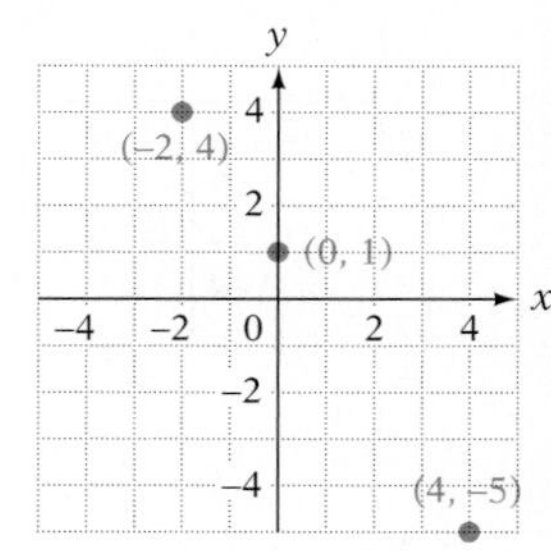

3. Does $y = \frac{1}{2}x - 3$ define y as a function of x for $x \in \{-2, 0, 4\}$?
Yes [12.1C]

4. Given $f(t) = t^2 + t$, find $f(2)$.
6 [12.1D]

5. Given $f(x) = x^2 - 2x$, find $f(-1)$.
3 [12.1D]

6. **Emergency Response** For seven homes, the distance of the house from a fire station and the amount of damage the house sustained in a fire are given in the following table. Write a relation in which the first coordinate of the ordered pair is the distance, in miles, from the fire station and the second coordinate is the amount of damage in thousands of dollars. Is the relation a function?

Distance (in miles)	3.5	4.0	5.2	5.0	4.0	6.3	5.4
Damage (in thousands of dollars)	25	30	45	38	42	12	34

{(3.5, 25), (4.0, 30), (5.2, 45), (5.0, 38), (4.0, 42), (6.3, 12), (5.4, 34)}; no [12.1C]

7. Graph $y = 3x + 1$.

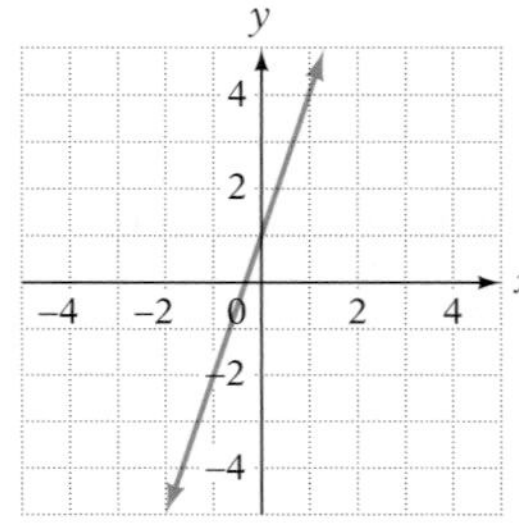

[12.2A]

8. Graph $y = -\frac{3}{4}x + 3$.

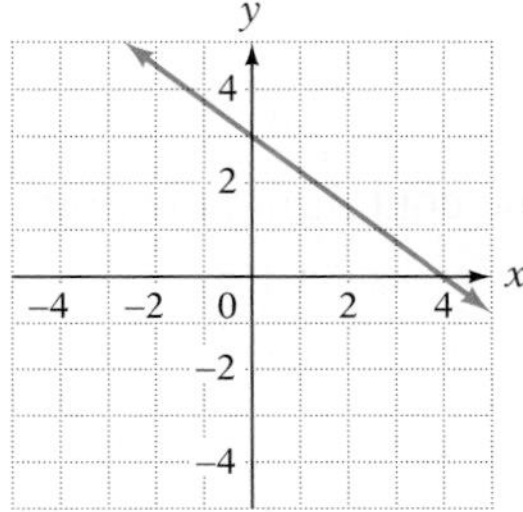

[12.2A]

9. Graph $3x - 2y = 6$.

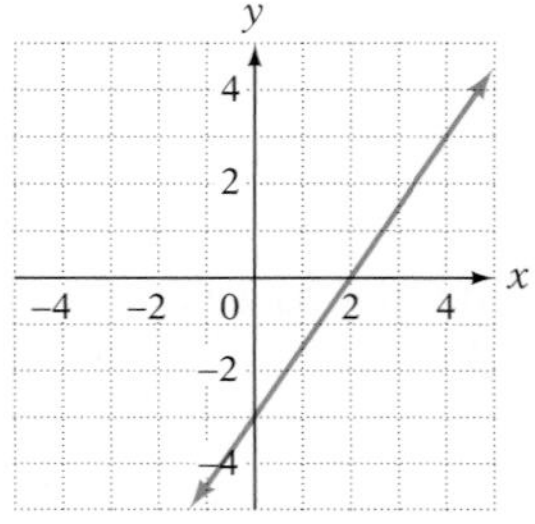

[12.2B]

10. Graph $x + 3 = 0$.

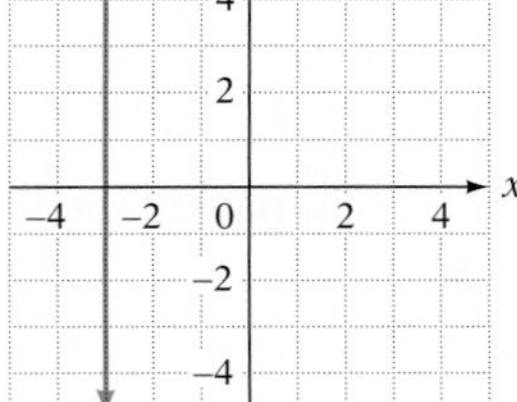

[12.2B]

11. Graph the line that has slope $-\frac{2}{3}$ and y-intercept $(0, 4)$.

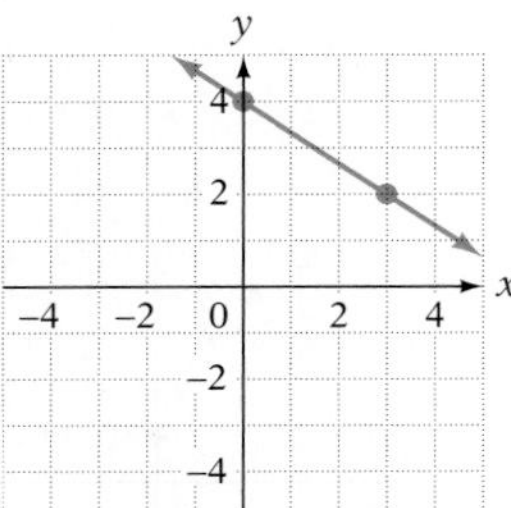

[12.3C]

12. Graph the line that has slope 2 and y-intercept -2.

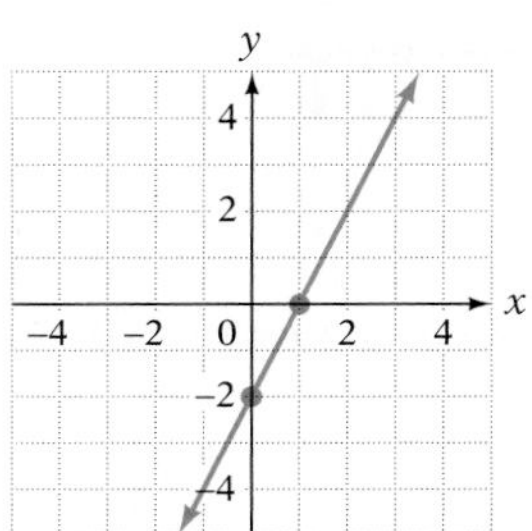

[12.3C]

13. **Sports** The equation for the speed of a ball that is thrown straight up with an initial speed of 128 ft/s is $v = 128 - 32t$, where v is the speed of the ball after t seconds. Graph this equation for values of t from 0 to 4. The point whose coordinates are (1, 96) is on the graph. Write a sentence that describes the meaning of this ordered pair.
After 1 s, the ball is traveling 96 ft/s. [12.2C]

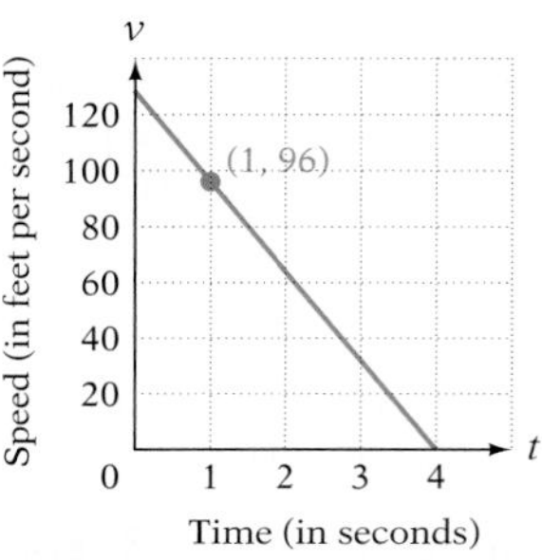

14. Find the x- and y-intercepts of $6x - 4y = 12$.
(2, 0), (0, −3) [12.3A]

15. Find the x- and y-intercepts of $y = \frac{1}{2}x + 1$.
(−2, 0), (0, 1) [12.3A]

16. Find the slope of the line containing the points $(2, -3)$ and $(4, 1)$.
2 [12.3B]

17. Is the line that passes through $(2, 5)$ and $(-1, 1)$ parallel, perpendicular, or neither parallel nor perpendicular to the line that passes through $(-2, 3)$ and $(4, 11)$?
Parallel [12.3B]

18. Find the slope of the line containing the points $(-5, 2)$ and $(-5, 7)$.
Undefined [12.3B]

19. Find the slope of the line whose equation is $2x + 3y = 6$.
$-\frac{2}{3}$ [12.3B]

20. Find the equation of the line that contains the point $(0, -1)$ and has slope 3.
$y = 3x - 1$ [12.4A]

21. Use the point-slope formula to find the equation of the line that contains the point $(-3, 1)$ and has slope $\frac{2}{3}$.
$y = \frac{2}{3}x + 3$ [12.4B]

22. Find the equation of the line that passes through the points $(5, -4)$ and $(-3, 1)$.
$y = -\frac{5}{8}x - \frac{7}{8}$ [12.4C]

23. Find the equation of the line that passes through the points $(-2, 0)$ and $(5, -2)$.
$y = -\frac{2}{7}x - \frac{4}{7}$ [12.4C]

Cumulative Review Exercises

1. Simplify: $12 - 18 \div 3 \cdot (-2)^2$
-12 [3.5A]

2. Evaluate $\frac{a-b}{a^2-c}$ when $a = -2$, $b = 3$, and $c = -4$.
$-\frac{5}{8}$ [4.1A]

3. Given $f(x) = \frac{2}{x-1}$, find $f(-2)$.
$f(-2) = -\frac{2}{3}$ [12.1D]

4. Solve: $2x - \frac{2}{3} = \frac{7}{3}$
$\frac{3}{2}$ [5.2A]

5. Solve: $3x - 2[x - 3(2 - 3x)] = x - 7$
$\frac{19}{18}$ [5.3B]

6. Write $6\frac{2}{3}\%$ as a fraction.
$\frac{1}{15}$ [6.3A]

7. Simplify: $(-2x^2y)^3(2xy^2)^2$
$-32x^8y^7$ [9.2B]

8. Simplify: $\frac{-15x^7}{5x^5}$
$-3x^2$ [9.4A]

9. Divide: $(x^2 - 4x - 21) \div (x - 7)$
$x + 3$ [9.5B]

10. Factor: $5x^2 + 15x + 10$
$5(x + 2)(x + 1)$ [10.2B]

11. Factor: $x(a + 2) + y(a + 2)$
$(a + 2)(x + y)$ [10.1B]

12. Solve: $x(x - 2) = 8$
4 and -2 [10.6A]

13. Multiply: $\frac{x^5y^3}{x^2 - x - 6} \cdot \frac{x^2 - 9}{x^2y^4}$
$\frac{x^3(x + 3)}{y(x + 2)}$ [11.1B]

14. Subtract: $\frac{3x}{x^2 + 5x - 24} - \frac{9}{x^2 + 5x - 24}$
$\frac{3}{x + 8}$ [11.3A]

15. Solve: $3 - \frac{1}{x} = \frac{5}{x}$
2 [11.5A]

16. Solve $4x - 5y = 15$ for y.
$y = \frac{4}{5}x - 3$ [11.6A]

17. Find the ordered-pair solution of $y = 2x - 1$ corresponding to $x = -2$.
$(-2, -5)$ [12.1B]

18. Find the slope of the line that contains the points $(2, 3)$ and $(-2, 3)$.
Zero [12.3B]

19. Find the equation of the line that contains the point $(2, -1)$ and has slope $\frac{1}{2}$.
$y = \frac{1}{2}x - 2$ [12.4A]

20. Find the equation of the line that contains the point $(0, 2)$ and has slope -3.
$y = -3x + 2$ [12.4A]

21. Use the point-slope formula to find the equation of the line that contains the point $(-1, 0)$ and has slope 2.
$y = 2x + 2$ [12.4B]

22. Use the point-slope formula to find the equation of the line that contains the point $(6, 1)$ and has slope $\frac{2}{3}$.
$y = \frac{2}{3}x - 3$ [12.4B]

23. Probability Four blue marbles, three red marbles, and two green marbles are placed in a bag. One marble is chosen at random. What is the probability that the marble chosen is not red?
$\frac{2}{3}$ [8.3A]

24. Geometry The measure of the first angle of a triangle is 3° more than the measure of the second angle. The measure of the third angle is 5° more than twice the measure of the second angle. Find the measure of each angle.
46°, 43°, 91° [7.1C]

25. Taxes The real estate tax on a home that costs \$500,000 is \$6250. At this rate, what is the value of a home for which the real estate tax is \$13,750?
\$1,100,000 [6.2B]

26. Business An electrician requires 6 h to wire a garage. An apprentice can do the same job in 10 h. How long would it take to wire the garage if both the electrician and the apprentice worked together?
$3\frac{3}{4}$ h [11.7A]

27. Graph $y = \frac{1}{2}x - 1$.

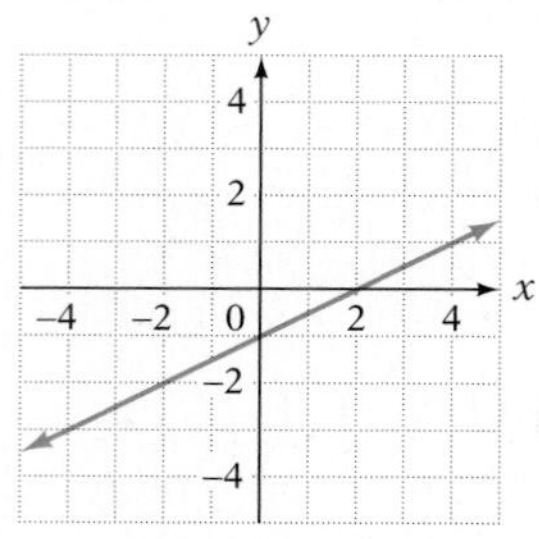

[12.2A]

28. Graph the line that has slope $-\frac{2}{3}$ and y-intercept 2.

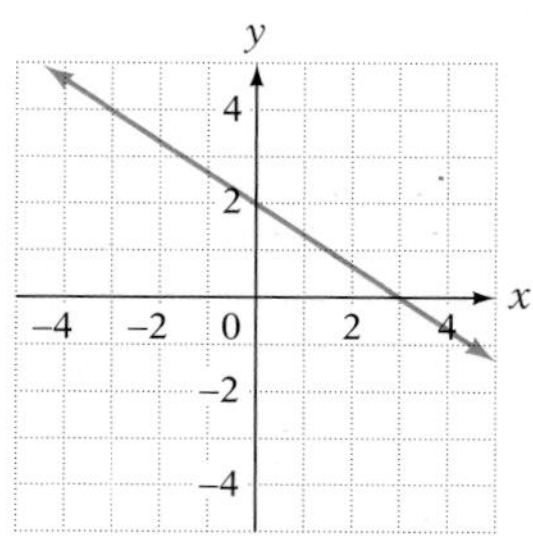

[12.3C]

Systems of Linear Equations

13

OBJECTIVES

SECTION 13.1

A To solve a system of linear equations by graphing

SECTION 13.2

A To solve a system of linear equations by the substitution method

B To solve investment problems

SECTION 13.3

A To solve a system of linear equations by the addition method

SECTION 13.4

A To solve rate-of-wind or rate-of-current problems

B To solve application problems using two variables

Focus on Success

What resources do you use when you need help in this course? You know to read and reread the text when you are having difficulty understanding a concept. Instructors are available to help you during their office hours. Most schools have a math center where students can get help. Some schools have a tutoring program. You might also ask a student who has been successful in this class for assistance. (See Habits of Successful Students, page AIM-6.)

© Monkey Business Images/Shutterstock.com

Prep Test

Are you ready to succeed in this chapter? Take the Prep Test below to find out if you are ready to learn the new material.

1. Solve $3x - 4y = 24$ for y.
   $y = \frac{3}{4}x - 6$ [11.6A]

2. Solve:
   $50 + 0.07x = 0.05(x + 1400)$
   1000 [5.3B]

3. Simplify:
   $-3(2x - 7y) + 3(2x + 4y)$
   $33y$ [4.2D]

4. Simplify: $4x + 2(3x - 5)$
   $10x - 10$ [4.2D]

5. Is $(-4, 2)$ a solution of $3x - 5y = -22$?
   Yes [12.1B]

6. Find the x- and y-intercepts of $3x - 4y = 12$.
   $(4, 0), (0, -3)$ [12.3A]

7. Are the graphs of $3x + y = 6$ and $y = -3x - 4$ parallel?
   Yes [12.3B]

8. Graph:
   $y = \frac{5}{4}x - 2$
   [12.3C]

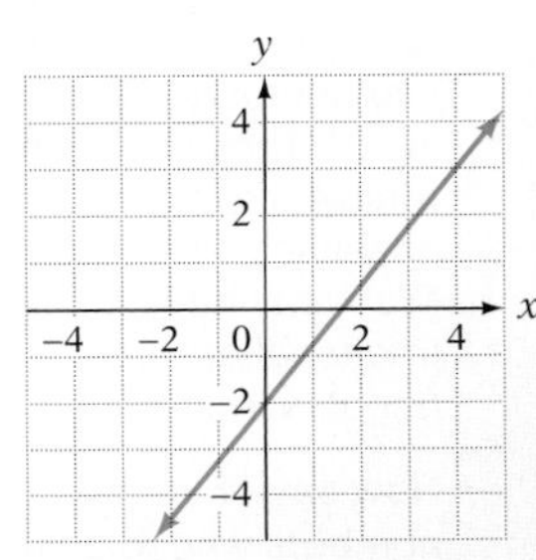

9. **Hiking** One hiker starts along a trail walking at 3 mph. One-half hour later, another hiker starts on the same walking trail at a speed of 4 mph. How long after the second hiker starts will the two hikers be side-by-side? 1.5 h [5.5B]

SECTION

13.1 Solving Systems of Linear Equations by Graphing

OBJECTIVE A *To solve a system of linear equations by graphing*

Two or more equations considered together are called a **system of equations.** Three examples of *linear* systems of equations in *two* variables are shown below, along with the graphs of the equations of each system.

System I

$$x - 2y = -8$$
$$2x + 5y = 11$$

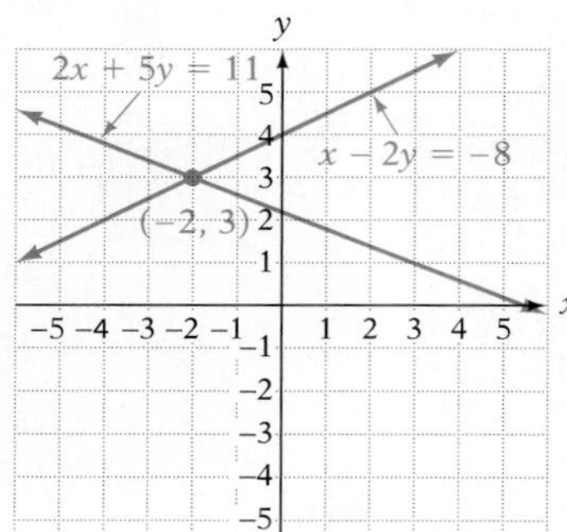

System II

$$4x + 2y = 6$$
$$y = -2x + 3$$

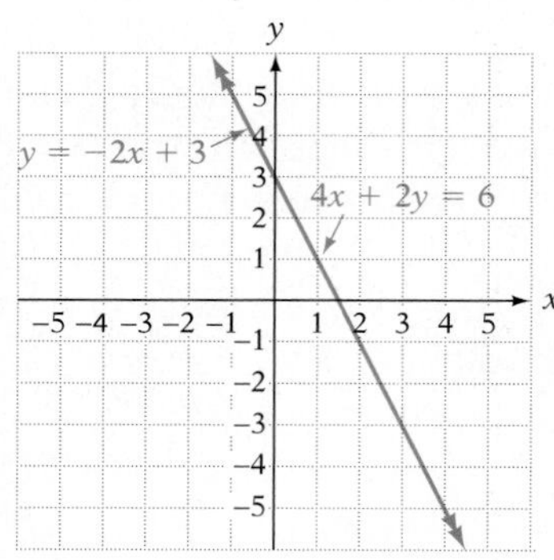

System III

$$4x + 6y = 12$$
$$6x + 9y = -9$$

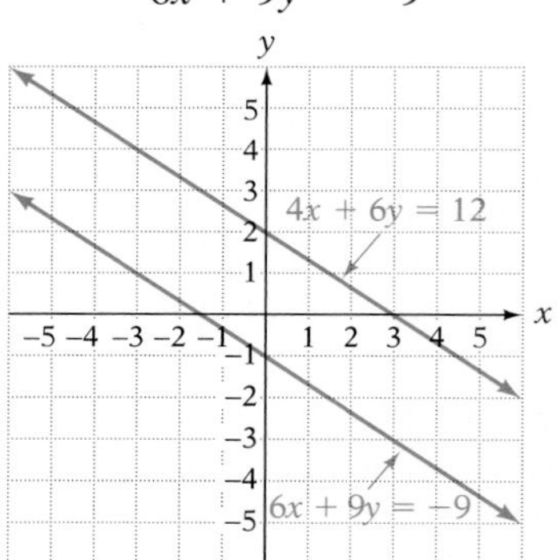

Take Note
The systems of equations above are called *linear systems of equations* because each of the equations in the system has a graph that is a line. Also, each equation has two variables. In future math courses, you will study equations that contain more than two variables.

For system I, the two lines intersect at a single point, $(-2, 3)$. Because this point lies on both lines, it is a solution of each equation of the system of equations. We can check this by replacing x by -2 and y by 3. The check is shown below.

$x - 2y = -8$		$2x + 5y = 11$	
$-2 - 2(3)$	-8	$2(-2) + 5(3)$	11
$-2 - 6$	-8	$-4 + 15$	11
$-8 = -8$ ✓		$11 = 11$ ✓	

• Replace x by -2 and replace y by 3.

A **solution of a system of equations in two variables** is an ordered pair that is a solution of each equation of the system. The ordered pair $(-2, 3)$ is a solution of system I.

INSTRUCTOR NOTE
One way to illustrate that more than one equation is sometimes necessary to yield a unique answer is to say to students, "Find two numbers whose sum is 10." They will soon realize that the number of possible solutions is infinite. (You may have to suggest fractional answers or negative numbers.)

Now say, "Find two numbers whose sum is 10 and whose difference is 6." Only the ordered pair (8, 2) satisfies both conditions. Ask students to create this system of equations.

HOW TO 1 Is $(-1, 4)$ a solution of the system of equations?

$$7x + 3y = 5$$
$$3x - 2y = 12$$

$7x + 3y = 5$		$3x - 2y = 12$	
$7(-1) + 3(4)$	5	$3(-1) - 2(4)$	12
$-7 + 12$	5	$-3 - 8$	12
$5 = 5$ ✓		$-11 \neq 12$	

• Replace x by -1 and replace y by 4.
• Does not check

Because $(-1, 4)$ is not a solution of both equations, $(-1, 4)$ is not a solution of the system of equations.

Using the system of equations above and the graph at the right, note that the graph of the ordered pair $(-1, 4)$ lies on the graph of $7x + 3y = 5$ but not on *both* lines. The ordered pair $(-1, 4)$ is *not* a solution of the system of equations. The graph of the ordered pair $(2, -3)$ does lie on both lines, and therefore the ordered pair $(2, -3)$ is a solution of the system of equations.

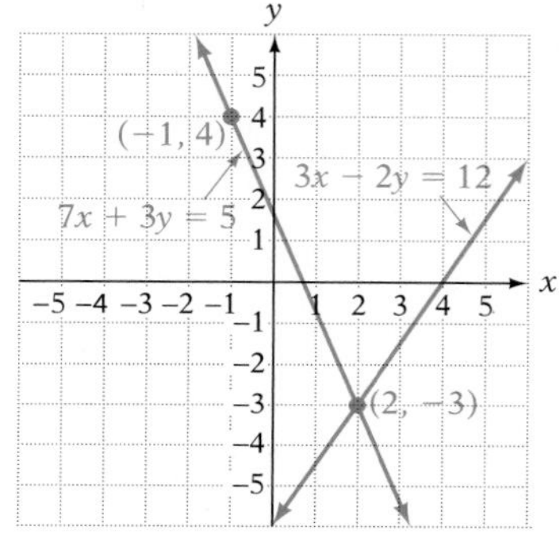

Take Note

The fact that there are an infinite number of ordered pairs that are solutions of the system at the right does not mean that *every* ordered pair is a solution. For instance, (0, 3), (−2, 7), and (2, −1) are solutions. However, (3, 1), (−1, 4), and (1, 6) are not solutions. You should verify these statements.

System II from the preceding page and the graph of the equations of that system are shown again at the right. Note that the graph of $y = -2x + 3$ lies directly on top of the graph of $4x + 2y = 6$. Thus the two lines intersect at an infinite number of points. Because the graphs intersect at an infinite number of points, there are an infinite number of solutions of this system of equations. Because each equation represents the same set of points, the solutions of the system of equations can be stated by using the ordered-pair solutions of either one of the equations. Therefore, we can say, "The solutions are the ordered pairs that satisfy $4x + 2y = 6$," or we can say "The solutions are the ordered pairs that satisfy $y = -2x + 3$."

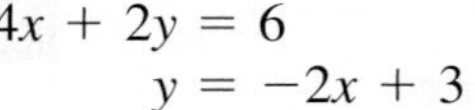

$$4x + 2y = 6$$
$$y = -2x + 3$$

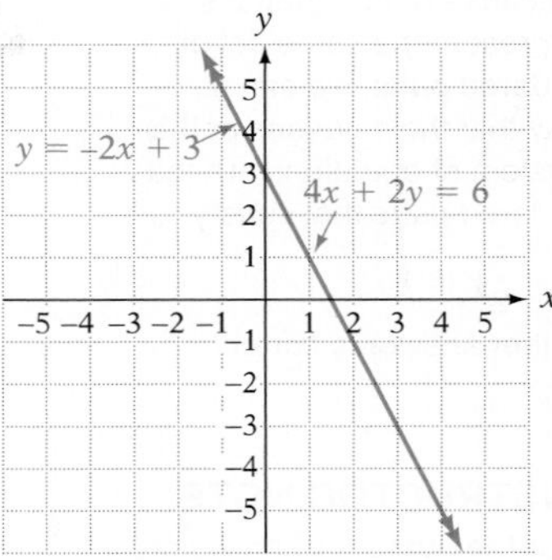

System III from the preceding page and the graph of the equations of that system are shown again at the right. Note that in this case, the graphs of the lines are parallel and do not intersect. Because the graphs do not intersect, there is no point that is on both lines. Therefore, the system of equations has no solution.

$$4x + 6y = 12$$
$$6x + 9y = -9$$

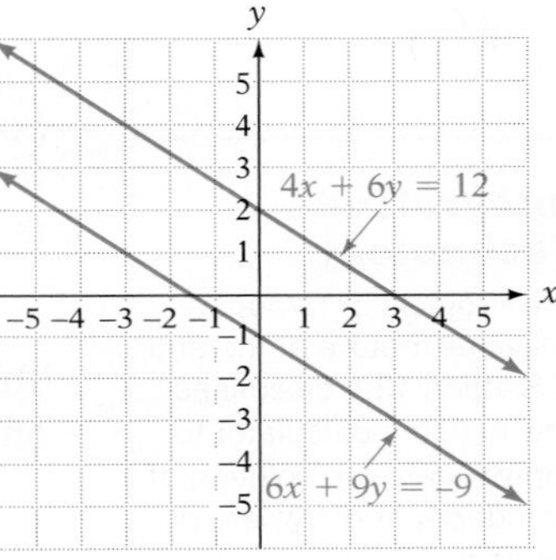

The preceding examples illustrate three types of systems of linear equations. An **independent system** has exactly one solution—the graphs intersect at one point. A **dependent system** has an infinite number of solutions—the graphs are the same line. An **inconsistent system** has no solution—the graphs are parallel lines.

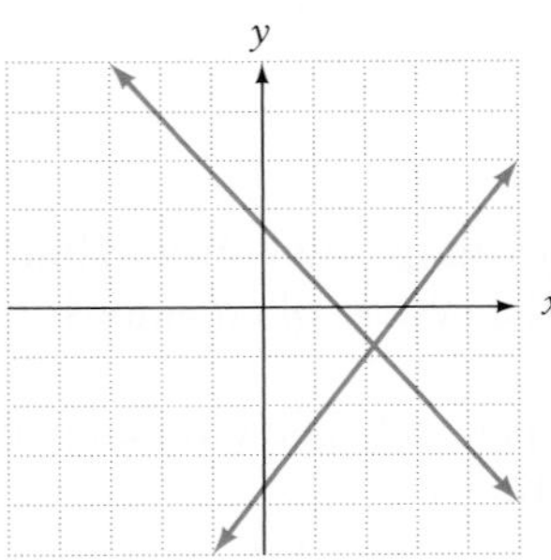

Independent system: one solution

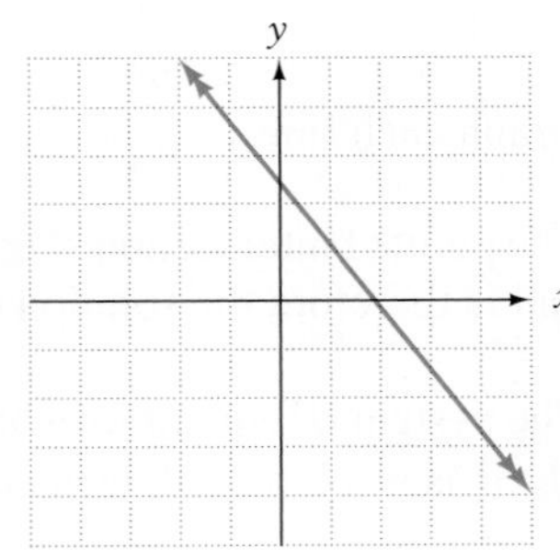

Dependent system: infinitely many solutions

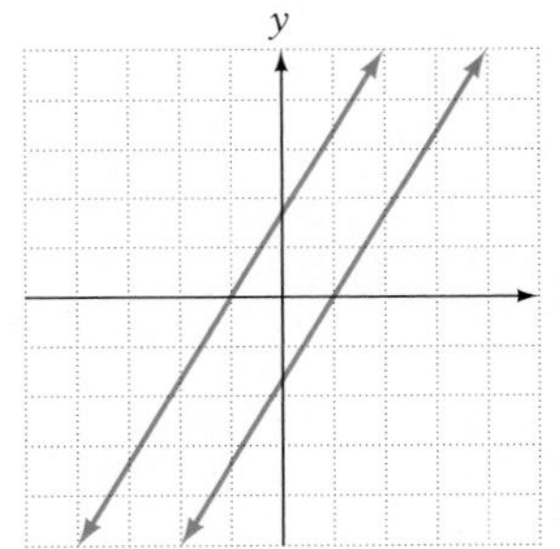

Inconsistent system: no solution

HOW TO 2 The graphs of the equations in the system of equations below are shown at the right. What is the solution of the system of equations?

$$2x + 3y = 6$$
$$2x + y = -2$$

The graphs intersect at $(-3, 4)$. This is an *independent* system of equations. The solution of the system of equations is $(-3, 4)$.

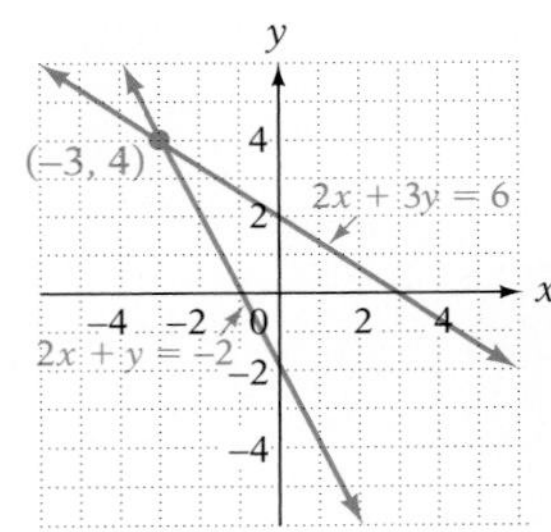

Take Note

Because both equations represent the same set of ordered pairs, we can also say that the solutions of the system of equations are the ordered pairs that satisfy $x = \frac{1}{2}y + 1$.

Either answer is correct.

INSTRUCTOR NOTE

For the system of equations at the right, emphasize that the solution of the system of equations can be stated as "the set of ordered pairs that satisfy $y = 2x - 2$ and $x = \frac{1}{2}y + 1$."

Integrating Technology

The Projects or Group Activities feature at the end of Section 13.4 discusses how to use a calculator to approximate the solution of an independent system of equations.

HOW TO 3 The graphs of the equations in the system of equations at the right are shown below. What is the solution of the system of equations?

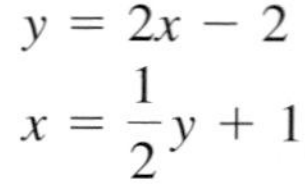

$$y = 2x - 2$$
$$x = \frac{1}{2}y + 1$$

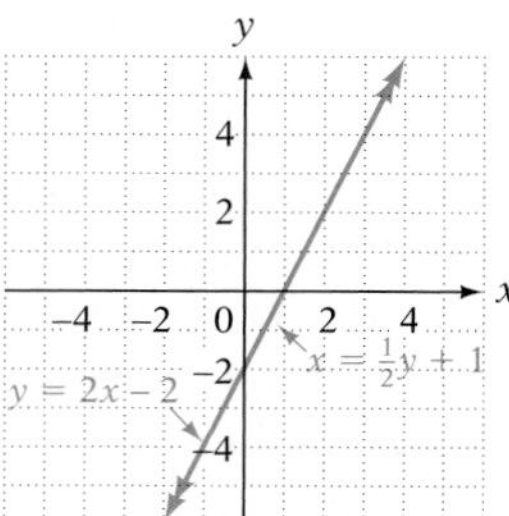

The two graphs lie directly on top of one another. Thus the two lines intersect at an infinite number of points, and the system of equations has an infinite number of solutions. This is a *dependent* system of equations. The solutions of the system of equations are the ordered pairs that satisfy $y = 2x - 2$.

Solving a system of equations means finding the ordered-pair solutions of the system. One way to do this is to draw the graphs of the equations in the system of equations and then determine where the graphs intersect.

To solve a system of linear equations in two variables by graphing, graph each equation on the same coordinate system, and then determine the point of intersection.

HOW TO 4 Solve by graphing: $2x - y = -1$
$x + 2y = 7$

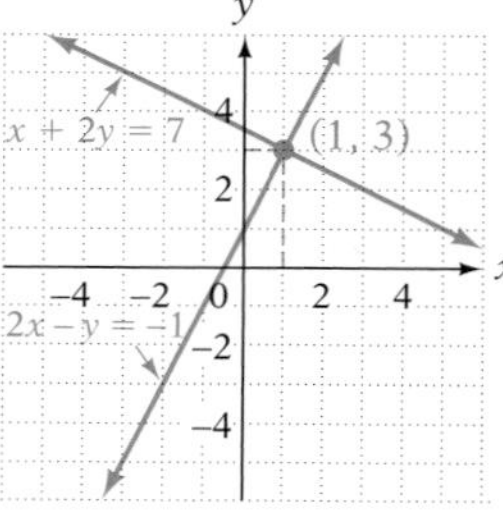

Graph each line.

The point of intersection of the two graphs lies on both lines and is therefore the solution of the system of equations.

The system of equations is independent. The ordered pair (1, 3) is a solution of each equation.

The solution is (1, 3).

HOW TO 5 Solve by graphing: $y = 2x + 2$
$4x - 2y = 4$

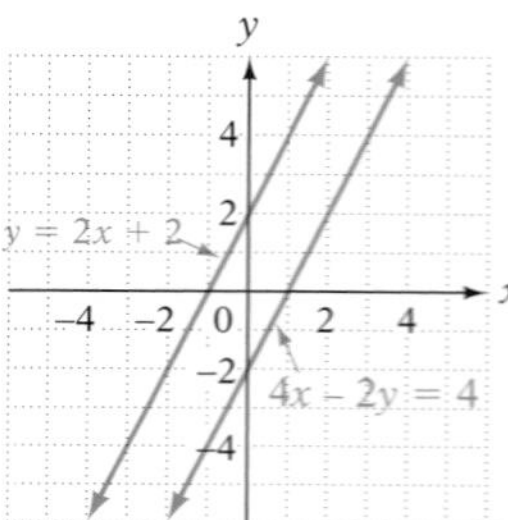

Graph each line.

The graphs do not intersect. The system of equations is inconsistent.

The system of equations has no solution.

EXAMPLE 1

Is $(1, -3)$ a solution of the following system?
$3x + 2y = -3$
$x - 3y = 6$

Solution

Replace x by 1 and y by -3.

$3x + 2y$	-3
$3 \cdot 1 + 2(-3)$	-3
$3 + (-6)$	-3
$-3 = -3$	

$x - 3y$	6
$1 - 3(-3)$	6
$1 - (-9)$	6
$10 \neq 6$	

No, $(1, -3)$ is not a solution of the system of equations.

YOU TRY IT 1

Is $(-1, -2)$ a solution of the following system?
$2x - 5y = 8$
$-x + 3y = -5$

Your solution

Yes

IN-CLASS EXAMPLES

1. Is $(3, -4)$ a solution of the system of equations?
$2x - 3y = 18$
$x - 4y = 19$
Yes
2. Solve by graphing: $x - 2y = 0$
$2x - y = -3$
(−2, −1)

EXAMPLE 2

Solve by graphing:
$x - 2y = 2$
$x + y = 5$

Solution

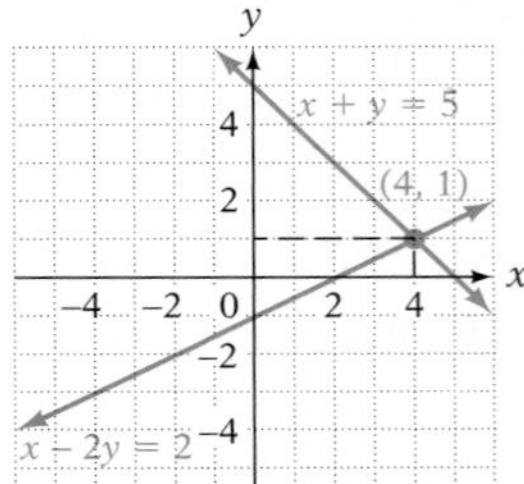

The solution is $(4, 1)$.

YOU TRY IT 2

Solve by graphing:
$x + 3y = 3$
$-x + y = 5$

Your solution

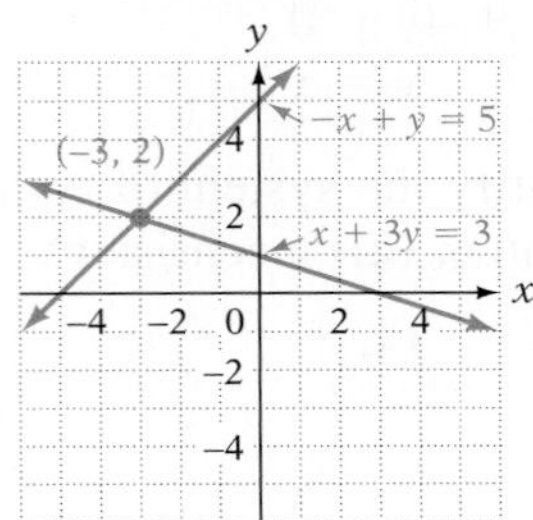

$(-3, 2)$

EXAMPLE 3

Solve by graphing:
$4x - 2y = 6$
$y = 2x - 3$

Solution

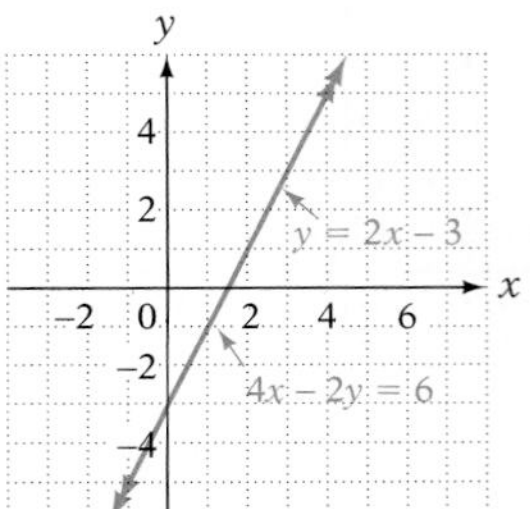

The solutions are the ordered pairs that satisfy the equation $y = 2x - 3$.

YOU TRY IT 3

Solve by graphing:
$y = 3x - 1$
$6x - 2y = -6$

Your solution

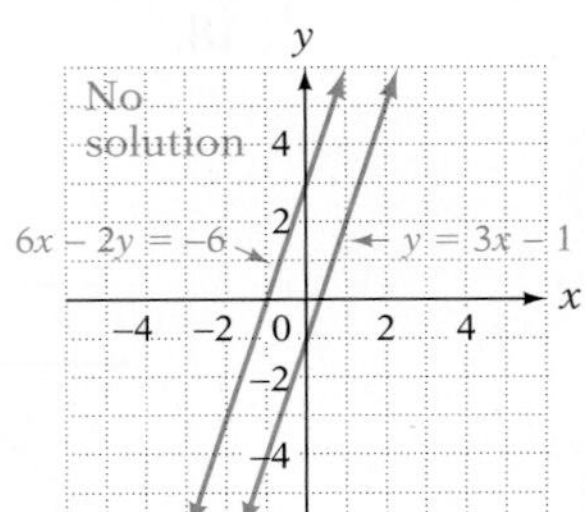

The system of equations is inconsistent and has no solution.

Solutions on pp. S31–S32

13.1 EXERCISES

SUGGESTED ASSIGNMENT:
Exercises 1–4; Exercises 5–41, odds; More challenging exercises: Exercises 44–47

Concept Check

Determine whether the statement is always true, sometimes true, or never true.

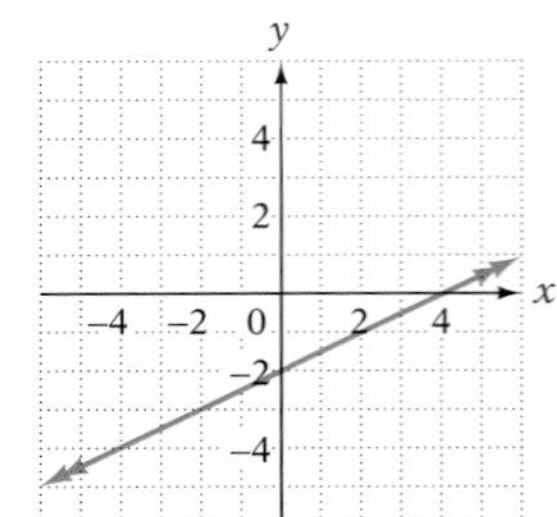

1. A solution of a system of linear equations in two variables is an ordered pair (x, y). Always true
2. Graphically, the solution of an independent system of linear equations in two variables is the point of intersection of the graphs of the two equations. Always true
3. The system of two linear equations graphed at the right has no solution. Never true
4. An independent system of equations has no solution. Never true

OBJECTIVE A To solve a system of linear equations by graphing

5. Is (2, 3) a solution of $\begin{matrix} 3x + 4y = 18 \\ 2x - y = 1 \end{matrix}$?
   Yes
6. Is (2, −1) a solution of $\begin{matrix} x - 2y = 4 \\ 2x + y = 3 \end{matrix}$?
   Yes
7. Is (4, 3) a solution of $\begin{matrix} 5x - 2y = 14 \\ x + y = 8 \end{matrix}$?
   No
8. Is (2, 5) a solution of $\begin{matrix} 3x + 2y = 16 \\ 2x - 3y = 4 \end{matrix}$?
   No
9. Is (2, −3) a solution of $\begin{matrix} y = 2x - 7 \\ 3x - y = 9 \end{matrix}$?
   Yes
10. Is (−1, −2) a solution of $\begin{matrix} 3x - 4y = 5 \\ y = x - 1 \end{matrix}$?
    Yes
11. Is (0, 0) a solution of $\begin{matrix} 3x + 4y = 0 \\ y = x \end{matrix}$?
    Yes
12. Is (3, −4) a solution of $\begin{matrix} 5x - 2y = 23 \\ 2x - 5y = 25 \end{matrix}$?
    No

For Exercises 13 to 16, identify the system of equations represented by the graph as **(i)** independent, **(ii)** dependent, or **(iii)** inconsistent.

13. iii

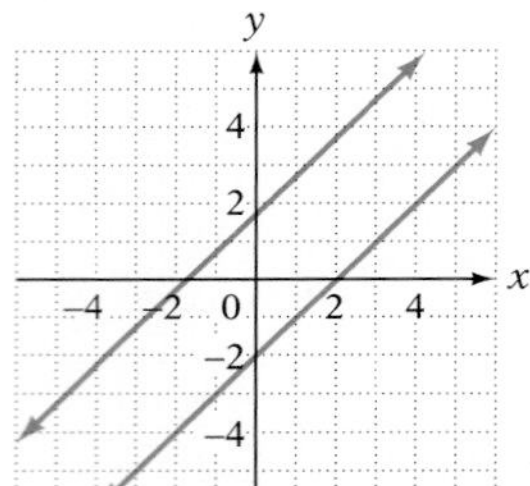

14. i

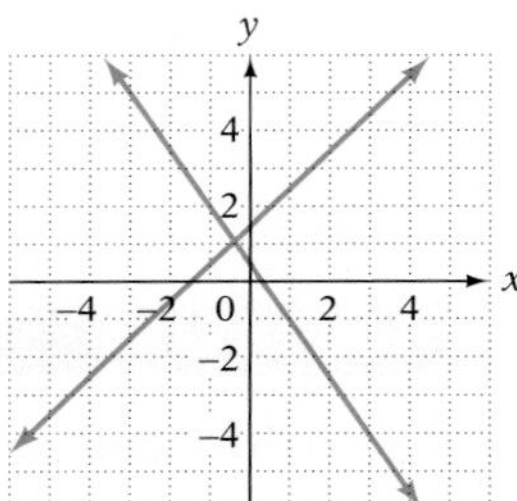

15. i

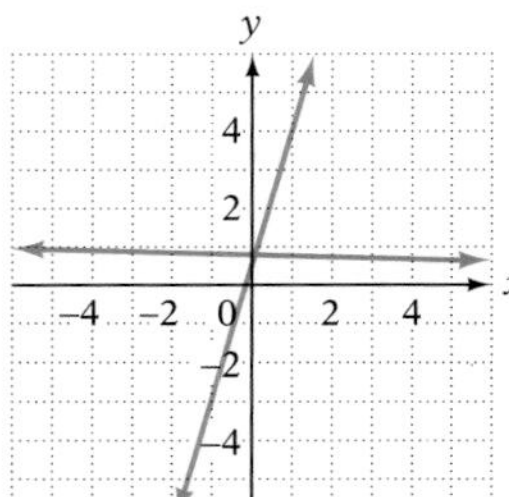

16. ii

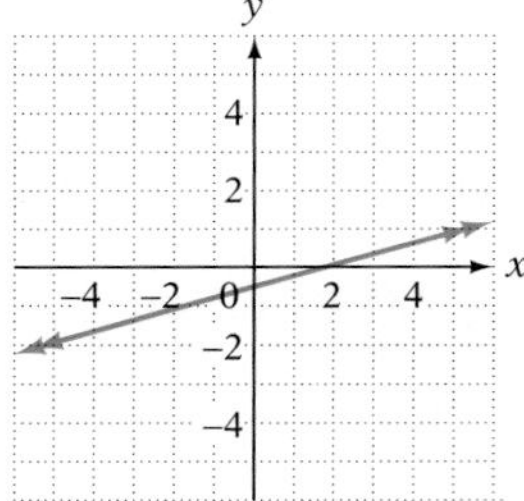

For Exercises 17 to 22, use the graphs of the equations of the system of equations to find the solution of the system of equations.

17.

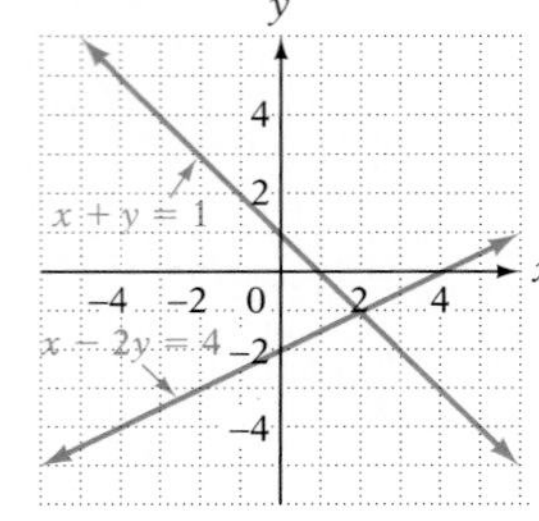

(2, −1)

18.

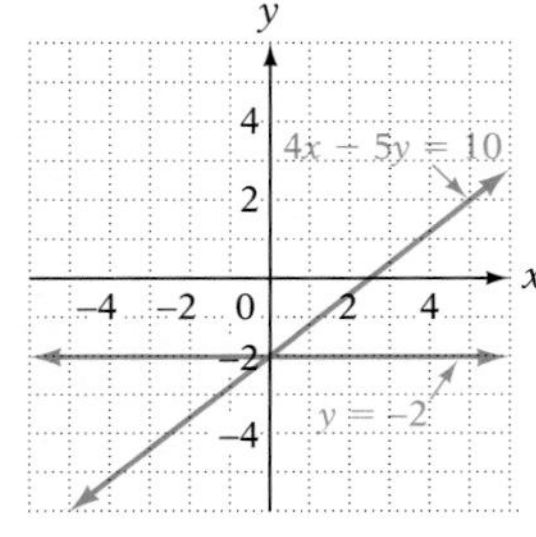

(0, −2)

19.

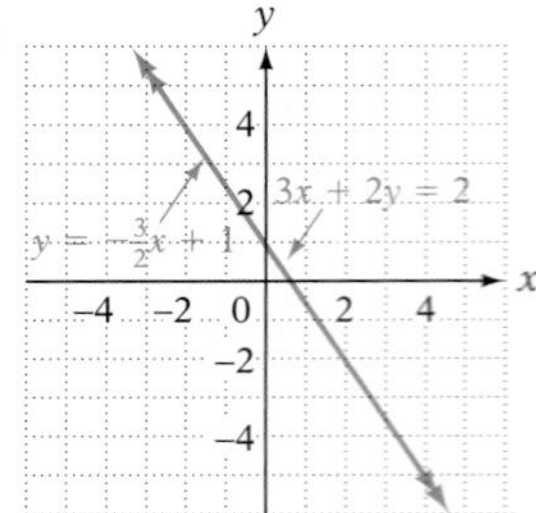

The ordered-pair solutions of $y = -\frac{3}{2}x + 1$

20.

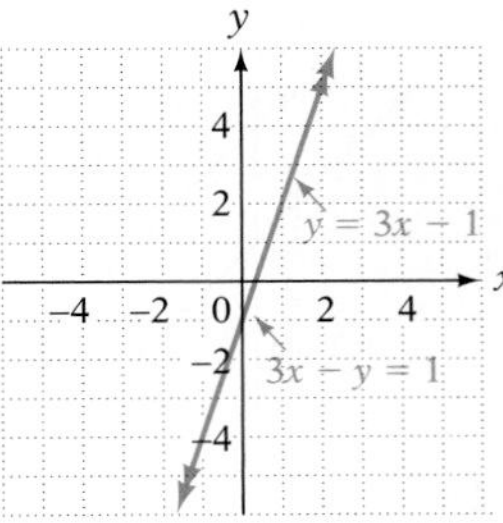

The ordered-pair solutions of $y = 3x - 1$

21.

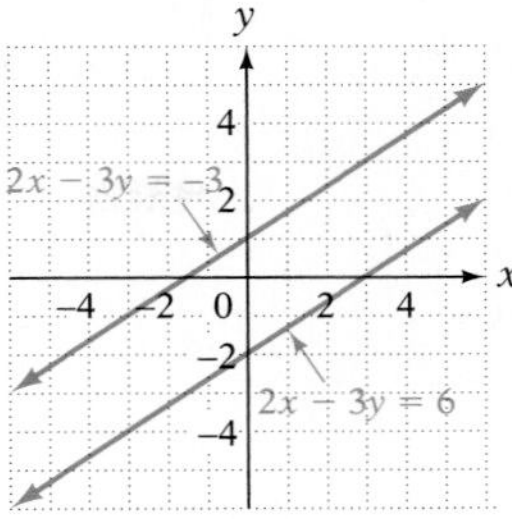

No solution

22.

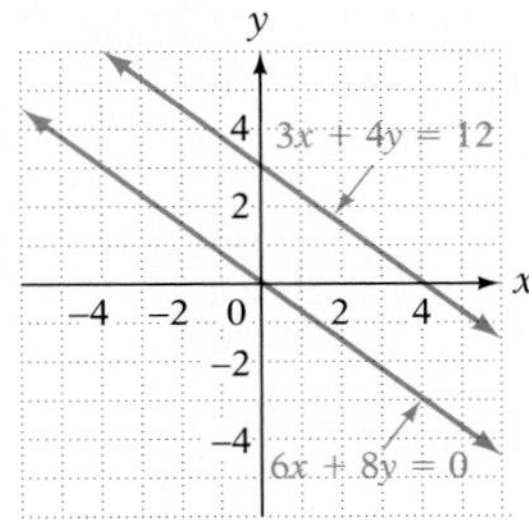

No solution

For Exercises 23 to 41, solve by graphing.

23. $2x - y = 4$
$x + y = 5$

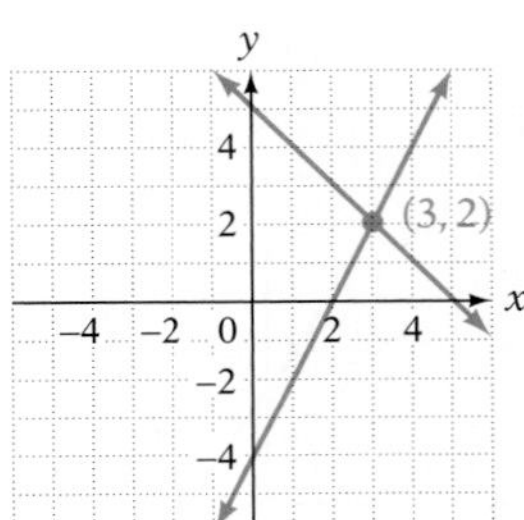

24. $x + 2y = 6$
$x - y = 3$

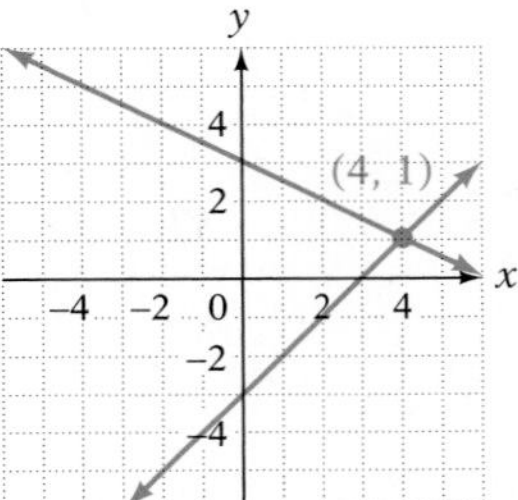

25. $3x - y = 3$
$2x + y = 2$

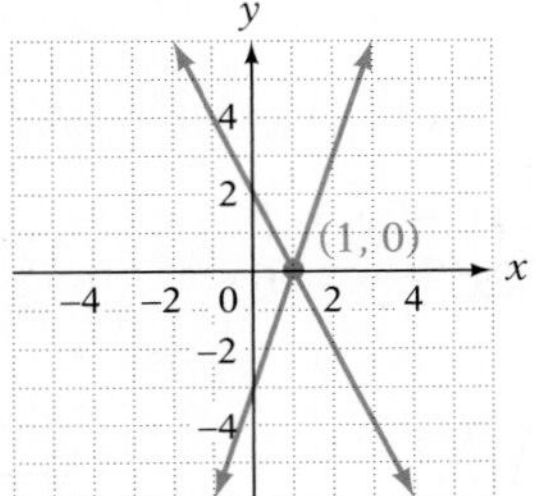

26. $3x - 2y = 6$
$y = 3$

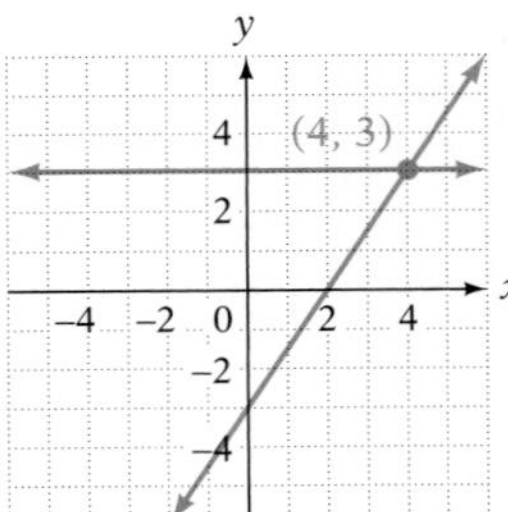

27. $x = 2$
$3x + 2y = 4$

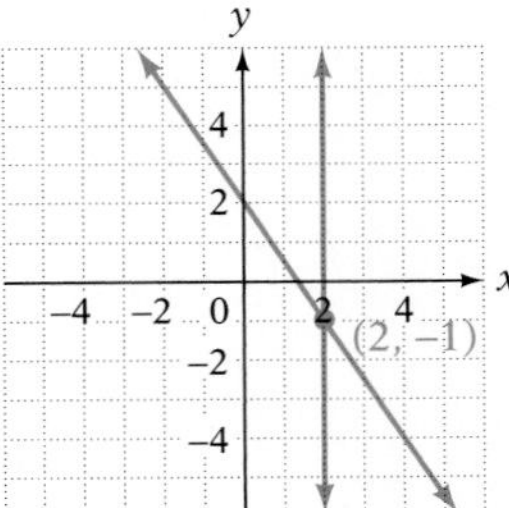

28. $x = 3$
$y = -2$

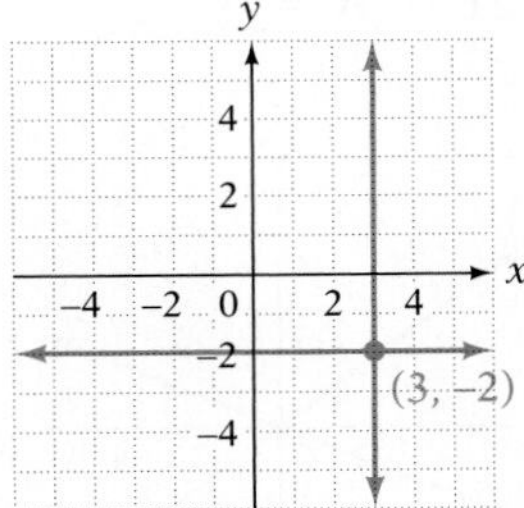

29. $x + 1 = 0$
$y - 3 = 0$

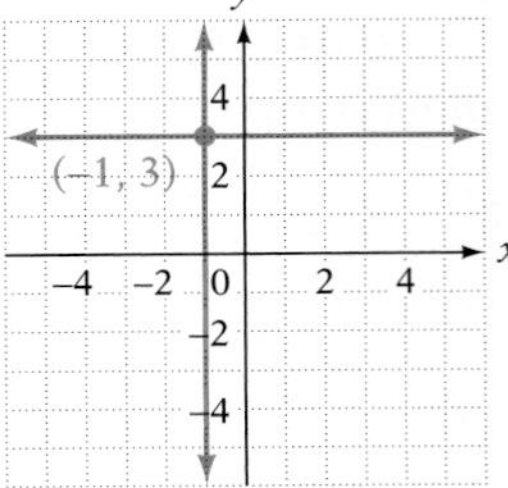

30. $y = 2x - 6$
$x + y = 0$

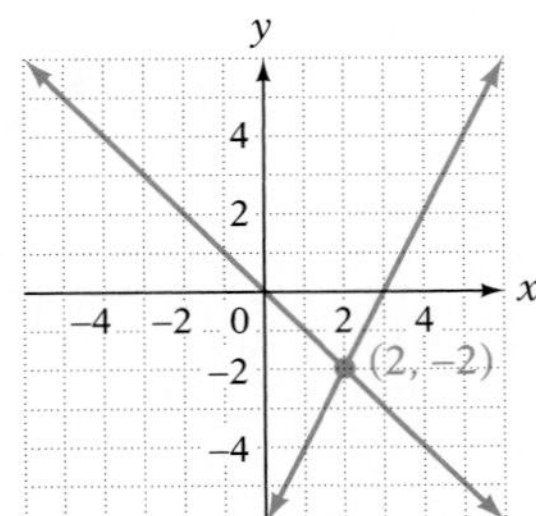

31. $5x - 2y = 11$
$y = 2x - 5$

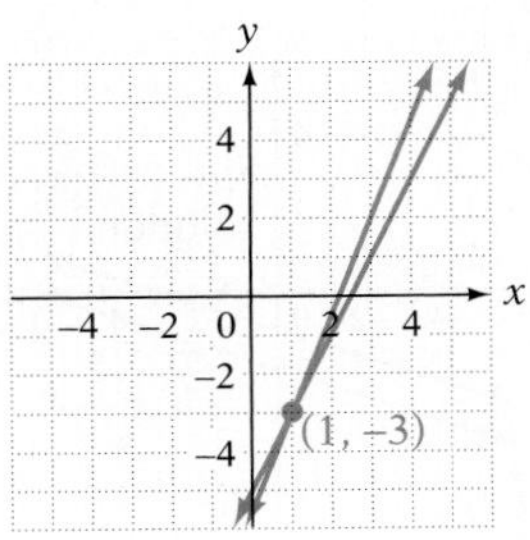

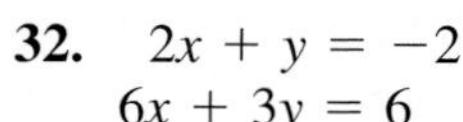

32. $2x + y = -2$
$6x + 3y = 6$

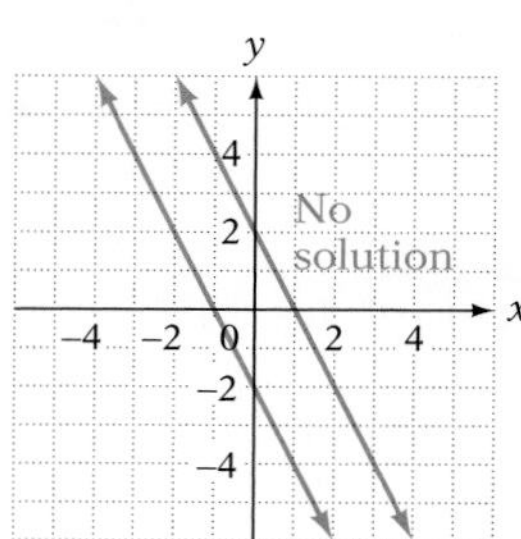

33. $x + y = 5$
$3x + 3y = 6$

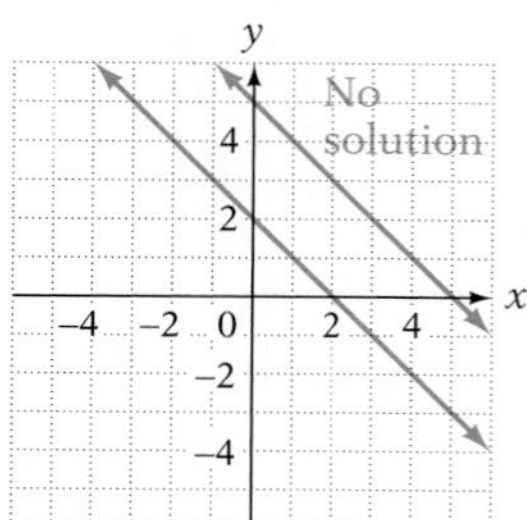

34. $y = 2x - 2$
$4x - 2y = 4$

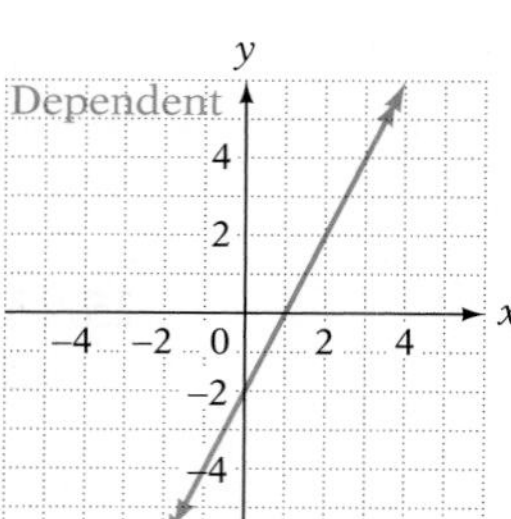
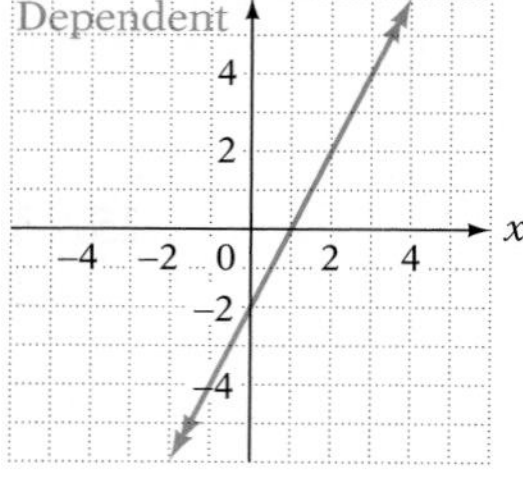

The ordered-pair solutions of $y = 2x - 2$

35. $y = -\frac{1}{3}x + 1$
$2x + 6y = 6$

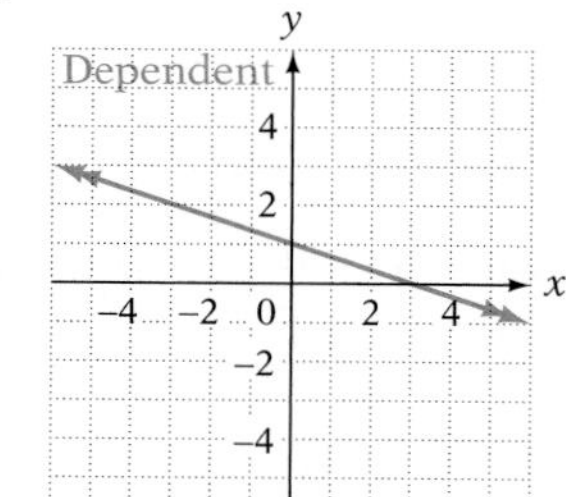

The ordered-pair solutions of $y = -\frac{1}{3}x + 1$

36. $x - y = 5$
$2x - y = 6$

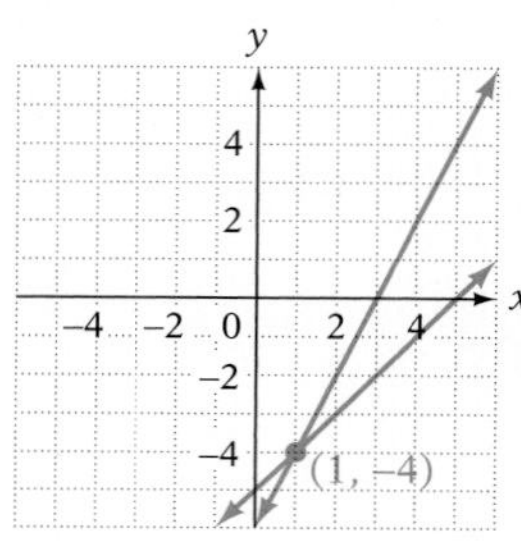

37. $5x - 2y = 10$
$3x + 2y = 6$

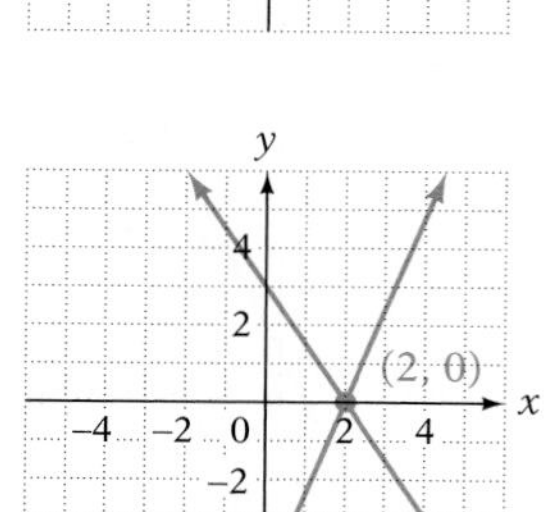

38. $3x + 4y = 0$
$2x - 5y = 0$

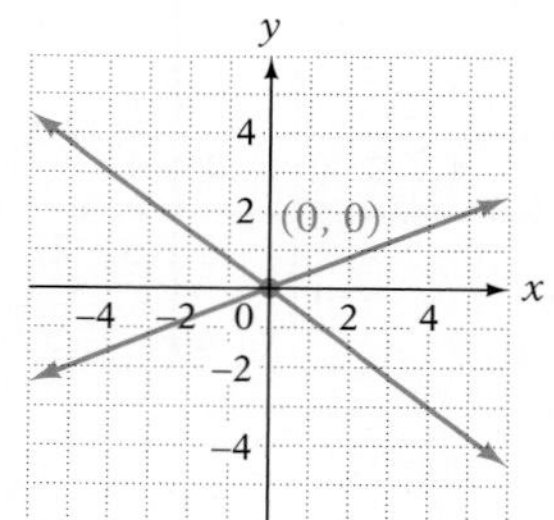

39. $2x - 3y = 0$
$y = -\frac{1}{3}x$

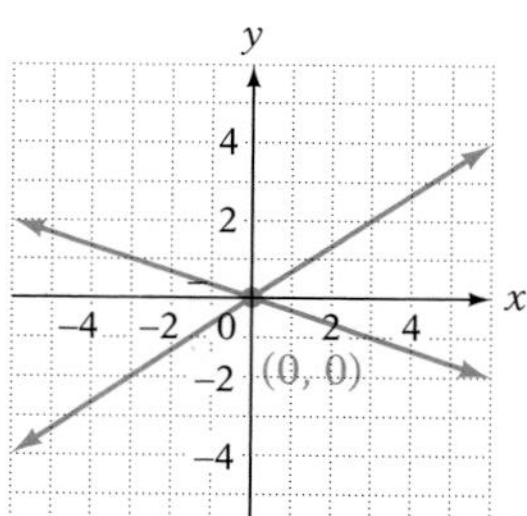

40. $x - 3y = 3$
$2x - 6y = 12$

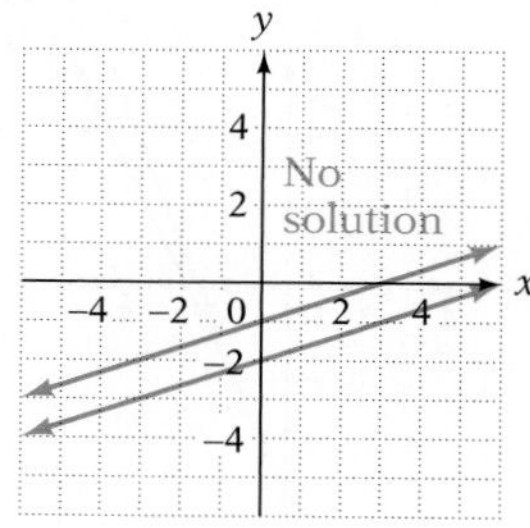

41. $4x + 6y = 12$
$6x + 9y = 18$

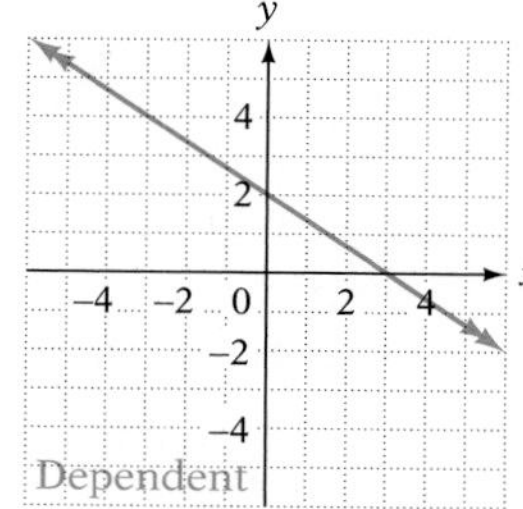

The ordered-pair solutions of $4x + 6y = 12$

For Exercises 42 and 43, A, B, C, and D are nonzero real numbers. State whether the system of equations is independent, inconsistent, or dependent.

42. $y = Ax + B$
$y = Ax + C, B \neq C$
Inconsistent

43. $x = C$
$y = D$
Independent

Critical Thinking

For Exercises 44 to 47, write a system of equations given the graph.

44.

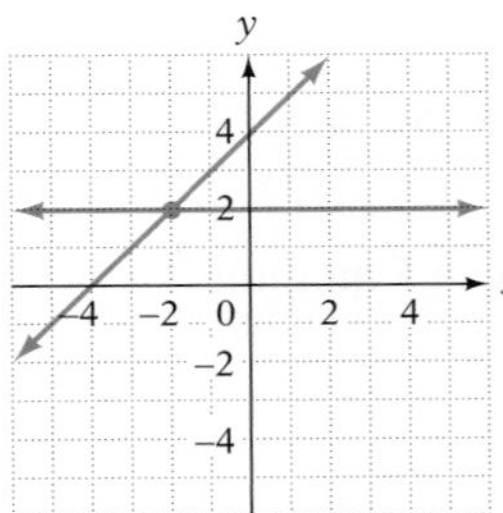

$y = 2$
$y = x + 4$

45.

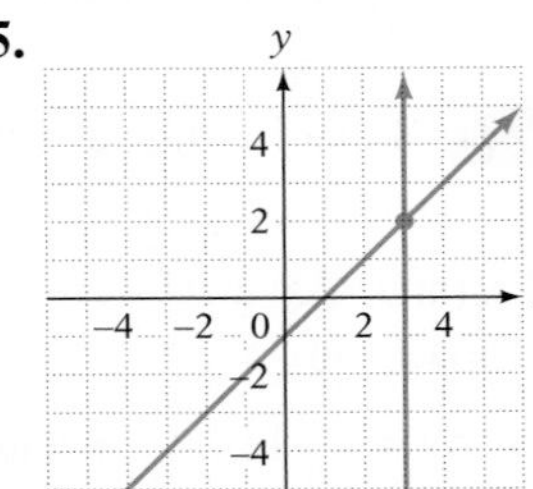

$x = 3$
$y = x - 1$

46.

$y = x$
$y = -x + 2$

47.

$y = 2x - 2$
$y = \frac{2}{3}x + \frac{2}{3}$

QUICK QUIZ

1. Is (3, −4) a solution of the following system of equations?
$2x - 3y = 18$
$-x + 4y = -19$
Yes [13.1A]
2. Solve by graphing:
$x + 2y = 6$
$2x - y = 7$
(4, 1) [13.1A]
3. Solve by graphing:
$x + 2y = 6$
$y = -\frac{1}{2}x + 1$
Inconsistent [13.1A]

Projects or Group Activities

48. Match each system of equations with its graph.

a. $2x - 3y = 6$
$2x - 5y = 10$

b. $3x - y = -5$
$x + y = 1$

c. $x + 2y = 10$
$y = x + 2$

d. $y = -3x + 5$
$y = 2x - 5$

i.

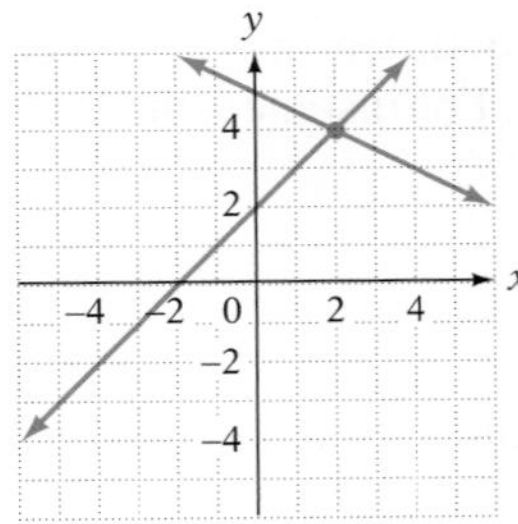

ii.

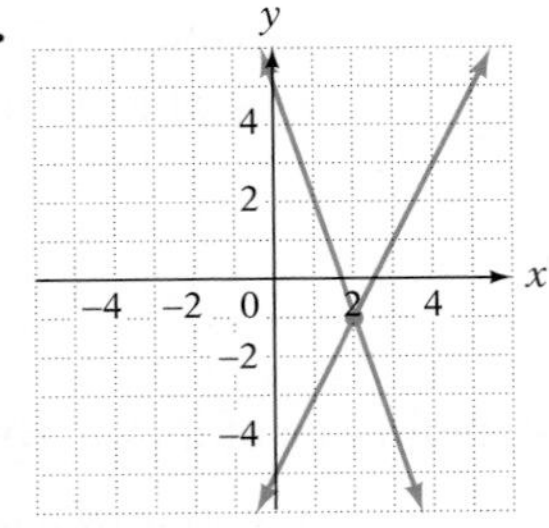

iii.

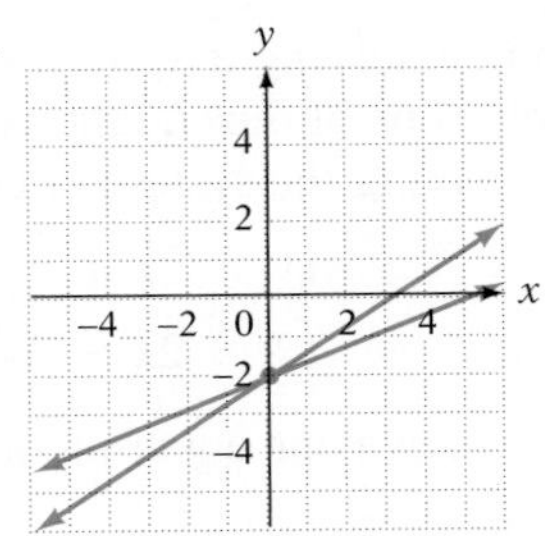

iv.

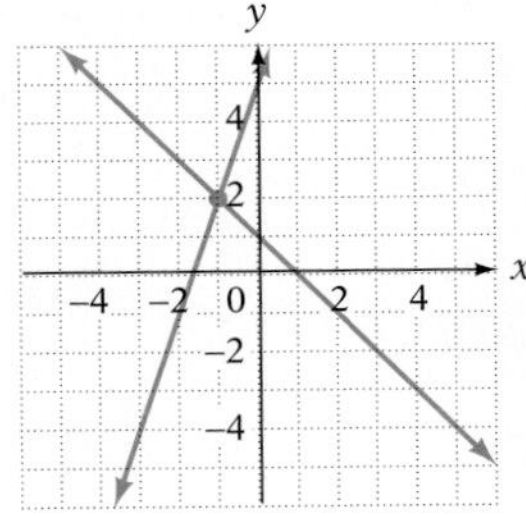

a and iii; b and iv; c and i; d and ii

49. Write three different systems of equations: **a.** one that has $(-3, 5)$ as its only solution, **b.** one for which there is no solution, and **c.** one that is a dependent system of equations.

Answers will vary. For example: **a.** $y = x + 8$, $y = -x + 2$ **b.** $y = 2x - 3$, $y = 2x + 4$ **c.** $y = 3x - 5$, $3x - y = 5$

SECTION

13.2 Solving Systems of Linear Equations by the Substitution Method

OBJECTIVE A *To solve a system of linear equations by the substitution method*

INSTRUCTOR NOTE
When students evaluate a variable expression, they replace a variable with a constant. Here, the student is replacing a variable with a variable expression. Mentioning this connection will help some students master the substitution method of solving a system of equations.

A graphical solution of a system of equations is found by approximating the coordinates of a point of intersection. Algebraic methods can be used to find an exact solution of a system of equations. The **substitution method** can be used to eliminate one of the variables in one of the equations so that we have one equation in one unknown.

HOW TO 1 Solve by the substitution method: (1) $2x + 5y = -11$
(2) $y = 3x - 9$

Equation (2) states that $y = 3x - 9$. Substitute $3x - 9$ for y in Equation (1). Then solve for x.

$2x + 5y = -11$ • This is Equation (1).
$2x + 5(3x - 9) = -11$ • From Equation (2), substitute $3x - 9$ for y.
$2x + 15x - 45 = -11$ • Solve for x.
$17x - 45 = -11$
$17x = 34$
$x = 2$

Now substitute the value of x into Equation (2) and solve for y.

$y = 3x - 9$ • This is Equation (2).
$y = 3(2) - 9$ • Substitute 2 for x.
$y = 6 - 9 = -3$

The solution is the ordered pair $(2, -3)$.

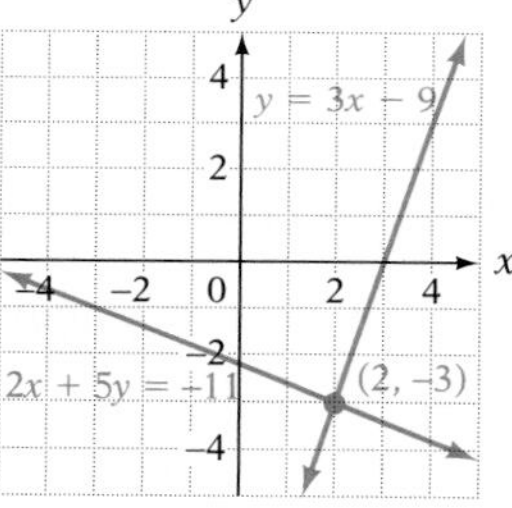

The graph of the system of equations given in HOW TO 1 is shown at the right. Note that the lines intersect at the point whose coordinates are $(2, -3)$, which is the algebraic solution we determined by the substitution method.

When solving a system of equations by the substitution method, we may first need to solve one of the equations in the system for one of its variables. For instance, the first step in solving the system of equations

(1) $x + 2y = -3$
(2) $2x - 3y = 5$

is to solve one equation of the system for one of its variables. Either equation can be used.

Solving Equation (1) for x:

$x + 2y = -3$
$x = -2y - 3$

Solving Equation (2) for x:

$2x - 3y = 5$
$2x = 3y + 5$
$x = \frac{3y + 5}{2} = \frac{3}{2}y + \frac{5}{2}$

Because solving Equation (1) for x does not result in fractions, it is the easier of the two equations to use.

Here is the solution of the system of equations given on the preceding page.

HOW TO 2 Solve by the substitution method: (1) $x + 2y = -3$
(2) $2x - 3y = 5$

To use the substitution method, we must solve one equation of the system for one of its variables. We will use Equation (1) because solving it for x does not result in fractions.

$x + 2y = -3$

(3) $x = -2y - 3$ • **Solve Equation (1) for x. This is Equation (3).**

Now substitute $-2y - 3$ for x in Equation (2) and solve for y.

$2x - 3y = 5$ • **This is Equation (2).**

$2(-2y - 3) - 3y = 5$ • **From Equation (3), substitute $-2y - 3$ for x.**

$-4y - 6 - 3y = 5$ • **Solve for y.**

$-7y - 6 = 5$

$-7y = 11$

$y = -\frac{11}{7}$

Substitute the value of y into Equation (3) and solve for x.

$x = -2y - 3$ • **This is Equation (3).**

$= -2\left(-\frac{11}{7}\right) - 3$ • **Substitute $-\frac{11}{7}$ for y.**

$= \frac{22}{7} - 3 = \frac{22}{7} - \frac{21}{7} = \frac{1}{7}$

The solution is $\left(\frac{1}{7}, -\frac{11}{7}\right)$.

The graph of the system of equations given in HOW TO 2 above is shown at the right. It would be difficult to determine the exact solution of this system of equations from the graphs of the equations.

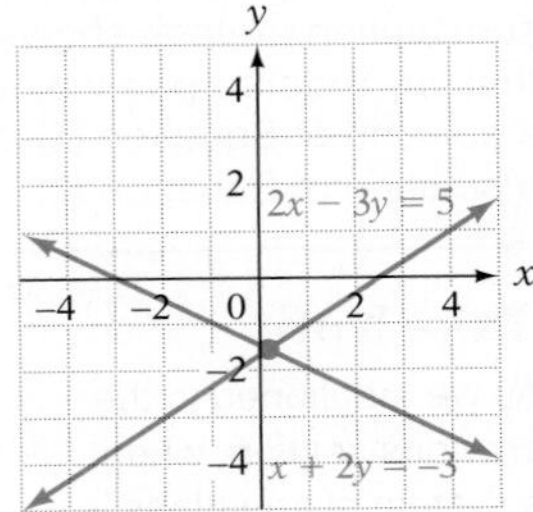

HOW TO 3 Solve by the substitution method: (1) $y = 3x - 1$
(2) $y = -2x - 6$

$y = -2x - 6$

$3x - 1 = -2x - 6$ • **Substitute $3x - 1$ for y in Equation (2).**

$5x = -5$ • **Solve for x.**

$x = -1$

Substitute this value of x into Equation (1) or Equation (2) and solve for y. Equation (1) is used here.

$y = 3x - 1$

$y = 3(-1) - 1 = -4$ • **Substitute -1 for x.**

The solution is $(-1, -4)$.

INSTRUCTOR NOTE

To prepare students for solving the inconsistent system of equations in HOW TO 4, try asking them whether 5 is a solution of $x + 2 = 8$. Most students will say no, because $7 \neq 8$. Now present students with the system of equations in HOW TO 4 and ask whether (3, 1) is a solution. They should determine that it is a solution of Equation (2) but not of Equation (1), and therefore is not a solution of the system. Now give a few more ordered pairs that are solutions of Equation (2), such as $(-3, 5)$, $(0, 3)$, and $(6, -1)$, and have students verify that they are not solutions of the system. Solving this system of equations by the substitution method shows that *any* ordered pair that is a solution of Equation (2) is not a solution of Equation (1).

A similar strategy can be used for dependent systems of equations. In this case, however, every solution of Equation (1) *is* a solution of Equation (2). Solving this system of equations by the substitution method shows that *any* ordered pair that is a solution of Equation (1) is a solution of Equation (2).

Take Note

As we mentioned in the previous section, when a system of equations is dependent, either equation can be used to write the ordered-pair solutions. Thus we could have said, "The solutions are the ordered pairs (x, y) that are solutions of $4x - 8y = 12$." Also note that, as we show at the right, if we solve each equation for y, the equations have the same slope-intercept form. This means that we could also say, "The solutions are the ordered pairs (x, y) that are solutions of $y = \frac{1}{2}x - \frac{3}{2}$." When a system of equations is dependent, there are several ways in which the solutions can be stated.

The substitution method can be used to analyze inconsistent and dependent systems of equations. If, when solving a system of equations algebraically, the variable is eliminated and the result is a false equation, such as $0 = 4$, the system of equations is inconsistent. If the variable is eliminated and the result is a true equation, such as $12 = 12$, the system of equations is dependent.

HOW TO 4 Solve by the substitution method: (1) $2x + 3y = 3$ (2) $y = -\frac{2}{3}x + 3$

$2x + 3y = 3$ • This is Equation (1).

$2x + 3\left(-\frac{2}{3}x + 3\right) = 3$ • From Equation (2), replace y with $-\frac{2}{3}x + 3$.

$2x - 2x + 9 = 3$ • Solve for x.

$9 = 3$ • This is a false equation.

Because $9 = 3$ is a false equation, the system of equations has no solution. The system is inconsistent.

Solving Equation (1) above for y, we have $y = -\frac{2}{3}x + 1$.

Comparing this equation with Equation (2) reveals that the slopes are equal and the y-intercepts are different. The graphs of the equations that make up this system of equations are parallel and thus never intersect. Because the graphs do not intersect, there are no solutions of the system of equations. The system of equations is inconsistent.

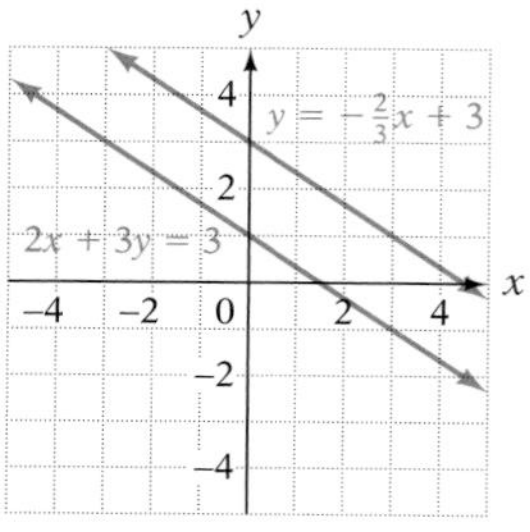

HOW TO 5 Solve by the substitution method: (1) $x = 2y + 3$ (2) $4x - 8y = 12$

$4x - 8y = 12$ • This is Equation (2).

$4(2y + 3) - 8y = 12$ • From Equation (1), replace x by $2y + 3$.

$8y + 12 - 8y = 12$ • Solve for y.

$12 = 12$ • This is a true equation.

The true equation $12 = 12$ indicates that any ordered pair (x, y) that satisfies one equation of the system satisfies the other equation. Therefore, the system of equations has an infinite number of solutions. The system is dependent. The solutions are the ordered pairs (x, y) that are solutions of $x = 2y + 3$.

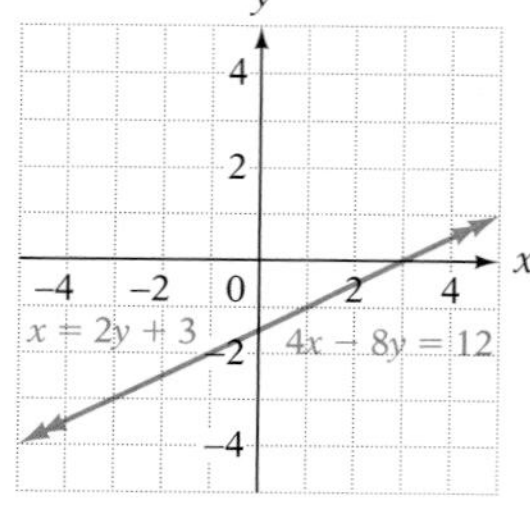

If we write Equation (1) and Equation (2) from HOW TO 5 in slope-intercept form, we have

$$x = 2y + 3 \qquad -2y = -x + 3 \qquad y = \frac{1}{2}x - \frac{3}{2}$$

$$4x - 8y = 12 \qquad -8y = -4x + 12 \qquad y = \frac{1}{2}x - \frac{3}{2}$$

The slope-intercept forms of the equations are the same, and therefore the graphs are the same. If we graph these two equations, we essentially graph one over the other, so the graphs intersect at an infinite number of points.

EXAMPLE 1

Solve by substitution:
(1) $3x + 4y = -2$
(2) $-x + 2y = 4$

Solution

$-x + 2y = 4$ • Solve Equation (2) for x.
$-x = -2y + 4$
$x = 2y - 4$

Substitute in Equation (1).
(1) $3x + 4y = -2$
$3(2y - 4) + 4y = -2$ • $x = 2y - 4$
$6y - 12 + 4y = -2$ • Solve for y.
$10y - 12 = -2$
$10y = 10$
$y = 1$

Substitute in $x = 2y - 4$.
$x = 2y - 4$
$x = 2(1) - 4$ • $y = 1$
$x = 2 - 4$
$x = -2$

The solution is $(-2, 1)$.

YOU TRY IT 1

Solve by substitution:
(1) $7x - y = 4$
(2) $3x + 2y = 9$

Your solution

(1, 3)

IN-CLASS EXAMPLES

1. Solve by substitution: $4x - 3y = 11$, $3x - y = 7$
   (2, −1)
2. Solve by substitution: $6x + 2y = 8$, $y = -3x + 1$
   No solution
3. Solve by substitution: $x - 2y = 8$, $y = \frac{1}{2}x - 4$
   Dependent. The solutions are the ordered-pair solutions of $y = \frac{1}{2}x - 4$.

EXAMPLE 2

Solve by substitution:
$4x + 2y = 5$
$y = -2x + 1$

Solution

$4x + 2y = 5$
$4x + 2(-2x + 1) = 5$ • $y = -2x + 1$
$4x - 4x + 2 = 5$ • Solve for x.
$2 = 5$ • A false equation

The system of equations is inconsistent and therefore has no solution.

YOU TRY IT 2

Solve by substitution:
$3x - y = 4$
$y = 3x + 2$

Your solution

No solution

EXAMPLE 3

Solve by substitution:
$y = 3x - 2$
$6x - 2y = 4$

Solution

$6x - 2y = 4$
$6x - 2(3x - 2) = 4$ • $y = 3x - 2$
$6x - 6x + 4 = 4$ • Solve for x.
$4 = 4$ • A true equation

The system of equations is dependent. The solutions are the ordered pairs that satisfy the equation $y = 3x - 2$.

YOU TRY IT 3

Solve by substitution:
$y = -2x + 1$
$6x + 3y = 3$

Your solution

The system of equations is dependent. The solutions are the ordered pairs that satisfy the equation $y = -2x + 1$.

Solutions on p. S32

OBJECTIVE B *To solve investment problems*

Recall from Section 6.5 that the annual simple interest earned by an investment is given by the equation $Pr = I$, where P is the principal, or the amount invested, r is the simple interest rate, and I is the simple interest.

INSTRUCTOR NOTE

Some students may recall the simple interest equation as $I = Prt$. Because we are discussing *annual* interest, $t = 1$. Thus we just write $I = Pr$.

For instance, if you invest $750 at a simple interest rate of 6%, then the interest earned after one year is calculated as follows:

$$Pr = I$$
$$750(0.06) = I$$ • Replace P by 750 and r by 0.06 (6%).
$$45 = I$$ • Simplify.

The amount of interest earned is $45.

Tips for Success

Word problems are challenging because we must read the problem, determine the quantity we must find, think of a method to find it, actually solve the problem, and then check the answer. In short, we must devise a *strategy* and then use that strategy to find the *solution*. See *AIM for Success* at the front of the book.

INSTRUCTOR NOTE

Students may not realize that investors do not always choose to put all of their money into the account with the greatest interest rate because that account usually has the most risk. Placing money in different accounts allows the investor to diversify.

HOW TO 6 A medical lab technician decides to open an Individual Retirement Account (IRA) by placing $2000 in two simple interest accounts. On one account, a corporate bond fund, the annual simple interest rate is 7.5%. On the second account, a real estate investment trust, the annual simple interest rate is 9%. If the technician wants annual earnings of $168 from the two investments, how much must be invested in each account?

Strategy for Solving Simple-Interest Investment Problems

1. For each amount invested, use the equation $Pr = I$. Write a numerical or variable expression for the principal, the interest rate, and the interest earned.

Amount invested at 7.5%: x
Amount invested at 9%: y

	Principal, P	·	Interest rate, r	=	Interest earned, I
Amount at 7.5%	x	·	0.075	=	$0.075x$
Amount at 9%	y	·	0.09	=	$0.09y$

2. Write a system of equations. One equation will express the relationship between the amounts invested. The second equation will express the relationship between the amounts of interest earned by the investments.

The total amount invested is $2000: $x + y = 2000$
The total annual interest earned is $168: $0.075x + 0.09y = 168$

Solve the system of equations.

(1) $x + y = 2000$
(2) $0.075x + 0.09y = 168$

Solve Equation (1) for y and substitute into Equation (2).

(3) $y = -x + 2000$

$$0.075x + 0.09(-x + 2000) = 168$$ • Substitute $-x + 2000$ for y.
$$0.075x - 0.09x + 180 = 168$$
$$-0.015x = -12$$
$$x = 800$$

Substitute the value of x into Equation (3) and solve for y.

$y = -x + 2000$
$y = -800 + 2000 = 1200$ • Substitute 800 for x.

The amount invested at 7.5% is $800. The amount invested at 9% is $1200.

EXAMPLE 4

A hair stylist invested some money at an annual simple interest rate of 5.2%. A second investment, \$1000 more than the first, was invested at an annual simple interest rate of 7.2%. The total annual interest earned was \$320. How much was invested in each account?

Strategy

- Amount invested at 5.2%: x
  Amount invested at 7.2%: y

	Principal	*Rate*	*Interest*
Amount at 5.2%	x	0.052	$0.052x$
Amount at 7.2%	y	0.072	$0.072y$

- The second investment is \$1000 more than the first investment:

  $y = x + 1000$

  The sum of the interest earned at 5.2% and the interest earned at 7.2% equals \$320.

  $0.052x + 0.072y = 320$

Solution

(1) $y = x + 1000$
(2) $0.052x + 0.072y = 320$

Replace y in Equation (2) by $x + 1000$ from Equation (1). Then solve for x.

$$0.052x + 0.072y = 320$$
$$0.052x + 0.072(x + 1000) = 320 \quad \bullet\ y = x + 1000$$
$$0.052x + 0.072x + 72 = 320 \quad \bullet\ \text{Solve for } x.$$
$$0.124x + 72 = 320$$
$$0.124x = 248$$
$$x = 2000$$

$$y = x + 1000$$
$$= 2000 + 1000 \quad \bullet\ x = 2000$$
$$= 3000$$

\$2000 was invested at an annual simple interest rate of 5.2%; \$3000 was invested at 7.2%.

YOU TRY IT 4

The manager of a city's investment income wishes to place \$330,000 in two simple interest accounts. The first account earns 6.5% annual interest, and the second account earns 4.5%. How much should be invested in each account so that both accounts earn the same annual interest?

Your strategy

Your solution

\$135,000 at 6.5%; \$195,000 at 4.5%

IN-CLASS EXAMPLES

4. A web page designer invested a total of \$10,000 in two accounts, a money market account and a high-yield corporate bond fund. The annual interest rate on the money market account was 3.5%, and the annual interest rate on the high-yield corporate bond fund was 9.25%. If the designer received annual interest income of \$723.75, how much was invested in each account? **\$3500 at 3.5%; \$6500 at 9.25%**

Solution on p. S32

13.2 EXERCISES

SUGGESTED ASSIGNMENT:
Exercises 1–6; Exercises 7–35, odds; Exercises 41–51, odds;
More challenging exercise: Exercise 58

Concept Check

1. When you solve a system of equations by the substitution method, how do you determine whether the system of equations is dependent? How do you determine whether the system of equations is inconsistent?

2. Use this system of equations: (1) $y = 3x - 5$
(2) $x = 2$

To solve the system by substitution, substitute __2__ for x in equation (1):
$y = 3(2) - 5 =$ __1__.

The solution of the system of equations is (__2__, __1__).

For Exercises 3 to 6, determine whether the statement is true or false.

3. For one year, you have x dollars deposited in an account that pays 7% annual simple interest. You will earn $0.07x$ in simple interest on this account. True

4. If you have a total of \$8000 deposited in two accounts and you represent the amount you have in the first account as x, then the amount in the second account is represented as $8000 - x$. True

5. The amount of interest earned on one account is $0.05x$, and the amount of interest earned on a second account is $0.08(9000 - x)$. If the two accounts earn the same amount of interest, then we can write the equation $0.05x + 0.08(9000 - x)$. False

6. If the amount of interest earned on one account is $0.06x$ and the amount of interest earned on a second account is $0.09(4000 - x)$, then the total interest earned on the two accounts can be represented as $0.06x + 0.09(4000 - x)$. True

OBJECTIVE A *To solve a system of linear equations by the substitution method*

For Exercises 7 to 36, solve by substitution.

7. $2x + 3y = 7$
$x = 2$
(2, 1)

8. $y = 3$
$3x - 2y = 6$
(4, 3)

9. $y = x - 3$
$x + y = 5$
(4, 1)

10. $y = x + 2$
$x + y = 6$
(2, 4)

11. $x = y - 2$
$x + 3y = 2$
(−1, 1)

12. $x = y + 1$
$x + 2y = 7$
(3, 2)

13. $y = 4 - 3x$
$3x + y = 5$
No solution

14. $y = 2 - 3x$
$6x + 2y = 7$
No solution

15. $x = 3y + 3$
$2x - 6y = 12$
No solution

16. $x = 2 - y$
$3x + 3y = 6$
Dependent. The solutions satisfy the equation $x = 2 - y$.

17. $3x + 5y = -6$
$x = 5y + 3$
$\left(-\frac{3}{4}, -\frac{3}{4}\right)$

18. $y = 2x + 3$
$4x - 3y = 1$
(−5, −7)

19. $3x + y = 4$
$4x - 3y = 1$
(1, 1)

20. $x - 4y = 9$
$2x - 3y = 11$
$\left(\frac{17}{5}, -\frac{7}{5}\right)$

21. $3x - y = 6$
$x + 3y = 2$
(2, 0)

22. $4x - y = -5$
$2x + 5y = 13$
$\left(-\frac{6}{11}, \frac{31}{11}\right)$

23. $3x - y = 5$
$2x + 5y = -8$
(1, −2)

24. $3x + 4y = 18$
$2x - y = 1$
(2, 3)

25. $4x + 3y = 0$
$2x - y = 0$
(0, 0)

26. $5x + 2y = 0$
$x - 3y = 0$
(0, 0)

27. $2x - y = 2$
$6x - 3y = 6$
Dependent. The solutions satisfy the equation $2x - y = 2$.

28. $3x + y = 4$
$9x + 3y = 12$
Dependent. The solutions satisfy the equation $3x + y = 4$.

29. $x = 3y + 2$
$y = 2x + 6$
(−4, −2)

30. $x = 4 - 2y$
$y = 2x - 13$
(6, −1)

31. $y = 2x + 11$
$y = 5x - 19$
(10, 31)

32. $y = 2x - 8$
$y = 3x - 13$
(5, 2)

33. $y = -4x + 2$
$y = -3x - 1$
(3, −10)

34. $x = 3y + 7$
$x = 2y - 1$
(−17, −8)

35. $x = 4y - 2$
$x = 6y + 8$
(−22, −5)

36. $x = 3 - 2y$
$x = 5y - 10$
$\left(-\frac{5}{7}, \frac{13}{7}\right)$

For Exercises 37 and 38, assume that A, B, and C are nonzero real numbers. State whether the system of equations is independent, inconsistent, or dependent.

37. $x + y = A$
$x = A - y$
Dependent

38. $x + y = B$
$y = -x + C, C \neq B$
Inconsistent

OBJECTIVE B *To solve investment problems*

For Exercises 39 and 40, use the system of equations at the right, which represents the following situation. Owen Marshall divides an investment of $10,000 between two simple interest accounts. One account earns 8% annual simple interest, and the second account earns 6.5% annual simple interest.

$$x + y = 10{,}000$$
$$0.08x + 0.065y = 710$$

39. What do the variables x and y represent? Explain the meaning of each equation in terms of the problem situation.
x = amount invested at 8%, y = amount invested at 6.5%; $x + y = 10{,}000$ represents the fact that the sum of the two investments is $10,000; $0.08x + 0.065y = 710$ represents the fact that the total interest earned by the two investments is $710.

40. Write a question that could be answered by solving the system of equations.
Answers will vary. For example, "How much money did Owen invest at 8%?"

41. An investment of \$3500 is divided between two simple interest accounts. On one account, the annual simple interest rate is 5%, and on the second account, the annual simple interest rate is 7.5%. How much should be invested in each account so that the total interest earned from the two accounts is \$215?
\$1900 at 5%; \$1600 at 7.5%

42. A mortgage broker purchased two trust deeds for a total of \$250,000. One trust deed earns 7% simple annual interest, and the second earns 8% simple annual interest. If the total annual interest earned from the two trust deeds is \$18,500, what was the purchase price of each trust deed?
7% trust deed: \$150,000; 8% trust deed: \$100,000

43. When Sara Whitehorse changed jobs, she rolled over the \$6000 in her retirement account into two simple interest accounts. On one account, the annual simple interest rate is 9%; on the second account, the annual simple interest rate is 6%. How much was invested in each account if the accounts earned the same amount of annual interest?
\$3600 at 6%; \$2400 at 9%

44. An animal trainer decided to take the \$15,000 won on a game show and deposit it in two simple interest accounts. Part of the winnings were placed in an account paying 7% annual simple interest, and the remainder was used to purchase a government bond that earns 6.5% annual simple interest. The amount of interest earned for one year was \$1020. How much was invested in each account?
\$9000 at 7%; \$6000 at 6.5%

45. A police officer has chosen a high-yield stock fund that earns 8% annual simple interest for part of a \$6000 investment. The remaining portion is used to purchase a preferred stock that earns 11% annual simple interest. How much should be invested in each account so that the amount earned on the 8% account is twice the amount earned on the 11% account?
\$4400 at 8%; \$1600 at 11%

46. To save for the purchase of a new car, a deposit was made into an account that earns 7% annual simple interest. Another deposit, \$1500 less than the first deposit, was placed in a certificate of deposit (CD) earning 9% annual simple interest. The total interest earned on both accounts for one year was \$505. How much money was deposited in the CD?
\$2500

47. The Pacific Investment Group invested some money in a certificate of deposit (CD) that earns 6.5% annual simple interest. Twice the amount invested at 6.5% was invested in a second CD that earns 8.5% annual simple interest. If the total annual interest earned from the two investments was \$4935, how much was invested at 6.5%?
\$21,000

48. A corporation gave a university \$300,000 to support product safety research. The university deposited some of the money in a 10% annual simple interest account and the remainder in an 8.5% annual simple interest account. How much should be deposited in each account so that the annual interest earned is \$28,500?
\$200,000 at 10%; \$100,000 at 8.5%

49. Ten coworkers formed an investment club, and each member deposited \$2000 in the club's account. The club decided to take the total amount and invest some of it in preferred stock that pays 8% annual simple interest and the remainder in a municipal bond that pays 7% annual simple interest. The amount of interest earned each year from the investments was \$1520. How much was invested in each?
\$12,000 at 8%; \$8000 at 7%

50. A financial consultant advises a client to invest part of \$30,000 in municipal bonds that earn 6.5% annual simple interest and the remainder of the money in 8.5% corporate bonds. How much should be invested in each so that the total interest earned each year is \$2190? \$18,000 at 6.5%; \$12,000 at 8.5%

51. Alisa Rhodes placed some money in a real estate investment trust that earns 7.5% annual simple interest. A second investment, which was one-half the amount placed in the real estate investment trust, was used to purchase a trust deed that earns 9% annual simple interest. If the total annual interest earned from the two investments was \$900, how much was invested in the trust deed? \$3750

QUICK QUIZ

Solve by substitution.

1. $3x - 4y = 9$
   $y = 2x - 1$
   $(-1, -3)$ [13.2A]
2. $2x + 7y = -5$
   $x + 4y = -3$
   $(1, -1)$ [13.2A]
3. $2x + 3y = 3$
   $y = -\frac{2}{3}x + 1$
   Dependent [13.2A]
4. A landscape architect invested a total of \$20,000 in two accounts, a municipal bond fund and a real estate investment trust. The annual interest rate on the municipal bond fund was 4.25%, and the annual interest rate on the real estate investment trust was 9%. If the architect received annual interest income of \$1230, how much was invested in each account? **\$12,000 at 4.25%; \$8000 at 9% [13.2B]**

Critical Thinking

For Exercises 52 to 57, rewrite each equation so that the coefficients are integers. Then solve the system of equations by the substitution method.

52. $0.1x - 0.6y = 0.5$
$-0.7x + 0.2y = 0.5$ $(-1, -1)$

53. $0.8x - 0.1y = 0.3$
$0.5x - 0.2y = -0.5$ $(1, 5)$

54. $0.4x + 0.5y = 0.2$
$0.3x - 0.1y = 1.1$ $(3, -2)$

55. $-0.1x + 0.3y = 1.1$
$0.4x - 0.1y = -2.2$ $(-5, 2)$

56. $1.2x + 0.1y = 1.9$
$0.1x + 0.3y = 2.2$ $(1, 7)$

57. $1.25x - 0.01y = 1.5$
$0.24x - 0.02y = -1.52$
$(2, 100)$

58. The following was offered as a solution of the system of equations.

(1) $y = \frac{1}{2}x + 2$

(2) $2x + 5y = 10$

$$2x + 5y = 10 \quad \text{• Equation (2)}$$

$$2x + 5\left(\frac{1}{2}x + 2\right) = 10 \quad \text{• Substitute } \tfrac{1}{2}x + 2 \text{ for } y.$$

$$2x + \frac{5}{2}x + 10 = 10 \quad \text{• Solve for } x.$$

$$\frac{9}{2}x = 0$$

$$x = 0$$

At this point the student stated that because $x = 0$, the system of equations has no solution. If this assertion is correct, is the system of equations independent, dependent, or inconsistent? If the assertion is not correct, what is the correct solution?
The assertion is not correct. The system of equations is independent. The solution is $(0, 2)$.

59. A financial manager invested 20% of a client's money in bonds paying 9% annual simple interest, 35% in an 8% simple interest account, and the remainder in 9.5% corporate bonds. Find the amount invested in each if the total annual interest earned is \$5325. \$12,000 at 9%; \$21,000 at 8%; \$27,000 at 9.5%

60. A plant manager invested \$3000 more in stocks than in bonds. The stocks paid 8% annual simple interest, and the bonds paid 9.5% annual simple interest. Both investments yielded the same income. Find the total annual interest received on both investments. \$3040

Projects or Group Activities

For Exercises 61 to 63, find the value of k for which the system of equations has no solution.

61. $2x - 3y = 7$
$kx - 3y = 4$
2

62. $8x - 4y = 1$
$2x - ky = 3$
1

63. $x = 4y + 4$
$kx - 8y = 4$
2

64. A bank offers a customer a 4-year certificate of deposit (CD) that earns 6.5% compound annual interest. This means that the interest earned each year is added to the principal before the interest for the next year is calculated. Find the value in 4 years of a nurse's investment of \$3000 in this CD. \$3859.40

65. A bank offers a customer a 5-year certificate of deposit (CD) that earns 7.5% compound annual interest. This means that the interest earned each year is added to the principal before the interest for the next year is calculated. Find the value in 5 years of an accountant's investment of \$2500 in this CD. \$3589.07

CHECK YOUR PROGRESS: CHAPTER 13

For Exercises 1 to 3, solve by graphing.

1. $x - y = 3$
$x + y = 5$ (4, 1) [13.1A]

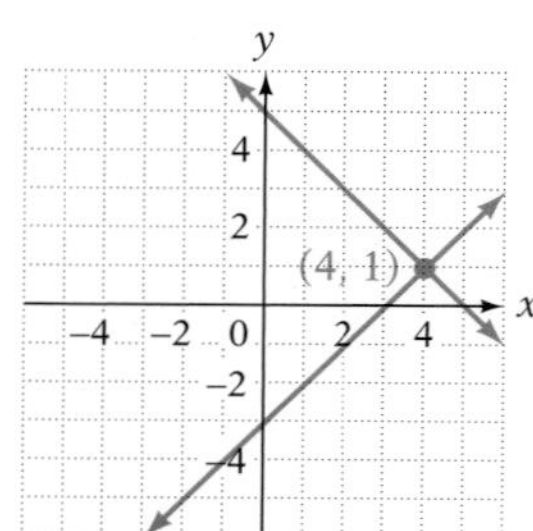

2. $4x + 3y = 12$
$y = -\frac{4}{3}x + 4$ The ordered-pair solutions of $y = -\frac{4}{3}x + 4$ [13.1A]

3. $y = \frac{1}{2}x + 2$
$x - 2y = 8$ No solution [13.1A]

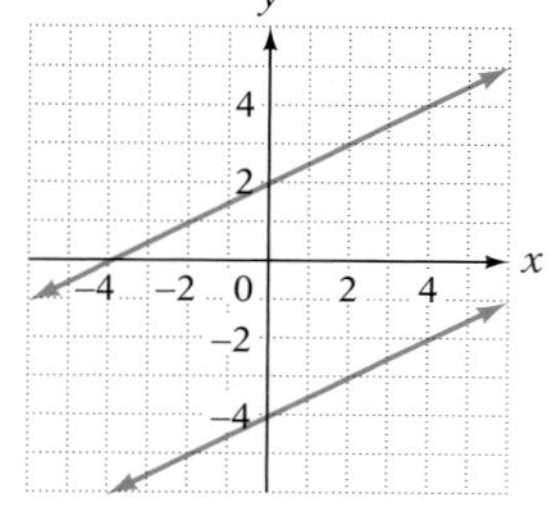

4. Is $(2, -3)$ a solution of the system $y = 2x - 7$
$y = 3x - 9$?
Yes [13.1A]

5. Solve by substitution:
$x - 3y = -14$
$3x + 8y = 26$
$(-2, 4)$ [13.2A]

6. Solve by substitution:
$x - 3y = -12$
$y = \frac{1}{3}x + 4$
The ordered-pair solutions of $y = \frac{1}{3}x + 4$ [13.2A]

7. Virak Ly invested part of \$30,000 in municipal bonds that earn 6.5% annual simple interest and the remainder of the money in 8.5% corporate bonds. How much is invested in each account if the total annual interest earned is \$2190?
\$18,000 at 6.5%; \$12,000 at 8.5% [13.2B]

SECTION

13.3 Solving Systems of Linear Equations by the Addition Method

OBJECTIVE A *To solve a system of linear equations by the addition method*

INSTRUCTOR NOTE

It may help some students if you review the Addition Property of Equations before starting this section. For instance, give them the equation $3x - 5 = 7$ and then add 5 to each side: $3x - 5 + 5 = 7 + 5$. Now simplify. Next, present this as the system of equations $\begin{array}{l} 3x - 5 = 7 \\ 5 = 5 \end{array}$. Add the two equations and simplify.

For the system $\begin{array}{l} 5x + 2y = 11 \\ 3x - 2y = 13 \end{array}$, the situation is similar. Add $3x - 2y$ to each side of Equation (1).

$$5x + 2y + (3x - 2y) = 11 + (3x - 2y)$$

Now use substitution to replace $3x - 2y$ on the right side of the equation by 13. After simplifying, we get $8x = 24$.

Another method of solving a system of equations is called the **addition method.** This method is based on the Addition Property of Equations.

Note, for the system of equations at the right, the effect of adding Equation (2) to Equation (1). Because $2y$ and $-2y$ are opposites, adding the equations results in an equation with only one variable.

$$\begin{array}{lr} (1) & 5x + 2y = 11 \\ (2) & \underline{3x - 2y = 13} \\ & 8x + 0y = 24 \\ & 8x = 24 \end{array}$$

Solving $8x = 24$ for x gives the first coordinate of the ordered-pair solution of the system of equations.

$$\frac{8x}{8} = \frac{24}{8}$$
$$x = 3$$

The second coordinate is found by substituting the value of x into Equation (1) or Equation (2) and then solving for y. Equation (1) is used here.

$$\begin{array}{lr} (1) & 5x + 2y = 11 \\ & 5(3) + 2y = 11 \\ & 15 + 2y = 11 \\ & 2y = -4 \\ & y = -2 \end{array}$$

The solution is $(3, -2)$.

Sometimes, adding the two equations of a system does not eliminate one of the variables. In this case, use the Multiplication Property of Equations to rewrite one or both of the equations so that the coefficients of one variable are opposites. Then add the equations and solve for the variables.

HOW TO 1 Solve by the addition method: (1) $4x + y = 5$ (2) $2x - 5y = 19$

Multiply Equation (2) by -2. The coefficients of x will then be opposites.

$-2(2x - 5y) = -2 \cdot 19$ • **Multiply Equation (2) by -2.**

(3) $-4x + 10y = -38$ • **Simplify. This is Equation (3).**

Add Equation (3) to Equation (1). Then solve for y.

(1) $4x + y = 5$

(3) $\underline{-4x + 10y = -38}$ • **Note that the coefficients of x are opposites.**

$11y = -33$ • **Add the two equations.**

$y = -3$ • **Solve for y.**

Substitute the value of y into Equation (1) or Equation (2) and solve for x. Equation (1) is used here.

(1) $4x + y = 5$

$4x + (-3) = 5$ • **Substitute -3 for y.**

$4x - 3 = 5$ • **Solve for x.**

$4x = 8$

$x = 2$

The solution is $(2, -3)$.

Sometimes each equation of a system of equations must be multiplied by a constant so that the coefficients of one variable are opposites.

HOW TO 2 Solve by the addition method:

(1) $3x + 7y = 2$
(2) $5x - 3y = -26$

To eliminate x, multiply Equation (1) by 5 and Equation (2) by -3. Note at the right how the constants are chosen.

$$5(3x + 7y) = 5 \cdot 2$$
$$-3(5x - 3y) = -3(-26)$$

• The negative is used so that the coefficients of x will be opposites.

$$\begin{aligned} 15x + 35y &= 10 \\ -15x + 9y &= 78 \\ \hline 44y &= 88 \\ y &= 2 \end{aligned}$$

• 5 times Equation (1)
• -3 times Equation (2)
• Add the equations.
• Solve for y.

Substitute the value of y into Equation (1) or Equation (2) and solve for x. Equation (1) is used here.

(1)
$$\begin{aligned} 3x + 7y &= 2 \\ 3x + 7(2) &= 2 \\ 3x + 14 &= 2 \\ 3x &= -12 \\ x &= -4 \end{aligned}$$

• Substitute 2 for y.
• Solve for x.

The solution is $(-4, 2)$.

For the system of equations in HOW TO 2, the system was solved for y, and the value of x was determined by substitution. The value of x could have been determined by eliminating y from the system.

$$\begin{aligned} 9x + 21y &= 6 \\ 35x - 21y &= -182 \\ \hline 44x \quad &= -176 \\ x &= -4 \end{aligned}$$

• 3 times Equation (1)
• 7 times Equation (2)
• Add the equations.
• Solve for x.

Note that this is the same value of x that we obtained by using substitution.

Take Note

When you use the addition method to solve a system of equations and the result is an equation that is always true (like the one in HOW TO 3), the system of equations is dependent. Compare this result with the result obtained in HOW TO 4.

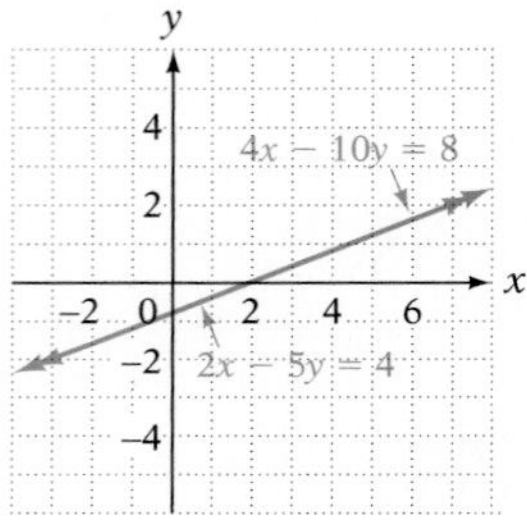

HOW TO 3 Solve by the addition method:

(1) $2x - 5y = 4$
(2) $4x - 10y = 8$

Eliminate x. Multiply Equation (1) by -2.

$$-2(2x - 5y) = -2(4)$$
(3) $-4x + 10y = -8$

• -2 times Equation (1)
• This is Equation (3).

Add Equation (3) to Equation (2) and solve for y.

(2) $4x - 10y = 8$
(3) $-4x + 10y = -8$

$$\begin{aligned} 0x + 0y &= 0 \\ 0 &= 0 \end{aligned}$$

The equation $0 = 0$ means that the system of equations is dependent. Therefore, the solutions of the system of equations are the ordered pairs that satisfy $2x - 5y = 4$.

The graphs of the two equations of the system in HOW TO 3 are shown at the left. One line is on top of the other; therefore, the lines intersect at an infinite number of points.

INSTRUCTOR NOTE

Show students that if the two equations in HOW TO 4 are both solved for y, then we have $y = -2x + 2$ and $y = -2x - \frac{5}{2}$.

Because the lines have the same slope but different y-intercepts, the graphs are parallel and do not intersect.

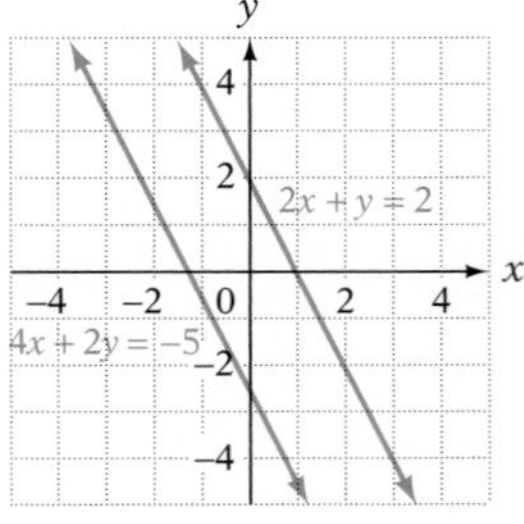

HOW TO 4 Solve by the addition method: (1) $2x + y = 2$ (2) $4x + 2y = -5$

Eliminate y. Multiply Equation (1) by -2.

$-2(2x + y) = -2 \cdot 2$ • −2 times Equation (1)

(3) $-4x - 2y = -4$ • This is Equation (3).

Add Equation (2) to Equation (3) and solve for x.

(3) $-4x - 2y = -4$

(2) $4x + 2y = -5$

$0x + 0y = -9$ • Add Equation (2) to Equation (3).

$0 = -9$ • This is a false equation.

The system of equations is inconsistent and therefore has no solution.

The graphs of the two equations of the system of equations in HOW TO 4 are shown at the left. Note that the graphs are parallel and therefore do not intersect. Thus the system of equations has no solution.

EXAMPLE 1

Solve by the addition method:

(1) $2x + 4y = 7$

(2) $5x - 3y = -2$

Solution

Eliminate x.

$5(2x + 4y) = 5 \cdot 7$ • 5 times Equation (1)

$-2(5x - 3y) = -2(-2)$ • −2 times Equation (2)

$10x + 20y = 35$

$-10x + 6y = 4$

$26y = 39$ • Add the equations.

$y = \frac{39}{26} = \frac{3}{2}$ • Solve for y.

Substitute $\frac{3}{2}$ for y in Equation (1).

(1) $2x + 4y = 7$

$2x + 4\left(\frac{3}{2}\right) = 7$ • Replace y by $\frac{3}{2}$.

$2x + 6 = 7$ • Solve for x.

$2x = 1$

$x = \frac{1}{2}$

The solution is $\left(\frac{1}{2}, \frac{3}{2}\right)$.

YOU TRY IT 1

Solve by the addition method:

(1) $2x - 3y = 1$

(2) $-3x + 4y = 6$

Your solution

(−22, −15)

IN-CLASS EXAMPLES

Solve by the addition method.

1. $3x + 4y = -5$
   $9x - 2y = 13$
   (1, −2)
2. $2x + 5y = 1$
   $3x + 1 = 2y + 12$
   (3, −1)
3. $x + 3y = 3$
   $3x + 9y = 9$
   Dependent. The solutions are the ordered pairs that satisfy $x + 3y = 3$.
4. $3x = 2y + 4$
   $6x - 4y = 5$
   No solution

Solution on p. S33

EXAMPLE 2

Solve by the addition method:

(1) $6x + 9y = 15$
(2) $4x + 6y = 10$

Solution

Eliminate x.

$4(6x + 9y) = 4 \cdot 15$ • **4 times Equation (1)**

$-6(4x + 6y) = -6 \cdot 10$ • **−6 times Equation (2)**

$24x + 36y = 60$

$-24x - 36y = -60$

$0x + 0y = 0$ • **Add the equations.**

$0 = 0$

The system of equations is dependent. The solutions are the ordered pairs that satisfy the equation $6x + 9y = 15$.

YOU TRY IT 2

Solve by the addition method:

$2x - 3y = 4$
$-4x + 6y = -8$

Your solution

The system of equations is dependent. The solutions are the ordered pairs that satisfy the equation $2x - 3y = 4$.

EXAMPLE 3

Solve by the addition method:

(1) $2x = y + 8$
(2) $3x + 2y = 5$

Solution

Write Equation (1) in the form $Ax + By = C$.

$2x = y + 8$

(3) $2x - y = 8$ • **This is Equation (3).**

Eliminate y.

$2(2x - y) = 2 \cdot 8$ • **2 times Equation (3)**

$3x + 2y = 5$ • **This is Equation (2).**

$4x - 2y = 16$

$3x + 2y = 5$

$7x = 21$ • **Add the equations.**

$x = 3$

Replace x in Equation (1).

(1) $2x = y + 8$

$2 \cdot 3 = y + 8$ • **Replace x by 3.**

$6 = y + 8$

$-2 = y$

The solution is $(3, -2)$.

YOU TRY IT 3

Solve by the addition method:

$4x + 5y = 11$
$3y = x + 10$

Your solution

$(-1, 3)$

Solutions on p. S33

13.3 EXERCISES

Concept Check

SUGGESTED ASSIGNMENT
Exercises 1 and 2; Exercises 3–37, odds

1. Use this system of equations: (1) $-3x - y = 5$
(2) $x - 4y = 7$

a. To eliminate x from the system of equations by using the addition method, multiply each side of equation (2) by __3__.

b. To eliminate y from the system of equations by using the addition method, multiply each side of equation (1) by __−4__.

2. Use this system of equations: (1) $2x - 3y = 3$
(2) $x + 6y = 9$

a. To eliminate x from the system of equations by using the addition method, multiply each side of equation (__2__) by (__−2__).

b. To eliminate y from the system of equations by using the addition method, multiply each side of equation (__1__) by (__2__).

OBJECTIVE A *To solve a system of linear equations by the addition method*

For Exercises 3 to 38, solve by the addition method.

3. $x + y = 4$
$x - y = 6$
(5, −1)

4. $2x + y = 3$
$x - y = 3$
(2, −1)

5. $x + y = 4$
$2x + y = 5$
(1, 3)

6. $x - 3y = 2$
$x + 2y = -3$
(−1, −1)

7. $2x - y = 1$
$x + 3y = 4$
(1, 1)

8. $x - 2y = 4$
$3x + 4y = 2$
(2, −1)

9. $4x - 5y = 22$
$x + 2y = -1$
(3, −2)

10. $3x - y = 11$
$2x + 5y = 13$
(4, 1)

11. $2x - y = 1$
$4x - 2y = 2$
Dependent. The solutions satisfy the equation $2x - y = 1$.

12. $x + 3y = 2$
$3x + 9y = 6$
Dependent. The solutions satisfy the equation $x + 3y = 2$.

13. $4x + 3y = 15$
$2x - 5y = 1$
(3, 1)

14. $3x - 7y = 13$
$6x + 5y = 7$
(2, −1)

15. $2x - 3y = 1$
$4x - 6y = 2$
Dependent. The solutions satisfy the equation $2x - 3y = 1$.

16. $2x + 4y = 6$
$3x + 6y = 9$
Dependent. The solutions satisfy the equation $2x + 4y = 6$.

17. $3x - 6y = -1$
$6x - 4y = 2$
$\left(\frac{2}{3}, \frac{1}{2}\right)$

18. $5x + 2y = 3$
$3x - 10y = -1$
$\left(\frac{1}{2}, \frac{1}{4}\right)$

19. $5x + 7y = 10$
$3x - 14y = 6$
(2, 0)

20. $7x + 10y = 13$
$4x + 5y = 6$
(−1, 2)

21. $3x - 2y = 0$
$6x + 5y = 0$
(0, 0)

22. $5x + 2y = 0$
$3x + 5y = 0$
(0, 0)

23. $2x - 3y = 16$
$3x + 4y = 7$
(5, −2)

24. $3x + 4y = 10$
$4x + 3y = 11$
(2, 1)

25. $5x + 3y = 7$
$2x + 5y = 1$
$\left(\frac{32}{19}, -\frac{9}{19}\right)$

26. $-2x + 7y = 9$
$3x + 2y = -1$
(−1, 1)

27. $3x + 4y = 4$
$5x + 12y = 5$
$\left(\frac{7}{4}, -\frac{5}{16}\right)$

28. $2x + 5y = 2$
$3x + 3y = 1$
$\left(-\frac{1}{9}, \frac{4}{9}\right)$

29. $8x - 3y = 11$
$6x - 5y = 11$
(1, −1)

30. $4x - 8y = 36$
$3x - 6y = 15$
No solution

31. $5x + 15y = 20$
$2x + 6y = 12$
No solution

32. $y = 2x - 3$
$3x + 4y = -1$
(1, −1)

33. $3x = 2y + 7$
$5x - 2y = 13$
(3, 1)

34. $2y = 4 - 9x$
$9x - y = 25$
(2, −7)

35. $2x + 9y = 16$
$5x = 1 - 3y$
(−1, 2)

36. $3x - 4 = y + 18$
$4x + 5y = -21$
$\left(\frac{89}{19}, -\frac{151}{19}\right)$

37. $2x + 3y = 7 - 2x$
$7x + 2y = 9$
(1, 1)

38. $5x - 3y = 3y + 4$
$4x + 3y = 11$
(2, 1)

For Exercises 39 to 41, assume that A, B, and C are nonzero real numbers, where $A \neq B \neq C$. State whether the system of equations is independent, inconsistent, or dependent.

39. $Ax + By = C$
$2Ax + 2By = 2C$
Dependent

40. $x - Ay = B$
$3x - 3Ay = 3C$
Inconsistent

41. $Ax + By = C$
$Bx + Ay = 2C$
Independent

Critical Thinking

42. The point of intersection of the graphs of the equations $Ax + 2y = 2$ and $2x + By = 10$ is $(2, -2)$. Find A and B.
$A = 3$; $B = -3$

43. The point of intersection of the graphs of the equations $Ax - 4y = 9$ and $4x + By = -1$ is $(-1, -3)$. Find A and B.
$A = 3$; $B = -1$

Projects or Group Activities

44. Find an equation such that the system of equations formed by your equation and the equation $3x - 4y = 10$ has $(2, -1)$ as a solution.
Answers will vary. $2x + 3y = 1$ is a possibility.

QUICK QUIZ

Solve by the addition method.

1. $2x - 5y = 19$
   $3x + 4y = -6$
   (2, −3) [13.3A]
2. $4x + 5y = 20$
   $8x + 10y = 40$
   The ordered-pair solutions of $4x + 5y = 20$ [13.3A]
3. $3x + 5y = 1$
   $3x = -5y + 12$
   Inconsistent [13.3A]

SECTION

13.4 Application Problems in Two Variables

OBJECTIVE A To solve rate-of-wind or rate-of-current problems

Take Note
See Section 5.1 for a discussion of how the rate of a current affects the speed of a boat traveling on a river.

We normally need two variables to solve motion problems that involve an object moving with or against a wind or current.

HOW TO 1 Flying with the wind, a small plane can fly 600 mi in 3 h. Flying against the wind, the plane can fly the same distance in 4 h. Find the rate of the plane in calm air and the rate of the wind.

Strategy for Solving Rate-of-Wind or Rate-of-Current Problems

1. Choose one variable to represent the rate of the object in calm conditions and a second variable to represent the rate of the wind or current. Using these variables, express the rate of the object traveling with and against the wind or current. Use the equation $rt = d$ to write expressions for the distance traveled by the object. The results can be recorded in a table.

Rate of plane in calm air: p
Rate of wind: w

	Rate	·	Time	=	Distance
With the wind	$p + w$	·	3	=	$3(p + w)$
Against the wind	$p - w$	·	4	=	$4(p - w)$

2. Determine how the expressions for distance are related.

The distance traveled with the wind is 600 mi.
The distance traveled against the wind is 600 mi.
Solve the system of equations.

$$3(p + w) = 600$$
$$4(p - w) = 600$$

$$3(p + w) = 600 \longrightarrow \frac{1}{3} \cdot 3(p + w) = \frac{1}{3} \cdot 600 \longrightarrow p + w = 200$$

$$4(p - w) = 600 \longrightarrow \frac{1}{4} \cdot 4(p - w) = \frac{1}{4} \cdot 600 \longrightarrow p - w = 150$$

$$2p = 350$$
$$p = 175$$

$$p + w = 200$$
$$175 + w = 200 \quad \text{• } p = 175$$
$$w = 25$$

The rate of the plane in calm air is 175 mph.
The rate of the wind is 25 mph.

EXAMPLE 1

A 450-mile trip from one city to another takes 3 h when a plane is flying with the wind. The return trip, against the wind, takes 5 h. Find the rate of the plane in still air and the rate of the wind.

Strategy

- Rate of the plane in still air: p
  Rate of the wind: w

	Rate	*Time*	*Distance*
With wind	$p + w$	3	$3(p + w)$
Against wind	$p - w$	5	$5(p - w)$

- The distance traveled with the wind is 450 mi. The distance traveled against the wind is 450 mi.

Solution

$3(p + w) = 450 \qquad \frac{1}{3} \cdot 3(p + w) = \frac{1}{3} \cdot 450$

$5(p - w) = 450 \qquad \frac{1}{5} \cdot 5(p - w) = \frac{1}{5} \cdot 450$

$$p + w = 150$$
$$p - w = 90$$
$$2p = 240$$
$$p = 120$$

$$p + w = 150$$
$$120 + w = 150 \qquad \bullet\ p = 120$$
$$w = 30$$

The rate of the plane in still air is 120 mph. The rate of the wind is 30 mph.

YOU TRY IT 1

A canoeist paddling with the current can travel 15 mi in 3 h. Rowing against the current, it takes the canoeist 5 h to travel the same distance. Find the rate of the current and the rate of the canoeist in calm water.

Your strategy

Your solution

Rate of current: 1 mph
Rate of canoeist in calm water: 4 mph

IN-CLASS EXAMPLES

1. Traveling with the current, a boat went 22 mi in 2 h. Traveling against the current, the boat traveled 10 mi in 2 h. Find the rate of the boat in calm water and the rate of the current.
   Rate of boat in calm water: 8 mph; rate of current: 3 mph

Solution on p. S33

OBJECTIVE B *To solve application problems using two variables*

The application problems in this section are varieties of the types of problems solved earlier in the text. Each of the strategies for the problems in this section will result in a system of equations.

© Yuri Arcurs/Shutterstock.com

HOW TO 2 A jeweler purchased 5 oz of a gold alloy and 20 oz of a silver alloy for a total cost of \$540. The next day, at the same prices per ounce, the jeweler purchased 4 oz of the gold alloy and 25 oz of the silver alloy for a total cost of \$450. Find the cost per ounce of the gold and silver alloys.

Strategy for Solving an Application Problem in Two Variables

1. Choose one variable to represent one of the unknown quantities and a second variable to represent the other unknown quantity. Write numerical or variable expressions for all of the remaining quantities. The results can be recorded in two tables, one for each of the conditions.

Cost per ounce of gold alloy: g
Cost per ounce of silver alloy: s

First day:

	Amount	·	Unit Cost	=	Value
Gold	5	·	g	=	$5g$
Silver	20	·	s	=	$20s$

Second day:

	Amount	·	Unit Cost	=	Value
Gold	4	·	g	=	$4g$
Silver	25	·	s	=	$25s$

Point of Interest

The Babylonians had a method for solving a system of equations. Here is an adaptation of a problem from an ancient Babylonian text (around 1500 B.C.). "There are two silver blocks. The sum of $\frac{1}{7}$ of the first block and $\frac{1}{11}$ of the second block is one sheqel (a weight). The first block diminished by $\frac{1}{7}$ of its weight equals the second diminished by $\frac{1}{11}$ of its weight. What are the weights of the two blocks?"

2. Determine a system of equations. Each table will give one equation of the system.

The total value of the purchase on the first day was \$540. $\quad 5g + 20s = 540$

The total value of the purchase on the second day was \$450. $\quad 4g + 25s = 450$

INSTRUCTOR NOTE
The weights of the blocks described in the Point of Interest above are $\frac{35}{8}$ sheqels and $\frac{33}{8}$ sheqels.

Solve the system of equations.

$$5g + 20s = 540 \qquad 4(5g + 20s) = 4 \cdot 540 \qquad 20g + 80s = 2160$$
$$4g + 25s = 450 \qquad -5(4g + 25s) = -5 \cdot 450 \qquad -20g - 125s = -2250$$
$$-45s = -90$$
$$s = 2$$

$$5g + 20s = 540$$
$$5g + 20(2) = 540 \qquad \bullet\ s = 2$$
$$5g + 40 = 540$$
$$5g = 500$$
$$g = 100$$

The cost per ounce of the gold alloy was \$100.
The cost per ounce of the silver alloy was \$2.

EXAMPLE 2

A store owner purchased 20 halogen light bulbs and 30 fluorescent bulbs for a total cost of \$630. A second purchase, at the same prices, included 30 halogen bulbs and 10 fluorescent bulbs for a total cost of \$560. Find the cost of a halogen bulb and of a fluorescent bulb.

Strategy

Cost of a halogen bulb: h
Cost of a fluorescent bulb: f

First purchase:

	Amount	*Unit Cost*	*Value*
Halogen	20	h	$20h$
Fluorescent	30	f	$30f$

Second purchase:

	Amount	*Unit Cost*	*Value*
Halogen	30	h	$30h$
Fluorescent	10	f	$10f$

The total cost of the first purchase was \$630.
The total cost of the second purchase was \$560.

Solution

$$20h + 30f = 630$$
$$30h + 10f = 560$$

$$20h + 30f = 630$$
$$-3(30h + 10f) = -3(560)$$

$$20h + 30f = 630$$
$$-90h - 30f = -1680$$
$$-70h = -1050$$
$$h = 15$$

$$20h + 30f = 630$$
$$20(15) + 30f = 630 \quad \bullet\ h = 15$$
$$300 + 30f = 630$$
$$30f = 330$$
$$f = 11$$

The cost of a halogen light bulb is \$15.
The cost of a fluorescent light bulb is \$11.

YOU TRY IT 2

A citrus grower purchased 25 orange trees and 20 grapefruit trees for \$2900. The next week, at the same prices, the grower bought 20 orange trees and 30 grapefruit trees for \$3300. Find the cost of an orange tree and the cost of a grapefruit tree.

Your strategy

Your solution

Orange tree: \$60
Grapefruit tree: \$70

IN-CLASS EXAMPLES

2. A jeweler purchased 5 oz of a gold alloy and 10 oz of a platinum alloy for a total cost of \$2375. In a second purchase at the same prices, the jeweler bought 8 oz of the gold alloy and 7 oz of the platinum alloy for a total cost of \$2225. What was the cost per ounce of the gold alloy and of the platinum alloy?
Gold: \$125 per ounce; platinum: \$175 per ounce

Solution on pp. S33–S34

13.4 EXERCISES

Concept Check

SUGGESTED ASSIGNMENT

Exercises 1–6; Exercises 7–33, odds; More challenging exercise: Exercise 34

For Exercises 1 to 4, determine whether the statement is true or false.

1. A plane flying with the wind is traveling faster than it would be traveling without the wind. True

2. The uniform motion equation $r = dt$ is used to solve rate-of-wind and rate-of-current problems. False

3. If b represents the rate of a boat in calm water and c represents the rate of the current, then $b + c$ represents the rate of the boat traveling against the current. False

4. If, in a system of equations, p represents the rate of a plane in calm air and w represents the rate of the wind, and $p = 100$, this means that the rate of the wind is 100. False

5. A contractor bought 100 yd of nylon carpet for x dollars per yard and 50 yd of wool carpet for y dollars per yard. How can you represent the total cost of the carpet? $100x + 50y$

6. A boat travels down a river for 2 h (traveling with the current), then turns around and takes 3 h to return (traveling against the current). Let b be the rate of the boat, in miles per hour, in calm water, and let c be the rate of the current in miles per hour. Complete the following table.

	Rate, r	·	Time, t	=	Distance, d
With current	$b + c$	·	2	=	$2(b + c)$
Against current	$b - c$	·	3	=	$3(b - c)$

OBJECTIVE A To solve rate-of-wind or rate-of-current problems

7. Traveling with the wind, a plane flies m miles in h hours. Traveling against the wind, the plane flies n miles in h hours. Is m less than, equal to, or greater than n? Greater than

8. Traveling against the current, it takes a boat h hours to go m miles. Traveling with the current, the boat takes k hours to go m miles. Is k less than, equal to, or greater than h? Less than

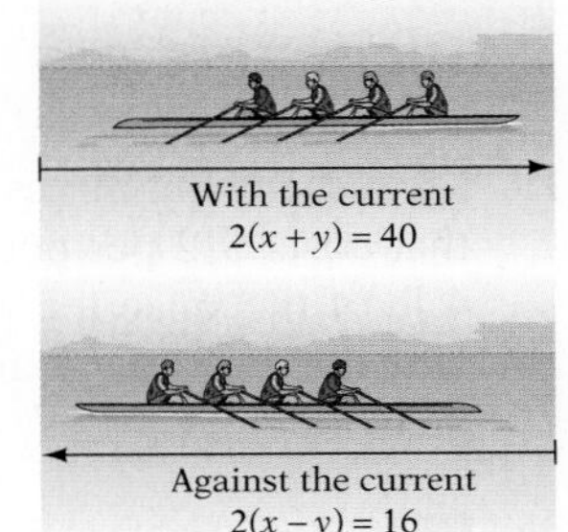

9. A rowing team rowing with the current traveled 40 km in 2 h. Rowing against the current, the team could travel only 16 km in 2 h. Find the rowing rate in calm water and the rate of the current. Rowing: 14 km/h; current: 6 km/h

10. A plane flying with the jet stream flew from Los Angeles to Chicago, a distance of 2250 mi, in 5 h. Flying against the jet stream, the plane could fly only 1750 mi in the same amount of time. Find the rate of the plane in calm air and the rate of the wind. Plane: 400 mph; wind: 50 mph

11. A whale swimming against an ocean current traveled 60 mi in 2 h. Swimming in the opposite direction, with the current, the whale was able to travel the same distance in 1.5 h. Find the speed of the whale in calm water and the rate of the ocean current.
Whale: 35 mph; current: 5 mph

© Sokolov Alexey/Shutterstock.com

12. The bird capable of the fastest flying speed is the swift. A swift flying with the wind to a favorite feeding spot traveled 26 mi in 0.2 h. On returning, now flying against the wind, the swift was able to travel only 16 mi in the same amount of time. What is the rate of the swift in calm air, and what was the rate of the wind?
Swift: 105 mph; wind: 25 mph

13. A private Learjet 31A was flying with a tailwind and traveled 1120 mi in 2 h. Flying against the wind on the return trip, the jet was able to travel only 980 mi in 2 h. Find the speed of the jet in calm air and the rate of the wind.
Jet: 525 mph; wind: 35 mph

14. A plane flying with a tailwind flew 300 mi in 2 h. Flying against the wind, the plane took 3 h to travel the same distance. Find the rate of the plane in calm air and the rate of the wind.
Plane: 125 mph; wind: 25 mph

© Karl R. Martin/Shutterstock.com

15. A Boeing Apache Longbow military helicopter traveling directly into a strong headwind was able to travel 450 mi in 2.5 h. The return trip, now with a tailwind, took 1 h 40 min. Find the speed of the helicopter in calm air and the rate of the wind.
Helicopter: 225 mph; wind: 45 mph

16. Rowing with the current, a canoeist paddled 14 mi in 2 h. Rowing against the current, the canoeist could paddle only 10 mi in the same amount of time. Find the rate of the canoeist in calm water and the rate of the current.
Canoeist: 6 mph; current: 1 mph

© Richard Paul Kane/Shutterstock.com

17. A motorboat traveling with the current went 35 mi in 3.5 h. Traveling against the current, the boat went 12 mi in 3 h. Find the rate of the boat in calm water and the rate of the current.
Boat: 7 mph; current: 3 mph

18. Throwing with the wind, a quarterback passes a football 140 ft in 2 s. Against the wind, the same pass would have traveled 80 ft in 2 s. Find the rate of the pass and the rate of the wind.
Pass: 55 ft/s; wind: 15 ft/s

OBJECTIVE B *To solve application problems using two variables*

19. A merchant mixes 4 lb of cinnamon tea with 1 lb of spice tea to create a mixture that costs $12 per pound. When the merchant mixes 1 lb of the cinnamon tea with 4 lb of the spice tea, the mixture costs $15 per pound. Is the cost per pound of the cinnamon tea less than, equal to, or greater than the cost per pound of the spice tea?
Less than

20. The total value of nickels and dimes in a bank is $2. If the nickels were dimes and the dimes were nickels, the total value would be $2.95. Is the number of nickels in the bank less than, equal to, or greater than the number of dimes in the bank?
Greater than

For Exercises 21 and 22, use the system of equations at the right, which represents the following situation. You spent \$320 on theater tickets for 4 adults and 2 children. For the same performance, your neighbor spent \$240 on tickets for 2 adults and 3 children.

$$4x + 2y = 320$$
$$2x + 3y = 240$$

21. What do the variables x and y represent? Explain the meaning of each equation in terms of the problem situation.
x = cost of an adult ticket, y = cost of a child ticket; $4x + 2y = 320$ represents the fact that you spent \$320 on 4 adult tickets and 2 child tickets; $2x + 3y = 240$ represents the fact that your neighbor spent \$240 on 2 adult tickets and 3 child tickets.

22. Write a question that could be answered by solving the system of equations.
Answers will vary. For example, "What is the cost of an adult ticket?"

Roberto Herrett/age fotostock

23. Flour Mixtures A baker purchased 12 lb of wheat flour and 15 lb of rye flour for a total cost of \$18.30. A second purchase, at the same prices, included 15 lb of wheat flour and 10 lb of rye flour. The cost of the second purchase was \$16.75. Find the cost per pound of the wheat flour and of the rye flour.
Wheat: \$.65; rye: \$.70

24. Consumerism For using a computerized financial news network for 50 min during prime time and 70 min during non-prime time, a customer was charged \$10.75. A second customer was charged \$13.35 for using the network for 60 min of prime time and 90 min of non-prime time. Find the cost per minute for using the financial news network during prime time. \$.11

25. Consumerism The employees of a hardware store ordered lunch from a local delicatessen. The lunch consisted of 4 turkey sandwiches and 7 orders of french fries, for a total cost of \$38.30. The next day, the employees ordered 5 turkey sandwiches and 5 orders of french fries totaling \$40.75. What does the delicatessen charge for a turkey sandwich? What is the charge for an order of french fries?
Turkey sandwich: \$6.25; order of french fries: \$1.90

26. Fuel Mixtures An octane number of 87 on gasoline means that it will fight engine "knock" as effectively as a reference fuel that is 87% isooctane, a type of gas. Suppose you want to fill an empty 18-gallon tank with some 87-octane gasoline and some 93-octane fuel to produce a mixture that is 89-octane. How much of each type of gasoline must you use?
87-octane: 12 gal; 93-octane: 6 gal

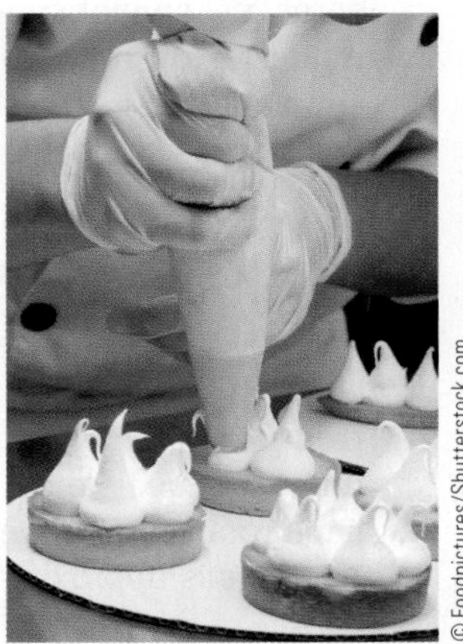
© Foodpictures/Shutterstock.com

27. Food Mixtures A pastry chef created a 50-ounce sugar solution that was 34% sugar from a 20% sugar solution and a 40% sugar solution. How much of the 20% sugar solution and how much of the 40% sugar solution were used?
20% solution: 15 oz; 40% solution: 35 oz

Ideal Body Weight There are various formulas for calculating ideal body weight. In each of the formulas in Exercises 28 and 29, W is ideal body weight in kilograms, and x is height in inches above 60 in.

28. J. D. Robinson gave the following formula for calculating ideal body weight for men: $W = 52 + 1.9x$. D. R. Miller published a slightly different formula for men: $W = 56.2 + 1.41x$. At what height do both formulas give the same ideal body weight? Round to the nearest whole number. 69 in.

29. J. D. Robinson gave the following formula for women: $W = 49 + 1.7x$. D. R. Miller published a slightly different formula for women: $W = 53.1 + 1.36x$. At what height do both formulas give the same ideal body weight? Round to the nearest whole number. 72 in.

30. **Fuel Economy** Read the article at the right. Suppose you use 10 gal of gas to drive a 2007 Ford Taurus 208 mi. Using the new miles-per-gallon estimates given in the article, find the number of city miles and the number of highway miles you drove. City: 108 mi; highway: 100 mi

31. **Stamps** Stolen in 1967, the famous "Ice House" envelope (named for the address shown on the envelope) was recovered in 2006. The envelope displays a Lincoln stamp, a Thomas Jefferson stamp, and a Henry Clay stamp.

a. The original postage value of three Lincoln stamps and five Jefferson stamps was \$3.20. The original postage value of two Lincoln stamps and three Jefferson stamps was \$2.10. Find the original value of the Lincoln stamp and of the Jefferson stamp. Lincoln stamp: \$.90; Jefferson stamp: \$.10

b. The total postage on the Ice House envelope was \$1.12. What was the original postage value of the Henry Clay stamp? \$.12

In the NEWS!

New Miles-per-Gallon Estimates

Beginning with model year 2008, the Environmental Protection Agency is using a new method to estimate miles-per-gallon ratings for motor vehicles. In general, estimates will be lower than before. For example, under the new method, ratings for a 2007 Ford Taurus would be lowered to 18 mpg in the city and 25 mpg on the highway.

Source: www.fueleconomy.gov

Critical Thinking

32. **Geometry** Two angles are supplementary. The measure of the larger angle is 15° more than twice the measure of the smaller angle. Find the measures of the two angles. (Supplementary angles are two angles whose sum is 180°.)
55° and 125°

33. **Geometry** Two angles are complementary. The measure of the larger angle is four times the measure of the smaller angle. Find the measures of the two angles. (Complementary angles are two angles whose sum is 90°.)
18° and 72°

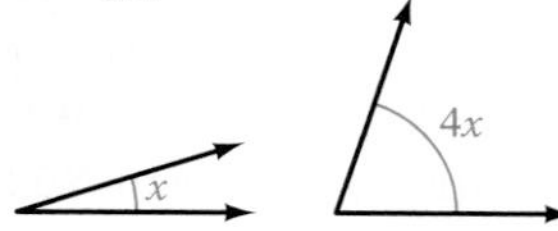

34. **Investments** An investor has \$5000 to invest in two accounts. The first account earns 8% annual simple interest, and the second account earns 10% annual simple interest. How much money should be invested in each account so that the total annual simple interest earned is \$600?
It is impossible to earn \$600 in interest.

Projects or Group Activities

35. Find the time t between successive alignments of the hour and minute hands on a clock. [*Hint:* Begin with the hands aligned at 12:00. Let $d°$ be the angle, measured from 12:00, at which the hands next align. The time t it takes for the hour hand to rotate $d°$ equals the time it takes for the minute hand to rotate $(d + 360)°$. The hour hand rotates at 30° per hour, and the minute hand rotates at 360° per hour.]
The time is approximately 65.5 min.

A graphing calculator can be used to approximate the solution of a system of equations in two variables. First graph each equation of the system of equations, and then approximate the coordinates of the point of intersection. The process by which you approximate the solution depends on what model of calculator you have. In all cases, however, you must first solve each equation of the system of equations for y.

QUICK QUIZ

1. Flying with the wind, a pilot was able to travel 600 mi in 2 h. Flying against the wind, it took the pilot 3 h to fly the same distance. Find the rate of the wind and the rate of the plane in calm air.
   Rate of wind: 50 mph; rate of plane in calm air: 250 mph [13.4A]
2. A chemist mixed 20 ml of reagent I with 30 ml of reagent II. The result was a solution that was 13% acetic acid. Using the same reagents, the chemist mixed 30 ml of reagent I with 20 ml of reagent II to make a solution that was 12% acetic acid. What percent acetic acid was reagent I?
   10% [13.4B]

Solve: $2x - 5y = 9$
$4x + 3y = 2$

$$\begin{aligned} 2x - 5y &= 9 \\ -5y &= -2x + 9 \\ y &= \frac{2}{5}x - \frac{9}{5} \end{aligned} \qquad \begin{aligned} 4x + 3y &= 2 \\ 3y &= -4x + 2 \\ y &= -\frac{4}{3}x + \frac{2}{3} \end{aligned}$$

• **Solve each equation for *y*.**

For the TI-84 Plus, press Y=. Enter one equation as Y1 and the other as Y2. The result should be similar to the screen at the left below. Press GRAPH. The graphs of the two equations should appear on the screen, as shown at the right below. If the point of intersection is not visible on the screen, adjust the viewing window by pressing the WINDOW key.

Take Note
The graphing calculator screens shown here are taken from a TI-84 Plus. Similar screens would display if we used a different model of graphing calculator.

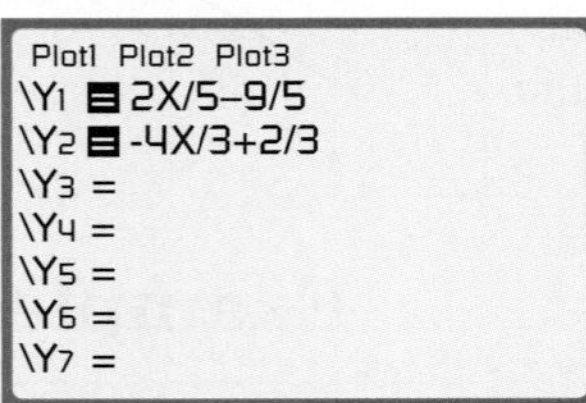

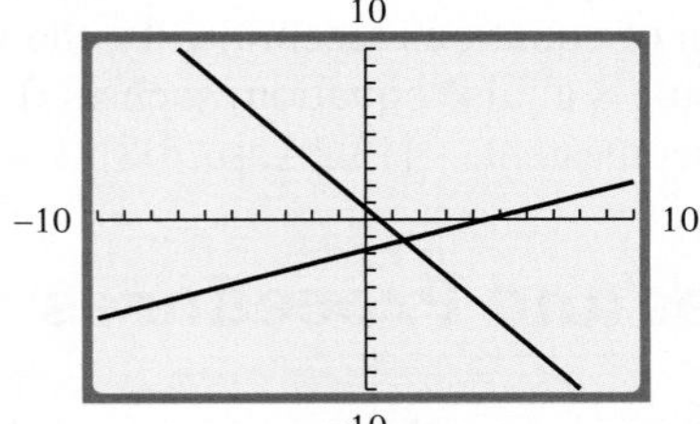

Press 2ND CALC 5 ENTER ENTER ENTER.
After a few seconds, the point of intersection will display at the bottom of the screen as X = 1.4230769, Y = −1.230769.

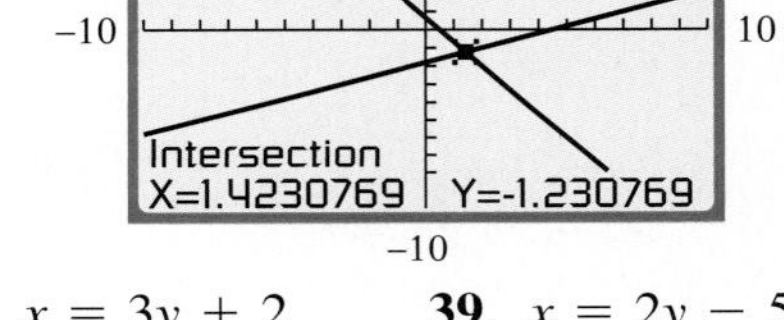

For Exercises 36 to 39, solve by using a graphing calculator.

36. $4x - 5y = 8$
$5x + 7y = 7$

37. $3x + 2y = 11$
$7x - 6y = 13$

38. $x = 3y + 2$
$y = 4x - 2$

39. $x = 2y - 5$
$x = 3y + 2$

36. (1.716981132, −0.2264150943)
37. (2.875, 1.1875)
38. (0.3636363636, −0.5454545455)
39. (−19, −7)

CHAPTER 13 Summary

Key Words	Examples
Two or more equations considered together are called a **system of equations.** [13.1A, p. 698]	An example of a system of equations is $2x - 3y = 9$, $3x + 4y = 5$
A **solution of a system of equations in two variables** is an ordered pair that is a solution of each equation of the system. [13.1A, p. 698]	The solution of the system of equations shown above is the ordered pair (3, −1) because it is a solution of each equation of the system of equations.
An **independent system** of linear equations has exactly one solution. The graphs of the equations in an independent system of linear equations intersect at one point. [13.1A, p. 699]	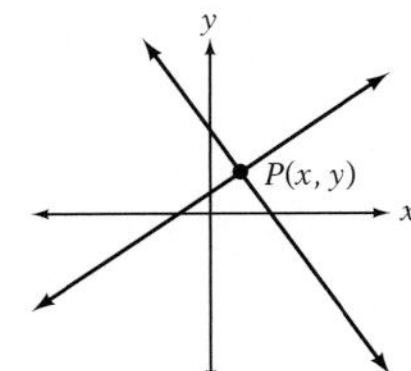

A **dependent system** of linear equations has an infinite number of solutions. The graphs of the equations in a dependent system of linear equations are the same line. [13.1A, p. 699]

If, when solving a system of equations algebraically, the variable is eliminated and the result is a true equation, such as $5 = 5$, the system of equations is dependent. [13.2A, p. 708]

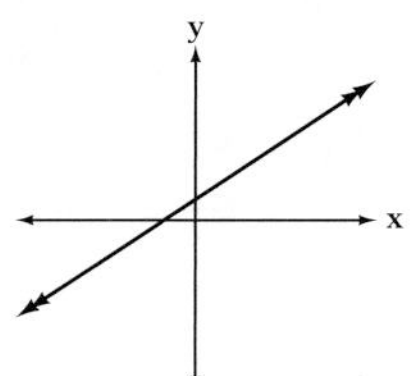

An **inconsistent system** of linear equations has no solution. The graphs of the equations of an inconsistent system of linear equations are parallel lines. [13.1A, p. 699]

If, when solving a system of equations algebraically, the variable is eliminated and the result is a false equation, such as $0 = 4$, the system of equations is inconsistent. [13.2A, p. 708]

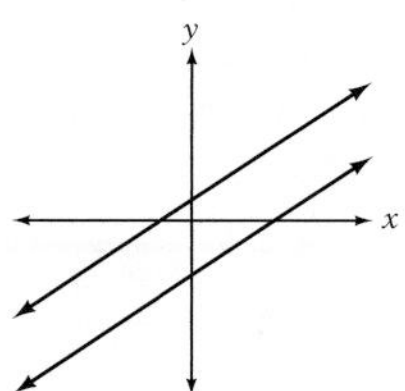

Essential Rules and Procedures

Examples

To solve a system of linear equations in two variables by graphing, graph each equation on the same coordinate system, and then determine the point of intersection. [13.1A, p. 700]

Solve by graphing:

$$x + 2y = 4$$
$$2x + y = -1$$

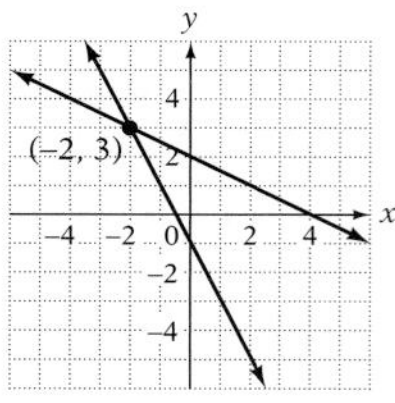

The solution is $(-2, 3)$.

To solve a system of linear equations by the substitution method, write one variable in terms of the other variable. [13.2A, p. 706]

Solve by substitution: (1) $2x + y = 5$
(2) $3x - 2y = 11$

$2x + y = 5$

$y = -2x + 5$ • Solve Equation (1) for y.

$3x - 2y = 11$

$3x - 2(-2x + 5) = 11$ • Substitute for y in Equation (2).

$3x + 4x - 10 = 11$

$7x = 21$

$x = 3$

$y = -2x + 5$

$y = -2(3) + 5$

$y = -1$ The solution is $(3, -1)$.

To solve a system of linear equations by the addition method, use the Multiplication Property of Equations to rewrite one or both of the equations so that the coefficients of one variable are opposites. Then add the equations and solve for the variables. [13.3A, p. 717]

Solve by the addition method:

(1) $2x + 5y = 8$

(2) $3x - 4y = -11$

$6x + 15y = 24$ • 3 times Equation (1)

$-6x + 8y = 22$ • −2 times Equation (2)

$23y = 46$ • Add the equations.

$y = 2$ • Solve for y.

$2x + 5y = 8$

$2x + 5(2) = 8$ • Replace y by 2 in Equation (1).

$2x + 10 = 8$ • Solve for x.

$2x = -2$

$x = -1$

The solution is $(-1, 2)$.

CHAPTER

13 Review Exercises

1. Is $(-1, -3)$ a solution of the system of equations?
$5x + 4y = -17$
$2x - y = 1$
Yes [13.1A]

2. Is $(-2, 0)$ a solution of the system of equations?
$-x + 9y = 2$
$6x - 4y = 12$
No [13.1A]

3. Solve by graphing:
$3x - y = 6$
$y = -3$

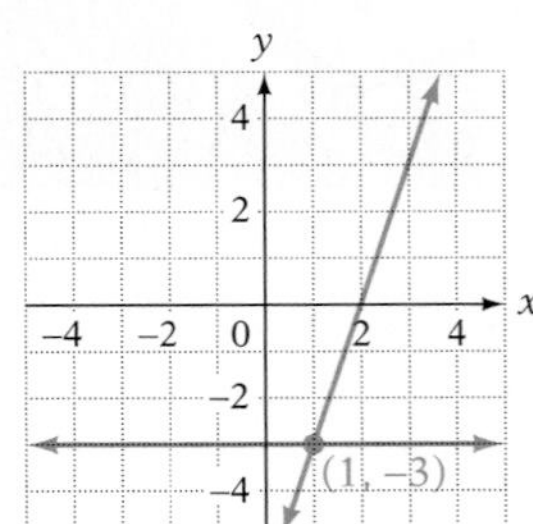

[13.1A]

4. Solve by graphing:
$4x - 2y = 8$
$y = 2x - 4$

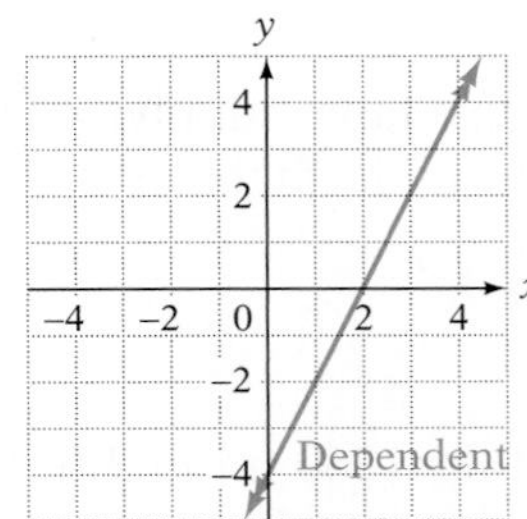

The solutions are the ordered pairs that satisfy the equation $y = 2x - 4$. [13.1A]

5. Solve by graphing:
$x + 2y = 3$
$y = -\frac{1}{2}x + 1$

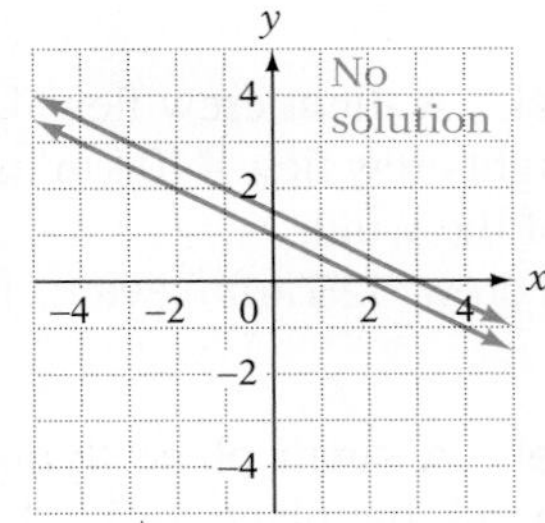

[13.1A]

6. Solve by substitution:
$4x + 7y = 3$
$x = y - 2$
$(-1, 1)$ [13.2A]

7. Solve by substitution:
$6x - y = 0$
$7x - y = 1$
$(1, 6)$ [13.2A]

8. Solve by the addition method:
$3x + 8y = -1$
$x - 2y = -5$
$(-3, 1)$ [13.3A]

9. Solve by the addition method:
$6x + 4y = -3$
$12x - 10y = -15$
$\left(-\frac{5}{6}, \frac{1}{2}\right)$ [13.3A]

10. Solve by substitution:
$12x - 9y = 18$
$y = \frac{4}{3}x - 3$
No solution [13.2A]

11. Solve by substitution:
$8x - y = 2$
$y = 5x + 1$
$(1, 6)$ [13.2A]

12. Solve by the addition method:
$4x - y = 9$
$2x + 3y = -13$
$(1, -5)$ [13.3A]

13. Solve by the addition method:
$5x + 7y = 21$
$20x + 28y = 63$
No solution [13.3A]

14. Solve by substitution:
$4x + 3y = 12$
$y = -\frac{4}{3}x + 4$
Dependent. The solutions satisfy the equation $y = -\frac{4}{3}x + 4$. [13.2A]

15. Solve by substitution:
$7x + 3y = -16$
$x - 2y = 5$
$(-1, -3)$ [13.2A]

16. Solve by the addition method:
$3x + y = -2$
$-9x - 3y = 6$
Dependent. The solutions satisfy the equation $3x + y = -2$. [13.3A]

17. Solve by the addition method:
$6x - 18y = 7$
$9x + 24y = 2$
$\left(\frac{2}{3}, -\frac{1}{6}\right)$ [13.3A]

18. Sculling A sculling team rowing with the current went 24 mi in 2 h. Rowing against the current, the sculling team went 18 mi in 3 h. Find the rate of the sculling team in calm water and the rate of the current.
Sculling team: 9 mph; current: 3 mph [13.4A]

© John Kropewnicki/Shutterstock.com

19. Investments An investor bought 1500 shares of stock, some at \$6 per share and the rest at \$25 per share. If \$12,800 worth of stock was purchased, how many shares of each kind did the investor buy?
1300 shares at \$6; 200 shares at \$25 [13.4B]

20. Travel A flight crew flew 420 km in 3 h with a tailwind. Flying against the wind, the flight crew flew 440 km in 4 h. Find the rate of the flight crew in calm air and the rate of the wind.
Flight crew: 125 km/h; wind: 15 km/h [13.4A]

21. Travel A small plane flying with the wind flew 360 mi in 3 h. Flying against a headwind, the plane took 4 h to fly the same distance. Find the rate of the plane in calm air and the rate of the wind.
Plane: 105 mph; wind: 15 mph [13.4A]

22. Consumerism An online computer service charges one hourly rate for regular use and a higher hourly rate for designated "premium" services. A customer was charged \$14.00 for 9 h of basic use and 2 h of premium use. Another customer was charged \$13.50 for 6 h of regular use and 3 h of premium use. What is the service charge per hour for regular and premium services?
Regular: \$1.00; premium: \$2.50 [13.4B]

23. Investments Terra Cotta Art Center receives an annual income of \$915 from two simple interest investments. One investment, in a corporate bond fund, earns 8.5% annual simple interest. The second investment, in a real estate investment trust, earns 7% annual simple interest. If the total amount invested in the two accounts is \$12,000, how much is invested in each account?
\$7000 at 7%; \$5000 at 8.5% [13.2B]

24. Grain Mixtures A silo contains a mixture of lentils and corn. If 50 bushels of lentils were added, there would be twice as many bushels of lentils as of corn. If 150 bushels of corn were added instead, there would be the same amount of corn as of lentils. How many bushels of each type of grain were originally in the silo?
350 bushels of lentils; 200 bushels of corn [13.4B]

25. Investments Mosher Children's Hospital received a \$300,000 donation that it invested in two simple interest accounts, one earning 5.4% and the other earning 6.6%. If each account earned the same amount of annual interest, how much was invested in each account?
\$165,000 at 5.4%; \$135,000 at 6.6% [13.2B]

CHAPTER 13 TEST

1. Is $(-2, 3)$ a solution of the system?
$2x + 5y = 11$
$x + 3y = 7$
Yes [13.1A]

2. Is $(1, -3)$ a solution of the system?
$3x - 2y = 9$
$4x + y = 1$
Yes [13.1A]

3. Solve by graphing: $3x + 2y = 6$
$5x + 2y = 2$

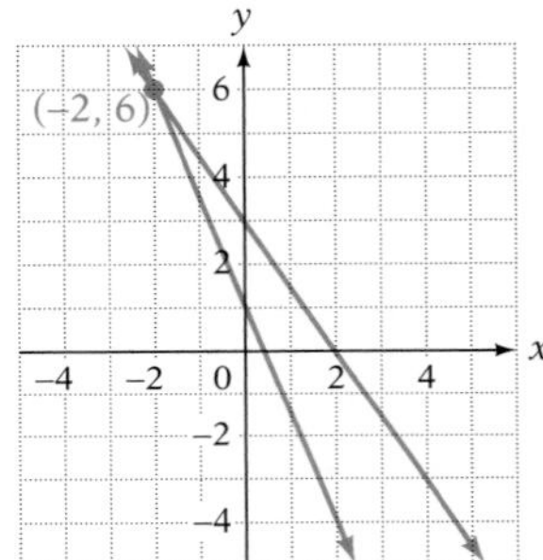

[13.1A]

4. Solve by substitution:
$4x - y = 11$
$y = 2x - 5$
(3, 1) [13.2A]

5. Solve by substitution:
$x = 2y + 3$
$3x - 2y = 5$
(1, −1) [13.2A]

6. Solve by substitution:
$3x + 5y = 1$
$2x - y = 5$
(2, −1) [13.2A]

7. Solve by substitution:
$3x - 5y = 13$
$x + 3y = 1$
$\left(\frac{22}{7}, -\frac{5}{7}\right)$ [13.2A]

8. Solve by substitution:
$2x - 4y = 1$
$y = \frac{1}{2}x + 3$
No solution [13.2A]

9. Solve by the addition method:
$4x + 3y = 11$
$5x - 3y = 7$
(2, 1) [13.3A]

10. Solve by the addition method:
$2x - 5y = 6$
$4x + 3y = -1$
$\left(\frac{1}{2}, -1\right)$ [13.3A]

11. Solve by the addition method:
$x + 2y = 8$
$3x + 6y = 24$
Dependent. The solutions satisfy the equation $x + 2y = 8$. [13.3A]

12. Solve by the addition method:
$7x + 3y = 11$
$2x - 5y = 9$
(2, −1) [13.3A]

13. Solve by the addition method:
$5x + 6y = -7$
$3x + 4y = -5$
(1, −2) [13.3A]

14. Travel Flying with the wind, a plane flies 240 mi in 2 h. Flying against the wind, the plane requires 3 h to travel the same distance. Find the rate of the plane in calm air and the rate of the wind.
Plane: 100 mph; wind: 20 mph [13.4A]

15. Entertainment For the first performance of a play in a community theater, 50 reserved-seat tickets and 80 general-admission tickets were sold. The total receipts were $980. For the second performance, 60 reserved-seat tickets and 90 general-admission tickets were sold. The total receipts were $1140. Find the price of a reserved-seat ticket and the price of a general-admission ticket.
Reserved seat: $10; general admission: $6 [13.4B]

16. Investments Bernardo Community Library received a $28,000 donation that it invested in two accounts, one earning 7.6% annual simple interest and the other earning 6.4% annual simple interest. If both accounts earned the same amount of annual interest, how much was invested in each account?
$15,200 at 6.4%; $12,800 at 7.6% [13.2B]

Cumulative Review Exercises

1. Evaluate $\frac{a^2 - b^2}{2a}$ when $a = 4$ and $b = -2$.
$\frac{3}{2}$ [4.1A]

2. Solve: $-\frac{3}{4}x = \frac{9}{8}$
$-\frac{3}{2}$ [5.1C]

3. Given $f(x) = x^2 + 2x - 1$, find $f(2)$.
7 [12.1D]

4. Multiply: $(2a^2 - 3a + 1)(2 - 3a)$
$-6a^3 + 13a^2 - 9a + 2$ [9.3B]

5. Simplify: $\frac{(-2x^2y)^4}{-8x^3y^2}$
$-2x^5y^2$ [9.4A]

6. Divide: $(4b^2 - 8b + 4) \div (2b - 3)$
$2b - 1 + \frac{1}{2b - 3}$ [9.5B]

7. Simplify: $\frac{8x^{-2}y^5}{-2xy^4}$
$-\frac{4y}{x^3}$ [9.4A]

8. Factor: $4x^2y^4 - 64y^2$
$4y^2(xy - 4)(xy + 4)$ [10.5A]

9. Solve: $(x - 5)(x + 2) = -6$
4, −1 [10.6A]

10. Divide: $\frac{x^2 - 6x + 8}{2x^3 + 6x^2} \div \frac{2x - 8}{4x^3 + 12x^2}$
$x - 2$ [11.1C]

11. Add: $\frac{x - 1}{x + 2} + \frac{2x + 1}{x^2 + x - 2}$
$\frac{x^2 + 2}{(x + 2)(x - 1)}$ [11.3B]

12. Simplify: $\frac{x + 4 - \frac{7}{x - 2}}{x + 8 + \frac{21}{x - 2}}$
$\frac{x - 3}{x + 1}$ [11.4A]

13. Solve: $\frac{x}{2x - 3} + 2 = \frac{-7}{2x - 3}$
$-\frac{1}{5}$ [11.5A]

14. Solve $A = P + Prt$ for r.
$r = \frac{A - P}{Pt}$ [11.6A]

15. Find the x- and y-intercepts of $2x - 3y = 12$.
x-intercept (6, 0); y-intercept (0, −4) [12.3A]

16. Find the slope of the line that passes through the points (2, −3) and (−3, 4).
$-\frac{7}{5}$ [12.3B]

17. Find the equation of the line that passes through the point (−2, 3) and has slope $-\frac{3}{2}$.
$y = -\frac{3}{2}x$ [12.4A]

18. Is (2, 0) a solution of the system?
$5x - 3y = 10$
$4x + 7y = 8$
Yes [13.1A]

19. Solve by substitution:
$3x - 5y = -23$
$x + 2y = -4$
(−6, 1) [13.2A]

20. Solve by the addition method:
$5x - 3y = 29$
$4x + 7y = -5$
(4, −3) [13.3A]

21. Graph: $2x - 3y = 6$.

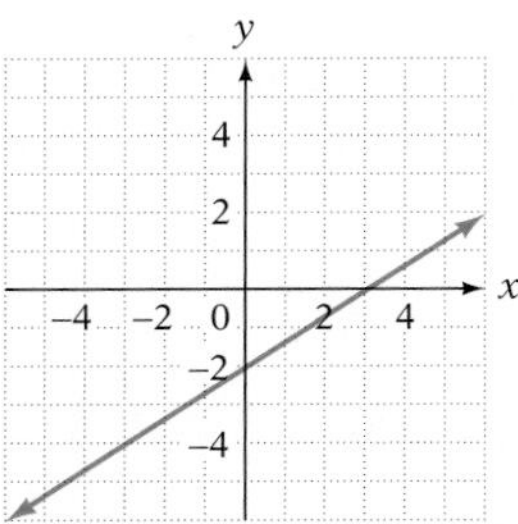

[12.2B]

22. Solve by graphing: 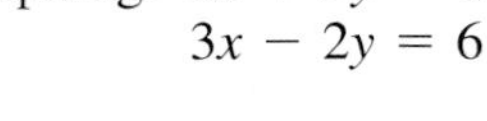 $3x + 2y = 6$
$3x - 2y = 6$

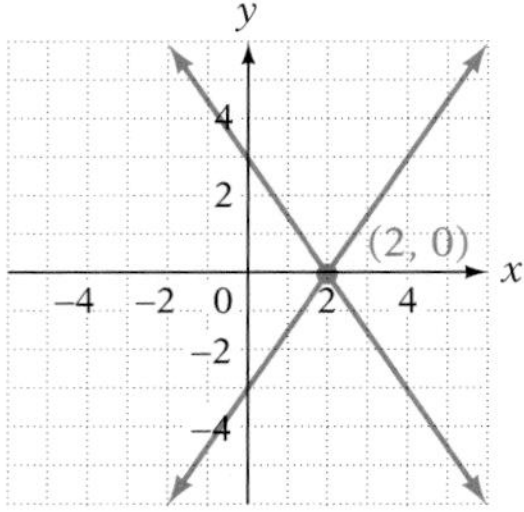

[13.1A]

23. Investments A total of $8750 is invested in two accounts. On one account, the annual simple interest rate is 9.6%; on the second account, the annual simple interest rate is 7.2%. How much should be invested in each account so that both accounts earn the same interest?
$3750 at 9.6%; $5000 at 7.2% [13.2B]

24. Travel A passenger train leaves a train depot $\frac{1}{2}$ h after a freight train leaves the same depot. The freight train is traveling 8 mph slower than the passenger train. Find the rate of each train if the passenger train overtakes the freight train in 3 h.
Freight train: 48 mph; passenger train: 56 mph [5.5B]

25. Geometry The length of each side of a square is extended 4 in. The area of the resulting square is 144 in^2. Find the length of a side of the original square.
8 in. [10.6B]

26. Travel A plane can travel 160 mph in calm air. Flying with the wind, the plane can fly 570 mi in the same amount of time it takes to fly 390 mi against the wind. Find the rate of the wind.
30 mph [13.4A]

27. Travel Traveling with the current, a motorboat can travel 48 mi in 3 h. Traveling against the current, the boat requires 4 h to cover the same distance. Find the rate of the boat in calm water.
14 mph [13.4A]

28. Registered Voters In a recent year, the U.S. voting-age population was 205 million people, but only 156 million Americans were registered to vote. (*Source*: The Election Center) What percent of the voting-age population was registered to vote? Round to the nearest percent. 76% [6.4C]

Inequalities

OBJECTIVES

SECTION 14.1

A To write a set using the roster method

B To write and graph sets of real numbers

SECTION 14.2

A To solve an inequality using the Addition Property of Inequalities

B To solve an inequality using the Multiplication Property of Inequalities

C To solve application problems

SECTION 14.3

A To solve general inequalities

B To solve application problems

SECTION 14.4

A To graph an inequality in two variables

Focus on Success

Why do you want to succeed in this course? Perhaps it is a course you need to pass in order to graduate. Maybe it is a prerequisite for another course you have to take. Perhaps math skills are important to success in your chosen career. When there is a reason to do a task, that task is easier to accomplish. When you are struggling, remind yourself why you are taking this class and let your reason be your motivation to succeed. (See Motivate Yourself, page AIM-3.)

© iStockphoto.com/Alejandro Rivera

Prep Test

Are you ready to succeed in this chapter? Take the Prep Test below to find out if you are ready to learn the new material.

1. Place the correct symbol, $<$ or $>$, between the two numbers.

   $-45 < -27$ [3.1A]

2. Simplify: $3x - 5(2x - 3)$

   $-7x + 15$ [4.2D]

3. State the Addition Property of Equations.

   The same number can be added to each side of an equation without changing the solution of the equation. [5.1B]

4. State the Multiplication Property of Equations.

   Each side of an equation can be multiplied by the same nonzero number without changing the solution of the equation. [5.1C]

5. **Nutrition** A certain grade of hamburger contains 15% fat. How many pounds of fat are in 3 lb of this hamburger? 0.45 lb [6.4C]

6. Solve:
   $7 - 2(2x - 3) = 3x - 1$

   2 [5.3B]

7. Graph: $y = \frac{2}{3}x - 3$ [12.2A]

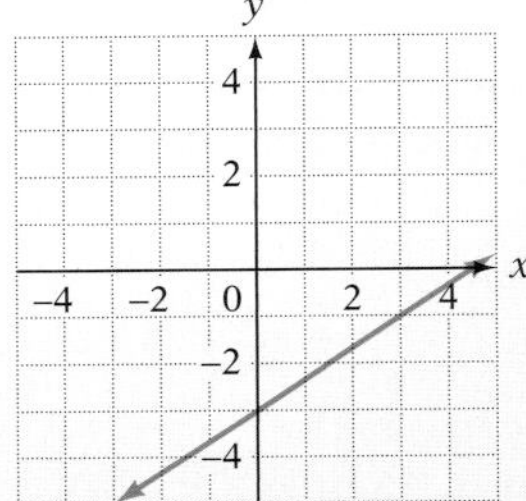

SECTION

14.1 Sets

OBJECTIVE A To write a set using the roster method

Recall that a *set* is a collection of objects, which are called the *elements* of the set. The **roster method** of writing a set encloses a list of the elements in braces.

The set of the positive integers less than 5 is written $\{1, 2, 3, 4\}$.

HOW TO 1 Use the roster method to write the set of integers between 0 and 10.

$A = \{1, 2, 3, 4, 5, 6, 7, 8, 9\}$ • **A set can be designated by a capital letter. Note that 0 and 10 are not elements of the set.**

HOW TO 2 Use the roster method to write the set of natural numbers.

$A = \{1, 2, 3, 4, \ldots\}$ • **The three dots mean that the pattern of numbers continues without end.**

INSTRUCTOR NOTE
Students want to write the empty set as $\{\varnothing\}$. It is very difficult to convince them that this is incorrect. Students, in general, have a difficult time with the idea that a set can be an element of another set.

The **empty set,** or **null set,** is the set that contains no elements. The symbol $\varnothing$ or $\{\ \}$ is used to represent the empty set.

The set of people who have run a 2-minute mile is the empty set.

Union and Intersection of Two Sets

The **union** of two sets, written $A \cup B$, is the set of all elements that belong to either set A *or* set B.

The **intersection** of two sets, written $A \cap B$, is the set that contains the elements that are common to both A and B.

EXAMPLES

Find $A \cup B$ and $A \cap B$, given $A = \{1, 2, 3, 4\}$ and $B = \{3, 4, 5, 6\}$.

$A \cup B = \{1, 2, 3, 4, 5, 6\}$ • **The union of A and B contains all the elements of A and all the elements of B. Elements in both sets are listed only once.**

$A \cap B = \{3, 4\}$ • **The intersection of A and B contains the elements common to A and B.**

EXAMPLE 1

Use the roster method to write the set of the odd positive integers less than 12.

Solution

$A = \{1, 3, 5, 7, 9, 11\}$

YOU TRY IT 1

Use the roster method to write the set of the odd negative integers greater than -10.

Your solution

$A = \{-9, -7, -5, -3, -1\}$

Solution on p. S34

EXAMPLE 2

Use the roster method to write the set of the even positive integers.

Solution

$A = \{2, 4, 6, \ldots\}$

YOU TRY IT 2

Use the roster method to write the set of the odd positive integers.

Your solution

$A = \{1, 3, 5, \ldots\}$

IN-CLASS EXAMPLES

1. Use the roster method to write the set of even integers between 20 and 30. $A = \{\mathbf{22, 24, 26, 28}\}$

EXAMPLE 3

Find $D \cup E$, given $D = \{6, 8, 10, 12\}$ and $E = \{-8, -6, 10, 12\}$.

Solution

$D \cup E = \{-8, -6, 6, 8, 10, 12\}$

YOU TRY IT 3

Find $A \cup B$, given $A = \{-2, -1, 0, 1, 2\}$ and $B = \{0, 1, 2, 3, 4\}$.

Your solution

$A \cup B = \{-2, -1, 0, 1, 2, 3, 4\}$

EXAMPLE 4

Find $A \cap B$, given $A = \{5, 6, 9, 11\}$ and $B = \{5, 9, 13, 15\}$.

Solution

$A \cap B = \{5, 9\}$

YOU TRY IT 4

Find $C \cap D$, given $C = \{10, 12, 14, 16\}$ and $D = \{10, 16, 20, 26\}$.

Your solution

$C \cap D = \{10, 16\}$

2. Find $A \cup B$ and $A \cap B$, given $A = \{a, e, i, o, u\}$ and $B = \{a, b, c, d, e\}$. $\{\mathbf{a, b, c, d, e, i, o, u}\}$; $\{\mathbf{a, e}\}$

EXAMPLE 5

Find $A \cap B$, given $A = \{1, 2, 3, 4\}$ and $B = \{8, 9, 10, 11\}$.

Solution

$A \cap B = \varnothing$

YOU TRY IT 5

Find $A \cap B$, given $A = \{-5, -4, -3, -2\}$ and $B = \{2, 3, 4, 5\}$.

Your solution

$A \cap B = \varnothing$

3. Find $C \cup D$ and $C \cap D$, given $C = \{10, 20, 30, 40\}$ and $D = \{5, 15, 25, 35\}$. $\{\mathbf{5, 10, 15, 20, 25, 30, 35, 40}\}$; $\varnothing$

Solutions on p. S34

OBJECTIVE B *To write and graph sets of real numbers*

Point of Interest

The symbol $\in$ was first used in the book *Arithmeticae Principia,* published in 1889. It is the first letter of the Greek word εστι, which means "is." The symbols for union and intersection were also introduced around the same time.

Another method of representing sets is called **set-builder notation.** This method of writing sets uses a rule to describe the elements of the set. Using set-builder notation, we represent the set of all positive integers less than 10 as

$\{x | x < 10, x \in \text{positive integers}\}$, which is read "the set of all positive integers x that are less than 10."

In addition to the inequality symbols for *is less than* and *is greater than*, there are also inequality symbols for **is less than or equal to (≤)** and **is greater than or equal to (≥).**

$7 \leq 15$ — 7 is less than or equal to 15. This is true because $7 < 15$.

$6 \leq 6$ — 6 is less than or equal to 6. This is true because $6 = 6$.

HOW TO 3 Use set-builder notation to write the set of integers less than or equal to 12.

$\{x | x \leq 12, x \in \text{integers}\}$ • **This is read "the set of all integers x that are less than or equal to 12."**

Take Note

Set-builder notation is mainly used to represent sets that have an infinite number of elements. The set $\{x|x > 4\}$ has an infinite number of elements and cannot be represented using the roster method.

HOW TO 4 Use set-builder notation to write the set of real numbers greater than 4.

$\{x|x > 4, x \in \text{real numbers}\}$ • **This is read "the set of all real numbers x that are greater than 4."**

For the remainder of this section, all variables will represent real numbers. Given this convention, $\{x|x > 4, x \in \text{real numbers}\}$ is written $\{x|x > 4\}$.

Some sets that are written in set-builder notation can be written in **interval notation.** For instance, the interval notation $[-3, 2)$ represents the set of real numbers between -3 and 2. The bracket means that -3 is included in the set, and the parenthesis means that 2 is *not* included in the set. Using set-builder notation, the interval $[-3, 2)$ is written

$\{x|-3 \le x < 2\}$ • **This is read "the set of all real numbers x between -3 and 2, including -3 but excluding 2."**

To indicate an interval that extends forever in the positive direction, we use the **infinity symbol, ∞;** to indicate an interval that extends forever in the negative direction, we use the **negative infinity symbol, $-\infty$.**

HOW TO 5 Write $\{x|x > 1\}$ in interval notation.

$\{x|x > 1\}$ is the set of real numbers greater than 1. This set extends forever in the positive direction. In interval notation, this set is written $(1, \infty)$.

HOW TO 6 Write $\{x|x \le -2\}$ in interval notation.

$\{x|x \le -2\}$ is the set of real numbers less than or equal to -2. This set extends forever in the negative direction. In interval notation, this set is written $(-\infty, -2]$.

When writing a set in interval notation, we always use a parenthesis to the right of ∞ and to the left of $-\infty$. Infinity is not a real number, so it cannot be represented as belonging to the set of real numbers by using a bracket.

HOW TO 7 Write $[1, 3]$ in set-builder notation.

This is the set of real numbers between 1 and 3, including 1 and 3. In set-builder notation, this set is written $\{x|1 \le x \le 3\}$.

We can graph sets of real numbers given in set-builder notation or in interval notation.

HOW TO 8 Graph: $(-\infty, -1)$

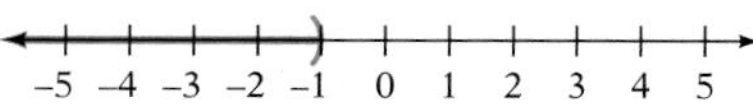

This is the set of real numbers less than -1, excluding -1. The parenthesis at -1 on the number line indicates that -1 is excluded from the set.

HOW TO 9 Graph: $\{x|x \ge 1\}$

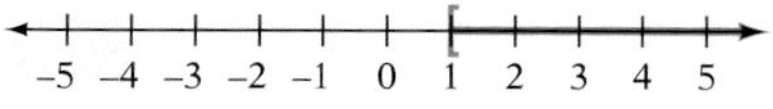

This is the set of real numbers greater than or equal to 1. The bracket at 1 indicates that 1 is included in the set.

EXAMPLE 6

Write in interval notation.
a. $\{x|x \geq 2\}$ **b.** $\{x|0 \leq x \leq 1\}$

Solution

a. $\{x|x \geq 2\}$ is the set of real numbers greater than or equal to 2. This set extends forever in the positive direction. In interval notation, this set is written $[2, \infty)$.
b. $\{x|0 \leq x \leq 1\}$ is the set of real numbers between 0 and 1, including 0 and 1. In interval notation, this set is written $[0, 1]$.

YOU TRY IT 6

Write in interval notation.
a. $\{x|x \leq 3\}$ **b.** $\{x|-5 \leq x \leq -3\}$

Your solution

a. $(-\infty, 3]$ b. $[-5, -3]$

IN-CLASS EXAMPLES

4. Write $\{x|x \leq -5\}$ in interval notation. $(-\infty, -5]$
5. Write $(8, \infty)$ in set-builder notation. $\{x|x > 8\}$

EXAMPLE 7

Write in set-builder notation.
a. $(-\infty, 0]$ **b.** $(-3, 3)$

Solution

a. The interval $(-\infty, 0]$ is the set of real numbers less than or equal to 0. In set-builder notation, this set is written $\{x|x \leq 0\}$.
b. The interval $(-3, 3)$ is the set of real numbers between -3 and 3, excluding -3 and 3. In set-builder notation, this set is written $\{x|-3 < x < 3\}$.

YOU TRY IT 7

Write in set-builder notation.
a. $(-3, \infty)$ **b.** $[0, 4)$

Your solution

a. $\{x|x > -3\}$ b. $\{x|0 \leq x < 4\}$

6. Graph: $[-3, \infty)$

7. Graph: $\{x|0 \leq x \leq 5\}$

EXAMPLE 8

Graph.
a. $\{x|-2 < x < 1\}$ **b.** $\{x|x < 4\}$

Solution

a. The graph is the set of real numbers between -2 and 1, excluding -2 and 1. Use parentheses at -2 and 1.
b. The graph is the set of real numbers less than 4. Use a parenthesis at 4.

YOU TRY IT 8

Graph.
a. $\{x|-4 \leq x \leq 4\}$ **b.** $\{x|x > -3\}$

Your solution

EXAMPLE 9

Graph: $(-\infty, 5)$

Solution

The graph is the set of real numbers less than 5. Use a parenthesis at 5.

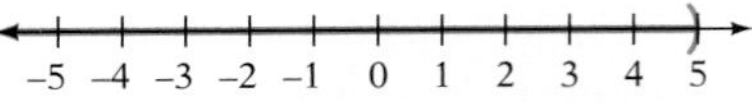

YOU TRY IT 9

Graph: $[2, 5]$

Your solution

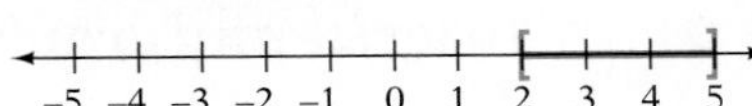

Solutions on p. S34

14.1 EXERCISES

Concept Check

SUGGESTED ASSIGNMENT:
Exercises 1 and 2; Exercises 3–57, odds

1. The set $\{1, 2, 3\}$ is written using the ___roster___ method. The set $\{x|x < 4, x \in \text{positive integers}\}$ is written using ___set-builder___ notation. The set $[-3, 2]$ is written in ___interval___ notation.

2. Explain how to find **a.** the union of two sets and **b.** the intersection of two sets.

OBJECTIVE A *To write a set using the roster method*

For Exercises 3 to 6, use the roster method to write the set.

3. The integers between 15 and 22
   $A = \{16, 17, 18, 19, 20, 21\}$

4. The integers between -10 and -4
   $A = \{-9, -8, -7, -6, -5\}$

5. The odd integers between 8 and 18
   $A = \{9, 11, 13, 15, 17\}$

6. The even integers between -11 and -1
   $A = \{-10, -8, -6, -4, -2\}$

For Exercises 7 to 12, find $A \cup B$.

7. $A = \{3, 4, 5\}$; $B = \{4, 5, 6\}$
   $A \cup B = \{3, 4, 5, 6\}$

8. $A = \{-3, -2, -1\}$; $B = \{-2, -1, 0\}$
   $A \cup B = \{-3, -2, -1, 0\}$

9. $A = \{-10, -9, -8\}$; $B = \{8, 9, 10\}$
   $A \cup B = \{-10, -9, -8, 8, 9, 10\}$

10. $A = \{\text{m, n, p, q}\}$; $B = \{\text{m, n, o}\}$
    $A \cup B = \{\text{m, n, o, p, q}\}$

11. $A = \{1, 3, 7, 9\}$; $B = \{7, 9, 11, 13\}$
    $A \cup B = \{1, 3, 7, 9, 11, 13\}$

12. $A = \{-3, -2, -1\}$; $B = \{-1, 1, 2\}$
    $A \cup B = \{-3, -2, -1, 1, 2\}$

For Exercises 13 to 18, find $A \cap B$.

13. $A = \{3, 4, 5\}$; $B = \{4, 5, 6\}$
    $A \cap B = \{4, 5\}$

14. $A = \{-4, -3, -2\}$; $B = \{-6, -5, -4\}$
    $A \cap B = \{-4\}$

15. $A = \{-4, -3, -2\}$; $B = \{2, 3, 4\}$
    $A \cap B = \varnothing$

16. $A = \{1, 2, 3, 4\}$; $B = \{1, 2, 3, 4\}$
    $A \cap B = \{1, 2, 3, 4\}$

17. $A = \{\text{a, b, c, d, e}\}$; $B = \{\text{c, d, e, f, g}\}$
    $A \cap B = \{\text{c, d, e}\}$

18. $A = \{\text{m, n, o, p}\}$; $B = \{\text{k, l, m, n}\}$
    $A \cap B = \{\text{m, n}\}$

OBJECTIVE B *To write and graph sets of real numbers*

For Exercises 19 to 24, use set-builder notation to write the set.

19. The negative integers greater than -5
    $\{x|x > -5, x \in \text{negative integers}\}$

20. The positive integers less than 5
    $\{x|x < 5, x \in \text{positive integers}\}$

21. The integers greater than 30
$\{x|x > 30, x \in \text{integers}\}$

22. The integers less than -70
$\{x|x < -70, x \in \text{integers}\}$

23. The real numbers greater than 8
$\{x|x > 8\}$

24. The real numbers less than 57
$\{x|x < 57\}$

For Exercises 25 to 33, write the set in interval notation.

25. $\{x|1 < x < 2\}$
$(1, 2)$

26. $\{x|-2 < x \le 4\}$
$(-2, 4]$

27. $\{x|x > 3\}$
$(3, \infty)$

28. $\{x|x \le 0\}$
$(-\infty, 0]$

29. $\{x|-4 \le x < 5\}$
$[-4, 5)$

30. $\{x|-3 \le x \le 0\}$
$[-3, 0]$

31. $\{x|x \le 2\}$
$(-\infty, 2]$

32. $\{x|x \ge -3\}$
$[-3, \infty)$

33. $\{x|-3 \le x \le 1\}$
$[-3, 1]$

For Exercises 34 to 42, write the interval in set-builder notation.

34. $[-4, 5]$
$\{x|-4 \le x \le 5\}$

35. $(-5, -3)$
$\{x|-5 < x < -3\}$

36. $(4, \infty)$
$\{x|x > 4\}$

37. $(-\infty, -2]$
$\{x|x \le -2\}$

38. $(4, 9]$
$\{x|4 < x \le 9\}$

39. $[-3, -2]$
$\{x|-3 \le x \le -2\}$

40. $[0, \infty)$
$\{x|x \ge 0\}$

41. $(-\infty, 6]$
$\{x|x \le 6\}$

42. $(-\infty, \infty)$
$\{x|-\infty < x < \infty\}$

For Exercises 43 to 58, graph the set.

43. $[-5, 4]$

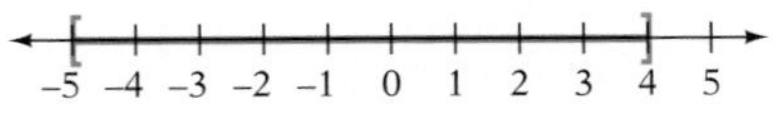

–5 –4 –3 –2 –1 0 1 2 3 4 5

44. $(-3, 5]$

–5 –4 –3 –2 –1 0 1 2 3 4 5

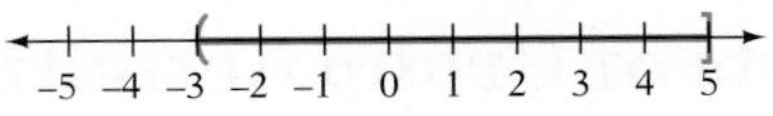

45. $\{x|x < 4\}$

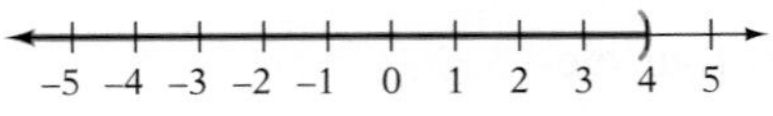

–5 –4 –3 –2 –1 0 1 2 3 4 5

46. $\{x|x \ge -3\}$

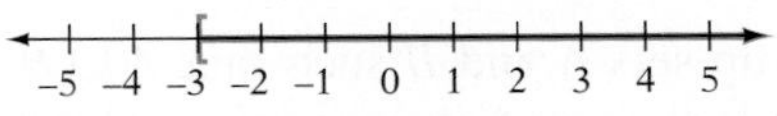

–5 –4 –3 –2 –1 0 1 2 3 4 5

47. $\{x|x \le -4\}$

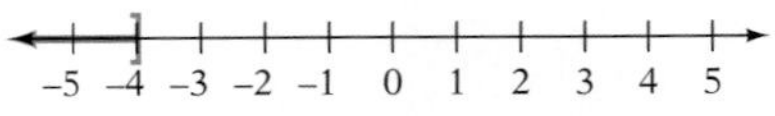

–5 –4 –3 –2 –1 0 1 2 3 4 5

48. $\{x|x > 0\}$

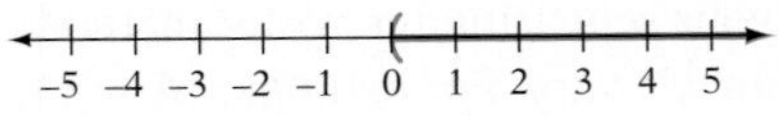

–5 –4 –3 –2 –1 0 1 2 3 4 5

49. $(-\infty, 3]$

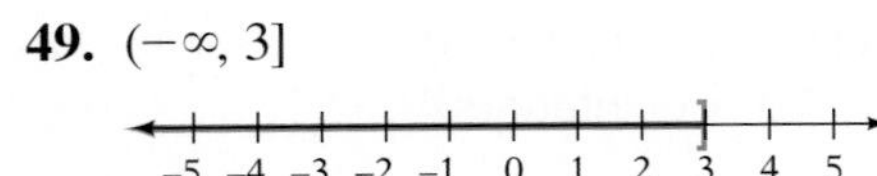

50. $(4, \infty)$

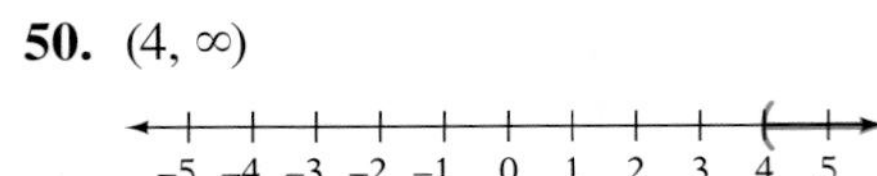

51. $[-1, 3)$

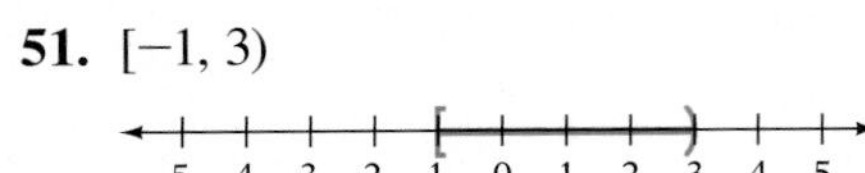

52. $(-3, 0]$

53. $\{x \mid -3 < x < 3\}$

54. $\{x \mid 0 \leq x < 4\}$

55. $\{x \mid 2 \leq x \leq 4\}$

56. $\{x \mid -4 < x < 1\}$

57. $\{x \mid -\infty < x < \infty\}$

58. $(-\infty, \infty)$

59. How many elements are in the set given in interval notation as $(4, 4)$?
None

60. How many elements are in the set given by $\{x \mid 4 \leq x \leq 4\}$?
One

Critical Thinking

For Exercises 61 and 62, write an inequality that describes the situation.

61. To avoid shipping charges, one must spend a minimum m of \$250.
$m \geq 250$

62. The temperature t never got above freezing (32°F).
$t \leq 32$

63. True or false? If $A \cup B = A$, then $A \cap B = B$.
True

QUICK QUIZ

1. Use the roster method to write the set of integers between −6 and 0.
$\{-5, -4, -3, -2, -1\}$ [14.1A]
2. Find $C \cup D$ and $C \cap D$, given $C = \{-3, -2, -1, 0\}$ and $D = \{0, 1, 2, 3\}$.
$\{-3, -2, -1, 0, 1, 2, 3\}$; $\{0\}$ [14.1A]
3. Write $\{x \mid x > -6\}$ in interval notation. **$(-6, \infty)$ [14.1B]**
4. Write $(-\infty, 7]$ in set-builder notation.
$\{x \mid x \leq 7\}$ [14.1B]
5. Graph: $(-\infty, 4)$ **[14.1B]**
6. Graph: $\{x \mid -4 < x < 2\}$ **[14.1B]**

Projects or Group Activities

64. Make up sets A and B such that $A \cup B$ has three elements and $A \cap B$ has no elements. Write your sets using the roster method.
Answers will vary. For example, $A = \{1, 2\}$ and $B = \{3\}$.

65. Make up sets A and B such that $A \cup B$ has four elements and $A \cap B$ has four elements. Write your sets using the roster method.
Answers will vary. For example, $A = \{1, 2, 3, 4\}$ and $B = \{1, 2, 3, 4\}$.

66. Make up sets A and B such that $A \cup B$ has five elements and $A \cap B$ has two elements. Write your sets using the roster method.
Answers will vary. For example, $A = \{1, 2, 3\}$ and $B = \{1, 2, 4, 5\}$.

SECTION

14.2 The Addition and Multiplication Properties of Inequalities

OBJECTIVE A *To solve an inequality using the Addition Property of Inequalities*

The inequality at the right is true if the variable is replaced by 7 or 9.3.

$$x + 5 > 8$$

$$\left.\begin{array}{r} 7 + 5 > 8 \\ 9.3 + 5 > 8 \end{array}\right\} \text{True inequalities}$$

The inequality $x + 5 > 8$ is false if the variable is replaced by 2 or $-\frac{1}{2}$.

$$\left.\begin{array}{r} 2 + 5 > 8 \\ -\frac{1}{2} + 5 > 8 \end{array}\right\} \text{False inequalities}$$

The **solution set of an inequality** is the set of numbers each element of which, when substituted for the variable, results in a true inequality. The values of x that will make the inequality $x + 5 > 8$ true are the numbers greater than 3. The solution set of $x + 5 > 8$ is $\{x \mid x > 3\}$. This set can also be written in interval notation as $(3, \infty)$.

At the right is the graph of the solution set of $x + 5 > 8$.

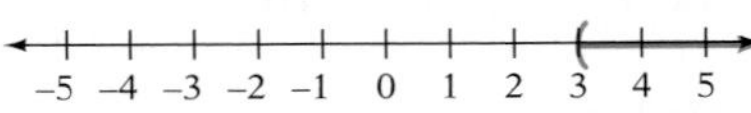

In solving an inequality, the goal is to rewrite the given inequality in the form *variable* $>$ *constant* or *variable* $<$ *constant*. The Addition Property of Inequalities is used to rewrite an inequality in this form.

Addition Property of Inequalities

The same term can be added to each side of an inequality without changing the solution set of the inequality.

If $a > b$, then $a + c > b + c$. If $a < b$, then $a + c < b + c$.

EXAMPLE

The inequality $x - 2 > 5$ has the same solution set as the inequality $x - 2 + 2 > 5 + 2$.

The Addition Property of Inequalities also holds true for an inequality containing the symbol $\geq$ or $\leq$. The Addition Property of Inequalities is used when, in order to rewrite an inequality in the form *variable* $>$ *constant* or *variable* $<$ *constant*, we must remove a term from one side of the inequality. Add the opposite of that term to each side of the inequality.

HOW TO 1 Solve and write the answer in set-builder notation: $x - 4 < -3$

$$x - 4 < -3$$

$$x - 4 + 4 < -3 + 4$$ • **Add 4 to each side of the inequality.**

$$x < 1$$ • **Simplify.**

$$\{x \mid x < 1\}$$ • **Write in set-builder notation.**

At the right is the graph of the solution set of $x - 4 < -3$.

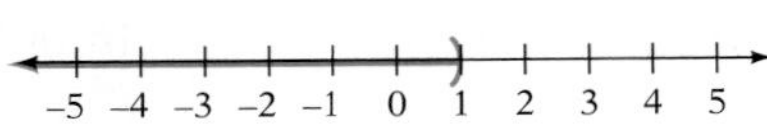

Because subtraction is defined in terms of addition, the Addition Property of Inequalities allows the same term to be subtracted from each side of an inequality.

HOW TO 2 Solve and write the answer in set-builder notation: $5x - 6 \le 4x - 4$

$5x - 6 \le 4x - 4$
$5x - 4x - 6 \le 4x - 4x - 4$ • **Subtract 4x from each side of the inequality.**
$x - 6 \le -4$ • **Simplify.**
$x - 6 + 6 \le -4 + 6$ • **Add 6 to each side of the inequality.**
$x \le 2$ • **Simplify.**
$\{x \mid x \le 2\}$ • **Write in set-builder notation.**

EXAMPLE 1

Solve. Write the solution set in set-builder notation and in interval notation.

$7x - 14 \le 6x - 16$

Solution

$7x - 14 \le 6x - 16$
$7x - 6x - 14 \le 6x - 6x - 16$ • **Subtract 6x from each side.**
$x - 14 \le -16$
$x - 14 + 14 \le -16 + 14$ • **Add 14 to each side.**
$x \le -2$
$\{x \mid x \le -2\}$ • **Set-builder notation**
$(-\infty, -2]$ • **Interval notation**

YOU TRY IT 1

Solve. Write the solution set in set-builder notation and in interval notation.

$5x + 3 > 4x + 5$

Your solution

$\{x \mid x > 2\}$; $(2, \infty)$

IN-CLASS EXAMPLES

Write answers in set-builder notation.

1. Solve and graph the solution set of $-6 \ge a - 3$. $\{a \mid a \le -3\}$

-3 0

2. Solve.
   a. $10x + 6 < 4 + 9x$ $\{x \mid x < -2\}$
   b. $3y - \frac{2}{5} > \frac{1}{10} + 2y$ $\left\{y \mid y > \frac{1}{2}\right\}$
   c. $5.3x \le 8 + 4.3x$ $\{x \mid x \le 8\}$

Solution on p. S34

OBJECTIVE B *To solve an inequality using the Multiplication Property of Inequalities*

Consider the two inequalities below and the effect of multiplying each inequality by 2, a *positive* number.

$$-3 < 7 \qquad 6 > 4$$
$$2(-3) < 2(7) \qquad 2(6) > 2(4)$$
$$-6 < 14 \qquad 12 > 8$$

In each case, the inequality symbol remains the same. Multiplying each side of an inequality by a **positive** number does not change the inequality.

Now consider the same inequalities and the effect of multiplying by -2, a *negative* number.

$$-3 < 7 \qquad 6 > 4$$
$$-2(-3) > -2(7) \qquad -2(6) < -2(4)$$
$$6 > -14 \qquad -12 < -8$$

In order for the inequality to be true, the inequality symbol must be reversed. If each side of an inequality is multiplied by a **negative** number, the inequality symbol must be reversed in order for the inequality to remain a true inequality.

Take Note

Any time an inequality is multiplied or divided by a negative number, the inequality symbol must be reversed. Compare the next two examples.

$2x < -4$ Divide each side by *positive* 2.

$\frac{2x}{2} < \frac{-4}{2}$

$x < -2$ Inequality *is not* reversed.

$-2x < 4$ Divide each side by *negative* 2.

$\frac{-2x}{-2} > \frac{4}{-2}$

$x > -2$ Inequality *is* reversed.

Multiplication Property of Inequalities—Part 1

Each side of an inequality can be multiplied by the same **positive** number without changing the solution set of the inequality. In symbols, this is stated as follows.

If $a < b$ and $c > 0$, then $ac < bc$. If $a > b$ and $c > 0$, then $ac > bc$.

Multiplication Property of Inequalities—Part 2

Multiplying each side of an inequality by the same **negative** number and reversing the inequality symbol does not change the solution set of the inequality. In symbols, this is stated as follows.

If $a < b$ and $c < 0$, then $ac > bc$. If $a > b$ and $c < 0$, then $ac < bc$.

EXAMPLES

The inequality $3x < 6$ has the same solution set as the inequality $\frac{3x}{3} < \frac{6}{3}$.

The inequality $-4x > 8$ has the same solution set as the inequality $\frac{-4x}{-4} < \frac{8}{-4}$.

In solving an inequality, the goal is to rewrite the given inequality in the form *variable* $>$ *constant* or *variable* $<$ *constant.* The Multiplication Property of Inequalities is used when, in order to rewrite an inequality in this form, we must remove a coefficient from one side of the inequality.

The Multiplication Property of Inequalities also holds true for an inequality containing the symbol $\geq$ or $\leq$.

HOW TO 3 Solve $-\frac{3}{2}x \leq 6$ and write the answer in set-builder notation. Graph the solution set.

$$-\frac{3}{2}x \leq 6$$

$$-\frac{2}{3}\left(-\frac{3}{2}x\right) \geq -\frac{2}{3}(6)$$

- **Multiply each side of the inequality by $-\frac{2}{3}$. Because $-\frac{2}{3}$ is a negative number, the inequality symbol must be reversed.**

$$x \geq -4$$

$$\{x | x \geq -4\}$$

- **Write in set-builder notation.**

-5 -4 -3 -2 -1 0 1 2 3 4 5

- **Graph $\{x | x \geq -4\}$.**

Because division is defined in terms of multiplication, the Multiplication Property of Inequalities allows us to divide each side of an inequality by a nonzero constant.

Take Note

As shown in HOW TO 4 at the right, the goal in solving an inequality can be *constant* $<$ *variable* or *constant* $>$ *variable.* We could have written the third line of HOW TO 4 as $x > -\frac{2}{3}$.

HOW TO 4 Solve $-4 < 6x$ and write the answer in set-builder notation.

$$-4 < 6x$$

$$\frac{-4}{6} < \frac{6x}{6}$$

- **Divide each side of the inequality by 6.**

$$-\frac{2}{3} < x$$

- **Simplify: $\frac{-4}{6} = -\frac{2}{3}$.**

$$\left\{x \,\middle|\, x > -\frac{2}{3}\right\}$$

- **Write in set-builder notation.**

EXAMPLE 2

Solve $-7x > 14$ and write the answer in interval notation. Graph the solution set.

Solution

$$-7x > 14$$

$$\frac{-7x}{-7} < \frac{14}{-7} \quad \text{• Divide by } -7\text{. Reverse the inequality symbol.}$$

$$x < -2$$

$(-\infty, -2)$

YOU TRY IT 2

Solve $-3x > -9$ and write the answer in interval notation. Graph the solution set.

Your solution

$(-\infty, 3)$

EXAMPLE 3

Solve $-\frac{5}{8}x \le \frac{5}{12}$ and write the answer in set-builder notation.

Solution

$$-\frac{5}{8}x \le \frac{5}{12}$$

$$-\frac{8}{5}\left(-\frac{5}{8}x\right) \ge -\frac{8}{5}\left(\frac{5}{12}\right) \quad \text{• Multiply by } -\frac{8}{5}\text{. Reverse the inequality symbol.}$$

$$x \ge -\frac{2}{3}$$

$$\left\{x \mid x \ge -\frac{2}{3}\right\}$$

YOU TRY IT 3

Solve $-\frac{3}{4}x \ge 18$ and write the answer in set-builder notation.

Your solution

$\{x \mid x \le -24\}$

IN-CLASS EXAMPLES

Write answers in interval notation.

3. Solve and graph the solution set of $-3y > -15$. **$(-\infty, 5)$**

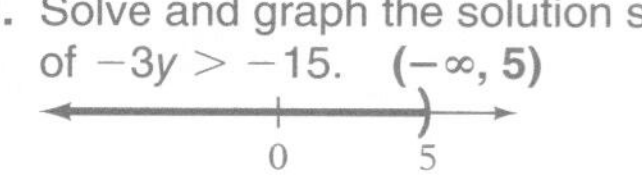

4. Solve.
   a. $0 \le 7n$ **$[0, \infty)$**
   b. $6 < -\frac{2}{5}x$ **$(-\infty, -15]$**
   c. $1.4a \ge -1.96$ **$[-1.4, \infty)$**

Solutions on p. S34

OBJECTIVE C *To solve application problems*

EXAMPLE 4

A student must have at least 450 points out of 500 points on five tests to receive an A in a course. One student's results on the first four tests were 94, 87, 77, and 95. What scores on the last test will enable this student to receive an A in the course?

Strategy

To find the scores, write and solve an inequality using N to represent the possible scores on the last test.

Solution

Total number of points on the five tests	is greater than or equal to	450

$$94 + 87 + 77 + 95 + N \ge 450$$

$$353 + N \ge 450 \quad \text{• Simplify.}$$

$$353 - 353 + N \ge 450 - 353 \quad \text{• Subtract 353.}$$

$$N \ge 97$$

The student's score on the last test must be greater than or equal to 97.

YOU TRY IT 4

A consumer electronics dealer will make a profit on the sale of an LCD HDTV if the cost of the TV is less than 70% of the selling price. What selling prices will enable the dealer to make a profit on a TV that costs the dealer $942?

Your strategy

Your solution

Any price greater than or equal to $1345.71

IN-CLASS EXAMPLES

5. One-fourth of a number is less than five-sixths. Find the largest integer that satisfies this inequality. **3**
6. In a person's daily diet, fat intake should be at most 30% of calorie intake. If a person who eats 2000 calories a day consumes 270 calories of fat at breakfast, how many more fat calories can this person consume during the rest of the day? **≤ 330 calories**

Solution on p. S34

14.2 EXERCISES

SUGGESTED ASSIGNMENT:
Exercises 1–6; Exercises 7–37, odds; Exercises 43–75, odds; Exercise 80; Exercises 81–87, odds

Concept Check

1. State whether or not you would need to reverse the inequality symbol when solving the inequality.

a. $x - 3 > 6$ No **b.** $3x < 6$ No **c.** $-3x > 6$ Yes

d. $3x \leq -6$ No **e.** $3 + x \geq -6$ No **f.** $-\frac{x}{3} < 6$ Yes

2. Which numbers are solutions of the inequality $x - 5 < -6$?
(i) 1 **(ii)** -1 **(iii)** 12 **(iv)** -5 iv

3. Which numbers are solutions of the inequality $-4x \leq 12$?
(i) 0 **(ii)** 3 **(iii)** -3 **(iv)** -4 i, ii, iii

Complete Exercises 4 and 5 by filling in the blank in the first statement with "includes" or "does not include." Fill in the blank in the second statement with the correct inequality symbol: $>$, $<$, $\geq$, or $\leq$.

4. The graph of the solution set shown at the right ___includes___ the number -2. The graph is of the solution set of the inequality x ___$\leq$___ -2.

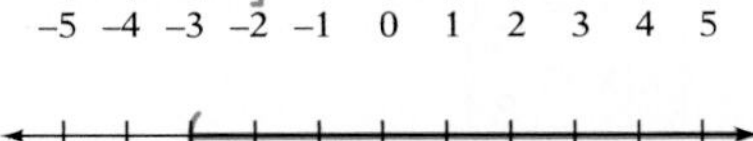

5. The graph of the solution set shown at the right ___does not include___ the number -3. The graph is of the solution set of the inequality x ___$>$___ -3.

6. In your own words, state the Addition Property of Inequalities and the Multiplication Property of Inequalities.

OBJECTIVE A *To solve an inequality using the Addition Property of Inequalities*

For Exercises 7 to 14, solve the inequality and write the answer in set-builder notation. Graph the solution set.

7. $x + 1 < 3$ $\{x|x < 2\}$

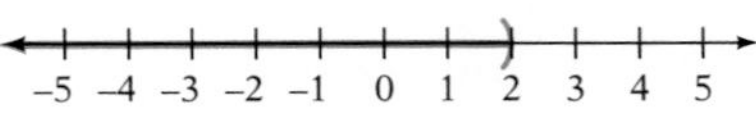

8. $y + 2 < 2$ $\{y|y < 0\}$

9. $x - 5 > -2$ $\{x|x > 3\}$

10. $x - 3 > -2$ $\{x|x > 1\}$

11. $7 \leq n + 4$ $\{n|n \geq 3\}$

12. $3 \leq 5 + x$ $\{x|x \geq -2\}$

13. $x - 6 \leq -10$ $\{x|x \leq -4\}$

14. $y - 8 \leq -11$ $\{x|x \leq -3\}$

For Exercises 15 to 26, solve and write the answer in interval notation.

15. $y - 3 \geq -12$
$[-9, \infty)$

16. $x + 8 \geq -14$
$[-22, \infty)$

17. $3x - 5 < 2x + 7$
$(-\infty, 12)$

18. $5x + 4 < 4x - 10$
$(-\infty, -14)$

19. $8x - 7 \geq 7x - 2$
$[5, \infty)$

20. $3n - 9 \geq 2n - 8$
$[1, \infty)$

21. $2x + 4 < x - 7$
$(-\infty, -11)$

22. $9x + 7 < 8x - 7$
$(-\infty, -14)$

23. $4x - 8 \le 2 + 3x$
$(-\infty, 10]$

24. $5b - 9 < 3 + 4b$
$(-\infty, 12)$

25. $6x + 4 \ge 5x - 2$
$[-6, \infty)$

26. $7x - 3 \ge 6x - 2$
$[1, \infty)$

For Exercises 27 to 38, solve and write the answer in set-builder notation.

27. $2x - 12 > x - 10$
$\{x|x > 2\}$

28. $3x + 9 > 2x + 7$
$\{x|x > -2\}$

29. $d + \frac{1}{2} < \frac{1}{3}$
$\left\{d \middle| d < -\frac{1}{6}\right\}$

30. $x - \frac{3}{8} < \frac{5}{6}$
$\left\{x \middle| x < \frac{29}{24}\right\}$

31. $x + \frac{5}{8} \ge -\frac{2}{3}$
$\left\{x \middle| x \ge -\frac{31}{24}\right\}$

32. $y + \frac{5}{12} \ge -\frac{3}{4}$
$\left\{y \middle| y \ge -\frac{7}{6}\right\}$

33. $x - \frac{3}{8} < \frac{1}{4}$
$\left\{x \middle| x < \frac{5}{8}\right\}$

34. $y + \frac{5}{9} \le \frac{5}{6}$
$\left\{y \middle| y \le \frac{5}{18}\right\}$

35. $2x - \frac{1}{2} < x + \frac{3}{4}$
$\left\{x \middle| x < \frac{5}{4}\right\}$

36. $x + 5.8 \le 4.6$
$\{x|x \le -1.2\}$

37. $x - 3.5 < 2.1$
$\{x|x < 5.6\}$

38. $x - 0.23 \le 0.47$
$\{x|x \le 0.70\}$

For Exercises 39 to 42, assume that n and a are both positive numbers. State whether the solution set of an inequality of the given form contains only negative numbers, only positive numbers, or both negative and positive numbers.

39. $x + n < a$, where $n > a$
Negative

40. $x + n > a$, where $n < a$
Positive

41. $x + n < a$, where $n < a$
Negative and positive

42. $x + n > a$, where $n > a$
Negative and positive

OBJECTIVE B *To solve an inequality using the Multiplication Property of Inequalities*

For Exercises 43 to 52, solve and write the answer in set-builder notation. Graph the solution set.

43. $3x < 12$ $\{x|x < 4\}$

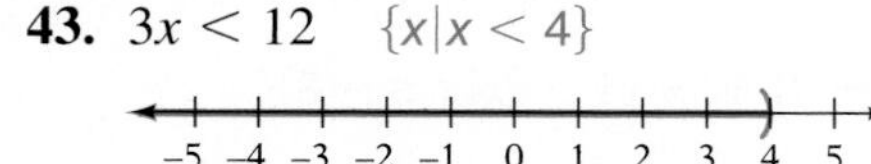

44. $8x \le -24$ $\{x|x \le -3\}$

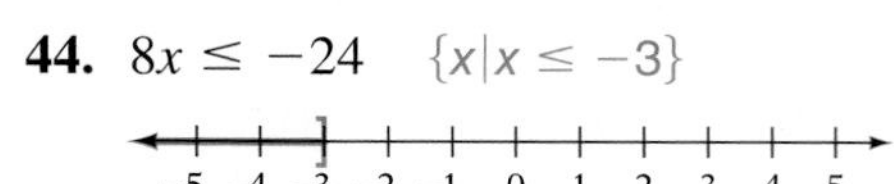

45. $15 \le 5y$ $\{y|y \ge 3\}$

46. $-48 < 24x$ $\{x|x > -2\}$

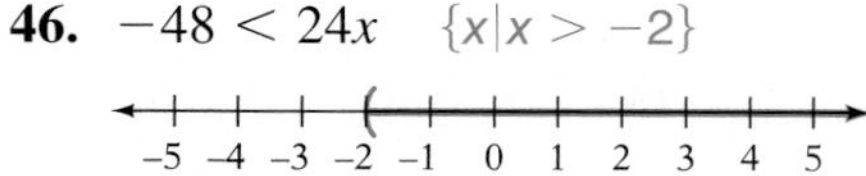

47. $16x \le 16$ $\{x|x \le 1\}$

48. $3x > 0$ $\{x|x > 0\}$

49. $-8x > 8$ $\{x|x < -1\}$

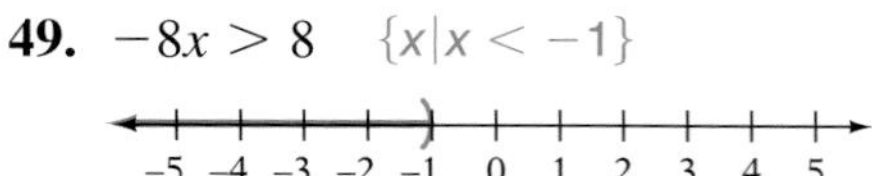

50. $-2n \le -8$ $\{n|n \ge 4\}$

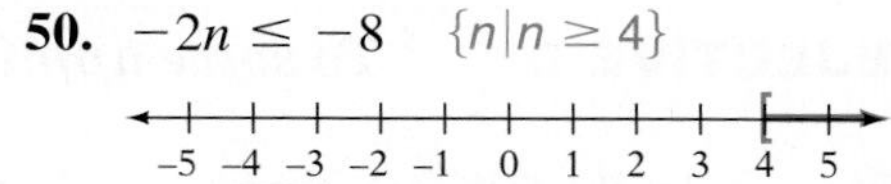

51. $-6b > 24$ $\{b|b < -4\}$

52. $-4x < 8$ $\{x|x > -2\}$

For Exercises 53 to 64, solve and write the answer in interval notation.

53. $-5y \ge 0$ $(-\infty, 0]$

54. $-3z < 0$ $(0, \infty)$

55. $7x > 2$ $\left(\frac{2}{7}, \infty\right)$

56. $6x \le -1$ $\left(-\infty, -\frac{1}{6}\right]$

57. $-x \ge 3$ $(-\infty, -3]$

58. $-y < 4$ $(-4, \infty)$

59. $2 > -y$ $(-2, \infty)$

60. $-5 \le -x$ $(-\infty, 5]$

61. $\frac{5}{6}n < 15$ $(-\infty, 18)$

62. $\frac{3}{4}x < 12$ $(-\infty, 16)$

63. $10 \le \frac{5}{8}x$ $[16, \infty)$

64. $4 \ge \frac{2}{3}x$ $(-\infty, 6]$

For Exercises 65 to 76, solve and write the answer in set-builder notation.

65. $-\frac{2}{11}b \ge -6$ $\{b|b \le 33\}$

66. $-\frac{4}{7}x \ge -12$ $\{x|x \le 21\}$

67. $-\frac{3}{5}x < 0$ $\{x|x > 0\}$

68. $-\frac{2}{3}x \ge 0$ $\{x|x \le 0\}$

69. $-\frac{3}{8}x \ge \frac{9}{14}$ $\left\{x|x \le -\frac{12}{7}\right\}$

70. $-\frac{3}{5}x < -\frac{6}{7}$ $\left\{x|x > \frac{10}{7}\right\}$

71. $-\frac{4}{5}x < -\frac{8}{15}$ $\left\{x|x > \frac{2}{3}\right\}$

72. $-\frac{8}{9}x \ge -\frac{16}{27}$ $\left\{x|x \le \frac{2}{3}\right\}$

73. $1.5x \le 6.30$ $\{x|x \le 4.2\}$

74. $2.3x \le 5.29$ $\{x|x \le 2.3\}$

75. $4.25m > -34$ $\{m|m > -8\}$

76. $-3.9x \ge -19.5$ $\{x|x \le 5\}$

For Exercises 77 to 79, without actually solving the inequality or using a calculator, determine which of the following statements is true.
(i) n must be positive. **(ii)** n must be negative. **(iii)** n can be positive, negative, or zero.

77. $-0.8157n > 7.304$ ii

78. $3.978n \le 0.615$ iii

79. $-917n \ge -10{,}512$ iii

OBJECTIVE C To solve application problems

80. Consider the following statement: Today's high temperature will be at least 10 degrees lower than yesterday's high temperature. If the inequality $T \leq t - 10$ correctly represents this statement, what does the variable t represent?
Yesterday's high temperature

81. **Mortgages** See the news clipping at the right. Suppose a couple's mortgage application is approved. Their monthly mortgage payment is $2050. What is the couple's monthly household income? Round to the nearest dollar.
$5395 or more

In the NEWS!

New Federal Standard for Mortgages

A new federal regulation states that the purchaser of a house is not to be approved for a monthly mortgage payment that is more than 38% of the purchaser's monthly household income.
Source: US News & World Report

82. **Sports** To be eligible for a basketball tournament, a basketball team must win at least 60% of its remaining games. If the team has 17 games remaining, how many games must the team win to qualify for the tournament?
11 or more games

83. **Health** A health official recommends a maximum cholesterol level of 200 units. By how many units must a patient with a cholesterol level of 275 units reduce her cholesterol level to satisfy the recommended maximum level?
75 or more units

84. **Recycling** A service organization will receive a bonus of $200 for collecting more than 1850 lb of aluminum cans during its four collection drives. On the first three drives, the organization collected 505 lb, 493 lb, and 412 lb. How many pounds of cans must the organization collect on the fourth drive to receive the bonus?
More than 440 lb

85. **Grading** To pass a course with a B grade, a student must have an average of 80 points on five tests. The student's grades on the first four tests were 75, 83, 86, and 78. What scores can the student receive on the fifth test to earn a B grade?
78 or higher

Alternative Energy For Exercises 86 to 88, use the information in the article at the right.

In the NEWS!

New Law Eases Restrictions on Small Wind Systems

A research project created by students in the University of New Hampshire's Environmental Politics class has led to a change in New Hampshire state law. Under the new law, a small wind turbine installed on a residential property must be set back from the property line by a distance greater than 150% of the turbine height. Individual towns may lower the 150% requirement, but they may not increase it.
Source: www.gencourt.state.nh.us

86. **a.** A couple living in a town that has not changed the set-back requirement wants to install an 80-foot wind turbine on their property. How far back from the property line must the turbine be set? More than 120 ft

b. Suppose the town lowers the 150% requirement to 125%. How far back from the property line must the turbine be set? More than 100 ft

87. You live in a town that has not changed the set-back requirement. You want to install a wind turbine 68 ft from your property line. To the nearest foot, what is the height of the tallest wind turbine you can install? 45 ft

88. You live in a town that has changed the set-back requirement to 115%. A good spot for a wind turbine on your property is 75 ft from the property line. To the nearest foot, what is the height of the tallest wind turbine you can install? 65 ft

Critical Thinking

89. How does the solution set of $x \leq 4$ differ from the solution set of $x < 4$?
$x \leq 4$ includes the element 4; $x < 4$ does not.

90. True or false: The solution set of $x \geq 4$ is the set $\{4, 5, 6, 7, 8, 9, \ldots\}$ False

For Exercises 91 and 92, write an inequality that describes the graph.

91. 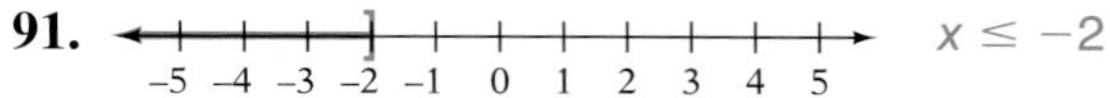

$x \leq -2$

92. –5 –4 –3 –2 –1 0 1 2 3 4 5 $x > -4$

Projects or Group Activities

For Exercises 93 to 96, graph the solution set.

93. $|x| < 3$ –5 –4 –3 –2 –1 0 1 2 3 4 5

94. $|x| < 4$ –5 –4 –3 –2 –1 0 1 2 3 4 5

95. $|x| > 2$ –5 –4 –3 –2 –1 0 1 2 3 4 5

96. $|x| > 1$ –5 –4 –3 –2 –1 0 1 2 3 4 5

QUICK QUIZ

1. Solve. Write answers in set-builder notation.
   a. $7n - 3 \geq 2 + 6n$ $\{n|n \geq 5\}$
   b. $b + \frac{1}{6} < -\frac{3}{4}$ $\left\{b|b < -\frac{11}{12}\right\}$ **[14.2A]**

Write answers in interval notation.

2. Solve and graph the solution set of $-2 \leq 2x$. **$[-1, \infty)$**

[14.2B]

3. Solve. a. $\frac{3}{7} < \frac{9}{14}x$ $\left(\frac{2}{3}, \infty\right)$
   b. $-5a > 0$ **$(-\infty, 0)$ [14.2B]**

4. To earn an A in a course, a student must have an average of 90 or more on five tests. One student's first four test scores were 78, 88, 92, and 95. What scores can the student receive on the fifth test to earn an A?
   97 or more [14.2C]

CHECK YOUR PROGRESS: CHAPTER 14

1. Use the roster method to write the set of integers between -12 and -9. $\{-11, -10\}$ [14.1A]

2. Find $A \cup B$, given $A = \{4, 8, 16, 20\}$ and $B = \{8, 16, 24\}$.
$A \cup B = \{4, 8, 16, 20, 24\}$ [14.1A]

3. Find $A \cap B$, given $A = \{10, 20, 30, 40\}$ and $B = \{20, 40, 60, 80\}$.
$A \cap B = \{20, 40\}$ [14.1A]

4. Find $A \cap B$, given $A = \{-3, -2, -1, 0\}$ and $B = \{1, 2, 3\}$.
$A \cap B = \varnothing$ [14.1A]

5. Write $\{x|-1 \leq x \leq 3\}$ in interval notation.
$[-1, 3]$ [14.1B]

6. Write $\{x|x > 8\}$ in interval notation.
$(8, \infty)$ [14.1B]

7. Write $[-9, \infty)$ in set-builder notation.
$\{x|x \geq -9\}$ [14.1B]

8. Write $(-4, 7]$ in set-builder notation.
$\{x|-4 < x \leq 7\}$ [14.1B]

9. Graph: $(-5, \infty)$

–5 –4 –3 –2 –1 0 1 2 3 4 5 [14.1B]

10. Graph: $\{x|-3 \leq x < 5\}$

–5 –4 –3 –2 –1 0 1 2 3 4 5 [14.1B]

11. Solve $x - 5 \geq -3$ and write the answer in set-builder notation. Graph the solution set.

$\{x|x \geq 2\}$ 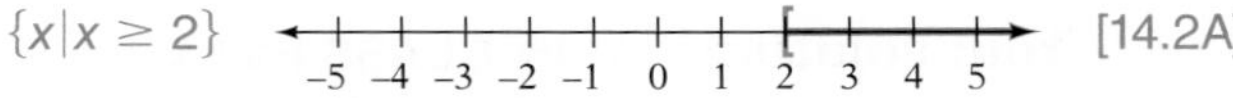

[14.2A]

12. Solve $4 < x + 7$ and write the answer in interval notation. Graph the solution set.

$(-3, \infty)$ 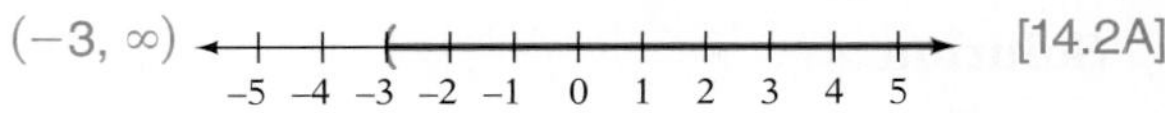

[14.2A]

13. Solve $10x - 15 \leq 9x - 20$ and write the answer in set-builder notation.
$\{x|x \leq -5\}$ [14.2A]

14. Solve $-12 \leq -3x$ and write the answer in interval notation.
$(-\infty, 4)$ [14.2B]

15. **Grading** A student must have at least 400 points out of 500 points on five tests to receive an A in a course. One student's results on the first four tests were 88, 91, 83, and 76. What scores on the last test will enable the student to receive an A in the course? 62 or higher [14.2C]

SECTION

14.3 General Inequalities

OBJECTIVE A *To solve general inequalities*

Solving an inequality frequently requires application of both the Addition and Multiplication Properties of Inequalities.

HOW TO 1 Solve and write the answer in interval notation: $4y - 3 \geq 6y + 5$

$4y - 3 \geq 6y + 5$

$4y - 6y - 3 \geq 6y - 6y + 5$ • **Subtract 6*y* from each side of the inequality.**

$-2y - 3 \geq 5$ • **Simplify.**

$-2y - 3 + 3 \geq 5 + 3$ • **Add 3 to each side of the inequality.**

$-2y \geq 8$ • **Simplify.**

$\dfrac{-2y}{-2} \leq \dfrac{8}{-2}$ • **Divide each side of the inequality by −2. Because −2 is a negative number, the inequality symbol must be reversed.**

$y \leq -4$

$(-\infty, -4]$ • **Write in interval notation.**

Take Note
When an inequality contains parentheses, one of the steps in solving the inequality is to use the Distributive Property.

HOW TO 2 Solve and write the answer in set-builder notation: $-2(x - 7) > 8 - 4(2x - 3)$

$-2(x - 7) > 8 - 4(2x - 3)$

$-2x + 14 > 8 - 8x + 12$ • **Use the Distributive Property.**

$-2x + 14 > -8x + 20$ • **Simplify.**

$-2x + 8x + 14 > -8x + 8x + 20$ • **Add 8*x* to each side of the inequality.**

$6x + 14 > 20$ • **Simplify.**

$6x + 14 - 14 > 20 - 14$ • **Subtract 14 from each side of the inequality.**

$6x > 6$ • **Simplify.**

$\dfrac{6x}{6} > \dfrac{6}{6}$ • **Divide each side of the inequality by 6.**

$x > 1$

$\{x \mid x > 1\}$ • **Write in set-builder notation.**

EXAMPLE 1

Solve and write the answer in interval notation:
$7x - 3 \leq 3x + 17$

Solution

$7x - 3 \leq 3x + 17$

$7x - 3x - 3 \leq 3x - 3x + 17$ • **Subtract 3*x* from each side.**

$4x - 3 \leq 17$

$4x - 3 + 3 \leq 17 + 3$ • **Add 3 to each side.**

$4x \leq 20$

$\dfrac{4x}{4} \leq \dfrac{20}{4}$ • **Divide each side by 4.**

$x \leq 5$

$(-\infty, 5]$

YOU TRY IT 1

Solve and write the answer in interval notation:
$5 - 4x > 9 - 8x$

Your solution

$(1, \infty)$

IN-CLASS EXAMPLES
Solve. Write answers in interval notation.

1. $0.3(70 + x) \leq x$ **$[30, \infty)$**
2. $9 - 5(1 - 2x) > 6(x + 4)$ **$(5, \infty)$**
3. $-3(8x + 2) < 5(8 - 4x)$ $\left(-\dfrac{23}{2}, \infty\right)$

Solution on p. S35

EXAMPLE 2

Solve and write the answer in set-builder notation: $3(3 - 2x) \geq -5x - 2(3 - x)$

Solution

$$3(3 - 2x) \geq -5x - 2(3 - x)$$
$$9 - 6x \geq -5x - 6 + 2x \quad \text{• Distributive Property}$$
$$9 - 6x \geq -3x - 6$$
$$9 - 6x + 3x \geq -3x + 3x - 6 \quad \text{• Add } 3x \text{ to each side.}$$
$$9 - 3x \geq -6$$
$$9 - 9 - 3x \geq -6 - 9 \quad \text{• Subtract 9 from each side.}$$
$$-3x \geq -15$$
$$\frac{-3x}{-3} \leq \frac{-15}{-3} \quad \text{• Divide each side by } -3.$$
$$x \leq 5$$
$$\{x \mid x \leq 5\}$$

YOU TRY IT 2

Solve and write the answer in set-builder notation: $8 - 4(3x + 5) \leq 6(x - 8)$

Your solution

$\{x \mid x \geq 2\}$

Solution on p. S35

OBJECTIVE B *To solve application problems*

EXAMPLE 3

A rectangle is 10 ft wide and $(2x + 4)$ ft long. Express as an integer the maximum length of the rectangle when the area is less than 200 ft^2. (The area of a rectangle is equal to its length times its width.)

Strategy

To find the maximum length:
- Replace the variables in the area formula by the given values and solve for x.
- Replace the variable in the expression $2x + 4$ with the value found for x.

Solution

Length times width	is less than	200 ft^2

$$10(2x + 4) < 200$$
$$20x + 40 < 200 \quad \text{• Distributive Property}$$
$$20x + 40 - 40 < 200 - 40 \quad \text{• Subtract 40 from each side.}$$
$$20x < 160$$
$$\frac{20x}{20} < \frac{160}{20} \quad \text{• Divide each side by 20.}$$
$$x < 8$$

The length is $(2x + 4)$ ft. Because $x < 8$, $2x + 4 < 2(8) + 4 = 20$. Therefore, the length is less than 20 ft. The maximum length is 19 ft.

YOU TRY IT 3

Company A rents cars for \$8 a day and \$.10 for every mile driven. Company B rents cars for \$10 a day and \$.08 per mile driven. You want to rent a car for one week. What is the maximum number of miles you can drive a Company A car if it is to cost you less than a Company B car?

Your strategy

Your solution

699 mi

IN-CLASS EXAMPLES

4. The label on a bottle of juice says that the drink is at least 15% real fruit juice. If the manufacturer begins with 450 oz of real juice, how many ounces of water and other ingredients can be added while still keeping the final mixture at least 15% real juice? **2550 oz or less**

Solution on p. S35

14.3 EXERCISES

Concept Check

SUGGESTED ASSIGNMENT:
Exercises 1–4; Exercises 5–31, odds

Determine whether the statement is true or false.

1. Both "is greater than" and "is more than" are represented by the inequality symbol $\geq$. False
2. A minimum refers to a lower limit, whereas a maximum refers to an upper limit. True
3. Given that $x > \frac{32}{6}$, the minimum integer that satisfies the inequality is 6. True
4. Given that $x < \frac{25}{4}$, the maximum integer that satisfies the inequality is 7. False

OBJECTIVE A To solve general inequalities

For Exercises 5 to 13, solve and write the answer in interval notation.

5. $4x - 8 < 2x$ $(-\infty, 4)$
6. $7x - 4 < 3x$ $(-\infty, 1)$
7. $2x - 8 > 4x$ $(-\infty, -4)$
8. $3y + 2 > 7y$ $\left(-\infty, \frac{1}{2}\right)$
9. $8 - 3x \leq 5x$ $[1, \infty)$
10. $10 - 3x \leq 7x$ $[1, \infty)$
11. $3x + 2 > 5x - 8$ $(-\infty, 5)$
12. $2n - 9 \geq 5n + 4$ $\left(-\infty, -\frac{13}{3}\right]$
13. $5x - 2 < 3x - 2$ $(-\infty, 0)$

For Exercises 14 to 24, solve and write the answer in set-builder notation.

14. $8x - 9 > 3x - 9$ $\{x|x > 0\}$
15. $0.1(180 + x) > x$ $\{x|x < 20\}$
16. $x > 0.2(50 + x)$ $\{x|x > 12.5\}$
17. $2(2y - 5) \leq 3(5 - 2y)$ $\left\{y|y \leq \frac{5}{2}\right\}$
18. $2(5x - 8) \leq 7(x - 3)$ $\left\{x|x \leq -\frac{5}{3}\right\}$
19. $5(2 - x) > 3(2x - 5)$ $\left\{x|x < \frac{25}{11}\right\}$
20. $4(3d - 1) > 3(2 - 5d)$ $\left\{d|d > \frac{10}{27}\right\}$
21. $4 - 3(3 - n) \leq 3(2 - 5n)$ $\left\{n|n \leq \frac{11}{18}\right\}$
22. $15 - 5(3 - 2x) \leq 4(x - 3)$ $\{x|x \leq -2\}$
23. $2x - 3(x - 4) \geq 4 - 2(x - 7)$ $\{x|x \geq 6\}$
24. $4 + 2(3 - 2y) \leq 4(3y - 5) - 6y$ $\{y|y \geq 3\}$
25. Which of the following inequalities are equivalent to the inequality $-7x - 2 > -4x + 1$?
(i) $-3 > -11x$ **(ii)** $3x > 3$ **(iii)** $-3 > 3x$ **(iv)** $3x < -3$ iii and iv

OBJECTIVE B To solve application problems

© iStockphoto.com/Sean Locke

26. An automatic garage door opener costs \$325 plus an installation labor charge of \$30 per hour, with a minimum of 1 h and a maximum of 3 h of labor. Which of the following are *not* possible amounts for the total cost of the door and installation?
(i) \$355 **(ii)** \$450 **(iii)** \$325 **(iv)** \$415 **(v)** \$350 ii, iii, and v

27. **Compensation** A sales agent for a jewelry company is offered a flat monthly salary of \$3200 or a base salary of \$1000 plus an 11% commission on the selling price of each item sold by the agent. If the agent chooses the \$3200 flat salary, what dollar amount does the agent expect to sell in one month?
\$20,000 or less

28. **Compensation** A baseball player is offered an annual salary of \$200,000 or a base salary of \$100,000 plus a bonus of \$1000 for each hit over 100 hits. How many hits must the baseball player make to earn more than \$200,000?
201 or more hits

29. **Comparing Services** A site licensing fee for a computer program is \$1500. Paying this fee allows the company to use the program at any computer terminal within the company. Alternatively, the company can choose to pay \$200 for each individual computer it owns. How many individual computers must a company own for the site license to be the more economical choice for the company?
8 or more computers

30. **Transportation** A shuttle service taking skiers to a ski area charges \$8 per person each way. Four skiers are debating whether to take the shuttle bus or rent a car for \$45 plus \$.25 per mile. Assuming that the skiers will share the cost of the car and that they want the least expensive method of transportation, how far away is the ski area if they choose the shuttle service?
More than 38 mi

© Photobac/Shutterstock.com

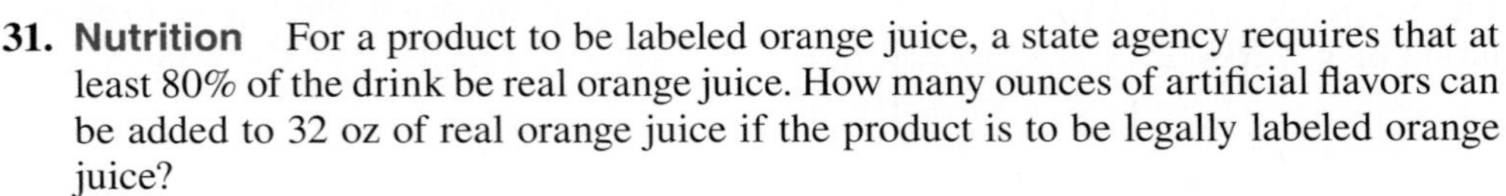

31. **Nutrition** For a product to be labeled orange juice, a state agency requires that at least 80% of the drink be real orange juice. How many ounces of artificial flavors can be added to 32 oz of real orange juice if the product is to be legally labeled orange juice?
8 oz or less

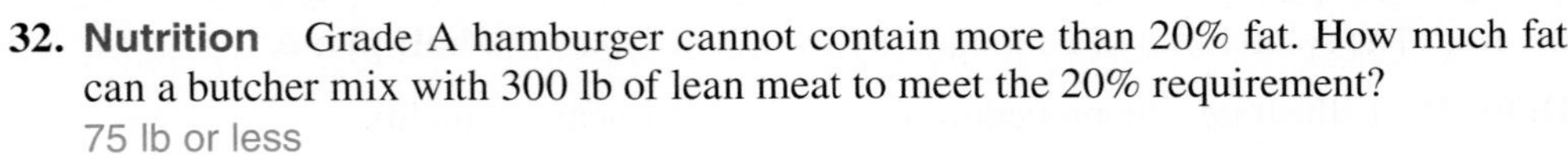

32. **Nutrition** Grade A hamburger cannot contain more than 20% fat. How much fat can a butcher mix with 300 lb of lean meat to meet the 20% requirement?
75 lb or less

Critical Thinking

33. What number is a solution of $3x - 4 \geq 5$ but not a solution of $3x - 4 > 5$? 3

34. What number is a solution of $8 - 2(x + 6) \leq 4$ but not a solution of $8 - 2(x + 6) < 4$? -4

35. A theorem from geometry called the Triangle Inequality Theorem states that the sum of the lengths of two sides of a triangle must be greater than the length of the third side. Suppose two sides of a triangle measure 10 in. and 18 in. Let x be the length of the third side. What are the possible values for x? Between 8 in. and 28 in.

Projects or Group Activities

36. Determine whether the statement is always true, sometimes true, or never true, given that a, b, and c are real numbers.
    a. If $a > b$, then $-a > -b$. Never true
    b. If $a < b$, then $ac < bc$. Sometimes true
    c. If $a > b$, then $a + c > b + c$. Always true
    d. If $a \neq 0$, $b \neq 0$, and $a > b$, then $\frac{1}{a} > \frac{1}{b}$. Sometimes true

QUICK QUIZ

Solve. Write answers in set-builder notation.

1. $3x - 7 \leq 7x + 11$
$\left\{x \mid x \geq -\frac{9}{2}\right\}$ **[14.3A]**
2. $4(5 - x) > 3(2x + 10)$
$\{x \mid x < -1\}$ **[14.3A]**
3. $12 - 3(4x - 1) \geq 6(4 - 3x)$
$\left\{x \mid x \geq \frac{3}{2}\right\}$ **[14.3A]**
4. A telephone company offers two plans: a flat monthly fee of \$36, or a monthly fee of \$6 with a charge of \$.15 per minute of calling time. How many minutes of calling time per month must a person use for the flat fee of \$36 to be the less expensive option?
More than 200 min [14.3B]

SECTION

14.4 Graphing Linear Inequalities

OBJECTIVE A *To graph an inequality in two variables*

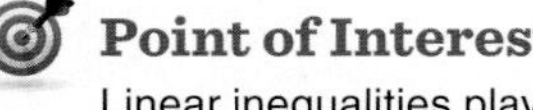

Point of Interest

Linear inequalities play an important role in applied mathematics. They are used in a branch of mathematics called *linear programming,* which was developed during World War II to help with the logistics of supplying the Air Force with the machine parts necessary to keep planes flying. Today, linear programming applications extend to many other disciplines.

Tips for Success

Be sure to do all you need to do in order to be successful at graphing linear inequalities: Read through the introductory material, work through the HOW TO example, study the paired examples, do the You Try Its, and check your solutions against those in the back of the book. See *AIM for Success* at the front of the book.

INSTRUCTOR NOTE

Show students that as long as the graph of an equation does not pass through the origin, the ordered pair (0, 0) affords an easy check of the correct region to shade. If (0, 0) satisfies the linear inequality, then the point (0, 0) should be included in the shaded region. If (0, 0) does not satisfy the inequality, the point (0, 0) should not be in the shaded region.

The graph of the linear equation $y = x - 2$ separates a plane into three sets:
the set of points on the line,
the set of points above the line, and
the set of points below the line.

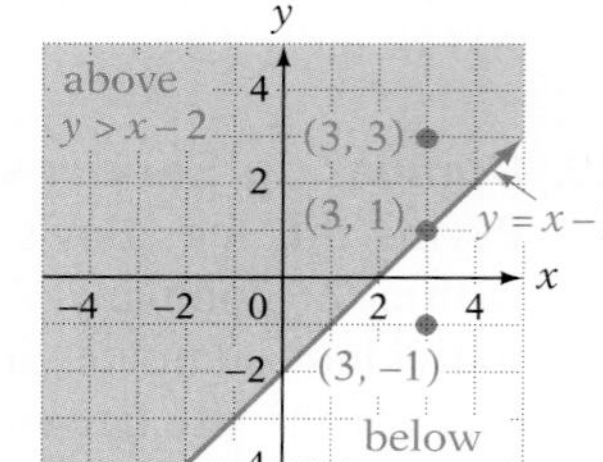

The point (3, 1) is a solution of $y = x - 2$.

$$\begin{array}{c|c} \multicolumn{2}{c}{y = x - 2} \\ \hline 1 & 3 - 2 \\ \multicolumn{2}{c}{1 = 1} \end{array}$$

The point (3, 3) is a solution of $y > x - 2$.

$$\begin{array}{c|c} \multicolumn{2}{c}{y > x - 2} \\ \hline 3 & 3 - 2 \\ \multicolumn{2}{c}{3 > 1} \end{array}$$

Any point above the line is a solution of $y > x - 2$.

The point $(3, -1)$ is a solution of $y < x - 2$.

$$\begin{array}{c|c} \multicolumn{2}{c}{y < x - 2} \\ \hline -1 & 3 - 2 \\ \multicolumn{2}{c}{-1 < 1} \end{array}$$

Any point below the line is a solution of $y < x - 2$.

The solution set of $y = x - 2$ is all points on the line. The solution set of $y > x - 2$ is all points above the line. The solution set of $y < x - 2$ is all points below the line. The solution set of an inequality in two variables is a **half-plane.**

HOW TO 1 illustrates the procedure for graphing a linear inequality.

HOW TO 1 Graph the solution set of $2x + 3y \leq 6$.

Solve the inequality for y.

$$2x + 3y \leq 6$$
$$2x - 2x + 3y \leq -2x + 6 \quad \text{• Subtract } 2x \text{ from each side.}$$
$$3y \leq -2x + 6 \quad \text{• Simplify.}$$
$$\frac{3y}{3} \leq \frac{-2x + 6}{3} \quad \text{• Divide each side by 3.}$$
$$y \leq -\frac{2}{3}x + 2 \quad \text{• Simplify.}$$

Change the inequality to an equality and graph $y = -\frac{2}{3}x + 2$. If the inequality is $\geq$ or $\leq$, the line is part of the solution set and is shown by a solid line. If the inequality is $>$ or $<$, the line is not part of the solution set and is shown by a dashed line.

If the inequality is $>$ or $\geq$, shade the upper half-plane. If the inequality is $<$ or $\leq$, shade the lower half-plane.

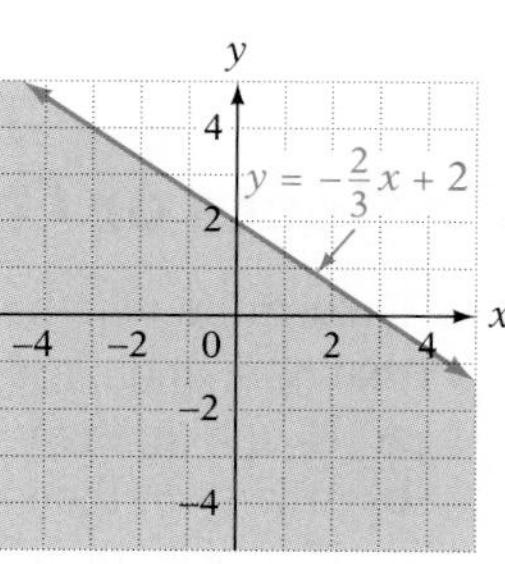

EXAMPLE 1

Graph the solution set of $3x + y > -2$.

Solution

$$3x + y > -2$$
$$3x - 3x + y > -3x - 2$$
$$y > -3x - 2$$

• Subtract $3x$ from each side.

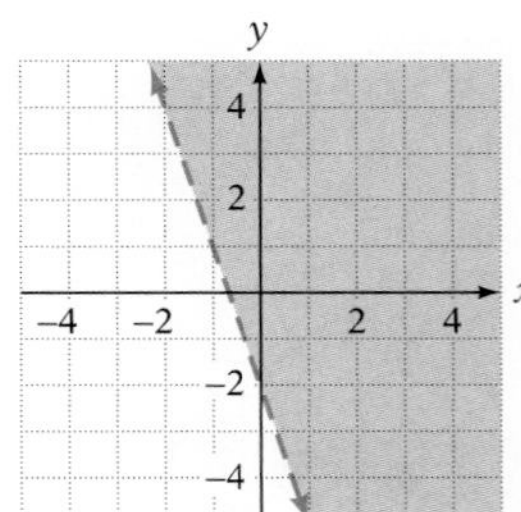

• Graph $y = -3x - 2$ as a dashed line. Shade the upper half-plane.

YOU TRY IT 1

Graph the solution set of $x - 3y < 2$.

Your solution

$y > \frac{1}{3}x - \frac{2}{3}$

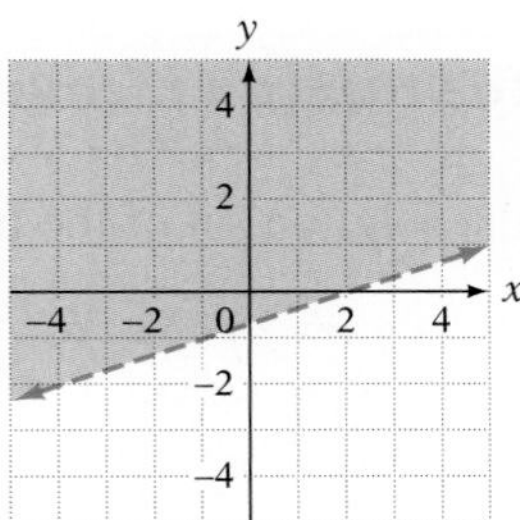

IN-CLASS EXAMPLES

Graph the solution set.

1. $x - y < -2$
2. $3x + 4y \leq -12$
3. $x \geq -1$

EXAMPLE 2

Graph the solution set of $2x - y \geq 2$.

Solution

$$2x - y \geq 2$$
$$2x - 2x - y \geq -2x + 2$$
$$-y \geq -2x + 2$$
$$-1(-y) \leq -1(-2x + 2)$$
$$y \leq 2x - 2$$

• Subtract $2x$ from each side.

• Multiply each side by -1.

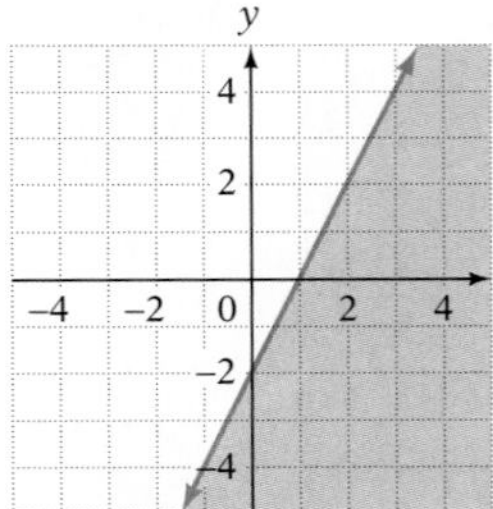

• Graph $y = 2x - 2$ as a solid line. Shade the lower half-plane.

YOU TRY IT 2

Graph the solution set of $2x - 4y \leq 8$.

Your solution

$y \geq \frac{1}{2}x - 2$

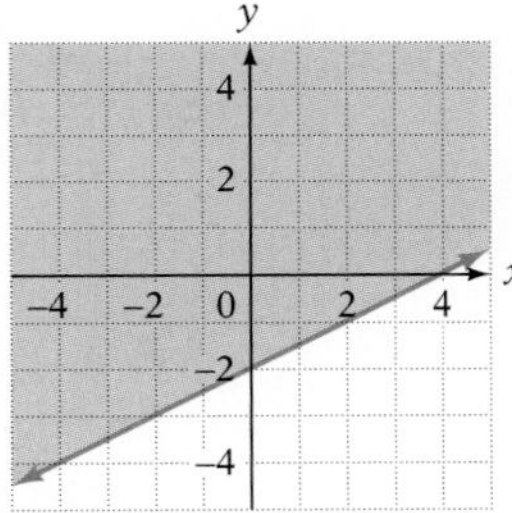

EXAMPLE 3

Graph the solution set of $y > -1$.

Solution

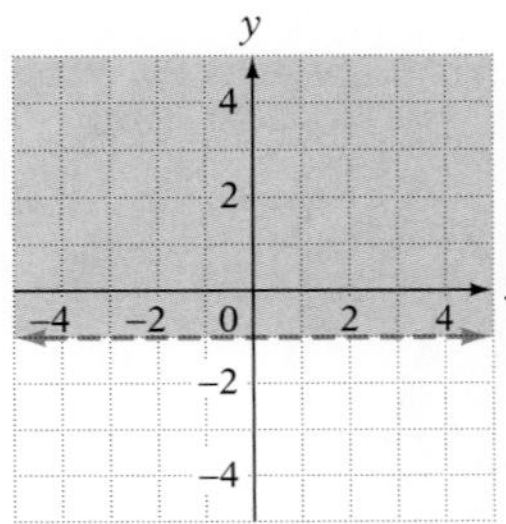

• Graph $y = -1$ as a dashed line. Shade the upper half-plane.

YOU TRY IT 3

Graph the solution set of $x < 3$.

Your solution

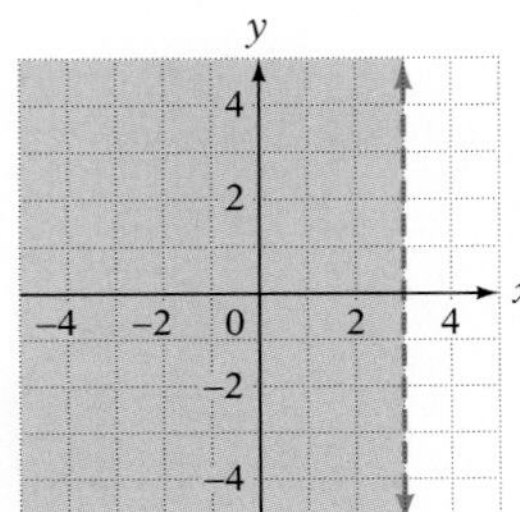

Solutions on p. S35

14.4 EXERCISES

Concept Check

SUGGESTED ASSIGNMENT:
Exercises 1–4; Exercises 5–21, odds

For Exercises 1 to 4, determine whether (0, 0) is a solution of the inequality.

1. $y < -5x + 2$ Yes **2.** $y > x + 1$ No **3.** $y \le \frac{1}{4}x - 5$ No **4.** $y \ge -\frac{2}{3}x - 6$ Yes

OBJECTIVE A *To graph an inequality in two variables*

For Exercises 5 to 22, graph the solution set of the inequality.

5. $y > -x + 4$

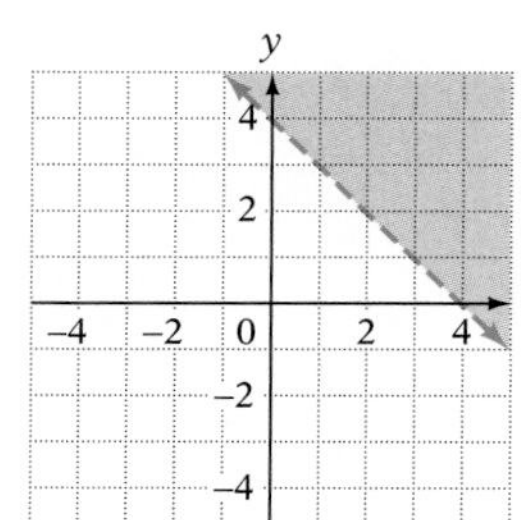

6. $y < x + 3$

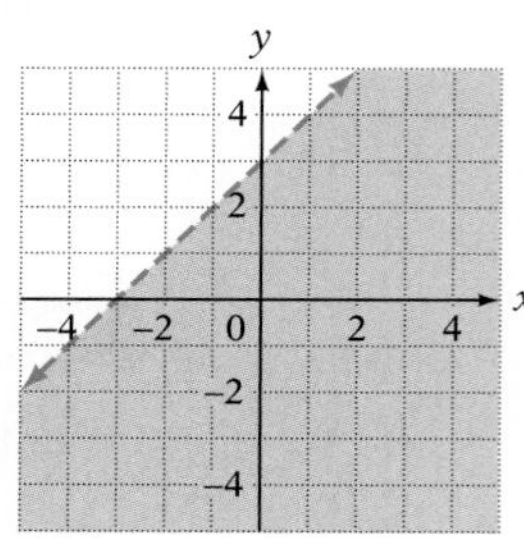

7. $y > 2x + 3$

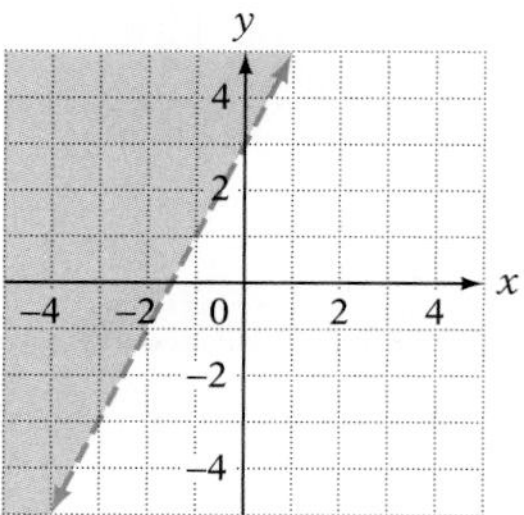

8. $y > 3x - 9$

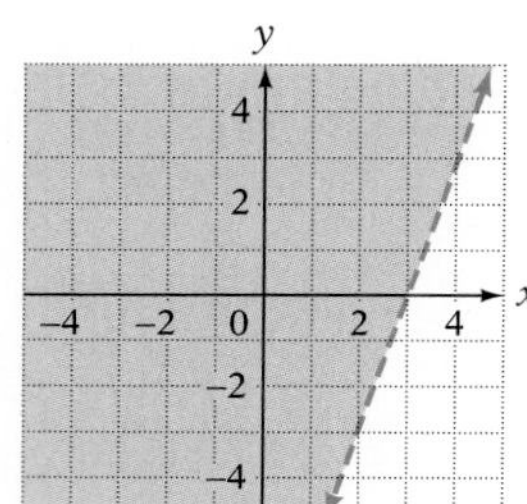

9. $2x + y \ge 4$

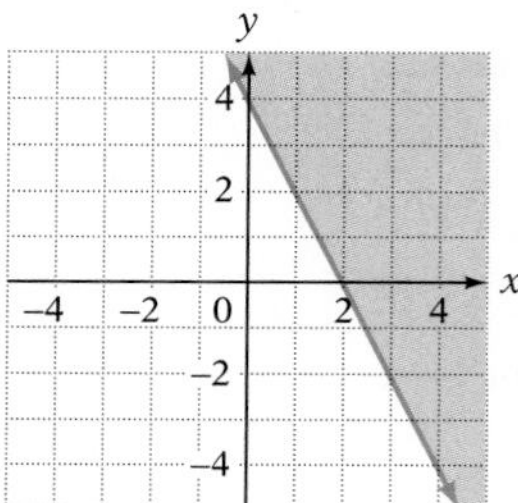

10. $3x + y \ge 6$

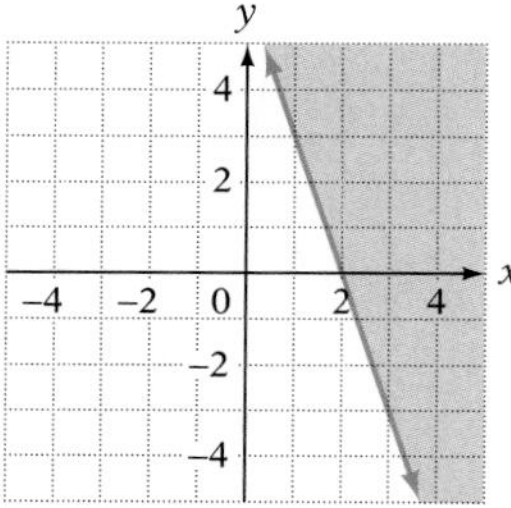

11. $y \le -2$

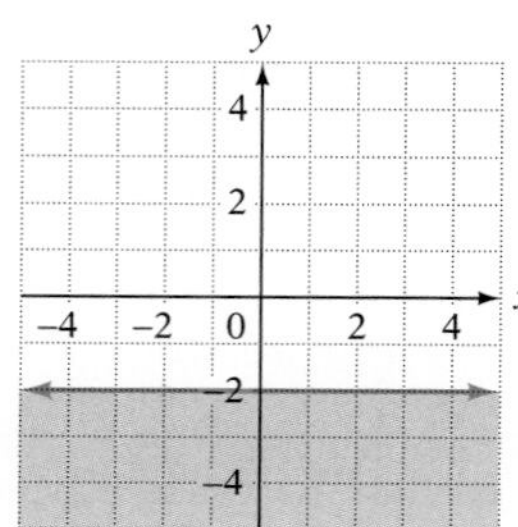

12. $y > 3$

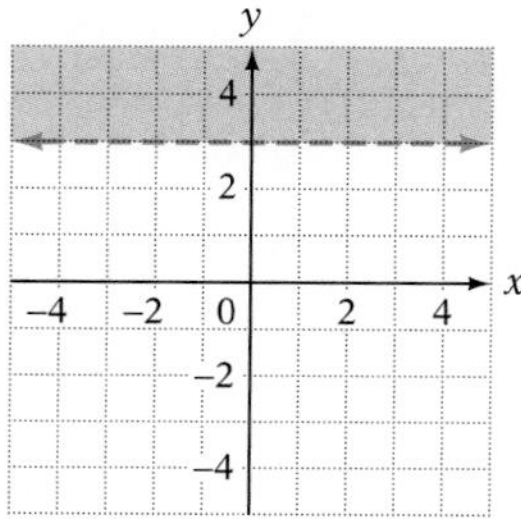

13. $3x - 2y < 8$

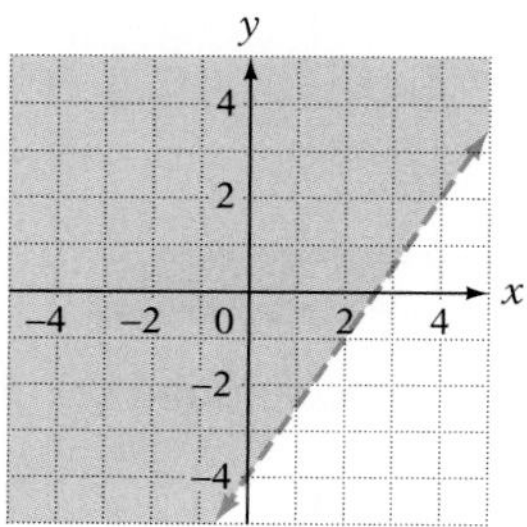

14. $5x + 4y > 4$

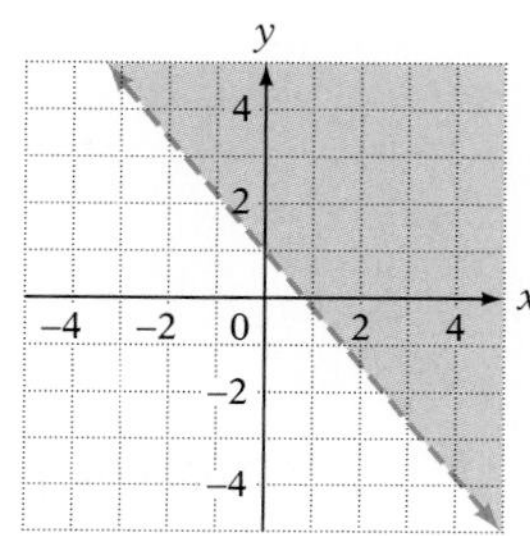

15. $-3x - 4y \ge 4$

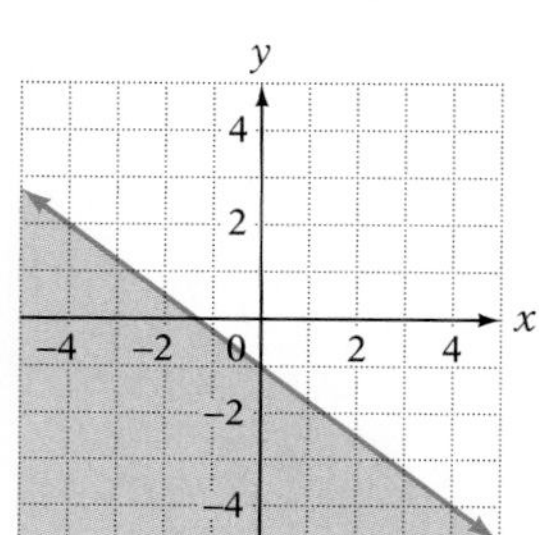

16. $-5x - 2y \ge 8$

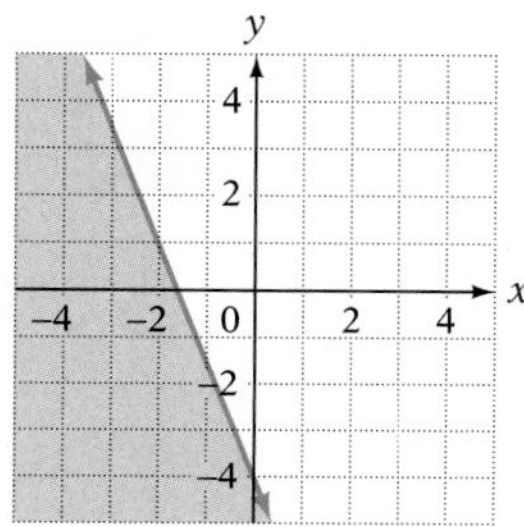

17. $6x + 5y \leq -10$

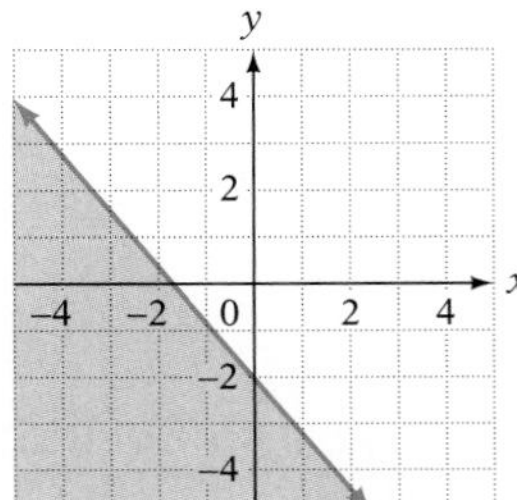

18. $2x + 2y \leq -4$

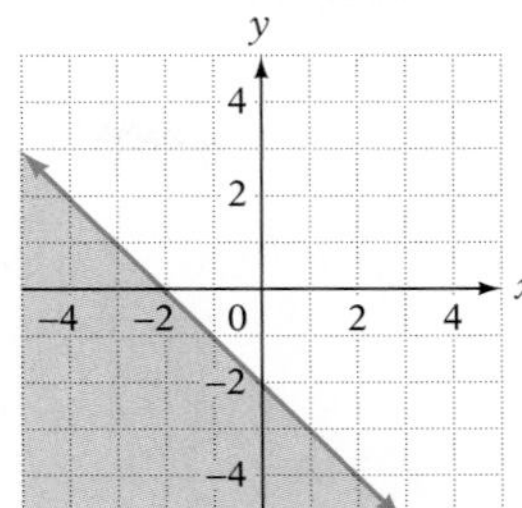

19. $-4x + 3y < -12$

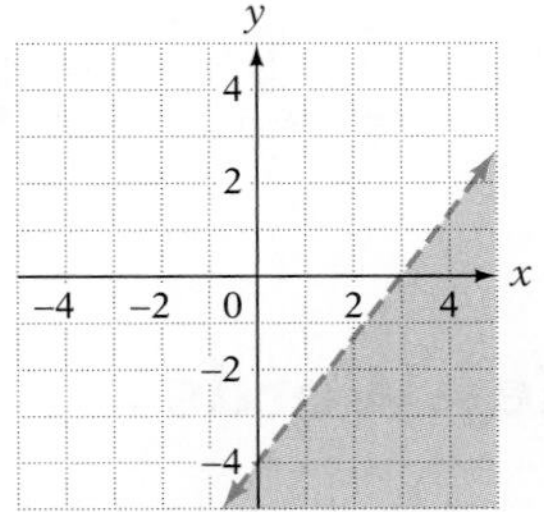

20. $-4x + 5y < 15$

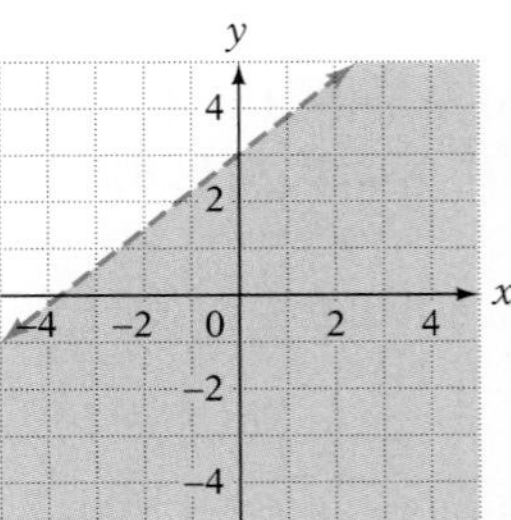

21. $-2x + 3y \leq 6$

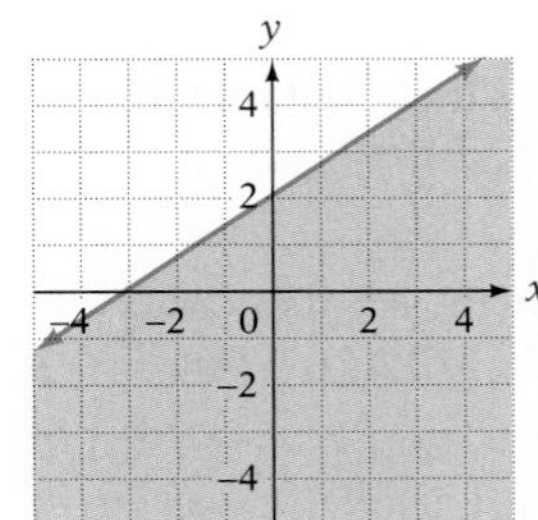

22. $3x - 4y > 12$

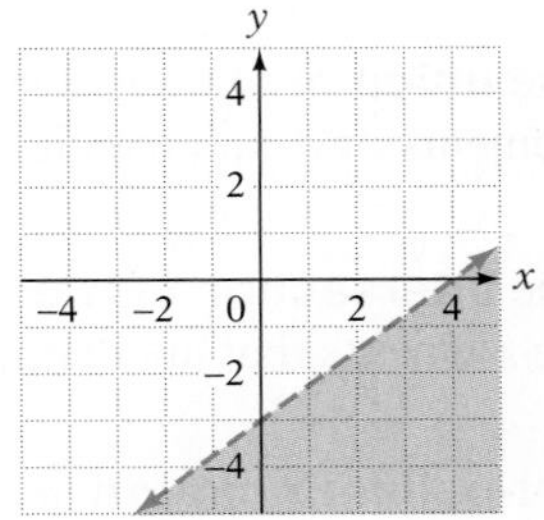

23. Suppose (0, 0) is a point on the graph of the linear inequality $Ax + By > C$, where C is not zero. Is C positive or negative? Negative

24. Suppose $Ax + By < C$, where C is a negative number. Is (0, 0) a point on the graph of $Ax + By < C$? No

Critical Thinking

For Exercises 25 to 27, write the inequality given its graph.

25.

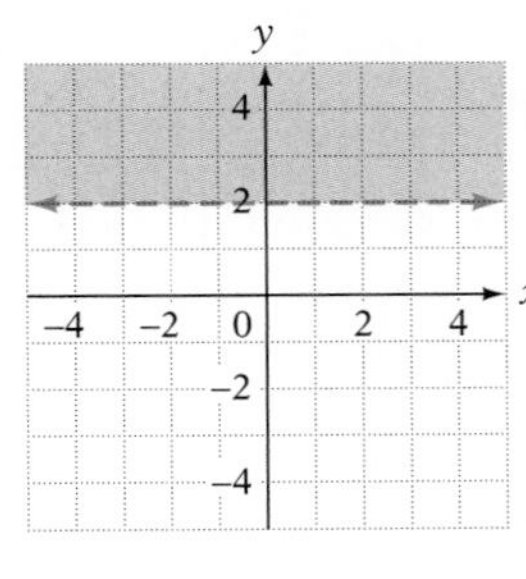

$y > 2$

26.

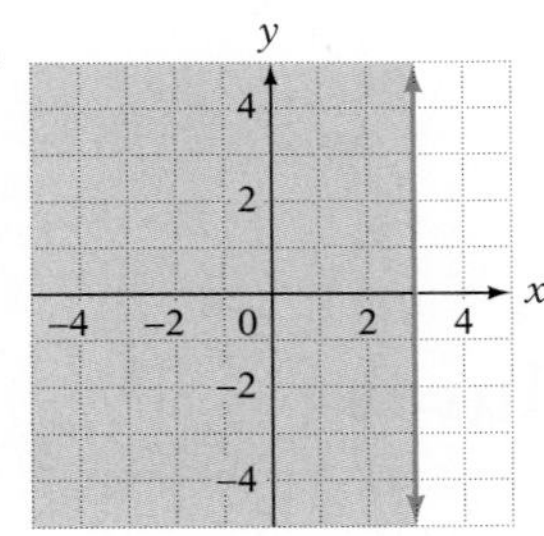

$x \leq 3$

27.

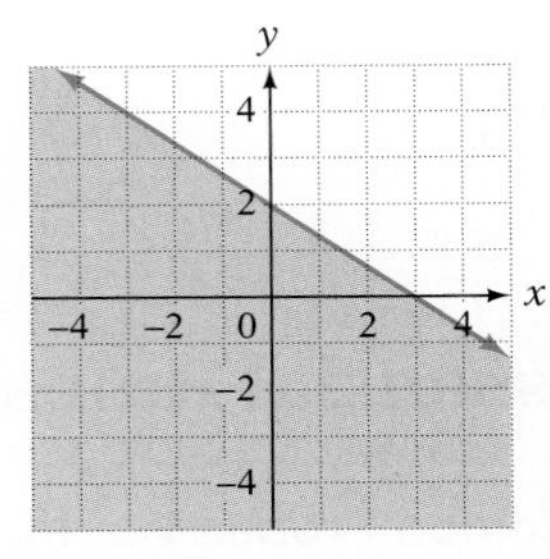

$y \leq -\frac{2}{3}x + 2$

Projects or Group Activities

28. Does an inequality in two variables define a relation? Why or why not? Does an inequality in two variables define a function? Why or why not?

29. Are there any points whose coordinates satisfy both $y < 2x - 3$ and $y > -\frac{1}{4}x + 1$? If so, give the coordinates of three such points. If not, explain why not.

30. Are there any points whose coordinates satisfy both $y > 3x + 1$ and $y < 3x - 4$? If so, give the coordinates of three such points. If not, explain why not.

QUICK QUIZ

Graph the solution set.

1. $x - 2y \geq 2$ **[14.4A]**
2. $y > -x + 3$ **[14.4A]**
3. $y < 1$ **[14.4A]**

CHAPTER 14 Summary

Key Words

The **roster method** of writing a set encloses a list of the elements in braces. The **empty set** or **null set,** written $\emptyset$, is the set that contains no elements. [14.1A, p. 740]

Example: The set of positive integers less than 5 is $\{1, 2, 3, 4\}$. The set of positive integers less than 1 is $\emptyset$.

The **union** of two sets, written $A \cup B$, is the set that contains the elements of A and the elements of B. [14.1A, p. 740]

Example: Let $A = \{2, 4, 6, 8\}$ and $B = \{0, 1, 2, 3, 4\}$. Then $A \cup B = \{0, 1, 2, 3, 4, 6, 8\}$.

The **intersection** of two sets, written $A \cap B$, is the set that contains the elements that are common to both A and B. [14.1A, p. 740]

Example: Let $A = \{2, 4, 6, 8\}$ and $B = \{0, 1, 2, 3, 4\}$. Then $A \cap B = \{2, 4\}$.

Set-builder notation and **interval notation** are used to describe the elements of a set. [14.1B, pp. 741–742]

Example: The set of real numbers greater than 2 is written in set-builder notation as $\{x \mid x > 2\}$ and in interval notation as $(2, \infty)$.

The **solution set of an inequality** is a set of numbers each element of which, when substituted for the variable, results in a true inequality. The solution set of an inequality can be graphed on a number line. [14.2A, p. 747]

Example: The solution set of $3x - 1 < 5$ is $\{x \mid x < 2\}$. The graph of the solution set is

−5 −4 −3 −2 −1 0 1 2 3 4 5

The solution set of a linear inequality in two variables is a **half-plane.** [14.4A, p. 760]

Example: The solution set of $3x + 4y \geq 12$ is the half-plane shown at the right.

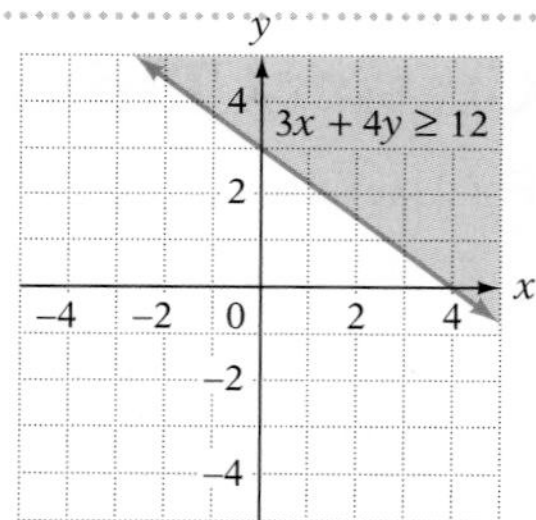

Essential Rules and Procedures

Addition Property of Inequalities [14.2A, p. 747]
The same term can be added to each side of an inequality without changing the solution set of the inequality.

If $a > b$, then $a + c > b + c$.
If $a < b$, then $a + c < b + c$.

Example:

$$x - 3 < -7$$
$$x - 3 + 3 < -7 + 3$$
$$x < -4$$

Multiplication Property of Inequalities [14.2B, p. 749]
Each side of an inequality can be multiplied by the same positive number without changing the solution set of the inequality.

If each side of an inequality is multiplied by the same negative number and the inequality symbol is reversed, then the solution set of the inequality is not changed.

Examples:

$$4x > -8 \qquad \frac{4x}{4} > \frac{-8}{4} \qquad x > -2$$

$$-2x < 6 \qquad \frac{-2x}{-2} > \frac{6}{-2} \qquad x > -3$$

CHAPTER 14 Review Exercises

1. Solve and write the solution in set-builder notation: $2x - 3 > x + 15$
$\{x|x > 18\}$ [14.2A]

2. Find $A \cap B$, given $A = \{0, 2, 4, 6, 8\}$ and $B = \{-2, -4\}$.
$A \cap B = \varnothing$ [14.1A]

3. Use set-builder notation to write the set of odd integers greater than -8.
$\{x \mid x > -8, x \in \text{odd integers}\}$ [14.1B]

4. Find $A \cup B$, given $A = \{6, 8, 10\}$ and $B = \{2, 4, 6\}$.
$A \cup B = \{2, 4, 6, 8, 10\}$ [14.1A]

5. Use the roster method to write the set of odd positive integers less than 8.
$A = \{1, 3, 5, 7\}$ [14.1A]

6. Solve and write the solution set in interval notation: $12 - 4(x - 1) \le 5(x - 4)$
$[4, \infty)$ [14.3A]

7. Graph: $\{x \mid x > 3\}$

−5 −4 −3 −2 −1 0 1 2 3 4 5 [14.1B]

8. Solve and write the solution set in set-builder notation: $3x + 4 \ge -8$
$\{x|x \ge -4\}$ [14.3A]

9. Graph: $3x + 2y \le 12$

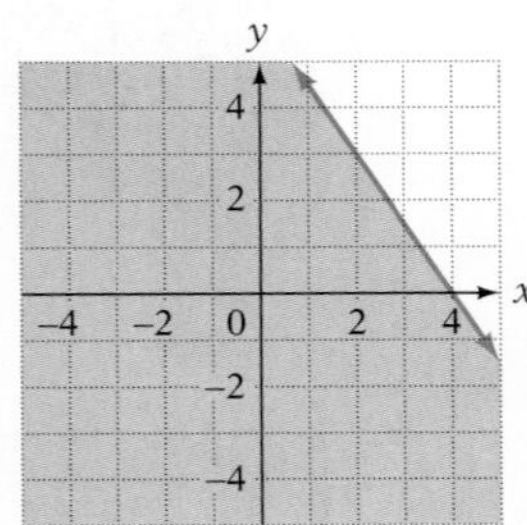

[14.4A]

10. Graph: $5x + 2y < 6$

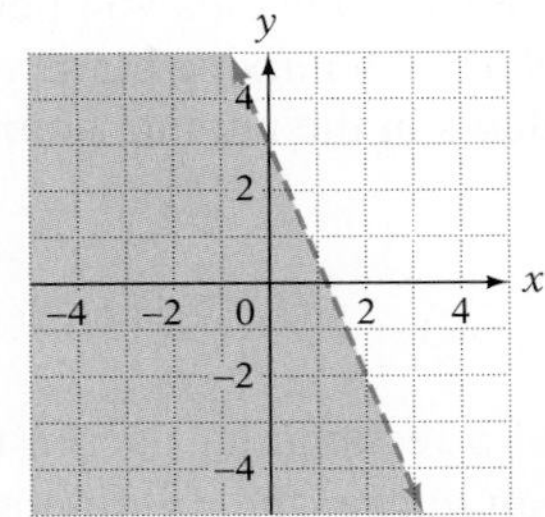

[14.4A]

11. Write the set $\{x \mid x > -4\}$ in interval notation.
$(-4, \infty)$ [14.1B]

12. Solve $x - 3 > -1$ and write the solution set in interval notation. Graph the solution set.

−5 −4 −3 −2 −1 0 1 2 3 4 5 $(2, \infty)$ [14.2A]

13. Find $A \cap B$, given $A = \{1, 5, 9, 13\}$ and $B = \{1, 3, 5, 7, 9\}$.
$A \cap B = \{1, 5, 9\}$ [14.1A]

14. Graph the interval $[1, 4]$.

−5 −4 −3 −2 −1 0 1 2 3 4 5 [14.1B]

15. Graph: $\{x | -1 < x \le 2\}$

-5 -4 -3 -2 -1 0 1 2 3 4 5 [14.1B]

16. Solve and write the solution set in set-builder notation: $-15x \le 45$
$\{x | x \ge -3\}$ [14.2B]

17. Solve and write the solution set in interval notation: $6x - 9 < 4x + 3(x + 3)$
$(-18, \infty)$ [14.3A]

18. Solve and write the solution set in set-builder notation: $5 - 4(x + 9) > 11(12x - 9)$
$\left\{x \middle| x < \frac{1}{2}\right\}$ [14.3A]

19. Solve and write the solution set in set-builder notation: $-\frac{3}{4}x > \frac{2}{3}$
$\left\{x \middle| x < -\frac{8}{9}\right\}$ [14.2B]

20. Solve and write the solution set in interval notation: $7x - 2(x + 3) \ge x + 10$
$[4, \infty)$ [14.3A]

21. Graph: $2x - 3y < 9$

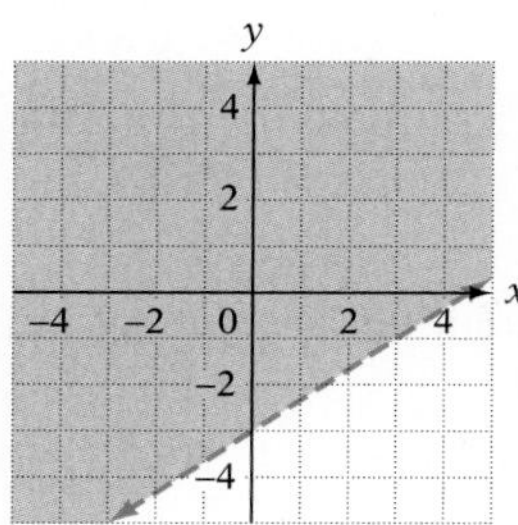

[14.4A]

22. **Floral Delivery** Florist A charges a \$6 delivery fee plus \$70 per bouquet delivered. Florist B charges a \$18 delivery fee plus \$64 per bouquet delivered. A church wants to supply each resident of a small nursing home with a bouquet for Grandparents Day. Find the number of residents in the nursing home if using florist B is more economical than using florist A.
3 or more [14.3B]

© ElenaGaak/Shutterstock.com

23. **Gardens** The width of a rectangular garden is 12 ft. The length of the garden is $(3x + 5)$ ft. Express as an integer the minimum length of the garden when the area is greater than 276 ft^2. (The area of a rectangle is equal to its length times its width.)
24 ft [14.3B]

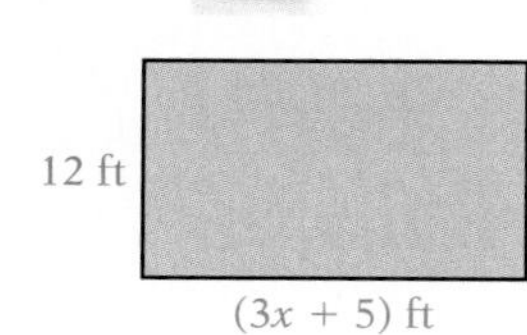

24. **Integer Problem** Six less than a number is greater than twenty-five. Find the smallest integer that will satisfy the inequality.
32 [14.2C]

25. **Grading** A student's grades on five sociology tests were 68, 82, 90, 73, and 95. What is the lowest score the student can receive on the next test and still be able to attain a minimum of 480 points?
72 [14.2C]

CHAPTER 14 TEST

1. Graph the interval (0, 5).

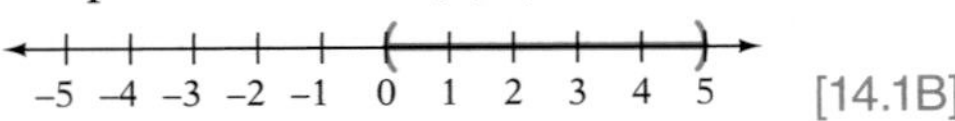

[14.1B]

2. Use set-builder notation to write the set of positive integers less than 50.
$\{x \mid x < 50, x \in \text{positive integers}\}$ [14.1B]

3. Use the roster method to write the set of the even positive integers between 3 and 9.
$A = \{4, 6, 8\}$ [14.1A]

4. Solve and write the solution set in interval notation: $3(2x - 5) \geq 8x - 9$
$(-\infty, -3]$ [14.3A]

5. Solve and write the solution set in set-builder notation: $x + \frac{1}{2} > \frac{5}{8}$
$\left\{x \middle| x > \frac{1}{8}\right\}$ [14.2A]

6. Graph: $\{x \mid x > -2\}$

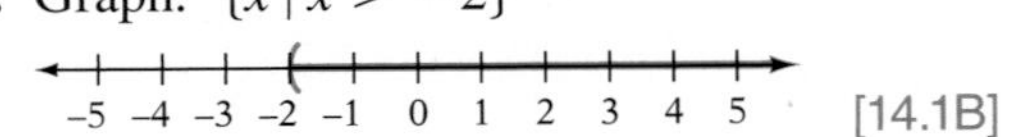

[14.1B]

7. Solve and write the solution set in interval notation: $5 - 3x > 8$
$(-\infty, -1)$ [14.3A]

8. Use set-builder notation to write the set of real numbers greater than -23.
$\{x \mid x > -23\}$ [14.1B]

9. Graph the solution set of $3x + y > 4$.

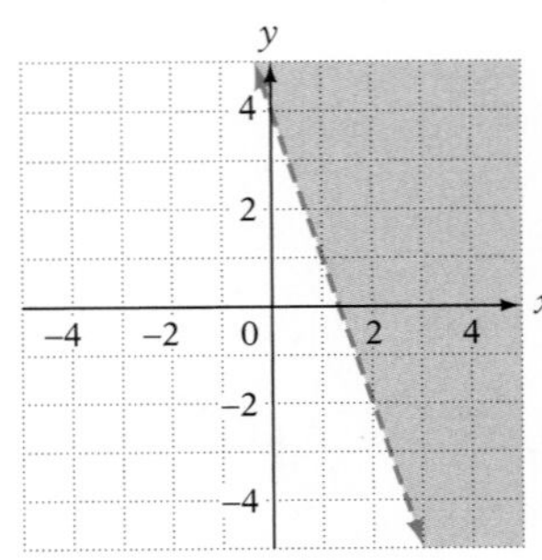

[14.4A]

10. Graph the solution set of $4x - 5y \geq 15$.

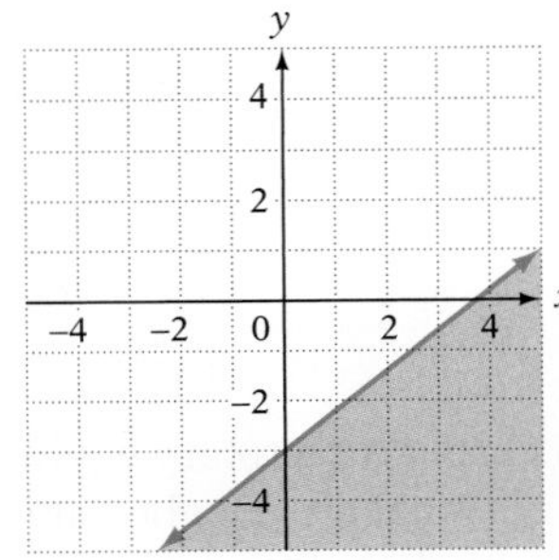

[14.4A]

11. Find $A \cap B$, given $A = \{6, 8, 10, 12\}$ and $B = \{12, 14, 16\}$.
$A \cap B = \{12\}$ [14.1A]

12. Solve $4 + x < 1$ and write the solution set in set-builder notation. Graph the solution set.

–5 –4 –3 –2 –1 0 1 2 3 4 5

$\{x \mid x < -3\}$ [14.2A]

13. Solve and write the solution set in set-builder notation: $-\frac{3}{8}x \leq 5$
$\left\{x \middle| x \geq -\frac{40}{3}\right\}$ [14.2B]

14. Solve and write the solution set in interval notation: $6x - 3(2 - 3x) < 4(2x - 7)$
$\left(-\infty, -\frac{22}{7}\right)$ [14.3A]

15. Solve $\frac{2}{3}x \geq 2$ and write the solution set in interval notation. Graph the solution set.

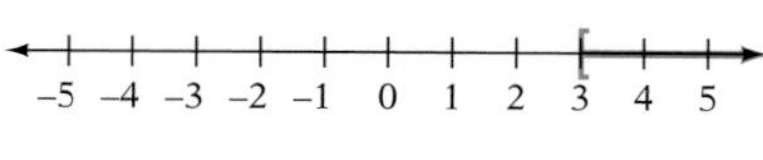

[3, ∞) [14.2B]

16. Solve and write the solution set in set-builder notation: $2x - 7 \leq 6x + 9$

$\{x|x \geq -4\}$ [14.3A]

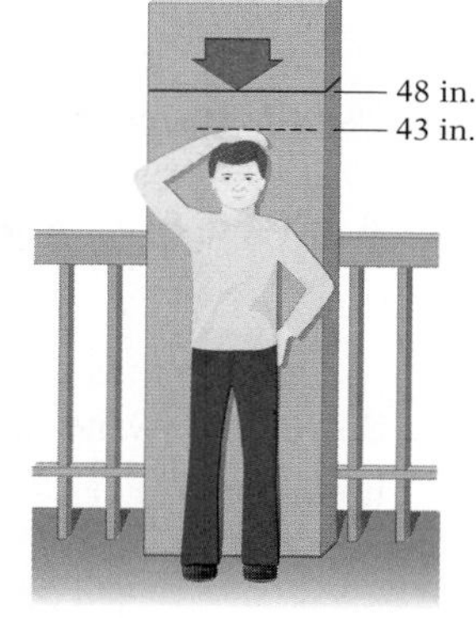

17. **Safety** To ride a certain roller coaster at an amusement park, a person must be at least 48 in. tall. How many inches must a child who is 43 in. tall grow to be eligible to ride the roller coaster?

5 in. or more [14.2C]

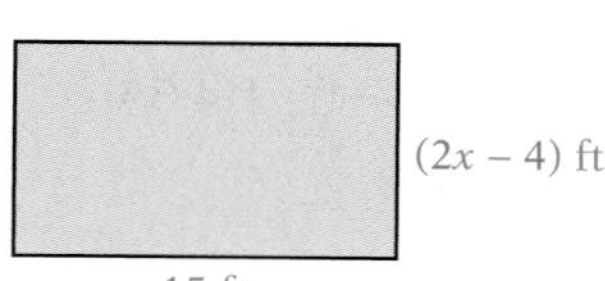

18. **Geometry** A rectangle is 15 ft long and $(2x - 4)$ ft wide. Express as an integer the maximum width of the rectangle if the area is less than 180 ft^2. (The area of a rectangle is equal to its length times its width.)

11 ft [14.3B]

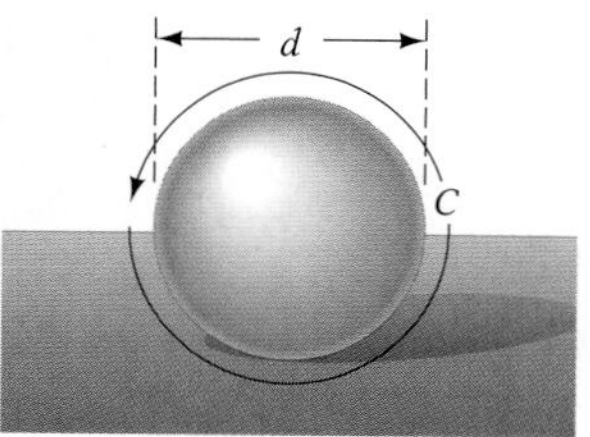

19. **Machining** A ball bearing for a rotary engine must have a circumference between 0.1220 in. and 0.1240 in. What are the allowable diameters for the bearing? Round to the nearest ten-thousandth. Recall that $C = \pi d$. Use 3.14 for π.

Between 0.0389 in. and 0.0395 in. [14.2C]

20. **Compensation** A stockbroker receives a monthly salary that is the greater of $5000 or $1000 plus 2% of the total value of all stock transactions the broker processes during the month. What dollar amounts of transactions did the broker process in a month for which the broker's salary was $5000?

$200,000 or less [14.3B]

Cumulative Review Exercises

1. Simplify: $2[5a - 3(2 - 5a) - 8]$
$40a - 28$ [4.2D]

2. Solve: $\frac{5}{8} - 4x = \frac{1}{8}$
$\frac{1}{8}$ [5.2A]

3. Solve: $2x - 3[x - 2(x - 3)] = 2$
4 [5.3B]

4. Simplify: $(-3a)(-2a^3b^2)^2$
$-12a^7b^4$ [9.2B]

5. Simplify: $\frac{27a^3b^2}{(-3ab^2)^3}$
$-\frac{1}{b^4}$ [9.4A]

6. Divide: $(16x^2 - 12x - 2) \div (4x - 1)$
$4x - 2 - \frac{4}{4x - 1}$ [9.5B]

7. Given $f(x) = x^2 - 4x - 5$, find $f(-1)$.
0 [12.1D]

8. Factor: $27a^2x^2 - 3a^2$
$3a^2(3x - 1)(3x + 1)$ [10.5A]

9. Divide: $\frac{x^2 - 2x}{x^2 - 2x - 8} \div \frac{x^3 - 5x^2 + 6x}{x^2 - 7x + 12}$
$\frac{1}{x + 2}$ [11.1C]

10. Subtract: $\frac{4a}{2a - 3} - \frac{2a}{a + 3}$
$\frac{18a}{(2a - 3)(a + 3)}$ [11.3B]

11. Solve: $\frac{5y}{6} - \frac{5}{9} = \frac{y}{3} - \frac{5}{6}$
$-\frac{5}{9}$ [11.5A]

12. Solve $R = \frac{C - S}{t}$ for C.
$C = S + Rt$ [11.6A]

13. Find the slope of the line that passes through the points $(2, -3)$ and $(-1, 4)$.
$-\frac{7}{3}$ [12.3B]

14. Find the equation of the line that passes through the point $(1, -3)$ and has slope $-\frac{3}{2}$.
$y = -\frac{3}{2}x - \frac{3}{2}$ [12.4A]

15. Solve by substitution.
$x = 3y + 1$
$2x + 5y = 13$
(4, 1) [13.2A]

16. Solve by the addition method.
$9x - 2y = 17$
$5x + 3y = -7$
(1, −4) [13.3A]

17. Find $A \cup B$, given $A = \{0, 1, 2\}$ and $B = \{-10, -2\}$.
$A \cup B = \{-10, -2, 0, 1, 2\}$ [14.1A]

18. Use set-builder notation to write the set of real numbers less than 48.
$\{x \mid x < 48\}$ [14.1B]

19. Write $\{x \mid x < 4\}$ in interval notation.
$(-\infty, 4)$ [14.1B]

20. Graph the solution set of $\frac{3}{8}x > -\frac{3}{4}$.

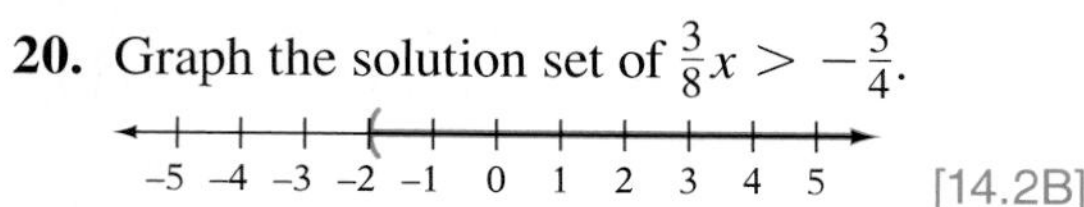

[14.2B]

21. Solve: $-\frac{4}{5}x > 12$
$x < -15$ [14.2B]

22. Solve: $15 - 3(5x - 7) < 2(7 - 2x)$
$x > 2$ [14.3A]

23. Graph: $y = 2x - 1$

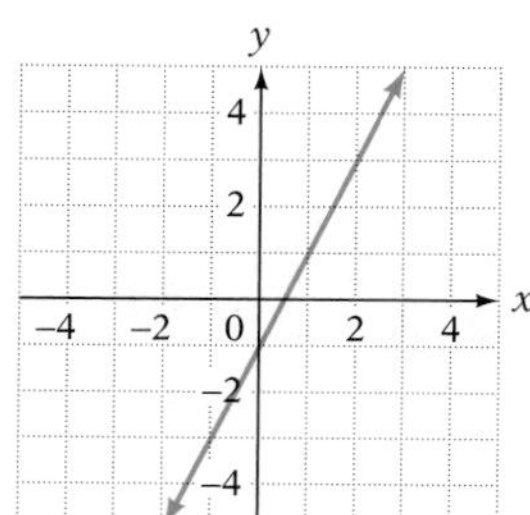

[12.2A]

24. Graph the solution set of $6x - 3y \geq 6$.

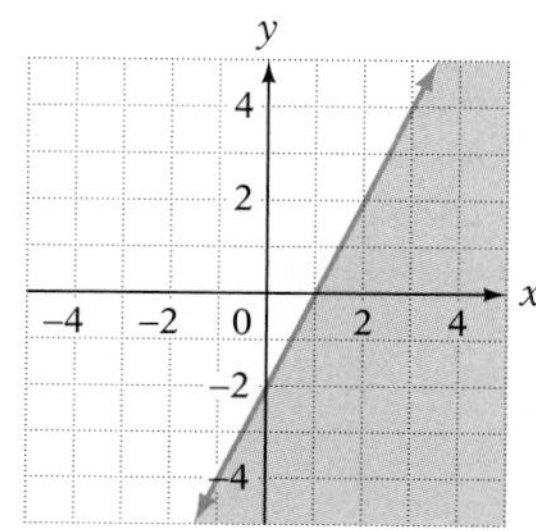

[14.4A]

25. Integer Problem Three-fifths of a number is less than negative fifteen. What integers satisfy this inequality? Write the answer in set-builder notation.
$\{x \mid x \leq -26, x \in \text{integers}\}$ [14.2C]

26. Rental Agencies Company A rents cars for \$6 a day and \$.25 for every mile driven. Company B rents cars for \$15 a day and \$.10 per mile driven. You want to rent a car for 6 days. What is the maximum number of miles you can drive a Company A car if it is to cost you less than a Company B car?
359 mi [14.3B]

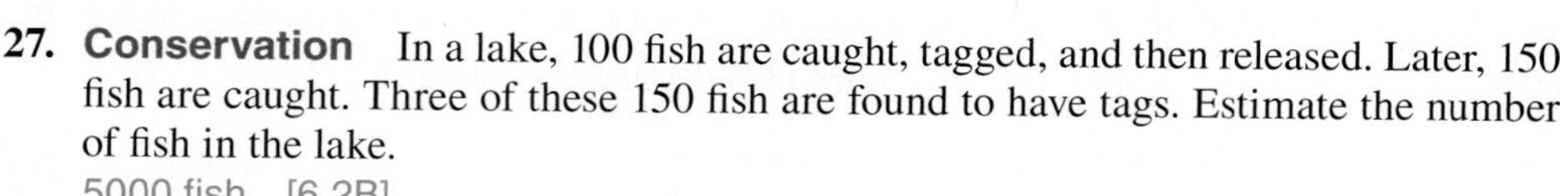

27. Conservation In a lake, 100 fish are caught, tagged, and then released. Later, 150 fish are caught. Three of these 150 fish are found to have tags. Estimate the number of fish in the lake.
5000 fish [6.2B]

© Dmitrijs Bindemanis/Shutterstock.com

28. Geometry The measure of the first angle of a triangle is 30° more than the measure of the second angle. The measure of the third angle is 10° more than twice the measure of the second angle. Find the measure of each angle.
65°, 35°, and 80° [7.1C]

Radical Expressions

OBJECTIVES

SECTION 15.1

A To simplify numerical radical expressions

B To simplify variable radical expressions

SECTION 15.2

A To add and subtract radical expressions

SECTION 15.3

A To multiply radical expressions

B To divide radical expressions

SECTION 15.4

A To solve an equation containing a radical expression

B To solve application problems

Focus on Success

Remember to prepare your brain for the material you will learn in this chapter. Read the list of objectives on this page. Look through the entire chapter, noting words that are in bold. Read the rules and definitions that appear in boxes. Getting an overview of the material presented provides a foundation for learning it. (See Understand the Organization, page AIM-8.)

Prep Test

Are you ready to succeed in this chapter? Take the Prep Test below to find out if you are ready to learn the new material.

1. Evaluate: $-|-14|$
-14 [3.1C]

2. Simplify: $3x^2y - 4xy^2 - 5x^2y$
$-2x^2y - 4xy^2$ [4.2A]

3. Solve: $1.5h = 21$
14 [5.1C]

4. Solve: $3x - 2 = 5 - 2x$
$\frac{7}{5}$ [5.3A]

5. Simplify: $x^3 \cdot x^3$
x^6 [9.2A]

6. Expand: $(x + y)^2$
$x^2 + 2xy + y^2$ [9.3D]

7. Expand: $(2x - 3)^2$
$4x^2 - 12x + 9$ [9.3D]

8. Multiply: $(2 - 3v)(2 + 3v)$
$4 - 9v^2$ [9.3D]

9. Multiply: $(a - 5)(a + 5)$
$a^2 - 25$ [9.3D]

10. Simplify: $\frac{2x^4y^3}{18x^2y}$
$\frac{x^2y^2}{9}$ [9.4A]

SECTION

15.1 Introduction to Radical Expressions

OBJECTIVE A To simplify numerical radical expressions

Point of Interest

The radical symbol was first used in 1525, when it was written as √. Some historians suggest that the radical symbol also developed into the symbols for "less than" and "greater than." Because typesetters of that time did not want to make additional symbols, the radical was rotated to the position > and used as a "greater than" symbol and rotated to < and used as the "less than" symbol. Other evidence, however, suggests that the "less than" and "greater than" symbols were developed independently of the radical symbol.

A **square root** of a positive number a is a number whose square is a.

A square root of 16 is 4 because $4^2 = 16$.

A square root of 16 is -4 because $(-4)^2 = 16$.

Every positive number has two square roots, one positive and one negative. The symbol $\sqrt{\ }$, called a **radical sign,** is used to indicate the positive or **principal square root** of a number. For example, $\sqrt{16} = 4$ (the principal square root of 16 is 4) and $\sqrt{25} = 5$ (the principal square root of 25 is 5). The number under the radical sign is called the **radicand.**

When the negative square root of a number is to be found, a negative sign is placed in front of the radical. For example, $-\sqrt{16} = -4$ and $-\sqrt{25} = -5$.

The square of an integer is a **perfect square.** For instance, 49, 81, and 144 are perfect squares. The principal square root of a perfect-square integer is a positive integer.

$7^2 = 49$ $\quad \sqrt{49} = 7$

$9^2 = 81$ $\quad \sqrt{81} = 9$

$12^2 = 144$ $\quad \sqrt{144} = 12$

If a number is not a perfect square, its square root can only be approximated. For example, 2 and 7 are not perfect squares. The square roots of these numbers are *irrational numbers.* Their decimal approximations never terminate or repeat.

$\sqrt{2} \approx 1.4142135\ldots$

$\sqrt{7} \approx 2.6457513\ldots$

Take Note

Recall that a factor of a number divides the number evenly. For instance, 6 is a factor of 18. The perfect square 9 is also a factor of 18. It is a *perfect-square factor* of 18. The number 6 is not a perfect-square factor of 18 because 6 is not a perfect square.

A radical expression is in *simplest form* when the radicand contains no factor greater than 1 that is a perfect square. For instance, $\sqrt{50}$ is not in simplest form because 25 is a perfect-square factor of 50. The radical expression $\sqrt{15}$ is in simplest form because there are no perfect-square factors of 15 that are greater than 1.

A knowledge of perfect squares and the Product Property of Square Roots are used to simplify radicands that are not perfect squares. The chart below shows the square roots of some perfect squares.

Square Roots of Perfect Squares			
$\sqrt{1} = 1$	$\sqrt{16} = 4$	$\sqrt{49} = 7$	$\sqrt{100} = 10$
$\sqrt{4} = 2$	$\sqrt{25} = 5$	$\sqrt{64} = 8$	$\sqrt{121} = 11$
$\sqrt{9} = 3$	$\sqrt{36} = 6$	$\sqrt{81} = 9$	$\sqrt{144} = 12$

The Product Property of Square Roots

If a and b are positive real numbers, then $\sqrt{ab} = \sqrt{a} \cdot \sqrt{b}$.

EXAMPLE

Simplify: $\sqrt{72}$

$\sqrt{72} = \sqrt{36 \cdot 2}$ • **Write the radicand as the product of a perfect square and a factor that does not contain a perfect square.**

$= \sqrt{36}\sqrt{2}$ • **Use the Product Property of Square Roots to write the expression as a product. Then simplify.**

$= 6\sqrt{2}$

INSTRUCTOR NOTE

If students are having difficulty finding a perfect-square factor, have them write the prime factorization of the radicand. For instance,

$\sqrt{288} = \sqrt{2^5 3^2} = \sqrt{(2^4 3^2)2}$
$= \sqrt{2^4 3^2}\sqrt{2} = 2^2 \cdot 3\sqrt{2}$
$= 12\sqrt{2}$

Note in the example above that 72 must be written as the product of a perfect square and *a factor that does not contain a perfect square.* Therefore, it would not be correct to simplify $\sqrt{72}$ as $\sqrt{9 \cdot 8}$. Although 9 is a perfect-square factor of 72, 8 also contains a perfect-square factor ($8 = 4 \cdot 2$). Therefore, $\sqrt{8}$ is not in simplest form. Remember to find the largest perfect-square factor of the radicand.

$\sqrt{72} = \sqrt{9 \cdot 8}$
$= \sqrt{9} \cdot \sqrt{8}$
$= 3\sqrt{8}$
Not in simplest form

HOW TO 1 Simplify: $\sqrt{360}$

$\sqrt{360} = \sqrt{36 \cdot 10}$ • **Write the radicand as the product of a perfect square and a factor that does not contain a perfect square.**

$= \sqrt{36}\sqrt{10}$ • **Use the Product Property of Square Roots to write the expression as a product.**

$= 6\sqrt{10}$ • **Simplify.**

From HOW TO 1, note that $\sqrt{360} = 6\sqrt{10}$. The two expressions are different representations of the same number. Using a calculator, we find that $\sqrt{360} \approx 18.973666$ and $6\sqrt{10} \approx 18.973666$.

HOW TO 2 Simplify: $\sqrt{-16}$

Because the square of any real number is positive, there is no real number whose square is -16. $\sqrt{-16}$ is not a real number.

EXAMPLE 1

Simplify: $3\sqrt{90}$

Solution

$3\sqrt{90} = 3\sqrt{9 \cdot 10}$ • **9 is the largest perfect-square factor.**

$= 3\sqrt{9}\sqrt{10}$ • **Product Property of Square Roots**

$= 3 \cdot 3\sqrt{10}$

$= 9\sqrt{10}$

YOU TRY IT 1

Simplify: $\sqrt{216}$

Your solution

$6\sqrt{6}$

IN-CLASS EXAMPLES

Simplify.

1. $7\sqrt{48}$ **$28\sqrt{3}$**
2. $\sqrt{675}$ **$15\sqrt{3}$**
3. $3\sqrt{12}$ **$6\sqrt{3}$**

EXAMPLE 2

Simplify: $\sqrt{252}$

Solution

$\sqrt{252} = \sqrt{36 \cdot 7}$ • **36 is the largest perfect-square factor.**

$= \sqrt{36}\sqrt{7}$ • **Product Property of Square Roots**

$= 6\sqrt{7}$

YOU TRY IT 2

Simplify: $-5\sqrt{32}$

Your solution

$-20\sqrt{2}$

Solutions on p. S35

OBJECTIVE B *To simplify variable radical expressions*

Variable expressions that contain radicals do not always represent real numbers. For example, if $a = -4$, then

$$\sqrt{a^3} = \sqrt{(-4)^3} = \sqrt{-64}$$

and $\sqrt{-64}$ is not a real number.

Now consider the expression $\sqrt{x^2}$. Evaluate this expression for $x = -2$ and $x = 2$.

$$\sqrt{x^2} \qquad \sqrt{x^2}$$
$$\sqrt{(-2)^2} = \sqrt{4} = 2 = |-2| \qquad \sqrt{2^2} = \sqrt{4} = 2 = |2|$$

This suggests the following rule:

For any real number a, $\sqrt{a^2} = |a|$. If $a \geq 0$, then $\sqrt{a^2} = a$.

In order to avoid variable expressions that do not represent real numbers, and so that absolute value signs are not needed for certain expressions, the variables in this chapter will represent *positive* numbers unless otherwise stated.

A variable raised to a power or a product of variables written in exponential form is a perfect square when each exponent is an even number. To find the square root of a perfect square, remove the radical sign and multiply each exponent by $\frac{1}{2}$.

HOW TO 3 Simplify: $\sqrt{a^6}$

$\sqrt{a^6} = a^3$ • **The exponent, 6, is an even number. Remove the radical sign and multiply 6 by $\frac{1}{2}$.**

A variable radical expression is in simplest form when the radicand contains no factor greater than 1 that is a perfect square.

HOW TO 4 Simplify: $\sqrt{x^7}$

$\sqrt{x^7} = \sqrt{x^6 \cdot x}$ • **Write x^7 as the product of a perfect square and x.**

$= \sqrt{x^6}\sqrt{x}$ • **Use the Product Property of Square Roots.**

$= x^3\sqrt{x}$ • **Simplify the perfect square.**

HOW TO 5 Simplify: $3x\sqrt{8x^3y^{13}}$

$3x\sqrt{8x^3y^{13}} = 3x\sqrt{4x^2y^{12}(2xy)}$ • **Write the radicand as the product of perfect squares and factors that do not contain a perfect square.**

$= 3x\sqrt{4x^2y^{12}}\sqrt{2xy}$ • **Use the Product Property of Square Roots.**

$= 3x \cdot 2xy^6\sqrt{2xy}$ • **Simplify.**

$= 6x^2y^7\sqrt{2xy}$

INSTRUCTOR NOTE
As a class exercise, have students verify that $\sqrt{a^2 + b^2} \neq a + b$ by using $a = 3$ and $b = 4$.

HOW TO 6 Simplify: $\sqrt{25(x + 2)^2}$

$\sqrt{25(x + 2)^2} = 5(x + 2)$ • 25 is a perfect square. $(x + 2)^2$ is a perfect square

$= 5x + 10$ • Distributive Property

EXAMPLE 3

Simplify: $\sqrt{b^{15}}$

Solution

$\sqrt{b^{15}} = \sqrt{b^{14} \cdot b}$ • b^{14} is a perfect square.

$= \sqrt{b^{14}} \cdot \sqrt{b} = b^7\sqrt{b}$

YOU TRY IT 3

Simplify: $\sqrt{y^{19}}$

Your solution

$y^9\sqrt{y}$

EXAMPLE 4

Simplify: $\sqrt{24x^5}$

Solution

$\sqrt{24x^5} = \sqrt{4x^4(6x)}$ • 4 and x^4 are perfect squares.

$= \sqrt{4x^4}\sqrt{6x}$

$= 2x^2\sqrt{6x}$

YOU TRY IT 4

Simplify: $\sqrt{45b^7}$

Your solution

$3b^3\sqrt{5b}$

EXAMPLE 5

Simplify: $2a\sqrt{18a^3b^{10}}$

Solution

$2a\sqrt{18a^3b^{10}}$

$= 2a\sqrt{9a^2b^{10}(2a)}$ • 9, a^2, and b^{10} are perfect squares.

$= 2a\sqrt{9a^2b^{10}}\sqrt{2a}$

$= 2a \cdot 3ab^5\sqrt{2a}$

$= 6a^2b^5\sqrt{2a}$

YOU TRY IT 5

Simplify: $3a\sqrt{28a^9b^{18}}$

Your solution

$6a^5b^9\sqrt{7a}$

IN-CLASS EXAMPLES

Simplify.

4. $\sqrt{b^{11}}$ $b^5\sqrt{b}$
5. $\sqrt{80a^{15}}$ $4a^7\sqrt{5a}$
6. $8x\sqrt{72x^7y^{19}}$ $48x^4y^9\sqrt{2xy}$
7. $\sqrt{81(x + 4)^2}$ $9x + 36$
8. $\sqrt{a^2 + 12a + 36}$ $a + 6$

EXAMPLE 6

Simplify: $\sqrt{16(x + 5)^2}$

Solution

$\sqrt{16(x + 5)^2} = 4(x + 5) = 4x + 20$

YOU TRY IT 6

Simplify: $\sqrt{25(a + 3)^2}$

Your solution

$5a + 15$

EXAMPLE 7

Simplify: $\sqrt{x^2 + 10x + 25}$

Solution

$\sqrt{x^2 + 10x + 25} = \sqrt{(x + 5)^2} = x + 5$

YOU TRY IT 7

Simplify: $\sqrt{x^2 + 14x + 49}$

Your solution

$x + 7$

Solutions on p. S36

15.1 EXERCISES

Concept Check

SUGGESTED ASSIGNMENT
Exercises 1–4; Exercises 5–77, odds; Exercises 83 and 84

1. In the expression $\sqrt{a}$, the symbol $\sqrt{\ }$ is called the radical sign, and a is called the radicand.

2. $16x^6y^8$ is a perfect square because $16 = (4)^2$, $x^6 = (x^3)^2$, and $y^8 = (y^4)^2$.

3. How can you tell whether a variable exponential expression is a perfect square?

4. Explain why $2\sqrt{2}$ is in simplest form and $\sqrt{8}$ is not in simplest form.

OBJECTIVE A To simplify numerical radical expressions

For Exercises 5 to 28, simplify.

5. $\sqrt{16}$ 4 **6.** $\sqrt{64}$ 8 **7.** $\sqrt{49}$ 7 **8.** $\sqrt{144}$ 12 **9.** $\sqrt{32}$ $4\sqrt{2}$ **10.** $\sqrt{50}$ $5\sqrt{2}$

11. $\sqrt{8}$ $2\sqrt{2}$ **12.** $\sqrt{12}$ $2\sqrt{3}$ **13.** $-6\sqrt{18}$ $-18\sqrt{2}$ **14.** $-3\sqrt{48}$ $-12\sqrt{3}$ **15.** $5\sqrt{40}$ $10\sqrt{10}$ **16.** $2\sqrt{28}$ $4\sqrt{7}$

17. $\sqrt{15}$ $\sqrt{15}$ **18.** $\sqrt{21}$ $\sqrt{21}$ **19.** $\sqrt{29}$ $\sqrt{29}$ **20.** $\sqrt{13}$ $\sqrt{13}$ **21.** $-9\sqrt{72}$ $-54\sqrt{2}$ **22.** $-11\sqrt{80}$ $-44\sqrt{5}$

23. $\sqrt{45}$ $3\sqrt{5}$ **24.** $\sqrt{225}$ 15 **25.** $\sqrt{0}$ 0 **26.** $\sqrt{210}$ $\sqrt{210}$ **27.** $6\sqrt{128}$ $48\sqrt{2}$ **28.** $9\sqrt{288}$ $108\sqrt{2}$

For Exercises 29 to 32, find consecutive integers m and n such that the given number is between m and n, or state that the given number is not a real number. Do not use a calculator.

29. $-\sqrt{115}$ -11 and -10 **30.** $-\sqrt{-90}$ Not a real number **31.** $\sqrt{\sqrt{64}}$ 2 and 3 **32.** $\sqrt{200}$ 14 and 15

For Exercises 33 to 38, find the decimal approximation rounded to the nearest thousandth.

33. $\sqrt{240}$ 15.492 **34.** $\sqrt{300}$ 17.321 **35.** $\sqrt{288}$ 16.971 **36.** $\sqrt{600}$ 24.495 **37.** $\sqrt{350}$ 18.708 **38.** $\sqrt{500}$ 22.361

OBJECTIVE B To simplify variable radical expressions

For Exercises 39 to 78, simplify.

39. $\sqrt{x^{14}}$ x^7 **40.** $\sqrt{x^{12}}$ x^6 **41.** $\sqrt{y^{15}}$ $y^7\sqrt{y}$ **42.** $\sqrt{y^{11}}$ $y^5\sqrt{y}$

43. $\sqrt{a^{20}}$ a^{10} **44.** $\sqrt{a^{16}}$ a^8 **45.** $\sqrt{x^4y^4}$ x^2y^2 **46.** $\sqrt{x^{12}y^8}$ x^6y^4

47. $\sqrt{4x^4}$
$2x^2$

48. $\sqrt{25y^8}$
$5y^4$

49. $\sqrt{24x^2}$
$2x\sqrt{6}$

50. $\sqrt{x^3y^{15}}$
$xy^7\sqrt{xy}$

51. $\sqrt{60x^5}$
$2x^2\sqrt{15x}$

52. $\sqrt{72y^7}$
$6y^3\sqrt{2y}$

53. $\sqrt{49a^4b^8}$
$7a^2b^4$

54. $\sqrt{144x^2y^8}$
$12xy^4$

55. $\sqrt{18x^5y^7}$
$3x^2y^3\sqrt{2xy}$

56. $\sqrt{32a^5b^{15}}$
$4a^2b^7\sqrt{2ab}$

57. $\sqrt{40x^{11}y^7}$
$2x^5y^3\sqrt{10xy}$

58. $\sqrt{72x^9y^3}$
$6x^4y\sqrt{2xy}$

59. $\sqrt{80a^9b^{10}}$
$4a^4b^5\sqrt{5a}$

60. $\sqrt{96a^5b^7}$
$4a^2b^3\sqrt{6ab}$

61. $-2\sqrt{16a^2b^3}$
$-8ab\sqrt{b}$

62. $-5\sqrt{25a^4b^7}$
$-25a^2b^3\sqrt{b}$

63. $x\sqrt{x^4y^2}$
x^3y

64. $y\sqrt{x^3y^6}$
$xy^4\sqrt{x}$

65. $-4\sqrt{20a^4b^7}$
$-8a^2b^3\sqrt{5b}$

66. $-5\sqrt{12a^3b^4}$
$-10ab^2\sqrt{3a}$

67. $3x\sqrt{12x^2y^7}$
$6x^2y^3\sqrt{3y}$

68. $4y\sqrt{18x^5y^4}$
$12x^2y^3\sqrt{2x}$

69. $2x^2\sqrt{8x^2y^3}$
$4x^3y\sqrt{2y}$

70. $3y^2\sqrt{27x^4y^3}$
$9x^2y^3\sqrt{3y}$

71. $\sqrt{25(a+4)^2}$
$5a + 20$

72. $\sqrt{9(x+2)^2}$
$3x + 6$

73. $\sqrt{4(x+2)^4}$
$2x^2 + 8x + 8$

74. $\sqrt{81(x+y)^4}$
$9x^2 + 18xy + 9y^2$

75. $\sqrt{x^2 + 4x + 4}$
$x + 2$

76. $\sqrt{b^2 + 8b + 16}$
$b + 4$

77. $\sqrt{y^2 + 2y + 1}$
$y + 1$

78. $\sqrt{a^2 + 6a + 9}$
$a + 3$

For Exercises 79 to 82, assume that a is a positive integer that is not a perfect square. State whether the expression represents a rational number or an irrational number.

79. $\sqrt{100a^6}$
Rational

80. $\sqrt{9a^9}$
Irrational

81. $\sqrt{\sqrt{25a^{16}}}$
Irrational

82. $\sqrt{\sqrt{81a^8}}$
Rational

Critical Thinking

83. **Credit Cards** See the news clipping at the right. The equation $N = 2.3\sqrt{S}$, where S is a student's year in college, can be used to find the average number of credit cards N that a student has. Use this equation to find the average number of credit cards for **a.** a first-year student, **b.** a sophomore, **c.** a junior, and **d.** a senior. Round to the nearest tenth.

a. 2.3 credit cards b. 3.3 credit cards c. 4.0 credit cards d. 4.6 credit cards

In the NEWS!

Student Credit Card Debt Grows

With each advancing year in college, students acquire more credit cards and accumulate more debt. The average credit card balance for a first-year student is $1585, for a sophomore is $1581, for a junior is $2000, and for a senior or fifth-year student is $2864.

Source: Nellie Mae

84. Given $f(x) = \sqrt{2x - 1}$, find each of the following. Write your answer in simplest form.

a. $f(1)$ **b.** $f(5)$ **c.** $f(14)$

1 3 $3\sqrt{3}$

QUICK QUIZ

Simplify.

1. $\sqrt{36}$ 6 [15.1A]
2. $\sqrt{18}$ $3\sqrt{2}$ [15.1A]
3. $6\sqrt{75}$ $30\sqrt{3}$ [15.1A]
4. $\sqrt{x^{10}}$ x^5 [15.1B]
5. $\sqrt{x^{15}}$ $x^7\sqrt{x}$ [15.1B]
6. $8\sqrt{45x^5y^9}$ $24x^2y^4\sqrt{5xy}$ [15.1B]

Projects or Group Activities

85. **Automotive Safety** Traffic accident investigators can estimate the speed S, in miles per hour, at which a car was traveling from the length of its skid mark by using the formula $S = \sqrt{30fl}$, where f is the coefficient of friction (which depends on the type of road surface) and l is the length, in feet, of the skid mark. Say the coefficient of friction is 1.2 and the length of a skid mark is 60 ft.

a. Determine the speed of the car as a radical expression in simplest form.

b. Write the answer to part (a) as a decimal rounded to the nearest integer.

a. $12\sqrt{15}$ mph b. 46 mph

SECTION

15.2 Addition and Subtraction of Radical Expressions

OBJECTIVE A *To add and subtract radical expressions*

INSTRUCTOR NOTE
Operations with radical expressions are similar to operations with variable expressions. Making this connection for students may help them with simplifying radical expressions.

The Distributive Property is used to simplify the sum or difference of radical expressions with like radicands.

$5\sqrt{2} + 3\sqrt{2} = (5 + 3)\sqrt{2} = 8\sqrt{2}$

$6\sqrt{2x} - 4\sqrt{2x} = (6 - 4)\sqrt{2x} = 2\sqrt{2x}$

Radical expressions that are in simplest form and have unlike radicands cannot be simplified by the Distributive Property.

$2\sqrt{3} + 4\sqrt{2}$ cannot be simplified by the Distributive Property.

To simplify the sum or difference of radical expressions, first simplify each radical expression.

HOW TO 1 Simplify: $4\sqrt{8} - 10\sqrt{2}$

$$\begin{aligned} 4\sqrt{8} - 10\sqrt{2} &= 4\sqrt{4 \cdot 2} - 10\sqrt{2} \\ &= 4\sqrt{4}\sqrt{2} - 10\sqrt{2} \\ &= 4 \cdot 2\sqrt{2} - 10\sqrt{2} \\ &= 8\sqrt{2} - 10\sqrt{2} \\ &= (8 - 10)\sqrt{2} \\ &= -2\sqrt{2} \end{aligned}$$

- The radical expressions have unlike radicands. Use the Product Property of Square Roots to simplify $\sqrt{8}$.
- The radical expressions now have like radicands. Simplify the expression by using the Distributive Property.

HOW TO 2 Simplify: $8\sqrt{18x} - 2\sqrt{32x}$

$$\begin{aligned} 8\sqrt{18x} - 2\sqrt{32x} &= 8\sqrt{9 \cdot 2x} - 2\sqrt{16 \cdot 2x} \\ &= 8\sqrt{9}\sqrt{2x} - 2\sqrt{16}\sqrt{2x} \\ &= 8 \cdot 3\sqrt{2x} - 2 \cdot 4\sqrt{2x} \\ &= 24\sqrt{2x} - 8\sqrt{2x} \\ &= (24 - 8)\sqrt{2x} \\ &= 16\sqrt{2x} \end{aligned}$$

- The radical expressions have unlike radicands. Use the Product Property of Square Roots to simplify each radical expression.
- The radical expressions now have like radicands. Simplify the expression by using the Distributive Property.

EXAMPLE 1

Simplify: $5\sqrt{2} - 3\sqrt{2} + 12\sqrt{2}$

Solution

$5\sqrt{2} - 3\sqrt{2} + 12\sqrt{2}$ • The radical expressions have like radicands.

$= (5 - 3 + 12)\sqrt{2}$ • Distributive Property

$= 14\sqrt{2}$

YOU TRY IT 1

Simplify: $9\sqrt{3} + 3\sqrt{3} - 18\sqrt{3}$

Your solution

$-6\sqrt{3}$

IN-CLASS EXAMPLES
Simplify.
1. $7\sqrt{11} + 8\sqrt{11} - 2\sqrt{11}$ **$13\sqrt{11}$**
2. $9\sqrt{18} + 5\sqrt{50}$ **$52\sqrt{2}$**
3. $5\sqrt{24x^5} + 3x\sqrt{54x^3}$ **$19x^2\sqrt{6x}$**
4. $3ab\sqrt{45b} + 2a\sqrt{80b^3} - 7\sqrt{20a^2b^3}$ **$3ab\sqrt{5b}$**

Solution on p. S36

EXAMPLE 2

Simplify: $3\sqrt{12} - 5\sqrt{27}$

Solution

$3\sqrt{12} - 5\sqrt{27}$

$= 3\sqrt{4 \cdot 3} - 5\sqrt{9 \cdot 3}$ • Unlike radicands • Simplify $\sqrt{12}$ and $\sqrt{27}$.

$= 3\sqrt{4}\sqrt{3} - 5\sqrt{9}\sqrt{3}$

$= 3 \cdot 2\sqrt{3} - 5 \cdot 3\sqrt{3}$

$= 6\sqrt{3} - 15\sqrt{3}$ • Like radicands

$= (6 - 15)\sqrt{3}$ • Distributive Property

$= -9\sqrt{3}$

YOU TRY IT 2

Simplify: $2\sqrt{50} - 5\sqrt{32}$

Your solution

$-10\sqrt{2}$

EXAMPLE 3

Simplify: $3\sqrt{12x^3} - 2x\sqrt{3x}$

Solution

$3\sqrt{12x^3} - 2x\sqrt{3x}$ • Unlike radicands

$= 3\sqrt{4x^2 \cdot 3x} - 2x\sqrt{3x}$ • Simplify $\sqrt{12x^3}$.

$= 3\sqrt{4x^2}\sqrt{3x} - 2x\sqrt{3x}$

$= 3 \cdot 2x\sqrt{3x} - 2x\sqrt{3x}$

$= 6x\sqrt{3x} - 2x\sqrt{3x}$ • Like radicands

$= (6x - 2x)\sqrt{3x}$ • Distributive Property

$= 4x\sqrt{3x}$

YOU TRY IT 3

Simplify: $y\sqrt{28y} + 7\sqrt{63y^3}$

Your solution

$23y\sqrt{7y}$

EXAMPLE 4

Simplify: $2x\sqrt{8y} - 3\sqrt{2x^2y} + 2\sqrt{32x^2y}$

Solution

$2x\sqrt{8y} - 3\sqrt{2x^2y} + 2\sqrt{32x^2y}$

$= 2x\sqrt{4 \cdot 2y} - 3\sqrt{x^2 \cdot 2y} + 2\sqrt{16x^2 \cdot 2y}$

$= 2x\sqrt{4}\sqrt{2y} - 3\sqrt{x^2}\sqrt{2y} + 2\sqrt{16x^2}\sqrt{2y}$

$= 2x \cdot 2\sqrt{2y} - 3 \cdot x\sqrt{2y} + 2 \cdot 4x\sqrt{2y}$

$= 4x\sqrt{2y} - 3x\sqrt{2y} + 8x\sqrt{2y}$

$= 9x\sqrt{2y}$

YOU TRY IT 4

Simplify: $2\sqrt{27a^5} - 4a\sqrt{12a^3} + a^2\sqrt{75a}$

Your solution

$3a^2\sqrt{3a}$

Solutions on p. S36

15.2 EXERCISES

Concept Check

SUGGESTED ASSIGNMENT
Exercises 1–6; Exercises 7–61, odds

1. Which of the numbers 2, 9, 20, 25, 50, 81, and 100 are *not* perfect squares?
2, 20, 50

2. Write down a number that has a perfect-square factor that is greater than 1.
Answers will vary; for instance, 50.

For Exercises 3 to 6, determine whether the expression can be simplified.

3. $5\sqrt{3} + 6\sqrt{3}$
Yes

4. $3\sqrt{5} + 3\sqrt{6}$
No

5. $4\sqrt{2x} - 8\sqrt{2x}$
Yes

6. $3\sqrt{5x} + 5\sqrt{3x}$
No

OBJECTIVE A *To add and subtract radical expressions*

For Exercises 7 to 62, simplify.

7. $2\sqrt{2} + \sqrt{2}$
$3\sqrt{2}$

8. $3\sqrt{5} + 8\sqrt{5}$
$11\sqrt{5}$

9. $-3\sqrt{7} + 2\sqrt{7}$
$-\sqrt{7}$

10. $4\sqrt{5} - 10\sqrt{5}$
$-6\sqrt{5}$

11. $-3\sqrt{11} - 8\sqrt{11}$
$-11\sqrt{11}$

12. $-3\sqrt{3} - 5\sqrt{3}$
$-8\sqrt{3}$

13. $2\sqrt{x} + 8\sqrt{x}$
$10\sqrt{x}$

14. $3\sqrt{y} + 2\sqrt{y}$
$5\sqrt{y}$

15. $8\sqrt{y} - 10\sqrt{y}$
$-2\sqrt{y}$

16. $-5\sqrt{2a} + 2\sqrt{2a}$
$-3\sqrt{2a}$

17. $-2\sqrt{3b} - 9\sqrt{3b}$
$-11\sqrt{3b}$

18. $-7\sqrt{5a} - 5\sqrt{5a}$
$-12\sqrt{5a}$

19. $3x\sqrt{2} - x\sqrt{2}$
$2x\sqrt{2}$

20. $2y\sqrt{3} - 9y\sqrt{3}$
$-7y\sqrt{3}$

21. $2a\sqrt{3a} - 5a\sqrt{3a}$
$-3a\sqrt{3a}$

22. $-5b\sqrt{3x} - 2b\sqrt{3x}$
$-7b\sqrt{3x}$

23. $3\sqrt{xy} - 8\sqrt{xy}$
$-5\sqrt{xy}$

24. $-4\sqrt{xy} + 6\sqrt{xy}$
$2\sqrt{xy}$

25. $\sqrt{45} + \sqrt{125}$
$8\sqrt{5}$

26. $\sqrt{32} - \sqrt{98}$
$-3\sqrt{2}$

27. $2\sqrt{2} + 3\sqrt{8}$
$8\sqrt{2}$

28. $4\sqrt{128} - 3\sqrt{32}$
$20\sqrt{2}$

29. $5\sqrt{18} - 2\sqrt{75}$
$15\sqrt{2} - 10\sqrt{3}$

30. $5\sqrt{75} - 2\sqrt{18}$
$25\sqrt{3} - 6\sqrt{2}$

31. $5\sqrt{4x} - 3\sqrt{9x}$
$\sqrt{x}$

32. $-3\sqrt{25y} + 8\sqrt{49y}$
$41\sqrt{y}$

33. $3\sqrt{3x^2} - 5\sqrt{27x^2}$
$-12x\sqrt{3}$

34. $-2\sqrt{8y^2} + 5\sqrt{32y^2}$
$16y\sqrt{2}$

35. $2x\sqrt{xy^2} - 3y\sqrt{x^2y}$
$2xy\sqrt{x} - 3xy\sqrt{y}$

36. $4a\sqrt{b^2a} - 3b\sqrt{a^2b}$
$4ab\sqrt{a} - 3ab\sqrt{b}$

37. $3x\sqrt{12x} - 5\sqrt{27x^3}$
$-9x\sqrt{3x}$

38. $2a\sqrt{50a} + 7\sqrt{32a^3}$
$38a\sqrt{2a}$

39. $4y\sqrt{8y^3} - 7\sqrt{18y^5}$
$-13y^2\sqrt{2y}$

40. $2a\sqrt{8ab^2} - 2b\sqrt{2a^3}$
$2ab\sqrt{2a}$

41. $b^2\sqrt{a^5b} + 3a^2\sqrt{ab^5}$
$4a^2b^2\sqrt{ab}$

42. $y^2\sqrt{x^5y} + x\sqrt{x^3y^5}$
$2x^2y^2\sqrt{xy}$

43. $4\sqrt{2} - 5\sqrt{2} + 8\sqrt{2}$
$7\sqrt{2}$

44. $3\sqrt{3} + 8\sqrt{3} - 16\sqrt{3}$
$-5\sqrt{3}$

45. $5\sqrt{x} - 8\sqrt{x} + 9\sqrt{x}$
$6\sqrt{x}$

46. $\sqrt{x} - 7\sqrt{x} + 6\sqrt{x}$
0

47. $8\sqrt{2} - 3\sqrt{y} - 8\sqrt{2}$
$-3\sqrt{y}$

48. $8\sqrt{3} - 5\sqrt{2} - 5\sqrt{3}$
$3\sqrt{3} - 5\sqrt{2}$

49. $8\sqrt{8} - 4\sqrt{32} - 9\sqrt{50}$
$-45\sqrt{2}$

50. $2\sqrt{12} - 4\sqrt{27} + \sqrt{75}$
$-3\sqrt{3}$

51. $-2\sqrt{3} + 5\sqrt{27} - 4\sqrt{45}$
$13\sqrt{3} - 12\sqrt{5}$

52. $-2\sqrt{8} - 3\sqrt{27} + 3\sqrt{50}$
$11\sqrt{2} - 9\sqrt{3}$

53. $4\sqrt{75} + 3\sqrt{48} - \sqrt{99}$
$32\sqrt{3} - 3\sqrt{11}$

54. $2\sqrt{75} - 5\sqrt{20} + 2\sqrt{45}$
$10\sqrt{3} - 4\sqrt{5}$

55. $\sqrt{25x} - \sqrt{9x} + \sqrt{16x}$
$6\sqrt{x}$

56. $\sqrt{4x} - \sqrt{100x} - \sqrt{49x}$
$-15\sqrt{x}$

57. $3\sqrt{3x} + \sqrt{27x} - 8\sqrt{75x}$
$-34\sqrt{3x}$

58. $5\sqrt{5x} + 2\sqrt{45x} - 3\sqrt{80x}$
$-\sqrt{5x}$

59. $2a\sqrt{75b} - a\sqrt{20b} + 4a\sqrt{45b}$
$10a\sqrt{3b} + 10a\sqrt{5b}$

60. $2b\sqrt{75a} - 5b\sqrt{27a} + 2b\sqrt{20a}$
$-5b\sqrt{3a} + 4b\sqrt{5a}$

61. $x\sqrt{3y^2} - 2y\sqrt{12x^2} + xy\sqrt{3}$
$-2xy\sqrt{3}$

62. $a\sqrt{27b^2} + 3b\sqrt{147a^2} - ab\sqrt{3}$
$23ab\sqrt{3}$

63. Which expression is equivalent to $\sqrt{2ab} + \sqrt{2ab}$?
(i) $2\sqrt{ab}$ **(ii)** $\sqrt{4ab}$ **(iii)** $2ab$ **(iv)** $\sqrt{8ab}$ iv

Critical Thinking

For Exercises 64 to 66, simplify.

64. $\frac{1}{4}\sqrt{48ab^2} + \frac{1}{5}\sqrt{75ab^2}$
$2b\sqrt{3a}$

65. $\frac{a}{3}\sqrt{54ab^3} + \frac{b}{4}\sqrt{96a^3b}$
$2ab\sqrt{6ab}$

66. $\frac{x}{6}\sqrt{72xy^5} + \frac{y}{7}\sqrt{98x^3y^3}$
$2xy^2\sqrt{2xy}$

67. **Geometry** The length of a rectangle is $3\sqrt{2}$ cm. The width is $\sqrt{2}$ cm. Find the perimeter of the rectangle. $8\sqrt{2}$ cm

$3\sqrt{2}$ cm
$\sqrt{2}$ cm

68. Given $G(x) = \sqrt{x+5} + \sqrt{5x+3}$, write $G(3)$ in simplest form.
$5\sqrt{2}$

Projects or Group Activities

69. Write a paragraph that compares adding two monomials to adding two radical expressions. For example, compare the addition of $5x + 3x$ to the addition of $5\sqrt{x} + 3\sqrt{x}$.

QUICK QUIZ

Simplify.

1. $6\sqrt{15} + 7\sqrt{15} - 10\sqrt{15}$
   $\mathbf{3\sqrt{15}}$ **[15.2A]**
2. $8\sqrt{12} + 2\sqrt{18}$
   $\mathbf{16\sqrt{3} + 6\sqrt{2}}$ **[15.2A]**
3. $3\sqrt{72x^{15}} + 8x^4\sqrt{8x^7}$
   $\mathbf{34x^7\sqrt{2x}}$ **[15.2A]**

SECTION

15.3 Multiplication and Division of Radical Expressions

OBJECTIVE A *To multiply radical expressions*

The Product Property of Square Roots is used to multiply radical expressions.

$\sqrt{2x}\sqrt{3y} = \sqrt{2x \cdot 3y} = \sqrt{6xy}$

HOW TO 1 Simplify: $\sqrt{2x^2}\sqrt{32x^5}$

$$\begin{aligned}\sqrt{2x^2}\sqrt{32x^5} &= \sqrt{2x^2 \cdot 32x^5} && \bullet \text{ Use the Product Property of Square Roots.}\\ &= \sqrt{64x^7} && \bullet \text{ Multiply.}\\ &= \sqrt{64x^6 \cdot x} && \bullet \text{ Simplify.}\\ &= \sqrt{64x^6}\sqrt{x} = 8x^3\sqrt{x}\end{aligned}$$

HOW TO 2 Simplify: $\sqrt{2x}(x + \sqrt{2x})$

$$\begin{aligned}\sqrt{2x}(x + \sqrt{2x}) &= \sqrt{2x}(x) + \sqrt{2x}\sqrt{2x} && \bullet \text{ Use the Distributive Property to remove parentheses.}\\ &= x\sqrt{2x} + \sqrt{4x^2} && \bullet \text{ Simplify.}\\ &= x\sqrt{2x} + 2x\end{aligned}$$

Use FOIL to multiply radical expressions with two terms.

HOW TO 3 Simplify: $(\sqrt{2} - 3x)(\sqrt{2} + x)$

$$\begin{aligned}(\sqrt{2} - 3x)(\sqrt{2} + x) &= \sqrt{2}\sqrt{2} + x\sqrt{2} - 3x\sqrt{2} - 3x^2 && \bullet \text{ Use the FOIL method to remove parentheses.}\\ &= \sqrt{4} + (x - 3x)\sqrt{2} - 3x^2\\ &= 2 - 2x\sqrt{2} - 3x^2\end{aligned}$$

The expressions $a + b$ and $a - b$, which differ only in the sign of one term, are called **conjugates.** Recall that $(a + b)(a - b) = a^2 - b^2$.

Take Note
For $x > 0$, $(\sqrt{x})^2 = x$ because $(\sqrt{x})^2 = \sqrt{x} \cdot \sqrt{x} = \sqrt{x^2} = x$.

HOW TO 4 Simplify: $(3 + \sqrt{y})(3 - \sqrt{y})$

$$\begin{aligned}(3 + \sqrt{y})(3 - \sqrt{y}) &= 3^2 - (\sqrt{y})^2 && \bullet\ (3 + \sqrt{y})(3 - \sqrt{y}) \text{ is the product of conjugates.}\\ &= 9 - y\end{aligned}$$

EXAMPLE 1

Simplify: $\sqrt{3x^4}\sqrt{2x^2y}\sqrt{6xy^2}$

Solution

$$\begin{aligned}&\sqrt{3x^4}\sqrt{2x^2y}\sqrt{6xy^2}\\ &= \sqrt{36x^7y^3} && \bullet \text{ Product Property of Square Roots}\\ &= \sqrt{36x^6y^2 \cdot xy} && \bullet \text{ Simplify.}\\ &= \sqrt{36x^6y^2}\sqrt{xy}\\ &= 6x^3y\sqrt{xy}\end{aligned}$$

YOU TRY IT 1

Simplify: $\sqrt{5a}\sqrt{15a^3b^4}\sqrt{20b^5}$

Your solution $10a^2b^4\sqrt{15b}$

IN-CLASS EXAMPLES
Simplify.

1. $\sqrt{30y^5}\sqrt{6y^8}\sqrt{10y^6}$ $\mathbf{30y^9\sqrt{2y}}$
2. $\sqrt{8mn}(\sqrt{2m} - \sqrt{3n})$ $\mathbf{4m\sqrt{n} - 2n\sqrt{6m}}$
3. $(3\sqrt{5ab} - 7c)(3\sqrt{5ab} + 7c)$ $\mathbf{45ab - 49c^2}$
4. $(5\sqrt{a} + 3\sqrt{b})(2\sqrt{a} - \sqrt{b})$ $\mathbf{10a + \sqrt{ab} - 3b}$

Solution on p. S36

EXAMPLE 2

Simplify: $\sqrt{3ab}(\sqrt{3a} + \sqrt{9b})$

Solution

$\sqrt{3ab}(\sqrt{3a} + \sqrt{9b})$

$= \sqrt{9a^2b} + \sqrt{27ab^2}$ • Distributive Property

$= \sqrt{9a^2 \cdot b} + \sqrt{9b^2 \cdot 3a}$ • Simplify.

$= \sqrt{9a^2}\sqrt{b} + \sqrt{9b^2}\sqrt{3a}$

$= 3a\sqrt{b} + 3b\sqrt{3a}$

YOU TRY IT 2

Simplify: $\sqrt{5x}(\sqrt{5x} - \sqrt{25y})$

Your solution

$5x - 5\sqrt{5xy}$

EXAMPLE 3

Simplify: $(\sqrt{x} - 2\sqrt{y})(4\sqrt{x} + \sqrt{y})$

Solution

$(\sqrt{x} - 2\sqrt{y})(4\sqrt{x} + \sqrt{y})$

$= 4(\sqrt{x})^2 + \sqrt{xy} - 8\sqrt{xy} - 2(\sqrt{y})^2$ • FOIL

$= 4x - 7\sqrt{xy} - 2y$

YOU TRY IT 3

Simplify: $(3\sqrt{x} - \sqrt{y})(5\sqrt{x} - 2\sqrt{y})$

Your solution

$15x - 11\sqrt{xy} + 2y$

EXAMPLE 4

Simplify: $(\sqrt{a} - \sqrt{b})(\sqrt{a} + \sqrt{b})$

Solution

$(\sqrt{a} - \sqrt{b})(\sqrt{a} + \sqrt{b})$ • Product of conjugates

$= (\sqrt{a})^2 - (\sqrt{b})^2$

$= a - b$

YOU TRY IT 4

Simplify: $(2\sqrt{x} + 7)(2\sqrt{x} - 7)$

Your solution

$4x - 49$

Solutions on p. S36

OBJECTIVE B *To divide radical expressions*

The Quotient Property of Square Roots, given below, states that the square root of a quotient is equal to the quotient of the square roots.

The Quotient Property of Square Roots

If a and b are positive real numbers, then $\sqrt{\frac{a}{b}} = \frac{\sqrt{a}}{\sqrt{b}}$ and $\frac{\sqrt{a}}{\sqrt{b}} = \sqrt{\frac{a}{b}}$.

EXAMPLE

Simplify: $\sqrt{\frac{4x^2}{z^6}}$

$\sqrt{\frac{4x^2}{z^6}} = \frac{\sqrt{4x^2}}{\sqrt{z^6}}$ • Rewrite the radical expression as a quotient of square roots.

$= \frac{2x}{z^3}$ • Simplify.

Point of Interest

A radical expression that occurs in Einstein's Theory of Relativity is

$$\frac{1}{\sqrt{1-\frac{v^2}{c^2}}}$$

where v is the velocity of an object and c is the speed of light.

HOW TO 5 Simplify: $\sqrt{\frac{24x^3y^7}{3x^7y^2}}$

$\sqrt{\frac{24x^3y^7}{3x^7y^2}} = \sqrt{\frac{8y^5}{x^4}}$ • Simplify the radicand.

$= \frac{\sqrt{8y^5}}{\sqrt{x^4}}$ • Rewrite the radical expression as a quotient of square roots.

$= \frac{\sqrt{4y^4 \cdot 2y}}{\sqrt{x^4}}$ • Simplify.

$= \frac{\sqrt{4y^4}\sqrt{2y}}{\sqrt{x^4}}$

$= \frac{2y^2\sqrt{2y}}{x^2}$

The Quotient Property of Square Roots is used to divide radical expressions.

HOW TO 6 Simplify: $\frac{\sqrt{4x^2y}}{\sqrt{xy}}$

$\frac{\sqrt{4x^2y}}{\sqrt{xy}} = \sqrt{\frac{4x^2y}{xy}}$ • Use the Quotient Property of Square Roots.

$= \sqrt{4x}$ • Simplify the radicand.

$= \sqrt{4}\sqrt{x}$ • Simplify the radical expression.

$= 2\sqrt{x}$

The previous examples all result in radical expressions written in simplest form.

Simplest Form of a Radical Expression

For a radical expression to be in simplest form, three conditions must be met:

1. The radicand contains no factor greater than 1 that is a perfect square.
2. There is no fraction under the radical sign.
3. There is no radical in the denominator of a fraction.

The procedure used to remove a radical from a denominator is called **rationalizing the denominator.**

INSTRUCTOR NOTE

Rationalizing the denominator is another case in which the Multiplication Property of One is used. Students do not always believe that $\frac{2}{\sqrt{3}}$ and $\frac{2\sqrt{3}}{3}$ are equal. Have these students use a calculator to verify, to the limits of the calculator, that the two expressions are equal.

HOW TO 7 Simplify: $\frac{2}{\sqrt{3}}$

$\frac{2}{\sqrt{3}} = \frac{2}{\sqrt{3}} \cdot \boxed{\frac{\sqrt{3}}{\sqrt{3}}}$ • To rationalize the denominator, multiply the expression by $\frac{\sqrt{3}}{\sqrt{3}}$, which equals 1.

$= \frac{2\sqrt{3}}{(\sqrt{3})^2}$

$= \frac{2\sqrt{3}}{3}$ • Simplify.

When the denominator contains a radical expression with two terms, rationalize the denominator by multiplying the numerator and denominator by the conjugate of the denominator.

HOW TO 8 Simplify: $\dfrac{\sqrt{2y}}{\sqrt{y}+3}$

$$\frac{\sqrt{2y}}{\sqrt{y}+3} = \frac{\sqrt{2y}}{\sqrt{y}+3}\cdot\frac{\sqrt{y}-3}{\sqrt{y}-3}$$

• Multiply the numerator and denominator by $\sqrt{y}-3$, the conjugate of $\sqrt{y}+3$.

$$= \frac{\sqrt{2y^2}-3\sqrt{2y}}{(\sqrt{y})^2-3^2} = \frac{y\sqrt{2}-3\sqrt{2y}}{y-9}$$

EXAMPLE 5

Simplify: $\dfrac{\sqrt{4x^2y^5}}{\sqrt{3x^4y}}$

Solution

$$\frac{\sqrt{4x^2y^5}}{\sqrt{3x^4y}} = \sqrt{\frac{4x^2y^5}{3x^4y}} = \sqrt{\frac{4y^4}{3x^2}} = \frac{\sqrt{4y^4}}{\sqrt{3x^2}}$$

$$= \frac{2y^2}{x\sqrt{3}} = \frac{2y^2}{x\sqrt{3}}\cdot\frac{\sqrt{3}}{\sqrt{3}}$$

• Rationalize the denominator.

$$= \frac{2y^2\sqrt{3}}{3x}$$

YOU TRY IT 5

Simplify: $\dfrac{\sqrt{15x^6y^7}}{\sqrt{3x^7y^9}}$

Your solution

$\dfrac{\sqrt{5x}}{xy}$

EXAMPLE 6

Simplify: $\dfrac{\sqrt{2}}{\sqrt{2}+\sqrt{6}}$

Solution

$$\frac{\sqrt{2}}{\sqrt{2}+\sqrt{6}}$$

$$= \frac{\sqrt{2}}{\sqrt{2}+\sqrt{6}}\cdot\frac{\sqrt{2}-\sqrt{6}}{\sqrt{2}-\sqrt{6}}$$

• Multiply the numerator and denominator by the conjugate of the denominator.

$$= \frac{(\sqrt{2})^2-\sqrt{12}}{2-6} = \frac{2-2\sqrt{3}}{-4}$$

$$= \frac{2(1-\sqrt{3})}{-4} = \frac{1-\sqrt{3}}{-2} = -\frac{1-\sqrt{3}}{2}$$

YOU TRY IT 6

Simplify: $\dfrac{\sqrt{3}}{\sqrt{3}-\sqrt{6}}$

Your solution

$-1-\sqrt{2}$

EXAMPLE 7

Simplify: $\dfrac{3-\sqrt{y}}{2+3\sqrt{y}}$

Solution

$$\frac{3-\sqrt{y}}{2+3\sqrt{y}} = \frac{3-\sqrt{y}}{2+3\sqrt{y}}\cdot\frac{2-3\sqrt{y}}{2-3\sqrt{y}}$$

• Rationalize the denominator.

$$= \frac{6-9\sqrt{y}-2\sqrt{y}+3(\sqrt{y})^2}{4-9y}$$

$$= \frac{6-11\sqrt{y}+3y}{4-9y}$$

YOU TRY IT 7

Simplify: $\dfrac{5+\sqrt{y}}{1-2\sqrt{y}}$

Your solution

$\dfrac{5+11\sqrt{y}+2y}{1-4y}$

IN-CLASS EXAMPLES

Simplify.

5. $\dfrac{\sqrt{12x^3y^3}}{\sqrt{24xy^6}}$ $\dfrac{x\sqrt{2y}}{2y^2}$

6. $\dfrac{\sqrt{5}}{\sqrt{5}-\sqrt{10}}$ $-1-\sqrt{2}$

7. $\dfrac{2+\sqrt{7x}}{6+\sqrt{7x}}$ $\dfrac{12+4\sqrt{7x}-7x}{36-7x}$

Solutions on p. S36

15.3 EXERCISES

Concept Check

SUGGESTED ASSIGNMENT
Exercises 1–10; Exercises 11–45, odds; Exercises 49–77, odds; Exercises 81 and 86

For Exercises 1 to 3, determine the conjugate of the expression.

1. $3 + \sqrt{5}$
$3 - \sqrt{5}$

2. $6 - \sqrt{x}$
$6 + \sqrt{x}$

3. $\sqrt{2a} - 8$
$\sqrt{2a} + 8$

For Exercises 4 and 5, find the product of the expression and its conjugate.

4. $4 + \sqrt{3}$
13

5. $5 - \sqrt{y}$
$25 - y$

For Exercises 6 to 8, by what form of 1 should the expression be multiplied to rationalize the denominator?

6. $\frac{2}{\sqrt{6}}$ $\frac{\sqrt{6}}{\sqrt{6}}$

7. $\frac{3}{\sqrt{x}}$ $\frac{\sqrt{x}}{\sqrt{x}}$

8. $\frac{2 - \sqrt{x}}{\sqrt{y}}$ $\frac{\sqrt{y}}{\sqrt{y}}$

9. Why is $\frac{\sqrt{3}}{3}$ in simplest form but $\frac{1}{\sqrt{3}}$ not in simplest form?

10. Why can we multiply $\frac{2}{\sqrt{5}}$ by $\frac{\sqrt{5}}{\sqrt{5}}$ without changing the value of $\frac{2}{\sqrt{5}}$?

OBJECTIVE A *To multiply radical expressions*

For Exercises 11 to 46, simplify.

11. $\sqrt{5} \cdot \sqrt{5}$
5

12. $\sqrt{11} \cdot \sqrt{11}$
11

13. $\sqrt{3} \cdot \sqrt{12}$
6

14. $\sqrt{2} \cdot \sqrt{8}$
4

15. $\sqrt{x} \cdot \sqrt{x}$
x

16. $\sqrt{y} \cdot \sqrt{y}$
y

17. $\sqrt{xy^3} \cdot \sqrt{x^5y}$
x^3y^2

18. $\sqrt{a^3b^5} \cdot \sqrt{ab^5}$
a^2b^5

19. $\sqrt{3a^2b^5} \cdot \sqrt{6ab^7}$
$3ab^6\sqrt{2a}$

20. $\sqrt{5x^3y} \cdot \sqrt{10x^2y}$
$5x^2y\sqrt{2x}$

21. $\sqrt{6a^3b^2} \cdot \sqrt{24a^5b}$
$12a^4b\sqrt{b}$

22. $\sqrt{8ab^5} \cdot \sqrt{12a^7b}$
$4a^4b^3\sqrt{6}$

23. $\sqrt{2ac} \cdot \sqrt{5ab} \cdot \sqrt{10cb}$
$10abc$

24. $\sqrt{3xy} \cdot \sqrt{6x^3y} \cdot \sqrt{2y^2}$
$6x^2y^2$

25. $\sqrt{2}(\sqrt{2} - \sqrt{3})$
$2 - \sqrt{6}$

26. $3(\sqrt{12} - \sqrt{3})$
$3\sqrt{3}$

27. $\sqrt{x}(\sqrt{x} - \sqrt{y})$
$x - \sqrt{xy}$

28. $\sqrt{b}(\sqrt{a} - \sqrt{b})$
$\sqrt{ab} - b$

29. $\sqrt{5}(\sqrt{10} - \sqrt{x})$
$5\sqrt{2} - \sqrt{5x}$

30. $\sqrt{6}(\sqrt{y} - \sqrt{18})$
$\sqrt{6y} - 6\sqrt{3}$

31. $\sqrt{3a}(\sqrt{3a} - \sqrt{3b})$
$3a - 3\sqrt{ab}$

32. $\sqrt{5x}(\sqrt{10x} - \sqrt{x})$
$5x\sqrt{2} - x\sqrt{5}$

33. $(\sqrt{x} - 3)^2$
$x - 6\sqrt{x} + 9$

34. $(2\sqrt{a} - y)^2$
$4a - 4y\sqrt{a} + y^2$

35. $(\sqrt{5} + 3)(2\sqrt{5} - 4)$
$-2 + 2\sqrt{5}$

36. $(2 - 3\sqrt{7})(5 + 2\sqrt{7})$
$-32 - 11\sqrt{7}$

37. $(4 + \sqrt{8})(3 + \sqrt{2})$
$16 + 10\sqrt{2}$

38. $(6 - \sqrt{27})(2 + \sqrt{3})$
3

39. $(2\sqrt{x} + 4)(3\sqrt{x} - 1)$
$6x + 10\sqrt{x} - 4$

40. $(5 + \sqrt{y})(6 - 3\sqrt{y})$
$30 - 9\sqrt{y} - 3y$

41. $(3\sqrt{x} - 2y)(5\sqrt{x} - 4y)$
$15x - 22y\sqrt{x} + 8y^2$

42. $(5\sqrt{x} + 2\sqrt{y})(3\sqrt{x} - \sqrt{y})$
$15x + \sqrt{xy} - 2y$

43. $(3 + \sqrt{5})(3 - \sqrt{5})$
4

44. $(1 + \sqrt{6})(1 - \sqrt{6})$
-5

45. $(3\sqrt{x} - 4)(3\sqrt{x} + 4)$
$9x - 16$

46. $(\sqrt{x} - y)(\sqrt{x} + y)$
$x - y^2$

47. For $a > 0$, is $(\sqrt{a} - 1)(\sqrt{a} + 1)$ less than, equal to, or greater than a?
Less than

48. For $a > 0$, is $\sqrt{a}(\sqrt{2a} - \sqrt{a})$ less than, equal to, or greater than a?
Less than

OBJECTIVE B *To divide radical expressions*

For Exercises 49 to 78, simplify.

49. $\frac{\sqrt{32}}{\sqrt{2}}$
4

50. $\frac{\sqrt{45}}{\sqrt{5}}$
3

51. $\frac{\sqrt{98}}{\sqrt{2}}$
7

52. $\frac{\sqrt{48}}{\sqrt{3}}$
4

53. $\frac{\sqrt{27a}}{\sqrt{3a}}$
3

54. $\frac{\sqrt{72x^5}}{\sqrt{2x}}$
$6x^2$

55. $\frac{\sqrt{15x^3y}}{\sqrt{3xy}}$
$x\sqrt{5}$

56. $\frac{\sqrt{40x^5y^2}}{\sqrt{5xy}}$
$2x^2\sqrt{2y}$

57. $\frac{\sqrt{2a^5b^4}}{\sqrt{98ab^4}}$
$\frac{a^2}{7}$

58. $\frac{\sqrt{48x^5y^2}}{\sqrt{3x^3y}}$
$4x\sqrt{y}$

59. $\frac{\sqrt{9xy^2}}{\sqrt{27x}}$
$\frac{y\sqrt{3}}{3}$

60. $\frac{\sqrt{4x^2y}}{\sqrt{3xy^3}}$
$\frac{2\sqrt{3x}}{3y}$

61. $\frac{\sqrt{16x^3y^2}}{\sqrt{8x^3y}}$
$\sqrt{2y}$

62. $\frac{\sqrt{2}}{\sqrt{8} + 4}$
$\frac{-1 + \sqrt{2}}{2}$

63. $\frac{1}{\sqrt{2} - 3}$
$-\frac{\sqrt{2} + 3}{7}$

64. $\frac{5}{\sqrt{7} - 3}$
$-\frac{5\sqrt{7} + 15}{2}$

65. $\frac{3}{5 + \sqrt{5}}$
$\frac{15 - 3\sqrt{5}}{20}$

66. $\frac{\sqrt{3}}{5 - \sqrt{27}}$
$-\frac{5\sqrt{3} + 9}{2}$

67. $\frac{7}{\sqrt{2} - 7}$
$-\frac{7\sqrt{2} + 49}{47}$

68. $\frac{-6}{4 + \sqrt{2}}$
$\frac{-12 + 3\sqrt{2}}{7}$

69. $\frac{-\sqrt{15}}{3 - \sqrt{12}}$
$\sqrt{15} + 2\sqrt{5}$

70. $\frac{-12}{\sqrt{6} - 3}$
$4\sqrt{6} + 12$

71. $\frac{\sqrt{xy}}{\sqrt{x} - \sqrt{y}}$
$\frac{x\sqrt{y} + y\sqrt{x}}{x - y}$

72. $\frac{\sqrt{x}}{\sqrt{x} - \sqrt{y}}$
$\frac{x + \sqrt{xy}}{x - y}$

73. $\frac{3 - \sqrt{6}}{5 - 2\sqrt{6}}$
$3 + \sqrt{6}$

74. $\frac{6 - 2\sqrt{3}}{4 + 3\sqrt{3}}$
$-\frac{42 - 26\sqrt{3}}{11}$

75. $\frac{\sqrt{2} + 2\sqrt{6}}{2\sqrt{2} - 3\sqrt{6}}$
$-\frac{20 + 7\sqrt{3}}{23}$

76. $\frac{2\sqrt{3} - \sqrt{6}}{5\sqrt{3} + 2\sqrt{6}}$
$\frac{14 - 9\sqrt{2}}{17}$

77. $\frac{3 + \sqrt{x}}{2 - \sqrt{x}}$
$\frac{6 + 5\sqrt{x} + x}{4 - x}$

78. $\frac{\sqrt{a} - 4}{2\sqrt{a} + 2}$
$\frac{a - 5\sqrt{a} + 4}{2a - 2}$

79. For $a > 0$, is $\frac{a}{\sqrt{a}}$ less than, equal to, or greater than $\sqrt{a}$?
Equal to

80. For $a > 0$ and $b > 0$, is $\frac{a-b}{\sqrt{a}-\sqrt{b}}$ less than, equal to, or greater than $\sqrt{a}$?
Greater than

Critical Thinking

81. Geometry Find the area of the rectangle shown at the right. All dimensions are given in meters.
59 m^2

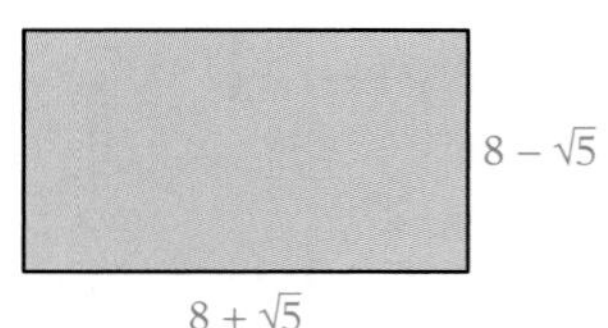

For Exercises 82 to 85, simplify.

82. $-\sqrt{1.3}\sqrt{1.3}$ -1.3

83. $\sqrt{\frac{5}{8}}\sqrt{\frac{5}{8}}$ $\frac{5}{8}$

84. $-\sqrt{\frac{16}{81}}$ $-\frac{4}{9}$

85. $\sqrt{1\frac{9}{16}}$ $\frac{5}{4}$

86. Show that 2 is a solution of the equation $\sqrt{x+2} + \sqrt{x-1} = 3$.

87. Show that $1 + \sqrt{6}$ and $1 - \sqrt{6}$ are solutions of the equation $x^2 - 2x - 5 = 0$.

Projects or Group Activities

88. The number $\frac{\sqrt{5}+1}{2}$ is called the golden ratio. Research the golden ratio and write a few paragraphs about this number and its applications.

QUICK QUIZ

Simplify.

1. $\sqrt{3a^5}\sqrt{6a^3}\sqrt{18a^4}$
$18a^6$ [15.3A]
2. $\sqrt{2x}(\sqrt{2x} - \sqrt{8})$
$2x - 4\sqrt{x}$ [15.3A]
3. $(4\sqrt{b} - 5)(4\sqrt{b} + 5)$
$16b - 25$ [15.3A]
4. $\frac{\sqrt{72x^7}}{\sqrt{2x}}$ **$6x^3$ [15.3B]**
5. $\frac{1+\sqrt{6a}}{3+\sqrt{6a}}$
$\frac{3 + 2\sqrt{6a} - 6a}{9 - 6a}$ [15.3B]

CHECK YOUR PROGRESS: CHAPTER 15

For Exercises 1 to 14, simplify.

1. $\sqrt{300}$ $10\sqrt{3}$ [15.1A]

2. $5\sqrt{180}$ $30\sqrt{5}$ [15.1A]

3. $\sqrt{64x^{10}}$ $8x^5$ [15.1B]

4. $\sqrt{18x^5y^4}$ $3x^2y^2\sqrt{2x}$ [15.1B]

5. $5\sqrt{5} - 8\sqrt{5}$ $-3\sqrt{5}$ [15.2A]

6. $5\sqrt{a^3b} + a\sqrt{4ab} - 3\sqrt{49a^3b}$
$-14a\sqrt{ab}$ [15.2A]

7. $\sqrt{2a^3b^5}\sqrt{32ab^5}$ $8a^2b^5$ [15.3A]

8. $\sqrt{8}(\sqrt{2} - \sqrt{5})$ $4 - 2\sqrt{10}$ [15.3A]

9. $(\sqrt{a} - 3)(3\sqrt{a} + 2)$ $3a - 7\sqrt{a} - 6$ [15.3A]

10. $(\sqrt{2y} + 5)(\sqrt{2y} - 5)$ $2y - 25$ [15.3A]

11. $\frac{\sqrt{50}}{\sqrt{2}}$ 5 [15.3B]

12. $\frac{6}{\sqrt{12x}}$ $\frac{\sqrt{3x}}{x}$ [15.3B]

13. $\frac{7}{7-\sqrt{2}}$ $\frac{49 + 7\sqrt{2}}{47}$ [15.3B]

14. $\frac{5+\sqrt{2}}{3-\sqrt{2}}$ $\frac{17 + 8\sqrt{2}}{7}$ [15.3B]

SECTION

15.4 Solving Equations Containing Radical Expressions

OBJECTIVE A To solve an equation containing a radical expression

An equation that contains a variable expression in a radicand is a **radical equation.**

$$\left.\begin{aligned}\sqrt{x} &= 4\\ \sqrt{x+2} &= \sqrt{x-7}\end{aligned}\right\}\text{ Radical equations}$$

The following property of equality states that if two numbers are equal, the squares of the numbers are equal. This property is used to solve radical equations.

INSTRUCTOR NOTE

As a class discussion, ask students whether $a^2 = b^2$ means that $a = b$. The negative answer to this question will lead students to see why it is necessary to check solutions of radical equations.

Property of Squaring Both Sides of an Equation

If a and b are real numbers and $a = b$, then $a^2 = b^2$.

EXAMPLES

1. If $\sqrt{x} = 7$, then $(\sqrt{x})^2 = 7^2$, or $x = 49$.
2. If $\sqrt{x+1} = 5$, then $(\sqrt{x+1})^2 = 5^2$, or $x + 1 = 25$.

Procedure for Solving a Radical Equation

1. Write the equation with a radical alone on one side.
2. Square both sides of the equation (Property of Squaring Both Sides of an Equation).
3. Solve for the variable.
4. Check the solution(s) in the original equation.

Tips for Success

Always check a solution. You should substitute the solution into the *original* equation. Below is the check for the equation in HOW TO 1.

Check:

$$\begin{array}{r|l}\multicolumn{2}{c}{\sqrt{x-2}-7=0}\\ \hline \sqrt{51-2}-7 & 0\\ \sqrt{49}-7 & 0\\ 7-7 & 0\\ 0 = 0 & \end{array}$$

A true equation

HOW TO 1 Solve: $\sqrt{x-2} - 7 = 0$

$\sqrt{x-2} - 7 = 0$ • Isolate the radical by adding 7 to both sides of the equation.

$\sqrt{x-2} = 7$

$(\sqrt{x-2})^2 = 7^2$ • Square both sides of the equation.

$x - 2 = 49$ • Solve the resulting equation.

$x = 51$

The check is shown at the left. The solution is 51.

When both sides of an equation are squared, the resulting equation may have a solution that is not a solution of the original equation. Checking a proposed solution of a radical equation, as we did at the left, is a necessary step.

HOW TO 2 Solve: $\sqrt{2x-5} + 3 = 0$

$\sqrt{2x-5} + 3 = 0$ • Isolate the radical by subtracting 3 from both sides of the equation.

$\sqrt{2x-5} = -3$

$(\sqrt{2x-5})^2 = (-3)^2$ • Square both sides of the equation.

$2x - 5 = 9$ • Solve for x.

$2x = 14$

$x = 7$

Take Note

Any time each side of an equation is squared, you *must* check the proposed solution of the equation.

Here is the check for the equation from HOW TO 2 on the preceding page.

Check:

$$\sqrt{2x-5}+3=0$$

$\sqrt{2\cdot 7-5}+3$	0
$\sqrt{14-5}+3$	0
$\sqrt{9}+3$	0
$3+3$	0

$$6\neq 0$$

7 does not check as a solution. The equation has no solution.

EXAMPLE 1

Solve: $\sqrt{3x}+2=5$

Solution

$\sqrt{3x}+2=5$

$\sqrt{3x}=3$ • Isolate $\sqrt{3x}$.

$(\sqrt{3x})^2=3^2$ • Square both sides.

$3x=9$

$x=3$ • Solve for x.

Check:

$$\sqrt{3x}+2=5$$

$\sqrt{3\cdot 3}+2$	5
$\sqrt{9}+2$	5
$3+2$	5

$$5=5$$

The solution checks. The solution is 3.

YOU TRY IT 1

Solve: $\sqrt{4x}+3=7$

Your solution

4

EXAMPLE 2

Solve: $1=\sqrt{x}-\sqrt{x-5}$

Solution

When an equation contains two radicals, isolate the radicals one at a time.

$1=\sqrt{x}-\sqrt{x-5}$

$1+\sqrt{x-5}=\sqrt{x}$ • Isolate $\sqrt{x}$.

$(1+\sqrt{x-5})^2=(\sqrt{x})^2$ • Square both sides.

$1+2\sqrt{x-5}+(x-5)=x$ • Expand the left side.

$2\sqrt{x-5}=4$ • Simplify.

$\sqrt{x-5}=2$ • Isolate $\sqrt{x-5}$.

$(\sqrt{x-5})^2=2^2$ • Square both sides.

$x-5=4$

$x=9$ • Solve for x.

Check:

$$1=\sqrt{x}-\sqrt{x-5}$$

1	$\sqrt{9}-\sqrt{9-5}$
1	$\sqrt{9}-\sqrt{4}$
1	$3-2$

$$1=1$$

The solution is 9.

YOU TRY IT 2

Solve: $\sqrt{x}+\sqrt{x+9}=9$

Your solution

16

IN-CLASS EXAMPLES

Solve.

1. $\sqrt{2x}+5=9$ **8**
2. $\sqrt{5-4x}-2=3$ **−5**
3. $5=8-\sqrt{6x}$ $\frac{3}{2}$
4. $\sqrt{x+11}+\sqrt{x}=11$ **25**
5. $1=9+\sqrt{2x}$ **No solution**

Solutions on p. S37

OBJECTIVE B *To solve application problems*

Pythagoras
(c. 580 B.C.–520 B.C.)

A **right triangle** is a triangle that contains a 90° angle. The side opposite the 90° angle is called the **hypotenuse.** The other two sides are called **legs.**

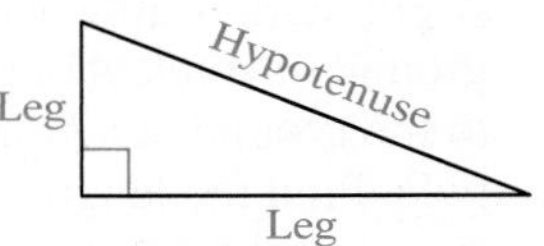

Pythagoras, a Greek mathematician who lived around 550 B.C., is given credit for the Pythagorean Theorem. It states that the square of the hypotenuse of a right triangle is equal to the sum of the squares of the two legs. Actually, this theorem was known to the Babylonians around 1200 B.C.

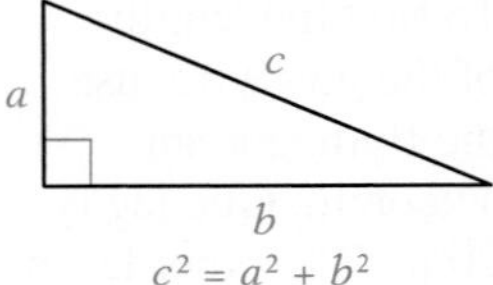

Pythagorean Theorem

If a and b are the lengths of the legs of a right triangle and c is the length of the hypotenuse, then $c^2 = a^2 + b^2$.

Using this theorem, we can find the hypotenuse of a right triangle when we know the two legs. Use the formula

$$\begin{aligned} \text{Hypotenuse} &= \sqrt{(\text{leg})^2 + (\text{leg})^2} \\ c &= \sqrt{a^2 + b^2} \\ &= \sqrt{(5)^2 + (12)^2} \\ &= \sqrt{25 + 144} \\ &= \sqrt{169} \\ &= 13 \end{aligned}$$

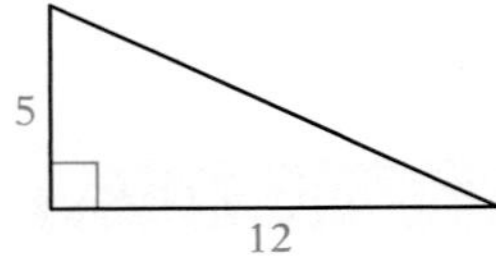

The leg of a right triangle can be found when one leg and the hypotenuse are known. Use the formula

$$\begin{aligned} \text{Leg} &= \sqrt{(\text{hypotenuse})^2 - (\text{leg})^2} \\ a &= \sqrt{c^2 - b^2} \\ &= \sqrt{(25)^2 - (20)^2} \\ &= \sqrt{625 - 400} \\ &= \sqrt{225} \\ &= 15 \end{aligned}$$

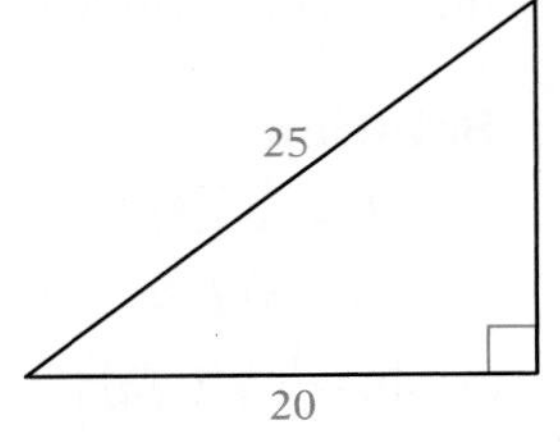

Example 3 and You Try It 3 on the following page illustrate the use of the Pythagorean Theorem. Example 4 and You Try It 4 illustrate other applications of radical equations.

EXAMPLE 3

A guy wire is attached to a point 20 m above the ground on a telephone pole. The wire is anchored to the ground at a point 8 m from the base of the pole. Find the length of the guy wire. Round to the nearest tenth.

Strategy

To find the length of the guy wire, use the Pythagorean Theorem. One leg is 20 m. The other leg is 8 m. The guy wire is the hypotenuse. Solve the Pythagorean Theorem for the hypotenuse.

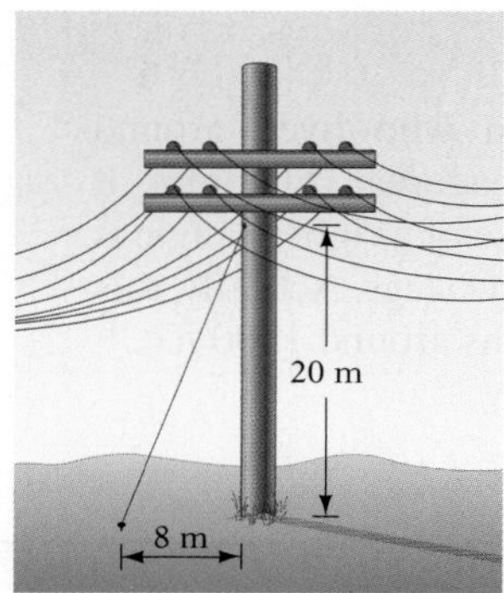

Solution

$c = \sqrt{a^2 + b^2}$

$= \sqrt{(20)^2 + (8)^2}$ • $a = 20, b = 8$

$= \sqrt{400 + 64} = \sqrt{464} \approx 21.5$

The guy wire has a length of approximately 21.5 m.

YOU TRY IT 3

A ladder 8 ft long is resting against a building. How high on the building will the ladder reach when the bottom of the ladder is 3 ft from the building? Round to the nearest hundredth.

Your strategy

Your solution

7.42 ft

IN-CLASS EXAMPLES

6. Can a straight line 7 in. long be drawn on the bottom of a box that is 5 in. wide, 5 in. long, and 1 in. high? **Yes. The diagonal of the 5-inch by 5-inch box is approximately 7.07 in.**
7. The maximum distance d, in kilometers, that one can see from the top of a tall building is given by the formula $d = 1.117\sqrt{10h}$, where h is the height of the building in meters. If a person at the top of the Canadian National Tower in Toronto can see 65.7 km, determine the height of the National Tower to the nearest meter. **346 m**

EXAMPLE 4

How far above the water must a submarine's periscope be for a lookout to see a ship 4 mi away? The equation for the distance in miles that the lookout can see is $d = \sqrt{1.5h}$, where h is the periscope's height in feet above the surface of the water. Round to the nearest hundredth.

Strategy

To find the height above the water, replace d in the equation with the given value and solve for h.

Solution

$d = \sqrt{1.5h}$

$4 = \sqrt{1.5h}$ • $d = 4$

$4^2 = (\sqrt{1.5h})^2$

$16 = 1.5h$

$10.67 \approx h$

The periscope must be approximately 10.67 ft above the water.

YOU TRY IT 4

Find the length of a pendulum that makes one swing in 2.5 s. The equation for the time of one swing is $T = 2\pi\sqrt{\frac{L}{32}}$, where T is the time in seconds and L is the length in feet. Use 3.14 for π. Round to the nearest hundredth.

Your strategy

Your solution

5.07 ft

Solutions on p. S37

15.4 EXERCISES

Concept Check

SUGGESTED ASSIGNMENT
Exercises 1–10; Exercises 11–67, odds

For Exercises 1 to 4, determine whether the equation is a radical equation.

1. $8 = \sqrt{5}x$ No

2. $\sqrt{x - 7} = 9$ Yes

3. $\sqrt{x} + 4 = 6$ Yes

4. $12 = \sqrt{3}x$ No

For Exercises 5 to 8, determine whether the statement is always true, sometimes true, or never true.

5. A radical equation is an equation that contains a radical. Sometimes true

6. We can square both sides of an equation without changing the solution(s) of the equation. Sometimes true

7. We use the Property of Squaring Both Sides of an Equation to eliminate a radical expression from an equation. Always true

8. The first step in solving a radical equation is to square both sides of the equation. Sometimes true

9. In a right triangle, the hypotenuse is the side opposite the ___90°___ angle. The other two sides are called ___legs___.

10. Label the right triangle shown at the right. Include the right angle symbol, the three angles, the two legs, and the hypotenuse.

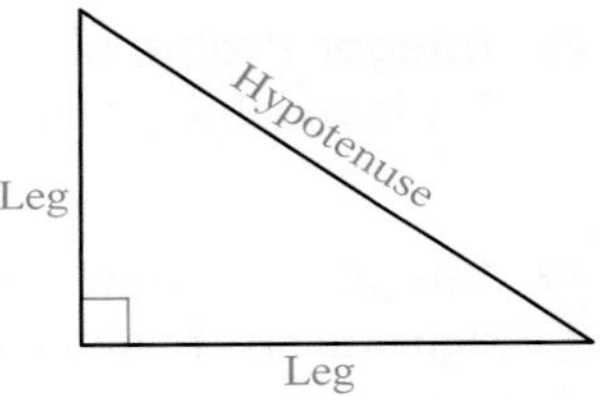

OBJECTIVE A *To solve an equation containing a radical expression*

For Exercises 11 to 46, solve and check.

11. $\sqrt{x} = 5$ 25

12. $\sqrt{y} = 7$ 49

13. $\sqrt{a} = 12$ 144

14. $\sqrt{a} = 9$ 81

15. $\sqrt{5x} = 5$ 5

16. $\sqrt{3x} = 4$ $\frac{16}{3}$

17. $\sqrt{4x} = 8$ 16

18. $\sqrt{6x} = 3$ $\frac{3}{2}$

19. $\sqrt{2x} - 4 = 0$ 8

20. $3 - \sqrt{5x} = 0$ $\frac{9}{5}$

21. $\sqrt{4x} + 5 = 2$ No solution

22. $\sqrt{3x} + 9 = 4$ No solution

23. $\sqrt{3x - 2} = 4$ 6

24. $\sqrt{5x + 6} = 1$ -1

25. $\sqrt{2x + 1} = 7$ 24

26. $\sqrt{5x + 4} = 3$ 1

27. $\sqrt{5x + 2} = 0$ $-\frac{2}{5}$

28. $\sqrt{3x - 7} = 0$ $\frac{7}{3}$

29. $\sqrt{3x} - 6 = -4$ $\frac{4}{3}$

30. $\sqrt{5x} + 8 = 23$ 45

31. $0 = 2 - \sqrt{3 - x}$ -1

32. $0 = 5 - \sqrt{10 + x}$ 15

33. $0 = \sqrt{3x - 9} - 6$ 15

34. $0 = \sqrt{2x + 7} - 3$ 1

35. $\sqrt{5x - 1} = \sqrt{3x + 9}$ 5

36. $\sqrt{3x + 4} = \sqrt{12x - 14}$ 2

37. $\sqrt{5x - 3} = \sqrt{4x - 2}$ 1

38. $\sqrt{5x - 9} = \sqrt{2x - 3}$ 2

39. $\sqrt{x^2 - 5x + 6} = \sqrt{x^2 - 8x + 9}$ 1

40. $\sqrt{x^2 - 2x + 4} = \sqrt{x^2 + 5x - 12}$ $\frac{16}{7}$

41. $\sqrt{x} = \sqrt{x + 3} - 1$ 1

42. $\sqrt{x + 5} = \sqrt{x} + 1$ 4

43. $\sqrt{2x + 5} = 5 - \sqrt{2x}$ 2

44. $\sqrt{2x} + \sqrt{2x + 9} = 9$ 8

45. $\sqrt{3x} - \sqrt{3x + 7} = 1$ No solution

46. $\sqrt{x} - \sqrt{x + 9} = 1$ No solution

47. Without solving the equations, identify which equation has no solution.
(i) $-\sqrt{2x - 5} = -3$ **(ii)** $\sqrt{2x} - 5 = -3$ **(iii)** $\sqrt{2x - 5} = -3$ iii

OBJECTIVE B *To solve application problems*

48. **Integer Problem** Five added to the square root of the product of four and a number is equal to seven. Find the number. 1

49. **Integer Problem** Two added to the square root of the sum of a number and five is equal to six. Find the number. 11

50. A 20-foot ladder leans against the side of a building with its bottom d feet from the building. The ladder reaches a height of h feet. Which of the following distances is not possible as a value for h?
(i) 4 ft **(ii)** 10 ft **(iii)** 16 ft **(iv)** 22 ft iv

Geometry For Exercises 51 to 53, solve. Round to the nearest hundredth.

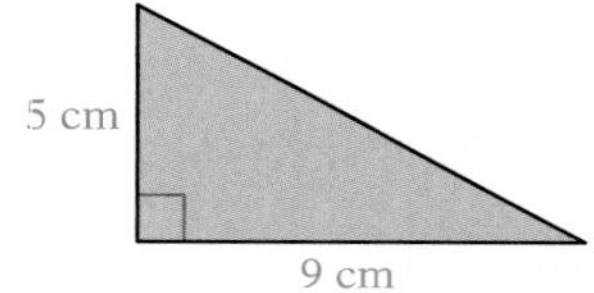

51. The two legs of a right triangle measure 5 cm and 9 cm. Find the length of the hypotenuse. 10.30 cm

52. The two legs of a right triangle measure 8 in. and 4 in. Find the length of the hypotenuse. 8.94 in.

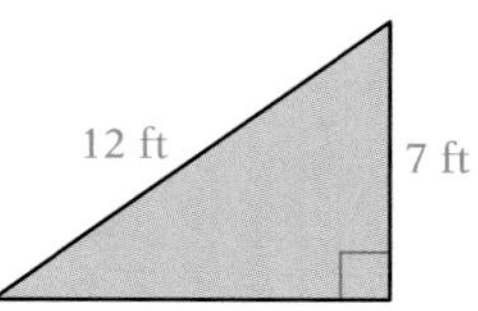

53. The hypotenuse of a right triangle measures 12 ft. One leg of the triangle measures 7 ft. Find the length of the other leg of the triangle. 9.75 ft

54. The hypotenuse of a right triangle measures 20 cm. One leg of the triangle measures 16 cm. Find the length of the other leg of the triangle. 12 cm

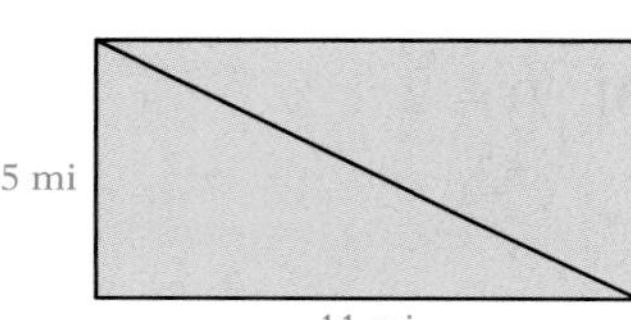

55. A diagonal of a rectangle is a line drawn from one vertex to the opposite vertex. Find the length of the diagonal in the rectangle shown at the right. Round to the nearest tenth. 12.1 mi

56. Education One method used to "curve" the grades on an exam is to use the formula $R = 10\sqrt{O}$, where R is the revised score and O is the original score. Use this formula to find the original score on an exam that has a revised score of 75. Round to the nearest whole number. 56

57. Physics A formula used in the study of shallow-water wave motion is $C = \sqrt{32H}$, where C is the wave velocity in feet per second and H is the depth in feet. Use this formula to find the depth of the water when the wave velocity is 20 ft/s. 12.5 ft

58. Physics See the news clipping at the right. The time it takes an object to fall a certain distance is given by the equation $T = \sqrt{\frac{d}{16}}$, where T is the time in seconds and d is the distance in feet. Use this equation to find the height from which the hay was dropped. 576 ft

In the NEWS!

Hay Drop for Stranded Cattle

The Wyoming and Colorado National Guards have come to the aid of thousands of cattle stranded by the blizzard that has paralyzed southeastern Colorado. Flying low over the cattle, the guardsmen drop bales of hay that 6 s later smash into the ground, break apart, and provide food for the animals, which would otherwise starve.

Sources: The Denver Post; www.af.mil

59. Sports The infield of a softball diamond is a square. The distance between successive bases is 60 ft. The pitcher's mound is on the diagonal between home plate and second base at a distance of 46 ft from home plate. Is the pitcher's mound more or less than halfway between home plate and second base? More than halfway

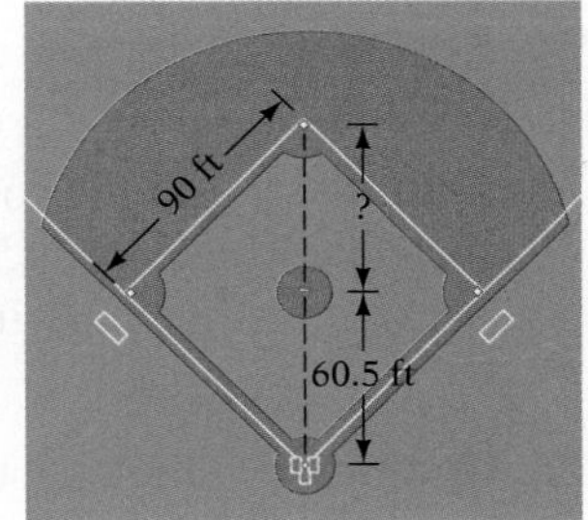

60. Sports The infield of a baseball diamond is a square. The distance between successive bases is 90 ft. The pitcher's mound is on the diagonal between home plate and second base at a distance of 60.5 ft from home plate. Is the pitcher's mound more or less than halfway between home plate and second base? Less than halfway

61. Communications Marta Lightfoot leaves a dock in her sailboat and sails 2.5 mi due east. She then tacks and sails 4 mi due north. The walkie-talkie Marta has on board has a range of 5 mi. Will she be able to call a friend on the dock from her location using the walkie-talkie? Yes

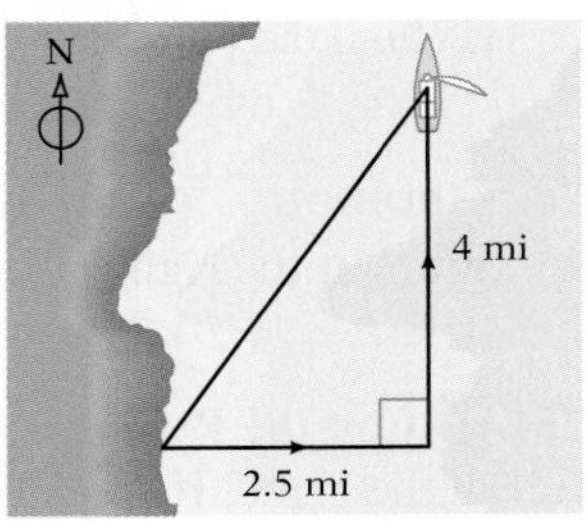

62. Navigation How far above the water would a submarine's periscope have to be for the lookout to see a ship 5 mi away? The equation for the distance in miles that the lookout can see is $d = \sqrt{1.5h}$, where h is the periscope's height in feet above the surface of the water. Round to the nearest hundredth. 16.67 ft

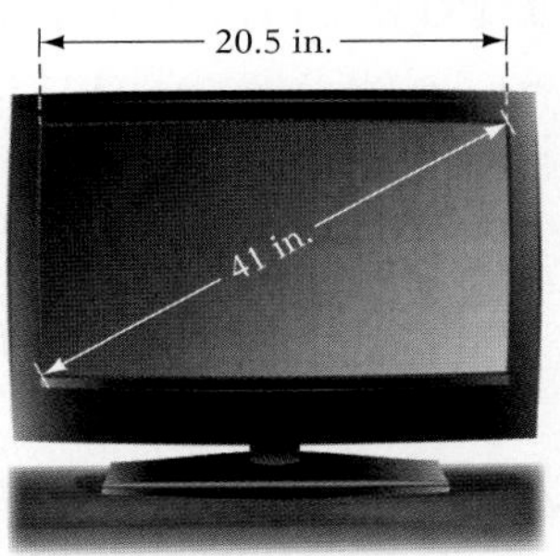

63. Home Entertainment The measure of a television screen is given by the length of a diagonal across the screen. A 41-inch television has a width of 20.5 in. Find the height of the screen to the nearest tenth of an inch. 35.5 in.

64. Physics The speed of a child riding a merry-go-round at a carnival is given by the equation $v = \sqrt{12r}$, where v is the speed in feet per second and r is the distance in feet from the center of the merry-go-round to the rider. If a child is moving at 15 ft/s, how far is the child from the center of the merry-go-round? 18.75 ft

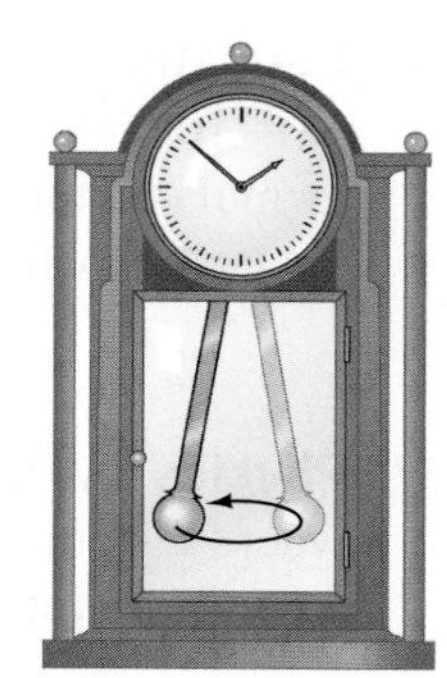

65. Physics Find the length of a pendulum that makes one swing in 1.5 s. The equation for the time of one swing is $T = 2\pi\sqrt{\frac{L}{32}}$, where T is the time in seconds and L is the length in feet. Use 3.14 for π. Round to the nearest hundredth. 1.83 ft

66. Aviation A commuter plane leaves an airport and travels due south at 400 mph. Another plane leaves at the same time and travels due east at 300 mph. Find the distance between the two planes after 2 h. 1000 mi

67. Physics A stone is dropped from a bridge and hits the water 2 s later. How high is the bridge? The equation for the distance an object falls in T seconds is $T = \sqrt{\frac{d}{16}}$, where d is the distance in feet. 64 ft

68. Physics A stone is dropped into a mine shaft and hits the bottom 3.5 s later. How deep is the mine shaft? The equation for the distance an object falls in T seconds is $T = \sqrt{\frac{d}{16}}$, where d is the distance in feet. 196 ft

QUICK QUIZ

Solve.

1. $\sqrt{2x - 1} + 4 = 7$
   5 [15.4A]
2. $\sqrt{2x + 6} = 4$
   No solution [15.4A]
3. What is the measure of a diagonal of a rectangle that has a width of 4 in. and a length of 9 in.? Round to the nearest tenth. **9.8 in. [15.4B]**

Critical Thinking

For Exercises 69 to 71, solve.

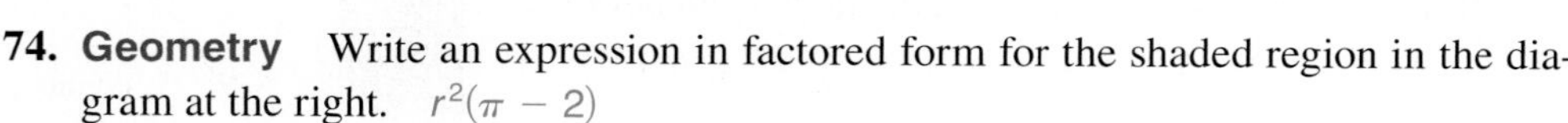

69. $\sqrt{\frac{5y + 2}{3}} = 3$ 5

70. $\sqrt{\frac{3y}{5}} - 1 = 2$ 15

71. $\sqrt{9x^2 + 49} + 1 = 3x + 2$ 8

72. Geometry In the coordinate plane, a triangle is formed by drawing lines between the points (0, 0) and (5, 0), (5, 0) and (5, 12), and (5, 12) and (0, 0). Find the number of units in the perimeter of the triangle. 30 units

73. Geometry The hypotenuse of a right triangle is $5\sqrt{2}$ cm, and the length of one leg is $4\sqrt{2}$ cm.

a. Find the perimeter of the triangle. $12\sqrt{2}$ cm

b. Find the area of the triangle. 12 cm^2

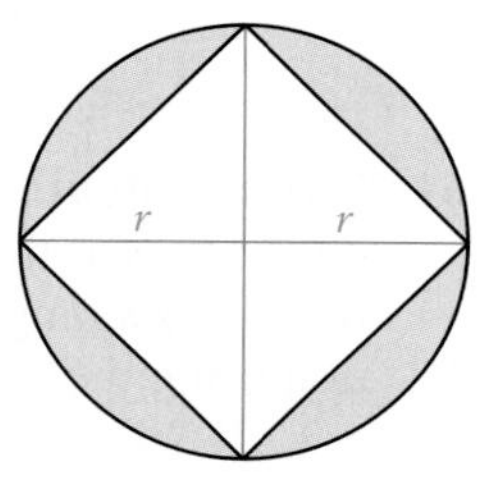

74. Geometry Write an expression in factored form for the shaded region in the diagram at the right. $r^2(\pi - 2)$

75. Can the Pythagorean Theorem be used to find the length of side c of the triangle at the right? If so, determine c. If not, explain why the theorem cannot be used.

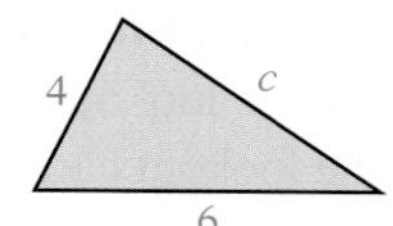

Projects or Group Activities

76. The length of a side of the outer square in the diagram at the right is $2x$ inches. The corners of the inner square are the midpoints of the sides of the outer square.

a. What is the length of a side of the inner square? $x\sqrt{2}$ inches

b. What is the area of the inner square? $2x^2$ square inches

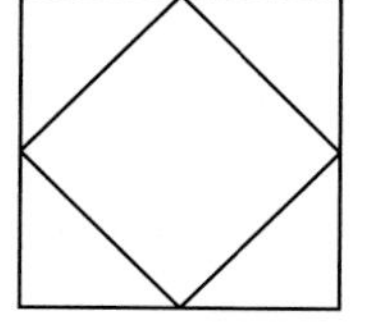

77. Three squares are lined up along the x-axis as shown at the right. Find AB. Round to the nearest tenth. 6.4 units

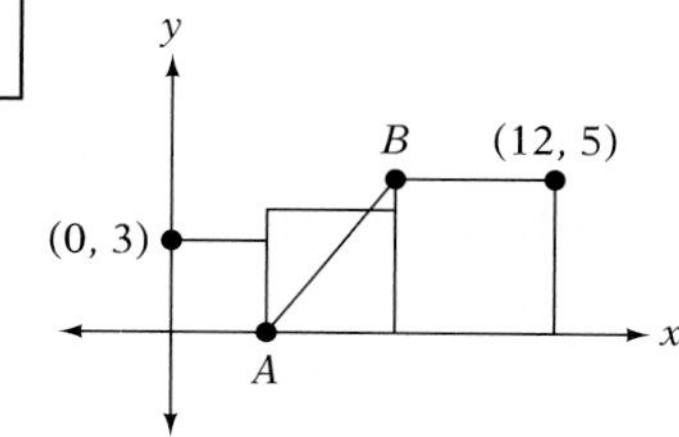

CHAPTER 15 Summary

Key Words

A **square root** of a positive number a is a number whose square is a. Every positive number has two square roots, one positive and one negative. The square root of a negative number is not a real number. [15.1A, p. 772]

Examples

A square root of 49 is 7 because $7^2 = 49$.

A square root of 49 is -7 because $(-7)^2 = 49$.

$\sqrt{-9}$ is not a real number.

The symbol $\sqrt{\ }$ is called a **radical sign** and is used to indicate the positive or **principal square root** of a number. The negative square root of a number is indicated by placing a negative sign in front of the radical. The **radicand** is the expression under the radical sign. [15.1A, p. 772]

$\sqrt{49} = 7$

$-\sqrt{49} = -7$

In the expression $\sqrt{49xy}$, $49xy$ is the radicand.

The square of an integer is a **perfect square.** If a number is not a perfect square, its square root can only be approximated. Such square roots are **irrational numbers.** Their decimal representations never terminate or repeat. [15.1A, p. 772]

1, 4, 9, 16, 25, 36, 49, 64, ... are examples of perfect squares.

7 is not a perfect square. $\sqrt{7}$ is an irrational number.

Conjugates are expressions with two terms that differ only in the sign of one term. The expressions $a + b$ and $a - b$ are conjugates. [15.3A, p. 782]

$-5 + \sqrt{11}$ and $-5 - \sqrt{11}$ are conjugates.

$\sqrt{x} - 3$ and $\sqrt{x} + 3$ are conjugates.

A **radical equation** is an equation that contains a variable expression in a radicand. [15.4A, p. 789]

$\sqrt{2x} + 5 = 9$ is a radical equation.

$2x + \sqrt{5} = 9$ is not a radical equation.

A **right triangle** is a triangle that contains a 90° angle. The side opposite the 90° angle is called the **hypotenuse.** The other two sides are called **legs.** [15.4B, p. 791]

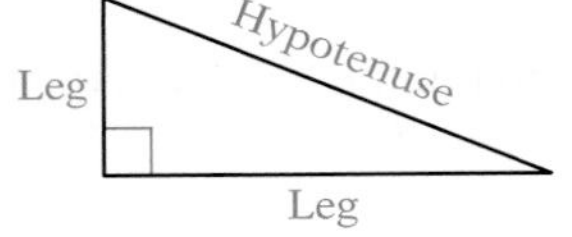

Essential Rules and Procedures

Examples

The Product Property of Square Roots [15.1A, p. 772]
If a and b are positive real numbers, then $\sqrt{ab} = \sqrt{a} \cdot \sqrt{b}$.
Use the Product Property of Square Roots and a knowledge of perfect squares to simplify radicands that are not perfect squares.

$\sqrt{28} = \sqrt{4 \cdot 7} = \sqrt{4} \cdot \sqrt{7} = 2\sqrt{7}$

$\sqrt{9x^7} = \sqrt{9x^6 \cdot x} = \sqrt{9x^6}\sqrt{x} = 3x^3\sqrt{x}$

Adding or Subtracting Radical Expressions [15.2A, p. 778]
The Distributive Property is used to simplify the sum or difference of radical expressions with like radicands.

$8\sqrt{2x} - 3\sqrt{2x} = (8 - 3)\sqrt{2x} = 5\sqrt{2x}$

Multiplying Radical Expressions [15.3A, p. 782]
The Product Property of Square Roots is used to multiply radical expressions.
Use FOIL to multiply radical expressions with two terms.

$\sqrt{2y}(\sqrt{3} - \sqrt{x}) = \sqrt{6y} - \sqrt{2xy}$

$(3 - \sqrt{x})(5 + \sqrt{x})$
$= 15 + 3\sqrt{x} - 5\sqrt{x} - (\sqrt{x})^2$
$= 15 - 2\sqrt{x} - x$

The Quotient Property of Square Roots [15.3B, p. 783]

If a and b are positive real numbers, then $\sqrt{\frac{a}{b}} = \frac{\sqrt{a}}{\sqrt{b}}$ and $\frac{\sqrt{a}}{\sqrt{b}} = \sqrt{\frac{a}{b}}$.

The Quotient Property of Square Roots is used to divide radical expressions.

$\frac{\sqrt{27}}{\sqrt{3}} = \sqrt{\frac{27}{3}} = \sqrt{9} = 3$

$\frac{\sqrt{3x^5y}}{\sqrt{75xy^3}} = \sqrt{\frac{3x^5y}{75xy^3}} = \sqrt{\frac{x^4}{25y^2}} = \frac{x^2}{5y}$

Simplest Form of a Radical Expression [15.3B, p. 784]
For a radical expression to be in simplest form, three conditions must be met:

1. The radicand contains no factor greater than 1 that is a perfect square.
2. There is no fraction under the radical sign.
3. There is no radical in the denominator of a fraction.

$\sqrt{12}$, $\sqrt{\frac{3}{4}}$, and $\frac{1}{\sqrt{3}}$ are not in simplest form.

$5\sqrt{3}$ and $\frac{\sqrt{3}}{3}$ are in simplest form.

Rationalizing the Denominator [15.3B, p. 784]
The procedure used to remove a radical from a denominator is called **rationalizing the denominator.**

$\frac{5}{\sqrt{7}} = \frac{5}{\sqrt{7}} \cdot \frac{\sqrt{7}}{\sqrt{7}} = \frac{5\sqrt{7}}{7}$

Property of Squaring Both Sides of an Equation [15.4A, p. 789]
If a and b are real numbers and $a = b$, then $a^2 = b^2$.

$\sqrt{x} = 5$
$(\sqrt{x})^2 = 5^2$
$x = 25$

Procedure for Solving a Radical Equation [15.4A, p. 789]

1. Write the equation with the radical alone on one side.
2. Square both sides of the equation.
3. Solve for the variable.
4. Check the solution(s) in the original equation.

$\sqrt{2x} - 1 = 5$
$\sqrt{2x} = 6$ • Isolate the radical.
$(\sqrt{2x})^2 = 6^2$ • Square both sides.
$2x = 36$
$x = 18$ • Solve for x.

The solution checks.

Pythagorean Theorem [15.4B, p. 791]
If a and b are the lengths of the legs of a right triangle and c is the length of the hypotenuse, then $c^2 = a^2 + b^2$.

Two legs of a right triangle measure 4 cm and 7 cm. Find the length of the hypotenuse.

$c = \sqrt{a^2 + b^2}$
$c = \sqrt{4^2 + 7^2}$ • $a = 4, b = 7$
$c = \sqrt{16 + 49}$
$c = \sqrt{65}$

The length of the hypotenuse is $\sqrt{65}$ cm.

CHAPTER

15 Review Exercises

1. Simplify: $\sqrt{3}(\sqrt{12} - \sqrt{3})$
3 [15.3A]

2. Simplify: $3\sqrt{18a^5b}$
$9a^2\sqrt{2ab}$ [15.1B]

3. Simplify: $2\sqrt{36}$
12 [15.1A]

4. Simplify: $\sqrt{6a}(\sqrt{3a} + \sqrt{2a})$
$3a\sqrt{2} + 2a\sqrt{3}$ [15.3A]

5. Simplify: $\dfrac{12}{\sqrt{6}}$
$2\sqrt{6}$ [15.3B]

6. Simplify: $2\sqrt{8} - 3\sqrt{32}$
$-8\sqrt{2}$ [15.2A]

7. Simplify: $(3 - \sqrt{7})(3 + \sqrt{7})$
2 [15.3A]

8. Solve: $\sqrt{x + 3} - \sqrt{x} = 1$
1 [15.4A]

9. Simplify: $\dfrac{2x}{\sqrt{3} - \sqrt{5}}$
$-x\sqrt{3} - x\sqrt{5}$ [15.3B]

10. Simplify: $-3\sqrt{120}$
$-6\sqrt{30}$ [15.1A]

11. Solve: $\sqrt{5x} = 10$
20 [15.4A]

12. Simplify: $5\sqrt{48}$
$20\sqrt{3}$ [15.1A]

13. Simplify: $\dfrac{\sqrt{98x^7y^9}}{\sqrt{2x^3y}}$
$7x^2y^4$ [15.3B]

14. Solve: $3 - \sqrt{7x} = 5$
No solution [15.4A]

15. Simplify: $6a\sqrt{80b} - \sqrt{180a^2b} + 5a\sqrt{b}$
$18a\sqrt{5b} + 5a\sqrt{b}$ [15.2A]

16. Simplify: $4\sqrt{250}$
$20\sqrt{10}$ [15.1A]

17. Simplify: $2x\sqrt{60x^3y^3} + 3x^2y\sqrt{15xy}$
$7x^2y\sqrt{15xy}$ [15.2A]

18. Simplify: $(4\sqrt{y} - \sqrt{5})(2\sqrt{y} + 3\sqrt{5})$
$8y + 10\sqrt{5y} - 15$ [15.3A]

19. Simplify: $3\sqrt{12x} + 5\sqrt{48x}$
$26\sqrt{3x}$ [15.2A]

20. Solve: $\sqrt{2x - 3} + 4 = 0$
No solution [15.4A]

21. Simplify: $\dfrac{8}{\sqrt{x} - 3}$
$\dfrac{8\sqrt{x} + 24}{x - 9}$ [15.3B]

22. Simplify: $4y\sqrt{243x^{17}y^9}$
$36x^8y^5\sqrt{3xy}$ [15.1B]

23. Simplify: $y\sqrt{24y^6}$
$2y^4\sqrt{6}$ [15.1B]

24. Solve: $2x + 4 = \sqrt{x^2 + 3}$
-1 [15.4A]

25. Simplify:
$2x^2\sqrt{18x^2y^5} + 6y\sqrt{2x^6y^3} - 9xy^2\sqrt{8x^4y}$
$-6x^3y^2\sqrt{2y}$ [15.2A]

26. Simplify: $\dfrac{16}{\sqrt{a}}$
$\dfrac{16\sqrt{a}}{a}$ [15.3B]

27. Surveying To find the distance across a pond, a surveyor constructs a right triangle as shown at the right. Find the distance d across the pond. Round to the nearest foot.
43 ft [15.4B]

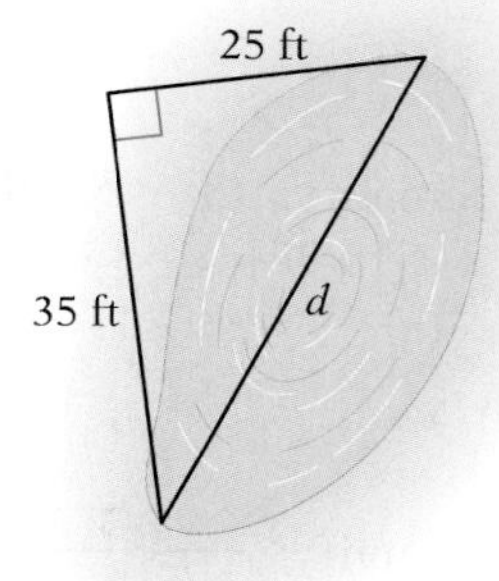

28. Space Exploration The weight of an object is related to the object's distance above the surface of Earth. An equation for this relationship is $d = 4000\sqrt{\frac{W_0}{W_d}} - 4000$, where W_0 is an object's weight on the surface of Earth and W_d is the object's weight at a distance of d miles above Earth's surface. If a space explorer weighs 36 lb at a distance of 4000 mi above the surface of Earth, how much does the explorer weigh on the surface of Earth?
144 lb [15.4B]

29. Tsunamis A tsunami is a great sea wave produced by underwater earthquakes or volcanic eruption. The velocity of a tsunami as it approaches land depends on the depth of the water and can be approximated by the equation $v = 3\sqrt{d}$, where d is the depth of the water in feet and v is the velocity of the tsunami in feet per second. Find the depth of the water if the velocity of a tsunami is 30 ft/s.
100 ft [15.4B]

30. Bicycle Safety A bicycle will overturn if it rounds a corner too sharply or too fast. An equation for the maximum velocity at which a cyclist can turn a corner without tipping over is $v = 4\sqrt{r}$, where v is the velocity of the bicycle in miles per hour and r is the radius of the corner in feet. What is the radius of the sharpest corner that a cyclist can safely turn while riding at 20 mph?
25 ft [15.4B]

© mypokcik/Shutterstock.com

CHAPTER 15 TEST

1. Simplify: $\sqrt{121x^8y^2}$
$11x^4y$ [15.1B]

2. Simplify: $\sqrt{3x^2y}\sqrt{6xy^2}\sqrt{2x}$
$6x^2y\sqrt{y}$ [15.3A]

3. Simplify: $5\sqrt{8} - 3\sqrt{50}$
$-5\sqrt{2}$ [15.2A]

4. Simplify: $\sqrt{45}$
$3\sqrt{5}$ [15.1A]

5. Simplify: $\dfrac{\sqrt{162}}{\sqrt{2}}$
9 [15.3B]

6. Solve: $\sqrt{9x} + 3 = 18$
25 [15.4A]

7. Simplify: $\sqrt{32a^5b^{11}}$
$4a^2b^5\sqrt{2ab}$ [15.1B]

8. Simplify: $\dfrac{\sqrt{98a^6b^4}}{\sqrt{2a^3b^2}}$
$7ab\sqrt{a}$ [15.3B]

9. Simplify: $\dfrac{2}{\sqrt{3} - 1}$
$\sqrt{3} + 1$ [15.3B]

10. Simplify: $\sqrt{8x^3y}\sqrt{10xy^4}$
$4x^2y^2\sqrt{5y}$ [15.3A]

11. Solve: $\sqrt{x-5} + \sqrt{x} = 5$
9 [15.4A]

12. Simplify: $3\sqrt{8y} - 2\sqrt{72x} + 5\sqrt{18y}$
$21\sqrt{2y} - 12\sqrt{2x}$ [15.2A]

13. Simplify: $\sqrt{72x^7y^2}$
$6x^3y\sqrt{2x}$ [15.1B]

14. Simplify: $(\sqrt{y} - 3)(\sqrt{y} + 5)$
$y + 2\sqrt{y} - 15$ [15.3A]

15. Simplify: $2x\sqrt{3xy^3} - 2y\sqrt{12x^3y} - 3xy\sqrt{xy}$
$-2xy\sqrt{3xy} - 3xy\sqrt{xy}$ [15.2A]

16. Simplify: $\dfrac{2 - \sqrt{5}}{6 + \sqrt{5}}$
$\dfrac{17 - 8\sqrt{5}}{31}$ [15.3B]

17. Simplify: $\sqrt{a}(\sqrt{a} - \sqrt{b})$
$a - \sqrt{ab}$ [15.3A]

18. Simplify: $\sqrt{75}$
$5\sqrt{3}$ [15.1A]

19. Physics Find the length of a pendulum that makes one swing in 3 s. The equation for the time of one swing of a pendulum is $T = 2\pi\sqrt{\frac{L}{32}}$, where T is the time in seconds and L is the length in feet. Use 3.14 for π. Round to the nearest hundredth.
7.30 ft [15.4B]

20. Camping A support rope for a tent is attached to the top of a pole and then secured to the ground as shown in the figure at the right. If the rope is 8 ft long and the pole is 4 ft high, how far x from the base of the pole should the rope be secured? Round to the nearest foot.
7 ft [15.4B]

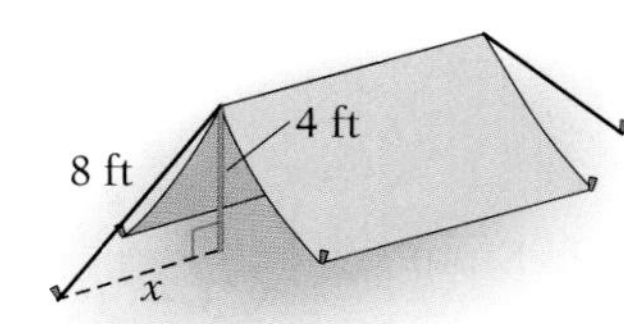

Cumulative Review Exercises

1. Simplify:
$\left(\frac{2}{3}\right)^2 \cdot \left(\frac{3}{4} - \frac{3}{2}\right) + \left(\frac{1}{2}\right)^2$
$-\frac{1}{12}$ [3.5A]

2. Simplify:
$-3[x - 2(3 - 2x) - 5x] + 2x$
$2x + 18$ [4.2D]

3. Solve:
$2x - 4[3x - 2(1 - 3x)] = 2(3 - 4x)$
$\frac{1}{13}$ [5.3B]

4. Simplify: $(-3x^2y)(-2x^3y^4)$
$6x^5y^5$ [9.2A]

5. Simplify: $\frac{12b^4 - 6b^2 + 2}{-6b^2}$
$-2b^2 + 1 - \frac{1}{3b^2}$ [9.5A]

6. Given $f(x) = \frac{2x}{x - 3}$, find $f(-3)$.
1 [12.1D]

7. Factor: $2a^3 - 16a^2 + 30a$
$2a(a - 5)(a - 3)$ [10.2B]

8. Multiply: $\frac{3x^3 - 6x^2}{4x^2 + 4x} \cdot \frac{3x - 9}{9x^3 - 45x^2 + 54x}$
$\frac{1}{4(x + 1)}$ [11.1B]

9. Subtract: $\frac{x + 2}{x - 4} - \frac{6}{(x - 4)(x - 3)}$
$\frac{x + 3}{x - 3}$ [11.3B]

10. Solve: $\frac{x}{2x - 5} - 2 = \frac{3x}{2x - 5}$
$\frac{5}{3}$ [11.5A]

11. Find the equation of the line that contains the point $(-2, -3)$ and has slope $\frac{1}{2}$.
$y = \frac{1}{2}x - 2$ [12.4A]

12. Solve by substitution:
$4x - 3y = 1$
$2x + y = 3$
(1, 1) [13.2A]

13. Solve by the addition method:
$5x + 4y = 7$
$3x - 2y = 13$
$(3, -2)$ [13.3A]

14. Solve: $3(x - 7) \geq 5x - 12$
$x \leq -\frac{9}{2}$ [14.3A]

15. Simplify: $\sqrt{108}$
$6\sqrt{3}$ [15.1A]

16. Simplify: $3\sqrt{32} - 2\sqrt{128}$
$-4\sqrt{2}$ [15.2A]

17. Simplify: $2a\sqrt{2ab^3} + b\sqrt{8a^3b} - 5ab\sqrt{ab}$
$4ab\sqrt{2ab} - 5ab\sqrt{ab}$ [15.2A]

18. Simplify: $\sqrt{2a^9b}\sqrt{98ab^3}\sqrt{2a}$
$14a^5b^2\sqrt{2a}$ [15.3A]

19. Simplify: $\sqrt{3}(\sqrt{6} - x)$
$3\sqrt{2} - x\sqrt{3}$ [15.3A]

20. Simplify: $\dfrac{\sqrt{320}}{\sqrt{5}}$
8 [15.3B]

21. Simplify: $\dfrac{3}{2 - \sqrt{5}}$
$-6 - 3\sqrt{5}$ [15.3B]

22. Solve: $\sqrt{3x - 2} - 4 = 0$
6 [15.4A]

23. Markup The selling price of a book is \$59.40. The markup rate used by the bookstore is 20%. Find the cost of the book. Use the formula $S = C + rC$, where S is the selling price, C is the cost, and r is the markup rate.
\$49.50 [5.2B]

24. Uniform Motion Two cyclists start from the same point and ride in opposite directions. One cyclist rides 4 mph faster than the other. In 2 h, they are 52 mi apart. Find the rate of the faster cyclist.
15 mph [5.5B]

25. Number Problem The sum of two numbers is twenty-one. The product of the two numbers is one hundred four. Find the two numbers.
8, 13 [10.6B]

26. Work Problem A small water pipe takes twice as long to fill a tank as does a larger water pipe. With both pipes open, it takes 16 h to fill the tank. Find the time it would take the small pipe, working alone, to fill the tank.
48 h [11.7A]

27. 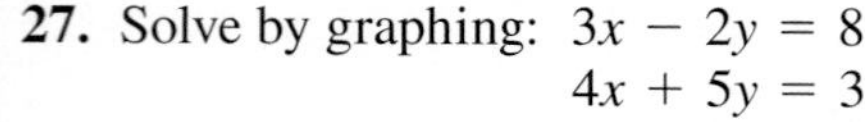
Solve by graphing: $3x - 2y = 8$
$4x + 5y = 3$

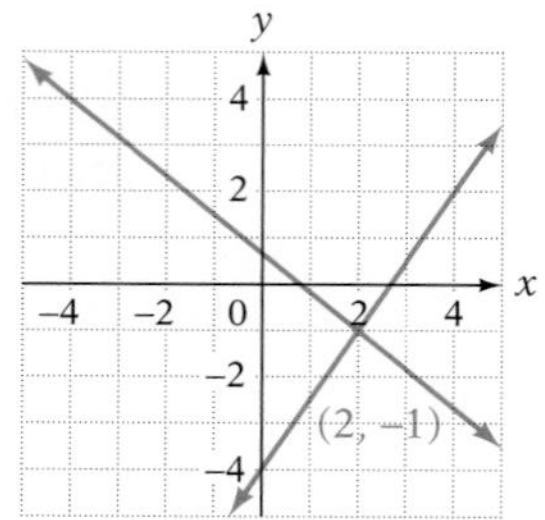

[13.1A]

28. Graph the solution set of $3x + y \leq 2$.

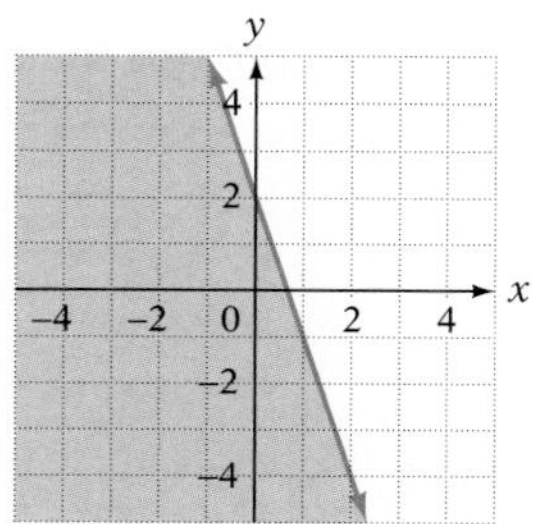

[14.4A]

29. Integer Problem The square root of the sum of two consecutive integers is equal to 9. Find the smaller integer.
40 [15.4B]

30. Physics A stone is dropped from a building and hits the ground 5 s later. How tall is the building? The equation for the distance an object falls in T seconds is $T = \sqrt{\dfrac{d}{16}}$, where d is the distance in feet.
400 ft [15.4B]

Quadratic Equations

OBJECTIVES

SECTION 16.1

A To solve a quadratic equation by factoring

B To solve a quadratic equation by taking square roots

SECTION 16.2

A To solve a quadratic equation by completing the square

SECTION 16.3

A To solve a quadratic equation by using the quadratic formula

SECTION 16.4

A To graph a quadratic equation of the form $y = ax^2 + bx + c$

SECTION 16.5

A To solve application problems

Focus on Success

The end of the semester is generally a very busy and stressful time. You may be dealing with the anxiety of taking final exams. You have covered a great deal of material in this course, and reviewing all of it may be daunting. You might begin by reviewing the Chapter Summary for each chapter that you were assigned during the term. Then take the Final Exam on page 845. The answer to each exercise is given at the back of the book. (See Ace the Test, page AIM-11.)

© F.C.G./Shutterstock.com

Prep Test

Are you ready to succeed in this chapter? Take the Prep Test below to find out if you are ready to learn the new material.

1. Evaluate $b^2 - 4ac$ when $a = 2$, $b = -3$, and $c = -4$.
41 [4.1A]

2. Solve: $5x + 4 = 3$
$-\frac{1}{5}$ [5.2A]

3. Factor: $x^2 + x - 12$
$(x + 4)(x - 3)$ [10.2A]

4. Factor: $4x^2 - 12x + 9$
$(2x - 3)^2$ [10.4A]

5. Is $x^2 - 10x + 25$ a perfect square trinomial?
Yes [10.4A]

6. Solve: $\frac{5}{x - 2} = \frac{15}{x}$
3 [11.5A]

7. Graph: $y = -2x + 3$
[12.2A]

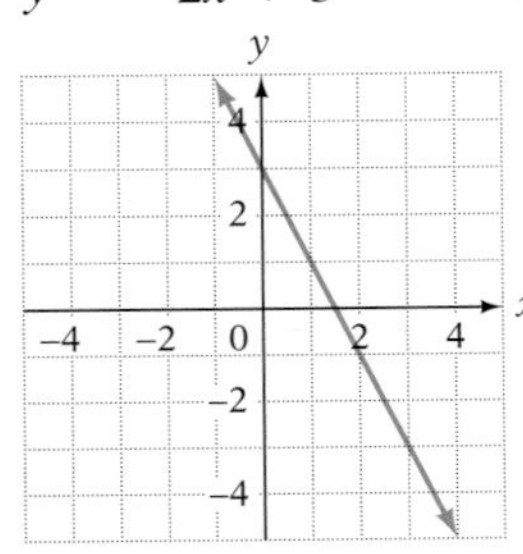

8. Simplify: $\sqrt{28}$
$2\sqrt{7}$ [15.1A]

9. If a is *any* real number, simplify $\sqrt{a^2}$. $|a|$ [15.1B]

10. **Exercising** Walking at a constant speed of 4.5 mph, Lucy and Sam walked from the beginning to the end of a hiking trail. When they reached the end, they immediately started back along the same path at a constant speed of 3 mph. If the round-trip took 2 h, what is the length of the hiking trail? 3.6 mi [5.5B]

SECTION

16.1 Solving Quadratic Equations by Factoring or by Taking Square Roots

OBJECTIVE A *To solve a quadratic equation by factoring*

INSTRUCTOR NOTE
As a class discussion, ask students why the condition $a \neq 0$ is placed on the quadratic equation.

An equation of the form $ax^2 + bx + c = 0$, where a, b, and c are real numbers and $a \neq 0$, is a **quadratic equation.**

$4x^2 - 3x + 1 = 0$, $a = 4, b = -3, c = 1$

$3x^2 - 4 = 0$, $a = 3, b = 0, c = -4$

$\frac{x^2}{2} - 2x + 4 = 0$, $a = \frac{1}{2}, b = -2, c = 4$

A quadratic equation is also called a **second-degree equation.**

A quadratic equation is in **standard form** when the polynomial is in descending order and equal to zero. $3x^2 + 5x - 2 = 0$ is a quadratic equation in standard form.

INSTRUCTOR NOTE
Quadratic equations were solved by factoring earlier in the text. This objective is completely self-contained so that if this is the first introduction for students, all the necessary information is included here.

Recall that the Principle of Zero Products states that if the product of two factors is zero, then at least one of the factors must be zero.

If $a \cdot b = 0$,
then $a = 0$ or $b = 0$.

The Principle of Zero Products can be used to solve quadratic equations by factoring. Write the equation in standard form, factor the polynomial, apply the Principle of Zero Products, and solve for the variable.

HOW TO 1 Solve by factoring: $2x^2 - x = 1$

$$2x^2 - x = 1$$

$$2x^2 - x - 1 = 0$$ • Write the equation in standard form.

$$(2x + 1)(x - 1) = 0$$ • Factor.

$$2x + 1 = 0 \qquad x - 1 = 0$$ • Use the Principle of Zero Products to set each factor equal to zero.

$$2x = -1 \qquad x = 1$$ • Solve each equation for x.

$$x = -\frac{1}{2}$$

Take Note
You should always check your proposed solutions by substituting them back into the *original* equation.

Check:

$2x^2 - x = 1$	
$2\left(-\frac{1}{2}\right)^2 - \left(-\frac{1}{2}\right)$	1
$2 \cdot \frac{1}{4} + \frac{1}{2}$	1
$\frac{1}{2} + \frac{1}{2}$	1
$1 = 1$	

$2x^2 - x = 1$	
$2(1)^2 - 1$	1
$2 \cdot 1 - 1$	1
$2 - 1$	1
$1 = 1$	

The solutions are $-\frac{1}{2}$ and 1.

HOW TO 2 Solve by factoring: $3x^2 - 4x + 8 = (4x + 1)(x - 2)$

$3x^2 - 4x + 8 = (4x + 1)(x - 2)$

$3x^2 - 4x + 8 = 4x^2 - 7x - 2$ • **Multiply the factors on the right side of the equation.**

$0 = x^2 - 3x - 10$ • **Write the equation in standard form.**

$0 = (x - 5)(x + 2)$ • **Factor.**

$x - 5 = 0 \qquad x + 2 = 0$ • **Use the Principle of Zero Products to set each factor equal to zero.**

$x = 5 \qquad x = -2$ • **Solve each equation for x.**

Check:

$3x^2 - 4x + 8$	$= (4x + 1)(x - 2)$
$3(5)^2 - 4(5) + 8$	$(4[5] + 1)(5 - 2)$
$3(25) - 4(5) + 8$	$(20 + 1)(3)$
$75 - 20 + 8$	$(21)(3)$
63	$= 63$

$3x^2 - 4x + 8$	$= (4x + 1)(x - 2)$
$3(-2)^2 - 4(-2) + 8$	$(4[-2] + 1)(-2 - 2)$
$3(4) - 4(-2) + 8$	$(-8 + 1)(-4)$
$12 + 8 + 8$	$(-7)(-4)$
28	$= 28$

The solutions are 5 and -2.

INSTRUCTOR NOTE

For an equation in one variable, the highest exponent on the variable is the same as the number of solutions of the equation. For example, for quadratic equations, the highest exponent on a variable is 2, and the number of solutions is 2. It is for this reason that double roots are emphasized.

HOW TO 3 Solve by factoring: $x^2 - 10x + 25 = 0$

$x^2 - 10x + 25 = 0$

$(x - 5)(x - 5) = 0$ • **Factor.**

$x - 5 = 0 \qquad x - 5 = 0$ • **Use the Principle of Zero Products.**

$x = 5 \qquad x = 5$ • **Solve each equation for x.**

The solution is 5.

In HOW TO 3, 5 is called a **double root** of the quadratic equation.

EXAMPLE 1

Solve by factoring: $\dfrac{z^2}{2} - \dfrac{z}{4} - \dfrac{1}{4} = 0$

Solution

$\dfrac{z^2}{2} - \dfrac{z}{4} - \dfrac{1}{4} = 0$ • **The equation is in standard form.**

$4\left(\dfrac{z^2}{2} - \dfrac{z}{4} - \dfrac{1}{4}\right) = 4(0)$ • **Multiply each side by 4 to clear fractions.**

$2z^2 - z - 1 = 0$

$(2z + 1)(z - 1) = 0$ • **Factor.**

$2z + 1 = 0 \qquad z - 1 = 0$ • **Principle of Zero Products**

$2z = -1 \qquad z = 1$

$z = -\dfrac{1}{2}$

The solutions are $-\frac{1}{2}$ and 1.

YOU TRY IT 1

Solve by factoring: $\dfrac{3y^2}{2} + y - \dfrac{1}{2} = 0$

Your solution

$\dfrac{1}{3}, -1$

IN-CLASS EXAMPLES

Solve by factoring.

1. $x(x - 1) = 12$ **$-3, 4$**
2. $5x^2 + 9x - 2 = 0$ **$\frac{1}{5}, -2$**
3. $\dfrac{x^2}{2} + \dfrac{5x}{6} + \dfrac{1}{3} = 0$ **$-\frac{2}{3}, -1$**

Solution on p. S37

OBJECTIVE B *To solve a quadratic equation by taking square roots*

Consider a quadratic equation of the form $x^2 = a$. This equation can be solved by factoring.

$$x^2 = 25$$
$$x^2 - 25 = 0$$
$$(x - 5)(x + 5) = 0$$
$$x - 5 = 0 \qquad x + 5 = 0$$
$$x = 5 \qquad x = -5$$

The solutions are 5 and -5. The solutions are plus or minus the same number, which is frequently written by using $\pm$; for example, "the solutions are ± 5." An alternative method of solving this equation is suggested by the fact that ± 5 can be written as $\pm\sqrt{25}$.

Take Note
Recall that the solution of the equation $|x| = 5$ is ± 5. This principle is used when solving an equation by taking square roots. Remember that $\sqrt{x^2} = |x|$. Therefore,

$x^2 = 25$
$\sqrt{x^2} = \sqrt{25}$
$|x| = 5$ • $\sqrt{x^2} = |x|$
$x = \pm 5$ • If $|x| = 5$, then $x = \pm 5$.

Principle of Taking the Square Root of Each Side of an Equation

If $x^2 = a$, then $x = \pm\sqrt{a}$.

EXAMPLE

Solve by taking square roots: $x^2 = 25$

$x^2 = 25$
$\sqrt{x^2} = \sqrt{25}$ • Take the square root of each side of the equation. Then simplify.
$x = \pm\sqrt{25}$
$x = \pm 5$

The solutions are 5 and -5.

Take Note
Here is a check for HOW TO 4 at the right.

Check:

$3x^2 = 36$	
$3(2\sqrt{3})^2$	36
$3(12)$	36
$36 = 36$	

$3x^2 = 36$	
$3(-2\sqrt{3})^2$	36
$3(12)$	36
$36 = 36$	

HOW TO 4 Solve by taking square roots: $3x^2 = 36$

$3x^2 = 36$
$x^2 = 12$ • Solve for x^2. Divide each side by 3.
$\sqrt{x^2} = \sqrt{12}$ • Take the square root of each side.
$x = \pm\sqrt{12}$ • Simplify.
$x = \pm 2\sqrt{3}$

The solutions are $2\sqrt{3}$ and $-2\sqrt{3}$.

HOW TO 5 Solve by taking square roots: $49y^2 - 25 = 0$

$49y^2 - 25 = 0$
$49y^2 = 25$ • Solve for y^2. Add 25 to each side.
$y^2 = \frac{25}{49}$ • Divide each side by 49.
$\sqrt{y^2} = \sqrt{\frac{25}{49}}$ • Take the square root of each side.
$y = \pm\frac{5}{7}$ • Simplify.

The solutions are $\frac{5}{7}$ and $-\frac{5}{7}$.

An equation that contains the square of a binomial can be solved by taking square roots.

Take Note

Here is a check for one of the solutions in HOW TO 6 at the right. You should check all solutions.

Check:

$$\begin{array}{r|l} 2(x-1)^2-36 & 0 \\ \hline 2(1+3\sqrt{2}-1)^2-36 & 0 \\ 2(3\sqrt{2})^2-36 & 0 \\ 2(18)-36 & 0 \\ 36-36 & 0 \\ 0 = 0 & \end{array}$$

HOW TO 6 Solve by taking square roots: $2(x-1)^2 - 36 = 0$

$2(x-1)^2 - 36 = 0$

$2(x-1)^2 = 36$ • Solve for $(x-1)^2$. Add 36 to each side.

$(x-1)^2 = 18$ • Divide each side by 2.

$\sqrt{(x-1)^2} = \sqrt{18}$ • Take the square root of each side.

$x - 1 = \pm\sqrt{18}$

$x - 1 = \pm 3\sqrt{2}$ • Simplify.

$x = 1 \pm 3\sqrt{2}$ • Solve for x.

The solutions are $1 + 3\sqrt{2}$ and $1 - 3\sqrt{2}$.

EXAMPLE 2

Solve by taking square roots:
$x^2 + 16 = 0$

Solution

$x^2 + 16 = 0$

$x^2 = -16$ • Solve for x^2.

$\sqrt{x^2} = \sqrt{-16}$ • Take square roots.

$\sqrt{-16}$ is not a real number.

The equation has no real number solution.

YOU TRY IT 2

Solve by taking square roots:
$x^2 + 81 = 0$

Your solution

No real number solution

EXAMPLE 3

Solve by taking square roots:
$5(y-4)^2 = 25$

Solution

$5(y-4)^2 = 25$

$(y-4)^2 = 5$ • Solve for $(y-4)^2$.

$\sqrt{(y-4)^2} = \sqrt{5}$ • Take square roots.

$y - 4 = \pm\sqrt{5}$ • Simplify.

$y = 4 \pm \sqrt{5}$ • Solve for y.

The solutions are $4 + \sqrt{5}$ and $4 - \sqrt{5}$.

YOU TRY IT 3

Solve by taking square roots:
$7(z+2)^2 = 21$

Your solution

$-2 \pm \sqrt{3}$

IN-CLASS EXAMPLES

Solve by taking square roots.

4. $x^2 - 8 = 0$ **$\pm 2\sqrt{2}$**
5. $y^2 + 64 = 0$ **No real number solution**
6. $11(x+3)^2 = 66$ **$-3 \pm \sqrt{6}$**

Solutions on p. S37

16.1 EXERCISES

Concept Check

SUGGESTED ASSIGNMENT:
Exercises 1–5; Exercises 7–37, odds; Exercises 41–65, odds

1. By the Principle of Zero Products, if $(3x + 4)(x - 7) = 0$, then $\underline{3x + 4} = 0$ or $\underline{x - 7} = 0$.

2. The solutions of an equation are $x = \pm 6$. This means that $x = \underline{6}$ or $x = \underline{-6}$.

For Exercises 3 to 5, write the quadratic equation in standard form.

3. $x^2 - 8 = 3x$ $\quad x^2 - 3x - 8 = 0$
4. $2x^2 = 4x - 1$ $\quad 2x^2 - 4x + 1 = 0$
5. $x + 5 = x(x - 3)$ $\quad x^2 - 4x - 5 = 0$

OBJECTIVE A To solve a quadratic equation by factoring

For Exercises 6 to 8, solve for x.

6. $x(x - 7) = 0$ $\quad 0, 7$
7. $(2x + 5)(3x - 1) = 0$ $\quad -\frac{5}{2}, \frac{1}{3}$
8. $(x - 4)(2x - 7) = 0$ $\quad \frac{7}{2}, 4$

For Exercises 9 to 38, solve by factoring.

9. $x^2 + 2x - 15 = 0$ $\quad -5, 3$
10. $t^2 + 3t - 10 = 0$ $\quad -5, 2$
11. $z^2 - 4z + 3 = 0$ $\quad 1, 3$
12. $s^2 - 5s + 4 = 0$ $\quad 1, 4$
13. $p^2 + 3p + 2 = 0$ $\quad -2, -1$
14. $v^2 + 6v + 5 = 0$ $\quad -5, -1$
15. $x^2 - 6x + 9 = 0$ $\quad 3$
16. $y^2 - 8y + 16 = 0$ $\quad 4$
17. $12y^2 + 8y = 0$ $\quad -\frac{2}{3}, 0$
18. $6x^2 - 9x = 0$ $\quad 0, \frac{3}{2}$
19. $r^2 - 10 = 3r$ $\quad -2, 5$
20. $t^2 - 12 = 4t$ $\quad -2, 6$
21. $3v^2 - 5v + 2 = 0$ $\quad \frac{2}{3}, 1$
22. $2p^2 - 3p - 2 = 0$ $\quad -\frac{1}{2}, 2$
23. $3s^2 + 8s = 3$ $\quad -3, \frac{1}{3}$
24. $3x^2 + 5x = 12$ $\quad \frac{4}{3}, -3$
25. $\frac{3}{4}z^2 - z = -\frac{1}{3}$ $\quad \frac{2}{3}$
26. $\frac{r^2}{2} = 1 - \frac{r}{12}$ $\quad -\frac{3}{2}, \frac{4}{3}$
27. $4t^2 = 4t + 3$ $\quad -\frac{1}{2}, \frac{3}{2}$
28. $5y^2 + 11y = 12$ $\quad -3, \frac{4}{5}$
29. $4v^2 - 4v + 1 = 0$ $\quad \frac{1}{2}$
30. $9s^2 - 6s + 1 = 0$ $\quad \frac{1}{3}$
31. $x^2 - 9 = 0$ $\quad -3, 3$
32. $t^2 - 16 = 0$ $\quad -4, 4$
33. $4y^2 - 1 = 0$ $\quad -\frac{1}{2}, \frac{1}{2}$
34. $9z^2 - 4 = 0$ $\quad -\frac{2}{3}, \frac{2}{3}$
35. $x + 15 = x(x - 1)$ $\quad -3, 5$
36. $p + 18 = p(p - 2)$ $\quad -3, 6$
37. $r^2 - r - 2 = (2r - 1)(r - 3)$ $\quad 1, 5$
38. $s^2 + 5s - 4 = (2s + 1)(s - 4)$ $\quad 0, 12$

39. Let a be a positive integer. Which equation has a positive double root?
(i) $x^2 - a^2 = 0$ **(ii)** $x^2 + 2ax + a^2 = 0$ **(iii)** $x^2 - 2ax + a^2 = 0$ iii

OBJECTIVE B To solve a quadratic equation by taking square roots

For Exercises 40 to 66, solve by taking square roots.

40. $x^2 = 36$
± 6

41. $y^2 = 49$
± 7

42. $v^2 - 1 = 0$
± 1

43. $z^2 - 64 = 0$
± 8

44. $4x^2 - 49 = 0$
$\pm\frac{7}{2}$

45. $9w^2 - 64 = 0$
$\pm\frac{8}{3}$

46. $9y^2 = 4$
$\pm\frac{2}{3}$

47. $4z^2 = 25$
$\pm\frac{5}{2}$

48. $16v^2 - 9 = 0$
$\pm\frac{3}{4}$

49. $25x^2 - 64 = 0$
$\pm\frac{8}{5}$

50. $y^2 + 81 = 0$
No real number solution

51. $z^2 + 49 = 0$
No real number solution

52. $w^2 - 24 = 0$
$\pm 2\sqrt{6}$

53. $v^2 - 48 = 0$
$\pm 4\sqrt{3}$

54. $(x - 1)^2 = 36$
$-5, 7$

55. $(y + 2)^2 = 49$
$-9, 5$

56. $2(x + 5)^2 = 8$
$-3, -7$

57. $4(z - 3)^2 = 100$
$-2, 8$

58. $9(x - 1)^2 - 16 = 0$
$-\frac{1}{3}, \frac{7}{3}$

59. $4(y + 3)^2 - 81 = 0$
$-\frac{15}{2}, \frac{3}{2}$

60. $49(v + 1)^2 - 25 = 0$
$-\frac{12}{7}, -\frac{2}{7}$

61. $81(y - 2)^2 - 64 = 0$
$\frac{10}{9}, \frac{26}{9}$

62. $(x - 4)^2 - 20 = 0$
$4 \pm 2\sqrt{5}$

63. $(y + 5)^2 - 50 = 0$
$-5 \pm 5\sqrt{2}$

64. $(x + 1)^2 + 36 = 0$
No real number solution

65. $2\left(z - \frac{1}{2}\right)^2 = 12$
$\frac{1}{2} \pm \sqrt{6}$

66. $3\left(v + \frac{3}{4}\right)^2 = 36$
$-\frac{3}{4} \pm 2\sqrt{3}$

For Exercises 67 to 70, assume that a and b are both positive numbers. For each equation, state the number of real number solutions.

67. $(x + a)^2 = 0$
One

68. $ax^2 - b = 0$
Two

69. $(x + a)^2 = b$
Two

70. $ax^2 + b = 0$
Zero

Critical Thinking

71. Evaluate $2n^2 - 7n - 4$, given $n(n - 2) = 15$.
11, 35

72. Evaluate $3y^2 + 5y - 2$, given $y(y + 3) = 28$.
66, 110

Projects or Group Activities

73. Investments The value A of an initial investment of P dollars after 2 years is given by $A = P(1 + r)^2$, where r is the annual interest rate earned by the investment. If an initial investment of \$1500 grew to a value of \$1782.15 in 2 years, what was the annual interest rate? 9%

QUICK QUIZ

1. Solve by factoring: $x(x + 8) = 2x - 9$
−3 [16.1A]
2. Solve by taking square roots: $9x^2 - 4 = 0$
$\pm\frac{2}{3}$ **[16.1B]**

SECTION

16.2 Solving Quadratic Equations by Completing the Square

OBJECTIVE A *To solve a quadratic equation by completing the square*

INSTRUCTOR NOTE
This section is very difficult for students. Writing an outline of the procedure on the board and allowing students to use it to solve some quadratic equations will help many students. Then erase the procedure and ask students to recreate it on paper for themselves. Go over their procedures to be sure they have a workable plan.

Recall that a perfect-square trinomial is the square of a binomial.

Perfect-Square Trinomial		Square of a Binomial
$x^2 + 6x + 9$	=	$(x + 3)^2$
$x^2 - 10x + 25$	=	$(x - 5)^2$
$x^2 + 8x + 16$	=	$(x + 4)^2$

For each perfect-square trinomial, the square of $\frac{1}{2}$ of the coefficient of x equals the constant term.

$x^2 + 6x + 9$, $\quad \left(\frac{1}{2} \cdot 6\right)^2 = 9$

$x^2 - 10x + 25$, $\quad \left[\frac{1}{2}(-10)\right]^2 = 25$

$x^2 + 8x + 16$, $\quad \left(\frac{1}{2} \cdot 8\right)^2 = 16$

Adding to a binomial the constant term that makes it a perfect-square trinomial is called **completing the square.**

HOW TO 1 Complete the square on $x^2 - 8x$. Write the resulting perfect-square trinomial as the square of a binomial.

$\left[\frac{1}{2}(-8)\right]^2 = 16$ • Find the constant term.

$x^2 - 8x + 16$ • Complete the square on $x^2 - 8x$ by adding the constant term.

$x^2 - 8x + 16 = (x - 4)^2$ • Write the resulting perfect-square trinomial as the square of a binomial.

HOW TO 2 Complete the square on $y^2 + 5y$. Write the resulting perfect-square trinomial as the square of a binomial.

$\left(\frac{1}{2} \cdot 5\right)^2 = \left(\frac{5}{2}\right)^2 = \frac{25}{4}$ • Find the constant term.

$y^2 + 5y + \frac{25}{4}$ • Complete the square on $y^2 + 5y$ by adding the constant term.

$y^2 + 5y + \frac{25}{4} = \left(y + \frac{5}{2}\right)^2$ • Write the resulting perfect-square trinomial as the square of a binomial.

A quadratic equation that cannot be solved by factoring can be solved by completing the square. When the quadratic equation is in the form $x^2 + bx = c$, add to each side of the equation the term that completes the square on $x^2 + bx$. Factor the perfect-square trinomial, and write it as the square of a binomial. Take the square root of each side of the equation, and then solve for x.

Tips for Success

This is a new skill and one that is difficult for many students. Be sure to do all you need to do in order to be successful at solving quadratic equations by completing the square: Read through the introductory material, work through the How To examples, study the paired examples, do the You Try Its, and check your solutions against the ones given in the back of the book. See *AIM for Success* at the front of the book.

HOW TO 3 Solve by completing the square: $x^2 + 8x - 2 = 0$

$$x^2 + 8x - 2 = 0$$

$$x^2 + 8x = 2$$ • Add 2 to each side of the equation.

$$x^2 + 8x + \left(\frac{1}{2}\cdot 8\right)^2 = 2 + \left(\frac{1}{2}\cdot 8\right)^2$$ • Complete the square on $x^2 + 8x$. Add $\left(\frac{1}{2}\cdot 8\right)^2$ to each side of the equation.

$$x^2 + 8x + 16 = 2 + 16$$ • Simplify.

$$(x+4)^2 = 18$$ • Factor the perfect-square trinomial.

$$\sqrt{(x+4)^2} = \sqrt{18}$$ • Take the square root of each side of the equation.

$$x + 4 = \pm\sqrt{18}$$ • Solve for x.

$$x + 4 = \pm 3\sqrt{2}$$

$$x = -4 \pm 3\sqrt{2}$$

Check:

$x^2 + 8x - 2 = 0$	
$(-4+3\sqrt{2})^2 + 8(-4+3\sqrt{2}) - 2$	0
$16 - 24\sqrt{2} + 18 - 32 + 24\sqrt{2} - 2$	0
$0 = 0$	

$x^2 + 8x - 2 = 0$	
$(-4-3\sqrt{2})^2 + 8(-4-3\sqrt{2}) - 2$	0
$16 + 24\sqrt{2} + 18 - 32 - 24\sqrt{2} - 2$	0
$0 = 0$	

The solutions are $-4 + 3\sqrt{2}$ and $-4 - 3\sqrt{2}$.

If the coefficient of the second-degree term is not 1, a necessary step in completing the square is to multiply each side of the equation by the reciprocal of that coefficient.

HOW TO 4 Solve by completing the square: $2x^2 - 3x + 1 = 0$

$$2x^2 - 3x + 1 = 0$$

$$2x^2 - 3x = -1$$ • Subtract 1 from each side of the equation.

$$\frac{1}{2}(2x^2 - 3x) = \frac{1}{2}\cdot(-1)$$ • In order to complete the square, the coefficient of x^2 must be 1. Multiply each side of the equation by $\frac{1}{2}$.

$$x^2 - \frac{3}{2}x = -\frac{1}{2}$$

$$x^2 - \frac{3}{2}x + \left[\frac{1}{2}\left(-\frac{3}{2}\right)\right]^2 = -\frac{1}{2} + \left[\frac{1}{2}\left(-\frac{3}{2}\right)\right]^2$$ • Complete the square. Add $\left[\frac{1}{2}\left(-\frac{3}{2}\right)\right]^2$ to each side of the equation.

$$x^2 - \frac{3}{2}x + \frac{9}{16} = -\frac{1}{2} + \frac{9}{16}$$ • Simplify.

$$\left(x - \frac{3}{4}\right)^2 = \frac{1}{16}$$ • Factor the perfect-square trinomial.

$$\sqrt{\left(x - \frac{3}{4}\right)^2} = \sqrt{\frac{1}{16}}$$ • Take the square root of each side of the equation.

$$x - \frac{3}{4} = \pm\frac{1}{4}$$ • Solve for x.

$$x = \frac{3}{4} \pm \frac{1}{4}$$

$$x = \frac{3}{4} + \frac{1}{4} = 1 \qquad x = \frac{3}{4} - \frac{1}{4} = \frac{1}{2}$$

The solutions are $\frac{1}{2}$ and 1.

EXAMPLE 1

Solve by completing the square:
$2x^2 - 4x - 1 = 0$

Solution

$2x^2 - 4x - 1 = 0$

$2x^2 - 4x = 1$ • Add 1.

$\frac{1}{2}(2x^2 - 4x) = \frac{1}{2} \cdot 1$ • Multiply by $\frac{1}{2}$.

$x^2 - 2x = \frac{1}{2}$ • The coefficient of x^2 is 1.

Complete the square.

$x^2 - 2x + 1 = \frac{1}{2} + 1$ • $\left[\frac{1}{2} \cdot (-2)\right]^2 = [-1]^2 = 1$

$(x - 1)^2 = \frac{3}{2}$ • Factor.

$\sqrt{(x - 1)^2} = \sqrt{\frac{3}{2}}$ • Take square roots.

$x - 1 = \pm\frac{\sqrt{6}}{2}$ • Solve for x.

$x = 1 \pm \frac{\sqrt{6}}{2}$

$x = 1 + \frac{\sqrt{6}}{2} = \frac{2 + \sqrt{6}}{2}$ $\qquad x = 1 - \frac{\sqrt{6}}{2} = \frac{2 - \sqrt{6}}{2}$

Check:

$2x^2 - 4x - 1$	$= 0$
$2\left(\frac{2 + \sqrt{6}}{2}\right)^2 - 4\left(\frac{2 + \sqrt{6}}{2}\right) - 1$	0
$2\left(\frac{4 + 4\sqrt{6} + 6}{4}\right) - 2(2 + \sqrt{6}) - 1$	0
$2 + 2\sqrt{6} + 3 - 4 - 2\sqrt{6} - 1$	0
0	$= 0$

$2x^2 - 4x - 1$	$= 0$
$2\left(\frac{2 - \sqrt{6}}{2}\right)^2 - 4\left(\frac{2 - \sqrt{6}}{2}\right) - 1$	0
$2\left(\frac{4 - 4\sqrt{6} + 6}{4}\right) - 2(2 - \sqrt{6}) - 1$	0
$2 - 2\sqrt{6} + 3 - 4 + 2\sqrt{6} - 1$	0
0	$= 0$

The solutions are $\frac{2 + \sqrt{6}}{2}$ and $\frac{2 - \sqrt{6}}{2}$.

YOU TRY IT 1

Solve by completing the square:
$3x^2 - 6x - 2 = 0$

Your solution

$\frac{3 \pm \sqrt{15}}{3}$

Solution on p. S38

IN-CLASS EXAMPLES

Solve by completing the square.

1. $x^2 + 14x = -24$ **−12, −2**
2. $2x^2 + 6x - 1 = 0$ $\frac{-3 \pm \sqrt{11}}{2}$
3. $x^2 + 5x + 14 = 0$ **No real number solution**

EXAMPLE 2

Solve by completing the square:
$x^2 + 4x + 5 = 0$

Solution

$x^2 + 4x + 5 = 0$

$x^2 + 4x = -5$ • **Subtract 5.**

Complete the square.

$x^2 + 4x + 4 = -5 + 4$ • $\left(\frac{1}{2} \cdot 4\right)^2 = 2^2 = 4$

$(x + 2)^2 = -1$ • **Factor.**

$\sqrt{(x + 2)^2} = \sqrt{-1}$ • **Take square roots.**

$\sqrt{-1}$ is not a real number.

The quadratic equation has no real number solution.

YOU TRY IT 2

Solve by completing the square:
$x^2 + 6x + 12 = 0$

Your solution

No real number solution

EXAMPLE 3

Solve $x^2 = -6x - 4$ by completing the square. Approximate the solutions to the nearest thousandth.

Solution

$x^2 = -6x - 4$

$x^2 + 6x = -4$ • **Add 6x.**

Complete the square.

$x^2 + 6x + 9 = -4 + 9$ • $\left(\frac{1}{2} \cdot 6\right)^2 = 3^2 = 9$

$(x + 3)^2 = 5$ • **Factor.**

$\sqrt{(x + 3)^2} = \sqrt{5}$ • **Take square roots.**

$x + 3 = \pm\sqrt{5}$

$x + 3 = \sqrt{5}$ $\qquad$ $x + 3 = -\sqrt{5}$

$x = -3 + \sqrt{5}$ $\qquad$ $x = -3 - \sqrt{5}$

$\approx -3 + 2.236$ $\qquad$ $\approx -3 - 2.236$

≈ -0.764 $\qquad$ ≈ -5.236

The solutions are approximately -0.764 and -5.236.

YOU TRY IT 3

Solve $x^2 + 8x + 8 = 0$ by completing the square. Approximate the solutions to the nearest thousandth.

Your solution

$-1.172, -6.828$

Solutions on p. S38

16.2 EXERCISES

SUGGESTED ASSIGNMENT:
Exercises 1–6; Exercises 7–55, odds

Concept Check

1. When we square a binomial, the result is a ____________. perfect-square trinomial

2. When solving the equation $x^2 - 8x + 16 = 18$ by completing the square, the next step after writing the equation in the form $(x - 4)^2 = 18$ is to ____________. take the square root of each side of the equation

For Exercises 3 to 6, complete the square on the binomial. Write the resulting trinomial as the square of a binomial.

3. $x^2 - 6x$
$x^2 - 6x + 9, (x - 3)^2$

4. $x^2 + 6x$
$x^2 + 6x + 9, (x + 3)^2$

5. $x^2 - 5x$
$x^2 - 5x + \frac{25}{4}, \left(x - \frac{5}{2}\right)^2$

6. $x^2 - 3x$
$x^2 - 3x + \frac{9}{4}, \left(x - \frac{3}{2}\right)^2$

OBJECTIVE A *To solve a quadratic equation by completing the square*

For Exercises 7 to 47, solve by completing the square.

7. $x^2 + 2x - 3 = 0$
$-3, 1$

8. $y^2 + 4y - 5 = 0$
$-5, 1$

9. $z^2 - 6z - 16 = 0$
$-2, 8$

10. $w^2 + 8w - 9 = 0$
$-9, 1$

11. $x^2 = 4x - 4$
2

12. $z^2 = 8z - 16$
4

13. $v^2 - 6v + 13 = 0$
No real number solution

14. $x^2 + 4x + 13 = 0$
No real number solution

15. $y^2 + 5y + 4 = 0$
$-4, -1$

16. $v^2 - 5v - 6 = 0$
$-1, 6$

17. $w^2 + 7w = 8$
$-8, 1$

18. $y^2 + 5y = -4$
$-4, -1$

19. $v^2 + 4v + 1 = 0$
$-2 \pm \sqrt{3}$

20. $y^2 - 2y - 5 = 0$
$1 \pm \sqrt{6}$

21. $x^2 + 6x = 5$
$-3 \pm \sqrt{14}$

22. $w^2 - 8w = 3$
$4 \pm \sqrt{19}$

23. $\frac{z^2}{2} = z + \frac{1}{2}$
$1 \pm \sqrt{2}$

24. $\frac{y^2}{10} = y - 2$
$5 \pm \sqrt{5}$

25. $p^2 + 3p = 1$
$\frac{-3 \pm \sqrt{13}}{2}$

26. $r^2 + 5r = 2$
$\frac{-5 \pm \sqrt{33}}{2}$

27. $t^2 - 3t = -2$
1, 2

28. $z^2 - 5z = -3$
$\frac{5 \pm \sqrt{13}}{2}$

29. $v^2 + v - 3 = 0$
$\frac{-1 \pm \sqrt{13}}{2}$

30. $x^2 - x = 1$
$\frac{1 \pm \sqrt{5}}{2}$

31. $y^2 = 7 - 10y$
$-5 \pm 4\sqrt{2}$

32. $v^2 = 14 + 16v$
$8 \pm \sqrt{78}$

33. $r^2 - 3r = 5$
$\frac{3 \pm \sqrt{29}}{2}$

34. $s^2 + 3s = -1$
$\frac{-3 \pm \sqrt{5}}{2}$

35. $t^2 - t = 4$
$\frac{1 \pm \sqrt{17}}{2}$

36. $y^2 + y - 4 = 0$
$\frac{-1 \pm \sqrt{17}}{2}$

37. $x^2 - 3x + 5 = 0$
No real number solution

38. $z^2 + 5z + 7 = 0$
No real number solution

39. $2t^2 - 3t + 1 = 0$
$\frac{1}{2}, 1$

40. $2x^2 - 7x + 3 = 0$
$\frac{1}{2}, 3$

41. $2r^2 + 5r = 3$
$-3, \frac{1}{2}$

42. $2y^2 - 3y = 4$
$\frac{3 \pm \sqrt{41}}{4}$

43. $2s^2 = 7s - 1$
$\frac{7 \pm \sqrt{41}}{4}$

44. $4v^2 + 4v - 1 = 0$
$\frac{-1 \pm \sqrt{2}}{2}$

45. $6s^2 + s = 3$
$\frac{-1 \pm \sqrt{73}}{12}$

46. $6z^2 = z + 2$
$-\frac{1}{2}, \frac{2}{3}$

47. $6p^2 = 5p + 4$
$-\frac{1}{2}, \frac{4}{3}$

For Exercises 48 and 49, without using a calculator, determine if both of the given solutions are negative, both are positive, or one is negative and one is positive.

48. A quadratic equation has solutions $-3 \pm \sqrt{5}$.
Both negative

49. A quadratic equation has solutions $2 \pm \sqrt{7}$.
One negative and one positive

For Exercises 50 to 53, solve by completing the square. Approximate the solutions to the nearest thousandth.

50. $y^2 + 3y = 5$
−4.193, 1.193

51. $w^2 + 5w = 2$
−5.372, 0.372

52. $2z^2 - 3z = 7$
−1.266, 2.766

53. $2x^2 + 3x = 11$
−3.212, 1.712

QUICK QUIZ

Solve by completing the square.

1. $x^2 - 6x - 7 = 0$
−1, 7 [16.2A]
2. $2x^2 - 2x = 1$
$\frac{1 \pm \sqrt{3}}{2}$ [16.2A]
3. $x^2 - 6x + 16 = 6$
No real number solution [16.2A]

Critical Thinking

54. If $(x + 6)^2 = 9$, then $x + 6$ is equal to what number(s)? −3 or 3

55. Find the solutions of the quadratic equation $ax^2 + bx + c = 0$ in which $a = 1$, $b = 8$, and $c = -14$.
$-4 \pm \sqrt{30}$

For Exercises 56 to 58, solve.

56. $\sqrt{2x + 7} - 4 = x$
−3

57. $\frac{x + 1}{2} + \frac{3}{x - 1} = 4$
$4 \pm \sqrt{3}$

58. $\frac{x - 2}{3} + \frac{2}{x + 2} = 4$
$6 \pm \sqrt{58}$

Projects or Group Activities

59. Explain why the equation $(x - 2)^2 = -4$ does not have a real number solution.

60. What number is equal to three less than its square? $\frac{1 + \sqrt{13}}{2}$ or $\frac{1 - \sqrt{13}}{2}$

61. Baseball A ball player hits a ball. The height of the ball above the ground after t seconds can be approximated by the equation $h = -16t^2 + 76t + 5$. When will the ball hit the ground? *Hint:* The ball strikes the ground when $h = 0$ ft.
After 4.81 s

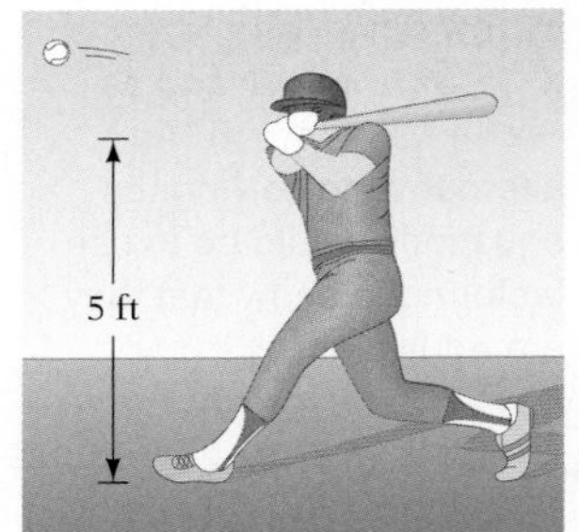

SECTION

16.3 Solving Quadratic Equations by Using the Quadratic Formula

OBJECTIVE A

To solve a quadratic equation by using the quadratic formula

INSTRUCTOR NOTE
Students wonder why we discuss the different ways in which a quadratic equation can be solved. Explain to students that factoring, when the factors are easily determined, is the quickest way. The method of completing the square has other uses besides being used to derive the quadratic formula and is rarely used to solve an equation. The quadratic formula is used for those equations that do not factor.

Any quadratic equation can be solved by completing the square. Applying this method to the standard form of a quadratic equation produces a formula that can be used to solve any quadratic equation.

Solve $ax^2 + bx + c = 0$ by completing the square.

$$ax^2 + bx + c = 0$$

Add the opposite of the constant term to each side of the equation.

$$ax^2 + bx + c + (-c) = 0 + (-c)$$
$$ax^2 + bx = -c$$

Multiply each side of the equation by the reciprocal of a, the coefficient of x^2.

$$\frac{1}{a}(ax^2 + bx) = \frac{1}{a}(-c)$$
$$x^2 + \frac{b}{a}x = -\frac{c}{a}$$

Complete the square by adding $\left(\frac{1}{2} \cdot \frac{b}{a}\right)^2$ to each side of the equation.

$$x^2 + \frac{b}{a}x + \left(\frac{1}{2} \cdot \frac{b}{a}\right)^2 = \left(\frac{1}{2} \cdot \frac{b}{a}\right)^2 - \frac{c}{a}$$
$$x^2 + \frac{b}{a}x + \frac{b^2}{4a^2} = \frac{b^2}{4a^2} - \frac{c}{a}$$

Simplify the right side of the equation.

$$x^2 + \frac{b}{a}x + \frac{b^2}{4a^2} = \frac{b^2}{4a^2} - \left(\frac{c}{a} \cdot \frac{4a}{4a}\right)$$
$$x^2 + \frac{b}{a}x + \frac{b^2}{4a^2} = \frac{b^2}{4a^2} - \frac{4ac}{4a^2}$$
$$x^2 + \frac{b}{a}x + \frac{b^2}{4a^2} = \frac{b^2 - 4ac}{4a^2}$$

Factor the perfect-square trinomial on the left side of the equation.

$$\left(x + \frac{b}{2a}\right)^2 = \frac{b^2 - 4ac}{4a^2}$$

Take the square root of each side of the equation.

$$\sqrt{\left(x + \frac{b}{2a}\right)^2} = \sqrt{\frac{b^2 - 4ac}{4a^2}}$$
$$x + \frac{b}{2a} = \pm\frac{\sqrt{b^2 - 4ac}}{2a}$$

Solve for x.

$$x + \frac{b}{2a} = \frac{\sqrt{b^2 - 4ac}}{2a} \qquad x + \frac{b}{2a} = -\frac{\sqrt{b^2 - 4ac}}{2a}$$
$$x = -\frac{b}{2a} + \frac{\sqrt{b^2 - 4ac}}{2a} \qquad x = -\frac{b}{2a} - \frac{\sqrt{b^2 - 4ac}}{2a}$$
$$= \frac{-b + \sqrt{b^2 - 4ac}}{2a} \qquad = \frac{-b - \sqrt{b^2 - 4ac}}{2a}$$

INSTRUCTOR NOTE
It may help to have students determine a, b, and c for different equations. Here are some suggestions:
$2x = x^2 - 3$
$4x - 3x^2 + 3 = 0$
$2x^2 - x = 0$
Students will ask whether it matters to which side of the equation a term is moved. To convince these students that it does not matter, have them solve $3x = x^2 - 4$ by rewriting it as $x^2 - 3x - 4 = 0$ and as $-x^2 + 3x + 4 = 0$. An alternative to solving the equations would be to use factoring to show that they are equivalent.
$-x^2 + 3x + 4 = 0$
$\rightarrow -(x^2 - 3x - 4) = 0$
$\rightarrow x^2 - 3x - 4 = 0$

The Quadratic Formula

The solutions of the quadratic equation $ax^2 + bx + c = 0$, $a \neq 0$, are

$$x = \frac{-b \pm \sqrt{b^2 - 4ac}}{2a}$$

HOW TO 1 Solve by using the quadratic formula: $2x^2 = 4x - 1$

$$2x^2 = 4x - 1$$
$$2x^2 - 4x + 1 = 0$$

- **Write the equation in standard form. Subtract $4x$ from each side and add 1 to each side.**

$$x = \frac{-b \pm \sqrt{b^2 - 4ac}}{2a}$$

- **The quadratic formula**

$$= \frac{-(-4) \pm \sqrt{(-4)^2 - (4 \cdot 2 \cdot 1)}}{2 \cdot 2}$$

- **$a = 2, b = -4, c = 1$. Replace a, b, and c by their values.**

$$= \frac{4 \pm \sqrt{16 - 8}}{4} = \frac{4 \pm \sqrt{8}}{4}$$

- **Simplify.**

$$= \frac{4 \pm 2\sqrt{2}}{4} = \frac{2 \pm \sqrt{2}}{2}$$

The solutions are $\frac{2 + \sqrt{2}}{2}$ and $\frac{2 - \sqrt{2}}{2}$.

Take Note

$$\frac{4 \pm 2\sqrt{2}}{4} = \frac{2(2 \pm \sqrt{2})}{2 \cdot 2} = \frac{2 \pm \sqrt{2}}{2}$$

EXAMPLE 1

Solve by using the quadratic formula:
$2x^2 - 3x + 1 = 0$

Solution

$$2x^2 - 3x + 1 = 0$$

- **Standard form**

$$x = \frac{-(-3) \pm \sqrt{(-3)^2 - 4(2)(1)}}{2 \cdot 2}$$

- **$a = 2, b = -3, c = 1$**

$$= \frac{3 \pm \sqrt{9 - 8}}{4} = \frac{3 \pm \sqrt{1}}{4} = \frac{3 \pm 1}{4}$$

$$x = \frac{3 + 1}{4} = 1 \qquad x = \frac{3 - 1}{4} = \frac{1}{2}$$

The solutions are 1 and $\frac{1}{2}$.

YOU TRY IT 1

Solve by using the quadratic formula:
$3x^2 + 4x - 4 = 0$

Your solution

$\frac{2}{3}, -2$

EXAMPLE 2

Solve by using the quadratic formula: $\frac{x^2}{2} = 2x - \frac{5}{4}$

Solution

$$\frac{x^2}{2} = 2x - \frac{5}{4}$$

$$4\left(\frac{x^2}{2}\right) = 4\left(2x - \frac{5}{4}\right)$$

- **Multiply by 4.**

$$2x^2 = 8x - 5$$
$$2x^2 - 8x + 5 = 0$$

- **Standard form**

$$x = \frac{-(-8) \pm \sqrt{(-8)^2 - 4(2)(5)}}{2 \cdot 2}$$

- **$a = 2, b = -8, c = 5$**

$$= \frac{8 \pm \sqrt{64 - 40}}{4} = \frac{8 \pm \sqrt{24}}{4}$$

$$= \frac{8 \pm 2\sqrt{6}}{4} = \frac{4 \pm \sqrt{6}}{2}$$

The solutions are $\frac{4 + \sqrt{6}}{2}$ and $\frac{4 - \sqrt{6}}{2}$.

YOU TRY IT 2

Solve by using the quadratic formula: $\frac{x^2}{4} + \frac{x}{2} = \frac{1}{4}$

Your solution

$-1 \pm \sqrt{2}$

IN-CLASS EXAMPLES

Solve by using the quadratic formula.

1. $4x^2 - 9x - 9 = 0$ **$3, -\frac{3}{4}$**
2. $x^2 - 4x = 1$ **$2 \pm \sqrt{5}$**
3. $2x^2 + x + 5 = 0$ **No real number solution**
4. $(2x - 1)(x + 2) = 25$ **$-\frac{9}{2}, 3$**

Solutions on p. S38

16.3 EXERCISES

Concept Check

SUGGESTED ASSIGNMENT
Exercises 1–4; Exercises 5–33, odds; Exercises 37–45, odds

1. If a quadratic equation is solved by using the quadratic formula and the result is $x = \frac{1 \pm \sqrt{13}}{2}$, what are the solutions of the equation? $\frac{1 + \sqrt{13}}{2}$ and $\frac{1 - \sqrt{13}}{2}$
2. If a quadratic equation is solved by using the quadratic formula and the result is $x = \frac{2 \pm 6}{4}$, what are the solutions of the equation? -1 and 2
3. Explain what the quadratic formula is used for.
4. Write the quadratic formula. Explain what each letter in the formula represents.

OBJECTIVE A *To solve a quadratic equation by using the quadratic formula*

For Exercises 5 to 34, solve by using the quadratic formula.

5. $x^2 - 4x - 5 = 0$
   $-1, 5$
6. $y^2 + 3y + 2 = 0$
   $-2, -1$
7. $y^2 = 2y + 3$
   $-1, 3$
8. $w^2 = 3w + 18$
   $-3, 6$
9. $2y^2 - y - 1 = 0$
   $-\frac{1}{2}, 1$
10. $2t^2 - 5t + 3 = 0$
    $1, \frac{3}{2}$
11. $w^2 + 3w + 5 = 0$
    No real number solution
12. $x^2 - 2x + 6 = 0$
    No real number solution
13. $4y^2 + 4y = 15$
    $-\frac{5}{2}, \frac{3}{2}$
14. $6y^2 + 5y - 4 = 0$
    $-\frac{4}{3}, \frac{1}{2}$
15. $2x^2 + x + 1 = 0$
    No real number solution
16. $3r^2 - r + 2 = 0$
    No real number solution
17. $\frac{1}{2}t^2 - t = \frac{5}{2}$
    $1 \pm \sqrt{6}$
18. $y^2 - 4y = 6$
    $2 \pm \sqrt{10}$
19. $\frac{1}{3}t^2 + 2t - \frac{1}{3} = 0$
    $-3 \pm \sqrt{10}$
20. $z^2 + 4z + 1 = 0$
    $-2 \pm \sqrt{3}$
21. $w^2 = 4w + 9$
    $2 \pm \sqrt{13}$
22. $y^2 = 8y + 3$
    $4 \pm \sqrt{19}$
23. $9y^2 + 6y - 1 = 0$
    $\frac{-1 \pm \sqrt{2}}{3}$
24. $9s^2 - 6s - 2 = 0$
    $\frac{1 \pm \sqrt{3}}{3}$
25. $4p^2 + 4p + 1 = 0$
    $-\frac{1}{2}$

26. $9z^2 + 12z + 4 = 0$
$-\frac{2}{3}$

27. $\frac{x^2}{2} = x - \frac{5}{4}$
No real number solution

28. $r^2 = \frac{5}{3}r - 2$
No real number solution

29. $4p^2 + 16p = -11$
$\frac{-4 \pm \sqrt{5}}{2}$

30. $4y^2 - 12y = -1$
$\frac{3 \pm 2\sqrt{2}}{2}$

31. $4x^2 = 4x + 11$
$\frac{1 \pm 2\sqrt{3}}{2}$

32. $4s^2 + 12s = 3$
$\frac{-3 \pm 2\sqrt{3}}{2}$

33. $9v^2 = -30v - 23$
$\frac{-5 \pm \sqrt{2}}{3}$

34. $9t^2 = 30t + 17$
$\frac{5 \pm \sqrt{42}}{3}$

35. True or false? If you use the quadratic formula to solve $ax^2 + bx + c = 0$ and get rational solutions, then you could have solved the equation by factoring. True

36. True or false? If the value of $b^2 - 4ac$ in the quadratic formula is 0, then $ax^2 + bx + c = 0$ has only one solution, a double root. True

For Exercises 37 to 45, solve by using the quadratic formula. Approximate the solutions to the nearest thousandth.

37. $x^2 - 2x - 21 = 0$
$-3.690, 5.690$

38. $y^2 + 4y - 11 = 0$
$-5.873, 1.873$

39. $s^2 - 6s - 13 = 0$
$-1.690, 7.690$

40. $w^2 + 8w - 15 = 0$
$-9.568, 1.568$

41. $2p^2 - 7p - 10 = 0$
$-1.089, 4.589$

42. $3t^2 - 8t - 1 = 0$
$-0.120, 2.786$

43. $4z^2 + 8z - 1 = 0$
$-2.118, 0.118$

44. $4x^2 + 7x + 1 = 0$
$-1.593, -0.157$

45. $5v^2 - v - 5 = 0$
$-0.905, 1.105$

Critical Thinking

46. Find the solutions of the quadratic equation in which $a = 4$, $b = -8$, and $c = 1$. $\frac{2 \pm \sqrt{3}}{2}$

47. Find the difference between the larger root and the smaller root of $x^2 - 6x = 14$. $2\sqrt{23}$

For Exercises 48 to 50, solve.

48. $\sqrt{x^2 + 2x + 1} = x - 1$
No solution

49. $\frac{x + 2}{3} - \frac{4}{x - 2} = 2$
$3 \pm \sqrt{13}$

50. $\frac{x + 1}{5} - \frac{3}{x - 1} = 2$
$5 \pm \sqrt{31}$

51. Explain why the equation $0x^2 + 3x + 4 = 0$ cannot be solved by using the quadratic formula.

52. Basketball A basketball player shoots at a basket 25 ft away. The height of the ball above the ground at time t is given by $h = -16t^2 + 32t + 6.5$. How many seconds after the ball is released does it hit the basket? *Hint:* When the ball hits the basket, $h = 10$ ft. Round to the nearest hundredth. 1.88 s

Projects or Group Activities

For a quadratic equation of the form $x^2 + bx + c = 0$, the sum of the solutions is equal to the opposite of b, and the product of the solutions is equal to c. For example, the solutions of the equation $x^2 + 5x + 6 = 0$ are -2 and -3. The sum of the solutions is -5, the opposite of the coefficient of x. The product of the solutions is 6, the constant term. This is one way to check the solutions of a quadratic equation. For Exercises 53 to 56, use this method to determine whether the given numbers are solutions of the equation. If they are not solutions of the equation, find the solutions.

QUICK QUIZ

Solve by using the quadratic formula.

1. $x^2 - 3x - 18 = 0$ **$-3, 6$ [16.3A]**
2. $x^2 - 2x = 4$ **$1 \pm \sqrt{5}$ [16.3A]**
3. $2x^2 + 3x - 1 = 0$ **$\frac{-3 \pm \sqrt{17}}{4}$ [16.3A]**

53. $x^2 - 4x - 21 = 0$; -3 and 7 Yes

54. $x^2 - 4x - 3 = 0$; $2 + \sqrt{7}$ and $2 - \sqrt{7}$ Yes

55. $x^2 - 4x + 1 = 0$; $2 + \sqrt{3}$ and $2 - \sqrt{3}$ Yes

56. $x^2 - 8x - 14 = 0$; $-4 + \sqrt{15}$ and $-4 - \sqrt{15}$ No. The solutions are $4 \pm \sqrt{30}$.

57. Factoring, completing the square, and using the quadratic formula are three methods of solving quadratic equations. Describe each method, and cite the advantages and disadvantages of each.

CHECK YOUR PROGRESS: CHAPTER 16

1. Solve for x: $(x - 9)(x + 11) = 0$

$-11, 9$ [16.1A]

2. Solve by factoring: $6r^2 = 12 - r$

$-\frac{3}{2}, \frac{4}{3}$ [16.1A]

3. Solve by taking square roots: $2(x + 1)^2 = 50$
$-6, 4$ [16.1B]

4. Solve by completing the square:
$y^2 - 2y - 5 = 0$ $1 \pm \sqrt{6}$ [16.2A]

5. Solve by using the quadratic formula:
$t^2 - 2t = 6$ $1 \pm \sqrt{7}$ [16.3A]

6. Solve for x: $(2x - 7)(3x + 4) = 0$

$-\frac{4}{3}, \frac{7}{2}$ [16.1A]

7. Solve by taking square roots:
$(x - 4)^2 = 20$ $4 \pm 2\sqrt{5}$ [16.1B]

8. Solve by completing the square:
$x^2 + 6x + 4 = 0$ $-3 \pm \sqrt{5}$ [16.2A]

9. Solve by using the quadratic formula:
$4t^2 - 12t - 15 = 0$ $\frac{3 \pm 2\sqrt{6}}{2}$ [16.3A]

10. Solve by taking square roots:
$y^2 - 12 = 0$ $\pm 2\sqrt{3}$ [16.1B]

11. Solve by factoring: $5y^2 + 11y = 12$

$-3, \frac{4}{5}$ [16.1A]

12. Solve by completing the square:
$2y^2 - 4y = 1$ $\frac{2 \pm \sqrt{6}}{2}$ [16.2A]

13. Solve by using the quadratic formula:
$\frac{x^2}{2} = 3x - \frac{7}{2}$ $3 \pm \sqrt{2}$ [16.3A]

14. Solve by taking square roots:
$(x + 2)^2 + 49 = 0$

No real number solution [16.1B]

15. Solve $4x^2 + 6x - 1 = 0$ by using the quadratic formula. Approximate the solutions to the nearest thousandth. $0.151, -1.651$ [16.3A]

SECTION

16.4 Graphing Quadratic Equations in Two Variables

OBJECTIVE A *To graph a quadratic equation of the form $y = ax^2 + bx + c$*

Take Note

For the equation $y = 3x^2 - x + 1$, $a = 3$, $b = -1$, and $c = 1$.

Point of Interest

Mirrors in some telescopes are ground into the shape of a parabola. The mirror at the Palomar Mountain Observatory is 2 ft thick at the ends and weighs 14.75 tons. The mirror has been ground to a true paraboloid (the three-dimensional version of a parabola) to within 0.0000015 in. A possible equation of the mirror is $y = 2640x^2$.

Take Note

One of the equations at the right was written as $y = 2x^2 + 3x - 2$, and the other was written using function notation as $f(x) = -x^2 + 3x + 2$. Remember that y and $f(x)$ are different symbols for the same quantity.

An equation of the form $y = ax^2 + bx + c$, $a \neq 0$, is a **quadratic equation in two variables.** Examples of quadratic equations in two variables are shown at the right.

$$y = 3x^2 - x + 1$$
$$y = -x^2 - 3$$
$$y = 2x^2 - 5x$$

For these equations, y is a function of x, and we can write $f(x) = ax^2 + bx + c$. This equation represents a **quadratic function.**

HOW TO 1 Evaluate $f(x) = 2x^2 - 3x + 4$ when $x = -2$.

$f(x) = 2x^2 - 3x + 4$

$f(-2) = 2(-2)^2 - 3(-2) + 4$ • **Replace x by -2.**

$= 2(4) + 6 + 4 = 18$ • **Simplify.**

The value of the function when $x = -2$ is 18.

The graph of $y = ax^2 + bx + c$ or $f(x) = ax^2 + bx + c$ is a **parabola.** The graph is U-shaped, and opens up when a is positive and down when a is negative. The graphs of two parabolas are shown below.

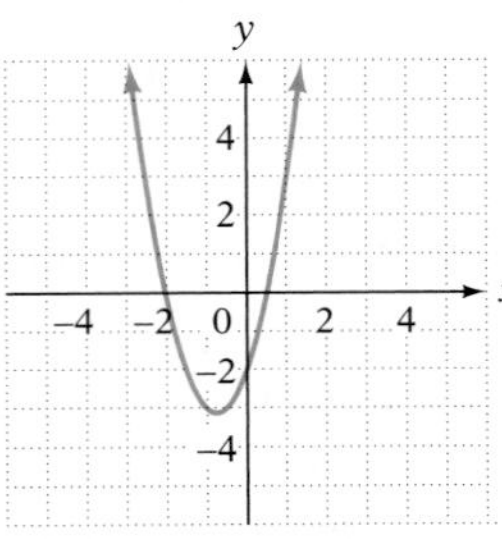

$y = 2x^2 + 3x - 2$
$a = 2$, a positive number
Parabola opens up.

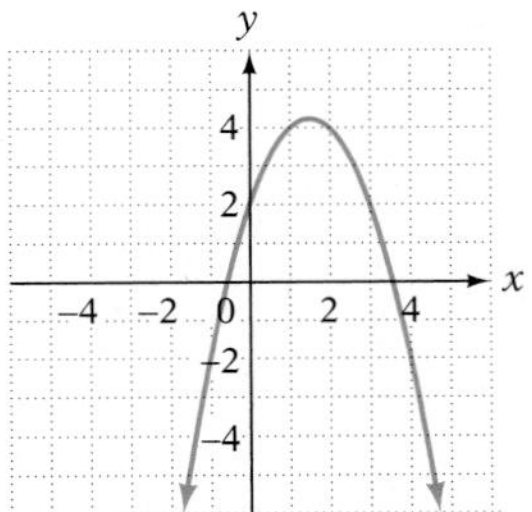

$f(x) = -x^2 + 3x + 2$
$a = -1$, a negative number
Parabola opens down.

HOW TO 2 Graph $y = x^2 - 2x - 3$.

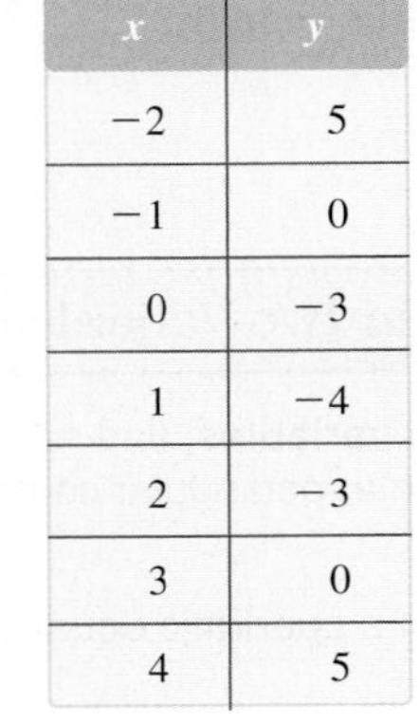

x	y
−2	5
−1	0
0	−3
1	−4
2	−3
3	0
4	5

• **Find several solutions of the equation. Because the graph is not a straight line, several solutions must be found in order to determine the U-shape. Record the ordered pairs in a table.**

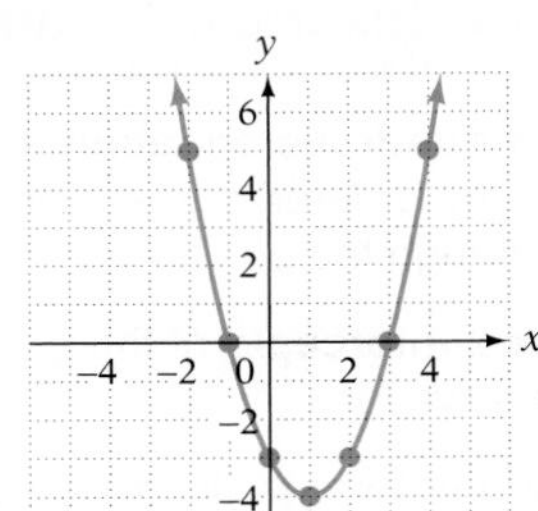

• **Graph the ordered-pair solutions on a rectangular coordinate system. Draw a parabola through the points.**

Note that the graph of $y = x^2 - 2x - 3$, shown again below, crosses the x-axis at $(-1, 0)$ and $(3, 0)$. This is also confirmed from the table for the graph. From the table, note that $y = 0$ when $x = -1$ and when $x = 3$. The x-intercepts of the graph are $(-1, 0)$ and $(3, 0)$.

x	y
−2	5
−1	0
0	−3
1	−4
2	−3
3	0
4	5

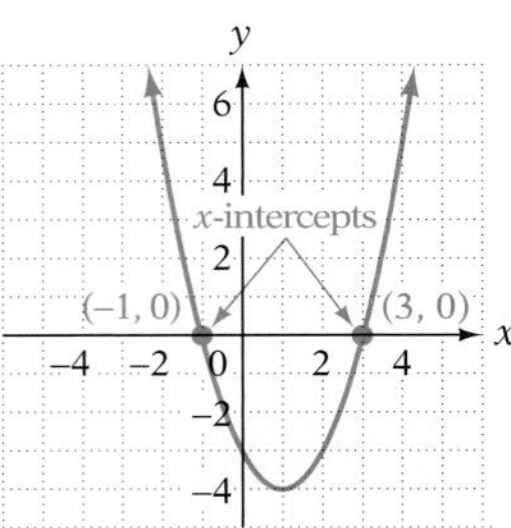

The y-intercept is the point at which the graph crosses the y-axis. At this point, $x = 0$. From the graph, we can see that the y-intercept is $(0, -3)$.

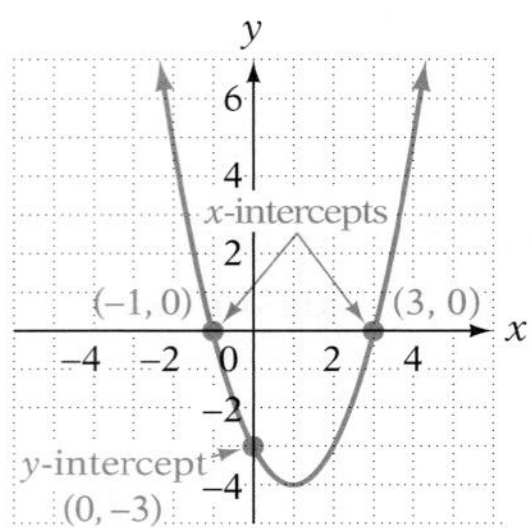

We can find the x-intercepts algebraically by letting $y = 0$ and solving for x.

$y = x^2 - 2x - 3$

$0 = x^2 - 2x - 3$ • **Replace y by 0 and solve for x.**

$0 = (x + 1)(x - 3)$ • **This equation can be solved by factoring. However, it will be necessary to use the quadratic formula to solve some quadratic equations.**

$x + 1 = 0 \qquad x - 3 = 0$

$x = -1 \qquad x = 3$

The x-intercepts are $(-1, 0)$ and $(3, 0)$.

We can find the y-intercept algebraically by letting $x = 0$ and solving for y.

$y = x^2 - 2x - 3$

$y = 0^2 - 2(0) - 3$ • **Replace x by 0 and simplify.**

$= -3$

The y-intercept is $(0, -3)$.

Integrating Technology

One of the Projects or Group Activities at the end of the exercise set for this section shows how to use a graphing calculator to draw the graph of a parabola and find the x-intercepts. You may want to verify the graphs you draw in this section by drawing them on a graphing calculator.

Graph of a Quadratic Equation in Two Variables

To graph a quadratic equation in two variables, find several solutions of the equation. Graph the ordered-pair solutions on a rectangular coordinate system. Draw a parabola through the points.

To find the x-intercepts of the graph of a quadratic equation in two variables, let $y = 0$ and solve for x.

To find the *y*-intercept, let $x = 0$ and solve for y.

EXAMPLE 1

Graph $y = x^2 - 2x$.

Solution

x	y
−1	3
0	0
1	−1
2	0
3	3

• Find several solutions of the equation.

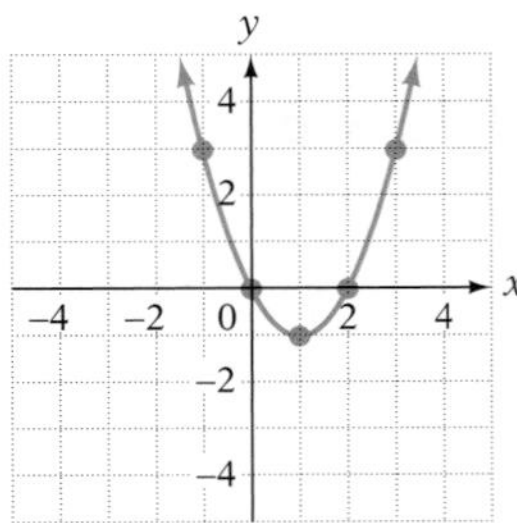

• Graph the ordered-pair solutions. Draw a parabola through the points.

YOU TRY IT 1

Graph $y = x^2 + 2$.

Your solution

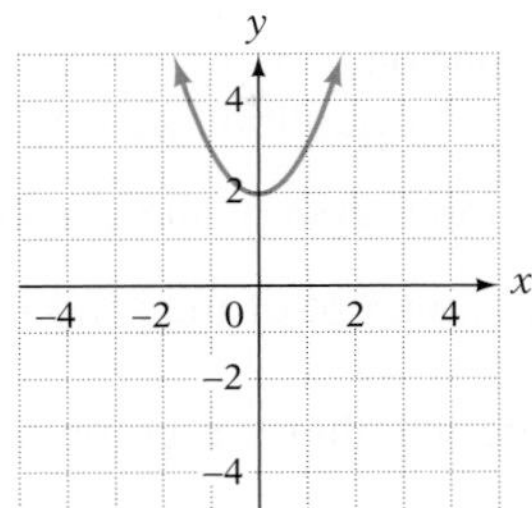

EXAMPLE 2

Find the x- and y-intercepts of the graph of $y = x^2 - 2x - 5$.

Solution

To find the x-intercepts, let $y = 0$ and solve for x. This gives the equation $0 = x^2 - 2x - 5$, which is not factorable over the integers. Use the quadratic formula.

$$x = \frac{-b \pm \sqrt{b^2 - 4ac}}{2a}$$

$$= \frac{-(-2) \pm \sqrt{(-2)^2 - 4(1)(-5)}}{2(1)}$$ • $a = 1, b = -2, c = -5$

$$= \frac{2 \pm \sqrt{24}}{2} = \frac{2 \pm 2\sqrt{6}}{2}$$

$$= 1 \pm \sqrt{6}$$

The x-intercepts are $(1 - \sqrt{6}, 0)$ and $(1 + \sqrt{6}, 0)$.

To find the y-intercept, let $x = 0$ and solve for y.

$$y = x^2 - 2x - 5$$
$$= 0^2 - 2(0) - 5$$ • Replace x by 0.
$$= -5$$

The y-intercept is $(0, -5)$.

YOU TRY IT 2

Find the x- and y-intercepts of the graph of $f(x) = x^2 - 6x + 9$.

Your solution

x-intercept: (3, 0)
y-intercept: (0, 9)

IN-CLASS EXAMPLES

Graph.

1. $y = x^2 - 4x + 3$

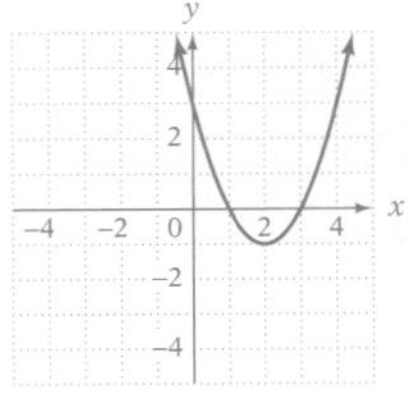

2. $y = -x^2 + 4$

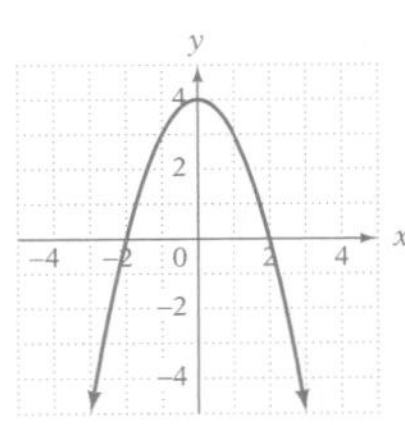

Solutions on pp. S38–S39

16.4 EXERCISES

SUGGESTED ASSIGNMENT:
Exercises 1–8; Exercises 9–41, odds; Exercises 44–50

Concept Check

1. What is the name of the graph of a quadratic equation in two variables? Parabola
2. What is the clue in the equation $y = x^2 - 4x + 3$ that the graph will be a parabola and not a straight line? The equation has an x^2 term.
3. Explain how to find the x-intercepts of the graph of $y = x^2 - 4x + 3$. Let $y = 0$ and solve for x.
4. Explain how to find the y-intercept of the graph of $y = x^2 - 5x + 4$. Let $x = 0$ and solve for y.

For Exercises 5 to 8, determine whether the graph of the equation opens up or down.

5. $y = -\frac{1}{3}x^2$ Down
6. $y = x^2 - 2x - 3$ Up
7. $f(x) = 2x^2 - 4$ Up
8. $f(x) = 3 - 2x - x^2$ Down

OBJECTIVE A *To graph a quadratic equation of the form $y = ax^2 + bx + c$*

For Exercises 9 to 14, evaluate the function for the given value of x.

9. $f(x) = x^2 - 2x + 1; x = 3$ 4
10. $f(x) = 2x^2 + x - 1; x = -2$ 5
11. $f(x) = 4 - x^2; x = -3$ −5
12. $f(x) = x^2 + 6x + 9; x = -3$ 0
13. $f(x) = -x^2 + 5x - 6; x = -4$ −42
14. $f(x) = -2x^2 + 2x - 1; x = -3$ −25

For Exercises 15 to 29, graph.

15. $y = x^2$

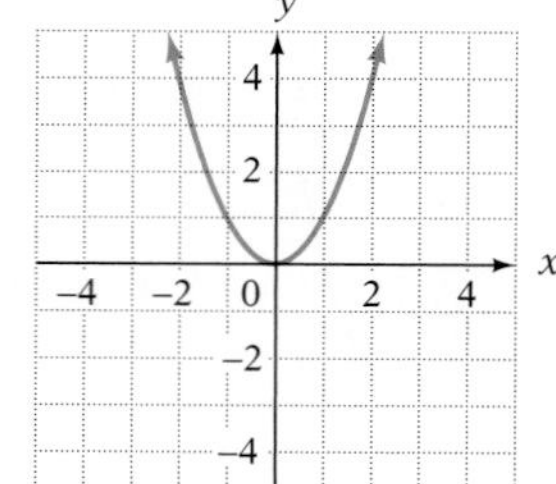

16. $y = -x^2$

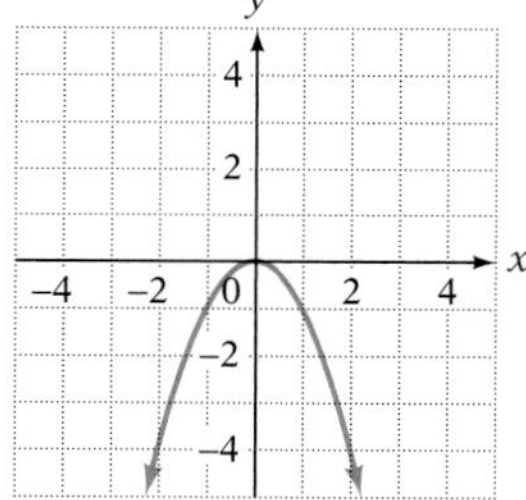

17. $y = -x^2 + 1$

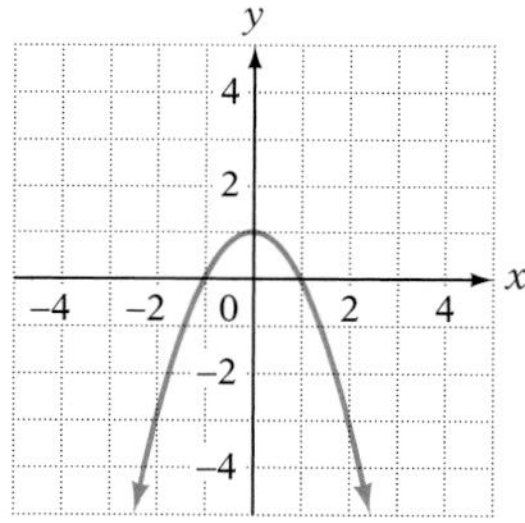

18. $y = x^2 - 1$

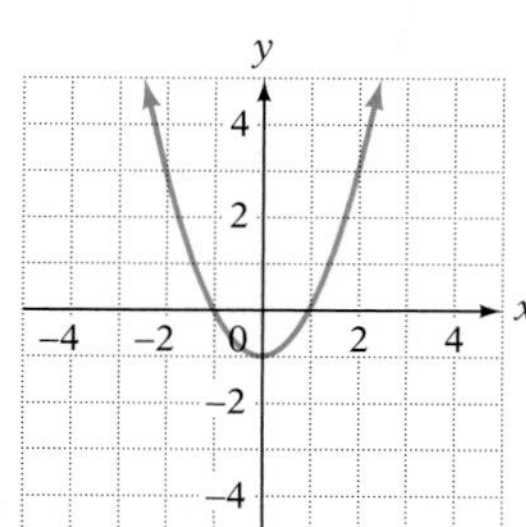

19. $f(x) = 2x^2$

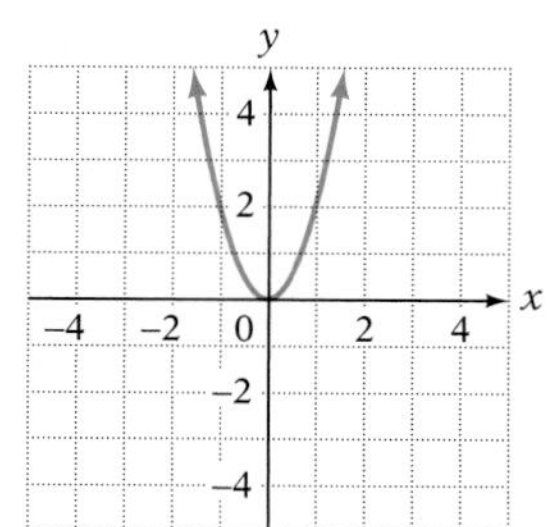

20. $f(x) = \frac{1}{2}x^2$

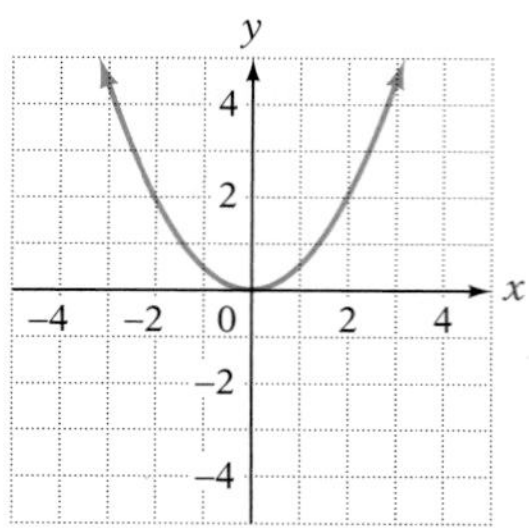

21. 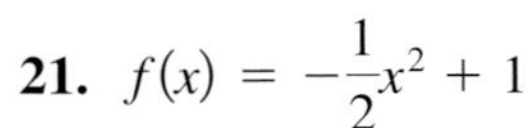 $f(x) = -\frac{1}{2}x^2 + 1$

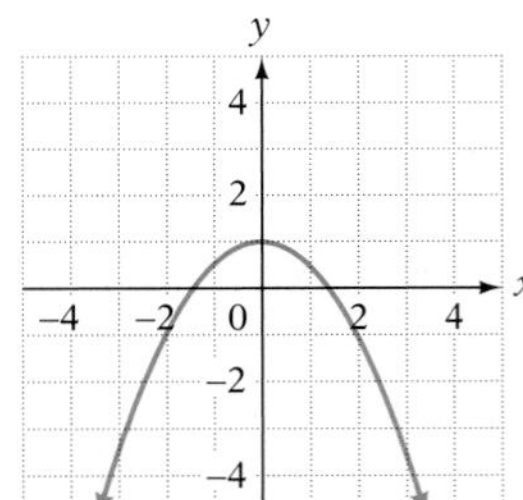

22. $f(x) = 2x^2 - 1$

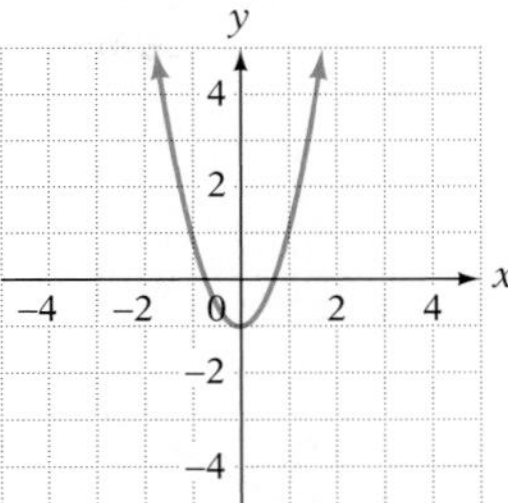

23. $y = x^2 - 4x$

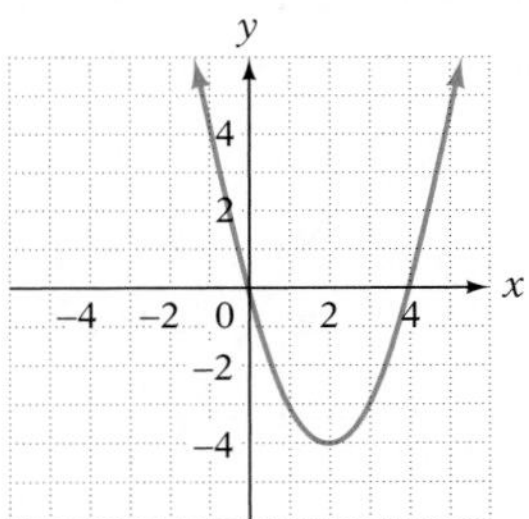

24. $y = x^2 + 4x$

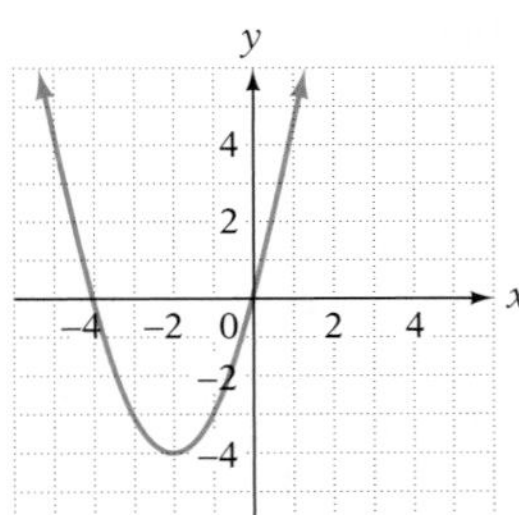

25. $y = x^2 - 2x + 3$

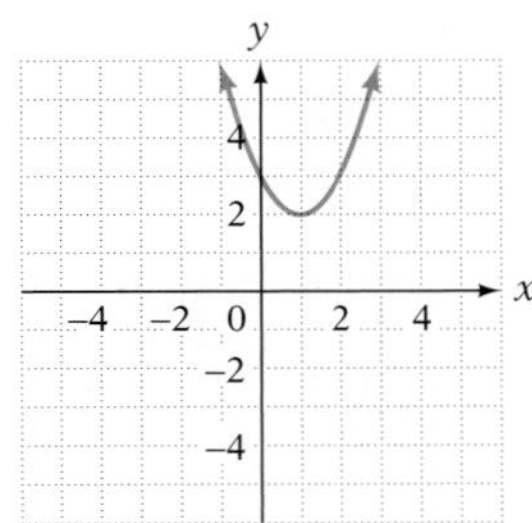

26. $y = x^2 - 4x + 2$

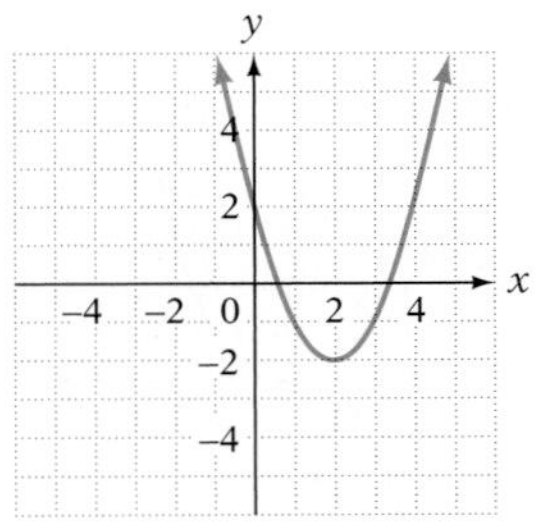

27. $y = -x^2 + 2x + 3$

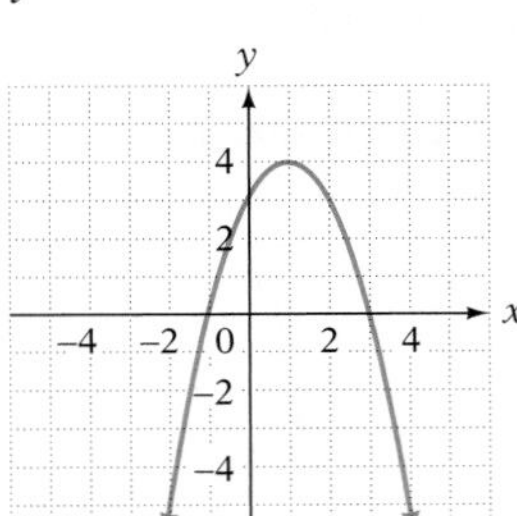

28. $y = -x^2 - 2x + 3$

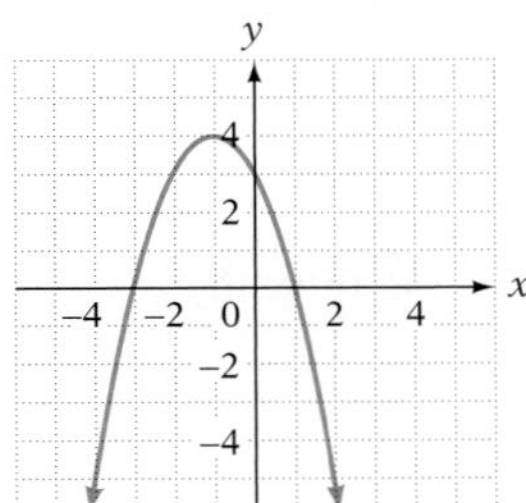

29. $y = -x^2 + 4x - 4$

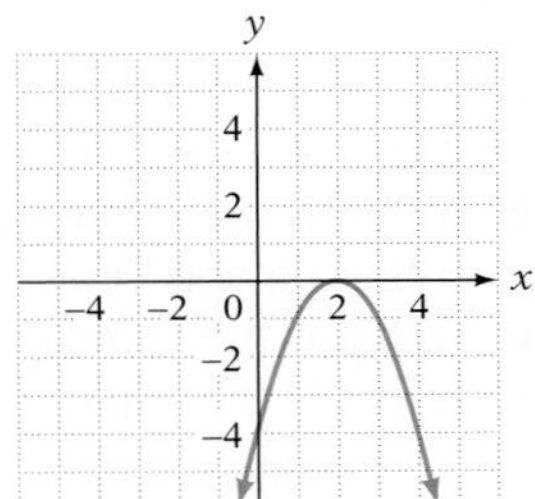

For Exercises 30 to 41, determine the x- and y-intercepts.

30. $y = x^2 - 5x + 6$
(2, 0), (3, 0); (0, 6)

31. $y = x^2 + 5x - 6$
(−6, 0), (1, 0); (0, −6)

32. $f(x) = 9 - x^2$
(−3, 0), (3, 0); (0, 9)

33. $f(x) = x^2 + 12x + 36$
(−6, 0); (0, 36)

34. $y = x^2 + 2x - 6$
$(-1 \pm \sqrt{7}, 0)$, (0, −6)

35. $f(x) = x^2 + 4x - 2$
$(-2 \pm \sqrt{6}, 0)$, (0, −2)

36. $y = x^2 + 2x + 3$
No x-intercepts; (0, 3)

37. $y = x^2 - x + 1$
No x-intercepts; (0, 1)

38. $f(x) = 2x^2 - x - 3$
$\left(\frac{3}{2}, 0\right)$, (−1, 0); (0, −3)

39. $f(x) = 2x^2 - 13x + 15$
$\left(\frac{3}{2}, 0\right)$, (5, 0); (0, 15)

40. $y = 4 - x - x^2$
$\left(\frac{-1 \pm \sqrt{17}}{2}, 0\right)$; (0, 4)

41. $y = 2 - 3x - 3x^2$
$\left(\frac{-3 \pm \sqrt{33}}{6}, 0\right)$; (0, 2)

42. What is the y-intercept of the parabola with equation $y = ax^2 + bx + c$? (0, c)

43. Suppose the graph of $y = ax^2 + bx + c$, $c \neq 0$, is a parabola with only one x-intercept, and a is negative. Is c positive or negative? Negative

Critical Thinking

For Exercises 44 to 49, state whether the graph is the graph of a linear function, a quadratic function, or neither.

44.

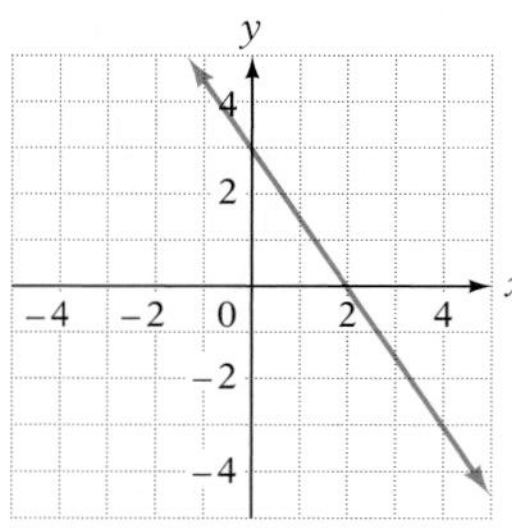

Linear

45.

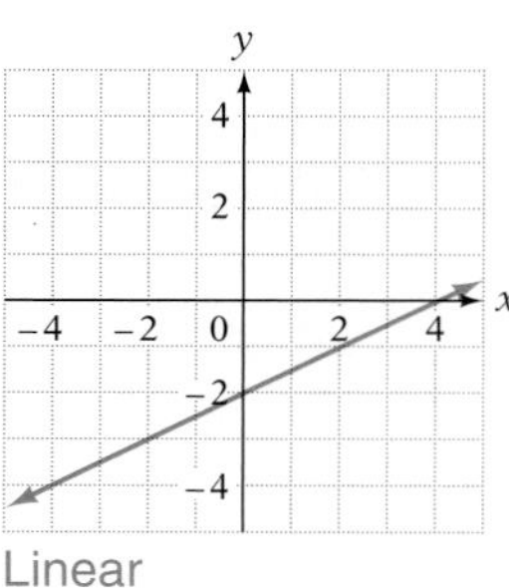

Linear

46.

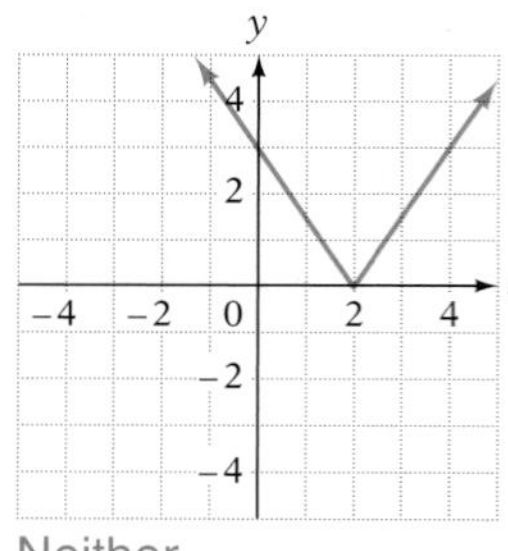

Neither

47.

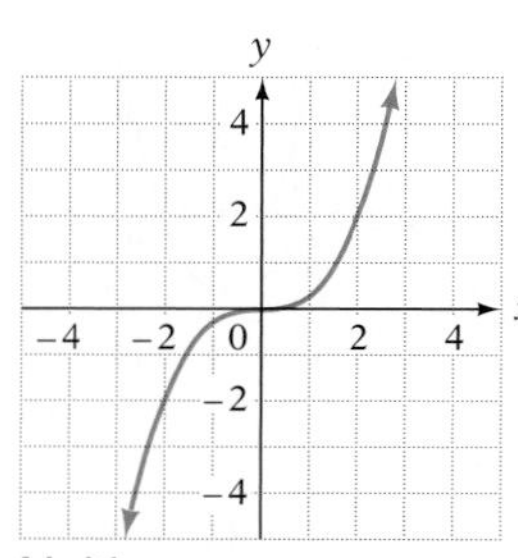

Neither

48.

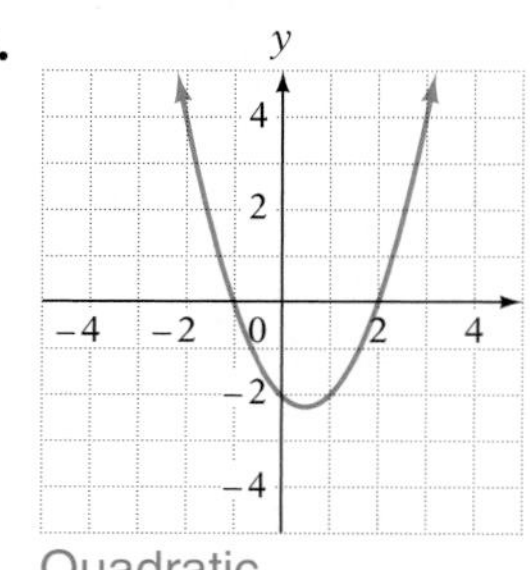

Quadratic

49.

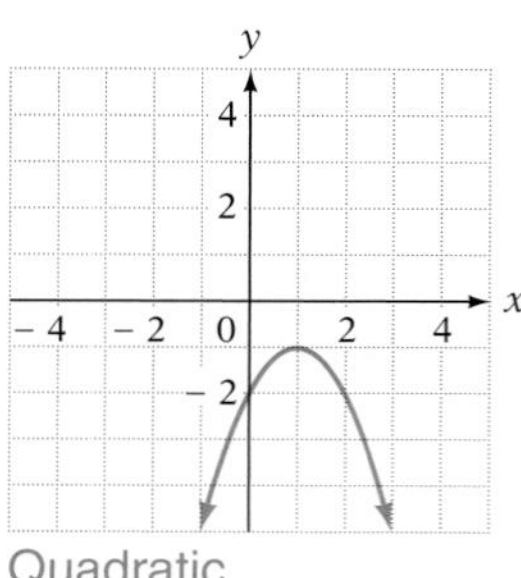

Quadratic

50. Consider the graph shown at the right.

a. What are the x-intercepts? $(-1, 0)$, $(1, 0)$

b. What is the y-intercept? $(0, 2)$

c. What do you know about the value of a? It is negative.

d. What is the value of x when $y = 2$? 0

e. What is the value of y when $x = 1$? 0

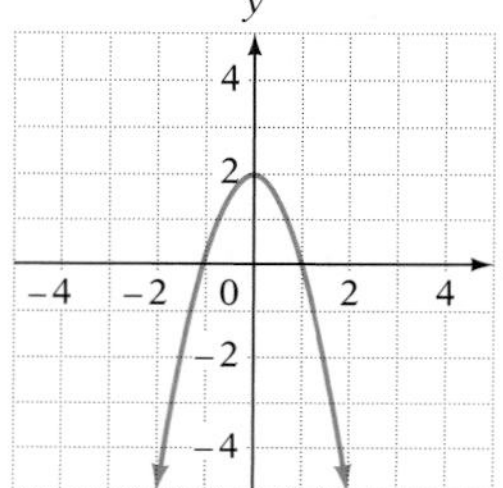

QUICK QUIZ

1. Graph: $y = -x^2 - 1$

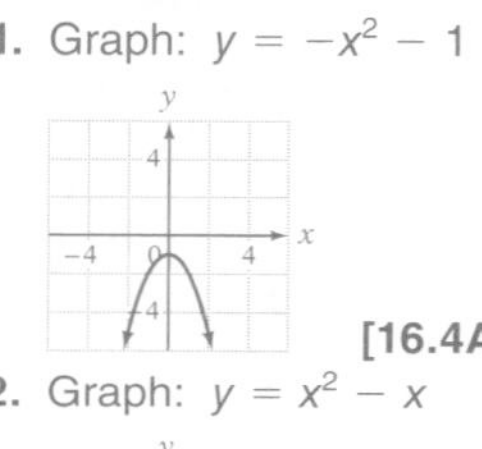

[16.4A]

2. Graph: $y = x^2 - x$

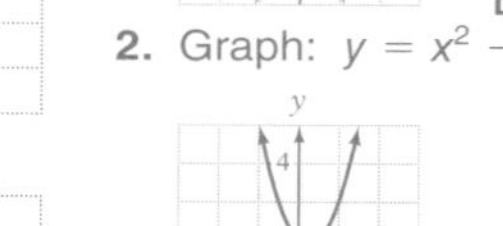

[16.4A]

3. Find the x- and y-intercepts of the graph of $y = x^2 - 2x - 3$. $(-1, 0)$, $(3, 0)$; $(0, -3)$ [16.4A]

51. Consider the graph shown at the right.

a. What are the x-intercepts? $(-2, 0)$, $(2, 0)$

b. What is the y-intercept? $(0, -4)$

c. What do you know about the value of a? It is positive.

d. What is the value of x when $y = -4$? 0

e. What is the value of y when $x = -1$? -3

Projects or Group Activities

52. Draw a parabola that opens up and has $(-2, -4)$ as its vertex.
Sample graph: $y = x^2 + 4x$

53. Draw a parabola that opens down and has $(3, 1)$ as its vertex.
Sample graph: $y = -x^2 + 6x - 8$

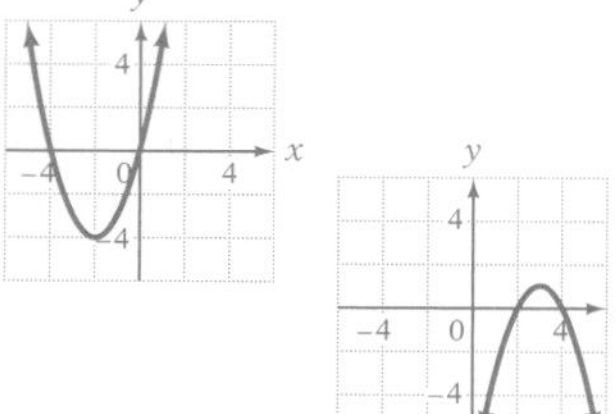

54. The point whose coordinates are (x_1, y_1) lies in quadrant I and is a point on the graph of the equation $y = 2x^2 - 2x + 1$. Given $y_1 = 13$, find x_1. 3

55. The point whose coordinates are (x_1, y_1) lies in quadrant II and is a point on the graph of the equation $y = 2x^2 - 3x - 2$. Given $y_1 = 12$, find x_1. -2

Graphical Solutions of Quadratic Equations A real number x is called a **zero of a function** if the function evaluated at x is equal to zero. That is, if $f(x) = 0$, then x is called a zero of the function. For instance, evaluating $f(x) = x^2 + x - 6$ when $x = -3$, we have

$$f(x) = x^2 + x - 6$$
$$f(-3) = (-3)^2 + (-3) - 6 \quad \text{• Replace } x \text{ by } -3.$$
$$f(-3) = 9 - 3 - 6 = 0$$

For this function, $f(-3) = 0$, so -3 is a zero of the function.

Verify that 2 is a zero of $f(x) = x^2 + x - 6$ by showing that $f(2) = 0$.

The graph of $f(x) = x^2 + x - 6$ is shown at the right. Note that the graph crosses the x-axis at -3 and 2, the two zeros of the function. The points $(-3, 0)$ and $(2, 0)$ are x-intercepts of the graph.

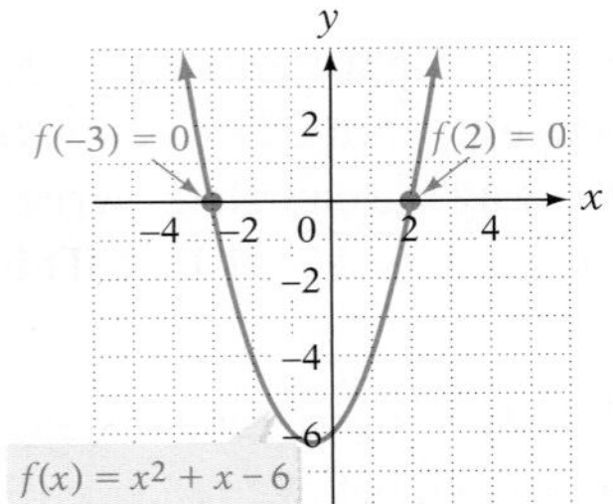

Consider the equation $0 = x^2 + x - 6$, which is $f(x) = x^2 + x - 6$ with $f(x)$ replaced by 0. Solving $0 = x^2 + x - 6$, we have

$$0 = x^2 + x - 6$$
$$0 = (x + 3)(x - 2) \quad \text{• Solve by factoring and using the Principle of Zero Products.}$$
$$x + 3 = 0 \qquad x - 2 = 0$$
$$x = -3 \qquad x = 2$$

Observe that the solutions of the equation are the zeros of the function. This important connection among the real zeros of a function, the x-intercepts of its graph, and the solutions of the equation is the basis for using a graphing calculator to solve an equation.

The following method of solving a quadratic equation by using a graphing calculator is based on a TI-84 Plus calculator. Other calculators will require a slightly different approach.

HOW TO Approximate the solutions of $x^2 + 4x = 6$ by using a graphing calculator.

1. Write the equation in standard form: $x^2 + 4x - 6 = 0$.
2. Press Y= and enter $x^2 + 4x - 6$ for Y1.
3. Press GRAPH. If the graph does not appear on the screen, press ZOOM 6.
4. Press 2ND CALC 2. Note that the selection for 2 says zero. This will begin the calculation of the zeros of the function, which are the solutions of the equation.

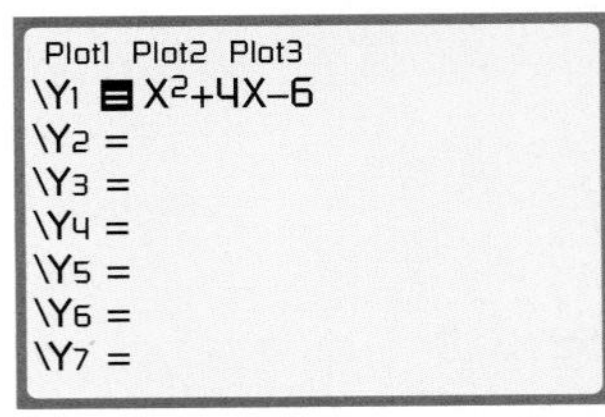

Step 2

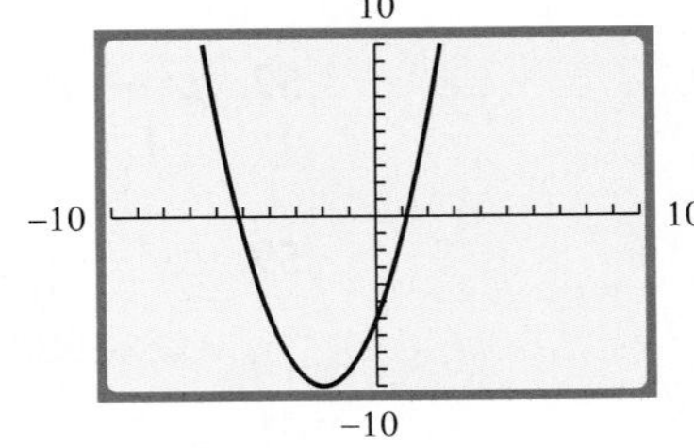

Step 3

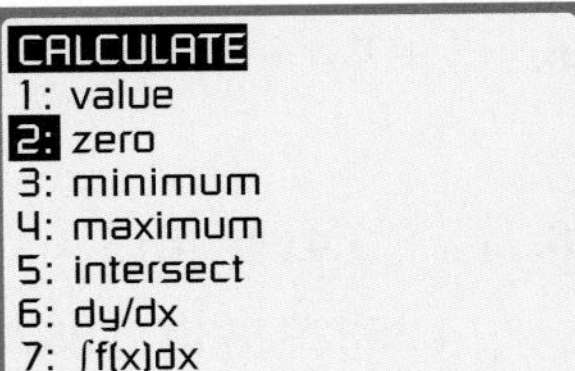

Step 4

5. At the bottom of the screen you will see **LeftBound?** This is asking you to move the blinking cursor so that it is to the *left* of the first x-intercept. Use the left arrow key to move the cursor to the left of the first x-intercept. The values of x and y that appear on your calculator may be different from the ones shown here. Just be sure that you are to the left of the x-intercept. When you are done, press ENTER.

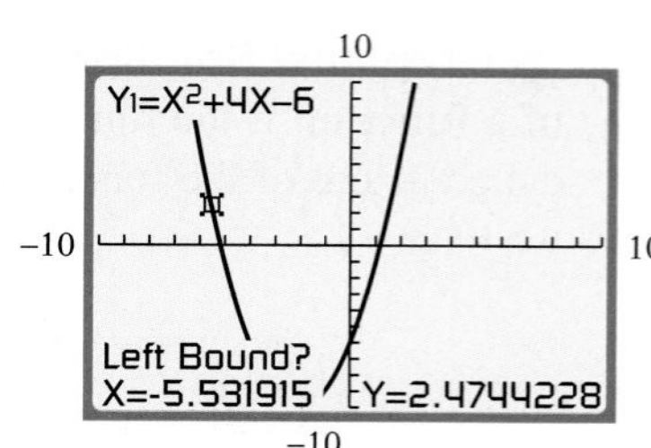

Step 5

6. At the bottom of the screen you will see **RightBound?** This is asking you to move the blinking cursor so that it is to the *right* of the x-intercept. Use the right arrow key to move the cursor to the right of the x-intercept. The values of x and y that appear on your calculator may be different from the ones shown here. Just be sure that you are to the right of the x-intercept. When you are done, press ENTER.

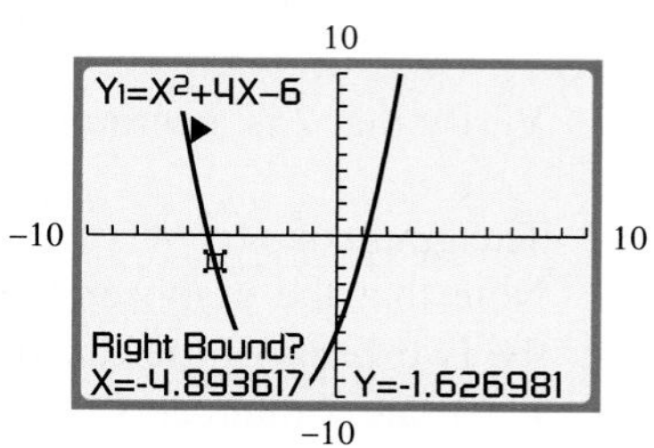

Step 6

7. At the bottom of the screen you will see **Guess?** Press ENTER.

8. The zero of the function is approximately -5.162278. Thus one solution of $x^2 + 4x = 6$ is approximately -5.162278. Also note that the value of y is given as $Y1 = {}^{-}1E^{-}12$. This is the way the calculator writes a number in scientific notation. We would normally write $Y1 = -1 \times 10^{-12}$. This number is very close to zero.

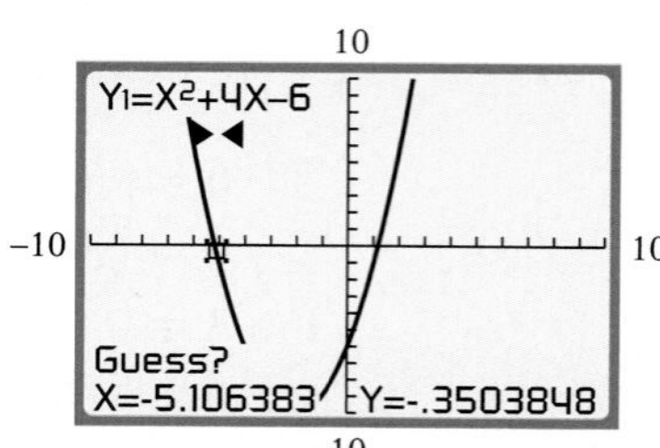

Step 7

To find the other solution of $x^2 + 4x = 6$, we repeat Steps 4 through 8. The screens for Steps 5 through 8 are shown below.

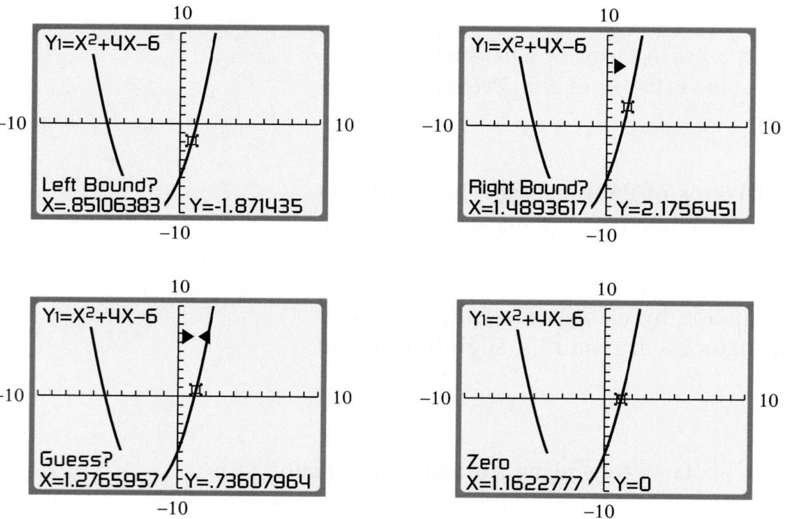

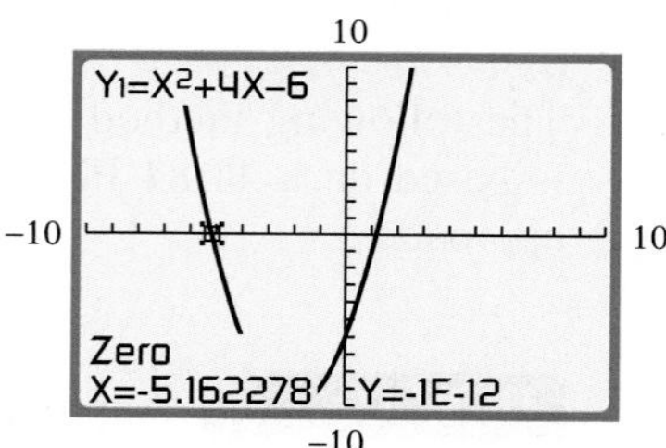

Step 8

A second zero of the function is approximately 1.1622777. Thus the two solutions of $x^2 + 4x = 6$ are $x \approx -5.162278$ and $x \approx 1.1622777$.

INSTRUCTOR NOTE

For Step 8, it may help some students to write out the decimal equivalent of -1×10^{-12}.

For Exercises 56 to 61, use a graphing calculator to approximate the solutions of the equation.

56. $x^2 + 3x - 4 = 0$
$-4, 1$

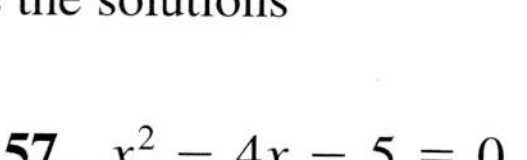

57. $x^2 - 4x - 5 = 0$
$-1, 5$

58. $x^2 + 3.4x = 4.15$
$-4.353299832, 0.9532998323$

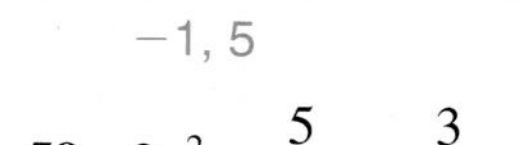

59. $2x^2 - \frac{5}{9}x = \frac{3}{8}$
$0.5936307095, -0.3158529318$

60. $\pi x^2 - \sqrt{17}x - 2 = 0$
$-0.3768579289, 1.689283211$

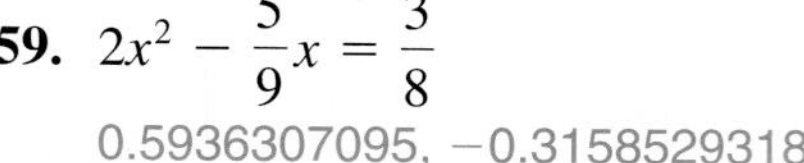

61. $\sqrt{2}x^2 + x - \sqrt{7} = 0$
$-1.766291404, 1.059184622$

SECTION

16.5 Application Problems

OBJECTIVE A *To solve application problems*

The application problems in this section are varieties of the types of problems solved earlier in the text. Each of the strategies for the problems in this section will result in a quadratic equation.

© iStockphoto.com/AVAVA

HOW TO 1 In 5 h, two campers paddled 12 mi down a stream and then paddled back to their campsite. The rate of the stream's current was 1 mph. Find the rate at which the campers paddled.

Strategy for Solving an Application Problem

1. Determine the type of problem. For example, is it a uniform motion problem, a geometry problem, or a work problem?

The problem is a uniform motion problem.

2. Choose a variable to represent the unknown quantity. Write numerical or variable expressions for all the remaining quantities. The results can be recorded in a table.

The unknown rate of the campers: r

	Distance	÷	*Rate*	=	*Time*
Downstream	12	÷	$r + 1$	=	$\frac{12}{r+1}$
Upstream	12	÷	$r - 1$	=	$\frac{12}{r-1}$

3. Determine how the quantities are related.

The time going downstream plus the time going upstream is equal to 5 h.

$$\frac{12}{r+1} + \frac{12}{r-1} = 5$$

Solve for r.

$$(r+1)(r-1)\left(\frac{12}{r+1} + \frac{12}{r-1}\right) = (r+1)(r-1)5$$
$$(r-1)12 + (r+1)12 = (r^2-1)5$$
$$12r - 12 + 12r + 12 = 5r^2 - 5$$
$$24r = 5r^2 - 5$$
$$0 = 5r^2 - 24r - 5$$
$$0 = (5r+1)(r-5)$$

$$5r + 1 = 0 \qquad r - 5 = 0$$
$$5r = -1 \qquad r = 5$$
$$r = -\frac{1}{5}$$

The rate cannot be a negative number; therefore, the solution $-\frac{1}{5}$ is not possible.

The paddling rate was 5 mph.

EXAMPLE 1

Working together, a painter and the painter's apprentice can paint a room in 2 h. Working alone, the apprentice requires 3 more hours to paint the room than the painter requires working alone. How long does it take the painter, working alone, to paint the room?

Strategy

- This is a work problem.
- Time for the painter to paint the room: t
  Time for the apprentice to paint the room: $t + 3$

	Rate	*Time*	*Part*
Painter	$\frac{1}{t}$	2	$\frac{2}{t}$
Apprentice	$\frac{1}{t+3}$	2	$\frac{2}{t+3}$

- The sum of the parts of the task completed must equal 1.

Solution

$$\frac{2}{t} + \frac{2}{t+3} = 1$$

- **The parts completed by the painter and the apprentice must equal 1.**

$$t(t+3)\left(\frac{2}{t} + \frac{2}{t+3}\right) = t(t+3) \cdot 1$$

- **Multiply by $t(t + 3)$.**

$$(t+3)2 + t(2) = t(t+3)$$

$$2t + 6 + 2t = t^2 + 3t$$

- **Quadratic equation**

$$4t + 6 = t^2 + 3t$$

$$0 = t^2 - t - 6$$

- **Standard form**

$$0 = (t-3)(t+2)$$

- **Factor.**

$$t - 3 = 0 \qquad t + 2 = 0$$

$$t = 3 \qquad t = -2$$

- **Set each factor equal to zero.**

The solution $t = -2$ is not possible.

The time is 3 h.

YOU TRY IT 1

The length of a rectangle is 2 m more than the width. The area is 15 m^2. Find the width.

Your strategy

Your solution

3 m

IN-CLASS EXAMPLES

1. It took a boat 2 h more to travel 90 mi against the current than to go 90 mi with the current. The rate of the current was 6 mph. Find the rate of the boat in calm water. **24 mph**
2. A tank is emptied by two drains. The larger drain can empty the tank in half the amount of time it takes the smaller drain to empty the tank. Using both drains, the tank can be emptied in 2 h. How long would it take the larger drain, working alone, to empty the tank? **3 h**

Solution on p. S39

16.5 EXERCISES

SUGGESTED ASSIGNMENT:
Exercises 1–4; Exercises 5–29, odds

Concept Check

1. If the length of a rectangle is three more than twice the width and the width is represented by W, then the length is represented by ______. $2W + 3$

2. If it takes one pipe 15 min longer to fill a tank than it does a second pipe, and the rate of work for the second pipe is represented by $\frac{1}{t}$, then the rate of work for the first pipe can be represented by ______. $\frac{1}{t + 15}$

3. If a plane's rate of speed is r and the rate of the wind is 30 mph, then the plane's rate of speed flying with the wind is $r + 30$, and the plane's rate of speed flying against the wind is ______. $r - 30$

4. When using the quadratic formula to solve the equation $2 = -16t^2 + 24t + 4$ for t, substitute ______ (-16) for a in the quadratic formula, ______ (24) for b, and ______ (2) for c.

OBJECTIVE A *To solve application problems*

5. **Geometry** The height of a triangle is 2 m more than twice the length of the base. The area of the triangle is 20 m^2. Find the height of the triangle and the length of the base.
Height: 10 m; length: 4 m

6. **Geometry** The length of a rectangle is 4 ft more than twice the width. The area of the rectangle is 160 ft^2. Find the length and width of the rectangle.
Length: 20 ft; width: 8 ft

7. **Sports** The area of the batter's box on a major-league baseball field is 24 ft^2. The length of the batter's box is 2 ft more than the width. Find the length and width of the rectangular batter's box.
Length: 6 ft; width: 4 ft

© Mike Liu/Shutterstock.com

8. **Sports** The length of the batter's box on a softball field is 1 ft more than twice the width. The area of the batter's box is 21 ft^2. Find the length and width of the rectangular batter's box.
Length: 7 ft; width: 3 ft

9. **Work Problem** A tank has two drains. One drain takes 16 min longer to empty the tank than does the second drain. With both drains open, the tank is emptied in 6 min. How long would it take each drain, working alone, to empty the tank?
First drain: 24 min; second drain: 8 min

10. **Work Problem** One computer takes 21 min longer than a second computer to calculate the value of a complex expression. Working together, the computers can complete the calculation in 10 min. How long would it take each computer, working alone, to calculate the value?
First computer: 35 min; second computer: 14 min

11. **Sports** The length of a swimming pool is twice the width. The area of the pool is 5000 ft^2. Find the length and width of the pool.
Length: 100 ft; width: 50 ft

12. **Sports** Read the article at the right. The Longhorns' old scoreboard was a rectangle with a length 30 ft greater than its width. Find the length and width of the old scoreboard.
Length: 70 ft; width: 40 ft

In the NEWS!

Long Board for the Longhorns

The University of Texas Longhorns have replaced their stadium's old 2800-square-foot scoreboard with a new, state-of-the-art, 7370-square-foot scoreboard designed and built by local business Daktronics, Inc.

Sources: Business Wire, www.engadget.com

13. **Transportation** Using one engine of a ferryboat, it takes 6 h longer to cross a channel than it does using a second engine alone. With both engines operating, the ferryboat can make the crossing in 4 h. How long would it take each engine, working alone, to power the ferryboat across the channel?
First engine: 12 h; second engine: 6 h

14. **Work Problem** An apprentice mason takes 8 h longer than an experienced mason to build a small fireplace. Working together, the masons can build the fireplace in 3 h. How long would it take the experienced mason, working alone, to build the fireplace?
4 h

15. **Uniform Motion** It took a small plane 2 h longer to fly 375 mi against the wind than it took to fly the same distance with the wind. The rate of the wind was 25 mph. Find the rate of the plane in calm air.
100 mph

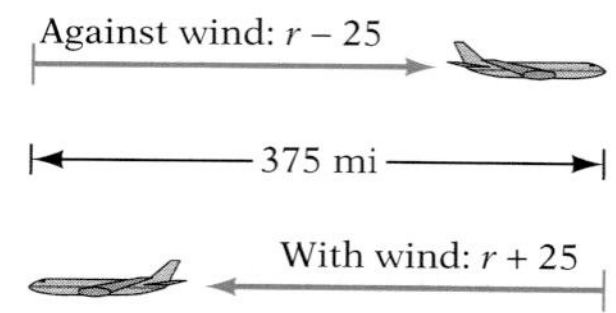

16. **Uniform Motion** It took a motorboat 1 h longer to travel 36 mi against the current than it took to travel 36 mi with the current. The rate of the current was 3 mph. Find the rate of the boat in calm water.
15 mph

© Ljupco Smokovski/Shutterstock.com

17. **Uniform Motion** A motorcycle traveled 150 mi at a constant rate before its speed was decreased by 15 mph. Another 35 mi was driven at the decreased speed. The total time for the 185-mile trip was 4 h. Find the cyclist's rate during the first 150 mi.
50 mph

18. **Uniform Motion** A cruise ship sailed through a 20-mile inland passageway at a constant rate before its speed was increased by 15 mph. Another 75 mi was traveled at the increased rate. The total time for the 95-mile trip was 5 h. Find the rate of the ship during the last 75 mi.
25 mph

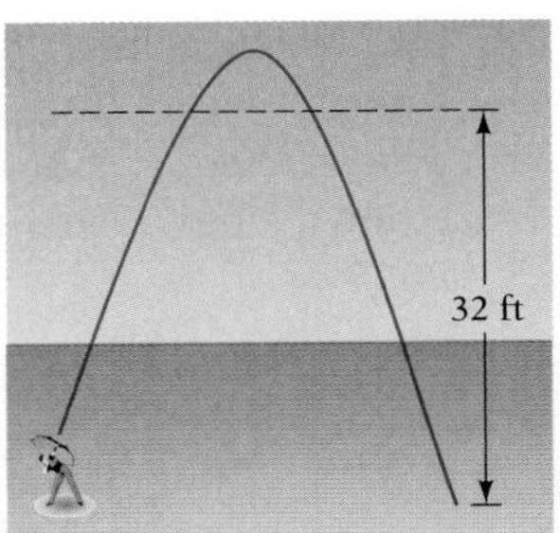

19. Physics An arrow is projected into the air with an initial velocity of 48 ft/s. At what times will the arrow be 32 ft above the ground? Use the equation $h = 48t - 16t^2$, where h is the height, in feet, above the ground after t seconds.
1 s, 2 s

20. Physics A model rocket is launched with an initial velocity of 200 ft/s. The height h of the rocket t seconds after launch is given by $h = -16t^2 + 200t$. How many seconds after launch will the rocket be 300 ft above the ground? Round to the nearest hundredth.
1.74 s, 10.76 s

21. Botany Botanists have determined that some species of weeds grow in a circular pattern. For one such weed, the area of growth A, in square meters, can be approximated by $A(t) = 0.005\pi t^2$, where t is the time in days after the growth of the weed first can be observed. How many days after the growth is first observed will this weed cover an area of 10 m^2? Round to the nearest whole number.
25 days

22. Physics The kinetic energy of a moving body is given by $E = \frac{1}{2}mv^2$, where E is the kinetic energy, m is the mass, and v is the velocity in meters per second. What is the velocity of a moving body whose mass is 5 kg and whose kinetic energy is 250 newton-meters?
10 m/s

In the NEWS!

Boomers Turn 65

By the time the last baby boomer turns 65, the population of people aged 65 and older will have more than doubled, from 35 million to 71 million.
Source: Census Bureau

23. Demography See the news clipping at the right. Approximate the year in which there will be 50 million people aged 65 and older in the United States. Use the equation $y = 0.03x^2 + 0.36x + 34.6$, where y is the population, in millions, in year x, where $x = 0$ corresponds to the year 2000.
2017

24. Sports A basketball player shoots at a basket 25 ft away. The height h, in feet, of the ball above the ground at time t, in seconds, is given by $h = -16t^2 + 32t + 6.5$. How many seconds after the ball is released does it hit the basket? Round to the nearest hundredth. (*Hint:* When the ball hits the basket, $h = 10$ ft.)
1.88 s

25. Sports In a slow-pitch softball game, the height of the ball thrown by a pitcher can be modeled by the equation $h = -16t^2 + 24t + 4$, where h is the height of the ball in feet and t is the time, in seconds, since it was released by the pitcher. If the batter hits the ball when it is 2 ft off the ground, for how many seconds has the ball been in the air? Round to the nearest hundredth.
1.58 s

In the NEWS!

Alzheimer's Diagnoses Rising

As the population of senior citizens grows, so will the number of people diagnosed with Alzheimer's, the disease that afflicted former president Ronald Reagan for the last 10 years of his life.
Source: The Alzheimer's Association

26. Alzheimer's See the news clipping at the right. Find the year in which 15 million Americans are expected to have Alzheimer's. Use the equation $y = 0.002x^2 + 0.05x + 2$, where y is the population with Alzheimer's, in millions, in year x, where $x = 0$ corresponds to the year 1980.
2049

27. Sports The hang time of a football that is kicked on the opening kickoff is given by $s = -16t^2 + 88t + 1$, where s is the height, in feet, of the football t seconds after leaving the kicker's foot. What is the hang time of a kickoff that hits the ground without being caught? Round to the nearest tenth.
5.5 s

28. **The Internet** See the news clipping at the right. Find the year in which consumer Internet traffic will reach 55 million terabytes per month. Use the equation $y = 0.932x^2 - 12.6x + 49.4$, where y is consumer Internet traffic in millions of terabytes per month and x is the year, where $x = 10$ corresponds to the year 2010. 2014

In the NEWS!

72 Million Years of Video

Transmission of video content through the Internet is increasing so quickly that before long you will need 72 million years to watch the video content that will be transmitted in one year. Total consumer Internet traffic is projected to reach 55 million terabytes per month before 2015, with over 90% of that traffic being video content.

Source: businessweek.com

Complete Exercises 29 and 30 *without* writing and solving an equation. Use this situation: A small pipe takes 12 min longer to fill a tank than does a larger pipe. Working together, the pipes can fill the tank in 4 min.

29. True or false? The amount of time it takes for the larger pipe to fill the tank is less than 4 min. False

30. True or false? The amount of time it takes for the small pipe to fill the tank is greater than 16 min. True

Critical Thinking

31. **Geometry** The hypotenuse of a right triangle measures $\sqrt{13}$ cm. The length of one leg is 1 cm shorter than twice the length of the other leg. Find the lengths of the legs of the right triangle. 2 cm and 3 cm

32. **Integer Problem** The sum of the squares of four consecutive integers is 86. Find the four integers. −6, −5, −4, and −3, or 3, 4, 5, and 6

33. **Geometry** Find the radius of a right circular cone that has a volume of 800 cm^3 and a height of 12 cm. Round to the nearest hundredth. 7.98 cm

12 cm

34. **Food Industry** The radius of a large pizza is 1 in. less than twice the radius of a small pizza. The difference between the areas of the two pizzas is 33π in^2. Find the radius of the large pizza. 7 in.

35. **Food Industry** A square piece of cardboard is to be formed into a box to transport pizzas. The box is formed by cutting 2-inch-square corners from the cardboard and folding them up as shown in the figure at the right. If the volume of the box is 512 in^3, what are the dimensions of the cardboard? 20 in. by 20 in.

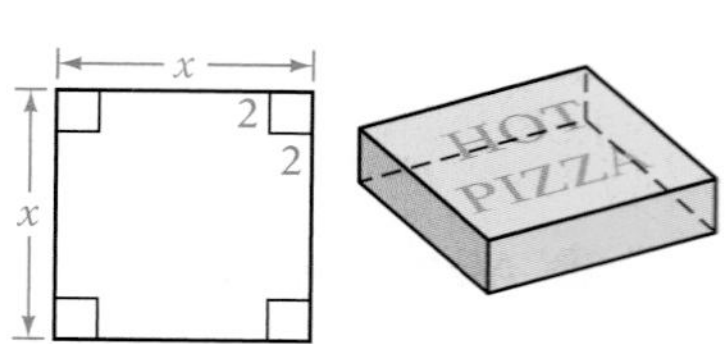

Projects or Group Activities

36. **Metalwork** A wire 8 ft long is cut into two pieces. A circle is formed from one piece and a square is formed from the other. The total area of both figures is given by $A = \frac{1}{16}(8 - x)^2 + \frac{x^2}{4\pi}$. What is the length of each piece of wire if the total area is 4.5 ft^2? Round to the nearest thousandth. 7.507 ft, 0.493 ft

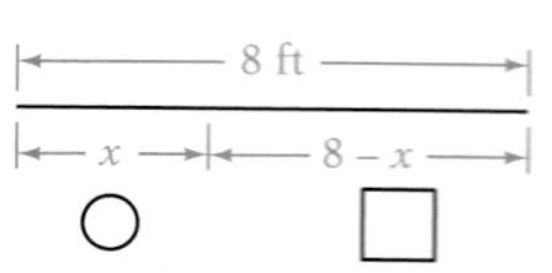

37. Geometry Consider the two rectangles shown below. The rectangles have the same perimeter but different areas.

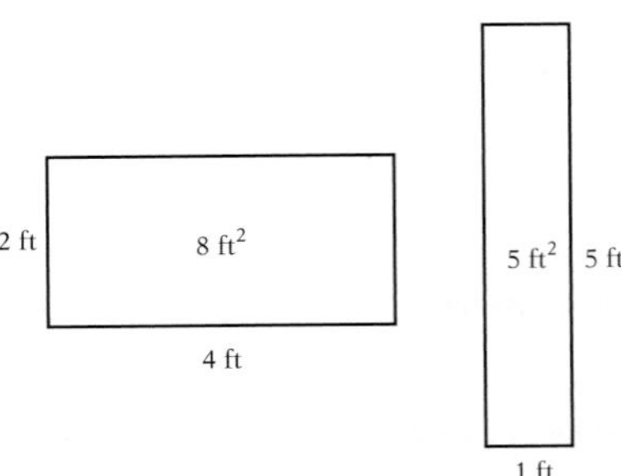

a. Using L for the length and W for the width, write the perimeter formula for a rectangle whose perimeter is 12 ft. $12 = 2L + 2W$

b. Using A for the area, L for the length, and W for the width, write the formula for the area of a rectangle. $A = LW$

c. Solve the formula in part (a) for L. Substitute your expression for L into the formula in part (b). Then simplify. $L = 6 - W$; $A = (6 - W)W$; $A = -W^2 + 6W$

d. The formula you wrote in part (c) gives the area of a rectangle in terms of the width. Experiment with this formula until you find the dimensions of the rectangle of perimeter 12 ft that has the largest area. Length: 3 ft; width: 3 ft

QUICK QUIZ

1. The length of a rectangle is 4 ft more than twice the width. The area of the rectangle is 48 ft². Find the length and the width of the rectangle. **Length: 12 ft, width: 4 ft [16.5A]**
2. A tank is emptied by two drains. The smaller drain can empty the tank in twice the amount of time it takes the larger drain to empty the tank. Using both drains, the tank can be emptied in 2 h. How long would it take the larger drain, working alone, to empty the tank? **3 h [16.5A]**

CHAPTER

16 Summary

Key Words

A **quadratic equation** is an equation that can be written in the form $ax^2 + bx + c = 0$, where a, b, and c are real numbers and $a \neq 0$. [16.1A, p. 806]

A quadratic equation is in **standard form** when the polynomial is in descending order and equal to zero. [16.1A, p. 806]

Adding to a binomial the constant term that makes it a perfect-square trinomial is called **completing the square**. [16.2A, p. 812]

An equation of the form $y = ax^2 + bx + c$, $a \neq 0$, is a **quadratic equation in two variables**. [16.4A, p. 823]

Examples

$3x^2 - 5x - 3 = 0$ is a quadratic equation. For this equation, $a = 3$, $b = -5$, and $c = -3$.

$2x - 4 + 5x^2 = 0$ is not in standard form. The same equation in standard form is $5x^2 + 2x - 4 = 0$.

Adding to $x^2 - 8x$ the constant term 16 results in a perfect square trinomial: $x^2 - 8x + 16 = (x - 4)^2$.

$y = 2x^2 + 3x - 4$ is a quadratic equation in two variables.

The graph of an equation of the form $y = ax^2 + bx + c$, $a \neq 0$, is a **parabola**. The graph is U-shaped, and opens up when $a > 0$ and down when $a < 0$. [16.4A, p. 823]

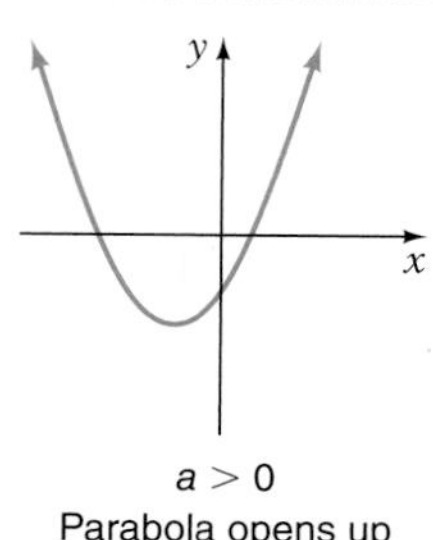

$a > 0$
Parabola opens up

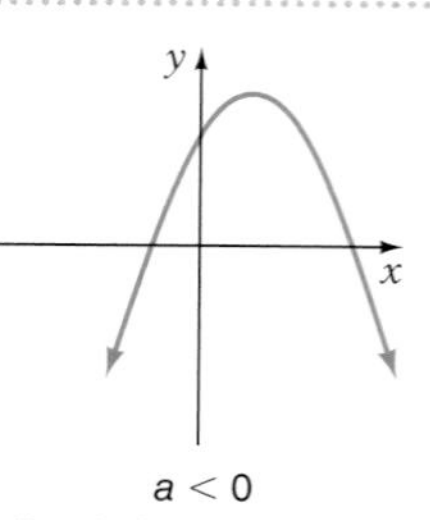

$a < 0$
Parabola opens down

Essential Rules and Procedures

Examples

Solving a Quadratic Equation by Factoring [16.1A, p. 806]
Write the equation in standard form, factor the polynomial, apply the Principle of Zero Products, and solve for the variable.

$$x^2 - 3x = 10$$
$$x^2 - 3x - 10 = 0$$
$$(x + 2)(x - 5) = 0$$
$$x + 2 = 0 \qquad x - 5 = 0$$
$$x = -2 \qquad x = 5$$

Principle of Taking the Square Root of Each Side of an Equation [16.1B, p. 808]
If $x^2 = a$, then $x = \pm\sqrt{a}$.
This principle is used to solve quadratic equations by taking square roots.

$$2x^2 - 36 = 0$$
$$2x^2 = 36$$
$$x^2 = 18$$
$$\sqrt{x^2} = \sqrt{18}$$
$$x = \pm\sqrt{18} = \pm 3\sqrt{2}$$

Solving a Quadratic Equation by Completing the Square [16.2A, p. 812]
When a quadratic equation is in the form $x^2 + bx = c$, add to each side of the equation the term that completes the square on $x^2 + bx$. Factor the perfect-square trinomial, and write it as the square of a binomial. Take the square root of each side of the equation, and solve for x.

$$x^2 + 6x = 5$$
$$x^2 + 6x + 9 = 5 + 9$$
$$(x + 3)^2 = 14$$
$$\sqrt{(x + 3)^2} = \sqrt{14}$$
$$x + 3 = \pm\sqrt{14}$$
$$x = -3 \pm \sqrt{14}$$

The Quadratic Formula [16.3A, p. 818]
The solutions of the quadratic equation $ax^2 + bx + c = 0$, $a \neq 0$, are $x = \dfrac{-b \pm \sqrt{b^2 - 4ac}}{2a}$.

$$2x^2 + 3x - 6 = 0$$
$$x = \frac{-b \pm \sqrt{b^2 - 4ac}}{2a}$$
$$= \frac{-3 \pm \sqrt{(3)^2 - 4(2)(-6)}}{2(2)}$$
$$= \frac{-3 \pm \sqrt{9 + 48}}{4} = \frac{-3 \pm \sqrt{57}}{4}$$

Graph of a Quadratic Equation in Two Variables [16.4A, p. 824]
To graph a quadratic equation in two variables, find several solutions of the equation. Graph the ordered-pair solutions on a rectangular coordinate system. Draw a parabola through the points.
To find the x-intercepts of the graph of a quadratic equation in two variables, let $y = 0$ and solve for x.
To find the y-intercept, let $x = 0$ and solve for y.

$y = x^2 - x - 2$

x	y
−2	4
−1	0
0	−2
1	−2
2	0
3	4

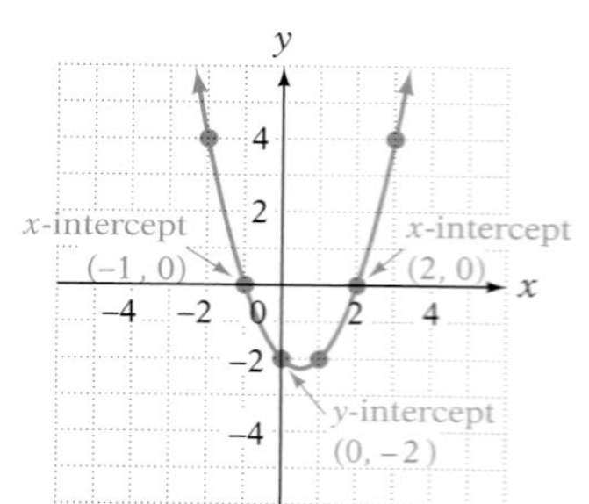

CHAPTER

16 Review Exercises

1. Solve by factoring: $6x^2 + 13x - 28 = 0$

   $-\frac{7}{2}, \frac{4}{3}$ [16.1A]

2. Solve by taking square roots:
   $49x^2 = 25$

   $\pm\frac{5}{7}$ [16.1B]

3. Solve by completing the square:
   $x^2 + 2x - 24 = 0$

   $-6, 4$ [16.2A]

4. Solve by using the quadratic formula:
   $x^2 + 5x - 6 = 0$

   $-6, 1$ [16.3A]

5. Solve by completing the square:
   $2x^2 + 5x = 12$

   $-4, \frac{3}{2}$ [16.2A]

6. Solve by factoring: $12x^2 + 10 = 29x$

   $2, \frac{5}{12}$ [16.1A]

7. Solve by taking square roots:
   $(x + 2)^2 - 24 = 0$

   $-2 \pm 2\sqrt{6}$ [16.1B]

8. Solve by using the quadratic formula:
   $2x^2 + 3 = 5x$

   $1, \frac{3}{2}$ [16.3A]

9. Solve by factoring: $6x(x + 1) = x - 1$

   $-\frac{1}{2}, -\frac{1}{3}$ [16.1A]

10. Solve by taking square roots:
    $4y^2 + 9 = 0$

    No real number solution [16.1B]

11. Solve by completing the square:
    $x^2 - 4x + 1 = 0$

    $2 \pm \sqrt{3}$ [16.2A]

12. Solve by using the quadratic formula:
    $x^2 - 3x - 5 = 0$

    $\frac{3 \pm \sqrt{29}}{2}$ [16.3A]

13. Solve by completing the square:
    $x^2 + 6x + 12 = 0$

    No real number solution [16.2A]

14. Solve by factoring: $(x + 9)^2 = x + 11$

    $-10, -7$ [16.1A]

15. Solve by taking square roots:
    $\left(x - \frac{1}{2}\right)^2 = \frac{9}{4}$

    $-1, 2$ [16.1B]

16. Solve by completing the square:
    $4x^2 + 16x = 7$

    $\frac{-4 \pm \sqrt{23}}{2}$ [16.2A]

17. Solve by using the quadratic formula:
$x^2 - 4x + 8 = 0$

No real number solution [16.3A]

18. Solve by using the quadratic formula:
$2x^2 + 5x + 2 = 0$

$-2, -\frac{1}{2}$ [16.3A]

19. Graph $y = -3x^2$.

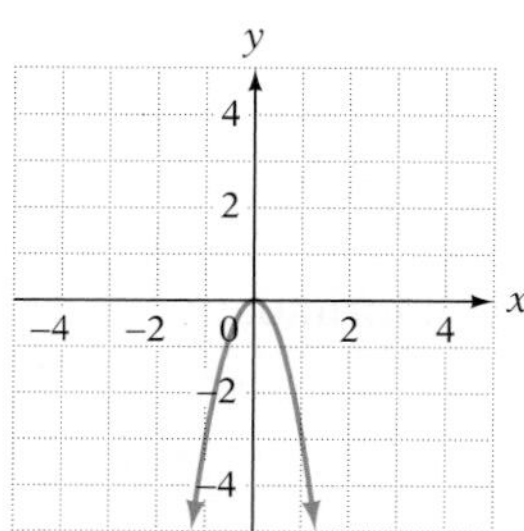

[16.4A]

20. Graph $y = -\frac{1}{4}x^2$.

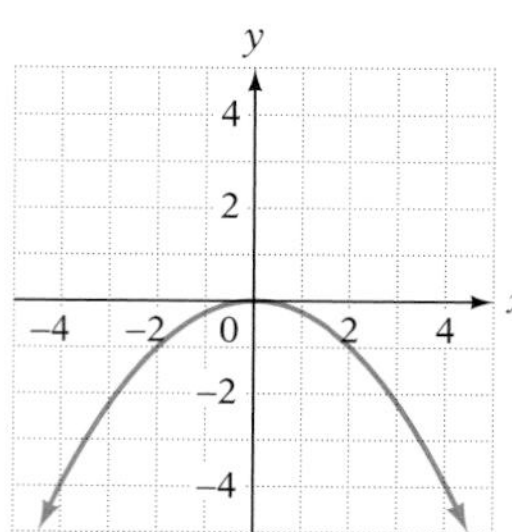

[16.4A]

21. Graph $y = 2x^2 + 1$.

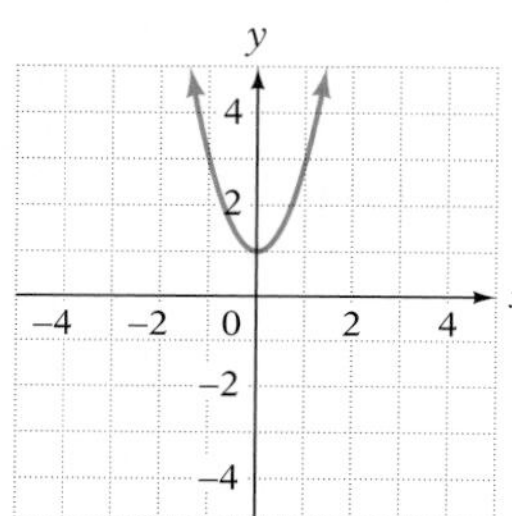

[16.4A]

22. Graph $y = x^2 - 4x + 3$.

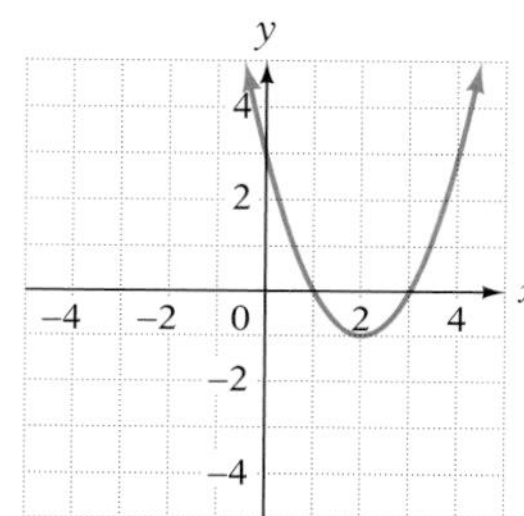

[16.4A]

23. Graph $y = -x^2 + 4x - 5$.

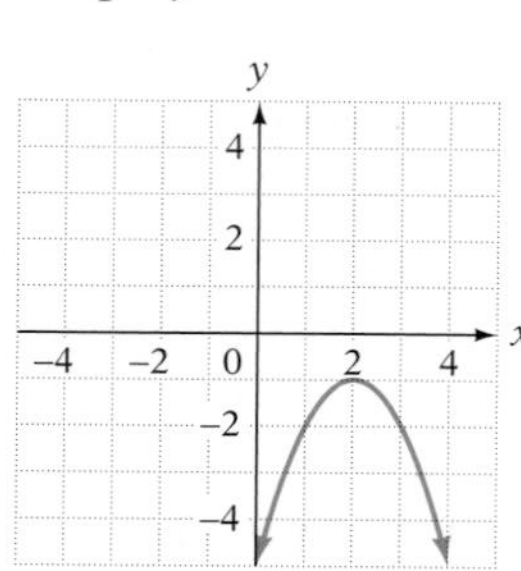

[16.4A]

24. Find the x- and y-intercepts of the graph of $y = x^2 - 2x - 15$.

x-intercepts: $(-3, 0)$, $(5, 0)$

y-intercept: $(0, -15)$ [16.4A]

25. Uniform Motion It took a hawk half an hour longer to fly 70 mi against the wind than to fly 40 mi with the wind. The rate of the wind was 5 mph. Find the rate of the hawk in calm air.
75 mph [16.5A]

CHAPTER 16 TEST

1. Solve by factoring: $x^2 - 5x - 6 = 0$
   $-1, 6$ [16.1A]

2. Solve by factoring: $3x^2 + 7x = 20$
   $-4, \frac{5}{3}$ [16.1A]

3. Solve $2x^2 + x = 0$ by factoring.
   $-\frac{1}{2}, 0$ [16.1A]

4. Solve $4x^2 - 9 = 0$ by taking square roots.
   $\pm\frac{3}{2}$ [16.1B]

5. Solve by taking square roots:
   $2(x - 5)^2 - 50 = 0$
   $0, 10$ [16.1B]

6. Solve by taking square roots:
   $3(x + 4)^2 - 60 = 0$
   $-4 \pm 2\sqrt{5}$ [16.1B]

7. Solve by completing the square:
   $x^2 + 4x - 16 = 0$
   $-2 \pm 2\sqrt{5}$ [16.2A]

8. Solve by completing the square:
   $x^2 + 3x = 8$
   $\frac{-3 \pm \sqrt{41}}{2}$ [16.2A]

9. Solve by completing the square:
   $2x^2 - 6x + 1 = 0$
   $\frac{3 \pm \sqrt{7}}{2}$ [16.2A]

10. Solve by completing the square:
    $2x^2 + 8x = 3$
    $\frac{-4 \pm \sqrt{22}}{2}$ [16.2A]

11. Solve by using the quadratic formula:
    $x^2 + 4x + 2 = 0$
    $-2 \pm \sqrt{2}$ [16.3A]

12. Solve by using the quadratic formula:
    $x^2 - 3x = 6$
    $\frac{3 \pm \sqrt{33}}{2}$ [16.3A]

13. Solve by using the quadratic formula:
$2x^2 - 5x - 3 = 0$
$-\frac{1}{2}, 3$ [16.3A]

14. Solve by using the quadratic formula:
$3x^2 - x = 1$
$\frac{1 \pm \sqrt{13}}{6}$ [16.3A]

15. Solve $4x^2 + 6x - 1 = 0$ by using the quadratic formula. Approximate the solutions to the nearest thousandth.
$-1.651, 0.151$ [16.3A]

16. Solve $3x^2 + 2x - 3 = 0$ by using the quadratic formula. Approximate the solutions to the nearest thousandth.
$-1.387, 0.721$ [16.3A]

17. Graph $y = x^2 + 2x - 4$.

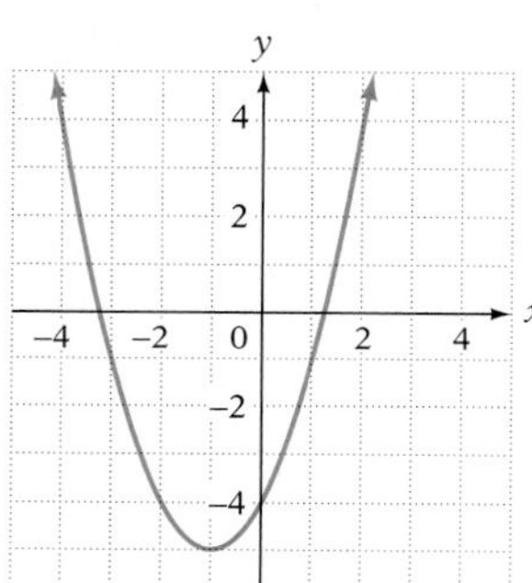

[16.4A]

18. Find the x- and y-intercepts of the graph of $f(x) = x^2 + x - 12$.
x-intercepts: $(-4, 0), (3, 0)$
y-intercept: $(0, -12)$ [16.4A]

19. Geometry The length of a rectangle is 2 ft less than twice the width. The area of the rectangle is 40 ft^2. Find the length and width of the rectangle.
Length: 8 ft; width: 5 ft [16.5A]

© Yuriy Chertok/Shutterstock.com

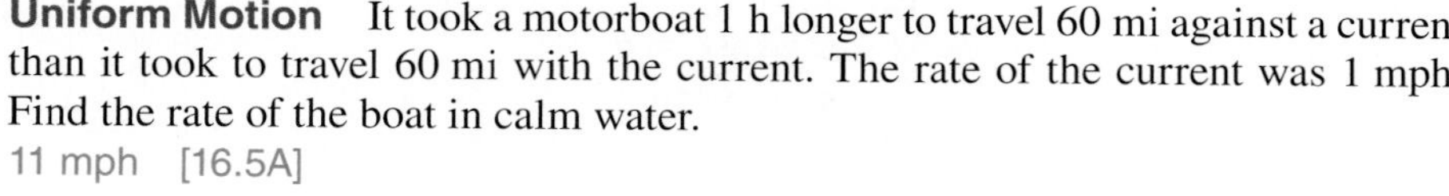
20. Uniform Motion It took a motorboat 1 h longer to travel 60 mi against a current than it took to travel 60 mi with the current. The rate of the current was 1 mph. Find the rate of the boat in calm water.
11 mph [16.5A]

Cumulative Review Exercises

1. Simplify: $2x - 3[2x - 4(3 - 2x) + 2] - 3$
$-28x + 27$ [4.2D]

2. Solve: $-\frac{3}{5}x = -\frac{9}{10}$
$\frac{3}{2}$ [5.1C]

3. Solve: $2x - 3(4x - 5) = -3x - 6$
3 [5.3B]

4. Simplify: $(2a^2b)^2(-3a^4b^2)$
$-12a^8b^4$ [9.2B]

5. Divide: $(x^2 - 8) \div (x - 2)$
$x + 2 - \frac{4}{x - 2}$ [9.5B]

6. Factor: $3x^3 + 2x^2 - 8x$
$x(3x - 4)(x + 2)$ [10.3A/10.3B]

7. Divide: $\frac{3x^2 - 6x}{4x - 6} \div \frac{2x^2 + x - 6}{6x^3 - 24x}$
$\frac{9x^2(x - 2)^2}{(2x - 3)^2}$ [11.1C]

8. Subtract: $\frac{x}{2(x - 1)} - \frac{1}{(x - 1)(x + 1)}$
$\frac{x + 2}{2(x + 1)}$ [11.3B]

9. Simplify: $\dfrac{1 - \frac{7}{x} + \frac{12}{x^2}}{2 - \frac{1}{x} - \frac{15}{x^2}}$
$\frac{x - 4}{2x + 5}$ [11.4A]

10. Find the x- and y-intercepts of the graph of $4x - 3y = 12$.
x-intercept: (3, 0); y-intercept: (0, -4) [12.3A]

11. Find the equation of the line that contains the point $(-3, 2)$ and has slope $-\frac{4}{3}$.
$y = -\frac{4}{3}x - 2$ [12.4A/12.4B]

12. Solve the system of equations by substitution:
$3x - y = 5$
$y = 2x - 3$
(2, 1) [13.2A]

13. Solve the system of equations by the addition method:
$3x + 2y = 2$
$5x - 2y = 14$
(2, -2) [13.3A]

14. Solve: $2x - 3(2 - 3x) > 2x - 5$
$x > \frac{1}{9}$ [14.3A]

15. Simplify: $(\sqrt{a} - \sqrt{2})(\sqrt{a} + \sqrt{2})$
$a - 2$ [15.3A]

16. Simplify: $\frac{\sqrt{108a^7b^3}}{\sqrt{3a^4b}}$
$6ab\sqrt{a}$ [15.3B]

17. Simplify: $\dfrac{\sqrt{3}}{5 + 2\sqrt{3}}$

$\dfrac{-6 + 5\sqrt{3}}{13}$ [15.3B]

18. Solve: $3 = 8 - \sqrt{5x}$

5 [15.4A]

19. Solve by factoring: $6x^2 - 17x = -5$

$\dfrac{5}{2}, \dfrac{1}{3}$ [16.1A]

20. Solve by taking square roots:
$2(x - 5)^2 = 36$

$5 \pm 3\sqrt{2}$ [16.1B]

21. Solve by completing the square:
$3x^2 + 7x = -3$

$\dfrac{-7 \pm \sqrt{13}}{6}$ [16.2A]

22. Solve by using the quadratic formula:
$2x^2 - 3x - 2 = 0$

$-\dfrac{1}{2}, 2$ [16.3A]

23. Food Mixtures Find the cost per pound of a mixture made from 20 lb of cashews that cost \$4.90 per pound and 50 lb of peanuts that cost \$2.10 per pound.

\$2.90 per pound [5.5A]

24. The Stock Market A stock investment of 100 shares paid a dividend of \$215. At this rate, how many additional shares must the investor own to earn a dividend of \$752.50?

250 additional shares [6.2B]

25. Uniform Motion A 720-mile trip from one city to another takes 3 h when a plane is flying with the wind. The return trip, against the wind, takes 4.5 h. Find the rate of the plane in still air and the rate of the wind.

Plane in still air: 200 mph; wind: 40 mph [13.4A]

26. Grading A student received a 70, a 91, an 85, and a 77 on four tests in a mathematics class. What scores on the last test will enable the student to receive a minimum of 400 points?

77 or more points [14.2C]

27. Integer Problem The sum of the squares of three consecutive odd integers is 83. Find the middle odd integer.

−5 or 5 [16.5A]

28. Exercise A jogger ran 7 mi at a constant rate and then reduced the rate by 3 mph. An additional 8 mi was run at the reduced rate. The total time spent jogging the 15 mi was 3 h. Find the jogger's rate for the last 8 mi.

4 mph [16.5A]

29. Graph the solution set of $2x - 3y > 6$.

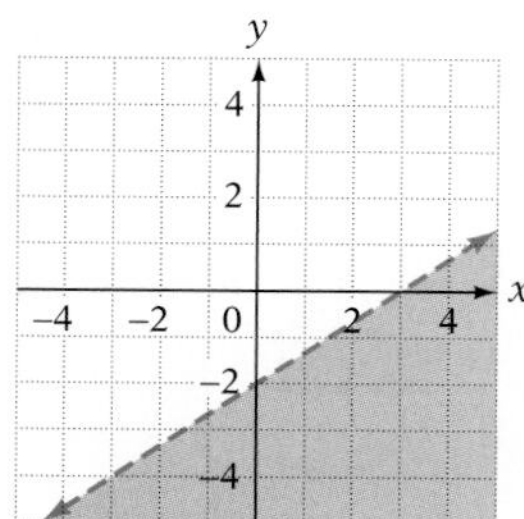

[14.4A]

30. Graph $y = x^2 - 2x - 3$.

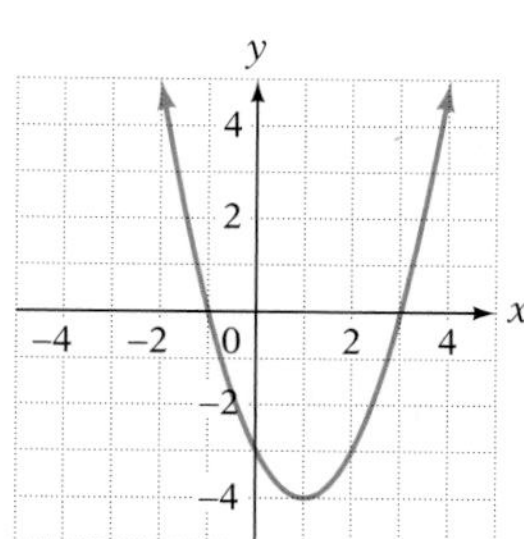

[16.4A]

FINAL EXAM

1. Evaluate $-|-3|$.
-3 [3.1C]

2. Subtract: $-15 - (-12) - 3$
-6 [3.2B]

3. Simplify: $-\frac{4}{5} - \left(-\frac{3}{10}\right)$
$-\frac{1}{2}$ [3.4A]

4. Simplify: $-7 - \frac{12 - 15}{2 - (-1)} \cdot (-4)$
-11 [3.5A]

5. Evaluate $\frac{a^2 - 3b}{2a - 2b^2}$ when $a = 3$ and $b = -2$.
$-\frac{15}{2}$ [4.1A]

6. Simplify: $6x - (-4y) - (-3x) + 2y$
$9x + 6y$ [4.2A]

7. Simplify: $(-15z)\left(-\frac{2}{5}\right)$
$6z$ [4.2B]

8. Simplify: $-2[5 - 3(2x - 7) - 2x]$
$16x - 52$ [4.2D]

9. Solve: $20 = -\frac{2}{5}x$
-50 [5.1C]

10. Solve: $4 - 2(3x + 1) = 3(2 - x) + 5$
-3 [5.3B]

11. Write $\frac{1}{8}$ as a percent.
12.5% [6.3B]

12. Find 19% of 80.
15.2 [6.4A/6.4B]

13. Subtract: $(2x^2 - 5x + 1) - (5x^2 - 2x - 7)$
$-3x^2 - 3x + 8$ [9.1B]

14. Simplify: $(-3xy^3)^4$
$81x^4y^{12}$ [9.2B]

15. Multiply: $(3x^2 - x - 2)(2x + 3)$
$6x^3 + 7x^2 - 7x - 6$ [9.3B]

16. Simplify: $\frac{(-2x^2y^3)^3}{(-4xy^4)^2}$
$-\frac{x^4y}{2}$ [9.4A]

17. Divide: $\frac{12x^2y - 16x^3y^2 - 20y^2}{4xy^2}$
$\frac{3x}{y} - 4x^2 - \frac{5}{x}$ [9.5A]

18. Divide: $(5x^2 - 2x - 1) \div (x + 2)$
$5x - 12 + \frac{23}{x + 2}$ [9.5B]

19. Simplify: $(4x^{-2}y)^2(2xy^{-2})^{-2}$
$\frac{4y^6}{x^6}$ [9.4A]

20. Given $f(t) = \frac{t}{t + 1}$, find $f(3)$.
$\frac{3}{4}$ [12.1D]

21. Factor: $x^2 - 5x - 6$
$(x - 6)(x + 1)$ [10.2A]

22. Factor: $6x^2 - 5x - 6$
$(3x + 2)(2x - 3)$ [10.3A/10.3B]

23. Factor: $8x^3 - 28x^2 + 12x$
$4x(2x - 1)(x - 3)$ [10.5A]

24. Factor: $25x^2 - 16$
$(5x - 4)(5x + 4)$ [10.4A]

25. Factor: $2a(4 - x) - 6(x - 4)$
$2(a + 3)(4 - x)$ [10.1B]

26. Factor: $75y - 12x^2y$
$3y(5 - 2x)(5 + 2x)$ [10.5A]

27. Solve: $2x^2 = 7x - 3$
$\frac{1}{2}, 3$ [10.6A]

28. Multiply: $\frac{2x^2 - 3x + 1}{4x^2 - 2x} \cdot \frac{4x^2 + 4x}{x^2 - 2x + 1}$
$\frac{2(x + 1)}{x - 1}$ [11.1B]

29. Subtract: $\frac{5}{x + 3} - \frac{3x}{2x - 5}$
$\frac{-3x^2 + x - 25}{(2x - 5)(x + 3)}$ [11.3B]

30. Simplify: $x - \frac{1}{1 - \frac{1}{x}}$
$\frac{x^2 - 2x}{x - 1}$ [11.4A]

31. Solve: $\frac{5x}{3x - 5} - 3 = \frac{7}{3x - 5}$
2 [11.5A]

32. Solve $a = 3a - 2b$ for a.
$a = b$ [11.6A]

33. Find the slope of the line that contains the points $(-1, -3)$ and $(2, -1)$.
$\frac{2}{3}$ [12.3B]

34. Find the equation of the line that contains the point $(3, -4)$ and has slope $-\frac{2}{3}$.
$y = -\frac{2}{3}x - 2$ [12.4A/12.4B]

35. Solve the system of equations by substitution:
$y = 4x - 7$
$y = 2x + 5$
(6, 17) [13.2A]

36. Solve the system of equations by the addition method:
$4x - 3y = 11$
$2x + 5y = -1$
$(2, -1)$ [13.3A]

37. Solve: $4 - x \geq 7$
$x \leq -3$ [14.2A]

38. Solve: $2 - 2(y - 1) \leq 2y - 6$
$y \geq \frac{5}{2}$ [14.3A]

39. Simplify: $\sqrt{49x^6}$
$7x^3$ [15.1B]

40. Simplify: $2\sqrt{27a} + 8\sqrt{48a}$
$38\sqrt{3a}$ [15.2A]

41. Simplify: $\frac{\sqrt{3}}{\sqrt{5} - 2}$
$\sqrt{15} + 2\sqrt{3}$ [15.3B]

42. Solve: $\sqrt{2x - 3} + 4 = 5$
2 [15.4A]

43. Solve by factoring:
$3x^2 - x = 4$
$-1, \frac{4}{3}$ [16.1A]

44. Solve by using the quadratic formula:
$4x^2 - 2x - 1 = 0$
$\frac{1 \pm \sqrt{5}}{4}$ [16.3A]

45. Translate and simplify "the sum of twice a number and three times the difference between the number and two."
$2x + 3(x - 2)$; $5x - 6$ [4.3B]

46. Depreciation Because of depreciation, the value of an office machine is now $4800. This is 80% of its original value. Find the original value.
$6000 [6.4C]

47. Meteorology A city's average monthly snowfall amounts, in inches, for January through December were 5.8, 5.2, 4.3, 1.2, 0.8, 0, 0, 0, 0, 0.3, 2.4, 4.3. Find the mean, median, and mode of the data.
Mean: 2.025 in., median: 1 in., mode: 0 in. [8.2A]

48. Investment An investment of $3000 is made at an annual simple interest rate of 8%. How much additional money must be invested at 11% so that the total interest earned is 10% of the total investment?
$6000 [13.2B]

© Olga Popova/Shutterstock.com

49. Food Mixtures A grocer mixes 4 lb of peanuts that cost $2.50 per pound with 2 lb of walnuts that cost $7 per pound. What is the cost per pound of the resulting mixture?
$4 per pound [5.5A]

50. Probability Four aces, two kings, and three queens are removed from a deck of cards and placed in a pile. One card is chosen at random from the pile. What is the probability that the card chosen is not a queen?
$\frac{2}{3}$ [8.3A]

51. Travel At 2 P.M., a small plane had been flying for 1 h when a change of wind direction doubled its average ground speed. The complete 860-kilometer trip took 2.5 h. How far did the plane travel in the first hour?
215 km [5.5B]

52. Geometry The angles of a triangle are such that the measure of the second angle is 10° more than the measure of the first angle, and the measure of the third angle is 10° more than the measure of the second angle. Find the measures of the three angles.
50°, 60°, 70° [7.1C]

© michaeljung/Shutterstock.com

53. Integer Problem The sum of the squares of three consecutive integers is 50. Find the middle integer.
4 or −4 [16.5A]

54. Food Preparation It takes a chef 1 h to prepare a dinner. The chef's apprentice can prepare the dinner in 1.5 h. How long would it take the chef and the apprentice, working together, to prepare the dinner?
0.6 h [11.7A]

55. Geometry The length of a rectangle is 5 m more than the width. The area of the rectangle is 50 m^2. Find the dimensions of the rectangle.
Width: 5 m; length: 10 m [10.6B]

56. Paint Mixtures A paint formula requires 2 oz of dye for every 15 oz of base paint. How many ounces of dye are required for 120 oz of base paint?
16 oz [6.2B]

57. Travel Traveling with the current, a motorboat travels 50 mi in 2.5 h. Traveling against the current, the boat takes twice as long to go 50 mi. Find the rate of the boat in calm water and the rate of the current.
Boat in calm water: 15 mph; current: 5 mph [13.4A]

58. Travel Flying against the wind, it took a pilot $\frac{1}{2}$ h longer to travel 500 mi than it took flying with the wind. The rate of the plane in calm air is 225 mph. Find the rate of the wind.
25 mph [16.5A]

59. Graph $\{x|x > -4\}$.

−5 −4 −3 −2 −1 0 1 2 3 4 5

[14.1B]

60. Graph $y = -\frac{3}{2}x + 4$.

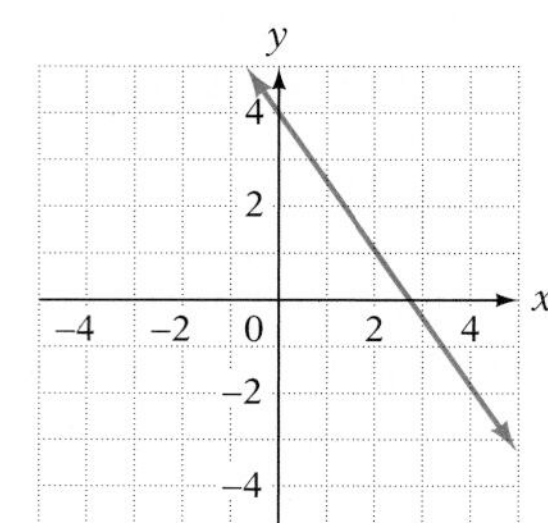

[12.2A]

61. Graph $x - 4y = 4$.

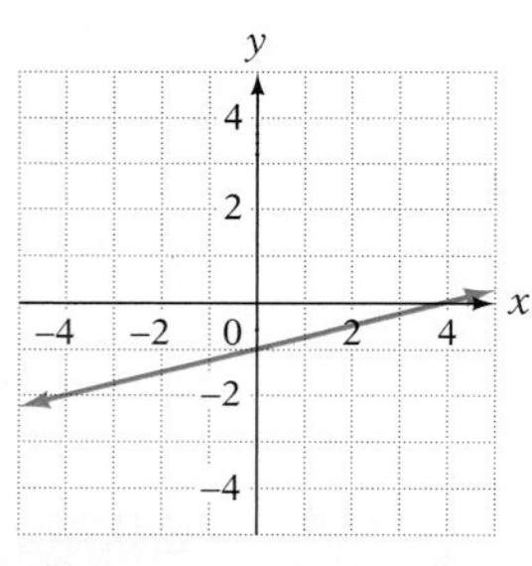

[12.2B]

62. Graph the line that has slope $-\frac{1}{2}$ and y-intercept $(0, -3)$.

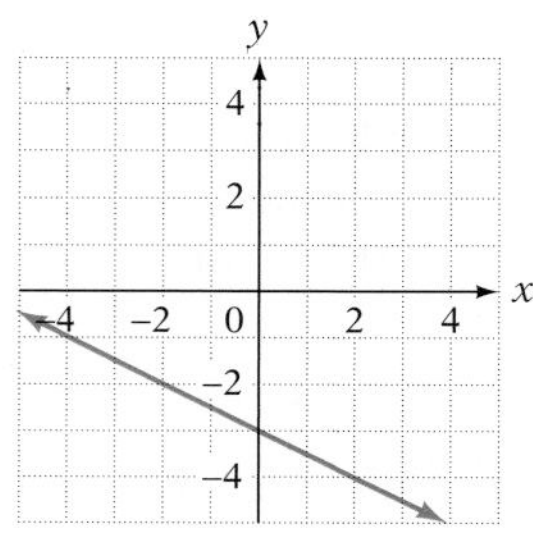

[12.3C]

63. Graph $5x - 2y < 10$.

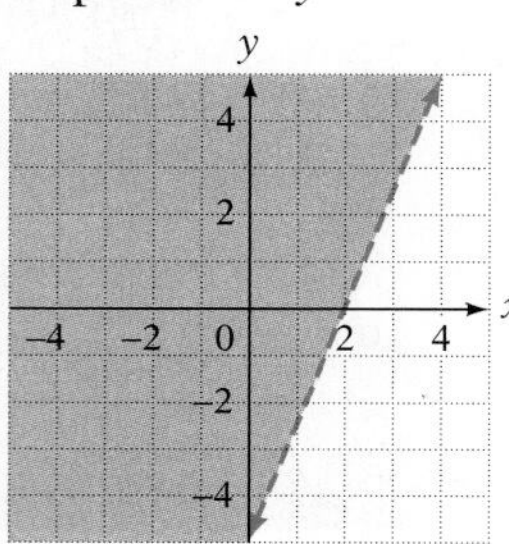

[14.4A]

64. Graph $y = x^2 - 4x + 3$.

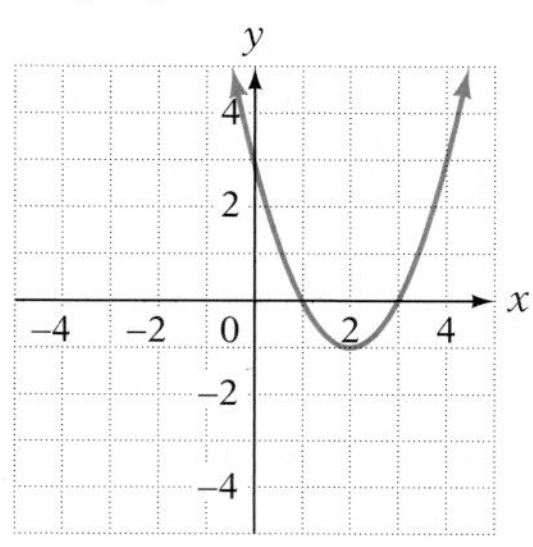

[16.4A]

Transitioning to Algebra

OBJECTIVES

SECTION T.1
A To add and subtract fractions
B To multiply and divide fractions

SECTION T.2
A To add and subtract integers
B To multiply and divide integers

SECTION T.3
A To add and subtract rational numbers
B To multiply and divide rational numbers
C To evaluate exponential expressions
D To use the Order of Operations Agreement to simplify expressions

SECTION T.4
A To solve a first-degree equation in one variable

Focus on Success

Reviewing concepts and skills that you have studied is one way to strengthen your ability to use those concepts and skills to solve problems. This transition chapter provides you with an opportunity to review material that you have studied in the PreAlgebra chapters of this text. As you begin the Introductory Algebra chapters of the text, also review the study skills that you and other students have used to be successful. Read through Chapter A, AIM for Success.

Prep Test

Are you ready to succeed in an algebra course? Take the Prep Test below to find out if you are ready to review some of the skills you will need.

1. Find the sum of 28 and 43.
   71 [1.2A]

2. Evaluate $x - y$ when $x = 3005$ and $y = 387$.
   2618 [1.2B]

3. Evaluate $3xy$ when $x = 5$ and $y = 9$.
   135 [1.3A]

4. Find the quotient of 96 and 6.
   16 [1.3C]

5. Find the prime factorization of 78.
   $2 \cdot 3 \cdot 13$ [1.3D]

6. Find the least common multiple (LCM) of 24 and 36.
   72 [2.1A]

7. Find the greatest common divisor (GCD) of 24 and 36.
   6 [2.1A]

8. Place the correct symbol, $<$ or $>$, between two numbers.
   $-37 < -28$ [3.1A]

9. Evaluate: $|-27|$
   27 [3.1C]

10. What is the opposite of -4?
    4 [3.2B]

SECTION

T.1 Fractions

OBJECTIVE A To add and subtract fractions

2.3A Add fractions

When we add two fractions with the same denominator, we add the numerators. The denominator remains the same. Then we write the answer in simplest form.

$$\frac{2}{9} + \frac{4}{9} = \frac{2+4}{9} = \frac{6}{9} = \frac{2}{3}$$

Addition of Fractions

To add fractions with the same denominator, add the numerators and place the sum over the common denominator.

$\frac{a}{b} + \frac{c}{b} = \frac{a+c}{b}$, where $b \neq 0$

2.1A Find the least common multiple (LCM)

Before two fractions can be added, the fractions must have the same denominator. To add fractions with different denominators, first rewrite the fractions as equivalent fractions with a common denominator. The common denominator is the least common multiple (LCM) of the denominators of the fractions. The LCM of denominators is sometimes called the least common denominator (LCD).

HOW TO 1 Add: $\frac{2}{3} + \frac{1}{4}$

$\frac{2}{3} + \frac{1}{4} = \frac{8}{12} + \frac{3}{12}$

- The common denominator is the LCM of 3 and 4, which is 12. Write the fractions as equivalent fractions with the common denominator.

$= \frac{8+3}{12} = \frac{11}{12}$

- Add the fractions. $\frac{11}{12}$ is in simplest form.

2.3B Subtract fractions

When we subtract two fractions with the same denominator, we subtract the numerators. The denominator remains the same. Then we write the answer in simplest form.

$$\frac{7}{9} - \frac{4}{9} = \frac{7-4}{9} = \frac{3}{9} = \frac{1}{3}$$

Subtraction of Fractions

To subtract fractions with the same denominator, subtract the numerators and place the difference over the common denominator.

$\frac{a}{b} - \frac{c}{b} = \frac{a-c}{b}$, where $b \neq 0$

To subtract fractions with different denominators, first rewrite the fractions as equivalent fractions with a common denominator. As with addition of fractions, the common denominator is the least common multiple (LCM) of the denominators of the fractions.

HOW TO 2 Subtract: $\frac{2}{3} - \frac{5}{8}$

$\frac{2}{3} - \frac{5}{8} = \frac{16}{24} - \frac{15}{24}$

- The common denominator is the LCM of 3 and 8, which is 24. Write the fractions as equivalent fractions with the common denominator.

$= \frac{16 - 15}{24} = \frac{1}{24}$

- Subtract the fractions. $\frac{1}{24}$ is in simplest form.

EXAMPLE 1

Add: $\frac{3}{8} + \frac{7}{12}$

Solution

$\frac{3}{8} + \frac{7}{12} = \frac{9}{24} + \frac{14}{24}$

- The LCM of 8 and 12 is 24.

$= \frac{23}{24}$

- Add the numerators. Place the sum over the common denominator.

YOU TRY IT 1

Add: $\frac{5}{12} + \frac{9}{16}$

Your solution

$\frac{47}{48}$

EXAMPLE 2

Add: $\frac{2}{3} + \frac{3}{5} + \frac{5}{6}$

Solution

$\frac{2}{3} + \frac{3}{5} + \frac{5}{6}$

- The LCM of 3, 5, and 6 is 30.

$= \frac{20}{30} + \frac{18}{30} + \frac{25}{30}$

- Write equivalent fractions using the LCM.

$= \frac{63}{30}$

- Add the numerators. Place the sum over the common denominator.

$= \frac{21}{10} = 2\frac{1}{10}$

- Simplify.

YOU TRY IT 2

Add: $\frac{3}{4} + \frac{4}{5} + \frac{5}{8}$

Your solution

$2\frac{7}{40}$

EXAMPLE 3

Subtract: $\frac{11}{16} - \frac{5}{12}$

Solution

$\frac{11}{16} - \frac{5}{12} = \frac{33}{48} - \frac{20}{48}$

- The LCM of 16 and 12 is 48.

$= \frac{13}{48}$

- Subtract the numerators. Place the difference over the common denominator.

YOU TRY IT 3

Subtract: $\frac{5}{6} - \frac{1}{4}$

Your solution

$\frac{7}{12}$

Solutions on p. S39

OBJECTIVE B *To multiply and divide fractions*

To multiply two fractions, multiply the numerators and multiply the denominators.

2.4A Multiply fractions

Multiplication of Fractions

The product of two fractions is the product of the numerators over the product of the denominators.

$\frac{a}{b} \cdot \frac{c}{b} = \frac{ac}{bd}$, where $b \neq 0$ and $d \neq 0$

Note that fractions do not need to have the same denominator in order to be multiplied.

HOW TO 3 Multiply: $\frac{2}{3} \cdot \frac{4}{5}$

$\frac{2}{3} \cdot \frac{4}{5} = \frac{2 \cdot 4}{3 \cdot 5}$ • Multiply the numerators. Multiply the denominators.

$= \frac{8}{15}$

After multiplying two fractions, write the product in simplest form, as illustrated in the example below.

HOW TO 4 Multiply: $\frac{3}{4} \cdot \frac{14}{15}$

$\frac{3}{4} \cdot \frac{14}{15} = \frac{3 \cdot 14}{4 \cdot 15}$ • Multiply the numerators. Multiply the denominators.

$= \frac{3 \cdot 2 \cdot 7}{2 \cdot 2 \cdot 3 \cdot 5}$ • Express the fraction in simplest form by first writing the prime factorization of each number.

$= \frac{\overset{1}{\cancel{3}} \cdot \overset{1}{\cancel{2}} \cdot 7}{\underset{1}{\cancel{2}} \cdot 2 \cdot \underset{1}{\cancel{3}} \cdot 5}$ • Divide by the common factors.

$= \frac{7}{10}$ • Write the product in simplest form.

Division is defined as multiplication by the reciprocal. Fractions are divided by applying this definition.

2.4B Divide fractions

Division of Fractions

To divide two fractions, multiply the first fraction by the reciprocal of the second fraction.

$\frac{a}{b} \div \frac{c}{d} = \frac{a}{b} \cdot \frac{d}{c}$, where $b \neq 0$, $c \neq 0$, and $d \neq 0$

HOW TO 5 Divide: $\frac{2}{3} \div \frac{3}{4}$

$$\frac{2}{3} \div \frac{3}{4} = \frac{2}{3} \cdot \frac{4}{3}$$

- Multiply the first fraction by the reciprocal of the second fraction.

$$= \frac{2 \cdot 4}{3 \cdot 3}$$

- Multiply the numerators. Multiply the denominators.

$$= \frac{2 \cdot 2 \cdot 2}{3 \cdot 3} = \frac{8}{9}$$

- There are no common factors in the numerator and denominator.

EXAMPLE 4

Multiply: $\frac{4}{15} \cdot \frac{5}{28}$

Solution

$$\frac{4}{15} \cdot \frac{5}{28} = \frac{4 \cdot 5}{15 \cdot 28}$$

- Multiply the numerators. Multiply the denominators.

$$= \frac{2 \cdot 2 \cdot 5}{3 \cdot 5 \cdot 2 \cdot 2 \cdot 7}$$

- Write the prime factorization of each number.

$$= \frac{\overset{1}{\cancel{2}} \cdot \overset{1}{\cancel{2}} \cdot \overset{1}{\cancel{5}}}{3 \cdot \underset{1}{\cancel{5}} \cdot \underset{1}{\cancel{2}} \cdot \underset{1}{\cancel{2}} \cdot 7}$$

- Divide by the common factors.

$$= \frac{1}{21}$$

- Write the product in simplest form.

YOU TRY IT 4

Multiply: $\frac{4}{21} \cdot \frac{7}{44}$

Your solution

$\frac{1}{33}$

EXAMPLE 5

Multiply: $\frac{3}{16} \cdot 4$

Solution

$$\frac{3}{16} \cdot 4 = \frac{3}{16} \cdot \frac{4}{1}$$

- Write 4 as $\frac{4}{1}$.

$$= \frac{3 \cdot 4}{16 \cdot 1}$$

- Multiply the fractions.

$$= \frac{3 \cdot \overset{1}{\cancel{2}} \cdot \overset{1}{\cancel{2}}}{\underset{1}{\cancel{2}} \cdot \underset{1}{\cancel{2}} \cdot 2 \cdot 2 \cdot 1}$$

- Divide by the common factors.

$$= \frac{3}{4}$$

- Write the product in simplest form.

YOU TRY IT 5

Multiply: $\frac{2}{15} \cdot 5$

Your solution

$\frac{2}{3}$

EXAMPLE 6

Divide: $\frac{3}{4} \div \frac{9}{10}$

Solution

$$\frac{3}{4} \div \frac{9}{10} = \frac{3}{4} \cdot \frac{10}{9}$$

- Multiply the first fraction by the reciprocal of the second fraction.

$$= \frac{3 \cdot 10}{4 \cdot 9} = \frac{\overset{1}{\cancel{3}} \cdot \overset{1}{\cancel{2}} \cdot 5}{\underset{1}{\cancel{2}} \cdot 2 \cdot \underset{1}{\cancel{3}} \cdot 3} = \frac{5}{6}$$

YOU TRY IT 6

Divide: $\frac{1}{6} \div \frac{4}{9}$

Your solution

$\frac{3}{8}$

Solutions on p. S39

T.1 EXERCISES

OBJECTIVE A *To add and subtract fractions*

For Exercises 1 to 36, add or subtract.

1. $\frac{2}{7} + \frac{1}{7}$
$\frac{3}{7}$

2. $\frac{3}{11} + \frac{5}{11}$
$\frac{8}{11}$

3. $\frac{1}{2} + \frac{1}{2}$
1

4. $\frac{1}{3} + \frac{2}{3}$
1

5. $\frac{3}{8} + \frac{7}{8} + \frac{1}{8}$
$1\frac{3}{8}$

6. $\frac{5}{12} + \frac{7}{12} + \frac{1}{12}$
$1\frac{1}{12}$

7. $\frac{1}{2} + \frac{2}{3}$
$1\frac{1}{6}$

8. $\frac{2}{3} + \frac{1}{4}$
$\frac{11}{12}$

9. $\frac{3}{14} + \frac{5}{7}$
$\frac{13}{14}$

10. $\frac{7}{10} + \frac{3}{5}$
$1\frac{3}{10}$

11. $\frac{8}{15} + \frac{7}{20}$
$\frac{53}{60}$

12. $\frac{1}{6} + \frac{7}{9}$
$\frac{17}{18}$

13. $\frac{3}{20} + \frac{7}{30}$
$\frac{23}{60}$

14. $\frac{5}{12} + \frac{7}{30}$
$\frac{13}{20}$

15. $\frac{1}{3} + \frac{5}{6} + \frac{7}{9}$
$1\frac{17}{18}$

16. $\frac{2}{3} + \frac{5}{6} + \frac{7}{12}$
$2\frac{1}{12}$

17. $\frac{2}{3} + \frac{1}{5} + \frac{7}{12}$
$1\frac{9}{20}$

18. $\frac{3}{4} + \frac{4}{5} + \frac{7}{12}$
$2\frac{2}{15}$

19. $\frac{11}{12} - \frac{7}{12}$
$\frac{1}{3}$

20. $\frac{13}{15} - \frac{4}{15}$
$\frac{3}{5}$

21. $\frac{3}{4} - \frac{1}{8}$
$\frac{5}{8}$

22. $\frac{2}{3} - \frac{1}{6}$
$\frac{1}{2}$

23. $\frac{5}{9} - \frac{4}{15}$
$\frac{13}{45}$

24. $\frac{11}{12} - \frac{2}{3}$
$\frac{1}{4}$

25. $\frac{9}{20} - \frac{7}{20}$
$\frac{1}{10}$

26. $\frac{48}{55} - \frac{13}{55}$
$\frac{7}{11}$

27. $\frac{11}{24} - \frac{5}{24}$
$\frac{1}{4}$

28. $\frac{23}{30} - \frac{13}{30}$
$\frac{1}{3}$

29. $\frac{5}{7} - \frac{3}{14}$
$\frac{1}{2}$

30. $\frac{5}{9} - \frac{7}{15}$
$\frac{4}{45}$

31. $\frac{8}{15} - \frac{7}{20}$
$\frac{11}{60}$

32. $\frac{7}{9} - \frac{1}{6}$
$\frac{11}{18}$

33. $\frac{5}{6} - \frac{3}{4}$
$\frac{1}{12}$

34. $\frac{4}{5} - \frac{2}{3}$
$\frac{2}{15}$

35. $\frac{7}{8} - \frac{2}{3}$
$\frac{5}{24}$

36. $\frac{5}{12} - \frac{1}{3}$
$\frac{1}{12}$

OBJECTIVE B *To multiply and divide fractions*

For Exercises 37 to 72, multiply or divide.

37. $\frac{2}{3} \cdot \frac{7}{8}$ $\frac{7}{12}$

38. $\frac{1}{2} \cdot \frac{2}{3}$ $\frac{1}{3}$

39. $\frac{15}{16} \cdot \frac{7}{15}$ $\frac{7}{16}$

40. $\frac{3}{8} \cdot \frac{6}{7}$ $\frac{9}{28}$

41. $\frac{2}{5} \cdot \frac{5}{6}$ $\frac{1}{3}$

42. $\frac{11}{12} \cdot \frac{3}{5}$ $\frac{11}{20}$

43. $\frac{3}{5} \cdot \frac{10}{11}$ $\frac{6}{11}$

44. $\frac{6}{7} \cdot \frac{14}{15}$ $\frac{4}{5}$

45. $\frac{8}{9} \cdot \frac{27}{4}$ 6

46. $\frac{3}{5} \cdot \frac{3}{10}$ $\frac{9}{50}$

47. $\frac{3}{8} \cdot \frac{5}{12}$ $\frac{5}{32}$

48. $\frac{3}{2} \cdot \frac{4}{9}$ $\frac{2}{3}$

49. $\frac{7}{8} \cdot \frac{3}{14}$ $\frac{3}{16}$

50. $\frac{5}{12} \cdot \frac{6}{7}$ $\frac{5}{14}$

51. $\frac{5}{6} \cdot \frac{4}{15}$ $\frac{2}{9}$

52. $\frac{5}{7} \cdot \frac{14}{15}$ $\frac{2}{3}$

53. $\frac{2}{3} \cdot \frac{5}{4} \cdot \frac{1}{9}$ $\frac{5}{54}$

54. $\frac{3}{4} \cdot \frac{5}{6} \cdot \frac{8}{9}$ $\frac{5}{9}$

55. $\frac{2}{3} \cdot 6$ 4

56. $14 \cdot \frac{5}{7}$ 10

57. $\frac{3}{7} \div \frac{3}{2}$ $\frac{2}{7}$

58. $\frac{3}{7} \div \frac{3}{7}$ 1

59. $0 \div \frac{1}{2}$ 0

60. $\frac{5}{24} \div \frac{15}{36}$ $\frac{1}{2}$

61. $\frac{2}{15} \div \frac{3}{5}$ $\frac{2}{9}$

62. $\frac{1}{9} \div \frac{2}{3}$ $\frac{1}{6}$

63. $\frac{2}{5} \div \frac{4}{7}$ $\frac{7}{10}$

64. $\frac{3}{8} \div \frac{5}{12}$ $\frac{9}{10}$

65. $\frac{1}{2} \div \frac{1}{4}$ 2

66. $\frac{1}{3} \div \frac{1}{9}$ 3

67. $\frac{4}{15} \div \frac{2}{5}$ $\frac{2}{3}$

68. $\frac{7}{15} \div \frac{14}{5}$ $\frac{1}{6}$

69. $4 \div \frac{2}{3}$ 6

70. $\frac{2}{3} \div 4$ $\frac{1}{6}$

71. $\frac{3}{2} \div 3$ $\frac{1}{2}$

72. $3 \div \frac{3}{2}$ 2

SECTION

T.2 Integers

OBJECTIVE A *To add and subtract integers*

The rule for adding two integers depends on whether the signs of the integers are the same or different.

3.2A Add integers

Rule for Adding Two Integers

To add two integers with the same sign, add the absolute values of the numbers. Then attach the sign of the addends.

To add two integers with different signs, find the absolute values of the numbers. Subtract the smaller absolute value from the larger absolute value. Then attach the sign of the addend with the larger absolute value.

HOW TO 1 Add: $(-5) + (-11)$

$(-5) + (-11) = -16$

- The signs of the addends are the same. Add the absolute values of the numbers. $|-5| = 5$, $|-11| = 11$, $5 + 11 = 16$ Attach the sign of the addends. (Both addends are negative. The sum is negative.)

HOW TO 2 Add: $-16 + (-32)$

$-16 + (-32) = -48$

- The signs of the addends are the same. Add the absolute values of the numbers. Attach the sign of the addends.

HOW TO 3 Add: $7 + (-20)$

$7 + (-20) = -13$

- The signs of the addends are different. Find the absolute values of the numbers. $|7| = 7$, $|-20| = 20$ Subtract the smaller absolute value from the larger absolute value. $20 - 7 = 13$ Attach the sign of the number with the larger absolute value. ($|-20| > |7|$. Attach the negative sign.)

HOW TO 4 Add: $82 + (-136)$

$82 + (-136) = -54$

- The signs are different. Find the difference between the absolute values of the numbers. $136 - 82 = 54$ Attach the sign of the number with the larger absolute value.

Opposites are used to rewrite subtraction problems as related addition problems. Notice below that the subtraction of two whole numbers is the same as addition of the opposite number.

Subtraction		*Addition of the Opposite*	
$9 - 5$	$=$	$9 + (-5)$	$= 4$
$7 - 4$	$=$	$7 + (-4)$	$= 3$
$8 - 3$	$=$	$8 + (-3)$	$= 5$

Subtraction of integers can be written as the addition of the opposite number. To subtract two integers, rewrite the subtraction expression as the first number plus the opposite of the second number.

3.2B Subtract integers

Rule for Subtracting Two Integers

To subtract two integers, add the opposite of the second integer to the first integer.

HOW TO 5 Subtract: $(-14) - 62$

$(-14) - 62$
$= (-14) + (-62)$ • **Rewrite the subtraction operation as the first number plus the opposite of the second number. The opposite of 62 is -62.**
$= -76$ • **Add.**

HOW TO 6 Subtract: $7 - (-5)$

$7 - (-5)$
$= 7 + 5$ • **Rewrite the subtraction operation as the first number plus the opposite of the second number. The opposite of -5 is 5.**
$= 12$ • **Add.**

HOW TO 7 Subtract: $9 - 18$

$9 - 18$
$= 9 + (-18)$ • **Rewrite the subtraction operation as the first number plus the opposite of the second number. The opposite of 18 is -18.**
$= -9$ • **Add.**

When subtraction occurs several times in an expression, rewrite each subtraction as addition of the opposite, and then add.

HOW TO 8 Subtract: $-23 - 7 - (-5)$

$-23 - 7 - (-5)$ • **Rewrite each subtraction as addition of the opposite.**
$= -23 + (-7) + 5$
$= -30 + 5$ • **Add.**
$= -25$

EXAMPLE 1

Add.

a. $-6 + 17$ **b.** $-15 + (-8)$ **c.** $19 + (-26)$

Solution

a. $-6 + 17 = 11$

- The signs are different. Subtract the absolute values. The sum has the same sign as the number with the larger absolute value.

b. $-15 + (-8) = -23$

- The signs are the same. Add the absolute values. The sum has the same sign as the addends.

c. $19 + (-26) = -7$

- The signs are different. Subtract the absolute values. The sum has the same sign as the number with the larger absolute value.

YOU TRY IT 1

Add.

a. $-25 + 13$ **b.** $-41 + (-60)$ **c.** $37 + (-9)$

Your solution

a. -12 b. -101 c. 28

EXAMPLE 2

Subtract.

a. $-9 - 18$ **b.** $-25 - (-13)$

c. $17 - (-40)$ **d.** $10 - (-3) - 7 + 6$

Solution

a. $-9 - 18 = -9 + (-18) = -27$

- -9 minus $18 = -9$ plus the opposite of 18. The opposite of 18 is -18.

b. $-25 - (-13) = -25 + 13 = -12$

- -25 minus $-13 = -25$ plus the opposite of -13. The opposite of -13 is 13.

c. $17 - (-40) = 17 + 40 = 57$

- 17 minus $-40 = 17$ plus the opposite of -40. The opposite of -40 is 40.

d. $10 - (-3) - 7 + 6$

$= 10 + 3 + (-7) + 6$

- Rewrite each subtraction as addition of the opposite.

$= 13 + (-7) + 6$

- Add the numbers.

$= 6 + 6$

$= 12$

YOU TRY IT 2

Subtract.

a. $-27 - 18$ **b.** $-34 - (-90)$

c. $8 - 42$ **d.** $-12 + 9 - (-5) - 4$

Your solution

a. -45 b. 56 c. -34 d. -2

Solutions on pp. S39–S40

OBJECTIVE B *To multiply and divide integers*

The rule for multiplying two integers depends on whether the signs of the integers are the same or different.

3.3A Multiply integers

Rule for Multiplying Two Integers

To multiply two integers with the same sign, multiply the absolute values of the numbers. The product is positive.

To multiply two integers with different signs, multiply the absolute values of the numbers. The product is negative.

HOW TO 9 Multiply: $-3(-12)$

$-3(-12) = 36$

- **The signs of the factors are the same (they are both negative). Multiply the absolute values of the factors.** $|-3| = 3$, $|-12| = 12$, $3(12) = 36$ **The product is positive.**

HOW TO 10 Multiply: $-6(30)$

$-6(30) = -180$

- **The signs of the factors are different. Multiply the absolute values of the factors. The product is negative.**

The rule for dividing two integers depends on whether the signs of the integers are the same or different.

3.3B Divide integers

Rule for Dividing Two Integers

To divide two integers with the same sign, divide the absolute values of the numbers. The quotient is positive.

To divide two integers with different signs, divide the absolute values of the numbers. The quotient is negative.

HOW TO 11 Divide: $(-24) \div (-8)$

$(-24) \div (-8) = 3$

- **The signs of the numbers are the same. Divide the absolute values of the numbers.** $|-24| = 24$, $|-8| = 8$, $24 \div 8 = 3$ **The quotient is positive.**

HOW TO 12 Divide: $(-44) \div 11$

$(-44) \div 11 = -4$

- **The signs of the numbers are different. Divide the absolute values of the numbers. The quotient is negative.**

EXAMPLE 3

Multiply.

a. $(-5)(-12)$ **b.** $4(-9)$ **c.** $(-2)(3)(8)(-10)$

Solution

a. $(-5)(-12) = 60$

- **The signs are the same. The product is positive.**

b. $4(-9) = -36$

- **The signs are different. The product is negative.**

c. $(-2)(3)(8)(-10)$
$= -6(8)(-10)$
$= -48(-10)$
$= 480$

- **Multiply the first two numbers. Then multiply the product by the third number. Continue until all the numbers have been multiplied.**

YOU TRY IT 3

Multiply.

a. $-25(4)$ **b.** $-4(-61)$ **c.** $(-4)(5)(-3)(-1)$

Your solution

a. -100 b. 244 c. -60

EXAMPLE 4

Divide.

a. $-18 \div (-18)$ **b.** $16 \div (-4)$ **c.** $\frac{-20}{-5}$

Solution

a. $-18 \div (-18) = 1$

- **The signs are the same. The quotient is positive.**

b. $16 \div (-4) = -4$

- **The signs are different. The quotient is negative.**

c. $\frac{-20}{-5} = 4$

- **The fraction bar can be read "divided by."** $\frac{-20}{-5} = (-20) \div (-5)$ **The signs are the same. The quotient is positive.**

YOU TRY IT 4

Divide.

a. $(-30) \div 6$ **b.** $(-50) \div (-25)$ **c.** $\frac{32}{-8}$

Your solution

a. -5 b. 2 c. -4

Solutions on p. S40

T.2 EXERCISES

OBJECTIVE A *To add and subtract integers*

For Exercises 1 to 46, add or subtract.

1. $4 + (-9)$
-5

2. $6 + (-7)$
-1

3. $(-5) + (-12)$
-17

4. $(-8) + (-11)$
-19

5. $-5 + 8$
3

6. $-8 + 5$
-3

7. $-14 + (-6)$
-20

8. $-17 + (-3)$
-20

9. $-6 + 6$
0

10. $-19 + 19$
0

11. $64 + (-43)$
21

12. $-78 + 51$
-27

13. $8 - 15$
-7

14. $7 - 10$
-3

15. $-8 - 3$
-11

16. $-10 - 5$
-15

17. $7 - (-1)$
8

18. $4 - (-5)$
9

19. $-9 - (-9)$
0

20. $-13 - (-13)$
0

21. $-10 - 15$
-25

22. $-8 - 7$
-15

23. $(-11) - (-2)$
-9

24. $(-8) - (-5)$
-3

25. $6 - (-16)$
22

26. $4 - (-26)$
30

27. $(-12) - (-6)$
-6

28. $-3 - (-17)$
14

29. $8 - (-8)$
16

30. $(-32) - 46$
-78

31. $45 - 77$
-32

32. $-82 - (-16)$
-66

33. $0 + (-15)$
-15

34. $-18 + 0$
-18

35. $(-21) - (-7)$
-14

36. $-13 - (-4)$
-9

37. $5 - (-6)$
11

38. $12 - (-2)$
14

39. $6 - (-10)$
16

40. $13 - (-5)$
18

41. $7 + 3 - (-3)$
13

42. $(-9) - 8 + (-6)$
-23

43. $-2 + (-5) - (-12)$
5

44. $-3 - 5 + 8 - 1$
-1

45. $-4 + 6 - 9 - 2$
-9

46. $7 - (-3) - 6 + 5$
9

OBJECTIVE B *To multiply and divide integers*

For Exercises 47 to 94, multiply or divide.

47. $-3 \cdot 7$
-21

48. $-6 \cdot 8$
-48

49. $-5(-7)$
35

50. $-9(-2)$
18

51. $4(-9)$
-36

52. $3(-11)$
-33

53. $-10(5)$
-50

54. $-8(4)$
-32

55. $(-7)(-7)$
49

56. $(-4)(-7)$
28

57. $(-9)(0)$
0

58. $-16(1)$
-16

59. $15(4)$
60

60. $42(3)$
126

61. $-21(6)$
-126

62. $-14(2)$
-28

63. $(-3)(-27)$
81

64. $(-6)(-32)$
192

65. $8(-24)$
-192

66. $7(-30)$
-210

67. $-5 \cdot (17)$
-85

68. $-6 \cdot (22)$
-132

69. $-7(-14)$
98

70. $-4(-62)$
248

71. $2 \cdot (-8) \cdot 5$
-80

72. $5 \cdot 6 \cdot (-1)$
-30

73. $-2(-6)(-3)(4)$
-144

74. $-1(4)(-9)(-2)$
-72

75. $12 \div (-4)$
-3

76. $18 \div (-6)$
-3

77. $(-81) \div (-9)$
9

78. $(-48) \div (-6)$
8

79. $0 \div (-4)$
0

80. $-36 \div 1$
-36

81. $77 \div (-7)$
-11

82. $-50 \div (-10)$
5

83. $\frac{36}{-4}$
-9

84. $\frac{40}{-8}$
-5

85. $\frac{-66}{-3}$
22

86. $\frac{-100}{-20}$
5

87. $-84 \div (-6)$
14

88. $-112 \div (-7)$
16

89. $-48 \div 0$
Undefined

90. $(-210) \div (-210)$
1

91. $-126 \div 6$
-21

92. $-160 \div (-5)$
32

93. $(-240) \div 6$
-40

94. $(-96) \div (-8)$
12

SECTION

T.3 Rational Numbers

OBJECTIVE A *To add and subtract rational numbers*

In this section, operations with rational numbers are discussed. A **rational number** is the quotient of two integers.

Rational Numbers

A rational number is a number that can be written in the form $\frac{a}{b}$, where a and b are integers and $b \neq 0$.

3.4A Add or subtract rational numbers

We begin by reviewing addition of rational numbers in fractional form. If an addend is a fraction containing a negative sign, rewrite the fraction with the negative sign in the numerator. Then add the numerators and place the sum over the common denominator.

HOW TO 1 Add: $-\frac{5}{6} + \frac{3}{8}$

$$-\frac{5}{6} + \frac{3}{8} = -\frac{20}{24} + \frac{9}{24}$$

- The LCM of the denominators 6 and 8 is 24. Write each fraction with a denominator of 24.

$$= \frac{-20}{24} + \frac{9}{24}$$

- Write the negative sign in the numerator.

$$= \frac{-20 + 9}{24}$$

- Add the fractions.

$$= \frac{-11}{24}$$

- Simplify the numerator.

$$= -\frac{11}{24}$$

- Write the negative sign in front of the fraction.

HOW TO 2 Add: $-\frac{3}{5} + \left(-\frac{1}{3}\right)$

$$-\frac{3}{5} + \left(-\frac{1}{3}\right) = -\frac{9}{15} + \left(-\frac{5}{15}\right)$$

- The LCM of the denominators 5 and 3 is 15. Write each fraction with a denominator of 15.

$$= \frac{-9}{15} + \frac{-5}{15}$$

- Write the negative signs in the numerators.

$$= \frac{-9 + (-5)}{15}$$

- Add the fractions.

$$= \frac{-14}{15}$$

- Simplify the numerator.

$$= -\frac{14}{15}$$

- Write the negative sign in front of the fraction.

To subtract fractions with negative signs, rewrite the fractions with the negative signs in the numerators.

HOW TO 3 Subtract: $-\frac{2}{3} - \frac{5}{8}$

$-\frac{2}{3} - \frac{5}{8} = -\frac{16}{24} - \frac{15}{24}$
- The LCM of the denominators 3 and 8 is 24. Write each fraction with a denominator of 24.

$= \frac{-16}{24} + \frac{-15}{24}$
- Rewrite subtraction as addition of the opposite. Write the negative signs in the numerators.

$= \frac{-16 + (-15)}{24}$
- Add the fractions.

$= \frac{-31}{24}$
- Simplify the numerator.

$= -\frac{31}{24} = -1\frac{7}{24}$
- Write the negative sign in front of the fraction.

HOW TO 4 Subtract: $-\frac{1}{6} - \left(-\frac{2}{9}\right)$

$-\frac{1}{6} - \left(-\frac{2}{9}\right) = -\frac{1}{6} + \frac{2}{9}$
- Rewrite subtraction as addition of the opposite.

$= -\frac{3}{18} + \frac{4}{18}$
- Write the fractions as equivalent fractions with a common denominator.

$= \frac{-3}{18} + \frac{4}{18}$
- Write the negative sign in the numerator.

$= \frac{-3 + 4}{18}$
- Add the fractions.

$= \frac{1}{18}$
- Simplify the numerator.

The sign rules for adding and subtracting decimals are the same rules used to add and subtract integers.

HOW TO 5 Simplify: $-29.871 + 34.06$

$34.06 - 29.871 = 4.189$
- The signs of the addends are different. Subtract the smaller absolute value from the larger absolute value.

$|34.06| > |-29.871|$
$-29.871 + 34.06 = 4.189$
- Attach the sign of the number with the larger absolute value. The sum is positive.

Recall that the opposite of n is $-n$ and the opposite of $-n$ is n. To find the opposite of a number, change the sign of the number.

HOW TO 6 Simplify: $-3.92 - 21.7$

$$
\begin{aligned}
&-3.92 - 21.7 \\
&\quad = -3.92 + (-21.7) \\
&\quad = -25.62
\end{aligned}
$$

- **Rewrite subtraction as addition of the opposite. The opposite of 21.7 is −21.7.**
- **The signs of the addends are the same. Add the absolute values of the numbers. Attach the sign of the addends.**

EXAMPLE 1

Add: $-\frac{17}{20} + \frac{4}{5}$

Solution

$-\frac{17}{20} + \frac{4}{5} = -\frac{17}{20} + \frac{16}{20}$ • **Write the fractions with a common denominator.**

$= \frac{-17}{20} + \frac{16}{20}$ • **Write the negative sign in the numerator.**

$= \frac{-17 + 16}{20}$ • **Add the fractions.**

$= \frac{-1}{20}$ • **Simplify the numerator.**

$= -\frac{1}{20}$ • **Write the negative sign in front of the fraction.**

YOU TRY IT 1

Add: $-\frac{1}{4} + \left(-\frac{3}{8}\right)$

Your solution

$-\frac{5}{8}$

EXAMPLE 2

Subtract: $-\frac{7}{20} - \frac{1}{5}$

Solution

$-\frac{7}{20} - \frac{1}{5} = -\frac{7}{20} - \frac{4}{20}$ • **Write the fractions with a common denominator.**

$= \frac{-7}{20} + \frac{-4}{20}$ • **Rewrite subtraction as addition of the opposite. Write the negative signs in the numerators.**

$= \frac{-7 + (-4)}{20}$ • **Add the fractions.**

$= \frac{-11}{20}$ • **Simplify the numerator.**

$= -\frac{11}{20}$ • **Write the negative sign in front of the fraction.**

YOU TRY IT 2

Subtract: $-\frac{3}{8} - \left(-\frac{1}{6}\right)$

Your solution

$-\frac{5}{24}$

Solutions on p. S40

EXAMPLE 3

Simplify: $-3.97 - (-10.8)$

Solution

$-3.97 - (-10.8)$

$= -3.97 + 10.8$ • Rewrite subtraction as addition of the opposite.

$= 6.83$ • Subtract the absolute values of the numbers. The sum has the same sign as the number with the larger absolute value.

YOU TRY IT 3

Simplify: $4.69 - 12.5$

Your solution

-7.81

Solution on p. S40

OBJECTIVE B *To multiply and divide rational numbers*

3.4B Multiply or divide rational numbers

The product of two rational numbers written in fractional form is the product of the numerators over the product of the denominators. The sign rules are the same rules used to multiply integers.

The product of two numbers with the same sign is positive.

The product of two numbers with different signs is negative.

HOW TO 7 Multiply: $-\frac{3}{8} \cdot \frac{4}{15}$

$-\frac{3}{8} \cdot \frac{4}{15} = -\left(\frac{3}{8} \cdot \frac{4}{15}\right)$ • The signs are different. The product is negative.

$= -\frac{3 \cdot 4}{8 \cdot 15}$ • Multiply the numerators. Multiply the denominators.

$= -\frac{3 \cdot 2 \cdot 2}{2 \cdot 2 \cdot 2 \cdot 3 \cdot 5}$ • Write the product is simplest form.

$= -\frac{1}{10}$

The sign rules for dividing rational numbers are the same rules used to divide integers.

The quotient of two numbers with the same sign is positive.

The quotient of two numbers with different signs is negative.

HOW TO 8 Divide: $-\frac{3}{8} \div \left(-\frac{4}{5}\right)$

$$-\frac{3}{8} \div \left(-\frac{4}{5}\right) = \frac{3}{8} \div \frac{4}{5}$$

- The signs are the same. The quotient is positive.

$$= \frac{3}{8} \cdot \frac{5}{4}$$

- Rewrite division as multiplication by the reciprocal.

$$= \frac{3 \cdot 5}{8 \cdot 4}$$

- Multiply the fractions.

$$= \frac{3 \cdot 5}{2 \cdot 2 \cdot 2 \cdot 2 \cdot 2}$$

$$= \frac{15}{32}$$

The sign rules for multiplying and dividing decimals are the same rules used to multiply and divide integers.

HOW TO 9 Multiply: $(-3.25)(-10.1)$

$$(-3.25)(-10.1) = 32.825$$

- The signs are the same. The product is positive. Multiply the absolute values of the numbers.

HOW TO 10 Divide: $-29.4 \div 3.5$

$$-29.4 \div 3.5 = -8.4$$

- The signs are different. The quotient is negative. Divide the absolute values of the numbers.

EXAMPLE 4

Multiply: $\left(-\frac{5}{8}\right)\left(-\frac{3}{5}\right)$

Solution

$$\left(-\frac{5}{8}\right)\left(-\frac{3}{5}\right) = \left(\frac{5}{8}\right)\left(\frac{3}{5}\right)$$

- The signs are the same. The product is positive.

$$= \frac{5 \cdot 3}{8 \cdot 5}$$

- Multiply the numerators. Multiply the denominators.

$$= \frac{5 \cdot 3}{2 \cdot 2 \cdot 2 \cdot 5}$$

- Write the product in simplest form.

$$= \frac{3}{8}$$

YOU TRY IT 4

Multiply: $\frac{10}{11}\left(-\frac{2}{5}\right)$

Your solution

$-\frac{4}{11}$

Solution on p. S40

EXAMPLE 5

Divide: $-\frac{9}{16} \div \frac{3}{4}$

Solution

$$-\frac{9}{16} \div \frac{3}{4} = -\left(\frac{9}{16} \div \frac{3}{4}\right)$$

- The signs are different. The quotient is negative.

$$= -\left(\frac{9}{16} \cdot \frac{4}{3}\right)$$

- Rewrite division as multiplication by the reciprocal.

$$= -\frac{9 \cdot 4}{16 \cdot 3}$$

- Multiply the fractions.

$$= -\frac{3 \cdot 3 \cdot 2 \cdot 2}{2 \cdot 2 \cdot 2 \cdot 2 \cdot 3}$$

$$= -\frac{3}{4}$$

YOU TRY IT 5

Divide: $-\frac{3}{8} \div \left(-\frac{1}{2}\right)$

Your solution

$\frac{3}{4}$

EXAMPLE 6

Multiply: $(-8.9)(0.25)$

Solution

$(-8.9)(0.25) = -2.225$

- The signs are different. The product is negative. Multiply the absolute values of the numbers.

YOU TRY IT 6

Multiply: $(-3.6)(-1.45)$

Your solution

5.22

EXAMPLE 7

Divide: $(-16.2) \div (-3.6)$

Solution

$(-16.2) \div (-3.6) = 4.5$

- The signs are the same. The quotient is positive. Divide the absolute values of the numbers.

YOU TRY IT 7

Divide: $5.04 \div (-8.4)$

Your solution

-0.6

Solutions on pp. S40–S41

OBJECTIVE C *To evaluate exponential expressions*

Recall that an exponent indicates repeated multiplication of the same factor. For example,

$$3^5 = 3 \cdot 3 \cdot 3 \cdot 3 \cdot 3$$

The **exponent,** 5, indicates how many times the **base,** 3, occurs as a factor in the multiplication.

The base of an exponential expression can be any rational number, for example, 0.5^4. To evaluate this expression, write the factor as many times as indicated by the exponent and then multiply.

$$0.5^4 = 0.5(0.5)(0.5)(0.5) = 0.25(0.5)(0.5) = 0.125(0.5) = 0.0625$$

EXAMPLE 8

Simplify: $\left(-\frac{3}{4}\right)^3 \cdot 8^2$

Solution

$\left(-\frac{3}{4}\right)^3 \cdot 8^2$

$= \left(-\frac{3}{4}\right)\left(-\frac{3}{4}\right)\left(-\frac{3}{4}\right) \cdot 8 \cdot 8$ • Write each factor the number of times indicated by the exponent.

$= -\left(\frac{3}{4} \cdot \frac{3}{4} \cdot \frac{3}{4} \cdot \frac{8}{1} \cdot \frac{8}{1}\right)$ • The product is negative.

$= -\frac{3 \cdot 3 \cdot 3 \cdot 8 \cdot 8}{4 \cdot 4 \cdot 4 \cdot 1 \cdot 1}$ • Multiply the fractions.

$= -27$ • Simplify.

YOU TRY IT 8

Simplify: $\left(\frac{2}{9}\right)^2 \cdot (-3)^4$

Your solution

4

Solution on p. S41

OBJECTIVE D *To use the Order of Operations Agreement to simplify expressions*

Whenever an expression contains more than one operation, the operations must be performed in a specified order, as listed on the next page in the Order of Operations Agreement.

3.5A Use the Order of Operations Agreement

The Order of Operations Agreement

Step 1	Do all operations inside grouping symbols. Grouping symbols include parentheses ( ), brackets [ ], and absolute value symbols | |.
Step 2	Simplify any numerical expressions containing exponents.
Step 3	Do multiplication and division as they occur from left to right.
Step 4	Do addition and subtraction as they occur from left to right.

The Order of Operations Agreement is used to simplify the expression in the following example.

HOW TO 11 Simplify: $0.2(2.5 - 5.6) + (1.4)^2$

$0.2(2.5 - 5.6) + (1.4)^2$

$= 0.2(-3.1) + (1.4)^2$ • Perform operations inside parentheses.

$= 0.2(-3.1) + 1.96$ • Simplify the exponential expression.

$= -0.62 + 1.96$ • Do the multiplication.

$= 1.34$ • Do the addition.

EXAMPLE 9

Simplify: $3 \div \left(\frac{1}{4} - \frac{1}{2}\right)^2 - 5$

Solution

$3 \div \left(\frac{1}{4} - \frac{1}{2}\right)^2 - 5$ • Use the Order of Operations Agreement.

$= 3 \div \left(-\frac{1}{4}\right)^2 - 5$ • Perform the operation inside the parentheses.

$= 3 \div \frac{1}{16} - 5$ • Simplify the exponential expression.

$= 3(16) - 5$ • Rewrite division as multiplication by the reciprocal.

$= 48 - 5$ • Do the multiplication.

$= 43$ • Do the subtraction.

YOU TRY IT 9

Simplify: $7 \div \left(\frac{1}{7} - \frac{3}{14}\right) - 9$

Your solution

-107

Solution on p. S41

T.3 EXERCISES

OBJECTIVE A *To add and subtract rational numbers*

For Exercises 1 to 27, simplify.

1. $-\frac{3}{4}+\frac{2}{3}$

$-\frac{1}{12}$

2. $-\frac{5}{12}+\frac{3}{8}$

$-\frac{1}{24}$

3. $\frac{2}{5}+\left(-\frac{11}{15}\right)$

$-\frac{1}{3}$

4. $\frac{1}{4}+\left(-\frac{1}{7}\right)$

$\frac{3}{28}$

5. $-\frac{1}{2}-\frac{3}{8}$

$-\frac{7}{8}$

6. $-\frac{5}{6}-\frac{1}{9}$

$-\frac{17}{18}$

7. $-\frac{3}{10}-\frac{4}{5}$

$-1\frac{1}{10}$

8. $-\frac{5}{12}-\left(-\frac{2}{3}\right)$

$\frac{1}{4}$

9. $-\frac{5}{8}-\left(-\frac{7}{12}\right)$

$-\frac{1}{24}$

10. $-\frac{3}{4}-\left(-\frac{5}{16}\right)$

$-\frac{7}{16}$

11. $-\frac{2}{3}+\left(-\frac{1}{12}\right)$

$-\frac{3}{4}$

12. $-\frac{2}{5}+\left(-\frac{4}{15}\right)$

$-\frac{2}{3}$

13. $\frac{3}{8}+\left(-\frac{1}{2}\right)+\frac{7}{12}$

$\frac{11}{24}$

14. $-\frac{7}{12}+\frac{2}{3}+\left(-\frac{4}{5}\right)$

$-\frac{43}{60}$

15. $\frac{2}{3}+\left(-\frac{5}{6}\right)+\frac{1}{4}$

$\frac{1}{12}$

16. $-\frac{5}{8}+\frac{3}{4}+\frac{1}{2}$

$\frac{5}{8}$

17. $-42.1-8.6$

-50.7

18. $-6.57-8.933$

-15.503

19. $5.73-9.042$

-3.312

20. $-31.894+7.5$

-24.394

21. $1.09-(-8.3)$

9.39

22. $-8-(-10.37)$

2.37

23. $-19-(-2.65)$

-16.35

24. $3.18-5.72-6.4$

-8.94

25. $-12.3-4.07+6.82$

-9.55

26. $-8.9+7.36-14.2$

-15.74

27. $-5.6-(-3.82)-17.409$

-19.189

28. Without simplifying, which is greater, $\frac{5}{8} - \left(-\frac{5}{6}\right)$ or $-\frac{5}{6} - \frac{5}{9}$? Explain.

$\frac{5}{8} - \left(-\frac{5}{6}\right)$, because $\frac{5}{8} - \left(-\frac{5}{6}\right) = \frac{5}{8} + \frac{5}{6}$, so the difference is positive, whereas the difference $-\frac{5}{6} - \frac{5}{9}$ is negative.

29. Without simplifying, which is greater, $-\frac{1}{8} - \frac{3}{4}$ or $\frac{11}{12} - \left(-\frac{1}{4}\right)$? Explain.

$\frac{11}{12} - \left(-\frac{1}{4}\right)$, because $\frac{11}{12} - \left(-\frac{1}{4}\right) = \frac{11}{12} + \frac{1}{4}$, so the difference is positive, whereas the difference $-\frac{1}{8} - \frac{3}{4}$ is negative.

OBJECTIVE B *To multiply and divide rational numbers*

For Exercises 30 to 68, simplify.

30. $-\frac{6}{7} \cdot \frac{11}{12}$

$-\frac{11}{14}$

31. $\frac{3}{8} \cdot \left(-\frac{2}{3}\right)$

$-\frac{1}{4}$

32. $\frac{5}{6} \cdot \left(-\frac{2}{5}\right)$

$-\frac{1}{3}$

33. $\left(-\frac{4}{15}\right)\left(-\frac{3}{8}\right)$

$\frac{1}{10}$

34. $\left(-\frac{3}{4}\right)\left(-\frac{2}{9}\right)$

$\frac{1}{6}$

35. $-\frac{3}{4} \cdot \frac{1}{2}$

$-\frac{3}{8}$

36. $-\frac{8}{15} \cdot \frac{5}{12}$

$-\frac{2}{9}$

37. $-\frac{7}{12} \cdot \frac{5}{8} \cdot \frac{16}{25}$

$-\frac{7}{30}$

38. $\frac{5}{12} \cdot \left(-\frac{1}{3}\right) \cdot \left(-\frac{8}{15}\right)$

$\frac{2}{27}$

39. $\left(-\frac{3}{5}\right) \cdot \frac{1}{2} \cdot \left(-\frac{5}{8}\right)$

$\frac{3}{16}$

40. $\frac{5}{6} \cdot \left(-\frac{2}{3}\right) \cdot \frac{3}{25}$

$-\frac{1}{15}$

41. $12 \cdot \left(-\frac{5}{8}\right)$

$-7\frac{1}{2}$

42. $24\left(-\frac{3}{8}\right)$

-9

43. $-9 \cdot \frac{7}{15}$

$-4\frac{1}{5}$

44. $\frac{1}{3} \cdot (-9)$

-3

45. $-\frac{5}{2} \cdot 4$

-10

46. $\frac{4}{7} \div \left(-\frac{4}{7}\right)$

-1

47. $\left(-\frac{3}{8}\right) \div \frac{7}{8}$

$-\frac{3}{7}$

48. $-\frac{5}{16} \div \left(-\frac{3}{8}\right)$

$\frac{5}{6}$

49. $\left(-\frac{3}{4}\right) \div \left(-\frac{5}{6}\right)$

$\frac{9}{10}$

50. $\frac{3}{4} \div (-6)$

$-\frac{1}{8}$

51. $-\frac{2}{3} \div 8$

$-\frac{1}{12}$

52. $\frac{5}{12} \div \left(-\frac{15}{32}\right)$

$-\frac{8}{9}$

53. $\frac{3}{8} \div \left(-\frac{5}{12}\right)$

$-\frac{9}{10}$

54. $-5.2(0.8)$
-4.16

55. $(-2.1)(-0.7)$
1.47

56. $(-6.3)(-2.4)$
15.12

57. $(1.9)(-3.7)$
-7.03

58. $-1.3(4.2)$
-5.46

59. $-8.1(-7.5)$
60.75

60. $1.31(-0.006)$
-0.00786

61. $-10(0.59)$
-5.9

62. $(-100)(4.73)$
-473

63. $27.08 \div (-0.4)$
-67.7

64. $-8.919 \div 0.9$
-9.91

65. $(-3.312) \div (-0.8)$
4.14

66. $84.66 \div (-1.7)$
-49.8

67. $-2.501 \div 0.41$
-6.1

68. $1.003 \div (-0.59)$
-1.7

For Exercises 69 to 71, divide. Round to the nearest tenth.

69. $-6.824 \div 0.053$
-128.8

70. $0.0416 \div (-0.53)$
-0.1

71. $(-31.792) \div (-0.86)$
37.0

72. Without simplifying, which is greater, $\left(-\frac{8}{9}\right)\left(-\frac{3}{4}\right)$ or $-\frac{5}{16} \div \frac{3}{8}$? Explain.

$\left(-\frac{8}{9}\right)\left(-\frac{3}{4}\right)$, because the product is positive, whereas the quotient $-\frac{5}{16} \div \frac{3}{8}$ is negative.

73. Without simplifying, which is greater, $-\frac{5}{6} \div (-5)$ or $-\frac{3}{4}\left(\frac{2}{9}\right)$? Explain.

$-\frac{5}{6} \div (-5)$, because the quotient is positive, whereas the product $-\frac{3}{4}\left(\frac{2}{9}\right)$ is negative.

OBJECTIVE C To evaluate exponential expressions

For Exercises 74 to 81, simplify.

74. $\left(-\frac{1}{6}\right)^3$

$-\frac{1}{216}$

75. $\left(-\frac{2}{7}\right)^3$

$-\frac{8}{343}$

76. $(2.25)^2$

5.0625

77. $(3.5)^2$

12.25

78. $\left(\frac{4}{5}\right)^4 \cdot \left(-\frac{5}{8}\right)^3$

$-\frac{1}{10}$

79. $\left(-\frac{9}{11}\right)^2 \cdot \left(\frac{1}{3}\right)^4$

$\frac{1}{121}$

80. $-4 \cdot \left(\frac{4}{7}\right)^2 \cdot \left(-\frac{3}{4}\right)^3$

$\frac{27}{49}$

81. $-3 \cdot \left(\frac{2}{5}\right)^2 \cdot \left(-\frac{1}{6}\right)^2$

$-\frac{1}{75}$

OBJECTIVE D To use the Order of Operations Agreement to simplify expressions

For Exercises 82 to 93, simplify.

82. $(0.2)^2 \cdot (-0.5) + 1.72$

1.7

83. $0.3(1.7 - 4.8) + (1.2)^2$

0.51

84. $(1.8)^2 - 2.52 \div (1.8)$

1.84

85. $(1.65 - 1.05)^2 \div 0.4 + 0.8$

1.7

86. $\frac{7}{12} + \frac{5}{6}\left(\frac{1}{6} - \frac{2}{3}\right)$

$\frac{1}{6}$

87. $-\frac{3}{4}\left(\frac{11}{12} - \frac{7}{8}\right) + \frac{5}{16}$

$\frac{9}{32}$

88. $\frac{11}{16} - \left(-\frac{3}{4}\right)^2 + \frac{7}{8}$

1

89. $\left(-\frac{2}{3}\right)^2 - \frac{7}{18} + \frac{5}{6}$

$\frac{8}{9}$

90. $\left(-\frac{1}{3}\right)^2 \cdot \left(-\frac{9}{4}\right) + \frac{3}{4}$

$\frac{1}{2}$

91. $\left(-\frac{2}{3}\right)^2 + \left(-\frac{1}{6}\right) \div \frac{3}{8}$

0

92. $\left(\frac{1}{3} - \frac{5}{6}\right) + \frac{7}{8} \div \left(-\frac{1}{2}\right)^3$

$-7\frac{1}{2}$

93. $\left(-\frac{1}{4}\right)^2 \div \left(\frac{1}{2} - \frac{3}{4}\right) + \frac{3}{8}$

$\frac{1}{8}$

94. Arrange the expressions in order from greatest value to least value.

$16 - 3(3 - 8) \div 5$
$4(-3) \div [2(6 - 7)^2]$
$18 \div (-2) + (-3)^2 - (-15)$

$16 - 3(3 - 8) \div 5 > 18 \div (-2) + (-3)^2 - (-15) > 4(-3) \div [2(6 - 7)^2]$; $[19 > 15 > -6]$

95. Arrange the expressions in order from greatest value to least value.

$20 \div (6 - 2^4) + (-5)$
$18 \div |2^3 - 9| + (-3)$
$16 + 15 \div (-5) - (-4)$

$16 + 15 \div (-5) - (-4) > 18 \div |2^3 - 9| + (-3) > 20 \div (6 - 2^4) + (-5)$; $[17 > 15 > -7]$

SECTION T.4 Equations

OBJECTIVE A To solve a first-degree equation in one variable

An **equation** expresses the equality of two mathematical expressions. Each of the equations below is a **first-degree equation in one variable.** *First degree* means that the variable has an exponent of 1.

$$x + 11 = 14$$
$$3a + 5 = 8a$$
$$2(6y - 1) = 3$$

A **solution** of an equation is a number that, when substituted for the variable, results in a true equation.

3 is a solution of the equation $x + 4 = 7$ because $3 + 4 = 7$.
9 is not a solution of the equation $x + 4 = 7$ because $9 + 4 \neq 7$.

5.1B, 5.1C, 5.2A, 5.3A, 5.3B
Solve first-degree equations in one variable

To **solve an equation** means to find a solution of the equation. In solving an equation, the goal is to rewrite the given equation with the variable alone on one side of the equation and a constant term on the other side of the equation; the constant term is the solution of the equation. The following properties of equations are used to rewrite equations in this form.

Addition Property of Equations

The same number can be added to each side of an equation without changing the solution of the equation. In symbols, the equation $a = b$ has the same solution as the equation $a + c = b + c$.

Multiplication Property of Equations

Each side of an equation can be multiplied by the same nonzero number without changing the solution of the equation. In symbols, if $c \neq 0$, then the equation $a = b$ has the same solution as the equation $ac = bc$.

Take Note
Subtraction is defined as addition of the opposite.

$$a - b = a + (-b)$$

The Addition Property of Equations is used to remove a term from one side of an equation by adding the opposite of that term to each side of the equation. Because subtraction is defined in terms of addition, the Addition Property of Equations also makes it possible to subtract the same number from each side of an equation without changing the solution of the equation.

For example, to solve the equation $t + 9 = -4$, subtract the constant term (9) from each side of the equation.

$$t + 9 = -4$$
$$t + 9 - 9 = -4 - 9$$
$$t = -13$$

Now the variable is alone on one side of the equation and a constant term (-13) is on the other side. The solution is the constant. The solution is -13.

Take Note
Division is defined as multiplication by the reciprocal.

$$a \div b = a \cdot \frac{1}{b}$$

The Multiplication Property of Equations is used to remove a coefficient by multiplying each side of the equation by the reciprocal of the coefficient. Because division is defined in terms of multiplication, each side of an equation can be divided by the same nonzero number without changing the solution of the equation.

Take Note
When using the Multiplication Property of Equations, multiply each side of the equation by the reciprocal of the coefficient when the coefficient is a fraction. Divide each side of the equation by the coefficient when the coefficient is an integer or a decimal.

For example, to solve the equation $-5q = 120$, divide each side of the equation by the coefficient -5.

$$-5q = 120$$
$$\frac{-5q}{-5} = \frac{120}{-5}$$
$$q = -24$$

Now the variable is alone on one side of the equation and a constant (-24) is on the other side. The solution is the constant. The solution is -24.

In solving more complicated first-degree equations in one variable, use the following sequence of steps.

Steps for Solving a First-Degree Equation in One Variable

Step 1	Use the Distributive Property to remove parentheses.
Step 2	Combine any like terms on the right side of the equation and any like terms on the left side of the equation.
Step 3	Use the Addition Property to rewrite the equation with only one variable term.
Step 4	Use the Addition Property to rewrite the equation with only one constant term.
Step 5	Use the Multiplication Property to rewrite the equation with the variable alone on one side of the equation and a constant on the other side of the equation.

If one of the above steps is not needed to solve a given equation, proceed to the next step.

EXAMPLE 1

Solve: $3x + 5 - 4x = 6$

Solution

$$
\begin{aligned}
3x + 5 - 4x &= 6 \\
5 - x &= 6 && \bullet \text{ Step 2} \\
5 - 5 - x &= 6 - 5 && \bullet \text{ Step 4} \\
-x &= 1 \\
\frac{-x}{-1} &= \frac{1}{-1} && \bullet \text{ Step 5} \\
x &= -1
\end{aligned}
$$

The solution is -1.

YOU TRY IT 1

Solve: $5x + 3 - 7x = 9$

Your solution

-3

EXAMPLE 2

Solve: $5x + 9 = 23 - 2x$

Solution

$$
\begin{aligned}
5x + 9 &= 23 - 2x \\
5x + 2x + 9 &= 23 - 2x + 2x && \bullet \text{ Step 3} \\
7x + 9 &= 23 \\
7x + 9 - 9 &= 23 - 9 && \bullet \text{ Step 4} \\
7x &= 14 \\
\frac{7x}{7} &= \frac{14}{7} && \bullet \text{ Step 5} \\
x &= 2
\end{aligned}
$$

The solution is 2.

YOU TRY IT 2

Solve: $4x + 3 = 7x + 9$

Your solution

-2

EXAMPLE 3

Solve: $8x - 3(4x - 5) = -2x + 6$

Solution

$$
\begin{aligned}
8x - 3(4x - 5) &= -2x + 6 \\
8x - 12x + 15 &= -2x + 6 && \bullet \text{ Step 1} \\
-4x + 15 &= -2x + 6 && \bullet \text{ Step 2} \\
-4x + 2x + 15 &= -2x + 2x + 6 && \bullet \text{ Step 3} \\
-2x + 15 &= 6 \\
-2x + 15 - 15 &= 6 - 15 && \bullet \text{ Step 4} \\
-2x &= -9 \\
\frac{-2x}{-2} &= \frac{-9}{-2} && \bullet \text{ Step 5} \\
x &= \frac{9}{2}
\end{aligned}
$$

The solution is $\frac{9}{2}$.

YOU TRY IT 3

Solve: $4 - (5x - 8) = 4x + 3$

Your solution

1

Solutions on p. S41

T.4 EXERCISES

OBJECTIVE A *To solve a first-degree equation in one variable*

For Exercises 1 to 36, solve.

1. $x + 7 = -5$
   -12

2. $9 + b = 21$
   12

3. $-9 = z - 8$
   -1

4. $b - 11 = 11$
   22

5. $-48 = 6z$
   -8

6. $-9a = -108$
   12

7. $-\frac{3}{4}x = 15$
   -20

8. $\frac{5}{2}x = -10$
   -4

9. $-\frac{x}{4} = -2$
   8

10. $\frac{2x}{5} = -8$
    -20

11. $3x + 8 = 17$
    3

12. $2 + 5a = 12$
    2

13. $5 = 3x - 10$
    5

14. $4 = 3 - 5x$
    $-\frac{1}{5}$

15. $\frac{2}{3}x + 5 = 3$
    -3

16. $-\frac{1}{2}x + 4 = 1$
    6

17. $2b + 6 - 3b = 4$
    2

18. $3x + 4 - 5x = 8$
    -2

19. $4 - 2b = 2 - 4b$
    -1

20. $4y - 10 = 6 + 2y$
    8

21. $5x - 3 = 9x - 7$
    1

22. $5x + 7 = 8x + 5$
    $\frac{2}{3}$

23. $2 - 6y = 5 - 7y$
    3

24. $4b + 15 = 3 - 2b$
    -2

25. $2(x + 1) + 5x = 23$
    3

26. $9n - 15 = 3(2n - 1)$
    4

27. $7a - (3a - 4) = 12$
    2

28. $5(3 - 2y) = 3 - 4y$
    2

29. $9 - 7x = 4(1 - 3x)$
    -1

30. $2(3b + 5) - 1 = 10b + 1$
    2

31. $2z - 2 = 5 - (9 - 6z)$
    $\frac{1}{2}$

32. $4a + 3 = 7 - (5 - 8a)$
    $\frac{1}{4}$

33. $5(6 - 2x) = 2(5 - 3x)$
    5

34. $4(3y + 1) = 2(y - 8)$
    -2

35. $2(3b - 5) = 4(6b - 2)$
    $-\frac{1}{9}$

36. $3(x - 4) = 1 - (2x - 7)$
    4

Appendix

The Metric System of Measurement

International trade, or trade among nations, is a vital and growing segment of business in the world today. The United States, as a nation, is dependent on world trade. And world trade is dependent on internationally standardized units of measurement: the metric system. The Third International Mathematics and Science Study (TIMSS) compared the performance of half a million students from 41 countries at five different grade levels on tests of their mathematics and science knowledge. One area of mathematics in which the U.S. average was below the international average was measurement, due in large part to the fact that the units cited in the questions were metric units. Because the United States has not yet converted to the metric system, its citizens are less familiar with it.

Point of Interest

To learn more about these tests, go to **www.ed.gov.** Use the search feature and enter TIMSS.

In this Appendix, we present the metric system of measurement and explain how to convert between different units.

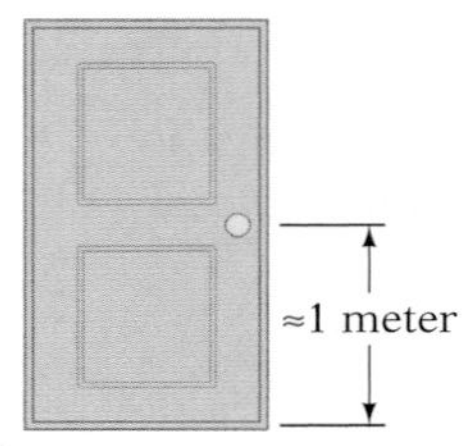

The basic unit of *length,* or distance, in the metric system is the **meter** (m). One meter is approximately the distance from a doorknob to the floor. All units of length in the metric system are derived from the meter. Prefixes to the basic unit denote the length of each unit. For example, the prefix *centi-* means "one-hundredth"; therefore, 1 centimeter is 1 one-hundredth of a meter (0.01 m).

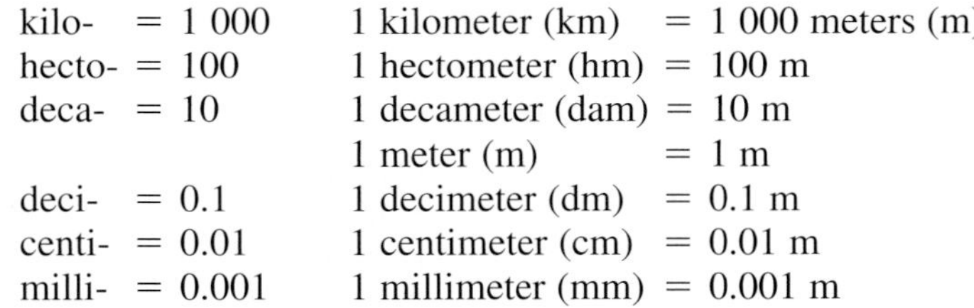

kilo-	= 1 000	1 kilometer (km)	= 1 000 meters (m)
hecto-	= 100	1 hectometer (hm)	= 100 m
deca-	= 10	1 decameter (dam)	= 10 m
		1 meter (m)	= 1 m
deci-	= 0.1	1 decimeter (dm)	= 0.1 m
centi-	= 0.01	1 centimeter (cm)	= 0.01 m
milli-	= 0.001	1 millimeter (mm)	= 0.001 m

Point of Interest

Originally the meter (spelled *metre* in some countries) was defined as $\frac{1}{10,000,000}$ of the distance from the equator to the North Pole. Modern scientists have redefined the meter as 1,650,753.73 wavelengths of the orange-red light given off by the element krypton.

Note in this list that 1000 is written as 1 000, with a space between the 1 and the zeros. **When writing numbers using metric units, each group of three numbers is separated by a space instead of a comma.** A space is also used after each group of three numbers to the right of a decimal point. For example, 31,245.2976 is written 31 245.297 6 in metric notation.

Mass and weight are closely related. *Weight* is a measure of how strongly gravity is pulling on an object. Therefore, an object's weight is less in space than on Earth's surface. However, the amount of material in the object, its *mass,* remains the same. On the surface of Earth, the terms *mass* and *weight* can be used interchangeably.

The basic unit of mass in the metric system is the **gram** (g). If a box that is 1 centimeter long on each side is filled with water, the mass of that water is 1 gram.

1 cm
1 cm
1 cm

1 gram = the mass of water in a box that is 1 centimeter long on each side

The units of mass in the metric system have the same prefixes as the units of length.

1 kilogram (kg)	=	1 000 grams (g)
1 hectogram (hg)	=	100 g
1 decagram (dag)	=	10 g
1 gram (g)	=	1 g
1 decigram (dg)	=	0.1 g
1 centigram (cg)	=	0.01 g
1 milligram (mg)	=	0.001 g

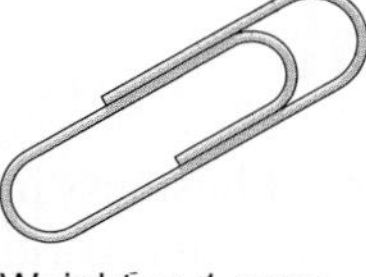
Weight ≈ 1 gram

The gram is a very small unit of mass. A paperclip weighs about 1 gram. In applications, the kilogram (1 000 grams) is a more useful unit of mass. This textbook weighs about 1 kilogram.

Liquid substances are measured in units of *capacity*.

The basic unit of capacity in the metric system is the **liter** (L). One liter is defined as the capacity of a box that is 10 centimeters long on each side.

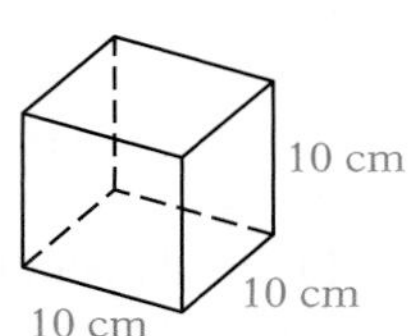

1 liter = the capacity of a box that is 10 centimeters long on each side

The units of capacity in the metric system have the same prefixes as the units of length.

1 kiloliter (kl)	=	1 000 liters (L)
1 hectoliter (hl)	=	100 L
1 decaliter (dal)	=	10 L
1 liter (L)	=	1 L
1 deciliter (dl)	=	0.1 L
1 centiliter (cl)	=	0.01 L
1 milliliter (ml)	=	0.001 L

Point of Interest

The definition of 1 inch has been changed as a consequence of the wide acceptance of the metric system. One inch is now exactly 25.4 mm.

Converting between units in the metric system involves moving the decimal point to the right or to the left. Listing the units in order from largest to smallest will indicate how many places to move the decimal point in which direction.

To convert 3 800 cm to meters, write the units of length in order from largest to smallest.

km hm dam m dm cm mm

2 positions

- **Converting from centimeters to meters requires moving two places to the left.**

3 800 cm = 38.00 m

2 places

- **Move the decimal point the same number of places in the same direction.**

Take Note
In the metric system, all prefixes represent powers of 10. Therefore, when converting between units, we are multiplying or dividing by a power of 10.

HOW TO 1 Convert 27 kg to grams.

kg hg dag g dg cg mg

3 positions

- Write the units of mass in order from largest to smallest.
- Converting from kg to g requires moving three positions to the right.

27 kg = 27 000 g

3 places

- Move the decimal point the same number of places and in the same direction.

EXAMPLE 1

Convert 4.08 m to centimeters.

Solution

Write the units of length from largest to smallest.

km hm dam (m) dm (cm) mm

Converting meters to centimeters requires moving two positions to the right.

4.08 m = 408 cm

YOU TRY IT 1

Convert 1 295 m to kilometers.

Your solution

1.295 km

EXAMPLE 2

Convert 5.93 g to milligrams.

Solution

Write the units of mass from largest to smallest.

kg hg dag (g) dg cg (mg)

Converting grams to milligrams requires moving three positions to the right.

5.93 g = 5 930 mg

YOU TRY IT 2

Convert 7 543 g to kilograms.

Your solution

7.543 kg

EXAMPLE 3

Convert 82 ml to liters.

Solution

Write the units of capacity from largest to smallest.

kl hl dal (L) dl cl (ml)

Converting milliliters to liters requires moving three positions to the left.

82 ml = 0.082 L

YOU TRY IT 3

Convert 6.3 L to milliliters.

Your solution

6 300 ml

Solutions on p. S41

EXAMPLE 4

Convert 9 kl to liters.

Solution

Write the units of capacity from largest to smallest.

(kl) hl dal (L) dl cl ml

Converting kiloliters to liters requires moving three positions to the right.

9 kl = 9 000 L

YOU TRY IT 4

Convert 2 kl to liters.

Your solution

2 000 L

Solution on p. S41

As a result of technological advances in the computer industry, other prefixes in the metric system are becoming more common. For example,

tera- = 1 000 000 000 000
giga- = 1 000 000 000
mega- = 1 000 000

micro- = 0.000 001
nano- = 0.000 000 001
pico- = 0.000 000 000 001

The amount of memory in a computer hard drive is generally measured in gigabytes. The speed of a computer is measured in picoseconds.

Here are a few more examples of how these prefixes are used.

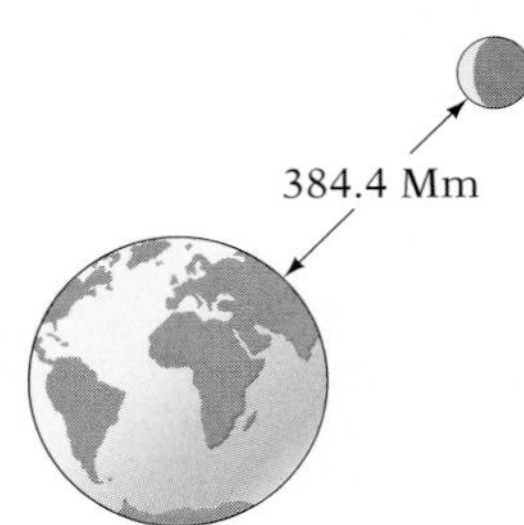

The mass of Earth gains 40 Gg (gigagrams) each year from captured meteorites and cosmic dust.

The average distance from Earth to the moon is 384.4 Mm (megameters), and the average distance from Earth to the sun is 149.5 Gm (gigameters).

The wavelength of yellow light is 590 nm (nanometers).

The diameter of a hydrogen atom is about 70 pm (picometers).

There are additional prefixes in the metric system, representing both larger and smaller units. We may hear them more and more often as computer chips hold more and more information, as computers get faster and faster, and as we learn more and more about objects in our universe that are great distances away.

The U.S. Metric Association (USMA) advocates U.S. conversion to the metric system, which is also referred to as the International System of Units, abbreviated SI. The process of changing measurement units to the metric system is called **metric transition** or **metrication.**

EXERCISES

1. In the metric system, what is the basic unit of length? Of liquid measure? Of weight?
Meter, liter, gram

2. a. Explain how to convert meters to centimeters.
b. Explain how to convert milliliters to liters.

For Exercises 3 to 26, name the unit in the metric system that would be used to measure each.

3. The distance from New York to London
Kilometer

4. The weight of a truck
Kilogram

5. A person's waist
Centimeter

6. The amount of coffee in a mug
Milliliter

7. The weight of a thumbtack
Gram

8. The amount of water in a swimming pool
Kiloliter

9. The distance a baseball player hits a baseball
Meter

10. A person's hat size
Centimeter

11. The amount of fat in a slice of cheddar cheese
Gram

12. A person's weight
Kilogram

13. The maple syrup served with pancakes
Milliliter

14. The amount of water in a water cooler
Liter

15. The amount of vitamin C in a vitamin tablet
Milligram

16. A serving of cereal
Gram

17. The width of a hair
Millimeter

18. A person's height
Centimeter

19. The amount of medication in an aspirin
Milligram

20. The weight of a lawnmower
Kilogram

21. The weight of a slice of bread
Gram

22. The contents of a bottle of salad dressing
Milliliter

23. The amount of water a family uses monthly
Kiloliter

24. The newspapers collected at a recycling center
Kilogram

25. The amount of liquid in a bowl of soup
Milliliter

26. The distance to the bank
Kilometer

For Exercises 27 to 56, convert the given measure.

27. 42 cm = 420 mm
28. 91 cm = 910 mm
29. 360 g = 0.360 kg
30. 1 856 g = 1.856 kg
31. 5 194 ml = 5.194 L
32. 7 285 ml = 7.285 L
33. 2 m = 2 000 mm
34. 8 m = 8 000 mm
35. 217 mg = 0.217 g
36. 34 mg = 0.034 g
37. 4.52 L = 4 520 ml
38. 0.029 7 L = 29.7 ml
39. 8 406 m = 8.406 km
40. 7 530 m = 7.530 km
41. 2.4 kg = 2 400 g
42. 9.2 kg = 9 200 g
43. 6.18 kl = 6 180 L
44. 0.036 kl = 36 L
45. 9.612 km = 9 612 m
46. 2.35 km = 2 350 m
47. 0.24 g = 240 mg
48. 0.083 g = 83 mg
49. 298 cm = 2.98 m
50. 71.6 cm = 0.716 m
51. 2 431 L = 2.431 kl
52. 6 302 L = 6.302 kl
53. 0.66 m = 66 cm
54. 4.58 m = 458 cm
55. 243 mm = 24.3 cm
56. 92 mm = 9.2 cm

57. a. Complete the table.

Metric System Prefix	*Symbol*	*Magnitude*	*Means Multiply the Basic Unit by:*
tera-	T	10^{12}	1 000 000 000 000
giga-	G	10^{9}	1 000 000 000
mega-	M	10^{6}	1 000 000
kilo-	k	10^{3}	1 000
hecto-	h	10^{2}	100
deca-	da	10^{1}	10
deci-	d	$\frac{1}{10}$	0.1
centi-	c	$\frac{1}{10^2}$	0.01
milli-	m	$\frac{1}{10^3}$	0.001
micro-	μ (mu)	$\frac{1}{10^6}$	0.000 001
nano-	n	$\frac{1}{10^9}$	0.000 000 001
pico-	p	$\frac{1}{10^{12}}$	0.000 000 000 001

b. How can the magnitude column in the table above be used to determine how many places to move the decimal point when converting to the basic unit in the metric system?

58. The Olympics

a. One of the events in the summer Olympics is the 50 000-meter walk. How many kilometers do the entrants in this event walk?

b. One of the events in the winter Olympic Games is the 10 000-meter speed skating event. How many kilometers do the entrants in this event skate?

a. 50 km **b.** 10 km

59. Gemstones A carat is a unit of weight equal to 200 mg. Find the weight in grams of a 10-carat precious stone.

2 g

60. Fabric How many pieces of material, each 75 cm long, can be cut from a bolt of fabric that is 6 m long?

8 pieces

61. Swimming Pools An athletic club uses 800 ml of chlorine each day for its swimming pool. How many liters of chlorine are used in a month of 30 days?

24 L

62. Carpentry Each of the four shelves in a bookcase measures 175 cm. Find the cost of the shelves when the price of lumber is $15.75 per meter.

$110.25

63. Serving Size The printed label from a container of milk is shown at the right. To the nearest whole number, how many 230-milliliter servings are in the container?
16 servings

Dairy Hill
Skim Milk
Vitamin A & D Added
Pasteurized • Homogenized
INGREDIENTS: PASTEURIZED SKIM MILK, NONFAT MILK SOLIDS, VITAMIN A PALMITATE AND VITAMIN D3 ADDED.
0 15400 20209 1
1 GAL. (3.78 L)

64. Serving Size A 1.19-kilogram container of Quaker Oats contains 30 servings. Find the number of grams in one serving of the oatmeal. Round to the nearest gram.
40 g

65. Nutrition A patient is advised to supplement her diet with 2 g of calcium per day. The calcium tablets she purchases contain 500 mg of calcium per tablet. How many tablets per day should the patient take?
4 tablets

66. Chemistry A laboratory assistant is in charge of ordering acid for three chemistry classes of 30 students each. Each student requires 80 ml of acid. How many liters of acid should be ordered? The assistant must order by the whole liter.
8 L

67. Consumerism A case of 12 one-liter bottles of apple juice costs $19.80. A case of 24 cans, each can containing 340 ml of apple juice, costs $14.50. Which case of apple juice costs less per milliliter?
The case containing 12 one-liter bottles

68. Construction A column assembly is being constructed in a building. The components are shown in the diagram at the right. What length column must be cut?
215.5 cm

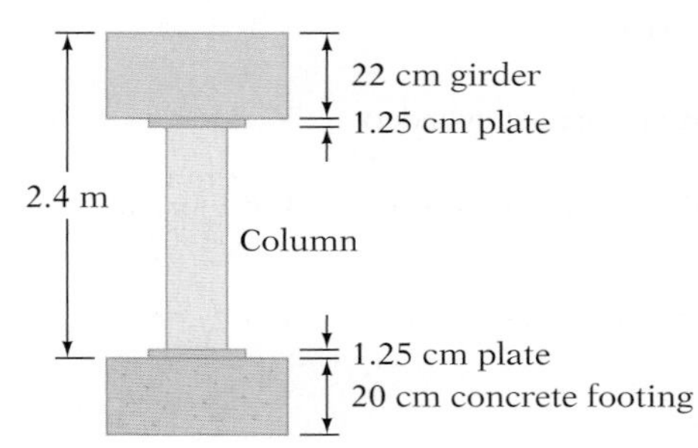

69. Astronomy The distance between Earth and the sun is 150 000 000 km. Light travels 300 000 000 m in 1 s. How long does it take for light to reach Earth from the sun?
500 s

70. Why is it necessary to have internationally standardized units of measurement?

Critical Thinking

71. Business A service station operator bought 85 kl of gasoline for $38,500. The gasoline was sold for $.658 per liter. Find the profit on the 85 kl of gasoline.
$17,430

72. Business For $149.50, a cosmetician buys 5 L of moisturizer and repackages it in 125-milliliter jars. Each jar costs the cosmetician $.55. Each jar of moisturizer is sold for $8.95. Find the profit on the 5 L of moisturizer.
$186.50

73. Business A health food store buys nuts in 10-kilogram containers and repackages the nuts for resale. The store packages the nuts in 200-gram bags, costing $.06 each, and sells them for $2.89 per bag. Find the profit on a 10-kilogram container of nuts costing $75.
$66.50

Projects or Group Activities

74. Form two debating teams. One team should argue in favor of changing to the metric system in the United States, and the other should argue against it.

Table of Geometric Formulas and Properties

PERIMETER

Triangle: $P = a + b + c$

Rectangle: $P = 2L + 2W$

Square: $P = 4s$

Circle: $C = \pi d$ or $C = 2\pi r$

AREA

Triangle: $A = \frac{1}{2}bh$

Rectangle: $A = LW$

Square: $A = s^2$

Circle: $A = \pi r^2$

Parallelogram: $A = bh$

Trapezoid: $A = \frac{1}{2}h(b_1 + b_2)$

VOLUME

Rectangular solid: $V = LWH$

Cube: $V = s^3$

Sphere: $V = \frac{4}{3}\pi r^3$

Right circular cylinder: $V = \pi r^2 h$

Right circular cone: $V = \frac{1}{3}\pi r^2 h$

Regular pyramid: $V = \frac{1}{3}s^2 h$

SURFACE AREA

Rectangular solid: $SA = 2LW + 2LH + 2WH$

Cube: $SA = 6s^2$

Sphere: $SA = 4\pi r^2$

Right circular cylinder: $SA = 2\pi r^2 + 2\pi rh$

Right circular cone: $SA = \pi r^2 + \pi rl$

Regular pyramid: $SA = s^2 + 2sl$

TRIANGLES

Sum of the measures of the interior angles $= 180°$

Sum of an interior and corresponding exterior angle $= 180°$

An **isosceles triangle** has two sides equal in length; the angles opposite the equal sides are of equal measure.

In an **equilateral triangle**, the three sides are of equal length; the three angles are of equal measure.

A **scalene triangle** has no two sides of equal length; no two angles are of equal measure.

An **acute triangle** has three acute angles.

An **obtuse triangle** has one obtuse angle.

A **right triangle** has a right angle.

In **similar triangles**:

The ratios of corresponding sides are equal.

The ratio of corresponding heights is equal to the ratio of corresponding sides.

Rules used to determine **congruent triangles**: SSS rule, SAS rule, ASA rule.

PYTHAGOREAN THEOREM

If a and b are the legs of a right triangle and c is the length of the hypotenuse, then $c^2 = a^2 + b^2$.

Solutions to "You Try It"

Solutions to Chapter 1 "You Try It"

SECTION 1.1

You Try It 1

0 1 2 3 4 5 6 7 8 9 10 11 12

You Try It 2

7 is 4 units to the left of 11.

You Try It 3 **a.** $47 > 19$ **b.** $26 > 0$

You Try It 4 0, 3, 17, 52, 68, 94

You Try It 5 forty-six million thirty-two thousand seven hundred fifteen

You Try It 6 920,008

You Try It 7 $70{,}000 + 6000 + 200 + 40 + 5$

You Try It 8

Given place value

529,374

$9 > 5$

529,374 rounded to the nearest ten-thousand is 530,000.

You Try It 9

Given place value

7985

$8 > 5$

7985 rounded to the nearest hundred is 8000.

You Try It 10

Strategy To find the sport named by the greatest number of people, find the largest number given in the circle graph.

Solution The largest number given in the graph is 80.

The sport named by the greatest number of people was football.

You Try It 11

Strategy To find the shorter distance, compare the numbers 347 and 387.

Solution $347 < 387$

The shorter distance is between Los Angeles and San Jose.

You Try It 12

Strategy To determine which state has fewer sanctioned league bowlers, compare the numbers 239,951 and 239,010.

Solution $239{,}010 < 239{,}951$

Ohio has fewer sanctioned league bowlers.

You Try It 13

Strategy To find the land area to the nearest thousand square miles, round 3,851,809 to the nearest thousand.

Solution 3,851,809 rounded to the nearest thousand is 3,852,000.

To the nearest thousand, the land area of Canada is 3,852,000 mi^2.

SECTION 1.2

You Try It 1

6285	→	6000
3972	→	4000
5140	→	+ 5000
		15,000

You Try It 2 The Addition Property of Zero

You Try It 3

$$\begin{array}{r} 125{,}500{,}000 \\ 68{,}200{,}000 \\ 18{,}200{,}000 \\ +\quad 2{,}000{,}000 \\ \hline 213{,}900{,}000 \end{array}$$

A total of 213,900,000 cases of eggs were produced during the year.

You Try It 4 $x + y + z$

$1692 + 4783 + 5046$

$$\begin{array}{r} {\scriptstyle 1\,2\,1} \\ 1692 \\ 4783 \\ +\ 5046 \\ \hline 11{,}521 \end{array}$$

You Try It 5

$$\begin{array}{c|c} 13 = b + 6 & \\ \hline 13 & 7 + 6 \end{array}$$

$13 = 13$

Yes, 7 is a solution of the equation.

You Try It 6

$$\begin{array}{r} {\scriptstyle 8\ \ 9\ \ 9\ \ 12} \\ 4\,\not{9},\not{0}\,\not{0}\,\not{2} \\ -3\,1{,}8\,6\,5 \\ \hline 1\,7{,}1\,3\,7 \end{array} \qquad \textit{Check:}\ \begin{array}{r} 31{,}865 \\ +\ 17{,}137 \\ \hline 49{,}002 \end{array}$$

You Try It 7

$$\begin{array}{l} 8544 \longrightarrow \\ 3621 \longrightarrow \end{array} \begin{array}{r} 9000 \\ -4000 \\ \hline 5000 \end{array} \qquad \begin{array}{r} 8544 \\ -3621 \\ \hline 4923 \end{array}$$

You Try It 8 2025: 652 quadrillion Btu

2015: 563 quadrillion Btu

$$\begin{array}{r} 652 \\ -563 \\ \hline 89 \end{array}$$

The difference is 89 quadrillion Btu.

You Try It 9 $x - y$

$7061 - 3229$

$$\begin{array}{r} {\scriptstyle 6\ 10\ 5\ 11} \\ \not{7}\,\not{0}\,\not{6}\,\not{1} \\ -3\,2\,2\,9 \\ \hline 3\,8\,3\,2 \end{array}$$

You Try It 10

$$\begin{array}{c|c} 46 = 58 - p & \\ \hline 46 & 58 - 11 \end{array}$$

$46 \neq 47$

No, 11 is not a solution of the equation.

You Try It 11

Strategy To find how many more taste genes the mosquito has than the fruit fly:

- ▶ Find the number of taste genes in the mosquito.
- ▶ Find the number of taste genes in the fruit fly.
- ▶ Subtract the smaller number from the larger number.

Solution Taste genes in a mosquito: 76

Taste genes in a fruit fly: 68

$76 - 68 = 8$

The mosquito has 8 more taste genes than the fruit fly.

You Try It 12

Strategy To find the price, replace C by 148 and M by 74 in the given formula, and solve for P.

Solution $P = C + M$

$P = 148 + 74$

$P = 222$

The price of the leather jacket is $222.

You Try It 13

Strategy Draw a diagram.

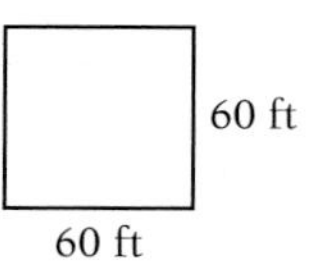

To find the length of fencing needed, use the formula for the perimeter of a rectangle, $P = L + W + L + W$. $L = 60$ and $W = 60$.

Solution $P = L + W + L + W$

$P = 60 + 60 + 60 + 60$

$P = 240$

240 ft of fencing are needed.

SECTION 1.3

You Try It 1 The average monthly savings in France is $175.

$$\begin{array}{r} 175 \\ \times\ 12 \\ \hline 350 \\ 175 \\ \hline 2100 \end{array}$$

The average annual savings of individuals in France is $2100.

You Try It 2

$$\begin{array}{r} 8704 \longrightarrow 9000 \\ 93 \longrightarrow 90 \end{array}$$

$9000 \cdot 90 = 810{,}000$

You Try It 3 $5xy$

$$\begin{aligned} 5(20)(60) &= 100(60) \\ &= 6000 \end{aligned}$$

You Try It 4 $90(7000) = 630{,}000$

You Try It 5 $0 \cdot 10 = 0$

You Try It 6

$$\begin{array}{r|l} 7a & = 77 \\ \hline 7 \cdot 11 & 77 \\ 77 & = 77 \end{array}$$

Yes, 11 is a solution of the equation.

You Try It 7 $2 \cdot 2 \cdot 2 \cdot 3 \cdot 3 \cdot 3 \cdot 3 = 2^3 \cdot 3^4$

You Try It 8

$$\begin{aligned} 6^4 &= 6 \cdot 6 \cdot 6 \cdot 6 = 36 \cdot 6 \cdot 6 \\ &= 216 \cdot 6 = 1296 \end{aligned}$$

You Try It 9 $10^8 = 100{,}000{,}000$

You Try It 10 x^4y^2

$$\begin{aligned} 1^4 \cdot 3^2 &= (1 \cdot 1 \cdot 1 \cdot 1) \cdot (3 \cdot 3) \\ &= 1 \cdot 9 \\ &= 9 \end{aligned}$$

You Try It 11

$$\begin{array}{r} 320 \text{ r}14 \\ 24\overline{)\,7694} \\ -72 \\ \hline 49 \\ -48 \\ \hline 14 \\ -\ 0 \\ \hline 14 \end{array}$$

Check: $(320 \cdot 24) + 14 = 7680 + 14$
$= 7694$

You Try It 12 The annual expense for food is $7200.

$7200 \div 12 = 600$

The monthly expense for food is $600.

You Try It 13

$216{,}936 \longrightarrow 200{,}000$
$207 \longrightarrow 200$

$200{,}000 \div 200 = 1000$

You Try It 14 $\dfrac{x}{y}$

$$\frac{672}{8} = 84$$

You Try It 15

$$\frac{60}{y} = 2$$

$$\begin{array}{c|c} \frac{60}{12} & 2 \\ 5 \neq 2 & \end{array}$$

No, 12 is not a solution of the equation.

You Try It 16

$30 \div 1 = 30$
$30 \div 2 = 15$
$30 \div 3 = 10$
$30 \div 4$ Does not divide evenly.
$30 \div 5 = 6$
$30 \div 6 = 5$ The factors are repeating.

The factors of 30 are 1, 2, 3, 5, 6, 10, 15, and 30.

You Try It 17

$$\begin{array}{r} 11 \\ 2\overline{)22} \\ 2\overline{)44} \\ 2\overline{)88} \end{array}$$

$88 = 2 \cdot 2 \cdot 2 \cdot 11 = 2^3 \cdot 11$

You Try It 18

$$\begin{array}{r} 59 \\ 5\overline{)295} \end{array}$$

$295 = 5 \cdot 59$

You Try It 19

Strategy To find how many times more expensive a stamp was, divide the cost in 1997 (32) by the cost in 1960 (4).

Solution $32 \div 4 = 8$

A stamp was 8 times more expensive in 1997.

You Try It 20

Strategy Draw a diagram.

6 m

To find the amount of carpet that should be purchased, use the formula for the area of a square, $A = s^2$, with $s = 6$.

Solution

$A = s^2$
$A = 6^2$
$A = 36$

36 m^2 of carpet should be purchased.

You Try It 21

Strategy To find the speed, replace d by 486 and t by 9 in the given formula, and solve for r.

Solution
$$r = \frac{d}{t}$$
$$r = \frac{486}{9}$$
$$r = 54$$

You would need to travel at a speed of 54 mph.

SECTION 1.4

You Try It 1
$$\begin{aligned} 4 \cdot (8 - 3) \div 5 - 2 &= 4 \cdot 5 \div 5 - 2 \\ &= 20 \div 5 - 2 \\ &= 4 - 2 \\ &= 2 \end{aligned}$$

You Try It 2
$$\begin{aligned} 16 + 3(6 - 1)^2 \div 5 &= 16 + 3(5)^2 \div 5 \\ &= 16 + 3(25) \div 5 \\ &= 16 + 75 \div 5 \\ &= 16 + 15 \\ &= 31 \end{aligned}$$

You Try It 3
$$(a - b)^2 + 5c$$
$$\begin{aligned} (7 - 2)^2 + 5(4) &= 5^2 + 5(4) \\ &= 25 + 5(4) \\ &= 25 + 20 \\ &= 45 \end{aligned}$$

Solutions to Chapter 2 "You Try It"

SECTION 2.1

You Try It 1

	2	3	5
12 =	(2 · 2)	3	
27 =		(3 · 3 · 3)	
50 =	2		(5 · 5)

The LCM = 2 · 2 · 3 · 3 · 3 · 5 · 5 = 2700.

You Try It 2

	2	3	5
36 =	(2 · 2)	3 · 3	
60 =	2 · 2	(3)	5
72 =	2 · 2 · 2	3 · 3	

The GCF = 2 · 2 · 3 = 12.

You Try It 3

	2	3	5	11
11 =				11
24 =	2 · 2 · 2	3		
30 =	2	3	5	

Because no numbers are circled, the GCF = 1.

SECTION 2.2

You Try It 1 $\frac{19}{6}; 3\frac{1}{6}$

You Try It 2
$$\begin{array}{r} 8 \\ 3\overline{)\,26} \\ -24 \\ \hline 2 \end{array} \qquad \frac{26}{3} = 8\frac{2}{3}$$

You Try It 3
$$\begin{array}{r} 9 \\ 4\overline{)\,36} \\ -36 \\ \hline 0 \end{array} \qquad \frac{36}{4} = 9$$

You Try It 4 $9\frac{4}{7} = \frac{(7 \cdot 9) + 4}{7} = \frac{63 + 4}{7} = \frac{67}{7}$

You Try It 5 $3 = \frac{3}{1}$

You Try It 6 $48 \div 8 = 6$
$$\frac{5}{8} = \frac{5 \cdot 6}{8 \cdot 6} = \frac{30}{48}$$
$\frac{30}{48}$ is equivalent to $\frac{5}{8}$.

You Try It 7 $8 = \frac{8}{1}$ $\quad 12 \div 1 = 12$
$$8 = \frac{8}{1} = \frac{8 \cdot 12}{1 \cdot 12} = \frac{96}{12}$$
$\frac{96}{12}$ is equivalent to 8.

You Try It 8 $\frac{21}{84} = \frac{3 \cdot 7}{2 \cdot 2 \cdot 3 \cdot 7} = \frac{1}{4}$

You Try It 9 $\frac{32}{12} = \frac{2 \cdot 2 \cdot 2 \cdot 2 \cdot 2}{2 \cdot 2 \cdot 3} = \frac{8}{3}$

You Try It 10 $\frac{11t}{11} = \frac{11 \cdot t}{11} = t$

You Try It 11 The LCM of 9 and 21 is 63.

$$\frac{4}{9} = \frac{28}{63} \qquad \frac{8}{21} = \frac{24}{63}$$

$$\frac{28}{63} > \frac{24}{63}$$

$$\frac{4}{9} > \frac{8}{21}$$

You Try It 12 The LCM of 24 and 9 is 72.

$$\frac{17}{24} = \frac{51}{72} \qquad \frac{7}{9} = \frac{56}{72}$$

$$\frac{51}{72} < \frac{56}{72}$$

$$\frac{17}{24} < \frac{7}{9}$$

SECTION 2.3

You Try It 1 $\frac{7}{12} + \frac{3}{8} = \frac{14}{24} + \frac{9}{24} = \frac{23}{24}$

You Try It 2

$$\frac{3}{5} + \frac{2}{3} + \frac{5}{6} = \frac{18}{30} + \frac{20}{30} + \frac{25}{30} = \frac{63}{30}$$

$$= 2\frac{3}{30} = 2\frac{1}{10}$$

You Try It 3 $16 + 8\frac{5}{9} = 24\frac{5}{9}$

You Try It 4

$$\frac{2}{3} + z = \frac{23}{24}$$

$\frac{2}{3} + \frac{3}{8}$	$\frac{23}{24}$
$\frac{16}{24} + \frac{9}{24}$	$\frac{23}{24}$

$$\frac{25}{24} \neq \frac{23}{25}$$

No, $\frac{3}{8}$ is not a solution of $\frac{2}{3} + z = \frac{23}{24}$.

You Try It 5

$$x + y + z$$

$$3\frac{5}{6} + 2\frac{1}{9} + 5\frac{5}{12} = 3\frac{30}{36} + 2\frac{4}{36} + 5\frac{15}{36}$$

$$= 10\frac{49}{36}$$

$$= 11\frac{13}{36}$$

You Try It 6

$$\frac{5}{6} - \frac{7}{9} = \frac{5}{6} - \frac{7}{9}$$

$$= \frac{15}{18} - \frac{14}{18}$$

$$= \frac{15 - 14}{18}$$

$$= \frac{1}{18}$$

You Try It 7 $9\frac{7}{8} - 5\frac{2}{3} = 9\frac{21}{24} - 5\frac{16}{24} = 4\frac{5}{24}$

You Try It 8 $6 - 4\frac{2}{11} = 5\frac{11}{11} - 4\frac{2}{11} = 1\frac{9}{11}$

You Try It 9

$$\frac{2}{3} - v = \frac{11}{12}$$

$\frac{2}{3} - \frac{1}{4}$	$\frac{11}{12}$
$\frac{2}{3} - \frac{1}{4}$	$\frac{11}{12}$
$\frac{8}{12} - \frac{3}{12}$	$\frac{11}{12}$

$$\frac{5}{12} \neq \frac{11}{12}$$

No, $\frac{1}{4}$ is not a solution of the equation.

You Try It 10

Strategy To find the fraction of the respondents who did not name glazed, filled, or frosted:

- Add the three fractions to find the fraction that named glazed, filled, or frosted.
- Subtract the fraction that named glazed, filled, or frosted from 1, the entire group surveyed.

Solution

$$\frac{2}{5} + \frac{8}{25} + \frac{3}{20} = \frac{40}{100} + \frac{32}{100} + \frac{15}{100}$$

$$= \frac{87}{100}$$

$$1 - \frac{87}{100} = \frac{100}{100} - \frac{87}{100} = \frac{13}{100}$$

$\frac{13}{100}$ of the respondents did not name glazed, filled, or frosted as their favorite type of doughnut.

SECTION 2.4

You Try It 1 $\frac{5}{12} \cdot \frac{9}{35} \cdot \frac{7}{8} = \frac{5 \cdot 9 \cdot 7}{12 \cdot 35 \cdot 8}$

$$= \frac{5 \cdot 3 \cdot 3 \cdot 7}{2 \cdot 2 \cdot 3 \cdot 5 \cdot 7 \cdot 2 \cdot 2 \cdot 2}$$

$$= \frac{3}{32}$$

You Try It 2 $\frac{y}{10} \cdot \frac{z}{7} = \frac{y \cdot z}{10 \cdot 7} = \frac{yz}{70}$

You Try It 3 $\frac{8}{9} \cdot 6 = \frac{8}{9} \cdot \frac{6}{1} = \frac{8 \cdot 6}{9 \cdot 1}$

$$= \frac{2 \cdot 2 \cdot 2 \cdot 2 \cdot 3}{3 \cdot 3 \cdot 1} = \frac{16}{3} = 5\frac{1}{3}$$

You Try It 4 $3\frac{6}{7} \cdot 2\frac{4}{9} = \frac{27}{7} \cdot \frac{22}{9} = \frac{27 \cdot 22}{7 \cdot 9}$

$$= \frac{3 \cdot 3 \cdot 3 \cdot 2 \cdot 11}{7 \cdot 3 \cdot 3} = \frac{66}{7} = 9\frac{3}{7}$$

You Try It 5 x^4y^3

$$\left(2\frac{1}{3}\right)^4 \cdot \left(\frac{3}{7}\right)^3 = \left(\frac{7}{3}\right)^4 \cdot \left(\frac{3}{7}\right)^3$$

$$= \frac{7}{3} \cdot \frac{7}{3} \cdot \frac{7}{3} \cdot \frac{7}{3} \cdot \frac{3}{7} \cdot \frac{3}{7} \cdot \frac{3}{7}$$

$$= \frac{7 \cdot 7 \cdot 7 \cdot 7 \cdot 3 \cdot 3 \cdot 3}{3 \cdot 3 \cdot 3 \cdot 3 \cdot 7 \cdot 7 \cdot 7} = \frac{7}{3} = 2\frac{1}{3}$$

You Try It 6 $\frac{5}{6} \div \frac{10}{27} = \frac{5}{6} \cdot \frac{27}{10} = \frac{5 \cdot 27}{6 \cdot 10}$

$$= \frac{5 \cdot 3 \cdot 3 \cdot 3}{2 \cdot 3 \cdot 2 \cdot 5} = \frac{9}{4} = 2\frac{1}{4}$$

You Try It 7 $4\frac{3}{8} \div 3\frac{1}{2} = \frac{35}{8} \div \frac{7}{2} = \frac{35}{8} \cdot \frac{2}{7} = \frac{35 \cdot 2}{8 \cdot 7}$

$$= \frac{5 \cdot 7 \cdot 2}{2 \cdot 2 \cdot 2 \cdot 7} = \frac{5}{4} = 1\frac{1}{4}$$

You Try It 8 $4 \div \frac{6}{7} = \frac{4}{1} \cdot \frac{7}{6}$

$$= \frac{4 \cdot 7}{1 \cdot 6}$$

$$= \frac{2 \cdot 2 \cdot 7}{1 \cdot 2 \cdot 3} = \frac{14}{3} = 4\frac{2}{3}$$

You Try It 9 $\frac{x}{8} \div \frac{y}{6} = \frac{x}{8} \cdot \frac{6}{y}$

$$= \frac{x \cdot 6}{8 \cdot y} = \frac{x \cdot 2 \cdot 3}{2 \cdot 2 \cdot 2 \cdot y} = \frac{3x}{4y}$$

You Try It 10 $x \div y$

$$2\frac{1}{4} \div 9 = \frac{9}{4} \div \frac{9}{1} = \frac{9}{4} \cdot \frac{1}{9} = \frac{9 \cdot 1}{4 \cdot 9}$$

$$= \frac{3 \cdot 3 \cdot 1}{2 \cdot 2 \cdot 3 \cdot 3} = \frac{1}{4}$$

You Try It 11 $\dfrac{\frac{5}{6}}{\frac{5}{12} - \frac{1}{3}} = \dfrac{\frac{5}{6}}{\frac{1}{12}}$

$$= \frac{5}{6} \div \frac{1}{12}$$

$$= \frac{5}{6} \cdot \frac{12}{1}$$

$$= 10$$

You Try It 12 $\frac{x}{y - z}$

$$\frac{2\frac{4}{9}}{3 - 1\frac{1}{3}} = \frac{\frac{22}{9}}{\frac{5}{3}} = \frac{22}{9} \div \frac{5}{3} = \frac{22}{9} \cdot \frac{3}{5}$$

$$= \frac{22}{15} = 1\frac{7}{15}$$

You Try It 13

Strategy To find the amount of felt needed, use the formula for the area of a triangle, $A = \frac{1}{2}bh$. $b = 18$ and $h = 9$.

Solution $A = \frac{1}{2}bh$

$$A = \frac{1}{2}(18)(9)$$

$$A = 81$$

81 in^2 of felt are needed.

You Try It 14

Strategy To find the total cost:

- Multiply the amount of material per sash $\left(1\frac{3}{8}\right)$ by the number of sashes (22) to find the total number of yards of material needed.
- Multiply the total number of yards of material needed by the cost per yard (12).

Solution

$$1\frac{3}{8} \cdot 22 = \frac{11}{8} \cdot \frac{22}{1} = \frac{11 \cdot 22}{8 \cdot 1} = \frac{11 \cdot 2 \cdot 11}{2 \cdot 2 \cdot 2 \cdot 1}$$

$$= \frac{121}{4} = 30\frac{1}{4}$$

$$30\frac{1}{4} \cdot 12 = \frac{121}{4} \cdot \frac{12}{1} = \frac{121 \cdot 12}{4 \cdot 1}$$

$$= \frac{11 \cdot 11 \cdot 2 \cdot 2 \cdot 3}{2 \cdot 2 \cdot 1} = 363$$

The total cost of the material is $363.

SECTION 2.5

You Try It 1 The digit 4 is in the thousandths place.

You Try It 2 $\frac{501}{1000} = 0.501$
(501 thousandths)

You Try It 3 $0.67 = \frac{67}{100}$ (67 hundredths)

You Try It 4 fifty-five and six thousand eighty-three ten-thousandths

You Try It 5 806.00491
(1 — hundred-thousandths place)

You Try It 6
$0.065 = 0.0650$
$0.0650 < 0.0802$
$0.065 < 0.0802$

You Try It 7
3.03, 0.33, 0.30, 3.30, 0.03
0.03, 0.30, 0.33, 3.03, 3.30
0.03, 0.3, 0.33, 3.03, 3.3

You Try It 8
3.675849 (5 — Given place value; 4 < 5)

3.675849 rounded to the nearest ten-thousandth is 3.6758.

You Try It 9
48.907 (9 — Given place value; 0 < 5)

48.907 rounded to the nearest tenth is 48.9.

You Try It 10
31.8652 (1 — Given place value; 8 > 5)

31.8652 rounded to the nearest whole number is 32.

You Try It 11

Strategy To determine who had more home runs for every 100 times at bat, compare the numbers 7.03 and 7.09.

Solution $7.09 > 7.03$

Ralph Kiner had more home runs for every 100 times at bat.

You Try It 12

Strategy To determine the average annual precipitation to the nearest inch, round the number 2.65 to the nearest whole number.

Solution 2.65 rounded to the nearest whole number is 3.

To the nearest inch, the average annual precipitation in Yuma is 3 in.

SECTION 2.6

You Try It 1

$$\begin{array}{r} \overset{1\,1\,1}{8.64} \\ 52.7 \\ +\ 0.39105 \\ \hline 61.73105 \end{array}$$

You Try It 2 $9.378 - 4.002 = 5.376$

You Try It 3

$$\begin{array}{r} 2\overset{4}{\cancel{5}}.\overset{9}{\cancel{0}}\overset{10}{\cancel{0}} \\ -\ 4.91 \\ \hline 20.09 \end{array} \qquad \textit{Check:} \quad \begin{array}{r} 4.91 \\ +20.09 \\ \hline 25.00 \end{array}$$

You Try It 4

$$\begin{array}{lr} 6.514 \longrightarrow & 7 \\ 8.903 \longrightarrow & 9 \\ 2.275 \longrightarrow & +\ 2 \\ \hline & 18 \end{array}$$

You Try It 5

$x + y + z$
$7.84 + 3.05 + 2.19$
$= 10.89 + 2.19$
$= 13.08$

You Try It 6

$$\begin{array}{r|l} m + 16.9 = 40.7 & \\ \hline 23.8 + 16.9 & 40.7 \\ 40.7 = 40.7 & \end{array}$$

• Replace m with 23.8.

Yes, 23.8 is a solution of the equation.

You Try It 7

$$\begin{array}{r} 0.000081 \\ \times \quad 0.025 \\ \hline 405 \\ 162 \\ \hline 0.000002025 \end{array}$$

0.000081 ← 6 decimal places
0.025 ← 3 decimal places
0.000002025 ← 9 decimal places

You Try It 8

$6.407 \longrightarrow 6$
$0.959 \longrightarrow \times 1$

6

You Try It 9

Move the decimal point 4 places to the right.
$1.756 \cdot 10^4 = 17{,}560$

You Try It 10

$25xy$
$25(0.8)(0.6) = 20(0.6) = 12$

You Try It 11

$$\begin{array}{r} 48.2 \\ 6.53.\overline{)\ 314.74.6} \\ -261\ 2 \\ \hline 53\ 54 \\ -52\ 24 \\ \hline 1\ 30\ 6 \\ -1\ 30\ 6 \\ \hline 0 \end{array}$$

• Move the decimal point 2 places to the right.

You Try It 12

$62.7 \longrightarrow 60$
$3.45 \longrightarrow 3$
$60 \div 3 = 20$

You Try It 13

$$\begin{array}{r} 6.0391 \approx 6.039 \\ 86\overline{)\ 519.3700} \\ -516 \\ \hline 3\ 3 \\ -\ \ 0 \\ \hline 3\ 37 \\ -2\ 58 \\ \hline 790 \\ -774 \\ \hline 160 \\ -\ 86 \\ \hline 74 \end{array}$$

You Try It 14

Move the decimal point 2 places to the left.
$63.7 \div 100 = 0.637$

You Try It 15

$\dfrac{x}{y}$

$\dfrac{40.6}{0.7} = 58$

You Try It 16

$$\begin{array}{c|c} 2 = \dfrac{0.6}{d} & \\ \hline 2 & \dfrac{0.6}{1.2} \end{array}$$

• Replace d with 1.2.

$2 \neq 0.5$

No, 1.2 is not a solution of the equation.

You Try It 17

$5\overline{)4.0}$ with quotient 0.8 $\qquad \dfrac{4}{5} = 0.8$

You Try It 18

$6\overline{)5.0000}$ with quotient 0.8333 $\qquad 1\dfrac{5}{6} = 1.8\overline{3}$

You Try It 19

$6.2 = 6\dfrac{2}{10} = 6\dfrac{1}{5}$

You Try It 20

$\dfrac{7}{12} \approx 0.5833$

$0.5880 > 0.5833$

$0.588 > \dfrac{7}{12}$

You Try It 21

Strategy

To find the change you receive:

- ▶ Multiply the number of stamps (12) by the cost of each stamp (45¢) to find the total cost of the stamps.
- ▶ Convert the total cost of the stamps to dollars and cents.
- ▶ Subtract the total cost of the stamps from $10.

Solution

$12(45) = 540$ • The stamps cost 540¢.
$540¢ = \$5.40$ • The stamps cost $5.40.
$10 - 5.40 = 4.60$

You receive $4.60 in change.

You Try It 22

Strategy

To find the insurance premium due, replace B by 276.25 and F by 1.8 in the given formula, and solve for P.

Solution

$P = BF$
$P = 276.25(1.8)$
$P = 497.25$

The insurance premium due is $497.25.

SECTION 2.7

You Try It 1

$$\begin{aligned}&(1.2 - 0.8)^2 + (1.5)(6)\\&= (0.4)^2 + (1.5)(6)\\&= 0.16 + (1.5)(6)\\&= 0.16 + 9\\&= 9.16\end{aligned}$$

You Try It 2

$$\left(\frac{1}{2}\right)^3 \cdot \frac{7-3}{9-4} + \frac{4}{5}$$

$$= \left(\frac{1}{2}\right)^3 \cdot \frac{4}{5} + \frac{4}{5}$$ • Simplify $\frac{7-3}{9-4}$.

$$= \frac{1}{8} \cdot \frac{4}{5} + \frac{4}{5}$$ • Simplify $\left(\frac{1}{2}\right)^3$.

$$= \frac{1}{10} + \frac{4}{5} = \frac{1}{10} + \frac{8}{10} = \frac{9}{10}$$

Solutions to Chapter 3 "You Try It"

SECTION 3.1

You Try It 1

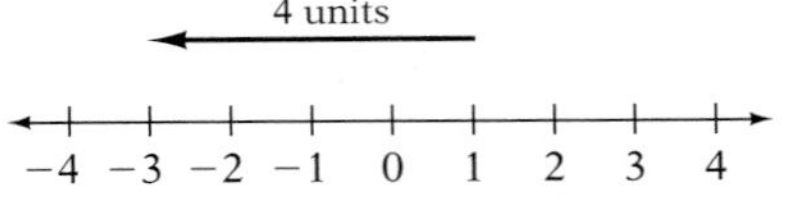

-3 is 4 units to the left of 1.

You Try It 2

−5 −4 −3 −2 −1 0 1 2 3

A is -5 and C is -3.

You Try It 3

a. 2 is to the right of -5 on the number line.
$2 > -5$

b. -4 is to the left of 3 on the number line.
$-4 < 3$

You Try It 4 $-7, -1, 0, 4, 8$

You Try It 5 **a.** -24 **b.** 13 **c.** b

You Try It 6
a. negative three minus twelve
b. eight plus negative five

You Try It 7 **a.** $-(-59) = 59$ **b.** $-(y) = -y$

You Try It 8 **a.** $|-8| = 8$ **b.** $|12| = 12$

You Try It 9 **a.** $|0| = 0$ **b.** $-|35| = -35$

You Try It 10 $|-y| = |-2| = 2$

You Try It 11
$|6| = 6, |-2| = 2, -(-1) = 1,$
$-|-8| = -8$
$-8, -4, 1, 2, 6$
$-|-8|, -4, -(-1), |-2|, |6|$

You Try It 12

Strategy To find the player who came in second, find the player with the second lowest number for a score.

Solution $-14 < -12 < -10$

The second lowest number among the scores is -12.

Day and Scott tied for second.

You Try It 13

Strategy To determine which is closer to blastoff, find the absolute value of each number. The number with the smaller absolute value is closer to zero and, therefore, closer to blastoff.

Solution $|-9| = 9, |-7| = 7$

$7 < 9$

-7 s and counting is closer to blastoff than -9 s and counting.

SECTION 3.2

You Try It 1 $-38 + (-62) = -100$

You Try It 2 $47 + (-53) = -6$

You Try It 3
$$\begin{aligned}-36 + 17 + (-21) &= -19 + (-21)\\&= -40\end{aligned}$$

You Try It 4 $-154 + (-37) = -191$

You Try It 5
$$\begin{aligned}&-x + y\\&-(-3) + (-10) = 3 + (-10)\\&\qquad\qquad\qquad\;\; = -7\end{aligned}$$

You Try It 6
$$\begin{array}{c|c}\multicolumn{2}{c}{2 = 11 + a}\\ \hline 2 & 11 + (-9)\end{array}$$
$2 = 2$

Yes, -9 is a solution of the equation.

You Try It 7
$$\begin{aligned}-35 - (-34) &= -35 + 34\\&= -1\end{aligned}$$

You Try It 8
$$\begin{aligned}83 - (-29) &= 83 + 29\\&= 112\end{aligned}$$

You Try It 9

The boiling point of xenon is -108.
The melting point of xenon is -112.

$$\begin{aligned}-108 - (-112) &= -108 + 112\\&= 4\end{aligned}$$

The difference is 4°C.

You Try It 10
$$\begin{aligned}-8 - 14 &= -8 + (-14)\\&= -22\end{aligned}$$

You Try It 11 $25 - 68 = 25 + (-68)$
$= -43$

You Try It 12 $-4 - (-3) + 12 - (-7) - 20$
$= -4 + 3 + 12 + 7 + (-20)$
$= -1 + 12 + 7 + (-20)$
$= 11 + 7 + (-20)$
$= 18 + (-20)$
$= -2$

You Try It 13 $x - y$
$-9 - 7 = -9 + (-7)$
$= -16$

You Try It 14

$a - 5 = -8$	
$-3 - 5$	-8
$-3 + (-5)$	-8

$-8 = -8$

Yes, -3 is a solution of the equation.

You Try It 15

Strategy To find the difference, subtract the lowest melting point shown (-259) from the highest melting point shown (181).

Solution $181 - (-259) = 181 + 259$
$= 440$

The difference is 440°C.

You Try It 16

Strategy To find the temperature, add the increase (10) to the previous temperature (-3).

Solution $-3 + 10 = 7$

The temperature is 7°C.

You Try It 17

Strategy To find the difference, subtract the lower temperature (-70) from the higher temperature (59).

Solution $59 - (-70) = 59 + 70$
$= 129$

The difference between the average temperatures is 129°F.

You Try It 18

Strategy To find d, replace a by -6 and b by 5 in the given formula, and solve for d.

Solution $d = |a - b|$
$d = |-6 - 5|$
$d = |-11|$
$d = 11$

The distance between the two points is 11 units.

SECTION 3.3

You Try It 1 $-38(51) = -1938$

You Try It 2 $-7(-8)(9)(-2) = 56(9)(-2)$
$= 504(-2)$
$= -1008$

You Try It 3 $-9y$
$-9(20) = -180$

You Try It 4

$12 = -4a$	
12	$-4(-3)$

$12 = 12$

Yes, -3 is a solution of the equation.

You Try It 5 $0 \div (-17) = 0$

You Try It 6 $\frac{84}{-6} = -14$

You Try It 7 Any number divided by 1 is the number.
$x \div 1 = x$

You Try It 8 $\frac{a}{-b}$

$\frac{-14}{-(-7)} = \frac{-14}{7} = -2$

You Try It 9 $\frac{-6}{y} = -2$

$\frac{-6}{-3}$	-2

$2 \neq -2$

No, -3 is not a solution of the equation.

You Try It 10

Strategy To find the average daily high temperature:
- ▶ Add the seven temperature readings.
- ▶ Divide by 7.

Solution

$-7 + (-8) + 0 + (-1) + (-6) + (-11) + (-2) = -35$

$-35 \div 7 = -5$

The average daily high temperature was $-5°$.

SECTION 3.4

You Try It 1
$$-\frac{5}{12}+\frac{5}{8}+\left(-\frac{1}{6}\right)=\frac{-5}{12}+\frac{5}{8}+\frac{-1}{6}$$
$$=\frac{-10}{24}+\frac{15}{24}+\frac{-4}{24}$$
$$=\frac{-10+15+(-4)}{24}$$
$$=\frac{1}{24}$$

You Try It 2
$$-\frac{5}{6}-\frac{4}{9}=\frac{-15}{18}-\frac{8}{18}$$
$$=\frac{-15-8}{18}$$
$$=\frac{-23}{18}$$
$$=-1\frac{5}{18}$$

You Try It 3 $5.007-8.289=-3.282$

You Try It 4
$x+y+z$
$-6.07+(-4.26)+3.84$
$=-10.33+3.84$
$=-6.49$

You Try It 5
$$\frac{2}{3}-y=\frac{11}{12}$$

$\frac{2}{3}-\left(-\frac{1}{4}\right)$	$\frac{11}{12}$
$\frac{2}{3}+\frac{1}{4}$	$\frac{11}{12}$
$\frac{8}{12}+\frac{3}{12}$	$\frac{11}{12}$

• Replace y by $-\frac{1}{4}$.

$$\frac{11}{12}=\frac{11}{12}$$

Yes, $-\frac{1}{4}$ is a solution of the equation.

You Try It 6
$$-\frac{1}{3}\left(-\frac{5}{12}\right)\left(\frac{8}{15}\right)=\frac{1}{3}\cdot\frac{5}{12}\cdot\frac{8}{15}$$
$$=\frac{1\cdot5\cdot8}{3\cdot12\cdot15}$$
$$=\frac{1\cdot5\cdot2\cdot2\cdot2}{3\cdot2\cdot2\cdot3\cdot3\cdot5}$$
$$=\frac{2}{27}$$

You Try It 7
$$3\frac{6}{7}\cdot\left(-\frac{4}{9}\right)=-\left(\frac{27}{7}\cdot\frac{4}{9}\right)$$
$$=-\frac{27\cdot4}{7\cdot9}$$
$$=-\frac{3\cdot3\cdot3\cdot2\cdot2}{7\cdot3\cdot3}$$
$$=-\frac{12}{7}$$
$$=-1\frac{5}{7}$$

You Try It 8
$$8\div\left(-\frac{6}{7}\right)=-\left(\frac{8}{1}\div\frac{6}{7}\right)$$
$$=-\left(\frac{8}{1}\cdot\frac{7}{6}\right)$$
$$=-\frac{8\cdot7}{1\cdot6}$$
$$=-\frac{2\cdot2\cdot2\cdot7}{1\cdot2\cdot3}=-\frac{28}{3}=-9\frac{1}{3}$$

You Try It 9 $(-0.7)(-5.8)=4.06$

You Try It 10 The quotient is negative.
$-25.7\div0.31\approx-82.9$

You Try It 11
xy
$$5\frac{1}{8}\cdot\frac{2}{3}=\frac{41}{8}\cdot\frac{2}{3}$$
$$=\frac{41\cdot2}{8\cdot3}$$
$$=\frac{41\cdot2}{2\cdot2\cdot2\cdot3}$$
$$=\frac{41}{12}=3\frac{5}{12}$$

You Try It 12
$$\frac{x}{y}$$
$$\frac{-33.6}{-0.7}=48$$

You Try It 13
$25xy$
$25(-0.6)(0.6)=-15(0.6)=-9$

You Try It 14 $-2 = \dfrac{y}{-0.6}$

$$\begin{array}{c|c} -2 & \dfrac{-1.2}{-0.6} \end{array}$$ • Replace y with -1.2.

$-2 \neq 2$

No, -1.2 is not a solution of the equation.

You Try It 15

Strategy To find how many degrees the temperature fell, subtract the lower temperature (-13.33) from the higher temperature (12.78).

Solution
$$\begin{aligned} 12.78 - (-13.33) &= 12.78 + 13.33 \\ &= 26.11 \end{aligned}$$

The temperature fell 26.11°C in the 15-minute period.

SECTION 3.5

You Try It 1
$$\begin{aligned} 8 \div 4 \cdot 4 - (-2)^2 &= 8 \div 4 \cdot 4 - 4 \\ &= 2 \cdot 4 - 4 \\ &= 8 - 4 \\ &= 4 \end{aligned}$$

You Try It 2
$$\begin{aligned} &(-2)^2(3-7)^2 - (-16) \div (-4) \\ &= (-2)^2(-4)^2 - (-16) \div (-4) \\ &= (4)(16) - (-16) \div (-4) \\ &= 64 - (-16) \div (-4) \\ &= 64 - 4 \\ &= 60 \end{aligned}$$

You Try It 3
$$\begin{aligned} &3a - 4b \\ 3(-1.7) - 4(4.5) &= -5.1 - 4(4.5) \\ &= -5.1 - 18 \\ &= -5.1 + (-18) \\ &= -23.1 \end{aligned}$$

You Try It 4
$$\begin{aligned} &(-6)(2) + |-1 - 7| \\ &= (-6)(2) + |-8| \\ &= (-6)(2) + 8 \\ &= -12 + 8 \\ &= -4 \end{aligned}$$

Solutions to Chapter 4 "You Try It"

SECTION 4.1

You Try It 1 -4 is the constant term.

You Try It 2
$$\begin{aligned} &2xy + y^2 \\ &2(-4)(2) + (2)^2 \\ &= 2(-4)(2) + 4 \\ &= (-8)(2) + 4 \\ &= (-16) + 4 \\ &= -12 \end{aligned}$$

You Try It 3
$$\begin{aligned} &\frac{a^2 + b^2}{a + b} \\ \frac{5^2 + (-3)^2}{5 + (-3)} &= \frac{25 + 9}{5 + (-3)} \\ &= \frac{34}{2} \\ &= 17 \end{aligned}$$

You Try It 4
$$\begin{aligned} &x^3 - 2(x + y) + z^2 \\ &(2)^3 - 2[2 + (-4)] + (-3)^2 \\ &= 8 - 2(-2) + 9 \\ &= 8 + 4 + 9 \\ &= 12 + 9 \\ &= 21 \end{aligned}$$

SECTION 4.2

You Try It 1 $3a - 2b - 5a + 6b = -2a + 4b$

You Try It 2 $-3y^2 + 7 + 8y^2 - 14 = 5y^2 - 7$

You Try It 3 $-5(4y^2) = -20y^2$

You Try It 4 $-7(-2a) = 14a$

You Try It 5 $-\dfrac{3}{5}\left(-\dfrac{7}{9}a\right) = \dfrac{7}{15}a$

You Try It 6 $5(3 + 7b) = 15 + 35b$

You Try It 7 $(3a - 1)5 = 15a - 5$

You Try It 8 $-8(-2a + 7b) = 16a - 56b$

You Try It 9 $3(12x^2 - x + 8) = 36x^2 - 3x + 24$

You Try It 10 $3(-a^2 - 6a + 7) = -3a^2 - 18a + 21$

You Try It 11
$$\begin{aligned} 3y - 2(y - 7x) &= 3y - 2y + 14x \\ &= y + 14x \end{aligned}$$

You Try It 12
$$\begin{aligned} -2(x - 2y) - (-x + 3y) &= -2x + 4y + x - 3y \\ &= -x + y \end{aligned}$$

You Try It 13
$$\begin{aligned} 3y - 2[x - 4(2 - 3y)] &= 3y - 2[x - 8 + 12y] \\ &= 3y - 2x + 16 - 24y \\ &= -2x - 21y + 16 \end{aligned}$$

SECTION 4.3

You Try It 1 the difference between twice n and the *square* of n

$2n - n^2$

You Try It 2 the quotient of 7 less than b and 15

$\dfrac{b - 7}{15}$

You Try It 3 the unknown number: x
the difference between the number and sixty: $x - 60$
$5(x - 60)$
$= 5x - 300$

You Try It 4 the unknown number: n
the cube of the number: n^3
the total of ten and the cube of the number: $10 + n^3$
$-4(10 + n^3)$

You Try It 5 the speed of the older model: s
the speed of the new jet plane is twice the speed of the older model: $2s$

You Try It 6 the length of the longer piece: y
the length of the shorter piece: $6 - y$

Solutions to Chapter 5 "You Try It"

SECTION 5.1

You Try It 1

$10x - x^2 = 3x - 10$	
$10(5) - (5)^2$	$3(5) - 10$
$50 - 25$	$15 - 10$

$25 \neq 5$

No, 5 is not a solution.

You Try It 2

$$26 = y - 14$$
$$26 + 14 = y - 14 + 14$$
$$40 = y - 0$$
$$40 = y$$

The solution is 40.

You Try It 3

$$-\frac{2x}{5} = 6$$
$$\left(-\frac{5}{2}\right)\left(-\frac{2}{5}x\right) = \left(-\frac{5}{2}\right)(6)$$
$$x = -15$$

The solution is -15.

You Try It 4

$$4x - 8x = 16$$
$$-4x = 16$$
$$\frac{-4x}{-4} = \frac{16}{-4}$$
$$x = -4$$

The solution is -4.

You Try It 5

Strategy To find the distance, solve the equation $d = rt$ for d. The time is 3 h. Therefore, $t = 3$. The plane is moving against the wind, which means the headwind is slowing the actual speed of the plane. 250 mph $-$ 25 mph $=$ 225 mph. Thus $r = 225$.

Solution

$$d = rt$$
$$d = 225(3) \quad \bullet\ r = 225, t = 3$$
$$= 675$$

The plane travels 675 mi in 3 h.

SECTION 5.2

You Try It 1

$$5x + 7 = 10$$
$$5x + 7 - 7 = 10 - 7 \quad \bullet \text{ Subtract 7.}$$
$$5x = 3$$
$$\frac{5x}{5} = \frac{3}{5} \quad \bullet \text{ Divide by 5.}$$
$$x = \frac{3}{5}$$

The solution is $\frac{3}{5}$.

You Try It 2

$$2 = 11 + 3x$$
$$2 - 11 = 11 - 11 + 3x \quad \bullet \text{ Subtract 11.}$$
$$-9 = 3x$$
$$\frac{-9}{3} = \frac{3x}{3} \quad \bullet \text{ Divide by 3.}$$
$$-3 = x$$

The solution is -3.

You Try It 3

$$\frac{5}{8} - \frac{2x}{3} = \frac{5}{4}$$
$$\frac{5}{8} - \frac{5}{8} - \frac{2}{3}x = \frac{5}{4} - \frac{5}{8} \quad \bullet \text{ Recall that } \frac{2x}{3} = \frac{2}{3}x.$$
$$-\frac{2}{3}x = \frac{5}{8}$$
$$-\frac{3}{2}\left(-\frac{2}{3}x\right) = -\frac{3}{2}\left(\frac{5}{8}\right) \quad \bullet \text{ Multiply by } -\frac{3}{2}.$$
$$x = -\frac{15}{16}$$

The solution is $-\frac{15}{16}$.

You Try It 4

$$\frac{2}{3}x + 3 = \frac{7}{2}$$
$$6\left(\frac{2}{3}x + 3\right) = 6\left(\frac{7}{2}\right)$$
$$6\left(\frac{2}{3}x\right) + 6(3) = 6\left(\frac{7}{2}\right) \quad \text{• Distributive Property}$$
$$4x + 18 = 21$$
$$4x + 18 - 18 = 21 - 18 \quad \text{• Subtract 18.}$$
$$4x = 3$$
$$\frac{4x}{4} = \frac{3}{4} \quad \text{• Divide by 4.}$$
$$x = \frac{3}{4}$$

The solution is $\frac{3}{4}$.

You Try It 5

$$x - 5 + 4x = 25$$
$$5x - 5 = 25$$
$$5x - 5 + 5 = 25 + 5$$
$$5x = 30$$
$$\frac{5x}{5} = \frac{30}{5}$$
$$x = 6$$

The solution is 6.

You Try It 6

Strategy Given: $P = 45$
Unknown: D

Solution

$$P = 15 + \frac{1}{2}D$$
$$45 = 15 + \frac{1}{2}D$$
$$45 - 15 = 15 - 15 + \frac{1}{2}D$$
$$30 = \frac{1}{2}D$$
$$2(30) = 2 \cdot \frac{1}{2}D$$
$$60 = D$$

The depth is 60 ft.

SECTION 5.3

You Try It 1

$$5x + 4 = 6 + 10x$$
$$5x - 10x + 4 = 6 + 10x - 10x \quad \text{• Subtract } 10x.$$
$$-5x + 4 = 6$$
$$-5x + 4 - 4 = 6 - 4 \quad \text{• Subtract 4.}$$
$$-5x = 2$$
$$\frac{-5x}{-5} = \frac{2}{-5} \quad \text{• Divide by } -5.$$
$$x = -\frac{2}{5}$$

The solution is $-\frac{2}{5}$.

You Try It 2

$$5x - 10 - 3x = 6 - 4x$$
$$2x - 10 = 6 - 4x \quad \text{• Combine like terms.}$$
$$2x + 4x - 10 = 6 - 4x + 4x \quad \text{• Add } 4x.$$
$$6x - 10 = 6$$
$$6x - 10 + 10 = 6 + 10 \quad \text{• Add 10.}$$
$$6x = 16$$
$$\frac{6x}{6} = \frac{16}{6} \quad \text{• Divide by 6.}$$
$$x = \frac{8}{3}$$

The solution is $\frac{8}{3}$.

You Try It 3

$$5x - 4(3 - 2x) = 2(3x - 2) + 6$$
$$5x - 12 + 8x = 6x - 4 + 6 \quad \text{• Distributive Property}$$
$$13x - 12 = 6x + 2$$
$$13x - 6x - 12 = 6x - 6x + 2 \quad \text{• Subtract } 6x.$$
$$7x - 12 = 2$$
$$7x - 12 + 12 = 2 + 12 \quad \text{• Add 12.}$$
$$7x = 14$$
$$\frac{7x}{7} = \frac{14}{7} \quad \text{• Divide by 7.}$$
$$x = 2$$

The solution is 2.

You Try It 4

$$-2[3x - 5(2x - 3)] = 3x - 8$$
$$-2[3x - 10x + 15] = 3x - 8 \quad \text{• Distributive Property}$$
$$-2[-7x + 15] = 3x - 8$$
$$14x - 30 = 3x - 8$$
$$14x - 3x - 30 = 3x - 3x - 8 \quad \text{• Subtract } 3x.$$
$$11x - 30 = -8$$
$$11x - 30 + 30 = -8 + 30 \quad \text{• Add 30.}$$
$$11x = 22$$
$$\frac{11x}{11} = \frac{22}{11} \quad \text{• Divide by 11.}$$
$$x = 2$$

The solution is 2.

You Try It 5

Strategy Given: $F_1 = 45$
$F_2 = 80$
$d = 25$
Unknown: x

Solution

$$F_1x = F_2(d - x)$$
$$45x = 80(25 - x)$$
$$45x = 2000 - 80x$$
$$45x + 80x = 2000 - 80x + 80x$$
$$125x = 2000$$
$$\frac{125x}{125} = \frac{2000}{125}$$
$$x = 16$$

The fulcrum is 16 ft from the 45-pound force.

SECTION 5.4

You Try It 1

Strategy

The total of three times the smaller number and six	amounts to	seven less than the product of four and the larger number

The smaller number: n
The larger number: $12 - n$

Solution

$$\begin{aligned} 3n + 6 &= 4(12 - n) - 7 \\ 3n + 6 &= 48 - 4n - 7 \\ 3n + 6 &= 41 - 4n \\ 3n + 4n + 6 &= 41 - 4n + 4n \\ 7n + 6 &= 41 \\ 7n + 6 - 6 &= 41 - 6 \\ 7n &= 35 \\ \frac{7n}{7} &= \frac{35}{7} \\ n &= 5 \end{aligned}$$

$12 - n = 12 - 5 = 7$

The smaller number is 5.

The larger number is 7.

You Try It 2

Strategy

- First integer: n
  Second integer: $n + 1$
  Third integer: $n + 2$
- The sum of the three integers is -6.

Solution

$$\begin{aligned} n + (n + 1) + (n + 2) &= -6 \\ 3n + 3 &= -6 \\ 3n &= -9 \\ n &= -3 \end{aligned}$$

$n + 1 = -3 + 1 = -2$
$n + 2 = -3 + 2 = -1$

The three consecutive integers are -3, -2, and -1.

You Try It 3

Strategy

To find the number of tickets purchased, write and solve an equation using x to represent the number of tickets purchased.

\$3.50 plus \$17.50 for each ticket	is	\$161

Solution

$$\begin{aligned} 3.50 + 17.50x &= 161 \\ 3.50 - 3.50 + 17.50x &= 161 - 3.50 \\ 17.50x &= 157.50 \\ \frac{17.50x}{17.50} &= \frac{157.50}{17.50} \\ x &= 9 \end{aligned}$$

You purchased 9 tickets.

You Try It 4

Strategy

To find the length, write and solve an equation using x to represent the length of the shorter piece and $22 - x$ to represent the length of the longer piece.

The length of the longer piece	is	4 in. more than twice the length of the shorter piece

Solution

$$\begin{aligned} 22 - x &= 2x + 4 \\ 22 - x - 2x &= 2x - 2x + 4 \\ 22 - 3x &= 4 \\ 22 - 22 - 3x &= 4 - 22 \\ -3x &= -18 \\ \frac{-3x}{-3} &= \frac{-18}{-3} \\ x &= 6 \end{aligned}$$

$22 - x = 22 - 6 = 16$

The length of the shorter piece is 6 in.

The length of the longer piece is 16 in.

SECTION 5.5

You Try It 1

Strategy

- Pounds of \$.75 fertilizer: x

	Amount	*Cost*	*Value*
\$.90 fertilizer	20	0.90	0.90(20)
\$.75 fertilizer	x	0.75	$0.75x$
\$.85 fertilizer	$20 + x$	0.85	$0.85(20 + x)$

- The sum of the values before mixing equals the value after mixing.

Solution

$$\begin{aligned} 0.90(20) + 0.75x &= 0.85(20 + x) \\ 18 + 0.75x &= 17 + 0.85x \\ 18 - 0.10x &= 17 \\ -0.10x &= -1 \\ x &= 10 \end{aligned}$$

10 lb of the \$.75 fertilizer must be added.

You Try It 2

Strategy

► Rate of the first train: r
Rate of the second train: $2r$

	Rate	Time	Distance
1st train	r	3	$3r$
2nd train	$2r$	3	$3(2r)$

► The sum of the distances traveled by the two trains equals 288 mi.

Solution

$$3r + 3(2r) = 288$$
$$3r + 6r = 288$$
$$9r = 288$$
$$r = 32$$
$$2r = 2(32) = 64$$

The first train is traveling at 32 mph.
The second train is traveling at 64 mph.

You Try It 3

Strategy

► Time spent flying out: t
Time spent flying back: $5 - t$

	Rate	Time	Distance
Out	150	t	$150t$
Back	100	$5 - t$	$100(5 - t)$

► The distance out equals the distance back.

Solution

$$150t = 100(5 - t)$$
$$150t = 500 - 100t$$
$$250t = 500$$
$$t = 2 \quad \text{(The time out was 2 h.)}$$

The distance out $= 150t = 150(2)$
$= 300$

The parcel of land was 300 mi away.

Solutions to Chapter 6 "You Try It"

SECTION 6.1

You Try It 1

$$\frac{12}{20} = \frac{3}{5}$$
$$12:20 = 3:5$$
12 to 20 = 3 to 5

You Try It 2

$$\frac{20 \text{ bags}}{8 \text{ acres}} = \frac{5 \text{ bags}}{2 \text{ acres}}$$

You Try It 3

$$\frac{\$8.96}{3.5 \text{ lb}}$$
$$8.96 \div 3.5 = 2.56$$

The unit rate is \$2.56/lb.

SECTION 6.2

You Try It 1

$$\frac{50}{3} \diagup\!\!\!\!\diagdown \frac{250}{12} \quad \begin{array}{l} \rightarrow 3 \cdot 250 = 750 \\ \rightarrow 50 \cdot 12 = 600 \end{array}$$
$$750 \neq 600$$

The proportion is not true.

You Try It 2

$$\frac{7}{12} = \frac{42}{x}$$
$$12 \cdot 42 = 7 \cdot x$$
$$504 = 7x$$
$$72 = x$$

You Try It 3

$$\frac{5}{n} = \frac{3}{322}$$
$$n \cdot 3 = 5 \cdot 322$$
$$3n = 1610$$
$$\frac{3n}{3} = \frac{1610}{3}$$
$$n \approx 536.67$$

You Try It 4

$$\frac{4}{5} = \frac{3}{x - 3}$$
$$5 \cdot 3 = 4(x - 3)$$
$$15 = 4x - 12$$
$$27 = 4x$$
$$6.75 = x$$

You Try It 5

Strategy

To find the number of gallons, write and solve a proportion using n to represent the number of gallons needed to travel 832 mi.

Solution

$$\frac{396 \text{ mi}}{11 \text{ gal}} = \frac{832 \text{ mi}}{n \text{ gal}}$$
$$11 \cdot 832 = 396 \cdot n$$
$$9152 = 396n$$
$$23.1 \approx n$$

To travel 832 mi, approximately 23.1 gal of gas are needed.

You Try It 6

Strategy

To find the number of defective transmissions, write and solve a proportion using n to represent the number of defective transmissions in 120,000 cars.

Solution

$$\frac{15 \text{ defective transmissions}}{1200 \text{ cars}} = \frac{n \text{ defective transmissions}}{120{,}000 \text{ cars}}$$
$$1200 \cdot n = 15 \cdot 120{,}000$$
$$1200n = 1{,}800{,}000$$
$$n = 1500$$

1500 defective transmissions would be found in 120,000 cars.

SECTION 6.3

You Try It 1 33% means 33 out of 100.
33 out of every 100 Americans carry balances up to \$10,000 on their credit cards.

You Try It 2 $110\% = 110\left(\frac{1}{100}\right) = \left(\frac{110}{100}\right) = 1\frac{1}{10}$

$110\% = 110(0.01) = 1.10$

You Try It 3 $33\frac{1}{3}\% = 33\frac{1}{3}\left(\frac{1}{100}\right) = \frac{100}{3}\left(\frac{1}{100}\right)$

$= \frac{100}{300} = \frac{1}{3}$

You Try It 4 $0.8\% = 0.8(0.01) = 0.008$

You Try It 5 $\frac{5}{7} = \frac{5}{7}(100\%) = \frac{500}{7}\% = 71\frac{3}{7}\%$

You Try It 6 $1\frac{5}{9} = \frac{14}{9} = \frac{14}{9}(100\%) = \frac{1400}{9}\% \approx 155.6\%$

You Try It 7 $\frac{3}{5} = \frac{3}{5}(100\%) = \frac{300}{5}\% = 60\%$
60% of consumers have a rewards credit card.

You Try It 8 $0.038 = 0.038(100\%)$
$= 3.8\%$

SECTION 6.4

You Try It 1 To find the amount, use the basic percent equation. Percent $= 66\frac{2}{3}\% = \frac{2}{3}$, base $= 45$, amount $= n$

Percent · base = amount

$$\frac{2}{3}(45) = n$$
$$30 = n$$

30 is $66\frac{2}{3}\%$ of 45.

You Try It 2 To find the percent, use the basic percent equation. Percent $= n$, base $= 40$, amount $= 25$

Percent · base = amount

$$n \cdot 40 = 25$$
$$\frac{40n}{40} = \frac{25}{40}$$
$$n = 0.625 = 62.5\%$$

25 is 62.5% of 40.

You Try It 3 To find the base, use the basic percent equation. Percent $= 16\frac{2}{3}\% = \frac{1}{6}$, base $= n$, amount $= 15$

Percent · base = amount

$$\frac{1}{6} \cdot n = 15$$
$$6 \cdot \frac{1}{6}n = 15 \cdot 6$$
$$n = 90$$

$16\frac{2}{3}\%$ of 90 is 15.

You Try It 4 Percent $= 25$, base $= n$, amount $= 8$

$$\frac{25}{100} = \frac{8}{n}$$
$$25 \cdot n = 100 \cdot 8$$
$$25n = 800$$
$$\frac{25n}{25} = \frac{800}{25}$$
$$n = 32$$

8 is 25% of 32.

You Try It 5 Percent $= 0.74$, base $= 1200$, amount $= n$

$$\frac{0.74}{100} = \frac{n}{1200}$$
$$100 \cdot n = 0.74 \cdot 1200$$
$$100n = 888$$
$$\frac{100n}{100} = \frac{888}{100}$$
$$n = 8.88$$

0.74% of 1200 is 8.88.

You Try It 6 Percent $= n$, base $= 180$, amount $= 54$

$$\frac{n}{100} = \frac{54}{180}$$
$$n \cdot 180 = 100 \cdot 54$$
$$180n = 5400$$
$$\frac{180n}{180} = \frac{5400}{180}$$
$$n = 30$$

30% of 180 is 54.

You Try It 7

Strategy To find the percent, use the basic percent equation. Percent $= n$, base $= 4330$, amount $= 649.50$

Solution Percent · base = amount

$$n \cdot 4330 = 649.50$$
$$\frac{4330n}{4330} = \frac{649.50}{4330}$$
$$n = 0.15$$

15% of the instructor's salary is deducted for income tax.

You Try It 8

Strategy To find the number, use the basic percent equation.

Percent = 19% = 0.19, base = 2.4 million, amount = n

Solution Percent · base = amount

$$0.19 \cdot 2.4 = n$$
$$0.456 = n$$

0.456 million = 456,000

There are approximately 456,000 female surfers in this country.

You Try It 9

Strategy To find the increase in the hourly wage:

- ► Find last year's wage. Solve the basic percent equation.

  Percent = 115% = 1.15, base = n, amount = 30.13

- ► Subtract last year's wage from this year's wage.

Solution Percent · base = amount

$$1.15 \cdot n = 30.13$$
$$\frac{1.15n}{1.15} = \frac{30.13}{1.15}$$
$$n = 26.20$$

$30.13 - 26.20 = 3.93$

The increase in the hourly wage is $3.93.

SECTION 6.5

You Try It 1

Strategy To calculate the maturity value:

- ► Find the simple interest due on the loan by solving the simple interest formula for I.

  $t = \frac{8}{12}$, $P = 12{,}500$, $r = 9.5\% = 0.095$

- ► Use the formula for the maturity value of a simple interest loan, $M = P + I$.

Solution $I = Prt$

$$I = 12{,}500(0.095)\left(\frac{8}{12}\right)$$
$$I \approx 791.67$$

$$M = P + I$$
$$M = 12{,}500 + 791.67$$
$$M = 13{,}291.67$$

The total amount due on the loan is $13,291.67.

Solutions to Chapter 7 "You Try It"

SECTION 7.1

You Try It 1

$$QR + RS + ST = QT$$
$$24 + RS + 17 = 62 \quad \text{• } QR = 24, ST = 17, QT = 62$$
$$41 + RS = 62 \quad \text{• Add 24 and 17.}$$
$$RS = 21 \quad \text{• Subtract 41 from each side.}$$

$RS = 21$ cm

You Try It 2

$$AC = AB + BC$$
$$AC = \frac{1}{4}(BC) + BC \quad \text{• } AB \text{ is one-fourth } BC.$$
$$AC = \frac{1}{4}(16) + 16 \quad \text{• } BC = 16$$
$$AC = 4 + 16$$
$$AC = 20$$

$AC = 20$ ft

You Try It 3

Strategy Supplementary angles are two angles whose sum is 180°. To find the supplement, let x represent the supplement of a 129° angle. Write an equation and solve for x.

Solution

$$x + 129^\circ = 180^\circ$$
$$x = 51^\circ$$

The supplement of a 129° angle is a 51° angle.

You Try It 4

Strategy To find the measure of $\angle a$, write an equation using the fact that the sum of the measure of $\angle a$ and 68° is 118°. Solve for $\angle a$.

Solution

$$\angle a + 68^\circ = 118^\circ$$
$$\angle a = 50^\circ$$

The measure of $\angle a$ is 50°.

You Try It 5

Strategy The angles labeled are adjacent angles of intersecting lines and are therefore supplementary angles. To find x, write an equation and solve for x.

Solution

$$(x + 16^\circ) + 3x = 180^\circ$$
$$4x + 16^\circ = 180^\circ$$
$$4x = 164^\circ$$
$$x = 41^\circ$$

You Try It 6

Strategy $3x = y$ because corresponding angles have the same measure. $y + (x + 40°) = 180°$ because adjacent angles of intersecting lines are supplementary angles. Substitute $3x$ for y and solve for x.

Solution
$$3x + (x + 40°) = 180°$$
$$4x + 40° = 180°$$
$$4x = 140°$$
$$x = 35°$$

You Try It 7

Strategy
- To find the measure of angle b, use the fact that $\angle b$ and $\angle x$ are supplementary angles.
- To find the measure of angle c, use the fact that the sum of the interior angles of a triangle is 180°.
- To find the measure of angle y, use the fact that $\angle c$ and $\angle y$ are vertical angles.

Solution
$$\angle b + \angle x = 180°$$
$$\angle b + 100° = 180°$$
$$\angle b = 80°$$
$$\angle a + \angle b + \angle c = 180°$$
$$45° + 80° + \angle c = 180°$$
$$125° + \angle c = 180°$$
$$\angle c = 55°$$
$$\angle y = \angle c = 55°$$

You Try It 8

Strategy To find the measure of the third angle, use the fact that the measure of a right angle is 90° and the fact that the sum of the measures of the interior angles of a triangle is 180°. Write an equation using x to represent the measure of the third angle. Solve the equation for x.

Solution
$$x + 90° + 34° = 180°$$
$$x + 124° = 180°$$
$$x = 56°$$

The measure of the third angle is 56°.

SECTION 7.2

You Try It 1

Strategy To find the perimeter, use the formula for the perimeter of a square. Substitute 60 for s and solve for P.

Solution
$$P = 4s$$
$$P = 4(60)$$
$$P = 240$$

The perimeter of the infield is 240 ft.

You Try It 2

Strategy To find the length of molding needed, use the formula for the perimeter of a rectangle. Substitute 12 for L and 8 for W, and solve for P.

Solution
$$P = 2L + 2W$$
$$P = 2(12) + 2(8)$$
$$P = 24 + 16$$
$$P = 40$$

The length of decorative molding needed to edge the tops of the walls is 40 ft.

You Try It 3

Strategy To find the circumference, use the circumference formula that involves the diameter. Leave the answer in terms of π.

Solution
$$C = \pi d$$
$$C = \pi(9)$$
$$C = 9\pi$$

The circumference is 9π in.

You Try It 4

Strategy

To find the number of rolls of wallpaper to be purchased:
- Use the formula for the area of a rectangle to find the area of one wall.
- Multiply the area of one wall by the number of walls to be covered (2).
- Divide the area of wall to be covered by the area one roll of wallpaper will cover (30).

Solution

$A = LW$

$A = 12 \cdot 8 = 96$ • The area of one wall is 96 ft^2.

$2(96) = 192$ • The area of the two walls is 192 ft^2.

$192 \div 30 = 6.4$

Because a portion of a seventh roll is needed, 7 rolls of wallpaper should be purchased.

You Try It 5

Strategy To find the area, use the formula for the area of a circle. An approximation is asked for; use the π key on a calculator. $r = 11$

Solution
$$A = \pi r^2$$
$$A = \pi(11)^2$$
$$A = 121\pi$$
$$A \approx 380.13$$

The area is approximately 380.13 cm^2.

SECTION 7.3

You Try It 1

Strategy To find the measure of the other leg, use the Pythagorean Theorem. $a = 2, c = 6$

Solution

$$a^2 + b^2 = c^2$$
$$2^2 + b^2 = 6^2$$
$$4 + b^2 = 36$$
$$b^2 = 32$$
$$b = \sqrt{32}$$ • The Principal Square Root Property
$$b \approx 5.66$$

The measure of the other leg is approximately 5.66 m.

You Try It 2

Strategy To find FG, write a proportion using the fact that, in similar triangles, the ratio of corresponding sides equals the ratio of corresponding heights. Solve the proportion for FG.

Solution

$$\frac{AC}{DF} = \frac{CH}{FG}$$
$$\frac{10}{15} = \frac{7}{FG}$$
$$10(FG) = 15(7)$$
$$10(FG) = 105$$
$$FG = 10.5$$

The height FG of triangle DEF is 10.5 m.

You Try It 3

Strategy To determine whether the triangles are congruent, determine whether one of the rules for congruence is satisfied.

Solution $PR = MN$, $QR = MO$, and $\angle QRP = \angle OMN$. Two sides and the included angle of one triangle equal two sides and the included angle of the other triangle.

The triangles are congruent by the SAS Rule.

SECTION 7.4

You Try It 1

Strategy To find the volume, use the formula for the volume of a cube. $s = 2.5$

Solution

$$V = s^3$$
$$V = (2.5)^3 = 15.625$$

The volume of the cube is 15.625 m^3.

You Try It 2

Strategy To find the volume:

- Find the radius of the base of the cylinder. $d = 8$
- Use the formula for the volume of a cylinder. Leave the answer in terms of π.

Solution

$$r = \frac{1}{2}d = \frac{1}{2}(8) = 4$$
$$V = \pi r^2 h = \pi(4)^2(22) = \pi(16)(22) = 352\pi$$

The volume of the cylinder is 352π ft^3.

You Try It 3

Strategy To find the surface area:

- Find the radius of the base of the cylinder. $d = 6$
- Use the formula for the surface area of a cylinder. An approximation is asked for; use the π key on a calculator.

Solution

$$r = \frac{1}{2}d = \frac{1}{2}(6) = 3$$
$$SA = 2\pi r^2 + 2\pi rh$$
$$SA = 2\pi(3)^2 + 2\pi(3)(8)$$
$$= 2\pi(9) + 2\pi(3)(8)$$
$$= 18\pi + 48\pi$$
$$= 66\pi$$
$$\approx 207.35$$

The surface area of the cylinder is approximately 207.35 ft^2.

You Try It 4

Strategy To find the surface area, use the formula for the surface area of a cube. $s = 10$

Solution

$$SA = 6s^2$$
$$SA = 6(10)^2$$
$$= 6(100)$$
$$= 600$$

The surface area of the cube is 600 cm^2.

Solutions to Chapter 8 "You Try It"

SECTION 8.1

You Try It 1

Strategy **a.** To find the ratio:

- From the graph, find the percent of lane-change accidents and the percent of road-departure accidents.
- Write the ratio in fractional form. Simplify.

b. To find the number of accidents that occurred at intersections:

- ▶ From the graph, find the percent of accidents that occurred at intersections.
- ▶ Solve the basic percent equation for amount. The base is 4300.

Solution **a.** Lane-change accidents: 9%
Road-departure accidents: 21%

$$\frac{9\%}{21\%} = \frac{3}{7}$$

The ratio is $\frac{3}{7}$.

b. Accidents that occurred at intersections:
26% = 0.26

$$\text{Percent} \cdot \text{base} = \text{amount}$$
$$0.26 \cdot 4300 = n$$
$$1118 = n$$

1118 accidents occurred at intersections in Twin Falls in 2005.

SECTION 8.2

You Try It 1

Strategy To find the mean amount spent by the 12 customers:

- ▶ Find the sum of the numbers.
- ▶ Divide the sum by the number of customers (12).

Solution 11.01 + 10.75 + 12.09 + 15.88 + 13.50 + 12.29 + 10.69 + 9.36 + 11.66 + 15.25 + 10.09 + 12.72 = 145.29

$$\bar{x} = \frac{145.29}{12} \approx 12.11$$

The mean amount spent by the 12 customers was $12.11.

You Try It 2

Strategy To find the median weight loss:

- ▶ Arrange the weight losses from least to greatest.
- ▶ Because there is an even number of values, the median is the mean of the middle two numbers.

Solution 10, 14, 16, 16, 22, 27, 29, 31, 31, 40

$$\text{Median} = \frac{22 + 27}{2} = \frac{49}{2} = 24.5$$

The median weight loss was 24.5 pounds.

You Try It 3

Strategy To draw the box-and-whiskers plot:

- ▶ Find the median, Q_1, and Q_3.
- ▶ Use the least value, Q_1, the median, Q_3, and the greatest value to draw the box-and-whiskers plot.

Solution 4 7 7 8 8 9 13

(Q_1 = 7, Median = 8, Q_3 = 9)

a.

Median
Q_1 Q_3
4 7 8 9 13

b. Answers about the spread of the data will vary. For example, in You Try It 3, the values in the interquartile range are all very close to the median. They are not so close to the median in Example 3. The whiskers are long with respect to the box in You Try It 3, whereas they are short with respect to the box in Example 3. This shows that the data values outside the interquartile range are closer together in Example 3 than in You Try It 3.

SECTION 8.3

You Try It 1

Strategy To find the probability:

- ▶ List the outcomes of the experiment in a systematic way. We will use a table.
- ▶ Use the table to count the number of possible outcomes of the experiment.
- ▶ Count the number of outcomes of the experiment that are favorable to the event of two true questions and one false question.
- ▶ Use the probability formula.

Solution

Question 1	Question 2	Question 3
T	T	T
T	T	F
T	F	T
T	F	F
F	T	T
F	T	F
F	F	T
F	F	F

There are 8 possible outcomes:

S = {TTT, TTF, TFT, TFF, FTT, FTF, FFT, FFF}

There are 3 outcomes favorable to the event:

{TTF, TFT, FTT}

Probability of an event

$$= \frac{\text{number of favorable outcomes}}{\text{number of possible outcomes}} = \frac{3}{8}$$

The probability of two true questions and one false question is $\frac{3}{8}$.

Solutions to Chapter 9 "You Try It"

SECTION 9.1

You Try It 1

$$\begin{aligned}&(-4x^3 + 2x^2 - 8) + (4x^3 + 6x^2 - 7x + 5)\\&= (-4x^3 + 4x^3) + (2x^2 + 6x^2) + (-7x) + (-8 + 5)\\&= 8x^2 - 7x - 3\end{aligned}$$

You Try It 2

$$\begin{array}{r}6x^3 \qquad\quad + 2x + 8\\ -9x^3 + 2x^2 - 12x - 8\\ \hline -3x^3 + 2x^2 - 10x \quad\end{array}$$

You Try It 3

a. $$\begin{aligned}&(-4w^3 + 8w - 8) - (3w^3 - 4w^2 - 2w - 1)\\&= (-4w^3 + 8w - 8)\\&\quad + (-3w^3 + 4w^2 + 2w + 1)\\&= -7w^3 + 4w^2 + 10w - 7\end{aligned}$$

b. $$\begin{array}{r}13y^3 \qquad\quad - 6y - 7\\ - 4y^2 + 6y + 9\\ \hline 13y^3 - 4y^2 \qquad\quad + 2\end{array}$$

SECTION 9.2

You Try It 1

$$\begin{aligned}&(12p^4q^3)(-3p^5q^2)\\&= [12(-3)](p^4 \cdot p^5)(q^3 \cdot q^2)\\&= -36p^9q^5\end{aligned}$$

• Multiply coefficients. Add exponents with the same base.

You Try It 2

$$\begin{aligned}(-xy^4)(-2x^3y^2)^2 &= (-xy^4)[(-2)^{1\cdot 2}x^{3\cdot 2}y^{2\cdot 2}]\\&= (-xy^4)[(-2)^2x^6y^4]\\&= (-xy^4)(4x^6y^4)\\&= -4x^7y^8\end{aligned}$$

• Rule for Simplifying the Power of a Product

SECTION 9.3

You Try It 1

$$(-2y + 3)(-4y) = -2y(-4y) + 3(-4y) = 8y^2 - 12y$$

You Try It 2

$$\begin{aligned}-a^2(3a^2 + 2a - 7) &= -a^2(3a^2) + (-a^2)(2a) - (-a^2)(7)\\&= -3a^4 - 2a^3 + 7a^2\end{aligned}$$

You Try It 3

$$\begin{array}{rl}2y^3 + 2y^2 \qquad - 3 & \\ 3y - 1 & \\ \hline -2y^3 - 2y^2 \qquad + 3 & = -1(2y^3 + 2y^2 - 3)\\ 6y^4 + 6y^3 \qquad - 9y \quad & = 3y(2y^3 + 2y^2 - 3)\\ \hline 6y^4 + 4y^3 - 2y^2 - 9y + 3 & \end{array}$$

You Try It 4

$$\begin{aligned}(4y - 5)(2y - 3) &= 8y^2 - 12y - 10y + 15\\&= 8y^2 - 22y + 15\end{aligned}$$

You Try It 5

$$\begin{aligned}(3b + 2)(3b - 5) &= 9b^2 - 15b + 6b - 10\\&= 9b^2 - 9b - 10\end{aligned}$$

You Try It 6 $(2a + 5c)(2a - 5c) = 4a^2 - 25c^2$

You Try It 7 $(3x + 2y)^2 = 9x^2 + 12xy + 4y^2$

You Try It 8

Strategy To find the area, replace the variable r in the equation $A = \pi r^2$ by $(x - 4)$ and solve for A.

Solution

$$\begin{aligned}A &= \pi r^2\\A &= \pi(x - 4)^2\\A &= \pi(x^2 - 8x + 16)\\A &= \pi x^2 - 8\pi x + 16\pi\end{aligned}$$

The area of the circle is $(\pi x^2 - 8\pi x + 16\pi)$ ft^2.

SECTION 9.4

You Try It 1

$$\begin{aligned}&(-2x^2)(x^{-3}y^{-4})^{-2}\\&= (-2x^2)(x^6y^8)\\&= -2x^8y^8\end{aligned}$$

• Rule for Simplifying the Power of a Product

You Try It 2

$$\begin{aligned}&\frac{(6a^{-2}b^3)^{-1}}{(4a^3b^{-2})^{-2}}\\&= \frac{6^{-1}a^2b^{-3}}{4^{-2}a^{-6}b^4}\\&= 4^2(6^{-1}a^8b^{-7})\\&= \frac{16a^8}{6b^7} = \frac{8a^8}{3b^7}\end{aligned}$$

• Rule for Simplifying the Power of a Product

• Rule for Dividing Exponential Expressions

You Try It 3

$$\left[\frac{6r^3s^{-3}}{9r^3s^{-1}}\right]^{-2} = \left[\frac{2r^0s^{-2}}{3}\right]^{-2} = \frac{2^{-2}s^4}{3^{-2}} = \frac{9s^4}{4}$$

You Try It 4 $290{,}000{,}000{,}000 = 2.9 \times 10^{11}$

You Try It 5 $0.000000961 = 9.61 \times 10^{-7}$

You Try It 6 $7.329 \times 10^6 = 7{,}329{,}000$

You Try It 7 $1.802 \times 10^{-12} = 0.000000000001802$

SECTION 9.5

You Try It 1

$$\begin{aligned}\frac{24x^2y^2 - 18xy + 6y}{6xy} &= \frac{24x^2y^2}{6xy} - \frac{18xy}{6xy} + \frac{6y}{6xy}\\&= 4xy - 3 + \frac{1}{x}\end{aligned}$$

You Try It 2

$$\begin{array}{r} x^2 + 2x - 1 \\ 2x - 3\overline{)2x^3 + x^2 - 8x - 3} \\ \underline{2x^3 - 3x^2} \\ 4x^2 - 8x \\ \underline{4x^2 - 6x} \\ -2x - 3 \\ \underline{-2x + 3} \\ -6 \end{array}$$

$$(2x^3 + x^2 - 8x - 3) \div (2x - 3)$$
$$= x^2 + 2x - 1 - \frac{6}{2x - 3}$$

You Try It 3

$$\begin{array}{r} x^2 + x - 1 \\ x - 1\overline{)x^3 + 0x^2 - 2x + 1} \\ \underline{x^3 - x^2} \\ x^2 - 2x \\ \underline{x^2 - x} \\ -x + 1 \\ \underline{-x + 1} \\ 0 \end{array}$$

$$(x^3 - 2x + 1) \div (x - 1) = x^2 + x - 1$$

Solutions to Chapter 10 "You Try It"

SECTION 10.1

You Try It 1 The GCF is $7a^2$.

$$14a^2 - 21a^4b = 7a^2(2) + 7a^2(-3a^2b)$$
$$= 7a^2(2 - 3a^2b)$$

You Try It 2 The GCF is 9.

$$27b^2 + 18b + 9$$
$$= 9(3b^2) + 9(2b) + 9(1)$$
$$= 9(3b^2 + 2b + 1)$$

You Try It 3

The GCF is $3x^2y^2$.

$$6x^4y^2 - 9x^3y^2 + 12x^2y^4$$
$$= 3x^2y^2(2x^2) + 3x^2y^2(-3x) + 3x^2y^2(4y^2)$$
$$= 3x^2y^2(2x^2 - 3x + 4y^2)$$

You Try It 4

$$2y(5x - 2) - 3(2 - 5x)$$
$$= 2y(5x - 2) + 3(5x - 2)$$
$$= (5x - 2)(2y + 3)$$

- **$5x - 2$ is the common factor.**

You Try It 5

$$a^2 - 3a + 2ab - 6b$$
$$= (a^2 - 3a) + (2ab - 6b)$$
$$= a(a - 3) + 2b(a - 3)$$
$$= (a - 3)(a + 2b)$$

- **$a - 3$ is the common factor.**

You Try It 6

$$2mn^2 - n + 8mn - 4$$
$$= (2mn^2 - n) + (8mn - 4)$$
$$= n(2mn - 1) + 4(2mn - 1)$$
$$= (2mn - 1)(n + 4)$$

- **$2mn - 1$ is the common factor.**

You Try It 7

$$3xy - 9y - 12 + 4x$$
$$= (3xy - 9y) - (12 - 4x)$$
$$= 3y(x - 3) - 4(3 - x)$$
$$= 3y(x - 3) + 4(x - 3)$$
$$= (x - 3)(3y + 4)$$

- **$-12 + 4x = -(12 - 4x)$**
- **$-(3 - x) = (x - 3)$**
- **$x - 3$ is the common factor.**

SECTION 10.2

You Try It 1

Find the positive factors of 20 whose sum is 9.

Factors	Sum
1, 20	21
2, 10	12
4, 5	**9**

$$x^2 + 9x + 20 = (x + 4)(x + 5)$$

You Try It 2

Find the factors of -18 whose sum is 7.

Factors	Sum
+1, −18	−17
−1, +18	17
+2, −9	−7
−2, +9	**7**
+3, −6	−3
−3, +6	3

$$x^2 + 7x - 18 = (x + 9)(x - 2)$$

You Try It 3

The GCF is $-2x$.

$$-2x^3 + 14x^2 - 12x = -2x(x^2 - 7x + 6)$$

Factor the trinomial $x^2 - 7x + 6$. Find two negative factors of 6 whose sum is -7.

Factors	Sum
−1, −6	**−7**
−2, −3	−5

$$-2x^3 + 14x^2 - 12x = -2x(x - 6)(x - 1)$$

You Try It 4

The GCF is 3.

$3x^2 - 9xy - 12y^2 = 3(x^2 - 3xy - 4y^2)$

Factor the trinomial.

Find the factors of -4 whose sum is -3.

Factors	Sum
+1, −4	**−3**
−1, +4	3
+2, −2	0

$3x^2 - 9xy - 12y^2 = 3(x + y)(x - 4y)$

SECTION 10.3

You Try It 1

Factor the trinomial $2x^2 - x - 3$.

Positive factors of 2: 1, 2

Factors of -3: $+1, -3$; $-1, +3$

Trial Factors	Middle Term
$(x + 1)(2x - 3)$	$-3x + 2x = \mathbf{-x}$
$(x - 3)(2x + 1)$	$x - 6x = -5x$
$(x - 1)(2x + 3)$	$3x - 2x = x$
$(x + 3)(2x - 1)$	$-x + 6x = 5x$

$2x^2 - x - 3 = (x + 1)(2x - 3)$

You Try It 2

The GCF is $-3y$.

$-45y^3 + 12y^2 + 12y = -3y(15y^2 - 4y - 4)$

Factor the trinomial $15y^2 - 4y - 4$.

Positive factors of 15: 1, 15; 3, 5

Factors of -4: $1, -4$; $-1, 4$; $2, -2$

Trial Factors	Middle Term
$(y + 1)(15y - 4)$	$-4y + 15y = 11y$
$(y - 4)(15y + 1)$	$y - 60y = -59y$
$(y - 1)(15y + 4)$	$4y - 15y = -11y$
$(y + 4)(15y - 1)$	$-y + 60y = 59y$
$(y + 2)(15y - 2)$	$-2y + 30y = 28y$
$(y - 2)(15y + 2)$	$2y - 30y = -28y$
$(3y + 1)(5y - 4)$	$-12y + 5y = -7y$
$(3y - 4)(5y + 1)$	$3y - 20y = -17y$
$(3y - 1)(5y + 4)$	$12y - 5y = 7y$
$(3y + 4)(5y - 1)$	$-3y + 20y = 17y$
$(3y + 2)(5y - 2)$	$-6y + 10y = 4y$
$(3y - 2)(5y + 2)$	$6y - 10y = \mathbf{-4y}$

$-45y^3 + 12y^2 + 12y = -3y(3y - 2)(5y + 2)$

You Try It 3

Factors of −14 [2(−7)]	Sum
+1, −14	−13
−1, +14	**13**
+2, −7	−5
−2, +7	5

$$\begin{aligned} 2a^2 + 13a - 7 &= 2a^2 - a + 14a - 7 \\ &= (2a^2 - a) + (14a - 7) \\ &= a(2a - 1) + 7(2a - 1) \\ &= (2a - 1)(a + 7) \end{aligned}$$

$2a^2 + 13a - 7 = (2a - 1)(a + 7)$

You Try It 4

The GCF is $5x$.

$15x^3 + 40x^2 - 80x = 5x(3x^2 + 8x - 16)$

Factors of -48 $[3(-16)]$	Sum
$+1, -48$	-47
$-1, +48$	47
$+2, -24$	-22
$-2, +24$	22
$+3, -16$	-13
$-3, +16$	13
$+4, -12$	-8
$-4, +12$	**8**

$$\begin{aligned}3x^2 + 8x - 16 &= 3x^2 - 4x + 12x - 16\\ &= (3x^2 - 4x) + (12x - 16)\\ &= x(3x - 4) + 4(3x - 4)\\ &= (3x - 4)(x + 4)\end{aligned}$$

$$\begin{aligned}15x^3 + 40x^2 - 80x &= 5x(3x^2 + 8x - 16)\\ &= 5x(3x - 4)(x + 4)\end{aligned}$$

SECTION 10.4

You Try It 1

$$\begin{aligned}25a^2 - b^2 &= (5a)^2 - b^2 && \text{• Difference of two squares}\\ &= (5a + b)(5a - b)\end{aligned}$$

You Try It 2

$$\begin{aligned}n^4 - 81 &= (n^2)^2 - 9^2 && \text{• Difference of two squares}\\ &= (n^2 + 9)(n^2 - 9) && \text{• Difference of two squares}\\ &= (n^2 + 9)(n + 3)(n - 3)\end{aligned}$$

You Try It 3 Because $16y^2 = (4y)^2$, $1 = 1^2$, and $8y = 2(4y)(1)$, the trinomial is a perfect-square trinomial.

$16y^2 + 8y + 1 = (4y + 1)^2$

You Try It 4 $x^2 = (x)^2$ and $36 = 6^2$

Because $2(x)(6) \neq 15x$, the trinomial is not a perfect-square trinomial. Try to factor the trinomial by another method.

$x^2 + 15x + 36 = (x + 3)(x + 12)$

SECTION 10.5

You Try It 1

The GCF is $4x$.

$$\begin{aligned}&4x^3 + 28x^2 - 120x\\ &= 4x(x^2 + 7x - 30) && \text{• Factor out the GCF, } 4x.\\ &= 4x(x + 10)(x - 3) && \text{• Factor the trinomial.}\end{aligned}$$

SECTION 10.6

You Try It 1

$2x(x + 7) = 0$

$$\begin{aligned}2x &= 0 \qquad & x + 7 &= 0 && \text{• Principle of Zero Products}\\ x &= 0 & x &= -7\end{aligned}$$

The solutions are 0 and -7.

You Try It 2

$$\begin{aligned}4x^2 - 9 &= 0 && \text{• Difference of two squares}\\ (2x - 3)(2x + 3) &= 0\end{aligned}$$

$$\begin{aligned}2x - 3 &= 0 \qquad & 2x + 3 &= 0 && \text{• Principle of Zero Products}\\ 2x &= 3 & 2x &= -3\\ x &= \frac{3}{2} & x &= -\frac{3}{2}\end{aligned}$$

The solutions are $\frac{3}{2}$ and $-\frac{3}{2}$.

You Try It 3

$$\begin{aligned}(x + 2)(x - 7) &= 52\\ x^2 - 5x - 14 &= 52\\ x^2 - 5x - 66 &= 0\\ (x + 6)(x - 11) &= 0\end{aligned}$$

$$\begin{aligned}x + 6 &= 0 \qquad & x - 11 &= 0 && \text{• Principle of Zero Products}\\ x &= -6 & x &= 11\end{aligned}$$

The solutions are -6 and 11.

You Try It 4

Strategy First consecutive positive integer: n

Second consecutive positive integer: $n + 1$

The sum of the squares of the two consecutive positive integers is 61.

Solution

$$\begin{aligned}n^2 + (n + 1)^2 &= 61\\ n^2 + n^2 + 2n + 1 &= 61\\ 2n^2 + 2n + 1 &= 61\\ 2n^2 + 2n - 60 &= 0\\ 2(n^2 + n - 30) &= 0\\ 2(n - 5)(n + 6) &= 0\end{aligned}$$

$$\begin{aligned}n - 5 &= 0 \qquad & n + 6 &= 0 && \text{• Principle of Zero Products}\\ n &= 5 & n &= -6\end{aligned}$$

Because -6 is not a positive integer, it is not a solution.

$n = 5$

$n + 1 = 5 + 1 = 6$

The two integers are 5 and 6.

You Try It 5

Strategy Width $= x$

Length $= 2x + 4$

The area of the rectangle is 96 in^2.

Use the equation $A = L \cdot W$.

Solution

$$A = L \cdot W$$
$$96 = (2x + 4)x$$
$$96 = 2x^2 + 4x$$
$$0 = 2x^2 + 4x - 96$$
$$0 = 2(x^2 + 2x - 48)$$
$$0 = 2(x + 8)(x - 6)$$

$x + 8 = 0 \quad x - 6 = 0$ • Principle of Zero Products

$x = -8 \quad x = 6$

Because the width cannot be a negative number, -8 is not a solution.

$x = 6$

$2x + 4 = 2(6) + 4 = 12 + 4 = 16$

The length is 16 in. The width is 6 in.

Solutions to Chapter 11 "You Try It"

SECTION 11.1

You Try It 1

$$\frac{6x^5y}{12x^2y^3} = \frac{\overset{1}{\cancel{2}} \cdot \overset{1}{\cancel{3}} \cdot x^5y}{\underset{1}{\cancel{2}} \cdot 2 \cdot \underset{1}{\cancel{3}} \cdot x^2y^3} = \frac{x^3}{2y^2}$$

You Try It 2

$$\frac{x^2 + 4x - 12}{x^2 - 3x + 2} = \frac{\overset{1}{\cancel{(x - 2)}}(x + 6)}{(x - 1)\underset{1}{\cancel{(x - 2)}}} = \frac{x + 6}{x - 1}$$

You Try It 3

$$\frac{x^2 + 2x - 24}{16 - x^2} = \frac{\overset{-1}{\cancel{(x - 4)}}(x + 6)}{\underset{1}{\cancel{(4 - x)}}(4 + x)}$$
$$= -\frac{x + 6}{x + 4}$$

• $\frac{x - 4}{4 - x} = \frac{x - 4}{-1(x - 4)} = -1$

You Try It 4

$$\frac{12x^2 + 3x}{10x - 15} \cdot \frac{8x - 12}{9x + 18} = \frac{3x(4x + 1)}{5(2x - 3)} \cdot \frac{4(2x - 3)}{9(x + 2)}$$
$$= \frac{\overset{1}{\cancel{3}}x(4x + 1) \cdot 4\overset{1}{\cancel{(2x - 3)}}}{5\underset{1}{\cancel{(2x - 3)}} \cdot \underset{1}{\cancel{3}} \cdot 3(x + 2)}$$
$$= \frac{4x(4x + 1)}{15(x + 2)}$$

You Try It 5

$$\frac{x^2 + 2x - 15}{9 - x^2} \cdot \frac{x^2 - 3x - 18}{x^2 - 7x + 6}$$
$$= \frac{(x - 3)(x + 5)}{(3 - x)(3 + x)} \cdot \frac{(x + 3)(x - 6)}{(x - 1)(x - 6)}$$ • Factor.
$$= \frac{\overset{-1}{\cancel{(x - 3)}}(x + 5) \cdot \overset{1}{\cancel{(x + 3)}}\overset{1}{\cancel{(x - 6)}}}{\underset{1}{\cancel{(3 - x)}}\underset{1}{\cancel{(3 + x)}} \cdot (x - 1)\underset{1}{\cancel{(x - 6)}}} = -\frac{x + 5}{x - 1}$$

You Try It 6

$$\frac{a^2}{4bc^2 - 2b^2c} \div \frac{a}{6bc - 3b^2}$$
$$= \frac{a^2}{4bc^2 - 2b^2c} \cdot \frac{6bc - 3b^2}{a}$$ • Multiply by the reciprocal.
$$= \frac{a^2 \cdot 3\overset{1}{\cancel{b}}\overset{1}{\cancel{(2c - b)}}}{2\underset{1}{\cancel{b}}c\underset{1}{\cancel{(2c - b)}} \cdot a} = \frac{3a}{2c}$$

You Try It 7

$$\frac{3x^2 + 26x + 16}{3x^2 - 7x - 6} \div \frac{2x^2 + 9x - 5}{x^2 + 2x - 15}$$
$$= \frac{3x^2 + 26x + 16}{3x^2 - 7x - 6} \cdot \frac{x^2 + 2x - 15}{2x^2 + 9x - 5}$$ • Multiply by the reciprocal.
$$= \frac{\overset{1}{\cancel{(3x + 2)}}(x + 8) \cdot \overset{1}{\cancel{(x + 5)}}\overset{1}{\cancel{(x - 3)}}}{\underset{1}{\cancel{(3x + 2)}}\underset{1}{\cancel{(x - 3)}} \cdot (2x - 1)\underset{1}{\cancel{(x + 5)}}} = \frac{x + 8}{2x - 1}$$

SECTION 11.2

You Try It 1

$8uv^2 = 2 \cdot 2 \cdot 2 \cdot u \cdot v \cdot v$

$12uw = 2 \cdot 2 \cdot 3 \cdot u \cdot w$

$\text{LCM} = 2 \cdot 2 \cdot 2 \cdot 3 \cdot u \cdot v \cdot v \cdot w = 24uv^2w$

You Try It 2

$m^2 - 6m + 9 = (m - 3)(m - 3)$

$m^2 - 2m - 3 = (m + 1)(m - 3)$

$\text{LCM} = (m - 3)(m - 3)(m + 1)$

You Try It 3

The LCM is $36xy^2z$.

$$\frac{x - 3}{4xy^2} = \frac{x - 3}{4xy^2} \cdot \frac{9z}{9z} = \frac{9xz - 27z}{36xy^2z}$$
$$\frac{2x + 1}{9y^2z} = \frac{2x + 1}{9y^2z} \cdot \frac{4x}{4x} = \frac{8x^2 + 4x}{36xy^2z}$$

You Try It 4

The LCM is $(x + 2)(x - 5)(x + 5)$.

$$\frac{x + 4}{x^2 - 3x - 10} = \frac{x + 4}{(x + 2)(x - 5)} \cdot \frac{x + 5}{x + 5}$$
$$= \frac{x^2 + 9x + 20}{(x + 2)(x - 5)(x + 5)}$$
$$\frac{2x}{25 - x^2} = \frac{2x}{-(x^2 - 25)} = -\frac{2x}{(x - 5)(x + 5)} \cdot \frac{x + 2}{x + 2}$$
$$= -\frac{2x^2 + 4x}{(x + 2)(x - 5)(x + 5)}$$

SECTION 11.3

You Try It 1

$$\frac{2x^2}{x^2 - x - 12} - \frac{7x + 4}{x^2 - x - 12}$$
$$= \frac{2x^2 - (7x + 4)}{x^2 - x - 12} = \frac{2x^2 - 7x - 4}{x^2 - x - 12}$$
$$= \frac{(2x + 1)\overset{1}{\cancel{(x - 4)}}}{(x + 3)\underset{1}{\cancel{(x - 4)}}} = \frac{2x + 1}{x + 3}$$

You Try It 2

$$\frac{x^2-1}{x^2-8x+12}-\frac{2x+1}{x^2-8x+12}+\frac{x}{x^2-8x+12}$$

$$=\frac{(x^2-1)-(2x+1)+x}{x^2-8x+12}=\frac{x^2-1-2x-1+x}{x^2-8x+12}$$

$$=\frac{x^2-x-2}{x^2-8x+12}=\frac{(x+1)\overset{1}{\cancel{(x-2)}}}{\underset{1}{\cancel{(x-2)}}(x-6)}=\frac{x+1}{x-6}$$

You Try It 3

The LCM of the denominators is $24y$.

$$\frac{z}{8y}-\frac{4z}{3y}+\frac{5z}{4y}$$

$$=\frac{z}{8y}\cdot\frac{3}{3}-\frac{4z}{3y}\cdot\frac{8}{8}+\frac{5z}{4y}\cdot\frac{6}{6}$$ • Write each fraction using the LCM.

$$=\frac{3z}{24y}-\frac{32z}{24y}+\frac{30z}{24y}$$

$$=\frac{3z-32z+30z}{24y}=\frac{z}{24y}$$ • Combine the numerators.

You Try It 4 The LCM is $x-3$.

$$2-\frac{1}{x-3}=2\cdot\frac{x-3}{x-3}-\frac{1}{x-3}$$

$$=\frac{2x-6}{x-3}-\frac{1}{x-3}$$

$$=\frac{2x-6-1}{x-3}$$

$$=\frac{2x-7}{x-3}$$

You Try It 5

$2-x=-(x-2)$; therefore, $\frac{3}{2-x}=\frac{-3}{x-2}$.

$$\frac{5x}{x-2}+\frac{3}{2-x}=\frac{5x}{x-2}+\frac{-3}{x-2}$$ • The LCM is $x-2$.

$$=\frac{5x+(-3)}{x-2}=\frac{5x-3}{x-2}$$ • Combine the numerators.

You Try It 6

The LCM is $(3x-1)(x+4)$.

$$\frac{4x}{3x-1}+\frac{9}{x+4}=\frac{4x}{3x-1}\cdot\frac{x+4}{x+4}+\frac{9}{x+4}\cdot\frac{3x-1}{3x-1}$$

$$=\frac{4x^2+16x}{(3x-1)(x+4)}+\frac{27x-9}{(3x-1)(x+4)}$$

$$=\frac{(4x^2+16x)+(27x-9)}{(3x-1)(x+4)}$$

$$=\frac{4x^2+16x+27x-9}{(3x-1)(x+4)}$$

$$=\frac{4x^2+43x-9}{(3x-1)(x+4)}$$

You Try It 7

$$\frac{2}{5-x}=\frac{-2}{x-5}$$

The LCM is $(x+5)(x-5)$.

$$\frac{2x-1}{x^2-25}+\frac{2}{5-x}=\frac{2x-1}{(x+5)(x-5)}+\frac{-2}{x-5}$$

$$=\frac{2x-1}{(x+5)(x-5)}+\frac{-2}{x-5}\cdot\frac{x+5}{x+5}$$

$$=\frac{2x-1}{(x+5)(x-5)}+\frac{-2(x+5)}{(x+5)(x-5)}$$

$$=\frac{2x-1+(-2)(x+5)}{(x+5)(x-5)}$$

$$=\frac{2x-1-2x-10}{(x+5)(x-5)}$$

$$=\frac{-11}{(x+5)(x-5)}$$

$$=-\frac{11}{(x+5)(x-5)}$$

You Try It 8

The LCM is $(3x+2)(x-1)$.

$$\frac{2x-3}{3x^2-x-2}+\frac{5}{3x+2}-\frac{1}{x-1}$$

$$=\frac{2x-3}{(3x+2)(x-1)}+\frac{5}{3x+2}\cdot\frac{x-1}{x-1}$$

$$-\frac{1}{x-1}\cdot\frac{3x+2}{3x+2}$$

$$=\frac{2x-3}{(3x+2)(x-1)}+\frac{5x-5}{(3x+2)(x-1)}$$

$$-\frac{3x+2}{(3x+2)(x-1)}$$

$$=\frac{(2x-3)+(5x-5)-(3x+2)}{(3x+2)(x-1)}$$

$$=\frac{2x-3+5x-5-3x-2}{(3x+2)(x-1)}$$

$$=\frac{4x-10}{(3x+2)(x-1)}=\frac{2(2x-5)}{(3x+2)(x-1)}$$

SECTION 11.4

You Try It 1

The LCM of 3, x, 9, and x^2 is $9x^2$.

$$\frac{\frac{1}{3}-\frac{1}{x}}{\frac{1}{9}-\frac{1}{x^2}}=\frac{\frac{1}{3}-\frac{1}{x}}{\frac{1}{9}-\frac{1}{x^2}}\cdot\frac{9x^2}{9x^2}=\frac{\frac{1}{3}\cdot 9x^2-\frac{1}{x}\cdot 9x^2}{\frac{1}{9}\cdot 9x^2-\frac{1}{x^2}\cdot 9x^2}$$ • Multiply by the LCM.

$$=\frac{3x^2-9x}{x^2-9}=\frac{3x\overset{1}{\cancel{(x-3)}}}{\underset{1}{\cancel{(x-3)}}(x+3)}=\frac{3x}{x+3}$$

You Try It 2

The LCM of x and x^2 is x^2.

$$\frac{1+\frac{4}{x}+\frac{3}{x^2}}{1+\frac{10}{x}+\frac{21}{x^2}} = \frac{1+\frac{4}{x}+\frac{3}{x^2}}{1+\frac{10}{x}+\frac{21}{x^2}}\cdot\frac{x^2}{x^2}$$ • Multiply by the LCM.

$$= \frac{1\cdot x^2+\frac{4}{x}\cdot x^2+\frac{3}{x^2}\cdot x^2}{1\cdot x^2+\frac{10}{x}\cdot x^2+\frac{21}{x^2}\cdot x^2}$$ • Distributive Property

$$= \frac{x^2+4x+3}{x^2+10x+21} = \frac{(x+1)\overset{1}{\cancel{(x+3)}}}{\underset{1}{\cancel{(x+3)}}(x+7)}$$

$$= \frac{x+1}{x+7}$$

You Try It 3

The LCM is $x - 5$.

$$\frac{x+3-\frac{20}{x-5}}{x+8+\frac{30}{x-5}} = \frac{x+3-\frac{20}{x-5}}{x+8+\frac{30}{x-5}}\cdot\frac{x-5}{x-5}$$

$$= \frac{(x+3)(x-5)-\frac{20}{x-5}\cdot(x-5)}{(x+8)(x-5)+\frac{30}{x-5}\cdot(x-5)}$$

$$= \frac{x^2-2x-15-20}{x^2+3x-40+30} = \frac{x^2-2x-35}{x^2+3x-10}$$

$$= \frac{\overset{1}{\cancel{(x+5)}}(x-7)}{(x-2)\underset{1}{\cancel{(x+5)}}} = \frac{x-7}{x-2}$$

SECTION 11.5

You Try It 1

$$\frac{x}{x+6} = \frac{3}{x}$$ • The LCM is $x(x + 6)$.

$$\frac{x\overset{1}{\cancel{(x+6)}}}{1}\cdot\frac{x}{\underset{1}{\cancel{x+6}}} = \frac{x(x+6)}{1}\cdot\frac{3}{x}$$ • Multiply by the LCM.

$$x^2 = (x+6)3$$ • Simplify.

$$x^2 = 3x + 18$$

$$x^2 - 3x - 18 = 0$$ • Standard form

$$(x+3)(x-6) = 0$$ • Factor.

$x + 3 = 0 \qquad x - 6 = 0$ • Principle of Zero Products

$x = -3 \qquad x = 6$

Both -3 and 6 check as solutions.

The solutions are -3 and 6.

You Try It 2

$$\frac{5x}{x+2} = 3 - \frac{10}{x+2}$$ • The LCM is $x + 2$.

$$\frac{(x+2)}{1}\cdot\frac{5x}{x+2} = \frac{(x+2)}{1}\left(3-\frac{10}{x+2}\right)$$ • Clear denominators.

$$\frac{\overset{1}{\cancel{x+2}}}{1}\cdot\frac{5x}{\underset{1}{\cancel{x+2}}} = \frac{x+2}{1}\cdot 3 - \frac{\overset{1}{\cancel{x+2}}}{1}\cdot\frac{10}{\underset{1}{\cancel{x+2}}}$$

$$5x = (x+2)3 - 10$$ • Solve for x.

$$5x = 3x + 6 - 10$$

$$5x = 3x - 4$$

$$2x = -4$$

$$x = -2$$

-2 does not check as a solution.

The equation has no solution.

SECTION 11.6

You Try It 1

$$5x - 2y = 10$$

$$5x - 5x - 2y = -5x + 10$$ • Subtract $5x$.

$$-2y = -5x + 10$$

$$\frac{-2y}{-2} = \frac{-5x+10}{-2}$$ • Divide by -2.

$$y = \frac{5}{2}x - 5$$

You Try It 2

$$s = \frac{A+L}{2}$$

$$2\cdot s = 2\left(\frac{A+L}{2}\right)$$ • Multiply by 2.

$$2s = A + L$$

$$2s - A = A - A + L$$ • Subtract A.

$$2s - A = L$$

You Try It 3

$$S = a + (n-1)d$$

$$S = a + nd - d$$ • Distributive Property

$$S - a = a - a + nd - d$$ • Subtract a.

$$S - a = nd - d$$

$$S - a + d = nd - d + d$$ • Add d.

$$S - a + d = nd$$

$$\frac{S-a+d}{d} = \frac{nd}{d}$$ • Divide by d.

$$\frac{S-a+d}{d} = n$$

You Try It 4

$$S = rS + C$$
$$S - rS = rS - rS + C \quad \text{• Subtract } rS.$$
$$S - rS = C$$
$$(1 - r)S = C \quad \text{• Factor.}$$
$$\frac{(1 - r)S}{1 - r} = \frac{C}{1 - r} \quad \text{• Divide by } 1 - r.$$
$$S = \frac{C}{1 - r}$$

SECTION 11.7

You Try It 1

Strategy

► Time for one printer to complete the job: t

	Rate	Time	Part
1st printer	$\frac{1}{t}$	2	$\frac{2}{t}$
2nd printer	$\frac{1}{t}$	5	$\frac{5}{t}$

► The sum of the parts of the task completed must equal 1.

Solution

$$\frac{2}{t} + \frac{5}{t} = 1$$
$$t\left(\frac{2}{t} + \frac{5}{t}\right) = t \cdot 1$$
$$2 + 5 = t$$
$$7 = t$$

Working alone, one printer takes 7 h to print the payroll.

You Try It 2

Strategy

► Rate sailing across the lake: r
Rate sailing back: $3r$

	Distance	Rate	Time
Across	6	r	$\frac{6}{r}$
Back	6	$3r$	$\frac{6}{3r}$

► The total time for the trip was 2 h.

Solution

$$\frac{6}{r} + \frac{6}{3r} = 2$$
$$3r\left(\frac{6}{r} + \frac{6}{3r}\right) = 3r(2) \quad \text{• Multiply by the LCM, } 3r.$$
$$3r \cdot \frac{6}{r} + 3r \cdot \frac{6}{3r} = 6r$$
$$18 + 6 = 6r \quad \text{• Solve for } r.$$
$$24 = 6r$$
$$4 = r$$

The rate sailing across the lake was 4 km/h.

Solutions to Chapter 12 "You Try It"

SECTION 12.1

You Try It 1

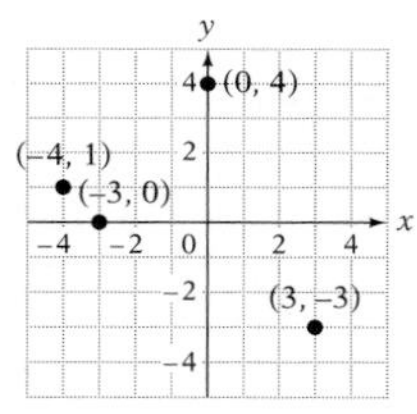

You Try It 2

$A(4, -2)$, $B(-2, 4)$
The abscissa of D is 0.
The ordinate of C is 0.

You Try It 3

$x - 3y$	$= -14$
$-2 - 3(4)$	-14
$-2 - 12$	-14
-14	$= -14$

Yes, $(-2, 4)$ is a solution of $x - 3y = -14$.

You Try It 4

$$x + 2y = 4$$
$$2y = -x + 4$$

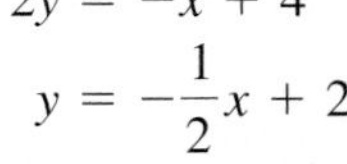

$$y = -\frac{1}{2}x + 2$$

x	y
−4	4
−2	3
0	2
2	1

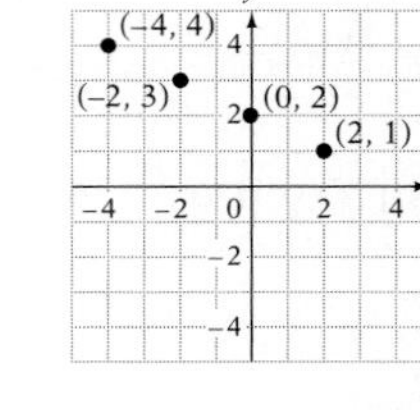

You Try It 5

$\{(145, 140), (140, 125), (150, 130), (165, 150), (140, 130)\}$
No, the relation is not a function. The two ordered pairs $(140, 125)$ and $(140, 130)$ have the same first coordinate but different second coordinates.

You Try It 6 Determine the ordered pairs defined by the equation. Replace x in $y = \frac{1}{2}x + 1$ by the given values and solve for y: $\{(-4, -1), (0, 1), (2, 2)\}$.
Yes, y is a function of x.

You Try It 7

$$H(x) = \frac{x}{x - 4}$$

$$H(8) = \frac{8}{8 - 4} \qquad \bullet \text{ Replace } x \text{ by } 8.$$

$$H(8) = \frac{8}{4} = 2$$

SECTION 12.2

You Try It 1

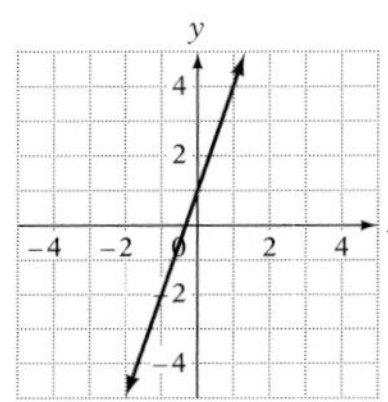

You Try It 2

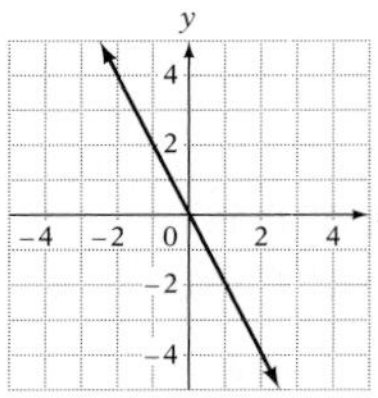

You Try It 3

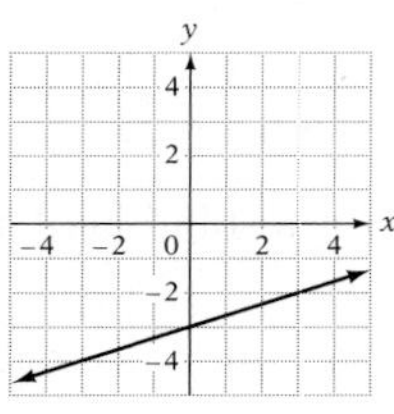

You Try It 4

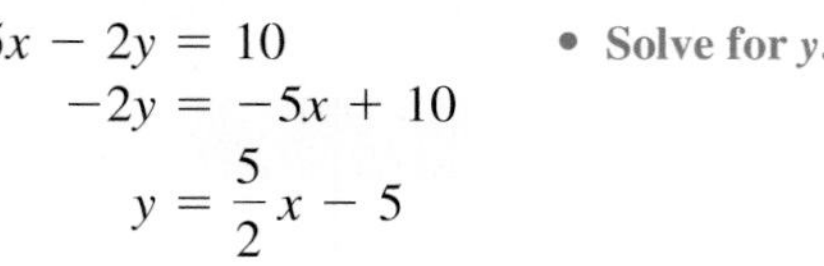

$$5x - 2y = 10 \qquad \bullet \text{ Solve for } y.$$

$$-2y = -5x + 10$$

$$y = \frac{5}{2}x - 5$$

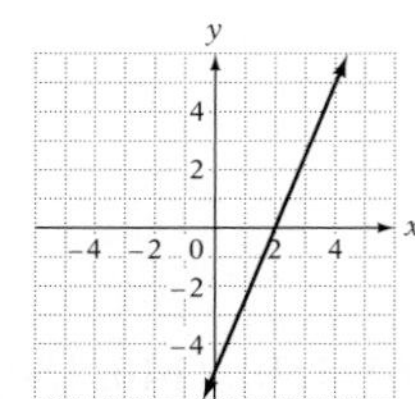

You Try It 5

$$x - 3y = 9 \qquad \bullet \text{ Solve for } y.$$

$$-3y = -x + 9$$

$$y = \frac{1}{3}x - 3$$

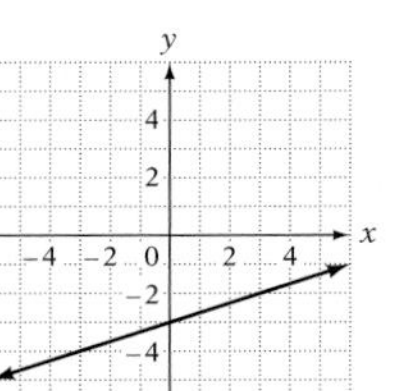

You Try It 6

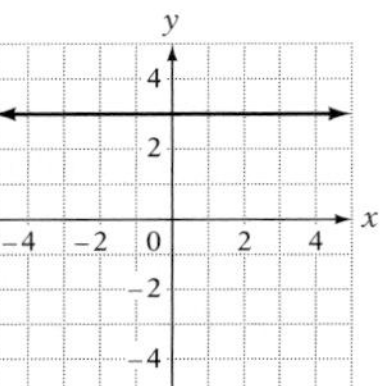

You Try It 7

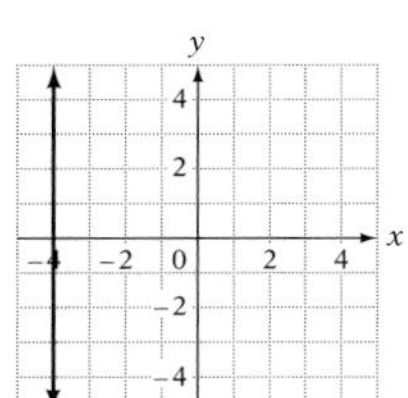

You Try It 8 The ordered pair $(3, 120)$ means that in 3 h, the car will have traveled 120 mi.

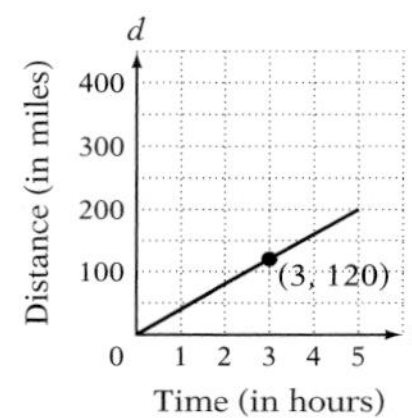

SECTION 12.3

You Try It 1

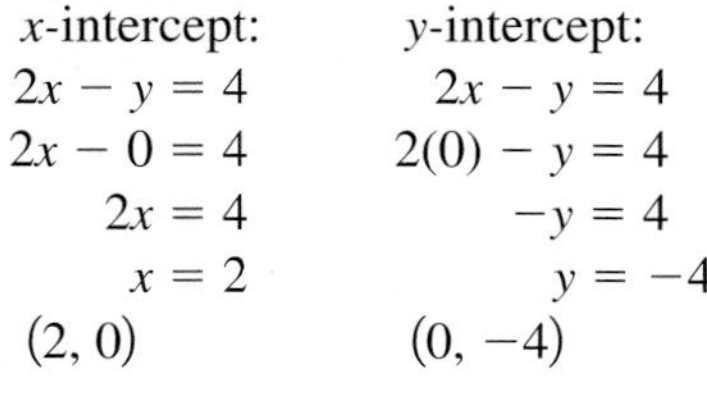

x-intercept:	y-intercept:
$2x - y = 4$	$2x - y = 4$
$2x - 0 = 4$	$2(0) - y = 4$
$2x = 4$	$-y = 4$
$x = 2$	$y = -4$
$(2, 0)$	$(0, -4)$

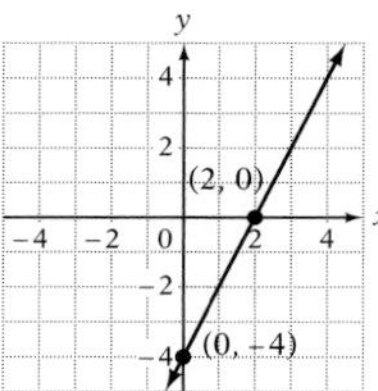

You Try It 2 Let $P_1 = (1, 4)$ and $P_2 = (-3, 8)$.

$$m = \frac{y_2 - y_1}{x_2 - x_1} = \frac{8 - 4}{-3 - 1} = \frac{4}{-4} = -1$$

The slope is -1.

You Try It 3 Let $P_1 = (-1, 2)$ and $P_2 = (4, 2)$.

$$m = \frac{y_2 - y_1}{x_2 - x_1} = \frac{2 - 2}{4 - (-1)} = \frac{0}{5} = 0$$

The slope is 0.

You Try It 4 $m = \dfrac{8650 - 6100}{1 - 4} = \dfrac{2550}{-3}$

$m = -850$

A slope of -850 means that the value of the car is decreasing at a rate of \$850 per year.

You Try It 5 y-intercept $= (0, b) = (0, -1)$

$m = -\dfrac{1}{4}$

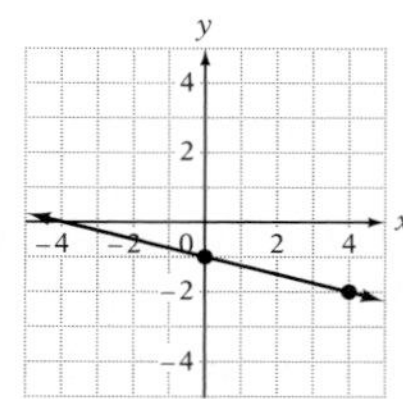

You Try It 6 Solve the equation for y.

$$x - 2y = 4$$
$$-2y = -x + 4$$
$$y = \frac{1}{2}x - 2$$

y-intercept $= (0, b) = (0, -2)$

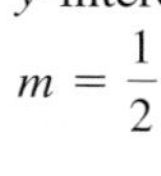

$m = \dfrac{1}{2}$

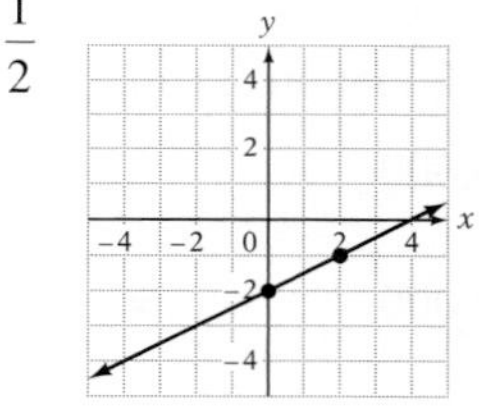

SECTION 12.4

You Try It 1 Because the slope and y-intercept are known, use the slope-intercept formula, $y = mx + b$.

$y = mx + b$

$y = \dfrac{5}{3}x + 2$ • $m = \dfrac{5}{3}; b = 2$

You Try It 2

$y = mx + b$ • **Slope-intercept form**

$y = \dfrac{3}{2}x + b$ • $m = \dfrac{3}{2}$

$-2 = \dfrac{3}{2}(4) + b$ • $(x, y) = (4, -2)$

$-2 = 6 + b$ • **Solve for** b.

$-8 = b$

$y = \dfrac{3}{2}x - 8$ • $m = \dfrac{3}{2}; b = -8$

The equation of the line is $y = \frac{3}{2}x - 8$.

You Try It 3 $m = \dfrac{3}{4}$ $(x_1, y_1) = (4, -2)$

$$y - y_1 = m(x - x_1)$$
$$y - (-2) = \frac{3}{4}(x - 4)$$
$$y + 2 = \frac{3}{4}x - 3$$
$$y = \frac{3}{4}x - 5$$

The equation of the line is $y = \frac{3}{4}x - 5$.

You Try It 4 Find the slope of the line between the two points.

$P_1 = (-6, -2), P_2 = (3, 1)$

$$m = \frac{y_2 - y_1}{x_2 - x_1} = \frac{1 - (-2)}{3 - (-6)} = \frac{3}{9} = \frac{1}{3}$$

Use the point-slope formula.

$y - y_1 = m(x - x_1)$

$y - (-2) = \dfrac{1}{3}[x - (-6)]$ • $y_1 = -2;$ $x_1 = -6$

$y + 2 = \dfrac{1}{3}x + 2$

$y = \dfrac{1}{3}x$

The equation of the line is $y = \frac{1}{3}x$.

Solutions to Chapter 13 "You Try It"

SECTION 13.1

You Try It 1

$2x - 5y = 8$		$-x + 3y = -5$	
$2(-1) - 5(-2)$	8	$-(-1) + 3(-2)$	-5
$-2 + 10$	8	$1 + (-6)$	-5
$8 = 8$		$-5 = -5$	

Yes, $(-1, -2)$ is a solution of the system of equations.

You Try It 2

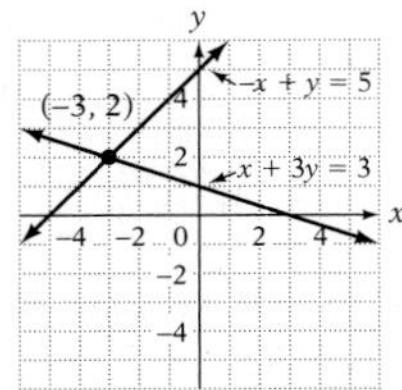

The solution is $(-3, 2)$.

You Try It 3

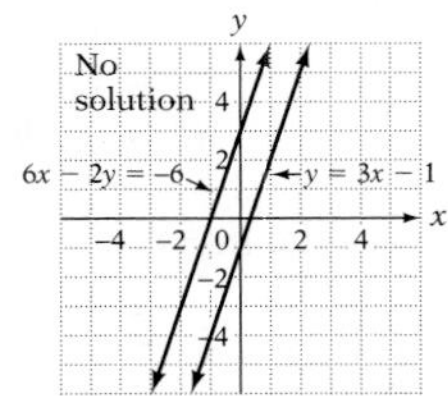

The lines are parallel. The system of equations is inconsistent and has no solution.

SECTION 13.2

You Try It 1

$$(1) \quad 7x - y = 4$$
$$(2) \quad 3x + 2y = 9$$

Solve Equation (1) for y.

$$7x - y = 4$$
$$-y = -7x + 4$$
$$y = 7x - 4$$

Substitute in Equation (2).

$$3x + 2y = 9$$
$$3x + 2(7x - 4) = 9 \quad \bullet\ y = 7x - 4$$
$$3x + 14x - 8 = 9$$
$$17x - 8 = 9$$
$$17x = 17$$
$$x = 1$$

Substitute in Equation (1).

$$7x - y = 4$$
$$7(1) - y = 4 \quad \bullet\ x = 1$$
$$7 - y = 4$$
$$-y = -3$$
$$y = 3$$

The solution is $(1, 3)$.

You Try It 2

$$(1) \quad 3x - y = 4$$
$$(2) \quad y = 3x + 2$$
$$3x - y = 4$$
$$3x - (3x + 2) = 4 \quad \bullet\ y = 3x + 2$$
$$3x - 3x - 2 = 4$$
$$-2 = 4$$

This is a false equation. The system of equations is inconsistent and therefore has no solution.

You Try It 3

$$(1) \quad y = -2x + 1$$
$$(2) \quad 6x + 3y = 3$$
$$6x + 3y = 3$$
$$6x + 3(-2x + 1) = 3 \quad \bullet\ y = -2x + 1$$
$$6x - 6x + 3 = 3$$
$$3 = 3$$

The system of equations is dependent. The solutions are the ordered pairs that satisfy the equation $y = -2x + 1$.

You Try It 4

Strategy

► Amount invested at 6.5%: x
Amount invested at 4.5%: y

	Principal	*Rate*	*Interest*
Amount at 6.5%	x	0.065	$0.065x$
Amount at 4.5%	y	0.045	$0.045y$

► The sum of the two investments is \$330,000: $x + y = 330{,}000$.
The interest earned at 6.5% equals the interest earned at 4.5%: $0.065x = 0.045y$

Solution

$$(1) \quad x + y = 330{,}000$$
$$(2) \quad 0.065x = 0.045y$$

Solve Equation (2) for y.

$$(3) \quad y = \frac{13}{9}x$$

Replace y by $\frac{13}{9}x$ in Equation (1) and solve for x.

$$x + y = 330{,}000$$
$$x + \frac{13}{9}x = 330{,}000 \quad \bullet\ y = \frac{13}{9}x$$
$$\frac{22}{9}x = 330{,}000$$
$$x = 135{,}000$$

Replace x by 135,000 in Equation (3) and solve for y.

$$y = \frac{13}{9}x$$
$$= \frac{13}{9}(135{,}000) = 195{,}000 \quad \bullet\ x = 135{,}000$$

\$135,000 should be invested at 6.5%, and \$195,000 should be invested at 4.5%.

SECTION 13.3

You Try It 1

(1) $2x - 3y = 1$
(2) $-3x + 4y = 6$

Eliminate x.

$3(2x - 3y) = 3(1)$ • Multiply by 3.
$2(-3x + 4y) = 2(6)$ • Multiply by 2.

$6x - 9y = 3$
$-6x + 8y = 12$ • Add the equations.
$-y = 15$
$y = -15$

Replace y in Equation (1).

$2x - 3(-15) = 1$ • $y = -15$
$2x + 45 = 1$
$2x = -44$
$x = -22$

The solution is $(-22, -15)$.

You Try It 2

(1) $2x - 3y = 4$
(2) $-4x + 6y = -8$

Eliminate y.

$2(2x - 3y) = 2 \cdot 4$ • Multiply by 2.
$-4x + 6y = -8$

$4x - 6y = 8$
$-4x + 6y = -8$
$0x + 0y = 0$ • Add the equations.
$0 = 0$

The system of equations is dependent. The solutions are the ordered pairs that satisfy the equation $2x - 3y = 4$.

You Try It 3

(1) $4x + 5y = 11$
(2) $3y = x + 10$

Write equation (2) in the form $Ax + By = C$.

$3y = x + 10$
$-x + 3y = 10$

Eliminate x.

$4x + 5y = 11$
$4(-x + 3y) = 4 \cdot 10$ • Multiply by 4.

$4x + 5y = 11$
$-4x + 12y = 40$ • Add the equations.
$17y = 51$
$y = 3$

Replace y in Equation (1).

$4x + 5y = 11$
$4x + 5 \cdot 3 = 11$ • $y = 3$
$4x + 15 = 11$
$4x = -4$
$x = -1$

The solution is $(-1, 3)$.

SECTION 13.4

You Try It 1

Strategy

► Rate of the current: c
Rate of the canoeist in calm water: r

	Rate	Time	Distance
With current	$r + c$	3	$3(r + c)$
Against current	$r - c$	5	$5(r - c)$

► The distance traveled with the current is 15 mi.
The distance traveled against the current is 15 mi.

Solution

$3(r + c) = 15 \quad \frac{1}{3} \cdot 3(r + c) = \frac{1}{3} \cdot 15$ • Multiply by $\frac{1}{3}$.

$5(r - c) = 15 \quad \frac{1}{5} \cdot 5(r - c) = \frac{1}{5} \cdot 15$ • Multiply by $\frac{1}{5}$.

$r + c = 5$
$r - c = 3$
$2r = 8$
$r = 4$

$r + c = 5$
$4 + c = 5$ • $r = 4$
$c = 1$

The rate of the current is 1 mph.
The rate of the canoeist in calm water is 4 mph.

You Try It 2

Strategy

► Cost of an orange tree: x
Cost of a grapefruit tree: y

First purchase:

	Amount	Unit Cost	Value
Orange trees	25	x	$25x$
Grapefruit trees	20	y	$20y$

Second purchase:

	Amount	Unit Cost	Value
Orange trees	20	x	$20x$
Grapefruit trees	30	y	$30y$

► The total cost of the first purchase was $2900.
The total cost of the second purchase was $3300.

Solution

$25x + 20y = 2900 \qquad 4(25x + 20y) = 4 \cdot 2900$ • **Multiply by 4.**

$20x + 30y = 3300 \qquad -5(20x + 30y) = -5 \cdot 3300$ • **Multiply by −5.**

$$\begin{aligned} 100x + 80y &= 11{,}600 \\ -100x - 150y &= -16{,}500 \\ \hline -70y &= -4900 \\ y &= 70 \end{aligned}$$

$$\begin{aligned} 25x + 20y &= 2900 \\ 25x + 20(70) &= 2900 \quad \bullet\ y = 70 \\ 25x + 1400 &= 2900 \\ 25x &= 1500 \\ x &= 60 \end{aligned}$$

The cost of an orange tree is $60.
The cost of a grapefruit tree is $70.

Solutions to Chapter 14 "You Try It"

SECTION 14.1

You Try It 1 $A = \{-9, -7, -5, -3, -1\}$

You Try It 2 $A = \{1, 3, 5, \ldots\}$

You Try It 3 $A \cup B = \{-2, -1, 0, 1, 2, 3, 4\}$

You Try It 4 $C \cap D = \{10, 16\}$

You Try It 5 $A \cap B = \varnothing$

You Try It 6 **a.** $\{x|x \le 3\}$ is the set of real numbers less than or equal to 3. This set extends forever in the negative direction. In interval notation, this set is written $(-\infty, 3]$.

b. $\{x|-5 \le x \le -3\}$ is the set of real numbers between −5 and −3, including −5 and −3. In interval notation, this set is written $[-5, -3]$.

You Try It 7 **a.** The interval $(-3, \infty)$ is the set of real numbers greater than −3. In set-builder notation, this set is written $\{x|x > -3\}$.

b. The interval $[0, 4)$ is the set of real numbers between 0 and 4, including 0 and excluding 4. In set-builder notation, this set is written $\{x|0 \le x < 4\}$.

You Try It 8 **a.** The graph is the set of real numbers between −4 and 4, including −4 and 4. Use brackets at −4 and 4.

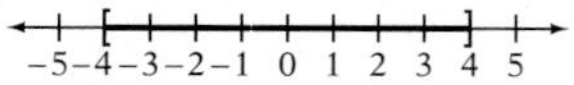

−5 −4 −3 −2 −1 0 1 2 3 4 5

b. The graph is the set of real numbers greater than −3. Use a parenthesis at −3.

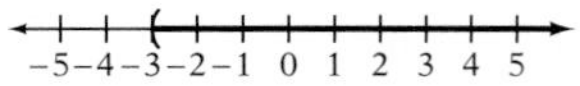

−5 −4 −3 −2 −1 0 1 2 3 4 5

You Try It 9 The graph is the set of real numbers between 2 and 5, including 2 and 5. Use brackets at 2 and 5.

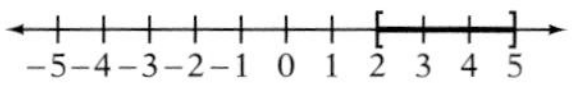

−5 −4 −3 −2 −1 0 1 2 3 4 5

SECTION 14.2

You Try It 1

$$\begin{aligned} 5x + 3 &> 4x + 5 \\ 5x - 4x + 3 &> 4x - 4x + 5 \quad \bullet \text{ Subtract } 4x. \\ x + 3 &> 5 \\ x + 3 - 3 &> 5 - 3 \quad \bullet \text{ Subtract 3.} \\ x &> 2 \\ \{x|x &> 2\} \quad \bullet \text{ Set-builder notation} \\ (2&, \infty) \quad \bullet \text{ Interval notation} \end{aligned}$$

You Try It 2

$$\begin{aligned} -3x &> -9 \\ \frac{-3x}{-3} &< \frac{-9}{-3} \quad \bullet \text{ Divide by } -3. \\ x &< 3 \end{aligned}$$

$(-\infty, 3)$

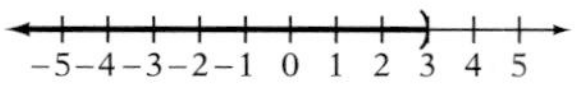

−5 −4 −3 −2 −1 0 1 2 3 4 5

You Try It 3

$$\begin{aligned} -\frac{3}{4}x &\ge 18 \\ -\frac{4}{3}\left(-\frac{3}{4}x\right) &\le -\frac{4}{3}(18) \quad \bullet \text{ Multiply by } -\frac{4}{3}. \\ x &\le -24 \end{aligned}$$

$\{x|x \le -24\}$

You Try It 4

Strategy To find the selling prices, write and solve an inequality using p to represent the possible selling prices.

Solution

$$\begin{aligned} 0.70p &> 942 \\ p &> 1345.71 \quad \bullet \text{ Divide by 0.70. Round to the nearest hundredth.} \end{aligned}$$

The dealer will make a profit with any selling price greater than or equal to $1345.71.

SECTION 14.3

You Try It 1

$$5 - 4x > 9 - 8x$$
$$5 - 4x + 8x > 9 - 8x + 8x \quad \text{• Add } 8x.$$
$$5 + 4x > 9$$
$$5 - 5 + 4x > 9 - 5 \quad \text{• Subtract 5.}$$
$$4x > 4$$
$$\frac{4x}{4} > \frac{4}{4} \quad \text{• Divide by 4.}$$
$$x > 1$$
$$(1, \infty)$$

You Try It 2

$$8 - 4(3x + 5) \le 6(x - 8)$$
$$8 - 12x - 20 \le 6x - 48 \quad \text{• Distributive Property}$$
$$-12 - 12x \le 6x - 48$$
$$-12 - 12x - 6x \le 6x - 6x - 48 \quad \text{• Subtract } 6x.$$
$$-12 - 18x \le -48$$
$$-12 + 12 - 18x \le -48 + 12 \quad \text{• Add 12.}$$
$$-18x \le -36$$
$$\frac{-18x}{-18} \ge \frac{-36}{-18} \quad \text{• Divide by } -18.$$
$$x \ge 2$$
$$\{x | x \ge 2\}$$

You Try It 3

Strategy To find the maximum number of miles:

- ▶ Write an expression for the cost of each car, using x to represent the number of miles driven during the week.
- ▶ Write and solve an inequality.

Solution

Cost of a Company A car	is less than	cost of a Company B car

$$8(7) + 0.10x < 10(7) + 0.08x$$
$$56 + 0.10x < 70 + 0.08x$$
$$56 + 0.10x - 0.08x < 70 + 0.08x - 0.08x \quad \text{• Subtract } 0.08x.$$
$$56 + 0.02x < 70$$
$$56 - 56 + 0.02x < 70 - 56 \quad \text{• Subtract 56.}$$
$$0.02x < 14$$
$$\frac{0.02x}{0.02} < \frac{14}{0.02} \quad \text{• Divide by 0.02.}$$
$$x < 700$$

The maximum number of miles is 699 mi.

SECTION 14.4

You Try It 1

$$x - 3y < 2$$
$$x - x - 3y < -x + 2 \quad \text{• Subtract } x.$$
$$-3y < -x + 2$$
$$\frac{-3y}{-3} > \frac{-x + 2}{-3} \quad \text{• Divide by } -3.$$
$$y > \frac{1}{3}x - \frac{2}{3}$$

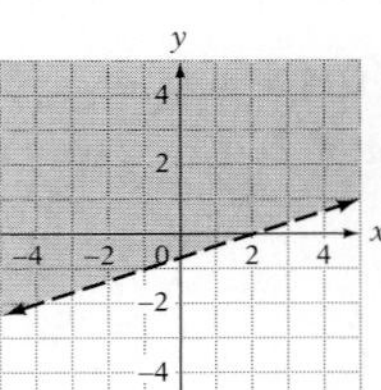

You Try It 2

$$2x - 4y \le 8$$
$$2x - 2x - 4y \le -2x + 8 \quad \text{• Subtract } 2x.$$
$$-4y \le -2x + 8$$
$$\frac{-4y}{-4} \ge \frac{-2x + 8}{-4} \quad \text{• Divide by } -4.$$
$$y \ge \frac{1}{2}x - 2$$

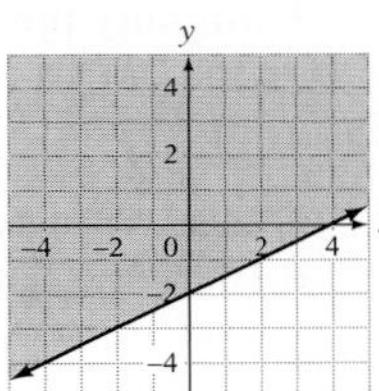

You Try It 3 $x < 3$

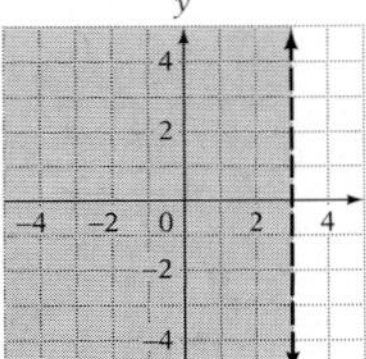

Solutions to Chapter 15 "You Try It"

SECTION 15.1

You Try It 1

$$\sqrt{216} = \sqrt{36 \cdot 6} \quad \text{• 36 is the largest perfect square.}$$
$$= \sqrt{36}\sqrt{6} = 6\sqrt{6}$$

You Try It 2

$$-5\sqrt{32} = -5\sqrt{16 \cdot 2} \quad \text{• 16 is the largest perfect square.}$$
$$= -5\sqrt{16}\sqrt{2}$$
$$= -5 \cdot 4\sqrt{2} = -20\sqrt{2}$$

You Try It 3

$\sqrt{y^{19}} = \sqrt{y^{18} \cdot y}$ • y^{18} is a perfect square.

$= \sqrt{y^{18}}\sqrt{y} = y^9\sqrt{y}$

You Try It 4

$\sqrt{45b^7} = \sqrt{9b^6 \cdot 5b}$ • $9b^6$ is a perfect square.

$= \sqrt{9b^6}\sqrt{5b} = 3b^3\sqrt{5b}$

You Try It 5

$3a\sqrt{28a^9b^{18}} = 3a\sqrt{4a^8b^{18}(7a)}$ • $4a^8b^{18}$ is a perfect square.

$= 3a\sqrt{4a^8b^{18}}\sqrt{7a}$

$= 3a \cdot 2a^4b^9\sqrt{7a} = 6a^5b^9\sqrt{7a}$

You Try It 6 $\sqrt{25(a+3)^2} = 5(a+3) = 5a + 15$

You Try It 7 $\sqrt{x^2 + 14x + 49} = \sqrt{(x+7)^2} = x + 7$

SECTION 15.2

You Try It 1

$9\sqrt{3} + 3\sqrt{3} - 18\sqrt{3} = (9 + 3 - 18)\sqrt{3} = -6\sqrt{3}$

You Try It 2

$2\sqrt{50} - 5\sqrt{32}$ • Unlike radicands

$= 2\sqrt{25 \cdot 2} - 5\sqrt{16 \cdot 2}$ • Simplify the radicands.

$= 2\sqrt{25}\sqrt{2} - 5\sqrt{16}\sqrt{2}$

$= 2 \cdot 5\sqrt{2} - 5 \cdot 4\sqrt{2}$

$= 10\sqrt{2} - 20\sqrt{2}$ • Like radicands

$= (10 - 20)\sqrt{2}$ • Distributive Property

$= -10\sqrt{2}$

You Try It 3

$y\sqrt{28y} + 7\sqrt{63y^3}$ • Unlike radicands

$= y\sqrt{4 \cdot 7y} + 7\sqrt{9y^2 \cdot 7y}$ • Simplify the radicands.

$= y\sqrt{4}\sqrt{7y} + 7\sqrt{9y^2}\sqrt{7y}$

$= y \cdot 2\sqrt{7y} + 7 \cdot 3y\sqrt{7y}$

$= 2y\sqrt{7y} + 21y\sqrt{7y}$ • Like radicands

$= (2y + 21y)\sqrt{7y}$ • Distributive Property

$= 23y\sqrt{7y}$

You Try It 4

$2\sqrt{27a^5} - 4a\sqrt{12a^3} + a^2\sqrt{75a}$

$= 2\sqrt{9a^4 \cdot 3a} - 4a\sqrt{4a^2 \cdot 3a} + a^2\sqrt{25 \cdot 3a}$

$= 2\sqrt{9a^4}\sqrt{3a} - 4a\sqrt{4a^2}\sqrt{3a} + a^2\sqrt{25}\sqrt{3a}$

$= 2 \cdot 3a^2\sqrt{3a} - 4a \cdot 2a\sqrt{3a} + a^2 \cdot 5\sqrt{3a}$

$= 6a^2\sqrt{3a} - 8a^2\sqrt{3a} + 5a^2\sqrt{3a} = 3a^2\sqrt{3a}$

SECTION 15.3

You Try It 1 $\sqrt{5a}\sqrt{15a^3b^4}\sqrt{20b^5}$

$= \sqrt{1500a^4b^9} = \sqrt{100a^4b^8 \cdot 15b}$

$= \sqrt{100a^4b^8} \cdot \sqrt{15b}$

$= 10a^2b^4\sqrt{15b}$

You Try It 2

$\sqrt{5x}(\sqrt{5x} - \sqrt{25y})$

$= \sqrt{25x^2} - \sqrt{125xy}$ • Distributive Property

$= \sqrt{25x^2} - \sqrt{25 \cdot 5xy} = \sqrt{25x^2} - \sqrt{25}\sqrt{5xy}$

$= 5x - 5\sqrt{5xy}$

You Try It 3

$(3\sqrt{x} - \sqrt{y})(5\sqrt{x} - 2\sqrt{y})$

$= 15(\sqrt{x})^2 - 6\sqrt{xy} - 5\sqrt{xy} + 2(\sqrt{y})^2$ • FOIL

$= 15(\sqrt{x})^2 - 11\sqrt{xy} + 2(\sqrt{y})^2$

$= 15x - 11\sqrt{xy} + 2y$

You Try It 4

$(2\sqrt{x} + 7)(2\sqrt{x} - 7)$

$= 4(\sqrt{x})^2 - 7^2$ • Product of conjugates

$= 4x - 49$

You Try It 5

$$\frac{\sqrt{15x^6y^7}}{\sqrt{3x^7y^9}} = \sqrt{\frac{15x^6y^7}{3x^7y^9}} = \sqrt{\frac{5}{xy^2}} = \frac{\sqrt{5}}{\sqrt{xy^2}}$$

$$= \frac{\sqrt{5}}{y\sqrt{x}} = \frac{\sqrt{5}}{y\sqrt{x}} \cdot \frac{\sqrt{x}}{\sqrt{x}}$$ • Rationalize the denominator.

$$= \frac{\sqrt{5x}}{xy}$$

You Try It 6

$$\frac{\sqrt{3}}{\sqrt{3} - \sqrt{6}} = \frac{\sqrt{3}}{\sqrt{3} - \sqrt{6}} \cdot \frac{\sqrt{3} + \sqrt{6}}{\sqrt{3} + \sqrt{6}}$$ • Rationalize the denominator.

$$= \frac{3 + \sqrt{18}}{3 - 6} = \frac{3 + 3\sqrt{2}}{-3}$$

$$= \frac{3(1 + \sqrt{2})}{-3} = -1(1 + \sqrt{2})$$

$$= -1 - \sqrt{2}$$

You Try It 7

$$\frac{5 + \sqrt{y}}{1 - 2\sqrt{y}} = \frac{5 + \sqrt{y}}{1 - 2\sqrt{y}} \cdot \frac{1 + 2\sqrt{y}}{1 + 2\sqrt{y}}$$ • Rationalize the denominator.

$$= \frac{5 + 10\sqrt{y} + \sqrt{y} + 2(\sqrt{y})^2}{1 - 4y}$$

$$= \frac{5 + 11\sqrt{y} + 2y}{1 - 4y}$$

SECTION 15.4

You Try It 1

$$\sqrt{4x} + 3 = 7$$
$$\sqrt{4x} = 4 \quad \bullet \text{ Isolate } \sqrt{4x}.$$
$$(\sqrt{4x})^2 = 4^2 \quad \bullet \text{ Square both sides.}$$
$$4x = 16$$
$$x = 4 \quad \bullet \text{ Solve for } x.$$

Check:
$$\sqrt{4x} + 3 = 7$$
$$\sqrt{4 \cdot 4} + 3 \mid 7$$
$$\sqrt{16} + 3 \mid 7$$
$$4 + 3 \mid 7$$
$$7 = 7$$

The solution is 4.

You Try It 2

$$\sqrt{x} + \sqrt{x+9} = 9$$
$$\sqrt{x} = 9 - \sqrt{x+9} \quad \bullet \text{ Isolate } \sqrt{x}.$$
$$(\sqrt{x})^2 = (9 - \sqrt{x+9})^2 \quad \bullet \text{ Square both sides.}$$
$$x = 81 - 18\sqrt{x+9} + (x+9)$$
$$-90 = -18\sqrt{x+9}$$
$$5 = \sqrt{x+9} \quad \bullet \text{ Isolate } \sqrt{x+9}.$$
$$5^2 = (\sqrt{x+9})^2 \quad \bullet \text{ Square both sides.}$$
$$25 = x + 9$$
$$16 = x \quad \bullet \text{ Solve for } x.$$

Check:
$$\sqrt{x} + \sqrt{x+9} = 9$$
$$\sqrt{16} + \sqrt{16+9} \mid 9$$
$$\sqrt{16} + \sqrt{25} \mid 9$$
$$4 + 5 \mid 9$$
$$9 = 9$$

The solution is 16.

You Try It 3

Strategy To find the distance, use the Pythagorean Theorem. The hypotenuse is the length of the ladder. One leg is the distance from the bottom of the ladder to the base of the building. The distance along the building from the ground to the top of the ladder is the unknown leg.

Solution

$$a = \sqrt{c^2 - b^2}$$
$$= \sqrt{(8)^2 - (3)^2} \quad \bullet\ c = 8, b = 3$$
$$= \sqrt{64 - 9}$$
$$= \sqrt{55}$$
$$\approx 7.42$$

The distance is approximately 7.42 ft.

You Try It 4

Strategy To find the length of the pendulum, replace T in the equation with the given value and solve for L.

Solution

$$T = 2\pi\sqrt{\frac{L}{32}}$$
$$2.5 = 2(3.14)\sqrt{\frac{L}{32}} \quad \bullet\ T = 2.5$$
$$2.5 = 6.28\sqrt{\frac{L}{32}}$$
$$\frac{2.5}{6.28} = \sqrt{\frac{L}{32}}$$
$$\left(\frac{2.5}{6.28}\right)^2 = \left(\sqrt{\frac{L}{32}}\right)^2$$
$$\frac{6.25}{39.4384} = \frac{L}{32}$$
$$(32)\left(\frac{6.25}{39.4384}\right) = (32)\left(\frac{L}{32}\right)$$
$$\frac{200}{39.4384} = L$$
$$5.07 \approx L$$

The length of the pendulum is approximately 5.07 ft.

Solutions to Chapter 16 "You Try It"

SECTION 16.1

You Try It 1

$$\frac{3y^2}{2} + y - \frac{1}{2} = 0$$
$$2\left(\frac{3y^2}{2} + y - \frac{1}{2}\right) = 2(0) \quad \bullet \text{ Multiply each side by 2.}$$
$$3y^2 + 2y - 1 = 0$$
$$(3y - 1)(y + 1) = 0 \quad \bullet \text{ Factor.}$$
$$3y - 1 = 0 \qquad y + 1 = 0 \quad \bullet \text{ Principle of Zero Products}$$
$$3y = 1 \qquad y = -1$$
$$y = \frac{1}{3}$$

The solutions are $\frac{1}{3}$ and -1.

You Try It 2

$$x^2 + 81 = 0$$
$$x^2 = -81 \quad \bullet \text{ Solve for } x^2.$$
$$\sqrt{x^2} = \sqrt{-81} \quad \bullet \text{ Take square roots.}$$

$\sqrt{-81}$ is not a real number.

The equation has no real number solution.

You Try It 3

$$7(z+2)^2 = 21$$
$$(z+2)^2 = 3 \quad \bullet \text{ Solve for } (z+2)^2.$$
$$\sqrt{(z+2)^2} = \sqrt{3} \quad \bullet \text{ Take square roots.}$$
$$z + 2 = \pm\sqrt{3}$$
$$z = -2 \pm \sqrt{3} \quad \bullet \text{ Solve for } z.$$

The solutions are $-2 + \sqrt{3}$ and $-2 - \sqrt{3}$.

SECTION 16.2

You Try It 1

$3x^2 - 6x - 2 = 0$

$3x^2 - 6x = 2$ • Add 2.

$\frac{1}{3}(3x^2 - 6x) = \frac{1}{3} \cdot 2$ • Multiply by $\frac{1}{3}$.

$x^2 - 2x = \frac{2}{3}$ • The coefficient of x^2 is 1.

Complete the square.

$x^2 - 2x + 1 = \frac{2}{3} + 1$ • $\left[\frac{1}{2}(-2)\right]^2 = [-1]^2 = 1$

$(x - 1)^2 = \frac{5}{3}$ • Factor.

$\sqrt{(x-1)^2} = \sqrt{\frac{5}{3}}$ • Take square roots.

$x - 1 = \pm\sqrt{\frac{5}{3}}$ • Solve for x.

$x = 1 \pm \sqrt{\frac{5}{3}}$

$x = 1 \pm \frac{\sqrt{15}}{3}$

$x = \frac{3 \pm \sqrt{15}}{3}$

The solutions are $\frac{3 + \sqrt{15}}{3}$ and $\frac{3 - \sqrt{15}}{3}$.

You Try It 2

$x^2 + 6x + 12 = 0$

$x^2 + 6x = -12$ • Subtract 12.

$x^2 + 6x + 9 = -12 + 9$ • $\left(\frac{1}{2} \cdot 6\right)^2 = 3^2 = 9$

$(x + 3)^2 = -3$ • Factor.

$\sqrt{(x+3)^2} = \sqrt{-3}$ • Take square roots.

$\sqrt{-3}$ is not a real number.

The quadratic equation has no real number solution.

You Try It 3

$x^2 + 8x + 8 = 0$

$x^2 + 8x = -8$ • Subtract 8.

$x^2 + 8x + 16 = -8 + 16$ • $\left(\frac{1}{2} \cdot 8\right)^2 = 4^2 = 16$

$(x + 4)^2 = 8$ • Factor.

$\sqrt{(x+4)^2} = \sqrt{8}$ • Take square roots.

$x + 4 = \pm\sqrt{8}$

$x + 4 = \pm 2\sqrt{2}$

$x = -4 \pm 2\sqrt{2}$

$x = -4 + 2\sqrt{2}$ $\quad$ $x = -4 - 2\sqrt{2}$

$\approx -4 + 2(1.414)$ $\quad$ $\approx -4 - 2(1.414)$

$\approx -4 + 2.828$ $\quad$ $\approx -4 - 2.828$

≈ -1.172 $\quad$ ≈ -6.828

The solutions are approximately -1.172 and -6.828.

SECTION 16.3

You Try It 1

$3x^2 + 4x - 4 = 0$

$a = 3, b = 4, c = -4$

$$x = \frac{-(4) \pm \sqrt{(4)^2 - 4(3)(-4)}}{2 \cdot 3}$$

$$= \frac{-4 \pm \sqrt{16 + 48}}{6}$$

$$= \frac{-4 \pm \sqrt{64}}{6} = \frac{-4 \pm 8}{6}$$

$x = \frac{-4 + 8}{6}$ $\quad$ $x = \frac{-4 - 8}{6}$

$= \frac{4}{6} = \frac{2}{3}$ $\quad$ $= \frac{-12}{6} = -2$

The solutions are $\frac{2}{3}$ and -2.

You Try It 2

$\frac{x^2}{4} + \frac{x}{2} = \frac{1}{4}$

$4\left(\frac{x^2}{4} + \frac{x}{2}\right) = 4\left(\frac{1}{4}\right)$ • Multiply by 4.

$x^2 + 2x = 1$ • Standard form

$x^2 + 2x - 1 = 0$

$a = 1, b = 2, c = -1$

$$x = \frac{-(2) \pm \sqrt{(2)^2 - 4(1)(-1)}}{2 \cdot 1}$$

$$= \frac{-2 \pm \sqrt{4 + 4}}{2} = \frac{-2 \pm \sqrt{8}}{2}$$

$$= \frac{-2 \pm 2\sqrt{2}}{2} = -1 \pm \sqrt{2}$$

The solutions are $-1 + \sqrt{2}$ and $-1 - \sqrt{2}$.

SECTION 16.4

You Try It 1

$y = x^2 + 2$

x	y
−2	6
−1	3
0	2
1	3
2	6

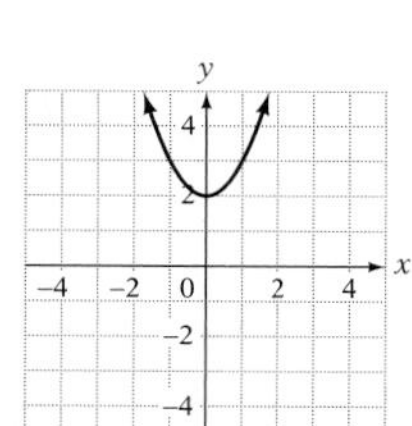

You Try It 2 To find the x-intercept, let $f(x) = 0$ and solve for x.

$$f(x) = x^2 - 6x + 9$$
$$0 = x^2 - 6x + 9$$
$$0 = (x - 3)(x - 3) \quad \bullet \text{ Factor.}$$
$$x - 3 = 0 \qquad x - 3 = 0 \quad \bullet \text{ Principle of Zero Products}$$
$$x = 3 \qquad x = 3$$

The x-intercept is $(3, 0)$.

There is only one x-intercept. The equation has a double root.

To find the y-intercept, evaluate the function at $x = 0$.

$$f(x) = x^2 - 6x + 9$$
$$f(0) = 0^2 - 6(0) + 9 = 9$$

The y-intercept is $(0, 9)$.

SECTION 16.5

You Try It 1

Strategy

- This is a geometry problem.
- Width of the rectangle: W
  Length of the rectangle: $W + 2$
- Use the equation $A = L \cdot W$.

Solution

$$A = L \cdot W$$
$$15 = (W + 2)W \quad \bullet\ A = 15, L = W + 2$$
$$15 = W^2 + 2W$$
$$0 = W^2 + 2W - 15$$
$$0 = (W + 5)(W - 3) \quad \bullet \text{ Factor.}$$
$$W + 5 = 0 \qquad W - 3 = 0 \quad \bullet \text{ Principle of Zero Products}$$
$$W = -5 \qquad W = 3$$

The solution -5 is not possible.
The width is 3 m.

Solutions to Chapter T "You Try It"

SECTION T.1

You Try It 1

$$\frac{5}{12} + \frac{9}{16} = \frac{20}{48} + \frac{27}{48} \quad \bullet \text{ The LCM of 12 and 16 is 48.}$$
$$= \frac{47}{48} \quad \bullet \text{ Add the numerators. Place the sum over the common denominator.}$$

You Try It 2

$$\frac{3}{4} + \frac{4}{5} + \frac{5}{8}$$
$$= \frac{30}{40} + \frac{32}{40} + \frac{25}{40} \quad \bullet \text{ The LCM of 4, 5, and 8 is 40. Write equivalent fractions using the LCM.}$$
$$= \frac{87}{40} \quad \bullet \text{ Add the numerators. Place the sum over the common denominator.}$$
$$= 2\frac{7}{40}$$

You Try It 3

$$\frac{5}{6} - \frac{1}{4} = \frac{10}{12} - \frac{3}{12} \quad \bullet \text{ The LCM of 6 and 4 is 12.}$$
$$= \frac{7}{12} \quad \bullet \text{ Subtract the numerators. Place the difference over the common denominator.}$$

You Try It 4

$$\frac{4}{21} \cdot \frac{7}{44} = \frac{4 \cdot 7}{21 \cdot 44} \quad \bullet \text{ Multiply the numerators. Multiply the denominators.}$$
$$= \frac{2 \cdot 2 \cdot 7}{3 \cdot 7 \cdot 2 \cdot 2 \cdot 11} \quad \bullet \text{ Write the prime factorization of each number.}$$
$$= \frac{\overset{1}{\cancel{2}} \cdot \overset{1}{\cancel{2}} \cdot \overset{1}{\cancel{7}}}{3 \cdot \underset{1}{\cancel{7}} \cdot \underset{1}{\cancel{2}} \cdot \underset{1}{\cancel{2}} \cdot 11} \quad \bullet \text{ Divide by the common factors.}$$
$$= \frac{1}{33} \quad \bullet \text{ Write the fraction in simplest form.}$$

You Try It 5

$$\frac{2}{15} \cdot 5 = \frac{2}{15} \cdot \frac{5}{1} \quad \bullet \text{ Write 5 as } \frac{5}{1}.$$
$$= \frac{2 \cdot 5}{15 \cdot 1} \quad \bullet \text{ Multiply the fractions.}$$
$$= \frac{2 \cdot \overset{1}{\cancel{5}}}{3 \cdot \underset{1}{\cancel{5}} \cdot 1} \quad \bullet \text{ Divide by the common factors.}$$
$$= \frac{2}{3} \quad \bullet \text{ Write the fraction in simplest form.}$$

You Try It 6

$$\frac{1}{6} \div \frac{4}{9} = \frac{1}{6} \cdot \frac{9}{4} \quad \bullet \text{ Multiply the first fraction by the reciprocal of the second fraction.}$$
$$= \frac{1 \cdot 9}{6 \cdot 4}$$
$$= \frac{1 \cdot \overset{1}{\cancel{3}} \cdot 3}{2 \cdot \underset{1}{\cancel{3}} \cdot 2 \cdot 2}$$
$$= \frac{3}{8}$$

SECTION T.2

You Try It 1

a. $-25 + 13 = -12$ • The signs are different. Subtract the absolute values. The sum has the same sign as the number with the larger absolute value.

b. $-41 + (-60) = -101$ • The signs are the same. Add the absolute values. The sum has the same sign as the addends.

c. $37 + (-9) = 28$ • The signs are different. Subtract the absolute values. The sum has the same sign as the number with the larger absolute value.

You Try It 2

a. $-27 - 18 = -27 + (-18)$
$= -45$

• −27 minus 18 = −27 plus the opposite of 18. The opposite of 18 is −18.

b. $-34 - (-90) = -34 + 90$
$= 56$

• −34 minus −90 = −34 plus the opposite of −90. The opposite of −90 is 90.

c. $8 - 42 = 8 + (-42)$
$= -34$

• 8 minus 42 = 8 plus the opposite of 42. The opposite of 42 is −42.

d. $-12 + 9 - (-5) - 4$
$= -12 + 9 + 5 + (-4)$

• Rewrite each subtraction as addition of the opposite.

$= -3 + 5 + (-4)$
$= 2 + (-4)$
$= -2$

• Add the numbers.

You Try It 3

a. $-25(4) = -100$

• The signs are different. The product is negative.

b. $-4(-61) = 244$

• The signs are the same. The product is positive.

c. $(-4)(5)(-3)(-1)$
$= (-20)(-3)(-1)$
$= 60(-1)$
$= -60$

• Multiply the first two numbers. Then multiply the product by the third number. Continue until all the numbers have been multiplied.

You Try It 4

a. $(-30) \div 6 = -5$

• The signs are different. The quotient is negative.

b. $(-50) \div (-25) = 2$

• The signs are the same. The quotient is positive.

c. $\frac{32}{-8} = -4$

• The fraction bar can be read "divided by."
$\frac{32}{-8} = (32) \div (-8)$
The signs are different. The quotient is negative.

SECTION T.3

You Try It 1

$$-\frac{1}{4} + \left(-\frac{3}{8}\right) = -\frac{2}{8} + \left(-\frac{3}{8}\right)$$

• Write the fractions with a common denominator.

$$= \frac{-2}{8} + \frac{-3}{8}$$

• Write the negative signs in the numerators.

$$= \frac{-2 + (-3)}{8}$$

• Add the fractions.

$$= \frac{-5}{8}$$

• Simplify the numerator.

$$= -\frac{5}{8}$$

• Write the negative sign in front of the fraction.

You Try It 2

$$-\frac{3}{8} - \left(-\frac{1}{6}\right) = -\frac{3}{8} + \frac{1}{6}$$

• Rewrite subtraction as addition of the opposite.

$$= -\frac{9}{24} + \frac{4}{24}$$

• Write the fractions with a common denominator.

$$= \frac{-9}{24} + \frac{4}{24}$$

• Write the negative sign in the numerator.

$$= \frac{-9 + 4}{24}$$

• Add the fractions.

$$= \frac{-5}{24}$$

• Simplify the numerator.

$$= -\frac{5}{24}$$

• Write the negative sign in front of the fraction.

You Try It 3

$4.69 - 12.5 = 4.69 + (-12.5)$

• Rewrite subtraction as addition of the opposite.

$= -7.81$

• Subtract the absolute values of the numbers. The sum has the same sign as the number with the larger absolute value.

You Try It 4

$$\frac{10}{11}\left(-\frac{2}{5}\right) = -\left(\frac{10}{11} \cdot \frac{2}{5}\right)$$

• The signs are different. The product is negative.

$$= -\frac{10 \cdot 2}{11 \cdot 5}$$

• Multiply the numerators. Multiply the denominators.

$$= -\frac{2 \cdot 5 \cdot 2}{11 \cdot 5}$$

• Write the product in simplest form.

$$= -\frac{4}{11}$$

You Try It 5

$$-\frac{3}{8} \div \left(-\frac{1}{2}\right) = \frac{3}{8} \div \frac{1}{2}$$

• The signs are the same. The quotient is positive.

$$= \frac{3}{8} \cdot \frac{2}{1}$$

• Rewrite division as multiplication by the reciprocal.

$$= \frac{3 \cdot 2}{8 \cdot 1}$$

• Multiply the fractions.

$$= \frac{3 \cdot 2}{2 \cdot 2 \cdot 2 \cdot 1}$$

$$= \frac{3}{4}$$

You Try It 6

$(-3.6)(-1.45) = 5.22$

• The signs are the same. The product is positive. Multiply the absolute values of the numbers.

You Try It 7

$5.04 \div (-8.4) = -0.6$

- The signs are different. The quotient is negative. Divide the absolute values of the numbers.

You Try It 8

$$\left(\frac{2}{9}\right)^2 \cdot (-3)^4$$

$$= \left(\frac{2}{9}\right)\left(\frac{2}{9}\right) \cdot (-3)(-3)(-3)(-3)$$

- Write each factor the number of times indicated by the exponent.

$$= \left(\frac{2}{9}\right)\left(\frac{2}{9}\right) \cdot (3)(3)(3)(3)$$

- The product is positive.

$$= \frac{2 \cdot 2 \cdot 3 \cdot 3 \cdot 3 \cdot 3}{3 \cdot 3 \cdot 3 \cdot 3}$$

- Multiply.

$$= 4$$

You Try It 9

$$7 \div \left(\frac{1}{7} - \frac{3}{14}\right) - 9$$

- Use the Order of Operations Agreement.

$$= 7 \div \left(-\frac{1}{14}\right) - 9$$

- Perform the operation inside the parentheses.

$$= 7(-14) - 9$$

- Rewrite division as multiplication by the reciprocal.

$$= -98 - 9$$

- Do the multiplication.

$$= -98 + (-9)$$

- Do the subtraction.

$$= -107$$

SECTION T.4

You Try It 1

$$5x + 3 - 7x = 9$$
$$3 - 2x = 9 \quad \text{• Step 2}$$
$$3 - 3 - 2x = 9 - 3 \quad \text{• Step 4}$$
$$-2x = 6$$
$$\frac{-2x}{-2} = \frac{6}{-2} \quad \text{• Step 5}$$
$$x = -3$$

The solution is -3.

You Try It 2

$$4x + 3 = 7x + 9$$
$$4x - 7x + 3 = 7x - 7x + 9 \quad \text{• Step 3}$$
$$-3x + 3 = 9$$
$$-3x + 3 - 3 = 9 - 3 \quad \text{• Step 4}$$
$$-3x = 6$$
$$\frac{-3x}{-3} = \frac{6}{-3} \quad \text{• Step 5}$$
$$x = -2$$

The solution is -2.

You Try It 3

$$4 - (5x - 8) = 4x + 3$$
$$4 - 5x + 8 = 4x + 3 \quad \text{• Step 1}$$
$$-5x + 12 = 4x + 3 \quad \text{• Step 2}$$
$$-5x - 4x + 12 = 4x - 4x + 3 \quad \text{• Step 3}$$
$$-9x + 12 = 3$$
$$-9x + 12 - 12 = 3 - 12 \quad \text{• Step 4}$$
$$-9x = -9$$
$$\frac{-9x}{-9} = \frac{-9}{-9} \quad \text{• Step 5}$$
$$x = 1$$

The solution is 1.

Solutions to Appendix "You Try It"

You Try It 1 1 295 m = 1.295 km

You Try It 2 7 543 g = 7.543 kg

You Try It 3 6.3 L = 6 300 ml

You Try It 4 2 kl = 2 000 L

Answers to Selected Exercises

Answers to Chapter 1 Selected Exercises

PREP TEST

1. 8 **2.** 1 2 3 4 5 6 7 8 9 10 **3.** a and D; b and E; c and A; d and B; e and F; f and C **4.** 0 **5.** Fifty

SECTION 1.1

1. is greater than **3.** thousand **5.** less
7. 0 1 2 3 4 5 6 7 8 9 10 11 12 **9.** 0 1 2 3 4 5 6 7 8 9 10 11 12 **11.** 0 1 2 3 4 5 6 7 8 9 10 11 12
13. 5 **15.** 5 **17.** 0 **19.** $27 < 39$ **21.** $0 < 52$ **23.** $273 > 194$ **25.** $2761 < 3857$ **27.** $4610 > 4061$
29. $8005 < 8050$ **31.** Yes **33.** 11, 14, 16, 21, 32 **35.** 13, 48, 72, 84, 93 **37.** 26, 49, 77, 90, 106
39. 204, 399, 662, 736, 981 **41.** 307, 370, 377, 3077, 3700 **43.** five hundred eight **45.** six hundred thirty-five
47. four thousand seven hundred ninety **49.** fifty-three thousand six hundred fourteen **51.** two hundred forty-six thousand fifty-three
53. three million eight hundred forty-two thousand nine hundred five **55.** 496 **57.** 53,340 **59.** 502,140 **61.** 9706
63. 5,012,907 **65.** 8,005,010 **67.** 7000 + 200 + 40 + 5 **69.** 500,000 + 30,000 + 2000 + 700 + 90 + 1
71. 5000 + 60 + 4 **73.** 20,000 + 300 + 90 + 7 **75.** 400,000 + 2000 + 700 + 8 **77.** 8,000,000 + 300 + 10 + 6
79. Tens **81.** 7110 **83.** 5000 **85.** 28,600 **87.** 7000 **89.** 94,000 **91.** 630,000 **93.** 350,000 **95.** Sometimes true
97. Never true **99.** Billy Hamilton had more stolen bases than Ty Cobb. **101.** *Fiddler on the Roof* had more performances than *Hello Dolly.*
103. Two tablespoons of peanut butter have more calories than two tablespoons of grape jelly. **105a.** Enrollment was the lowest in 1980.
b. Enrollment increased between 1990 and 2000. **107a.** The complaint mentioned most often was people talking. **b.** The complaint mentioned the least was uncomfortable seats. **109.** Subway had more restaurants. **111.** The acreage of the Appalachian Trail to the nearest ten-thousand acres is 160,000 acres. **113.** The population of the United States on April 10, 2010, to the nearest million, was 309,000,000 people.
115. 999; 10,000 **117.** Asia, Africa, North America, South America, Antarctica, Europe, Australia

SECTION 1.2

1. 24; 15; 39 **3.** thousand; ten-thousand **5.** addition **7.** 1,383,659 **9.** 6043 **11.** 12,548 **13.** 199,556 **15.** 327,473
17. 168,574 **19.** 7947 **21.** 99,637 **23.** There are a total of 1872 undergraduate students. **25.** 15,040; 15,000
27. 1,388,917; 1,400,000 **29.** 1998; 2000 **31.** 329,801; 307,000 **33.** 1272 **35.** 12,150 **37.** 89,900 **39.** 1572
41. 14,591 **43.** 56,010 **45.** The Commutative Property of Addition **47.** The Associative Property of Addition
49. The Addition Property of Zero **51.** 28 **53.** 4 **55.** 15 **57.** The Commutative Property of Addition **59.** No **61.** Yes
63. No **65.** 353 **67.** 467 **69.** 103 **71.** 658 **73.** 2786 **75.** 2127 **77.** 4738 **79.** 61,757 **81.** 1336 **83.** 11,279
85. $x - y$ **87.** The eruption of the Giant is 25 ft higher than that of Old Faithful. **89.** 6736; 7000 **91.** 33,573; 30,000
93. 39,244; 40,000 **95.** 845,181; 870,000 **97.** 47 **99.** 426 **101.** 627 **103.** 4302 **105.** 438 **107.** 48,148 **109.** Yes
111. No **113.** Yes **115.** The difference is 901. **117.** The total number of calories consumed is 370.
119. The perimeter of the rectangle is 78 m. **121.** The perimeter of the triangle is 43 in. **123.** The amount in your checking account is $1924.
125. The amount owed is $544. **127.** Your car has been driven approximately 20,000 mi during the past year.
129. Car sales increased the most from January to February in 2015. The amount of increase was 24 cars.
131. There are 115 million households in the United States. **133.** The number of electric car sales is projected to increase the most between 2016 and 2017. **135.** The value of the investment is $13,275. **137.** The mortgage loan amount is $261,000.
139. The ground speed is 350 mph. **141.** No **143.** $b - a$; $b - a$ represents how much longer the side of length b is than the side of length a.
145. 90; 900 **147.**

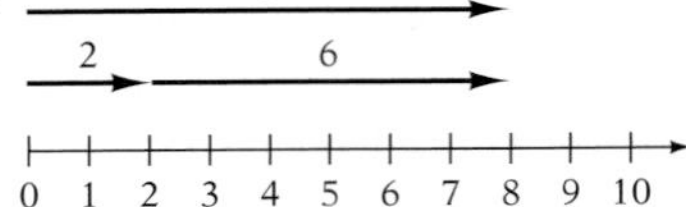

CHECK YOUR PROGRESS: CHAPTER 1*

1. 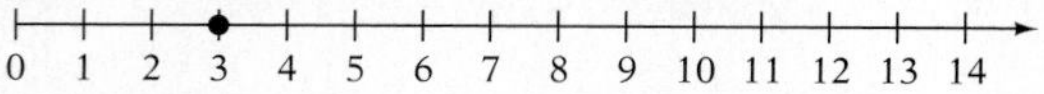 [1.1A] **2.** 199, 247, 462, 506, 831 [1.1A] **3a.** 397 > 246 **b.** 898 < 1594 [1.1A] **4.** 3 [1.1A] **5.** six thousand seven hundred two [1.1B] **6.** 32,518 [1.1B] **7.** 900,000 + 3000 + 400 + 80 + 7 [1.1B] **8.** 16,000 [1.1C] **9.** 433,000 [1.1C] **10.** 172,621 [1.2A] **11.** 1683 [1.2A] **12.** 1900 [1.2A] **13.** The Associative Property of Addition [1.2A] **14.** 97 [1.2A] **15.** No [1.2A] **16.** 1819 [1.2B] **17.** 5249 [1.2B] **18.** 10,000 [1.2B] **19.** 425 [1.2B] **20.** Yes [1.2B] **21.** The difference between the most expensive and the least expensive Audi Duo is $930. [1.2C] **22.** The total amount of her charitable contributions for the six months was $130. [1.2C] **23.** The planet Neptune is smaller than the planet Uranus. [1.1C] **24.** The perimeter of the triangle is 27 m. [1.2C] **25.** The price is $198. [1.2C]

SECTION 1.3

3. 3; 4; 3; 3; 3; 3; 81 **5.** 495; 6 **7.** factors; 1, 3, 5, 15 **9.** division **11.** 1143 **13.** 46,963 **15.** 470,152 **17.** 48,493 **19.** 324,438 **21.** 3,206,160 **23.** 1500 **25.** 2000 **27.** 0 **29a.** You would burn 2238 calories. **b.** You would burn 4236 calories. **31.** 550,935; 540,000 **33.** 4,315,403; 4,200,000 **35.** 39,312; 36,000 **37.** 612,792; 600,000 **39.** 9525 **41.** 2292 **43.** 4000 **45.** 12,540 **47.** Answers will vary. For example, 20 and 500 **49.** The Associative Property of Multiplication **51.** The Multiplication Property of Zero **53.** 5 **55.** 1 **57.** No **59.** Yes **61.** No **63.** $3^6 \cdot 5^3$ **65.** $7^2 \cdot 11^3 \cdot 19^4$ **67.** d^3 **69.** a^2b^4 **71.** 64 **73.** 1,000,000,000 **75.** 144 **77.** 1600 **79.** 0 **81.** 4050 **83.** 216 **85.** 121 **87.** t^5 **89.** 36 **91.** 448 **93.** 125,000 **95.** 540 **97.** 204 r4 **99.** 8700 **101.** 21 r18 **103.** 180 r21 **105.** 200 r7 **107.** 609 **109.** 40 r27 **111.** 908 **113.** 461 r4 **115a.** The average monthly claim for theft was $25,000. **b.** The average monthly claim for all sources combined was $95,000. **117.** 1072; 1000 **119.** 21,968; 20,000 **121.** 222 r26; 200 **123.** 1951; 2000 **125.** 1 **127.** 0 **129.** 5400 **131.** Yes **133.** No **135.** 1, 2, 4, 5, 10, 20 **137.** 1, 3, 9 **139.** 1, 2, 4, 8, 16 **141.** 1, 17 **143.** 1, 2, 3, 4, 6, 8, 12, 24 **145.** 1, 2, 3, 4, 6, 9, 12, 18, 36 **147.** 1, 3, 5, 9, 15, 45 **149.** 1, 2, 4, 8, 16, 32 **151.** 1, 2, 4, 8, 16, 32, 64 **153.** 1, 3, 5, 15, 25, 75 **155.** $2^3 \cdot 3$ **157.** 3^3 **159.** $2^2 \cdot 3^2$ **161.** $2 \cdot 5^2$ **163.** Prime **165.** $2^4 \cdot 5$ **167.** 7^2 **169.** 3^4 **171.** Prime **173.** $2^3 \cdot 3 \cdot 5$ **175.** There are an average of 28 funerals each day at Arlington National Cemetery. **177a.** Each week, 3794 marriages occur between eHarmony members. **b.** Each year, 197,830 marriages occur between eHarmony members. **179.** The length of fencing needed is 220 ft. **181.** The area of the patio is 81 ft^2. **183.** The total cost of the order is approximately $16,000. **185.** Melissa's monthly starting salary is $5754. **187.** The total wages paid by Carlos are $2760. **189.** The total amount paid on the loan is $6840. **191.** It would take 9 h to drive 513 mi. **193.** The value per share of the fund is $21. **195.** 87,312 **197a.** 1, 3, 7, 9 **b.** Answers will vary. For example, 21, 33, 27, and 39 **199.** 2, 3, 5, 7, 11, 13, 17, 19, 23, 29, 31, 37, 41, 43, 47, 53, 59, 61, 67, 71, 73, 79, 83, 89, and 97

SECTION 1.4

1. to multiply 7 times 2 **3.** 4 **5.** 29 **7.** 13 **9.** 19 **11.** 11 **13.** 6 **15.** 61 **17.** 54 **19.** 19 **21.** 24 **23.** 186 **25.** 39 **27.** 18 **29.** 14 **31.** 14 **33.** 2 **35.** 57 **37.** 8 **39.** 68 **41.** 16 **43.** $12 + (9 - 5) \cdot 3 > 11 + (8 + 4) \div 6\ [24 > 13]$ **45.** $5 + 7 \cdot (3 - 1)$ **47.** $5 + (7 \cdot 3) - 1$ **49.** 97 **51.** $3 + 3^3$

CHAPTER 1 REVIEW EXERCISES

1. 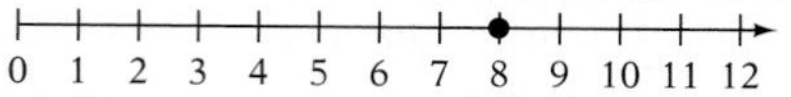 [1.1A] **2.** 10,000 [1.3B] **3.** 2583 [1.2B] **4.** $3^2 \cdot 5^4$ [1.3B] **5.** 1389 [1.2A] **6.** 38,700 [1.1C] **7.** 247 > 163 [1.1A] **8.** 32,509 [1.1B] **9.** 700 [1.3A] **10.** 2607 [1.3C] **11.** 4048 [1.2B] **12.** 1500 [1.2A] **13.** 1, 2, 5, 10, 25, 50 [1.3D] **14.** Yes [1.2B] **15.** 18 [1.4A] **16.** The Commutative Property of Addition [1.2A] **17.** four million nine hundred twenty-seven thousand thirty-six [1.1B] **18.** 675 [1.3B] **19a.** There were 16 times more PG-13 films released than NC-17 films. **b.** There were 61 times more R-rated films released than NC-17 films. [1.3E] **20.** 67 r70 [1.3C] **21.** 2636 [1.3A] **22.** 137 [1.2B] **23.** $2 \cdot 3^2 \cdot 5$ [1.3D] **24.** 80 [1.3C] **25.** 1 [1.3A] **26.** 10 [1.4A] **27.** 932 [1.2A] **28.** 432 [1.3A] **29.** 56 [1.5A] **30.** Kareem Abdul-Jabbar had more rebounds than Elvin Hayes. [1.1D] **31.** The total cost of the contractor's work is $238,000. [1.3E] **32a.** The perimeter is 74 m. **b.** The area is 300 m^2. [1.2C, 1.3E] **33.** The projected growth is 283,000 adults. [1.2C] **34.** The distance traveled is 42 mi. [1.3E] **35.** The markup on the copy machine is $449. [1.2C]

CHAPTER 1 TEST

1. 329,700 [1.3A; You Try It 4] **2.** 16,000 [1.3B; Example 10] **3.** 4029 [1.2B; HOW TO 11] **4.** x^4y^3 [1.3B; You Try It 7] **5.** Yes [1.2A; Example 5] **6.** 3000 [1.1C; Example 9] **7.** 7177 < 7717 [1.1A; Example 3] **8.** 8490 [1.1B; Example 6] **9.** three hundred eighty-two thousand nine hundred four [1.1B; Example 5] **10.** 2000 [1.2A; Example 1] **11.** 11,008 [1.3A; HOW TO 1] **12.** 2,400,000 [1.3A; Example 2] **13.** 1, 2, 4, 23, 46, 92 [1.3D; HOW TO 16] **14.** $2^4 \cdot 3 \cdot 5$ [1.3D; Example 18]

*Note: The numbers in brackets following the answers in the Check Your Progress are a reference to the objective that corresponds to that problem. For example, the reference [1.2A] stands for Section 1.2, Objective A. This notation will be used for all Prep Tests, Check Your Progress, Chapter Reviews, Chapter Tests, and Cumulative Reviews throughout the text.

15. 30,866 [1.2B; Example 9] **16.** The Commutative Property of Addition [1.2A; Example 2] **17.** 897 [1.3C; Example 15] **18.** 26 [1.4A; Example 2] **19.** Girls grow the most between birth and age 1. [1.2B; Example 8] **20.** 7 [1.4A; HOW TO 1] **21.** 3000 + 900 + 70 + 2 [1.1B, Example 7] **22.** 56 [1.5A; Example 3] **23.** 7 [1.2A; Example 2] **24.** 720 [1.3A; HOW TO 5] **25.** The balance in your account after making the purchase is \$556. [1.2C; Example 11] **26a.** The perimeter is 96 cm. **b.** The area is 576 cm^2. [1.3E; HOW TO 19, HOW TO 21] **27.** The diver's monthly take-home pay is \$4456. [1.2C; Example 11] **28.** There are 465 million more registered users on Facebook than on Twitter. [1.2C; Example 11] **29.** The commission earned is \$1440. [1.3E; Example 21] **30.** The value per share of the fund is \$11. [1.3E; Example 22]

Answers to Chapter 2 Selected Exercises

PREP TEST

1. 20 [1.3A] **2.** 120 [1.3A] **3.** 9 [1.3A] **4.** 10 [1.2A] **5.** 7 [1.2B] **6.** 2 r3 [1.3C] **7.** 1, 2, 3, 4, 6, 12 [1.3C] **8.** 59 [1.4A] **9.** 7 [1.2A] **10.** $44 < 48$ [1.1A]

SECTION 2.1

1. 5, 10, 15, 20 **3.** 10, 20, 30, 40 **5.** Multiples of 6: 6, 12, 18, 24, 30, 36, 42, 48, 54, 60; multiples of 8: 8, 16, 24, 32, 40, 48, 56, 64, 72, 80; common multiples: 24, 48; least common multiple: 24 **7.** 1, 2, 4, 5, 10, 20 **9.** 1, 2, 4, 7, 14, 28 **11.** 40 **13.** 24 **15.** 12 **17.** 24 **19.** 60 **21.** 56 **23.** 32 **25.** 36 **27.** 660 **29.** 9384 **31.** 24 **33.** 30 **35.** 24 **37.** 576 **39.** 420 **41.** True **43.** 1 **45.** 3 **47.** 5 **49.** 25 **51.** 1 **53.** 4 **55.** 4 **57.** 4 **59.** 1 **61.** 7 **63.** 5 **65.** 8 **67.** 1 **69.** 25 **71.** 8 **73.** True **75.** They will have another day off together in 12 days. **79a.** No **b.** Yes **c.** Yes **d.** Yes

SECTION 2.2

1a. 9; 4 **b.** improper **c.** divided by; 9; 4 **3.** 3; 2; 17; 17; 5 **5.** 1; 2 **7.** $\frac{4}{5}$ **9.** $\frac{1}{4}$ **11.** $\frac{4}{3}$; $1\frac{1}{3}$ **13.** $\frac{13}{5}$; $2\frac{3}{5}$ **15.** $3\frac{1}{4}$ **17.** 4 **19.** $2\frac{7}{10}$ **21.** 7 **23.** $1\frac{8}{9}$ **25.** $2\frac{2}{5}$ **27.** 18 **29.** $2\frac{2}{15}$ **31.** 1 **33.** $9\frac{1}{3}$ **35.** $\frac{9}{4}$ **37.** $\frac{11}{2}$ **39.** $\frac{14}{5}$ **41.** $\frac{47}{6}$ **43.** $\frac{7}{1}$ **45.** $\frac{33}{4}$ **47.** $\frac{31}{3}$ **49.** $\frac{55}{12}$ **51.** $\frac{8}{1}$ **53.** $\frac{64}{5}$ **55.** $a > b$ **57.** $\frac{6}{12}$ **59.** $\frac{9}{24}$ **61.** $\frac{6}{51}$ **63.** $\frac{24}{32}$ **65.** $\frac{108}{18}$ **67.** $\frac{30}{90}$ **69.** $\frac{14}{21}$ **71.** $\frac{42}{49}$ **73.** $\frac{8}{18}$ **75.** $\frac{28}{4}$ **77.** $\frac{1}{4}$ **79.** $\frac{3}{4}$ **81.** $\frac{1}{6}$ **83.** $\frac{8}{33}$ **85.** 0 **87.** $\frac{7}{6}$ **89.** 1 **91.** $\frac{3}{5}$ **93.** $\frac{4}{15}$ **95.** $\frac{3}{5}$ **97.** $\frac{2m}{3}$ **99.** $\frac{y}{2}$ **101.** $\frac{2a}{3}$ **103.** c **105.** $6k$ **107.** ii **109.** iii; One example is $\frac{5}{6}$ and $\frac{15}{18}$. **111.** $\frac{5}{7} > \frac{2}{3}$ **113.** $\frac{7}{12} < \frac{5}{8}$ **115.** $\frac{11}{14} > \frac{3}{4}$ **117.** $\frac{11}{12} > \frac{7}{9}$ **119.** $\frac{5}{8} > \frac{4}{7}$ **121.** $\frac{11}{30} > \frac{7}{24}$ **123.** $\frac{9}{11} < \frac{7}{8}$ **125.** $\frac{3}{4} < \frac{11}{13}$ **127.** $\frac{2}{3} < \frac{7}{10}$ **129.** $\frac{3}{10} > \frac{7}{25}$ **131.** One example is $\frac{4}{7}$ and $\frac{3}{5}$. **133.** More people chose a fast-food restaurant on the basis of location. **135.** You answered more than $\frac{8}{10}$ of the questions correctly. **137a.** $\frac{3}{a}$ **b.** $\frac{6}{b}$ and $\frac{7}{b}$ **139a.** $\frac{1}{4}$ of a standard deck of cards is spades. **b.** $\frac{1}{13}$ of a standard deck of cards is aces.

SECTION 2.3

1. denominators **3.** $\frac{1}{2}$; $\frac{3}{7}$ **5.** subtraction **7.** $\frac{9}{11}$ **9.** 1 **11.** $1\frac{2}{3}$ **13.** $1\frac{1}{6}$ **15.** $\frac{16}{b}$ **17.** $\frac{9}{c}$ **19.** $\frac{11}{x}$ **21.** $\frac{11}{12}$ **23.** $\frac{11}{12}$ **25.** $1\frac{7}{12}$ **27.** $2\frac{2}{15}$ **29.** $15\frac{2}{3}$ **31.** $5\frac{2}{3}$ **33.** $15\frac{1}{20}$ **35.** $10\frac{7}{36}$ **37.** $7\frac{5}{12}$ **39.** $\frac{3}{4}$ **41.** $12\frac{5}{18}$ **43.** $6\frac{5}{24}$ **45.** $1\frac{2}{5}$ **47.** $1\frac{13}{18}$ **49.** $1\frac{5}{24}$ **51.** $11\frac{2}{3}$ **53.** $14\frac{3}{4}$ **55.** Yes **57.** $\frac{31}{50}$ of the money borrowed on home equity loans is spent on debt consolidation and home improvement. **59.** iii **61.** $\frac{1}{6}$ **63.** $\frac{1}{6}$ **65.** $\frac{5}{d}$ **67.** $\frac{5}{n}$ **69.** $\frac{1}{14}$ **71.** $\frac{1}{2}$ **73.** $\frac{1}{4}$ **75.** $2\frac{1}{3}$ **77.** $6\frac{3}{4}$ **79.** $1\frac{1}{12}$ **81.** $3\frac{3}{8}$ **83.** $5\frac{1}{9}$ **85.** $2\frac{3}{4}$ **87.** $1\frac{17}{24}$ **89.** $4\frac{19}{24}$ **91.** $1\frac{7}{10}$ **93.** $\frac{5}{24}$ **95.** $6\frac{5}{12}$ **97.** $\frac{1}{3}$ **99.** $\frac{1}{6}$ **101.** $1\frac{1}{9}$ **103.** $4\frac{2}{5}$ **105.** $2\frac{2}{9}$ **107.** $4\frac{11}{12}$ **109.** Yes **111.** i **113.** You own $1\frac{3}{4}$ acres.

115. You are still required to do $7\frac{3}{4}$ h of community service. **117.** $\frac{5}{12}$ of the job remains to be done. Yes, the roofer and the apprentice can complete the job in one more day. **119.** You need $29\frac{1}{2}$ ft of fencing. **121a.** The hikers plan to travel $17\frac{17}{24}$ mi the first two days. **b.** There will be $9\frac{19}{24}$ mi left to travel on the third day. **123.** The difference is $\frac{1}{32}$ in. **125.** The boxer must gain $6\frac{3}{4}$ lb. **127.** Answers will vary. **129.** Not possible **131.** A possible answer is $\frac{4}{6} + \frac{4}{3} = 2$. **133.** Not possible

SECTION 2.4

1a. can **b.** product; product **3.** three **5.** division **7.** $\frac{3}{5}$ **9.** $\frac{4}{5}$ **11.** 0 **13.** $\frac{1}{9}$ **15.** $\frac{63}{xy}$ **17.** $\frac{yz}{30}$ **19.** 1 **21.** 6 **23.** 0 **25.** 19 **27.** 42 **29.** $5\frac{1}{2}$ **31.** $\frac{7}{10}$ **33.** $1\frac{4}{5}$ **35.** A typical U.S. household spends \$13,000 on housing per year. **37.** $\frac{7}{48}$ **39.** $3\frac{1}{2}$ **41.** $\frac{1}{5}$ **43.** $\frac{1}{6}$ **45.** $3\frac{2}{3}$ **47.** No **49.** Less than **51.** $\frac{9}{16}$ **53.** $\frac{5}{128}$ **55.** $\frac{4}{45}$ **57.** $1\frac{1}{7}$ **59.** $\frac{16}{81}$ **61.** $\frac{2}{3}$ **63.** $1\frac{11}{14}$ **65.** 0 **67.** 8 **69.** $\frac{1}{8}$ **71.** Undefined **73.** $\frac{8}{9}$ **75.** $\frac{32}{xy}$ **77.** $\frac{bd}{30}$ **79.** $5\frac{1}{3}$ **81.** $\frac{1}{2}$ **83.** $5\frac{2}{7}$ **85.** $1\frac{29}{31}$ **87.** There are 32 servings in a box of Kellogg Honey Crunch Corn Flakes. **89.** $1\frac{1}{5}$ **91.** $\frac{7}{26}$ **93.** $\frac{1}{12}$ **95.** 48 **97.** Greater than **99.** $\frac{3}{4}$ **101.** $\frac{1}{6}$ **103.** 6 **105.** $\frac{18}{35}$ **107.** $1\frac{7}{25}$ **109.** $3\frac{3}{11}$ **111.** 17 **113.** 1 **115.** 1 **117.** 0 **119.** The length of time in four chukkers is 30 min. **121.** There are $16\frac{1}{2}$ ft in one rod; There are 198 in. in one rod. **123.** The average couple spends 234 h per year cleaning house. **125.** The developer plans to build 30 houses. **127.** The asteroid's distance from Earth at its closest point is 225,000 mi. **129.** The area of the vegetable garden is $136\frac{1}{2}$ ft^2. **131.** Two bags of seed should be purchased. **133.** The pressure on the diver is $21\frac{1}{4}$ pounds per square inch. **135.** There are 1250 mi between the two cities.

CHECK YOUR PROGRESS: CHAPTER 2

1. 60 [2.1A] **2.** 26 [2.1B] **3.** $3\frac{1}{3}$ [2.2A] **4.** 9 [2.2A] **5.** $\frac{13}{4}$ [2.2A] **6.** $\frac{17}{1}$ [2.2A] **7.** $\frac{8}{12}$ [2.2B] **8.** $\frac{3}{8}$ [2.2B] **9.** $\frac{2}{3} > \frac{5}{8}$ [2.2C] **10.** $\frac{2}{3}$ [2.3A] **11.** $5\frac{7}{12}$ [2.3A] **12.** $\frac{3}{5}$ [2.3B] **13.** $\frac{27}{40}$ [2.3B] **14.** $2\frac{3}{4}$ [2.4A] **15.** $\frac{1}{15}$ [2.4A] **16.** $\frac{30}{mn}$ [2.4B] **17.** $\frac{1}{3}$ [2.4B] **18.** $\frac{1}{2}$ [2.4C] **19.** $1\frac{7}{11}$ [2.3B] **20.** Yes [2.4A] **21.** $\frac{1}{2}$ [2.4B] **22.** $\frac{6}{7}$ [2.4C] **23.** The length of the exercise course is $68\frac{1}{6}$ yd. [2.3C] **24.** The dimensions of the board are 14 in. by 7 in. by $1\frac{3}{4}$ in. [2.4D]

SECTION 2.5

1. hundredths; thousandths; hundred-thousandths; millionths **3.** and; thousandths **5.** $<$; $<$ **7.** thousandths **9.** ten-thousandths **11.** hundredths **13.** 0.3 **15.** 0.21 **17.** 0.461 **19.** 0.093 **21.** $\frac{1}{10}$ **23.** $\frac{47}{100}$ **25.** $\frac{289}{1000}$ **27.** $\frac{9}{100}$ **29.** thirty-seven hundredths **31.** nine and four tenths **33.** fifty-three ten-thousandths **35.** forty-five thousandths **37.** twenty-six and four hundredths **39.** 3.0806 **41.** 407.03 **43.** 246.024 **45.** 73.02684 **47.** $0.7 > 0.56$ **49.** $3.605 > 3.065$ **51.** $9.004 < 9.04$ **53.** $9.31 > 9.031$ **55.** $4.6 < 40.6$ **57.** $0.07046 > 0.07036$ **59.** 0.609, 0.66, 0.696, 0.699 **61.** 1.237, 1.327, 1.372, 1.732 **63.** 21.78, 21.805, 21.87, 21.875 **65.** $0.62 > 0.062$ **67.** 5.4 **69.** 30.0 **71.** 413.60 **73.** 6.062 **75.** 97 **77.** 5440 **79.** 0.0236 **81a.** The cost to mint a penny is greater than the face value of a penny. **b.** The cost to mint a penny is 2¢. **c.** The cost to mint a nickel is greater than the face value of a nickel. **d.** The cost to mint a nickel is 8¢. **83.** An entrant who completes the Boston Marathon runs 26.2 mi. **85a.** The shipping cost is \$2.40. **b.** The shipping cost is \$3.60. **c.** The shipping cost is \$6.00. **d.** The shipping cost is \$7.00. **e.** The shipping cost is \$4.70. **f.** The shipping cost is \$2.40. **g.** The shipping cost is \$2.40. **87.** Answers will vary. For example, **a.** 0.15 **b.** 1.05 **c.** 0.001

SECTION 2.6

1. $\begin{array}{r} 2.391 \\ 45. \\ +\ 13.0784 \\ \hline 60.4694 \end{array}$ **3.** 1; 2; 3; 1.113 **5.** two; whole; $304.\overset{1.2}{\overline{)364.8}}$ **7.** 5; 4; terminating **9.** 65.9421 **11.** 190.857 **13.** 21.26
15. 21.26 **17.** 2.768 **19.** 56.361 **21.** 53.67 **23.** 12.325; 12 **25.** 33.63; 40 **27.** 0.303; 0.3 **29.** 38.618; 40
31a. The total number of children in grades K–12 is 56.7 million. **b.** There are 43.4 million more children in public school than in private school.
33. 25.653 **35.** 1.321 **37.** 7.01 − 2.325 **39.** 19.35 − 8.967 **41.** 1.70 **43.** 0.03316 **45.** 4250 **47.** 67,100
49. 7.5537; 8.0 **51.** 68.5936; 70 **53.** 32.1485; 30 **55.** 12,534 British pounds would be exchanged for 20,000 U.S. dollars. **57.** 50.16
59. Yes **61.** Two **63.** 32.3 **65.** 67.7 **67.** 6.3 **69.** 5.8 **71.** 0.81 **73.** 0.08 **75.** 5.278 **77.** 0.4805
79. 11.17; 10 **81.** 1.16; 1 **83.** 58.90; 50 **85.** 7.20; 6 **87.** The sales in 2010 were 8 times greater than in 1997. **89.** 5.06
91. Yes **93.** No **95.** Three **97.** 0.375 **99.** $0.\overline{72}$ **101.** $0.58\overline{3}$ **103.** 1.75 **105.** 1.5 **107.** $4.1\overline{6}$ **109.** 2.25
111. 3.8 **113.** $\frac{1}{5}$ **115.** $\frac{3}{4}$ **117.** $\frac{1}{8}$ **119.** $2\frac{1}{2}$ **121.** $4\frac{11}{20}$ **123.** $1\frac{18}{25}$ **125.** $\frac{9}{200}$ **127.** $\frac{9}{10} > 0.89$
129. $\frac{4}{5} < 0.803$ **131.** $0.444 < \frac{4}{9}$ **133.** $0.13 > \frac{3}{25}$ **135.** $\frac{5}{16} > 0.312$ **137.** $\frac{10}{11} > 0.909$ **139.** $\frac{3}{5}$
141. iii and iv **143.** The new balance is $473.72. **145.** A U.S. homeowner's average annual cost of electricity is $1147.92.
147a. The amount of the payments over 36 months is $17,982. **b.** The total cost of the car is $22,982.
149a. The difference for women is 5.3 years. **b.** The difference for men is 5.0 years. **151.** The amount received for the 400 cans is $14.06.
153. You will pay $5.83 in taxes. **155.** Your family will use 0.1 ton of coal in one year.
157a. The reduction in solid waste per month would be 133,333,333 tons. **b.** The reduction in greenhouse gas emissions per month would be 175,000 tons. **159.** The profit on 5 L of cough syrup is $127.80. **161.** The perimeter is 15.5 in. **163.** The area is 14.625 in^2.
165. The perimeter is 13.95 m. **167.** The employee's federal earnings are $562.20. **169.** The force is 41.65 newtons.
171. $1.3 \times 2.31 = \frac{13}{20} \times \frac{231}{100} = \frac{3003}{1000} = 3.003$ **173.** × **175.** × **177.** ÷

SECTION 2.7

1. Addition, division, subtraction **3.** $1\frac{1}{5}$ **5.** $\frac{5}{36}$ **7.** $\frac{11}{32}$ **9.** 1 **11.** 4 **13.** $\frac{8}{9}$ **15.** 1.72 **17.** 1.84 **19.** 2.04
21. $1\frac{3}{10}$ **23.** $1\frac{1}{9}$ **25.** $1\frac{15}{16}$ **27.** $\frac{1}{2}$ **29.** 1 **31.** 18.09 **33.** 30.5 **35.** $\frac{11}{20}$

CHAPTER 2 REVIEW EXERCISES

1. $9\frac{1}{2}$ [2.2A] **2.** $2\frac{5}{6}$ [2.3B] **3.** $1\frac{1}{2}$ [2.4B] **4.** 5.034 [2.5A] **5.** $\frac{7}{25}$ [2.6D] **6.** $2\frac{2}{3}$ [2.4A] **7.** 8.039 < 8.31 [2.5B]
8. $\frac{3}{5} > \frac{7}{15}$ [2.2C] **9.** 150 [2.1A] **10.** 91,800 [2.6B] **11.** $3\frac{1}{3}$ [2.4A] **12.** $\frac{10}{7}$; $1\frac{3}{7}$ [2.2A] **13.** $\frac{3}{7} < 0.429$ [2.6D]
14. $\frac{3}{5}$ [2.4C] **15.** $\frac{32}{72}$ [2.2B] **16.** $\frac{1}{3}$ [2.4A] **17.** $\frac{2}{7}$ [2.7A] **18.** 21 [2.1B] **19.** 0.0142 [2.6C] **20.** 0.1 [2.6C]
21. $\frac{5}{6}$ [2.4B] **22.** 0.11 [2.6C] **23.** 440 [2.6A] **24.** 2.4622 [2.6B] **25.** 50.743 [2.6A] **26.** $2\frac{1}{4}$ [2.4A] **27.** $9\frac{1}{12}$ [2.3A]
28. $\frac{2}{7}$ [2.2B] **29.** $4\frac{7}{10}$ [2.3B] **30.** 6.143 [2.6C] **31.** The cost per ounce is $1.68. [2.6E] **32.** The price of the treadmill is $1499.50. [2.6E] **33.** The wrestler must gain $6\frac{1}{4}$ lb. [2.3C] **34a.** The difference in cost is $2.72 trillion. **b.** The cost of the Vietnam war was 1.5 times greater than the cost of World War I. [2.6E] **35.** The employee's overtime pay is $150. [2.4D]
36. The final velocity is 496 ft/s. [2.4D]

CHAPTER 2 TEST

1. $2\frac{4}{7}$ [2.2A; Example 2] **2.** $3\frac{11}{12}$ [2.3B; HOW TO 9] **3.** $22\frac{1}{2}$ [2.4A; You Try It 4] **4.** $\frac{7}{12}$ [2.4A; Example 3]
5. 90 [2.1A; Example 1] **6.** 9.033 [2.5A; Example 5] **7.** $2\frac{11}{32}$ [2.4A; HOW TO 6] **8.** $\frac{19}{5}$ [2.2A; You Try It 4]
9. $\frac{7}{9}$ [2.4B; Example 6] **10.** 4.003 < 4.009 [2.5B; HOW TO 1] **11.** 7 [2.4C; You Try It 12] **12.** 18 [2.1B; Example 2]
13. $\frac{1}{6}$ [2.3B; HOW TO 6] **14.** $\frac{4}{5}$ [2.2B; Example 8] **15.** $2\frac{17}{24}$ [2.3A; You Try It 5] **16.** $\frac{5}{6} > \frac{11}{15}$ [2.2C; Example 11]
17. $3\frac{16}{25}$ [2.7A; HOW TO 3] **18.** $0.22 < \frac{2}{9}$ [2.6D; HOW TO 20] **19.** 6.051 [2.5C; Example 8] **20.** $1\frac{1}{2}$ [2.4B; Example 10]

21. 22.753 [2.6A; HOW TO 4] **22.** 70 [2.6A; HOW TO 6] **23.** 14.497 [2.6A; HOW TO 1] **24.** 64 [2.6B; You Try It 10]

25. $\frac{12}{28}$ [2.2B; Example 6] **26.** 0.8496 [2.6C; HOW TO 14] **27.** The gross from *Thunderball* was $40.8 million greater than the gross from *On Her Majesty's Secret Service*. [2.6E; You Try It 21] **28.** The patient must lose $10\frac{5}{24}$ lb. [2.3C; You Try It 10]

29. You should buy $17\frac{1}{2}$ lb of hamburger meat. [2.4D; Example 14] **30.** 120 in^2 of felt are needed to make the pennant. [2.4D; You Try It 13]

31. You are required to do 10 more hours of community service. [2.3C; You Try It 10]

32. The perimeter of the triangle is 18.5 m. [2.6E; Example 22]

CUMULATIVE REVIEW EXERCISES

1. 39 [1.4A] **2.** $3\frac{1}{2}$ [2.4A] **3.** $8\frac{11}{18}$ [2.3A] **4.** 0.03879 [2.6C] **5.** 36 [2.1B] **6.** 16 [2.4A] **7.** $1\frac{1}{9}$ [2.4B]

8. 0.76 [2.6D] **9.** 9 [2.4C] **10.** $\frac{7}{11} < \frac{4}{5}$ [2.2C] **11.** $1\frac{22}{27}$ [2.4B] **12.** $\frac{1}{15}$ [2.4A] **13.** 2 [2.4A]

14. $7\frac{1}{28}$ [2.3B] **15.** 18.42 [2.6A] **16.** $1\frac{7}{12}$ [2.7A] **17.** 30 [2.6B] **18.** $6\frac{3}{16}$ [2.3A] **19.** 8,072,092 [1.1B] **20.** $4\frac{5}{9}$ [2.2A]

21. $\frac{1}{7}$ [2.3B] **22.** $\frac{3}{28}$ [2.4A] **23.** 2.8 [2.6C] **24.** 11,272 [1.2A] **25.** 48 [1.4A] **26.** $\frac{3}{10}$ [2.4C]

27. 20,000 [1.2B] **28.** $1\frac{1}{2}$ [2.4B] **29.** $\frac{31}{4}$ [2.2A] **30.** $2^2 \cdot 5 \cdot 7$ [1.3D] **31.** You would burn 40 more calories. [1.3E]

32. The increase in the population is 522,348 people. [1.2C] **33.** The charge for having 75 pages copied is $10.31. [2.6E]

34. The length of fencing needed is 66 ft. [2.4D] **35.** The bicyclist traveled $4\frac{1}{8}$ mi. [2.4D]

36. The pressure on the diver is $22\frac{3}{8}$ pounds per square inch. [2.4D]

Answers to Chapter 3 Selected Exercises

PREP TEST

1. $54 > 45$ [1.1A] **2.** 4 units [1.1A] **3.** 15,847 [1.2A] **4.** 3779 [1.2B] **5.** 26,432 [1.3A] **6.** 6 [1.3C] **7.** $1\frac{4}{15}$ [2.3A]

8. $\frac{7}{16}$ [2.3B] **9.** 11.058 [2.6A] **10.** 3.781 [2.6A] **11.** $\frac{2}{5}$ [2.4A] **12.** $\frac{5}{9}$ [2.4B] **13.** 9.4 [2.6B] **14.** 0.4 [2.6C]

15. 31 [1.4A]

SECTION 3.1

1a. left **b.** right **3.** negative; positive **5.** absolute value **7.** −6 −5 −4 −3 −2 −1 0 1 2 3 4 5 6

9. −6 −5 −4 −3 −2 −1 0 1 2 3 4 5 6 **11.** −6 −5 −4 −3 −2 −1 0 1 2 3 4 5 6

13. −6 −5 −4 −3 −2 −1 0 1 2 3 4 5 6 **15.** 1 **17.** −1 **19.** 3 **21.** *A* is −4. *C* is −2. **23.** *A* is −7. *D* is −4.

25. $-2 > -5$ **27.** $3 > -7$ **29.** $-42 < 27$ **31.** $53 > -46$ **33.** $-51 < -20$ **35.** $-131 < 101$

37. −7, −2, 0, 3 **39.** −5, −3, 1, 4 **41.** −4, 0, 5, 9 **43.** −10, −7, −5, 4, 12 **45a.** Never true **b.** Sometimes true

c. Sometimes true **d.** Always true **47.** −45 **49.** 88 **51.** $-n$ **53.** d **55.** the opposite of negative thirteen

57. the opposite of negative p **59.** five plus negative ten **61.** negative fourteen minus negative three **63.** negative thirteen minus eight

65. m plus negative n **67.** 7 **69.** −46 **71.** 73 **73.** z **75.** $-p$ **77.** Negative **79.** 4 **81.** 9 **83.** 11 **85.** 12

87. 23 **89.** −27 **91.** 25 **93.** −41 **95.** −93 **97.** 10 **99.** 8 **101.** 6 **103.** $|-12| > |8|$ **105.** $|6| < |13|$

107. $|-1| < |-17|$ **109.** $|x| = |-x|$ **111.** $-|6|, -(4), |-7|, -(-9)$ **113.** $-9, -|-7|, -(5), |4|$

115. $-|10|, -|-8|, -(-2), -(-3), |5|$ **117.** The USPS loss as a negative number is −329,000,000.

119. The loss was greater during the first quarter. **121a.** The predicted earnings per share for Mycopen in 2015 are −27¢.

b. The predicted earnings per share for Mycopen in 2017 are −40¢. **123.** Yes, Mycopen is predicted to have a profit in 2018.

125. The stock that showed the least net change is Stock B. **127.** The wind chill factor is −9°F. **129.** The cooling power is −35°F.

131. A temperature of −30°F with a 5-mile-per-hour wind would feel colder than a temperature of −20°F with a 10-mile-per-hour wind.

133. 11, −11 **135.** −6, −5, −4, −3, −2, −1, 0, 1, 2, 3, 4, 5, 6 **137a.** −2 and 6 **b.** −2 and 8 **139.** Answers will vary.

SECTION 3.2

1. the same; negative **3.** Negative; negative **5.** Negative; minus **7.** (-5) **9.** -11 **11.** -5 **13.** 8 **15.** -4 **17.** -2 **19.** -9 **21.** 1 **23.** -15 **25.** 0 **27.** -21 **29.** -14 **31.** 19 **33.** -5 **35.** -30 **37.** 9 **39.** -12 **41.** -28 **43.** -13 **45.** -18 **47.** 11 **49.** 1 **51.** $x + (-7)$ **53a.** The total of the U.S. balance of trade with Japan and Mexico is $-\$126,500,000,000$. **b.** The total of the U.S. balance of trade with Canada and Mexico is $-\$94,900,000,000$. **c.** The total of the U.S. balance of trade with Japan and China is $-\$333,200,000,000$. **55.** 5 **57.** -2 **59.** -11 **61.** -17 **63.** The Addition Property of Zero **65.** The Associative Property of Addition **67.** 0 **69.** 18 **71.** No **73.** Yes **75.** No **77.** Sometimes true **79.** Always true **81.** -3 **83.** -13 **85.** 7 **87.** 0 **89.** -17 **91.** -3 **93.** 12 **95.** 27 **97.** -106 **99.** -67 **101.** -6 **103.** -15 **105.** The difference between the highest and lowest temperatures ever recorded in South America is 82°C. **107.** -9 **109.** 11 **111.** 0 **113.** -138 **115.** 26 **117.** 13 **119.** -8 **121.** 5 **123.** 2 **125.** -6 **127.** 12 **129.** -3 **131.** 18 **133.** Yes **135.** No **137.** Yes **139.** Sometimes true **141a.** The difference in elevation between Mt. Aconcagua and Death Valley is 7046 m. **b.** The difference in elevation between Mt. Kilimanjaro and Lake Assal is 6051 m. **143.** Europe has the smallest difference between highest and lowest elevations. **145.** The difference between the average temperatures at 12,000 ft and 40,000 ft is 86°. **147.** The golfer's score relative to par is -3. **149a.** The difference between the high and low temperatures in the United States on April 2, 2010, was 107°F. **b.** The difference between the high and low temperatures in the contiguous 48 states on April 2, 2010, was 100°F. **151.** The distance is 19 units. **153.** Answers will vary. Possible answers include -1 and -6, -2 and -5, and -3 and -4.

CHECK YOUR PROGRESS: CHAPTER 3

1. 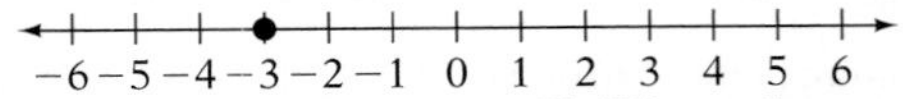

[3.1A] **2.** -3 [3.1A] **3.** $-12 > -16$ [3.1A] **4.** $-19, -8, 4, 7$ [3.1A] **5a.** 11 **b.** -13 **c.** m [3.1B] **6.** negative five minus negative seven [3.1B] **7a.** 42 **b.** $-t$ [3.1B] **8a.** 18 **b.** 37 [3.1C] **9a.** 51 **b.** -67 [3.1C] **10.** -2 [3.1C] **11.** $|-19| > |7|$ [3.1C] **12.** $-|12|, -|-8|, |3|, |-5|, -(-6)$ [3.1C] **13.** -20 [3.2A] **14.** 10 [3.2A] **15.** -35 [3.2B] **16.** -16 [3.2B] **17.** 23 [3.2B] **18.** -27 [3.2B] **19.** -1 [3.2A] **20.** 4 [3.2A] **21.** 2 [3.2B] **22.** No [3.2B] **23.** The colder temperature is -16°F. [3.1D] **24.** The new temperature is 5°C. [3.2C] **25.** The distance between the points is 14 units. [3.2C]

SECTION 3.3

1a. different; negative **b.** the same; positive **3.** $\frac{-63}{9}$ **5.** -24 **7.** 6 **9.** 18 **11.** -20 **13.** -16 **15.** 25 **17.** 0 **19.** 42 **21.** -128 **23.** 208 **25.** -243 **27.** -115 **29.** 238 **31.** -96 **33.** -210 **35.** -224 **37.** -40 **39.** 180 **41.** $-qr$ **43a.** The projected 2011 annual net income for Sears Holdings is $-\$680,000,000$. **b.** The projected 2011 annual net income for Rite Aid is $-\$296,000,000$. **45.** The Multiplication Property of One **47.** The Associative Property of Multiplication **49.** -6 **51.** 1 **53.** -24 **55.** -60 **57.** 357 **59.** -56 **61.** -1600 **63.** No **65.** No **67.** Yes **69.** Positive **71.** -6 **73.** 8 **75.** -49 **77.** 8 **79.** -11 **81.** 14 **83.** 13 **85.** 1 **87.** 26 **89.** 23 **91.** -110 **93.** 111 **95.** $\frac{-9}{x}$ **97.** The average monthly net income for Delta Air Lines was $-\$106$ million. **99.** -9 **101.** 9 **103.** -6 **105.** 6 **107.** Yes **109.** No **111.** Yes **113.** $\frac{a}{b}$ **115.** $-\frac{a}{b}$ **117.** The average score of the four golfers was -3. **119.** The average record low temperature for the first three months of the year is -63°F. **121.** The average U.S. trade deficit for March, April, and May 2011 was $-\$47$ billion. **123.** The average daily low temperature for the week is -4°. **125.** Answers will vary. A possible answer is $(-3)(2) = -3 + (-3) = -6$. **127.** -2; $-16, 32, -64, 128$ **129.** 5; $-125, -625, -3125, -15{,}625$

SECTION 3.4

1a. Integers: 0, -3 **b.** Rational numbers: $-\frac{15}{2}, 0, -3, 2.3\overline{3}$ **c.** Irrational numbers: π, 4.232232223…, $\frac{\sqrt{5}}{4}$, $\sqrt{7}$ **d.** all **3.** $-\frac{5}{24}$ **5.** $-\frac{19}{24}$ **7.** $\frac{5}{26}$ **9.** $\frac{7}{24}$ **11.** $-\frac{19}{60}$ **13.** $-\frac{11}{8}$ **15.** $\frac{3}{4}$ **17.** $-\frac{47}{48}$ **19.** $\frac{3}{8}$ **21.** $-\frac{7}{60}$ **23.** $\frac{13}{24}$ **25.** -3.4 **27.** -8.89 **29.** -8.0 **31.** -0.68 **33.** -11.03 **35.** -6.8 **37.** -20.7 **39.** -37.19 **41.** -34.99 **43.** $-\frac{5}{48}$ **45.** $-1\frac{5}{36}$ **47.** $1\frac{3}{10}$ **49.** -649.36 **51.** $-\frac{1}{6}$ **53.** $-1\frac{5}{24}$ **55.** -25.665 **57.** $-1\frac{1}{3}$ **59.** $\frac{1}{12}$ **61.** -27.553 **63.** -1.412 **65.** Yes **67.** Yes **69.** Negative **71.** $\frac{1}{21}$ **73.** $\frac{2}{9}$ **75.** $-\frac{2}{9}$ **77.** $-\frac{45}{328}$ **79.** $\frac{2}{3}$ **81.** $\frac{15}{64}$ **83.** $-\frac{3}{7}$ **85.** $-\frac{10}{9}$ **87.** $\frac{5}{6}$ **89.** $-\frac{16}{7}$ **91.** $-\frac{27}{2}$ **93.** 31.15 **95.** -112.97 **97.** 0.0363 **99.** 97 **101.** 2.2 **103.** $-\frac{1}{12}$ **105.** $-\frac{1}{21}$ **107.** $-1\frac{1}{24}$ **109.** -131.328 **111.** -25.4 **113.** $-17\frac{1}{2}$ **115.** -8 **117.** -48 **119.** $-1\frac{3}{5}$ **121.** $-1\frac{1}{2}$

123. 10.5 **125.** −1.7 **127.** Yes **129.** No **131.** False **133.** The temperature fell 32.22°C in 27 min. **135.** The difference is greater than 4.8. **137.** The difference is 14.06°C. **139a.** True **b.** True **c.** False **d.** False **141.** $-\frac{7}{8} < -\frac{5}{6}$ **143.** $-\frac{3}{4} < -0.7$

SECTION 3.5

1. division **3.** −6 **5.** −5 **7.** 2 **9.** 1 **11.** 14 **13.** −5 **15.** −6 **17.** 0.21 **19.** −0.29 **21.** −1 **23.** $-\frac{5}{8}$ **25.** −1 **27.** 74 **29.** 12 **31.** 4 **33.** −3 **35.** 1.35 **37.** $\frac{1}{9}$ **39.** $\frac{3}{8}$ **41.** 2 **43.** 1 **45.** 15 **47.** 32 **49.** 1 **51.** 28 **53.** 1 **55.** 20 **57.** Negative **59.** −4 **61a.** No **b.** Yes **63.** $6 - 12 \div 2 \cdot (3 - 5)^2$

CHAPTER 3 REVIEW EXERCISES

1. eight minus negative one [3.1B] **2.** −36 [3.1C] **3.** 200 [3.3A] **4.** −9 [3.3B] **5.** −14 [3.2A] **6.** 13 [3.1B] **7.** (number line from −6 to 6 with a dot at −2) −6 −5 −4 −3 −2 −1 0 1 2 3 4 5 6 [3.1A] **8.** −98.38 [3.4A] **9.** 17 [3.3B] **10.** −210 [3.3B] **11.** −2 [3.2B] **12.** −18 [3.3A] **13.** −1 [3.2A] **14.** −72 [3.3A] **15.** −4 [3.5A] **16.** −2 [3.2B] **17.** The difference between Tom Lehman's score and Mark Calcavecchia's score is 18 points. [3.2C] **18.** 13 [3.2B] **19.** $\frac{2}{7}$ [3.4B] **20.** Yes [3.2B] **21.** 14 [3.2B] **22.** 0 [3.3B] **23.** −60 [3.3A] **24.** −12 [3.2A] **25.** 5 [3.5A] **26.** −8 > −10 [3.1A] **27.** 21 [3.2A] **28.** 27 [3.1C] **29.** −2.8 [3.4B] **30.** $-\frac{5}{48}$ [3.4A] **31.** 9 [3.5A] **32.** The colder temperature is −12°C. [3.1D] **33.** The boiling point of neon is −238°C. [3.3C] **34.** The new temperature is −3°C. [3.2C] **35.** The distance between the points is 12 units. [3.2C]

CHAPTER 3 TEST

1. negative three plus negative five [3.1B; Example 6] **2.** −34 [3.1C; Example 9B] **3.** 18 [3.2B; Example 10] **4.** −20 [3.2A; HOW TO 7] **5.** 24 [3.3A; HOW TO 3] **6.** $-\frac{7}{18}$ [3.4A; HOW TO 1] **7.** 12 [3.3B; You Try It 6] **8.** 2 [3.2A; HOW TO 6] **9.** 16 > −19 [3.1A; Example 3B] **10.** −2 [3.2B; HOW TO 12] **11.** −3 [3.2B; HOW TO 14] **12.** 49 [3.1B; Example 7] **13.** −250 [3.3A; Example 1] **14.** −|5|, −(3), |−9|, −(−11) [3.1C; You Try It 11] **15.** No [3.2B; Example 14] **16.** −3 [3.1A; Example 1] **17.** The difference between Taylor Leon's score and Yani Tseng's score is 21 points. [3.2C; Example 17] **18.** 0 [3.3B; You Try It 5] **19.** 19 [3.5A; HOW TO 2] **20.** −25 [3.1B; Example 5] **21.** −11.613 [3.4A; You Try It 3] **22.** −11 [3.2B; HOW TO 11] **23.** 24 [3.3B; Example 6] **24.** 10 [3.5A; You Try It 1] **25.** −7 [3.3B; Example 8] **26.** 60 [3.3A; HOW TO 3] **27.** −27 [3.4B; Example 8] **28.** −10 [3.2B; You Try It 10] **29.** −107 [3.5A; HOW TO 2] **30.** −1.53 [3.4B; Example 13] **31.** −15.31 [3.4A; HOW TO 6] **32.** The new temperature is 5°C. [3.2C; Example 16] **33.** The wind chill factor is −64°F. [3.3A; Apply the Concept, p. 116] **34.** The temperature fell by 5.25°C. [3.4C; You Try It 15] **35.** The distance between the points is 16 units. [3.2C; Example 15]

CUMULATIVE REVIEW EXERCISES

1. 5 [3.2B] **2.** 12,000 [1.3A] **3.** 32.3 [2.6C] **4.** 2 [1.4A] **5.** −82 [3.1C] **6.** 309,480 [1.1B] **7.** 2400 [1.3A] **8.** 21 [3.3B] **9.** −11 [3.2B] **10.** −40 [3.2A] **11.** 1, 2, 4, 11, 22, 44 [1.3D] **12.** 1 [2.4A] **13.** 630,000 [1.1C] **14.** 1300 [1.2A] **15.** 9 [3.2B] **16.** −2500 [3.3A] **17.** 8.77 [2.6A] **18.** $5\frac{2}{3}$ [2.3A] **19.** −32 [3.5A] **20.** −4 [3.3B] **21.** $1\frac{1}{5}$ [2.4B] **22.** −62 < 26 [3.1A] **23.** 126 [3.3A] **24.** 4.14 [3.4B] **25.** $2^5 \cdot 7^2$ [1.3B] **26.** 47 [1.4A] **27.** 10,062 [1.2A] **28.** −26 [3.2B] **29.** 5000 [1.2B] **30.** 2025 [1.3B] **31.** The land area of the United States immediately after the Louisiana Purchase was 1,722,685 mi^2. [1.2C] **32.** Albert Einstein was 76 years old when he died. [1.2C] **33.** The amount still owed for the car is $27,650. [1.2C] **34.** The total cost of the land is $281,750. [1.3E] **35.** The new temperature is −5°C. [3.2C] **36a.** The difference between the record high and record low temperatures for Arizona is 168°F. **b.** The difference between the record high and record low temperatures is the greatest in Alaska. [3.2C] **37.** Your fourth-quarter sales must be $24,900. [1.2C] **38.** The golfer's score relative to par is −8. [3.2C]

Answers to Chapter 4 Selected Exercises

PREP TEST

1. 3 [3.2B] **2.** 4 [3.3B] **3.** $\frac{1}{12}$ [3.4A] **4.** $-\frac{4}{9}$ [2.4B] **5.** $\frac{3}{10}$ [3.4B] **6.** −16 [3.5A] **7.** $\frac{8}{27}$ [2.4A] **8.** 48 [1.4A] **9.** 1 [1.4A] **10.** 12 [3.5A]

SECTION 4.1

1. $2x^2, 5x, \underline{-8}$ **3.** $-a^4, \underline{6}$ **5.** $7x^2y, \underline{6xy^2}$ **7.** $1, -9$ **9.** $1, -4, -1$ **13.** 10 **15.** 32 **17.** 21 **19.** 16 **21.** -9 **23.** 41 **25.** -7 **27.** 13 **29.** -15 **31.** 41 **33.** 1 **35.** 5 **37.** 1 **39.** 57 **41.** 5 **43.** 8 **45.** -3 **47.** -2 **49.** -4 **51.** Positive **53.** Negative **55.** 41 **57.** 1 **59.** -23 **61a.** 2 **b.** 5 **c.** 6 **d.** 7; $n^x > x^n$ if $x > n$ or $x > n + 1$

SECTION 4.2

1. Commutative **3.** reciprocal (or multiplicative inverse) **7.** $14x$ **9.** $5a$ **11.** $-6y$ **13.** $7 - 3b$ **15.** $5a$ **17.** $-2ab$ **19.** $5xy$ **21.** 0 **23.** $-\frac{5}{6}x$ **25.** $6.5x$ **27.** $0.45x$ **29.** $7a$ **31.** $-14x^2$ **33.** $-\frac{11}{24}x$ **35.** $17x - 3y$ **37.** $-2a - 6b$ **39.** $-3x - 8y$ **41.** $-4x^2 - 2x$ **43.** iv and v **45.** $60x$ **47.** $-10a$ **49.** $30y$ **51.** $72x$ **53.** $-28a$ **55.** $108b$ **57.** $-56x^2$ **59.** x^2 **61.** x **63.** a **65.** b **67.** x **69.** n **71.** $2x$ **73.** $-2x$ **75.** $-15a^2$ **77.** $6y$ **79.** $3y$ **81.** $-2x$ **83.** $-9y$ **85.** $8x - 6$ **87.** $-2a - 14$ **89.** $-6y + 24$ **91.** $-x - 2$ **93.** $35 - 21b$ **95.** $2 - 5y$ **97.** $15x^2 + 6x$ **99.** $2y - 18$ **101.** $-15x - 30$ **103.** $-6x^2 - 28$ **105.** $-6y^2 + 21$ **107.** $3x^2 - 3y^2$ **109.** $-4x + 12y$ **111.** $-6a^2 + 7b^2$ **113.** $4x^2 - 12x + 20$ **115.** $\frac{3}{2}x - \frac{9}{2}y + 6$ **117.** $-12a^2 - 20a + 28$ **119.** $12x^2 - 9x + 12$ **121.** $10x^2 - 20xy - 5y^2$ **123.** $-8b^2 + 6b - 9$ **125.** iii **127.** $a - 7$ **129.** $-11x + 13$ **131.** $-4y - 4$ **133.** $-2x - 16$ **135.** $14y - 45$ **137.** $a + 7b$ **139.** $6x + 28$ **141.** $5x - 75$ **143.** $4x - 4$ **145.** $2x - 9$ **147.** $1.24x + 0.36$ **149.** $-0.01x + 40$ **153a.** Yes; for example, $3 \otimes 2 = (3 \cdot 2) - (3 + 2) = 6 - 5 = 1$ and $2 \otimes 3 = (2 \cdot 3) - (2 + 3) = 6 - 5 = 1$. **b.** No; for example, $[3 \otimes 2] \otimes 4 = 1 \otimes 4 = -1$ but $3 \otimes [2 \otimes 4] = 3 \otimes 2 = 1$.

CHECK YOUR PROGRESS: CHAPTER 4

1. -12 [4.1A] **2.** 46 [4.1A] **3.** 7 [4.1A] **4.** -2 [4.1A] **5.** 6 [4.1A] **6.** -1 [4.1A] **7.** $-3y$ [4.2A] **8.** $3a + 4b$ [4.2A] **9.** $-40a$ [4.2B] **10.** z [4.2B] **11.** $36 - 24b$ [4.2C] **12.** $6x^2 - 8x + 10$ [4.2C] **13.** $-5x + 20$ [4.2D] **14.** $9a - 46$ [4.2D] **15.** $-18x + 23$ [4.2D]

SECTION 4.3

1. sum, times **3.** total, divided by **5.** $25 - x$ **7.** $8 + y$ **9.** $t + 10$ **11.** $z + 14$ **13.** $x^2 - 20$ **15.** $\frac{3}{4}n + 12$ **17.** $8 + \frac{n}{4}$ **19.** $3(y + 7)$ **21.** $t(t + 16)$ **23.** $\frac{1}{2}x^2 + 15$ **25.** $5n^3 + n^2$ **27.** $r - \frac{r}{3}$ **29.** $x^2 - (x + 17)$ **31.** $9(z + 4)$ **33.** Answers will vary. For example: The product of 5 and 1 more than the square of n, or 5 times the sum of 1 plus the square of n **35.** $\frac{x}{18}$ **37.** $x + 20$ **39.** $11x - 8$ **41.** $\frac{7}{5 + x}$ **43.** $40 - \frac{x}{20}$ **45.** $x^2 + 2x$ **47.** $10(x - 50)$; $10x - 500$ **49.** $x - (x + 3)$; -3 **51.** $(2x - 4) + x$; $3x - 4$ **53.** $x - (3x - 8)$; $-2x + 8$ **55.** $3x + x$; $4x$ **57.** $(x + 6) + 5$; $x + 11$ **59.** $x - (x + 10)$; -10 **61.** $\frac{1}{6}x + \frac{4}{9}x$; $\frac{11}{18}x$ **63.** s represents the number of students enrolled in fall-term science classes.
65. Let M be the number of visitors to the Metropolitan Museum of Art; the number of visitors to the Louvre is $M + 3{,}800{,}000$.
67. Let d be the noise level, in decibels, of a car horn; the noise level of an ambulance siren is $d + 10$.
69. Let T be U2's concert ticket sales; Bruce Springsteen and the E Street Band's concert ticket sales are $T - 28{,}500{,}000$.
71. Let N be the number of bones in your body; the number of bones in your foot is $\frac{1}{4}N$.
73. Let d be the diameter of a baseball; diameter of a basketball is $4d$.
75. Let B be the attendance at major league basketball games; the attendance at major league baseball games is $B + 50{,}000{,}000$.
77. Let L be the measure of the largest angle; the measure of the smallest angle is $\frac{1}{2}L - 10$.
79. Let h be the number of hours of labor; the amount of the repair bill is $238 + 89h$.
81. Let x be the distance traveled by the slower car; the distance traveled by the faster car is $200 - x$.
83. The number of hydrogen atoms in the pound of sugar in terms of the number of oxygen atoms is $2x$.
87. Answers will vary. For example: 16 less than d; the difference between d and 16; d decreased by 16; 16 subtracted from d.
89. Answers will vary. For example: y divided by 5; the quotient of y and 5; the ratio of y to 5.

CHAPTER 4 REVIEW EXERCISES

1. $3x^2 - 24x - 21$ [4.2C] **2.** $11x$ [4.2A] **3.** $8a - 4b$ [4.2A] **4.** $-5n$ [4.2B] **5.** 79 [4.1A] **6.** $10x - 35$ [4.2C] **7.** $-42x^2$ [4.2B] **8.** $-63 - 36x$ [4.2C] **9.** $-5y$ [4.2A] **10.** -4 [4.1A] **11.** $-6x - 1$ [4.2D] **12.** $-40a + 40$ [4.2D] **13.** $24y + 30$ [4.2D] **14.** $9c - 5d$ [4.2A] **15.** $20x$ [4.2B] **16.** $7x + 46$ [4.2D] **17.** $-4x^2 + 6x$ [4.2A] **18.** $-90x + 25$ [4.2D] **19.** $-0.2x + 150$ [4.2D] **20.** $-\frac{1}{12}x$ [4.2A] **21.** $28a^2 - 8a + 12$ [4.2C] **22.** -7 [4.1A] **23.** $36y$ [4.2B] **24.** $\frac{2}{3}(x + 10)$ [4.3A] **25.** $x - 6$ [4.3A]

26. $x + 2x$; $3x$ [4.3B] **27.** $2x - \frac{1}{2}x$; $\frac{3}{2}x$ [4.3B] **28.** $3x + 5(x - 1)$; $8x - 5$ [4.3B] **29.** Let A be the number of American League players' cards; the number of National League players' cards is $5A$. [4.3C]
30. Let T be the number of ten-dollar bills; the number of five-dollar bills is $35 - T$. [4.3C]
31. Let a be the number of calories in an apple; the number of calories in the candy bar is $2a + 8$. [4.3C]
32. Let w be the width of the Parthenon; the length of the Parthenon is $1.6w$. [4.3C]
33. Let h be the person's kneeling height; the person's standing height is $1.3h$. [4.3C]

CHAPTER 4 TEST

1. $5x$ [4.2A; HOW TO 1] **2.** $-6x^2 + 21y^2$ [4.2C; HOW TO 9] **3.** $-x + 6$ [4.2D; Example 11]
4. $-7x + 33$ [4.2D; Example 13] **5.** $-9x - 7y$ [4.2A; Example 1] **6.** 22 [4.1A; HOW TO 1]
7. $2x$ [4.2B; Example 5] **8.** $7x + 38$ [4.2D; Example 12] **9.** $-10x^2 + 15x - 30$ [4.2C; Example 9]
10. $-2x - 5y$ [4.2A; Example 1] **11.** 3 [4.1A; Example 3] **12.** $3x$ [4.2B; HOW TO 7]
13. y^2 [4.2A; Example 2] **14.** $-4x + 8$ [4.2C; You Try It 8] **15.** $-10a$ [4.2B; Example 5]
16. $2x + y$ [4.2D; Example 13] **17.** $36y$ [4.2B; You Try It 4] **18.** $15 - 35b$ [4.2C; Example 6]
19. $a^2 - b^2$ [4.3A; HOW TO 2] **20.** $10(x - 3) = 10x - 30$ [4.3B; HOW TO 3]
21. $x + 2x^2$ [4.3B; Example 4] **22.** $\frac{6}{x} - 3$ [4.3B; HOW TO 3] **23.** $b - 7b$ [4.3A; Example 2]
24. Let d be the distance from Earth to the sun; the distance from Neptune to the sun is $30d$. [4.3C; You Try It 5]
25. Let x be the length of the shorter piece; the length of the longer piece is $4x - 3$. [4.3C; Example 5]

CUMULATIVE REVIEW EXERCISES

1. -7 [3.2A] **2.** 5 [3.2B] **3.** 24 [3.3A] **4.** -5 [3.3B] **5.** $2 \cdot 5 \cdot 11$ [1.3D] **6.** $\frac{11}{48}$ [3.4C]
7. $-\frac{1}{6}$ [3.4B] **8.** $\frac{1}{4}$ [3.4B] **9.** 1300 [1.2A] **10.** -5 [3.5A] **11.** $-\frac{27}{26}$ [3.5A] **12.** 16 [4.1A]
13. $5x^2$ [4.2A] **14.** $-7a - 10b$ [4.2A] **15.** 8.357 [2.5A] **16.** 96 ft [1.3E] **17.** $24 - 6x$ [4.2C]
18. $6y - 18$ [4.2C] **19.** 10 [2.6A] **20.** 8.7 [2.5C] **21.** $-8x^2 + 12y^2$ [4.2C]
22. $-9y^2 + 9y + 21$ [4.2C] **23.** $-7x + 14$ [4.2D] **24.** $5x - 43$ [4.2D] **25.** $17x - 24$ [4.2D]
26. $-3x + 21y$ [4.2D] **27.** $\frac{1}{2}b + b$ [4.3A] **28.** $\frac{10}{y - 2}$ [4.3A] **29.** $8 - \frac{x}{12}$ [4.3B]
30. $x + (x + 2)$; $2x + 2$ [4.3B] **31.** The area is 3600 ft^2. [1.3E] **32.** Let w be the speed of the wildebeest; the speed of the peregrine falcon is $4w$. [4.3C]

Answers to Chapter 5 Selected Exercises

PREP TEST

1. 1 [3.4B] **2.** 1 [3.4B] **3.** $7y$ [4.2A] **4.** -9 [4.2A] **5.** $\frac{7}{6}x$ [4.2A] **6.** $9x - 18$ [4.2C] **7.** -5 [4.1A]
8. $5 - 2n$ [4.3B] **9.** Let s be the speed of the old card. The speed of the new card is $5s$. [4.3C]
10. The length of the shorter piece in terms of x is $5 - x$. [4.3C]

SECTION 5.1

1a. Equation **b.** Expression **c.** Expression **d.** Equation **e.** Expression **3.** i, ii, and iv are equations of the form $x + a = b$; you would subtract a from both sides. **5.** Keith had the greater average speed. **7.** Yes **9.** No **11.** No **13.** Yes **15.** No **17.** Yes **19.** Yes **21.** No **25.** 2 **27.** 15 **29.** 6 **31.** 3 **33.** 0 **35.** -7 **37.** -7 **39.** -12 **41.** -5 **43.** 15 **45.** 9 **47.** 14 **49.** -1 **51.** 1 **53.** $-\frac{1}{2}$ **55.** $-\frac{7}{12}$ **57.** 0.6529 **59.** 9.257 **61.** -3 **63.** 0 **65.** -2 **67.** 180 **69.** 0 **71.** 6 **73.** -10 **75.** 12 **77.** -12 **79.** 0 **81.** -24 **83.** $\frac{1}{3}$ **85.** 4.745 **87.** 2.06 **89.** 7 **91.** 4 **93.** 3 **95.** Positive **97.** Negative **99a.** The distance biked by Emma is equal to the distance biked by Morgan. **b.** The time spent biking by Emma is less than the time spent biking by Morgan. **101.** The dietician's average rate of speed is 30 mph. **103.** Marcella's average rate of speed is 36 mph. **105.** It would take Palmer 2.5 h to walk the same course. **107.** The two joggers will meet in 40 min. **109.** The two cyclists are 8.5 mi apart. **111.** The two trains are 30 mi apart. **113.** -15 **115.** 5 **117.** 6 **119.** One possible answer is $x + 7 = 9$. **121.** $\frac{7}{11}$

SECTION 5.2

1a. i **b.** iii **c.** ii **d.** iv **3.** 5; 8 **5.** 3 **7.** 6 **9.** -1 **11.** -3 **13.** 2 **15.** 2 **17.** 5 **19.** -3 **21.** 6 **23.** 3 **25.** 1 **27.** 6 **29.** -7 **31.** 0 **33.** $\frac{3}{4}$ **35.** $\frac{4}{9}$ **37.** $\frac{1}{3}$ **39.** $-\frac{1}{2}$ **41.** $-\frac{3}{4}$ **43.** $\frac{1}{3}$ **45.** $-\frac{1}{6}$ **47.** 0 **49.** 0.15 **51.** $-\frac{3}{2}$ **53.** 18 **55.** 8 **57.** -16 **59.** 25 **61.** $\frac{3}{4}$ **63.** $\frac{3}{8}$ **65.** $\frac{16}{9}$ **67.** $\frac{1}{18}$ **69.** $\frac{15}{2}$ **71.** $-\frac{18}{5}$ **73.** 2 **75.** 3 **77.** Negative **79.** Negative **81.** The average crown spread of the baldcypress is 57 ft. **83.** There are 9 g of protein in an 8-ounce serving of the yogurt. **85.** The initial velocity is 8 ft/s. **87.** The depreciated value will be $38,000 after 2 years. **89.** The approximate length is 31.8 in. **91.** The distance the car will slide is 168 ft. **93.** ii **95.** $x = 4$ **97.** $y = -6$ **99.** -11 **101.** One possible answer is $2x + 5 = -1$.

SECTION 5.3

1. True **3.** True **5.** -2 **7.** 3 **9.** -2 **11.** -3 **13.** 2 **15.** -2 **17.** -0.2 **19.** 0 **21.** -2 **23.** -2 **25.** -2 **27.** 4 **29.** $\frac{3}{4}$ **31.** $\frac{3}{2}$ **33.** -14 **35.** 7 **37.** ii **39.** 1 **41.** 4 **43.** -1 **45.** -1 **47.** 24 **49.** 495 **51.** $\frac{1}{2}$ **53.** $-\frac{1}{3}$ **55.** $\frac{10}{3}$ **57.** $-\frac{1}{4}$ **59.** 0 **61.** The customer was driven 6 mi. **63a.** The fulcrum is 5 ft from the other person. **b.** The person who is 3 ft from the fulcrum is heavier. **c.** No, the seesaw will not balance. **65.** The fulcrum must be placed 10 ft from the child. **67.** The fulcrum must be placed 4.8 ft from the 90-pound child. **69.** The force on the lip of the can is 1770 lb. **71.** The break-even point is 260 barbecues. **73.** The break-even point is 520 recorders. **75.** The oxygen consumption is 54.8 ml/min. **77.** 4 **79.** No solution **83.** 6 **85.** Hampton's population at the beginning of the 1990s was 30,000 people.

CHECK YOUR PROGRESS: CHAPTER 5

1. Yes [5.1A] **2.** -11 [5.1B] **3.** 9 [5.1C] **4.** 4 [5.2A] **5.** Yes [5.1A] **6.** $-\frac{1}{2}$ [5.1B] **7.** 1 [5.3B] **8.** -1 [5.3A] **9.** No [5.1A] **10.** 100 [5.1B] **11.** $\frac{4}{5}$ [5.1C] **12.** 28 [5.2A] **13.** $\frac{4}{3}$ [5.1C] **14.** 3 [5.3B] **15.** -7 [5.3A] **16.** 1 [5.3B] **17.** The trip lasts 6 h. [5.1D] **18.** The passenger was driven 5 mi. [5.3C] **19.** No, the seesaw is not balanced. [5.3C]

SECTION 5.4

1. True **3.** True **5.** equals **7.** 1; 2; 2 **9.** $x - 15 = 7$; 22 **11.** $9 - x = 7$; 2 **13.** $5 - 2x = 1$; 2 **15.** $2x + 5 = 15$; 5 **17.** $4x - 6 = 22$; 7 **19.** $3(4x - 7) = 15$; 3 **21.** $3x = 2(20 - x)$; 8, 12 **23.** $2x - (14 - x) = 1$; 5, 9 **25.** 15, 17, 19 **27.** -1, 1, 3 **29.** 4, 6 **31.** iii **33.** The length of the Golden Gate Bridge is 1280 m. **35.** The U. S. gross national product in 1937 was $91 billion. **37.** The lengths of the sides of the triangle are 6 ft, 6 ft, and 11 ft. **39.** The intensity of the sound of a jet engine is 140 decibels. **41.** The area of Greenland is 840,000 mi^2. **43.** The number of kilowatt-hours used is 515 kWh. **45.** The executive used the phone for 951 min. **47.** The customer pays $.15 per text message over 300 messages. **49.** The perimeter of the larger square is 8 ft. **51.** The cyclist will complete the entire trip in $\frac{1}{3}$ additional hour. **53.** The integers are -12, -10, -8, and -6. **55.** Any three consecutive odd integers **57.** even **59.** even **61.** even **63.** even **65.** odd

SECTION 5.5

1. $10.50 **3.** $.76 **7.** 2 lb of dog food and 3 lb of vitamin supplement should be used to make the 5-pound mixture. **9.** 8 lb of chamomile tea must be used. **11.** The cost per pound of the mixture is $6.98. **13.** The amount of herbs costing $1 per ounce is 20 oz. **15.** The amount of pepper cheese is 1.5 kg; the amount of Pennsylvania Jack is 3.5 kg. **17.** The amount of meal costing $.80 per pound is 300 lb. **19.** 37 lb of almonds and 63 lb of walnuts were used. **21.** The cost per pound of the breakfast cereal is $1.40. **23.** The parks department bought 8 bundles of seedlings and 6 bundles of container-grown plants. **25.** The cost per ounce of the sunscreen is $3. **27.** The first plane is flying at 105 mph and the second plane is flying at 130 mph. **29.** The second skater will overtake the first skater 40 s after the second skater starts. **31.** Michael's boat will be alongside the tour boat 2 h after the tour boat leaves. **33.** The distance from the airport to the corporate offices is 120 mi. **35.** The sailboat traveled 36 mi in the first 3 h. **37.** The passenger train is traveling at 50 mph and the freight train is traveling at 30 mph. **39.** It takes 1 h for the second ship to catch up to the first ship. **41.** The rate of the faster car is 95 km/h. **43.** The second car will not overtake the first car. **45.** The bus overtakes the car 180 mi from the starting point. **47.** The plane flew 2 h at 115 mph and 3 h at 125 mph. **49.** The mixture contains 10 lb of walnuts and 20 lb of cashews. **51.** The campers turned around downstream at 10:15 A.M. **53.** The cyclist's average speed for the trip was $13\frac{1}{3}$ mph. **55.** The round trip was 8 mi.

CHAPTER 5 REVIEW EXERCISES

1. 21 [5.1B] **2.** 10 [5.3B] **3.** 7 [5.2A] **4.** No [5.1A] **5.** 20 [5.1C] **6.** −2 [5.3B] **7.** −4 [5.1B] **8.** 4 [5.3A] **9.** −1 [5.3B] **10.** 4 [5.3A] **11.** $-\frac{5}{2}$ [5.3A] **12.** $\frac{5}{4}$ [5.1C] **13.** 10 [5.2A] **14.** $\frac{4}{3}$ [5.3B] **15.** The force is 24 lb. [5.3C] **16.** The average speed on the winding road was 32 mph. [5.5B] **17.** 2 [5.4B] **18.** 10 [5.4B] **19.** The amount of cranberry juice is 7 qt; the amount of apple juice is 3 qt. [5.5A] **20.** The three integers are −1, 0, and 1. [5.4A] **21.** $5n - 4 = 16$; 4 [5.4A] **22.** The height of the Eiffel Tower is 1063 ft. [5.4B] **23.** 37.8° C [5.2B] **24.** The jet overtakes the propeller-driven plane 600 mi from the starting point. [5.5B] **25.** The numbers are 8 and 13. [5.4A] **26.** The farmer harvested 25,300 bushels of corn. [5.4B]

CHAPTER 5 TEST

1. −5 [5.3A; HOW TO 1] **2.** −5 [5.1B; HOW TO 2] **3.** −3 [5.2A; Example 1] **4.** 2 [5.3B; HOW TO 2] **5.** No [5.1A; Example 1] **6.** 5 [5.2A; Example 2] **7.** $-\frac{1}{2}$ [5.2A; Example 2] **8.** $-\frac{1}{3}$ [5.3B; HOW TO 2] **9.** 2 [5.3A; Example 2] **10.** −12 [5.1C; HOW TO 4] **11.** 95 [5.2A; HOW TO 1] **12.** $\frac{16}{5}$ [5.3A; Example 1] **13.** −3 [5.2A; Example 5] **14.** 11 [5.3B; HOW TO 2] **15.** The amount of rye is 10 lb; the amount of wheat is 5 lb. [5.5A; HOW TO 1] **16.** 200 calculators were produced. [5.2B; Example 6] **17.** The numbers are 10, 12, and 14. [5.4A; HOW TO 2] **18.** 4000 clocks were made. [5.2B; Example 6] **19.** $3x - 15 = 27$; 14 [5.4A; HOW TO 1] **20.** The rate of the snowmobile was 6 mph. [5.5B; HOW TO 2] **21.** The company makes 110 LCD flat-panel TVs each day. [5.4B; Example 3] **22.** The smaller number is 8; the larger number is 10. [5.4A; Example 1] **23.** The distance between the airports is 360 mi. [5.5B; You Try It 3] **24.** The time required is 11.5 s. [5.2B; You Try It 6] **25.** The final temperature is 60°C. [5.3C; Example 5]

CUMULATIVE REVIEW EXERCISES

1. 6 [3.2B] **2.** −48 [3.3A] **3.** $-\frac{19}{48}$ [3.4A] **4.** −2 [3.4B] **5.** 54 [3.5A] **6.** 24 [3.5A] **7.** 6 [4.1A] **8.** $-17x$ [4.2A] **9.** $-5a - 2b$ [4.2A] **10.** $2x$ [4.2B] **11.** $36y$ [4.2B] **12.** $2x^2 + 6x - 4$ [4.2C] **13.** $-4x + 14$ [4.2D] **14.** $6x - 34$ [4.2D] **15.** Yes [5.1A] **16.** No [5.1A] **17.** $\frac{11}{18}$ [3.5A] **18.** −25 [5.1C] **19.** −3 [5.2A] **20.** 3 [5.2A] **21.** 0.047383 [2.6B] **22.** 7 [1.2B] **23.** 13 [5.3B] **24.** 2 [5.3B] **25.** −3 [5.3A] **26.** $\frac{1}{2}$ [5.3A] **27.** The final temperature is 60°C. [5.3C] **28.** $12 - 5x = -18$; 6 [5.4A] **29.** The area of the garage is 600 ft^2. [5.4B] **30.** 20 lb of oat flour are needed for the mixture. [5.5A] **31.** $3n + 4$ [4.3B] **32.** The number is 2. [5.4B] **33.** The length of the track is 120 m. [5.5B]

Answers to Chapter 6 Selected Exercises

PREP TEST

1. $\frac{19}{100}$ [2.4A] **2.** 0.23 [2.6B] **3.** 47 [2.6B] **4.** 2850 [2.6B] **5.** 4000 [2.6C] **6.** $\frac{4}{5}$ [2.2B] **7.** 62.5 [3.4B] **8.** $66\frac{2}{3}$ [2.2A] **9.** 1.75 [2.6C]

SECTION 6.1

1. are not; are **3.** $\frac{1}{5}$; 1:5; 1 to 5 **5.** $\frac{2}{1}$; 2:1; 2 to 1 **7.** $\frac{3}{8}$; 3:8; 3 to 8 **9.** $\frac{1}{1}$; 1:1; 1 to 1 **11.** $\frac{7}{10}$; 7:10; 7 to 10 **13.** $\frac{80 \text{ mi}}{3 \text{ h}}$ **15.** 1 **17.** 1 **19.** $4250/month **21.** 250 words/page **23.** 52.4 miles/hour **25.** $3.25/pound **27.** The ratio of the number of National Basketball Association rookies to the number of college seniors playing college basketball is $\frac{1}{56}$. **29.** In 2009, each user receives approximately 148.6 messages. In 2011, each user receives approximately 183.3 messages. In 2013, each user receives approximately 240.6 messages. **31.** For television advertising rates, the unit "dollars" is in the numerator and the unit "seconds" is in the denominator.

SECTION 6.2

1. proportion; *a*; *d*; *b*; *c*; equal **3.** $\frac{n \text{ mi}}{30 \text{ min}}$ **5.** Not true **7.** True **9.** True **11.** Not true **13.** 10 **15.** 2.4 **17.** 4.5 **19.** 17.14 **21.** 25.6 **23.** 20.83 **25.** 4.35 **27.** 10.97 **29.** 1.15 **31.** 38.73 **33.** 0.5 **35.** 10 **37.** 0.43 **39.** −1.6 **41.** 6.25 **43.** 32 **45.** 6.2 **47.** 5.8 **49.** Answers will vary. **a.** One example is $\frac{2}{9} = \frac{4}{18}$. **b.** One example is $\frac{2}{4} = \frac{4}{8}$. **51.** A 174-pound person would weigh 29 lb on the moon. **53.** 24 robes can be made from 26 yd of material. **55.** The property tax on a home appraised at $280,000 is $6720. **57.** The car would travel 406 mi on 14.5 gal of gasoline. **59.** 438 light fixtures are needed for an office building of 35,000 ft^2. **61.** It will take 60 weeks for the dieter to lose 36 lb. **63.** A person would need to walk 26.92 mi to lose 1 lb. **65.** 160,000 people are expected to vote in the election. **67.** The actual distance between the two points is 20 mi. **69.** No, it is not possible. **71.** The first person's share of the winnings was $1,250,000. **73.** Reardon's ERA for 1979 was 1.71. **75.** Halladay's ERA was lower in 2008 than in 2009. His ERA was 0.01 lower. **77.** Answers will vary.

CHECK YOUR PROGRESS: CHAPTER 6

1. $\frac{1}{2}$; 1 : 2; 1 to 2 [6.1A] **2.** $\frac{2}{3}$; 2 : 3; 2 to 3 [6.1A] **3.** $\frac{\$13}{2 \text{ T-shirts}}$ [6.1A] **4.** $\frac{28 \text{ feet}}{3 \text{ seconds}}$ [6.1A] **5.** $3225/month [6.1A] **6.** $4.24/lb [6.1A] **7.** True [6.2A] **8.** No [6.2A] **9.** 3 [6.2A] **10.** 17.5 [6.2A] **11.** 16.67 [6.2A] **12.** 0.6 [6.2A] **13.** The ratio is $\frac{9}{13}$. [6.1A] **14.** The ratio is $\frac{2}{3}$. [6.1A] **15.** The rate of travel is 462 mph [6.1A] **16.** The annual dividend would be $666. [6.2B] **17.** The cost is $170.40. [6.2B]

SECTION 6.3

1. 29 figures should be circled. **5.** 0.01; 0.01; 0.53 **7.** $\frac{1}{100}$; $\frac{1}{100}$; $\frac{4}{5}$ **9.** 100%; 100%; 46% **11.** 100%; 100%; 30% **13.** $\frac{1}{20}$, 0.05 **15.** $\frac{3}{10}$, 0.30 **17.** $\frac{5}{2}$, 2.50 **19.** $\frac{7}{25}$, 0.28 **21.** $\frac{7}{20}$, 0.35 **23.** $\frac{29}{100}$, 0.29 **25.** $\frac{1}{9}$ **27.** $\frac{3}{8}$ **29.** $\frac{2}{3}$ **31.** $\frac{1}{15}$ **33.** $\frac{1}{200}$ **35.** $\frac{1}{16}$ **37.** 0.073 **39.** 0.158 **41.** 0.003 **43.** 1.212 **45.** 0.6214 **47.** 0.0825 **49.** $\frac{13}{20}$ of teachers have one or more English-language learners in the classroom. **51.** greater than **53.** It represents $\frac{1}{2}$ of the regular price. **55.** 37% **57.** 2% **59.** 12.5% **61.** 136% **63.** 96% **65.** 7% **67.** 83% **69.** 33.3% **71.** 44.4% **73.** 45% **75.** 250% **77.** 16.7% **79.** 68% **81.** $56\frac{1}{4}$% **83.** $262\frac{1}{2}$% **85.** $283\frac{1}{3}$% **87.** $23\frac{1}{3}$% **89.** $22\frac{2}{9}$% **91.** $\frac{3}{4}$; 75% **93.** 0.375; 37.5% **95.** $\frac{9}{16}$; 0.5625 **97.** $\frac{13}{25}$; 52% **99.** 0.18; 18% **101.** 75% of Americans ages 17 to 24 cannot enlist in the military. **103.** Greater than **105.** $\frac{1}{4}$, 0.25, 25%; $\frac{3}{4}$, 0.75, 75% **107a.** False **b.** Answers will vary. For example, 200% × 4 = 2 × 4 = 8

SECTION 6.4

1. 0.12; *n*; 68 **3.** 0.08; 450; *n* **5.** 36; *n*; 25 **7.** 21 of the 30 squares should be shaded. **9.** 25 of the 40 squares should be shaded. **11.** 5 of the 30 squares should be shaded. **13.** 27 of the 48 people should be circled. **15.** 8 **17.** 0.075 **19.** $16\frac{2}{3}$% **21.** 37.5% **23.** 100 **25.** 1200 **27.** 51.895 **29.** 13 **31.** 2.7% **33.** 400% **35.** 7.5 **37.** 6232 respondents did not answer yes to the question. **39.** 15.8 million travelers allowed their children to miss school to go on a trip. **41.** $x < y$ **43.** 27 **45.** 22% **47.** 150 **49.** 1500% **51.** 875 **53.** 72 **55.** 46.2% **57.** 196.65 **59.** 8 **61.** 14.3 **63.** 250% **65.** 0.4% of the total energy production was generated by wind machines. **67.** ii **69.** True **71.** The value of fireworks imported from China represented 96.4% of the value of fireworks imported to the United States. **73.** 12.2% of the deaths occurred during training. **75.** There were 50 million students in the United States that year. **77.** There are 5 million opposite-sex cohabitating couples who maintain households in the United States. **79a.** $175 million is generated from the sales of Thin Mints. **b.** $63 million is generated from the sales of Trefoil shortbread cookies. **81.** 51% of the total cranberry crop was produced in Wisconsin. **83.** 14,000,000 oz of gold were mined in the United States that year. **85.** 27.5% is spent on food. **87.** Approximately 13.2 million people in the United States aged 18 to 24 do not have health insurance. **89.** 29.8% of Americans with diabetes have not been diagnosed with the disease. **91.** 5451 fewer faculty members described their views as conservative than as middle-of-the-road. **93.** No **95a.** 1 lb **b.** 1 lb **c.** 50 lb **d.** 50 lb **e.** 25 lb **f.** 25 **g.** 70 squares should be shaded. **h.** 70% **97a.** 0.2 lb **b.** 0.2 lb **c.** 10 lb **d.** 10 lb **e.** 5 lb **f.** 5 **g.** 40 squares should be shaded. **h.** 40%

SECTION 6.5

3. Row 1: 5000, 0.06, $\frac{1}{12}$, \$25; Row 2: 5000, 0.06, $\frac{2}{12}$, \$50; Row 3: 5000, 0.06, $\frac{3}{12}$, \$75; Row 4: 5000, 0.06, $\frac{4}{12}$, \$100; Row 5: 5000, 0.06, $\frac{5}{12}$, \$125 **5.** You can multiply the interest due on the 1-month loan by 7. **7.** The simple interest due on the loan is \$69.35. **9.** The simple interest due on the loan is \$1166.67. **11.** The interest owed to the credit union is \$16. **13.** The simple interest that Kara owes is \$168.75. **15.** The maturity value of the loan is \$27,050. **17.** The maturity value of the car loan is \$5517.50. **19.** The annual simple interest rate that Michele paid on the loan was 7.5%. **21.** Don paid an annual simple interest rate of 5.84% on the loan. **23a.** The difference between the maturity values of the two loans is \$125. **b.** The difference between the monthly payments for the two loans is \$20.83.

CHAPTER 6 REVIEW EXERCISES

1. $\frac{1}{1}$, 1:1, 1 to 1 [6.1A] **2.** $\frac{\text{2 roof supports}}{\text{1 ft}}$ [6.1A] **3.** \$15.70/h [6.1A] **4.** $\frac{8}{15}$ [6.1A] **5.** 1.6 [6.2A] **6.** $\frac{\text{5 lb}}{\text{4 trees}}$ [6.1A] **7.** 57 mph [6.1A] **8.** 6.86 [6.2A] **9.** $\frac{8}{25}$ [6.3A] **10.** 0.22 [6.3A] **11.** $\frac{1}{4}$, 0.25 [6.3A] **12.** $\frac{17}{500}$ [6.3A] **13.** 17.5% [6.3B] **14.** 128.6% [6.3B] **15.** 280% [6.3B] **16.** 21 [6.4A/6.4B] **17.** 500% [6.4A/6.4B] **18.** 66.7% [6.4A/6.4B] **19.** 30 [6.4A/6.4B] **20.** 15.3 [6.4A/6.4B] **21.** 562.5 [6.4A/6.4B] **22.** 5.625% [6.4A/6.4B] **23.** The ratio is $\frac{1}{5}$. [6.1A] **24.** \$12,000 must be invested to earn \$780 in dividends. [6.2B] **25.** 2.75 lb of plant food should be used on a lawn of 275 ft^2. [6.2B] **26.** The other attorney receives \$64,000. [6.2B] **27.** 34.0% of the tourists projected to visit the listed countries will be visiting China. [6.4C] **28.** The company spent \$8400 on advertising. [6.4C] **29.** 3952 telephones were not defective. [6.4C] **30.** Cable households spend 36.5% of the week watching TV. [6.4C] **31.** The simple interest due on the loan is \$31.81. [6.5A] **32.** The corporation paid a 9.00% annual simple interest rate. [6.5A] **33.** The maturity value of the loan is \$10,405. [6.5A]

CHAPTER 6 TEST

1. $\frac{1}{8}$, 1:8, 1 to 8 [6.1A; You Try It 1] **2.** $\frac{\text{1 oz}}{\text{4 cookies}}$ [6.1A; Example 2] **3.** 0.6 mi/min [6.1A; Example 3] **4.** $\frac{2}{1}$ [6.1A; Example 1] **5.** 0.75 [6.2A; HOW TO 2] **6.** 2 ft/s [6.1A; Example 3] **7.** 476.67 ft^2/h [6.1A; Example 3] **8.** 3.56 [6.2A; You Try It 2] **9.** 0.864 [6.3A; Example 4] **10.** 40% [6.3B; HOW TO 4] **11.** 125% [6.3B; You Try It 6] **12.** $\frac{5}{6}$ [6.3A; Example 3] **13.** $\frac{8}{25}$ [6.3A; HOW TO 1] **14.** 118% [6.3B; Example 8] **15.** 90 [6.4A/6.4B; Example 3] **16.** 49.64 [6.4A/6.4B; HOW TO 1] **17.** 56.25% [6.4A/6.4B; Example 2] **18.** 200 [6.4A/6.4B; You Try It 4] **19.** The ratio of the lung capacity of an inactive male to that of an athletic male is $\frac{1}{2}$ or 1 : 2 or 1 to 2. [6.1A; You Try It 1] **20.** The sales tax on the car is \$3136. [6.2B; HOW TO 3] **21.** 243,750 registered voters would vote in the election. [6.2B; You Try It 5] **22.** The room is 50 ft long. [6.2B; You Try It 6] **23.** 33 accidents are expected for a company that employs 1500 people. [6.4C; You Try It 8] **24.** The student answered 82.2% of the questions correctly. [6.4C; Example 7] **25.** The increase in the assistant's weekly wage over last year is \$80. [6.4C; You Try It 9] **26.** The percent is 600%. [6.4C; HOW TO 6] **27.** The simple interest due on the loan is \$202.50. [6.5A; HOW TO 1] **28.** The maturity value of the loan is \$41,027.40. [6.5A; Example 1] **29.** The simple interest rate on the loan is 8.4%. [6.5A; HOW TO 2]

CUMULATIVE REVIEW EXERCISES

1. 57 [3.5A] **2.** 625 [1.3B] **3.** $3\frac{31}{36}$ [2.3B] **4.** $1\frac{2}{3}$ [2.7A] **5.** -114 [3.3B] **6.** 22 [3.5A] **7.** 4 [5.2A] **8.** 3 [5.3B] **9.** 100,500 [2.6B] **10.** $\frac{23}{24}$ [3.5A] **11.** 21 [3.5A] **12.** $-\frac{3}{8}$ [3.5A] **13.** 4 [3.2B] **14.** $8a - 3$ [4.2D] **15.** $2\frac{4}{5}$ [2.4B] **16.** $-4y^2 - 3y$ [4.2A] **17.** -12 [5.1C] **18.** $\frac{3}{10}$ [6.1A] **19.** \$3885/month [6.1A] **20.** 24.954 [2.6A] **21.** 32 [6.2A] **22.** $\frac{10}{11}$ [2.4C] **23.** 8.3% [6.4A/6.4B] **24.** 67.2 [6.4A/6.4B] **25.** The difference between the average amount spent monthly in the northeast and in the south is \$28.67. [2.6E] **26.** The number is 12. [5.4A] **27.** $4x - 3(x + 2)$; $x - 6$ [4.3B] **28.** There are 64 mi left to drive. [1.2C] **29.** The new balance is \$265.48. [2.6E] **30.** $\frac{4}{15}$ of the job is left to be finished on the third day. [2.3C] **31.** $\frac{1}{10}$ of the population aged 75–84 is affected by Alzheimer's disease. [6.3A] **32.** 35 mi were traveled per gallon of gas. [6.1A] **33.** The rpm of the engine in third gear is 3750 rpm. [5.4B]

Answers to Chapter 7 Selected Exercises

PREP TEST

1. 56 [1.4A] **2.** 56.52 [4.1A] **3.** 113.04 [4.1A] **4.** 43 [5.1B] **5.** 51 [5.1B] **6.** 14.4 [6.2A]

SECTION 7.1

1. 12; 5; x; 4 **3.** 160°; 140°; 360° **5.** a; b **7.** c; d; 180° **9a.** $\angle a$, $\angle b$, and $\angle c$ **b.** $\angle y$ and $\angle z$ **c.** $\angle x$ **11.** 40°; acute **13.** 115°; obtuse **15.** 90°; right **17.** 28° **19.** 18° **21.** 14 cm **23.** 28 ft **25.** 30 m **27.** 86° **29.** 30° **31.** 36° **33.** 71° **35.** 127° **37.** 116° **39.** 20° **41.** 20° **43.** 20° **45.** 141° **47.** $90° - x$ **49.** 106° **51.** 11° **53.** $\angle a = 38°$, $\angle b = 142°$ **55.** $\angle a = 47°$, $\angle b = 133°$ **57.** 20° **59.** False **61.** True **63.** The measure of $\angle x$ is 155° and the measure of $\angle y$ is 70°. **65.** The measure of $\angle a$ is 45° and the measure of $\angle b$ is 135°. **67.** The measure of the third angle is 60°. **69.** The measure of the third angle is 35°. **71.** True **73.** Point D, or 3.5, is halfway between two other points. **75.** The largest angle is 105°. **79.**

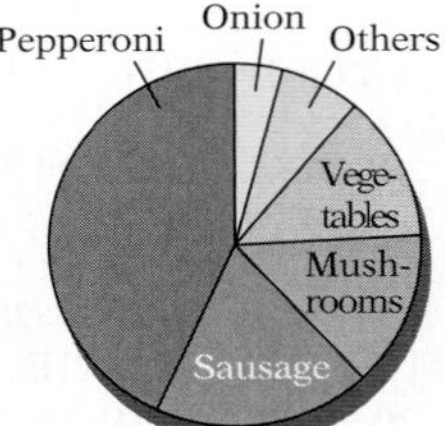

SECTION 7.2

1. hexagon **3.** pentagon **5.** scalene **7.** equilateral **9.** obtuse **11.** acute **13.** 56 in. **15.** 14 ft **17.** 47 mi **19.** 8π cm; 25.13 cm **21.** 11π mi; 34.56 mi **23.** 17π ft; 53.41 ft **25.** The perimeter is 17.4 cm. **27.** The perimeter is 8 cm. **29.** The perimeter is 24 m. **31.** The perimeter is 17.5 in. **33.** The perimeter is 48.8 cm. **35.** The circumference is 1.5π in. **37.** The circumference is 226.19 cm. **39.** 60 ft of fencing should be purchased. **41.** 44 ft of carpet must be nailed down. **43.** The length of the playground is 120 ft. **45.** The length of the third side is 10 in. **47.** Each side of the frame is 12 in. **49.** A diameter of the circle is 2.55 cm. **51.** The length of molding needed is 13.19 ft. **53.** The bicycle travels 50.27 ft. **55.** The circumference of Earth is 39,935.93 km. **57.** A square whose side is 1 ft has the greater perimeter. **59.** 60 ft^2 **61.** 20.25 in^2 **63.** 546 ft^2 **65.** 16π cm^2; 50.27 cm^2 **67.** 30.25π mi^2; 95.03 mi^2 **69.** 72.25π ft^2; 226.98 ft^2 **71.** The area is 156.25 cm^2. **73.** The area is 570 in^2. **75.** The area is 192 in^2. **77.** The area is 13.5 ft^2. **79.** The area is 330 cm^2. **81.** The area is 25π in^2. **83.** The area of the reserve in the Congo is approximately 10,500 mi^2. **85.** The area watered by the irrigation system is 2500π ft^2. **87.** The area of the patio is 72.25 m^2. **89.** 7500 yd^2 of artificial turf must be purchased. **91.** The width is 10 in. **93.** The length of the base is 20 m. **95.** You should buy 2 qt of stain. **97.** The cost to wallpaper the two walls is $148. **99.** You should select the 10×20 unit. **101.** The increase in area is 339.29 cm^2. **103.** You will spend $59.96 on paint. **105.** 80 ft^2 of material must be purchased to make the drapes. **107.** The area of the resulting rectangle is 4 times larger. **109.** A rectangle that is 5 units by 5 units will have the greatest possible area.

CHECK YOUR PROGRESS: CHAPTER 7

1. 20 ft [7.1A] **2.** 168° [7.1A] **3.** $\angle b = 138°$, $\angle c = 42°$, $\angle d = 138°$ [7.1B] **4.** The third angle measures 67°. [7.1C] **5.** The area of the square quilt is 1600 in^2. [7.2B] **6.** 20° [7.1A] **7.** The circumference is 37.70 cm. [7.2A] **8.** $\angle a = 135°$, $\angle b = 45°$ [7.1B] **9.** The length of the base is 5 m. [7.2B] **10.** The area is 98 m^2. [7.2B] **11.** The length of a side is 9.5 in. [7.2A] **12.** $\angle x = 24°$, $\angle y = 156°$ [7.1C] **13.** The length of the rectangle is 16 m. [7.2B] **14.** The perimeter is 36 in. [7.2A] **15.** The area is 1.96π m^2, or approximately 6.16 m^2. [7.2B] **16.** The area is 72 cm^2. [7.2B] **17.** The length of molding needed is 37 ft. [7.2A]

SECTION 7.3

1. the hypotenuse; a leg **3.** FD; BA **5.** $\frac{1}{2}$ **7.** $\frac{3}{4}$ **9.** $\angle E$ **11.** 5 in. **13.** 8.6 cm **15.** 11.2 ft **17.** 4.5 cm **19.** 12.7 yd **21.** iii **23.** The ladder reaches a height of 7.4 m on the building. **25.** The perimeter is 24.3 cm. **27.** 7.2 cm **29.** 3.3 m **31.** 12 m **33.** 12 in. **35.** 56.3 cm^2 **37.** The height of the flagpole is 18 ft. **39.** The height of the building is 16 m. **41.** Yes, SAS Rule **43.** Yes, SSS Rule **45.** Yes, ASA Rule **47.** Yes, SAS Rule **49.** No **51.** No **53.** Yes

SECTION 7.4

1a. cone **b.** cube **c.** sphere **d.** cylinder **3.** $s^2 + 2sl$; l; s **5.** 840 in^3 **7.** 15 ft^3 **9.** 4.5π cm^3; 14.14 cm^3 **11.** The volume is 34 m^3. **13.** The volume is 15.625 in^3. **15.** The volume is 36π ft^3. **17.** The volume is 8143.01 cm^3. **19.** The volume is 392.70 cm^3. **21.** The volume is 216 m^3. **23.** The height of the aquarium is 8.5 in. **25.** The height of the cylinder is 15.01 cm. **27.** The volume of the portion of the silo that is not being used for storage is 1507.96 ft^3. **29.** The volume of the lock is 6,600,000 ft^3. **31.** Yes **33.** No **35.** The volume of the guacamole is 172,800 ft^3. **37.** 94 m^2 **39.** 56 m^2 **41.** 96π in^2; 301.59 in^2 **43.** The surface area is 184 ft^2. **45.** The surface area is 69.36 m^2.

47. The surface area is 225π cm^2. **49.** The surface area is 402.12 in^2. **51.** The surface area is 6π ft^2. **53.** The surface area is 297 in^2. **55.** The width is 3 cm. **57.** 3217 ft^2 of fabric was used to construct the balloon. **59.** 456 in^2 of glass is needed to make the fish tank. **61a.** Always true **b.** Never true **c.** Sometimes true **63.** The cone should be filled with water three times.

CHAPTER 7 REVIEW EXERCISES

1. $\angle x = 22°$, $\angle y = 158°$ [7.1C] **2.** 24 in. [7.3B] **3.** 168 in^3 [7.4A] **4.** 68° [7.1B] **5.** Yes, by the SAS Rule [7.3C] **6.** 125.66 m^2 [7.4B] **7.** 44 cm [7.1A] **8.** 19° [7.1A] **9.** 32 in^2 [7.2B] **10.** 96 cm^3 [7.4A] **11.** 42 in. [7.2A] **12.** $\angle a = 138°$, $\angle b = 42°$ [7.1B] **13.** 220 ft^2 [7.4B] **14.** 9.75 ft [7.3A] **15.** The volume is 42.875 in^3. [7.4A] **16.** The supplement is 148°. [7.1A] **17.** The volume is 39 ft^3. [7.4A] **18.** The third angle measures 95°. [7.1C] **19.** The length of the base is 8 cm. [7.2B] **20.** The volume is 288π mm^3. [7.4A] **21.** The length of each side of the frame is 21.5 cm. [7.2A] **22.** 4 cans of paint must be purchased in order to paint the cylinder. [7.4B] **23.** 208 yd of fencing are needed to surround the park. [7.2A] **24.** The area of the patio is 90.25 m^2. [7.2B] **25.** The area of the walkway is 276 m^2. [7.2B]

CHAPTER 7 TEST

1. 7.55 cm [7.3A; HOW TO 1] **2.** Yes, by the SAS Rule [7.3C; You Try It 3] **3.** The area is 111 m^2. [7.2B; HOW TO 5] **4.** The area is 42 ft^2. [7.2B; HOW TO 8] **5.** The volume is $\frac{784\pi}{3}$ cm^3. [7.4A; You Try It 2] **6.** The surface area is 75 m^2. [7.4B; Example 3] **7.** 4618.14 cm^3 [7.4A; You Try It 2] **8.** 159 in^2 [7.2B; HOW TO 9] **9.** 20° [7.1B; HOW TO 4] **10.** 75 m^2 [7.4B; Example 3] **11.** 34° [7.1B; Example 5] **12.** Octagon [7.2A; HOW TO 1] **13.** Not necessarily congruent [7.3C; Example 3] **14.** 168 ft^3 [7.4A; You Try It 1] **15.** 8.06 m [7.3A; Example 1] **16.** 143° [7.1B; HOW TO 4] **17.** 500π cm^2 [7.4B; You Try It 3] **18.** 61° [7.1C; Example 7] **19.** 6.67 ft [7.3B; You Try It 2] **20.** 4.27 ft [7.3B; HOW TO 2] **21.** The perimeter is 20 m. [7.2A; HOW TO 3] **22.** The perimeter is 26 cm. [7.2A; HOW TO 2] **23.** The perimeter is 51.6 ft. [7.3A; Example 1] **24.** The third angle measures 102°. [7.1C; Example 8] **25.** The supplement is 139°. [7.1A; Example 3]

CUMULATIVE REVIEW EXERCISES

1. 204 [6.4A/6.4B] **2.** 1, 2, 3, 6, 13, 26, 39, 78 [1.3D] **3.** $\frac{5}{6}$ [2.4B] **4.** 18 [3.1C] **5.** 12.8 [2.6C] **6.** -2 [3.2B] **7.** 131° [7.1B] **8.** 26 cm [7.3A] **9.** 56 in^2 [7.2B] **10.** 40° [7.1B] **11.** $1\frac{11}{30}$ [2.3A] **12.** $\frac{1}{2}$ [5.3B] **13.** The third angle measures 58°. [7.1C] **14.** 75 [3.3A] **15.** $7x + 18$ [4.2D] **16.** -2 [4.1A] **17.** $\frac{4}{5}$ [4.1A] **18.** $2 \cdot 3 \cdot 13$ [1.3D] **19.** 5 [5.3A] **20.** 37.5% [6.3B] **21.** $8(2n)$; $16n$ [4.3B] **22.** The rates of the two cars are 50 mph and 55 mph. [5.5B] **23.** The simple interest due is $1313.01. [6.5A] **24.** 24 oz of the silver alloy that costs $3.50 per ounce must be used. [5.5A] **25.** You sent or received 22 text messages. [5.4B] **26.** The sales tax is $4.50. [6.2B] **27.** The increase is $.08 trillion. [2.6E] **28.** The height of the box is 3 ft. [7.4A] **29.** The depth is 40 ft. [5.2B] **30.** The wrestler must lose $2\frac{1}{4}$ lb. [2.3C]

Answers to Chapter 8 Selected Exercises

PREP TEST

1. 95 trillion emails were spam. [6.4A/6.4B] **2a.** The greatest cost increase is between 2009 and 2010. **b.** Between those years, there was an increase of $5318. [1.2C] **3.** The ratio is $\frac{11}{7}$. [6.1A] **4.** $\frac{4}{25}$ of the women in the military are in the Marine Corps. [6.3A]

SECTION 8.1

1. $\frac{1}{4}$ **5.** The ratio of the number of units needed in finance to the number of units needed in accounting is $\frac{1}{3}$. **7.** $6,324,000,000 was spent on video game hardware in 2010. **9.** $\frac{4}{25}$ of the total money spent was spent on accessories. **11.** The estimated population in 2030 is more than 8 billion people. **13.** The change in world population between 1990 and 2010 was about 1.6 billion people. **15.** Women ages 75 and older have the lowest recommended number of Calories. **17.** True

19.

	Wind Power Capacity (in megawatts)	
Year	Iowa	California
2000	200	1600
2001	300	1700
2002	400	1800
2003	500	2000
2004	600	2100
2005	800	2200
2006	900	2400
2007	1300	2400
2008	2800	2500
2009	3600	2800
2010	3700	3300

20.

Year	Greater capacity	Difference (megawatts)
2000	California	1400
2001	California	1100
2002	California	1400
2003	California	1500
2004	California	1500
2005	California	1400
2006	California	1500
2007	California	1100
2008	Iowa	300
2009	Iowa	800
2010	Iowa	400

The wind power capacity of Iowa exceeded that of California in 2008–2010.

SECTION 8.2

3a. Median **b.** Mean **c.** Mode **d.** Median **e.** Mode **f.** Mean **5.** The mean number of seats filled is 381.5625 seats. The median number of seats filled is 394.5 seats. Since each number occurs only once, there is no mode. **7.** The mean cost is $85.615. The median cost is $85.855. **9.** The mean monthly rate is $403.625. The median monthly rate is $404.50. **11a.** The mean life expectancy is 75.0 years. **b.** The median life expectancy is 74.4 years. **13.** Median **15.** The mean of the new data set is 5 more than the mean of the original data set. **17.** Lowest is $37,985. Highest is $66,707. Q_1 = $44,243. Q_3 = $55,528. Median = $49,177. Range = $28,722. Interquartile range= $11,285. **19a.** There were 40 adults who had cholesterol levels above 217. **b.** There were 60 adults who had cholesterol levels below 254. **c.** There are 20 cholesterol levels in each quartile. **d.** 25% of the adults had cholesterol levels of 198 or less. **21a.** Range = 5.6 million metric tons. Q_1 = 0.59 million metric tons. Q_3 = 1.52 million metric tons. Interquartile range = 0.93 million metric tons.

b.

0.45 0.59 1.035 1.52 6.05

c. 6.05 **23a.** No, the difference in the means is not greater than 1 inch.

b. The difference in medians is 0.3 inch. **c.**

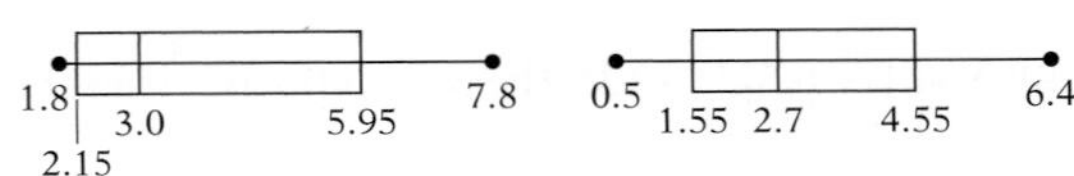

25. Answers will vary. For example, 55, 55, 55, 55, 55, or 50, 55, 55, 55, 60 **27.** Answers will vary. For example, 20, 21, 22, 24, 26, 27, 29, 31, 31, 32, 32, 33, 33, 36, 37, 37, 39, 40, 41, 43, 45, 46, 50, 54, 57

CHECK YOUR PROGRESS: CHAPTER 8

1a. Most people in the survey selected chocolate. **b.** 180 people preferred mint chocolate chip. **c.** 60 more people chose cookie dough than chose mint chocolate chip. [8.1A] **2a.** The population of New York City is more than twice the population of Los Angeles. **b.** The combined populations of Los Angeles and Chicago are less than the population of New York. **c.** The sum of the population of the three least-populated cities is 4.8 million people. [8.1A] **3a.** A gallon of gasoline cost $1.60 in 2008. **b.** The price of a gallon of gasoline was lowest in 2008. **c.** The price was less in 2006, 2008, 2009, and 2010. [8.1A] **4.** The mean of the salaries is $41,300. The median of the salaries is $41,250. [8.2A] **5.** The mode is 23 bags of flour. [8.2A] **6a.** The range is 47 Calories. **b.** The interquartile range is 12.5 Calories. [8.2B]

c.

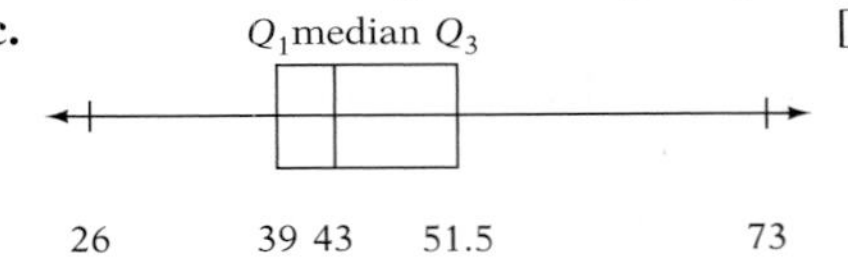

SECTION 8.3

1. {3, 6, 9} **3.** {(HHHH), (HHHT), (HHTT), (HHTH), (HTTT), (HTHH), (HTTH), (HTHT), (TTTT), (TTTH), (TTHH), (THHH), (TTHT), (THHT), (THTT), (THTH)} **5.** {(1, 1), (1, 2), (1, 3), (1, 4), (2, 1), (2, 2), (2, 3), (2, 4), (3, 1), (3, 2), (3, 3), (3, 4), (4, 1), (4, 2), (4, 3), (4, 4)} **7.** {1, 2, 3, 4, 5, 6, 7, 8} **9a.** The probability that the sum is 5 is $\frac{1}{9}$. **b.** The probability that the sum is 15 is 0. **c.** The probability that the sum is less than 15 is 1. **11a.** The probability that the sum is 4 is $\frac{3}{16}$. **b.** The probability that the sum is 6 is $\frac{3}{16}$. **13.** The probability of throwing a sum of 5 is greater. **15.** The probability of choosing a red marble is greater.

17. The empirical probability that a person prefers a cash discount is 0.39. **19.** The probability is $\frac{185}{377}$ that a customer rated the service as satisfactory or excellent. **21a.** 56 **b.** 28 **c.** 256 **d.** $\frac{35}{128}$ **e.** $\frac{1}{32}$ **f.** $\frac{93}{256}$ **g.** $\frac{255}{256}$ **h.** 1

CHAPTER 8 REVIEW EXERCISES

1. The agencies spent $349 million on maintaining websites. [8.1A] **2.** The ratio is $\frac{9}{8}$. [8.1A] **3.** NASA spent 8.9% of the total amount of money. [8.1A] **4.** Texas had the larger population. [8.1A] **5.** The population of California was 12.5 million people more than the population of Texas. [8.1A] **6.** The Texas population increased the least from 1925 to 1950. [8.1A] **7.** The difference was 50 days. [8.1A] **8.** The percent is 50%. [8.1A] **9.** The Southeast had the lowest number of days of full operation. This region had 30 days of full operation. [8.1A] **10.** The mean is 7.17 lb. The median is 7.05 lb. [8.2A] **11.** [8.2B]

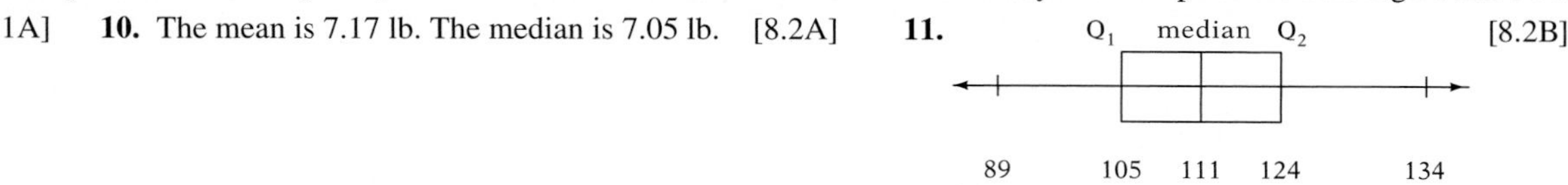

12. There are 12 elements in the sample space. [8.3A] **13.** The probability is $\frac{1}{500}$. [8.3A] **14.** $Q_1 = 1$; $Q_3 = 3$ [8.2B] **15.** The probability is $\frac{1}{6}$. [8.3A] **16.** The probability is $\frac{5}{14}$. [8.3A] **17a.** The mean is 91.6 heartbeats per minute. The median is 93.5 heartbeats per minute. The mode is 96 heartbeats per minute. [8.2A] **b.** The range is 36 heartbeats per minute. The interquartile range is 15 heartbeats per minute. [8.2B]

CHAPTER 8 TEST

1. During 1995 and 1996, the numbers of fatalities were the same. [8.1A; Example 1] **2.** There were 32 fatal accidents from 1991 to 1999. [8.1A; Example 1] **3.** There were 4 more fatalities from 1995 to 1998. [8.1A; Example 1] **4.** There were 355 more films rated R. [8.1A; Example 1] **5.** There were 16 times more films rated PG-13. [8.1A; Example 1] **6.** The percent of films rated G was 5.6%. [8.1A; Example 1] **7.** The student enrollment increased the least during the 1990s. [8.1A; Example 1] **8.** The increase in enrollment was 17 million students. [8.1A; Example 1] **9.** The median response time was 14 min. [8.2A; HOW TO 2] **10.** The modal response was "very good." [8.2A; p. 466] **11a.** The range is 22 days. **b.** The median is 14 vacation days. [8.2B; HOW TO 3]

12.

Q_1 median Q_3

68 70 72.5 74 80

[8.2B; You Try It 3] **13.** The probability is $\frac{3}{10}$ that the ball chosen is red. [8.3A; HOW TO 2]

14. The probability is $\frac{4}{31}$. [8.3A; HOW TO 2] **15.** The probability is $\frac{1}{3}$. [8.3A; HOW TO 3] **16.** The probability is $\frac{1}{8}$. [8.3A; Example 1]

17a. The mean time is 2.53 hours. [8.2A; Example 1] **b.** The median time is 2.55 hours. [8.2A; Example 2]

c.

2.0 2.35 2.55 2.8 3.1

[8.2B; Example 3]

CUMULATIVE REVIEW EXERCISES

1. 540 [1.3B] **2.** 14 [1.4A] **3.** 120 [2.1A] **4.** $\frac{5}{12}$ [2.2B] **5.** $12\frac{3}{40}$ [2.3A] **6.** $4\frac{17}{24}$ [2.3B] **7.** 2 [2.4A] **8.** $\frac{64}{85}$ [2.4B] **9.** $8\frac{1}{4}$ [2.7A] **10.** 209.305 [2.5A] **11.** 2.82348 [2.6B] **12.** $16.\overline{6}$ [2.6D] **13.** 26.4 miles/gallon [6.1A] **14.** 3.2 [6.2A] **15.** 80% [6.3B] **16.** 80 [6.4A/6.4B] **17.** 16.34 [6.4A/6.4B] **18.** 40% [6.4A/6.4B] **19.** The salesperson's income for the week was $650. [6.4C] **20.** The cost is $407.50. [6.2B] **21.** The interest due is $3750. [6.5A] **22.** The price of the compact disc player is $279. [6.4C] **23.** The amount budgeted for food is $855. [8.1A] **24.** The difference in the number answered correctly is 12 problems. [8.1A] **25.** The mean high temperature is 69.6°F. [8.2A] **26.** The probability is $\frac{5}{36}$ that the sum of the dots on the upward faces is 8. [8.3A]

Answers to Chapter 9 Selected Exercises

PREP TEST

1. 1 [3.2B] **2.** −18 [3.3A] **3.** $\frac{2}{3}$ [3.3B] **4.** 48 [4.1A] **5.** 0 [1.3C] **6.** No [4.1A]
7. $5x^2 - 9x - 6$ [4.2A] **8.** 0 [4.2A] **9.** $-6x + 24$ [4.2C] **10.** $-7xy + 10y$ [4.2D]

SECTION 9.1

1. Yes **3.** No **5.** No **7.** Binomial **9.** Trinomial **11.** None of these **13.** Binomial **15.** $5x^2 + 8x$ **17.** $7x^2 + xy - 4y^2$ **19.** $3a^2 - 3a + 17$ **21.** $5x^3 + 10x^2 - x - 4$ **23.** $3r^3 + 2r^2 - 11r + 7$ **25.** $-2x^2 + 3x$ **27.** $5x^2 + 7x + 20$ **29.** $x^3 + 2x^2 - 6x - 6$ **31.** $2a^3 - 3a^2 - 11a + 2$ **33.** iv **35.** $-y^2 - 13xy$ **37.** $2x^2 - 3x - 1$ **39.** $-2x^3 + x^2 + 2$ **41.** $3a^3 - 2$ **43.** $4y^3 + 2y^2 + 2y - 4$ **45.** $3y^2 - 4y - 2$ **47.** $-7x - 7$ **49.** $4x^3 + 3x^2 + 3x + 1$ **51.** $y^3 + 5y^2 - 2y - 4$ **53.** $x^2 + 9x - 11$ **55.** $2x^3 + x^2 - 5x + 6$ **57.** $x^3 - x^2 + 2x + 6$ **59.** Answers will vary. For example, $3x^2 - 4x + 7$ and $-3x^2 + 5x - 2$

SECTION 9.2

1. Product **3.** Power **5.** Power **7.** Product **9.** No **11.** No **13.** $30x^3$ **15.** $-42c^6$ **17.** $9a^7$ **19.** x^3y^4 **21.** $-10x^9y$ **23.** $12x^7y^8$ **25.** $-6x^3y^5$ **27.** x^4y^5z **29.** $a^3b^5c^4$ **31.** $-30a^5b^8$ **33.** $6a^5b$ **35.** $40y^{10}z^6$ **37.** $x^3y^3z^2$ **39.** $-24a^3b^3c^3$ **41.** $8x^7yz^6$ **43.** $30x^6y^8$ **45.** $-36a^3b^2c^3$ **47.** No **49.** Yes **51.** x^{15} **53.** x^{14} **55.** x^8 **57.** y^{12} **59.** $-8x^6$ **61.** x^4y^6 **63.** $9x^4y^2$ **65.** $-243x^{15}y^{10}$ **67.** $-8x^7$ **69.** $24x^8y^7$ **71.** a^4b^6 **73.** $64x^{12}y^3$ **75.** $-18x^3y^4$ **77.** $-8a^7b^5$ **79.** $-54a^9b^3$ **81.** $12x^2$ **83.** $2x^6y^2 + 9x^4y^2$ **85.** 0 **87.** $17x^4y^8$ **89.** $-120x^{15}$

SECTION 9.3

1. Always true **3.** Sometimes true **5.** Always true **7.** Sometimes true **9.** Sometimes true **11.** $x^2 - 2x$ **13.** $-x^2 - 7x$ **15.** $3a^3 - 6a^2$ **17.** $-5x^4 + 5x^3$ **19.** $-3x^5 + 7x^3$ **21.** $12x^3 - 6x^2$ **23.** $6x^2 - 12x$ **25.** $3x^2 + 4x$ **27.** $-x^3y + xy^3$ **29.** $2x^4 - 3x^2 + 2x$ **31.** $2a^3 + 3a^2 + 2a$ **33.** $3x^6 - 3x^4 - 2x^2$ **35.** $-6y^4 - 12y^3 + 14y^2$ **37.** $-2a^3 - 6a^2 + 8a$ **39.** $6y^4 - 3y^3 + 6y^2$ **41.** $x^3y - 3x^2y^2 + xy^3$ **43.** ii and iii **45.** $x^3 - 4x^2 + 11x - 14$ **47.** $2x^3 - 9x^2 + 19x - 15$ **49.** $-2a^3 + 7a^2 - 7a + 2$ **51.** $-2a^3 - 3a^2 + 8a - 3$ **53.** $2y^3 + y^2 - 10y$ **55.** $2y^4 + 7y^3 - 4y^2 - 16y + 8$ **57.** $12y^3 + 3y^2 - 29y + 15$ **59.** $18b^4 - 33b^3 + 5b^2 + 42b - 7$ **61.** $4a^4 - 12a^3 + 13a^2 - 8a + 3$ **63.** $x^2 + 4x + 3$ **65.** $a^2 + a - 12$ **67.** $y^2 - 5y - 24$ **69.** $y^2 - 10y + 21$ **71.** $2x^2 + 15x + 7$ **73.** $3x^2 + 11x - 4$ **75.** $4x^2 - 31x + 21$ **77.** $3y^2 - 2y - 16$ **79.** $9x^2 + 54x + 77$ **81.** $21a^2 - 83a + 80$ **83.** $6a^2 - 25ab + 14b^2$ **85.** $2a^2 - 11ab - 63b^2$ **87.** $100a^2 - 100ab + 21b^2$ **89.** $15x^2 + 56xy + 48y^2$ **91.** $14x^2 - 97xy - 60y^2$ **93.** $56x^2 - 61xy + 15y^2$ **95.** $12x^2 - x - 20$ **97.** $y^2 - 36$ **99.** $16x^2 - 49$ **101.** $81x^2 - 4$ **103.** $16x^2 - 81y^2$ **105.** $y^2 - 6y + 9$ **107.** $36x^2 - 60x + 25$ **109.** $x^2 - 4xy + 4y^2$ **111.** $4a^2 - 36ab + 81b^2$ **113.** Negative **115.** Positive **117.** The area of the rectangle is $(18x^2 + 12x + 2)$ in². **119.** The area of the circle is $(\pi x^2 + 8\pi x + 16\pi)$ cm². **121.** The total area of the softball diamond and the base paths is $(90x + 2025)$ ft². **123a.** The length of the Water Cube is $(5h + 22)$ ft. **b.** The area of one exterior wall of the Water Cube is $(5h^2 + 22h)$ ft². **125.** $4ab$ **127.** $9a^4 - 24a^3 + 28a^2 - 16a + 4$ **129.** $24x^3 - 3x^2$ **131.** 1024 **133.** $12x^2 - x - 20$ **135.** $-x^3 - 1$ **137.** $-x^5 - 1$ **139.** $-x^7 - 1$

CHECK YOUR PROGRESS: CHAPTER 9

1. $4x^2 - x - 5$ [9.1A] **2.** $3y^2 + 8y - 35$ [9.3C] **3.** $20y^2 - 12y^4$ [9.3A] **4.** $-6a^5b^5$ [9.2A] **5.** $100x^2 - 9$ [9.3D] **6.** $2x^3 - 15x^2 + 23x - 30$ [9.3B] **7.** $6x^{11}y^8$ [9.2A] **8.** $81x^{24}y^{20}$ [9.2B] **9.** $2x^4 - 5x^3 - 3x^2 + 12x + 6$ [9.3B] **10.** $b^2 - 22b + 121$ [9.3D] **11.** $-32b^7$ [9.2B] **12.** $2x^3 + x^2 - 2x - 6$ [9.1B] **13.** $15x^4 - 5x^3 + 35x^2$ [9.3A] **14.** $12a^2 - 35a + 18$ [9.3C] **15.** $25 - 36y^2$ [9.3D] **16.** $9a^2 - 30ab + 25b^2$ [9.3D] **17.** The area of the rectangle is $(12x^2 - 8x)$ in². [9.3E] **18.** The area of the square is $(16x^2 + 40x + 25)$ ft². [9.3E]

SECTION 9.4

3. False **5.** True **7.** False **9.** 1; 1; 1; −2 **11.** No. 39.4 is not between 1 and 10. **13.** No. 2.4 is not an integer. **15.** y^4 **17.** a^3 **19.** p^4 **21.** $2x^3$ **23.** $2k$ **25.** m^5n^2 **27.** $\frac{3r^2}{2}$ **29.** $-\frac{2a}{3}$ **31.** $\frac{1}{y^5}$ **33.** $\frac{1}{a^6}$ **35.** $\frac{1}{3x^3}$ **37.** $\frac{2}{3x^5}$ **39.** $\frac{y^4}{x^2}$ **41.** $\frac{2}{5m^3n^8}$ **43.** $\frac{1}{p^3q}$ **45.** $\frac{1}{2y^3}$ **47.** $\frac{7xz}{8y^3}$ **49.** $\frac{p^2}{2m^3}$ **51.** $\frac{1}{25}$ **53.** 64 **55.** $\frac{1}{27}$ **57.** 2 **59.** $\frac{1}{x^2}$ **61.** a^6 **63.** $\frac{4}{x^7}$ **65.** $\frac{2}{3z^2}$ **67.** $5b^8$ **69.** $\frac{x^2}{3}$ **71.** 1 **73.** −1 **75.** $-\frac{8x^3}{y^6}$ **77.** $\frac{9}{x^2y^4}$ **79.** $\frac{2}{x^4}$ **81.** $-\frac{5}{a^8}$ **83.** $-\frac{a^5}{8b^4}$ **85.** $\frac{10y^3}{x^4}$ **87.** $\frac{1}{2x^3}$ **89.** $\frac{3}{x^3}$ **91.** $\frac{1}{2x^2y^6}$ **93.** $\frac{1}{x^6y}$ **95.** $\frac{a^4}{y^{10}}$ **97.** $-\frac{1}{6x^3}$

99. $-\frac{a^2b}{6c^2}$ **101.** $-\frac{7b^6}{a^2}$ **103.** $\frac{s^8t^4}{4r^{12}}$ **105.** $\frac{125p^3}{27m^{15}n^6}$ **107.** False **109.** True **111.** 8; left; 8 **113.** 3.24×10^{-9}
115. 3×10^{-18} **117.** 3.2×10^{16} **119.** 1.22×10^{-19} **121.** 5.47×10^{8} **123.** 0.000167 **125.** 68,000,000 **127.** 0.0000305
129. 0.00000000102 **131.** $-n - 1$ **133.** 1.5×10^{-8} m **135.** 5.98×10^{24} **137.** 6.65×10^{-13} **139.** 2.45×10^{9}
141. 3.9×10^{-19} **143.** 1.6×10^{10} **145.** $\frac{3}{64}$ **147.** $\frac{1}{4}, \frac{1}{2}, 1, 2, 4; 4, 2, 1, \frac{1}{2}, \frac{1}{4}$ **149.** 0.0625 **151.** 1 **153.** 0
157a. If every person in the world moved to Texas, every person would have 1047.6 ft^2 of land. **b.** If every person in the United States moved to Rhode Island, each person would have 90 ft^2 of land. **c. i.** 57,900 people would fit in a square mile. **ii.** 120,900 mi^2 of land would be required to accommodate the entire world population. **d.** If the total land area of Earth were divided equally, each person would be allocated 5.2 acres of land. **e.** The carrying capacity of Earth would be 3300 billion people.

SECTION 9.5

1. $15x^2 + 12x = 3x(5x + 4)$ **3.** True **5.** $3y; 3y; 6y^4; 1$ **7.** $2a - 5$ **9.** $3a + 2$ **11.** $x - 2$ **13.** $-x + 2$
15. $x^2 + 3x - 5$ **17.** $x^4 - 3x^2 - 1$ **19.** $xy + 2$ **21.** $-3y^3 + 5$ **23.** $3x - 2 + \frac{1}{x}$ **25.** $-3x + 7 - \frac{6}{x}$
27. $4a - 5 + 6b$ **29.** $9x + 6 - \frac{3}{y}$ **31.** Multiply $4x$ and $2x^2 - 3x - 1$, $4x(2x^2 - 3x - 1) = 8x^3 - 12x^2 - 4x$ **33.** $x + 2$
35. $2x + 1$ **37.** $x + 1 + \frac{2}{x - 1}$ **39.** $2x - 1 - \frac{2}{3x - 2}$ **41.** $b - 5 - \frac{24}{b - 3}$ **43.** $3x + 17 + \frac{64}{x - 4}$ **45.** $5y + 3 + \frac{1}{2y + 3}$
47. $3x - 5$ **49.** $x^2 + 2x + 3 + \frac{5}{x + 1}$ **51.** $x^2 - 3$ **53.** False **55.** $4y^2$ **57.** $x^3 - 4x^2 + 11x - 2$ **59.** $x^2 + 2x - 3$

CHAPTER 9 REVIEW EXERCISES

1. $8b^2 - 2b - 15$ [9.3C] **2.** $21y^2 + 4y - 1$ [9.1A] **3.** $x^4y^8z^4$ [9.2A] **4.** $\frac{2x^3}{3}$ [9.4A]
5. $-8x^3 - 14x^2 + 18x$ [9.3A] **6.** $-\frac{1}{2a}$ [9.4A] **7.** $16u^{12}v^{16}$ [9.2B] **8.** 64 [9.2B] **9.** $2x^2 + 3x - 8$ [9.1B]
10. $\frac{b^6}{a^4}$ [9.4A] **11.** $-108x^{18}$ [9.2B] **12.** $25y^2 - 70y + 49$ [9.3D] **13.** $100a^{15}b^{13}$ [9.2B] **14.** $4b^4 + 12b^2 - 1$ [9.5A]
15. $-\frac{1}{16}$ [9.4A] **16.** $13y^3 - 12y^2 - 5y - 1$ [9.1B] **17.** $-x + 2 + \frac{1}{x + 3}$ [9.5B] **18.** $2ax - 4ay - bx + 2by$ [9.3C]
19. $6y^3 + 17y^2 - 2y - 21$ [9.3B] **20.** $b^2 + 5b + 2 + \frac{7}{b - 7}$ [9.5B] **21.** $8a^3b^3 - 4a^2b^4 + 6ab^5$ [9.3A]
22. $4a^2 - 25b^2$ [9.3D] **23.** $12b^5 - 4b^4 - 6b^3 - 8b^2 + 5$ [9.3B] **24.** $2x^3 + 9x^2 - 3x - 12$ [9.1A] **25.** $-4y + 8$ [9.5A]
26. $a^2 - 49$ [9.3D] **27.** 3.756×10^{10} [9.4B] **28.** 14,600,000 [9.4B] **29.** $-54a^{13}b^5c^7$ [9.2A] **30.** $2y - 9$ [9.5B]
31. $\frac{x^4y^6}{9}$ [9.4A] **32.** $10a^2 + 31a - 63$ [9.3C] **33.** 1.27×10^{-7} [9.4B] **34.** 0.0000000000032 [9.4B]
35. The area is $(2w^2 - w)$ ft^2. [9.3E] **36.** The area is $(9x^2 - 12x + 4)$ in^2. [9.3E]

CHAPTER 9 TEST

1. $4x^3 - 6x^2$ [9.3A; HOW TO 1] **2.** $4x - 1 + \frac{3}{x^2}$ [9.5A; HOW TO 1] **3.** $-\frac{4}{x^6}$ [9.4A; HOW TO 12]
4. $-6x^3y^6$ [9.2A; HOW TO 1] **5.** $x - 1 + \frac{2}{x + 1}$ [9.5B; Example 3] **6.** $x^3 - 7x^2 + 17x - 15$ [9.3B; HOW TO 2]
7. $-8a^6b^3$ [9.2B; Example 2] **8.** $\frac{9y^{10}}{x^{10}}$ [9.4A; Example 2] **9.** $a^2 + 3ab - 10b^2$ [9.3C; Example 4]
10. $4x^4 - 2x^2 + 5$ [9.5A; HOW TO 1] **11.** $x + 7$ [9.5B; HOW TO 2] **12.** $6y^4 - 9y^3 + 18y^2$ [9.3A; HOW TO 1]
13. $-4x^4 + 8x^3 - 3x^2 - 14x + 21$ [9.3B; You Try It 3] **14.** $16y^2 - 9$ [9.3D; Example 6] **15.** a^4b^7 [9.2A; You Try It 1]
16. $8ab^4$ [9.4A; HOW TO 12] **17.** $4a - 7$ [9.5A; HOW TO 1] **18.** $-5a^3 + 3a^2 - 4a + 3$ [9.1B; You Try It 3]
19. $4x^2 - 20x + 25$ [9.3D; Example 7] **20.** $2x + 3 + \frac{2}{2x - 3}$ [9.5B; HOW TO 3] **21.** $-2x^3$ [9.4A; Example 2]
22. $10x^2 - 43xy + 28y^2$ [9.3C; HOW TO 5] **23.** $3x^3 + 6x^2 - 8x + 3$ [9.1A; HOW TO 1] **24.** 3.02×10^{-9} [9.4B; You Try It 5]
25. The area of the circle is $(\pi x^2 - 10\pi x + 25\pi)$ m^2. [9.3E; You Try It 8]

CUMULATIVE REVIEW EXERCISES

1. $\frac{5}{144}$ [3.4A] **2.** $\frac{5}{3}$ [3.5A] **3.** $\frac{25}{11}$ [3.5A] **4.** $-\frac{22}{9}$ [4.1A] **5.** $5x - 3xy$ [4.2A] **6.** $-9x$ [4.2B]
7. $-18x + 12$ [4.2D] **8.** -16 [5.1C] **9.** -16 [5.3A] **10.** 15 [5.3B] **11.** 22% [6.4A/6.4B]
12. $4b^3 - 4b^2 - 8b - 4$ [9.1A] **13.** $3y^3 + 2y^2 - 10y$ [9.1B] **14.** a^9b^{15} [9.2B] **15.** $-8x^3y^6$ [9.2A]

16. $6y^4 + 8y^3 - 16y^2$ [9.3A] **17.** $10a^3 - 39a^2 + 20a - 21$ [9.3B] **18.** $15b^2 - 31b + 14$ [9.3C]
19. $\frac{1}{2b^2}$ [9.4A] **20.** $a - 7$ [9.5B] **21.** 0.0000609 [9.4B] **22.** $8x - 2x = 18; 3$ [5.4B]
23. The cost of the fruit drink is $.13 per ounce. [5.5A] **24.** The car overtakes the cyclist 25 mi from the starting point. [5.5B]
25. The length is 15 m and the width is 6 m. [7.2A]

Answers to Chapter 10 Selected Exercises

PREP TEST

1. $2 \cdot 3 \cdot 5$ [1.3D] **2.** $-12y + 15$ [4.2C] **3.** $-a + b$ [4.2C] **4.** $-3a + 3b$ [4.2D] **5.** 0 [5.1C]
6. $-\frac{1}{2}$ [5.2A] **7.** $x^2 - 2x - 24$ [9.3C] **8.** $6x^2 - 11x - 10$ [9.3C] **9.** x^3 [9.4A] **10.** $3x^3y$ [9.4A]

SECTION 10.1

1. 4 **3a.** x **b.** $2x - 1$ **5.** $(2x^3 - x^2) + (6x - 3)$ **7.** $5(a + 1)$ **9.** $8(2 - a^2)$ **11.** $4(2x + 3)$ **13.** $x(7x - 3)$
15. $a^2(3 + 5a^3)$ **17.** $2x(x^3 - 2)$ **19.** $2x^2(5x^2 - 6)$ **21.** $4a^5(2a^3 - 1)$ **23.** $xy(xy - 1)$ **25.** $3xy(xy^3 - 2)$
27. $3x(x^2 + 2x + 3)$ **29.** $2x^2(x^2 - 2x + 3)$ **31.** $2x(x^2 + 3x - 7)$ **33.** $y^3(2y^2 - 3y + 7)$ **35.** $xy(x^2 - 3xy + 7y^2)$
37. $5y(y^2 + 2y - 5)$ **39.** $3b^2(a^2 - 3a + 5)$ **41.** x^c **43.** $(b + 4)(x + 3)$ **45.** $(y - x)(a - b)$ **47.** $(x - 2)(x - y)$
49. $(2m - 3n)(8c - 1)$ **51.** $(x + 2)(x + 2y)$ **53.** $(p - 2)(p - 3r)$ **55.** $(a + 6)(b - 4)$ **57.** $(2z - 1)(z + y)$
59. $(2x - 5)(x - 3y)$ **61.** $(y - 2)(3y - a)$ **63.** $(3x - y)(y + 1)$ **65.** $(3s + t)(t - 2)$ **67.** -1 **69.** $b - 3a$

SECTION 10.2

1. -8 **3.** -2 and 6 **5.** Different **7.** $(x + 1)(x + 2)$ **9.** $(x + 1)(x - 2)$ **11.** $(a + 4)(a - 3)$ **13.** $(a - 1)(a - 2)$
15. $(a + 2)(a - 1)$ **17.** $(b - 3)(b - 3)$ **19.** $(b + 8)(b - 1)$ **21.** $(y + 11)(y - 5)$ **23.** $(y - 2)(y - 3)$
25. $(z - 5)(z - 9)$ **27.** $(z + 8)(z - 20)$ **29.** $(p + 3)(p + 9)$ **31.** $(x + 10)(x + 10)$ **33.** $(b + 4)(b - 5)$
35. $(y + 3)(y - 17)$ **37.** $(p + 3)(p - 7)$ **39.** Nonfactorable over the integers **41.** $(x - 5)(x - 15)$ **43.** $(p + 3)(p + 21)$
45. $(x + 2)(x + 19)$ **47.** Nonfactorable over the integers **49.** $(a + 4)(a - 11)$ **51.** $(a - 3)(a - 18)$ **53.** $(z + 21)(z - 7)$
55. $(c + 12)(c - 15)$ **57.** $(p + 9)(p + 15)$ **59.** $(c + 2)(c + 9)$ **61.** $(x + 15)(x - 5)$ **63.** $(x + 25)(x - 4)$
65. $(b - 4)(b - 18)$ **67.** $(a + 45)(a - 3)$ **69.** $(b - 7)(b - 18)$ **71.** $(z + 12)(z + 12)$ **73.** $(x - 4)(x - 25)$
75. $(x + 16)(x - 7)$ **77.** Positive **79.** $3(x + 2)(x + 3)$ **81.** $-(x + 6)(x - 2)$ **83.** $a(b + 8)(b - 1)$ **85.** $x(y + 3)(y + 5)$
87. $-2a(a + 1)(a + 2)$ **89.** $4y(y + 6)(y - 3)$ **91.** $2x(x^2 - x + 2)$ **93.** $6(z + 5)(z - 3)$ **95.** $3a(a + 3)(a - 6)$
97. $(x + 7y)(x - 3y)$ **99.** $(a - 5b)(a - 10b)$ **101.** $(s + 8t)(s - 6t)$ **103.** Nonfactorable over the integers
105. $z^2(z + 10)(z - 8)$ **107.** $b^2(b + 2)(b - 5)$ **109.** $3y^2(y + 3)(y + 15)$ **111.** $-x^2(x - 12)(x + 1)$ **113.** $3y(x + 3)(x - 5)$
115. $-3x(x - 3)(x - 9)$ **117.** $(x - 3y)(x - 5y)$ **119.** $(a - 6b)(a - 7b)$ **121.** $(y + z)(y + 7z)$ **123.** $3y(x + 21)(x - 1)$
125. $3x(x + 4)(x - 3)$ **127.** $2(t - 5s)(t - 7s)$ **129.** $3(a + 3b)(a - 11b)$ **131.** $5x(x + 2y)(x + 4y)$ **133a.** Yes **b.** No
135. $-2x$ **137.** $y(x + 6)(x - 9)$ **139.** $3p(p + 8)(p - 4)$ **141.** 19, 11, 9, -9, -11, -19 **143.** 15, 9, -9, -15 **145.** 6, 10, 12
147. 6, 10, 12 **149.** 4, 6

SECTION 10.3

1. $2x + 5$ **3.** $4x - 3$ **5.** 4, -5 **7.** $-2x - 6x$ **9.** $(x + 1)(2x + 1)$ **11.** $(y + 3)(2y + 1)$ **13.** $(a - 1)(2a - 1)$
15. $(b - 5)(2b - 1)$ **17.** $(x + 1)(2x - 1)$ **19.** $(x - 3)(2x + 1)$ **21.** $(t + 2)(2t - 5)$ **23.** $(p - 5)(3p - 1)$
25. $(3y - 1)(4y - 1)$ **27.** Nonfactorable over the integers **29.** $(2t - 1)(3t - 4)$ **31.** $(x + 4)(8x + 1)$
33. Nonfactorable over the integers **35.** $(3y + 1)(4y + 5)$ **37.** $(z - 14)(2z + 1)$ **39.** $(p + 8)(3p - 2)$ **41.** $2(x + 1)(2x + 1)$
43. $5(y - 1)(3y - 7)$ **45.** $x(x - 5)(2x - 1)$ **47.** $b(a - 4)(3a - 4)$ **49.** Nonfactorable over the integers
51. $-3x(x + 4)(x - 3)$ **53.** $4(4y - 1)(5y - 1)$ **55.** $z(2z + 3)(4z + 1)$ **57.** $y(2x - 5)(3x + 2)$ **59.** $5(t + 2)(2t - 5)$
61. $p(p - 5)(3p - 1)$ **63.** $2(z + 4)(13z - 3)$ **65.** $2y(y - 4)(5y - 2)$ **67.** $yz(z + 2)(4z - 3)$ **69.** $3a(2a + 3)(7a - 3)$
71. $y(3x - 5y)(3x - 5y)$ **73.** $xy(3x - 4y)(3x - 4y)$ **75.** Odd **77.** $(2x - 3)(3x - 4)$ **79.** $(b + 7)(5b - 2)$
81. $(2a - 3)(3a + 8)$ **83.** $(z + 2)(4z + 3)$ **85.** $(2p + 5)(11p - 2)$ **87.** $(y + 1)(8y + 9)$ **89.** $(3t + 1)(6t - 5)$
91. $(b + 12)(6b - 1)$ **93.** $(3x + 2)(3x + 2)$ **95.** $(2b - 3)(3b - 2)$ **97.** $(3b + 5)(11b - 7)$ **99.** $(3y - 4)(6y - 5)$
101. $(3a + 7)(5a - 3)$ **103.** $(2y - 5)(4y - 3)$ **105.** $(2z + 3)(4z - 5)$ **107.** Nonfactorable over the integers
109. $(2z - 5)(5z - 2)$ **111.** $(6z + 5)(6z + 7)$ **113.** $(x + y)(3x - 2y)$ **115.** $(a + 2b)(3a - b)$ **117.** $(y - 2z)(4y - 3z)$
119. $-(z - 7)(z + 4)$ **121.** $-(x - 1)(x + 8)$ **123.** $3(x + 5)(3x - 4)$ **125.** $4(2x - 3)(3x - 2)$ **127.** $a^2(5a + 2)(7a - 1)$
129. $5(b - 7)(3b - 2)$ **131.** $(x - 7y)(3x - 5y)$ **133.** $3(8y - 1)(9y + 1)$ **135.** One positive, one negative
137. One positive, one negative **139.** $(x - 2)(x + 3)$ **141.** $y(y + 1)$ **143.** $(3a + 2)(a + 3)$ **145.** $2y(y - 3)(4y - 1)$
147. $ab(a + 4)(a - 6)$ **149.** 7, -7, 5, -5 **151.** 7, -7, 5, -5 **153.** 11, -11, 7, -7

CHECK YOUR PROGRESS: CHAPTER 10

1. $5(4b + 1)$ [10.1A] **2.** $(b + 7)(2x - y)$ [10.1B] **3.** $(x + 10)(x + 10)$ [10.2A] **4.** $y(x + 4)(x - 6)$ [10.2B] **5.** $-(x - 7)(x + 5)$ [10.2B] **6.** Nonfactorable over the integers [10.2A] **7.** $(7x + 2y)(3x - 7)$ [10.1B] **8.** $3a(2b + 3)$ [10.1A] **9.** $(y - 4)(5y - 2)$ [10.3A] **10.** $(3x + 1)(4x + 9)$ [10.3B] **11.** $x(9 - 5x)$ [10.1A] **12.** $(2x + 1)(x + y)$ [10.1B] **13.** $(2a + b)(4a - 3b)$ [10.3B] **14.** $(b + 4)(b + 5)$ [10.2A] **15.** $2a(a + 9)(a + 3)$ [10.2B] **16.** $(a - 5)(11a + 1)$ [10.3A] **17.** $4(9y + 1)(10y - 1)$ [10.3B] **18.** $y(14y^2 + 5y + 11)$ [10.1A] **19.** $(x - 2)(x - 5)$ [10.2A] **20.** Nonfactorable over the integers [10.2B] **21.** $(b + 8)(b + 5)$ [10.2A] **22.** $(2x - 5)(x - 3y)$ [10.1B] **23.** $xy(x - y^2 + x^2)$ [10.1A] **24.** $(b + 4)(3b + 4)$ [10.3A] **25.** $(x + 3)(x - 14)$ [10.2A]

SECTION 10.4

1. 4; $25x^6$; $100x^4y^4$ **3.** i and iv **5.** Sometimes true **7.** Always true **9.** $3x$; 2 **11.** Answers will vary. For example: **a.** $x^2 - 16$ **b.** $(x + 7)(x - 7)$ **c.** $x^2 + 10x + 25$ **d.** $(x - 3)^2$ **e.** $x^2 + 36$ **13.** $(x + 2)(x - 2)$ **15.** $(a + 9)(a - 9)$ **17.** $(y + 1)^2$ **19.** $(a - 1)^2$ **21.** $(2x + 1)(2x - 1)$ **23.** $(x^3 + 3)(x^3 - 3)$ **25.** Nonfactorable over the integers **27.** $(x + y)^2$ **29.** $(2a + 1)^2$ **31.** $(3x + 1)(3x - 1)$ **33.** $(1 + 8x)(1 - 8x)$ **35.** Nonfactorable over the integers **37.** $(3a + 1)^2$ **39.** $(b^2 + 4a)(b^2 - 4a)$ **41.** $(2a - 5)^2$ **43.** $(3a - 7)^2$ **45.** $(5z + y)(5z - y)$ **47.** $(ab + 5)(ab - 5)$ **49.** $(5x + 1)(5x - 1)$ **51.** $(2a - 3b)^2$ **53.** $(2y - 9z)^2$ **55.** (i) and (iii) **57.** 9 **59.** 1 **61.** 25

SECTION 10.5

1. common **3.** $x^2 - 81$ **5.** Determine whether the polynomial is a perfect square trinomial or try to "UNFOIL" the trinomial. **9.** $12(n + 2)(n - 2)$ **11.** $r(2s - 1)^2$ **13.** $(9 + t^2)(3 + t)(3 - t)$ **15.** $(x + 2)(x + 8)$ **17.** $4c^2(3c - 2)^2$ **19.** $2(4s^2 + 1)(2s + 1)(2s - 1)$ **21.** $(3 + 4a)^2$ **23.** $4x(x + 5)$ **25.** $(2x + 3 + 2y)(2x + 3 - 2y)$ **27.** $2(x + 3)(x - 3)$ **29.** $y(y - 5)^2$ **31.** $a^2(a - 3)(a - 8)$ **33.** $6(y - 2)(y - 6)$ **35.** Nonfactorable over the integers **37.** $3b(a + 9)(a - 2)$ **39.** $b(b^2 - 8b - 7)$ **41.** $3(y + 7)(y - 7)$ **43.** $3(2a - 3)^2$ **45.** $a^2(b + 11)(b - 8)$ **47.** $4(2x - y)(2x - 3y)$ **49.** $-2(x + 6)(x - 6)$ **51.** $b^2(a + 3)^2$ **53.** $xy(x - 2y)(2x - 3y)$ **55.** $2a(3a + 2)^2$ **57.** $3(25 + 9y^2)$ **59.** $3x(2x - 5)(4x - 1)$ **61.** $2a(a - 2b)^2$ **63.** $b^2(a - 3)^2$ **65.** $-x^2(2x - 3)(x + 7)$ **67.** $b^2(b + a)(b - a)$ **69.** $2x(4y - 3)^2$ **71.** $-y^2(x - 3)(x + 5)$ **73.** $3(x + 3y)(x - 3y)$ **75.** $y(y + 3)(y - 3)$ **77.** $x^2y^2(5x + 4y)(3x - 5y)$ **79.** $2(x - 1)(a + b)$ **81.** $(x - 2)(x + 1)(x - 1)$ **83.** $(x + 2)(x - 2)(a + b)$ **85.** $(x - 5)(2 + x)(2 - x)$ **87.** $(4x - 3 + y)(4x - 3 - y)$ **89.** $(x - 2 + y)(x - 2 - y)$ **91.** 19 **93.** (middle number)$^2 - 1 =$ (first number) · (third number)
Let the numbers be $n - 1$, n, and $n + 1$. Then $n^2 - 1 = (n + 1)(n - 1)$.

SECTION 10.6

1a. Yes **b.** No **c.** Yes **3a.** Yes **b.** Yes **c.** No **d.** Yes **e.** No **f.** Yes **5.** $-3, -2$ **7.** 7, 3 **9.** 0, 5 **11.** 0, 9 **13.** $0, -\frac{3}{2}$ **15.** $0, \frac{2}{3}$ **17.** $-2, 5$ **19.** $9, -9$ **21.** $\frac{7}{2}, -\frac{7}{2}$ **23.** $\frac{1}{3}, -\frac{1}{3}$ **25.** $-4, -2$ **27.** $2, -7$ **29.** $-\frac{1}{2}, 5$ **31.** $-\frac{1}{3}, -\frac{1}{2}$ **33.** 0, 3 **35.** 0, 7 **37.** $-1, -4$ **39.** 2, 3 **41.** $\frac{1}{2}, -4$ **43.** $\frac{1}{3}, 4$ **45.** 3, 9 **47.** $9, -2$ **49.** $-1, -2$ **51.** $5, -9$ **53.** $4, -7$ **55.** $-2, -3$ **57.** $-8, 9$ **59.** 1, 4 **61.** $-5, 2$ **63.** Less than **65.** The number is 6. **67.** The numbers are 2 and 4. **69.** ii **71.** The numbers are 4 and 5. **73.** The numbers are 15 and 16. **75.** The base of the triangle is 18 ft. The height is 6 ft. **77.** The length of the rectangle is 18 ft. The width is 8 ft. **79.** The length of a side of the original square is 4 m. **81.** The radius of the original circle is 3.81 in. **83.** The dimensions are 4 in. by 7 in. **85.** The width of the lane is 16 ft. **87.** The object will hit the ground in 4 s. **89.** There are 15 consecutive natural numbers beginning with 1 that will give a sum of 120. **91.** There are 10 teams in the league. **93.** The golf ball will return to the ground in 3 s. **95.** $\frac{3}{2}, -4$ **97.** $-1, -9$ **99.** 0, 7 **101.** 18, 1 **103.** 2 or -128 **107.** The length of the piece of cardboard is 20 in. The width is 10 in.

CHAPTER 10 REVIEW EXERCISES

1. $(b - 3)(b - 10)$ [10.2A] **2.** $(x - 3)(4x + 5)$ [10.1B] **3.** Nonfactorable over the integers [10.3A] **4.** $5x(x^2 + 2x + 7)$ [10.1A] **5.** $7y^3(2y^6 - 7y^3 + 1)$ [10.1A] **6.** $(y - 4)(y + 9)$ [10.2A] **7.** $(2x - 7)(3x - 4)$ [10.3A] **8.** $3ab(4a + b)$ [10.1A] **9.** $(a^3 + 10)(a^3 - 10)$ [10.4A] **10.** $n^2(n + 1)(n - 3)$ [10.2B] **11.** $(6y - 1)(2y + 3)$ [10.3A] **12.** $2b(3b - 4)(2b - 7)$ [10.5A] **13.** $(3y^2 + 5z)(3y^2 - 5z)$ [10.4A] **14.** $(c + 6)(c + 2)$ [10.2A] **15.** $(6a - 5)(3a + 2)$ [10.3B] **16.** $\frac{1}{4}, -7$ [10.6A] **17.** $4x(x - 6)(x + 1)$ [10.2B] **18.** $3(a + 2)(a - 7)$ [10.2B] **19.** $(2a + 5)(a - 12)$ [10.3B] **20.** $-3, 7$ [10.6A] **21.** $(3a - 5b)(7x + 2y)$ [10.1B] **22.** $(ab + 1)(ab - 1)$ [10.4A] **23.** $(2x + 5)(5x + 2y)$ [10.1B] **24.** $5(x + 2)(x - 3)$ [10.2B] **25.** $3(x + 6)^2$ [10.5A] **26.** $(3x - 2)(x - 5)$ [10.3B] **27.** The length is 100 yd. The width is 60 yd. [10.6B] **28.** The distance is 20 ft. [10.6B] **29.** The width of the frame is 1.5 in. or $1\frac{1}{2}$ in. [10.6B] **30.** The two integers are 4 and 5. [10.6B]

CHAPTER 10 TEST

1. $(b + 6)(a - 3)$ [10.1B; Example 6] **2.** $2y^2(y + 1)(y - 8)$ [10.2B; Example 3] **3.** $4(x + 4)(2x - 3)$ [10.3B; Example 4] **4.** $(2x + 1)(3x + 8)$ [10.3A; HOW TO 2] **5.** $(a - 3)(a - 16)$ [10.2A; Example 1] **6.** $2x(3x^2 - 4x + 5)$ [10.1A; HOW TO 2] **7.** $(x + 5)(x - 3)$ [10.2A; Example 2] **8.** $\frac{1}{2}, -\frac{1}{2}$ [10.6A; Example 2] **9.** $5(x^2 - 9x - 3)$ [10.1A; HOW TO 2] **10.** $(p + 6)^2$ [10.4A; Example 3] **11.** 3, 5 [10.6A; Example 3] **12.** $3(x + 2y)^2$ [10.5A; Example 1] **13.** $(b + 4)(b - 4)$ [10.4A; You Try It 1] **14.** $3y^2(2x + 1)(x + 1)$ [10.3B; Example 4] **15.** $(p + 2)(p + 3)$ [10.2A; You Try It 1] **16.** $(x - 2)(a + b)$ [10.1B; Example 4] **17.** $(p + 1)(x - 1)$ [10.1B; Example 4] **18.** $3(a + 5)(a - 5)$ [10.5A; Example 1] **19.** Nonfactorable over the integers [10.3B; HOW TO 6] **20.** $(x + 3)(x - 12)$ [10.2A; HOW TO 2] **21.** $(2a - 3b)^2$ [10.4A; HOW TO 3] **22.** $(2x + 7y)(2x - 7y)$ [10.4A; Example 1] **23.** $\frac{3}{2}, -7$ [10.6A; HOW TO 1] **24.** The two numbers are 3 and 7. [10.6B; Example 4] **25.** The length is 15 cm. The width is 6 cm. [10.6B; You Try It 5]

CUMULATIVE REVIEW EXERCISES

1. 7 [3.2B] **2.** 4 [3.5A] **3.** -7 [4.1A] **4.** $15x^2$ [4.2B] **5.** 12 [4.2D] **6.** $\frac{2}{3}$ [5.1C] **7.** $\frac{7}{4}$ [5.3A] **8.** 3 [5.3B] **9.** 45 [6.4A/6.4B] **10.** $9a^6b^4$ [9.2B] **11.** $x^3 - 3x^2 - 6x + 8$ [9.3B] **12.** $4x + 8 + \frac{21}{2x - 3}$ [9.5B] **13.** $\frac{y^6}{x^8}$ [9.4A] **14.** $(a - b)(3 - x)$ [10.1B] **15.** $5xy^2(3 - 4y^2)$ [10.1A] **16.** $(x - 7y)(x + 2y)$ [10.2A] **17.** $(p - 10)(p + 1)$ [10.2A] **18.** $3a(2a + 5)(3a + 2)$ [10.5A] **19.** $(6a - 7b)(6a + 7b)$ [10.4A] **20.** $(2x + 7y)^2$ [10.4A] **21.** $(3x - 2)(3x + 7)$ [10.3A] **22.** $2(3x - 4y)^2$ [10.5A] **23.** $(x - 3)(3y - 2)$ [10.1B] **24.** $\frac{2}{3}, -7$ [10.6A] **25.** The shorter piece is 4 ft long. The longer piece is 6 ft long. [5.4B] **26.** The sale price is 60% of the regular price. [6.4C] **27.** The measure of $\angle a$ is 72°. The measure of $\angle b$ is 108°. [7.1B] **28.** The distance to the resort is 168 mi. [5.5B] **29.** The integers are 10, 12, and 14. [5.4A] **30.** The length of the base of the triangle is 12 in. [10.6B]

Answers to Chapter 11 Selected Exercises

PREP TEST

1. 36 [2.1A] **2.** $\frac{3x}{y^3}$ [9.4A] **3.** $-\frac{5}{36}$ [3.4A] **4.** $-\frac{10}{11}$ [3.4B] **5.** No [1.3C] **6.** $\frac{19}{8}$ [5.2A] **7.** $(x - 6)(x + 2)$ [10.2A] **8.** $(2x - 3)(x + 1)$ [10.3A] **9.** 9:40 A.M. [5.5B]

SECTION 11.1

5. $\frac{3}{4x}$ **7.** $\frac{1}{x + 3}$ **9.** -1 **11.** $\frac{2}{3y}$ **13.** $-\frac{3}{4x}$ **15.** $\frac{a}{b}$ **17.** $-\frac{2}{x}$ **19.** $\frac{y - 2}{y - 3}$ **21.** $\frac{x + 5}{x + 4}$ **23.** $\frac{x + 4}{x - 3}$ **25.** $-\frac{x + 2}{x + 5}$ **27.** $\frac{2(x + 2)}{x + 3}$ **29.** $\frac{2x - 1}{2x + 3}$ **31.** $-\frac{x + 7}{x + 6}$ **33.** $\frac{2}{3xy}$ **35.** $\frac{8xy^2ab}{3}$ **37.** $\frac{2}{9}$ **39.** $\frac{y^2}{x}$ **41.** $\frac{y(x + 4)}{x(x + 1)}$ **43.** $\frac{x^3(x - 7)}{y^2(x - 4)}$ **45.** $-\frac{y}{x}$ **47.** $\frac{x + 3}{x + 1}$ **49.** $\frac{x - 5}{x + 3}$ **51.** $-\frac{x + 3}{x + 5}$ **53.** $-\frac{x + 3}{x - 12}$ **55.** $\frac{x + 2}{x + 4}$ **57.** 1 **59.** 1 **61.** $\frac{7a^3y^2}{40bx}$ **63.** $\frac{4}{3}$ **65.** $\frac{3a}{2}$ **67.** $\frac{x^2(x + 4)}{y^2(x + 2)}$ **69.** $\frac{x(x - 2)}{y(x - 6)}$ **71.** $-\frac{3by}{ax}$ **73.** $\frac{(x + 6)(x - 3)}{(x + 7)(x - 6)}$ **75.** 1 **77.** $-\frac{x + 8}{x - 4}$ **79.** $\frac{2n + 1}{2n - 3}$ **81.** Yes **83.** No **85.** 5, -1 **87.** $\frac{4}{25}$ **89.** $\frac{x + 4}{x - 3}$ and $\frac{2x - 1}{3x + 1}$ or $\frac{x + 4}{3x + 1}$ and $\frac{2x - 1}{x - 3}$

SECTION 11.2

1. True **3.** False **5.** $24x^3y^2$ **7.** $6x^2y(x + 4)$ **9.** $36x(x + 2)^2$ **11.** $6(x + 1)^2$ **13.** $(x - 1)(x + 2)(x + 3)$ **15.** $(2x + 3)^2(x - 5)$ **17.** $(x - 1)(x - 2)$ **19.** $(x - 3)(x + 2)(x + 4)$ **21.** $(x + 4)(x + 1)(x - 7)$ **23.** $(x - 6)(x + 6)(x + 4)$ **25.** $(2x - 1)(x - 3)(x + 1)$ **27.** $(x + 2)(x - 3)$ **29.** $\frac{4x}{x^2}, \frac{3}{x^2}$ **31.** $\frac{4x}{12y^2}, \frac{3yz}{12y^2}$ **33.** $\frac{xy}{x^2(x - 3)}, \frac{6x - 18}{x^2(x - 3)}$ **35.** $\frac{9x}{x(x - 1)^2}, \frac{6x - 6}{x(x - 1)^2}$ **37.** $\frac{3x}{x(x - 3)}, -\frac{5}{x(x - 3)}$ **39.** $\frac{x^2 - 6x + 8}{(x + 3)(x - 4)}, \frac{x^2 + 3x}{(x + 3)(x - 4)}$ **41.** $\frac{3}{(x + 2)(x - 1)}, \frac{x^2 - x}{(x + 2)(x - 1)}$ **43.** $\frac{x^2 - 3x}{(x + 3)(x - 3)(x - 2)}, \frac{2x^2 - 4x}{(x + 3)(x - 3)(x - 2)}$ **45.** $\frac{300}{10^4}; \frac{5}{10^4}$ **47.** $\frac{b^2}{b}; \frac{5}{b}$

SECTION 11.3

1. False **3.** False **5.** $\frac{11}{y^2}$ **7.** $-\frac{7}{x+4}$ **9.** $\frac{8x}{2x+3}$ **11.** $\frac{5x+7}{x-3}$ **13.** $\frac{2x-5}{x+9}$ **15.** $\frac{-3x-4}{2x+7}$ **17.** $\frac{1}{x+5}$ **19.** $\frac{1}{x-6}$ **21.** $\frac{3}{2y-1}$ **23.** $\frac{1}{x-5}$ **25.** i and iv **27.** $\frac{4y+5x}{xy}$ **29.** $\frac{19}{2x}$ **31.** $\frac{5}{12x}$ **33.** $\frac{19x-12}{6x^2}$ **35.** $\frac{52y-35x}{20xy}$ **37.** $\frac{13x+2}{15x}$ **39.** $\frac{7}{24}$ **41.** $\frac{x+90}{45x}$ **43.** $\frac{x^2+2x+2}{2x^2}$ **45.** $\frac{2x^2+3x-10}{4x^2}$ **47.** $\frac{-x^2-4x+4}{x+4}$ **49.** $\frac{4x+7}{x+1}$ **51.** $\frac{4x^2+9x+9}{24x^2}$ **53.** $\frac{3x-1-2xy-3y}{xy^2}$ **55.** $\frac{20x^2+28x-12xy+9y}{24x^2y^2}$ **57.** $\frac{9x^2-3x-2xy-10y}{18xy^2}$ **59.** $\frac{7x-23}{(x-3)(x-4)}$ **61.** $\frac{-y-33}{(y+6)(y-3)}$ **63.** $\frac{3x^2+20x-8}{(x-4)(x+6)}$ **65.** $\frac{3(4x^2+5x-5)}{(x+5)(2x+3)}$ **67.** $\frac{-4x+5}{x-6}$ **69.** $\frac{2(y+2)}{(y-4)(y+4)}$ **71.** $-\frac{4x}{(x+1)^2}$ **73.** $\frac{2x-1}{(1+x)(1-x)}$ **75.** $\frac{14}{(x-5)^2}$ **77.** $\frac{-2(x+7)}{(x+6)(x-7)}$ **79.** $\frac{x-4}{x-6}$ **81.** $\frac{2x+1}{x-1}$ **83.** $\frac{-3(x^2+8x+25)}{(x-3)(x+7)}$ **85.** $\frac{5}{a}+\frac{4}{b}$ **87.** $\frac{3}{y^2}+\frac{4}{xy}$ **89a.** $\frac{44{,}400}{x}$ dollars **b.** $\frac{222{,}000}{x(x+5)}$ dollars **c.** You will save \$296 in one year.

SECTION 11.4

1. $\frac{2}{2}$ **3.** $\frac{(x-1)(x+4)}{(x-1)(x+4)}$ **5.** True **7.** $\frac{x}{x-3}$ **9.** $\frac{2}{3}$ **11.** $\frac{y+3}{y-4}$ **13.** $\frac{2(2x+13)}{5x+36}$ **15.** $\frac{x+2}{x+3}$ **17.** $\frac{x-6}{x+5}$ **19.** $\frac{-x+2}{x+1}$ **21.** $x-1$ **23.** $\frac{1}{2x-1}$ **25.** $\frac{x-3}{x+5}$ **27.** $\frac{x-7}{x-8}$ **29.** $\frac{2y-1}{2y+1}$ **31.** $\frac{x-2}{2x-5}$ **33.** $\frac{-x-1}{4x-3}$ **35.** $\frac{x+1}{2(5x-2)}$ **37.** True **39.** $\frac{8}{5}$ **41.** $-\frac{1}{y}$ **43.** y^2-x^2 **45.** The total resistance in the circuit is $\frac{6}{5}$ ohms.

CHECK YOUR PROGRESS: CHAPTER 11

1. $\frac{x+2}{x+5}$ [11.1A] **2.** $\frac{5}{3}$ [11.1B] **3.** $\frac{b^4x^2y}{a^2}$ [11.1C] **4.** $\frac{a^2(a+4)}{b^5(a+2)}$ [11.1C] **5.** $30x^4y^2$ [11.2A] **6.** $8x^2(x+2)$ [11.2A] **7.** $\frac{3x}{x^2(x+2)}, \frac{4x+8}{x^2(x+2)}$ [11.2B] **8.** $-\frac{2a}{3a-1}$ [11.3A] **9.** $\frac{a+3}{a+5}$ [11.3B] **10.** $\frac{19x+6}{8x-15}$ [11.4A]

SECTION 11.5

1. Multiplication Property of Equations **3.** We can clear denominators in an *equation*, as in part (a), but not in an *expression*, as in part (b). **5.** $-1, 2$ **7.** $0, 9$ **9.** 1 **11.** 3 **13.** 2 **15.** 2 **17.** $\frac{2}{3}$ **19.** 4 **21.** -3 **23.** $\frac{3}{4}$ **25.** 7 **27.** -7 **29.** -1 **31.** -1 **33.** No solution **35.** $2, -6$ **37.** $-\frac{2}{3}, 5$ **39.** $-1, 6$ **41.** 0 **43.** $0, -\frac{2}{3}$ **45.** The intensity of the illumination is 4 lm. **47.** A 320-candela-light source is needed. **49.** The light source must be placed 2 m from the desk surface.

SECTION 11.6

1. True **3.** R **5.** $t=\frac{d}{r}$ **7.** $T=\frac{PV}{nR}$ **9.** $l=\frac{P-2w}{2}$ **11.** $b_1=\frac{2A-hb_2}{h}$ **13.** $h=\frac{3V}{A}$ **15.** $S=C-Rt$ **17.** $P=\frac{A}{1+rt}$ **19.** $w=\frac{A}{S+1}$ **21.** $y=-3x+10$ **23.** $y=4x-3$ **25.** $y=-\frac{3}{2}x+3$ **27.** $y=\frac{2}{5}x-2$ **29.** $y=-\frac{2}{7}x+2$ **31.** $y=-\frac{1}{3}x+2$ **33.** $x=-3y+6$ **35.** $x=\frac{1}{3}y+1$ **37.** $x=-\frac{5}{2}y+5$ **39.** $x=2y-1$ **41a.** Yes **b.** Yes **43.** $R_2=\frac{RR_1}{R_1-R}$

SECTION 11.7

3. $\frac{1}{x}$ **5.** Jen has the greater rate of work. **7a.** Chris's rate of work is $\frac{1}{x}$ of the job per hour. **b.** Chris can lay $\frac{3}{x}$ of the floor in 3 h. **9.** The faster printer printed $\frac{h}{5}$ of the brochures. **11a.** The speed of the boat traveling with the current is 12 mph. **b.** The speed of the boat traveling against the current is 4 mph. **13.** Row 1: $\frac{1}{10}, t, \frac{t}{10}$; Row 2: $\frac{1}{12}, t, \frac{t}{12}$ **15.** It will take 2 h to fill the fountain with both sprinklers operating. **17.** With both skiploaders working together, it would take 3 h to transfer the earth. **19.** It would take both computers, working together, 30 h to solve the problem. **21.** With both air conditioners working, it would take 24 min to cool the room 5°F. **23.** It would take the second welder, working alone, 15 h to complete the task. **25.** It would take the second pipeline, working alone, 90 min to fill the tank.

27. It would take 3 h to harvest the field using only the older reaper. **29.** It will take the second technician 3 h to complete the wiring. **31.** It would take the small unit, working alone, $14\frac{2}{3}$ h to heat the pool. **33.** It will take the apprentice, working alone, 3 h to complete the repairs. **35.** t is less than k. **37a.** Row 1: 1440, $380 - r$, $\frac{1440}{380 - r}$; Row 2: 1600, $380 + r$, $\frac{1600}{380 + r}$ **b.** $\frac{1440}{380 - r}$; $\frac{1600}{380 + r}$
39. The camper hiked at 4 mph. **41.** The rate of the jet is 360 mph. **43.** The rate of the boat for the first 15 mi was 7.5 mph. **45.** The technician traveled at 20 mph through the congested traffic. **47.** The family can travel 21.6 mi down the river and still return the boat in 3 h. **49.** The rate of the river's current is 5 mph. **51.** The rate of the freight train is 30 mph, and the rate of the express train is 50 mph. **53.** The rate of the current is 2 mph. **55.** The rate of the jet stream is 50 mph. **57.** The rate of the current is 5 mph. **59.** It would take $1\frac{1}{19}$ h to fill the tank with all three pipes operating. **61.** The amount of time spent traveling by canoe was 2 h. **63.** The bus usually travels at 60 mph.

CHAPTER 11 REVIEW EXERCISES

1. $\frac{b^3y}{10ax}$ [11.1C] **2.** $\frac{7x + 22}{60x}$ [11.3B] **3.** $\frac{2xy}{5}$ [11.1B] **4.** $\frac{2xy}{3(x + y)}$ [11.1C] **5.** $\frac{x - 2}{3x - 10}$ [11.4A]
6. $-\frac{x + 6}{x + 3}$ [11.1A] **7.** $\frac{2x^4}{3y^7}$ [11.1A] **8.** 62 [11.5A] **9.** $\frac{(3y - 2)^2}{(y - 1)(y - 2)}$ [11.1C] **10.** $x = \frac{5}{3a - 1}$ [11.6A]
11. 8 [11.5A] **12.** $\frac{x^2 + 3y}{xy}$ [11.3B] **13.** $y = -\frac{5}{4}x + 5$ [11.6A] **14.** $\frac{by^3}{6ax^2}$ [11.1B] **15.** $\frac{x}{x - 7}$ [11.4A]
16. $\frac{3x^2 - x}{(2x + 3)(6x - 1)(3x - 1)}, \frac{24x^3 - 4x^2}{(2x + 3)(6x - 1)(3x - 1)}$ [11.2B] **17.** $a = \frac{T - 2bc}{2b + 2c}$ [11.6A] **18.** 2 [11.5A]
19. $\frac{2x + 1}{3x - 2}$ [11.4A] **20.** $\frac{x^2 + 5}{(x - 5)(x - 2)}$ [11.3B] **21.** $c = \frac{100m}{i}$ [11.6A] **22.** No solution [11.5A]
23. $\frac{1}{x^2}$ [11.1C] **24.** $\frac{2y - 3}{5y - 7}$ [11.3B] **25.** $\frac{1}{x + 3}$ [11.3A] **26.** $(5x - 3)(2x - 1)(4x - 1)$ [11.2A]
27. $y = -\frac{4}{9}x + 2$ [11.6A] **28.** $\frac{2x + 1}{x + 2}$ [11.1B] **29.** 5 [11.5A] **30.** $\frac{3x - 1}{x - 5}$ [11.3B] **31.** 10 [11.5A] **32.** 12 [11.5A]
33. It would take 6 h to fill the pool. [11.7A] **34.** The rate of the car is 45 mph. [11.7B] **35.** The rate of the wind is 20 mph. [11.7B]

CHAPTER 11 TEST

1. $\frac{x^2 - 4x + 5}{(x - 2)(x + 3)}$ [11.3B; Example 6] **2.** -1 [11.5A; You Try It 1B] **3.** $\frac{(x - 5)(2x - 1)}{(x + 3)(2x + 5)}$ [11.1B; Example 5]
4. $\frac{2x^3}{3y^3}$ [11.1A; Example 1] **5.** $t = \frac{d - s}{r}$ [11.6A; Example 3] **6.** 2 [11.5A; Example 2] **7.** $-\frac{x + 5}{x + 1}$ [11.1A; Example 3]
8. $3(2x - 1)(x + 1)$ [11.2A; HOW TO 1] **9.** $\frac{5}{(2x - 1)(3x + 1)}$ [11.3B; Example 6] **10.** $\frac{x + 5}{x + 4}$ [11.1C; Example 7]
11. $\frac{x - 3}{x - 2}$ [11.4A; Example 2] **12.** $\frac{3x + 6}{x(x - 2)(x + 2)}, \frac{x^2}{x(x - 2)(x + 2)}$ [11.2B; Example 4] **13.** $\frac{2}{x + 5}$ [11.3A; Example 1]
14. $y = \frac{3}{8}x - 2$ [11.6A; Example 1] **15.** No solution [11.5A; HOW TO 2] **16.** $\frac{x + 1}{x^3(x - 2)}$ [11.1B; Example 4] **17.** $\frac{6b^4x}{ay^3}$ [11.1C; You Try It 6] **18.** $\frac{1}{x^2y}$ [11.3A; Example 1] **19.** It would take 4 h to fill the pool. [11.7A; HOW TO 1]
20. The rate of the wind is 20 mph. [11.7B; HOW TO 2] **21.** It will take 3 h until the run can be opened. [11.7A; HOW TO 1]
22. The rate of the current is 5 mph. [11.7B; HOW TO 2]

CUMULATIVE REVIEW EXERCISES

1. $\frac{31}{30}$ [2.7A] **2.** 21 [4.1A] **3.** $5x - 2y$ [4.2A] **4.** $-8x + 26$ [4.2D] **5.** $-\frac{9}{2}$ [5.2A] **6.** -12 [5.3B]
7. 10 [6.4A/6.4B] **8.** a^3b^7 [9.2A] **9.** $a^2 + ab - 12b^2$ [9.3C] **10.** $3b^3 - b + 2$ [9.5A] **11.** $x^2 + 2x + 4$ [9.5B]
12. $(4x + 1)(3x - 1)$ [10.3A] **13.** $(y - 6)(y - 1)$ [10.2A] **14.** $a(2a - 3)(a + 5)$ [10.3A] **15.** $4(b + 5)(b - 5)$ [10.5A]
16. $-3, \frac{5}{2}$ [10.6A] **17.** $\frac{2x^3}{3y^5}$ [11.1A] **18.** $-\frac{x - 2}{x + 5}$ [11.1A] **19.** 1 [11.1C] **20.** $\frac{3}{(2x - 1)(x + 1)}$ [11.3B]
21. $\frac{x + 3}{x + 5}$ [11.4A] **22.** 4 [11.5A] **23.** 3 [11.5A] **24.** $t = \frac{f - v}{a}$ [11.6A] **25.** $5x - 13 = -8; x = 1$ [5.4A]
26. The school-age population is 50 million people. [6.4C] **27.** The base is 10 in. The height is 6 in. [10.6B] **28.** The cost of a \$5000 policy is \$80. [6.2B] **29.** It would take both pipes 6 min to fill the tank. [11.7A] **30.** The rate of the current is 2 mph. [11.7B]

Answers to Chapter 12 Selected Exercises

PREP TEST

1. 3 [3.5B] **2.** -1 [4.1A] **3.** $-3x + 12$ [4.2C] **4.** -2 [5.2A] **5.** $x = 5$ [5.2A] **6.** $y = -2$ [5.2A]
7. $-4x + 5$ [9.5A] **8.** 4 [6.2A] **9.** $y = \frac{3}{5}x - 3$ [11.6A] **10.** $y = -\frac{1}{2}x - 5$ [11.6A]

SECTION 12.1

1. Quadrant II **3.** y-axis **5.** Answers will vary. For example, $(-3, 2)$ and $(5, 2)$ **7.** right; down
9. $(6, -5)$ **11.** x; y **13.** ordered pairs; domain; range **15.**

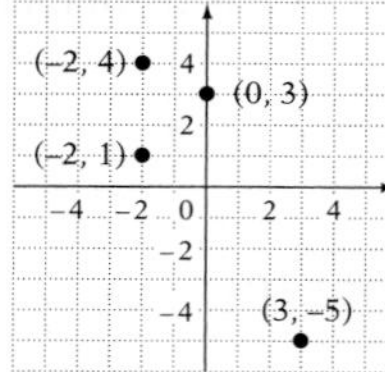

17.

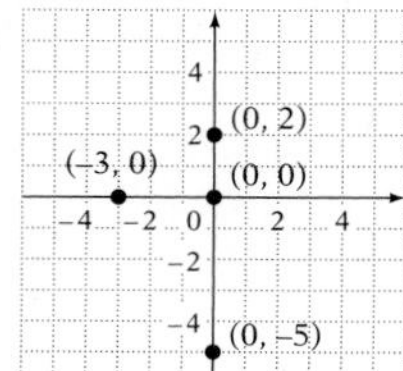

19.

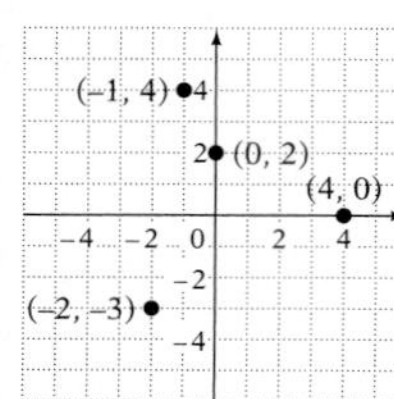

21. $A(2, 3)$, $B(4, 0)$, $C(-4, 1)$, $D(-2, -2)$

23. $A(-2, 5)$, $B(3, 4)$, $C(0, 0)$, $D(-3, -2)$ **25a.** $2, -4$ **b.** $1, -3$ **27a.** I **b.** II **c.** IV **d.** III **29.** Yes **31.** No
33. No **35.** Negative **37.**

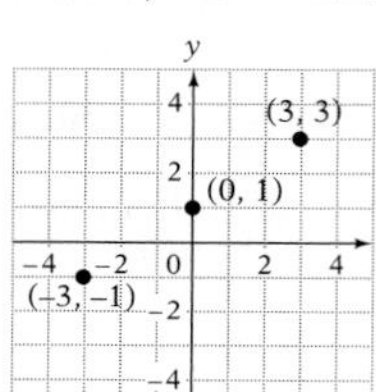

39.

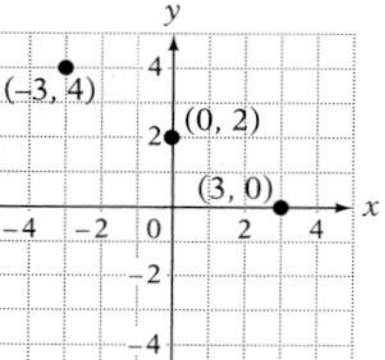

41.

43. No **45.** $\{(35, 7.50), (45, 7.58), (38, 7.63), (24, 7.78), (47, 7.80), (51, 7.86), (35, 7.89), (48, 7.92)\}$ No, the relation is not a function.
47. $\{(1600, 18), (2000, 20), (2200, 24), (2500, 25), (2800, 31)\}$ Yes, the relation is a function. **49.** D: $\{0, 2, 4, 6\}$; R: $\{0\}$; yes
51. D: $\{2\}$; R: $\{2, 4, 6, 8\}$; no **53.** Yes **55.** Yes **57.** 11 **59.** 0 **61.** 6 **63.** $-\frac{4}{3}$ **65.** 11 **67.** $\frac{6}{7}$ **69.** Either
71. Positive **73.** 4 units **75.** 2 units **77.** 5 units

SECTION 12.2

1. i and ii **3.** b and d are graphs of straight lines. **5.** Multiples of 3, such as $-3, 0, 3$, and 6

7.

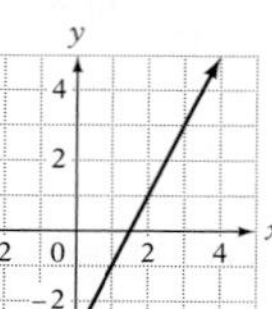

9.

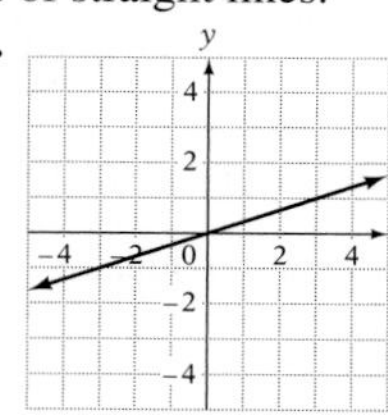

11.

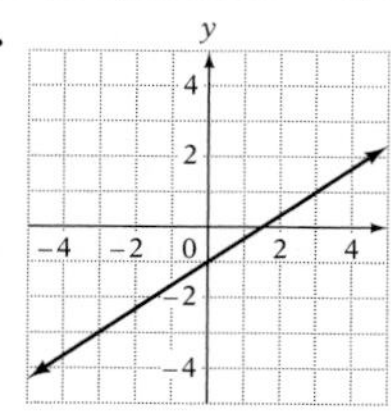

13.

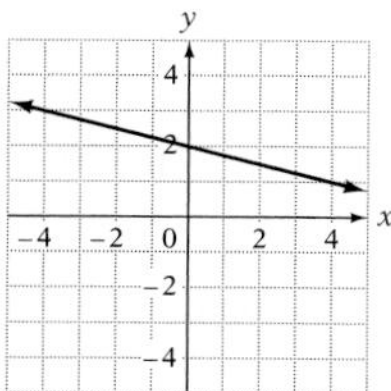

15.

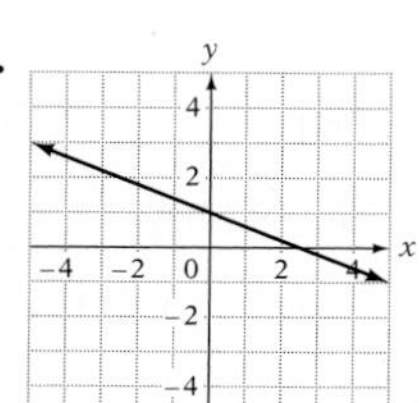

17.

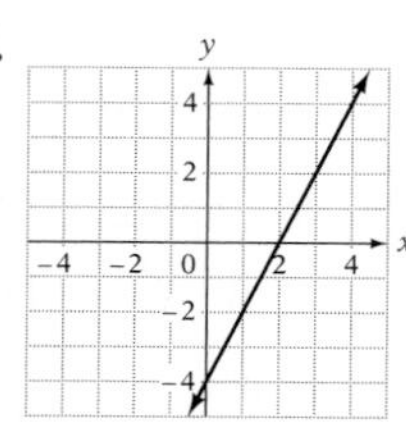

19.

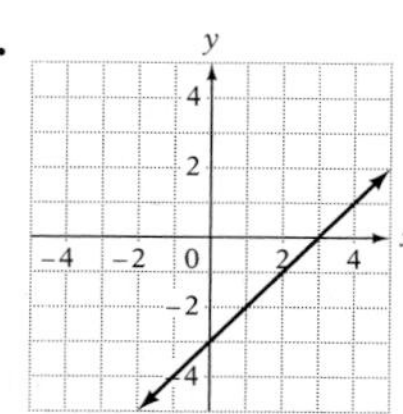

21.

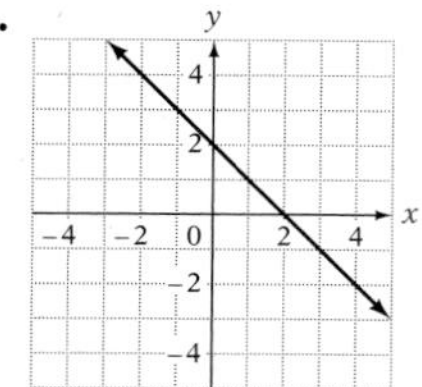

23.
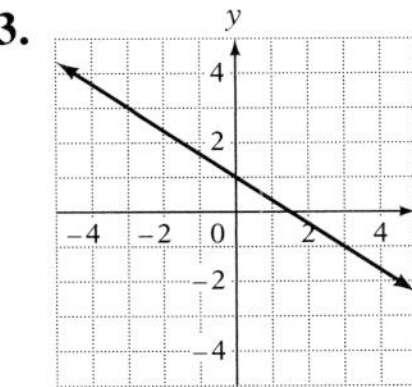

25. 0 **27.** $y = -2x + 5$ **29.** $y = 5x - 7$ **31.** $y = -\frac{2}{3}x + 3$ **33.** $y = \frac{5}{2}x - 2$ **35.** $y = \frac{6}{5}x - 2$ **37.** $y = \frac{1}{4}x - 3$

39.
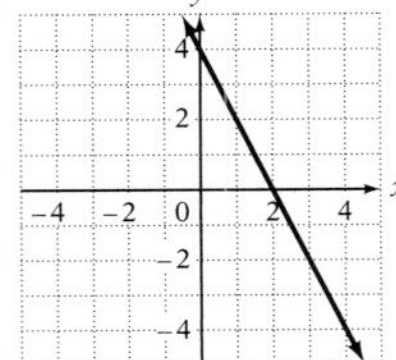

41.
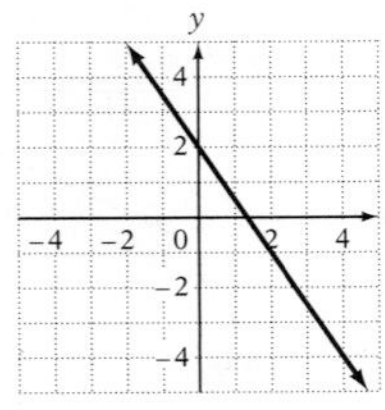

43.
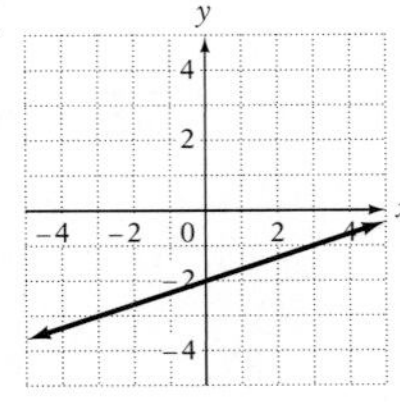

45.
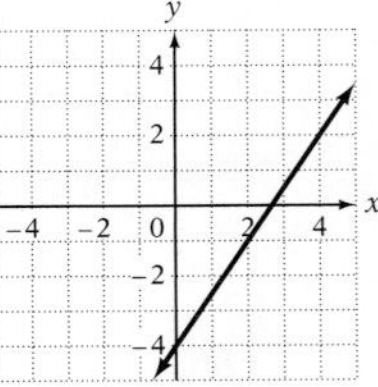

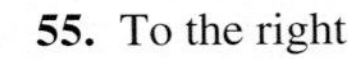

47.
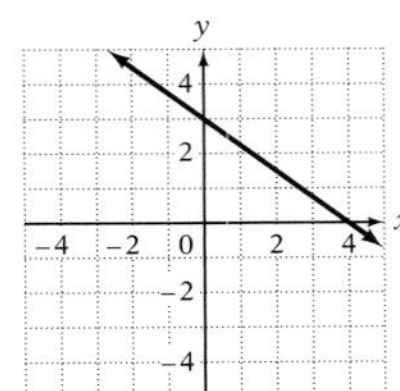

49.
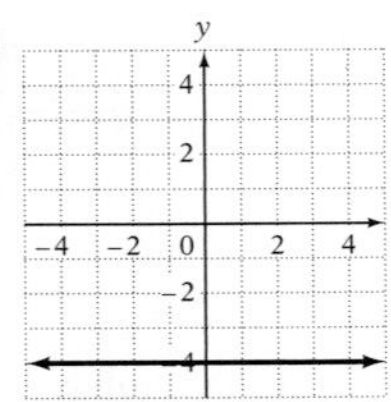

51.
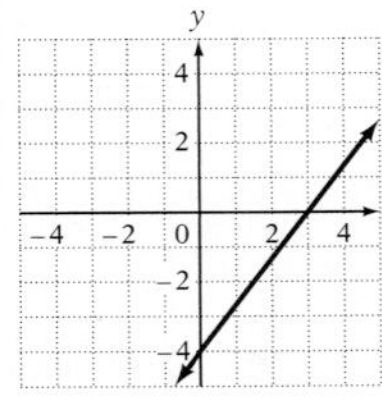

53. *A* **55.** To the right

57. A custom sign 15 ft^2 in area costs \$182.50.

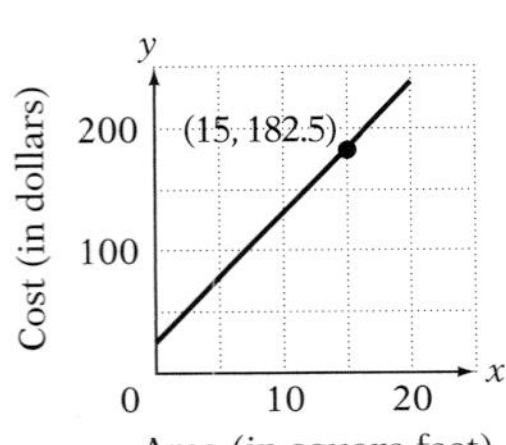

59. A dog 6 years old is equivalent in age to a human 40 years old.

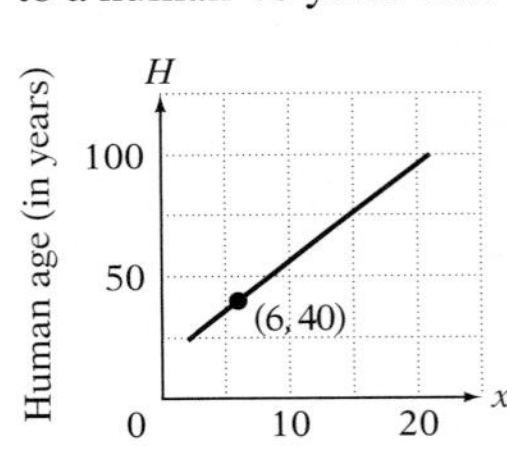

61. Answers will vary. For example, $y = 2x$

CHECK YOUR PROGRESS: CHAPTER 12

1. [12.1A]
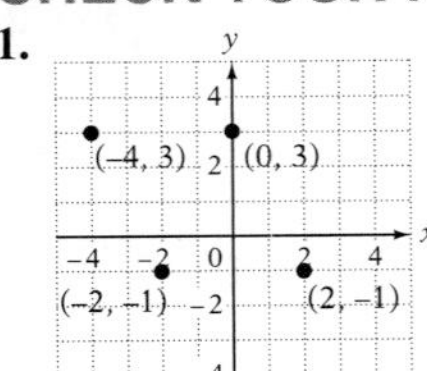

2. [12.2A]
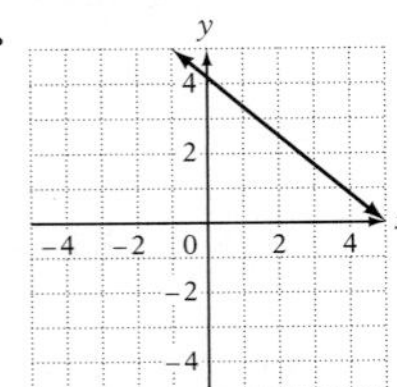

3. [12.2B]
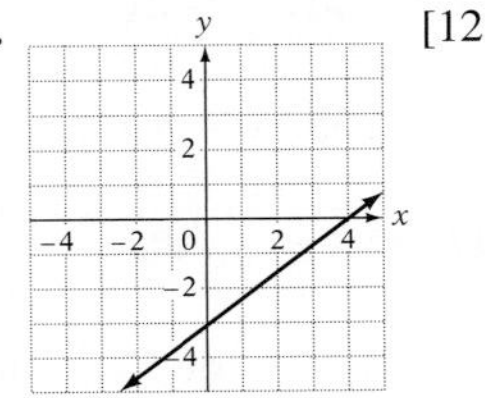

4. $(-1, 5), (0, 2), (1, -1), (2, -4)$ [12.1B] **5.** The graph is a vertical line passing through $(-5, 0)$. [12.2B]
6. D: $\{-3, -2, -1\}$; R: $\{-2, -1, 0\}$; yes [12.1C] **7.** 0 [12.1D] **8.** Yes [12.1B] **9.** Yes [12.1C]

SECTION 12.3

1. *m* **3a.** positive **b.** negative **c.** zero **d.** undefined **5.** *x*-coordinate **7.** 2; −4; 3; 1 **9.** Vertical
11. $\frac{6}{5}$ **13.** (3, 0), (0, −3) **15.** (2, 0), (0, −6) **17.** (10, 0), (0, −2) **19.** (−4, 0), (0, 12) **21.** (0, 0), (0, 0) **23.** (6, 0), (0, 3)

25.
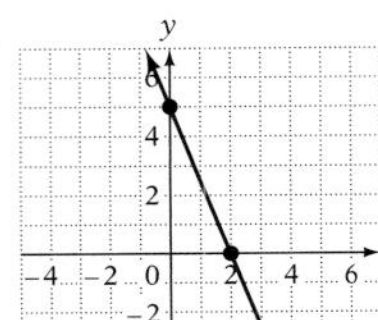

27.
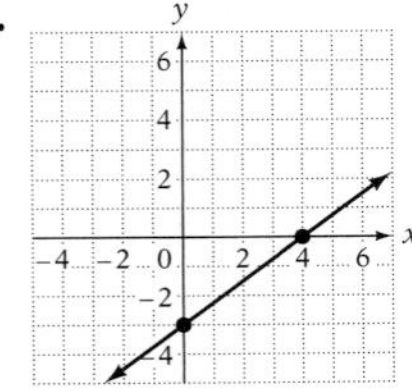

29.
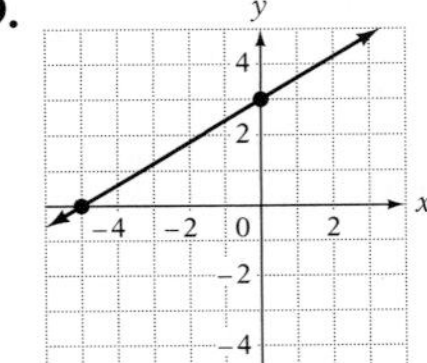

31. Above the *x*-axis **33.** −2

35. $\frac{1}{3}$ **37.** $-\frac{5}{2}$ **39.** Undefined **41.** Zero **43.** $-\frac{1}{3}$ **47.** $b = d, a \neq c$ **49.** No **51.** No

53. Parallel **55.** Perpendicular **57.** Neither **59.** Perpendicular **61.** $m = -\frac{19}{30}$. The water in the lock decreases by $0.6\overline{3}$ million gallons each minute. **63.** $m = 70$. Walking burns 70 calories per mile. **65.** $m = 2.25$. The percent of people using seat belts has increased by 2.25% per year. **67.** $m = -\frac{3}{8}$, (0, 5) **69.** $m = \frac{2}{3}$, (0, −2) **71.** $m = -\frac{2}{5}$, (0, 2) **73.** $m = \frac{1}{4}$, (0, 0)

75.

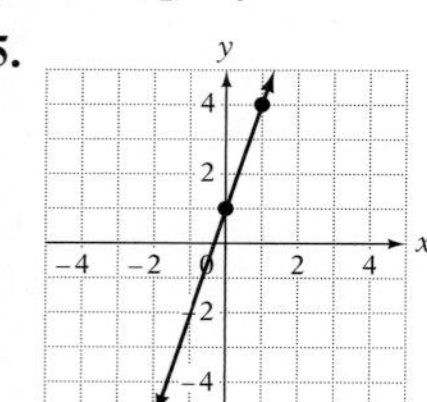

77.

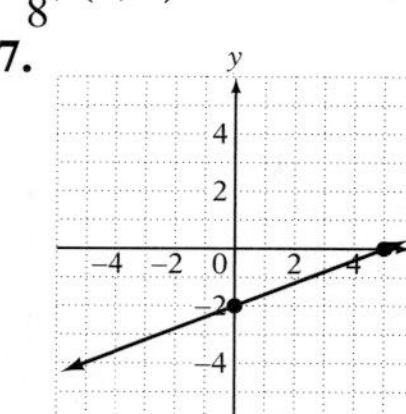

79.

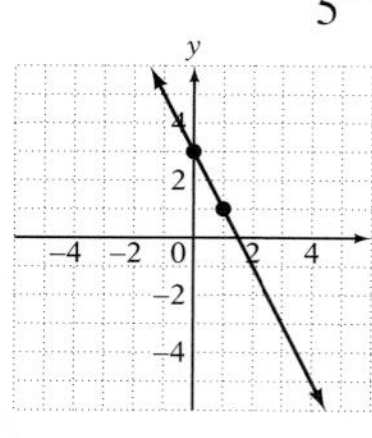

81.

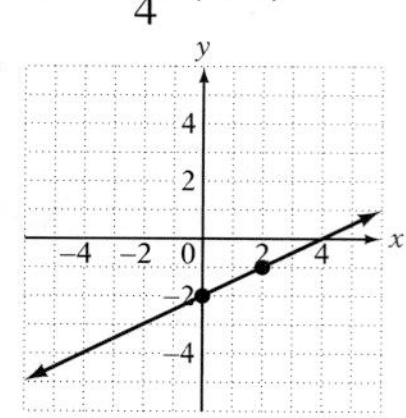

83.

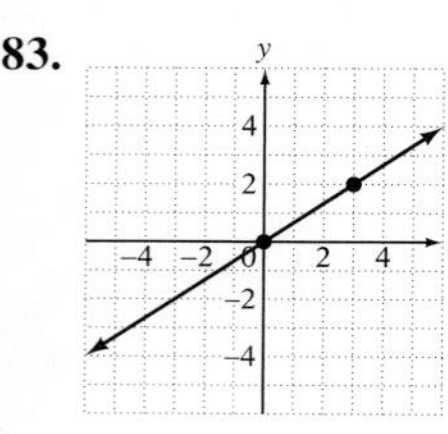

85.

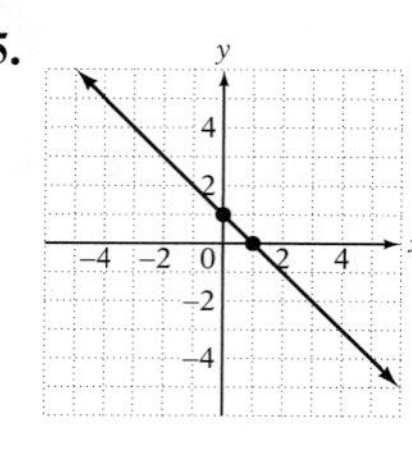

87.

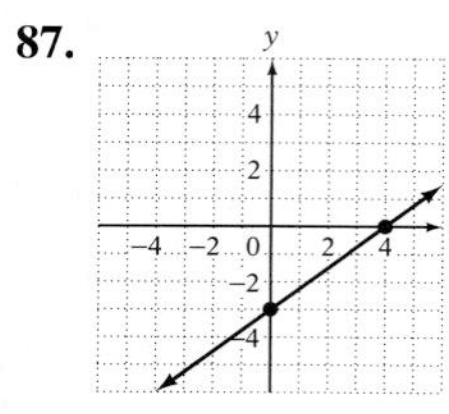

89.

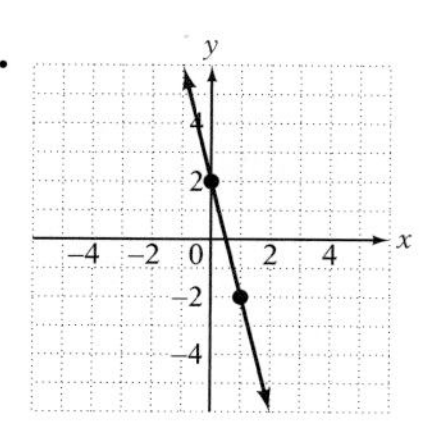

91. Above; upward to the right **93.** Decreases the slope **95.** Decreases the y-coordinate of the y-intercept **97.** No; for example, $x = 2$ **99.** Line a slants upward to the right. Line b slants downward to the right. **101.** Line a has a y-intercept of (0, 5). Line b has a y-intercept of (0, −5). **103.** Line a is a horizontal line. Line b is a vertical line.

105.

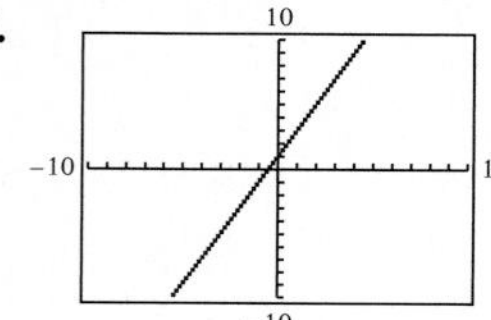

107.

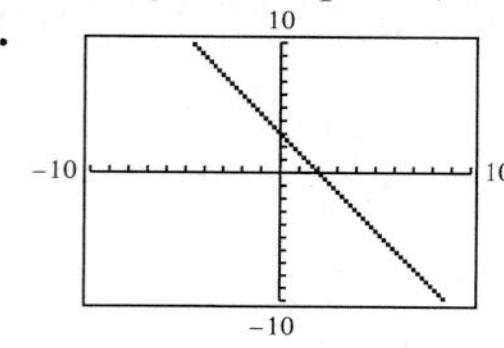

SECTION 12.4

1. 5; 7 **3.** 0; 2 **5.** 3; 1; $3x + 1$ **7.** $y = 2x + 2$ **9.** $y = -3x - 1$ **11.** $y = \frac{1}{3}x$ **13.** $y = \frac{3}{4}x - 5$ **15.** $y = -\frac{3}{5}x$ **17.** $y = \frac{1}{4}x + \frac{5}{2}$ **19.** $y = -\frac{2}{3}x - 7$ **21.** $y = 2x - 3$ **23.** $y = -2x - 3$ **25.** $y = \frac{2}{3}x$ **27.** $y = \frac{1}{2}x + 2$ **29.** $y = -\frac{3}{4}x - 2$ **31.** $y = \frac{3}{4}x + \frac{5}{2}$ **33.** $y = -\frac{4}{3}x - 9$ **35.** $y = mx + b$ **37.** $y = 3x + 4$ **39.** $y = -x - 4$ **41.** $y = -\frac{6}{5}x + 5$ **43.** $y = -\frac{2}{5}x - 7$ **45.** $y = 5$ **47.** $x = 5$ **49.** $y = \frac{4}{5}x + 8$ **51.** $y = -\frac{1}{2}x - 2$ **53.** $y = -\frac{4}{3}x - 3$ **55.** $y = 3x - 3$ **57.** $y = 3x$ **59.** $x = 3$ **61.** 2 **63.** Yes; $y = \frac{1}{2}x - 3$ **65.** Yes; $y = -\frac{1}{3}x$ **67.** 1 **69.** −8 **71a.** (3, 0) **b.** (0, 2) **c.** $-\frac{2}{3}$ **d.** $y = -\frac{2}{3}x + 2$ **73a.** (−1, 0) **b.** (0, −2) **c.** −2 **d.** $y = -2x - 2$

CHAPTER 12 REVIEW EXERCISES

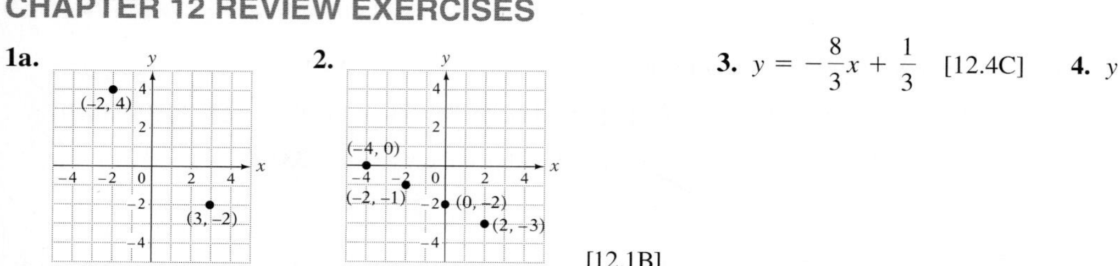

b. −2

c. −4 [12.1A]

3. $y = -\frac{8}{3}x + \frac{1}{3}$ [12.4C] **4.** $y = -\frac{5}{2}x + 16$ [12.4A]

5. 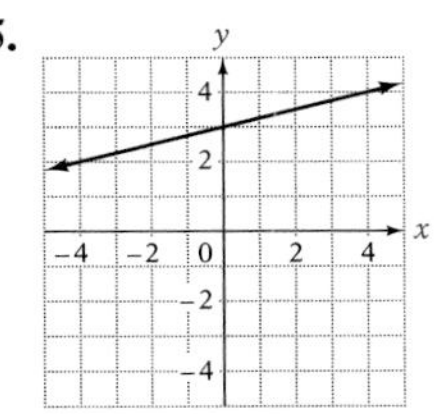 [12.2A]

6. 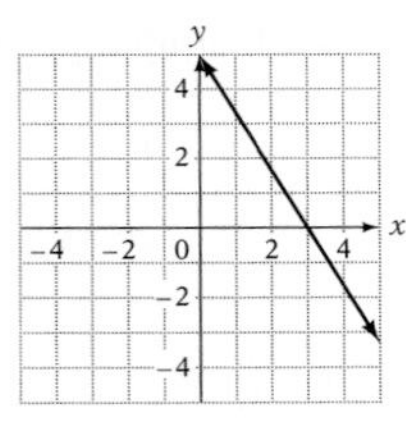 [12.2B]

7. Neither [12.3B] **8.** −1 [12.1D]

9. Yes [12.1C] **10.** $\frac{7}{11}$ [12.3B] **11.** (8, 0), (0, −12) [12.3A] **12.** 0 [12.3B]

13. 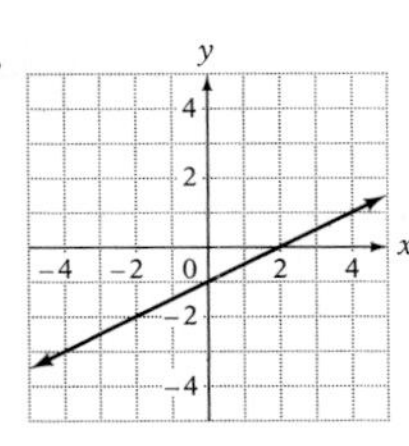 [12.3C]

14. 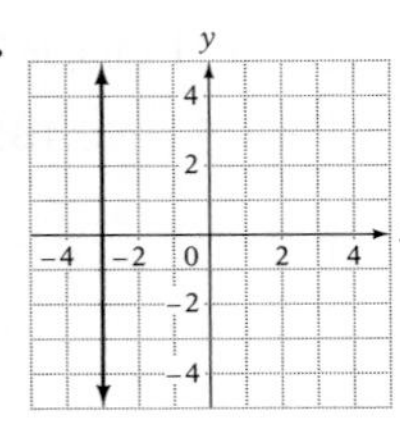 [12.2B]

15. 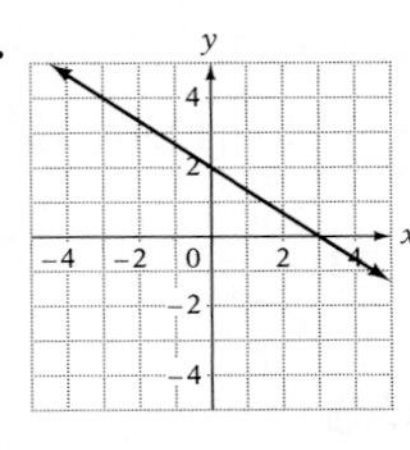 [12.3C]

16. 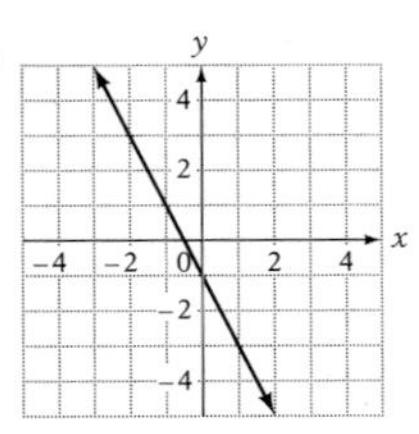 [12.2A]

17. 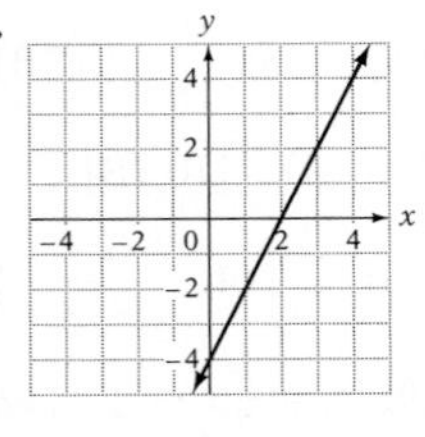 [12.3C]

18. 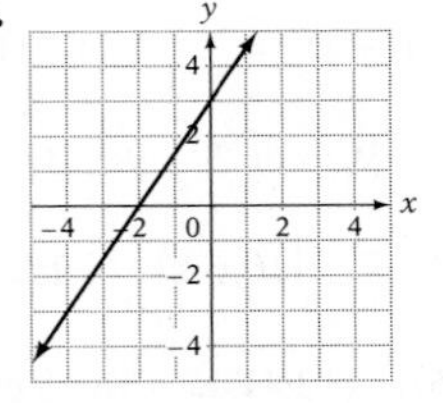 [12.2B]

19. {(55, 95), (57, 101), (53, 94), (57, 98), (60, 100), (61, 105), (58, 97), (54, 95)}; no [12.1C]

20. The cost of 50 min of access time for one month is \$97.50.

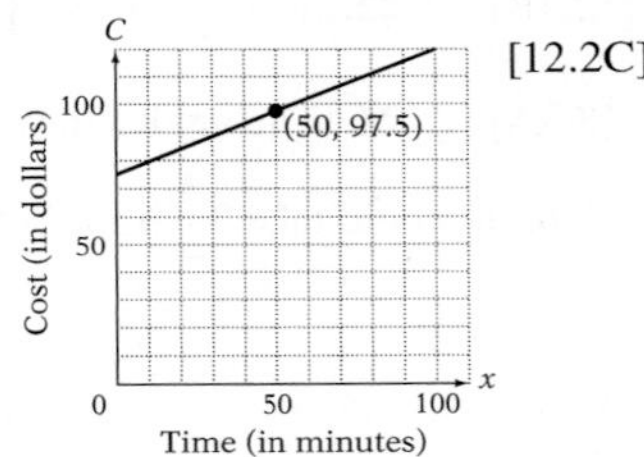

[12.2C]

CHAPTER 12 TEST

1. (3, −3) [12.1B; HOW TO 2]

2. 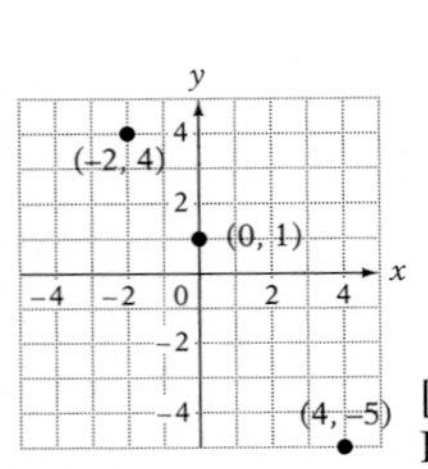

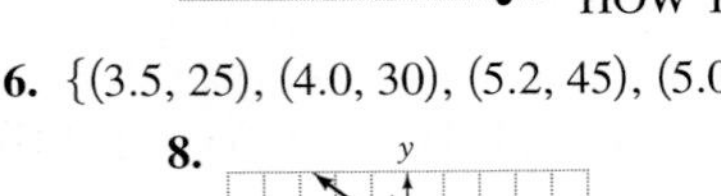

[12.1B; HOW TO 3]

3. Yes [12.1C; Example 6] **4.** 6 [12.1D; HOW TO 4]

5. 3 [12.1D; HOW TO 4] **6.** {(3.5, 25), (4.0, 30), (5.2, 45), (5.0, 38), (4.0, 42), (6.3, 12), (5.4, 34)}; no [12.1C; Example 5]

7. 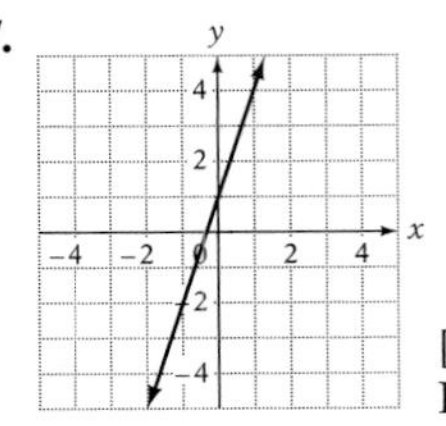 [12.2A; Example 1]

8. 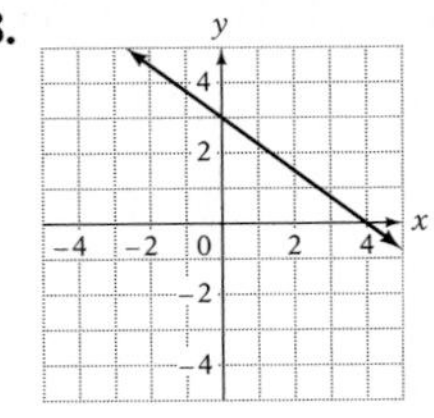 [12.2A; Example 3]

9. 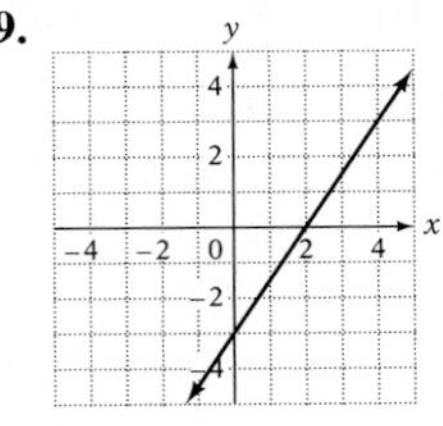 [12.2B; Example 4]

10. 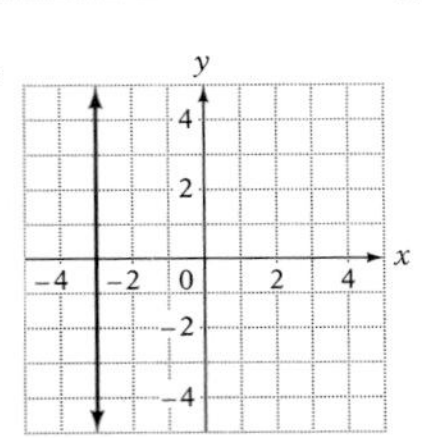 [12.2B; You Try It 7]

11. 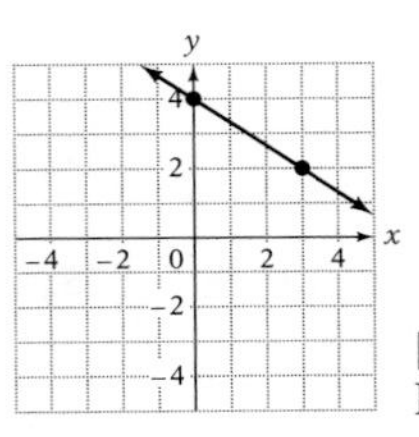 [12.3C; Example 5]

12. 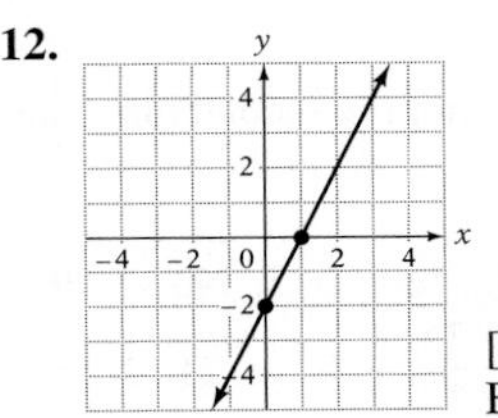 [12.3C; Example 5]

13. After 1 s, the ball is traveling 96 ft/s. [12.2C; Example 8] **14.** (2, 0), (0, −3) [12.3A; Example 1]

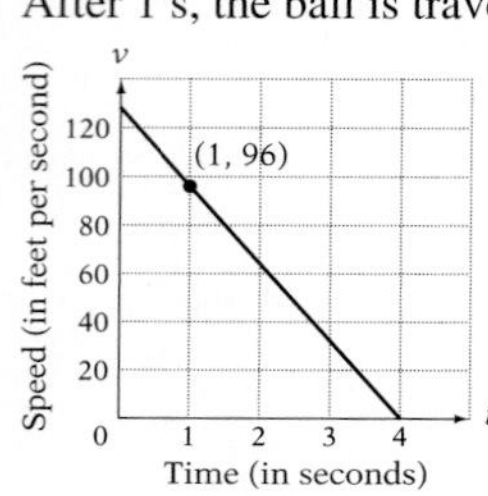

15. (−2, 0), (0, 1) [12.3A; Example 1] **16.** 2 [12.3B; Example 2] **17.** Parallel [12.3B; Example 2] **18.** Undefined [12.3B; Example 3] **19.** $-\frac{2}{3}$ [12.3B; HOW TO 2] **20.** $y = 3x - 1$ [12.4A; Example 1] **21.** $y = \frac{2}{3}x + 3$ [12.4B; You Try It 3] **22.** $y = -\frac{5}{8}x - \frac{7}{8}$ [12.4C; HOW TO 3] **23.** $y = -\frac{2}{7}x - \frac{4}{7}$ [12.4C; Example 4]

CUMULATIVE REVIEW EXERCISES

1. −12 [3.5A] **2.** $-\frac{5}{8}$ [4.1A] **3.** $f(-2) = -\frac{2}{3}$ [12.1D] **4.** $\frac{3}{2}$ [5.2A] **5.** $\frac{19}{18}$ [5.3B] **6.** $\frac{1}{15}$ [6.3A] **7.** $-32x^8y^7$ [9.2B] **8.** $-3x^2$ [9.4A] **9.** $x + 3$ [9.5B] **10.** $5(x + 2)(x + 1)$ [10.2B] **11.** $(a + 2)(x + y)$ [10.1B] **12.** 4 and −2 [10.6A] **13.** $\frac{x^3(x + 3)}{y(x + 2)}$ [11.1B] **14.** $\frac{3}{x + 8}$ [11.3A] **15.** 2 [11.5A] **16.** $y = \frac{4}{5}x - 3$ [11.6A] **17.** (−2, −5) [12.1B] **18.** Zero [12.3B] **19.** $y = \frac{1}{2}x - 2$ [12.4A] **20.** $y = -3x + 2$ [12.4A] **21.** $y = 2x + 2$ [12.4B] **22.** $y = \frac{2}{3}x - 3$ [12.4B] **23.** The probability that the marble is not red is $\frac{2}{3}$. [8.3A] **24.** The angles measure 46°, 43°, and 91°. [7.1C] **25.** The value of the home is $1,100,000. [6.2B] **26.** It would take $3\frac{3}{4}$ h for both, working together, to wire the garage. [11.7A]

27.

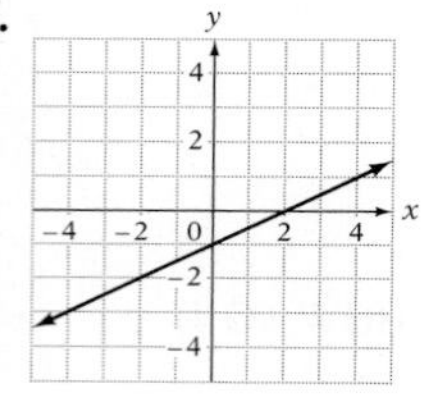

[12.2A]

28.

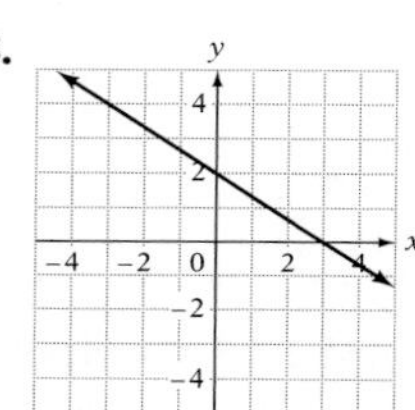

[12.3C]

Answers to Chapter 13 Selected Exercises

PREP TEST

1. $y = \frac{3}{4}x - 6$ [11.6A] **2.** 1000 [5.3B] **3.** $33y$ [4.2D] **4.** $10x - 10$ [4.2D] **5.** Yes [12.1B] **6.** (4, 0), (0, −3) [12.3A] **7.** Yes [12.3B] **8.**

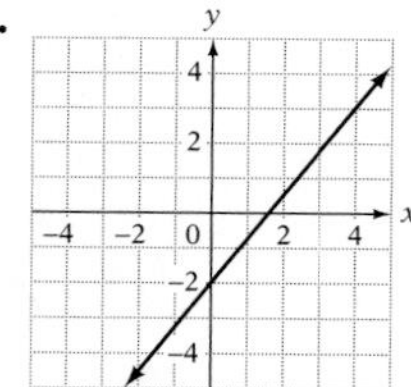

[12.3C]

9. The hikers will be side-by-side 1.5 h after the second hiker starts. [5.5B]

SECTION 13.1

1. Always true **3.** Never true **5.** Yes **7.** No **9.** Yes **11.** Yes **13.** iii **15.** i **17.** (2, −1) **19.** The ordered-pair solutions of $y = -\frac{3}{2}x + 1$ **21.** No solution

23. 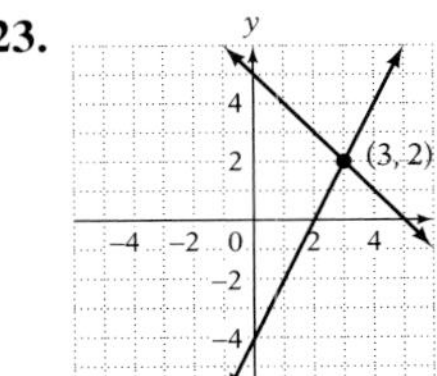

25. 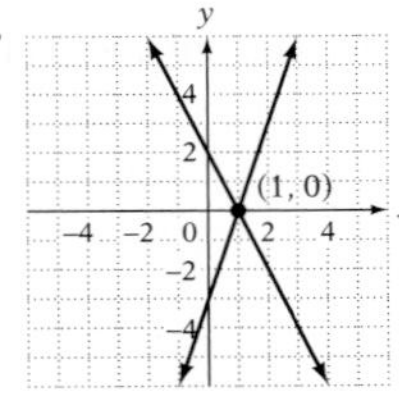

27. 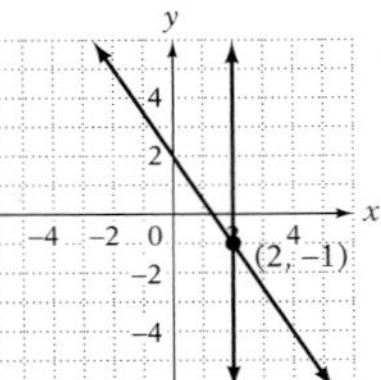

29. 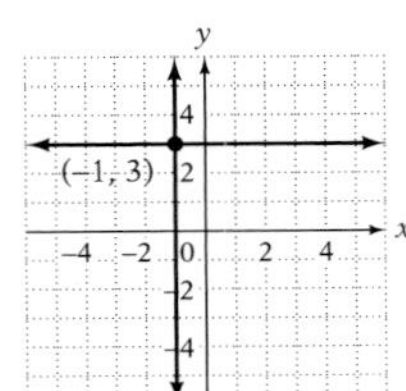

31. 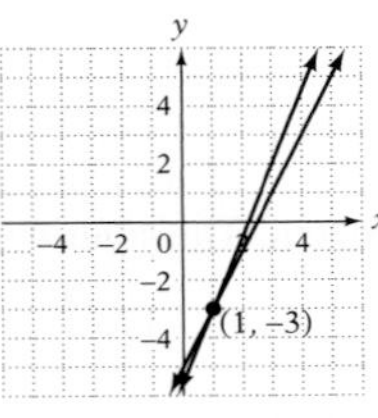

33. 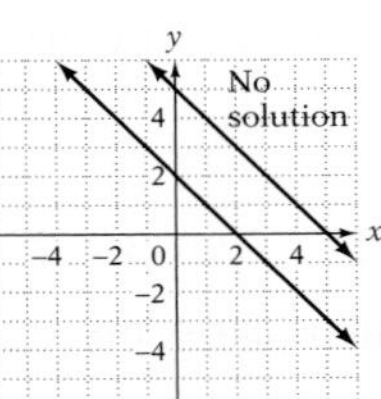

35. 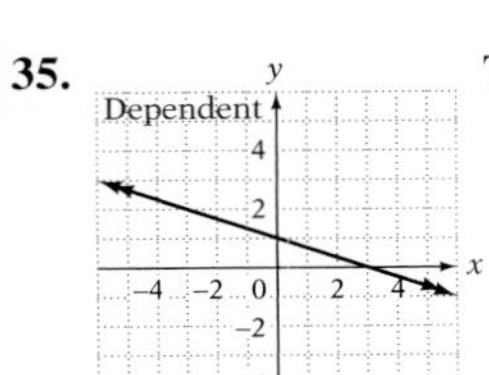

The ordered-pair solutions of $y = -\frac{1}{3}x + 1$

37. 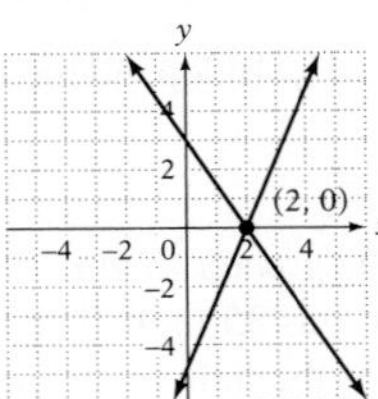

39. 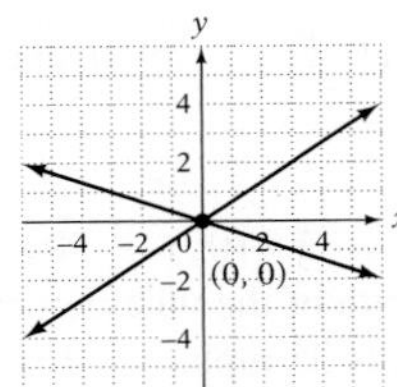

41. 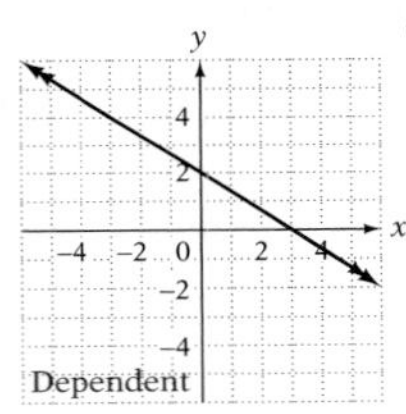

The ordered-pair solutions of $4x + 6y = 12$ **43.** Independent **45.** $x = 3$, $y = x - 1$

47. $y = 2x - 2$, $y = \frac{2}{3}x + \frac{2}{3}$ **49.** Answers will vary. For example: **a.** $y = x + 8$, $y = -x + 2$ **b.** $y = 2x - 3$, $y = 2x + 4$ **c.** $y = 3x - 5$, $3x - y = 5$

SECTION 13.2

3. True **5.** False **7.** (2, 1) **9.** (4, 1) **11.** (−1, 1) **13.** No solution **15.** No solution **17.** $\left(-\frac{3}{4}, -\frac{3}{4}\right)$ **19.** (1, 1) **21.** (2, 0) **23.** (1, −2) **25.** (0, 0) **27.** Dependent. The solutions satisfy the equation $2x - y = 2$. **29.** (−4, −2) **31.** (10, 31) **33.** (3, −10) **35.** (−22, −5) **37.** Dependent **39.** x = amount invested at 8%, y = amount invested at 6.5%; $x + y = 10{,}000$ represents the fact that the sum of the two investments is \$10,000; $0.08x + 0.065y = 710$ represents the fact that the total interest earned by the two investments is \$710. **41.** The amounts invested should be \$1900 at 5% and \$1600 at 7.5%. **43.** The amounts invested were \$3600 at 6% and \$2400 at 9%. **45.** The amounts invested should be \$4400 at 8% and \$1600 at 11%. **47.** The amount invested at 6.5% was \$21,000. **49.** The amounts invested were \$12,000 at 8% and \$8000 at 7%. **51.** The amount invested in the trust deed was \$3750. **53.** (1, 5) **55.** (−5, 2) **57.** (2, 100) **59.** The amounts invested were \$12,000 at 9%, \$21,000 at 8%, and \$27,000 at 9.5%. **61.** 2 **63.** 2 **65.** The value of the CD in 5 years is \$3589.07.

CHECK YOUR PROGRESS: CHAPTER 13

1. 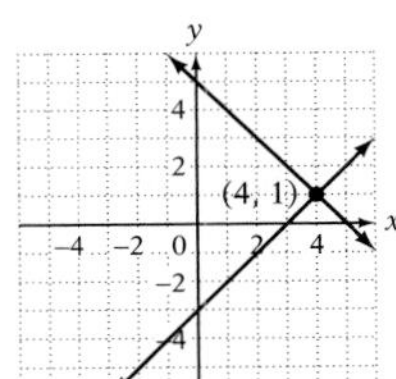

(4, 1) [13.1A]

2. 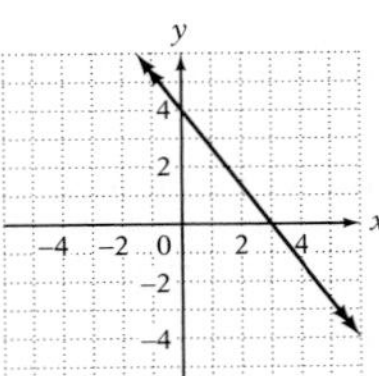

The ordered pair solutions of $y = -\frac{4}{3}x + 4$. [13.1A]

3. 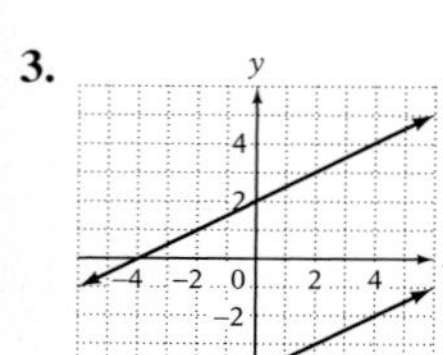
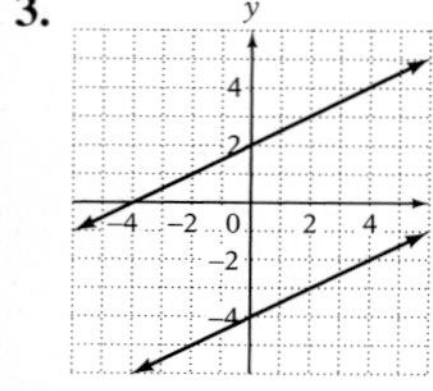
No solution [13.1A] **4.** Yes [13.1A] **5.** $(-2, 4)$ [13.2A] **6.** The ordered-pair solutions of $y = \frac{1}{3}x + 4$ [13.2A]

7. The amounts invested were $18,000 at 6.5% and $12,000 at 8.5%. [13.2B]

SECTION 13.3

1a. 3 **b.** -4 **3.** $(5, -1)$ **5.** $(1, 3)$ **7.** $(1, 1)$ **9.** $(3, -2)$ **11.** Dependent. The solutions satisfy the equation $2x - y = 1$. **13.** $(3, 1)$ **15.** Dependent. The solutions satisfy the equation $2x - 3y = 1$. **17.** $\left(\frac{2}{3}, \frac{1}{2}\right)$ **19.** $(2, 0)$ **21.** $(0, 0)$ **23.** $(5, -2)$ **25.** $\left(\frac{32}{19}, -\frac{9}{19}\right)$ **27.** $\left(\frac{7}{4}, -\frac{5}{16}\right)$ **29.** $(1, -1)$ **31.** No solution **33.** $(3, 1)$ **35.** $(-1, 2)$ **37.** $(1, 1)$ **39.** Dependent **41.** Independent **43.** $A = 3$; $B = -1$

SECTION 13.4

1. True **3.** False **5.** $100x + 50y$ **7.** m is greater than n. **9.** The rowing rate in calm water was 14 km/h. The rate of the current was 6 km/h. **11.** The rate of the whale in calm water was 35 mph. The rate of the current was 5 mph. **13.** The rate of the Learjet was 525 mph. The rate of the wind was 35 mph. **15.** The rate of the helicopter in calm air was 225 mph. The rate of the wind was 45 mph. **17.** The rate of the boat in calm water was 7 mph. The rate of the current was 3 mph. **19.** Less than **21.** x = cost of an adult ticket, y = cost of a child ticket; $4x + 2y = 320$ represents the fact that you spent $320 on four adult tickets and two child tickets; $2x + 3y = 240$ represents the fact that your neighbor spent $240 on two adult tickets and three child tickets. **23.** The cost per pound of the wheat flour was $.65. The cost per pound of the rye flour was $.70. **25.** The delicatessen charges $6.25 for a turkey sandwich and $1.90 for an order of fries. **27.** The pastry chef used 15 oz of the 20% solution and 35 oz of the 40% solution. **29.** Both formulas give the same ideal body weight at 72 in. **31a.** The original postage value of the Lincoln stamp was $.90. The original postage value of the Jefferson stamp was $.10. **b.** The original postage value of the Henry Clay stamp was $.12. **33.** The measures of the two angles are 18° and 72°. **35.** The time is approximately 65.5 min. **37.** $(2.875, 1.1875)$ **39.** $(-19, -7)$

CHAPTER 13 REVIEW EXERCISES

1. Yes [13.1A] **2.** No [13.1A] **3.** 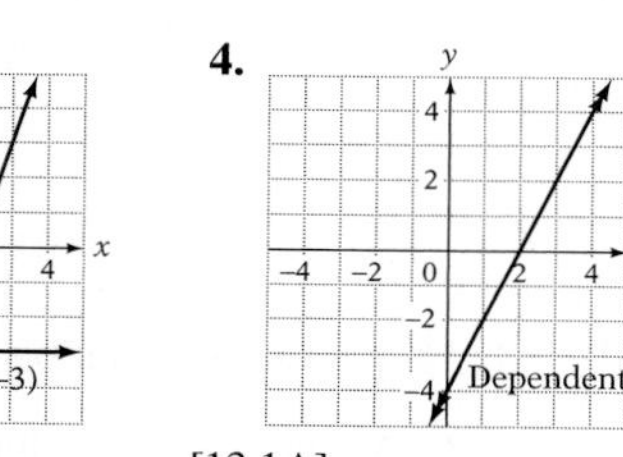

[13.1A] **4.** The solutions are the ordered pairs that satisfy the equation $y = 2x - 4$. [13.1A]

5. [13.1A] **6.** $(-1, 1)$ [13.2A] **7.** $(1, 6)$ [13.2A] **8.** $(-3, 1)$ [13.3A] **9.** $\left(-\frac{5}{6}, \frac{1}{2}\right)$ [13.3A]

10. No solution [13.2A] **11.** $(1, 6)$ [13.2A] **12.** $(1, -5)$ [13.3A] **13.** No solution [13.3A] **14.** Dependent. The solutions satisfy the equation $y = -\frac{4}{3}x + 4$. [13.2A] **15.** $(-1, -3)$ [13.2A] **16.** Dependent. The solutions satisfy the equation $3x + y = -2$. [13.3A] **17.** $\left(\frac{2}{3}, -\frac{1}{6}\right)$ [13.3A] **18.** The rate of the sculling team in calm water was 9 mph. The rate of the current was 3 mph. [13.4A] **19.** The investor bought 1300 $6 shares, and 200 $25 shares. [13.4B] **20.** The rate of the flight crew in calm air was 125 km/h. The rate of the wind was 15 km/h. [13.4A] **21.** The rate of the plane in calm air was 105 mph. The rate of the wind was 15 mph. [13.4A] **22.** The service charge per hour for regular service is $1.00. The service charge per hour for premium service is $2.50. [13.4B] **23.** The amounts invested are $7000 at 7% and $5000 at 8.5%. [13.2B] **24.** There were originally 350 bushels of lentils and 200 bushels of corn in the silo. [13.4B] **25.** The amounts invested were $165,000 at 5.4% and $135,000 at 6.6%. [13.2B]

CHAPTER 13 TEST

1. Yes [13.1A; Example 1] **2.** Yes [13.1A; Example 1] **3.** [13.1A, Example 2] **4.** $(3, 1)$ [13.2A; HOW TO 1]

5. $(1, -1)$ [13.2A; HOW TO 1] **6.** $(2, -1)$ [13.2A; Example 1] **7.** $\left(\frac{22}{7}, -\frac{5}{7}\right)$ [13.2A; You Try It 1]

8. No solution [13.2A; Example 2] **9.** $(2, 1)$ [13.3A; Example 1] **10.** $\left(\frac{1}{2}, -1\right)$ [13.3A; Example 1]

11. Dependent. The solutions satisfy the equation $x + 2y = 8$. [13.3A; Example 2] **12.** $(2, -1)$ [13.3A; Example 3]

13. $(1, -2)$ [13.3A; You Try It 3] **14.** The rate of the plane in calm air is 100 mph. The rate of the wind is 20 mph. [13.4A; Example 1]

15. The price of a reserved-seat ticket was \$10. The price of a general-admission ticket was \$6. [13.4B; Example 2]

16. The amounts invested were \$15,200 at 6.4% and \$12,800 at 7.6%. [13.2B; You Try It 4]

CUMULATIVE REVIEW EXERCISES

1. $\frac{3}{2}$ [4.1A] **2.** $-\frac{3}{2}$ [5.1C] **3.** 7 [12.1D] **4.** $-6a^3 + 13a^2 - 9a + 2$ [9.3B] **5.** $-2x^5y^2$ [9.4A]

6. $2b - 1 + \frac{1}{2b - 3}$ [9.5B] **7.** $-\frac{4y}{x^3}$ [9.4A] **8.** $4y^2(xy - 4)(xy + 4)$ [10.5A] **9.** 4, -1 [10.6A]

10. $x - 2$ [11.1C] **11.** $\frac{x^2 + 2}{(x + 2)(x - 1)}$ [11.3B] **12.** $\frac{x - 3}{x + 1}$ [11.4A] **13.** $-\frac{1}{5}$ [11.5A] **14.** $r = \frac{A - P}{Pt}$ [11.6A]

15. x-intercept: $(6, 0)$; y-intercept: $(0, -4)$ [12.3A] **16.** $-\frac{7}{5}$ [12.3B] **17.** $y = -\frac{3}{2}x$ [12.4A] **18.** Yes [13.1A]

19. $(-6, 1)$ [13.2A] **20.** $(4, -3)$ [13.3A] **21.** [12.2B] **22.**

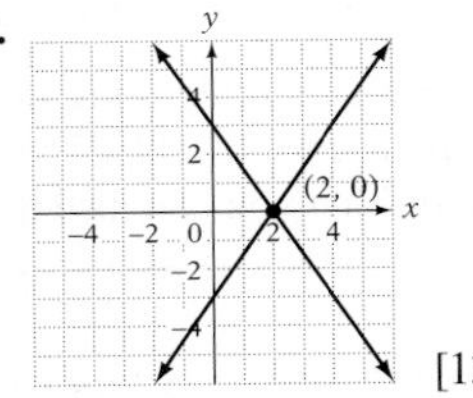

[13.1A]

23. The amounts invested should be \$3750 at 9.6% and \$5000 at 7.2%. [13.2B]

24. The rate of the freight train is 48 mph. The rate of the passenger train is 56 mph. [5.5B]

25. The length of a side of the original square is 8 in. [10.6B] **26.** The rate of the wind is 30 mph. [13.4A]

27. The rate of the motorboat in calm water is 14 mph. [13.4A] **28.** 76% of the voting-age population was registered to vote. [6.4C]

Answers to Chapter 14 Selected Exercises

PREP TEST

1. $-45 < -27$ [3.1A] **2.** $-7x + 15$ [4.2D] **3.** The same number can be added to each side of an equation without changing the solution of the equation. [5.1B] **4.** Each side of an equation can be multiplied by the same nonzero number without changing the solution of the equation. [5.1C] **5.** There is 0.45 lb of fat in 3 lb of this grade of hamburger. [6.4C]

6. 2 [5.3B] **7.**

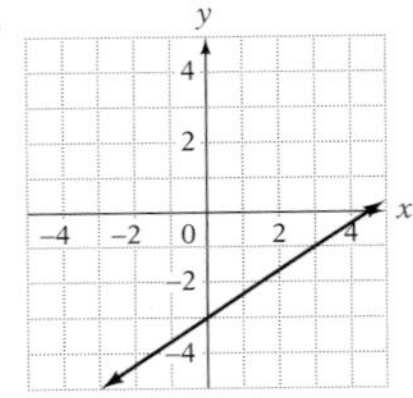

[12.2A]

SECTION 14.1

1. roster; set-builder; interval **3.** $A = \{16, 17, 18, 19, 20, 21\}$ **5.** $A = \{9, 11, 13, 15, 17\}$ **7.** $A \cup B = \{3, 4, 5, 6\}$ **9.** $A \cup B = \{-10, -9, -8, 8, 9, 10\}$ **11.** $A \cup B = \{1, 3, 7, 9, 11, 13\}$ **13.** $A \cap B = \{4, 5\}$ **15.** $A \cap B = \varnothing$ **17.** $A \cap B = \{c, d, e\}$ **19.** $\{x | x > -5, x \in \text{negative integers}\}$ **21.** $\{x | x > 30, x \in \text{integers}\}$ **23.** $\{x | x > 8\}$ **25.** $(1, 2)$ **27.** $(3, \infty)$ **29.** $[-4, 5)$ **31.** $(-\infty, 2]$ **33.** $[-3, 1]$ **35.** $\{x | -5 < x < -3\}$ **37.** $\{x | x \le -2\}$ **39.** $\{x | -3 \le x \le -2\}$ **41.** $\{x | x \le 6\}$ **43.** −5 −4 −3 −2 −1 0 1 2 3 4 5 **45.** −5 −4 −3 −2 −1 0 1 2 3 4 5 **47.** −5 −4 −3 −2 −1 0 1 2 3 4 5 **49.** −5 −4 −3 −2 −1 0 1 2 3 4 5 **51.** −5 −4 −3 −2 −1 0 1 2 3 4 5 **53.** −5 −4 −3 −2 −1 0 1 2 3 4 5 **55.** −5 −4 −3 −2 −1 0 1 2 3 4 5 **57.** −5 −4 −3 −2 −1 0 1 2 3 4 5 **59.** None **61.** $m \ge 250$ **63.** True

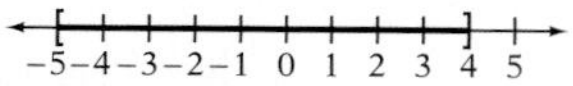

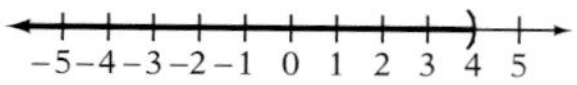

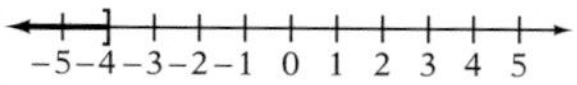

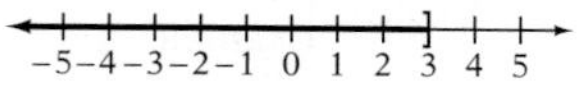

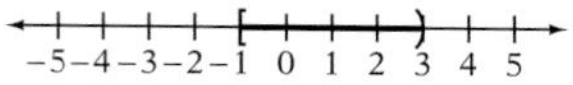

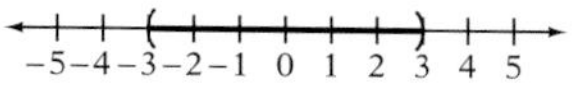

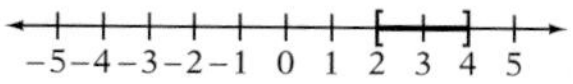

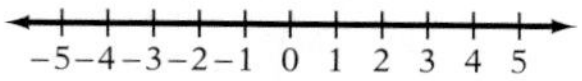

65. Answers will vary. For example, $A = \{1, 2, 3, 4\}$ and $B = \{1, 2, 3, 4\}$

SECTION 14.2

1a. No **b.** No **c.** Yes **d.** No **e.** No **f.** Yes **3.** i, ii, iii **5.** does not include; $>$ **7.** $\{x | x < 2\}$ −5 −4 −3 −2 −1 0 1 2 3 4 5 **9.** $\{x | x > 3\}$ −5 −4 −3 −2 −1 0 1 2 3 4 5 **11.** $\{n | n \ge 3\}$ −5 −4 −3 −2 −1 0 1 2 3 4 5 **13.** $\{x | x \le -4\}$ −5 −4 −3 −2 −1 0 1 2 3 4 5 **15.** $[-9, \infty)$ **17.** $(-\infty, 12)$ **19.** $[5, \infty)$ **21.** $(-\infty, -11)$ **23.** $(-\infty, 10]$ **25.** $[-6, \infty)$ **27.** $\{x | x > 2\}$ **29.** $\left\{d \middle| d < -\frac{1}{6}\right\}$ **31.** $\left\{x \middle| x \ge -\frac{31}{24}\right\}$ **33.** $\left\{x \middle| x < \frac{5}{8}\right\}$ **35.** $\left\{x \middle| x < \frac{5}{4}\right\}$ **37.** $\{x | x < 5.6\}$ **39.** Negative **41.** Negative and positive **43.** $\{x | x < 4\}$ −5 −4 −3 −2 −1 0 1 2 3 4 5 **45.** $\{y | y \ge 3\}$ −5 −4 −3 −2 −1 0 1 2 3 4 5 **47.** $\{x | x \le 1\}$ −5 −4 −3 −2 −1 0 1 2 3 4 5 **49.** $\{x | x < -1\}$ −5 −4 −3 −2 −1 0 1 2 3 4 5 **51.** $\{b | b < -4\}$ −5 −4 −3 −2 −1 0 1 2 3 4 5 **53.** $(-\infty, 0]$ **55.** $\left(\frac{2}{7}, \infty\right)$ **57.** $(-\infty, -3]$ **59.** $(-2, \infty)$ **61.** $(-\infty, 18)$ **63.** $[16, \infty)$ **65.** $\{b | b \le 33\}$ **67.** $\{x | x > 0\}$ **69.** $\left\{x \middle| x \le -\frac{12}{7}\right\}$ **71.** $\left\{x \middle| x > \frac{2}{3}\right\}$ **73.** $\{x | x \le 4.2\}$ **75.** $\{m | m > -8\}$ **77.** ii **79.** iii **81.** The couple's monthly household income is \$5395 or more. **83.** The patient must reduce his cholesterol level by 75 or more units. **85.** The student must receive a grade of 78 or higher. **87.** The height of the tallest wind turbine you can install is 45 ft. **89.** $x \le 4$ includes the element 4; $x < 4$ does not. **91.** $x \le -2$ **93.** −5 −4 −3 −2 −1 0 1 2 3 4 5 **95.** −5 −4 −3 −2 −1 0 1 2 3 4 5

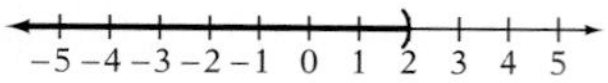

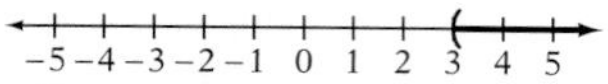

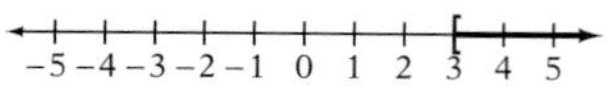

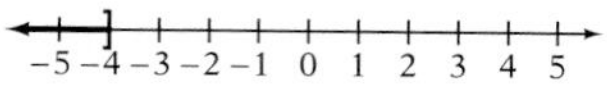

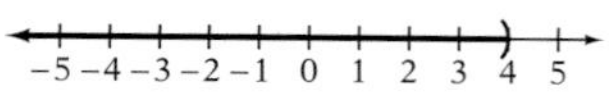

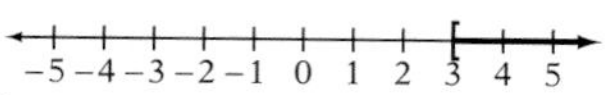

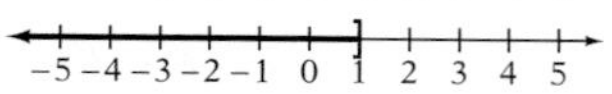

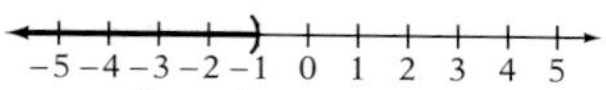

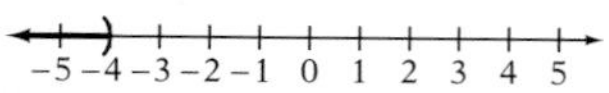

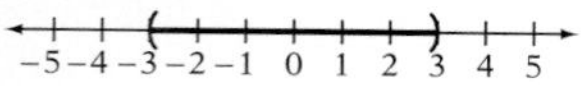

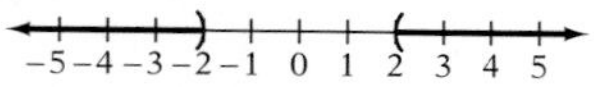

CHECK YOUR PROGRESS: CHAPTER 14

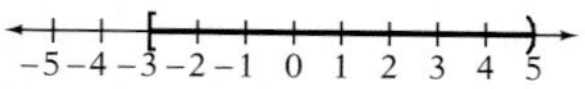

1. $\{-11, -10\}$ [14.1A] **2.** $A \cup B = \{4, 8, 16, 20, 24\}$ [14.1A] **3.** $A \cap B = \{20, 40\}$ [14.1A] **4.** $A \cap B = \varnothing$ [14.1A] **5.** $[-1, 3]$ [14.1B] **6.** $(8, \infty)$ [14.1B] **7.** $\{x | x \ge -9\}$ [14.1B] **8.** $\{x | -4 < x \le 7\}$ [14.1B] **9.** −5 −4 −3 −2 −1 0 1 2 3 4 5 [14.1B] **10.** −5 −4 −3 −2 −1 0 1 2 3 4 5 [14.1B] **11.** $\{x | x \ge 2\}$ −5 −4 −3 −2 −1 0 1 2 3 4 5 [14.2A] **12.** $(-3, \infty)$ −5 −4 −3 −2 −1 0 1 2 3 4 5 [14.2A] **13.** $\{x | x \le -5\}$ [14.2A] **14.** $(-\infty, 4)$ [14.2B] **15.** The student must get a 62 or higher on the last test to receive an A in the course. [14.2C]

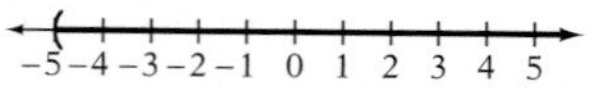

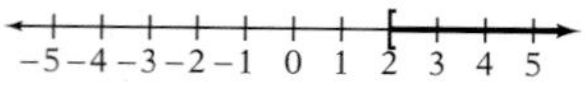

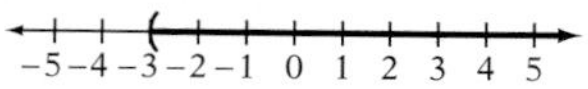

SECTION 14.3

1. False **3.** True **5.** $(-\infty, 4)$ **7.** $(-\infty, -4)$ **9.** $[1, \infty)$ **11.** $(-\infty, 5)$ **13.** $(-\infty, 0)$ **15.** $\{x | x < 20\}$ **17.** $\left\{y \middle| y \le \frac{5}{2}\right\}$ **19.** $\left\{x \middle| x < \frac{25}{11}\right\}$ **21.** $\left\{n \middle| n \le \frac{11}{18}\right\}$ **23.** $\{x | x \ge 6\}$ **25.** iii and iv **27.** In one month, the agent expects to make sales totaling \$20,000 or less. **29.** The company must own 8 or more individual computers for the site license to be the more economical choice. **31.** The amount of artificial flavors that can be added is 8 oz or less. **33.** 3 **35.** Between 8 in. and 28 in.

SECTION 14.4

1. Yes **3.** No

5.
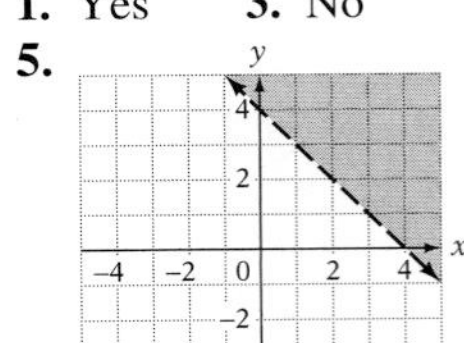

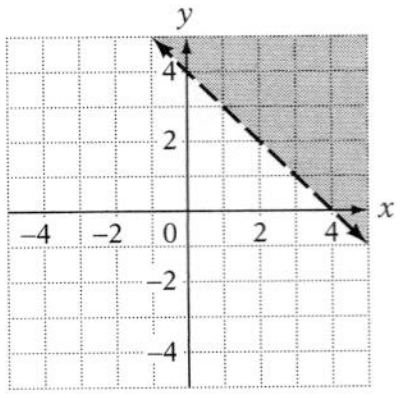

7.
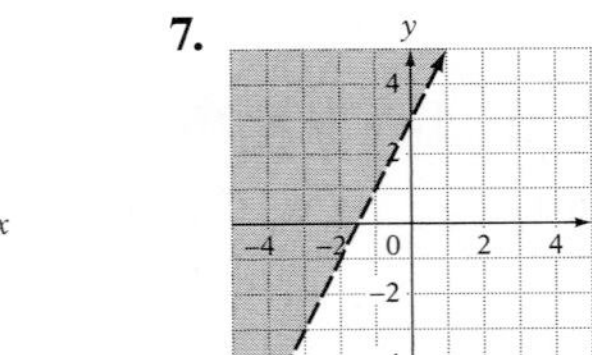

9.
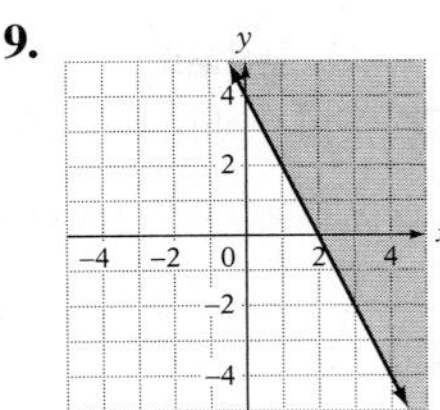

11.
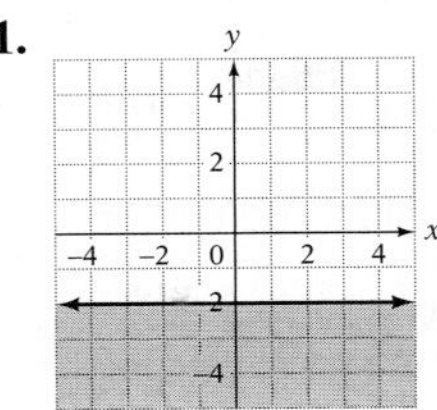

13.
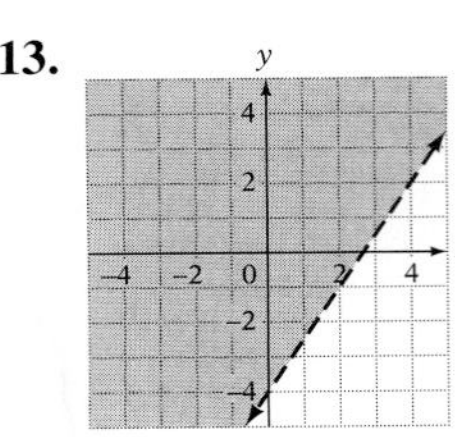

15.
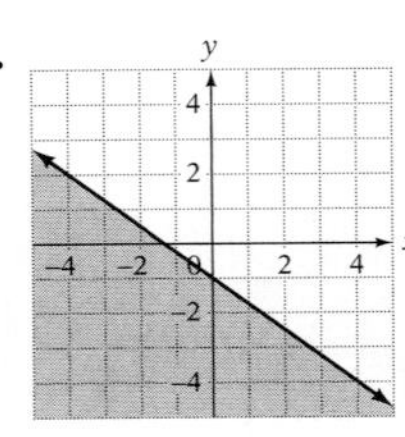

17.
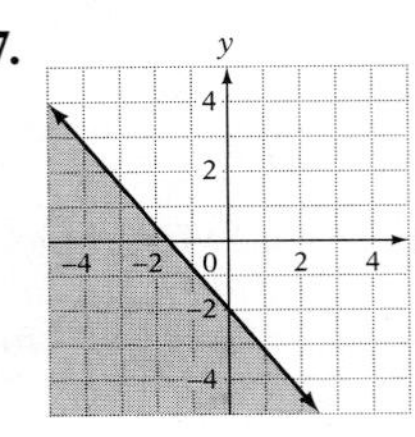

19.
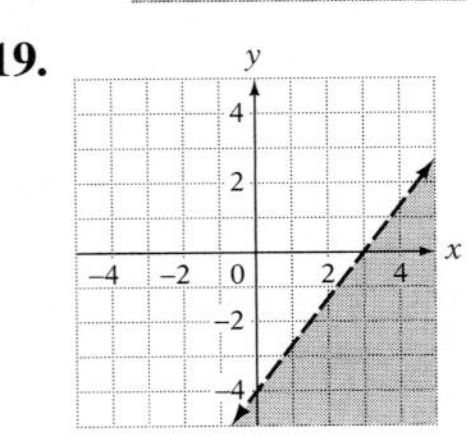

21.
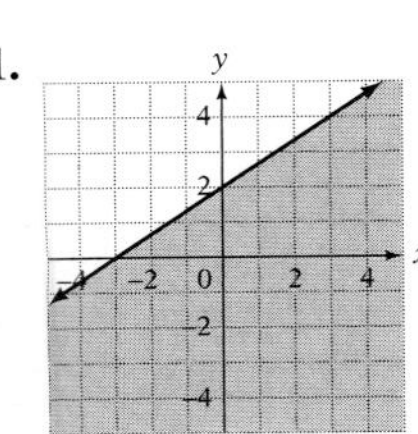

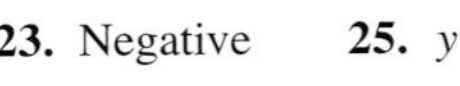
23. Negative **25.** $y > 2$ **27.** $y \leq -\frac{2}{3}x + 2$

CHAPTER 14 REVIEW EXERCISES

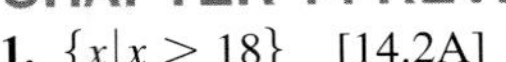
1. $\{x|x > 18\}$ [14.2A] **2.** $A \cap B = \varnothing$ [14.1A] **3.** $\{x|x > -8, x \in \text{odd integers}\}$ [14.1B]

4. $A \cup B = \{2, 4, 6, 8, 10\}$ [14.1A] **5.** $A = \{1, 3, 5, 7\}$ [14.1A] 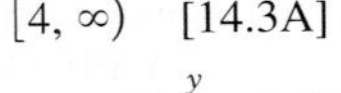
6. $[4, \infty)$ [14.3A]

7. [number line −5 to 5] [14.1B] **8.** $\{x|x \geq -4\}$ [14.3A] **9.**
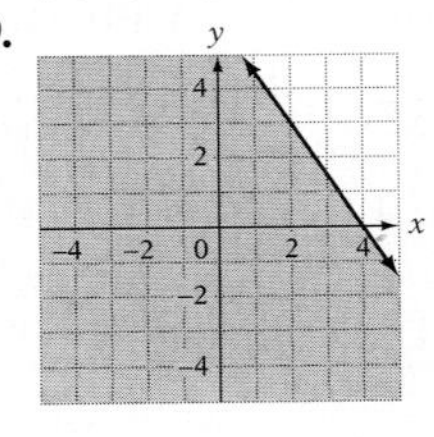
[14.4A]

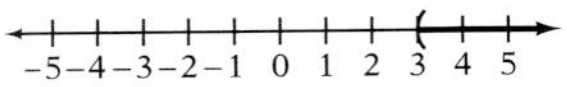

10.
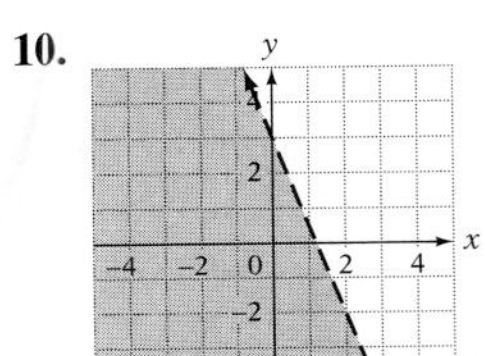
[14.4A]

11. $(-4, \infty)$ [14.1B] **12.** $(2, \infty)$ [number line −5 to 5] [14.2A]

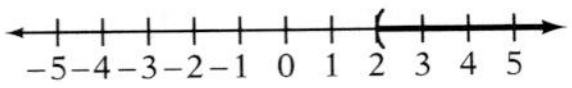

13. $A \cap B = \{1, 5, 9\}$ [14.1A] **14.**
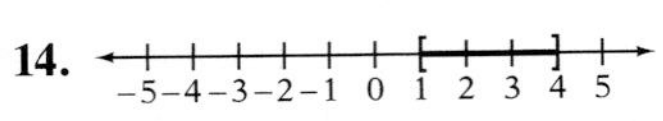
[14.1B] **15.**
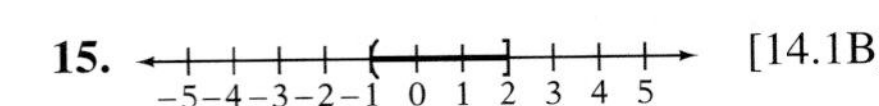
[14.1B]

16. $\{x|x \geq -3\}$ [14.2B] **17.** $(-18, \infty)$ [14.3A] **18.** $\left\{x\middle|x < \frac{1}{2}\right\}$ [14.3A] **19.** $\left\{x\middle|x < -\frac{8}{9}\right\}$ [14.2B]

20. $[4, \infty)$ [14.3A] **21.** [graph] [14.4A]

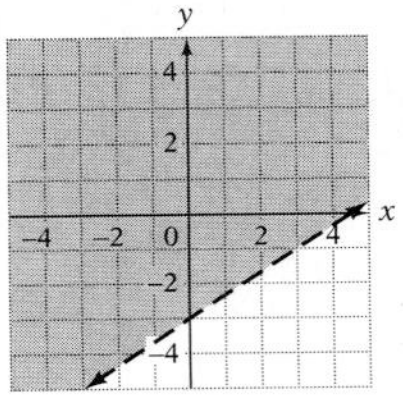

22. For florist B to be more economical, there must be 3 or more residents in the nursing home. [14.3B]

23. The minimum length is 24 ft. [14.3B] **24.** The smallest integer that satisfies the inequality is 32. [14.2C]

25. 72 is the lowest score that the student can receive and still attain a minimum of 480 points. [14.2C]

CHAPTER 14 TEST

1. [14.1B; Example 9] **2.** $\{x|x < 50, x \in \text{positive integers}\}$ [14.1B; HOW TO 3]

3. $A = \{4, 6, 8\}$ [14.1A; Example 1] **4.** $(-\infty, -3]$ [14.3A; Example 1] **5.** $\left\{x|x > \frac{1}{8}\right\}$ [14.2A; HOW TO 1]

6. [14.1B; You Try It 8b] **7.** $(-\infty, -1)$ [14.3A; You Try It 1]

8. $\{x|x > -23\}$ [14.1B; HOW TO 4] **9.**

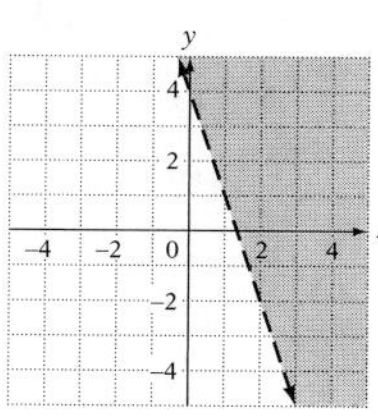

[14.4A; Example 1]

10. [14.4A; You Try It 2]

11. $A \cap B = \{12\}$ [14.1A; Example 4]

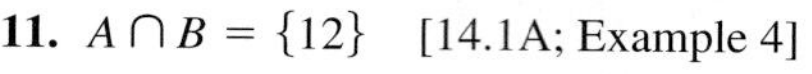

12. $\{x|x < -3\}$ [14.2A; HOW TO 1] **13.** $\left\{x|x \geq -\frac{40}{3}\right\}$ [14.2B; HOW TO 3]

14. $\left(-\infty, -\frac{22}{7}\right)$ [14.3A; Example 2] **15.** $[3, \infty)$ [14.2B; Example 2]

16. $\{x|x \geq -4\}$ [14.3A; Example 2] **17.** The child must grow 5 in. or more. [14.2C; Example 4] **18.** The maximum width is 11 ft. [14.3B; Example 3] **19.** The diameter must be between 0.0389 in. and 0.0395 in. [14.2C; You Try It 4] **20.** The total value of the stock processed by the broker was \$200,000 or less. [14.3B; Example 3]

CUMULATIVE REVIEW EXERCISES

1. $40a - 28$ [4.2D] **2.** $\frac{1}{8}$ [5.2A] **3.** 4 [5.3B] **4.** $-12a^7b^4$ [9.2B] **5.** $-\frac{1}{b^4}$ [9.4A]

6. $4x - 2 - \frac{4}{4x - 1}$ [9.5B] **7.** 0 [12.1D] **8.** $3a^2(3x - 1)(3x + 1)$ [10.5A] **9.** $\frac{1}{x + 2}$ [11.1C]

10. $\frac{18a}{(2a - 3)(a + 3)}$ [11.3B] **11.** $-\frac{5}{9}$ [11.5A] **12.** $C = S + Rt$ [11.6A] **13.** $-\frac{7}{3}$ [12.3B]

14. $y = -\frac{3}{2}x - \frac{3}{2}$ [12.4A] **15.** $(4, 1)$ [13.2A] **16.** $(1, -4)$ [13.3A] **17.** $A \cup B = \{-10, -2, 0, 1, 2\}$ [14.1A]

18. $\{x|x < 48\}$ [14.1B] **19.** $(-\infty, 4)$ [14.1B] **20.** [14.2B]

21. $x < -15$ [14.2B] **22.** $x > 2$ [14.3A] **23.** **24.**

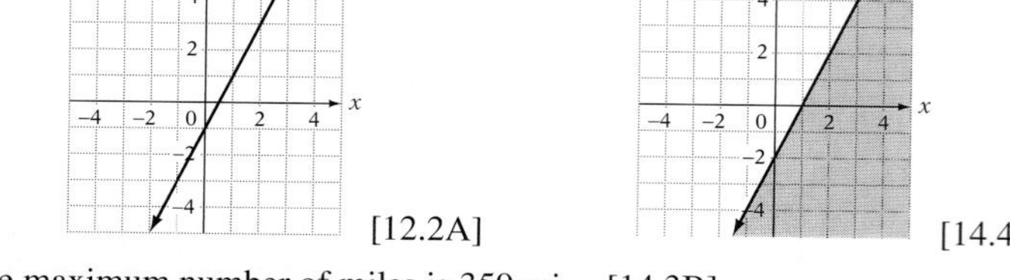

[12.2A] [14.4A]

25. $\{x|x \leq -26, x \in \text{integers}\}$ [14.2C] **26.** The maximum number of miles is 359 mi. [14.3B] **27.** There are an estimated 5000 fish in the lake. [6.2B] **28.** The angle measures are 65°, 35°, and 80°. [7.1C]

Answers to Chapter 15 Selected Exercises

PREP TEST

1. -14 [3.1C] **2.** $-2x^2y - 4xy^2$ [4.2A] **3.** 14 [5.1C] **4.** $\frac{7}{5}$ [5.3A] **5.** x^6 [9.2A] **6.** $x^2 + 2xy + y^2$ [9.3D]

7. $4x^2 - 12x + 9$ [9.3D] **8.** $4 - 9v^2$ [9.3D] **9.** $a^2 - 25$ [9.3D] **10.** $\frac{x^2y^2}{9}$ [9.4A]

SECTION 15.1

1. radical sign; radicand **5.** 4 **7.** 7 **9.** $4\sqrt{2}$ **11.** $2\sqrt{2}$ **13.** $-18\sqrt{2}$ **15.** $10\sqrt{10}$ **17.** $\sqrt{15}$ **19.** $\sqrt{29}$ **21.** $-54\sqrt{2}$ **23.** $3\sqrt{5}$ **25.** 0 **27.** $48\sqrt{2}$ **29.** -11 and -10 **31.** 2 and 3 **33.** 15.492 **35.** 16.971 **37.** 18.708 **39.** x^7 **41.** $y^7\sqrt{y}$ **43.** a^{10} **45.** x^2y^2 **47.** $2x^2$ **49.** $2x\sqrt{6}$ **51.** $2x^2\sqrt{15x}$ **53.** $7a^2b^4$ **55.** $3x^2y^3\sqrt{2xy}$ **57.** $2x^5y^3\sqrt{10xy}$ **59.** $4a^4b^5\sqrt{5a}$ **61.** $-8ab\sqrt{b}$ **63.** x^3y **65.** $-8a^2b^3\sqrt{5b}$ **67.** $6x^2y^3\sqrt{3y}$ **69.** $4x^3y\sqrt{2y}$ **71.** $5a + 20$ **73.** $2x^2 + 8x + 8$ **75.** $x + 2$ **77.** $y + 1$ **79.** Rational **81.** Irrational **83a.** The average number of credit cards for a first-year student is 2.3. **b.** The average number of credit cards for a sophomore is 3.3. **c.** The average number of credit cards for a junior is 4.0. **d.** The average number of credit cards for a senior is 4.6. **85a.** The speed of the car was $12\sqrt{15}$ mph. **b.** 46 mph

SECTION 15.2

1. 2, 20, and 50 **3.** Yes **5.** Yes **7.** $3\sqrt{2}$ **9.** $-\sqrt{7}$ **11.** $-11\sqrt{11}$ **13.** $10\sqrt{x}$ **15.** $-2\sqrt{y}$ **17.** $-11\sqrt{3b}$ **19.** $2x\sqrt{2}$ **21.** $-3a\sqrt{3a}$ **23.** $-5\sqrt{xy}$ **25.** $8\sqrt{5}$ **27.** $8\sqrt{2}$ **29.** $15\sqrt{2} - 10\sqrt{3}$ **31.** $\sqrt{x}$ **33.** $-12x\sqrt{3}$ **35.** $2xy\sqrt{x} - 3xy\sqrt{y}$ **37.** $-9x\sqrt{3x}$ **39.** $-13y^2\sqrt{2y}$ **41.** $4a^2b^2\sqrt{ab}$ **43.** $7\sqrt{2}$ **45.** $6\sqrt{x}$ **47.** $-3\sqrt{y}$ **49.** $-45\sqrt{2}$ **51.** $13\sqrt{3} - 12\sqrt{5}$ **53.** $32\sqrt{3} - 3\sqrt{11}$ **55.** $6\sqrt{x}$ **57.** $-34\sqrt{3x}$ **59.** $10a\sqrt{3b} + 10a\sqrt{5b}$ **61.** $-2xy\sqrt{3}$ **63.** iv **65.** $2ab\sqrt{6ab}$ **67.** The perimeter is $8\sqrt{2}$ cm.

SECTION 15.3

1. $3 - \sqrt{5}$ **3.** $\sqrt{2a} + 8$ **5.** $25 - y$ **7.** $\dfrac{\sqrt{x}}{\sqrt{x}}$ **11.** 5 **13.** 6 **15.** x **17.** x^3y^2 **19.** $3ab^6\sqrt{2a}$ **21.** $12a^4b\sqrt{b}$ **23.** $10abc$ **25.** $2 - \sqrt{6}$ **27.** $x - \sqrt{xy}$ **29.** $5\sqrt{2} - \sqrt{5x}$ **31.** $3a - 3\sqrt{ab}$ **33.** $x - 6\sqrt{x} + 9$ **35.** $-2 + 2\sqrt{5}$ **37.** $16 + 10\sqrt{2}$ **39.** $6x + 10\sqrt{x} - 4$ **41.** $15x - 22y\sqrt{x} + 8y^2$ **43.** 4 **45.** $9x - 16$ **47.** Less than **49.** 4 **51.** 7 **53.** 3 **55.** $x\sqrt{5}$ **57.** $\dfrac{a^2}{7}$ **59.** $\dfrac{y\sqrt{3}}{3}$ **61.** $\sqrt{2y}$ **63.** $-\dfrac{\sqrt{2}+3}{7}$ **65.** $\dfrac{15-3\sqrt{5}}{20}$ **67.** $-\dfrac{7\sqrt{2}+49}{47}$ **69.** $\sqrt{15} + 2\sqrt{5}$ **71.** $\dfrac{x\sqrt{y}+y\sqrt{x}}{x-y}$ **73.** $3 + \sqrt{6}$ **75.** $-\dfrac{20+7\sqrt{3}}{23}$ **77.** $\dfrac{6+5\sqrt{x}+x}{4-x}$ **79.** Equal to **81.** The area is 59 m^2. **83.** $\dfrac{5}{8}$ **85.** $\dfrac{5}{4}$

CHECK YOUR PROGRESS CHAPTER 15

1. $10\sqrt{3}$ [15.1A] **2.** $30\sqrt{5}$ [15.1A] **3.** $8x^5$ [15.1B] **4.** $3x^2y^2\sqrt{2x}$ [15.1B] **5.** $-3\sqrt{5}$ [15.2A] **6.** $-14a\sqrt{ab}$ [15.2A] **7.** $8a^2b^5$ [15.3A] **8.** $4 - 2\sqrt{10}$ [15.3A] **9.** $3a - 7\sqrt{a} - 6$ [15.3A] **10.** $2y - 25$ [15.3A] **11.** 5 [15.3B] **12.** $\dfrac{\sqrt{3x}}{3}$ [15.3B] **13.** $\dfrac{49+7\sqrt{2}}{47}$ [15.3B] **14.** $\dfrac{17+8\sqrt{2}}{7}$ [15.3B]

SECTION 15.4

1. No **3.** Yes **5.** Sometimes true **7.** Always true **9.** 90°; legs **11.** 25 **13.** 144 **15.** 5 **17.** 16 **19.** 8 **21.** No solution **23.** 6 **25.** 24 **27.** $-\dfrac{2}{5}$ **29.** $\dfrac{4}{3}$ **31.** -1 **33.** 15 **35.** 5 **37.** 1 **39.** 1 **41.** 1 **43.** 2 **45.** No solution **47.** iii **49.** The number is 11. **51.** The length of the hypotenuse is 10.30 cm. **53.** The length of the other leg of the triangle is 9.75 ft. **55.** The length of the diagonal is 12.1 mi. **57.** The depth of the water is 12.5 ft. **59.** The pitcher's mound is more than halfway between home plate and second base. **61.** Yes, she will be able to call a friend on the dock. **63.** The height of the screen is 35.5 in. **65.** The length of the pendulum is 1.83 ft. **67.** The bridge is 64 ft high. **69.** 5 **71.** 8 **73a.** The perimeter of the triangle is $12\sqrt{2}$ cm. **b.** The area of the triangle is 12 cm^2. **77.** AB is 6.4 units.

CHAPTER 15 REVIEW EXERCISES

1. 3 [15.3A] **2.** $9a^2\sqrt{2ab}$ [15.1B] **3.** 12 [15.1A] **4.** $3a\sqrt{2} + 2a\sqrt{3}$ [15.3A] **5.** $2\sqrt{6}$ [15.3B] **6.** $-8\sqrt{2}$ [15.2A] **7.** 2 [15.3A] **8.** 1 [15.4A] **9.** $-x\sqrt{3} - x\sqrt{5}$ [15.3B] **10.** $-6\sqrt{30}$ [15.1A] **11.** 20 [15.4A] **12.** $20\sqrt{3}$ [15.1A] **13.** $7x^2y^4$ [15.3B] **14.** No solution [15.4A] **15.** $18a\sqrt{5b} + 5a\sqrt{b}$ [15.2A] **16.** $20\sqrt{10}$ [15.1A] **17.** $7x^2y\sqrt{15xy}$ [15.2A] **18.** $8y + 10\sqrt{5y} - 15$ [15.3A] **19.** $26\sqrt{3x}$ [15.2A] **20.** No solution [15.4A] **21.** $\dfrac{8\sqrt{x}+24}{x-9}$ [15.3B] **22.** $36x^8y^5\sqrt{3xy}$ [15.1B] **23.** $2y^4\sqrt{6}$ [15.1B] **24.** -1 [15.4A] **25.** $-6x^3y^2\sqrt{2y}$ [15.2A] **26.** $\dfrac{16\sqrt{a}}{a}$ [15.3B] **27.** The distance across the pond is approximately 43 ft. [15.4B] **28.** The explorer weighs 144 lb on the surface of Earth. [15.4B] **29.** The depth of the water is 100 ft. [15.4B] **30.** The radius of the sharpest corner is 25 ft. [15.4B]

CHAPTER 15 TEST

1. $11x^4y$ [15.1B; Example 5] **2.** $6x^2y\sqrt{y}$ [15.3A; Example 1] **3.** $-5\sqrt{2}$ [15.2A; Example 2] **4.** $3\sqrt{5}$ [15.1A; HOW TO 1] **5.** 9 [15.3B; HOW TO 7] **6.** 25 [15.4A; Example 1] **7.** $4a^2b^5\sqrt{2ab}$ [15.1B; Example 5] **8.** $7ab\sqrt{a}$ [15.3B; HOW TO 7] **9.** $\sqrt{3} + 1$ [15.3B; HOW TO 9] **10.** $4x^2y^2\sqrt{5y}$ [15.3A; HOW TO 1] **11.** 9 [15.4A; You Try It 2] **12.** $21\sqrt{2y} - 12\sqrt{2x}$ [15.2A; Example 4] **13.** $6x^3y\sqrt{2x}$ [15.1B; Example 5] **14.** $y + 2\sqrt{y} - 15$ [15.3A; HOW TO 3] **15.** $-2xy\sqrt{3xy} - 3xy\sqrt{xy}$ [15.2A; Example 4] **16.** $\frac{17 - 8\sqrt{5}}{31}$ [15.3B; Example 7] **17.** $a - \sqrt{ab}$ [15.3A; Example 2] **18.** $5\sqrt{3}$ [15.1A; HOW TO 1] **19.** The length of the pendulum is 7.30 ft. [15.4B; You Try It 4] **20.** The rope should be secured about 7 ft from the base of the pole. [15.4B; Example 3]

CUMULATIVE REVIEW EXERCISES

1. $-\frac{1}{12}$ [3.5A] **2.** $2x + 18$ [4.2D] **3.** $\frac{1}{13}$ [5.3B] **4.** $6x^5y^5$ [9.2A] **5.** $-2b^2 + 1 - \frac{1}{3b^2}$ [9.5A] **6.** 1 [12.1D] **7.** $2a(a - 5)(a - 3)$ [10.2B] **8.** $\frac{1}{4(x + 1)}$ [11.1B] **9.** $\frac{x + 3}{x - 3}$ [11.3B] **10.** $\frac{5}{3}$ [11.5A] **11.** $y = \frac{1}{2}x - 2$ [12.4A] **12.** (1, 1) [13.2A] **13.** (3, −2) [13.3A] **14.** $x \le -\frac{9}{2}$ [14.3A] **15.** $6\sqrt{3}$ [15.1A] **16.** $-4\sqrt{2}$ [15.2A] **17.** $4ab\sqrt{2ab} - 5ab\sqrt{ab}$ [15.2A] **18.** $14a^5b^2\sqrt{2a}$ [15.3A] **19.** $3\sqrt{2} - x\sqrt{3}$ [15.3A] **20.** 8 [15.3B] **21.** $-6 - 3\sqrt{5}$ [15.3B] **22.** 6 [15.4A] **23.** The cost of the book is \$49.50. [5.2B] **24.** The rate of the faster cyclist is 15 mph. [5.5B] **25.** The numbers are 8 and 13. [10.6B] **26.** It would take the small pipe, working alone, 48 h. [11.7A]

27.

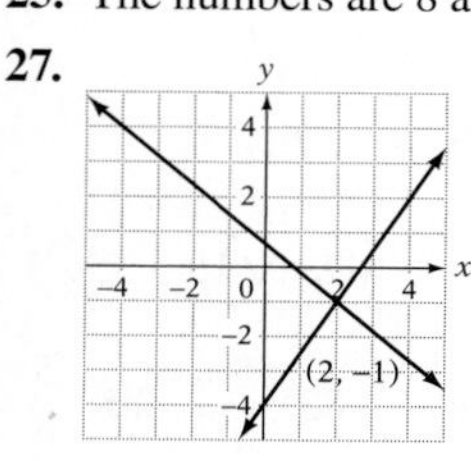

[13.1A]

28.

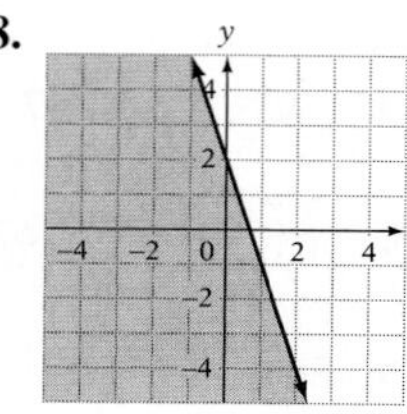

[14.4A]

29. The smaller integer is 40. [15.4B]
30. The height of the building is 400 ft. [15.4B]

Answers to Chapter 16 Selected Exercises

PREP TEST

1. 41 [4.1A] **2.** $-\frac{1}{5}$ [5.2A] **3.** $(x + 4)(x - 3)$ [10.2A] **4.** $(2x - 3)^2$ [10.4A] **5.** Yes [10.4A] **6.** 3 [11.5A]

7. [12.2A]

8. $2\sqrt{7}$ [15.1A] **9.** $|a|$ [15.1B] **10.** The length of the hiking trail is 3.6 mi. [5.5B]

SECTION 16.1

1. $3x + 4, x - 7$ **3.** $x^2 - 3x - 8 = 0$ **5.** $x^2 - 4x - 5 = 0$ **7.** $-\frac{5}{2}, \frac{1}{3}$ **9.** −5, 3 **11.** 1, 3 **13.** −2, −1 **15.** 3 **17.** $-\frac{2}{3}, 0$ **19.** −2, 5 **21.** $\frac{2}{3}, 1$ **23.** $-3, \frac{1}{3}$ **25.** $\frac{2}{3}$ **27.** $-\frac{1}{2}, \frac{3}{2}$ **29.** $\frac{1}{2}$ **31.** −3, 3 **33.** $-\frac{1}{2}, \frac{1}{2}$ **35.** −3, 5 **37.** 1, 5 **39.** iii **41.** ±7 **43.** ±8 **45.** $\pm\frac{8}{3}$ **47.** $\pm\frac{5}{2}$ **49.** $\pm\frac{8}{5}$ **51.** No real number solution **53.** $\pm 4\sqrt{3}$ **55.** −9, 5 **57.** −2, 8 **59.** $-\frac{15}{2}, \frac{3}{2}$ **61.** $\frac{10}{9}, \frac{26}{9}$ **63.** $-5 \pm 5\sqrt{2}$ **65.** $\frac{1}{2} \pm \sqrt{6}$ **67.** One **69.** Two **71.** 11, 35 **73.** The annual interest rate was 9%.

SECTION 16.2

1. perfect-square trinomial **3.** $x^2 - 6x + 9, (x - 3)^2$ **5.** $x^2 - 5x + \frac{25}{4}, \left(x - \frac{5}{2}\right)^2$ **7.** $-3, 1$ **9.** $-2, 8$ **11.** 2 **13.** No real number solution **15.** $-4, -1$ **17.** $-8, 1$ **19.** $-2 \pm \sqrt{3}$ **21.** $-3 \pm \sqrt{14}$ **23.** $1 \pm \sqrt{2}$ **25.** $\frac{-3 \pm \sqrt{13}}{2}$ **27.** 1, 2 **29.** $\frac{-1 \pm \sqrt{13}}{2}$ **31.** $-5 \pm 4\sqrt{2}$ **33.** $\frac{3 \pm \sqrt{29}}{2}$ **35.** $\frac{1 \pm \sqrt{17}}{2}$ **37.** No real number solution **39.** $\frac{1}{2}, 1$ **41.** $-3, \frac{1}{2}$ **43.** $\frac{7 \pm \sqrt{41}}{4}$ **45.** $\frac{-1 \pm \sqrt{73}}{12}$ **47.** $-\frac{1}{2}, \frac{4}{3}$ **49.** There is one negative and one positive solution. **51.** $-5.372, 0.372$ **53.** $-3.212, 1.712$ **55.** $-4 \pm \sqrt{30}$ **57.** $4 \pm \sqrt{3}$ **61.** The ball will hit the ground in 4.81 s.

SECTION 16.3

1. $\frac{1 + \sqrt{13}}{2}$ and $\frac{1 - \sqrt{13}}{2}$ **5.** $-1, 5$ **7.** $-1, 3$ **9.** $-\frac{1}{2}, 1$ **11.** No real number solution **13.** $-\frac{5}{2}, \frac{3}{2}$ **15.** No real number solution **17.** $1 \pm \sqrt{6}$ **19.** $-3 \pm \sqrt{10}$ **21.** $2 \pm \sqrt{13}$ **23.** $\frac{-1 \pm \sqrt{2}}{3}$ **25.** $-\frac{1}{2}$ **27.** No real number solution **29.** $\frac{-4 \pm \sqrt{5}}{2}$ **31.** $\frac{1 \pm 2\sqrt{3}}{2}$ **33.** $\frac{-5 \pm \sqrt{2}}{3}$ **35.** True **37.** $-3.690, 5.690$ **39.** $-1.690, 7.690$ **41.** $-1.089, 4.589$ **43.** $-2.118, 0.118$ **45.** $-0.905, 1.105$ **47.** $2\sqrt{23}$ **49.** $3 \pm \sqrt{13}$ **53.** Yes **55.** Yes

CHECK YOUR PROGRESS: CHAPTER 16

1. $-11, 9$ [16.1A] **2.** $-\frac{3}{2}, \frac{4}{3}$ [16.1A] **3.** $-6, 4$ [16.1B] **4.** $1 \pm \sqrt{6}$ [16.2A] **5.** $1 \pm \sqrt{7}$ [16.3A] **6.** $-\frac{4}{3}, \frac{7}{2}$ [16.1A] **7.** $4 \pm 2\sqrt{5}$ [16.1B] **8.** $-3 \pm \sqrt{5}$ [16.2A] **9.** $\frac{3 \pm 2\sqrt{6}}{2}$ [16.3A] **10.** $\pm 2\sqrt{3}$ [16.1B] **11.** $-3, \frac{4}{5}$ [16.1A] **12.** $\frac{2 \pm \sqrt{6}}{2}$ [16.2A] **13.** $3 \pm \sqrt{2}$ [16.3A] **14.** No real number solution [16.1B] **15.** $0.151, -1.651$ [16.3A]

SECTION 16.4

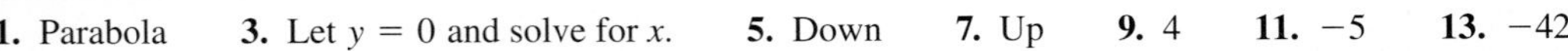

1. Parabola **3.** Let $y = 0$ and solve for x. **5.** Down **7.** Up **9.** 4 **11.** -5 **13.** -42

15. **17.**

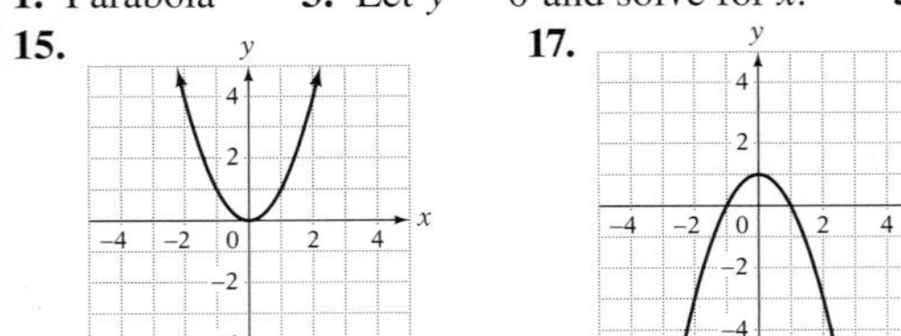

19. **21.** **23.** **25.**

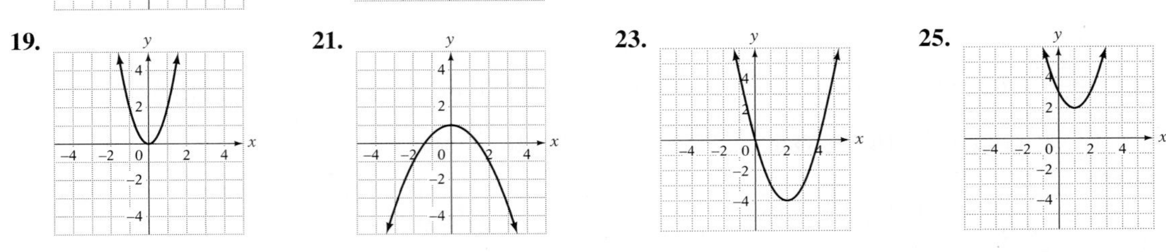

27. **29.**

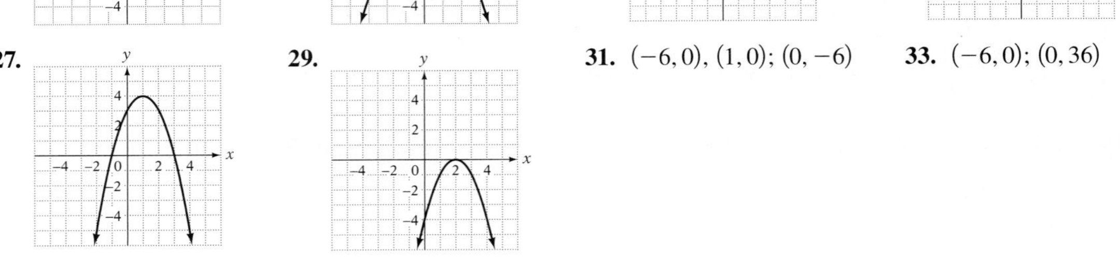

31. $(-6, 0), (1, 0); (0, -6)$ **33.** $(-6, 0); (0, 36)$ **35.** $(-2 - \sqrt{6}, 0), (-2 + \sqrt{6}, 0); (0, -2)$ **37.** No x-intercepts; $(0, 1)$ **39.** $\left(\frac{3}{2}, 0\right), (5, 0); (0, 15)$

41. $\left(\frac{-3-\sqrt{33}}{6}, 0\right), \left(\frac{-3+\sqrt{33}}{6}, 0\right)$; $(0, 2)$ **43.** Negative **45.** Linear **47.** Neither **49.** Quadratic
51a. $(-2, 0), (2, 0)$ **b.** $(0, -4)$ **c.** It is positive. **d.** 0 **e.** -3 **53.** Answers will vary. For example, the graph of $y = -x^2 + 6x - 8$. **55.** -2 **57.** $-1, 5$ **59.** 0.5936307095, -0.3158529318 **61.** -1.766291404, 1.059184622

SECTION 16.5

1. $2W + 3$ **3.** $r - 30$ **5.** The height of the triangle is 10 m. The length of the base is 4 m. **7.** The length is 6 ft. The width is 4 ft. **9.** Working alone, the first drain would take 24 min to empty the tank. Working alone, the second drain would take 8 min. **11.** The length is 100 ft. The width is 50 ft. **13.** It would take the first engine 12 h and the second engine 6 h to power the ferryboat across the channel. **15.** The rate of the plane in calm air was 100 mph. **17.** The cyclist's rate during the first 150 mi was 50 mph. **19.** The arrow will be 32 ft above the ground at 1 s and at 2 s. **21.** The weed will cover an area of 10 m^2 after 25 days. **23.** There will be 50 million people aged 65 or older in the year 2017. **25.** The ball has been in the air for 1.58 s. **27.** The hang time is 5.5 s. **29.** False **31.** The lengths of the legs are 2 cm and 3 cm. **33.** The radius of the cone is 7.98 cm. **35.** The dimensions of the cardboard are 20 in. by 20 in. **37a.** $12 = 2L + 2W$ **b.** $A = LW$ **c.** $L = 6 - W$; $A = (6 - W)W$; $A = -W^2 + 6W$
d. Length: 3 ft; width: 3 ft

CHAPTER 16 REVIEW EXERCISES

1. $-\frac{7}{2}, \frac{4}{3}$ [16.1A] **2.** $\pm\frac{5}{7}$ [16.1B] **3.** $-6, 4$ [16.2A] **4.** $-6, 1$ [16.3A] **5.** $-4, \frac{3}{2}$ [16.2A]
6. $2, \frac{5}{12}$ [16.1A] **7.** $-2 \pm 2\sqrt{6}$ [16.1B] **8.** $1, \frac{3}{2}$ [16.3A] **9.** $-\frac{1}{2}, -\frac{1}{3}$ [16.1A] **10.** No real number solution [16.1B]
11. $2 \pm \sqrt{3}$ [16.2A] **12.** $\frac{3 \pm \sqrt{29}}{2}$ [16.3A] **13.** No real number solution [16.2A] **14.** $-10, -7$ [16.1A]
15. $-1, 2$ [16.1B] **16.** $\frac{-4 \pm \sqrt{23}}{2}$ [16.2A] **17.** No real number solution [16.3A] **18.** $-2, -\frac{1}{2}$ [16.3A]

19. [16.4A]

20. 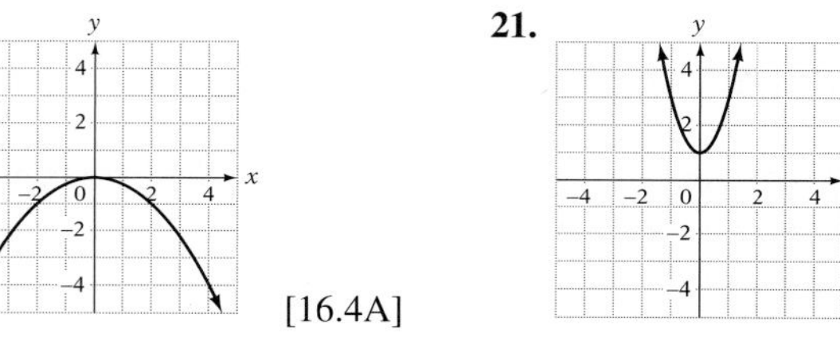 [16.4A] **21.** [16.4A]

22. 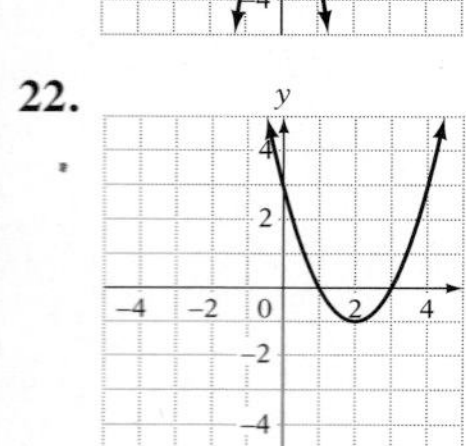 [16.4A] **23.** 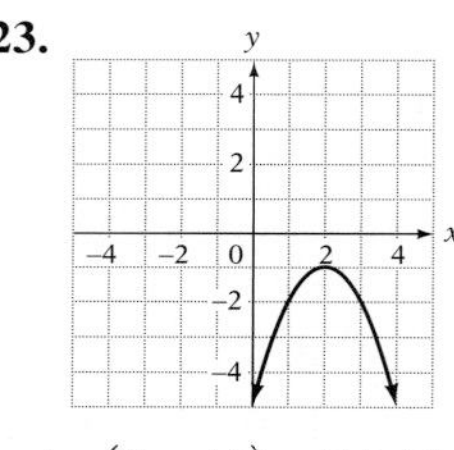 [16.4A]

24. x-intercepts: $(-3, 0), (5, 0)$; y-intercepts: $(0, -15)$ [16.4A] **25.** The rate of the hawk in calm air is 75 mph. [16.5A]

CHAPTER 16 TEST

1. $-1, 6$ [16.1A; HOW TO 1] **2.** $-4, \frac{5}{3}$ [16.1A; HOW TO 1] **3.** $-\frac{1}{2}, 0$ [16.1A; HOW TO 1] **4.** $\pm\frac{3}{2}$ [16.1B; HOW TO 5]
5. 0, 10 [16.1B; HOW TO 6] **6.** $-4 \pm 2\sqrt{5}$ [16.1B; HOW TO 6] **7.** $-2 \pm 2\sqrt{5}$ [16.2A; HOW TO 3]
8. $\frac{-3 \pm \sqrt{41}}{2}$ [16.2A; HOW TO 3] **9.** $\frac{3 \pm \sqrt{7}}{2}$ [16.2A; Example 1] **10.** $\frac{-4 \pm \sqrt{22}}{2}$ [16.2A; Example 1]
11. $-2 \pm \sqrt{2}$ [16.3A; HOW TO 1] **12.** $\frac{3 \pm \sqrt{33}}{2}$ [16.3A; HOW TO 1] **13.** $-\frac{1}{2}, 3$ [16.3A; You Try It 1]
14. $\frac{1 \pm \sqrt{13}}{6}$ [16.3A; HOW TO 1] **15.** $-1.651, 0.151$ [16.3A; Example 1] **16.** $-1.387, 0.721$ [16.3A; You Try It 1]

17. 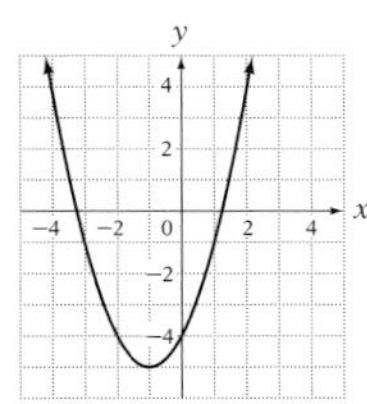
[16.4A; HOW TO 2]

18. x-intercepts: $(-4, 0)$, $(3, 0)$; y-intercept: $(0, -12)$ [16.4A; Example 2]

19. The length is 8 ft. The width is 5 ft. [16.5A; You Try It 1] **20.** The rate of the boat in calm water is 11 mph. [16.5A; HOW TO 1]

CUMULATIVE REVIEW EXERCISES

1. $-28x + 27$ [4.2D] **2.** $\frac{3}{2}$ [5.1C] **3.** 3 [5.3B] **4.** $-12a^8b^4$ [9.2B] **5.** $x + 2 - \frac{4}{x-2}$ [9.5B]
6. $x(3x - 4)(x + 2)$ [10.3A/10.3B] **7.** $\frac{9x^2(x-2)^2}{(2x-3)^2}$ [11.1C] **8.** $\frac{x+2}{2(x+1)}$ [11.3B] **9.** $\frac{x-4}{2x+5}$ [11.4A]
10. x-intercept: $(3, 0)$; y-intercept: $(0, -4)$ [12.3A] **11.** $y = -\frac{4}{3}x - 2$ [12.4A/12.4B] **12.** $(2, 1)$ [13.2A] **13.** $(2, -2)$ [13.3A]
14. $x > \frac{1}{9}$ [14.3A] **15.** $a - 2$ [15.3A] **16.** $6ab\sqrt{a}$ [15.3B] **17.** $\frac{-6 + 5\sqrt{3}}{13}$ [15.3B] **18.** 5 [15.4A]
19. $\frac{5}{2}, \frac{1}{3}$ [16.1A] **20.** $5 \pm 3\sqrt{2}$ [16.1B] **21.** $\frac{-7 \pm \sqrt{13}}{6}$ [16.2A] **22.** $-\frac{1}{2}, 2$ [16.3A]
23. The cost of the mixture is $2.90 per pound. [5.5A] **24.** 250 additional shares are required. [6.2B] **25.** The rate of the plane in still air is 200 mph. The rate of the wind is 40 mph. [13.4A] **26.** The score on the last test must be 77 or more points. [14.2C] **27.** The middle odd integer can be -5 or 5. [16.5A] **28.** The rate for the last 8 mi is 4 mph. [16.5A]

29. 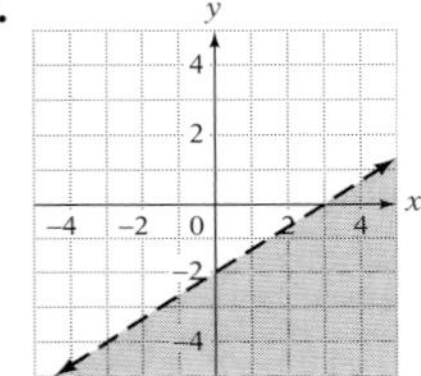
[14.4A]

30. 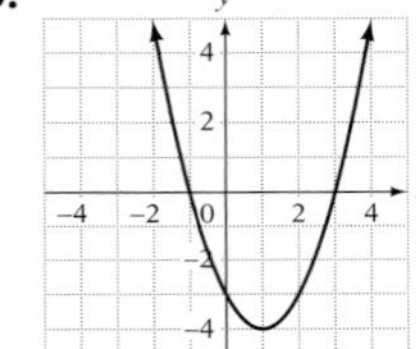
[16.4A]

FINAL EXAM

1. -3 [3.1C] **2.** -6 [3.2B] **3.** $-\frac{1}{2}$ [3.4A] **4.** -11 [3.5A] **5.** $-\frac{15}{2}$ [4.1A] **6.** $9x + 6y$ [4.2A]
7. $6z$ [4.2B] **8.** $16x - 52$ [4.2D] **9.** -50 [5.1C] **10.** -3 [5.3B] **11.** 12.5% [6.3B] **12.** 15.2 [6.4A/6.4B]
13. $-3x^2 - 3x + 8$ [9.1B] **14.** $81x^4y^{12}$ [9.2B] **15.** $6x^3 + 7x^2 - 7x - 6$ [9.3B] **16.** $-\frac{x^4y}{2}$ [9.4A]
17. $\frac{3x}{y} - 4x^2 - \frac{5}{x}$ [9.5A] **18.** $5x - 12 + \frac{23}{x+2}$ [9.5B] **19.** $\frac{4y^6}{x^6}$ [9.4A] **20.** $\frac{3}{4}$ [12.1D]
21. $(x - 6)(x + 1)$ [10.2A] **22.** $(3x + 2)(2x - 3)$ [10.3A/10.3B] **23.** $4x(2x - 1)(x - 3)$ [10.5A]
24. $(5x - 4)(5x + 4)$ [10.4A] **25.** $2(a + 3)(4 - x)$ [10.1B] **26.** $3y(5 - 2x)(5 + 2x)$ [10.5A] **27.** $\frac{1}{2}, 3$ [10.6A]
28. $\frac{2(x+1)}{x-1}$ [11.1B] **29.** $\frac{-3x^2 + x - 25}{(2x-5)(x+3)}$ [11.3B] **30.** $\frac{x^2 - 2x}{x - 1}$ [11.4A] **31.** 2 [11.5A] **32.** $a = b$ [11.6A]
33. $\frac{2}{3}$ [12.3B] **34.** $y = -\frac{2}{3}x - 2$ [12.4A/12.4B] **35.** $(6, 17)$ [13.2A] **36.** $(2, -1)$ [13.3A] **37.** $x \le -3$ [14.2A]
38. $y \ge \frac{5}{2}$ [14.3A] **39.** $7x^3$ [15.1B] **40.** $38\sqrt{3a}$ [15.2A] **41.** $\sqrt{15} + 2\sqrt{3}$ [15.3B] **42.** 2 [15.4A]
43. $-1, \frac{4}{3}$ [16.1A] **44.** $\frac{1 \pm \sqrt{5}}{4}$ [16.3A] **45.** $2x + 3(x - 2)$; $5x - 6$ [4.3B] **46.** The original value is $6000. [6.4C]
47. The mean is 2.025 in. The median is 1 in. The mode is 0 in. [8.2A] **48.** $6000 must be invested at 11%. [13.2B]
49. The cost of the mixture is $4 per pound. [5.5A] **50.** The probability that the card is not a queen is $\frac{2}{3}$. [8.3A]
51. The distance traveled in the first hour was 215 km. [5.5B] **52.** The angles measure 50°, 60°, and 70°. [7.1C]
53. The middle integer can be -4 or 4. [16.5A] **54.** Working together, it would take them 36 min or 0.6 h. [11.7A]

55. The width is 5 m. The length is 10 m. [10.6B] **56.** 16 oz of dye are required. [6.2B]
57. The rate of the boat in calm water is 15 mph. The rate of the current is 5 mph. [13.4A]
58. The rate of the wind is 25 mph. [16.5A] **59.** –5 –4 –3 –2 –1 0 1 2 3 4 5 [14.1B]

60. 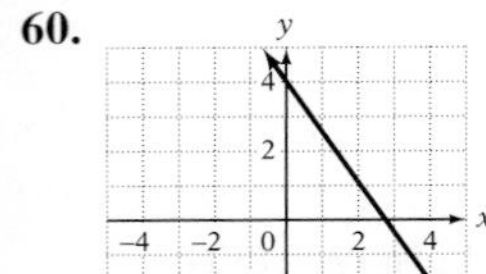 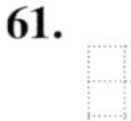 [12.2A] **61.** 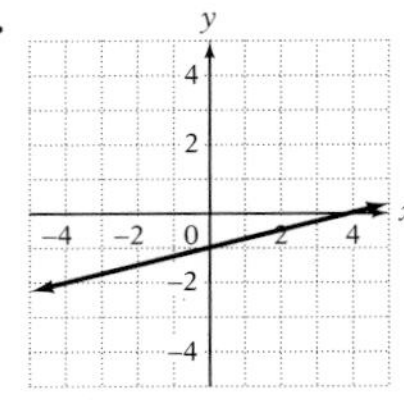  [12.2B] **62.** 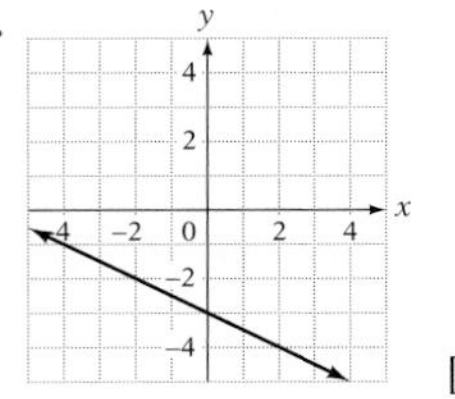 [12.3C]

63. 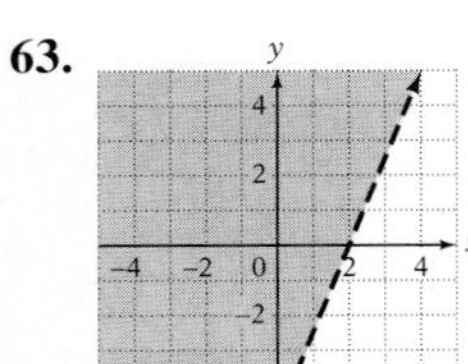 [14.4A] **64.** 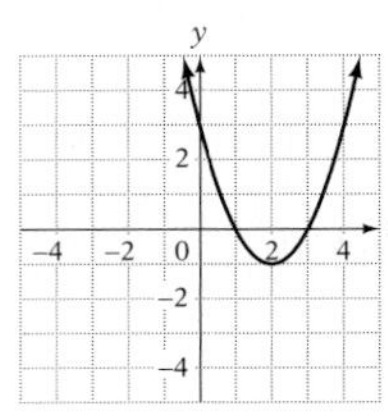 [16.4A]

Answers to Chapter T Selected Exercises

PREP TEST

1. 71 [1.2A] **2.** 2618 [1.2B] **3.** 135 [1.3A] **4.** 16 [1.3C] **5.** $2 \cdot 3 \cdot 13$ [1.3D] **6.** 72 [2.1A]
7. 6 [2.1A] **8.** $-37 < -28$ [3.1A] **9.** 27 [3.1C] **10.** 4 [3.2B]

SECTION T.1

1. $\frac{3}{7}$ **3.** 1 **5.** $1\frac{3}{8}$ **7.** $1\frac{1}{6}$ **9.** $\frac{13}{14}$ **11.** $\frac{53}{60}$ **13.** $\frac{23}{60}$ **15.** $1\frac{17}{18}$ **17.** $1\frac{9}{20}$ **19.** $\frac{1}{3}$ **21.** $\frac{5}{8}$ **23.** $\frac{13}{45}$
25. $\frac{1}{10}$ **27.** $\frac{1}{4}$ **29.** $\frac{1}{2}$ **31.** $\frac{11}{60}$ **33.** $\frac{1}{12}$ **35.** $\frac{5}{24}$ **37.** $\frac{7}{12}$ **39.** $\frac{7}{16}$ **41.** $\frac{1}{3}$ **43.** $\frac{6}{11}$ **45.** 6 **47.** $\frac{5}{32}$
49. $\frac{3}{16}$ **51.** $\frac{2}{9}$ **53.** $\frac{5}{54}$ **55.** 4 **57.** $\frac{2}{7}$ **59.** 0 **61.** $\frac{2}{9}$ **63.** $\frac{7}{10}$ **65.** 2 **67.** $\frac{2}{3}$ **69.** 6 **71.** $\frac{1}{2}$

SECTION T.2

1. −5 **3.** −17 **5.** 3 **7.** −20 **9.** 0 **11.** 21 **13.** −7 **15.** −11 **17.** 8 **19.** 0 **21.** −25
23. −9 **25.** 22 **27.** −6 **29.** 16 **31.** −32 **33.** −15 **35.** −14 **37.** 11 **39.** 16 **41.** 13 **43.** 5
45. −9 **47.** −21 **49.** 35 **51.** −36 **53.** −50 **55.** 49 **57.** 0 **59.** 60 **61.** −126 **63.** 81
65. −192 **67.** −85 **69.** 98 **71.** −80 **73.** −144 **75.** −3 **77.** 9 **79.** 0 **81.** −11 **83.** −9
85. 22 **87.** 14 **89.** Undefined **91.** −21 **93.** −40

SECTION T.3

1. $-\frac{1}{12}$ **3.** $-\frac{1}{3}$ **5.** $-\frac{7}{8}$ **7.** $-1\frac{1}{10}$ **9.** $-\frac{1}{24}$ **11.** $-\frac{3}{4}$ **13.** $\frac{11}{24}$ **15.** $\frac{1}{12}$ **17.** −50.7 **19.** −3.312
21. 9.39 **23.** −16.35 **25.** −9.55 **27.** −19.189 **29.** $\frac{11}{12} - \left(-\frac{1}{4}\right)$, because $\frac{11}{12} - \left(-\frac{1}{4}\right) = \frac{11}{12} + \frac{1}{4}$, so the difference is positive, whereas the difference $-\frac{1}{8} - \frac{3}{4}$ is negative. **31.** $-\frac{1}{4}$ **33.** $\frac{1}{10}$ **35.** $-\frac{3}{8}$ **37.** $-\frac{7}{30}$ **39.** $\frac{3}{16}$ **41.** $-7\frac{1}{2}$ **43.** $-4\frac{1}{5}$
45. −10 **47.** $-\frac{3}{7}$ **49.** $\frac{9}{10}$ **51.** $-\frac{1}{12}$ **53.** $-\frac{9}{10}$ **55.** 1.47 **57.** −7.03 **59.** 60.75 **61.** −5.9 **63.** −67.7
65. 4.14 **67.** −6.1 **69.** −128.8 **71.** 37.0 **73.** $-\frac{5}{6} \div (-5)$, because the quotient is positive, whereas the product $-\frac{3}{4}\left(\frac{2}{9}\right)$ is negative. **75.** $-\frac{8}{343}$ **77.** 12.25 **79.** $\frac{1}{121}$ **81.** $-\frac{1}{75}$ **83.** 0.51 **85.** 1.7 **87.** $\frac{9}{32}$ **89.** $\frac{8}{9}$ **91.** 0 **93.** $\frac{1}{8}$
95. $16 + 15 \div (-5) - (-4) > 18 \div |2^3 - 9| + (-3) > 20 \div (6 - 2^4) + (-5)$; $[17 > 15 > -7]$

SECTION T.4

1. -12 **3.** -1 **5.** -8 **7.** -20 **9.** 8 **11.** 3 **13.** 5 **15.** -3 **17.** 2 **19.** -1 **21.** 1 **23.** 3
25. 3 **27.** 2 **29.** -1 **31.** $\frac{1}{2}$ **33.** 5 **35.** $-\frac{1}{9}$

Answers to Appendix Selected Exercises

1. Meter, liter, gram **3.** Kilometer **5.** Centimeter **7.** Gram **9.** Meter **11.** Gram **13.** Milliliter
15. Milligram **17.** Millimeter **19.** Milligram **21.** Gram **23.** Kiloliter **25.** Milliliter **27.** 420 mm
29. 0.360 kg **31.** 5.194 L **33.** 2 000 mm **35.** 0.217 g **37.** 4 520 ml **39.** 8.406 km **41.** 2 400 g
43. 6 180 L **45.** 9 612 m **47.** 240 mg **49.** 2.98 m **51.** 2.431 kl **53.** 66 cm **55.** 24.3 cm
57. a. Column 2: k, c, m; column 3: 10^9, 10^3, 10^2, $\frac{1}{10^3}$, $\frac{1}{10^{12}}$; column 4: 1 000 000, 10, 0.1, 0.01, 0.000 001, 0.000 000 001
59. The weight is 2 g. **61.** 24 L of chlorine are used in a month of 30 days. **63.** There are 16 servings in the container.
65. The patient should take 4 tablets per day. **67.** The case containing 12 one-liter bottles costs less per milliliter.
69. It takes light 500 s to reach Earth from the sun. **71.** The profit is \$17,430. **73.** The profit is \$66.50.

Glossary

abscissa The first number in an ordered pair. It measures a horizontal distance and is also called the first coordinate. [12.1]
absolute value of a number The distance between zero and the number on the number line. [3.1]
acute angle An angle whose measure is between 0° and 90°. [7.1]
acute triangle A triangle that has three acute angles. [7.2]
addend In addition, one of the numbers added. [1.2]
addition The process of finding the total of two numbers. [1.2]
addition method An algebraic method of finding an exact solution of a system of linear equations. [13.3]
Addition Property of Zero Zero added to a number does not change the number. [1.2]
additive inverses Numbers that are the same distance from zero on the number line, but on opposite sides; also called opposites. [3.1; 4.2]
adjacent angles Two angles that share a common side. [7.1]
alternate exterior angles Two nonadjacent angles that are on opposite sides of the transversal and outside the parallel lines. [7.1]
alternate interior angles Two nonadjacent angles that are on opposite sides of the transversal and between the parallel lines. [7.1]
analytic geometry Geometry in which a coordinate system is used to study the relationships between variables. [12.1]
angle An angle is formed when two rays start at the same point; it is measured in degrees. [1.2; 7.1]
area A measure of the amount of surface in a region. [1.3; 7.2]
Associative Property of Addition Numbers to be added can be grouped (with parentheses, for example) in any order; the sum will be the same. [1.2]
Associative Property of Multiplication Numbers to be multiplied can be grouped (with parentheses, for example) in any order; the product will be the same. [1.3]
average The sum of all the numbers divided by the number of those numbers. [8.2]
axes The two number lines that form a rectangular coordinate system; also called coordinate axes. [12.1]
bar graph A graph that represents data by the height of the bars. [1.1; 8.1]
base In exponential form, the factor that is multiplied the number of times shown by the exponent. [1.3]
base of a triangle The side that the triangle rests on. [2.4; 7.2]
binomial A polynomial of two terms. [9.1]
binomial factor A factor that has two terms. [10.1]
box-and-whiskers plot A graph that shows the smallest value in a set of numbers, the first quartile, the median, the third quartile, and the greatest value. [8.2]
broken-line graph A graph that represents data by the position of the lines and shows trends and comparisons. [1.1; 8.1]
circle A plane figure in which all points are the same distance from point O, which is called the center of the circle. [7.2]
circle graph A graph that represents data by the size of the sectors. [1.1; 8.1]
circumference The distance around a circle. [7.2]
clearing denominators Removing denominators from an equation that contains fractions by multiplying each side of the equation by the LCM of the denominators. [5.2]
combining like terms Using the Distributive Property to add the coefficients of like variable terms; adding like terms of a variable expression. [4.2]
common factor A number that is a factor of two or more numbers is a common factor of those numbers. [2.1]
common multiple A number that is a multiple of two or more numbers is a common multiple of those numbers. [2.1]
Commutative Property of Addition Two numbers can be added in either order; the sum will be the same. [1.2]
Commutative Property of Multiplication Two numbers can be multiplied in either order; the product will be the same. [1.3]
complementary angles Two angles whose sum is 90°. [7.1]
completing the square Adding to a binomial the constant term that makes it a perfect-square trinomial. [16.2]
complex fraction A fraction whose numerator or denominator contains one or more fractions. [2.4; 11.4]
composite number A number that has natural number factors besides 1 and itself. For instance, 18 is a composite number. [1.3]
congruent objects Objects that have the same shape and the same size. [7.3]
congruent triangles Triangles that have the same shape and the same size. [7.3]
conjugates Binomial expressions that differ only in the sign of a term. The expressions $a + b$ and $a - b$ are conjugates. [15.3]
consecutive even integers Even integers that follow one another in order. [5.4]
consecutive integers Integers that follow one another in order. [5.4]
consecutive odd integers Odd integers that follow one another in order. [5.4]
constant term A term that includes no variable part; also called a constant. [4.1]
coordinate axes The two number lines that form a rectangular coordinate system; also simply called axes. [12.1]
coordinates of a point The numbers in an ordered pair that is associated with a point. [12.1]
corresponding angles Two angles that are on the same side of the transversal and are both acute angles or are both obtuse angles. [7.1]
counting numbers The numbers 1, 2, 3, 4, 5, ... [1.1]
cube A rectangular solid in which all six faces are squares. [7.4]
cylinder A geometric solid in which the bases are circles and are perpendicular to the height. [7.4]
data Numerical information. [8.1]
decimal A number written in decimal notation. [2.5]
decimal notation Notation in which a number consists of a whole number part, a decimal point, and a decimal part. [2.5]
decimal part In decimal notation, that part of the number that appears to the right of the decimal point. [2.5]
decimal point In decimal notation, the point that separates the whole number part from the decimal part. [2.5]

degree Unit used to measure angles; one complete revolution is 360°. [1.2; 7.1]
degree of a polynomial in one variable The largest exponent that appears on the variable. [9.1]
denominator The part of a fraction that appears below the fraction bar. [2.2]
dependent system A system of equations that has an infinite number of solutions. [13.1]
dependent variable In a function, the variable whose value depends on the value of another variable known as the independent variable. [12.1]
descending order The terms of a polynomial in one variable arranged so that the exponents on the variable decrease from left to right. The polynomial $9x^5 - 2x^4 + 7x^3 + x^2 - 8x + 1$ is in descending order. [9.1]
diameter of a circle A line segment with endpoints on the circle and going through the center. [7.2]
diameter of a sphere A line segment with endpoints on the sphere and going through the center. [7.4]
difference In subtraction, the result of subtracting two numbers. [1.2]
difference of two squares A polynomial of the form $a^2 - b^2$. [10.4]
dividend In division, the number into which the divisor is divided to yield the quotient. [1.3]
division The process of finding the quotient of two numbers. [1.3]
divisor In division, the number that is divided into the dividend to yield the quotient. [1.3]
domain The set of first coordinates of the ordered pairs in a relation. [12.1]
double-bar graph A graph used to display data for purposes of comparison. [1.1]
element of a set One of the objects in a set. [12.1]
empirical probability The ratio of the number of observations of an event to the total number of observations. [8.3]
empty set The set that contains no elements; also called the null set. [14.1]
endpoint A point at which a ray starts. Either of two points marking the end of a line segment. [1.2; 7.1]
equation A statement of the equality of two numerical or variable expressions. [1.2; 5.1]
equilateral triangle A triangle that has three sides of equal length; the three angles are also of equal measure. [7.2]
equivalent fractions Equal fractions with different denominators. [2.2]
estimate An approximation. [1.2]
evaluating a function Replacing x in $f(x)$ with some value and then simplifying the numerical expression that results. [12.1]
evaluating a variable expression Replacing the variable or variables with numbers and then simplifying the resulting numerical expression. [1.2; 4.1]
even integer An integer that is divisible by 2. [5.4]
event One or more outcomes of an experiment. [8.3]
expanded form The number 46,208 can be written in expanded form as 40,000 + 6000 + 200 + 8. [1.1]
experiment Any activity that has an observable outcome. [8.3]
exponent In exponential form, the raised number that indicates how many times the base occurs in the multiplication. [1.3]
exponential form The expression 2^5 is in exponential form. [1.3]
exterior angle An angle adjacent to an interior angle in a triangle. [7.1]
extremes in a proportion The first and fourth terms in a proportion. [6.2]
factor a polynomial To write the polynomial as a product of other polynomials. [10.1]
factor a trinomial of the form $x^2 + bx + c$ To express the trinomial as the product of two binomials. [10.2]
factor by grouping Process of grouping and factoring terms in a polynomial in such a way that a common binomial factor is found. [10.1]
factor completely Refers to writing a polynomial as a product of factors that are nonfactorable over the integers. [10.2]
factors In multiplication, the numbers that are multiplied. [1.3]
favorable outcomes The outcomes of an experiment that satisfy the requirements of a particular event. [8.3]
first coordinate The first number in an ordered pair. It measures a horizontal distance and is also called the abscissa. [12.1]
first-degree equation in two variables An equation of the form $y = mx + b$, where m is the coefficient and b is a constant; also called a linear equation in two variables or a linear function. [12.2]
first quartile In a set of numbers, the number below which one-quarter of the data lie. [8.2]
FOIL A method of finding the product of two binomials; the letters stand for First, Outer, Inner, and Last. [9.3]
formula A literal equation that states rules about measurements. [11.6]
fraction The notation used to represent the number of equal parts of a whole. [2.2]
fraction bar The bar that separates the numerator of a fraction from the denominator. [2.2]
function A relation in which no two ordered pairs that have the same first coordinate have different second coordinates. [12.1]
function notation A function designated by $f(x)$, which is the value of the function at x. [12.1]
geometric solid A figure in space. [7.4]
graph A display that provides a pictorial representation of data. [8.1]
graph a point in the plane To place a dot at the location given by the ordered pair; also called plotting a point in the plane. [12.1]
graph of a relation The graph of the ordered pairs that belong to the relation. [12.1]
graph of a whole number A heavy dot placed directly above that number on the number line. [1.1]
graph of an equation in two variables A graph of the ordered-pair solutions of the equation. [12.2]
graph of an ordered pair The dot drawn at the coordinates of the point in the plane. [12.1]
greater than A number that appears to the right of a given number on the number line is greater than the given number. [1.1]
greater than or equal to The symbol $\geq$ means "is greater than or equal to." [14.1]
greatest common factor (GCF) The largest common factor of two or more numbers. [2.1; 10.1]
greatest common factor (GCF) of two or more monomials The product of the GCF of the coefficients and the common variable factors. [10.1]
half-plane The solution set of an inequality in two variables. [14.4]
height of a parallelogram The distance between parallel sides. [7.2]
height of a triangle A line segment perpendicular to the base from the opposite vertex. [2.4; 7.2]
hypotenuse The side opposite the right angle in a right triangle. [7.3; 15.4]
improper fraction A fraction greater than or equal to 1. [2.2]
inconsistent system A system of equations that has no solution. [13.1]
independent system A system of equations that has one solution. [13.1]
independent variable In a function, the variable that varies independently and whose value determines the value of the dependent variable. [12.1]
inequality An expression that contains the symbol $<$, $>$, $\geq$ (is greater than or equal to), or $\leq$ (is less than or equal to). [1.1]
integers The numbers . . . , −3, −2, −1, 0, 1, 2, 3, ... [3.1; 5.4]
interest Money paid for the privilege of using someone else's money. [6.5]
interest rate The percent used to determine the amount of interest. [6.5]
interior angles The angles within the region enclosed by a triangle. [7.1]
interquartile range The difference between the third quartile and the first quartile. [8.2]
intersecting lines Lines that cross at a point in the plane. [1.2; 7.1]
intersection of sets *A* and *B* The set that contains the elements that are common to both A and B. [14.1]
inverting a fraction Interchanging the numerator and denominator. [2.4]

irrational number The decimal representation of an irrational number never repeats or terminates and can only be approximated. [15.1]
isosceles triangle A triangle that has two sides of equal length; the angles opposite the equal sides are of equal measure. [7.2]
least common multiple (LCM) The smallest common multiple of two or more numbers. [2.1]
least common multiple (LCM) of two or more polynomials The polynomial of least degree that contains all the factors of each polynomial. [11.2]
legs of a right triangle The sides opposite the acute angles in a right triangle. [7.3; 15.4]
less than A number that appears to the left of a given number on the number line is less than the given number. [1.1]
less than or equal to The symbol $\leq$ means "is less than or equal to." [14.1]
like terms Terms of a variable expression that have the same variable part. [4.2]
line A line extends indefinitely in two directions in a plane; it has no width. [1.2; 7.1]
linear equation in two variables An equation of the form $y = mx + b$, where m and b are constants; also called a linear function or a first-degree equation in two variables. [12.2]
linear function An equation of the form $y = mx + b$, where m and b are constants; also called a linear equation in two variables or a first-degree equation in two variables. [12.2]
literal equation An equation that contains more than one variable. [11.6]
line segment Part of a line; it has two endpoints. [1.2; 7.1]
maturity value of a loan The principal of a loan plus the interest owed on it. [6.5]
mean The sum of all values divided by the number of those values; also known as the average value. [8.2]
means in a proportion The second and third terms in a proportion. [6.2]
median The value that separates a list of values in such a way that there is the same number of values below the median as above it. [8.2]
minuend In subtraction, the number from which another number (the subtrahend) is subtracted. [1.2]
mixed number A number greater than 1 that has a whole number part and a fractional part. [2.2]
mode In a set of numbers, the value that occurs most frequently. [8.2]
monomial A number, a variable, or a product of numbers and variables; a polynomial of one term. [9.1]
multiples of a number The products of that number and the numbers 1, 2, 3, ... [2.1]
multiplication The process of finding the product of two numbers. [1.3]
Multiplication Property of One The product of a number and one is the number. [1.3]
Multiplication Property of Zero The product of a number and zero is zero. [1.3]
multiplicative inverse The reciprocal of a number. [4.2]
natural numbers The numbers 1, 2, 3, 4, 5, . . . [1.1]
negative integers The numbers . . . , −5, −4, −3, −2, −1. [3.1]
negative numbers Numbers less than zero. [3.1]
negative slope A property of a line that slants downward to the right. [12.3]
nonfactorable over the integers A polynomial that does not factor using only integers. [10.2]
null set The set that contains no elements; also called the empty set. [14.1]
number line A line on which a number can be graphed; also called the real number line. [1.1]
numerator The part of a fraction that appears above the fraction bar. [2.2]
numerical coefficient The number part of a variable term. When the numerical coefficient is 1 or −1, the 1 is usually not written. [4.1]
obtuse angle An angle whose measure is between 90° and 180°. [7.1]
obtuse triangle A triangle that has one obtuse angle. [7.2]
odd integer An integer that is not divisible by 2. [5.4]
opposite numbers Two numbers that are the same distance from zero on the number line, but on opposite sides. [3.1]
opposite of a polynomial The polynomial created when the sign of each term of the original polynomial is changed. [9.1]
ordered pair Pair of numbers of the form (a, b) that can be used to identify a point in the plane determined by the axes of a rectangular coordinate system. [12.1]
Order of Operations Agreement A set of rules that tells us in what order to perform the operations that occur in a numerical expression. [1.5; 2.7; 3.5]
ordinate The second number in an ordered pair. It measures a vertical distance and is also called the second coordinate. [12.1]
origin The point corresponding to 0 on the number line. Also the point of intersection of the two coordinate axes that form a rectangular coordinate system. [3.1; 12.1]
parabola The graph of a quadratic equation in two variables. [16.4]
parallel lines Lines that never meet; the distance between them is always the same. [1.2; 7.1; 12.3]
percent Parts per hundred. [6.3]
perfect square The square of an integer. [15.1]
perfect-square trinomial A trinomial that is the product of a binomial and itself. [10.4; 16.2]
perimeter The distance around a plane figure. [1.2; 7.2]
period In a number written in standard form, each group of digits separated from other digits by a comma or commas. [1.1]
perpendicular lines Intersecting lines that form right angles. [7.1; 12.3]
pictograph A graph that uses symbols to represent information. [1.1]
place value The position of each digit in a number written in standard form determines that digit's place value. [1.1; 2.5]
place-value chart A chart that indicates the place value of every digit in a number. [1.1]
plane A flat surface. [1.2; 7.1; 12.1]
plane figures Figures that lie totally in a plane. [1.2; 7.1]
plot a point in the plane To place a dot at the location given by the ordered pair; to graph a point in the plane. [12.1]
point-slope formula If (x_1, y_1) is a point on a line with slope m, then $y - y_1 = m(x - x_1)$. [12.4]
polygon A closed figure determined by three or more line segments that lie in a plane. [1.2; 7.2]
polynomial A variable expression in which the terms are monomials. [9.1]
positive integers The numbers 1, 2, 3, 4, 5, . . . ; also called the natural numbers. [3.1]
positive numbers Numbers greater than zero. [3.1]
positive slope A property of a line that slants upward to the right. [12.3]
prime factorization The expression of a number as the product of its prime factors. [1.3]
prime number A number whose only natural number factors are 1 and itself. For instance, 13 is a prime number. [1.3]
principal The amount of money originally deposited or borrowed. [6.5]
principal square root The positive square root of a number. [15.1]
probability A number from 0 to 1 that tells us how likely it is that a certain outcome of an experiment will happen. [8.3]
product In multiplication, the result of multiplying two numbers. [1.3]
proper fraction A fraction less than 1. [2.2]
proportion An equation that states the equality of two ratios or rates. [6.2]
Pythagorean Theorem The square of the hypotenuse of a right triangle is equal to the sum of the squares of the two legs. [7.3; 15.4]
quadrant One of the four regions into which the two axes of a rectangular coordinate system divide the plane. [12.1]
quadratic equation An equation of the form $ax^2 + bx + c = 0$, where a, b, and c are constants and a is not equal to zero; also called a second-degree equation. [10.6; 16.1]

quadratic equation in two variables An equation of the form $y = ax^2 + bx + c$, where a is not equal to zero. [16.4]
quadratic function A quadratic function is given by $f(x) = ax^2 + bx + c$, where a is not equal to zero. [16.4]
quadrilateral A four-sided polygon. [1.2; 7.2]
quartiles One of the three points that divide a range of data into four equal parts. [8.2]
quotient In division, the result of dividing the divisor into the dividend. [1.3]
radical equation An equation that contains a variable expression in a radicand. [15.4]
radical sign The symbol $\sqrt{\ }$, which is used to indicate the positive, or principal, square root of a number. [15.1]
radicand In a radical expression, the expression under the radical sign. [15.1]
radius of a circle A line segment going from the center to a point on the circle. [7.2]
radius of a sphere A line segment going from the center to a point on the sphere. [7.4]
range of a data set In a set of numbers, the difference between the largest and smallest values. [8.2]
range of a relation The set of second coordinates of the ordered pairs in a relation. [12.1]
rate A comparison of two quantities that have different units. [6.1]
rate of work That part of a task that is completed in one unit of time. [11.7]
ratio A comparison of two quantities that have the same units. [6.1]
rational expression A fraction in which the numerator and denominator is a polynomial. [11.1]
rationalizing the denominator The procedure used to remove a radical from the denominator of a fraction. [15.3]
rational number A number that can be written in the form $\frac{a}{b}$, where a and b are integers and b is not equal to zero. [3.4]
ray A ray starts at a point and extends indefinitely in one direction. [1.2; 7.1]
reciprocal of a fraction The fraction with the numerator and denominator interchanged. [2.4]
reciprocal of a rational expression A rational expression in which the numerator and denominator have been interchanged. [11.1]
rectangle A quadrilateral in which opposite sides are parallel, opposite sides are equal in length, and all four angles are right angles. [1.2]
rectangular coordinate system System formed by two number lines, one horizontal and one vertical, that intersect at the zero point of each line. 12.1]
rectangular solid A solid in which all six faces are rectangles. [7.4]
regular polygon A polygon in which each side has the same length and each angle has the same measure. [7.2]
relation Any set of ordered pairs. [12.1]
remainder In division, the quantity left over when it is not possible to separate objects or numbers into a whole number of equal groups. [1.3]
repeating decimal A decimal in which a block of one or more digits repeats forever. [2.6]
right angle A 90° angle. [1.2; 7.1]
right triangle A triangle that contains one right angle. [7.2; 7.3; 15.4]
roster method Method of writing a set by enclosing a list of the elements in braces. [12.1; 14.1]
rounding Giving an approximate value of an exact number. [1.1]
sample space All the possible outcomes of an experiment. [8.3]
scalene triangle A triangle that has no sides of equal length; no two of its angles are of equal measure. [7.2]
scientific notation Notation in which each number is expressed as the product of two factors, one a number between 1 and 10 and the other a power of 10. [9.4]
second coordinate The second number in an ordered pair. It measures a vertical distance and is also called the ordinate. [12.1]
second-degree equation An equation of the form $ax^2 + bx + c = 0$, where a, b, and c are constants and a is not equal to zero; also called a quadratic equation. [16.1]
set A collection of objects. [12.1]
set-builder notation A method of designating a set that makes use of a variable and a certain property that only elements of that set possess. [14.1]
sides of a polygon The line segments that form the polygon. [1.2; 7.2]
similar objects Objects that have the same shape but not necessarily the same size. [7.3]
similar triangles Triangles that have the same shape but not necessarily the same size. [7.3]
simple interest Interest computed on the original principal. [6.5]
simplest form of a fraction A fraction is in simplest form when the numerator and denominator have no common factors other than 1. [2.2]
simplest form of a rate A rate is in simplest form when the numbers that make up the rate have no common factor other than 1. [6.1]
simplest form of a ratio A ratio is in simplest form when the two numbers do not have a common factor other than 1. [6.1]
simplest form of a rational expression A rational expression is in simplest form when the numerator and denominator have no common factors other than 1. [11.1]
slope The measure of the slant of a line. The symbol for slope is m. [12.3]
slope-intercept form The slope-intercept form of an equation of a straight line is $y = mx + b$. [12.3]
solution of an equation A number that, when substituted for the variable, results in a true equation. [1.2; 5.1]
solution of an equation in two variables An ordered pair whose coordinates make the equation a true statement. [12.1]
solution of a system of equations in two variables An ordered pair that is a solution of each equation of the system. [13.1]
solution set of an inequality A set of numbers, each element of which, when substituted for the variable, results in a true inequality. [14.2]
solving an equation Finding a solution of the equation. [5.1]
sphere A solid in which all points are the same distance from point O, which is called the center of the sphere. [7.4]
square A rectangle that has four equal sides. [1.3]
square of a binomial A polynomial that can be expressed in the form $(a + b)^2$. [9.3; 16.2]
square root A square root of a positive number x is a number a for which $a^2 = x$. [7.3; 15.1]
standard form of a linear equation in two variables An equation of the form $Ax + By = C$, where A and B are coefficients and C is a constant. [12.2]
standard form of a number A whole number is in standard form when it is written using the digits 0, 1, 2, . . . , 9. An example is 46,208. [1.1]
standard form of a quadratic equation A quadratic equation is in standard form when the polynomial is in descending order and equal to zero. $ax^2 + bx + c = 0$ is in standard form. [10.6; 16.1]
statistics The branch of mathematics concerned with data, or numerical information. [8.1]
straight angle A 180° angle. [7.1]
substitution method An algebraic method of finding an exact solution of a system of equations. [13.2]
subtraction The process of finding the difference between two numbers. [1.2]
subtrahend In subtraction, the number that is subtracted from another number (the minuend). [1.2]
sum In addition, the total of the numbers added. [1.2]
supplementary angles Two angles whose sum is 180°. [7.1]
surface area The total area on the surface of a solid. [7.4]
system of equations Equations that are considered together. [13.1]
terminating decimal A decimal that has a finite number of digits after the decimal point, which means that it comes to an end and does not go on forever. [2.6]

terms in a proportion Each of the four numbers in a proportion. [6.2]
terms of a variable expression The addends of the expression. [4.1]
theoretical probability A fraction with the number of favorable outcomes of an experiment in the numerator and the total number of possible outcomes of the experiment in the denominator. [8.3]
third quartile In a set of numbers, the number above which one-quarter of the data lie. [8.2]
transversal A line intersecting two other lines at two different points. [7.1]
triangle A three-sided polygon. [1.2; 7.1]
trinomial A polynomial of three terms. [9.1]
undefined slope A property of a vertical line. [12.3]
uniform motion The motion of a moving object whose speed and direction do not change. [5.1; 11.7]
union of sets *A* and *B* The set that contains all the elements of *A* and all the elements of *B*. [14.1]
unit rate A rate in which the number in the denominator is 1. [6.1]
value of a function at *x* The result of evaluating a variable expression, represented by the symbol $f(x)$. [12.1]
value of a variable The number assigned to the variable. [4.1]
variable A letter used to stand for a quantity that is unknown or that can change. [1.1; 1.2; 4.1]
variable expression An expression that contains one or more variables. [1.2; 4.1]
variable part In a variable term, the variable or variables and their exponents. [4.1]
variable term A term composed of a numerical coefficient and a variable part. [4.1]
vertex The common endpoint of two rays that form an angle. [7.1; 7.4]
vertical angles Two angles that are on opposite sides of the intersection of two lines. [7.1]
volume A measure of the amount of space inside a closed surface. [7.4]
whole numbers The whole numbers are 0, 1, 2, 3, ... [1.1]
***x*-coordinate** The abscissa of an ordered pair in an *xy*-coordinate system. [12.1]
***x*-intercept** The point at which a graph crosses the *x*-axis. [12.3]
***xy*-coordinate system** A rectangular coordinate system in which the horizontal axis is labeled *x* and the vertical axis is labeled *y*. [12.1]
***y*-coordinate** The ordinate of an ordered pair in an *xy*-coordinate system. [12.1]
***y*-intercept** The point at which a graph crosses the *y*-axis. [12.3]
zero of a function A value of *x* for which $f(x) = 0$. [16.4]
zero slope A property of a horizontal line. [12.3]

Index

Common Core Correlation Guide

THE NUMBER SYSTEM	
• Understand and apply properties of operations and the relationship between addition and subtraction.	1.2 Addition and Subtraction of Whole Numbers; 3.2 Addition and Subtraction of Integers; 4.2 Simplifying Variable Expressions
• Work with addition and subtraction equations.	1.2 Addition and Subtraction of Whole Numbers; 5.1 Introduction to Equations
• Represent and solve problems involving multiplication and division.	1.3 Multiplication and Division of Whole Numbers; 2.4 Multiplication and Division of Fractions; 2.6 Operations on Decimals; 3.3 Multiplication and Division of Integers; 3.4 Operations with Rational Numbers
• Find a percent of a quantity as a rate per 100 (30% of a quantity means 30/100 times the quantity); solve problems involving finding the whole, given a part and the percent.	6.4 The Basic Percent Equation
Numbers and Operations in Base Ten	
• Understand the place value system.	1.1 Introduction to Whole Numbers
• Perform operations with multi-digit whole numbers and with decimals to hundredths.	1.2 Addition and Subtraction of Whole Numbers; 1.3 Multiplication and Division of Whole Numbers; 2.6 Operations on Decimals
Numbers and Operations—Fractions	
• Use equivalent fractions as a strategy to add and subtract fractions.	2.3 Addition and Subtraction of Fractions
• Apply and extend previous understandings of multiplication and division to multiply and divide fractions.	2.4 Multiplication and Division of Fractions
• Apply and extend previous understandings of multiplication and division to divide fractions by fractions.	2.4 Multiplication and Division of Fractions
• Compute fluently with multi-digit numbers and find common factors and multiples.	1.2 Addition and Subtraction of Whole Numbers; 1.3 Multiplication and Division of Whole Numbers; 2.1 The Least Common Multiple and Greatest Common Factor
• Apply and extend previous understandings of numbers to the system of rational numbers.	3.1 Introduction to Integers; 3.4 Operations with Rational Numbers
• Apply and extend previous understandings of operations with fractions to add, subtract, multiply, and divide rational numbers.	3.4 Operations with Rational Numbers
• Know that there are numbers that are not rational, and approximate them by rational numbers.	3.4 Operations with Rational Numbers; 15.4 Solving Equations Containing Radical Expressions
The Real Number System	
• Use properties of rational and irrational numbers.	3.4 Operations with Rational Numbers; 15.1 Introduction to Radical Expressions
Quantities	
• Reason quantitatively and use units to solve problems.	6.1 Ratios and Rates; 6.2 Proportions; 7.2 Plane Geometric Figures; 7.4 Solids; and elsewhere in the text

Ratios and Proportional Relationships/Measurement and Data	
• Convert like measurement units within a given measurement system.	Appendix: The Metric System of Measurement
• Represent and interpret data.	1.1 Introduction to Whole Numbers; 8.1 Statistical Graphs; 8.2 Statistical Measures
• Geometric measurement: understand concepts of volume and relate volume to multiplication and to addition.	7.4 Solids
• Understand ratio concepts and use ratio reasoning to solve problems.	6.1 Ratios and Rates; 6.2 Proportions; 7.3 Triangles
• Analyze proportional relationships and use them to solve real-world and mathematical problems.	6.2 Proportions; 6.4 The Basic Percent Equation; 7.3 Triangles
ALGEBRA	
Operations and Algebraic Thinking	
• Write and interpret numerical expressions.	4.3 Translating Verbal Expressions into Variable Expressions
• Analyze patterns and relationships.	For example: Critical Thinking and Projects or Group Activities, pages 39, 83, 220, 253, 320, 349, 426, 482, 507, 567, 593, 667, 730, 759, 796
Expressions and Equations	
• Apply and extend previous understandings of arithmetic to algebraic expressions.	4.2 Simplifying Variable Expressions; 9.1 Addition and Subtraction of Polynomials; 9.2 Multiplication of Monomials; 9.3 Multiplication of Polynomials; 9.5 Division of Polynomials
• Reason about and solve one-variable equations and inequalities.	5.1 Introduction to Equations; 5.2 General Equations - Part I; 5.3 General Equations - Part II; 14.2 The Addition and Multiplication Properties of Inequalities; 14.3 General Inequalities
• Represent and analyze quantitative relationships between dependent and independent variables.	12.1 The Rectangular Coordinate System; 12.2 Linear Equations in Two Variables
• Use properties of operations to generate equivalent expressions.	4.2 Simplifying Variable Expressions; 9.1 Addition and Subtraction of Polynomials; 9.2 Multiplication of Monomials; 9.3 Multiplication of Polynomials; 9.5 Division of Polynomials
• Solve real-life and mathematical problems using numerical and algebraic expressions and equations.	For example: 1.2 Addition and Subtraction of Whole Numbers; 1.3 Multiplication and Division of Whole Numbers; 3.4 Operations with Rational Numbers; 5.4 Translating Sentences into Equations; 5.5 Mixture and Uniform Motion Problems; 6.4 The Basic Percent Equation; Chapter 7 Geometry; 11.7 Application Problems; 13.4 Application Problems in Two Variables
• Work with radicals and integer exponents.	9.4 Integer Exponents and Scientific Notation; 15.1 Introduction to Radical Expressions; 15.2 Addition and Subtraction of Radical Expressions; 15.3 Multiplication and Division of Radical Expressions
• Understand the connections between proportional relationships, lines, and linear equations.	6.2 Proportions; 12.3 Intercepts and Slopes of Straight Lines
• Analyze and solve linear equations and pairs of simultaneous linear equations.	5.1 Introduction to Equations; 5.2 General Equations - Part I; 5.3 General Equations - Part II; Chapter 13 Systems of Linear Equations
Seeing Structure in Expressions	
• Interpret the structure of expressions.	4.2 Simplifying Variable Expressions; 9.1 Addition and Subtraction of Polynomials; 10.4 Special Factoring
• Write expressions in equivalent forms to solve problems.	4.3 Translating Verbal Expressions into Variable Expressions; 9.3 Multiplication of Polynomials; 10.4 Special Factoring; 10.6 Solving Equations

Arithmetic with Polynomials and Rational Expressions	
• Perform arithmetic operations on polynomials.	9.1 Addition and Subtraction of Polynomials; 9.2 Multiplication of Monomials; 9.3 Multiplication of Polynomials; 9.5 Division of Polynomials
• Understand the relationship between zeros and factors of polynomials.	16.4 Graphing Quadratic Equations in Two Variables (Projects or Group Activities)
• Rewrite rational expressions.	11.1 Multiplication and Division of Rational Expressions; 11.2 Expressing Fractions in Terms of the LCM of the Denominators; 11.4 Complex Fractions
Creating Equations	
• Create equations that describe numbers or relationships.	5.4 Translating Sentences into Equations; 6.2 Proportions; 6.4 The Basic Percent Equation
Reasoning with Equations and Inequalities	
• Understand solving equations as a process of reasoning and explain the reasoning.	5.1 Introduction to Equations; 5.2 General Equations - Part I; 5.3 General Equations - Part II
• Solve equations and inequalities in one variable.	5.1 Introduction to Equations; 5.2 General Equations - Part I; 5.3 General Equations - Part II; 14.2 The Addition and Multiplication Properties of Inequalities; 14.3 General Inequalities
• Solve systems of equations.	Chapter 13 Systems of Linear Equations
FUNCTIONS	
Functions	
• Define, evaluate, and compare functions.	12.1 The Rectangular Coordinate System; 16.4 Graphing Quadratic Equations in Two Variables
• Use functions to model relationships between quantities.	12.2 Linear Equations in Two Variables; 12.3 Intercepts and Slopes of Straight Lines
Interpreting Functions	
• Understand the concept of a function and use function notation.	12.1 The Rectangular Coordinate System; 16.4 Graphing Quadratic Equations in Two Variables
• Interpret functions that arise in applications in terms of the context.	12.2 Linear Equations in Two Variables; 12.3 Intercepts and Slopes of Straight Lines
• Analyze functions using different representations.	12.1 The Rectangular Coordinate System
GEOMETRY	
Geometry	
• Graph points on the coordinate plane to solve real-world and mathematical problems.	12.1 The Rectangular Coordinate System; 12.2 Linear Equations in Two Variables; 12.3 Intercepts and Slopes of Straight Lines
• Classify two-dimensional figures into categories based on their properties.	7.2 Plane Geometric Figures; 7.3 Triangles
• Solve real-world and mathematical problems involving area, surface area, and volume.	1.3 Multiplication and Division of Whole Numbers; 7.2 Plane Geometric Figures; 7.4 Solids
• Solve real-life and mathematical problems involving angle measure, area, surface area, and volume.	7.1 Introduction to Geometry; 7.2 Plane Geometric Figures; 7.3 Triangles; 7.4 Solids
• Understand congruence and similarity using physical models, transparencies, or geometry software.	7.3 Triangles
• Understand and apply the Pythagorean Theorem.	7.3 Triangles; 15.4 Solving Equations Containing Radical Expressions
• Solve real-world and mathematical problems involving volume of cylinders, cones and spheres.	7.4 Solids

Geometric Measurement and Dimension	
• Explain volume formulas and use them to solve problems.	7.4 Solids
• Visualize relationships between two-dimensional and three-dimensional objects.	7.4 Solids
STATISTICS AND PROBABILITY	
Statistics and Probability	
• Develop understanding of statistical variability.	8.2 Statistical Measures
• Summarize and describe distributions.	8.1 Statistical Graphs; 8.2 Statistical Measures
• Draw informal comparative inferences about two populations.	8.2 Statistical Measures
• Investigate chance processes and develop, use, and evaluate probability models.	8.3 Introduction to Probability
Interpreting Categorical and Quantitative Data	
• Summarize, represent, and interpret data on a single count or measurement variable.	8.1 Statistical Graphs; 8.2 Statistical Measures

TI-30X IIS

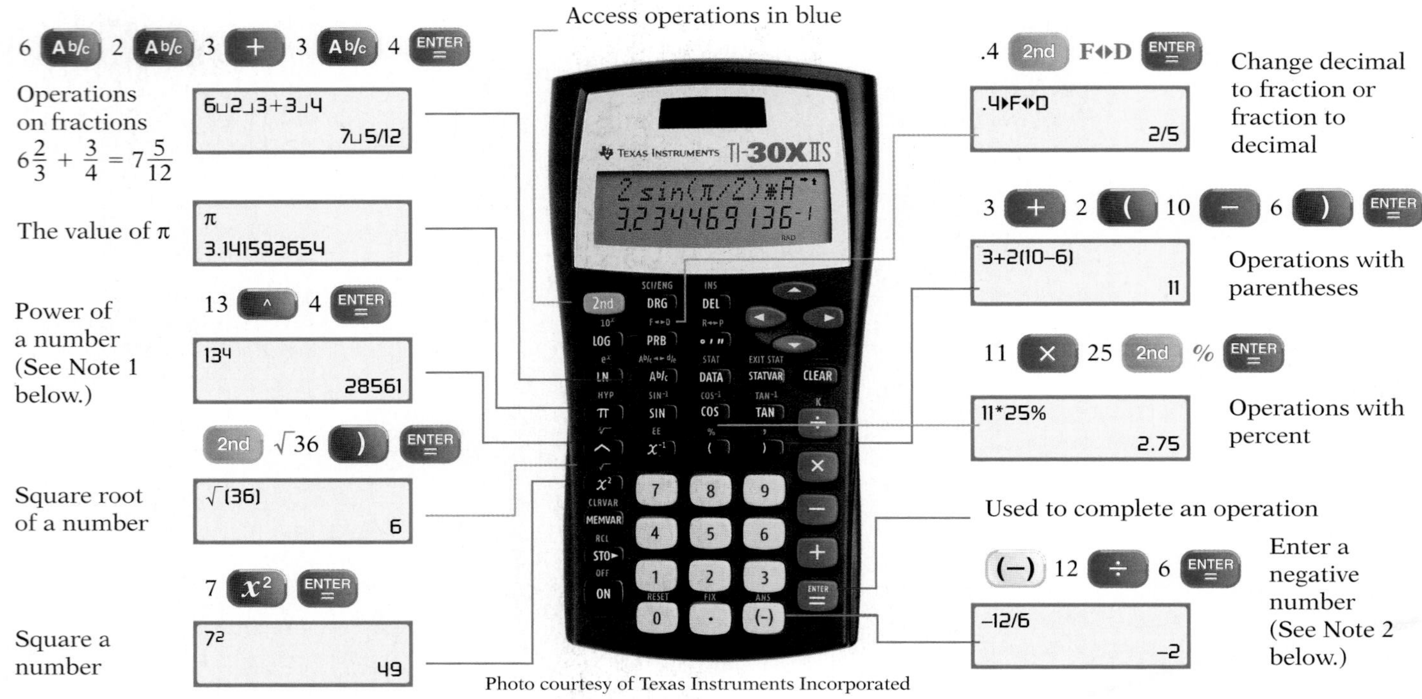

Photo courtesy of Texas Instruments Incorporated

fx-300MS

Access operations in gold

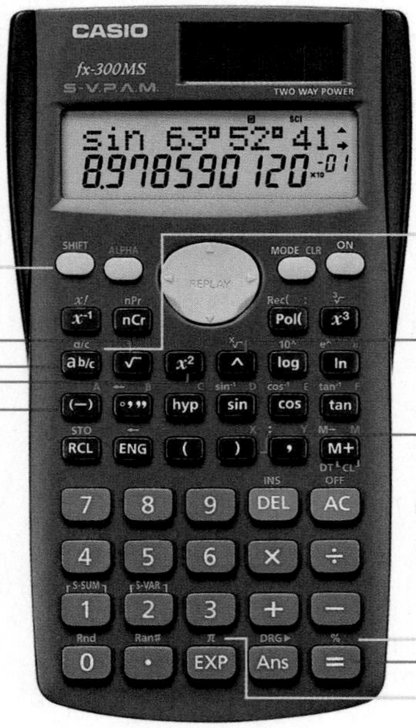

√ 36 =

Square root of a number

√36
6

6 a b/c 2 a b/c 3 + 3 a b/c 4 =

Operations on fractions $6\frac{2}{3} + \frac{3}{4} = 7\frac{5}{12}$

6⌟2⌟3+3⌟4
7⌟5⌟12

7 x^2 =

Square a number

7²
49

(−) 12 ÷ 6 =

Enter a negative number (See Note 2 below.)

−12÷6
−2

.4 = SHIFT d/c

.4
2⌟5

Change decimal to fraction

13 ∧ 4 =

13^4
28561

Power of a number (See Note 1 below.)

3 + 2 (10 − 6) =

3+2(10−6)
11

Operations with parentheses

11 × 25 SHIFT % =

11x25%
2.75

Operations with percent

Used to complete an operation

SHIFT π =

π
3.141592654

The value of π

Photo courtesy of Casio, Inc.

NOTE 1: Some calculators use the y^x key to calculate a power. For those calculators, enter 13 y^x 4 = to evaluate 13^4.

NOTE 2: Some calculators use the +/− key to enter a negative number. For those calculators, enter 12 +/− ÷ 6 = to calculate −12 ÷ 6.